4

ATHLETICS 2006

THE INTERNATIONAL TRACK AND FIELD ANNUAL

BY PETER MATTHEWS

ASSOCIATION OF TRACK & FIELD STATISTICIANS

Published by SportsBooks Ltd

SportsBooks Limited
PO Box 422
Cheltenham
GL50 2YN
United Kingdom
Tel: 01242 2565755
Fax: 01242 254694
e-mail randall@sportsbooks.ltd.uk
Website www.sportsbooks.ltd.uk

This publication incorporates the ATFS Annual.

Photographs supplied by Mark Shearman, 22 Grovelands Road, Purley, Surrey, CR8 4LA.
Tel: 0208-660-0156 Fax: 0208-660-3437

British Library Cataloguing in Publication Data

Athletics: the international track and
field annual – 2006
1. Athletics. Track & Field events –
Serials
1. International athletics annual (London)
796.4'2'05

ISBN 1899807 34 9

Cover design: Katherine Northam

Printed by Compass Press.

CONTENTS

INTRODUCTION

AS EVER this Annual contains reviews and results of the past year, detailed records, an extensive biographical section and the deep world lists compiled in association with ATFS members.

While it takes a long time to work on the 2005 lists so that they can be as accurate as possible – and even now there are some unresolved problems – I endeavour to ensure that this Annual is as topical as possible.

At the back of the book you will find leading results from the 2006 Commonwealth Games, World Indoor Championships and World Cross-Country, the latter held in early April, just a month prior to books being received in stock. I was delighted to provide TV commentary for the IAAF at the World Indoors in Moscow, so very different a city from my previous visits for the 1980 Olympics and 1986 European Cup. Then I followed the Commonwealth Games avidly from home, watching on BBC Television. The extraordinary support for sport from the Australian public brought back memories of Sydney 2000 and the use of the Melbourne Cricket Ground rekindled thoughts of my earliest essays into athletics statistics.

The MCG was last used for athletics when it staged the 1956 Olympic Games. It was then that I first bought the British monthly *World Sports* and this had excellent coverage of athletics. A few months later I saw advertised therein the International Athletics Annual 1957, published by World Sports at 7 shillings and 6 pence. I sent off for this and the 208-page volume arrived. I was at first disappointed as it seemed so small, but that changed rapidly as I 'devoured' the statistics that packed this volume. In the next couple of years two marvellous volumes hugely augmented my historical data: the European Track and Field Handbook (1958) and the All-Time World List (1959). Common to all of these books was General Editor R.L.Quercetani, and I am particularly delighted that Roberto, the doyen of international athletics statisticians, has contributed an article of this 2006 Annual. In this he examines the huge changes in the balance of powers by continent in middle and long distance events over the past 70 years.

Bob Phillips, credited as Assistant Editor from 1966 to 1973, joined Roberto on the World Sports Annual. Bob, who broadcast so knowledgably on athletics for BBC Radio for nearly 20 years, now lives in France and does a brilliant job as editor of the NUTS Quarterly Track Stats. He, too, contributes again this year with a fascinating article on the Olympic Games of 100 years ago in Athens 1906.

As I work on the detailed world lists every year, I find it fascinating to see how standards and national successes vary over the years. In general 2005 levels in depth were below those of Olympic year 2004 as can be seen from the Trends detailed on pages 519-520. Over the 21 years that I have been editing this book there has been remarkably little change in the world top 150-200 standards across the range of events compared to the huge increase in standards in the 1950s, 1960s and 1970s. But there have been huge changes in the composition of world lists with the surge of numbers and standards by distance runners from Africa matched by the considerable decline in these events in particular by Europeans. In the men's shot in 1984 we listed 170 men to 18.75 in the shot, in 2005 134 men did so and we list to lower standards in all the men's and women's throws, illustration of the socio-economic changes in Eastern Europe and of course of the far tougher drug testing regime we have nowadays. Just a little of the thoughts that come from detailed study of the statistics.

With the sport in decline in many developed nations, there are many calls for changes to competitions and their presentation. I am as keen as anyone for our sport to be well staged and presented, but I hope that there will not be excessive tinkering, which can actually detract from the essence of our sport – head-to-head competition. I look forward to giving all the details in our 2007 Annual.

Peter Matthews
7 April 2006

Please send me information, results, corrections etc. to 10 Madgeways Close, Great Amwell, Ware, Herts SG12 9RU, England. Email: p.jmatthews@tisacli.co.uk

Information or requests re sales, distribution, publication etc. to our publisher, Randall Northam, SportsBooks Ltd, 1 Evelyn Court, Cheltenham GL50 2JP. Fax 44 (0)1242 254694. Email: randall@sportsbooks.ltd.uk

ABBREVIATIONS

Meeting Abbreviations

The following abbreviations have been used for meetings with, in parentheses, the first year that they were held.

AAA (GBR) Amateur Athletic Association Championships (1880)
AAU (USA) Amateur Athletic Union Championships (1888) (now TAC)
Af-AsG Afro-Asian Games (2003)
AfCh African Championships (1979)
AfG African Games (1965)
Af-J African Junior Championships
AmCp America's Cup (World Cup Trial)
APM Adriaan Paulen Memorial, Hengelo
AsiC Asian Championships (1973)
AsiG Asian Games (1951)
Asi-J Asian Junior Championships (1990)
ASV Weltklasse in Köln, ASV club meeting (1934)
Athl Athletissima, Lausanne (1976)
Balk Balkan Games (1929), C - Championships
Barr (Cuba) Barrientos Memorial (1950)
BGP Budapest Grand Prix (1978)
Bisl Bislett Games, Oslo (1965) (Bergen 2004)
BrGP British Grand Prix
CAC Central American and Caribbean Championships (1967)
CAG Central American and Caribbean Games (1926)
CalR California Relays (1942)
C.Asian Central Asian Championships
CAU Inter-counties, GBR (1934)
CISM International Military Championships (1946)
CG Commonwealth Games (1930)
DNG DN Galan, Stockholm (1966)
Drake Drake Relays (1910)
EAsG East Asian Games (1993)
EC European Championships (1934)
ECCp European Clubs Cup (1975)
EChall European Challenge (10,000m 1997, Throws 2001)
ECp European Cup - track & field (1965), multi-events (1973)
EI European Indoor Championships (1970, Games 1966-9)
EICp European Indoor Cup (2003)
EJ European Junior Championships (1970)
EU23 European Under-23 Championships (1997) and European Under-23 Cup (1992-4)
FBK Fanny Blankers-Koen Games, Hengelo (formerly APM)
FlaR Florida Relays (1939)
FOT (USA) Final Olympic Trials (1920)
Franc Francophone Games
Gaz Gaz de France meeting, FRA (1968)
GGala Golden Gala, Roma (from 1980), Verona (1988), Pescara (1989), Bologna (1990)
GNR Great North Run – Newcastle to South Shields, GBR (1981)
GO Golden Oval, Dresden
GP Grand Prix
GPF IAAF Grand Prix Final (1985)
GS Golden Spike, Ostrava (1969)
Gugl Zipfer Gugl Grand Prix, Linz (1988)
GWG Goodwill Games (1986)
Herc Herculis, Monte Carlo, Monaco (1987)
IAAF International Amateur Athletic Federation
IAC IAC meeting (1968), formerly Coca-Cola
IAU International Association of Ultrarunners
IbAm Ibero-American Championships (1983)
ISTAF Internationales Stadionfest, Berlin (1921)
Jen Bruce Jenner Classic, San Jose (1979)
Jerome Harry Jerome Track Classic (1984)
JUCO Junior Colleges Championships, USA
KansR Kansas Relays, Lawrence (1923)
Kuso Janusz Kusocinski Memorial (1954)
Kuts Vladimir Kuts Memorial
Macc Maccabiah Games, Israel
MAI Malmö AI Galan, Sweden (formerly Idag) (1958)
Mal Malinowski Memorial, Poland
Mast Masters pole vault, Grenoble (1987)
MedG Mediterranean Games (1951)
Mill Millrose Games, New York indoors (1908)
ModR Modesto Relays
MSR Mt. San Antonio College Relays (1959)
NA Night of Athletics, Heusden (2000) formerly Hechtel
NACAC North American, XCentral American & Caribbean Ch (2003)
NC National Championships
NC-w National Winter Championships
NCAA National Collegiate Athletic Association Championships, USA (1921)
NCAA-r NCAA Regional Championships (2003)
NCp National Cup
NG National Games
Nik Nikaïa, Nice (1976)
NM Narodna Mladezhe, Sofia (1955)
N.Sch National Schools
Nurmi Paavo Nurmi Games (1957)
NYG New York Games (1989)
OD Olympischer Tag (Olympic Day)
Oda Mikio Oda Memorial Meeting, Hiroshima
OG Olympic Games (1896)
OT Olympic Trials
Owens Jesse Owens Memorial (1981)
PAm Pan American Games (1951)
PArab Pan Arab Championships (G- Games)
PennR Pennsylvania Relays (1895)
PG Peugeot (Talbot) Games (1980), Royal Mail Parcels Games 1989-90, Parcelforce Games 1991
Prav (URS) Pravda Cup
PTS Pravda Televízia Slovnaft, Bratislava (1957) (now GPB)
Pre Steve Prefontaine Memorial (1976)
RdVin Route du Vin Half Marathon, Luxembourg

RomIC Romanian International Championships (1948)
Ros Evzen Rosicky Memorial, Praha (1947)
R-W Rot-Weiss meeting, Koblenz
SACh South American Championships (1919)
SAsG South Asian Games
SEAG South East Asia Games
SEC Southeast Conference Championships
SGP IAAF Super Grand Prix
Slovn Slovnaft, Bratislava (formerly PTS) (1990)
Spark Sparkassen Cup, Stuttgart (indoor) (1987)
Spart (URS) Spartakiad (1956)
Stra Stramilano Half marathon, Milan
TexR Texas Relays (1925)
USOF US Olympic Festival
VD Ivo Van Damme Memorial, Brussels (1977)
Veniz Venizelia, Haniá, Crete
WAC Western Athletic Conference Championships
WAF World Athletics Finals, Monaco (2003)
WAfC West African Championships
WAsG West Asian Games
WCh World Championships (1983)
WCp World Cup - track & field (1977), marathon (1985)
Walking – Lugano Trophy – men (1961), Eschborn Cup – women (1979)
WCT World Championships Trial
WG World Games, Helsinki (1961)
WI World Indoor Championships (1987), World Indoor Games (1985)
WJ World Junior Championships (1986)
WK Weltklasse, Zürich (1962)
WMilG World Military Games
WUG World University Games (1923)
WY World Youth Championships (1999)
Zat Emil Zátopek Classic, Melbourne
Znam Znamenskiy Brothers Memorial (1958)
-j, -y, -23 Junior, Youth or under-23

Dual and triangular matches are indicated by "v" (versus) followed by the name(s) of the opposition. Quadrangular and larger inter-nation matches are denoted by the number of nations and -N; viz 8-N designates an 8-nation meeting.

Events

CC cross-country
Dec decathlon
DT discus
h hurdles
Hep heptathlon
HJ high jump
HMar half marathon
HT hammer
JT javelin
LJ long jump
Mar marathon
Pen pentathlon
PV pole vault
R relay
SP shot
St steeplechase
TJ triple jump
W walk
Wt weight

Miscellaneous abbreviations

+ Intermediate time in longer race
= Tie (ex-aequo)
A Made at an altitude of 1000m or higher
b date of birth
D Made in decathlon competition
dnf did not finish
dnq did not qualify
dns did not start
exh exhibition
h heat
H Made in heptathlon competition
hr hour
i indoors
kg kilograms
km kilometres
m metres
M mile
m/s metres per second
mx Made in mixed men's and women's race
nh no height
O Made in octathlon
P Made in pentathlon
pb personal best
Q Made in qualifying round
qf quarter final (or q in lists)
r Race number in a series of races
sf semi final (or s in lists)
w wind assisted
WIR world indoor record
WR world record or best
y yards
* Converted time from yards to metres:
For 200m: 220 yards less 0.11 second
For 400m: 440 yards less 0.26 second
For 110mh: 120yh plus 0.03 second

Countries

(IAAF membership reached 211 in 2003)

After the 2000 Olympic Games, the IAAF determined to align their abbreviations with those of the IOC, so we switched also. Former IAAF abbreviations are shown in brackets in this list.

AFG Afghanistan
AHO Netherlands Antilles
AIA Anguilla (ANG)
ALB Albania
ALG Algeria
AND Andorra
ANG Angola (ANO)
ANT Antigua & Barbuda
ARG Argentina
ARM Armenia
ARU Aruba
ASA American Samoa (AMS)
AUS Australia
AUT Austria
AZE Azerbaijan
BAH Bahamas
BAN Bangladash
BAR Barbados
BDI Burundi (BUR)
BEL Belgium
BEN Benin
BER Bermuda
BHU Bhutan
BIH Bosnia Herzegovina (BSH)
BIZ Belize
BLR Belarus
BOL Bolivia
BOT Botswana
BRA Brazil

BRN Bahrain (BHR)
BRU Brunei
BUL Bulgaria
BUR Burkina Faso (BKF)
CAF Central African Republic
CAM Cambodia
CAN Canada
CAY Cayman Islands
CGO Congo
CHA Chad
CHI Chile
CHN People's Republic of China
CIV Côte d'Ivoire (Ivory Coast)
CMR Cameroon
COD Democratic Republic of Congo (ex ZAI Zaïre)
COK Cook Islands (CKI)
COL Colombia
COM Comoros
CPV Cape Verde Islands (CVD)
CRC Costa Rica
CRO Croatia
CUB Cuba
CYP Cyprus
CZE Czech Republic
DEN Denmark
DJI Djibouti
DMA Dominica (DMN)
DOM Dominican Republic
ECU Ecuador
EGY Egypt
ENG England
ERI Eritrea
ESA El Salvador
ESP Spain
EST Estonia
ETH Ethiopia
FIJ Fiji
FIN Finland
FRA France
FRG Federal Republic of Germany (1948-90)
FSM Micronesia
GAB Gabon
GAM The Gambia
GBR United Kingdom of Great Britain & Northern Ireland
GBS Guinea-Bissau
GDR German Democratic Republic (1948-90)
GEO Georgia
GEQ Equatorial Guinea
GER Germany (pre 1948 and from 1991)
GHA Ghana
GIB Gibraltar
GRE Greece
GRN Grenada
GUA Guatemala
GUI Guinea
GUM Guam
GUY Guyana
HAI Haiti
HKG Hong Kong, China
HON Honduras
HUN Hungary
INA Indonesia
IND India
IRI Iran (IRN)
IRL Ireland
IRQ Iraq
ISL Iceland
ISR Israel
ISV US Virgin Islands
ITA Italy
IVB British Virgin Islands (BVI)
JAM Jamaica
JOR Jordan
JPN Japan
KAZ Kazakhstan (KZK)
KEN Kenya
KGZ Kyrgyzstan
KIR Kiribati
KOR Korea
KSA Saudi Arabia (from SAU)
KUW Kuwait
LAO Laos
LAT Latvia
LBA Libya
LBR Liberia
LCA St Lucia (STL)
LES Lesotho
LIB Lebanon
LIE Liechtenstein
LTU Lithuania (LIT)
LUX Luxembourg
MAC Macao
MAD Madagascar
MAR Morocco
MAS Malaysia
MAW Malawi
MDA Moldova (MOL)
MDV Maldives (MLD)
MEX Mexico
MGL Mongolia
MKD Former Yugoslav Republic of Macedonia
MLI Mali
MLT Malta
MNT Montserrat
MON Monaco
MOZ Mozambique
MRI Mauritius
MSH Marshall Islands
MTN Mauritania
MYA Myanmar (formerly BIR Burma)
NAM Namibia
NCA Nicaragua
NED Netherlands (HOL)
NEP Nepal
NFI Norfolk Islands
NGR Nigeria
NGU Papua New Guinea (PNG)
NI Northern Ireland
NIG Niger
NMA Northern Marianas Islands
NOR Norway
NRU Nauru (NAU)
NZL New Zealand
OMA Oman
PAK Pakistan
PAN Panama
PAR Paraguay
PER Peru
PHI Philippines
PLE Palestine (PAL)
PLW Palau
PNG Papua New Guinea
POL Poland
POR Portugal
PRK North Korea (DPR Korea)
PUR Puerto Rico
PYF French Polynesia
QAT Qatar
ROM Romania
RSA South Africa
RUS Russia
RWA Rwanda
SAM Samoa
SCG Serbia & Montenegro (Crna Gora)
SCO Scotland
SEN Sénégal
SEY Seychelles
SIN Singapore
SKN St Kitts & Nevis (STK)
SLE Sierra Leone
SLO Slovenia
SMR San Marino
SOL Solomon Islands
SOM Somalia
SRI Sri Lanka
STP São Tomé & Principé
SUD Sudan
SUI Switzerland
SUR Surinam
SVK Slovakia
SWE Sweden
SWZ Swaziland
SYR Syria
TAN Tanzania
TCH Czechoslovakia (to 1991)
TGA Tonga (TON)
THA Thailand
TJK Tadjikistan
TKM Turkmenistan
TKS Turks & Caicos Islands
TLS East Timor
TOG Togo
TPE Taiwan (Chinese Taipei)
TRI Trinidad & Tobago
TUN Tunisia
TUR Turkey
UAE United Arab Emirates
UGA Uganda
UKR Ukraine
URS Soviet Union (to 1991)
URU Uruguay
USA United States
UZB Uzbekistan
VAN Vanuatu
VEN Venezuela
VIE Vietnam
VIN St Vincent & the Grenadines (STV)
WAL Wales
YEM Republic of Yemen
YUG Yugoslavia (to 2002)
ZAM Zambia
ZIM Zimbabwe

ACKNOWLEDGEMENTS

THIS BOOK, the supreme compilation of information on our sport, is made possible by help that I get from a worldwide collection of experts, and as always I thank them for their help.

Many members of the ATFS members work very hard on our key work of compiling the annual world lists. As they have been throughout the 22 years that I have produced the Annual, Jirí Havlín and Richard Hymans have been in the forefront of this work as has Milan Skocovsky for juniors, and I am indebted to them for their careful and expert attention to detail. Mirko Jalava has established an amazing depth of performance details for athletes and great topicality on his web site www.tilastopaja.net so that this is a wonderful reference source for us enthusiasts. Thanks also to such specialist contributors as Carlos Fernández for distance running, Dr. David E Martin, marathons, Emmerich Götze, walks and relays, and Winfried Kramer for national records and widespread probing for results. Throughout the year the area specialists contribute invaluable work: *Africa*: Yves Pinaud, *Asia*: Heinrich Hubbeling, *Central and South America*: Eduardo Biscayart and Luis Vinker.

The following specialists supplied information for their respective areas of interest and countries:

Records György Csiki, *Ultrarunning* Andy Milroy, *Indoors* Ed Gordon, *Men's middle and long distance* Ian Smith, *Shot* Norbert Heinrich, *Multi events:* Hans van Kuijen, Enn Endjärv.

Australia: Paul Jenes and David Tarbotton; *Austria*: Dr Karl Graf; *Belgium*: André de Hooghe and Alain Monet; *Bulgaria*: Alexander Vangelov; *Caribbean*: Néstor Calixto; *Canada*: Cecil Smith; *China*: Mirko Jalava and Shen Xinsheng; *Cuba*: Basilio Fuentes and Alfredo Sánchez; *Czech Republic*: Milan Skocovsky, Jirí Havlín, Milan Urban and Vaclav Klvana; *Denmark*: Erik Laursen; *Estonia*: Erlend Teemägi and Enn Endjärv; *Finland*: Juhani Jalava, Mirko Jalava and Matti Hannus; *France*: Alain Bouillé, Jean Gilbert, and José Guilloto; *Germany*: Sven Kuus, Eberhard Vollmer and Klaus Amrhein; *Greece*: Thomas Konstas; *Hungary*: György Csiki and Gabriel Szabó; *Iceland*: Fridrik Oskarsson; *India*: R Murali Krishnan; *Ireland*: Pierce O'Callaghan; *Israel*: David Eiger; *Italy*: Raul Leoni; *Japan*: Yoshimasa Noguchi, Akihiro Onishi and Ken Nakamura; *Latvia*: Andris Stagis; *Lithuania*: Stepas Misiunas; *Luxembourg*: Georges Klepper; *Netherlands*: Wilmar Kortleever; *New Zealand*: Peter Heidenstrom; *Norway*: Tore Johansen and Børre Lilloe; *Poland*: Zbigniew Jonik, Janusz Rozum and Tadeusz Wolejko; *Portugal:* Manuel Arons Carvalho; *Romania*: Alexandru Boriga; *Russia*: Sergey Tikhonov; *Serbia & CG*: Ozren Karamata; *Slovakia*: Alfons Juck; *Slovenia*: Zdravko Peternelj; *South Africa:* Gert le Roux and Riël Haumann; *Spain*: José Luis Hernández, Carles Baronet and the AEEA team; *Sweden*: A.Lennart Julin, Owe Fröberg and Peter Larsson; *Switzerland*: Alberto Bordoli and Antonin Hejda; *Syria and Arab world*: Fouad Habbash; *Trinidad:* Bernard Linley, *Turkey*: Meric Tafolar; *Ukraine*: Oleg Cherkasenko; *UK*: Peter Matthews, Tony Miller and Ian Hodge; *Uruguay*: José María Lombardo; *USA*: Scott Davis, Garry Hill, Marty Post and *Track Newsletter*. Also various national federation lists and to those who post results or ranking lists to various web sites.

Also to Marco Buccellato, Mark Butler, Ottavio Castellini (IAAF), Richard Cooper, Eric Cowe, Carole Fuchs, José Maria García, Arild Gjerde, Grzegorz Gladzikowski, Stan Greenberg, Norbert Heinrich, Bob Hersh, Ove Karlsson, Alan Lindop, Rooney Magnusson, Bill Mallon, Pino Mappa, David Martin, Phil Minshull, Walt Murphy, Jirí Ondracek, Lionel Peters, Bob Phillips, Roberto Quercetani, Chris Turner and Pierre-Jean Vazel. And, as ever, to Rob Whittingham for his computer expertise and advice.

My apologies to anybody whose name I may have missed or who have corresponded with other key ATFS personnel, but all help, however small is deeply appreciated.

Keep the results flowing

During the year Mel Watman and I publish all marks that we know about to ATFS standards in *Athletics International*, of which there are 26 issues per year. This serves as a base from which the lists in this book can be compiled, together with information from the major magazines that are published around the world, such as *Track & Field News* (USA) with its email results spin-off *Track Newsletter*, and *Leichtathletik* (Germany) and the newsletters with particular spheres of interest such as Yves Pinaud's *Lettre de l'Athlétisme*, *Atletismo en España* by Francisco J Ascorbe and José Luis Hernández, and Luis Vinker's *South America Bulletin*.

Many of the national contributors to *Athletics International* are included in the list above. In order to ensure that the record of 2006 is as complete as possible I urge results contribution worldwide to AI, and then in turn our lists in *Athletics 2007* will be as comprehensive as we can make them.

Peter Matthews

THE ASSOCIATION OF TRACK & FIELD STATISTICIANS

The ATFS was founded in Brussels (at the European Championships) in 1950 and ever since has built upon the work of such key founding members as Roberto Quercetani, Don Potts and Fulvio Regli to produce authoritative ranking lists in the International Athletics Annual and elsewhere,

Current Executive Committee
President
Paul Jenes AUS
Vice-President
A.Lennart Julin SWE
Secretary General
Scott Davis USA
Treasurer
Rob Whittingham GBR
Past Presidents
Rooney Magnusson SWE
Dr Roberto Quercetani ITA

Committee
Jírí Havlín CZE
Nejat Kök TUR
Gert le Roux RSA
Bernard Linley TRI
Peter J Matthews GBR
Yves Pinaud FRA
Tatsumi Senda JPN
Luis R Vinker ARG

For details of ATFS Membership which is open to keen statisticians, apply to the secretary: Scott Davis, 4432 Snowbird Circle, Cerritos, California 90703 USA; EMail: ssd@aol.com

Internet – Web sites

Sites of international and national federations or other comprehensive sites for athletics: (all start – http://)

IAAF	www.iaaf.org
CAC Confederation	www.athlecac.org
European AA	www.european-athletics.org
World Mountain Running Association	www.wmra.info
World Masters Athletics	www.world-masters-athletics,org
Africa	www.africathle.com
Andorra	www.faa.ad
Argentina	www.cada-atletismo.org
Australia	www.athletics.org.au
Austria	www.oelv.at
Bahamas	www.bahamastrack.com
Belgium	www.val.be
	www.lbfa.be
Bermuda	www.bermudatracknfield.com
Bolivia	www.atle-bolivia.com
Brazil	www.cbat.org.br
Bulgaria	www.bfla.org
magazine	www.athletics.netbg.com
Canada	www.athleticscanada.com
Caribbean	www.cac-athletics.org ?
Chile	www.fedachi.cl
China	www.athletics.org.cn
Croatia	www.has.hr
Czech Republic	www.atletika.cz
Denmark	www.dansk-atletik.dk
Estonia	www.ekjl.ee
Finland	www.sul.fi
France	www.athle.org
Georgia	www.geo-athletic.de
Germany	www.leichtathletik.de
Great Britain	www.ukathletics.net
deeper statistics	www.britishathletics.info
Greece	www.segas.gr
also for results	www.athletix.org
Hong Kong	www.hkaaa.com
Hungary	www.masz.hu
Iceland	www.fri.is
India	www.aafindia.com
Ireland	www.athleticsireland.ie
Israel	www.iaa.co.il
	http://members.tripod.com/~eiger
Italy	www.fidal.it
Jamaica	www.jaaa.org.jm
Japan	www.rikuren.or.jp
Kenya	www.athleticskenya.org
Korea	www.kaf.go.kr
Kuwait	www.kaaf.net
Latvia	www.lat-athletics.lv
Lithuania	www.laf.lt
Luxembourg	www.fla.lu
Macedonia	www.afm.org.mk
Malta	www.athleticsmalta.net
Mauritius	www.maaa.intnet.mu
Monaco	www.fma.mc
Netherlands	www.atletiek.nl
New Zealand	www.athletics.org.nz
Nigeria	www.afn.org.ng
Northern Ireland	www.niathletics.org
Norway	www.friidrett.no
Poland	www.pzla.pl
Portugal	www.fpatletismo.pt
Puerto Rico	www.fapur.net
Romania	www.fra.ro
Russia	www.rusathletics.ru
Saudi Arabia	www.saaaf.com
Scotland	www.scottishathletics.org.uk
Serbia & Montenegro	www.asj.org.yu
Singapore	www.singaporeathletics.org.sg
Slovakia	www.saz.sk
Slovenia	www.atletska-zveza.si
South Africa	www.athletics.org.za
Spain	www.rfea.es
Sweden	www.friidrott.se
Switzerland	www.swiss-athletics.ch
Turkey	www.taf.org.tr
Ukraine	www.uaf.org.ua
USA	www.usatf.org
Venezuela	www.feveatletismo.org
Wales	www.welshathletics.org

Other recommended sites for statistics and results

AIMS	www.aims-association.org
ARRS	www.arrs.net
Mirko Jalava	www.tilastopaja.com
Martin Rix	www.gbrathletics.com
Masters Track & Field	www.masterstrack.co
Men's shot put	www.menshotput.com
Running Stats	www.runningstats.com
Runners World	www.runnersworld.com
Tracklion	sportslion.net/tracklion_e.html
Track & Field News	www.trackandfieldnews.com
Ultrarunning	www.iau.org.tw
US colleges	www.fansonly.com
World junior news	www.wjan.org
News (mainly US)	/www.newsnow.co.uk/newsfeed ?name=Athletics

DIARY OF 2005
by Peter Matthews

January

21 **Reno, USA**. Brad Walker added 1cm to his best with 5.83 at the annual USATF Pole Vault summit. The women's winner was Stacy Dragila 4.55.

22 **Hustopece, Czech Republic**. Jaroslav Bába added 1cm to his pb with 2.35 to win the first of a three-meeting Tour of Moravia High Jump series.

28 **Chapel Hill**, USA. Erin Gilreath added 16cm to her world best for the 20lb weight with 24.11 (x, 24.11, 23.34, x, x, 22.49).

29 **Boston (Roxbury)**, USA. Tirunesh Dibaba took 6.36 secs of the world indoor record for 5000m with 14:32.93 (kms 2:56.0, 2:55.2, 3:00.0, 2:55.0 and 2:46.7) and Meseret Defar just missed the world 3000m record as she won in 8:30.05 at the Reebok Boston Indoor Games. Dibaba followed Yelena Kaneles (1000m 2:55.8 and 2000m 5:50.9), fell behind for 3000m in 8:51.2 and 4000m 11:46.2, but covered the final 1000m in a remarkable 2:46.7. On his American debut Kenenisa Bekele misjudged the finish and produced his finishing kick with a lap to go so had to yield to Alistair Cragg who won the 3000m in 7:39.89. Laban Rotich ran a Kenyan record 3:53.18 to win the mile from Bernard Lagat 3:53.61. This meeting, with the Millrose Games, Tyson Invitational and US Championships, made up the USATF's Visa Championship Series.

29 **Glasgow**, GBR. The Russian women's team of Yekaterina Kondratyeva, Irina Khabarova, Yuliya Pechonkina and Yuliya Gushchina took 0.14 secs off the world 4x200m record (of 1988 and 1999) with 1:32.41. After 22 successive wins in 2004 Stefan Holm was beaten in the high jump by Aleksey Dmitrik, 2.34 to 2.32. Russia was again the winning team in the Norwich Union International at Kelvin Hall with 63 from GBR 48, France 47, Sweden 48 and Italy 33.

29 **Stuttgart**, Germany. Berhane Adere won the 3000m at the 19th Sparkassen Cup meeting, but her 8:37.91 fell well short of her world record target. Ruslan Yeremenko pole vaulted 5.84, a 4cm pb and the world lead.

30 **Osaka**, Japan. Jelena Prokopcuka won the international women's marathon in a Latvian record 2:22:56 with Mari Ozaki 2nd in 2:23:59.

February

3 **Göteborg**, Sweden. Yaroslav Rybakov beat Stefan Holm 2.35 to 2.33 in the high jump and Carolina Klüft long jumped 6.84 in the third edition of the "EuroJump" meeting.

4 98th **Millrose Games, New York**, USA. On the 148m track, Bernard Lagat won the Wanamaker Mile in 3:52.87 to break the 3:53.00 Games record set by Eamonn Coghlan in 1981. The shot putters took centre stage with Rees Hoffa winning with a pb 21.62 in the last round to overhaul John Godina 21.17 with Adam Nelson 3rd 21.00 and Christian Cantwell 4th 20.37.

5 **Arnstadt**, Germany. Yaroslav Rybakov beat Jaroslav Bába on count-back as both men jumped a meeting record 2.37 at the 29th High Jump with Music competition. Stefan Holm was 3rd at 2.35 and Andrey Sokolovskiy 4th 2.31, while Anna Chicherova was the women's winner with 2.00.

6 **Gent**, Belgium. Ronald Pognon ran a French record 6.51 for 60m at the Flanders Indoor meeting.

11 **Fayetteville**, USA. 18 year-old LaShawn Merritt ran the second fastest ever 400m indoors with 44.93 at the Tyson Invitational. The previous world junior best was 45.90 and Merritt added a 20.40 world junior indoor best 200m the following day. Bernard Lagat ran the third fastest ever mile indoors with a US record 3:49.89.

12 **Donetsk**, Ukraine. Yelena Isinbayeva started her year with a 4.87 world indoor record at the 15th Pole Vault Stars meeting. Anna Rogowska improved her Polish record to 4.75 with compatriot Monika Pyrek 3rd 4.70. Men's winner was Derek Miles 5.85.

12-13 **AAA Indoor Championships**. Sheffield. In his first indoor triple jump since 14.20 as an 18 year-old Phillips Idowu won with 17.30 and Jason Gardener won his fifth AAA 60m title with 6.60.

13 **Karlsruhe**, Germany. Ronald Pognon took 0.01 off the European 60m record with 6.45 from Leonard Scott 6.53 and Dwight Phillips 6.55 after equalling his French record with a 6.51 heat. The newly emergent Daniel Kipchirchir Komen ran the year's fastest indoor 1500m, 3:33.08.

15 **Stockholm**, Sweden. The 16th GE Globen Galen meeting included a Russian high jump record 2.38 by Yaroslav Rybakov with Jaroslav Bába second 2.34.

18 **Birmingham**, GBR. Yelena Isinbayeva won a $30,000 bonus for her latest world indoor record – 4.88 – at this Norwich Union GP, clearing on her second attempt by a very substantial margin. Svetlana Feofanova was 2nd at 4.70 in what proved to be her last competition of 2005. Veronica Campbell's 22.38 for 200m was much the fastest indoor time of the year. Three men were disqualified in the final of the 60m, drawing attention once again to the inadequacy of the "new" false start rule, but Leonard Scott still won in a fast 6.49 ahead of Kim Collins and Maurice Greene, both 6.54. Markos Geneti beat Kenenisa Bekele at 2 miles 8:14.28 to 8:15.49. Home winners included Kelly Holmes, 1000m 2:35.39, and Jo Pavey, 3000m 8:41.43.

22 **Balkan Indoor Championships, Athens (Peanía)**, Greece. Top marks included a 4.50 Bulgarian indoor women's PV by Tania Stefanova and 2.31 HJ by Dragutin Topic.

24 **Madrid, Spain**. Dwight Phillips improved his best from 6.55 to 6.47 to win the 60m from Francis Obikwelu 6.54.

25-27 **US Indoor Championships**, Boston (Roxbury). John Godina, with a world leading shot put and indoor pb of 21.83, and Angela Daigle, who improved from 7.21 to 7.09 to tie Veronica Campbell's fastest 60m time of the year, won a bonus of $25,000 each for the best performances of the 2005 US indoor circuit based on IAAF scoring tables. Rees Hoffa improved his best to 21.74 for 2nd and Adam Nelson was 3rd at 21.59 in the shot. Erin Gilreath threw 24.46, as against her world indoor best of 24.23 in the women's 20lb weight, but a record was disallowed as the implement was too long when remeasured after the throw.

25-27 **Chinese Walks Championships**. Terrific depth in standards included wins for Yu Chaohong. 20k 1:19:08, Han Yucheng, 50k 3:36:20 Asian record with three more men under 3:40, and Jiang Jing, women's 20k 1:27:19.

26 **Liévin**, France. Yelena Isinbayeva cleared 4.89 on her first attempt for another world indoor vault record. En route to his French record 7.43 win in the 60m hurdles, Ladji Doucouré was timed in a European record 6.36 at 50m; Allen Johnson was 2nd in 7.49. Christine Arron won at 60m/200m in 7.10/22.69 and Leonard Scott improved to 6.46 at 60m.

26 **Perth**, Australia. Paul "Budgie" Burgess became the 13th man to pole vault six metres at a low-key inter-club competition after previous pbs in 2005 at 5.91 and 5.95.

27 **Kumamoto**, Japan. Takayuki Matsumiya ran 30k in 1:28:00 to improve his own world record on the same out and back course on which he set the previous record, 1:28:36 in 2003.

27 **Yokohama**, Japan. Japan won the 23rd women's international Ekiden in 2:13:40 from Russia 2:14:21 and Ethiopia 2:14:37.

March

4-6 28th **European Indoor Championships,** Madrid, Spain, in the recently rebuilt and well attended Palacio de Deportas Communidad de Madrid. Yelena Isinbayeva set another world indoor pole vault record (4.90), Carolina Klüft was close to a world record pentathlon with 4948, and Stefan Holm cleared 2.40 to equal the highest any person has jumped over his own head of 59cm (also Franklin Jacobs USA when he cleared 2.32 in 1978) in a classic high jump duel with Yaroslav Rybakov 2.38. All eight HJ finalists cleared 2.30, the highest qualifying mark ever. Other championship records were set in the 1500m (Ivan Heshko 3:36.70), pole vault (Igor Pavlov 5.90) and women's 4x400m (Russia 3:28.00), while world indoor bests for 2005 were registered in the HJ, PV, LJ (Joan Lino Martínez 8.37), heptathlon (Roman Sebrle 6232), women's 400m (Svetlana Pospelova 50.41), 1500m (Elena Iagar 4:03.09), 60m hurdles (Susanna Kallur 7.80), HJ (Anna Chicherova 2.01), PV, TJ (Viktoriya Gurova 14.74), shot (Nadezhda Ostapchuk 19.37), pentathlon and 4x400m. The only athletes to retain the titles they won in 2002 were Jason Gardener (third 60m win), Sebrle and Kim Gevaert (60m). Russia was easily the top nation with 9 wins and 17 medals. Sweden had three winners, while on medals Spain (12) and Britain (7) were 2nd and 3rd. *For leading results see Athletics 2005 p.606.*

5 **Oudtshoorn**, South Africa. Jacques Freitag responded to an unexpected clearance of 2.30 by 19 year-old Ramsay Carelse (1.80m tall) by equalling the Commonwealth record of 2.38, adding 1cm to his 2002 African record.

11-12 **NCAA Indoor Championships**, Fayetteville, Arkansas. Kerron Clement took 0.06 off Michael Johnson's world record for 400m with 44.57 and Wallace Spearmon set US records in heat (20.21) and final (20.10) of the 200m. Arkansas were men's team champions for the 40th overall title of coach John McDonnell's career (1984-2005) and Tennessee, led by Tianna Madison, long jump winner with a pb 6.78, took the women's title for the first time.

12-13 **European Winter Throwing Cup**, Mersin, Turkey. Renamed from the previous Throws Challenge, this competition again provided top class competition for many of Europe's top throwers. Rutger Smith won the shot with a Dutch record 21.00. *See Championships section for leading results.*

12-13 **Russian Winter Walks Championships, Adler**. Vladimir Kanaykin equalled his 2004 world best with 2:23:17 for 35km and improved that for 30km en route to 2:01:47. 20km winners were Vladimir Parvatkin 1:18:06 and Iraida Pudovkina 1:26:28 with the usual outstanding depth of times.

13 **Lisbon**, Portugal. The 15th edition of

this race lived up to its reputation as four men bettered the hour and Paul Tergat won in 59:10, the second fastest ever time for a half marathon, just 4 secs outside his 2000 time although ineligible for records on this slightly downhill (69m) course. Conditions were ideal on a windless day. The reigning world champions at marathon, Jaouad Gharib, and half marathon, Paul Kirui, came 6th and 7th. There were 3943 finishers and 30,000 took part in the accompanying 7km race – including the President and Prime Minister of Portugal.

19-20 **World Cross-Country Championships**, Saint-Galmier, France. Kenenisa Bekele won his fourth successive short and long course double and Tirunesh Dibaba won both women's races as they led to Ethiopia to a sweep of the senior team titles. Kenya was second in all four, but beat Ethiopia into second in both the junior races where the individual champions were Augustine Choge (Kenya 1-2-3-4-5) and Gelete Burka ETH. With their ex-Kenyans, Qatar took all three men's team bronze medals. For the Ethiopian women Werknesh Kidane took her tally of World CC medals to 20 and Gete Wami to 19. *See Athletics 2005 p.608.*

20-21 **Tijuana**, Mexico. Nathan Deakes was an impressive winner with 1:21:48 in the 20km in first stage of the IAAF Race Walking Challenge. Trond Nymark won the 50km 3:46:05 and Melanie Seeger the women's 20km 1:30:48.

26 **Dudince**, Slovakia. Chinese walkers starred at the 24th annual international meeting with meetings records at 20km by Zhu Hongjun 1:18:37 and Song Hongjuan 1:28:37 and Han Yucheng won the 50km in 3:40:30.

26 **New Orleans**, USA. Isabella Ochichi ran the second fastest ever time by a woman for 10km on the roads as she won the Crescent City race in 30:27 from Paula Radcliffe 30:45.

April

2 **European Cup 10,000m**, Barakaldo, Spain. Formerly the European Challenge, winners were Juan Carlos de la Ossa 27:27.80 and Sabrina Mockenhaupt 31:21.28.

2 **Rio Maior**, Portugal. Winners of the IAAF Race Walking Challenge 20km races were Francisco Fernández 1:19:02 and Margarita Turova in a Belarus record 1:27:19.

2 **São Paulo**, Brazil. Irving Saladino jumped an Panamanian record 8.18 in the long jump before unleashing a mighty 8.51w/+2.3.

10 **Beijing**, China. International Ekiden winners were men: Kenya 2:04:17, women: Ethiopia 2:18:08.

10 **Paris Marathon**, France. Salim Kipsang won in 2:08:04 and the women's winner was Lidiya Grigoryeva 2:27:01.

10 **Rotterdam Marathon**, Netherlands. Jimmy Muindi won in 2:07:50, 12 secs ahead of Jackson Koech, although after 15k in 44:36, times were slowed by rain and cold. Lorna Kiplagat won the women's race by a huge margin in 2:27:36 for her first Dutch marathon title.

12-14 1st **Islamic Solidarity Games**, Makkah, Saudi Arabia. Mohamed Salim Al-Kuwalidi produced the top mark with an Asian record long jump of 8.44.

14-15 **Columbia, Missouri**, USA. Austra Skujyte set a new world decathlon record of 8358 points (originally announced as 8366 but 100m time later corrected), winning by 1545 points from Breanna Eveland.

15-16 **South African Championships**, Durban. Chris Harmse improved his Commonwealth hammer record to 80.83; this was also his 14th African record. Godfrey Mokoena smashed the RSA triple jump record with 17.25 and 19 year-old Louis van Zyl won the 400m hurdles in 48.39. *See South Africa section.*

15-17 **Mt SAC Relays**, Walnut, California, USA. Wallace Spearmon ran 19.97 for 200m and Breaux Greer missed the US javelin record by just 3cm with 87.65. Marion Jones, starting her season as usual at this meeting, was tailed off in the 400m to finish last in 55.03. She later ran just a few 100m races in 2005 with a best of 11.28.

17 **London Marathon**. Paula Radcliffe was at her best as she won by a full mile in a world best for a women-only race and the third quickest ever time of 2:17:42. Her record bonus of $125,000 brought her total prize money for the race to $255,000 ... as well as an appearance fee rumoured to be $500,000. She reached 10k in 32:17, 20k in 64:55 and halfway in 68:27, then 25k 1:21:03, 30k 1:37:27 and 20M 1:44:35 (sub-16 pace) before slowing with stomach cramps, going on to 40k 2:10:26 and 25M 2:11:13. She became the first women to have four sub-2:20 times. Constantina Tomescu broke the Romanian record with 2:22:50 and Susan Chepkemei was 3rd in 2:24:00. Martin Lel headed a stellar men's field with 2:07:26 from Jaouad Gharib 2:07:49 and Hendrick Ramaala 2:08:32. Abdelkader El Mouaziz was 4th in 2:09:25 for a record 13th sub-2:10 time. New race records were set with 35,557 starters and 35,105 finishers.

18 **Boston Marathon**, USA. Catherine Ndereba, 2:25:13, became the first woman to win the Boston Marathon for a fourth time and men's winner was Hailu Negussie 2:11:45, times slowed by the hot weather. With 20,453 runners this was the second largest field in race history.

23 **Cixi**, China. The third leg of the IAAF Race Walking Challenge resulted in amazing depth of performance. The men's 20km was won in a Commonwealth and Oceania record 1:17:33 by Nathan Deakes followed by the best ever times for all places 2-24, with 17 men under 1:20. Zhu Hongjun was 2nd in an Asian record 1:17:41, then Cui Zhide 1:17:53 and Li Gaobo 1:18:07, a world U17 best and Asian U20 record.

Eleven women, headed by Jiang Jing 1:27:56, broke 1:30 in the women's 20km.

23-24 **Kobe, Japan.** Teenage Kenyan runners, Martin Irungu Mathathi 27:08.42 and Lucy Wangui 31:22.37, headed excellent depth of 10,000m times at the 52nd Hyogo Relays.

24 **Hamburg Marathon**, Germany. Julio Rey won in 2:07:38, maintaining marvellous consistency following previous wins in 2:07:46 (2001) and 2:07:27 (2003). Edith Masai had a winning marathon debut with 2:27:06.

27-29 **Gulf Championships**, Manama, Bahrain. *See Championships section for winners.*

28-30 **Penn Relays**, Philadelphia, USA. A crowd of 44,612 attended the final day that featured a 'USA v The World' relay series. Top mark was the US women's 4x400m 3:22.93 and both USA (Allyson Felix 200m, Kia Davis 200m, Debbie Dunn 400m 51.3, Hazel Clark 800m 2:00.0) 3:37.42 and Jamaica 3:37.87 (Kenia Sinclair 800m 1:59.5) broke the previous world best for the 1600m medley relay. The University of Michigan team, with 16:04.54, broke the Collegiate record for 4 x 1 mile.

30 **Fort-de-France**, Martinique. IAAF GP II meeting. Maurice Greene won the 100m in 10.03 and there was a thrilling 110mh won by Allan Johnson 13.18w from Terrence Trammell and Dominique Arnold, both 13.19.

May

7 **Kingston**, Jamaica. Asafa Powell won the 100m in 9.84 to tie the Commonwealth record and further sprint victories came from Usain Bolt, 200m 20.14, Sherrone Simpson, 100m 11.03, and Veronica Campbell, 200m 22.53. American LaShawn Merritt won the 400m in a world age-18 best of 44.66.

7 64th **Modesto Relays**, USA. Toby Stevenson won the pole vault with 5.85, but did not get close on his tries at 6.04 and Anwar Moore improved his 110mh by 0.12 to 13.23.

7 **Osaka** GP, Japan. Liu Xiang won the 110mh at this IAAF GP I meeting in 13.12.

7-8 **Pan-American Race Walking Cup**, Lima, Peru. Rolando Saquipay set a pb and championship best of 1:19:21 to win the 20km. *See Championships section for medallists.*

13 **Doha**, Qatar. Early season world-leading marks in this IAAF Super GP included 3:30.77 for 1500m by Daniel Kipchirchir Komen and the top three marks of the year for 3000m, Eliud Kipchoge 7:28.56 from Augustine Choge, world junior record 7:28.76, and Ben Limo 7:29.60; Jamal Bilal Salem was 4th in an Asian record 7:30.76. Saïf Saaeed Shaheen ran the second fastest ever time for 2000m steeplechase time with 5:14.53, missing the world mark by just 0.10. Dorcus Inzikuru set Commonwealth and African women's records with her 9:28.50 for 3000m steeplechase.

13-15 **Nashville**, USA. The Southeastern Conference (SEC) is now well established as providing the highest level of competition on the US Collegiate scene. Xavier Carter beat Wallace Spearmon and Tyson Gay to win the 200m in 20.16, Kerron Clement ran 48.49 for 400mh and Tianna Madison long jumped 6.92w.

15 **Rio de Janeiro**, Brazil. Jadel Gregório, who had a mark of 17.71 two weeks earlier, again starred in this IAAF GP II meeting with a 17.58 triple jump. Valerie Vili added 20cm to her New Zealand shot record with 19.52.

21 **European Walking Cup**, Naumburg, Germany. Russia won four of the five team competitions and provided all the individual winners, including Aleksey Voyevodin, 50km 3:41:03, and Olimpiada Ivanova, women's 20km 1:28:18. *See Championships section.*

21 **Halle**, Germany. Virgilijus Alekna starred with a 68.04 discus win at the annual throwers' meeting. Other winners were: SP: Ralf Bartels 20.91, HT: Vadim Devyatovskiy 79.64, JT: Christian Nicolay 81.45; women – SP: Petra Lammert 18.99, DT: Franka Dietzsch 66.29, HT: Betty Heidler 71.61, JT: Steffi Nerius 65.49.

22 **Belém**, Brazil. With a big crowd of 35,000, Jadel Gregório was again in form in this IAAF GP, as he beat Walter Davis 17.40 to 17.29 in the triple jump. He, Lashinda Demus (53.56 for 400mh), Trecia Kaye-Smith TJ and Valerie Vili SP won here as well as at Rio and Fortaleza.

22 **adidas Track Classic, Carson, USA**. Bershawn Jackson improved his 400mh best from 47.86 to a world-leading 47.62 and John Godina took his 6 year-old shot pb from 22.02 to 22.20. Other world-pacing marks for 2005: Jeremy Wariner 400m 44.53, Veronica Campbell 100m 10.96, Allyson Felix 200m 22.14 (a sea level pb) and Joanna Hayes 100mh 12.64.

26-27 **Sochi**, Russia. Injured later in the year, Irina Simagina produced a 2005 world women's long jump best of 7.04.

27-28 **NCAA Regional Championships** were held at Bloomington (Mid-East), Eugene (West), Norman (Mid-West) and Randall's Island, New York (East) as qualification meetings for the NCAA Nationals. Top marks included a US junior 100m record of 10.06 by Walter Dix (East), and a 200m in which Xavier Carter beat Tyson Gay 20.02 to 20.10 (Mid-East).

28-29 **European Champion Clubs Cup**, Lagos, Portugal. Sports Club Luch of Moscow had a ninth successive win in the women's event while Fiamme Galle Roma were the men's champions. The only Cup records were set by Elvan Abeylegesse of the Turkish club Enka – at both 3000m (8:54.00) and 5000m (15:08.59), apart from an inaugural record of 10:02.60 in the women's steeplechase by Clarisse Cruz. *See Championships section.*

28-29 **Götzis**, Austria. Carolina Klüft extended her heptathlon win streak to 12 (from 2001) at the Hypo meeting. Her 6824 (with pbs in

100mh, HJ and 800m) won from Kelly Sotherton 6547, Hyleas Fountain 6502 (a pb by 467 points), Margaret Simpson 6423 African record and Austra Skujyte 6386. Roman Sebrle had a record fifth successive win here in the decathlon, although with 8534 he was pushed by Attila Zsivoczky 8480 and Aleksandr Pogorelov 8429. Bryan Clay, 9th 7961, had a disaster in the long jump and injured his rib cage in the javelin.

29 **Fanny Blankers-Koen Games, Hengelo**, Netherlands. IAAF GP. Kenenisa Bekele ran the fourth fastest ever 10,000m time, 26:28.72, but "it was too cold and there was too much wind" for the world record. He was followed by Abebe Dinkesa 26:30.74, improving from his 27:23.60 here in 2004, Abderrahim Goumri a pb 27:02.62 and Bernard Kipyego Kiprop 27:04.45, just 0.45 outside the world junior record. Other world-leading marks were set by Brimin Kipruto 3000mSt 8:09.53 (by 0.30 from Paul Koech) and Isabella Ochichi 5000m 14:50.96. Isaac Songok outkicked Eliud Kipchoge 7:30.14 to 7:30.56 in the 3000m with Daniel Kipchirchir Komen third 7:31.98.

29-30 **Payton Jordan US Open, Stanford**, USA. IAAF GP II. Werknesh Kidane won the women's 10,000m in 30:19.39 for a US all-comers record and her fiancée Gebre-egziabher Gebremariam won the men's race in 27:11.57.

June

1 **Milan**, Italy. IAAF GP II. Dorcus Inzikuru of Uganda ran a world best 6:04.46 for women's 2000m steeplechase (although Gulnara Samitova had passed 2000m in 5:59.4 during her 3000m 9:01.59 world record in 2004).

3 **Memorial Primo Nebiolo, Turin**, Italy. IAAF GP II. Veronica Campbell extended her winning streak at 200m to 27, clocking her season's best of 22.35.

4 **La Coruña**, Spain. In 20km races at this IAAF Walking Challenge event Francisco Fernández beat Ilya Markov 1:17:52 to 1:19:36 and the women's winner Cristina López was just outside the CAC record of 1:30:08.

4 **Seville**, Spain. Meeting records in this IAAF GP were set by Daniel Kipchirchir Komen, a 1500m win over Ivan Heshko 3:31.46 to 3:32.81, Craig Mottram, 5000m 13:04.06, and Christian Cantwell, in top form with 21.67 in the shot. World fastest times of the year were set by Amine Laâlou (1:44.22 800m), Mottram and Paul K Koech (8:06.26 steeple).

4 30th **Prefontaine Classic, Eugene**, USA. Justin Gatlin just beat Asafa Powell at 100m with both men timed in a 9.84w. Eliud Kipchoge set a US all-comers 2 miles record of 8:07.68 from Alan Webb, American record 8:11.48. Alex Kipchirchir won the mile in a world-leading 3:50.91 ahead of Rashid Ramzi, Bahrain record 3:51.33, and the now-US citizen Bernard Lagat 3:51.53. Other world leading marks came from Tonique Williams-Darling (400m 49.95 just ahead of Sanya Richards 49.98) and Liu Xiang 13.06 for 110mh ahead of Terrence Trammell 13.12 with Allen Johnson disqualified on a false start. Maria Mutola won the 800m (1:59.95) for the 13th consecutive year.

4-5 **Arles**, France. With a world-leading 6889 Eunice Barber added 28 points to the French record that she had set when winning the 1999 World title; she won by 610 points from Natalya Dobrynska. The men's decathlon winner Kristjan Rahnu added 323 points to his best with 8526, well clear of Attila Zsivoczky 8302.

5 **Bydgoszcz**, Poland. The European Athletics Festival was marred by strong winds and cold weather after torrential rain just prior to the meeting. However, Anna Jesien took the 20 year-old Polish record for 400m hurdles and beat Sandra Glover 54.22 to 54.53.

5 **Glasgow (Scotstoun)** GBR. Russia won the Norwich Union International with 118 from USA 108 and GBR 92. In her first outdoor race of the year Dame Kelly Holmes won the 1500m in impressive style in 4:06.52. Allyson Felix shot off in the 400m and, though slowing considerably, held on to win in 51.12, a brilliant pb in the cool and windy conditions.

8-11 **NCAA Championships**, Sacramento, USA. There were Collegiate records from Monique Henderson, 400m 50.10 from a pb of 50.53, Kerron Clement, a world-leading 47.56 for 400m hurdles from Bennie Brazell 47.67 (their previous pbs 48.29 and 48.05 respectively) and the LSU 4x400m team, 2:59.59. Wallace Spearmon won the 200m in a world-leading 19.91 into an 0.7m wind from Xavier Carter 20.08 and Tyson Gay 20.16 (after a 19.93 semi-final win) and Darold Williamson won the 400m in 44.51 (pb of 44.27 in his semi) and later ran a 43.49 anchor leg for Baylor. Arkansas retained the men's team title with 60 points from Florida 49 and LSU 36 and Texas were women's champions at 55 from South Carolina and UCLA 48. *See USA section for winners*.

9 **Ostrava**, Czech Republic. Asafa Powell smashed the meeting record with an extraordinary 9.85 for 100 metres at the Golden Spike IAAF Super GP meeting. Level with Olusoji Fasuba for the first half of the race, he then powered away from the field in sensational fashion to win by 3.5m; the wind was +0.6 but it was cool and still drizzling from heavy rain earlier. Sergey Makarov set a 2005 world-leading mark in the javelin with his first throw of 88.84.

11 **Reebok Grand Prix, New York (Randalls Island)**, USA. Held in the new Icahn Stadium. Allen Johnson won the 110m hurdles in 13.03 from Dominique Arnold pb 13.05 and Liu Xiang 13.11, and Michelle Perry improved by 0.20 to 12.45 to burst past Joanna Hayes, second in 12.47, in the last three strides of the 100mh. Three more women set world-leading marks:

Tirunesh Dibaba, 5000m 14:32.42, Meseret Defar, 3000m 8:33.57, and Kenia Sinclair 800m, Jamaican record 1:59.10. Adam Nelson returned to form in the shot with 21.58, but John Godina, whose first throw was a foul in the region of 22m, sprained his ankle on his second attempt (21.40) and did not throw again.

12 51st **Kusocinski Memorial, Warsaw**, Poland. Top mark was Natalya Sadova 65.84 in the women's discus.

12 **Villeneuve d'Ascq**, France. Vanessa Boslak set a French pole vault record of 4.56 at this IAAF GP meeting.

14 **Athens**, Greece. Asafa Powell took the world record for 100m in the IAAF Super GP with 9.77. Aziz Zakari was second in 9.99 and the following wind was 1.6 m/s. Dorcus Inzikuru improved her Commonwealth and African record for 3000m steeplechase from 9:28.50 to 9:15.04 for second on the world all-time list and in second Wioletta Janowska ran 9:25.09 on her debut at the event. World-leading marks also came in the men's 800m, Mbulaeni Mulaudzi 1:44.12, 3000m steeplechase, Saïf Saaeed Shaheen 7:57.28, women's 1500m, Maryam Jamal 3:59.13 from a previous best of 4:06.60, and 400m hurdles – Jana Pittman 53.44.

16-19 **Brazil Championships**, São Paulo. Jadel Gregório triple jumped a season's best 17.71. *See Brazil section.*

17-19 **European Cup Super League**, Firenze, Italy. Germany retained the men's Cup and Russia took a ninth consecutive women's victory by a huge margin of 37.5 points over Poland, winning 10 of the 20 events. The inaugural Athlete of the SPAR European Cup awards went to Italian javelin thrower Francesco Pignata (3rd 81.67, his first time over 80m) and Christine Arron, winner of the 100m 11.09 and 200m 22.84. Top men's mark was 13.16 for 110m hurdles by Ladji Doucouré and the one new Cup record was 9:35.95 for 3000m steeplechase by Cristina Casandra. *See Championships section.*

18-19 **European Cup First Leagues**. At Gävle, Sweden, promotion was won by Finland (men), for whom Tero Pitkämäki improved his javelin pb to 85.90, and Sweden (women). For the hosts Kajsa Bergqvist continued her great comeback with a world-leading high jump of 2.01 and Carolina Klüft long jumped 6.91w/2.1. At Leiria the winners were Ukraine (men) and Britain (women). *See Championships section.*

18 **Sidoarjo**, Indonesia. First of three Asian GP meetings – followed by Jun 21, Singapore and Jun 24, Songkha, Thailand.

21-22 **European Cup Second Leagues**, Tallinn, EST and Istanbul TUR.

23-26 **USA Championships,** Carson. Justin Gatlin became the first man for 20 years to complete the 100/200m double, but only after being allowed progress to the semi-finals after disqualification for a false start in his heat. 19 year-old Kerron Clement ran the fastest 400m hurdles time since 1998 with 47.24 for sixth on the world all-time list, Erin Gilreath improved her US hammer record to 73.87, and other world-leading performances came from Allyson Felix, 200m 22.13, Jeremy Wariner and Sanya Richards, 400m 44.20 and 49.28, Michelle Perry, 100mh 12.43 (in a semi), and Allen Johnson, whose 12.99 was a record tenth career sub-13 sec time for 110mh. Behind him Dominique Arnold ran 13.01 and Terrence Trammell 13.02, the fastest ever for third place. Clement and Richards each won a cash prize of $25,000 for the best men's and women's performances on the IAAF Scoring Tables. Lashinda Demus was just one point behind Richards with 53.35 for 400mh and Stacy Dragila won a seventh successive pole vault title (and ninth in all).

24-26 **Chinese Women's Championships,** Changsha. Zhang Wenxiu set an Asian record, also a world junior record, of 73.24 in the hammer. *See China section.*

24-26 **Jamaican Championships**, Kingston. Veronica Campbell won the sprint double in 10.97 and 22.53. *See Jamaica section.*

25 **Znamenskiy Memorial**, Kazan, Russia. IAAF GP II. Svetlana Cherkasova ran a world-leading 1:56.93 for 800m, well ahead of Zulia Calatayud 1:58.07, and Olga Yegorova won the 1500m in 3:59.47.

25-26 **Italian Championships**, Bressanone. Ester Balassini set her 17th Italian hammer record with 73.59. *See Italy section.*

26 **Kuortane**, Finland. Tero Pitkämäki, with a previous best of 85.95, shot to the top of the world javelin rankings with a throw of 91.53 for sixth on the world all-time list.

26 **100km World Cup**, Yubetsu, Lake Saroma, Japan. Contested by teams from 20 nations. *See Championships section for details.*

27 **Odlozil Memorial, Prague**, Czech Republic. IAAF GP II. 66.81 by Vera Cechlová for the women's discus was the 2005 world best and Sileshi Sihine won the 10,000m in 26:57.27.

28 **Sollentuna**, Sweden. Tirunesh Dibaba won on her debut at 10,000m in 30:15.67 from sister Ejegayehu 30:18.39.

29- Jul 2 15th **Mediterranean Games**, Almeria, Spain. Top mark was Baya Rahouli's Algerian record 14.94 triple jump.

July

1 **Meeting Gaz de France Paris Saint-Denis**, France. Kenenisa Bekele ran the fourth fastest ever 5000m with 12:40.18 and his 18 year-old brother Tariku took 12.84 off his pb with 12:59.03. The enthusiastic crowd was announced as a Golden League record 74,000. Christine Arron won the 100m in 11.03 and Ladji Doucouré set a French record 13.02 as he dipped ahead of Allen Johnson 13.04, Liu Xiang

13.06 and Dominique Arnold 13.10 (the fastest ever 4th place). Tatyana Lebedeva started her successful season with 15.11 TJ. Daniel Kipchirchir Komen maintained his progress with 3:30.01 for 1500m and in sixth place Nick Willis shaded the great John Walker's New Zealand record of 3:32.4 set in 1975.

2-3 **German Championships**, Bochum-Wattenscheid. Having won the 100m in a pb 10.16 on the first day, Tobias Unger took the 20 year-old German record (Frank Emmelmann 20.24) with 20.20 for 200m. Eighth titles were won by Karsten Kobs, HT, Tim Lobinger, PV, and Franka Dietzsch, DT, and Charles Friedek won his seventh at TJ. *See Germany section.*

2-4 **Belarus Championships**, Brest. Ivan Tikhon came within one centimetre of Yuriy Sedykh's 1986 world hammer record with a final round throw of 86.73. Vadim Devyatovskiy was 2nd with 83.69. *See Belarus section.*

3-4 **European Cup Combined Events**. Estonia retained the men's Cup and Belarus won the women's for the first time in the Super League. The best performance came in the First League at Jyväskylä as Carolina Klüft won the heptathlon with 6688 and the Second League events were held at Maribor, Slovenia.

4-8 **European Youth Olympic Festival**, Lignano, Italy.

5 30th **Athletissima, Lausanne**, Switzerland. Yelena Isinbayeva made her outdoor debut and soared over 4.93 for yet another world pole vault record. Although the bar quivered, she was way above it at her high point. There were three other world-leading marks as Marian Oprea jumped a Romanian record 17.81 on his only one valid TJ effort, Virgilijus Alekna threw the discus 70.53 and fast starting Chandra Sturrup (33) took 0.02 from her five year-old Bahamian 100m record with 10.84 from Lauryn Williams 10.91 and Christine Arron 10.94. Ronald Pognon scored an upset 100m win with a French record 9.99 over Aziz Zakari 10.02 and Justin Gatlin 10.03 and the closest race was the 110m hurdles in which Liu Xiang outdipped Terrence Trammell, both given 13.05.

6 **Salamanca**, Spain. Sonia Bisset achieved a rare win over Osleidys Menéndez with a pb 67.67 to 66.02.

8 25th **Golden Gala, Roma**, Italy. Only three of the 12 Golden League winners from Saint-Denis kept in the Jackpot hunt: Christine Arron 100m, Lashinda Demus 400mh and Tatyana Lebedeva TJ. Stefan Holm had seemed a prime contender, but even though he improved his 2005 outdoor best to 2.33 and 2.36 he was outjumped by the often-inconsistent Andrey Sokolovskiy who led with first-time clearances at 2.33, 2.36 and a pb 2.38; Jaroslav Bába tied Holm and the Czech record at 2.36. Tirunesh Dibaba won the 5000m in 14:32.57, as she, Berhane Adere and Meseret Defar ran the last lap in under 60 secs. There were records for six women under 14:40 and 13 under 14:55 (compared to a previous best of eight), while 8 under 14:50 and 13 under 15 minutes tied the records. The men's 5000m also had great depth, with the best ever times for places 14 and 15 (13:12.35); Isaac Songok confirmed the success of his move up as he followed his win at the Kenyan Trials with a superb win in 12:52.29 compared to a previous pb of 13:06.22, speeding around the last lap in 53.8. Rashid Ramzi ran an Asian 1500m record of 3:30.00 to beat Daniel Kipchirchir Komen 3:30.37 and Bernard Lagat 3:31.09 and Saïf Saaeed Shaheen (58.93 last lap) just held off Paul Kipsiele Koech in a great 3000m steeplechase 7:56.34 to 7:56.37.

9-10 **AAA Championships**, Manchester, England. Nathan Douglas, who had set a pb with 16.95 to win here a year earlier, moved up to 17.64. *See UK section.*

9-11 20th **CAC Championships**, Nassau, Bahamas. Eleven championships records included 20.03 for 200m by Usain Bolt, both Darrel Brown and Marc Burns running 10.02 for 100m and Chandra Sturrup 11.02 for 100m. Cuba was easily the most successful nation.

10 **European Mountain Running Championships**, Heiligenblut, Austria.

10 **Réthimno**, Greece. EAA Permit. Yelena Isinbayeva had the bar up at a world record height of 4.94 and at her third attempt thought she had cleared successfully ... only to see the bar tumble belatedly. Virgilijus Alekna extended his world-leading discus mark to 70.58 and Michelle Perry just missed her best with 12.45 for 100m hurdles.

10-13 **Russian Championships**, Tula. Tatyana Lysenko equalled the Russian hammer record of 75.95 that she had set at the Moscow Championships on June 30 and other women's world-leading marks came from Yuliya Pechonkina, 400mh 53.01, Tatyana Andrianova, 800m 1:56.07 with four more women under 1:58, and Yuliya Chizhenko, 1500m 3:58.68. Yelena Slesarenko was back in form with a 2.00 high jump and Natalya Sadova won her eighth Russian discus title. *See Russia section.*

11 **Zagreb**, Croatia. IAAF GP. Kajsa Bergqvist continued her comeback with another 2.00 win and Manuela Montebrun set a French hammer record, 74.66 to beat Yipsi Moreno 73.88.

13-17 **World Youth Championships**, Marrakech, Morocco. The one individual double gold medallist was Harry Aikines-Aryeetey at 100m and 200m. Championship bests were set in 17 events with two winners exceeding the world U17 bests: Yordani García with 6462 points for octathlon and Tareq Mubarak Taher, 5:23.95 for 2000m steeplechase. However, while Mubarak was entered by Bahrain with a birthdate of 1.12.89, we have an alternative for him, the former Denis Keter of Kenya, of 23.3.84. Similarly another Bahrain entrant Bilal Mansoor Ali (formerly the Kenyan John Yego) was a brilliant winner of the 1500m in 3:36.98 but a birthdate of 17.10.88 compared to one to 17.10.83. 15 year-olds (thus eligible for the next Championships in 2007) won the 3000m and women's pole vault, long jump, hammer and walk, and Kenya's Sheila Chepkirui (14), took the 1500m! The given dates of birth of athletes from certain countries should be treated with caution. *See Championships section for medallists.*

14-16 **French Championships**, Angers. Ladji Doucouré took 0.05 off his recent French record with 12.97, the world best 110mh of 2005. Christine Arron won the 200m in 22.38 and Vanessa Boslak vaulted a French record 4.60.

14-17 **European U23 Championships**, Erfurt, Germany. Three men's and six women's championship bests were set, with the top mark 11.03 for 100m by María Karastamáti. Carolina Klüft retained her long jump title with 6.79. Russia (15 gold, 10 silver and 6 bronze medals) and Germany 4/14/8) were much the most successful nations. *See Championships section.*

15 **Kuts Memorial, Moscow**, Russia. Tatyana Lysenko smashed the world record for the hammer (Mihaela Melinte's 76.07 in 1999) with a stunning 77.06 in the final round after a Russian record 76.05 in the third round.

16 **Madrid**, Spain. IAAF Super GP meeting. Yelena Isinbayeva added 2cm to her world vault record with a second attempt clearance at 4.95 and there were world-leading performances from Dwight Phillips, LJ 8.47, and Virgilijus Alekna with 70.67. Tatyana Kotova had four windy long jumps over 7m topped by 7.20w; and Kamila Skolimowska smashed her Polish hammer record with a final round 74.27 to overtake Yipsi Moreno 71.75. Zulia Calatayud (1:58.81) had a significant 800m victory over Hasna Benhassi and Maria Mutola, and Joachim Olsen raised his season's shot best to 21.32.

16-17 **World 24 Hours Challenge**, Wörschach, Austria. Both individual events and the women's team went to Russia with Japan taking the men's team title. *See Championships section.*

17 **Thessaloníki**, Greece. IAAF GP II. Jan Zelezny returned with a 83.43 javelin win.

21 **Minsk**, Belarus. Nadezhda Ostapchuk produced a world leading shot mark of 21.09 at the Ovsyanik Memorial.

21-24 **European Junior Championships**, Kaunas, Lithuania. Vera Sokolova set a world junior record in the 10,000m walk of 43:11.34 after leading for most of the race, yet she had been passed on the last lap and left well behind by Yelena Ladanova who crossed the line in 42:59.30 – only to be disqualified. The most clear-cut win was by Greg Rutherford who set a British junior record of 8.14 for a 41cm winning margin in the long jump. Russians dominated the championships with eight gold, 12 silver and four bronze medals from Britain 6/5/3 and Germany 5/7/4. *See Championships section.*

21-24 **South American Championships**, Calí, Colombia. Juan Ignacio Cerra won a fifth title at hammer and Gilmar Mayo a fourth at high jump. *See Championships section.*

22 **London Grand Prix**, London (CP), GBR. IAAF Super GP. Once again Yelena Isinbayeva benefited from the $50,000 bonus offered by British sponsors Norwich Union. But this time not once but twice, for after adding a centimetre to take her world record to 4.96 she cleared superbly on her first attempt at the landmark height of 5 metres (42 years after Brian Sternberg became the first man to do so). Asafa Powell and Justin Gatlin won their 100m heats in 10.02 and 10.01 but Powell pulled up after five strides in the final as Gatlin went on to overhaul fast-starting Leonard Scott (pb 9.94) for a clear-cut victory in 9.89, breaking Powell's UK all-comers record of 9.91 here in 2004. Three men broke 20 secs for 200m as Wallace Spearmon ran 2005's fastest time of 19.89 from Usain Bolt and Tyson Gay, both 19.99. As in 2004 Craig Mottram ran a brilliant 5000m but again he was beaten by a great Ethiopian; this time Kenenisa Bekele in 12:55.55 to 12:56.13. A run of 42 winning races (28 finals) at 200m from 2001 by Veronica Campbell was ended, as she had to yield to Allyson Felix, 22.16w to 22.29.

23 **Heusden-Zolder**, Belgium. KBC Night of Athletics (IAAF GP II). From 13:21.11 in 2003 and then a Saudi Arabian record 13:08.64 at Saint-Denis on 1 July, Mohamed Al-Outaibi won the 5000m in an Asian record 12:58.58 followed by five Africans under 13:05.

23 **Sesto San Giovanni**, Italy, Ivano Brugnetti took 4 secs off the world best for 10,000m track walk with 37:58.6.

23-24 **Balkan Championships**, Novi Sad, SCG. Romania was the top nation for both men and women. *See Championships section.*

25 **Helsinki**, Finland. Four world-leading marks for the year were set in this IAAF GP. In the Olympic Stadium Mbulaeni Mulaudzi ran 800m in 1:44.08, in 4x100m relays Trinidad clocked 38.38 and the USA 42.65, while the previous evening at the warm-up track Osleidys Menéndez threw the javelin 68.47.

26 **DN Galan, Stockholm**, Sweden. IAAF Super GP. One-carat diamonds worth $10,000 for setting a stadium record went to Isaac Songok, who sped round the last lap in 54.22 to take the 3000m in 7:35.84, and Yelena Isinbayeva pole vault 4.79 before she had a couple of narrow failures at the world record height of 5.01. Local heroes, Stefan Holm (2.33) and Kajsa Bergqvist (1.95) had high jump victories.

29 **Bislett Games, Oslo**, Norway. There was a 15,400 capacity crowd at the rebuilt Bislett Stadium opened by the Mayor of Oslo, Per

Ditlev-Simonsen, in the presence of the King and Queen of Norway and IAAF President Lamine Diack. Top moment was a third-round javelin throw of 87.66 by Andreas Thorkildsen to add nearly a metre to his Norwegian record. That took the lead from Aleksandr Ivanov's opening 83.93, but was surpassed by Tero Pitkämäki, a fourth-round 90.54, and Sergey Makarov, 87.76 in the final round. Maryam Yusuf Jamal was a hugely impressive winner of the women's 3000m in a 2005 world best time of 8:28.87. The Dream Mile provided the seven fastest times of the year, six men under 3:50 tied the world record, and there were best ever times for places 5, 9 and 10. Daham Najim Bashir won in an Asian record 3:47.97 from Bernard Lagat, Daniel Kipchirchir Komen, Alan Webb and Craig Mottram, Oceania record 3:48.98, with a South American record by Hudson de Souza, 8th in 3:51.05. Lashinda Demus buckled just before the line when leading in the 400mh and lost her chance of the Golden League Jackpot, leaving just two three-time winners, Tatyana Lebedeva and Christine Arron.

29-31 **Pan-American Junior Championships**, Windsor, Canada. Top mark was a CAC junior record of 13.46 for 110m hurdles by Dayron Robles. *See Championships section.*

August

6-14 **World Championships**, Helsinki, Finland. Three world records highlighted another great Championships, 22 years after the first in the IAAF series in the same stadium, despite wind and heavy rain that marred several days. The incomparable Yelena Isinbayeva won the women's vault by the amazing margin of 41cm in clearing 5.01, Olimpiada Ivanova walked 20km in 1:25:41 for the fastest time able to be ratified and Osleidys Menéndez added 16cm to her 4-year old javelin mark. Three athletes achieved marvellous doubles: Justin Gatlin, 100m and 200m by huge margins of 0.17 and 0.16 secs, Rashid Ramzi, the first since Peter Snell in 1964 to win both 800m and 1500m at a global championships, and Tirunesh Dibaba with her devastating finishes, the first to win both women's 5000m and 10,000m. The were the first ever 1-2-3-4 sweeps in the men's 100m (USA) and women's 5000m (Ethiopia).

15-20 **World University Games**, Izmir, Turkey. The event suffered by the close proximity of the Worlds for the second WUG running and the absence of an American team detracted from the worth of many titles. However, there were championships records from Björn Otto, 5.80 PV, Kim Smith, 5000m 15:29.18, and Jiang Qiuyan, 20kmW 1:33:13, and perhaps the best performances came in the final round of the women's hammer as Kamila Skolimowska produced a winner of 72.75 against Liu Yinghui's pb 72.51. Wilson Busienei won an amazing triple, with 10,000m, 5000m and half marathon – in that order – within four days. Lyudmila Blonska, her two-year drugs ban recently completed, won the heptathlon with 6297.

16 **Tallinn**, Estonia. Virgilijus Alekna suffered his one discus defeat of the year as Frantz Kruger edged ahead 65.97 to 65.91.

18-21 15th **Bolivar Games**, Armenia, Colombia. 26 championship records were set at this high altitude venue.

19 **Weltklasse**, **Zürich**, Switzerland. Despite running in the height of the rainstorm, which marred all but the start of the meeting, Sanya Richards beat Tonique Williams-Darling (49.30) in a stunning 48.92, a pb by 0.36, for ninth on the world all-time list and the world's fastest since 1996 as well as being, at 20, the youngest ever to break 49 secs. While Tatyana Lebedeva won again, Christine Arron lost her chance of the Golden League jackpot. She ran 10.99, but was well beaten by Veronica Campbell 10.85 and Lauryn Williams 10.88. Several world champions won again, and making up for Helsinki disappointment Maryam Jamal won the 3000m in 8:29.45 and Daniel Kipchirchir Komen the 1500m in 3:30.49. Saïf Saaeed Shaheen won the steeplechase in 8:02.69 despite falling at the final water jump.

20-21 **Eberstadt**, Germany. High jump winners were Vyacheslav Voronin 2.33 and Irina Mikhalchenko 1.91.

21 **British Grand Prix, Sheffield**, GBR. Kelly Holmes was given a rousing send-off on the occasion of her final track race in Britain but an Achilles injury meant that she came in 8th in the 800m in 2:06.69. A UK all-comers record was set in the discus by Virgilijus Alekna at 69.22 and equalled by Kajsa Bergqvist with the world's best high jump of the year, 2.03. Miguel Pate rebounded from just 7.70 in Helsinki to win the long jump with 8.45 and beat Dwight Phillips (8.38) for the second time in 2005. Michael East became the first British winner of the Emsley Carr Mile with 3:52.50.

22- 3 Sep **World Masters Championships**, San Sebastián, Spain. Kip Janvrin set a world M40 decathlon record of 8623 on the Masters tables – or 7525 on the normal IAAF decathlon tables an improvement of 883 on the previous record! Two days later he won the 400m hurdles in 54.68. In the triple jump the great Willie Banks was second with 14.64 to Germany's Wolfgang Knabe 14.78.

23 **Linz**, Austria. IAAF GP. Dwight Phillips returned to top form with an 8.57 long jump and Tatyana Tomashova produced the quickest 1000m time of the year, 2:34.91.

26 29th **Van Damme Memorial, Brussels**, Belgium. Kenenisa Bekele took 2.78 secs off his world record for 10,000m with kilometre splits of 2:40.6, 5:16.4, 7:53.3, 10:30.4, 13:09.4, 15:44.66, 18:23.98, 21:04.63, 23:45.09 and 26:17.53 after a 57.1 last lap. Robert García led through the first 2k in

2:39.85 and 5:16.63, and Tariku Bekele at 7:53.02, 10:29.98 and 13:09.19 for 5000m before Kenenisa took over. He ran the last 1500m in 3:52.6 – the time that Paavo Nurmi had run for his world record at that distance in 1924. A record six men beat 27 minutes and there were best ever times for places 5-6-7. In second, 20 year-old Boniface Kiprop took 30.23 secs off his Ugandan record with 26:39.77 and the third, Samuel Wanjiru, reduced the world junior record from Kiprop's 27:04.00 to 26:41.75 in his first race in Europe. Saïf Saaeed Shaheen just failed in a record bid at 3000m steeplechase, but ended with the third fastest ever time of 7:55.51. Meseret Defar ran an African record and world best for 2005 with 14:28.98 for 5000m; she might have achieved a record but for the pace slowing in the middle part of the race and her last 200m was 28.4. Tatyana Lebedeva maintained her bid for the Golden League Jackpot – and her recovery from her ankle injury – with a triple jump win at 14.94.

27-28 **Sweden v Finland**, Göteborg, Sweden. Finland's men beat Sweden 212 to 197 but Sweden had a clear win 230-179 for women. Carolina Klüft won the long jump with 6.92w and helped the Kallur twins to Swedish 1-2-3 at 100m and 200m; these three also helped Sweden to a national record 43.61 at 4x100m and Susanna completed a treble (11.42/23.32/12.89) by beating Jenny Kallur to win the 100mh, but in that Klüft pulled up with an injury. Robert Kronberg won the 110mh for the eighth time in nine years and Anna Söderberg won the discus for the 12th time since 1992. This annual match was first held in 1925 and its popularity remains with over 20,000 spectators each day.

28 **Banská Bystrica**, Slovakia. Seven meeting records from 13 events were headed by Yipsi Moreno, who achieved a season's best of 74.95 as four women beat 70m in the hammer.

28 **Rieti**, Italy. The 35th edition of this GP maintained its reputation for super times with three world-leading marks in the middle distance races – plus a meeting record 5.96 by Brad Walker in the pole vault. Wilfred Bungei ran 1:43.70 for 800m, six women, headed by Maryam Jamal 3:56.79, broke 4 minutes for 1500m and Bernard Lagat won the men's 1500m in 3:29.30 for the first 2005 sub-3:30 time and a US record to beat Sydney Maree's 3:29.77 of 1985. Ten of the first 13 in this race set pbs. Dorcus Inzikuru maintained her clear superiority at 3000m steeplechase with a 9:16.46 win (record six women under 9:40) and Sileshi Sihine took over 11 secs off his 3000m pb to win by a huge margin in 7:29.92.

30 **Rovereto**, Italy. EAA Permit. In 800m races Youssef Saad Kamel clocked the year's second fastest time with 1:43.96, while Janeth Jepkosgei, who hadn't broken 2 min before 2005, set a Kenyan women's record 1:57.82.

September

1-4 **African Junior Championships**, Radès, Tunisia. Kabelo Kgosimang won the high jump, setting Botswana records at 2.06, 2.10, 2.12, 2.14 and 2.16! *See Championships section for winners.*

1-4 **Asian Championships**, Inchon, Korea. Asian records were set by Ehsan Hadidi, DT 65.25, and Gao Shuying, PV 4.53, and six more championship records included 13.30 for 110mh by Liu Xiang, 65.15 DT by Song Aimin, and an Asian junior record 800m of 1:44.27 by Majid Saeed Sultan. *See Championships section.*

3 **DécaNation**, Paris (Charléty), France. The format of this novel international match was that eight nations fielded one athlete each in the ten events that make up the decathlon. Russia came out on top ahead of France for whom Vanessa Boslak equalled her national pole vault record of 4.60 and Ronald Pognon and Christine Arron scored quick 100m victories in 10.02w and 10.95. 1. RUS 127, 2. FRA 120, 3. POL 110, 4. USA 103, 5= GBR & ESP 82, 7. ITA 75.

3 **World Athletics Final – Hammer, Szombathely**, Hungary. Ivan Tikhon maintained his unbeaten record with 81,70 and women's winner, Yipsi Moreno was just below her season's best with 74.75. *See WAF results.*

4 **ISTAF, Berlin**, Germany. Tatyana Lebedeva achieved her goal of winning at all six Golden League meetings, the only athlete to do so this year – and thus reaped the huge reward of taking the $1 million jackpot. She won with 14.85 as Yamilé Aldama came, with 14.82, closer to her than any other athlete during the series. A season of great javelin competitions continued as Andreas Thorkildsen threw his fourth Norwegian record of the year (87.75) in the final round to overtake Sergey Makarov 88.14, only for Tero Pitkämäki to end with 89.32. Tim Lobinger thrilled the crowd with season's best vault clearances at 5.83 and 5.93 and Bernard Lagat was delighted to take over 15 secs off his best as he won the 5000m in 12:59.29. Christine Arron took her fifth 100m GL race of the year, as she came from well down on fast-starting Chandra Sturrup to win 11.01 to 11.02, and Daniel Kipchirchir Komen broke 3:30 for the first time in taking his fourth GL win of the season, running the world's second fastest time of the year 3:29.72. *See Championships section for all Golden League event winners.*

4 **Russian Challenge**, Moscow, Russia. There was a men's win for USA 54-42 and a women's win for Russia 101-56 in this mini-international.

4 **Tilburg**, Netherlands. Haile Gebrselassie took 21 secs off the best time for 10 miles on the roads with 44:24. His 5k splits were 13:46, 27:35 and 41:22 – seven secs better than the world record. The course was nearly a complete loop.

9-10 3rd **IAAF World Athletics Final**, Monaco. Although once again there were few spectators, there were 15 new meeting records, testimony to the standard of competition, excellent prize money and near-perfect conditions. Amongst these Tyree Washington ran 400m in 44.51 – from a previous 2005 best of 45.02, Adam Nelson added 19cm to his season's best with 21.92 in the shot and the surprise world high jump champion Victor Moya set a pb at 2.32 before sealing his victory with 2.35. Another great javelin competition was won by Tero Pitkämäki with 91.33 from Andreas Thorkildsen, Norwegian record 89.60, and Meseret Defar won the 3000m/5000m double. Three women, Dorcus Inzikuru, Kajsa Bergqvist and Yelena Isinbayeva maintained unbeaten season's records at their events. At the World Athletics Gala held after the meeting, Kenenisa Bekele and Yelena Isinbayeva were announced as the 2005 Athletes of the Year, with awards for the Performances of the Year going to Justin Gatlin and Tirunesh Dibaba for their double World triumphs. Harry Akines-Aryeetey, World Youth 100m & 200m champion, was awarded the Rising Star Award and Wilson Kipketer and Lasse Viren were honoured for lifetime achievements.

11 **European 100km Championship**, Winschoten, Netherlands. *See Championships section for medallists.*

11 **Rotterdam**, Netherlands. Samuel Wanjiru ran 59:16 for half marathon, taking a second off the world record that Paul Tergat had set in Milan in 1998.

15-18 14th **Arab Championships**, Radès, Algeria. Maryam Jamal won a treble with 800m, 1500m and 5000m. *See Championships section.*

17 **Shanghai**, China. Liu Xiang had a big win over Allen Johnson, 13.05 to 13.20, at the inaugural Grand Prix here watched by a crowd of c.40,000. Dwight Phillips won the long jump with 8.39 but was given a strong challenge by Ignisious Gaisah, whose fourth round 8.34 tied his Ghanaian record. Kenenisa Bekele won the 3000m in 7:36.36 as his brother Tariku was 2nd in a pb 7:36.63.

17-18 **Talence**, France. Roman Sebrle's 8326 decathlon win ensured him success in the IAAF Combined Events Challenge for 2005. Eunice Barber, despite an injured right leg at the start of day two, won the women's heptathlon with 6675 by 397 points from Kelly Sotherton and Lyudmila Blonska, but she fell just 11 behind Carolina Klüft's three meeting total for the overall Challenge title. Sotherton beat Blonska here by being ahead in five of the seven events.

18 **Great North Run, Newcastle to South Shields**, GBR. Zersenay Tadesse, 59:05, took a second off the world best for half marathon on an 'aided' course, in this case 30.5m downhill, unacceptable for records. Tadesse and Dejene Berhanu reached 5k in 13:34 and 10k in 27:38, but Tadesse went away with 7th and 8th miles in 4:15 and 4:17. He slowed to 15k in 41:27 and 10M 44:34 and at 20k his 56:03 was 15 sec better than Tergat when he ran 59:06 at Lisbon in 2000. Berhanu was 2nd 60:44 and Hendrick Ramaala 3rd 62:25. Derartu Tulu was first woman in 67:33 from Werknesh Kidane 68:09 and Jelena Prokopcuka 68:11 with Edith Masai improving her W35 world best to 68:19.

18 **Philadelphia**, USA. Deena Kastor took 41 sec off Joan Benoit's 1984 US record with 67:53 for half marathon.

19 **Yokohama**, Japan. A win streak of 19 was ended as a tired Yelena Isinbayeva failed to clear her opening height of 4.50. Allyson Felix improved her 100m best from 11.14 to 11.05 and Liu Xiang had a clear hurdles win in 13.08.

24 **Fifth Avenue Mile**, New York. Craig Mottram surged past Alan Webb over 100m from the finish and won this road race, once again a glamour event, in 3:49.9 to 3:51.4.

25 **Berlin Marathon**, Germany. In her first marathon since winning the 2004 Olympic title, Mizuki Noguchi ran an Asian record 2:19:12, winning by a huge margin from Luminita Zaituc 2:27:34. Noguchi set world records at 25k 1:22:13 and 30k 1:38:49 (Paula Radcliffe had run faster times in London, but that course is slightly downhill to 25k – OK overall). Kenyans, led by Philip Manyim 2:07:41, took the first five places in the men's race. There were 30,506 finishers.

25 **World Mountain Running Trophy**, Wellington, New Zealand. Jonathan Wyatt took the men's title for a record fifth time. Italy won the senior men's team title for the 13th successive year and the senior women's for the 5th year in a row. *See Championships section.*

October

1 **World Half Marathon Championships**, Edmonton, Canada. Fabiano Joseph won in 61:08, but he was lucky because Qatar's Mubarak Hassan Shami (the former Richard Yatich of Kenya) made the elementary error of celebrating too soon and was pipped at the post by a second. Yonas Kifle was 3rd in 61:11, and Sileshi Sihine, 4th in 61:14, led Ethiopia to the team title. Constantina Tomescu dominated the women's race to win by 1:02 in 69:17 and led Romania to team victory.

1-2 **South American Junior Championships**, Santa Fé, Argentina. *See Championships section for winners.*

9 28th LaSalle **Chicago Marathon**, USA. Kenyan domination reached new levels as they took the top ten placings with five men inside 2:08. Felix Limo 2:07:02, Ben Maiyo 2:07:09 pb and Daniel Njenga 2:07:14 with the 2004-05 winner Evans Rutto 4th in 2:07:28. Deena Kastor looked certain to break her American women's record of 2:21:16 before slowing

drastically in the last mile and only just hanging on in 2:21:25 ahead of Constantina Tomescu's Romanian record 2:21:30. Kastor passed 25k in 1:21:57 and 30k in 1:38:29, faster than Mizuki Noguchi's splits in Berlin (1:22:13 & 1:38:49), but as the distance markers were not certified the times cannot be ratified as world records.

16 ING **Amsterdam Marathon**, Netherlands. Haile Gebrselassie ran the world's quickest time of the year and a course record, knocking 15 sec off his own Ethiopian record with 2:06:20. He was on world record schedule through 10k in 29:39, 20k in 58:49 and halfway in 62:03, but he slowed thereafter through 30k in 1:28:57, 25k 1:43:50 and 40k 1:59:16.

16 **Beijing Marathon**, China. Despite a sore knee Sun Yingjie ran 2:21:01, the third fastest marathon of 2005 by a woman to win for the fourth successive year, but only just managed to shake off Zhou Chunxiu, whose 2:21:11 took two minutes off her pb and was her fourth sub-2:30 marathon of the year. Benson Cherono finished in 2:06:55, but he ran 800m short due to a mistake by the lead car in sight of the National Stadium where the race ended; the competition management decided to declare him the winner anyway because of his big lead.

16 IAU **European 50km Trophy**, Palermo, Italy. Inaugural event. Winners of the IAU 50km challenge trophy were determined on the aggregate time from one of the nine qualifying races and this final and the men's trophy went to Sandor Barcza, runner-up to Oleg Kharitonov here. The women's winner was Heather Foundling-Hawker in just her second 50km race. *See Championships section for medallists.*

17-22 10th **Chinese National Games,** Nanjing. Just one day after their fast marathons Sun Yingjie and Zhou Chunxiu came 2nd and 3rd in the 10,000m in 31:03.90 and 31:09.03, behind Xing Huina 31:00.73. Xing then ran in the 1500m, and reduced her best from 4:09.01 to 4:03.98, but she was disqualified for obstructing 19 year-old Liu Qing over the final 200m. Both Sun and Xing ran heats and final of the 5000m, Xing going on to an easy win in the final, and Liu ran 1:59.74 for 800m. But Sun tested positive for drugs and was disqualified – claiming later her drink had been spiked. The greatest depth of top-class marks came in the walks. In the men's 50k, Yu Chaohong broke the Asian record with 3:36:06, just ahead of Zhao Chenliang 3:36:13. 18 year-old Bai Yanmin won the women's 20k by 37 secs in 1:27:37 with six women under 1:30. Many more brilliant performances by young athletes were headed by 16 year-old Li Gaobo's win in the 20k in 1:18:22, just 15 secs short of the world youth record that he had set at Cixi in April, as he led three other men under 1:20, and two world junior records: Ni Liang 3:41:30 in the 50k walk and Wang Xing (also world age 18 best) when 2nd to Huang Xiaoxiao (54.18) in 54.40 in the women's 400m hurdles.

November

1-4 4th **East Asian Games,** Macau, China. *See Championships section for winners.*

6 ING **New York City Marathon**, USA. Paul Tergat and Hendrick Ramaala had one of history's most thrilling races with Tergat just prevailing in a dip finish in 2:09:30. He won a $100,000 first prize plus $25,000 time bonus, but Jelena Prokopcuka exceeded that. For the first time the women's winner was paid more ($130,000), thanks to a special bonus by the sponsors, to which she added $30,000 for breaking 2:25 (2:24:41). Susan Chepkemei was 2nd in 2:24:55. New records were set with 36,856 finishers (24,794 men and 12,062 women) from 37,597 starters.

13-15 1st **Asian Indoor Games**, Pattaya, Thailand. The first indoor meeting ever held in Thailand – in a new air-conditioned stadium.

20 **Nijmegen**, Netherlands. Haile Gebrselassie won the Seven Hills 15k race in 41:57 from Zersenay Tadesse 42:17 and women's winner was Berhane Adere 47:48.

20 **Tokyo Women's Marathon**, Japan. Naoko Takahashi won in 2:24:39 after a two-year absence from marathon running.

20-26 **Colac**, Australia. Yiannis Kouros added 13.6k to the world record for 6 days of running that he had set at the same venue in 1984! He covered 1036.8k in all after 254.4k in the first 24 hours and 590.8k at halfway.

23 **Chiba Ekiden Relays**, Japan. Kenya's men broke Morocco's 1994 world marathon road relay record of 1:57:56 in the Chiba Ekiden in 1:57:06 – although this time was well short of the 1:55:59 by Ethiopia in this race (then five stages) in 2003. The Kenyan team was Josephat Ndambiri 5k 13:24, Martin Mathathi 10k 27:12, Daniel Mwangi 5k 13:59, Mekubo Mogusu 10k 27:56, Onesmus Nyerre 5k 14:36, John Kariuki 7.195k 19:59. Japan was 2nd in an Asian record 1:58:38 and USA 3rd in a North American record 1:59:08. Kenya won the women's event in 2:13:33.

27-30 **South East Asian Games**, Manila, Philippines. *See Championships section for winners.*

December

4 **Fukuoka**, Japan. Dmitriy Baranovskiy won the 59th annual International Marathon in a Ukrainian record 2:08:29.

7-9 **West Asian Games**, Doha, Qatar. *See Championships section for winners.*

11 **European Cross-country Championships**, Tilburg, Netherlands. Sergey Lebed, who has contested all 12 editions of this race, won the men's title for a record sixth time and Lornah Kiplagat won the women's race. Barnabás Bené defended his junior men's title in fine style. As in 2004, four different nations won team titles. *See Cross-country section.*

11-16 5th **Francophone Games**, Naimey, Niger. Times were affected by very hot weather.

ATHLETES OF 2005

By Peter Matthews

In the assessments of the year's form much weight is placed of course on the World Championships, and after that, as in 2003 and 2004 the World Athletics Finals (WAF) brought together most of the world's very best even though some were tired and past their past at the end of the season. The six Golden League meetings were also vital for many events. Honours won, win-loss records and sequence of performances are evaluated.

The rankings concentrate on outdoor form, but I also give rankings where appropriate with indoor form included as well, although with the exception of events such as the high jump the general world level of indoor competition was lower than usual in 2005 and fewer top-class athletes competed.

Pretty much universal choices as athletes of the year were Kenenisa Bekele and Yelena Isinbayeva – just as they were in 2004.

Amongst the top men just three world champions went through the season undefeated: Kenenisa Bekele at 5000m and 1000m, Saïf Saaeed Shaheen at steeplechase and Ivan Tikhon at hammer. Just two men set world records at the standard track and field events – Asafa Powell at 100m and Kenenisa Bekele at 10,000m. Very strong seasons were also compiled by two men who lost just once: Bershawn Jackson in 13 competitions at 400mh and Virgilijus Alekna in 19 at discus and Justin Gatlin won 12 of 14 at 100m and 4 of 5 at 200m, including that brilliant Worlds double. Dwight Phillips won 14 of 16 at long jump and was one of 12 world champions to win again at the WAF.

Kenenisa Bekele overcame the tragic death of his fiancée Alem Techale on 4 January while running with Bekele in a forest outside Addis Ababa, to win the World CC double for the fourth successive year and to have a perfect outdoor season. Years ago the great Haile Gebrselassie identified him as his successor and so it has proved.

Male Athlete of the Year

My selection of the top 10 athletes of 2005 together with the list compiled by international experts polled by *Track & Field News* and those of *Athletics International* readers (who voted for top five) is as follows:

	PJM	T&FN	AI
Kenenisa Bekele	1	1	1
Justin Gatlin	2	5	2,
Saïf Saaeed Shaheen	3	2	5
Virgilijus Alekna	4	4	4
Ivan Tikhon	5	3	6
Dwight Phillips	6	7	-
Rashid Ramzi	7	9	3
Jeremy Wariner	8	8	7
Bershawn Jackson	9	6	-
Bryan Clay	10	11	9
Ladji Doucouré		10	
Asafa Powell		15	8
Adam Nelson		13	10
Tero Pitkämäki		12	
Bernard Lagat		14	

European AA: 1. Alekna, 2. Doucouré, 3= Tikhon & Stefan Holm; 5= Yuriy Borzakovskiy & Roman Sebrle

100 Metres

ASAFA POWELL looked awesome when he ran 9.84 on a cold and damp June evening at Ostrava and it was no surprise when he took the world record with 9.77 in ideal conditions (+1.6 wind) at Athens a week later. But he suffered a groin injury and was unable to prove whether he could take on such form to beat all comers at the World Championships, as he had failed to do in 2004 at the Olympics. He had, however, been narrowly beaten by Justin Gatlin as both ran 9.84w at Eugene five days before Ostrava. Although Powell had the three fastest

Kenenisa Bekele in 2005

29 Jan	BIG	Boston	3000m	2	7:41.42i
18 Feb	GP	Birmingham	2M	2	8:15.49i
19 Mar	WCh	St-Galmier	4.2k CC	1	11:33
20 Mar	WCh	St-Galmier	12.02k CC	1	35:06
29 May	FBK	Hengelo	10000m	1	26:28.72
1 Jul	GL	Saint-Denis	5000m	1	12:40.18
5 Jul	Athl	Lausanne	3000m	1	7:34.57
22 Jul	LGP	London (CP)	5000m	1	12:55.55
8 Aug	WCh	Helsinki	10000m	1	27:08.33
19 Aug	WK	Zürich	3000m	1	7:32.59
26 Aug	VD	Bruxelles	10000m	1	26:17.53 WR
17 Sep		Shanghai	3000m	1	7:36.36

times of the year, Gatlin was clearly the world's no.1 as he went on to win the World title by a record margin of 0.17 secs in 9.88 despite cool (18°C) weather and 0.4 wind in Helsinki, He lost just twice in 14 meetings: third in Doha behind Francis Obikwelu and Shaun Crawford and in his opening race in Europe with 10.03 for 3rd in Lausanne behind Ronald Pognon (French record 9.99) and Aziz Zakari 10.02. Crawford and Leonard Scott were 2-3 at the US Champs but Crawford was way below form through injury at the Worlds, where Michael Frater took a surprise silver medal from Kim Collins, ever at his best in the championships, but who made the final by just 0.01 from Jason Gardener. Zakari came last in the Helsinki final, maintaining his dreadful record at global events, but he had an excellent Golden League season (1-2-2-1-3-6) and was 2nd at the WAF in 10.01 behind Marc Burns (7th Worlds) 10.00 and ahead of the other top Caribbean sprinters, Dwight Thomas (5th Worlds) and Darrel Brown (7sf) with Pognon (8sf) 5th. Brown had beaten Burns for the CAC title after vice-versa in the Trinidad Championships and Thomas's fine finish to the season included wins at Linz 10.00 and Berlin 10.01. Obikwelu was 4th at the Worlds and 6th WAF with Scott 6th and 7th in these races. Overall Thomas was 5-5 v Zakari, 4-3 v Frater and 4-1 v Burns, Frater beat Burns 2-0, Burns was 6-5 v Obikwelu and 5-3 v Scott, and Obikwelu 3-1 v Burns and Collins, and 5-2 v Scott. Gardener ended the season well, 3-0 v Brown, but his best of 10.08 was but 17= on the world list.

Maurice Greene had a win over Crawford in New York, but after a winning 10.01 in his semi pulled up with a left hamstring pull in the final of the US Champs, and is not ranked after nine successive years in the top ten (five as no.1).

Most times at 10.05 or faster: Gatlin 10+1w, Zakari 8+1w, Powell 6+1w, Thomas 4, Brown, Collins & Scott 3+1w, Burns, Frater & Obikwelu 3, Pognon 2+2w. There were 16 'legal times under 10.00 (there had been 33 in 2004).

1. Gatlin, 2. Powell, 3. Thomas, 4. Zakari, 5. Frater, 6. Burns, 7. Obikwelu, 8. Scott, 9. Collins, 10. Pognon

200 Metres

THE USA made World Championships history as Justin Gatlin, Wallace Spearmon, John Capel and Tyson Gay came in 1-2-3-4. Gatlin won by 0.16 in 20.04 and had won his previous 200m races in Monterrey in 20.00 and at the US Champs in 20.04. After Helsinki he won at Sheffield in 20.04 and although he was only 4th at the WAF in 20.25, he is the obvious world no.1. There were seven 'legal' sub-20 second times, three of them coming at the London GP where Spearmon won in 19.89 from Usain Bolt and Gay, both 19.99. Spearmon had run 19.97 at Walnut and then the year's second fastest time, 19.91 to win the NCAA title from Gay's pb 19.93, but he was only 4th at the US Championship in 20.16 behind Gatlin, Gay and Shaun Crawford. Fortunately for him Crawford ceded his World place due to injury. Gay also ran a third sub-20 when he won the WAF race in 19.99 from Chris Williams 20.19 and Spearmon 20.23. Overall Spearmon edged Gay 4-3. Bolt won the CAC title in 20.03 but pulled up injured in the World Final when in fifth place after a good run around the turn in lane one. Williams, 2nd to Bolt in the Jamaican Champs, was 5th in his semi at the Worlds, but ended with excellent series of runs, including a win in Berlin and beat Capel (who ran at the Worlds with a wild card as defending champion) 4-0. Fifth fastest on times was Xavier Carter, only 7th at the US Champs, but with an excellent college season and 3-1 v Gay and 2-2 v Spearmon. As usual many sprinters preferred to contest prestige 100m races, and thus had thin records at 200m. Stéphane Buckland was 5th at both Worlds and WAF, and Christian Malcolm was Europe's fastest with his 20.15 at the European Cup. Tobias Unger was 2m behind then but made the World final (7th) while Malcolm was a poor 7th in his semi.

Most times at 20.30 or better: Gay 9, Spearmon 8, Gatlin 5, Bolt & Carter 4, Walter Dix, Unger & Williams 2.

1. Gatlin, 2. Spearmon, 3. Gay, 4, Bolt, 5. Williams, 6. Carter, 7. Buckland, 8. Capel, 9. Unger, 10. Malcolm

400 Metres

JUST AS he had at the 2004 Olympic Games, Jeremy Wariner showed that is he an athlete of rare talent as he improved his best to 43.93, the world's fastest time for five years, when winning the World title. He won 8 of his 12 races at 400m, including taking the US title in 44.20 from Darold Williamson 44.62 and Andrew Rock 44.80. He lost twice to Williamson in early season and also to Tim Benjamin in London before running out of steam and coming last at the WAF. Williamson was 7th at the Worlds in 45.12 and this was the fastest of his five races in Europe, but Rock went on to take his best down to 44.35 for the World silver medal, 0.09 ahead of Tyler Christopher. Tyler, however, beat Rock in Padua and Zürich and impressed with three Canadian records. Chris Brown and Benjamin were 4th and 5th at the Worlds and both made excellent progress, with the order reversed in 2-3 at the WAF. Benjamin had an overall 3-2 advantage, and he was 3-1 over the Jamaicans Brandon Simpson (World 6th) and Michael Blackwood. The surprising winner at the WAF was Tyree Washington in 44.51; his previous season's best was 45.01 when he won in Rome and he had been only 7th at the US

Champs but he beat Simpson 4-2. Lansford Spence beat Simpson and Blackwood to win the Jamaican title and also won the CAC title, but ran poorly in other major races as the other top ten spots are contested by LaShawn Merritt (4th US Champs), and World semi-finalists Gary Kikaya and Alleyne Francique. Williamson and Blackwood went 2-2.

Most sub-45.00 times: Wariner 8, Benjamin, Rock, Simpson, Tyler & Williamson 5, Brown 4, Blackwood 3.

1. Wariner, 2. Christopher, 3. Rock, 4. Benjamin, 5. Brown, 6. Simpson, 7. Williamson, 8. Washington, 9. Blackwood, 10. Kikaya

800 Metres

RASHID RAMZI completed the first global 800m/1500m double since Peter Snell at the 1964 Olympics, by following his 1500m success with another impressive run as he set pbs at 1:44.30 (semi) and 1:44.24 (final). He had earlier had a good win in Lausanne in 1:44.73, a second ahead of William Yiampoy. However, his only other two 800m races were 4th in Berlin (1:44.99) and 8th in Shanghai following the Championships, so he is very difficult to rank. Until late August it looked as if 2005 might be the first year since 1982 in which there was no sub-1:44 time, but then Wilfred Bungei ran 1:43.70 at Rieti (still the slowest world lead for 23 years) and Youssef Saad Kamel (the former Gregory Konchellah) 1:43.96 at Rovereto. As usual Bungei had an excellent competitive record and after 4th at the Worlds won all his five subsequent races, including Zürich and WAF; he regains the top ranking he had in 2003. Both Bungei and Mbulaeni Mulaudzi were 3-1 against Yuriy Borzakovskiy, but Borzakovskiy and Yiampoy took the World silver and bronze medals while Mulaudzi and Kamel were surprisingly eliminated in the semis.

Mulaudzi's generally good record was also shown by his record of 5-1 v Kamel and 3-2 v Yiampoy and his three of the top six times. Kamel, Borzakovskiy, Yiampoy and Mulaudzi came 2-5 behind Bungei at the WAF. The next best athletes on series of times were the WAF 6-8: Alfred Kirwa, Antonio Reina and Gary Reed, with Reed the only one of this group to make the World finals. Finishing 5-7 in Helsinki were Djabir Saïd-Guerni (just one sub-1:45 time and best placing of 4th). Mehdi Baala (with just four 800m races) and Mansoor Bilal Ali, who, if his age given by Bahrain were to be believed set a world U-18 record of 1:44.34 in June.

Most times sub-1:45: Bungei, Kamel & Mulaudzi 8, Borzakovskiy 7, Reed & Reina 5, Kirwa, Ramzi, Khadevis Robinson & Yiampoy 4.

1. Bungei, 2. Borzakovskiy, 3. Mulaudzi, 4. Kamel, 5. Ramzi, 6. Yiampoy, 7. Reed, 8. Kirwa, 9. Reina, 10. Saïd-Guerni

1500 Metres

RASHID RAMZI showed impressive speed to take the World title after slow early laps had been followed by an ultimately suicidal mid-race burst from Alan Webb. Ramzi had a season's record of three wins and three seconds before a poor 8th at the WAF, but deserves top ranking as he had set a then season's best and Asian record of 3:30.00 in winning in Rome ahead of two men that he was perhaps fortunate not to meet in the World final: Daniel Kipchirchir Komen 3:30.37 and Bernard Lagat 3:31.09. Komen badly misjudged his heat at the Worlds to be eliminated in 6th place, but won four of the six Golden League races and was 5th at the WAF. He was 3-2 v Lagat, ineligible at the Worlds due to his switch to the USA and these two men ran the two sub-3:30 times of the year: Lagat 3:29.30 at Rieti and Komen 3:29.72 at Berlin. Lagat was 2-2 v Ivan Heshko, who followed his World 4th with wins at the World University Games and WAF, where he was followed home by Lagat, Alex Kipchirchir, Sulaiman Simotwo and Daham Najim Bashir (formerly David Nyaga). Webb faded to 9th at the Worlds but had win-loss advantage over Simotwo and Bashir and was 1-1 with Kipchirchir. The top seven mile times of 2005 came at the Bislett Games in Oslo, won by Bashir in 3:47.97 from Lagat, Komen, Webb, Craig Mottram and Tarek Boukensa, who all broke 3:50. Kipchirchir at Eugene and Michael East, Emsley Carr Mile at Sheffield, won the other major mile races. Rui Silva took the World bronze medal and had been a good 5th in Rome in 3:32.91 but was no better than 9th in four big 1500m races post-Helsinki and was beaten 5-1 by both Simotwo and Bashir. Mehdi Baala was third at St-Denis in 3:30.80 behind Komen and Lagat but was 8th in his World semi and had just five 1500m races. Isaac Songok ran just two 1500m races, but broke 3:32 in both (4th Doha and 2nd Berlin).

Most times sub-3:34 or 3:51M: Komen 9+1i, Heshko & Lagat 8, Kipchirchir 5, Bashir, Simotwo & Webb 4.

1. Ramzi, 2. Komen, 3. Lagat, 4. Heshko, 5. Kipchirchir, 6. Webb, 7. Simotwo, 8. Bashir, 9. Silva, 10. Baala.

3000 Metres/2 Miles

THE THREE fastest times of the year were run at Doha where Eliud Kipchoge, Augustine Choge and Benjamin Limo broke 7:30, as did Sileshi Sihine at Rieti (in his only 3000m). Kipchoge also ran the year's fastest 2 miles – 8:07.68 at Eugene, but he was second to Isaac Songok at Hengelo and to Bernard Lagat, in his one 3000m race of the year, at the WAF (with Choge 3rd, Limo 4th). Songok also won at Nairobi and Stockholm (from Limo and Choge), but was 7th in Zürich, where Kenenisa Bekele won from Ali Saïdi-Sief, Craig Mottram and Limo. Mottram won the Sheffield 2 miles in 8:11.27. After two second places indoors, Bekele won each of his three outdoor 3000m races in 7:32-7:36 times and also was timed at 7:32.71 en route to 5000m at St-Denis.

5000 Metres

BEN LIMO took full advantage of the opportunity to sprint to the World title from Sileshi Sihine and Craig Mottram, but, as his winning time of 13:32.55 might indicate, this was a most unsatisfactory race. Limo ran consistently in a full racing programme, with two sub 13-minute runs: 7th at Rome and 3rd at Brussels, but Sihine had just one other 5000m race as he beat a top field at the WAF in an even slower time than in Helsinki – 13:39.40 – and that makes it hard to rank him against the 17 men who broke 13 minutes in 2005 (he ran 13:13.04 in his heat and the second 5000m in the World 10000m in 13:17.77!). Kenenisa Bekele decided not to double in Helsinki, but was by ten seconds the fastest of the year as he won in St-Denis in 12:40.18, and he also won in London in 12:55.55. Mottram was second in that race in 12:56.13 and won his three other 5000m races. Eliud Kipchoge, 4th at the Worlds, won in Brussels in 12:50.22 and was 2nd to Isaac Songok at Rome with Gebre Gebremariam, Augustine Choge, Dejene Berhanu, Boniface Kiprop and Limo making seven under 13 minutes. Songok had won the Kenyan Trial (from Limo, John Kibowen and Kipchoge) and was 2nd to Mottram in Seville, but was only 10th in the Worlds before 3rd WAF (2. Kiprop, 4. Gebremariam). Bernard Lagat is another man who is hard to rank, but he won both his 5000m races, including when running 12:59.29 in Berlin ahead of Limo, Sammy Kipketer and Choge. Kibowen won in Oslo and was 6th at the Worlds, a place behind Ali Saïdi-Sief with Tariku Bekele 7th, Berhanu 8th and Kiprop 11th. Markos Geneti with four (1st Stanford, 7 St-Denis, 9th Rome and 5th Berlin) and Limo, Bekele (including his time en route to the 10,000m WR) and Abderrahim Goumri (2nd Brussels 12:50.25, 4th Seville and 11th Rome) were the only men to run three sub-13:10 times.

1. K Bekele, 2. Mottram, 3. B Limo, 4. Kipchoge, 5. Sihine, 6. Songok, 7. Lagat, 8. Gebremariam, 9. Choge, 10. T Bekele

10,000 Metres

Kenenisa Bekele is top for the third successive year. He ran and won three 10,000m races in 2005: first the fourth fastest ever time of 26:28.72 at Hengelo, then the World title by adding a 13:15.9 second half after 13:52.4 at 5000m for 27:08.33 and finally he took 2.78 seconds off his 2004 world record with 26:17.53 (13:09.4 + 13:08.1) in Brussels. Sihine and Mosop were the other World medallists, and Mosop ran a great 27:51.8 to win the Kenyan trial in Nairobi (worth perhaps a minute faster at low altitude). As usual the Brussels race dominates the world lists with seven (1, 4-8 and 12) of the top 12 times (under 27:05). Four times from Hengelo and one from Prague, Sileshi Sihine 26:57.27, complete those times. Despite the steady start, the World Championships race then provided nine times from 14th to 25th on the world performances list. Boniface Kiprop moved to tenth on the world all-time list with 26:39.77 when 2nd at Brussels after 6th at Hengelo and 4th Worlds, and Samuel Wanjiru set a world junior record of 26:41.75 for 3rd in Brussels after winning four races in Japan. Another Kenyan based in Japan was Martin Irungu Mathathi who had two wins there and was 5th at the Worlds and 3rd in the Kenyan trial (2nd was Charles Kamathi, 12th Worlds). Brussels 4-7 were Nicholas Kemboi (9th Worlds), Sammy Kipketer (4th Kenyan Trial), Mark Bett (only 10k race) and Zersenay Tadesse (6th Worlds). The Hengelo 2-4 were Abebe Dinkesa (26:30.74), who was later 7th at the Worlds, Abderrahim Goumri (8th Worlds) and Bernard Kiprop Kipyego (8th Brussels). Gebre Gebremariam beat Dinkesa for the Ethiopian title and won at Stanford but faded to 15th at the Worlds.

1. Bekele, 2. Sihine, 3. Mosop, 4. B Kiprop, 5. Dinkesa, 6. Mathathi, 7. Wanjiru, 8. Kemboi, 9. Kipketer, 10. Tadesse

Half Marathon

THE JUNIOR Samuel Wanjiru set a new world record for the distance with 59:16 at Rotterdam (from Patrick Ivuti 59:47 and Paul Kimaiyo 60:15) in September and two months earlier had won in 59:43 at Sendai. Paul Tergat had gone even faster on the 69m downhill course in Lisbon, where he won in 59:10, followed under the hour by Robert K Cheruiyot, Wilson Kiprotich and Martin Lel, and on the 30.5m downhill point-to-point course of the Great North Run, Zersenay Tadesse ran the fastest ever time for the full distance of 59:05, leaving Dejene Berhanu well behind in 60:45. The World Championship race was at Edmonton and times were good considering the highish altitude and cold weather as Fabiano Joseph ran 61:08 to just beat Mubarak Hassan Shami (ex Richard Yatich) with Yonas Kifle and Sileshi Sihine (on his debut at the distance) close behind. Joseph had earlier been 4th in Milan in 61:00, behind W Kiprotich 60:11, John Yuda (6th Worlds) and Lawrence Kiprotich, and 6th in Rotterdam in 61:07. Joseph later won in Lagos.

Marathon

AS USUAL we had the Spring and Autumn big city races and the major championship in midsummer, although this year we had more temperate conditions in Helsinki than more most recent World and Olympic races. Again many of the world's top marathoners, particularly the Kenyans, did not contest the World Championships, making ranking comparisons very difficult. Although he missed the world record by 1:35, Haile Gebrselassie ran easily the fastest time of 2005 to win at Amsterdam in 2:06:20. The next fastest was Felix Limo 2:07:04 at Chicago, the race with the greatest depth of top times, as Benjamin Maiyo (also 2nd Los Angeles), Daniel Njenga, Evans Rutto (9th London) and Patrick Ivuti all ran 2:07s. The other races won in such times were: London, where Martin Lel won in 2:07:26 from Jaouad Gharib 2:07:46, Hamburg – Julio Rey 2:07:38, Tokyo – Toshinari Takaoka 2:07:41, Berlin – Philip Manyim 2:07:41 and Rotterdam – Jimmy Muindi 2:07:50 (from Jackson Koech and Felix Limo). Gharib went on to a splendid victory at the World Championships, his winning time of 2:10:10 slowed by the twisting and hilly course, from the surprising Christopher Isegwe, whose other marathon was 2nd at Mumbai in 2:13:29, Tsuyoshi Ogata and Takaoka; Rey was 12th and Muindi (who also won at Honolulu) did not finish. Paul Tergat won the closest ever New York marathon in 2:09:30 by just a metre from Hendrick Ramaala, after these two men had been 8th and 3rd in London. Overall the number of sub-2:10 and sub-2:08 times was at 64 and 12 almost identical to 2004 (59 and 12) but down from the 81 and 25 in the record year of 2003.

1. Gharib, 2. Gebrselassie, 3. F Limo, 4. Lel, 5. Takaoka, 6. Manyim, 7. Maiyo, 8. Rey, 9. Isegwe, 10. Muindi

3000 Metres Steeplechase

SAÏF SAAEED SHAHEEN ranked as the worlds' number one for the fourth successive year and was unbeaten at steeplechase for the third successive year for an unbroken run of 20 victories. He was truly a class apart, winning the World title as he pleased and running four of the world's five fastest times of the year, his best coming at Brussels with 7:55.51, although that missed his targeted world record by just under two seconds. He was, however, run close by Paul Koech in Rome,7:56.37 to Shaheen's 7:56.34. Koech was only 5th behind Ezekiel Kemboi, Brimin Kipruto, Michael Kipyego and David Chemweno at the Kenyan Trials, and although selected for the Worlds was only 7th there. He returned to form, however, to win at the WAF, from the World 2nd and 3rd placers, Kemboi and Kipruto and was 2-2 and 3-4 respectively against these men, with Kemboi 4-0 v Kipruto.

Behind the Kenyans these men placed at both Worlds and WAF: Brahim Boulami 4th and 6th, Simon Vroemen 5th and 9th, Bob Tahri 8th and 5th, and Moussa Omar Obaid 9th and 7th. Boulami won at the Mediterranean Games, Omar Obaid took the Asian title and Vroemen, at the age of 36, made the European record his sole possession with 8:04.95 behind Shaheen at Brussels with Boulami, Kemboi and Tahri 2-5 and Kipruto only 10th. Kipkirui Misoi, Chemweno, Wilson Boit Kipketer and Wesley Kiprotich complete 8 Kenyans in the world top 12 on best times.

The top five rankings are the same as for 2004, except that Koech and Kemboi swap places.

Most times under 8:15: Kipruto, Koech & Shaheen 6, Kemboi, Misoi & Obaid 5, Boulami & Tahri 4, Kiprotich 3.

1. Shaheen, 2. Koech, 3. Kemboi, 4. Kipruto, 5. Boulami, 6. Vroemen, 7. Tahri, 8. Obaid, 9. Misoi, 10. Chemweno

110 Metres Hurdles

FIVE MEN ran the 23 times of 13.10 or better and took the top five places at the World Championships when they finished in the order: Ladji Doucouré, Liu Xiang, Allen Johnson, Dominque Arnold and Terrence Trammell. They stay in that order on win-loss throughout the year with Doucouré, world leader with his French record 12.97, 2-1 v Liu and 4-1 v Johnson, although he showed poor form after the Worlds. Liu was 4-2 v Johnson, Johnson 7-5 v Arnold and 7-3 v Trammell, and Arnold, who hit top form with a pb 13.01 at age 31, 8-4 v Trammell. Johnson completed 11 successive years running 13.05 or faster and ranks in the top five for the 12th successive year. Stanislav Olijar started the year with 13.11 and ended with 13.17 for 4th at the WAF, a place ahead of Maurice Wignall (7th Worlds), but was not quite so good in mid-season and 11th best at the Worlds. The US Champs 4th placer Joel Brown was 6th at the Worlds and 2-2 v Wignall, and in close contention for the final top ten places were Anwar Moore, Thomas Blaschek, Ron Bramlett, Arend Watkins, Matheus Inocéncio (8th Worlds and WUG champion) and Shi Dongpeng.

Most times under 13.30: Arnold 14+2w, Liu 14, Trammell 10+2w, Johnson 10+1w, Doucouré 10, Brown 5, Olijar 4, Moore 2+1w, Wignall 2.

1. Doucouré, 2. Liu, 3. Johnson, 4. Arnold, 5. Trammell, 6. Olijar, 7. Brown, 8. Wignall, 9. Moore, 10. Blaschek

400 Metres Hurdles

KERRON CLEMENT won the NCAA title in 47.56 and the US title in 47.24, the world's fastest time since 1998, but the brilliant 19 year-old missed his stride pattern in both semi and final of the Worlds to finish 4th in 48.18. Way ahead of him, Bershawn Jackson and James Carter (2nd and 3rd in the US Champs) took gold and silver in pbs 47.30 and 47.42 despite the wind and rain in Helsinki. Jackson went on to complete a brilliant season with 12 wins in 13 races including the WAF and 9 of the top 18 times. Dai Tamesue took the World bronze medal, but his overall record is perhaps a little inferior to that of WAF 2nd placer Kemel Thompson. They did not meet as Thompson missed a World final spot by one place. Félix Sánchez, who had dominated world 400m hurdling 2001-04, had his season ruined by injury and ran only twice pre-Helsinki. There, however, he excelled to run a season's best of 48.24 in the semi before breaking down again in the final. Bennie Brazell (2nd NCAA and 4th US) and Bayano Kamani (7th Worlds and 6th WAF) joined Clement, Jackson and Carter in breaking 48 seconds but ahead of them in the rankings come L.J.van Zyl, who followed his World 6th with 3rd at the WAF in a pb 48.11, and Naman Keïta, 5th Worlds and 4th WAF. Danny McFarlane beat Brazell 2-0, but had slower top times and was 5th in his Worlds semi, two places behind Kenji Narisako, who went on to win the World Universities title and finished the season with 48.09 at the Japanese National Sports Festival to join Thompson as 6th equal on the year list.

Most times under 48.50: Jackson 12, Carter 8, Clement 6, Keïta & van Zyl 4, Brazell, Kamani, Narisako & Thompson 3, Sánchez & Tamesue 2.

1. Jackson, 2. Carter, 3. Clement, 4. Thompson, 5. Tamesue, 6. van Zyl, 7. Keïta, 8. Kamani, 9. Brazell, 10. Narisako

High Jump

STEFAN HOLM was unbeaten in 2003 and 2004, but his win streak was ended when he was beaten 2.34 to 2.32 by Aleksey Dmitrik indoors in Glasgow in January. Holm lost three more indoor competitions but then equalled the world best of 59cm cleared above own head with his 2.40 to win the European Indoor title. While always a major contender he was, however, a little below his best outdoors and was surprisingly only seventh at 2.29 at the World Championships, that strange competition in which there were 23 consecutive failures by the eight men left in at 2.32 until unheralded Yuriy Krymarenko popped over at that height, just 1cm below his best. Indoors Yaroslav Rybakov beat Holm 3-1 and Vyacheslav Voronin 5-0 and set Russian records at 2.37 and 2.38 twice, including when he won the European Indoor silver. Outdoors he was 2= at the Worlds and 3rd WAF, but had a best of only 2.33, and was beaten 4-3 by Voronin (8 Worlds, 2 WAF) and 5-3 by Holm (who was 5-3 v Voronin). Moving swiftly to the top was Victor Moya. The Cuban, from a 2004 best of 2.25, improved to 2.28 in January and 2.29 in March, tying that pb for 2= at the Worlds.

Then came 2.30 for 2= at Eberstadt, 2.31 to win at Brussels and 2.32 and 2.35 to win at the WAF; he beat Holm 5-1 to ensure top ranking on outdoor form. The year's best outdoors was 2.38 by both Jacques Freitag (African record) and Andrey Sokolovskiy. Freitag did this in March and won the South African title with 2.35, but again had injury problems and only once (2= at Eberstadt behind Voronin 2.33) jumped 2.30 in an extensive European campaign; he did not qualify for the World final and was 6th WAF. Sokolovskiy excelled to win the year's best competition when he cleared 2.38 at Rome, from Holm and Jaroslav Bába 2.36 and Rybakov 2.33, but had a best of 2.29 (5th WAF) thereafter and was 13th at the Worlds. Bába heads both those 2.38 men on win-loss outdoors and was another who was better in the indoor season. Michael Bieniek had successes at 2.36 and 2.34 by had no support for such levels at major meetings and was 7= at the European U23s at 2.23.

Most competitions over 2.30m (outdoors/in): Rybakov 6/9, Holm 7/7, Bába 3/8, Voronin 7, Sokolovskiy 3/2, Ton 2/3, Dragutin Topic 1/4, Freitag & Moya 4, Bieniek 3/1, Dmitrik 1/3, Pavel Fomenko 0/4, Krymarenko 3, Andrey Tereshin 1/2.

1. Moya (3), 2. Holm (2), 3. Voronin (5), 4. Rybakov (1), 5. Krymarenko (6), 6. Bába (4), 7. Sokolovskiy, 8. Freitag, 9. Ton, 10. Nieto; Topic (10). (Including indoors).

Pole Vault

JUST ONE man cleared 6m in 2005 – Paul Burgess, but after excellent marks in Perth in January-March he had just one more competition through injury. Igor Pavlov topped the world rankings indoors with 5.90 to win the European Indoor title, but was less impressive outdoors apart from his 5.80 to win the Russian title and 5.65 for 4th at the Worlds. Abysmal conditions in Helsinki severely marred the World Championships, but all credit to Rens Blom for winning at 5.80, just 1cm below his all-time best. However, Blom was well behind several men on win-loss; Tim Lobinger beat him 8-3, Toby Stevenson 5-1 and Brad Walker 5-2, although he was 5-1 v Pavlov. Walker, never previously in the top ten rankings, takes top spot; he was US and WAF champion and 2nd at the Worlds. From 5.82 in 2004 he improved to 5.83 indoors, 5.90 in June and 5.96 in August, He beat Lobinger (3 Eur Indoors, 5= Worlds, 2 WAF) 2-0 indoors and 5-2 outdoors . Lobinger ended the year in top form with a 5.93 win at Berlin and had a 4-3 (1 tie) advantage over Giuseppe Gibilisco (5= Worlds and 3= WAF) and 4-1 v Stevenson, who cleared 5.90 twice but who pulled out of the World final at the last minute with a sore hamstring.

Pavel Gerasimov took the World bronze medal at 5.65 and beat Pavlov 3-1, but his best was 5.70 (world list 29=) when he won at the DécaNation meeting. Derek Miles had an important win with 5.85 at the Donetsk Masters indoors, with Pavlov 2nd, Denys Yurchenko 3rd and Walker 4th, and was consistently good indoors and out (5 WAF), but did not compete at the US Champs; he was 5-2 v Stevenson outdoors and 4-2 indoors. Daichi Sawano improved the Japanese record to 5.83 and was 3-0 v Tim Mack, who fell back a little from his 5.85 in May.

Most competitions over 5.80m (outdoors/in): Walker 6/1, Burgess 6, Lobinger 5/1, Miles 3/3, Stevenson 4, Pavlov 1/3, Gibilisco 3, Daniel Ryland & Yurchenko 0/3, Blom 2.

1. Walker, 2. Lobinger, 3. Gibilisco, 4. Stevenson (7), 5. Blom, 6. Miles (4), 7. Gerasimov (8), 8. Burgess (9), 9. Pavlov (6), 10. Sawano. (Including indoors).

Long Jump

FOR THE third successive year Dwight Phillips was clearly the world's best. He won 14 of his 16 competitions and, as in 2004, had a season's best of 8.60. This came at the Worlds after 8.59w in qualifying, and he had eight of the top ten marks of the year. His two losses were both to Miguel Pate (8.35 to 8.25 at the US Champs and 8.45 to 8.38 at Sheffield), but he beat Pate on the other eight occasions they met. Pate was only a non-qualifying 16th at the Worlds, but returned for 2nd at the WAF and was 5-2 v Ignisious Gaisah (2nd Worlds, 4th WAF). Mohamed Al-Khuwalidi jumped 8.44 in April for third on the world list but had only one other competition. Some way behind the top three, the best were Tommy Evilä (3rd World and 6th WAF), James Beckford (9th World, 3rd WAF), and Salim Sdiri (5th Worlds & WAF). Competing less often against the world's best were Joan Lino Martínez and Irving Saladino, 4th and 6th at the Worlds after Saladino had impressed with Panamanian records at 8.22, 8.26 and 8.29 and a windy 8.51 in São Paulo. Martínez beat the US 3rd placer Brian Johnson 2-0, although Johnson has two jumps over 8.30 to the legal best outdoors of 8.17 by Martínez, who, however won the European Indoor title with 8.37. The World 7th placer, Godfrey Mokoena, had top marks of 8.37 and 8.27 at high altitude. Overall standards were down with 27 men over 8.15 compared to 31, 33 and 34 in the years 2002-04.

Most competitions over 8.15m (outdoors/in): Phillips 11+2w, Pate 7/1, Gaisah 5+1w, Johnson 4/1, Evilä 3+2w, Mokoena & Saladino 3+1w, Sdiri 2+1w/1, Beckford 1+3w, Martínez 1+1w/1.

1. Phillips, 2. Pate, 3. Gaisah, 4. Evilä, 5, Beckford (6), 6. Sdiri (7), 7. Saladino (8), 8. Martínez (5), 9. Johnson, 10. Mokoena. (Including indoors).

Triple Jump

CHRISTIAN OLSSON missed the whole season through injury and there was no clear-cut choice for World No. 1. Walter Davis won the World title from Yoandri Betanzos and Martin Oprea, Betanzos won the WAF from Jadel Gregório and Davis, Oprea produced the year's best with 17.81 at Lausanne and Gregório, 6th at the Worlds, had three of the top five performances. Davis won both his indoor events, including his 2005 best of 17.62 and was US champion indoors and out, but was beaten 3-2 by Betanzos and 5-1 by Gregório, with Betanzos beating Gregório in both majors, although Gregório was 2-0 indoors. With good depth of marks and 3-1 v Gregório, Oprea just takes top spot. Behind the top four Leevan Sands was 4th Worlds and 5th WAF, while Alexander Martínez won 7 of his 8 competitions but did not contest the Worlds or WAF and his one loss was 7th in Lausanne. Sands was 2-1 and Martínez 1-1 v Nathan Douglas, whose 17.64 at the AAAs was put him third on the world list but who was only 15th at the Worlds and 6th WAF. Another below his best in those events was Igor Spasovkhodskiy (16th and 7th) but who had good marks and was Russian champion indoors and out with a 3-1 record (0-1 indoors) against Danila Burkenya, who was 2nd in the European Cup to Charles Friedek and 4th WAF. Karl Taillepierre had fewer top marks but was 5th at the Worlds where 7-9 were Kenta Bell, David Giralt and Viktor Yastrebov.

Most competitions over 17.15 (outdoors/in): Gregório 10/1, Oprea 9, Davis 6/2, Betanzos 4+2w, Martínez 4, Spasovkhodskiy 3/1, Douglas & Konstadínos Zalaggítis 3, Sands 2+1w.

1. Oprea, 2. Betanzos, 3. Gregório, 4. Davis, 5. Sands, 6. Martínez, 7. Douglas, 8. Spasovkhodskiy, 9. Burkenya, 10. Taillepierre.

Shot

ADAM NELSON won the World gold medal after silvers at the last two Worlds and two Olympics. Although beaten by Christian Cantwell for the US title, he also had a good series of marks with five of the top ten performances outdoors topped by his 21.92 to win the WAF title. John Godina had the top marks, 22.20 and 21.93 in May following a world-leading 21.83 to win the US indoor title, but injury limited him to two competitions after mid-June and he managed only 19.54 for 17th at the Worlds; including indoors he is in the top five for the ninth year. Rutger Smith took the World silver medal and also the European Indoor silver (behind Manuel Martínez); although he competed only six times outdoors he was 2-0 (and 1-1 indoors) against Joachim Olsen, who won the European Indoors and was 2nd at the WAF although 7th at the Worlds. Olsen had the advantage against top Americans, 4-1 v Rees Hoffa and 3-1 (0-1 indoors) v Cantwell. Hoffa was 2nd at the US Indoors with his year's best of 21.74 and ended the year with WAF 3rd place. He was 5th at the US Champs behind Cantwell, Nelson, Godina and Sheldon Battle, but had a strong season, 4-3 out and 2-1 in v Cantwell and 4-0 v World bronze medallist Ralf

Bartels. Hoffa was 1-1 v Godina outdoors and 1-2 indoors. Cantwell was 5th at the Worlds, a place behind Yuriy Bilonog, and was beaten 3-1 by Bartels, but was 3-1 v Godina (1-2 indoors). Bilonog was also 6th WAF and beat Andrey Mikhnevich (6th Worlds, 7th WAF) 2-1. Jamie Beyer (6th US Champs) had better marks and beat the World 8th placer Ville Tiisanoja at their one meeting. Tomasz Majewski was 9th at the Worlds and then on to win at the World Universities and DécaNation.

Most competitions over 20.80 (outdoors/ in): Hoffa 11/2, Cantwell 9/2, Godina 8/3, Bartels 10, Olsen 8/2, Nelson 5 (all over 21.50)/3, Beyer & Smith 3, Bilonog & Mikhnevich 2.

1. Nelson, 2. Olsen, 3. Hoffa, 4. Smith (6), 5, Bartels (7), 6. Cantwell (4), 7. Godina (5), 8. Bilonog, 9. Mikhnevich, 10. Beyer. (Including indoors).

Discus

VIRGILIJUS ALEKNA is top for the fifth time in six years (and sixth overall) and ever more dominant as he won 18 of his 19 competitions, Frantz Kruger beating him by 6cm at Tallinn in August. Alekna (15) and Gerd Kanter (6) shared the 21 performances over 68m and Kanter, who set an Estonian record at 70.10, was second to Alekna at both Worlds and WAF. Third in these competitions was taken by Michael Möllenbeck (8th WAF) and Zoltán Kövágó (10th Worlds), with Aleksandr Tammert 4th in both and Kruger 6th and 5th. Tammert was 6-2 v Kruger and 3-3 v Kövágó, and Kruger 4-3 v Kövágó.

Lars Riedel (9th World) was 6-2 against his German colleague Möllenbeck. who was also 1-5 against Mario Pestano (11th Worlds, 6th WAF). Ian Waltz and Jared Rome were 1-2 at the US Champs and were 5th and 7th at the Worlds, with Waltz 11-6 ahead in their many clashes. Canadian champion Jason Tunks (8th Worlds) was 3-3 v Rome and 3-2 v Waltz.

Most competitions over 65m: Kanter 22, Alekna 20, Kövágó, Tammert & Tunks 7, Kruger & Riedel 5, Pestano & Waltz 4, Möllenbeck 3, Rome & Varga 2.

1. Alekna, 2. Kanter, 3. Tammert, 4. Kruger, 5. Kövágó, 6. Riedel, 7. Pestano, 8. Möllenbeck, 9. Waltz, 10. Rome

Hammer

IVAN TIKHON missed Yuriy Sedykh's world record by just 1cm when he won the Belarus title with 86.73 after a previous national record of 84.80. His next best was 83.89 to win the World title and he won all his nine competition, all by over a metre. His compatriot Vadim Devyatovskiy was 2nd to him at the Worlds, won the WUG, and was 3rd behind Tikhon and Ola-Pekka Karjalainen (5th Worlds) at the WAF. Karjalainen was 4-3 against Szymon Ziólkowski but 1-2 against Markus Esser, the men who were 3rd and 4th at the Worlds and 5th and 7th WAF. Krisztián Pars (7th Worlds, 4th WAF) was 3-3 v Ziólkowski but down 2-3 to Karjalainen and 2-4 to Esser. Esref Apak was third on the world list with 81.45, but this was nearly 3m better than his next best, and he did not make the World final.

Aleksey Zagorniy was 2nd to Tikhon at the early-season European Throws Cup, ahead of Ilya Konovalov, Esser and Apak, and he won the Russian Winter title at 80.81, but his performances fell back in mid-summer, whereas Konovalov won the Russian and European Cup meetings and was 6th Worlds and 8th WAF.

Libor Charfreitag was twice over 80m and 9th Worlds/6th WAF and Karsten Kobs won the German title (Esser 3rd) but did not compete at the world events. Andrey Skvaruk competed only three times: he won the Ukrainian title with 81.00 and was 10th at the Worlds. Last year's top man, Koji Murofushi, was restricted to just one competition in 2005, taking the Japanese title with 76.47.

Most competitions over 80m/78.50m: Tikhon 8/10, Devyatovskiy 7/13, Charfreitag 2/3, Pars 1/5, Konovalov 1/4, Esser 0/7, Karjalainen 0/5, Ziólkowski 0/4, Kobs & Artyom Rubanko 0/3.

1. Tikhon, 2. Devyatovskiy, 3. Karjalainen, 4. Ziólkowski. 5, Esser, 6, Pars, 7. Konovalov, 8. Charfreitag, 9. Kobs, 10. Skvaruk

Javelin

THREE MEN had a series of marvellous competitions in 2005 sharing the 14 best performances of the year between them, with Tero Pitkämäki (three times) and Sergey Makarov over 90m and Andreas Thorkildsen just below that mark but with five Norwegian records during the year. I rank them in the order that they finished in their final clash at the WAF: Pitkämäki, Thorkildsen, Makarov, with Pitkämäki beating his rivals 8-2 and 6-3 respectively with 12 wins in 16 competitions. Makarov was 5-3 v Thorkildsen but the latter was 2nd and Makarov 3rd with Pitkämäki, the least able it seemed to handle the conditions, 4th at the Worlds, where they were all upstaged by Andrus Värnik with 87.17, two cm short of his season's best.

Värnik also beat the big three in Rome but had some poor competitions, including 8th WAF. The only other man to exceed 85m was Breaux Greer with early season marks at 87.65 and 85.75 but, after 6th in Doha and winning the US title, he was unable to compete through injury and is difficult to rank. Jan Zelezny only competed five times and missed the Worlds but was WAF 4th and beat Mark Frank (1st European Cup, 8th Worlds, 5th WAF) 3-0 and Aleksandr Ivanov (2nd European Cup, 5th Worlds, 7th WAF) 3-1. Frank was 4-2 v Ivanov and 8-6 against German champion Christian Nicolay, who was only 14th at the Worlds. Eriks

Rags was 6th and Ainars Kovals 7th in Helsinki, with Rags 4-1 ahead overall. Although 10th at the Worlds Guillermo Martínez had win-loss advantage, but World 9th Aki Parviainen competed only in a few Finnish meetings after a fine win at 83.79 in Doha.

Most competitions over 84m/82.50m: Pitkämäki 13/15, Makarov 10/13, Thorkildsen 10/12, Värnik 3/5, Zelezny 0/4, Frank & Martínez 0/3, Greer & Ivanov 0/2.

1. Pitkämäki, 2. Thorkildsen, 3. Makarov, 4. Värnik, 5. Zelezny, 6. Frank, 7. Ivanov, 8. Martínez, 9. Rags, 10. Kovals

Decathlon

BRYAN CLAY was only 9th at Götzis with 7961, but won the US title with 8506 and took the World title with 8732, when in better conditions he might have challenged the US record. Roman Sebrle scored 8524 to win at Götzis and 8521 for World silver with a win at Talence (8326) to retain the IAAF Combined Events Challenge. Attila Zsivoczky contested five decathlons with bests of 8480 for 2nd at Götzis and 8385 for World bronze. Kristjan Rahnu had the world's third best score, 8526 at Arles but with 6th and 3rd he was a place behind Aleksandr Pogorelov (3rd Götzis 8429) at both Worlds and Talence.

André Niklaus took sixth on the world list with 8316 for 4th Worlds after 7th Götzis and a win at Ratingen. Although Qi Haifeng (4th Götzis) and Maurice Smith (1st NACAC) had scores of over 8200 they both failed to finish at the Worlds and Romain Barras ranks next due to his consistent form: 1st Mediterranean Games, 5th Götzis and Talence and 7th Worlds the European Cup. Russian and European U23 champion Aleksandr Drozdov (10th Worlds) had four 8000 plus scores. Tomás Dvorák was 8th at the Worlds and won the European Cup First League but dnf at Götzis and was 8th at Talence. Just 19 men exceeded 8000 points in 2005 compared to 23, 22 and 33 in the preceding three years,

1. Clay, 2. Sebrle, 3. Zsivoczky, 4. Pogorelov, 5. Rahnu, 6. Niklaus, 7. Barras, 8. Drozdov, 9. Dvorák, 10. Qi Haifeng

20 Kilometres Walk

JEFFERSON PÉREZ added a second World title to his Olympic gold and three World Cup wins. His supremacy in Helsinki with a win in the South American Champs is enough to secure top ranking, although he was only 64th in Cixi and allowed his compatriot Rolando Saquipay (who had helped him at the Worlds and won at the Pan Am Cup) to finish ahead at the Bolivar Games.

Francisco Fernández took the IAAF World Race Walking Challenge with wins at Rio Maior, Sesto SG and La Coruña before winning the Mediterranean Games title and taking World silver, while Nathan Deakes could but wonder what might have happened if he had not had to withdraw through injury from the Worlds, after four wins including a world-leading 1:17:33 at Cixi and 2nd at Rio Maior. Although his best time of 1:19:44 for World bronze was only 26th on the world list, Juan Manuel Molina had an excellent series of results in eight 20k races. He was 2-2 v Ilya Markov (dq World) and these two were 3-4 in the Challenge. Markov won at the European Cup from Molina and Vladimir Stankin (6th Worlds). Markov and Stankin were 2-3 at the Russian Winter Championships behind Vladimir Parvatkin, who also won the Russian summer title, but who did not finish at the European Cup or World University Games.

Seventeen men beat 1:20 at Cixi, the Chinese race in the IAAF Challenge series and the 2nd man there Zhu Hongjun was 9th at the Worlds with other fast times when 1st at Dudince (from Lu Ronghua and Yu Chaohong, 9th and 6th at Cixi) and 2nd at the Chinese National Games, where the winner was Li Gaobo (4th Cixi) and Yu was 3rd. Yu won the Chinese winter and East Asian titles but was disqualified at the Worlds. André Höhne and Hatem Ghoula were 4th and 5th at the Worlds.

1. Pérez, 2. Fernández, 3. Deakes, 4. Markov, 5. Molina, 6. Stankin, 7. Zhu, 8. Li, 9. Yu, 10. Ghoula

50 Kilometres Walk

MOST OF the top times came in Chinese races, but the top men were undoubtedly Sergey Kirdyapkin and Aleksey Voyevodin who took gold and silver at the Worlds, the reverse of their European Cup places. Yu Chaohong headed the world list with his Asian record 3:36:06 at the Chinese National Games, 13 seconds ahead of Zhao Chenliang with Gadasu Alatan third, and four of the seven times under 3:40 in 2005 came at Nanning in February when the order was Han Yucheng, Xing Shucai, Zhao C and Dong Jimin with Yu 6th and Gadasu 9th. At the Worlds Zhao was 5th as the other Chinese walkers Han (who also won at Dudince from Gadasu) and Xing failed to finish. Alex Schwazer first broke 4 hours with 3:56:59 to win the Italian title and then improved fast to 3:49:42 when 6th at the European Cup and to 3:41:54 for World bronze, when 4th was Trond Nymark, who won his other two 50k races –Tijuana (2nd Jesús Ángel García, 3rd Omar Zepeda) and Nordic Champs. Zepeda was 6th at the Worlds where García was disqualified. Vladimir Kanaykin was Russian champion in 3:40:40 but dnf European Cup and dq Worlds and Mikel Odriozola won the Spanish title in 3:41:57 but was also dq Worlds. Yuriy Andronov was 3rd in the European Cup in his only 50k of the year.

1. Kirdyapkin, 2. Voyevodin, 3. Schwazer, 4. Nymark, 5. Zhao, 6. Yu, 7. Han, 8. Gadasu, 9. Xing, 10. Zepeda

WOMEN ATHLETES OF 2005

Yelena Isinbayeva was clearly the woman athlete of the year with her nine pole vault world records and an unbeaten season until no heighting in her last competition of the year in Shanghai. See the lists for details of all her pole vault marks. The most surprising thing about her in 2005 was that at the end of such a brilliant year, and now with the top eleven vaults ever, she dismissed her career-long coach Yevgeniy Trofimov and announced plans to train with Vitaliy Petrov, the former coach of the great Sergey Bubka.

Of the women ranked at number one, seven had unbeaten seasons at their main event: Tirunesh Dibaba at 10000m and Paula Radcliffe at marathon, but each with just two races at those distances (and beaten at others), Allyson Felix 200m, Dorcus Inzikuru steeplechase, Kajsa Bergqvist high jump, Nadezhda Ostapchuk shot and Carolina Klüft at multi-events (one indoor pentathlon, three heptathlons). Apart from Isinbayeva, world records went at standard events to Osleidys Menéndez, javelin, and Tatyana Lysenko at hammer.

100 Metres

LAURYN WILLIAMS won the world title from Veronica Campbell, Christine Arron and Chandra Sturrup, and Arron won five of the six Golden League races, but Campbell is my choice as number one. She won her other seven finals at 100m including at Zürich in 10.85 from Williams, Sturrup and Arron, a race scuppering Arron's chance of the jackpot, and ended the season with another top win at the WAF from Arron, Williams and Sturrup. These women were very much the top four of 2005, with CAC champion Sturrup running the year's fastest time, 10.84 at Lausanne ahead of Williams and Arron. Sturrup and Arron both beat Williams 5-3. Me'Lisa Barber was a surprise US champion (from Muna Lee and Williams) but confirmed that form with 5th at Worlds and WAF, and Sherone Simpson, 2nd to Campbell at the Jamaican Champs, was 6th in both those races. Lee was 7th and Yuliya Nesterenko 8th at the Worlds. That last represented quite a feat for the Olympic champion as her only previous race was 11.47 for 7th in Eugene, but she showed fairly solid form thereafter. Ivet Lalova had fast wins in her three races: 11.04w, 11.03 and 11.09 but was then sidelined with a serious injury, and there were fast times also for María Karastamáti, 11.03 to win the European U20s, Allyson Felix, an excellent win in 11.05 in Yokohama over Barber, and LaTasha Colander, 11.06.

Most times under 11.10 (11.00): Arron 13+1w (7+1w), Sturrup 11 (2), Williams 7+1w (3), Barber 7+1w (1w), Campbell 6+2w (5+2w), Simpson 4 (1), Lalova 2+1w.

1. Campbell, 2. Arron, 3. Williams, 4. Sturrup, 5. Barber, 6. Simpson, 7. Lee, 8. Nesterenko, 9. Felix, 10. Colander

Woman Athlete of the Year

My selection of the top 10 athletes of 2005 together with the list compiled by international experts polled by *Track & Field News* and those of *Athletics International* readers (who voted for top five) is as follows:

	PJM	*T&FN*	*AI*
Yelena Isinbayeva	1	1	1
Tirunesh Dibaba	2	2	2
Osleidys Menéndez	3	4	5
Carolina Klüft	4	6	4
Kajsa Bergqvist	5	3	6
Paula Radcliffe	6	7	3
Dorcus Inzikuru	7	12	10
Allyson Felix	8	5	7
Tatyana Lebedeva	9	10	8
Nadezhda Ostapchuk	10	8	
Olimpiada Ivanova		18	9
Sanya Richards		9	
Michelle Perry		11	
Meseret Defar		13	
Maryan Jamal		14	

European AA: 1. Isinbayeva, 2. Klüft, 3= Lebedeva & Radcliffe, 5. Bergqvist, 6. Christine Arron

200 Metres

AT 19 YEARS of age, Allyson Felix is beginning to fulfil her enormous potential. She was unbeaten in ten 200m finals, exhibiting the coolness and smoothness of a veteran, and headed the world list with her 22.13 at the US Champs. She was followed at US and World Championships by Rachelle Smith (née Boone), who improved from 22.67 in 2004 to 22.22. Christine Arron was 3rd in both Worlds and WAF, with Veronica Campbell 4th and 2nd in these races. The remaining World finalists were LaTasha Colander, Yuliya Gushchina, Kim Gevaert and Cydonie Mothersill, with the last three finishing in the reverse order for WAF 4-5-6. Mothersill, also CAC champion, beat Gevaert 3-1 and Gevaert was 2-1 v Gushchina. Although she ran only four 200m races, Lauryn Williams comes into contention with 22.27 behind Felix 22.14 at Carson, ahead of 22.39 by the US Champs third placer Colander, and she also beat Mothersill and Gevaert at Sheffield behind Felix. Other fast times from limited races at the distance came from Me'Lisa Barber, 22.37 for 4th US Champs with Muna Lee 5th, and Svetlana Pospelova, 22.39 at the Russian Cup.

The year's fastest times indoors were run by Campbell 22.38 and Arron 22.69, with Ivet Lalova winning at the European Indoors in 22.91.

Most times under 22.80 (indoors): Felix 9+1w, Smith 7, Colander 6+2w, Campbell 5+1w (1), Arron 5 (1), Gushchina 6, Barber, Gevaert & Lee 3, Mothersill & Williams 2+1w.

1. Felix, 2. Smith, 3. Arron, 4. Campbell,
5. Colander, 6. Williams, 7. Mothersill,
8. Gevaert, 9. Gushchina, 10. Barber.

400 Metres

IN 2004 Tonique Williams-Darling had been clearly the world's number one but in 2005 she was challenged hard by the brilliant 20 year-old American Sanya Richards. After trading wins at Eugene and Lausanne, Williams-Darling won the World title in appalling conditions in Helsinki in 49.55 to 49.74, with the World No. 1 of 2001-03 Ana Guevara third in 49.81 and the top European Svetlana Pospelova 4th in 50.11. But Richards ended the year with three successive wins over W-D – as both ran their best times, 48.92 and 49.30, in Zürich and then in Sheffield and at the WAF. After a win at Hermosillo, Guevara had four 2nds and two 3rd places and Pospelova was Russian champion although only 7th at the WAF, where Trotter was 3rd and Amy Mbacké Thiam, Christine Amertil and Monique Hennagan 4-5-6. Trotter and Henderson were 2-3 at the US Championships with Moushami Robinson and Hennagan 4-5. Amertil was 3rd in her World semi-final and was 4-2 v Hennagan, who had win-loss advantage at 5-3 v Trotter and 3-1 v Thiam. Trotter, however was 5th at the Worlds with Olesya Zykina 6th, Henderson 7th and Thiam 8th. Olga Zaytseva was the second fastest Russian at 50.06 and she won the European U23 title and beat Thiam in her only clash. Another to place 3rd in her semi at the Worlds was Natalya Antyukh, who won at the European Cup and was 2-1 against Zykina but 0-3 v Thiam. Svetlana Pospelova won the European Indoor title in 50.41 from Svetlana Usovich.

Most times under 51.00 (50.00): Richards 12 (9), Williams 11 (7), Hennagan 11, Pospelova 8+1i (2), Guevara & Trotter 8 (1), Henderson 5 (1), Amertil 5, Antyukh, Tatyana Firova, Olesya Krasnomovets, Thiam, Zaytseva & Zykina 3.

1. Richards, 2. Williams-Darling, 3. Guevara,
4. Pospelova, 5. Trotter, 6. Henderson, 7. Amertil,
8. Hennagan, 9. Zaytseva, 10. Thiam

800 Metres

ALTHOUGH ONLY seventh fastest of the year, Zuliya Calatayud pulled well clear in the final straight to win the World title and she went on to further major victories in Zürich, Berlin and WAF for an overall record of 9 wins in 12 races. She was 2nd to Svetlana Cherkasova at Kazan and St-Denis and 5th in Stockholm. Tatyana Andrianova ran the two fastest times, 1:56.07 for the Russian title and 1:56.91 in Oslo, both in July, but her form fell away after 3rd in the Worlds. Hasna Benhassi was 2nd in Worlds, Zürich and WAF and beat Andrianova 3-1. Five of the top nine outdoor times of the year came at the Russian Championships where 2-5 were Larisa Chzhao, Svetlana Klyuka, Cherkasova and Olga Kotlyarova. Chzhao had shown impressive form indoors, her five wins including the European Indoor title, and was 6th Worlds and 5th WAF, but Cherkasova was the second best Russian to Andrianova, who beat her 5-2. Cherkasova was 3-1 against Maria Mutola, who was some way below her usual form with a bests of 1:58.49 indoors and 1:58.96 outdoors, but battled hard for World 4th. Mayte Martínez, who was 5th Worlds and 3rd WAF after 2nd European Indoors, had a best of 1:59.40 so lacked the fast times of the top Russians but beat Cherkasova 3-2, Chzhao 4-0 outdoors and Kotlyarova 3-1; she was 1-3 v Mutola. Despite winning the Kenyan Trials race, Janeth Jepkosgei was not selected for the Worlds, but made good progress with six successive wins in mid-season and another newcomer was Jamaican champion Kenia Sinclair. She beat the US champion Hazel Clark (8th Worlds, 7th WAF) 3-1, but was 0-3 v Kotlyarova.

Most times under 2:00: Calatayud 11, Benhassi 9, Cherkasova 9, Mutola 7+2i, Kotlyarova 6, Andrianova, Clark & Sinclair 5, Chzhao 4+4i, Klyuka 4, Jepkosgei, Martínez 3.

1. Calatayud, 2. Benhassi, 3. Andrianova,
4. Cherkasova, 5. Mutola, 6. Martínez, 7. Chzhao,
8. Jepkosgei, 9. Kotlyarova, 10. Sinclair

1500 Metres

TATYANA TOMASHOVA retained her world title but this was her only win in five 1500m competitions, as she fell in Eugene, was 8th in Athens, 3rd in Rieti and 2nd WAF. Maryam Jamal (newly recruited for Bahrain, formerly the Swiss-based, Ethiopian born Tola Kotu Zenebech) improved from 4:07.78 in 2004 to 4:06.60 in May and then to 3:59.13 when winning in Athens and to the year's best of the year, 3:56.79 in Rieti. She showed her tactical naiveté and suffered from being pushed aside in the World final by Yuliya Chizhenko, who was disqualified after finishing second. but her record was 6/7 at 1500m with further wins at Lausanne, WAF and Arab Championships and she was 3-1 v Tomashova. Natalya Yevdokimova was only 6th at the Russian Championships, where Chizhenko won from Olga Yegorova and Yelena Soboleva, but ran the year's 2nd fastest time of 3:57.73 behind Jamal in Rieti and was WAF 3rd. She was 2-2 v Yegorova who took the World silver medal with Bouchra Ghezielle elevated to bronze after Chizhenko's dq. Ghezielle had nipped past Soboleva and Jamal on the finish line. Chizhenko had beaten Maria Cioncan and Ghezielle at the European Cup but was beaten by Ghezielle again at the DécaNation and 4th to 6th at the WAF. Six of the ten sub-4-minute times of 2005 came at Rieti, where Natalia Rodríguez (6th Worlds, 8th WAF), Gelete Burka (8th Worlds) and Chizhenko were 4-5-6, followed by Hind Dehiba (5th WAF), Anna Jakubczak (7th Worlds), Ghezielle and Carmen Douma-Hussar (9th Worlds). The three Russians in 2-3-4 in my rankings retain their positions from 2004. Kelly Holmes, no. 1 in 2004, won her only 1500m races in 2005, one indoors, one out (4:06.52 in Glasgow) but was unable to compete after that through injury.

Most times under 4:04: Chizhenko & Jamal 5, Ghezielle, Yegorova & Yevdokimova 4; Dehiba, Rodríguez, Soboleva & Tomashova 3.

1. Jamal, 2. Tomashova, 3. Yegorova,
4. Yevdokimova, 5. Chizhenko, 6. Ghezielle,
7. Soboleva, 8. Rodríguez, 9. Burka, 10. Dehiba.

3000 Metres

Maryam Jamal ran the two fastest times of the year: 8:28.87 at Oslo and 8:29.45 at Zürich, after two previous Bahrain records, 8:42.84 when 5th in Doha and 8:41.30 at Aix-les-Bains. Meseret Defar won her five 3000m races – the two fastest of the year indoors (8:30.05 Boston and 8:33.05 Birmingham) and at Doha, New York and WAF outdoors. Following her at Doha were Berhane Adere, Gelete Burka and Prisca Jepleting, and in the WAF: Burka, Zakia Mrisho, Isabella Ochichi and Meselech Melkamu. Edith Masai was second fastest outdoors with 8:31.27 in the Paris St-Denis Golden League meeting with Ochichi and Jo Pavey 2-3 and under 8:35 both in this race and in Oslo. Adere was 2nd in Zürich in 8:31.89 with Ochichi and Melkamu also under 8:35.

5000 Metres

TIRUNESH DIBABA completed a scintillating double at the World Championships, running a 58.19 last lap in the 5000m (and 58.4 in the 10,000m) and Meseret Defar, Ejegayehu Dibaba and Meselech Melkamu completed a unique women's 1-2-3-4 for Ethiopia. T Dibaba and Defar, with Berhane Adere between them, had shown sub-60 finishing speed earlier in the Rome Golden Gala meeting (4. Edith Masai, 5. E Dibaba, 6. Melkamu), and in a slightly more slowly run race at the WAF Defar produced a 57.5 finish to beat T Dibaba and Adere. That was Tirunesh's one loss in six 5000m races with a best of 14:32.42 in New York, while Defar and Adere headed the world list with 14:28.98 and 14:31.09 in Brussels, where E Dibaba was 3rd and Isabella Ochichi (8th Worlds) 4th. Xing Huina, Zakia Mrisho and Prisca Jepleting took places 5-6-7 at the Worlds. Xing won both major Chinese races and was 5th in Shanghai behind Defar, Melkamu, Gelete Burka and Ines Chenonge (4th WAF). Masai's run in Rome was her only 5000 race of the year and Jo Pavey, 7th there in 14:40.71 much the fastest by a European in 2005, was ill when she ran in the World final. Russian champion Liliya Shobukhova was 9th and Olga Kravtsova 10th at the Worlds. Kravtsova set Belarus records in beating Paula Radcliffe in the European Cup 1B and twice in Helsinki. Ochichi won the Kenyan Trial with Jepleting 3rd and Chenonge 4th and Mrisho was 2nd in Stockholm (to Irene Kwambai) and Berlin (to Adere) before 7th in Shanghai. Ethiopians take the top five rankings.

Most times under 15 mins: T Dibaba 6, Defar & E Dibaba 5, Adere & Susanne Wigene 4, Melkamu, Mrisho & Ochichi 3.

1. T Dibaba, 2. Defar, 3. Adere, 4. E Dibaba,
5. Melkamu, 6. Ochichi, 7. Xing, 8. Mrisho,
9. Jepleting, 10. Shobukhova

10,000 Metres

TIRUNESH DIBABA made her 10,000m debut at Sollentuna in June, winning in 30:15.67 from her sister Ejegayehu 30:18.39, and Werknesh Kidane ran 30:19.39 at Stanford in May. These times remained the best of the year, with the next fastest nine all coming in the World Championships at Helsinki, where Berhane Adere split the Dibaba sisters for an Ethiopian clean sweep of the medals. Xing Huina, Edith Masai, Kidane, Sun Yingjie, Galina Bogomolova, Paula Radcliffe and Irene Kwambai made up the top ten, all under 31 minutes The only other such times in 2005 came at Utrecht, where Masai won on her track debut from Kwambai. Bogomolova ran 31:04.61 for the Russian title and Xing and Sun were just outside 31 mins at the Chinese National Games, but Sun's positive test there disqualified her from that race and my rankings. The 10th place is thus taken by Kayoko Fukushi, 11th at the Worlds just ahead of Jelena Prokopcuka and winner of two other 10,000m races in Japan. Alice Timbilil beat Kwambai and Masai at the Kenyan Trials in 31:45.4 worth much better at low altitude, but dropped out of the Kenyan Worlds team.

1. T Dibaba, 2. Adere, 3. E Dibaba, 4. Kidane,
5. Xing, 6. Masai, 7. Bogomolova, 8. Radcliffe,
9. Kwambai, 10. Fukushi

Half Marathon

DEENA KASTOR ran the year's fastest time on a course acceptable for records with 67:53 at Philadelphia. although Derartu Tulu ran faster, 67:33, on the slightly downhill Great North Run course when she was followed in 68+ times by Werknesh Kidane, Jelena Prokopcuka and Edith Masai. Susan Chepkemei won on the similarly downhill course in Lisbon in 68:47 and, although she did not contest a half marathon in 2005, Paula Radcliffe ran the first half of the London marathon in 68:27 for the other sub-69 time. Constantina Tomescu won the World title at Edmonton in 69:17 with Lornah Kiplagat and Chepkemei taking the other medals.

Marathon

PAULA RADCLIFFE, recovered from her Olympic trauma, returned to the top with superb wins at London (2:17:42, over five minutes ahead of the 2nd) and at the World Championships (2:20:57, 1:04 ahead of 2nd). Olympic champion Mizuki Noguchi, in her one marathon of the year, won in Berlin in the year's second fastest time of 2:19:12. Next quickest were Sun Yingjie 2:21:01 and Zhou Chunxiu 2:21:11, only for Sun to be discredited by her drugs dq from her 10,000m the following day. Zhou had earlier won in Seoul and at the Chinese Champs and was 5th at the Worlds. Catherine Ndereba won in Boston and was 2nd at the Worlds, and Constantina Tomescu had a splendid year with the World bronze (2:23:19) between 2nd places at London (2:22:50) and Chicago (2:21:30). Deena Kastor won that last race in 2:21:25, ranking lower as it was her only marathon of the year. Jelena Prokopcuka, Susan Chepkemei and Derartu Tulu were 1-2-3 in a splendidly competitive New York race, all having previous good form. Prokopcuka won at Osaka from Mari Ozaki and Harumi Hiroyama, respectively 15th and 8th at the Worlds, Chepkemei was 3rd in London, and Tulu 3rd at Nagano and 4th Worlds. Masako Chiba won at Hokkaido and was third in Chicago, and Yukiko Hara won at Nagoya and was 6th Worlds. Naoko Takahashi won at Tokyo in 2:24:39 in her first marathon for two years.

1. Radcliffe, 2. Ndereba, 3. Tomescu,
4. Prokopcuka, 5. Noguchi, 6. Zhou,
7. Chepkemei, 8. Tulu, 9. Kastor, 10. Hara

3000 Metres Steeplechase

ALTHOUGH HER best of 9:15.04 was well short of the world record of 9:01.59 set by Gulnara Samitova, who did not compete in 2005, Dorcus Inzikuru was easily the top woman steeplechaser, winning all her six races at 3000m, including the four fastest times of the year, and setting a world best of 6:04.46 for 2000m at Milan. The only women to attempt to go with her at the World Championships (1st km 2:57.98) were two with excellent flat race pedigree – Yelena Zadorozhnaya and Wioletta Janowska, but they paid for the pace by fading to 6th and 14th respectively. Yekaterina Volkova ran a much more even pace and gained a lot of ground to take the silver with 9:20.49; she also won the Russian title and was second at Rieti, in which a record six women broke 9:38. Jeruto Kiptum was the World bronze medallist and Janowska ran 9:25 times when 2nd to Inzikuru at both Athens and WAF. The Jamaican pair of Korine Hinds and Mardrea Hyman traded wins and at CAC Champs, Worlds, Rieti and WAF were respectively 2/4/3/6 and 1/8/4/3. Zadorozhnaya, still with much to learn about hurdling, was 5th at both Rieti and WAF with the WUG champion Livia Tóth, 4th and 6th in these races and the experienced Cristina Casandra 7th in both and at the Worlds, and US champion Elizabeth Jackson 9th at Worlds and Rieti and 8th WAF. Salome Chepchumba was 5th at the Worlds and 10th WAF and had a good earlier series of races, including 3rd at Athens behind Inzikuru and Janowska and ahead of Tóth. The number of women under 10 minutes grew to 55 compared to 47 in 2004, 33 in 2003, 26 in 2002, 19 in 2001 and 7 in 2000.

Most times under 9:40: Inzikuru 7 (all under 9:30), Casandra 6, Hinds, Hyman & Zadorozhnaya 5; Chepchumba, Tóth & Volkova 4, Janowska 3, Kiptum 2.

1. Inzikuru, 2. Volkova, 3. Kiptum, 4. Janowska,
5. Hinds, 6. Hyman, 7. Chepchumba,
8. Zadorozhnaya, 9. Tóth, 10. Casandra

100 Metres Hurdles

ALTHOUGH HER season was not perfect (10 wins from 15 competitions), Michelle Perry was a most worthy number one. Never having previously been in the world top ten (best 12.74 in 2004), she had the three fastest times of the year (12.43 and two 12.45s) and won the US, World and WAF titles. Behind her the top women were closely matched, with Brigitte Foster-Hylton and Deloreen Ennis-London 3/2 and 2/3 at Worlds and WAF and with the former having a 5-3 win-loss advantage. Ennis-London was 3-2 v Joanna Hayes, who was the world's second fastest (12.47 when 2nd to Perry in New York) and US 2nd but who fell while challenging for a medal in the World final and was 6th WAF. Top of the next group was Kirsten Bolm (4th Worlds and 8th WAF). She was 3-1 v Perdita Felicien and 2-1 v Susanna Kallur and Anjanette Kirkland, who was only 5th at the US Champs but ran well in Europe and, like Kallur, was 3-3 v Felicien but 4-0 v Kallur. Lacena Golding-Clarke was 4th at the Jamaican Championships but both she and French champion and European Cup winner Linda Khodadin had better times than Mariya Koroteyeva (5th Worlds). Kallur and Glory Alozie were unfortunate to run in the third semi at the Worlds where a strong adverse wind made making qualifying spots on time impossible, but they were 4th and 5th at the WAF. Virginia Powell had an excellent college season in the USA, leading to taking the NCAA title, and was 3rd in the US champs, but fared less well in Europe.

Most times at 12.70 or faster: Perry 14, Foster-Hylton 9, Hayes & Kirkland 5, Ennis-London 4, Felicien 3, Bolm 2+1w.

1. Perry, 2. Foster-Hylton, 3. Ennis-London, 4. Hayes, 5. Bolm, 6. Felicien, 7. Kirkland, 8. S Kallur, 9. Golding-Clarke, 10. Khodadin

400 Metres Hurdles

YULIYA NOSOVA-PECHONKINA has disappointed at some major events in the past, but excelled with a clear win in 52.90 at the 2005 Worlds. Her 53.05 at Tula and 53.01 for the Russian title gave her the three fastest times of the year and in all she won 6/8, as post-Helsinki she won in Zürich but was 3rd in Brussels to the World silver and bronze medallists Lashinda Demus and Sandra Glover and was beaten again by Demus, with Glover 3rd, at the WAF. That gave Demus a 2-1 win-loss record against Pechonkina and she had an 8-1 record against Glover, who again had a superbly consistent season. Jana Pittman was next fastest at 53.44 behind the top three, but injury ended her season in early July after just six races, and then with a Polish record 53.96 came Anna Jesien, who was 1-1 v Pittman and 4th to the top three at Worlds, Zürich, Brussels and WAF. The remaining World finalists (5-8) were Huang Xiaoxiao, Andrea Blackett, Tatyana Tereshchuk and Malgorzata Pskit. Huang won all her other races in Asia, including the Asian and East Asian and two Chinese titles, and Blackett was WAF 5th. Running significantly better marks than the World 7-8 were two Americans Shauna Smith (1st NCAA and 2nd US) and Sheena Johnson (2-2 against each other) and Surita Febbraio (sf Worlds, 8th WAF). Johnson was only 4th at the US Champs but beat Tereshchuk 4-2 and was 1-1 against Febbraio. Pskit was consistent at just over 55 seconds and beat Tereshchuk 4-2, including 6th to 7th at WAF. Olympic champion Faní Halkía did not compete in 2005.

Most times under 54.0/55.0: Pechonkina 9/10, Demus 8/15, Glover 4/19, Pittman 2/3, Jesien 1/12, Smith -/4, Febbraio & Huang -/3.

1. Pechonkina, 2. Demus. 3. Glover, 4. Jesien, 5. Pittman, 6. Huang, 7. Blackett, 8. Smith, 9. Febbraio, 10. Johnson

High Jump

IT WAS a delight to see Kajsa Bergqvist back in action after her career-threatening Achilles tendon injury. With Hestrie Cloete taking at least a sabbatical and Yelena Slesarenko competing just three times (1.85, 1.89 and 2.00 to win the Russian title), Bergqvist dominated, winning all her 12 competitions, seven of then at 2.00 or more with a best of 2.03 at Sheffield and regains the top ranking she had in 2000 (including indoors) and 2002. Just four women cleared 2.00m in 2005 compared to 13 in 2004; Anna Chicherova twice indoors, including 2.01 for the European Indoor title with an outdoor best of 1.98, and Chaunte Howard broke new ground with three clearances at 2.00, including for the World silver medal behind Bergqvist's 2.02. Emma Green took a surprise World bronze medal at 1.96, a height also cleared in Helsinki by Chicherova, with Vita Palamar, Tia Hellebaut and Viktoriya Styopina placing 5-6-7 at 1.93. Green improved to 1.97 when winning the Swedish title and also won the European U23 silver medal behind Tatyana Kivimyagi. Palamar and Iryna Mikhalchenko (12th Worlds) tied for WAF second at 1.93, with Howard, Styopina and Kivimyagi 4-5-6 at the same height. Venelina Veneva and Kivimyagi tied for fifth on the world outdoor list with 1.98, but Ruth Beitia jumped 1.99 indoors for the European Indoor silver, 2cm ahead of Veneva (bronze). Beitia was 2nd at the DécaNation meeting with 1.97 behind Chicherova 1.99, but was below 1.90 at Worlds and WAF. Blanka Vlasic had just two competitions, with 1.95 for the Croatian title. Adding indoor form makes the ranking of those 4th to 10th even more equal than on outdoor form alone.

Most competitions over 1.97m (indoors/out): Bergqvist 10, Chicherova 2/3, Howard 4, Veneva 1/1.

1. Bergqvist, 2. Howard, 3. Chicherova, 4. Green, 5. Palamar (6), 6. Veneva (4), 7. Mikhalchenko, 8. Kivimyagi (10), 9. Beitia (9), 10. Styopina (8). (Including indoors).

Pole Vault

YELENA ISINBAYEVA added four world records indoors (4.87 to 4.90) and five outdoors (4.93 to 5.01) to add to her rapidly growing collection. She achieved the historic 5m clearance at the London Grand Prix and added a centimetre for the World title, when she was an astonishing 41 cm ahead of the silver medallist Monika Pyrek. In all she won 4/4 indoors and all 11 outdoors until a no-height at Yokohama. Anna Rogowska was only 6th at the Worlds and 7th WAF with 4.35, but had much the next best set of marks, setting Polish records twice indoors at 4.75 and outdoors at 4.80, 4.82 and 4.83. She beat Pyrek 4-2 indoors, including when they were 2nd and 3rd to Isinbayeva at the European Indoors, but Pyrek won 5-2 outdoors and was splendidly consistent, including 2nd at Worlds and WAF as well as beating Rogowska to win Polish titles indoors and out. Pavla Hamácková, Tatyana Polnova and Gao Shuying were World 3-4-5, all at 4.50, and the same height was enough at the WAF for Polnova 3rd and Vanessa Boslak (World 8th) 4th. Gao won the Asian title with a season's best 4.53. Carolin Hingst cleared 4.65 for European Indoor 4th with two other indoor events at 4.60, but was 10th at the Worlds and had a best of 4.50 (2nd European Cup to Rogowska) outdoors. Polnova (indoors) and Tracy O'Hara, Mary Sauer, Stacy Dragila and Boslak (outdoors) had 4.60 bests. Dragila won the US title but just missed the World final despite clearing

4.40; she was, however, 2-1 (plus 1-0 indoors) v Dana Ellis (6= Worlds). Ellis went 4-4 (1 tie) v Hamácková and 3-3 v Jillian Schwartz (who beat O'Hara 7-3 outdoors). Svetlana Feofanova missed the outdoor season through injury after 4.70 and 4.53 in her indoor competitions.

Most competitions over 4.50m (outdoors/ in): Pyrek 14/10, Isinbayeva 11/4, Rogowska 9/8, Polnova 6/5, Boslak 5, Dragila 3/2, Hamácková & Schwartz 3/1, Hingst 1/4.

1. Isinbayeva, 2. Pyrek, 3. Rogowska, 4. Polnova, 5. Boslak (6), 6. Hamácková (5), 7. Gao, 8. Dragila, 9. Ellis (-), 10. Schwartz (-). Hingst (9), Feofanova (10). (Including indoors)

Long Jump

TATYANA KOTOVA jumped 7.20w in Madrid but Irina Simagina (twice) was the one woman to jump over 7m without excess wind in 2005. Simagina won her first five meetings, including at the European Cup, but injuries curtailed her season and she was not fully fit when reappearing for 7th 6.47 at the WAF. In her absence the 19 year-old Tianna Madison overcame adverse conditions to win the World title from Kotova and Eunice Barber. Madison had a best of 6.60 in 2004 and improved that to 6.69, 6.71 and 6.76 indoors and to 6.82 and 6.92w in the USA with 6.83 in qualifying and 6.89 in the final of the Worlds. She lost just two of her ten competitions, both to Grace Upshaw – when both jumped 6.70 at the US Champs and by 2cm in Stockholm. Upshaw herself was 7th at the Worlds and 3rd WAF. Kotova's WAF win gave her 7 wins in 8 competitions. Carolina Klüft led the world indoor list at 6.84 and jumped 6.87 to Barber's 6.75 in the World heptathlon and won 5/6 at long jump. Yargelis Savigne successfully doubled long and triple jumping, and at this event won the CAC title and was 4th at the Worlds, a place ahead of Anju Bobby George, who showed her consistency with 6.66 there and 6.65 to win the Asian title before a season's best 6.75 for WAF 2nd. Upshaw was 3-2 v George. Oksana Udmurtova had three performances over 6.80m, but ranks lower off her 6th at both Worlds and WAF. She was 2-2 v Upshaw and 2-1 v Lyudmila Kolchanova, the World University Games champion who beat Upshaw in their one meeting. Concepción Montaner was third on the world list at 6.92, but her next best was 6.67 and she was 11th at the Worlds. Last year's number one, Tatyana Lebedeva, had just two long jump competitions.

Most competitions over 6.70m (outdoors/ in): Kotova 7 +1w, Simagina 5, Savigne 4+1w, Udmurtova 4, Madison 3/2, Barber 3+2w, Kolchanova 3+1w, Yuliya Zinovyeva 3, Klüft 2+2w/1, Upshaw 2+1w.

1. Kotova, 2. Madison, 3. Simagina, 4. Klüft, 5. Barber, 6. Savigne, 7. Upshaw, 8. George, 9. Udmurtova, 10. Kolchanova.

Triple Jump

TATYANA LEBEDEVA started her season with 15.11 at the St-Denis meeting, but then got steadily worse! She followed with 15.05 in Lausanne and 15.03 in Rome, but thereafter had 14.85-14.94 marks to win. She also aggravated an Achilles tendon injury at Oslo and this caused her to drop out of the World final (after qualifying with a modest 14.15), but she came back and magnificently held off all challengers to take sole possession of the Golden League $1 million jackpot. She had seven wins in all before finishing 3rd cm behind the 14.79 of Hrysopiyi Devetzí at the WAF. In Lebedeva's absence Trecia Smith won the World title by a 29 cm margin with 15.11, but she was beaten 7-0 by Lebedeva. Yargelis Savigne and Anna Pyatykh were 2nd and 3rd at the Worlds and 3rd and 5th at WAF (Smith 4th), with Savigne beating Pyatykh, who won at the European Cup for the fourth successive year, 4-0, with 4-3 for Pyatykh over Devetzí and Devetzí over Yamilé Aldama (4th Worlds/6th WAF). Aldama was 5-1 v Magdelin Martínez (8th/7th), who in turn was 4-1 v Baha Rahouli (7th/8th). Kéne Ndoye was 6th at the Worlds, three places ahead of Huang Qiuyan, but the latter had better marks, as did European U23 champion Simona La Mantia (dnq 14th Worlds). Viktoriya Gurova jumped 14.74 to win the European Indoor title from Martínez, but was 10th Worlds and had an outdoor best of 14.38. Overall standards were well down on 2004.

Most competitions over 14.60m (outdoors/ in): 11+1w, Lebedeva 8, Pyatykh 7, Devetzí 4, Savigne 3, Rahouli 2+2w, Aldama 2.

1. Lebedeva, 2. Smith, 3. Savigne, 4. Pyatykh, 5. Devetzí, 6. Aldama, 7. Martínez, 8. Rahouli, 9. Huang (9), 10. Ndoye (-). Gurova (10) (Including indoors).

Shot

NADEZHDA OSTAPCHUK had the top five marks of the year, her leading 21.09 compared to the next best of 20.24 by Svetlana Krivelyova, and she won all her ten competitions, the European Indoors and nine outdoors, with an 87cm winning margin at the Worlds and 89cm at WAF. Olga Ryabinkina and 20 year-old Valerie Vili won silver and bronze at the Worlds with Vili 2nd and Ryabinkina 4th WAF and Vili 2-1 ahead. Nadine Kleinert (5th Worlds, 6th WAF) was the third woman over 20m and beat Krivelyova 3-1, but as in 2004 the latter (4th Worlds) lost form though injury at the end of the year. Olympic champion Yumileidi Cumbá could not match her 2004 form but was consistent up to her best of 19.06 and was 6th Worlds and 7th WAF. She had a 3-2 advantage over Natalya Khoroneko, who won the World University Games title between 8th Worlds and 3rd WAF. Second at the WUG was World 7th placer Li

Meiju, who won the Asian, East Asian and both Chinese titles. 21 year-old Petra Lammert had improved from an outdoor best of 17.16 to 18.01 indoors in December 2004 and maintained that progress up to 19.81 in 2005, when she won the European U23 title and was 5th WAF, but she was 15th in qualifying at the Worlds. Completing the rankings is World 10th and WUG 3rd Misleydis González, just ahead of the Germans Astrid Kumbernuss, retiring after a most distinguished career (14 years in the top ten, four top), and Christina Schwanitz, World 9th and European U23 2nd. Kryzstyna Zabawska was 2nd at the European Indoors (Ryabinkina 3rd. Lammert 4th) but only had three outdoor competitions (in May).

Most competitions over 19m: Vili 12, Ostapchuk 10+1, Kleinert 6, Ryabinkina 5, Krivelyova 3, Khoroneko 2.

1. Ostapchuk, 2. Vili, 3. Ryabinkina, 4. Kleinert, 5. Krivelyova, 6. Cumbá, 7. Khoroneko, 8. Li, 9. Lammert, 10. González. Kumbernuss (10). (Including indoors)

Discus

AT HER eighth World Championships, Franka Dietzsch regained the title she won in 1999 and had a fine season with 12 wins and four second places in her 16 competitions. Those four losses were all to World silver medallist Natalya Sadova, who had a 4-2 advantage overall, won the Russian and WAF titles and had slightly the better marks. Vera Cechlová (3rd Worlds, 4th WAF) was a clear third although beaten 7-0 by Dietzsch and 5-2 by Sadova. Beatrice Faumuina was 4th and Nicoleta Grasu 5th at the Worlds with Grasu also 5th WAF and 2-1 v Faumuina, who only competed three times in Europe. Olena Antonova was 4th on the world list with 65.89 and 2nd to Dietzsch, with Polish champion Marzena Wysocka 3rd and Grasu 4th, at the European Cup, but after a series of good marks fell to below 60m at Worlds (8th) and WAF (7th). Song Aimin was only 10th at the Worlds but excelled in Chinese meetings, was twice over 65m and won Asian and East Asian titles. She was also 2nd at the World University Games to Wioletta Potepa (dnq 19th Worlds, 6th WAF). Aretha Thurmond had a disaster (with just 47.15) at the Worlds, but came back with 3rd at the WAF. Cuban champion Yania Ferrales takes the final ranking spot with a 2-0 advantage over Potepa and better marks than the youngest contender 23 year-old Dragana Tomasevic, Mediterranean Games and Balkan champion and 3rd WUG.

Most competitions over 63m: Dietzsch 15, Sadova 11, Cechlová 10, Song 6, Wysocka 4, Antonova, Ferrales, Grasu & Thurmond 3, Faumuina 2.

1. Sadova, 2. Dietzsch, 3. Cechlová, 4. Grasu, 5. Faumuina, 6. Antonova, 7. Song, 8. Thurmond, 9. Wysocka, 10. Ferrales.

Hammer

TATYANA LYSENKO improved from 71.54 in 2004 to set Russian records at 75.95 at Moscow in June and again two weeks later at the Russian Champs before 76.05 and a world record 77.06 at the Kuts Memorial meeting a further two days later. However the 21 year-old ranks third, as she was 3rd at the Worlds (72.46) and 4th at WAF (72.34) as the top two shared those big events. Olga Kuzenkova, who had been 2nd at the Russian Champs with 73.59, won the World title with a season's best 75.10 and was 3rd WAF with a 4-1 record v Lysenko; she has been in the top three for each of the 11 years the event was been ranked, having earlier set world bests in 1992-4. Yipsi Moreno won the WAF title after World 2nd and she was 4-0 v Lysenko. Olga Tsander had a 76.66 in Minsk, but her next best was 70.82 and she was 14th at the Worlds, so the next two are Manuèla Montebrun and Kamila Skolimowska, 2-2 on win loss with both over 74m and respectively 4th/7th and 7th/2nd at World/WAF. Zhang Wenxiu was 5th at the Worlds and won the Chinese, Asian and East Asian titles, although beaten by her compatriot Liu Yinghui at the Chinese National Games. Liu was also 2nd to Skolimowska at the World University Games, with Ester Balassini (dnq Worlds, 5th WAF) 3rd. Yekaterina Khoroshikh had three no throws in the World qualifying, but won the European U23 title from German champion Betty Heidler and beat Lysenko 5-2. Overall standards continue to improve with a record 23 women over 70m.

Most competitions over 73m/70m: Moreno 5/10, Lysenko 3/13, Montebrun 3/10, Kuzenkova 2/9, Skolimowska 1/11, Zhang 1/8, Khoroshikh 1/7, Heidler 0/9, Balassini 0/8, Erin Gilreath 1/4, Tsander 1/3, Susanne Keil 0/4.

1. Kuzenkova, 2. Moreno, 3. Lysenko, 4. Montebrun, 5. Skolimowska, 6. Zhang, 7. Khoroshikh, 8. Heidler, 9. Balassini, 10. Liu

Javelin

The World Championships provided an extraordinary competition as first Osleidys Menéndez improved her world record to 71.70 and then Christina Obergföll improved her pb from 64.59 to a European record 70.03. Steffi Nerius, who had thrown in pb 66.52 in qualifying, was isolated at 65.96 in third. Menéndez lost just two of her 12 competitions in 2005, one each to Nerius and World 7th placer Sonia Bisset and Nerius beat Obergföll on the other five times they met. Bisset (3rd WAF behind Menéndez and Nerius) had clearly the fourth best series of marks, with Barbora Spotáková (dnq 13th at the Worlds) the only other thrower (twice) over 64m. Fourth to sixth at the Worlds were Christina Scherwin (Danish records in the final at 62.32 and 63.43), Zahra Bani and Paula Tarvainen, but Laverne Eve, CAC champion and 10th Worlds, was 4th at the WAF followed as 5-8 by Spotáková, Scherwin, Aggelikí Tsiolakoúdi (World 8th) and Bani. Barbara Madejczyk was 6th in the world list at 63.03 but was beaten 2-0 by Tarvainen. Ranking positions 1-2-4-6 are the same as in 2004.

Most competitions over 62m: Nerius 15, Menéndez 12, Bisset & Obergföll 6, Spotáková 4, Bani 3, Tsiolakoúdi 2.

1. Menéndez, 2. Nerius, 3. Obergföll, 4. S Bisset, 5. Spotáková, 6. Eve, 7. Scherwin, 8. Tsiolakoúdi, 9. Bani, 10. Tarvainen.

Heptathlon

FOR THE fourth successive year Carolina Klüft won all her three heptathlons (Götzis 6824, European Cup 1 6688 and Worlds 6887), and ranks as world number one; she won her third successive IAAF Combined Events Challenge. Her top score was however two points short of the 6889 totalled at Arles by Eunice Barber, who made a splendid return to top form and also won at Talence with 6675. Crucially, despite having to protect a damaged ankle (holding her back to 1.82 in the high jump) and an earlier knee injury, Klüft beat Barber by 65 points in Helsinki. The top two were over 300 points clear of the next best Kelly Sotherton, who scored 6547 for 2nd at Götzis and was also 2nd at Talence although she slipped to 5th at the Worlds, behind Margaret Simpson and Austra Skujyte, who had been 4th and 5th in Götzis. The Götzis third placer, Hyleas Fountain was the fourth woman over 6500 points and won the US title but was only 12th at the Worlds. Lyudmila Blonska returned from a drugs ban to win at WUG and Woerden and she was 3rd at Talence. In the top positions at Götzis, Worlds and Talence were: Karin Ruckstuhl 6-5-7, Natalya Dobrynska 7-8-4 and Marie Collonvillé 15-6-6, and the last also won at the Mediterranean Games. The World 7th placer Naide Gomes also won at Logroño.

1. Klüft, 2. Barber, 3. Sotherton, 4. Simpson, 5. Skujyte, 6. Blonska, 7. Fountain, 8. Ruckstuhl, 9. Dobrynska, 10. Collonvillé

20 Kilometres Walk

ALTHOUGH SHE raced the distance only twice, Olimpiada Ivanova had a perfect record, winning at the European Cup and setting a world record 1:25:41 at the Worlds. Then Ryta Turava was an obvious choice for second ranking, as although she did not finish the European Cup race, she won at Rio Maior and Sesto San Giovanni and was 2nd at La Coruña and Worlds. The world lists are dominated by fast times from races in China (5th under 1:30 in Nanning, 11 in Cixi and 6 in Nanjing) and Russia (7 sub-1:30 in Adler) but those recording such times were not always able to reproduce this form in the big European races without getting disqualified. Walkers needed three races to qualify for the IAAF World Race Walking Challenge, which excluded Ivanova, but 1-6 in that were: 1. Turava, 2. Susanna Feitor (3rd Worlds), 3. Claudia Stef (8th), 4. Elisa Rigaudo (7th), 5. Melanie Seeger (11th), 6. Jane Saville (20th) with the top Chinese woman 7. Song Hongjuan (9th). Jiang Jing was 1st, 1st and 2nd in those big Chinese races (Bai Yanmin won at the Chinese National Games), and was also 2nd to Song at Dudince but was disqualified at the Worlds. Maria Vasco as usual showed consistent form, with 4th at the Worlds and 2nd at the Spanish Champs and Mediterranean Games (won by Rigaudo).

There were a record 35 women under 1:30 in 2004 from the previous best of 27 in 2000.

1. Ivanova, 2. Turava, 3. Feitor, 4. Song, 5. Rigaudo, 6. Stef, 7. Jiang, 8. Vasco, 9. Wang Liping, 10. Bai Yanmin

Progress of Women's Pole Vault World Record

THE IAAF first ratified a world record for the women's pole vault in 1995 – this was 4.05m by Sun Caiyun (Chn) in 1992. Diane Bragg (USA), sister of the 60 Olympic champion Don Bragg, was noted to have vaulted 8ft 6in (2.59) in 1952 and Irene Spieker (USA) improved this mark from 2.60 in 1978 to 3.05 at Louisville in 1979 and Jana Edwards (USA) made rapid improvements in 1983 up to 3.59 at Fort Wayne. From 1988 Chinese vaulters led the way before the event gained international approval.

Most absolute WRs ratified by IAAF:

14 Yelena Isinbayeva RUS 4.82-5.01 (2003-06), 11 Emma George AUS 4.25-4.60 (1995-9), 10 Dániela Bartová CZE 4.10-4.22 (1995), 10 Stacy Dragila USA 4.60-4.81 (1999-2001)

First athletes to succeed at each 10cm:

3.70	Zhang Chunzen CHN	3.72	20 Apr 88
3.80	Zhang Chunzen CHN	3.80	9 Sep 89
4.00	Zhang Chunzen CHN	4.00	24 Mar 91
4.10	Sun Caiyun CHN	4.11	21 Mar 93
4.20	Dániela Bartová CZE	4.20	18 Aug 95
4.30	Emma George AUS	4.30	28 Jan 96
4.40	Emma George AUS	4.41	28 Jan 96
4.50	Emma George AUS	4.50	8 Feb 97
4.60	Emma George AUS	4.60	20 Feb 99
4.70	Stacy Dragila USA	4.70	11 Jun 00
4.80	Stacy Dragila USA	4.81	9 Jun 01
4.90	Yelena Isinbayeva RUS	4.90	30 Jul 04
5.00	**Yelena Isinbayeva RUS**	**5.00**	**22 Jul 05**

IAAF WORLD RANKINGS

THE IAAF world rankings were trialed in 2000 and formally adopted by the IAAF council in November 2000. They are now updated and issued every week, with the intention of giving statisticians, journalists and fans an image of how the leading athletes of our sport are performing. They can be seen at: www.iaaf.org

Here are positions as at the end of 2005 – the top 50 men and women overall and the top 20 for each event.

Overall Ranking List

Events shown are main ones – but points may have been gained at others.

Men

1	Kenenisa Bekele ETH	1451	3/5/10000m/CC
2	Justin Gatlin USA	1435	100m/200m
3	Saïf Saaeed Shaheen QAT	1433	3000mSt
4	Virgilijus Alekna LTU	1408	DT
4	Bershawn Jackson USA	1408	400mh
6	Dominique Arnold USA	1401	110mh
6	Ladji Doucouré FRA	1401	110mh/60mh
8	Daniel Kipchirchir Komen KEN	1399	1500m
9	Dwight Phillips USA	1394	LJ/60m
10	Allen Johnson USA	1390	110mh
11	Liu Xiang CHN	1389	110mh
12	Rashid Ramzi BRN	1385	800m/1500m
13	Bernard Lagat USA	1378	1500m-5000m
14	James Carter USA	1377	400mh
15	Brad Walker USA	1376	PV
16	Tero Pitkämäki FIN	1372	JT
17	Paul Kipsiele Koech KEN	1370	3000mSt
18	Eliud Kipchoge KEN	1366	3/5000m
19	Jeremy Wariner USA	1362	400m
20	Terrence Trammell USA	1357	110mh
21	Brimin Kipruto KEN	1354	3000mSt
22	Aziz Zakari GHA	1353	100m
23	Benjamin Limo KEN	1351	3/5000m
24	Ivan Heshko UKR	1349	1500m
25	Yaroslav Rybakov RUS	1346	HJ
25	Stefan Holm SWE	1346	HJ
25	Tyson Gay USA	1346	100m/200m
28	Francisco J Fernández ESP	1345	20km Walk
29	Sileshi Sihine ETH	1343	5/10000m/HM
29	Andreas Thorkildsen NOR	1343	JT
29	Isaac Songok KEN	1343	1500m/5000m
32	Wallace Spearmon USA	1342	200m
32	Gerd Kanter EST	1342	DT
34	Ivan Tikhon BLR	1341	HT
34	Yuriy Borzakovskiy RUS	1341	800m
34	Sergey Makarov RUS	1341	JT
37	Dwight Thomas JAM	1340	100m
38	Marian Oprea ROM	1338	TJ
39	Ezekiel Kemboi KEN	1336	3000mSt
40	Roman Sebrle CZE	1335	Dec/Hep
41	L.J. Van Zyl RSA	1334	400mh
41	Boniface Kiprop UGA	1334	5/10000m/CC
41	Naman Keïta FRA	1334	400mh
44	Abebe Dinkesa ETH	1333	5/10000m/HM
44	Asafa Powell JAM	1333	100m
46	Joachim Olsen DEN	1332	SP
46	Adam Nelson USA	1332	SP
48	Kerron Clement USA	1331	400mh/400m
48	Daham Najim Bashir QAT	1331	1500m/3000m
50	Tim Benjamin GBR	1330	400m
50	Brandon Simpson JAM	1330	400m
50	Jaouad Gharib MAR	1330	Mar/HMar
50	Ronald Pognon FRA	1330	100m/60m
50	Tim Lobinger GER	1330	PV

Women

1	Yelena Isinbayeva RUS	1453	PV
2	Tirunesh Dibaba ETH	1445	5/10000m/CC
3	Carolina Klüft SWE	1421	Hep/Pen
4	Lashinda Demus USA	1402	400mh
5	Veronica Campbell JAM	1398	100m/200m
6	Meseret Defar ETH	1397	3/5000m
7	Berhane Adere ETH	1395	3/5/10000m
8	Sanya Richards USA	1394	400m
9	Christine Arron FRA	1389	100m/200m
10	Tonique W-Darling BAH	1383	400m
11	Paula Radcliffe GBR	1380	Mar/10 km
11	Michelle Perry USA	1380	100mh
13	Yuliya Pechonkina RUS	1378	400mh
14	Eunice Barber FRA	1376	Hep
15	Sandra Glover USA	1374	400mh
16	Maryam Yusuf Jamal BRN	1373	1500m/3000m
17	Ejegayehu Dibaba ETH	1370	5/10000m
18	Allyson Felix USA	1369	100m,200m
19	Tatyana Lebedeva RUS	1367	TJ
20	Constantina Tomescu ROM	1361	HMar/Mar
21	Kajsa Bergqvist SWE	1360	HJ
22	Zulia Calatayud CUB	1359	800m
23	Brigitte Foster-Hylton JAM	1357	100mh
24	Lauryn Williams USA	1356	100m
25	Trecia Smith JAM	1347	TJ
26	Chandra Sturrup BAH	1343	100m
27	Osleidys Menéndez CUB	1341	JT
27	Isabella Ochichi KEN	1341	3/5000m/CC
29	Dell. Ennis-London JAM	1339	100mh
30	Anna Jesien POL	1338	400mh
31	Hasna Benhassi MAR	1333	800m
32	Dorcus Inzikuru UGA	1331	3000mSt
32	Zhou Chunxiu CHN	1331	Marathon
34	Margarita Turava BLR	1330	20km Walk
35	Ana Guevara MEX	1329	400m
36	Tatyana Kotova RUS	1325	LJ
36	Tatyana Andrianova RUS	1325	800m
38	Svetlana Pospelova RUS	1324	400m
39	Kirsten Bolm GER	1321	100mh/60mh
39	Catherine Ndereba KEN	1321	Mar/HMar
41	Lisa Barber USA	1320	100m
42	Edith Masai KEN	1319	3/5/10000m/Mar
43	Yargelis Savigne CUB	1318	LJ/TJ
43	Bouchra Ghezielle FRA	1318	1500m/3000m
45	Svetlana Cherkasova RUS	1315	800m
46	Meselech Melkamu ETH	1314	3/5000m/CC
47	Susanna Kallur SWE	1311	100mh/60mh
47	Anna Pyatykh RUS	1311	TJ
49	Nadezhda Ostapchuk BLR	1307	SP
49	Perdita Felicien CAN	1307	100mh
49	Maria Mutola MOZ	1307	800m
49	DeeDee Trotter USA	1307	400m

Event Ranking Lists

100m (50m - 55m - 60m)

1	Justin Gatlin	USA	1405
2	Aziz Zakari	GHA	1353
3	Dwight Thomas	JAM	1340
4	Asafa Powell	JAM	1333
5	Ronald Pognon	FRA	1330
6	Francis Obikwelu	POR	1325
7	Leonard Scott	USA	1322
8	Kim Collins	SKN	1321
9	Marc Burns	TRI	1319
10	Michael Frater	JAM	1314
11	Jason Gardener	GBR	1283
12	Darrel Brown	TRI	1271
13	Olusoji Fasuba	NGR	1243
14	Maurice Greene	USA	1230
15	Shawn Crawford	USA	1227
16	Uchenna Emedolu	NGR	1221
17	Coby Miller	USA	1212
18	Tyson Gay	USA	1206
19	John Capel	USA	1201
19	Deji Aliu	NGR	1201

200m

1	Tyson Gay	USA	1343
2	Wallace Spearmon	USA	1342
3	Justin Gatlin	USA	1339
4	Tobias Unger	GER	1280
5	Chris Williams	JAM	1277
6	Usain Bolt	JAM	1266
7	Stéphane Buckland	MRI	1256
8	Aaron Armstrong	TRI	1245
9	John Capel	USA	1242
10	Xavier Carter	USA	1230
11	André D. da Silva	BRA	1225
12	Marlon Devonish	GBR	1213
13	Omar Brown	JAM	1206
14	Christian Malcolm	GBR	1205
15	Walter Dix	USA	1203
16	Rodney Martin	USA	1201
17	Guus Hoogmoed	NED	1200
18	Leo Bookman	USA	1196
18	Daniel Batman	AUS	1196
20	Joshua J. Johnson	USA	1195

400m (300m - 500m ind.)

1	Jeremy Wariner	USA	1362
2	Tim Benjamin	GBR	1330
2	Brandon Simpson	JAM	1330
4	Tyler Christopher	CAN	1326
5	Christopher Brown	BAH	1322
6	Tyree Washington	USA	1304
7	Andrew Rock	USA	1303
8	Michael Blackwood	JAM	1281
8	Gary Kikaya	COD	1281
10	Darold Williamson	USA	1274
11	Alleyne Francique	GRN	1265
12	Davian Clarke	JAM	1263
13	Carlos Santa	DOM	1253
14	LaShawn Merritt	USA	1252
15	Derrick Brew	USA	1242
16	Sanjay Ayre	JAM	1236
17	N. El-Abubakr	SUD	1219
18	Leonard Byrd	USA	1217
19	Marc Raquil	FRA	1209
20	Young T. Nyongani	ZIM	1205

800m (600m - 1000m)

1	Yuriy Borzakovskiy	RUS	1341
2	Mbulaeni Mulaudzi	RSA	1329
3	Wilfred Bungei	KEN	1324
4	William Yiampoy	KEN	1308
5	Youssef Kamel	BRN	1300
6	Gary Reed	CAN	1294
7	Antonio M. Reina	ESP	1291
8	Alfred Kirwa Yego	KEN	1289
9	Mehdi Baala	FRA	1277
10	Rashid Ramzi	BRN	1275
11	Amine Laâlou	MAR	1264
12	Khadevis Robinson	USA	1262
13	Mouhssin Chéhibi	MAR	1249
14	Djabir Saïd-Guerni	ALG	1239
15	Mohammed Al Salhi	KSA	1233
16	Dmitriy Bogdanov	RUS	1231
17	Dmitrijs Milkevics	LAT	1224
18	Fabiano Peçanha	BRA	1219
19	James McIlroy	GBR	1217
20	Joseph Mutua	KEN	1213

1500m (Mile - 2000m)

1	Daniel Kip. Komen	KEN	1399
2	Bernard Lagat	USA	1367
3	Ivan Heshko	UKR	1349
4	Rashid Ramzi	BRN	1325
5	Alex Kipchirchir	KEN	1319
6	Daham Najim Bashir	QAT	1318
7	Suleiman Simotwo	KEN	1316
8	Rui Silva	POR	1292
9	Alan Webb	USA	1290
10	Antar Zerguelaine	ALG	1271
10	Juan Carlos Higuero	ESP	1271
12	Laban Rotich	KEN	1268
13	Tarek Boukensa	ALG	1244
14	William Chirchir	KEN	1241
15	Mehdi Baala	FRA	1236
16	Elkanah Angwenyi	KEN	1235
17	Belal Mansoor Ali	BRN	1229
18	Michael East	GBR	1219
19	Hudson de Souza	BRA	1213
20	Arturo Casado	ESP	1204

5000 - 10,000m (3000m - 2M - CC)

1	Kenenisa Bekele	ETH	1451
2	Eliud Kipchoge	KEN	1366
3	Benjamin Limo	KEN	1351
4	Boniface Kiprop	UGA	1334
5	Augustine Choge	KEN	1327
6	Isaac Songok	KEN	1323
7	Sileshi Sihine	ETH	1322
8	Craig Mottram	AUS	1314
9	Abebe Dinkesa	ETH	1311
10	Moses Mosop	KEN	1294
11	Boniface Songok	KEN	1287
12	Zersenay Tadesse	ERI	1282
12	Markos Geneti	ETH	1282
12	Tariku Bekele	ETH	1282
15	Abderrahim Goumri	MAR	1280
16	Geb. Gebremariam	ETH	1278
17	Dejene Birhanu	ETH	1274
18	Sammy Kipketer	KEN	1272
19	John Kibowen	KEN	1251
20	Ali Saidi-Sief	ALG	1249

Road Running - Marathon (10-100k)

1	Jaouad Gharib	MAR	1330
2	Martin Lel	KEN	1305
3	Haile Gebrselassie	ETH	1301
4	Fabiano Joseph	TAN	1288
5	Felix Limo	KEN	1285
6	Paul Tergat	KEN	1280
7	Julio Rey	ESP	1278
8	Mubarak Shami	QAT	1275
9	Jackson Koech	KEN	1265
10	Philip Manyim	KEN	1262
11	Robert K Cheruiyot	KEN	1259
12	Hendrick Ramaala	RSA	1258
13	Patrick Ivuti	KEN	1250
14	Chris. Cheboiboch	KEN	1249
15	William Kipsang	KEN	1242
16	Paul Biwott	KEN	1241
17	Jason Mbote	KEN	1236
18	John Yuda	TAN	1235
18	Daniel Njenga	KEN	1235
18	Luke Kibet	KEN	1235

3000mSC (2000mSC)

1	Saïf S. Shaheen	QAT	1433
2	Paul K. Koech	KEN	1370
3	Brimin Kipruto	KEN	1354
4	Ezekiel Kemboi	KEN	1336
5	Bouabdallah Tahri	FRA	1329
6	Brahim Boulami	MAR	1327
7	Wesley Kiprotich	KEN	1320
8	Kipkurui Misoi	KEN	1296
9	Obaid Musa Amer	QAT	1288
10	Antonio Jiménez	ESP	1264
11	Simon Vroemen	NED	1257
12	Mustafa Mohamed	SWE	1250
13	David Chemweno	KEN	1241
14	Linus Chumba	KEN	1230
15	Richard Matelong	KEN	1229
16	Ronald Kipchumba	KEN	1226
17	Julius Nyamu	KEN	1216
18	Michael Kipyego	KEN	1209
19	Gaël Pencreach	FRA	1199
20	Radoslaw Poplawski	POL	1195

110mH (50mH - 55mH - 60mH)

1	Dominique Arnold	USA	1401
1	Ladji Doucouré	FRA	1401
3	Allen Johnson	USA	1390
4	Liu Xiang	CHN	1389
5	Terrence Trammell	USA	1357
6	Stanislav Olijar	LAT	1317
7	Joel Brown	USA	1312
8	Maurice Wignall	JAM	1310
9	Ron Bramlett	USA	1289
10	Thomas Blaschek	GER	1282
11	Matheus Inocêncio	BRA	1279
12	Anwar Moore	USA	1274
13	Redelén dos Santos	BRA	1273
14	Arend Watkins	USA	1267
15	Robert Kronberg	SWE	1257
16	Serhiy Demidyuk	UKR	1253
17	Shi Dongpeng	CHN	1243
18	David Oliver	USA	1226
19	Elmar Lichtenegger	AUT	1224
20	Felipe Vivancos	ESP	1221

400mH

1	Bershawn Jackson	USA	1408
2	James Carter	USA	1377
3	L.J. Van Zyl	RSA	1334
3	Naman Keïta	FRA	1334
5	Kerron Clement	USA	1318
5	Bayano Kamani	PAN	1318
7	Kemel Thompson	JAM	1306
8	Dai Tamesue	JPN	1301
9	Periklis Iakovákis	GRE	1276
10	Ian Weakley	JAM	1253
10	Bennie Brazell	USA	1253
12	Danny McFarlane	JAM	1252
13	Kenji Narisako	JPN	1247
14	Kenneth Ferguson	USA	1245
15	Pieter de Villiers	RSA	1241
16	Hadi S. Al Somaily	KSA	1238
17	Llewellyn Herbert	RSA	1236
18	Gianni Carabelli	ITA	1235
19	Ockert Cilliers	RSA	1231
20	Dean Griffiths	JAM	1227

High Jump

1	Yaroslav Rybakov	RUS	1346
1	Stefan Holm	SWE	1346
3	Víctor Moya	CUB	1325
4	Jaroslav Bába	CZE	1315
5	Vyacheslav Voronin	RUS	1294
6	Andriy Sokolovskiy	UKR	1253
7	Jacques Freitag	RSA	1248
8	Yuriy Krymarenko	UKR	1242
9	Svatoslav Ton	CZE	1233
10	Jamie Nieto	USA	1223
11	Nicola Ciotti	ITA	1213
12	Dragutin Topic	SCG	1212
13	Aleksey Dmitrik	RUS	1200
14	Jesse Williams	USA	1199
15	Michal Bieniek	POL	1197
16	Grzegorz Sposób	POL	1191
17	Mark Boswell	CAN	1184
18	Kyriakos Ioannou	CYP	1178
19	Andrey Tereshin	RUS	1173
20	Giulio Ciotti	ITA	1165

Pole Vault

1	Brad Walker	USA	1376
2	Tim Lobinger	GER	1330
3	Rens Blom	NED	1298
4	Giuseppe Gibilisco	ITA	1289
5	Derek Miles	USA	1282
6	Toby Stevenson	USA	1280
7	Igor Pavlov	RUS	1278
8	Denys Yurchenko	UKR	1255
9	Daichi Sawano	JPN	1248
10	Paul Burgess	AUS	1245
11	Björn Otto	GER	1244
12	Pavel Gerasimov	RUS	1241
12	Nick Hysong	USA	1241
12	Steven Hooker	AUS	1241
15	Konst. Filippídis	GRE	1240
16	Timothy Mack	USA	1238
17	Lars Börgeling	GER	1230
18	Oleksandr Korchmid	UKR	1220
19	Dmitri Markov	AUS	1216
19	Daniel Ecker	GER	1216

Long Jump

1	Dwight Phillips	USA	1394
2	Miguel Pate	USA	1294
3	Ignisious Gaisah	GHA	1292
4	Joan Lino Martínez	ESP	1260
5	Tommi Evilä	FIN	1256
6	Salim Sdiri	FRA	1247
7	James Beckford	JAM	1241
8	Irving Saladino	PAN	1234
9	Volodimir Zyuskov	UKR	1231
10	Godfrey Mokoena	RSA	1227
11	Brian Johnson	USA	1210
12	Nils Winter	GER	1189
13	Loúis Tsátoumas	GRE	1187
14	Vitaliy Shkurlatov	RUS	1185
15	Arnaud Casquette	MRI	1179
16	Erivaldo Vieira	BRA	1178
17	Issam Nima	ALG	1171
18	John Moffitt	USA	1170
19	Bogdan Tarus	ROM	1167
20	Gaspar Araújo	POR	1163
20	Tim Parravicini	AUS	1163

Triple Jump

1	Marian Oprea	ROM	1338
2	Jadel Gregório	BRA	1324
3	Walter Davis	USA	1322
4	Francis Betanzos	CUB	1305
5	Nathan Douglas	GBR	1266
6	Leevan Sands	BAH	1261
7	Igor Spasovkhodskiy	RUS	1248
8	Danila Burkenya	RUS	1242
9	Dmitrij Valukevic	SVK	1241
10	Viktor Yastrebov	UKR	1232
11	Karl Taillepierre	FRA	1227
11	Alexander Martínez	CUB	1227
13	Kenta Bell	USA	1226
14	Momchil Karailiev	BUL	1218
15	David Giralt	CUB	1216
16	Konst. Zalaggítis	GRE	1213
17	Aleksandr Sergeyev	RUS	1194
18	Rodrigo Mendes	BRA	1192
19	Aleksandr Petrenko	RUS	1186
20	Mykola Savolainen	UKR	1185

Shot

1	Joachim Olsen	DEN	1332
1	Adam Nelson	USA	1332
3	Reese Hoffa	USA	1318
4	Christian Cantwell	USA	1310
5	Ralf Bartels	GER	1293
6	Rutger Smith	NED	1274
6	John Godina	USA	1274
8	Yuriy Bilonoh	UKR	1255
9	Andrey Mikhnevich	BLR	1238
10	Mikulás Konopka	SVK	1233
11	Ville Tiisanoja	FIN	1226
12	Gheorghe Guset	ROM	1211
13	Tomasz Majewski	POL	1209
14	Daniel Taylor	USA	1208
14	Manuel Martínez	ESP	1208
16	Jamie Beyer	USA	1203
17	Edis Elkasevic	CRO	1200
18	Petr Stehlík	CZE	1198
19	Carl Myerscough	GBR	1195
20	Khalid Al Suwaidi	QAT	1181

Discus

1	Virgilijus Alekna	LTU	1408
2	Gerd Kanter	EST	1342
3	Aleksander Tammert	EST	1274
4	Frantz Kruger	RSA	1260
5	Zoltán Kövágó	HUN	1252
6	Mario Pestano	ESP	1242
7	Jason Tunks	CAN	1223
7	Michael Möllenbeck	GER	1223
9	Ian Waltz	USA	1217
10	Jarred Rome	USA	1210
11	Gábor Máté	HUN	1186
12	Lars Riedel	GER	1179
13	Roland Varga	HUN	1174
14	Andrzej Krawczyk	POL	1156
15	Carl Brown	USA	1154
16	Ehsan Hadadi	IRI	1152
16	Piotr Malachowski	POL	1152
18	Frank Casañas	CUB	1151
19	Robert Harting	GER	1150
20	Vikas Gowda	IND	1144

Hammer

1	Ivan Tikhon	BLR	1341
2	Vadim Devyatovskiy	BLR	1318
3	Olli-Pekka Karjalainen	FIN	1263
4	Szymon Ziólkowski	POL	1262
5	Krisztián Pars	HUN	1242
6	Markus Esser	GER	1229
7	Ilya Konovalov	RUS	1223
8	Libor Charfreitag	SVK	1216
9	Esref Apak	TUR	1190
10	Karsten Kobs	GER	1184
11	Chris Harmse	RSA	1178
11	Vadim Khersontsev	RUS	1178
11	Aleksey Zagorniy	RUS	1178
14	Holger Klose	GER	1176
15	Artem Rubanko	UKR	1173
16	Alex. Papadimitríou	GRE	1167
17	Mohamed Al Zinkavi	KUW	1166
18	Andras Haklits	CRO	1163
19	Sergey Kirmasov	RUS	1160
20	Dilshod Nazarov	TJK	1157

Javelin

1	Tero Pitkämäki	FIN	1372
2	Andreas Thorkildsen	NOR	1343
3	Sergey Makarov	RUS	1341
4	Andrus Värnik	EST	1262
5	Aleksandr Ivanov	RUS	1226
6	Mark Frank	GER	1213
7	Eriks Rags	LAT	1183
8	Guillermo Martínez	CUB	1176
9	Ainars Kovals	LAT	1167
10	Christian Nicolay	GER	1145
11	Esko Mikkola	FIN	1129
11	Aki Parviainen	FIN	1129
13	Vadims Vasilevskis	LAT	1128
14	Li Rongxiang	CHN	1124
15	Tero Järvenpää	FIN	1116
16	Brian Chaput	USA	1105
17	Stefan Wenk	GER	1102
18	Björn Lange	GER	1096
19	Tomas Intas	LTU	1091
20	Jarkko Koski-Vähälä	FIN	1089

Decathlon (Heptathlon indoor)

1	Roman Sebrle	CZE	1335
2	Attila Zsivoczky	HUN	1283
3	Bryan Clay	USA	1274
4	Aleksandr Pogorelov	RUS	1269
5	Kristjan Rahnu	EST	1244
6	André Niklaus	GER	1237
7	Romain Barras	FRA	1206
8	Aleksey Drozdov	RUS	1192
9	Tomás Dvorák	CZE	1181
10	Ryan Harlan	USA	1169
11	Jaakko Ojaniemi	FIN	1168
12	Aleks. Parkhomenko	BLR	1164
13	Paul Terek	USA	1160
14	Mikk Pahapill	EST	1159
15	Qi Haifeng	CHN	1155
16	Hamdi Dhouibi	TUN	1143
17	Maurice Smith	JAM	1141
18	Rudy Bourguignon	FRA	1140
19	Phil McMullen	USA	1139
20	Roland Schwarzl	AUT	1138

Race Walking - 20km-50km (10km-30km)

1	Franc. J. Fernández	ESP	1345
2	Trond Nymark	NOR	1297
2	Zhao Chengliang	CHN	1297
4	Jefferson Pérez	ECU	1293
5	Nathan Deakes	AUS	1282
6	Juan Manuel Molina	ESP	1280
7	Alex Schwazer	ITA	1275
8	Zhu Hongjun	CHN	1272
9	Han Yucheng	CHN	1268
10	Yu Chaohong	CHN	1262
11	Vladimir Stankin	RUS	1260
12	Ilya Markov	RUS	1255
13	Hatem Ghoula	TUN	1252
14	Cui Zhide	CHN	1250
15	Liu Yunfeng	CHN	1244
16	Roman Magdziarczyk	POL	1238
17	Benjamin Kucinski	POL	1237
18	Eder Sánchez	MEX	1235
19	Xing Shucai	CHN	1234
20	Omar Zepeda	MEX	1232

WOMEN

100m (50m - 55m - 60m)

1 Christine Arron FRA 1376
2 Veronica Campbell JAM 1364
3 Lauryn Williams USA 1356
4 Chandra Sturrup BAH 1343
5 Me'Lisa Barber USA 1320
6 Sherone Simpson JAM 1297
7 Yuliya Nesterenko BLR 1289
8 Kim Gevaert BEL 1268
9 Muna Lee USA 1265
10 Allyson Felix USA 1244
11 Zhanna Block UKR 1239
12 LaTasha Colander USA 1235
13 Angela Daigle USA 1231
14 Olga Fyodorova RUS 1230
14 Aleen Bailey JAM 1230
16 Rachelle Smith USA 1228
17 María Karastamáti GRE 1227
18 Yeorgia Koklóni GRE 1220
19 Lucimar de Moura BRA 1215
20 Tayna Lawrence JAM 1195

200m

1 Allyson Felix USA 1367
2 Veronica Campbell JAM 1331
3 Christine Arron FRA 1324
4 Cydonie Mothersill CAY 1293
5 Kim Gevaert BEL 1285
6 LaTasha Colander USA 1275
7 Rachelle Smith USA 1269
8 Yuliya Gushchina RUS 1264
9 Lucimar de Moura BRA 1233
10 Fabienne Feraez BEN 1229
11 Christine Amertil BAH 1220
12 Karin Mayr-Krifka AUT 1199
13 Peta-Gaye Dowdie JAM 1197
13 Stephanie Durst USA 1197
15 Marina Maydanova UKR 1195
16 Jacqueline Poelman NED 1192
17 Anna Pacholak POL 1191
18 Yekat. Kondratyeva RUS 1190
18 Donna Fraser GBR 1190
20 Natalya Ivanova RUS 1189

400m (300m - 500m ind.)

1 Sanya Richards USA 1394
2 Tonique W-Darling BAH 1383
3 Ana Guevara MEX 1329
4 Svetlana Pospelova RUS 1324
5 DeeDee Trotter USA 1307
6 Monique Hennagan USA 1301
7 Christine Amertil BAH 1286
8 Amy Mbacké Thiam SEN 1278
9 Olesya Zykina RUS 1249
10 Monique Henderson USA 1242
11 Natalya Antyukh RUS 1235
11 Olesya Krasnomovets RUS 1235
13 Antonina Yefremova UKR 1228
14 Moushaumi Robinson USA 1218
15 Svetlana Usovich BLR 1217
16 Ilona Usovich BLR 1214
17 Lorraine Fenton JAM 1213
18 Christine Ohuruogu GBR 1212
19 Tiandra Ponteen SKN 1207
20 Olga Zaytseva RUS 1201
20 Shericka Williams JAM 1201
20 Kaltouma Nadjina CHA 1201

800m (600m - 1000m)

1 Zulia Calatayud CUB 1359
2 Hasna Benhassi MAR 1333
3 Tatyana Andrianova RUS 1325
4 Svetlana Cherkasova RUS 1315
5 Maria Mutola MOZ 1307
6 Mayte Martínez ESP 1301
7 Larisa Chzhao RUS 1297
8 Hazel Clark USA 1283
9 Olga Kotlyarova RUS 1269
10 Kenia Sinclair JAM 1259
11 Svetlana Klyuka RUS 1244
11 Agnes Samaria NAM 1244
11 Laetitia Valdonado FRA 1244
14 Janet Jepkosgei KEN 1226
15 Diane Cummins CAN 1220
16 Mina Aït Hammou MAR 1215
17 Svetlana Usovich BLR 1206
18 Natalya Tsyganova RUS 1205
19 Jolanda Ceplak SLO 1201
20 Virginie Fouquet FRA 1197

1500m (Mile - 2000m)

1 Maryam Yusuf Jamal BRN 1332
2 Olga Yegorova RUS 1298
3 Bouchra Ghezielle FRA 1296
4 Hind Dehiba FRA 1292
5 Natalya Yevdokimova RUS 1279
6 Yuliya Chizhenko RUS 1273
7 Alesya Turava BLR 1265
8 C. Douma-Hussar CAN 1258
9 Nancy Chebet Lagat KEN 1253
10 Helen Clitheroe GBR 1236
11 Yelena Soboleva RUS 1234
12 Gelete Burka ETH 1230
13 Natalia Rodríguez ESP 1225
14 Anna Jakubczak POL 1219
15 Mestawet Tadesse ETH 1218
16 Wioletta Janowska POL 1216
17 Corina Dumbravean ROM 1209
18 Jennifer Toomey USA 1201
19 Treniere Clement USA 1188
19 Olesya Chumakova RUS 1188

5000 - 10,000m (3000m - 2 Miles - CC)

1 Tirunesh Dibaba ETH 1445
2 Meseret Defar ETH 1397
3 Berhane Adere ETH 1395
4 Ejegayehu Dibaba ETH 1370
5 Isabella Ochichi KEN 1341
6 Meselech Melkamu ETH 1314
7 Prisca Jepleting KEN 1302
8 Edith Masai KEN 1300
9 Zakia Mrisho TAN 1298
9 Werknesh Kidane ETH 1298
11 Susanne Wigene NOR 1291
12 Xing Huina CHN 1277
13 Irene Kwambai KEN 1275
14 Ines Chenonge KEN 1271
15 Joanne Pavey GBR 1268
15 Alice Timbilil KEN 1268
17 Liliya Shobukhova RUS 1265
18 Lucy Wangui KEN 1262
18 Sab. Mockenhaupt GER 1262
20 Sun Yingjie CHN 1245

Road Running - Marathon (10-100k)

1 Paula Radcliffe GBR 1380
2 Constantina Tomescu ROM 1361
3 Zhou Chunxiu CHN 1331
4 Catherine Ndereba KEN 1321
5 Derartu Tulu ETH 1301
6 Jelena Prokopcuka LAT 1287
7 Yumiko Hara JPN 1274
8 Susan Chepkemei KEN 1272
8 Lornah Kiplagat NED 1272
10 Harumi Hiroyama JPN 1254
11 Megumi Oshima JPN 1249
12 Edith Masai KEN 1243
13 Lidiya Grigoryeva RUS 1229
14 Helen Kimutai KEN 1228
15 Luminita Zaituc GER 1222
16 Naoko Takahashi JPN 1221
17 Masako Chiba JPN 1214
18 Elfenesh Alemu ETH 1213
19 Lidia Simon ROM 1212
20 Rosaria Console ITA 1211
20 Zivilé Balciunaité LTU 1211

3000mSC (2000mSC)

1 Dorcus Inzikuru UGA 1331
2 Mardrea Hyman JAM 1226
3 Korene Hinds JAM 1223
4 Lívia Tóth HUN 1222
5 Cristina Casandra ROM 1219
6 Salome Chepchumba KEN 1207
7 Elizabeth Jackson USA 1157
8 Lisa Galaviz USA 1134
9 Roisin Mcgettigan IRL 1117
10 Türkan Erismis TUR 1115
11 Carrie Messner USA 1113
12 Steph. De Croock BEL 1111
12 Briana Shook USA 1111
14 Jo Ankier GBR 1110
15 Clarisse Cruz POR 1109
16 Victoria Mitchell AUS 1103
17 Rosa Morató ESP 1101
18 Valentina Horpinich UKR 1100
19 Miranda Boonstra NED 1098
20 Verena Dreier GER 1092

100mh (50mh - 55mh - 60mh)

1 Michelle Perry USA 1380
2 Brigitte Foster-Hylton JAM 1357
3 Dell. Ennis-London JAM 1339
4 Kirsten Bolm GER 1321
5 Susanna Kallur SWE 1311
6 Perdita Felicien CAN 1307
7 Joanna Hayes USA 1298
8 Anjanette Kirkland USA 1293
9 Glory Alozie ESP 1290
10 Irina Shevchenko RUS 1283
11 Jenny Kallur SWE 1282
12 Linda Khodadin FRA 1273
13 L. Golding-Clarke JAM 1263
14 Vonette Dixon JAM 1262
14 Danielle Carruthers USA 1262
16 Mariya Koroteyeva RUS 1255
17 Aurelia Trywianska POL 1236
18 Lolo Jones USA 1232
18 Olena Krasovska UKR 1232
20 Sarah Claxton GBR 1230

400mH

1 Lashinda Demus USA 1402
2 Yuliya Pechonkina RUS 1378
3 Sandra Glover USA 1374
4 Anna Jesien POL 1338
5 Andrea Blackett BAR 1296
6 Malgorzata Pskit POL 1279
7 Tetyana Tereshchuk UKR 1274
8 Huang Xiaoxiao CHN 1273
9 Surita Febbraio RSA 1256
10 Sheena Johnson USA 1251
11 Benedetta Ceccarelli ITA 1240
12 Shauna Smith USA 1234
13 Debbie-Ann Parris JAM 1213
14 Claudia Marx GER 1206
15 Marjolein de Jong NED 1201
16 Marta Chrust-Rozej POL 1194
17 Brenda Taylor USA 1190
17 Tiff. Ross-Williams USA 1190
19 Cora Olivero ESP 1188
19 Monika Niederstätter ITA 1188

High Jump

1	Kajsa Bergqvist	SWE	1360
2	Anna Chicherova	RUS	1275
3	Chaunte Howard	USA	1259
4	Vita Palamar	UKR	1258
5	Vita Styopina	UKR	1223
6	Venelina Veneva	BUL	1222
7	Ruth Beitia	ESP	1218
8	Emma Green	SWE	1211
9	Irina Mikhalchenko	UKR	1208
10	Tatyana Kivimyagi	RUS	1202
11	Oana Pantelimon	ROM	1185
12	Marta Mendía	ESP	1183
13	Tatyana Efimenko	KGZ	1175
13	Amy Acuff	USA	1175
15	Melanie Skotnik	FRA	1168
16	Yek. Aleksandrova	RUS	1164
17	Tia Hellebaut	BEL	1160
18	Viktoriya Seryogina	RUS	1154
19	Erin Aldrich	USA	1153
20	Ifoma Jones	USA	1151

Pole Vault

1	Yelena Isinbayeva	RUS	1453
2	Monika Pyrek	POL	1284
3	Anna Rogowska	POL	1275
4	Tatyana Polnova	RUS	1207
5	Pavla Hamácková	CZE	1197
6	Vanessa Boslak	FRA	1177
7	Dana Ellis	CAN	1163
8	Carolin Hingst	GER	1154
9	Stacy Dragila	USA	1151
10	Gao Shuying	CHN	1150
11	Jillian Schwartz	USA	1136
12	Thórey Elisdóttir	ISL	1126
13	Tracy O'hara	USA	1119
14	Janine Whitlock	GBR	1105
15	Mary Sauer	USA	1097
16	Zhao Yingying	CHN	1096
17	Krisztina Molnár	HUN	1093
18	Anzhela Balakhonova	UKR	1086
18	Silke Spiegelburg	GER	1086
20	Kirsten Belin	SWE	1078

Long Jump

1	Tatyana Kotova	RUS	1325
2	Grace Upshaw	USA	1241
3	Oksana Udmurtova	RUS	1236
4	Anju Bobby George	IND	1234
5	Tianna Madison	USA	1232
6	Yargelis Savigne	CUB	1206
7	Eunice Barber	FRA	1202
8	Carolina Klüft	SWE	1201
9	Irina Simagina	RUS	1200
10	Elva Goulbourne	JAM	1182
11	Lyudmila Kolchanova	RUS	1178
12	Rose Richmond	USA	1176
13	Jackie Edwards	BAH	1171
14	Ineta Radevica	LAT	1170
15	Bianca Kappler	GER	1165
16	Concepción Montaner	ESP	1162
16	Stilianí Pilátou	GRE	1162
18	Tünde Vaszi	HUN	1158
18	Naide Gomes	POR	1158
20	Niurka Montalvo	ESP	1155

Triple Jump

1	Tatyana Lebedeva	RUS	1367
2	Trecia Smith	JAM	1347
3	Anna Pyatykh	RUS	1311
4	Hrysopiyi Devetzí	GRE	1300
5	Yargelis Savigne	CUB	1293
6	Yamilé Aldama	SUD	1291
7	Baya Rahouli	ALG	1246
8	Magdelín Martínez	ITA	1241
9	Simona La Mantia	ITA	1203
10	Viktoriya Gurova	RUS	1198
11	Yelena Oleynikova	RUS	1196
12	Carlota Castrejana	ESP	1194
13	Natalya Safronova	BLR	1191
14	Kène Ndoye	SEN	1185
15	Huang Qiuyan	CHN	1181
16	Anast. Zhuravlyeva	UZB	1172
17	Xie Limei	CHN	1163
18	Sárka Kaspárková	CZE	1162
19	Iríni Dimitráki	GRE	1161
20	Nadezhda Bazhenova	RUS	1160

Shot

1	Nadezhda Ostapchuk	BLR	1307
2	Valerie Vili	NZL	1238
3	Olga Ryabinkina	RUS	1231
4	Nadine Kleinert	GER	1212
5	Natalya Khoroneko	BLR	1204
6	Yumileidi Cumbá	CUB	1181
7	Petra Lammert	GER	1177
8	Li Meiju	CHN	1168
9	Svetlana Krivelyova	RUS	1151
10	Misleidis González	CUB	1123
11	Astrid Kumbernuss	GER	1121
12	Christina Schwanitz	GER	1109
13	Lieja Tunks	NED	1107
13	Krystyna Zabawska	POL	1107
15	Assunta Legnante	ITA	1106
16	Li Ling	CHN	1092
17	Olga Ivanova	RUS	1083
18	Zhang Guirong	SIN	1077
18	Kristin Heaston	USA	1077
18	Kimberly Barrett	JAM	1077

Discus

1	Natalya Sadova	RUS	1286
2	Franka Dietzsch	GER	1281
3	Vera Cechlová	CZE	1244
4	Nicoleta Grasu	ROM	1204
5	Song Aimin	CHN	1174
6	Aretha Thurmond	USA	1167
7	Beatrice Faumuina	NZL	1166
8	Olena Antonova	UKR	1162
9	Marzena Wysocka	POL	1157
10	Dragana Tomaäevic	SCG	1139
11	Wioletta Potepa	POL	1133
12	Yania Ferrales	CUB	1126
13	Ma Shuli	CHN	1104
14	Nataliya Fokina	UKR	1096
15	Ellina Zvereva	BLR	1095
16	Becky Breisch	USA	1089
17	Elizna Naude	RSA	1087
18	Anna Söderberg	SWE	1082
18	Joanna Wisniewska	POL	1082
20	Sun Taifeng	CHN	1073

Hammer

1	Yipsi Moreno	CUB	1283
2	Tatyana Lysenko	RUS	1260
3	Kamila Skolimowska	POL	1259
4	Olga Kuzenkova	RUS	1244
5	Manuela Montebrun	FRA	1232
6	Zhang Wenxiu	CHN	1222
7	Ester Balassini	ITA	1187
8	Betty Heidler	GER	1178
9	Susanne Keil	GER	1153
10	Yekaterina Khoroshikh	RUS	1151
11	Olga Tsander	BLR	1150
12	Erin Gilreath	USA	1149
13	Mihaela Melinte	ROM	1146
14	Ivana Brkljacic	CRO	1134
15	Liu Yinghui	CHN	1132
15	Candice Scott	TRI	1132
17	Clarissa Claretti	ITA	1124
18	Kathrin Klaas	GER	1120
19	Irina Sekachova	UKR	1115
20	Gu Yuan	CHN	1110

Javelin

1	Osleidys Menéndez	CUB	1341
2	Steffi Nerius	GER	1272
3	Sonia Bisset	CUB	1224
4	Christina Obergföll	GER	1209
5	Barbora Spotáková	CZE	1165
6	Laverne Eve	BAH	1162
7	Zahra Bani	ITA	1149
8	Christina Scherwin	DEN	1135
8	Angelikí Tsiolakoúdi	GRE	1135
10	Goldie Sayers	GBR	1110
11	Barbara Madejczyk	POL	1106
12	Paula Tarvainen	FIN	1099
13	Nikolett Szabó	HUN	1096
14	Felicia Moldovan	ROM	1085
15	Mikaela Ingberg	FIN	1079
16	Taina Kolkkala	FIN	1078
17	Ma Ning	CHN	1071
18	Xue Juan	CHN	1065
19	Olha Ivankova	UKR	1060
19	Mercedes Chilla	ESP	1060

Heptathlon (Pentathlon Ind.)

1	Carolina Klüft	SWE	1421
2	Eunice Barber	FRA	1376
3	Kelly Sotherton	GBR	1300
4	Margaret Simpson	GHA	1260
5	Austra Skujyté	LTU	1248
6	Karin Ruckstuhl	NED	1232
7	Nataliya Dobrynska	UKR	1228
8	Marie Collonvillé	FRA	1218
9	Hyleas Fountain	USA	1204
10	Sonja Kesselschläger	GER	1197
11	Jessica Zelinka	CAN	1150
11	Laurien Hoos	NED	1150
13	Lilli Schwarzkopf	GER	1149
14	Virginia Miller	USA	1148
15	Kylie Wheeler	AUS	1146
16	Fiona Asigbee	USA	1144
17	Claudia Tonn	GER	1140
18	Tatyana Alisevich	BLR	1128
18	Yvonne Wisse	NED	1128
20	Diana Koritskaya	RUS	1125
20	Yuliya Akulenko	UKR	1125

Race Walking - 20km (5km-10km-50km)

1	Margarita Turava	BLR	1330
2	Susana Feitor	POR	1296
3	Elisa Rigaudo	ITA	1254
4	María Vasco	ESP	1252
4	Claudia Stef	ROM	1252
6	Jiang Jing	CHN	1250
7	Song Hongjuan	CHN	1244
8	Barbora Dibelková	CZE	1237
9	Melanie Seeger	GER	1230
10	Sabine Zimmer	GER	1229
11	He Dan	CHN	1226
12	Wang Liping	CHN	1224
13	Jiang Qiuyan	CHN	1223
14	Tang Yinghua	CHN	1219
14	Shi Na	CHN	1219
16	Bai Yanmei	CHN	1218
17	Yuliya Voyevodina	RUS	1217
18	Yelena Ginko	BLR	1212
19	Cristina López	ESA	1211
20	Irina Pudovkina	RUS	1205

CROSS-COUNTRY - NATIONAL CHAMPIONS 2005

	MEN (longer distance)	**WOMEN** (longer distance)
Australia	Martin Dent	Susan Michelsson
Austria	Günther Weidlinger	Andrea Mayr
Belgium	Tom Van Hooste	Mounia Aboulahcen
Brazil	Ubiratan dos Santos	Lucelia Peres
Bulgaria	Stanislev Lambev	Rumyana Panovska
Canada (Dec)	Simon Bairu	Carmen Douma-Hussar
Chile	Roberto Echeverría	Susana Robolledo
Czech Republic (Nov)	David Gerych	Vendula Frintová
Denmark (Oct)	Steen Walter	Louise Mørch
Ecuador	Franklin Tenorio	Rosa Chacha
England	Glynn Tromans	Hayley Yelling
Estonia	Aleksei Saveljev	Maria Sahharova
Ethiopia	Abebe Dinkessa	Tirunesh Dibaba
Finland	Tuomo Lehtinen	Maija Oravamäki
France	Driss El Himer	Maria Martins
Germany (Nov)	Jens Borrmann	Sabrina Mockenhaupt
Greece	Hristóforos Meroúsis	María Protópappa
Hungary	Miklós Németh	Krisztina Papp
Ireland	Gary Murray	Jolene Byrne
Israel	Haile Satayin	Nili Avramski
Italy	Maurizio Leone	Patrizia Tisi
Kenya	Eliud Kipchoge	Rose Chepchumba
Latvia	Valerijs Zolnerovics	Daniela Fetcere
Lithuania	Vitalij Gorlukovic	Irina Krakoviak
Luxembourg	Thierry Hübsch	Pascale Schmoetten
Netherlands	Kamiel Maase	Adriënne Herzog
New Zealand	Phil Costley	Kate McIlroy
Northern Ireland	Steve Cairns	Jill Shannon
Norway	Trond Idland	Anita Evertsen
Poland	Jakub Czaja	Justyna Lesman
Portugal	Fernando Silva	Anália Rosa
Romania (Nov)	Marius Ionescu	Ana Maria Bordea
Russia	Dmitriy Maksimov	Albina Ivanova
Scotland	Robert Russell	Colette Fagan
Serbia & CG	Mirko Petrovic	Azra Eminovic
Slovakia	Marcel Matanin	Zuzana Novacková
Slovenia	Borut Veber	Spela Krzan
South Africa	Norman Dlomo	Lebogang Phalula
Spain	Carlos de la Ossa	Jacqueline Martín
Sweden	Mustafa Mohamed	Ida Nilsson
Switzerland	Bruno Heuberger	Simone Niggli-Luder
Turkey	Abdülakdir Türk	Lale Öztürk
UK	Glynn Tromans	Hayley Yelling
Ukraine (Mar)	Dmitriy Baranovskiy	Margarita Luchinina
(Nov)	Leonid Rybak	Nataliya Berkut
USA Winter	Darren Ritzenhein	Colleen De Reuck
Wales	Ian Mitchell	Catherine Dugdale
Asian	Hang Geng CHN	Li Helan CHN
Team	Qatar	China
Balkan	Abdülakdir Türk TUR	Cristina Casandra ROM
East African	Richard Limo KEN	Doris Changeywo KEN
European Clubs	Zersenay Tadesse ERI/ESP	Fernanda Rbeiro POR
Teams	C.A.Adidas ESP	Maratona Maia, POR
NCAA (Nov)	Simon Bairu CAN	Johanna Nilsson SWE
Nordic (Nov)	Henrik Ahnström SWE	Louise Mørch DEN
South American	William Naranjo COL	Lucilia Peres BRA
Southern Africa	Lewis Masundo ZIM	Poppy Mlambo RSA
World Universities	Günther Weidlinger AUT	M Alaoui Selsouli MAR
Team	Morocco	GBR

	MEN (short distance)	**WOMEN** (short distance)
Austria	Günther Weidlinger	
Belgium	Mario Van Waeyenberghe	Liesbeth Van De Velde
Brazil	Hudson de Souza	Maria Vieira
Bulgaria	Ivaylo Ignatov	Rumyana Panovska
Chile	Roberto Echeverría	Susana Robolledo

Czech Republic (Nov)	Jirí Miler	
Denmark	Claus Bugge	Louise Mørch
Etsonia	Ergo Kilki	
Ethiopia	Dejene Berhanu	Meselech Melkamu
Finland	Simo Wannas	
France	Mokhtar Benhari	Bouchra Ghézielle
Germany (Nov)	Dominik Burkhardt	
Hungary	Balázs Csillag	
Israel	Kokav Bitao	
Italy	Luciano Di Pardo	Federica Dal Ri
Kenya	Isaac Songok	Priscah Jepleting
Netherlands	Simon Vroemen	Lesley van Miert
New Zealand	Ben Ruthe	Kate McIlroy
Norway	Bård Kvalheim	Susanne Wigene
Poland	Marcin Chabowski	
Portugal	Ricardo Ribas	Anália Rosa
Romania (Nov)	Marius Ionescu	Ana Maria Bordea
Russia	Andrey Khramov	Alevtina Ivanova
Scotland	Robert Russell	Colette Fagan
Slovakia	Miroslav Vanko	
Slovenia	Cne Subic	
South Africa	Emmanuel Mkhabela	
Spain	Roberto García	Rosa Morató
Sweden	Mustafa Mohamed	Ida Nilsson
Switzerland	Ueli Koch	Christina Caruzzo
UK	Steve Vernon	Lisa Dobriskey
Ukraine (Mar)	Vitaliy Rybak	Yuliya Ruban
(Nov)	Mykola Labovsky	
USA Winter	Tim Broe	Shalane Flanagan
East African	Dennis Ndiso KEN	Nancy Wambui KEN
South American	Israel dos Anjos BRA	Susana Rebolledo CHI
Southern Africa	Ruben Ramolefi RSA	Dinahrose Phalula RSA

Winners of EAA and IAAF Permit Cross-Country Races 2005

8 Jan	Belfast (IAAF)	Darren Ritzenhein USA	Etalemahu Kidane ETH
9 Jan	Amorebieta (EAA)	Abdullah Ahmad Hassan QAT	Benita Johnson AUS
15 Jan	Edinburgh (IAAF)	Eliud Kipchoge KEN	Tirunesh Dibaba ETH
16 Jan	Sevilla (IAAF)	Maregu Zewdie ETH	Werknesh Kidane ETH
23 Jan	Hannut (EAA)	Luke Kipkosgei KEN	Benita Johnson AUS
23 Jan	Tourcoing (IAAF)	Sergey Lebed UKR	Susan Chepkemei KEN
30 Jan	Albufeira (IAAF)	Moses Mosop KEN	Nancy Kiprop KEN
6 Feb	San Vittore (IAAF)	Saïf Saaeed Shaheen QAT	Benita Johnson AUS
12 Feb	Nairobi (IAAF)	Eliud Kipchoge KEN	Rose Chepchumba KEN
13 Feb	Diekirch (IAAF)	Sultan Khamis Zaman QAT	Natalie Harvey GBR
20 Feb	Chiba (IAAF)	Samuel Wanjiru KEN	Miwako Yamanaka JPN
6 Mar	Fukuoka (IAAF)	Samuel Wanjiru KEN	Mesaret Defar ETH
17 Oct	Pardubice (EAA)	Elisha Sawe KEN	Justyna Bak POL
13 Nov	Amora-Seixal (EAA)	Adam Ismael BRN	Leonor Carneiro
13 Nov	Tilburg (EAA)	Aïssa Dghoughi MAR	Anikó Kálovics HUN
19 Nov	Oeiras (IAAF)	Ronald Rutto KEN	Elisabeth Rumokol KEN
20 Nov	Soria (EAA)	Boniface Songok KEN	Rose Chepchumba KEN
27 Nov	Llodio (IAAF)	Tariku Bekele ETH	Anikó Kálovics HUN
27 Nov	Leffinckroucke (EAA)	Denis Ndiso KEN	Teyiba Erkesso ETH
27 Nov	Torres Vedra (EAA)	Adam Ismael BRN	Nancy Kiprop KEN
27 Nov	Roeselare (EAA)	Tom Van Hooste BEL	Veerle DeJaeghere BEL
18 Dec	Brussels (IAAF)	Abebe Dinkessa ETH	Teyiba Erkesso ETH

European Cross-Country Championships 2005

At Tilburg, Netherlands 11 December.

Senior Men (9.44k)
1. Sergiy Lebid UKR 27:09
2. Alberto García ESP 27:21
3. Driss Maazouzi FRA 27:26
4. Bouabdellah Tahri FRA 27:27
5. Günther Weidlinger AUT 27:28
6. Mokhtar Benhari FRA 27:35
7. Tom Van Hooste BEL 27:36
8. Khalid Zoubaa FRA 27:36
9. Juan Carlos de la Ossa ESP 27:36
10. José Rios ESP 27:37
11. Fernando Silva POR 27:39
12. Gary Murray IRL 27:41
13. Driss El Himer FRA 27:43
14. Mustafa Mohamed SWE 27:44
15. Gabrielle De Nard ITA 27:45

88 finished.

Teams: 1. FRA 21, 2. ESP 64, 3. UKR 71, 4. ITA 75, 5. POR 92, 6. RUS 123, 7. GBR 129, 8. IRL 139, 9. SWE 178, 10. AUT 178, 11. BEL 186, 12. NED 198, 13. GER 200, 14. TUR 203, 15. MDA 338.

Junior Men (6.5k)
1. Barnabás Bene HUN 18:41
2. Andy Vernon GBR 18:42
3. Dusan Markesevic SCG 18:42
4. Mohamed Elbendir ESP 18:50

5. Ciprian Suhanea ROM 18:50
6. Stefan Patru ROM 18:52
7. Siarhei Chabiarak BLR 18:53
8. Marcin Chabowski POL 18:54
9. Martin Dematteis ITA 18:54
10. Arkadiusz Gardzielewski POL 18:54
101 finished.
Teams: 1. POL 60, 2. GBR 68, 3. ROM 71, 4. ITA 101, 5. POR 115, 6. ESP 120, 7. RUS 130, 8. GER 141, 9. BLR 175, 10. FRA 179, 11. TUR 183, 12. HUN 194, 13. IRL 204, 14. NED 208, 15. UKR 220, 16. BEL 258, 17. SUI 324.
Senior Women (6.5k)
1. Lornah Kiplagat NED 19:55
2. Sabrina Mockenhaupt GER 20:00
3. Johanna Nilsson SWE 20:01
4. Olivera Jevtic SCG 20:04
5. Anikó Kálovics HUN 20:15
6. Hayley Yelling GBR 20:16
7. Inga Abitova RUS 20:16
8. Liz Yelling GBR 20:17
9. Rosa María Morató ESP 20:18
10. Marina Konovalova RUS 20:18
11. Mary Cullen IRL 20:22
12. Veerle Dejaeghere BEL 20:24
13. Latifa Essarokh FRA 20:25
14. Lidiya Grigoryeva RUS 20:26
15. Adrienne Herzog NED 20:28.
71 finished.
Teams: 1. RUS 52, 2. GBR 54, 3. FRA 73, 4. POR 87, 5. IRL 106, 6. NED 109, 7. GER 126, 8. BEL 157, 9. ESP 169, 10. ITA 171, 11. DEN 269
Junior Women (4.83k)
1. Ancuta Bobocel ROM 15:23
2. Emily Pidgeon GBR 15:25
3. Susan Kuijken NED 15:33
4. Linda Byrne IRL 15:39
5. Galina Maksimova RUS 15:40
6. Morag MacLarty GBR 15:42
7. Stephanie Twell GBR 15:45
8. Yuliya Ivanova RUS 15:47
9. Azra Eminovic SCG 15:50
10. Larisa Arcip ROM 15:51
80 finished.
Teams: 1. GBR 30, 2. ROM 49, 3. RUS 60, 4. IRL 98, 5. BEL 123, 6. GER 124, 7. ESP 152, 8. FRA 170, 9. ITA 172, 10. TUR 183, 11. SUI 196, 12. UKR 200, 13. NED 206.

See ATHLETICS 2005 page 608 for results of the 2005 World Cross-Country Championships.

2005 WORLD ROAD RACE REVIEW

By David E Martin

WHERE THERE are runners, there are road races. It's perhaps the running world's simplest form of competition, going either from one point to another or out-and-back, with a stopwatch and clipboard all that's required to keep score. In today's sophisticated world, however, with upwards of 50,000 participants in many events, and high stakes at the front of the pack in the form of prize money, with the possibility of doping control to ensure a clean competition, these events are as complex to stage as a track meeting.

The accompanying list summarizes the men and women winners of 167 major races, over distances from 4.7 to 30 kilometers. Perusal gives a view of the global scope of road racing. The venues include 29 nations on six continents. Among the women winners, 31 countries are represented, with Kenya predominant on the victory stand (31.4%), followed by Ethiopia (13.6%), Russia and the USA (each 6%). Thus, 4 nations account for 96 winners of the 154 races listed. For the men, 18 nations are represented, but there is far greater Kenyan domination on the victory podium: 90 of the 153 listed races, or 59%, compared to runner-up Ethiopia with 17 (11%).

While the road racing scene remains full of vitality, there are a few sources of confusion. One concerns the implementation of the IAAF point system for identifying numerically the degree of excellence of a given result. Courses with beneficial terrain are excluded from the rankings. Thus, courses having a downslope greater than 1 m/km, or a start/finish separation greater than 50% of the course distance, are ineligible for record consideration. Some, however, suggest that 30% S/F separation will better 'protect' the risk of favorable course terrain causing an inappropriate bias in finish times. Lists of performances should compare athlete excellence rather than course difficulty. The debate continues.

A second source of confusion arises when runners change nationalities and even more importantly, change their identity because of an accompanying name change. Thus, Qatar's Mubarak Hassan Shami was once Kenya's Richard Yatich. Similarly, Bahrain's Abel Yagout Jawher once was Kenya's Abel Cheruiyot. This phenomenon is of course occurring among distance runners in the track world as well.

The road-racing world has its own IAAF world championships, typically contested around October over the half-marathon distance. It is of the highest quality, but this year's event was a combination of challenges: altitude (643 m), cold weather (5°C), rain, and remoteness (Edmonton).

Among the men, the winner was teenager Fabiano Joseph of Tanzania, runner-up the past two years, with a sprint finish (61:08) over Qatar's Shami (61:09). With the women, the top two spots went to athletes whose performances were excellent tune-ups for upcoming marathons: Constantina Dita (69:17 - Chicago) and Lornah Kiplagat (70:19 - New York).

Leading Road Races 2005

Date	Race	Men	Women
6 Jan	Maldonado 10km	Robert Cheruiyot KEN 28:37	Lydia Cheromei KEN 32:30
6 Jan	Miyazaki HMar	Women only	Lidia Simon ROM 69:58
9 Jan	Egmond aan Zee HMar	Robert Cheboror KEN 63:35	Mizuki Noguchi JPN 67:47*
16 Jan	Houston HMar	Julius Kibet KEN 63:17	Olga Romanova RUS 72:36
23 Jan	Naples HMar	John Korir KEN 65:22	Lyubov Denisova RUS 74:26
30 Jan	Almeria HMar	Haile Gebrselassie ETH 61:46	Men only
6 Feb	Coamo HMar	James Kwambai KEN 63:45	Elfenesh Alemu ETH 72:57
6 Feb	Granollers HMar	Haile Gebrselassie ETH 61:33	Men only
6 Feb	Marugame HMar	Laban Kagika KEN 61:36	Takako Kotorida JPN 69:34
11 Feb	Himeji 10M	Terukazu Omori JPN 46:23*	Men only
13 Feb	Schoorl 10km	Kamiel Maase NED 28:54	Lornah Kiplagat NED 33:09
20 Feb	Ferrara HMar	Women only	Helena Javornik SLO 69:53
20 Feb	Ome 30km	Takehisa Okino JPN 1:31:37	Mika Okunaga JPN 1:46:11
27 Feb	Carolina 10km	John Korir KEN 27:56	Lornah Kiplagat NED 32:11
27 Feb	Kumamoto 30km	Takayuki Matsumiya JPN 1:28:00WR	Men only
27 Feb	Ostia HMar	James Kwambai KEN 60:45	Rosalba Console ITA 69:34=CR
6 Mar	Alphen aan den Rijn 20km	Felix Limo KEN 58:34	Kirsten Otterbu NOR 69:05
6 Mar	Barcelona HMar	Edwin Kibet KEN 63:04	Isabel Eizmendi ESP 73:01
6 Mar	Paris HMar	Denis Ndiso KEN 62:34	Linah Cheruiyot KEN 71:56
6 Mar	Reading HMar	Julius Kimutai KEN 61:51	Catherine Mutwa KEN 73:09
12 Mar	Jacksonville 15km Nat. Ch	Ryan Shay USA 43:52	Jennifer Rhines USA 49:21
13 Mar	Kyoto HMar	Koichi Mitsuyuki JPN 62:34	Rie Ueno JPN 70:54
13 Mar	Lisboa HMar	Paul Tergat KEN 59:10	Susan Chepkemei KEN 68:47
13 Mar	Liverpool HMar	Simon Kasimili KEN 64:15	Debbie Mason GBR 73:02
13 Mar	Ribarroja del Turia HMar	Julius Rotich KEN 62:51	Malgorzata Sobanska POL 75:57
13 Mar	Yamaguchi HMar	Daniel Njenga KEN 61:31	Terumi Asoshina JPN 69:54
13 Mar	Zapopan HMar	Anthony Korir KEN 64:00	Dorota Gruca POL 73:29
19 Mar	Azkoitia HMar	Simon Kiprop KEN 61:53	Yesenia Centeno ESP 74:12
19 Mar	Den Haag HMar	Moses Kigen KEN 61:45	Mary Ptikany KEN 70:18
19 Mar	Mobile 10km	Luke Kipkosgei KEN 28:37	Sally Barsosio KEN 32:28
19 Mar	Virginia Beach 8km	Eric Chirchir KEN 23:37	Tetyana Hladyr UKR 25:49
20 Mar	Hamilton 30km	Joseph Nderitu KEN 1:38:48	Kate McNamara CAN 1:58:08
20 Mar	Matsue HMar	Women only	Miki Ohira JPN 71:06
20 Mar	Palma de Mallorca HMar	Edwin Kibet KEN 63:36	Alemayehu Mersha ETH 73:26
26 Mar	New Orleans 10km	Sammy Kipketer KEN 27:47	Isabella Ochichi KEN 30:27*
26 Mar	New York 8km USA Ch	Jorge Torres USA 22:47	Deena Kastor USA 25:05
26 Mar	Paderborn 10km	Moses Kigen KEN 28:33	Eunice Jepkorir KEN 32:16
26 Mar	Paderborn HMar	Elijah Sang KEN 61:49*	Beatrice Omwanza KEN 71:32
28 Mar	Berkane 10km	Benjamin Limo KEN 28:29	Zhor El Kamch MAR 16:13
28 Mar	Dongio 10/5km	Paul Kimulgul KEN 28:35	Alice Timbilil KEN 15:31
28 Mar	Stadskanaal 10km	John Kipchumba KEN 27:53*	Pauline Wangui KEN 32:39*
2 Apr	Praha HMar	Silas Kirui KEN 61:07	Susan Kirui KEN 72:49
3 Apr	Barcelona 10km	Sahle Warga ETH 28:35	Irene Kwambai KEN 31:25
3 Apr	Berlin HMar	Paul Kimulgul KEN 61:04	Luminita Zaituc GER 71:04
3 Apr	Brunssum 10km	John Kibowen KEN 27:51	Eunice Jepkorir KEN 32:19
3 Apr	Carlsbad 5km	Dejene Berhanu ETH 13:10	Tirunesh Dibaba ETH 14:51 =WR
3 Apr	Chicago 8km	Brian Sell USA 23:17	Deena Kastor USA 24:36
3 Apr	Washington 10M	John Kipkoech Korir KEN 46:54	Nuta Olaru ROM 52:01
9 Apr	Dublin 10km	Craig Mottram AUS 28:35	Amy Rudolph USA 32:16*
9 Apr	Richmond 10km	Ernest Meli Kimeli KEN 28:43	Tatyana Petrova RUS 32:46
10 Apr	Korschenbroich 10/5km	Moses Kigen KEN 28:36	Sabrina Mockenhaupt GER 15:47
10 Apr	Madrid HMar	Edwin Kibet KEN 63:15	Muliye Lemma ETH 74:38
10 Apr	Milano HMar	Wilson Kiprotich Kebenei KEN 60:11	Anikó Kálovics HUN 71:57
10 Apr	Vilamoura HMar	Tesfaye Tola ETH 61:56	Jelena Prokopcuka LAT 70:13
16 Apr	Brugnera HMar	Rachid Amour TUN 61:53	Jane Kariuki KEN 72:33

17 Apr	Hilversum 10km	Musa Kipkemboi Cheruti KEN 28:07	Peninah Arusei KEN 32:53
17 Apr	Monterrey HMar	George Okworo KEN 62:03	Grace Momanyi KEN 70:20
17 Apr	Vancouver 10km	Michael Power AUS 29:26	Nicole Stevenson CAN 32:30
17 Apr	Vitry-sur-Seine HMar	Evans Cheruiyot KEN 61:01	Jane Auro Ekimat KEN 70:39
24 Apr	Heillecourt 8.7/4.7km	John Korir KEN 24:17	Isabella Ochichi KEN 14:13
24 Apr	Maastricht 15km	John Kelai KEN 43:16	Fatiha Baouf BEL 50:24
24 Apr	Nice HMar	Benson Barus KEN 61:14	Irina Permitina RUS 72:20
1 May	Breda HMar	Jeroen van Damme NED 46:07	Nadezhda Wijenberg NED 52:47
1 May	Marseille 10km	John Kipkoech Korir KEN 28:07	Rose Cheruiyot KEN 32:25
1 May	Spokane 12km	John Korir KEN 34:26	Asmae Leghzaoui MAR 39:33
7 May	Indianapolis HMar	Wesley Ochoro KEN 63:31	Albina Ivanova RUS 73:35
8 May	Berlin 25km	Luke Kibet KEN 1:13:51	Rose Cheruiyot KEN 1:24:46
8 May	Edinburgh 10km	Juan Carlos de la Ossa ESP 28:22	Jelena Prokopcuka LAT 32:42
14 May	Grand Rapids 25km	Simon Wangui KEN 1:13:55*	Colleen De Reuck USA 1:25:15
15 May	Glasgow 10km	Women only	Lornah Kiplagat NED 31:44
15 May	San Francisco 12km	Gilbert Okari KEN 34:49	Asmae Leghzaoui MAR 38:22*
15 May	Santos 10km	Marilson G dos Santos BRA 28:30	Margaret Karie KEN 33:38
21 May	Göteborg HMar	Silas Sang KEN 63:18	Susan Kirui KEN 72:34
21 May	New York 10km	Craig Mottram AUS 28:28	Alemtsehay Misganaw ETH 35:10
22 May	Casablanca 10km	Women only	Zakia Mrisho TAN 32:49
22 May	Cleveland 10km	Julius Kibet KEN 28:44	Asmae Leghzaoui MAR 31:10*
22 May	Coban HMar	John Korir KEN 63:45	Grace Momanyi KEN 73:10
22 May	Manchester 10km	Haile Gebrselassie ETH 27:25*	Lornah Kiplagat NED 31:28
28 May	Ottawa 10km	George Kirwa Misoi CAN 28:56	Grace Momanyi KEN 31:25*
30 May	Boulder 10km @	Gudisa Shentema ETH 29:21	Elva Dryer USA 32:51
4 Jun	Albany 5km	Women only	Asmae Leghzaoui MAR 15:18*
4 Jun	Groesbeek 10km	Ahmed El Baday MAR 28:41	Doris Changeywo KEN 33:02
5 Jun	Gardena 5km	Eric Chirchir KEN 13:41	Men only
11 Jun	New York 10km	Women only	Lornah Kiplagat NED 31:44
11 Jun	Peoria 4M	Shadrack Kosgei KEN 17:45	Constantina Tomescu ROM 20:47
12 Jun	Wien 5km	Women only	Sabrina Mockenhaupt GER 15:43
19 Jun	Kaiserslautern 5km	Musir Jawher BRN 13:43	Margaret Chirchir KEN 16:07
22 Jun	Darmstadt 7.6/5.5km	Sammy Kipruto KEN 22:23	Grazyna Syrek POL 18:27
25 Jun	Appingedam 10km	Thomas Chemitei KEN 28:49	Genet Getaneh ETH 33:32
3 Jul	Sapporo HMar	Megubo Mogusu KEN 61:28	Catherine Ndereba KEN 69:24
3 Jul	Southport HMar	Patrick Nyangelo KEN 63:35	Yuko Sato JPN 72:49
4 Jul	Atlanta 10km	Gilbert Okari KEN 28:18	Lornah Kiplagat NED 31:17
4 Jul	Cedar Rapids 8km	Julius Kiptoo KEN 23:03	Atalelech Ketema ETH 26:56
10 Jul	Sendai HMar	Samuel Wanjiru KEN 59:43	Tegla Loroupe KEN 72:50
10 Jul	Utica 15km	Gilbert Okari KEN 43:22	Sally Barsosio KEN 50:11
11 Jul	Oelde 10km	Gebo Burka ETH 28:28	Carolyne Kiptoo KEN 33:03
16 Jul	Kingsport 8km	Tibebu Yenew ETH 23:06	Viktoriya Klimina RUS 26:15
20 Jul	Voorthuizen 10km	Sammy Kipruto KEN 28:47	Carolyne Kiptoo KEN 32:50
24 Jul	Capitola 6M	Wilson Kigen KEN 27:36	Sally Barsosio KEN 31:17
30 Jul	Davenport 7M	Gilbert Okari KEN 32:24	Nuta Olaru ROM 36:53
31 Jul	Bogotá HMar@	James Kwambai KEN 63:10*	Adriana Fernández MEX 75:02
6 Aug	Cape Elizabeth 10km	Gilbert Okari KEN 27:39	Lornah Kiplagat NED 31:35
14 Aug	Falmouth 7.04M	Gilbert Okari KEN 31:59	Lornah Kiplagat NED 36:09
14 Aug	Rio de Janeiro HMar	Stephen Biwott KEN 62:46	Solange S de Pinho BRA 74:21
14 Aug	Sydney 14km	Patrick Nyangelo TAN 41:12	Kerryn McCann AUS 46:27
21 Aug	Bishop Auckland 10km	Micah Kogo KEN 28:49	Olga Kimaiyo KEN 32;45
21 Aug	Configno 8.5km	Sergey Lebid UKR 23:43	Rose Chepchumba KEN 27:59
21 Aug	Toa Baja 10km	Gilbert Okari KEN 28:41	Lourdes Cruz PUR 37:52
27 Aug	Flint 10M	Fabiano Joseph TAN 47:46	Alevtina Ivanova RUS 53:34
28 Aug	Sululta HMar ETH Ch @	Solomon Tsige ETH 61:37	Merima Hashim ETH 71:52
3 Sep	Lille HMar	James Kibocha Theury KEN 60:54	Merima Denboba ETH 71:37
4 Sep	London 5km	Women only	Derartu Tulu ETH 15:30

4 Sep	Tilburg 10M/10km	Haile Gebrselassie ETH 44:24 WR*	Edith Masai KEN 31:37
4 Sep	Virginia Beach HMar	James Mwangi Macharia KEN 60:42*	Werknesh Kidane ETH 69:48
5 Sep	New Haven 20km USA Ch	Abdihakim Abdirahman USA 58:42	Blake Russell USA 66:43
5 Sep	Park Forest 10M	Alene Amere ETH 47:24	Tatyana Chulakh RUS 55:37
11 Sep	Pila HMar	Michael Karonei KEN 64:55	Natalia Berkut UKR 73:30
11 Sep	Providence 5km	Mohammed Amyn MAR 13:44	Olga Kravtsova RUS 15:43
11 Sep	Rotterdam HMar	Samuel Wanjiru KEN 59:16 WR*	Bizunesh Bekele ETH 71:54
11 Sep	Zaragoza HMar ESP Ch	Toni Peña ESP 62:38	Yesenia Centeno ESP 72:14
17 Sep	Uster HMar	Women only	Joyce Chepchumba KEN 71:45
18 Sep	Newcastle HMar	Zersenay Tadesse ERI 59:05 WB	Derartu Tulu ETH 67:33
18 Sep	Philadelphia HMar	Gudisa Shentema ETH 62:23	Deena Kastor USA 67:53
18 Sep	Torino HMar	Nicholas Kemboi KEN 62:10	Zaituni Nkoki TAN 73:25
18 Sep	Zaandam 10M	William Kipsang KEN 46:04	Isabella Ochichi KEN 51:07
25 Sep	Lisboa HMar	Martin Lel KEN 61:37	Rose Cheruiyot KEN 72:49
25 Sep	Remich HMar	Wilson Chebet KEN 62:19	Joan Aiyabei KEN 72:36
25 Sep	Udine HMar	Robert Kipchumba KEN 61:13	Pamela Chepchumba KEN 69:06
25 Sep	Versailles 16.3km	Wesley Ochoro KEN 49:00	Irina Permitina RUS 56:19
1 Oct	Edmonton HMar IAAF Ch	Fabiano Joseph TAN 61:08	Constantina Tomescu ROM 69:17
2 Oct	St. Denis HMar	Denis Ndiso KEN 61:59	Josca Obare KEN 72:20
8 Oct	Trento 10km ITA Ch	Paul Kimulgul KEN 28:00	Bruna Genovese ITA 33:15
9 Oct	Groningen 4M	Eliud Kipchoge KEN 17:10 WB*	Gelete Burka ETH 19:51
9 Oct	Portsmouth 10M	John Yuda TAN 46:45	Derartu Tulu ETH 51:27
10 Oct	Boston 10km USA Ch	Women only	Katie McGregor USA 32:26
16 Oct	Chihuahua HMar	Reuben Cheruiyot KEN 62:29	Susan Muthoni KEN 71:47
16 Oct	London 10km	Women only	Paula Radcliffe GBR 32:19
16 Oct	New Delhi HMar	Philip Rugut KEN 61:54	Irina Timofeyeva RUS 70:35
16 Oct	Paris 20km	Evans Cheruiyot KEN 57:19	Dire Tune ETH 68:17
23 Oct	Chula Vista 5km	Paul Morrison CAN 13:58	Emilie Mondor CAN 15:37
23 Oct	Durban 10km	Shadrack Hoff RSA 28:34	Poppy Mlambo RSA 33:48
23 Oct	Reims HMar	Kimwole Kimutai KEN 62:27	Teyebe Erkesso ETH 70:00
30 Oct	Cassis 20.308km	Wm. Chebon Chebor KEN 60:40	Fatiha Fauvel Klileh FRA 72:53
30 Oct	Milano 10km	Viktor Röthlin SUI 28:38	Silvia Sommaggio ITA 33:51
30 Oct	Torreón 10km	Reuben Cheruiyot KEN 28:48	Adriana Fernández MEX 32:58*
5 Nov	Mobile 10km USA Ch	Dathan Ritzenhein USA 28:11	Katie McGregor USA 32:51
6 Nov	Boulogne Billancourt HMar	David Langat KEN 60:47	Miriam Wangari KEN 72:00
6 Nov	Ourense 10km	Peter Kamais KEN) 28:50	Beatrice Jepchumba KEN 33:34
11 Nov	Issy les Moulineaux 10km	Aïssa Dehoughi MAR 28:19	Caroline Kwambai KEN 33:18
13 Nov	Pietramurata HMar	Eliap Kiplagat Kurgat KEN 61:18	Ivana Iozzia ITA 73:51
19 Nov	Lagos HMar	Fabiano Joseph TAN 62:20*	Millicent Doadi GHA 76:31
20 Nov	La Habana HMar	Aguelmis Rojas CUB 63:40*	Mariela González CUB 77:33
20 Nov	Nijmegen 15km	Haile Gebrselassie ETH 41:57	Berhane Adere ETH 47:48
24 Nov	Nagoya HMar	Julius Maina KEN 61:43	Mie Ueda JPN 71:39
26 Nov	Basel 10/7.8km	Günther Weidlinger AUT 28:35	Aster Bacha ETH 25:13
27 Nov	Addis Ababa 10km @	Ketema Negussie ETH 28:25*	Genet Getaneh ETH 33:06*
27 Nov	Madrid 10km	Ronaldo Kipchumba KEN 28:33	Belainesh Zemedkun ETH 32:57
4 Dec	Heerenberg 15km	Hailu Mekonnen ETH 43:09	Bezunesh Bekele ETH 48:32*
4 Dec	Mazatlán HMar	Isaac Kimaiyo KEN 63:16*	Genoveva Jelagat Kigen KEN 70:22*
11 Dec	Kosa 10M	Samuel Wanjiru KEN 45:10	Men only
18 Dec	Los Palacios HMar	Festus Langat KEN 61:58	Caroline Kwambai KEN 74:54
23 Dec	Okayama 10km	Women only	Benita Johnson AUS 32:26
23 Dec	Okayama 21.1km	Women only	Evelyne Kimwei KEN 70:47
31 Dec	Bolzano 10/5km	Abebe Dinkesa ETH 28:39	Isabella Ochichi KEN 15:54
31 Dec	Luanda 15km	Paul Tergat KEN 45::23	Margaret Okayo KEN 49:12
31 Dec	Madrid 10km	Eliud Kipchoge KEN 27:34*	Paula Radcliffe GBR 31:16*
31 Dec	São Paulo 15km	Marilson G dos Santos BRA 44:21	Olivera Jevtic SCG 51:38

@=altitude > 1000m, * course record

See also major championships and national championships sections

2005 WORLD MARATHON REVIEW

By David E Martin

THE YEAR 2005 may be remembered in marathoning annals as the year of the sprint finish. The most notable example, of course, was the globally televised epic battle in the men's race between defending champion South African Hendrick Ramaala and world record-holder Paul Tergat at New York in November. It was the closest finish in the race's 36-year history: Tergat in 2:09:29.90 by just 0.32 seconds over Ramaala. IAAF rules require rounding upward of such decimals to the next full second, so Tergat's margin increased to a full second.

One month earlier, the 22nd edition of the marathon at Eindhoven in the Netherlands was held in such ideal weather (cloudy, 14°C) that two Kenyans broke the course record by 20 seconds. Boniface Usisivu and Philip Singoei were less than a step apart, and given the same time (2:08:45), with Usisivu declared the winner.

However, five months earlier, in May, the inaugural edition of the city marathon in Geneva, Switzerland had not only a three-man Ethiopian sweep of the medals but only 0.6 seconds separating first and third. Tesfaye Eticha was won (2:15:29.3) from Tesfaye Direba (2:15:29.6) and Urgessa Weyessa (2:15:29.9). [For the record, the closest 3-way finish in marathon history occurred at Moskva on 29 July 1979 with only 0.4 seconds separating Leonid Moseyev (2:13:19.6) from Shigeru Soh (2:13:19.8) and Viktor Zubov (2:13:20.0).]

Among the women, a similarly close finish occurred in December, when in the inaugural Las Vegas marathon – staged along its famous "Strip" or main street – Mexico's Adriana Fernandez and Russian debutante Galina Bogomolova each ran 2:31:54, with Poland's Dorota Gruca only one second behind (2:31:55).

Just as notable as these close finishes, however, were the unusually wide winning margins, especially among the women, at some of the world's most prestigious races. At Berlin, Mizuki Noguchi's 2:19:12 was 8:22 ahead of runner-up Luminita Zaituc. At London, Paula Radcliffe's 2:17:42 (a women's-only world record) was 6:08 faster than Constantina Tomescu's Romanian record of 2:22:50. Paula and Constantina met again in 2005 at the World Championships in Helsinki. Although Catherine Ndereba was runner-up to Radcliffe, with Tomescu in third, Paula's winning margin against this incredible competition was still 64 seconds. Earlier in the year, at Boston, Ndereba's winning margin over Elfenesh Alemu was a sizable 1:50. At the end of 2005, Ndereba's record of 11 sub-2:26:00 lifetime performançes remained unequalled.

Marathon racing continues its global growth. The table gives one indication of this by tabulating the number of finishers at the very largest races. Note the continuing trend for European marathons to have far fewer female participants than North American marathons. Despite the difficulty in completing the marathon distance, most races report a high percentage of finishes. Perhaps the best example of this is the New York marathon, which reported that 37,597 runners crossed its starting line, and after ten hours of racing, 98.0% had finished – it was history's largest marathon.

With obscure results still arriving as the publisher's deadline approaches, some characteristics of marathon participation at the top end can nevertheless be made. For men, the

The Largest Marathons in 2005

Date	*Venue*	*number men*	*percent men*	*number Women*	*percent Women*	*Total*
6 Nov	New York	24,794	67.3	12,062	32.7	36,856
17 Apr	London	24,690	70.0	10,571	30.1	35,261
9 Oct	Chicago	18,673	56.6	14,322	43.4	32,995
25 Sep	Berlin	24,573	80.6	5,933	19.4	30,506
10 Apr	Paris	24,655	85.5	4,202	14.5	28,857
11 Dec	Honolulu	12,763	52.7	11,456	47.3	24,219
6 Mar	Los Angeles	12,409	62.1	7,576	37.9	19,985
30 Oct	Washington	11,293	59.1	7,817	40.9	19,110
24 Apr	Hamburg	14,161	80.7	3,396	19.3	17,557
18 Apr	Boston	10,894	62.1	6,655	37.9	17,549
5 Jun	San Diego	7,467	46.9	8,467	53.1	15,934
4 Hub	Stockholm	10,0333	79.0	2,665	21.0	12,698
11 Sep	Köln	8,865	81.8	2,206	18.2	11,071

current tally shows 1087 performances under the time-honored 2:20:00 barrier, achieved by 762 different athletes from 60 countries. The 500th fastest men's performance is 2:15:46 (402 performances under 2:15:00), and the 1000th fastest performance is 2:19:29. For women, the 1000th fastest performance is 2:49:45, and the 500th fastest is 2:40:42 (471 under 2:40:00).

An analysis of winners of fastest men's (146) and women's (144) marathons shows some additional demographic trends. The men winners represent 24 nations, but Kenyan men are supremely dominant on the victory platform – their 72 wins comprising 49% of the total! Ethiopian men were far behind with only 13 victories (9%). The women winners, on the other hand, represent many more nations (34), but the dominant nations are Russia (39 victories), Kenya (20), and Ethiopia (13).

The Kenyan male marathon 'army' continues to 'rule the world' in both numbers and excellence – their domination is unprecedented. 472 of the 1087 sub-2:20:00 men's performances in 2005 were by Kenyans –43.4% of the total! In second place is Japan (94 performances for 8.6%), followed by Ethiopia (88, 8.1%). Even more astounding is the quality of Kenyan marathon achievements: of the 402 sub-2:15:00 marks, 200 are by Kenyan athletes. Thus, essentially half of the world's fastest marathon performances were achieved during 2005 by athletes of one small, but very talented country. And there will be more when the lists are complete. Amazing!

Results of 2005 Marathons

6 Jan	Tiberias	Habtamu Bekele ETH	2:18:08	Nili Avramski ISR	2:44:50
7 Jan	Dubai	Dejene Guta ETH	2:10:49	Deribe Hunde ETH	2:39:08
9 Jan	Tempe	Terefe Yae ETH	2:14:24	Shitaye Gemechu ETH	2:32:51
16 Jan	Houston	David Cheruiyot KEN	2:14:50	Kelly Keane USA	2:32:27
16 Jan	Marrakech	Abderahim Benradouane MAR	2:15:16	Hafida Narmouch MAR	2:40:58
16 Jan	Mumbai	Julius Sugut KEN	2:13:20	Mulu Seboka ETH	2:35:03
30 Jan	Lahore	Tseko Mpolokeng RSA	2:16:57	Jane Kariuki KEN	2:43:03
30 Jan	Miami	Elias Rodrigues Bastos BRA	2:17:26	Sandra Ruales ESP	2:37:02
30 Jan	Las Vegas #	Gilbert Koech KEN	2:13:45	Olga Kovpotina RUS	2:31:54
30 Jan	Osaka	*Women only*		Jelena Prokopcuka LAT	2:22:56
6 Feb	Oita	Satoshi Irifune JPN	2:09:58	*Men only*	
6 Feb	Tampa	Zepherinus Joseph STL	2:18:48	Firiya Zhdanova RUS	2:38:18
13 Feb	Austin #	Mikhail Khobotov RUS	2:12:38	Tatyana Borisova KGZ	2:31:01
13 Feb	Tokyo	Toshinari Takaoka JPN	2:07:41	*Men only*	
20 Feb	Durban	Johannes Kekana RSA	2:19:16	Dimakatsi Morobi RSA	2:50:14
20 Feb	Nobeoka	Kodai Fukunaga JPN	2:13:09	*Men only*	
20 Feb	Senshu	Kazuya Nakamori JPN	2:18:13	Kaori Shinjo JPN	2:44:21
20 Feb	Valencia	Rachid El Ghanmouni MAR	2:14:03	Natalya Zolotaryeva RUS	2:43:24
27 Feb	Hong Kong	Samson Loywapet KEN	2:15:21	Dai Yanyan CHN	2:34:41
27 Feb	Sevilla	Noah Kiplagat Serem KEN	2:22:15	Liliya Yadzhak RUS	2:45:18
6 Mar	Los Angeles	Mark Saina KEN	2:09:35	Lyubov Denisova RUS	2:26:11
6 Mar	Otsu	Joseph Riri KEN	2:09:00	*Men only*	
6 Mar	Piacenza	Sammy Rotich KEN	2:17:56	Tiziana Di Sessa ITA	2:51:43
6 Mar	Torreón	George Okworo KEN	2:11:47	Dulce María Rodríguez MEX	2:29:00
6 Mar	Treviso	Denis Curzi ITA	2:11:37	Zinesh Alemu ETH	2:40:53
13 Mar	Casablanca	Amos Matui KEN	2:14:34	Esther Jepkoech Saina KEN	2:39:59
13 Mar	Nagoya	*Women only*		Yumiko Hara JPN	2:24:19
13 Mar	Roma	Alberico di Cecco ITA	2:08:02	Silviya Skvortsova RUS	2:28:01
13 Mar	Seoul	William Kipsang KEN	2:08:53	Zhou Chunxiu CHN	2:23:24
20 Mar	Brescia	Richard Kiprono Maiyo KEN	2:11:47	Natalya Cerches MDA	2:47:04
26 Mar	Xiamen	Raymond Kipkoech KEN	2:09:49	Zhou Chunxiu CHN	2:29:58
27 Mar	Santa Rosa	Oscar Cortinez ARG	2:19:56	Veronica Paez ARG	2:50:53
27 Mar	Taipei	David Kariuki KEN	2:16:41	Hu Xiuying CHN	2:51:23
28 Mar	Utrecht	Giorgio Calcaterra ITA	2:19:37	Tatyana Perepelkina RUS	2:40:51
3 Apr	Russi	Joshua Kipchumba Rop KEN	2:17:37	Faustina Bianco ITA	2:50:20
3 Apr	Zürich	Stanley Leleito KEN	2:10:17	Claudia Oberlin SUI	2:34:39
8 Apr	Jeonju	Kim Ye-yong KOR	2:13:04	Choi Kyong-hee KOR	2:35:56
10 Apr	Bonn	Peter Kimeli Chemei KEN	2:15:06	Valentina Delion MDA	2:36:50

10 Apr	Debno	Rafal Wojcik POL	2:14:47	Halina Karnatsevich BLR	2:39:53
10 Apr	Debrecen	Tesfaye Bogale ETH	2:15:59	Ida Kovács HUN	2:43:15
10 Apr	Paris	Salim Kipsang KEN	2:08:04	Lidiya Grigoryeva RUS	2:27:01
10 Apr	Pyongyang	Ri Kyong-chol PRK	2:11:36	Ham Bong-sil PRK	2:31:46
10 Apr	Rotterdam	Jimmy Muindi KEN	2:07:50	Lornah Kiplagat DEN	2:27:36
10 Apr	Vitoria	Antoni Bernado AND	2:14:30	Marie José Pueyo ESP	2:37:05
17 Apr	Essen	Moses Ndiema Masai KEN	2:10:13	Mary Ptikany KEN	2:30:22
17 Apr	Leipzig	Julius Kiptum Rop KEN	2:16:22	Judy Kiplimo KEN	2:46:06
17 Apr	Lisboa	Philemon Kemei KEN	2:15:42	Fatima Silva POR	2:33:48
17 Apr	London	Martin Lel KEN	2:07:26	Paula Radcliffe GBR	2:17:42
17 Apr	Nagano	Isaac Macharia KEN	2:10:59	Albina Ivanova RUS	2:28:21
17 Apr	São Paulo	José Telles de Souza BRA	2:19:47	Marcia Narloch BRA	2:40:39
17 Apr	Torino	Danilo Goffi ITA	2:11:13	Beatrice Omwanza KEN	2:30:41
17 Apr	Würzburg	Elijah Sang KEN	2:20:45	Olga Nevkapsa UKR	2:38:42
18 Apr	Boston #	Hailu Negussie ETH	2:11:45	Catherine Ndereba KEN	2:25:13
23 Apr	Beograd	Derbe Badede ETH	2:12:10	Inga Abitova RUS	2:38:21
23 Apr	Salt Lake City #	Araya Haregot ETH	2:15:14	Dorota Gruca POL	2:30:08
24 Apr	Albi	Aleksandr Krestianinov RUS	2:18:08	Esther Jepkoech Saina KEN	2:36:40
24 Apr	Hamburg	Julio Rey ESP	2:07:38	Edith Masai KEN	2:27:06
24 Apr	Madrid	Daniel Rono KEN	2:12:29	Larisa Malikova RUS	2:33:27
24 Apr	Padova	Paul Lokira KEN	2:11:26	Ivana Iozzia ITA	2:35:55
24 Apr	Wroclaw	Reuben Toroitich KEN	2:14:55	Svetlana Nekhorosh UKR	2:38:13
30 Apr	Nashville	Nephat Kinyanjui KEN	2:15:37	Irina Safarova RUS	2:33:53
1 May	Vancouver	Kassahun Kabiso ETH	2:15:40	Rimma Dubovik UKR	2:44:05
7 May	Kraków	Piotr Gladki POL	2:19:30	Janina Malska POL	2:43:20
8 May	Düsseldorf	Alan Bomfin Silva BRA	2:17:21	Luminita Zaituc GER	2:26:46
8 May	Enschede	John Ekiru Kelai KEN	2:11:44	Tigist Abedi ETH	2:33:01
8 May	Génève	Tesfaye Eticha ETH	2:15:30	Chawlla Keneni ETH	2:43:53
8 May	Hannover	Simon Lopuyet KEN	2:15:36	Emily Kimuria KEN	2:48:21
8 May	Mainz	Marek Dryja POL	2:16:53	Yelena Tikhonova RUS	2:38:05
8 May	Trieste	Migidio Bourifa ITA	2:10:48	Rosita Rota Gelpi ITA	2:39:28
22 May	Green Bay	Wilson Komen KEN	2:17:32	Larisa Malikova RUS	2:41:01
22 May	Moskva	Aleksey Sokolov RUS	2:17:35	Nina Podnebesnova RUS	2:40:46
22 May	Praha	Stephen Cheptot KEN	2:10:42	Salina Kosgei KEN	2:28:42
22 May	Wien	Mubarak Hassan Shami QAT	2:12:20	Florence Barsosio KEN	2:31:40
29 May	Ottawa	David Cheruiyot KEN	2:14:20	Lidiya Vassilevskaya RUS	2:31:53
29 May	Porto Alegre	José Ferreira BRA	2:17:46	Rosa Jussara Barbosa BRA	2:41:31
5 Jun	Stockholm	Kasirai Sita ZIM	2:13:30	Faustina María ESP	2:41:28
5 Jun	San Diego	Christopher Cheboiboch KEN	2:09:17	Getenesh Wami ETH	2:30:55
12 Jun	Caen	William Kipchumba KEN	2:14:18	Elisabeth Mongudhi NAM	2:41:37
12 Jun	Edinburgh	Zachary Kihara KEN	2:15:26	Zinaida Semyonova RUS	2:33:36
18 Jun	Duluth	Wesley Ngetich KEN	2:13:18	Halina Karnatsevich BLR	2:28:43
3 Jul	Southport	Dickson Marwa TAN	2:16:14	Jackie Fairweather AUS	2:34:45
7 Aug	Omsk	Mikhail Khobotov RUS	2:20:23	Liliya Yadzhak RUS	2:39:14
13 Aug	Blumenau	Jean Carlos da Silva BRA	2:19:28	Ilda Alves dos Santos BRA	2:42:38
13/14 Aug	Helsinki	Jaouad Gharib MAR	2:10:10	Paula Radcliffe GBR	2:20:57
28 Aug	Basel	Tesfaye Eticha ETH	2:13:46	Tsege Worku ETH	2:35:05
28 Aug	Bruxelles	Samson Kosgei KEN	2:12:03	Rose Kerubo Nyangacha KEN	2:37:48
28 Aug	Ciudad Mexico @	Reuben Chesang KEN	2:19:35	Alicia Rodríguez MEX	2:42:31
28 Aug	Sapporo	Tomonori Watanabe JPN	2:14:50	Masako Chiba JPN	2:25:46
11 Sep	Cape Town	Edward Kgosiemang RSA	2:16:06	Gwen van Lingen RSA	2:52:52
11 Sep	Köln	Joseph Kadon Epetet KEN	2:11:55	Claudia Dreher GER	2:31:43
11 Sep	Moskva	Andrey Naumov RUS	2:18:19	Nadezhda Slobodchikova RUS	2:51:09
18 Sep	Karlsruhe	Gideon Koech KEN	2:18:48	Dorota Ustianowska POL	2:39:24
18 Sep	Ravenna	Francesco Ingargiola ITA	2:18:17	Sara Ferrari ITA	2:49:35
18 Sep	Warszawa	Grzegorz Gajdus POL	2:14:50	Nina Kolyaseva RUS	2:34:53
25 Sep	Berlin	Philip Manyim KEN	2:07:41	Mizuki Noguchi JPN	2:19:12
25 Sep	Odense	Josephat Kipchoge Rop KEN	2:14:49	Irina Songerlainen RUS	2:41:25

25 Sep	Toronto	Simon Bor KEN	2:11:57	Anastasha Ndereba KEN	2:36:31
1 Oct	Akron	Charles Kamindo KEN	2:18:48	Maria Portillo Cruz PER	2:39:09
2 Oct	Istanbul	Joseph Mutunga Mbithi KEN	2:15:13	Madina Biktagirova RUS	2:34:25
2 Oct	Kosice	David Maiyo KEN	2:16:07	Edyta Lewandowska POL	2:37:48
2 Oct	Le Havre	Michael Chemchir KEN	2:19:12	Yelena Kozhevnikova RUS	2:48:09
2 Oct	St. Paul	Mbarak Hussein USA	2:18:28	Nicole Aish USA	2:40:21
8 Oct	Hartford	Moses Kemboi KEN	2:16:34	Abeba Tolla ETH	2:47:22
9 Oct	Buenos Aires	Geovanni Santos BRA	2:15:53	Roxana Preussler ARG	2:49:49
9 Oct	Chicago	Felix Limo KEN	2:07:02	Deena Kastor USA	2:21:25
9 Oct	Eindhoven	Boniface Usisivu KEN	2:08:45	Tatyana Perepelkina RUS	2:38:27
9 Oct	Graz	Henry Kapkiai KEN	2:13:20	Eva-Maria Gradwohl AUT	2:40:18
15 Oct	Baltimore	Mykola Antonenko UKR	2:15:40	Ramilya Burangulova RUS	2:42:00
16 Oct	Amsterdam	Haile Gebrselassie ETH	2:06:20	Kutre Dulecha ETH	2:30:06
16 Oct	Beijing	Benson Cherono KEN	-	Sun Yingjie CHN	2:21:01
16 Oct	Carpi #	Stephen Biwott	2:11:16	Romina Sedoni ITA	2:36:45
16 Oct	Columbus	Teren Jameson USA	2:18:37	Lyudmila Pushkina RUS	2:29:56
16 Oct	Poznan	Leszek Beblo POL	2:17:07	Natalya Kravets BLR	2:40:47
16 Oct	Toronto	David Cheruiyot KEN	2:17:13	Lyudmila Kortchaguina CAN	2:37:18
23 Oct	Chunchon	Elijah Chemwelo Mutai KEN	2:09:27	Yun Sun-sook KOR	2:37:25
23 Oct	Detroit	Andrey Gordeyev BLR	2:14:59	Wioletta Kryza POL	2:40:46
23 Oct	Dresden	Moses Kimeli Arusel KEN	2:16:49	Yelena Tikhonova RUS	2:42:45
23 Oct	Lausanne	Tesfaye Eticha ETH	2:12:41	Sandra Annen Lenard SUI	3:01:03
23 Oct	Ljubljana	Samuel Njoroge KEN	2:15:47	Daneja Grandovec SLO	2:50:42
23 Oct	Nairobi @	Samson Barmao KEN	2:12:15	Caroline Cheptanui KEN	2:36:08
23 Oct	Reims	Kasine Adillo ETH	2:12:02	Zekiros Adanech ETH	2:35:55
23 Oct	Venezia	Mubarak Hassan Shami QAT	2:09:22	Emily Kimuria KEN	2:28:42
30 Oct	Dalian	Qiu Mingjun CHN	2:20:55	Zhu Xiaolin CHN	2:36:04
30 Oct	Frankfurt	Wilfred Kibet Kigen KEN	2:08:29	Alevtina Biktamirova RUS	2:25:12
31 Oct	Dublin	Dmytro Osadchyi UKR	2:13:14	Zinaida Semyonova RUS	2:32:53
6 Nov	Athína	James Saina KEN	2:16:05	Sisay Measo ETH	2:38:39
6 Nov	New York	Paul Tergat KEN	2:09:30	Jelena Prokopcuka LAT	2:24:41
6 Nov	Seoul	William Kiplagat KEN	2:08:27	Kwan Keun-young KOR	2:49:09
12 Nov	Richmond	Andrey Gordeyev BLR	2:14:32	Marina Bychkova RUS	2:42:40
13 Nov	Beirut	Francis Kamau KEN	2:19:20	Jane Omoro KEN	2:42:19
13 Nov	Livorno	Ahmed Nasef MAR	2:17:50	Ilaria Bianchi ITA	2:52:32
20 Nov	Tokyo	*Women only*		Naoko Takahashi JPN	2:24:39
27 Nov	Firenze	Samson Kosgei KEN	2:11:27	Alice Chelangat KEN	2:30:46
27 Nov	La Rochelle	Elijah Kiplagat Kurgat KEN	2:12:17	Elizabeth Chemweno KEN	2:34:50
27 Nov	Tsukuba	Akihiro Oshikiri JPN	2:17:03	Hiroko Sho JPN	2:42:11
3 Dec	Memphis	Kassahun Kabiso ETH	2:16:48	Jenny Deweese USA	2:49:11
4 Dec	Fukuoka	Dmytro Baranovskiy UKR	2:08:29	*Men only*	
4 Dec	Las Vegas	Stephen Kiogora KEN	2:11:58	Adriana Fernández MEX	2:31:54
4 Dec	Lisboa	Phillip Biwott KEN	2:18:22	Yelena Kozhevnikova RUS	2:41:57
4 Dec	Macau	Phillip Bandawe ZIM	2:19:49	Natalya Volguina RUS	2:40:59
4 Dec	Mazatlan	Francisco Bautista MEX	2:15:58	Luci Muhami KEN	2:34:51
4 Dec	Milano	Helder Ornelas POR	2:10:00	Hellen Kimaiyo Kimutai KEN	2:28:49
4 Dec	Sacramento #	Sergey Fedotov RUS	2:18:30	Yelena Orlova RUS	2:37:38
4 Dec	Singapore	Amos Matui KEN	2:15:57	Irina Timofeyeva RUS	2:34:42
4 Dec	West Palm Beach	Simon Sawe KEN	2:18:31	Tatyana Belovol UKR	2:44:32
11 Dec	Dallas	Pavel Andreyev RUS	2:15:24	Lyudmila Kortchaguina CAN	2:30:03
11 Dec	Honolulu	Jimmy Muindi KEN	2:12:00	Olesya Nurgalyeva RUS	2:30:24
11 Dec	Reggio Emilia	Mohamed Hadji MAR	2:14:08	Silvia Sommaggio ITA	2:40:32
16 Dec	Niamey	Rachid Kisri MAR	2:17:03	Celine Cormerais FRA	2:45:28
18 Dec	Taipei	Luke Kibet KEN	2:11:54	Jane Ekimat KEN	2:33:39

@ = altitude > 1000m, # = downslope > 1 m/km

Ultra Summary

by Andy Milroy

INCREASINGLY IN recent years ultrarunning has become focused upon championships. Without the commercial prize money races to balance the equation, to provide other opportunities for elite runners, this has meant an inevitable decline in quality in other events. South Africa is an exception to this trend, with its rich Comrades races in particular, but since RSA do not send teams to international ultra championships, once again the equation is unbalanced.

The decline in Western distance running is a fact, and ultrarunning, rooted as it is in Western Europe and North America, cannot be immune from this. The emergence of the Eastern Asian nations in ultrarunning is due in part to the contrasting continued strength of their distance running cultures. The prominence of Russian ultrarunning is likewise a reflection of their strong distance running overall. The clash between the Japanese and the Russians, particularly the male runners, was a key feature of the year. Without significant African presence at the 100km this looks set to continue.

Russian Grigoriy Murzin has established himself as one of the most consistent 100km over much of the last decade. He has shown the ability to run under 6:30 year after year, so his win in the world event in Saroma in Japan did not come as a surprise – he won the last time the event was held in that country back in 1998. His time on the point-to-point course was 6:24:15, well clear of the Spaniard Jorge Aubeso, with third Tsutomu Sassa, who led the Japanese to the team trophy. A Russian also took the European 100km title at Winschoten in the Netherlands, with Oleg Kharitonov clocking 6:30:31 ahead of last year's dominant 100km racer Mario Ardemagni of Italy. Murzin reinforced his credentials as the world No. 1 by setting the fastest time of the year, 6:23:48, at Santa Cruz de Bezaña in Spain in October. With five 100km marks under 6:25 in his career, Murzin has a record in the event second to none, including that of the great Konstantin Santalov.

Assessing second place at 100km is more difficult. Kharitonov, second fastest performer and winner of the European, passed up the World 100km in favour of the Comrades where he finished second. However Aubeso was also beaten twice during the year and so has to give way to Kharitonov, and take the third spot. The team results in the championships showed the same pattern, with France also coming into the picture.

The Italian men did not make the same impact last year as they had in 2004, but Monica Casiraghi continued to be strong in the women's event. Hiroko Syou of Japan won the women's World 100km in 7:53.41, from the American Anne Riddle Lundblad (7:54.22), but the fastest times came in the European event where Casiraghi clocked 7:53.25 to beat Birgit Schönherr-Hölscher of Germany by just three seconds.

With the usually dominant Russian women missing from both the World and the European events, the World No 1 has to be Syou from Riddle Lundblad with Casiraghi third.

Although the European men did better in the World 24 Hours at Wörschach, Austria in 2005, the Japanese still took the team title. The vastly experienced Russian Anatoliy Kruglikov claimed the individual title with 268.065km, from Austrian Ewald Eder's 263.810km racing on home soil, with Germany's Jens Lukas in third. Fourth placed Ryoichi Sekiya also ran the greatest track distance of the year, 264.410km. The rankings for year would be Kruglikov in first place, Eder second and Sekiya third.

The Russians and the Japanese met head to head in the women 24 Hour World event. With 242.229km, Russia's Lyudmila Kalinina held off her fellow countrywoman Galina Yeremina (239.874). Japan's Sumie Inagaki, winner in 2004, came third but another Russian, Irina Koval, took fourth. Perhaps significantly fifth went to Korea's Kim Jung-ok. With Kalinina also running the second best distance of the year with 241.521km on the track in Moscow, the world No. 1 is clear. Yeremina also produced a solid second mark in Moscow, and so is a strong No.2. Inagaki also competed well internationally, so takes third.

A couple of pointers for the future: There were two Koreans in the top ten 24 hour performers this year and the veteran Brazilian Maria Venancio, a medallist in the 1998 World 100km, also moved up to the 24 hour in 2005, and has the potential to go much further in the longer event.

The Japanese had also set their sights on the longer 48 Hour event, with wins in the two major races, indoors at Brno in the Czech Republic, Kenji Okiyama with 407.343km, and outdoors on the track at Surgères in France, Masayuki Otaki 405.639km. The greatest distance within 48 hours was to come in the longer

6-day race at Colac, Australia where Yiannis Kouros ran 432.400km.

The Russian/Japanese women's struggle also extended in the 48-hour event. Irina Koval ran the greatest distance of the year in Brno with 369.146km, ahead of her fellow Russian Galina Yeremina 368.788km. Close behind was Masae Kamura JPN with 364.342km. Koval also won at Surgères, where Nina Mitrofanova UKR was the main opposition.

There was a revival of the 6-Day event in 2004 and this continued into 2005, with the best performances seen for many years. In August Claude Hardel of France became the 10th best track performer of modern times with 923.210km at Erkrath in Germany, but in Colac, Australia in November Yiannis Kouros GRE/AUS was to break his own world track mark, and surpass the indoor mark of Jean-Gilles Boussiquet, with 1036.800km; his 1000km time was 5d17:41:57. The women's performances of 2005 were not as strong. Christine Bodet FRA ran 773.480km at Erkrath on the track and Dipali Cunningham AUS 762.829km on the road in New York.

The longest race on a certified course was once again over 3100 miles in New York and won by the Serbo-Montenegran Srdjan Stojanovich in 46 days 10:51:16, with Suprabha Beckjord USA clocking 63:04:23:28. There were 14 starters and 13 finishers!

The traditional point-to-point ultras are still a major attraction for many runners. Arguably the oldest, the 87.08km London to Brighton, was won by South African Johannes Oosthuizen in 5:50:30, denying a fourth victory for Brian Hennessey GBR, second in 6:08:31 (faster than in 2004) just ahead of Matthew Lynas 6:08:47 . The first woman was once again Vicky Skelton in 7:17:10, from Ulla Korenjak 7:34:01 and Nicola Brenchley 7:36:50. The biggest is the South African Comrades Marathon, in 2005 downhill from Pietermaritzburg to Durban, a distance of 89.17 km. The winner was Sipho Ngomane RSA in 5:27:10, well clear of Oleg Kharitonov RUS 5:29:15 with former winner Andrew Kelehe RSA third with 5:31:44. The Russian women, so obviously missing from the 100km event, showed up in force in the Comrades. First was Tatyana Zhirkova in 5:58:50, with the Nurgalyeva twins, Olesya and Yelena, second 6:10:39 and third 6:12:18. Farwa Mentoor RSA finished fourth, with further Russians in places 5-7 and 9.

The Athens to Sparta race, commemorating Pheidippidies' run to gain help from the Spartans before the Battle of Marathon, was won for the second year running by the German Jens Lukas in 24:26:39 from Jean-Jacques Moros FRA 25:03:30 and Austrian Markus Thalmann 26:33:42. The strength of the Japanese in such events is evident with Kimie Noto winning for the second year running (30:23:07) from the German pair Elke Streicher 32:19:59 and Anke Drescher 32:52:23.

One of the longest point-to-point races was the 18-stage race across France, "La Transe Gaule" from Roscoff to Gruissan-Plage covering some 1166 km. The winner was Janne Kankaansyrjä FIN in an elapsed time of 98:08:52 from Trond Sjåvik NOR 111:39:27 and Bernard Constant FRA 113:22:03. The first woman was Hiroko Okiyama JPN in 116:43:48.

Ultrarunning is currently largely dominated by Eastern Europeans and the Japanese, with Koreans gradually gaining in stature. This is in stark contrast to the rest of world distance running where runners from Africa dominate. This divide is not based on physiological differences, but to purely to economics. African runners seldom have any financial incentives to run beyond 50km.

South African runners have shown over the 90km distance of the Comrades that they can be competitive with elite Russian ultrarunners. In 2005 Ngomane's 5:27:10 equates to a 100km time of around 6:17:35. Admittedly the 2005 Comrades course was substantially downhill (a drop of 7.5 metres per km) but this does not detract from the fact that potentially African runners like Ngomane have the ability to make a very major impact on the 100km event and probably beyond given the financial incentive to do so.

Continental 24 Hour Records

Oce	303,306	Yiannis KOUROS	AUS	Adelaide	1-2 Mar 97
Eur	283.600	Yiannis KOUROS	GRE	Montauban	5-16 Mar 85
SAm	273.828	Valmir NUNES	BRA	Soochow	10-11 Mar 03
Asi	271.750	Masayumi OTAKI	JPN	Soochow	28 Mar 04
NAm	265,932	Rae CLARK	USA	Portland	28-29 Sep 90
Afr	256.400	Wally HAYWARD	RSA	Motspur Park	20 Nov 53
Women					
Eur	250.106	Edit BERCES	HUN	Verona	21-22 Sep 02
Asi	237.154	Sumie INAGAKI	JPN	Brno	24 Oct 04
Oce	229.080	Helen STANGER	AUS	Coburg	22-23 Aug 98
NAm	223.634	Pam REED	USA	San Diego	8 Nov 03
SAm	213.181t	M.Auxiliadora VENÂNCIO	BRA	São Caetano do Sul	11 Dec 05
Afr	188.647	Yvonne SUMNER	RSA	Durban	10 Oct 86

WORLD CHAMPIONSHIPS 2005

Medals and Points Table – 2005 World Championships

Points: 8 for 1st to 1 for 8th. 61 nations placed athletes in the top eight, 40 won medals, 21 won gold medals.

Nation	G	S	B	Medals	Points
USA	14	8	3	25	249
RUS	7	8	5	20	214
JAM	1	5	2	8	84
ETH	3	4	2	9	83
FRA	2	1	4	7	82
KEN	1	2	4	7	82
GER	1	1	3	5	69
CUB	2	4	-	6	55
CHN	-	1	-	1	43
BLR	2	2	1	5	41
ESP	-	1	1	2	41
POL	-	1	1	2	40
UKR	1	-	-	1	35
GBR	1	-	2	3	34
BAH	1	1	-	2	30
CZE	-	1	2	3	28
MAR	1	2	-	3	28
SWE	2	-	1	3	27
JPN	-	-	2	2	24
EST	1	1	-	2	23
BRN	2	-	-	2	22
ITA	-	-	1	1	21
NED	1	1	-	2	20
FIN	-	-	1	1	19
POR	-	-	2	2	19
ROM	-	-	2	2	19
CAN	-	-	1	1	16
UGA	1	-	-	1	16
AUS	-	-	1	1	14
GHA	-	1	1	2	14
TAN	-	1	-	1	14
LTU	1	-	-	1	13
NOR	-	1	-	1	12
ALG	-	-	-	-	11
NZL	-	-	1	1	11
MEX	-	-	1	1	10
TRI	-	1	-	1	10
ECU	1	-	-	1	8
QAT	1	-	-	1	8
HUN	-	-	1	1	8
BRA	-	-	-	-	8
GRE	-	-	-	-	8
RSA	-	-	-	-	8

Points: 7 DEN, 6 SKN, 5 BEL, LAT, 4 TUN; 3 BAR, COL, ERI, AHO; 2 NGR, SCG; 1 CAY

THERE WAS some muttering early on about the level of performances, but by the end of the nine days of action – and with the fine days at the end – there came a growing realisation that, despite the awful weather in the middle days, this had been a very successful meeting, well-managed and with the thrills of real championship action – more than enough to make Helsinki 2005 a most worthy successor to the nine previous World Championships.

World records were broken in three women's events: the incomparable Yelena Isinbayeva with her 5.01 in the pole vault in the pole vault, Olimpiada Ivanova in the 20km walk and Osleidys Menéndez in the javelin, the event so beloved of Finns.

Other highlights included the marvellous doubles by Justin Gatlin, Rashid Ramzi and Tirunesh Dibaba. Gatlin's 100m run of 9.88 in 18°C surely rates as superior to the world record and he showed great maturity in coming back to lead a unique US 1-2-3-4 in the 200m. The Ethiopian women matched that in the 5000m after 1-2-3 in the 10,000m and Dibaba showed awesome finishing speed after fast races in both. Her sub 60-second last laps were more than Tatyana Tomashova could produce in the 1500m! There were many notable young champions (the average age of the US medallists was 23 compared to 29 at the Olympics), including the first ever teenage champion in an individual sprint at World Championships – Allyson Felix – and another American 19 year-old, Tianna Madison, won the long jump with supreme confidence. Also super-star qualities were shown by 21 year-old Jeremy Wariner and 22 year-old Carolina Klüft in her epic struggle with Eunice Barber.

Then there was Bryan Clay, magnificent throughout the decathlon, the triumph on the last throw by Virgilijus Alekna, gold at last from Kajsa Bergqvist, the outstanding run by Dorcus Inzikuru to become the first ever women's world steeplechase champion, the superb final exchange by the French 4x100m men, and the joy in seeing the marvellous Paula Radcliffe showing everybody that she is not just the greatest ever female marathon runner, but fully capable of winning gold medals when it matters most in a global event.

There were very few poor events (men's 5000m and high jump?) although some were severely affected by the wind and heavy rain, not least the men's javelin where Finnish hopes were so high for Tero Pitkämäki. But the crowd got the medal they so deserved with a most impressive display of character and ability from Tommi Evilä in the long jump.

Torrential rain of an intensity rarely seen at such an event caused a two-hour delay on 9 August and came again the following day. The wind conditions made qualifying by the next fastest times grossly unfair in some events. In the men's 200m heat 6 had a wind benefitting the athletes all around the bend and at +4.3 in the straight and all seven runners ran 20.40 or better, whereas other heats had -2.7 and -2.5 readings. And take the Kallur twins in the women's 100m hurdles – Susanna always beats Jenny, yet Jenny progressed to the final with 12.88 from heat 1 (-0.5) while Susanna was slowed to 13.05 in heat 3 (-3.3).

At the first World Championships in 1983 the USSR topped the table with 229.5 points from the USA 225, and in 2005 the USA headed the list with 249 from Russia alone 214. Other top nations, however, slipped badly: From the 41 events on the 1983 programme (47 now) the GDR scored 220 and the FRG 113.5, but the combined Germany scored just 69 here. Britain had its lowest ever World Champs points score, at 34 (14th nation) – less than a third of the 104 points (5th nation) totalled in 1983. 61 nations placed athletes in the top eight compared to 39 nations in 1983. Kenya's score grew from 2 in 1983 to 82, Ethiopia's from 9 to 83 and Jamaica's from 32 to 84. One might note also that Greece took no medals in Helsinki, after five at the Athens Olympics.

884 drugs tests were completed in Helsinki, with two positives: Naswant J Singh (dnq 19th women's discus) and Vladislav Piskunov (12th men's hammer).

• Four athletes won at 2003 & 2005 Worlds and at 2004 Olympics: Bekele 10,000m, Phillips DT, Alekna DT, Klüft W Hep
• Six more athletes won individual titles at both 2004 Olympics and 2005 Worlds: Gatlin 100m, Wariner 400m, Williams W 400m, Isinbayeva W PV, Kuzenkova W HT, Menéndez W JT
• Four more athletes retained titles won in 2003: Gharib Mar, Shaheen 3000mSC, Tikhon HT, Dibaba W 5000m
• Competing at 8th Championship (to equal record of Jan Zelezny): Men: Tim Berrett, Yevgeniy Misyulya, Lars Riedel; Women: Laverne Eve, Yelena Nikolayeva, Franka Dietzsch, Jackie Edwards, Susana Feitor, Fiona May, Beverly McDonald, Maria Mutola

MEN

100 Metres (h, qf 6th, sf, F 7th +0.4)

GATLIN BECAME the fifth man to be both a world and Olympic 100m champion, running a brilliant 9.88 despite a -0.4m wind and cool weather (18°C). Scott led early on, but Gatlin pulled well away from the field from 60m and his winning margin of 0.17 was the biggest ever in a World 100m final. The other two men on the podium had ranked only 8th and 9th among the entrants on 2005 times. Frater ran just 0.02 off his pb while defending champion Collins had only reached the semis as a fastest loser and then scraped into the final with 10.07, 0.01 ahead of Jason Gardener. Scott was fastest in round 1 with 10.12 and in round 2, Darrel Brown 10.10 and Ronald Pignon 10.11 were quickest, but these two were 7th and 8th in semi no.2, as Scott won the first in 10.08 (with Shaun Crawford last, hampered by a bad foot) and Gatlin the second in 9.99 from Zakari 10.00. The latter was last in the final ... but at least that was better than the Olympic finals of 2000 and 2004 when he pulled up each time with cramp.

1. Justin Gatlin USA	9.88
2. Michael Frater JAM	10.05
3. Kim Collins SKN	10.05
4. Francis Obikwelu POR	10.07
5. Dwight Thomas JAM	10.09
6. Leonard Scott USA	10.13
7. Marc Burns TRI	10.14
8. Aziz Zakari GHA	10.20

200 Metres (h 9th, qf, sf 10th, F 11th -0.5)

THE US made World Champs history by filling the first four places, something which has only been possible since the IAAF decreed that from 2001 defending champions could be automatic entrants. It last happened at an Olympics, before the maximum of three per event was introduced in 1932, in 1920 when Finns took first four positions in, of course, the javelin. It also happened in the 200m, in the St Louis Games of 1904, but then nearly all the competitors were American anyway. Most impressive during the rounds was Gay with an easing up 19.99w in his heat (a very fast one with a 4.3m tailwind whereas a later heat was run into a 2.7m wind), followed by the fastest times also in the quarters (20.64) and semis (20.27). In the final, however, he looked too tense and was edged out of the bronze medal position by defending champion Capel.

Second was Spearmon, world's fastest of 2005, yet running only because Crawford had given up his place, but even he finished nearly 2m down as Gatlin replicated Maurice Greene's 1999 feat by completing a World Champs sprint double. His 20.04 was into an 0.5m wind in light rain and a temperature of only 15°C, Bolt, drawn in lane 1, ran a good turn and was a close fifth when he pulled up injured.

1. Justin Gatlin USA	20.04
2. Wallace Spearmon USA	20.20
3. John Capel USA	20.31

4. Tyson Gay USA 20.34
5. Stéphane Buckland MRI 20.41
6. Patrick Johnson AUS 20.58
7. Tobias Unger GER 20.81
8. Usain Bolt JAM-J 26.27

400 Metres (h 9th, sf 10th, F 12th)

WARINER DISPLAYED great maturity to win in 43.93, the world's quickest time for five years. He reached the 200 mark in 21.1 before running a great third 100 in 10.8 for a 300 time of 31.9. At that point he was followed by Christopher 32.2, Rock 32.4, Brown and Benjamin 32.5. Rock finished strongly for the silver medal and pb from Christopher and Brown, who both set national records. Benjamin had been the fastest heat winner with 44.85, easing down in windy conditions, but, drawn in lane 1, admitted he "struggled a bit" to take fifth place after he been a close third in much the toughest of the semis, which were slowed by wind and heavy rain (fastest Christopher 45.47).

1. Jeremy Wariner USA 43.93
2. Andrew Rock USA 44.35
3. Tyler Christopher CAN 44.44
4. Christopher Brown BAH 44.48
5. Tim Benjamin GBR 44.93
6. Brandon Simpson JAM 45.01
7. Darold Williamson USA 45.12
8. John Steffensen AUS 45.46

800 Metres (h 11th, sf 12th, F 14th)

BORZAKOVSKIY LOOKED in top form as he won the first semi in 1:44.26 with Ramzi (fastest in the heats at 1:46.17) setting a pb at his favourite event of 1:44.30 (from 1:44.70) two days after his 1500m victory. Mansour Bilal Ali won the second semi in 1:45.35 with Mbulaeni Mulaudzi, 3rd 1:45.73, surprisingly run out of a qualifying place and Reed set a Canadian record of 1:44.33 in the third semi ahead of Bungei as Kamel failed to advance as a fastest loser with 1:44.90. In the final Ali led at 200m in 24.96 (Ramzi 7th 25.8, Borzavovskiy 8th 25.9) and 400m in 52.48 with the whole field close behind. Bungei led at 600m in 1:18.24 before Ramzi sprinted home with a second 400m in 51.4 to become the first man since Peter Snell at the 1964 Olympics to take global titles at both 800 and 1500. Borzakovskiy ran into trouble as he was 6m down at 600m and blocked by Baala; he lost his rhythm and, by the time he took up the chase, it was too late to win but he nipped past Yiampoy and Bungei for the silver.

1. Rashid Ramzi BRN 1:44.24
2. Yuriy Borzakovskiy RUS 1:44.51
3. William Yiampoy KEN 1:44.55
4. Wilfred Bungei KEN 1:44.98
5. Djabir Saïd-Guerni ALG 1:45.31
6. Mehdi Baala FRA 1:45.32
7. Bilal Mansoor Ali BRN 1:45.55
8. Gary Reed CAN 1:46.20

1500 Metres (h 6th, sf 8th, F 10th)

THE SUCCESSOR to Morceli and El Guerrouj as World 1500m champion was another North African, Ramzi (né Khoula from Morocco), albeit representing Bahrain (their first athlete ever to place in the top eight at the Worlds). The Asian record holder with his 3:30.00 in July, Ramzi atoned for his failure to reach the Olympic final with a well judged victory in a somewhat bizarre race, chased home by another Moroccan, Kaouch, with Silva adding to his medal collection with a late charge for bronze. The final started very slowly (Estévez 60.73, 2:03.78), before at precisely 800m Webb sprinted away into a 10m lead, covering the backstraight 100 in an ultimately suicidal 12.3. The American was ahead of Ramzi and Kipchirchir at the bell in 2:43.69, having run 39.91 for 300 but with a full lap to go! Webb eventually slid back to ninth and Ramzi, followed closely now by Heshko, was ahead before 1200 (2:57.52) for a 53.74 third lap and he finished with a 40.36 300 and 1:49.1 last 800m. Even faster were Silva 1:48.6 and Kaouch 1:48.8. Daniel Kipchirchir Komen misjudged his heat to finish 6th in 3:41.88 and another favourite, Mehdi Baala, was 8th in 3:41.34 in the first semi in which the last 300 was covered by Kaouch in 38.72. In contrast Ramzi won the second semi in 3:34.69, the fastest ever preliminary in a World Champs, from Webb 3:36.07 and Boukensa 3:36.14.

1. Rashid Ramzi BRN 3:37.88
2. Adil Kaouch MAR 3:38.00
3. Rui Silva POR 3:38.02
4. Ivan Heshko UKR 3:38.71
5. Arturo Casado ESP 3:39.45
6. Juan Carlos Higuero ESP 3:40.34
7. Alex Kipchirchir KEN 3:40.43
8. Tarek Boukensa ALG 3:41.01
9. Alan Webb USA 3:41.04
10. Daham Najim Bashir QAT 3:43.48
11. Reyes Estévez ESP 3:46.65
12. Yassine Bensghir MAR 3:50.19

5000 Metres (h 11th, F 14th)

WITHOUT KENENISA BEKELE there was no clear-cut favourite, and the final was one of those unsatisfactory races, the slowest in World Champs history, with everybody waiting for a final burst. The kilometres were run in 2:54.47 (Limo), 2:44.93 and 2:48.34 (Joseph 8:27.74) with laps of 67-70 secs apart from the fourth of 62.04, before Bakken injected some life into the proceedings with a kilometre in 2:33.6 from 3400m to 4400m through 4k in 11:06.41. Sihine led at the bell in 12:38.56 ahead of Kipchoge and Mottram and was still in front with 200 to go (13:06.62). In the final straight Limo sprinted from fourth to first with Mottram edging Kipchoge for bronze, the first medal in this event by a non-African born runner since 1987. Limo's last lap was 53.8

with his last 1600m in 3:57.5 and he became the seventh Kenyan winner of this event at the ten World Championships – for the only Kenyan gold this year in Helsinki. Songok won the first heat in 13:20.36 and then seven runners, led by Kipchoge 13:12.86, ran faster in the second.

1. Benjamin Limo KEN 13:32.55
2. Sileshi Sihine ETH 13:32.81
3. Craig Mottram AUS 13:32.96
4. Eliud Kipchoge KEN 13:33.04
5. Ali Saïdi-Sief ALG 13:33.25
6. John Kibowen KEN 13:33.77
7. Tariku Bekele ETH-J 13:34.76
8. Dejene Berhanu ETH 13:34.98
9. Moukheld Al-Outaibi KSA 13:35.29
10. Isaac Songok KEN 13:37.10
11. Boniface Kiprop UGA 13:37.73
12. Marius Bakken NOR 13:38.63
13. James Kwalia QAT 13:38.90
14. Zersenay Tadesse ERI 13:40.27
15. Fabiano Joseph TAN 13:42.50

10,000 Metres (8th)

THE FIELD of 23, comprising two Europeans, two Japanese and 19 African-born runners, got away to a cautious start and halfway was reached in 13:51.10 (kilo splits 2:49.05, 2:47.62, 2:46.53, 2:45.39 and 2:42.51). For most of the race the top three Ethiopians shared pacemaking duties with Bekele apparently dictating the strategy. The tempo continued to quicken with kilos of 2:41.32 and 2:39.13 before levelling out at 2:40.26 and then slowing to 2:47.55 as the nine men still in contention drew breath before the final onslaught. At the bell (26:14.09) the pack was led by the Ethiopian trio plus Mosop. Bekele was just in front with 200 to go, pursued by Sihine and Mosop, and he sprinted the last lap in 54.0 (28.2 & 25.8, 39.7 for the last 300m) with the final kilometre in 2:28.4 for halves of 13:51.7 and 13:16.6. Bekele thus brought his total of world titles, cross country included, to eleven (plus an Olympic gold) ... and he only turned 23 in June. The top seven finishers were all from East Africa and the depth was unprecedented for a championship race with eight inside 27:15, all of them covering the second half inside 13:24, and there were the fastest ever times for places 16 to 20 (28:12.59).

1. Kenenisa Bekele ETH 27:08.33
2. Sileshi Sihine ETH 27:08.87
3. Moses Mosop KEN 27:08.96
4. Boniface Kiprop UGA 27:10.98
5. Martin Irungu Mathathi KEN 27:12.51
6. Zersenay Tadesse ERI 27:12.82
7. Abebe Dinkesa ETH 27:13.09
8. Abderrahim Goumri MAR 27:14.64
9. Nicholas Kemboi QAT 27:16.22
10. Juan Carlos de la Ossa ESP 27:33.42
11. Yonas Kifle ERI 27:35.72
12. Charles Kamathi KEN 27:37.82
13. Abdi Abdirahman USA 27:52.01
14. Christian Belz SUI 27:53.16
15. Gebre Gebremariam ETH 27:53.19

Marathon (13th)

GHARIB BECAME just the fifth man to have won two global marathon titles. An extraordinary 34 of the 95 starters failed to finish in humid conditions on a tough course that included four 10k laps with several sharp turns and some ups and downs. Gharib ran 10k splits of 30:23, 30:48, 30:44 and 31:12 (+ 7:13) for halves of 64:17 and 65:53. He made his move at 1:28 into the race and pulled clear shortly after 30k (1:31:45). By 35k (1:47:00) he held a 22 sec lead over Ramadhani with his Tanzanian colleague Isegwe, an early leader, in fifth place. Isegwe, with a previous best of 2:10:56, moved into second after 36k and was narrowing Gharib's lead (30 secs at 35k, 21 at 40k, 11 at the finish) for an unexpected silver. Ogata, in third place with good support from the more favoured Takaoka (who recoverd from a bad patch in mid race), led Japan to World Cup team victory, for which Tanzania was in strong contention until their third man, Getula Bayo, dropped out late in the race. Olympic champion Baldini dropped out suffering from a hamstring problem after having been up with the leaders for over 30k.

1. Jaouad Gharib MAR 2:10:10
2. Christopher Isegwe TAN 2:10:21
3. Tsuyoshi Ogata JPN 2:11:16
4. Toshinari Takaoka JPN 2:11:53
5. Samson Ramadhani TAN 2:12:08
6. Alex Malinga UGA 2:12:12
7. Paul Biwott KEN 2:12:39
8. Julio Rey ESP 2:12:51
9. Brian Sell USA 2:13:27
10. Marilson dos Santos BRA 2:13:40
11. Robert Cheboror KEN 2:14:08
12. Dan Robinson GBR 2:14:26
13. Gudisa Shentama ETH 2:15:13
14. Wataru Okutani JPN 2:15:30
15. Luc Krotwaar NED 2:15:47

World Cup: 1. JPN 6:38:39, 2. KEN 6:46:38, 3. ETH 6:52:14, 4. USA 6:53:55, 5. BRA 6:57:57, 6. ESP 6:58.04, 7. POR 6:58:51, 8. ISR 7:03:21

3000 Metres Steeplechase (h 7th, F 9th)

SHAHEEN RETAINED his title easily with a final kilometre in 2:32.92 in a final delayed by 80 minutes and run in heavy rain,. Blanco was the leader after a slow first kilo in 2:52.13, with Boulami and Shaheen reaching 2000m in 5:40.39 (2:48.26). Shaheen struck with 600 to go and at the bell (7:15.63) led by a couple of metres from Kemboi with Boulami an equal distance behind. Shaheen stretched the gap to over 10m while a spectacular late run enabled Kipruto to catch the Moroccan. Six of the finalists were born in Kenya, two running for Qatar and one for Bahrain. The heats were fast with 13 men under 8:20; Shaheen won the first in 8:11.79 (last lap 57.68) from Kemboi 8:11.90 and Vroemen 8:13.08, and Koech the second in 8:16.42.

1. Saïf Saaeed Shaheen QAT	8:13.31
2. Ezekiel Kemboi KEN	8:14.95
3. Brimin Kipruto KEN	8:15.30
4. Brahim Boulami MAR	8:15.32
5. Simon Vroemen NED	8:16.76
6. Antonio Jiménez ESP	8:17.69
7. Paul K Koech KEN	8:19.14
8. Bouabdallah Tahri FRA	8:19.96
9. Obaid Musa Amer QAT	8:20.22
10. Mustafa Mohamed SWE	8:20.26
11. Luis Miguel Martín ESP	8:22.13
12. Günther Weidlinger AUT	8:22.84
13. Daniel Lincoln USA	8:23.89
14. José Luis Blanco ESP	8:24.62
15. Tareq M Taher BRN-J?	8:37.62

110 Metres Hurdles

(h 10th, sf 11th, F 12th -0.2)

JUST 0.03 covered the medallists in a thrilling final, with Doucouré (lane 5) just prevailing over the fast-finishing Liu (lane 2), who dived desperately for the tape and Johnson (lane 4), who hit six hurdles and was not aware of Liu, but whose bronze equalled the record of five medals in the same men's track event held by El Guerrouj and Gebrselassie. The US quartet (Johnson had a wild card) finished 3-4-5-6. Liu had been fast in the first round in a modest 13.73 and the semi-final winners were Doucouré 13.35, Trammell 13.31 and Johnson 13.23. All the races in heats and semis, as well as the final, had headwinds.

1. Ladji Doucouré FRA	13.07
2. Liu Xiang CHN	13.08
3. Allen Johnson USA	13.10
4. Dominique Arnold USA	13.13
5. Terrence Trammell USA	13.20
6. Joel Brown USA	13.47
7. Maurice Wignall JAM	13.47
8. Mateus Inocéncio BRA	13.48

400 Metres Hurdles

(h 6th, sf 7th, F 9th)

Despite the rain and wind, Jackson and Carter ran remarkable personal bests in taking gold and silver as Tamesue held on for bronze after taking the early lead. The 2001 and 2003 champion Sánchez, who had suffered from hamstring, calf and foot problems, did well to qualify for the final with a season's best 48.24 in his semi but he broke down early in the final in which Jackson (l6) powered away from Carter (l3) off the final hurdle. The 19 year-old Clement, world leader at 47.24, messed up his approach to the final hurdle and lost the bronze by easing off in the last few strides. Clement, at 48.98, had been the one man under 49 secs in the first round, and the semis were won by Carter 47.78 (from Kamani's South American record 47.84) and van Zyl 48.16.

1. Bershawn Jackson USA	47.30
2. James Carter USA	47.43
3. Dai Tamesue JPN	48.10
4. Kerron Clement USA	48.18
5. Naman Keita FRA	48.28
6. L.J. van Zyl RSA	48.54
7. Bayano Kamani PAN	50.18
dnf. Felix Sánchez DOM	–

High Jump (Q 2.29 12th, F 14th)

THERE WAS a totally unheralded champion, as with eight men left in the final with the bar at 2.32, the first 23 attempts were failures before on the very last chance Krymarenko just made it. Silver medals went to Moya and Rybakov who had clean sheets up to that point. The favourite Holm said "I don't know why I didn't have any power in my legs today." 2.27 proved enough to make the final and Frösén and Rybakov got in with 2.24 jumps, but Jacques Freitag managed only 2.20.

1. Yuriy Krymarenko UKR	2.32
2= Victor Moya CUB	2.29
2= Yaroslav Rybakov RUS	2.29
4. Mark Boswell CAN	2.29
5= Jaroslav Bába CZE	2.29
5= Nicola Ciotti ITA	2.29
7. Stefan Holm SWE	2.29
8. Vyacheslav Voronin RUS	2.29
9. Dragutin Topic SCG	2.25
10. Kyriakos Ioannou CYP	2.25
11= Matt Hemingway USA	2.20
11= Oskari Frösen FIN	2.20
13. Andrey Sokolovskiy UKR	2.20

Pole Vault (Q 5.60 9th, F 11th)

THE ABYSMAL conditions (especially for the qualifying round with six men finding 5.45 enough for a final place) were reminiscent of the 1983 Championships in Helsinki when an outsider, Sergey Bubka, scored the first of what would be six world titles ... and again the formbook was cast to the winds. Only four managed to clear 5.65 and the two Russians found 5.75 beyond them. Walker was first over, at the second attempt, but Blom tied for the lead minutes later and after an initial failure by Walker, Blom made 5.80, just 1cm below his lifetime best, at his first attempt on this blustery evening. The American took his two remaining attempts unsuccessfully at 5.85 and so Holland could celebrate its first ever world champion. Toby Stevenson had to withdraw after just one warm-up attempt in qualifying.

1. Rens Blom NED	5.80
2. Brad Walker USA	5.75
3. Pavel Gerasimov RUS	5.65
4. Igor Pavlov RUS	5.65
5= Nick Hysong USA	5.50
5= Tim Lobinger GER	5.50

5= Giuseppe Gibilisco ITA 5.50
8. Daichi Sawano JPN 5.50
9. Patrik Kristiansson SWE 5.50
10. Kevin Rans BEL 5.35
nh. Dmitri Markov AUS –
nh. Danny Ecker GER –

Long Jump (Q 8.10 12th, F 13th)

PHILLIPS LEAPT a windy 8.59 in qualifying (in which his three American colleagues, Pate, Davis and Johnson went out) and 8.60 in just the fourth jump of the final. Nobody got close to that and Phllips, striving too hard in his attempt to threaten the world record, proceeded to foul all of his remaining attempts, but there was a great battle for silver and bronze. Gaisah jumped a Ghanaian record 8.34 in the second round and, to the huge delight of the fans, Finland at last had a medallist. Evilä had broken the 39 year-old national record with 8.18 in qualifying and in the final he followed up two fouls with 8.16 in the third round and moved into bronze medal position with 8.25w in round 5 to overtake the 8.20 by Sdiri in the first round and the 8.24w by Martínez in round 4. Sdiri's last jump was just short at 8.21w and another frustrated athlete was 20 year-old Mokoena whose third round 8.11w came with 21cm to spare on the board. Iván Pedroso, in a record 7th Worlds, failed to register a jump in qualifying.

1. Dwight Phillips USA 8.60/1.6
2. Ignisious Gaisah GHA 8.34/0.2
3. Tommi Evilä FIN 8.25w/2.9
4. Joan Lino Martínez ESP 8.24w/2.9
5. Salim Sdiri FRA 8.21w/2.4
6. Irving Saladino PAN 8.20w/2.8
7. Godfrey Mokoena RSA 8.11w/2.6
8. Volodomyr Zyuskov UKR 8.06w/2.3
9. James Beckford JAM 8.02/0.1
10. Vitaliy Shkurlatov RUS 7.88/1.4
11. Issam Nima ALG 7.73/0.6
12. Nils Winter GER 7.72w/3.2

Triple Jump (Q 17.00 10th, F 11th)

FOUR MEN exceeded 17m in qualifying: Betanzos 17.40w, Sands 17.21, Gregório 17.20 and Davis 17.08. Davis was the first round leader in the final with 17.22w but was passed in the second round by Taillepierre 17.27 and Sands 17.39. Gregório, who had opened at 17.11 with 30cm to spare on the board, produced an enormous leap which would have been a clear winner had he not fouled, but thereafter could do no better than 17.20. In the third round Davis bounded out to 17.57. Betanzos reached 17.42 in round 4 (and again in round 6) and with his final effort Oprea knocked Sands out of the medals with 17.40. Given the driving rain, the standard was excellent.

1. Walter Davis USA 17.57/0.3
2. Yoandri Betanzos CUB 17.42/0.4
3. Marian Oprea ROM 17.40/2.0
4. Leevan Sands BAH 17.39w/2.3
5. Karl Taillepierre FRA 17.27/2.0
6. Jadel Gregório BRA 17.20/0.0
7. Kenta Bell USA 17.11/2.0
8. David Giralt CUB 17.09/0.7
9. Vyktor Yastrebov UKR 16.90w/2.3
10. Dmitrij Valukevic SVK 16.79w/2.8
11. Momchil Karailev BUL 16.70w/2.2
12. Anders Møller DEN 16.16w/2.7

Shot (Q 20.25 & F 6th)

NELSON, THE 1994 world junior champion, finally struck gold as a senior after silvers in the last two Olympics, two World Champs and the 2001 World Indoors. He passed Smith's 21.29 with a season's best of 21.73 in the first round and no one, other than himself with a third round 21.68, came close to that. Bartels, who uses the glide technique while the top two are spinners, took the bronze from Bilonog with his final throw of 20.99. Leading qualifiers (all 12 beat 20m) were Cantwell 21.11 and Olsen 20.85. Godina, three times the world champion, was 17th with 19.54 – he was 5kg underweight as a result of a stomach virus and had suffered a seres of injuries in the previous two months.

1. Adam Nelson USA 21.73
2. Rutger Smith NED 21.29
3. Ralf Bartels GER 20.99
4. Yuriy Bilonog UKR 20.89
5. Christian Cantwell USA 20.87
6. Andrey Mikhnevich BLR 20.74
7. Joachim Olsen DEN 20.73
8. Ville Tiisanoja FIN 20.57
9. Tomasz Majewski POL 20.23
10. Tepa Reinikainen FIN 20.09
11. Mikulás Konopka SVK 19.72
12. Carl Myerscough GBR 19.67

Discus (Q 63.50 6th, F 7th)

ALEKNA SHOWED his extraordinary competitive ability for his fourth World medal and fifth successive top 4 finish. He had been easily the longest qualifier at 68.79 from Riedel 66.22 and Kanter 65.76, and led the final with 67.90 and 68.10 in rounds two and three, but in round four Kanter unleashed a throw of 68.57. Alekna replied with 66.75 and a foul before his final throw, the last of the competition, sailed out to 70.17. This was first ever 70m throw in a global championship. Möllenbeck was a delighted third with 65.95 and Riedel, although below par in the final, set a record by becoming the first athlete in any event to reach a final in eight editions of the World Championships.

1. Virgilijus Alekna LTU 70.17*
2. Gerd Kanter EST 68.57
3. Michael Möllenbeck GER 65.95
4. Aleksander Tammert EST 64.84
5. Ian Waltz USA 64.27
6. Frantz Kruger RSA 64.23
7. Jarred Rome USA 64.22

8. Jason Tunks CAN	63.77
9. Lars Riedel GER	63.05
10. Zoltán Kövágó HUN	62.94
11. Mario Pestano ESP	62.75
12. Andrzej Krawczyk POL	62.71

Hammer (Q 77.50 6th, F 8th)

DEVYATOVSKIY LED the qualifiers (75.92 or better) with 81.20 qualifier as the favourite Tikhon put pressure on himself with 71.80 and a foul before producing a safe 79.26. In the final, held in wet conditions, Tikhon opened with two fouls before taking the lead with 80.97 ahead of Devyatovskiy (80.45) and Ziólkowski (79.35). Later in the third round Devyatovskiy struck back with 82.60 only for Tikhon to regain the advantage in round 4 with 83.89. That was the second longest throw ever in a global championship (best 84.80 in the 1988 Olympics by Sergey Litvinov, who is Tikhon's coach), and Tikhon emulated Litvinov (1983/87) in successfully defending a world title. The top two emphasised their superiority to the rest as in the final round Tikhon threw 81.52 and Devyatovskiy 82.19.

1. Ivan Tikhon BLR	83.89*
2. Vadim Devyatovskiy BLR	82.60
3. Symon Ziólkowski POL	79.35
4. Markus Esser GER	79.16
5. Olli-Pekka Karjalainen FIN	78.77
6. Ilya Konovalov RUS	78.59
7. Krisztian Pars HUN	78.03
8. Vadim Khersontsev RUS	77.59
9. Libor Charfreitag SVK	76.05
10. Andriy Skvaruk UKR	76.01
11. Holger Klose GER	74.80
drugs dq (12) Vladyslav Piskunov UKR	74.78

Javelin (Q 81.00 9th, F 10th)

DEFENDING CHAMPION Makarov, who had led the qualifiers with 85.08, set the early pace with 80.77 and 83.30 until Thorkildsen went ahead with a third round 83.41. It was the fourth round which decided the final positions. Värnik unleashed a mighty 87.17, close to his best ever of 87.83, for the lead; Makarov improved slightly to 83.48 (and 83.54 in round 6) and Thorkildsen overtook him for second with 85.71, which he consolidated with 86.18 in the fifth round. Pitkämäki was the hope of the fans, but, after 82.21 in qualifying, could not cope well with the conditions in the final. Värnik became Estonia's first world champion,

1. Andrus Värnik EST	87.17
2. Andreas Thorkildsen NOR	86.18
3. Sergey Makarov RUS	83.54
4. Tero Pitkämäki FIN	81.27
5. Aleksandr Ivanov RUS	79.14
6. Eriks Rags LAT	78.77
7. Ainars Kovals LAT	77.61
8. Mark Frank GER	77.56
9. Aki Parviainen FIN	74.86
10. Guillermo Martínez CUB	72.68
11. Tomas Intas LTU	70.11
12. Scott Russell CAN	68.59

Decathlon (9th-10th)

IN THEIR seventh decathlon contest, Clay beat Sebrle fot the first time in an enthralling competition. During the first six events it could have swung either way. Clay started with 10.43w for 100m but Sebrle closed with 7.86 LJ and 16.29 shot, before taking the lead in the high jump. But Clay had raised his pb in all three rounds of the shot (15.49, 15.67, 16.25), and ended the day with a 14 point lead (4527-4513) after a 47.78 pb 400m. Rahnu was third on 4404. Clay was never again headed and achieved a great score, highlighted by 53.68 discus and 72.00 pb javelin, despite poor conditions. After nine events Pogorelov was third with 7707 ahead of Rahnu's 7662 and Zsivoczky's 7655 but the Hungarian ran himself to a standstill in the 1500m to claim the bronze, his first medal since winning the world junior title in 1996. Dmitriy Karpov was disqualified for two false starts in the 100m.

1. Bryan Clay USA	8732
2. Román Sebrle CZE	8521
3. Attila Zsivoczky HUN	8385
4. André Niklaus GER	8316
5. Aleksandr Pogorelov RUS	8246
6. Kristian Rahnu EST	8223
7. Romain Barras FRA	8087
8. Tomás Dvorák CZE	8068
9. Jaakko Ojaniemi FIN	8042
10. Aleksey Drozdov RUS	8038
11. Hamdi Dhouibi TUN	8023
12. Mikk Pahapill EST	8003
13. Paul Terek USA	7921
14. Frédéric Xhonneux BEL	7616
15. Roland Schwarzl AUT	7549

4 x 100 Metres Relay (h 12th, F 13th)

THE USA team for the final was going to be Scott, Greene, Gay and Gatlin, but, as in 1995 and 1997, a bungled exchange in the heats ended American hopes. At the first change Mardy Scales was unable to pass the baton successfully to Scott. The consequence was that France won the heat in a world-leading 38.34 with Trinidad taking the other heat in a national record of 38.28. In the final great baton changing by the French squad of Doucouré , Pognon, de Lépine and Dovy (much slower on paper than leading rivals) took them to a narrow victory over Trinidad (another national record), anchored by Brown, while the British squad – with only Gardener at the top of his form – took the bronze by inches as Frater and Johnson for Australia made up a huge amount of ground on Lewis-Francis. Ths was the first time that a non-North American team had won this gold.

1. FRA	38.08	Doucouré, Pognon, De Lépine, Dovy
2. TRI	38.10	Pierre, Burns, Harper, Brown
3. GBR	38.27	Gardener, Devonish, Malcolm, Lewis-Francis
4. JAM	38.28	
5. AUS	38.32	
6. AHO	38.45	
7. GER	38.48	
8. JPN	38.77	

4 x 400 Metres Relay (h 13th, F 14th)

The US team won as expected although they were pushed much more closely than might have been anticipated. The Bahamas were fastest in the heats in 2:59.73 and in the final they ran so strongly to set a national record that Wariner needed to run 43.49 on the anchor to stay ahead of Brown 43.42 with a world-leading time of 2:56.91. Rock (44.7e) took the lead from Ayre, McKinney and Benjamin and Brew (44.3e) took the lead to 5m over Bahamas, closely followed by Jamaica and Britain (44.9 by 18 year-old Rooney). Williamson (44.40) extended the US lead by another metre or two with 0.3 sec gaps at the end of the third leg between Bahamas, Jamaica and Britain. The gaps widened on the final leg as Clarke anchored Jamaica and Davis brought Britain home for the fastest ever fourth place time. Quickest splits in the heats were Spence & Clarke 44.33 for Jamaica's 2:59.75.

1. USA	2:56.91	Rock, Brew, Williamson, Wariner
2. BAH	2:57.32	McKinney, Moncur, A Williams, Brown
3. JAM	2:58.07	Ayre, Simpson, Spence, D Clarke
4. GBR	2:58.82	
5. POL	3:00.58	
6. FRA	3:03.10	
7. RUS	3:03.20	
dq. TRI		

20 Kilometres Walk (6th)

PÉREZ WON in brilliant style to add to his 1996 Olympic, 2003 World and three World Cup wins. He had Fernández for company to 15k in 59:10; they had left the pack at 13k after 19:47 at 5k and 39:31. Pérez increased his pace for a final 5k of 19:25 and Fernández was dropped by a minute and had to settle for another silver to add to those won at the 2003 Worlds and 2004 Olympics. Molina took the bronze in personal best time. Afterwards Perez paid tribute to his training partner Saquipay (dq with 2km to go) for helping him burn off Fernández. 32 finished, 7 dq (inc. Ilya Markov and Bernardo Segura) and 3 dnf inc. Olympic champion Ivano Brugnetti).

1. Jefferson Pérez ECU	1:18:35
2. Francisco J. Fernández ESP	1:19:36
3. Juan Manuel Molina ESP	1:19:44
4. André Höhne GER	1:20:00
5. Hatem Ghoula TUN	1:20:19
6. Vladimir Stankin RUS	1:20:25
7. Benjamin Kucinski POL	1:20:34
8. Eder Sánchez MEX	1:20:45
9. Zhu Hongjun CHN	1:21:01
10. Luke Adams AUS	1:21:43
11. Andriy Yurin UKR	1:22:15
12. Luis Fernando López COL	1:22:28
13. Erik Tysse NOR	1:22:45
14. Lorenzo Civallero ITA	1:22:52
15. Sérgio Galdino BRA	1:23:03

50 Kilometres Walk (12th)

THE RUSSIANS took 1-2 from Kirdyapkin and Voyevodin. They walked abreast at 20k in 1:28:02 with a handsome 37 sec margin over Zhao and at halfway Kirdyapkin (1:50:05) was just ahead of his compatriot (1:50:07) with three Chinese next: Zhao 1:50:26, Han 1:51:17 and Xing 1:51:34 (the last two would fail to finish). By 30k Kirdyapkin (2:11:47) had established a 26 sec lead over Voyevodin with Zhao on 2:12:32 and at 40k (2:54:39) that advantage had stretched to nearly two minutes. In the closing kilometres Zhao fell from third to fifth, as the 20 year-old Schwazer took the bronze medal in 3:41:54, a national record and pb by nearly 8 minutes. Kirdyapkin, who received no warnings in a race with 14 of the 44 starters disqualified, reduced his best time by 3:03 for tenth on the world all-time list.

1. Sergey Kirdyapkin RUS	3:38:08
2. Aleksey Voyevodin RUS	3:41:25
3. Alex Schwazer ITA	3:41:54
4. Trond Nymark NOR	3:44:04
5. Zhao Chengliang CHN	3:44:45
6. Omar Zepeda MEX	3:49:01
7. Roman Magdziarczyk POL	3:49:55
8. Yuki Yamazaki JPN	3:51:15
9. Horacio Nava MEX	3:53:57
10. Peter Korcok SVK	3:55:02
11. Tim Berrett CAN	3:55:48
12. Julio Martínez GUA	3:57:56
13. Marco De Luca ITA	3:58:32
14. Denis Langlois FRA	3:59:31
15. Ken Akashi JPN	3:59:35

WOMEN

100 Metres (h, qf 7th; sf, F 8th)

Arron and Sturrup were fastest in the first round at 11.15, and Arron led the 2nd round with 11.03 and beat Campbell 10.96 to 11.00 in the first semi with Williams winning the other in 11.03. In the final, run in torrential rain, Arron ran 10.98 but that proved good enough only for third place as once more she paid the penalty for too slow a start. Sturrup was quickest away but faded to fourth as the big three came through. Williams took the gold 0.02 ahead of Campbell.

1. Lauryn Williams USA	10.93
2. Veronica Campbell JAM	10.95
3. Christine Arron FRA	10.98
4. Chandra Sturrup BAH	11.09
5. Me'Lisa Barber USA	11.09
6. Sherrone Simpson JAM	11.09
7. Muna Lee USA	11.09
8. Yuliya Nesterenko BLR	11.13

200 Metres (h 10th, sf 11th, F 12th +0.2)

FELIX CAME from third around the bend to run a brilliant straight and become the first teenager to win an individual World sprint title. Campbell ran such a fast bend in lane 7 that she was out of control as she came off the curve and drifted out into lane 8 for a few steps before fading to 4th. Arron, who had never before made her mark at 200m in a major championship, had a good race and at 150m looked a possible winner but she tied up a little in the closing stages to wind up third in 22.31, her quickest for six years. In a photo finish she was pipped for silver by the fast-finishing Smith. Just 27 women contested the event. Gushchina had been fastest in the heats with 22.53 and Arron in the semis, where her 22.45 was despite a 2.7 m/s head wind.

1. Allyson Felix USA	22.16
2. Rachelle Smith USA	22.31
3. Christine Arron FRA	22.31
4. Veronica Campbell JAM	22.38
5. LaTasha Colander USA	22.66
6. Yuliya Gushchina RUS	22.75
7. Kim Gevaert BEL	22.86
8. Cydonie Mothersill CAY	23.00

400 Metres (h 7th, sf 8th, F 10th)

POSPELOVA WAS fastest in round one with 50.80 and won her semi in 50.34, as the two favourites, Richards 50.05 and Williams-Darling 49.69 were impressive winners of the other two semi-finals. The conditions for the final were deplorable; it was cold (15°C), windy and the rain was cascading down, but that didn't inhibit Richards, who blazed off in lane 3. By 300 she held a slim lead in 35.6, over Williams-Darling (lane 6) 35.7 with Pospelova (lane 5) third 35.8, but Williams-Darling – with a much more even race – was too strong in the closing stages and became the first Bahamian woman to win individual world gold in a season's best of 49.55 with Guevara also finishing strongly and almost catching Richards for second. Both Guevara and Thiam were in their third successive world final.

1. Tonique Williams-Darling BAH	49.55
2. Sanya Richards USA	49.74
3. Ana Guevara MEX	49.81
4. Svetlana Pospelova RUS	50.11
5. DeeDee Trotter USA	51.14
6. Olesya Zykina RUS	51.24
7. Monique Henderson USA	51.77
8. Amy Mbacké Thiam SEN	52.22

800 Metres (h 6th, sf 7th, F 9th)

CHZHAO WAS the one runner to beat 2 minutes in the heats with 1;59.07 and seven women did so in the semis, with Kenia Sinclair (3s2 1:59.45) not making the final. Clark won the first semi in 1:59.00 and Calatayud was a most impressive winner of the second in 1:57.92 after a 59.11 first lap by 40 year-old Letitia Vriesde, but the third was slow with Andrianova and Benhassi 1-2 in over 2:01, so Mutola (3s1 1:59.29) made the final as a fastest loser. She led in the final through 200 in 28.42 and 400 in 60.72 with Calatayud close behind and shared the lead with Andrianova at 600 in 1:30.75 with the 25 year-old Cuban a metre back (1:30.9) and Benhassi starting to challenge after being at the rear of the field at the bell. Andrianova came through on the inside, and fought it out with Calatayud around the final turn, only for Calatayud to pull well clear in the straight for victory with a second lap in 58.1 and the final 100m in just 14.0. Benhassi stole second place, as in the Olympics, while Andrianova held off Mutola, whose fourth was her worst World Champs placing (except for 1995 when she was dq'ed for stepping inside her lane) since she set a world junior record of 1:57.63 for fourth back in 1991.

1. Zuliya Calatayud CUB	1:58.82
2. Hasna Benhassi MAR	1:59.42
3. Tatyana Andrianova RUS	1:59.60
4. Maria Mutola MOZ	1:59.71
5. Mayte Martínez ESP	1:59.99
6. Larisa Chzhao RUS	2:00.25
7. Svetlana Cherkasova RUS	2:00.71
8. Hazel Clark USA	2:01.52

1500 Metres (h 12th, F 14th)

A Russian 1-2-3-4 looked possible – but they had to settle for 1-2-4 with Tomashova retaining her title. Soboleva led through 400m in 66.28, 800m in 2:12.68. the bell in 2:59.44 and 1200m in 3:16.97 with the other three Russians in close attendance. Jamal went ahead but along the back straight Chizhenko forced her way past on the inside, knocking Jamal off stride. With 200 to go Jamal was seemingly impeded again by Chizhenko and Tomashova and eventually came home a dispirited sixth, promoted subsequently to fifth. A 43.38 final 300m took Tomashova past Chizhenko in the final straight. Next came Yegorova and there was a bonus for Moroccan-born Ghezielle as her fourth place (just nipping past Soboleva on the line) turned into third when Chizhenko (fastest in the heats at 4:07.26) was disqualified following a protest by the Bahrain officials.

1. Tatyana Tomashova RUS	4:00.35
2. Olga Yegorova RUS	4:01.46
3. Bouchra Ghezielle FRA	4:02.45
4. Yelena Soboleva RUS	4:02.48
5. Maryam Yusuf Jamal BRN	4:02.49
6. Natalia Rodríguez ESP	4:03.06
7. Anna Jakubczak POL	4:03.38
8. Gelete Burka ETH-J	4:04.77
9. Carmen Douma-Hussar CAN	4:05.08
10. Helen Clitheroe GBR	4:05.19
11. Irina Krakoviak LTU	4:08.18
dq. (2) Yuliya Chizhenko RUS	(4:00.93)

5000 Metres (h 10th, F 13th)

TIRUNESH DIBABA became the first athlete since Miruts Yifter at the 1980 Olympics to win a global 5000m/10,000m double and the first ever woman. She had four days rest after the 10,000m before winning her heat in 14:50.98 and another three to the final. The race started slowly (Kravtsova leading in laps of 71.71 and 73.78) but Sun stepped up the pace from just before 1000m (3:02.53) with a second kilo of 2:51.32. Sun remained an unwilling leader during a much slower third kilo of 2:58.77 for 3000m in 8:52.62 from T Dibaba 8:52.8, E Dibaba 8:52.9, Defar 8:53.1 and the fourth Ethiopian, Melkamu, 8:53.3. The next kilo, with T Dibaba leading mostly, was even slower at 3:01.78 (Ochichi 11:54.40). Xing was ahead at the bell (13:40.40) but with just over 300m remaining T Dibaba shot ahead, followed by her compatriots. With 200 to go (14:10.55) Defar was at Dibaba's shoulder and they were locked in battle along the home straight but it was Defar who gave way to Dibaba, who covered the last kilo in 2:44.0, 400m in 58.19 and 200m in 28.04! Defar ended with 59.0 (28.8), E Dibaba with 61.8 and Melkamu with 62.6 to ensure first four places for Ethiopia, emulating the USA's feat in the men's 200m. The Dibabas became the first siblings to win medals in a single individual event in the same year – in both 10,000m and 5000m. The runners who finished 5th to 10th all set pbs, including second national records in three days by Mrisho and Kravtsova and there were the fastest ever times for places 8-11 and 14. Top European Pavey was sadly out of sorts in the final, losing touch even by 3000m (8:56.0).

1. Tirunesh Dibaba ETH	14:38.59*
2. Meseret Defar ETH	14:39.54
3. Ejegayehu Dibaba ETH	14:42.47
4. Meselech Melkamu ETH	14:43.47
5. Xing Huina CHN	14:43.64
6. Zakia Mrisho TAN	14:43.87
7. Prisca Jepleting KEN	14:44.00
8. Isabella Ochichi KEN	14:45.14
9. Liliya Shobukhova RUS	14:47.07
10. Olga Kravtsova BLR	14:47.75
11. Sun Yingjie CHN	14:51.19
12. Kayoko Fukushi JPN	14:59.92
13. Susene Wigene NOR	15:00.23
14. Marta Domínguez ESP	15:02.30
15. Jo Pavey GBR	15:14.37

10,000 Metres (6th)

RADCLIFFE, RUNNING in flats as the marathon was her main objective, produced kilometres of 3:02.50, 3:01.78, 3:02.96, 3:04.57 and 3:04.48 for a decent but unthreatening halfway time of 15:16.29 with ten women close behind her. Such a pace led to a record number of ten athletes breaking 31 min and 20 under 32 min and best ever times for places 8-23. Masai and Kidane took over through kilos of 3:07.36 and 3:04.11 before Radcliffe went back in front approaching 8000m, reached in 24:30.76 (3:03.00). She led for one more lap before Sun Yingjie took over. The 9000m mark was passed in 27:35.19 (3:04.43) and at the bell (29:25.50) defending champion Adere (at her seventh worlds) burst away from the Dibaba sisters, but even though she ran a superb 60.0 last lap she was no match for the extraordinary finish of Tirunesh Dibaba – a final 400m in 58.4 (27.8!/30.6). Covering the last kilometre in 2:48.8, she added the 10,000m title to the world 5000m championship she won two years ago ... and she's still only 20! Her 5000m splits were 15:17.0 and 15:07.0 and her only previous 10,000m was a 30:15.67 victory in Sollentuna on June 28. The 38 year-old Masai set a Kenyan record, but Radcliife took 75.6 for the last 400m to come in ninth.

1. Tirunesh Dibaba ETH	30:24:02
2. Berhane Adere ETH	30:25.41
3. Ejegayehu Dibaba ETH	30:26:00
4. Xing Huina CHN	30:27.18
5. Edith Masai KEN	30:30.26
6. Werknesh Kidane ETH	30:32.47
7. Sun Yingjie CHN	30:33.53
8. Galina Bogomolova RUS	30:33.75
9. Paula Radcliffe GBR	30:42.75
10. Irene Kwambai KEN	30:55.80
11. Kayoko Fukushi JPN	31:03.75
12. Jelena Prokopcuka LAT	31:04.55
13. Alla Zhilyayeva RUS	31:17.97
14. Katie McGregor USA	31:21.20

Marathon (14th)

RADCLIIFE TOOK her sixth win in seven marathons, and at last had a World title to add to those she had won at cross country and half marathon. Her run-out in the 10,000m proved to her she was fit and she put aside her horrendous Athens 2004 to demonstrate, as she has in every other marathon of her career, that she is a class apart. Despite the tough course (see the men's race), although with good climatic conditions (16°C and drizzling at the start), such was the pace that Radcliffe set (comfortable for her) – 10k in 33:23, 20k in 66:16 and halfway in 69:49 – that times in depth were excellent and, in a race in which 51 of 57 finished, ten women set pbs. Initially Hara and Gigi followed in her footsteps, with a group led by Ndereba 3-5 seconds behind, and at 48 min into the race Tomescu bridged the gap to join the top four, but by halfway only Ndereba, Kimutai and Tomescu remained close, with Zhou 30 seconds behind followed by Asha Gigi (who ended 16th 2:30:38) and Hara. Tomescu caught Radcliffe just before 25k, but at 27k Radcliffe started to pull away and at 30k it was: Radcliffe 1:39:22, Tomescu 1:39:33, Ndereba 1:39:38, Kimutai 1:40:30. A kilometre later Ndereba moved past Tomescu into second place but Radcliffe continued to draw ever further away: 30 sec at 37k, 47 sec at 40k, 64 sec by the finish which she reached in the fastest ever time in an international championship race. Another distinction for Radcliffe is that she is the first Briton of either sex to win a world or Olympic marathon title; she also helped Britain to place third in the World Cup team race behind Kenya and Japan but ahead of Ethiopia for whom Tulu (33), who in the early 1990s laid the foundation for that country's female track distance running supremacy, was first home, running a pb for a strong finishing fourth. There were best ever marks for places 10-13 and 16.

1. Paula Radcliffe GBR	2:20:57*
2. Catherine Ndereba KEN	2:22:01
3. Constantina Tomescu ROM	2:23:19
4. Derartu Tulu ETH	2:23:30
5. Zhou Chunxiu CHN	2:24:12
6. Yumiko Hara JPN	2:24:20
7. Rita Jeptoo KEN	2:24:22
8. Harumi Hiroyama JPN	2:25:46
9. Helen Kimutai KEN	2:26:14
10. Megumi Oshima JPN	2:26:29
11. Madaí Pérez MEX	2:26:50
12. Halina Karnatsevich BLR	2:27:14
13. Doruta Gruca POL	2:27:46
14. Jong Yong-ok PRK	2:29:43
15. Mari Ozaki JPN	2:30:28

World Cup: (three to score) 1. KEN 7:12:37, 2. JPN 7:16:35, 3. GBR 7:27:04, 4. ETH 7:28.09, 5. PRK 7:38:25, 6. USA 7:49.44, 7. NZL 8:07.26

3000 Metres Steeplechase (h 6th, F 8th)

INZIKURU TOOK the lead from the start in the final and became the first Ugandan to win a World title. She simply destroyed the opposition with an opening kilometre of 2:57.98, accompanied only by the novices at the event, Zadorozhnaya and Janowska. Janowska blew up to finish 14th, while Zadorozhnaya stayed in medal contention for much longer but she is small and her appalling technique, virtually coming to a standstill as she landed two-footed at each water jump, cancelled out her flat speed and she faded to sixth. Inzikuru covered the second kilo in 3:07.22 and the third in 3:13.04. Volkova, running a much more even race, made up a lot of ground for a 12 sec improvement on her best and 4th place on the all-time list and Kiptum took bronze with a Kenyan record (after one at 9:29.1 in her heat). A could be expected for a new event, there were best ever marks for every position from 2nd to 13th except for 4th. Zadorozhnaya won the first heat in 9:32.98, an inaugural championship record which Inzikuru improved in the final heat to 9:27.85.

1. Dorcus Inzikuru UGA	9:18.24*
2. Yekaterina Volkova RUS	9:20.49
3. Jeruto Kiptum KEN	9:26.95
4. Korene Hinds JAM	9:33.30
5. Salome Chepchumba KEN	9:37.39
6. Yelena Zadorozhnaya RUS	9:37.91
7. Cristina Casandra ROM	9:39.52
8. Mardrea Hyman JAM	9:39.66
9. Elizabeth Jackson USA	9:46.72
10. Bouchra Chaabi MAR	9:47.62
11. Yamina Bouchaouante FRA	9:48.48
12. Minori Hayakari JPN	9:48.97
13. Inês Monteiro POR	9:50.35
14. Wioletta Janowska POL	10:00.03
15. Carrie Messner USA	10:11.20

100 Metres Hurdles (h 9th, sf 10th, F 11th)

THERE WAS a delay of 90 minutes for the storm after the first heat, but all but two of the 24 qualifiers beat 13 seconds, headed by Perry and Foster-Hylton 12.64. The semis were severely affected by changing winds. Defending champion Felicien made a bad mistake at the seventh hurdle and was 4th in semi 1, and the Kallur twins both came 3rd, looking to qualify on time, but Susanna was slowed to 13.05 by a -3.3 wind in s3 while Jenny ran 12.85/-0.5 in s1. Foster was quickest with 12.65/+0.5 in s2. Perry was ahead by halfway in the final and sped to victory in 12.66, a good time into a 2.0m wind and a metre behind the two Jamaicans practically dead-heated. Hayes was in medal contention when she clipped the ninth hurdle and got entangled with the tenth. She did extricate herself to cross the line last, in tears, but was disqualified anyway.

1. Michelle Perry USA	12.66
2. Delloreen Ennis-London JAM	12.76
3. Brigitte Foster-Hylton JAM	12.76
4. Kirsten Bolm GER	12.82
5. Mariya Koroteyeva RUS	12.93
6. Jenny Kallur SWE	12.95
7. Irina Shevchenko RUS	12.97
dq. Joanna Hayes USA	(13.57)

400 Metres Hurdles (h 10th, sf 11th, F 13th)

PECHONKINA, WHO had under-performed previously on big occasions, won her heat (53.77 to next best of 55.31) and semi (53.86), and took the gold medal in her second quickest time. Demus, unsighted in lane 8, went out too fast over the first half but Pechonkina (lane 4) put in a strong third 100 to lead into the final straight, holding on well from Demus and Glover, who both ran lifetime bests. The USA delegation filed a protest when it appeared from TV replays that Pechonkina's lead leg had gone round instead of over the first hurdle, but the appeal was rejected.

1. Yuliya Pechonkina RUS	52.90
2. Lashinda Demus USA	53.27
3. Sandra Glover USA	53.32
4. Anna Jesien POL	54.17
5. Huang Xiaoxiao CHN	54.57
6. Andrea Blackett BAR	55.06
7. Tatyana Tereshchuk UKR	55.09
8. Malgorzata Pskit POL	55.58

High Jump (Q 1.93 6th, F 8th)

BERGQVIST WAS delighted to win this title after returning from a career-threatening Achilles tendon injury. The surprising Green cleared a pb 1.96 at the second attempt to take bronze. Howard also made 1.96 second time but she went on to clear 1.98 at the second attempt and a pb equalling 2.00 at the third to pressurise Bergqvist who kept a clean card until she incurred one failure at 2.00. She was over on the second try and made an outdoor world leading mark of 2.02 first time before trying the world record height of 2.10, an immense 35cm above her head. Olympic champion Slesarenko was a non-starter after injuring herself warming up

1. Kajsa Bergqvist SWE	2.02
2. Chaunte Howard USA	2.00
3. Emma Green SWE	1.96
4. Anna Chicherova RUS	1.96
5. Viktoriya Palamar UKR	1.93
6. Tia Hellebaut BEL	1.93
7. Viktoriya Styopina UKR	1.93
8. Amy Acuff USA	1.89
9. Dóra Györffy HUN	1.89
10. Venelina Veneva BUL	1.85
11. Iva Straková CZE	1.85
12. Iryna Mikhalchenko UKR	1.85

Pole Vault (Q 4.45 7th, F 12th)

ISINBAYEVA WON by a huge margin of 41cm and her 18th world record 5.01 (cleared with plenty to spare on her second attempt) earned her a $100,000 bonus on top of her first place prize money of $60,000. She had massive clearances at 4.40 and 4.45 in qualifying in which eliminated two-time champion Dragila missed out narrowly, clearing 4.40 at the third attempt. Rogowska surprisingly failed at 4.50, which Isinbayeva and Hamácková made first time, Pyrek cleared 4.60 first time (as did Isinbayeva) and that ensured second place. Isinbayeva then soared over 4.70 while Pyrek missed twice and exited at 4.75 and went on to the world record despite conditions for the final (already delayed for two days by the bad weather) that were far from ideal.

1. Yelena Isinbayeva RUS	5.01*
2. Monika Pyrek POL	4.60
3. Pavla Hamácková CZE	4.50
4. Tatyana Polnova RUS	4.50
5. Gao Shuying CHN	4.50
6= Dana Ellis CAN	4.35
6= Anna Rogowska POL	4.35
8. Vanessa Boslak FRA	4.35
9. Naroa Agirre ESP	4.35
10. Carolin Hingst GER	4.35
11. Jillian Schwartz USA	4.20
12. Tatiana Grigorieva AUS	4.00
nh. Tracy O'Hara USA	-

Long Jump (Q 6.65 9th, F 10th)

THE RUSSIANS had entered three of the four longest jumpers of the year but world leader Simagina withdrew with a hamstring injury and only one medal was won. That was silver by a deeply disappointed Kotova, who had finished second also in the two previous World Champs as well as third in the 2004 Olympics. The winner was 19 year-old Madison, whose pb of 6.83 to lead the qualifiers proved to be a harbinger of what would happen in the final when distances held down by the cold, damp and ever changing winds. Kotova led with 6.76 in the first round and 6.79 in the thirdto lead from 6.69 by Madison and Savigne. Defending champion Barber jumped into second with her fourth round 6.70 but in round 5 Madison landed at 6.89. Barber finished with a windy 6.76 for bronze and a complete set of World Champs medals, having previously won two golds and two silvers. Fiona May, who had two golds, a silver and a bronze 1995-2001, was 14th in qualifying at 6.51.

1. Tianna Madison USA	6.89/1.1
2. Tatyana Kotova RUS	6.79/1.5
3. Eunice Barber FRA	6.76w/2.3
4. Yargelis Savigne CUB	6.69/0.1
5. Anju Bobby George IND	6.66/1.4
6. Oksana Udmurtova RUS	6.53/1.0
7. Grace Upshaw USA	6.51/1.4
8. Kelly Sotherton GBR	6.42w/5.4
9. Jackie Edwards BAH	6.42w/2.9
10. Tünde Vaszi HUN	6.32/1.7
11. Concepción Montaner ESP	6.21/-1.7
12. Elva Goulbourne JAM	6.21/-1.7

Triple Jump (Q 14.35 6th, F 7th)

DEVETZÍ 14.72 and Smith 14.69w led the qualifiers, but Lebedeva had come into the Championships with an Achilles tendon injury and took only one jump, a modest 14.15, well below the standard of 14.35 and good for only 10th place; perhaps with an eye on the Golden League jackpot, she then withdrew from the final. There Aldama opened with 14.72, but that was surpassed in round 2 by Pyatykh at 14.75 with Savigne setting a pb of 14.73 and Smith reaching 14.67 despite 24cm to spare on the board. Smith, despite having hurt her ankle, went on to jump 14.91 (from almost 40cm behind the take-off line!) to take the lead in round 4, 15.11 in round 5 to equal Lebedeva's world-leading mark of the year and 15.01 on her final attempt. Savigne nailed second place with her fifth round 14.82 just ahead of Pyatykh who finished with 14.77 and 14.78.

1. Trecia Smith JAM	15.11/0.8
2. Yargelis Savigne CUB	14.82/0.7
3. Anna Pyatykh RUS	14.78/-0.5
4. Yamilé Aldama SUD	14.72/0.8
5. Hrysopiyí Devetzí GRE	14.64/0.3
6. Kène Ndoye SEN	14.47/0.5
7. Baya Rahouli ALG	14.40/1.1
8. Magdelín Martínez ITA	14.31/1.4
9. Huang Qiuyan CHN	14.21/0.6
10. Viktoriya Gurova RUS	13.96/0.2
11. Carlotta Castrejana ESP	13.86/1.6
dns. Tatyana Lebedeva RUS	–

Shot (Q 18.30 12th, F 13th)

VILI LED the qualifiers with an Oceania record 19.87, from Ostapchuk 19.65 and Krivelyova 19.65, and threw well again in the final to take the bronze, two cm behind Ryabinkina. But Ostapchuk was in a class of her own as she opened with 20.30, added 20.13 and 20.23 with two fouls, and completed her series with 20.51.

1. Nadezhda Ostapchuk BLR	20.51
2. Olga Ryabinkina RUS	19.64
3. Valerie Vili NZL	19.62
4. Svetlana Krivelyova RUS	19.16
5. Nadine Kleinert GER	19.07
6. Yumeileidi Cumbá CUB	18.64
7. Li Meiju CHN	18.35
8. Natalya Khoroneko BLR	18.34
9. Christina Schwanitz GER	18.02
10. Misleydis González CUB	18.01
11. Lieja Tunks NED	17.83
12. Assunta Legnante ITA	16.99

Discus (Q 61.00 7th, F 11th)

NONE OF the other ten athletes who equalled Jan Zelezny's record of eight World Champs appearances could match Franka Dietzsch's achievement of winning in Helsinki. Placed 13th (dnq) in 1991, 8th in 1993, 7th in 1995, no mark in the qualifying in 1997, winner in 1999, 4th in 2001 and dnq (14th) in 2003, she came good again at the age of 37. The final was postponed after just four throws for two days because of the dire weather on Aug 9 and Dietzsch led the opening round with 64.89 from Olympic champion Sadova 64.33. That was as close as anyone would get as Dietzsch ("normally I hate the rain, but I think from this day on I will love it") produced an excellent series, over 64m five times topped by a season's best of 66.56 in the fourth round. Cechlová, who had led the qualifiers with 64.26 from Song 64.15, took third with 63.00 in the second round and sealed bronze with 63.19 in the fifth. Aretha Thurmond was the major casualty of the qualifying as she threw only 47.15

1. Franka Dietzsch GER	66.56
2. Natalya Sadova RUS	64.33
3. Vera Cechlová CZE	63.19
4. Beatrice Faumuina NZL	62.73
5. Nicoleta Grasu ROM	62.05
6. Ma Shuli CHN	61.33
7. Dragana Tomasevic SCG	60.56
8. Olena Antonova UKR	59.37
9. Natalya Fokina UKR	58.44
10. Song Aimin CHN	57.90
11. Anna Söderberg SWE	57.41
12. Joanna Wisniewska POL	57.06

Hammer (Q 70.00 10th, F 12th)

THE QUALIFYING round eliminated three women who had thrown over 73m in 2005: Olga Tsander, Ester Balassini and Yekaterina Khoroshikh, as Moreno led with 72.67. Moreno, the champion in 2001 and 2003, led after two rounds of the final with 70.39. In the third round Kuzenkova threw 70.70 and Moreno responded with 70.88; Lysenko was third at 70.30. With her fourth throw Montebrun seized the lead with 71.41 but her delight was short-lived as in round 5 Lysenko reached 72.46, followed immediately by a season's best of 74.03 from Kuzenkova and Moreno throwing 73.08. In the final round Kuzenkova stretched her lead to 75.10 for the second longest of her career and Moreno threw 73.04. Kuzenkova thus won gold after three World silver medals.

1. Olga Kuzenkova RUS	75.10
2. Yipsi Moreno CUB	73.08
3. Tatyana Lysenko RUS	72.46
4. Manuèla Montebrun FRA	71.41
5. Zhang Wenxiu CHN-J	69.82
6. Iryna Sekachova UKR	69.65
7. Kamila Skolimowska POL	68.96
8. Candice Scott TRI	66.55
9. Clarissa Claretti ITA	64.76
10. Erin Gilreath USA	64.54
11. Mihaela Melinte ROM	64.31
12. Susanne Keil GER	63.25

Javelin (Q 60.50 12th, F 14th)

The last time an officially ratified world javelin record was achieved in the Olympic Stadium was in 1982 when Tiina Lillak, who would so memorably capture the inaugural world title there the following year, threw the old specification implement 72.40. Now Menéndez threw a mighty 71.70, adding 16cm to her 2001 world record as the last of the first round after Nerius had opened the event with 65.96. Menéndez grabbed a Cuban flag and began to celebrate as if already on her lap of honour and indeed it was surely all over in terms of the gold medal. However, Obergföll, the German second string who had improved this year from 63.34 to 64.59 but only made it to the final on her final throw, having opened with a modest 61.55, suddenly became the world's second longest thrower since the javelin specification was changed in 1999 with an astonishing breakthrough to 70.03, adding 55cm to the European record. She passed her next three throws and had a final 59.67. Menéndez had a second best of 65.53 and Scherwin in fourth place twice broke her Danish record. Nerius led the qualifying with a pb 66.52 from Menéndez 65.77 and Bisset 64.50 with defending champion Mirela Manjani having three fouls.

1. Osleidys Menéndez CUB 71.70*
2. Christina Obergföll GER 70.03
3. Steffi Nerius GER 65.96
4. Christina Scherwin DEN 63.43
5. Zahra Bani ITA 62.75
6. Paula Tarvainen FIN 62.64
7. Sonia Bisset CUB 61.75
8. Aggeliki Tsiolakoúdi GRE 57.99
9. Mihaela Ingberg FIN 57.54
10. Laverne Eve BAH 57.10
11. Rumyana Karapetyova BUL 57.06
12. Goldie Sayers GBR 54.44

Heptathlon (6th/7th)

KLÜFT, WHO had earlier been bothered by a knee injury, damaged her left ankle in training on the eve of competition, but still competed with her usual verve to win a great duel with Barber. After Barber took the early lead with 12.94 for 100mh to Klüft's 13.19, the Swede found high jumping difficult and 1.82 (far below her 1.94pb) left her well short of Barber (1.91). Klüft, however, raised her shot pb from 14.77 to 15.02 and with 23.70 for 200m into a strong wind ended the first day just two points behind Barber: 3971 to 3973, from Sotherton 3817, Skujyte 3778, Dobrynska 3697.

Klüft's terrific opening jump of 6.87 was spot on the board (a French protest was turned down). Barber replied with 6.75 but Klüft was in the lead for the rest of the event ending with a pb 2:08.80 for 800m behind the 2:07.96 by Sotherton who lost her chance of a medal with a pathetic 33.09 JT. Simpson held off Skujyte for bronze after a pb javelin throw of 56.36 took her from 10th to 3rd.

1. Carolina Klüft SWE 6887
2. Eunice Barber FRA 6824
3. Margaret Simpson GHA 6375
4. Austra Skujyte LTU 6360
5. Kelly Sotherton GBR 6325
6. Marie Collonvillé FRA 6248
7. Nadia Gomes POR 6189
8. Karin Ruckstuhl NED 6174
9. Natalya Dobrynska UKR 6144
10. Sonja Kesselschläger GER 6113
11. Jessica Zelinka CAN 6097
12. Hyleas Fountain USA 6055
13. Lilly Schwarzkopf GER 5993
14. Irina Naumenko KAZ 5991
15. Kylie Wheeler AUS 5919

4 x 100 Metres Relay (ht 12th, F 13th)

THE US team were easily the fastest in the heats with 42.16 and ran a world-leading team of 41.78 to win the final with Campbell making up some ground with a fine anchor leg for Jamaica, second in 41.99. Belarus set a national record of 42.56 for third. The Bahamians and Russians missed a medal winning opportunity as in the heats Sturrup fell over while preparing to receive the baton, and Kruglova and 39 year-old Khabarova failed to transfer at the last changeover. Carolina Klüft helped her team set a Swedish record of 43.67 for third in heat 1.

1. USA 41.78 Daigle, Lee, Barber, L Williams
2. JAM 41.99 Browning, Simpson, Bailey, Campbell (McDonald ran in heat)
3. BLR 42.56 Nesterenko, Sologub, Nevmerzhitskaya, Dragun
4. FRA 42.85
5. BRA 42.99
6. COL 43.07
7. NGR 43.25
8. POL 43.49

4 x 400 Metres Relay (h 13th, F 14th)

THE CLASH between the USA and Russia was awaited with keen interest but the US team was disqualified after winning the second heat in 3:23.38 as Suziann Reid ran out of her lane. Before that the Russians had run the fastest ever heat time and world leading mark of 3:20.32 with Antyukh running the fastest leg in 49.4 and they went on to win the final easily in a slightly slower time. Jamaica dropped the baton at the last change in heat 2 but got through as a fastest loser and went on to take silver medals. Britain just held off Poland (national record) for the bronze medals.

1. RUS 3:20.95 Pechonkina, Krasnomovets, Antyukh, Pospelova (Fireva & Zykina ran in heats)
2. JAM 3:23.29 S Williams, N Williams, R Smith, Fenton
3. GBR 3:24.44 McConnell, Fraser, Sanders, Ohuruogu
4. POL 3:24.49
5. UKR 3:28.00

6. GER 3:28.39
dq. BLR (3:27.00)
dq. BRA (3:27.40)

20 Kilometres Walk (7th)

IVANOVA COLLECTED $60,000 for winning and a $100,000 bonus for breaking the world record with 1:25:41. This bettered the officially ratified 1:26:22 although there are six quicker times which were never recognised by the IAAF, headed by Ivanova's 1:24:50 in 2001. Only Jiang Jing made a serious bid to stay with Ivanova in the early stages as they went through 5k in 21:43 with Turava next at 22:02. However, the Chinese teenager was disqualified, leaving Ivanova 42:54 with an immense lead at halfway over Turava 43:59, Vasco, Rigaudo and Tsoumeléka 44:05 and Feitor 44:25. Ivanova walked the second half even quicker (42:47), reaching 15k in 1:04:05 ahead of Turava 1:05:26, Rigaudo 1:05:55, Tsoumeléka 1:06:04, Vasco 1:06:10 and Feitor 1:06:28, who moved through to take bronze. Turava, sister of the former world steeplechase record holder, broke her Belarus record in second place. Olympic champion Tsoumeléka was disqualified after 15km when in fourth place and defending champion Nikolayeva dropped out early in the race.

1. Olimpiada Ivanova RUS 1:25:41*
2. Rita Turava BLR 1:27:05
3. Susana Feitor POR 1:28:44
4. María Vasco ESP 1:28:51
5. Barbora Dibelková CZE 1:29:05
6. Athiná Papayiánni GRE 1:29:21
7. Elisa Rigaudo ITA 1:29:52
8. Claudia Stef ROM 1:30:07

2005 CHAMPIONSHIPS

IAAF World Half Marathon Championships

At Edmonton, Canada, October 1

Men

1. Fabiano Joseph TAN 61:08
2. Mubarak Hassan Shami QAT 61:09 rec
3. Yonas Kifle ERI 61:13
4. Sileshi Sihine ETH 61:14
5. Abebe Dinkesa ETH 61:53
6. John Yuda TAN 62:11
7. James Mwangi KEN 62:25
8. Kazuo Ietani JPN 62:26
9. Yared Asmerom ERI 62:44
10. Norman Dlomo RSA 62:45
11. Takayuki Matsumiya JPN 62:45
12. Tesfayohannes Mesfin ERI 63:08
13. Leshane Yegezu ETH 63:11
14. Wilson Busienei UGA 63:12
15. Ryan Shay USA 63:13
16. Paul Kimaiyo KEN 63:17
17. Takanobu Otsubo JPN 63:19
18. Solomon Tsege ETH 63:23
19. Sultan Khamis Zaman QAT 63:31
20. Jason Hartmann USA 63:32

81 of 87 finished

Teams: 1. ETH 3:06:18, 2. ERI 3:07:05, 3. JPN 3:08:30, 4. QAT 3:08:46, 5. KEN 3:09:32, 6. USA 3:11:38, 7. RSA 3:12:15, 8. ESP 3:14:56, 9. BOT 3:17:27, 10. UGA 3:18:47, 11. CAN 3:20:10, 12. CHI 3:21:34, 13. ISR 3:21:43, 14. JAM 3:41:22, 15. TRI 3:56:29

Women

1. Constantina Tomescu ROM 69:17
2. Lornah Kiplagat NED 70:19
3. Susan Chepkemei KEN 70:20
4. Galina Bogomolova RUS 70:34
5. Mihaela Botezan ROM 70:36
6. Madai Pérez MEX 70:37
7. Lidiya Grigoryeva RUS 71:01
8. Nuta Olaru ROM 71:07
9. Merima Hashim ETH 71:09
10. Adriana Pîrtea ROM 71:10
11. Irina Timofeyeva RUS 71:30
12. Terumi Asoshina JPN 71:45
13. Hiromi Ominami JPN 71:57
14. Yoko Yagi JPN 72:00
15. Derartu Tulu ETH 72:12
16. Caroline Cheptanui KEN 72:13
17. Akane Taira JPN 72:23
18. Mara Yamauchi GBR 72:40
19. Letay Nagash ETH 72:43
20. Nina Rillstone NZL 73:03

64 of 69 finished

Teams: 1. ROM 3:31:00, 2. RUS 3:33:05, 3. JPN 3:35:42, 4. ETH 3:36:04, 5. GBR 3:40:08, 6. CAN 3:42:39, 7. ITA 3:43:55, 8. ESP 3:49:21, 9. USA 3:49:50

4th IAAF World Youth Championships

At Marrakech, Morocco, July 13-17

Men

100m	1. Harry Aikines-Aryeetey GBR 10.35
(0.8)	2. Alex Nelson GBR 10.36
	3. Keston Bledman TRI 10.55
200m	1. Harry Aikines-Aryeetey GBR 20.91
(0.7)	2. Jorge Valcárcel CUB 21.08
	3. Matteo Galvan ITA 21.14
400m	1. Adam Mohamed Al-Noor SUD 46.56
	2. Julius Kirwa KEN 46.70
	3. Bryshon Nellum USA 46.81
800m	1. Gilbert Keter KEN 1:48.42*
	2. Jackson Kivuna KEN 1:48.57
	3. Jan Masenamela RSA 1:49.73
1500m	1. Bilal Mansoor Ali BRN 3:36.98

2. Bader Khalil Ibrahim BRN 3:43.70
3. Abubaker Kaki SUD 3:45.06

3000m 1. Abreham Feleke Cherkos ETH 8:00.90
2. Ibrahim Jellan Gashu ETH 8:04.21
3. Saleh Marzooq Bakheet BRN 8:04.78

2000mSC 1. Tareq Mubarak Taher BRN 5:23.95*
2. Abel Mutai KEN 5:24.69
3. Bisluke Kiplagat KEN 5:24.87

110mh (91.4cm) (1.1) 1. Cordera Jenkins USA 13.35
2. Ryan Brathwaite BAR 13.44
3. Gianni Frankis GBR 13.48

400mh (84cm) 1. Abdulagadir Idriss SUD 50.78
2. Mohammed Daak KSA 50.90
3. David Klech USA 50.90

HJ 1. Huang Haiqiang CHN 2.27*
2. Oleksandr Nartov UKR 2.18
3. Alex Soto ESP 2.18

PV 1. Yang Yansheng CHN 5.25*
2. Scott Roth USA 5.25*
3. Albert Vélez ESP 5.20

LJ 1. Chris Noffke AUS 7.97w/2.2 (7.95/0.8*)
2. Tiberiu Talnar ROM 7.53w/2.1
3. Claiton Sabino BRA 7.49/1.2

TJ 1. Héctor Fuentes CUB 16.63/1.4*
2. Ilya Yefremov RUS 16.45/1.5
3. Zhivko Petkov BUL 16.20/0.5

SP (5kg) 1. Jan Hoffman RSA 20.99
2. Vladislav Tulácek CZE 19.97
3. Rosen Karamfilov BUL 19.86

DT (1.5kg) 1. Ali Shahrokhi IRI 61.07
2. Osmel Charlot CUB 60.17
3. António Vital e Silva POR 59.30

HT (5kg) 1. Sándor Pálhegyi HUN 81.89*
2. Artem Vynnyk UKR 77.88
3. Alex Smith GBR 73.77

JT (700g) 1. Noël Meyer RSA 80.52
2. Roman Avramenko UKR 79.22
3. Victor Fatecha PAR 77.21

Oct 1. Yordani Garcia CUB 6482*
2. Matthias Prey GER 6282
3. Claiton Sabino BRA 6218

10kmW 1. Sergey Morozov RUS 42:26.92
2. Vladimir Akhmetov RUS 42:32.81
3. Yusuke Suzuki JPN 42:43.22

MedR 1. USA (Green, Mays, Chandy, Nellum) 1:51.19
2. TRI 1:52.51
3. KSA 1:52.89

Women

100m (-0.1) 1. Bianca Knight USA 11.38
2. Ebony Collins USA 11.44
3. Schillonie Calvert JAM 11.44

200m (0.7) 1. Aymée Martínez CUB 22.99*
2. Bianca Knight USA 23.33
3. Latoya King JAM 23.57

400m 1. Nawal Al-Jack SUD 51.19*
2. Danijela Grgic CRO 51.30
3. Aymeé Martínez CUB 52.04

800m 1. Flavious Kwamboka KEN 2:07.42
2. Winny Chebet KEN 2:08.15
3. Katherine Katsanevakis AUS 2:08.35

** = Championships or Games record throughout the championships section*

1500m 1. Sheila Chepkirui KEN 4:12.29*
2. Yuriko Kobayashi JPN 4:13.96
3. Bizunesh Urgesa ETH 4:19.34

3000m 1. Veronica Wanjiru KEN 9:01.61*
2. Pauline Korikwiang KEN 9:05.42
3. Hitomi Niiya JPN 9:10.34

100mh (76.2cm) (1.1) 1. April Williams USA 13.23
2. Natasha Ruddock JAM 13.38
3. Theresa Lewis USA 13.39

400mh 1. Ebony Collins USA 55.96*
2. Lauren Boden AUS 58.30
3. Aya Miyahara JPN 59.62

HJ 1. Gu Biwei CHN 1.87
2. Sophia Begg AUS 1.85
3. Yekaterina Yevseyeva KAZ 1.85

PV 1. Ekateríni Stefanídi GRE 4.30*
2. Keisa Monterola VEN 4.30*
3. Yu Shuo CHN 4.20

LJ 1. Arantxa King BER 6.39/2.0
2. Eloyse Lesueur FRA 6.28/0.3
3. Cornelia Deiac ROM 6.25/1.6

TJ 1. Sha Li CHN 13.81/1.8
2. Kaire Leibak EST 13.74/0.3
3. Cristina Bujin ROM 13.23/-0.5

SP 1. Simoné du Toit RSA 16.33
2. Li Bo CHN 15.92
3. Dani Samuels AUS 15.53

DT 1. Dani Samuels AUS 54.09*
2. Simoné du Toit RSA 52.10
3. Kamorean Hayes USA 49.64

HT 1. Bianca Perie ROM 62.27
2. Anna Bulgakova RUS 62.05
3. Dóra Lévai HUN 58.80

JT 1. Zhang Li CHN 56.66
2. Vira Rebryk UKR 56.16
3. Yanet Cruz CUB 51.66

Hep 1. Tatyana Chernova RUS 5875* (76.2m 100mh)
2. Yana Panteleyeva RUS 5611
3. Diana Rach GER 5481

5kmW 1. Tatyana Kalmykova RUS 22:14.47*
2. Elmira Alembekova RUS 22:27.17
3. Chai Xue CHN 22:34.28

MedR 1. USA (Carter, Collins, Knight, Cross) 2:03.93
2. AUS 2:06.58
3. BRA 2:06.60

Medal and Points table

Country	*G*	*S*	*B*	*Points*
USA	6	3	4	126
KEN	4	5	1	82
RUS	3	5	-	79
CHN	5	1	2	70
AUS	2	3	2	68
RSA	3	1	1	61
GBR	2	1	2	60
JPN	-	1	3	57
CUB	3	2	2	55
SUD	3	-	1	47
GER	-	1	1	46
ROM	1	1	2	42
BRN	2	1	1	39
UKR	-	4	-	36
JAM	-	1	2	30
KSA	-	1	1	30

BRA	-	-	2	28
POL	-	-	-	26
ETH	1	1	1	25
ESP	-	-	2	22

36 nations won medals (16 gold) and 71 placed athletes in the top 8.

23rd World University Games 2005

At Izmir, Turkey August 15-20

Men

100m (0.7) 1. Hu Kai CHN 10.30
2. Andrey Yepishin RUS 10.43
3. Sandro Viana BRA 10.49

200m (1.1) 1. Leigh Julius RSA 20.56
2. Shinji Takahira JPN 20.93
3. Paul Hession IRL 21.02

400m 1. Marvin Essor JAM 45.99
2. DeWayne Barrett JAM 46.14
3. Yuki Yamaguchi JPN 46.15

800m 1. Fabiano Peçanha BRA 1:46.01
2. Slahattin Cobanoglu TUR 1:47.49
3. Maksim Adamovich RUS 1:47.50

1500m 1. Ivan Heshko UKR 3:49.49
2. Andrew Baddeley GBR 3:50.90
3. Vincent Rono KEN 3:51.48

5000m 1. Wilson Busienei UGA 13:38.51
2. Reid Coolsaet CAN 13:39.90
3. Simon Ndirang KEN 13:43.47

10,000m 1. Wilson Busienei UGA 28:27.57
2. Fadil Mohamed MAR 28:31.86
3. Karim El-Mabchour MAR 28:43.15

HMar 1. Wilson Busienei UGA 63:47
2. Takayuki Tagami JPN 63:48
3. Fadil Mohamed MAR 63:52

3000mSC 1. Halil Akkas TUR 8:30.16
2. Ivan Luchianov MDA 8:30.66
3. Ruben Ramolefi RSA 8:31.53

110mh (0.4) 1. Mateus Inocêncio BRA 13.45
2. Jared MacLeod CAN 13.67
3. Sergey Demydyuk UKR 13.69

400mh 1. Kenji Narisako JPN 48.96
2. Takayuki Koike JPN 49.75
3. Gregory Little JAM 49.77

HJ 1. Aleksander Walerianczyk POL 2.30
2. Gennadiy Moroz BLR 2.26
3. Martyn Bernard GBR 2.23

PV 1. Björn Otto GER 5.80*
2. Konstadínos Filippídis GRE 5.75
3. Aleksandr Korchmyd UKR 5.70

LJ 1. Vladimir Zyuskov UKR 8.06/0.1
2. Issam Nima ALG 8.02/0.9
3. Stefano Dacastello ITA 7.95/0.4

TJ 1. Aleksandr Sergeyev RUS 16.72/0.2
2. Steven Shalders GBR 16.67/1.3
3. Nikolay Savolaynen UKR 16.67/-0.6

SP 1. Tomasz Majewski POL 20.60
2. Taavi Peetre EST 20.02
3. Anton Lyuboslavskiy RUS 19.40

DT 1. Gerd Kanter EST 65.29
2. Omar El-Ghazely EGY 62.68
3. Gábor Máté HUN 61.91

HT 1. Vadim Devyatovskiy BLR 79.13
2. Esref Apak TUR 76.18
3. Valeriy Sviatokho BLR 74.71

JT 1. Ainars Kovals LAT 80.67
2. Tero Järvenpää FIN 79.61
3. Stefan Müller SUI 78.57

Dec 1. Aleksandr Parkhomenko BLR 8051
2. François Gourmet BEL 7792
3. Nadir El Fassi FRA 7724

4x100m 1. ITA (Verdecchia, Rocco, Donati, Anceschi) 39.25
2. JPN (Kitamura, Aikawa, Minami, Takahira) 39.29
3. GBR (Eastman, Edgar, Chin, Abeyie) 39.41

4x400m 1. POL (Wieruszewski, Dabrowski, Kedzia, Klimczak) 3:02.57
2. JPN (Ota, Horigome, Yamaguchi, Narisako) 3:03.20
3. RUS (Petrov, Borshchenko, Svechkar, Frolov) 3:03.33

20kmW 1. Juan Manuel Molina ESP 1:24:06
2. Kim Hyun-sup KOR 1:24:42
3. Koichiro Morioka JPN 1:25:18

Women

100m (1.1) 1. Olga Khalandyreva RUS 11.64
2. Ailis McSweeney IRL 11.68
3. Nikolett Listár HUN 11.71

200m (-1.0) 1. Natalya Ivanova RUS 23.28
2. Yelena Yakovleva RUS 23.45
3. Elodie Ouédraogo BEL 23.62

400m 1. Natalya Nazarova RUS 51.31
2. Fatou Binetou Fall SEN 51.33
3. Tatyana Roslanova KAZ 52.46

800m 1. Svetlana Klyuka RUS 2:00.80
2. Binnaz Uslu TUR 2:01.42
3. Marilyn Okoro GBR 2:01.90

1500m 1. Olesya Syreva RUS 4:12.69
2. Tatyana Holovchenko UKR 4:12.73
3. Liu Qing CHN 4:12.76

5000m 1. Kimberley Smith NZL 15:29.18*
2. Tatyana Holovchenko UKR 15:44.92
3. Jolene Byrne IRL 15:56.01

10,000m 1. Eri Sato JPN 34:12.06
2. Zeng Guang CHN 34:57.57
3. Mary Davies NZL 35:58.20

HMar 1. Lee Eun-jeong KOR 74:31
2. Ryoko Kizaki JPN 74:34
3. Jong Song-ok PRK 74:50

3000mSC 1. Lívia Tóth HUN 9:40.37
2. Victoria Mitchell AUS 9:47.54
3. Türkan Erismis TUR 9:50.32

100mh (0.5) 1. Mirjam Liimask EST 12.96
2. Tatyana Pavliy RUS 13.01
3. Derval O'Rourke IRL 13.02

400mh 1. Marina Shiyan RUS 55.14
2. Benedetta Ceccarelli ITA 55.22
3. Marta Chrust-Rozej POL 55.49

HJ 1. Anna Chicherova RUS 1.90
2. Irina Kovalenko UKR 1.88
3. Ariane Friedrich GER 1.88

PV 1. Julia Hütter GER 4.25
2. Nadine Rohr SUI 4.20
3. Dímitra Emmanouíl GRE 4.20

LJ 1. Lyudmila Kolchanova RUS 6.79/0.1
2. Naide Gomes POR 6.56/-0.2
3. Natalya Lebusova RUS 6.51/0.0

TJ 1. Wang Ying CHN 14.12/0.4
2. Olga Saladuha UKR 13.96/-0.3
3. Nadezhda Bazhenova RUS 13.90/-0.5
SP 1. Natalya Khoroneko BLR 18.86
2. Li Meiju CHN 18.48
3. Misleidis González CUB 18.26
DT 1. Wioletta Potepa POL 62.10
2. Song Aimin CHN 61.74
3. Dragana Tomasevic SCG 59.92
HT 1. Kamila Skolimowska POL 72.75
2. Liu Yinghui CHN 72.51
3. Ester Balassini ITA 70.13
JT 1. Barbora Spotáková CZE 60.73
2. Ma Ning CHN 59.18
3. Justine Robbeson RSA 58.70
Hep 1. Lyudmila Blonska UKR 6297
2. Simone Oberer SUI 5996
3. Jessica Ennis GBR 5910
20kmW 1. Jiang Qiuyan CHN 1:33:13*
2. Vera Santos POR 1:33:54
3. Tatyana Sibileva RUS 1:34:16
4x100m 1. RUS (Polyakova, Khalandyreva, Yakovleva, Chermoshanskaya) 43.62
2. FRA (Vouaux, Kassambara, Thélamon, Lamalle) 43.73
3. IRL (O'Rourke, Boyle, McSweeney, Maher) 44.69
4x400m 1. RUS (Ovchinnikova, Migunova, Kostetskaya, N Nazarova) 3:27.47
2. POL (Bejnar, Setowska, Chrust-Rozej, Prokopek) 3:27.71
3. UKR (Yefremova, Zavhorodnya, Pyhyda, Pilyuhina) 3:28.23

Asian Championships 2005

At Inchon, Korea 1-4 September

Men

100m (-0.4) 1. Yahya Saeed Al-Kahes KSA 10.39
2. Shingo Suetsugu JPN 10.42
3. Khalid Al-Obaidli QAT 10.45
200m (1.8) 1. Hamed Hamadan Al-Bishi 20.66
2. TatsuroYoshino JPN 20.68
3. Yang Yaozu CHN 20.85
400m 1. Yuzo Kanemaru JPN 46.04
2. Prasanna Amarasekara SRI 46.48
3. Rohan Pradeep Kumara SRI 46.52
800m 1. Majid Saeed Sultan QAT 1:44.27*
2. Abdulrahman Sulaiman QAT 1:44.73
3. Sajad Moradi IRI 1:44.74
1500m 1. Ali Abubaker Kamal QAT 3:44.24
2. Adnan Taees Akkar IRQ 3:44.57
3. Nasser Shams Kareem QAT 3:46.09
5000m 1. James Kwalia QAT 14:08.56
2. Daham Najim Bashir QAT 14:15.92
3. Wu Wen-Chien TPE 14:32.43
10,000m 1. Essa Ismail Rashed QAT 29:03.60
2. Moukhled Al-Outaibi KSA 29:04.85
3. Ali Saadiun Al-Dawoodi QAT 29:05.93
3000mSC 1. Moussa Omar Obaid QAT 8:33.62
2. Moustafa Shebto QAT 8:40.86
3. Wu Wen-Chien TPE 8:42.96
110mh (0.0) 1. Liu Xiang CHN 13.30*
2. Shi Dongpeng CHN 13.44
3. Rouhollah Ashgari IRI 13.89
400mh 1. Hadi Sou'an Al-Somaily KSA 49.16
2. Yevgeniy Meleshenko KAZ 49.18
3. Zhang Shibao CHN 49.65
HJ 1. Manjula K Wijesekara SRI 2.27
2. Naoyuki Daigo JPN 2.23
3. Zhang Shufeng CHN 2.23
PV 1. Daichi Sawano JPN 5.40
2. Zhang Hongwei CHN 5.20
3. Takehiro Ariki JPN 5.20
LJ 1. Ahmad Fayaz Marzouk KSA 7.98/0.4
2. Oh Sang-won KOR 7.87/0.2
3. Zhou Can CHN 7.83/0.2
TJ 1. Gu Junjie CHN 16.90w/2.6
2. Kazuyoshi Ishikawa JPN 16.88/1.1
3. Kim Duk-hyun KOR 16.78/-0.6
SP 1. Khalid H Al-Suwaidi QAT 19.45
2. Navpreet Singh IND 19.40
3. Zhang Qi CHN 19.02
DT 1. Ehsan Hadadi IRI 65.25*
2. Vikas Gowda IND 59.95
3. Anil Kumar IND 59.95
HT 1. Ali Mohamed Al-Zankawi KUW 71.74
2. Dilshod Nazarov TJK 71.38
3. Hiroaki Doi JPN 69.50
JT 1. Li Rongxiang CHN 78.28
2. Jung Sang-jin KOR 76.85
3. Jagdish Singh IND 74.83
Dec 1. Pavel Andreyev UZB 7744
2. Kim Kun-woo KOR 7694
3. Hiromasa Tanaka JPN 7351
20kmW 1. Li Ronghua CHN 1:25:30
2. Kum Hyun-sup KOR 1:25:41
3. Zhang Hong 1:27:14
4x100m 1. JPN 39.10
2. THA 39.23
3. KSA 39.25
4x400m 1. JPN 3:03.51
2. SRI 3:04.12
3. IND 3:07.45

Women

100m (0.3) 1. Qin Wangping CHN 11.47
2. Guzel Khubbieva UZB 11.56
3. Liang Yi CHN 11.62
200m (0.9) 1. Damyanthi Dharsha SRI 23.21
2. Guzel Khubbieva 23.43
3. Ni Xiaoli CHN 23.58
400m 1. Manjit Kaur IND 51.50
2. Sathi Geetha IND 51.75
3. Asami Tanno JPN 52.91
800m 1. Miho Sugimori JPN 2:01.84
2. Soundarajan Shanthi IND 2:04.01
3. Zamira Amirova UZB 2:04.22
1500m 1. Miho Sugimori JPN 4:12.69*
2. Svetlana Lukasheva KAZ 4:13.83
3. Yuriko Kobayashi JPN 4:14.15
5000m 1. Bai Xue CHN 15:40.89
2. Lee Eun-jung KOR 15:41.67
3. Yumi Sato JPN 15:47.14
10,000m 1. Bai Xue 33:34.74
2. Yumi Sato JPN 33:42.11
3. Ham Bong-sil PRK 34:35.30
100mh: (0.4) 1. Su Yiping CHN 13.30
2. Lee Yeon-kyoung KOR 13.38
3. Kumiko Ikeda JPN 13.54
400mh: 1. Huang Xiaoxiao CHN 55.63*
2. Norasheela Mohd Khalid MAS 56.39

	3. Makiko Yoshida JPN 56.85
HJ	1. Tatyana Efimenko KGZ 1.92
	2. Jing Xuezhu CHN 1.92
	3. Anna Ustinova KAZ 1.84
PV	1. Gao Shuying CHN 4.53*
	2. Chang Ko-Hsin TPE 4.10
	3. Roslinda Samsu MAS 4.10
LJ	1. Anju B George 6.65/0.1
	2. Marestella Torres PHI 6.63/0.5
	3. Kumiko Ikeda 6.52/0.0
TJ	1. Xie Limei CHN 14.38/-0.7
	2. Anastasiya Zhuravlyeva 14.14/1.1
	3. Huang Qiuyan CHN 13.75/0.5
SP	1. Li Meiju CHN 18.64
	2. Zhang Guirong SIN 18.57
	3. Li Ling CHN 18.04
DT	1. Song Aimin CHN 65.15*
	2. Sun Taifeng CHN 59.09
	3. Krishna Poonia IND 57.67
HT	1. Zhang Wenxiu CHN 70.05
	2. Gu Yuan CHN 63.89
	3. Yuka Murofushi 62.62
JT	1. Park Ho-hyun KOR 55.58
	2. Lee Young-sun KOR 55.29
	3. Anne Maheshi De Silva SRI 54.86
Hep	1. Soma Biswas IND 5377
	2. Sushmita Singha Roy IND 5308
	3. Watcharaporn Masim THA 5279
20kmW	1. He Dan CHN 1:34:25
	2. Tang Yinghua CHN 1:34:50
	3. Svetlana Tolstaya KAZ 1:36:39
4x100m	1. THA 44.18
	2. CHN 44.24
	3. JPN 44.85
4x400m	1. IND 3:30.93*
	2. KAZ 3:32.61
	3. JPN 3:33.54

Medal and points table

Country	*G*	*S*	*B*	*Points*
JPN	6	5	12	300
CHN	15	7	10	277
KOR	1	7	1	143
IND	4	5	4	139
KAZ	-	3	2	92
QAT	6	3	3	88
KSA	4	1	1	78
SRI	2	2	2	63
UZB	1	3	1	49
IRI	1	-	2	49
THA	1	1	1	47

12 nations won golds, 20 won medals.

European Under-23 Championships 2005

At Erfurt, Germany, July 14-17

Men

100m (2.4)	1. Oudere Kankarafou FRA 10.26w
	2. Eddy De Lépine FRA 10.30
	3. Stefan Wieser GER 10.32
200m (1.3)	1. David Alerte FRA 20.47
	2. Sebastian Ernst GER 20.58
	3. Koura Fantoni Kaba ITA 20.71
400m	1. Robert Tobin GBR 46.81
	2. Kamghe Gaba GER 47.07
	3. Daniel Dabrowski POL 47.44
800m	1. Kevin Hautcoeur FRA 1:51.29
	2. Manuel Olmedo ESP 1:51.47
	3. René Bauschinger GER 1:51.49
1500m	1. Arturo Casado ESP 3:47.02
	2. Stefan Eberhardt GER 3:48.09
	3. Francisco España ESP 3:48.16
5000m	1. Anatoliy Rybakov RUS 14:06.69
	2. Mohammed Farah GBR 14:10.96
	3. Aleksey Aleksandrov RUS 14:11.10
10,000m	1. Yevgeniy Rybakov RUS 29:30.76
	2. André Pollmächer GER 29:33.22
	3. Marius Ionescu ROM 29:34.52
3000mSC	1. Radoslaw Poplawski POL 8:32.61
	2. Halil Akkas TUR 8:37.38
	3. Pieter Desmet BEL 8:41.07
110mh (2.9)	1. David Hughes GBR 13.56w
	2. Willi Mathiszik GER 13.58
	3. Stanislav Sajdok CZE 13.66
400mh	1. Rhys Williams GBR 49.60
	2. Minás Alozídis GRE 50.04
	3. Ákos Dezsö HUN 50.31
HJ	1. Jaroslav Bába CZE 2.29
	2. Artyom Zaytsev BLR 2.27
	3. Yuriy Krimarenko UKR 2.27
PV	1. Damiel Dossevi FRA 5.75
	2. Fabian Schulze GER 5.65
	3= Jérôme Clavier FRA 5.60
	3= Matti Mononen FIN 5.60
LJ	1. Danut Simion ROM 8.12/0.8
	2. Dmitriy Sapinskiy RUS 8.01/1.1
	3. Povilas Mykolaitis LTU 8.00/1.1
TJ	1. Aleksandr Sergeyev RUS 17.11/0.0
	2. Aleksandr Petrenko RUS 17.03/0.6
	3. Nelson Évora POR 16.89/1.9
SP	1. Anton Lyuboslavskiy RUS 20.44*
	2. Taavi Peetre EST 19.85
	3. Mika Vasara FIN 19.84
DT	1. Robert Harting GER 64.50*
	2. Piotr Malachowski POL 63.99
	3. Dmitriy Sivakov BLR 60.62
HT	1. Pavel Krivitski BLR 73.72
	2. Aleksandr Kozulko BLR 73.60
	3. Andrey Azarenkov RUS 71.18
JT	1. Igor Janik POL 77.25
	2. Antti Ruuskanen FIN 76.82
	3. Magnus Arvidsson SWE 76.15
Dec	1. Aleksey Drozdov RUS 8196
	2. Aleksey Sysoyev RUS 8089
	3. Norman Müller GER 7989
20kW	1. Igor Yerokhin RUS 1:23:14
	2. Benjamín Sánchez ESP 1:23:30
	3. Nikolay Seredovich BLR 1:23:56
4x100m	1. FRA (Kankarafou, M'Barke, de Lépine, Alerte) 38.95*
	2. GER (Rentz, Broening, Ernst, Helmke) 39.12
	3. ITA (La Mastra, Rocco, Anceschi, Kaba Fantoni) 39.41
4x400m	1. POL (Banka, Zrada, Dabrowski, Kedzia) 3:04.41
	2. GBR (Steele, Williams, Davenport, Tobin) 3:04.83
	3. NED (Ward, de Wild, Kampen, Lathouwers) 3:04.99

Women

100m (1.5)
1. María Karastamáti GRE 11.03*
2. Lina Jacques-Sébastien FRA 11.46
3. Verena Sailer GER 11.53

200m (0.7)
1. Yelena Yakovleva RUS 22.99
2. Nikolett Listár HUN 23.19
3. Vincenza Calì ITA 23.31

400m
1. Olga Zaytseva RUS 50.72*
2. Christine Ohuruogu GBR 50.73
3. Yelena Migunova RUS 51.59

800m
1. Yevgeniya Zolotova RUS 2:06.00
2. Jemma Simpson GBR 2:06.16
3. Élodie Guégan FRA 2:06.29

1500m
1. Corina Dumbravean ROM 4:14.78
2. Olesya Syreva RUS 4:16.23
3. Antje Möldner GER 4:16.34

5000m
1. Binnaz Uslu TUR 15:57.21
2. Tatyana Petrova RUS 16:01.79
3. Silvia La Barbera ITA 16:07.01

10,000m
1. Tatyana Petrova RUS 33:55.99
2. Volga Minina BLR 34:03.55
3. Eva Maria Stöwer GER 34:05.03

3000mSC
1. Katarzyna Kowalska POL 9:54.17
2. Türkan Erismis TUR 9:55.45
3. Svetlana Ivanova RUS 9:56.44

100mh (0.9)
1. Mirjam Liimask EST 12.93
2. Tina Klein GER 12.97
3. Anna Yevdokimova RUS 13.12

400mh
1. Yelena Ildeykina RUS 56.43
2. Anastasiya Trifonova RUS 56.51
3. Sian Scott GBR 57.02

HJ
1. Tatyana Kivimyagi RUS 1.94
2. Emma Green SWE 1.92
3. Ariane Friedrich GER 1.90

PV
1. Nataliya Kushch UKR 4.30
2. Floé Kühnert GER 4.30
3. Julia Hütter GER 4.25

LJ
1. Carolina Klüft SWE 6.79/0.8
2. Yuliya Zinovyeva RUS 6.58/1.3
3. Adina Anton ROM 6.55/1.8

TJ
1. Simona La Mantia ITA 14.43/-0.6
2. Svetlana Bolshakova RUS 14.11/0.7
3. Athanasía Pérra GRE 13.94/0.3

SP
1. Petra Lammert GER 18.97
2. Christina Schwanitz GER 18.64
3. Chiara Rosa ITA 18.22

DT
1. Sabine Rumpf GER 60.75*
2. Darya Pishchalnikova RUS 59.45
3. Kateryna Karsak UKR 56.81

HT
1. Yekaterina Khoroshikh RUS 71.51*
2. Betty Heidler GER 69.64
3. Nataliya Zolotuhina UKR 67.75

JT
1. Annika Suthe GER 57.72
2. Katharina Molitor GER 57.01
3. Linda Brivule LAT 56.12

Hep
1. Laurien Hoos NED 6291*
2. Lilli Schwarzkopf GER 6196
3. Olga Levenkova RUS 5950

20km W
1. Irina Petrova RUS 1:33:24
2. Olga Kaniskina RUS 1:33:33
3. Barbora Dibelková CZE 1:34:44

4x100m
1. FRA (Vouaux, Jacques-Sébastien, Kamga, Ikuesan) 44.22
2. GER (K Köhler, Sailer, Kedzierski, Möllinger) 44.89
3. ITA (Baggio, Tomasini, Beri, Calì) 45.03

4x400m
1. RUS (Ovchinnikova, Kochetova, Migunova, Zaytseva) 3:27.27*
2. GBR (Wall, Scott, Miller, Ohuruogu) 3:31.64
3. FRA (Jemaa, Sigère, Monthe, Anacharsis) 3:31.91

Medal and Points table

Country	*G*	*S*	*B*	*Points*
RUS	15	10	6	270
GER	4	14	8	251
FRA	6	2	3	135.5
GBR	3	5	1	128
POL	4	1	1	97
BLR	1	3	2	82
ITA	1	0	6	72
UKR	1	-	3	63
ROM	2	-	2	46
ESP	1	2	1	46
GRE	1	1	1	45
FIN	-	1	2	43.5
CZE	1	-	2	30
NED	1	-	1	29
SWE	1	1	1	27
TUR	1	2	-	24
IRL	-	-	-	23
LTU	-	-	1	18
EST	1	1	-	17

22 nations won medals (16 gold) and 32 placed athletes in the top 8.

European Junior (U20) Championships 2005

At Kaunas, Lithuania, July 21-24

Men

100m
1. Craig Pickering GBR 10.51
2. Simeon Williamson GBR 10.52
3. Alex Nelson GBR 10.60

200m (-1.6)
1. Daniel Schnelting GER 21.12
2. Julian Thomas GBR 21.17
3. Wade Bennett-Jackson GBR 21.41

400m
1. Zeljko Vincek CRO 46.14
2. Martyn Rooney GBR 46.56
3. Dimítrios Régas GRE 46.79

800m
1. Mattias Claesson SWE 1:49.58
2. Lukas Rifesser ITA 1:50.79
3. Steve Fennell GBR 1:50.85

1500m
1. Colin Costello IRL 3:45.25
2. Danny Darcy IRL 3:46.07
3. Adrian Danilewicz POL 3:47.22

5000m
1. Barnabás Bene HUN 14:22.30
2. Dusan Markesevic SCG 14:24.04
3. László Tóth HUN 14:25.46

10,000m
1. Mugdat Öztürk TUR 30:10.60
2. Stepan Rogovtsev BLR 30:12.76
3. Carlos Gazapo ESP 30:24.18

3000mSC
1. Marcin Chabowski POL 8:40.88*
2. Albert Minczér HUN 8:45.82
3. Andrzej Pasternak POL 8:52.31

110mh (-2.4)
1. Garfield Darien FRA 13.77
2. Konstadínos Douvalídis GRE 13.99
3. Alexander John GER 14.10

400mh 1. Milan Kotur CRO 50.15
2. David Greene GBR 51.14
3. Fadil Bellaabouss FRA 51.31
HJ 1. Ivan Ukhov RUS 2.23
2. Wojciech Theiner POL 2.21
3. Niki Palli ISR 2.19
PV 1. Dmitriy Starodubtsev RUS 5.50
2= Mikhail Golovtsov RUS 5.45
2= Konstadínos Filippídis GRE 5.45
LJ 1. Greg Rutherford GBR 8.14/0.0
2. Sebastian Bayer GER 7.73/0.0
3. Mihaíl Mertzanídis-Despotéris GRE 7.63/-0.5
TJ 1. Stevens Marie-Sainte FRA 16.29/1.9
2. Zhivko Petkov BUL 15.98/0.4
3. Dmitriy Nikonov RUS 15.84/0.3
SP 6 kg 1. Remigius Machura CZE 20.09
2. Lajos Kürthy HUN 19.65
3. Maksim Sidorov RUS 19.32
DT 1.75 kg 1. Margus Hunt EST 62.19*
2. Lajos Kürthy HUN 59.75
3. Martin Wierig GER 59.04
HT 6kg 1. Kristóf Németh HUN 78.85*
2. Yevgeniy Aydamirov RUS 76.73
3. Yuriy Shayunov BLR 74.78
JT 1. Ioánnis-Yeóryios Smaliós GRE 77.25
2. Alexander Vieweg GER 75.85
3. Ari Mannio FIN 72.47
Dec 1. Andrei Krauchanka BLR 7997
(6kg SP) 2. Arthur Abele GER 7634
(1.75k DT) 3. MauriKaattari FIN 7427
10kmW 1. Andrey Ruzavin RUS 39:28.45*
2. Aleksandr Prokhorov RUS 40:43.67
3. Giorgio Rubino ITA 40:46.95
4x100m 1. GER (Sewald, Blum, Müller, Schnelting) 39.90
2. POL (Lewanski, Kuc, Drapal, Sienkiewicz) 40.03
3. FIN (Vilén, Hongisto, Salonen, Viiala) 40.29
4x400m 1. GBR (Buck, Osho, Strachan, Rooney) 3:06.67
2. RUS (Sigalovskiy, Buryak, Kokorin, Sergiyenkov) 3:07.19
3. POL (Baranowski, Dobek, Rys, Kozlowski) 3:09.75

Women

100m 1. Iwona Brzezinska POL 11.67
2. Lina Grincikaite LTU 11.69
3. Eleni Artymata CYP 11.74
200m 1. Yuliya Chermoshanskaya RUS 23.21
(0.5) 2. Jala Gangnus GER 23.57
3. Angela Morosanu ROM 23.71
400m 1. Danijela Grgic CRO 52.42
2. Kseniya Zadorina RUS 53.39
3. Angela Morosanu ROM 53.48
800m 1. Natalya Lupu UKR 2:02.78
2. Mariya Shapayeva RUS 2:03.00
3. Olga Cristea MDA 2:03.08
1500m 1. Morag MacLarty GBR 4:15.12
2. Yekaterina Martynova RUS 4:15.46
3. Azra Eminovic SCG 4:15.77
3000m 1. Adelina De Soccio ITA 9:20.89
2. Susan Kuijken NED 9:28.45
3. Barbara Maveau BEL 9:29.78
5000m 1. Silvia La Barbera ITA 15:52.20
2. Inna Poluskina LAT 15:55.69
3. Charlotte Dale GBR 16:07.26
3000mSC 1. Emily Pidgeon GBR 16:14.71
2. Tatyana Azorkina RUS 16:18.60
3. Svetlana Kudelich BLR 16:33.07
100mh 1. Eline Berings BEL 13.41
(-1.5) 2. Christina Vukicevic NOR 13.56
3. Cindy Billaud FRA 13.65
400mh 1. Zuzana Hejnová CZE 55.89*
2. Yekaterina Kostetskaya RUS 55.89*
3. Yuliya Bychkova RUS 58.12
HJ 1. Svetlana Shkolina RUS 1.91
2. Julia Hartmann GER 1.87
3. Iryna Kovalenko UKR 1.85
PV 1. Silke Spiegelburg GER 4.35
2. Svetlana Makarevich BLR 4.20
3. Elena Scarpellini ITA 4.15
LJ 1. Denisa Scerbová CZE 6.57/0.3
2. Amy Harris GBR 6.35/1.2
3. Anna Nazarova RUS 6.31/1.9
TJ 1. Tetyana Dyachenko UKR 14.04/0.7
2. Cristina Bujin ROM 13.72/1.3
3. Liliya Kulyk UKR 13.42/1.6
SP 1. Denise Hinrichs GER 17.55
2. Irina Tarasova RUS 16.53
3. Magdalena Sobieszek POL 16.24
DT 1. Kristina Gehrig GER 50.60
2. Liliana Cá POR 49.69
3. Marina Yakimova BLR 49.31
HT 1. Noémi Németh HUN 63.70
2. Valentina Srsa CRO 63.12
3. Laura Gibilisco ITA 62.58
JT 1. Mariya Abakumova RUS 57.11
2. María Zérva GRE 56.47
3. Sandra Schaffarzik GER 55.49
Hep 1. Jessica Ennis GBR 5891
2. Julia Mächtig GER 5830
3. Ksenja Balta EST 5747
10kmW 1. Vera Sokolova RUS 43:11.34*
2. Olga Mikhaylova RUS 45:31.49
3. Martina Gabrielli ITA 46:38.53
4x100m 1. POL (Ceglarek, Popowicz, Jeschke, Brzezinska) 44.65
2. RUS (Mekhti-Zade, Dashina, Kashina, Chermoshankaya) 44.70
3. FRA (Monne, Banco, Behi, Distel) 44.79
4x400m 1. RUS (Kuznetsova, Zadorina, Shlyapnikova, Kostetskaya) 3:32.63
2. GER (Ullmann, Meyer, Müller-Foell, Lindenberg) 3:36.63
3. UKR (Peitsheva, Shevchenko, Lupu, Karandyuk) 3:36.64

Medal and points table

Country	*G*	*S*	*B*	*Points*
RUS	8	12	4	232
GER	5	7	4	161.5
POL	3	2	4	148
GBR	6	5	3	140
HUN	3	3	1	75
BLR	1	2	3	71.5
FRA	2	-	3	67
UKR	2	-	3	66
GRE	1	3	2	61.5

ITA	1	1	4	57
ROM	-	2	2	53
FIN	-	-	3	53
CRO	3	1	-	34
CZE	3	-	-	34
IRL	1	1	-	29
ESP	-	-	1	26
EST	1	-	1	24
BUL	-	1	-	24
LTU	-	1	-	24
SWE	1	-	-	23
LAT	1	-	-	20
NED	-	1	-	19

31 nations won medals (19 gold) and 35 placed athletes in the top 8.

European Cup 2005

Super-League at Florence, Italy June 17-19

Men: 1. GER 113, 2. FRA 104, 3. ITA 98, 4. POL 94.5, 5. RUS 88, 6. ESP 86.5, 7. GBR 70, 8. CZE 63.

100m (2.1)
1. Ronald Pognon FRA 10.06w
2. Mark Lewis-Francis GBR 10.10
3. Simone Collio ITA 10.15

200m (-0.6)
1. Christian Malcolm GBR 20.15
2. Tobias Unger GER 20.36
3. Jirí Vojtík CZE 20.66

400m
1. Marc Raquil FRA 45.80
2. Simon Kirch GER 45.86
3. Andrey Rudnitskiy RUS 46.06

800m
1. Antonio Manuel Reina ESP 1:46.11
2. Grzegorz Krzosek POL 1:46.52
3. Dmitriy Bogdanov RUS 1:46.79

1500m
1. Juan Carlos Higuero ESP 3:41.72
2. Mounir Yemmouni FRA 3:42.10
3. Pawel Czapiewski POL 3:42.19

3000m
1. Jesús España ESP 8:16.48
2. Mohammed Farah GBR 8:17.28
3. Yared Shegumo POL 8:18.06

5000m
1. Juan Carlos de la Ossa ESP 13:30.97
2. Bouabdellah Tahri FRA 13:32.34
3. Jan Fitschen GER 13:33.46

3000mSC
1. Antonio Jiménez ESP 8:20.17
2. Radoslaw Poplawski POL 8:20.48
3. Vincent Le Dauphin FRA 8:22.03

110mh (2.0)
1. Ladji Doucouré FRA 13.16
2. Thomas Blaschek GER 13.44
3. Andrea Giaconi ITA 13.52

400mh
1. Naman Keïta FRA 48.77
2. Marek Plawgo POL 48.99
3. Gianni Carabelli ITA 49.04

HJ
1. Aleksey Dmitrik RUS 2.30
2. Nicola Ciotti ITA 2.30
3. Svatoslav Ton CZE 2.27

PV
1. Giuseppe Gibilisco ITA 5.80
2. Adam Ptácek CZE 5.60
3. Yevgeniy Mikhaylichenko RUS 5.50

LJ
1. Nils Winter GER 8.06/0.5
2. Salim Sdiri FRA 8.05w/2.3
3. Vitaliy Shkurlatov RUS 7.98/0.9

TJ
1. Charles Friedek GER 17.20/0.4
2. Danila Burkenya RUS 17.06/0.5
3. Sébastien Pincemail FRA 16.83/0.9

SP
1. Ralf Bartels GER 20.76
2. Manuel Martínez ESP 20.28
3. Petr Stehlík CZE 20.24

DT
1. Mario Pestano ESP 66.29
2. Michael Möllenbeck GER 64.12
3. Diego Fortuna ITA 61.06

HT
1. Szymon Ziólkowski POL 79.14
2. Ilya Konovalov RUS 76.78
3. Markus Esser GER 76.11

JT
1. Mark Frank GER 82.38
2. Aleksandr Ivanov RUS 81.96
3. Francesco Pignata ITA 81.67

4x100m
1. GBR (Gardener, Devonish, Malcolm, Lewis-Francis) 38.67
2. ITA (Verdecchia, Collio, Torrieri, Fantoni Kaba) 38.69
3. FRA (Dovy, Pognon, Doucouré, M'Barke) 38.78

4x400m
1. GBR (Tobin, Hedman, Davis, Benjamin) 3:00.51
2. POL (Klimczak, Marciniszyn, Mackowiak, Plawgo) 3:01.33
3. FRA (El Haouzy, Keïta, Maunier, Raquil) 3:01.65

Women: 1. RUS 131.5, 2. POL 94, 3. GER 93, 4. FRA 90.5, 5. UKR 86, 6. ROM 85, 7. ITA 77, 8. GRE 62

100m (1.3)
1. Christine Arron FRA 11.09
2. Olga Fyodorova RUS 11.21
3. María Karastamáti GRE 11.30

200m (-0.6)
1. Christine Arron FRA 22.84
2. Yelena Bolsun RUS 23.00
3. Maryna Mindareva UKR 23.01

400m
1. Natalya Antyukh RUS 50.67
2. Antonina Yefremova UKR 51.56
3. Dímitra Dóva GRE 51.89

800m
1. Maria Cioncan ROM 2:00.88
2. Monika Gradzki GER 2:01.00
3. Svetlana Klyuka RUS 2:01.02

1500m
1. Yuliya Chizhenko RUS 4:06.76
2. Maria Cioncan ROM 4:07.39
3. Bouchra Ghezielle FRA 4:08.02

3000m
1. Yelena Zadorozhnaya RUS 8:57.08
2. Maria Martins FRA 9:00.71
3. Tetyana Kryvobok UKR 9:01.65

5000m
1. Liliya Shobukhova RUS 15:01.15
2. Wioletta Janowska POL 15:08.38
3. Mihaela Botezan ROM 15:13.36

3000mSC
1. Cristina Casandra ROM 9:35.95*
2. Lyubov Ivanova RUS 9:46.63
3. Justyna Bak POL 9:51.51

100mh (-1.3)
1. Linda Khodadin FRA 12.73
2. Kirsten Bolm GER 12.79
3. Flóra Redoúmi GRE 13.03

400mh
1. Anna Jesien POL 54.90
2. Yekaterina Bikert RUS 55.73
3. Claudia Marx GER 55.84

HJ
1. Tatyana Kivimägi RUS 1.98
2. Vita Palamar UKR 1.92
3. Melanie Skotnik FRA 1.92

PV
1. Anna Rogowska POL 4.60
2. Carolina Hingst GER 4.50
3. Nataliya Kushch UKR 4.30

LJ
1. Irina Simagina RUS 6.76/1.0
2. Fiona May ITA 6.43/0.1
3. Adina Anton ROM 6.35/0.0

TJ
1. Anna Pyatykh RUS 14.72/0.9
2. Hrisopiyí Devetzí GRE 14.62/1.0
3. Magdelin Martinez ITA 14.54w/2.2

SP 1. Olga Ryabinkina RUS 19.65
2. Nadine Kleinert GER 18.89
3. Assunta Legnante ITA 18.42

DT 1. Franka Dietzsch GER 64.38
2. Olena Antonova UKR 62.59
3. Marzena Wysocka POL 62.28

HT 1. Kamila Skolimowska POL 72.38
2. Manuela Montebrun FRA 71.10
3. Gulfiya Khanafeyeva RUS 70.06

JT 1. Steffi Nerius GER 64.59
2. Barbara Madejczyk POL 61.72
3. Zahra Bani ITA 61.66

4x100m 1. RUS (Fyodorova, Gushchina, Khabarova, Kondratyeva) 42.73
2. GER (Wakan, Möller, B Rockmeier, Sailer) 43.58
3. ITA (Sordelli, Calí, Grillo, Levorato) 43.83

4x400m 1. RUS (Gushchina, Levina, Lisnichenko, Antyukh) 3:23.56
2. POL (Radecka, Bejnar, Prokopek, Jesien) 3:24.61
3. UKR (Yefremova, Ilyushkina, Pilyugina, Pygyda) 3:26.72

First League Group A at Gävle, Sweden June 18-19

Men: 1. FIN 120, 2. SWE 118, 3. SUI 106, 4. HUN 99, 5. SLO 79, 6. EST 73, 7. CRO 69, 8. SVK 54. **Winners: 100m**: Matic Osovnikar SLO 10.63, **200m**: Tommi Hartonen FIN 21.31, **400m**: Zeljko Vincek CRO 46.61, **800m**: André Bucher SUI 1:51.70, **1500m**: Rizak Dirshe SWE 3:47.60, **3000m**: Christian Belz SUI 8:03.57, **5000m**: Henrik Skoog SWE 14:59.84, **3000mSC**: Mustafa Mohamed SWE 8:31.67, **110mh**: Robert Kronberg SWE 13.72, **400mh**: Mikael Jakobsson SWE 50.27, **HJ**: Stefan Holm SWE 2.27, **PV**: Patrik Kristiansson SWE 5.45, **LJ**: Tommi Evilä FIN 7.90, **TJ**: Jaanus Uudmäe EST 16.69w, **SP**: Ville Tiisanoja FIN 20.13, **DT**: Gerd Kanter EST 68.16, **HT**: Olli-Pekka Karjalainen FIN 78.16, **JT**: Tero Pitkämäki FIN 85.90, **4x100m**: SLO 39.78, **4x400m**: SWE 3:05.79.

Women: SWE 134, 2. ESP 131, 3. CZE 92, 4. FIN 90, 5. HUN 87.5, 6. SLO 69, 7. NOR 64, 8. CRO 52.5. **Winners: 100m**: Glory Alozie ESP 11.53, **200m**: Jenny Kallur 23.47, **400m**: Lena Aruhn SWE 52.40, **800m**: Mayte Martínez ESP 2:03.69, **1500m**: Johanna Risku FIN 4:21.04, **3000m**: Susanne Wigene NOR 9:01.31, **5000m**: Sonia Bejarano ESP 15:53.80, **3000mSC**: Livia Tóth HUN 9:39.97, **100mh**: Susanna Kallur SWE 13.03, **400mh**: Cora Olivero ESP 56.67, **HJ**: Kajsa Bergqvist SWE 2.01, **PV**: Pavla Hamácková CZE 4.50, **LJ**: Carolina Klüft SWE 6.91w, **TJ**: Carlota Castrejana ESP 13.85, **SP**: Martina de la Puente ESP 16.49, **DT**: Vera Cechlová CZE 61.23, **HT**: Ivana Brkljacic CRO 68.25, **JT**: Mercedes Chilla ESP 60.22, **4x100m**: SWE 44.09/3:31.28.

First League Group B at Leiria, Portugal June 18-19

Men: 1. UKR 115, 2. GRE 111, 3. NED 105, 4. POR 102, 5. BEL 99, 6. ROM 77, 7. IRL 65, 8. SCG 44. **Winners: 100m/200m**: Francis Obikwelu POR 10.14/20.48, **400m**: David Gillick IRL 45.96, **800m**: Tom Omey BEL 1:49.67, **1500m**: Manuel Damião POR 3:45.06, **3000m**: Rui Silva POR 8:10.26, **5000m**: Ricardo Ribas POR 14:24.47, **3000mSC**: Simon Vroemen NED 8:31.60, **110mh**: Marcel van der Westen NED 13.43, **400mh**: Perilkís Iakovákis GRE 50.08, **HJ**: Wilbert Pennings NED 2.21, **PV**: Vladyslav Revenko UKR 5.80, **LJ/TJ**: Marian Oprea ROM 7.73/17.22, **SP**: Gheorghe Guset ROM 20.07, **DT**: Jo Van Daele BEL 62.02, **HT**: Aléxandros Papadimitriou GRE 76.06, **JT**: Elefthérios Karasmanákis GRE 76.47, **4x100m/4x400m**: GRE 39.77/3:05.42

Women: 1. GBR 134.5, 2. BLR 107.5, 3. BEL 90, 4. NED 85, 5. POR 85, 6. BUL 83, 7. IRL 79, 8. SCG 53. **Winners: 100m/200m**: Kim Gevaert BEL 11.19/22.97, **400m**: Donna Fraser GBR 52.34, **800m**: Sandra Stals BEL 2:04.86, **1500m**: Helen Clitheroe GBR 4:07.42, **3000m**: Paula Radcliffe GBR 8:50.18, **5000m**: Olga Kravtsova BLR 15:10.14, **3000mSC**: Roisin McGettigan IRL 9:47.0, **100mh**: Sarah Claxton GBR 13.02, **400mh**: Liz Fairs GBR 56.65, **HJ**: Venelina Veneva BUL 1.92, **PV**: Janine Whitlock GBR 4.40, **LJ**: Karin Ruckstuhl 6.58, **TJ**: Natalya Safronova BLR 14.25w, **SP**: Lieja Tunks NED 18.20, **DT**: Dragana Tomasevic SCG 61.64, **HT**: Shirley Webb GBR 66.29, **JT**: Goldie Sayers GBR 61.37, **4x100m**: BLR 43.41, **4x400m**: GBR 3:27.03

Second League Group A at Tallinn, Estonia June 18-19

Men: 1. NOR 127, 2. AUT 109, 3. DEN 106, 4. LTU 101, 5. ISR 88.5, 6. LAT 88, 7. ISL 50, 8. LUX 40; **Women**: 1. LTU 110, 2. LAT 106, 3. EST 103, 4. AUT 101.5, 5. DEN 96.5, 6. SVK 87, 7. ISR 62, 8. ISL 51.

Second League Group B at Istanbul Turkey June 18-19

Men: 1. BLR 227, 2. TUR 225, 3. BUL 192, 4. MDA 171, 5. CYP 167, 6. BIH 153, 7. AZE 129, 8. GEO 104, 9. ARM 101, 10. AND 97, 11. AASE (Small States of Europe) 84, 12. ALB 68, 13. MKD 62; **Women**: 1. TUR 217, 2. SUI 199, 3. CYP 197, 4. MDA 176, 5. BIH 127, 6. ALB 118, 7. AAS 117, 8. GEO 114.5, 9. ARM 98, 10. AZE 71, 11. AND 66.5, 12. MKD 33.

2006 Matches – on June 28-29

Super League, Málaga, ESP

Men: ESP, FIN, FRA, GBR, GER, ITA, POL, RUS, UKR
Women: ESP, FRA, GBR, GER, POL, ROM, RUS, SWE, UKR

First League Group A, Prague, CZE

Men: AUT, BEL, BLR, CZE, EST, NOR, SUI, SWE
Women: BEL, BLR, CZE, FIN, IRL, ITA, LAT, SUI

First League Group B, Thessaloníki, GRE

Men: CRO, GRE, HUN, NED, POR, ROM, SLO, TUR
Women: BUL, GRE, HUN, LTU, NED, POR, SLO, TUR

Second League Group A, Banská Bystrika, SVK

Men: AND, BIH, IRL, ISL, ISR, LAT, MDA, SVK
Women: AND, BIH, CRO, ISL, ISR, MDA, NOR, SVK

Second League Group B, Novi Sad, SCG

Men: AASSE (Athletic Association of the Small States of Europe), ALB, ARM, AZE, BUL, CYP, DEN, GEO, LTU, LUX, MKD, SCG
Women: AASSE, ALB, ARM, AUT, AZE, CYP, DEN, EST, GEO, MKD, SCG
Nine teams, including the hosts Spain, will compete in the 2006 SPAR European Cup so Britain, as 7th placed men's team in 2005 in the Super League, was not relegated. Also only three teams were relegated from the European Cup First League instead of the usual four. The best seventh placed teams according to the IAAF scoring tables remained in the First League (men: Croatia, women: Ireland).

European Cup Combined Events 2005

Super League at Bydgoszcz, Poland July 2-3
Men Dec: 1. EST 23,139, 2. RUS 22,711, 3. ESP 22,482, 4. ITA 22,272, 5. FRA 22,204, 6. POL 22,190, 7. GER 22,036. Ind: 1. Mikk Pahapill EST 8149, 2. Nikolay Tishchenko RUS 7767, 3. David Gómez ESP 7698.
Women Hep: 1. BLR 17,626, 2. UKR 17,506, 3. RUS 17,487, 4. FIN 17,335, 5. GER 17,289, 6. POL 17,112, 7. GBR 16,984, 8. NED 16,279. Ind: 1. Tatyana Alisevich BLR 6173, 2. Yvonne Wisse NED 6026, 3. Diana Koritskaya RUS 5981.

First League at Jyväskylä, Finland July 2-3

Men Dec: 1. HUN 22,879, 2. FIN 22,771, 3. CZE 22,624, 4. UKR 22,128, 5. NED 21,893, 6. LAT 21,870, 7. GBR 21,411, 8. SUI 21,224. Ind: 1. Tomás Dvorák CZE 8105, 2. Attila Zsivoczky HUN 8105, 3. Jaakko Ojaniemi 7977.
Women Hep: 1. EST 17,070, 2. SWE 16,988, 3. ITA 16,892, 4. LTU 16,791, 5. GRE 16.693, 6. CZE 15,998, 7. FRA 15,186, 8. AUT 14,954. Ind: 1. Carolina Klüft SWE 6688, 2. Austra Skujyte LTU 6206, 3. Larisa Netseporuk EST 5910.

Second League at Maribor, Slovenia July 2-3

Men Dec: 1. BLR 22,604, 2. GRE 21.227, 3. SWE 19.318, 4. BEL 17.542, 5. CRO 17.099. Ind: Aleksandr Parkhomenko BLR 8025.
Women Hep: 1. SUI 15,587, 2. HUN 15,420, 3. LAT 14,917, 4. ESP 14,785. 5. SLO 13,449, 6. TUR 12,619. Ind: Esenija Volzankina LAT 5437.

2006 Matches on July 1-2

Super League, Arles, FRA
Men: ESP, EST, FIN, FRA, HUN, ITA, POL, RUS
Women: BLR, EST, FIN, GBR, POL, RUS, SWE, UKR
First League, Yalta, UKR
Men: AUT, BLR, CZE, GBR, GRE, LAT, NED, UKR
Women: CZE, FRA, GRE, HUN, ITA, LTU, NED, SUI
Second League, Monzon, ESP
Men: BEL, CRO, LTU, NOR, POR, SLO, SUI, SWE plus individuals from AZE, CRO, CYP, DEN, IRL, ISL, MDA, ROM, SCG, SVK, TUR
Women: AUT, ESP, LAT, POR, SLO, TUR plus individuals from BEL, CRO, DEN, IRL, ISL, ISR, NOR, ROM, SCG, SVK

The DLV has withdrawn Germany's teams, so that Britain's women were not relegated to the First League and the men not relegated to the Second League.

European Winter Throwing Cup 2005

March 12-13, Mersin, Turkey
Men: 1. RUS 8602, 2. GER 8286, 3. ITA 7959; **SP**: 1. Rutger Smith NED 21.00, 2. Gheorghe Guset ROM 20.75, 3. Manuel Martínez ESP 20.22; **DT**: 1. Gerd Kanter EST 66.05, 2. Gábor Máté HUN 64.17, 3. Rutger Smith 62.80; **HT**: 1. Ivan Tikhon BLR 80.79, 2. Aleksey Zagornyi RUS 78.11, 3. Ivan Konovalov RUS 77.35; **JT**: 1. Aleksandr Ivanov RUS 81.13, 2. Igor Sukhomlinov RUS 80.02, 3. Manuel Nau GER 76.76.
Women: 1. RUS 8334, 2. GER 8155, 3. ITA 7848, 4. UKR 7448; **SP**: 1. Olga Ryabinkina RUS 18.41, 2. Assunta Legnante ITA 17.98, 3. Kristin Marten GER 17.68; **DT**: 1. Natalya Sadova RUS 61.74, 2. Nicoleta Grasu ROM 60.75, 3. Jana Tucholke GER 57.84; **HT**: 1. Ivana Brkljacic CRO 71.00, 2. Mihaela Melinte ROM 70.40, 3. Olga Kuzenkova RUS 70.11; **JT**: 1. Steffi Nerius GER 61.01, 2. Mariya Abakumova RUS 59.06, 3. Vivian Zimmer GER 58.74; B: Lada Chernova RUS 60.05.

European Cup 10,000m 2005

April 2, Barakaldo, Spain
Men: 1. José Carlos de la Ossa ESP 27:27.80, 2. Carlos Castillejo ESP 28:06.88, 3, Ricardo Serrano 28:19.20; **Teams**: 1, ESP 1:25:53.88, 2. POR 1:27:04.86, 3, GER 1:28:32.82. **Women**: 1. Sabrina Mockenhaupt GER 31:21.28, 2. Fernanda Ribeiro POR 32:03.22, Viktoriya Klimina RUS 32:04.57; **Teams**: 1. POR 1:38:36.25, 2. ESP 1:40:20.45

European Cup of Race Walking 2005

At Miskolc, Hungary, May 21
Men 20km: 1. Ilya Markov RUS 1:20:50, 2. Juan Manuel Molina ESP 1:20:54, 3. Vladimir Stankin RUS 1:21:28, 4. Andrey Yurin UKR 1:22:13, 5. Stepan Yudin RUS 1:22:20, 6. Roman Magdziarczyk POL 1:22:26, 7. Silviu Casandra ROM 1:23:00, 8. Erik Tysse NOR 1:23:04, 9. Grzegorz Sudol POL 1:23:17, 10. Andrey Talashko BLR 1:23:59. 49 of 62 finished.
Teams: 1. RUS 9, 2. ESP 33, 3. UKR 42, 4. SVK 65, 5. BLR 77, 6. FRA 79.
Men 50km: 1. Aleksey Voyevodin RUS 3:41:03, 2. Sergey Kirdyapkin RUS 3:41:11, 3. Yuriy Andronov RUS 3:42:34, 4. Yohan Diniz FRA 3:45:17, 5. Denis Langlois FRA 3:47:31, 6. Alex Schwazer ITA 3:49:42, 7. Peter Korcok SVK 3:51:30. 8. Andrey Stepanchuk BLR 3:51:40, 9. Milos Bátovsky SVK 3:54:49, 10. David Boulanger FRA 3:55:117. 37 of 55 finished.
Teams: 1. RUS 6, 2. FRA 19, 3. ITA 30, 4, BLR 49, 5, POR 65, 6. UKR 66
U20 Men 10km: 1. Andrey Ruzavin RUS 39:57, 2, Giorgio Rubino ITA 40:46, 3. Aleksandr Prokhorov RUS 41:26. **Teams:** 1. RUS 4, 2. GER 11, 3. BLR 13, 4. UKR 18, 5, ITA 25, 6. SVK 29
Women 20km: 1. Olimpiada Ivanova RUS 1:28:18,

2. Susana Feitor POR 1:29:01, 3. Elisa Rigaudo ITA 1:29:26, 4. Claudia Stef ROM 1:30:11, 5. Yuliya Voyevodina RUS 1:30:34, 6. Sabine Zimmer GER 1:30:57, 7. Vera Santos POR 1:31:58, 8. Natalya Misyulya BLR 1:32:03, 9. Mayte Gargallo ESP 1:32:18, 10. Gisella Orsini ITA 1:32:23. 48 of 65 finished. **Teams:** 1. POR 25, 2. ITA 26, 3. ROM 30, 4. ESP 52, 5. LTU 77, 6. UKR 82.

U20 Women 10km: 1. Vera Sokolova RUS 44:09, 2. Tatyana Kalmykova RUS 45:02, 3. Yelena Rusak BLR 46:37. **Teams:** 1. RUS 3, 2. BLR 8, 3. ITA 23, 4. UKR 23, 5. IRL 32, 6. POR 33.

European Champion Clubs Cup 2005

At Lagos, Portugal 28-29 May

Group A: Men: 1. Fiamme Galle Roma ITA 115, 2. Luch Moskva RUS 113, 3. Sporting Clube POR 101.5, 4. Panellios GRE 101.5, 5. Dukla Praha CZE 94, 6. Montreuil FRA 76.5, 7. Puma Chapin Jérez ESP 72, 8. Amsterdam NED 45.5. **Women**: 1. SC Luch Moskva 125 (9th successive win), 2. Panellinos GRE 110, 3. Valencia ESP 108, 4. Enka TUR 91, 5. Sporting Clube POR 81, 6. Fondiari ITA 80, 7. USK Praha CZE 72, 8. Montreuil FRA 49. Meeting records: 3000m/5000m: Elvan Abeylegesse TUR 8:54.00/15:08.59, 3000mSC: Clarisse Cruz POR 10:02.60.

Group B Men: 1. AK Spartak SVK 50; 2, Maccabi ISR; 3, Crusaders IRL.

42nd South American Championships 2005

At Calí, Colombia 21-24 July

Men

100m	1. André da Silva BRA 10.32
(0.2)	2. Vicente de Lima BRA 10.37
	3. Heber Viera URU 10.43
200m	1. André da Silva BRA 20.33w(*)
(4.9)	2. Heber Viera URU 20.62
	3. Geronimo Goeloe AHO 20.80
400m	1. Andrés Silva URU 45.38
	2. Sanderlei Parrela BRA 45.83
	3. Gustavo Aguirre ARG 46.43
800m	1. Fabiano Peçanha BRA 1:47.02
	2. Diego Diniz Gomes BRA 1:48.30
	3. Jhon Chávez COL 1:48.65
1500m	1. Fabiano Peçanha BRA 3:41.51
	2. Byron Piedra ECU 3:41.90
	3. Javier Carriqueo ARG 3:45.53
5000m	1. Byron Piedra ECU 14:12.24
	2. Jacinto López COL 14:14.07
	3. Javier Carriqueo ARG 14:19.10
10,000m	1. José Alirio Carrasco COL 30:07.24
	2. Jhon Cusi PER 30:14.74
	3. Diego Colorado COL 30:15.55
3000mSC	1. Mariano Mastromarino ARG 9:02.89
	2. Fernando Fernandes BRA 9:04.46
	3. Sergio Lobos CHI 9:08.59
110mh	1. Redelen dos Santos BRA 13.46w
(3.4)	2. Paulo César Villar COL 13.49
	3. Matheus Inocêncio BRA 13.72
400mh	1. Tiago Bueno BRA 50.87
	2. Víctor Solarte VEN 51.00
	3. Cleverson Silva BRA 52.32
HJ	1. Gilmar Mayo COL 2.22 (4th win)
	2. Erasmo Jata ARG 2.19
	3. Rodrigo Assis Santos BRA 2.16
PV	1. Fábio Gomes da Silva BRA 5.20
	2. Javier Benítez ARG 5.20
	3. Germán Charaviglio ARG 5.10
LJ	1. Erivaldo Vieira BRA 8.15/0.3*
	2. Thiago Dias BRA 7.93/0.84
	3. Esteban Copland VEN 7.92/1.3
TJ	1. Jefferson Sabino BRA 16.24/0.0
	2. Hugo Chila ECU 15.91/0.3
	3. Carlos Carabalí VEN 7.92/1.3
SP	1. Marco Antonio Verni CHI 18.43
	2. Yojer Medina VEN 18.32
	3. Jhonny Rodríguez COL 18.22
DT	1. Jorge Balliengo ARG 60.97*
	2. Marcelo Pugliese ARG 56.76
	3. Ronald Julião BRA 56.51
HT	1. Juan Cerra ARG 72.03
	2. Wágner Domingos BRA 67.33
	3. Patricio Palma CHI 67.10
JT	1. Luiz F. da Silva BRA 79.44
	2. Júlio César de Oliveira BRA 73.60
	3. Noraldo Palacios COL 73.54
Dec	1. Jorge Naranjo CHI 7489
	2. Iván S. da Silva BRA 7437
	3. Andrés Mantilla COL 7383
20kmW	1. Jefferson Pérez ECU 1:22:54.4*
	2. Rolando Saquipay ECU 1:22:55.4
	3. Luis Fernando López COL 1:23:43.2
4x100m	1. BRA (A da Silva, Sena, Moreira, de Lima) 39.17
	2. COL 39.85
	3. ECU 40.45
4x400m	1. BRA (Ambrósio, Parrela, Chyaromont, W Souza) 3:04.15
	2. COL 3:05.94
	3. ARG 3:08.61

Women

100m	1. Lucimar de Moura BRA 11.25
(0.5)	2. Melisa Murillo COL 11.39
	3. Luciana A. dos Santos BRA 11.46
200m	1. Lucimar de Moura BRA 22.98w
(5.0)	2. Felipa Palacios COL 23.14
	3. Wilmary Álvarez VEN 23.14
400m	1. Maria Almirão BRA 52.32
	2. Geisa Coutinho BRA 52.94
	3. Wilmary Álvarez VEN 53.57
800m	1. Rosibel García COL 2:03.28
	2. Jenny Mejias VEN 2:04.93
	3. Perla dos Santos BRA 2:06.04
1500m	1. Rosibel García COL 4:29.63
	2. María Peralta ARG 4:30.37
	3. Valeria Rodriguez ARG 4:31.35
5000m	1. Bertha Sánchez COL 16:47.03
	2. Lucélia Peres BRA 167:03.55
	3. Nadir de Siquiera BRA 17:16.33
10,000m	1. Bertha Sánchez COL 34:34.40
	2. Lucélia Peres BRA 34:51.12
	3. Ruby Riativa COL 35:38.02
3000mSC	1. Patrícia Lobo BRA 10:36.21
	2. Mónica Amboya ECU 10:43.67
	3. Yolanda Caballero COL 10:48.36

100mh (0.1)	1. Maíla Machado BRA 13.18
	2. Princesa Oliveros COL 13.51
	3. Brigith Meriano COL 13.68
400mh	1. Perla dos Santos BRA 58.33
	2. Lucimar Teodoro BRA 59.27
	3. Lucy Jaramillo ECU 59.78
HJ	1. Katarina Ibargüen COL 1.93*
	2. Solange Witteveen ARG 1.88
	3. Eliana da Silva BRA 1.79
PV	1. Joana Ribeiro Costa BRA 4.20
	2. Fabiana Murer BRA 4.00
	3. Milena Agudelo COL 4.00
LJ	1. Luciana A. dos Santos BRA 6.39/0.1
	2. Keila Costa BRA 6.32/-1.3
	3. Katarina Ibargüen COL 6.30/-3.0
TJ	1. Gisela de Oliveira BRA 13.90/1.6
	2. Keila Costa BRA 13.75/0.0
	3. Katarina Ibargüen COL 13.59/1.3
SP	1. Andréa Pereira BRA 16.60
	2. Luz Dary Castro COL 16.27
	3. Rosario Ramos VEN 14.67
DT	1. Luz Dary Castro COL 53.49
	2. Rosario Ramos VEN 52.46
	3. Renata Figueirêdo BRA 51.74
HT	1. Jennifer Dahlgren ARG 65.05*
	2. Johana Moreno COL 61.65
	3. Rosa Rodríguez VEN 61.51
JT	1. Alessandra Resende BRA 56.06
	2. Zuleima Araméndiz COL 54.81
	3. Romina Maggi ARG 48.76
Hep	1. Elizete Gomes da Silva BRA 5429
	2. Andrea Bordalejo ARG 5249
	3. Daniela Crespo ARG 5170
20kmW	1. Sandra Zapata COL 1:40:52.6
	2. Morelba Useche VEN 1:48:24.9
	3. Marcela Pacheco CHI 1:49:50.1
4x100m	1. COL (M Murillo, Palacios, Obregón, N González) 43.17*
	2. BRA 44.35
	3. CHI 45.37
4x400m	1. BRA (Teodoro, Almirão, Coutinho, Fontes Dias) 3:29.24
	2. COL 3:36.95
	3. CHI 3:40.49

Medal and Points (8-7-6-5-4-3-2-1) Table

Nation	*1*	*2*	*3*	*Points*
BRA	25	15	10	478
COL	10	12	14	321
ARG	4	6	7	150
VEN	0	4	6	92
ECU	2	5	3	87
CHI	2	0	4	85
URU	1	1	0	20
PER	0	1	0	20

African Junior Championships 2005

September 1-4, Radès, Tunisia

Men: 100m: Katim Touré 10.68, **200m**/400: Nagmedin El Abubakr SUD 20.95/46.02, **800m/1500m**: Geoffrey Rono KEN 1:47.10/3:42.76, **5000m/10,000m**: Moses Masai KEN 13:45.37/28:30.27, **3000mSC**: Willy Komen KEN 8:35.82, **110mh**: Ruan de Vries RSA 14.12, **400mh**: Séléké Samake 51.32, **HJ**: Kabelo Kgosimang BOT 2.16, **PV**: Mohamed Abdelatif Djadoun 4.60, **LJ**: Mohamed Yassine Chaieb TUN 7.49w, **TJ**: Okba Ramoul ALG 15.60, **SP** 6kg: Mostafa Abdul El-Moaty EGY 18.26, **DT** 1.75kg: Mohamed Mansour Ouadhah LBA 54.72, **HT**: Khaled Chawki Wanis EGY 61.75, **JT**: Robert Oosthuizen RSA 75.94, **Dec** J: Guillaume Thierry MRI 6838, **10kmW:** Ali Amrouch ALG 45:31.13, **4x100m**: RSA 40.60, **4x400m**: SUD 3:09.00; **Women**: **100m**: Thandi Mngwevu RSA 12.08, **200m/400m/400mh**: Nawal El-Jack SUD 24.07/53.94/59.72, **800m**: Lydia Wafula KEN 2:02.84, **1500m**: Chahrazad Cheboub ALG 4:17.06, **3000m/3000mSC**: Mercy Njorege KEN 9:14.89/9:50.63, **5000m**: Beatrice Chebusit KEN 16:04.10, **100mh**: Félicité Traore BUR 14.31, **HJ**: Anika Smit RSA 1.89, **PV**: Nadia Mabrouk TUN 3.30, **LJ**: Lindi van Dyk RSA 5.80, **TJ**: Sahnoune Camélia Chiraz ALG 12.89, **SP/DT**: Marli Knoetze RSA 16.93/46.44, **HT**: Iman Al-Ashri EGY 54.59, **JT**: Riatha Jacobs RSA 47.29, **Hep**: Mona Jabir Ahmed SUD 4587, **10kmW:** Hendrik Botha RSA 52:15.22, **4x100m**: TUN 48.20, **4x400m**: SUD 3:40.24.

14th Arab Championships 2005

September 15-18, Radès, Tunisia

Men: 100m: Yahya Saeed Al Kahes KSA 10.28*, **200m**: Hamed Hamadan Al-Bishi KSA 20.96, **400m**: Nagmeldin El-Abubakr 45.66, **800m**: Youssef Saad Kamel BRN 1:47.36, **1500m**: Bilal Mansour Ali BRN 3:38.85*, **5000m/10,000m**: Aïssa Ismail Rashed QAT 13:53.15/28:36.39*, **HMar**: Khaled Khaled BRN 64:18, 3000SC: Tarek Mubarek BRN 8:40.16, **110mh**: Hamdi Mhirsi TUN 13.82, **400mh**: Kamel Tabbal TUN 50.94, **HJ**: Omar Moussa Al-Masrahi KSA 2.18, **PV**: Béchir Zaghouani TUN 5.00, **LJ**: Issam Nima ALG 8.09w, **TJ**: Ibrahim Aboubaker QAT 16.59, **SP**: Kha1ed Al-Suwaidi QAT 19.70*, **DT**: Omar El Ghazaly EGY 60.87, **HT**: Ali Mohamed Al-Zankawi KUW 76.10*, **JT**: Walid Abderrazak Mohamed EGY 74.18, **Dec**: Boualem Lamri 6832, **4x100m/4x400m**: KSA 39.88/3:05.77, 20,000W: Hassanine Sbii TUN 1:28:28*. **Women**: **100m**: Awatef Hamrouni TUN 11.90, **200m/400m**: Nawal Al-Jack SUD 23.97/53.43, **800m/1500m/5000m**: Maryam Jamal BRN 2:09.73/4:10.31/16:53.25, **10,000m/HMar**: Karima Saleh Jassem 34:45.47*/79:30*, **100mh**: Naïma Ben Tahar ALG 14.27, **400mh/Hep**: Mona Jabir Ahmed SUD 57.88/4977, **HJ/LJ/TJ**: Yamilé Aldama SUD 1.81*/6.19/14.05*, **PV**: Syrine Balti TUN 3.80*, **SP**: Amel Benkhaled TUN 15.36, **DT**: Monia Kari TUN 54.61*, **HT**: Marwa Ahmed Hussein EGY 62.52*, **JT**: Hana Ramadhan Omar EGY 52.00, **4x100m**: TUN 47.36, **4x400m**: SUD 3:41.43, **10kmW:** Ghania Amzal ALG 49:33*.

Leaders in medal table: TUN 9G-13S-12B, BRN 9-7-5, SUD 8-4-4, EGY 5-5-5, KSA 5-4-3, QAT 4-4-4, ALG 4-0-5. 11 nations won medals.

1st Asian Indoor Games 2005

November 13-15, Pattaya, Thailand

Men: 60m: Tang Yik Chun HKN 6.80, **400m**: Mohamed Akefian IRI 47.83, **800m**: Ghamanda Ram

IND 1:50.69, **1500m/3000m**: Kamal Ali Thamer QAT 3:50.28/8:05.03, **60mh:** Narongdech Janjal THA 7.93, **HJ**: Sergey Zasimovich KAZ 2.17, **PV**: Artyom Pilipenko KAZ 5.30, **LJ/TJ**: Roman Valiyev KAZ 7.84/16.51, **SP**: Navpreet Singh IND 18.80, **Hep**: Pavel Dubitskiy KAZ 5549, **4x400m**: THA 3:14.11. **Women**: **60m:** Nongnuch Saenrat THA 7.46, **400m**: Tatyana Roslanova KAZ 52.69, **800m**: Sunita Kanojia IND 2:06.07, **1500m/3000m**: O.P. Jaisha IND 4:15.75/9:38.43, **60mh**: Ji Fangqian CHN 8.37, **HJ**: Noengruthai Chaipetch THA 1.88, **PV**: Yang Jing CHN 4.31, **LJ**: Guan Yingan CHN 6.54, **TJ**: Olesya Belayeva 13.60, **SP**: Li Ling CHN 18.20, Pen: Olga Rypakova KAZ 3954, **4x400m**: IND 3:46.48.

60th Balkan Championships 2005

July 3-4, Istanbul, Turkey.

Men: **100m**: Yoran Ilinov BUL 10.40, **200m**: Panayiótis Sarrís GRE 20.69, **400m**: Dimítrios Grávelos GRE 47.22, **800m**: Catalin Mihu ROM 1:51.07, **1500m**: Darko Radomirovic SCG 3:45.25, **3000m**: Mirko Petrovic SCG 8:18.66, **5000m**: Marius Ionescu ROM 14:02.38, **3000mSC**: Ionet Enache ROM 9:01.86, **110mh**: Alexandru Mihailescu ROM 13.75, **400mh**: Pláton Gavélas GRE 51.35, **HJ**: Dragutin Topic SCG 2.26, **PV**: Igor Sarcevic SCG 5.00, **LJ**: Danut Simion ROM 7.89, **TJ**: Daniel Donovici ROM 16.55/-0.6, **SP**: Gheorghe Guset ROM 20.25, **DT**: Ercüment Olgundeniz TUR 60.79, **HT**: Spirídon Zoullién GRE 72.61, **JT**: Levente Bartha ROM 74.88, **4x100m**: GRE 40.25, **4x400m**: ROM 3:07.21; **Teams:** 1. ROM 150, 2. GRE 142, 3. SCG 129, 4. BIH 95, 5. MDA 90, 6. TUR 83, 7. BUL 70, 8. MKD 39, 9. ALB 37. **Women**: **100m**: (1.2) Yeoryía Kókloni GRE 11.36, **200m**: Klodiana Shala ALB 23.99, **400m**: Mariyana Dimitrova BUL 53.11, **800m/1500m**: Corina Dumbravean ROM 2:02.44/4:04.56, 5000: Adriana Pîrtea ROM 15:36.01, **3000mSC**: Claudia Colita ROM 10:08.51, **100mh**: Jelena Jotanovic SCG 13.63, **400mh**: Vanya Stambolova BUL 58.41, **HJ**: Inna Gliznutsa MDA 1.92, **PV**: Dímitra Emmanouil GRE 4.00, **LJ**: Stilianí Pilátou GRE 6.54, **TJ**: Athanasía Pérra GRE 13.71, **SP**: Elena Hila ROM 17.69, **DT**: Dragana Tomasevic SCG 62.43, **HT**: Mihaela Melinte ROM 69.64, **JT**: Monica Stoian ROM 49.26, **4x100m**; GRE 46.31, **4x400m**: BUL 3:35.49. **Teams:** ROM 157, 2. GRE 132, 3. SCG 119, 4. BUL 93, 5. BIH 79, 6. TUR 72, 7. MDA 60, 8. ALB 48, 9. MKD 34.

Walks Champs: at Préveza, Greece April 23: **20km:** Silviu Casandra 1:25:48, **Women 20km:** Evaggelía Xinoú 1:35:35.

Marathon Champs

at Istanbul, Turkey October 2:

Men: Iaroslav Musinschi MDA 2:20:42, **Women**: Natalia Cherches MDA 2:42:58

15th Bolivar Games 2005

August 18-21, Armenia, COL (A 1483m)

Men: **100m/200m**: Daniel Grueso COL 10.44/20.75*, **400m**: Carlos Andres Peña COL 46.65, **800m**: Simoncito Silvera VEN 1:51.26, **1500m**: Byron Piedra ECU 3:44.62*, **5000m/10,000m**: José Carrasco COL 14:23.61/30:06.24, **HMar**: Diego Colorado COL 67:18, **3000mSC**: Edmigio Delgado VEN 9:05.93, **110mh/400mh**: Paulo Villar COL 13.44*/50.61, **HJ**: Gilmar Mayo COL 2.26*, **PV**: David Rojas COL 4.70, **LJ**: Esteban Copland VEN 7.75, **TJ**: Jhonny Rodríguez VEN 16.10, **SP**: Yoger Medina VEN 18.74, **DT**: Jesús Parejo VEN 54.65, **HT**: Aldo Bello VEN 67.63*, **JT**: Noraldo Palacios COL 77.37*, **Dec**: Andres Mantilla COL 7352*, **4x100m/4x400m**: COL 39.80/3:07.99, **20kmW**: Rolando Saquipay ECU 1:22:51*, 50kmW: Xavier Moreno ECU 4:09:07*. **Women**: **100m/200m**: Felipa Palacios COL 11.18*/22.85*, **400m**: Norma González COL 53.08, **800m/1500m**: Rosibel García COL 2:01.57*/4:29.16, **5000m**: Bertha Sánchez COL 17:40.58, **10,000m**: Martha Tenorio ECU 34:36.66*, **HMar**: Sandra Ruales ECU 80:12*, **100mh**: Briggite Merlano COL 13.62*, **400mh**: Lucy Jaramillo ECU 57.58*, **HJ/LJ**: Katerina Ibargüen COL 1.91*/6.54*, **PV**: Milena Aguledo COL 4.21*, **TJ**: Johana Triviño COL 13.90*, **SP**: Luz Dary Castro COL 16.46*, **DT**: Rosario Ramos VEN 53.60 drugs dq, **HT**: Johana Ramírez COL 61.91*, **JT**: Zuleima Araméndiz COL 54.78, **Hep**: Taimara Rivas VEN 5461*, **4x100m/4x400m**: COL 45.61*/3:35.25*, **20kmW**: Geovana Irusta BOL 1:39:14.

20th Central American and Caribbean Championships 2003

July 9-11, Nassau, Bahamas

Men: **100m**: Darrel Brown TRI 10.02* (2. Marc Burns TRI 10.02*), **200m**: Usain Bolt JAM 20.03*, **400m**: Lansford Spence JAM 45.29, **800m**: Yeiman López CUB 1:47.64, **1500m**: Maurys Surel Castillo CUB 3:47.89, **5000m**: Juan Luis Barrios MEX 14:22.57, **10,000m**: Aquelmis Rojas 30:14.75, **3000mSC**: Alexander Greaux PUR 8:56.15, **110mh**: Yoel Hernández CUB 13.32w, **400mh**: Dean Griffiths JAM 48.99*, **HJ**: Victor Moya CUB 2.26, **PV**: Lázaro Borges CUB 4.80, **LJ**: Leevan Sands BAH 8.13, **TJ**: Yoandri Betanzos CUB 17.33w, **SP**: Dorian Scott JAM 20.21*, **DT**: Yunio Lastre CUB 60.10, **HT**: Iosvany Suárez CUB 69.47, **JT**: Emeterio González CUB 76.44, **Dec**: Claston Bernard JAM 7877*, **4x100m**: TRI (Armstrong, Burns, Harper, Brown) 38.47*, **4x400m**: BAH (Cleare, Williams, McKinney, Brown) 3:01.08, **20kmW**: Julio Martínez GUA 1:30:39. **Women**: **100m**: Chandra Sturrup BAH 11.02*, **200m**: Cydonie Mothersill CAY 22.26w, **400m**: Tonique Williams-Darling BAH 50.97, **800m**: Neisha Bernard-Thomas GRN 2:01.07, **1500m**: Yadira Vataille CUB 4:26.43, **5000m/10,000m**: Yudelkis Martínez CUB 17:12.58/34:53.50, **3000mSC**: Mardrea Hyman JAM 9:54.01*, **100mh**: Nadine Faustin-Parker HAI 12.83, **400mh**: Debbie-Ann Parris JAM 55.26, **HJ**: Lavern Spencer LCA 1.94, **PV**: Katiuska Pérez CUB 4.25*, **LJ**: Yargelis Savigne CUB 6.88w, **TJ:** Yarianna Martínez CUB 14.18, **SP**: Yumileidi Cumbá CUB 18.98*, **DT**: Yarelis Barrios CUB 56.59, **HT**: Candice Scott TRI 67.44*, **JT**: Laverne Eve BAH 61.11, **Hep**: Juana Castillo DOM 5760, **4x100m**: JAM (Browning, Brooks, McDonald, Dowdie) 43.21, **4x400m**: JAM (Thompson, Sutherland, S Williams, Beckford) 3:30.63, **10kmW:** Cristina López ESA 45:52.32*.

Medal Table & Point Leaders: CUB 403 (17G-13S-17B), JAM 224 (9-6-5), BAH 165 (5-4-6), TRI 117 (3-6-1), PUR 95 (1-4-3), MEX 77.5 (1-4-2), DOM 56.5 (1-1-0), GUA 50 (1-1-0), BAR 43 (0-1-1), HAI 28 (1-0-1), ESA 24 (1-0-1), GRN 23 (1-0-1); 19 nations won medals, 23 in points.

Central American Championships 2005

June 3-4, San José, Costa Rica

Men: **100m/200m**: Andrés Rodríguez PAN 11.12/21.77, **400m**: Nery Brenes CRC 46.42, **800m**: Marco Pérez CRC 1:52.57, **1500m**: Francis Jiménez ESA 4:02.43, **5000m**: Roy Vargas CRC 15:02.58, **10,000m**: José Amado García GUA 30:11.54, **3000mSC**: César Lizano CRC 9:31.22, **110mh**: David Umaña CRC 15.06, **400mh**: Jonathan Gibson PAN 52.78, **HJ**: Henry Linton CRC 2.09, **PV**: Pedro Fuentes ESA 4.40, **LJ**: Jonathan Romero PAN 7.18, **TJ**: Maxwell Álvarez GUA 15.15, **SP**: Henry Santos GUA 13.30, **DT/HT**: Raúl Rivera GUA 45.70/62.06, **JT**: Javier Ugarte NCA 67.12, **Dec**: Darwin Colón HON 5798, **20kmW**: Luis F García GUA 1:26:21.85, **4x100m**: HON 42.18, **4x400m**: CRC 3:15.52. **Women**: **100m/200m**: Tracy Joseph CRC 12.37/24.98, **400m/400mh**: Verónica Quijano ESA 55.75/60.57, **800m**: Wendy Zuñiga CRC 2:13.99, **1500m**: Gabriela Traña CRC 4:39.12, **5000m/10,000m**: Dina Judith Cruz 18:00.07/37:40.68, **3000mSC**: Melissa González CRC 12:56.14, **100mh**: Jeimy Bernardez HON 14.72, **HJ/TJ**: María Carrillo 1.68/12.49, **PV**: Peggy Ovalle GUA 3.30, **LJ**: Sabrina Asturias GUA 5.68, **SP**: Natyan Caetano PAN 12.82, **DT**: Aixa Midleton PAN 43.15, **HT**: Viviana Abarca CRC 41.73, **JT**: Dalila Rugama NCA 50.35, **Hep**: Dilian Ramírez CRC 3739, **10kmW**: Evelyn Núñez GUA 48:45.46, **4x100m**: CRC 48.17, **4x400m**: ESA 3:52.21.

4th East Asian Games 2005

November 1-4, Macau, China

Men: **100m**: Hu Kai 10.40, **200m**: Shinji Takahira JPN 20.88, **400m**: Yoshihiro Horigome JPN 46.44, **800m**: Lee Jae-hun KOR 1:48.60, **1500m**: Hiroyuki Morikawa JPN 3:48.27, **5000m/10,000m**: Yuki Nakamura JPN 14:05.77/31:59.69, **HMar**: Toshinari Fujimoto JPN 68:14, **3000mSC**: Yoshitaka Iwamizu JPN 8:40.16, **110mh**: Liu Xiang CHN 13.21*, **400mh**: Takayuki Koike JPN 50.85, **HJ**: Huang Haiqiang CHN 2.23, **PV**: Takuro Mori JPN 5.00, **LJ**: Song Jian CHN 7.77w, **TJ**: Kim Duk-hyung KOR 16.79, **SP**: Zhang Qi CHN 20.06*, **DT**: Wu Tao CHN 61.74, **HT**: Hiroaki Doi JPN 70.35, **JT**: Li Rongxiang CHN 79.75, **Dec**: Kim Kun-woo KOR 7754, **20kmW**: Yu Chaohong CHN 1:23:51, **4x100m/4x400m**: JPN 39.61/3:07.70. **Women**: **100m**: Qin Wangping CHN 11.65, **200m**: Chen Lisha CHN 23.78, **400m**: Asami Tanno JPN 52.69, **800m**: Liu Qing CHN 2:00.11*, **1500m**: Xie Sainan CHN 4:20.54, **5000m**: Xing Huina CHN 16:04.56, **10,000m**: Bao Guiying CHN 32:25.07, **HMar**: Yoshiko Ichikawa JPN 76:31, **100mh**: Feng Yun CHN 13.09*, **400mh**: Huang Xiaoxiao CHN 55.33*, **HJ**: Jing Xuezhu CHN 1.85, **PV**: Zhao Yingying CHN 4.40*, **LJ**: Kumiko Ikeda JPN 6.54, **TJ**: Huang Qiuyan CHN 14.08, **SP**: Li Meiju CHN 18.12, **DT**: Song Aimin CHN 64.32*, **HT**: Zhang Wenxiu CHN 72.23*, **JT**: Ma Ning CHN 61.95, **Hep**: Wang Hailian CHN 5932, **20kmW**: Wang Liping CHN 1:34:01, **4x100m**: JPN 44.88, **4x400m**: CHN 3:33.59.

5th Francophone Games 2005

December 11-16, Naimey, Niger

Men: **100m**: Idrissa Sanou BUR 10.48, **200m**: Ben Youssef Meité CIV 20.99, **400m**: Mathieu Gnanligo BEN 46.43, **800m/1500m**: Yassine Bensghir MAR 1:47.11/3:46.58, **5000m**: Adil Kaouch MAR 14:16.23, **10,000m**: Dieudonné Disi RWA 29:17.11, **Mar:** Rachid Kisri MAR 2:17:03*, **3000mSC**: Hamid Ezzine MAR 8:52.72, **110mh**: Cédric Lavanne FRA 13.68, **400mh**: Ibou Faye SEN 50.67, **HJ**: Mustapha Raïfak FRA 2.24, **PV**: Damiel Dossévi FRA 5.40, **LJ**: Salim Sdiri FRA 7.98, **TJ**: Tareq Bougtaïb MAR 16.91, **SP/DT**: Yves Niaré FRA 18.64/54.15, **HT**: Jim Steacy CAN 71.90, **JT**: David Brisseault FRA 71.64, **Dec**: Romain Barras FRA 8046, **4x100m**: CIV 39.79, **4x400m**: MAR 3:06.87, **20kmW**: Denis Langlois FRA 1:30:47. **Women**: **100m**: Véronique Mang FRA 11.40, **200m/400m**: Kaltouma Nadjina CHA 22.92/52.12, **800m/1500m**: Sultana Aït Hammou MR 2:04.63/4:34.32, **5000m/10,000m**: Zhor El Kamch MAR 16:19.71/33:41.28, **Mar:** Céline Cormerais FRA & Eléna Fétizon FRA 2:45:28, **100mh**: Joanna Bujak FRA 13.47, **400mh**: Sylvanie Morandais FRA 58.27, **HJ**: Whitney Evans CAN 1.83, **PV**: Kelsie Hendry CAN 4.15, **LJ**: Elise Vesanes FRA 6.42, **TJ**: Mariette Mien BUR 13.23, **SP**: Jessica Cérival FRA 16.32, **DT**: Ileana Brîndusoiu ROM 52.28, **HT**: Stéphanie Falzon FRA 65.12, **JT**: Lindy Leveau-Agricole SEY 53.92, **4x100m/4x400m**: FRA 44.61/3:37.91

Games of the Small States of Europe 2005

May 31- June 4, Andorra-la-Vella, Andorra

Men: 1. CYP 107, 2. LUX 91.5, 3. ISL 91, 4. MON 65, 5. AND 59.5, 6. MLT 59, 7. SMR 27, 8. LIE 6. **100m/200m**: Daniel Abenzoar LUX 10.42/21.38, **400m**: Johan Mordijck LUX 48.23, **800m**: Brice Etes MON 1:54.71, **1500m**: Victor Martínez AND 3:58.01, **5000m**: Antoni Bernadó AND 14:39.46, **10,000m**: Mustapha Tantan MON 31:30.69, **3000mSC**: Pascal Groben LUX 9:15.1, **110mh**: Claude Godart LUX 14.54, **400mh**: Bjorgvin Vikingsson ISL 53.49, **HJ**: Kyriacos Ioannou CYP 2.18, **PV**: Stefanos Demosthenous CYP 5.00, **LJ**: Andrei Mikhalkevitch LUX 7.62, **TJ**: Panagiotis Papavarnavas CYP 15.11, **SP**: Odinn Björn Thorsteinsson ISL 17.15, **DT**: Georgeos Aresti CYP 53.70, **JT**: Ioannis Stylianou CYP 64.06, **4x100m**: MLT 40.63, **4x400m**: CYP 3:15.85. **Women**: 1. CYP 125, 2. ISL 115, 3. MLT 79, 4. LUX 60, 5. AND 59, 6. SMR 19, 7. LIE 10, 8. MON 5. **100m/200m**: Eleni Artymata CYP 11.67/23.98, **400m**: Alissa Kallinikou CYP 55.04, **800m/1500m**: Anni Christofidou CYP 2:09.57/4:31.27, **5000m**: Iris Anna Skuladóttir ISL 17:55.39, **10,000m**: Carol Galea MLT 37:40.36, **100mh**: Morfo Baourda CYP 14.05, **HJ**: Iouilia Farmaka CYP 1.75, **PV**: Thórey Edda Elisdóttir

ISL 4.40, **LJ**: Irini Charalambous CYP 6.17, **TJ**: Maria Diikiti CYP 12.82, **SP**: Christina Strovolidou CYP 14.07, **DT/JT**: Asdis Hjálmsdóttir ISL 46.07/57.05, **HT**: Paraskevi Theodorou CYP 53.09, **4x100m/4x400m**: CYP 45.40/3:49.15.

11th Gulf Championships 2005

April 27-29, Manama, Bahrain.
Men: **100m**: Salem Al-Yami KSA 10.35, **200m**: Hamed Hamadan Al-Bishi KSA 21.16, **400m**: Hamdan Odha Al-Bishi KSA 46.69, **800m**: Mohammed Al-Salhi KSA 1:52.20, **1500m**: Daham Najim Bashir QAT 3:37.38, **5000m**: Essa Ismail Rashed QAT 13:54.35, **10,000m**: Mohamed Abdou Bakheet QAT 31:45.82, **HMar**: Mubarak Hassan Shami QAT 62:18, **3000mSC**: Nasser Kareem QAT 9:02.97, **110mh**: Mubarak Ata Mubarak KSA 14.07, **400mh**: Mubarak Al-Nubi QAT 50.37, **HJ**: Omar Moussa Al-Masrahi KSA 2.19, **PV**: Ali Makki Al-Sabagha KUW 4.70, **LJ**: Mohamed Al-Khuwalidi KSA 8.17, **TJ**: Salem Al-Ahmadi KSA 16.36, 6.95kg **SP**: Khaled Al-Suwaidi QAT 21.07, **DT**: Sultan Al-Dawoodi KSA 61.11, **HT**: Mohamed Al-Zankawi KUW 75.00, **JT**: Ahmad Hamad Abou Jalala QAT 66.09, **Dec**: Ibrahim Abou Al-Ainain QAT 6390, **10kmW:** Walid Ahmed Al-Sabahi QAT 44:29.65, **4x100m**: OMA 40.21, **4x400m**: KSA 3:08.12.

15th Mediterranean Games 2005

June 29 - July 2, Almeria, Spain
Men: **100m/200m**: Matic Osovnikar SLO 10.35/20.75, **400m**: Sofiane Labidi TUN 45.60, **800m**: Antonio M. Reina ESP 1.47.03, **1500m**: Arturo Casado ESP 3.45.61, **5000m**: Ali Saïdi Sief ALG 13:29:94, **10,000m**: Mohammed Amyn MAR 29:13:05, **HMar**: Saïd Belhout ALG 65:01, **3000mSC**: Brahim Boulami MAR 8:15:15, **110mh**: Felipe Vivancos ESP 13.53*, **400mh**: Gianni Carabelli ITA 49.32, **HJ**: Kyriacos Ioannou CYP 2.24, **PV**: Konstadínos Filippídis GRE 5.60, **LJ**: Salim Sdiri FRA 8.05, **TJ**: Hrístos Melétoglou GRE 17.09w, **SP**: Edis Elkasevic CRO 20.26, **DT**: Mario Pestano ESP 63.96, **HT**: Esref Apak TUR 77.88, **JT**: Vitoli Tipotio FRA 75.20, **Dec**: Romain Barras FRA 8127, **4x100m**: ITA 39.13, **4x400m**: ESP 3:03.65, **20kmW**: Francisco J. Fernández ESP 1:22:45. **Women**: **100m**: Véronique Mang FRA 11.44, **200m**: Alenka Bikar SLO 23.65, **400m**: Dímitra Dóva GRE 52.67, **800m**: Laetitia Valdonado FRA 2.01.71, **1500m**: Fatima Lanouar TUN 4:10:77, **5000m**: Margaret Maury FRA 15:22:59, **10,000m**: Souad Aït Salem ALG 32:55.48, **HMar**: Zhor El Kamch MAR 73:50, **100mh**: Glory Alozie ESP 12.90, **400mh**: Benedetta Ceccarelli ITA 55.76, **HJ**: Ruth Beitia 1.95, **PV**: Vanessa Boslak FRA 4.40, **LJ**: Fiona May ITA 6.64, **TJ**: Baya Rahouli ALG 14.98, **SP**: Cristiana Checchi ITA 18.59, **DT**: Dragan Tomasevic SCG 62.10, **HT**: Ester Balassini ITA 71.17, **JT**: Aggelikí Tsiolakoúdi GRE 62.61, **Hep**: Marie Collonvillé FRA 6017, **4x100m**: FRA 43.75, **4x400m**: ESP 3:31.45, **20kmW**: Elisa Rigaudo ITA 1:32:44.
Medal Table: FRA 9-13-7, ESP 9-10-6, ITA 7-8-7, GRE 4-2-6, ALG 4-1-1, MAR 3-6-1, SLO 3-1-2, TUN 2-0-3; 15 nations won medals.

NACAC Combined Events Championships 2005

May 28-29, San Juan, Puerto Rico
Men Dec: Maurice Smith JAM 8232. **Women Hep**: Fiona Asigbee USA 5868.

Pan-American Junior Championships 2005

July 29-31, Windsor, Canada
Men: **100m**: J-Mee Samuels USA 10.20*, **200m**: Otis McDaniel USA 20.67w, **400m**: Justin Oliver USA 46.73, **800m**: Gilder Barboza VEN 1:50.76, **1500m**: Mike Woods CAN 3:45.72*, **5000m**: Daniel Nunn USA 14:55.17, **10,000m**: Neal Naughton USA 30:12.14, **3000mSC**: José Sánchez CUB 8:43.96*, **110mh**: Dayron Robles CUB 13.46*, **400mh**: Reuben McCoy USA 50.28, **HJ**: Dustin Jonas USA 2.21, **PV**: Germán Chiaraviglio ARG 5.40, **LJ**: Robert Rands USA 7.60, **TJ**: Deraliz Fernández CUB 16.80w, 6k **SP**/1.75k **DT**: Ryan Whiting USA 19.75/61.40*, 6k **HT**: Boldiszar Kocsor USA 68.15, **JT**: Julio de Oliveira BRA 72.35, Jnr **Dec**: Andrés Silva URU 7671*, **4x100m/4x400m**: USA 39.36/3:05.34, **10kmW:** Marco Rodríguez ESA 44:49.62. **Women**: **100m**: Cleo Tyson USA 11.52, **200m**: Ammeisha McLaughlin JAM 23.00, **400m**: Natasha Hastings USA 52.15, **800m**: Rebekah Noble USA 2:04.07, **1500m**: Sarah Bowman USA 4:17.61, **3000m**: Alyson Kohlmeier CAN 9:25.09, **5000m**: Inés Melchor PER 16:48.06, **3000mSC**: Sabine Heitling BRA 10:04.71*, **100mh**: Latoya Greaves JAM 13.38w, **400mh**: Nickiesha Wilson JAM 57.40, **HJ**: Rhonda Watlins TRI 1.79, **PV**: Keisa Monterola VEN 4.10*, **LJ**: Arantxa King BER 6.21, **TJ**: Yanelis Veranes CUB 13.54, **SP**: Sarah Stevens USA 16.10, **DT**: Lisandra Rodríguez CUB 49.86, **HT**: Arasay Thondike CUB 64.80*, **JT**: Rachel Yurkovich USA 52.58*, **Hep**: Lauren Stewart USA 5333, **4x100m/4x400m**: USA 43.97/3:32.82, **10kmW:** Jamy Franco GUA 49:36.25*.
Medal Table: USA 22-24-11, CUB 6-4-3, JAM 3-5-3, CAN 2-5-11, BRA 2-1-7, VEN 2-0-1, TRI 1-1-1, BER & PER 1-1-0, ARG & GUA 1-0-1, 8 more nations won 1 medal.

Pan-American Race Walking Cup 2005

May 7-8, Lima, Peru.
Men: **20km:** 1. Rolando Saquipay ECU 1:19:21*, 2. Luís Fernando López COL 1:20:26, 3. Sergio Galdino BRA 1:21:29; **50km**: 1. Miguel Solis MEX 3:54:24, 2. Horacio Nava MEX 3:59:26, 3. Claudio Vargas 4:03:03. **Women 20km:** 1. Cristina López ESA 1:30:35*, 2 Miriam Ramón MEX 1:31:25; 3. Graciela Mendoiza MEX 1:33:04.

36th South American Junior Championships 2005

October 1-2, Rosario, Argentina
Men: **100m**: Rafael Ribeiro BRA 10.33*, **200m**: Hawer Murillo COL 21.04, **400m**: Rodrigo Bargas BRA 47.04, **800m/1500m**: Gilder Barboza VEN 1:52.03/3:55.54,

5000m: Marvin Blanco VEN 15:01.94, **10,000m**: Alexander Meléndez VEN 31:02.07, **3000mSC**: Mario Bazan PER 8:57.23, **110mh**: Éder de Souza BRA 13.95, **400mh**: Víctor José Solarte VEN 51.30, **HJ**: Fábio Baptista BRA 2.09, **PV**: Tomás González CHI 4.60, **LJ**: Hilton da Silva BRA 7.42, **TJ**: Hugo Chila ECU 15.57, 6k **SP**: Maximiliano Alonso CHI 17.33, 1.75k **DT**: Raoni de Morães BRA 54.96, 6k **HT**: Rhaony Caldas BRA 61.21, **JT**: Júlio César de Oliveira BRA 71.46*, Jnr **Dec**: Gonzalo Barroilhet CHI 7304*, **4x100m/4x400m**: BRA 40.48/3:09.95, **10kmW:** Robinson Vivar ECU 43:01.55, **Women**: **100m/200m**: Franciela Krasucki BRA 11.39*/23.54w, **200m**: Wilmary Álvarez VEN 23.68, **400m**: María Alejandra Idrobo COL 54.20, **800m**: Muriel Coneo COL 2:10.57, **1500m**: Geisiane de Lima BRA 4:35.38, **3000m/5000m**: Inés Melchor PER 9:50.87/17:05.78, **3000mSC**: Sabine Heitling BRA 10:41.11, **100mh**: Fabiana Morães BRA 14.01w, **400mh**: Dalelque Ferreira BRA 60.55, **HJ**: Marierlis Rojas VEN 1.76, **PV**: Keisa Monterola VEN 3.60, **LJ**: Eliane Martins BRA 6.41*, **TJ**: Tania F da Silva BRA 13.31w, **SP/DT**: Rocío Comba ARG 14.98/51.97*, **HT**: Rosa Rodríguez VEN 57.90*, **JT**: Jucilene de Lima 46.04, **Hep**: Jaílma de Lima BRA 4962, **4x100m**: BRA 45.25, **4x400m**: COL 3:44.80, **10kmW:** Ingrid Hernández COL 49:49.64.

Medal Table Leaders: BRA 20G-20S-16B, VEN 8-6-5, COL 5-5-7, PER 5-5-2, CHI 3-3-5, ARG 3-1-5, ECU 2-2-3.

South East Asian Games 2005

November 27-30, Manila, Philippines

Men: **100m**: Wachara Sondee THA 10.47, **200m**: Sittichai Suwonprateep THA 20.94, **400m**: Jimar Aing PHI 47.03, **800m**: Le Van Duong VIE 1:51.15, **1500m**: Aung Thi Ha MYA 3:49.25, **5000m/10,000m**: Srisung Boonthung THA 14:15.09/29:29.59, **Mar:** Booncho Chandacha THA 2:29:27, **3000mSC**: Rene Herrera PHI 8:56.14, **110mh**: Mohd Robani Hassan MAS 14.08, **400mh**: Shahadan Jamaluddin MA 51.28, **HJ**: Nguyen Duy Bang VIE 2.14, **PV**: Amnat Kunpadit THA 4.90, **LJ**: Henry Dagmil PHI 7.81*, **TJ**: Theerayut Philakong THA 16.00, **SP**: Chatchawal Polyemg THA 17.06, **DT**: James Wong Tuck Yim SIN 55.11, **HT**: Arniel Ferrera PHI 60.47*, **JT**: Danilo Fresnido PHI 70.20, **Dec**: Vu Van Huyen VIE 7139, **20kmW**: Mohd Shahrul Haizy MAS 1:35:46, **4x100m**: THA 39.74, **4x400m**: PHI 3:09.15. **Women**: **100m**: Vu Thi Huong VIE 11.49, **200m**: Kay Khine Lwin MYA 23.77, **400m**: Yin Yin Khine MYA 52.69, **800m**: Do Thi Bong VIE 2:03.65*, **1500m**: Truong Thanh Hang VIE 4:18.50*, **5000m**: Oliva Sadi INA 16:34.94, **10,000m**: Mercedita Manipol PHI 35:38.04, **Mar:** Christabel Martes PHI 2:47:07, **100mh**: Moh Siew Wei MAS 13.54, **400mh**: Vassanee Vinatho THA 57.20, **HJ**: Bui Thi Nhung VIE 1.89*, **PV**: Roslinda Samsu MAS 4.10*, **LJ**: Marestella Torres PHI 6.47, **TJ**: Ngew Sin Mei MAS 13.61*, **SP**: Zhang Guirong SIN 17.40, **DT**: Du Xianhui SIN 49.48, **HT**: Siti Shahidah Abdullah MAS 53.35*, **JT**: Buaban Phamang THA 55.06*, **Hep**: Nguyen Thi Thu Cuc VIE 5350, **20kmW**: Yuan Yufang MAS 1:42:53, **4x100m**: THA 44.30, **4x400m**: MYA 3:35.68*.

Medal Table Leaders: THA 12G-13S-19B, PHI 9-11-9, VIE 8-8-4, MAS 8-3-4, MYA 4-3-1, SIN 3-1-3, INA 1-6-5.

West Asian Games 2005

December 7-9, Doha, Qatar

Men: **100m**: Yahya Saeed Al-Kahes KSA 10.39, **200m**: Hamoud Al-Saad KUW 21.31, **400m**: Fawzi Al-Shammari KUW 47.58, **800m**: Majed Saeed Sultan QAT 1:46.86, **1500m**: Bilal Mansoor Ali BRN 3:40.84, **5000m**: Essa Ismail Rasheed QAT 13:33.07, **10,000m**: Jamal Bilal Salem QAT 28:40.99, **HMar**: Mubarak Hassan Shami QAT 62:21, **3000mSC**: Moussa Omar Obaid QAT 8:19.46, **110mh**: Bader Abou Al-Ainain KSA 14.14, **400mh**: Mubarak Al-Nubi QAT 50.37, **HJ**: Moh. Abd. Abbas Derouiche UAE 2.16, **PV**: Abdullah Ghanem Saoud QAT 5.00, **LJ**: Saleh Al-Haddad KUW 7.50, **TJ**: Mohamed Hazouri SYR 16.48, **SP**: Bilal Saad Mubarak QAT 17.54, **DT**: Ehsan Hadadi IRI 63.63, **HT**: Ali Mohamed Al-Zinkawi KUW 76.25, **JT**: Mohamed Ibrahim Al-Khalifa QAT 71.73, **Dec**: Ali Feizi IRI 6445, **20kmW**: Mabrouk Saleh Nasser QAT 1:33:04, **4x100m**: KUW 40.48, **4x400m**: QAT 3:09.81. **Women**: **100m**: Roqaya Al-Gassra BRN 12.28, **200m**: Mounira Al-Saleh SYR 23.89 (drugs dq), **HJ**: Zahra Nabizadeh IRI 1.70, **LJ**: Rima Taha Farid JOR 5.82, **4x100m**: SYR 49.41.

Medals: QAT 11G-10S-5B, KUW 5-2-0, IRI 3-4-5, SYR 3-3-2, KSA 2-3-4, BRN 2-1-1, JOR 1-2-4, UAE 1-0-2, OMA 0-2-0, IRQ 0-0-3.

IAU 100km WORLD CUP 2005

July 16-17, Wörschach, Austria

Men: 1. Grigoriy Murzin RUS 6:24:15, 2. Jorge Aubeso ESP 6:33:03, 3. Tsutomu Sassa JPN 6:40:20, 4. Sandor Barcza FRA 6:44:45, 5. Yoshiaki Kobayashi JPN 6:49:43; **Teams:** 1. JPN 20:34:07, 2. FRA 20:43.27, 3. GER 21:25:19; **Women**: 1. Hiroki Syou JPN 7:53:41, 2. Anne Riddle-Lundblad USA 7:54:22, 3. Yoko Yamazawa JPN 8:10;27, 4. Laurence Fricottea ITA 8:12:02, 5. Magali Reymoneng FRA 8:18:52; **Teams:** 1. USA 24:46:39, 2. FRA 25:01:07, 3. JPN 25:17:40.

IAU World 24 Hours Challenge 2005

July 16-17, Wörschach, Austria

Men: 1. Anatoliy Kruglikov RUS 268.065km, 2. Ewald Eder AUT 263.810, 3. Jens Lukas GER 256.368, 4. Ryiochi Sekiya JPN 250.618, 5. Sergio Orsi ITA 249.876; **Teams:** 1. JPN 734.498, 2. RUS 731.229, 3. ITA 725.897; **Women**: 1. Lyudmila Kalinina RUS 242.228, 2. Galina Yeremina RUS 239.874, 3. Sumie Inagaki JPN 238.251, 4. Irina Koval RUS 227.469, 5. Kim Jung-ok KOR 223.109; **Teams:** 1. RUS 709. 573, JPN 654.385, 3. USA 604.514.

IAU European 50km Trophy 2005

October 16, Palermo, Italy

Men: 1. Oleg Kharitonov RUS 3:02:01, 2. Sandor Barcza FRA 3:02:21, 3. Stefano Sartori ITA 3:12:40; **Women**: 1, Heather Foundling-Hawker GBR 3:44:55; 2. Monica Casiraghi ITA 3:48:06, 3. Lorena Di Vito ITA 3:48:08

European 100km Championship 2005

September 11, Winschoten, Netherlands

Men: 1. Oleg Kharitonov RUS 6:30:31, 2. Mario Ardemagni ITA 6:40:39, 3. Pascal Fétizon FRA 6:50:22; **Teams:** 1. RUS 20:21:40, 2. FRA 20:56:35, 3. GER 21:19:12. **Women**: 1. Monica Casiraghi ITA 7:53:25, 2. Birgit Schönherr-Hölscher GER 7:53:28, 3. Karine Herry FRA 7:55:33; **Teams:** 1. FRA 24:11:42, 2. GER 24:37:14, 3. ITA 25:30:58.

21st WMRA World Mountain Running Trophy 2005

September 25, Wellington, New Zealand

Men (13.5km, 930m height difference): 1. Jonathan Wyatt NZL 53:23 (5th win), 2. Gabriele Abate ITA 55:35, 3. Davide Chicco ITA 55:41, 4. Marco Gaiardo ITA 56:08, 5. Helmut Schiessl GER 56:22. **Teams:** 1. ITA 17, 2. NZL 75, 3. FRA 101, 4. ENG 106, 5. SUI 114. **Women** (9.1km, 620m HD): 1. Kate McIlroy NZL 39:40, 2. Tracey Brindley SCO 41:42, 3. Anna Pichrtová CZE 41:59, 4. Mary Wilkinson ENG 42:39, 5. Isabelle Guillot FRA 42:47. **Teams:** 1. ITA 25, 2. SCO 38, 3. CZE 48, 4. ENG 48, 5, NZL 48; Junior **Men** (9.1km, 620m HD): Vedal Gunen TUR 36:48, **Teams:** TUR 12; Junior **Women** (3.57km, 447m HD): Yuliya Mochalova RUS 21:50, **Teams:** SLO 6.

4th European Mountain Running Championships 2005

July 16-17, Heiligenblut, Austria

Men (12.95km, 1520m height difference) 1. Florian Heinzle AUT 1:11:36, 2. Helmut Schiessl GER 1:12:16, 3. Mario De Gaspari 1:12:35; **Teams:** 1. ITA 20, 2. GBR 31, 3. FRA 36; **Women** (10.06km, 1335m HD): 1. Andrea Mayr AUT 1:07:42, 2. Anna Pichrtová CZE 1:09:38, 3. Angeline Joly-Flueckieger SUI 1:10:44; **Teams:** 1. GBR 34, 2. ITA 34, 3. CZE 41.

World Athletics Final 2005

September 9-10, Monaco.

Prize Money for each event: 1st $30,000, 2nd $20,000, 3rd $12,000, 4th $7000, 5th $5000, 6th $4000, 7th $3000, 8th $2000. Also at 1500m, 5000m, 3000mSC: 9th to 12th each $1000. Women's steeple 50% of above.

Men

100 Metres (-0.6)
1. Marc Burns TRI 10.00
2. Aziz Zakari GHA 10.01
3. Dwight Thomas JAM 10.01
4. Darrel Brown TRI 10.05
5. Ronald Pognon FRA 10.07
6. Francis Obikwelu POR 10.09
7. Leonard Scott USA 10.18

200 Metres (a) (-1.5)
1. Tyson Gay USA 19.96*
2. Chris Williams JAM 20.19
3. Wallace Spearmon USA 20.21
4. Justin Gatlin USA 20.25
5. Stéphan Buckland MRI 20.64
6. Aaron Armstrong TRI 20.75
7. André D. da Silva BRA 20.81
8. John Capel USA 21.04

400 Metres (a)
1. Tyree Washington USA 44.51*
2. Tim Benjamin GBR 44.56
3. Chris Brown BAH 44.68
4. Brandon Simpson JAM 44.86
5. Michael Blackwood JAM 44.88
6. Carlos Santa DOM 45.06
7. Alleyne Francique GRN 45.78
8. Jeremy Wariner USA 46.37

800 Metres
1. Wilfred Bungei KEN 1:47.05
2. Youssef Saad Kamel BRN 1:47.13
3. Yuriy Borzakovskiy RUS 1:47.18
4. William Yiampoy KEN 1:47.20
5. Mbulaeni Mulaudzi RSA 1:47.22
6. Alfred Kirwa KEN 1:47.39
7. Antonio Manuel Reina ESP 1:48.18
8. Gary Reed CAN 1:49.60

1500 Metres
1. Ivan Heshko UKR 3:33.50*
2. Bernard Lagat USA 3:33.55
3. Alex Kipchirchir KEN 3:33.71
4. Suleiman Simotwo KEN 3:33.71
5. Daniel Kipchirchir Komen KEN 3:33.72
6. Dahame Najem Bashir QAT 3:34.56
7. Anter Zerguelaine ALG 3:36.34
8. Rashid Ramzi BRN 3:36.88
9. Laban Rotich KEN 3:39.99
10. Juan Carlos Higuero ESP 3:45.45
11. Rui Silva POR 3:50.17

3000 Metres (a)
1. Bernard Lagat USA 7:38.00
2. Eliud Kipchoge KEN 7:38.95
3. Augustine Choge KEN 7:39.99
4. Benjamin Limo KEN 7:40.22
5. Tariku Bekele ETH 7:40.30
6. Shadrack Korir KEN 7:40.97
7. Boniface Songok KEN 7:40.98
8. Ali Saïdi-Sief ALG 7:41.61
9. Markos Geneti ETH 7:41.76
10. Abderrahim Goumri MAR 7:43.93
11. Mounir Yemmouni FRA 8:10.57

5000 Metres
1. Sileshi Sihine ETH 13:39.40
2. Boniface Kiprop UGA 13:40.03
3. Isaac Songok KEN 13:40.24
4. Gebregziabher Gebremariam ETH 13:40.59
5. Sammy Kipketer KEN 13:41.06
6. James Kwalia QAT 13:41.10
7. Boniface Songok KEN 13:42.25
8. John Kibowen KEN 13:44.81
9. Abebe Dinkesa ETH 13:46.51
10. Mark Bett KEN 13:50.94
11. Robert Sigei KEN 13:59.65

3000 Metres Steeplechase (a)
1. Paul Kipsiele Koech KEN 8:07.91
2. Ezekiel Kemboi KEN 8:09.04
3. Brimin Kipruto KEN 8:09.20
4. Wesley Kiprotich KEN 8:09.43
5. Bouabdellah Tahri FRA 8:10.13
6. Brahim Boulami MAR 8:14.43
7. Moussa Omar Obaid QAT 8:14.92
8. Kipkurui Misoi KEN 8:21.01
9. Simon Vroemen NED 8:23.97
10. Richard Matelong KEN 8:29.00
11. Antonio Jiménez ESP 8:29.28

110 Metres Hurdles (-1.4)
1. Allen Johnson USA 13.09*
2. Dominique Arnold USA 13.10

3. Terrence Trammell USA 13.17
4. Stanislav Olijar LAT 13.17
5. Maurice Wignall JAM 13.20
6. Ladji Doucouré FRA 13.27
7. Joel Brown USA 13.28
8. Ron Bramlett USA 13.32

400 Metres Hurdles

1. Bershawn Jackson USA 48.05
2. Kemel Thompson JAM 48.09
3. L.J. van Zyl RSA 48.11
4. Naman Keïta FRA 48.36
5. James Carter USA 48.62
6. Bayano Kamani PAN 49.30
7. Gianni Carabelli ITA 49.84
8. Ian Weakley JAM 50.72

High Jump

1. Víctor Moya CUB 2.35*
2. Vyacheslav Voronin RUS 2.32
3. Yaroslav Rybakov RUS 2.32
3. Stefan Holm SWE 2.32
5. Andriy Sokolovsky UKR 2.29
6. Jacques Freitag RSA 2.29
7. Jaroslav Bába CZE 2.20
8. Yuriy Krimarenko UKR 2.20

Pole Vault (a)

1. Brad Walker USA 5.86
2. Tim Lobinger GER 5.70
3. Giuseppe Gibilisco ITA 5.60
3. Igor Pavlov RUS 5.60
5. Derek Miles USA 5.60
6. Tim Mack USA 5.60
7. Toby Stevenson USA 5.60
8. Rens Blom NED 5.45

Long Jump

1. Dwight Phillips USA 8.46*/0.8
2. Miguel Pate USA 8.30/1.6
3. James Beckford JAM 8.28/0.3
4. Ignisious Gaisah GHA 8.23/1.2
5. Salim Sdiri FRA 8.05/1.9
6. Tommi Evilä FIN 8.00/1.6
7. Volodymyr Zyuskov UKR 7.70/1.3
8. Nils Winter GER 7.37w/2.1

Triple Jump (a)

1. Yoandri Betanzos CUB 17.46/0.1
2. Jadel Gregório BRA 17.32/1.0
3. Walter Davis USA 17.23/0.0
4. Danila Burkenya RUS 17.10/0.0
5. Leevan Sands BAH 16.93/0.0
6. Nathan Douglas GBR 16.81/0.4
7. Igor Spasovkhodskiy RUS 16.55/0.1
8. Kenta Bell USA 16.38/0.1

Shot

1. Adam Nelson USA 21.92*
2. Joachim Olsen DEN 21.03
3. Reese Hoffa USA 20.87
4. Ralf Bartels GER 20.53
5. Christian Cantwell USA 20.09
6. Yuriy Bilonoh UKR 20.04
7. Andrei Mikhnevich BLR 19.61
8. Mikulás Konopka SVK 19.29

Discus (a)

1. Virgilijus Alekna LTU 67.64
2. Gerd Kanter EST 66.01
3. Zoltán Kövágó HUN 65.65
4. Aleksander Tammert EST 65.22
5. Frantz Kruger RSA 63.19
6. Mario Pestano ESP 62.97
7. Jason Tunks CAN 61.24
8. Michael Möllenbeck GER 59.27

Hammer *(at Szombathely 3 Sep)*

1. Ivan Tikhon BLR 81.70
2. Ola-Pekka Karjalainen FIN 79.81
3. Vadim Devyatovskiy BLR 78.98
4. Krisztian Pars HUN 78.32
5. Szymon Ziólkowski POL 77.49
6. Libor Charfreitag SVK 76.59
7. Markus Esser GER 75.88
8. Ivan Konovalov RUS 72.66

Javelin

1. Tero Pitkämäki FIN 91.33*
2. Andreas Thorkildsen NOR 89.60
3. Sergey Makarov RUS 86.69
4. Jan Zelezny CZE 83.98
5. Mark Frank GER 81.81
6. Eriks Rags LAT 79.86
7. Aleksandr Ivanov RUS 78.32
8. Andrus Värnik EST 76.11

Women

100 Metres (a) (-0.2)

1. Veronica Campbell JAM 10.92
2. Christine Arron FRA 10.93
3. Lauryn Williams USA 11.04
4. Chandra Sturrup BAH 11.07
5. Me'Lisa Barber USA 11.09
6. Sherone Simpson JAM 11.21
7. Yuliya Nesterenko BLR 11.23
8. Kim Gevaert BEL 11.42

200 Metres (-0.6)

1. Allyson Felix USA 22.27*
2. Veronica Campbell JAM 22.37
3. Christine Arron FRA 22.43
4. Cydonie Mothersill CAY 22.92
5. Kim Gevaert BEL 22.93
6. Yuliya Gushchina RUS 23.18
7. Fabienne Feraez BEN 23.21
8. Lucimar de Moura BRA 23.57

400 Metres

1. Sanya Richards USA 49.52
2. Tonique Williams-Darling BAH 49.54
3. Dee Dee Trotter USA 50.64
4. Ami Mbacké Thiam SEN 50.69
5. Christine Amertil BAH 51.23
6. Monique Hennagan USA 51.31
7. Svetlana Pospelova RUS 51.50
8. Natalya Antyukh RUS 51.90

800 Metres

1. Zulia Calatayud CUB 1:59.07*
2. Hasna Benhassi MAR 1:59.86
3. Mayte Martínez ESP 2:00.36
4. Olga Kotlyarova RUS 2:00.94
5. Larisa Chzhao RUS 2:01.63
6. Svetlana Cherkasova RUS 2:01.93
7. Hazel Clark USA 2:04.04
8. Tatyana Andrianova RUS 2:08.10

1500 Metres (a)

1. Maryam Jamal BRN 3:59.35
2. Tatyana Tomashova RUS 4:00.28
3. Natalya Yevdokimova RUS 4:00.60
4. Bouchra Ghezielle FRA 4:01.28
5. Hind Dehiba FRA 4:02.08
6. Yuliya Chizhenko RUS 4:02.83
7. Carmen Douma-Hussar CAN 4:03.10
8. Natalia Rodríguez ESP 4:03.72
9. Olga Yegorova RUS 4:07.71
10. Helen Clitheroe GBR 4:09.41
11. Alesya Turava BLR 4:11.42

3000 Metres

1. Meseret Defar ETH 8:47.26*
2. Gelete Burka ETH 8:48.65
3. Zakia Mrisho TAN 8:49.63

4. Isabella Ochichi KEN 8:49.79
5. Meselech Melkamu ETH 8:50.42
6. Edith Masai KEN 8:50.78
7. Susanne Wigene NOR 8:51.41
8. Priscila Jepleting KEN 8:53.18
9. Carmen Douma-Hussar CAN 8:53.83
10. Liliya Shobukhova RUS 9:02.23
11. Derebe Alemu ETH 9:04.98

5000 Metres (a)
1. Meseret Defar ETH 14:45.87*
2. Tirunesh Dibaba ETH 14:46.84
3. Berhane Adere ETH 14:46.91
4. Ines Chenonge KEN 14:54.43
5. Lucy Wangui KEN 15:00.20
6. Sabrina Mockenhaupt GER 15:12.43
7. Kim Smith NZL 15:14.91
8. Derebe Alemu ETH 15:17.13
9. Irene Kwambai KEN 15:23.22
10. Krisztina Papp HUN 15:43.19
dnf. Ejagayou Dibaba ETH

3000 Metres Steeplechase (a)
1. Dorcus Inzikuru UGA 9:21.80*
2. Wioletta Janowska POL 9:25.47
3. Mardrea Hyman JAM 9:27.21
4. Lívia Tóth HUN 9:30.20
5. Yelena Zadorozhnaya RUS 9:32.41
6. Korine Hinds JAM 9:33.46
7. Cristina Casandra ROM 9:46.06
8. Elizabeth Jackson USA 9:46.10
9. Roísín McGettigan IRL 9:46.12
10. Salome Chepchumba KEN 9:53.83
11. Jo Ankier GBR 9:56.16
12. Lisa Galaviz USA 10:05.01

100 Metres Hurdles (-0.8)
1. Michelle Perry USA 12.54
2. Brigitte Foster-Hylton JAM 12.55
3. Delloreen Ennis-London JAM 12.57
4. Susanna Kallur SWE 12.74
5. Glory Alozie ESP 12.76
6. Joanna Hayes USA 12.78
7. Perdita Felicien CAN 12.80
8. Kirsten Bolm GER 12.84

400 Metres Hurdles (a)
1. Lashinda Demus USA 53.37*
2. Yuliya Pechonkina RUS 53.80
3. Sandra Glover USA 54.09
4. Anna Jesien POL 55.22
5. Andrea Blackett BAR 55.25
6. Malgorzata Pskit POL 55.72
7. Tetyana Tereshchuk UKR 56.28
8. Surita Febbraio RSA 56.83

High Jump (a)
1. Kajsa Bergqvist SWE 2.00
2. Iryna Myhalchenko UKR 1.93
2. Vita Palamar UKR 1.93
4. Chaunte Howard USA 1.93
5. Viktoriya Styopina UKR 1.93
6. Tatyana Kivimyagi RUS 1.93
7. Ruth Beitia ESP 1.89
7. Anna Chicherova RUS 1.89

Pole Vault
1. Yelena Isinbayeva RUS 4.74
2. Monika Pyrek POL 4.62
3. Tatyana Polnova RUS 4.50
4. Vanessa Boslak FRA 4.50
5. Dana Ellis CAN 4.35
5. Pavla Hamácková CZE 4.35
7. Anna Rogowska POL 4.35
8. Thórey Edda Elísdóttir ISL 4.20

Long Jump (a)
1. Tatyana Kotova RUS 6.83/0.8
2. Anju B. George IND 6.75/0.5
3. Grace Upshaw USA 6.67/0.9
4. Eunice Barber FRA 6.51/0.2
5. Tatyana Lebedeva RUS 6.49/1.1
6. Oksana Udmurtova RUS 6.48/0.4
7. Irina Simagina RUS 6.47/1.1

Triple Jump
1. Hrisopiyí Devetzí GRE 14.89/1.7
2. Tatyana Lebedeva RUS 14.86/0.8
3. Yargelis Savigne CUB 14.81/1.5
4. Trecia Smith JAM 14.69/0.4
5. Anna Pyatykh RUS 14.65/0.8
6. Yamilé Aldama SUD 14.26/0.8
7. Magdelin Martinez ITA 14.24/1.2
8. Baya Rahouli ALG 13.85/0.9

Shot (a)
1. Nadezhda Ostapchuk BLR 20.44*
2. Valerie Vili NZL 19.55
3. Natallia Khoroneko BLR 18.80
4. Olga Ryabinkina RUS 18.64
5. Petra Lammert GER 18.49
6. Nadine Kleinert GER 18.46
7. Yumileidi Cumbá CUB 18.44
8. Svetlana Krivelyova RUS 17.33

Discus
1. Natalya Sadova RUS 63.40
2. Franka Dietzsch GER 61.91
3. Aretha Thurmond USA 60.68
4. Vera Cechlová CZE 58.38
5. Nicoleta Grasu ROM 58.25
6. Wioletta Potepa POL 57.93
7. Olena Antonova UKR 56.57
8. Marzena Wysocka POL 55.08

Hammer *(at Szombathely 3 Sep)*
1. Yipsi Moreno CUB 74.75
2. Kamila Skolimowska POL 72.73
3. Olga Kuzenkova RUS 72.46
4. Tatyana Lysenko RUS 72.34
5. Ester Balassini ITA 70.63
6. Betty Heidler GER 69.95
7. Manuela Montebrun FRA 69.70
8. Olga Tsander BLR 68.35

Javelin (a)
1. Osleidys Menéndez CUB 67.24*
2. Steffi Nerius GER 66.35
3. Sonia Bisset CUB 63.56
4. Laverne Eve BAH 61.96
5. Barbora Spotáková CZE 61.60
6. Christina Scherwin DEN 60.19
7. Aggelikí Tsiolakoúdi GRE 58.42
8. Zahra Bani ITA 55.02

IAAF World Race Walking Challenge 2005

First held in 2003. 2005 events were: Tijuana MEX, Rio Maior POR, Cixi CHN, Sesto San Giovanni ITA and La Coruña ESP, World Championships (Helsinki). Final positions were based on the best positions from any three of the Challenge competitions, with 10 points for a win, nine for second, eight for third, and so on, down to 10th position. Prize money was awarded to the first eight – from $30,000 for 1st to $5000 for 8th

Men: 1. Francisco Fernández ESP 30 pts (3 wins – Rio Maior, Sesto SG. La Coruña), 2. Nathan Deakes

AUS 29 (2 wins – Tijuana, Cixi – and 2nd Rio Maior), 3. Juan Manuel Molina ESP 19, 4. Ilya Markov RUS 18, 5. Trond Nymark NOR 17, 6. Hatem Ghoula TUN 17, 7. Omar Zepeda MEX 13, 8. Zhu Hongjun CHN 11

Women: 1. Ryta Turava BLR 29 (2 wins – Rio Maior. Sesto SG, 2nd La C & WCh), 2. Susana Feitor POR 24, 3. Claudia Stef ROM 22, 4. Elisa Rigaudo ITA 20, 5. Melanie Seeger GER 17, 6. Jane Saville AUS 15, 7. Song Hongjuan CHN 11, 8= Jiang Jing CHN, Cristina López ESA 10.

IAAF World Athletics Tour

The IAAF have agreed upon a new global circuit of one-day meetings – the World Athletics Tour – for 2006. Under the IAAF brand there are 24 of these higher quality meetings in 2006 compared to 34 in 2005. At least one meeting from each Continental area is included in the Tour. Tour points will be earned from these meetings and also from 28 designated Continental Permit meetings to determine qualifictaion for the season-capping World Athletics Final. to be held in Stuttgart, GER on 9-10 Sep 2006.

IAAF World Combined Events Challenge 2005

Ranking based on the sum of the best scores achieved in any three of the designated competitions.

Men Decathlon					
1	Roman Sebrle CZE	25,381	8534 Götzis	8521 World Ch	8326 Talence
2	Bryan Clay USA	25,199	7961 Götzis	8506 World Ch	8732 World Ch
3	Attila Zsivóczky HUN	25,185	8480 Götzis	8320 Arles	8385 World Ch
4	Aleksandr Pogorelov RUS	24,922	8429 Götzis	8246 World Ch	8247 Talence
5	Kristjan Rahnu EST	24,873	8526 Arles	8223 World Ch	8124 Talence
6	André Niklaus GER	24,583	8074 Götzis	8193 Ratingen	8316 World Ch
7	Romain Barras FRA	24,366	8185 Götzis	8087 World Ch	8060 Talence
8	Tomás Dvorák CZE	24,169	8105 Eur Cup I	8068 World Ch	7996 Talence
9	Mikk Pahapil EST	24,146	8149 Eur Cup S	8003 World Ch	7994 Talence
10	Jaakko Ojaniemi FIN	24,095	8076 Arles	7977 Eur Cup 1	8042 World Ch
Women Heptathlon					
1	Carolina Klüft SWE	20,399	6824 Götzis	6688 Eur Cup 1	6887 World Ch
2	Eunice Barber FRA	20,388	6889 Arles	6824 World Ch	6675 Talence
3	Kelly Sotherton GBR	19,150	6547 Götzis	6325 World Ch	6278 Talence
4	Austra Skujyte LTU	18,952	6386 Götzis	6206 Eur Cup 1	6360 World Ch
5	Nataliya Dobrynska UKR	18,813	6299 Götzis	6279 Arles	6235 Talence
6	Margaret Simpson GHA	18,804	6006 Salo'	6423 Götzis	6375 World Ch
7	Hyleas Fountain USA	18.765	6502 Götzis	6208 US Ch	6055 World Ch
8	Karin Ruckstuhl NED	18,621	6318 Götzis	6174 World Ch	6129 Talence
9	Marie Collonvillé FRA	18,444	6022 Götzis	6248 World Ch	6174 Talence
10	Jessica Zelinka CAN	18,322	6137 Götzis	6088 Arles	6097 World Ch

Prize Money for the IAAF World Combined Events Challenge: 1st place $30,000, 2nd $20,000, 3rd $15,000, 4th $10,000, 5th $8000, 6th $7000, 7th $6000, 8th $5000.

IAAF Golden League 2005

There were six meetings in the TDK Golden League 2005, The $1 million jackpot was taken by triple jumper Tatyana Lebedeva, the one athlete to win at each meeting. Winners of Golden League events:

Event	*St-Denis 1/7*	*Rome 8/7*	*Oslo 29/7*	*Zürich 19/8*	*Brussels 26/8*	*Berlin 4/9*
Men						
100m	A Zakari	J Gatlin	A Zakari	J Gatlin	J Gatlin	D Thomas
800m	W Yiampoy	A Kirwa	M Mulaudzi	W Bungei	Y Borzakovskiy	M Mulaudzi
1500m	D K Komen	R Ramzi	D N Bashir	D K Komen	D K Komen	D K Komen
3/5000m	K Bekele	I Songok	J Kibowen	K Bekele	E Kipchoge	B Lagat
110mh	L Doucouré	D Arnold	L Doucouré	D Arnold	A Johnson	D Arnold
HJ	S Holm	A Sokolovskiy	S Holm	S Ton	V Moya	T Rybakov
JT	T Pitkämäki	A Värnik	T Pitkämäki	T Pitkämäki	S Makarov	T Pitkämäki
Women						
100m	C Arron	C Arron	C Arron	V Campbell	C Arron	C Arron
800m	S Cherkasova	H Benhassi	T Andrianova	Z Calatayud	M Martínez	Z Calatayud
3/**5000m**	E Masai	T Dibaba	M Jamal	M Jamal	M Defar	B Adere
400mh	L Demus	L Demus	S Glover	Y Pechonkina	L Demus	S Glover
TJ	T Lebedeva	T Lebedeva	T Lebedeva	T Lebedeva	T Lebedeva	T Lebedeva

There will be eleven IAAF Golden League events contested at each of the six meetings in the 2006 series. The designated "golden" events are men's 100m, 400m, 1500m, 3000m/5000m, long jump and javelin, and women's 100m, 400m, 3000/5000m, 100m hurdles and high jump.

Grand Prix meetings 2005 - World Athletics Tour 2006

The 24 World Athletics Tour meetings for 2006 are designated: GL – Golden League, SGP – Super Grand Prix, GP – Grand Prix. Qualifying Continental Permit Meetings are shown as APM.*

2005 date		*Meeting*	*2006 date*	
5 Feb		Telstra A Series, Canberra, AUS	26 Jan	APM
17 Feb	GP II	Telstra A Series, Melbourne, AUS	9 Mar	GP
5 Feb		Telstra A Series, Brisbane, AUS	3 Mar	APM
3 Apr		Grand Prix de Dakar	29 Apr	GP
30 Apr	GP II	Conseil General, Fort-de-France, Martinique		
–		CAA Grand Prix, Abuja, NGR	6 May	APM
7 May		Jamaica International, Kingston, JAM	6 May	APM
7 May	GP	Osaka, JPN	7 May	GL
–		Gold Meeting Porto Alegre, BRA	7 May	APM
13 May	SGP	Qatar Athletic Super Grand Prix, Doha	12 May	SGP
15 May	GP II	Gold Meeting Rio de Athletismo, Rio de Janeiro, BRA	14 May	APM
18 May		Gold Meeting Caixa Fortaleza, BRA	17 May	APM
22 May	GP	Grande Premio Brasil de Atletismo, Belém BRA	21 May	GP
22 May		Adidas Track Classic, Carson, USA	21 May	APM
–		Asian Grand Prix, Bangalore, IND	22 May	APM
–		Asian Grand Prix, Pune, IND	26 May	APM
29 May	GP	Thales FBK Games, Hengelo, NED	28 May	GP
30 May	GP II	US Open, Stanford, California, USA		
1 Jun	GP II	GP Regione Lombardia, Milan, ITA		
3 Jun	GP II	Memorial Primo Nebiolo, Turin, Italy	6 Jun	APM
4 Jun	GP	Prefontaine Classic, Eugene, Oregon, USA	28 May	GP
4 Jun	GP	Gran Premio, Seville, ESP		
5 Jun		Athletics Festival, Bydgoszcz, POL	4 Jun	APM
7 Jun		Huelva, ESP (Ibero-American meeting 2005)	3 Jun	APM
9 Jun	SGP	Golden Spike, Ostrava, CZE	30 May	GP
11 Jun		Reebok Grand Prix, New York, USA	3 Jun	APM
12 Jun	GP	Lille Métropole, Villeneuve d'Ascq, FRA	10 Jun	APM
12 Jun		Janusz Kusocinski Memorial, Warsaw, POL	18 Jun	APM
14 Jun		Luzern Spitzenleichtathletik, SUI	13 Jun	APM
14 Jun	SGP	Athens Super Grand Prix, Athens, GRE	14 Jun	SGP
18 Jun		CAA Grand Prix, Rabat, MAR	17 Jun	APM
23 Jun		CAA Grand Prix, Alger, ALG	22 Jun	APM
24 Jun		Asian Grand Prix, Bangkok, THA (Songkha in 2005)	18 May	APM
24 Jun		Gobierno de Arragorn, Zaragoza, ESP	20 Jun	APM
25 Jun	GP II	Znamenskiy Memorial, Kazan, RUS	24 Jun	APM
27 Jun	GP II	Josef Odlozil Memorial, Prague, CZE	5 Jun	APM
1 Jul	GL	Gaz de France Paris Saint-Denis, FRA	7 Jul	GL
2 Jul		Cork City Games, Cork, IRL	1 Jul	APM
5 Jul	SGP	Athletissima, Lausanne, SUI	11 Jul	SGP
8 Jul	GL	Golden Gala, Rome, ITA	14 Jul	GL
10 Jul		Vardinoyiannia, Réthimno, GRE	21 Jul	APM
11 Jul	GP	Grand Prix Zagreb, CRO	31 Aug	GP
16 Jul	SGP	Madrid 2012, ESP	17 Jul	GP
17 Jul	GP II	Thessaloniki, Greece	24 Jul	APM
22 Jul	SGP	Norwich Union London Grand Prix, (CP), GBR	28 Jul	SGP
23 Jul	GP II	Night of Athletics, Heusden-Zolder, BEL	22 Jul	APM
25 Jul	GP II	Helsinki Grand Prix, FIN	26 Jul	GP
26 Jul	SGP	DN Galan, Stockholm, SWE	25 Jul	SGP
29 Jul	GL	Bislett Games, Oslo, NOR	2 Jun	GL
16 Aug		Tallinn, EST	28 Jul	APM
19 Aug	GL	Weltklasse, Zürich, SUI	18 Aug	GL
21 Aug	SGP	Norwich Union British GP, Sheffield 05 Gateshead 06, GBR	11 Jun	GP
23 Aug	GP	Gugl Meeting, Linz, AUT	22 Aug	APM
26 Aug	GL	Memorial Ivo van Damme, Brussels, BEL	25 Aug	GL
28 Aug	GP	Rieti, ITA	27 Aug	GP
31 Aug		Palio Citta della Quercia, Rovereto, ITA	30 Aug	APM
4 Sep	GL	ISTAF, Berlin, GER	3 Sep	GL
9-10 Sep		Herculis (World Athletics Final 2005), Monaco, MON	20Aug	SGP

* also Hamilton, NZL 14 **Dec** 2005.

Other IAAF Permit Meetings 2006: 14 May Olympia, GRE and 23 Sep Shanghai, CHN

80 YEARS OF CAC GAMES 1926-2006

By Bernard Linley

THE XX Central American and Caribbean (CAC) Games, scheduled to be held in Cartagena de Indias, Colombia, 15-30 July 2006, will mark the 80th birthday of this multi-sport event.

Sanctioned by the IOC during its 1924 Congress in Paris to provide sportsmen of the region with a regular competition to better prepare themselves for the quadrennial Olympics, the CAC Games have been held regularly between the summer Olympic Games since 1926. In that year, the first edition was held in Mexico City, opening on 12 October, the date chosen to commemorate the first landing of Christopher Columbus in the New World and the initial Meeting of Two Cultures. Unfortunately only three eligible countries participated (Cuba. Guatemala and Mexico), but track and field athletics was one of eight sports contested, along with basketball, baseball, diving, fencing, shooting, swimming and tennis.

The Games grew gradually over the years and now more than 30 countries regularly participate in more than 30 sports. The cycle of regular four-year intervals was broken just once (when World War II caused the cancellation of the 1942 celebration). In addition three Games were held in odd-numbered years: 1935 instead of 1934 (postponed following an earthquake in host country El Salvador), 1959 instead of 1958 (after political elections were called for the same December 1958 dates originally fixed by host country Venezuela), and 1993 instead of 1994 (advanced to coincide with the 500th anniversary of the arrival of Columbus in the host country Puerto Rico).

In the 19 editions to date eighteen athletes have won three gold medals in the same event. That fourteen of these are from Cuba illustrates clearly the domination of that island over the other countries. The other four multiple champions came from Guatemala (high jumper Teodoro Palacios Flores 1959-62-66), Mexico (20km walker Ernesto Canto 1982-86-90), Puerto Rico (pole vaulter Rolando Cruz 1959-62-66, with his brother Ruben Cruz second each time) and Surinam (Letitia Vriesde 800m 1993-98-2002).

Cuban 100m specialist Rafael Fortun was the first to accomplish the feat (1946-50-54), before being emulated by high hurdler Alejandro Casañas (1970-74-78), steeplechaser José Cobo (1974-78-82, after being 6th in 1970), discus thrower Luis Mariano Delis (1978-82-86) and high jumper Javier Sotomayor (1990-93-98). In addition, Leandro Peñalver (1982-86-90) and Andrés Simon (1986-90-93) were on winning Cuban 4x100m relay teams . The Cuban female heroes to date include Miguelina Cobian, the first woman to win three titles (100m in 1962-66-70), javelin thrower Caridad Colón (1978-82-86, plus a silver medal in 1990), and discus throwers Carmen Romero (1970-74-78, who was also 3rd in 1966 and 2nd in 1982) and Eloina Echevarría (1990-93-98).

Liliana Allen won 100m and 200m titles in 1990-93 representing Cuba then, after switching to Mexican colours, was 8th in the 1998 100m final before winning her third 100m/200m double in 2002. As she was also on the winning Cuban 4x100m relay teams in 1990 and 1993, her gold medal collection totals eight. The other Cuban women in this list recorded their wins in the 4x400m relay: Julia Duporty (1990-93-98) and Ana Fidelia Quirot, who was actually on four winning relay teams (1978-82-86-90).

Quirot won nine CAC Games medals, the most by any woman athlete, in a career stretching from 1978 to 1998 (when she was 4th in the 800m), as she also scored 400m/800m victories in 1986-90, and was 2nd in the 800m final of 1993.

The main multiple medallist among men is Jamaican sprinter/quarter miler George Rhoden, with ten medals, all collected in eight years: 1946: gold in 4x400m relay, bronze in 400m; 1950: gold in 800m, silvers in 400m and 4x100m relay, bronze in 4x400m relay; 1954: golds in both relays, silvers in 400m and 800m.

One athlete that we cannot overlook in this brief look back at the CAC Games over the past 80 years is Teofilo Colon of Puerto Rico. A top level regional athlete for no less than 21 years, he was 2nd in the 110m hurdles at the 1938 Games, and again at the 1959 Games. In the intervening years he competed in two more 110m hurdles finals, finishing 2nd in 1946 and 4th in 1950.

The CAC region covers all countries in Central America and the Caribbean, as well as those nations on the north coast of South America bordering the Caribbean Sea. The 19 editions held until 2002 have been held in 10 countries. Mexico has hosted the Games three times (1926, 1954 and 1990, always in Mexico City), but in 2006 it will be joined by Colombia (1946 in Barranquilla and 1978 in Medellín). Six countries have held the Games twice: Cuba (Havana in 1930 and 1982), El Salvador (San Salvador 1935 and 2002), Panama (Panama City 1938 and 1970), Venezuela (Caracas 1959 and Maracaibo 1998), Puerto Rico (San Juan 1966 and Ponce 1993) and Dominican Republic (Santo Domingo 1974 and Santiago de los Caballeros 1986). Guatemala (1950) and Jamaica (1962) each hosted one edition, in their respective capitals.

Barring accidents, Cuba and the Caribbean islands will maintain their supremacy over the continental countries and win the most track and field medals in 2006. However, any such prediction for the 2010 Games, which have been allocated to Mayaguez in Puerto Rico, is more problematic.

EUROPEAN CHAMPIONSHIPS 2006

THE FIRST European Championships were staged at the Stadio Comunale, Torino, Italy in 1934 for men only. Women's championships were held separately in 1938, but men's and women's events were combined at one venue from 1946. The championships are held at four-yearly intervals, although there was a break in that pattern when they were held in 1969 and 1971. The 19th Championships will be held in Göteborg, Sweden 7-13 August, 2006, based at the Ullevi Stadium, the venue for the World championships in 1995.

Championship Records

Men

100m	9.96	Dwain Chambers GBR	2002
200m	19.85	Konstadinos Kedéris GRE	2002
400m	44.52	Iwan Thomas GBR	1998
800m	1:43.84	Olaf Beyer GDR	1978
1500m	3:35.27	Fermín Cacho ESP	1994
5000m	13:10.15	Jack Buckner GBR	1986
10,000m	27:30.99	Martti Vainio FIN	1978
Mar	2:10:31	Martín Fiz ESP	1994
3000mSt	8:12.66	Francesco Panetta ITA	1990
110mh	13.02	Colin Jackson GBR	1998
400mh	47.48	Harald Schmid FRG	1982
HJ	2.35	Steinar Hoen NOR	1994
PV	6.00	Rodion Gataullin URS	1994
LJ	8.41	Robert Emmiyan URS	1986
	8.41w	Lutz Dombrowski GDR	1982
TJ	17.99	Jonathan Edwards GBR	1998
SP	22.22	Werner Günthör SUI	1986
DT	68.83	Róbert Fazekas HUN	2002
HT	86.74	Yuriy Sedykh URS	1986
JT	89.72	Steve Backley GBR	1998
Dec	8811	Daley Thompson GBR	1986
4x100mR	37.79	France	1990
4x400mR	2:58.22	GBR	1990
20 kmW	1:18:37	Franc. Fernández ESP	2002
50 kmW	3:36:39	Rob. Korzeniowski POL	2002

Women

100m	10.73	Christine Arron FRA	1998
200m	21.71	Heike Drechsler GDR	1986
400m	48.15	Marita Koch GDR	1982
800m	1:55.41	Olga Minayeva URS	1982
1500m	3:57.80	Olga Dvirna URS	1982
3000m	8:30.28	Svetlana Ulmasova URS	1982
5000m	14:57.65+	Paula Radcliffe GBR	2002
10,000m	30:01.09	Paula Radcliffe GBR	2002
Mar	2:26:05	Maria Guida ITA	2002
100mh	12.38	Yordanka Donkova BUL	1986
400mh	53.32	Marina Styepanova URS	1986
HJ	2.02	Ulrike Meyfarth FRG	1982
PV	4.60	Svetlana Feofanova RUS	2002
LJ	7.30	Heike Drechsler GDR	1990
TJ	14.89	Anna Biryukova RUS	1994
	15.00w	Ashia Hansen GBR	2002
SP	21.69	Viktoriya Pavlysh UKR	1998
DT	71.36	Diane Sachse GDR	1986
HT	72.94	Olga Kuzenkova RUS	2002
JT	77.44	Fatima Whitbread GBR	q1986
new spec	67.47	Miréla Manjani GRE	2002
Hep	6717	Anke Behmer GDR	1986
4x100mR	41.68	GDR	1990
4x400mR	3:16.87	GDR	1986
20kmW	1:26:42	Olimpiada Ivanova RUS	2002

Four Successive Titles

Men

4 Janis Lusis URS JT 1962-66-69-71
4 Steve Backley GBR JT 1990-94-98-2002
4 Colin Jackson GBR 110mh 1990-94-98-2002

Women

4 Nadezhda Chizhova URS SP 1966-69-71-74
4 Heike Drechsler GDR/GER 1986-90-94-98

Most gold medals at all events

Men: 5 Harald Schmid FRG, Roger Black GBR
Women: 6 Marita Koch GDR, Fanny Blankers-Koen NED, Irena Szewinska POL, Marlies Göhr GDR, Heike Drechsler GDR/GER, Grit Breuer GDR/GER

Most Medals

Men: 6 Harald Schmid FRG 1978-86, Pietro Mennea ITA 1971-4, Roger Black GBR 1986-94

Women: 10 Irena Szewinska POL 1966-78, 8 Fanny Blankers-Koen NED 1938-50, Renate Stecher GDR 1969-74; 7 Marlies Göhr GBR 1978-86; 6 Yevgeniya Sechenova USS 1946-50, Marita Koch GDR 1978-86, Heike Drechsler GDR/GER 1986-98, Irina Privalova RUS 1994-8, Grit Breuer GDR/GER 1990-2002

Medals By Nation 1934-2002

Nation	*Men* G	S	B	*Women* G	S	B	*Total*
USSR	65	69	60	54	41	43	332
GDR	39	37	32	51	45	33	237
UK	71	40	44	14	19	24	212
FR Germany	27	24	36	9	20	18	134
France	28	31	22	10	6	12	109
Poland	21	24	22	14	8	20	109
Italy	27	30	21	5	6	15	104
Germany *	19	16	18	15	17	13	98
Finland	26	25	30	4	2	5	92
Sweden	20	31	31	3	3	2	90
Russia	9	8	6	14	18	16	71

26 other nations have won medals

* Germany - 1934 and 1938 Championships. The Federal Republic took part from 1954 and the GDR from 1958. Germany again from 1994.

The European nations from the ex-USSR, Czech Republic and Slovakia from Czechoslovakia and the ex-constituent nations of Yugoslavia competed from 1994.

Timetable and Qualifying Standards

QUALIFYING standards must be achieved in bona fide competition (indoors or outdoors) between 1 January 2005 to 28 July 2006 (the closing date for final entries). A maximum of three athletes by any one EAA Member Federation may compete provided that each athlete has reached the qualifying standard. Provided that any EAA Member Federation enters only one athlete for any event such athlete shall not be required to have reached the qualifying standard for that event. Every EAA Member may enter one team in each relay event. Seven days of competition are scheduled. Dates of successive rounds (all in August)

Event	*Days*	*Qual. standards*
Men		A
100m	7-7-8-8	10.50
200m	9-9-10-10	21.10
400m	7-8-9	46.75
800m	10-11-13	1:47.20
1500m	7-9	3:41.00
5000m	10-13	13:42.00
10,000m	8	28:50.00
Mar	13	none
3000mSt	9-11	8:35.00
110mh	11-12-12	13.88
400mh	8-9-10	50.60
HJ	7-9	2.25
PV	10-13	5.55
LJ	7-8	7.95
TJ	10-12	16.50
SP	7-7	18.90
DT	10-12	62.00
HT	9-11	75.00
JT	7-9	77.00
Dec	10/11	7800
4x100m	12-13	none
4x400m	12-13	none
20 kmW	8	1:24:00
50 kmW	10	4:00:00

Women		
100m	8-8-9-9	11.60
200m	10-10-11-11	2375
400m	8-9-10	53.40
800m	7-8-10	2:02.50
1500m	11-13	4:13.00
5000m	9-12	15:40.00
10,000m	7	33:20.00
Mar	12	none
3000mSt	6-8	10:05.00
100mh	10-11-11	13.45
400mh	7-8-9	57.80
HJ	8-11	1.89
PV	10-12	4.20
LJ	11-13	6.50
TJ	8-9	13.65
SP	11-12	16.55
DT	8-10	56.00
HT	7-8	64.50
JT	12-13	55.50
Hep	7/8	5750
4x100m	12-13	none
4x400m	12-13	none
20kmW	9	1:33:30

Wheelchair: men's 800m 10-11, women's 800m 10th

Most Championships Contested

6 Ludvik Danek TCH 1962-78
6 Abdon Pamich ITA 1954-71
6 Nenad Stekic YUG 1971-90

Most Medals at One Event

5 Igor Ter-Ovanesyan URS long jump 3/2/0 1958-71

Most Medals at one Championship

Men

4 John Regis GBR 2/1/1 1990

Women

4 Fanny Blankers-Koen HOL 3/1/0 1950
4 Irena Kirszenstein/Szewinska POL 3/1/0 1966
4 Stanislawa Walasiewicz POL 2/2/0 1938

MAJOR INTERNATIONAL EVENTS 2006-2010

2006

IAAF World Indoor Championships – Moscow, Russia (10-12 March)
Commonwealth Games – Melbourne, Australia (19-25 March)
IAAF World Cross Country Championships – Fukuoka, Japan (1-2 April)
IAAF World Race Walking Cup – La Coruña, Spain (13-14 May)
Ibero-American Championships – Ponce, Puerto Rico (26-28 May)
CAC Championships – San Pedro Sula, Honduras (16-18 June)
European Cup – Super League – Málaga, Spain (28-29 June)
European Cup for Combined Events (1-2 July)
NACAC U23 Championships – Santo Domingo, Dominican Republic (7-9 July)
Central American & Caribbean Games – Cartagena, Colombia (25-30 July)
IAAF World Junior Championships – Beijing, China (15-20 August)
European Championships – Göteborg, Sweden (7-13 August)
African Championships – Réduit, Mauritius (9-13 August)
IAAF World Athletics Final – Stuttgart, Germany (9-10 September)
IAAF World Cup – Athens, Greece (16-17 September)
IAU 100km World Challenge – Seoul, Korea (8 October)
IAAF World Road Running Championships (20km) – Debrecen, Hungary (8 October)
South American U23 Championships – Montevideo, Uruguay (14-15 October)
Asian Junior Championships – Macao, China (23-26 November)
Asian Games – Doha, Qatar (7-15 December)
European Cross Country Championships – San Georgio su Legnano, Italy (10 Dec)

2007

European Indoor Championships – Birmingham, GBR (2-4 March)
IAAF World Cross Country Championships – Mombasa, Kenya
European Cup of Race Walking – Leamington Spa, GBR (20 May)
Pan-American Junior Championships – Fortaleza, Brazil (6-8 July)
IAAF World Youth Championships – Ostrava, Czech Republic (11-15 July)
European U23 Championships – Debrecen, Hungary (12-15 July)
African Games – Alger, Algeria (15-19 July)
European Junior Championships – Hengelo, Netherlands (19-22 July)
European Youth Olympic Festival, Belgrade, SCG (23-27 Jul)
Pan-American Games – Rio de Janeiro, Brazil (23-29 July)
Afro-Asian Games – Alger, Algeria (26 Jul - 3 Aug)
World University Games – Bangkok, Thailand (9-14 August)
IAAF World Championships – Osaka, Japan (25 Aug - 2 Sep)
IAAF World Athletics Final – Stuttgart, Germany (22-23 Sep tbc)
Asian Junior Championships – Jakarta, Indonesia
IAAF World Road Running Championships (Half Marathon) – Udine, Italy (14 Oct)
European Cross Country Championships – Toro, Spain (9 December)

2008

IAAF World Indoor Championships – Valencia, Spain (7-9 Mar)
IAAF World Race Walking Cup – Cheboksary, Russia (10-11 May)
IAAF World Junior Championships – Bydgoszcz, Poland
Olympic Games – Beijing (8-24 August)
IAAF World Athletics Final – Stuttgart, Germany
IAAF World Road Running Championships – Rio de Janeiro, Brazil (5 Oct)

2009

IAAF World Championships – Berlin, Germany (15-23 Aug)
Mediterranean Games – Pescara, Italy
World Masters Games – Sydney, Australia (October)

2010

IAAF World Junior Championships – Moncton, Canada
Commonwealth Games – New Delhi, India
IAAF World Cup – Split, Croatia

OBITUARY 2005

See ATHLETICS 2005 for obituaries of the following who died in early 2005: Olle Åkerberg, Mikko Ala-Leppilampi, Henry Bagnall-Oakeley, Artidoro Berti, Per Borten, George Coleman, José Luis Martínez, Ekkehard zur Megede, Paul Messner, Philip Ndoo, Neville Scott, Alemu Techale and Nettie Witziers-Timmer.

Boris ACQUADRO (Switzerland) (b. 18 Jun 1929) on 9 June. An IAAF Press and TV Commission member since 1987, he had been a TV journalist since 1954, covering 18 Summer and Winter Olympic Games. Head of Sport at Swiss Television (French language) 1962-94, he was a former chairman of the Sports Programme Commission of the European Broadcasting Union. He received the Olympic Order in 1997.

Altti ALAROTU (Finland) (b. 30 Sep 1945) of pneumonia on 8 April. A colourful athlete and world class pole vaulter, he briefly held the European indoor best of 5.18 in 1968. In 1967 he became the fourth Finn to clear 5m and he set five Finnish outdoor records from 5.05 in 1967 to 5.31 in 1970 (at Turku when he beat Bob Seagren). He never won a national championship (2nd in 1967 and 1971) and was 13th in the 1966 Europeans, 14th at the 1968 Olympics, 10th in the 1971 Europeans and 4th in the 1967 European Indoors. He studied sports science at Brigham Young in the USA. His uncle Martti Alarotu had a shot pb of 15.75 (1933) and brother Aaro Alarotu had pbs of 2.15 HJ (1973) and 6977 decathlon (1975).

Terry ALBRITTON (USA) (b. 14 Jan 1955) died suddenly on 1 September in Phnom Penh, Cambodia apparently of asthma. Known as a "free spirit", he had lived and worked in Thailand for several years before moving to Cambodia. He was a shot putting prodigy, setting a world junior record of 20.38 in 1974 after a massive 21.05 indoors and a world record of 21.85 at Honolulu on 21 Feb 1976 just a month after his 21st birthday. He was AAU champion in 1977 and indoors in 1974 and 1976 and won the NCAA title in 1977 and indoors in 1976, was 3rd in the 1975 Pan-American Games and 4th in the 1977 World Cup. He went to college at Stanford on a football scholarship in 1973, but, disillusioned with that sport, he transferred to Hawaii, before returning to Stanford when Hawaii dropped its track programme just after his world record.

Annual progression (position on world list): 1972- 16.84, 1973- 18.85 (66), 1974- 21.05i/20.38 (11), 1975- 20.75 (10), 1976- 21.85 (3), 1977- 21.50i/20.90 (2), 1978- 19.31i (67=), 1980- 19.61 (68).

Jean-Claude ARIFON (France) (b. 16 Nov 1926 Marseille) on 8 July in Nîmes. He made 9 international appearances for France 1946-8, and at 400mh was World Student Games champion in 1947 and fourth in his semi (52.2) at the 1948 Olympics. He set three French records: 52.3 and 52.1 in 1947 and 51.6 to equal the European record in Paris on 9 Sep 1948, taking second on the world lists each year. He was French champion in 1948, but his career ended after that.

Georges AUDOUY (France) (b. 18 May 1926 Liesse) on 30 March. In 1946 he was French high jump champion and 8th at the European Championships. Pb 1.945 (1949).

Belén AZPEITIA (Spain) (b. 12 Dec 1952 San Sebastián) in Paz in August. At 800m she was Spanish champion 1971-2 and set a national record with 2:06.03 in 1971 and at 1500m she set six Spanish records from 4:24.2 in 1971 to 4:18.6 in 1972. Pb 3000m 10:01.0 (1973). She was 15th the International CC in 1971.

Messias José BAPTISTA (Brazil) (b. 24 May 1968) from leukaemia on 11 September in São Paulo. South American triple jump champion in 1995 (and 2nd in 2001), in 1996 he competed at the Olympics and won the Ibero-American title in Medellín with his personal best of 16.99A. Pb LJ 7.56 (1993).

Frederick BARRY-BROWN (Australia) in late June at the age of 92. He was 6th in his heat of the 1 mile in the 1938 Empire Games, having been 2nd in the 1937 Australian Champs 1 mile in 4.22.4e. He served in the Air Force in World War II.

Sandor BEREC (SCG) (b. 3 Nov 1922) on 14 September. He made nine international appearances for Yugoslavia at the hammer, with a best of 53.58 in 1951. He turned to rugby in 1954 and was a member of the international team until 1962.

Carlo BERTOCCHI (Italy) (b. 13 Mar 1916 Molinella, Bologna) on 30 April. Italian 3000m steeplechase champion 1942 and international 1940-2. Pbs: 1500m 3:55.2, 5000m 15:14.6, 3000mSt 9:32.0 (all 1942).

Colette BESSON (France) (b. 7 Apr 1946 St Georges-de-Didonne) of cancer in La Rochelle on 9 August. One of the most glamorous as well as successful athletes of the late 1960s, she produced one of the shock results of the 1968 Olympics in Mexico City when, having run no faster than 53.8 before the Games, she edged past Lillian Board in the final few strides of the 400m to win the gold medal in a European record of 52.03. At the following year's European Champs in Athens she shared in a world record of 51.7 with her compatriot Nicole Duclos, the title going to Duclos in an electrically timed 51.77 with Besson registering 51.79. Later Besson ran the anchor leg in a memorable 4x400m relay. She went out too fast and was pipped on the line by Board with Britain and France sharing the world record time of 3:30.8. In 1970 she set a world best for the rarely run 500m with 69.9 at altitude in Font Romeu. Other results: OG: '72- qf; EC: '71- 7; EI: '69- 1, '70- 3. French champion 400 1968 1971, 800m 1970, CC 1971; MedG 400m 1971. She set three French records at 400m and two at 400mh. Other pbs: 100m 11.7 (1968), 11.6w (1970); 200m 23.4 (1969), 800m 2:03.3 (1971), 1000m 2:42.6 (1975), 1500m 4:25.4 (1975), 3000m 9:48.8 (1975), 400mh 59.91 (1977), pentathlon 4286 (1970).

Annual progression at 400m (position on world list): 1966- 54.2 (16=), 1967- 55.2 (43=), 1968- 52.03A (1), 1969- 51.79 (2), 1970- 52.6 (7=), 1971- 52.5 (3=), 1972- 52.6 (22=), 1973- 56.1, 1974- 53.5 (53=), 1975- 54.7, 1977- 54.3.

Tage (Andersson) **BJUREFELDT** (Sweden) (b. 22 Dec 1918 Bollnäs) on 12 November. He was 5th in the Swedish 400m in 1941 and had a pb of 49.3 (1944) before winning the first world title in modern pentathlon in 1949.

Charles BOUVET-BIONDA (France) (b. 18 Oct 1918 Allinges) on 26 May. He made five international appearances for France at pole vault, including 17= in qualifying at the 1948 Olympic Games. Pb 3.92 (1945).

Ivar BREDHOLT (Norway) (b. 28 Jul 1945) on 27 October. A Norwegian PV (pb 4.30 '69) and Decathlon (6639 '70) international, he was third in the NOR decathlon in 1972 when his brothers Arild (1st) and Knut (2nd) completed a family 1-2-3.

Audrey Kilner **BROWN** (GBR) (b. 24 May 1913 India) (later Court) on 11 June. A graduate of Birmingham University and member of Birchfield Harriers, she won an Olympic silver medal in 1936 at 4x100m and went out in the heats of the 100m, after placing 3rd in the WAAA 100m that year. She ran a 200m pb of 25.4 for 2nd in an international in Paris in 1937 and also ran at the 1938 Europeans in Vienna (sf 100m after pb 12.3 in heat, hts 200m, dq 4x100m). She was awarded the MBE for services to the community. She was the sister of Godfrey Brown (gold and silver) at the 1936 Olympics and Ralph Kilner Brown (bronze 1934 Empire Games 440yh).

Michel BUTET (France) (b. 19 Jun 1947) on 3 September. He set a French junior javelin record with 75.42, the second best in the world by a junior in 1966 and had a pb of 79.72 in 1973. He was French champion in 1969, with 18 internationals 1966-74. He became a handball leader and president of l'ACBB.

Don CANHAM (USA) (b. 27 Apr 1918 Chicago) in a car accident near Saline, Michigan on 3 May. He tied for the 1940 NCAA high jump with a pb 2.01 (sixth on the world list that year) for the University of Michigan and after war service in the Air Force was there for nearly 40 years from 1949, first as head track and field coach and then as athletic director. He wrote several books on training and technique and conducted coaching clinics in many parts of the world.

Torsten CARLIUS (Sweden) (b. 15 Mar 1939 Helsingborg) on 23 November while in Shanghai. He was a member of the board of the Swedish AA 1972-85 (for several years with his father Nils, who was president 1958-64). In 1988 he was appointed vice president of the European Veterans AA and became a member of the board of the WAVA, becoming secretary general and in 1997 president of the WAVA (now WMA – World Masters Association). He then left the EVAA, where he had by then became president, only to make a come back in 2003 as a member of the EVAA Council. He was a member of the IAAF Committee for Veterans athletics from 1995.

Wally CHISHOLM (Australia) on 28 December. Coached winners of 20 Australian pole vault titles including Ray Boyd (12 wins 1970-83), his son Robert Chisholm (1984) and the first Australians over 15ft (Ross Filshie), 16 ft (Eddie Johnson) and 17ft (Mike Sullivan).

Gilbert CRUTER (USA) (b. 16 Feb 1915 Trinidad, Colorado) in Denver on 25 July. He was one of the first African-American varsity student-athletes at the University of Colorado and for them tied for the NCAA high jump title in 1937 and 1938. On the latter occasion he jumped an outdoor best of 6-8 ¾ and with Dave Albritton topped the world list that year. 6ft 5in tall with a barrel-roll style, he had set a world indoor best of 6- 8 7/8 two years earlier at Fort Collins.

He worked as a track coach, as a teacher and for the US State department as a goodwill ambassador to West Africa before spending four years in Africa as a cultural affairs attaché. He was Executive Director of the Department of Community Schools in Denver from 1982 to his retirement.

Annual progression at HJ (position on world list): 1933- 1.84, 1934- 1.93 (35=), 1936- 2.054i/1.97 (4), 1937- 2.00 (11=), 1938- 2.051 (1=).

James '**Jim**' **DINGWALL** (GBR) (b. 30 May 1949) on 22 July of bowel cancer. He was 18th in the marathon at the 1978 Commonwealth Games and had a best of 2:11:44 for 5th in London (3rd AAA) in 1983. He was Scottish champion at 10,000m 1974 and 1976-7 and marathon in 1977. He went to Edinburgh University, worked as a research chemist for BP and competed for Falkirk Victoria Harriers. Pbs: 1500m 3:45.8 (1973), 3000m 7:578 (1975), 2M 8:43.7 (1976), 5000m 13:48.0 (1975), 10,000m 28:45.25 (1978).

Jacques DOHEN (France) (b. 4 May 1930 Paris) on 9 May. French champion six times at 110m hurdles (1954-8 and 1961), he set five French records with 14.4 in 1955, three times at 14.3 and then 14.2 in 1957 (a pb he equalled in 1961), and competed in 39 internationals 1952-64. He competed at the 1952 Olympics (heat) and was a semi-finalist at the 1954 and 1958 Europeans.

Kenneth Sandilands '**Sandy**' **DUNCAN** (GBR) (b. 26 Apr 1912 Haslingden, Lancashire) on 18 June. He led the British teams at all the Olympic Games from 1952 to 1972 as Secretary General of the British Olympic Association 1949-75. He was also honorary secretary of the Commonwealth Games Federation, overseeing the Games from 1954 to 1982, and was awarded the OBE in 1975. At the long jump he was 4th at the 1934 Empire Games and competed in seven internationals for Britain 1933-7. In the LJ first six at the AAAs each year 1932-7, his best was 2nd in 1934 and he was also 6th at shot 1938-9 and discus 1938.

He captained the England team at the 1938 Empire Games and although eliminated in the heats of the 100y and failing to qualify for the long jump final, he won a silver medal at 4x110y. After Oxford University, where he was also a soccer blue, he served in the Royal Artillery in WW II (ending as a major) and then became a schoolmaster at Bradfield, setting up the national coaching scheme under Geoff Dyson. Pbs: 100y 9.8 (1936), 100m 10.7 (1937), LJ 7.21 (1937), SP 13.60 (1939), DT 38.76 (1938).

Tage EKFELDT (Sweden) (b. 14 Jun 1926 Konungsund) on 28 December. He was Swedish champion at 400m 1952 and 800m 1952-3 and set Swedish 800m records at 1:49.2 and 1:49.0 in 1953. 15 internationals for Sweden 1950-4, winning 7 of 11 races at 800m. He ran at the 1952 Olympics (400m and 4x400m) and at the European Championships in 1950 (3rd 4x400m) and 1954 (7th 800m, 4th 4x400m). Other pbs: 400m 47.6 (1952), 1000m 2:26.0 (1953), 1500m 3:50.4 (1953).

William Thomas '**Willie**' **FARRELL** (South Africa) (b. 8 Jun 1951) in March. He had a marathon best of 2:13:43 when 3rd in the South African Champs in 1980. Other pbs: 5000m 13:58.6 (1976), 10,000m 29:28.80 (1980), 1Hr 19,916mA (1977).

Othilie '**Tilly**' **FLEISCHER** (Germany) (b. 2 Oct 1911 Frankfurt-am-Main) on 14 July. She set her pb for javelin of 45.18 in winning the 1936 Olympic gold medal in Berlin. At the 1932 Olympics she placed third in the javelin, fourth in the discus and sixth in the 4x100m relay and at the Women's World Games won silver medals at discus in 1930 and shot in 1934. She was German javelin champion in 1932 and 1936 and set unratified world records in the shot (12.40 in 1929, 12.88 in 1930) and relay (49.0 in 1929) and had a discus best of 38.71 (1935).

Annual progression at javelin (position on world list): 1928- 36.07 (10), 1929- 38.25 (2), 1931- 39.92 (3), 1932- 44.25 (3), 1933- 41.57 (3), 1934- 42.09 (5), 1935- 43.55 (3), 1936- 45.18 (4).

Marian FOIK (Poland) (b. 6 Oct 1933 Bielszowice/Katowice) on 20 May in Warsaw. A top sprinter of the 1950/1960s, he won a silver medal at 4x100m at his third Olympic Games in 1964; and was 4th in 1960 and 6th in 1964 at 200m. At European Championships he won silver medals at 200m and 4x100m in 1962 and was 6th at 100m in 1958 and 1962. He was Polish champion at 100m in 1955, 1957-8, 1960-1 and 1964 and at 200m 1955, 1958-9, 1961, 1963-4. He set nine Polish records at 100m from 10.5 in 1956 to 10.2 in 1961 and 1962 and three at 200m: 21.0 and 20.9 in 1959 and 20.6 in 1960. Pb 400m 48.9 (1963).

Piotr GLADKI (Poland) (b. 8 Feb 1972 Gdansk) in a car accident near Kartizy on 27 June while returning from a road race in which he had placed third. He competed at the 2000 Olympic Games (dnf marathon) and was twice Polish champion at 5000m (1998-9) and once at 3000m indoors. Pbs: 3000m 7:57.07 (2001), 5000m 13:36.50 (1994), 10,000m 28:38.41 (1998), HMar 61:35 (2000), Mar 2:11:06 (2000).

Ragnar GRAEFFE (Finland) (b. 16 Sep 1929 Hanko) on 28 August at Lohja. A member of Finnish 4x400 relay bronze team at Berne in 1954, he competed in the Helsinki Olympic Games in the 400m hurdles and the relay. Second in the Finnish 400m in 1950, 1952 and 1954, his pb was 48.5 (1954) and 54.6 (1952) for 400mh.

Hendrickson HAREWOOD (Trinidad) (b. 1923) in South Trinidad in September. Having taken up athletics in his 20s he ran his best times in his 30s, including 10.4 to win the 100m at the first two editions of the British West Indies Championships in 1957-8. He was Trinidad champion at 100y in 1954 and 1957 and at 220y in 1957, and reached the second round of the 1951 Pan-Am 100m and 1958 Empire Games 100m (heats of 200m/220y in each case). Pbs: 100y 9.7 (1954), 100m 10.4 (1956), 200m 21.3 (1954).

David HEDMAN (Sweden) (b. 25 Jun 1914 Skellefteå) on 9 October. He was 5th in the World University Championships 200m in 1939, competed in one international and had a 200m pb 22.2 (1939).

Daniel HÉRICÉ (France) (b. 7 Sep 1921 Saint-Émilion) on 28 June. French champion at decathlon 1942-3 and discus 1945. Pb DT 44.89 (1946). He played in one international for France at rugby union in 1950 as a flanker and later at rugby league.

Margareta HOLM (Sweden) (b. 8 May 1924 Vetlanda) on 14 March. Swedish champion at discus 1950, two internationals and pb 39.33 (1948).

Harry HOLMQVIST (Sweden) (b. 26 Aug 1907 Stockholm) on 11 April. He competed at 3000m steeplechase (dnf in final) at the 1936 Olympic Games and had three internationals. Pbs: 3000mSt 9:30.2 (1936), 9:20.2 (1936, no water jump); 3000m 8:40.4 (1935), 5000m 14:59.6 (1935), 10,000m 32:35.0 (1941).

Robert JOANBLANQ (France) (b. 21 Feb 1917 Aldudes) on 23 December. He was French champion at long jump in 1937-8 and 1943-4 and triple jump in 1941-3 and 1944-5. He made 11 international appearances at LJ/relay 1937-46 with 10th at long jump in the 1938 European Championships. He set French triple jump records at 14.18 and 14.315 in 1941, LJ pb 7.30 (1941). He became a rugby league professional and international.

Tauno KARLSSON (Finland) (b. 17 Feb 1925 Vaasa) on 6 September in Helsinki. Despite nearly losing his throwing arm in the Russian War in 1944, he became Finnish discus champion in 1950 and 1952 and competed in 12 internationals 1948-56, pb 50.39 (1955). He won a Finnish archery silver medal in 1972.

Gerhard KELLER (Germany) (b. 4 Aug 1927 Süssen/Krs. Göppingen) at the age of 78. FRG javelin champion in 1956 with a pb of 74.70 in 1957. He competed in the 1954 Europeans and won the javelin and pentathlon at the 1953 FISU World University Games.

Larry KENNEDY (USA) (b. 6 Aug 1942) in California on 8 October after a long battle with kidney disease. He won the 1964 NCAA discus title while at the University of New Mexico, and had a best of 64.34 in 1976.

Humphrey KHOSI (South Africa) (b. 1939) on 2 May at his home in Fochville. The first black athlete to set a South African athletics record, he suffered from the Apartheid system, having to run in separate trials from white athletes, but he was the first South African to beat 1:50 for the half mile with three official RSA records: 1:48.9 and 1:48.7 in 1964 and 1:48.60 in 1967. He was selected for the 1964 Olympics but the Japanese authorities denied visas to SA sportsmen. He won ten national titles at the SA Non-White Championships (5 each at 440y and 880y) 1962-70. Pb 440y 46.8 (1965).

Mauno KOSKI (Finland) (b.21 Feb 1930 Raisio) on 2 November in Turku. Finnish 200m champion at age 19 in a pb 22.3 in 1949 when he also competed in two internationals. Later a University professor in Turku, he co-authored, with coach Paavo Karikko, Paavo Nurmi´s excellent biography "Yksin aikaa vastaan" (Alone against time) in 1965. Other pbs: 100m 10.9 (1949), 400m 49.6 (1953).

Janusz KOTLINSKI (Poland) (b. 8 Jan 1932 Dobrzelin/Kutno) in Lublin on 19 October. He set Polish records for 110mh 14.7 and 14.4 (1957), 200mh 24.4 (1955), and 400mh 52.6 (1956) and 51.7 (1957). He was Polish champion at 110mh 1955, 200mh 1955-6 and 1958, and 400mh 1958 and went out in the heats of the 1958 European Champs. Other pbs: 400m 48.8 (1957), 200mh 23.9 (1958).

Mihaíl KOÚSIS (Greece) (b. 10 Oct 1953 Agrínio) on 24 May. He took part in the marathon at three Olympics (1976- 29, 1980- 20, 1984- 26) and two Europeans (1978- 10, 1982- 20) after 24th in the European 10,000m in 1974. He won Balkan Games titles at 5000m 1978, marathon 1979 and 1981, the Mediterranean Games marathon in 1975, 1979 (in 2:06:53 before the course was found to be c.900m short) and 1983, and eight Greek titles, 3 each at 5000m and 10,000m and 2 at marathon and was the first Greek runner to break 29 minutes for 1000m and 2:20 for the marathon. Coached by Mihály Iglói, he set eight Greek records, 3 each at 5000m and marathon, 1 each at 3000m and 10,000m. Pbs: 1500m 3:44.1 (1974), 3000m 7:57.2 (1975), 5000m 13:35.4 (1978), 10,000m 28:44.4 (1974), marathon 2:14:36 (1982).

Pierre LEGRAIN (France) (b. 18 Feb 1920 La Neuville) on 20 June. He competed in 43 internationals for France at hammer 1948-59 including at the 1952 Olympics and 1950 and 1954 Europeans. He set four French hammer records from 51.28 in 1949 to 53.30 in 1954. Coach at l'Etoile d'Oignies and later at AC Douai, his most notable protégé was 1976 Olympic 110m hurdles champion Guy Drut.

Charles MAYS (USA) (b. 3 Feb 1941) on 11 April in Jersey City. He had the misfortune to foul out in the memorable final at the 1968 Olympics in Mexico City, won by Bob Beamon with a staggering world record of 8.90, and one of those no-jumps was reportedly in the region of 8.60, which would easily have secured the silver medal. His personal best was 8.01 in 1964 (he placed 4th in the US Olympic Trials that year) plus 8.16w at altitude in 1968. He was US indoor LJ champion 1962-4 and outdoors was

2nd in 1964 and 1966 and 3rd in 1963 and 1968. He went to Maryland State University.

Annual progression (position on world list): 1961- 7.50i (68=), 1962- 7.66 (35=), 1963- 7.87 (9=), 1964- 8.01 (7), 1965- 7.81i/7.78 (14=), 1966- 8.00 (8), 1967- 7.64 (69=), 1968- 7.85/8.16Aw (27=), 1969- 7.67i/7.81dh (80=), 1970- 7.86 (29=). Other pbs: 200m 21.1 (1968), 440y 48.2 (1961), HJ 1.95 (1961), TJ 14.79 (1964).

Silvano MECONI (Italy) (b. 28 Oct 1931 Cortona) in Firenze on 22 September. He set 13 Italian shot records from 15.82 (1955) to 18.82 (1960); these included three European records (18.03, 18.19 and 18.48) in 1959. Meconi was not at his best on occasions that mattered most – he was 10th in the 1956 Olympics and when at his peak was only 13th with 16.73 at the 1960 Olympics in Rome. He was also 5th in the 1958 European Champs and failed to reach the final at the 1962 Europeans and 1964 Olympics. A giant of 1.88m and 115kg, he also had a discus best of 48.72. He made 47 international appearances 1955-69 and was Italian shot champion 1955-65 and 1967-8.

Colleen MILLS (New Zealand) (née Knight, b. 1933) on 14 October. After marrying the 1966 Commonwealth discus champion Les Mills, she returned to competition 20 years after competing as a teenage hurdler, and took up 400m running, with 58.4 in her first race, She improved rapidly to a world masters' record 54.02 to win the NZ 400m title at age 40. With son Phillip and daughter Donna she represented NZ at the 1974 Commonwealth Games (out in heat due to a stress fracture). (The only one of the family not in the team was Les, who had competed in 1958, 1962, 1966 and 1970 and won five medals), Colleen later won seven world masters' titles, including four in 1979 in sprints, hurdles, and pentathlon. With Les she was mayoress of NZ's largest city, Auckland 1990-8. Earlier they held the same (honorary) positions in the athletes' village at the 1990 Commonwealth Games in Auckland (a very popular appointment). President of Athletics NZ 1997.

Jan MULAK (Poland) (b. 28 Mar 1914 Warszawa) in Warszawa on 31 January. Coach and one of the creators of the Polish "Wunderteam". He was editor in chief of the monthly *Lekka Atletyka* 1957-70 and Chairman of the Polish Athletic Federation 1984-8. Doctor honoris causa of PE Academy of Poznan 1995, Senator 1993-7. Pbs: 400mh 53.3 (1937), 800m 1:58.4 (1935), 1000m 2:34.0 (1937), 1500m 4:10.7 (1935), 3000m 9:20.0 (1938).

Leslie John **PERRY** (Australia) (b. 29 Jan 1923) on 17 September. He set Australian records from 3000m to 10,000m and was Australian champion at 3 miles 1950-3 and at cross-country in 1950. He was 7th in the 3 miles in the 1950 Empire Games, and at the Olympic Games 6th at 5000m (dnf 10,000m) in 1952 and dnf marathon in 1956. Inspired by Emil Zátopek's achievements in Helsinki, he helped to set up the Victorian Marathon Club, which started the Zátopek 10,000m, held annually in Melbourne. Pbs: 1M 4:11.4 (1953), 3000m 8:19.8 (1952), 2M 8:55.2 (1954), 3M 13:50.7 (1955), 5000m 14:23.6 (1952), 6M 29:18.4 (1952), 10,000m 30:23.0 (1953).

Charles **'Chuck' PETERS** (USA) (b. 23 May 1927) on 21 December in Bloomington, Indiana. He was the only man to have reached the NCAA 100 & 200m finals for four years (1947-50); competing for Indiana University, his best placing was 2nd at 220y in 1947. In 1948 he ranked second on the world list to Mel Patton with 20.9 for 220y (turn) but was 4th in his heat at the US Olympic Trials. Other pbs: 100y 9.5 (1947 at altitude, 1948 & 1950), 100m 10.4 (1949 four times), 220y straight 20.7 (1949). He was 3rd at 100m and 2nd at 200m in the 1949 AAUs.

Vernetta ROLLE (Bahamas) (b. 9 Jan 1976) of cancer in Houston on 10 May. She won five silver and two bronze medals at U17 and U20 in the Carifta Games and set the Bahamas 800m record at 2:04.82 in 1998. pb 400m 53.75 (1998).

Fritz SCHILGEN (Germany) (b. 8 Sep 1906 Kronberg) at his birthplace near Frankfurt on 12 September. He carried the Olympic torch around the track and lit the Olympic flame at the 1936 Games in Berlin. He was third in the German 1500m in 1929, 1931 and 1933 and his finest achievement was a win at 1500m over Séra Martin and Otto Peltzer for Germany against France in 1932. He ran on relay teams that set German records at 4x1500m in 1931 and 4x1 mile in 1929. Pbs: 1500m 3:59.2 (1931), 3000m 8:37.2 (1932), 5000m 15:10.4 (1935), 3000mSt 9:53.4 (1935).

Edward F SHEEHAN, Jr (USA) (b. 18 Jun 1958) on 6 May while on a training run in Weymouth, Massachussets. He ran a 2:13:46 marathon in 1982 and was former head coach at the Boston Athletic Association.

Anna-Liisa SILENIUS (Finland) (née Kurki, b. 11 Sep 1926) on 12 February. In her brief career she won the Finnish 800m title in 1949 in her second ever race on the distance, plus another in 1950 and a bronze in her final season 1951. In September 1950, improving exactly 10 seconds from the previous year, she won in Bucharest in a Finnish record time of 2:17.2 for 9th place on the world list behind eight Russians.

Nchenami SIWANE (Botswana) (b. 10 Jan 1986 Goshwe) committed suicide on 2 July. He was 49th in the 2005 World CC Championships.

Zdobyslaw STAWCZYK (Poland) (b. 1 Jun 1923 Czestochowa) in Poznan on 1 September. He competed at the 1952 Olympics (qf 200m, sf 4x100m) and 1954 European Championships (sf 100m, heats 200m and 4x100m). He was Polish champion at 100m 1948 and 1950, and 200m 1949-51 and 1954, and set Polish records of 21.6 and 21.2 for 200m in 1949, when he also set a 100m pb of 10.6. Other pbs: 400m 49.4 (1953), LJ 7.04 (1954). PE professor and rector (president) of PE Academy of Poznan 1987-90.

Gertrude STELLING WILHELMSEN (USA) (b. 16 Jan 1913 Puyallup, Washington) on 19 March in Puyallup. She placed 7th in the javelin (pb 37.35) and 8th in the discus at the 1936 Olympics. As she was German-speaking she played a key role on the Olympic team, acting as a de facto translator for the team and meeting with German officials. She later played pro baseball and as a golfer boasted five career holes-in-one in competition. She married Andrew Wilhelmsen in 1932 after placing 4th at javelin at the US Olympic Trials and was a also an excellent golfer.

Matic SUSTERSIC (SLO) (b. 27 Feb 1980), a member of the Slovenian 4x100m relay team in the Sydney Olympics, pb 100m 10.36 (2000), 10.34w (2004), was one of three young athletes who died in a car crash in Ljubljana on 11-12 June.

Lajos SZENTGÁLI (Hungary) (b. 7 Jun 1932) on 2 November. He had a wonderful month at 800m in August 1954. First he set a national record at 1:49.0, then he took the World University Games title and 20 days later won a superb race at the European Championships in 1:47.1, as the first four men set times bettered only by Rudolf Harbig's 1:46.6 in 1939. He won the World University Games title again in 1955, was 5th in the European 800m in 1958 and competed at the Olympic Games in 1952 (ht 4x400m) and 1956 (ht 800m). His 1:47.1 remained the Hungarian record for 26 years and he competed in 50 internationals, winning Hungarian titles at 800m in 1954, 1956-59 and 1961; 1500m 1961. Other pbs: 400m 48.0 (1955), 1500m 3:43.0 (1961).

Annual progression at 800m (position on world list): 1948- 2:02.5, 1950- 1:57.7, 1951- 1:54.7, 1952- 1:56.3, 1953- 1:50.1 (18), 1954- 1:47.1 (1), 1955- 1:48.1 (12). 1956- 1:47.8 (8), 1957- 1:48.9 (34), 1958- 1:47.7 (11=), 1959- 1:48.7 (27=), 1960- 1:49.4 (69=), 1961- 1:49.1 (45=), 1962- 1:52.8.

David TEE (South Africa) (b. 23 June 1932 Uitenhage) in Port Elizabeth on 6 July. He was RSA 440y champion in 1957 and represented South Africa in test matches against West German touring teams in 1955 and 1959. A popular but reserved person, he ran on teams that twice set SA records for 4x440y in 1959 and ran his pbs for 440y 47.3 sec and 880y 1:51.2 sec on the same day, 11 Nov. 1959, at Queenstown.

Volker TULZER (Austria) (b. 24 Jan 1940) on 13/14 October in Vienna. Austrian champion at 800m 1965, 1967 and 1970, he was a semi-finalist at 800m at the 1962 Europeans and competed at 1500m at the 1964 Olympics. Pbs: 800m 1:48.7 (1965), 1000m 2:22.2 (1963), 1500m 3:42.2 (Austrian record 1963)

Carol Joan **TYSON** (GBR) (b. 15 Dec 1957 Birmingham) on 24 June in Perth, Scotland. She set world records for 5000m walk at 23:11.2 on 30 Jun 1979 and for 3000m at 13:25.2 a week later, both at Östersund, Sweden, before women's walks records were officially recognised. Later that year she was second to her compatriot Marion Fawkes in 22:59 for 10km road to help Britain to win the Eschborn Cup. She had previously set five more British records at 3000m from 14:10.2 in 1976 and two at 5000m in 1977 and one at 10,000m – 49:59.0 in 1978, with a later pb of 48:34.5 in 1981. She won the UK 5000m walk in 1980 and 1981 and was WAAA champion at 5000m in 1978 and 1981 and 10,000m in 1978. Running pbs: 800m 2:21.6 (1974), 1500m 4:43.9 (1977), 3000m 10:02.2i (1978). She qualified as a doctor at King's College. London and competed for Lakeland AC.

Cornelius 'Sonny' **van ANTWERP** (South Africa) (b. 7 Oct 1942 Johannesburg). He was 38th in the International CC in 1967 and RSA champion at 6M and marathon in 1965. With DeVilliers Lamprecht he set the inaugural RSA record at 10,000m, 30:14.4 in 1964, and also set RSA records at 10M (49:45.2) and 1 hour (12M 99y/19.346m) at altitude in Germiston in 1966. Other pbs: 5000m 14:32.4A (1968), 6M 28:40.0 (1967), 10,000m 29:42.3 (1968), Mar 2:30:44 (1965).

Eijo VESANEN (Finland) (b. 6 May 1912 at Vihti) on 29 July at Helsinki. Third in the Finnish PV in 1934 and 1936-7 with three internationals, he had a pb of 3.95 in Stockholm 1935. Professor and Doctor of Philosophy, he became an eminent expert of seismology, working at Washington University at Seattle in 1948-52 and later at Helsinki University. In 1965-6 he was working for Unesco at International Earthquake Research Institute at Tokyo. In the midst of all these achievements he somehow found time for studies to become a dentist!

Pauli VESTERINEN (Finland) (b. 20 Nov 1923 Kanneljärvi, Karelia, now part of Russia) on 8 August at Nurmijärvi. Just 1.73m and 70kg, he became the smallest world class javelin thrower of his era and, in the opinion of great Matti Järvinen, also "technically the best in the world". Having received valuable coaching in his youth from his neighbour Yrjö Nikkanen (WR

1938), Vesterinen was 4th in the 1948 Olympics (won by film star team mate Tapio Rautavaara) but never won the Finnish title (3rd in 1947-8 and 1950-2). A police constable in Helsinki, he had his greatest win in Sep 1955 at the Helsinki Olympic Stadium with a pb 75.72 ahead of all the leading Finns. During his long career 1945-70 he competed some 600 times, more than 100 of them taking place at his favourite venue, Zoological Gardens grounds (warm-up track for the 2005 World Championships). At age 42 in 1966 he still threw 67.26.

Denis WATTS (GBR) (b. 31 July 1920 Solihull) on 10 June. He was a hugely respected figure in British athletics. Formerly a teacher, for 30 years from 1948 he was one of the AAA's professional coaches – responsible for the Northern Area. He coached Dorothy Hyman, Ann Packer and Lillian Board to the highest of world class levels, and his other top internationals included Janet Simpson, Andy Carter and Tom Farrell. In 1978 he retired as one of the two Principal National Coaches. He competed in four internationals for Britain in 1945-7, including at the 1946 European Championships at which he was 6th at long jump and 9th at triple jump. He won the AAA LJ in 1946 and TJ in 1946 and 1947. Pbs: LJ 7.28 (1946), TJ 14.37 (1948), HJ 1.83 (1947). He also played rugby union for Hertfordshire and London Welsh.

John Charles Malcolm **WILKINSON** (GBR) (b. 17 Jan 1929 Epsom, Surrey) in August. An England schoolboy international at rugby union, he was only 18 and a medical student at Oxford when in 1947 he clocked his best times of 10.5 for 100m and 21.3 for 200m (twice). That 100m time ranked him equal fastest among European-born sprinters that season while the 200m mark rated him no 1 and he won the World University Games titles at both distances in Paris. Injuries blighted his career and cost him his chance of competing in the 1948 Olympics. In 1951, his last year of international competition, he ran a 440y pb of 49.1. He was 2nd in the AAA 100y in 1947 and at 100y and 220y in 1950 and competed in five UK international matches 1947-51. He made the news again in 1956 during his RAF National Service while operating as a doctor with an SAS (Special Air Service) jungle rescue team based in Singapore. In answer to an emergency call over 1000miles away, he parachuted in very difficult conditions onto Christmas Island to save the life of a British woman. He was awarded the Air Force Cross for showing "courage and determination of a very high order." He later became a consultant psychiatrist and worked in forensic psychiatry at Rampton Hospital for the criminally insane before retiring to live in the South of France.

Herbert WILLNY (Sweden) (b. 4 Sep 1918 Oskarshamn) on 10 May. Swedish champion at shot 1943-5, four internationals in each of which he won the shot; pb 15.22 (1945).

Walter ZAMPARELLI (Italy) (b. 7 Mar 1944 Arenzano) on 18 December. He was Italian high jump champion in 1961 and set national records at 2.03 and 2.04 in 1962 with pb 2.06 (1964). He competed in seven internationals 1961-5.

ZORA SINGH (India) (b. 15 Jun 1929) on 15 October. He was eighth in the 1960 Olympic 50km walk in 4:37:45. Later he became a coach in the sports department of Punjab state until his death.

Died in 2006

István ÁRVA (Hungary) (b. 26 Dec 1948 Ujpest) on 12 February in Budapest. He won 13 Hungarian titles in hurdles and relays and had pbs: 110mh 14.5 (1973), 200mh 24.5 (1969), 400mh 50.4 91973), 50.76 (1977).

Larry BLACK (USA) (b. 20 Jul 1951 Miami) on 9 February of an aneurysm. He won the silver medal at 200m in 20.19 and a gold medal as he led off the US 4x100m team that set a world record of 38.24 at the 1972 Olympic Games in Munich and won the NCAA 220y for North Carolina Central University in 1971. He became director of the parks and recreation department in Miami and at the time of his death was a personal trainer in Coral Gables, Florida.

Annual progression at 200m (* 220y less 0.1/0.12 secs) (position on world list): 1970- 20.4* (4=), 1971- 20.4* (6=), 1972- 20.0/20.19 (2), 1974- 20.6*/20.90* (32=). Pbs: 100y 9.3 (1974), 440y 46.6 (1970).

Otis CHANDLER (USA) (b. 23 Nov 1927, Los Angeles), on 27 February in Ojai, California. One of the world's foremost shot putters in the early 1950s, he achieved far wider renown as the go-ahead publisher of the *Los Angeles Times* between 1960 and 1980, transforming it into one of America's most prestigious newspapers. A graduate of Stanford University, he was one of the first track and field athletes to incorporate serious weightlifting in his training. He ranked 8th in the world in 1948 with 16.34, 3rd in 1949 with 17.08 and 2nd to world record holder Jim Fuchs in 1950 with 17.48 (for third place on the world all-time list) and in 1951 with 17.10. He continued to compete until 1956 but never reached 17m again. He was 2nd to Fuchs at AAU and NCAA in 1950.

Ibolya CSÁK (Hungary) (b. 6 Jan 1915, Budapest) on 10 February in Budapest. She was Hungary's first female Olympic athletics champion, with the high jump in Berlin in 1936, when she cleared a pb 1.62 in a jump-off with Dorothy Tyler. She improved to 1.63 in 1937 and 1.64 in 1938 when ostensibly finishing second in the European Champs in Vienna. However, the title passed to her when the German "winner", Dora Ratjen, turned out to be a man. She won nine Hungarian titles (seven HJ, two LJ) and set eight Hungarian records at HJ and one at LJ, 5.35 (1939).

Annual progression at HJ: 1933- 1.49, 1934- 1.55, 1935- 1.56, 1936- 1.61, 1937-1.63, 1938- 1.64.

Elisabeth **'Lisa' GELIUS** (Germany) (b. 23 Jul 1909 München) on 14 January in Kreuth/ Krs. Misebach. She set five world records: 11.6 at Breslau on 30 Jul 1938 for 80mh, three at 4x100m on TSV München teams 1928-30 and with 62.43 for both hands combined javelin in 1934, a European 100m record of 12.1 in 1929 and a German javelin record of 45.22 in 1936. At the Women's World Games in 1930 she won gold at 4x100m, silver at 60m and bronze at 100m, and in 1934 she won the javelin. She was European javelin champion in 1938, when she also took the 80mh silver medal in 11.7 behind the world record 11.6 of Claudia Testoni. She was German champion at 100m 1929-30, 200m 1929, 80mh 1938, javelin 1937-40 and pentathlon 1940.

Annual progression at javelin (position on world list): 1928- 31.66 1929- 32.48, 1930- 36.15 (11), 1932- 40.02 (7), 1933- 39.32 (9), 1934- 42.33 (3=), 1935- 42.95 (4), 1936- 45.22 (3), 1937- 43.41 (5), 1938- 45.74 (2), 1939- 45.07 (3), 1940- 44.19 (3), 1941- 43.97 (2), 1942- 40.26 (14), 1943- 40.77 (11), 1948- 36.76, 1949- 39.15, 1950- 40.51, 1951- 39.11, 1952- 37.53. Other pbs: 50m 6.8 (1932), 60m 7.8 (1930), 200m 25.3w (1930), SP 12.24 (1932), DT 37.09 (1932), Pen 3999 (1938).

István GYULAI (Hungary) (b. 21 Mar 1943) on 12 Marchin Monte Carlo after a long illness. He was a Hungarian international 1961-9 and won at 400m won three Hungarian titles (1963-4 and 1966) and had a pb of 47.3 (1963 and 1965-6). He also won 13 HUN relay titles. At the World University Games he won a gold medal at 4x100m in 1963 and silver at 4x400m in 1965 and was 5th in the 400m in 1963; he also competed in the 1964 Olympics and 1966 Europeans. Other pbs: 100m 10.5 (1965), 200m 21.2 (1963). He became Head of Sport for Hungarian TV, combining that career with important positions in Hungarian and international sport. He was a member of the IAAF Council from 1984 until 2001, and was IAAF General Secretary from 1991, working tirelessly and with great imagination for the cause of world athletics. His son Miklós was also an athletics Olympian in the 4x100m in 2000 and competed at bobsleigh at the Winter Olympics.

Jess JARVER (Australia) (b. Lembit Jarver 3 Mar 1922 Tallinn, Estonia) on 11 February in Adelaide. He edited *Modern Athlete & Coach* for 40 years and was a former President of the Australian Track & Field Coaches Association.

Louis Woodward **JONES** III (USA) (b. 15 Jan 1932 New Rochelle, NY) on 2 February in New York. He set a world record for 400m of 45.4 at the Pan-American Games in Mexico City, benefitting, as was then little understood, from the 2247m high altitude. His previous pb had been 2nd to Jim Lea, 46.7 to 46.6 for 440y at the 1954 AAU. Jones went on to faster under 'normal' conditions, however, as he improved the world record to 45.2 when winning the 1956 Olympic Trials in Los Angeles, going through 200m in 21.3. He had a poor Olympic Games, however, only just qualifying for the final in which he was 5th in 48.35, fading badly after leading at 300m in 33.4.

He gained some consolation with a gold medal at 4x400m, leading off the US team. In pre-Olympic meetings he ran on the US teams that set world records for 4x400y of 3:08.6 (unratified) and 3:07.3. He won the AAU indoor 600y in 1956. A business administration graduate of Manhattan College, he became a high school teacher in New York and later a dean at Manhattan College and assistant professor at Queensborough Community College.

Annual progression at 400m (* 440y less 0.3 secs) (position on world list): 1949- 49.2*, 1950- 48.9*, 1951- 48.1*, 1952- 47.7 (29=), 1953- 47.7* (24=), 1954- 46.4* (3), 1955- 45.4A (1). 1956- 45.2 (1). Pbs: 500y 57.4i (1956), 600y 1:10.6i (1956).

Hans Jørgen MOESGAARD-KJELDSEN (Denmark) (b. 1924) on 31 January in Tunbridge Wells, UK. He came to England after World War II and, a member of Polytechnic Harriers, won the AAA decathlon each year 1947-9. His best was 6137 points (5857 on current tables) in 1949.

Heinz ROSENDAHL (Germany) (b. 24 Jul 1920 Langerfeld) on 27 February in Leverkusen. He was German discus champion in 1953 and father of 1972 Olympic long jump and 4x100m relay champion Heide Rosendahl and grandfather of 6m pole vaulter Danny Ecker. Pbs: DT 51.71 (1954), SP 14.62 (1948), HT 44.60 (1948), JT 60.97 (1941).

Matti SALMENKYLA (Finland) (b. 4 Oct 1930 Helsinki) on 9 February in Helsinki. The esteemed athletics journalist was Press Chief for the Local Organising Committee at the first ever IAAF World Championships in Helsinki in 1983 and acted as IAAF and AIPS Press Delegate at the 1987, 1995 and 1997 editions, and was Press Chief at the 1994 European Championships in Helsinki. He was a member of the Executive Committee of the International Sports Press Association (AIPS) from 1977 and was General Secretary 1991-2001.

Hans SCHENK (Germany) (b. 1 Jan 1936 Muldschen/Krs. Gerdauen) on 19 January in Leverkusen. At the javelin he was 7th at the

1958 Europeans and 12th at the 1964 Olympics with a pb of 78.12 (1964), and competed in 16 internationals for FRG 1956-65. He was the German javelin coach, responsible for such stars as Klaus Wolfermann and Klaus Tafelmeier.

Angelina SEPHOOA (b. 25 May 1975, née Pitso) on 22 January. She set a Lesotho marathon record at 2:40:45 in 1999 and achieved greatest success at ultramarathoning. She was one of only two women to score three consecutive victories in the Two Oceans race.

Rolf von der LAAGE (Germany) (b. 23 Aug 1932) on 14 January in Köln. The distinguished journalist and Asian athletics had covered athletics from the 1954 European Championships that he reported on for a newspaper in Aachen. Up to his death he was a member of the IAAF Press Commission. With his wife Gladys Chai he set up the photo agency ASVOM in Köln in 1979. He organised the early ASV Grand Prix meetings in Köln and wrote studies of sport in China. He also published Asian annuals and most infomative news bulletins about Asian athletics

Ian WARD (GBR) (b. 24 Feb 1929) on 8 March in Todmorden. He made 16 international appearances for Britain at pole vault 1953-60 and was AAA champion in 1956 and 1957 and 5th at the 1958 Empire Games; pb 4.20 (1960). He became a senior lecturer at Madeley College of Education and a leading coach.

William Dennis WEAVER (USA) (b. 6 Jun 1924, Joplin, Missouri) on 24 February in Ridgeway, Colorado. Dennis Weaver was a very well known actor. Starting with *The Raider* (1952) he became famous for his television roles in *Gunsmoke*, *McCloud* and *Stone* and starred in Stephen Spielberg's first film *Duel*. He was known as Billy Weaver when he was 6th in the decathlon with 6488 points (6189 on current tables) in the 1948 US Olympic Trials. He was then at the University of Oklahoma.

Teresa Wieczorek-CIEPLY (Poland) (b. 19 Oct.1937) on 8 March in Bydgoszcz. She won bronze at 4x100m in 1960 and gold at 4x100m (in a world record 43.6) and silver at 80mh in 1964 at the Olympic Games, and also won three European medals – gold at 80mh and 4x100m and bronze at 100m in 1962. She was Polish champion at 100m 1960-2 and 80mh 1961-2 and 1964-5 and set six Polish records at 11.6/11.5 for 100m (1961-2) and six at 80mh from 10.9 (1961) to 10.5 (1964, unverified world best). Other pbs: 200m 24.7 (1960), LJ 6.22 (1962), Pentathlon 4420 (1960). She was married to Olgierd Cieply (5th 1960 and 8th 1964 in the Olympics at hammer).

Jürgen SCHOCH (Germany) (b. 10 Apr 1962 Ludwigsburg) on 16 March in Kornwestheim. He competed in 11 internationals for FRG as a hurdler 1983-8, including at three European Indoor Championships at 60mh, reaching one final: 7th in 1984. He was 2nd in the German 110mh in 1983, 1984 and 1985 and ran a pb of 13.78 for 3rd in 1988. Other pbs: 100 10.56 (1982), 10.4 (1983); 60mh 7.90i (1988).

Died in 2004

Thore TILLMAN (Sweden) (b. 9 Aug 1915) on 12 August in Östersund. In 1939 he set Swedish records at 5000m (14:24.8) and 10,000m (30:42.2 to beat Edwin Wide's 1924 mark and 30:37.6); he improved his 10,000m best to 30:15.2 in 1945. He was 5th in the European 10,000m in 1938 (dnf 1946 after 2nd at 5k) and Swedish champion at 10,000m 1938-9.

Progression at 10,000m (position on world list): 1938- 31:04.0 (15), 1939- 30:37.6 (6), 1940- 30:50.4 (18), 1941- 30:28.0 (3), 1942- 30:21.4 (1942), 1944- 30:34.4 (3), 1945- 30:15.2 (4), 1946- 30:37;8 (5), 1947- 30:18.4 (3), 1948- 30:37.8 (11). pb 3000m 8:25.6 (1942).

Anne VIALLIX (France) (b. 23 Sep 1962 Gradignan) in June. She went missing and her body was found in the Alps in December. She was the World Universities CC champion in 1986 and won medals with the French team at the World Championships – bronze in 1986 and silver in 1987 when she was respectively 26th and 18th individual. Pbs: 1500m 4:19.83 (1985), 3000m 9:20.14 (1985).

DRUGS BANS

The IAAF has a longstanding history in the fight against doping and continues to take a lead in the world of sport, conducting far more tests than any other international federation. It has recently expanded its' Medical and Anti-Doping Department and recruited staff from some of the world's leading National Anti-Doping Agencies to help manage the testing programme and plans to conduct in excess of 3000 doping controls both in-competition and out-of-competition during the current year.

The following cases were reported of athletes receiving drugs bans in 2005

Suspension: Life - life ban, y = years, m = months, W = warning and disqualification, P = pending hearing

Leading athletes

Men	Name	Date
Vladimir Andreyev RUS	27 Jan	1y
Harálobos Arsoniádis GRE	10 Jun	2y
Leo Bookman USA	7 May	W
Arnaud Casquette MRI	12 Dec	6m
Sébastien Denis FRA	25 Jun	W
Hristóforos Hoídis GRE	10 Jun	2y
Jacek Kazimierowski POL	11 Jul	W
Mark Lewis-Francis GBR	5 Mar	W
Artur Osman POL	24 Apr	2y
Serhiy Pavlyuchenko UKR	30 Jul	2y
Vladyslav Piskunov UKR	8 Aug	L
Hristos Polihroníou GRE	22 Feb	2y
Khaled Chawki Wanis EGY	2 Sep	2y
Aleksandr Zyabrev RYS	18 May	2y
Women		
Mounira Al-Saleh SYR	9 Dec	2y
Vukosava Djapic SCG	30 Jun	
Suzette Lee JAM	21 Jul	W
Evelina Licenco ROM	2 Jul	2y
Gladys Lukhwareni RSA	4 Sep	2y
Natasha Mayers VIN	21 Apr	2y
Yelena Mironova RUS	10 Feb	2y
María Papadopoúlou GRE	29 Jul	2y
Lyubov Perepelova UZB	26 Apr	2y
Qin Aihua CHN	25 May	2y
Rosario Ramos VEN	19 Aug	2y
Darya Safonova RUS	10 Feb	2y
Neelam Jaswant Singh IND	7 Aug	
Sun Hongfeng CHN	12 Sep	
Sun Yingjie CHN	17 Oct	2y
Anna Tkach ISR	20 Jun	2y
Wang Lina CHN	27 Aug	

Life: Inis Viviers RSA 11 Feb

3 years: Ionela Casile ROM 28 Aug

2 years: Oksana Clerc FRA 20 Nov, Senem Eser TUR 25 Jun, Nilay Essen TUR 25 Jun, Robert Gindera POL 18 Mar, Aleksey Gneushev RUS 22 May, Edward Kgosimang RSA 5 Oct, Igor Klimenko RUS 11 Feb, Aleksandra Kokorina RUS 25 Apr, Andrey Mezhevov RUS 19 Feb, Merriam Mooki RSA 29 Sep, Niu Nana CHN 27 Aug, Darya Safanova RUS 10 Feb, Najibe Marco Salmi ALG 16 May, Christian Schmitt GER 9 Jul, Svetlana Sedunova RUS 25 Apr, Adeo Soares BRA 27 Jun, Michel Tremouille FRA 10 Sep, Vito Votoni ITA 27 May, Mariya Yenkina RUS 12 Jul, Maxwell Zungu RSA 29 Sep

1 year: Valeriy Borchin RUS 13 Mar

6 months: Ludovic Delferière FRA 4 Jun, Daniel Miszkurko POL 5 Jul

3 months: Rose-Audrey Ndje FRA 16 Jan

Public warning: Michal Bernardelli POL 6 Jul, Roberto Bertolini ITA 13 Feb, Narul Eftihah MAS 8 Jul, Galatoula Hrysovalandi GRE 18 Jun, Laïla Khouja FRA 17 Apr, Leny Yee Yi MAS 2 Jul, Cyril Maetie FRA 29 Jan, Henry Moyo MAW 6 Mar, Akpa Njoku NGR 8 Jul, Thavanesan Ramvah MAS 3 Jul, Stéphane Ruiz FRA 9 Oct, Xavier Sabourin FRA 25 Sep, Hairul bin Abu Shah MAS 31 Jul

Balco Conspiracy

Tim Montgomery USA and Chryste Gaines USA were given 2-year bans from 6.6.05.

8-year ban for Michelle Collins USA was reduced to 4 years from 16.07.04.

2006

Men		
Gergely Palágy HUN	25 Jan	2y
Women		
Ibifuro Tobin-West NGR	Feb	

Add to athletes failing drug tests in 2004

Men Name	Date	
Adrián Annus HUN	27 Aug	2y
LaMark Carter USA	15 Jul	W
Róbert Fazekas HUN	23 Aug	2y
Raul Fernández ESP	11 May	2y
Vladimir Sasimovich BLR	20 Jun	2y
Larry Wade USA	11 May	2y
Women		
Süreyya Ayhan TUR	13/25 Jul	2y
Yelena Fedoseyeva RUS	24 Jun	2y
Natalya Iosifidi RUS	23 May	2y
Irina Korzhanenko RUS	14 Aug	L
Amaia Piedra ESP	26 Jun	2y
Galina Sharova RUS	24 Jun	2y
Olga Shukina UZB	14 Aug	2y

2 years: Martin Bren CZE 25 Jun, José Luis Delgado ESP 12 Sep, Mostafa Errebbah ITA 28 Nov, Ricardo Fernández ESP 23 Jul, Klaus Liedtke GER 11 Sep, Ilya Lisigor RUS 23 Jun, Luciano Santos Mello BRA 18 May, Javier Moro Moreno ESP 21 Aug, Josef Muschinski GER 11 Sep, Daniel Otosson SWE 6 Dec, Mark Pacqué BEL 7 Nov, Ralf Prochnau GER 11 Sep.

6 months: Abdellah Daoui MAR 5 Feb, Damien Rouquet FRA 28 Nov, Lionel Saint-Amand FRA 26 Dec.

3 months: Geoffrey Bex BEL 19 Dec, David Prieto Diaz ESP 27 Jun

Public warning: Yahya Habeeb KSA 23 Jun, Alexandre Landenne BEL 19 Dec

AFRICA STILL RULES THE ROOST IN MIDDLE & LONG DISTANCE RUNNING

(But new challengers may be round the corner)

By Roberto L. Quercetani

EUROPE WAS for many years the dominant power in middle and long distance running, but for occasional yet notable interferences from several other parts of the world. The picture changed rather abruptly in the last decade of the XX century under the mounting pressure of the "African wave". By 2000 the balance of powers had shifted completely in favour of runners from the "Dark Continent".

Changes in the balance of powers are shown in the adjoining tables, which give the number of entries for each continent in the World Year lists of the Top 20 for the following events – 800, 1500, 5000, 10,000 metres and 3000m steeplechase. The years taken as reference points are: 1936, 1960, 1980, 2000 and 2005. The reason why we chose 1936 rather than 1940 is easily explained: by 1940 quite a few countries were involved in the throes of WW2 and their athletic activities were understandably at a low ebb, whereas 1936, year of the Berlin Olympics, seemed to offer a more adequate reference point.

The first five years of the new century have seen no dramatic changes, yet 2005 in particular offered signs of new possible trends for the near future. Quite revealing, in this respect, may be the fact that last year Asia excelled Africa, 7 entries to 6, for entries in the 800m Top 20 list. Such a tally was assured by athletes from South-West Asia or rather what we Europeans call the Middle East, namely Bahrain (3), Qatar (2), Saudi Arabia and Iran (one each). Out of this group there came an athlete, Rashid Ramzi, who won 800 and 1500metres for Bahrain at the World Championships in Helsinki, a double last scored in a "global" championship by Peter Snell of New Zealand at the 1964 Olympics! We are living in a fast moving and changing world and "transfers of loyalty" have something to do with such a trend. Ramzi was a Moroccan in the early years of his life and actually won the 1500metre silver medal for Morocco at the 1999 African Junior Championships. By the end of 2001 he gained Bahraini citizenship. Another middle distance ace, Youssef Saad Kamel, also representing Bahrain and no.2 in the 2005 World List for the 800m (1:43.96), was originally a Kenyan, actually the son of Billy Konchellah, who won two 800m titles at the World Championships (1987 and 1991).

Many years ago Scandinavian fans were upset when news came that Edvin Wide, at birth a Swedish language Finn, had chosen to take the Swedish nationality. He competed for "gamla Sverige" (old Sweden) in three editions of the Olympic Games, but as a sign of respect for his mother country he always abstained from taking part in the Sweden vs. Finland dual, which in the two countries concerned is always referred to simply as "The Match".

The flow of talents from Africa towards the Middle East has chiefly developed along the Kenya-to-Qatar route. The most famous example is that of Saïf Saaeed Shaheen, the former Stephen Cherono of Kenya, who won three "global" titles in the 3000m steeplechase (2003 and '05 Worlds, 2004 Olympics) after transferring allegiance to Qatar. Prior to his move, Kenya had provided the winner of the steeplechase event in eleven "global" meets (Olympics 1984-2000; Worlds 1991-2001). As everybody surmised, it took a former Kenyan to bring such a series to an end.

The demise of Europe in the middle and long distance department knows very few exceptions – Spain, which is virtually new to the medium/high ranks of the sport, has if anything shown progress vis-à-vis her former standards; and France, whose ability in using her patrimony from the "térritoires d'outre-mer" is very well known. Most other countries – Great Britain, Germany, Italy and the whole of Scandinavia, as well as the countries from the former USSR – have not only lost precious ground vis-à-vis Africa, but as often as not they seem unable to reedit their former record marks. In other words, even clock-wise the present British élite still has to reach the onetime standards of Coe and Cram. Ditto for present Italian distance runners in relation to their predecessors Cova and Antibo. Through my contacts with several European countries I have recently heard that "lack of vocations" may be one of the reasons, if not the chief reason, of such a problem. In other words, present-day youngsters from European countries seem generally unwilling to train long enough and hard enough in order to emerge in athletics. Of course, ball games in general and football in particular may offer better economic incentives. Add that even some of the best distance runners, in Europe and USA, are sometimes tempted to leave the track for more lucrative prospects in road events, particularly in the marathon, which now evolves in a "planet" of its own.

(Even apart from middle and long distance events, I wouldn't be surprised if Asia were to make the headlines more and more often in the years that lie ahead. The 2007 Worlds in Osaka and the 2008 Olympics in Beijing may act as a powerful incentive in that respect).

The balance of powers by continent in middle and long distance events

	Afr	Eur	NoAm	C&SAm	Asia	Oce
800m						
1936	-	5	15	-	-	-
1960	-	10	6	1	-	3
1980	2	13	4	-	-	1
2000	14	6	-	-	-	-
2005	6	5	2	-	7	-
1500m						
1936	-	14	5	-	-	1
1960	1	14	4	-	-	1
1980	2	14	3	-	-	1
2000	12	6	2	-	-	-
2005	8	5	2	1	2	2
5000m						
1936	-	18	1	-	1	-
1960	1	16	1	-	-	2
1980	7	10	2	-	-	1
2000	18	2	-	-	-	-
2005	16	-	1	-	2	1
10,000m						
1936	-	16	1	2	1	-
1960	-	17	1	-	-	2
1980	4	9	2	-	3	2
2000	17	2	1	-	-	-
2005	18	1	-	-	1	-
3000m St						
1936	-	16	4	-	-	-
1960	-	19	1	-	-	-
1980	5	9	5	-	1	-
2000	11	7	2	-	-	-
2005	12	4	1	-	3	-

IAAF RULE CHANGES 2006

By Robert Hersch

AT ITS 2005 Congress, held in Helsinki just before the World Championships, the IAAF approved a number of amendments to the Rules of Competition. Some of them were quite technical, dealing with specifications for such things as hammer cages and certain lines on the track.

A number of the amendments, however, will have some significance to statisticians and others who are not competition officials but who follow the sport closely. Some of the important ones are summarised below. Officials and others who need to know the precise language of the rules can, as always, order a rule book from the IAAF or download the text from www.iaaf.org.

Statistics: The rule change that will have the most obvious importance for statisticians are the lowering of the height of the Junior men's 110m hurdles from 1.067m (42 inches) to 0.995m (39 inches) (Rule 168.3)

Those who keep Masters statistics will have to deal with the lowering of the age that defines the category. Men will now become masters at 35, rather than 40. (Rule 141)

Amendments to Rules 144 and 145 provide that if an athlete is disqualified, his/her performances up to the time of the disqualification shall be invalid. However, performances accomplished in qualifying rounds of the same event remain valid. (Violation of doping rules, however, nullify all performances in the competition).

Spectators: The most significant change intended solely to enhance the effective presentation involves the competition order in the throws and horizontal jumps. Ten years ago, the IAAF adopted the procedure of re-ordering the field after the third round so that the athletes thereafter compete in the inverse order of their placings after Round 3. In the future, in major international competition, the field will again be re-ordered after Round 5 to maximise the drama of the last round. This procedure will be optional at Invitational meetings. (Rule 180.5)

Spectators at major international championships will particularly welcome one change. A sentence was added to the uniform rule (143.1) that states that athletes' vests should have the same colour on the front and back.

Also, in competitions other than major championships and cups, athletes' bibs can identify the athletes by their name, rather than an arbitrary number that appears in the programme. (Rule 143.7)

Spectators may not notice this, but the rules will now provide for an Event Presentation Manager, a senior level official whose job will be to co-ordinate all elements of the in-stadium presentation of the event. This role has always existed at major competition, but the creation of a new official position emphasises its importance to the IAAF. (Rule 124)

A potential negative for spectators, coaches and journalists is an amendment that will permit umpires to communicate apparent violations to the referee by means other than a yellow flag. They can now use technical devices (or even hand-written notes) that alert the referee, but nobody else, of a possible disqualification. (Rule 127.3)

Running Events: In an effort to provide a uniformly high standard at major championships and cups, new Rule 110(h) creates the position "International Starter" and Rule 118 adds the International Starter to International Photo Finish Judge as positions appointed by the IAAF or Area Associations.

A new note to Rule 162.3 provides that in competition under Rule 1.1(a) and (b) (Olympic Games, IAAF World Championships and Cups and Area, Regional and Group Championships), the starting commands must be given in English only.

The Track Referee was given the power to disregard the false start detection apparatus if he/she determines that it is "obviously inaccurate." (Rule 125.2)

Under amendments to Rule 165, transponder timing may now be used for all running, walking, and cross-country events not held entirely on a stadium track. New notes to Rules 261 and 262 make it clear, however, that transponder timing is not acceptable for records. Video-based timing systems are no longer recognised as official,

A new note to Rule 166.2 codifies the existing practice of departing from the heat formation tables in the World Championships and Olympic Games.

Field Events: Hammer throwers may now do what had formerly been prohibited. Under the new Rule 191.2, when the hammer touches the ground during the thrower's preliminary swings, he/she may stop and begin the throw again, assuming that no other rule (e.g., the time limit) has been violated.

An amendment to Rule 187.2 will give athletes greater latitude in using personal implements, other than the models supplied by the Organising Committee, provided that those implements are IAAF certified.

The use by throwers of weights attached to the body are now specifically prohibited (Rules 187.4(a)). Roughening the surface of the throwing circle is now specifically prohibited (Rule 187.8).

Combined Events: Rule 200.8 now provides that in the Combined Events, all of the component events shall be seeded so that athletes with similar performances in a pre-determined period shall be placed in the same heat or group.

Race Walking: The nomenclature of the race walking rules was simplified by eliminating the dichotomy between two words – caution and warning – that have the very similar meanings. The new Rule 230 replaces "warning" with "Red Card." Red cards from three different judges result in disqualification. Another change involving walking provides that three (rather than two) judges from the IAAF Panel must have officiated at an event in order for a World Record to be recognised.

Facilities and Equipment: An amendment to Rule 148 provides that all steel tapes, bars or scientific measuring apparatus must have been certified by the IAAF. An amendment to Rule 163.10 provides the same for wind gauge equipment.

An amendment to Rule 183.1 provides that the line marking the back end of the pole vault box shall appear on the surface of the landing bed. Thus, any movement of the landing pads on the sides of the box will require that the pads be repositioned.

The deletion of the former Rule 185.4 means that the sprinkling of sand is no longer an acceptable alternative to plasticine. The new 185.8 expands the width of the plasticine from 3mm to 10mm and suggests that the plasticine be a third colour, different from both the take-off board and the plasticine indicator board.

The arc marking the foul line in the javelin must now be made only of wood; metal arcs are not permitted. (Rule 182.9)

National Affiliation: The Congress dealt with the transfer of allegiance issue that has generated some controversy in recent years. Under the new Rule 5.2, athletes may not represent their new country in major international competition until three years after the acquisition of their new citizenship (or one year if the athlete's former country agrees. It should be noted, however, that the rule applies only to athletes who have previously represented the original country in certain major international competitions. Thus, the new rule does nothing to slow down the inter-federation recruiting of Youth and Junior athletes who have not previously competed for their country.

THE OLYMPIC GAMES OF 100 YEARS AGO

By Bob Phillips

"INTERCALATED" IS an uncommon word in the English language and appears to have had only one particular usage – as a description of the 1906 Olympic Games. According to the Concise Oxford Dictionary, "intercalated" means "interim" or "interposed", and presumably the Edwardian ear preferred the more formal-sounding term to any other. Those Games of a century ago were devised by the Greeks to celebrate the 10th anniversary of the establishment of the modern Olympic era and were intended to be held every four years thereafter, but economic and political circumstances soon put an end to that ambition.

Whatever the prefix, the pity is that the 1906 Olympics have rarely been given their full due, and instead have been regarded largely as unofficial and have frequently been ignored in historical perspective. Yet there is every good reason to believe that it was these Games which were the ones to gave credibility to Baron de Coubertin's Olympic ideal, rather than those of London and Stockholm which immediately followed. Certainly, neither in Athens in 1896, nor in Paris in 1900, nor in St Louis in 1904 were the Games in any way universally representative – and in the case of the latter two venues they were little more than disjointed and characterless sideshows. The eminent British coach of the inter-war years, F.A.M. Webster, was to write of the 1906 Games that "they formed by far the most important gathering of athletes which had ever up to that time been brought together".

The United States and Great Britain were much the dominant athletic nations in 1906, reflecting their Worldwide importance by every criterion, and both countries for the first time paid sufficient respect to the challenge of an Olympic Games to select their representatives on merit. The athletics events in Athens took place from 25 April to 1 May, and so the US contingent of 31 which set out on the 16-day journey to Greece included the holders of eight AAU titles from the previous year. Of the 20 British athletes, seven were from Oxford or Cambridge Universities and were therefore well accustomed to a competitive season which reached its peak early in the year. One of the three Irishmen in the team, Jack Daly, had placed 4th in the previous month's International Cross-Country Championship behind three Englishmen who were not track practitioners of note or marathon aspirants and so were not considered for the team to go to Athens.

Daly was also among those who had taken part in the 1904 Games, where he had finished 2nd in the steeplechase. His conqueror on that occasion (and also winner of the 800 and 1500m) had been James Lighbody, who was again a member of the immensely strong US team, as also were three other triple champions from St Louis – Archie Hahn, at 60, 100 and 200m; Harry Hillman at 400m, 200m hurdles and 400m hurdles, and Ray Ewry for the standing versions of the high jump, long jump and triple jump. Also title-winners at those US-dominated Games had been Myer Prinstein (long jump and triple jump), Martin Sheridan (discus), Paul Pilgrim and Howard Valentine (both in the four miles team race), and to set against this formidable array Britain's most noted challengers were Daly's versatile fellow-Irishmen, Con Leahy and Peter O'Connor. Among those few whose absence from Athens could have been truly regretted were the great American throwers, Ralph Rose and Wesley Coe, and the leading English milers, AAA champion George Butterfield and Inter-Varsity winner Charles Hamilton-Henderson.

It would be another six years before the establishment of the IAAF and official recognition of World records, but Lightbody, Ewry, Sheridan, O'Connor and the inaugural Olympic triple-jump champion, James Connolly, were current holders competing in Athens, together with a German-domiciled South African, Vincent Duncker, at 100m; the French pole-vaulter, Fernand Gonder; and the Swedish javelin-thrower, Eric Lemming. In all there were at least 235 athletes from 18 nations taking part, as follows (numbers of athletes in brackets): Australia (3), Austria (10), Belgium (2), Bohemia (5), Canada (3), Denmark (3), Egypt (1), Finland (3), France (12), Germany (14), Great Britain (20), Greece (88), Hungary (12), Italy (6), Norway (8), Sweden (13), Turkey (1), USA (31). There were certainly 30 Greeks who ran in the marathon and the host team may have been more than 100-strong.

As expected, the USA was by far the most successful nation with 23 medals, followed by Great Britain (nine) and Greece (seven), but of assuredly greater significance was the fact that eight other countries also won medals. Americans took the 100m, 400m, 800m and 1500m, 110m hurdles, long jump, standing high jump, standing long jump, shot, discus and 1500m walk; Britons won the five miles, high jump and triple jump; Swedes won the javelin and pentathlon. The five remaining titles among the 21 events went to Canada (marathon), Hungary (3000m walk), France (pole vault), Finland (Greek-style discus) and Greece (stone throw). Had there been a chosen "Athlete of the Games", then the chief candidates would have been American double winners Paul Pilgrim (400m and 800m), Ray Ewry (standing jumps) and Martin Sheridan (shot and discus), or perhaps Sweden's Eric Lemming, who set the only World record of the meeting, in the javelin. Large and enthusiastic crowds of more than 60,000 a day attended throughout and the organisation was generally regarded as excellent.

On the opening day (25 April) there were 28 starters in the five miles, which was won by a British army officer, Henry Hawtrey, from Johan Svanberg, of Sweden, and Britain would have had a second medal but for the disqualification of the Irishman, Daly, for obstruction. Quite why a distance of five miles was chosen and not 5000m, which had been contested at the 1900 Paris Olympics, must remain a matter of conjecture. The pole vault was won by Gonder, the World record-holder, with the AAU champion, Edward Glover, only 3rd, and it was no surprise in the discus that another World record-holder, Sheridan, was the first US champion of the Games, as he had also won in 1904 (and would so again in 1908). An historic Olympic medal for Finland was earned in 3rd place by Venne Järvinen, who would become father to an Olympic champion and World record-holder in the javelin (Matti) and a double silver-medallist in the decathlon (Akilles).

Four Americans, including Hahn, qualified for the 100m final, and another four, including Lightbody, reached the 800m final, but there were considerable British hopes in the latter event as Wyndham Halswelle, the AAA champion at 440 yards, and Reginald Crabbe, who had run 1:55.8 for 880 yards at the Cambridge University Sports the previous month, had both got through. Even allowing for athletes conserving their energies, the fastest 100m time of 11.2 and the fastest 800m of 2:05.4 seemed clear indication of the slowness and tightness of the traditionally-built Panathenaikon Stadium track with its 333.33-metre circumference of soft cinders and severe turns.

The next day's javelin final (26 April) was a totally one-sided contest which Eric Lemming, of Sweden, could have won easily with his first throw of 49.66. All credit to him, therefore, for persevering and beating his own World record of almost three years previously by 11cm with 53.90. Between 1899 and 1911 Lemming was to make 13 successive improvements to the World record, from 49.32 to 58.27, and after briefly losing the record to a Finn in 1912 he won it back later in the year with the first 62m-plus throw. He was also Olympic champion in 1908 and 1912. It seems odd that the javelin was the only event decided that day, but there remain differing versions of the timetable of events.

By contrast, the third day of competition (27 April) was a full one, featuring the finals of the 100m, long jump and standing long jump, shot and stone throw, and the completion of the pentathlon. For Hahn, triple winner in St Louis, there was only the one sprint event to contest in Athens, and the official results show that he won by one-tenth (11.2) from another American, Fay Moulton, though a photo of the finish suggests the margin was rather greater than that. Two months later a US absentee from Athens, Daniel Kelly, ran 100 yards in 9.6, which was eventually recognised as the first official World record. Less convincingly in August the man who finished last in the Athens 100m, Knut Lindberg, of Sweden, was twice credited with unratified World records of 10.8, though he does have the distinction of having run in an Olympic track final and won a silver medal in a field event (the javelin the day before). John Morton, AAA 100 yards champion every year from 1904 to 1907, would certainly have been a sprint medal contender, had he been in Athens.

The long jump had promised to be the outstanding event of the Games, bringing together the Irishman, Peter O'Connor, and the American, Myer Prinstein, who were the World's foremost exponents of the event. O'Connor had set five World records during 1900-01, culminating in 24ft 11¾in (7.61), and had been AAA champion every year from 1902 to 1905. Prinstein, the defending Olympic champion, had held the previous World record at 24-7¼ (7.50) and had been three times AAU title-winner. As it happens, O'Connor had persistent problems with his run-up and Prinstein won with his opening leap of 7.20. All 27 competitors each took three jumps and only the leading three were permitted to continue, with O'Connor placing 2nd and the AAU champion, Hugo Friend, 3rd.

It would be a mistake to assume that the standing long jump was a lesser event because it actually attracted three more competitors than the conventional version, though none of the leaders in either attempted both. Ray Ewry the defending champion and World record-holder, led a US clean-sweep with ease and the other medals went to the enviably athletic weightsman, Sheridan, and to Lawson Robertson, who had run in the 100m final and would gain fame in later years as a renowned coach. Sheridan won his second gold medal of the Games the same day in the shot, though he benefited from the absence of both the defending champion and former World-record-holder, Ralph Rose, and the man who had beaten Rose's record at the AAU Championships the previous August, Wesley Coe.

The pentathlon was based on the Ancient Greek model, with the standing long jump, discus and javelin on the first day and a sprint of 192 metres (the original distance) and Greco-Roman wrestling on the second day. Only the leading six competitors took part in all five events and the winner was Hjalmar Mellander, of Sweden, with the javelin champion, Lemming, in 3rd place, but among the intrepid Americans who took up the challenge was Lawson Robertson, thus completing his ninth individual effort of the Games so far and finishing a valiant 5th overall. Equally tireless was Martin Sheridan, tackling his fifth event (including a brief appearance in the pentathlon) and placing 2nd to the Greek, Nikolaos Georgantas, in the 6.4kg stone throw.

The fourth day (29 April) was given over to no more than two finals, at 400m and 1500m. Only the winners of each of six heats two days previously had advanced to the 400 final, together with two others from a repechage, comprising in all four Americans, two Britons, a Frenchman and an Australian. Wyndham Halswelle had won the previous year's AAA 440 yards in 50.8 and the best of the Americans seemed obviously to be Harry Hillman, the 1904 Olympic champion in 49.2, but a time of fully four seconds slower proved sufficient to win the title in a race in which dexterity on a crowded track counted as much as sheer speed. The unexpected new champion was Paul Pilgrim, who had run in the 1904 final but had paid his own way to Athens after not being included in the US team, while Halswelle took 2nd place and the Australian, Nigel Barker, won bronze, as he had at 100m.

Henry Hawtrey, the five miles winner on the opening day, had been highly thought of for the 1500m but had failed to finish his heat because of an ankle injury. This left James Lightbody as clear favourite and the Irish-born Scotsman, John McGough, who had given the great Alfred Shrubb and then George Butterfield close races in successive AAA mile finals, as the nearest challenger. So it proved, with Lightbody winning by 0.6sec in a time which was a respectable seven seconds outside his World record. The 1500m was still then a rarely run event and performances in no way compared with the best for one mile by an amateur (4:15.6 by Tommy Conneff, of the USA, in 1895). Lightbody's time in winning the 1905 AAU mile had been the slowest since 1878 – 4:48.8!

Lightbody took to the track again the next day (30 April) for the 800m final but lost by one-tenth to Paul Pilgrim (2:01.5), who thus became a triple Olympic champion (including 1904) without ever having won an American title. Halswelle, Olympic champion-to-be at 400m in 1908, and Crabbe, a future Bishop of Mombasa, were 3rd and 4th for Britain. Lightbody had run 1:56.0 when winning at the St Louis Olympics, but the World record for this event had stood at 1:53.4 for the longer 880 yards (804.67m) by Charles Kilpatrick in the celebrated New York AC-v-London AC match of 1895, and when Mel Sheppard won the AAU half-mile title later in 1906 in 1:55.4 it made the Olympic race seem rather ordinary. In Pilgrim's defence it should be said that his time was undoubtedly worth several seconds faster, allowing for the difficult track conditions.

The high jump and triple jump provided a double for the Irish. Con Leahy, one of seven brothers who were all reputable athletes, was the AAA champion and among those he beat was the AAU title-holder, Herbert Kerrigan, in equal 3rd place. Leahy also came close to winning the triple jump, leading until Peter O'Connor superceded him in the final round. The World record-holder and Olympic champion from 1896, James Connolly, also competed but was very much out of sorts, registering no valid performance, and the best of the Americans was another with an Irish-sounding name, Thomas Cronan, in 3rd place. Myer Prinstein, winner at St Louis, had two no-jumps and was surprisingly only 11th.

Walking events made their first Olympic appearance in the sort of controversial circumstances which were to come to characterise the discipline – or perhaps one should say in this instance 'lack of discipline'. The event was won by Robert Wilkinson for Great Britain from Austria's Eugen Spiegler, but both were disqualified after crossing the finish-line. An American, George Bonhag, who had placed 4th in the five miles and 6th at 1500m and then taken some impromptu race-walk coaching from the Canadian specialist, Don Linden, was next to finish, but he, too, met with the displeasure of two of the four judges. It then seemed logical that the generous-spirited Linden, in 4th place, would be elevated to the title. Not so – as a compromise a re-walk was ordered for the following day, only for the officials to renege on the deal and allow Bonhag to keep the title despite failing to put in an appearance !

Nor did Bonhag and – more surprisingly – Linden line up for he 3000m walk on that final day of competition (1 May), and Wilkinson and Spiegler duly finished 1st and 2nd again, with György Sztantics, of Hungary, little more than two seconds behind in a desperately close race. Yet once more the leading two were disqualified, and so the Hungarian was awarded the title. For the marathon the Canadian 10 miles champion, Billy Sherring, had arrived in Athens two months before and his preparations paid off with victory by almost seven minutes from the Swede, Johan Svanberg, winning his second silver medal. A famous photograph shows Sherring wearing a jaunty fedora hat as he nears the finish, excitedly accompanied by the uniformed Prince Giorgios of Greece. The best of His Highness's numerous compatriots in the race arrived more than 18 minutes later in 5th position and among nine non-finishers was a lone Italian named Dorando Pietri. Sherring was presented with $7000 by civic authorities when he returned home to Hamilton, Ontario, and never competed again.

The fact that the Greeks were still using the Julian Calendar, rather than the Gregorian Calendar which was 13 days in advance, has no doubt contributed to the confusion regarding the precise dates of some of the finals. None of this matters very much, except that it seems certain that the 3000m walk and the marathon could not have taken place on the same day, and the explanation is simple. In 2nd place in the walk was Hermann Müller, of Germany, which must have come as full compensation for his experience in the five miles running race, in which he had been lapped and ordered off the track. The indefatigable Herr Müller was also 9th in the marathon and it is somewhat unlikely that he would have contested a walking race the same day.

In the 110m hurdles Hugo Friend, the AAU champion (as he was in the long jump), was beaten into 4th place and the title went to another American, Robert Leavitt, who was never to be an AAU winner. Ray Ewry won a further gold to add to his mounting collection (which would reach 10 in all by 1908) in the standing high jump, in which the ubiquitous Martin Sheridan and Lawson Robertson shared 2nd place, and the Games ended ignominiously for the hosts with the Finn, Venne Järvinen, beating the local heroes in the Greek-style discus throw just as the American, Robert Garrett, had done in 1896.

It had been a memorable Olympic celebration. The vast majority of titles had been won by some of the finest athletes of their generation – Hahn, Pilgrim, Lightbody, Hawtrey, Sherring, Leahy, Gonder, Prinstein, O'Connor, Ewry, Sheridan, Järvinen, Lemming. Two years later, at the London Games, Halswelle, Ewry, Sheridan and Lemming would win further honours.

Even when the Games returned at last to Athens in 2004 the prestigious French sports daily, *L'Equipe*, continued to give short shrift to the celebration of 1906, devoting to it only two pages of a lavish 570-page Olympic history. In Athens 100 years ago the Olympic Games came to maturity and deserve better remembrance than that.

Olympic champions in 1906 and the current World record-holders

100m: 11.2 Archie Hahn (USA). WR – 10.8 Walter Tewkesbury (USA) 1900, Carl Ljung (Sweden) 1900, Eric Frick (Sweden) 1903, Vincent Duncker (South Africa/Germany) 1905.
400m: 53.2 Paul Pilgrim (USA). WR – 47.8 Maxey Long (USA) 1900.
800m: 2:01.5 Paul Pilgrim (USA). WR – 1:53.4y Charles Kilpatrick (USA) 1895.
1500m: 4:12.0 James Lightbody (USA). WR – 4:05.4 Lightbody 1904.
5 miles: 26:11.8 Henry Hawtrey (Great Britain). WR – 24:33.4 Alfred Shrubb (Great Britain) 1904.
Marathon: (41.860km): 2:51:23.6 Billy Sherring (Canada).
110m hurdles: 16.2 Robert Leavitt (USA). WR – 15.0y Thaddeus Shideler (USA) 1904.
High jump: 1.775 Con Leahy (Great Britain). WR – 6ft 5 5/8in (1.97) Mike Sweeney (USA) 1895.
Pole vault: 3.50 Fernand Gonder (France). WR – 3.74 Gonder 1905.
Long jump: 7.20 Myer Prinstein (USA). WR – 24ft 11¾ (7.61) Peter O'Connor (Great Britain) 1901.
Triple jump: 14.075 Peter O'Connor (Great Britain). WR – 49ft 0¼in (14.94) James Connolly (USA) 1896.
Standing high jump: 1.56 Ray Ewry (USA). WR – 5ft 5¼in (1.66) Ewry 1901.
Standing long jump: 3.30 Ray Ewry (USA). WR – 11ft 4 7/8in (3.47) Ewry 1904.
Shot: 12.325 Martin Sheridan (USA). WR – 49ft 6in (15.08) Wesley Coe (USA) 1905.
Discus: 41.46 Martin Sheridan (USA). WR – 143ft 4in (43.69) Sheridan 1905.
Discus (Greek style): 35.17 Venne Järvinen (Finland).
Javelin: 53.90 Eric Lemming (Sweden). WR – 53.79 Lemming 1903.
Stone throw (6.4kg): Nikolaos Georgantas (Greece).
1500m walk: 7:12.6 George Bonhag (USA). WR (1 mile) – 6:26.0 George Larner (Great Britain) 1904.
3000m walk: 15:13.2 György Sztantics (Hungary). WR – 12:17.0 (estimated time in two miles event) George Larner (Great Britain) 1904.
Pentathlon (standing long jump, discus, javelin, 192m, wrestling): Hjalmar Mellander (Sweden).
Note: times are given in decimals for convenience sake, rather than in the form of fractions, as was the widespread practice at the time.

NOTES FROM THE EDITOR

The European Challenge

STUDY OF world lists over many years shows quite clearly that European standards have been declining for many years, This is most noticeable, as I have demonstrated in previous Annuals, in distance running events where comfortable Western lifestyles and severe decline in physical activity by children simply do not match those of the "hungry fighters" from Africa. The European AA are addressing this from a number of angles and have proposed making the European Championships a biennial affair (as they were in 1969 and 1971) , but clearly this will pose many problems given three global championships in each four-year cycle.

In my view, factors that need to be taken into account include the over-reliance on individuals and on record breaking. For sure stars will bring in the crowds in any sport, but with such a developed sport and its worldwide spread over the past fifty years, building meetings on world-record breaking attempts is doomed to failure far too often. World records are increasingly rare commodities and need to be treasured all the more when they happen.

I would like to see much more emphasis on team competition. We moved substantially away from the international dual meetings that were such a stable for the sport in the 1950s and 1960s to the Grand Prix type meetings with the emphasis on individual professional athletes. But many people get bored with seeing the same groupe of athletes going from meeting to meeting – unless of course there can be real meaning in head-to-head clashes. And if we look at other sports, we will soon see that for most support of a team is an essential prerequisite.

Many of those old dual meetings lacked sufficient interest for general fans, but I believe that, for instance, an annual Britain v France or Germany (or both) match could be hugely popular. People who know little about the sport can be attracted to battles between old rivals, particularly at an international level. Of course, the matches need to be meaningful and have to become a 'must-do' meeting for all the big names. It would take years to build such a tradition. But there is a shining example in the annual Finland v Sweden matches, attracting sell-out crowds for year after year and a meeting in which all the top stars love to compete.

The series of USA - Russia matches in the late 1950s and early 1960s were also a huge success, attracting vast crowds. But we must avoid the thinking which has seen meetings falsely, to my mind, presented as internationals when they are contested by teams far from representative of the nations concerned and containing only a small proportion of the full programme of events. For sure some meetings can be snappy two-three hour Grand Prix style events, but let us not be frightened of events which take much longer, because the international matches that I would love to see back on the calendar must be staged for the whole range of events and thus take much longer, probably over two days. But then there are plenty of examples in the wide range of sports of events hugely supported by the public that are day-long and taking several days. We are not all constrained by football mania.

Age Problems

THE IAAF introduced World Youth Championships, to be held on a biennial basis, in 1999. They have provided the first taste of top international competition for many athletes and the fourth such Championships were staged successfully in Marrakech this year. There were many exceptional performances despite extremely high temperatures and tough weather conditions.

A most disturbing feature, however, is the possibility that two of the titles were won by athletes who might be significantly older than that allowed for this event.

This is not a new problem as there have been rumours for years of athletes running in Junior Championships who were ineligible due to their age. In some cases there may well have been deliberate fraud involved. But such is very difficult to prove, because in some parts of the world, particularly in Africa, there is no universal birth registration. Thus, how can one be sure how old an athlete is? In some cases they simply do not know their date of birth – and do not have one until it is provided (invented?) for a passport. There is also no doubt that many athletes display amazing ability at very early ages. This is particularly true for the distance runners who emanate from the Rift Valley region of East Africa. Young men and women from the highlands have made a huge impact on world athletics, not least because the harnessing of their abilities and life-style enables them, with dedicated hard work, to break out of their environment and earn a lot of money. The "hungry fighters"...

Recently oil-rich Middle Eastern nations have recruited many East Africans. Qatar was probably the first to do this, attracting youngsters from Somalia. There has been a huge escalation in this, and now athletes who have already reached a high standard are attracted to change nationality for high reward. This has been the subject of much international discussion and the IAAF has tightened its rules regarding change of nationality. While some might look askance at such a practice, it must be pointed out that such is the depth of talent in Kenya, for instance, that athletes who might never have had the chance to make the national team are being given opportunities to compete on a world stage.

But along with this recruitment has come changes of names and, it seems, the issuing of dates of birth that may well be seriously wrong. This was shown when Gregory Konchellah changed nationality to Bahrain and his name to Youssef Saad Kamel. He was entered by Bahrain at the Olympic Games with a date of birth of 29 March 1987, thus making him 17 at the time and eligible for junior championships in 2005 and 2006. However the athlete himself insisted that he was much older and we had shown him our lists as born in 1983 when he first appeared in world lists in 2003 as a Kenyan.

So, to look at those World Youth champions for Bahrain in 2005: Tareq Mubarak Taher won the 2000m steeplechase title in 5:23.95 for a world youth record. He was entered with documents showing his date of birth as 1 February 1989. Yet we believe that he was formerly Denis Kipkirui Keter of Kenya who was prominent in world lists in 2002 (5000m 13:32.71) and 2003 (3000m 7:48.82 and 5000m 13:30.52) with a date of birth of 24 March 1984. Surely he was not just 13 when he ran 13:32.17! Bilal Mansour Ali, entered as born on 17 October 1988, won the 2005 World Youth 1500m title in 3:36.98, well ahead of the runner-up, another Bahrain athlete, Bader Khalil Ibrahim, who ran 3:43.70. But Mansour Ali was formerly John Yego who was a successfully cross-country runner in Kenya from 2002 and again surely much older than his new date of birth would indicate. Indeed reports from Kenya stated that he was "approaching 25 years". Bader Khalil Ibrahim (above) was formerly Tesfu Bikila of Ethiopia who won the African JUNIOR title in 2003. He was then thought to have been born in 1986, but now entered as born in 1989. I understand that the Asian AA have refused to recognise the above marks as Asian junior records.

There are other examples, and as mentioned before, we cannot be sure of dates of birth in all too many cases. There also may be problems with different calendars and solutions are far from easy given the lack of reliable data, but surely governing bodies need to be resolute to act firmly in this matter because otherwise the credibility of events such as the World Youth and World Junior Championships is in doubt.

Kenenisa Bekele

In ATHLETICS 2005 I listed the successive cross-country races won by Kenenisa Bekele. The last two races in that list (on page 116) should have been dated in 2005 and we have found one additional race:

6 Apr 03 Alí dei Sardi

Now Bekele has said that he may race no more on the country, so to complete that list – now 25 successive wins – add:

14 Jan 06 Edinburgh
1 Apr 06 Fukuoka – World SC
2 Apr 06 Fukuoka – World LC

Javelin Breakthrough

Christina Obergföll's amazing breakthrough at the 2005 World Championships when she improved her personal best for the javelin from 64.59 to a European record 70.03 struck me at the time as surely being one of the most amazing improvements to have happened at a major championship. But then the javelin is just the sort of event when suddenly everything can come together and the thrower can "hit it' just right. And there were two previous improvements that were even greater:

Anna Pazera won the gold medal for Australia at the 1958 Commonwealth Games with a world record 57.40 from a previous best of 50.60 in 1956 (when she was Anna Wojtasek of Poland).

Charles Clover won the gold medal for England at the 1974 Commonwealth Games with a British and Commonwealth record (also a European Junior record) of 84.92 from a previous best of 77.68 .

World Athletics Final

The IAAF introduced the World Athletics Final in 2003 and it was held then and in the next two years in Monaco, the venue switching to Stuttgart from 2006. The move should surely attract larger crowds than attended in the Stade Louis II in Monaco. While such an end-of-season event will always suffer from many athletes being tired from their competitive efforts throughout the year, usually peaking for the Worlds, Olympics , Europeans etc., there can be little doubt that the prize money on offer (from $30,000 for winners) has improved the standards previously seen in Grand Prix Finals.

Allen Johnson (110m hurdles) is the only athlete to have won at all three WAF events to date. The athletes to have won most IAAF Grand Prix titles (1985-2002) were:

Men

5 Mike Conley TJ 1986-94
5 Lars Riedel GER 1991-9
5 Jan Zelezny CZE 1991-2001
4 Noureddine Morceli ALG 1500m/1M 1990-4
4 Hicham El Guerrouj MAR 1996-2002
4 Sergey Bubka USSR/UKR PV 1985-1993

Women

7 Merlene Ottey JAM 100m (5), 200m (2) 1987-96
5 Sonia O'Sullivan IRL 3000m/5000m 1992-2000
5 Marion Jones USA 100m (3), 200m (1), LJ (1) 1997-2002
4 Ana Fidelia Quirot CUB 1987-97
4 Maria Mutola MOZ 800m 1993-2001 (and WAF 2003)
4 Ilke Wyludda GDR/GER 1990-6

Note that events usually staged every other years, although middle distances nearly every year.

Facts from the Lists

I referred in my Introduction to the way that standards in world athletics have generally remained fairly constant over the past couple of decades, but that there have been many changes within that framework. A study of the trends shows many interesting developments. Here are a few more observations:

Every year I examine the standards to which we publish performances in Athletics International and which form the base for list compilation. If there are large increases on depth of marks then I cut some of the lower marks – not going beyond 200 deep. Thus in the marathon (an event which has shown improving depth consistently over the years) I cut the men's lists at 2:13:07 and the women's at 2:36:44 in 2004, and at 2:13:20 and 2:36:20 in 2005.

The **marathon** is an event at which many changes are made each year to all-time lists, but there were three events for which no changes were needed in 2005 for the world top 50s published in this Annual: men's 800 metres and women's long jump and discus. Indeed for the last there were no changes in the top 100. And for three events there was only one change in the top 50s: men's decathlon and women's 800m and shot.

The drop in **men's 800m** standards in 2005 was particularly noticeable. For much of the year it even looked as though there would be no sub-1:44 time – until Wilfred Bungei ran 1:43.70 in Rieti at the end of August, followed two days later by Youssef Saad Kamel 1:43.96 at Rovereto. But just two such marks was a far cry from the record of 44 performances by 15 men in 1996. The world record was first taken under 1:44 by the South-African born Italian Marcelo Fiasconaro with 1:43.7 at Milano in 1973 and after Sebastian Coe had taken the world record down to 1:41.71 in 1981 there was another great year for the event in 1984 when Joaquim Cruz (1:41.7) led 10 men to run 23 performances under 1:44.

The decline in athletics in the developed world is illustrated by the sad decline in the **multi-events**. 125 men achieved our standard of 7400 points in 2005 (with 95 over 7500). Back in 1984, when the current scoring tables were introduced there 181 men over 7500 points. From that figure the number over 7500 dropped to 151, 140, 135 and 142 in the years 1985-8 and we lowered our standard of 7500 points to 7450, although the 100th best man scored 7702 points, a record figure almost matched by 7701 in 1996. By then, however, we had lowered our standard to 7400, achieved by 174 men that year. Since then there has been a pretty steady decline, with the 100th best mark in 2005 of 7490 being much the lowest with the current tables. The story is not quite so drastic in the women's heptathlon, but again numbers of class performers have dropped with 144 women over 5450 points compared to 180 in 2000, However, the 100th best mark of 5650 in 2005 is actually better than in a few recent years although below the peaks of 5701, 5741 and 5703 achieved in 1987, 1988 and 1990.

In contrast the 'new' women's events are increasingly popular. The **3000m steeplechase** had lagged behind, but now seems to be catching on as several athletes with top-class credentials on the flat at events from 1500m to 5000m, such as Yelena Zadorozhnaya and Wioletta Janowska in 2005, are now trying the event. So the world 100th best has improved from 10:23.76 in 2003 to 10:18.55 in 2004 and 10:13.00. Nonetheless there is still some way to go, as the gap between 10th (9:35.51) and 100th best in 2005 was 37.49 secs compared to 23.94 secs in the men's event. The world record of 9:01.59 by Gulnara Samitova in 2004 is undoubtedly an excellent one, as might be expected from an athlete who is world-class on the flat, but even though Dorcus Inzikuru had a terrific season in 2005 her best of 9:15.04 was much slower. Even if one allowed as much as a 40 second differential between flat and steeplechase times it is fascinating to speculate what world-class runners such as those towards the top of the flat 3000m lists and who have also shown the ability to cope with the changing rhythms and obstacles of cross-country courses, for instance Paula Radcliffe, the Dibaba sisters and Edith Masai could do for steeplechase. Some might not be able to handle hurdling technique – we saw how Zadorozhnaya struggled in 2005 – but times around 9 minutes would surely be on. And just think what Wang Junxia, with her fantastic 8:06.11 3000m world record in 1993, or other Chinese runners of that generation, might have done!

Note that the International Olympic Committee has accepted the addition of the women's 3000m steeplechase to the Olympic programme from 2008.

For the first time the world **hammer** 100th best mark for women did not increase in 2005 (63.14 to 63.73 in 2004) which might indicate that the event is settling down at these levels, but, on the other hand, the 10th best rose from a record 72.57 in 2004 to 73.08 in 2005. The hammer is now a far more popular event for women than shot and discus, making it all the more extraordinary that is was not until 1998 that it was added to the international programme.

Although Yelena Isinbayeva continues to take **women's pole vaulting** to new levels, passing the 5m barrier in 2005, the 10th best has stuck 4.60m each year 2002-06, but standards in depth continue to rise with the number of women clearing 4.05 or higher growing as follows: 1997- 30, 1998- 54, 1999- 78, 2000- 106, 2001- 114, 2002- 139, 2003- 151, 2004- 179, 2005- 213.

Longevity

Athletes who maintain world-class form over many years are the subject of special admiration. One example in 2005 was that Pat Manson pole vaulted over 18ft (5.48m) over the 20th successive year. It was 19 years (1987-2005) over 5.50m as he had a best of 5.49 in 1986. The previous best was 18 years by Earl Bell 1975-92 (all but one over 5.50). Jeff Hartwig is the current master of the event at the highest level, clearing 5.85 indoors in 2006 at the age of 38, but he has fewer years at the top as he did not jump over 18ft or 5.50 until 1992, when he was 25.

Kip Janvrin smashed the world over-40 masters record as his 7525 points to win the World Masters title in San Sebastián in 2005 added 883 to the pre-season record. He graduated from Simpson College in Missouri in 1988 and this year the Simpson Twilight Open has been renamed the Kip Janvrin Open in his honour. He has a world record 78 decathlon scores over 7000 points, with a US record 26 scores over 8000 topped by 8462 for the USA v Germany in 1996. He was won the Drake Relays decathlon a record 15 times. He has been a part of the coaching staff at Central Missouri State since 1988 and co-head coach for the past 11 years.

In ATHLETICS 2004 I featured the career of Maria Mutola. To the end of March 2006 she has now run 179 races at 800m in under two minutes and her ability to sustain top world-class form over a long period is shown by her 12 successive wins at the Weltklasse in Zürich 1993-2004 and her 13 successive at the Steve Prefontaine Classic in Eugene 1993-2005. Her Zürich run came to an end with 4th place in 2005, but her hold on the World Indoor title remained as she had a record eighth win at the event in 2006 (compared to the next best of five titles by Iván Pedroso at long jump and Stefka Kostadinova at high jump.

In ATHLETICS 2005 I noted four athletes who had been ranked in the world top 100 for 20 successive years: Merlene Ottey (25 at 100m), Igor Astapkovich (22 HT), Mick Hill (20 JT) and Anna Romanova (20 W SP), but all these missed the 2005 lists.

I also listed six athletes who had missed just one year from 1985 and of these three remain: Jan Zelezny JT 1984-97, 1999-2005 (including 19 years in the top ten)); Irina Yatchenko DT 1985-93, 1995-2005 (10 in top 10) and Olga Chernyavskaya DT 1985-86, 1998-2005 (10 in top 10).

WORLD LISTS 1956

As I mentioned in the Introduction, 1956 was the first year that I became engrossed by world athletics statistics. It was an era in which there were great advances in standards as European nations recovered from the years of austerity following World War II and the boom in living standards in the USA continued. It was also the start of the spread of the sport to embraces athletes all over the world. Here are the top sixes of 1956 for events on the international programme.

! = world record (lots of them this year)

100 YARDS

9.3!	Leamon King USA	1	Fresno	12 May
9.3!	David Sime USA	1	Raleigh	19 May
9.4	Bobby Morrow USA	1	Melbourne	4 Jan
9.4	Ed Waters USA	1	Baltimore	12 May
9.4	Ken Kave USA	2	Baltimore	12 May
	9.3w	1	Lincoln Un	14 Apr
9.2w	Bobby Whilden USA	1	Fayetteville	12 May
9.3w	Thane Baker USA	1	Columbus	12 Apr

10th best 9.5, 99 to 9.7

100 METRES

10.1!	Willie Williams USA	1	Berlin	3 Aug
10.1!	Ira Murchison USA	1	Berlin	4 Aug
10.1!	Leamon King USA	1	Berlin	5 Aug
10.2	Bobby Morrow USA	1	Houston	19 May
10.2	Thane Baker USA	2	Los Angeles	29 Jun
10.2	David Sime USA	1	New Orleans	30 Dec

10th best 10.3, 100th 10.6

200 METRES (* 220y less 0.1 sec.)

20.6*	Thane Baker USA	1	Riverside	9 Jun
20.6	Bobby Morrow USA	1	Berkeley	16 Jun
20.6	Andrew Stanfield USA	2	Bakersfield	23 Jun
20.7	Theodius Bush USA	3	Bakersfield	23 Jun
20.9	Manfred Germar GER	1	Berlin	18 Aug
20.9w	Vilem Mándlík TCH	1	Ostrava	25 Aug

10th best 21.5, 100th 21.5

Half turn

20.7	Ardalion Ignatyev URS	1	Kiev	14 Jul
20.7	Karl-Friedrich Haas FRG	1	Köln	14 Oct

220 YARDS (Straight Track)

20.0!	David Sime USA	1	Sanger	9 Jun
20.1	Michael Agostini TRI	1	Bakersfield	17 Mar
20.4	Art Pollard USA	1	University Pk	19 May
20.6	James Lea USA	2	Bakersfield	17 Ma
20.4w	Bobby Whilden USA	1	Dallas	27 Apr

400 METRES (* 440y less 0.3 sec.)

45.2!	Louis Jones USA	1	Los Angeles	30 Jun
45.5*	James Lea USA	1	Modesto	26 May
45.8	Thomas Courtney USA	1	Bakersfield	23 Jun
45.9*	J.W. Masburn USA	2	Modesto	26 May
46.1	Charles Jenkins USA	3	Los Angeles	30 Jun
46.1	Voitto Hellsten FIN	2	Melbourne	29 Nov

10th best 46.4, 100th 47.9

800 METRES (* 880y less 0.7 sec.)

1:46.4	Thomas Courtney USA	1	Los Angeles	30 Jun
1:46.4	Auden Boysen NOR	1	Oslo	30 Jul
1:46.7	Arnold Sowell USA	1	Berkeley	16 Jun
1:47.2	Roger Moens BEL	1	Berlin	30 Jun
1:47.5	Brian Hewson GBR	1	Glasgow	15 Sep
1:47.6	Lonnie Spurrier USA	3	Los Angeles	30 Jun

10th best 1:48.0, 100th 1:50.9

1000 METRES

2:19.1	Stanislav Jungwirth CZE	1	St. Boleslav	27 Sep
2:19.6	Roger Moens BEL	1	Malmö	4 Sep
2:19.9	Brian Hewson GBR	1	Manchester	22 Sep

1500 METRES

3:40.5	István Rozsavölgyi HUN	1	Tata	3 Aug
3:41.2	Ingvar Ericsson SWE	1	Budapest	29 Sep
3:41.2	Ron Delany IRL	1	Melbourne	1 Dec

3:41.3	Dan Waern SWE	2	Göteborg	30 Sep
3:41.8	Siegfried Herrmann GDR	1	Erfurt	30 Jul
3:42.0	Olavi Salsola FIN	1	Gävle	23 Jul
3:42.0	László Tábori HUN	2	Budapest	29 Sep
3:42.0	Klaus Richtzenhain GDR	2	Melbourne	1 Dec
3:42.0	John Landy AUS	3	Melbourne	1 Dec

10th best 3:42.4, 100th 3:49.6

1 MILE

3:58.6	John Landy AUS	3	Melbourne	28 Jan
3:58.6	James Bailey AUS	1	Los Angeles	5 May
3:59.0	Ron Delany IRL	1	Compton	1 Jun
3:59.0	István Rozsavölgyi HUN	1	Budapest	26 Aug
3:59.1	Gunnar Nielsen DEN	2	Compton	1 Jun
3:59.4	Derek Ibbotson GBR	1	London (WC)	6 Aug

10th best 4:01.8, 100th 4:12.4

3000 METRES

7:52.8!	Gordon Pirie GBR	1	Malmö	4 Sep
7:53.4	István Rozsavölgyi HUN	2	Malmö	4 Sep
7:56.4	Jerzy Chromik POL	2	Trondheim	22 Jun
7:59.0	Siegfried Herrmann GDR	1	Berlin	30 Jun
7:59.4	Sándor Iharos HUN	1	Warszawa	10 Jun
8:00.8	László Tábori HUN	2	Warszawa	10 Jun

10th best 8:05.0, 50th 8:19.0

5000 METRES

13:36.8!	Gordon Pirie GBR	1	Bergen	19 Jun
13:39.6	Vladimir Kuts SU	2	Bergen	19 Jun
13:46.6	Sándor Iharos HUN	1	Stockholm	1 Sep
13:51.0	Jerzy Chromik POL	2	Poznan	7 Jul
13:54.4	Miklós Szabó HUN	2	Stockholm	1 Sep
13:54.4	Derek Ibbotson GBR	3	Melbourne	28 Nov

10th best 14:01.8, 100th 14:25.6

10,000 METRES

28:30.4!	Vladimir Kuts SU	1	Moskva	11 Sep
28:42.8!	Sándor Iharos HUN	1	Budapest	15 Jul
28:52.4	József Kovács HUN	2	Melbourne	23 Nov
28:53.6	Allan Lawrence AUS	3	Melbourne	23 Nov
29:05.0	Zdzislaw Krzyszkowiak POL	4	Melbourne	23 Nov
29:10.0	Jerzy Chromik POL	1	Warszawa	9 Sep

10th best 29:21.6, 100th 30:40.8

MARATHON

2:18:05	Paavo Kotila FIN	1	Pieksamäki	12 Aug
2:18:51	Eino Oksanen FIN	2	Pieksamäki	12 Aug
2:18:57	Veikko Karvonen FIN	3	Pieksamäki	12 Aug
2:19:27	Eino Pulkkinen FIN	4	Pieksamäki	12 Aug
2:20:06	Ivan Filin URS	1	Moskva	12 Aug
2:20:16	Ronald Clark GBR	1	Chiswick	16 Jun

10th best 2:21:09

3000m STEEPLECHASE

8:35.6!	Sándor Rozsnyói HUN	1	Budapest	16 Sep
8:39.8!	Semyon Rzhishchin URS	1	Moskva	14 Aug
8:40.8	László Jeszensky HUN	1	Budapest	16 Jul
8:41.2	Chris Brasher GBR	1	Melbourne	29 Nov
8:42.4	Ernst Larsen NOR	1	Trondehim	5 Sep
8:42.4	Ilkka Auer FIN	3	Budapest	20 Sep

10th best 8:47.4, 100th 9:13.0

110m HURDLES (y = 120y h)

13.4!	Jack Davis USA	1	Bakersfield	22 Jun
13.5	Lee Calhoun USA	1	Melbourne	28 Nov
13.6y	Milton Campbell USA	2	Bendigo	17 Nov
13.7y	Joel Shankle USA	2	Sanger	9 Jun
13.8	Charles Pratt USA	1	Compton	6 Jun
13.8	Rafer Johnson USA	2	Berkeley	16 Jun
13.8y	Elias Gilbert USA	2	Baltimore	12 May
13.8yw	Ed Roberts USA	1	Tulsa	12 May

10th best 14.0, 100th 14.6

220y HURDLES (Straight Track)

22.2!	David Sime USA	1	Durham, NC	5 May
22.5	Ancel Robinson USA	1	Fresno	21 Apr
	22.2w	1	Fresno	7 Apr
22.7	Rafer Johnson USA	1	Los Angeles	24 Mar
	22.6w	1	Los Angeles	28 Apr

400m HURDLES (* 440y less 0.3 sec.)

49.5!	Glenn Davis USA	1	Los Angeles	29 Jun
49.7	Eddie Southern USA	2	Los Angeles	29 Jun
50.4	Yuriy Lituyev SU	1	Tashkent	14 Oct
50.6	John Culbreath USA	3	Los Angeles	29 Jun
50.7	Igor Ilin URS	1	Kiev	28 Jul
50.9	Aubrey Lewis USA	2	Milwaukee	9 Jun

10th best 51.4, 100th 53.7

HIGH JUMP

2.15!	Charles Dumas USA	1	Los Angeles	29 Jun
2.10	Igor Kashkarov RUS	1	Tashkent	21 Oct
2.10	Charles Porter AUS	2	Melbourne	23 Nov
2.09	Bengt Nilsson SWE	1	Stockholm	2 Sep
2.09	Donald Stewart USA	1	Dallas	3 May
2.08i	Phil Reavis USA	1	Philadelphia	20 Jan
2.08	Ernst Shelton USA	1	Los Angeles	5 May

10th best 2.07, 100th 1.98

POLE VAULT

4.70i	Don Bragg USA	1	New York	3 Mar
	4.66	1	Stockton	2 Jun
4.70	Robert Richards USA	1=	Santa Ana	27 Oct
4.70	Robert Gutowski USA	1=	Santa Ana	27 Oct
4.57i	Jerry Welbourn USA	2	Milwaukee	10 Mar
4.57	Ronald Morris USA	1=	Compton	1 Jun
4.53	George Mattos USA	2	Los Angeles	30 Jun
4.51	Eeles Landström FIN	1	Hamburg	23 Sep

10th best 4.48, 100th 4.20

LONG JUMP

8.09	Gregory Bell USA	1	Ontario, CA	20 Oct
7.98	Henk Visser NED	1	Bucuresti	17 Sep
7.95	Ernest Shelby USA	1	Bakersfield	22 Jun
7.83	John Bennett USA	1=	Los Angeles	29 Jun
7.77	Jorma Valkama FIN	1	Turku	16 Sep
7.76	Rafer Johnson USA	1	Los Angeles	5 May
7.76	Oleg Fyedoseyev URS	1	Tashkent	21 Oct

10th best 7.73, 100th 7.30

TRIPLE JUMP

16.48	Teruji Kogake JPN	1	Sendai	7 Oct
16.46	Leonid Shcherbakov URS	1	Moskva	4 Jul
16.35	Adhemar da Silva BRA	1	Melbourne	27 Nov
16.26	Vilhjálmur Einarsson ISL	2	Melbourne	27 Nov
16.02	Vitold Kreer URS	3	Melbourne	27 Nov
15.95	Yevgeniy Chen URS	1	Tashkent	22 Oct

10th best 15.88, 100th 14.88

SHOT

19.25!	Parry O'Brien USA	1	Los Angeles	1 Nov
18.38	William Nieder USA	1	Manhattan	19 May
18.30	Kenneth Bantum USA	1	Berkeley	15 Jun
17.76	Jirí Skobla TCH	4	Ostrava	25 Aug
17.67	Vartan Ovsepyan URS	1	Tashkent	30 Oct
17.60	Charles Butt USA	1	Berkeley	19 May

10th best 17.38, 100th 15.82

DISCUS

57.21	Fortune Gordien USA	1	Los Angeles	30 Jun
56.85	Adolfo Consolini ITA	1	Verona	25 Apr
56.68	Karel Merta TCH	1	Praha	22 Jul
56.46	Parry O'Brien USA	1	Honolulu	12 May
56.36	Al Oerter USA	1	Melbourne	27 Nov
55.48	Kim Bukhantsev URS	1	Tashkent	21 Oct

10th best 54.85, 100th 49.18

HAMMER

68.54!	Harold Connolly USA	1	Los Angeles	2 Nov
67.32!	Mikhail Krivonosov SU	1	Tashkent	22 Oct
65.95	Clifford Blair USA	1	Needham	4 Jul
65.03	Anatoliy Samotsvetov URS	1	Bucuresti	17 Sep
63.98	Stanislav Nyenashev SU	1	Baku	16 Dec
63.57	Tadeusz Rut POL	1	Oslo	31 Aug

63.57	Dmitriy Yegorov URS	1	Tashkent	30 Aug

10th best 62.80, 100th 55.49

JAVELIN

85.71!	Egil Danielsen NOR	1	Melbourne	26 Nov
83.66	Janusz Sidlo POL	1	Milano	30 Jun
83.56	Soini Nikkinen FIN	1	Kuhmoinen	24 Jun
82.29	Franklin Held USA	1	Pasadena	22 Sep
81.12	Jan Kopyto POL	1	Warszawa	9 Sep
80.22	Heiner Will FRG	1	Köln	22 Oct
79.89	Viktor Tsibulenko URS	2	Bucuresti	16 Sep

10th best 78.75, 100th 69.15

DECATHLON (1952 tables)

7937	Milton Campbell USA (7565 on current tables)	1	Melbourne	30 Nov
7755	Rafer Johnson USA	1	Crawfordville	14 Jul
7733	Vasiliy Kuznetsov URS	1	Moskva	15 Aug
7393	Yuriy Kutyenko URS	2	Moskva	15 Aug
7201	Martin Lauer FRG	1	Hamburg	23 Sep
7194	Robert Mathias USA	1	Los Angeles	16 Jun

20 KILOMETRES WALK

1:27:59.2t!	Mikhail Lavrov RUS	1	Moskva	13 Aug
1:28:01.8t	Leonid Spirin RUS	2	Moskva	13 Aug
1:28:04.6t	Bruno Junk URS	1	Kiev	13 Oct
1:28:19.6t	Antanas Mikenas URS	2	Kiev	13 Oct
1:29:15.8t	Yuriy Kulkov URS	3	Kiev	13 Oct
1:29:59.8	Josef Dolezal TCH	1	Praha	25 Jul

50 KILOMETRES WALK

4:05:12.2!	Grigoriy Klimov URS	1	Moskva	10 Aug
4:08:57	Yevg. Maskinskov URS	2	Moskva	10 Aug
4:09:47	Mikhail Lavrov URS	3	Moskva	10 Aug
4:11:23	Vladimir Ukhov URS	4	Moskva	10 Aug
4:12:54.4	Abdon Pamich ITA	1	Podebrady	26 Aug
4:15:08	Anatoliy Vedyakov URS	5	Moskva	10 Aug

WOMEN

100 YARDS

10.5	Marlene Mathews AUS	1	Sydney	21 Jan
10.6	Betty Cuthbert AUS	1	Sydney	25 Feb
10.5w	Joyce Crotty NZL	1hc	Te Puke	24 Mar
10.5w	Isabelle Daniels USA	1	Sydney	2 Dec

100 METRES

11.4	Giuseppina Leone ITA	1	Bologna	21 Oct
11.4	Betty Cuthbert AUS	1	Melbourne	24 Nov
	11.2w	1	Sydney	7 Oct
11.5	Marlene Mathews AUS	1	Sydney	10 Mar
	11.2w	2	Sydney	7 Oct
11.5	Gisela Köhler GDR	1	Berlin	30 Jun
11.5	Bertha van Duyne NED	1	Frechen	29 Jul
11.5	Galina Popova URS	1	Moskva	10 Aug
11.5	Christa Stubnick GDR	1	Dresden	30 Sep
11.3w	Fleur Mellor AUS	3	Sydney	7 Oct

10th best 11.6, 50th 11.9

200 METRES

23.2!	Betty Cuthbert AUS	1	Sydney	16 Sep
23.4	Maria Itkina URS	1	Tashkent	13 Oct
23.5	Christa Stubnick GDR	1	Riesa	9 Sep
23.5	Norma Croker AUS	1	Brisbane	6 Oct
23.8	Barbara Lerczak POL	1	Bucuresti	17 Sep
23.8	Marlene Mathews AUS		Melbourne	30 Nov

Half turn

23.7	June Paul GBR	1	Budapest	30 Sep
23.8	Jean Scrivens GBR	2	Budapest	30 Sep

10th best 1:48.0, 100th 1:50.9

400 METRES

55.3	Nona Paltseva URS	1	Moskva	27 Jul
55.5	Nina Otkalenko URS	1	Kiev	20 May

800 METRES

2:05.3	Ludmila Lysenko SU	1	Moskva	16 Aug
2:05.8+	Nina Otkalenko SU	1	Moskva	10 Jun
2:06.9	Dzidra Levitska URS	3	Moskva	16 Aug
2:07.3	Phyllis Perkins GBR	1	Budapest	29 Sep
2:07.4	Aida Lapshina URS	4	Moskva	16 Aug
2:07.5	Ursula Donath	1	London (WC)	12 Sep

10th best 2:08.7, 50th 2:12.6

1500 METRES

4:35.4	Phyllis Perkins GBR	1	Hornchurch	17 May

80m HURDLES

10.6!	Zenta Gastl FRG	1	Frechen	29 Jul
10.7	Nina Vinogradova URS	1	Moskva	14 Aug
10.7	Galina Bystrova URS	1	Tashkent	22 Oct
10.7	Mariya Golubnichaya URS	2	Tashkent	22 Oct
10.7	Shirley Strickland AUS	1	Melbourne	28 Nov
10.8	Erika Frish FRG	2	Frechen	29 Jul
10.8	Gisela Köhler GDR	1	Leipzig	2 Sep
10.8w	Norma Thrower AUS		Melbourne	27 Nov

10th best 10.9, 50th 11.3

HIGH JUMP

1.76!	Mildred McDaniel USA	1	Melbourne	1 Dec
1.75!	Iolanda Balas ROM	1	Bucuresti	14 Jul
1.74!	Thelma Hopkins GBR	1	Belfast	5 May
1.72	Micheline Mason AUS		Melbourne	17 Nov
1.70	Valentina Balode URS	1	Bucuresti	17 Sep
1.70	Mariya Grigalka URS		Tashkent	29 Oct

10th best 1.67, 50th 1.59

LONG JUMP

6.35!	Elzbieta Krzesinska POL	1	Budapest	20 Aug
6.19	Erika Fisch FRG	1	Berlin	19 Aug
6.19	Marga Weidner FRG	2	Berlin	19 Aug
6.15	Nadezhda Dvalishvili URS	1	Tashkent	13 Oct
6.14	Sheila Hoskin GBR	1	London (TB)	5 May
	6.26w	1	Maidstone	7 Jul
6.14	Galina Segen URS	1	Kiev	24 Jun
6.14	Lidiya Radchenko URS		Kiev	28 Jul

10th best 6.11, 50th 5.81

SHOT

16.76!	Galina Zybina SU	1	Tashkent	13 Oct
16.60	Zinaida Doynikova SU		Tashkent	21 Oct
16.59	Tamara Tishkyevich SU	1	Melbourne	30 Nov
15.79	Mariya Kuznetsova SU		Tashkent	21 Oct
15.67	Marianne Werner FRG	1	Düsseldorf	22 Jul
15.34	Valerie Sloper NZL	5	Melbourne	30 Nov

10th best 15.01, 50th 13.67

DISCUS

54.76	Nina Ponomaryeva SU	1	Kiev	16 Jun
53.69	Olga Fikotova TCH	1	Melbourne	23 Nov
52.71	Irina Begyakova SU		Tashkent	30 Oct
52.27	Nina Dumbadze SU	1	Tbilisi	
51.40	Jirina Voborilová TCH		Praha	15 Oct
51.35	Earlene Brown USA	4	Melbourne	23 Nov

10th best 50.33, 50th 45.57

JAVELIN

53.86	Inese Jaunzeme URS	1	Melbourne	28 Nov
53.32	Virve Roolaid SU	1	Tallinn	27 May
52.83	Almut Brömmel FRG	1	Nürnberg	7 Oct
52.69	Erszebet Vigh HUN	1	Budapest	29 Sep
52.24	Dana Zátopková TCH	1	Praha	17 Jun
52.16	Aleksandra Chudina URS	1	Moskva	13 Aug

10th best 51.05, 50th 44.98

PENTATHLON (1954 tables)

4767	Nina Vinogradova URS	1	Moskva	12 Aug
4632	Aleksandra Chudina URS	2	Moskva	12 Aug
4570	Nilia Besedina URS	3	Moskva	12 Aug
4555	Galina Bystrova URS	4	Moskva	12 Aug
4548	Sofia Burdelenko URS	1	Kiev	
4413	Yevgeniya Gurvich URS	1	Minsk	5 Jul

Amendments to ATHLETICS 2005

p.27 110mh: Larry Wade drugs dq, so loses 4th place ranking; move up the rest
p.87 World Athletics Final 2004
p.88 WAF Women 100m dq 8. Gaines

Obituaries:
p.98 Ratu MARA pb HJ 1.83 (1946) in NZ.
p.102 Paul MESSNER pb 1500m 3:55.0 (1946).
p.103 **Drugs Bans**: delete Awatef Ben Hassine in men's lists (in women's)
p.116 Kenenise Bekele – additional CC win 6 Apr 2003 Alá dei Sardi, last two wins in 2005
p.120 5th best men's shot all-time to end 1955 should be 17.68 Charles Fonville (1948),

National Champions 2004:

SWITZERLAND. Men: 10000mW/20kmW/35kmW: Nicolas Perrier 44:20.6/1:34:43/2:53:59, 50kmW: Bruno Grandjean 4:38:24. **Women** 5000mW/10kmW/20kmW: Marie Polli 23:02.2/48:11/1:41:25.

WORLD LISTS 2004

Men

100m: 9.93 Crawford 3 NC/OT, 10.01 Scott 3s2, 10.04 Williams 4s2, 10.08 Montgomery ¶ to drugs dq (all marks from 31 Mar 2001 annulled), 10.11 Egbele 1st, 10.21 Sousa 3 & 10.26 Williams 4th, 10.23w Jenkins 7.4.83; Jnr: 10.1w Harris 17.9.86, delete 10.1 Bonno (was 10.2)
200m: 20.40 0.4 Edwards, 20.57/20.48w Vaden 15.9.78 (& 400m), 20.82/20.79w Blakely 28.9.81 (& 400m 46.25); hand: 20.6A Vincent Mumo KEN 3.3.82 19 Jun
400m: 44.58 Banda 16.8.82 (& 200m 20.59), 46.23 Weatherborne 19.5.81
800m: 1:47.15 Litei 2.6.83, 147.7A Chepkonga .79; Jnr: 1:48.0A Kiprono Boit 4, 1:48.4 Kipchirchir & Choge
1000m: 2:18.6+ Benjamin Kipkurui KEN 28.12.80 23 Jul
1500m: 3:40.12 Hamoumraoui .83, 3:40.34 Brooks 10.1.78 (& 3000mSt 8:36.30), 3:41.29 Schmidt 21.8.82
1M: 3:59.35 Isaac Sang KEN 24.8.78 25 Jun
2000m: Indoors: 5:01.2+ Sileshi Sihine ETH 29.1.83 2 in 3k Stuttgart 31 Jan
3000m: 7:37.86 Bellani 15.9.79 (& 5k 13:05.72), 7:51.56 Philemon Tanui, 7:52.20i Chirchir 20.11.83
5000m: 13:19.92 James Kipkemboi Katui 12.9.78, 13:32.69 Ridha El Amri (& 62:10 HMar)
10000m: 27:07.29 Masai 1.6.86 (5000m 13:25.5), 27:41.49 Martínez 10, 27:46.06 Robert Kipngetich Sigei (& 7:48.15/7:43.09i, 5000m 13:27.03), 28:34.8 David Ndegwa 17.12.72
10kmRd: 28:33 Eliud Tanui 8.8.83
HMar: 60:00 Luke Kibet 19.6.83, 61:41 Kenduiywo 28.12.74, 62:14 Riri 21.10.73, 62:28 Azzouzi 8.5.79
Mar: 2:12:58 Laâroussi .70
2000mSt: 5:39.00 Meziane 23.5.86
3000mSt: 8:37.1 Noureddine Moufti MAR 12.1.79 17 Jun, 8:38.4A Amos Kipchirchir KEN-J 18.4.85, 8:39.24 Moumen Bouchiba ALG .82 8 Apr
110mh: Larry Wade ¶ drugs dq from 13 May, so remove 13.14 and 13.12w marks to footnote; 13.71/-1.1 Tucker 12 Jun (delete at 13.54), 13.84 Tinsley 21.4.84, 13.90 -1.4 Kai Doczynski 21 Aug (delete at 13.84)
400mh: 50.58 Collier 14.1.81, 50.64 Poll 30.7.83, 50.71 Hutcherson 18.11.71; Jnr: 51.18 Couto also 51.1 1 Maputo 27 Jul
HJ: 2.22 McKinney 4.4.82, 2.20 Littleton 14.10.83
PV: 5.60 King 18.3.82, 5.36 Litchfield 27.11.80
LJ: 8.32 Gaisah 19 Sep
TJ: 16.98 Ishikawa 6.11.82, 16.89w Kazimierowski 2.9
SP: 21.14 Verni 1st, 20.07i/19.93 Al-Suwaidi 10.10.84
TJ: 16.33 Mendes 21.6.78
SP: 19.73 Frank (in US)/Francisco (in MEX) Guzmán, 18.64 Máté; Jnr: 18.45 Shahrokhi 23.5.85; 6.25kg: Lajos Kürthy (and in DT lists)
DT: Jnr DT: 62.24 Haddadi 21.1.85
HT: 69.85 Mohamed 12.2.80, 69.55 D Smith 3.8.79, 68.23 Samir Haouam ALG 20.6.68 12 Jul; 6kg: 74.65 Kristóf Németh HUN 17.9.87 1 Szombathely 6 May
JT: Vasilevskis 24 Sep series: 76.92, 77.18, 84.68, 82.00, x, p
Dec: 8225 Bernard SP 14.80, 8085w Moore 400m 47.80, 8043 Tishchenko SP 14.50, 7940 Gómez 400m 48.60
4x100m: hand timed 39.8A KEN 25 Jun; **4x110mh**

Women

100m: 11.06 Gaines ¶ to drugs dq, 11.14 Mayers 5th; 11.41 Fant 2.12.81, 11.52 Patient Emen Edem NGR 15.10.83 & Beatrice Nwaogwugwu NGR 19.1.82 8 Jul, 11.35w Tyson 1.5.86, 11.49w Ratcliff 9.4.82; hand: 11.3 Fatumata Coly SEN 3.1.84 27 Jun
200m: 22.34 Khabarova at NC, 22.91 Perry 1.5.79, 23.34A/23.41 Tyson 1.5.86, 23.28 Gaines ¶ to drugs dq;
800m: 2:03.25 Morgan 21.9.80, Indoor – delete 2:03.27 Cook
1500m: 4:11.04 Amane Gobena 1.9.82 (not J) (& 5000m 15:19:50), 4:13.53 (not A) Quispe
1500m: 4:06.10 Burka, 4:15.24 Woodworth 14.8.81
5000m: To disqualified: 15:21.43 Piedra, best before: 15:39.01 19 Jun; 100th best 15:27.20
10000m: 32:45.78 Newberry 31.08.78
Mar: dh 2:34:02 Vinitskaya 23.8.73
3000mSt: NC not NC/OT for US marks, 10:09.75 Rudkin 15.5.80, 10:19.01 Hull 2.10.81
100mh: 13.25 Wells 16.7.82, 13.26 Tyson 8.9.77
400mh: 56.62 Melaine Walker
HJ: 1.85 Kerin 29.4.79, 1.84 Beth Ann Castagno 6.11.78
PV: 4.17 Sowa 1 Gdansk 5 Sep, 4.31 OK? Sabine Schulte 3 Trosidorf 5 Sep (not by Anna Schultze – shown as Exhibition), 4.11 Canino & Olson 28 May, 4.01 Marino 23.4.81; delete 4.10i Eveland (best 4.05 outdoors)
LJ: 6.62 0.0 Sofia Schulte 1 Olpe 11 Aug (from 6.60), 6.50i Anna Nazarova RUS 14.3.86 22 Jan, 6.46 1.0 Deák, 6.41 Harris 17.11.84, 6.35 Éva Miklós
TJ: 14.03 Dubina – false mark? best 13.55, 13.52 Nkiruka 28.8.85, 13.46 Edwards 6.7.80; delete repeated marks 13.66 Sha Li & Spencer, 199 in list
SP: 18.38i Irina Khudoroshkina ¶ RUS 13.10.68 3 Moskva 1 Feb (prior to drugs ban), 17.86 Breisch on 10 Jun, 17.21 Kekhishvili – false mark? Best out: 16.90 Yepimashko 1H Minsk 21 May
DT: 58.26 Matejková uncertified track - replace with 57.58 3 IbAm Huelva 7 Aug
HT: Moreno – 73.65 was on 27 Feb, 64.21 Guzmán CUB Ch, 63.46 Smith 20 May, delete 61.02 de Jesús (at 61.48), 60.41 Godsey-J 1.1.86, 60.06 McClain 1 Apr; 199 in list
JT: 53.15 Pounds 5.6.84
Hep: 5700 Gnezdilov
4x400m: 3:40.46 ISR 20 Jun Tkach ¶ drugs dq
p.595 final line for 300mh belongs in women's lists.

World Indoor Lists 2005

Men: 60m: 6.59 drugs dq Lewis-Francis #, best 6.61 18 Feb; **800m**: 1:46.97 Hicks 7.11.84; **3000m**: 7:48.3+

M Bett 6 Feb; **60mh**: 7.43 Doucouré 1 26 Feb; **PV**: add 5.61 Daichi Sawano JPN 16.9.80 5 Mar; **LJ**: delete 8.00 Harris

Old World Lists

2003

Men SP: add to Jnr perfs: G Johnson 18.58i 1 Chapel Hill 21 Feb; **HT**: Tikhon series at WUG: x, 78.63, 82.13, 82.77, 79.52, x; Jnr perfs: Al-Zankawai 70.64 21 Sep; **Dec**: Jnrs: top mark 7544 Trey Hardee as in main list and 7468 5 NCAA Sacramento 12 Jun. **Women 100m**: 11.44w Lisa Montiner 1 Miami c.12 Jun, 11.51w Tamara Rigby BAH-J 1s1 Miami c.12 Jun

2002: Women 100mh: delete 13.19 Candice Davis (was Kia); add wa: 13.51w 2.3 Candice Davis USA-J 26.10.83 3 NC-j Stanford 22 Jun

Shot: **1966**: Bianco 3.5.44, **1978**: 19.34 White .55, **1996**: 19.01 Heimerman 9.5.74 180/120

European Indoor Championships 2005

Men 60m: dq 2 Mark Lewis-Francis. move up rest: 2. Pognon 3. Vasyukov etc.

Amendments to previous Championships results

2000 Olympics: 4x400m: Jerome Young was officially disqualified by the IOC from the 4x400 relay and loses a gold medal. But he ran only in the heat and the CAS ruled that the winning USA team in the final should NOT be disqualified despite a recommendation to this effect by the IAAF.

Drugs ban on Tim Montgomery and annulment of all his results from 31 Mar 2001 mean:

2001 Worlds: 100m: dq 2 Montgomery, so 2. Williams, 3. Boldon etc.; 4x100m: dq 1 USA, so. 1. RSA, 2. TRI, 3. AUS

2001 US Champs: 100m champion Bernard Williams 9.98w

2002 GP Final: 100m: dq 1 Montgomery – loses WR 9.78

2003 Worlds: 100m: dq 4/5 Chambers/Montgomery. so 4. Williams, 5. Aliu, 6. Emedolu

With thanks to Alberto Sánchez Traver, Juan Maiu Iriondo (corrections to biographies), José M.García, Marty Post and other correspondents.

Marriages

Mark Carroll IRL	Amy Rudolph USA 7 Oct 05
Gebre Gebremariam ETH	Werksnesh Kidane ETH 4 Feb 06
Ryan Hall USA	Sara Bei USA 25 Sep 05
Ato Mobido TRI	Cydonie Mothersill CAY
Phill Sharpe GBR	Kara Nwidobie GBR
Reedus Thurmond USA	Aretha Hill USA April 05

Further recent women's name changes

Original	*married name*
Yekaterina Aleksandrova RUS	Savchenk
Olga Alekseyeva KAZ	Rypakova
Olga Andreyeva UKR	Daniv
Tawa Babatunde CAN	Dortch
Mishael Bertrand USA	Berger
Rachelle Boone USA	Smith
Cleopatra Borel TRI	Borel-Brown
Dawn Cleary USA	Cromer
Michelle Griffith GBR	Robinson
Beth Hinshaw USA	Spearman
Oksana Ilyushkina UKR	Kochetkova
Anastasiya Ivanova RUS	Shvedova
Brooke Krueger AUS	Billett
Susan Jones GBR	Moncrieff
Natalya Kresova RUS	Rusakova
Daniela Lincoln SWE	Saavedra
Rasa Michniovaite LTU	Troup
Eloise Poppett AUS	Wellings
Tiffany Ross USA	Ross-Williams
Mihaela Stancescu ROM	Neascu
Lyudmila Starovoytova BLR	Kupriyanova
Natalya TomashevskayaUKR	Yastrebova
Donna Tyberek AUS	MacFarlane

Change of nationality

Men

Aaron Armstrong USA to TRI
Ambrose Ezenwa NGR to AUS April 2005
Arthémon Hatungimana BUR to FRA
Nicholas Kemboi KEN to QAT
James Kibocha Theuri KEN to FRA (23 Feb 2006)
Francis Kirwa KEN to FIN
Germaine Mason JAM to GBR
Simon Munyuto KEN to FRA (23 Feb 2006)
Kevon Pierre SKN to TRI
Jackson Quiñonez ECU to ESP
Allen Simms USA to PUR
Frank Vicet CUB to ESP (29 Jun 2005)

Women

Sylvie Mballa Eloundou FRA to CMR
Bouchra Ghezielle MAR to FRA
Zolia Gómez MEX to USA (22 Sep 2005)
Taneisha Robinson-Scanlon IRL to GBR (October 2005)
Irina Sustelo POR to BEL
Estle Viljoen RSA to GBR (2006)

and names

Men

Moses Chirchir KEN	Salem Amer Al-Badri QAT
Abel Cheruiyot KEN	Abel Yagout Jawher BRN
Daniel Kemboi Kipkosgei KEN	Essa Ismail Rasheed QAT
David Nyaga KEN	Daham Najim Bashir QAT
Richard Yatich KEN	Mubarak Hassan Shami QAT
John Yego KEN	Bilal Mansoor Ali BRN

Women

Tola Kotu Zenebech ETH	Maryam Jamal BRN

Retiring

It is always difficult to be sure about athletes and retirement. Some announce such, but come back after a break, others drift away, perhaps never getting back to full fitness. But these prominent athletes are amongst those who declared their retirement in the last year:

Jamie Baulch, Mark Crear, Kelly Holmes, Monica Iagar, Sárka Kaspárková, Martin Keino, Wilson Kipketer, Bob Kennedy, Astrid Kumbernuss, Denise Lewis, Beverly McDonald, Fiona May, Katharine Merry, Elana Meyer, Debbie-Ann Parris, Gabriela Szabo, Niki Xánthou.

ATHLETICS REFERENCE BOOKS

Reviewed by Peter Matthews

Biographisches Handbuch zur Geschichte der deutschen Leichtathletik 1898-2005. By Klaus Amrhein. Two A5 volumes totalling 1388 pages. This fantastic compendium presents biographical profiles (naming 11,277 in all!) of athletes and other important figures in the history of German athletics, thus bringing together and up dating the author's previous works. The detailed stats include personal details, performances in national and international championships, personal bests and annual progressions. Wonderful – and terrific value at euro 24.95 for the two volumes plus a CD from Klaus Amrhein, Lindenweg 3, 64846 Klein-Zimmern, German.

Early Women's Athletics: Statistics & History, Vol 2, by Eric L Cowe. A5 182pp. The author continues his prodigious work in unearthing the early history of women's athletics as this volume deals with the sport's development in the USA from the late 19th century to the mid-1930s. This is a welcome and fascinating addition to a previously under-documented area. Contents include detailed US all-time lists to the end of 1921 and year lists for 1922-32, followed by a special section on Helen Stephens and her career to 1937.

Order from the author at 4 Preston Terrace, Crossflatts, Bingley BD16 2SE, UK (e-mail: ericcowe@blueyonder.co.uk); UK – £20 (cash or cheque), rest of europe – 30 euros (cash only); USA – $40 (cash only). Special offer: Vol 1, dealing with early British women's athletics, and Vol 2 together for £26 (UK), 40 euros or $55.

A World History of The One-Lap Race 1850-2004 by Roberto L. Quercetani; published by SEP Editrice, Milan; 19.5 x 24cm, 285 pp. I have not seen this book, but it is sure to be a masterpiece. £29 inc. postage, £35 for rest of world – add £3 for credit card payments) from Athletics International, 13 Garden Court, Marsh Lane, Stanmore, Middlesex HA7 4TE. UK.

Cuban Athletes. Basilio Fuentes has compiled a book about Cuba's athletes classified into the first 100 of the world for 1950-2002 year by year and by event, with a foreword by Alberto Juantorena, world records by Cubans, Cuban all-time lists and national records, and personal data on 523 athletes. $20 US, 20 euros or £15 from Marianela Collishaw, 4651 SW 153 PL, Kendall, Miami, FLA 33185, USA.

The Lexicon – "From Adamczak To Zaslona" by Henryk Kurzynski, Stefan Pietkiewicz and Marian Rynkowski. 244x169mm, 260pp, over 100 photos. Detailed statistical profiles of top Polish athletes 1920-39. 20 euros + postage from Janusz Rozum, Angorska Str. 14/23, 03-913 Warszawa, Poland. jrozum@poczta.onet.pl

Najbolji Rezultati Jugosovenskih Athleticara. 204pp. Part 2 (women) of deep Yugoslav all-time performance lists (with index of competitors) by Ozren Karamata. Similar to the previous one with men's results, but with somewhat deeper lists, adding indoor sprint and hurdle events for men and women. Price inc. postage 25 euros by cash from Ozren Karamata, Karamatina 17, 11080 Zemun, Serbia and Crna Gora. 35 euros for both men's and women's books.

Statistical Handbook – European Athletics U23 Championships. By Jirí Ondrácek for the European AA. A5 98 pages. This booklet, produced for the 2005 Championships at Erfurt, includes complete results of the previous four championships, European national U23 records and 30-deep European U23 lists.

World All-Time Lists. A4 272pp. Luis Leite has updated to the end of 2005 his world lists – 300 deep for men and 250 deep for women with top 50 performances. He also shows the best performances using his scoring tables. 20 euro within europe, 25 euro elsewhere from Luis at Av. Alm. Gago Coutinho 154, 1700-033 Lisboa, Portugal.

TAFWA All-Time Indoor List 2006. A5 216pp. Ed Gordon's excellent annual compilation of world all-time indoor lists of performers (over 200 deep) and performances (c. 150 deep) for all events, men and women was updated to include the 2005 season. New editions appear in December each year – in book form and on CD. Contact ed@gordon007.net.

World Junior Athletics Annual 2004/2005, by Lionel Peters. A5, 143pp. Complete results of the 2004 World Junior Champs, deep 2004 lists, world junior records progression since 1945 compiled by Alain Bouillé and world age bests (from 12 to 19) compiled by Robert Martin. From Lionel Peters, 40 Berkeley Road, London NW9 9DG; £10 (UK), £11 (rest of europe), £12 (rest of world). E-mail: lionel@wjan.org.

World Junior Indoor Athletics Handbook 2005/2006, by Lionel Peters. A5, 60pp. The

4th edition of this booklet contains details of junior performances indoors: world and junior records, 10-20 deep all-time and 2005 lists, juniors at World Indoor Championships, worldwide results in 2005, and world and European junior records progression. £8 europe, £10 elsewhere – as above.

World Junior Cross Country Annual 2005/2006, by Lionel Peters. A5, 52pp. The 5th edition of this booklet contains details of junior performances at cross-country including top ten junior placings at all IAAF World CC races and medals at European Junior CC with best placings by country etc.; also full details for 2004-05 races. £5 europe, £6 elsewhere – as above.

Sporting Eye by Fionnbar Callanan. Subtitled "Fifty Years of Irish and International Sports Photography", this handsome 144-page hardback contains the best work of a splendid photographer – specialising in athletics – from 1948. Irish greats and international stars of the past are pictured. Fionnbar, also a distinguished athletics writer and long-serving ATFS member, was himself a notable athlete and in 1955 long jumped 7.44. Order at www.libertiespress.com for 25 euros, US $30 or £16.90.

IAAF Handbooks

Part of a long list of productions from the IAAF, 17 rue Princesse Florestine, BP 359, MC 98007, Monaco. Prices (by Visa, Master Card or eurocard) include postage by airmail. email to: headquarters@iaaf.org. Payment by credit card (Visa, Mastercard or eurocard only), quoting name on card, number of card, expiry date, name and address and signature.

IAAF Statistics Handbook, Helsinki 2005. A5 630 pages. Mark Butler has again done a wonderful job in this the latest in his series of handbooks for the major IAAF Championships. The book starts with full results of World Championships 1983-2003 with tables of multiple medallists, most appearances, youngest and oldest, national placings, performance trends etc. and best placings for each nation and all their medallists.

Listed are medallists at other IAAF World Series events and Olympic Games, gold medallists at the World University Games, Commonwealth Games and major continental championships, world and continental records plus world junior, youth, over-35 and over-40 with world teenage bests by age. 30-deep world all-time lists are followed by Winfried Kramer's national records and best World Championships placings at each event for each nation, a concise progression of official world records and biographies of over 1000 current world-class athletes. As I said of the 2003 edition – truly a monumental work of reference. $20.

IAAF Statistics Handbook, Moscow 2006. A5 316pp. Another superb work by Mark Butler, this covers similar ground to the above, except for indoor athletics, being a guide for the 11th IAAF World Indoor championships. $16.

IAAF Magazine/Newsletter. The quarterly magazine is a top-quality colour production (A4, 60 plus pages) with reports and results of major competitions and articles by leading authorities. The regular newsletters are generally 16 pages. $80 subscription for text in English and French.

IAAF Competition Rules 2006-07. 169 x114mm. 212pp. Rules and regulations in English, French or Spanish editions. Each $10.

IAAF Directory and Calendar 2006. A5, 280 pages. Contact details for officials, organisations and national federations, with calendar and lists of records and champions. $16.

IAAF World Rankings Yearbook 2005. A5 602pp. Packed with comprehensive details of the rankings, with 100 deep lists and season's records for the top 20 athletes at each event for the year to 4 October 2004. $20.

The IAAF also sells videos of highlights of its World Series meetings, including all World Championships from 1991.

SportsBooks, publishers of the ATFS annual, are selling the official book of the 10th **World Championships** in Helsinki. Cost inc. p&p 56 euros (europe), 57 euros (rest of the world). or by cheque for £38 (if outside the UK please pay in sterling drawn on a UK bank) to SportsBooks, PO Box 422, Cheltenham, GL50 2JR. No eurocheques please. Payment can also be by Mastercard or Visa and will be charged in euros.

ANNUALS

For most Annuals below referring to 2004/05, there will be new issues covering 2005/06.

Combined Events Annual 2005 by Hans van Kuijen. A5. The 13th edition of this attractively produced annual includes top 200 men's decathlon and women's heptathlon lists (with deep performances) for 2005 with indoor multis lists and deep all-time world lists. Also results of major events, profiles and complete career details of the world's top multi-eventers, records, best performances by event etc. In europe: 25 euro or £20 sterling cash (add £7.5 for cheques or payments to bank account

52.31.27.898 of ABN-AMRO, Helmond, BIC code ABNANL2A). Outside europe: US $35 cash or $47.50 cheques – from Hans van Kuijen, de Bergen 66, 5706 RZ Helmond, Netherlands. email: hvankuijen@wxs.nl. Back numbers for 1995, 1997, 1999-2003: 15 euro each.

L'Athlétisme Africain/African Athletics 2005. A5, 152p. By Yves Pinaud. 24th edition of this splendid book has 100 deep men's and women's lists for Africa for 2004, with all-time lists, national championships and major meetings results. 20 euro or US $25 from Éditions Polymédias, 103 rue de Paris, 94220 Charenton le Pont, France. (Previous annuals 1979-2004 available at various prices).

Asian Athletics 2004 rankings. A5 97 pages. By Heinrich Hubbeling. Asian records and top 30s for athletes from Asian nations, with continuation lists for countries other than China and Japan and all new national records set during the year. euro 15/US $18 in cash or by International Money Order from the author, Haydnstrasse 8, 48691 Vreden, Germany. Copies also available for 1998, 2000, 2003 at euro 10/US $12 each.

British Athletics 2005. The NUTS Annual, edited by Rob Whittingham and Peter Matthews. 432 pages including 16 of colour photographs. Deep UK ranking lists for all age groups in 2004, top 12 merit rankings, all-time lists, results etc. £16 UK, £18 rest of europe, £20 outside europe; from Umbra Athletics Ltd, Unit 1, Bredbury Business Park, Bredbury Park Way, Stockport, SK6 2SN, England. All orders by credit card to www.umbraathletics.com sent worldwide post-free for £16.

CAC 2004 – The Central American & Caribbean Athletics Annual. A5 256pp. Produced and edited by Nestor Calixto with the collaboration of Bernard Linley, the doyen of CAC statistics. After yearly leaders, records and results, the book has 100-deep performer and 50-deep performance lists for CAC athletes in 2004. It thus builds upon Bernard's great series of annuals to provide the most comprehensive publication ever produced for the region. Orders in europe to Polymédias, 103 rue de Paris, F-94220 Charenton-le-Pont, France (www.polymedias.fr) or outside europe, $20 to Nestor Calixto, 8015 NW 8th St #A-110, Miami, FL 33126, USA (www.athlecac.org).

Laursens Store Lommebog 2004. A5 86p. Erik Laursen's annual compilation of Danish indoor and outdoor lists for 2004. Also included are indoor all-time lists and a continuation of his special feature of annual Danish lists for men's 1500m with 1980-4. Price 50 DK plus postage (21 in europe, 35 elsewhere). From Erik Laursen (erik.laursen@privat.dk), Sandbakken 95, 8270 Højbjerg, Denmark.

Deutsche Bestenliste 2004 A5 190 pp. 30 DM or US $20. Edited by Klaus Amrhein for the Deutschen Gesellschaft für Leichtathletik-Dokumentation (DGLD). Deep performance and performer year lists, indoors and out, for Germany for 2004. See DGLD details.

DLV Leichtathletik Jahrbuch 2005. A5 376pp. The official yearbook of the German Federation. Directory and review, with articles on top athletes, detailed results of 2005 meetings, records and top tens, also many illustrations in colour. euro 18 plus postage, from Deutsche Leichtathletik Marketing GmbH, Postfach 10 04 63, 64219 Darmstadt, Germany.

DLV Leichtathletik Bestenliste 2005. A5 432pp. The DLV's ranking lists for 2005 for all events compiled by Eberhard Vollmer, generally 50-deep for seniors and Jugend-A, 30-deep for other age groups. Also German records. euro 15 as above,

European Athletics Yearbook 2004-05. A5 530pp. The EAA's splendidly informative review of 2004 and look ahead to 2005 includes 100-deep European year lists, plus under-23s and juniors, all-time lists and results of the major EAA events. 25 euro (in europe) or 30 euro elsewhere. Order forms from the 'Publications' section on www.European-athletics.org or from Ph. Reinheimer, Druckerei GmbH & Co. KG, c/o EAA, Alsfelder Strasse 27, 64289 Darmstadt, Germany.

Payment by cash or by bank transfer to – account: Justus von Liebig Verlag Darmstadt, bank: Postgiroamt Ffm, BLZ: 500 100 60, account no: 51 889-604.

Suomen Yleisurheilu 2005. A5 656pp. The Finnish Yearbook, published by the Finnish AA and compiled by Juhani and Mirko Jalava, contains not only every conceivable statistic for Finnish athletics in 2005 but also world indoor, outdoor and junior lists for the year as at November. 25 euros or £17 including postage in europe, and for the rest of the world $35. Orders by e-mail to juhani@tilastopaja.fi

Athlérama 2004. A5, 608pp. The French Annual, edited by Jean Gilbert and Patricia Doilin with a strong team of compilers, is again a superb reference book. Packed with information on French athletics – deep year lists, indexes, athlete profiles, results and all-time lists for all age groups. Extras include French top ten lists for 1954 and top marks for 1904. Also many colour photos. 25 euros from the FFA, 33 avenue Pierre de Coubertin, 75640 Paris CEDEX 13, France.

Greek Athletics Annual 2004. A5 350pp. Published by SEGAS. 50 deep performers and 20 deep performances, with 10 deep all-time lists (indoors and out) and biographical profiles of leading Greek athletes, records and results. Colour photographs. In Greek characters.

Indian Athletics Results & Records 2004. A5, 172pp. Results of championships meetings and national records. Published by the Athletics Federation of India. See www.indianathletics.org

Israeli Athletics 2005/6 Annual. 240 x 170mm, 54pp. By David Eiger and Arik Cooks. Records, championship results, 2005 top 20s and all-time lists, with profiles of leading Israeli athletes. 7 euro or US $8 from David Eiger, 10 Ezra Hozsofer Str, Herzliya 46 371, Israel.

Latvijas Vieglatletikas Gadagramata 2006. A5 352 pp. Comprehensive coverage of Latvian athletics, including 2005 lists and records, all-time lists, results and biographies, compiled by Andris Stagis. From the Latvian Athletic Association, Augsiela 1, Riga LV-1009, Latvia.

Annuare FLA 2005. A4 144p. The splendid Luxembourg Annual, edited by Georges Klepper has every possible detail for this nation. 15 euros in europe, 20 euros elsewhere to account no. LU32 1111 0200 0321 0000. See www.fla.lu.

KNAU Statistisch jaarboek 2004. A5 252pp. Compiled by Remko Riebeek, the Netherlands yearbook includes detailed year lists for seniors and juniors with all-time top tens and championship and international results. 25 euros in europe and 30 outside europe; cash (euros only) to: KNAU, Afdeling Verkoop, Postbox 230, 3400 AE Ijsselstein, The Netherlands.

Pacific Statistics. Compiled by Tony Isaacs. **No.25**: 44pp. Melanesia results and rankings 2004; Oceania Senior and Youth Championships, Oceania Grand Prix and National Championship. This and other booklets in the series: £5 sterling or euros 10 in banknotes from Tony Isaacs, 43 St.Georges Road, Felixstowe, Suffolk IP11 9PN, UK, England. E-mail: tony.isaacs2@tinyworld.co.uk.

Scottish Athletics Yearbook 2005. A5 268p. Edited by Arnold Black for the SATS. Comprehensive review of Scottish athletics with articles, deep Scottish lists for all age groups, event reviews and championship results with all-time lists and records and a 4-page section of colour photographs. £6 (£7.50 inc. postage in the UK, £8.50 europe, £9 elsewhere), sterling cheques only, payable to S.A.T.S. From Arnold Black, 19 Millbrae Crescent, Langside, Glasgow G42 9UW, UK.

South African Athletics Annual 2006. A5 208 pages. Edited by Gert le Roux. The 55th edition of this Annual includes 2005 and all-time lists, records and results. Order from Gert le Roux, PO Box 35209, Menlo Park, South Africa at 70 SA Rand per copy (surface mail) and 100 SA Rand (by airmail)…or the equivalent in US Dollars, euros or Sterling. No cheques.

Spanish Athletics Annual 2004/2005. 840pp. Surely the largest national annual ever, this has everything about Spanish athletics with immense depth of results and annual lists for 2005 as well as records, all-time lists, details of all Spanish champions, lists of Spanish international matches and all Spanish performances at major championships, with biographies of current stars and colour photographs. 22 euros inc. postage from: Federación Española de Atletismo (RFEA), Avda. Valladolid 81 - 1° - 28.008 Madrid SPAIN. E-mail: publicaciones@rfea.es.

Annuario 2004/2005 – Pista Cubierta y Campo a Través. A5 392pp. Comprehensive details for the Spanish cross country and indoor seasons with lists and results, all-time lists, progressive records, lists of previous champions and colour photographs. 10 euros plus postage (€6 in Spain, €12 elsewhere) from RFEA as above.

Friidrott 2004. A5 384pp. The 12th edition of this attractive annual edited by Göran Lenz covering world and Scandinavian athletics. Detailed championships results with narrative and world outdoor top 50 year and all-time lists, top 25 Scandinavian year and all-time lists plus indoor top tens. $49 europe, $52 rest of the world. 355 kr. Details from Gordons Förlag, Bärnstensvägen 2, 226 51 Lund, Sweden. email: goran.lenz@swipnet.se

Sverige Bästa 2004. A5 276p. Edited by Jonas Hedman. Detailed Swedish lists with all-time top tens. Published by the Svenska Friidrottsförbundet, Box 11, 171 18 Solna, Sweden.

Swiss Athletics 2004. A5 324p. The 31st edition of this Annual provides the usual comprehensive compilation of Swiss records, results, year lists and all-time top tens. There are also statistical profiles of 13 top athletes. From the Schweizerischer Leichtathletik Verband (SLV), Postfach 8222, CH 3001, Bern.

2005 Turkish Top Lists. 230x16mm. 50 deep per event, from Meric Tafolar (tafolar@yahoo.com) for postage cost only. Includes results of major meetings, national records for age groups and colour photos of top Turkish athletes.

2005 USA Track & Field Media Guide & FAST Annual (general editors: Jill Geer & Scott

Davis). A5 682pp. The 27th edition of the FAST Annual was again combined with the USATF Media Guide (first 244 pages includes detailed profiles on top athletes and lists of all US champions from 1985) to present a mighty tome on US athletics. The US lists for 2004 and the senior all-time lists are as usual 50-deep, with junior top 10s and 12-deep all-time junior and college lists. The final index section includes annual progressions etc. for all top American athletes (with distances in Imperial only!). Price $24 ($32 airmail) from Scott Davis, 4432 Snowbird Circle, Cerritos, CA 90703, USA.

Track Stats Historical Series: the NUTS event booklets series – giving great historical coverage of British athletics. Progressive UK records (senior and U20), indoors and out, age bests, very deep UK performer and performance all-time lists, best performances for each decade and yearly bests from 1827, results of all British and English internationals, all British performances at major international championships, national and area champions, and biographies of leading athletes. Price for each booklet inc. postage: £5 in UK, $8 or 8 euro in cash in sterling or Money Orders from outside Britain from Dave Terry, 34 Windmill Hill, Ruislip, Middlesex HA4 8PX, UK

(Email mdterry@dial.pipex.com). The two latest (by Ian Tempest, series editor Peter Matthews) are:

No. 9 Long Jump (men and women). A5 96pp. Published at end of 2004.

No. 10 Shot Put (men and women). A5 88pp. Published at end of 2005.

Statistical bulletins

The **DGLD – German** statistical group, the Deutschen Gesellschaft für Leichtathletik-Dokumentation produces annual national ranking lists (see **Deutsche Bestenliste**) for Germany and most impressive bulletins of up to 268 pages, packed with historical articles and statistical compilations. Each issue (three per year) includes statistical profiles of athletes born in that quarter 70 years ago, 75, 80, 85, 90 etc.

No. **42**. 196 pp. A special issue by Otto Verhoeven on German athletics in 1947 with championship results, year lists, records and articles. Profiled as athletes of the year were Heinz Ulzheimer and Marga Petersen.

No. **43**. 152 pp. Progressive German indoor records Men's 1500m-5000m, GDR all-time lists continued. miscellaneous profiles and corrections.

Membership, with free Deutsche Bestenliste euro 55 per year. Contact Hans Waynberg, Grefrather Weg 100, 41464 Neuss/Rh, Germany. Website: www.leichtathletik-dgld.de

The DGLD is also publishing a series of books dealing with the history of 100 years of athletics in Germany, event-by-event. The latest to be published is Band 5 – 1500m-Lauf Männer (275 pages, price euro 15 from Hans Waynberg. above). Editions covering men's Mar, HJ, SP, 110mh, 400mh and both men's and women's Walks are still available (DT sold out).

TRACK STATS. The NUTS quarterly bulletin, edited by Bob Phillips, includes a wealth of fascinating statistics and articles. A5, c.80 pages. Annual subscription (4 issues) is £17 (UK), £21 (rest of europe) or £26 (elsewhere); contact Liz Sissons, 9 Fairoak Lane, Chessington, Surrey KT9 2NS, UK.

May 2005: included an interview with 400m international and former MP Terry (now Lord) Higgins, a study of British javelin throwing 1920s-1940s and features on Audrey Williamson, Jim Thorpe, Bob Tisdall, George Saling and Voitto Hellsten.

August 2005: David Thurlow interviewed Chris Chataway and there are the world's leading performers in 1900 by Hubert Hamacher; the beginnings of indoor athletics in Britain, a profile of Joe Schatzle and a history of the one hour run by Andy Milroy.

November 2005: included features on Mal Whitfield and Hermine Bauma, John Wilkinson and Bert Cooper and a very detailed biography by Riël Hauman of the South African 1912 Olympic marathon winner Kennedy McArthur. Also pole vault bests with bamboo or metal poles by Leonid Nikitin, world all-time men's 5000m performers by Ian Smith and Estonian javelin throwing.

February 2006: included features on Heroic American Milers, features on Dorothy Manley/Hall, Mike Ellis, Ali Irfan, Tom Carruthers and Basil Ince, part 1 of Ian Tempest's statistical history of the AAA Indoor Championships.

The **Spanish group**, the **AEEA** continues to produce magnificent statistical publications. Membership for 2006 (four bulletins per year) is 55 euros from AEEA secretary Ignacio Mansilla E-mail: imc987@terra.es

No. 73: Mediterranean Games History Handbook. A5 124 pages. Published for the 2005 Games at Almeria. Raul Leoni updated his complete results of the Mediterranean Games and Györgi Csiki compiled an index of all medallists and national records for all the

Mediterranean countries. 12 euros inc. postage from Ignacio Mansilla, Urbanización Encina del Rey, Parcela n°18 - 28450 Collado Mediano Madrid, SPAIN. email ranking@rfea.es

No. 74: Historia de los 100 metros en los Juegos Olimpicos. A5 246 pages. This well-illustrated book includes complete details (by Enric Plá) of all the 100m competitions at the Olympic Games, but there is so much more... with profiles of all the champions, facts and feats and statistical summaries of each 4-year period leading up to the Games, including year leaders, lists for the period, international championship finals results and national champions of the major powers for the men's 100m.

Polymédias, 103 rue de Paris, 94220 Charenton le Pont, France will handle subscriptions for the major athletics magazines including their own **la letter de l'athlétisme** (42 euro outside France), **Leichtathletik** (Germany), **Track and Field News** (USA), and **Athletics International** (UK). www.polymedias.fr. Their catalogue of athletics books and magazine **la mémoire du sport** includes a large list of publications (including rare historical items) available.

Umbra Athletics have a wealth of invaluable books for the statistician. List from Unit 1, Bredbury Business Park, Bredbury Park Way, Stockport, SK6 2SN, England (email: julie@umbra.co.uk). These include books that Rob Whittingham (Treasurer) holds for the ATFS. Includes: IAAF Statistics Handbooks, some ATFS Annuals. Also: National Athletics records – various editions 1975-98, Race Walking World Statistics (many in the 1980s), British Athletics Annuals 1990-2006, and other national publications. ATFS Track & Field Performances Through The Years Volumes 2, 3 and 4 (£20 each).

HALL OF FAME 2006

The following athletes are included in our Hall of Fame (introduced in 2001).

Men: Abebe Bikila ETH, Valeriy Brumel RUS, Sergey Bubka UKR, Ron Clarke AUS, Sebastian Coe GBR, Jonathan Edwards GBR, Hicham El Guerrouj MAR, Herb Elliott AUS, Haile Gebrselassie ETH, Vladimir Golubnichiy RUS, Gunder Hägg SWE, Colin Jackson GBR, Michael Johnson USA, Kip Keino KEN, Robert Korzeniowski POL, Carl Lewis USA, Noureddine Morceli ALG, Edwin Moses USA, Paavo Nurmi FIN, Parry O'Brien USA, Al Oerter USA, Jesse Owens USA, Viktor Saneyev RUS, Yuriy Sedykh RUS, Peter Snell NZL, Daley Thompson GBR, Lasse Viren FIN, Cornelius Warmerdam USA, Emil Zátopek CZE, Jan Zelezny CZE.
Women: Iolanda Balas ROM, Fanny Blankers-Koen NED, Nadezhda Chizhova RUS, Gail Devers USA, Heike Drechsler GER, Ruth Fuchs GDR, Jackie Joyner-Kersee USA, Tatyana Kazankina RUS, Marita Koch GDR, Ingrid Kristiansen NOR, Faina Melnik RUS, Maria Mutola MOZ, Merlene Ottey JAM, Paula Radcliffe GBR, Gabriela Szabo ROM, Irena Szewinska POL.

Each year we add five new athletes – a mix of past and current stars, taking special consideration of athletes who have just retired. Any current stars can only be included if they have already had at least ten years in international competition.

This year I asked several experts for their choices for five newcomers, but their selections varied widely, so that of ten people who nominated athletes three names came up on top, with three votes each! They were Bob Beamon, Rudolf Harbig and Grete Waitz – and to those names I have added one athlete who is newly retired, Wilson Kipketer, and the fastest woman of all-time, the late Flo-Jo.

Our five 2006 additions are:

Bob BEAMON (USA) (b. 29 Aug 1946) – Beamon's long jump of 8.90m to win the Olympic title in 1968 was long regarded as a contender for a perpetual world record. At 2½ inches over 29 feet, it was not only the first 29 ft jump, but also the first over 28 ft. Beamon, who was the favourite for the title but known as an inconsistent jumper, took full advantage of the maximum permitted wind aid and the 2247m high altitude of Mexico City to add an amazing 55cm to the world record and nearly two feet to his own best of 8.33m (27ft 4 in).

No other athlete bettered even 28 feet (8.53m) until 1980, and the record was eventually bettered when Mike Powell jumped 8.95m at Tokyo in 1991. Beamon himself, having achieved everything in just a few seconds activity, never again jumped over even 27ft, falling an inch short in 1969, in which year he suffered a serious hamstring injury. He was second in the 1967 Pan-American Games and was AAU champion outdoors in 1968 and 1969 and indoors in 1967 and 1968. While at North Carolina A&T he was NCAA champion indoors at long and triple jumps in 1968, and he graduated from the University of Texas at El Paso in 1970. He became a social worker. Other bests: 100y 9.5 (1966), triple jump 16.02i (1968).

Florence GRIFFITH-JOYNER (USA) (b. 21 Dec 1959, d. 21 Sep 1998) – 'Flo-Jo', an extraordinarily talented athlete, captured the headlines in 1988 with her amazing series of runs at the US Trials, especially her world record time of 10.49 in the quarter-final of the 100m, which was followed by a US record of 21.77 for 200m. The wind for the 100m was shown and officially accepted as 0.0, but seems nearly certain to have been strongly wind-assisted at c.4-5m/s. She won the final in 10.61 and it may be that this is the 'true' world record. She showed equally brilliant form at the Olympics, where she won the 100m in 10.54w, then set two more world records at the 200m, 21.56 in the semi-final and 21.34 in the final.

She completed triple gold at the sprint relay and then earned a silver at 4x400m relay with a 48.07 leg. Her four medals equalled the women's Olympic record. Her attire that year was equally impressive, as she revealed a series of colourful, clinging body-suits, and she formerly had six-inch long painted fingernails on her left hand! She then retired – surprisingly in view of the rewards she could have earned – and her world records seem out of sight for women sprinters that have followed her. Allegations of drug use were rife, yet unsubstantiated, and there can be no doubt of her speed and allure.

She had just missed the Olympic team in the

boycott year of 1980 as she was 4th at 200m in the US Trials. While at UCLA she won NCAA titles at 200m in 1982 and at 400m in 1983. At 200m she won the silver medal at the 1984 Olympics and 1987 Worlds (where she won a gold at sprint relay). Her best time for 400m was 50.89 in 1985. She was the Sullivan Award winner in 1988.
She married Al Joyner, the 1984 Olympic triple jump champion, in October 1987 and their daughter Mary Ruth was born on 14 Nov 1990.

Rudolf HARBIG (Germany) (b. 3 Nov 1913, d. 8 Mar 1944) – Harbig was an immensely gifted runner but deprived of Olympic opportunity due to the War, in which he was killed on the Eastern Front. He took the bronze medal at 4x400m at the 1936 Olympics, after going out in a heat of the 800m. He won 55 consecutive races at various distances 1938-40, including the gold medal at 800m (and 4x400m relay) at the 1938 European Championships.
He reached his pinnacle of form with 800m in 1:46.6 for Germany against Italy at Milan on 15 July 1939, and this remained a world record for 16 years. A month later Harbig added the world record for 400m with 46.0, again convincingly beating his arch-rival Mario Lanzi, and in 1941 he added further world records, 1000m in 2:21.5 and at 4x800m relay. Harbig, German champion at 400m 1942 and 800m 1936-41 and coached by Waldemar Gerschler, remains the last man to have held world records for both 400m and 800m.

Wilson KIPKETER (Denmark) (b. 12 July 1970 Kenya) – Kipketer, a pupil of the renowned Father Colm O'Connell at St Patrick's School in Kenya, went to Denmark in 1990 to study electrical engineering, and stayed there, eventually gaining Danish citizenship. Having run for Kenya in the World Junior Championships of 1988 and 1990 (4th), he won the World 800m for Denmark in 1995, 1997 and 1999 and the European title in 2002.
He was not permitted, however, to run for Denmark at the Olympic Games in 1996, when he was clearly the world number one, winning all his 14 races, with six 1:42s and a close attempt at the world record with 1:41.83, but after injuries and illness won Olympic silver in 2000 and bronze in 2004. He was at his best in 1997, starting with a superb performance at the World Indoor Championships. In his heat he smashed the world indoor record of 1:44.84 with his 1:43.96 and in the final broke it again with 1:42.67. Outdoors, showing for the first time real commitment to a fast pace throughout his race, he tied Sebastian Coe's 16 year-old world record of 1:41.73 at Oslo in July, and In August set world records with 1:41.24 in Zürich and, 11 days later, 1:41.11 in Köln.
Other best times: 400m 46.85 (1994), 1000m 2:14.96i (1000), 2:16.29 (1995); 1500m 3:42.80 (1993), 1M 3:59.57 (1993).

Grete WAITZ (Norway) (b. 1 Oct 1953, née Andersen) – Waitz was the first world champion at the women's marathon in 1983, fitting recognition of her ability and her pioneering role in women's distance running. She ran world bests in her first three marathons annually at New York from 1978 to 1980, her times 2:32:29.8, 2:27:32.6 and 2:25:41.
She set a fourth world best with 2:25:29 in London on 17 April 1983 and went on to complete nine wins in the New York Marathon, winning each year 1982-6 and in 1988. In all she won 13 of her 19 marathons 1978-90, including London again in 1986 in her best ever time of 2:24:54. She was also runner-up to Joan Benoit in the first women's Olympic marathon in 1984.
She first competed in the European Championships in 1971 at 800m and 1500m, and in the Olympics at 1500m in 1972. On the track she set a European junior 1500m record in 1971 and two world records at 3000m: 8:46.6 in 1975 and 8:45.4 in 1976, with a European 5000m record of 15:08.80 in 1982. She had a World Cup win at 3000m in 1977 and took European bronze medals at 1500m in 1974 and at 3000m in 1978. She was at her best in road races, where her first ever loss was to Maricica Puica in 1981, and at cross-country, where she was unbeaten for twelve years and achieved a record five wins (1978-81 and 1983) in the World Championships (also third in 1982 and 1984).
She won 33 Norwegian senior titles from 1971 to 1983 and set 23 Norwegian records at track events from 800m to 5000m. A statue of her was erected outside the Bislett Stadium in Oslo in 1984. Other bests: 800m 2:03.1 (1975), 1500m 4:00.55 (1978), 1 mile 4:26.90 (1979), 3000m 8:31.75 (1979).

Bob Beamon soars into history at the 1968 Olympics with the world's first 29ft jump. (courtesy Track and Field News)

Florence Griffiths Joyner – still the world record holder for 100m and 200m.

Rudolf Harbig – whose 800m world record lasted for 16 years.
(courtesy Track and Field News)

Grete Waitz – won the New York Marathon nine times.

Wilson Kipketer – three times World 800m champion outdoors and once indoors.

Taytana Lebedeva – Golden League jackpot winner at triple jump

Olimpiada Ivanova – world record at 20km walk at Worlds

Tirunesh Dibaba - 5000m/10,000m double at Helsinki and double World CC champion

NATIONAL CHAMPIONS 2005 and BIOGRAPHIES OF LEADING ATHLETES

By Peter Matthews

THIS SECTION incorporates biographical profiles of 765 of the world's top athletes, 416 men and 349 women, listed by nation. Also listed are national champions at standard events in 2005 for the leading countries prominent in athletics (for which I have such details).

The athletes profiled have, as usual, changed quite considerably from the previous year, not only that all entries have been updated, but also that many newcomers have been included to replace those who have retired or faded a little from the spotlight.

The choice of who to include is always invidious, but I have concentrated on those who are currently in the world's top 10-15 per event, those who have the best championship records and some up-and-coming athletes who I consider may make notable impact during the coming year.

Since this section was introduced in the 1985 Annual, biographies have been given for a total of 3335 different athletes (1939 men and 1396 women).

The ever continuing high turnover in our sport is reflected in the fact that there are many more newcomers than usual (76 men, 68 women) to this section, as well as 15 (9 men, 6 women) reinstated from previous Annuals. The athletes to have had the longest continuous stretch herein are Jan Zelezny at 19 years, Gail Devers 18 years, Franka Dietzsch and Yelena Nikolayeva 17 years.

No doubt some of those dropped from this compilation will also again make their presence felt; the keen reader can look up their credentials in previous Annuals, and, of course, basic details may be in the athletes' index at the end of this book.

Athletes included in these biographies are identified in the index at the end of this Annual by * for those profiled in this section and by ^ for those who were included in previous Annuals.

The biographical information includes:

a) Name; date and place of birth; height (in metres); weight (in kilograms).
b) Previous name(s) for married women; club or university; occupation.
c) Major championships record – all placings in such events as the Olympic Games, World Championships, European Championships, Commonwealth Games, World Cup and European Cup Super League; leading placings in finals of the World Indoor Championships, European or World Junior Championships, European Under-23 Championships and other Continental Championships; and first three to six in European Indoors or World University Games.
IAAF Grand Prix first three at each event or overall.
World Athletics Final (WAF) winners
d) National (outdoor) titles won or successes in other major events.
e) Records set: world, continental and national; indoor world records/bests (WIR/WIB).
f) Progression of best marks over the years at each athlete's main event(s).
g) Personal best performances at other events.
h) Other comments.

See Introduction to this Annual for lists of abbreviations used for events and championships.

Note that for comparison purposes decathlons and heptathlons made before the introduction of the current tables have been rescored using the 1984 IAAF Tables, except those marked *, for which event breakdowns were unavailable. Women's pentathlons (p) have not been rescored.

Information given is as known at 5 April 2006 (to include performances at the World Indoor Championships, Commonwealth Games and the World Cross-country Championships as well as some early outdoor events of 2006).

I am most grateful to various ATFS members who have helped check these details. Additional information or corrections would be welcomed for next year's Annual.

Peter Matthews

ALGERIA

Governing body: Fédération Algerienne d'Athlétisme, BP n°61, Dely-Ibrahim, Alger. Founded 1963.

National Champions 2005: **Men**: 200m: Mailk Louahla 20.90, 800m: Anter Zerguelaine 1:50.17, 1500m: Tarek Boukensa 3:36.05, 5000m: Khoudir Aggoune 13:43.63, LJ: Issam Nima 7.76. **Women**: 800m: Chahrazad Cheboub 2:07.51, 1500m: Fatiha Azzouhoum 4:18.76, 5000m: Souad Aït Salem 16:26.37, 100mh: Sarah Bouaoudia 13.71.

Djabir SAÏD-GUERNI b. 29 Mar 1977 Algers 1.87m 70kg. Army sergeant.

At 800m: OG: '00- 3, '04- 7; WCh: '99- 3, '03- 1, '05- 5; WJ: '96- h; AfCh: '98- 3, '00- 1/1R, '02- 1; WUG: '99- 4; WCp: '02- 2.

Two Algerian 800m records 1999.

Progress at 800m: 1997- 1:46.84, 1998- 1:45.72, 1999- 1:43.09, 2000- 1:43.25, 2001- 1:44.55, 2002- 1:44.03, 2003- 1:44.60, 2004- 1:44.44, 2005- 1:44.80. pbs: 400m 46.15 '00, 46.1 '03; 1000m 2:14.52 '99.

Made huge breakthrough at 1999 World Champs, when he reduced his pb of 1:45.72 to 1:45.65, 1:45.17 and 1:44.18 in successive rounds to the bronze medal. Then 3rd in Brussels in 1:43.09. Formerly married to Wassila Rédoune, African champion who competed at the 2000 Olympic Games at fencing. His older brother Chakib ran on the team that was 2nd at 4x100m in the 1994 African Junior Champs.

Ali SAÏDI SIEF b. 15 Mar 1978 Constantine 1.80m 68kg. ENA d'Angers, France.

At 1500m: WCh: '97- h, '99- sf; WJ: '96- 7; AfCh: '98- 3. At 3000m: WI: '99- 9; 2nd GP 2000. At 5000m: OG: '00- 2, '04- 10; WCh: '01- dq 2, '05- 5; AfCh: '00- 1; won Med G 2005. World CC: '97- 17J, '00- 16 (4k).

World junior 2000m record 1997. Algerian records 3000m and 5000m 2000, 2000m 2001.

Progress at 1500m, 5000m: 1996- 3:41.6, 1997- 3:37.47, 1998- 3:35.87, 1999- 3:30.91, 13:39.5; 2000- 3:30.82, 12:50.86; 2001- 3:29.51, 13:02.16; 2003- 3:40.22, 2004- 3:32.46, 13:07.37; 2005- 3:34.48, 13:13.50. pbs: 1M 3:48.23 '01, 2000m 4:46.88 '01, 3000m 7:25.02 '00.

Tested positive for Nandrolene after taking second place in World 5000m 2001 and served two-year drugs ban, On his return in 2003 had a major win at 3000m in Brussels in 7:30.79.

Women

Baya RAHOULI b. 27 Jul 1979 Bab el Oued 1.79m 64kg.

At TJ(/LJ): OG: '00- 5, '04- 6; WCh: '99- 10, '03- 11, '05- 7; WJ: '96- 10, '98- 1; WI: '03- 7, '04- 10; WCp: '98- 6; AfG:'95- 4, '99- 2/6; AfCh: '98- 1/3, '00- 1; Af-J: '94- 1, '95- 1/2, '97- 1/2 (1 100mh); WUG: '99- 4; won MedG 2001, 2005; Pan Arab 100m, 100mh, LJ & TJ 2004.

Six African triple jump records 1998-9. ALG records 100m 1999, LJ 1998-9, TJ 1998-2005.

Progress at TJ: 1993- 11.76, 1994- 12.05, 1995- 13.09, 1996- 13.48, 1997- 13.55, 1998- 14.04, 1999- 14.64A/14.30, 2000- 14.30/14.42w, 2001- 13.88/14.30w, 2002- 14.02, 2003- 14.48, 2004- 14.89, 2005- 14.98. pbs: 60m 7.45i '99, 100m 11.1/11.62/11.51w '99, 100mh 13.49 '04, LJ 6.70 '99.

Brother Hamimed Rahouli set African 50km walk record of 4:19:15 in 1987.

ARGENTINA

Governing body: Confederación Argentina de Atletismo, 21 de Noviembre No. 207. 3260 Concepción del Uruguay, Entre Ríos. Founded 1954 (original governing body founded 1919).

National Championships first held in 1920 (men), 1939 (women). **2005 Champions: Men**: 100m/200m: Iván Carlos Altamirano 10.32w/21.80, 400m: Esteban Brandán 48.47, 800m: Leonardo Price 1:51.70, 1500m: Javier Carriqueo 3:49.68, 5000m: Cristian Alfonsín 14:34.43, 10,000m: Juan Osvaldo Suárez 29:33.24, HMar: Gastón Fuentealba 68:52, Mar: Oscar Cortínez 2:19:56, 3000mSt: Mariano Mastromarino 8:49.77, 110mh/Dec: Leandro Peyrano 14.35w/6773, 400mh: Christian Deymonnaz 52.42, HJ: Ersamo Jara 2.15, PV: Javier Benitez 5.15, LJ: Eric Kerwitz 7.42, TJ: Martin Falico 14.61, SP: Germán Lauro 17.37, DT: Jorge Balliengo 60.37, HT: Juan Cerra 68.90, JT: Pablo Pietrobelli 67.70, 20000mW: Jorge Lorefice 1:45:20.3. **Women**: 100m/200m: Vanesa Wohlgemuth 11.94/24.94, 400m: María Andrea Rossotti 55.82/2:13.03, 1500m: Valeria Rodríguez 4:24.96, 5000m: Sandra Amarillo 16:55.73, 10,000m: Roxana Preussler 35:36.37, HMar: Sandra Torres Álvarez 78:35, Mar: Verónica Páez 2:50:53, 3000mSt: María Peralta 10:36.73, 100mh: Maria de la Paz Azatto 14.10, 400mh: Verónica Barraza 63.17, HJ: Solange Witteveen 1.84, PV: Alejandra García 4.15, LJ: Andrea Bordalejo 5.89, TJ: Dayana Sastre URU 12.48, SP/DT: Rocío Comba 15.05/41.60, HT: Karina Moya 62.36, JT: Romina Maggi 45.78, Hep: Andrea Bordalejo 4970, 20000mW: Lidia Carriego 2:04:47.3.

AUSTRALIA

Governing body: Athletics Australia, Suite 22, Fawkner Towers, 431 St.Kilda Rd, Melbourne, Victoria 3004. Founded 1897.

National Championships first held in 1893 (men) (Australasian until 1927), 1930 (women). **2005 Champions: Men**: 100m: Joshua Ross 10.22, 200m: Daniel Batman 20.76, 400m: Ben Offereins 46.37, 800m: Nick Bromley 1:48.09, 1500m: Lachlan Chisholm 3:45.18, 5000m: Craig Mottram 14:01.38, 10,000m (held Dec 2004): David Ruschena 28:59.55, HMar: Damon Harris 67:05, Mar: Brett Cartwright 2:18:16, 3000mSt: Peter Nowill 8:30.16, 110mh: Greg Eyears 14.39, 400mh: Brendan Cole 51.29, HJ: Nick Moroney 2.18, PV: Paul Burgess

5.60, LJ: Chris Noffke 8.00w, TJ: Michael Perry 16.60w, SP: Clay Cross 18.78, DT: Scott Martin 59.20, HT: Stuart Rendell 74.35, JT: Oliver Dziubak 77.39, Dec: Erik Surjan 7621, 20kmW/50kmW: Nathan Deakes 1:19:39/3:47:51. **Women**: 100m: Sally McLellan 11.77, 200m: Lauren Hewitt 23.55, 400m: Tamsyn Lewis 52.44, 800m: Katherine Katsanevakis 2.04.72, 1500m: Sarah Jamieson 4:09.42, 5000m: Benita Johnson 15:46.53, 10,000m (held Dec 2004): Haley McGregor 32:41.10, HMar: Kate Smyth 78:45, Mar: Jackie Fairweather 2:34:45, 3000mSt: Kristy Villis 10:27.23, 100mh: Fiona Cullen & Sally McLellan 13.41, 400mh: Lauren Boden 58.59, HJ: Sophia Begg 1.86, PV: Kym Howe 4.40, LJ: Kerrie Taurima 6.59w, TJ: Jeanette Bowles 12.81, SP: Alifatou Djibril TOG 15.72, DT: Dani Samuels 55.78, HT: Bronwyn Eagles 65.43, JT: Kim Mickle 55.91, Hep: Kylie Wheeler 59.74, 20kmW: Jane Saville 1:32:49.

Luke ADAMS b. 22 Oct 1976 Myumi, Tanzania 1.89m 70kg. Bankstown. Studied industrial design.
At 20kmW: OG: '04- 16; WCh: '03- 5, '05- 10; CG: '02- 2, '06- 2; WCp: '04- 14. At 10,000mW: WJ: '94- 24. Won AUS 20kmW 2003, 30kmW 1998.
Progress at 20kmW: 1995- 1:30:21, 1996- 1:25:27, 1999- 1:23:52, 2000- 1:24:18, 2001- 1:26:31, 2002- 1:23:56, 2003- 1:19:35, 2004- 1:21:24, 2005- 1:19:19, 2006- 1:20:49. pbs: 3000mW 11:48.4 '95. 5000mW 19:34.68 '00, 10,000mW 40:04.88 '05, 30kmW 2:17:33 '02; 50kmW 4:04:03 '02.

Paul BURGESS b. 14 Aug 1979 Perth 1.84m 83kg. Stirling Swans.
At PV: OG: '00- dnq 16=, '04- 11=; CG: '98- 2, '02- 2; WJ: '96- 1, '98- 3=; WCp: '98- 7, '02- 5=. AUS champion 2000, 2002, 2005-06.
Oceania indoor pole vault record 5.80 in 2006.
Progress at PV: 1994- 3.90, 1995- 5.25, 1996- 5.35, 1997- 5.51, 1998- 5.60, 1999- 5.50, 2000- 5.60, 2001- 5.71, 2002- 5.75, 2003- 5.70, 2004- 5.77, 2005- 6.00, 2006- 5.85. Former gymnast.

Nathan DEAKES b. 17 Aug 1977 Geelong 1.83m 66kg. Bellarine.
At 20kmW(/50kmW): OG: '00- 8/6, '04- 3/dq; WCh: '99- 7, '01- 4/dq; CG: '98- 3, '02- 1/1, '06- 1/1; WCp: '04- 3. At 10,000mW: WJ: '96- 3. Won GWG 20000mW 2001, AUS 20kmW 2000-02, 2004-06; 50kmW 1999 (t), 2005-06.
Commonwealth & Oceania walk records at 20km 2001 & 2005, 20,000m track (1:19:48.1) 2001, 50km 2003. 5000m 2006.
Progress at 20kmW, 50kmW: 1996- 1:26:27, 1997- 1:23:58, 1998- 1:23:25, 1999- 1:20:15, 3:52:53; 2000- 1:21:03, 3:47:29; 2001- 1:18:14, 3:43:43; 2002- 1:21:07, 3:52:40; 2003- 3:39:43, 2004- 1:19:11, 2005- 1:17:33, 3:47.51; 2006- 1:19:55, 3:42:53. pbs: 3000mW 11:17.0 '98, 5000mW 18:45.19 '06, 10,000m 38:44.87 '02, 30kmW 2:10:57 '04, 35kmW 2:35:05 '00.
Unable to compete at 2005 Worlds due to a hamstring injury, returned for second Commonwealth Games double in 2006.

Steve HOOKER b. 16 Jul 1982 Melbourne 1.87m 82kg. Box Hill.
At PV: OG: '04- 28=; WCh: '04- dnq 17=; CG: '06- 1; WJ: '00- 4.
Progress at PV: 1999- 5.00, 2000- 5.20, 2001- 5.30, 2002- 5.25, 2003- 5.45, 2004- 5.65, 2005- 5.87, 2006- 5.91. pbs: 100m 10.6, 10.68w '05, 200m 21.1 '05, LJ 7.10 '05.
Played Australian Rules football before taking up pole vaulting. His father Bill was 6th CG 800m 1974, had pbs: 800m 1:45.36 '73, 400mh pb 50.6 '69, and his mother Erica (née Nixon) was 6th LJ, 4th Pen 1974 and 2nd LJ 1978 (in pb 6.58) at CG.

Patrick JOHNSON b. 26 Sep 1972 near Cairns 1.77m 73kg. AIS. Was at Australian National University. Administrative officer with the Department of Foreign Affairs and Trade.
At 100m/(200m)/4x100mR: OG: '00- qf/qf, '04- 6R; WCh: '97- (h), '03- qf/qf, '05- qf/6; CG: '02- 3R, '06- 6/4. Won AUS 100m 2003, 200m 2001, 2003, 2006.Oceania 100m record 2003.
Progress at 100m: 1996- 10.47w, 1997- 10.39/10.27w, 1998- 10.43, 1999- 10.17, 2000- 10.10, 2001- 10.25/10.13w, 2002- 10.26, 2003- 9.93/9.88w, 2004- 10.28/10.24w, 2005- 10.20/10.01w, 2006- 10.18. pb 200m 20.49 '06, 20.25w '03.
Aboriginal mother, Irish father.

Dmitri MARKOV b. 14 Mar 1975 Vitebsk, Belarus 1.82m 82kg. SASI.
At PV: OG: '96- 6, '00- 5=, '04- dnq 22=; WCh: '97- nh, '99- 2, '01- 1, '03- 4, '05- nh; CG: '02- 4=, '06- 2; EI: '96- 1; WJ: '94- 2; EJ: '93- 6. 3rd GP 1999. AUS champion 1998, 2001, 2003-04.
Commonwealth pole vault record 2001, four BLR records 1996-8, four AUS 1999-2001.
Progress at PV: 1991- 4.80, 1992- 5.10, 1993- 5.42, 1994- 5.50, 1995- 5.65, 1996- 5.86, 1997- 5.95, 1998- 6.00, 1999- 5.95, 2000- 5.85, 2001- 6.05, 2002- 5.65, 2003- 5.86, 2004- 5.80, 2005- 5.75, 2006- 5.70. pb LJ 7.31w/7.24 '03.
Became an Australian citizen in May 1999, a month after his wife Valentina, who was granted citizenship as a result of spending two consecutive years in Australia after becoming a permanent resident in April 1997.

Craig MOTTRAM b. 18 Jun 1980 Frankston, Victoria 1.88m 73kg. Deakin. Degree from Deakin University
At 5000m (1500m): OG: '00- h, '04- 8; WCh: '01- (sf), '05- 3; CG: '02- 6, '06- 2 (9). At 3000m: WI: '01- 8, '04- 10; WCp: '02- 1. World CC: '99- 17J, 4k: '01-02-04-06: 8/5/9/11; 12k: '04-05: 13/22. Won AUS 1500m 2002, 5000m 2002, 2004-06; 10,000m 2001.
Oceania records 3000m 2002, 5000m (4) 2002-04, 2M 2005.
Progress at 5000m: 1999- 13:40.48, 2000- 13:26.20, 2001- 13:23.94, 2002- 13:12.04, 2003- 13:17.81, 2004- 12:55.76, 2005- 12:56.13. pbs: 800m 1:52.90, 1500m: 3:34.80/3:32.7e '05, 1M 3:48.98 '05,

2000m 5:06.97 '01, 3000m 7:37.30 '02, 2M 8:11.27 '05, 10,000m 27:50.55 '03.
Former AUS junior triathlon champion. British parents, father Brian played football for Wimbledon.

John STEFFENSEN b. 30 Aug 1982 Perth 1.80m 71kg. University of Western Australia.
At LJ: OG: '04- 2R; WCh: '03- hR, '05- 8; CG: '06- 1/1R. Australian champion 2006.
Progress at 400m: 2002- 47.14, 2003- 46.07, 2004- 45.63, 2005- 45.31, 2006- 44.73. pbs: 200m 20.88 '05, LJ 7.18/7.28w '02.
Was a state champion boxer.

Women

Brooke BILLETT b. 9 Jul 1980 Tailem Bend, SA 1.80m 125kg. née Krueger. Enfield H. Primary school teacher.
At HT: OG: '04- dnq 33; WCh: '03- dnq 17; CG: '02- 4, '06- 1; WJ: '98- dnq. Won AUS 2003, 2006.
Progress at HT: 1995- 31.09, 1996- 49.54, 1997- 52.62, 1998- 56.89, 1999- 54.80, 2000- 61.89, 2001- 62.64, 2002- 67.87, 2003- 67.40, 2004- 68.78, 2005- 68.25, 2006- 70.72.
Married hammer thrower Darren Billett (pb 66.32 '06) in 2004. Her uncle was Test cricketer Brian Booth.

Tatyana GRIGORIEVA b. 8 Oct 1975 St Petersburg, Russia 1.80m 64kg. SA Sports Institute. Model.
At PV: OG: '00- 2; WCh: '99- 3, '01- 4, '05- 12; CG: '02- 1, '06- 2; WI: '99- 9=; WCp: '02- nh. Won AUS 1999, 2001-02, 2006.
Progress at PV: 1997- 3.90, 1998- 4.35, 1999- 4.50/4.55ex, 2000- 4.55, 2001- 4.56, 2002- 4.46, 2003- 4.23, 2004- 4.30, 2005- 4.47, 2006- 4.45. pbs: 100y 11.3w '98, 400mh 58.54 '96.
She moved with her husband pole-vaulter Viktor Chistiakov (now separated) from Russia to Australia in 1997 and then took up vaulting.

Kym HOWE-NADIN b. 12 Jun 1980 1.77m 64kg. née Howe. Curtin. Child care worker.
At PV: OG: '04- dnq 16; WCh: '99- 3, '01- 4, '05- 12; CG: '02- 2, '06- 1; WJ: '98- 11. Won AUS 1999, 2004-05.
Two Commonwealth & Oceania pole vault records 2006.
Progress at PV: 1997- 3.60, 1998- 3.90, 1999- 4.16, 2000- 4.20, 2001- 4.30, 2002- 4.45, 2003- 4.30, 2004- 4.40, 2005- 4.40, 2006- 4.62.
Member of Western Australian junior gymnastics team 1993-6.

Benita JOHNSON b. 6 May 1979 Mackay, QLD 1.66m 50kg. née Willis. University of Queensland.
At 3000m: WI: '01- 6, '03- 7. At 5000m (1500m): OG: '00- h; WCh: '01- 12; CG: '02- 6 (h); WJ: '98- (7); WUG: '99- (5); WCp: '02- 4. At 10,000m: OG: '04- 24; WCh: '03- 8, '05- 19; CG: '06- 4. World HMar: '03- 3; CC: 4km: '01-02-03-06: 6/4/5/4; 8km: '04-05-06: 1/7/4. Won AUS 5000m 2003, 2005-06; 10,000m 2004, 2006.
Oceania records: 3000m (2) 2001-03, 5000m (3) 2001-02, 2000m & 10,000m 2003.
Progress at 5000m, 10,000m, Mar: 1997- 16:11.57, 1998- 16:31.2, 2000- 15:21.37, 2001- 15:04.18, 2002- 14:47.60, 2003- 14:54.52, 30:37.68; 2004- 15:16.61, 31:49.9, 2:38:03; 2005- 15:21.02, 31:55.15, 2:26:32. pbs: 800m 2:05.41 '00, 1500m 4:07.05 '00, 1M 4:32.61 '06, 2000m 5:37.71 '03, 3000m 8:38.06 '03, HMar 67:55 '04.
Became Australia's first World CC champion in 2004 and later won Great North Run half marathon. Under-18 international at hockey. Married Cameron Johnson 2 Feb 2002. Her younger sister Caitlin Willis has 400m pb 52.75 '06 (1R CG '06).

Donna MacFARLANE b. 18 Jun 1977 Melbourne 1.76m 57kg. née Tyberek. Sandy Bay. Radio producer
At 3000mSt: CG: '06- 3.
Progress at 3000mSt: 2000- 10:31.10. 2005- 9:51.60, 2006- 9:25.05. pbs: 800m 2:06.39 '06, 1500m 4:15.83 '06, 1M 4:15.83 '06, 5000m 16:43.30 '99, 3000m 8:50.65 '06.
Australian junior 1500m champion 1997, retired to start a family; made dramatic return 2005/06.

Jana PITTMAN b. 9 Nov 1982 Sydney 1.81m 68kg. Multelink Hills and Panellínios GRE.
At 400mh(/400m): OG: '00- h; '04- 5; WCh: '03- 1; CG: '02- 1/1R, '06- 1/1R; WJ: '00- 1/1; WY: '99- 1/7; WCp: '02- 3. AUS champion 2001-03.
Equalled official world junior record 400mh 2000. Oceania 300m best 2003.
Progress at 400mh: 1998- 59.75, 1999- 56.23, 2000- 55.20A/55.63, 2001- 55.93, 2002- 54.14, 2003- 53.22, 2004- 53.43, 2005- 53.44, 2006- 53.82. pbs: 100m 11.77 '03, 200m 23.52 '03, 300m 36.34 '03, 400m 50.43 '03, 800m 2:04.03 '05, 100mh 13.92 '00.
Won the 400m/400mh double at the 2000 World Juniors, the first woman to achieve this feat at an IAAF/IOC event. Named the IAAF Rising Star for 2000. Set world age 19 400mh record in 2002. World champ at Yth, Jnr, Snr. Had arthroscopic knee surgery just a couple of weeks before OG 2004. Married British 400m hurdler Chris Rawlinson (1 CG 2002) on 31 Mar 2006.

Melissa ROLLISON b. 13 Apr 1983 Adelaide 1.66m 50kg. Victory Sports. Medical massage therapist.
At 3000mSt: CG: '06- 2; Won GWG 2001, AUS champion 1999-2000, 2002, 2006. At 1500m: WJ: '00- 8. World CC: '02- 9J, '06- 11 4k.
Three world junior records 1999-2001, four Oceania 1999-2006 at 3000mSt.
Progress at 3000mSt: 1999- 10.15.73, 2000- 10:10.73, 2001- 9:30.70, 2002- 9:56.92, 2006- 9:24.29. pbs: 800m 2:05.72 '02, 1500m 4:09.80 '02, 1M 4:31.88 '06, 3000m 8:54.86 '06, 5000m 15:55.19 '04, 2000mSt 6:32.23 '01.

Jane SAVILLE b. 5 Nov 1974 Sydney 1.64m 53kg. Randwick Botany H.
At 20kmW: OG: '00- dq, '04- 3: WCh: '99- 7, '01-

dq, '03- 11, '05- 20; CG: '02- 1. '06- 1; WCp: '04- 4. At 10kmW: OG: '96- 26; WCh: '97- h; CG: '94- 8, '98- 1, '02- 1. At 5000mW: WJ: '92- 2. Won AUS 5000mW 1997, 10kmW 1991-2, 1997-8, 20kmW 2000, 2002-06.
Oceania & Commonwealth 20km walk records 2000 & 2004.
Progress at 10kmW, 20kmW: 1990- 52:24, 1991- 47:10, 1992- 46:02, 1993- 47:29.1, 1994- 46:04, 1995- 45:10, 1996- 45:22, 1997- 42:59, 1998- 43:38, 1:37:53; 1999- 42:15, 1:31:58; 2000- 44:06, 1:28:56; 2001- 44:40, 1:31:20; 2002- 1:34:18, 2003- 44:43, 1:30:51; 2004- 44:06, 1:27:44; 2005- 44:58, 1:29:33. pbs: 3000mW 12:27.74 '93, 5000mW 21:32.26 '97.
Disqualified when leading just outside stadium at Sydney Olympics. Married to Matt White, who competed at cycling for Australia at the 1998 Commonwealth Games. Her sister **Natalie** (b. 7 Sep 1978) was 2nd to her at 2006 CG (4th 2002), pbs: 10kmW 45:10 '97, 20kmW 1:31:34 '04.

Bronwyn THOMPSON b. 29 Jan 1978 Rockhampton, Queensland 1.77m 68kg. Southern Suburbs. Paediatric physiotherapist.
At LJ: OG: '00- dnq 16, '04- 4; WCh: '03- 7; CG: '02- 6, '06- 1. Australian champion 2002-03, 2006.
Oceania long jump records 2001 & 2002.
Progress at LJ: 1992- 5.42, 1993- 5.60, 1994- 6.04/6.14w, 1995- 6.10; 1996- 6.10/6.15w, 1997- 5.95, 2000- 6.56/6.64w, 2001- 6.88, 2002- 7.00, 2003- 6.73/6.75w, 2004- 6.96, 2005- 6.59/6.73w, 2006- 6.97. pbs: 100m 11.77 '03, 200m 24.19 '03.
Serious knee injury after 2004 Olympics. Three jumps over 6.90 at 2006 CG, despite jumping from behind the board (7.15 from jump to take-off on best jump).

Kylie WHEELER b. 17 Jan 1980 Perth 1.80m 63kg. University of Western Australia.
At Hep: WCh: '05- 15; CG: '02- 2, '06- 2; WUG: '03- 1. At 400mh: WJ: '98- sf. Won AUS Hep 2003-06.
Progress at Hep: 1996- 4700, 1997- 4586, 1998- 4859, 1999- 5059, 2000- 5583, 2001- 5702, 2002- 5962, 2003- 6031, 2004- 6296, 2005- 6231, 2006- 6298. pbs: 100m 12.15 '05, 11.81w '05, 11.6w '02; 200m 23.99 '05, 400m 54.49 '99, 800m 2:09.98 '05, 100mh 13.63 '06, 400mh 58.11 '00, HJ 1.86 '05, LJ 6.57 '03, 6.66w '04; SP 13.19 '05, JT 37.88 '06.

AUSTRIA

Governing body: Österreichischer Leichtathletik Verband, 1040 Vienna, Prinz Eugenstrasse 12. Founded 1902.
National Championships first held in 1911 (men), 1918 (women). **2005 Champions**: **Men**: 100m: Sergey Osivic 10.55, 200m: Roland Kwitt 21.41, 400m: Ralf Hegny 47.30, 800m: Georg Mlynek 1:53.73, 1500m: Daniel Spitzl 3:54.49, 5000m/10,000m: Günther Weidlinger 14:20.14/ 29:22.97, HMar: Markus Hohenwarter 65:30, Mar: Erich Kokaly 2:22:30, 3000mSt: Martin Pröll 8:46.17, 110mh: Elmar Lichtenegger 13.65, 400mh: Gotthard Schöpf 52.22, HJ: Pavel Vanicek 2.05, PV: Thomas Ager 5.00, LJ: Isagani Peychär 7.76, TJ: Michael Mölschl 15.40, SP: Gerhard Zillner 17.50, DT: Gerhard Mayer 60.19, HT: Benjamin Siart 63.31, JT: Klaus Ambrosch 69.96, Dec: Markus Walser 7106, 20kmW: Norbert Jung 1:52:09. 50kmW: Dietmar Hirschmugl 5:09:33. **Women**: 100m/200m: Karin Mayr-Krifka 11.59/23.80, 400m/400mh: Sabine Kreiner 55.53/58.87, 800m: Elisabeth Niedereder 2:11:50, 1500m/5000m/10,000m: Susanne Pumper 4:23.26 /16:01.88/32:12.33, HMar/Mar: Eva-Maria Gradwohl 74:56/2:40:16, 100mh: Daniela Wöckinger 13.34, HJ: Monika Gollner 1.70, PV: Doris Auer 3.70, LJ: Bianca Durr 6.06, TJ: Olivia Wöckinger 13.20, SP/DT: Veronika Watrez 14.51/53.30, HT: Claudia Stern 54.60, JT: Andrea Lindenthaler 47.44, Hep: Victoria Schreibis 5299, 10kmW/20kmW: Gabriela Winkler 55:19/1:49:23.

Günther WEIDLINGER b. 5 Apr 1978 Braunau 1.69m 54kg. SU IGLA Harmonie Linz. Soldier.
At 3000mSt: OG: '00- 8; WCh: '99- 9, '03- h, '05- 12; EC: '98- h, '02- 12; WJ: '96- 4; EU23: '99- 1; EJ: '95- 8, '97- 1. At 3000m: WI: '03/06- 10; EI: '05- 4. At 5000m: OG: '04- h. Eur CC: '97-8-02-04-05: 2J/4/10/4/5. Won World Univs CC 2000. Won AUT 1500m 1999-2000, 5000m 2004-05, 10,000m 2003-05, 3000mSt 1998-9; CC 2001-02.
Austrian records: 1500m 2000, 3000mSt (3) 1999, 2M & 5000m 2005.
Progress at 3000mSt: 1995- 9:02.15, 1996 8:38.97, 1997- 8:31.43, 1998- 8:23.13, 1999- 8:10.83, 2000- 8:11.51, 2001- 8:23.62, 2002- 8:23.91, 2003- 8:17.90, 2005- 8:12.26. pbs: 1500m 3:34.69 '00, 3000m 7:44.19i '03, 7:48.46 '04; 2M 8:21.88 '05, 5000m 13:13.44 '05, 10,000m 29:03.64 '02, 10kmRd 28:35 '05.

BAHAMAS

Governing body: Bahamas Association of Athletics Associations, P.O.Box SS 5517, Nassau. Founded 1952.
National Champions 2005: **Men**: 100m: Derrick Atkins 10.28, 200m: Dominic Demeritte 20.77, 400m: Andrae Williams 45.33, 800m: Ramon Miller 1:53.4, 1500m: Oniel Williams 3:57.64, 5000m: Jason Williams 16:28.45, 110mh: Christophe Bethel 14.64, 400mh: Douglas Lynes-Bell 50.7, HJ: Trevor Barry 2.14, PV: Kenny Moxey 4.42, LJ: Leevan Sands 7.94, TJ: Antonio Saunders 15.89, SP/DT: Reginald Sands 15.10/41.08, HT: Mark Sterling 41.00, JT: Ramon Farrington 60.17. **Women**: 100m: Chandra Sturrup 11.12, 200m: Tonique Darling 23.03, 400m: Christine Amertil 51.40, 800m/1500m: Shelly Rolle 2:21.8/5:11.16, 100mh: Krystal Bodie 15.03, HJ: Krishanda Campbell 1.73, LJ: Jackie Edwards 6.65, TJ: Donnovette Martin 12.33, SP: Aymara Albury 16.49, DT/HT: Chafree Bain 45.12/55.00, JT: Laverne Eve 60.02.

Christopher BROWN b. 15 Oct 1978 1.78m

68kg. Was at Norfolk State University.
At 400m/4x400mR: OG: '00- qf/4R, '04- sf; WCh: '01- h/2R, '03- sf/3R, '05- 4/2R; CG: '02- 7/3R, '06- 4; CAC: '98- 3R, '99- 1R, '03- 2/1R; WI: '06- 3; BAH champion 2002, 2004. At 800m: CG: '98- h.
Progress at 400m: 1997- 47.46, 1998- 46.44, 1999- 45.96, 2000- 45.08, 2001- 45.45, 2002- 45.11, 2003- 44.94A/45.16, 2004- 45.09, 2005- 44.48. pbs: 200m 21.05 '03, 800m 1:49.54 '98 (BAH record).
Had fastest split (43.42 anchor leg) in 2005 World 4x400m.

Leevan SANDS b. 16 Aug 1981 1.90m 75kg. Student at Auburn University, USA.
At TJ (LJ): OG: '04- dnq 27; WCh: '03- 3, '05- 4 (dnq); CG: '02- 3; WJ: '98- dnq, '00- 5 (dnq 19); PAm: '99- 6; won CAC LJ 2005, TJ 2003, CAm-J 1998, 2000; NCAA LJ 2003 & TJ 2004, BAH LJ 2003. Bahamas triple jump record 2002.
Progress at TJ: 1998- 15.70, 1999- 16.00/16.02w, 2000- 16.22, 2001- 16.39, 2002- 17.50, 2003- 17.40, 2004- 17.41, 2005- 17.30/17.39w. pb LJ 8.13 '05, 8.28w '03.

Women

Christine AMERTIL b. 18 Aug 1979 Nassau 1.68m 53kg. Studied accountancy at Southeastern Louisiana University, USA.
At 400m: OG: '00- h, '04- 7; WCh: '03- sf, '05- sf (h 200m); CG: '02- 8, '06- 4; WI: '03- 2, '06- 3. At 4x100mR: CAC: '03- 1R. Won BAH 400m 2004-05.
Progress at 400m: 1999- 52.99, 2000- 52.00, 2001- 52.70, 2002- 50.82, 2003- 51.11i/51.25, 2004- 50.17, 2005- 50.09, 2006- 50.34i. pbs: 60m 7.50i '03, 100m 11.49 '05, 200m 22.58 '05.

Tonique DARLING b. 17 Jan 1976 Nassau 1.68m 59kg. née Williams. Was at University of Georgia, then South Carolina.
At 400m: OG: '00- h, '04- 1; WCh: '97- qf, '99- h, '03- 5, '05- 1; CG: '06- 2; PAm: '99- h; CAC: '99- 2, '05- 1; WI: '04- 3. At 200m: CAC: '03- 3.
Three BAH 400m records 2004, CAC indoor 400m record 50.87 '04.
Progress at 400m: 1994- 53.72, 1995- 52.40, 1996- 52.42, 1997- 52.15, 1998- 51.99, 1999- 52.01, 2000- 52.35, 2003- 50.24, 2004- 49.07, 2005- 49.30. pbs: 55m 6.99i '97, 60m 7.49i '97, 100m 11.72 '97, 200m 22.77 '04, 300m 35.6+ '04.
Married sprinter Dennis Darling (pb 400m 45.82 '97) on 11 April 2003. Won $500,000 as share of Golden League jackpot 2004.

Laverne EVE b. 16 Jun 1965 Nassau 1.79m 77kg. Louisiana State TC, was at Louisiana State University.
At JT: OG: '88- dnq 16, '96- dnq 17, '00- dnq 16, '04- 6; WCh: '91/5/7/9/01- dnq 22/15/16/18/17, '03- 8, '05- 10; CG: '94- 7, '02- 1, '06- 2; PAm: '87- 5, '95- 2, '99- 3, '03- 2; CAG: '98- 3; WCp: '89- 3. At SP: CAG: '93- 3. Won NCAA 1987, TAC 1989, CAC 1989, 1991, 1999, 2001, 2003, 2005; PAm-J shot 1984.
Bahamas records for shot, discus and javelin. New javelin Commonwealth best 1999. World W40 javelin record 2005.
Progress at JT: 1982- 48.62, 1983- 50.22, 1984- 53.50, 1986- 53.54, 1987- 62.42, 1988- 60.02, 1989- 64.78, 1990- 59.12, 1991- 58.06, 1992- 56.74, 1993- 56.90, 1994- 57.26, 1995- 63.24, 1996- 58.48, 1997- 60.42. 1998- 60.66; new 1999- 62.94, 2000- 63.73, 2001- 60.26, 2002- 58.46, 2003- 62.89, 2004- 62.77, 2005- 61.96. pbs: SP 16.20i '93, 15.82 '94; DT 52.52 '90, HT 54.90 '99, Hep 5197w '94.

Chandra STURRUP b. 12 Sep 1971 Nassau 1.63m 55kg. Studied business management at Norfolk State University, USA.
At 100m(/200m/4x100mR): OG: '96- 4/6/2R, '00- 6/qf/1R, '04- qf/4R; WCh: '99- 7/sf/1R, '01- 4, '03- 3, '05- 4; CG: '98- 1, '02- 1R; PAm: '99- 1; CAG: '93- 3/5, '98- 1; WJ: '88- sf/sf, '90- sf/6; WCp: '98- 2/2R. At 60m: WI: '97- 2, '01- 1. Won CAC 100m 2005.
BAH records 100m (4) 1996-2005, 200m 1996.
Progress at 100m, 200m: 1987- 11.75, 1988- 11.93/11.70w, 23.96w; 1989- ?, 1990- 11.62, 23.77; 1992- 11.54, 23.55; 1993- 11.20, 22.85; 1994- 11.75, 1995- 11.39/11.35w/11.1w, 23.31/23.14w; 1996- 11.00, 22.33; 1997- 11.26, 22.77; 1998- 10.95, 23.52/22.64w; 1999- 10.96/10.94w, 22.75; 2000- 10.86, 22.57; 2001- 10.95, 22.99; 2002- 11.01, 2003- 10.89/10.88w, 23.56; 2004- 11.37, 2005- 10.84. pbs: 50m 6.11+ '99, 55m 6.73i '96, 60m 7.05i '01, 300m 37.95 '01, 400m 54.77 '00, LJ 6.70 '00, 6.80w '95. Former volleyball player.

BAHRAIN

Governing body: Bahrain Athletics Association, PO Box 29269, Manama. Founded 1974.

Mushir Salim JAWHER formerly Leonard Mucheru (KEN) b. 13 Jun 1978 Kenya 1.82m 66kg.
At 3000m: WI: '03- 7. World 4km CC: '00- 4.
Progress at 5000m: 2000- 13:21.14, 2001- 13:14.94, 2002- 13:21.68, 2003- 13:01.76, 2004- 13:00.40, 2005- 12:59.79. pbs: 1500m 3:33.79 '01, 1M 3:49.75 '01, 3000m 7:35.35 '01.
Eligible to compete for Bahrain from 16 March 2006.

Youssef Saad KAMEL formerly Gregory Konchellah (KEN) b. 29 Mar 1983 Kenya 1.90m 73kg.
At 800m: OG: '04- h; WCh: '05- sf. Won WAF 2004, Pan Arab 2004-05.
Asian and three BRN 800m records 2004
Progress at 800m: 2003- 1:45.88, 2004- 1:43.11, 2005- 1:43.96. pbs: 600m 1:16.01 '03, 1000m 2:19.71 '03, 1500m 3:40.7A '05.
Son of Billy Konchellah (world 800m champion 1987 and 1991), he changed nationality to Bahrain in 2003.

Rashid Mohamed **RAMZI** b. 17 Jul 1980 Morocco 1.75m 58kg. Army corporal.

At (800m)/1500m: OG: '04- sf; WCh: '05- 1/1; WI: '04- (2); AsiG: '02- 1; AsiC: '02- 2, '03- 1; Af-J: '99- 2.

Three Asian 1500m records 2004-05, Bahrain 1M 2005.

Progress at 800m, 1500m: 1998- 1:51.49, 1999- 3:47.13, 2001- 3:43.2, 2002- 1:46.5, 3:44.85; 2003- 1:47.56, 3:39.30 (3:37.26?); 2004- 1:46.15i, 3:30.25; 2005- 1:44.24, 3:30.00. pb 1M 3:51.33 '05.

In 2005 he became the first man to win a global 800m/1500m double since Peter Snell OG 1964. He won the 1500m silver medal for Morocco at the 1999 African Junior Championships, but he seemed unable to break into top flight athletics and was unemployed when a friend of his recommended he relocate to Bahrain. He moved at the end of 2001 and gained Bahraini citizenship on joining the armed forces. Coached by Khalid Boulami, he is compiling an excellent championships record and after surprisingly winning the 2004 World Indoor silver he made an amazing breakthrough at 1500m, taking his pb from 3:39.30 to Asian records of 3:31.87 and 3:30.25 with major wins in Algiers and Rome.

Women

Maryam JAMAL YUSUF b. 16 Sep 1984 1.55m 44kg. Stade Lausanne, Switzerland.

At 1500m: WCh: '05- 5; WI: '06- 3. Won Swiss CC 2003, P.Arab 800m, 1500m & 5000m 2005.

Bahrain records 2005: 800m, 1500m (3), 3000m (3), 5000m. Asian indoor record 1500m (4:01.82) 2006.

Progress at 1500m, 5000m: 2003- 4:18.12, 2004- 4:07.78, 15:19.45mx; 2005- 3:56.79, 14:51.68; 2006- 4:01.82i. pbs: 800m 1:59.69 '05, 2000m 5:41.9 '05, 3000m 8:28.87 '05, HMar 71:43 '04

Formerly Ethiopian Zenebech Kotu Tola, based in Switzerland, ran series of fast times after converting to Jamal of Bahrain in 2005. Married to Mnashu Taye (now Tareq Yaqoob BRN).

BARBADOS

Governing body: Amateur Athletic Association of Barbados, P.O.Box 46, Bridgetown. Founded 1947.

Women

Andrea BLACKETT b. 24 Jan 1976 London, GBR 1.60m 54kg. Was at Rice University, USA.

At 400mh/4x400mR: OG: '00- sf, '04- h; WCh: '97- 8, '99- 4, '01- h, '03- 6, '05- 6; CG: '98- 1, '02- h; PAm: '99- 2/3R, '03- 3; CAG: '98- 2/3R; WJ: '94- h; WCp: '98- 2R; 2nd GP 1999; won CAC 1997 (3rd 100mh), 1999; 2nd 1998.

Barbadian 400mh records 1994-9, 100mh 1997-2003.

Progress at 400mh: 1994- 58.75, 1995- 58.59, 1996- 57.35A, 1997- 54.74, 1998- 53.74, 1999- 53.36, 2000- 54.41, 2001- 55.68, 2002- 56.95, 2003- 53.71, 2004- 55.41, 2005- 54.79. pbs: 200m 23.73 '00, 600m 1:27.78 '04, 800m 2:10.47 '99, 55mh 7.65Ai '97, 60mh 8.37i '03, 100mh 13.39 '03, 13.2 '98.

BELARUS

Governing body: Belarus Athletic Federation, 2 Surganov Street, Minsk 220012. Founded 1991.

National Champions 2005. **Men**: 100m/200m: Maksim Piskunov 10.72/21.50, 400m: Sergey Kozlov 47.00, 800m: Aleksandr Trutko 1:50.65, 1500m: Mark Romanchuk 3:51.45, 5000m: Aleksandr Donchenko 14:22.98, 10,000m: Ruslan Sadovskiy 30:14.97, 3000mSt: Vitaliy Piskun 8:48.34, 110mh: Maksim Lynsha 13.92, 400mh: Leonid Vershinin 50.27, HJ: Aleksandr Veryutin 2.24, PV: Igor Alekseyev 5.50, LJ: Aleksey Postupaylo 7.39, TJ: Dmitriy Detsuk 16.16, SP: Andrey Mikhnevich 21.08, DT: Aleksandr Malashevich 60.51, HT: Ivan Tikhon 86.73, JT: Nikolay Vasiltsov 76.10, Dec: Aleksandr Korzun 7384, 20kmW: Andrey Talashko 1:20:33. **Women**: 100m/200m: Natalya Sologub 11.30/22.82, 400m: Anna Kozak 52.41, 800m: Svetlana Klimkovich 2;02.01, 1500m: Olga Kravtsova 4:05.76, 5000m: Irina Kunakhovets 16:43.60, 10,000m: Galina Karnatsevich 33:17.30, 3000mSt: Natalya Grigoryeva 10:30.10, 100mh: Yevgeniya Likhuta 13.77, 400mh: Inna Kalinina 58.39, HJ: Irina Chuyko 1.75, PV: Yekaterina Arkhipova 3.40, LJ: Anzhela Zhalnerchik 6.00, TJ: Olesya Lesun 13.40, SP: Natalya Khoroneko 19.78, DT: Ellina Zvereva 61.10, HT: Olga Tsander 70.49, JT: Natalya Shimchuk 57.65, Hep: Tatyana Alisevich 5842, 20kmW: Tatyana Zuyeva 1:43:29.

Vadim DEVYATOVSKIY b. 20 Mar 1977 Novopolotsk 1.94m 120kg. Brest.

At HT: OG: '04- 4; WCh: '03- 7, '05- 2; WJ: '94- 5, '96- 2; EU23: '99- 4; WUG: '05- 1. BLR champion 2000.

Progress at HT: 1994- 67.20, 1995- 68.82?/64.60, 1996- 74.18, 1997- 69.64, 1998- 75.00, 1999- 76.77, 2000- 81.36, 2003- 79.90, 2004- 82.91, 2005- 84.90.

Two year drugs ban from positive test on 18 Sep 2000.

Vasiliy KAPTYUKH b. 27 Jun 1967 Molodechno 1.97m 120kg. Minsk TR. Sports instructor.

At DT: OG: '96- 3, '00- 4, '04- 4; WCh: '91- dns, '93- 7, '95- 3, '97- 11, '01- 6, '03- 3, '05- dnq 20; EC: '90- 4; WJ: '86- 3; EJ: '85- 3. BLR champion 1992, 2003-04.

Progress at DT: 1985- 57.18, 1986- 60.24, 1988- 61.60, 1989- 62.92, 1990- 63.72, 1991- 62.88, 1992- 63.34, 1993- 66.18, 1994- 58.86, 1995- 66.30, 1996- 66.92, 1997- 65.52, 2000- 67.59, 2001- 67.48, 2003- 66.51, 2004- 65.45, 2005- 62.80. pb SP 17.26 '00.

Father Boris (1950s) and aunt Vera Kaptyukh (1960s, Pen) were prominent athletes.

Andrey MIKHNEVICH b. 12 Jul 1976 Bobruysk 2.02m 127kg.

At SP: OG: '00- 9, '04- 5; WCh: '01- dq 10, '03- 1, '05- 6; EC: '98- dnq 17; WUG: '97- 6, '03- 1; WI: '99- 8, '04- 6, '06- 2. BLR champion 2000, 2005.

Progress at SP: 1994- 16.74, 1995- 17.36, 1996- 19.24, 1997- 19.27, 1998- 20.07i/19.90, 1999- 20.52i/20.30, 2000- 20.48i/20.12, 2001- 20.92,

2003- 21.69, 2004- 21.23, 2005- 21.08, 2006- 21.37i. Two year drugs ban from positive test on 4 Aug 2001, when he lost 10th place at the World Champs. Threw 21.66 four days after return from ban in August 2003, world title 2 weeks later.

Ivan TIKHON b. 24 Jul 1976 Slonim 1.86m 110kg.
At HT: OG: '00- 4, '04- 2; WCh: 97- nt (12), '01- dnq 22, '03- 1, '05- 1; EC: '98- dnq 30, '02- 9; EU23: 97- 1; EJ: '95- 9; WUG: '03- 1. Won WAF 2005, BLR 2001-05.
Two Belarus hammer records 2005.
Progress at HT: 1994- 62.66, 1995- 66.84, 1996- 75.32, 1997- 77.46, 1998- 78.03, 1999- 70.37, 2000- 79.85, 2001- 78.73, 2002- 79.04, 2003- 84.32, 2004- 84.46, 2005- 86.73.

Women

Natalya KHORONEKO b. 25 May 1982 1.80m 81kg.
At SP: OG: '04- 5; WCh: '05- 8; WJ: '00- 3; WY: '99- 2; EJ: '01- 1; EU23: '03- 1; WI: '04- 9, '06- 1; WUG: '05- 1. BLR champion 2001, 2004-05.
Progress at SP: 1999- 16.12, 2000- 16.58, 2001- 17.25, 2002- 17.20, 2003- 18.05, 2004- 20.04, 2005- 19.78, 2006- 19.84i.

Yuliya NESTERENKO b. 15 Jun 1979 1.73m 61kg. née Bartsevich.
At 100m/4x100mR: OG: '04- 1; WCh: '03- 7R, '05- 8/3R: EC: '02- sf. At 60m: WI: '04-3. Won BLR 100m 2002.
Three Belarus 100m records 2004.
Progress at 100m: 2000- 11.87, 2001- 11.53/11.32w/11.1, 2002- 11.29, 2003- 11.45, 2004- 10.92, 2005- 11.08. pbs: 60m 7.10i '04, 200m 22.91 '04.
Married to 400m runner Dmitriy Nesterenko (47.19 '02).

Nadezhda OSTAPCHUK b. 12 Oct 1980 1.80m 90kg. Luch Moskva, RUS.
At SP: OG: '04- 4; WCh: '99- dnq 17, '01- 7, '03- 2, '05- 1; EC: '02- 5; WJ: '98- 1; EJ: '99- 1; EU23: '01- 1; WI: '01-03-04-06: 2/2/7/6, EI: '00- 6, '05- 1; Won WAF 2004, 2nd GP 2001. Won WAF 2005, BLR 1999-2000.
Two Belarus shot records 2005.
Progress at SP: 1997- 14.23, 1998- 18.23, 1999- 18.73, 2000- 19.13i/18.83, 2001- 19.73, 2002- 19.40, 2003- 20.56i/20.12, 2004- 20.36, 2005- 21.09, 2006- 20.86i.

Olga TSANDER b. 18 May 1976 Grodno 1.74m 83kg. Sports instructor.
At HT: OG: '00- dnq, '04- 6; WCh: '01- 10, '03- dnq, '05- dnq 14; EC: '02- dnq 22; WUG: '01- 4; ECp: '01- 1; BLR champion 2002-05. At DT: WJ: '94- 5; EJ: '95- 2.
Three BLR hammer records 2002-04.
Progress at HT: 1998- 58.88, 1999- 64.56, 2000- 69.81, 2001- 68.94, 2002- 70.11, 2003- 70.02, 2004- 74.72, 2005- 76.66. pbs: SP 15.18 '94, DT 59.82 '97.

Alesya TUROVA b. 6 Dec 1979 1.80m 64kg.
At 1500m: WCh: '01- 7, '03- sf, '05- h; EC: '02- 7; WJ: '98- h; EU23: '99- 5, '01- 1; EJ: '97- 11; WI: '01-03-04: 6/7/7; EI: '02- 3, '05- 5; ECp: '01- 4.
Two world 3000m steeple records 2002; BLR records: 2000m & 3000m (3), 5000m 2000-01.
Progress at 1500m, 3000mSt: 1997- 4:24.64, 1998- 4:21.53, 1999- 4:12.8, 2000- 4:05.99, 2001- 4:07.25, - 3:59.89, 9:16.51; 2003- 4:03.32, 9:20.28; 2004- 4:04.42i, 2005- 4:02.21. pbs: 800m 2:02.11i '03, 2:04.52 '99; 1M 4:33.88i '02, 2000m 5:42.55 '01, 3000m 8:32.89 '01, 5000m 15:23.84 '00.
Sister of Rita (b. 28 Dec 1980) – see below.

Margarita 'Rita' TUROVA b. 28 Dec 1980 1.74m 55kg.
At 20kmW: OG: '04- 4; WCh: '05- 2. At 5000mW: WJ: '98- 5; EJ: '97-12, '99- 3.
World indoor best 5000m walk 2005, BLR 20km walk record 2005.
Progress at 20kmW: 2001- 1:29:31, 2004- 1:29:06, 2005- 1:27:05. pbs: 5000mW 20:32.77i '05, 21:48.11 '99; 10kmW 42:05 '05.
Won IAAF Race Walking Challenge 2005. Two year drugs ban from 20 May 2000.

BELGIUM

Governing bodies: Ligue Royale Belge d'Athlétisme, Stade Roi Baudouin, avenue du Marathon 199B, 1020 Bruxelles (KBAB/LRBA). Vlaamse Atletiekliga (VAL); Ligue Belge Francophone d'Athlétisme (LBFA). Original governing body founded 1889.

National Championships first held in 1889 (women 1921). **2005 Champions**: **Men**: 100m: Anthony Ferro 10.50, 200m: Kristof Beyens 20.45, 400m: Cédric Van Branteghem 45.59, 800m: Tom Vanchaze 1:47.77, 1500m: Joeri Jansen 3:57.49, 5000m: Stefan Van Den Broeck 14:16.34, 10,000m: Guy Fays 29:30.94, HMar: Rik Ceulemans 65:54, Mar: Eric Gérôme 2:21:57, 3000mSt: Koen Wilssens 8:53.86, 110mh: Jonathan Nsenga 13.87, 400mh: Piet Deveughele 50.70, HJ: Stijn Stroobants 2.11, PV: Kevin Rans 5.40, LJ: Gert Messiaen 7.57, TJ: Gert Brijs 14.70, SP: Wim Blondeel 18.35, DT: Jo Van Daele 59.97, HT: Walter De Wyngaert 62.26, JT: Marc Van Mensel 68.83, Dec: Hans Van Alphen 7064, 20000mW: Frank Buytaert 1:35:52.2, 50kmW: Dirk Nicque 4:48:47. **Women**: 100m/200m: Kim Gevaert 11.24/22.68, 400m: Sandra Stals 53.30, 800m: Shana Major 2:04.25, 1500m: Veerle Dejaeghere 4:14.40, 5000m: Nathalie De Vos 16:22.25, 10,000m: Anja Smolders 34:50.34, HMar: Nathalie Loubele 80:03, Mar: Sandrine Van den Haesevelde 2:53:29, 3000mSt: Sigrid Vanden Bempt 10:01.49, 100mh: Elisabeth Davin 13.82, 400mh: Joke Mortier 58.94, HJ: Tia Hellebaut 1.90, PV: Irena Dufour 4.20, LJ/TJ: Jessica Van De Steene 6.18/13.08, SP/DT: Veerle Blondeel 15.74/54.22, HT: Irina Sustelo 51.34, JT: Cindy Stas 47.16, Hep: Sara Aerts 5045, 10,000mW: Caroline Housmans 63:10.7.

Women

Kim GEVAERT b. 5 Aug 1978 Leuven 1.70m 60kg. VAC.
At (100m/)200m): OG: '00- dnq 15, '04- sf/6; WCh: '99- qf/qf, '01- qf/sf, '03- sf/sf, '05- sf/7; EC: '98- h/sf, '02- 2/2; WJ: '96- sf/7; EU23: '99- 3/5; EJ: '95- (6), '97- 5; WUG: '99- 4/1, '01- 2; WCp: '02- (8). At 60m: WI: '04- 2, '06- 3; EI: '00-02-05: 6/1/1. Won BEL 100m 1996, 1998-2005; 200m 1995-2001, 2004-05.
Belgian records: 100m (10) 1998-2005, 200m (7) 1999-2004, 400m 2005.
Progress at 100m, 200m: 1994- 12.02, 1995- 11.63, 23.92; 1996- 11.68/11.60w, 23.59; 1997- 11.52, 23.84/ 23.58w; 1998- 11.40, 23.10; 1999- 11.17, 23.03; 2000- 11.34, 23.09; 2001- 11.26, 22.94; 2002- 11.15, 22.53; 2003- 11.21, 22.64; 2004- 11.14, 22.48; 2005- 11.12, 22.68. pbs: 60m 7.11i '06, 400m 51.45 '05, TJ 11.67 '03.
'La Gazelle de Kampenhout', who was an award-winning classical pianist, set ten Belgian records in 2002 and 2004. Member of EAA Athletes Commission 2002-06.

Tia HELLEBAUT b. 16 Feb 1978 Antwerpen 1.82m 62kg. AT84.
At HJ: OG: '04-12; WCh: '05- 6; WI: '06- 6. At Hep: WCh: '01- 14, '03- dnf; EJ: '97- 11; EU23: '99- 6. At Pen: WI: '04- 5. Won BEL HJ 2000, 2002-03, 2005; Hep 1999-2000, 2002.
Belgian records: HJ (2) 2004, Indoor HJ (2) 2006, Indoor LJ 2006).
Progress at HJ, Hep: 1992- 1.56, 1993- 1.70, 1994- 1.73, 4731; 1995- 1.76, 5167; 1996- 1.78, 5104; 1997- 1.75+, 5197; 1998- 1.81, 5381; 1999- 1.87i/1.82, 5629; 2000- 1.89, 5646; 2001- 1.89i/1.87, 5859; 2002- 1.85, 5584; 2003- 1.91, 6019; 2004- 1.95, 5954; 2005- 1.93, 2006- 1.97i. pbs: 200m 25.32 '03, 800m 2:14.86 '03, 50mh 7.34i '04, 60mh 8.50i '06, 100mh 13.98 '04, LJ 6.36i '06, 6.07/6.18w '03; TJ 12.54i '01, SP 13.26i '06, 13.10 '99; JT 44.37 '01, Pen 4589i '03.

BRAZIL

Governing body: Confederação Brasileira de Atletismo (CBAt), Avenida Rio Purus No. 103 - Conj. Vieiralves, Bairro N.Sra das Graças, Manaus, AM 69053-050. Founded 1914 (Confederação 1977).

2005 National Champions: Men: 100m/200m: Vicente de Lima 10.23/20.44 400m: Sanderlei Parrela 45.92, 800m/1500m: Fabiano Peçanha 1:47.00/3:45.38, 5000m: Hudson de Souza 13:51.10, 10,000m: Franck de Almeida 29:16.21, 3000mSt: Fernando A Fernandes 8:43.34, 110mh: Matheus Inocêncio 13.34, 400mh: Tiago Bueno 49.59, HJ: Fábio Baptista 2.19, PV: Fábio Gomes da Silva 5.40, LJ: Erivaldo Vieira 7.96, TJ: Jadel Gregório 17.73, SP: Daniel Freire 17.04, DT: Ronald Julião 55.31, HT: Wágner Domingos 66.91, JT: Luiz F. da Silva 74.58, Dec: Ivan S. da Silva 7711, 20000mW/20kmW: Sérgio Galdino 1:23:31.6/1:28:19, 50kmW:. **Women:** 100m/200m: Lucimar de Moura 11.26/22.75, 400m/400mh: Lucimar Teodoro 51.23/56.12, 800m: Christiane dos Santos 2:04.38, 1500m: Juliana de Azevedo 4:17.60, 5000m: Fabiana da Silva 16:13.36, 10,000m: Lucélia Peres 34:03.73, 3000mSt: Michelle da Costa 10:00.54, 100mh: Maíla Machado 12.89, HJ: Eliana da Silva 1.82, PV: Fabiana Murer 4.23, LJ/TJ: Keila Costa 6.63/13.84, SP: Andrea Pereira 16.02, DT: Renata de Figueiredo 51.42, HT: Josiane Soares 59.92, JT: Alessandra Resende 55.09, Hep: Lucimara da Silva 5378, 20000mW/20kmW: Alessandra Picagevicz 1:45:46.2/1:44:22.

Jadel GREGÓRIO b. 16 Sep 1980 Jandaia do Sul, Paraná 2.02m 102kg. BM&F Atletismo.
At TJ: OG: '04- 5 (dnq 32 LJ); WCh: '03- 5, '05- 6; PAm: '03- 2; SACh: '01- 1, 03- 1; WI: '03-04-06: 6/2/2; WUG: '01- 3. Won Ib-Am 2002; BRA TJ 2001-05, LJ 2002, 2004.
South American indoor triple jump records 2002 & 2004.
Progress at TJ: 1999- 16.07, 2000- 16.48, 2001- 17.13, 2002- 17.35i/17.08, 2003- 17.11/17.37w, 2004- 17.72, 2005- 17.73, 2006- 17.56i. pbs: HJ 2.10 '99, LJ 8.22 '04.

Matheus Facho **INOCÊNCIO** b. 17 May 1981 Patrocínio Paulista, SP 1.92m 93kg. Patrocinense. Economics student.
At 110mh: OG: '04- 7; WCh: '03- sf, '05- 8; SACh: '03- 3, '05- 3; IbAm: '02- 2, '04- 2; WJ: '00- sf; WUG: '05- 1. Won SAm-J 2000, BRA 2005.
Progress at 110mh: 2000- 14.22, 2001- 14.12, 2002- 13.47, 2003- 13.42A/13.43, 2004- 13.33, 2005- 13.34. pbs: 100m 10.52 '02, 10.43w '04; 200m 21.62 '04, 60mh 7.67i '06, LJ 7.65 '05.

Redelen Melo **dos SANTOS** b. 24 Apr 1976 São Paulo 2.00m 96kg. BM&F Atletismo.
At 110mh: WCh: '03/05- sf; PAm: '03- 4; SACh: '01- 2, '03- 1, '05- 1; IbAm: '00- 2. Won BRA 2003-04. Four South American and Brazilian records 2003-04.
Progress at 110mh: 1996- 14.13, 1997- 14.34, 1999- 13.90, 2000- 13.59, 2001- 13.67, 2002- 13.71, 2003- 13.34, 2004- 13.29, 2005- 13.30. pb 60mh: 7.65i '06.
Missed 2004 Olympic Games due to injury after three South American records.

BULGARIA

Governing body: Bulgarian Athletic Federation, 75 bl. Vassil Levski, Sofia 1000. F'd 1924.

National Championships first held in 1926 (men), 1938 (women). **2005 Champions**: **Men**: 100m: Desislav Gunev 10.55, 200m: Yordan Ilinov 21.39, 400m: Krasimir Braykov 47.81, 800m: Boyan Kodinov 1:56.93, 1500m: Stefan Stefanov 4:04.86, 5000m: Yolo Nikolov 14:52.64, 10,000m/HMar: Stanislav Lambev 31:09.61/69:22, Mar: Aleksandar Panovski 2:27:08, 3000mSt. Georgi Georgiev 9:17.86, 110mh/400mh: Rumen Lotsi 14.29/51.71,

HJ: Stoyan Kekov 2.05, PV: Iliyan Efremov 5.65, LJ: Atanas Rusenov 7.88, TJ: Momchil Karailiev 17.19, SP: Galin Kostadinov 18.68, DT: Encho Shterev 53.96, HT: Andrian Andreev 67.28, JT: Kolyo Neshev 68.30, Dec: Borislav Borisov 5626, 20kmW: Georgi Simeonov Georghiev 1:46:07. **Women**: 100m: Ivet Lalova 11.09, 200m: Tezdzhyan Naimova 24.18, 400m: Mariyana Dimitrova 52.68, 800m: Teodora Kolarova 2:04.35, 1500m/5000m/HMar: Vanya Koleva Stoyanova 4:28.94/16:40.26/68:24, 10,000m/HMar: Milka Mikhaylova 35:12.00/2:46:57, 3000mSt: Dobrinka Shalamanova 10:25.93, 100mh: Desislava Mutafchieva 13.62, 400mh: Vanya Stambolova 56.91, HJ: Elena Denkova 1.76, PV: Tanya Stefanova 4.35, LJ: Darinka Yotova 6.26, TJ: Mariya Dimitrova 13.97, SP: Radoslava Mavrodieva 15.11, DT: Tsvetanka Khristova 52.53, HT: Siyana Kirilova 54.70, JT: Rumyana Karapetrova 52.94, Hep: Kristina Damyanova 4235, 20kmW: Iliyana Nyagalova 1:53:59.

Women

Ivet LALOVA b. 18 May 1984 Sofia 1.68m 56kg. Levski Sofia, Panellínios GRE.

At 100m/200m: OG: '04- 4/5; WJ: '02- sf/-; WY: '01- h/sf; EJ: '03: 1/1; EI: '05- -/1. Won BUL 100m 2004-05, 200m 2004.

Bulgarian 100m record 2004.

Progress at 100m, 200m: 1998- 13.0, 27.2; 1999- 12.71, 2000- 12.14, 25.24; 2001- 11.72, 24.03; 2002- 11.59, 24.4; 2003- 11.14, 22.87; 2004- 10.77, 22.51/22.36w; 2005- 11.03, 22.76. pb 60m 7.21i '04.

Father Miroslav Lalov had 100m pb 10.4 (1966) and mother Liliya Lalova was a heptathlete.

Tereza MARINOVA b. 5 Sep 1977 Pleven 1.73m 56kg. Chendini.

At TJ: OG: '00- 1; WCh: '97- 6, '01- 3; EC: '98- 3; WJ: '94- dnq 15, '96- 1; EJ: '95- 1; WI: '97-9-01-06: 8/4/1/6; EI: '02- 1; E23: '94- 6; won GP 2001. Balkan champion 1996, 2000; BUL 1998.

Two world junior triple jump records (one unofficial) 1996. Bulgarian TJ record 2000.

Progress at TJ: 1993- 12.18, 1994- 13.23/13.51w, 1995- 13.90, 1996- 14.62, 1997- 14.34/14.53w, 1998- 14.67, 1999- 14.76i/14.64, 2000- 15.20, 2001- 14.91i/14.77, 2002- 14.81i, 2003- 14.40i/14.27, 2004- 14.43i, 2006- 14.49i. pb LJ 6.53i '02, 6.46 '00, 6.63w '01.

Set pbs when winning European (1995) and World (1996) Junior gold medals and again to win 2000 Olympic title. Had Achilles surgery in April 2002 and June 2004. Her father Moncho Marinov set a Bulgarian 800m record of 1:47.7 in 1974 and brother Tsvetomir (b. 10 Jul 1976) was 3rd in the 1995 European Junior 400m.

Vanya STAMBOLOVA b. 28 Nov 1983 Varna. Klasa Sofiya.

At 400m: WI: '06- 2. Won BUL 400mh 2002, 2005.

Progress at 400m: 1998- 57.91, 1999- 57.45, 2000- 58.82, 2001- 57.86, 2002- 58.30, 2005- 52.99, 2006- 50.21i. pb 200m 23.51i '06, 400mh 56.29 '05.

Huge improvement in 2006 indoor season. Former footballer.

Venelina VENEVA b. 13 Jun 1974 Ruse 1.79m 61kg. Universal.

At HJ: OG: '96- dnq 29=, '00- 9=, '04- dnq 15; WCh: '91-5-9: dnq 21=/14/14=, '01- 4, '03- 4, '05- 10; EC: '98- 5; EJ: '91- 2; WI: '01- 3, '04- 7; EI: '00- 4, '05- 3. BUL champion 1995, 2004; Balkan 2003.

Progress at HJ: 1987- 1.68, 1988- 1.80, 1989- 1.86, 1990- 1.93i/1.90, 1991- 1.91, 1992- 1.91, 1993- 1.89i/1.85, 1994- 1.90, 1995- 1.94, 1996- 1.94i/1.88, 1998- 2.03, 1999- 1.90, 2000- 2.01, 2001- 2.04, 2002- 2.02i, 2003- 2.01, 2004- 2.01, 2005- 1.98. pbs: LJ 6.17 '90, TJ 12.51 '95.

Daughter Neapola born in 1997. World age-15 best of 1.93i in 1990.

Daniela YORDANOVA b. 8 Mar 1976 Slivnitsa 1.65m 52kg. CMA Varna.

At 1500m/(5000m): OG: '00- (10), '04- 5; WCh: '01- sf/h, '03- 7, '05- h; EC: '02- 5; WI: '04- 4; EI: '02- 5. At 3000m: EI: '00- 5. Won BUL 1500m 1999, 5000m 1998.

Bulgarian records 2000m 2004, 3000m (2) 2001, 5000m (3) 2000.

Progress at 1500m, 5000m: 1994- 4:48.94, 19:10.48; 1995- 4:39.59, 17:42.73; 1996- 4:43.26i, 17:50.77; 1997- 17:13.25, 1998- 4:08.83, 16:16.46; 1999- 4:11.93, 16:07.28; 2000- 4:03.83, 14:56.95; 2001- 4:01.68, 2002- 4:00.65, 2003- 4:01.83, 2004- 3:59.10, 2005- 4:11.64. pbs: 800m 2:03.02 '01, 2000m 5:35.83 '04, 3000m 8:30.59 '01, 10,000m 37:30.21 '95.

CAMEROON

Governing body: Fédération Camerounaise d'Athlétisme, BP 353, Yaoundé. Founded 1957.

Françoise MBANGO Etone b. 14 Apr 1976 Yaoundé 1.72m 63kg.

At TJ(/LJ): OG: '00- 10, '04- 1; WCh: '99- dnq 13, '01- 2, '03- 2; CG: '98- 2/10, '02- 2, AfG: '99- 1/2; AfCh: '96-8-00-02: 3/2/1/1 (02- 1); WI: '03- 2, '04- 6; WCp: '02- 1/8. French champion 1999, 2001-02.

Ten African triple jump records 1999-2004, CMR records LJ from 1993, TJ from 1997.

Progress at TJ: 1994- 12.18, 1995- 11.92, 1996- 12.59, 1997- 13.75A, 1998- 14.02, 1999- 14.70A/14.65, 2000- 14.18, 2001- 14.65, 2002- 14.95, 2003- 15.05, 2004- 15.30, 2005- 14.07. pbs: 100m 12.00 '04, 11.5w '00, LJ 6.55A/6.43 '99, 6.68w '02.

First athlete from CMR to win World and Commonwealth medals.

CANADA

Governing body: Athletics Canada, Suite 300-2197 Riverside Drive, Ottawa, Ontario K1H 7X3. Formed as Canadian AAU in 1884.

National Championships first held in 1884 (men), 1925 (women). **2005 champions: Men**: 100m: Pierre Browne 10.67, 200m: Anson Henry 21.05w, 400m: Nathan Vadeboncoeur 46.12, 800m: Gary Reed 1:46.94; 1500m: Kevin Sullivan 3:48.07, 5000m: Reid Coolsaet 13:52.66, 10,000m/HMar: Mark Bomba 29:25.22/66:47, Mar: Jim Finlayson 2:18:21, 110mh: Karl Jennings 13.79, 400mh: Adam Kunkel 49.90, HJ: Kwaku Boateng 2.22; PV: Jason Wurster 5.20, LJ: Maurice Ennis 7.39, TJ: Marlon Nagle 15.43, SP: Dylan Armstrong 18.77; DT: Jason Tunks 65.89, HT: Jim Steacy 69.94, JT: Scott Russell 77.57, Dec: James Holder 7264, 20kmW: Tim Berrett 1:27:26. **Women**: 100m: Toyin Olupona 11.35, 200m: Adrienne Power 23.41w, 400m: Esther Akinsulie 53.88, 800m: Diane Cummins 2:02.59, 1500m: Carmen Douma-Hussar 4:15.58, 5000m: Megan Metcalfe 16:00.45, 10,000m/HMar: Tara Quinn-Smith 33:34.05/74:32, Mar: Lyudmila Korchagina RUS 2:32:19, 100mh: Perdita Felicien 12.82, 400mh: Tawa Dortch 56.40, HJ: Whitney Evans 1.82, PV: Dana Ellis 4.51, LJ: Alice Falaiye 6.54w, TJ: Althea Williams 12.99, SP: Caroline Larose 14.65, DT: Marie Josee Le Jour McDonagh 50.45, HT: Jennifer Joyce 67.03, JT: Dominique Bilodeau 53.63, Hep: Jessica Zelinka 5753, 20kmW: Marina Crivello 1:46:01.

Mark BOSWELL b. 28 Jul 1977 Mandeville, Jamaica 1.89m 77kg. Lightning T&F. Was at University of Texas.
At HJ: OG: '00- 6=, '04- 7; WCh: '99- 2, '01- 6=, '03- 3, '05- 4; WJ: '96: 1; CG: '02- 1, '06- 1; PAm: '99- 1=; WUG: '99- 2; WI: '03- 5; WCp: '02- 2; Won NCAA 1999-2000, Canadian 1997, 2000-04.
Five Canadian high jump records 1999-2002.
Progress at HJ: 1994- 2.10, 1995- 2.00, 1996- 2.24, 1997- 2.28, 1998- 2.29, 1999- 2.35, 2000- 2.35, 2001- 2.33, 2002- 2.35, 2003- 2.32, 2004- 2.30, 2005- 2.29.
Moved to Canada in 1988.

Tyler CHRISTOPHER b. 3 Oct 1983 Chilliwack, British Columbia 1.88m 84kg. Edmonton International.
At 400m: WCh: '03- hR, '05- 3. Canadian champion 2004. At 200m: WJ: '02- sf.
Canadian records 300m 2004, 400m (3) 2005.
Progress at 400m: 2002- 46.53, 2003- 45.61, 2004- 45.25, 2005- 44.44. pbs: 60m 6.75i '04, 200m 20.49 '05, 300m 31.77 '04.
Former long and triple jumper.

Gary REED b. 25 Oct 1981 Corpus Christie, Texas, USA 1.75m 66kg. Kamloops.
At 800m: OG: '04- sf; WCh: '01- hR; '03- h, '05- 8; CG: '06- ht; Canadian champion 2003-05.
Three Canadian 800m records 2005.
Progress at 800m: 2002- 1:48.08, 2003- 1:45.34, 2004- 1:44.92, 2005- 1:44.33. pbs: 400m 46.68A '02, 600m 1:14.72 '03. Began as long/triple jumper. then a decathlete (4th PAm Jnrs 1999).

Jason TUNKS b. 7 May 1975 London, Ontario 2.00m 125kg. London Western. Was at Southern Methodist University, USA.
At DT (SP): OG: '96- dnq 33, '00- 6, '04- dnq 15; WCh: '97- 9, '99- dnq 20, '01- 9, '03- 11, '05- 8; WJ: '94- 8 (10); CG: '98-02-06: 3/2/2; PAm: '99- 3 (5), '03- 1; WCp: '02- 5. Won NCAA 1997; Canadian SP 1997, DT 1995, 1997-2005.
Commonwealth & 2 CAN discus records 1998.
Progress at DT: 1992- 48.38, 1993- 51.52, 1994- 58.76, 1995- 58.66, 1996- 63.86, 1997- 65.20, 1998- 67.88, 1999- 65.54, 2000- 66.28, 2001- 67.70, 2002- 66.50, 2003- 65..84/66.55dh, 2004- 66.15, 2005- 66.59, 2006- 66.50. pb SP 19.06 '97.
Was married to Teri Steer (USA, pb SP 19.21 '01). Now married to **Lieja Koeman** (NED, b. 10 Mar 1976, pb 18.82 '03, 3 EI 02, 11 OG 04 & WCh 05).

Women

Diane CUMMINS b. 19 Jan 1974 Durban, South Africa 1.65m 50kg. Pacific Sport.
At 800m/4x400m (1500m): OG: '04- sf; WCh: '01- 5, '03- 6, '05- sf; CG: '98- sf/3R, '02- 2 (9), '06- 5; PAm: '99- 5; won CAN 800m 1998, 2000-05.
Canadian records: 800m 2001, 1000m 2002.
Progress at 800m: 1997- 2:08.65, 1998- 2:03.45, 1999- 2:02.14, 2000- 2:01.95, 2001- 1:58.39, 2002- 1:58.79, 2003- 1:58.89, 2004- 1:59.22, 2005- 2:00.10. pbs: 400m 53.89 '01, 1000m 2:34.14 '02, 1500m 4:05.02 '01, 1M 4:42.42i '02.
Came to Canada from South Africa in November 1994.

Carmen DOUMA-HUSSAR b. 12 Mar 1977 Cambridge, Ontario 1.72m 57kg. née Douma. Graduate of Villanova University, USA.
At 1500m: OG: '04- 9; WCh: '05- 9; CG: '06- 5; WI: '04- 2. Won NCAA 1998 (and indoor mile 1998, 2000), Canadian 2003, 2005.
Progress at 1500m: 1995- 4:28.42, 1996- 4:26.59, 1998- 4:16.04, 1999- 4:19.69, 2000- 4:16.09, 2001- 4:40.84M, 2002- 4:14.60, 2003- 4:08.09, 2004- 4:02.31, 2005- 4:02.29. pbs: 800m 2:02.43 '04, 1000m 2:36:26 '05, 1M 4:28.43i '05, 4:33.62 '03, 3000m 8:53.83 '05.
Married Christopher Hussar December 2001.

Dana ELLIS b. 7 Dec 1979 Kitchener, Ontario 1.62m 57kg. KWTF. Was at University of Waterloo.
At PV: OG: '04- 6=; WCh: '05- 6=; CG: '02- 6, '06- 4=; PAm: '03- 6. Canadian champion 2004-05
Five Canadian pole vault records 2004-05.
Progress at PV: 1998- 3.35, 1999- 3.65, 2000- 4.02A, 2001- 4.10, 2002- 4.20A, 2003- 4.30, 2004- 4.47, 2005- 4.51, 2006- 4.40i.
She was a member of the Canadian gymnastics team for seven years and took up vaulting after injuries. Married to US pole vaulter Ross Buller (pb 5.81 '01).

Perdita FELICIEN b. 29 Aug 1980 Oshawa, Ontario 1.65m 63kg. Phoenix TC. Studied kinesiology at University of Illinois, USA.

At 100mh: OG: '00- h, '04- dnf; WCh: '01- sf, '03- 1, '05- sf; PAm: '03- 2. At 60mh: WI: '04- 1. Won FrancG 2001, CAN 2000, 2002-05, NCAA 2002-03.
Canadian 100mh records 2003 & 2004.
Progress at 100mh: 1998- 13.69/13.47w, 1999- 13.69, 2000- 12.91, 2001- 12.73, 2002- 12.83/12.77w, 2003- 12.53, 2004- 12.46/12.45w, 2005- 12.58. pbs: 60m 7.37i '02, 100m 11.62 '01, 200m 24.21 '02, 50mh 6.80i '04, 60mh 7.75i '04.
Improved her best from 12.68 to 12.53 to win World 100mh in 2003 and from 7.90 to 7.75 to win World Indoor 60mh in 2004. Fell in 2004 Olympic final.

Angela WHYTE b. 22 May 1980 Edmonton 1.70m 57kg. Graduate of University of Idaho, USA.
At 100mh: OG: '04- 6; WCh: '01- h, '03/05- sf; CG: '02- 5, '06- 2; PAm: '03- 5. Canadian champion 2001.
Progress at 100mh: 1999- 13.97/13.43Aw, 2000- 13.37A/13.58, 2001- 13.09/12.82w, 2002- 13.03/13.00w, 2003- 12.78, 2004- 12.69, 2005- 12.88, 2006- 12.80. pbs: 60m 7.52i '05, 100m 11.63 '03, 11.37w '04; 200m 23.74 '03, 55mh 7.48iA '03, 60mh 8.01i '06, 400mh 60.56 '00, LJ 5.86 '03, Hep 5745 '03.

CAYMAN ISLANDS

Governing Body: Cayman Islands Amateur Athletic Association, PO Box 527, George Town, Grand Cayman. Founded 1980.

Women

Cydonie MOTHERSILL b. 19 Mar 1978 Kingston, Jamaica 1.70m 54kg. Was at Clemson University, USA.
At 200m(/100m): OG: '96- (h), '00- qf/qf, '04- sf; WCh: '97- (h), '01- 4, '03- sf, '05- 8; WJ: '96- sf/6; CG: '02- 5, '06- 4; PAm: '99- 5, '03- 2; PAm-J: '97- 3/3; WI: '03- 4; won CAC 2001, 2003, 2005.
Cayman Islands records 100m 1994-2005. 200m 1994-05, 400m 1998-9.
Progress at 200m: 1994- 24.31, 1995- 23.83, 1996- 23.65, 1997- 23.80, 1998- 23.48, 1999- 22.81, 2000- 22.66, 2001- 22.54, 2002- 22.76, 2003- 22.45/22.41w, 2004- 22.40, 2005- 22.39/22.26w, 2006- 22.57. pbs: 60m 7.36i '03, 100m 11.24 '05, 11.15w '04; 300m 35.82 '00, 400m 53.13 '99.
Married to Ato Modibo TRI (400m 44.87 '01).

CHILE

Governing body: Federación Atlética de Chile, Calle Santo Toribio No 660, Ñuñoa, Santiago de Chile. Founded 1917.
2005 National Champions: **Men**: 100m: Kael Becerra 10.67, 200m: Roberto Cortés 21.41, 400m: Mauricio Mery 47.58, 800m: Steven Mwangi KEN 1:51.15 (Pablo Navarette 1:52.10), 1500m/5000m: Leslie Encina 3:56.48/14:42.50, 10,000m: Leónidas Rivadeneira 30:41.22, 3000mSt: Sergio Lobos 9:01.61, 110mh: Gonzalo Barroilhet 14.41, 400mh: Carlos Zbinden 53.85 HJ: Jacques Laborde 1.95, PV: Juan Pablo Valdevieso 4.00, LJ: Luis Zepeda 7.20, TJ Alejandro Horn 14.77, SP: Daniel Muñoz 16.09, DT: Bernardo Heiremans 47.90, HT: Patricio Palma 67.54, JT: Diego Moraga 70.97, Dec Sebastián Rosselot 6097, 20kmW: Hugo Aros 1:32:42. **Women**: 100m: Daniela Riderelli 12.14, 200m: María José Echeverría 24.32, 400m/800m: Nicole Manríquez 55.04/2:14.15, 1500m: Susana Aburto 4:46.37, 5000m: Luz Eliana Silva 16:49.97 10,000m: Mónica Regonesi 37:51.12, 3000mSt: Belén Rojas 13:04.92, 100mh: Francisca Guzmán 14.14, 400mh: Karen Sauterel 66.38, HJ: Kerstin Weiss 1.72, PV: Carolina González 3.00, LJ: Melanie Chávez 5.18, TJ: Macarena Reyes 12.54, SP: Natalia Ducó 14.41, DT: Marianne Berndt 48.58, HT: Odette Palma 59.62, JT: Bárbara Pino 36.20, Hep: Natalia Depassier 4213, 20kmW: Josette Sepúlveda 1:49:39.

CHINA

Governing body: Athletic Association of the People's Republic of China, 9 Tiyuguan Road, Beijing 100763.
National Championships first held in 1910 (men), 1959 (women). **2005 Champions**. **Men**: 100m: Hu Kai 10.27, 200m: Liu Haitao 20.98, 400m: Wang Liangyu 46.47, 800m: Li Guangming 1:49.27, 1500m: Gu Ming 3:46.92, 5000m/10,000m: Zhang Yunshan 13:57.80/30:10.49, Mar: Li Jianfei 2:14:56, 3000mSt: Sun Wenyong 8:46.55, 110mh: Liu Xiang 13.21, 400mh: Zhang Shibao 49.69, HJ: Zhang Shufeng 2.27, PV: Zhang Hongwei 5.30, LJ: Li Runrun 7.85, TJ: Zhu Shujing 16.78, SP: Jia Peng 19.49, DT: Wu Tao 62.65, HT: Zhao Yihai 69.94, JT: Chen Qi 79.31, Dec: Qi Haifeng 7910, 20kmW: Yu Chaohong 1:19:08, 50kmW: Han Yucheng 3:36:20. **Women**: 100m/200m: Qin Wangping 11.33/23.38, 400m: Tang Xiaoyin 53.05, 800m/1500m: Liu Qing 2:04.91/4:16.37, 5000m: Xing Huina 15:31.10, 10,000m/Mar: Zhou Chunxiu 32:40.77/2:29:58, 100mh: Feng Yun 12.99, 400mh: Wang Xing 55.39, HJ: Jing Xuezhu 1.88, PV: Zhao Yingying 4.30, LJ: Wang Lina 6.56, TJ: Huang Qiuyan 14.15, SP: Li Meiju 19.05, DT: Sun Taifeng 59.63, HT: Zhang Wenxiu 73.24, JT: Xue Juan 59.72, Hep: Shen Shengfei 5834, 20kmW: Jiang Jiang 1:27:19.
National Games 2005: Men: 100m: Gong Wei 10.24w, 200m: Yang Yaozu 20.73, 400m: Wang Liangyu 46.15, 800m: Li Xiangyu 1:48.21, 1500m: Dou Zhaobo 3:40.88, 5000m: Sun Wenyong 13:58.02, 10,000m: Chen Mingfu 28:16.40, 3000mSt: Sun Wenli 8:32.36, 110mh: Liu Xiang 13.10, 4000mh: Meng Yan 49.19, HJ: Zhang Shufeng 2.24, PV: Liu Feiliang 5.60, LJ: Zhang Xin 7.99, TJ: Li Yanxi 16.95, SP: Zhang Qi 20.15, DT: Li Shaojie 62.85, HT: Ye Kuigang 71.93, JT: Li Rongxiang 81.06, Dec: Qi Haifeng 7854, 20kmW: Li Gaobo 1:18:22, 50kmW: Yu Chaohong 3:36:06. **Women**: 100m/200m: Qin

Wangping 11.34/23.50, 400m/400mh: Huang Xiaoxiao 51.95/54.18, 800m: Liu Qing 1:59.74, 1500m: Liu Qing 4:04.00, 5000m/10,000m: Xing Huina 15:20.09/31:00.73, 1100mh: Liu Jing 12.96, HJ: Jing Xuezhu 1.92, PV: Zhao Yingying 4.40, LJ: Guan Yingnan 6.65, TJ: Huang Qiuyan 14.54, SP: Li Meiju 18.88, DT: Li Qiumei 64.89, HT: Liu Yinghui 72.17, JT: Ma Ning 60.64, Hep: Shen Shengfei 6165, 20kmW: Bai Yanmin 1:27:37.

CUI Zhide b. 11 Jan 1983 Qinghai 1.82m 73kg. Army.
Progress at 20kmW, 50kmW: 2001- 1:28:40, 4:11:59; 2002- 1:25:20, 2003- 1:23:47, 3:59:37; 2004- 1:20:12, 3:45:36; 2005- 1:17:53, 3:44:20.

GADASU Alatan b. 27 Jan 1984 1.73m 60kg. Inner Mongolia.
At 50kmW: OG: '04- 10; WCp: '04- 5.
Progress at 20kmW, 50kmW: 2001- 1:30:34, 4:08:51; 2002- 1:30:17, 2003- 1:25:06, 3:54:21; 2004- 1:24:05, 3:45:41; 2005- 1:23:52, 3:40:23.

HAN Yucheng b. 16 Dec 1978 1.75m 63kg. Liaoning.
At 20kmW (50kmW): OG: '04- 40 (dnf); WCh: '05- (dnf); WCp: '04- 4, AsiC: '03- 1. Won CHN 20kmW 2004, 50kmW 2004-05.
Asian 50km records 2004 & 2005.
Progress at 20kmW, 50kmW: 2003- 1:20:00, 3:54:45; 2004- 1:19:30, 3:39:10; 2005- 1:18:31, 3:36:20. pb 30kmW 2:12:39 '05.

LIU Xiang b. 13 Jul 1983 Shanghai 1.89m 82kg.
At 110mh: OG: '04- 1; WCh: '01- sf, '03- 3, '05- 2; WJ: '00- 4; WUG: '01- 1; AsiG: '02- 1; AsiC: '02- 1, '05- 1; WCp: '02- dnf. Won CHN 2002, 2004-05; CHN NG 2005, E.Asian 2001, 2005. At 60mh: WI: '03- 3, '04- 2.
Tied world 110mh record 2004, World junior records 110mh 2002, indoors 50mh (6.53 and 6.52) & 60mh (7.61 and 7.55). Six Asian indoor 60mh records 2002-04.
Progress at 110mh: 1999- 14.19, 2000- 13.75, 2001- 13.32, 2002- 13.12, 2003- 13.17, 2004- 12.91, 2005- 13.05. pbs: 200m 21.27 '02. 50mh 6.52i '02, 60mh 7.43i '04, HJ 2.04 '98.
With his brilliant 110mh win in 2004 he become the first Chinese man to win a global athletics gold medal. Set world age records 16 (13.94)-17-18 in 2000-02.

QI Haifeng b. 7 Aug 1983 1.86m 78kg. Liaoning.
At Dec: OG: '04- 18; WCh: '03- 7, '05- dnf; AsiG: '02- 1; AsiC: '02- 5; WUG: '03- 1; won CHN 2001-05, CHN NG 2005.
Six Chinese decathlon records 2002-05.
Progress at Dec: 1999- 7437, 2000- 7430, 2001- 8021, 2002- 8041, 2003- 8126, 2004- 7960, 2005- 8290. pbs: 60m 7.14i '04, 100m 10.87 '05, 400m 48.72 '05, 1000m 2:43.41i '02, 1500m 4:23.22 '01, 60mh 8.26i '04, 110mh 14.40 '03, HJ 2.06 '02, PV 4.80 '02, LJ 7.52 '02, 7.58w '03; SP 13.78i '04, 13.73 '05; DT 48.57 '05, JT 64.53 '05, Hep 5763i '06. World age bests at 15 (7119) and 16 in 1999.

SHI Dongpeng b. 6 Jan 1984 1.92m 75kg. Hebei.
At 110mh: OG: '04- h; WCh: '03- 6, '05- sf; WJ: '02- 2; AsiG: '02- 4; AsiC: '03- 1, '05- 2; Won CHN 2003.
World U18 110mh record 2001.
Progress at 110mh: 2000- 14.10, 2001- 13.43, 2002- 13.50, 2003- 13.40, 2004- 13.50, 2005- 13.29. pbs: 50mh 6.75i '04, 60mh 7.63i '06.

XING Shucai b. 4 Aug 1984 1.72m 60kg. Yunnan.
At 50kmW: WCh: '05- dnf; WCp: '04- 14.
Progress at 20kmW, 50kmW: 2003- 1:22:58, 4:24:46; 2004- 1:21:53, 3:40:22; 2005- 1:18:27, 3:37:58. pb 10,000mW 40:55.42 '04.

YU Chaohong b. 12 Dec 1976 1.75m 63kg. Yunnan.
At 20kmW: WCh: '03- 15, '05- dq; WCp: '99- 16; AsiG: '02- 2. At 50kmW: OG: '04- 4; WCp: '04- 2. Won E.Asian 20kmW 2005, CHN 20kmW 2002-03, 2005; 50kmW 2003, NG 50kmW 2005
Asian 50km walk record 2005.
Progress at 20kmW, 50kmW: 1995- 1:25:33, 1997- 4:00:47, 1999- 1:23:09, 2000- 1:23:35, 3:58:44; 2001- 1:21:04, 3:47:04, 2002- 1:21:45, 3:58:57; 2003- 1:18:56, 3:44:11; 2004- 1:21:04, 3:42:28; 2005- 1:18:30, 3:36:06. pbs: 30kmW 2:10:58 '04, 35kmW 2:33:04 '04.

ZHAO Chengliang b. 1 Jun 1984 1.70m 62kg. Yunnan.
At 50kmW: WCh: '05- 5; WCp: '04- 19.
Progress at 20kmW, 50kmW: 2003- 1:26:55, 2004- 1:23:03, 3:43:09; 2005- 1:20:20, 3:36:13. pbs: 30kmW 2:12:32 '05, 35kmW 2:34:33 '05.

ZHU Hongjun b. 18 Aug 1983 Qinghai 1.75m 68kg. Liaoning.
At 20kmW: OG: '04- 6; WCh: '05- 9; Chinese champion 2003. Won AsiJ 10,000mW 2001.
Asian 20km walk record 2001.
Progress at 20kmW: 2000- 1:23:34, 2001- 1:21:58, 2002- 1:21:48, 2003- 1:18:43, 2004- 1:20:10, 2005- 1:17:41. pbs: 30kmW 2:20:28 '01, 50kmW 4:07:47 '98.

Women

GAO Shuying b. 28 Oct 1979 1.80m 63kg. Shanghai.
At PV: OG: '00- 10, '04- dnq 24=; WCh: '01- 5, '03- 9, '05- 5; WJ: '98- 8; AsiG: '02- 1; AsiC: '02/03/05- 1/4/1; WUG: '01- 1; WCp: '02- 4. Won CHN 2000-02, 2004; E.Asian & CHN NG 2001.
Eight Asian pole vault records 2000-05.
Progress at PV: 1996- 3.30, 1997- 3.70, 1998- 3.90, 1999- 4.10, 2000- 4.35, 2001- 4.52, 2002- 4.45i/4.43, 2003- 4.40, 2004- 4.45, 2005- 4.53.

GU Yuan b. 9 May 1982 1.71m 85kg. Shaanxi.
At HT: OG: '04- 10; WCh: '03- 4, '05- dnq; AsiG: '02- 1; AsiC: '98-02-03-05: 1/1/1/2; WCp: '02- 1. Won CHN 2003, NG 2001.
Ten CHN hammer records 1998-2003, five Asian 2001-03, five Asian junior 1999-2001.

Progress at HT: 1998- 62.28, 1999- 63.38, 2000- 64.72, 2001- 66.97, 2002- 71.10, 2003- 72.03, 2004- 72.36, 2005- 69.69.

GUAN Yingnan b. 25 Apr 1977 Shanghai 1.77m 60kg.
At LJ: OG: '00-04: dnq 19/19; WCh: '99- dnq 17, '01- 9, '03- dnq 13; WJ: '96- 1; AsiG: '98- 1; AsiC: '98- 1; WI: '99-01-04: 6/7/4; WUG: '01- 2; WCp: '98- 3. Won Asi-J 1996, CHN 1998-2000, 2004; E.Asian 2001.
Progress at LJ: 1994- 6.11, 1995- 6.48, 1996- 6.68, 1997- 6.86, 1998- 6.91, 1999- 6.80, 2000- 6.95, 2001- 6.77, 2003- 6.72, 2004- 6.80i/6.75, 2005- 6.78. pbs: 100mh 14.53A '95, HJ 1.80 '94, JT 39.64A '95, Hep 5637A '95.

HUANG Qiuyan b. 25 Jan 1980 1.72m 66kg. Guangxi.
At LJ: OG: '00-04: dnq 19/19; WCh: '99- dnq 17, '01- 9, '03- dnq 13, '05- 9; WJ: '96- 1; AsiG: '98- 1; AsiC: '98- 1, '05- 3; WI: '99-01: 6/7; WUG: '01- 2; WCp: '98- 3. Won Asi-J 1996, CHN 1998-2000, 2004-05 & NG 1997, 2001, 2005; E.Asian 2001, 2005.
World youth TJ record 1997, Asian record 2001.
Progress at TJ: 1997- 14.57, 1998- 14.36, 1999- 13.68, 2000- 13.76, 2001- 14.72, 2002- 14.60, 2003- 14.39, 2004- 14.66, 2005- 14.58. pb LJ 6.26 '97.
World age-17 best in 1997.

HUANG Xiaoxiao b. 3 Mar 1983 1.81m 62kg. Shandong.
At 400mh: OG: '04- sf; WCh: '05- 5; AsiC: '03- 1; WUG: '03- 2. Won E.Asian 2005, CHN 400mh 2003, CHN NG 400m 2003, 2005; 400mh 2005.
Progress at 400mh: 2001- 55.15, 2002- 56.96, 2003- 55.10, 2004- 54.83, 2005- 54.18. pbs: 200m 24.28 '00, 400m 51.93 '03.

JIANG Jing b. 23 Oct 1985 1.64m 51kg. Jiangsu.
At 20kmW: OG: '04- 32; WCh: '05- dq; WCp: '04- 2. Chinese champion 2004-05.
Progress at 20kmW: 2003- 1:29:42, 2004- 1:27:34, 2005- 1:27:19. pb 10kmW 44:07 '04.

LI Meiju b. 23 Jan 1981 1.73m 85kg. Hebei.
At SP: OG: '04- 9; WCh: '03- 11, '05- 7; WJ: '00- 2; AsiG: '02- 1, AsiC: '03- 1, '05- 1; WI: '04- 5; WUG: '05- 2. Won CHN 2002, 2004-05; NG 2001, 2005; Af-AsG 2003.
Progress at SP: 1998- 15.89, 1999- 16.62, 2000- 17.48, 2001- 18.92, 2002- 18.95, 2003- 18.96, 2004- 18.89, 2005- 19.05.

SONG Aimin b. 15 Mar 1978 1.78m 90kg. Hebei.
At DT: OG: '04- dnq 25; WCh: '03- 7, '05- 10; AsiG: '02- 2; AsiC: '05- 1; WUG: '05- 2. Won Asi-J 1997, E.Asian 2005, CHN 2001-03.
Progress at DT: 1997- 55.84, 1998- 56.64, 1999- 60.50, 2000- 60.39, 2001- 62.34, 2002- 62.28, 2003- 65.33, 2004- 64.90, 2005- 65.23.

SONG Hongjuan b. 4 Jul 1984 1.66m 50kg. Jilin.
At 20kmW: OG: '04- 14; WCh: '03- dq, '05- 9; WCp: '04- 6; Chinese champion 2003-04.
World junior records 20,000m walk (1:29:23.4) and 20km road 2003.
Progress at 20kmW: 2000- 1:43:04, 2001- 1:40:38, 2003- 1:27:16, 2004- 1:26:46, 2005- 1:28:26. pb 10kmW 43:44 '04.

SUN Yingjie b. 3 Oct 1977 1.65m 50kg. Railway
At 5000m/10,000m: OG: '04- 8/6; WCh: '03- 9/3, '05- 11/7. AsiG: '02- 1/1; AsiC: '03- 1/1 At Mar: WCh: '99- 12. At HMar: WCh: '04- 1 Won CHN 5000m 2002-03, 10,000m 2002-04 Mar 1998.
Asian marathon record 2003, Chinese half marathon record 2004.
Progress at 5000m, 10,000m, Mar: 1997- 2:30:10 1998- 15:47.87, 32:34.48, 2:25:45; 1999- 15:32.14 32:12.7, 2:30:12; 2000- 2:26:36, 2001- 15:02.70 31:49.47, 2:29:16; 2002- 14:40.41, 30:28.26, 2:21:21 2003- 14:46.73, 30:07.20, 2:19:39; 2004- 15:03.00 30:54.37; 2005- 14:51.19, 30:33.53, 2:21:01. pbs 1500m 4:16.01 '03, 3000m 8:50.34 '03, HMar 68:40 '04.
In October 2002 followed Asian Games records at 5000m and 10,000m with 2nd in Beijing marathon (later 1st after Wei Yanan disqualified for drugs positive three weeks earlier). Seven wins in 19 marathons: Tianjin and Dalian 1998 Tianjin 2003, Beijing 2002-05.

WANG Liping b. 8 Jul 1976 Liaoning Province 1.65m 48kg.
At 20kmW: OG: '00- 1, '04- 8; WCh: '05- dnf Won E.Asian 2005, CHN 2000. At 10kmW WCp: '97- 10, '04- 10; WUG: '01- 3.
Progress at 10kmW, 20kmW: 1994- 1:35:09, 1995- 46:19.83t, 1:29:26; 1997- 42:53, 1:36:22; 1998- 45:12 2000- 44:55, 1:28:33; 2001- 44:01, 1:26:23; 2003- 1:32:40, 2004- 44:07. 1:28:58; 2005- 45:05, 1:27:24.
Married to Zou Menghui (pb 50kmW 3:48:12 '97), baby born November 2002.

XING Huina b. 25 Feb 1984 Weifang, Shandong province 1.66m 50kg.
At (5000m)/10,000m: OG: '04- 9/1; WCh: '03- 7 '05- 5/4; AsiG: '02- 4/3. Won CHN 1500m 2003-04, 5000m 2004-05, CHN NG 5000m & 10,000m 2005.
World junior 10,000m record 2003.
Progress at 5000m, 10,000m: 2000- 16:11.09 2001- 14:56.15, 36:38.91; 2002- 15:42.99, 31:42.58 2003- 15:00.02, 30:31.55; 2004- 14:56.01, 30:24.36 2005- 14:43.64, 30:27.18. pb 1500m 4:03.98dq '05 4:09.01 '03, 3000m 8:53.5 '05.

ZHANG Wenxiu b. 22 Mar 1986 Dalian 1.82m 102kg. Army.
At HT: OG: '04- 7; WCh: '01- 11, '03- dnq 14, '05- 5; WJ: '02- dnq 20; AsiC: '05- 1. Won Asi-J 2002 CHN 2004, NG 2003.
Three Asian hammer records 2001-05, world youth record 2003, two world junior record 2004-05.
Progress at HT: 2000- 60.30, 2001- 66.30, 2002- 67.13, 2003- 70.60, 2004- 72.42, 2005- 73.24.
World age bests at 15-16-18.

ZHOU Chunxiu b. 8 Mar 1979 Jiangsu province 1.62m 51kg. Henan.
At Mar: OG: '04- 33; WCh: '05- 5; Chinese champion 2003-05. World HMar: '04- 12.
Progress at 10,000m, Mar: 2000- 33:14.63, 2003- 2:23:41, 32:13.96; 2004- 2:23:28, 33:03.04; 2005- 2:21:11, 31:09.03. pbs: 1500m 4:16.59 '98, 3000m 9:34.68 '00, 5000m 15:22.46 '03, HMar 72:52 '04.
Three wins in nine marathons to April 2006. Four sub 2:30 marathons in 2005 (first woman to do so in one year), won Seoul in pb 2:23:24 and improved by 2:13 for 2nd in Beijing.

COLOMBIA

Governing body: Federación Colombiana de Atletismo, Calle 28 No. 25-18, Apartado Aéreo 5024, Santafé de Bogotá. Founded 1937.
2005 Champions. Men: 100m/200m: Daniel Grueso 10.39/21.11, 400m: Carlos Peña 46.81, 800m/1500m: John Chávez 1:49.62/3:50.46, 5000m: Rolando Ortiz 14:36.97, 10,000m: Jason Gutiérrez 30:46.29, HMar: Herder Vásquez 64:18, 3000mSt: Wilder Álvarez 9:24.68, 110mh: Paulo César Villar 14.66w, 400mh: Oscar Candanoza 52.20, HJ: Gilmar Mayo 2.11, PV: Víctor Medina 4.50, LJ: Lewis Asprilla 7.35, TJ: Carlos Carabalí 16.08, SP/DT: Jhonny Rodríguez 18.40/49.21, HT: Freiman Arias 57.16, JT: Noraldo Palacios 70.54, Dec: José Gómez 6415, 20000mW/20kmW: Luis Fernando López 1:24:05.0/1:25:59. **Women:** 100m: Yomara Hinestroza 11.68, 200m: Darlenis Obregón 23.54, 400: Norma González 54.38, 800m/1500m: Rosibel García 2:05.29/4:31.47, 5000m/10,000m/HMar: Bertha Sánchez 17:24.44/34:59.18/77:09, 3000mSt: Ángela Figueroa 10:49.57, 100mh: Brigith Merlano 13.70w, 400mh: Dinelba Hinestroza 63.13, HJ/TJ: Katarina Ibargüen 1.88/13.62, PV: Karina Quejada 3.60, LJ: Helena Guerrero 6.20, SP/DT: Luz Dary Castro 16.05/53.11, HT: Johana Ramírez 59.16, JT: Tatiana Valencia 44.16, Hep: Nasly Perea 4997, 20000mW: Sandra Zapata 1:42:35.0, 20kmW: Magnolia Rojas 1:43:08.

DEMOCRATIC REPUBLIC OF CONGO

Governing Body: Fédération d'Athlétisme du Congo, BP 1527 Kinshasa 1. Founded 1949.

Gary KIKAYA b. 4 Feb 1978 Congo 1.84m 75kg. Studied sociology at University of Tennessee.
At 400m: OG: '04- sf; WCh: '03/05- sf; WI: '04- 3; Won NCAA 2002, indoor 2003.
COD records 200m 2001-05, 400m 2001-03.
Progress at 400m: 2000- 46.51A, 2001- 45.58A, 2002- 44.53, 2003- 44.99, 2004- 44.80, 2005- 44.81. pbs: 55m 6.20i '05, 200m 20.56 '05, 300m 31.95 '05.
His World Indoor bronze was the first ever global medal for his country. Lived in South Africa for a decade as his father was Congo's ambassador there.

CROATIA

Governing body: Hrvatski Atletski Savez, Tg Sportova 11, 10000 Zagreb. Founded 1912.
2005 Champions: **Men**: 100m/200m: Josip Soprek 10.53/21.09, 400m: Ivan Rimac 48.22, 800m: Igor Jankovic 1:50.74, 1500m/5000m: Slavko Petrovic 3:50.12/14:48.93, 3000m: Dario Nemec 8:53.28, Mar: Janez Maroevic 2:37:42, 3000mSt: Duje Pedisic 9:57.83, 110mh: Nenad Varda 14.84, 400mh: Milan Kotur 51.87, HJ: Jure Simundic 2.14, PV: Nenad Pavlicek 4.70, LJ: Ivan Pucelj 7.71, TJ: Ivan Mitrovic 14.75, SP: Edis Elkasevic 20.04, DT: Martin Maric 55.93, HT: Andras Haklits 75.23, JT: Martin Maric 70.22, 10,000mW: Zeljko Konosic 63:20.1. **Women**: 100m: Ria Ergotic 11.96, 200m/400m: Danijela Grgic 24.06/54.41, 800m: Vanja Perisic 2:06.43, 1500m: Maja Cikatic 4:49.22, 3000m/5000m: Ljiljana Culibrk 9:41.46/16:33.22, Mar: Lidija Rajaic 2:51:15, 100mh: Andrea Ivancevic 13.89, 400mh: Sandra Parlov 64.90, HJ: Blamka Vlasic 1.95, PV: Ivona Jerkovic 4.05, LJ: Petra Karanikic 5.98, TJ: Mateja Posavec 12.44, SP: Martina Masic 13.71, DT: Vera Begic 56.85, HT: Ivana Brkljacic 69.91, JT: Ivana Vukovic 47.57.

Women

Ivana BRKLJACIC b. 25 Jan 1983 Vinningen-Schweningen, Germany 1.70m 65kg. Mladost Zagreb.
At HT: OG: '00- 11, '04- dnq 13; WCh: '01- 8, '03/05- dnq 36/15; EC: '02- dnq 17; WJ: '98- dnq 15, '00- 1, '02- 1; WY: '99- 3; EU23: '03- 8; EJ: '99- 5, '01- 1. CRO champion 1999, 2001-02, 2004.
Croatian hammer record from 1998.
Progress at HT: 1998- 56.84, 1999- 58.51, 2000- 68.18, 2001- 66.49, 2002- 66.54, 2003- 68.03, 2004- 69.38, 2005- 71.00. pbs: SP 12.90 '04, DT 42.84 '04.

Blanka VLASIC b. 8 Nov 1983 Split 1.92m 75kg. ASK PK Split.
At HJ: OG: '00- dnq 17, '04- 11; WCh: '01- 6, '03- 7, '05- dnq 19=; EC: '02- 5=; WJ: '00- 1, '02- 1; WY: '99- 8; EU23: '03- 1; EJ: '01- 7; WI: '03-04-06: 4/3/2. Won MedG 2001, CRO 2001-02, 2005.
Two Croatian high jump records 2003.
Progress at HJ: 1998- 1.68, 1999- 1.80, 2000- 1.93, 2001- 1.95, 2002- 1.96, 2003- 2.01, 2004- 2.03, 2005- 1.95, 2006- 2.05i.
Her father Josko set the Croatian decathlon record with 7659 (1983).

CUBA

Governing body: Federación Cubana de Atletismo, Calle 13 y C Vedado 601, Zona Postal 4, La Habana 10400. Founded 1922.
National Champions 2005 Men: 100m/200m: Luis Reyes 10.59/21.03, 400m: Williams Collazo 46.40, 800m: Yeimar López 1:46.61, 1500m: Maury Castillo 3:44.36, 5000m: Liván Luque

14:36.29, 10,000m: Agüelmis Rojas 30:10.18, 3000mSt: Osmani Calzado 8:53.78, 110mh: Anier García 13.63, 400mh: Sergio Hierrezuelo 49.81, HJ: Lisvany Pérez 2.29, PV: Lázaro Borges 5.00, LJ: Iván Pedroso 7.79w, TJ: Yoandri Betanzos 16.93, SP: Alexis Paumier 18.80, DT: Frank Casañas 60.61, HT: Erik Jiménez 72.60, JT: Guillermo Martínez 81.36, Dec: Alexis Chivás 7518, 20kmW: Loisel Gutiérrez 1:29:23. **Women**: 100m: Virgen Benavides 11.39, 200m: Roxana Díaz 23.54, 400m: Libania Grenot 52.43, 800m/1500m: Adriana Muñoz 2:04.37/4:17.85, 5000m: Yudelkis Martínez 16:28.04, 10,000m: Mariela González 34:45.72, 100mh: Anay Tejeda 13.24, 400mh: Yaniuska Pérez 58.99, HJ: Yariadnis Argüelles 1.90, PV: Katiuska Pérez 4.20, LJ: Yudelkis Fernández 6.53, TJ: Yusmay Bicet 14.54, SP: Yumileidi Cumbá 18.80, DT: Yania Ferrales 60.52, HT: Yunaika Crawford 69.30, JT: Osleidys Menéndez 64.29, Hep: Yasmiany Pedroso 5512, 20kmW: Yarelis Sánchez 1:41:49.

Yoandri BETANZOS b. 15 Feb 1982 Ciego de Ávila 1.79m 71kg.
At TJ: OG: '04- 4; WCh: '03- 2, '05- 2; WJ: '00- 2; WY: '99- 2; PAm: '03- 1; WUG: '01- 5; WI: '04- 3, '06- 3; Won WAF & CAC 2005, PAm-J 2001, Cuban 2002-06.
Progress at TJ: 1999- 15.94/16.07w, 2000- 16.82, 2001- 16.84/16.86w, 2002- 17.29, 2003- 17.28, 2004- 17.53, 2005- 17.46, 2006- 17.63.

Anier Octavio **GARCÍA** b. 9 Mar 1976 Santiago de Cuba 1.89m 85kg.
At 110mh: OG: '96- qf, '00- 1, '04- 3; WCh: '97- sf, '99- 2, '01- 2, '05- sf; WJ: '94- 5; PAm: '99- 1, '03- h; CAG: '98- 1; WCp: '98- 3, '02- 1. Won GP 2001, PAm-J 1995, IbAm 1996, Cuban 1997-2000, 2005. At 60mh: WI: '97-9-01-03: 1/6/2/2.
Five CAC & Cuban 110mh records 1997-2000. CAC indoor records at 50mh & 60mh 2000.
Progress at 110mh: 1993- 14.61, 1994- 13.91, 1995- 13.63/13.6, 1996- 13.39A/13.43, 1997- 13.11, 1998- 13.14A/13.24, 1999- 13.07, 2000- 13.00, 2001- 13.07, 2002- 13.03, 2003- 13.55, 2004- 13.20, 2005- 13.61. pbs: 50mh 6.36i '00, 60mh 7.37i '00.
World number one in 2002. His father Pedro was an international 400mh runner and his mother Barbara Ortíz was a heptathlete.

David GIRALT b. 26 Aug 1984 Santiago de Cuba 1.82m 72kg.
At TJ: OG: '04- dnq 17; WCh: '03- 4, '05- 8; WJ: '02- 1, WY: '01- 2. Won PAm-J 2003 (2 LJ).
Progress at TJ: 2000- 15.23, 2001- 16.33, 2002- 16.84, 2003- 17.31, 2004- 17.12, 2005- 17.14. pb LJ 7.70 '02.
Father (also David) had LJ pbs 8.22/8.32w and was third in the World Cup in 1979.

Yoel HERNÁNDEZ b. 12 Dec 1977 Manacas, Villa Clara 1.84m 77kg.
At 110mh: OG: '00/04- sf; WCh: '99- 6, '01- 4, '03- 7; WJ: '94- sf, '96- 1; PAm: '99- 2; Won Cuban 2002, IbAm 2004. At 60mh: WI: '01- 5, '04- 7.
Progress at 110mh: 1994- 14.20, 1995- 13.81, 1996- 13.81/13.72w, 1997- 13.70, 1998- 13.45, 1999- 13.24, 2000- 13.24/13.20w, 2001- 13.30, 2002- 13.30, 2003- 13.49, 2004- 13.29/13.28w, 2005- 13.39/13.32w. pbs: 100m 10.69 '99, 200m 21.10 '02, 50mh 6.42i '00, 60mh 7.40i '00.

Yuniel HERNÁNDEZ b. 28 Mar 1981 Caimit 1.83m 76kg.
At 110mh: OG: '04- sf; WCh: '01/05- sf; WJ '00- 1; PAm: '03- 1. CAC champion 2005, Cuban 2003-04. At 60mh: WI: '04- 5, '06- 8.
At 110mh: 1997- 14.78, 1998- 14.17, 1999 13.99/13.81w, 2000- 13.60/13.5, 2001- 13.26 2002- 13.63, 2003- 13.35, 2004- 13.46/13.24w 2005- 13.78/13.6. pbs: 100m 10.43 '01, 200m 21.24 '05, 50mh 6.56i '01, 60mh 7.54i '02.

Guillermo MARTÍNEZ b. 28 Jun 1981 Camagüey 1.90m 101kg.
At TJ: OG: '04- dnq 17; WCh: '05- 10; Cuban champion 2004-06.
Progress at TJ: 1999- 64.66, 2000- 70.82, 2001 73.50, 2002- 75.90, 2003- 75.35, 2004- 81.45, 2005 84.06, 2006- 83.33.

Victor MOYA b. 24 Oct 1982 Santiago de Cuba 1.96m 80kg.
At HJ: WCh: '05- 2=, '06- 4; Won WAF & CAC 2005, Cuban 2006.
Progress at HJ: 1999- 2.00, 2000- 2.05, 2001- 2.10 2002- 2.21, 2003- 2.18, 2004- 2.25, 2005- 2.35 2006- 2.31.
Set pbs at 2.32 and 2.35 to win 2005 WAF title.

Iván Lázaro **PEDROSO** b. 17 Dec 1972 Habana del Este, La Habana 1.76m 70kg. Adidas.
At LJ: OG: '92- 4, '96- 12, '00- 1, '04- 7; WCh: '93- nj '95- 1, '97- 1, '99- 1, '01- 1, '03- nj, '05- dnq; WI: '93 5-7-9-01-04: 1/1/1/1/1/8; WJ: '90- 4; WUG: '97- 1 PAm: '91-5-9-03: 3/1/1/1; CAG: '98- 1; WCp: '92 1, '98- 1, '02- 2. Won GP 1995, 1997, 1999; GWG 1998, 2001; PAm J 1991, IbAm 1992, CAC 1997 Cuban 1992-3, 1995, 1997-8, 2000, 2005.
Three CAC & Cuban long jump records 1992-5
Progress at LJ: 1988- 7.43, 1989- 7.43, 1990- 8.06 1991- 8.22, 1992- 8.53/8.79w, 1993- 8.49, 1994 8.26i/8.16, 1995- 8.71/8.96Aw, 1996- 8.46i/8.32 1997- 8.63, 1998- 8.54, 1999- 8.62i/8.60, 2000 8.65, 2001- 8.43i/8.40, 2002- 8.30, 2003- 8.31 2004- 8.23, 2005- 8.22. pb TJ 16.05 '91.
Won fifth successive World Indoor title and fourth successive outdoor title in 2001. Clearl the world top long jumper in 1995, when h had a narrow foul at 9.03 at the Pan-America Games and jumped 8.96 at Sestriere. This wa given a wind of just 1.2 m/s, but an official had stood in front of the gauge and the mark wa not recognised. Unbeaten in 26 LJ competition 1995 to Jan 1996. Hamstring surgery in 199 meant that he was not fully fit at the Olympics but he won 84/99 competitions in 1997-2001 Cousin of Aliuska López (Pedroso).

Harry Aikines-Aryeetey – World Youth champion at 100m & 200m and winner of IAAF Rising Star award.

And it's supposed to be a summer sport! The effects of a cloud burst at the Helsinki World Championships

The US clean sweep in the Helsinki 200m (from left) Justin Gatlin (1st), Tyson Gay (4th), John Capel (3rd) and Wallace Spearmon (2nd).

Osleidys Menéndez – world javelin record at Worlds.

Tero Pitkämäki – world's top male javelin thrower of 2005.

Carolina Klüft – still supreme at heptathlon.

Christine Arron – winner of five out of six Golden League 100m races and the European Cup 100m/200m double.

Ivan Tikhon – World hammer champion

Double world champion Rashid Ramzi (right) wins the 1500m from Adil Kaouch (centre) and Rui Silva (left).

Adam Nelson – World and World Athletics Final shot champion

Dorcus Inzikuru – World steeplechase champion

Yoelbi Luis **QUESADA** b. 4 Aug 1973 Trinidad, Sancti Spíritus 1.81m 71kg. Adidas.
At TJ: OG: '92- 6, '96- 3, '00- 4, '04- 8; WCh: '91- 7, '93- 12, '95- 4, '97- 1, '99- 10, '03- 9; WI: '93-5-9-03: 5/2/4/3; WJ: '90- 2, '92- 1; WUG: '97- 1, '99- 1; WCp: '94- 1, '98- 3; PAm: '91-5-9-03: 1/1/1/3; CAG: '93- 1, '98- 1. Won CAC-J 1990, PAmJ 1991, IbAm 1992, Cuban 1991-5, 1997-8, 2002. 2nd GP 1996.
Cuban triple jump record 1997.
Progress at TJ: 1989- 16.11, 1990- 16.68, 1991- 17.13, 1992- 17.23, 1993- 17.68, 1994- 17.61, 1995- 17.67/17.97w, 1996- 17.75, 1997- 17.85, 1998- 17.43i/17.27, 1999- 17.40, 2000- 17.37, 2001- 16.55, 2002- 17.42, 2003- 17.27i/16.97, 2004- 17.13, 2005- 17.03. 2006- 17.38w. pb LJ 7.88 '94.
World age bests for each age 15-19 in 1989-93.

Dayron ROBLES b. 19 Nov 1986 Guantánamo 1.89m 74kg.
At 110mh: WCh: '05- sf; WJ: '04- 2, WY: '03- 6. At 60mh: WI: '06- 2. Cuban champion 2006.
Progress at 110mh: 2003- 14.30, 2004- 13.75, 2005- 13.46/13.2/13.41w, 2006- 13.56. pbs: 100m 10.71 '05, 200m 22.08 '05, 60mh 7.46i '06.

Women

Sonia BISSET b. 1 Apr 1971 Palma Soriano, Santiago de Cuba 1.71m 69kg.
At JT: OG: '00- 5, '04- 5; WCh: '97- 6, '99- 6, '01- 3, '03- 6, '05- 7; PAm: '03- 5; CAG: '98- 1; WUG: '97- 2; WCp: '98- 2. CAC champion 1995, IbAm 1996, Cuban 1998, GP 2000.
Progress at JT: 1987- 50.40, 1988- 58.28, 1989- 55.94, 1990- 55.20, 1991- 57.64, 1992- 58.38, 1993- 59.52, 1994- 61.42, 1995- 62.52, 1996- 64.54, 1997- 68.24, 1998- 67.59; new: 1999- 63.52, 2000- 65.87, 2001- 66.54, 2002- 65.52, 2003- 60.75, 2004- 65.93, 2005- 67.67.

Zulia Inés **CALATAYUD** b. 9 Nov 1979 Playa, La Habana 1.69m 59kg.
At 800m: OG: '00- 6, '04- 8; WCh: '99- h, '01- sf, '05- 1; PAm: '99- 2; WCp: '02- 4; Won WAF 2005, Ib-Am 2004. At 400m: WJ: '98- sf. Won Cuban 400m 1999, 800m 1999-2001.
Progress at 800m: 1995- 2:18.9, 1996- 2:13.80, 1997- 2:12.7, 1999- 2:00.67, 2000- 1:58.66, 2001- 1:58.60, 2002- 1:56.09, 2004- 1:59.21, 2005- 1:57.92. pbs: 200m 24.33/24.2 '98, 400m 50.87 '01, 1000m 2:34.31 '02, 1500m 4:23.84 '05.
Missed 2003 season with shin injuries.

Yunaika CRAWFORD b. 2 Nov 1982 Marianao, La Habana 1.65m 75kg.
At HT: OG: '04- 3; WCh: '03/05- dnq 20/26; WJ: '00- 3; WY: '99- 2; PAm: '03- 2; Won PAm-J 2001, CAC 2001, Cuban 2005-06.
Progress at HT: 1995- 38.86, 1997- 48.98, 1998- 58.92, 1999- 62.71, 2000- 65.88, 2001- 65.67, 2002- 70.62, 2003- 70.69, 2004- 73.16, 2005- 69.30, 2006- 71.92.

Yumileidi CUMBÁ b. 11 Feb 1975 Guantánamo 1.83m 100kg. PE student.
At SP: OG: '96- dnq 13, '00- 6, '04- 1; WCh: '99- 6, '01- 8, '03- dnq 13, '05- 6; PAm: '95- 3, '99- 2, '03- 1; CAG: '93- 2, '98- 1; WJ: '92- 4, '94- 2; WI: '99-01-03-04-06: 6/5/6/2/5; WUG: '99- 1, '01- 1; WCp: '98- 4, '02- 2. Won CAC 2005, Cuban 1994-5, 1998, 2000-06; IbAm 2002, 2004.
Progress at SP: 1990- 14.53, 1991- 15.84, 1992- 17.44, 1993- 17.70, 1994- 18.78, 1995- 19.11, 1996- 18.57, 1998- 19.20, 1999- 19.29, 2000- 19.48, 2001- 19.10i/19.00, 2002- 19.39, 2003- 19.31, 2004- 19.97, 2005- 19.06, 2006- 19.52. pb DT 42.84 '93.

Yania FERRALES b. 28 Jul 1977 Morón, Ceigo de Avila 1.80m 86kg.
At DT: OG: '04- nt; WCh: '05- dnq 14; PAm: '03- 3. CAC champion 2001, 2003; Ibero-American 2004, Cuban 2000-01, 2004-06.
Progress at DT: 1995- 45.64, 1996- 51.94, 1997- 53.82, 1998- 56.40, 1999- 56.94, 2000- 57.40, 2001- 56.90, 2002- 59.04, 2003- 61.34, 2004- 62.88, 2005- 64.52, 2006- 66.00.

Mabel GAY b. 5 May 1983 Santiago de Cuba 1.86m 71kg.
At TJ: WCh: '03- 5, '05- dnq 18; WJ: '02- 1; WY: '99- 1; PAm: '03- 1; WI: '04- 9; Won CAC-J 2002, IbAm 2002, Cuban 2003-04, 2006.
Progress at TJ: 1997- 13.00, 1998- 13.48, 1999- 13.82, 2000- 14.02, 2001- 14.05, 2002- 14.29, 2003- 14.52, 2004- 14.57i/14.20, 2005- 14.21/14.44w, 2006- 14.27.
World age 17 record in 1999.

Osleidys MENÉNDEZ b. 14 Nov 1979 Martí, Matanzas 1.78m 80kg.
At JT: OG: '00- 3, '04- 1; WCh: '97- 7, '99- 4, '01- 1, '03- 5, '05- 1; WJ: '96- 1, '98- 1; WUG: '01- 1; PAm: '99- 1, '03- 3; CAG: '98- 2; WCp: '02- 1. Won GWG 2001, IbAm 2004, PAm-J 1995, 1997; Cuban 1997, 1999-2002-06; CAC 1997, GP 2002 (3rd 2000), WAF 2004-05.
World javelin records 2001 & 2005. Eight CAC bests and one world (66.45 '99) new javelin 1999-2001.
Progress at JT: 1994- 53.98, 1995- 54.30, 1996- 62.54, 1997- 66.92, 1998- 68.17, 1999- 67.59; new 1999- 66.49, 2000- 67.83, 2001- 71.54, 2002- 67.40, 2003- 63.96, 2004- 71.53, 2005- 71.70.
On 1 July 2001 she became the first Cuban woman to set a world record in athletics. World age 19 best in 1999.

Yipsi MORENO b. 19 Nov 1980 Camagüey 1.68m 70kg.
At HT: OG: '00- 4, '04- 2; WCh: '99- 18, '01- 1, '03- 1, '05- 2; WJ: '98- 4; PAm: '99- 2, '03- 1; WUG: '01- 2; WCp: '02- 2. Won WAF 2003, 2005, PAm-J 1997, IbAm 2004, Cuban 2000-04.
World junior hammer record 1999, 20 CAC records 1999-2004.
Progress at HT: 1996- 53.94, 1997- 61.96, 1998- 61.00, 1999- 66.34, 2000- 69.36, 2001- 70.65, 2002- 71.47, 2003- 75.14, 2004- 75.18, 2005- 74.95.

Yargelis SAVIGNE b. 13 Nov 1984 Niceto Pérez, Guantánamo 1.65m 53kg.

At LJ/(TJ): WCh: '05- 4/2; WJ: '02- dnq; PAm: '03- 3; WI: 6/5. Won CAC LJ & TJ 2005, Cuban LJ 2006. Cuban triple jump record 2005.
Progress at LJ, TJ: 1998- 12.13, 1999- 5.60, 12.65; 2000- 5.92, 12.70; 2001- 6.24, 13.03; 2002- 6.46, 2003- 6.63, 2004- 6.60A/6.52, 2005- 6.77/6.88w, 14.82; 2006- 6.81w, 14.72i.

Anay TEJEDA b. 3 Apr 1983 Marianao, La Habana 1.65m 59kg
At 100mh: OG: '04- h; WCh: '05- sf; WJ: '00- 7, '02- 1; WY: '99- 3; PAm: '03- 8. Won Cuban 2002-05.
Progress at 100mh: 1998- 14.00, 1999- 13.56, 2000- 13.38, 2001- 13.20/13.07w, 2002- 12.89/12.6/12.81w, 2003- 12.99, 2004- 12.74, 2005- 12.95. pbs: 60m 7.51i '05, 100m 11.92, 11.55w '04; 200m 24.2 '02, 50mh 6.91i '05, 60mh 7.96i '05.

CZECH REPUBLIC

Governing body: Cesky atleticky svaz, Diskarská 100, 169 00 Praha 6 -Strahov, PO Box 40. AAU of Bohemia founded in 1897.
National Championships first held in 1907 (Bohemia), 1919 (Czechoslovakia), 1993 CZE. **2005 Champions**: **Men**: 100m: Jan Stokláska 10.58, 200m: Jirí Vojtík 20.77, 400m: Karel Bláha 46.37; 800m: Michal Sneberger 1:46.94, 1500m: Vladimír Bartunek 3:52.53, 5000m/HMar/Mar: Jan Bláha 14:45.10/68:10/2:17:59, 10,000m: Pavel Faschingbauer 29:41.17, 3000mSt: Michael Nejedly 8:58.80, 110mh: Stanislav Sajdok 13.90, 400mh: Michal Uhlík 49.43, HJ: Jaroslav Bába 2.28, PV: Ales Honcl 5.40, LJ: Stepán Wagner 7.72, TJ: Tomás Cholensky 16.31, SP: Petr Stehlík 19.71, DT: Libor Malina 61.71, HT: Vladimír Maska 73.90, JT: Petr Belunek 72.82, Dec: Josef Karas 7252, 20kmW: Milos Holusa 1:24:45, 50kmW: David Snajdr 4:40:52. **Women**: 100m: Stepánka Klapácová 11.76, 200m: Denisa Scerbová 24.05, 400m: Jitka Bartonícková 54.93, 800m: Petra Lochmanová 2:07.69, 1500m: Marcela Lustigová 4:22.90, 5000m/10,000m: Petra Kamínková 16:50.32/ 34:18.34, HMar: Jana Klimesová 79:14, Mar: Ivana Martincová 2:58:00, 3000mSt: Barbora Kuncová 10:13.48, 100mh: Lucie Martincová 13.09, 400mh: Alena Rücklová 57.07, HJ: Iva Straková 1.90, PV: Pavla Hamácková 4.30, LJ/TJ: Martina Darmovzalová 6.66/13.36, SP: Jana Kárníková 16.40, DT: Vera Cechlová 65.35, HT: Lucie Vrbenská 62.78, JT: Barbora Spotáková 61.91, Hep: Michaela Hejnová 5596, 20kmW: Barbora Dibelková 1:33:16.

Jaroslav BÁBA b. 2 Sep 1984 Karviná 1.96m 82kg. SSK Vítkovice.
At HJ: OG: '04- 3; WCh: '03- 11, '05- 5=; WJ: '02- 8; WY: '01- 10=; EU23: '05- 1; EJ: '03- 1; WI: '03- 9, '04- 3=; EI: '05- 4. Won CZE 2003, 2005.
Czech high jump record 2005.
Progress at HJ: 1997- 1.72i, 1998- 1.81i/1.75, 1999- 1.93i/1.92, 2000- 1.95, 2001- 2.16i/2.15, 2002- 2.27/2.28et, 2003- 2.32i/2.30, 2004- 2.34, 2005- 2.37i/2.36. pb TJ 15.43 '03.

Tomás DVORÁK b. 11 May 1972 Gottwaldov (now Zlín) 1.86m 88kg. Dukla Praha. Soldier.
At Dec: OG: '96- 3 (h 110mh), '00- 6, '04- dnf; WCh: '93- 10, '95- 5, '97- 1, '99- 1, '01- 1, '03- 4, '05- 8; EC: '94- 7, '98- 5, '02- dnf; ECp: '94- 3, '95- 1, '99- 1; WJ: '90- 17; EJ: '91- 2; won GWG 2001. At Hep: WI: '95-7-9-03: 2/dnf/4/5; EI: '94-6-8-00-02: 4/2/4/1/2. Won Czech 110mh 1994-2001, Dec 1991.
World decathlon record 1999, three Czech 1996-9. European indoor heptathlon record 2000.
Progress at Dec: 1989- 6999, 1990- 7251w/7138, 1991- 7748, 1992- 7392, 1993- 8054, 1994- 8313, 1995- 8347, 1996- 8664, 1997- 8837, 1998- 8592, 1999- 8994, 2000- 8900, 2001- 8902, 2002- 8226, 2003- 8242, 2004- 8211, 2005- 8105. pbs: 60m 6.90i '97, 100m 10.54 '99, 200m 21.39 '98, 400m 47.56 '97, 1000m 2:34.60i '98, 1500m 4:27.63 '03, 50mh 6.59i '96, 60mh 7.76i '00, 110mh 13.61/13.6 '97, HJ 2.09 '00, PV 5.00 '97, LJ 8.07 '01, SP 16.88 '00, DT 50.28 '00, JT 72.32 '99, Hep 6424i '00.
Set four pbs en route to Olympic bronze in 1996 and six pbs when he won World gold in 1997. In 1999 he won all his four decathlons and added 103 points to Dan O'Briens' world record, missing 9000 by just six points and setting five pbs. After 2nd 1996-8, won at Götzis 1999 and 2000 and Talence 2000 before injury held him back to sixth in Sydney. Won the IAAF Combined Events Challenge in 1999 and 2001. Has 34 decathlons over 8000 points 1993-2005. Married Gabriela Vánová (pb LJ 6.28/6.30w '93, daughter of his ex-coach).

Jirí MUZÍK b. 1 Sep 1976 Plzen 1.81m 75kg. Dukla Praha.
At 400mh (400m): OG: '00/04- sf; WCh: '97- 8, '99- sf, '01- 7, '03- sf, '05- h; EC: '98- 7, '02- 2; EU23: '97- 4/2R; WUG: '97- 4; ECp: '99- 7 (7), "05- 5. At 400m: EJ: '95- h; EI: '00- 1R, '02- 5. Won CZE 400mh 1997, 2001-02, 2004.
Three Czech 400mh records 1997.
Progress at 400mh: 1997- 48.27, 1998- 48.83, 1999- 49.15, 2000- 48.71, 2001- 48.53, 2002- 48.43, 2003- 48.63, 2004- 48.85, 2005- 48.83. pbs: 100m 10.72 '03, 200m 21.06 '03, 400m 45.78 '98, 800m 1:52.73i '04, LJ 7.26 '93, TJ 15.55 '96.
Ran first 400mh race on 1 June 1997 and reached World final three months later. His father Jirí had LJ best of 7.75 '75.

Roman SEBRLE b. 26 Nov 1974 Lanskroun 1.86m 88kg. Dukla Praha. Soldier.
At Dec: OG: '00- 2, '04- 1; WCh: '97- 9, '99- dnf, '01- 10, '03- 2, '05- 2; EC: '98- 6, '02- 1; WUG: '97- 1; ECp: '97-8-9: 1/2/2. At Hep: WI: '99-01-03-04-06: 3/1/3/1/3; EI: '00-02-05: 2/1/1. At 110mh: ECp: '99- 6. At LJ: ECp: '05- 7. Won Czech Dec 1996, LJ 1998.
World decathlon record 2001, European indoor heptathlon record 2004.
Progress at Dec: 1991- 5187, 1992- 6541, 1993- 7066, 1994- 7153, 1995- 7642, 1996- 8210, 1997- 8380, 1998- 8589, 1999- 8527, 2000- 8757, 2001-

9026, 2002- 8800, 2003- 8807, 2004- 8893, 2005- 8534. pbs: 60m 6.87i '02, 100m 10.64 '01, 200m 21.74 '04, 400m 47.76 '99, 1000m 2:37.86i '01, 1500m 4:21.98 '01, 60mh 7.84i '02, 110mh 13.79 '99, 13.68w '01; HJ 2.15 '00, PV 5.20 '03, LJ 8.11 '01, SP 16.36 '04, DT 49.37 '03, JT 71.10 '04, Hep 6438i '04.

Married Eva Kasalová (b. 4 Dec 1976, pb 800m 2:02.79 '98), on 14 Oct 2000. At Götzis in 2001 he became the first decathlete to exceed 9000 points with the current scoring tables, setting five personal bests. Won again at Götzis 2002-05 and at Talence in 2004-05, and he won IAAF Combined Challenge in 2004 and 2005. Has 17 decathlons over 8500 and 33 over 8000 (58 in all to Talence 2005).

Svatoslav TON b. 20 Oct 1978 Brno 1.92m 75kg. Dukla Praha.

At HJ: OG: '04- 8; WCh: '05- dnq 21; EC: '02- 6; WJ: '96- 2=; EU23: '01- 7; EJ: '95- dnq, '97- 10; EI: '05- 7; ECp: '05- 3. Czech champion 2004.

Progress at HJ: 1992- 1.64, 1993- 1.86, 1994- 2.08i/2.05, 1995- 2.16, 1996- 2.24i/2.21, 1997- 2.27i/2.25, 1998- 2.20, 1999- 2.20, 2000- 5.61, 2001- 2.26, 2002- 2.30i/2.28, 2004- 2.33, 2005- 2.33i/2.30, 2006- 2.33i. pb LJ 7.74 '97.

Jan ZELEZNY b. 16 Jun 1966 Mladá Boleslav 1.86m 88kg. Dukla Praha.

At JT: OG: '88- 2, '92- 1, '96- 1, '00- 1, '04- 9; WCh: '87- 3, '91- dnq 18, '93- 1, '95- 1, '97- 9, '99- 3, '01- 1, '03- 4; EC: '86- dnq 18, '90- dnq 13, '94- 3, '02- nt; EJ: '83- 6, '85- 4; WCp: '92- 1; ECp: '87-89-91-3: 3/2/1/1. Won GP JT 1991, 1993, 1995, 1997 (2nd overall first 3 years), 2001; 2nd 1999. Won CS 1986, 1990, CZE 1992, 1994, 1996.; GWG 2001.

Five world javelin records 1987-96, eight CS records 1986-93, five CZE records 1992-6.

Progress at JT: 1979- 44.44, 1982- 57.22, 1983- 74.34, 1984- 80.32, 1985- 84.68, new: 1986- 82.48, 1987- 87.66, 1988- 86.88, 1989- 84.74, 1990- 89.66, 1991- 90.72, 1992- 94.74, 1993- 95.66, 1994- 91.82, 1995- 92.28, 1996- 98.48, 1997- 94.02, 1999- 89.06, 2000- 90.59A, 2001- 92.80, 2002- 87.77, 2003- 89.06, 2004- 86.12, 2005- 83.98.

His third successive Olympic gold in 2000 surely sealed Zelezny's place as the greatest ever javelin thrower. He won 114 of 148 competitions 1991-2003. In his career with the new javelin 1986-2003 his competition bests averaged 85.50, with 59 throws over 90m and 142 in all over 88m. His 100 best throws averaged 90.71m, 200 best 89.27, 300 best 88.17 and 500 best 86.08. His 94.74 throw in 1992 was made with a new 'Németh' javelin, later ruled illegal by the IAAF. In 1993 he added 4.08m to Steve Backley's world record with 95.54 at Pietersburg, RSA in April, and threw 95.56 at Sheffield in August. Suffered a fractured vertebra at the end of 1989, but recovered to regain the world record in 1990. In 1991 he was most unlucky not to qualify for the World final, when he fell, perhaps over the line, on a long throw. Serious injury cost him the 1998 season amid fears that he might not compete again, but he was back in full training by the end of the year. In December 1999 he was amongst the first group of ten active participants to be elected a member of the IOC, having already been a member of its athletes' commission, but he resigned in December 2001. Relected 2004.

His father, Jaroslav, threw the javelin 68.46m in 1969 and his mother Jana 43.23 in 1959.

Women

Nikola BREJCHOVÁ b. 25 Jun 1974 Gottwaldov (now Zlín) 1.80m 77kg. née Tomecková. PSK Olymp Praha. Sports instructor.

At JT: OG: '96- dnq 25, '00- 8; WCh: '93- dnq 22, '95- dnq 17, '97- dnq 26, '99- dnq 21, '01- 4; EC: '98- dnq 13, '02- dnq 14; WJ: '92- 11; EJ: '91- 2, '93- 5; WUG: '01- 2; ECp: '98-9-01: 2/5/2; E23Cp: '94- 5. Czech champion 1993-2002.

11 Czech new javelin records 1999-2004.

Progress at JT: 1987- 32.22, 1988- 39.80, 1989- 42.24, 1990- 49.22, 1991- 55.80, 1992- 59.78, 1993- 57.48, 1994- 56.68, 1995- 63.80, 1996- 64.50, 1997- 62.96, 1998- 64.18; new: 1999- 60.92A, 2000- 64.19, 2001- 65.71, 2002- 61.43, 2004- 65.91.

Married in 2002, daughter Valerie b. 13 Dec 2005.

Véra CECHLOVÁ-POSPISILOVÁ b. 19 Nov 1978 Litomerice 1.78m 78kg. née Pospísilová. PSK Olymp Praha.

At (SP/)DT: OG: '04- 4; WCh: '01- 6, '03- 5, '05- 3; EC: '02- 4; EU23: '99- 3; EJ: '97- 12/8; ECp: '01- 7/4; Won WAF 2003-04, 2nd GP 2002. Won CZE SP 2001-02, DT 2003-05.

Progress at DT: 1992- 28.24, 1993- 34.28, 1994- 39.48, 1995- 40.24, 1996- 45.72, 1997- 50.00, 1998- 54.67, 1999- 58.17, 2000- 58.28, 2001- 63.20, 2002- 64.10, 2003- 67.71, 2004- 66.42, 2005- 66.81. pb SP 16.92 '01.

Married wrestler Jakub Cechl on 17 Oct 2003.

Pavla HAMÁCKOVÁ b. 20 May 1978 Chomutov 1.70m 68kg. Dukla Praha.

At PV: OG: '00- dnq 22=, '04- 11; WCh: '99- 6=, '01- 8, '05- 3; EC: '98- 12=; EJ: '97- 5; EU23: '99- 7=; WUG: '99- 1; WI: '99- 7, '01- 1; EI: '00-02-05: 1/6/6; ECp: '99- 3, '01- 3. Czech champion 1999, 2003, 2005.

Czech pole vault record 2003.

Progress at PV: 1993- 2.40i, 1994- 3.20, 1995- 3.21i/3.28i exh, 1997- 3.95, 1998- 4.15, 1999- 4.40, 2000- 4.45, 2001- 4.56i/4.47, 2002- 4.56i/4.30A, 2003- 4.60, 2004- 4.45, 2005- 4.55i/4.51.

Barbora SPOTÁKOVÁ b. 30 Jun 1981 Jablonec 1.82m 80kg. Dukla Praha.

At JT: OG: '04- dnq 23; WCh: '05- dnq 13; EC: '02- dnq 17; EU23: '03- 6; WUG: '05- 1; Czech champion 2003, 2005. At Hep: WJ: '00- 4.

Progress at JT: 1997- 37.28, 1998- 44.56, new: 1999- 41.69, 2000- 54.15, 2001- 51.97, 2002-

56.76, 2003- 56.65, 2004- 60.95, 2005- 65.74. pbs: 200m 25.11w '00, 800m 2:18.29 '00, 100mh 13.99 '00, 400mh 62.68 '98, HJ 1.78 '00, LJ 5.60 '00, SP 14.12 '04, DT 36.80 '02, Dec 6749 '04, Hep 5873 '00.

DENMARK

Governing body: Dansk Athletik Forbund, Idraettens Hus, Brøndby Stadion 20, DK-2605 Brøndby. Founded 1907.

National Championships first held in 1894. **2005 Champions**: **Men**: 100m/LJ: Morten Jensen 10.40/7.80w, 200m: Mads Bangsø 21.89, 400m: Steffen Jørgensen 48.03, 800m: Eddie Andersen 1:56.69, 1500m: Mikkel Kleis 3:55.43, 5000m: Flemming Bjerre 14:47.03, 10,000m: Christian Olsen 28:48.54, HMar (c.20.9k)/Mar: Søren Palshøj 66:38/2:23:63, 3000mSt: Morten Tjalve 9:22.49, 110mh/TJ: Thomas Flensborg 15.05/15.79, 400mh: Andreas Bube 52.90, HJ/Dec: Anders Black 2.06/6976, PV: Lars Haukohl 4.55, SP: Simon Stewart USA 18.10, DT: Magnus Hallgrimsson ISL 51.37, HT: Jan Bielecki 68.13, JT: Richard A Knudsen 74.78, 5000mW: Andreas Nielsen 24:06.71, 10,000mW/20kmW/30kmW: Jacob Sorensen 48:31.7/1:36:54/2:04:01. **Women**: 100m: Sabrina Søndergaard 12.14, 200m: Sunna Gestsdottir 24.98, 400m/800m: Rikke Rønholt 54.83/2:07.40, 1500m: Louise Mørch 4:26.54, 5000m/Mar: Gitte Karlshøj 17:04.7/2:42:18, 10,000m: Anne Mette Aagaard 35:04.16, HMar (c.20.9k): Annemette Jensen 72:00, 100mh: Anne Møller 14.63, 400mh: Sara Petersen 58.21, HJ: Signe Vest 1.70, PV: Anita Tørring 3.95, LJ: Julie Flensborg-Madsen 5.61, TJ: Lotte Thiesen 12.59w, SP/JT: Christina Scherwin 14.21/61.72, DT: Anne Marie Gausel 41.67, HT: Vanessa Mortensen 56.70, Hep: Tina Bach Ejlersen 4692, 3000mW/5000mW: Pia M.Christensen 17:28.90/32:02.5.

Joachim B **OLSEN** b. 31 May 1977 Aalborg 1.84m 142kg. Studied history at the University of Idaho, USA. Århus 1900.
At SP: OG: '00- dnq 17, '04- 3; WCh: '99- dnq 22, 01- 10, '03- dns, '05- 7; EC: '02- 2; EU23: '99- 2; WI: '03-04-06: 8/3/3; EI: '02- 2, '05- 1. At DT: WJ: '96- dnq 23. Won WAF 2004, NCAA 2000, DEN SP 1997-2003, DT 1999-03.
Five Danish shot records 2000-02 (and 14 indoor 1999-2004).
Progress at SP: 1994- 13.27, 1995- 14.54, 1996- 14.89, 1997- 17.11, 1998- 18.40, 1999- 19.75, 2000- 20.88, 2001- 20.43, 2002- 21.57, 2003- 20.85, 2004- 21.63i/21.46, 2005- 21.32. pb DT 60.67 '02.

Women

Christina SCHWERIN b. 11 Jul 1976 Viborg 1.76m 67kg. IF Sparta.
At JT: OG: '04- dnq 29; WCh: '05- dnq 13; EC: '02- dnq 18; WJ: '94- 5; WUG: '03- 2; won Danish JT 2000, 2002-03, 2005; SP 2002-3, 2005. At Hep: WJ: '00- 4.
Danish records: Javelin (5+) 2000-05, Shot 2003.
Progress at JT: 1991- 44.04, 1992- 45.46, 1993- 53.48, 1994- 55.70, 1995- 43.48, 1996- 50.78, 1997- 52.10, 1998- 53.63, new: 1999- 53.61, 2000- 59.00, 2002- 55.99, 2003- 56.80, 2004- 59.36, 2005- 63.43. pb SP 14.64 '03.

DOMINICAN REPUBLIC

Governing body: Federación Dominicana de Asociaciones de Atletismo. Avenida J.F. Kennedy, esquina Ortega y Gasset. Centro Olímpico "Juan Pablo Duarte". Santo Domingo. Founded 1953.

Félix SÁNCHEZ b. 30 Aug 1977 New York, USA 1.78m 73kg. Was at University of Southern California.
At 400mh: OG: '00- sf, '04- 1; WCh: '99- ht, '01- 1, '03- 1, '05- dnf; PAm: '99- 4, '03- 1/3R; CAG: '02- 1R; WCp: '02- 1R. Won NCAA 2000, GWG 2001, GP 2002 (3rd overall), WAF 2003.
Three CAC 400mh records 2001-03. DOM records: 400mh (11) 1997-2003, 400m (3) 2001-02.
Progress at 400m, 400mh: 1995- 51.33, 1996- 51.19, 1997- 46.36, 50.01; 1998- 51.30, 1999- 48.60, 2000- 48.33, 2001- 44.90, 47.38; 2002- 45.14, 47.35; 2003- 45.22A/45.33, 47.25; 2004- 46.28, 47.63; 2005- 46.32, 48.24. pbs: 100m 10.45 '05, 200m 20.87 '01, 800m 1:49.36 '04.
Born in New York and raised in California, he first competed for the Dominican Republic, where his parents were born, in 1999 after placing 6th in US 400mh. Unbeaten in nine 400mh races in 2002 including GP Final and won 43 successive 400mh races (including 7 heats) from loss to Dai Tamesue on 2 Jul 2001 until he pulled up in Brussels on 3 Sep 2004.

ECUADOR

Governing body: Federación Ecuatoriana de Atletismo, Casilla 01-01-736, Cuenca. F'd 1925.

National Champions 2005: **Men:** 100m: Luis Morán 10.3, 200m: Oscar Mina 20.9, 400m: Francisco Aguirre 48.1, 800m: Cristian Matute 1:53.2, 1500m: Byron Piedra 4:00.1, 5000m: Wladimir Guerra 14:52.9, 10,000m: Franklin Tenorio 31:38.9, 3000mSt: Gerardo Villacrés 9:40.0, 100mh: David González 14.8, 400mh: Esteban Lucero 52.9, HJ: Cristian Calle 2.00, PV: Lenin Zambrano 4.46, LJ: Carlos Jaramillo 7.66, TJ: Hugo Chila 16.35, SP: Mario Zambrano 14.03, DT: Gabriel Hugo 45.88, HT: Lenin Proaño 50.26, JT: Xavier Mercado 59.28, Dec: Félix Sánchez 5752, 20000mW: Xavier Moreno 1:31:10.0. **Women:** 100m/LJ: Ana Mariuxi Caicedo 11.8/6.04, 200m: Jéssica Perea 24.2, 400m/800m/400mh: Lucy Jaramillo 53.6/2:10.7/61.3, 1500m: Mónica Amboya 4:45.5, 5000m: Rosalba Chacha 17:18.3, 10,000m: Martha Tenorio 35:28.4, 3000mSt: Alexandra Anangonó 12:16.9, 100mh/Hep: Virna Zalazar 14.7/4209, HJ: Francisca Ortiz 1.65, PV: Lorena Ortiz 3.35, TJ: María Batallas 12.24, SP/DT/HT:

Karina Díaz 13.29/46.16/48.08, JT: Jenny Llulluna 43.72, 20000mW: Tatiana Orellana 1:49:04.0.

Jefferson PÉREZ b. 1 Jul 1974 Cuenca 1.74m 59kg. Graduate of business management from University of Azuay.

At 20kmW: OG: '92- dnf, '96- 1, '00- 4, '04- 4 (12 50kmW); WCh: '95- 32, '97- 14, '99- 2, '01- 8, '03- 1, '05- 1; WCp: '97-02-04: 1/1/1; PAm: '95- 1, '99- 3, '03- 1; SAmCh: '93- 1, '05- 1. Won IbAm 2002, SAm Cup 1994-5, 1997-8; PAm Cup 2003. At 10kmW: WJ: '90- 3, '92- 1; won SAm-J 1989-93, PAm-J 1993. At 50km: WCp: '99- dnf.

World best 20km walk 2003, South American record 1997 & 2003, 9 Ecuador records 20kmW 1992-2003, 50kmW 2003 & 2004.

Progress at 20kmW, 50kmW: 1992- 1:25:50.5, 1993- 1:24:03, 1994- 1:23:27, 1995- 1:22:53, 1996- 1:20:07/1:20:55.4t, 1997- 1:18:24, 1998- 1:19:19, 1999- 1:20:46, 2000- 1:20:18, 2001- 1:22:20, 2002- 1:19:08, 2003- 1:17:21, 3:56:04; 2004- 1:18:42, 3:53:04; 2005- 1:18:35. pbs: 5000mW 19:49.54i '90, 10,000mW 39:50.73 '93, 10kmW 38:24 '02, 35kmW 2:38:04 '04.

In 1996 he became the youngest ever Olympic walking champion and Ecuador's first medallist at any sport. He then walked 459km from Quito, along the Pan-American Freeway at an altitude of 2500 to 4800m, to his home-town of Cuenca, as a religious promise. The Ecuador postal authorities issued a stamp with his picture. Tied record with third World Cup win in 2004. Set world age 16 best for 10,000m walk with 40:08.23 in 1990.

ERITREA

Yonas KIFLE b. 8 Feb 1982 1.60m 56kg. C.A. Adidas. Madrid, Spain.

At 10,000m: OG: '00- h, '04- 16; WCh: '05- 11; At 5000m: WCh: '99-h, '01- h, AfCH: '02- 6. World CC: 2002-04-05-06: 8/9/15/7; HMar: '02-04-05: 4/11/3. Eritrean record HMar 2002.

Progress at 10,000m: 2000- 28:07.15, 2004- 27:40.92, 2005- 27:35.72. pbs: 3000m 7:53.02 '02, 5000m 13:17.72 '02, Rd: 15km 43:28 '05, HMar 61:05 '02.

Zersenay TADESSE b. 8 Feb 1982 1.60m 56kg. C.A. Adidas. Madrid, Spain.

At 5000m/(10,000m): OG: '04- 7/3; WCh: '03- 8, '05- 14/6; AfG: '02- (6). World CC: 2002-03-04-05-06: 30/9/6/2/4; HMar: '02-03: 21/7.

Eritrean records 5000m and HMar 2003, 10,000m (3) 2004-05, 3000m 2005.

Progress at 5000m, 10,000m: 2002- 13:48.79, 28:47.29; 2003- 13:05.57, 28:42.79; 2004- 13:13.74, 27:22.57; 2005- 13:12.23, 27:04.70. pbs: 3000m 7:39.93 '05, Road: 15km 41:27 '05, 20km 56:03 '05, HMar 59:05 '05.

Won Eritrea's first medal at Olympics in 2004 and World CC in 2005. Ran 59:05 for the fastest ever half marathon to win the Great North Run (slightly downhill overall) in 2005. Won a national road cycling title in 2001 before taking up athletics. His younger brother Kidane was 16th in 2005 World Junior CC.

ESTONIA

Governing body: Eesti Kergejôustikuliit, Pirita tee 12, Tallinn 10127. Founded 1920.

National Championships first held in 1917. **2005 Champions: Men**: 100m: Henri Sool 10.86, 200m/400m: Martin Vihmann 21.38/47.63, 800m: Priit Lehismets 1:51.09, 1500m/5000m: Tiidrek Nurme 4:00.04/15:11.59, 10,000m: Margus Pirksaar 30:57.29, HMar: Pavel Loskutov 64:59, Mar: Margus Lehtna 2:34:34, 3000mSt: Aleksei Saveljev 9:15.02, 110mh: Tarmo Jallai 14.17, 400mh: Indrek Tustit 51.78, HJ: Marko Aleksejev 2.13, PV: Gert Rahnel 4.80, LJ/TJ: Jaanus Uudmäe 7.50/16.18, SP: Taavi Peetre 19.46, DT: Gerd Kanter 66.05, HT: Marek Vähi 59.29, JT: Andrus Värnik 80.97, Dec: Andres Raja 7608, 20kmW/50kmW: Margus Luik 1:36:57.2/4:25:51. **Women**: 100m: Katrin Käärt 11.86, 200m/100mh: Kadri Viigipuu 24.39/13.49, 400m: Jekaterina Duman 55.55, 800m: Maria Sahharova 2:09.70, 1500m/5000m: Jekaterina Patjuk 4:33.22/17:21.60, HMar/Mar: Tiina Tross 80:50/2:55:50, 400mh: Veera Duman 62.26, HJ: Anja Iljustsenko 1.73, PV: Kristina Ulitina 3.70, LJ: Kristel Bedrendsen 6.38, TJ: Veera Baranova 13.63w, SP/DT: Eha Rünne 14.85/51.26, HT: Maris Röngelep 56.42, JT: Moonika Aava 56.48, Hep: Ksenia Balta 5794, 10,000mW: Jekaterina Jutkina 55:57.2, 20kmW: Ragle Raudsepp 2:12:01.

Gerd KANTER b. 6 May 1979 Tallinn 1.96m 120kg. Altius, Pärnu. Business management graduate.

At DT: OG: '04- dnq 19; WCh: '03- dnq 25, '05- 2; EC: '02- 12; EU23: '01- 5. Estonian champion 2004-05.

Three Estonian discus records 2004-05.

Progress at DT: 1998- 47.37, 1999- 49.65, 2000- 57.68, 2001- 60.47, 2002- 66.31, 2003- 67.13, 2004- 68.50, 2005- 70.10. pb SP 17.31i '04, 16.11 '00.

Kristjan RAHNU b. 29 Aug 1979 Kadrina 1.92m 90kg.

At Dec: OG: '04- dnf; WCh: '03- dnf, '05- 6; WJ: '98- dnf. At Hep: WI: '06- 4.

Progress at Dec: 1996- 5541, 1997- 7157, 1998- 7335, 2001- 7534, 2002- 8081, 2003- 8203, 2004- 8062w/7784, 2005- 8526. pbs: 60m 6.80i '05, 100m 10.48/10.43w '02, 400m 48.58 '05, 1000m 2:48.74i '06, 1500m 4:52.18 '05, 60mh 7.85i '05, 110mh 14.20 '03, 14.04w '05; HJ 2.08 '97, PV 4.95 '05, LJ 7.58 '05, SP 16.58 '02, DT 53.16 '02, JT 65.02 '03, Hep 6062i '06.

Improved best by 323 points to win at Arles in 2005.

Aleksander TAMMERT b. 2 Feb 1973 Tartu 1.96m 126kg. Audentes, Tallinn. Was at Southern Methodist University, USA.

At DT: OG: '96- dnq 25, '00- 9, '04- 3; WCh:

'95- dnq 23, '97- 12, '99- 10, '01- dnq 16, '03- 7, '05- 4; EC: '98- dnq 20, '02- 5; WUG: '97- 5, '99- 4, '01- 1. Won EST SP 1998, 2002, DT 1993-5, 1997-2003, 2005.
Eight Estonian discus records 1998-2002.
Progress at DT: 1990- 42.06, 1991- 48.24, 1992-51.12, 1993- 54.54, 1994- 55.50, 1995- 60.24, 1996- 64.80, 1997- 64.78, 1998- 65.35, 1999- 66.95, 2000- 67.41, 2001- 67.10, 2002- 67.75, 2003- 66.63, 2004- 68.48, 2005- 67.93. pbs: SP 18.41 '01, HT 52.09 '99.
Father (also Aleksander) won 1966 European Junior shot, pbs: SP 19.41 '76, DT 54.98 '77.

Andrus VÄRNIK b. 27 Sep 1977 Anstla 1.82m 100kg. Löunalövi, Vöru.
At JT: OG: '00- dnq 15, '04- 6; WCh: '03- 2, '05- 1; EC: '02- dnq 21. EST champion 1999-2000, 2003-05.
Two Estonian javelin records 2002-03.
Progress at JT: 1994- 65.22, 1995- 62.28, 1996-68.36, 1997- 72.20, 1998- 69.96, 1999- 77.19, 2000-82.16, 2001- 80.83, 2002- 85.47, 2003- 87.83, 2004-87.58, 2005- 87.19. pb SP: 14.20 '03.
Became Estonia's first world champion in 2005.

ETHIOPIA

Governing body: Ethiopian Athletic Federation, Addis Ababa Stadium, PO Box 3241, Addis Ababa. Founded 1961.
2005 Champions: **Men**: 100m/200m: Wetere Gelelcha 10.3/21.0, 400m: Habtamu Abeje 46.6, 800: Abiyot Abebe 1:48.6, 1500m: Kumsh Adugna 3:43.4, 5000m/10,000m: Gebre-egziabher Gebremariam 13:45.7/28:39.0, 3000mSt: Roba Gari 8:41.9, 110mh/400mh: Ubang Abaya 14.7/52.4, HJ: Ugula Ubang 2.05, LJ: Girmay Gebretsadik 6.95, SP/DT: Tsegaye Woldesenbet 12.70/34.97, HT: Sisay Mekonnen 27.58, JT: Abdissa Tadesse 64.73, 20kmW: Ashenafi Merach 1:35:42. **Women**: 100m/200m: Atekelt Wubshet 11.8/?, 400m: ?, 800m: Mestawot Tadesse 2:05.0, 1500m/5000m: Gelete Burka 4:10.1/15:39.2, 3000m: Belaynesh Zemedkun 9:30.3, 10,000m: Werknesh Kidane 32:50.6, 100mh: Netsanet Bekele 16.8, 400mh: Mendaye Lemma 61.3, HJ: Mekdes Bekele 1.48, LJ/TJ: Emebet Tilahun ?/11.81, SP: Roman Abera 11.31, DT: Mersit Gebreegziabher 36.18, 10,000mW: Hanna Haileselassie 55:26.6.

Abiyote ABATE b. 20 Nov 1980 1.74m 56kg.
At 5000m: WCh: '01- 7, '03- 11. At 3000m: WI: '03- 5, '04- 11. World CC (4k): '99-00-02: 4J/11/15. Won ETH 5000m 2001, 4k CC 1998.
Progress at 5000m, 10,000m: 1999- 13:23.41, 2000-13:10.7, 2001- 13:00.36, 2002- 13:11.80, 2003- 13:05.13, 2004- 13:03.33, 2005- 13:43.66, 27:45.56. pbs: 3000m 7:32.38 '01, 2M 8:14.77i '04, 10kmRd 28:14 '99.

Kenenisa BEKELE b. 13 Jun 1982 near Bekoji, Arsi Province 1.60m 54kg.
At 5000m(/10,000m): OG: '04- 2/1; WCh: '03-3/1, '05- (1); WJ: '00- 2; AfG: '03- 1. At 3000m: WY: '99- 2; WI: '06- 1. World CC: '99- 9J, 4k: '01- 1J/2 4k, '02-03-04-05-06: all 1/1. Won WAF 3000m 2003.
World records: 5000m 2004, 10,000m 2004 & 2005, indoor 5000m (12:49.60) 2004; World junior record 3000m 2001.
Progress at 5000m, 10,000m: 2000- 13:20.57, 2001- 13:13.33, 2002- 13:26.58, 2003- 12:52.26, 26:49.57; 2004- 12:37.35, 26:20.31; 2005- 12:40.18, 26:17.53. pbs: 1M 4:01.57i '06, 2000m 5:00.32i '04, 3000m 7:30.67 '01, 2M 8:05.12i '06, Rd 15km 42:42 '01.
Has won a record 18 (11 individual, 7 team) world CC gold medals from his record winning margin of 33 seconds for the World Juniors in 2001, a day after coming second in senior 4km. He is the only man to win both World senior CC races in the same year, and has now done so five times, unbeaten in 25 CC races from Dec 2001 to April 2006. Has won all his seven 10,000m track races including three major gold medal, from a brilliant debut win over Haile Gebrselassie at Hengelo in June 2003. He ran 3000m in 7:30.77 on his indoor debut in 2004 to win in Stuttgart and then broke the world indoor record for 5000m in Birmingham, adding outdoor WRs in the summer.
His fiancée Alem Techale (b. 13.12.87, the 2003 World Youth 1500m champion) died of a heart attack on 4 Jan 2005.

Tariku BEKELE b. 21 Jan 1987 near Bekoji 1.60m 52kg.
At 5000m: WCh: '05- 7; WJ: '04- 3. At 3000m: WY: '03- 2; WI: '06- 6. World CC: '05- 6J, '06- 3J. World junior indoor 2M best 2006.
Progress at 5000m: 2004- 13:11.97, 2005- 12:59.03. pbs: 3000m 7:36.63 '05, 2M 8:13.32i '06.
Younger brother of Kenenisa Bekele.

Dejene BERHANU b. 12 Dec 1980 Addis Alem 1.82m 64kg.
At 5000m: WCh: '05- 8. At 10,000m: OG: '04- 5; AfCh: '00- 2, '02- 5; AfG: '03- 3. World CC: '03-20, '05- 6; 4k: '04- 11, '05- 7. Won ETH CC 2001, 4k CC 2005; E.Afr 4k 2004.
Ethiopian half marathon record 2004.
Progress at 5000m, 10,000m: 2000- 13:36.58, 28:41.11; 2002- 13:26.74, 28:46.21; 2003- 13:14.05, 27:14.61; 2004- 12:54.15, 28:21.38A '04; 2005-12:56.24, 27:12.22. pbs: 1500m 3:44.65 '00, HMar 59:37 '04, Mar 2:11:48 '05.
Brilliant winner of Great North Run in 2004 in 59:37 and 2nd in 2005.

Abebe DINKESA Negera b. 6 Mar 1984 Dendhi, near Ambo 1.69m 55kg.
At 10,000m: WCh: '05- 7; AfCh: '04- 2. World HMar: '04- 10, CC: '05- 4. Won ETH CC 2005-06.
Progress at 5000m, 10,000m: 2002- 13:40.33, 2004- 13:23.85, 27:23.60; 2005- 12:55.58, 26:30.74. pbs: 3000m 7:32.9+ '05, 2M 8:28.22i '06; Road: 15km 43:28 '05, HMar 61:53 '05.
Ran 10,000m pbs at Hengelo with 27:23.60 in 2004 and 26:30.74 in 2005. Won Great Ethiopian Run 2004.

Gebre-egziabher GEBREMARIAM b. 10 Sep 1984 Tsenkanet, Tigray region 1.78m 56kg.
At 10,000m (5000m): OG: '04- (4); WCh: '03- (6), '05- 15; WJ: '02- 1 (3); AfG: '03- 2. World CC: '02- 1J, '03- 3, 04- 2/2, '05- 9(4k), '06- 13. Won ETH CC 2003, 5000m & 10,000m 2005. E.Afr 2004.
Progress at 5000m, 10,000m: 2001- 14:13.74A, 31:04.61A; 2002- 13:12.14, 27:25.61; 2003- 12:58.08, 28:03.03; 2004- 12:55.59, 26:53.73; 2005- 12:52.80, 27:11.57. pbs: 3000m 7:39.48 '05, Mar 2:12:01 '04, 3000mSt 8:57.7A '02.
Married Worknesh Kidane on 4 Feb 2006.

Haile GEBRSELASSIE b. 18 Apr 1973 Arssi 1.64m 53kg.
At 10,000m (5000m): OG: '96- 1, '00- 1, '04- 5; WCh: '93- 1 (2), '95- 1, '97- 1, '99- 1, '01- 3, '03- 2; WJ: '92- 1 (1); AfG: '93- 3 (2). At 3000m: WI: '97- 1, '99- 1 (1 1500m), '03- 1. Won GP 3000m 1995, 1998. World CC: '91-2-3-4-5-6: 8J/2J/7/3/4/5; HMar: '01- 1; Rd Rly team: '94- 2.
World records 5000m (4) 1994-8, 10,000m (3) 1995-8, 10km road (27:02) 2002, 10M road (44:24) 2005, 20km, HMar & 25km 2006; Indoors 2000m 1998, 3000m (7:30.72 '96, 7:26.15 '98), 5000m (13:10.98 '96, 12:59.04 '97, 12:50.38 '99); World best 2M 1995 (8:07.46) & 1997, indoors 8:04.69 (2003). ETH records 1993-9: 1500m (2), 1M (1), 3000m (6), 5000m (5), 10,000m (3), marathon 2002 & 2005.
Progression at 5000m, 10,000m, marathon: 1992- 13:36.06, 28:03.99; 1993- 13:03.17, 27:30.17; 1994- 12:56.96, 27:15.00; 1995- 12:44.39, 26:43.53; 1996- 12:52.70, 27:07.34; 1997- 12:41.86, 26:31.32; 1998- 12:39.36, 26:22.75; 1999- 12:49.64, 27:57.27; 2000- 12:57.95, 27:18.20; 2001- 27:54.41, 2002- 28:16.50+, 2:06:35; 2003- 12:54.36, 26:29.22; 2004- 12:55.51, 26:41.58; 2005- 2:06:20. pbs: 800m 1:49.35i '97, 1000m 2:20.3+i '98, 1500m 3:31.76i '98, 3:33.73 '99; 1M 3:52.39 '99, 2000m 4:52.86i '98, 4:56.1 '97; 3000m 7:25.09 '98, 2M 8:01.08 '97; Road: 15km 41:22 '05, 10M 44:24 '05, 20km 55:48 '06, 25km 1:11:37 '06, HMar 58:55 '06.
A beautifully smooth runner, perhaps the greatest ever. After finishing a place behind Ismael Kirui at two successive World Junior CC championships, he outkicked his rival for a brilliant double at the 1992 World Juniors. He set the first of his 20 world records in Hengelo in 1994 at 5000m and in 1995 he took 8.7 secs off the 10,000m WR and regained the 5000m record by taking 10.91 secs off Kiptanui's mark. Between these feats he won the World 10,000m, with 25.1 for the last 200m!. He ran the second 5000m in c.13:11.6 to win the 1996 Olympic 10,000m and in 1997 took 6.76 secs off the world 10,000m record in Oslo. In 1998 he regained both the 5000m and 10,000m world records. From 1992 to 2004 he had 13 wins in 19 races at 10,000m, 26/28 at 3000m/2M, and 28/36 at 5000 including 16 successive 1996 to 2000. He has 7/7 wins at half marathon 2001-07. He had run c.2:48 for the marathon at the age of 15, but made his senior debut at the distance at London 2002, when he was third in 2:06:35 and won at Amsterdam in 2:06:20 in 2005. After missing the 2002 summer season through injury he set a world 10km road record of 27:02 at Doha, Qatar in December for a reward of $1 million.
Based during the summer in the Netherlands. His brother Tekeye had marathon pb 2:11:45 '94 and was 13th in 1991 World Cup.

Markos GENETI b. 30 May 1984 Walega 1.75m 55kg.
At 5000m: WJ: '02- 2; AfG: '03- 4. At 3000m: WY: '01- 1; WI: '04- 3. At 1500m: '05- sf.
Progress at 5000m: 2001- 13:50.14, 2002- 13:28.83, 2003- 13:11.87, 2004- 13:17.57, 2005- 13:00.25. pbs: 1500m 3:33.83 '05, 3000m 7:37.0i '04, 7:38.11 '05; 2M 8:08.39i '04.

Sileshi SIHINE b. 29 Jan 1983 Sheno 1.71m 55kg.
At (5000m)/10,000m: OG: '04- 2; WCh: '03- 3, '05- 2/2; WJ: '02- 2; AfG: '03- 1. World CC: '02-03-04-06: 6J/7/3/2 & 12 4k. World HMar: '05- 4. Won WAF 5000m 2004-05, Ethiopian 5000m 2003, 10,000m 2003-04, Af-AsG 10,000m 2003.
Progress at 5000m, 10,000m: 2002- 13:21.81, 27:26.12; 2003- 13:06.53, 26:58.76; 2004- 12:47.04, 26:39.69; 2005- 13:13.04, 26:57.27; 2006- 13:06.72i. pbs: 2000m 5:01.2i+ '04, 5:02.2 '05; 3000m 7:29.92 '05, 2M 8:27.03i '06; Road: 15km 41:38 '04, HMar 61:14 '05.

Mulugeta WONDIMU b. 28 Dec 1985 1.73m 57kg.
At 1500m: OG: '04- 10; WCh: '05- h. At 5000m: Af-J '03- 3 (2 10,000m). World CC: '04- 5J.
Two Ethiopian 1500m records 2004.
Progress at 1500m, 5000m: 2003- 13:26.73, 2004- 3:31.13, 12:57.05; 2005- 3:37.00, 13:03.40. pbs: 3000m 7:37.97 '05, 2M 8:19.81 '05, 10,000m 29:17.43 '03.

Women

Berhane ADERE b. 21 Jul 1973 Shewa District 1.70m 48kg.
At 10,000m (5000m): OG: '96- 18, '00- 12; WCh: '95- h, '97- 4, '99- 7, '01- 2, '03- 1 (10), '05- 2; AfCh: '93- 1 (5 3000m). At 5000m: AfCh: '98- 1, '02- 1; WCp: '98- 3. At 3000m: WI: '03- 1, '04- 2; WCp: '02- 1; 3rd GP 2002. World CC: '96-7-00: 10/14/14; HMar: '01-02-03: 3/1/2. Won Rd Rly team '96, ETH 3000m & 10,000m 1993.
Records: African 5000m and 10,000m 2003, World indoor 3000m (8:29.15) 2002, 5000m 2004, African indoor 5000m 2003; Ethiopian 2000m 2003, 3000m 1997 and 2001.
Progress at 5000m, 10,000m: 1992- 34:13.3, 1993- 32:48.52, 1995- 15:44.46, 32:02.94; 1996- 14:59.17, 32:21.09; 1997- 15:08.22, 31:48.95; 1998- 15:22.34, 32:06.42; 1999- 14:54.88, 31:32.51; 2000- 14:52.61, 30:51.30; 2001- 14:51.67, 31:32.70; 2002- 14:33.65, 2003- 14:29.32, 30:04.18; 2004- 14:36.92; 2005- 14:31.09, 30:25.41. pbs: 1500m 4:05.54i, 4:06.46

'02; 2000m 5:35.62 '03; 3000m 8:25.62 '01; road: 15km 48:11 '01, 10M 53:16 '98, HMar 67:32 '03, Mar 2:41:50 '01.
Married to Lemme Erpassa (five team medals at World CC 1988-97), son Aleme born in 1994.

Elfenesh ALEMU b. 10 Jun 1975 Lemo Arya, Aris region 1.71m 57kg.
At Mar: OG: '00- 6, '04- 4; WCh: '99- 5, '01- dnf, '03- 6; WCp: '95- 18; AfG: '95- 3.
Progress at Mar: 1993- 2:57:32A, 1994- 3:08:05, 1995- 2:40:04, 1996- 2:36:29, 1997- 2:37:37, 1998- 2:30:19; 1999- 2:28:52, 2000- 2:24:47, 2001- 2:24:29, 2002- 2:26:01, 2003- 2:24:47, 2004- 2:24:43, 2005- 2:26:50. pb HMar 69:46 '00.
Broke 2:25 for marathon twice in 2000: 4th Osaka, 1st Nagano before 2:26:45 at Olympics. Won Nagano 2001 when also 5th London and 2nd Chicago. Won Tokyo 2003, 2nd Boston 2004-05 (3rd 2002). Married Gezahegne Abera (won OG marathon 2000, WCh 2001) in June 2003.

Gelete BURKA Bati b. 15 Feb 1986 Kofele 1.65m 45kg.
At 1500m: WCh: '05- 8. World CC: '03-05-06: 3J/1J/1 4k. Won ETH 1500m 2004-05, 5000m 2005, 4k CC 2006.
African junior 1500m record 2005.
Progress at 1500m, 5000m: 2003- 4:10.82, 16:23.8A, 2004- 4:06.10, 2005- 3:59.60, 14:51.47. pbs: 800m 2:07.05 '03, 1M 4:30.81 '03, 3000m 8:39.90 '05.

Meseret DEFAR b. 19 Nov 1983 Addis Ababa 1.55m 42kg.
At 5000m: OG: '04- 1; WCh: '03- h, '05- 2; WJ: '00- 2, '02- 1; AfG: '03- 1; AfCh: '00- 2. At 3000m: WJ: '02- 1; WY: '99- 2; WI: '03-04-06: 3/1/1. Won WAF 3000m 2004-05, 5000m 2005. World CC: '02- 13J.
African 5000m record 2005.
Progress at 3000m, 5000m: 1999- 9:02.08, 2000- 8:59.90, 15:08.36; 2001- 8:52.47, 15:08.65; 2002- 8:40.28, 15:26.45; 2003- 8:38.31, 14:40.34; 2004- 8:33.44i/8:36.46, 14:44.81; 2005- 8:30.05i/8:33.57, 14:28.98; 2006- 8:30.72i. pbs: 1500m 4:22.1+ '03, 1M: 4:28.5ei '06, 2000m 5:34.74i '06.

Ejegayehu DIBABA b. 25 Jun 1982 Chefe, Arsi region 1.60m 46kg.
At (5000m/)10,000m: OG: '04- 2; WCh: '03- 9, '05- 3/3; AfG: '03- 1; won Af-AsG 2003. At 5000m: AfCh: '02- 3. World CC 4k: '03-04: 9/10/14; 8k:'04-06: 2/14.
Progress at 5000m, 10,000m: 2001- 15:32.31, 32:24.20; 2002- 15:56.02, 2003- 14:41.67, 31:01.07; 2004- 14:32.74, 30:24.98; 2005- 14:37.34, 30:18.39. pbs: 2000m 5:46.6+ '05, 3000m 8:42.8e '05.
Older sister of Tirunesh Dibaba.

Tirunesh DIBABA b. 1 Jun 1985 Chefe, Arsi region 1.60m 47kg.
At 5000m(/10,000m): OG: '04- 3; WCh: '03- 1, '05- 1/1; WJ: '02- 2; AfG: '03- 4. World CC: '01-02-03-05-06: 5J/2J/1J/1/1; 4k: '04- 05: 2/1. Won ETH 4k CC & 5000m 2003. 8k CC 2005.
World indoor 5000m record 2005, World junior 5000m records 2003-04, indoor best 8:33.56 '04, world road 5k best 14:51 '05.
Progress at 5000m: 2002- 14:49.90, 2003- 14:39.94, 2004- 14:30.88, 2005- 14:32.42, 30:15.67. pbs: 2000m 5:42.7 '05, 3000m 8:33.56i '04, 8:38.9 '05.
In 2003 she became, at 18 years 90 days, the youngest ever world champion at an individual event and in 2005 the first woman to win the 5000m/10,000m double (with last laps of 58.19 and 58.4) at a global event after earlier in the year winning both World CC titles. Younger sister of Ejagayou Dibaba.

Kutre DULECHA b. 22 Aug 1978 1.68m 48kg.
At 1500m (800m): OG: '96- sf (h), '00- 4, '04- sf; WCh: '97- 9, '99- 3, '03- sf; WI: '97-9-03-04: 8/8/9/1; WJ: '94- 5 (3), '96- 1; AfG: '95- 1 (3), '99- 1, '03- 1; Af-J: '94- 2 (2); 2nd GP 1998, 2000. World CC: '96- 1J, 4k: '98-9-00: 3/12/1.
Ethiopian records: 1500m (5) 1997-8, 800m & 1000m 1999. World junior record indoor 1500m 1997, African indoor 1500m record 4:01.90 '04.
Progress at 1500m: 1994- 4:15.59, 1995- 4:08.70, 1996- 4:07.69, 1997- 4:05.67, 1998- 3:58.38, 1999- 4:00.96, 2000- 3:59.02, 2001- 4:05.75i, 2003- 4:02.74, 2004- 4:01.90i/4:06.95. pbs: 800m 1:59.17i/1:59.37 '99, 1000m 2:37.82 '99, 1M 4:23.33i '01, 4:39.04 '97; 10kmRd 32:29 '02, HMar 70:54 '05, Mar 2:30:06 '05.
Won Amsterdam Marathon 2005. Son Hailegebrale born 30 Nov 2001.

Sentayehu EJIGU b. 21 Jun 1985 Debremarkos 1.60m 45kg.
At 1500m: WY: '01- 3. At 3000m: WI: '06- 4. At 5000m: OG: '04- 10; AfG: '03- 5. World CC: '03- 6J.
Progress at 5000m: 2002- 14:53.99, 2003- 15:00.53, 2004- 14:35.18, 2005- 14:51.11. pbs: 1500m 4:15.89 '01, 1M 4:40.43i '03, 3000m 8:42.63 '04.

Werknesh KIDANE b. 21 Nov 1981 Mayshie district, Tigray region 1.58m 42kg.
At 10,000m: OG: '04- 4; WCh: '03- 2, '05- 6; AfG: '03- 2; At 5000m: OG: '00- 7; WCh: '01- h; WJ: '98- 6; AfG: '99- 4. At 3000m: WI: '01- 9. World CC: '97-8-9-00-01-03-04-05: 13J/3J/1J/9J/1/3/3; 4k: '01-02-03-04-05: 5/2/2/4/2. Won ETH 10,000m 2003, 2005; 4k CC 2001-02, E.Afr 4k & 8k CC 2004.
Progress at 5000m, 10,000m: 1998- 15:50.10, 1999- 15:24.56, 2000- 14:47.40, 33:48.7A; 2001- 15:29.96, 31:43.41; 2002- 14:43.53, 2003- 14:33.04, 30:07.15; 2004- 14:38.05, 30:28.30; 2005- 15:01.6, 30:19.39. pbs: 1500m 4:17.0A '03, 3000m 8:36.39 '05, HMar 68:09 '05.
Has won 20 team and individual medals at World CC. Married Gebre Gebremariam on 4 Feb 2006.

Meselech MELKAMU b. 19 Apr 1985 Debre Markos 1.58m 47kg.
At 5000m: WCh: '05- 4; WJ: '04- 1. World CC: '03-04-05-06: 4J/1J/4 & 6/3 & 3. Won ETH

5000m 2004, 4k CC 2005, CC 2006.
Progress at 5000m: 2003- 15:27.93, 2004- 15:00.02, 2005- 14:38.97. pbs: 1500m 4:09.77 '03, 1M 4:33.94 '03, 3000m 8:34.73 '05.

Derartu TULU b. 21 Mar 1972 Bejoki, Arusi province 1.55m 45kg. Employed by the prison police in Addis Ababa.
At 10,000m (3000m): OG: '92- 1, '96- 4, '00- 1, '04- 3; WCh: '91- 8, '95- 2, '97- h, '01- 1, '03- dnf; WJ: '90- 1; AfG: '91- 1; AfCh: '90- 1 (1), '92- 1 (1); WCp: '92- 1 (1). At Mar: WCh: '05- 4. World CC: '89-90-1-5-6-7-00-04: 23/15/2/1/4/1/1/16; HMar: '99-05: 14/15. Won GWG 10,000m 2001.
Three African 10,000m records 1992-2000. World junior 10,000m record 1991 (32:08.74), Ethiopian records 1500m, 5000m (4), 10,000m (5) 1991-2000, HMar 1995 & 2000.
Progress at 5000m, 10,000m, Mar: 1990- 16:56.7, 32:56.26; 1991- 15:21.29, 31:45.95; 1992- 15:36.5, 31:06.02; 1994- 15:40.29, 31:48.93; 1995- 14:57.65, 31:08.10; 1996- 14:50.88, 31:10.46; 1997- 33:25.99, 2:30:28; 1999- 2:40:55, 2000- 14:44.57, 30:17.49, 2:26:09; 2001- 31:48.19, 2:23:57; 2002- 15:26.73, 2:28:37; 2003- 14:44.22, 2:26:33; 2004- 14:46.51, 30:26.42, 2:30:21; 2005- 2:23:30. pbs: 1500m 4:12.08 '92, 3000m 8:46.32 '00, Road: 10M 51:27 '05, HMar 67:03 '01.
Undefeated on the track in 1992 when she won her first Olympic title. Married decathlete Zewde Deboba in 1988, daughter Tsion born 1998. Returned to road racing in 1999 and to a third world CC title and second Olympic title in 2000. 5th Boston on marathon debut 1997; 6th London and 3rd Tokyo in 2000, won London and Tokyo marathons 2001. Won Great North Run 2005.

Getenesh WAMI b. 11 Dec 1974 Debre Birhan 1.54m 45kg.
At 10,000m (5000m): OG: '96- 3, '00- 2 (3); WCh: '95- 18, '97- dnf, '99- 1, '01- 3; WJ: '92- 2; AfG: '95- 3, '99- 1; AfCh: '92- 4. Won GP 3000m 1998, 2nd 5000m 1996. World CC: '91-2: 5J/9J, '95-6-7-8-9-00-01-05: 5/1/3/3/1/2/2 &1 4k/8; Rd Rly team: '96/8- 1/1.
African records 5000m 2000, 10,000m 1999. ETH 3000m 1998, 5000m (4) 1996-8, Mar 2002.
Progress at 5000m, 10,000m, Mar: 1992- 32:34.68, 1994- 36:15.0A, 1995- 15:28.65, 32:17.41; 1996- 14:46.45, 31:06.65; 1997- 14:54.05, 32:05.73; 1998- 14:36.08, 34:23.4A; 1999- 15:25.5, 30:24.56; 2000- 14:30.88, 30:22.48; 2001- 14:31.69, 31:49.98; 2002- 2:22:20, 2004- 2:32:07, 2005- 14:58.58, 2:27:40; 2006- 2:25:26. pbs: 1500m 4:01.47 '98, 2000m 5:39.9 '01, 3000m 8:27.62 '01, 10M Rd 51:30 '05.
Has won 19 individual and team medals at World CC. After missing the 2002 track season, she became the second fastest ever marathon debutante when winning at Amsterdam. Married Geteneh Tessema November 1999, daughter Eva born August 2003. 2nd Los Angeles Marathon 2006.

FINLAND

Governing body: Suomen Urheiluliitto, Radiokatu 20, SF-00240 Helsinki. Founded 1906.
National Championships first held in 1907 (men), 1913 (women). **2005 Champions**: **Men**: 100m: Markus Pöyhönen 10.54, 200m: Visa Hongisto 21.21, 400m: Antti Toivonen 47.35, 800m: Juha Kukkamo 1:49.69, 1500m: Jonas Hamm 3:46.52, 5000m: Francis Kirwa 14:14.28,10,000m: Tuomo Lehtinen 29:29.06; HMar: Jussi Utriainen 65:54, Mar: Petri Saavalainen 2:24:37, 3000mSt: Jukka Keskisalo 8:31.77, 110mh: Juha Sonck 13.86, 400mh: Ari-Pekka Lattu 49.76, HJ: Oskari Frösén 2.27, PV: Mikko Latvala 5.50, LJ: Tommi Evilä 8.11, TJ: Johan Meriluoto 16.32, SP: Ville Tiisanoja 20.42, DT: Timo Tompuri 60.73, HT: Olli-Pekka Karjalainen 78.06, JT: Tero Pitkämäki 87.63, Dec: Aki Heikkinen 7508, 20kmW: Antti Kempas 1:28:54, 50kmW: Timo Viljanen 4:37:27. **Women**: 100m: Heidi Hannula 11.60, 200m/400m: Kirsi Mykkänen 23.53/52.99, 800m: Suvi Myllymäki 2:06:47, 1500m: Johanna Risku 4:22.09, 5000m/10,000m: Annemari Sandell-Hyvärinen 16:25.71/34:26.36, HMar: Maija Oravamäki 76:26, Mar: Mira Tuominen 2:49:08, 3000mSt: Anni Tuimala 10:17.56, 100mh: Hanna Korell 13.33, 400mh: Ilona Ranta 58.02, HJ: Hanna Mikkonen 1.86, PV: Aino-Maija Karvinen 4.00, LJ: Niina Saarman-Bartholdi 6.37, TJ: Natalia Kilpeläinen 13.79, SP/DT: Niina Kelo 14.79/51.06, HT: Sini Pöyry 66.16, JT: Mikaela Ingberg 59.87, Hep: Sanna Saarman 5509, 10kmW/20kmW: Outi Sillanpää 48:40/1:37:34.

Tommi EVILÄ b. 6 Apr 1980 Tampere 1.94m 83kg. Tampereen Pyrintö. Student at Technical University of Tampere.
At LJ: OG: '04- 6; WCh: '05- 3; WJ: '98- 10; EU23: '01- 5; EI: '05- 4. Finnish champion 2001. 2003-05.
Two Finnish long jump records 2005.
Progress at LJ: 1995- 6.42, 1996- 6.85, 1997- 7.48, 1998- 7.48/7.51w, 1999- 7.45/7.49w, 2000- 7.69/7.80w, 2001- 8.04/8.11w, 2002- 7.76/7.88w, 2003- 7.96, 2004- 8.15, 2005- 8.19/8.25w. pbs: 60m 6.97i '01, 100m 10.89 '01, LJ 15.55i/15.53 '03.
Finland's one medallist at 2006 Worlds.

Olli-Pekka KARJALAINEN b. 7 Mar 1980 Töysä 1.94m 110kg. Töysän Veto. Political science student at University of Helsinki.
At HT: OG: '00/04- dnq 34/15; WCh: '99- 11, '01- 10, '03- dnq 14, "05- 5; EC: '02- 8; WJ: '98- 1; EJ: '97- 3, '99- 1; EU23: '01- 2; ECp: '02- 1. Won WAF 2004, Finnish 1998-2005.
World junior hammer record 2000, three Finnish 2002-04.
Progress at HT: 1995- 48.26, 1996- 58.80, 1997- 69.84, 1998- 75.08, 1999- 78.33, 2000- 80.55, 2001- 80.54, 2002- 81.70, 2003- 80.20, 2004- 83.30, 2005- 79.81.

Frantz KRUGER b. 22 May 1975 Kempton Park, RSA 2.03m 125kg. Former medical student at Free State University, Bloemfontein. Rentmeester-Tuks.
At DT: OG: '00- 3, '04- 5; WCh: '99- dnq 17, '01- 8, '03- 6, '05- 6; CG: '98- 2, '02- 1; WJ: '94- 1; AfG: '99- 1; AfCh: '98- 1, '04- 1; WUG: '97- 6, '99- 1; WCp: '98- 3. Won GWG 2001, RSA DT 1996, 1999-2005; Af-J SP & DT 1994.
Three African and Commonwealth discus records 2000-02.
Progress at DT: 1993- 58.28, 1994- 58.52, 1995- 60.06, 1996- 60.66, 1997- 61.64, 1998- 65.73, 1999- 67.38, 2000- 69.75A, 2001- 69.96, 2002- 70.32, 2003- 66.70, 2004- 66.59, 2005- 67.30.
Set RSA U13 record for 200m individual medley swimming. Married **Heli Koivula** (b. 27 Jun 1975; 2 EC TJ 2002, pb 14.39 '03, 14.83w '02) on 28 June 2003 and had taken Finnish nationality.

Aki PARVIAINEN b. 26 Oct 1974 Helsinki 1.92m 100kg. Joensuun Kataja.
At JT: OG: '00- 5; WCh: '95- 9, '97- 8, '99- 1, '01- 2, '03- 5, '05- 9; EC: '98- 9, '02- 8; WJ: '92- 1; EJ: '91- 3; ECp: '98- 3. Finnish champion 1998-2003.
Finnish javelin records 1998 and 1999.
Progress at JT: 1990- 63.50, 1991- 79.96, 1992- 80.94, 1993- 78.18i/69.94, 1994- 78.76, 1995- 85.60, 1996- 84.96, 1997- 87.48, 1998- 90.88, 1999- 93.09, 2000- 90.97, 2001- 92.41, 2002- 82.48, 2003- 83.30, 2004- 79.32, 2005- 83.79. pbs: SP 12.26 '96, DT 36.78 '96.
Set world age records at 14-16-17. The first Finn to win world titles at junior and senior level. Missed most of 1993-4 seasons through an arm injury and had to have knee and elbow operations at the end of the 2003 season. Older brother Mika threw 80.26 in 1992.

Tero PITKÄMÄKI b. 19 Dec 1982 Ilmajoki 1.95m 92kg. Nurmon Urheilijat. Electrical engineering student.
At JT: OG: '04- 8; WCh: '05- 4; E23: '03- 3; EJ: '01- 6. Won WAF 2005, Finnish 2004-05.
Progress at JT: 1999- 66.83, 2000- 73.75, 2001- 74.89, 2002- 77.24, 2003- 80.45, 2004- 84.64, 2005- 91.53.

Tepa REINIKAINEN b. 16 Mar 1976 Kangasniemi 1.98m 147kg. Kangasniemen Kalske. Was at UTEP, USA.
At SP: OG: '04- dnq 13; WCh: '03- 6, '05- 10; EJ: '95- 1; WI: '03- 6; EI: '00- 7. Finnish champion 2003-04.
Progress at SP: 1992- 13.30, 1993- 13.70, 1994- 16.16, 1995- 17.69, 1996- 17.74, 1997- 17.68, 1998- 18.87, 1999- 19.53, 2000- 20.11, 2001- 20.88, 2002- 20.43, 2003- 20.69i/20.55, 2004- 20.50, 2005- 20.43. pbs: DT 50.18 '99, JT 60.81 '99.

Ville TIISANOJA b. 24 Dec 1975 Vantaa 1.92m 119kg. Kenttäurheilijat-58 Vantaa.
At SP: OG: '00/04- dnq 15/19; WCh: '99- 8, '01- 9, '03- 7, '05- 8; EC: '02- 6; WJ: '94- 3 (10 DT); EU23: '97- 4; EJ: '93- 7; EI: '02- 4, '05- 4; ECp: '02- 2. Finnish champion 1999, 2005.
Progress at SP: 1992- 16.41, 1993- 17.35, 1994- 17.90, 1995- 19.10, 1996- 18.29, 1997- 19.40, 1998- 19.13, 1999- 20.49, 2000- 20.76, 2001- 20.78, 2002- 21.09, 2003- 20.37, 2004- 20.90, 2005- 20.64. pbs: DT 54.10 '94, HT 51.36 '94.
Exonerated after a suspension in June 2003 due to a small quantity of illegal drugs having been found by French police near Lyon in 2002 in the car he shared with discus thrower Timo Tompuri.

Women

Mikaela INGBERG b. 29 Jul 1974 Vaasa 1.74m 75kg. Vasa Idrottssällskap.
At JT: OG: '96- 7, '00- 9, '04- dnq 13; WCh: '95- 3, '97- 4, '99- 9, '01- 6, '03- 4, '05- 9; EC: '94- dnq 16, '98- 3, '02- 3; EJ: '91- 15, '93- 1; WCp: '98- 3, '02- 3; 2nd GP 2002. Finnish champion 1994, 1999-2000, 2002, 2004-05.
Finnish javelin record 2000.
Progress at JT: 1987- 33.70, 1988- 41.78, 1989- 43.92, 1990- 51.96, 1991- 52.30, 1992- 54.00, 1993- 58.26, 1994- 58.70, 1995- 65.16, 1996- 65.66, 1997- 67.32, 1998- 66.43; new 1999- 61.50, 2000- 64.03, 2001- 63.13, 2002- 63.50, 2003- 63.55, 2004- 62.53, 2005- 61.06. pbs: HJ 1.57 '88, SP 12.67 '99, DT 39.56 '95.

Taina KOLKKALA b. 24 Oct 1976 Pori 1.73m 74kg. née Uppa. Porin Tarmo.
At JT: OG: '96- dnq 19, '00- dnq 20, '04- 10; WCh: '95- dnq 24, '97- dnq 20, '99- 10, '01- 12, '03- 10; EC: '94- 10, '98- dnq 14, '02- 7; EU23: '94- 4Cp, '97- 1; WJ: '94- 1; EJ: '95- 1.
Finnish javelin record 2000.
Progress at JT: 1990- 39.58, 1991- 49.78, 1992- 54.78, 1993- 52.08, 1994- 61.78, 1995- 66.00, 1996- 63.78, 1997- 61.00, 1998- 62.31; new 1999- 63.63, 2000- 64.06, 2001- 60.55, 2002- 62.86, 2003- 61.96, 2004- 61.46, 2005- 59.69.
Baby born on 14 Feb 2006.

Paula TARVAINEN b. 17 Feb 1973 Pori 1.67m 68kg. née Huhtaniemi. Noormarkun Nopsa.
At JT: OG: '04- dnq 28; WCh: '01-03: dnq 13/20; '05- 6; EC: '02- 10. Finnish champion 2001, 2003.
Finnish javelin record 2003.
Progress at JT: 1990- 33.84, 1991- 48.34, 1992- 52.50, 1993- 57.34, 1994- 51.64, 1995- 56.68, 1996- 55.24, 1997- 56.08, 1998- 58.10; new 1999- 58.44, 2000- 61.01, 2001- 63.05, 2002- 62.35, 2003- 64.90, 2004- 62.63, 2005- 62.64.

FRANCE

Governing body: Fédération Française d'Athlétisme, 33 avenue Pierre de Coubertin, 75640 Paris cedex 13. Founded 1920.
National Championships first held in 1888 (men), 1918 (women). **2005 Champions: Men**: 100m: Lueyi Dovy 10.24, 200m: Ronald Pognon

20.34, 400m: Marc Raquil 45.88, 800m:Florent Lacasse 1:46.25, 1500m: Mehdi Baala 3:43.36, 5000m: Loïc Letellier 13:50.33, 10,000m: Driss El Himer 28:30.80, HMar: David Ramard 65:16, Mar: David Antoine 2:24:58, 3000mSt: Gaël Pencréach 8:27.79, 110mh: Ladji Doucouré 12.97, 400mh: Naman Keïta 49.19, HJ: Grégory Gabella 2.28, PV: Pierre-Charles Peuf 5.60, LJ: Salim Sdiri 8.25, TJ: Karl Taillepierre 17.45, SP: Yves Niaré 18.65, DT: Jean-Claude Retel 57.35, HT: Nicolas Figère 74.51, JT: David Brisseault 77.03, Dec: Romain Barras 8024, 20000mW: Denis Langlois 1:28:02.9, 50kmW: Yohan Diniz 4:00:14. **Women**: 100m: Sylvie Mballa Eloundou 11.13, 200m: Christine Arron 22.38, 400m: Amy Mbacké Thiam SEN 51.47, 800m: Bouchra Ghezielle 2:00.29, 1500m: Hind Dehiba 4:16.46, 5000m: Margaret Maury 15:49.66, HMar: Hafida Gadi 74:47, Mar: Corinne Raux 2:40:30, 3000mSt: Yamina Bouchaouante 10:01.87, 100mh: Linda Khodadin 12.66, 400mh: Sylvanie Morandais 56.22, HJ: Mélanie Skotnik 1.94, PV: Vanessa Boslak 4.60, LJ: Céline Nyanga 6.34w, TJ: Amy Zongo 13.88w, SP: Laurence Manfrédi 17.04, DT: Mélina Robert-Michon 53.82, HT: Manuèla Montebrun 72.01, JT: Sarah Walter 55.27, Hep: Gertrud Bacher ITA 5744 ?, 20000mW: Christine Guinaudeau 1:38:01.0.

Mehdi BAALA b. 17 Aug 1978 Strasbourg 1.83m 65kg. ASPTT Strasbourg.

At 1500m (800m): OG: '00- 4, '04- h; WCh: '01- 12, '03- 2, '05- sf (6); EC: '02- 1; WJ: '96- h; EU23: '99- 3; EJ: '97- 7; EI: '00- 3; WCp: '02- 3; ECp: '00-01-02-04: 1 (1)/2/1/1. Won FRA 800m 2001, 1500m 2002, 2005.

French records 800m 2002, 1000m (2) 2002-03, 1500m (2) 2003, 2000m 2005.

Progress at 800m, 1500m: 1994- 1:56.5, 4:08.1; 1995- 1:53.76, 3:48.74; 1996- 1:49.62, 3:43.50; 1997- 1:50.08, 3:45.34; 1998- 1:49.57, 3:41.86; 1999- 1:46.41, 3:34.83; 2000- 1:46.24, 3:32.05; 2001- 1:46.94, 3:31.97; 2002- 1:43.15, 3:32.03; 2003- 1:44.17, 3:28.98; 2004- 1:45.52, 3:31.25; 2005- 1:44.74, 3:30.80. pbs: 1000m 2:13.96 '03, 2000m 4:53.12 '05, 3000m 8:08.06i '98, 8:23.69 '98.

Married Hanane Sabri (ht WC 1500m '01, FRA champion 2001) in September 2000. His elder brother Samir won 2002 French marathon.

Romain BARRAS b. 1 Aug 1980 Calais 1.93m 84kg. SO Calais.

At Dec: OG: '04- 13; WCh: '05- 7; EU23: '01- 4; WUG: '01- 5, 03- 1; ECp: '03- 1; won MedG & Franc G 2005.

Progress at Dec: 1998- 6505, 1999- 7147, 2000- 7609, 2001- 7876, 2002- 7835, 2003- 8196, 2004- 8067, 2005- 8185. pbs: 60m 7.25i '06, 100m 11.02 '03, 400m 48.63 '05, 1000m 2:39.89i '06, 1500m 4:24.65 '05, 50mh 7.09i '04, 6.8i '03; 60mh 8.14i '01, 110mh 14.24 '02, HJ 2.01 '03, PV 5.00i '06, 4.90 '05; LJ 7.35 '05, SP 15.35 '04, DT 47.21 '05, JT 65.84 '05, Hep 5895i '06.

Leslie DJHONE b. 18 Mar 1981 Abidjan, CIV 1.87m 72kg. Neuilly Plaisance Sports.

At 400m/4x400m: OG: '04- 7; WCh: '03- 5/1R, '05- h; EC: '02- 3R; EU23: '03- 1; ECp: '04- 3. At LJ/4x100m: WJ: '98- dnq, '00- 2R; EU23: '01- 4/4R, '03- 2R; EJ: '99- 1/1R. At 200m: ECp: '03- 5. Won FRA 200m 2004.

French 400m record 2004.

Progress at 400m: 2001- 47.01, 2002- 45.63, 2003- 44.83, 2004- 44.64, 2005- 45.56. pbs: 100m 10.52 '03, 200m 20.51i '03, 20.67 '04; 300m 32.18 '03, LJ: 7.92 '99, 8.06w '01.

Ladji DOUCOURÉ b. 28 Mar 1983 Juvisy-sur-Orge 1.83m 75kg. Viry Nord Sud Evry Essonne.

At 110mh/4x100mR: OG: '04- 8; WCh: '03- sf, '05- 1; WJ: '00- 3/2R; EU23: '03- 1; ECp: '01- 7, '03- 1, '05- 1/3R; French champion 2004-05. At 100mh: WY: '99- 1. At 60mh: WI: '03- 4; EI: '05- 1. At Dec: EJ: '01- 1/2R.

Four French 110mh records 2004-05. European indoor 50mh record 2005.

Progress at 110mh: 2000- 13.75, 2001- 13.58, 2002- 13.87/13.73w, 2003- 13.23, 2004- 13.06, 2005- 12.97. pbs: 60m 6.78i '00, 100m 10.48 '01, 200m 20.75 '01, 400m 46.82 '01, 50mh 6.36i '05, 55mh 7.14i '04, 60mh 7.42i '05, PV 4.45 '01, LJ 7.82i '01, 7.57/7.73w '01, SP 12.97 '03, Dec 7794 '01.

Improved from 7.64 to 7.61 and 7.58 (for surprise fourth place) at 60mh at 2003 World Indoors. Set two French records (13.18 and 13.06) at 2004 Olympics before smashing into a hurdle in final and two more French records (13.02 and 12.97) before winning World title in 2005. Father came from Mali, mother from Sénegal.

Laurent HERNU b. 22 Aug 1976 Creil 1.90m 85kg. Stade Nogent-sur-Oise.

At Dec: OG: '00- 19, '04- 7; WCh: '01- 8, '03- 5; EC: '02- 7; ECp: '00-01-02-04: 2/3/6/2. French champion 2000, 2002-03. At Hep: WI: '03- 7; EI: '05- 7.

Progress at Dec: 1996- 6277, 1997- 5975, 1998- 7566w/7390, 1999- 7937, 2000- 8178, 2001- 8280, 2002- 8108, 2003- 8219, 2004- 8237, 2005- dnf (6788). pbs: 50m 6.18i '04, 60m 7.11i '03, 100m 10.93 '04, 400m 48.62 '04, 1000m 2:40.72i '05, 1500m 4:24.35 '04, 50mh 6.90i '04, 60mh 7.96i '00, 110mh 14.01/13.94w '01, HJ 2.10 '00, PV 5.15 '01, LJ 7.56 '03, SP 14.99i '04, 14.80 '01; DT 48.32 '04, JT 60.14 '01, Hep 6109i '03.

Won Talence decathlon 2003.

Naman KEÏTA b. 9 Apr 1978 Paris 1.96m 86kg. Avia, Issy-les-Moulineaux.

At 400mh/4x400mR: OG: '04- 3; WCh: '03- sf/1R, '05- 5; EC: '02- h/3R; ECp: '04- 2, '05- 1/3R. French champion 2003-05.

Progress at 400mh: 1996- 54.54, 1997- 51.86, 1998- 51.59, 1999- 50.95, 2000- 50.40, 2001- 50.39, 2002- 49.60, 2003- 48.86, 2004- 48.17, 2005- 48.27. pbs: 300m 33.01 '04, 400m 45.74 '04, HJ 2.07 '96.

Driss MAAZOUZI b. 15 Oct 1969 Meknès, Morocco 1.80m 65kg. Coquelicot 42 St-Etienne.
At 1500m: OG: '96- 10, '00- 11; WCh: '97- sf, '99- 8, '01- 3; WI: '03- 1. At 3000m: ECp: '99-00-01-02: 3/1/1/1. World 4k CC: '02-03: 10/14; Eur CC: '04- 3, '05- 3. Won FRA 1500m 1997-2001, 4k CC 1998-2000, 2002; MedG 1500m 1997.
French records 1000m (2), 1500m (3) 1998-2002, 2000m 2001.
Progress at 1500m: 1990- 3:45.8, 1991- 3:42.12, 1993- 3:43.3, 1994- 3:37.04, 1995- 3:35.45, 1996- 3:34.08, 1997- 3:35.26, 1998- 3:31.59, 1999- 3:31.51, 2000- 3:32.01, 2001- 3:31.54, 2002- 3:31.45, 2003- 3:36.93i, 2004- 3:36.35, 2005- 3:37.18. pbs: 800m 1:46.3 '96, 1000m 2:15.26 '99, 1M 3:51.79 '00, 2000m 4:55.55 '01, 3000m 7:36.21 '98, 2M 8:28.26i '03, 5000m 13:30.34 '02, 10km Rd 29:42 '01, HMar 64:44 '95, 3000mSt 9:08.6 '91.
Competed for Morocco to 1997, then switched allegiance (naturalised for France 23/7/96), but unable to compete for France until clearance granted by Morocco for 1999.

Romain MESNIL b. 13 Jul 1977 Le Plessis Bouchard 1.88m 79kg. ECLA Albi. Engineer.
At PV: OG: '00/04- dnq 31/18; WCh: '99- nh, '01- 5, '03- dnq; EC: '02- dnq; EU23: '99-1; WJ: '96- dnq 13=; WI: '99-01-03-04: 6=/3/7/7; ECp: '00-03-04: 5/1/1. French champion 2000-03.
Progress at PV: 1993- 4.30, 1994- 4.65, 1995- 5.15, 1996- 5.30, 1997- 5.40, 1998- 5.80, 1999- 5.93, 2000- 5.75, 2001- 5.86i/5.85, 2002- 5.75, 2003- 5.95, 2004- 5.80, 2005- 5.75, 2006- 5.75i. pb Dec 5724 '98.
Former gymnast. Married to Karine Bénézech (PV 3.75i '99).

Ronald POGNON b. 16 Nov 1982 Lamentin, Martinique 1.85m 75kg. ES Montgeron.
At 100m/(200m)/4x100mR: OG: '04- sf; WCh: '03- sf, '05- sf/qf/1R; EC: '02- (sf); WJ: '00- (qf)/ 2R; EJ: '01- (1)/2R; EU23: '03- 1, ECp: '04- 2/4, '05- 1/3R. At 60m: WI: '06- 6; EI: '05- 2. Won French 200m 2005.
European indoor 60m record & French 100m record 2005.
Progress at 100m, 200m: 1998- 11.13, 22.50; 1999- 11.07, 22.09; 2000- 10.50, 21.25; 2001- 10.52, 20.80/20.4w; 2002- 10.24, 20.77; 2003- 10.13/10.12w, 20.54; 2004- 10.11, 20.49; 2005- 9.99, 20.34. pbs: 50m 5.67i '05, 60m 6.45i '05.

Marc RAQUIL b. 2 Apr 1977 Créteil 1.91m 81kg. Neuilly Plaisance Sports.
At 400m/4x400mR: OG: '00- qf/4R; WCh: '99- 5R, '01- sf, '03- 3/1R, '05- 6R; EC: '02- sf; EU23: '97- 4R, '99- 3/4R; EI: '00- 3, '05- 1R; ECp: '99-01-03-05: 6/1/1/1 (3R '05). French champion 2002-05. Three French records 2001-03.
Progress at 400m: 1995- 49.12, 1996- 47.92, 1997- 47.13, 1998- 46.39, 1999- 45.82, 2000- 45.31, 2001- 44.95, 2002- 45.39, 2003- 44.79, 2004- 46.21, 2005- 45.57. pbs: 200m 21.03 '01, 300m 32.60 '99, 800m 1:50.90 '03.

Salim SDIRI b. 26 Oct 1978 Ajaccio, Corsica 1.85m 80kg, USM Montargis.
At LJ: OG: '04- 12; WCh: '03- dnq 13, '05- 5; EC: '02- 7; WI: '03- 7; ECp: '02-04-05: 3/2/2; won Med G 2005, French 2003-05.
Progress at LJ: 1999- 7.37, 2000- 7.95, 2001- 7.83, 2002- 8.23, 2003- 8.29w, 2004- 8.24, 2005- 8.25, 2006- 8.27i. pbs: 100m 10.6w '01, TJ 16.10 '00.

Bouabdellah 'Bob' TAHRI b. 20 Dec 1978 Metz 1.90m 65kg. ASPTT Metz.
At 3000mSt: OG: '00- h, '04- 7; WCh: '99- 12, '01- 5, '03- 4, '05- 8; EC: '98- 10, '02- 4; WJ: '96- 7; ECp: '00-01-02-04: 1/1/1/1. At 5000m: EJ: '97- 1; ECp: '05- 2. At 1500m: ECp: '03- 4. World CC: '97-04: 22J/15 4k; Eur CC: '05- 4. Won FRA 1500m 2004, 3000mSt 1998.
European record 3000mSt 2003, best 2000mSt 2002.
Progress at 3000mSt: 1996- 8:44.65, 1998- 8:19.75, 1999- 8:12.24, 2000- 8:16.14, 2001- 8:09.23, 2002- 8:10.83, 2003- 8:06.91, 2004- 8:14.26, 2005- 8:09.58. pbs: 800m 1:48.96 '01, 1000m 2:20.34 '05, 1500m 3:34.85 '02, 1M 3:52.95 '02. 2000m 4:57.58 '02, 3000m 7:41.41i '02, 7:42.49 '05; 5000m 13:24.05 '99, 10km Rd 29:53 '04, HMar 66:12 '03, 2000mSt 5:15.96 '02.

Karl TAILLEPIERRE b. 13 Aug 1976 Pointe-à-Pitre, Guadeloupe 1.76m 64kg. Neuilly-Plaisance Sports.
At TJ: OG: '04- dnq 42; WCh: '01- dnq 15, '05- 5; French champion 2001, 2004-05.
Progress at TJ: 1993- 13.69, 1994- 15.15, 1995- 15.29, 1996- 16.28, 1997- 15.24, 1998- 16.00, 1999- 16.17, 2000- 16.62, 2001- 17.10, 2002- 16.88i/16.83, 2003- 16.96/16.99w, 2004- 17.16, 2005- 17.45. pbs: 100m 10.94 '05, LJ 7.79 '05.

Women

Christine ARRON b. 13 Sep 1973 Abymes, Guadeloupe 1.77m 64kg. Neuilly Plaisance Sports.
At 100m/4x100m (200m): OG: '00- sf/4R, '04- sf/3R (sf); WCh: '97- 4/3R, '99- 6/2R, '03- 5/1R, '05- 3/3/4R; EC: '98- 1/1R, ECp: '97-8-9-00-03-04-05: 2R/2&3R/1&1R/2&1R/1&1R/1&1R (1 200m '97)/1&1; WJ: '92- sf. At 60m: WI: '04- 7, '06- 4. Won French 100m 2000, 2003-04; 200m 1997, 2004-05. MedG 200m 1997.
European and four French 100m records 1998.
Progress at 100m, 200m: 1988- 12.04, 1989- 11.64/11.6, 25.43; 1990- 12.41/12.3/12.0w, 1991- 11.97, 24.4; 1992- 11.51, 23.75; 1993- 11.93/11.92w, 1994- 24.18, 1995- 23.92, 1996- 23.26, 1997- 11.03, 22.62/22.57w, 1998- 10.73, 22.95i; 1999- 10.97, 22.26; 2000- 10.99/10.89w, 2001- 11.15, 23.42/23.14w; 2003- 11.01/10.95w, 22.92; 2004- 10.95, 22.60; 2005- 10.93/10.82w, 22.31. pbs: 50m 6.05+ '99, 60m 7.00+ '99, 7.06i '06; 400m 53.76 '95.
The superstar of the 1998 European Championships followed a majestic 100m victory in a

European record 10.73 with an awesome final sprint relay leg to take France to gold. She first set French age records at 14 in 1988 (for 80m and 150m). Won five of six Golden League 100m races in 2005. Breakthrough in 1997, setting a French indoor 200m record (23.13), stepping in for Marie-José Pérec to win European Cup 200m and placing 4th in World 100m. Son Ethan born 28 Jun 2002.

Eunice BARBER b. 17 Nov 1974 Freetown, Sierra Leone 1.75m 68kg. EFS Reims.
At Hep (100mh): OG: '92- 26 (h), '96- 5 (dnq LJ), '00- dnf, '04- dnq LJ; WCh: '93- dnf, '95- 4, '97- dnf, '99- 1 (qf), '01- dnf, '03- 2 (1 LJ), '05- 2 (3 LJ); WJ: '92- 14. At Pen: WI: '97- 6. At LJ: AfG: '95- 1; ECp: '99-01-03: 1/2/1; won WAF 2003.
French records: LJ 1999 & 2003, heptathlon record 1999 & 2005. African heptathlon record 1996. SLE records 100mh, HJ, LJ, SP, JT, Hep 1992-8.
Progress at LJ, Hep: 1990- 5.47, 1991- 5.66, 1992- 6.02, 5048; 1993- 5.94, 5308; 1994- 5.93, 5378; 1995- 6.57/6.70Aw, 6340; 1996- 6.59/6.66w, 6416; 1997- 6.70, 1998- 6.86i/6.75/6.90w, 1999- 7.01, 6861; 2000- 6.85, 6842; 2001- 6.97, 6736; 2003- 7.05, 6755; 2004- 6.61i/6.37, 2005- 6.80, 6889. pbs: 60m 7.36i '00, 100m 11.90 '99, 200m 23.53 '99, 800m 2:10.55 '01, 60mh 8.11i '00, 100mh 12.78 '01, 12.62w '05; 200mh 27.47 '99, HJ 1.93 '99, SP 13.99 '03, JT 53.10 '05, Pen 4558i '97.
Became a French citizen in February 1999, having previously represented Sierra Leone, but living in Reims from 1992. After concentrating on the long jump for a couple of years and taking the French record to 7.01, she returned in 1999 to the heptathlon where she had wins at 6461 (Arles) and 6505 (European Cup) before adding 356 points to her pb in Seville to take the world title. Another win at Talence (6514) secured her the IAAF Combined Events Challenge award. Won at Götzis with world's best score of 2000, but then held back by injuries; returned for Olympics but unable to continue beyond long jump in heptathlon. In 2001 she won again at Götzis, and started the World Championships heptathlon in great form with a clear lead after two events, but then made the terrible of error of having three no throws in the shot and withdrew. Back at her best in 2005 after injury in 2004.

Vanessa BOSLAK b. 11 Jun 1982 Lesquin 1.69m 57kg. ASPTT Lille. Physiotherapy student.
At PV: OG: '04- 6=, WCh: '05- 8; EC: '02- 11=; WJ: '98- 6; '00- 3=; EU23: '03- 2; EJ: '01- 3; WI: '04- 5=, '06- 5; ECp: '01-02-04: 5/3/5; won Med G 2005, French 2001, 2003-05.
Ten French pole vault records 2002-05.
Progress at PV: 1995- 3.25, 1996- 3.76, 1997- 3.90, 1998- 4.10, 1999- 4.15i/4.11, 2000- 4.32, 2001- 4.33i/4.30, 2002- 4.46, 2003- 4.50, 2004- 4.51, 2005- 4.60, 2006- 4.65i. pb JT 44.27 '99.

Marie COLLONVILLÉ b. 23 Nov 1973 Amiens 1.63m 54kg. Amiens UC
At Hep: OG: '04- 7; WCh: '97-99-01-05: 12/9/11/6; EC: '98- 8; WUG: '97- 3 (3 HJ); ECp: '96-7-8-00: 6/4/1/5. At Pen: WI: '97- 8, '03- 3; EI: '98- 5, '05- 6. Won MedG Hep 2005, FRA HJ 1997, Hep 1995, 1999, 2002.
Inugural world decathlon record 2004.
Progress at Hep: 1991- 4882, 1992- 5233, 1993- 5638, 1994- 5995, 1995- 5833, 1996- 6143, 1997- 6350, 1998- 6218, 1999- 6188, 2000- 6119, 2001- 5887, 2002- 6083, 2003- 6007, 2004- 6279, 2005- 6248. pbs: 60m 8.09i '04, 100m 12.44 '05, 200m 24.71 '97, 24.68w '04; 400m 56.15 '04, 800m 2:10.90 '99, 1500m 5:06.09 '04, 50mh 7.33i '04, 60mh 8.48i '05, 100mh 13.52 '00, 13.2w '98; 400mh 59.56 '95, HJ 1.94 '97, PV 3.64i '05, 3.60 '02; LJ 6.40i '03, 6.32 '96; SP 12.87i '03, 12.58 '05; DT 35.28 '04, JT 50.74 '97, Pen 4644i '03, Dec 8150 '04.
Accomplished pianist.

Hind DEHIBA b. 17 Mar 1979 Khouribga, Morocco 1.62m 44kg. née Chahyd. CA Montreuil.
At 1500m: OG: '04- h; WCh: '05- h; WI: '06- 4; EI: '05- 3. French champion 2005.
French 1500m record 2005.
Progress at 1500m: 1995- 4:21.0, 1998- 4:11.3, 1999- 4:27.50, 2003- 4:21.52, 2004- 4:03.72, 2005- 4:00.49. pbs: 800m 1:59.75 '05, 1M 4:40.23 '03, 3000m 8:52.21 '05.
Ex Morocco, naturalised French citizen 2004.

Bouchra GHÉZIELLE b. 19 May 1979 Khemisset, Morocco 1.65m 47kg. EA Franconville. née Benthami.
At 1500m: WCh: '05- 3; WJ: '96- 11, '98- 3; AfCh: '98- 3; ECp: '05- 3. Won French 800m 2005, Sh CC 2002-03, 2005.
French records 1500m & 3000m 2005.
Progress at 1500m: 1995- 4:25.68, 1996- 4:18.82, 1997- 4:18.7, 1998- 4:11.40, 1999- 4:10.91, 2004- 4:04.19, 2005- 4:01.28. pbs: 800m 2:00.29 '05, 3000m 8:35.41 '05, 10km Rd 32:49 '02.
Formerly Morocco, for whom she competed in the World CC each year 1996-9, became French citizen in 2005.

Muriel HURTIS b. 25 Mar 1979 Bondy 1.80m 68kg. AC Bobigny.
At (100m)/200m/4x100m: OG: '00- sf/4R, '04- qf/3R; WCh: '99- sf/2R, '01- 2R, '03- 3/1R; EC: '02- 1/1R; WJ: '98- 1/2R; EJ: '97- 2/4R; EU23: '99- 2/1R; WI: '01- 5, '03- 1; EI: '00- 1, '02- 1; WCp: '02- 2; ECp: '00-02-03-04: 1&1R/1&1R/3&1R/1&1R (1 100m '02). At 60m: WI: '04- 5. Won WAF 200m 2003, French 200m 2000, 2002.
Progress at 100m, 200m: 1995- 11.95, 23.91/23.76w; 1996- 11.89/11.8, 23.92; 1997- 11.80, 23.79; 1998- 11.43, 22.76/22.72w, 1999- 11.33/11.3, 22.31; 2000- 11.36/11.28w, 22.70; 2001- 11.51, 23.06i/23.35/23.14w; 2002- 10.96, 22.43/22.35w, 2003- 11.08/10.97w, 22.41; 2004- 11.21, 22.76. pbs: 50m 6.14i '03, 60m 7.09i '03, 400m 54.44 '98, LJ 6.04i '97, 5.86 '95. Son Leyhan born 21 March 2005.

Linda KHODADIN b. 24 Dec 1976 Paris 1.69m 51kg. née Ferga. US Créteil.
At 100mh (/LJ): OG: '00- 7/4R, '04- h; WCh: '97- (dnq), '01- 7, '03/05- sf; EC: '98- 8/7, '02- sf; EJ: '95- 3/1; EI: '98- (3); ECp: '00-01-04-05: 1&1R/2/6/1 (LJ: '97-8: 5/3). At 60mh: WI: '99-01-03-04: 5/6/5/3; EI: '00- 1, '02- 1. Won FRA LJ 1997, 100mh 2005
Progress at 100mh: 1994- 14.12, 1995- 13.61, 1996- 13.32/13.2, 1997- 13.34/13.02w, 1998- 12.95, 1999- 12.98/12.84w, 2000- 12.81/12.77w, 2001- 12.67, 2002- 12.84, 2003- 12.86/12.84w, 2004- 12.75, 2005- 12.66. pbs: 50m 6.29i '05, 60m 7.23i '97, 100m 11.35 '98, 50mh 6.80i '03, 60mh 7.82i '04, LJ 6.80 '97, 6.82w '98.
Ruptured right Achilles in Helsinki 2005.

Manuèla MONTEBRUN b. 13 Nov 1979 Laval 1.75m 92kg. Stade Laval. Student.
At HT: OG: '00/04- dnq 24/15; WCh: '99- 12, '01- 5, '03- 3, '05- 4; EC: '98- dnq 26, '02- 3; WJ: '98- 5; EU23: '99- 4, '01- 1; WUG: '99- 3, '01- 1; ECp: '00-01-02-03-04-05: 3/4/2/1/5/2. French champion 2000-05.
Ten French hammer records 1999-2005.
Progress at HT: 1996- 47.34, 1997- 52.58, 1998- 62.79, 1999- 68.11, 2000- 71.18, 2001- 70.28, 2002- 72.54, 2003- 74.50/75.20dh, 2004- 72.73, 2005- 74.66. pb SP 13.99 '99.

GERMANY

Governing body: Deutscher Leichtathletik Verband (DLV), Alsfelder Str. 27, 64289 Darmstadt. Founded 1898.
National Championships first held in 1891. **2005 Champions**: **Men**: 100m/200m: Tobias Unger 10.16/20.20, 400m: Simon Kirch 45.80, 800m: René Herms 1:45.39, 1500m: Franek Haschke 3:40.39, 5000m/10,000m: Jan Fitschen 13:39.71/29:55.44, HMar: Stefan Koch 64:45, Mar: Dirk Nürnberger 2:22:48, 30000mSt: Filmon Ghirmai 8:34.10, 110mh: Thomas Blaschek 13.49, 400mh: Christian Duma 49.69, HJ: Eike Onnen 2.26, PV: Tim Lobinger 5.75, LJ: Nils Winter 8.03, TJ: Andreas Pohle 16.99, SP: Charles Friedek 16.89, SP: Ralf Bartels 20.67, DT: Michael Möllenbeck 64.12, HT: Karsten Kobs 78.13, JT: Christian Nicolay 81.73, Dec: Jacob Minah 7652, 10,000mW: Jan Albrecht 39:48.94, 20kmW: André Höhne 1:21:49, 50kmW Frank Werner 4:12:40. **Women**: 100m/200m: Birgit Rockmeier 11.33/23.05, 400m: Claudia Hoffmann 52.51, 800m: Monika Gradzki 2:03.51, 1500m: Antje Möldner 4:12.38, 5000m/10,000m: Sabrina Mockenhaupt 15:09.39/34:36.43, HMar: Luminita Zaituc 73:39, Mar: Monika Schuri 2:39:17, 3000mSt: Verena Dreier 10:06.51, 100mh: Kirsten Bolm 12.84, 400mh: Claudia Marx 56.14, HJ: Daniela Rath 1.84, PV: Silke Spiegelburg 4.40, LJ: Bianca Kappler 6.49, TJ: Silvia Otto 13.56, SP: Nadine Kleinert 18.68, DT: Franke Dietzsch 64.19, HT: Betty Heidler 70.34, JT: Steffi Nerius 64.54, Hep: Sonja Kesselschläger 5998, 5000mW/20kmW: Sabine Zimmer 20:11.45/1:29:07.

Ralf BARTELS b. 21 Feb 1978 Malchin 1.86m 125kg. SC Neubrandenburg. Soldier.
At SP: OG: '04- 8; WCh: '01- dnq 17, '03- 5, '05- 3; EC: '02- 3; WJ: '96- 1; EU23: '99- 6; EJ: '95- 4, '97- 1; WCp: '02- 3; ECp: '01-02-03-04-05: 4/4/5/3/1. German champion 2002-05.
Progress at SP: 1995- 17.63, 1996- 18.71, 1997- 18.35, 1998- 18.50, 1999- 18.95, 2000- 19.34, 2001- 20.30, 2002- 20.85, 2003- 20.67, 2004- 20.88, 2005- 21.36, 2006- 21.43i.

Thomas BLASCHEK b. 5 Apr 1981 Gera 1.89m 83kg. LAZ Leipzig.
At 110mh: WCh: '05- sf; WJ: '00- 2; EJ: '99- 3; EU23: '03- sf; ECp: '05- 2. At 60mh: WI: '06- 6; EI: '05- 5. Won German 110mh 2005, 60mh indoors 2005.
Progress at 110m: 1999- 13.93, 2000- 13.78, 2001- 13.81, 2002- 13.84, 2003- 13.66, 2004- 13.62, 2005- 13.31. pb 60mh 7.56i '06.

Lars BÖRGELING b. 16 Apr 1979 Neuss 1.89m 86kg. TSV Bayer 04 Leverkusen. Student.
At PV: OG: '04- 6; WCh: '03- dnq 13, '05- dnq; EC: '02- 2; WJ: '96- 8=, '98- 2; EU23: '99- 2, '01- 1; EJ: '97- 1; EI: '02- 3; WCp: '02- 3; ECp: '03- 3, '04- 3=. German champion 2002.
Progress at PV: 1993- 3.83, 1994- 4.30, 1995- 4.60, 1996- 5.20, 1997- 5.50, 1998- 5.62, 1999- 5.80, 2000- 5.75ex/5.70, 2001- 5.80, 2002- 5.85, 2003- 5.80, 2004- 5.80, 2005- 5.77. pbs: Dec 6478 '99.

Danny ECKER b. 21 Jul 1977 Leverkusen 1.92m 80kg. TSV Bayer 04 Leverkusen.
At PV: OG: '00- 8, '04- 5; WCh: '99- 4=, '01- 11, '05- nh; EC: '98- 4; WI: '99- 3; EI: '98- 3; WJ: '96- 3; ECp: '98- 4. GER champion 2004.
Progress at PV: 1990- 2.90, 1991- 3.30, 1992- 3.80, 1993- 4.40, 1994- 4.70, 1995- 5.12, 1996- 5.61, 1997- 5.72i/5.71, 1998- 5.93, 1999- 5.90, 2000- 5.90, 2001- 6.00i/5.85, 2002- 5.82i/5.70, 2004- 5.75, 2005- 5.75. pbs: HJ 2.00 '99, LJ 6.83 '99.
Son of Heide Rosendahl, 1972 Olympic LJ champion (and 2nd Pen) (WR 6.84 '70), and US basketball player John Ecker.

Andreas ERM b. 12 Mar 1976 Berlin 1.84m 70kg. SC Potsdam. Soldier.
At 20kmW: OG: '96- 24, '00- 5; WCh: '97- dq, '99/01- dnf; EC: '98- 4; EU23: '97- 5; ECp: '98-00-01 4/2/3. At 50kmW: OG: '04- dq; WCh: '03- 3. At 10,000mW: WJ: '94- 9; EJ: '95- 1. Won GER 20kmW 1998-2002, 2004; 10,000mW 2000-01, 2004; 50kmW 2002-03.
German records 20km walk 2000, 50km 2003; world best indoor 3000m walk 2001.
Progress at 20kmW, 50kmW: 1994- 1:26:41, 1995- 1:23:20, 1996- 1:22:16, 1997- 1:21:05, 1998- 1:20:57, 1999- 1:19:24, 2000- 1:18:42, 2001- 1:19:32, 2002- 1:22:04, 3:45:28; 2003- 1:28:49, 3:37:46; 2004- 1:20:13, 2005- 1:29:47. pbs: 3000mW 10:31.42i '01,

11:10.20 '01; 5000mW 18:22.25i '01, 10,000mW 38:51.51 '04, 35kmW 2:37:04 '05.

Markus ESSER b. 3 Feb 1980 Leverkusen 1.82m 99kg. TSV Bayer 04 Leverkusen. Soldier.
At HT: OG: '00- dnq 35; WCh: '05- 4; WJ: '98- 12; EJ: '99- 3; EU23: '01- 7; ECp: '04- 2, '05- 3.
Progress at HT: 1997- 64.78, 1998- 73.10, 1999- 70.29, 2000- 76.66, 2001- 75.69, 2002- 76.94, 2003- 78.13, 2004- 79.01, 2005- 80.00.

Mark FRANK b. 21 Jun 1977 Neustrelitz 1.87m 91kg. 1.LAV Rostock. Soldier.
At JT: WCh: '05- 8; EU23: '99- 3; ECp: '05- 1; World Military champion 2002.
Progress at JT: 1995- 71.58, 1996- 68.98, 1998- 72.96, 1999- 77.62. 2000- 65.17, 2001- 77.83, 2002- 83.24, 2003- 80.55, 2004- 81.21, 2005- 84.88.
Son-in-law of Anita Weiss (4 OG 1976, 1 EI 1975 at 800m).

Charles-Michael **FRIEDEK** b. 26 Aug 1971 Giessen 1.84m 80kg. TSV Bayer 04 Leverkusen. Law student.
At TJ: OG: '96- dnq 14, '00- nj (12), '04- dnq; WCh: '97- 11, '99- 1, '05- dnq 26; EC: '98- 6, '02- 2; WJ: '90- 12; EJ: '89- dnq; WI: '97- 4, '99- 1, '01- 4; EI: '98- 2, '00- 1; WUG: '97- 5, '99- 2; WCp: '98- 1, '02- 4; ECp: '96-7-8-01-02-05: 4/3/3/8/3/1. Won GP 1998, GER 1996-2000, 2002, 2005.
Progress at TJ: 1987- 13.67, 1988- 15.13, 1989- 15.85, 1990- 16.34, 1991- 15.77, 1992- 16.10, 1993- 16.32i/16.26/16.51w, 1994- 16.31, 1995- 16.34/16.60w, 1996- 17.10, 1997- 17.59, 1998- 17.42A/17.38, 1999- 17.59, 2000- 17.41, 2001- 17.13i/16.90, 2002- 17.33, 2003- 16.53, 2004- 17.40, 2005- 17.39. pbs: 100m 11.01 '92, 200m 22.23 '89, LJ 7.66 '97.

Boris HENRY b. 14 Dec 1973 Völklingen 1.93m 108kg. SV Saar 05 Saarbrücken. Army staff sergeant.
At JT: OG: '96- 5, '00- 7; WCh: '93- dnq, '95- 3, '97- 6, '99- 6, '01- 6, '03- 3; EC: '94- 11, '02- 3; WJ: '92- 2; EJ: '91- 4; WCp: '02- 2; ECp: '97-8-00-02: 3/1/3/3. 2nd/3rd GP 1997/99. GER champion 1995, 1997-8, 2000, 2003-04.
Progress at JT: 1989- 58.20, 1990- 65.86, 1991- 74.78, 1992- 76.92, 1993- 84.12, 1994- 82.02, 1995- 88.46, 1996- 88.00, 1997- 90.44, 1998- 89.21, 1999- 88.62, 2000- 86.65, 2001- 86.53, 2002- 86.67, 2003- 88.10, 2004- 86.86, 2005- 65.91. pbs: SP 14.37 '94, DT 46.24 '94, Pen 3503 '93.
For several years wore a red baseball cap given to him as an 18th birthday present, now sports a white one. World teenage best 84.12 '93. Missed 2005 season through injury.

René HERMS b. 17 Jul 1982 Dohna 1.95m 80kg. LG Asics Pirnadent.
At 800m: OG: '04- sf; WCh: '03/05- sf; EC: '02- 7; EU23: '03- 1; EJ: '01- 1; ECp: '03-04-05: 3/2/4. German champion 2001-05.
Progress at 800m: 2001- 1:46.81, 2002- 1:45.85, 2003- 1:45.35, 2004- 1:44.14, 2005- 1:44.71. pbs: 200m 22.40 '99, 400m 47.51 '01, 1000m 2:19.43 '04, 1500m 3:51.25 '04.

André HÖHNE b. 10 Mar 1978 Berlin 1.85m 72kg. SCC Berlin. Soldier.
At 20kmW: OG: '04- 8 (dnf 50km); WCh: '01- dnf, '03- 13, '05- 4; EC: '98- 23, '02- 11; EU23: '99- 12; WCp: '04- 15. At 10,000mW: EJ: '97- 2. German champion 10kmW 2002, 20kmW 2005
Progress at 20kmW: 1996- 1:36:12, 1997- 1:31:00, 1998- 1:25:04, 1999- 1:24:22, 2000- 1:22:05, 2001- 1:22:49, 2002- 1:21:38, 2003- 1:20:44, 2004- 1:21:27, 2005- 1:20:00. pbs: 3000mW 11:31.76i '05, 5000mW 19:12.33i '06, 19:51.0 '04; 10,000mW 39:24.9 '04, 35kmW 2:38:58 '04, 50kmW 3:49:00 '04.

Karsten KOBS b. 16 Sep 1971 Dortmund 1.96m 125kg. Teutonia Lanstrop.
At HT: OG: '96/00- dnq 18/31, '04- 8; WCh: '93-95-03: dnq 16/16/17, '97- 9, '99- 1; EC: '94- 10, '98- 3, '02- dnq 14; WJ: '90- 4; EJ: '89- 10; WCp: '02- 3; ECp: '93-5-6-9-00-01-02-03: 7/3/1/3/3/5/5/1; E23Cp: '92- 2. German champion 1996, 1999-2005. 3rd GP 2000.
Progress at HT: 1988- 59.80, 1989- 65.02, 1990- 70.02, 1991- 71.82, 1992- 74.36, 1993- 75.94, 1994- 76.30, 1995- 76.80, 1996- 78.92, 1997- 79.08, 1998- 81.21, 1999- 82.78, 2000- 80.21, 2001- 79.15, 2002- 81.49, 2003- 80.63, 2004- 79.11, 2005- 79.46. pb SP 15.53 '98.
Improved every year of his career until he reached the world number one ranking in 1999. His father, Reiner, had HT pb of 58.90 (1974).

Tim LOBINGER b. 3 Sep 1972 Rheinbach 1.93m 87kg. ASV Köln.
At PV: OG: '96- 7, '00- 13, '04- 11=; WCh: '93- dnq, '95- 11, '97- 4, '99- 6, '03- 5, '05- 5=; EC: '94- dnq 21=, '98- 2, '02- 3; WI: '97-03-04-06: 5/1/5/3; EI: '96-98-02-05: 6/1/1/3; WJ: '90- dnq; EJ: '91- 3; WCp: '98- 2; ECp: '93-4-5-6-7-00-02: 5/3/nh/2/3/2/1; E23Cp: '92- 1, '94- 4. Won WAF 2003, GP 2000, 3rd 1997, 2002; German champion 1993-4, 1997-2000, 2003, 2005.
Three German pole vault records 1997-9.
Progress at PV: 1986- 3.46, 1987- 3.90, 1988- 4.60, 1989- 4.85, 1990- 5.32, 1991- 5.35, 1992- 5.50, 1993- 5.55, 1994- 5.60, 1995- 5.70, 1996- 5.91, 1997- 6.00, 1998- 5.92, 1999- 6.00, 2000- 5.95i/5.85, 2001- 5.80, 2002- 5.90, 2003- 5.91, 2004- 5.80, 2005- 5.93. pbs: 110mh 14.78 '99, HJ 1.97 '99, DT 42.76 '99, Dec 7346 '99.
Set (then) world decathlon PV best of 5.75 in 7346 decathlon at Leverkusen 1999. His ex-wife **Petra** (b. 24 Jan 1967 Siegen-Weidenau, née Laux) set four German indoor TJ records from 14.15 '96 to 14.36 '97 (5 WI), outdoor pb 14.31/14.35w '97; German champion 1992, 1996-7, 10 WCh 1997.

Michael MÖLLENBECK b. 12 Dec 1969 Wesel 2.00m 130kg. TV Wattenscheid. Businessman.
At DT: OG: '96- dnq, '00- 10, '04- dnq 20; WCh: '95- dnq 16, '99- 6, '01- 3, '03- 5, '05- 3; EC: '02- 3;

WJ: '88- 9; EJ: '87- 6; WCp: '02- 4; ECp: '02-03-04-05: 1/2/1/2. Won GER 2002, 2004-05.
Progress at DT: 1988- 53.00, 1989- 59.26, 1990- 60.16, 1991- 58.86, 1992- 62.12, 1993- 62.82, 1994- 58.26, 1995- 65.78, 1996- 67.44, 1997- 66.66, 1998- 67.18, 1999- 67.00, 2000- 65.49, 2001- 67.61, 2002- 67.64, 2003- 67.42, 2004- 66.36, 2005- 66.56. pb SP 16.78 '95.
Threw pb in first round of 2001 World DT final. Married discus thrower Anja Gündler (1 EJ 91, 5 WCh 93, pb 64.63 '98) in 1996.

Christian NICOLAY b. 4 Mar 1976 Bassenheim 1.89m 88kg. TV Wattenscheid. Economics graduate.
At JT: OG: '04- dnq 16; WCh: '03- 6, '05- dnq 14; WJ: '94- 5; EU23: '97- 3; EJ: '95- 1; ECp: '03- 2. German champion 2005.
Progress at PV: 1993- 68.34, 1994- 73.80, 1995- 76.88, 1996- 79.96, 1997- 78.36, 1998- 75.71, 1999- 78.23, 2000- 80.19, 2001- 71.41, 2002- 81.90, 2003- 84.54, 2004- 83.02, 2005- 83.20.

André NIKLAUS b. 30 Aug 1981 Berlin 1.90m 82kg. LG Nike Berlin.
At Dec: WCh: '03- 8, '05- 4; WJ: '00- 3; EU23: '01- 1, '03- 1; EJ: '99- 4; ECp: '04- 4. At Hep: WI:'06- 1.
Progress at Dec: 1996- 7368, 1997- 7835, 1998- 7979, 1999- 8363, 2000- 7847, 2001- 8206, 2002- dnf, 2003- 8060, 2004- 8343, 2005- 8316. pbs: 60m 7.06i '06, 100m 10.91 '03, 400m 48.55 '00, 1000m 2:40.38i '06, 1500m 4:19.09 '04, 60mh 8.17i '03, 110mh 14.33 '01, HJ 2.03 '01, PV 5.40i '03, 5.30 '05; LJ 7.64i 06, 7.48 '04; SP 14.41i '06, 14.24 '05; DT 46.13 '05, JT 61.74 '05, Hep 6192i '06.

Lars RIEDEL b. 28 Jun 1967 Zwickau 1.99m 115kg. LAC Chemnitz. Computer salesman.
At DT: OG: '92- dnq 14, '96- 1, '00- 2, '04- 7; WCh: '91-3-5-7-9-01-03-05: 1/1/1/1/3/1/4/9; EC: '90- dnq 15, '94- dns, '98- 1; WJ: '86- 4; WUG: '93- 1; WCp: '98- 2; ECp: '93-5-7-00-01: 1/1/1/1/1. GER champion 1992-8, 2000-01, 2003. Won GP 1993, 1995, 1997 (2nd overall), 1999; 2nd 1991.
Progress at DT: 1985- 52.02, 1986- 58.66, 1988- 62.26, 1989- 60.84, 1990- 64.86, 1991- 67.78, 1992- 68.66, 1993- 68.42, 1994- 66.08, 1995- 69.08, 1996- 71.06, 1997- 71.50, 1998- 68.21, 1999- 69.18, 2000- 69.72, 2001- 69.72, 2002- 66.72, 2003- 69.50, 2004- 68.05, 2005- 66.39. pbs: SP 15.93 '91, JT 61.14 '93, Dec 6087 '93.
The top discus thrower of the 1990s with four world titles (and a fifth in 2001) and the 1996 Olympic gold. In 1992 improved to 67.90, but failed at the Olympics before making a fine comeback with four throws over 68m at the ISTAF meeting. In 1994 a bad back caused his withdrawal from European final. He exceeded 70m for the first time in Zürich in 1995.

Tobias UNGER b. 10 Jul 1979 München 1.81m 70kg. LAZ Salamander Kornwestheim/ Ludwigsburg. Economics student at University of Nürtingen.
At 200m/4x100m: OG: '04- 7; WCh: '01- h, '05- 7; EU23: '01- 7; WJ: '98- qf/3R; WI: '04- 3; EI: '05- 1; ECp: '05- 2. Won German 100m 2005, 200m 2003-05.
German 200m record 2005.
Progress at 200m: 1995- 22.35, 1996- 22.13, 1997- 22.31, 1998- 21.68, 1999- 21.11, 2000- 20.96, 2001- 20.68, 2002- 21.36, 2003- 20.41, 2004- 20.30, 2005- 20.20. pbs: 60m 6.60i '05, 100m 10.16/10.11w '05.

Women

Kirsten BOLM b. 4 Mar 1975 Frechen 1.81m 70kg. MTG Mannheim. Was at Brigham Young University, USA.
At 100mh: OG: '04- sf; WCh: '99- qf, '01- h, '05- 4; EC: '02- h; WJ: '92- 5, '94- 1 (5 LJ); WUG: '99- 5/3R; WCp: '02- 7; ECp: '99-01-02-04-05: 6/3/2/7/2; Won German 2000-02, 2004-05. At 60mh: WI: '06- 5; EI: '02- 2, '05- 3.
Progress at 100mh: 1991- 13.49, 1992- 13.42, 1993- 13.52, 1994- 13.26, 1995- 13.60, 1996- 13.57, 1998- 13.75, 1999- 13.04/12.86Aw, 2000- 12.92, 2001- 12.98. 2002- 12.84, 2004- 12.80/12.66w, 2005- 12.59. pbs: 60m 7.41i '02, 100m 11.68A '00, 200m 24.05i '02, 24.12A '00; 50mh 7.12i '01, 60mh 7.89i '02, HJ 1.81 '00, LJ 6.55 '94.

Franka DIETZSCH b. 22 Jan 1968 Wolgast 1.83m 92kg. SC Neubrandenburg. Bank employee.
At DT: OG: '92- 12, '96- 4, '00- 6, '04- dnq 27; WCh: '91- dnq 13, '93- 8, '95- 7, '97- dnq, '99- 1, '01- 4, '03- dnq 14, '05- 1; EC: '94- 9, '98- 1; WJ: '86- 2; WUG: '89- 4; WCp: '98- 1; ECp: '97-9-01-02-03-04-05: 2/3/1/3/4/2/1; Won GP 2000, 2nd 1998. GER champion 1997-2001, 2003-05.
Progress at DT: 1981- 27.70, 1982- 43.80, 1983- 50.04, 1984- 51.16, 1985- 56.94, 1986- 64.34, 1987- 66.34, 1988- 65.56, 1989- 68.26, 1990- 67.42, 1991- 61.22, 1992- 64.64, 1993- 62.06, 1994- 62.76, 1995- 62.26, 1996- 66.66, 1997- 67.66, 1998- 68.91, 1999- 69.51, 2000- 68.06, 2001- 65.87A, 2002- 64.12, 2003- 66.00, 2004- 66.12, 2005- 66.56. pb SP 15.02 '85.

Betty HEIDLER b. 14 Oct 1983 Berlin 1.75m 81kg. LG Eintracht Frankfurt. Student.
At HT: OG: '04- 4; WCh: '03- 11, '05- dnq 29; EU23: '03- 4; WJ: '00/02- dnq 19/17; EJ: '01- 9, ECp: '04- 3. German champion 2005.
German hammer record 2004.
Progress at HT: 1999- 42.07, 2000- 56.02, 2001- 60.54, 2002- 63.38, 2003- 70.42, 2004- 72.73, 2005- 72.19.

Carolin HINGST b. 18 Sep 1980 Donauwörth 1.74m 60kg. USC Mainz.
At PV: OG: '04- dnq 22=; WCh: '01- 10, '03- dnq 15=, '05- 10; EC: '02- dnq 13=; EU23: '01- 3; WI: '04- dnq 9; EI: '05- 4; ECp: 04- nh, '05- 2. German champion 2004.
Progress at PV: 1999- 3.60, 2000- 4.01, 2001- 4.50, 2002- 4.50, 2003- 4.51, 2004- 4.66, 2005- 4.65i/4.50. pbs: 100mh 14.54 '98, HJ 1.75 '98, LJ 5.81 '98.

Susanne KEIL b. 18 May 1978 Frankfurt-am-

Main 1.72m 69kg. TSV Bauer 04 Leverkusen.
At HT: OG: '04- dnq 21; WCh: '01- dnq 14, '03- 5, '05- 12; EC: '02- 10; EJ: '97- 3; WUG: '01- 6; WCp: '02- 6; ECp: '03- 5, '05- 5. German champion 2002-03.
Three German hammer records 2003-05.
Progress at HT: 1994- 47.56, 1995- 52.00, 1996- 58.16, 1997- 60.94, 1998- 64.50, 1999- 64.40, 2000- 64.04, 2001- 68.07, 2002- 68.17, 2003- 71.93, 2004- 68.05, 2005- 72.74.
Her sister Alexandra has 100mh best of 13.4 '97, 13.65 '00.

Sonja KESSELSCHLÄGER b. 20 Jan 1978 Finsterwalde 1.78m 66kg. SC Neubrandenburg.
At Hep: OG: '04- 6; WCh: '03- 8, '05- 10; EC: '02- 9; WJ: '96- 7; EJ: '97- 3; EU23: '99- 3; WUG: '01- 3; ECp: '01- 2, '02- 3; German champion 2005. At Pen: WI: '03- 4, '06- 4; EI: '00-02-05: 6/5/5.
Progress at Hep: 1994- 5005, 1995- 5236, 1996- 5620, 1997- 5753, 1998- 5763, 2000- 6039, 2001- 6064, 2002- 6205, 2003- 6175, 2004- 6287, 2005- 6221. pbs: 200m 24.52 '02, 400m 55.94i '05, 800m 2:11.95 '04, 60mh 8.35i '04, 100mh 13.34 '03, HJ 1.85 '00, LJ 6.42 '04, SP 14.53 '04, JT 46.06 '96, Pen 4586i '06.

Nadine KLEINERT b. 20 Oct 1975 Magdeburg 1.90m 90kg. SC Magdeburg.
At SP: OG: '00- 8, '04- 2; WCh: '97- 7, '99- 2, '01- 2, '03- 7, '05- 5; EC: '98- 6, '02- 6; WJ: '92- 12, '94- 6; EU23: '94- 3Cp, '97- 1; EJ: '93- 2; WI: '99-01-04-06: 5/4/3/2; EI: '96-98-00: 5/5/2; ECp: '99-01-04-05: 2/1/3/2. Won GP 1999. German champion 1998, 2000-01, 2005.
Progress at SP: 1990- 13.85, 1991- 15.08, 1992- 16.32, 1993- 17.07, 1994- 17.44, 1995- 17.13, 1996- 18.37, 1997- 18.91, 1998- 19.22, 1999- 19.61, 2000- 19.81, 2001- 19.86, 2002- 19.24, 2003- 19.33i/19.14, 2004- 19.55, 2005- 20.06, 2006- 19.64i. pb DT 50.99 '01.

Petra LAMMERT b. 3 Mar 1984 Freudenstadt 1.82m 85kg. SC Neubrandenberg.
At SP: WCh: '05- dnq 15; EJ: '03- 3; EU23: '05- 1; WI: '06- 4; EI: '05- 4.
Progress at SP: 2001- 13.55, 2002- 15.18, 2003- 16.23, 2004- 18.01i/17.16, 2005- 19.81.

Irina MIKITENKO b. 23 Aug 1972 Bakankas, Kazakhstan 1.58m 49kg. née Volynskaya. TV Wattenscheid 01.
At 5000m: OG: '96- h, '00- 5, '04- 7; WCh: '99- 4, '01- 5, '03- h; ECp: '99-00-03: 2/2/4. At 10,000m: EC: '98- 8; WCp: '98- 5. 3rd GP 3000m 1999. World 4k CC: '00- 19. Won Central Asian 1500m 1995; German 10,000m 1998, 5000m 1999-2000.
German records 3000m 2000, 5000m (3) 1999.
Progress at 5000m, 10,000m: 1995- 15:47.85, 1996- 15:49.59, 1997- 15:48.29, 1998- 15:18.86, 32:10.61; 1999- 14:42.03, 31:38.68; 2000- 14:43.59; 2001- 14:53.00, 31:29.55; 2003- 14:56.64, 31:38.48; 2004- 14:55.43, 32:04.86. pbs: 800m 2:09.97 '98, 1500m 4:06.08 '01, 2000m 5:40.6 '01, 3000m 8:30.39 '00
German parents; changed nationality from Kazakhstan to Germany in March 1998. Son Alexander.

Sabrina MOCKENHAUPT b. 6 Dec 1980 Siegen 1.56m 46kg. Kölner Verein für Marathon.
At 10,000m: OG: '04- 15; WCh: '03- dnf, '05- 17; EC: '02- 10; EU23: '01- 4; ECp: '05- 1. At 5000m: EJ: '99- 4 (8 3000m); WCp: '02- 7; ECp: '02-04-05: 4/3/4; World Military champion 2002. At 3000m: WI: '04- 7; EI: '02- 8, '05- 4; ECp: '01-03-04: 6/3. Eur CC: '00-03-05: 17/15/2. WQon GER 5000m 2001-05, 10,000m 2003-05, CC 2005.
Progression at 10,000m: 2000- 33:12.97mx, 2001- 32:38.1, 2002- 32:08.52, 2003- 32:11.95, 2004- 31:23.35, 2005- 31:21.28. pbs: 1500m 4:14.93 '05, 2000m 5:44.98i '05, 3000m 8:44.65 '03, 5000m 15:03.47 '04.

Steffi NERIUS b. 1 Jul 1972 Bergen/Rügen 1.78m 72kg. TSV Bayer 04 Leverkusen. PE teacher.
At JT: OG: '96- 9, '00- 4, '04- 2; WCh: '93- 9, '95- 11, '99- dnq 16, '01- 5, '03- 3, '05- 3; EC: '98- 6, '02- 2; EJ: '91- 3; WUG: '97- 5; WCp: '92- 6, '02- 4; ECp: '95-01-02-03-04-05: 1/2/3/1/2/1. 2nd GP 1996. German champion 2001, 2003-05.
Progress at JT: 1985- 30.12, 1987- 45.16, 1988- 48.00, 1989- 56.88, 1990- 56.14, 1991- 60.02, 1992- 59.46, 1993- 63.88, 1995- 68.42, 1996- 69.42, 1997- 64.58, 1998- 67.33; new: 1999- 61.56. 2000- 65.76, 2001- 63.72, 2002- 64.55, 2003- 64.42, 2004- 65.82, 2005- 66.52.
Was a GDR youth volleyball champion. Threw personal best in last round of 2004 Olympics to move from 4th to 2nd.

Christina OBERGFÖLL b. 28 Aug 1981 Lahr (Baden) 1.75m 71kg. LG Offenburg. Student.
At JT: OG: '04-dnq 15; WCh: '05- 2; EU23: '01- 9, '03- 8; WJ: '00- 8.
European javelin record 2005.
Progress at JT: 1997- 49.20, 1998- 48.52, new: 1999- 50.57, 2000- 54.50, 2001- 56.83, 2002- 60.61, 2003- 57.40, 2004- 63.34, 2005- 70.03.
Made a wondrous breakthrough at the 2005 World Champs to take her pb from 64.59 to a European record 70.03 and the silver medal.

Melanie SEEGER b. 8 Jan 1977 Brandenburg/Havel 1.69m 55kg. SC Potsdam.
At 20kmW: OG: '04- 5; WCh: '99- 33, '01- 7, '03- 8, '05- 11; EC: '98- dnf, '02- 14; EU23: '97- 8, '99- 3; WCp: '04- 9; ECp: '03- 9. At 5000mW: WJ: '96- 4; EJ: '93- 10, '95- 4. Won German 5000mW 2001-05, 20kmW 2001, 2005.
Four German records 20km walk 2001-04.
Progress at 20kmW: 1999- 1:34:17, 2000- 1:32:10, 2001- 1:30:41, 2002- 1:31:08, 2003- 1:29:44, 2004- 1:28:17, 2005- 1:30:21, 2006- 1:29:15. pbs: 3000mW 11:50.48i '04, 12:49.62 '02, 5000mW 20:18.87i '04, 20:56.19 '03; 10kmW 43:12 '02.

Silke SPIEGELBURG b. 17 Mar 1986 1.73m 62kg. TSV Bayer 04 Leverkusen.
At PV: OG: '04- dnq 13; WJ: '02- 8; WY: '01- 1; EJ:

'03- 1, '05- 1; WI: '06- 8. German champion 2005. World junior pole vault record 2005.
Progress at PV: 1999- 3.30, 2000- 3.75, 2001- 4.00, 2002- 4.20, 2003- 4.20i/4.15, 2004- 4.40, 2005- 4.48i/4.42, 2006- 4.45i.
Her brother **Richard** (b. 12 Aug 1977) has PV pb 5.85 '01; 6= WCh 01, 1 WUG 99.

GHANA

Governing body: Ghana Athletic Association, National Sports Council, PO Box 1272, Accra. Founded 1944.

Ignisious GAISAH b. 20 Jun 1983 1.86m 70kg. Formerly known as Anthony Essuman. Lives in the Netherlands.
At LJ: OG: '04- 6; WCh: '03- 4, '05- 2; CG: '06- 1; AfG: '04- 1; WI: '06- 1. Won WAF 2004.
Eight Ghana long jump records 2003-05.
Progress at LJ: 1998- 7.35, 1999- 7.42, 2000- 7.40, 2002- 8.12, 2003- 8.30, 2004- 8.32, 2005- 8.34, 2006- 8.36i/8.20.

Abdul **Aziz ZAKARI** b. 2 Sep 1976 Accra 1.78m 73kg.
At 100m(/200m): OG: '00/04- dnf; WCh: '97- qf, '01- 7, '03- h, '05- 8; CG: '98- sf/sf, '02- sf/5, '06- 5; AfG: '03- 7/3/1R; AfCh: '98- (4), '00-1/1/1R, '02- -/2; WCp: '02- 3R.
Progress at 100m, 200m: 1995- 10.4, 21.36/21.0; 1996- 10.30, 20.90; 1997- 10.26, 20.88; 1998- 10.29, 20.62; 1999- 10.35/10.08w, 20.84; 2000- 10.06, 20.23; 2001- 10.04, 20.27; 2002- 10.15/10.13w, 20.29; 2003- 10.07/9.98w, 20.34; 2004- 10.00, 20.61; 2005- 9.99. pb 60m 6.63i '03.
Was due to run at 1996 Olympics, but 4x100m team not permitted to race due to an ineligible runner, then twice a non-finisher in Olympic finals due to cramp.

Women

Margaret Esi **SIMPSON** b. 31 Dec 1981 Kumasi 1.62m 53kg.
At Hep: OG: '04- 9; WCh: '01- 13, '03- dnf, '05- 3; CG: '02- 3; WJ: '00- dnf; AfG: '03- 1; AfCh: '00- 5, '02- 1, '04- 1. Won Af-J 1999.
African heptathlon record 2005, Ghana records at HJ, JT and eight heptathlon 1999-2004.
Progress at Hep: 1999- 5366, 2000- 5543, 2001- 5836, 2002- 6105w/6004, 2003- 6152, 2004- 6306, 2005- 6423. pbs: 200m 24.54 '04, 800m 2:17.02 '05, 100mh 13.41 '05, HJ 1.85 '05, LJ 6.32 '05, SP 13.01 '05, JT 56.36 '05.
Expecting a baby in July 2006.

GREECE

Governing body: Hellenic Amateur Athletic Association (SEGAS), 137 Siggroú Avenue, 171 21 Nea Smirni, Athens. Founded 1897.
National Championships first held in 1896 (men), 1930 (women). **2005 Champions**: **Men**: 100m: Panayiótis Sarrís 10.34, 200m: Anastásios Goúsis 20.98, 400m: Dimítrios Grávalos 46.24, 800m: Pávlos Faroúggias 1:51.95, 1500m: Panayiótis Ikonómou 3:54.42, 5000m: Anastásios Frággos 14:22.16, 10,000m: Mihail Yelasákis 29:44.37, Mar: Yerásimos Kókotos 2:24:52, 3000mSt: Aléxandros-Arbédo Lítsis 9:03.04, 110mh: Aléxandros Theofánov 13.62, 400mh: Periklís Iakovákis 49.31, HJ: Kyriacos Ioannou CYP 2.24, PV: Konstadínos Filippídis 5.25, LJ: Loúis Tsátoumas 8.01, TJ: Konstadínos Zalaggítis 16.80, SP: Andréas Anastasópoulos 18.88, DT: Stéfanos Kónstas 60.33, HT: Aléxandros Papadimitríou 75.45, JT: Elefthérios Karasmanákis 76.37, Dec: Mihail Papaioánnou 7328, 20kmW: Theódoros Koupídis 1:28:44, 50kmW: Konstadínos Stefanópoulos 4:08:48. **Women**: 100m: María Karastamáti 11.27, 200m: Eleni Artymata CYP 24.10, 400m: Dímitra Dóva 52.21, 800m: Eléni Filándra 2:06.79, 1500m: Konstadína Efedáki 4:35.81, 5000m: María Protópappa 16:27.00, 10,000m: Ekateríni Asimakopoúlou 34:55.51, Mar: Yeoryía Abatzídou 2:42:50, 3000mSt: María Pardaloú 10:13.04, 100mh: Flóra Redoúmi 13.12, 400mh: Hristína Hantzí-Neag 57.20, HJ: María Papayeoryíou 1.85, PV: Afrodíti Skafída 4.48, LJ: Ioánna Kafetzí 6.62, TJ: Hrisopiyí Devetzí 14.59, SP/HT: Stilianí Papadopoúlou 16.11/68.14, DT: Aretí Abatzí 54.51, JT: Miréla Manjani 59.22, Hep: Aryiró Stratáki 5822, 20kmW: Evaggelía Xinoú 1:38:10.

Konstadínos FILIPÍDDIS b. 26 Nov 1986 1.87m 73kg. Panellínios YS Athens. Student of Economics at University of Athens.
At PV: WCh: '05- dnq 14=; WJ: '04- 4; WY: '03- 4; EJ: '05- 2; WUG: '05- 2; Won MedG 2005; Greek champion 2005.
Five Greek pole vault records 2005.
Progress at PV: 2001- 3.70, 2002- 4.80, 2003- 5.22, 2004- 5.50, 2005- 5.75.
Switched from gymnastics to pole vault in 2001.

Periklís IAKOVÁKIS b. 24 Mar 1979 Pátra 1.85m 76kg. Olympiakós SF Piraeus. Student of Economics at University of Athens. Air Force officer.
At 400mh/4x400mR: OG: '00- h, '04- sf; WCh: '99- h, '01- sf, '03- 3, '05- sf; EC: '98- hR, '02- 5; WJ: '98- 1; EJ: '97- 2/2R; EU23: '99- 3, '01- 2; WUG: '01- 4; ECp: '99-00-03: 6/4/2 (2R '03). Greek champion 1998-2005, Med.Games 2001. At 400m: WJ: '96- h; ECp: '97- 8.
Five Greek 400mh records 2002-03.
Progress at 400mh: 1997- 51.6, 1998- 49.82, 1999- 49.53, 2000- 49.35, 2001- 48.87, 2002- 48.66, 2003- 48.17, 2004- 48.47, 2005- 48.24. pbs: 100m 11.1 '96, 200m 21.62 '97, 400m 46.35 '02. 110mh 15.09 '02. LJ 6.58 '95.
Older brother Thomás (b. 1976), pbs 100m 10.89 '03, 200m 21.39 '99, 400m 47.96 '98; younger brother Sotírios (b. 1982), pbs 400m 47.79 '04, 400mh 49.9 '05.

Aléxandros PAPADIMITRÍOU b. 18 J1un 1973 Lárisa 1.85m 115kg. AEK Athens. MSc in kinesiology at UTEP, Texas, USA. Harbour guard officer.

At HT: OG: '96- dnq 16; '00- 12, '04- dnq 17; WCh: '97-9-01-05: dnq 19/27/16/12, '03- 8; EC: '98- dnq 27, '02- 3; WJ: '92- 6; EJ: '91- 7; ECp: '97-00-03: 3/2/3; E23Cp: '94- 2. Greek champion 1994-7, 2000, 2002-05; Balkan 1997, 2000-01, 2003, 2005.

Two Greek hammer records 1996-2000.

Progress at HT: 1989- 53.74, 1990- 61.72, 1991- 65.82, 1992- 69.48, 1993- 70.74, 1994- 73.74, 1995- 74.80, 1996- 77.84, 1997- 76.72, 1998- 77.60, 1999- 78.88, 2000- 80.45, 2001- 79.52, 2002- 80.21, 2003- 79.52, 2004- 80.35, 2005- 78.28.

Women

Hrisopiyí DEVETZÍ b. 2 Jan 1976 Alexandroúpoli 1.70m 57kg. Olympiakós SF Piraeus. Physiotherapist. Air Force officer.

At TJ: OG: '04- 2; WCh: '03- 8, '05- 5; EC: '02- 7; WI: '04- 3; EI: '02- dnq 16; ECp: '03-04-05: 4/2/2. Won WAF TJ 2005, Greek TJ 2002-05, Balkan LJ 2000.

Greek triple jump record 2004.

Progress at TJ: 1992- 11.76, 1993- 12.48, 1994- 12.52, 1995- 12.52/12.83w, 1996- 12.72i/12.69/12.77w, 1997- 12.70i/12.59, 1998- 13.44, 1999- 13.61/13.66w, 2000- 13.48, 2001- 14.00/14.12w, 2002- 14.15, 2003- 14.84i/14.34, 2004- 15.32, 2005- 14.89. pbs: HJ 1.64 '96, LJ 6.56 '05, JT 32.26 '92.

She won national championship medals in gymnastics as a child.

Faní HALKIÁ b. 2 Feb 1979 Lárisa 1.75m 64kg. Olympiakós SF Piraeus. Air Force officer.

At 400mh/4x400mR: OG: '04- 1; WCh: '03- hR; WJ: '98- h; EJ: '97- h; ECp: '04- 1/3R. Greek champion 1998, 2004, Balkan 1997. At 400m: WI: '04- 6.

Greek records 400mh (7) 2003-04, 400m 2004.

Progress at 400mh: 1995- 62.37, 1996- 61.40, 1997- 59.17, 1998- 59.99, 1999- 61.99, 2002- 58.80, 2003- 56.40, 2004- 52.77. pbs: 100m 12.47/12.2 '03, 200m 24.48 '02, 400m 50.56 '04, 100mh 14.45 '03, HJ 1.55 '94.

Having been a promising junior, she had many injuries and gave up athletics for two years after a poor year in 1999. In this time she worked mainly as a journalist. Coached by Yeóryios Panayiotópoulos, she made rapid progress to her triumphant year in 2004 when she set Greek 400mh records at 54.88, 54.16 and 53.99 before 53.85 and 52.77 at the Olympic Games before winning the gold medal with 52.82. Missed almost all 2005 season with a foot injury.

María KARASTAMÁTI b. 10 Dec 1984 Pireás 1.72m 63kg. Olympiakós SF Piraeus.

At 100m: OG: '04- h R; WCh: '03- sf; EU23: '05- 1; ECp: '05- 3. At 60m: EI: '05- 3. Greek champion 100m 2005.

Progress at 100m: 1999- 12.59, 2000- 12.59, 2001- 12.63, 2002- 12.13, 2003- 11.67, 2004- 11.48, 2005- 11.03. pbs: 60m 7.19i '05, 200m 24.25 '04.

Miréla MANJANI b. 21 Dec 1976 Dirráhio (Durrës), Albania 1.65m 64kg, Olympiakós SF Piraeus. Naval sub-lieutenant.

At JT: OG: '96- dnq 24, '00- 2, '04- 3; WCh: '95- 12, '97- 11, '99- 1, '01- 2, '03- 1, '05- dnq; EC: '94- dnq 22, '98- 9, '02- 1; WJ: '94- 8; EJ: '95- 2; ECp: '00-03-05: 3/2/6. Greek champion 1999, 2001, 2005; Balkan 1994, 1997.

Two World records (64.99 and 67.09) new javelin 1999. Seven Greek records 1999-2000.

Progress at JT: 1993- 54.86, 1994- 57.20, 1995- 62.40, 1996- 62.46 (still Albanian record), 1997- 63.50, 1998- 65.14, new spec: 1999- 67.09, 2000- 67.51, 2001- 66.70, 2002- 67.47, 2003- 66.52, 2004- 64.29, 2005- 59.22.

Switched from Albania to become Greek citizen in 1997. Married to weightlifter Yeóryios Tzelílis (4th 1996 Olympics 64kg, 2nd 1999 Worlds 69kg) from November 1996 until late 2001.

Aggelikí TSIOLAKOÚDI b. 10 May 1976 Alexandroúpoli 1.67m 72kg. Olympiakós SF Piraeus. Was at University of Texas at El Paso, USA, now PE student at University of Athens.

At JT: OG: '00/04- dnq 18/19; WCh: '97- dnq 25, '01- 8, '03- dnq 17, '05- 8; EC: '02- 5; WJ: '94- 7; EJ: '95- 3; WUG: '01- 4; ECp: '04- 1. Won MedG 2005, NCAA 2000, Greek 2000, 2002.

Progress at JT: 1991- 43.30, 1992- 47.80, 1993- 58.42, 1994- 57.04, 1995- 57.44, 1996- 53.30, 1997- 63.32, 1998- 58.68; new: 1999- 56.91, 2000- 60.26, 2001- 62.90, 2002- 63.14, 2003- 56.66, 2004- 62.80, 2005- 62.72. pb DT 30.42 '03.

Athanasía TSOUMELÉKA b. 2 Jan 1982 Préveza 1.58m 48kg. FS Astéras Prevézis. Student of psychology at University of Athens. Naval sub-lieutenant.

At 20kmW: OG: '04- 1; WCh: '03- 7, '05- dq; WCp: '04- 14; EC: '02- 9; EU23: '03- 1. At 10,000mW: WJ: '00- 4; EJ: '01- 2. Greek champion 20kmW 2002-03.

Greek walks records 3000m 2000, 10,000m (2) 2003-04, 10km 2005, 20km (2) 2002-03.

Progress at 20kmW: 2002- 1:31:25, 2003- 1:29:34, 2004- 1:29:12, 2005- 1:35:11. pbs: 3000mW 13:37.15 '00, 5000mW 22:04.90 '03, 10,000mW 44:10.02 '04, 44:05R '05.

Ólga-Anastasia VASDÉKI b. 26 Sep 1973 Vólos 1.75m 60kg. Panellínios (Athens). Harbour guard officer. PE graduate of Athens University.

At TJ: OG: '96- 5, '00- 7, '04- 11; WCh: '97- 4, '99- 3, '03- 12; EC: '98- 1; EI: '96- 3, '98- 4; WCp: '98- 1. Won GRE 1993, 1995-6, 1998; MedG 1997.

Eleven Greek triple jump records 1993-8.

Progress at TJ: 1992- 12.77, 1993- 13.37, 1994- 13.25i, 1995- 13.45/13.73w, 1996- 14.48/14.51w, 1997- 14.62, 1998- 14.64A/14.59, 1999- 14.67, 2000- 14.26, 2002- 13.82, 2003- 14.50, 2004- 14.54, 2005- 13.21. pb LJ 6.60 '98, 6.66w '99.

Huge improvement in 1996. Married to her coach Panayiótis Markianídis (b. 1966) pbs 100m 10.61 '94, 200m 21.81 '89, Dec 6981 '92. Her brother Spirídon Vasdékis (b. 23 Jan 1970) had LJ best of 8.19 '95 and 8.29Aw '96, 3 EI '96, 8 WI '97, 16 OG '92, 14 OG '96.

GRENADA

Governing body: Grenada Athletic Assocation, PO Box 419, St George's. Founded 1924.

Alleyne FRANCIQUE b. 7 Jun 1976 Grenada 1.88m 75kg. Was at Louisiana State University.
At 400m: OG: '96- hR, '04- 4; WCh: '99- h, '01- 7, '03- 7, '05- sf; CG: '02- 5, '06- 2; PAm: '03- 3; WI: '04- 1, '06- 1. Won CAC 2003, NCAA indoor 400m 2002.
Five Grenada 400m records 2001-04. Commonwealth indoor 400m record 45.35 '02.
Progress at 400m: 1998- 47.30, 1999- 46.46, 2000- 47.14, 2001- 44.91, 2002- 44.72, 2003- 44.78, 2004- 44.47, 2005- 44.60, 2006- 45.09. pbs: 200m 20.83 '03, 600m 1:18.25i '00.
Awarded OBE in 2005.

HAITI

Governing body: Fédération Haitienne d'Athlétisme Amateur, BP 2405, Port-au-Prince. Founded 1969.

Dudley DORIVAL b. 1 Sep 1975 Elizabeth, New Jersey, USA 1.85m 77kg. Sales consultant, studied sociology at University of Connecticut,
At 110mh: OG: '00- 7, '04- sf; WCh: '99- sf, '01- 3, '03/05- sf; WJ: '94- 2; PAm: '03- 5; CAG: '02- 1; WUG: '97- 3. At 60mh: WI: '01- 7.
Six Haitian 110mh records from three at 13.42 in 1999 to 2001.
Progress at 110mh: 1994- 13.79/13.65w, 1995- 13.53A, 1996- 13.60/13.59w, 1997- 13.48, 1998- 13.30, 1999- 13.38/13.29w, 2000- 13.33, 2001- 13.25, 2002- 13.50, 2003- 13.41, 2004- 13.39, 2005- 13.58/13.50w. pbs: 100m 10.45 '98, 200m 20.64w '98, 50mh 6.50i '01, 55mh 7.16i '96, 60mh 7.55i '01.
Switched from USA to take up Haiti (the land of his) from July 1999. At the 2001 Worlds he won Haiti's first global medal since Silvio Cator won the Olympic long jump in 1928.

HUNGARY

Governing body: Magyar Atlétikai Szövetség, 1146 Budapest, Istvánmezei út 1-3. Founded 1897.

National Championships first held in 1896 (men), 1932 (women). **2005 Champions**. **Men**: 100m: Gábor Dobos 10.63, 200m: Roland Németh 21.01, 400m: Zoltán Borsányi 47.01, 800m: Dávid Takács 1:49.90, 1500m: Gábor Csaja 3:57.02, 5000m/10,000m: Barnabás Bene 14:25.64/29:37.70, HMar: András Juhász 65:57, Mar: Miklós Zatykó 2:22:58, 3000mSt: Albert Minczér 8:54.67, 110mh: Daniel Kiss 13.65, 400mh: Ákos Dezsö 50.00, HJ: László Boros 2.28, PV/Dec: Péter Skoumal 5.30/7309, LJ: Pál Babicz 7.80, TJ: János Farkas 15.47, SP: Zsolt Biber 19.12, DT: Zoltán Kövágó 65.80, HT: Krisztián Pars 78.76, JT: Gergely Horváth 75.34, 20kmW: Gyula Dudás 1:29:01, 50kmW: János Tóth 4:01:53. **Women**: 100m: Enikö Szabó 11.82, 200m: Nikolett Listár 23.60, 400m: Barbara Petráhn 52.92, 800m: Kitti Cziráki 2:07.90, 1500m/5000m/10,000m: Krisztina Papp 4:12.26/16:00.76/32:39.61, HMar: Eszter Erdélyi 76:10, Mar: Ida Kovács 2:43:15, 3000mSt: Lívia Tóth 9:55.65, 100mh: Edit Vári 13.93, 400mh: Andrea Pék 58.80, HJ: Dóra Györffy 1.89, PV: Krisztina Molnár 4.45, LJ: Tünde Vaszi 6.69, TJ: Zita Ajkler 13.52, SP: Éva Kürti 15.68, DT: Katalin Divós 54.44, HT: Éva Orbán 66.38, JT: Nikolett Szabó 58.72, Hep: Zita Óvári 5539, 10kmW/20kmW: Ildikó Ilyés 49:21/1:43:13.

Zoltán KÖVAGÓ b. 10 Apr 1979 Szolnok 2.04m 127kg. Budapesti Honvéd SE. Army lieutenant.
At DT: OG: '00- dnq, '04- 2; WCh: '01-03: dnq 20/19, '05- 10; EC: '02- 7; WJ: '96- 4, '98- 1; EJ: '97- 3; EU23: '99- 6, '01- 1. HUN champion 2001, 2004-05.
Progress at DT: 1995- 49.78, 1996- 59.70, 1997- 62.16, 1998- 60.27, 1999- 63.23, 2000- 66.76, 2001- 66.93, 2002- 65.98, 2003- 66.03, 2004- 68.93, 2005- 66.00. pb SP 15.93 '01.

Krisztián PARS b. 18 Feb 1982 Körmend 1.88m 104kg. Dobó SE.
At HT: OG: '04- 5; WCh: '05- 7; WY: '99- 1; EJ: '01- 1; EU23: '03- 1. HUN champion 2005.
World junior records with 6kg hammer: 80.64 & 81.34 in 2001.
Progress at HT: 1998- 54.00, 1999- 61.92, 2000- 66.80, 2001- 73.09, 2002- 74.18, 2003- 78.81, 2004- 80.90, 2005- 80.03. pbs: SP 15.60 '05, DT 52.07 '05.

Roland VARGA b. 22 Oct 1977 Budapest 1.97m 102kg. Pécsi VSK.
At DT: WCh: '01- 7, '05- dnq 15; EC: '02- dnq 13; WJ: '96- 2; EU23: '99- 2; WUG: '01- 4, '03- 4.
Progress at DT: 1993- 43.60, 1994- 48.18, 1995- 52.88, 1996- 55.20, 1997- 58.70, 1998- 60.33, 1999- 62.78, 2000- 65.39, 2001- 65.86, 2002- 67.38, 2003- 61.71, 2004- 66.73, 2005- 65.24. pbs: 100m 11.2 '94, 11.46 '95; 400m 50.65 '95, 1500m 4:54.31 '95, 110mh 17.14 '95, HJ 1.84 '95, PV 3.90 '94, LJ 6.64w/6.49 '95; SP 16.33 '02, HT 53.70 '96, Dec 6782 '95.

Attila ZSIVOCZKY b. 29 Apr 1977 Budapest 1.93m 82kg. Debreceni SC. Was at Kansas State University, USA.
At Dec: OG: '00- 8, '04- 6; WCh: '99- 10, '01- 4, '03- dnf, '05- 3; EC: '98- 16; WJ: '96- 1; EU23: '97- 4, '99- 1; ECp: '98-9-01: 5/5/2. At Hep: EI: '00-02-05: 4/5/5.
Hungarian decathlon record 2000.
Progress at Dec: 1995- 7242, 1996- 7582, 1997- 7804, 1998- 8103, 1999- 8379, 2000- 8554, 2001- 8371, 2002- 8175, 2003- 7923, 2004- 8287, 2005- 8480. pbs: 60m 7.11i '00, 100m 10.90 '05, 10.64w '00; 400m 47.93 '00, 1000m 2:34.79i '98, 1500m 4:20.94 '99, 60mh 8.14i '06, 110mh 14.52w/14.63 '05, HJ 2.23i '98, 2.22 '94; PV 4.91i '02, 4.90 '01;

LJ 7.31 '99, SP 15.96 '05, DT 49.58 '05, JT 65.87 '00, Hep 6033i '00.

Son of Gyula Zsivótzky (OG: 60- 2, 64- 2, 68- 1, 72- 5; EC: 58- 3, 62- 1, 66- 2, 69- 4) who set two world hammer records – 73.74 in 1965 and 73.76 in 1968.

Women

Dóra GYÖRFFY b. 23 Feb 1978 Budapest 1.76m 58kg. BEAC. Political science graduate of Harvard University, USA.
At HJ: OG: '00- dnq 18=; WCh: '01- 7=, '05- 9; EC: '98- dnq 19, '02- 12; WJ: '94- 7=, '96- 2; EJ: '95- 5=, '97- 5; EU23: '99- 5; WUG: '03- 1; WI: '01- 5=; EI: '02- 2=. HUN champion 1998-2003, 2005.
Two Hungarian high jump records 2001.
Progress at HJ: 1991- 1.69, 1992- 1.76, 1993- 1.71, 1994- 1.84, 1995- 1.87, 1996- 1.92, 1997- 1.93, 1998- 1.92, 1999- 1.94, 2000- 1.97i/1.95, 2001- 2.00, 2002- 1.97i/1.91, 2003- 1.96i/1.94, 2004- 1.95i, 2005- 1.93. pbs: LJ 5.88 '95, TJ 13.05 '01.

Nikolett SZABÓ b. 3 Mar 1980 Budapest 1.68m 65kg. FTC.
At JT: OG: '00/04- dnq 14/16; WCh: '97- dnq 19, '01- dnq 14, '03- 12, '05- dnq 20; EC: '98- 8, '02- 8; WJ: '96- 2, '98- 4; EU23: '01- 1; EJ: '95-7-9: 7/1/1. HUN champion 1997-2001, 2003-05.
Three HUN records new javelin 1999-2001.
Progress at JT: 1993- 45.28, 1994- 49.78, 1995- 55.32, 1996- 58.88, 1997- 61.76, 1998- 65.10; new: 1999- 61.79, 2000- 61.23, 2001- 64.62, 2002- 63.25, 2003- 62.88, 2004- 63.19, 2005- 61.68. pbs: SP 12.92 '95, DT 36.43 '98.

Livia TÓTH b. 7 Jan 1980 Veszprém 1.76m 57kg. VEDAC.
At 3000mSt: WCh: '05- h; EU23: '01- 2; WUG: '05- 1. At 1500m: EC: '02- h. Hungarian champion 1500m 2001-02, 2004; 3000mSt 2002-05.
Three Hungarian 3000m steeplechase records 2004-05.
Progress at 3000mSt: 2001- 10:04.99, 2002- 9:51.38, 2003- 10:00.93, 2004- 9:39.84, 2005- 9:30.20. pbs: 800m 2:04.86 '03, 1500m 4:09.28 '03, 3000m 8:58.53 '02, 5000m 16:35.54 '01, 10,000m 35:06.56 '01, HMar 80:13 '00, 2000mSt 6:22.61 '05 (HUN record).

Tünde VASZI b. 18 Apr 1972 Piskolt, Romania 1.70m 60kg. Budapesti Honvéd SE
At LJ: OG: '96- 8, '00- 8, '04- 8; WCh: '95/97/99- dnq, '01- 4, '03- 6, '05- 10; EC: '98- 4, '02- 3; WI: '97-9-03: 9/5/8; EI: '00- 5; WCp: '98- 5; 3rd GP 2002. Won HUN 100m 1999, LJ 1996-9, 2001-05; TJ 1995.
Hungarian long jump record 2001.
Progress at LJ: 1990- 5.80, 1991- 6.05, 1992- 6.22, 1993- 5.81/6.04w, 1994- 6.43/6.46w, 1995- 6.58, 1996- 6.73/6.82Aw, 1997- 6.76/6.78w, 1998- 6.77/6.82w, 1999- 6.82i/6.66, 2000- 6.70, 2001- 6.86, 2002- 6.78, 2003- 6.76, 2004- 6.70/6.78w, 2005- 6.69/6.72w. pbs: 60m 7.49i '97, 100m 11.50 '96, 200m 24.11 '96, 400m 58.31 '96, 100mh 13.84 '95, HJ 1.63 '96, PV 4.40i '06, 4.15 '99; TJ 13.39i '97, 13.38 '95.

ICELAND

Governing body: Frjálsíthróttasamband Islands, Engjavegur 6, IS-104 Reykjavik. Founded 1947.
National Championships first held in 1927.
2005 Champions: Men: 100m: Reynir Logi Ólafsson 11.32, 200m: Sveinn Elias Eliasson 22.58, 400m: Halldór Lárusson 50.17, 800m: Björn Margeirsson 1:51.95, 1500m/10,000m: Sigurbjörn Árni Arngrímsson 4:10.26/35:45.43, 5000m/HMar: Kári Steinn Karlsson 15:20.33/72:07, Mar: Trausti Valdimarsson 3:10:24, 3000mSt: Stefán Gudmundsson 9:41.18, 110mh/PV/LJ: Jón Arnar Magnússon 15.38/4.00/7.25, 400mh: Björgvin Víkingsson 53.58, HJ: Gauti Ásbjörnsson 1.90, TJ: Thorsteinn Ingvarsson 14.55, SP/DT: Ódinn Björn Thorsteinsson 17.16/50.46, HT: Bergur Ingi Pétursson 60.20, JT/Dec: Jónas Hlynur Hallgrimsson 61.95/6638.
Women: 100m/200m/400m/100mh/400mh: Silja Úlfarsdóttir 12.32/24.82/57.53/14.60/61.36, 800m: Birna Björnsdóttir 2:16.09, 1500m: Iris Anna Skúladóttir 4:40.34, HMar: Martha Ernstdóttir 1:22:08, Mar: Bryndis Ernstdóttir 2:55:39, HJ: Helga Margrét Thorsteinsdóttir 1.67, PV: Fanney Bkörk Tryggvadóttir 3.20, LJ/TJ: Jóhanna Ingadóttir 5.69/12.21, SP/DT/JT: Ásdís Hjálmsdóttir 12.48/44.94/52.70, HT: Kristbjörg Helga Ingvarsdóttir 43.17, Hep: Kristín Birna Ólafsdóttir 4922.

Thórey Edda ELISDOTTIR b. 30 Jun 1977 1.81m 64kg. Was at University of Georgia, USA.
At PV: OG: '00- dnq 22=, '04- 5; WCh: '99- 13, '01- 6, '03- nh, '05- dnq 17=; EC: '98- dnq 22, '02- 11=; EU23: '97- 9, '99- 5. ISL champion 2001-04.
Two ISL pole vault records 2004.
Progress at PV: 1997- 3.80, 1998- 4.21, 1999- 4.37i/4.22, 2000- 4.30, 2001- 4.51i/4.45, 2002- 4.41, 2003- 4.50i/4.48, 2004- 4.60, 2005- 4.50.
Member of EAA Athletes Commission 2002-06.

INDIA

Governing body: Athletics Federation of India, Room No.1148, Gate No 28, East Block, Jawaharlal Nehru Stadium, Lodi Complex, New Delhi 110003. Founded 1946.
National Championships first held as Indian Games in 1924. **2005 National Champions: Men**: 100m: Anil Kumar 10.46, 200m: Alaguvel Arvind 21.28, 400m: P.S.Sreejith 47.33, 800m: Ghamanda Ram 1:46.67, 1500m: Pritam Kumar Bind 3:48.46, 5000m/10,000m: Jagannath Lakade 14:16.58/31:23.65, 3000mSt: Arun D'Souza 9:00.38, 110mh: Naunidh Singh 14.05, 400mh: Joseph G.Abraham 50.87, HJ: Hari Shankar Roy 2.10, PV: V.V.Geesh Kumar 5.05, LJ: Shiv Shankar Yadav 7.81, TJ: Renjith Maheshwary 16.39, SP: Navpreet Singh 18.19, DT: Amrit Pal Singh

53.75, HT: Nirbhay Singh 65.85, JT: Anil Kumar 76.31, Dec: Kulwinder Singh 7257, 20kW: Gurmeet Singh 1:30:50, 50kmW: Gurdev Singh 4:16:22. **Women**: 100m: Poonam Tomar 11.80, 200m: Babita B.Singh 24.01, 400m/800m: Pinki Parmanik 53.29/2:04.30, 1500m/5000m: O.P.Jaisha 4:17.78/17:08.76, 10,000m: L.Aruna Devi 36:51.13, 3000mSt: L.Manjula 11:10.12, 100mh: Anuradha Biswal 13.99, 400mh: Pooja Jakhar 58.61, HJ: Tessymol Joseph 1.70, PV: Chetna Solanki 3.70, LJ: M.A.Prajusha 5.97/0.2, TJ: Tessymol Joseph 12.96, SP: Nicholas Latha 14.31, DT: Saroj Kumari Sihag 55.16, HT: Ritu Rani 55.41, JT: Gurmeet Kaur 53.77, Hep: M. B.Shinimol 4310, 20kmW: Amandeep Kaur 1:43:49.

Anju Bobby GEORGE b. 19 Apr 1977 Cheeranchira, Kerala 1.77m 62kg. née Markose. Customs & Excise officer.
At LJ: OG: '04- 6; WCh: '03- 3, '05- 5; CG: '02- 3, '06- 6, AsiG: '02- 1 (4 TJ); AsiC: '05- 1; WI: '03- 7; won Af-AsG 2003.
Indian records LJ (6) 1999–2004, TJ 2001.
Progress at LJ: 1996- 6.13, 1997- 6.20, 1998- 6.12, 1999- 6.37, 2000- 6.59, 2001- 6.74, 2002- 6.74, 2003- 6.70, 2004- 6.83, 2005- 6.75. pb TJ 13.67 '02.
Married triple jumper Bobby George in 2001.

IRELAND

Governing Body: The Athletic Association of Ireland (AAI), 11 Prospect Road, Glasnevin, Dublin 9. Founded in 1999. Original Irish AAA founded in 1885.

National Championships first held in 1873. **2005 champions**: **Men**: 100m: Gary Ryan 10.37w, 200m: Paul Brizzel 21.08, 400m: Tomas Coman 46.48, 800m: Ciaran O'Connell 1:50.73, 1500m: Gary Murray 3:47.57, 5000: Martin Fagan 14:11.44, 10,000m: Joseph McAlister 30:18.80, HMar: Gerry Ryan 64:05, Mar: Gary Crossan 2:23:19, 3000mSt: Eugene O'Neill 9:03.73, 110mh: Peter Coghlan 13.91w, 400mh: Antoine Burke 52.41, HJ: Simon Phelan GBR 2.05, PV: Ruairi O'Briain 4.75, LJ: Darragh O'Farrell 7.12, TJ: Patrick Shannon 14.44, SP: Paul Crowe 16.92, DT: John Menton 52.01, HT: Mark Hanily 56.33, JT: Michael McConkey 63.69, Dec: Kevin Burke 5899, 10,000mW: Robert Heffernan 40:32.74, 20kmW: Pat Ryan 1:50:48, 30kmW: Colin Griffin 2:23:46. **Women**: 100m: Anna Boyle 11.53, 200m: Emily Maher 23.39, 400m: Karen Shinkins 52.49, 800m: Aoife Byrne 2:06.14, 1500m: Jolene Byrne 4:11.72, 5000m: Mary Cullen 16:02.05, HMar: Orla O'Mahoney 75:43, Mar: Pauline Curley 2:42:16, 100mh: Derval O'Rourke 12.95w, 400mh: Michelle Carey 59.14, HJ: Rosemary Daniels 1.75, PV: Claire Wilkinson 2.90, LJ: Donna Hosford 5.63, TJ: Aoife Hoey 11.73w, SP: Eva Massey GBR 15.11, DT/HT: Eileen O'Keeffe 43.34/62.44, JT: Laura Kerr GBR 45.94, Hep: Kelly Proper 4709, 5000mW/20kmW: Olive Loughnane 21:52.56/1:32:28.

Alistair CRAGG b. 13 Jun 1980 Johannesburg, South Africa 1.83m 59kg. Clonliffe H. Studied marketing at University of Arkansas.
At 5000m: OG: '04- 12; At 3000m: WI: '06- 4; EI: '05- 1. World 4k CC: '04- 16. Won Irish 1500m 2004, NCAA 5000m 2003, 10,000m 2004 (indoor 3000m 2003-04, 5000m 2002-04).
Progress at 5000m: 1998- 14:27.82, 1999- 14:25.04, 2000- 13:49.25, 2002- 13:22.07, 2003- 13:25.59, 2004- 13:12.74. pbs 1500m 3:39.24 '03, 1M 3:55.04i '06, 4:03.70 '02; 3000m 7:38.59i, 7:38.96 '04; 10,000m 28:20.29 '03.
Ran for South Africa at 1998 & 1999 World Junior CC, but held Irish passport through two Irish grandparents. Missed summer season after winning 2005 European Indoor title.

Women

Derval O'ROURKE b. 28 May 1981 1.68m 57kg. Leevale. Graduate of University College Dublin; sports administrator for Dublin City University.
At 100mh: OG: '04- h; WCh: '05- sf; WJ: '00- sf; EU23: '01- 7, '03- 4; EJ: '99- sf; WUG: '05- 3; Irish champion 2001-02, 2004-05. At 60mh: WI: '06- 1.
Irish 100mh record 2003.
Progress at 100mh: 1998- 14.29, 1999- 13.82, 2000- 13.49, 2001- 13.57, 2002- 13.38, 2003- 12.96, 2004- 13.39, 2005- 13.00/12.95w pbs: 60m 7.59i '05, 100m 11.54 '05, 50mh 6.80i '06, 60mh 7.84i '06.
Set six Irish records at 60mh from 8.02 to 7.84 to win World Indoor title in 2006.

ISRAEL

Governing body: Israeli Athletic Association, PO Box 24190, Tel Aviv 61241. Founded as Federation for Amateur Sport in Palestine 1931.

National Championships first held in 1935. **2005 Champions**: 100m: Ram Mor 10.61, 200m: Tal Mor 21.26, 400m: Naor Greene 47.29, 800m: Gezacho Yoseph 1:52.62, 1500m: Itai Maggidi 3:48.92, 5000m: Haile Satayin 14:07.05, 10,000m: Vodage Zvadya 29:44.04, Mar: Asaf Bimro 2:20:02, 3000mSt: Yamharan Yossef 9:38.24, 110mh: Yevgeniy Minenko 14.48, 400mh: Yurie Pelles 52.05, HJ: Niki Palli 2.23, PV: Alex Averbukh 5.65, LJ: Yochai Halevi 7.74, TJ: Ran Gil'adi 14.87, SP: Shai Shalev 16.01, DT: Lior Peretz 54.27, HT: Issar Yazbin 60.25, JT: Vadim Bavikin 69.89, Dec: Yevgeniy Olkhovskiy 6049. **Women**: 100m: Orly Lettos 12.33, 200m/400mh: Liat Anav 25.37.61.90, 400m/LJ/Hep: Svetlana Gnezdilov 54.92/6.00/5364, 800m/1500m: Duha Suliman 2:13.14/4:39.37, 5000m/10,000m/Mar: Nili Avramski 16:49.17/35:07.60/2:44:50, 3000mSt: Irina Weingarten 10:57.04, 100mh: Irina Lenskiy 13.74, HJ: Khen Edri 1.76, PV: Olga Dogadko 3.95, TJ: Niva Ziv 12.82, SP/DT: Sivan Jean 15.65/50.55, HT: Yevgeniya Zabolotniy 44.90, JT: Khen Edri 40.88.

Alex AVERBUKH b. 1 Oct 1974 Irkutsk. Siberia 1.78m 76kg. Maccabi Tel-Aviv.
At PV: OG: '00- 10=, '04- 8; WCh: '99- 3, '01- 2, '03- dnq; EC: '02- 1. WI: '01- 4, '06- 4=; EI: '00- 1; EJ: '93- dnq; WUG: '01- 1; 2nd GP 2002. EI Hep: '98- . Won ISR PV 2000-02, 2004-05; RUS Dec 1997.
Six ISR pole vault records 1999-2003 (from 5.80).
Progress at PV, Dec: 1991- 4.95, 1993- 5.30, 1994- 5.20, 1995- 5.50, 7598w; 1996- 5.40, 7716; 1997- 5.60, 8084; 1998- 5.70, 7658; 1999- 5.81, 2000- 5.85, 2001- 5.91, 2002- 5.85, 2003- 5.93, 2004- 5.85, 2005- 5.65. pbs: 60m 6.89i '98, 6.6i '97; 100m 10.64 '00, 400m 48.74 '98, 1500m 4:33.79 '97, 60mh 8.36i '98, 8.2i '97; 110mh 14.14 '97, HJ 2.06 '95, LJ 7.53i/7.50 '97, SP 15.12 '98, DT 41.51 '00, JT 53.26 '97, Hep 6144i '98.
His father Valeriy had a decathlon best of 7557 points and his brother Yevgeniy (died 1996 in a car crash) an 800m best of 1:48.18. Emigrated from Russia to Israel, and became a citizen on 3 August 1999, just in time to compete at World Championships. In Munich 2002 he became Israel's first European outdoor champion in athletics.

ITALY

Governing Body: Federazione Italiana di Atletica Leggera (FIDAL), Via Flaminia Nuova 830, 00191 Roma. Constituted 1926. First governing body formed 1896.
National Championships first held in 1897 (one event)/1906 (men), 1927 (women). **2005 champions**: **Men**: 100m: Simone Collio 10.50, 200m: Koura Kaba Fantoni 20.58, 400m: Andrea Barberi 45.89, 800m: Andrea Longo 1:51.21, 1500m: Christian Obrist 3:45.14, 5000m: Simone Zanon 14:03.99, 10,000m: Giuliano Battocletti 28:39.26, HMar: Fabio Mascheroni 64:58, Mar: Vincenzo Modica 2:14:03, 3000mSt: Yuri Floriani 8:44.08, 110mh: Andrea Giaconi 14.12, 400mh: Gianni Carabelli 49.05, HJ: Nicola Ciotti 2.28, PV: Giorgio Piantella 5.30, LJ: Stefano Dacastello 7.82, TJ: Paolo Camossi 16.86, SP: Marco Dodoni 18.93, DT: Hannes Kirchler 60.84, HT: Nicola Vizzoni 74.29, JT: Francesco Pignata 78.36, Dec: Paolo Mottadelli 7344, 10,000mW: Enrico Lang 41:42.49, 20kmW: Giorgio Rubino 1:24:01, 50kmW: Alex Schwazer 3:56:59. **Women**: 100m/200m: Vincenza Calì 11.59/23.22, 400m: Daniela Reina 53.47, 800m: Elisa Cusma 2:03.60, 1500m: Eleonora Berlanda 4:13.66, 5000m: Silvia Wessteiner 16:14.11, 10,000m: Renate Rungger 33:15.96, HMar: Bruna Genovese 74:40, Mar: Ivana Iozzia 2:35:55, 3000mSt: Elena Romagnolo 10:22.25, 100mh: Micol Cattaneo 13.49, 400mh: Benedetta Ceccarelli 55.66, HJ: Stefania Cadamuro 1.89, PV: Sara Bruzzese 4.10, LJ: Fiona May 6.50, TJ: Simona La Mantia 14.62, SP: Chiara Rosa 18.69, DT: Cristiana Checchi 53.60, HT: Ester Balassini 73.59, JT: Zahra Bani 59.30, Hep: Elisa Trevisan 5744, 5000mW: Sibilla Di Vincenzo 22:17.60, 20kmW: Elisa Rigaudo 1:33:46.

Stefano BALDINI b. 25 May 1971 Castelnovo di Sotto, Reggio Emilia 1.76m 60kg. Works for Corradini Excelsior Rubiera.
At Mar: OG: '00- dnf, '04- 1; WCh: '01- 3, '03- 3, '05- dnf; EC: '98- 1. At 10,000m (5000m): OG: '96- 18 (sf); WCh: '95- 18, '97- 9; EC: '94- 20, '02- 4; WJ: '90- (6); EJ: '89- (9); ECp: '95- 1. World HMar: '96- 1, '97- 9. Eur CC: '99- 10. Won ITA 10,000m 1993-6, 2001-02; HMar 1995, 1998, 2001, 2004.
Italian records: half marathon 1997 & 2000, marathon 1997 & 2002.
Progress at 10,000m, Mar: 1990- 29:48.5, 1992- 28:50.16, 1993- 28:25.98, 1994- 27:57.86, 1995- 27:50.17, 2:11:01sh; 1996- 27:43.98; 1997- 28:07.81, 2:07:57; 1998- 27:55.92, 2:09:33; 2000- 2:09:45, 2001- 28:21.38, 2:08:51; 2002- 27:50.98, 2:07:29; 2003- 2:07:56, 2004- 2:08:37, 2005- 2:09:25. pbs: 1500m 3:45.7 '91, 3000m 7:43.14 '96, 5000m 13:23.43 '96, HMar 60:50w '00, 60:56 '97.
Four wins in 19 marathons: Rome and EC 1998, Madrid 2001, OG 2004; 2nd London 1997 & 2003, 3rd New York 1997. On 9 Oct 1999 married **Virna De Angeli** (b. 27 Feb 1976) (2 WJ 400mh 1994, Italian record 400m 51.31 '97), but they are now separated. Older brother Marco (b. 14 May 1968) had marathon best of 2:16:32 sh '95.

Ivano BRUGNETTI b. 1 Sep 1976 Milano 1.75m 62kg. Fiamme Gialle Ostia.
At 20kmW: OG: '04- 1; WCh: '05- dnf; WCp: '04- 6. At 50kmW: OG: '00- dnf; WCh: '99- 1; WCp: '99- 26. At 10,000mW: EJ: '95- 14. Won ITA 10,000mW 1999, 20kmW 2003-04.
Progress at 20kmW, 50kmW: 1995- 1:30:33, 1997- 1:26:51, 4:06:43; 1998- 1:25:12, 4:02:15; 1999- 1:25:44, 3:47:54; 2000- 1:21:21, 2001- 1:24:38, 4:08:35; 2002- 1:26:08, 2003- 1:22:01, 2004- 1:19:40, 2005- 1:22:50. pbs: 5000mW 18:42.80i '04, 10,000mW 37:58.6 '05 (world best), 30kmW: 2:10:06 '99, 35kmW 2:33:43 '99.
He finished second at the 1999 World Championships, but two years later the winner German Skurygin (Rus) received a two-year ban from a positive drugs test in Seville, and Brugnetti was awarded the gold.

Fabrizio DONATO b. 14 Aug 1976 Latina 1.89m 82kg. Fiamme Galle.
At TJ: OG: '00/04- dnq 25/21; WCh: '03- dnq 13; EC: '02- 4; EJ: '95- 5; WI: '01- 6; EI: '02- 4; ECp: '00-02-03-04: 2/2/1/6. Won MedG 2001, Italian 2000, 2004.
Italian triple jump record 2000.
Progress at TJ: 1992- 12.88, 1993- 14.36, 1994- 15.27, 1995- 15.81, 1996- 16.35, 1997- 16.40A, 1998- 16.73, 1999- 16.66i/16.53w, 2000- 17.60, 2001- 17.05, 2002- 17.17, 2003- 17.16, 2004- 16.90, 2005- 16.65/16.68w, 2006- 17.33i. pb LJ 7.80 '04, 7.88w '00.
He married Patrizia Spuri (400m pb 51.74 '98, 8 EC 98) on 27 Sep 2003.

Giuseppe GIBILISCO b. 5 Jan 1979 Siracusa, Sicily 1.83m 78kg. Fiamme Galle.
At PV: OG: '00- 10=, '04- 3; WCh: '01- dnq, '03-

1, '05- 5=; EC: '02- 10; WJ: '98- 3=; EU23: '99- 9, '01- 3; EJ: '97- nh; WI: '04- 6; ECp: '00-02-03-05: 4/2=/2/1. Four Italian records 2003.
Progress at PV: 1993- 3.50, 1994- 3.80, 1995- 4.80, 1996- 5.05, 1997- 5.30, 1998- 5.30, 1999- 5.60, 2000- 5.70, 2001- 5.60i/5.50, 2002- 5.70, 2003- 5.90, 2004- 5.85, 2005- 5.83.
Set two Italian vault records in 2003 at both Golden Gala (5.77 & 5.82) and World Champs (5.85 & 5.90).

Andrew HOWE b. 12 May 1985 Los Angeles, USA 1.84m 73kg. Aeronautica Militare.
At (200m)/LJ: OG: '04- (h); WCh: '05- (qf); WJ: '02- 5 4x100mR, '04- 1/1; WY: '01- 3; WI: '06- 3. European Junior 200m record 2004.
Progress at 200m, LJ: 1999- 6.51, 2000- 7.52, 2001- 20.99/20.91w, 7.61; 2002- 21.15/21.0, 7.38; 2003- 21.03, 7.63i/7.47; 2004- 20.28, 8.11; 2005- 20.52, 8.02; 2006- 8.19i. pbs: 100m 10.24w '04, 10.58 '03; 150m 15.3 '04, 300m 33.7 '04, 110mh 14.65 '02, HJ 2.06 '00, TJ 16.27 '02.
Left the USA with his mother Renée Felton (100mh 13.72 '81) at age five in 1990 – she married an Italian, Ugo Besozzi. He has set many Italian age group records. From a previous best of 7.61 he set Italian junior LJ records with 7.93, 8.01, 8.04 and 8.07 in 2004. improving to 8.11 to win World Junior gold. He followed this with a pb 20.86 in his heat, then a national junior record 20.72 in his semi and then an amazing European junior record 20.28 to win the 200m.

Alex SCHWAZER b. 26 Dec 1984 Vipitano (Bolzano) 1.85m 73kg. Carabinieri Bologna.
At 50kmW: WCh: '05- 3; ECp: '05- 6. Italian champion 2005. At 20km: EU23: '05- dnf.
Italian 50km walk record 2005.
Progress at 50kmW: 2004- 4:00:51, 2005- 3:41:54. pbs: 20kmW 1:21:38 '06, 30kmW: 2:12:20 '04, 35kmW 2:36:40 '05.
Rapid improvement in 2005 with 3:56:59 in January, 3:49:42 in May and 3:41:54 to win the World bronze medal at the age of 20 in August.

Women

Ester BALASSINI b. 20 Oct 1977 Bologna 1.73m 74kg. Fiamme Gialle.
At HT: OG: '00- dnq, '04- dnq 26; WCh: '01/05- dnq; EC: '98- dnq 20, '02- 6; EU23: '97- 10, '99- 5; ECp: '98-9-00-01-02-03-05: 4/7/6/5/4/4/4; Won MedG 2005, ITA 1998-2002, 2005.
17 Italian hammer records 1998-2005.
Progress at HT: 1996- 46.64, 1997- 56.04, 1998- 61.73, 1999- 64.44, 2000- 66.17, 2001- 68.50, 2002- 68.54, 2003- 70.43, 2004- 71.28, 2005- 73.59, 2006- 72.11. pb DT 38.52.
Formerly a rollerskate dancer. Engaged to Cristiano Andrei (DT 64.49 '03).

Zahra BANI b. 31 Dec 1979 Mogadishu (Somalia) 1.73m 71kg. Fiamme Azzurre Roma.
At JT: WCh: '05- 5; WJ: '98- dnq 26; EU23: '99- 6; WUG: '05- 6, ECp: '05- 3. Italian champion 2005.
Progression: 1995- 39.12, 1996- 43.66, 1997- 47.92, 1998- 51.35, 1999- 53.78, new: 2000- 54.26 2001- 54.98, 2002- 55.34, 2003- 56.50, 2004- 59.10 2005- 62.75.
She was born in Somalia to old colonial family from Livorno/Tuscany. The family went to Italy/Turin in 1989, due to the Somali civil war

Rossella GIORDANO b. 1 Dec 1972 Asti 1.70m 51kg. Fiamme Azzurre Roma.
At 20kmW: OG: '04- 11; WCh: '99- 27, '03- 6 WCp: '02- 9; ECp: '03- 12. At 10kmW: OG: '96- 5; WCh: '95- 6; WCp: '95- 7, '97- 5; ECp: '96- 2 WUG: '93- 4, '95- 2, '97- 2, '99- 2. At 5000mW WJ: '90- 18; EJ: '89- 7, '91- 6. Won ITA 10kmW 1996, 1998.
World record 20,000m track walk (1:30:48.3) 2000
Progress at 10kmW, 20kmW: 1988- 50:42, 1989 50:02, 1990- 48:22, 1991- 48:07, 1992- 46:35.2 1:37:06; 1993- 45:28.1, 1994- 44:20, 1995- 42:26 1996- 42:20, 1997- 41:38, 1:29:12; 1998- 43:21 1999- 43:14, 1:31:02; 2000- 43:36, 1:29:47; 2001 45:18, 1:36:13; 2002- 43:14, 1:31:10; 2003- 43:36.82t 1:29:14; 2004- 44:39, 1:30:28; 2005- 43:51. pbs 3000mW 12:18.16 '96, 5000mW 20:48.11 '97 10,000mW 42:56.9 '96, 1HrW 13.240k '04 (world best).

Magdelin MARTINEZ b. 10 Feb 1976 Camagüey, Cuba 1.78m 63kg. Assindustria Padova.
At TJ: OG: '04- 7; WCh: '01- 4, '03- 3, '05- 8 EC: '02- 6; WJ: '94- 9; PAm: '99- 3; WI: '03- 5 '04- 5; EI: '05- 2; ECp: '02-03-05: 3/2/3. Italian champion 2002.
Five Italian triple jump records 2002-04.
Progress at TJ: 1992- 12.82, 1993- 13.07, 1994 13.60, 1995- 13.74, 1996- 14.13/14.17w, 1997- 13.78/14.96w, 1998- 14.26, 1999- 14.14/14.18w 2000- 14.40, 2001- 14.59, 2002- 14.73, 2003- 14.90, 2004- 15.03/15.24Aw, 2005- 14.69. pb LJ 6.67/6.74w '04.
Changed nationality from Cuba to Italy in 2001 after marrying an Italian, Beppe Picotti in 1999.

Elisa RIGAUDO b. 17 Jun 1980 Cuneo 1.68m 56kg. Fiamme Galle.
At 20kmW: OG: '04- 6; WCh: '03- 10, '05- 7 EU23: '03- 1; WCp: '02-04: 16/5. At 5000mW WJ: '98- 7; EJ: '99-6. Won MedG 20kmW 2005 Italian 5000mW 2004, 20kmW 2004-05.
Progress at 20kmW: 1999- 1:42:40. 2000- 1:32:50 2001- 1:29:54, 2002- 1:30:42, 2003- 1:30:34, 2004- 1:27:49, 2005- 1:29:26. pbs: 3000mW 11:57.00 '04, 12:28.92 '02; 5000mW 20:56.29 '02, 10kmW 43:06.4t '04.

JAMAICA

Governing body: Jamaica Amateur Athletic Association, PO Box 272, Kingston 5. Founded 1932. **2005 Champions**: **Men**: 100m: Asafa Powell 10.04, 200m: Usain Bolt 20.27, 400m: Lansford Spence 44.77, 800m: Aldwyn Sappleton 1:49.40

1500m: Alex Morgan 3:56.70, 5000m/10,000m: Wainard Talbert 15:07.19/31:41.47, 110mh: Maurice Wignall 13.54, 400mh: Kemel Thompson 48.14, HJ: Germaine Mason 2.10, PV: Dwayne Brownr 3.30, LJ: James Beckford 7.63, TJ: Wilbert Walker 16.17, SP: Dorian Scott 18.68, DT: Maurice Smith 52.25. **Women**: 100m/200m: Veronica Campbell 10.97/22.53, 400m: Shericka Williams 50.97, 800m: Kenia Sinclair 2:00.37, 1500m: Nicola Maye 4:39.57, 3000mSt: Mardrea Hyman 9:36.14, 100mh: Delloreen-Ennis-London & Brigitte Foster-Hylton 12.60, 400mh: Debbie Parris 55.45, HJ: Sheree Francis 1.89, LJ: Elva Goulbourne 6.47, TJ: Trecia Smith 14.63, SP: Kim Barrett 16.83, DT: Kesheila Reid 41.13, HT: Nicky Grant 57.88, JT: Olivia McKoy 60.49.

James BECKFORD b. 9 Jan 1975 St Mary 1.83m 73kg. Was a PE student at Blinn JC, USA.
At LJ (TJ): OG: '96- 2, '00- dnq 14, '04- 4; WCh: '95- 2 (6/4R), '97- 4, '01- 7, '03- 2, '05- 9; CG: '02- nj; WI: '97-9-04: 5/5/2; CAG: '98- 1. 2nd GP LJ 1997, 1999 (3rd 1995). Won JAM LJ 1995-8, 2000, 2002, 2004-05; TJ 1995.
Commonwealth records: LJ 1995 & 1997, TJ 1995, Jamaican records: LJ (5), TJ (4) 1994-7.
Progress at LJ, TJ: 1993- 7.53, 15.70; 1994- 8.13/8.29w, 17.29; 1995- 8.45/8.68w, 17.92; 1996- 8.52, 16.43i; 1997- 8.62, 1998- 8.60/8.61w, 16.09; 1999- 8.50, 2000- 8.42, 2001- 8.41, 2002- 8.21/8.25w, 2003- 8.28, 2004- 8.31, 2005- 8.28/8.36w. pbs: 60m 6.79i '04, 100m 10.78 '05.
An outstanding long/triple jumper, now concentrating on the long jump.

Michael BLACKWOOD b. 29 Aug 1976 Kingston 1.90m 79kg. Studied graphic design at Oklahoma University, USA.
At 400m/4x400mR: OG: '00- 3R, '04- 8; WCh: '01- res 3R, '03- 4/2R, '05- sf/res(3)R; CG: '02- 1; WI: '01- 3R, '03- 2R; WCp: '02- 1/1R. Won GP 2002, WAF 2004, JAM 400m 2002-03.
Progress at 400m: 1996- 47.04, 1997- 46.25, 1998- 45.45, 1999- 45.33, 2000- 44.69, 2001- 45.66, 2002- 44.60, 2003- 44.74, 2004- 44.74, 2005- 44.84. pbs: 200m 21.17 '99, 800m 1:50.00 '99.
His sister, Catherine Scott (b. 27 Aug 1973) won 2000 OG silver and 2001 World gold at 4x400m.

Usain BOLT b. 21 Aug 1986 Trelawny 1.96m 86kg. Student.
At 200m/4x100mR: OG: '04- h; WCh: '05- 8; WJ: 02- 1/2R/2R; WY: '01- sf, '03- 1; Won PAm-J: 2003, JAM & CAC 2005.
WJR 200m 2003 & 2004. World U18 200m record 2003.
Progress at 200m, 400m: 2001- 21.81, 48.28; 2002- 20.58, 47.12; 2003- 20.13, 45.35; 2004- 19.93, 2005- 19.99.
In 2002, after running 20.61 to win the CAC U17 200m title, he became the youngest ever male world junior champion at 15y 332d and set a world age best with 20.5, with further age records for 16 and 17 in 2003-04. Won IAAF 'Rising Star' award for men in 2002 and again in 2003. Missed 2006 CG through injury.

Omar O. **BROWN** b. 21 Jun 1982 Trelawny 1.77m 70kg. University of Arkansas, USA.
At 200m/4x100mR: WCh: '05- h; CG: '06- 1; WJ: '00- 4; WY: 2/1R (3 100m).
Progress at 200m: 1998- 21.47, 1999- 21.09, 2000- 20.89, 2003- 21.02i, 2004- 20.66/20.36w, 2005- 20.43, 2006- 20.47. pbs: 60m 6.72i '04, 100m 10.27/10.20w '00, 300m 33.20i '06, 400m 46.00 '05.

Davian CLARKE b. 30 Apr 1976 St Catherine 1.80m 77kg. Was at University of Miami, USA.
At 400m/4x400mR: OG: '96- 7/3R, '00- sf, '04- 6; WCh: '95- sf/2R, '97- sf/3R, '99- 3R, '03- h/2R, '05- 3R; CG: '98- 7/1R, '02- hR, "06- sf/3R; PAm: '99- 1R, '03- 8/1R; WJ: '92/4- 2R; WI: '01-03-04-06: 3R/2R/2 & 1R/4. Won NCAA & Jamaican 1996.
Progress at 400m: 1993- 46.56, 1994- 46.61, 1995- 45.21, 1996- 44.87, 1997- 45.01, 1998- 45.06, 1999- 45,44, 2000- 45.06, 2001- 44.98, 2002- 45.62, 2003- 45.18, 2004- 44.83, 2005- 44.92. pb 200m 20.72 '99, 20.66w '97.
At 19, he was the youngest male medallist at the 1995 World Championships. Ran 43.51 split at 1997 Worlds. Husband of Lucena Golding.

Michael FRATER b. 6 Oct 1982 Manchester 1.70m 67kg. Graduate of Texas Christian University.
At 100m: OG: '04- sf; WCh: '03- sf, '05- 2; CG: '02- sf, '06- sf/1R; PAm: '03- 1; WJ: '00- 5. 2nd NCAA 100m 2003-04.
Progress at 100m: 1999- 10.73/10.47w, 2000- 10.46, 2001- 10.26, 2002- 10.21/10.05w, 2003- 10.13, 2004- 10.06, 2005- 10.03. pbs: 60m 6.64i '02, 200m 20.63, 20.45w '02.
Older brother Lindel was former Jamaican champion, pb 100m 10.07 '00, 9.9w '98.

Dean GRIFFITHS b. 27 Jan 1980 St Andrew 1.80m 72kg. Degree in Management Information Systems from Auburn University, USA.
At 400mh: OG: '04- sf; WCh: '03/05- sf; CG: '06- 6; PAm: '03- 3. Won NCAA 2003, CAC 2005.
Progress at 400mh: 1999- 51.87, 2000- 51.75, 2001- 51.21, 2002- 49.90, 2003- 48.55, 2004- 48.70, 2005- 48.78. pb 400m 46.69 '02.

Danny McFARLANE b. 14 Feb 1972 St Mary 1.85m 81kg. Was at University of Oklahoma, USA.
At 400m/4x400mR: OG: '00- 8/3R; WCh: '93- 7R, '95- sf/2R, '97- 3R, '99- sf/3R, '01- 3R; CG: '02- dnf R; WI: '01- 3/3R, '03- 2R; PAm: '99- 1R. Won CAC 1997, 2001. At 400mh: OG: '04- 2; WCh: '03- 4/2R, '05- sf. Won JAM 400mh 2003-04.
Progress at 400m, 400mh: 1993- 45.82, 1994- 45.74, 1995- 44.90, 1996- 46.18i/46.23, 1997- 45.47, 1998- 45.61, 1999- 45.37, 2000- 45.26, 2001- 45.20A/45.59, 2002- 45.66, 2003- 45.72, 48.30; 2004- 46.86, 48.00, 2005- 48.53. pb 200m 21.17 '95.

Asafa POWELL b. 11 Nov 1982 St Catherine 1.90m 88kg. Sports medicine student at Kingston

University of Technology.
At 100m/4x100mR: OG: '04- 5 (dns 200); WCh: '03- dq; CG: '02- sf/2R, '06- 1/1R; PAm-J: '01- 2R. Won JAM 100m 2003-05, WAF 100m & 200m 2004.
World 100m record, four Jamaican 2004-5, two CAC & Commonwealth 2005.
Progress at 100m, 200m: 2001- 10.50, 2002- 10.12, 20.48; 2003- 10.02/9.9, 2004- 9.87, 20.06; 2005- 9.77, 2006- 10.03. pb 60m 6.56i '04.
Disqualified for false start in World quarters 2003 after fastest time (10.05) in heats. In 2004 he tied the record of nine sub-10 second times in a season and in 2005 he took the world record for 100m at Ostrava. His elder brother Donovan Powell (b. 31 Oct 1971) won the 1996 US indoor 60m and was 6th WI 60m 1999 (pbs 60m 6.51i '96, 100m 10.07/9.7 '95).

Brandon SIMPSON b. 6 Sep 1981 Kingston 1.85m 79kg. Was at Texas Christian University, USA.
At 400m/4x400mR: OG: '04- 5; WCh: '01- 3R, '03- sf/2R, '05- 6/3R; WJ: '00- 2/1R; CAC: '01- 2; PAm-J: '99- 1R. Jamaican champion 2004.
Progress at 400m: 1999- 47.22, 2000- 45.73, 2001- 45.46A/45.68, 2002- 45.11, 2003- 44.84, 2004- 44.76, 2005- 44.70. pb 200m 21.32 '04.
Plans to switch nationality to USA.

Dwight THOMAS b. 23 Sep 1980 Kingston 1.85m 82kg. adidas.
At 100m/4x100mR: OG: '04- sf; WCh: '03- sf, '05- 5; CG: '02- 4=/2R; PAm: '99- 3R; WJ: '98- 3/1R. At 200m: OG: '00- qf/4R. At 60m: WI: '03- sf. At 60mh: WI: '04- 8. Won CAC-J 110mh 1998, PAm-J 100m & 200m 1999, Jamaican 100m & 200m 2002.
Progress at 100m: 1998- 10.38, 1999- 10.37, 2000- 10.12, 2001- 10.19, 2002- 10.15, 2003- 10.19, 2004- 10.12, 2005- 10.00. pbs: 55m 6.27i '01, 60m 6.61i '03, 200m 20.41 '04, 60mh 7.59i '04, 110mh 13.34 '04.

Kemel THOMPSON b. 25 Sep 1974 Kingston 1.80m 75kg. Took masters degree in sports science at Loughborough University, UK, was at South Florida University, USA.
At 400mh: OG: '00- h, '04- sf; WCh: '99- sf, '03- 5, '05- sf; CG: '98- 6, '06- 3; Jamaican champion 1999-2000, 2002, 2005.
Progress at 400mh: 1996- 50.52, 1997- 49.71, 1998- 49.39, 1999- 48.82, 2000- 48.56, 2002- 48.57, 2003- 48.05, 2004- 48.06, 2005- 48.09, 2006- 48.59. pbs: 400m 46.97 '99, 300mh 35.22 '02.
Lived in USA from age 13 and in Britain from 2001.

Maurice WIGNALL b. 17 Apr 1976 St Andrew 1.86m 75kg. Was at George Mason University, USA. Graphic designer.
At 110mh (LJ): OG: '04- 4; WCh: '97- (nj), '01- h, '05- 7; CG: '02- 3, '06- 1; PAm: '99- 7 (6); WUG: '01- 5. At 60mh: WI: '04- 3, '06- 4=. Won JAM 110mh 1997, 1999, 2001-05; LJ 1999.
Four Jamaican records 110mh 2002-04.
Progress at 110mh: 1993- 14.56, 1994- 14.59/14.2, 1995- 13.93, 1996- 13.98, 1997- 13.75, 1999- 13.66, 2000- 13.71, 2001- 13.70, 2002- 13.49, 2003- 13.28, 2004- 13.17, 2005- 13.20, 2006- 13.26. pbs: 60mh 7.48i '04, LJ 8.09 '97.
Formerly a long jumper (won NCAA indoor 1999), now concentrating on hurdling.

Christopher WILLIAMS b. 15 Mar 1972 Manchester 1.78m 68kg. Went to Riverside CC, USA.
At 200m/4x400mR (100m): OG: '00- sf/3R (qf, 4x100m), '04- sf; WCh: '99- sf, '01- 2/3R, '03- qf, '05- sf; CG: '02- dq h/2R, '06- 3/1R; PAm: '99- 7 (3 4x100m), '03- 2; WI: '01- 4; WCp: '02- 2R. Won CAC 1999, JAM 100m 2001, 200m 1999-2001, 2004.
Progress at 200m: 1996- 20.69, 1997- 20.95, 1999- 20.48/20.40w, 2000- 20.02, 2001- 20.11, 2002- 20.84, 2003- 20.54, 2004- 20.34, 2005- 20.19. pbs: 60m 6.61i '01, 100m 10.05/10.04w '00, 400m 46.30 '96.

Women

Aleen BAILEY b. 25 Nov 1980 St Mary 1.70m 64g. Student at University of South Carolina.
At 100m/(200m)/4x100mR: OG: '04- 5/4/1R, WCh: '01- (h), '03- 6, '05- sf/2R; WJ: '96- 2R, '98- 3R; PAmJ: '99- 1/1. Won NCAA 100m & 200m (and indoor 200m) 2003, Jamaican 100m & 200m 2001, 2003.
Progresion at 100m, 200m: 1995- 12.10, 1996- 11.67, 23.99; 1997- 11.60/11.55w, 23.65; 1998- 11.37, 23.96/23.16w, 1999- 11.41, 23.37; 2000- 11.47/11.38w, 23.45/22.86w; 2001- 11.14, 22.59; 2002- 11.33, 22.54; 2003- 11.07, 22.59; 2004- 11.04, 22.33; 2005- 11.07, 23.00/22.75w. pb 60m 7.23i '03.

Sheri-Ann BROOKS b. 11 Feb 1983 Manchester 1.70m 64kg. Zion TC. Florida International University.
At (100m)/200m/4x100mR: WCh: '05- h; CG: '06- 1/5/1R. Won NCAA 200m 2005.
Progress at 100m, 200m: 2003- 11.85, 2004- 11.52, 24.11/23.98w; 2005- 11.24/11.23w, 22.80/22.74w; 2006- 11.19, 23.07. pbs: 55m 6.75i '05, 60m 7.29i '05.

Veronica CAMPBELL b. 15 May 1982 Trelawny 1.63m 61kg. Student at University of Arkansas, USA.
At 100m/4x100mR (200m): OG: '00- 2R, '04- 3/1/1R; WCh: '05- 2/4/2R; CG: '02- 2/2R, '06- (2); WJ: '98- qf, '00- 1/2R (1); WY: '99- 1/1R. Won WAF 100m 2004-05, 200m 2004, CAC-J 100m 2000, JAM 100m 2002, 2004-05; 200m 2004-05.
Progress at 100m, 200m: 1999- 11.49, 23.73; 2000- 11.12/11.1, 22.87; 2001- 11.13/22.92; 2002- 11.00, 22.39; 2004- 10.91, 22.05; 2005- 10.85, 22.35/22.29w. pbs: 60m 7.04i '06, 400m 52.24i '05.
In 2000 became the first woman to become World Junior champion at both 100m and 200m. Unbeaten at 200m in 28 finals (42 races in all) from 11 March 2000 to 22 July 2005 (lost to

Alyson Felix).

Vonette DIXON b. 26 Nov 1975 Hanover 1.70m 62kg. Graduate of Auburn University, USA.
At 100mh: WCh: '01- 8, '03- 9, '05- sf; CG: '02- 2.
Progress at 100mh: 1994- 15.13/15.0, 1995- 14.29, 1996- 13.52/13.30w, 1997- 13.26, 1998- 13.52, 1999- 13.40, 2000- 12.90, 2001- 12.83, 2002- 12.83/12.82w, 2003- 12.72, 2004- 12.76, 2005- 12.67. pbs: 55m 6.79i '00, 60m 7.33i '00, 100m 11.47/11.40w '00, 200m 23.57/23.48w '00, 50mh 6.85i '02, 55mh 7.55i '00, 60mh 7.92i '02.

Delloreen ENNIS-LONDON b. 5 Mar 1975 St Catherine 1.78m 67kg. née Ennis. Business management graduate of Abilene Christian University, USA.
At 100mh: OG: '00- 4, '04- sf; WCh: '99- 7, '05- 2; CG: '06- 3; WJ: '92- sf. 3rd GP 2000. Jamaican champion 1999-2001, 2004, 2005 (tie); CAC 2003. CAC 100mh record 2000.
Progress at 100mh: 1992- 13.81, 1994- 13.96, 1996- 13.53/13.30w, 1997- 13.60/13.51w, 1998- 13.27/13.1w, 1999- 12.71/12.60w, 2000- 12.52, 2001- 12.57, 2003- 12.70, 2004- 12.51, 2005- 12.57. pbs: 60m 7.39i '99, 100m 11.50 '99, 11.30w '04; 55mh 7.56i '99, 60mh 7.92i '04, 400mh 62.75 '98.
Coached by her husband Lincoln London.

Lorraine FENTON b. 8 Sep 1973 Mandeville 1.74m 59kg. née Graham. Graduated in criminal justice from Lincoln University, USA.
At 400m/4x400mR: OG: '00- 2/2R; WCh: '97- sf/3R, '99- 3, '01- 2/1R, '03- 2/3R, '05- sf/2R; CG: '02- dnf R. Won JAM 400m 1997, 1999-2003. Won GP 2000 (2nd 2002).
Progress at 400m: 1994- 53.31, 1995- 53.63, 1996- 51.85, 1997- 50.69, 1998- 50.23, 1999- 49.92, 2000- 49.58, 2001- 49.88, 2002- 49.30, 2003- 49.43, 2005- 50.95. pbs: 100m 11.73 '99, 200m 22.63 '01, 300m 36.00+ '00.
Missed 2004 season with a thigh injury.

Brigitte FOSTER-HYLTON b. 7 Nov 1974 St Elizabeth 1.70m 62kg. Was at Southwest Texas State University, USA.
At 100mh: OG: '00- 8, '04- sf; WCh: '01- sf, '03- 2, '05- 3; CG: '98- 5/2R, '02- dns, '06- 1; PAm: '03- 1; WCp: '02- 2; 2nd GP 2002. JAM champion 2002-03, 2005 (tie). At 60mh: WI: '03- 6.
Three CAC 100mh records 2002-03.
Progress at 100mh: 1993- 14.22, 1996- 13.34, 1998- 13.19/13.13w/12.9w, 1999- 13.35, 2000- 12.70, 2001- 12.70, 2002- 12.49, 2003- 12.45, 2004- 12.56, 2005- 12.55, 2006- 12.65. pbs: 60m 7.32i '04; 100m 11.17 '03, 200m 23.51/23.35w '98, 400m 53.84 '05, 60mh 7.96i '03, 400mh 64.62 '93.

Michelle FREEMAN b. 5 May 1969 St Catherine 1.70m 63kg. Was at University of Florida, now assistant coach at University of Texas.
At 100mh/4x100mR: OG: '92- qf, '96- 6/R, '00- qf; WCh: '91- sf, '93- 7/3R, '95- sf/res R (2), '97- 3; CG: '94- 1; WJ: '88- h (sf 100m); PAm: '91- 5. At 100m: CG: '90- h. At 60mh: WI: '93/5/7/01- dnf/7/1/2. Won JAM 100mh 1991-4, 1997; NCAA 1992. Won GP 100mh 1998 (3rd 1992), 3rd overall 1996.
WIR 55mh 1992. Eight JAM 100mh records 1990-8, inc. five Commonwealth 1992-8 and four CAC 1996-8.
Progress at 100mh: 1988- 13.70, 1989- 13.61/13.4, 1990- 13.18/13.09w, 1991- 12.98, 1992- 12.75, 1993- 12.77, 1994- 12.93/12.74w, 1995- 12.98, 1996- 12.57, 1997- 12.52/12.40w, 1998- 12.52, 2000- 12.57, 2001- 12.89, 2004- 13.03. pbs: 55m 6.66i '93, 60m 7.12i '98, 100m 11.16 '93, 11.13w '92; 200m 22.87 '92, 50mh 6.75i '96, 55mh 7.34i '92, 60mh 7.74i '98.
Had to withdraw from 1988 Olympic team through injury. Missed 1999 season due to multiple stress fractures in her left shin. Daughter Tamya born December 2003.

Lacena GOLDING-CLARKE b. 20 Mar 1975 Clarendon 1.68m 57kg. Was at Auburn University, USA.
At 100mh/4x100mR: OG: '04- 5; WCh: '03- 8; CG: '02- 1, '06- 4; PAm: '03- 3/3R. At LJ: OG: '96- dnq; WCh: '95- dnq 20, '97- dnq 18; CG: '98- 4; WJ: '92- 6, '94- 8; CAG: '98- 1; CAC: '99- 1; PAm-J '93- 1. At 60mh: WI: '01-03-04-06: 8/4/6/6; Won JAM LJ 1994, 1996-9.
Progress at 100mh: 1994- 13.98, 1995- 13.22/13.19w/13.0w, 1997- 13.05/13.04w, 1998- 13.00, 1999- 13.11, 2000- 12.93, 2001- 12.97, 2002- 12.74/12.70w, 2003- 12.72, 2004- 12.69, 2005- 12.68/12.67w. pbs: 55m 6.89i '97, 100m 11.69/11.64w '97, 200m 23.99 '98, 50mh 6.83i '00, 55mh 7.37Ai '98, 60mh 7.83i '06, HJ 1.71i '94, 1.70 '95; LJ 6.87 '98, TJ 12.03 '98, JT 41.02 '95, Hep 5750 '98.
Married to 400m runner **Davian Clarke**.

Elva GOULBOURNE b. 21 Jan 1980 St Ann 1.70m 50kg. Was at Auburn University, USA.
At LJ/4x100mR: OG: '00- 10; WCh: '01- 10 (3 res R), '03- dnq 20, '05- 12; CG: '02- 1/2R, '06- 9; PAm: '99- 3. Won PAm-J 1997/99, CAC-J 1998, CAC 2001, 2003; JAM 2000-05, NCAA 2002-03.
Commonwealth indoor LJ record 2002.
Progress at LJ: 1997- 6.10, 1998- 6.47, 1999- 6.49, 2000- 6.74/6.79w, 2001- 6.86/6.90w, 2002- 6.91i/6.82/6.87w, 2003- 6.83/6.96w, 2004- 7.16A/6.62, 2005- 6.64/6.81w. pbs: 55m 6.73i '03, 60m 7.23i '03, 100m 11.20 '03, 200m 22.98 '03, TJ 13.78i '03.

Korene HINDS b. 18 Jan 1976 Spanish Town 1.63m 54kg. Post-graduate degree in education from Kansas State University, USA.
At 3000mSt: WCh: '05- 4.
Five CAC 3000m steeplechase records 2002-05.
Progress at 3000mSt: 2002- 9:58.9, 2003- 10:00.44, 2004- 9:50.64, 2005- 9:30.12. pbs: 600m 1:29.43 '98, 800m 2:03.72 '00, 1500m 4:17.00 '02, 1M 4:40.78i '01, 3000m 9:08.55i '03, 9:10.10 '00.
Ran in 1991 World CC as a 15 year-old. First ran the steeplechase in 2002. Lives in Albuquerque.

Mardrea HYMAN b. 22 Dec 1972 Clarendon 1.68m 52kg. Graduated in kinesiology from UTEP, USA.
At 3000mSt: WCh: '05- 8; CG: '06- 9. At 1500m (800m): OG: '00- sf; WCh: '01- 10; CG: '98- (4), 02- 6; CAG: '98- 1 (3); WCp: '02- 9. Won JAM 800m 1996, 1998, 1500m 1996-8, 2001-02, 2004, 3000mSt 2005.
Two CAC 3000m steeplechase records 2005.
Progress at 1500m, 3000mSt: 1993- 4:34.7, 1994- 4:17.8, 1995- 4:25.8, 1996- 4:19.98, 1997- 4:17.00, 1998- 4:18.53, 1999- 4:22.61, 2000- 4:09.83, 2001- 4:05.25, 2002- 4:06.80, 2003- 4:06.36, 2004- 4:11.55, 2005- 4:07.96, 9:27.21. pbs: 800m 1:59.71 '98, 1000m 2:39.08 '01, 1500m 4:05.25 '01, 1M 4:33.90 '00, 3000m 9:17.83 '00, 2M 9:49.32 '02, 5000m 16:02.41 '00.
After a useful middle-distance career took up steeplechasing with great success in 2005.

Sherone SIMPSON b. 12 Aug 1984 Manchester, Jamaica 1.60m 50kg. Kingston University of Technology.
At 100m/(200m)/4x100mR: OG: '04- 6/1R; WCh: '05- 6/2R; CG: '06- (1)/1R; WJ: '02- 1R; PAm-J: '03- 2.
Progress at 100m, 200m: 2002- 11.60, 24.21; 2003- 11.37/11.1, 23.60; 2004- 11.01, 22.70; 2005- 10.97, 22.54; 2006- 22.59. pbs: 400m 53.24 '06, 100mh 14.10 '02.

Kenia SINCLAIR b. 14 July 1980 St Catherine 1.67m 54kg. Was at Seton Hall University, USA.
At 800m: WCh: '05- sf; CG: '06- 2; WI: '06- 2. Jamaican champion 2005.
Three Jamaican 800m records 2005.
Progress at 800m: 2002- 2:05.26i/2:07.39, 2003- 2:03.21, 2005- 1:58.88, 2006- 1:58.16. pbs: 1000m 2:37.37 '05, 1500m 4:07.11 '05, 1M 4:32.33i '05, 3000m 9:52.71i '02.
Based in Gainesville, Florida.

Trecia-Kaye SMITH b. 5 Nov 1975 Westmoreland 1.85m 77kg. Graduated in physiotherapy from University of Pittsburgh, USA.
At TJ: OG: '04- 4; WCh: '97- dnq 31, '01- 8, '05- 1; CG: '02- 3, '06- 1; WI: '04- 4, '06- 4; WCp: '02- 4. At LJ: WJ: '94- 11. Won NCAA LJ 1997, 1999; TJ 1998; JAM TJ 2001-02, 2004-05.
Commonwealth triple jump record 2004. Six Jamaican records 1997-2004.
Progress at TJ: 1996- 13.55/13.58w, 1997- 14.22, 1998- 14.05i/13.98, 1999-14.02i/13.91/13.95w, 2000- 13.76/13.92w, 2001- 14.12A/14.88w, 2002- 14.32, 2003- 13.96i/13.55/13.89w, 2004- 15.16, 2005- 15.11. pbs: 200m 24.39 '97, 60mh 8.10i '98, 100mh 14.48 '97, 14.36w '99; HJ 1.81 '97, LJ 6.74 '01, 6.84w '97; SP 14.74 '98, DT 44.20 '98, JT 44.52 '98, Pen 4080i '99, Hep 5931 '97.
Set national TJ records of 14.57 in qualifying and 14.70 and 14.71 in final at 2004 World Indoors and outdoors improved from 14.34 to 15.16.

Novlene WILLIAMS b. 26 Apr 1982 St Ann 1.67m 55kg. Studied recreation at University of Florida, USA.
At 400m/4x400mR: OG: '04- sf/3R; WCh: '05 2R; CG: '06- 3; PAm: '03- 6/2R; WI: '06- 5.
Progress at 400m: 1999- 55.62, 2000- 53.90, 2001 54.99, 2002- 52.05, 2003- 51.93, 2004- 50.59, 2005 51.09, 2006- 51.03. pbs: 200m 24.08 '04.

JAPAN

Governing body: Nippon Rikujo-Kyog Renmei, 1-1-1 Jinnan, Shibuya-Ku, Tokyo 150 8050. Founded 1911.
National Championships first held in 191 (men), 1925 (women). **2005 Champions**: **Men** 100m: Shinya Saburi 10.40, 200m: Shinji Takahir 20.89, 400m: Yuzo Kanemaru 45.86, 800m: Yoshihiro Shimodaira 1:48.54, 1500m: Fumikazu Kobayashi 3:40.15, 5000m: Tomohiro Seto 13:51.42 10,000m: Yu Mitsuya 28:09.89, Ma: Toshinar Takaoka 2:07:41, 3000mSt: Yoshitaka Iwamiz 8:32.41, 110mh: Satoru Tanigawa 13.61, 400mh Dai Tamesue 49.27, HJ: Naoyuki Daigo 2.18, PV Satoru Yasuda 5.40, LJ: Shin-ichi Terano 7.78, TJ Kazuyoshi Ishikawa 16.92, SP: Satoshi Hatas 17.93, DT: Shigeo Hatakeyama 54.25, HT: Koj Murofushi 76.47, JT: Yukifumi Murakami 79.79 Dec: Hiromasa Tanaka 7477, 20kmW: Takyuk Tanii 1:21:06, 50kmW: Yuki Yamazaki 3:50:40 **Women**: 100m: Tomoko Ishida 11.84, 200m Sakie Nobuoka 23.64, 400m: Asami Tanno 51.93 800m: Miho Sugimori 2:00.45, 1500m: Yurik Kobayashi 4:14.55, 5000m/10,000m: Kayok Fukushi 15:15.27/31:30.82, Mar: Naok Takahashi 2:24:39, 100m/LJ: Kumiko Iked 13.47/6.69, 400mh: Rika Sakurai 57.99, HJ: Yok Hannicutt 1.86, PV: Takayo Kondo 4.10, TJ Fumiyo Yoshida 13.28, SP: Yoko Toyonaga 16.69 DT/HT: Yuka Murofushi 54.88/61.61, JT Harumi Yamamoto 52.85, Hep: Yuki Nakat 5905, 20kmW: Mayumi Kawasaki 1:31:51.

Shigeru ABURAYA b. 8 Feb 1977 Yamaguch pref. 1.63m 52kg. Chugoku Electric Power.
At Mar: OG: '04- 5; WCh: '01- 5, '03- 5; JPN champion 2001. At HMar: WCh: '99- 23.
Progress at Mar: 2000- 2:10:48, 2001- 2:07:52 2003- 2:09:26, 2004- 2:13:11. pbs: 5000m 13:39.3 '02, 10,000m 28:13.76 '00, HMar 61:54 '02.
2nd Tokyo marathon 2003. Three consecutive fifths in global marathons.

Koji MUROFUSHI b. 8 Oct 1974 Shizuoka 1.87m 97kg. Graduate of Chukyo University. Mizuno.
At HT: OG: '00- 9, '04- 1; WCh: '95- dnq, '97- 10 '99- dnq 14, '01- 2, '03- 3; WJ: '92- 8; AsiG: '94- 2 '98- 1, '02- 1; AsiC: '93-5-8-02: 2/2,/2/1; WCp '02- 2 (9 DT). Won GWG 2001, GP 2002 (2nd 2000) Won E.Asian 1997, 2001; Japanese 1995-2005.
18 Japanese hammer records 1998-2003, Asian records 2001 & 2003.
Progress at HT: 1991- 61.76, 1992- 66.30, 1993- 68.00, 1994- 69.54, 1995- 72.32, 1996- 73.82 1997- 75.72, 1998- 78.57, 1999- 79.17, 2000- 81.08 2001- 83.47, 2002- 83.33, 2003- 84.86, 2004- 83.15,

2005- 76.47. pb DT 44.64 '96.

His father Shigenobu Murofushi won a record five Asian Games gold medals 1970-86 and held the Japanese hammer record with 75.96 (Los Angeles 1984) until Koji broke it for the first time on 26 Apr 1998. His mother was a Romanian javelin thrower. His sister **Yuka** (b. 11 Feb 77) holds Japanese records: DT 56.84 '99 and HT 67.77 '04. 6th WJ DT 1996.

Kenji NARISAKO b. 25 Jul 1984 1.85m 74kg. Student at University of Tsukuba.

At 400mh: WCh: '05- sf; WJ: '02- h; WY: '01- 3; WUG: '05- 1.

Progress at 400mh: 2001- 51.33, 2002- 51.49, 2003- 50.53, 2004- 48.54, 2005- 48.09. pbs: 400m 46.02 '05, 110mh 14.77/14.62w '02.

Tsuyoshi OGATA b. 11 May 1973 Arusha 1.65m 50kg. Chugoko Electric Power.

At Mar: WCh: '03- 12, '05- 3.

Progress at Mar: 1999- 2:15:22, 2000- 2:11:43, 2002- 2:09:15, 2003- 2:08:37, 2004- 2:10:56, 2005- 2:11:16. pbs: 3000m 8:01.86 '04, 5000m 13:31.46 '03, 10,000m 28:05.76 '04, HMar 61:50 '02.

Won Fukuoka marathon 2004.

Daichi SAWANO b. 16 Sep 1980 1.82m 68kg. Nishi Sports. Was at Nihon University.

At PV: OG: '04- 13=; WCh: '03- dns, '05- 8; AsiC: '02- 1, '05- 1; WCp: '02- nh. JPN champion 1999-2000, 2003-04.

Three Japanese pole vault records 2003-05.

Progress at PV: 1994- 3.80, 1995- 4.30, 19960 4.80, 1997- 5.25, 1998- 5.40, 1999- 5.50, 2000- 5.45, 2001- 5.52, 2002- 5.51, 2003- 5.75, 2004- 5.80, 2005- 5.83.

Shingo SUETSUGU b. 2 Jun 1980 Kumamoto pref. 1.78m 68kg. Mizuno. Was at Tokai University.

At 200m/4x100mR (100m): OG: '00- sf, '04- (qf)/4R; WCh: '01- sf, '03- 3, '05- sf; AsiG: '02- 1/2R; AsiC: '05- (2). Won E.Asian 2001, JPN 100m 2003-04; 200m 2001, 2003.

Asian 200m record 2003.

Progress at 100m, 200m: 1996- 10.63, 21.62; 1997- 10.52, 21.37; 1998- 10.37, 21.08; 1999- 10.46, 21.36; 2000- 10.19, 20.26; 2001- 10.31, 20.30; 2002- 10.05, 20.37; 2003- 10.03, 20.03; 2004- 10.10, 2005- 10.15, 20.55. pb 400m 45.99 '02.

Toshinari TAKAOKA b. 24 Sep 1970 Yamashiro, Kyoto 1.86m 64kg. Kanebo. Graduate of Ryukoku University.

At 10,000m (/5000m): OG: '96- h, '00- 7/15; WCh: '93- (h), '97- dns, '99- 12/h, '01- 15; AsiG: '94- 1/1, AsiC: '98- (1); WUG: '93- (3). At Mar: WCh: '05- 4. Won E.Asian 5000m 2001, JPN 5000m 2002, 10,000m 1996, 1999; Mar 2005.

Asian records 5000m 1998, 10,000m 2001, marathon 2002. Japanese records: 3000m 1999, 5000m 1992 (13:20.43) and 1998

Progress at 5000m, 10,000m, Mar: 1986- 14:53.7, 1987- 14:58.4, 1988- 15:00.09, 1989- 14:40.6, 1990- 14:25.55, 30:50.15; 1991- 13:57.4, 1992- 13:20.43, 1993- 13:23.98, 28:28.1; 1994- 13:33.31, 27:59.72; 1995- 13:54.66, 1996- 13:45.52, 27:49.89; 1997- 13:27.56, 27:53.03; 1998- 13:13.40, 27:50.08; 1999- 13:21.08, 27:53.37; 2000- 13:15.34, 27:40.44; 2001- 13:38.87, 27:35.09, 2:09:41; 2002- 13:29.77, 28:17.29, 2:06:16; 2003- 13:24.66, 28:03.62, 2:07:59; 2004- 13:45.90, 28:00.90, 2:07:50; 2005- 13:37.40, 28:04.80, 2:07:41; 2006- 2:09:31. pbs: 1500m 3:40.20 '99, 3000m 7:41.87 '99, HMar 61:07 '03, 30000m 1:29:23 '01.

After a successful track career, he was third in his first four marathons: Fukuoka 2001 and 2003, Chicago 2002 and 2004 before winning at Tokyo 2005 (2nd 2006).

Dai TAMESUE b. 3 May 1978 Hiroshima pref. 1.70m 67kg. Graduate of Hosei University.

At 400mh: OG: '00- h, '04- sf; WCh: '01- 3, '03- sf, '05- 3; AsiG: '02- 3. Japanese champion 2001-05. At 400m: WJ: '96- 4/2R.

Two Japanese records 2001.

Progress at 400mh: 1996- 49.09, 1998- 49.19, 1999- 49.12, 2000- 48.47, 2001- 47.89, 2002- 48.69, 2003- 48.94, 2004- 48.46, 2005- 48.10. pbs: 200m 21.23 '96, 400m 45.94 '96.

One of the shortest ever top-class 400m hurdlers. Has set national records at each age group.

Women

Masako CHIBA b. 18 Jul 1976 Uji City, Kyoto pref. 1.56m 39kg. Toyota Industries.

At 10,000m: OG: '96- 5; WCh: 97- 3. At Mar: '03- 3. World CC: '95- 16J. Won E.Asian 10,000m 1997.

World half marathon record 1999, Japanese 10,000m record 1996.

Progress at 5000m, 10,000m. Mar: 1993- 16:15.6, 1994- 16:01.1, 1995- 15:52.4, 31:43.7; 1996- 15:20.13, 31:20.46; 1997- 15:20.58, 31:31.85; 1998- 2:37:44, 1999- 15:29.65, 31:38.02, 2:29:00; 2001- 2:30:39, 2002- 2:25:11, 2003- 2:21:45, 2004- 2:26:50, 2005- 2:25:46. pbs: 3000m 9:20.50 '95, HMar 66:43 '97.

Ran a 30:55 leg for 10k in the International Chiba Ekiden 1996. Her 66:43 half marathon at Tokyo in January 1997 was just 4 secs off the fastest ever mark, by Ingrid Kristiansen, which was not able to be accepted as a world best. Chiba passed 20km in a world best 63:14. Won Hokkaido Marathon 2004-05, 2nd Rotterdam 2002, Osaka 2003-04; 3rd Chicago 2005.

Kayoko FUKUSHI b. 25 Mar 1982 Aiomori pref. 1.61m 45kg. Wacoal.

At 5000m/(10,000m): OG: '04- (26); WCh: '03- h/11, '05- 12/11; WJ: '00- 4. AsiG: '02- 2/2; World CC: '02- 15, '06- 6. Won JPN 5000m 2002, 2004-05; 10,000m 2002-05.

World 15km record & Asian half marathon record 2006, Japanese records: 3000m 2002, 5000m (4) 2002-05.

Progress at 5000m, 10,000m: 1998- 16:56.35, 1999- 16:38.69, 35:37.54; 2000- 15:29.70, 2001- 15:10.23, 31:42.05; 2002- 14:55.19, 30:51.81; 2003- 15:09.02, 31:10.57; 2004- 14:57.73, 31:05.68; 2005- 14:53.22, 31:03.75. pbs: 3000m 8:44.40 '02, 15km 46:55 '06,

HMar 67:26 '06.
Set Japanese junior records at 3000m, 5000m and 10,000m in 2001.

Yumiko HARA b. 9 Jan 1982 Tochigi prefecture 1.63m 43kg. Kyocera.
At Mar: WCh: '05- 6.
Progress at 10,000m, Mar: 1999- 33:13.99, 2000- 34:02.90, 2001- 31:48.50, 2002- 32:31.59, 2003- 31:51.80, 2004- 32:15.86, 2005- 31:24.33, 2:24:19. pbs: 5000m 15:38.81 '04, HMar 69:28 '02.
Won at Nagoya in 2005 on marathon debut.

Harumi HIROYAMA b. 2 Sep 1968 Tokushima pref. 1.60m 47kg. née Suzuki. Graduate of Kokushikan University. Shiseido.
At Mar: WCh: '05- 8; AsiG: '02- 2. At 10,000m: OG: '00- 20, '04- 18; WCh: '99- 4. At 5000m: OG: '96- h; WCh: '97- 8. At 3000m: WCh: '93- h (h 1500m); AsiG: '94- 2. Won E.Asian 5000m 1997, JPN 1500m 1992, 3000m 1992-3, 10,000m 1997, 1999, Mar 2000.
Japanese records: 1500m 1992 and 1994, 3000m (2) 1994, 5000m 1997 and 1998.
Progress at 5000m, 10,000m, Mar: 1990- 17:18.21, 1991- 16:55.0, 2:51:36; 1993- 15:30.78, 1994- 15:33.53, 1995- 15:28.17, 32:03.35; 1996- 15:09.69, 31:43.99; 1997- 15:07.75, 31:22.72; 1998- 15:03.67, 2:28:12; 1999- 15:21.04, 31:26.84; 2000- 15:20.36, 31:59.60, 2:22:56; 2001- 15:29.73, 31:39.80, 2:29:01; 2002- 2:24:34, 2003- 15:31.78, 31:32.27; 2004- 15:25.70, 31:34.08, 2:31:07; 2005- 15:42.52, 31:24.79, 2:25:46; 2006- 2:23:26. pbs: 800m 2:06.19 '94, 1500m 4:11.10 '94, 3000m 8:50.40 '94, HMar 69:41 '01.
Won Nagoya marathon 2006 (3rd 1998), 2nd Osaka 2000 and 2002 (3rd 2005). Married to Tsutomu Hiroyama (b. 22 Oct 1966, Mar pb 2:11:37 '90).

Mizuki NOGUCHI b. 3 Jul 1978 Ise, Mie pref. 1.50m 41kg. Globary.
At 10,000m: WCh: '01- 13. At Mar: OG: '04- 1; WCh: '03- 2. World HMar: '99-00-01-02: 2/4/4/9. Won Asian CC 1999, E.Asian HMar 2001, JPN Mar 2003.
Asian marathon record 2005. World road records 25km 1:22:12 & 30km 1:38:48 in 2005 Berlin Marathon.
Progress at 10,000m, Mar: 1999- 33:09.98, 2000- 32:05.23, 2001- 31:51.13, 2002- 31:50.18, 2:25:35; 2003- 31:59.28, 2:21:18; 2004- 31:21.03, 2:26:20, 2005- 31:44.29, 2:19:12. pbs: 3000m 9:24.51 '98, 5000m 15:34.36 '99, Rd: 15km 48:11 '01, HMar 67:43 '06, 30km 1:39:09 '04.
Formerly excelling at half marathon, she won the Nagoya marathon on debut in 2002 and won again at Osaka in January 2003, at the Olympics in 2004 and in Berlin 2005.

Mari OZAKI b. 16 Jul 1975 Hirakata, Osaka pref. 1.62m 48kg. Noritz.
At 10,000m: WCh: '01- 19, '05- 15. Won JPN 5000m 2003.
Progress at 10,000m, Mar: 1999- 31:58.05, 2000- 32:03.00, 2001- 31:50.56, 2002- 32:44.9, 2003 31:46.57, 2:23:30, 2004- 31:47.47, 2005- 31:34.15 2:23:59. pbs: 3000m 8:59.4 '00, 5000m 15:12.7 '03, HMar 69:33 '02.
Ran 2:23:30 for fifth on debut at Osaka 200 (fifth fastest ever debut) and was second a Osaka 2005 in her second marathon.

Naoko SAKAMOTO b. 14 Nov 1980 Hyog pref. 1.60m 44kg. Tenmaya.
At Mar: OG: '04- 7; WCh: '03- 4.
Progress at Mar: 2003- 2:21:51, 2004- 2:25:29 pbs: 3000m 9:33.93 '98, 5000m 15:45.75 '02 10,000m 33:06.17 '03, HMar 69:27 '01.
Ran 2:21:51 for third on debut at Osaka 200 and won at Osaka 2004 in her third marathon.

Yoko SHIBUI b. 14 Mar 1979 Kuroiso, Tochig pref. 1.65m 48kg. Mitsui-Sumitomo.
At Mar: WCh: '01- 4. At 10,000m: WCh: '03- 14. Japanese records 10,000m 2002, Marathon 2004
Progress at 10,000m, Mar: 1997- 33:53.20, 1999- 32:43.02, 2000- 31:48.89, 2001- 31:48.73, 2:23:11 2002- 30:48.89, 2:21:22; 2003- 31:42.01, 2004 32:17.72, 2:19:41; 2005- 32:34.11, 2:27:40; 2006- 2:23:58. pbs: 3000m 9:11.37 '96, 5000m 15:18.9 '02, 15km 49:07 '02, HMar 69:17+ '02.
Ran the fastest ever debut marathon by a woma with 2:23:11 to win at Osaka in January 2001 Her breakthrough came with a 31:59 ekide road relay leg in January 2000 and she had shown brilliant form with 10km legs of 31:0 and 31:11 in November 2000. She was third in the 2002 Chicago Marathon and returned from injuries to win the Berlin Marathon in 2004 in 2:19:41. 2nd Nagoya 2006.

Naoko TAKAHASHI b. 6 May 1972 Gifu 1.63m 46kg. Skynet Asia Airlines. Graduate of Osaka Gakuin University.
At Mar: OG: '00- 1; AsiG: '98- 1. At 5000m: WCh: '97- 13. Won JPN marathon 1998, 2005.
World marathon record 2001, Asian and two Japanese records 1998.
Progress at 10,000m, Mar: 1994- 34:02.02, 1996- 31:48.23, 1997- 32:34.50, 2:31:32; 1998- 31:55.95, 2:21:47; 2000- 2:22:19, 2001- 2:19:46, 2002- 2:21:49, 2003- 2:27:21, 2005- 2:24:39. pbs: 800m 2:11.73 '94, 1500m 4:22.89 '94, 3000m 9:13.00 '94, 5000m 15:21.15 '98, HMar 68:55 '00.
Made her marathon debut with 7th at Osaka in 1997 and then had six successive marathon wins until second in Tokyo 2003. The two-year break until winning Tokyo 2005. After graduating from University she joined the Recruit team coached by Yoshio Koide and later followed him to the Sekisui team. In 1998 she set national records, 2:25:48 at Nagoya in March, and then a superb 2:21:47, on her own all the way and despite slowing in intense heat and humidity, to win the Asian Games gold medal in December. Withdrew, injured, from 1999 World Champs on the eve of the race, but returned with 2:22:19 (69:39 second half) to win at Nagoya in March 2000 and later

took the Olympic gold in great style. She won at Berlin in 2001, when she became the first women to break 2:20, and in 2002.

Reiko TOSA b. 11 Jun 1976 Ehime pref. 1.67m 45kg. Mitsui Sumitomo. Graduate of Matsuyama University.

At Mar: OG: '04- 5; WCh: '01- 2. Japanese champion 2004. At HMar: WCh: '99- 5.

Progress at Mar: 1998- 2:54:57, 2000- 2:24:36, 2001- 2:26:06, 2002- 2:22:46, 2004- 2:23:57. pbs: 3000m 9:43.00 '98, 5000m 15:37.08 '00, 10,000m 32:15.63 '00, HMar 69:36 '99.

Won Nagoya Marathon 2004, 2nd Nagoya (2:24:36) and Tokyo (2:24:47) 2000; 4th London 2002.

KAZAKHSTAN

Governing body: Athletic Federation of the Republic of Kazakhstan, Abai Street 48, 480072 Almaty. Founded 1959.

2005 National Champions: Men: 100m/200m: Vyacheslav Muravyov 10.46/21.21, 400m: Denis Rypakov 47.74, 800m: Grigoriy Aksenov 1:51.50, 1500m: Mikhail Kolganov 3:54.47, 5000m: Artyom Zhigalov 15:06.0, 10,000m: Takhir Mamashayev 32:11.9, HMar: Serek Azimbayev 74:55, 3000mSt: Andrey Konyushak 9:37.24, 110mh: Oleg Normatov UZB 14.50, 400mh: Yevgeniy Meleshenko 49.49, HJ: Sergey Zasimovich 2.12, PV: Artyom Pilipenko 5.40, LJ: Zhandos Akhmedov 7.61, TJ: Roman Valiyev 16.60, SP: Sergey Rubtsov 16.20, DT: Yevgeniy Labutov 54.03, JT: Yaroslav Yeliseyev 54.71, Dec: Pavel Dubitskiy 7553, 20000mW: Rustam Kuvatov 1:33:23.8. **Women:** 100m: Natalya Ivoninskaya 11.85w, 200m/400m: Anna Gavryushenko 24.21/53.89, 800m: Viktoriya Yalovtseva 2:04.12, 1500m: Svetlana Lukasheva 4:19.84, 5000m: Galina Kirilyuk KGZ 18:31.3, 10,000m: Zharkynay Kolisenova 41:51.9, HMar: Rashida Sarbassova 81:28, 100mh: Natalya Ivoninskaya 13.48, 400mh: Natalya Alimzhanova 56.70, HJ: Svetlana Stavskaya 1.85, PV: Viktoriya Loshankova 3.50, LJ: Olga Rypakova 6.36, TJ: Yelena Parfenova 14.23, SP: Iolanta Ulyeva 16.01, DT: Kseniya Shkirenko 38.80, HT: Natalya Kozylenkova 45.37, JT: Olga Sasonova 43.23, Hep: Yuliya Mishutina 4937, 10,000mW: Anna Makovosova 55:35.20.

Dmitriy KARPOV b. 23 Jul 1981 Karaganda 1.98m 92kg.

At Dec: OG: '04- 3; WCh: '03- 3, '05- dnf; WJ: '00- 4; AsiG: '02- 2; won E.Asian 2001. At Hep: WI: '04- 4. At 110mh: AsiC: '02- 5. Won KAZ 200m 2003, Dec 1999.

Two Asian decathlon records 2004.

Progress at Dec: 1999- 7105, 2000- 7620, 2001- 7567, 2002- 7995, 2003- 8374, 2004- 8725. pbs: 60m 7.04i '04, 100m 10.72 '03, 10.50w; '04; 400m 46.81 '04, 1000m 2:42.34i '04, 1500m 4:34.49 '01, 60mh 7.87i '04, 110mh 13.93 '02, HJ 2.12 '03, PV 4.92 '04, LJ 8.05 '02, SP 15.93 '04, DT 52.33 '04, JT 55.54 '04, Hep 6155i '04 (Asian record).

Set national record of 8253 to win at Desenzano in 2003 from previous best of 7995. Then three pbs en route to World bronze and another KAZ record with 8374. In 2004 he was third at Götzis with 8512 and set three pbs in his 8725 for Olympic bronze. Did not compete in 2005 apart from two false starts in World Champs decathlon 100m.

KENYA

Governing body: Kenya Amateur Athletic Association, PO Box 46722, 00100 Nairobi. Founded 1951.

2005 National Champions: **Men**: 100m: Kipkemboi Soi 10.84, 200m: Vincent Mumo 21.56, 400m: Thomas Musembi 46.03, 800m: Suleiman Simotwo 1:45.5, 1500m: Churchill Kipsang 3:40.2, 5000m: Benjamin Limo 13:23.3, 10,000m: Barnabas Koskei 28:05.6, 3000mSt: Caleb Ngetich 8:27.1, 110mh: Daniel Kosgei 14.56, 400mh: Julius Bungei 50.24, HJ: Justus Musembi 2.05, LJ: Luka Kiprop 7.62, TJ: Silas Kosgei 15.73, DT: Joshua Pondo 49.09, HT: Morris Omoro 52.06, JT: Sammy Keskeny 68.22, c.19kmW: David Kimutai 1:16:07. **Women**: 100m/200m/400m: Elizabeth Muthoka 11.97/24.0/52.75, 800m: Caroline Chepkwony 2:03.7, 1500m: Mary Wangari 4:14.2, 5000m: Sally Barsosio 15:42.3, 10,000m: Catherine Ndereba 33:22.27, 3000mSt: Jeruto Kiptum 9:43.0, 100mh/400mh: Florence Wasike 14.6/57.73, LJ: Hellen Chemtai 5.63, TJ: Janet Chepchumba 11.82, JT: Cecilia Kiplagat 48.55, c.19kmW: Grace Wanjiru 1:32:20.

Mark BETT b. 22 Dec 1976 1.80m 64kg.

At 5000m: AfCh: 02- 11. 3rd GP 3000m 2002. World CC: '95- 8J.

World indoor 10,000m best 2002.

Progress at 5000m, 10,000m: 1997- 13:15.97, 27:41.14; 1998- 13:22.36, 27:18.66; 1999- 13:14.27, 27:38.64; 2000- 12:55.63, 28:15.98; 2001- 12:58.72, 27:24.68; 2002- 13:00.38, 27:50.29i; 2003- 13:16.42, 2004- 13:07.80, 27:02.00; 2005- 13:16.2+, 26:52.93. pbs: 3000m 7:36.66 '01, 2M 8:20.65 '05.

Paul BITOK b. 26 Jun 1970 Kilibwoni 1.73m 58kg. Nandi. Airman (SPTE).

At 5000m: OG: '92- 2, '96- 2; WCh: '93- 8, '97- 13; WJ: '88- 9; AfG: '93- 4; AfCh: '02- 1. At 3000m: WI: '97- 2, '99- 2, '01- 10; WCp: '02- 4. Won GP 5000m 1992, 3000m 2001 (2nd 1999, 2002); GWG 5000m 2001. World Rd Rly team: '92- 1.

Progress at 5000m: 1988- 14:08.8, 1992- 13:08.89, 1993- 13:08.68, 1994- 13:07.30, 1995- 13:16.39, 1996- 13:04.48, 1997- 13:04.74, 1998- 13:14.26, 1999- 13:15.22i/13:31.01; 2000- 13:04.15, 2001- 13:00.10, 2002- 12:58.94, 2003- 13:14.03, 2004- 13:12.78. pbs: 1500m 3:31.96 '01, 1M 3:56.39i '00, 3:59.6 '96; 2000m 4:54.36 '99, 3000m 7:28.41 '96, 2M 8:13.28i '01, 8:16.44 '99; 10,000m 28:20.31i '02, 28:51.6 '95; Rd 10km 28:31 '93.

Ten years after winning his first GP title, he at

last broke 13 minutes for 5000m in 2002. Won the Paavo Nurmi Challenge 1997 with 1500m in 3:36.87 followed by 5000m in 13:26.25. Married to **Pauline Konga** (b. 10 Apr 1970), 2nd Olympic 5000m 1996, pbs 3000m 8:37.76 '96 (then KEN record), 5000m 14:47.51 '96, HMar 69:33 '96.

Wilson BOIT KIPKETER b. 6 Oct 1973 1.67m 52kg. Keiyo.
At 3000mSt: OG: '00- 2; WCh: '97- 1, '99- 2; AfG: '99- 2; AfCh: '02- 2; WCp: '02- 1. 2nd GP 1999. World CC: '98- 5.
World 3000m steeplechase record 1997.
Progress at 3000mSt: 1993- 8:39.0A, 1994- 8:27.90A, 1995- 8:33.6A, 1996- 8:11.29, 1997- 7:59.08, 1998- 8:01.05, 1999- 8:07.10, 2000- 8:07.33, 2001- 8:01.73, 2002- 8:00.56, 2003- 8:09.16, 2004- 8:16.27, 2005- 8:09.32. pbs: 1500m 3:40.29 '00, 2000m 5:02.1e '97, 3000m 7:33.96 '97, 10,000m 28:43.89A '97.

Wilfred Kipkemboi **BUNGEI** b. 24 Jul 1980 Kabirisang, near Kapsabet 1.72m 60kg. Nandi (Kalenjin).
At 800m: OG: '04- 5; WCh: '01- 2, '05- 4; WJ: '98- 2; WI: '03- 3, '06- 1. Won WAF 2003, 2005.
Progress at 800m: 1998- 1:47.21, 1999- 1:45.14, 2000- 1:44.23, 2001- 1:42.96, 2002- 1:42.34, 2003- 1:42.52, 2004- 1:43.06, 2005- 1:43.70. pbs: 400m 47.08 '05, 600m 1:14.94 '99, 1000m 2:18.60 '02.

Abrahim CHEBII Kosgei b. 23 Dec 1979 Kaptabuk, near Kapsowar 1.72m 63kg. Keiyo.
At 5000m: OG: '04- dnf; WCh: '03- 5; Won GP 3000m 2002. World 4k CC: '00-04-05: 5/19/2.
Progress at 5000m, 10,000m: 1999- 13:30.41, 2000- 13:01.9, 2001- 13:12.53, 27:04.20; 2002- 12:58.98, 2003- 12:52.99, 2004- 13:08.01, 2005- 13:22.53. pbs: 1500m 3:38.5A '04, 1M 3:55.31 '00, 3000m 7:36.11 '02.
Won 2002 GP 3000m final with 50.68 last lap and outsprinted Gebrselassie in Paris and both Geb and Bekele in Rome in 2003 5000m races.

David CHEMWENO b. 18 Dec 1981 1.75m 58kg.
At 3000mSt: WJ: '00- 2; AfCh: '04- 1.
Progress at 3000mSt: 2000- 8:31.95, 2001- 8:30.12, 2002- 8:49.2A, 2003- 8:14.14, 2004- 8:11.44, 2005- 8:09.09. pbs: 1M 3:56.60 '01, 3000m 7:41.35 '04.

Robert Kipkoech CHERUIYOT b. 26 Sep 1978.
Progress at Mar: 2003- 2:10:11, 2004- 2:12:14, 2005- 2:11:01. pbs: 10km 27:57 '04, HMar 59:21 '05.
Great record in Lisbon half marathon: 3-3-2-2in 2003-06, the last three sub 1 hour. Won Boston Marathon 2003.

Cornelius CHIRCHIR b. 5 Jun 1983 Bomet 1.72m 58kg. Kipsigis.
At 1500m: WJ: '00- 1; WY: '99- 1; WI: '03- 4; AfCh: '02- 4; Won Afr-J 800m & 1500m 2001. 3rd GP 2002.
World junior 1500m record 2002.
Progress at 1500m: 1999- 3:44.02, 2000- 3:35.16, 2001- 3:34.53, 2002- 3:30.24, 2003- 3:31.17, 2004- 3:30.60, 2005- 3:40.33. pbs: 800m 1:44.98 '01, 1000m 2:18.24i '03, 1M 3:50.40 '03.
World age-16 best in 2000 (and 1M 3:59.3). Younger brother of William Chirchir.

William CHIRCHIR b. 6 Feb 1979 Bomet 1.75m 55kg. Kipsigis.
At 800m: WJ: '98- 1. At 1500m: OG: '00- h; WCh: '01- 4; CG: '02- 2; 3rd GP 2001. Won Kenyan 1500m 2001.
Ratified world junior 1500m record 1998.
Progress at 800m, 1500m: 1997- 1:47.08, 3:35.44, 1998- 1:44.69, 3:33.24; 1999- 1:43.33, 3:36.22, 2000- 1:43.84, 3:31.02; 2001- 1:44.02, 3:29.29; 2002- 3:30.88, 2003- 1:45.14, 3:31.70; 2004- 1:44.65, 3:32.10; 2005- 1:45.88A, 3:32.93. pbs: 100m 11. '97, 1000m 2:14.99 '99, 1M 3:47.94 '00, 3000m 7:55.78 '97, HJ 1.90 '97.
Won Kenyan Schools decathlon in 1997.

Augustine Kiprono **CHOGE** b. 21 Jan 198? Kipsigat, Nandi 1.62m 53kg.
At 5000m: CG: '06- 1; WJ: '04- 1. At 3000m: WY: '03- 1. At 1500m: WCh: '05- h. World CC: '03- 4J, '05- 1J, '06- 7 4k. Won E.African Youth 800m/1500m/3000m 2003, Junior 1500m 2004.
World youth 5000m record 2004, world junior 3000m record 2005.
Progress at 1500m, 5000m: 2003- 3:37.48, 13:20.08, 2004- 3:36.64, 12:57.01, 2005- 3:33.99, 12:53.66, 2006- 12:56.41. pbs: 800m 1:48.4 '04, 3000m 7:28.78 '05, 10,000m 29:06.5A '02.

Patrick Mutuku **IVUTI** b. 30 Jun 1978 Machakos 1.65m 52kg.
At 10,000m: OG: '00- 4. World CC: '96-7-9-00-01-03: 9J/6J/2/4/7/2.
Progress at 5000m, 10,000m, Mar: 1999- 28:48.0A, 2000- 13:02.68, 27:09.79; 2001- 13:24.48, 28:53.7A, 2002- 13:21.91, 27:05.88; 2004- 28:24.6A, 2005- 2:07:46. pbs: 3000m 7:38.69 '02, HMar 59:31 '00.
Fifth in Chicago marathon on debut in 2005.

Charles KAMATHI b. 18 May 1978 Mathari, Nyeri 1.65m 51kg. Police corporal.
At 10,000m: OG: '04- 13; WCh: '01- 1, '03- 7, '05- 12; AfCh: '04- 1. World CC: '00-01-02-04-05: 7/3/5/5/10; HMar: '02- 9. Won KEN 5000m 2004, 10,000m 2001.
Progress at 5000m, 10,000m: 1999- 13:05.29, 26:51.49; 2000- 13:23.24; 2001- 13:05.16, 27:22.58, 2002- 13:02.51, 28:20.98A; 2003- 13:15.33, 27:29.12; 2004- 13:11.41, 26:59.93; 2005- 13:11.98, 27:28.35. pbs: 1500m 3:41.6? '99, 3000m 7:41.8? '03, road: 10M 46:01 '03, HMar 60:22 '02.
Made a sensational debut in European competition when he won at 10,000m in 26:51.49 in Brussels in September 1999. He had won in India in July at 3000m 7:56.56 and 5000m 13:45.91 in his only previous races outside Kenya, where he had been 2nd at 5000m and 10,000m in the Kenyan Police Championships (c. 14:01 and 28:57) and had a 5000m best of c.13:43.

Ezekiel KEMBOI Cheboi b. 25 May 1982 Matira near Kapsowar, Marakwet District 1.75m 62kg.
At 3000mSt: OG: '04- 1; WCh: '03- 2, '05- 2; CG

'02- 2, '06- 1; AfG: '03- 1; AfCh: '02- 4; Afr-J: '01- 1. Kenyan champion 2003.
Progress at 3000mSt: 2001- 8:23.66, 2002- 8:06.65, 2003- 8:02.49, 2004- 8:02.98, 2005- 8:09.04. pbs: 1500m 3:40.8A '04, 3000m 7:56.8A '05.

John Kemboi **KIBOWEN** b. 21 Apr 1969 Changach 1.75m 64kg. Nandi. Air Force corporal.
At 5000m: OG: '04- 6; WCh: '01- 3, '03- 4, '05- 6; AfG: '03- 3. At 1500m: WCh: '97- h; CG: '98- 4. World CC 4k: '98-00-01-03-04: 1/1/7/2/32; 12k: '06- 12; Rd Rly team: '98- 1. Won KEN 1500m 1998, 4k CC 2003.
Commonwealth 2000m record 1998.
Progress at 1500m, 5000m: 1996- 3:38.6, 13:48.5; 1997- 3:30.44, 1998- 3:30.18, 2000- 3:33.04, 2001- 12:59.97, 2002- 12:58.61, 2003- 12:54.07, 2004- 13:01.32, 2005- 13:07.74. pbs: 800m 1:47.74 '97, 1M 3:47.88 '97, 2000m 4:48.74 '98, 3000m 7:29.09 '98, 10kmRd 27:40 '03.
Trained as an aircraft technician 1992-5 before concentrating on running. Missed 1999 season through injury.

Alex KIPCHIRCHIR Rono b. 26 Nov 1984 Uasin Gishu 1.88m 63kg.
At 800m: WJ: '02- 1; CG: '06- 1. At 1500m: WCh: '05- 7.
World junior 1 mile record 2003.
Progress at 1500m: 2002- 3:32.95, 2003- 3:31.42, 2004- 3:30.46, 2005- 3:30.82. pbs: 800m 1:45.5A '02, 1:45.54 '05; 1000m 2:16.94 '05, 1M 3:50.25 '03. World age 18 1500m best 2003.

Daniel KIPCHIRCHIR KOMEN b. 27 Nov 1984 1.75m 60kg.
At 1500m: WCh: '05- h; WI: '06- 2. At 5000m: Af-J: '03- 2.
Progress at 1500m: 2004- 3:34.66, 2005- 3:29.72. pbs: 800m 1:47.3A '05, 1000m 2:18.19i '06, 1M 3:48.49 '05, 3000m 7:31.98 '05, 5000m 13:16.26 '04.
Four Golden League wins in 2005.

Eliud KIPCHOGE b. 5 Nov 1984 Kapsisiywa, Nandi 1.67m 52kg.
At 5000m: OG: '04- 3; WCh: '03- 1, '05- 4. At 3000m: WI: '06- 3. World CC: '02-03-04-05: 5J/1J/4/5. Won WAF 5000m 2003, 3000m 2004, Kenyan CC 2005.
World junior 5000m record 2003. World road best 4M 17:10 '05.
Progress at 1500m, 5000m: 2002- 13:13.03, 2003- 3:36.17, 12:52.61; 2004- 3:33.20, 12:46.53; 2005- 3:33.80, 12:50.22. pbs: 1M 3:50.40 '04, 2000m 4:59.?+ '04, 3000m 7:27.72 '04, 2M 8:07.68 '05. 10km Rd 27:34 '05.
Kenyan Junior CC champion 2002-03, followed World Junior CC win by winning the World 5000m title, becoming at 18 years 298 days the second youngest world champion. Age 19 bests for 3000m & 5000m 2004.

Sammy KIPKETER b. 29 Sep 1981 Keiyo 1.66m 52kg.
At 5000m: WCh: '01- 6; CG: '02- 1. At 10,000m: AfG: '03- 6. 3rd GP 3000m 2000. World CC: '99- 6J, '03- 14; 4k: '00-01-02: 2/4/4. Won KEN 4k CC 2002.
Official world junior record 3000m 1999. World road bests 5km 13:00 2000 & 2001, 10km 27:18 '01, 27:11 '02.
Progress at 5000m, 10,000m: 1999- 12:58.10, 2000- 12:54.07, 2001- 12:59.34, 2002- 12:56.99, 26:49.38; 2003- 12:52.33, 27:13.42; 2004- 13:25e+, 27:03.61; 2005- 13:01.55, 26:52.60. pbs: 1500m 3:40.0A '01, 2000m 5:00.0e '99, 3000m 7:33.62 '01.
World age-17 bests at 3000m and 5000m 1999.

Raymond KIPKOECH Chemwelo b. 19 Apr 1978 Marakwet.
Progress at Mar: 1999- 2:16:43, 2000- 2:10:52, 2001- 2:12:41, 2002- 2:06:47, 2003- 2:09:21, 2004- 2:09:54. 2005- 2:09:49.
In 2002 he won his sixth and seventh marathons: Enschede and Berlin, when he improved his best by 4 minutes. Won Venice 2004, Xiamen 2005.

Benjamin KIPKURUI b. 28 Dec 1980 Molo 1.74m 57kg. Kipsigis.
At 1500m (/800m): WJ: '98- 2; AfG: '99- (4), '03- 3; Af-J: '97- 1/1.
World junior records 1000m and 1500m 1999.
Progress at 800m, 1500m: 1997- 1:49.3, 3:44.17; 1998- 1:44.71, 3:35.35, 1999- 1:44.56, 3:33.16; 2000- 1:46.30, 3:30.73; 2001- 1:44.80, 3:30.67; 2002- 3:37.17, 2003- 1:48.35, 3:32.42; 2004- 3:33.22, 2005- 1:46.86, 3:36.17. pbs: 600m 1:18.71 '00, 1000m 2:15.00 '99, 1M 3:49.34 '00, 2000m 5:00.21 '03.
World age-17 bests at 800m and 1500m in 1998.

Wesley KIPROTICH b. 31 Jul 1979 1.79m 64kg.
At 3000mSt: CG: '06- 2.
Progress at 3000mSt: 2004- 8:05.68, 2005- 8:09.43. pbs: 1500m 3:43.37 '05, 3000m 7:57.00 '00, 5000m 14:05.64 '05, 2000mSt 5:16.46 '05.

Brimin KIPRUTO b. 31 Jul 1985 Korkitony, Marakwet District 1.76m 54kg.
At 3000mSt: OG: '04- 2; WCh: '05- 3; Af-J: '03- 2. At 1500m: WJ: '04- 3. At 2000St: WY: '01- 2; World 4k CC: '06- 18.
Progress at 3000mSt: 2002- 8:33.0A, 2003- 8:34.5A, 2004- 8:05.52; 2005- 8:04.22. pbs: 1500m 3:35.96 '04, 3000m 7:55.54 '05.
First name is actually Firmin, but he has stayed with the clerical error of Brimin written when he applied for a birth certificate in 2001.

Timothy KIPTANUI Too b. 5 Jan 1980 Kapiptui, Nandi 1.82m 60kg.
At 1500m: OG: '04- 4.
Progress at 800m, 1500m: 2002- 3:41.1A. 2003- 1:46.03, 3:34.07; 2004- 1:44.49, 3:30.04; 2005- 3:38.3A. pbs: 1000m 2:16.19 '03, 2000m 4:59.52 '03, 400mh 52.0u '01.
Former volleyball player, took up running seriously in 2002.

Bernard Kiprop KIPYEGO b. 16 Jul 1986.
At 10,000m: Afr-J: '03- 7. World CC: '05- 2J.

Progress at 10,000m: 2003- 29:29.09, 2004- 28:18.94, 2005- 27:04.45. pbs: 3000m 7:54.91 '05, 5000m 13:09.96 '05, 15km Rd 43:23 '04.

Paul KIRUI b. 5 Feb 1980.
World HMar: '02- 10, '04- 1.
pbs: 10km 28:37 '03, HMar: 60:22 '04, Mar 2:11:28 '05.
Had four wins in five half marathons 2003-04. 2nd Milan marathon 2005.

Alfred KIRWA Yego b. 28 Nov 1986 1.88m 63kg.
At 800m: WCh: '05- h; WJ: '04- 2.
Progress at 800m: 2004- 1:47.39, 2005- 1:44.45. pbs: 1500m 3:37.95 '04.

Justus KOECH b. 19 Mar 1980 Uasin Gashu district 1.75m 60kg.
At 800m: WCh: '03- 6; AfG: '03- 3.
Progress at 800m: 2002- 1:46.10A, 2003- 1:44.16A, 2004- 1:44.19, 2005- 1:45.73. pb 1000m 2:19.83 '03.

Paul Kipsiele **KOECH** b. 10 Nov 1981 Cheplanget. Buret District 1.68m 57kg.
At 3000mSt: OG: '04- 3; WCh: '05- 7; AfG: '03- 2. Won WAF 2005.
Progress at 3000mSt: 2001- 8:15.92, 2002- 8:05.44, 2003- 7:57.42, 2004- 7:59.65, 2005- 7:56.37. pbs: 1500m 3:38.87 '01, 3000m 7:33.93 '05, 5000m 13:11.26 '05.

John Cheruiyot **KORIR** b. 13 Dec 1981 Kiramwok, Bomet district 1.72m 57kg. Army private.
At 10,000m: OG: '00- 5, '04- 6; WCh: '01- 8, '03- 5; CG: '02- 4; AfCh: '02- 2. World CC: '00-01-03-04-05: 3J/28/6/11/9; HMar: '03- 4, '04- 4. Won Kenyan 10,000m 2000, 2003; CC 2001, 2003.
Progress at 5000m,10,000m: 1999- 13:24.22, 27:38.86; 2000- 13:09.58, 27:24.75; 2001- 13:19.58, 27:49.34A; 2002- c.13:24+, 26:52.87; 2003- 13:17.7, 27:17.24; 2004- 13:20.31, 27:05.14; 2005- 27:30.46. pbs: 3000m 7:43.35 '00, HMar 61:02 '03.
Ran fastest ever 10,000m at high altitude, 27:48.42, to win 2000 Kenyan title.

Paul Kipketer **KORIR** b. 15 Jul 1977 Kipkoror, Nandi District 1.80m 64kg. Nandi.
At 1500m: WCh: '03- 4; AfG: '03- 1; AfCh: '04- 1; WI: '04- 1. Won WAF 1500m 2003, Kenyan 800m 2001.
Progress at 800m, 1500m: 1999- 1:47.6, 2000- 1:44.21, 3:41.3A; 2001-1:45.02, 3:41.3A; 2002- 1:45.55, 3:39.18; 2003- 3:30.72, 2004- 3:31.10, 2005- 3:35.84. pbs: 800m 1:47.05A '05, 1000m 2:17.07i '04, 2:18.2 '03; 1M 3:48.17 '03.

Sammy KORIR b. 12 Dec 1971 1.60m 61kg. FILA Milan.
At HMar: WCh: '99- 11.
Progress at Mar: 1996- 2:12:33, 1997- 2:08:02, 1998- 2:08:13, 1999- 2:08:27, 2001- 2:08:14, 2002- 2:08:10, 2003- 2:04:56, 2004- 2:06:49, 2005- 2:10:53, 2006- 2:10:07. pb HMar 60:15 '98.
Has won seven of his 17 marathons: Florence and Cancun 1996, Amsterdam 1997 and 1998, Turin 1999; Beppu and San Diego 2002, Second, just one second behind Paul Tergat's world record at Berlin 2003 and 2nd London 2004. 3rd Rotterdam 1997 and Tokyo 2006.

Paul KOSGEI Malakwen b. 22 Apr 1978 Marakwet 1.75m 57kg.
At 3000mSt: WCh: '99- 7. At 10,000m: WCh: '01- 7; CG: '02- 2; AfCh: '02- 1. At 5000m: WCp: '02- 2. World CC: '97- 3J, 4k: '98-9-00: 3/2/3; 12k: '01- 5; HMar: '02- 1; Rd Rly team: '98- 1. Won KEN 10,000m 2002, 4km CC 1999.
World junior record 3000m steeplechase 1997, Kenyan HMar record in Berlin 2006.
Progress at 5000m, 10,000m, 3000mSt: 1997- 8:07.69, 1998- 8:07.86, 1999- 8:07.13, 2000- 13:05.44, 27:38.22, 8:29.57; 2001- 13:06.29, 27:51.87A; 2002- 13:20.92, 27:44.14A; 2003- 27:21.56. pbs: 1500m: 3:42.7A '00, 2000m 5:03.1+ '00, 3000m 7:39.15 '00, HMar 59:06 '06, 2000mSt 5:19.78 '98.
Won his heat at 1999 World Champs in 8:10.34, the fastest ever time in a preliminary round, but stopped steeplechasing in 2000 due to a knee injury. Ran world road best 10km 27:03 in 2000, and won the World Half marathon title in his first major race at the distance followed by the fastest ever 10,000m at high altitude, 27:44.14 to win the Kenyan title, and Great North Run half marathon win in 59:58 in 2002.

Reuben KOSGEI b. 2 Aug 1979 Kapsabet 1.70m 55kg.
At 3000mSt: OG: '00- 1; WCh: '01- 1, '03- dnf; CG: '06- 3; WJ: '98- 1; Afr-J: '97- 1. Kenyan champion 2000.
Progress at 3000mSt: 1998- 8:23.76, 1999- 8:12.33, 2000- 8:03.92, 2001- 7:57.29, 2002- 8:05.87, 2003- 8:09.65, 2005- 8:12.57. pbs: 1500m 3:37.24 '00, 3000m 7:41.86i '00, 10,000m 29:09.6A '02.
After his World Championship win in 2001, he improved his best ever time to 8:03.22 at Zürich and to 7:57.29, fourth fastest of all-time at the event, at Brussels, behind Brahim Boulami. Had two years of Achilles problems before good return in 2005-06.

Martin LEL b. 29 Oct 1978 1.71m 54kg.
World HMar: '03- 1.
Progress at Mar: 2002- 2:10:02, 2003- 2:10:30, 2004- 2:13:38, 2005- 2:07:26. pbs: 10km 28:39 '03, 15km 43:26 '03, HMar 59:30 '06.
Marathons: dnf Prague and 2nd in Venice 2002, 3rd Boston 2003-04, 1st New York 2003 and London 2005. Ran exclusively on the roads in 2003, winning all three half marathons.

Benjamin LIMO b. 23 Aug 1974 Chepkongony, Keiyo 1.78m 65kg. Army engineer.
At 5000m: WCh: '99- 2, '05- 1; CG: '02- 2, '06- 3, AfG: '03- 7; AfCh: '02- 2. Won GP 3000m 1999. World 4k CC: '98-9-01-03-06: 4/1/3/3/4; Rd Rly team: '98- 1. Won KEN 5000m 2002, 2005.
Progress at 5000m: 1998- 13:07.38, 1999- 12:55.86, 2000- 12:55.82, 2001- 12:59.53, 2002- 12:57.24,

2003- 12:54.99, 2004- 13:31.25, 2005- 12:55.26. pbs: 1500m 3:37.59 '99, 2000m 4:59.2e '99, 3000m 7:28.67 '99, 10,000m 27:42.43 '04.

Only began running seriously in November 1997. Has great finishing speed. Uncle of Sally Barsosio (1997 World 10,000m champion).

Felix LIMO b. 22 Aug 1980 Nandi 1.74m 58kg.

World best for 15km road with 41:29 at Nijmegen 2001.

Progress at 10,000m, Mar: 1998- 28:48A, 1999- 28:23.30, 2000- 27:04.54, 2001- 27:26.86; 2003- 2:06:42, 2004- 2:06:14, 2005- 2:07:02. pbs: 3000m 7:40.67 '01, 5000m 13:16.42 '01, HMar 61:15 '02.

Made second fastest ever marathon debut when 2nd at Amsterdam in 2003. Won at Rotterdam (2:06:14) and Berlin (2:06:44) in 2004 and at Chicago 2005, 3rd Rotterdam 2005.

Richard Kipkemei **LIMO** b. 18 Nov 1980 Cheptigit 1.67m 53kg. Kalenjin.

At 5000m: OG: '00- 10; WCh: '01- 1, '03- 7; CG: '98- 3; AfG: '99- 6. At 3000mSt: AfCh: '98- 2. World CC: '98-9-02-03-04: 2J/2J/4/4/32. Won KEN 5000m 2001, CC 2002.

World junior records 3000m 1998, 2M 1999.

Progress at 5000m, 10,000m: 1998- 13:21.59, 1999- 12:58.15, 2000- 12:58.70, 2001- 12:56.72, 27:25.27; 2002- 12:57.52, 26:50.20; 2003- 13:01.13, 26:56.63; 2004- 12:59.37, 27:09.61; 2005- 13:09.52, 28:16.7A. pbs: 1500m 3:43.3A '02, 2000m 5:00.6 '99, 3000m 7:32.23 '01, 2M 8:13.47 '99, 3000mSt 8:20.67 '98.

Benjamin MAIYO b. 6 Oct 1978 Trans Nzoia 1.75m 58kg.

At 10,000m: WCh: '99- 7; AfG: '99- 5; AfCh: '02- 3.

Progress at 5000m, 10,000m, Mar: 1998- 13:18.98, 27:34.38; 1999- 13:02.38, 28:01.8A; 2000- 13:02.28, 28:28.7A; 2001- 13:05.43, 27:07.55; 2002- 13:02.95, 28:06.0A; 2003- 13:14.75, 29:07.7A; 2004- 27:30.30, 2:13:07; 2005- 2:07:09. pbs: 1500m 3:42.30 '99, 2000m 5:01.9+ '00; 3000m 7:32.36 '00, HMar 61:59 '02, Mar 2:13:17 '04.

2nd Los Angeles and Chicago marathons 2005.

Martin Irungu **MATHATHI** b. 25 Dec 1985 1.65m 45kg. Suzuki.

At 10,000m: WCh: '05- 5. World CC: '06- 3.

Progress at 5000m, 10,000m: 2003- 14:09.3A, 27:43.16; 2004- 13:03.84, 27:22.46; 2005- 13:05.99, 27:08.42. pbs: 10M Rd 44:51 '04.

Posted a brilliant series of times in road races in Japan at the end of 2004.

Kipkirui MISOI b. 23 Dec 1978 Bomet 1.77m 59kg.

At 3000mSt: CG: '98- 3; WJ: '96- 2; AfG: '99- 1. World CC: '98- 8 4k.

World junior record 3000m steeplechase 1998.

Progress at 3000mSt: 1995- 8:56.0A, 1996- 8:33.31, 1997- 8:16.76, 1998- 8:09.46, 1999- 8:08.62, 2000- 8:07.21, 2001- 8:01.69, 2002- 8:13.47, 2003- 8:07.74, 2004- 8:12.99, 2005- 8:08.15. pbs: 1500m 3:39.17 '98, 1M 4:01.12 '01, 3000m 7:40.93 '00, 5000m 13:26.83 '98, 2000mSt 5:26.08 '03.

Moses MOSOP (or Kimosop) b. 17 Jul 1985 Kamasia, Marakwet 1.72m 57kg.

At 10,000m: OG: '04- 7; WCh: '05- 3. World CC: '02-03-05: 10J/7J/18.

Progress at 5000m, 10,000m: 2002- 29:38.6A, 2003- 13:11.75, 27:13.66; 2004-13:09.68, 27:30.66; 2005- 13:06.83, 27:08.96. pbs: 3000m 7:41.78 '04.

Joseph Mwengi MUTUA b. 10 Dec 1978 1.70m 58kg.

At 800m: OG: '00- h, '04- sf; WJ: '96- 1; CG: '02- 2; WI: '04- 6. Won KEN 800m 2002-04.

Commonwealth and African indoor 800m record 1:44.71 04.

Progress at 800m: 1995- 1:48.3A, 1996- 1:46.3A, 1997- 1:48.0A, 1998- 1:47.81, 1999- 1:48.8A, 2000- 1:45.49A, 2001- 1:43.63, 2002- 1:43.33, 2003- 1:43.52, 2004- 1:43.35, 2005- 1:45.58. pbs: 400m 46.68A '04, 46.6A '02; 600m 1:13.72 '03, 1000m 2:17.55 '02, 1500m 3:43.17 '99.

Ranked as world number two at 800m in 2002, when, at Zürich, he was the only man to beat Wilson Kipketer outdoors.

Noah Kiprono **NGENY** b. 2 Nov 1978 Kabenas 1.82m 68kg.

At 1500m: OG: '00- 1; WCh: '99- 2; WI: '01- 3; WJ: '96- 8 (tripped on final lap). Won GP 1999-2000, KEN 1500m 1999-2000, GWG 1M 2001.

Records: World and two African records 1000m 1999, World Junior 1500m (2) and 1M records 1997, Commonwealth: 1500m (3), 1M 1999-2000.

Progress at 1500m: 1996- 3:42.44, 1997- 3:32.91, 1998- 3:30.34, 1999- 3:28.73/3:28.6+u, 2000- 3:28.12, 2001- 3:31.94, 2002- 3:33.02, 2003- 3:33.96, 2004- 3:33.38. pbs: 800m 1:44.49 '00, 1000m 2:11.96 '99, 1M 3:43.40 '99, 2000m 4:50.08 '99, 3000m 7:35.46 '00.

Tripped on the first lap in the final of the 1996 World Juniors, sprinted to the front and led for three laps before being tripped again with 200m to go and losing his rhythm. Came through in 1997 to run world junior records. Although beaten three times by Hicham El Guerrouj, he had a wonderful season in 1999, following his World silver medal at 1500m, with the world record for 1000m (beating Seb Coe's 1981 mark) and a win in the Grand Prix Final 1500m. Then he ended El Guerrouj's winning run with Olympic gold in 2000. Brother of **Philip Kibitok** (b. 23 Mar 1971) pb 800m 1:43.55 '96.

Daniel NJENGA b. 7 May 1976 1.76m 61kg.

World Junior record when winning Japanese 3000m steeplechase title in 1994.

Progress at 3000mSt, Mar: 1993- 8:41.46, 1994- 8:19.21, 1995- 8:27.03, 2:20:28; 1996- 8:28.67, 1997- 8:30.50, 1998- 8:32.14, 1999- 2:11:49, 2001- 2:20:58, 2002- 2:06:16, 2003- 2:07:41, 2004- 2:07:44, 2005- 2:07:14. pbs: 1500m 3:43.43 '94, 5000m 13:36.55 '96, 10,000m 27:51.83 '02, HMar 60:39 '96.

Based in Japan. Huge breakthough when 2nd at Chicago 2002 in his seventh marathon, and was third in 2003 and 2005 and second 2004. Won Tokyo 2004.

Julius NYAMU b. 1 Dec 1977 Nyeri 1.78m 66kg.
World 4k CC: '02- 6.
Progress at 3000mSt: 2001- 8:07.59, 2002- 8:11.13, 2003- 8:09.06, 2004- 8:11.29, 2005- 8:15.29. pb 2000mSt 5:25.47 '03.

Laban ROTICH 20 Jan 1969 Mosoriot 1.63m 45kg. Fireman in Kenyan Air Force. Nandi.
At 1500m: OG: '96- 4; WCh: '97- 11, '99- 6, '01- sf; CG: '98- 1; AfCh: '98- 1, '02- 2; WI: '99-01-04: 2/4/3; WCp: '98- 1. 2nd GP 1998, 3rd 1996 & 1999. Won Kenyan 1500m 1997.
KEN records 1500m (3) 1996-7, 1000m & 1M 1997.
Progress at 800m, 1500m: 1995- 3:39.85, 1996- 1:45.8A, 3:31.06; 1997- 1:44.47, 3:30.13; 1998- 1:43.65, 3:29.91; 1999- 3:31.60, 2000- 1:48.14, 3:32.93; 2001- 3:31.38, 2002- 1:48.40, 3:32.82; 2003- 3:33.91, 2004- 3:32.81, 2005- 3:33.83. pbs: 1000m 2:14.43 '97, 1M 3:47.65 '97, 2000m 4:56.09i '99, 4:57.63 '96, 3000m 7:47.97i '04, 7:58.46 '03; 2M 8:28.25i '03.
World high altitude best 1500m 3:33.1 '98.

Evans RUTTO b. 8 Apr 1978 Marakwet 1.68m 56kg.
World CC: 1999- 5; HMar: '01- 6.
Progress at 5000m, 10,000m, Mar: 1999- 13:24.84, 28:06.60; 2000- 13:02.71, 27:21.32; 2001- 13:28.25, 2003- 2:05:50, 2004- 2:06:16. 2005- 2:07:28. pbs: 2000m 5:02.3+ '99; 3000m 7:36.38 '00; Road: 10km 28:19 '02, 15km 43:15 '01; 10M 46:26 '01, HMar 60:30 '01.
Ran fastest ever debut marathon when he won at Chicago 2003 and won again at London (2:06:19) and Chicago (2:06:16) 2004. 10th London and 4th Chicago 2005.

Suleiman SIMOTWO b. 21 Apr 1980 1.82m 70kg. PE instructor in Kenyan Police.
Won Kenyan 800m 2005.
Progress at 1500m: 2002- 3:42.2A. 2003- 3:36.98, 2004- 3:34.48, 2005- 3:31.85. pbs: 800m 1:45.5A '05, 1000m 2:19.31 '04, 1M 3:50.82 '05, 2000m 4:59.06 '03, 3000m 7:48.38 '03.

Boniface Kiprotich **SONGOK** b. 25 Dec 1980 1,72m 57kg.
At 5000m: AfCh: '04- 2. At World 4k CC: '04- 21.
Progress at 5000m: 2004- 13:00.62, 2005- 12:55.85. pbs: 1500m 3:41.0A '01, 3000m 7:30.62 '04, 2M 8:12.86 '05, 10km Rd 28:45 '04.

Isaac Kiprono **SONGOK** b. 25 Apr 1984 Kaptel, near Kapasbet, Nandi region 1.76m 54kg.
At 1500m: OG: '04- 12; WCh: '03- 9; WJ: '02- 7; WY: '01- 1; At 5000m: WCh: '05- 10. World 4k CC: '04-05-05: 7/3/2. Won KEN 1500m 2003, 4k CC 2005.
World U18 records 1M (3:54.56) & 2000m (4:56.86, also U20 record) 2001.
Progress at 1500m, 5000m: 2001- 3:35.55, 13:37.3A; 2002- 3:34.20, 2003- 3:31.54, 2004- 3:30.99, 2005- 3:31.72, 12:52.29. pbs: 800m 1:50.5A '03, 1M 3:54.56 '01, 2000m 4:56.86 '01, 3000m 7:30.14 '05.
National primary school champion at 5000m in 1999 and 2000.

Paul TERGAT b. 17 Jun 1969 Kabarnet, Barango 1.82m 62kg. Air Force sergeant (SPTE). Tugen.
At 10,000m: OG: '96- 2, '00- 2; WCh: '95- 3 '97- 2, '99- 2. At Mar: OG: '04- 10. World HMar '92-4-9-00: 5/11/1/1. World CC: '93-4-5-6-7-8-9 00: 10/4/1/1/1/1/1/3. Won Kenyan CC 1992 1995-6.
World records: 10,000m 1997, marathon 2003 World road best 15km 1994 (42:13), half mara thon 59:17 '98 and 59:06 '00 (40m dh at Lisbon) 58:51 at Milano 1996 was on a course 49m short Two Kenyan marathon record 2002-03.
Progress at 5000m, 10,000m, Mar: 1991- 29:46.8A 1992- 13:48.64, 1993- 13:20.16, 27:18.43; 1994 13:15.07, 27:23.89; 1995- 13:07.49, 27:14.08; 1996 12:54.72, 26:54.41; 1997- 12:49.87, 26:27.85; 1998 12:58.74, 26:44.44; 1999- 12:55.37, 27:10.08; 2000 12:55.18, 27:03.87; 2001- 2:08:15, 2002- 2:05:48 2003- 2:04:55, 2004- 2:14:45, 2005- 2:09:30. pbs 1500m 3:42.3 '96, 1M 3:58.4 '96, 2000m 4:57.4 '96 3000m 7:28.70 '96, HMar 59:06 '00, 58:51sh '96.
Former basketball player who made a majo impact when he won the Kenyan CC in 1992, bu missed the Worlds through injury. Won a recor five successive World Cross-country titles. Wo the Stramilano half marathon each year 1994- and unbeaten at that distance 1995-2000. On th track he won four silver medals and a bronz behind the great Haile Gebrselassie in glob 10,000m races. He was 2nd in his first thre marathons: London (2:08:15), Chicago (2:08:5 2001 and London (2:05:48) 2002 and then fourt at Chicago (2:06:18) 2002 and London 200 before his world record 2:04:55 at Berlin 200 He won the New York Marathon in 2005.

Samuel WANJIRU Kamau b. 10 Nov 198 1.63m 52kg. Toypota Yushu Company.
At 10,000m: Japanese champion 2005.
World half marathon record 2005, juni 10,000m 2005.
Progress at 10,000m: 2002- 28:36.08, 2003- 28:20.0 2004- 28:00.14, 2005- 26:41.75. pbs: 1500m 3:49. '03, 5000m 13:09.5+ '05, 15km 42:08 '05, 10 45:10 '05, HMar 59:16 '05.
Left Kenya in 2002 to go to school in Japan ar that year ran world age 15 record for 10,000m

William Oloonkishu **YIAMPOY** b. 17 May 19 Emarti, near Kilgoris 1.83m 70kg. Masai.
At 800m: OG: '00- sf; WCh: '01- 4, '05- 3; AfC '02- 2, '04- 1; WI: '04- 5. Kenyan & GWG char pion 2001.
Progress at 800m: 1999- 1:44.38, 2000- 1:44.2 2001- 1:43.00, 2002- 1:42.91, 2003- 1:45.01A, 200 1:43.29, 2005- 1:44.51. pbs: 1000m 2:14.41 '9 1500m 3:34.12 '01.
Joined Kenya Police 1990, began running 199

Women

Selina (Sally) BARSOSIO b. 21 Mar 1978 Keiyo 1.65m 46kg. Elgeyo Marakwet.
At 10,000m (5000m): OG: '96- 10, '00- 17, 04- 17; WCh: '93- 3, '95- (11), '97- 1; WJ: '92- 3; AfG: '95- 1; AfCh: '92- 5 (5), '98- (2). Won GP 5000m 1997 (3rd 3000m 2000), KEN 5000m 1998, 2005; 10,000m 1993, 1997; CC 1996-7, African Junior 1500m & 3000m 1994. World CC: '93-4-5-6-7-8-00-01-04: 3J/1J/3/11/5/10/8 (4k)/18/10; Rd Rly team: '98- 2.
World Junior records: 10,000m 1993 (not ratified as no drugs test) and 1997, 3000m 1997; Kenyan records 10,000m 1993, 5000m 1996, 3000m 1997.
Progress at 5000m, 10,000m: 1992- 32:41.76, 1993- 31:15.38, 1994- 15:42.45; 1995- 15:05.75, 32:22.26, 1996- 14:47.81, 31:36.00; 1997- 14:46.71, 31:32.92; 1998- 15:27.22, 32:50.16; 1999- 15:42.79, 32:26.28; 2000- 14:53.61, 31:57.41; 2003- 16:22.71A, 34:36.0A; 2004- 15:24.49, 31:18.72; 2005- 15:43.2A. pbs: 1500m 4:13.11 '00, 2000m 5:39.4 '97, 3000m 8:35.89 '97, HMar 72:05 '05.
A prodigious talent at 15 (18 according to some sources, including her mother!), but fortunate to be reinstated after disqualification in the 1993 World 10,000m to become the youngest ever World Championship medallist. She had caused havoc during the race by continually baulking Elana Meyer and running across several other runners. Four years later she became Kenya's first senior woman track world champion. Missed 1999 season through injury. Son Ricky born 18 Feb 2002.
Her elder sister Jepkemboi (**Florence**) Barsosio (b. 11 Aug 1976) was 6th World marathon and won Paris marathon 2001, pb 2:27:00 '00; Kenyan champion and 13th World 5000m 1995, World CC: '96- 16, '97- 13. Niece of Paul Koech.

Joyce CHEPCHUMBA Koech b. 6 Nov 1970 Kericho 1.60m 52kg. Kenyan postal service.
At Mar: OG: '96- dnf, '00- 3; WCh: '03- 7. World HMar: '97-8-9-01: 4/6/4/18; CC: '94- 18.
Kenyan marathon record 1997.
Progress at Mar: 1995- 2:33:51, 1996- 2:29:38, 1997- 2:26:51, 1998- 2:23:57, 1999- 2:23:22, 2000- 2:24:02, 2001- 2:24:12, 2002- 2:25:56, 2003- 2:26:06, 2004- 2:26:21, 2005- 2:27:01. pbs: 800m 2:11.2 '94, 1500m 4:36.3A '91, 3000m 9:23.26 '95, 5000m 15:26.19 '00, 10,000m 32:07.50 '99, road 5km 15:52 '94, 10km 32:19 '96, 15km 49:21 '97, 10M 54:27 '95, HMar 68:11 '04.
Six major wins in 25 marathons (20 sub 2:30, record 17 sub 2:28): London 1997 and 1999 (when she won the then biggest ever prize of $230,000) (also 2nd 1996, 3rd 1998, 2000-01, 6th 2002, 7th 2005), Chicago 1998 and 1999, Tokyo 2000 (2nd 1997), New York 2002 (4th on marathon debut 1995, 3rd 1996, 4th 2001, 6th 2003). 18 successive marathons all under 2:30 to 2004. Won Great North Run 1999. Has a training base in Dettmond, Germany. Son born in 1991.

Salome CHEPCHUMBA b. 29 Sep 1982 1.74m 57kg. North Rift.
At 3000mSt: WCh: '05- 5. World 4k CC: '01- 34. Kenyan champion 2000mSt 2003, 3000mSt 2004. Kenyan 3000m steeplechase record 2004.
Progress at 3000mSt: 2004- 9:29.81, 2005- 9:31.44. pbs: 1500m 4:21.95 '04, 3000m 8:51.5A '00, 5000m 16:13.13 '05, 2000mSt 6:21.93 '05.

Susan CHEPKEMEI Kapkama b. 25 Jun 1975 West Pokot Region 1.64m 48kg.
At 5000m: WCp: '02- 5; at 10,000m: CG: '02- 2; AfCh: '02- 1. World HMar: '00-01-02-03-05: 2/2/2/8/3; CC: '98-9-00-01: 12/5/3/4; Rd Rly team: '98- 2. Won Kenyan 10,000m 2001-02.
Progress at 10,000m, Mar: 1995- 34:57.40A, 1996- 34:21.0A, 1997- 34:27.2A, 1998- 33:30.6A, 2:28:19, 1999- 33:01.2A, 2:26:38; 2000- 33:20.6A, 2001- 33:03.7A, 2:25:12; 2002- 31:32.04, 2:23:19; 2003- 35:45.2A, 2:23:12; 2004- 2:23:13, 2005- 32:24.5A, 2:24:00. pbs: 1500m 4:20.6A '01, 3000m 8:43.95 '01, 5000m 14:55.27 '01; Road: 10km 31:13 '03, 15km 47:54 '01, 10M 51:13 '05, HMar 65:44 '01.
Second in her first two marathons: Berlin 1998 and Rotterdam 1999, In 2001 at half marathon she ran a world best on the slightly downhill Lisbon course and won the Great North Run with the second of three successive World silvers and won the Rotterdam marathon. 2nd New York Marathon 2001 & 2004-05; 4th 2003, 3rd 2005 in London. Based in the Netherlands.

Janeth JEPKOSGEI b. 13 Feb 1978 1.67m 47kg. North Rift.
At 800m: CG: '06- 1; WJ: '02- 1; WY: '99- h.
Kenyan 800m record 2005.
Progress at 800m: 1999- 2:11.0A, 2001- 2:06.21, 2002- 2:00.80, 2003- 2:03.05, 2004- 2:00.52, 2005- 1:57.82, 2006- 1:57.88. pbs: 1000m 2:37.98 '02, 1500m 4:11.91 '04.

Priscah JEPLETING Ngetich b. 26 Jun 1980 1.62m 39kg.
At 5000m: WCh: '05- 7; WJ: '98- 7; AfCh: '04- 2. Kenyan champion 2004. World CC J/4k: '97-8-02-03-04-06: 2J/11J/18/11/4/2.
Progress at 5000m: 1996- 15:39.1A, 1998- 16:07.12, 1999- 16:24.4A, 2001- 16:42.4A, 2002- 15:41.13A, 2003- 15:35.7A, 2004- 14:54.24, 2005- 14:44.00. pbs: 800m 2:07.8A '99, 1500m 4:23.7A '00, 3000m 8:41.85 '05, 10km Rd 31:53 '02.

Jeruto KIPTUM b. 29 Sep 1982 1.66m 50kg.
At 3000mSt: WCh: '05- 3; CG: '06- 6. World 4k CC: '01- 34. Kenyan champion 2000mSt 2003, 3000mSt 2004.
Two Kenyan 3000m steeplechase records 2005.
Progress at 3000mSt: 2005- 9:26.95. pbs: 800m 2:06.1A '99, 1500m 4:08.6A '00, 3000m 9:01.90 '99.

Selina KOSGEI b. 16 Nov 1976 Simotwo, Keiyo district 1.62m 58kg. Corporal in Kenya Prisons Service.
At 10,000m: WCh: '03- 19; CG: '02- 1. At 800m: CG: '94- 5. Won Kenyan 10,000m 2003.

Progress at 5000m, 10,000m, Mar: 1998- 15:50.43, 2002- 15:20.17, 31:27.83; 2003- 15:01.79, 32:09.15; 2004- 32:49.0A, 2:24:32; 2005- 2:25:30. pbs: 800m 2:03.38 '94, 1500m 4:19.9 '98, 3000m 9:34.35 '02, HMar 67:52 '06.

Won four successive Kenyan Schools titles at heptathlon, as well as at 200m, 800m and on both winning relay teams in her final year. Won Paris marathon on debut 2004 and Prague 2005. Married (1995) Barnabas Kinyor (3rd Commonwealth 400mh 1994). Children born 1996 and 2001.

Edith Chewanjel **MASAI** b. 4 Apr 1967 Chepkoya, Mt Elgon 1.68m 55kg. Police sergeant.

At 5000m: OG: '04- dnf; WCh: '01- 7, '03- 3; CG: '02- 2; AfG: '03- 6. At 10,000m: WCh: '05- 5. World 4km CC: '01-02-03-04: 3/1/1/1. Won WAF 3000m 2003, KEN 1500m 2004, 5000m 2001-03, 4km CC 2002.

African 3000m record 2002, Kenyan 5000m & 10,000m 2005.

Progress at 5000m, 10,000m: 2001- 14:45.86, 2002- 14:48.14, 2003- 14:45.35, 2004- 14:42.64, 2005- 14:37.20, 30:30.26. pbs: 1500m 4:18.6A '04, 2000m 5:40.3 '01, 3000m 8:23.23 '02; Road: 15km 48:37 '01, 10M 52:45 '02, HMar 67:16 '06, Mar 2:27:06 '05.

Son born 1990. Ran successfully in primary school, but only started running seriously after she separated from her husband in 1999. Won third successive World 4k CC title in 2004. Ran 31:27 for road 10km in 2001 but did not make track debut at 10,000m until 2005, when she also won at Hamburg on her marathon debut.

Catherine NDEREBA b. 21 Jul 1972 Nyeri 1.60m 45kg.

At Mar: OG: 04- 2; WCh: '03- 1, '05- 2. At HMar: WCh: '99- 3. Won Kenyan 10,000m 2005.

World marathon record in Chicago 2001.

Progress at Mar: 1999- 2:27:34, 2000- 2:21:33, 2001- 2:18:47, 2002- 2:19:26, 2003- 2:19:55, 2004- 2:24:27, 2005- 2:22:01, 2006- 2:25:05. pbs: 1500m 4:22.1A '01, 3000m 9:25.10 '99, 5000m 15:27.84 '00, 10,000m 32:17.58 '00; Road 5km 15:07 '98, 10km 31:02 '01, 15km 48:06 '01, 10M 52:25 '98, HMar 67:54 '01.

Married to Anthony Maina. Has had great success on the US road running circuit, where she was top ranked in 1996 and 1998, having had a baby, Jane, in 1997. Sixth in Boston on her debut, 8 wins in 16 marathons: Boston and Chicago in both 2000 and 2001 before 2003 Worlds, and Boston 2004-05, Osaka 2006. 2nd in New York 1999 and 2003 (2:23:03), in Boston (2:21:12) and Chicago 2002 and London 2003. Record 10 sub-2:26 marathons. Her sister **Anastasha** (b. 27 Sep 1974) won marathons in 2002 at Turin in 2:29:27 and Venice in 2:29:03, making them the fastest marathoning sisters.

Isabella Bosibori **OCHICHI** b. 28 Oct 1979 Keroka, Kisii 1.62m 48kg. Police corporal.

At 5000m: OG: '04- 2; WCh: '03- 6, '05- 8; CG: '06- 1; AfG: '03- 3. World CC: 4k: '02-03-04-05-06: 3/4/5/3/10; 8k: '05- 5; HMar: '01- 8. Won Kenyan CC 2003.

Progress at 5000m: 1997- 16:24.46, 2000- 16:54.1A, 2001- 16:34.0A, 2002- 15:01.42, 2003- 14:47.70, 2004- 14:46.42, 2005- 14:38.21, 2006- 14:57.84. pbs: 800m 2:09.1A '02, 1500m 4:14.5A '05, 2000m 5:39.47 '04, 3000m 8:31.32 '04, Road: 10km 30:27 '05, 15km 47:54 '01, 10M 51:08 '05, HMar 68:38 '01.

Married to marathoner David Maina. European base in Brest, France.

Margaret OKAYO b. 30 May 1976 Kisii 1.50m 39kg. Sergeant in police service.

At Mar: OG: '04- dnf. At HMar: WCh: '99- 13.

Progress at Mar: 1999- 2:26:00, 2000- 2:26:36, 2001- 2:24:21, 2002- 2:20:43, 2003- 2:22:31, 2004- 2:22:35, 2005- 2:25:22. pb: 5000m 15:30.0A '01, Road: 10km 32:32 '99, 15km 49:09 '99, HMar 67:23 '03.

7 wins in 15 marathons. Made a brilliant debut with 2:26:00 for 2nd at Chicago 1999, and won at San Diego 2000 and 2001, New York 2001 and 2003 (3rd 2000, 4th 2004, 6th 2002), Boston and Milan 2002, London 2004 (4th 2005).

Alice TIMBILIL b. 16 Jun 1983 1.55m 45kg.

At 10,000m: OG: '00- 14, '04- 16; WCh: '99- dnf. At 3000m: WY: '99- 1. World CC: '00-01-03-04-05: 2J/16J/14/4/2. Won KEN 10,000m 1999.

Progress at 5000m, 10,000m: 1998- 34:28.0A, 1999- 32:02.2A, 2000- 16:19.04, 31:50.22; 2001- 33:52.7A, 2002- 16:16.6A, 32:54.0A; 2003- 32:45.2, 2004- 14:53.17, 31:23.99; 2005- 14:47.06, 31:45.4A. pbs: 3000m 8:40.76 '05.

Lucy WANGUI b. 24 Mar 1984 Uasin Gishu 1.55m 42kg. Suzuki, Japan.

At (5000m)/10,000m: OG: '04- 9; CG: '06- 3/1. World 4k CC: '05- 5.

Progress at 10,000m: 2002- 32:54.70, 2003- 31:06.20, 2004- 31:05.90, 2005- 31:22.37, 2006- 31:29.66. pbs: 1500m 4:09.60 '02, 3000m 8:57.19 '02, 5000m 14:57.09 '04, HMar 69:47 '04.

KOREA

Governing body: Korea Amateur Athletic Federation, 10 Chamshil Dong, Songpa-Gu, Seoul. Founded 1945. **National Champions 2005**: **Men:** 100m/200m: Jeon Duk-hyung 10.51/20.98, 400m: Park Se-hyun 47.77, 800m: Lee Jae-hoon 1:47.90, 1500m: Kim Nam-jin 3:52.15, 5000m: Eumhyo-suk 14:25.58, 10,000m: Huh Jang-kyu 29:41.39, Mar: Kim Yi-yong 2:13:04, 3000mSt: Kim Young-jin 8:55.90, 110mh: Lee Jung-yun 14.08, 400mh: Lee Dong-jae 52.27, HJ: Oh Jin-wook 2.15, PV: Kim Se-in 5.30, LJ: Oh Sang-won 7.59, TJ: Kim Duk-hyung 16.21, SP: Hwang In-sung 18.01, DT: Choi Jong-bum 54.95, HT: Lee Yun-chol 65.89, JT: An Hyuk-yun 77.07, Dec: Kim Kun-woo 7774, 20kmW: Lee Dae-ro 1:22:16. **Women**: 100m/200m: Kimhyun-ran 11.91/24.52, 400m: Lee Mi-hee 56.86, 800m: Huh

Yeon-jung 2:10.45, 1500m/10,000m/Mar: Choi Kyung-hee 4:36.90/33:59.97/2:35:56, 5000m: Bae Hae-jin 16:45.04, 100mh: Lee Yeon-kyung 13.33, 400mh: Park Mi-jin 60.35, HJ: Park Jin-hee 1.75, PV: Choi Yun-hee 3.90, LJ: Jung Soon-ok 6.27, TJ: Chung Hye-kyong 13.39, SP: Lee Mi-young 17.09, DT: Lee Yun-kyong 48.35, HT: Chang Bok-shim 56.82, JT: Lee Young-sun 54.68, Hep: Lee Eun-im 5342, 20kmW: Park Ha-na 1:44:00.

LATVIA

Governing body: Latvian Athletic Association, 1 Augsiela Str, Riga LV-1009. Founded 1921.

National Championships first held in 1920 (men), 1922 (women). **2005 Champions**: **Men**: 100m/200m: Sandis Sabajevs 10.66/21.53w, 400m: Girts Lamba 48.50, 800m: Normunds Silins 1:52.28, 1500m: Girts Azis 3:55.14, 3000m: Valerijs Zolnerovics 8:34.56, 5000m: Armands Bucs 14:56.5, 10,000m: Viktors Slesarenoks 30:10.1, HMar: Normunds Duksis 71:06, Mar: Andris Dudels 2:38:48, 3000mSt: Dmitrijs Slesarenoks 9:33.88, 110mh: Maris Grenins 14.65, 400mh: Gatis Spunde 52.72, HJ: Normunds Pupols 2.15, PV: Mareks Arents 4.70, LJ: Arturs Abolins 7.71, TJ: Maksims Tkacovs 15.90w, SP: Maris Urtans 18.18, DT: Oskars Silcenoks 48.78, HT: Igors Sokolovs 70.53, JT: Ainars Kovals 82.22, Dec: Atis Vaisjuns 7442, 20kmW/50kmW: Ingus Janevics 1:27:34/4:19:33. **Women**: 100m: Olga Mirzagitova 12.02w, 200m/Hep: Esenija Volzankina 23.91/5303, 400m/400mh: Ieva Zunda 52.76/57.83, 800m: Anna Anfinogentova 2:07.35, 1500m: Jelena Stina 4:27.64, 5000m: Jelena Prokopcuka 16:03.14, 10,000m/HMar: Inna Poluskina 35:30.2/81:02, Mar: Svetlana Ivanova 2:56:21, 3000mSt: Irina Stula- Pankoka 10:57.32, 100mh: Zanda Grava 14.17, HJ: Agnese Seglina 1.74, PV: Alise Dimante 3.60, LJ: Ineta Radevica 6.39, TJ: Olga Savenkova 12.85w, SP: Laura Ludevika 12.44, DT: Dace Ruskule 53.28, HT: Vaira Godmane 51.67, JT: Inga Kozarenoka 55.46, 10kmW/20kmW: Jolanta Dukure 44:49sh/1:37:53.

Aigars FADEJEVS b. 27 Dec 1975 Valmiera 1.75m 59kg. "Tele 2".

At 20kmW (/50kmW): OG: '96- 6, '00- 14/2, '04- 9/11; WCh: '97- dnf, '99- dnf /dq, '01- dnf/4, '03 (dq), '05- 17/dq; EC: '94- 17, '98- 2, '02- (dq); EU23: '97- 1; WCp: '97- 15, '99- (9); ECp: '98-00-01: 3/6/8. At 10kmW: EJ: '93- 11; WJ: '94- dq. Won LAT 50kmW 1998.

Latvian records 10,000mW (2) 1998-2002, 20kmW (3) 1996-2002, 30kmW 2002, 50kmW 1998.

Progress at 20kmW, 50kmW: 1993- 1:36:19, 1994- 1:23:41, 4:02:18; 1995- 1:22:56, 1996- 1:20:40, 1997- 1:19:36, 1998- 1:19:44, 3:43:18; 1999- 1:20:31, 3:46:36; 2000- 1:20:18, 3:43:40; 2001- 1:19:53, 3:46:20; 2002- 1:19:25; 2003- 1:20:56, 3:46:03; 2004- 1:22:08, 3:52:52; 2005- 1:20:55. pbs: 5000mW 18:48.30 '98, 10,000mW 39:00.42 '02, 30kmW 2:06:01 '02, 35kmW 2:34:36 '02, Mar (run) 2:27:20 '01.

Stanislav(s) OLIJAR(S) b. 22 Mar 1979 Chelyabinsk, Russia 1.90m 80kg. ASK.

At 110mh: OG: '00- sf, '04- 5; WCh: '97- qf, '99- sf, '03- h, '05- sf; EC: '98- sf, '02- 2; WJ: '96- h (dnq LJ), '98- 1; EJ: '97- 2; EU23: '99- 2; WCp: '02- 3. At 60mh: WI: '01-03-04-06: 8/6/4/4=; EI: '00-02-05: 1/3/dq. Won LAT 100m 1999, 110mh 2002.

Five Latvian 110mh records 2002-03.

Progress at 110mh: 1996- 14.52, 1997- 13.62, 1998- 13.49, 1999- 13.28, 2000- 13.25, 2001- 13.29, 2002- 13.15A/13.22, 2003- 13.08, 2004- 13.20, 2005- 13.11. pbs: 60m 6.70i '98, 6.6i '01; 100m 10.42/10.33w '02, 200m 20.91A '03, 20.95 '02; 400m 46.66 '00, 50mh 6.46i '03, 60mh 7.49i '02, LJ 7.94i '00, 7.57A '97.

Hamstring injury caused him to pull up in heats of 2003 Worlds. His mother (and coach) Ludmila Olijar (b. 5 Feb 1958) set the Latvian record holder for 100mh 12.90 (1989).

Eriks RAGS b. 1 Jun 1975 Ventspils 1.83m 93kg. Ventspils.

At JT: OG: '00- dnq 26, '04- 7; WCh: '97- dnq 22, '99- 10, '01- 8, '03- dnq 17, '05- 6; EC: '98- dnq 21, '02- 4; WJ: '94- dnq 28; EU23: '97- 4; WUG: '99- 1, '01- 1. 2nd GP 2001. Latvian champion 1997, 1999-2003.

Five Latvian javelin records 1999-2001.

Progress at JT: 1991- 63.50, 1992- 60.90, 1993- 65.22, 1994- 68.42, 1995- 75.32, 1996- 76.92, 1997- 79.04, 1998- 80.50, 1999- 83.78, 2000- 83.61, 2001- 86.47, 2002- 86.44, 2003- 86.32A, 2004- 85.83, 2005- 82.35.

Vadims VASILEVSKIS b. 5 Jan 1982 Riga 1.87m 82kg. ASK.

At JT: OG: '04- 2; WCh: '05- dnq 16; EC: '02- dnq 16; WJ: '00- 8; EU23: '03- 7; EJ: '01- 7.

Progress at JT: 1998- 59.17, 1999- 63.82, 2000- 73.07, 2001- 73.25, 2002- 81.92, 2003- 77.81, 2004- 84.95, 2005- 81.30.

Set personal bests in qualifying (84.43) and final at 2004 Olympics.

Women

Jelena PROKOPCUKA b. 21 Sep 1976 Riga 1.68m 51kg. née Chelnova. Arkadija/ASK.

At 5000m (/10,000m): OG: '96- h, '00- 9/19, '04- (7); WCh: '97- h, '03- (10), '05- (12); EC: '98- 16, '02- (5); EU23: '97- 5/6. At 3000m (/10,000m): WJ: '94: h/13; EJ: '95- 5/4; EI: '98- 4, '00- 4. World HMar: '01- 5, '02- 3. Won LAT 1500m 1994, 1997-8, 2003, 3000m 1992-3, 1998-9, 2002; 5000m 1995-7, 2002, 2005; 10,000m 2003-04, HMar 1995, 1999, 2003; CC 2001-02.

Latvian records 3000m 2000, 5000m (4) 1997-2000, 10,000m (4) 2000-04, 1 Hour 2003, HMar 2001 & 2005, Mar (3) 2002-05.

Progress at 5000m, 10,000m, Mar: 1994- 35:22.44, 1995- 16:20.7, 34:21.84; 1996- 15:59.00, 33:59.9; 1997- 15:40.68, 33:41.51; 1998- 15:30.76, 33:29.04; 1999- 16:09.22, 2000- 14:47.71, 31:27.86; 2001- 15:14.73, 32:02.96; 2002- 15:08.28, 31:17.72, 2:29:36;

2003- 15:02.04, 31:06.14, 2:24:01; 2004- 31:04.10, 2:26:51; 2005- 15:03.10, 31:04.55, 2:22:56. pbs: 400m 60.46 '98, 800m 2:05.82 '00, 1500m 4:12.36 '00, 3000m 8:44.66i/8:46.97 '00, 15km 48:47 '01, 1 Hour 17,776m '03, HMar 68:11 '05.

43 Latvian titles including indoors. Married to Aleksandrs Prokopchuks (LAT marathon record 2:15:56 '95). Marathons: 7th London & 3rd Chicago 2003, 4th Boston & 5th New York 2004, won Osaka and New York 2005.

LITHUANIA

Governing body: Athletic Federation of Lithuania, Statybininku 12/10, Vilnius LT 03201. Founded 1921.

National Championships first held in 1921 (women 1922). **2005 Champions: Men**: 100m: Justas Buragas 10.62, 200m/400m: Raimundas Turla 21.24/47.29, 800m/1500m: Mindaugas Norbutas 1:52.23/3:49.31, 5000m: Egidijus Rupsys 14:32.59, 10,000m/3000mSt: Mindaugas Pukstas 30:35.53/8:53.84, HMar/Mar: Tomas Venckunas 69:45/2:30:47, 110mh: Rolandas Stanionis 14.39, 400mh: Arturas Kulnis 52.50, HJ: Nerijus Buzas 2.14, PV: Saulius Birmanas 4.60, LJ: Vytautas Seliukas 7.80, TJ: Andrius Gricevicius 15.85, SP: Vytas Druktenis 17.23, DT: Virgilijus Alekna 69.21, HT: Zydrunas Vasiliauskas 65.24, JT: Tomas Intas 76.65, Dec: Aivaras Aksionovas 6842, 20kmW: Tadas Suskevicius 1:27:11, 50kmW: Daugvinas Zujus 4:10:31. **Women**: 100m: Audra Dagelyte 11.68, 200m: Lina Grincikaite 23.60, 400m: Jurate Kudirkaite 54.20, 800m: Irina Krakoviak 2:02.19, 1500m/3000mSt: Liubov Novosad 4:47.12/11:24.07, 5000m: Zivile Balciunaite 16:02.56, 10,000m: Remalda Kergyte 39:05.22, HMar: Egle Kristaponyte 86:50, Mar: Modesta Drungiliene 3:02:57, 100mh/HJ/LJ/SP: Austra Skujyte 14.42/1.82/6.13/17.03, 400mh: Vlada Musvydaite 59.47, PV: Edita Grigelionyte 3.70, TJ: Asta Dauksaite 12.81, DT: Zinaida Sendriute 54.62, HT: Natalija Venckute 50.21, JT: Inga Stasiulionyte 62.27, Hep: Erika Baliutaviciute 3853, 20kmW: Kristina Saltanovic 1:35:37.

Virgilijus ALEKNA b. 13 Feb 1972 Terpeikiai, Kupiskis 2.00m 130kg. Graduate of Lithianian Axademy of Physical Culture and (from 1995) guard of the Lithuanian president.

At DT: OG: '96- 5, '00- 1, '04- 1; WCh: '95- dnq 19, '97- 2, '99- 4, '01- 2, '03- 1, '05- 1; EC: '98- 3, '02- 2; WCp: '98- 1. Won WAF 2003, 2005; GP 2001 (2nd 1999). LTU champion 1998, 2000-05.

Four Lithuanian discus records 2000.

Progress at DT: 1990- 52.84, 1991- 57.16, 1992- 60.86, 1993- 62.84, 1994- 64.20, 1995- 62.78, 1996- 67.82, 1997- 67.70, 1998- 69.66A, 1999- 68.25, 2000- 73.88, 2001- 70.99, 2002- 66.90, 2003- 69.69, 2004- 70.97, 2005- 70.67. pb SP: 19.99 '97.

His 72.35 and 73.88 at the 2000 LTU Championships were the second and third longest ever discus throws. His 70.17 to win the 2005 World title (coming from 2nd at 68.10 with the last throw) was the first ever 70m throw at a global championships. On 4 Mar 2000 he married Kristina Šablovskyte (pb LJ 6.14 '96, T 12.90 '97, sister of Remigija Nazaroviene).

Women

Austra SKUJYTE b. 12 Aug 1979 Birzai 1.88m 80kg. Graduated in kinesiology from Kansas State University, USA (now assistant coach).

At Hep: OG: '00- 12, '04- 2; WCh: '01- 6, '03- 10, '05- 4; EC: '02- 4; WJ: '98- 6; EU23: '99- 6, '01- 3. At Pen: WI: '04- 3. Won NCAA 2001-02; LTU 100mh 2000, 2005; HJ & LJ 2005, SP 2001-02, 2004-05; Hep 1997. World decathlon record 2005.

Progress at Hep: 1997- 4930, 1998- 5606, 1999- 5724, 2000- 6104, 2001- 6150w, 2002- 6275, 2003- 6213, 2004- 6435, 2005- 6386. pbs: 100m 12.4' '05, 200m 24.82 '04, 400m 57.19 '05, 800m 2:15.9 '04, 1500m 5:15.86 '05, 60mh 8.69i '04, 100mh 14.02/13.83w '04; HJ 1.85 '00, 1.89i '06; PV 3.1 '05, LJ 6.39i '05, 6.32 '04, 6.40w '01; SP 17.03 '02 DT 51.30 '02, JT 51.02 '02, Pen 4679i '04, Dec 8358 '05.

Set three pbs in 2004 Olympics, including two seconds off 800m best to secure silver.

LUXEMBOURG

Governing body: Fédération Luxembourgeoise d'Athlétisme, BP 503, L-2015 Luxembourg. Founded 1928.

2005 National Champions: **Men**: 100m/200m: Daniel Abenzoar 10.79/21.34, 400m: Raoul Peti 49.51, 800m/1500m: Mike Schumacher 1:53.16/4:00.81, 5000m/10,000m: Thierry Hübsch 15:03.09/31:54.10, HMar: Vincent Nothum 69:53, Mar: Alain Kieffer 2:34:04 3000mSt: Pascal Groben 9:13.28, 110mh: Claude Godart 14.36, 400mh: Jeff Steffen 56.03, HJ: Jacques Heyen 1.90, PV: Mike Gira 4.75, LJ: Patrick Hansen 7.08, TJ: Benjamin Kraemer 13.31, SP: Fernand Heintz 14.19, DT: Gast Main 39.06, HT: Gilles Lorang 53.30, JT: Christian Marche 53.30. **Women**: 100m/200m/LJ: Chantal Hayen 12.38/25.08/5.38, 400m/400mh/JT/Hep: Mandy Charlet 59.28/64.55/34.56/4837, 800m: Valérie Wagner 2:20.86, 1500m/3000m: Marys Scheller 5:06.08/10:20.57, 10,000m/HMar/Mar: Pascale Schmoetten 36:37.30/86:12/2:52:30 3000mSt: Anne Logelin 11:50.01, 100mh: Kim Reuland 14.73, HJ: Tammy Kieffer 1.65, PV: Stephanie Vieillevoye 3.20, TJ: Laurence Kipgen 11.23, SP: Kim Schaertz 12.49, DT: Vanessa Bignoli 39.16, HT: Tessy Biver 38.28.

MAURITIUS

Governing body: Mauritius Amateur Athletic Association, Nebiolo House, Maryse Justin Stadium, Réduit. Founded 1952.

Stéphan BUCKLAND b. 20 Jan 1977 Floréal 1.87m 73kg.

At (100m)/200m: OG: '00- qf/sf, '04- 6; WCh: '99- (qf), '01- 6, '03- 5, '05- 5; CG: '02- sf, '06- 2; AfG: '99- (8); AfCh: '00- (2).
MRI records: 100m from 1997, 200m from 1996.
Progress at 100m, 200m: 1994- 10.5, 1995- 10.61/10.4, 1996- 10.49/10.4, 21.14/21.0; 1997- 10.47, 1998- 10.47, 1999- 10.22/10.0A, 2000- 10.16, 20.31; 2001- 10.13, 20.15; 2002- 10.13, 20.29; 2003- 10.20, 20.06; 2004- 10.21/10.15w, 20.20; 2005- 10.28, 20.39. pbs: 60m 6.72i '04, 300m 33.41 '01.

MEXICO

Governing body: Federación Mexicana de Atletismo, Anillo Periférico y Av. del Conscripto, 11200 México D.F. Founded 1933.

2005 National Champions: Men: 100m: Jesús Domínguez 10.66, 200m: Juan Pedro Toledo 20.97, 400m: Alejandro Cárdenas 47.90, 800m: Amado Amador 1:49.29, 1500m: Juan Luis Barrios 3:44.14, 5000m: Alejandro Suárez 14:19.00, 10,000m: Juan Carlos Romero 30:14.14, 3000mSt: Salvador Miranda 9:01.65, 110mh: Norhiher Marín 14.67, 400mh: Oscar Juanz 52.48, HJ: Gerardo Martínez 2.20, PV: Giovanni Lanaro 5.65, LJ: Israel Rergis 16.95, TJ: Luis Rivera 15.42, SP: Daniel Ríos 16.19, DT: Mauricio Serna 50.65, HT: Luis García 61.53, JT: Frank Rodríguez 64.45, Dec: Juan Pedro Santarrosa 6591, 20kmW: Bernardo Segura 1:24:55. **Women:** 100m: Astrid Nassar 11.70, 200m: Ruth Grajeda 24.06, 400m: Mayra González 52.98, 800m: Yamilé Alaluf 2:09.58, 1500m: Dulce Rodríguez 4:26.84, 5000m: América Mateos 16:47.56, 10,000m: Angélica Sánchez 34:46.22, 3000mSt: Violeta Gómez 11:18.18, 100mh: Violeta Ávila 14.17, 400mh: Lourdes Escalona 60.15, HJ: Romary Rifka 1.80, PV: Cecilia Villar 3.40, LJ: Claude Martínez 5.86, TJ: Claudia Lugo 13.02, SP: Tamara Lechuga 14.13, DT: Flor Acosta 43.75, HT: Jéssica Ponce 56.40, JT: Ana Gutiérrez 51.32, 20kmW: Ariana Aquino 1:42:24.

Noé HERNÁNDEZ b. 15 Mar 1978 Chimalhuacán, Estado de México 1.75m 64kg.
At 20kmW: OG: '00- 2, '04- dq; WCh: '01- dq, '03- 4; WCp: '02- 4. Won CAC 1999, IbAm 2000, 2nd PAm Cup 2000, MEX 2001.
Progress at 20kmW: 1998- 1:26:17, 1999- 1:20:12, 2000- 1:19:03, 2001- 1:23:03, 2002- 1:21:46A, 2003- 1:18:14, 2004- 1:20:32, 2005- 1:18:51. pb 50kmW 4:11:35 02.

Bernardo SEGURA Rivera b. 11 Feb 1970 San Mateo Atenco, Estado de México. 1.75m 62kg.
At 20kmW: OG: '96- 3, '00- dq, '04- dnf; WCh: '93/03/05- dq, '95/9- dnf; WCp: '95- 3, '99- 1; PAm: '95- dq, '99- 1, '03- 2; CAG: '98- 2; WUG: '93- 3. Won America's Cup 1992, PAmCp 1994, 2000; GWG 1994.
World record 20,000m track walk 1994.
Progress at 20kmW: 1991- 1:22:01, 1992- 1:24:09, 1993- 1:19:39, 1994- 1:17:25.6t, 1995- 1:19:09, 1996- 1:19:05, 1997- 1:23:19, 1998- 1:19:46, 1999- 1:20:17, 2000- 1:22:47, 2002- 1:22:46, 2003- 1:19:06, 2004- 1:20:42, 2005- 1:21:46. pbs: 3000mW 19:05.5 91, 10,000mW 38:24.0 '94, 1HrW: 15,577.3m '94, 50kmW 4:03:51 '94.
Disqualified after 'winning' the Olympic 20km walk in 2000 and taking his lap of honour. Director of the National Sports Institute. He has named his son Jefferson Daniel Segura after the last two 20kmW Olympic gold medallists. His brother **Jorge** (b. 23 Apr 1975) won the world junior 10,000m walk title in 1994 and at 20km was CAC champion 1995, pb 1:22:50 '95.

Women

Ana Gabriela **GUEVARA** b. 4 Mar 77 Nogales, Sonora 1.73m 61kg.
At 400m/4x400m (800m): OG: '00- 5, '04- 2; WCh: '99- sf, '01- 3, '03- 1, '05- 3; WI: '99- 4. WJ: '96- sf; PAm: '99- 1, '03- 1; CAG: '98- 2 (2), '02- 1/1R; WUG: '97- (6); WCp: '02- 1. Won WAF 2003-04, GP 2002 (3rd overall), GWG 2001, IbAm 1998.
Four CAC 400m records 2002-03, MEX records 400m (9) 1998-2003, 800m (2) 1998. World best 300m 2003.
Progress at 400m, 800m: 1996- 54.75A, 2:09.80; 1997- 52.46A, 2:02.90; 1998- 50.65, 2:01.12; 1999- 50.70, 2:03.69, 2000- 49.70A/49.96, 2:02.88; 2001- 49.97; 2002- 49.16, 2003- 48.89, 2004- 49.53, 2005- 49.81. pbs: 200m: 23.78A '98, 300m 35.30A '03, 35.7+ '04, 35.92 '01.
She became the first Mexican woman to win a medal at any IAAF World Championship in track when 3rd in Edmonton 400m. Unbeaten in 24 successive 400m finals from then to loss to Tonique Williams-Darling in Rome on 2 July 2004, including 12 in 2002, when she shared the Golden League jackpot, and 8 in 2003. Played semi-professional basketball to December 1995.

MOROCCO

Governing Body: Fédération Royale Marocaine d'Athlétisme, Complex Sportif Prince Moulay Abdellah, PO Box 1778 R/P, Rabat. Founded 1957.

Mohammed AMYN b. 25 Mar 1976 1.68m 56kg.
At 5000m: WCh: '01- 12; AfCh: '02- 3 (1500m 11). At 3000m: WI: '04- 8. At 10,000m: OG: '04- 18; WCh: '05- 20; won MedG 2005. World CC: '95- 17J, 99- 10 4k; '06- 15.
Progress at 5000m, 10,000m: 1997- 13:29.2, 1998- 13:33.19, 2000- 13:40.89, 2001- 13:05.44, 2002- 13:01.98, 2003- 13:25.34, 2004- 13:10.18, 27:44.24; 2005- 13:30.50, 27:22.67. pbs: 1500m 3:34.81 '99, 1M 3:52.66 '99, 2000m 4:59.91i '99, 5:04.2 '98; 3000m 7:35.35 '01, 2M 8:19.57i '02, HMar 62:30 '05.

Brahim BOULAMI b. 20 Apr 1972 Safi 1.80m 64kg.
At 3000mSt: OG: '96- 7, 00- 7; WCh: '97- 10, '01- 10, '05- 4; AfCh: '98- 3, '02- 1; won MedG 1997, 2005; GWG & GPF 2001. World CC: '97- 22, 4k: '98-01: 6/7. Won Moroccan CC 1997.

Two World 3000m steeplechase records 2001, four Moroccan 2000-01.
At 3000mSt: 1995- 8:20.64, 1996- 8:18.49, 1997- 8:10.84, 1998- 8:11.30, 2000- 8:02.90, 2001- 7:55.28, 2002- 7:53.17dq/7:58.09, 2004- 8:02.66, 2005- 8:04.92. pbs: 3000m 7:38.18 '02, 5000m 13:28.06 '98.
Younger brother of Khalid Boulami (b. 7 Aug 1969, 5000m: 3 OG 1996, 2 WCh 1995 & 1997, pb 12:53.41 '97). Succeeded Ali Ezzine as fastest ever non-Kenyan steeplechaser in 2000 and in 2001 became the first non-Kenyan to set a world record for the event for 25 years. He ran even faster at Zürich in 2002 only to test positive for EPO and serve 2-year ban. On his first race back, he was 2nd at Brussels in 2004 in 8:02.66.

Mouhcine CHÉHIBI b. 28 Jan 1978 1.82m 70kg. Efs Reims, France.
At 800m: OG: '00- sf, '04- 4; WCh: '99/03- h, '05- sf; AfCh: '00- 3; WUG: '01- 6.
Progress at 800m: 1999- 1:46.15, 2000- 1:46.2, 2001- 1:46.54, 2002- 1:47.15, 2003- 1:45.73, 2004- 1:44.62. 2005- 1:44.46. pbs: 600m 1:18.86 '00, 1000m 2:20.43i '05, 2:21.43 '03; 1500m 3:45.84 '04.
Disqualified for pushing at 2003 Worlds. Married to Hasna Benhassi (2 OG 800m 2004).

Hicham EL GUERROUJ b. 14 Sep 1974 Berkane 1.76m 58kg.
At 1500m (/5000m): OG: '96- 12, '00- 2, '04- 1/1; WCh: '95- 2, '97- 1, '99- 1, '01- 1, '03- 1/2; WJ: '92- (3). WI: '95- 1, '97- 1. At 3000m: WI: '01- 1. World Rd Rly team: '94- 1. World CC: '92- 14J. Won GP 1500m 1996, 1998 and 2001-02 (2nd 1M 1997), 2nd overall 2002.
World records: 1500m 1998, 1M and 2000m 1999. World indoor records 1500m (3:31.18) and 1M (3:48.45) 1997. Moroccan records: 1500m & 1M 1997 and 1998, 2000m 1998.
Progress at 1500m, 1M, 5000m: 1992- 13:46.79, 1994- 3:33.61, 3:53.71; 1995- 3:31.16, 3:48.69; 1996- 3:29.05, 1997- 3:28.91, 3:44.90; 1998- 3:26.00, 3:44.60; 1999- 3:27.65, 3:43.13; 2000- 3:27.21, 3:45.96; 2001- 3:26.12, 3:44.95; 2002- 3:26.89, 3:48.28; 2003- 3:28.40, 3:50.20, 12:50.24; 2004- 3:27.64, 13:14.39. pbs: 1000m 2:16.85 '95, 2000m 4:44.79 '99, 3000m 7:23.09 '99, 2M 8:06.61i '03.
At last won Olympic gold in 2004, having won 84 of 89 races at 1500m or 1M from 1996. He won the 5000m bronze medal at the 1992 World Juniors and broke through in 1994 to run 3:33.61 for 1500m at Nice with no known form at this event. At Stuttgart on 2 Feb 1997 he took 2.98 secs off Morceli's world indoor 1500m record, in 1998 he took 1.37 secs off Morceli's 1500m WR with a majestic run at Rome, and a year later added world records at 1M and 2000m. His unbeaten record in 1999 included the second best ever 3000m time of 7:23.09 at Brussels in 1999, from a previous best of 7:49.84 (1994) and a time-trial 7:39.74 in 1996. Missed 2005 season.

Abdelkader EL MOUAZIZ b. 1 Jan 1969 Settat 1.72m 58kg.
At Mar: OG: '96- 44, '00- 7; WCh: '97- dnf '01- 6.
Progress at Mar: 1994- 2:15:45, 1995- 2:14:45 1996- 2:09:50, 1997- 2:09:50, 1998- 2:08:07, 1999- 2:07:57, 2000- 2:07:33, 2001- 2:07:11, 2002- 2:06:46 2003- 2:08:03, 2004- 2:09:42, 2005- 2:09:03. pb HMar 61:06 '04.
Eight wins in 26 marathons. He had won at Marrakech in 1996 and 1997 in the same time of 2:09:50 and again in 1999 in 2:08:15. Won London 1999 and 2001, 2nd 1998 and 2000, won New York 2000. Twice improved pb in 2002: 4th London 2:06:52, 5th Chicago 2:06:46. His 4th in London 2005 was his record 13th sub-2:10 time. Spent four years 1990-4 in Granada, Spain.
Younger brother **Hamid** (b. 17 Feb 1979) has 1500m pb 3:38.04 '01.

Ali EZZINE b. 3 Sep 1978 Ain Taouajtat, Meknès 1.76m 63kg.
At 3000mSt: OG: '00- 3, '04- 8; WCh: '99- 3, '01- 2, '03- 10; WJ: '96- 3. World CC: '97- 11J; 4k: '98- 12, '00- 13.
Three MAR 3000m steeple records 1999-2000.
Progress at 3000mSt: 1996- 8:34.2, 1997- 8:23.18, 1998- 8:15.85, 1999- 8:06.70, 2000- 8:03.57, 2001- 8:10.23, 2002- 8:27.98, 2003- 8:13.31, 2004- 8:12.93. pbs: 1500m 3:43.8 '98, 2000m 5:00.84 '98, 3000m 7:45.9 '04, 5000m 13:32.56 '97.
Became the then fastest ever non-Kenyan steeplechaser in 1999 with 8:07.31 in Paris and 8:06.70 in Berlin.

Jaouad GHARIB b. 22 May 1972 Khenifra province 1.76m 60kg.
At Mar: OG: '04- 11; WCh: '03- 1, '05- 1. At 10,000m: WCh: '01- 11; AfCh: '02- 8. At 3000m: WI: '03- 11. World HMar: '01- 9, '02- 2; CC: '02- 10. Won MedG 10,000m 2001.
Progress at 5000m, 10,000m, Mar: 2001- 13:19.69, 27:29.51; 2002- 13:20.59, 28:02.09i/28:57.12; 2003- 2:08:31, 2004- 2:07:02 (2:07:12?), 2005- 2:07:49. pbs: 3000m 7:39.22 '01, 15km 43:08 '01, HMar 59:56 '04.
Made sudden emergence into top class in 2001. Sixth in 2:09:15 at Rotterdam 2003 on marathon debut and won world title in next marathon; London: 3rd 2004, 2nd 2005.

Abderrahim GOUMRI b. 21 May 1976 Safi 1.67m 60kg.
At 5000m: OG: '04- 13; WCh: '03- 10. At 10,000m: WCh: '01- 16, '05- 8; AfCh: '02- 4. At 3000m: WI: '03- 9. World CC: '95-02-03-04-06: 25J/7/15/14/11; 4k: '03- 10, '05- 18; HMar: '03- 12.
Progress at 5000m, 10,000m: 1999- 13:20.70, 2001- 13:03.60, 27:26.01; 2002- 13:00.76, 27:52.62i/28:45.92; 2003- 13:05.81, 2004- 12:59.04, 2005- 12:50.25, 27:02.62. pbs: 1500m 3:39.80 '98, 1M 4:02.46 '99, 2000m 5:04.8 '02, 3000m 7:32.36 '01, HMar 61:19 '01.

Adil KAOUCH b. 1 Jan 1979 1.70m 60kg.
At 1500m: OG: '04- 9; WCh: '99- 11, '01- 11, '05- 2; WJ: '98- 1; WI: '99-7, 03- 5. World CC: '97-8: 19J/10J, 4k: '99-01-04-06: 11/11/10/3. Won P.Arab & Franc G 5000m 1999.
Progress at 1500m: 1998- 3:36.67, 1999- 3:34.28, 2000- 3:34.41, 2001- 3:36.01, 2004- 3:32.86, 2005- 3:38.00. pbs: 1M 3:51.62 '99, 2000m 4:58.56i '99, 3000m 7:39.52 '00, 2M 8:35.22i '04, 5000m 14:05.71 '99.
Paced El Guerrouj in 1999 and 2001 World finals. Two knee operations before return in 2004.

Women

Amina AÏT HAMMOU b. 18 Jul 1978 Kenitra 1.65m 49kg.
At 800m: OG: '00- h, '04- sf; WCh: '03- 4, '05- sf; AfCh: '02- 3; WUG: '99- 7; At 3000m: WJ: '98- 12. Won World Miltary 800m 2001.
Progress at 800m: 1999- 2:03.76, 2000- 2:03.16, 2001- 2:00.47, 2002- 2:01.03; 2003- 1:57.82, 2004- 1:58.92, 2005- 1:59.91. pbs: 400m 53.36 '04, 600m 1:27.47 '00, 1000m 2:39.61i '05, 3000m 8:59.2 '98.
Formerly played football and handball. Her younger sister **Seltana** (b. 21 May 1980) won Mediterranean Games 800m in 2001, OG sf 2004, pb 1:59.74 '03.

Hasna BENHASSI b. 1 Jun 1978 Marrakech 1.66m 55kg. Panellínios, Greece.
At 800m: OG: '00- 8, '04- 2 (12 1500m); WCh: '97- sf, '05- 2; AfCh: '98- 2, '00- 1; WJ: '96- sf; WI: '99- 5, '06- 3; won WAF 2004, MedG 1997, Moroccan 1996. At 1500m: WI: '01- 1, '03- 8; AfCh: '02- 3.
MAR records 800m (4), 1000m, 1500m (2) 1998-2004.
Progress at 800m, 1500m: 1995- 2:11.0, 1996- 2:04.6, 4:31.4; 1997- 2:00.48, 4:27.1; 1998- 1:58.47, 4:05.15; 1999- 1:57.45, 4:05.29; 2000- 1:58.47, 4:14.28; 2001- 1:59.86i, 4:04.48i; 2002- 4:05.28, 2003- 2:01.08, 4:02.54; 2004- 1:56.43, 4:04.42; 2005- 1:58.41. pbs: 400m 54.04 '00, 1000m 2:33.15 '99, 1M 4:32.99 '98.
Married to Mouhcine Chéhibi, daughter Farah born on 7 Dec 2001.

Asmae LEGHZAOUI b. 30 Aug 1976 1.55m 40kg.
At 10,000m (/5000m): OG: '00- 18; WCh: '99- h, '01- 7; AfCh: '00- (1), 02- (4). At 3000m: WI: '01- 10. World 4km CC: '99-01-03: 7/9/12; HMar: '02- 10. Won MedG 10,000m 2001, Arab 1999.
Three Moroccan 10,000m records 1999-01, world road 10km best 2002.
Progress at 5000m, 10,000m: 1996- 37:33.1, 1999- 32:18.1, 2000- 14:48.31, 31:59.21; 2001- 14:49.32, 31:16.94; 2002- 14:51.71, 2005- 15:23.30, 32:59.24. pbs: 2000m 5:41.3 '01, 3000m 8:33.85 '00, Rd: 10km 30:29 '02, 15km 48:56 '01, 10M 52:21 '02, HMar 68:34 '99.
Suspended for two years after positive test for EPO at 2003 World CC Champs.

MOZAMBIQUE

Governing body: Federaçao Moçambicana de Atletismo,Parque dos Continuardores, CP 1094, Maputo. Founded 1978.

Maria de Lurdes **MUTOLA** b. 27 Oct 1972 Maputo 1.62m 61kg.
At 800m (1500m): OG: '88- h, '92- 5 (9), '96- 3, '00- 1, '04- 4; WCh: '91- 4, '93- 1, '95 dq sf, '97- 3, '99- 2, '01- 1, '03- 1, '05- 4; WI: '93-5-7-9-01-03-04-06: 1/1/1/2/1/1/1/1; CG: '98- 1, '02- 1, '06- 3; AfCh: '88-90-3-8-02: 2/1/1/1/1 (1 1500m 90); AfG: '91- 1, '95- 1, '99- 1; WCp: '92- 1/3R, '94- 1, '98- 1, '02- 1. Won WAF 2003, GWG 1994, 2001; GP 1993, 1995 (won overall), 1999 (2nd overall), 2001; 2nd 1997.
Records: World 1000m 1995, two WIR 1000m (2:32.08 '96 and 2:30.94 '99). African: 800m (8) 1991-4, 1000m (4) 1993-5; Commonwealth 800m 1997. African junior 800m (3) and 1500m 1991. MOZ 200m to 3000m.
Progress at 800m, 1500m: 1988- 2:04.36, 1989- 2:05.7, 4:31.5; 1990- 2:13.54, 4:25.27; 1991- 1:57.63, 4:12.72; 1992- 1:57.49, 4:02.60; 1993- 1:55.43, 4:04.97; 1994- 1:55.19, 4:13.93; 1995- 1:55.72, 4:01.6mx; 1996- 1:57.07, 4:01.63; 1997- 1:55.29, 4:09.1mx; 1998- 1:56.11, 1999- 1:56.04, 2000- 1:56.15, 4:02.39; 2001- 1:56.85, 2002- 1:56.16, 4:01.50; 2003- 1:55.55, 2004- 1:56.51, 4:07.57; 2005- 1:58.49i/1:58.96, 2006- 1:58.77. pbs: 200m 23.86 '94, 300m 37.16mx '94, 400m 51.37 '94, 600m 1:22.87 '02, 1000m 2:29.34 '95, 1M 4:36.09 '91, 2000m 6:03.84 '92, 3000m 9:27.37 '91, 5000m 18:15.1 '90; Rd 1M 4:32.4 '95.
A star soccer player at school in Maputo, she was enabled to attend school in Eugene, Oregon, USA by a grant from the Olympic Solidarity Committee. She had 50 successive wins in 800m finals 1992-6, excluding her disqualification for stepping out of her lane after finishing first in her World semi-final, ending with her Olympic bronze in 1996, and 39 successive wins at 800m including 12 heats in 2002-04. She became Mozambique's first ever CG champion in 1998, following her country's admittance to the Commonwealth. She became the first athlete ever to win four individual World Cup titles in 2002, won World titles indoors and out and was the sole winner of the Golden League jackpot of £1 million in 2003, and now has a record seven World indoor titles. Her 1:56.36 for 800m in 1998 was disallowed as a world indoor record as she ran inside the lane. 12 successive wins at Zürich 1993-2004. She has run 179 sub-2 minute 800m times from 1991 to March 2006.

NETHERLANDS

Governing body: Koninklijke Nederlandse Atletiek Unie (KNAU), Postbus 230, 3400 AE IJsselstein. Founded 1901.
National Championships first held in 1910 (men), 1921 (women). **2005 Champions**: **Men**:

100m/200m: Guus Hoogmoed 10.36/20.41w, 400m: Robert Lathouwers 46.52, 800m: Arnoud Okken 1:49.53; 1500m: Casper Dirks 3:55.71, 5000m: Sander Schutgens 14:03.92, 10,000m: Khalid Choukoud 30:12.06, HMar: Luc Krotwaar 62:20, Mar: Kamiel Maase 2:12:51, 3000mSt: Simon Vroemen 8:54.08, 110mh: Gregory Sedoc 13.62, 400mh: Bram Kempkens 52.22, HJ: Jan-Peter Larsen 2.22, PV: Rens Blom 5.70, LJ: Jurgen Cools 7.85w, TJ: Ellsworth Manuel 14.78, SP/DT: Rutger Smith 20.59/65.51, HT: Ronald Gram 65.63, JT: Björn Blommerde 68.96, Dec: Ludo van der Plaat 7490, 50kmW: Pedro Huitjens 4:49:35. **Women**: 100m/200m: Jacqueline Poelman 11.61/23.06w, 400m: Henrieke Krommendijk 54.80, 800m: Lotte Visschers 2:12.86, 1500m: Adrienne Herzog 4:23.82, 5000m: Anita Looper 16:07.07, 10,000m: Kristyna Loonen 34:16.09, HMar: Selma Borst 71:23, Mar: Lornah Kiplagat 2:27:36, 100mh: Rosina Hodde 13.58, 400mh: Marjolein de Jong 56.07, HJ: Yvonne Wisse 1.79, PV: Galiart 4:10, LJ: Mirjam Boxhoorn 6.03, TJ: Francien Vierkant 12.17, SP/DT: Lieja Tunks 18.55/55.58, HT: Debby van der Schilt 57.90, JT: Bregje Crolla 51.21, Hep: Yvonne Wisse 5870.

Rens BLOM b. 1 Mar 1977 Munstergeleen 1.78m 75kg. AV Unitas & TSV Bayer 04 Leverkusen, GER.
At PV: OG: '00- dnq 15, '04- 9=; WCh: '01- nh, '03- dnq 14, '05- 1; EU23: '97- 10, '99- 5=; WI: '03- 3, '04- nh; EI: '00- 3; WUG: '97- 4; ECp: '04- 6. Dutch champion 2001-05.
Three Dutch pole vault records 1997-2004.
Progress at PV: 1990- 3.41, 1991- 3.90, 1992- 4.05, 1993- 4.70, 1994- 5.10i, 1995- 5.00, 1996- 5.40, 1997- 5.62, 1998- 5.60i/5.55, 1999- 5.70i/5.50, 2000- 5.75, 2001- 5.70, 2002- 5.65, 2003- 5.75, 2004- 5.81, 2005- 5.80.
In 2005 he became the first Dutch athlete to won gold at the World Championships, after which he was appointed a Knight in the Order of Orange-Nassau. Father Wim set pbs in 1967 of 100m 10.5, 200m 21.4/21.1w.

Gert-Jan LIEFERS b, 26 Sep 1978 Apeldoorn 1.87m 71kg. AV '34.
At 1500m: OG: '04- 8; WCh: '99- sf, '01- 9, '03- 7; WJ: '96- 4; EU23: '99- 2; EJ: '95- 3, '97- 1. At 3000m: WI: '03- 6, '04- 6; ECp: '04- 2. Eur CC: '97- 1J. Won Dutch 1500m 1998-9, 2004; 4k CC 2004.
Dutch records: 1500m & 2000m 2001, 1M 2003, 3000m 2002 & 2005.
Progress at 1500m: 1992- 4:05.35, 1993- 3:57.2, 1994- 3:53.4, 1995- 3:46.6, 1996- 3:40.47, 1997- 3:38.07, 1998- 3:34.27, 1999- 3:35.20, 2000- 3:42.77, 2001- 3:32.89, 2002- 3:37.77, 2003- 3:33.99, 2004- 3:33.87, 2005- 3:35.29. pbs: 800m 1:45.47 '98, 1M 3:51.39 '03, 2000m 4:56.56 '01, 3000m 7:37.48 '05, 5000m 13:22.26 '05.
Younger brother Arnoud was Dutch 400m junior champion in 2000. His mother Marjon Dekker was a Dutch CC champion.

Rutger SMITH b. 9 Jul 1981 Groningen 1.97m 124kg. Groningen Atletiek.
At SP/(DT): OG: '04- dnq 14/16; WCh: '03- dnq 25/15, '05- 2; EC: '02- 8; WJ: '00- 1/3; EU23: '03- 3/1; EJ: '99- 1/1; WI: '03- dnq 10; EI: '05- 2; ECp: '04- 2/2. Won NED SP 2000, 2002-05, DT 2002-05.
Two Dutch shot records 2005.
Progress at SP, DT: 1998- 15.23, 51.18; 1999- 18.27, 53.81; 2000- 19.48, 58.74; 2001- 18.92i/18,21, 59.96; 2002- 20.52, 64.69; 2003- 20.52, 62.70; 2004- 20.94, 63.79; 2005- 21.41, 65.51.

Simon VROEMEN b. 11 May 1969 Delft 1.89m 68kg. Oil company reservoir engineer, PhD in microbiology. AV Sprint, Breda
At 3000mSt: OG: '00- 12, '04- 6; WCh: '97- sf, '99/01- h, '03- 7, '05- 5; EC: '02- 2. Won NED 1500m 1991, 1994; 3000mSt 1995, 1997, 1999-2005.
European 3000m steeplechase records 2002 & 2005, Three Dutch records 200-05.
Progress at 3000mSt: 1994- 8:36.61; 1995- 8:33.52; 1996- 8:37.36, 1997- 8:19.16, 1998- 8:45.70, 1999- 8:19.52, 2000- 8:13.45, 2001- 8:20.67, 2002- 8:06.91, 2003- 8:09.18, 2004- 8:13.25, 2005- 8:04.95. pbs: 800m 1:48.87 '94, 1000m 2:20.9 '91, 1500m 3:39.19 '94, 1M 4:04.19 '92, 3000m 7:58.38 '01, 2M 8:46.10 '95, 5000m 13:50.77 '97, 2000mSt 5:26.08 '02.
Twin brother Casper has 3000mSt pb 8:35.18 '96.

Women

Lornah KIPLAGAT b. 20 Mar 1974 Kabeimit, Kenya 1.66m 49kg. AV Hylas. Married to Pieter Langerhorst NED.
At 10,000m: OG: '04- 5; WCh: '03- 4. World HMar: '05- 2; CC: '04-06: 6/5 (4k) & 2; Eur CC: '05- 1. Won Dutch Mar 2005.
World road best 10 miles 2002. Dutch records 10,000m & Marathon 2003.
Progress at 10,000m, Mar: 1997- 2:33:50, 1998- 2:34:03, 1999- 2:25:29, 2000- 2:22:36, 2001- 2:27:56, 2002- 2:23:55, 2003- 30:12.53, 2:22:22; 2004- 30:31.92, 2:28:21; 2005- 2:28:10. pbs: 3000m 8:52.82 '00, 5000m 14:51.95mx '02, 14:56.43 '03; Road: 5M 25:09 '97 (former world best), 10km 30:32 '02, 15km 47:28 '02, 10M 50:54 '02, HMar 66:34 '01.
Four wins in 15 marathons: Los Angeles 1997 and 1998, Amsterdam 1999, Osaka 2002. Capped a series of fine road runs with second in Chicago marathon 2000. Fourth Boston 2001, 4th Osaka and 3rd New York 2003. Switched from Kenyan to Dutch (citizen from 23 July 2003).

Karin RUCKSTUHL b. 2 Nov 1980 Baden, Switzerland 1.81m 65kg. Hellas Utrecht. PhD student in geophysics.
At Hep: OG: '04- 16; WCh: '05- 8; EC: '02- 14; EU23: '01- 13. At Pen: WI: '04- 4, '06- 2; EI: '05- 4. Won NED HJ 2004, LJ 2001, 2003-04, TJ 1999, 2001.
Dutch heptathlon record 2005.
Progress at Hep: 1998- 4836, 1999- 5329, 2000-

5269, 2001- 5735, 2002- 5858, 2003- 6017, 2004- 6206, 2005- 6318. pbs: 200m 24.27 '05, 800m 2:12.89 '04, 60mh 8.39i '04, 100mh 13.26 '05, HJ 1.85 '04, LJ 6.58 '05, SP 14.06 '04, JT 43.61 '05, Pen 4683i '06.

NEW ZEALAND

Governing body: Athletics New Zealand, PO Box 741, Wellington.

National Championships first held in 1887 (men), 1926 (women). **2005 Champions: Men**: 100m/200m: James Dolphin 10.53/20.88, 400m/TJ: Tim Hawkes 47.50/15.05, 800m: Gareth Hyett 1:53.90, 1500m: Paul Hamblyn 3:51.59, 5000m: Dale Warrander 14:17.19, 10,000m: Jonathan Wyatt 29:44.01, HMar: Kim Hogarth 68:58, Mar: Matthew Dravitzki 2:22:03, 3000mSt: Grant Schmid-Lechner 8:46.58, 110mh: James Mortimer 14.05, 400mh: Nicholas O'Brien 54.80, HJ: Ben Giles 2.08, PV: J.G.Nel 4.90, LJ/Dec: Brent Newdick 7.17/7260, SP: Shaka Sola 18.06, DT: Bertrand Vili 56.52, HT: Philip Jensen 65.72, JT: Stuart Farquhar 69.93, 3000mW/10kmW: Craig Barrett 11:49.17/45:35, 20kmW/50kmW: Tony Sargisson 1:33:33/4:05:59. **Women**: 100m/LJ: Chantal Brunner 11.83/6.46, 200m: Anna Smythe 24.19, 400m: Jane Arnott 55.47, 800m/1500m: Melissa Thomas 2:10.35/4:25.27, 5000m: Melissa Moon 17:01.89, 10,000m:, HMar: Nicole Cope 75:47, Mar: Shireen Crumpton 2:37:24, 3000mSt: Renee Holtom 11:36.75, 100mh/Hep: Rebecca Wardell 14.18/4986, 400mh: Sarah O'Connell 63.17, HJ: Angela McKee 1.88, PV: Melina Hamilton 4.31, TJ: Véroque Boyer 12.51, SP: Valerie Vili 19.32, DT: Beatrice Faumuina 62.39, HT: Debie McCaw 50.98, JT: Serafina Akeli 50.20, 3000mW: Gabrielle Gorst 14:12.07, 10kmW: Michelle Lei 54:42, 20kmW: Amelia De Lorenzo 1:55:30.

Nick WILLIS b. 25 Apr 1983 Lower Hutt 1.83m 68kg. Economics graduate of University of Michigan, USA.
At 1500m: OG: '04- sf, WCh: '05- sf; CG: '06-1; WJ: '02- 4. NZ champion 2006, NCAA indoor 2005. NZ 1500m record 2005.
Progress at 1500m: 2001- 3:43.54, 2002- 3:42.69, 2003- 3:36.58, 2004- 3:32.64, 2005- 3:32.38. pbs: 800m 1:45.54 '04, 1M 3:52.75 '06, 3000m 7:44.90i '04, 7:45.97 '05; 5000m 13:27.54 '05.
His brother Steve (b. 25 Apr 1975) had pbs: 1500m 3:40.29 '99, 1M 3:59.04 '00.

Women

Beatrice FAUMUINA b. 23 Oct 1974 Auckland 1.85m 115kg. Auckland City.
At DT (SP): OG: '96- dnq 23, '00- 12, '04- 7; WCh: '95- dnq 28, '97- 1, '99- 5, '03- 13, '05- 4; CG: '94- 2 (9), '98- 1 (4), '02- 1, '06- 4; WJ: '92- 5; WCp: '98- 4, '02- 1. 3rd GP 2000. Won NZ DT 1993-2000, 2002-06; SP 1994, 1997-9; AUS SP 1998, DT 1997-8, 2003.
Eleven NZ discus records 1993-7.
Progress at DT: 1990- 45.06, 1991- 46.04, 1992- 53.02, 1993- 55.20, 1994- 57.94, 1995- 60.28, 1996- 64.04, 1997- 68.52, 1998- 67.58, 1999- 64.62, 2000- 65.41A, 2001- 61.54, 2002- 65.05, 2003- 65.53 irreg/65.35, 2004- 66.08, 2005- 65.09. pbs: SP 16.96 '98, HT 44.24 '95.
First major success was winning 1992 Pacific Schools Games DT. 37 successive wins at discus 1997-8. Parents came from Western Samoa.

Valerie VILI b. 6 Oct 1984 Rotorua 1.93m 123kg. née Adams. Auckland City.
At SP: OG: '04- 8; WCh: '03- 5, '05- 3; CG: '02- 2, '06- 1; WJ: '02- 1; WY: '99- 10, '01- 1; WCp: '02- 6; WI: '04- 10. Won NZL SP 2001-06, DT 2004, HT 2003.
Three Oceania shot records 2005-06, 16 NZ 2002-06.
Progress at SP: 1999- 14.83, 2000- 15.72, 2001- 17.08, 2002- 18.40, 2003- 18.93, 2004- 19.29, 2005- 19.87, 2006- 20.20. pbs: DT 58.12 '04, HT 58.75 '02.
She matched her age with metres at the shot from 14 to 18 and missed that at 19 by only two months. Her father came from England and her mother from Tonga. She married New Caledonia thrower Bertrand Vili (SP 17.81 '02, DT 59.61 '05) in November 2004.

NIGERIA

Governing body: The Athletic Federation of Nigeria, P.O.Box 211, Marina, Lagos. F'd 1944.

2005 National Champions: **Men**: 100m: Uchenna Emedolu 10.13, 200m: Enefiok Udo-Obong 20.85, 400m: Joshua Godday 45.64, 800m: Lucky Iyoha 1:52.78, 1500m: Michael Haruna 4:00.81, 5000m: Jurbe Stephen 14:52.10, 10,000m/HMar: Kufkudi Danjuma 32:01.52/69:45, 3000mSt: Wilson Eku 9:31.65, 110mh: Chinedu Elekwa 14.27, 400mh: Moruf Lawal 51.70, HJ: Obiora Arinze 2.15, PV: Francis Gabriel 3.90, LJ: Tunde Suleiman 7.76, TJ: Akpa Njoku 16.12, SP/DT: Chima Ugwu 16.82/56.09, HT: John Osazuwa 61.59, JT: James Ayewoh 63.77, Dec: Lee Okoroafor 7078, 20kmW: Kazeem Adeyemi 1:45:34.01. **Women**: 100m: Endurance Ojokolo 11.29, 200m: Mercy Nku 23.47, 400m: Christy Ekpukpon 52.16, 800m: Joy Eze 2:03.93, 1500m: Grace Ebor 4:21.98, 5000m/10,000m: Alex Meprwmwa 17:28.47/35:02.00, HMar: Cecilia Cyril 1:26:06, 100mh: Joy Digha 13.87, 400mh: Omolade Akinremi 58.64, HJ: Nneka Ukuh 1.80, PV: Victoria Idodo 2.80, LJ: Esther Aghatise 6.47, TJ: Chinoye Ohadugba 13.81, SP/DT: Vivian Chukwuemeka 17.89/52.32, HT: Funke Adeoye 57.01, JT: Sorochukwu Ihuefo 50.02, Hep: Patience Okoro 5231, 20kmW: Kafayat Babalola 2:06:26.48.

Uchenna EMEDOLU b. 17 Sep 1976 Adazi-Ani, Aniocha 1.83m 79kg. Benfica, Portugal.
At 100m/(200m): OG: '00- (qf), '04- sf/3R; WCh: '01- sf/sf, '03- 6/8, '05- sf/qf; CG: '02- 2/qf; AfG: '03- 2/1; AfCh: '02- 2; WCp: '02- 1/3R.

Won NGR 200m 2001-03, 2005.
Progress at 100m, 200m: 1999- 21.08, 2000- 10.54/10.2, 20.69, 2001- 10.11/10.06w, 20.34; 2002- 10.06/10.00w, 20.31; 2003- 9.97, 20.38; 2004- 10.05/9.99w, 20.39; 2005- 10.13, 20.55/20.22w. pb 60m 6.66i '02.

Olusoji FASUBA b. 9 Jul 1984 1.75m 72kg.
At 100m/(200m)/4x100m: OG: '04- 3R; WCh: '03- 4R, '05- sf/qf; CG: '06- 2; AfCh: '04- 1. Won Af-AsG 2003. At 60m: WI: '06- 5. Won NGR 100m 2006.
Progress at 100m: 2002- 10.52/10.1, 2003- 10.15, 2004- 10.09, 2005- 10.09A/10.08w/9.8A, 2006- 10.11. pbs: 60m 6.50i '04, 200m 20.52 '04.

NORWAY

Governing body: Norges Fri-Idrettsforbund, Serviceboks 1, Ullevaal Stadium, 0840 Oslo. Founded 1896.

National Championships first held in 1897 (men), 1947 (women). **2005 Champions**: **Men**: 100m: Martin Rypdal 10.51, 200m: John Ertzgaard 21.61, 400m: Quincy Douglas 47.10, 800m: Ådne Svahn Dæhlin 1:53.02, 1500m: Bård Kvalheim3:49.18, 5000m: Marius Bakken 13:48.21, 10,000m/HMar: Uriga Buta ETH 29:23.02/64:26, Mar: Jan Helgesen 2:26:09, 3000mSt: Bjørnar Ustad Kristensen 8:44.54, 110mh/PV: Benjamin Jensen 14.05/5.00, 400mh: Ragnar Bergheim 51.64, HJ: Andreas Aune Viken 2.07, LJ: Thomas Mellin Olsen 7.57, TJ: Lars Eric Sæther 15.24, SP: Gjøran Sørli 18.64, DT: Gaute Myklebust 60.71, HT: Anders Halvorsen 59.70, JT: Andreas Thorkildsen 83.63, Dec: Hans Olav Uldal 7752,5000mW/20kmW: Erik Tysse 18:41.83/1:22:52, 10,000mW: Trond Nymark 41:56.0, 50kmW: Trond Nymark 3:49:36. **Women**: 100m: Ezinne Okparaebo 11.71, 200m: Elisabeth Slettum 23.96, 400m: Stine Meland Tomb 55.45, 800m/1500m: Ragnhild Kvarberg 2:05.56/4:20.54, 5000m: Susanne Wigene 15:01.05, 10,000m: Siri Merete Alfheim Espin 34:48.83, HMar: Turi Malme 80:08, Mar: Sofie van der Vlist Spiten NED 2:54:08, 3000mSt: Hanne Lyngstad 10:19.98, 100mh: Christina Vukicevic 14.09, 400mh: Lise Margareth Jensen 58.43, HJ: Anne Gerd Eieland 1.86, PV: Cathrine Larsåsen 3.71, LJ: Margrethe Renstrøm 6.11, TJ: Cecilie Rise 13.14, SP: Maren Romstad 14.39, DT: Grete Etholm Snyder 54.49, HT: Mona Holm 62.82, JT: Grethe Kleggetveit 48.78, Hep: Ellen Strøm 4621, 3000mW: Kjersti Tysse Plätzer 14:30.72, 5000mW/10kmW: Hanne Liland 26:14.0/54:23.

Marius BAKKEN b. 27 Mar 1978 Sandefjord 1.83m 63kg. IL Runar, Sandefjord.
At 5000m: OG: '00/04- h, WCh: '99- h, '01- 9, '05- 12; EC: '02- 14; EU23: '99- 2. Won NOR 1500m 2001, 2003-04, 5000m 2003, 2005.
Norwegian records 3000m (2), 5000m (4) 2000-04, 2000m 2003.
Progress at 5000m: 1999- 13:22.58, 2000- 13:11.30, 2001- 13:09.19, 2002- 13:57.89, 2003- 13:33.78, 2004- 13:06.39, 2005- 13:07.63. pbs: 800m 1:51.19 '97, 1500m 3:38.84 '05, 2000m 5:01.48 '03, 3000m 7:40.77 '01, 10,000m 28:26.36 '00.

Trond NYMARK b. 28 Dec 1976 Bergen 1.80m 64kg. TIF Viking, Bergen.
At 50kmW: OG: '04- 13; WCh: '99/01- dnf, '03- 8 '05- 4; EC: '02- 5. At 20kmW: EC: '98- 19; EU23 '97- 14. Won NOR 10,000m W 1997-8, 20kmW 1997, 2000, 2004; 50kmW 1998-9, 2004-05.
NOR record 30km walk 2000, 50km walk 2005.
Progress at 50kmW: 1998- 3:57:52, 1999- 3:54:36 2000- 3:53:10, 2002- 3:49:27, 2003- 3:46:14, 2004 3:44:55, 2005- 3:44:04. pbs: 3000mW 11:47.0 '00 5000mW 19:53.44i '02, 20:07.11 '00; 10,000mW 42:17.2 '02, 20kmW 1:22:52.4t '04, 30kmW 2:12:56 '00, 35kmW 2:36:40 '05.

Andreas THORKILDSEN b. 1 Apr 1982 Kristiansand 1.88m 90kg. Kristiansands IF.
At JT: OG: '04- 1; WCh: '01- dnq 26, '03- 11, '05- 2; EC: '02- dnq 15; WJ: '00- 2; EU23: '03- 5; EJ '99- 7, '01- 2; EY: '97- 1. Norwegian champion 2001, 2003-05.
World junior javelin record 2001, five Norwegian records 2005.
Progress at JT: 1996- 53.82, 1998- 61.57, 1999- 72.11, 2000- 77.48, 2001- 83.87, 2002- 83.43, 2003- 85.72, 2004- 86.50, 2005- 89.60.
His mother Bente Amundsen was a Norwegian champion at 100mh (pb 14.6), father Tomm was a junior international with bests of 100m 10.9 and javelin 71.64.

Women

Kjersti TYSSE PLÄTZER b. 18 Jan 1972 Os, Bergen 1.74m 54kg. née Tysse. IL Norna-Salhus, Bergen.
At 20kmW: OG: '00- 2, '04- 12; WCh: '99- 9, '01/03- dq; EC: '94- 16, '98- 9, '02- dq; WCp: '02- 5; ECp: '00- 3, '03- 6. At 5000mW: WJ: '86- 5. Won NOR 3000mW 2002, 2004-05; 5000mW 1985-7, 1992, 1994-6, 1998-2002, 10kmW 1994-5, 1998, 2000-02; 20kmW 1998-9, 2004.
World bests 1M walk 2001, 1500m walk 2002, 3km road (11:41) 2003. NOR walks records: 3000m (3), 5000m (4), 10km (6), 10,000m, 20km (4) 1996-2002.
Progress at 10kmW, 20kmW: 1986- 48:01, 1987- 45:45, 1994- 46:10, 1995- 45:12, 1996- 44:40, 1:39:36; 1998- 42:44, 1:32:55; 1999- 41:54, 1:28:35; 2000- 43:21.1t, 1:27:53; 2001- 42:23, 1:29:55, 2002- 41:16, 1:28:55; 2003- 43:59, 1:28:49; 2004- 42:52, 1:30:49. pbs: 1500mW 5:47.03 '02, 1MW 6:16.45 '01, 3000mW 11:59.3i '04, 12:01.91 '02; 5000mW 20:37.83 '01, 20:08R '03, 15kmW 1:05:12 '00; running: 3000m 10:43.19 '01, 5000m 17:57.55 '01.
Married to Stephan Plätzer GER (b. 12 Sep 66), pbs 800m 1:46.53 '89, 1500m 3:40.26 '89. Daughter Kiara Lea born 13 Oct 1997, son Sebastian born 5 Jun 2005. Her brother **Erik** (b. 4 Dec 1980) was 13th in the 2005 World 20km and set NOR records with 18:41.83 for 5000m and 1:21:11 for 20km in 2005.

Susanne WIGENE b. 12 Feb 1978 1.68m 50kg. IK Tjalve.
At 5000m: WCh: 05- 13; EU23: '99- 8; At 3000m: EJ: '97- 5. Won NOR 1500m 1999, 5000m 1998, 2004-05,. 3000mSt 2000; Nordic CC 2004.
Four Norwegian 3000mSt records 2000-04.
Progress at 5000m: 1998- 15:57.44, 1999- 15:41.57, 2000- 16:20.72, 2002- 16:04.24, 2003- 15:42.02, 2004- 15:12.27, 2005- 14:48.53. pbs: 1500m 4:13.01 '05, 3000m 8:40.23 '05, 10,000m 32:58.68 '00, 3000mSt 9:45.31 '04, 20km Rd 68:16 '04.

PANAMA

Bayano KAMANI b. 17 Apr 1980 Houston, USA 1.88m 79kg. Was at Baylor University.
At 400mh: OG '04- 5; WCh: '03- h, '05- 7; SACh: '03- 1; WUG: '99- 2; NCAA champion 1999, 2001.
South American 400mh record 2005, Six Panama records 2004-05.
Progress at 400mh: 1996- 51.71, 1997- 50.82, 1998- 49.86, 1999- 48.68, 2000- 48.43, 2001- 48.99, 2002- 50.05, 2003- 49.82, 2004- 48.23, 2005- 47.84. pb 400m 46.20i '01, 46.26 '05; 55mh 7.56i '97, 60mh 8.09i '98.
Lives in Los Angeles. Opted for his father's Panamanian nationality in 2003; his mother came from Barbados.

Irving SALADINO b. 23 Jan 1983 Ciudad de Colón 1.83m 70kg
At LJ: OG: '04- dnq 36; WCh: '05- 6; WJ: '02- dnq; SACh: '03- 3; WI: '06- 2; won SAm U23 2004.
Panama LJ records 2002-05.
Progress at LJ: 2002- 7.51A/7.39, 2003- 7.46, 2004- 8.12A/7.74, 2005- 8.29/8.51w, 2006- 8.29i. pbs: 100m 10.4 '04, TJ 14.47 '04.
Set South American indoor record in qualifying and four more in final of WI 2006.

POLAND

Governing body: Polski Zwiazek Lekkiej Atletyki (PZLA), 01-809 Warszawa, ul. Kopernika 30. Founded 1919.
National Championships first held in 1920 (men), 1922 (women). **2005 Champions**: **Men**: 100m: Michal Bielczyk 10.42, 200m: Marcin Jedrusinski 20.86, 400m: Marcin Marciniszyn 45.69, 800m: Pawel Czapiewski 1:47.10, 1500m: Miroslaw Formela 3:39.41, 5000m: Radoslaw Poplawski 13:46.80, 10,000m: Arkadiusz Sowa 28:48.29, HMar: Adam Dobrzynski 65:14, Mar: Rafal Wójcik 2:14:47, 3000mSt: Jakub Czaja 8:22.68, 110mh: Tomasz Scigaczewski 13.66, 400mh: Marek Plawgo 50.60, HJ: Michal Bieniek 2.34, PV: Adam Kolasa 5.60, LJ: Tomasz Mateusiak 7.91, TJ: Jacek Kazimierowski 16.52, SP: Tomasz Majewski 20.13, DT: Piotr Malachowski 64.74, HT: Szymon Ziólkowski 77.75, JT: Dariusz Trafas 77.55, Dec: Lukasz Placzek 7289, 20kmW: Benjamin Kucinski 1:20:45, 50kmW: Kamil Kalka 4:04:23. **Women**: 100m: Daria Onysko 11.44, 200m/400m: Anna Guzowska 23.02/51.29, 800m: Ewelina Setowska 2:02.17, 1500m: Wioletta Janowska 4:10.23, 5000m: Justyna Bak 17:09.53, 10,000m/HMar: Grazyna Syrek 33:21.73/74:56, Mar: Janina Malska 2:41:43, 3000mSt: Katarzyna Kowalska 10:11.07, 100mh: Aurelia Trywianska 13.05, 400mh: Anna Jesien 54.53, HJ: Anna Ksok 1.88, PV: Monika Pyrek 4.70, LJ: Malgorzata Trybanska 6.32, TJ: Aleksandra Fila 13.63, SP: Magdalena Sobieszek 15.97, DT: Marzena Wysocka 63.75, HT: Kamila Skolimowska 72.43, JT: Barbara Madejczyk 61.05, Hep: Magdalena Szczepanska 6090, 20kmW: Agnieszka Olesz 1:37:47.

Michal BIENIEK b. 17 May 1984 Gryfino 1.94m 72kg. AZS-AWF Wroclaw. Student at Academy of PE in Wroclaw.
At HJ: WCh: '03- dnq 22; WJ: '02- 13; WY: '01- 4; EJ: '03- 5, '05- 7. Polish champion 2005.
Progress at HJ: 1999- 1.85, 2000- 2.10, 2001- 2.19, 2002- 2.24, 2003- 2.30, 2004- 2.27, 2005- 2.36. pb LJ 7.22 '03.

Andrzej KRAWCZYK b. 11 Apr 1976 Plonsk 1.95m 112kg. AZS-AWF Biala Podlaska. PE teacher.
At DT: WCh: '05- 12; EC: '98- dnq 21; WJ: '94- 4; EU23: '97- 1; EJ: '95- 1; WUG: '03- 2; ECp: '99-03-04-05: 7/3/4/6. Polish champion 1996-8, 2002-04.
Progress at DT: 1992- 40.30, 1993- 49.90, 1994- 55.68, 1995- 58.22, 1996- 59.90, 1997- 60.12, 1998- 61.96, 1999- 63.60, 2000- 63.56, 2001- 63.11, 2002- 63.67, 2003- 62.79, 2004- 63.10, 2005- 65.56. pb SP 16.39 '99.

Roman MAGDZIARCZYK b. 5 Jul 1977 Walbrzych 1.80m 70kg. AZS-AWFiS Gdansk. PE student.
At 50kmW: OG: '00- 8, '04- 6; WCh: '99- 19, '01- dq, '03- 7, '05- 7; WCp: '02- 12. At 20kmW: EC: '02- 14; ECp: '05- 6. Won POL 50km 1998.
Progress at 50kmW: 1998- 4:06:42, 1999- 3:51:20, 2000- 3:48:17, 2002- 3:51:15, 2003- 3:44:53, 2004- 3:48:11, 2005- 3:49:55. pbs: 5000mW 19:34.13i '05, 19:34.15 '00; 20kmW 1:20:47 '05, 35kmW 2:37:33 '04.

Tomasz MAJEWSKI b. 30 Aug 1981 Nasielsk 2.04m 135kg. AZS-AWF Warszawa. Studying politics at Cardinal Wyszynski University.
At SP: OG: '04- dnq 18; WCh: '05- 9; EU23: '03- 4; WI: '04- 4, '06- 7; EI: '05- dnq 10; WUG: '03- 5, '05- 1; ECp: '03-04-05: 4/4/4. Polish champion 2002-05.
Progress at SP: 1998- 12.91, 1999- 15.77, 2000- 17.77, 2001- 18.34, 2002- 19.33, 2003- 20.09, 2004- 20.83i/20.52, 2005- 20.64, 2006- 20.60i.

Marek PLAWGO b. 25 Feb 1981 Ruda Slaska 1.81m 72kg. Warszawianka. Studying at University of Economics.
At 400mh: OG: '04- 6; WCh: '01- sf; WJ: '00- 1/3R; EU23: '03- 1/1R; EJ: '99- 4; ECp: '01: 2, '05- 2/2R. Won POL 2001, 2003, 2005. At

400m/4x400m: EC: '02- 4; EI: '02- 1/1R; ECp: '02- 3.
Polish 400mh records 2001 & 2004, 600m 2005.
Progress at 400mh: 1999- 51.97, 2000- 49.23, 2001- 48.16, 2002- 48.25, 2003- 48.45, 2004- 48.16, 2005- 48.99. pbs: 100m 10.60 '01, 200m 20.61 '02, 300m 32.77 '02, 400m 45.35 '02, 600m 1:16.03 '05.
Ran Polish indoor records 45.49 and 45.39 at 2002 European Indoors.

Grzegorz SPOSÓB b. 12 Feb 1976 Swidnik 2.00m 87kg. Start Lublin. Student at Technical University.
At HJ: OG: '04- dnq 20=; WCh: '01- dnq 21=, '03- 6, '05- 18=; EC: '02- dns; WUG: '01- 4; ECp: '01-02-03-04-05: 2/3/3/2/5=. Polish champion 2001-02.
Progress at HJ: 1998- 2.05, 1999- 2.16, 2000- 2.25, 2001- 2.30, 2002- 2.30, 2003- 2.30, 2004- 2.34, 2005- 2.30.

Grzegorz SUDOL b. 28 Aug 1978 Nowa Deba 1.76m 63kg. AZS-AWF Kraków. PE student.
At 50kmW: OG: '04- 7; WCh: '03/05- dq; EC: '02- 10. At 20kmW: ECp: '05- 9. At 10,000mW: WJ: '96- 7, EJ: '97- 10. Won POL 50km 2002.
Progress at 50kmW: 2002- 3:50:37, 2003- 3:55:40, 2004- 3:49:09, 2006- 3:50:24. pbs: 3000mW 11:25.93i/11:29.20 '05, 5000mW 18:55.01i/19:10.53 '05, 10kmW 39:01 '05, 20kmW 1:21:03 '05.

Aleksander WALERIANCZYK b. 1 Sep 1982 Kraków 1.95m 78kg. Wawel Kraków. PE student.
At HJ: WCh: '03- 10; EC: '02- 13=; EU23: '03- 1; WUG: '05- 1. Polish champion 2003.
Progress at HJ: 1999- 2.04, 2000- 2.10i/2.06, 2001- 2.15i/2.14, 2002- 2.27, 2003- 2.36, 2004- 2.27, 2005- 2.30.
World best mark of 2003. His brother Tomasz (b. 1981) has 400mh pb 52.90 '04.

Szymon ZIÓLKOWSKI b. 1 Jul 1976 Poznan 1.92m 120kg. AZS Poznan. Student.
At HT: OG: '96- 10, '00- 1, '04- dnq 13; WCh: '95- dnq 22, '99- dnq 23, '01- 1, '05- 3; EC: '98- 5, '02- dnq 15; WJ: '94- 1; EJ: '93- 7, '95- 1; EU23: '97- 2; ECp: '95-6-9-01-04-05: 6/2/2/1/1/1. Polish champion 1996-7, 1999-2002, 2004-05.
Six Polish hammer records 2000-01.
Progress at HT: 1991- 55.96, 1992- 63.84, 1993- 67.34, 1994- 72.48, 1995- 75.42, 1996- 79.52, 1997- 79.14, 1998- 79.58, 1999- 79.01, 2000- 81.42, 2001- 83.38, 2002- 79.78, 2003- 76.97, 2004- 79.41, 2005- 79.35. pbs: SP 15.25 '95, DT 49.58 '00.
His sister Michalina (b. 1983) was second in the 2000 Polish U18 Championships, pb 58.33 '04. Married javelin thrower (50.90 '98) Joanna Domagala in December 2000.

Women

Lidia CHOJECKA b. 25 Jan 1977 Siedlce 1.63m 51kg. Pogon Siedlce. Teacher.
At 1500m (3000m): OG: '00- 5, '04- 6; WCh: '99- 9, '01- 5; EC: '98- 6, '02- 9; WJ: '94- 7, '96- 5; EJ: '95- 1; EU23: '97- 2, '99- 1; WUG: '97- 3; WI: '97-9-04-06: 3/3/8/(3); EI: '98- 2, '00- (2), '05- (1); ECp: '99- (2), '02- 2 (3), 04- (2). Eur CC: '02- 13. Won POL 800m 1996, 1500m 1999-2000, 2002.
POL records: 1500m 2000, 3000m (4) 1999-2002, 5000m 2002.
Progress at 1500m: 1993- 4:40.84, 1994- 4:18.70, 1995- 4:15.27, 1996- 4:11.36, 1997- 4:05.74, 1998- 4:03.32, 1999- 4:01.36, 2000- 3:59.22, 2001- 4:03.51, 2002- 4:04.84, 2003- 4:03.58i/4:08.73, 2004- 3:59.27, 2005- 4:04.84i. pbs: 800m 1:59.97 '99, 1000m 2:36.97i '03, 2:40.49 '98; 1M 4:24.44i '00, 4:25.18 '98; 2000m 5:48.15 '02, 3000m 8:31.69 '02, 5000m 15:04.88 '02.
Former married name Okninska (12 May 2001).

Anna JAKUBCZAK b. 2 Feb 1973 Zamosc 1.67m 53kg. Agros Zamosc.
At 1500m: OG: '00- 6, '04- 7; WCh: '99- 7, '05- 7; EC: '98- 4; ECp: '99-04-05: 2/7/4. At 800m: ECp: '02- 7. Won POL 800m 1994, 1997, 1999; 1500m 1998, 2004.
Progress at 1500m: 1990- 4:38.54, 1991- 4:36.73, 1992- 4:32.62, 1993- 4:17.84, 1994- 4:14.72, 1995- 4:21.54, 1996- 4:13.84, 1997- 4:13.71, 1998- 4:03.63, 1999- 4:01.43, 2000- 4:06.49, 2002- 4:08.12, 2003- 4:09.51, 2004- 4:00.15, 2005- 4:00.59. pbs: 800m 2:00.78 '99, 1000m 2:35.96 '00, 1M 4:44.87 '02, 2000m 5:54.21 '02, 3000m 9:17.75 '98.
Son Filip born 2001.

Wioletta JANOWSKA b. 9 Jun 1977 Piotrków Trybunalski 1.77m 58kg. née Frankiewicz. AZS-AWF Kraków.
At 1500m (3000mSt): OG: '04- sf; WCh: '05- h (14). At 5000m: ECp: '05- 2. Won Polish 1500m 2002, 2004-05, 5000m 2002, 2004.
Progress at 1500m, 3000mSt: 1995- 4:41.98, 1996- 4:24.27, 1997- 4:21.49, 1998- 4:37.47, 1999- 4:21.73, 10:18.10; 2002- 4:07.84, 2003- 4:10.31, 2004- 4:03.09, 2005- 4:03.68, 9:25.09. pbs: 800m 2:06.67i '04, 2:06.86 '03; 1000m 2:36.97 '04, 2:43.04i '03; 3000m 8:44.42 '05, 5000m 15:08.38 '05, 10,000m 32:16.27 '04.

Anna JESIEN b. 10 Dec 1978 Sokolow Podlaski 1.68m 57kg. née Olichwierczuk. Skra Warszawa. Economist.
At 400mh: OG: '00/04- h; WCh: '01- sf, '03- h, '05- 4; EC: '02- 3; ECp: '99-02-05: 7/2&3R/2&2R. Polish champion 1999-2000, 2002-03, 2005.
Two Polish 400mh records 2005.
Progress at 400mh: 1995- 66.84, 1996- 61.34, 1997- 58.97, 1998- 58.21, 1999- 56.43, 2000- 55.75, 2001- 55.61, 2002- 55.11, 2003- 55.38, 2004- 55.85, 2005- 53.96. pbs: 100m 12.14 '01, 200m 24.19 '00, 300m 38.33 '02, 400m 52.43 '05, 100mh 14.1 '05, 14.49 '99.
Coached by her husband (ammriwd on 8 Oct 2001) Pawel Jesien (400mh pb 51.08 '00).

Malgorzata PSKIT b. 25 May 1976 Lódz 1.75m 61kg. AZS-AWF Wroclaw. Student.

At 400mh: OG: '04- sf; WCh: '01/03- sf, '05- 8; EC: '02- 6/3R; EU23: '97- 3; WUG: '01- 2; WI: '06- 4R; EI: '05- 2R; ECp: '04- 3. Polish champion 1998, 2001, 2004. At TJ: EJ: '95- 13.
Progress at 400mh: 1996- 58.67, 1997- 57.29, 1998- 58.07, 1999- 57.65, 2000- 55.86, 2001- 55.04, 2002- 56.03, 2003- 55.18, 2004- 54.75, 2005- 55.03. pbs: 200m 24.86 '01, 400m 53.10 '02, 600m 1:29.93 '03, 800m 2:02.65i '05, 2:04.88 '01; TJ 12.80 '95.

Monika PYREK b. 11 Aug 1980 Gdynia 1.74m 52kg. MKL Szczecin. Graduated in pedagogy from Lódz University.
At PV: OG: '00- 7, '04- 4; WCh: '01- 3, '03- 4=, '05- 2; EC: '98- 7, '02- dnq 13=; WJ: '98- 2=; EU23: '01- 1; EJ: '97- 10, '99- 4; WI: '03-04-06: 3/5=/4; EI: '02- 3, '05- 3; ECp: '02-04: 4/2. Polish champion 1999-2002, 2004-05 and indoors 1998-2006. 41 Polish pole vault records 1996-2004 (and 28 indoors 1996-2006), European record 2001.
Progress at PV: 1995- 2.30, 1996- 3.60, 1997- 3.83, 1998- 4.15, 1999- 4.21i/4.16, 2000- 4.40, 2001- 4.61, 2002- 4.62, 2003- 4.60, 2004- 4.72, 2005- 4.70, 2006- 4.76i. pb HJ 1.72 '03.

Anna ROGOWSKA b. 21 May 1981 Gdynia 1.71m 55kg. SKLA Sopot. PE student.
At PV: OG: '04- 3; WCh: '03- 7, '05- 6=; EC: '02- 7=; EU23: '03- 3; WI: '03- 6=, '04- 7; WI: '06- 2; EI: '05- 2; ECp: '05- 1.
Nine Polish pole vault records 2004-05.
Progress at PV: 1997- 2.60, 1998- 2.90, 1999- 3.40, 2000- 3.60, 2001- 3.90, 2002- 4.40, 2003- 4.47i/4.45, 2004- 4.71, 2005- 4.83, 2006- 4.80i.
Coached by fiancé Jacek Torlinski (pb PV 4.85 '97).

Kamila SKOLIMOWSKA b. 4 Nov 1982 Warszawa 1.80m 105kg. Gwardia Warszawa. Graduate of Warsaw University.
At HT: OG: '00- 1, '04- 5; WCh: '99- 21, '01- 4, '03- 8, '05- 7; EC: '98- 7, '02- 2; WJ: '98- dnq, '00- dnq 20; WY: '99- 1; EU23: '03- 1; EJ: '97- 1; WUG: '05- 1; WCp: '02- 5; ECp: '99-02-04-05: 4/6/4/1; Won GPF & GWG 2001. Polish champion 1996-7, 1999-2005.
Five World junior hammer records 1999-2001, 14 Polish hammer records 1996-2005.
Progress at HT: 1996- 47.66, 1997- 63.48, 1998- 62.72, 1999- 66.62, 2000- 71.16, 2001- 71.71, 2002- 72.60, 2003- 71.38, 2004- 72.57, 2005- 74.27, 2006- 73.32.
Youngest ever Polish champion and record holder (at 13y 229d), won European Junior title at 14y 264d and became the youngest Olympic champion in Sydney 2000 at 17y 331d. Set world age bests at each age 14-19. Father, Robert, was junior world champion at weightlifting in 1976 and 7th at super-heavyweight at the 1980 Olympics (his weight 155kg). Mother, Teresa Wenta, had DT pb 40.32 '77 as a junior.

Aurelia TRYWIANSKA b. 9 May 1976 Szczecin 1.74m 59kg. AZS-AWF Warszawa. Political science graduate of Iowa State University, USA.
At 100mh: OG: '04- h; WCh: '03- 5, '05- sf; EC: '02- sf; EU23: '97- 4; EJ: '95- h/3R; ECp: '02-04-05: 6/5/4. Won POL 2002-05.
Progress at 100mh: 1992- 14.79, 1993- 14.25, 1994- 13.80, 1995- 13.84, 1996- 13.68, 1997- 13.50, 1998- 13.68, 1999- 13.70, 2000- 13.36/13.32w, 2001- 13.49, 2002- 12.97, 2003- 12.74, 2004- 12.79, 2005- 12.77. pbs: 60m 7.36i '03, 100m 11.59 '03, 200m 24.07 '97, 60mh 7.93i '06, LJ 6.32 '04, TJ 12.49i '00.
Married her coach, Korey Kollasch, on 1 Jun 2002.

Krystyna ZABAWSKA b. 14 Jan 1968 Dabrowa Bialostocka 1.83m 92kg. née Danilczyk. Podlasie Bialystok. PE student.
At SP: OG: '92- 10, '00- 5, '04- 6; WCh: '91- 12, '93 dnq 17, '97- 8, '99- 8, '01- 10, '03- 6; EC: '94- 9, '98- 11, '02- 7; WI: '99-01-04: 2/8/4; EI: '94-8-00-05: 6/4/5/2; ECp: '91-3-9-02-04: 5/5/1/3/4. Polish champion 1991-4, 1996-2004 (and 14 indoors).
Progress at SP: 1985- 10.98, 1986- 12.20, 1987- 14.48, 1988- 15.70, 1989- 16.22, 1990- 18.31, 1991- 19.03, 1992- 19.42, 1993- 18.31, 1994- 19.23, 1995- 16.38, 1996- 18.62, 1997- 19.06, 1998- 19.24, 1999- 19.26i/19.23, 2000- 19.18, 2001- 19.10, 2002- 18.73, 2003- 18.95, 2004- 19.00i/18.93, 2005- 18.96i/18.79.
Coached by husband Przemyslaw Zabawski, Polish shot champion 1997 & 2000, pb 19.63 '01; Daughter Daria born 1995.

PORTUGAL

Governing body: Federação Portuguesa de Atletismo, Largo da Lagoa, 1799-538 Linda-a-Velha. Founded in 1921.

National Championships first held in 1910 (men), 1937 (women). **2005 Champions**: **Men**: 100m: Francis Obikwelu 10.39w, 200m: Paulo Ferreira 21.47, 400m/400mh: Edivaldo Monteiro 47.77/50.65, 800m: Rui Silva 1:47.94, 1500m: Hélio Gomes 3.55.42, 5000m: Rui Pedro Silva 14.39.97, 10,000m: Manuel Magalhães 29:28.44, Mar: João Marques 2:24:54, 3000mSt: Mário Teixeira 8:42.19; 110mh: Luis Sá 13.99, HJ: Rafael Gonçalves 2.08, PV: João André 5.15, LJ: Gaspar Araújo 7.75, TJ: Américo Castelbranco 15.28w, SP: Marco Fortes 17.35, DT: Paulo Bernardo 60.61, HT: Vítor Costa 74.21, JT: Filipe Ventura 65.48, Dec: Tiago Marto 6328, 20000mW: João Vieira 1:23:46.7, 50kmW: Pedro Martins 4:03:08. **Women**: 100m/200m: Carla Tavares 11.87/24.57w, 400m/400mh: Patrícia Lopes 54.50/60.01, 800m/1500m: Sandra Teixeira 2:03.12/4:15.06, 5000m: Inês Monteiro 16:05.58, 10,000m: Dina Malheiro 35:37.35, Mar: Fatima Silva 2:45:50, 3000mSt: Clarisse Cruz 10:04.44, 100mh: Naide Gomes 13.50, HJ: Sónia Carvalho 1.77, PV: Elisabete Tavares 4.13, LJ: Carina Gomes 5.87, TJ: Susana Costa 13.06w, SP: Antónia Borges 15.77, DT: Teresa Machado 53.99, HT: Vânia Silva 62.94, JT: Sílvia Cruz 52.03, Hep:

Carina Gomes 5010, 10,000mW: Ana Cabecinha 44.25.36, 20kmW: Vera Santos 1:32:44.

Francis Obiorah **OBIKWELU** b. 22 Nov 1978 Nigeria 1.95m 74kg. Sporting Club de Portugal.
At (100m/)200m: OG: '96- sf, '00- sf, '04- 2/5; WCh: '97- 2R (sf), '99- 3/3R, '03- h, '05- (4); EC: '02- 2/2; WI: '97- 3, '99- 4; WJ: '96- 1/1; AfG: '99- 2/1/1R; WCp: '02- 3/1. 3rd GP 200m 1999, 2001. At 400m: WJ: '94- sf; Af-J: '94- 2. At 60m: WI: '04- 6. Won NGR 100m 1999, 200m 1997, 1999; POR 100m 2004-05, 200m 2002-03.
European 100m record 2004; Two Nigerian 200m records 1999; POR records: 100m (5), 200m (6) 2002-04.
Progress at 100m, 200m: 1994- 21.16, 1995- 10.31, 21.22; 1996- 10.12, 20.24; 1997- 10.10, 20.53/20.27Aw; 1998- 10.01, 20.17; 1999- 10.01A/10.13/10.11w, 19.84; 2000- 9.97, 20.01; 2001- 9.98, 20.33; 2002- 10.01, 20.18; 2003- 10.11, 20.41; 2004- 9.86, 20.12; 2005- 10.04, 20.48. pbs: 50m 5.79i '04, 60m 6.54i '05, 400m 46.29 '98.
An Ibo, and thus in an ethnic minority group in Nigeria, he emigrated to Portugal in 1994 and became a Portuguese citizen on 26 October 2001.

Rui SILVA b. 3 Aug 1977 Vila Chã de Ourique 1.75m 65kg. Sporting Club de Portugal.
At 1500m: OG: '00- h, '04- 3; WCh: '99- sf (fell), '01- 7, '03- 5, '05- 3; EC: '98- 2, '02- 3; WJ: '96- 6; EJ: '95- 8; EU23: '99- 1; WI: '99- 5, '01- 1; EI: '98- 1, '02- 1; WCp: '98- 2. At 3000m: WI: '04- 2; EI: '00- 2. Won POR 800m 2002-05, 1500m 1999, 2001; CC sh 2000-02.
Portuguese records 1998-2002: 800m, 1500m (6), 1000m, 1M (2), 2000m.
Progress at 1500m: 1994- 3:50.9, 1995- 3:44.8, 1996- 3:40.09, 1997- 3:44.6, 1998- 3:34.00, 1999- 3:30.88, 2000- 3:32.60, 2001- 3:30.36, 2002- 3:30.07, 2003- 3:32.97, 2004- 3:30.90, 2005- 3:32.91. pbs: 800m 1:44.91 '02, 1000m 2:16.30 '99, 1M 3:49.50 '02, 2000m 4:54.66 '99, 3000m 7:39.44i '00, 7:46.41 '04; 5000m 13:19.20 '04, 10km Rd 28:07 '05.

Women

Susana FEITOR b. 28 Jan 1975 Alcobertas 1.60m 52kg. C Natação Rio Maior.
At 20kmW: OG: '00- 14, '04- 20; WCh: '99- 4, '01- dq, '03- 9, '05- 3; EC: '02- dnf; WCp: '99- 9, '02- 14; ECp: '03- 5, '05- 2. At 10kmW: OG: '92- dq, '96- 13; WCh: '91- 13, '93- 11, '95- 17, '97- h; EC: '94- 8, '98- 3; EU23: '97- 3; WUG: '95- 4, '97- 4, '01- 2; WCp: '93- 8, '95- 15; ECp: '96- 3. At 5000mW: WJ: '90- 1, '92- dq, 94- 2; EJ: '89- 6, '91- 2, '93- 1. Won POR 10kmW 1992, 1994-2000, 2002-04, 20kmW 1998-9, 2001-04.
POR walks records 1989-2001: 3000m (10), 5000m (9), 10km (9), 20km (3), 20,000m track (1:29:36.4 WR '01). World junior 5000m best (21:01.8) '93.
Progress at 10kmW, 20kmW: 1991- 45:37, 1992- 45:24, 1993- 43:44, 1994- 43:30, 1995- 44:05, 1996- 43:37, 1997- 44:26, 1998- 42:55, 1:31:03, 1999- 44:36, 1:30:13; 2000: 43:55, 1:28:19; 2001- 42:39, 1:27:55; 2002- 44:24, 1:31:12; 2003- 44:07.80t, 1:29:08; 2004- 44:31.21t, 1:29:13; 2005- 44:25+, 1:28:44. Track pbs: 3000mW 12:08.30 '01, 5000mW 20:40.24 '01, 10,000mW 44:07.80 '03.
Had a hugely successful junior career to her world silver medal in front of her home crowd in 1994, four years after she had won this title.

Naide GOMES b. 20 Nov 1979 São Tome e Principe 1.81m 70kg. Sporting Club de Portugal.
At Hep (LJ): OG: '04- 13; WCh: '05- 7/dnq 17; EC: '02- 18 (10); AfrG: '99- 5; WUG: '05- (2); WI: '06- (3); EI: '05- (1). At Pen: WI: '03- 5, '04- 1; EI: '02- 2. At 100mh: OG: '00- h. Won POR Hep 2001, 100mh 2004-05, HJ 2002, LJ 2002, 2004.
Portuguese records LJ (4), Heptathlon (2) 2002-05, indoor HJ & Pen 2004, LJ 2005.
Progress at LJ, Hep: 1996- 5.60, 1997- 5.63, 4578; 1998- 5.80, 1999- 5.81, 4964; 2000- 6.15, 5671; 2001- 6.36, 5606w; 2002- 6.57, 6160; 2003- 6.53, 6120; 2004- 6.51, 6151; 2005- 6.72, 6230; 2006- 6.76i. 60m 7.84i '04, 200m 24.87 '05, 400m 57.91 '05, 800m 2:16.31 '05, 60mh 8.39i '05, 100mh 13.50 '05, HJ 1.88i '04, 1.86 '02; TJ 11.73 '99, SP 15.08i/14.71 '04, JT 42.86 '00, Pen 4759i '04.
Changed nationality from São Tome e Principe to Portugal in 2001. Set pbs at HJ (Portuguese record) and SP en route to WI gold in 2004.

Fernanda RIBEIRO b. 23 Jun 1969 Penafiel 1.61m 48kg. Valencia Terra i Mar, Spain,
At 10,000m (5000m): OG: '96- 1, '00- 3, '04- dnf; WCh: '93- 10, '95- 1 (2), '97- 2 (3), '99/03- dnf; EC: '90- dnf, '94- 1, '98- 2, '02- dnf; WCp: '94- 2; won E.Chall '98, '03. At 3000m: OG: '88- h, '92- h; WCh: '87- h, '91- h; WI: '97- 3; EC: '86- h, '90- h; EI: '94- 1, '96- 1, '98- 2; WJ: '86- 4, '88- 2; EJ: '83- 11, '85- 4, '87- 1. World CC: '94- 10, '96- 6, '00- 10 (4k); Rd Rly team: '92- 1. Eur CC: '94- 6, '98- 4. Won IbAm 5000m 2000, 2004; POR 1500m 1989-90, 1995, 1998-9; 3000m 1985, 1993; 5000m 2000, 2002-04, 10,000m 1992, 1996; CC 1996-9, 2003, 4k CC 2003.
World 5000m record 1995. Portuguese records: 3000m (3), 5000m (3), 10,000m (4) 1994-2000.
Progress at 3000m, 5000m, 10,000m: 1982- 9:53.7, 1983- 9:21.71, 1984- 9:11.62, 1985- 9:14.19, 1986- 9:09.39, 1987- 8:56.33, 1988- 9:00.38, 1989- 9:04.33, 32:38.07; 1990- 9:03.35, 32:39.34; 1991- 8:57.64, 33:45.45; 1992- 8:56.10, 32:22.70; 1993- 8:51.91, 31:50.51; 1994- 8:42.13, 15:06.91, 31:04.25; 1995- 8:41.99, 14:36.45, 31:04.99; 1996- 8:39.49i/8:45.56, 14:41.07, 31:01.63; 1997- 8:37.14, 14:53.25, 31:39.15; 1998- 8:42.95, 15:22.8, 30:48.06; 1999- 8:30.66, 14:52.59; 2000- 8:34.99, 15:01.49, 30:22.88, 2001- 8:53.41i, 2002- 8:56.51i, 15:17.62, 31:40.80; 2003- 8:49.39i, 15:16.8+, 31:13.42; 2004- 8:51.92, 15:19.43, 31:32.28; 2005- 9:04.20, 15:38.34, 32:03.22. pbs: 800m 2:05.83 '94, 1000m 2:44.8 '92, 1500m 4:05.97 '97, 1M 4:32.66 '99, 2000m 5:37.34i '96, HMar 68:23 '00, Mar 2:37:04 '02.

At 11 was second in a half marathon in 1:24:02, just 4 secs behind Rosa Mota. Made international debut at 13 and set national age records each age 13-22 at 3000m and 14-18 and 20 at 1500m. She fulfilled her long-time promise in 1994 with brilliant performances to win European titles indoors and out, and added World and Olympic titles in the following years.

PUERTO RICO

Governing body: Federación de Athletismo Amateur de Puerto Rico, PO Box 9023464, San Juan, PR 00902-3464. Founded 1947.

2005 National Champions: **Men**: 100m/200m: Jorge Richardson 10.59/21.47, 400m: Félix Martínez 47.38, 800m: José Vargas 1:50.63, 1500m: David Freeman 3:48.82, 110mh: Enrique Llanos 13.81, 400mh: Javier Culson 50.62, 3000mSt: Johan Mendez 9:20.32, HJ: Eduardo Santos 1.95, PV: Abiezer Vega 4.50, LJ: Jonathan Vazquez 7.05, TJ: Jesef Aponte 14.61, SP/JT: Jerry Roman 14.00/56.96, DT: Alfredo Romero 50.17, HT: Santos Vega 62.69. **Women**: 100m/200m: Jenifer Gutierrez 12.31/25.00, 400m: Wilmary Álveraez VEN 53.91, 800m: Sandra Moya 2:08.20, 1500m: Roselyn Concepcion DOM 4:45.99, 100mh: Zolymar Febles 14.11, 400mh: Dayianne Vazquez 64.83, HJ: Jhoris Luque 1.80, PV: Denisse Orengo 4.00, LJ/TJ: Jennifer Arvelaez 5.71/13.04, SP/DT: Melissa Mojica 12.64/43.90, HT: Amarilys Alméstica 60.94, JT: Francia Manzanill DOM 44.86.

QATAR

Governing body: Qatar Association of Athletics Federation, PO Box 8139, Doha. Founded 1963.

Daham Najim BASHIR b. 8 Nov 1978 1.71m 60kg. Formerly David Nyaga (Kenya).
At 1500m: WCh: '05- 10. At 5000m: AsiC: '05- 2. Asian 1M record 2005, Qatar 1500m record 2005.
Progress at 1500m: 2001- 3:44.5A, 2002- 3:35.47, 2003- 3:37.19, 2004- 3:36.08, 2005- 3:31.04. pbs: 800m 1:48.56 '05, 1M 3:47.97 '05, 3000m 7:41.83 '05, 5000m 14:15.92; 3000mSt 8:32.48 '04.
Switched from Kenya to Qatar in 2005 and showed major improvement at 1500m from best of 3:35.47 (2002) to 3:31.04 at Doha in May.

Abdullah Ahmad HASSAN b. 4 Apr 1981 Keiyo, Kenya 1.70m 54kg. Formerly Albert CHEPKURUI KEN.
At 10,000m: WCh: '03- 4; AsiC: '03- 1. World CC: '99-02-05-06: 5J/6/3/14; 4k: '01-04-05: 6/4/8; HMar: '04- 3.
Asian records 5000m (2) (13:04.65 '03, 2004), 10,000m (2) 2003.
Progress at 5000m, 10,000m: 1998- 13:49.48, 1999- 13:25.18, 2000- 12:59.90, 2001- 13:18.71, 28:06.86; 2002- 13:12.22, 26:50.67; 2003- 12:56.27, 26:38.76; 2004- 13:02.03, 26:59.54; 2005- 13:27.61. pbs: 1500m 3:42.42 '00, 3000m 7:43.01 '99.
Three Asian records in month after transferring from Kenya to Qatar on 9 Aug 2003. He had been 4th in Kenyan 10,000m Trials on 26 July 2003! Tendon injury curtailed his 2005 season.

Nicholas KEMBOI b. 25 Nov 1983 Kericho 1.63m 50kg.
At 10,000m: WCh: '05- 9; World CC: '01- 4J, '02- 7J.
Progress at 5000m, 10,000m: 2000- 13:41.5A, 2001- 13:26.36, 2003- 13:01.14, 26:30.03; 2004- 13:19.65, 27:17.12; 2005- 13:10.36, 26:51.87. pbs: 3000m 7:50.99 '05, HMar 60:31 '03, 3000mSt 8:53.5A '02.
After 28:19.77 in June improved to 26:30.03 for second at Brussels in September 2003. Switched from Kenya to Qatar 2005.

James KWALIA Chepkurui b. 12 Jun 1984 1.71m 59kg.
At 5000m: WCh: '05- 13; AsiC: '05- 1. At 3000m: WY: '01- 3. World junior 1 mile record 2003.
Progress at 5000m: 2001- 13:44.3, 2002- 13:14.34, 2003- 12:54.58, 2004- 13:02.24, 2005- 13:21.36. pbs: 1500m 3:38.67 '03, 1M 3:50.39 '03, 2000m 4:59.11 '03, 3000m 7:28.28 '04.
Kenyan who received Qatar passport on 5 Aug 2004 and IAAF agreement to his transfer of allegiance from 28 Oct 2004.

Moussa OMAR OBAID b. 18 Apr 1985 1.85m 68kg. Formerly Moses Kimutai KEN.
At 3000mSt: OG:'04- 4; WCh: '05- 9; WJ: '04- 2; AsiC: '05- 1. Won Asi-J 10,000m & 3000mSt 2004, W.Asian 3000mSt 2005.
Three Asian junior 3000mSt records 2004.
Progress at 3000mSt: 2003- 8:35.1A, 2004- 8:07.18, 2005- 8:11.75. pbs: 3000m 7:45.89 '05, 5000m 14:03.83 '04, 10,000m 30:31.22 '04.

Saïf Saeed SHAHEEN b. 15 Oct 1982 Keiyo, Kenya 1.77m 64kg. Formerly Stephen Cherono KEN.
At 3000mSt: WCh: '03- 1, '05- 1; CG: '02- 1; AfCh: '02- 3; won KEN 2002, WAF 2003-04, 3rd GP 2001. At 2000mSt: WY: '99- 1. At 1500m/5000m: AsiC: '03- 2/2. At 3000m: WI: '06- 2. World CC: 4k: '04-05-06: 5/4/9; 12k: '05- 8.
World record 3000m steeplechase 2004, world junior record 2001; four Asian records 2003-04. Asian 3000m record 2004, indoor 3000m (7:39.77) 2006.
Progress at 5000m, 3000mSt: 1997- 8:43.0A, 1999- 8:19.12, 2000- 8:16.27, 2001- 7:58.66, 2002- 13:11.55, 7:58.10, 2003- 12:48.81, 7:57.38; 2004- 13:14.65, 7:53.63; 2005- 7:55.51. pbs: 1500m 3:35.15 '03, 2000m 5:03.06 '01, 3000m 7:34.67 '04, 2M 8:18.80 '99.
World age 17-18-19 records for 3000mSt 2000-02. 24 succcessive steeplechase wins (inc. 2 heats) from 16 Aug 2002 to end of 2005. Controversially transferred allegiance to Qatar and set first Asian record (3000mSt 8:02.48) nine days after citizenship granted (9 Aug 2003). Brother of **Abraham Cherono** (b. 21 Jul 1980): 3 CG 02,

5 WCh 03, pb 8:10.33 '03, and **Christopher Kosgei** (b. 14 Aug 1974): WCh: 95- 2, 99- 1; pb 8:05.43 '99.

Mubarak Hassan SHAMI b. 2 Dec 1980 Baringo, Kenya 1.63m 50kg. Formerly Richard Yatich KEN.
At HMar: WCh: '05- 2. Won Gulf & W.Asian HMar 2005.
Qatar half marathon record 2005.
Progress at Mar: 2005- 2:09:22. pbs: 10km 28:17 '03, 15km 43:28 '05, HMar 60:31 '04.

ROMANIA

Governing body: Federatia Romana de Atletism, Str. Dr Primo Nebiolo nr.2, Bucuresti 71331. Founded 1912.
National Championships first held in 1914 (men), 1925 (women). **2005 Champions**: **Men**: 100m: Catalin Cîmpeanu 10.42, 200m/400m: Florin Suciu 20.93/47.12, 800m: Catalin Mihu 1:49.49, 1500m: Cosmin Suteu 3:47.37, 5000m: Marius Ionescu 14:14.53, 10,000m/3000mSt: Ionut Enache 30:32.49/9:04.36, HMar: Valeriu Vlas 68:27, Mar: Maricel Gaman 2:33:01, 110mh: Alexandru Mihailescu 13.84, 400mh: Gilberto Vadeanu 52.15, HJ: Stefan Vasilache 2.22, PV: Tiberiu Agoston 4.60, LJ: Danut Simion 7.59, TJ: Marian Oprea 17.40, SP: Gheorghe Guset 20.28, DT: Mihai Grasu 54.19, HT: Cosmin Sorescu 71.40, JT: Levente Bartha 70.00, Dec: Nicolae Istrate 6549, 20kmW: Silviu Casandra 1:23:41, 50kmW: Ciprian Deac 4:17:36; **Women**: 100m/200m/400m: Angela Morosanu 11.54/23.39/52.48, 800m/1500m: Corina Dumbravean 2:03.23/4:08.25, 5000m: Adriana Pîrtea 15:50.43, 10,000m: Simona Fodor 33:44.47, HMar: Paula Todoran 75:35, Mar: Alina Gherasim 2:49:38, 3000mSt: Cristina Casandra 9:39.22, 100mh: Viorica Tigau 13.59, 400mh: Iuliana Popescu 60.56, HJ: Monica Iagar 1.92, PV: Alina Cantea 3.40, LJ: Adina Anton 6.38, TJ: Mariana Solomon 13.77, SP: Elena Hila 17.85, DT: Nicoleta Grasu 64.25, HT: Mihaela Melinte 69.04, JT: Felicia Moldovan 59.74, Hep: Otilia Dantis 5134, 10kmW: Ana-Maria Groza 44:19, 20kmW: Alina Olaru 1:34:46.

Gheorghe GUSET b. 28 May 1968 Zalau 1.85m 142kg. CSM Armatura Zalau.
At SP: OG: '00/04- dnq 30/15; WCh: '99-01-03-05: dnq 18/14/17/13; EC: '98- 10, '02- 7; ECp: '94- dq 3; WI: '01-03-06: 9/dq/5; EI: '00- 4, '05- 5. Balkan champion 1999-2002, 2004-05; ROM 1990, 1992-3, 1998-2005.
Five Romanian shot records 1990-9 (indoors 2005).
Progress at SP: 1984- 12.60i/12.48, 1985- 15.17, 1986- 16.51, 1987- 17.66, 1988- 18.66, 1989- 18.57i, 1990- 19.71, 1991- 20.33, 1992- 19.63, 1993- 19.81, 1994- 19.56i/19.97dq, 1998- 20.27, 1999- 20.84, 2000- 20.76i/20.66, 2001- 20.68i/20.39, 2002- 20.40, 2003- 20.48, 2004- 20.54, 2005- 20.93i/20.75, 2006- 21.04i. Four-year drugs ban 1994-8.

Marian OPREA b. 6 Jun 1982 Pitesti 1.90m 80kg. Rapid Bucuresti & CSM-PAB Arad. Sports teacher.
At TJ: OG: '04- 2; WCh: '01- dnq 13, '03- dnq 17, '05- 3; EC: '02- dnq 14; WJ: '00- 1, WY: '99- 4; EU23: '03- 2; EJ: '99- 3, '01- 1; WI: '03-04-06: 8/5/4; EI: '02- 2; WUG: '01- 2. ROM champion 2001, 2003-05; Balkan 2001-03.
Romanian TJ records 2003 and 2005.
Progress at TJ: 1997- 14.37, 1998- 14.78, 1999- 15.98, 2000- 16.49, 2001- 17.11/17.13w, 2002- 17.29i/17.11/17.39w, 2003- 17.63, 2004- 17.55, 2005- 17.81, 2006- 17.74i. pb LJ 7.73 '05.
Silver medal in 2004 was best ever Olympic placing by a Romanian male.

Women

Mihaela BOTEZAN b. 21 Nov 1976 Ocna Mures 1.62m 49kg. CSU Cluj-Napoca & Steaua Bucuresti. Sports teacher.
At (5000m)/10,000m: OG: '04- 11; WCh: '01- 5, '03- 13 (51 Mar), '05- 23; EC: '02- 6/4; ECp: '01-02-03: (3)/(6)/(3), At 3000m: ECp: '03- 4, '05- 4. World HMar: '00-01-02-04-05: 6/10/4/10/5. Eur CC: '01- 11, '04- 4. Won ROM 5000m 2003, 10,000m 2001.
Romanian 10,000m records 2002 & 2004.
Progress at 5000m, 10,000m: 1995- 16.29.14, 1996- 16.34.72, 1997- 17.05.6, 34.58.83; 1998- 17.16.6, 35.26.45; 1999- 15:54.86, 34.33.01; 2000- 34.00.27; 2001- 15.08.78, 31.45.06; 2002- 15:19.12, 31:13.96; 2003- 15:10.69, 31:28.72; 2004- 15:20.13, 31:11.24; 2005- 15:13.36, 32:28.29. pbs: 1500m 4:26.18 '95, 3000m 9:02.61 '03; Rd: 15km 49:35 '01, HMar 69:24 '02, Mar 2:25:32 '03, 3000mSt 10:08.46 '99.
Smashed her best when she won the European 10,000m Challenge 2002.

Cristina CASANDRA b. 1 Feb 1977 Zalău 1.68m 50kg. née Iloc. Steaua Bucuresti. Sports teacher.
At 3000mSt: WCh: '05- 7; ECp: '02-03-05: 2/2/1. At 5000m: WJ: '96- 3. Won ROM 3000mSt 2000-05; Balkan 2002-03.
Two world 3000m steeplechase bests 2000, five ROM records 2002-05.
Progress at 3000mSt: 2000- 9:40.20, 2001- 9:45.12, 2002- 9:33.16, 2003- 9:40.49, 2004- 9:31.96, 2005- 9:35.95. pbs: 1500m 4:20.46 '96, 2000m 5:56.82 '00, 5000m 15:22.64 '99, 2000mSt 6:16.58 '05 (ROM rec).
Married to her coach Silviu Casandra (b. 27 Oct 1975) 20kmW pb 1.21.35 '00.

Maria CIONCAN b. 19 Jun 1977 Maieru 1.72m 51kg. CSM-PAB Arad & Dinamo Bucuresti.
At (800m)/1500m (800m): OG: '04- 7/3; WCh: '03- sf/9; EU23: '99- 7; ECp: '02- 1, '03- 2/4, '05- 1/2. Won ROM 800m 2003, 1500m 2003-04.
Progress at 800m, 1500m: 1998- 4:13.36, 1999- 2:04.37, 4:11.18; 2000- 4:06.20, 2001- 4:07.89i/4:12.24, 2002- 4:02.10, 2003- 1:59.68,

4:02.80, 2004- 1:59.44, 3:58.39; 2005- 2:00.88, 4:07.39. pbs: 1000m 2:38.91 '05, 2000m 5:49.72i '02, 5:53.16 '01; 3000m 8:57.71 '02.

Set pbs at both 800m and 1500m at 2004 Olympics.

Adelina GAVRILA b. 26 Nov 1978 Brãila 1.75m 56kg. CSM Brãila & Farul Constanta. Sports teacher.

At TJ: OG: '04- 15; WCh: '99- 11, '01- dnq 15, '03- 9; EC: '98- 11; WJ: '96- 3; EJ: '97- 1; EU23: '99- 3; WUG: '99- 3; WI: '01-03-04: 8/8/7; EI: '05- 5; ECp: '03- 3. Won Balkan 1999, 2001, ROM 2000, 2003-04.

Progress at TJ: 1995- 13.69: 1996- 13.50, 1997- 13.62, 1998- 14.53, 1999- 14.71, 2000- 14.44, 2001- 14.18, 2002- 14.29i/14.13w, 2003- 14.76i/14.75, 2004- 14.71, 2005- 14.58i/14.23. pb LJ 6.24 '01.

Nicoleta GRASU b. 11 Sep 1971 Secuieni 1.76m 88kg. née Gradinaru. Administration officer. Dinamo Bucuresti & Enka TUR.

At DT: OG: '92- dnq 13, '96- 7, '00- dnq 19, '04- 6; WCh: '93- 7, '95- dnq 18, '97- 10, '99- 3, '01- 2, '05- 5; EC: '94- 4, '98- 3; WJ: '90- 6; WUG: '97- 3, '99- 1; WCp: '98- 2; ECp: '97-9-00-01-02-05: 4/2/1/3/2/4; E23Cp: '92- 1. Won Balkan 1992, 1997, 1999; ROM 1992-3, 1995-7, 1999-2002, 2004-05. 3rd GP 1996.

Progress at DT: 1985- 36.02, 1986- 43.56, 1987- 50.82, 1988- 51.06, 1989- 52.54, 1990- 56.02, 1991- 59.90, 1992- 65.66, 1993- 65.16, 1994- 64.40, 1995- 64.62, 1996- 65.26, 1997- 64.68, 1998- 67.80, 1999- 68.80, 2000- 68.70, 2001- 68.31, 2002- 64.90, 2004- 64.92, 2005- 64.89. pb SP 15.00i '92, 14.56 '91.

Married her coach Costel Grasu (b. 5 Jul 1967) DT pb 67.08 '92; 4 OG 1992.

Elena IAGAR b. 16 Jan 1975 Brasov 1.73m 54kg. née Buhaianu. Steaua Bucuresti, Civil servant.

At 1500m (800m): OG: '00- sf, '04- h; WCh: '99- 6, '01- h, EC: '98- 10 (h), '02- h; WI: '03- 6; EI: '02- 2, '05- 1; WUG: '99- 1 (3); ECp: '99- (4), '00- 6, '01- (8), '02- (5). Won ROM 800m 1998, 2000-02; 1500m 1998-2000, 2002; CC 1997, Balkan 800m 2002, 2004; 1500m 1999, 2004.

Progress at 800m, 1500m: 1992- 2:15.16i, 4:37.51; 1993- 2:07.08, 4:30.74; 1994- 2:07.96, 4:27.71i; 1995- 2:08.89, 4:20.46; 1996- 2:05.69, 1997- 2:04.32, 4:16.67; 1998- 2:01.44, 4:08.11; 1999- 2:00.26, 4:04.27; 2000- 2:01.29, 4:06.57; 2001- 2:04.03, 4:09.25; 2002- 2:00.80, 4:02.90; 2003- 2:02.09i, 4:07.44i; 2004- 1:59.43, 4:03.25; 2005- 2:03.02i, 4:03.09i/4:13.07. pbs: 400m 55.59 '05, 1M 4:30.62 '99, 1000m 2:42.97 '05, 2000m 5:49.78 '01, 3000m 8:59.99i '01, HMar 78:42 '97.

Mihaela MELINTE b. 27 Mar 1975 Bacau 1.74m 92kg. SCM Bacau. Sports teacher.

At HT: WCh: '99- 1, '03- 6, '05- 11; EC: '98- 1; WUG: '97- 1, '99- 1; EU23: '97- 1; ECp: '97-9-00-03-05: 2/1/dq/2/6 ROM champion 1992-2000, 2003-05; Balkan 2003, 2005.

Eight world hammer records 1995-9, 21 ROM records 1992-9, three world junior records 1992-4.

Progress at HT: 1991- 37.76, 1992- 58.70, 1993- 62.52, 1994- 65.48, 1995- 66.86, 1996- 69.42, 1997- 71.24, 1998- 73.14, 1999- 76.07, 2000- 72.90/74.80dq, 2003- 71.15, 2004- 71.26, 2005- 71.95. pbs: SP 13.98 '94, DT 43.12 '97.

Won 42 successive hammer competitions between losses to Olga Kuzenkova on 27 Jun 1997 and 25 Jun 2000. Positive drugs test (on 7 June 2000) announced just as she was about to compete at the Olympic Games. Returned to competition in 2003.

Felicia MOLDOVAN b. 29 Sep 1967 Mîgura Ilvei 1.69m 70kg. née Tilea. Steaua Bucuresti. Teacher.

At JT: OG: '96- 10, '00- dnq 15, '04- 11; WCh: '93- 8, '95- 2, '97- 5, '99- 11, '01/05- dnq 16/23; EC: '90- dq (9), '94- 3, '98- 10, '02- 9; WUG: '95- 1; ECp: '93-4-6-7-02-05: 1/3/1B/2/2/5. ROM champion 1990, 1994, 1996-8, 2004-05.

Romanian JT record 1996, new spec (2) 2000.

Progress at JT: 1981- 36.62, 1982- 44.00, 1983- 48.40, 1984- 46.80, 1985- 47.74, 1986- 51.42, 1987- 51.44, 1988- 47.42, 1989- 59.54, 1990- 64.02, 1993- 65.62, 1994- 66.40, 1995- 65.22, 1996- 69.26, 1997- 65.76, 1998- 65.10, 1999- 65.27; new: 60.97, 2000- 63.12, 2001- 62.27, 2002- 63.89, 2004- 63.01, 2005- 61.65.

Two-year drugs ban after positive test for steroids when 9th at 1990 Europeans. Married rowing coach Doru Moldovan in June 1997.

Oana PANTELIMON b. 27 Sep 1972 Tecuci 1.79m 61kg. née Musunoi. Steaua Bucuresti. Administration officer.

At HJ: OG: '00- 3=, '04- 7; WCh: '01- 9, '03/05- dnq 14/13; EC: '02- 4; WJ: '90- dnq, WI: '03- 9; EI: '05- 9; ECp: '01-02-03-05: 5/2/6=/6; E23Cp: '92- 3. ROM champion 1999, 2001, 2003; Balkan 2000, 2002.

Progress at HJ: 1987- 1.78, 1988- 1.86, 1989- 1.90, 1990- 1.85, 1991- 1.87i/1.86, 1992- 1.94, 1993- 1.91i/1.87, 1994- 1.88, 1995- 1.92, 1996- 1.92, 1997- 1.93, 1999- 1.80+, 2000- 1.99, 2001- 1.93, 2002- 1.94, 2003- 1.95i/1.92, 2004- 1.93, 2005- 1.95i/1.93.

Her bronze medal at the 2000 Olympics was in her first major championship; after matching her pb of 1.94 to qualify she raised it with 1.96 and 1.99 in the final.

Lidia SIMON b. 4 Sep 1973 Târgu Cârbunesti 1.57m 44kg. née Slavuteanu. Dinamo Bucuresti. Administration officer.

At Mar: OG: '96- 6, '00- 2, '04- dnf; WCh: '95- 10, '97- 3, '99- 3, '01- 1; EC: '94- 10; WCp: '95- 2; won Balkan 1994. At 10,000m: EC: '98- 3. World HMar: '96-7-8-00: 2/3/3/3.

Three Romanian marathon records 1997-2000, half marathon 2000.

Progress at 10,000m, Mar: 1990- 2:58:18, 1991- 34:23.52, 2:52:20; 1993- 2:56:10, 1994- 2:32:38, 1995- 2:31:46, 1996- 2:30:13, 1997- 2:27:04, 1998- 31:32.64, 2:28:31; 1999- 2:23:24, 2000- 2:22:54,

2001- 2:24:15, 2003- 2:40:54, 2004- 2:30:40, 2005- 2:27:01. pbs: 1500m 4:22.57 '91, 3000m 9:25.84 '91, HMar 68:34 '00.

Won marathons at Kastoria and Lyon 1994. Took over 3 minutes off her pb for 3rd in Osaka (2:27:04), almost matched that when 3rd in London (2:27:11) and had third 3rd of 1997 at the Worlds. Won Osaka 1998, 1999 (in ROM record 2:23:24, the then fastest ever in a women's only race on an out and back course), and in 2000, when she moved to eighth on world all-time list with 2:22:54. 2nd London 2000 and 4th 2001. Married to her coach Liviu Simon, their son Cristian born 24 Dec 2002.

Claudia STEF b. 25 Feb 1978 Craiova 1.60m 48kg. née Iovan. CSM Craiova & Steaua Bucuresti. Sports teacher.

At 20kmW: WCh: '99- 11, '03- 5, '05- 8; EC: '02- 5; WCp: '99-02-04: 6/6/12; ECp: '05- 4EU23: '99- 1. At 10kmW: EC: 98- 12; ECp: '98- 3; WUG: '99- 1. At 5000mW: WJ: '96- 3; EJ: '97- 1. Won ROM 10kmW 1998.

World indoor best 3000mW 1999.

Progress at 10kmW, 20kmW: 1996- 44:52, 1997- 43:52, 1998- 43:11, 1999- 42:37, 1:29:39; 2000- 44:35dq/4:52, 1:29:39; 2002- 42:35, 1:29:57; 2003- 44:12, 1:29:09; 2004- 44:08, 1:27:41; 2005- 44:43, 1:29:54; 2006- 1:30:00. pbs: 3000mW 12:24.47 '97, 11:40.33i '99; 5000mW 20:30.8 '98.

Two year drugs ban from 20 May 2000.

Ionela TÎRLEA-MANOLACHE b. 9 Feb 1976 Horezu 1.69m 54kg. CSM-PAB Arad. Sports teacher. Married Daniel Manolache on 20 Mar 2004.

At 400mh/4x400mR (200m): OG: '96- 7, '00- 6, '04- 2; WCh: '95- 7, '01- 6, '03- 4; EC: '94- 7, '98- 1/4, '02- 1; WJ: '94- 1/3R; EJ: '93- 1, '95- 1; WUG: '95- 2; WCp: '98- 4, '02- 4; ECp: '93- (7), '94- 7 (8), '97- 8, '99- 3R (4, 1-400, 4-100), '01- 2 (2), '02 (5), '03- 1 (2), '05- (2); WI: '97- 4, '99- (1); E23Cp: '94- 1 (2). At 400m: WUG: '99- 1; WJ: '92- 3/1R; WI: '97- 4, '04- 4/3R; EI: '94- 4, '96- 4, '98- 2; E23Cp: '92- 2 (4). Won ROM 100m 1998, 2001; 200m 1998-9, 2002; 400m 1996, 1999; 400mh 1994-6; Balkan 200m 2002.

Romanian records: 100m (2) 1998-9, 200m (3) 1998-9, 400m (2) 1998-9, 400mh (6) 1996-9. European Junior 400mh record 1995.

Progress at 200m, 400m, 400mh: 1991- 24.51, 1992- 23.84, 52.13; 1993- 23.49, 56.30H; 1994- 23.60, 56.25H; 1995- 23.54, 55.26H; 1996- 54.40, 1997- 23.07, 52.06i, 55.04; 1998- 22.65/22.5A, 50.32, 53.37; 1999- 22.35, 49.88, 53.25; 2000- 51.84, 54.35; 2001- 22.77, 52.64i, 54.65; 2002- 23.04, 54.61; 2003- 22.78, 52.19, 53.87; 2004- 23.13, 50.48, 53.32; 2005- 23.26, 52.09. pbs: 60m 7.24i '99, 100m 11.30 '99, 300m 36.20A '03.

Constantina TOMESCU b. 23 Jan 1970 Turburea 1.65m 48kg. née Dita. CSM Drobeta Turnu Severin. Sports teacher.

At 10,000m: EC: '02- 7. At Mar: OG: '04- 20; WCh: '99- 19, '01- 10, '03- dnf, '05- 3; EC: '98- 17; World CC: '98- 16; HMar: 99-03-04-05 12/5/3/1; Eur CC: '99- 2. Won ROM 10,000m 1998, HMar 2002 CC 1998; Balkan 5000m 2002 10,000m 1997-8.

Two Romanian marathon records 2005.

Progress at Mar: 1997- 2:35:32, 1998- 2:34:35 1999- 2:36:28, 2000- 2:37:57, 2001- 2:26:39, 2002- 2:23:54, 2003- 2:23:35, 2004- 2:23:45, 2005- 2:21:30 pbs: 5000m 15:28.91 '00, 10,000m 31:53.61 '02 Road: 15km 48:42 '05, HMar 68:10 '02.

Son Raphael born 1995. Led World marathon by almost 2 mins at 20k in 2001 and by 32sec at 5k in 2003. Stayed in lead to win Chicago 2004 (2nd 2003 and 2005); 2nd London 2005 (3rd 2004). Married to her coach Valeriu Tomescu.

RUSSIA

Governing body: All-Russia Athletic Federation Luzhnetskaya Nab. 8, Moscow 119992. Founded 1911.

National Championships first held 1908 USSR women from 1922. **2005 Champions Men**: 100m: Andrey Yepishin 10.32, 200m: Oleg Sergeyev 21.04, 400m: Dmitriy Forshev 46.28 800m: Dmitriy Bogdanov 1:47.12, 1500m: Yuriy Borzakovskiy 3:40.28, 5000m: Pavel Shapovalov 13:34.53, 10,000m: Dmitriy Maksimov 28:41.17 HMar: Sergey Davydov 66:38, Mar: Aleksey Sokolov 2:17:35, 3000mSt: Roman Usov 8:26.96 110mh: Igor Peremota 13.51, 400mh: Mikhail Lipskiy 50.13, HJ: Yaroslav Rybakov 2.30, PV Igor Pavlov 5.80, LJ: Vitaliy Shkurlatov 8.07, TJ Igor Spasovkhodskiy 17.30, SP: Ivan Yushkov 20.57, DT: Bogdan Pishchalnikov 63.57, HT: Ilya Konovalov 78.76, JT: Sergey Makarov 90.33 Dec: Aleksey Drozdov 8120, 20kmW: Vladimir Parvatkin 1:21:24, 50kmW: Vladimir Kanaykin 3:40:40. **Women**: 100m: Olga Fyodorova 11.25 200m: Yuliya Gushchina 22.62, 400m: Svetlana Pospelova 49.80, 800m: Tatyana Andrianova 1:56.07, 1500m: Yuliya Chizhenko 3:58.68, 5000m Liliya Shobukova 15:16.73, 10,000m: Galina Bogomolova 31:04.61, HMar: Irina Timofeyeva 73:52, Mar: Nina Podnebesnova 2:40:46, 3000mSt Yekaterina Volkova 9:36.12, 100mh: Mariya Koroteyeva 12.81, 400mh: Yuliya Pechonkina 53.01, HJ: Yelena Slesarenko 2.00, PV: Tatyana Pavlova 4.50, LJ: Tatyana Kotova 6.96, TJ Nadezhda Bazhenova 14.28, SP: Olga Ryabinkina 19.60, DT: Natalya Sadova 65.63, HT: Tatyana Lysenko 75.95, JT: Mariya Yakovenko 60.83, Hep Natalya Roshchupkina 6003, 20kmW: Tatyana Gudkova 1:29:02.

Note: Clubs abbreviations: Dyn – Dynamo, TU – Trade Union sports society, VS – Army, YR – Yunest Rossii.

Yuriy BORZAKOVSKIY b. 12 Apr 1981 Kratovo Moskva reg. 1.82m 72kg. Zhukovskiy Dyn Student.

At 800m/4x400mR: OG: '00- 6, '04- 1; WCh: '03- 2, '05- 2; EC: '02- 2R; EJ: '99- 1; WI: '01- 1, '06- 3

EI: '00- 1; ECp: '99- 1, '02- 1; 2nd GP 2001. At 400m: EC: '02- sf; EU23: '01- 1; At 1500m: ECp: '03- 3. Won Russian 800m 2004, 1500m 2005.
Records: Two world junior indoor 800m 2000, European Junior 800m (2) & 1000m 2000; four Russian 800m 2001.
Progress at 800m: 1997- 1:52.8i/1:53.69, 1998- 1:47.71, 1999- 1:46.13, 2000- 1:44.33, 2001- 1:42.47, 2002- 1:44.20, 2003- 1:43.68, 2004- 1:43.92, 2005- 1:44.18. pbs: 200m 22.56 '99, 400m 45.84 '00, 1000m 2:17.40 '00, 1500m 3:40.28 '05, 3000m 8:32 '99.
He won at the World Youth Games in 1998, and at the age of 18 had a startling victory when he sprinted to victory in the European Cup 800m. In January 2000 he set a hugely impressive Russian senior and world junior record 1:44.38 in Dortmund. He typically leaves himself a tremendous amount to do on the second lap of his 800m races and curiously did not compete at the 2001 Worlds or 2002 Europeans at this event, although he ran a 44.75 last leg in the European 4x400m. Olympic success in 2004 came from a remarkably even-paced race.

Viktor BURAYEV b. 23 Aug 1982 Zarechnyi, Penza Reg. 1.76m 58kg. Saransk VS.
At 20kmW: OG: '04- 22; WCh: '01- 3, '03- dq, '05- dnf; EC: '02- 4; WCp: '04- 7; ECp: '01- 1. At 10kmW: WJ: '00- 3. Won RUS 20kmW 2002-03.
World junior walks records 10,000m 2000, 20km 2001.
Progress at 20kmW: 1999- 1:28:18, 2001- 1:18:06, 2002- 1:20:36, 2003- 1:20:56, 2004- 1:20:14, 2005- 1:18:48. pbs: 5000mW 19:12.0 '02, 10,000mW 38:46.4 '00.
At 18 years 264 days he became the youngest ever men's walk medallist at the World Championships – and he was the only junior to win a medal in 2001.

Danila BURKENYA b. 20 Jul 1978 Ashkhabad, Turkmenistan 1.98m 82kg. Luch Moskva
At TJ: OG: '04- 3; WCh: '05- dnq 19; WI: '04- 7; EJ: '97- 9; ECp: '04- 2, '05- 2. At LJ: OG: '00- dnq 26; WCh: '01/03- dnq 19/30; EC: '02- 5; EJ: '97- 5; EI: '98- 4; ECp: '01- 1, '02- 4. Won RUS LJ 2000-02, TJ 2004.
Progress at LJ, TJ: 1994- 6.18, 13.73; 1995- 6.77, 15.28; 1996- 7.08, 14.87; 1997- 7.81, 16.29; 1998- 7.68, 16.36/16.40w; 1999- 8.07i/8.00, 16.30i; 2000- 8.12, 16.14; 2001- 8.31, 2002- 8.19/8.35w '02, 2003- 8.23, 16.58i; 2004- 7.84, 17.68; 2005- 17.10. pb 100m 10.98 '97.

Aleksey DMITRIK b. 12 Apr 1984 1.91m 69kg. St Petersburg YR.
At HJ: WJ: '02- 14; WY: '01- 1; EJ: '03- 2; EU23: '05- 6; ECp: '05- 1.
Progress at HJ: 2000- 2.08, 2001- 2.23, 2002- 2.26, 2003- 2.28, 2004- 2.30, 2005- 2.34i/2.30.

Aleksey DROZDOV b. 3 Dec 1983 Bryansk 1.84m 80kg. Bryansk VS.
At Dec: WCh: '05- 10; EU23: '03- 8, '05- 1; Russian champion 2005. At Hep: WI: '06- 5; EI: '05- 6.
Progress at Dec: 2002- 7037, 2003- 7536, 2004- 7805, 2005- 8196. pbs: 60m 6.7i '05, 6.94i '06; 100m 11.18, 400m 50.67 '04, 1000m 2:43.17i '05, 1500m 4:34.85 '05, 60mh 8.0i '05, 8.19i "06; 110mh 14.86 '05, HJ 2.09i/2.07 '05, PV 4.90i/4.70 '05, LJ 7.58i '06, 7.35; SP 16.98i '06, 15.56 '04; DT 51.68 '05, JT 67.08 '05, Hep 6225i '06.

Pavel GERASIMOV b. 29 May 1979 Aleksin, Tula reg. 1.90m 80kg. Luch Moskva.
At PV: OG: '00- dnq 26=, '04- 13=; WCh: '03- dnq 17, '05- 3; EC: '02- 12; WJ: '98- 1; EJ: '97- 2; WI: '01- 5, EI: '02- 6. Russian champion 2000.
Progress at PV: 1995- 4.40, 1996- 5.10i/5.00, 1997- 5.30, 1998- 5.55, 1999- 5.65/5.70ex, 2000- 5.90, 2001- 5.81i/5.50, 2002- 5.80i/5.60, 2003- 5.67, 2004- 5.77i/5.75, 2005- 5.70.

Viktor GUSHCHINSKIY b. 12 Aug 1978 Chervonograd, UKR 2.02m 95kg. Luch Moskva.
At TJ: OG: '04- 7; WCh: '05- dnq 17; WJ: '96- 8; EJ: '97- 1. Russian champion 2001.
Progress at TJ: 1994- 15.55, 1995- 15.72, 1996- 16.56, 1997- 16.78, 1998- 16.31i, 1999- 16.42i, 2000- 16.56i, 2001- 16.91, 2002- 16.97i/16.30, 2003- 16.91i/16.87, 2004- 17.22, 2005- 17.10. pb LJ 7.54 '01.

Aleksandr IVANOV b. 25 May 1982 Leningrad 1.94m 110kg. Luch Moskva.
At JT: OG: '04- 5; WCh: '01- 10, '03- 12, '05- 5; EC: '02- 6; EU23: '03- 1; EJ: '01- 1; WJ: '00- 6; WY: '99- 3; ECp: '04- 1, '05- 2. Russian champion 2002, 2004, World Military 2003.
Progress at JT: 1998- 67.97, 1999- 71.76, 2000- 77.11, 2001- 83.55, 2002- 87.62, 2003- 88.90, 2004- 87.73, 2005- 84.24.
Mother Valentina had JT best of 59.10 in 1980.

Vladimir KANAYKIN b. 21 Mar 1985 Mordoviya 1.70m 60kg. Saransk VS.
At 50kmW: WCh: '05- dq; RUS champion 2005. At 10,000mW: WJ: '02- 1, '04- 2; WY: '02- 1.
Three world bests 30km & 35km walk 2004-06 (each to win Russian winter 35k).
Progress at 20kmW. 50kmW: 2003- 1:21:23, 2004- 1:22:00, 3:40:40; 2005- 1:21:11, 3:40:40. pbs: 5000mW 20:20.26 '03, 10,000mW: 40:58.48 '04, 10kmW: 38:16 '04, 30kmW 2:01:13 '06, 35kmW 2:21:31 '06.
Disqualified when well clear of field in 2004 at World Cup junior 10km.

Vadim KHERSONTSEV b. 8 Jul 1974 Kursk region 1.92m 106kg. Luch Moskva.
At HT: OG: '96- dnq 15; WCh: '97- 7, '99- 8, '05- 8; EC: '02- 16; EJ: '93- 3; WUG: '97- 4; ECp: '97- 2, '02- 6. Russian champion 1996.
Progress at HT: 1990- 56.72, 1991- 61.80, 1992- 68.58, 1993- 72.72, 1994- 76.78, 1995- 76.94, 1996- 80.68, 1997- 78.58, 1998- 79.10, 1999- 78.82, 2000- 78.16, 2001- 81.26, 2002- 78.80, 2003- 78.89, 2004- 77.32, 2005- 79.47, 2006- 78.54.

Sergey KIRDYAPKIN b. 16 Jan 1980 Mordoviya 1.78m 67kg. Saransk VS.
At 50kmW: WCh: '05- 1; ECp: '05- 2.
Progress at 50kmW: 2001- 4:08:16, 2002- 3:52:09, 2004- 3:43:20, 2005- 3:38:08; pbs: 20kmW 1:23:07 '05, 30kmW 2:05:06 '03, 35kmW 2:25:57 '05.

Sergey KIRMASOV b. 25 Mar 1970 Mtsensk. Oryol region 1.80m 118kg. Oryol VS. Soldier.
At HT: OG: '04- dnq 16; WCh: '01/03/05- dnq 15/20/nt; EC: '98- dnq 18; EJ: '89- 1; ECp: '99-00-04: 7/5/4. Russian champion 1992, 1998, 2001.
Progress at HT: 1988- 71.20, 1989- 75.52, 1990- 77.66, 1991- 81.14, 1992- 79.92, 1993- 82.54, 1994- 79.20dq, 1998- 82.62, 1999- 79.55, 2000- 78.44, 2001- 80.07, 2002- 79.19, 2003- 79.62, 2004- 78.84, 2005- 78.97. Four year drugs ban 1994-8.

Sergey KLYUGIN b. 24 Mar 1974 Kineshma, Ivanova region 1.92m 82kg. Luch Moskva. Teacher.
At HJ: OG: '00- 1; WCh: '97- 11, '99- dnq 24, '01- 4=; EC: '98- 3; WJ: '92- 5=, EJ: '91- 2; EU23Cp: '94- 2; ECp: '97-8-00: 2/1/3=. Russian champion 2000-01.
Progress at HJ: 1986- 1.55, 1987- 1.65, 1988- 1.80, 1989- 1.98, 1990- 2.16, 1991- 2.27, 1992- 2.28i/2.24, 1993- 2.26i/2.24, 1994- 2.28i/2.26, 1995- 2.26, 1996- 2.28, 1997- 2.31i/2.30, 1998- 2.36, 1999- 2.33, 2000- 2.35, 2001- 2.31, 2002- 2.24, 2003- 2.25, 2004- 2.28i/2.22, 2005- 2.28.
Two knee operations in winter 2001/02.

Ilya KONOVALOV b. 4 Mar 1971 Efrosimovka, Kursk region 1.92m 120kg. Kursk Dyn. Soldier.
At HT: OG: '96- 6, '00- 5, '04- dnq 12; WCh: '95- 7, '97- 6, '99- 10, '01- 3, '03- 6, '05- 6; EC: '98- 9, '02- dnq 20; WUG: '97- 3; ECp: '95-98-05: 1/2/2. Won RUS 1995, 1999, 2002-05.
Progress at HT: 1988- 63.10, 1989- 71.30, 1990- 74.66, 1991- 76.26, 1992- 77.04, 1993- 77.44, 1994- 78.30, 1995- 79.66, 1996- 79.46, 1997- 78.92, 1998- 79.82, 1999- 80.51, 2000- 81.93, 2001- 80.27, 2002- 81.81, 2003- 82.28, 2004- 80.36, 2005- 79.92.

Sergey MAKAROV b. 19 Mar 1973 Lyubertsy 1.92m 100kg. Moskva Dyn.
At JT: OG: '96- 6, '00- 3, '04- 3; WCh: '97- 5, '99- 9, '01- 7, '03- 1, '05- 3; EC: '98- 4, '02- 2; WCp: '98- 2, '02- 1; ECp: '96-7-8-9-00-01-02-03: 2/4/2/2/2/2/1/1; E23Cp: '94- 2. Won GWG 1998, WAF 2003, RUS 1996-7, 2000-01, 2003, 2005.
Six Russian records 1996-2002.
Progress at JT: 1991- 73.48, 1992- 76.08, 1993- 75.78, 1994- 82.54, 1995- 84.42, 1996- 88.86, 1997- 88.54, 1998- 86.96, 1999- 89.93, 2000- 89.92, 2001- 88.42, 2002- 92.61, 2003- 90.11, 2004- 86.19, 2005- 90.33.
Married to Oksana Ovchinnikova (b. 21 Jul 1971, Russian 'old' javelin record 68.72 '96. 2 WJ 1990). His father Aleksandr Makarov (b. 11 Feb 1951) was 2nd in the 1980 Olympic JT with a pb 89.64 (old javelin).

Ilya MARKOV b. 19 Jun 1972 Asbest, Sverdlovsk reg. 1.74m 65kg. Asbest VS. Soldier.
At 20kmW: OG: '96- 2, '00- 15; WCh: '95- 4, '97- dq, '99- 1, '01- 2, '03- 8, '05- dq; EC: '94- 18, '98- 1; WUG: '97- 1; WCp: '95-3-9: 30/3/7; ECp: '03- 5, '05- 1. Won RUS 1995, GWG 1998. At 10kmW: WJ: '90- 1; EJ: '91- 1.
Progress at 20kmW: 1991- 1:33:46, 1992- 1:23:27, 1993- 1:20:19, 1994- 1:24:07, 1995- 1:18:53, 1996- 1:18:48, 1997- 1:18:30, 1998- 1:19:46, 1999- 1:18:50, 2000- 1:20:53, 2001- 1:19:36, 2003- 1:20:05, 2004- 1:19:25, 2005- 1:18:17. pbs: 3000mW 11:08.2i '92, 5000mW 18:36.71i '99, 18:46.96 '01; 10,000mW 39:15.6 '98.

Denis NIZHEGORODOV b. 26 Jul 1980 Saransk 1.80m 61kg. Saransk TU.
At 50kmW: OG: '04- 2; WCh: '03- 5; Russian champion 2003-04. At 20kmW: EU23: '01- 5, WUG: '01- 4; ECp: '00- 17, '01- 7.
World best (no drugs test) 50km walk 2004.
Progress at 20kmW, 50kmW: 2000- 1:21:47, 2001- 1:18:20; 2003- 1:23:23, 3:38:23; 2004- 3:35:29, 2005- dnf. pbs: 30kmW 2:05:08 '06, 35kmW 2:24:50 '06.

Vladimir PARVATKIN b. 10 Oct 1984 Insar Mordoviya 1.75m 65kg. Saransk VS.
At 20kmW: OG: '04- 38; RUS champion 2004-05. At 10,000mW: EJ: '03- 1.
Progress at 20kmW: 2004- 1:18:17, 2005- 1:18:06, pbs: 3000mW 11:45.0 '05, 10kmW 38:25 '04, 10,000mW 40:26.2 '05.

Igor PAVLOV b. 18 Jul 1979 Moskva 1.87m 83kg. Moskva VS.
At PV: OG: '04- 4; WCh: '05- 4; WI: '04- 1; EI: '05- 1; WUG: '03- 2. Russian champion 2005.
Progress at PV: 1998- 5.10, 1999- 5.30i, 2000- 5.55/5.70sq, 2001- 5.60i, 2002- 5.40, 2003- 5.65/5.75ex, 2004- 5.80, 2005- 5.90i/5.80.

Aleksandr POGORELOV b. 10 Jan 1980 Zheleznogorsk, Kursk region 2.01m 97kg Bryansk Dyn.
At Dec: OG: '04- 11; WCh: '03- dnf, '05- 5; EC: '02- 8; EJ: '99- dnf; ECp: '02- 5, '03- 2. At Hep: WI: '03-04-06: 6/6/6 EI: '05- 2.
Progress at Dec: 1997- 5750, 1998- 6356, 1999- 6895, 2001- 7354, 2002- 8163, 2003- 8072, 2004- 8084, 2005- 8429. pbs: 60m 6.90i '06, 100m 10.86 '05, 400m 50.16 '05, 1000m 2:52.30i '03, 1500m 4:47.00 '04, 60mh 7.93i '06, 110mh 14.14 '05, HJ 2.15 '02, PV 5.10 '05, LJ 7.74 '02, SP 16.12i/16.07 '05, DT 48.44 '05, JT 60.72 '03, Hep 6229i '06.

Vladimir POTEMIN b. 15 Jan 1980 Insar Morodoviya 1.77m 69kg. Saransk VS.
At 50kmW: WCh: '01- 5; WCp: '02- 17; ECp: '01- 3. At 20kmW: OG: '00- 26. 10,000mW: EJ: '99- 2 World U23 best 50km walk 2000.
Progress at 50kmW: 2000- 3:39:21, 2001- 3:46.12, 2002- 3:57:18, 2003- 3:45:27, 2004- 3:39:34, 2005- 3:51:34. pbs: 10,000mW 39:46.1 '05, 20kmW 1:23:37 '03, 30kmW 2:08:05 '01, 35kmW 2:29:03 '01.

Roman RASSKAZOV b. 28 Apr 1979 Kovylkino (Mordoviya) 1.86m 64kg. Saransk VS. Student.
At 20kmW: OG: '00- 6; WCh: '99- dnf, 01- 1, '03- 3. RUS champion 1999-2001. At 10,000mW: WJ: '98- 1.
World best and two RUS records 20km walk 2000.
Progress at 20kmW: 1997- 1:31:24, 1999- 1:19:36, 2000- 1:17:46, 2001- 1:20:31, 2002- 1:21:01, 2003- 1:18:07, 2004- 1:18:35. pbs: 5000mW 19:02.1i '00, 19:11.5 '02; 10kmW 37:11 (world best) '00.

Yaroslav RYBAKOV b. 22 Nov 1980 Mogilyev, Belarus 1.98m 82kg. Luch Moskva.
At HJ: OG: '04- 6; WCh: '01- 2=, '03- 9, '05- 2=; EC: '02- 1; WJ: '98- 5; EJ: '99- 3; WI: '01-03-04-06: 7/2/2/1; EI: '02- 3, '05- 2; WCp: '02- 1; ECp: '01-02-03: 1/2/1; Won WAF 2003, 2nd GP 2002. Russian champion 2002-04.
Progress at HJ: 1997- 2.10i/2.09, 1998- 2.20, 1999- 2.19i/2.18, 2000- 2.28, 2001- 2.33, 2002- 2.31, 2003- 2.34, 2004- 2.32, 2005- 2.38i/2.33, 2006- 2.37i. pbs: LJ 7.44i '98, Hep 5570i '98.

Vitaliy SHKURLATOV b. 25 May 1979 Volgograd 1.82m 80kg. Volgograd VS.
At LJ: OG: '04- 9; WCh: '01- 12, '03- dnq 18, '05- 10; WJ: '98- 8; EU23: '99- 2; EJ: '97- 4; WI: '01- 8, '04- 3; EI: '00- 3, '02- 7; ECp: '00-04-05: 1/3/3. Russian champion 2003-05.
Progress at LJ: 1995- 6.84, 1996- 7.64, 1997- 7.92, 1998- 7.79i, 1999- 8.06, 2000- 8.38i/8.22, 2001- 8.18, 2002- 8.15i/8.13, 2003- 8.23, 2004- 8.28i/8.21, 2005- 8.15. pb 60m 6.4/6.78i '02.

Pavel SOFIN b. 4 Sep 1981 Lyubertsky. Moskva region 2.01m 120kg. Moskva TU.
At SP: OG: '04- dnq; WCh: '03- dnq; WJ: '00- 7; EU23: '03- 2; EJ: '99- 6; WI: '06- 4; ECp: '05- 6.
Progress at SP: 1999- 17.12, 2000- 18.42, 2001- 18.44, 1002- 19.63, 2003- 20.33, 2004- 19.89, 2005- 20.05, 2006- 20.68i/20.19.

Igor SPASOVKHODSKIY b. 1 Aug 1979 Moskva 1.91m 91kg. Luch Moskva.
At TJ: OG: '00- dnq 32; WCh: '01- 3, '03/05- dnq 20/16; EC: '02- dnq 16; EU23: '01- 2; EJ: '99- 6; WI: '06- 5; EI: '02- 7, '05- 1; WUG: '01- 4; ECp: '02- 5. Russian champion 2005.
Progress at TJ: 1997- 14.42, 1998- 15.37, 1999- 16.32, 2000- 16.86, 2001- 17.44, 2002- 17.39/17.42w, 2003- 16.95, 2004- 17.09i/17.04, 2005- 17.40, 2006- 17.31i. pb LJ 7.58 '03.

Vladimir STANKIN b. 2 Jan 1974 Mordoviya 1.84m 71kg. Chelyabinsk TU.
At 20kmW: WCh: '05- 6; WCp: '04- 11; ECp: '05- 3.
Russian 20km walk record 2004.
Progress at 20kmW: 1992- 1:23:58, 1995- 1:21:43, 1996- 1:20:22, 1998- 1:22:06, 1999- 1:20:21, 2000- 1:20:31, 2001- 1:19:14. 2002- 1:22:07, 2003- 1:21:32, 2004- 1:17:23, 2005- 1:18:22. pbs: 5000mW 19:29.9i '06, 10kmW 38:50 '01, 10,000mW 40:35.20 '92, 30kmW 2:06:51 '97, 35kmW 2:29:26 '97.

His sister **Irina** became, at 18 years 135 days, the youngest ever world champion (at 10km walk) in 1995 and was World Junior 5000m walk champion in 1994 and 1996.

Andrey TERESHIN b. 15 Dec 1982 Kineshma, Ivanovo Reg. 1.95m 77kg. Moskva VS.
At HJ: WCh: '05- dnq 23=; EU23: '03- 2; WI: '06- 2; EI: '05- 8; WUG: '03- 6=.
Progress at HJ: 2000- 2.15, 2001- 2.18, 2002- 2.24, 2003- 2.24, 2004- 2.28i/2.26, 2005- 2.32, 2006- 2.36i.

Ivan UKHOV b. 29 Mar 1986 Chelyabinsk 1.92m 83kg. Sverdlovsk TU.
At HJ: WJ: '04- dnq 13; EJ: '05- 1; WUG: '05- 4.
Progress at HJ: 2004- 2.15, 2005- 2.30, 2006- 2.37i.
Former discus thrower.

Vyacheslav VORONIN b. 5 Apr 1974 Vladikavkaz 1.91m 78kg. Moskva Dyn.
At HJ: OG: '00- 10, '04- 9; WCh: '99- 1, '01- 2=, '05- 8; EJ: '93- 2; WI: '99- 2, '01- 9; EI: '98- 2, '00- 1; ECp: '99- 2, '04- 5=. Won GP 2000, RUS champion 1999, 2005.
Russian high jump record 2000.
Progress at HJ: 1990- 1.85, 1991- 2.07, 1992- 2.15, 1993- 2.18, 1995- 2.18, 1996- 2.29, 1997- 2.26/2.30sq, 1998- 2.32i/2.28, 1999- 2.37, 2000- 2.40, 2001- 2.37, 2002- 2.26i, 2003- 2.24i/2.21, 2004- 2.32, 2005- 2.33.

Aleksey VOYEVODIN b. 9 Aug 1970 Marat, Penza Reg. 1.78m 65kg. Luch Moskva.
At 50kmW: OG: '04- 3; WCh: '95- 15, '97- 10, '01- dnf, '03- 4, '05- 2; EC: '02- 2; WCp: '95-02-04: 10/1/1; ECp: '98-01-03-05: 4/6/2/1. Won RUS 50kmW 2001-02.
Progress at 50kmW: 1993- 4:04:44, 1994- 3:52:36, 1995- 3:48:55, 1996- 3:45:37, 1997- 3:41:33, 1998- 3:46:31, 1999- 3:51:43, 2000- 3:50:27, 2001- 3:44:32, 2002- 3:40:16, 2003- 3:38:01, 2004- 3:42:44, 2005- 3:41:03. pbs: 5000mW 19:19.0 '02, 10,000mW 39:22.0i '01, 20kmW 1:19:31 '98, 30kmW 2:05:18 '04, 35kmW 2:26:25 '04.
His wife **Yuliya Voyevodina** (b. 7.10.71) has 20kmW pb 1:27:53 '04, 13 OG 14, 10 WCh 05.

Aleksey ZAGORNYI b. 31 May 1978 Yaroslavl 1.97m 130kg. Luch Moskva.
At HT: OG: '00- dnq 22; WCh: '03- dnq 22; EC: '02- 11; EJ: '97- 5; EU23: '99- 7; WUG: '01- 4.
Progress at HT: 1994- 59.90, 1995- 71.00, 1996- 71.94, 1997- 71.30, 1998- 77.03, 1999- 77.20, 2000- 79.68, 2001- 80.80, 2002- 83.43, 2003- 80.13, 2004- 78.79, 2005- 80.81.

Women

Tatyana ANDRIANOVA b. 10 Dec 1979 Yaroslavl 1.73m 61kg. Moskva TU.
At 800m: OG: '04- 5; WCh: '05- 3; WI: '04- 5. Russian champion 2004-05.
Progress at 800m: 1998- 2:06.20, 2001- 2:04.09, 2003- 2:00.96, 2004- 1:56.23, 2005- 1:56.07. pbs: 400m 54.77 '03, 600m 1:26.81i '04, 1000m 2:45.22i '03, 1500m 4:12.02 '05.

Natalya ANTYUKH b. 26 Jun 1981 Leningrad 1.82m 73kg. Moskva VS.
At 400m/4x400mR: OG: '04- 3/2R; WCh: '05- sf/1R; EC: '02- 2R; WI: '03-04-06: 1R/GR/1R; EI: '02- 1; WCp: '02- 3R; ECp: '01- 3/1R, '05- 1/1R. At 200m: ECp: '04- 2.
Progress at 400m: 2000- 54.79, 2001- 51.19, 2002- 51.17i/51.24, 2003- 51.73i/52.28, 2004- 49.85, 2005- 50.67. pbs: 200m 22.75 '04, 300m 36.0+ '04, 400mh 58.30 '00.

Nadezhda BAZHENOVA b. 22 Sep 1978 Vladimir 1.76m 63kg. Vladimir TU.
At TJ: WCh: '03/05- dnq 23/20; WUG: '05- 3; EI: '02- 4. Russian champion 2003, 2005.
Progress at TJ: 1997- 13.21, 1998- 13.04, 1999- 14.25, 2000- 14.13, 2001- 14.60, 2002- 14.65i/14.31, 2003- 14.35, 2004- 14.23, 2005- 14.31. pb LJ 6.58 '01.

Yekaterina BIKERT b. 13 May 1980 Kachkanar, Sverdlovsk region 1.82m 68kg. Yekaterinburg TU.
At 400mh: OG: '04- 6; ECp: '04- 2, '05- 2.
Progress at 400mh: 2000- 60.55, 2001- 57.61, 2002- 59.87, 2003- 57.89, 2004- 53.72, 2005- 55.72. pbs: 400m 51.26 '04, 100mh 14.17 '00.
Huge improvement in 2004.

Galina BOGOMOLOVA b. 15 Oct 1977 Beloretsk, Bashkorstan 1.59m 43kg. Beloretsk VS.
At 10,000m (5000m): OG: '00- h, '04- 22; WCh: '03- 6, '05- 8; WJ: '96- 12 (h 3000m); EU23: '97- 7/7. At 3000m: WI: '03- 6; ECp: '00- 2. World HMar: '03- 17, '05- 4. Eur CC: '02- 2, '03- 10. Won RUS 10,000m 2000, 2003, 2005.
Russian 10,000m record (30:46.48) 2003.
Progress at 5000m. 10,000m: 1996- 16:29.56, 1997- 15:53.45, 33:34.44; 1998- 16:18.06, 33:56.04; 1999- 15:52.72, 2000- 15:08.61, 31:29.66; 2002- 15:39.14, 2003- 15:13.08, 30:26.20; 2004- 14:59.72, 32:15.31; 2005- 30:33.75. pbs: 1500m 4:10.00 '04, 3000m 8:42.03 '05, Road: 15km 49:56 '05, HMar 70:34 '05, Mar 2:31:54 '05.

Svetlana CHERKASOVA b. 20 May 1978 Belogorsk, Khabarovsk region 1.70m 52kg. née Belosurova. Luch Moskva.
At 800m: OG: '04- sf; WCh: '01- sf, '05- 7; EC: '02- sf; EI: '02- 5; WCp: '02- 5. Russian champion 2001.
Progress at 800m: 1998- 2:07.75, 1999- 2:00.91, 2000- 1:59.23, 2001- 1:57.59, 2002- 1:58.84, 2003- 1:59.28, 2004- 1:57.50, 2005- 1:56.93, 2006- 1:58.34i. pbs: 400m 52.76 '05, 600m 1:26.84i '02, 1000m 2:34.08 '01, 1500m 4:05.55 '03.
Husband Aleksey Cherkasov has 2.15 HJ best.

Anna CHICHEROVA b. 22 Jul 1982 Yerevan 1.80m 56kg. Moskva VS.
At HJ: OG: '04- 6; WCh: '03- 6, '05- 4; WJ: '00- 4; WY: '99- 1; EJ: '01- 2; WUG: '05- 1; WI: '04- 2; EI: '05- 1. Russian champion 2004.
Progress at HJ: 1998- 1.80, 1999- 1.89, 2000- 1.90, 2001- 1.92, 2002- 2.00i/1.89, 2003- 2.04i/2.00, 2004- 2.04i/1.98, 2005- 2.01i/1.99.

Yuliya CHIZHENKO b. 30 Aug 1979 Arkhangelsk 1.66m 54kg. St Petersburg VS.
At 1500m: WCh: 05- dq; WI: '06- 1; EI: '05- h; ECp: '05- 1. Russian champion 2005.
Progress at 1500m: 2002- 4:16.79, 2003- 4:07.21, 2004- 4:04.58, 2005- 3:58.68. pbs: 800m 2:01.08 '05, 1000m 2:32.16i '06, 2:35.20 '05; 2000m 5:50.95i '03, 3000m 8:53.80i '05, 9:01.22 '03; 5000m 16:27.19 '01.
Finished 2nd in World 1500m in 2005, but then disqualified for baulking Miryam Jamal.

Larisa CHZHAO b. 4 Feb 1971 Kirgizstan 1.75m 58kg. Formerly Panchik, née Popova. Yekaterinburg Dyn.
At 800m: WCh: '05- 6; EI: '05- 1.
Progress at 800m: 1990- 2:05.50, 1993- 2:01.33, 1994- 2:01.56, 1995- 2:03.46, 1996- 2:01.60, 1997- 2:04.57, 2000- 2:02.36, 2001- 2:04.42, 2002- 1:59.85, 2003- 1:58.71, 2004- 2:00.38, 2005- 1:57.33. pbs: 400m 52.72 '05, 1000m 2:35.34i '05, 1500m 4:09.71 '05.
Came to the fore in 2005, but 7/3/4/7 in Russian Champs 1994/2002/03/04.

Svetlana FEOFANOVA b. 16 Jul 1980 Moskva 1.64m 52kg. Luch Moskva.
At PV: OG: '00- dnq, '04- 2; WCh: '01- 2, '03- 1; EC: '02- 1; WI: '01-03-04-06: 2/1/3/3; EI: '02- 1, WCp: '02- 2; ECp: '00-02: 1/1; 2nd GP 2001. Russian champion 2001.
World pole vault record 2004, 9 European records 2001-04, 11 Russian 2000-04, 9 world indoor 2002-04 (4.71-4.85), 13 European indoor 2001-04.
Progress at PV: 1998- 3.90, 1999- 4.10, 2000- 4.50, 2001- 4.75, 2002- 4.78, 2003- 4.80i/4.75, 2004- 4.88, 2005- 4.70i, 2006- 4.70i.
Was a top gymnast, winning Russian titles at youth, junior and U23 level at asymmetric bars and floor exercises. Set five indoor world records in a month in 2002. Missed 2005 outdoor season due to a herniated disc.

Lidiya GRIGORYEVA b. 21 Jan 1974 Smychka, Chuvashiya 1.64m 58kg. Novocheboksarsk TU.
At 10,000m: OG: '00- 9, '04- 8; WCh: '03- 16. World HMar: '00-03-05: 11/4/7. Won Russian 10,000m 2004, CC 1998.
Progress at 10,000m, Mar: 1997- 34:32.08, 1998- 2:41:04; 1999- 32:49.64, 2:35:38; 2000- 31:21.27, 2:32:40; 2001- 32:36.6, 2003- 30:57.83, 2004- 31:01.15, 2:34:39; 2005- 31:20.58, 2:27:01; 2006- 2:25:10. pbs: 1M 4:36.82 '04, 3000m 8:45.73 '04, 5000m 15:17.21 '04, HMar 69:32 '03.
Won Paris marathon 2005, Los Angeles 2006 (when she collected $155,000 plus a Honda Accord car).

Tatyana GUDKOVA b. 23 Dec 1978 Magnitogorsk 1.70m 60kg. Magnitogorsk TU. Teacher.
At 20kmW: OG: '00- 8; WCh: '03- 4, '05- 18.

Russian champion 2000, 2002 (track), 2003, 2005. World best 20km walk 2000.
Progress at 10kmW, 20kmW: 1996- 47:07, 1997- 45:46, 1998- 44:42, 1999- 42:51, 1:33:05; 2000- 42:42, 1:25:18; 2001- 43:17, 1:30:12; 2002- 43:20, 1:30:20.1t; 2003- 44:01, 1:28:37; 2004- 43:46, 1:30:05; 2005- 44:19, 1:29:02.

Viktoriya GUROVA b. 22 May 1982 Sochi 1.78m 63kg. Krasnodar TU.
At TJ: OG: '04- dnq 21; WCh: '05- 10; EU23: '03- 1; EJ: '01- 3; WUG: '03- 2; EI: '05- 1.
Progress at TJ: 1998- 12.56, 1999- 13.02, 2000- 13.44, 2001- 13.75/13.92w, 2002- 14.22, 2003- 14.37, 2004- 14.65, 2005- 14.74i/14.38. pb LJ 6.49i '03.

Yuliya GUSHCHINA b. 4 Mar 1983 Novocherkask 1.75m 62kg. Rostov-na-Danu VS.
At 200m/4x400mR: WCh: '05- 6; WJ: '02- 3R; EU23: '03- 3; WI: '06- GR; ECp: '05- 1R (1 4x100mR). Won Russian 200m 2005.
World indoor records 4x200m 2005, 4x400m 2006.
Progress at 200m: 2002- 23.92/23.88w, 2003- 23.58, 2004- 23.06, 2005- 22.62. pbs: 60m 7.29i '04, 7.2i '03; 100m 11.50 '05, 400m 51.94 '03.

Yelena ISINBAYEVA b. 3 Jun 1982 Volgograd 1.74m 66kg. Volgograd VS.
At PV: OG: '00- dnq, '04- 1; WCh: '03- 3, '05- 1; EC: '02- 2; WJ: '98- 9, '00- 1, WY: '99- 1; EU23: '03- 1; EJ: '99- 5, '01- 1; WI: '01-03-04-06: 7/2/1/1; EI: '05- 1. Won WAF 2005, Russian 2002.
11 outdoor world pole vault records 2003-05, WIR (8) 2004-06 (inc. 3 absolute WR), world junior indoor records 2000 and 2001.
Progress at PV: 1997- 3.30, 1998- 4.00, 1999- 4.20, 2000- 4.45i/4.40, 2001- 4.47i/4.46, 2002- 4.60/4.65ex, 2003- 4.82, 2004- 4.92, 2005- 5.01, 2006- 4.91i.
Former gymnast. Set world age bests at 17-18-19 in 2000-02. World titles as Youth, junior and senior. World indoor records in all four competitions 2005 and a further five outdoors in 2005. These included the first 5m vault by a woman (at the London GP) followed by 5.01 to win the World title by 41 cm.

Lyubov IVANOVA b. 2 Mar (11 Jun?) 1981. Moskva VS.
At 3000mSt: EU23: '03- 1. RUS champion 2004.
World best 3000m steeplechase indoors 9:21.37 '04.
Progress at 3000mSt: 10:14.60, 2003- 9:24.78, 2004- 9:28.02, 2005- 9:46.63. pbs: 800m 2:03.30i '04, 2:05.52 '03; 1000m 2:39.27i '04, 1500m 4:11.49 '03, 3000m 8:53.58i/9:11.34 '04, 2000mSt 6:23.04 '05.

Olimpiada IVANOVA b. 26 Aug 1970 Munsyuty, Chuvashiya 1.68m 54kg. Moskva VS.
At 20kmW: OG: '04- 2; WCh: '03- dnf, '05- 1; EC: '02- 1; WCp: '02- 2; ECp: '00- 1; RUS champion 2004. At 10kmW: WCh: '97- drugs dq (2); WCp: '93- 12, '97- 2; won GWG 1994. At 5000mW: EJ: '85- 9.
World best 20km walk 2001, world record 2005.
Progress at 10kmW, 20kmW: 1987- 45:15, 1992- 45:18, 1993- 42:24, 1994- 42:30.31t, 1995- 41:30, 1996- 41:46, 1:30:58; 1997- 41:24, 1999- 43:31, 1:28:21; 2000- 42:43, 1:26:08; 2001- 42:34, 1:24:50; 2002- 43:26, 1:26:42; 2004- 43:46, 1:26:54; 2005- 42:54, 1:25:41. pbs: 3000mW 12:02.2 '95, 2MW 12:54.98i '96, 5000mW 20:50.6i '97, 20:56.10 '94, 20:51R '97.
Lost her 1997 World silver medal when she tested positive for Stanozolol, receiving a two-year ban. World best 20km walk time when she won Russian winter championship in March 2001 and official record to win 2005 World title.

Gulfiya KHANAFEYEVA b. 4 Jun 1982 1.83m 83kg. née Tauryanina. Moskva Dyn.
At HT: EU23: '03- 3; EJ: '01- 10; WUG: '03- 2; ECp: '05- 3.
Progress at HT: 1998- 51.10, 1999- 53.80, 2000- 56.46, 2001- 61.10, 2002- 62.19/64.50dq, 2003- 68.92, 2004- 72.71, 2005- 70.76, 2006- 75.35.

Yekaterina KHOROSHIKH b. 21 Jan 1983 Shakhty, Rostov Reg. 1.65m 75kg. Rostov VS.
At HT: WCh: '05- dnq; WJ: '02- 11; EU23: '05- 1.
Progress at HT: 2001- 48.78, 2002- 61.73, 2003- 64.42, 2004- 68.44, 2005- 73.08, 74.31 irreg.

Natalya KHRUSHCHELYOVA b. 30 May 1973 Tavda, Sverdlovsk reg. 1.71m 59kg. Yekaterinburg Dyn.
At 400m/4x400mR: EC: '94- 2R, '98- 2R; WJ: '92- 8R; WUG: '95- 1R, '99- 2R, '01- 7; EU23Cp: '94- 2; WCp: '98- 3R; ECp: '97-8- 1R/1R. At 800m: OG: '04- sf; WCh: '03- 3; ECp: '03- 4. Won RUS 800m 2003.
Progress at 400m, 800m: 1992- 53.56, 1994- 51.73, 1995- 52.43/52.3, 1996- 51.74, 1997- 52.66, 1998- 51.87, 1999- 52.78, 2000- 51.49, 2001- 52.06, 2002- 52.90, 1:59.77; 2003- 1:58.05, 2004- 1:56.59. pbs: 200m 23.28 '94, 22.8 '96; 500m 1:10.50i '02, 600m 1:25.15i '04, 1000m 2:44.29i '04.
Married to coach Vladimir Kazanin.

Svetlana KLYUKA b. 27 Dec 1978 Belogorsk, Khabarovsk reg. 1.70m 62kg. Moskva VS.
At 800m: WCh: '03- sf; WUG: '05- 1; ECp: '05- 3.
Progress at 800m: 2002- 2:00.97, 2003- 1:58.47, 2004- 1:59.55, 2005- 1:57.35. pbs: 400m 53.18 '05, 1000m 2:43.92i '05.

Yelena KONEVTSOVA b. 11 Mar 1981 Klin 1.83m 83kg. née Tauryanina. Moskva Dyn.
At HT: OG: '04- dnq 16; WCh: '03- dnq 24; EC: '02- dnq 23.
Progress at HT: 1997- 48.44, 1998- 55.19, 1999- 53.75, 2000- 60.41, 2001- 63.85, 2002- 67.35, 2003- 69.59, 2004- 73.68, 2005- 67.51.

Mariya KOROTEYEVA b. 10 Nov 1981 Kashira 1.75m 63kg. Moskva Dyn.
At 100mh: OG: '04- 4; WCh: '03- sf, '05- 5; EC: '02- sf; WJ: '00- sf; E23: '01- 6, '03- 3; EJ: '99- 7; ECp: '02- 3, '05- 7. Russian champion 2005.
Progress at 100mh: 1998- 14.20, 1999- 13.64,

2000- 13.36, 2001- 13.10, 2002- 12.94, 2003- 12.95, 2004- 12.60, 2005- 12.73. pbs: 50m 6.2i '04, 60mh 8.05i '04.

Olga KOTLYAROVA b. 12 Apr 1976 Sverdlovsk 1.80m 65kg. Student. Yekaterinburg TU.
At 400m/4x400mR: OG: '96- qf/5R, '00- 8/3R; WCh: '97- sf, '99- 8/1R; EC: '98- 3/2R; WJ: '94- 4R; EJ: '95- 1/2R; EU23: '97- 2R; WI: '97- 1R, '99- 1R, '01- 2/1R, '04- 1R; EI: '96- 2; WUG: '97- 2/1R; WCp: '98- 3R; ECp: '96-7-9-04: 4&3R/3&1R/2&1R/1. Russian champion 1998. At 800m: WI: '06- 5.
World indoor 4x400m record 1997, 1999, 2004.
Progress at 400m, 800m: 1994- 53.67, 1995- 52.03/51.8, 1996- 51.17, 1997- 50.63, 1998- 50.38, 1999- 50.32, 2000- 49.95, 2:05.17, 2001- 50.42i/50.81A, 2003- 52.86, 2004- 49.77, 1:57.96; 2005- 52.00, 1:57.55. pbs: 200m 23.35A '98, 300m 36.91+ '99, 500m 1:07.68i '03, 600m 1:23.44i '04 (world best).
Gave birth to daughter Tatyana in 2002.

Tatyana KOTOVA b. 11 Dec 1976 Kokand, Uzbekistan 1.82m 59kg. Luch Moskva.
At LJ: OG: '00- 4, '04- 3; WCh: '99- dnq 13, '01- 2, '03- 2, '05- 2; EC: '02- 1; WI: '99-01-03-04-06: 1/2/1/2/1; EU23: '97- 1; WCp: '02- 1; ECp: '02- 1; 2nd GP 2002. Won WAF 2005, Russian 1999-2001, 2005.
Progress at LJ: 1994- 6.32, 1995- 6.32, 1996- 6.65, 1997- 6.76, 1998- 6.82/6.97w, 1999- 6.99/7.01w, 2000- 7.04 (7.05iu), 2001- 7.12, 2002- 7.42, 2003- 6.94, 2004- 7.05, 2005- 6.96/7.20w, 2006- 7.00i. pbs: HJ 1.75 '95, TJ 13.69i/13.64 '98.
Born in Uzbekistan, she moved to Taboshari (Tajikistan) and now lives in Central Siberia. Her father came from Cherkassy in the Ukraine. Shared Golden League jackpot 2000. Achieved the world's best long jump for eight years in 2002.

Olesya KRASNOMOVETS b. 8 Jul 1979 Nizhniy Tagil, Sverdlovsk 1.71m 60kg. Nizhniy Tagil TU.
At 400m/4x400mR: OG: '04- 2R; WCh: '05- 1R; WI: '04- 2/1R, '06- 1/1R.
World indoor 4x400m record 2004.
Progress at 400m: 2001- 53.31, 2003- 53.77, 2004- 50.19, 2005- 50.77, 2006- 50.04i. pbs: 200m 23.09 '05, 300m 36.62i '04, 500m 1:08.84i '04.
Breakthrough in 2004 indoor season to win EI Cup and take silver and gold at World Indoors. Married to Dmitriy Forshev (b.30 May 1976) – 400m 45.62 '03, Russian champion 2005.

Svetlana KRIVELYOVA b. 13 Jun 1969 Bryansk 1.84m 94kg. Moskva Dyn. Teacher.
At SP: OG: '92- 1, '96- dnq 15, '00- 4, '04- 3; WCh: '91- 3, '93- 2, '97- 10, '99- 3, '01- 9, '03- 1, '05- 4; EC: '98- 4, '02- 3; WJ: '88- 4; WI: '91-3-9-01-03-04: 8/1/1/3/5/1; EI: '00- 4; WUG: '91- 1; ECp: '96-9-02-03: 3/3/1/2; Won GP 1993 (3rd 2001). USSR champion 1991, Russian 1992, 1998-2000, 2002-03.
Progress at SP: 1985- 15.18, 1986- 16.76, 1987- 17.51, 1988- 18.35, 1989- 18.36, 1990- 19.70, 1991- 20.36, 1992- 21.06, 1993- 20.84, 1996- 18.97, 1997- 19.32i/19.18, 1998- 20.53, 1999- 20.69i/20.26, 2000- 20.72, 2001- 20.17, 2002- 20.53, 2003- 20.77, 2004- 20.69, 2005- 20.24.
Took World Student Games gold medal in 1991 after Sui Xinmei disqualified, World Indoor gold in 1999 after both Pavlysh and Korzhanenko disqualified, and World Indoor in 2004 after Pavlysh disqualified.

Marina KUPTSOVA b. 22 Dec 1981 Moskva 1.85m 68kg. Luch Moskva.
At HJ: OG: '00- dnq 26=; WCh: '03- 2; EC: '02- 2; WJ: '98- 1, '00- 2; EU23: '01- 2=; EJ: '97- 2, '99- 3; EI: '02- 1; WCp: '02- 3; ECp: '02-03: 4=/3. Russian champion 2000, 2002-03.
Progress at HJ: 1995- 1.78i, 1996- 1.89, 1997- 1.90, 1998- 1.95i/1.90, 1999- 1.94, 2000- 1.96, 2001- 1.91i/1.90, 2002- 2.03i/2.00, 2003- 2.02, 2004- 1.94i, 2005- 1.92, 2006- 1.92i.
Was a talented swimmer and basketball player. Her 2.03i in 2002 is the best ever by a 20 year-old woman. Her father and coach Gennadiy was a decathlete and discus thrower,

Olga KUZENKOVA b. 4 Oct 1970 Smolensk 1.76m 76kg. Smolensk Dyn. Army Officer, has a diploma in physical education.
At HT: OG: '00- 2, '04- 1; WCh: '99- 2, '01- 2, '03- 2, '05- 1; EC: '98- 2, '02- 1; WUG: '97- 2, ECp: '97-8-9-00-02-03-04: 1/1/2/1/1/3/2; 3rd GP 2001. RUS champion 1992-4, 1997-2004; CIS 1992, WAF 2004.
Eleven world hammer records 1992-8 (six officially ratified), inc. unratified 69.46 '96 and 73.80 '98 due to no drugs testing procedures; 66.84 in 1994 was the first record for the event accepted by the IAAF. 14 Russian records 1993-2000.
Progress at HT: 1990- 59.50, 1991- 61.52, 1992- 65.40, 1993- 64.64, 1994- 66.84, 1995- 68.16, 1996- 69.46, 1997- 73.10, 1998- 73.80, 1999- 74.30, 2000- 75.68, 2001- 73.62, 2002- 73.07, 2003- 74.98, 2004- 75.02, 2005- 75.10.
Became the first 70m hammer thrower in 1997. After five championship silver medals at last won gold at the 2002 Europeans.

Tatyana LEBEDEVA b. 21 Jul 1976 Sterlitamsk, Bashkortostan 1.71m 61kg. Volgograd VS.
At TJ (/LJ): OG: '00- 2, '04- 3/1; WCh: '99- 4, '01- 1, '03- 1, '05- dns; EC: '98- 5; WJ: '94- 3/10; EJ: '95- 2/6; WI: '01- 2, '04- 1/1, '06- 1; EI: '00- 1; WUG: '01- 1; WCp: '98- 2; ECp: '00-01: 1/1. GP: 3rd 1999, 2nd 2001. Won WAF 2003, GWG 2001, Russian TJ 1998-2001, LJ 2004.
Three Russian triple jump records 2000-04.
Progress at LJ, TJ: 1991- 12.91, 1992- 13.03, 1993- 6.17, 13.13i/12.94; 1994- 6.65, 13.69; 1995- 13.88, 1996- 13.62, 1997- 13.89i/13.56, 1998- 14.45/14.58w, 1999- 14.89, 2000- 15.32, 2001- 6.71i, 15.25; 2003- 6.82, 15.18; 2004- 7.33, 15.36i/15.34; 2005- 6.70, 15.11.
Won 2001 World gold by massive margin of

65cm. Married to Nikolay Medveyev (400mh), daughter Anastasiya born in August 2002. Set three world indoor records (15.16, 15,25, 15.36) at WI 2004, and next day completed unique double with LJ gold. Sole winner of the Golden League Jackpot for 6/6 wins at TJ in 2005.

Tatyana LYSENKO b. 9 Oct 1983 Bataisk, Rostov region 1.86m 81kg. Bataisk VS.
At HT: OG: '04- dnq 19; WCh: '05- 3; EU23: '03- 5; WUG: '03- 5. Russian champion 2005.
World hammer record, 4 Russian records 2005.
Progress at HT: 2000- 49.08, 2001- 55.73, 2002- 61.85, 2003- 67.19. 2004- 71.54, 2005- 77.06.

Natalya NAZAROVA b. 26 May 1979 Moskva 1.68m 57kg. Luch Moskva.
At 400m/4x400mR: OG: '00- sf/3resR, '04- 8/2R; WCh: '99- 6/1R, '03- 4/2R; EC: '02- 2R; WJ: '98- 1/2R; WI: '99- 1R, '03- 1/1R, '04- 1/1R, '06- 4/1R; EI: '00- 2; EJ: '97- 7; WUG: '05- 1; WCp: '02- 3R; ECp: '99- 1R. Russian champion 1999-2000, 2003-04.
World indoor 4x400m world records 1999 & 2004.
Progress at 400m: 1995- 55.79, 1996- 54.59, 1997- 52.94, 1998- 51.50, 1999- 50.48, 2000- 50.10, 2002- 51.15, 2003- 49.78, 2004- 49.65, 2005- 51.31. pbs: 100m 11.57 '99, 200m 23.01/22.9 '99, 300m 36.3+ '03, 500m 1:07.36i '04 (world best), 600m 1:26.35i '00.
Plays violin and piano.

Yelena NIKOLAYEVA b. 1 Feb 1966 Akshiki Chuvashia 1.64m 58kg. née Kuznetsova. Cheboksary VS. Member of the state parliament in Cheboksary.
At 20kmW: OG: '04- 17; WCh: '99- 12, '01- dq, '03- 1, '05- dnf; EC: '02- 2; WCp: '99-02-04: 4/4/1; ECp: '01- 5, '03- 1. At 10kmW: OG: '92- 2, '96- 1; WCh: '87- 5, '93- 7, '95- 3, '97- 9; EC: '94- 3; WCp: '87-93-5: 5/3/2. Won GWG 1998, USSR champion 1987-8, CIS 1992, RUS 1996. Won RUS 2001-02. At 3000mW: WI: '91- 5, '93- 1; EI: '94- 4.
Three world 10km track walk records 1986-8, road best 1996, European records 3000m 1992, 5000m: 21:32.4 '87, 21:08.65 '88.
Progress at 10kmW, 20kmW: 1984- 48:29.1, 1985- 46:37, 1986- 44:32.50t, 1987- 43:57, 1988- 43:36.41t, 1991- 43:25, 1992- 42:40, 1993- 43:11, 1994- 42:43, 1995- 42:20, 1996- 41:04, 1997- 41:41, 1998- 43:51.97t, 1999- 42:04, 1:28:01; 2000- 45:55, 2001- 42:55, 1:27:49.3t; 2002- 43:20, 1:27:02; 2003- 43:26, 1:26:22; 2004- 43:29, 1:27:24. pbs: 3000mW 11:49.73i '93, 11:57.68 '96; 5000mW 20:54.65 '02, 20:48R '94.

Yuliya NOSOVA b. 21 Apr 1978 Krasnoyarsk 1.80m 66kg. Moskva reg. VS.
At 400mh/4x400mR: OG: '00- sf, '04- 8; WCh: '01- 2/3R, '03- 3/2R, '05- 1/1R; EC: '98- h; WJ: '96- h; EJ: '97- 6; WCp: '02- 1/3R; ECp: '01- 1/2R, '02- 1. RUS champion 1999, 2001, 2003-05. At 400m: WI: '01- 1R, '03- 1R; EI: '02- 5, '05- 1R.
World record 400m hurdles 2003, indoor 4x200m 2005.
Progress at 400mh: 1993- 63.47, 1994- 60.86, 1995- 60.30, 1996- 57.04, 1997- 57.53, 1998- 56.13, 1999- 53.98, 2000- 54.31, 2001- 53.84, 2002- 53.10, 2003- 52.34, 2004- 53.31, 2005- 52.90. pbs: 200m 23.26i '05, 300m 37.09i '05, 400m 51.00i '03, 500m 1:09.69i '03.
Married **Yevgeniy Pechonkin** (b. 9 Oct 1973, 110mh: 1 WJ 92, 2 EJ 91, pb 13.38 '96) on 15 Aug 2001; now separated. Remarried 2005.

Yelena OLEYNIKOVA b. 9 Dec 1976 Zernograd, Rostov-na-Donu reg. 1.78m 57kg. Luch Moskva.
At TJ: WCh: '01- dnq 14, '03- 14; EC: '02- 3; EI: '02- 3, '05- 7; WUG: '01- 3; WCp: '02- 6.
Progress at TJ: 1995- 12.79, 1996- 13.22, 1997- 13.38, 1998- 13.58, 1999- 13.85, 2000- 14.25, 2001- 14.59, 2002- 14.83, 2003- 14.56/14.70w, 2004- 14.57/14.63w, 2005- 14.33i/14.29.

Lyudmila PETROVA b. 7 Oct 1968 Karakly, Chuvashiya 1.60m 44kg. née Yakimova. Novocheboksary TU.
At 10,000m: OG: '96- 14; WCh: '01- 6. At Mar: OG: '04- 8; EC: '98- 9. World HMar: '97-9-02: 7/18/13. Won RUS 10,000m 1996.
Progress at 10,000m, Mar: 1995- 33:41.40, 1996- 31:58.84, 1997- 32:14.39, 2:39:26; 1998- 2:30:26, 1999- 2:29:13, 2000- 31:52.75, 2:25:45; 2001- 32:04.94, 2:26:18; 2002- 2:22:33, 2003- 31:36.76, 2:23:14; 2004- 2:26:02, 2005- 2:26:29. pbs: 3000m 8:59.15i/9:00.2 '96, 5000m 15:20.44 '96, Rd 15km 48:31 '98, HMar 69:26 '00.
Two wins in 18 marathons: Moscow 1998, New York 2000. 3rd 2002 and 2nd 2004 at London. Did not run 1987-94, when her two children were born. Husband killed in a car crash in 2005.

Tatyana POLNOVA b. 20 Apr 1979 Slavyansk-na-Kubani 1.73m 64kg. née Zaykova. Krasnodar TU.
At PV: WCh: '05- 4; WJ: '98- 10; WUG: '03- 1; EI: '05- 5; ECp: '03-04: 2/3. Won WAF 2003.
Progress at PV: 1995- 3.00, 1996- 3.75, 1997- 3.85, 1998- 4.10i/3.90, 2000- 4.20, 2001- 4.20, 2002- 4.60, 2003- 4.70, 2004- 4.78, 2005- 4.60i/4.52.
Former gymnast, coached by her husband Sergey Polnov. She competed for Turkey 1998-2000, but has now reverted to Russia.

Svetlana POSPELOVA b. 24 Dec 1979 Leningrad 1.68m 65kg. St Petersburg Dyn.
At 400m/4x400mR: OG: '00- dq h; WCh: '03- 8/res (2)R, '05- 4/1R; WJ: '98- h/2R; EU23: '99- 1R; EI: '00- 1/1R, '05- 1/1R; ECp: '00- 1, '03- 1/1R. Won Russian 200m 2000, 400m 2005.
Progress at 400m: 1996- 56.50, 1997- 55.17, 1998- 53.80, 1999- 52.58, 2000- 50.47, 2003- 50.70, 2004- 51.69. 2005- 49.80. pbs: 60m 7.20i '05, 100m 11.32 '05, 200m 22.39 '05, 300m 35.8+ '05.
Two-years drugs ban from positive test after elimination in Olympic 400m heat 2000.

Yelena PROKHOROVA b. 16 Apr 1978 Kemerovo 1.71m 59kg. Kemerovo VS. Student.
At Hep: OG: '00- 2, '04- 5; WCh: '01- 1, '03- 4; EU23: '99- 2; ECp: '99- 6, '03- 1. At Pen: WI: '01- 2; EI: '00- 5, '02- 1. Won RUS Hep 2000.
Progress at Hep: 1994- 4919, 1995- 4621, 1996- 5152, 1997- 5600, 1998- 5776, 1999- 6132, 2000- 6765, 2001- 6694, 2003- 6452, 2004- 6354. pbs: 200m 23.37 '00, 400m 54.25 '03, 800m 2:04.27 '00, 60mh 8.46i '01, 100mh 13.54 '00, HJ 1.88 '01, LJ 6.72 '00, SP 14.30 '00, JT 50.73 '01, Pen 4711i '01.
Won IAAF Combined Events Challenge in 2001. Missed 2002 outdoor season with a serious knee injury.

Anna PYATYKH b. 4 Apr 1981 Moskva 1.76m 64kg. Luch Moskva.
At TJ: OG: '04- 8; WCh: '03- 4, '05- 3; EC: '02- 8; WJ: '00- 2; EJ: '99- 3; WI: '03- 4, '06- 2; ECp: '02-03-04-05: 1/1/1/1. Russian champion 2004.
Progress at TJ: 1998- 12.98, 1999- 13.59, 2000- 14.19, 2001- 14.21/14.22w, 2002- 14.67, 2003- 14.79, 2004- 14.85, 2005- 14.88, 2006- 14.93i. pb LJ 6.57i/6.53 '05.

Olga RASPOPOVA b. 27 Dec 1978 Barabinsk, Novosibirsk reg 1.76m 62kg. Novosibirsk Dyn. Student.
At 800m: OG: '00- h; EC: '02- sf; WI: '04- 6; ECp: '04- 1. Russian champion 2002.
Progress at 800m: 1997- 2:12.0, 1999- 2:03.88, 2000- 1:56.85, 2001- 1:58.77, 2002- 1:58.63, 2003- 1:59.94, 2004- 1:58.28. pb 1000m 2:34.68i '04, 2:34.77 '01.

Oksana ROGOVA b. 7 Oct 1978 Tambov 1.80m 60kg. Tambov Sp. Student, Tambov University.
At TJ: OG: '00- 8; WCh: '99- 9; WJ: '96- 4; EU23: '99- 2; WI: '01- 5; EI: '00- 5; WUG: '03- 1.
Progress at TJ: 1993- 11.52, 1994- 12.48, 1995- 13.14, 1996- 13.49, 1997- 13.31, 1998- 14.14, 1999- 14.59/14.65w, 2000- 14.28i/14.27, 2001- 14.37i/14.20/14.23w; 2002- 14.70i/14.59, 2003- 14.16, 2004- 14.50, 2005- 14.25i. pb LJ 6.79 '02.

Natalya ROSHCHUPKINA b. 13 Jan1978 Lipetsk 1.82m 70kg. Lipetsk Dyn. Teacher.
At Hep: OG: '00- 6; WCh: '99- 10, '01- 4, '03- 13; EC: '98- 9; WJ: '96- 5; EU23: '99- 1; ECp: '98- 2, '00- 1; Russian champion 2003, 2005; won GWG 2001. At Pen: WI: '99- 7, '01- 4.
World junior indoor hep record (4513) 1997.
Progress at Hep: 1993- 4772, 1994- 5191, 1995- 5383, 1996- 5767, 1997- 5920, 1998- 6370h, 1999- 6219, 2000- 6633, 2001- 6551, 2002- 6029, 2003- 6170, 2005- 6003. pbs: 200m 23.27/22.84w '01, 800m 2:06.67 '01, 60mh 8.60i '01, 100mh 13.70 '00, HJ 1.91 '00, LJ 6.45 '00, SP 14.96 '01, JT 45.65 '01, Pen 4664i '01.

Olga RYABINKINA b. 24 Sep 1976 Bryansk 1.90m 87kg. St. Petersburg Dyn. Teacher.
At SP: OG: '00- 10, '04- dnq 13; WCh: '03- dnq 16, '05- 2; EJ: '95- 3 (4 DT); WI: '06- 3; EI: '05- 3; ECp: '04- 1, '05- 1. Russian champion 2005.
Progress at SP: 1993- 15.61, 1994- 16.52, 1995- 17.40, 1996- 17.75, 1997- 17.98, 1998- 17.51, 1999- 17.99, 2000- 19.32, 2001- 17.85, 2002- 19.36, 2003- 19.36i/19.07, 2004- 19.12, 2005- 19.65, 2006- 19.24i. pb DT 61.66 '98.

Natalya SADOVA b. 15 Jun 1972 Gorkiy 1.80m 100kg. née Koptyukh. Nizhniy Novgorod TU. Teacher.
At DT: OG: '96- 2, '00- 4, '04- 1; WCh: '95- 5, '97- 3, '99- 4, '01- dq (1), '03- 6, '05- 2; EC: '94- 11, '98- 2, '02- 2; WJ: '90- 1; EJ: '89- 5; WUG: '95- 1, '97- 1; WCp: '98- 3, '02- 3; ECp: '95-7-8-9-01-02-03: 1/1/1/1/2/1/3; E23Cp: '94- 1. Won GP 1998, 2002, WAF 2005, Russian 1995-6, 1999-2001, 2003-05.
Progress at DT: 1988- 53.02, 1989- 55.34, 1990- 61.44, 1991- 59.10, 1992- 57.82, 1993- 58.14, 1994- 62.12, 1995- 66.86, 1996- 67.22, 1997- 67.72, 1998- 68.50, 1999- 70.02, 2000- 67.33, 2001- 68.57, 2002- 67.73, 2003- 69.38, 2004- 68.63, 2005- 66.29. pb SP 14.21 '99.
Has a daughter Viktoriya. It was only discovered in January 2005 that she had lost the 2001 World gold due to a positive test for caffeine.

Gulnara SAMITOVA b. 9 Jul 1978 Naberezhnye Chelny, Tatarstan 1.74m 55kg. Naberezhnye Chelny TU.
At 1500m: WI: '04- 3; At 5000m: OG: '04- 6; WCh: '03- 7. At 3000m: ECp: '04- 1. At 3000mSt: ECp: '03- 1. Won RUS 1500m 2004, 5000m 2003-04, 3000mSt 2003, indoor 1500m & 3000m 2004.
Two World records and four Russian records 3000m steeplechase 2003-04.
Progress at 5000m, 3000mSt: 2003- 14:54.38, 9:08.33; 2004- 14:53.70, 9:01.59. pbs: 1000m 2:35.91i '04, 1500m 4:01.29 '04, 1M 4:22.68 '04, 3000m 8:41.72i/8:49.48 '04.
Great breakthrough in 2003, starting with world indoor 3000mSt best of 9:29.54.

Yekaterina SAVCHENKO b. 3 Jun 1977 Omsk 1.80m 60kg. née Aleksandrova.
At HJ: WCh: '01- dnq; WI: '06- 2; EI: '05- 6; WJ: '94- 7=; EJ: '95- 7; WUG: '99- 5. Russian champion 2001.
Progress at HJ: 1994- 1.88, 1995- 1.90, 1996- 1.94, 1997- 1.93, 1998- 1.96i/1.90, 1999- 1.92, 2000- 1.90, 2001- 1.96, 2003- 1.97, 2004- 1.98i, 2005- 1.97, 2006- 1.98i.

Viktoriya SERYOGINA b. 22 May 1973 Bryansk 1.80m 60kg. Bryansk Dyn.
At HJ: EC: '02- 10; WI: '99- 7.
Progress at HJ: 1992- 1.75, 1993- 1.84, 1994- 1.88, 1995- 1.91, 1996- 1.95, 1997- 1.85i, 1998- 1.97, 1999- 1.98i/1.96/1.97sq, 2000- 1.97i/1.93, 2001- 1.96i/1.90, 2002- 2.00, 2003- 2.00i/1.97, 2004- 2.00, 2005- 1.95. pb LJ 6.65 '98.

Irina SHEVCHENKO b. 2 Sep 1975 Frunze, Kirgizstan 1.75m 65kg. née Korotya. Moskva reg. Dyn.
At 100mh: OG: '04- dnf; WCh: '97- h, '99- sf, '01- sf, '05- 7; EC: '98- 3; EU23: '97- 1 (2 4x100mR);

WUG: '97- 4; WCp: '98- 3; ECp: '01- 1, '04- 2. Russian champion 1998-9, 2004. At 60mh: WI: '99- 8; EI: '05- 5.
Progress at 100mh: 1996- 13.47, 1997- 12.97, 1998--12.84/12.77Aw, 1999- 12.82, 2001- 12.81, 2003- 13.18, 2004- 12.67, 2005- 12.76. pbs: 200m 23.84 '96, 60mh 7.90i '05.
Unfortunately brought down by Perdita Felicien in Olympic 100mh final 2004.

Liliya SHOBUKHOVA b. 13 Nov 1977 Beloretsk, Bashkortostan 1.69m 50kg. née Volkova. Beloretsk VS.
At 5000m: OG: '04- 13; WCh: '05- 9; EC: '02- 17; ECp: '04- 2, '05- 1. At 3000m: WI: '06- 2; EI: '02- 5, '05- 6; ECp: '01- 4. World 4km CC: '02- 23. Eur CC: '02- 17, '04- 11. Russian champion 5000m 2002, 2005.
World indoor 3000m record 2006.
Progress at 5000m: 1998- 16:50.64, 2001- 15:42.0, 2002- 15:25.00, 2004- 14:52.19, 2005- 14:47.07. pbs: 800m 2:05.33 '05, 1000m 2:39.81i '06, 1500m 4:03.78 '04, 1M 4:22.14 '04, 2000m 5:45.05i '06, 3000m 8:27.86i '06, 8:34.85 '04; 10km Rd 33:11 '01.

Irina SIMAGINA b. 25 May 1982 Ryazan 1.71m 60kg. Luch Moskva.
At LJ: OG: '04- 2; WJ: '00- 6; WY: '99- 5; EU23: '03- 2; WUG: '03- 1; EI: '02- 4; ECp: '04- 1, '05- 1. Won WAF 2004.
Progress at LJ: 1999- 6.32i/6.12, 2000- 6.38, 2001- 6.41i/6.11, 2002- 6.74i/6.58, 2003- 6.83, 2004- 7.27, 2005- 7.04.

Yelena SLESARENKO b. 28 Feb 1982 Volgograd 1.78m 57kg. née Sivushenko. Volgograd VS.
At HJ: OG: '04- 1; EU23: '03- 2; EJ: '01- 4; WUG: '03- 3; WI: '04- 1, '06- 1; EI: '02- 5=; ECp: '04- 1. Won WAF 2004, Russian 2005.
Progress at HJ: 1999- 1.82, 2000- 1.88, 2001- 1.94i/1.88, 2002- 1.97, 2003- 1.98i/1.96, 2004- 2.06, 2005- 2.00, 2006- 2.02i.
Tied Russian indoor record to win gold at 2004 World Indoors and set a Russian record of 2.06 to win Olympic gold.

Yelena SOBOLEVA b. 3 Oct 1982 Bryansk 1.76m 66kg. Luch Moskva.
At 1500m: WCh: '05- 4; EU23: '03- 7; WI: '06- 2. WIR 1500m 2006.
Progress at 1500m: 2003- 4:12.02, 2004- 4:11.98, 2005- 4:01.14, 2006- 3:58.28i. pbs: 800m 1:58.53i '06, 2:00.59 '05; 1000m 2:32.40i '06, 2:36.50 '05; 3000m 8:55.89 '05.

Svetlana SOKOLOVA b. 9 Jan 1981 Baku, Azerbaijan 1.76m 70kg. Staryi Oskol VS.
At Hep: OG: '04- 10; EC: '02- 5; WJ: '98- 4; EU23: '01- 2; WUG: '01- 2; ECp: '01- 1. Russian champion 2002, 2004.
Progress at Hep: 1997- 5424, 1998- 5828h, 1999- 5761, 2000- 5369, 2001- 6270w/6179, 2002- 6150, 2004- 6591, 2005- 5689. pbs: 200m 24.02 '04, 23.62w '01, 23.9 '98; 800m 2:07.23 '04, 60mh 8.3i '00, 100mh 13.56 '04, HJ 1.82 '04, LJ 6.26 '04, SP 15.09 '04, JT 47.86 '04, Pen 4371i '02.

Tatyana TOMASHOVA b. 1 Jul 1975 Perm 1.64m 50kg. Perm VS.
At 1500m: OG: '04- 2; WCh: '03- 1, '05- 1; EC: '02- 3; WCp: '02- 2; ECp: '02- 3. At 5000m: OG: '00- 13; WCh: '01- 10; ECp: '00- 1. Won GP 3000m 2001 (2nd 2002), RUS 1500m 2001-03, 5000m 2000.
Progress at 1500m, 5000m: 1996- 4:17.97, 15:48.13; 1997- 4:16.39, 1998- 4:13.50, 1999- 4:08.5?, 15:26.67; 2000- 4:04.80, 14:53.00; 2001- 4:03.31, 14:39.22; 2002- 4:01.28, 14:47.85; 2003- 3:58.52, 2004- 3:58.12, 2005- 3:59.05. pbs: 800m 2:04.0 '99, 1000m 2:34.91 '05, 1M 4:38.13 '01, 2000m 5:43.3 '01, 3000m 8:25.56 '01, road 10km 32:48 '99.

Oksana UDMURTOVA b. 1 Feb 1982 Grakovo, Udmurtiya 1.72m 56kg. Volgograd VS.
At LJ: WCh: '05- 6; WI: '06- 7.
Progress at LJ: 2000- 6.29, 2001- 6.41, 2003- 6.78, 2004- 6.60, 2005- 6.86.

Yekaterina VOLKOVA b. 16 Feb 1978 Zheleznogorsk, Kursk region 1.69m 55kg. Zhelznogorsk TU.
At 3000mSt: WCh: '05- 2; ECp: '02- 7. Russian champion 2000-01, 2005.
Russian 3000m steeplechase record 2001.
Progress at 3000mSt: 1999- 10:04.46, 2000- 9:52.40, 2001- 9:41.54, 2002- 10:37.78, 2003- 9:32.31, 2005- 9:20.49. pbs: 1500m 4:09.03 '05, 1M 4:29.60 '05, 3000m 8:54.64 '05, 2000mSt 6:27.69 '00.

Olga YEGOROVA b. 28 Mar 1972 Novocheboksarsk, Chuvashiya 1.60m 48kg. Cheboksary Dyn. Economist.
At 1500m: OG: '04- 11; WCh: '05- 2; WJ: '90- 9; EJ: '91- 3. At 3000m: WI: '97/9/01- 6/6/1; EI: '00- 6; ECp: '98-9-03: 1/3/1. At 5000m: OG: '00- 8; WCh: '99- h, '01- 1, '03- h; EC: '98- 11, '02- 4; WCp: '02- 1; ECp: '02- 1; won RUS 1999, GWG 2001.
European 5000m record 2001, 2 Russian records 2000-01.
Progress at 1500m, 3000m, 5000m: 1989- 4:14.76, 1990- 4:18.26, 1991- 4:17.09, 1996- 16:00.07, 1997- 4:12.73i, 15:42.47, 1998- 15:32.74, 1999- 4:07.38, 8:33.02, 15:22.80; 2000- 4:04.75, 8:49.18i/8:53.76, 14:42.91; 2001- 4:02.76, 8:23.26, 14:29.32; 2002- 4:04.11, 8:46.24i, 14:48.29; 2003- 4:01.00, 8:38.00, 14:55.19; 2004- 4:01.15, 2005- 3:59.47. pbs: 800m 2:06.01 '03, 1M 4:25.54i '00, 2000m 5:39.30i '00, 5:39.9 '01; 2000mSt 6:28.2 '96.
Daughter Yevgeniya born June 1994.

Natalya YEVDOKIMOVA b. 17 Mar 1978 Leningrad 1.74m 65kg. St Petersburg YR.
At 1500m: OG: '04- 4; EJ: '97- 1. At 800m: WCh: '03- sf; WJ: '96- 8; EJ: '95- 8.
Progress at 800m, 1500m: 1993- 2:07.60, 4:29.2; 1995- 2:04.61, 4:20.29; 1996- 4:24.86, 1997- 2:06.18, 4:20.28; 2000- 2:01.51, 4:04.61; 2002- 2:03.15, 4:09.50i/4:09.65; 2003- 1:58.75, 4:04.61; 2004- 3:59.05, 2005- 2:00.34, 3:57.73. pbs: 1M 4:24.40 '03.
Formerly competed for Ukraine.

Yelena ZADOROZHNAYA b. 3 Dec 1977 Ust-Kut, Irkutsk reg. 1.57m 42kg. Irkutsk VS.
At 5000m (1500m): OG: '04- 4; WCh: '01- 6, '03- 4 (8); EC: '02- 3; ECp: '01- 1, '03- 1. At 3000m: WI: '01- 3, '04- 6; EI: '02- 3; WCp: '02- 3; ECp: '02- 2, '05- 3. At 1500m: EU23: '99- 2; ECp: '00- 2; won GP 2002. At 3000mSt: WCh: '05- 6.
Russian 5000m record 2001.
Progress at 1500m, 5000m, 3000mSt: 1998- 4:12.70, 1999- 4:09.3, 2000- 4:03.32, 2001- 4:02.16, 14:40.47; 2002- 3:59.94, 15:15.22; 2003- 4:00.12, 14:51.61; 2004- 4:01.38, 14:55.31; 2005- 4:03.65, 15:15.85, 9:32.41. pbs: 800m 2:01.74 '98, 1000m 2:37.71i '04, 1M 4:24.11i '01, 2000m 5:41.61i '02, 5:43.38 '03; 3000m 8:25.40 '01.
Took up steeplechasing in 2005.

Svetlana ZAKHAROVA b. 15 Sep 1970 Atayeva, Chuvashiya 1.58m 48kg. née Vasilyeva. Cheboksary.
At Mar: OG: '00- 3, '04- 9; WCh: '03- 9. World HMar: '97-8-02: 10/13/12.
Two Russian marathon records 2002.
Progress at Mar: 1994- 2:46+, 1995- 2:40:11, 1996- 2:35:36, 1997- 2:33:14, 1998- 2:36:44, 1999- 2:27:08, 2000- 2:28:11, 2001- 2:24:04, 2002- 2:21:31, 2003- 2:23:07, 2004- 2:25:01, 2005- 2:26:55. pbs: 10,000m 32:49.01 '97, HMar 69:48 '02.
Won Honolulu Marathon 1997 and 2002 (2nd 1998-2000), Boston & Chicago 2003, 2nd Los Angeles 1999, London 2001-02; 3rd New York 2001, 3rd Chicago 2004 (4th 2002). Her husband Nikolay Zakharov was an international cross-country skier.

Olga ZAYTSEVA b. 29 Jul 1975 Leningrad 1.76m 67kg. St Peterburg YR.
At 400m/4x400mR: EU23: '05- 1/1R.
Progress at 400m: 2004- 51.09, 2005- 50.06, 2006- 50.15. pbs: 200m 23.04 '05, 600m 1:06.76i '06.

Alla ZHILYAYEVA b. 5 Feb 1969 Verkhniy Dubovets, Kursk reg. 1.63m 50kg. née Shumakova. Kursk YR. Teacher.
At 10,000m: WCh: '95- 7, '03- 5, '05- 13; EC: '98- dnf; ECp: '95- 3. At Mar: OG: '96- dnf. World HMar: '94-5-6-03: 14/5/18/6; 4k CC: '03- 8. Eur CC: '94- 4, '95- 5. Won RUS 10,000m & HMar 1998.Russian 10,000m record 2003.
Progress at 10,000m, Mar: 1995- 31:52.15, 2:27:38; 1996- 2:32:32, 1997- 2:31:55, 1998- 31:45.02, 2000- 2:28:27, 2001- 2:33:21, 2002- 2:36:32, 2003- 30:23.07, 2:37:00; 2004- 31:07.58, 2005- 31:14.27. pbs: 1500m 4:15.61 '04, 1M 4:34.73 '04, 3000m 8:47.46 '04, 5000m 14:59.46 '04, HMar 69:43 '98, 10kmW 45:19 '90.
Former race walker. Ran 2:27:38 to win at Reims on her marathon début, also won Monaco and Reims marathons 1999

Olesya ZYKINA b. 7 Oct 1980 Kaluga 1.70m 60kg. Tula TU.
At 400m/4x400m: OG: '00- res (3)R, '04- 2R; WCh: '01- 6/3R, '03- 6/2R, '05- 6/res(1)R; EC: '02- 1/2R; WJ: '98- 2R (8 100m); EJ: '99- 1/1R; WI: '01- 3/1R, '04- GR, '03- 1R; WCp: '02- 3/3R; ECp: '00- 1R. Russian champion 2001-02.
Progress at 400m: 1999- 51.31, 2000- 50.36, 2001- 50.15, 2002- 50.44, 2003- 50.39, 2004- 50.44, 2005- 50.73. pbs: 60m 7.47i '04, 100m 11.84 '98, 200m 22.55 '05, 22.3 '99; 300m 36.6+ '03, 36.69i '04, 36.70 '01.

SAINT KITTS & NEVIS

Governing body: Saint Kitts Amateur Athletic Association, PO Box 932, Basseterre, St Kitts. Founded 1961.

Kim COLLINS b. 5 Apr 1976 St Kitts 1.75m 64kg. Studied sociology at Texas Christian University, USA.
At 100m (/200m): OG: '96- qf, 00- 7/sf, '04- 6; WCh: '97- h, 99- h/h, '01- 6/3=, '03- 1, '05- 3; CG: '02- 1; CAC: '99- 2, '01- 1/1, '03- 1; WCp: '02- 2/2R. At 60m: WI: '03- 2. Won NCAA indoor 60m & 200m 2001.
SKN records: 100m from 1996, 200m from 1998, 400m 2000.
Progress at 100m, 200m: 1995- 10.63, 21.85; 1996- 10.27, 21.06; 1998- 10.18/10.16w, 20.88/20.78w; 1999- 10.21, 20.43, 2000- 10.13A/10.15/10.02w, 20.31A/20.18w; 2001- 10.04A/10.00?/9.99w, 20.20/20.08w; 2002- 9.98, 20.49; 2003- 9.99/9.92w, 20.40w; 2004- 10.00, 20.98; 2005- 10.00. pbs: 60m 6.53i '00, 400m 46.93 '00.
The first athlete from his country to make Olympic and World finals and in 2003 the first to win a World Indoor medal and a World title. There is now a 'Kim Collins Highway' in St Kitts.

SAUDI ARABIA

Governing body: Saudi Arabian Athletics Federation, PO Box 5802, Riyadh 11432. Founded 1963.

Hussein Taher **Al-SABEE** b. 14 Nov 1979 1.86m 82kg.
At LJ: OG: '00- dnq 18; WCh: '99- 12, '01- 10, '03- 5; AsiG: '02- 1; AsiC: '00-02=-3: 1/1/1; WI: '01- 11; WCp: '02- 4. Arab champion 1997, 1999, 2003; Gulf 2000, 2003.
Six KSA long jump records 1997-2000.
Progress at LJ: 1996- 7.25, 1997- 7.73A/8.01Aw, 1998- 7.70, 1999- 8.06, 2000- 8.33, 2001- 8.31, 2002- 8.14, 2003- 8.30, 2004- 8.35/8.41w, 2005- 7.86. pbs: 200m 21.04 '02, 21.1 '00; 300m 33.42 '00, TJ 15.98 '03.

Mohammed AL-SALHI b. 11 May 1986 1.72m 66kg.
At 800m: OG: '04- h; WCh: '05- sf; WY: '03- 1; Gulf champion 2005. At 400m: AsiG: '02- sf; Asi-J '04- 1.
Five KSA 800m records 2003-05, World U18 record 2003.
Progress at 800m: 2003- 1:46.48, 2004- 1:48.42, 2005- 1:44.80. pbs: 400m 45.75 '03, 1000m 2:24.50 '03.

Hadi Soua'an AL-SOMAILY b. 21 Aug 1976 Taïf 1.91m 72kg. Teacher.
At 400mh: OG: '96- h, '00- 2, '04- sf; WCh: '95/99- h, '01- 4, '03/05- sf; WJ: '94- sf; AsiG: '94- 6, '02- 1; AsiC: '00- 1, '05- 1. Pan-Arab champion 1995, 1999, 2004; Gulf 1996, 2002. 2nd GP 2000. Two Asian 400mh records 2000. Six KSA records 1994-2000.
Progress at 400mh: 1993- 52.28, 1994- 50.58, 1995- 49.30, 1996- 49.48, 1998- 51.1, 1999- 49.14/49.1A, 2000- 47.53, 2001- 47.99, 2002- 48.11, 2003- 48.97, 2004- 48.77, 2005- 49.02. pbs: 200m 21.17 '03, 400m 47.10 '95.
Lives in the mountainous area of Saudi Arabia. Coached by John Smith in Los Angeles.

SENEGAL

Governing body: Fédération Sénégalaise d'Athlétisme, BP 1737, Stade Iba Mar DIOP, Dakar. Founded 1960.

Women

Kène NDOYE b. 20 Nov 1978 1.64m 58kg.
At TJ (/LJ): OG: '00- dnq 14, '04- 14 (dnq 22); WCh: '99- dnq 17, '03- 10, '05- 6; AfG: '99- 3, '03- 1/4; AfCh: '96- 1/3, '98- 3, '00- 3/1, '02- 2/2, '04- 2/1; WJ: '98- dnq; WI: '03- 3.
SEN records LJ 1999-2004, TJ 1996-2004.
Progress at TJ: 1996- 12.99, 1997- 13.03, 1998- 13.39, 1999- 14.08A/13.99, 2000- 14.03, 2002- 14.28, 2003- 14.91, 2004- 15.00, 2005- 14.47. pbs: 60mh 8.50i '04, 100mh 13.76 '04, 13.72w '02, LJ 6.64/6.78w '04, Pen 3795i '04.

Amy Mbacké THIAM b. 10 Nov 1976 1.83m 70kg. Racing Club de France.
At 400m: OG: '00- sf, '04- h; WCh: '99- sf, '01- 1, '03- 3, '05- 8; Af G: '99- 3; AfCh: '98- 4. French champion 1998-2000, 2005.
Eight SEN 400m records 1999-2001.
Progress at 400m: 1996- 54.40, 1997- 53.25, 1998- 51.60, 1999- 50.77, 2000- 50.88, 2001- 49.86, 2002- 50.96, 2003- 49.95, 2004- 50.82, 2005- 50.69. pbs: 100m 11.84 '98, 200m 23.10 '05, 23.0A '99; 300m 36.0+ '03, 36.37 '00.
In 2001 she became the first athlete to win a world title for Senegal in any sport.

SERBIA & MONTENEGRO (CRNA GORA)

Governing body: Atletski Savez Srbije I Crne Gore, Strahinjica Bana 73a, 11000 Beograd. Founded in 1921.

National Championships first held in 1920 (men) and 1923 (women). **2005 champions**: **Men**: 100m/200m: Marko Jankovic 10.70/21.54, 400m: Darko Mandic 48.12, 800m: Milos Vuckovic 1:53.82, 1500m: Ivan Jankovic 3:55.66, 3000m: Velimir Bojovic 8:46.60, 5000m: Emir Koca 15:49.58, 10,000m: Dragoljub Koprivica 34:18.8, Mar: Goran Cegar 2:35:20, 3000mSt: Dejan Bogicevic 9:21.94, 110mh: Nenad Loncar 14.09, 400mh: Bojan Maljkovic 53.24, HJ: Branko Djuricic 2.10, PV: Igor Sarcevic 4.90, LJ: Danial Jahic 7.59, TJ: Kosta Randjic 15.32, SP: Dragan Peric 19.87, Luka Rujevic 18.53, DT: Dragan Peric 59.10, Luka Rujevic 58.31, HT: Laslo Eperjesi 62.04, JT: Jovan Djukic 61.89, Dec: Darko Raicevic 5659, 10,000mW: Predrag Krstovic 44:19.90, 20kmW: Predrag Filipovic 1:30:22. **Women**: 100m/200m/100mh: Jelena Jotanovic 12.11/25.56/13.83, 400m: Jelena Kocic 57.94, 800m: Ivana Popadic 2:11.49, 1500m: Ivana Cebic 4:45.69, 3000m: Biljana Jovic 10:07.53, 5000m/Mar: Marijana Lukic 17:24.57/2:42:48, 10,000m: Sladjana Pejovic 39:24.1, 3000mSt: Jelena Mimic 11:54.49, 400mH: Ana Pavic 64.57, HJ not held, PV: Jelena Radinovic-Vasic 3.40, LJ/Hep: Milena Milasevic 5.94/4611, TJ: Mirjana Djuric 12.11, SP: Dijana Sefcic 14.24, DT: Daria Zivanovic 41.18, HT: Milka Djordjevic 49.97, JT: Sonja Etinski 47.78.

Dragutin TOPIC b. 12 Mar 1971 Belgrade 1.97m 77kg. AC Vojvodina, Novi Sad. Was at Belgrade University of PE.
At HJ: OG: '92- 8=, '96- 4, '00- dnq 21=, '04- 10; WCh: '91- 9, '93- dnq, '95- 8=, '97- dnq, '99- 4, '05- 9; EC: '90- 1, '94- 5=, '98- 9=; WJ: '90- 1; EJ: '89- 4; WI: '97- 3, '03- 4; EI: '92-6-00-05: 3/1/3/5; WUG: '95- 1. 3rd GP 1994, 2000. YUG champion 1993, 1996, 1999-2000, S & M 2004; Balkan 1998, 2004-05.
World junior high jump record 1990, five Yugoslav records 1990-3.
Progress at HJ: 1985- 1.85, 1986- 1.95, 1987- 1.95, 1988- 2.06, 1989- 2.23, 1990- 2.37, 1991- 2.32/2.34i, 1992- 2.35, 1993- 2.38, 1994- 2.32, 1995- 2.29, 1996- 2.35, 1997- 2.32i/2.31, 1998- 2.33, 1999- 2.32, 2000- 2.34i/2.33, 2001- 2.27i/2.32i drugs dq, 2003- 2.33i/2.31, 2004- 2.29, 2005- 2.31i/2.30. pbs: LJ 7.48i '93, TJ 15.66 '92, Dec 6155h '93.
Won World Junior and European senior HJ titles in 1990. Was at high school in Illinois, USA for a year in 1987/8, but played basketball while there and did not compete as a high jumper. Drugs ban for positive test on 2 Feb 2001 and played basketball while serving two year ban.

Women

Olivera JEVTIC b. 24 Jul 1977 Titovo Uzice 1.74m 52kg. AC Mladost, Uzice.
At 10,000m (/5000m): OG: '00- 11/dnf; WCh: '97- h/h, '99- 10, '01- 12/h; EC: '98- 4/4, '02- 6/dnf; EU23: '97- 1, '99- 1/3; WJ: '94- (3000m 10), 96- -/2 (3000m 5); EJ: '95- 2 (3000m 3). At Mar: OG: '04- 6; WCh: '03- 8. World HMar: '98-99-01-02: 4/21/7/6; CC: '95-00-01-04: 17J/15/9/12; Eur CC: '96-7-8-9-00-01-03-05: 13/3/3/3/3/4/6/4. Won YUG 1500m & 5000m 1996, HMar 1998-9, 2002; CC 1994-7, 1999; Balkan 5000m 1998, CC 2002.
Yugoslav records: 5000m (7) 1995-2000, 10,000m (2) 1998-2000, HMar (3) 1998-2002, Mar 2003.
Progress at 5000m, 10,000m, Mar: 1995- 16:03.34,

33:48.61; 1996- 15:40.59, 32:38.0; 1997- 15:34.65, 32:43.42; 1998- 15:16.61, 31:34.26; 1999- 15:19.08, 31:57.67; 2000- 15:11.25, 31:29.65; 2001- 15:26.84, 31:33.08; 2002- 15:40.24, 31:47.82, 2:26:44dq; 2003- 2:25:23, 2004- 15:33.37, 2:27:34; 2005- 2:31:43. pbs: 800m 2:12.41 '93, 1500m 4:16.16 '98, 3000m 8:59.21 '98, Rd: 10km 31:31 '01, 15km 49:06 '01, HMar 69.18 '02.
Third in New York on marathon debut 2002, but disqualified (public warning) for positive test for ephedrine, won Rotterdam marathon 2003, 3rd Boston 2004.

Dragana TOMASEVIC b. 4.Jun 1982 Sremska Mitrovica 1.75m 80kg. AC Sirmijum, Sremska Mitrovica
at DT: OG: '04- dnq 26; WCh: '05- 7; EU23: '03- 11; EJ: '01- 10; WUG: 2005- 3; Won Balkan & MedG 2005, SCG 2001-03.
Three SCG discus records 2005,
Progress at DT: 1999- 34.93, 2000- 45.87/47.04dh, 2001-52.80/53.00dh, 2002- 54.41/55.33dh, 2003- 56.24/56.74dh, 2004- 59.52, 2005- 62.43. pb SP 14.81 '04.

SLOVAKIA

Governing body: Slovak Athletic Federation, Junácka 6, 832 80 Bratislava. Founded 1939.
National Championships first held in 1939. **2005 Champions: Men**: 100m: Peter Krcmárek 10.87, 200m: Roman Holly 21.75, 400m: Peter Znava 47.47, 800m: Matús Lajcák 1:52.15, 1500m: Peter Ondrus 4:07.06, 5000m: Milan Fedak 14:56.36, 10,000m: Imrich Pastor 31:31.9, HMar: Jan Krizak 70:42, Mar: Marcel Matanin 2:20:37, 3000mSt: Pavol Michalcik 9:17.98, 110mh: Slaven Dizdarevic 14.43, 400mh: Tomás Celko 53.51, HJ: Peter Horák 2.17, PV: Ondrej Durjak 4.40, LJ: Marián Hruska 7.15, TJ: Dmitrij Valukevic 16.70, SP: Mikulás Konopka 20.07, DT: Daniel Vanek 58.28, HT: Libor Charfreitag 77.87, JT: Marián Bokor 76.28, Dec: Slaven Dizdarevic 7083, 20kmW: Matej Tóth 1:23:26, 50kmW: Martin Pupis 4:05:04. **Women**: 100m: Slavomíra Vrlíková 12.05, 200m: Erika Brselová 25.25, 400m: Erika Kucerová 55.22, 800m/1500m: Barbora Ostrenková 2:21.98/4:45.40, 5000m/10,000m/HMar: Dana Janecková 17:25.07/36:58.0/83:53, Mar: Sylvia Biliková 3:07:58, 100mh: Zuzana Lunterová 14.98, 400mh: Sylvia Macalová 62.08, HJ: Diana Láznicková 1.85, PV: Slavomíra Slúková 3.70, LJ: Jana Veldáková 6.59, TJ: Dana Veldáková 13.98, SP: Martina Zatková 14.54, DT: Eva Charfreitagová 44.28, HT: Monika Královenská 58.17, JT: Petra Ihringova 39.46, 20kmW: Maria Galiková 1:40:51.

Libor CHARFREITAG b. 11 Sep 1977 Trnava 1.91m 117kg. Studied at Southern Methodist University, USA. ASK Slavia Trnava.
At HT: OG: '00- dnq 30, '04- 7; WCh: '99-01-03: dnq 32/18/13, '05- 9; EC: '02- 7; WJ: '96- dnq 13. NCAA champion 1998, 2000; SVK 1998-9, 2002-05.
12 SVK hammer records 1996-2003, six European indoor bests 35lb weight 2003-05.
Progress at HT: 1993- 49.42, 1994- 54.32, 1995- 56.90, 1996- 66.82, 1997- 66.44, 1998- 72.30, 1999- 75.18, 2000- 77.22, 2001- 77.65, 2002- 79.20, 2003- 81.81, 2004- 79.84, 2005- 80.85. pbs: SP 17.27i/16.69 '00, DT 51.88 '00; 35lb Wt 25.68i '05.

Mikulás KONOPKA b. 23 Jan 1979 Rimavska Sobota 1.93m 110kg. Dukla Banská Bystrica.
At SP: OG: '00- dnq 24, '04- 10; WCh: '01- dnq 22, '05- 11; EC: '98- dnq; EU23: '99- 1, '01- 1; WJ: '96- 5, '98- 1; EJ: '97- 2; EI: '02- (3)dq, '05- 6. SVK champion 2000, 2005.
Three Slovakian shot records 2001.
Progress at SP: 1995- 15.42, 1996- 17.35, 1997- 18.60, 1998- 19.68, 1999- 19.71, 2000- 19.94, 2001- 20.66, 2002- 20.87idq/19.61i, 2004- 20.34, 2005- 20.61. pb DT 51.42 '99.
2-years drugs disqualification after third place EI 2002. His twin brother **Miloslav** set SVK hammer record 78.58 '01, improving pb to 81.33 '04 after serving two years drugs ban 2002-04, 3 EU23 '01.

Dmitrij VALUKEVIC b. 31 May 1981 Vitrysland, Belarus 1.86m 78kg. Spartak Dubnica.
At TJ: OG: '04- dnq 30; WCh: '03- dnq 16, '05- 10; EU23: '03- 1; WI: '04- 4. BLR champion 2002, SVK 2005.
Four SVK triple jump records 2005.
Progress at TJ: 1998- 15.52, 2000- 16.39, 2001- 16.62, 2002- 16.68i/16.53, 2003- 17.57, 2004- 17.31i/16.78, 2005- 17.19. pb LJ 7.86 '05.
Dmitriy Valyukevich of Belarus until gaining Slovak nationality in January 2005, having trained with Aleksandr Beskrovniy in Slovakia for the previous three years. Improved from 16.81 to 16.83 in qualifying and then 17.16, 17.51 and 17.57 in the final of the European U23s in 2003. His father Gennadiy had best of 17.53 in 1986, won the 1979 EI title (2nd 1982 and 1983) and set world indoor bests that year at 17.19 and 17.29. His mother Irina had a long jump best of 7.17 '87 and was WUG champion in 1985.

SLOVENIA

Governing body: Atletska Zveza Slovenije, Vodnikova cesta 155, 1000 Ljubljana. Current organisation founded 1948.
2005 National Champions: **Men**: 100m/200m: Matic Osovnikar 10.27/20.80, 400m: Matija Sestak 48.16, 800m: Domen Znidaric 1:55.08, 1500m/3000m: Boris Spes 3:52.42/8:35.74, 5000m/10,000m: Borut Veber 15:16.22/32:01.36, HMar: Joze Ceh 75:28, Mar: Roman Kejzar 2:22:08, 3000mSt: Bostjan Buc 8:22.91, 110mh: Damjan Zlatnar 13.80, 400mh: Peter Sajn 52.94, HJ: Rozle Prezelj 2.20, PV: Andrej Poljanec 5.30, LJ: Jan Zumer 7.83, TJ: Bostjan Simunic 16.60w, SP: Miroslav Vodovnik 19.89, DT: Igor Primc 56.23, HT: Tomaz Bogovic 51.49, JT: Robert Tersek 68.94, Dec: Luka Krizaj 6322. **Women**: 100m/200m/

400m: Sabina Veit 11.77/23.86w/56.59, 800m: Brigita Langerholc 2:03.34, 1500m: Taja Naraks 4:37.05, 3000m/5000m: Petra Sink 9:53.18/17:27.10, 10,000m/3000mSt: Daneja Grandovec 37:20.21/10:23.17, HMar: Anica Zivko 1:30:02, Mar: Daneja Grandovec 2:50:42, 100mh: Radmila Vukmirovic 13.28, 400mh: Sara Oresnik 58.54, HJ: Monika Gollner AUT 1.75, PV: Teja Melink 4.20, LJ: Tina Carman 5.90w, TJ: Nina Simunic 12.48w, SP: Karlinca Potocnik 11.04, DT: Tamara Stojkovic 40.95, HT: Ana Susec 54.89, JT: Martina Ratej 50.86, Hep: Mija Rangus 4498.

Women

Jolanda CEPLAK b. 12 Sep 1976 Celje 1.68m 55kg. née Steblovnik. Velenje.

At 800m: OG: '00- h 4x400mR, '04- 3; WCh: 97- h, '01- sf; EC: '02- 1; EJ: '93- 4; WI: '01-03-04: 6/4/2; EI: '00- 4, '02- 1; WCp: '02- 3; ECp: '98- 8. At 1500m: WCh: '03- 12; EJ: '95- 3. Won SLO 800m 2000, 1500m 1993, 1996, 1999; 3000m 1996.

WIR 800m 2002, Slovenian records: 800m (3) 1997-2002, 1000m 2002, 1500m (2) 2002-03.

Progress at 800m, 1500m: 1989- 2:17.65, 4:48.08; 1990- 2:10.55, 4:34.03; 1991- 2:10.15, 4:33.76; 1992- 2:10.41, 4:31.90; 1993- 2:07.91, 4:31.97; 1994- 2:06.53, 4:25.80; 1995- 2:06.43, 4:20.22; 1996- 2:04.94, 4:17.82; 1997- 2:00.94, 1998- 2:02.71, 4:20.89; 1999- 2:02.53, 2000- 2:00.80, 2001- 1:58.71, 4:13.19; 2002- 1:55.19, 4:05.44i/4:05.59; 2003- 1:57.44, 4:02.44; 2004- 1:56.43, 4:04.44; 2005- 1:59.98. pbs: 400m 54.67 '00, 600m 1:26.68i '02, 1000m 2:31.66 '02, 1M 5:06.6 '98, 3000m 9:50.15 '96, HMar 83:55 '97, 400mh 63.81 '95.

Broke WIR 800m by 0.58 at European Indoors 2002, front-running to 600m and reclaiming lead from Steffi Graf in one of the great races of all-time. Had set SLO age-15 records at all distances from 400m to 1500m. Had an Achilles operation in October 2005.

SOUTH AFRICA

Governing body: Athletics South Africa, PO Box 2712, Houghton 2041. Original body founded 1894.

National Championships first held in 1894 (men), 1929 (women). **2005 Champions**: **Men**: 100m: Jean du Randt 10.34w, 200m: Leigh Julius 20.38, 400m: Jan van der Merwe 45.94, 800m: Mbulaeni Mulaudzi 1:44.96, 1500m: Johan Pretorius 3:43.33, 5000m/10,000m: Coolboy Ngamole 13:56.14/28:55.61, HMar: Hendrick Ramaala 61:33, Mar: Johannes Kekana 2:19:16, 3000mSt: Ruben Ramolefi 8:24.74, 110mh: Frikkie van Zyl 13.77, 400mh: Louis van Zyl 48.39, HJ: Jacques Freitag 2.35, PV: Okkert Brits 5.20, LJ/TJ: Godfrey Mokoena 8.26w/17.25, SP: Janus Robberts 19.89, DT: Frantz Kruger 61.01, HT: Chris Harmse 80.63, JT: Lohan Rautenbach 80.03, Dec: Francois Potgieter 7272, 20000mW: Marc Mundell 1:37:13.03, 50kmW: Colin van Blommestein 5:06:05. **Women**: 100m/200m: Geraldine Pillay 11.07/22.78w, 400m: Heide Seyerling 51.47, 800m: Lebogang Phalula 2:04.23, 1500m: Dinah Lebo Phalula 4:18.99, 5000m/10,000m: Poppy Mlambo 16:10.82/33:46.23, HMar: Tanith Maxwell 75:52, Mar: Dimakatso Morobi 2:50:14, 3000mSt: Tebogo Masehla 10:17.68, 100mh: Justine Robbeson 13.88, 400mh: Surita Febbraio 54.60, HJ: Dianie Wondergem 1.80, PV: Lindie Roux 4.02, LJ: Janice Josephs 6.30w, TJ: Charlene Wondergem 12.60w, SP: Marli Knoetze 16.30, DT: Elizna Naude 59.50, HT: Marilize Coetzee 50.43, JT: Ynthie Coetzee 57.92, 20000mW: Nicolene Cronje 1:42:51.5.

Jacques FREITAG b. 11 Jun 1982 Warrenton 2.07m 83kg. Rentmeester-Tuks.

At HJ: OG: '04- dnq 20=; WCh: '01- dnq 23, '03- 1, '05- dnq 18=; WJ: '00- 1; WY: '99- 1. RSA champion 2000, 2002, 2005.

4 African and 9 South African high jump records 2000-05 (three African Junior 2000-01).

Progress at HJ: 1998- 2.08, 1999- 2.25A; 2000- 2.30A, 2001- 2.31, 2002- 2.37, 2003- 2.35, 2004- 2.34, 2005- 2.38.

First athlete to win gold medals at World Youth, Junior and Senior Champs. RSA sportsman of the year 2003. Mother, Hendrina Pieters was SA high jump champion and had pb 1.74 in 1973.

Llewellyn HERBERT b. 21 Jul 1977 Bethal 1.85m 80kg. Rentmeester-Tuks, Pretoria.

At 400mh: OG: '96- h, '00- 3, '04- sf; WCh: '97- 2, '01- h, '03- 8, '05- sf; WJ: '96- 2; AfCh: '02- 1, '04- 1; WUG: '97- 1; WCp: '02- 7. Won SA 110mh 1996-7, 400mh 1996-2002.

Seven SA 400mh records 1997-2000.

Progress at 400mh: 1995- 51.25, 1996- 48.76A, 1997- 47.86, 1998- 48.43A/48.76, 1999- 47.83A/48.28, 2000- 47.81, 2001- 48.52A/48.77, 2002- 48.02A/48.83, 2003- 48.50, 2004- 48.03, 2005- 48.57. pbs: 100m 10.30A/10.20Aw '99; 200m 20.50wA/21.06 '99, 400m 46.15A '02, 110mh 13.91A '98, 13.7A '97; 300mh 35.43i '05, 35.56 '04.

Khotso Godfrey **MOKOENA** b. 6 Mar 1985 1.90m 73kg.

At (LJ)/TJ: OG: '04- dnq 29; WCh: '05- (7); CG: '06- 4/2; WJ: '02- (12), '04- 2/1; AfG: '03- 2; WI: '06- (5). At HJ: WY: '01- 5. Won RSA LJ 2005-06, TJ 2004-06.

RSA records LJ 2005, TJ (2) 2004-05, African junior TJ record 2004.

Progress at LJ, TJ: 2001- 7.17A, 2002- 7.82A, 16.03A; 2003- 7.84A/7.83, 16.28; 2004- 8.09, 16.96A/16.77; 2005- 8.37A/8.22, 17.25. pbs: HJ 2.10 '01.

Mbulaeni MULAUDZI b. 8 Sep 1980 Muduluni Village, Limpopo Province 1.71m 62kg. Vaal Technikon. Student.

At 800m: OG: '04- 2; WCh: '01- 6, '03- 3, '05- sf;

CG: '02- 1; AfG: '03- 2; AfCh: '00- 2, '02- 3; WI: '04- 1, '06- 2; Won AfrJ 1999, RSA 2001-03, 2005. Progress at 800m: 1998- 1:50.33A, 1999- 1:48.33A; 2000- 1:45.55, 2001- 1:44.01, 2002- 1:43.81, 2003- 1:42.89, 2004- 1:44.56, 2005- 1:44.08. pbs: 400m 47.20A '99, 600m 1:17.25i '05, 1000m 2:18.45A '03, 1500m 3:39.70 '02.

Alwyn MYBURGH b. 13 Oct 1980 Vanderbijlpark 1.88m 73kg. Mr Price AC.
At 400mh: OG: '00- sf, '04- 7; WCh: '01/03- sf; CG: '06- 2; WUG: '01- 1; AfJ: '99- 1.
Progress at 400mh: 1998- 52.48A, 1999- 50.15A; 2000- 49.07A/49.11, 2001- 48.09, 2002- 48.39A/49.80, 2003- 48.61, 2004- 48.21, 2005- 48.75, 2006- 48.23. pbs: 100m 10.66A '99, 200m 21.11A '01, 20.9A '06; 400m 46.28A '04.
His father Hugo Myburgh had a 400mh best of 50.04 in 1974 and his mother Hybré de Lange set South African records of 13.2 and 13.48 for 100mh, 26.36 for 200mh and 57.6 for 400mh in 1974.

Hendrick RAMAALA b. 2 Feb 1972 GaMalepo, Pietersburg 1.72m 58kg. Mr Price AC. Law graduate of Wits University.
At 10,000m: OG: '96- h; WCh: '95- 17, '97- 14, '99- 11; AfG: '99- 7. At Mar: OG: '00- 12, '04- dnf; WCh: '03- 9, '05- dnf. World HMar: '97-8-9-01-02: 4/2/2/4/15. Won SA 5000m 1995, 1999; 10,000m 1995, 1999-2001; HMar 1997, 2005; CC 1998.
SA records 10,000m (3) 1997-9, HMar 1997, 2000.
Progress at 10,000m, Mar: 1995- 27:54.59, 1996- 27:57.8, 1997- 27:36.30, 1998- 27:30.57, 1999- 27:29.94, 2000- 27:46.38, 2:09:43; 2001- 27:38.36, 2:11:18; 2002- 28:02.37, 2:10:06; 2003- 27:43.07, 2:08:58; 2004- 28:35.56, 2:09:28; 2005- 29:20.13, 2:08:32. pbs: 1500m 3:52.14 '03, 3000m 8:06.03A '04, 5000m 13:24.43 '98, HMar 59:20 '00 & RSA rec 60:07 '97.
Won Great North Run 1997 & 2003. Did not finish on his marathon debut at Chicago 1999, won Mumbai and New York 2004, 3rd London and 2nd New York 2005. Partner of French distance runner Rodica Moroianu.

Janus ROBBERTS b. 10 Mar 1979 Louis Trichardt 1.96m 130kg. Was at Southern Methodist University, USA.
At SP (/DT): OG: '00- 7, '04- dnq 21; WCh: '99- dnq 20, '01- 11, '03- dnq 26, '05- dnq; CG: '98- 5, '02- 2/7, '06- 1/9; WJ: '98- 2/7; AfG: '99- 2; AfCh: '02- 1/1, '04- 1; WCp: '02- 4. Won RSA SP 2004-06, NCAA SP 1999, 2001-02; DT 2002; Afr-J SP/DT 1997.
Three African and one Commonwealth shot records 2001. Official world junior record 1998, four African indoors 2000-01.
Progress at SP: 1997- 18.61, 1998- 20.39, 1999- 20.10, 2000- 20.34, 2001- 21.97, 2002- 21.60, 2003- 20.27, 2004- 21.24, 2005- 20.43, 2006- 21.06. pb DT 62.37 '02.
Led the qualifying at the 2001 Worlds with 21.26, but 20.18 for 11th in the final.

Louis J. van ZYL b. 20 Jul 1985 1.86m 75kg. Mr. Price AC. Student at University of Potchefstroom.
At 400mh: WCh: '05- 6; CG: '06- 1/2R; WJ: '02- 1, '04- 4/2R; WY: '01- 3; RSA champion 2003, 2005.
Progress at 400mh: 2001- 51.14A, 2002- 48.89, 2003- 49.22, 2004- 49.06, 2005- 48.11. pbs: 100m 10.3Aw '03, 10.5A '01; 200m 21.20A '05, 21.0A '03, 21.19w '05; 400m 46.28A '05, 300mh 35.76 '04.
Ran world U18 record of 48.89 to win World Junior title in 2002 after world age record at 15 in 2001. Commonwealth Games record to win 400mh gold and ran brilliant final leg in 4x400m to take RSA from fifth to second in 2006.

SPAIN

Governing body: Real Federación Española de Atletismo, Avda. Valladolid, 81 - 1°, 28008 Madrid, Spain. Founded 1918.
National Championships first held in 1917 (men), 1931 (women). **2005 Champions**: **Men**: 100m: Orkatz Beitia 10.41, 200m: David Canal 21.16, 400m/800m: Antonio M Reina 46.12/1:49.05, 1500m: Arturo Casado 3.48.75, 5000m: Jesús España 14.03.12, 10,000m: José Manuel Martínez 27:42.90, HMar: Antonio Peña 62:38, Mar: Roger Roca 2:18:43, 3000mSt: Antonio Jiménez 8:24.45, 110mh: Felipe Vivancos 13.61, 400mh: Eduardo Rodríguez 50.18, HJ: Javier Bermejo 2.16, PV: Javier Gazol 5.41, LJ: Joan Lino Martinez 8.17, TJ: Pere Joseph 16.08, SP: Manuel Martínez 19.89, DT: Mario Pestano 62.78, HT: Moisés Campeny 70.85, JT: Gustavo Dacal 73.16, Dec: Oscar Gonzalez 7710, 20kmW: Juan Manuel Molina 1:24.49, 50kmW: Mikel Odriozola 3:41:47. **Women**: 100m/200m: Belén Recio 11.64/23.75w, 400m: Julia Alba 53.22, 800m: Mayte Martínez 2:04.51, 1500m: Natalia Rodríguez 4:22.86, 5000m: Yesenia Centeno 15.49.87, 10,000m: Teresa Recio 32:44.19, HMar: Yesenia Centeno 72:14, Mar: María José Pueyo 2:37:05, 3000mSt: Rosa Morató 10:11.81, 100mh: Glory Alozie 12.89w, 400mh: Cora Olivero 55.83, HJ: Marta Mendía 1.94, PV: María del Mar Sánchez 4.10, LJ: Niurka Montalvo 6.49, TJ: Carlota Castrejana 14.26, SP: Martina de la Puente 16.71, DT: Alice Matejkova 56.59, HT: Berta Castells 66.84, JT: Mercedes Chilla 56.29, Hep: María Peinado 5478, 10000W: María Vasco 45.16.67, 20kmW: Marí José Poves 1:31:55.

Reyes ESTÉVEZ b. 2 Aug 1976 Barcelona 1.87m 70kg. Nike Bowerman.
At 1500m: OG: '96- sf, '04- 7; WCh: '97- 3, '99- 3, '01- 5, '03- 6, '05- 11; EC: '98- 1, '02- 2; WJ: '94- 4; EJ: '93- 1, '95- 1; EU23: '97- 1; WI: '01- 2; EI: '05- 3 (& 3000m 3); WCp: '02- 2; ECp: '98- 2. World CC: '94- 8J. Won Spanish 1500m 1997-8, 2004.
European Junior 1500m record 1995.
Progress at 1500m: 1992- 3:54.7, 1993- 3:42.36,

1994- 3:39.28, 1995- 3:35.51, 1996- 3:34.86, 1997- 3:33.40, 1998- 3:30.87, 1999- 3:30.57, 2000- 3:40.64, 2001- 3:32.34, 2002- 3:32.93, 2003- 3:32.86, 2004- 3:35.37, 2005- 3:36.51i/3:38.10. pbs: 800m 1:46.90 '96, 1000m 2:17.45 '00, 1M 3:51.82 '02, 2000m 5:05.68 '04, 3000m 7:43.80i '05, 7:44.87 '99; 5000m 14:08.8 '96.
Has won four European titles U20 to senior.

Francisco Javier FERNÁNDEZ b. 6 Mar 1977 Guadix, Granada 1.75m 65kg. Agropaejido.
At 20kmW: OG: '00- 7, '04- 2; WCh: '99- 15, '01- dnf, '03- 2, '05- 2; EC: '98- 3, '02- 1; WCp: '97- 47, '99- 12; EU23: '97- 2; ECp: '98-00-01-03: 1/3/4/1; won Med G 2005, Spanish 1998-2004. At 10kmW: WJ: '96- 1; EJ: '95- 2.
World 20km walk best 2002. Spanish walks records 1999-2002: 5000m (2), 10,000m, 10km (3), 20km (2).
Progress at 20kmW: 1997- 1:21:59, 1998- 1:20:31, 1999- 1:21:55, 2000- 1:18:56, 2001- 1:19:47, 2002- 1:17:22, 2003- 1:18:00, 2004- 1:19:19, 2005- 1:17:52. pbs: 3000mW 12:27.27 '02, 5000mW 18:48.23 '02, 10,000mW 38:42.38 '99, 10kmRd 37:52 '02 (all Spanish records).
Won IAAF Race Walking Challenge 2005.

Alberto GARCÍA b. 22 Feb 1971 Madrid 1.63m 45kg. C.A.Adidas.
At 5000m: OG: '00- h; WCh: '99- h, '01- 4, '05- h; EC: '98- 10, '02- 1; WCp: '02- 1; ECp: '98- 1, '01- 2; Won MedG 1997, Spanish 2001-02. At 3000m: WI: '01- 3, '03- 2; EI: '96-8-02: 6/3/1. World CC 4k: '00-01-02-03: 17/16/17/20dq; Eur CC: '05- 2.
Spanish 5000m record 1998 & 2001. European indoor 3000m & 5000m records 2003.
Progress at 5000m, 10,000m: 1990- 14:43.14, 1992- 14:25.23, 1993- 14:05.73, 1994- 14:09.70, 1995- 13:50.78, 1996- 13:31.19, 1997- 13:20.44, 1998- 13:04.64, 1999- 13:08.13, 27:46.12; 2000- 13:09.50, 28:01.11; 2001- 13:02.54, 2002- 13:10.90, 2003- 13:11.39i, 2005- 13:10.73. pbs: 1000m 2:23.99 '98, 1500m 3:35.69 '01, 1M 3:58.81 '98, 2000m 4:56.08 '97, 3000m 7:32.98i '03, 7:36.53 '01.
Won 1999 European Challenge on 10,000m debut. Two year drugs ban for positive test for EPO at 2003 World CC Champs.

Jesús Ángel GARCÍA b. 17 Oct 1969 Madrid 1.71m 62kg. Canal de Isabel II.
At 50kmW: OG: '92- 10, '96- dnf, '00- 12, '04- 5; WCh: '93-5-7-9-01-03-05: 1/5/2/dnf/2/6/dq; EC: '94- 4, '98- dq, '02- 3; WCp: '93-5-7-9-02-04: 2/2/1/4/dq/6; ECp: '96-8-00-01: 1/2/1/1. At 20kmW: WUG: '91- 5; ECp: '05- 14. Won SPA 50kmW 1997, 2000.
Progress at 50kmW: 1991- 4:05:10, 1992- 3:48:24, 1993- 3:41:41, 1994- 3:41:28, 1995- 3:41:54, 1996- 3:46:59, 1997- 3:39.54, 1998- 3:43:17, 1999- 3:40:40, 2000- 3:42:51, 2001- 3:43:07, 2002- 3:44:33, 2003- 3:43:56, 2004- 3:44:42, 2005- 3:48:19. pbs: 5000mW 19:33.3 '01, 10,000mW 40:32.85 '04, road: 10kmW 40:38 '91, 20kmW 1:23:09 '05, 30kmW 2:08:47 '01.
In 1997 he married Carmen Acedo, who won a rhythmic gymnastics world title in 1993.

Juan Carlos HIGUERO b. 3 Aug 1978 Aranda de Duero (Burgos) 1.80m 60kg. Promoaranda.
At 1500m: OG: '00- 8, '04- sf; WCh: '03- 11, '05- 6; EC: '02- 5; EU23: '99- h; WI: '01- 9, '03- 8; EI: '00-02-05: 6/2/2; ECp: '03- 1, '05- 1. At 5000m: EJ: '97- 3. Eur CC: '96-97: 3J/4J. Won Spanish 1500m 2000, 2002-03.
Progress at 1500m: 1997- 3:50.90, 1998- 3:41.24, 1999- 3:39.57, 2000- 3:36.63, 2001- 3:32.30, 2002- 3:33.72, 2003- 3:31.61, 2004- 3:32.95, 2005- 3:33.72. pbs: 800m 1:46.00 '03, 1M 3:52.49 '02, 2000m 5:04.26 '05, 3000m 7:48.46i '05, 7:59.76 '99; 5000m 14:08.35 '97, 10kmRd 28:37 '03, 3000mSt 9:51.34 '95.

Antonio David **JIMÉNEZ** b. 18 Feb 1977 Sevilla 1.78m 63kg. Reebok RC
At 3000mSt: OG: '04- 14; WCh: '01- 6, '05- 6, EC: '02- 1; EU23: '99- 3; ECp: '01-03-05: 2/4/1; Won MedG 2001. At 3000m: WI: '04- 4; EI: '02- 2. World 4k CC: '02- 7. Eur CC: '01- 3. Won Spanish 4k CC 2002, 3000mSt 2001-02, 2004-05.
Two Spanish records 2000mSt 2001-05.
Progress at 3000mSt: 1995- 9:24.74, 1996- 9:17.93, 1997- 9:19.3, 1998- 8:54.90, 1999- 8:37:29, 2000- 8:20:34, 2001- 8:11.52, 2002- 8:17.77, 2003- 8:15.82, 2004- 8:14.30, 2005- 8:14.05. pbs: 1500m 3:43.23 '02, 2000m 5:04.91 '02, 3000m 7:46.49i '02, 7:50.30 '00; 2000mSt 5:18.65 '05.

Eliseo MARTÍN b. 5 Nov 1973 Monzón, Huesca 1.72m 61kg. Adidas.
At 3000mSt: OG: '00- 6, '04- 9; WCh: '99- 6, '01- 12, '03- 3; EC: '98- 7, '02- 5. At 10,000m: WJ: '92- 7. Won Spanish 3000mSt 1999, 2003.
Progress at 3000mSt: 1992- 9:02.55, 1993- 8:45.77, 1994- 8:32.89, 1995- 8:31.27, 1996- 8:31.99, 1997- 8:30.50, 1998- 8:25.92, 1999- 8:13.59, 2000- 8:13.63, 2001- 8:19.20, 2002- 8:19.09, 2003- 8:09.09, 2004- 8:15.77, 2005- 8:16.11. pbs: 1500m 3:40.96 '00, 3000m 7:50.71 '03, 5000m 13:47.77 '01, 10,000m 28:39.11 '99, 2000mSt 5:22.93 '01.

Luis Miguel MARTÍN b. 11 Jan 1972 Madrid 1.80m 69kg. Nike Bowerman.
At 3000mSt: OG: '00- 5, '04- 5; WCh: '99- h, '01- 4, '03- 6, '05- 11; EC: '98- 4, '02- 3; WCp: '02- 2; won IbAm 1998, Spanish 2000. At 1500m: WJ: '90- h; EJ: '91- h.
Four Spanish records 3000mSt 1999-2002.
Progress at 3000mSt: 1998- 8:20.54, 1999- 8:11.18, 2000- 8:09.77, 2001- 8:08.74, 2002- 8:07.44, 2003- 8:13.52, 2004- 8:11.64, 2005- 8:17.47. pbs: 800m 1:48.40 '96, 1500m 3:36.11 '02, 2000m 5:10.63 '03, 3000m 7:50.27 '00, 5000m 13:54.35 '02, 2000mSt 5:20.52 '02.
He married Miriam Alonso (400mh 55.45A '96) in 2005.

Joan Lino MARTÍNEZ b. 17 Jan 1978 La Habana, Cuba 1.76m 69kg.

At TJ: OG: '04- 3; WCh: '05- 4; WJ: '96- 7; CAG: '98- 3; EI: '05- 1. Won PAm-J 1997, IbAm 2004, Cuban 1999, Spanish 2005.
Progress at LJ: 1995- 7.53, 1996- 7.65, 1997- 8.06, 1998- 8.19, 1999- 8.18/8.39irreg, 2000- 7.94/8.18w, 2001- 8.08/8.13w, 2002- 8.24, 2003- 8.20/8.32w, 2004- 8.32, 2005- 8.37i/8.17/8.24w. pbs: 60m 6.75i '04, 100m 10.47 '03.
Switched from Cuba to Spain.

José Manuel 'Chema' **MARTÍNEZ** b. 22 Oct 1971 Madrid 1.76m 63kg. Nike Bowerman.
At 10,000m: OG: '04- 9; WCh: '99- 19, '01- 12, EC: '02- 1; WUG: '99- 1. At Mar: WCh: '03- 16, '05- 13. Eur CC: '00- 9, '02- 15. Won Spanish 10,000m 2004-05, CC 2002.
Progress at 10,000m, Mar: 1993- 29:22.72, 1994- 29:19.42, 1995- 29:15.8, 1996- 28:51.97, 1997- 28:11.67, 1998- 28:16.39, 1999- 27:51.82, 2000- 27:53.9, 2001- 27:54.81, 2002- 27:41.76, 2:09:55; 2003- 27:30.56, 2:08:09; 2004- 27:41.49, 2:13:14; 2005- 27:42.90, 2:11:56. pbs: 1500m 3:48.49 '97, 2000m 5:06.33 '04, 3000m 7:39.64 '04, 5000m 13:13.57 '02, HMar 63:17 '04.
Third in Rotterdam on marathon debut 2002 and again in 2003. Won the European 10,000m with a 56.6 last lap. Wife Nuria Moreno was an international hockey player.

Manuel MARTÍNEZ b. 7 Dec 1974 León 1.85m 132kg. León C.A.
At SP: OG: '96- dnq 15, '00- 6, '04- 4; WCh: '93- 11, '95- dnq 21, '97- dnq 13, '01- 4, '03/05- dnq 15/16; EC: '94- dnq 14, '98- 7, '02- 5; WI: '95-7-9-01-03-04-06: 4/5/4/3/1/5/6; EI: '94-96-98-00-02-05: 4/7/6/2/1/3; WJ: '92- 2; EJ: '93- 1; WUG: '01- 1; WCp: '02- 6; ECp: '93-5-6-7-8-01-03-05: 7/4/4/3/3/1/1/2; E23Cp: '94- 1. Won Spanish 1993-8, 2000-05 (also indoors 1993-2006); IbAm 1998, 2000, 2004; MedG 2001.
16 Spanish shot records 1993-2002.
Progress at SP: 1991- 15.57, 1992- 18.14, 1993- 19.53, 1994- 20.16, 1995- 19.97i/19.69, 1996- 20.12, 1997- 20.37i/20.27, 1998- 20.50i/20.08; 1999- 20.79i/20.04, 2000- 20.55, 2001- 21.35, 2002- 21.47, 2003- 21.24i/21.08, 2004- 21.15, 2005- 20.51i/20.32. pb DT 48.04 '98.

Juan Manuel MOLINA b. 15 Mar 1979 Cieza, Murcia 1.73m 67kg. UCAM-Athleo.
At 20kmW: OG: '04- 5; WCh: '05- 3; EC: '02- 3; EU23: '99- 4, '01- 1; WUG: '01- 2, '05- 1; WCp: '02- 8, '04- 8; ECp: '01- 10, '05- 2. At 10kmW: WJ: '98- 4; EJ: '97- 6. Won Spanish 20kmW 2005.
Spanish record 20,000m walk 1:22:31.8 '01.
Progress at 20kmW: 1999- 1:23:39, 2000- 1:22:43, 2001- 1:21:51, 2002- 1:20:18, 2003- 1:21:57, 2004- 1:20:29, 2005- 1:19:44. pbs: 3000mW 12:31.20 '02, 5000mW 19:12.5 '05, 10,000mW 39:30.36 '04, 10kmW 39:18 '05, 30kmW 2:11:05 '00, 50kmW 3:55:12 '06.

Mikel ODRIOZOLA b. 25 May 1973 San Sebastián 1.80m 62kg. Real Sociedad FIACT.
At 20kmW: WCh: '99- 18. At 50kmW: OG: '00- 24; WCh: '01- 15, '03- 14, '05- dq; EC: '98- 4, '02- dq. Won Spanish 50kmW 2001-03, 2005-96.
Spanish record 30km walk 2003.
Progress at 50kmW: 1996- 4:11:45, 1997- 3:57:15, 1998- 3:47:24, 1999- 3:51:01, 2000- 3:45:57, 2001- 3:45:22, 2002- 3:47:55, 2003- 3:42:03, 2005- 3:41:47. pbs: 5000mW 19:28.9 '00, 10,000mW 42:43.1 '96, 10kmW 40:30 '05, 20kmW 1:22:29 '00, 30kmW 2:05:28 '03.

Juan Carlos de la OSSA b. 25 Nov 1976 Cuenca 1.68m 50kg. Joma Sport.
At 10,000m: WCh: '05- 10; ECp: '05- 1. At 5000m: WCh: '03- 9; ECp: '05- 1. World CC: '05-06: 24/17; Eur CC: 02-03-04-05: 6/2/2/9. Won Spanish CC 2004-05.
Progress at 10,000m: 1994- 33:10.0, 1995- 30:47.7, 1998- 30:42.55, 2001- 30:10.10, 2002- 29:06.77, 2003- 28:07.19, 2005- 27:27.80. pbs: 3000m 7:42.16 '05, 5000m 13:10.58 '05, 10kmRd 27:55 '05, HMar 67:30 '99.

Mario PESTANO b. 8 Apr 1978 Santa Cruz de Tenerife 1.95m 120kg. C.A.Arona.
At DT: OG: '04- dnq 12; WCh: '99/01- dnq 30/22, '03- 8, '05- 11; EC: '02- 4; EU23: '99- 3; EJ: '97- 11; WCp: '02- 3; ECp: '01-03-05: 2/5/1. Won WAF 2004, IbAm 2004, MedG 2005, Spanish 2001-05.
Five Spanish discus records 2001-04.
Progress at DT: 1995- 49.36, 1996- 50.56, 1997- 53.68, 1998- 54.96, 1999- 61.73, 2000- 61.63, 2001- 67.92, 2002- 67.46, 2003- 64.99, 2004- 68.00, 2005- 66.57. pb SP 18.75i '00, 18.64 '02.

Antonio Manuel REINA b. 13 Jun 1981 Osuna, Sevilla 1.86m 71kg. Nike Bowerman.
At 800m: OG: '04- sf; WCh: '01- h/7R, '03- sf/5R, '05- sf; EC: '02- sf; WJ: '00- 3; EU23: '01- 1; WI: '03- 4; EI: '02- 3, '05- 2; WCp: '02- 1; ECp: '03- 1, '05- 1; Won Med G 2005, Spanish 400m 2005, 800m 2001-05.
Two Spanish 800m records 2002
Progress at 800m: 1998- 1:54.44, 1999- 1:51.75, 2000- 1:47.33, 2001- 1:46.00, 2002- 1:43.83, 2003- 1:44.37, 2004- 1:43.89, 2005- 1:44.18. pbs: 200m 21.83 '05, 400m 45.98 '05, 1000m 2:20.50 '01, 1500m 3:59.6 '00.
Improved in 2002 from a best of 1:45.25 (3rd in European Indoors) to a Spanish outdoor record 1:44.11 at San Sebastián and then 1:43.83 in a thrilling World Cup victory in Madrid.

Julio REY b. 13 Jan 1972 Toledo 1.66m 51kg. Adidas.
At Mar: OG: '04- 58; WCh: '01- 37, '03- 2, '05- 8; EC: '02- 3. At 10,000m: WCh: '97- 8; EC: '98- dnf. World HMar: '02- 11. World CC: '97- 9; Eur CC: '97-8: 7/9. Won Spanish 10,000m 1997, HMar 2004, CC 1997-8.
Progress at 10,000m, Mar: 1995- 28:18.6, 1996- 28:00.79, 1997- 27:55.19, 1998- 27:47.33, 2:08:33; 1999- 2:07:37dq, 2001- 2:07:46, 2002- 27:51.59,

2:11:14; 2003- 2:07:27, 2004- 2:24:54, 2005- 2:07:38. pbs: 3000m 7:54.40 '97, 5000m 13:22.13 '98, HMar 62:10 '02.

Two year-drugs ban after 3rd Rotterdam marathon 1999. Won Hamburg marathon 2001, 2003 & 2005; 2nd Fukuoka 2005. His brother Fernando (b. 16 Apr 1980) has 10,000m pb 28:14.90 '04.

José RIOS b. 15 Mar 1974 Premià de Dalt (Barcelona) 1.70m 49kg. Adidas.

At 10,000m: OG: '00- 18; WCh: '01- 6; EC: '02- 3. At Mar: OG: '04- 27; WCh: '05- dnf. Eur CC: '05- 10. Won Spanish 10,000m 2000-03, EChall 2001.

Progress at 5000m, 10,000m, Mar: 1991- 15:04.82, 31:15.89; 1992- 14:26.50, 31:24.50; 1993- 14:25.76, 29:48.44, 1994- 14:23.37, 29:35.2; 1995- 14:03.30, 29:03.6; 1996- 13:49.44, 29:00.34; 1997- 13:51.32, 28:37.52; 1998- 14:11.52, 28:56.51; 1999- 13:41.03, 28:30.53; 2000- 13:07.59, 27:22.20; 2001- 13:09.83, 27:38.57; 2002- 13:08.60, 27:35.13; 2003- 13:19.58, 27:29.60; 2004- 14:17.71, 2:07:42; 2005- 30:38.81, 2:09:03; 2006- 2:09:15. pbs: 1500m 3:51.11 '01, 3000m 7:42.08 '02, HMar: 63:21 '05.

Was a butcher, massive breakthrough in 2000. Won Lake Biwa 2004 (and again 2006) after dnf Rotterdam in debut marathon 2003.

Women

Glory ALOZIE b. 30 Dec 1977 Amator, Nigeria 1.56m 52kg. Valencia Terra i Mar.

At 100mh (100m): OG: '00- 2, '04- sf; WCh: '99- 2, '03- 4, '05- sf; EC: '02- 1 (4); WJ: '96- 2; AfG: '99- 1/1R; AfCh: '96- 1, '98- 1, '00- 1; Af-J: '95- 2; WCp: '98- 1, '02- 3 (5); ECp: '03- 1 (3), '04- 3 (1). 2nd GP 2000, 3rd 1998. At 60mh: WI: '99-03-06: 2/2/2; EI: '02- 1g, '05- 4. Won NGR 100mh 1999-2000, ESP 100mh 2001-02, 2004-05; Med G 2005. Records: African: 100m 1999, 100mh (5) 1998-9; indoor 50mh (2) 2001, 60mh (2) 1999; two Commonwealth 100mh 1998-9, five Spanish 2001-04 (from 12.87).

Progress at 100mh: 1993- 14.99, 1994- 14.25, 1995- 13.86, 1996- 13.30, 1997- 12.96, 1998- 12.44/12.4w, 1999- 12.44, 2000- 12.54, 2001- 12.69, 2002- 12.60, 2003- 12.66, 2004- 12.57, 2005- 12.71/12.62w. pbs: 50m 6.3i exh '02, 60m 7.20i '99, 100m 10.90 '99; 200m 23.09 '01, 22.91w '98; 50mh 6.76i '01, 60mh 7.82i '99.

Based in Spain since January 1997, she became a Spanish citizen on 7 July 2001, but not allowed to retain European Indoor 60mh title in 2002, as ruled ineligible for international competition until later that year. Won 17 of 19 finals in 1998 at 100mh. Her fiancée, 400m runner Hyginus Anugo, was killed in a road accident in Sydney just prior to the 2000 Games.

Ruth BEITIA b.1 Apr 1979 Santander 1.92m 71kg. Valencia Terra i Mar.

At HJ: OG: '04- dnq 16=; WCh: '03- 11=, '05- dnq 19=; EC: '02- 11; WJ: '96- dnq, '98- 8, EU23: '01- 1; EJ: '97- 9; WI: '03- 5=, '06- 3; EI: '05- 2; WCp: '02- 6=; ECp: '03-04: 2/6; Won Med G 2005, Spanish 2003.

Seven Spanish HJ records 1998-2003.

Progress at HJ: 1989- 1.29, 1990- 1.39, 1991- 1.50, 1992- 1.55, 1993- 1.66, 1994- 1.74, 1995- 1.80, 1996- 1.85, 1997- 1.86, 1998- 1.89, 1999- 1.83, 2000- 1.86i/1.85, 2001- 1.94i/1.91, 2002- 1.94, 2003- 2.00, 2004- 2.00i/1.96, 2005- 1.99i/1.97, 2006- 1.98i. pbs: 200m 25.26 '02, 100mh 14.95 '97, 14.93w '00; LJ 6.04 '03, TJ 10.93 '99.

Marta DOMÍNGUEZ b. 3 Nov 1975 Palencia 1.63m 52kg. Nike Bowerman.

At 5000m: OG: '00- h; WCh: '99- 9, '01- 2, '03- 2, '05- 14; EC: '98- 3, '02- 1; EU23: '97- 3 (1500m 5); WCp: '02- 2. At 3000m: WI: '95-7-01-03-04: 6/5/4/2/4; EI: '96-8-00-02: 3/3/3/1; ECp: '96- 3. At 1500m: OG: '96- h; WCh: '95- sf; WJ: '94- 2; EJ: '93- 1. World 4k CC: '00- 14. Won Spanish 1500m 1996, 5000m 1998-2003.

Spanish record 3000m 2000.

Progress at 3000m, 5000m: 1990- 10:15.0, 1991- 9:47.03, 1993- 9:35.16, 1994- 9:24.10, 1995- 9:01.79i, 1996- 8:53.34i/9:06.27, 1997- 8:52.74i/9:01.96, 15:41.91; 1998- 8:44.10, 14:59.49; 1999- 8:46.14, 15:16.93; 2000- 8:28.80, 15:26.00; 2001- 8:36.33, 14:58.12; 2002- 8:47.93, 15:10.67; 2003- 8:41.14i/8:50.6+, 14:48.33; 2004- 8:51.05i, 2005- 9:05.56, 14:54.98. pbs: 800m 2:06.1 '95, 1000m 2:50.1 '91, 1500m 4:06.08 '00, 2000m 5:49.55i '98, 10kmRd 31:35dh '03.

Mayte MARTÍNEZ b. 17 May 1976 Valladolid 1.68m 56kg. Adidas.

At 800m: OG: '00/04- sf; WCh: '01- 7, '05- 5, EC: '02- 2, WJ: '94- h; EJ: '95- 6; WI: '03- 3; EI: '02- 4, '05- 2; WCp: '02- 2; ECp: '03- 3. Won Spanish 800m 2000-02, 2004-05.

Progress at 800m: 1991- 2:14.48, 1992- 2:13.09, 1993- 2:07.99, 1994- 2:05.68, 1995- 2:05.00, 1996- 2:08.81i, 1997- 2:06.84, 1998- 2:05.49i, 2000- 1:59.60, 2001- 1:59.76, 2002- 1:58.29, 2003- 1:59.53i/1:59.62, 2004- 1:58.58, 2005- 1:59.40. pbs: 400m 53.67 '03, 1000m 2:38.80i/2:43.68 '05, 1500m 4:05.05 '05.

Married her coach Juan Carlos Granado on 20 Sep 2003.

Concepción MONTANER b.14 Jan 1981 L'Eliana, Valencia 1.70m 56kg. C.A.L'Elianna.

At LJ: OG: '00- dnq, WCh: '03- 12, '05- 11; EC: '02- 4; WJ: '98- h 4x100m, '00- 1, EU23: '01- 2; EJ: '99- 2; WI: '03- 9, '04- 7, '06- 4; WCp: '02- 3; ECp: '03-04: 2/8. Spanish champion 2003-05.

Progress at LJ: 1996- 5.62/5.75w, 1997- 5.43/ 5.51w, 1998- 5.95/5.96w, 1999- 6.47, 2000- 6.64/ 6.79w, 2001- 6.61i/6.57/6.67w, 2002- 6.89, 2003- 6.78i/6.69/6.70w, 2004- 6.65i/6.59, 2005- 6.92, 2006- 6.76i. pbs: 60m 7.47i '01, 100m 11.71 '01, 200m 25.12i '00, TJ 11.98 '97.

Natalia RODRÍGUEZ b. 2 Jun 1979 Tarragona 1.64m 49kg. Adidas.

At 1500m: OG: '00- h, '04- 10; WCh: '01- 6, '03- sf, '05- 6, EC: '02- 6; EU23: '99- 4, '01- 2, WJ:

'98- 6, EJ: '97- 5; ECp: '03- 1. At 800m: WJ: '96- h. Won Spanish 1500m 2000-05.
Spanish 1500m record 2005.
Progress at 800m, 1500m: 1995- 4:42.4, 1996- 2:06.23, 1997- 2:04.15, 4:17.28; 1998- 2:02.78, 4:16.20; 1999- 2:01.66, 4:10.65; 2000- 2:05.76, 4:04.24; 2001- 2:01.35, 4:06.32; 2002- 2:01.76, 4:02.84; 2003- 2:01.54, 4:01.30; 2004- 4:03.01, 2005- 2:03.54, 3:59.51. pb 3000m 9:01.40i '03.

María VASCO b. 26 Dec 1975 Barcelona 1.56m 45kg. FC Barcelona.
At 20kmW: OG: '00- 3, '04- 7; WCh: '99- 10, '01- 5, '03- dnf, '05- 4; EC: '02- dnf; WCp: '99-02-04: 23/8/3; ECp: '01- 7, '03- 3. At 10kmW: OG: '96- 28; WCh: '95- 26; EC: '98- 5; EU23: '97- 2; WCp '95- 26, '97- 22. At 5000mW: WJ: '90- 15, '92- 6, '94- 4; EJ: '93- 4. Won Spanish 10kmW 1996 10,000mW (t) 1997-9, 2001-05; 20kmW 1998, 2001-04.
Spanish records 5000m (2) 1997-2004, 10,000m track (4) 1996-2001, 10km 1998, 20km (6) 1998-2004.
Progress at 10kmW, 20kmW: 1993- 47:11, 1994- 47:05, 1995- 44:53, 1996- 44:51.60t, 1997- 43:54, 1998- 43:02, 1:34:11; 1999- 43:35, 1:32:38; 2000- 43:33.92t, 1:30:20; 2001- 43:02.04t, 1:30:09; 2002- 43:51, 1:28:47; 2003- 44:22, 1:28:10; 2004- 44:07, 1:27:36; 2005- 43:59, 1:28:51. pbs: 3000mW 12:20.44 '04, 5kmW 21:04 '05, 5000mW 21:18.58 '04.

SRI LANKA

Governing body: Amateur Athletic Association of Sri Lanka, n°33 Torrington Avenue, Colombo 7. Founded 1922.
National Champions 2005: **Men:** 100m: R.U.D.S.Surendra 10.72, 200m: S.M.Weerasooriya 21.60, 400m: Prasanna Amarasekara 46.01, 800m: Mohamed Siprath 1:50.90, 1500m: Sunil Jayaweera 3:48.97, 5000m: M.Ajanthan 14:49.46, 10,000m/HMar: I.M.A.Cooray 30:31.90/65:35, Mar: Ajith Bandara 2:18:26, 3000mSt: Indika Bandara 9:03.58, 110mh: A.A.I.Kumara 14.47, 400mh: Harijan Rathnayake 51.75, HJ: Manjula Kumara Wijesekara 2.25, PV: Ruwan Pradeep Perera 4.50, LJ: Suresh Kuumara 7.47w, TJ: Sampath Weerasinghe 15.95, SP: W.U.L.O.R. Perera 14.49, DT: K.G.U.P.Jayawardane 52.31, JT: Harshana Gunathilake 70.76, Dec: R Ratheeshan 6164, 20kmW: Nishantha Nayanananda 1:42:31. **Women**: 100: Jani C De Silva 11.98, 200m: Damayanthi Dharsha 23.79, 400m: Menaka Wickramesinghe 53.69, 800m: Mangala Priyadharshani 2:08.24, 1500m: N.A.Rajasekara 4:33.06, 5000m: Dalugoda A.Inoka 17:05.13, 10,000m: J.H.A.T.S.Jayasekara 35:41.06, HMar: Mallika Chandrakanthi 81:47, Mar: K.G.S.Chandrani 2:56:49, 2000mSt: K.H/N. Damayanthi 7:25.79, 100mh: M.A.Shamali 15.17, 400mh: S.V.A. Kusumawathi 59.79, HJ: Madushani Peiris 1.67, PV: N.V.Hettiarachchi 2.15, LJ/Hep: N.C.D. Priyadharshani 6.08w/3903, TJ: Ruwini Rubasinghe 12.61, SP: M.N.D.Muthunayaka 12.77, DT: Padma Nandan 43.18, JT: Nadeeka Lakmali 54.00, 20kmW: Gallage Geetha Nandani 1:47:00.

SUDAN

Governing body: Sudan Athletic Associatio, PO Box 13274, 11 111 Khartoum. Founded 1959.

Yamilé ALDAMA b. 14 Aug 1972 La Habana 1.73m 62kg. married name Dodds. Shaftesbury Barnet Harriers, GBR.
At TJ: OG: '00- 4, '04- 5; WCh: '97- dnq 13, '99- 2, '05- 4; PAm: '99- 1; AfC: '04- 1; CAG: '98- 1; WI: '97-9-04-06: 6/7/2/3; WCp: '98- 3. Won IbAm 1996, 1998; Cuban 1997-2000, AAA 2003; P.Arab HJ, LJ & TJ 2005.
Nine CAC triple jump records 1999-2003 (if still eligible), CAC indoor (14.65 and 14.88) 2003, three African and Sudan records 2004. SUD LJ record 2005.
Progress at TJ: 1994- 13.92, 1995- 13.84, 1996- 14.43, 1997- 14.46, 1998- 14.55, 1999- 14.77, 2000- 14.47, 2001- 13.85i, 2002- 14.40/14.54w, 2003- 15.29, 2004- 15.28, 2005- 14.82, 2006- 14.86i. pbs: 100mh 14.97/14.8 '92, HJ 1.88 '92, LJ 6.22 '99, Hep 5246 '93.
Aldama, who last competed for Cuba in 2000, was immediately free to compete for Sudan in January 2004. She had moved to London with Scottish husband Andrew Dodds in 2001, in which year her son Amil was born, and hoped to be eligible for Britain but a three-year waiting period meant that she was unable to gain a passport in sufficient time to compete at the 2003 Worlds (or 2004 Olympics).

SWEDEN

Governing body: Svenska Friidrottsförbundet, Box 11, 171 18 Solna. Founded 1895.
National Championships first held in 1896 (men), 1927 (women). **2005 Champions**: **Men**: 100m: Per Strandquist 10.67, 200m: Christofer Sandin 21.22, 400m: Johan Wissman 46.46, 800m: Mattias Claesson 1:49.20, 1500m: Rizak Dirshe 3:50.86, 5000m: Mustafa Mohamed 14:05.34, 10,000m: Oskar Käck 29:41.87, HMar: Alfred Shemweta 67:13, Mar: Said Regragui 2:18:38, 3000mSt: Per Jacobsen, 110mh: Robert Kronberg 13.48, 400mh: Mikael Jakobsson 50.02, HJ: Stefan Holm 2.26, PV: Alhaji Jeng 5.61, LJ: Michel Tornéus 7.81, TJ: Johan Attersand 15.54, SP: Jimmy Nordin 19.14, DT: Staffan Jönsson 57.13, HT: Bengt Johansson 68.08, JT: Daniel Ragnvaldsson 78.54, Dec: Daniel Almgren 7265, 20kmW: Bengt Bengtsson 1:37:45, 10kmW/50kmW: Fredrik Svensson 4:08:23. **Women**: 100m/100mh: Susanna Kallur 11.67/12.99, 200m: Carolina Klüft 23.51, 400m: Lena Aruhn 53.56, 800m: Louise Fredriksson 2:06.34, 1500m: Hanna Karlsson 4:20.99, 5000m/3000mSt: Ida Nilsson 16:29.01/10:02.24, 10,000m: Lena Gavelin 34:44.82, HMar: Anna

Rahm 76:39, Mar: Malin Ewerlöf Krepp 2:44:43, 400mh: Louise Gundert 57.12, HJ/LJ: Emma Green 1.97/6.41, PV: Hanna-Mia Persson 4.36, TJ: Camilla Johansson 13.42, SP: Helena Engman 15.97, DT: Anna Söderberg 59.37, HT: Tracey Andersson 64.85, JT: Annika Petersson 50.85, Hep: Jessica Samuelsson 5513, 10,000mW/20kmW: Monica Svensson 48:46.0/1:39:10.

Stefan HOLM b. 25 May 1976 Forshaga 1.81m 70kg. Kils AIK.
At HJ: OG: '00- 4, '04- 1; WCh: '99- 10=, '01- 4=, '03- 2, '05- 7; EC: '98- 7, '02- 2; WJ: '94- 7=; EJ: '93- 11, '95- 6; WI: '97-9-01-03-04-06: 8=/6=/1/1/1/5; EI: '00-02-05: 4/2/1; WUG: '99- 4; ECp: '00-04: 1/1. Won GP 2002, WAF 2004, GWG 2001, Swedish 1998-2003, 2005.
Progress at HJ: 1987- 1.40, 1988- 1.51, 1989- 1.61, 1990- 1.83, 1991- 1.94, 1992- 2.09i/2.06, 1993- 2.14, 1994- 2.18, 1995- 2.21, 1996- 2.26, 1997- 2.30i/2.22, 1998- 2.33, 1999- 2.32, 2000- 2.34, 2001- 2.34i/2.33, 2002- 2.35, 2003- 2.36i/2.34, 2004- 2.37i/2.36, 2005- 2.40i/2.36. pbs: 60m 7.33i '03, 100m 11.42 '99, 110mh 16.23 '99, LJ 7.18 '99; TJ 12.35i '91.
One of the smallest top high jumpers, he equalled the world best of 59cm cleared above own head with his 2.40 to win the 2005 European Indoor title. Is 77-47 v Staffan Strand 1989-2004 per his web site www.scholm.com. Won 8/8 indoors in both 2003 and 2004, also unbeaten in 14 outdoor competitions 2004. 90 competitions over 2.30 from 1997 to March 2006.

Alhaji JENG b. 13 Dec 1981 Banjul, The Gambia 1.85m 77kg. Örgryte IS.
At PV: WJ: '00- 8; EU23: '01- 6; WI: '06- 2
Progress at PV: 1996- 3.90i/3.60, 1997- 4.27, 1998- 4.80, 1999- 5.30, 2000- 5.40, 2001- 5.49, 2002- 5.41, 2003- 5.56i/5.40, 2004- 5.61, 2005- 5.75, 2006- 5.80i. pbs: 60mh 8.53i '03, 110mh 15.43 '01, HJ 2.00i '03, 1.94 '97; LJ 7.07i '03, Hep 5668i '03.
Family moved to Swden when he was a few months old.

Patrik KRISTIANSSON b. 3 Jun 1977 Göteborg 1.92m 83kg. KA 2 IF.
At PV: OG: '00/04- dnq 20=/20; WCh: '99- dnq 29=, '01- dnq 14, '03- 3, '05- 9; EC: '98- nh, '02- 4; WJ: '96- 2; EJ: '95- 6; WI: '04- 4; EI: '02- 2; ECp: '00-04: 3/2. Swedish champion 1998, 2001-03.
Two Swedish pole vault records 2001-02.
Progress at PV: 1989- 2.20, 1990- 3.08, 1991-3.50, 1992- 4.40, 1993- 4.70/4.80ex, 1994- 5.06/5.10ex, 1995- 5.30, 1996- 5.31, 1997- 5.51i/5.45, 1998- 5.77, 1999- 5.71, 2000- 5.70, 2001- 5.83, 2002- 5.85, 2003- 5.85, 2004- 5.80, 2005- 5.73. pbs: 110mh 15.96 '99, HJ 1.88 '99, LJ 6.64 '01, Dec 6412 '99.

Robert KRONBERG b. 15 Aug 1976 Göteborg 1.81m 86kg. IF Kville.
At 110mh: OG: '00- 8, '04- sf; WCh: '97/99- qf, '01- 5, '03/05- sf; EC: '02- 7; WJ: '94- sf; EJ: '95- 2; WUG: '01- 3; ECp: '00-04: 3/1. At 60mh: WI: '01-03-04: 4/7/6; EI: '00-02-05: 6/5/3. Won Swedish 110mh 1997-2005.
Three Swedish 110mh records 2001.
Progress at 110mh: 1993- 15.09, 1994- 14.21, 1995- 14.06, 1996- 13.97, 1997- 13.63, 1998- 13.61, 1999- 13.58, 2000- 13.36, 2001- 13.35, 2002- 13.42, 2003- 13.46, 2004- 13.39, 2005- 13.43. pbs: 60m 6.77i '04, 100m 10.60 '04, 200m 22.31 '98, 50mh 6.46i '01, 60mh 7.54i '01, HJ 1.90 '95, LJ 7.52 '97, TJ 14.23 '94.

Christian OLSSON b. 25 Jan 1980 Göteborg 1.92m 74kg. Örgryte IS.
At TJ (/HJ): OG: '00- dnq 17, '04- 1; WCh: '01- 2, '03- 1; EC: '02- 1; EU23: '01- 1; EJ: '99- 2/1; WI: '03- 1, '04- 1; EI: '02- 1; WCp: '02- 3; ECp: '00-04: 4/1. Won WAF 2003, GP 2002, Swedish TJ 2000-01, 2003.
Six Swedish triple jump records 2001-04. WIR 2004.
Progress at TJ: 1995- 12.20w, 1996- 12.44, 1998- 14.48, 1999- 16.30/16.59w, 2000- 16.97, 2001- 17.49, 2002- 17.80i/17.64, 2003- 17.77/17.92w, 2004- 17.83i/17.79. pbs: 110mh 16.21 '98, HJ 2.28i '02, 2.28 '03; PV 4.04 '99, LJ 7.71 '02, 7.84w '03.
Considered himself a high jumper, but took his TJ best from 14.48 to 16.27w in his first competition of 1999 and had a superb season at his new event in 2001 when he was the only man to defeat Jonathan Edwards (and did so twice). He challenged Edwards again in 2002, losing 4-5, and was easily the world number one in 2003, when unbeaten outdoors. First jumped 17m on 14 June 2001, and from then has been under that just twice in 75 meetings to the end of 2004, with 208 17m jumps in all. Shared Golden League jackpot 2004. Missed 2005 season through injury.

Linus THÖRNBLAD b. 6 Mar 1985 Lund 1.80m 76kg. IFK Lund.
At HJ: OG: '04- dnq 24; WJ: '02- dnq, '04- 4; WY: '01- dnq; EU23: '05- 10; EJ: '03- 3; WI: '06- 3.
Progress at HJ: 2000- 1.90i, 2001- 2.06, 2002- 2.19, 2003- 2.30, 2004- 2.27, 2005- 2.31i/2.26, 2006- 2.34i.

Women

Kajsa BERGQVIST b. 12 Oct 1976 Sollentuna 1.75m 59kg. Turebergs FK. Was at Southern Methodist University, USA.
At HJ: OG: '96- dnq 14, '00- 3=; WCh: '95- dnq 17=, 97- 5=, '99- 4=, '01- 3, '03- 3, '05- 1; EC: '98- dnq 14, '02- 1; WJ: '94- 2; EU23: '97- 2; EJ: '93- 8, '95- 2; WI: '97-01-03: 8/1/1; EI: '00- 1, '02- 2=; WCp: '02- 2. Swedish champion 1997-2003, NCAA 1997, 1999.
WIR high jump 2006, ten Swedish records 1997-2003.
Progress at HJ: 1988- 1.38, 1989- 1.56, 1990- 1.61i/1.56, 1991- 1.61, 1992- 1.77, 1993- 1.84, 1994- 1.90, 1995- 1.92i/1.90, 1996- 1.93, 1997- 1.95, 1998- 1.93, 1999- 1.98A, 2000- 2.01, 2001-

2.00, 2002- 2.05, 2003- 2.06, 2004- 2.02i/1.80, 2005- 2.03, 2006- 2.08i. pbs: 100mh 14.98/14.8w '94, LJ 5.73 '95, TJ 11.74 '98, SP 11.85 '96, JT 36.80 '05, Hep 4952 '94.
She tore her left Achilles tendon on her outdoor debut in 2004 and was out for the year, returning with a brilliant unbeaten season in 2005 and extending that into 2006 when she matched the women's record by jumping 33m above her own head for a world indoor record 2.08 at Arnstadt. Her father Gunnar had a 110mh best of 15.0 (1972).

Emma GREEN b. 8 Dec 1984 Bergsjön 1.80m 62kg. Örgryte IS.
At HJ: WCh: '05- 3; WJ: '02- 9; EU23: '05- 2; EJ: '03- 3; EI: '05- 8. Won Swedish HJ 2005 (indoors 2004-05), LJ 2005.
Progress at HJ: 1999- 1.71, 2000- 1.75i/1.73, 2001- 1.82, 2002- 1.82, 2003- 1.86, 2004- 1.90, 2005- 1.97, 2006- 1.96i. pbs: 60m 7.42i '06, 100m 11.84 '06, 11.66w mx '05; 200m 24.16 '05, LJ 6.41 '05, TJ 13.69i '06, 13.39w '05.

Jenny KALLUR b. 16 Feb 1981 Huntington, New York, USA 1.70m 62kg. Falu IK. Was at University of Illinois, USA
At 100mh/4x100mR (200m): OG: '04- h; WCh: '03- hR, '05- 6; EC: '02- h (h); WJ: '98- (sf), '00- 6/3R; EU23: '01- 2, '03- 6; At 60mh: WI: '06- 8; EI: '05- 2. At 100m/200m: EJ: '99- 7/5; EY: '97- 1/-/2R. Swedish champion 100m & 200m 1998, 2002.
Progress at 100mh: 1998- 14.10, 1999- 13.70, 2000- 13.18, 2001- 13.15/13.11w, 2002- 13.42, 2003- 13.04, 2004- 12.88, 2005- 12.85. pbs: 60m 7.28i '05, 100m 11.43 '04, 200m 23.26 '04, 300m 39.57 '97, 60mh 7.92i '05, 400mh 64.78 '99, LJ 5.64 '99, 5.80w '97; Pen 3529i '99, Hep 5021 '01.
Twin sister of Susanna. Their father Anders played for the New York Islanders at ice hockey, winning Stanley Cup four times.

Susanna KALLUR b. 16 Feb 1981 Huntington, New York, USA 1.70m 61kg. Falu IK. Was at University of Illinois, USA,
At 100mh: OG: '04- sf; WCh: '01/03/05- sf; WJ: '98- 3, '00- 1/3R; EC: '02- 7; EU23: '01- 1, '03- 1; EJ: '99- 5. At 60mh: WI: '03-04-06: 7/5/3; EI: '05- 1. Won Swedish 100m 2005, 100mh 1998, 2000, 2002-05
Progress at 100mh: 1997- 14.11, 1998- 13.48, 1999- 13.41, 2000- 13.02, 2001- 12.74, 2002- 12.94, 2003- 12.88, 2004- 12.67, 2005- 12.65. pbs: 50m 6.56i '00, 60m 7.27i '06, 100m 11.42 '05, 200m 23.32 '05, 50mh 6.83i '03, 60mh 7.80i '04, HJ 1.72 '98, PV 3.00i '98, LJ 6.11 '01, TJ 11.67i '97, 11.22 '98; SP 10.80i '02, Pen 3917i '02, Hep 5282 '98.

Carolina KLÜFT b. 2 Feb 1983 Borås 1.78m 65kg. IFK Växjö.
At Hep: OG: '04- 1 (11 LJ); WCh: '03- 1, '05- 1; EC: '02-1; WJ: '00- 1, '02- 1; EJ: '01- 1. At Hep: WI: '03- 1; EI: '02- 3, '05- 1. At LJ: EU23: '03- 1, '05- 1; WI: '04- 3. Won SWE 100m 2003-04, 200m 2005, HJ 2004, LJ 2001-02, Hep 2001.
Two world junior heptathlon records 2002, six Swedish records 2002-03.
Progress at LJ, Hep: 1998- 5.75, 1999- 6.13, 5162; 2000- 6.23, 6056; 2001- 6.26/6.33w, 6022; 2002- 6.48/6.59w, 6542; 2003- 6.86, 7001; 2004- 6.97, 6952; 2005- 6.87/6.92w, 6887. pbs: 60m 7.40i '05, 100m 11.48 '04, 200m 22.98 '03, 400m 53.17 '02, 800m 2:08.89 '05, 60mh 8.19i '03, 100mh 13.15 '05, HJ 1.94 '03, PV 3.16 '01, TJ 13.87 '04, SP 15.02 '05, DT 33.96 '00, JT 50.24 '03, Pen 4948i '05.
Eleven gold medals and two bronze in 14 major championship competitions and won all her three heptathlons each year 2002-05. Won IAAF 'Rising Star' award for women in 2002, when she was the world's top heptathlete while still a junior. Added 398 points to her Swedish indoor record when she won 2003 World Indoor title with 4933, setting pbs at first four events. Won Götzis and set five pbs en route to winning World title (for third on world all-time list) in 2003. Won the IAAF Combined Events Challenge each year 2003-05. Her winning margin at the Athens Olympics was the widest ever, 517 points. Set Swedish LJ record at 6.92 twice at World indoors 2004. Her mother Ingalill had long jump pb 6.09/6.20w (1979).

SWITZERLAND

Governing body: Schweizerischer Leichtathletikverband (SLV), 43/Postfach 45, 3250 Lyss. Formed 1905 as Athletischer Ausschuss des Schweizerischen Fussball-Verbandes.

National Championships first held in 1906 (men), 1934 (women). **2005 Champions**: **Men**: 100m: Andreas Baumann 10.43, 200m: Marc Schneeberger 20.89, 400m: Pierre Lavanchy 45.49, 800m: Christian Niederberger 1:54.59, 1500m: Mirco Zwahlen 3:46.61, 5000m: Philipp Bandi 14:08.46, 10,000m: Philipp Rist 30:40.56, HMar: Jérôme Schaffner 66:58, Mar: Christoph Seiler 2:28:32, 3000mSt: Markus Hagmann 8:54.69, 110mh: Andreas Kundert 14.10, 400mh: Chritsian Grossenbacher 50.08, HJ: Martin Günther GER 2.18, PV: Boris Zengaffinen 5.20, LJ: Julien Fivaz 7.54, TJ: Alexander Martínez CUB 16.55, SP: Gerardo Maurer 15.80, DT: Peter Müller 50.24, HT: Patric Suter 74.69, JT: Felix Loretz 75.38, Dec: David Gervasi 7465. 10,000mW/20kmW/50kmW: Nicolas Perrier 45:32.1/1:31:32/4:27:04, 35kmW: Bruno Grandjean 2:59:32. **Women**: 100m: Fabienne Weyermann 11.75, 200m: Mirjam Hess 24.23, 400m: Renate Kohler 54.90, 800m: Sibylle Dürrenmatt 2:08.18, 1500m: Christina Carruzzo 4:20.52, 5000m: Vera Notz-Umberg 16:06.81, HMar: Sabine Fischer 76:06, Mar: Rita Born 2:53:47, 100mh: Sabrina Altermatt 13.47w, 400mh: Martina Naef 58.38, HJ: Corinne Müller 1.91, PV: Nadine Rohr 4.20, LJ: Claudine Müller 6.20, TJ: Daniela Miescher 12.95, SP: Valerie Glayre-Maes 13.71, DT: Karin Hagmann 53.08, HT: Margrit

Duss 52.10, JT: Catherine Manigley 47.68, Hep: Sylvie Dufour 5706, 5000mW/10kmW/20kmW: Laura Polli 22:42.2/47:18/1:39:09.

Alexander MARTÍNEZ b. 23 Aug 1977 Nueva Gerona, Isla de la Juventud 1.84m 82kg. LC Zürich.
At TJ: 3rd GP 2002.
Progress at TJ: 1995- 15.53, 1996- 15.88, 1998- 16.67, 1999- 16.50, 2000- 16.80, 2001- 17.06, 2002- 17.32, 2003- 17.06, 2004- 17.09, 2005- 17.51. pb LJ 7.60 '05.
Lives in Zürich, has a Swiss wife Marion (with whom he has won international salsa dancing competitions) and gained Swiss citizenship on 22 Feb 2006. He set a Swiss indoor record of 16.70 four days later.

TANZANIA

Governing body: Tanzania Amateur Athletic Association, PO Box 2172, Dar es Salaam. Founded 1954.
National Champions 2005: **Men**: 800m/1500m: Daniel Chopa 1:51.49/3:57.33, 5000m/10,000m: Fabiano Joseph 13:57.90/28:33.44, HMar: John Yuda 61:40, 3000mSt: Musanduki Mohamed 9:15.36, DT: Ally Sefu 47.50. **Women**: 800m: Lwiza John 2:07.87, 1500m: Ruhama Shauri 4:31.31, 5000m: Restituta Joseph 16:25.88.

Christopher ISEGWE Njug'unda b. 22 Feb 1976 Arusha 1.68m 56kg.
At Mar: WCh: '05- 2; CG: '06- dnf. World HMar: '96- 20.
Progress at Mar: 2004- 2:10:56, 2005- 2:10:21. pbs: 10,000m 29:41.12 '05, HMar 62:17 '03.
Won Belgrade marathon and 2nd Beijing 2004.

Fabiano JOSEPH Naasi b. 24 Dec 1985 Babati, Mbulu district 1.58m 48kg. Iraqw.
At 10,000m (/5000m): OG: '04- 10/h; WCh: '03- 13, '05- (15); CG: '06- 3/5; WJ: '04- (6). World HMar: '03-04-05: 2/2/1; CC: '03-04: 19/7. Won AAA 10,000m 2003.
Progress at 10,000m: 2002- 29:04.7, 2003- 27:32.63, 2004- 28:01.94, 2005- 28:33.44, 2006- 27:51.99. pbs: 3000m 7:54.12 '04, 5000m 13:15.90 '04, HMar 60:52 '03.

Samson RAMADHANI Nyonyi b. 22 Feb 1976 Arusha 1.68m 56kg.
At Mar: OG: '04- 40; WCh: '03- 15, '05- 5; CG: '06- 1. At 1500m: WJ: '00- h.
Equalled TAN marathon record 2003
Progress at Mar: 2003- 2:08:01, 2004- 2:10:38, 2005- 2:12:08, 2006- 2:11:29. pbs: 10km Rd 28:52 '01, HMar 61:05 '02.
Won Beppu marathon 2003.

John YUDA Msuri b. 9 Jun 1979 Dodoma 1.62m 53kg.
At 10,000m: OG: '04- dnf; WCh: '03- 12, '05- 18; CG: '02- 3. At 5000m: AfG: '03- 5. World HMar: 01-02-03-05: 3/3/5/6; CC: '01- 14 (4k), '02- 2. Won TAN HMar 2001.
Tanzanian records 5000m & 10,000m 2002.
At 5000m, 10,000m: 2002- 13:03.62, 27:06.17; 2003- 13:18.0, 27:09.83; 2005- 27:33.84. pbs: HMar 60:02 '02, Mar 2:10:13 '04.
Ninth on marathon debut, London 2004. Married Hawa Hamisi Hussein in September 2002.

Women

Zakia MRISHO b. 19 Feb 1984 1.65m 45kg. US Quercia Rovereto, Italy.
At 5000m: WCh: '05- 6; CG: '06- 8. World CC: '05- 20.
Tanzanian records 3000m & 5000m (3) 2005.
Progress at 5000m: 2002- 16:28.4, 2004- 15:40.00i/16:00.46, 2005- 14:43.87. pbs: 1500m 4:10.47 '05, 3000m 8:39.91 '05, 10,000m 33:19.25 '02, 10km Rd 32:30 '03.

TRINIDAD & TOBAGO

Governing body: National Amateur Athletic Association of Trinidad & Tobago, PO Box 605, Port of Spain, Trinidad. Fd. 1945, reformed 1971.
National Champions 2005: **Men**: 100m: Marc Burns 9.96, 200m: Aaron Armstrong 19.98w, 400m: Damion Barry 45.55, 800m: Sheridan Kirk 1:46.40, 1500m: Denzil Ramirez 3:58.38, 5000m: Curtis Cox 15:22.26, 110mh/400mh: Sanchez Ross 14.20/52.49, HJ: James Grayman ANT 2.03, LJ: Keita Cline IVB 7.53, TJ: Chris Hercules USA 16.01, SP: Adonson Shallow STV 15.28, DT: Eric Matthias IVB 50.96, JT: Andre Andrews 51.49. **Women**: 100m/200m: Kelliann Baptiste 11.17/22.94, 400m: Josanne Lucas 53.59, 800m: Melissa de Leon 2:04.09, 1500m: Pilar McShine 4:36.00, 3000m: Janil Williams ANT 10:37.53, 400mh: Aisha George 62.00, HJ/LJ: Rhonda Watkins 1.80/6.19w, TJ: Sheron Mark 12.54, SP: Candice Scott 16.38, DT: Annie Alexander 44.94, JT: Kwema Phillander 36.10, Hep: Cuquie Melville 4568.

Aaron ARMSTRONG b. 14 Oct 1977 1.73m 78kg. Rebirth. Studied sociology at University of Florida.
At 200m/4x100mR: WCh 05- sf/2R; CG: '06- 5. Won TRI 2005.
Progress at 200m: 1997- 20.90, 1998- 20.32w, 1999- 20.08, 2000- 20.63/20.42Aw, 2001- 20.58/20.37w, 2002- 20.49, 2003- 20.60, 2004- 20.50, 2005- 20.35/19.98w. pbs: 55m 6.21i '99, 60m 6.62i '05, 100m 10.04/10.00w '05, 9.8w '99; 400m 47.65 '98, 400mh 51.68 '02.
Son of TRI Olympian Ainsley Armstrong (sf 200m 1972 and 100m 1976) and Debra Edwards USA (OG: h 400m 1972, sf 200m 1976). He grew up in the USA but switched allegiance to TRI in 2005. Paternal grandfather Ernest Armstrong was TRI 100y champion 1951 with pbs were 100y 9.9 '52, 100m 11.0 '49 and 220y 22.6 '51/

Darrel BROWN b. 7 Jan 1983 Arima 1.84m 79kg. Silver Bullet/Nike. Student at Southern

Union CC, Alabama, USA.
At 100m/4x100mR: OG: '04- 7R; WCh: '01- 2R, '03- 2, '05- sf/2R; CG: '06- qf; WJ: '00- 4; 02- 1/3R; WY: '01- 1; PAm: '03- 2R. Won CAC 100m 2005, CAC-J 100m 2000, 2002; 200m 2000; TRI 100m 2001.
World junior 100m record 2003.
Progress at 100m, 200m: 1998- 10.79, 22.41; 1999- 10.67, 21.20; 2000- 10.34, 21.14/20.76w; 2001- 10.24, 20.41; 2002- 10.09, 20.97; 2003- 10.01, 2004- 10.11A, 2005- 9.99, 20.61. pbs: 55m 6.15i '03, 60m 6.59i '04.
Set world age records for 100m at 15, 16, 17 and 18, the last a WJR 10.01 in the quarter-finals before his silver medal in the final in 2003; the youngest 100m medallist in World Championship history. At 16 years 305 days for the 4x100m bronze he is the youngest ever World medallist. Elder brother Darron has 100m pb 10.49 '04.

Marc BURNS b. 7 Jan 1983 1.85m 79kg. Rebirth/ adidas.
At 100m/4x100mR: OG: '04- h; WCh: '01- 2R, '03- h, '05- 7/2R; CG: '06- 3; WJ: '00- 3; 02- 2/3R; PAm: '03- 2R. Won WAF 2005, PAm-J 2001, TRI 2002, 2005.
Progress at 100m: 1998- 10.51, 2000- 10.40, 2001- 10.28, 2002- 10.18, 2003- 10.24, 2004- 10.12/9.99w, 2005- 9.96. pbs: 60m 6.61i '04, 200m 20.57 '05.

Women

Candice SCOTT b. 17 Sep 1980 1.80m 100kg. Was at University of Florida.
At HT: OG: '04- 9; WCh: '03- 9, '05- 8; CG: '02- 5; PAm: '03- 3. Won CAC 2005, NCAA 2003-04, indoor Wt 2002, 2004.
TRI hammer records 2001-05, CAC 20lb Wt bests.
Progress at HT: 2001- 54.70, 2002- 63.26, 2003- 69.79, 2004- 69.94, 2005- 71.45. pbs: SP 17.65i '05, 17.28 '04; 20lbWt 24.21i '05.

TURKEY

Governing body: Türkiye Atletizm Federasyonu, 19 mayis Spor Kompleksi, Ulus-Ankara. Founded 1922.
National Champions 2005: **Men**: 100m/200m: Ismail Arslan 10.54/21.69, 400m/400mh: Tuncay Örs 48.55/51.78, 800m: Ali Dereli 1:52.93, 1500m/3000m: Halil Akkas 3:40.61/7:54.60, 5000m: Ali Topkara 14:36.68, 10,000m: Zekeriya Dikmener 32:38.08, HMar: Abdülkadir Türk 65:57, 3000mSt: Bilal Yerlikaya 9:18.87, 110mh: Demirhan Çemberci 14.46, HJ: Ilker Azazi 2.10, PV: Abdullah Sari 4.50, LJ/TJ: Ferhat Çiçek 7.81/16.14, SP: Yavuz Kalyoncu 14.80, DT: Kamil Ulas Övünc 45.41, HT: Ali Mert Bozkurt 48.34, JT: Sevket Tas 68.50, Dec: Serdar Demirci 5843, 20kmW: Recep Celik 1:32:30. **Women**: 100m: Saliha Özyurt 11.59, 200m: Birsen Yavuz-Bekgöz 24.01, 400m: Pınar Saka 54.33, 800m: Zeynep Aydemir 2:11.65, 1500m: Arzu Berk 4:30.96, 3000m: Aysen Özkul 10:13.20, 5000m: Nilay Esen 18:49.78, HMar: Lale Öztürk 78:54, 3000mSt: Fadime Suna 11:38.52, 100mh: Esen Kızılda 13.58, 400mh: Özge Gürler 57.98, HJ: Deniz Öz 1.75, PV: Songül Kilic 3.40, LJ: Nuray Bas 6.11, TJ: Aysegül Baklacı 13.09, SP: Filiz Kadogan 17.09, DT: Hediye Gürbüzogulları 52.25, HT: Zübeyde Yıldız 58.55, JT: Berna Demirci 54.13, Hep: Fatma Cakır 3880, 20kmW: Handan Kocyigit 1:53:40.

Esref APAK b. 3 Jan 1982 Kalecik 1.86m 100kg. ENKA.
At HT: OG: '04- 3; WCh: '05- dnq 18; WJ: '00- 1; EU23: '03- 2; EJ: '01- 3; WUG: '05- 2; won Med G 2005, Turkish 2001-03.
20 Turkish hammer records 2000-05.
Progress at HT: 1999- 57.93, 2000- 69.97, 2001- 72.82, 2002- 73.24, 2003- 77.57, 2004- 81.27, 2005- 81.45.

Women

Elvan ABEYLEGESSE b. 11 Sep 1982 Addis Adaba, Ethiopia 1.59m 40kg. Enka.
At (1500m)/5000m: OG: '04- 8/12; WCh: '03- 5; EC: '02- 7; WJ: '00- 6/6; WY: '99- (5 3000m); EU23: '03- 1; EJ: '99- 2, '01- 1/1. Won WAF 5000m 2003-04. World CC: '99- 9J; Eur CC: '00-01-02-03: 3J/1J/3/2.
World 5000m record 2004. Turkish records 2000m 2003, 3000m 2002.
Progress at 1500m, 5000m: 1999- 4:24.1, 16:06.40; 2000- 4:18.7, 16:33.77; 2001- 4:11.31, 15:21.12; 2002- 4:11.00, 15:00.49; 2003- 4:07.25, 14:53.56; 2004- 3:58.28, 14:24.68; 2005- 15:08.59. pbs: 800m 2:07.10 '04, 2000m 5:33.83 '03, 3000m 8:31.94 '02, 10,000m 33:29.20 '01.
Previously known as Hewan Abeye ETH, then as Elvan Can on move to Turkey. In 2004 she became the first Turkish athlete to set a world record.

UGANDA

Governing body: Uganda Athletics Federation, PO Box 22726, Kampala. Founded 1925.

Boniface KIPROP b. 12 Oct 1985 Kabchorwa District 1.67m 53kg. Kalenjin.
At (5000m)/10,000m): OG: '04- 4; WCh: '03- (h), '05- 11/4; CG: '06- 1; WJ: '04- 5/1; AfG: '03- 6/4; Af-J: '01- 1/2, '03- 1/1; World CC: '00-02-03-04-05-06: 27J/3J/2J/2J/7/22.
World junior 10,000m record 2004. Ugandan records 5000m (5) 10,000m (3) 2003-05.
Progress at 5000m, 10,000m: 2001- 14:06.93, 28:45.76; 2002-13:55.5, 2003- 13:16.21, 27:15.88; 2004- 13:05.47, 27:04.00; 2005- 12:58.43/26:39.77. pb 3000m 7:47.16 '03.
Set world age 17 and 18 age records for 10,000m 2003-04. Previously known as Boniface Toroitich Tirop. Brother Martin Toroitich (11 WJ CC 2002).

Women

Dorcus INZIKURU b. 2 Feb 1982 Veurra, Arua district 1.58m 49kg. Camelot, Italy.
At 3000mSt: WCh: '05- 1; CG: '06- 1. At 5000m: OG: '04- h; WCh: '03- h; WJ: '00- 1; CG: '02- 4; AfG: '99- 6, '03- 2; AfCh: '02- 2; won WAF 2005. At 3000m: WY: '99- 8. World CC: '00- 10J, '05- 18 4k.
Five African 3000mSt records 2003-05, Commonwealth 2004; Ugandan 3000m 2002-2003, 5000m 1999-2004.
Progress at 5000m, 3000mSt: 1998- 17:10.9, 1999- 16:05.5, 2000- 16:12.0, 2002- 15:18.01, 2003- 15:54.81, 9:39.51; 2004- 15:05.30, 9:29.30; 2005- 9:15.04, 2006- 9:19.51. pbs: 800m 2:03.00 '03, 1500m 4:14.90 '03, 1M 4:36.05 '03, 3000m 8:46.29 '03, 2000mSt 6:04.46 '05 (world best).
Uganda's first World and Comonwealth champion. Her father Jackson Luluwa was a leading distance runner in Uganda. Married to Martin Boscop Acidri, Italian doctor.

UKRAINE

Governing body: Ukrainian Athletic Federation, Esplanadnaya Str. 42, Kiev 19 (P.O. Box 607). Founded 1991. **National Champions 2005**: **Men**: 100m: Anatoliy Dovhal 10.33, 200m: Dmytro Hluschenko 20.83, 400m: Andriy Tverdostup 46.07, 800m: Ivan Heshko 1:46.19, 1500m: Serhiy Lebid 3:38.44, 5000/10,000mm: Vasyl Matviychuk 13:38.00/28:59.91, 3000mSt: Vadym Slobodenyuk 8:30.49, 110mh: Serhiy Demydyuk 13.89, 400mh: Hennadiy Horbenko 50.85, HJ: Yuriy Krimarenko 2.25, PV: Olexandr Korchmid 5.60, LJ: Volodymyr Zyuskov 8.31, TJ: Viktor Yastrebov 16.83, SP: Yuriy Bilonoh 20.76, DT: Kyrylo Chuprynin 59.34, HT: Andriy Skvaruk 81.00, JT: Oleh Statsenko 78.02, Dec: Yuriy Blonsky 7546, 20kmW: Andrey Kovenko 1:22:26, 50kmW: Aleksey Shelest 3:56:23. **Women**: 100m: Iryna Shtanhyeyeva 11.55, 200m: Maryna Maydanova 23.22, 400m: Antonina Yefremova 51.48, 800m: Nelya Neporadna 2:02.28, 1500m: Tetyana Kryvobok 4:06.94, 5000m: Maryna Dubrova 15:38.72, 10,000m: Nataliya Berkut 33:02.68, 3000mSt: Valentyna Horpynych 9:49.73, 100mh: Yevheniya Snihur 13.50, 400mh: Anastasiya Rabchenyuk 56.56, HJ: Iryna Myhalchenko 1.97, PV: Anzhela Balakhonova 4.20, LJ: Viktoriya Molchanova 6.59, TJ: Olexandra Stadnyuk 13.94, SP: Tetyana Nasonova 17.45, DT: Olena Antonova 61.88, HT: Iryna Sekachova 70.30, JT: Olha Ivankova 57.06, Hep: Yuliya Akulenko 6103, 20kmW: Vera Zolzilya 1:32:26.
Note that the names above use Ukrainian language spellings/transliterations, although at present we continue to use mostly Russian transliterations in lists in this Annual.

Yuriy BELONOG (Bilonog) b. 9 Mar 1974 Belopol'ye 2.00m 135kg. Odessa Dyn & Sporting Clube de Portugal. Sports instructor.
At SP: OG: '00- 5, '04- 1; WCh: '97- 4, '99- 5, '01- 6, '03- 3 (dnq DT), '05- 4; EC: '98- 3, '02- 1; WI: '95-7-9-01-03-04: 5/1/3/8/3/8; WJ: '92- 1; WUG: '95- 1, '97- 1, '01- 2; WCp: '02- 5; ECp: '96- 3, '02- 1. 2nd GP 1998, 2002; 2nd overall 2000. Won UKR SP 2001, 2003, 2005; DT 2001, 2003.
UKR shot records 2000 & 2003.
Progress at SP: 1990- 15.60, 1991- 17.91, 1992- 19.02, 1993- 18.39, 1994- 18.72, 1995- 20.05, 1996- 21.20i/20.05, 1997- 21.02i/20.75, 1998- 20.92, 1999- 20.89i/20.65, 2000- 21.64, 2001- 20.98, 2002- 21.37, 2003- 21.81, 2004- 21.16, 2005- 20.93. pb DT 65.53 '03.
Mother-in-law Valentina Korsak: DT 63.92 '84.

Ivan GESHKO (Heshko) b. 19 Aug 1979 Kitsmany 1.80m 70kg.
At 1500m (/800m): OG: '00- h, '04- 5/sf; WCh: '03- 3, '05- 4; EC: '02- h; WJ: '98- 11/h; EU23: '99- 4, '01- 2; WI: '03-04-06: 5/2/1; EI: '05- 1; WUG: '05- 1; ECp: '02- 5/8. Won WAF 1500m 2004-05, UKR 800m 2003, 2005; 1500m 2000-04.
UKR records at 1500m & 1M 2004.
Progress at 1500m: 1996- 3:54.94, 1997- 3:46.21, 1998- 3:43.56, 1999-3:42.33, 2000- 3:38.48, 2001- 3:37.10, 2002- 3:37.07, 2003- 3:32.01, 2004- 3:30.33, 2005- 3:31.91. pb 800m 1:45.41 '03, 1000m 2:19.04 '01, 1M 3:50.04 '04, 2000m 5:03.91 '00, 3000m 7:52.33 '01.

Yuriy KRIMARENKO b. 11 Aug 1983 1.87m 65kg.
At HJ: WCh: '05- 1; EU23: '05- 3. UKR champion 2005.
Progress at HJ: 2000- 2.05, 2001- 2.15, 2002- 2.15, 2003- 2.22, 2004- 2.23, 2005- 2.33.

Aleksandr KRYKUN b. 1 Mar 1968 Leipzig, GDR 1.94m 130kg. Kolos Uman.
At HT: OG: '96- 3, '00/04- dnq 20/18; WCh: '95- 10, '97- 8, '01/03- dnq 23/21; EC: '94- 6, '98- 11, '02- dnq 18; EJ: '87- 2; WUG: '95- 2. UKR champion 2002.
Progress at HT: 1986- 68.34, 1987- 71.74, 1988- 71.40, 1989- 71.36, 1990- 70.52, 1991- 73.32, 1992- 75.12, 1993- 80.36, 1994- 79.02, 1995- 77.06, 1996- 80.02, 1997- 79.34, 1998- 76.23, 2000- 79.52, 2001- 80.38, 2002- 81.59, 2003- 79.35, 2004- 81.66, 2005- 72.90.

Sergey LEBED (Serhiy Lebid) b. 15 Jul 1975 Pridneprovsk 1.80m 65kg. Donetsk ZS. Based in Italy.
At 5000m: OG: '00- 7, 04- h; WCh: '99/01/05- h; EC: '98- 15, '02- 3; WUG: '99- 1, '01- 1, '03- 1; EU23: '97- 7 (10,000m 2). At 3000m: EI: '98- 5; WCp: '02- 7. World CC: '00-01-05: 8/2/14; 4k: '01- 10; Eur CC: '95-7-8-9-00-01-02-03-04-05: 11/3/1/7/2/1/1/1/1/1. Won UKR 1500m 1998, 2005; 5000m 1995-6, 1999-2001, 2003-04; 10,000m 2003.
UKR records 3000m 2002, 5000m (2) 2001-02, HMar (2) 2003.
Progress at 5000m: 1993- 14:23.54, 1994- 14:11.27, 1995- 13:52.39, 1996- 13:39.31, 1997- 13:50.51,

1998- 13:30.23, 1999- 13:18.18, 2000- 13:27.53, 2001- 13:14.51, 2002- 13:10.78, 2003- 13:15.15, 2004- 13:13.03, 2005- 13:12.35. pbs: 1500m 3:38.44 '05, 3000m 7:35.06 '02, 10,000m 28:12.62 '03, HMar 61:49 '03.
Has run in all 12 European CC Championships with a record six wins. Married Yelena Gorodnichova (1500m 4:05.78 '99) on 23 April 2003.

Andrey SKVARUK b. 9 Mar 1967 Brodivski 1.84m 109kg. Rovno ZS.
At HT: OG: '96- 4, '00- 10; WCh: '93- nt, '97- 2, '99- 5, '01- 5, '03- 4, '05- 10; EC: '94- 11, '98- dnq 14, '02- 5; ECp: '93-4-02: 3/2/2. Won GP 2000. UKR champion 1992, 1994-6, 2001, 2003, 2005.
Progress at HT: 1985- 65.42, 1986- 72.54, 1989- 73.60, 1990- 77.24, 1991- 71.60, 1992- 80.22, 1993- 80.80, 1994- 81.72, 1995- 78.00, 1996- 80.52, 1997- 81.46, 1998- 78.96, 1999- 80.75, 2000- 81.43, 2001- 82.34, 2002- 82.62, 2003- 81.74, 2005- 81.00.

Andrey (Andriy) **SOKOLOVSKIY** b. 16 Jul 1978 Moskva, Russia 1.96m 80kg. Vinnista Dyn. Sports instructor.
At HJ: OG: '00- dnq 16=, '04- 5; WCh: '99/01- dnq 27=/21=, '03- 8, '05-= 13; WI: '99-01-03-04-06: 6=/2/8/7/6; EU23: '99- 2; EI: '02- 4; ECp: '02- 4. UKR champion 2000-01, 2003-04.
Progress at HJ: 1997- 2.10, 1998- 2.22, 1999- 2.32, 2000- 2.28, 2001- 2.35i/2.34, 2002- 2.36, 2003- 2.33, 2004- 2.35, 2005- 2.38.

Ruslan YEREMENKO b. 31 Jul 1978 Brovary 1.93m 78kg. Kyiv area Dyn.
At PV: OG: '04- 13=; UKR champion 2001, 2004.
Progress at PV: 1999- 5.20, 2000- 5.60sq/5.40, 2001- 5.70, 2002- 5.80i, 2003- 5.63i, 2004- 5.70, 2005- 5.84i/5.60/5.80ex, 2006- 5.70i.

Denis YURCHENKO b. 27 Jan 1978 Donetsk 1.74m 74kg. Donetsk Dyn.
At PV: OG: '00- dnq, '04- 9=; WCh: '03- 6=, '05- dnq 17=; EC: '02- 6=; EJ: '97- nh; WI: '03- 3, '06- nh; EI: '05- 2; ECp: '02- 2=. Won UKR 2000, 2002-03.
Progress at PV: 1997- 5.20, 1998- 5.50, 1999- 5.59, 2000- 5.72, 2001- 5.70i/5.65/5.71ex, 2002- 5.75, 2003- 5.81, 2004- 5.75i/5.70/5.75ex, 2005- 5.85i/5.75, 2006- 5.70i.

Volodomyr (Vladimir) **ZYUSKOV** b. 29 Aug 1981 Donetsk 1.90m 75kg. Donetsk Dyn.
At LJ: OG: '04- dnq 18; WCh: '03- 6, '05- 8; EC: '02- dnq; WJ: '00- 2; EU23: '01- 2, '03- 2; WI: '03- 5, '04- 5; EI: '02- 6, '05- 3; WUG: '01- 4, '05- 1. UKR champion 2001-05.
Progress at LJ: 1998- 6.97, 1999- 7.69, 2000- 7.84, 2001- 8.13, 2002- 8.10, 2003- 8.22, 2004- 8.23, 2005- 8.31. pb 100m 10.4 '03.

Women

Yelena (Olena) **ANTONOVA** b. 16 Jun 1972 Nikopol 1.82m 95kg. Dnepropetrovsk U.
At DT: OG: '96/00- dnq 29/13, '04- 5; WCh: '97- dnq 13, '99- 7, '01- dnq 16, '03- 4, '05- 8; EC: '98- 11; EJ: '91- 3; WUG: '97- 4; ECp: '97-8-00-05: 3/3/6/2. UKR champion 1995-2005.
Progress at DT: 1989- 55.84, 1990- 57.30, 1991- 57.12, 1992- 61.94, 1993- 58.34, 1994- 59.80, 1995- 61.54, 1996- 63.60, 1997- 61.62, 1998- 65.44, 1999- 64.32, 2000- 66.67, 2001- 64.20, 2002- 63.40, 2003- 65.90, 2004- 67.30, 2005- 65.89. pb HT 56.28 '95.

Zhanna BLOCK b. 6 Jul 1972 Nezhin, near Chernigov 1.64m 62kg. née Tarnopolskaya, then Pintusevich. Kiev Dyn.
At 100m (/200m): OG: '96- 8/qf, '00- 5/8, '04- sf; WCh: '93- sf, '95- 5/h, '97- 2/1, '99- 4/qf, '01- 1, '03- 2/4, '05- sf; EC: '94- 2/2/4R, '98- 4/2; EJ: '91- 1/1/4R/2 4x400mR; WCp: '98- 4/3; ECp: '93- 3/4, '94- 1/1R. At 60m: WI: '93-03-06: 3/1/6; EI: '92- 1. Won UKR 100m 1994-5.
WIR 50m at 6.09 for a few minutes in 1993. UKR records: 100m (5) 1994-2001, 200m 1997.
Progress at 100m, 200m: 1987- 11.8, 1988- 11.75/11.5, 23.75; 1989- 11.64/11.5, 24.03; 1990- 11.99, 1991- 11.29/11.0, 23.56; 1992- 11.17, 1993- 11.08, 22.79; 1994- 10.99, 22.66; 1995- 11.01, 22.71/22.64w; 1996- 11.07, 23.15; 1997- 10.85/10.6, 22.17A/22.32; 1998- 10.92/10.9A, 22.35A/22.46; 1999- 10.94, 22.42; 2000- 10.93, 22.66; 2001- 10.82, 22.74; 2002- 10.83, 22.24; 2003- 10.99, 22.61; 2004- 11.23, 2005- 11.18, 22.98. pbs: 50m 6.03+ '97, 60m 6.97+ '97, 7.04i '03.
She won the 1997 World title at 200m in 22.32, five days after she thought that she had won the 100m, only for the photo-finish to show that Marion Jones had held on to beat her 10.83 to 10.85. Four years later it was the other way round, as she beat Jones 10.82 to 10.85. Married athletics agent Mark Block in January 1999. Formerly married to Igor Pintusevich (3rd WJ 110mh 1992).

Lyudmila BLONSKA(YA) b. 9 Nov 1977 1.75m 62kg. née Shevchuk.
At Hep: EC: '02- 13; WUG: '05- 1. At Pen: WI: '06- 1.
Progress at Hep: 1997- 4809, 1998- 5590, 1999- 5765, 2000- 5592, 2002- 6039, 2003- 6316/6425 dq, 2005- 6378. pbs: 200m 23.97 '03, 800m 2:13.48 '05, 2:13.29dq '03; 60mh 8.29i '06, 100mh 13.38 '05, HJ 1.89 '99, LJ 6.76 '05, SP 13.03 '05, JT 46.17 '03, Pen 4685i '06.
Two-year drugs ban from 8 June 2003.

Natalya DOBRINSKA (Dobrynska) b. 29 May 1982 Khmelnitsky 1.82m 77kg. Vinnitsa K.
At Hep: OG: '04- 8; WCh: '05- 9; EU23: '03- 5; EJ: '01- 10. At Pen: WI: '04- 2; EI: '05- 3.
Progress at Hep: 1999- 5226, 2000- 5322, 2001- 5742, 2002- 5936, 2003- 5877, 2004- 6387, 2005- 6299. pbs: 100m 11.60/11.2 '95, 200m 24.84 '05, 24.61w '04; 800m 2:15.38 '04, 60mh 8.42i '05, 100mh 13.83 '04, 13.7 '03, 13.71w '05; HJ 1.85 '05, LJ 6.43i '04, 6.35/6.49w '05; SP 16.23 '04, JT 47.24 '04, Pen 4727i '04.
Four pbs en route to UKR pentathlon record 4727 and WI silver medal 2004.

Yelena (Olena) **KRASOVSKA(YA)** b. 17 Aug 1976 Kyiv 1.76m 65kg. née Ovcharova. Kyiv Dyn.
At 100mh: OG: '96- qf, '00- sf, '04- 2; WCh: '95/01/03- h, '05- sf; EC: '98- h, '02- 2; EJ: '95- 1; WUG: '95- 2, '99- 4; WCp: '02- 4; ECp: '95-02-04: 2/5/1. UKR champion 1995, 1998-2004. At 60mh: EI: '00- 3.
European Junior 100mh record 1995.
Progress at 100mh: 1992- 14.5, 1993- 13.98, 1994- 13.29/13.1, 1995- 12.88, 1996- 13.03, 1997- 13.39/12.8, 1998- 12.92/12.9, 1999- 12.99, 2000- 12.82, 2001- 12.87, 2002- 12.85/12.73w, 2003- 13.06, 2004- 12.45, 2005- 12.75. pbs: 60m 7.35i '01, 7.2i '98; 100m 11.53 '02, 11.2 '95; 200m 23.70 97, 50mh 60mh 8.01i '00, LJ 6.52i '99.

Irina LISHCHINSKA(YA) b. 15 Jan 1976 Makeevka 1.65m 53kg. née Nedelenko. Donetsk U.
At 800m: WCh: '99- h; EC: '98- h; WUG: '97- 1; EU23: '97- 1; ECp: '97- 2, '98- 2. At 1500m: OG: '04- h; WCh: '03- sf; EC: '02- 10; WJ: '94- 6; WI: '03- 5; ECp: '02- 5. Won UKR 800m 1999, 1500m 2001-02, 2004.
Progress at 800m, 1500m: 1993- 2:07.04, 1994- 2:02.6, 1996- 2:05.03, 1997- 2:00.16, 1998- 1:59.15, 1999- 2:00.01, 2001- 2:03.36, 4:05.38; 2002- 2:00.45, 4:03.78; 2003- 2:01.22, 4:02.60; 2004- 2:01.99, 4:03.74; 2005- 2:07.43i, 4:14.71i. pbs: 400m 53.88 '98, 1M 4:28.31 '02, 3000m 9:04.24i '03.

Irina MIKHALCHENKO b. 20 Jan 1972 1.79m 60kg. Kyiv ZS.
At HJ: OG: '00- dnq 29, '04- 5; WCh: '99- dnq 14=, '05- 12; EC: '98- dnq, '02- 9; WI: '03- 5=; ECp: '02-04: 1/2. UKR champion 1998, 2000, 2002, 2005.
Progress at HJ: 1988- 1.80, 1989- 1.86i/1.85, 1990- 1.90, 1991- 1.86, 1992- 1.93, 1993- 1.86, 1994- 1.96i/1.95, 1995- 1.91, 1996- , 1997- 1.94/1.90, 1998- 1.94, 1999- 1.96, 2000- 1.98, 2001- 1.94, 2002- 2.00, 2003- 1.99, 2004- 2.01, 2005- 1.97, 2006- 1.96i.

Viktoriya PALAMAR b. 12 Oct 1977 1.87m 66kg. Kyiv ZS.
At HJ: OG: '00- 7; WCh: '01- 5, '03- 5, '05- 5; WJ: '96- 6=; WI: '01- 5=, '03- 4; EI: '00- 5; WUG: '01- 1; ECp: '05- 2. UKR champion 2001.
Progress at HJ: 1992-, 1993- 1.83, 1994- 1.91, 1995- 1.88, 1996- 1.89, 1997- 1.88, 1998- 1.89, 1999- 1.93, 2000- 1.98, 2001- 1.99, 2002- 1.95, 2003- 2.01, 2004- 2.00i/1.94, 2005- 1.95.

Irina SEKACHOVA b. 21 Jul 1976 Vasil'kov 1.65m 72kg. Vasil'kov Dyn.
At HT: OG: '00- dnq 16, '04- 8; WCh: '03- dnq 23, '05- 6; EC: '98- dnq, 02- dnq 14; ECp: '00-02-04: 7/3/1. UKR champion 1996, 2000-05.
Eight Ukraine hammer records 1998-2004.
Progress at HT: 1995- 53.64, 1996- 55.42, 1997- 56.46, 1998- 62.83, 1999- 65.93, 2000- 69.53, 2001- 67.00, 2002- 68.70, 2003- 72.96, 2004- 74.16, 2005- 70.30.

Vita STYOPINA b. 21 Feb 1976 Zaporozhye 1.78m 58kg. Nikolayev U.
At HJ: OG: '96- dnq 19=, '04- 3, WCh: '99- 7, '03- 9=, '05- 7; EC: '98- 7; WJ: '94- 6; EJ: '95- 1; WI: '04- 8, '06- 7; ECp: '97-8: 4/4. UKR champion 1996, 1999, 2004.
Progress at HJ: 1992- 1.83, 1993- 1.89, 1994- 1.86, 1995- 1.92, 1996- 1.92, 1997- 1.93, 1998- 1.94, 1999- 1.96, 2000- 1.96, 2001- 1.94, 2002- 1.92, 2003- 2.00, 2004- 2.02, 2005- 1.95i/1.93.

Tetyana TERESHCHUK - Antipova. b. 11 Oct 1969 Lugansk 1.85m 63kg. Kyiv Dyn.
At 400mh: OG: '96- sf, '00- 5, '04- 3; WCh: '95- 5, '97- 4, '99- 7, '03- 5, '05- 7; EC: '94- 6, '98- 2; WUG: '97- 1; ECp: '94-5-6-8-00: 2/3/4/1/1. Won GWG 2001, 3rd/2nd GP 1997/2000. UKR champion 1994, 1996, 1999, 2001.
Five UKR 400mh records 1997-04.
Progress at 400mh: 1989- 57.58, 1990- 57.98, 1991- 57.19, 1993- 58.20/57.9, 1994- 54.96, 1995- 54.88, 1996- 54.68, 1997- 53.64, 1998- 53.40, 1999- 53.46, 2000- 53.98, 2001- 53.89A/54.01, 2002- 54.28A, 2003- 54.26, 2004- 53.37, 2005- 55.09. pbs: 200m 24.03 '97, 100mh 12.8 '95, 13.12A '98, 13.14 '97.
Set UKR 400mh records in four successive races in 12 days in 1997: World semi and final, then Zürich and Monaco. Missed 2001 Worlds & 2002 Europeans through injury. Fifth UKR record in Olympic semi 2004.

UNITED KINGDOM

Governing body: UK Athletics, Athletics House, Central Boulevard, Blythe Valley Park, Solihull. West Midlands B90 8LA. Founded 1999 (replacing British Athletics, founded 1991, which succeeded BAAB, founded 1932). The Amateur Athletic Association was founded in 1880 and the Women's Amateur Athletic Association in 1922.

National Championships (first were English Championships 1863-79). **AAA Championships** first held in 1880 (women 1922). **2005 Champions**: 100m: Jason Gardener 10.26, 200m: Christian Malcolm 20.65, 400m: Tim Benjamin 45.52, 800m: Tim Bayley 1:48.54, 1500m: Nick McCormick 3:37.05, 5000m: Mark Carroll IRL 13:48.90, 10,000m: Gavin Thompson 28:40.58, HMar: Huw Lobb 66:52, Mar: Jon Brown 2:09.31, 3000mSt: Andrew Lemoncello 8:33.93, 110mh: Allan Scott 13.62, 400mh: Matt Elias 49.67, HJ: Ben Challenger 2.27, PV: Nick Buckfield 5.50, LJ: Greg Rutherford 7.79, TJ: Nathan Douglas 17.64, SP/DT: Carl Myerscough 20.27/58.48, HT: Andy Frost 72.09, JT: Nick Nieland 78.30, Dec: Ben Hazell 7193, 5000mW: Colin Griffin IRL 20:44.45. **Women**: 100m: Laura Turner 11.55, 200m/400m: Donna Fraser 23.36/51.27, 800m: Susan Scott 2:02.97, 1500m: Helen Clitheroe 4:08.29, 5000m: Hayley Yelling 15:45.67, 10,000m: Kathy Butler 31:46.53, HMar: Jo Kelsey 78:19, Mar: Paula Radcliffe 2:17:42, 3000mSt: Tina Brown 10:01.57, 100mh: Sarah Claxton 12.96, 400mh: Nicola Sanders

55.61, HJ: Susan Jones 1.86, PV: Janine Whitlock 4.20, LJ: Kelly Sotherton 6.48, TJ: Taneisha Scanlon IRL 13.30, SP: Julie Dunkley 16.14, DT: Philippa Roles 57.01, HT: Shirley Webb 66.60, JT: Goldie Sayers 57.99, Hep: Kate Brewington 5041, 5000mW: Johanna Jackson 23:34.12.
National Road Walk Champions: Men: 10kmW: Dominic King 45:01, 20kmW: Daniel King 1:32:55, 50kmW: Scott Davis 4:47:34. Women: 10km: Johanna Jackson 48:37, 20km: Katie Stones 1:46:48.

Tim BENJAMIN b. 2 May 1982 Cardiff 1.83m 75kg. Belgrave Harriers
At 400m/4x400mR (200m): OG: '04- sf/5R; WCh: '01- 6R, '03- hR, '05- 5; EC: '02- dns; CG: '02- sf/2R; EJ: '01- 1/2R; EU23: '03- 2; WI: '03- 3R; WCp: '02- 6/6R; ECp: '02-03-04-05: 1R/1R/1/1R. At 200m/4x100mR: WJ: '98- sf, '00- 3/1R; WY: '99- 1; EJ: '99- 2/4R, '01- 1R. Won AAA 400m 2002, 2004-05.
Progress at 400m: 1997- 48.9, 1998- 48.5, 1999- 48.88i, 2001- 46.10, 2002- 45.73, 2003- 45.27, 2004- 45.04, 2005- 44.56. pbs: 60m 6.75i '00, 100m 10.48 '00, 10.36w '01; 200m 20.67 '01, 20.60w '99; 300m 32.5+ '05, 32.61 '02.

Dwain CHAMBERS b. 5 Apr 1978 London 1.80m 83kg. Belgrave H.
At 100m/4x100mR: OG: '00- 4; WCh: '97- resR, '99- 3/2R, '01- 4 (qf 200m), '03- dq (4/2R); EC: '98- 2/res 1R, '02- 1/1R; CG: '98- sf/1R, '02- 8; WJ: '96- 5; EJ: '95- 1/1R, '97- 1/1R; WCp: '98- 3/1R, '02- 5; ECp: '99- 1, '02- 1/1R. Won AAA 2000-1, 2003; GWG 2001; 2nd GP 2002.
World junior 100m record 1997, European 100m record 2002.
Progression at 100m: 1994- 10.75/10.56w, 1995- 10.41, 1996- 10.42, 1997- 10.06, 1998- 10.03rA/ 10.10, 1999- 9.97, 2000- 10.08, 2001- 9.99/9.97w?, 2002- 9.87, 2003- 10.03/10.0. pbs: 50m 5.57+ '99, 60m 6.41+ '99, 200m 20.27 '02.
Positive test for tetrahydrogestrinome (THG) 1 Aug 2003 which resulted in a two-year ban and annulment of results from then. Older sister Christine Chambers (b. 4 Mar 1969) was 8th at 100m at 1987 European Juniors. pbs: 60m 7.46i '92, 100m 11.84 '87, 11.68w '92.

Nathan DOUGLAS b. 4 Dec 1982 Oxford 1.83m 72kg. Oxford City. Sports science graduate of Loughborough University.
At TJ: OG: '04- dnq 13; WCh: '05- dnq 15; WI: '06- 7; EI: '05- 4; ECp: '05- 5. Won AAA 2004-05.
Progress at TJ: 1999- 14.31, 2000- 15.18, 2001- 15.50, 2002- 15.69/16.13w, 2003- 16.30, 2004- 16.95, 2005- 17.64, 2006- 17.05i. pbs: 60m 6.9i '02, 100m 10.74w '03, 10.7/10.6w '02; LJ 7.40 '02.

Michael EAST b. 20 January 1978 Reading 1.87m 68kg. Newham & Essex Beagles.
At 1500m: OG: '04- 6; WCh: '03/05- sf; EC: '02- 6; CG: '02- 1; WCp: '02- 6; EJ: '97- 12; WI: '04- dq (3rd); EI: '02- 3; ECp: '02-03-04: 2/3/2. Won AAA 2003.
Progress at 1500m: 1994- 4:02.60, 1996- 3:50.48, 1997- 3:47.48, 1998- 3:44.86, 1999- 3:42.37, 2000- 3:40.13, 2001- 3:38.94, 2002- 3:37.35, 2003- 3:35.49. 2004- 3:32.37, 2005- 3:33.32. pbs: 800m 1:46.27 '04, 1M 3:52.50 '05, 3000m 7:56.52i '03, 8:04.27 '00; 2000mSt 5:56.3 '98, Road 10km 29:23 '00.
Sensational victory in the 2002 Commonwealth Games 1500m with a strong late surge.

Jason GARDENER b. 18 Sep 1975 Bath 1.78m 70kg. Bath & Wessex.
At 100m/4x100mR: OG: '00- qf, '04- sf/1R; WCh: '95- sf R, '99- 7/2R, '05- sf/3R; EC: '02- sf; CG: '98- res (1)R, '02- 6/1R; WJ: '94- 2/1R; ECp: '95-7-9-05: 1R/3R/1R. At 60m: WI: '99-03-04: 3/3/1; EI: '98-00-02-05: 2/1/1/1. Won AAA 100m 1997, 1999, 2004-05.
European indoor records 50m 2000, 60m 1999 & 2004.
Progress at 100m: 1992- 11.0, 1993- 10.62/10.46w, 1994- 10.25, 1995- 10.33, 1996- 10.5/10.41w, 1997- 10.31/10.17w, 1998- 10.30/10.17w/10.0w, 1999- 9.98, 2000- 10.09/10.04w, 2001- 10.23, 2002- 10.13/10.11w, 2003- 10.17/10.11w, 2004- 10.12, 2005- 10.08. pbs: 50m 5.61i '00, 60m 6.46i '99, 200m 20.65 '99.
Broke Linford Christie's European record for 60m with 6.46 for 3rd in World Indoors 1999, and outdoors became the third European to break 10 seconds for 100m.

Phillips IDOWU b. 30 Dec 1978 Hackney, London 1.92m 89kg. Belgrave H.
At TJ: OG: '00- 6, '04- nj; WCh: '01- 9; EC: '02- 5; CG: '02- 2, '06- 1; EU23: '99-5; EJ: '97- 4; ECp: '04- 3. Won AAA 2000, 2002.
Progress at TJ: 1995- 13.90, 1996- 15.12/15.53w, 1997- 15.86/16.34w, 1998- 16.35, 1999- 16.41, 2000- 17.12, 2001- 17.33/17.38w, 2002- 17.68, 2004- 17.47, 2005- 17.30i/16.96; 2006- 17.45. pbs: 60m 6.81i '04, 100m 10.60 '06, LJ 7.83 '00.

Dean MACEY b. 12 Dec 1977 Rochford, Essex 1.96m 92kg. Harrow.
At Dec: OG: '00- 4, '04- 4; WCh: '99- 2, '01- 3; CG: '06- 1; WJ: '96- 2; EU23: '97/99- dnf.
Progress at Dec: 1994- 5648, 1995- 6662, 1996- 7480, 1999- 8556, 2000- 8567, 2001- 8603, 2004- 8414. pbs: 100m 10.69/10.65w '99, 400m 46.21 '01, 1500m 4:23.45 '00, 110mh 14.34 '01, HJ 2.15 '01, PV 4.80 '00, LJ 7.77 '00, TJ 14.26/14.53w '94, SP 15.83 '06, DT 48.34 '04, JT 64.03 '99.
Set six individual event pbs in his 8556 on his senior international debut at the 1999 Worlds. Earlier he had won at Arles with 8347, a huge improvement on his pb from his last completed decathlon, 7480 for 2nd at the 1996 World Juniors. He was heading for a similar score and a gold or silver medal when he fell in the 110mh at the European U23s after a first-day score of 4358 and 'legal' pbs at 100m and LJ. Despite only one competition pre-Sydney in 2000, he excelled to take fourth at the Olympics,

setting pbs at LJ, 400m, PV and 1500m but held back in the throws by elbow problems. In 2001 he improved his best again for bronze at the Worlds, despite a groin injury which meant that he very nearly withdrew before both 400m and 110mh, in both of which he set pbs! Did not compete in 2002-03 through injury and not again after 2004 OG until winning gold at 2006 CG. Keen fisherman.

Christian MALCOLM b. 3 Jun 1979 Cardiff 1.74m 67kg. Cardiff AAC.
At 200m/4x100mR (100m): OG: '00- 5, '04- sf; WCh: '01- 5 (6), '03- sf/dq R(2), '05- sf/3R; EC: '02- 4/1R; CG: '98- 2/4R, '02- 8, '06- (h); WJ: '96- sf, '98- 1 (1); EJ: '97- 1/1R (2); EU23: '99- 2/1R (2=); WI: '01- 2; EI: '00- 1, '02- 2; WCp: '02- 6R; ECp: '00-01-02-03-04-05: 1&1R/2R/1R/2&3R/ 1&1R/1&1R. Won AAA 200m 2005.
European Junior 200m record 1998.
Progress at 100m, 200m: 1993- 11.74, 1994- 10.88, 22.36/22.2; 1995- 10.85, 21.58/21.41w; 1996- 10.60/10.5, 21.27; 1997- 10.24, 20.83/20.48w; 1998- 10.12/10.10w, 20.29; 1999- 10.22/10.20w, 20.47; 2000- 10.29, 20.19; 2001- 10.11/10.09w?, 20.08; 2002- 10.29, 20.30/20.29w; 2003- 10.22, 20.25; 2004- 10.26/10.2w, 20.51; 2005- 10.25, 20.15. pbs: 50m 5.81i '02, 60m 6.64i '01.

Carl MYERSCOUGH b. 21 Oct 1979 2.09m 149kg. Blackpool & Fylde. Was at University of Nebraska, USA.
At SP(/DT): WCh: '03- dnq 19, '05- 12; CG: '02- 3, '06- 4/5; WJ: '96- dnq 22, '98- 3/6; EJ: '97- dnq/6; EU23: '99- 8/9; WI: '04- 7; WCp: '02- 7; ECp: '02-03-04-05: 6/2&7/1&3/5; Won AAA SP 2003-05 (dq 1999), DT 2005; NCAA SP 2003-04.
British shot record 2003.
Progress at SP: 1995- 13.20, 1996- 17.30, 1997- 17.66, 1998- 19.46, 1999- 18.97, 2002- 21.26i/20.72, 2003- 21.92, 2004- 20.92, 2005- 20.62. pb DT 65.10 '04.
Immediately after serving a two-year drugs ban, he took Geoff Capes's 26-year old British indoor record with 21.08 at Lincoln, Nebraska in 2002. Two weeks later he improved to 21.26 to win the NCAA indoor title. Third UK indoor record to win 2003 NCAA indoor shot and took Geoff Capes's 23-year-old outdoor record when he won NCAAs with 21.92. Married Melissa Price (USA) in July 2003 after she had won the US hammer title with a pb 70.34 (later dq).

Women

Natasha DANVERS-SMITH b. 19 Sep 1977 London 1.75m 61kg. Shaftesbury Barnet. Was at University of Southern California, USA. Married her coach Darrel Smith Jnr on 1 November 2003.
At 400mh/4x400mR: OG: '00- 8; WCh: '99/01- h, '03- sf; CG: '02- 7, '06- 2; EC: '98: h/3R res, '02- 7; CG: '98- 5; EU23: '99- 1; ECp: '00-01-02-03: 3R/8/3/2; WUG: '99- 5/3R, '01- 1/2R; AAA 1998, 2002; NCAA 2000. At 100mh: WJ: '96- 6; EJ: '95- 2; ECp: '03- 7.
Progression at 400mh: 1993- 66.9, 1997- 56.84, 1998- 55.69, 1999- 55.75, 2000- 54.95, 2001- 54.94, 2002- 55.68, 2003- 54.02, 2005- 57.47, 2006- 55.17. pbs: 200m 24.99 '00, 300m 37.80 '00, 400m 53.26 '98, 60mh 8.32i '96, 100mh 12.96 '03, 12.8w '99; HJ 1.82 '98.
Son Jaden born in December 2004.

Jessica ENNIS b. 28 Jan 1986 Sheffield 1.64m 57kg. Sheffield. Studying psychology at University of Sheffield.
At Hep: CG: '06- 3; WJ: '04- 8; WY: '03- 5; EJ: '05- 1; WUG: '05- 3.
Progress at Hep: 2001- 4801, 2002- 5194, 2003- 5116, 2004- 5542, 2005- 5910, 2006- 6269. pbs: 100m 12.0 '05, 200m 23.80 '06, 800m 2:12.66 '06, 100mh 13.26 '05, HJ 1.91 '06, LJ 6.22/6.25w '05; SP 12.26 '05, JT 36.39 '06.
Set four pbs in adding 359 points to best score for third at 2006 Commonwealth Games.

Jade JOHNSON b. 7 Jun 1980 London 1.85m 72kg. Herne Hill H.
At LJ: OG: '04- 7; WCh: '03- 4; EC: '02- 2; CG: '02- 2, '06- 5; EJ: '99- dnq 14; EU23: '01- 1; ECp: '00-01-02-03: 7/5/5/6. Won AAA 2002-04.
Progress at LJ: 1994- 5.68, 1995- 6.13/6.24w, 1996- 6.08, 1999- 6.52, 2000- 6.58, 2001- 6.59/6.68w, 2002- 6.73, 2003- 6.69/6.77w, 2004- 6.80, 2005- 6.52i, 2006- 6.63. pbs: 60m 7.43i '04, 100m 12.0/11.72w '98, 12.09 '00; 200m 24.31 '98, TJ 13.11 '01.

Lee McCONNELL b. 9 Oct 1978 Glasgow 1.78m 64kg. Shaftesbury Barnet.
At 400m/4x400m (HJ): OG: '04- sf/4R; WCh: '01- 5R, '03- 7, '05- sf/3R; EC: '02- 3/4R; CG: '02- 2/4R; WUG: '99- 3R (14=), '01- 6/2R; EI: '05- 3R; WCp: '02- 4/5R; ECp: '02-03: 1R/2&2R. Won AAA 2002. At 400mh: CG: '06- 3.
Progress at 400m: 1996- 56.4, 1997- 57.0, 1998- 54.74, 1999- 53.81, 2001- 52.05, 2002- 50.82, 2003- 51.06, 2004- 50.87, 2005- 51.15. At 400mh: 2005- 56.06, 2006- 55.25. pbs: 100m 12.2 '95, 12.19w '94; 200m 23.22 '05, 300m 37.57i '05, HJ 1.88 '00.
Former high jumper set 400m pbs at AAA, CG, EC and WCp in 2002.

Christine OHURUOGU b. 17 May 1984 1.75m 70kg. Newham & Essex Beagles. Studying linguistics at University College, London.
At 400m: OG: '04- sf/4R; WCh: '05- sf/3R; CG: '06- 1; EU23: '05- 2/2R; EJ: '03- 3; Won AAA 400m 2004.
Progress at 400m: 2001- 55.29, 2003- 54.21, 2004- 50.50, 2005- 50.73, 2006- 50.28. pbs: 60m 7.39i '06, 200m 23.40 '04.
Played for England U17 and U19 at netball. Relay dq denied her second CG gold in 2006.

Joanne PAVEY b. 20 Sep 1973 Honiton 1.62m 51kg. née Davis. Bristol.

At 5000m: OG: '00- 12, '04- 5 (h 1500m); WCh: '05- 15; EC: '02- 5; CG: '02- 5, '06- 2; WCp: '02- 3; ECp: '02-03: 2/2. At 3000m: WI: '04- 5. At 1500m: WCh: '97- sf, '03- 10. Eur CC: '04- 3. Won UK 1500m 1997, AAA 5000m 2001.
Commonwealth indoor 3000m record 2004.
Progress at 1500m, 3000m, 5000m: 1988- 4:27.9, 1989- 4:30.91, 1990- 4:26.7, 1993- 9:56.1, 1994- 4:23.36, 1995- 4:28.46, 1996- 4:21.14, 9:37.6; 1997- 4:07.28, 9:05.87; 1998- 8:58.2, 2000- 8:36.70, 14:58.27; 2001- 8:36.58, 15:00.56; 2002- 4:11.16, 8:31.27, 14:48.66; 2003- 4:01.79, 8:37.89, 15:09.04; 2004- 4:12.50, 8:34.55i/8:40.22, 14:49.11; 2005- 4:16.3i, 8:33.79, 14:40.71; 2006- 14:59.08. pbs: 800m 2:09.68 '90, 1M 4:30.77 '97, 2000m 5:41.6/5:41.4i '05, 10km road 32:34 '04.
Set a British under-15 record at 1500m with 4:27.9 in 1988 and won four national titles at U15/U17 level, but did not compete much in the early 1990s, also missing two years through injury 1998-2000. Married to middle-distance runner Gavin Pavey.

Paula RADCLIFFE b. 17 Dec 1973 Northwich 1.73m 54kg. Bedford & County. Degree in European languages from Loughborough University.
At 10,000m (Mar): OG: '00- 4, '04- dnf (dnf); WCh: '99- 2, '01- 4, '05- 9 (1); EC: '98- 5, '02- 1; At 5000m: OG: '96- 5; WCh: '95- 5, '97- 4; CG: '02- 1; ECp: '98-9-01-04: 1/1/2/1 (2 1500m '98); 3rd GP 1997. At 3000m: WCh: '93- 7; WJ: '92- 4; EJ: '91- 4; ECp: '97- 3. World HMar: '00-01-03: 1/1/1; CC: '91- 15J, '92- 1J, '93-5-6-7-8-9-00-01-02: 18/18/19/2/2/3/5 (4 4k)/1 (2 4k)/1. Eur CC: '98- 1, '03- 1. Won AAA 5000m 1996, 2000; Mar 2002-03; UK 5000m 1997, CC 1994-5.
Records: World marathon 2002 & 2003; half marathon 2003; Commonwealth & UK 1998-2004: 3000m (3), 5000m (4), 10,000m (5); UK 5000m (6) 1996-2004. European 10,000m 2002, HMar 2000 & 2001, Marathon 2002.
Progress at 1500m, 3000m, 5000m, 10,000m, Mar: 1988- 4:41.0, 1989- 4:34.9, 1990- 4:31.3, 9:41.4; 1991- 4:23.68, 9:23.29; 1992- 4:16.82, 8:51.78, 16:16.77i; 1993- 4:11.6, 8:40.40; 1994- 4:23.84, 1995- 4:06.84, 8:40.82, 14:49.27; 1996- 4:08.42, 8:37.07, 14:46.76; 1997- 4:06.93, 8:35.28, 14:45.51; 1998- 4:05.81, 8:38.84, 14:51.27, 30:48.58; 1999- 4:06.71, 8:27.40, 14:43.54, 30:27.13; 2000- 4:11.45, 8:28.85, 14:44.36, 30:26.97; 2001- 4:05.37, 8:26.97, 14:32.44, 30:55.80; 2002- 8:22.20, 14:31.42, 30:01.09, 2:17:18; 2003- 2:15:25, 2004- 8:39.08+, 14:29.11, 30:17.15, 2:23:10; 2005- 4:13.13, 8:50.18, 15:16.29+, 30:42.75, 2:17:42. pbs: 400m 58.9 '92, 800m 2:05.22 '95, 1000m 2:47.17 '93, 1M 4:24.94 '96, 2000m 5:37.1 '02, 2M 9:17.4e '04; Road: 15km 46:41 '03, 10M 50:01 '03, HMar 65:40 '03, 30km 1:36:36 '03, 20M 1:43:33 '03.
In 2002 she won World CC, Commonwealth and European track gold medals, set national records at 3000m, 5000m and 10,000m and improved the world marathon record by 1:27 with 2:17:18 in Chicago after winning the London marathon in 2:18:56. That beat the women's only world record by over three minutes and was by over four minutes the fastest debut marathon. In 2003 she ran a world road best of 30:21 in San Juan and a sensational world record 2:15:25 at the London Marathon, but missed the track season through illness and injury. Returned with world 5km road best of 14:51 in September and then fastest ever half marathon, 65:40 to win Great North Run before third world half marathon and second European CC titles. After the trauma of failing to finish at the Olympics she came back to win the New York Marathon in 2004. Improved women's only world best to win London marathon 2005 with fourth sub-2:20 time, 2:17:42 and made it six wins in seven marathons with the World gold.
Fastest ever track debut for 10,000m, 30:48.58 when 2nd in 1998 European Challenge, and improved this Commonwealth record to 30:40.70 to win this race in 1999 and in Seville to 30:27.13. There, forcing the pace despite searing heat, she was passed on the last lap by Gete Wami, but won a glorious silver medal. She set an even faster pace at the 2000 Olympics, but was outkicked and finished 4th. Followed that with European half marathon record to win Great North Run and won the World Half marathon by 33 secs. Won 5th Avenue Mile 1996 & 1997.
Her great aunt Charlotte Radcliffe won an Olympic swimming silver medal at 4x100m freestyle relay in 1920. Married Gary Lough (1500m 3:34.76 '95) on 15 April 2000.

Nicola SANDERS b. 23 Jun 1982 High Wycombe 1.71m 59kg. Windsor, Slough, Eton & Hounslow.
At 400mh/4x400mR: WCh: '05- sf/3R; CG: '05- 4; WUG: '05- 6/4R; WJ: '00- 5; WY: '99- 4; EJ: '99- 3; Won Comm Yth G 2000, AAA 2005.
Progress at 400m, 400mh: 1998- 56.30, 1999- 55.66, 58.96; 2000- 56.48, 59.68; 2001- 56.97i/57.07, 61.1; 2002- 56.54, 58.72; 2003- 58.99H, 2004- 53.77, 2005- 51.95, 55.61; 2006- 50.72i, 55.32. pbs: 100m 12.15/11.89w '98, 200m 24.18 '05, 100mh 15.0 '02, Hep 4285 '99.

Kelly SOTHERTON b. 13 November 1976 Newport, Isle of Wight 1.80m 66kg. Birchfield H.
At Hep (LJ): OG: '04- 3; WCh: '05- 5 (8); CG: '02- 7, '06- 1; EU23: '97- 10; ECp: 04- (2). At Pen: EI: '05- 2. Won AAA LJ 2005.
Commonwealth indoor pentathlon record 2005.
Progress at Hep: 1994- 4823, 1995- 4961, 1996- 4930, 1997- 5585, 1998- 4599 dnf, 2000- 5428, 2001- 5410, 2002- 5794, 2003- 6059, 2004- 6424, 2005- 6547, 2006- 6396. pbs: 60m 7.70i '02, 100m 11.85, 11.80w '97, 11.8 '02; 200m 23.57 '04, 400m 54.17 '97; 800m 2:07.94 '05, 60mh 8.26i '04, 100mh 13.27 '05; 400mh 58.30 '02, HJ 1.85 '04, LJ 6.68 '04, TJ 11.88, 11.95w '02; SP 14.22i/13.86 '05, JT 40.81 '04, Pen 4733i '05.

USA

Governing body: USA Track and Field, One RCA Dome, Suite #140, Indianapolis, IN 46225. Founded 1979 as The Athletics Congress, when it replaced the AAU (founded 1888) as the governing body.

National Championships first held in 1876 (men), 1923 (women). **2005 Champions**: **Men**: 100m/200m: Justin Gatlin 10.08/20.04, 400m: Jeremy Wariner 44.20, 800m: Khadevis Robinson 1:45.27, 1500m: Alan Webb 3:41.97, 5000m: Tim Broe 13:12.76, 10,000m: Abdi Abdirahman 28:10.38, HMar: Dan Browne 63:56, Mar: Mbarak Hussein 2:18:28, 3000mSt: Dan Lincoln 8:17.27, 110mh: Allen Johnson 12.99, 400mh: Kerron Clement 47.24, HJ: Matt Hemingway 2.27, PV: Brad Walker 5.75, LJ: Miguel Pate 8.35, TJ: Walter Davis 17.15, SP: Christian Cantwell 21.64, DT: Ian Waltz 64.54, HT: James Parker 74.15, JT: Breaux Greer 79.19, Dec: Bryan Clay 8506, 20000mW: Tim Seaman 1:26:41.36, 50kmW: Curt Clausen 4:09:35. **Women**: 100m: Me'Lisa Barber 11.10, 200m: Allyson Felix 22.13, 400m: Sanya Richards 49.28, 800m: Hazel Clark 1:59.74, 1500m: Treniere Clement 4:06.73, 5000m: Shalane Flanagan 15:10.96, 10,000m: Katie McGregor 31:33.82, Mar: Nicole Aish 2:40:21, 3000mSt: Elizabeth Jackson 9:39.78, 100mh: Michelle Perry 12.66, 400mh: Lashinda Demus 53.35, HJ: Amy Acuff 1.90, PV: Stacy Dragila 4.45, LJ: Grace Upshaw 6.70, TJ: Erica McLain 14.01, SP: Kristin Heaston 18.68, DT: Becky Breisch 62.92, HT: Erin Gilreath 73.87, JT: Kim Kreiner 58.95, Hep: Hyleas Fountain 6208, 20000mW: Teresa Vaill 1:33:28.15.

NCAA Championships first held in 1921 (men), 1982 (women). **2005 champions**: **Men**: 100m: Walter Dix 10.21, 200m: Wallace Spearmon 19.91, 400m: Darold Williamson 44.51, 800m: Dmitrijs Milkevics LAT 1:44.74, 1500m: Leonel Manzano 3:37.13, 5000m: Ryan Hall 13:22.32, 10,000m: Robert Cheseret KEN 28:20.11, 3000mSt: Mircea Bogdan ROM 8:27.29, 110mh: Josh Walker 13.39, 400mh: Kerron Clement 47.56, HJ: Jesse Williams 2.29, PV: Róbison Pratt MEX 5.50, LJ: Fabrice Lapierre AUS 8.15w, TJ: Rodrigo Mendes BRA 17.04w, SP: Edis Elkasevic CRO 20.88, DT: Michael Robertson 61.70, HT: Spiridon Zoulién GRE 70.43, JT: Gabriel Wallin SWE 78.76, Dec: Trey Hardee 7881. **Women**: 100m: Marshevet Hooker 11.16, 200m: Sheri-Ann Brooks JAM 22.85, 400m: Monique Henderson 50.10, 800m: Aneita Denton JAM 2:02.84, 1500m: Anne Shadle 4:11.37, 5000m: Megan Metcalfe CAN 16:31.88, 10,000m: Sara Slattery 33:02.21, 3000mSt: Victoria Mitchell AUS 9:54.32, 100mh: Virginia Powell 12.80, 400mh: Shauna Smith 54.32, HJ: Sharon Day 1.93, PV: Kate Soma 4.30, LJ: Tianna Madison 6.66, TJ: Candice Baucham 14.07, SP: Kim Barrett JAM 18.20, DT: Beth Mallory 59.35, HT: Loree Smith 68.47, JT: Dana Pounds 56.48, Hep: Lela Nelson 5878.

Dominique ARNOLD b. 14 Sep 1973 Compton, California 1.85m 76kg. Nike. Studied fine arts at Washington State University.
At 110mh: WCh: '05- 4; PAm: '99- 4. 3rd GP 2001. Won NCAA 1996. At 60mh: WI: '06- 3.
Progress at 110mh: 1992- 14.55, 1993- 14.17, 1995- 14.00, 1996- 13.46/13.32w, 1998- 13.54/13.5/13.48w, 1999- 13.21/13.2, 2000- 13.11, 2001- 13.14, 2002- 13.70A, 2003- 13.35, 2004- 13.31, 2005- 13.01. pbs: 200m 21.0 '99, 50mh 6.68i '98, 55mh 7.15i '98, 60mh 7.51i '00.

Kenwood **'Kenta' BELL** b. 16 Mar 1977 Kilgore, Texas 1.83m 77kg. Studied criminology at Northwestern State University, Louisiana.
At TJ: OG: '04- 9; WCh: '03- 6, '05-7; WI: '01- 9; WUG: '01- 1 (6 LJ); US champion 2003.
Progress at 110mh: 1998- 15.85i/16.02w, 1999- 16.52/16.67w, 2000- 17.22, 2001- 17.22, 2002- 17.63, 2003- 17.59, 2004- 17.58/17.76Aw, 2005- 17.11. pb LJ 8.05 '00.

Ron BRAMLETT b. 22 Oct 1979 Frankfurt, Germany 1.81m 68kg. Advertising graduate from University of Alabama, formerly Middle Tennessee State.
At 110mh: WUG: '01- 4; won NCAA 2001-02.
Progress at 110mh: 1998- 14.01/13.93w, 1999- 13.72, 2000- 13.47, 2001- 13.43/13.39w, 2002- 13.35, 2003- 13.27, 2004- 13.26, 2005- 13.31. pbs: 60m 6.74i '06, 100m 10.45 '03, 200m 21.24 '02, 50mh 6.50i '05, 55mh 7.03i '02, 60mh 7.52i '02.

Bennie BRAZELL b. 2 Jun 1982 Houston 1.85m 77kg. Studied journalism at Louisiana State University.
At 400mh: OG: '04- 8.
Progress at 400mh: 1999- 53.00, 2000- 51.04, 2002- 48.80, 2003- 48.97, 2004- 48.05, 2005- 47.67. Won national collegiate football title as a wide receiver at LSU in 2003.

Derrick BREW b. 28 Dec 1977 Houston 1.85m 82kg. Nike. Studied business management at Louisiana State University.
At 4x400mR: OG: '04- 3/1R; WCh: '01- 1R, 03- dq(1)R, '05- 1R; WUG: '99- 1R; WI: '03- res (1)R.
Progress at 400m: 1995- 47.40, 1996- 46.67, 1997- 45.21, 1998- 44.53, 1999- 44.29, 2000- 44.70, 2001- 44.80, 2002- 46.02A, 2003- 44.83A/45.02, 2004- 44.42, 2005- 44.96. pbs: 200m 20.42, 20.38Aw '99; 300m 32.4 '04.

Joel BROWN b. 31 Jan 1980 Baltimore 1.80m 75kg. Nike. Studied financial planning at Ohio State University.
At 110mh: WCh: '05- 6; PAm: '03- 2; WI: '03- 9; won US indoor 60mh 2005.
Progress at 110mh: 2000- 14.49, 2001- 14.04, 2003- 13.74/13.58w, 2004- 13.35, 2005- 13.22. pbs: 55m 6.24i '06, 60m 6.74i '05, 100m 10.33 '04, 10.32w '05; 200m 20.55 '05, 55mh 7.18i '03, 60mh 7.60i '05, 400mh 52.45 '98.

Christian CANTWELL b. 30 Sep 1980 Jefferson City, Missouri 1.98m 145kg. Studied hotel

and restaurant management at University of Missouri.
At SP: WCh: '05- 5; WI: '04- 1; won WAF 2003, US 2005. At DT: PAm-J: '99- 2.
Progress at SP: 1999- 15.85, 2000- 19.67, 2001- 19.71, 2002- 21.45, 2003- 21.62, 2004- 22.54, 2005- 21.67. pbs: DT 59.32 '01, HT 57.18 '01, Wt 22.04i '03.
After three competitions over 22m in 2004, was 4th in the US Olympic Trials.

John CAPEL b. 27 Oct 1978 Brooksville, Florida 1.80m 82kg. Was at University of Florida.
At 200m/4x100mR (100m): OG: 00- 8; WCh: '03- 1/1R, '05- 3; WUG: '99- (2)/1R. Won US 200m 2000, NCAA 200m 1999 (2nd 100m).
Progress at 100m, 200m: 1997- 10.46/10.2, 21.01; 1998- 10.40, 1999- 10.03, 19.87; 2000- 10.12, 19.85, 2003- 9.97, 20.17; 2004- 9.95, 20.24; 2005- 10.08, 20.31. pbs: 55m 6.14i '03, 60m 6.48i '03.
Promising footballer (wide receiver) at University of Florida, but withdrew in April 2000 to concentrate on trying for Olympic success. After running the fastest time in the semis (20.10), was left at start of Olympic 200m final. He was drafted by the Chicago Bears in 2001, but cut before training camp; and then tried out for the Kansas City Chiefs. He returned to track in 2003, but had to withdraw from WI team. However, he took two gold medals outdoors.

James CARTER b. 7 May 1978 Baltimore 1.86m 77kg. Nike. Was at Hampton College.
At 400mh: OG: 00- 4, '04- 4; WCh: '01- sf, '05- 2; WCp: '02- 1/2R; 3rd GP 2002. US champion 2002, 2004.
Progress at 400mh: 1998- 50.17, 1999- 49.45, 2000- 48.04, 2001- 48.44, 2002- 47.57, 2003- 48.88, 2004- 47.68, 2005- 47.43. pbs: 60m 6.79i '03, 200m 21.03i/21.20 '04, 400m 46.21 '01, 55mh 7.44i '99, 60mh 8.15 '99, LJ 7.25 '99, TJ 15.61i '99.

Xavier CARTER b. 8 Dec 1985 Palm Bay, Florida 1.90m 86kg. Nike. Student at Louisiana State University.
At 400mh: OG: 00- 4, '04- 4; WCh: '01- sf, '05- 2; WCp: '02- 1/2R; 3rd GP 2002. US champion 2002, 2004.
Progress at 200m, 400m: 2001- 46.95, 2002- 21.02, 46.90; 2003- 20.69. 45.88; 2004- 20.69i/20.72/20.5, 45.44/45.3; 2005- 20.02, 45.65. pbs: 60m 6.74i '05, 100m 10.38 '03.
American football wide receiver for LSU.

Bryan CLAY b.3 Jan 1980 Austin, Texas 1.80m 79kg. Nike. Was at Azusa Pacific University.
At Dec: OG: '04- 2; WCh: '01/03- dnf, '05- 1, PAm-J: '99- 1. US champion 2004-05. At Hep: WI: '04- 2, '06- 2.
Progress at Dec: 1999- 7312, 2000- 7373, 2001- 8169, 2002- 8230, 2003- 8482, 2004- 8820, 2005- 8732. pbs: 60m 6.65i '04, 100m 10.36 '05, 400m 47.76 '05, 1000m 2:49.41i '04, 1500m 4:38.93 '01, 60mh 7.77i '04, 110mh 13.78 '05, HJ 2.15 '04, PV 5.10 '04, LJ 7.96/8.06w '04, SP 16.25 '05, DT 55.87 '05, JT 72.00 '05, Hep 6365i '04.
Moved from Texas to Hawaii at age five. Brilliant breakthrough with four pbs in 2004 World Indoor heptathlon. Set decathlon discus WR with 55.87 during 2005 US Champs. Set pbs at SP, 400m and JT when winning World gold in 2005.

Kerron CLEMENT b. 31 Oct 1985 Port of Spain, Trinidad 1.88m 84kg. Nike. Student at University of Florida.
At 400mh/4x400mR: WCh: '05- 4; WJ: '04- 1/1R. US champion 2005, NCAA 2004-05.
World junior 4x400m record 2004, world indoor records: 400m 2005, 4x400m 2006.
Progress at 400m, 400mh: 2002- 49.77H, 2003- 50.13H, 2004- 45.90, 48.51; 2005- 44.57i, 47.24. pbs: 200m 20.40i '05, 20.82 '04; 300m 31.94i '06, 55mh 7.28i '05, 60mh 7.80i '04, 110mh 13.78 '04.
Born in Trinidad, moved to Texas in 1998, US citizenship confirmed in 2005. Ran world-leading 47.24, the world's fastest time since 1998, to win 2005 US 400mh title.

Shawn CRAWFORD b. 14 Jan 1978 Van Wyck, SC 1.81m 83kg. Nike. Was at Clemson University.
At 200m/4x100mR (100m): OG: '04- 1/2R (4); WCh: '01- 3=, '05- (sf); WI: '01- 1; Won US 2001, 2004; GWG & GP 2001, NCAA 2000. At 60m: WI: '04- 2.
Progress at 100m, 200m: 1996- 10.62, 21.57; 1997- 10.51w, 20.83; 1998- 10.34/10.15w, 20.44A/20.12w; 1999- 10.41, 20.39; 2000- 10.16, 20.09; 2001- 10.09, 20.17; 2002- 9.94, 19.85A/20.29; 2003- 10.07, 20.02; 2004- 9.88/9.86w, 19.79; 2005- 9.99/9.98w, 20.12. pb 60m 6.47i '04.
US indoor record 20.26 to win NCAA indoor 200m 2000. Disqualified in 2003 WI semis. Calls himself 'The Cheetah Man' after racing against a zebra and a cheetah on Fox TV in 2003.

Walter DAVIS b. 2 Jul 1979 LaFayette, Louisiana 1.88m 83kg. Nike. Studied sociology at Louisiana State University.
At TJ/(LJ): OG: '00- 11, '04- 11/dnq 23; WCh: '01- 5, '03- dnq 15/7, '05- 1/dnq 19; WI: '03- 2, '06- 1; WCp: '02- 2. Won US 2002, 2005; NCAA 2001-02 (& LJ 2002).
Progress at LJ, TJ: 1997- 7.24, 15.67; 1998- 15.29w, 1999- 7.88i/7.70, 16.38/16.47w; 2000- 8.16, 17.07/17.08w, 2001- 8.14i/8.13/8.19w, 17.22; 2002- 8.15i/8.12/8.15w, 17.59; 2003- 8.24, 17.55; 2004- 8.25, 17.63; 2005- 7.98, 17.62i/17.57; 2006- 17.73i. pbs: 60m 6.78i '01, 100m 10.44w '05, 200m 20.98 '96, 20.87w '95, 20.6w '94.
All-state basketball player in high school.

Walter DIX b. 31 Jan 1986 1.70m 73kg. Nike. Student at Florida State University.
World junior 200m indoor best (20.37) 2005.
Progress at 100m, 200m: 2002- 10.72/10.67w, 2003- 10.41/10.29w, 21.04/20.94w; 2004- 10.28, 20.62/20.54w; 2005- 10.06/9.96w, 20.18. pbs: 55m 6.23i '05, 60m 6.59i '06, LJ 7.39 '04.

Justin GATLIN b. 10 Feb 1982 Brooklyn, NY 1.85m

79kg. Nike. Was at University of Tennessee.
At 100m/200m/4x100mR: OG: '04- 1/3/2R; WCh: '05- 1/1. At 60m: WI: '03- 1. Won US 100m & 200m 2005 (indoor 60m 2003), NCAA 100m & 200m 2001-02 (& indoor 60m/200m 2002).
Progress at 100m, 200m: 2000- 10.36, 2001- 10.08, 20.29/19.86w; 2002: under international suspension 10.05/10.00w, 19.86; 2003- 9.97, 20.04; 2004- 9.85, 20.01; 2005- 9.88/9.84w, 20.00. pbs: 60m 6.45i '03, 55mh 7.39i '02, 60mh 7.86i '01, 110mh 13.41dq '02, 13.78/13.74w '01; LJ 7.21 '00, 7./34i '01.
Top hurdler in high school (110mh 13.66 and 300mh 36.74 on junior hurdles), now concentrating on sprints. Retained NCAA sprint titles while ineligible for international competition in 2002 after failing a drugs test in 2001 (when he won 100m, 200m and 110mh at the US Juniors) for a prescribed medication to treat Attention Deficit Disorder. Reinstated by IAAF in July 2002. Won 2005 World 100m title by biggest ever winning margin of 0.17.

Tyson GAY b. 9 Sep 1982 Lexington 1.83m 73kg. Marketing student at University of Arkansas.
At 200m: WCh: '05- 3. Won WAF 200m 2005, NCAA 100m 2004.
Progress at 100m, 200m: 2000- 10.56, 21.27; 2001- 10.28, 21.23; 2002- 10.27/10.08w, 20.88/20.21w; 2003- 10.01w, 21.15/20.31w; 2004- 10.06/10.10w, 20.07; 2005- 10.08, 19.93. pb 60m 6.55i '05.

John GODINA b. 31 May 1972 Fort Sill, Oklahoma 1.93m 129kg. adidas. Studied biology at UCLA.
At SP/(DT): OG: '96- 2/dnq 14, '00- 3/dnq 17, '04- 9; WCh: '95- 1/10, '97- 1/5, '99- 7/dnq 16, '01- 1/dnq 21, '03- 8, '05- dnq 17; WI: '97-9-01-03: 3/2/1/2; WCp: '98- 1/4. Won GP SP 1996 (3rd 2000), 3rd DT 1997. Won US SP 1998-9, 2001, 2003; DT 1997-8, NCAA SP 1995, DT 1994-5, PAm-J SP & DT 1991; GWG SP 1998.
Progress at SP, DT: 1990- 53.58, 1991- 17.75, 58.60; 1992- 19.68, 61.52; 1993- 20.03, 60.48; 1994- 20.03, 62.24; 1995- 22.00, 64.92; 1996- 21.25, 64.58; 1997- 21.75, 67.40; 1998- 21.78, 69.91; 1999- 22.02, 69.05; 2000- 21.51, 68.32; 2001- 21.95, 67.66; 2002- 21.91, 64.71; 2003- 21.23i/21.08, 64.03/66.38dh; 2004- 21.71, 2005- 22.20.
Four world shot gold medals. Undefeated in 24 shot competitions July 1997 to February 1999. 4th in the US trials shot in 1997, but gained World place with a 'wild card' for a defending champion; came second but took gold after the disqualification of Aleksandr Bagach. He achieved the best ever one day SP-DT double with 21.58 and 69.91 at Salinas in 1998. He stepped into the US Olympic shot team after the withdrawal of CJ Hunter in 2000 and took bronze.

Adam GOUCHER b. 18 Feb 1975 Hollywood, Florida 1.78m 64kg. Communications graduate of University of Colorado.
At 5000m: OG: '00- 13; WCh: '01- 10. World 4k CC: '99-12, '06- 6. Won US 5000m 1999-2000, 4k CC 2006; NCAA 5000m & CC 1998.
Progress at 5000m: 1995- 13:45.84, 1996- 13:33.3, 1997- 13:34.13, 1998- 13:31.64, 1999- 13:11.25, 2000- 13:24.34, 2001- 13:22.29, 2003- 13:35.67, 2004- 13:41.11, 2005- 13:10.19. pbs: 800m 1:49.12 '99, 1500m 3:36.64 '01, 1M 3:54.17 '99, 2000m 4:58.92 '99, 3000m 7:34.96 '01, 3000mSt 8:46.04 '95.
His wife Kara (b. 9 Jul 1978) won NCAA 3000m & 5000m in 2000, pb 5000m 15:17.55 '05.

Maurice GREENE b. 23 Jul 1974 Kansas City, Kansas 1.76m 80kg. Adidas/HSI.
At 100m(/200m)/4x100mR: OG: '00- 1/1R, '04- 3/2R; WCh: '95- qf, '97- 1, '99- 1/1/1R, '01- 1, '03- sf, '05- hR; Won US 100m 1997, 2000, 2002, 2004; 200m 1999; GWG 100m 1998. 2nd GP 200m 1999. At 60m: WI: '95- 4, '99- 1.
World 100m record 1999; three world indoor 60m records 1998-2001.
Progress at 100m, 200m: 1993- 10.43, 21.00; 1995- 10.19/9.88w, 1996- 10.08, 1997- 9.86, 19.86; 1998- 9.90/9.79w, 20.03/19.88w; 1999- 9.79, 19.90; 2000- 9.86, 20.02/19.93w, 2001- 9.82, 2002- 9.89/9.88w, 2003- 9.94, 20.16; 2004-9.87/9.78w, 2005- 10.01. pbs: 50m 5.55+ '97, 55m 6.15i '96, 60m 6.39i/6.39+ '98.
52 'legal' sub-10 times for 100m – easily the record for the event. Moved from Kansas to train with John Smith in Los Angeles in 1996. In 1997 ran 100m in 9.90 to win US Champs and twice in Athens before 9.86 to win World 100m title. Took 0.05 off world record for 100m at Athens in June 1999, and won World Champs treble (the first man to win 100m and 200m at World Champs). Despite hobbling at the finish, he ran 9.82 to win the 2001 world title at 100m with a wind of –0.2. His elder brother Ernest was a former US junior college champion at 200m (20.60 '92).

Breaux GREER b. 19 Oct 1976 Houston 1.88m 102kg. adidas. Was at Northeast Louisiana University.
At JT: OG: '00- 12, '04- 12; WCh: '01- 4, '03- dnq 14; PAm: '03- 3. Won WAF 2004, US 2000-05.
Two North American javelin records 2004.
Progress at JT: 1995- 70.92, 1996- 79.98, 1997- 78.12, 1998- 79.68, 2000- 82.63, 2001- 87.00, 2002- 81.78, 2003- 82.10, 2004- 87.68, 2005- 87.65.
Set five pbs in 2001, including those to win US title (85.23) and in first round of World final.

Otis HARRIS b. 30 Jun 1982 Edwards, Mississippi 1.86m 77kg. Nike. Student at the University of South Carolina.
At 4x400mR: OG: '04- 2/1R.
Progress at 400m: 1999- 47.73, 2000- 46.56, 2001- 45.79A/45.90, 2002- 45.42, 2003- 44.57, 2004- 44.16, 2005- 46.78. pb 300m 32.1+ '04.

Jeff HARTWIG b. 25 Sep 1967 St Louis 1.90m 82kg. Nike. Was at Arkansas State University.
At PV: OG: '96- 11=; WCh: '99- dnq 14=; WI: '99-

2, '06- nh; WCp: '98- 3, '02- 2. Won GWG 1998, US 1998-9, 2002-03; GP 2002 (2nd 1999).
Four US pole vault records 1998-2000.
Progress at PV: 1983- 3.35, 1984- 3.81, 1985- 4.42, 1986- 4.57, 1987- 4.90, 1988- 5.10, 1989- 5.34, 1990- 5.40i/5.35, 1991- 5.35, 1992- 5.60i/5.50, 1993- 5.35, 1994- 5.63, 1995- 5.72, 1996- 5.80, 1997- 5.85, 1998- 6.01, 1999- 6.02, 2000- 6.03, 2001- 5.90, 2002- 6.02i/5.90, 2003- 5.80i/5.70, 2004- 5.88i/5.86, 2005- 5.76i/5.68, 2006- 5.85i.
The first 6m-vaulter from the USA, Hartwig is also a snake rancher, with a herd of pythons and boa constrictors. Clearly headed world rankings in 2000, but failed to clear his opening height in the qualifying round of the US Trials, when he had problems with his eyes.

Matt HEMINGWAY b. 24 Oct 1972 San Pedro, California 2.01m 81kg. US West. Was at University of Arkansas. Sales manager.
At HJ: OG: '04- 2; WCh: '03- 12, '05- 11=; US champion 2005, NCAA 1996.
Progress at HJ: 1990- 2.08, 1991- 2.23, 1992- 2.10, 1993- 2.25, 1994- 2.17, 1995- 2.25i/2.21, 1996- 2.30, 1997- 2.21i/2.20, 2000- 2.38i/2.30, 2002- 2.32, 2003- 2.34, 2004- 2.34, 2005- 2.31i/2.27.
Having been out for the sport for two and a half years 'tired of everything about track', but keeping fit playing basketball, he returned in the 2000 indoor season with pb 2.32, then 2.36 and 2.38 to win the US indoor title. He had been 2nd in the NCAA and 4th in the US Trials in 1996. His grandfather was the cousin of author Ernest Hemingway.

Reese HOFFA b. 8 Oct 1977 Evans, Georgia 1.82m 133kg. New York AC. Was at University of Georgia.
At SP: OG: '04- dnq 22; WCh: '03- dnq; PAm: '03- 1; WI: '04- 2, '06- 1; WUG: '01- 9.
Progress at SP: 1998- 19.08, 1999- 19.35, 2000- 19.79, 2001- 20.22, 2002- 20.47, 2003- 20.95, 2004- 21.67, 2005- 21.74i/21.29, 2006- 22.11i. pbs: DT 58.46 '99, HT 60.05 '02.
Added 37cm to his best to win WI gold 2006.

Nick HYSONG b. 9 Dec 1971 Winslow, Arizona 1.83m 77kg. Nike. Marketing degree from Arizona State University.
At PV: OG: '00- 1; WCh: '99- 4=, '01- 3, '05- 5=; WJ: '90- 6; WI: '95- 5=, '99- 8. Won NCAA 1994. 2nd GP 2000.
Progress at PV: 1989- 4.87, 1990- 5.30, 1991- 5.45, 1992- 5.52, 1993- 5.57i/5.50, 1994- 5.70, 1995- 5.85i/5.70, 1996- 5.71A, 1997- 5.67A, 1998- 5.70, 1999- 5.85i/5.80, 2000- 5.90, 2001- 5.85, 2002- 5.75, 2003- 5.78, 2004- 5.81, 2005- 5.71Ai/5.70.

Bershawn JACKSON b. 8 May 1983 Miami 1.73m 69kg. Nike. Studying accountancy at St Augustine's University, Raleigh.
At 400mh: WCh: '03- h (dq), '05- 1; WJ: '02- 3/1R. Won WAF 2004-05, US 2003, US indoor 400m 2005.
Progress at 400mh: 2000- 52.17, 2001- 50.86, 2002- 50.00, 2003- 48.23, 2004- 47.86, 2005- 47.30. pbs: 200m 21.03/20.46w '04, 400m 45.45 '05, 60m 1:18.65i '06.

Allen JOHNSON b. 1 Mar 1971 Washington DC 1.78m 70kg. Nike. Was at University of North Carolina.
At 110mh: OG: '96- 1, '00- 4, '04- h (fell); WCh: '95- 1, '97- res (1) 4x400mR, '99- sf, '01- 1, '03- 1, '05- 3; WCp: '94- 2, '98- 2R, '02- 2; 2nd GP 1995 & 2001. Won WAF 2003-04, GWG 2001, US 1996-7, 2000-03, 2005. At 60mh: WI: '95-03-04: 1/1/1.
US 110mh record 1996 and indoor 60mh 2004.
Progress at 110mh: 1990- 14.4, 1991- 14.11, 1992- 13.63, 1993- 13.47/13.34w, 1994- 13.25/13.23Aw, 1995- 12.98, 1996- 12.92, 1997- 12.93, 1998- 12.98, 1999- 13.01, 2000- 12.97, 2001- 13.04, 2002- 13.04, 2003- 12.97, 2004- 13.05, 2005- 12.99. pbs: 60m 6.62i '98, 100m 10.41/10.10w '99, 200m 20.26 '97, 400m 48.27 '96, 50mh 6.40i '05, 55mh 7.03i '94, 60mh 7.36i '04, 400mh 52.00 '91, HJ 2.11 '89, LJ 8.14i/7.91w '93, 7.85 '91; TJ 14.83 '89.
Having leapt into world class in 1994, on 8 Feb 1995 in Madrid he ended Colin Jackson's string of 44 sprint hurdles victories. He went on to win world titles indoors and out, adding Olympic gold in 1996, when he missed the world record by just 0.01 at the US Trials, and another world gold in 1997. Had to withdraw from the 1999 World semis through injury, but came back to take his third title in 2001. Won his third World Indoor 60mh title in 2004 in 7.36 to tie the US record and improve his pb of 7.38 '95.

Joshua J JOHNSON b. 10 May 1976 Dallas 1.91m 91kg. Pioneer TC.
At 200m/4x100mR: WCh: '01- res (dq1)R, '03- 6/1R. Won WAF 200m 2003.
Progress at 100m, 200m: 2000- 10.24/10.19w, 20.60; 2001- 10.22/10.11w, 19.88; 2002- 9.95, 20.74; 2003- 10.05, 20.05; 2004- 10.11, 20.28; 2005- 10.09, 20.30. pbs: 60m 6.55i '02, 400m 47.66 '00.
Played basketball at Oklahoma Panhandle State University and after failing to make professional leagues joined IBM. He trained with coach Nicholson Scott of the Pioneer TC in Arlington, Texas and in 2001 was 7th in US 100m and ran in World 4x100m heats. Made a sensational improvement from 20.48 to 19.88 at Brussels in 2001 and ran brilliant last leg to bring US to gold in World 4x100m 2003. He tried out as a receiver with American Football team, the Oakland Raiders in 2002 but was let go at the final cut.

Meb(rahtom) **KEFLEZIGHI** b. 5 May 1975 Asmara, Eritrea 1.70m 58kg. Nike. Was at UCLA.
At Mar: OG: '04- 2; At 10,000m: OG: '00- 12; WCh: '01- 23, '03- 16, '05- dnf; PAm: '99- 5. At 5000m: WCp: '02- 4. World CC: '01-02-03: 13/14/11. Won US 10,000m 2000, 2002, 2004; CC 2001-02; NCAA 5000m, 10,000m & CC 1997.
US records: 10,000m 2001, 20km road 58:57 '03.
Progress at 10,000m, Mar: 1995- 30:41.24, 1996-

29:55.75, 1997- 28:26.55, 1998- 28:16.79, 1999- 28:29.27, 2000- 27:53.63, 2001- 27:13.98, 2002- 27:20.15, 2:12:35; 2003- 27:57.59, 2:10:03; 2004- 27:24.10, 2:09:53; 2005- 28:10.57, 2:09:56. pbs: 1500m 3:42.29 '98, 1M 4:02.24i/4:02.86 '98, 3000m 7:48.81 '03, 2M 8:27.2 '01, 5000m 13:11.77 '00, Road: 15km 42:48 '02.

Emigrated from war-torn Eritrea at age of 10, first to Italy and then to San Diego, USA in 1987. Became US citizen on 2 July 1998. 2nd New York Marathon 2004 (3rd 2005).

Bernard LAGAT b. 12 Dec 1974 Kapsabet, Kenya 1.75m 61kg. Studied business management at Washington State University, USA.

At 1500m: OG: '00- 3, '04- 2; WCh: '01- 2, '05- sf; WI: '03- 2; AfCh: '02- 1; WUG: '99- 1; WCp: '02- 1; 2nd GP 1999-2000-02. At 3000m: WI: '01- 6, '04- 1. Won WAF 3000m 2005, KEN 1500m 2002, NCAA 5000m 1999 (and indoor 1M/3000m).

Commonwealth and KEN 1500m record 2001, N.American record 2005.

Progress at 1500m, 5000m: 1996- 3:37.7A, 1997- 3:41.19, 13:50.33; 1998- 3:34.48, 13:42.73; 1999- 3:30.56, 13:36.12; 2000- 3:28.51, 13:23.46; 2001- 3:26.34, 13:30.54; 2002- 3:27.91, 13:19.14; 2003- 3:30.55, 2004- 3:27.40, 2005- 3:29.30, 12:59.29. pbs: 800m 1:46.00 '03, 1000m 2:18.70 '00, 1M 3:47.28 '01, 2000m 4:55.49 '99, 3000m 7:33.51 '00.

Gave up his final year of scholastic eligibility (as under NCAA rules no payments can be received) at his university in order to compete (for money) in the 1999 GP Final, in which he was 2nd. He was 2nd to Hicham El Guerrouj six times in 2001, including his 3:26.34 at Brussels for 2nd on the world all-time list, and six times in 2002. Withdrew from 2003 Worlds after testing positive for EPO, but this was later repudiated. Lives in Tucson, Arizona and revealed in 2005 that he had gained US citizenship.

His brother **Robert Cheseret** won the NCAA 5000m in 2004.

Tim MACK b. 15 Sep 1972 Cleveland 1.88m 78kg. Nike. Graduate of University of Tennessee.

At PV: OG: '04- 1; WCh: '01- 9, '03- 6=. Won WAF 2004, GWG 2001, US 2004.

Progress at PV: 1993- 5.31, 1994- 5.52, 1995- 5.60, 1996- 5.65, 1998- 5.70, 1999- 5.70i/5.43, 2000- 5.81, 2001- 5.81, 2002- 5.85i/5.84, 2003- 5.76, 2004- 6.01, 2005- 5.85.

Became the world's 11th 6m vaulter with 6.01 at the WAF after pbs of 5.90 to win US title and 5.95 to win Olympic title in 2004.

Casey MALONE b. 6 Apr 1977 Wheatridge, Colorado 2.03m 109kg. Nike. Was at Colorado State University (now assistant coach).

At DT: OG: '04- 6; WCh: '03- dnq 16; WJ: '96- 1. NCAA champion 1998.

Progress at DT: 1996- 59.50, 1997- 58.46A, 1998- 61.39, 1999- 61.49, 2000- 64.47A, 2001- 60.96, 2002- 66.58A, 2003- 64.43A, 2004- 65.60A, 2005- 61.87.

LaShawn MERRITT b. 27 Jun 1986 Portsmouth, Virginia 1.88m 82kg. Nike.

At 400m/4x400mR: WCh: '05- res(1)R; WJ: '04- 1/1R (1 at 4x100); WI: '06- 1R.

World junior records 4x100m and 4x400m 2004, World indoor 200m junior best 2005.

Progress at 200m, 400m: 2002- 21.46, 2003- 21.33, 47.9?; 2004- 20.72/20.69w, 45.25; 2005- 20.38, 44.66. pbs: 55m 6.33i '04, 60m 6.68 '06, 100m 10.47/10.38w '04, 300m 31.94i '06, 32.5 '05.

World age-18 400m record with 44.66 in 2005. Spent a year at East Carolina University before signing for Nike and returning home to Portsmouth.

Derek MILES b. 28 Sep 1972 Sacramento 1.91m 82kg. Bell Athletics. History graduate of University of South Dakota. Academic advisor at Arkansas State University.

At PV: OG: '04- 7; WCh: '03- 6=, WI: '03- 5.

Progress at PV: 1997- 5.50, 1998- 5.35, 1999- 5.40Ai/5.35, 2000- 5.65, 2001- 5.82, 2002- 5.82i/5.74, 2003- 5.81, 2004- 5.81, 2005- 5.85i/5.81.

John MOFFITT b. 21 Dec 1980 Winnsboro, Louisiana 1.85m 75kg. Louisiana State University.

At LJ: OG: '04- 2; NCAA champion 2004.

Progress at LJ: 2001- 7.68/7.92w, 2002- 7.83/7.95w, 2003- 8.08i/8.02, 2004- 8.47, 2005- 8.16i/7.96, 2006- 8.23i. pbs: TJ 16.79i/16.69w '04, 16.53 '03.

Anwar MOORE b. 5 Mar 1979 1.82m 75kg. Was at St. Augustine's University.

Progress at 110mh: 2000- 13.9/14.33w, 2001- 14.18, 2002- 13.66, 2003- 13.44, 2004- 13.35, 2005- 13.23/13.20w. pbs: 55m 6.25i '03, 60m 6.72i '03, 100m 10.42 '05, 200m 21.63 '04, 21.19w '02; 55mh 7.17i '03, 60mh 7.60i '05.

Adam NELSON b. 7 Jul 1975 Atlanta 1.81m 115kg. Graduate of Dartmouth University. Training as a financial consultant.

At SP: OG: '00- 2, '04- 2; WCh: '01- 2, '03- 2, '05- 1; WI: '01- 2; WJ: '94- 1; WUG: '99- 2; WCp: '02- 1. GP 2002 (2nd 2000 and 3rd overall). Won WAF 2005, PAm-J 1993, GWG 2001, NCAA 1997, US 2000, 2002, 2004.

Progress at SP: 1993- 16.56, 1994- 18.34, 1995- 18.27, 1996- 19.14, 1997- 19.62, 1998- 20.61, 1999- 20.64, 2000- 22.12, 2001- 21.53, 2002- 22.51, 2003- 21.29, 2004- 21.68, 2005- 21.92. pb DT 56.18 '96.

Had a great season in 2000, when he improved his best from 20.64 to 21.70 and then the world's longest throw for four years, 22.12 (to take the US title) in July. Further improvement as world number one in 2002. Small for a shot putter, but very fast and dynamic in the circle. Played American Football at high school and college.

James NIETO b. 2 Nov 1976 Seattle 1.93m 79kg. Nike. Business administration graduate of Eastern Michigan University.

At HJ: OG: '04- 4; WCh: '03- 7; PAm: '03- 2; WI:

'03- 9; US champion 2003-04.
Progress at HJ: 1994- 1.93, 1995- 2.06, 1996- 2.14, 1997- 2.15, 1998- 2.25, 1999- 2.30, 2000- 2.23, 2001- 2.27, 2002- 2.30, 2003- 2.31, 2004- 2.34, 2005- 2.30.

Tom PAPPAS b. 6 Sep 1976 Azalea, Oregon 1.93m 93kg. Nike. Was at University of Tennessee.
At Dec: OG: '00- 5, '04- dnf; WCh: '99- dnf, '03- 1. Won PAm-J 1995, NCAA 1999, US 2000, 2002-03. At Hep: WI: '03- 1.
Progress at Dec: 1995- 7198, 1996- 7499, 1997- 7677, 1999- 8463, 2000- 8467, 2001- 8323, 2002- 8583, 2003- 8784, 2004- 8732. pbs: 60m 6.89i '03, 100m 10.65 '03, 10.63w '04; 400m 47.58 '03, 1000m 2:49.32i '04, 1500m 4:35.14 '95, 55mh 7.27i '03, 60mh 7.80i '03, 110mh 13.90 '04, HJ 2.21 '00, PV 5.20 '02, LJ 7.96 '03, SP 16.48 '03, DT 52.18 '03, JT 66.56 '00, Hep 6361i '03.
Won Talence decathlon 2002 and IAAF Combined Events Challenge 2003. Four pbs in World Indoor heptathlon win 2003. Grandfather was a professional wrestler, father (Nick) set a world motor speed record. Younger brother Billy (b. 22 Feb 1979) has decathlon best of 7745 '03. Tom married Kim Shiemenz (heptathlon 6209A '03) in 2004.

Miguel PATE b. 13 Jun 1979 St Francisville, Louisiana 1.88m 84kg. Nike. Studying criminal justice at University of Alabama.
At LJ: WCh: '01- 4, '05- dnq 16; WI: '03- 3; WUG: '01- 1. Won US 2001, 2005; NCAA 2000-01.
Progress at LJ: 1997- 7.28, 1998- 7.68/7.73w, 1999- 7.63, 2000- 8.26, 2001- 8.20/8.48w, 2002- 8.59i/8.45, 2003- 8.46A/8.27, 2004- 7.96A, 2005- 8.45. pbs: 55m 6.39i '01, 100m 10.50 '02, 200m 21.41 '01, HJ 2.18i '00, 2.13 '97; TJ 16.52i '02, 16.48 '01.

Darvis PATTON b. 4 Dec 1977 Dallas 1.83m 75kg. adidas. Was at Texas Christian University.
At 200m/4x100m: OG: '04- res 2R; WCh: '03- 2/1R. Won US 200m 2003.
Progress at 100m, 200m: 1998- 10.3, 20.49w; 2000- 10.22w/10.09w, 20.29; 2001- 10.16/10.14w, 20.31; 2002- 10.14, 20.12; 2003- 10.00/9.97w, 20.03, 2004- 10.12/9.89w, 20.17/20.07w; 2005- 10.27. pbs: 60m 6.58i '03, LJ 8.12 '01, TJ 16.17i '98.
Turned to athletics after dislocating his hip playing American football as a teenager.

Dwight PHILLIPS b. 1 Oct 1977 Decatur, Georgia 1.81m 82kg. Nike. Was at University of Kentucky, then Arizona State University.
At LJ: OG: '00- 8, '04- 1; WCh: '01- 8, '03- 1, '05- 1; WI: '03- 1; PAm: '99- 7. Won WAF 2003, 2005; US 2003-04.
Progress at LJ: 1996- 7.14, 1997- 7.26, 1999- 8.18, 2000- 8.21/8.30w, 2001- 8.13/8.23w, 2002- 8.38, 2003- 8.44, 2004- 8.60, 2005- 8.60. pbs: 50m 5.70i '05, 60m 6.47i '05, 100m 10.14 '05, 10.11w '00, 200m 20.68 '02, 400m 46.80 '97, TJ 16.41 '99.
World number one 2003-05, winning 34 of 42 competitions in those three years.

Andrew ROCK b. 23 Jan 1982 Marshfield, Wisconsin 1.88m 75kg. adidas. Studied finance at Wisconsin La Crosse University.
At 400m/4x400m: WCh: '05- 2/1R; OG: '04- res (1)R.
Progress at 400m: 2001- 46.52, 2002- 46.08, 2003- 45.29, 2004- 44.66, 2005- 44.35. pbs: 200m 20.84 '03, 300m 32.4 '05, 600m 1:18.53i '04.
Won Olympic relay gold in 2004, having run third leg in the heat. Improved pb from 44.66 to 44.35 in taking 2005 World silver.

Jarred ROME b. 21 Dec 1976 Seattle 1.96m 145kg. Studied business education at Boise State University.
At DT: OG: '04- dnq 13; WCh: '05- 7; WUG: '01- 8. US champion 2004.
Progress at DT: 1996- 53.14, 1997- 59.46, 1998- 59.78, 1999- 56.86, 2000- 64.00, 2001- 65.53, 2002- 65.92, 2003- 62.24, 2004- 67.51, 2005- 67.39. pb SP 20.17 '02.
Was a quarterback in high school.

Duane ROSS b. 5 Dec 1972 Shelby, North Carolina 1.83m 78kg. GWE. Financial adviser. Graduate of Clemson University.
At 110mh: OG: '04- sf; WCh: '99- 3; Won NCAA 1995. At 60mh: WI: '97- 4, '99- 4.
Progress at 110mh: 1992- 13.97/13.61w, 1993- 13.74, 1994- 13.48, 1995- 13.32, 1996- 13.45, 1997- 13.50, 1998- 13.24, 1999- 13.12, 2000- 13.53, 2001- 13.54, 2002- 13.20, 2003- 13.17, 2004- 13.21, 2005- 13.41. pbs: 200m 21.35w '95, 50mh 6.36i '99, 55mh 7.12i '93, 60mh 7.43i '99.

Leonard SCOTT b. 19 Jan 1980 Zachary. Louisiana 1.81m 80kg. Nike. Studied sociology at the University of Tennessee.
At 100m: WCh: '05- 6. At 60m: WI: '06- 1.
Progress at 100m: 1997- 10.56, 1998- 10.34, 1999- 10.29/9.83w, 2000- 10.26A/10.18w, 2001- 10.05, 2002- 10.13, 2004- 10.01, 2005- 9.94. pbs: 50m 5.58i '05, 55m 6.07i '99, 60m 6.46i '05, 200m 20.34 '01, 20.08w '99.
He missed the 2003 season while with the Pittsburgh Steelers Football team, although he did not play a game in the NFL. Slimmed down from 89kg to 80kg in a year and a half on his return to track.

Wallace SPEARMON b. 24 Dec 1984 Chicago 1.88m 78kg. Student at University of Arkansas.
At 200m: WCh: '05- 2. NCAA champion 2004-05. At 4x400m: WI: '06- 1R.
WIR 4x400m 2006. Two US indoor 200m records 2005.
Progress at 200m: 2003- 21.05, 2004- 20.25/20.12w, 2005- 19.89. pbs: 60m 6.72i '05, 100m 10.38 '04, 10.21w '05; 300m 31.88i '06 (world best), 400m 46.16i '05.
His father (also Wallace, b. 3 Sep 1962) had pbs: of 100m 10.19 '97, 10.14w '86, 10.0w '81; 200m 20.27/20.20w '87. 1 WUG 200/4x100m, 3 PAm 200m 1987.

Toby STEVENSON b. 19 Nov 1976 Odessa, Texas 1.86m 82kg. ZMA. Economics graduate of Stanford University.
At PV: OG: '04- 2; PAm: '03- 1, won NCAA 1998.
Progress at PV: 1994- 4.87, 1995- 5.18, 1996- ?, 1997- 5.40i/5.37, 1998- 5.55, 1999- 5.55, 2000- 5.73A, 2001- 5.40, 2002- 5.74, 2003- 5.75, 2004- 6.00, 2005- 5.90.
Wears a protective helmet while vaulting. Withdrew after warm-up through injury at 2005 Worlds.

Savanté STRINGFELLOW b. 6 Nov 1978 Jackson, Miss. 1.91m 84kg. Nike. Studied sociology at University of Mississippi.
At LJ: OG: '00- dnq 22; WCh: '99- dnq 39, '01- 2, '03- dnq 19; PAm: '99- 8; WI: '04- 1; WCp: '02- 1. 2nd GP 2001. Won US 2001-02, NCAA 2000-01.
Progress at LJ: 1998- 7.32, 1999- 8.12, 2000- 8.30, 2001- 8.38/8.47w, 2002- 8.52, 2003- 8.46, 2004- 8.41i/8.31, 2005- 8.14i/8.02. pbs: 100m 10.53 '03, 10.43w '01; 200m 20.66 '01, HJ 2.14 '99, 2.18i '99?. A torn right Achilles in May 2004 cost him the rest of the season.

Angelo TAYLOR b. 29 Dec 1978 Albany, Georgia 1.88m 77kg. Nike. Was at Georgia Tech University.
At 400mh/4x400mR: OG: '00- 1/dq (res 1)R, '04- sf; WCh: '99- h/1R, '01- sf/1R; WJ: '96- 3; won GP 2000 (and overall), PAm-J 1997, NCAA 1998, US 1999-2001, US indoor 400m 1999
Progress at 400m, 400mh: 1995- -, 52.76, 1996- 46.7, 50.18; 1997- 46.19i/46.81, 48.72; 1998- 45.14, 47.90; 1999- 45.50i, 48.15; 2000- 44.89, 47.50; 2001- 44.68, 47.95; 2002- 44.85, 48.87; 2003- 46.32, 48.94; 2004- 45.85, 48.03. pbs: 200m 20.67 '97, 300m 32.67 '02, TJ 14.76 '96.
Brilliant year in 1998, with fastest ever time by a 19 year-old and losing just twice (to Bryan Bronson) at 400mh. Went out in his heat (misjudging the finish) when favourite for 1999 World 400mh, but took relay gold, and, after winning Olympic gold in 2000, stumbled off the last hurdle in 2001 World 400mh semi.

Dan TAYLOR b. 12 May 1982 Cleveland 1.98m 149kg. Student at Ohio State University.
At SP: PAm: '03- 4. Won NCAA indoor 2003-04.
Progress at SP: 2001- 18.31, 2002- 20.01i/19.15, 2003- 21.33i/20.44, 2004- 20.62, 2005- 20.75. pbs: DT 59.00 '03, HT 69.35 '04, Wt 24.01i '04.
Achieved unique NCAA SP/Wt double 2004.

Paul TEREK b. 20 Oct 1979 Dearborn, Michigan 1.86m 83kg. Mechanical engineering graduate of Michigan State University.
At Dec: OG: '04- 21; WCh: '03- 12, '05- 13. Won US indoor heptathlon 2003-04.
Progress at Dec: 1998- 7206, 1999- 7225, 2001- 7695, 2002- 8041, 2003- 8275, 2004- 8312, 2005- 7976. pbs: 60m 7.04i '04, 100m 10.83 '02, 400m 48.70 '05, 1000m 2:39.43i '05, 1500m 4:24.28 '04, 60mh 8.48i '04, 110mh 15.12 '04, HJ 2.08 '03, PV 5.70i '03, 5.50 '02; LJ 7.33i '05, 7.29 '04, 7.38w '03; SP 15.99i/15.66 '04, DT 49.24 '04, JT 61.14 '03, Hep 6040i '04.
Disqualified for pushing over hurdles in World Champs decathlon 2003; if his time had been allowed he would have scored 8253 for 4th.

Terrrence TRAMMELL b. 23 Nov 1978 Atlanta 1.88m 84kg. Mizuno. Studied retail management at University of South Carolina.
At 110mh/4x100m: OG: '00- 2, '04- 2; WCh: '01- sf, '03- 2, '05- 5; WUG: '99- 1/1R; Won US 2004, NCAA 1999-2000. At 60mh: WI: '01- 1, '06- 1 (60m 3).
Progress at 110mh: 1997- 13.87, 1998- 13.32, 1999- 13.28, 2000- 13.16, 2001- 13.23, 2002- 13.17, 2003- 13.17, 2004- 13.09, 2005- 13.02. pbs: 55m 6.12i '99, 60m 6.45Ai '00, 6.46i '03; 100m 10.04 '00, 200m 20.74 '98, 20.45w '99; 55mh 6.94i '99, 60mh 7.42i '03.
Injured in heats of World Indoor 60m 2003.

Brad WALKER b. 21 Jun 1981 Aberdeen, South Dakota 1.88m 86kg. Nike. Graduated in business administration from University of Washington
At PV: WCh: '05- 2; WI: '06- 1; Won WAF 2005, US indoors and out 2005, NCAA indoor 2003-04.
Progress at PV: 1999- 4.80, 2000- 5.12, 2001- 5.48i/5.36, 2002- 5.64, 2003- 5.80i/5.65, 2004- 5.82, 2005- 5.96, 2006- 5.80i.

Dawane WALLACE b. 30 Dec 1976 Arlington, Va. 1.90m 79kg. Nike. Was at University of Tennessee.
At 110mh: WCh: '01- 7; WUG: '99- 3.
Progress at 110mh: 1996- 14.04w, 1997- 13.88/13.73w, 1998- 13.79/13.65w, 1999- 13.57/13.34w, 2000- 13.22, 2001- 13.22, 2002- 13.22, 2003- 13.32, 2004- 13.22, 2005- 13.36/13.33w. pbs: 50mh 6.50i '02, 55mh 7.13i '00, 60mh 7.58i '02, LJ 7.19 '95.

Ian WALTZ b. 15 Apr 1977 Ashland, Oregon 1.86m 122kg. Studied kinesiology at Washington State University.
At DT: OG: '04- dnq 21; WCh: '05- 5; WJ: '96- 5 (6 SP). US champion 2005.
Progress at DT: 1996- 57.78, 1997- 59.85, 1998- 64.44, 1999- 58.50, 2000- 60.54, 2001- 60.30, 2002- 63.84, 2003- 62.55, 2004- 66.14, 2005- 66.95. pb SP 20.10 '02.
American footballer (defensive end) at school.

Jeremy WARINER b. 31 Jan 1984 Irving, Texas 1.88m 67kg. Student of outdoor recreation at Baylor University.
WIR 4x400m 2006.
At 400m/4x400mR: OG: '04- 1/1R; WCh: '05- 1/1R; PAm-J: '03- 2/1R. US Champion 2004-05, NCAA 400m 2004.
Progress at 400m: 2001- 46.68, 2002- 45.57, 2003- 45.13, 2004- 44.00, 2005- 43.93. pbs: 100m 10.52w '02, 200m 20.41w '02, 20.59 '04; 300m 31.9+ '04.
His 43.93 to win 2005 World title was world's fastest 400m time for five years.

Tyree WASHINGTON b. 28 Aug 1976 Riverside, California 1.85m 84kg. Was at San Bernardino Valley CC.
At 400m/4x400mR: WCh: '97- 3/1R, '03- 2/1R; WI: '03- 1/dq (1)R, '06- 1R. Won WAF 2005, US 2003. World record 4x400m 1998.
Progress at 200m, 400m: 1994- 47.49, 1995- 46.34, 1996- 20.88w, 46.00; 1997- 20.10, 44.38; 1998- 20.29, 44.29; 1999- 20.09, 45.50; 2000- 44.72, 2001- 44.28, 2003- 44.33, 2004- 45.14A/45.40, 2005- 20.43, 44.51. pbs: 100m 10.41 '05, 500y 55.6i '98. LJ 7.39 '95.
Made substantial breakthrough in 1997. Started as sprinter and won 1994 California prep LJ title. Ran world's fastest time for 400m but suffered hamstring injury at US Championships in 2001. Great comeback after missing 2002 season.

Alan WEBB b. 13 Jan 1983 Ann Arbor, Michigan 1.76m 64kg. Nike. Was at University of Michigan, now studying economics.
At 1500m: OG: '04- h; WCh: '05- 9. Won US 1500m 2004-05.
US 2 miles record 2005.
Progress at 1500m/1M: 1999- 4:06.94M, 2000- 3:47.4/4:03.33M, 2001- 3:38.26/3:53.43M, 2002- 3:41.46, 2003- 3:42.87/3:58.84M, 2004- 3:32.73/3:50.73M, 2005- 3:32.52/3:32.1u/3:48.92M. pbs: 800m 1:46.09 '04, 1000m 2:20.32 '05, 3000m 7:39.28 '05, 2M 8:11.48 '05, 5000m 13:10.86 '05.
Broke Jim Ryun's high school record for sophomores in 1999 and in 2001 became the first high schooler to break 4 minutes indoors and outdoors broke Ryun's 36 year-old high school record with 3:53.43.

Bernard WILLIAMS b. 19 Jan 1978 Baltimore 1.83m 81kg. Nike. Was at University of Florida, moving to UCLA.
At 100m/4x100mR (200m): OG: '00- 1R, '04- (2); WCh: '01- 2/dq(1)R, '03- 4/1R; PAm: '99- 1/4R. Won NCAA 2000, USA 2001, 2003, WAF 2003. 2nd GP 200m 2001.
Progress at 100m, 200m: 1997- 10.45, 21.13; 1998- 10.03, 20.46w; 1999- 10.08, 20.69Ai/20.71; 2000- 9.99, 20.03; 2001- 9.94, 20.01; 2002- 9.99, 20.19; 2003- 10.04/10.0, 20.01; 2004- 10.04, 20.01; 2005- 10.26, 20.62. pbs: 55m 6.08Ai '98, 60m 6.56iA '99, 6.59i '01.
Performs as a stand-up comedian using the name "Hollywood Williams".

Darold WILLIAMSON b. 19 Feb 1983 San Antonio, Texas 1.88m 77kg. Student of communications at Baylor University.
At 400m/4x400mR: OG: '04- 1R; WCh: '05- 7/1R; WJ: '02- 1/1R. Won NCAA 2005.
WIR 4x400m 2006.
Progress at 400m: 2000- 46.94, 2001- 46.12, 2002- 45.23, 2003- 44.95, 2004- 44.51, 2005- 44.27. pbs: 200m 20.91 '01, 300m 32.2+ '05.

Women

Amy ACUFF b. 14 Jul 1975 Port Arthur, Texas 1.88m 66kg. Asics. Graduate of UCLA (biology) and Academy of Oriental Medicine, Austin. Part-time model.
At HJ: OG: '96- dnq 24=, '00- dnq 31, '04- 4; WCh: '95- 8=, '97- dnq 14, '99- 9, '01- 10=, '03- 9=, '05- 8; WI: '01- 4, '03- 10; WJ: '92- 9, '94-3=; WUG: '97- 1. 3rd GP 2001. Won PAm-J 1993, NCAA 1995-6, US 1995, 1997, 2001, 2003, 2005.
Progress at HJ: 1988- 1.73, 1990- 1.83, 1991- 1.89, 1992- 1.90, 1993- 1.93, 1994- 1.89, 1995- 1.98, 1996- 1.94, 1997- 2.00, 1998- 1.94, 1999- 1.95, 2000- 1.91, 2001- 1.98, 2002- 1.95, 2003- 2.01, 2004- 2.00, 2005- 1.93, 2006- 1.95i.
Married **Tye Harvey** (b. 25 Sep 1974, PV: 2 WI 03, 5.93i '01, 5.80 '00) in October 2004.

Jenny ADAMS b. 8 Jul 1978 Tomball, Texas 1.65m 55kg. Nike. Corporate communications graduate of University of Houston.
At 100mh: WCh: '01- 5 (nj LJ), '03- 6. Won US LJ 2001, NCAA LJ 2000.
Progress at 100mh: 1995- 14.45w, 1996- 13.98/13.93w, 1997- 13.47, 1998- 13.25/13.22w, 1999- 12.98/12.86w, 2000- 12.86, 2001- 12.63/12.61w, 2002- 12.80/12.71w, 2003- 12.67, 2004- 12.66, 2005- 12.89/12.88w. pbs: 60m 7.47i '00, 100m 11.58 '00, 200m 23.51 '03, 60mh 7.95i '03, LJ 6.68i/6.75w '01, 6.64 '00.

Me'Lisa BARBER b. 4 Oct 1980 Livingston, New Jersey 1.60m 52kg. Nike. Was at University of South Carolina.
At 100m/4x100mR: WCh: '05- 5/1R. At 400m/4x400mR: WCh: '03- 1R; PAm: '03- 5/1R; WUG: '01- 3R. At 60m: WI: '06- 1. Won US 100m 2005.
Progress at 100m, 200m, 400m: 1997- 11.86/11.78w, 24.20; 1998- 11.57, 23.93/23.63w, 57.21i; 1999- 11.40, 23.57/23.16w; 2000- 11.59, 23.23; 2001- 11.46/11.44w, 23.43/23.06w, 52.18; 2002- 11.35, 23.01, 50.87; 2003- 23.51, 52.04; 2004- 51.95, 2005- 11.04/10.87w, 22.37. pbs: 60m 7.01i '06, 300m 37.54 '03.
Her twin sister **Miki** has pbs: 200m 23.05 '99, 22.71w '01; 400m 50.63 '01 and at 400m/4x400mR: WJ: '98- 8/3R; WUG: '99-2/1R, '01- 3/3R, 1 NCAA 2000.

Danielle CARRUTHERS b. 22 Dec 1979 Paducah, Kentucky 1.73m 62kg. Nike. Was at University of Indiana.
At 100mh: WUG: '01- 8. At 60mh: WI: '06- 4. Won US indoor 60mh 2005-06.
Progress at 100mh: 1998- 13.88/13.77w, 2000- 13.33, 2001- 12.96/12.79w, 2002- 12.68, 2003- 12.79, 2004- 12.56, 2005- 12.72/12.63w. pbs: 55m 6.79i '00, 60m 7.26i '02, 100m 11.43/11.42w '01, 200m 23.24 '01, 50mh 6.85i '02, 55mh 7.55i '00, 60mh 7.88i '06

Hazel CLARK b. 3 Oct 1977 Livingston, NJ 1.78m 55kg. Nike. Was at University of Florida.
At 800m: OG: '00- 7, '04- h; WCh: '01- sf, '05- 8; PAm: '03- 7. US champion 2005, NCAA 1998.

Progress at 800m: 1994- 2:10.24, 1995- 2:05.50, 1996- 2:05.08i/2:06.66, 1997- 2:01.42, 1998- 2:00.23, 1999- 2:01.77i/2:02.01, 2000- 1:58.75, 2001- 1:59.95, 2002- 2:05.24, 2003- 2:01.71, 2004- 1:59.32, 2005- 1:57.99. pbs: 400m 53.69 '98, 1000m 2:36.47 '01, 1500m 4:16.04 '00, 1M 4:40.82 '00.
Sister of **Joetta** (b. 1 Aug 1962) who competed at four Olympics 1988-2000 (7th 1992) and five World Champs (7th 1997) and ranked in US top ten at 800m for 22 successive years 1979-2000; pb 1:57.84 (1998). Their brother (and coach) J J Clark married Jearl Miles-Clark and their father is the celebrated school principal, Joe Clark, portrayed in the movie *Lean On Me*.

LaTasha COLANDER b. 23 Aug 1976 Portsmouth, Va 1.67m 52kg. née Colander, then Colander-Richardson. Nike. Was at University of North Carolina.
At 100m: OG: '04- 8. At 200m: WCh: '05- 5. At 400m/4x400mR: OG: '00- qf/1R. At 100mh: WJ: '94- 2. Won US 100m 2004, 400m 2000-01.
World record 4x200m 2000.
Progress at 100m, 200m, 400m: 1993- 12.01/11.74w, 23.99, 1994- 11.65, 23.56/23.3w; 1995- 11.64/11.60w, 23.80/23.60w; 1996- 23.26w, 1997- 11.76, 23.21; 1998- 23.50i, 2000- 22.49, 49.87; 2001- 11.68, 22.63, 50.79; 2002- 50.84, 2003- 11.08, 2004- 10.97, 22.37; 2005- 11.06, 22.34/22.30w. pbs: 55m 6.91i '97, 60m 7.21i '05, 300m 36.00 '00, 55mh 7.57i '95, 60mh 8.13i '99, 100mh 13.07 '96, 12.99w '97; 400mh 56.88 '99.
Formerly a hurdler, she won the US title in her first season at 400m in 2000. Unable to compete at 2001 World Champs. Married Roderick Richardson in February 2000.

Lashinda DEMUS b. 10 Mar 1983 Palmdale, California 1.70m 62kg. Nike. Student at University of South Carolina.
At 400mh/4x400mR: OG: '04- sf; WCh: '05- 2; WJ: '02- 1/1R. Won WAF 2005, PAm-J 1999, US 2005, NCAA 2002.
Two world junior records 400mh 2002.
Progress at 400mh: 1998- 64.61, 1999- 57.04, 2001- 55.76, 2002- 54.70, 2003- 55.65, 2004- 53.43, 2005- 53.27. pbs: 50m 6.64i '01, 60m 7.73i '01, 100m 11.5 '01, 200m 24.0 '01, 23.50w '05; 400m 51.24 '02, 500y 1:05.8i '01, 800m 2:08.91i '06, 2:09.16 '04; 55mh 7.65i '04, 60mh 8.11i '04, 100mh 13.08 '04, 12.93w '05.
Her mother, Yolanda Rich, had a 400m best of 52.19 in 1980.

Gail DEVERS b. 19 Nov 1966 Seattle 1.60m 55kg. Nike International. Studied sociology at UCLA.
At 100mh/4x100mR (100m): OG: '88- sf; '92- 5 (1), '96- 4/1R (1), '00- sf, '04- h (sf); WCh: '91- 2, '93- 1/2R (1), '95- 1, '97- 1R, '99- 1 (5), '01- 2, '03- sf (7); PAm: '87- (1)/1R; WCp: '02- 1/2R. At 60mh: WI: '03- 1, '04- 2. At 60m: WI: '93- 97-99-04: 1/1/2/1. Won NCAA 100m 1988, US 100m 1993-4, 100mh 1991-2, 1995-6, 1999-2001, 2003-04. Won GWG 100mh 2001; WAF 100mh 2003, GP 100mh 2000, 2002 (2nd 1992), 2nd 100m 1996. overall: 3rd 2000, 2nd 2002.
US records 100mh (6) 1988-2000, indoor 60m 1993, 60mh 2003.
Progress at 100m, 100mh: 1983- 11.69; 1984- 11.51/11.34w, 14.32; 1985- 11.19, 13.16/13.15w; 1986- 11.12/10.96w, 13.08; 1987- 10.98/10.85w, 13.28/13.1w; 1988- 10.97/10.86w, 12.61; 1991- 11.29, 12.48; 1992- 10.82, 12.55; 1993- 10.82, 12.46; 1994- 11.12/10.77w; 1995- 11.04/10.8w, 12.61; 1996- 10.83, 12.62; 1997- 10.88; 1999- 10.94, 12.37; 2000- 10.99, 12.33; 2001- 12.53, 2002- 11.45, 12.40/12.29w; 2003- 11.11, 12.45; 2004- 11.05, 12.50. pbs: 50m 6.00+ '99, 55m 6.74i '89, 60m 6.95i '93, 200m 22.71/22.55w '87, 400m 52.66 '87, 800m 2:11.07 '82, 55mh 7.58i '92, 60mh 7.74i '03, 400mh 59.26 '85, LJ 6.77 '88, TJ 12.97/13.31w '86.
The fastest ever woman sprinter-hurdler. The thyroid disorder Graves's Disease caused her to miss competition in 1989-90, but after being close to having to have a foot amputated she made an astonishing return in 1991 to win the TAC 100mh and World silver with a US record in Berlin. In 1992 she was a surprise winner of the Olympic 100m but tripped over the last hurdle when well clear of the field in the 100mh. Won 16 successive 100mh finals from 1993 to Olympic 4th 1996, having become only the second woman to retain Olympic 100m title. She won the 1999 World outdoor 100mh with her first US record for six years. She was a clear favourite to take the 2000 Olympic gold at 100mh, but, feeling a hamstring problem, pulled up after four hurdles in her semi final. She was also unable to run in the 4x100m, but started, heavily strapped, in the GP Final 100mh a week later to ensure a huge payday with a share of the Golden League jackpot and third in the overall Grand Prix. Set US records for 60mh at 7.78 and 7.74 in 2003 before winning the World Indoor title. Her World Indoor win at 60m in 2004 was her 12th global gold medal.
Married to Ron Roberts 1988-92 and now to Mike Phillips; daughter Karsen Anise born in 2005.

Stacy DRAGILA b. 25 Mar 1971 Auburn, California 1.72m 62kg. née Mikaelson. Nike. Graduate of Idaho State University.
At PV: OG: '00- 1, '04- dnq 18=; WCh: '99- 1, '01- 1, '03- 4=, '05- dnq 16; WI: '97-9-01-03-04: 1/8/4/dnq/2. Won GWG 2001, GP 2001, US 1996-7, 1999-2001, 2003-05.
7 world pole vault records 1999-2001 & world outdoor best 2004, 10 WIR 1997-2003. 18 US records 1996-2004 (and 24 indoors 1995-2004).
Progress at PV: 1995- 3.70, 1996- 4.20, 1997- 4.45, 1998- 4.48i/4.42A, 1999- 4.60, 2000- 4.70b/4.63, 2001- 4.81, 2002- 4.72, 2003- 4.78i/4.62, 2004- 4.83, 2005- 4.60. pbs: 55mh 8.30i '03, 100mh 13.88A '98, HJ 1.70 '97, LJ 5.89/6.07w '02; SP 10.80 '02, JT 44.28A '98, Hep 5488A '98.
Won first women's world vault titles both indoors 1997 and outdoors 1999 (both in world

records) and inaugural Olympic title.

Torri EDWARDS b. 31 Jan 1977 Fontana, Cal. 1.63m 52kg. Nike/HSI. Was at University of Southern California.

At 100m/(200m)/4x100mR: OG: '00- qf/sf/3R; WCh: '01- dq1 resR, '03- 1/2/2R; PAm: '99- 2R; WUG: '99- 5/1R. At 60m: WI: '03- 3, '04- 4.

Progress at 100m, 200m: 1994- 24.52, 1995- 11.84w, 23.94/23.60w; 1996- 11.48, 23.60/23.1; 1997- 11.55A/11.35w, 23.43; 1998- 11.11/11.05w, 22.88/22.87w; 1999- 11.10/11.05w, 22.89/22.84w; 2000- 11.06/10.92w, 22.65; 2001- 11.11/11.09w, 2002- 11.11, 2003- 10.93, 22.28; 2004- 11.00dq, 22.38dq. pbs: 50m 6.31i '02, 60m 7.12i '04.

She finished 2nd at 100m and 3rd at 200m at the 2003 Worlds, positions that were elevated to gold and silver through the disqualification of Kelli White for drugs abuse. Received drugs ban from 24 Apr 2004, but reinstated early in November 2005 as nikethamide downgraded to public warning and one year's ineligibility.

Allyson FELIX b. 18 Nov 1985 Los Angeles 1.68m 57kg. adidas. Student at University of Southern California.

At 200m: OG: '04- 2; WCh: '03- qf, '05- 1; WJ: '02- 5; PAm: '03- 3. At 100m: WY: '01- 1 (1 Medley R). Won WAF 200m 2005, US 200m 2004-05.

World junior record 200m 2004 after unratified (no doping test) at age 17 in 2003.

Progress at 100m, 200m: 2000- 12.19/11.99w, 23.90; 2001- 11.53, 23.31/23.27w; 2002- 11.40, 22.83/22.69w; 2003- 11.29/11.12w, 22.11A/22.51; 2004- 11.16, 22.18, 2005- 11.05, 22.13. pbs: 50m 6.43i '02, 60m 7.32i '04, 400m 51.12 '05.

First teenager to won a World sprint title. Unbeaten in ten 200m competitions 2005. Older brother Wes Felix won World Junior bronze at 200m and gold in WJR at 4x100m in 2002.

Hyleas FOUNTAIN b. 14 Jan 1981 Columbus, Georgia 1.70m 60kg. Nike. University of Georgia.

At Hep: WCh: '05- 12; US champion 2005. At Pen: WI: '06- 8. Won NCAA Hep 2003, LJ 2004; US Junior HJ 2000.

Progress at Hep: 2001- 4905, 2002- 5673w, 2003- 5999, 2004- 6035, 2005- 6502. pbs: 200m 23.53 '03, 800m 2:16.88 '05, 55mh 7.61i '05, 60mh 8.15i '04, 100mh 13.09 '05, HJ 1.88 '05, LJ 6.67 '05, TJ 13.40 '04, SP 12.28 '04, JT 46.90 '05, Pen 4417i '05.

Erin GILREATH b. 11 Oct 1980 Gainesville 1.77m 92kg. NYAC. University of Florida.

At OG: '04- dnq 20; WCh: '05- 10. US champion 2004-05.

Four world indoor bests 20lb weight 2004-05, Three US hammer records 2004-05.

Progress at HT: 2002- 54.28, 2003- 70.50, 2004- 72.12, 2005- 73.87. pbs: SP 16.04 '03, 20lbWt: 24.23i (and 24.46i chain over long) '05.

A 38-ft shot putter in high school in 1998, she did not throw for three years but has made very rapid progress.

Sandra GLOVER b. 30 Dec 1968 Palestine, Texas 1.73m 59kg. née Cummings. Nike. Teacher, graduate of University of Houston.

At 400mh: OG: '00- sf; WCh: '99- 5, '01- 8, '03- 2, '05- 3; WCp: '02- 2; Won WAF 2003-04, US 1999-2002. 3rd GP 1999, 2001.

Progress at 400mh: 1988- 61.08, 1989- 59.99, 1990- 57.68, 1991- 56.97, 1992- 55.77, 1993- 56.76, 1994- 56.66, 1995- 57.39, 1996- 56.31mx/56.92, 1997- 55.63, 1998- 55.11, 1999- 53.65, 2000- 53.33, 2001- 54.30, 2002- 54.40, 2003- 53.34, 2004- 53.40, 2005- 53.32. pbs: 200m 23.73 '00, 100mh 13.79/13.62w '91.

Made huge improvement in 1999 at the age of 30. Coached by her husband, Don Glover.

Joanna HAYES b. 23 Dec 1976 Williamsport, Pa. 1.65m 58kg. Sociology graduate of UCLA.

At 100mh: OG: '04- 1; WCh: '05- dq (fell); PAmJ: '95- 1; won WAF 2004. At 400mh: WCh: '99- h, '03- sf; PAm: '99- 5, '03- 1; WUG: '99- 2; won NCAA 1999. At 60mh: WI: '04- 4.

Progress at 100mh, 400mh: 1994- 14.02/13.80w, 59.12; 1995- 13.38/13.06w, 59.02; 1996- 13.15, 58.32; 1997- 13.04, 56.38; 1998- 12.93, 57.09; 1999- 12.89, 54.57; 2000- 12.67, 54.97; 2003- 12.83/12.65w, 54.66; 2004- 12.37, 55.74; 2005- 12.47. pbs: 100m 11.41 '04, 60mh 7.83i '04.

Missed Olympics in 2000 (4th at 400mh and 5th at 100mh in US Trials) and did not compete in 2001-02 while working at the Jackie Joyner-Kersee Youth Center in East St. Louis. Then returned to LA.

Monique HENDERSON b. 18 Feb 1983 San Diego 1.70m 54kg.Reebok. Student at UCLA.

At 400m/4x400m: OG: '04- 1R; WCh: '05- 7; WJ: '02- 1/1R. NCAA champion 2005.

Progress at 400m: 1996- 54.79, 1997- 53.83, 1998- 52.93, 1999- 51.96, 2000- 50.74, 2001- 51.34, 2002- 51.10, 2003- 51.96, 2004- 50.53, 2005- 49.96. pbs: 60m 7.50i '03, 100m 11.34 '05, 200m 22.71 '04, 300m 35.8 '05.

Monique HENNAGAN b. 26 May 1976 Columbia, SC 1.73m 57kg. Nike. Degree in psychology from University of North Carolina.

At 400m/4x400mR: OG: '00- qf/1R, '04- 4/1R; WCh: '01- sf, '05- hR; WI: '99- 3R, '01- 5/4R, '03- 5/3R; WJ: '92- sf/4R, '94- 2/1R; PAm-J: '93- 2/2R; WCp: '02- 2R. Won US 400m 2004-05, NCAA 800m 1996.

Progress at 400m: 1992- 53.58, 1993- 52.30, 1994- 52.19, 1995- 52.32, 1996- 51.44, 1997- 52.00, 1998- 51.11, 1999- 51.05, 2000- 50.82, 2001- 50.98, 2002- 51.04, 2003- 51.46, 2004- 49.56, 2005- 50.24. pbs: 60m 7.42i '04, 100m 11.26 '05, 200m 22.87 '05, 300m 36.52 '01, 800m 2:02.5 '96.

Aretha HILL-THURMOND b. 14 Aug 1976 Seattle 1.81m 98kg. Was at University of Washington.

At DT: OG: '96/04- dnq 34/19; WCh: '99/03/05: dnq 24/20/21; PAm: '99- 1, '03- 1; WUG: '97- 6.

US champion 2003-04.
Progress at DT: 1992- 43.38, 1993- 47.48, 1994- 50.52, 1995- 54.84, 1996- 60.50, 1997- 59.92, 1998- 65.62dh/63.68, 1999- 62.15, 2000- 62.91, 2001- 61.64, 2002- 65.21, 2003- 65.10/66.23dh, 2004- 65.86, 2005- 64.56. pb SP 15.91i/15.67 '98.
Withdrew due to a collapsed lung from 1999 WUG and Worlds after 2nd in US 200m. Married Reedus Thurmond (DT pb 62.34 '00) in May 2005.

Chaunte HOWARD b. 12 Jan 1984 Templeton, California 1.75m 59kg. Student at Georgia Tech University.
At HJ: OG: '04- dnq 26=; WCh: '05- 2; PAm-J: '03- 3; Won NCAA 2004, indoors 2004-05
Progress at HJ: 2000- 1.75, 2001- 1.84, 2002- 1.87, 2003- 1.89, 2004- 1.98A, 2005- 2.00. pbs: 100m 11.83 '05, 100mh 13.78 '04, LJ 6.26 '02, TJ 12.93 '04, 12.98w '05.

Sheena JOHNSON b. 1 Oct 1982 Camden, New Jersey 1.65m 58kg. Nike. Student at UCLA.
At 400mh: OG: '04- 4; WJ: '98- h. Won US 2004, NCAA 2003-04.
Progress at 400mh: 1998- 58.61, 1999- 59.12, 2000- 56.82, 2001- 56.02, 2002- 55.71, 2003- 54.24, 2004- 52.95, 2005- 54.72. pbs: 60m 7.47i '03, 100m 11.74 '00, 200m 24.14 '00, 400m 53.49 '00, 60mh 8.06i '04, 100mh 12.75 '04, LJ 6.10/6.16w '00, TJ 12.67 '00.

Marion JONES b. 12 Oct 1975 Los Angeles 1.78m 68kg. Nike. Studied journalism at University of North Carolina at Chapel Hill.
At 100m/4x100m (200m): OG: '00- 1/3R (1, 3 LJ, 1 4x400), '04- (5 LJ); WCh: '97- 1/1R (10 LJ), '99- 1 (sf, 3 LJ); '01- 2/dq1R (1); WJ: '92- 5/2R (7); WCp: '98- 1 (1, 2 LJ), '02- 1/2R. Won GP 100m 1998, 2000, 2002; 200m 1997; won overall 1998 & 2002. 2nd 2000. Won US 100m 1997-8, 2002; 200m 1998-9, 2001-02; LJ 1997-8, 2004; GWG 100m/200m 1998, 100m 2001.
World record 4x200m 2000.
Progress at 100m, 200m, 400m, LJ: 1988- 13.0, c.59.0; 1989- 12.01, 24.46/24.06w/23.8w, 56.73; 1990- 11.62, 23.70, 54.21; 1991- 11.17, 22.76, 52.91; 1992- 11.14, 22.58, 54.44; 1993- 11.28/11.2, 23.01/22.79w, 6.71/6.75w; 1994- 11.40, 23.32, 6.75; 1995- 11.68, 23.96w, 6.64; 1997- 10.76, 21.76, 6.93; 1998- 10.65A/10.71, 21.62A/21.80, 50.36, 7.31; 1999- 10.70, 21.81, 50.79, 7.01; 2000- 10.75/10.68w, 21.84, 49.59, 7.02; 2001- 10.84, 22.23; 2002- 10.84, 22.11, 50.46; 2004- 11.04/10.99w, 22.93, 7.11/7.13w; 2005- 11.28, 55.03. pbs: 50m 5.93+ '99, 60m 6.85+ '99, 300m 35.68 '01.
Won 59 of 60 100m finals 1997-2002, 42 successive then a loss to Zhanna Pintusevich-Block at the 2001 Worlds and 19 more to 2004. The woman athlete of 1998, when she won 34 individual events until her 2nd to Heike Drechsler in World Cup LJ. Had another brilliant season in 1999, with 5 wins at 100m to World gold and 10 at 200m until pulled up with back spasms in her semi at the Worlds. In 2000 she won a record five medals at the Olympic Games, including three golds, in 2001 she won two golds and a silver at the Worlds, and in 2002 was unbeaten at individual events – 14 at 100m, 3 at 200m and 1 at 400m. Had dual nationality as mother was born in Belize, but opted for the USA. US junior champion at 100m & 200m 1991-2. 5th at 100m and 4th at 200m in 1992 US Olympic Trials, but declined Olympic relay reserve place. World 100m age bests for age 14-15-16 and 200m 15-16. She played point guard on the North Carolina basketball team that won the NCAA Division 1 title 1994, but broke her left foot in August and December 1995. Married C J Hunter (1999 World SP champ) on 3 Oct 1998, but separated in 2001. Now partner of Tim Montgomery, their son Tim was born on 28 June 2003.

Deena KASTOR b. 14 Feb 1973 Waltham, Mass. née Drossin. 1.63m 48kg.Asics. Graduate of University of Arkansas.
At 10,000m: OG: '00- h; WCh: '99- 11, '01- 11, '03- 12; WUG: '97- 1. At Mar: OG: '04- 3. World CC: '99-00-01-02-03: 10/12/12/2/2; Won US 10,000m 2000-01, 2003-04; HMar 2004, CC 1997, 1999-2003.
N.American records: 10,000m 2002, 15km road & Mar 2003, 10M, 20k & HMar 2006.
Progress at 5000m, 10,000m, Mar: 1992- 16:21.47, 1993- 15:52.80i/16:07.73, 1994- 16:39.62, 34:10.89; 1996- 16:29.17, 34:13.75; 1997- 15:43.63, 32:47.44; 1998- 15:07.83, 1999- 14:56.84, 32:00.72; 2000- 14:51.62, 31:51.05; 2001- 15:08.02, 32:05.14, 2:26:58; 2002- 15:13.93, 30:50.32, 2:26:53; 2003- 15:08.14, 31:17.86. 2:21:16; 2004- 15:29.30, 31:09.65, 2:27:20; 2005- 15:52.0, 31:45.08, 2:21:25. pbs: 1500m 4:07.82 '00, 2000m 5:42.76 '01, 3000m 8:42.59 '00, 2M 9:35.89 '02; Road: 5km 14:54 '02, 15km 47:15 '03, 10M 51:31 '06, 20km 64:07 '06, HMar 67:34 '06, 25km 1:21:57 '05, 30km 1:38:29 '05.
Seventh in New York on marathon debut 2001. 3rd London Marathon 2003, won Chicago 2005. At latter race 25km and 30km splits were faster than official world records, but not ratifiable. Married her massage therapist Andrew Kastor on 14 September 2003.

Anjanette KIRKLAND b. 24 Feb 1974 Pineville, Louisiana 1.72m 66kg. Nike. Degree in agricultural education from Texas A & M University.
At 100mh: WCh: '97- sf, '01- 1, '03- h; 3rd GP 2002. At 60mh: WI: '01- 1.
Progress at 100mh: 1992- 13.99, 1993- 13.49/13.47w, 1994- 13.22, 1995- 13.09/12.89w, 1996- 13.24, 1997- 12.74/12.70w, 1998- 12.83, 1999- 12.91/12.68w, 2000- 12.63, 2001- 12.42, 2002- 12.62, 2003- 13.80, 2004- 12.90/12.79w, 2005- 12.57. pbs: 60m 7.60i '99, 50mh 6.83i '01, 55mh 7.61i '96, 60mh 7.85i '01, 400mh 57.75 '97.
Formerly partner of Bernard Williams, their daughter Jadin Williams born on 4 May 2003.

Muna LEE b. 30 Oct 1981 Little Rock, Arkansas

1.72m 50kg. Studied fashion and design at Louisiana State University.
At 100m/4x100mR: WCh: '05- 7/1R. At 200m: OG: '04- 7=. Won NCAA indoor 60m 2003-04, 200m 2002-03.
Progress at 100m, 200m: 1998- 24.72, 1999- 11.66, 24.08; 2000- 11.36, 23.83; 2001- 11.17/11.13w, 23.04i/23.12/22.53w; 2002- 11.19, 22.66/22.33w; 2003- 11.04/10.97w, 22.49i/22.74; 2004- 11.12/11.00w, 22.36/22.22w; 2005- 11.09/10.99w, 22.46. pbs: 55m 6.73i '03, 60m 7.11i '05.

Tianna MADISON b. 30 Aug 1985 Elyria, Ohio 1.68m 60kg. Student at University of Tennessee.
At LJ: WCh: '05- 1; WI: '06- 2; PAm-J: '03- 4, NCAA champion indoors and out 2005.
Progress at LJ: 2000- 5.73, 2001- 6.07, 2002- 6.20, 2003- 6.28, 2004- 6.60, 2005- 6.89/6.92w, 2006- 6.80i. pbs: 55m 6.75i '05, 60m 7.27i '05, 100m 11.41 '05, 11.35w '04; 200m 23.56i '05, 23.66 '04.
Set pbs in qualifying and final of 2005 Worlds.

Melissa MORRISON-HOWARD b. 9 Jul 1971 Mooresville, NC 1.63m 52kg. née Morrison. Adidas. Psychology graduate of Appalachian State University.
At 100mh: OG: '00- 3, '04- 3; WCh: '97- h; US champion 1997. At 60mh: WI: '97-9-03: 5/6/3.
Progress at 100mh: 1988- 14.37, 1989- 14.09, 1991- 13.63w, 1992- 13.24, 1993- 13.24, 1994- 13.24, 1995- 13.05A, 1996- 12.92/12.81w, 1997- 12.61, 1998- 12.53, 1999- 12.67/12.55w, 2000- 12.57, 2001- 13.00/12.82w, 2002- 12.79, 2003- 12.70, 2004- 12.53/12.44w, 2005- 12.86. pbs: 60m 7.40i '99, 100m 11.45A '93, 200m 23.98 '02, 23.82w '01; 50mh 6.81i '99, 55mh 7.64i '96, 60mh 7.83i '98, LJ 6.23 '93, TJ 12.55 '93.

Michelle PERRY b. 15 Dec 1979 Granada Hills, California 1.75m 67kg. Sociology at UCLA.
At 100mh: WCh: '05- 1; PAm: '03- 4. At Hep: OG: '04- 14. Won WAF & US 100mh 2005.
Progress at 100mh: 1995- 14.36, 1996- 14.37/13.19w, 1997- 13.87/13.82w, 1998- 13.41, 1999- 13.26/13.08w/12.9w, 2000- 13.15/13.03w, 2001- 13.18, 2003- 12.80, 2004- 12.74, 2005- 12.43. pbs: 100m 11.57 '01, 11.55w '97; 200m 22.91 '04, 400m 54.80 '03, 800m 2:12.81 '04, 60mh 7.86i '06, 400mh 56.23 '01, HJ 1.70 '04, LJ 6.14 '01, 6.23w '05; SP 12.07 '03, JT 40.73 '04, Hep 6126 '04.

Suzy POWELL-ROOS b. 3 Sep 1976 Modesto 1.78m 63kg. Asics. Was at UCLA.
At DT: OG: '96- dnq 33, '00- dnq 15; WCh: '97- dnq 21, '01- dnq 18, '03- 9; WJ: '92- 10, '94- 3; PAm: '03- 4; US champion 1996, PAm-J 1995.
Progress at DT: 1990- 46.31, 1991- 49.66, 1992- 51.72, 1993- 55.06, 1994- 57.40, 1995- 58.06, 1996- 60.58, 1997- 65.22, 1998- 65.05, 1999- 60.89, 2000- 65.30, 2001- 64.50, 2002- 69.44dh/65.48, 2003- 65.38, 2004- 63.58, 2005- 62.35. pb JT 54.62 '97.
Her 69.44 at La Jolla in 2002 was acclaimed as a US discus record but throwing area was later found to be downhill. Married Tim Roos in November 2004.

Sanya RICHARDS b. 26 Feb 1985 Kingston, Jamaica 1.75m 63kg. Nike. University of Texas.
At (200m)/400m/4x400m: OG: '04- 6/1R; WCh: '03- sf/1R, '05- 2; WJ: '02- 3/2. Won WAF 2005, US 2003, 2005; NCAA 2003.
World junior indoor bests 200m, 400m (2) 2004.
Progress at 200m, 400m: 1999- 23.84, 2000- 23.57, 54.34; 2001- 23.09, 53.49; 2002- 23.01, 50.69; 2003- 22.80i/22.86, 50.58; 2004- 22.49i/22.73, 49.89; 2005- 22.53, 48.92. pbs: 60m 7.21i '04, 100m 11.28 '03, 300m 35.6 '05, LJ 6.08 '01.
Left Jamaica at the age of 12 and gained US citizenship on 20 May 2002. Her 48.92 at Zürich in 2005 was the world's fastest 400m since 1996.

Jillian SCHWARTZ b. 19 Sep 1979 Evanston 1.73m 63kg. Nike. Was at Duke University.
At PV: OG: '04- dnq 17; WCh: '03- dnq 18=, '05- 11; WI: '04- 4.
Progress at PV: 1999- 3.56, 2000- 4.10, 2001- 4.20, 2002- 4.50, 2003- 4.45, 2004- 4.60, 2005- 4.55, 2006- 4.55i.

Rachelle SMITH b. 30 Jun 1981 Norfolk, Virginia 1.60m 52kg. née Boone. Nike. Was at Indiana University.
At 200m: WCh: '05- 2.
Progress at 100m, 200m: 1999- 3.56, 2000- 11.49/11.39w, 23.37; 2001- 11.22/11.32w, 23.29/22.94w; 2002- 11.53, 22.99i/23.35; 2003- 11.22, 22.87; 2004- 11.37/11.26w, 22.69; 2005- 11.17/11.02w, 22.22. pbs: 60m 7.21i '03, 400m 54.19 '05.

Shauna SMITH b. 10 Sep 1983 Sheridan, Wyoming 1.78m 63kg. University of Wyoming.
At 400mh: WCh: '05- sf; Won NCAA 2005.
Progress at 400mh: 2001- 59.70, 2002- 58.89, 2003- 57.09, 2004- 54.42, 2005- 54.21. pbs: 60m 7.54iA '05, 200m 23.53A '04, 400m 51.79i '04, 53.04A '02; 55mh 7.84iA '04, 60mh 8.33iA '04, 100mh 13.29 '04.

Jennifer STUCZYNSKI b. 6 Feb 1982 1.80m 64kg. adidas. Graduate of Roberts Wesleyan University.
At PV: US indoor champion 2005.
Progress at PV: 2002- 2.75, 2004- 3.49, 2005- 4.57, 2006- 4.68i. pbs: 55mh 8.07i '05, JT 46.82 '05.
All-time top scorer at basketball at her university, she has made very rapid progress since taking up vaulting.

Seilala SUA b. 25 Feb 1978 Fort Lauderdale 1.87m 109kg. Nike. Studied sociology at UCLA.
At DT/(SP): OG: '00- 10, '04- dnq; WCh: '99- 6, '01- 5/dnq 17, '05- dnq 16; WJ: '96- 2/8; PAm-J: '95- 2/1, '97- 1/1. Won US DT 1998-2001, SP 2001; NCAA SP 1999-2000, DT 1997-2000.
Progress at DT: 1994- 44.22, 1995- 53.84, 1996- 56.78, 1997- 63.44, 1998- 64.67, 1999- 64.89, 2000- 65.90, 2001- 65.64, 2002- 62.89, 2003- 61.93, 2004- 62.13, 2005- 61.82. pbs: SP 18.51 '02, HT

50.60 '00, JT 49.12 '99, 20lb Wt 20.52i '99.
With the discus 1997-2000, Sua is only the second woman ever to win four successive NCAA titles at the same event (after Suzy Hamilton 1500m 1987-90). Her 107 points at shot, discus and weight indoors (38) and out (69) is an NCAA record for any athlete.

Kellie SUTTLE b. 9 May 1973 St Peters, Missouri 1.70m 59kg. Nike. Was at Arkansas State University.
At PV: OG: '00- 11, '04- dnq 24=; WCh: '99- 9; WI: '01-03-06: 2=/4/7; PAm: '99- 2, '03- 4. Won US 1998.
Progress at PV: 1995- 3.71i/3.67, 1996- 3.85i/3.66, 1997- 3.90, 1998- 4.27, 1999- 4.46i/4.35, 2000- 4.53, 2001- 4.60, 2002- 4.50, 2003- 4.58, 2004- 4.67, 2005- 4.50i/4.41, 2006- 4.55i. pb LJ 5.86 '93.
Started pole vaulting in 1994 while working as a gymnastics instructor.

Brenda TAYLOR b. 9 Feb 1979 St. Louis 1.74m 63kg. Nike. Psychology/biology graduate of Harvard University.
At 400mh: OG: '04- 7; WCh: '01- sf; PAm: '03- 4. NCAA champion 2001.
Progress at 400mh: 1997- 60.80, 1999- 57.29, 2000- 56.64, 2001- 55.46, 2002- 55.03, 2003- 54.92, 2004- 53.36, 2005- 55.40. pbs: 400m 52.56 '03, 100mh 13.19 '04.

Nicole TETER b. 8 Nov 1973 San Diego 1.72m 57kg. Nike Farm Team. Merchandising manager. Was at University of Arkansas.
At 800m: OG: '04- sf; PAm-J: '91- 2. Won US 2002.
Progress at 800m: 1989- 2:11.15, 1990- 2:10.27, 1991- 2:05.61, 1992- 2:04.1, 1993- 2:04.13, 1994- 2:07.35, 1995- 2:03.71, 1996- 2:02.55, 1998- 2:02.56, 2000- 2:01.59, 2001- 2:01.32, 2002- 1:57.97, 2003- 1:59.91, 2004- 1:58.52. pbs: 400m 55.49 '89, 1500m 4:04.19 '02, 1M 4:32.71i '02, 2M 9:49.09 '02.
US junior champion in 1991, she made a great breakthrough in 2002 when she broke the American indoor 800m record to win US title in 1:58.71 and improved outdoors to 1:58.83 to win US title and then to 1:57.97.

Jennifer TOOMEY b. 19 Dec 1971 New Haven, CT 1.65m 51kg Nike. née Lincoln. Biology graduate of Tufts University.
At 800m: WCh: '03- sf; WI: '04- 4. Won US indoor 800m & 1500m 2004.
Progress at 800m: 1998- 2:14, 1999- 2:06.12, 2000- 2:03.58, 2001- 2:00.38, 2002- 2:00.12, 2003- 1:59.75, 2004- 1:59.64i/2:02.54, 2005- 1:59.96. pbs: 1000m 2:34.19i '04 (N.Am record), 2:36.46 '05; 1500m 4:06.24 '05, 1M 4:30.9i mx '04, 4:39.85 '02.
In 2004 she became the first woman to win the NCAA Indoor 800m and 1500m double. Was a state champion diver in high school and did not start running seriously until 1998. Married Michael Toomey 12 Sep 1998.

De'Hashia **'Dee Dee' TROTTER** b. 8 Dec 1982 Twentynine Palms, California 1.78m 60kg. adidas. Degree in criminal justice from University of Tennessee.
At 400m/4x400mR: OG: '04-5/1R; WCh: '03- sf/res (1)R, '05- 5; PAm: '03- 1R. Won NCAA 2004.
Progress at 400m: 1998- 58.61, 1999- 59.12, 2000- 56.82, 2001- 56.02, 2002- 53.66, 2003- 50.66, 2004- 50.00, 2005- 49.88. pbs: 55m 6.93i '04, 60m 7.46i '05, 100m 11.65 '02, 200m 23.12 '05, LJ 6.00 '02.

Grace UPSHAW b. 22 Sep 1975 Berkeley 1.78m 65kg. Graduated in American studies from University of California, Berkeley.
At LJ: OG: '04- 10; WCh: '03- 8, '05- 7. US champion 2003, 2005; indoors 2002.
Progress at LJ: 1994- 5.80, 1995- 5.79, 1996- 5.98/6.19w, 1997- 6.24, 2000- 6.47A/6.38, 2001- 6.62/6.70w, 2002- 6.60/6.75w, 2003- 6.73/6.99w, 2004- 6.84/6.88w, 2005- 6.73/6.87w. pbs: 60m 7.63i '04, 100m 11.81 '02, 200m 24.16 '02.
After graduating she did not compete in 1998-9, returning in 2000. Daughter of Monte Upshaw, who set a US high school long jump record of 7.72 in 1954 (second best in the world that year).

Lauryn WILLIAMS b. 11 Sep 1983 Pittsburgh 1.57m 57kg. Nike. Finance graduate of University of Miami.
At 100m/4x100mR: OG: '04- 2; WCh: '03- res (1)R, '05- 1/1R; WJ: '02- 1/2R; PAm: '03- 1/1R. Won NCAA 2004. At 60m: WI: '06- 1.
Progress at 100m, 200m: 1999- 12.00/11.6, 24.2; 2000- 11.70, 24.31; 2001- 11.65/11.60w, 23.85; 2002- 11.33, 23.64/23.63w; 2003- 11.12, 23.25; 2004- 10.96/10.94w, 22.46; 2005- 10.88, 22.27. pbs: 55m 6.70i '04, 60m 7.01i '06.

VENEZUELA

Governing body: Federación Venezolana de Atletismo, Apartado Postal 29059, Caracas. Founded 1948.

National Champions 2005: **Men**: 100m: Juan Morillo 10.72, 200m: Ellis Ollarves 21.46, 400m: Carlos Pérez, 800m: Simoncito Silvera 1:50.49, 1500m: Nico Herrera 3:48.83, 5000m: Manuel Bellorín 15:08.68, 10,000m: Ender Moreno 30:30.35, 3000mSt: Néstor Nieves 8:52.86, 110mh: Jonathan Davis 14.75, 400mh: Víctor Solarte 50.93, HJ: Beltrán Leon 2.15, PV: César González 4.60, LJ: Louis Tristan 7.43, TJ: Johnny Rodríguez, SP: Yojer Medina 18.37, DT: Jesús Parejo 53.05, HT: Aldo Bello 62.02, JT: Manuel Fuenmayor 71.87, Dec: Juan Jaramillo 6877, 20kmW: Jesús Chirinos 1:33:17. **Women**: 100m: Fiorella Molina 12.12, 200m: Wilmary Álvarez 23.67, 400m/800m: Jenny Mejías 54.25/2:09.17, 1500m/5000m: Valentina Medina 4:32.98/17:33.14, 10,000m: Zuleima Amaya 36:37.36, 3000mSt: Candy Rincón 12:00.28, 100mh: Sandrine Legenort 13.97, 400mh: Yusmely García 60.77, HJ: Marierlys Rojas 1.75, PV: Diana Vázquez 2.90, LJ: Jessica Morillo 5.77, TJ: Johana Trevino 13.60, SP: Ahymara Espinoza 15.55, DT: Rosario Ramos 50.27, HT: Rosa Rodríguez 58;90, JT: María de los A. González 46.02, Hep: Thaimara Rivas 5129, 20kmW: Carolina Flores 1:46:20.

INTRODUCTION TO WORLD LISTS AND INDEX

Records

World, World U20 and U18, Olympic, Continental and Area records are listed for standard events. In running events up to and including 400 metres, only fully automatic times are shown. Marks listed are those which are considered statistically acceptable by the ATFS, and thus may differ from official records where, for instance the performance was set indoors. These are followed by road bests and bests by masters / veterans.

World All-time and Year Lists

These lists are presented in the following format: Mark, Wind reading (where appropriate), Name, Nationality (abbreviated), Date of birth, Position in competition, Meeting name (if significant), Venue, Date of performance.

In standard events the best 30 or so performances are listed followed by the best marks for other athletes. Position, meet and venue details have been omitted for reasons of space beyond 100th in year lists.

In the all-time lists performances which have been world records (or world bests, thus including some unratified marks) are shown with WR against them – outdoor records only.

Juniors (U20) are shown with-J after date of birth, and Youths (U18) with -Y.

Indexes

These contain the names of all athletes ranked with full details in the world year lists for standard events (and others such as half marathon). The format of the index is as follows: Family name, First name, Nationality, Birthdate, Height (cm) and Weight (kg), 2005 best mark, Lifetime best (with year) as at the end of 2004.

* indicates an athlete who is profiled in the Biographies section, and ^ one who has been profiled in previous editions.

General Notes

Altitude aid

Marks set at an altitude of 1000m or higher have been suffixed by the letter "A".

Although there are no separate world records for altitude assisted events, it is understood by experts that in all events up to 400m in length (with the possible exclusion of the 110m hurdles), and in the horizontal jumps, altitude gives a material benefit to performances. For events beyond 800m, however, the thinner air of high altitude has a detrimental effect.

Supplementary lists are included in relevant events for athletes with seasonal bests at altitude who have low altitude marks qualifying for the main list.

Some leading venues over 1000m

Venue	Altitude
Addis Ababa ETH	2365m
Air Force Academy USA	2194
Albuquerque USA	1555
Antananarivo MAD	1350
Bloemfontein RSA	1392
Bogotá COL	2644
Boulder USA	1655
Bozeman USA	1467
Calgary CAN	1045
Cali COL	1046
Ciudad de Guatemala GUA	1402
Ciudad de México MEX	2247
Cochabamba BOL	2558
Colorado Springs USA	1823
Cuenca ECU	2561
Denver USA	1609
El Paso USA	1187
Flagstaff USA	2107
Font-Romeu FRA	1850
Fort Collins USA	1521
Germiston RSA	1661
Guadalajara MEX	1567
Harare ZIM	1473
Johannesburg RSA	1748
Krugersdorp RSA	1740
Logan USA	1372
Medellín COL	1541
Monachil ESP	2320
Nairobi KEN	1675
Pietersberg RSA	1230
Pocatello USA	1361
Potchefstroom RSA	1351
Pretoria RSA	1400
Provo USA	1380
Reno USA	1369
Roodepoort RSA	1720
Rustenburg RSA	1157
Salt Lake City USA	1321
Secunda RSA	1628
Segovia ESP	1000
Sestriere ITA	2050
Soría ESP	1056
South Lake Tahoe USA	1909
Toluca MEX	2700
Tsakhkadzor ARM	1980
Windhoek NAM	1725

Some others over 500m

Venue	Altitude
Almaty KZK	847
Ankara TUR	902
Bern SUI	555
Blacksburg USA	634
Boise USA	818
Canberra AUS	581
La Chaux-de-Fonds SUI	997
Caracas VEN	922
Edmonton CAN	652
Jablonec CZE	598
Las Vegas USA	619
Lubbock USA	988

Madrid ESP	640
Magglingen SUI	751
Malles ITA	980
Moscow, Idaho USA	787
München GER	520
Nampa, Idaho USA	760
Salamanca ESP	806
Santiago de Chile CHI	520
(Apoquindo)	950
São Paulo BRA	725
Sofia BUL	564
Spokane USA	576
Taiyuan CHN	780
Trípoli GRE	655
Tucson USA	728

350m-500m

Annecy FRA	448
Banská Bystrica SVK	362
Fayetteville USA	407
Genève SUI	385
Götzis AUS	448
Johnson City USA	499
Lausanne SUI	375
Rieti ITA	402
Sindelfingen GER	440
Stuttgart GER	415
Tashkent UZB	477
Zürich SUI	410

Automatic timing

In the main lists for sprints and hurdles, only times recorded by fully automatic timing devices are included.

Hand timing

In the sprints and hurdles supplementary lists are included for races which are hand timed. Any athlete with a hand timed best 0.01 seconds or more better than his or her automatically timed best has been included, but hand timed lists have been terminated close to the differential levels considered by the IAAF to be equivalent to automatic times, i.e. 0.24 sec. for 100m, 200m, 100mh, 110mh, and 0.14 sec. for 400m and 400mh. It should be noted that this effectively recognises bad hand timekeeping, for there should be no material difference between hand and auto times, but what happens is that badly trained timekeepers anticipate the finish, having reacted to the flash at the start.

In events beyond 400m, auto times are integrated with hand timed marks, the latter identifiable by times being shown to tenths. All-time lists also include some auto times in tenths of a second, identified with the symbol ′.

Indoor marks

Indoor marks are included in the main lists for field events and straightway track events, but not for other track events. This is because track sizes vary in circumference (200m is the international standard) and banking, while outdoor tracks are standardised at 400m. Outdoor marks for athletes whose seasonal bests were set indoors are shown in a supplemental list.

Mixed races

For record purposes athletes may not, except in road races, compete in mixed sex races. Statistically there would not appear to be any particular logic in this, and women's marks set in such races are shown in our lists - annotated with mx. In such cases the athlete's best mark in single sex competition is appended.

Field event series

Field event series are given (where known) for marks in the top 30 performances lists.

Tracks and Courses

As well as climatic conditions, the type and composition of tracks and runways will affect standards of performance, as will the variations in road race courses.

Wind assistance

Anemometer readings have been shown where available in the lists for sprints and horizontal jumps in metres per second to one decimal place. If the figure was given to two decimal places, it has been rounded to the next tenth upwards, e.g. a wind reading of +2.01m/s, beyond the IAAF legal limit of 2.0, is rounded to +2.1; or -1.22m/s is rounded up to -1.2.

For multi-events a wind-assisted mark in one in which an event is aided by a wind over 4.0m/s and the average of the three wind-measured events is > 2m/s.

Drugs bans

The IAAF have determined that its Council may decertify an athlete's records, titles and results if he or she is found to have used a banned substance before those performances. Performances at or after such a positive finding are shown in footnotes. Such athletes are shown with ¶ after their name in year lists, and in all-time lists if at any stage of their career they have served a drugs suspension of a year or more (thus not including athletes receiving public warnings or 3 month bans for stimulants etc., which for that year only are indicated with a #). This should not be taken as implying that the athlete was using drugs at that time. Nor have those athletes who have subsequently unofficially admitted to using banned substances been indicated; the ¶ is used only for those who have been caught.

Venues

From time to time place names are changed. Our policy is to use names in force at the time that the performance was set. Thus Leningrad prior to 1991, Sankt-Peterburg from its re-naming.

Amendments

Keen observers may spot errors in the lists. They are invited to send corrections as well as news and results for 2006.

Peter Matthews, 10 Madgeways Close, Great Amwell, Ware, Herts SG12 9RU, England
Email: p.jmatthews@tiscali.co.uk

WORLD & CONTINENTAL RECORDS

As at end of 2005. **Key**: W = World, Afr = Africa, Asi = Asia, CAC = Central America & Caribbean, Eur = Europe, NAm = North America, Oce = Oceania, SAm = South America, Com = Commonwealth, W20 = World Junior (U20), W18 = World Youth (U18, not officially ratified by IAAF).
Successive columns show: World or Continent, performance, name, nationality, venue, date.
A altitude over 1000m, + timing by photo-electric-cell, * awaiting ratification, § not officially ratified

100 METRES

W,CAC,Com	9.77	Assafa POWELL	JAM	Athína	14 Jun 2005
NAm	9.79	Maurice GREENE	USA	Athína	16 Jun 1999
Afr	9.86	Frank FREDERICKS	NAM	Lausanne	3 Jul 1996
Eur	9.86	Francis OBIKWELU	POR	Athína	22 Aug 2004
SAm	10.00A	Róbson da SILVA	BRA	Ciudad de México	22 Jul 1988
Asi	10.00	Koji ITO	JPN	Bangkok	13 Dec 1998
Oce	9.93	Patrick JOHNSON	AUS	Mito	5 May 2003
W20	10.01	Darrel BROWN	TRI	Saint-Denis	24 Aug 2003
W18	10.24	Darrel BROWN	TRI	Bridgetown	14 Apr 2001
	10.23 ?	Tamunoski ATORUDIBO	NGR	Enugu	23 Mar 2002

200 METRES

W, NAm	19.32	Michael JOHNSON	USA	Atlanta	1 Aug 1996
Afr	19.68	Frank FREDERICKS	NAM	Atlanta	1 Aug 1996
Eur	19.72A	Pietro MENNEA	ITA	Ciudad de México	12 Sep 1979
CAC	19.77	Ato BOLDON	TRI	Stuttgart	13 Jul 1997
Com	19.68	Frank FREDERICKS	NAM	Atlanta	1 Aug 1996
SAm	19.89	Claudinei da SILVA	BRA	München	11 Sep 1999
Oce	20.06A	Peter NORMAN	AUS	Ciudad de México	16 Oct 1968
Asi	20.03	Shingo SUETSUGU	JPN	Yokohama	7 Jun 2003
W20	19.93	Usain BOLT	JAM	Hamilton, BER	11 Apr 2004
W18	20.13	Usain BOLT	JAM	Bridgetown	20 Jul 2003

400 METRES

W, NAm	43.18	Michael JOHNSON	USA	Sevilla	26 Aug 1999
CAC	44.14	Roberto HERNÁNDEZ	CUB	Sevilla	30 May 1990
Afr, Com	44.17	Innocent EGBUNIKE	NGR	Zürich	19 Aug 1987
SAm	44.29	Sanderlei PARRELA	BRA	Sevilla	26 Aug 1999
Eur	44.33	Thomas SCHÖNLEBE	GER	Roma	3 Sep 1987
Oce	44.38	Darren CLARK	AUS	Seoul	26 Sep 1988
Asi	44.56	Mohamed AL-MALKY	OMN	Budapest	12 Aug 1988
W20	43.87	Steve LEWIS	USA	Seoul	28 Sep 1988
W18	45.14	Obea MOORE	USA	Santiago de Chile	2 Sep 1995

800 METRES

W, Eur	1:41.11	Wilson KIPKETER	DEN	Köln	24 Aug 1997
Com	1:41.73	Sebastian COE	GBR	Firenze	10 Jun 1981
SAm	1:41.77	Joaquim CRUZ	BRA	Koln	26 Aug 1984
Afr	1:42.28	Sammy KOSKEI	KEN	Koln	26 Aug 1984
NAm	1:42.60	Johnny GRAY	USA	Koblenz	28 Aug 1985
CAC	1:42.85	Norberto TELLEZ	CUB	Atlanta	31 Jul 1996
Asi	1:43.11	Youssef Saad KAMEL	KOR	Zürich	6 Aug 2004
Oce	1:44.3 m	Peter SNELL	NZL	Christchurch	3 Feb 1962
W20	1:43.64	Japheth KIMUTAI	KEN	Zürich	13 Aug 1997
W18	1:46.25	Benson ESHO	KEN	Pergine Valsugana	23 Jul 2004

1000 METRES

W, Afr, Com	2:11.96	Noah NGENY	KEN	Rieti	5 Sep 1999
Eur	2:12.18	Sebastian COE	GBR	Oslo	11 Jul 1981
NAm	2:13.9	Rick WOHLHUTER	USA	Oslo	30 Jul 1974
SAm	2:14.09	Joaquim CRUZ	BRA	Nice	20 Aug 1984
Oce	2:16.57	John WALKER	NZL	Oslo	1 Jul 1980
CAC	2:17.0	Byron DYCE	JAM	København	15 Aug 1973
Asi	2:18.91	Mohamed SULEIMAN	QAT	Lindau	28 Jul 1995
W20	2:15.00	Benjamim KIPKURUI	KEN	Nice	17 Jul 1999
W18	2:17.59	Japheth KIMUTAI	KEN	København	23 Aug 1995

1500 METRES

W, Afr	3:26.00	Hicham EL GUERROUJ	MAR	Roma	14 Jul 1998

Com	3:26.34	Bernard LAGAT	KEN	Bruxelles	24 Aug 2001
Eur	3:28.95	Fermin CACHO	ESP	Zürich	13 Aug 1997
NAm	3:29.30	Bernard LAGAT	USA	Rieti	28 Aug 2005
Asi	3:30.00	Rashid RAMZI	BRN	Roma	8 Jul 2005
Oce	3:31.96	Simon DOYLE	AUS	Stockholm	3 Jul 1991
SAm	3:33.25	Hudson Santos de SOUZA	BRA	Rieti	28 Aug 2005
CAC	3:36.60	Stephen AGAR (later CAN)	DMN	Abbotsford	2 Jun 1996
W20	3:30.24	Cornelius CHIRCHIR	KEN	Monaco	19 Jul 2002
W18	3:35.16	Cornelius CHIRCHIR	KEN	Rieti	3 Sep 2000

1 MILE

W, Afr	3:43.13	Hicham El GUERROUJ	MAR	Roma	7 Jul 1999
Com	3:43.40	Noah NGENY	KEN	Roma	7 Jul 1999
Eur	3:46.32	Steve CRAM	GBR	Oslo	27 Jul 1985
NAm	3:47.69	Steve SCOTT	USA	Oslo	7 Jul 1982
Asi	3:47.97	Daham Najim BASHIR	QAT	Oslo	29 Jul 2005
Oce	3:48.98	Craig MOTTRAM	AUS	Oslo	29 Jul 2005
SAm	3:51.05	Hudson de SOUZA	BRA	Oslo	29 Jul 2005
CAC	3:57.34	Byron DYCE	JAM	Stockholm	1 Jul 1974
W20	3:50.25	Alex KIPCHIRCHIR	KEN	Rieti	7 Sep 2003
W18	3:54.56	Isaac SONGOK	KEN	Linz	20 Aug 2001

2000 METRES

W, Afr	4:44.79	Hicham EL GUERROUJ	MAR	Berlin	7 Sep 1999
Com	4:48.74	John KIBOWEN	KEN	Hechtel	1 Aug 1998
Eur	4:51.39	Steve CRAM	GBR	Budapest	4 Aug 1985
Oce	4:51.52	John WALKER	NZL	Oslo	30 Jun 1976
NAm	4:52.44	Jim SPIVEY	USA	Lausanne	15 Sep 1987
Asi	4:55.57	Mohammed SULEIMAN	QAT	Roma	8 Jun 1995
W18, W20	4:56.86	Issac SONGOK	KEN	Berlin	31 Aug 2001
SAm	5:03.34	Hudson Santos de SOUZA	BRA	Manaus	6 Apr 2002
CAC	5:03.4	Arturo BARRIOS	MEX	Nice	10 Jul 1989

3000 METRES

W, Afr, Com	7:20.67	Daniel KOMEN	KEN	Rieti	1 Sep 1996
Eur	7:26.62	Mohammed MOURHIT	BEL	Monaco	18 Aug 2000
Asi	7:30.76	Jamal Bilal SALEM	QAT	Doha	13 May 2005
NAm	7:30.84	Bob KENNEDY	USA	Monaco	8 Aug 1998
CAC	7:35.71	Arturo BARRIOS	MEX	Nice	10 Jul 1989
Oce	7:37.30	Craig MOTTRAM	AUS	Monaco	19 Jul 2002
SAm	7:39.70	Hudson Santos de SOUZA	BRA	Lausanne	2 Jul 2002
W20	7:28.78	Augustine CHOGE	KEN	Doha	13 May 2005
W18	7:36.82	Augustine CHOGE	KEN	Rieti	5 Sep 2004

5000 METRES

W, Afr	12:37.35	Kenenisa BEKELE	ETH	Hengelo	31 May 2004
Com	12:39.74	Daniel KOMEN	KEN	Bruxelles	22 Aug 1997
Eur	12:49.71	Mohammed MOURHIT	BEL	Bruxelles	25 Aug 2000
Oce	12:55.76	Craig MOTTRAM	AUS	London	30 Jul 2004
NAm	12:58.21	Bob KENNEDY	USA	Zürich	14 Aug 1996
Asi	12:58.58	Moukhled AL-OUTAIBI	KSA	Heusden-Zolder	23 Jul 2005
CAC	13:07.79	Arturo BARRIOS	MEX	London (CP)	14 Jul 1989
SAm	13:19.64	Antonio SILIO	ARG	Roma	17 Jul 1991
W20	12:52.61	Eliud KIPCHOGE	KEN	Oslo	27 Jun 2003
W18	12:57.01	Augustine CHOGE	KEN	Berlin	12 Sep 2004

10,000 METRES

W, Afr	26:17.53	Kenenisa BEKELE	ETH	Bruxelles	26 Aug 2005
Com	26:27.85	Paul TERGAT	KEN	Bruxelles	22 Aug 1997
Asi	26:38.76	Abdullah Ahmad HASSAN	QAT	Bruxelles	5 Sep 2003
Eur	26:52.30	Mohammed MOURHIT	BEL	Bruxelles	3 Sep 1999
CAC	27:08.23	Arturo BARRIOS	MEX	Berlin	18 Aug 1989
NAm	27:13.98	Mebrahtom KEFLEZIGHI	USA	Stanford	4 May 2001
Oce	27:31.92	Shaun CREIGHTON	AUS	Melbourne	25 Nov 1996
SAm	27:38.72	Antonio SILIO	ARG	Bruxelles	3 Sep 1993
W20	26:41.75	Samuel WANJIRU	KEN	Bruxelles	26 Aug 2005
W18	27:25.55	Robert KIPCHUMBA	KEN	Bruxelles	24 Aug 2001

MARATHON

W. Afr, Com	2:04:55	Paul TERGAT	KEN	Berlin	28 Sep 2003
NAm	2:05:38	Khalid KHANNOUCHI (ex MAR)	USA	London	14 Apr 2002
SAm	2:06:05	Ronaldo da COSTA	BRA	Berlin	20 Sep 1998
Asi	2:06:16	Toshinari TAKAOKA	JPN	Chicago	13 Oct 2002
Eur	2:06:36	António PINTO	POR	London	16 Apr 2000
	2:06:36	Benoît ZWIERZCHLEWSKI	FRA	Paris	6 Apr 2003
CAC	2:07:19	Andrés ESPINOSA	MEX	Boston	18 Apr 1994
Oce	2:07:51	Rob DE CASTELLA	AUS	Boston	21 Apr 1986
W20	2:10:13	Moses MASAI	KEN	Essen	17 Apr 2005

Boston course has an overall net drop of 139m (0.33%), and in 1994 there was a strong following wind.

3000 METRES STEEPLECHASE

W,Asi	7:53.63	Saïf Saaeed SHAHEEN	QAT	Bruxelles	3 Sep 2004
Afr	7:55.28	Brahim BOULAMI	MAR	Bruxelles	24 Aug 2001
Com	7:55.72	Bernard BARMASAI	KEN	Köln	24 Aug 1997
Eur	8:04.95	Simon VROEMEN	NED	Helsinki	26 Aug 2005
NAm	8:09.17	Henry MARSH	USA	Koblenz	28 Aug 1985
Oce	8:14.05	Peter RENNER	NZL	Koblenz	29 Aug 1984
SAm	8:14.41	Wander MOURA	BRA	Mar del Plata	22 Mar 1995
CAC	8:25.69	Salvador MIRANDA	MEX	Barakaldo	9 Jul 2000
W20	7:58.66	Stephen CHERONO	KEN	Bruxelles	24 Aug 2001
W18	8:18.51	Ronald KIPCHUMBA	KEN	Bruxelles	3 Sep 2004

110 METRES HURDLES

W, Eur, Com	12.91	Colin JACKSON	GBR	Stuttgart	20 Aug 1993
W, Asi	12.91	LIU Xiang	CHN	Athína	27 Aug 2004
NAm	12.92	Roger KINGDOM	USA	Zürich	16 Aug 1989
	12.92	Allen JOHNSON	USA	Atlanta	23 Jun 1996
	12.92	Allen JOHNSON	USA	Bruxelles	23 Aug 1996
CAC	13.00	Anier GARCIA	CUB	Sydney	25 Sep 2000
Afr	13.26	Shaun BOWNES	RSA	Heusden	14 Jul 2001
Oce	13.29	Kyle VANDER-KUYP	AUS	Göteborg	11 Aug 1995
SAm	13.29	Redelen DOS SANTOS	BRA	Lisboa	13 Jun 2004
W20	13.12	LIU Xiang	CHN	Lausanne	2 Jul 2002
W18	13.43	SHI Dongpeng	CHN	Shanghai	5 May 2001
W 18 (3'0")	13.22	Konstadínos DOUVALIDIS	GRE	Skópelos	2 Oct 2004

400 METRES HURDLES

W, NAm	46.78	Kevin YOUNG	USA	Barcelona	6 Aug 1992
Afr, Com	47.10	Samuel MATETE	ZAM	Zürich	7 Aug 1991
CAC	47.25	Felix SÁNCHEZ	DOM	Saint-Denis	29 Aug 2003
Eur	47.37	Stéphane DIAGANA	FRA	Lausanne	5 Jul 1995
Asi	47.53	Hadi Sou'an AL-SOMAILY	KSA	Sydney	27 Sep 2000
SAm	47.84	Bayano KAMANI	PAN	Helsinki	7 Aug 2005
Oce	48.28	Rohan ROBINSON	AUS	Atlanta	31 Jul 1996
W20	48.02	Danny HARRIS	USA	Los Angeles	17 Jun 1984
W18	48.89	Louis VAN ZYL	RSA	Kingston	19 Jul 2002

HIGH JUMP

W, CAC	2.45	Javier SOTOMAYOR	CUB	Salamanca	27 Jul 1993
Eur	2.42	Patrik SJÖBERG	SWE	Stockholm	30 Jun 1987
	2.42 i§	Carlos THRÄNHARDT	GER	Berlin	26 Feb 1988
NAm	2.40 i§	Hollis CONWAY	USA	Sevilla	10 Mar 1991
		Charles AUSTIN	USA	Zürich	7 Aug 1991
Asi	2.39	ZHU Jianhua	CHN	Eberstadt	10 Jun 1984
Com	2.38i	Steve SMITH	GBR	Wuppertal	4 Feb 1994
	2.38	Troy KEMP	BAH	Nice	12 Jul 1995
Afr, Com	2.38	Jacques FREITAG	RSA	Oudtshoorn	5 May 2005
Oce	2.36	Tim FORSYTH	AUS	Melbourne	2 Mar 1997
SAm	2.33	Gilmar MAYO	COL	Pereira	17 Oct 1994
W20	2.37	Dragutin TOPIC	YUG	Plovdiv	12 Aug 1990
		Steve SMITH	GBR	Seoul	20 Sep 1992
W18	2.33	Javier SOTOMAYOR	CUB	La Habana	19 May 1984

POLE VAULT

W, Eur	6.15 i§	Sergey BUBKA	UKR	Donetsk	21 Feb 1993
	6.14 A	Sergey BUBKA	UKR	Sestriere	31 Jul 1994

Oce, Com	6.05	Dmitriy MARKOV	AUS	Edmonton	9 Aug 2001
Afr	6.03	Okkert BRITS	RSA	Köln	18 Aug 1995
NAm	6.03	Jeff HARTWIG	USA	Jonesboro	14 Jun 2000
Asi	5.92i	Igor POTAPOVICH	KAZ	Stockholm	19 Feb 1998
	5.90	Grigoriy YEGOROV	KAZ	Stuttgart 19 Aug 1993 & London (CP)	10 Sep 1993
	5.90	Igor POTAPOVICH	KAZ	Nice	10 Jul 1996
SAm	5.76	Tom HINTNAUS	BRA	Zürich	21 Aug 1985
CAC	5.70A	Dominic JOHNSON	LCA	El Paso	26 Aug 2000
	5.72A §	Paul BENAVIDES	MEX	El Paso	18 Jun 1994
W20	5.80	Maksim TARASOV	RUS	Bryansk	14 Jul 1989
W18	5.51	Germán CHIARAVIGLIO	ARG	Pôrto Alegre	1 May 2004

LONG JUMP

W, NAm	8.95	Mike POWELL	USA	Tokyo	30 Aug 1991
Eur	8.86 A	Robert EMMIYAN	ARM	Tsakhkadzor	22 May 1987
CAC	8.71	Iván PEDROSO	CUB	Salamanca	18 Jul 1995
Com	8.62	James BECKFORD	JAM	Orlando	5 Apr 1997
Oce	8.49	Jai TAURIMA	AUS	Sydney	28 Sep 2000
Afr	8.46	Cheikh TOURÉ	SEN	Bad Langensalza	15 Jun 1997
Asi	8.44 #	Mohamed AL-KHUWALIDI	KSA	Makkah	13 Apr 2005
	8.40	LAO Jianfeng	CHN	Zhaoqing	28 May 1997
SAm	8.40	Douglas de SOUZA	BRA	São Paulo	15 Feb 1995
W20	8.34	Randy WILLIAMS	USA	München	8 Sep 1972
W18	8.25	Luis Alberto BUENO	CUB	La Habana	28 Sep 1986

TRIPLE JUMP

W, Eur, Com	18.29	Jonathan EDWARDS	GBR	Göteborg	7 Aug 1995
NAm	18.09	Kenny HARRISON	USA	Atlanta	27 Jul 1996
CAC	17.92	James BECKFORD	JAM	Odessa, Texas	20 May 1995
SAm	17.89 A	João Carlos de OLIVEIRA	BRA	Ciudad de México	15 Oct 1975
Oce	17.46	Ken LORRAWAY	AUS	London (CP)	7 Aug 1982
Asi	17.35	Oleg SAKIRKIN	KAZ	Moskva	5 Jun 1994
Afr	17.34	Ndabezinhle MDHLONGWA	ZIM	Lafayette	28 Mar 1998
W20	17.50	Volker MAI	GER	Erfurt	23 Jun 1985
W18	16.89	GU Junjie	CHN	Dalian	5 May 1985

SHOT

W, NAm	23.12	Randy BARNES	USA	Westwood	20 May 1990
Eur	23.06	Ulf TIMMERMANN	GER	Hania	22 May 1988
Afr, Com	21.97	Janus ROBBERTS	RSA	Eugene	2 Jun 2001
SAm	21.14	Marco Antonio VERNI	CHI	Santiago de Chile	29 Jul 2004
CAC	20.78	Alexis PAUMIER	CUB	La Habana	29 Jul 2000
Asi	20.54	Khalid Habash AL-SUWAIDI	QAT	Stayki	25 Jun 2005
	20.60 §	Shakti SINGH (no doping test)	IND	Bangalore	5 Jul 2000
Oce	20.96	Justin ANLEZARK	AUS	Brisbane	5 Apr 2003
W20	21.05 i§	Terry ALBRITTON	USA	New York	22 Feb 1974
	20.65 §	Mike CARTER	USA	Boston	4 Jul 1979
	20.39	Janus ROBBERTS	RSA	Germiston	7 Mar 1998
W18	18.73	Karsten STOLZ	GER	Essen	2 Sep 1981
W20 6kg	21.96	Edis ELKASEVIC	CRO	Zagreb	20 Jun 2002

DISCUS

W, Eur	74.08	Jürgen SCHULT	GER	Neubrandenburg	6 Jun 1986
NAm	72.34 ¶	Ben PLUCKNETT	USA	Stockholm	7 Jul 1981
	71.32 §	Ben PLUCKNETT	USA	Eugene	4 Jun 1983
CAC	71.06	Luis DELIS	CUB	La Habana	21 May 1983
Afr, Com	70.32	Frantz KRUGER	RSA	Salon-de-Provence	26 May 2002
Oce	65.62 §	Werner REITERER	AUS	Melbourne	15 Dec 1987
	65.06	Wayne MARTIN	AUS	Newcastle	3 Jan 1979
Asi	65.25	Ehsan HADADI	IRI	Inchon	1 Sep 2005
SAm	64.69	Jorge BALLIENGO	ARG	Rosario	3 May 2005
W20	65.62 §	Werner REITERER	AUS	Melbourne	15 Dec 1987
	63.64	Werner HARTMANN	GER	Strasbourg	25 Jun 1978
W20 1.75kg	65.88	Omar Ahmed EL GHAZALI	EGY	Cairo	7 Nov 2003
W18	58.62	Michal HODUN	POL	Santiago de C hile	21 Oct 2000
W18 1.5kg	69.50	Margus HUNT	EST	Valmiera	30 Jul 2004

¶ Disallowed by the IAAF following retrospective disqualification for drug abuse, but ratified by the AAU/TAC

HAMMER

W, Eur	86.74	Yuriy SEDYKH	UKR/RUS	Stuttgart	30 Aug 1986
Asi	84.86	Koji MUROFUSHI	JPN	Praha	29 Jun 2003
NAm	82.52	Lance DEAL	USA	Milano	7 Sep 1996
Afr, Com	80.63	Chris HARMSE	RSA	Durban	15 Apr 2005
Oce	79.29	Stuart RENDELL	AUS	Varazdin	6 Jun 2002
CAC	77.78	Alberto SANCHEZ	CUB	La Habana	15 May 1998
SAm	76.42	Juan CERRA	ARG	Trieste	25 Jul 2001
W20	78.33	Olli-Pekka KARJALAINEN	FIN	Seinäjoki	5 Aug 1999
W20 6kg	81.34	Krisztian PARS	HUN	Szmobathely	2 Sep 2001
W18	73.66	Vladislav PISKUNOV	UKR	Live	11 Jun 1994

JAVELIN

W, Eur	98.48	Jan ZELEZNY	CZE	Jena	25 May 1996
Com	91.46	Steve BACKLEY	GBR	Auckland (NS)	25 Jan 1992
NAm	89.16 §	Tom PETRANOFF	USA	Potchefstroom	1 Mar 1991
	87.68	Breaux GREER	USA	Monaco	19 Sep 2004
Afr	88.75	Marius CORBETT	RSA	Kuala Lumpur	21 Sep 1998
Oce	88.20	Gavin LOVEGROVE	NZL	Oslo	5 Jul 1996
Asi	87.60	Kazuhiro MIZOGUCHI	JPN	San José	27 May 1989
CAC	87.12	Emeterio GONZALEZ	CUB	Jena	3 Jun 2000
SAm	84.70	Edgar BAUMANN	PAR	San Marcos	17 Oct 1999
W20	83.87	Andreas THORKILDSEN	NOR	Fana	7 Jun 2001
W18	79.96	Aki PARVIAINEN	FIN	Pyhäselkä	12 Sep 1991

DECATHLON

W,Eur	9026	Roman SEBRLE	CZE	Götzis	27 May 2001
NAm	8891	Dan O'BRIEN	USA	Talence	5 Sep 1992
Com	8847	Daley THOMPSON	GBR	Los Angeles	9 Aug 1984
Asi	8725	Dmitriy KARPOV	KAZ	Athína	24 Aug 2004
Oce	8490	Jagan HAMES	AUS	Kuala Lumpur	18 Sep 1998
CAC	8252	Ra'l DUANY	CUB	La Habana	24 Jul 2000
SAm	8291 m	Tito STEINER	ARG	Provo	23 Jun 1983
	8266	Pedro da SILVA	BRA	Walnut	24 Apr 1987
Afr	8023	Hamdi DHOUIBI	TUN	Helsinki	10 Aug 2005
W20	8397	Torsten VOSS	GER	Erfurt	7 Jul 1982
W18	8104h	Valter KÜLVET	EST	Viimsi	23 Aug 1981
	7829	Valter KÜLVET	EST	Stockholm	13 Sep 1981

4 X 100 METRES RELAY

W, NAm	37.40	USA (Marsh, Burrell, Mitchell, C.Lewis)	Barcelona	8 Aug 1992
	37.40	USA (Drummond, Cason, Mitchell, Burrell)	Stuttgart	21 Aug 1993
Com	37.69	CAN (Esmie, Gilbert, Surin, Bailey)	Atlanta	3 Aug 1996
Eur	37.73	GBR (Gardener, Campbell, Devonish, Chambers)	Sevilla	29 Aug 1999
SAm	37.90	BRA (V Lima, Ribeiro, A da Silva, Cl da Silva)	Sydney	30 Sep 2000
Afr	37.94	NGR (O Ezinwa, Adeniken, Obikwelu, D Ezinwa)	Athína	9 Aug 1997
CAC	38.00	CUB (Simón, Lamela, Isasi, Aguilera)	Barcelona	8 Aug 1992
Oce	38.17	AUS (Henderson, Jackson, Brimacombe, Marsh)	Göteborg	12 Aug 1995
Asi	38.31	JPN (Inoue, K Ito, Tsuchie, Asahara)	Athína	9 Aug 1997
	38.31	JPN (Kawabata, K ito, Suetsugu, Asahara)	Sydney	29 Sep 2000
W20	38.66	USA (Kimmons, Omole, Williams, Merritt)	Grosseto	18 Jul 2004
W18	40.03	JAM (W Smith, M Frater, Spence, O Brown)	Bydgoszcz	18 Jul 1999

4 X 400 METRES RELAY

W, NAm	2:54.20	USA (Young, Pettigrew, Washington, Johnson)	Uniondale, NY	22 Jul 1998
Eur	2:56.60	GBR (Thomas, Baulch, Richardson, Black)	Atlanta	3 Aug 1996
CAC, Com	2:56.75	JAM (McDonald, Haughton, McFarlane, Clarke)	Athína	10 Aug 1997
SAm	2:58.56	BRA (C da Silva, A J dosSantos, de Araújo, Parrela)	Winnipeg	30 Jul 1999
Afr	2:58.68	NGR (Chukwu, Monye, Nada, Udo-Obong)	Sydney	30 Sep 2000
Oce	2:59.70	AUS (Frayne, Clark, Minihan, Mitchell)	Los Angeles	11 Aug 1984
Asi	3:00.76	JPN (Karube, K Ito, Osakada, Omori)	Atlanta	3 Aug 1996
W20	3:01.09	USA (Johnson, Merritt, Craig, Clement)	Grosseto	18 Jul 2004
W18	3:12.05	POL (Zrada, Kedzia, Grzegorczyk, Kowalski)	Kaunas	5 Aug 2001

20 KILOMETRES WALK

W, SAm	1:17:21	Jefferson PÉREZ	ECU	Saint-Denis	23 Aug 2003
Eur	1:17:22	Francisco FERNÁNDEZ	ESP	Turku	28 Apr 2002
CAC	1:17:25.6 t	Bernardo SEGURA	MEX	Fana	7 May 1994

Oce, Com	1:17:33	Nathan DEAKES	AUS	Cixi	23 Apr 2005
Asi	1:17:41	ZHU Hongyu	CHN	Cixi	23 Apr 2005
Afr	1:19:02	Hatem GHOULA	TUN	Eisenhüttenstadt	10 May 1997
NAm	1:21:03	Arturo HUERTA	CAN	Etobicoke	7 Jul 2000
W20	1:18:06 §	Viktor BURAYEV	RUS	Adler	4 Mar 2001
W18	1:18:07	LI Gaobo	CHN	Cixi	23 Apr 2005

20,000 METRES TRACK WALK

W, CAC	1:17:25.6	Bernardo SEGURA	MEX	Fana	7 May 1994
Eur	1:18:35.2	Stefan JOHANSSON	SWE	Fana	15 May 1992
Oce, Com	1:19:48.1	Nathan DEAKES	AUS	Brisbane	4 Sep 2001
Asi	1:20:24.4	LI Mingcai	CHN	Jinan	15 Mar 1992
SAm	1:20:55.4	Jefferson PÉREZ	ECU	Fana	4 May 1996
NAm	1:22:27.0	Tim BERRETT	CAN	Edmonds, WA	9 Jun 1996
Afr	1:22:51.84	Hatem GHOULA	TUN	Leutkirch	8 Sep 1994
W20	1:21:29.2	Viktor BURAYEV	RUS	Brisbane	4 Sep 2001
W18	1:24:28.3	ZHU Hongjun	CHN	Xian	15 Sep 1999

50 KILOMETRES WALK

W, Eur	3:36:03	Robert KORZENIOWSKI	POL	Saint-Denis	27 Aug 2003
	3:35:29 #	Denis NIZHEGORODOV (no doping test)	RUS	Cheboksary	13 Jun 2004
Asi	3:36:06	YU Chaohong	CHN	Nanjing	22 Oct 2005
Oce, Com	3:39:43	Nathan DEAKES	AUS	Melbourne	7 Dec 2003
CAC	3:41:20	Raúl GONZÁLEZ	MEX	Praha-Podebrady	11 Jun 1978
NAm	3:47:48	Marcel JOBIN	CAN	Québec	20 Jun 1981
SAm	3:52:16	Héctor MORENO	COL	Naumberg	25 May 1997
Afr	3:59:56	Hatem GHOULA	TUN	Naumburg	5 May 2002
W20	3:41:30	NI Liang	CHN	Nanjing	22 Oct 2005
W18	3:45:46	YU Guoping	CHN	Guangzhou	23 Nov 2001

50,000 METRES TRACK WALK

W, Eur	3:40:57.9	Thierry TOUTAIN	FRA	Héricourt	29 Sep 1996
CAC	3:41:38.4	Raúl GONZÁLEZ	MEX	Fana	25 May 1979
Oce, Com	3:43:50.0	Simon BAKER	AUS	Melbourne	9 Sep 1990
Asi	3:48:13.7	ZHAO Yongshen	CHN	Fana	7 May 1994
NAm	3:56:13.0	Tim BERRETT	CAN	Saskatoon	21 Jul 1991
SAm	4:14:28.5	Jorge LOREFICE	ARG	Buenos Aires	9 May 1993
	4:14:28.5	Benjamin LOREFICE	ARG	Buenos Aires	9 May 1993
Afr	4:21:44.5	Abdelwahab FERGUÈNE	ALG	Toulouse	25 Mar 1984

World Records at other men's track & field events recognised by the IAAF

20km	56:55.6	Arturo BARRIOS (now USA)	MEX	La Flèche	30 Mar 1991
1 Hour	21,101 m	Arturo BARRIOS (now USA)	MEX	La Flèche	30 Mar 1991
25km	1:13:55.8	Toshihiko SEKO	JPN	Christchurch	22 Mar 1981
30km	1:29:18.8	Toshihiko SEKO	JPN	Christchurch	22 Mar 1981
4 x 200m	1:18.68	Santa Monica Track Club	USA	Walnut	17 Apr 1994
		(Michael Marsh, Leroy Burrell, Floyd Heard, Carl Lewis)			
4 x 800m	7:03.89	United Kingdom Team	GBR	London	30 Aug 1982
		(Peter Elliott, Garry Cook, Steve Cram, Sebastian Coe)			
4 x l500m	14:38.8 m	F.R.Germany Team	GER	Köln	17 Aug 1977
		(Thomas Wessinghage, Harald Hudak, Michael Lederer, Karl Fleschen)			

Track Walking

2 Hours	29,572m	Maurizio DAMILANO	ITA	Cuneo	4 Oct 1992
30km	2:01:44.1	Maurizio DAMILANO	ITA	Cuneo	4 Oct 1992

WOMEN

100 METRES

W, NAm	10.49	Florence GRIFFITH JOYNER	USA	Indianapolis	16 Jul 1988
Eur	10.73	Christine ARRON	FRA	Budapest	19 Aug 1998
CAC, Com	10.74	Merlene OTTEY	JAM	Milano	7 Sep 1996
Asi	10.79	LI Xuemei	CHN	Shanghai	18 Oct 1997
Afr	10.90	Glory ALOZIE	NGR	La Laguna	5 Jun 1999
	10.84 §	Chioma AJUNWA	NGR	Lagos	11 Apr 1992
Oce	11.12A	Melinda GAINSFORD/TAYLOR	AUS	Sestriere	31 Jul 1994
SAm	11.17A	Lucimar de MOURA	BRA	Bogotá (sf)	25 Jun 1999
	11.17A	Lucimar de MOURA	BRA	Bogotá	25 Jun 1999
W20	10.88	Marlies OELSNER/GÖHR	GER	Dresden	1 Jul 1977
W18	11.13	Chandra CHEESEBOROUGH	USA	Eugene	21 Jun 1976

200 METRES

W, NAm	21.34	Florence GRIFFITH JOYNER	USA	Seoul	29 Sep 1988
CAC, Com	21.64	Merlene OTTEY	JAM	Bruxelles	13 Sep 1991
Eur	21.71	Marita KOCH	GER	Chemnitz	10 Jun 1979
	21.71 §	Marita KOCH	GER	Potsdam	21 Jul 1984
	21.71	Heike DRECHSLER	GER	Jena	29 Jun 1986
	21.71 §	Heike DRECHSLER	GER	Stuttgart	29 Aug 1986
Asi	22.01	LI Xuemei	CHN	Shanghai	22 Oct 1997
Afr	22.06 A§	Evette DE KLERK	RSA	Pietersburg	8 Apr 1989
	22.07	Mary ONYALI	NGR	Zürich	14 Aug 1996
Oce	22.23	Melinda GAINSFORD-TAYLOR	AUS	Stuttgart	13 Jul 1997
SAm	22.60A	Lucimar de MOURA	BRA	Bogotá	26 Jun 1999
W20	22.18	Allyson FELIX	USA	Athína	25 Aug 2004
	22.11A §	Allyson FELIX (no doping control)	USA	Ciudad de México	3 May 2003
W18	22.58	Marion JONES	USA	New Orleans	28 Jun 1992

400 METRES

W, Eur	47.60	Marita KOCH	GER	Canberra	6 Oct 1985
Oce, Com	48.63	Cathy FREEMAN	AUS	Atlanta	29 Jul 1996
NAm	48.83	Valerie BRISCO	USA	Los Angeles	6 Aug 1984
Afr	49.10	Falilat OGUNKOYA	NGR	Atlanta	29 Jul 1996
CAC	48.89 #	Ana GUEVARA	MEX	Saint-Denis	27 Aug 2003
SAm	49.64	Ximena RESTREPO	COL	Barcelona	5 Aug 1992
Asi	49.81	MA Yuqin	CHN	Beijing	11 Sep 1993
W20	49.42	Grit BREUER	GER	Tokyo	27 Aug 1991
W18	50.01	LI Jing	CHN	Shanghai	18 Oct 1997

800 METRES

W, Eur	1:53.28	Jarmila KRATOCHVÍLOVÁ	CZE	München	26 Jul 1983
CAC	1:54.44	Ana Fidelia QUIROT	CUB	Barcelona	9 Sep 1989
Afr	1:55.19	Maria Lurdes MUTOLA	MOZ	Zürich	17 Aug 1994
Com	1:55.29	Maria Lurdes MUTOLA	MOZ	Köln	24 Aug 1997
Asi	1:55.54	LIU Dong	CHN	Beijing	9 Sep 1993
NAm	1:56.40	Jearl MILES CLARK	USA	Zürich	11 Aug 1999
SAm	1:56.68	Letitia VRIESDE	SUR	Göteborg	13 Aug 1995
Oce	1:58.25	Toni HODGKINSON	NZL	Atlanta	27 Jul 1996
W20, W18	1:57.18	WANG Yuan	CHN	Beijing	8 Sep 1993

1000 METRES

W, Eur	2:28.98	Svetlana MASTERKOVA	RUS	Bruxelles	23 Aug 1996
Afr	2:29.34	Maria Lurdes MUTOLA	MOZ	Bruxelles	25 Aug 1995
Com	2:29.66	Maria Lurdes MUTOLA	MOZ	Bruxelles	23 Aug 1996
NAm	2:31.80	Regina JACOBS	USA	Brunswick	3 Jul 1999
SAm	2:32.25	Letitia VRIESDE	SUR	Berlin	10 Sep 1991
CAC	2:33.21	Ana Fidelia QUIROT	CUB	Jerez de la Frontera	13 Sep 1989
Asi	2:33.6 §	Svetlana ULMASOVA	UZB	Podolsk	5 Aug 1979
Oce	2:38.54	Alison WRIGHT	NZL	Berlin	17 Aug 1979
W20	2:35.4a	Irina NIKITINA	RUS	Podolsk	5 Aug 1979
	2:35.4	Katrin WÜHN	GDR	Potsdam	12 Jul 1984
W18	2:38.58	Jo WHITE	GBR	London (CP)	9 Sep 1977

1500 METRES

W, Asi	3:50.46	QU Yunxia	CHN	Beijing	11 Sep 1993
Eur	3:52.47	Tatyana KAZANKINA	RUS	Zürich	13 Aug 1980
Afr	3:55.30	Hassiba BOULMERKA	ALG	Barcelona	8 Aug 1992
NAm	3:57.12	Mary DECKER/SLANEY	USA	Stockholm	26 Jul 1983
Com	3:57.41	Jackline MARANGA	KEN	Monaco	8 Aug 1998
Oce	4:01.34	Margaret CROWLEY	AUS	Oslo	5 Jul 1996
CAC	4:01.84	Yvonne GRAHAM	JAM	Monaco	25 Jul 1995
SAm	4:05.67	Letitia VRIESDE	SUR	Tokyo	31 Aug 1991
W20	3:51.34	LANG Yinglai	CHN	Shanghai	18 Oct 1997
W18	3:54.52	ZHANG Ling	CHN	Shanghai	18 Oct 1997

1 MILE

W, Eur	4:12.56	Svetlana MASTERKOVA	RUS	Zürich	14 Aug 1996
NAm	4:16.71	Mary SLANEY	USA	Zürich	21 Aug 1985
Com	4:17.57	Zola BUDD	GBR	Zürich	21 Aug 1985
Afr	4:20.79	Hassiba BOULMERKA	ALG	Oslo	6 Jul 1991

CAC	4:24.64	Yvonne GRAHAM	JAM	Zürich	17 Aug 1994
Oce	4:25.84	Margaret CROWLEY	AUS	Monaco	10 Aug 1996
SAm	4:30.05	Soraya TELLES	BRA	Praha	9 Jun 1988
Asi	4:34.81	Ikuko TAMURA	JPN	Amagasaki	15 Jun 2002
W20	4:17.57	Zola BUDD	GBR	Zürich	21 Aug 1985
W18	4:30.81	Gelete BURIKA	ETH	Heusden	2 Aug 2003

2000 METRES

W, Eur	5:25.36	Sonia O'SULLIVAN	IRL	Edinburgh	8 Jul 1994
Com	5:26.93	Yvonne MURRAY	GBR	Edinburgh	8 Jul 1994
Asi	5:29.43 §	WANG Junxia	CHN	Beijing	12 Sep 1993
NAm	5:32.7	Mary SLANEY	USA	Eugene	3 Aug 1984
Afr	5:35.62	Berhane ADERE	ETH	Ostrava	12 Jun 2003
Oce	5:37.71	Benita JOHNSON	AUS	Ostrava	12 Jun 2003
W20	5:33.15	Zola BUDD	GBR	London (CP)	13 Jul 1984
W18	5:46.5+	Sally BARSOSIO	KEN	Zürich	16 Aug 1995

3000 METRES

W, Asi	8:06.11	WANG Junxia	CHN	Beijing	13 Sep 1993
Eur	8:21.42	Gabriela SZABO	ROM	Monaco	19 Jul 2002
Com	8:22.20	Paula RADCLIFFE	Eng	Monaco	19 Jul 2002
Afr	8:23.23	Edith MASAI	KEN	Monaco	19 Jul 2002
NAm	8:25.83	Mary SLANEY	USA	Roma	7 Sep 1985
CAC	8:37.07	Yvonne GRAHAM	JAM	Zürich	16 Aug 1995
Oce	8:38.06	Benita JOHNSON	AUS	Gateshead	13 Jul 2003
SAm	9:02.37	Delirde BERNARDI	BRA	Linz	4 Jul 1994
W20	8:28.83	Zola BUDD	GBR	Roma	7 Sep 1985
W18	8:36.45	MA Ningning	CHN	Jinan	6 Jun 1993

5000 METRES

W, Eur	14:24.68	Elvan ABEYLEGESSE	TUR	Bergen (Fana)	11 Jun 2004
Asi	14:28.09	JIANG Bo	CHN	Shanghai	23 Oct 1997
Afr	14:28.98	Meseret DEFAR	ETH	Bruxelles	26 Aug 2005
Com	14:29.11	Paula RADCLIFFE	Eng	Bydgoszcz	20 Jun 2004
NAm	14:45.35	Regina JACOBS	USA	Sacramento	21 Jul 2000
Oce	14:47.60	Benita JOHNSON	AUS	Berlin (P)	6 Sep 2002
CAC	15:04.32	Adriana FERNÁNDEZ	MEX	Gresham	17 May 2003
SAm	15:22.01	Carmen de OLIVEIRA	BRA	Hechtel	31 Jul 1993
W20	14:30.88	Tirunesh DIBABA	ETH	Bergen (Fana)	11 Jun 2004
W18	14:45.71	SONG Liqing	CHN	Shanghai	21 Oct 1997

10,000 METRES

W, Asi	29:31.78	WANG Junxia	CHN	Beijing	8 Sep 1993
Eur, Com	30:01.09	Paula RADCLIFFE	GBR/Eng	München	6 Aug 2002
Afr	30:04.18	Berhane ADERE	ETH	Saint-Denis	23 Aug 2003
Oce	30:37.68	Benita JOHNSON	AUS	Saint-Denis	23 Aug 2003
NAm	30:50.32	Deena DROSSIN	USA	Stanford	3 May 2002
CAC	31:10.12	Adriana FERNANDEZ	MEX	Brunswick	1 Jul 2000
SAm	31:47.76	Carmen de OLIVEIRA	BRA	Stuttgart	21 Aug 1993
W20	30:31.55	XING Huina	CHN	Saint-Denis	23 Aug 2003
W18	31:11.26	SONG Liqing	CHN	Shanghai	19 Oct 1997

MARATHON

W, Eur, Com	2:15:25	Paula RADCLIFFE	GBR/Eng	London	13 Apr 2003
Afr	2:18:47	Catherine NDEREBA	KEN	Chicago	7 Oct 2001
Asi	2:19:12	Mizuki NOGUCHI	JPN	Berlin	25 Sep 2005
NAm	2:21:16	Deena DROSSIN	USA	London	13 Apr 2003
Oce	2:23:51	Lisa MARTIN/ONDIEKI	AUS	Osaka	31 Jan 1988
CAC	2:24:06	Adriana FERNANDEZ	MEX	London	18 Apr 1999
SAm	2:27:41	Carmen de OLIVEIRA	BRA	Boston (dh 139m & w)a	18 Apr 1994
W20	2:23:37	LIU Min	CHN	Beijing	14 Oct 2001

3000 METRES STEEPLECHASE

W, Eur	9:01.59	Gulnara SAMITOVA	RUS	Iráklio	4 Jul 2004
Afr,Com	9:15.04	Dorcus INZIKURU	UGA	Athína	14 Jun 2005
CAC	9:27.21	Mardrea HYMAN	JAM	Monaco	9 Sep 2005
NAm	9:29.32	Briana SHOOK	USA	Heusden	31 Jul 2004
W20, Oce	9:30.70	Melissa ROLLISON	AUS	Brisbane	4 Sep 2001
Asi	9:41.21	Minori HAYAKARI	JPN	Helsinki	6 Aug 2005

SAm	10:00.54	Michelle COSTA	BRA	São Paulo	17 Jun 2005
W18	9:49.03	Ancuta BOBOCEL	ROM	Grosseto	15 Jul 2004

100 METRES HURDLES

W, Eur	12.21	Yordanka DONKOVA	BUL	Stara Zagora	20 Aug 1988
NAm	12.33	Gail DEVERS	USA	Sacramento	23 Jul 2000
Asi	12.44	Olga SHISHIGINA	KAZ	Luzern	27 Jun 1995
Afr, Com	12.44	Glory ALOZIE	NGR	Monaco	8 Aug 1998
	12.44	Glory ALOZIE	NGR	Bruxelles	28 Aug 1998
	12.44	Glory ALOZIE	NGR	Sevilla	28 Aug 1999
CAC	12.45	Brigitte FOSTER	JAM	Eugene	24 May 2003
SAm	12.71	Maurren MAGGI	BRA	Manaus	19 May 2001
Oce	12.93	Pam RYAN	AUS	München	4 Sep 1972
W20	12.84	Aliuska LÓPEZ	CUB	Zagreb	16 Jul 1987
W18	12.95	Candy YOUNG	USA	Walnut	16 Jun 1979

400 METRES HURDLES

Eur, W	52.34	Yuliya PECHONKINA	RUS	Tula	8 Aug 2003
NAm	52.61	Kim BATTEN	USA	Göteborg	11 Aug 1995
Com	52.74	Sally GUNNELL	GBR	Stuttgart	19 Aug 1993
CAC	52.82	Deon HEMMINGS	JAM	Atlanta	31 Jul 1996
Afr	52.90	Nezha BIDOUANE	MAR	Sevilla	25 Aug 1999
Oce	53.17	Debbie FLINTOFF-KING	AUS	Seoul	28 Sep 1988
Asi	53.96	HAN Qing	CHN	Beijing	9 Sep 1993
	53.96	SONG Yinglan	CHN	Guangzhou	22 Nov 2001
SAm	55.94	Lucimar TEODORO	BRA	São Paulo	6 Jun 2004
W20	54.40	WANG Xing	CHN	Nanjing	21 Oct 2005
W18	55.15	HUANG Xiaoxiao	CHN	Guangzhou	22 Nov 2001

HIGH JUMP

W, Eur	2.09	Stefka KOSTADINOVA	BUL	Roma	30 Aug 1987
Afr, Com	2.06	Hestrie CLOETE	RSA	Saint-Denis	31 Aug 2003
CAC	2.04	Silvia COSTA	CUB	Barcelona	9 Sep 1989
NAm	2.03	Louise RITTER	USA	Austin	8 Jul 1988
		Louise RITTER	USA	Seoul	30 Sep 1988
Oce	1 98	Vanessa WARD	AUS	Perth	12 Feb 1989
	1.98	Alison INVERARITY	AUS	Ingolstadt	17 Jul 1994
Asi	1.97	JIN Ling	CHN	Hamamatsu	7 May 1989
	1.97*	Svetlana ZALEVSKAYA	KAZ	Pierre-Benité	14 Jun 1996
	1.97	Svetlana ZALEVSKAYA	KAZ	Lausanne	5 Jul 2000
	1.97	Tatyana EFIMENKO	KGZ	Roma	11 Jul 2003
SAm	1.96	Solange WITTEVEEN	ARG	Oristano	8 Sep 1997
W20	2.01	Olga TURCHAK	KAZ	Moskva	7 Jul 1986
	2.01	Heike BALCK	GER	Chemnitz	18 Jun 1989
W18	1.96A	Charmaine GALE	RSA	Bloemfontein	4 Apr 1981
	1.96	Olga TURCHAK	KAZ	Donetsk	7 Sep 1984

POLE VAULT

W, Eur	5.01	Yelena ISINBAYEVA	RUS	Helsinki	12 Aug 2005
NAm	4.83	Stacy DRAGILA	USA	Ostrava	8 Jun 2004
Oce, Com	4.60	Emma GEORGE	AUS	Sydney	20 Feb 1999
Asi	4.53	GAO Shuying	CHN	Inchon	2 Sep 2005
SAm	4.43	Alejandra GARCÍA	ARG	Santa Fé	3 Apr 2004
Afr	4.42	Elmarie GERRYTS	RSA	Wesel	12 Jun 2000
CAC	4.25	Katiuska PÉREZ	CUB	Nassau	9 Jul 2005
W20	4.48i	Silke SPIEGELBURG	GER	Münster	25 Aug 2005
W18	4.37	Ekateríni STEFANÍDI	GRE	Athína (P)	20 Feb 2005

LONG JUMP

W, Eur	7.52	Galina CHISTYAKOVA	RUS	Sankt-Peterburg	11 Jun 1988
NAm	7.49	Jackie JOYNER-KERSEE	USA	New York	22 May 1994
	7.49A*	Jackie JOYNER-KERSEE	USA	Sestriere	31 Jul 1994
SAm	7.26A	Maurren MAGGI	BRA	Bogotá	26 Jun 1999
CAC,Com	7.16A	Elva GOULBOURNE	JAM	Ciudad de México	22 May 2004
Afr	7.12	Chioma AJUNWA	NGR	Atlanta	1 Aug 1996
Asi	7.01	YAO Weili	CHN	Jinan	5 Jun 1993
Oce	7.00	Bronwyn THOMPSON	AUS	Melbouren	7 Mar 2002
W20	7.14	Heike DAUTE/Drechsler	GER	Bratislava	4 Jun 1983
W18	6.91	Heike DAUTE/Drechsler	GDR	Jena	9 Aug 1981

TRIPLE JUMP

W, Eur	15.50	Inessa KRAVETS	UKR	Göteborg	10 Aug 1995
Afr,Com	15.30	Françoise MBANGO ETONE	CMR	Athína (Round 2	23 Aug 2004
	15.30	Françoise MBANGO ETONE	CMR	Athína (Round 6)	23 Aug 2004
CAC	15.29	Yamilé ALDAMA	CUB	Roma	11 Jul 2003
Asi	14.72	HUANG Qiuyan	CHN	Guangzhou	22 Nov 2001
SAm	14.53	Maurren MAGGI	BRA	São Caetano do Sul	27 Apr 2003
NAm	14.45	Tiombé HURD	USA	Sacramento	11 Jul 2004
Oce	14.04	Nicole MLADENIS	AUS	Perth	7 Dec 2003
W20	14.62	Tereza MARINOVA	BUL	Sydney	25 Aug 1996
W18	14.57	HUANG Qiuyan	CHN	Shanghai	19 Oct 1997

SHOT

W, Eur	22.63	Natalya LISOVSKAYA	RUS	Moskva	7 Jun 1987
Asi	21.76	LI Meisu	CHN	Shijiazhuang	23 Apr 1988
CAC	20.96	Belsy LAZA	CUB	Ciudad de México	2 May 1992
NAm	20.18	Ramona PAGEL	USA	San Diego	25 Jun 1988
Oce, Com	19.87	Valerie VILI	NZL	Helsinki	12 Aug 2005
SAm	19.30	Elisângela ADRIANO	BRA	Tunja	14 Jul 2001
Afr	18.43	Vivianne CHUKWUEMEKA	NGR	Walnut	19 Apr 2003
W20	20.54	Astrid KUMBERNUSS	GER	Orimattila	1 Jul 1989
W18	19.08	Ilke WYLUDDA	GDR	Chemnitz	9 Aug 1986

DISCUS

W, Eur	76.80	Gabriele REINSCH	GER	Neubrandenburg	9 Jul 1988
Asi	71.68	XIAO Yanling	CHN	Beijing	14 Mar 1992
CAC	70.88	Hilda RAMOS	CUB	La Habana	8 May 1992
Oce, Com	68.72	Daniela COSTIAN	AUS	Auckland	22 Jan 1994
NAm	66.10	Carol CADY	USA	San José	31 May 1986
SAm	61.96	Elisângela ADRIANO	BRA	São Leopoldo	21 May 1998
Afr	63.17A	Elizna NAUDE	RSA	Bloemfontein	4 Mar 2005
W20	74.40	Ilke WYLUDDA	GER	Berlin	13 Sep 1988
W18	65.86	Ilke WYLUDDA	GDR	Neubrandenburg	1 Aug 1986

HAMMER

W, Eur	77.06	Tatyana LYSENKO	RUS	Moskva	15 Jul 2005
CAC	75.18	Yipsi MORENO	CUB	La Habana	25 Apr 2004
Asi,W20	73.24	ZHANG Wenxiu	CHN	Changsha	24 Jun 2005
NAm	73.87	Erin GILREATH	USA	Carson	25 Jun 2005
Oce, Com	71.12	Bronwyn EAGLES	AUS	Adelaide	6 Feb 2003
Afr	68.48	Marwa Ahmed HUSSEIN	EGY	Cairo	18 Feb 2005
SAm	67.07	Jennifer DAHLGREN	ARG	Athens, GA	23 Apr 2005
W18	70.60	ZHANG Wenxiu	CHN	Nanning	5 Apr 2003

JAVELIN

W, CAC	71.70	Osleidys MENÉNDEZ	CUB	Helsinki	14 Aug 2005
Eur	70.03	Christina OBEGFÖLL	GER	Helsinki	14 Aug 2005
Oce, Com	66.80	Louise CURREY	AUS	Gold Coast	5 Aug 2000
Asi	63.92	WEI Jianhua	CHN	Beijing	18 Aug 2000
SAm	62.62A	Sabina MOYA	COL	Ciudad de Guatemala	12 May 2002
Afr	61.59A	Sunette VILJOEN	RSA	Potchefstroom	5 Dec 2003
NAm	60.86	Kim KREINER	USA	Santo Domingo	7 Aug 2003
W20, W18	62.93	XUE Juan	CHN	Changsha	27 Oct 2003

HEPTATHLON

W, NAm	7291	Jackie JOYNER-KERSEE	USA	Seoul	24 Sep 1988
Eur	7007	Larisa NIKITINA	RUS	Bryansk	11 Jun 1989
Asi	6942	Ghada SHOUAA	SYR	Götzis	26 May 1996
Com	6831	Denise LEWIS	GBR	Talence	30 Jul 2000
Oce	6695	Jane FLEMMING	AUS	Auckland	28 Jan 1990
CAC	6527	Diane GUTHRIE-GRESHAM	JAM	Knoxville	3 Jun 1995
Afr	6423	Margaret SIMPSON	GHA	Götzis	29 May 2005
SAm	6017	Conceição GEREMIAS	BRA	Caracas	25 Aug 1983
W20	6542	Carolina KLÜFT	SWE	München	10 Aug 2002
W18	6185	SHEN Shengfei	CHN	Shanghai	18 Oct 1997

DECATHLON

W, Eur	8358	Austra SKUJYTE	LTU	Columbia, MS	15 Apr 2005

4 X 100 METRES RELAY

W, Eur	41.37	GDR (Gladisch, Rieger, Auerswald, Göhr)	Canberra	6 Oct 1985
NAm	41.47	USA (Gaines, Jones, Miller, Devers)	Athína	9 Aug 1997
CAC, Com	41.73	JAM (Lawrence, Simpson, Bailey, Campbell)	Athína	27 Aug 2004
Asi	42.23	Sichuan CHN (Xiao Lin, Li Yali, Liu Xiaomei, Li Xuemei)	Shanghai	23 Oct 1997
Afr	42.39	NGR (Utondu, Idehen, Opara-Thompson, Onyali)	Barcelona	7 Aug 1992
SAm	42.97A	BRA (Moura, de Jesús, dos Santos, Neto)	Bogotá	10 Jul 2004
Oce	42.99A	AUS (Massey, Broadrick, Lambert, Gainsford-Taylor)	Pietersburg	18 Mar 2000
W20	43.33 §	GDR (Breuer, Krabbe, Dietz, Henke)	Berlin	20 Jul 1988
	43.38	USA (A Joyce, Aleah Williams, Robinson, Buchanan)	Tampa	11 Jul 1999
W18	44.05	GDR (Koppetsch, Oelsner, Sinzel, Brehmer)	Athína	24 Aug 1975

4 X 400 METRES RELAY

W, Eur	3:15.17	URS (Ledovskaya, Nazarova, Pinigina, Bryzgina)	Seoul	1 Oct 1988
NAm	3:15.51	USA (D.Howard, Dixon, Brisco, Griffith Joyner)	Seoul	1 Oct 1988
Afr	3:21.04	NGR (Bisi Afolabi, Yusuf, Opara, Ogunkoya)	Atlanta	3 Aug 1996
Com	3:21.21	CAN (Crooks, Richardson, Killingbeck, Payne)	Los Angeles	11 Aug 1984
CAC	3:21.30	JAM (Turner, L Graham, Hemmings, Richards)	Athína	10 Aug 1997
Oce	3:23.81	AUS (Peris, Lewis, Gainsford-Taylor, Freeman)	Sydney	30 Sep 2000
Asi	3:24.28	CHN / Hebei (An, Bai, Cao, Ma)	Beijing	13 Sep 1993
SAm	3:26.82	BRA (Almirão, Coutinho, Tito, Teodoro)	Helsinki	13 Aug 2005
W20	3:27.60	USA (Anderson, Kidd, Smith, Hastings)	Grosseto	18 Jul 2004
W18	3:36.98	GBR (Ravenscroft, E McMeekin, Kennedy, Pettett)	Duisburg	26 Aug 1973

10 KILOMETRES WALK

W, Eur	41:04	Yelena NIKOLAYEVA	RUS	Sochi	20 Apr 1996
Asi	41:16	WANG Yan	CHN	Eisenhüttenstadt	8 May 1999
Oce, Com	41:30	Kerry SAXBY-JUNNA	AUS	Canberra	27 Aug 1988
CAC	42:42	Graciella MENDOZA	MEX	Naumburg	25 May 1997
NAm	44:17	Michelle ROHL	USA	Göteborg	7 Aug 1995
SAm	45:03	Geovanna IRUSTA	BOL	Podebrady	19 Apr 1997
Afr	45:06A	Susan VERMEULEN	RSA	Bloemfontein	17 Apr 1999
W20	41:55	Irina STANKINA	RUS	Adler	11 Feb 1995

10,000 METRES TRACK WALK

W, Eur	41:56.23	Nadyezhda RYASHKINA	RUS	Seattle	24 Jul 1990
Oce	41:57.22	Kerry SAXBY-JUNNA	AUS	Seattle	24 Jul 1990
Asi	42:30.13	GAO Hongmiao	CHN	Nanjing	24 Oct 1995
NAm	44:30.1 m	Alison BAKER	CAN	Fana	15 May 1992
	44:06 no kerb	Michelle ROHL	USA	Kenosha	2 Jun 1996
CAC	44:51.81	Graciela MENDOZA	MEX	Athína	4 Aug 1997
SAm	45:59.95	Geovanna IRUSTA	BOL	Rio de Janeiro	20 May 2000
Afr	47:32.54A	Nicolene CRONJE	RSA	Pretoria	19 Mar 2005
W20	42:49.7 §	GAO Hongmiao	CHN	Jinan	15 Mar 1992
	43:11.34	Vera SOKOLOVA	RUS	Kaunas	21 Jul 2005
W18	42:56.09t	GAO Hongmiao	CHN	Tangshan	27 Sep 1991

20,000 METRES TRACK WALK

W, Eur	1:26:52.3	Olimpiada IVANOVA	RUS	Brisbane	6 Sep 2001
Oce,Com	1:33:40.2	Kerry SAXBY-JUNNA	AUS	Brisbane	6 Sep 2001
CAC	1:34:56.7	Maria del Rosario SÁNCHEZ	MEX	Xalapa	16 Jul 2000
NAm	1:33:28.2	Teresa VAILL	USA	Carson	25 Jun 2005
SAm	1:35:33.4	Alessandra PICAGEVICZ	BRA	Itajai	15 May 2004
Asi	1:36:18.2	LI Yuxin	CHN	Qufu	27 Sep 1999
Afr	1:36:43.43A	Nicolene CRONJE	RSA	Germiston	20 Mar 2004
W20	1:29:32.4 #	SONG Hongjuan	CHN	Changsha	24 Oct 2003
W18	1:37:33.9	GAO Kelian	CHN	Xian	18 Sep 1999

20 KILOMETRES WALK

W, Eur	1:24:50 §	Olimpiada IVANOVA	RUS	Adler	4 Mar 2001
	1:25:41	Olimpiada IVANOVA	RUS	Helsinki	7 Aug 2005
Asi	1:26:22	WANG Yan	CHN	Guangzhou	19 Nov 2001
Oce,Com	1:27:44	Jane SAVILLE	AUS	Naumburg	2 May 2004
CAC	1:30:03	Graciela MENDOZA	MEX	Mézidon-Canon	2 May 1999
SAm	1:31:25	Miriam RAMÓN	ECU	Lima	7 May 2005
NAm	1:31:51	Michelle ROHL	USA	Kenosha	13 May 2000
Afr	1:36:18	Susan VERMEULEN	RSA	Mézidon-Canon	2 May 1999
W20	1:27:16	SONG Hongjuan	CHN	Yangzhou	14 Apr 2003
W18	1:30:52	JIANG Kun	CHN	Dandong	13 Apr 2001

World Records at other track & field events recognised by the IAAF

1 Hour	18,340 m	Tegla LOROUPE	KEN	Borgholzhausen	7 Aug 1998
20km	1:05:26.6	Tegla LOROUPE	KEN	Borgholzhausen	3 Sep 2000
25km	1:27:05.84	Tegla LOROUPE	KEN	Mengerskirchen	21 Sep 2002
30km	1:45:50.0	Tegla LOROUPE	KEN	Warstein	6 Jun 2003
Decathlon	8150	Marie COLLONVILLÉ	FRA	Talence	26 Sep 2004
4x200m	1:28.15	GDR (Göhr, R Müller, Wöckel, Koch)		Jena	9 Aug 1980
4x800m	7:50.17	USSR (Olizarenko, Gurina, Borisova, Podyalovskaya)		Moskva	5 Aug 1984

WORLD BESTS AT NON-STANDARD EVENTS

50m	5.53+	Bruny Surin	CAN	Sevilla (in 100m)	22 Aug 1999
	5.53+	Ben Johnson ¶	CAN	Rome (in 100m)	30 Aug 1987
	drugs dq 5.52	Ben Johnson		Seoul (in 100m)	24 Sep 1988
60m	6.38+	Bruny Surin	CAN	Sevilla (in 100m)	22 Aug 1999
	6.38+	Ben Johnson ¶	CAN	Roma (in 100m)	30 Aug 1987
drugs dq	6.37+	Ben Johnson	CAN	Seoul (in 100m)	24 Sep 1988
150m	14.8	Pietro Mennea	ITA	Cassino	22 May 1983
	14.93+	John Regis	GBR	Stuttgart (in 200m)	20 Aug 1993
300m	30.85A	Michael Johnson	USA	Pretoria	24 Mar 2000
	31.48	Danny Everett	USA	Jerez de la Frontera	3 Sep 1990
	31.48	Roberto Hernández	CUB	Jerez de la Frontera	3 Sep 1990
500m	1:00.08	Donato Sabia	ITA	Busto Arsizio	26 May 1984
600m	1:12.81	Johnny Gray	USA	Santa Monica	24 May 1986
2 miles	7:58.61	Daniel Komen	KEN	Hechtel	19 Jul 1997
2000m Steeple	5:14.43	Julius Kariuki	KEN	Rovereto	21 Aug 1990
200mh	22.55	Laurent Ottoz	ITA	Milano	31 May 1995
(hand time)	22.5	Martin Lauer	FRG	Zürich	7 Jul 1959
220yh straight	21.9	Don Styron	USA	Baton Rouge	2 Apr 1960
300mh	34.48	Chris Rawlinson	GBR	Sheffield	30 Jun 2002
35lb weight	25.41	Lance Deal	USA	Azusa	20 Feb 1993
Pentathlon	4282 points	Bill Toomey	USA	London (CP)	16 Aug 1969
(1985 tables)		(7.58, 66.18, 21.3, 44.52, 4:20.3)			
Double decathlon	14185 points	Kip Janvrin	USA	Turku	7/8 Sep 2002

11.42, 6.79, 200mh 25.31, 13.63, 5k 18:23.97, 2:02.46, 1.87, 400m 50642, HT 34.27, 3kSt 11:22.96
15.23, DT 40.91, 200m 22.56, 4.93, 10:13.16, 400mh 54.40, 58.31, 4:45.76, TJ 13.18, 10k 42:37.71

3000m track walk	10:47.11	Giovanni De Benedictis	ITA	San Giovanni Valdarno	19 May 1990
5000m track walk	18:05.49	Hatem Ghoula	TUN	Tunis	1 May 1997
10,000m track walk	37:58.6	Ivano Brugnetti	ITA	Sesto San Giovanni	23 Jul 2005
10 km road walk	37:11	Roman Rasskazov	RUS	Saransk	28 May 2000
100 km road walk	8:38:07	Viktor Ginko	BLR	Scanzorosciate	27 Oct 2002

Women

60m	5.93+	Marion Jones	USA	Sevilla (in 100m)	22 Aug 1999
60m	6.85+	Marion Jones	USA	Sevilla (in 100m)	22 Aug 1999
150m	16.10+	Florence Griffith-Joyner	USA	Seoul (in 200m)	29 Sep 1988
300m	34.1+	Marita Koch	GDR	Canberra (in 400m)	6 Oct 1985
500m	1:05.9	Tatána Kocembová	CZE	Ostrava	2 Aug 1984
600m	1:22.63	Ana Fidelia Quirot	CUB	Guadalajara	25 Jul 1997
2 miles	9:11.97 mx	Regina Jacobs	USA	Los Gatos	12 Aug 1999
2000m Steeple	6:04.46	Dorcus Inzikuru	UGA	Milano	1 Jun 2005
200mh	25.6	Patricia Girard	FRA	Nantes	23 Aug 2001
	25.82	Patricia Girard	FRA	Nantes	22 Sep 1999
300mh	39.00	Jana Pittman	AUS	Meilen	11 Jul 2004
	38.6	Mame Tacko Diouf	SEN	Dakar	21 Feb 1999
Double heptathlon	10798 pts	Milla Kelo	FIN	Turku	8 Sep 2002

100mh 14.89, HJ 1.51, 500m 5:03.74, 400mh 62.18, SP 12.73, 200m 25.16, 100m 12.59
LJ 5.73w, 400m 56.10, JT 32.69, 800m 2:23.94, 200mh 28.72, DT 47.86, 3000m 11:48.68

3000m track walk	11:48.24	Ileana Salvador	ITA	Padova	29 Aug 1993
5000m track walk	20:02.60	Gillian O'Sullivan	IRL	Dublin	13 Jul 2002
50 km road walk	4:12:16	Yelena Ginko	BLR	Scanzorosciate	17 Oct 2004
100 km road walk	10:13:56	Kora Boufflert	FRA	Roubaix	9 Oct 1994

LONG DISTANCE WORLD BESTS – MEN TRACK

	hr:min:sec	*Name*	*Nat*	*Venue*	*Date*
15 km	0:42:34.0	Arturo Barrios	MEX	La Flèche	30 Mar 1991
10 miles	0:45:57.6	Jos Hermens	NED	Papendal	14 Sep 1975
15 miles	1:11:43.1	Bill Rodgers	USA	Saratoga, Cal.	21 Feb 1979
20 miles	1:39:14.4	Jack Foster	NZL	Hamilton, NZ	15 Aug 1971
30 miles	2:42:00	Jeff Norman	GBR	Timperley, Cheshire	7 Jun 1980

50 km	2:48:06	Jeff Norman	GBR	Timperley, Cheshire	7 Jun 1980
40 miles	3:48:35	Don Ritchie	GBR	London (Hendon)	16 Oct 1982
50 miles	4:51:49	Don Ritchie	GBR	London (Hendon)	12 Mar 1983
100 km	6:10:20	Don Ritchie	GBR	London (CP)	28 Oct 1978
150 km	10:34:30	Denis Zhalybin	RUS	London (CP)	20 Oct 2002
100 miles	11:28:03	Oleg Kharitonov	RUS	London (CP)	20 Oct 2002
200 km	15:10:27	Yiannis Kouros	AUS	Adelaide	4-5 Oct 1997
200 miles	27:48:35	Yiannis Kouros	GRE	Montauban	15-16 Mar 1985
500 km	60:23.00 ??	Yiannis Kouros	GRE	Colac, Aus	26-29 Nov 1984
500 miles	105:42:09	Yiannis Kouros	GRE	Colac, Aus	26-30 Nov 1984
1000 km	136:17:00	Yiannis Kouros	GRE	Colac, Aus	26-31 Nov 1984
1500 km	10d 17:28:26	Petrus Silkinas	LTU	Nanango, Qld	11-21 Mar 1998
1000 mile	11d 13:54:58	Petrus Silkinas	LTU	Nanango, Qld	11-22 Mar 1998
2 hrs	37.994 km	Jim Alder	GBR	Walton-on-Thames	17 Oct 1964
12 hrs	162.400 km	Yiannis Kouros	GRE	Montauban	15 Mar 1985
24 hrs	303.506 km *	Yiannis Kouros	AUS	Adelaide	4-5 Oct 1997
48 hrs	473.797 km	Yiannis Kouros	AUS	Surgères	3-5 May 1996
6 days	1036.8 km	Yiannis Kouros	GRE	Colac, Aus	20-26 Nov 2005

LONG DISTANCE ROAD RECORDS & BESTS – MEN

Where superior to track bests (over 10km) and run on properly measured road courses. (I) IAAF recognition.

	hr:min:sec	*Name*	*Nat*	*Venue*	*Date*
10 km (I)	0:27:02	Haile Gebrselassie	ETH	Doha	11 Dec 2002
15 km (I)	0:41:22+ §	Haile Gebrselassie	ETH	Tilburg	4 Sep 2005
	0:41:29	Felix Limo	KEN	Nijmegen	11 Nov 2001
10 miles	0:44:24 §	Haile Gebrselassie	ETH	Tilburg	4 Sep 2005
	0:44:45	Paul Koech	KEN	Amsterdam-Zaandam	21 Sep 1997
20 km (I)	0:55:48+	Haile Gebrselassie	ETH	Phoenix	15 Jan 2006
Half mar (I)	0:58:55	Haile Gebrselassie	ETH	Phoenix	15 Jan 2006
25 km (I)	1:12:45	Paul Kosgei	KEN	Berlin	9 May 2004
	1:11:37 §	Haile Gebrselassie	ETH	Alphen aan den Rijn	12 Mar 2006
30 km (I)	1:28:00	Takayuki Matsumiya	JPN	Kumamoto	27 Feb 2005
20 miles	1:35:22+	Steve Jones	GBR	Chicago	10 Oct 1985
30 miles	2:37:31+	Thompson Magawana	RSA	Claremont-Kirstenbosch	12 Apr 1988
50km	2:43:38	Thompson Magawana	RSA	Claremont-Kirstenbosch	12 Apr 1988
40 miles	3:45:39	Andy Jones	CAN	Houston	23 Feb 1991
50 miles	4:50:21	Bruce Fordyce	RSA	London-Brighton	25 Sep 1983
100 km (I)	6:13:33	Takahiro Sunada	JPN	Yubetsu	21 Jun 1998
1000 miles	10d:10:30:35	Yiannis Kouros	GRE	New York	21-30 May 1988
Ekiden (6) (I)	1:57:06 #	Kenya	KEN	Chiba	23 Nov 2005
5 stages	1:55:59	Ethiopia	ETH	Chiba	24 Nov 2003
	10k Dejene Birhanu, 5k Hailu Mekonnen, 10k Gebr. Gebremariam, 5k Markos Geneti, 12.195k Sileshi Sihine				
12 hrs	162.543 km	Yiannis Kouros	GRE	Queen's, New York	7 Nov 1984

LONG DISTANCE WORLD BESTS – WOMEN TRACK

	hr:min:sec	*Name*	*Nat*	*Venue*	*Date*
15 km	0:49:44.0+	Silvana Cruciata	ITA	Roma	4 May 1981
10 miles	0:54:21.8	Lorraine Moller	NZL	Auckland	9 Jan 1993
20 miles	1:59:09 !	Chantal Langlacé	FRA	Amiens	3 Sep 1983
30 miles	3:12:25+	Carolyn Hunter-Rowe	GBR	Barry, Wales	3 Mar 1996
50 km	3:18:52+	Carolyn Hunter-Rowe	GBR	Barry, Wales	3 Mar 1996
40 miles	4:26:43	Carolyn Hunter-Rowe	GBR	Barry, Wales	7 Mar 1993
50 miles	5:48:12.0+	Norimi Sakurai	JPN	San Giovanni Lupatoto	27 Sep 2003
100 km	7:14:05.8	Norimi Sakurai	JPN	San Giovanni Lupatoto	27 Sep 2003
150 km	13:45:54	Hilary Walker	GBR	Blackpool	5-6 Nov 1988
100 miles	14:25:45+	Edit Bérces	HUN	San Giovanni Lupatoto	22 Sep 2002
200 km	18:31:43	Edit Bérces	HUN	San Giovanni Lupatoto	22 Sep 2002
200 miles	39:09:03	Hilary Walker	GBR	Blackpool	5-7 Nov 1988
500 km	77:53:46	Eleanor Adams	GBR	Colac, Aus.	13-16 Nov 1989
500 miles	130:59:58	Sandra Barwick	NZL	Campbelltown, AUS	18-23 Nov 1990
1000 km	8d 00:27:06+	Eleanor Robinson	GBR	Nanango, Qld	11-19 Mar 1998
1500 km	12d 06:52:12+	Eleanor Robinson	GBR	Nanango, Qld	11-23 Mar 1998
1000 miles	13d 02:16:49	Eleanor Robinson	GBR	Nanango, Qld	11-24 Mar 1998
2 hrs	32.652 km	Chantal Langlacé	FRA	Amiens	3 Sep 1983
12 hrs	147.600 km	Ann Trason	USA	Hayward, Cal	3-4 Aug 1991
24 hrs	250.106 km	Edit Bérces	HUN	San Giovanni Lupatoto	22 Sep 2002
48 hrs	377.892 km	Sue Ellen Trapp	USA	Surgères	2-4 May 1997
6 days	883.631 km	Sandra Barwick	NZL	Campbelltown, AUS	18-24 Nov 1990

! Timed on one running watch only, * lap recorded by computer

LONG DISTANCE ROAD RECORDS & BESTS - WOMEN

	hr:min:sec	Name	Nat	Venue	Date
10 km (l)	0:30:21	Paula Radcliffe	GBR	San Juan	23 Feb 2003
15 km (l)	0:46:55+	Kayoko Fukushi	JPN	Marugame	5 Feb 2006
	0:46:41+ dh	Paula Radcliffe	GBR	Newcastle	21 Sep 2003
10 miles	0:50:54	Lornah Kiplagat	KEN	Zaandam	22 Sep 2002
	0:50:01+ dh	Paula Radcliffe	GBR	Newcastle	21 Sep 2003
20 km (l)	1:03:26+	Paula Radcliffe	GBR	Bristol	6 Oct 2001
	1:02:21+ dh	Paula Radcliffe	GBR	London	13 Apr 2003
Half mar (l)	1:06:44	Elana Meyer	RSA	Tokyo	15 Jan 1999
	1:05:40 dh	Paula Radcliffe	GBR	South Shields	21 Sep 2003
25 km (l)	1:22:13	Mizuki Noguchi	JPN	Berlin	25 Sep 2005
	1:20:36e+ dh	Paula Radcliffe	GBR	London	13 Apr 2003
30 km (l)	1:38:49	Mizuki Noguchi	JPN	Berlin	25 Sep 2005
	1:36:36+ dh	Paula Radcliffe	GBR	London	13 Apr 2003
20 miles	1:43:33+	Paula Radcliffe	GBR	London	13 Apr 2003
30 miles	3:01:16+	Frith van der Merwe	RSA	Claremont-Kirstenbosch	25 Mar 1989
50 km	3:08:39	Frith van der Merwe	RSA	Claremont-Kirstenbosch	25 Mar 1989
40 miles	4:26:13+	Ann Trason	USA	Houston	23 Feb 1991
50 miles	5:40:18	Ann Trason	USA	Houston	23 Feb 1991
100 km (l)	6:33:11	Tomoe Abe	JPN	Yubetsu	25 Jun 2000
100 miles	13:47:41	Ann Trason	USA	Queen's, New York	4 May 1991
200 km	19:00:31	Eleanor Adams	GBR	Milton Keynes (indoor)	3-4 Feb 1990
1000 km	7d 01:11:00	Sandra Barwick	NZL	New York	16-23 Sep 1991
1000 miles	12d 14:38:40	Sandra Barwick	NZL	New York	16-29 Sep 1991
Ekiden (6 stages)	2:11:22	(l)	ETH	Chiba	24 Nov 2003
Berhane Adere, Tirunesh Dibaba, Eyerusalem Kuma, Ejegayou Dibaba, Meseret Defar, Werknesh Kidane					
12 hours	144.840 km	Ann Trason	USA	Queen's, New York	4 May 1991
24 hours	243.657 km	Sigrid Lomsky	GER	Basel	1-2 May 1993

100 KILOMETRES CONTINENTAL RECORDS

W, Asi	6:13:33	Takahiro SUNADA	JPN	Yubetsu	21 Jun 1998
Eur	6:16:41	Jean-Paul PRAET	BEL	Torhout	24 Jun 1989
SAm	6:18:09	Valmir NUNES	BRA	Winschoten	16 Sep 1995
Afr	6:25:07	Bruce FORDYCE	RSA	Stellenbosch	4 Feb 1989
Oce	6:29:23	Tim SLOAN	AUS	Ross-Richmond	23 Apr 1995
NAm	6:30:11	Tom JOHNSON	USA	Winschoten	16 Sep 1995
WOMEN					
W, Asi	6:33:11	Tomoe ABE	JPN	Yubetsu	25 Jun 2000
NAm	7:00:48	Ann TRASON	USA	Winschoten	16 Sep 1995
Eur	7:10:32	Tatyana ZHYRKOVA	RUS	Winschoten	11 Sep 2004
SAm	7:20:22	Maria VENANCIO	BRA	Cubatão	8 Aug 1998
Afr	7:31:47	Helena JOUBERT	RSA	Winschoten	16 Sep 1995
Oce	7:40:58	Linda MEADOWS	AUS	North Otago	18 Nov 1995

WORLD INDOOR RECORDS

to March 2006

Men					
50 metres	5.56A	Donovan Bailey	CAN	Reno	9 Feb 1996
60 metres	6.39	Maurice Greene	USA	Madrid	3 Feb 1998
	6.39	Maurice Greene	USA	Atlanta	3 Mar 2001
200 metres	19.92	Frank Fredericks	NAM	Liévin	18 Feb 1996
400 metres	44.57	Kerron Clement	USA	Fayetteville	12 Mar 2005
800 metres	1:42.67	Wilson Kipketer	KEN	Paris (Bercy)	9 Mar 1997
1000 metres	2:14.96	Wilson Kipketer	KEN	Birmingham	20 Feb 2000
1500 metres	3:31.18	Hicham El Guerrouj	MAR	Stuttgart	2 Feb 1997
1 mile	3:48.45	Hicham El Guerrouj	MAR	Gent	12 Feb 1997
2000 metres #	4:52.86	Haile Gebrselassie	ETH	Birmingham	16 Feb 1998
3000 metres	7:24.90	Daniel Komen	KEN	Budapest	6 Feb 1998
2 miles #	8:04.69	Haile Gebrselassie	ETH	Birmingham	21 Feb 2003
5000 metres	12:49.60	Kenenisa Bekele	ETH	Birmingham	20 Feb 2004
10000 metres #	27:50.29	Mark Bett	KEN	Gent	10 Feb 2002
50 m hurdles	6.25	Mark McKoy	CAN	Kobe	5 Mar 1986
60 m hurdles	7.30	Colin Jackson	GBR	Sindelfingen	6 Mar 1994
High jump	2.43	Javier Sotomayor	CUB	Budapest	4 Mar 1989
Pole vault	6.15	Sergey Bubka	UKR	Donetsk	21 Feb 1993
Long jump	8.79	Carl Lewis	USA	New York	27 Jan 1984
Triple jump	17.83	Aliecer Urrutia	CUB	Sindelfingen	1 Mar 1997
	17.83	Christian Olsson	SWE	Budapest	7 Mar 2004
Shot	22.66	Randy Barnes	USA	Los Angeles	20 Jan 1989

Javelin #	85.78	Matti Närhi	FIN	Kajaani	3 Mar 1996
35 lb weight #	25.86	Lance Deal	USA	Atlanta	4 Mar 1995
3000m walk #	10:31.42	Andreas Erm	GER	Halle	4 Feb 2001
5000m walk	18:07.08	Mikhail Shchennikov	RUS	Moskva	14 Feb 1995
4 x 200m	1:22.11	United Kingdom		Glasgow	3 Mar 1991
		(Linford Christie, Darren Braithwaite, Ade Mafe, John Regis)			
4 x 400m	3:01.96	USA		Fayetteville	11 Feb 2006
		(Kerron Clement, Wallace Spearmon, Darold Williamson, Jeremy Wariner)			
4 x 800m	7:13.94	USA/Global Athletics & Marketing		Boston (Roxbury)	6 Feb 2000
		(Joey Woody, Karl Paranya, Rich Kenah, David Krummenacker)			
Heptathlon	6476 points	Dan O'Brien	USA	Toronto	13/14 Mar 1993
	(6.67 60m, 7.84 LJ, 16.02 SP, 2.13 HJ, 7.85 60mh, 5.20 PV, 2:57.96 1000m)				

Women

50 metres	5.96+	Irina Privalova	RUS	Madrid	9 Feb 1995
60 metres	6.92	Irina Privalova	RUS	Madrid 11 Feb 1993 &	11 Feb 1993
200 metres	21.87	Merlene Ottey	JAM	Liévin	13 Feb 1993
400 metres	49.59	Jarmila Kratochvílová	CZE	Milano	7 Mar 1982
800 metres	1:55.82	Jolanda Ceplak	SLO	Wien	3 Mar 2002
1000 metres	2:30.94	Maria Lurdes Mutola	MOZ	Stockholm	25 Feb 1999
1500 metres	3:58.28	Yelena Soboleva	RUS	Moskva	18 Feb 2006
1 mile	4:17.14	Doina Melinte	ROM	East Rutherford	9 Feb 1990
2000 metres #	5:30.53	Gabriela Szabo	ROM	Sindelfingen	8 Mar 1998
3000 metres	8:27.86	Liliya Shobukhova	RUS	Moskva	17 Feb 2006
2 miles #	9:23.38	Regina Jacobs	USA	Boston (Roxbury)	27 Jan 2002
5000 metres	14:32.93	Tirunesh Dibaba	WETH	Boston (Roxbury)	29 Jan 2005
50 m hurdles	6.58	Cornelia Oschkenat	GDR	Berlin	20 Feb 1988
60 m hurdles	7.69	Lyudmila Narozhilenko	RUS	Chelyabinsk	4 Feb 1990
High jump	2.08	Kajsa Bergqvist	SWE	Arnstadt	4 Feb 2006
Pole vault	4.91	Yelena Isinbayeva	RUS	Donetsk	12 Feb 2006
Long jump	7.37	Heike Drechsler	GDR	Wien	13 Feb 1988
Triple jump	15.36	Tatyana Lebedeva	RUS	Budapest	5 Mar 2004
Shot	22.50	Helena Fibingerová	CZE	Jablonec	19 Feb 1977
Javelin #	61.29	Taina Uppa/Kolkkala	FIN	Mustasaari	28 Feb 1999
20 lb weight #	24.23	Erin Gilreath	USA	Bloomington	18 Feb 2005
3000m walk	11:35.34 #	Gillian O'Sullivan	IRL	Belfast	15 Feb 2003
	11:40.33	Claudia Iovan/Stef	ROM	Bucuresti	30 Jan 1999
5000m walk #	20:37.77	Margarita Turova	BLR	Minsk	13 Feb 2005
4 x 200m	1:32.41	Russia		Glasgow	29 Jan 2005
		(Yekaterina Kondratyeva, Irina Khabarova, Yuliya Pechonkina, Yuliya Gushchina)			
4 x 400m	3:23.37	Russia		Glasgow	28 Jan 2006
		(Yuliya Gushchina, Olga Kotlyarova, Olga Zaytseva, Olesya Krasnomovets)			
4 x 800m	8:18.71	Russia		Moskva	4 Feb 1994
		(Natalya Zaytseva, Olga Kuznetsova, Yelena Afanasyeva, Yekaterina Podkopayeva)			
Pentathlon	4991 points	Irina Belova	RUS	Berlin	14/15 Feb 1992
		(8.22 60mh, 1.93 HJ, 13.25 SP, 6.67 LJ, 2:10.26 800m)			

events not officially recognised by the IAAF
¶ The IAAF stripped Johnson of his records in January 1990, after he had admitted long-term steroid use.

WORLD VETERANS/MASTERS RECORDS

MEN – aged 35 or more

100 metres	9.97A	Linford Christie (2.4.60)	GBR	Johannesburg	23 Sep 1995
200 metres	20.11	Linford Christie (2.4.60)	GBR	Villeneuve d'Ascq	25 Jun 1995
400 metres	45.76	Ibrahima Wade (6.9.68)	FRA	Saint-Denis	23 Jul 2004
800 metres	1:43.36	Johnny Gray (19.6.60)	USA	Zürich	16 Aug 1995
1000 metres	2:18.8+	William Tanui (22.2.64)	KEN	Rome	7 Jul 1999
1500 metres	3:32.45	William Tanui (22.2.64)	KEN	Athína	16 Jun 1999
1 mile	3:52.04	Marcus O'Sullivan (22.12.61)	IRL	Berlin	26 Aug 1997
2000 metres	4:58.3+ e	# William Tanui (22.2.64	KEN	Monaco	4 Aug 1999
	4:57.31i	William Tanui		Sindelfingen	28 Feb 1999
3000 metres	7:37.23	John Kibowen (21.4.69)	KEN	Doha	14 May 2004
5000 metres	13:01.32	John Kibowen (21.4.69)	KEN	Roma	2 Jul 2004
10000 metres	27:17.48	Carlos Lopes (18.2.47)	POR	Stockholm	2 Jul 1984
Marathon	2:07:12	Carlos Lopes (18.2.47)	POR	Rotterdam	20 Apr 1985
3000m steeple	8:04.95	Simon Vroemen (11.5.69)	NED	Helsinki	26 Aug 2005
110m hurdles	13.11	Colin Jackson (18.2.67)	GBR	München	10 Aug 2002
400m hurdles	48.93	Nat Page (26.1.57)	USA	London (CP)	10 Jul 1992
High jump	2.30i	Charles Austin (19.12.67)	USA	Boston	2 Mar 2003
	2.27	Charles Austin (19.12.67)	USA	Austin	5 Apr 2003
Pole vault	5.88i	Jeff Hartwig (25.9.67)	USA	Jonesboro	22 Feb 2004

	5.86	Jeff Hartwig	USA	Jonesboro	4 Jul 2004
Long jump	8.50	Larry Myricks (10.3.56)	USA	New York	15 Jun 1991
	8.50	Carl Lewis (1.7.61)	USA	Atlanta	29 Jul 1996
Triple jump	17.92	Jonathan Edwards (10.5.66)	GBR	Edmonton	6 Aug 2001
Shot	22.67	Kevin Toth ¶ (29.12.67)	USA	Lawrence	19 Apr 2003
Discus	71.26	John Powell ((25.6.47)	USA	San Jose	9 Jun 1984
	71.26	Rickard Bruch (2.7.46)	SWE	Malmö	15 Nov 1984
Hammer	83.62	Igor Astapkovich (4.1.63)	BLR	Staiki	20 Jun 1998
Javelin	92.80	Jan Zelezny (16.6.66)	CZE	Edmonton	12 Aug 2001
Decathlon	8241	Kip Janvrin (8.7.65)	USA	Eugene	22 Jun 2001
		(10.98, 7.01, 14.21, 1.89, 48.41, 14.72, 45.59, 5.20, 60.41, 4:14.96)			
20 km	1:18:44	Vladimir Andreyev (7.9.66)	RUS	Cheboksary	12 Jun 2004
50 km	3:36:03	Robert Korzeniowski (30.7.68)	POL	Saint-Denis	27 Aug 2003

MEN – aged 40 or more

100 metres	10.29	Troy Douglas (30.11.62)	NED	Leiden	7 Jun 2003
200 metres	20.64	Troy Douglas (30.11.62)	NED	Utrecht	9 Aug 2003
400 metres	47.82	Enrico Saraceni (19.5.64)	ITA	Århus	25 Jul 2004
	47.5u	Lee Evans (25.2.47)	USA		Apr 1989
800 metres	1:50.69	Colm Rothery (28.1.60)	IRL	Stretford	5 Sep 2000
	1:48.81i	Johnny Gray (19.6.60)	USA	Atlanta	3 Mar 2001
1000 metres	2:26.71i	Eamonn Coghlan (21.11.52)	IRL	Gainesville	21 Jan 1994
1500 metres	3:44.89	Luiz José Gonçalves (4.12.58)	BRA	Rio de Janeiro	4 Jun 1999
1 mile	4:02.53	David Moorcroft (10.4.53)	GBR	Belfast	19 Jun 1993
	3:58.15i	Eamonn Coghlan (21.11.52)	IRL	Boston	20 Feb 1994
3000 metres	8:05.08	Martti Vainio (30.12.50)	FIN	Mikkeli	12 Jun 1991
5000 metres	13:43.15	Mohamed Ezzher (26.4.60)	FRA	Sotteville	3 Jul 2000
10000 metres	28:30.88	Martti Vainio (30.12.50)	FIN	Hengelo	25 Jun 1991
1 Hour	19.710k	Steve Moneghetti (26.9.62)	AUS	Geelong	17 Dec 2005
Marathon	2:08:46	Andrés Espinosa (4.2.63)	MEX	Berlin	28 Sep 2003
3000m steeple	8:38.40	Angelo Carosi (20.1.64)	ITA	Firenze	11 Jul 2004
110m hurdles	14.16	Carlos Sala (20.3.60)	ESP	Castellón	16 Aug 2000
	13.79 ?	Roger Kingdom (26.8.62)	USA	Slippery Rock	23 Jun 2004
400m hurdles	52.62	Antônio Eusébio Dias Ferreira (2.3.60)	BRA	Rio de Janeiro	23 Jul 2000
High jump	2.15	Glen Conley (9.1.57)	USA	Troy, New York	2 Aug 1997
Pole vault	5.50A ?	Larry Jessee (31.3.52)	USA	El Paso	24 Aug 1996
Long jump	7.68A	Aaron Simpson (20.9.61)	USA	Cedar City, UT	21 Jun 2002
	7.57	Hans Schicker (3.10.47)	FRG	Kitzingen	16 Jul 1989
Triple jump	16.58	Ray Kimble (19.4.53)	USA	Edinburgh	2 Jul 1993
Shot	21.41	Brian Oldfield (1.6.45)	USA	Innsbruck	22 Aug 1985
Discus	69.46	Al Oerter (19.9.36)	USA	Wichita	31 May 1980
Hammer	82.23	Igor Astapkovich (4.1.63)	BLR	Minsk	10 Jul 2004
Javelin	84.08	Peter Blank (10.4.62)	GER	Ulm	29 Jun 2003
Pentathlon	3510 pts	Werner Schallau (8.9.38)	FRG	Gelsenkirchen	24 Sep 1978
		6.74, 59.20, 23.0, 43.76, 5:05.7			
Decathlon	7525 pts	Kip Janvrin (8.7.65)	USA	San Sebastián	24 Aug 2005
		11.56, 6.78, 14.01, 1.80, 49.46, 15.40, 42.70, 4.70, 58.43, 4:25.87			
20 km walk	1:21:36	Willi Sawall (7.11.41)	AUS	Melbourne	4 Jul 1982
50 km walk	3:49:06	José Marín (21.1.50)	ESP	Badalona	22 Mar 1992
4x100m	42.20	SpeedWest TC	USA	Irvine	2 May 2004
		(Frank Strong, Cornell Stephenson, Kettrell Berry, Willie Gault)			
4x400m	3:20.83	S Allah, K Morning, E Gonera, R Blackwell	USA	Philadelphia	27 Apr 2001

WOMEN – aged 35 or more

100 metres	10.74	Merlene Ottey (10.5.60)	JAM	Milano	7 Sep 1996
200 metres	21.93	Merlene Ottey (10.5.60)	JAM	Bruxelles	25 Aug 1995
400 metres	50.27	Jearl Miles Clark (4.9.66)	USA	Madrid	20 Sep 2002
800 metres	1:56.53	Lyubov Gurina (6.8.57)	RUS	Hechtel	30 Jul 1994
1000 metres	2:31.5	Maricica Puica (29.7.50)	ROM	Poiana Brasov	1 Jun 1986
1500 metres	3:57.73	Maricica Puica (29.7.50)	ROM	Bruxelles	30 Aug 1985
1 mile	4:17.33	Maricica Puica (29.7.50)	ROM	Zürich	21 Aug 1985
2000 metres	5:28.69	Maricica Puica (29.7.50)	ROM	London	11 Jul 1986
3000 metres	8:23.23	Edith Masai (4.4.67)	KEN	Monaco	19 Jul 2002
5000 metres	14:37.20	Edith Masai (4.4.67)	KEN	Roma	8 Jul 2005
10000 metres	30:30.26	Edith Masai (4.4.67)	KEN	Helsinki	6 Aug 2005
Marathon	2:24:35	Katrin Dörre-Heinig (6.10.61)	GER	Hamburg	25 Apr 1999
3000m steeple	9:50.29	Natalya Cherepanova (9.3.67)	RUS	Tula	10 Aug 2003
100m hurdles	12.40	Gail Devers (19.11.66)	USA	Lausanne	2 Jul 2002
400m hurdles	52.94	Marina Styepanova (1.5.50)	RUS	Tashkent	17 Sep 1986
High jump	2.01	Inga Babakova (27.6.67)	UKR	Oslo	27 Jun 2003
Pole vault	4.22	Gabriela Mihalcea (27.1.64)	ROM	Dreux	11 Jun 1999
	4.25i	Gabriela Mihalcea (27.1.64)	ROM	Pireas	13 Feb 1999

Long jump	6.99	Heike Drechsler (16.12.64)	GER	Sydney	29 Sep 2000
Triple jump	14.42	Inessa Kravets (5.10.66)	UKR	Waszawa	15 Jun 2003
	14.44i	Inessa Kravets (5.10.66)	UKR	Moskva	30 Jan 2003
Shot	21.46	Larisa Peleshenko (29.2.64)	RUS	Moskva	26 Aug 2000
	21.47i	Helena Fibingerová (13.7.49)	CZE	Jablonec	9 Feb 1985
Discus	69.60	Faina Melnik (9.7.45)	RUS	Donetsk	9 Sep 1980
Hammer	69.17	Alla Davydova (21.5.66)	RUS	Valencia	24 May 2003
Javelin	66.00	Tayyana Shikolenko (10.5.68)	RUS	Tula	10 Aug 2003
Heptathlon	6533 pts	Jane Frederick (7.4.52)	USA	Talence	27 Sep 1987
		13.60, 1.82, 15.50, 24.73; 6.29, 49.70, 2:14.88			
5000m walk	20:12.41	Elisabetta Perrone (9.7.68)	ITA	Rieti	2 Aug 2003
10km walk	42:42+	Tamara Kovalenko (5.6.64)	RUS	Moskva	19 May 2000
10000m t walk	43:26.5	Elisabetta Perrone (9.7.68)	ITA	Saluzzo	4 Aug 2004
20km walk	1:25:41	Olimpiada Ivanova (5.5.70)	RUS	Helsinki	7 Aug 2005
20000m t walk	1:27:49.3	Yelena Nikolayeva (1.2.66)	RUS	Brisbane	6 Sep 2001
4x100m	48.63	Desmier, Sulter, Andreas, Apavou	FRA	Eugene	8 Jun 1989
4x400m	3:50.80	Mitchell, Mathews, Beadnall, Gabriel	GBR	Gateshead	8 Aug 1999

WOMEN – aged 40 or more

100 metres	10.99	Merlene Ottey (10.5.60)	JAM	Thessaloniki	30 Aug 2000
200 metres	22.72	Merlene Ottey (10.5.60)	SLO	Athína	23 Aug 2004
400 metres	53.05A	María Figueirêdo (11.11.63)	BRA	Bogotá	10 Jul 2004
	53.14	María Figueirêdo (11.11.63)	BRA	San Carlos, VEN	19 Jun 2004
800 metres	1:59.25	Yekaterina Podkopayeva (11.6.52)	RUS	Luxembourg	30 Jun 1994
1000 metres	2:36.16	Yekaterina Podkopayeva (11.6.52)	RUS	Nancy	14 Sep 1994
	2:36.08i	Yekaterina Podkopayeva (11.6.52	RUS	Liévin	13 Feb 1993
1500 metres	3:59.78	Yekaterina Podkopayeva (11.6.52)	RUS	Nice	18 Jul 1994
1 mile	4:23.78	Yekaterina Podkopayeva (11.6.52)	RUS	Roma	9 Jun 1993
3000 metres	9:11.2	Joyce Smith (26.10.37)	GBR	London	30 Apr 1978
	9:02.83i	Lyubov Kremlyova (21.12.61)	RUS	Moskva	22 Jan 2002
5000 metres	15:20.59	Elena Fidatov (24.7.60)	ROM	Bucuresti	7 Aug 2000
10000 metres	32:12.07	Nicole Lévêque (27.1.51)	FRA	Helsinki	13 Aug 1994
Marathon	2:26:51	Priscilla Welch (22.11.44)	GBR	London	10 May 1987
3000m steeple	10:38.98	Soraya Telles (15.9.58)	BRA	Rio de Janeiro	5 Jun 1999
100 m hurdles	13.55	Clova Court (10.2.60)	GBR	Bedford	19 Aug 2000
400 m hurdles	58.3	Gowry Retchakan (21.6.60)	GBR	Hoo	3 Sep 2000
	58.88	Maria José dos Santos (12.9.59)	BRA	Americana	3 Jun 2000
High jump	1.76	Debbie Brill (10.3.53) #	CAN	Gateshead	6 Aug 1999
Pole vault	3.60	Larissa Lowe (19.8.63)	NED	Kingston	24 Apr 2004
	3.60i	Carla Forcellini (7.11.59)	ITA	Sindelfingen	12 Mar 2004
	3.60i	Larissa Lowe (19.8.63)	NED	Sindelfingen	12 Mar 2004
Long jump	6.41	Vera Olenchenko (21.3.59)	RUS	Rostov-na-Donu	26 Jun 2000
Triple jump	12.49	Dana Urnánková (8.4.62)	CZE	Turnov	19 May 2002
Shot	19.05	Antonina Ivanova (25.12.32)	RUS	Oryol	28 Aug 1973
	19.16i	Antonina Ivanova	RUS	Moskva	24 Feb 1974
Discus	67.10	Ellina Zvereva (16.11.60)	BLR	Edmonton	11 Aug 2001
Hammer	59.29	Oneithea Lewis (11.6.60)	USA	Princeton	10 May 2003
Javelin	61.96	Laverne Eve (16.6.65)	BAH	Monaco	9 Sep 2005
(old)	64.06	Tessa Sanderson (14.3.56)	GBR	London (CP)	12 Jul 1996
Heptathlon	4359 pts	Conceição Geremias (23.7.56)	BRA	São Caetano do Sul	7 Sep 1997
		15.61, 1.57, 12.14, 28.26, 5.49, 32.08, 2:56.10			
5000m walk	22:49.06	Suzanne Griesbach (22.4.45)	FRA	Annecy	9 Aug 1987
10km walk	45:09+	Kerry Saxby-Junna (2.6.61)	AUS	Edmonton	9 Aug 2001
20km walk	1:33:40.2t	Kerry Saxby-Junna (2.6.61)	AUS	Brisbane	6 Sep 2001
4x100m	50.07	Horwedel, Fritsche, Grissmer, Stopka	GER	Gateshead	8 Aug 1999
4x400m	3:58.70	Foreman, Thompson, Board, Libal	GBR	Eugene	24 Aug 1996

 # W45 record

WORLD AND CONTINENTAL RECORDS SET IN 2005

OUTDOORS - MEN

Event	Record	Mark	Athlete	Nat	Venue	Date
100	CAC,Com	9.84	Asafa POWELL	JAM	Kingston	7 May 2005
	W,CAC,Com	9.77	Asafa POWELL	JAM	Athína	14 Jun 2005
1500	Asi	3:30.00	Rashid RAMZI	MAR	Roma	8 Jul 2005
	NAm	3:29.30	Bernard LAGAT	USA	Rieti	28 Aug 2005
	SAm	3:33.25	Hudson de SOUZA	BRA	Rieti	28 Aug 2005
1M	Asi	3:47.97	Daham Najim BASHIR	QAT	Oslo	29 Jul 2005
	Oce	3:48.98	Craig MOTTRAM	AUS	Oslo	29 Jul 2005
	SAm	3:51.05	Hudson de SOUZA	BRA	Oslo	29 Jul 2005
3000	W20	7:28.78	Augustine CHOGE	KEN	Doha	13 May 2005
	Asi	7:30.76	Jamal Bilal SALEM	QAT	Doha	13 May 2005
2M	N.Am	8:11.48	Allan WEBB	USA	Eugene	4 Jun 2005
	Oce	8:11.27	Craig MOTTRAM	AUS	Sheffield	21 Aug 2005
	SAm	8:21.67	Hudson de SOUZA	BRA	Linz	23 Aug 2005
5000	Asi	12:58.58	Moukhled AL-OUTAIBI	KSA	Heusden-Zolder	23 Jul 2005
10000	W,Afr	26:17.53	Kenenisa BEKELE	ETH	Bruxelles	26 Aug 2005
	W20	26:41.75	Samuel WANJIRU	KEN	Bruxelles	26 Aug 2005
15kRd	W	41:22 §	Haile GEBRSELASSIE	ETH	Tilburg	4 Sep 2005
10MRd	W	44:24 §	Haile GEBRSELASSIE	ETH	Tilburg	4 Sep 2005
20kRd	(W,Afr)	56:03 §	Zersenay TADESSE	ERI	South Shields	18 Sep 2005
30kRd	W	1:28:00	Takayuki MATSUMIYA	JPN	Kumamoto	27 Feb 2005
HMar	W,W20,Afr,Com	59:16	Samuel WANJIRU	KEN	Rotterdam	11 Sep 2005
	(W,Afr)	59:05 §	Zersenay TADESSE	ERI	South Shields	18 Sep 2005
Mar	W20	2:10:13	Moses MASAI	KEN	Essen	17 Apr 2005
Ekiden Marathon Relay 5k, 10k, 5k, 10k, 5k, 7.195k						
	W,Afr	1:57:06	Kenya	KEN	Chiba	23 Nov 2005
	Asi	1:58:38	Japan	JPN	Chiba	23 Nov 2005
	NAm	1:59:08	United States	USA	Chiba	23 Nov 2005
	Eur ??	2:02:34	Russia	RUS	Chiba	23 Nov 2005
2000SC	W20	5:20.44	Ronald KIPCHUMBA RUTTO	KEN	Doha	13 May 2005
	W18	5:24.69	Abel MUTAI	KEN	Marrakech	15 Jul 2005
3000SC	Eur,W35	8:04.95	Simon VROEMEN	NED	Helsinki	26 Aug 2005
400H	S.Am	47.84	Bayano KAMANI	PAN	Helsinki	7 Aug 2005
HJ	Afr,Com	2.38	Jacques FREITAG	RSA	Oudtshoorn	5 Mar 2005
LJ	Asi	8.44	Mohamed Salim AL-KHUWALIDI	KSA	Makkah	13 Apr 2005
SP	Asi	20.54	Khalid Habash AL-SUWAIDI	QAT	Stayki	25 Jun 2005
DT	SAm	64.69	Jorge BALLIENGO	ARG	Rosario	3 May 2005
	Asi	65.25	Ehsan HADADI	IRI	Inchon	1 Sep 2005
HT	Afr,Com	80.63	Chris HARMSE	RSA	Durban	15 Apr 2005
Oct	W18	6482	Yordani GARCÍA	CUB	Marrakech	14 Jul 2005
Dec	Afr	8023	Hamdi DHOUIBI	TUN	Helsinki	10 Aug 2005
10,000W	W,Eur	37:58.6	Ivano BRUGNETTI	ITA	Sesto San Giovanni	23 Jul 2005
10kRW	W20	39:52 §	Aleksandr PROKHOROV	RUS	Sochi	13 Mar 2005
	W20	39:32+	Eder SÁNCHEZ	MEX	Helsinki	6 Aug 2005
20kRW	Oce,Com	1:17:33	Nathan DEAKES	AUS	Cixi	23 Apr 2005
	Asi	1:17:41	ZHU Hongyu	CHN	Cixi	23 Apr 2005
	W18	1:18:07	LI Gaobo	CHN	Cixi	23 Apr 2005
30kW	W,Eur	2:01:47+	Vladmir KANAYKIN	RUS	Adler	13 Mar 2005
35kW	W,Eur	2:23:17	Vladmir KANAYKIN	RUS	Adler	13 Mar 2005
50kRW	Asi	3:36:20	HAN Yucheng	CHN	Nanning	27 Feb 2005
	Asi	3:36:06	YU Chaohong	CHN	Nanjing	22 Oct 2005
	W20	3:41:30	NI Liang	CHN	Nanjing	22 Oct 2005

OUTDOORS - WOMEN

Event	Record	Mark	Athlete	Nat	Venue	Date
5000	W35	14:37.20	Edith MASAI	KEN	Roma	8 Jul 2005
	Afr	14:28.98	Meseret DEFAR	ETH	Bruxelles	26 Aug 2005
10000	W35	30:51.99	Edith MASAI	KEN	Utrecht	17 Jun 2005
	W35	30:30.26	Edith MASAI	KEN	Helsinki	6 Aug 2005
HMar	W35	68:19 dh	Edith MASAI	KEN	South Shields	18 Sep 2005
	NAm	67:53	Deena KASTOR	USA	Philadelphia	18 Sep 2005
25k Rd	W,Asi	1:22:13	Mizuki NOGUCHI	JPN	Berlin	25 Sep 2005
30k Rd	W,Asi	1:38:49	Mizuki NOGUCHI	JPN	Berlin	25 Sep 2005
Mar	Asi	2:19:12	Mizuki NOGUCHI	JPN	Berlin	25 Sep 2005
2000SC	W,Afr,Com	6:04.46	Dorcus INZIKURU	UGA	Milano	1 Jun 2005
3000SC	Afr,Com	9:28.50	Dorcus INZIKURU	UGA	Doha	13 May 2005
	CAC	9:44.27	Korene HINDS	JAM	Rio de Janeiro	15 May 2005
	SAm	10:00.54	Michele da COSTA	BRA	São Paulo	17 Jun 2005
	Afr,Com	9:15.04	Dorcus INZIKURU	UGA	Athína	14 Jun 2005
	CAC	9:36.14	Mardrea HYMAN	JAM	Kingston	26 Jun 2005

	Asi	9:41.21	Minori HAYAKARI	JPN	Helsinki	6 Aug 2005
	CAC	9:33.30	Korene HINDS	JAM	Helsinki	8 Aug 2005
	CAC	9:30.12	Korene HINDS	JAM	Rieti	28 Aug 2005
	CAC	9:27.21	Mardrea HYMAN	JAM	Monaco	9 Sep 2005
400H	W20	54.40	WANG Xing	CHN	Nanjing	21 Oct 2005
PV	CAC	4.20	Katiuska PÉREZ	CUB	La Habana	17 Mar 2005
	W,Eur	4.93	Yelena ISINBAYEVA	RUS	Lausanne	5 Jul 2005
	CAC	4.25	Katiuska PÉREZ	CUB	Nassau	9 Jul 2005
	W,Eur	4.95	Yelena ISINBAYEVA	RUS	Madrid	16 Jul 2005
	W,Eur	4.96	Yelena ISINBAYEVA	RUS	London (CP)	22 Jul 2005
	W,Eur	5.00	Yelena ISINBAYEVA	RUS	London (CP)	22 Jul 2005
	W,Eur	5.01	Yelena ISINBAYEVA	RUS	Helsinki	12 Aug 2005
	Asi	4.53	GAO Shuying	CHN	Inchon	2 Sep 2005
SP	Oce,Com	19.87	Valerie VILI	NZL	Helsinki	12 Aug 2005
DT	Afr	63.17	Elizna NAUDE	RSA	Bloemfontein	4 Mar 2005
HT	Afr	68.48	Marwa Ahmed HUSSEIN	EGY	Cairo	18 Feb 2005
	SAm	67.07	Jenniefr DAHLGREN	ARG	Athens, GA	23 Apr 2005
	NAm	73.87	Erin GILREATH	USA	Carson	25 Jun 2005
	Asi,W20	73.24	ZHANG Wenxiu	CHN	Changsha	24 Jun 2005
	W,Eur	77.06	Tatyana LYSENKO	RUS	Moskva	15 Jul 2005
JT	W,CAC	71.70	Osleidys MENÉNDEZ	CUB	Helsinki	14 Aug 2005
	Eur	70.03	Christina OBEGFÖLL	GER	Helsinki	14 Aug 2005
Hep	Afr	6423	Margaret SIMPSON	GHA	Götzis	29 May 2005
Dec	W,Eur	8358	Austra SKUJYTE	LTU	Columbia. MS	15 Apr 2005
4x400	SAm	3:26.82	Brazil	BRA	Helsinki	12 Aug 2005
3000tW	W20	12:10.31	CHEN Zhou	CHN	Zhengzhou	28 Aug 2005
10000tW	Afr	47:32.54A	Nicolene CRONJE	RSA	Pretoria	19 Mar 2005
	W20	43:11.34	Vera SOKOLOVA	RUS	Kaunas	21 Jul 2005
20000tW	NAm	1:33:28.2	Teresa VAILL	USA	Carson	25 Jun 2005
20KRW	SAm	1:31:25	Miriam RAMÓN	ECU	Lima	7 May 2005
	W,Eur,W35	1:35:41	Olimpiada IVANOVA	RUS	Helsinki	7 Aug 2005
50kRW	W20	4:49:39	Déspina ZAPOUNÍDOU	GRE	Scanzoroscaite	16 Oct 2005

INDOORS - MEN

60	Eur	6.45	Ronald POGNON	FRA	Karlsruhe	13 Feb 2005
200	W20	20.40	LaShawn MERRITT	USA	Fayetteville	12 Feb 2005
	NAm	20.21	Wallace SPEARMON	USA	Fayetteville	11 Mar 2005
	W20	20.37	Walter DIX	USA	Fayetteville	11 Mar 2005
	NAm	20.10	Wallace SPEARMON	USA	Fayetteville	11 Mar 2005
400	SAm	46.26	Bayano KAMANI	PAN	Boston	29 Jan 2005
	W20	44.93	LaShawn MERRITT	USA	Fayetteville	11 Feb 2005
	W,NAm	44.57	Kerron CLEMENT	USA	Fayetteville	12 Mar 2005
1000	Oce	2:20.30	Mark FOUNTAIN	AUS	Fayetteville	21 Jan 2005
1500	NAm	3:33.34+	Bernard LAGAT	USA	Fayetteville	11 Feb 2005
Mile	W35	3:53.18	Laban ROTICH	KEN	Boston (R)	29 Jan 2005
	NAm	3:49.89	Bernard LAGAT	USA	Fayetteville	11 Feb 2005
50H	Eur	6.36+	Ladji DOUCOURÉ	FRA	Liévin	26 Feb 2005
LJ	W20	8.22	Viktor KUZNETSOV	UKR	Brovary	22 Jan 2005
35lb Wt	E	25.25 & 25.28	Libor CHARFREITAG	SVK	Nampa	4 Feb 2005
	E	25.68	Libor CHARFREITAG	SVK	Sterling	5 Mar 2005
	W20	20.97	Lars ARRHENIUS	SWE	Pocatello	5 Mar 2005
	Afr	22.58	Mohsen ANANI	EGY	Clemson	3 Dec 2005
Hep	CAC	6035	Maurice SMITH	JAM	Fayetteville	26 Feb 2005

INDOORS - WOMEN

500	W20	1:10.05	Natasha HASTINGS	USA	New York	26 Dec 2004
800m	CAC	2:01.95	Kenia SINCLAIR	JAM	Gainesville	6 Feb 2005
1500	Asi	4:12.70	XIE Sainan	CHN	Shanghai	21 Feb 2005
Mile	CAC	4:32.33	Kenia SINCLAIR	JAM	Gainesville	3 Mar 2005
5000	W,Afr	14:32.93	Tirunesh DIBABA	ETH	Boston (Roxbury)	29 Jan 2005
	Oce,Com	14:50.46	Kim SMITH	NZL	Boston (Allston)	11 Feb 2005
50H	W35	6.83+	Michelle FREEMAN	JAM	Liévin	26 Feb 2005
PV	CAC	4.15A	Denisse ORENGO	PUR	Reno	22 Jan 2005
	W,Eur	4.87	Yelena ISINBAYEVA	RUS	Donetsk	12 Feb 2005
	W,Eur	4.88	Yelena ISINBAYEVA	RUS	Birmingham	18 Feb 2005
	W18	4.32 & 4.37	Ekateríni STEFANÍDI	GRE	Athína (P)	20 Feb 2005
	Asi	4.45	ZHAO Yingying	CHN	Madrid	24 Feb 2005
	W,Eur	4.89	Yelena ISINBAYEVA	RUS	Liévin	26 Feb 2005
	W,Eur	4.90	Yelena ISINBAYEVA	RUS	Madrid	6 Mar 2005
	W20	4.48	Silke SPIEGELBURG	GER	Münster	25 Aug 2005
TJ	SAm	13.76	Gisela de OLIVEIRA	BRA	Fayetteville	12 Mar2005
20lb Wt	CAC	23.15	Candice SCOTT	TRI	Clemson	3 Dec 2004

Event	Record	Mark	Athlete	Nat	Venue	Date
	W,NAm	24.11	Erin GILREATH	USA	Chapel Hill	28 Jan 2005
	CAC	23.23	Candice SCOTT	TRI	Chapel Hill	28 Jan 2005
	SAm	22.27	Jennifer DAHLGREN	ARG	Blacksburg	11 Feb 2005
	CAC	23.26	Candice SCOTT	TRI	Fayetteville	12 Feb 2005
	W,NAm	24.23	Erin GILREATH	USA	Bloomington	18 Feb 2005
	CAC	23.78	Candice SCOTT	TRI	Bloomington	18 Feb 2005
	CAC	24.17	Candice SCOTT	TRI	Fayetteville	12 Mar 2005
Note outdoors:	CAC	23.52	Candice SCOTT	TRI	Gainesville	15 Jan 2005
Pen	Com	4733	Kelly SOTHERTON	GBR	Madrid	4 Mar 2005
5000W	W	20:37.77	Margarita TUROVA	BLR	Minsk	13 Feb 2005
	W20	21:30.1	Vera SOKOLOVA	RUS	Chelyabinsk	6 Jan 2005
10000W	W20	47:40.21	Tatyana VLASOVA	RUS	Sankt-Peterburg	27 Jan 2005
4x200	W,Eur	1:32.41	RUS (Kondratyeva, Khabarova, Pechonkina, Gushchina)		Glasgow	29 Jan 2005
4x400	Afr	3:49.52	Senegal	SEN	Tehran	27 Sep 2005

There were notably fewer indoor records this year as the indoor season was passed by many top athletes.

WORLD AND CONTINENTAL RECORDS SET IN JAN-MAR 2006

OUTDOORS - MEN

Event	Record	Mark	Athlete	Nat	Venue	Date
2000	Oce	4:50.76	Craig MOTTRAM	AUS	Melbourne	9 Mar 06
20k	W	55:48	Haile GEBRSELASSIE	ETH	Phoenix	15 Jan 06
HMar	W	58:55	Haile GEBRSELASSIE	ETH	Phoenix	15 Jan 06
25k	W	1:11:37	Haile GEBRSELASSIE	ETH	Alphen	12 Mar 06
24Hr	Asi	272,936	Ryoichi SEKIYA	JPN	Taipei	26 Feb 06
5000W	Oce	18:45.19	Nathan DEAKES	AUS	Melbourne	9 Mar 06
30kW	W	2:01:13+	Vladimir KANAYKIN	RUS	Adler	19 Feb 06
35kW	W	2:21:31	Vladimir KANAYKIN	RUS	Adler	19 Feb 06

OUTDOORS - WOMEN

Event	Record	Mark	Athlete	Nat	Venue	Date
15k	W	46:55+	Kayoko FUKUSHI	JPN	Marugame	5 Feb 06
20k	Asi	63:41+	Kayoko FUKUSHI	JPN	Marugame	5 Feb 06
HMar	Asi	67:26	Kayoko FUKUSHI	JPN	Marugame	5 Feb 06
3000SC	Oce	9:24.29	Melissa ROLLISON	AUS	Melbourne	22 Mar 06
PV	Oce	4.61	Kym HOWE-NADIN	AUS	Canberra	26 Jan 06
	Oce	4.62	Kym HOWE-NADIN	AUS	Melbourne	25 Mar 06
SP	Oce	20.11	Valerie VILI	NZL	Christchurch	27 Jan 06
	Oce	20.20	Valerie VILI	NZL	Christchurch	27 Jan 06
Wt	SAm	22.48	Jennifer DAHLGREN	ARG	Gainesville	5 Feb 06

INDOORS - MEN

Event	Record	Mark	Athlete	Nat	Venue	Date
60	SAm	6.60	Vicente deLIMA	BRA	Moskva	10 Mar 06
100	SAm	10.42	Vicente deLIMA	BRA	Tampere	4 Feb 06
300	W	31.88	Wallace SPEARMON	USA	Fayetteville	10 Feb 06
	Eur	32.61	Johan WISSMAN	SWE	Liévin	3 Mar 06
400	W40	48.96	Enrico SARACENI	ITA	Linz	20 Mar 06
M	W20=	3:58.60	Geoffrey KIPKOECH RONO	KEN	New York	21 Jan 06
	CAC	3:59.61	David FREEMAN	PUR	Fayetteville	10 Feb 06
3000	Asi	7:39.77	Saïf Saeed SHAHEEN	QAT	Pattaya	11 Feb 06
2M	W20	8:13.32	Tariku BEKELE	ETH	Birmingham	18 Feb 06
	W35	8:27.60	Paul BITOK	KEN	Birmingham	18 Feb 06
50H	SAm	6.57	Redelen DOS SANTOS	BRA	Groningen	28 Jan 06
60H	W40	7.95	Vincent CLARICO	FRA	Linz	19 Mar 06
	W40	7.85	Vincent CLARICO	FRA	Linz	19 Mar 06
PV	CAC	5.70	Robinson PRATT	MEX	Reno	28 Jan 06
	Oce	5.70	Paul BURGESS	AUS	Donetsk	12 Feb 06
	Oce	5.80	Paul BURGESS	AUS	Donetsk	12 Feb 06
	CAC	5.71	Giovanni LANARO	MEX	Flagstaff	18 Feb 06
LJ	Afr	8.36	Ignisious GAISAH	GHA	Stockholm	2 Feb 06
	SAm	8.10	Irving SALADINO	PAN	Moskva	10 Mar 06
	SAm	8.18	Irving SALADINO	PAN	Moskva	11 Mar 06
	SAm	8.19	Irving SALADINO	PAN	Moskva	11 Mar 06
	SAm	8.27	Irving SALADINO	PAN	Moskva	11 Mar 06
	SAm	8.29	Irving SALADINO	PAN	Moskva	11 Mar 06
TJ	SAm=	17.46	Jadel GREGÓRIO	BRA	Moskva	11 Mar 06
	SAm	17.56	Jadel GREGÓRIO	BRA	Moskva	12 Mar 06
SP/5	W18	21.16	Rosen KARAMFILOV	BUL	Sofia	28 Jan 06
	W18	21.17	Rosen KARAMFILOV	BUL	Sofia	4 Feb 06
	W18	21.24	Rosen KARAMFILOV	BUL	Sofia	4 Feb 06
	W18	21.25	Rosen KARAMFILOV	BUL	Sofia	4 Feb 06
SP	CAC	19.99	Dorian SCOTT	JAM	Gainesville	15 Jan 06
	CAC	20.49	Dorian SCOTT	JAM	Gainesville	5 Feb 06

	Asi	20.09	Khalid Habash AL-SUWAIDI	QAT	Schio	11 Feb 06
	CAC	20.52	Dorian SCOTT	JAM	Blacksburg	18 Feb 06
Wt	Afr	22.78	Mohsen ANANI	EGY	Blacksburg	24 Feb 06
	Afr	22.95	Mohsen ANANI	EGY	Blacksburg	24 Feb 06
	Afr	22.95	Mohsen ANANI	EGY	Blacksburg	24 Feb 06
4x400	W	3:01.96	Clement,Spearmon,Williamson,Wariner	USA	Fayetteville	11 Feb 06

INDOORS - WOMEN

300	W20	36.96	Francena McCORORY	USA	Blacksburg	28 Jan 06
400	CAC	50.34	Christine AMERTIL	BAH	Moskva	12 Mar 06
500	W	1:06.31	Olesya KRASNOMOVETS	RUS	Yekaterinburg	7 Jan 06
	W20	1:08.94	Kseniya ZADORINA	RUS	Moskva	12 Jan 06
800	CAC	2:01.81	Kenia SINCLAIR	JAM	Fayetteville	10 Feb 06
	CAC	2:00.06	Kenia SINCLAIR	JAM	Moskva	11 Mar 06
	CAC	1:59.54	Kenia SINCLAIR	JAM	Moskva	12 Mar 06
1000	Eur	2:32.16	Yuliya CHIZHENKO	RUS	Moskva	25 Jan 06
1500	Asi	4:01.82	Maryam JAMAL	BRN	Valencia	11 Feb 06
	W	3:58.28	Yelena SOBOLEVA	RUS	Moskva	18 Feb 06
2000	Afr	5:34.74+	Meseret DEFAR	ETH	Stuttgart	4 Feb 06
3000	W	8:27.86	Liliya SHOBUKHOVA	RUS	Moskva	17 Feb 06
2000SC	W20	6:10.63	Yuliya MOCHALOVA	RUS	Volgograd	5 Feb 06
3000SC	W	9:07.00	Tatyana PETROVA	RUS	Moskva	17 Feb 06
	W20	9:28.63	Yuliya MOCHALOVA	RUS	Moskva	17 Feb 06
	W35	9:27.82	Natalya CHEREPANOVA	RUS	Moskva	17 Feb 06
60H	SAm	8.09	Maila Paula MACHADO	BRA	Karlsruhe	29 Jan 06
	SAm	8.08	Maila Paula MACHADO	BRA	Moskva	11 Mar 06
HJ	W	2.08	Kajsa BERGQVIST	SWE	Arnstadt	4 Feb 06
PV	SAm=	4.25	Fabiana DE MURER	BRA	Wuppertal	27 Jan 06
	SAm	4.35	Fabiana DE MURER	BRA	Wuppertal	27 Jan 06
	SAm	4.41	Fabiana DE MURER	BRA	Wuppertal	27 Jan 06
	W	4.91	Yelena ISINBAYEVA	RUS	Donetsk	12 Feb 06
TJ	SAm	14.11	Keila COSTA	BRA	Moskva	10 Mar 06
SP	Afr	18.13	Vivian CHUKWUEMEKA	NGR	Flagstaff	4 Feb 06
Wt	SAm	22.30	Jennifer DAHLGREN	ARG	Fayetteville	10 Feb 06
	SAm	22.35	Jennifer DAHLGREN	ARG	Blacksburg	4 Mar 06
	SAm	23.03	Jennifer DAHLGREN	ARG	Fayetteville	10 Mar 06
	SAm	24.04	Jennifer DAHLGREN	ARG	Fayetteville	10 Mar 06
Pen	CAC	4014	Chelsea HAMMOND	JAM	Clemson	28 Jan 06
	(8.69, 1.75, 10.38, 6.03, 2:28.73)					
	Asi	4582	Olga RYPAKOVA	KAZ	Pattaya	10 Feb 06
	(8.68, 1.88, 12.90, 6.55, 2:23.26)					
	CAC	4086	Chelsea HAMMOND	JAM	Fayetteville	11 Mar 06
	(8.45, 1.73, 10.17, 6.16, 2:27.30)					
4x400	W	3:23.37	Gushchina,Kotlyarova,Zaytseva,Krasnomovets	RUS	Glasgow	28 Jan 06
	CAC	3:30.03	S.Williams,R.Smith,Thompson,Beckford	JAM	Moskva	12 Mar 06
	CAC	3:29.54	S.Williams,N.Williams,Thompson,Beckford	JAM	Moskva	12 Mar 06

SPLIT TIMES IN WORLD RECORDS

Men			400m	800m	1200m	1600m	2000m	2400m	2800m
800m	1:41.11	Kipketer 1997	49.3	1:41.11		(200m 23.8, 600m 1:14.6)			
1000m	2:11.96	Ngeny 1999	49.66	1:44.62		(200m 24.12, 600m 1:17.14)			
1500m	3:26.00	El Guerrouj 1998	54.3	1:50.7	2:46.4	(1000m 2:18.8)			
1M	3:43.13	El Guerrouj 1999	55.2	1:51.2	2:47.0	(1000m 2:19.2)			
2000m	4:44.79	El Guerrouj 1999	57.1	1:55.4	2:52.4	3:49.60			
3000m	7:20.67	Komen 1996	57.6	1:57.0	2:54.9	3:53.6	4:53.4	5:51.3	6:51.2
2M	7:58.61	Komen 1997	58.6	2:00.4		3:58.4	4:58.2	5:56.7	6:57.5
5000m	12:37.35	Bekele 2004	kms: 2:33.24, 5:05.47, 7:37.34, 10:07.93, last 400m 57.9						
10,000m	26:17.53	Bekele 2005	kms: 2:40.6, 5:16.4, 7:53.3, 10:30.4, 13:09.4, 15:44.66, 18:23.98, 21:04.63, 23:45.09, 26:17.53, last 400m 57.1						
3kmSt	7:53.63	Shaheen 2004	1000m 2:36.13, 2000m 5:18.09						

Women												
800m	1:53.28	Kratochvílová 1983	56.1	1:53.28		(600m 1:25.0)						
1000m	2:28.98	Masterkova 1996	58.3	1:59.8		(200m 28.4, 600m 1:29.1)						
1500m	3:50.46	Qu Yunxia 1993	57.2	2:00.8	3:05.2							
1M	4:12.56	Masterkova 1996	62.0	2:06.7	3:12.2	(1000m 2:39.5)						
2000m	5:25.36	O'Sullivan 1994	64.9	2:07.8	3:14.8	4:23.5	5:25.36					
			1km	2km	3km	4km	5km	6km	7km	8km	9km	
3000m	8:06.11	Wang J 1993	2:42.0	5:29.7	(last 400m 62.7)							
5000m	14:28.09	Jiang B 1997	2:53.4	5:45.95	8:41.09	11:40.6	14:28.09					
10000m	29:31.78	Wang J 1993	2:54.7	5:56.6	8:59.2	12:02.8	15:05.7	18:10.1	21:14.4	23:59.9	26:44.8	
3kmSt	9:01.59	Samitova 2004	1000m 2:58.9, 2000m 5:59.4									

WORLD MEN'S ALL-TIME LISTS

100 METRES

Mark	Wind	Name		Nat	Born	Pos	Meet	Venue	Date
9.77 WR	1.6	Asafa	Powell	JAM	11.11.82	1	SGP	Athína	14 Jun 05
9.79 WR	0.1	Maurice	Greene	USA	23.7.74	1rA	GP II	Athína	16 Jun 99
9.80	0.2		Greene			1	WCh	Sevilla	22 Aug 99
9.82	-0.2		Greene			1	WCh	Edmonton	5 Aug 01
9.84 WR	0.7	Donovan	Bailey	CAN	16.12.67	1	OG	Atlanta	27 Jul 96
9.84	0.2	Bruny	Surin	CAN	12.7.67	2	WCh	Sevilla	22 Aug 99
9.84	1.8		Powell			1		Kingston	7 May 05
9.85 WR	1.2	Leroy	Burrell	USA	21.2.67	1rA	Athl	Lausanne	6 Jul 94
9.85	0.8		Greene			1	GGala	Roma	7 Jul 99
9.85	0.6	Justin	Gatlin	USA	10.2.82	1	OG	Athína	22 Aug 04
9.85	0.6		Powell			1	GS	Ostrava	9 Jun 05
9.86 WR	1.2	Carl	Lewis	USA	1.7.61	1	WCh	Tokyo	25 Aug 91
9.86	-0.4	Frank	Fredericks	NAM	2.10.67	1rA	Athl	Lausanne	3 Jul 96
9.86	0.2		Greene			1	WCh	Athína	3 Aug 97
9.86	1.8	Ato	Boldon	TRI	30.12.73	1rA	MSR	Walnut	19 Apr 98
9.86	-0.4		Boldon			1		Athína	17 Jun 98
9.86	0.1		Boldon			2rA	GP II	Athína	16 Jun 99
9.86	0.4		Boldon			1rA	Athl	Lausanne	2 Jul 99
9.86	-0.2		Greene			1	ISTAF	Berlin	1 Sep 00
9.86	-0.6	Francis	Obikwelu (10)	POR	22.11.78	2	OG	Athína	22 Aug 04
9.87	0.3	Linford	Christie ¶	GBR	2.4.60	1	WCh	Stuttgart	15 Aug 93
9.87	1.9		Fredericks			1	WG	Helsinki	25 Jun 96
9.87	1.3		Boldon			1q1	WCh	Athína	2 Aug 97
9.87A	-0.2	Obadele	Thompson	BAR	30.3.76	1	WCp	Johannesburg	11 Sep 98
9.87	0.6		Greene			1	DNG	Stockholm	30 Jul 99
9.87	-0.3		Greene			1	OG	Sydney	23 Sep 00
9.87	2.0	Dwain	Chambers ¶	GBR	5.4.78	2	GPF	Paris (C)	14 Sep 02
9.87	0.6		Greene			3	OG	Athína	22 Aug 04
9.87	0.2		Powell			1	VD	Bruxelles	3 Sep 04
		(30 performances by 13 athletes)							
9.88	1.8	Shawn	Crawford	USA	14.1.78	1	Pre	Eugene	19 Jun 04
9.91	1.2	Dennis	Mitchell ¶	USA	20.2.66	3	WCh	Tokyo	25 Aug 91
9.92	0.3	Andre	Cason	USA	20.1.69	2	WCh	Stuttgart	15 Aug 93
9.92	0.8	Jon	Drummond	USA	9.9.68	1h3	NC	Indianapolis	12 Jun 97
9.92	0.2	Tim	Montgomery ¶	USA	28.1.75	2	NC	Indianapolis	13 Jun 97
9.92A	-0.2	Seun	Ogunkoya	NGR	28.12.77	2	WCp	Johannesburg	11 Sep 98
9.92	1.0	Tim	Harden	USA	27.1.74	1		Luzern	5 Jul 99
		(20)							
9.93A WR	1.4	Calvin	Smith	USA	8.1.61	1	USOF	USAF Academy	3 Jul 83
9.93	-0.6	Michael	Marsh	USA	4.8.67	1	MSR	Walnut	18 Apr 92
9.93	1.8	Patrick	Johnson	AUS	26.9.72	1		Mito	5 May 03
9.94	0.2	Davidson	Ezinwa ¶	NGR	22.11.71	1	Gugl	Linz	4 Jul 94
9.94	-0.2	Bernard	Williams	USA	19.1.78	2	WCh	Edmonton	5 Aug 01
9.94	1.0	Leonard	Scott	USA	19.1.80	2	LGP	London (CP)	22 Jul 05
9.95A WR	0.3	Jim	Hines	USA	10.9.46	1	OG	Ciudad de México	14 Oct 68
9.95A	1.9	Olapade	Adeniken	NGR	19.8.69	1A		El Paso	16 Apr 94
9.95	0.8	Vincent	Henderson	USA	20.10.72	1		Leverkusen	9 Aug 98
9.95	1.8	Joshua 'J.J.'	Johnson	USA	10.5.76	1r6	MSR	Walnut	21 Apr 02
		(30)							
9.95	0.6	Deji	Aliu	NGR	22.11.75	1	Afr G	Abuja	12 Oct 03
9.95	1.8	John	Capel	USA	27.10.78	3	Pre	Eugene	19 Jun 04
9.96	0.1	Mel	Lattany	USA	10.8.59	1r1		Athens, Ga.	5 May 84
9.96	1.2	Ray	Stewart	JAM	18.3.65	6	WCh	Tokyo	25 Aug 91
9.96	0.8	Kareem	Streete-Thompson	CAY/USA	30.3.73	2h3	NC	Indianapolis	12 Jun 97
9.96	1.0	Marc	Burns	TRI	7.1.83	1	NC	Port of Spain	25 Jun 05
9.97	0.6	Uchenna	Emedolu	NGR	17.9.76	2	Afr G	Abuja	12 Oct 03
9.98A	0.6	Silvio	Leonard	CUB	20.9.55	1	WPT	Guadalajara	11 Aug 77
9.98	0.3	Daniel	Effiong ¶	NGR	17.6.72	2s1	WCh	Stuttgart	15 Aug 93
9.98	1.4	Percy	Spencer	JAM	24.2.75	1	NC	Kingston	20 Jun 97
		(40)							
9.98	1.6	Leonard	Myles-Mills	GHA	9.5.73	1	NCAA	Boise	5 Jun 99
9.98	0.4	Jason	Gardener	GBR	18.9.75	3rA	Athl	Lausanne	2 Jul 99
9.98	0.4	Coby	Miller	USA	19.10.76	1s1	NCAA	Durham	2 Jun 00
9.98	0.2	Kim	Collins	SKN	5.4.76	1	CG	Manchester	27 Jul 02
9.99	0.5	Brian	Lewis	USA	5.12.74	1		Cayenne	4 May 02
9.99	1.5	Mickey	Grimes ¶	USA	10.10.76	1rB	WK	Zürich	15 Aug 03

MEN All-time

Mark	Wind	Name		Nat	Born	Pos	Meet	Venue	Date
9.99	1.6	Abdul Aziz	Zakari	GHA	2.9.76	2	GP	Athína	14 Jun 05
9.99	1.0	Darrel	Brown	TRI	11.10.84	2	NC	Port of Spain	25 Jun 05
9.99	1.8	Ronald	Pognon	FRA	16.11.82	1	Athl	Lausanne	5 Jul 05

10.00 Woronin POL, C Imo ¶ NGR, R da Silva BRA, K Ito JPN, E Nkansah GHA, D Patton USA, D Thomas JAM (56) 100th man 10.06, 200th 10.12, 300th 10.17, 400th 10.20

Faulty wind gauge – possibly wind assisted

Mark	Wind	Name		Nat	Born	Pos	Meet	Venue	Date
9.97		Mark	Lewis-Francis	GBR	4.9.82	1q3	WCh	Edmonton	4 Aug 01

Doubtful wind reading

Mark	Wind	Name		Nat	Born	Pos	Meet	Venue	Date
9.91	-2.3	Davidson	Ezinwa ¶	NGR	22.11.71	1		Azusa	11 Apr 92

Low altitude marks for athletes with lifetime bests at high altitude

Mark	Wind	Name	Pos	Meet	Venue	Date
9.94	0.1	Ogunkoya	1	AfCh	Dakar	19 Aug 98
9.96	0.6	O Thompson	2	DNG	Stockholm	30 Jul 99
9.97	1.6	C Smith	1	WK	Zürich	24 Aug 83
9.97	1.2	Adeniken	1	TexR	Austin	4 Apr 92

Wind-assisted – 20 performances to 9.86, performers listed to 9.95

Mark	Wind	Name		Nat	Born	Pos	Meet	Venue	Date
9.69A	5+	Obadele	Thompson	BAR	30.3.76	1		El Paso	13 Apr 96
9.78	5.2	Carl	Lewis	USA	1.7.61	1	OT	Indianapolis	16 Jul 88
9.78	3.7	Maurice	Greene	USA	23.7.74	1	GP II	Stanford	31 May 04
9.79	5.3	Andre	Cason	USA	20.1.69	1h4	NC	Eugene	16 Jun 93
9.79	4.5		Cason			1s1	NC	Eugene	16 Jun 93
9.79	2.9		Greene			1	Pre	Eugene	31 May 98
9.80	4.3		Lewis			1q2	WCh	Tokyo	24 Aug 91
9.83	7.1	Leonard	Scott	USA	19.1.80	1r1	Sea Ray	Knoxville	9 Apr 99
9.84	3.3		Greene			1h2	NC	New Orleans	19 Jun 98
9.84	3.5		Greene			1	Pre	Eugene	30 May 99
9.84	3.4	Justin	Gatlin	USA	10.2.82	1	Pre	Eugene	4 Jun 05
9.84	3.4		Powell			2	Pre	Eugene	4 Jun 05
9.85	5.3		Burrell			2h4	NC	Eugene	16 Jun 93
9.85	4.8		Cason			1	NC	Eugene	17 Jun 93
9.85	4.8	Dennis	Mitchell ¶	USA	20.2.66	2	NC	Eugene	17 Jun 93
9.85A	3.0	Frank	Fredericks	NAM	2.10.67	1		Nairobi	18 May 02
9.86	5.2		Mitchell			2	OT	Indianapolis	16 Jul 88
9.86	2.5		Burrell			1rA	TexR	Austin	9 Apr 94
9.86	2.6	Shawn	Crawford	USA	14.1.78	1	GP	Doha	14 May 04
9.86	4.6		Greene			1		Carson	22 May 04
9.87	11.2	William	Snoddy	USA	6.12.57	1		Dallas	1 Apr 78
9.87	4.9	Calvin	Smith	USA	8.1.61	1s2	OT	Indianapolis	16 Jul 88
9.87	2.4	Michael	Marsh	USA	4.8.67	1rA	MSR	Walnut	20 Apr 97
9.88	2.3	James	Sanford	USA	27.12.57	1		Los Angeles (Ww)	3 May 80
9.88	5.2	Albert	Robinson	USA	28.11.64	4	OT	Indianapolis	16 Jul 88
9.88	4.9	Tim	Harden	USA	27.1.74	1	NC	New Orleans	20 Jun 98
9.88	4.5	Coby	Miller	USA	19.10.76	1		Auburn	1 Apr 00
9.88	3.6	Patrick	Johnson	AUS	26.9.72	1		Perth	8 Feb 03
9.89	4.2	Ray	Stewart	JAM	18.3.65	1s1	PAm	Indianapolis	9 Aug 87
9.90	5.2	Joe	DeLoach	USA	5.6.67	5	OT	Indianapolis	16 Jul 88
9.90	7.1	Kenny	Brokenburr	USA	29.10.68	2r1	Sea Ray	Knoxville	9 Apr 99
9.91	5.3	Bob	Hayes	USA	20.12.42	1s1	OG	Tokyo	15 Oct 64
9.91	4.2	Mark	Witherspoon	USA	3.9.63	2s1	PAm	Indianapolis	9 Aug 87
9.91	3.7	Nicolas	Macrozonaris	CAN	22.8.80	1	NC	Edmonton	22 Jun 02
9.92A	4.4	Chidi	Imo ¶	NGR	27.8.63	1s1	AfG	Nairobi	8 Aug 87
9.92A	2.8	Olapade	Adeniken	NGR	19.8.69	1rA		Sestriere	29 Jul 95
9.92	2.8	Kim	Collins	SKN	5.4.76	1rA	Tex R	Austin	5 Apr 03
9.93	7.5	Pablo	Montes	CUB	23.11.47	1s1	CAC	Panama City	1 Mar 70
9.93	5.3	Erick	Wilson	USA	10.1.82	1	JUCO	Levelland	10 May 03
9.93A	2.2	Churandy	Martina	AHO	3.7.84	1		El Paso	16 Apr 05
9.94	2.7	Vitaliy	Savin	KZK	23.1.66	1	CIS Ch	Moskva	22 Jun 92
9.94	2.5	Daniel	Effiong ¶	NGR	17.6.72	2	TexR	Austin	9 Apr 94
9.94	7.0	Ousmane	Diarra	MLI	30.9.66	1		La Laguna	13 Jul 96
9.94	5.2	Osmond	Ezinwa	NGR	22.11.71	1		Pula	4 Sep 96
9.94	3.9	Vincent	Henderson	USA	20.10.72	1s1	WUG	Catania	29 Aug 97
9.94	2.8	Bryan	Howard	USA	7.10.76	2r7	MSR	Walnut	16 Apr 00
9.95	8.9	Willie	Gault	USA	5.9.60	1		Knoxville	2 Apr 83
9.95	2.4	Mel	Lattany	USA	10.8.59	1		Athens, Ga	7 May 83
9.95	7.1	Anthony	Jones	USA	12.12.71	3r1	Sea Ray	Knoxville	9 Apr 99
9.95	4.2	Marcus	Brunson	USA	24.4.78	1h1	GP	Doha	14 May 04

Disqualified for drug abuse

Mark	Wind	Name		Nat	Born	Pos	Meet	Venue	Date
9.78 WR	2.0	Tim	Montgomery ¶	USA	28.1.75	1	GPF	Paris (C)	14 Sep 02
9.79	1.1	Ben	Johnson ¶	CAN	30.12.61	-	OG	Seoul	24 Sep 88
9.83	1.0		Johnson			(1)	WCh	Roma	30 Aug 87
9.84	2.0		Montgomery			1	Bisl	Oslo	13 Jul 01
9.85	-0.2		Montgomery			2	WCh	Edmonton	5 Aug 01

Mark	Wind	Name		Nat	Born	Pos	Meet	Venue	Date
Rolling start									
9.89w	3.7	Patrick	Jarrett ¶	JAM	2.10.77	1	Pre	Eugene	27 May 01
Hand timing									
9.7	1.9	Donovan	Powell ¶	JAM	31.10.71	1rA		Houston	19 May 95
9.7	1.9	Carl	Lewis	USA	1.7.61	2rA		Houston	19 May 95
9.7	1.9	Olapade	Adeniken	NGR	19.8.69	3rA		Houston	19 May 95
9.7w	3.8	Osvaldo	Lara	CUB	13.7.55	1		Santiago de Cuba	24 Feb 82
9.7w	6.6	Rod	Mapstone	AUS	19.11.69	1r1		Perth	21 Dec 96
9.7w	8.1	Sayon	Cooper	LBR	24.4.74	1		Abilene	28 Mar 98
Drugs dq:	9.7w 3.5		Ben Johnson ¶	CAN	30.12.61	1		Perth	24 Jan 87

200 METRES

Mark	Wind	Name		Nat	Born	Pos	Meet	Venue	Date
19.32 WR	0.4	Michael	Johnson	USA	13.9.67	1	OG	Atlanta	1 Aug 96
19.66 WR	1.7		Johnson			1	NC	Atlanta	23 Jun 96
19.68	0.4	Frank	Fredericks	NAM	2.10.67	2	OG	Atlanta	1 Aug 96
19.71A	1.8		Johnson			1rA		Pietersburg	18 Mar 00
19.72A WR	1.8	Pietro	Mennea	ITA	28.6.52	1	WUG	Ciudad de México	12 Sep 79
19.73	-0.2	Michael	Marsh	USA	4.8.67	1s1	OG	Barcelona	5 Aug 92
19.75	1.5	Carl	Lewis	USA	1.7.61	1	TAC	Indianapolis	19 Jun 83
19.75	1.7	Joe	DeLoach	USA	5.6.67	1	OG	Seoul	28 Sep 88
19.77	0.6		Johnson			1	DNG	Stockholm	8 Jul 96
19.77	0.7	Ato	Boldon	TRI	30.12.73	1rA		Stuttgart	13 Jul 97
19.79	1.7		Lewis			2	OG	Seoul	28 Sep 88
19.79	1.0		Johnson			1	OT	New Orleans	28 Jun 92
19.79	0.5		Johnson			1	WCh	Göteborg	11 Aug 95
19.79	1.2	Shawn	Crawford	USA	14.1.78	1	OG	Athína	26 Aug 04
19.80	-0.9		Lewis			1	OG	Los Angeles	8 Aug 84
19.80	0.4		Boldon			3	OG	Atlanta	1 Aug 96
19.81	0.3		Fredericks			1	GPF	Fukuoka	13 Sep 97
19.82A	2.0		Lewis			1		Sestriere	11 Aug 88
19.82	1.1		Fredericks			1	Bisl	Oslo	5 Jul 96
19.82	1.6		Boldon			1rA	DNG	Stockholm	7 Jul 97
19.83A WR	0.9	Tommie	Smith	USA	12.6.44	1	OG	Ciudad de México	16 Oct 68
19.83	1.7		Johnson			1	GP I	Atlanta	18 May 96
19.84	0.2		Lewis			1q3	OT	Los Angeles	19 Jun 84
19.84	1.7	Francis	Obikwelu (10)	NGR	22.11.78	1s2	WCh	Sevilla	25 Aug 99
19.85	0.4		Johnson			1	IAC	Edinburgh	6 Jul 90
19.85	0.3		Fredericks			1	WCh	Stuttgart	20 Aug 93
19.85	-0.9		Boldon			1	Athl	Lausanne	3 Jul 96
19.85	1.1		Johnson			2	Bisl	Oslo	5 Jul 96
19.85	-0.3	John	Capel	USA	27.10.78	1	NC	Sacramento	23 Jul 00
19.85A	0.0		Crawford			1		Pretoria	12 Apr 02
19.85	-0.5	Konstadínos	Kedéris	GRE	11.7.73	1	EC	München	9 Aug 02
		(31/12)							
19.86A	1.0	Don	Quarrie	JAM	25.2.51	1	PAm	Cali	3 Aug 71
19.86	1.6	Maurice	Greene	USA	23.7.74	2rA	DNG	Stockholm	7 Jul 97
19.87	0.8	Lorenzo	Daniel	USA	23.3.66	1	NCAA	Eugene	3 Jun 88
19.87A	1.8	John	Regis	GBR	13.10.66	1		Sestriere	31 Jul 94
19.87	1.2	Jeff	Williams	USA	31.12.65	1		Fresno	13 Apr 96
19.88	-0.3	Floyd	Heard	USA	24.3.66	2	NC	Sacramento	23 Jul 00
19.88	0.1	Joshua 'J.J'	Johnson	USA	10.5.76	1	VD	Bruxelles	24 Aug 01
19.89	-0.8	Claudinei	da Silva	BRA	19.11.70	1	GPF	München	11 Sep 99
		(20)							
19.89	1.8	Wallace	Spearmon	USA	24.12.84	1	LGP	London (CP)	22 Jul 05
19.92A	1.9	John	Carlos	USA	5.6.45	1	FOT	Echo Summit	12 Sep 68
		above mark made with illegal brush spikes							
19.93	1.4	Usain	Bolt	JAM	21.8.86	1		Hamilton, BER	11 Apr 04
19.93	0.6	Tyson	Gay	USA	9.9.82	1s1	NCAA	Sacramento	9 Jun 05
19.96	-0.9	Kirk	Baptiste	USA	20.6.63	2	OG	Los Angeles	8 Aug 84
19.96	0.4	Robson	da Silva	BRA	4.9.64	1	VD	Bruxelles	25 Aug 89
19.96	-0.3	Coby	Miller	USA	19.10.76	3	NC	Sacramento	23 Jul 00
19.97	-0.9	Obadele	Thompson	BAR	30.3.76	1	Super	Yokohama	9 Sep 00
19.98	1.7	Marcin	Urbas	POL	17.9.76	2s2	WCh	Sevilla	25 Aug 99
19.99	0.6	Calvin	Smith	USA	8.1.61	1	WK	Zürich	24 Aug 83
		(30)							
20.00	0.0	Valeriy	Borzov	UKR	20.10.49	1	OG	München	4 Sep 72
20.00	0.0	Justin	Gatlin	USA	10.2.82	1		Monterrey	11 Jun 05
20.01	-1.0	Michael	Bates	USA	19.12.69	3rA	WK	Zürich	19 Aug 92
20.01	0.1	Bernard	Williams	USA	19.1.78	2	VD	Bruxelles	24 Aug 01

Mark	Wind	Name		Nat	Born	Pos	Meet	Venue	Date
20.02	1.7	Christopher	Williams	JAM	15.3.72	1r5	MSR	Walnut	16 Apr 00
20.02	0.0	Xavier	Carter	USA	8.12.85	1rA	NCAA-r	Bloomington	28 May 05
20.03	1.6	Clancy	Edwards	USA	9.8.55	1		Los Angeles (Ww)	29 Apr 78
20.03	1.5	Larry	Myricks ¶	USA	10.3.56	2	TAC	Indianapolis	19 Jun 83
20.03	1.2	Jon	Drummond	USA	9.9.68	1	VD	Bruxelles	22 Aug 97
20.03	0.6	Shingo	Suetsugu	JPN	2.6.80	1	NC	Yokohama	7 Jun 03
		(40)							
20.03	0.6	Darvis	Patton	USA	4.12.77	1s1	WCh	Saint-Denis	29 Aug 03
20.04	1.7	Kenny	Brokenburr	USA	29.10.68	2r5	MSR	Walnut	16 Apr 00
20.05	1.0	Roy	Martin	USA	25.12.66	3	OT	Indianapolis	20 Jul 88
20.05	1.0	Albert	Robinson	USA	28.11.64	4	OT	Indianapolis	20 Jul 88
20.05	-0.1	Ramon	Clay	USA	29.6.75	1	Athl	Lausanne	4 Jul 01
20.06A	0.9	Peter	Norman	AUS	15.6.42	2	OG	Ciudad de México	16 Oct 68
20.06	1.7	Silvio	Leonard	CUB	20.9.55	1	Kuso	Warszawa	19 Jun 78
20.06	0.7	Stéphane	Buckland	MRI	20.1.77	1q3	WCh	Saint-Denis	27 Aug 03
20.06	0.7	Asafa	Powell	JAM	11.11.82	1	WAF	Monaco	19 Sep 04
20.07		James	Mallard	USA	29.11.57	1		Tuscaloosa	20 Apr 79
		(50)	100th man 20.20, 200th man 20.34, 300th man 20.41						

Wind-assisted 5 performances to 19.83, performers listed to 20.01

Mark	Wind	Name		Nat	Born	Pos	Meet	Venue	Date
19.61	>4.0	Leroy	Burrell	USA	21.2.67	1	SWC	College Station	19 May 90
19.70	2.7		Johnson			1s1	NC	Atlanta	22 Jun 96
19.79A	4.0		Marsh			1		Sestriere	21 Jul 92
19.83	3.5		Johnson			1	NC	Sacramento	18 Jun 95
19.83	9.2	Bobby	Cruse	USA	20.3.78	1r2	Sea Ray	Knoxville	9 Apr 99
19.86	4.6	Roy	Martin	USA	25.12.66	1	SWC	Houston	18 May 86
19.86	4.0	Justin	Gatlin	USA	10.2.82	1h2	NCAA	Eugene	30 May 01
19.90	3.8	Steve	Mullings ¶	JAM	29.11.82	1		Fort Worth	17 Apr 04
19.91		James	Jett	USA	28.12.70	1		Morgantown	18 Apr 92
19.93	2.4	Sebastián	Keitel	CHI	14.2.73	1		São Leopoldo	26 Apr 98
19.94	4.0	James	Sanford	USA	27.12.57	1s1	NCAA	Austin	7 Jun 80
19.94	3.7	Chris	Nelloms	USA	14.8.71	1	Big 10	Minneapolis	23 May 92
19.94	2.3	Kevin	Little	USA	3.4.68	1s3	NC	Sacramento	17 Jun 95
19.95	3.4	Mike	Roberson	USA	25.3.56	1h3	NCAA	Austin	5 Jun 80
19.96	2.2	Rohsaan	Griffin	USA	21.2.74	1s1	NC	Eugene	26 Jun 99
19.98w	2.1	Aaron	Armstrong	TRI	14.10.77	1	NC	Port of Spain	26 Jun 05
19.99	2.7	Ramon	Clay	USA	29.6.75	2s1	NC	Atlanta	22 Jun 96
20.00A	3.4	Olapade	Adeniken	NGR	19.8.69	1		USAF Academy	23 May 92
20.01	2.5	Derald	Harris	USA	5.4.58	1		San José	9 Apr 77
20.03	6.5	Alvis	Whitted	USA	4.9.74	1		College Park	20 Apr 96
20.03	3.5	Stanford	Routt	USA	23.7.83	1	NCAA-r	College Station	29 May 04

Low altitude marks for athletes with lifetime bests at high altitude

19.94 0.3 Regis 2 WCh Stuttgart 20 Aug 93 | 19.96 0.0 Mennea 1 Barletta 17 Aug 80

20.06 0.4 Quarrie 1 WK Zürich 16 Aug 74

Suspended under IAAF rules

Mark	Wind	Name		Nat	Born	Pos	Meet	Venue	Date
19.86	1.5	Justin	Gatlin ¶	USA	10.2.82	1	SEC	Starkville	12 May 02

Hand timing *" during 220 yards race, * 220 yards less 0.1 seconds*

Mark	Wind	Name		Nat	Born	Pos	Meet	Venue	Date
19.7A		James	Sanford	USA	27.12.57	1		El Paso	19 Apr 80
19.7A	0.2	Robson C.	da Silva	BRA	4.9.64	1	AmCp	Bogotá	13 Aug 89
19.8" WR	1.3	Don	Quarrie	JAM	25.2.51	1	Pre	Eugene	7 Jun 75
19.8* WR	1.3	Steve	Williams	USA	13.11.53	2	Pre	Eugene	7 Jun 75
19.8	1.6	James	Mallard	USA	29.11.57	1	SEC	Tuscaloosa	13 May 79
19.8*w	9.0	Carl	Lawson	JAM	27.10.47	1		Moscow, ID	19 May 73
19.8*w	3.4	James	Gilkes	GUY	21.9.52	1	NCAA	Austin	8 Jun 74
19.8w	4.4	Desmond	Ross	USA	30.12.61	1	Big8	Manhattan	11 May 85

300 METRES

In 300m races only, not including intermediate times in 400m races

Mark	Name		Nat	Born	Pos	Meet	Venue	Date
30.85A	Michael	Johnson	USA	13.9.67	1		Pretoria	24 Mar 00
31.48	Danny	Everett	USA	1.11.66	1		Jerez de la Frontera	3 Sep 90
31.48	Roberto	Hernández	CUB	6.3.67	2		Jerez de la Frontera	3 Sep 90
31.56		Johnson			1		Salamanca	22 Jul 94
31.56	Doug	Walker ¶	GBR	28.7.73	1		Gateshead	19 Jul 98
31.61	Anthuan	Maybank	USA	30.12.69	1		Durham	13 Jul 96
31.67	John	Regis	GBR	13.10.66	1	Vaux	Gateshead	17 Jul 92
31.70	Kirk	Baptiste	USA	20.6.63	1	Nike	London (CP)	18 Aug 84
31.73	Thomas	Jefferson	USA	8.6.62	1	DCG	London (CP)	22 Aug 87
31.74	Gabriel	Tiacoh	CIV	10.9.63	1		La Coruña	6 Aug 86
31.77	Tyler	Christopher (10)	CAN	3.10.83	1		Sainte-Anne	20 May 04
31.82	Steve	Lewis	USA	16.5.69	2	Vaux	Gateshead	17 Jul 92
31.87	Mark	Richardson	GBR	26.7.72	2		Gateshead	19 Jul 98
31.88	Darren	Clark	AUS	6.9.65	1	UlstG	Belfast	30 Jun 86

400 METRES

Mark	Wind	Name		Nat	Born	Pos	Meet	Venue	Date
43.18	WR	Michael	Johnson	USA	13.9.67	1	WCh	Sevilla	26 Aug 99
43.29	WR	Butch	Reynolds ¶	USA	8.6.64	1	WK	Zürich	17 Aug 88
43.39			Johnson			1	WCh	Göteborg	9 Aug 95
43.44			Johnson			1	NC	Atlanta	19 Jun 96
43.49			Johnson			1	OG	Atlanta	29 Jul 96
43.50		Quincy	Watts	USA	19.6.70	1	OG	Barcelona	5 Aug 92
43.65			Johnson			1	WCh	Stuttgart	17 Aug 93
43.66			Johnson			1	NC	Sacramento	16 Jun 95
43.66			Johnson			1rA	Athl	Lausanne	3 Jul 96
43.68			Johnson			1	WK	Zürich	12 Aug 98
43.68			Johnson			1	NC	Sacramento	16 Jul 00
43.71			Watts			1s2	OG	Barcelona	3 Aug 92
43.74			Johnson			1	NC	Eugene	19 Jun 93
43.75			Johnson			1		Waco	19 Apr 97
43.76			Johnson			1	GWG	Uniondale, NY	22 Jul 98
43.81		Danny	Everett	USA	1.11.66	1	OT	New Orleans	26 Jun 92
43.83			Watts			1	WK	Zürich	19 Aug 92
43.84			Johnson			1	OG	Sydney	25 Sep 00
43.86A	WR	Lee	Evans	USA	25.2.47	1	OG	Ciudad de México	18 Oct 68
43.86			Johnson			1	Bisl	Oslo	21 Jul 95
43.87		Steve	Lewis	USA	16.5.69	1	OG	Seoul	28 Sep 88
43.88			Johnson			1	WK	Zürich	16 Aug 95
43.90			Johnson			1		Madrid	6 Sep 94
43.91			Reynolds			2	NC	Atlanta	19 Jun 96
43.92			Johnson			1	Athl	Lausanne	2 Jul 99
43.92			Johnson			1	Pre	Eugene	24 Jun 00
43.93			Reynolds			1	OT	Indianapolis	20 Jul 88
43.93			Reynolds			2	OG	Seoul	28 Sep 88
43.93		Jeremy	Wariner	USA	31.1.84	1	WCh	Helsinki	12 Aug 05
43.94			Johnson			1	ISTAF	Berlin	27 Aug 93
		(30/7)							
43.97A		Larry	James	USA	6.11.47	2	OG	Ciudad de México	18 Oct 68
44.09		Alvin	Harrison ¶	USA	20.1.74	3	NC	Atlanta	19 Jun 96
44.09		Jerome	Young ¶	USA	14.8.76	1	NC	New Orleans	21 Jun 98
		(10)							
44.13		Derek	Mills	USA	9.7.72	1	Pre	Eugene	4 Jun 95
44.14		Roberto	Hernández	CUB	6.3.67	2		Sevilla	30 May 90
44.15		Anthuan	Maybank	USA	30.12.69	1rB	Athl	Lausanne	3 Jul 96
44.17		Innocent	Egbunike	NGR	30.11.61	1rA	WK	Zürich	19 Aug 87
44.16		Otis	Harris	USA	30.6.82	2	OG	Athína	23 Aug 04
44.18		Samson	Kitur	KEN	25.2.66	2s2	OG	Barcelona	3 Aug 92
44.20A		Charles	Gitonga	KEN	5.10.71	1	NC	Nairobi	29 Jun 96
44.21		Ian	Morris	TRI	30.11.61	3s2	OG	Barcelona	3 Aug 92
44.21		Antonio	Pettigrew	USA	3.11.67	1		Nassau	26 May 99
44.26		Alberto	Juantorena	CUB	3.12.50	1	OG	Montreal	29 Jul 76
		(20)							
44.27		Alonzo	Babers	USA	31.10.61	1	OG	Los Angeles	8 Aug 84
44.27		Darold	Williamson	USA	19.2.83	1s1	NCAA	Sacramento	10 Jun 05
44.28		Andrew	Valmon	USA	1.1.65	4	NC	Eugene	19 Jun 93
44.28		Tyree	Washington	USA	28.8.76	1		Eagle Rock	12 May 01
44.29		Derrick	Brew	USA	28.12.77	1	SEC	Athens, Ga	16 May 99
44.29		Sanderlei	Parrela	BRA	7.10.74	2	WCh	Sevilla	26 Aug 99
44.30		Gabriel	Tiacoh	CIV	10.9.63	1	NCAA	Indianapolis	7 Jun 86
44.30		Lamont	Smith	USA	11.12.72	4	NC	Atlanta	19 Jun 96
44.31		Alejandro	Cárdenas	MEX	4.10.74	3	WCh	Sevilla	26 Aug 99
44.33		Thomas	Schönlebe	GDR	6.8.65	1	WCh	Roma	3 Sep 87
		(30)							
44.34		Darnell	Hall	USA	26.9.71	1	Athl	Lausanne	5 Jul 95
44.35		Andrew	Rock	USA	23.1.82	2	WCh	Helsinki	12 Aug 05
44.36		Iwan	Thomas	GBR	5.1.74	1	NC	Birmingham	13 Jul 97
44.37		Roger	Black	GBR	31.3.66	2rA	Athl	Lausanne	3 Jul 96
44.37		Davis	Kamoga	UGA	17.7.68	2	WCh	Athína	5 Aug 97
44.37		Mark	Richardson	GBR	26.7.72	1	Bisl	Oslo	9 Jul 98
44.38		Darren	Clark	AUS	6.9.65	3s1	OG	Seoul	26 Sep 88
44.40		Fred	Newhouse	USA	8.11.48	2	OG	Montreal	29 Jul 76
44.41A		Ron	Freeman	USA	12.6.47	3	OG	Ciudad de México	18 Oct 68
44.43A		Ezra	Sambu	KEN	4.9.78	1	WCT	Nairobi	26 Jul 03
		(40)							

Mark	Wind	Name		Nat	Born	Pos	Meet	Venue	Date
44.44		Tyler	Christopher	CAN	3.10.83	3	WCh	Helsinki	12 Aug
44.45A		Ronnie	Ray	USA	2.1.54	1	PAm	Ciudad de México	18 Oct
44.45		Darrell	Robinson	USA	23.12.63	2	Pepsi	Los Angeles (Ww)	17 May
44.45		Avard	Moncur	BAH	2.11.78	1		Madrid	7 Jul
44.45		Leonard	Byrd	USA	17.3.75	1	GP	Belém	5 May
44.47		Michael	Franks	USA	23.9.63	1	WCp	Canberra	5 Oct
44.47		David	Grindley	GBR	29.10.72	4s2	OG	Barcelona	3 Aug
44.47		Alleyne	Francique	GRN	7.6.76	1	GP	Osaka	8 May
44.48		Roddie	Haley	USA	6.12.65	1	SWC	Houston	18 May
44.48		Chris	Brown	BAH	15.10.78	4	WCh	Helsinki	12 Aug
		(50)	100th man 44.71, 200th man 45.01						
Hand timing									
44.1		Wayne	Collett	USA	20.10.49	1	OT	Eugene	9 Jul
44.2*		John	Smith	USA	5.8.50	1	AAU	Eugene	26 Jun
44.2		Fred	Newhouse	USA	8.11.48	1s1	OT	Eugene	7 Jul

600 METRES

Mark	Name		Nat	Born	Pos	Meet	Venue	Date
1:12.81	Johnny	Gray	USA	19.6.60	1		Santa Monica	24 May
1:13.2 + ?	John	Kipkurgat	KEN	16.3.44	1		Pointe-à-Pierre	23 Mar
1:13.49	Joseph	Mutua	KEN	10.12.78	1		Liège (NX)	27 Aug
1:13.80	Earl	Jones	USA	17.7.64	2		Santa Monica	24 May

800 METRES

Mark	Name		Nat	Born	Pos	Meet	Venue	Date
1:41.11 WR	Wilson	Kipketer	DEN	12.12.70	1	ASV	Köln	24 Aug
1:41.24 WR		Kipketer			1rA	WK	Zürich	13 Aug
1:41.73! WR	Sebastian	Coe	GBR	29.9.56	1		Firenze	10 Jun
1:41.73		Kipketer			1rA	DNG	Stockholm	7 Jul
1:41.77	Joaquim	Cruz	BRA	12.3.63	1	ASV	Köln	26 Aug
1:41.83		Kipketer			1	GP II	Rieti	1 Sep
1:42.17		Kipketer			1	TOTO	Tokyo	16 Sep
1:42.20		Kipketer			1	VD	Bruxelles	22 Aug
1:42.27		Kipketer			1	VD	Bruxelles	3 Sep
1:42.28	Sammy	Koskei	KEN	14.5.61	2	ASV	Köln	26 Aug
1:42.32		Kipketer			1	GP II	Rieti	8 Sep
1:42.33 WR		Coe			1	Bisl	Oslo	5 Jul
1:42.34		Cruz			1r1	WK	Zürich	22 Aug
1:42.34	Wilfred	Bungei	KEN	24.7.80	2	GP II	Rieti	8 Sep
1:42.41		Cruz			1	VD	Bruxelles	24 Aug
1:42.47	Yuriy	Borzakovskiy	RUS	12.4.81	1	VD	Bruxelles	24 Aug
1:42.49		Cruz			1		Koblenz	28 Aug
1:42.51		Kipketer			1	Nik	Nice	10 Jul
1:42.52		Bungei			1	VD	Bruxelles	5 Sep
1:42.54		Cruz			1	ASV	Köln	25 Aug
1:42.55	André	Bucher	SUI	19.10.76	1rA	WK	Zürich	17 Aug
1:42.57		Kipketer			1	Herc	Monaco	4 Aug
1:42.58	Vebjørn	Rodal	NOR	16.9.72	1	OG	Atlanta	31 Jul
1:42.59		Kipketer			1	Herc	Monaco	10 Aug
1:42.60	Johnny	Gray	USA	19.6.60	2r1		Koblenz	28 Aug
1:42.61		Kipketer			1rA	WK	Zürich	14 Aug
1:42.61		Kipketer			1rA	Athl	Lausanne	2 Jul
1:42.62	Patrick	Ndururi	KEN	12.1.69	2rA	WK	Zürich	13 Aug
1:42.65		Gray			1	WK	Zürich	17 Aug
1:42.69	Hezekiél	Sepeng	RSA	30.6.74	2	VD	Bruxelles	3 Sep
1:42.69	Japheth	Kimutai	KEN	20.12.78	3	VD	Bruxelles	3 Sep
	(31/12)							
1:42.79	Fred	Onyancha	KEN	25.12.69	3	OG	Atlanta	31 Jul
1:42.81	Jean-Patrick	Nduwimana	BDI	9.5.78	2rA	WK	Zürich	17 Aug
1:42.85	Norberto	Téllez	CUB	22.1.72	4	OG	Atlanta	31 Jul
1:42.88	Steve	Cram	GBR	14.10.60	1rA	WK	Zürich	21 Aug
1:42.89	Mbulaeni	Mulaudzi	RSA	8.9.80	2	VD	Bruxelles	5 Sep
1:42.91	William	Yiampoy	KEN	17.5.74	3	GP II	Rieti	8 Sep
1:42.97	Peter	Elliott	GBR	9.10.62	1		Sevilla	30 May
1:42.98	Patrick	Konchellah	KEN	20.4.68	2	ASV	Köln	24 Aug
	(20)							
1:43.03	Kennedy/Kenneth	Kimwetich	KEN	1.1.73	2		Stuttgart	19 Jul
1:43.06	Billy	Konchellah	KEN	20.10.62	1	WCh	Roma	1 Sep
1:43.08	José Luiz	Barbosa	BRA	27.5.61	1		Rieti	6 Sep
1:43.09	Djabir	Saïd Guerni	ALG	29.3.77	5	VD	Bruxelles	3 Sep
1:43.11	Youssef Saad	Kamel	BRN	29.3.83	1rB	WK	Zürich	6 Aug

Mark	Wind	Name		Nat	Born	Pos	Meet	Venue	Date
1:43.15		Mehdi	Baala	FRA	17.8.78	5	GP II	Rieti	8 Sep 02
1:43.16		Paul	Ereng	KEN	22.8.67	1	WK	Zürich	16 Aug 89
1:43.17		Benson	Koech	KEN	10.11.74	1		Rieti	28 Aug 94
1:43.20		Mark	Everett	USA	2.9.68	1rA	Gugl	Linz	9 Jul 97
1:43.22		Pawel	Czapiewski	POL	30.3.78	5rA	WK	Zürich	17 Aug 01
		(30)							
1:43.26		Sammy	Langat (Kibet)	KEN	24.1.70	1rB	WK	Zürich	14 Aug 96
1:43.30		William	Tanui	KEN	22.2.64	2		Rieti	6 Sep 91
1:43.31		Nixon	Kiprotich	KEN	4.12.62	1		Rieti	6 Sep 92
1:43.33		Robert	Chirchir	KEN	26.11.72	3		Stuttgart	19 Jul 98
1:43.33		William	Chirchir	KEN	6.2.79	6	VD	Bruxelles	3 Sep 99
1:43.33		Joseph Mwengi	Mutua	KEN	10.12.78	1rA	WK	Zürich	16 Aug 02
1:43.35		David	Mack	USA	30.5.61	3r1		Koblenz	28 Aug 85
1:43.38		David (Singoei)	Kiptoo	KEN	26.6.65	2	Herc	Monaco	10 Aug 96
1:43.38		Rich	Kenah	USA	4.8.70	3rA	WK	Zürich	13 Aug 97
1:43.38		Arthémon	Hatungimana	BDI	21.1.74	3	VD	Bruxelles	24 Aug 01
		(40)							
1:43.44	WR	Alberto	Juantorena	CUB	3.12.50	1	WUG	Sofiya	21 Aug 77
1:43.50		Mahjoub	Haïda	MAR	1.7.70	2	GGala	Roma	14 Jul 98
1:43.5*	WR	Rick	Wohlhuter	USA	23.12.48	1		Eugene	8 Jun 74
1:43.54		William	Wuyke	VEN	21.5.58	2		Rieti	7 Sep 86
1:43.55		Philip	Kibitok	KEN	23.3.71	3	GP II	Rieti	1 Sep 96
1:43.56		Rob	Druppers	NED	29.4.62	4	ASV	Köln	25 Aug 85
1:43.57		Mike	Boit	KEN	6.1.49	1	ISTAF	Berlin	20 Aug 76
1:43.57		Joseph	Tengelei	KEN	8.12.72	3rB	WK	Zürich	16 Aug 95
1:43.60		Abdi	Bile	SOM	28.12.62	3	WK	Zürich	16 Aug 89
1:43.62		Earl	Jones	USA	17.7.64	2r1	WK	Zürich	13 Aug 86
		(50)	100th man 1:44.24, 200th man 1:44.98, 300th man 1:45.4						
			! photo-electric cell time						
Indoors									
1:42.67			Kipketer			1	WI	Paris (B)	9 Mar 97

1000 METRES

Mark	Wind	Name		Nat	Born	Pos	Meet	Venue	Date
2:11.96	WR	Noah	Ngeny	KEN	2.11.78	1	GP II	Rieti	5 Sep 99
2:12.18	WR	Sebastian	Coe	GBR	29.9.56	1	OsloG	Oslo	11 Jul 81
2:12.66			Ngeny			1	Nik	Nice	17 Jul 99
2:12.88		Steve	Cram	GBR	14.10.60	1		Gateshead	9 Aug 85
2:13.40	WR		Coe			1	Bisl	Oslo	1 Jul 80
2:13.56		Kenneth	Kimwetich	KEN	1.1.73	2	Nik	Nice	17 Jul 99
2:13.73		Noureddine	Morceli	ALG	28.2.70	1	BNP	Villeneuve d'Ascq	2 Jul 93
2:13.9	WR	Rick	Wohlhuter	USA	23.12.48	1	King	Oslo	30 Jul 74
2:13.96		Mehdi	Baala	FRA	17.8.78	1		Strasbourg	26 Jun 03
2:14.09		Joaquim	Cruz	BRA	12.3.63	1	Nik	Nice	20 Aug 84
2:14.28		Japheth	Kimutai	KEN	20.12.78	1	DNG	Stockholm	1 Aug 00
2:14.41		William	Yampoy (10)	KEN	19.5.74	2	GP II	Rieti	5 Sep 99
2:14.43		Laban	Rotich	KEN	20.1.69	1	Nik	Nice	16 Jul 97
2:14.50		Abdi	Bile	SOM	28.12.62	1		Jerez de la Frontera	13 Sep 89

1500 METRES

Mark	Wind	Name		Nat	Born	Pos	Meet	Venue	Date
3:26.00	WR	Hicham	El Guerrouj	MAR	14.9.74	1	GGala	Roma	14 Jul 98
3:26.12			El Guerrouj			1	VD	Bruxelles	24 Aug 01
3:26.34		Bernard	Lagat	KEN/USA	12.12.74	2	VD	Bruxelles	24 Aug 01
3:26.45			El Guerrouj			1 rA	WK	Zürich	12 Aug 98
3:26.89			El Guerrouj			1	WK	Zürich	16 Aug 02
3:26.96			El Guerrouj			1	GP II	Rieti	8 Sep 02
3:27.21			El Guerrouj			1	WK	Zürich	11 Aug 00
3:27.34			El Guerrouj			1	Herc	Monaco	19 Jul 02
3:27.37	WR	Noureddine	Morceli	ALG	28.2.70	1	Nik	Nice	12 Jul 95
3:27.40			Lagat			1rA	WK	Zürich	6 Aug 04
3.27.52			Morceli			1	Herc	Monaco	25 Jul 95
3:27.64			El Guerrouj			2rA	WK	Zürich	6 Aug 04
3:27.65			El Guerrouj			1	WCh	Sevilla	24 Aug 99
3:27.91			Lagat			2	Herc	Monaco	19 Jul 02
3:28.12		Noah	Ngeny	KEN	2.11.78	2	WK	Zürich	11 Aug 00
3:28.21+			El Guerrouj			1	in 1M	Roma	7 Jul 99
3.28.37			Morceli			1	GPF	Monaco	9 Sep 95
3:28.37			El Guerrouj			1	Herc	Monaco	8 Aug 98
3:28.38			El Guerrouj			1	GP	Saint-Denis	6 Jul 01
3:28.40			El Guerrouj			1	VD	Bruxelles	5 Sep 03
3:28.51			Lagat			3	WK	Zürich	11 Aug 00

Mark	Wind	Name		Nat	Born	Pos	Meet	Venue	Date
3:28.57			El Guerrouj			1rA	WK	Zürich	11 Aug 9
3:28.6+			Ngeny			2	in 1M	Roma	7 Jul 9
3:28.73			Ngeny			2	WCh	Sevilla	24 Aug 9
3:28.84			Ngeny			1	GP	Paris (C)	21 Jul 9
3:28.86	WR		Morceli			1		Rieti	6 Sep 9
3:28.91			El Guerrouj			1rA	WK	Zürich	13 Aug 9
3:28.92			El Guerrouj			1	VD	Bruxelles	22 Aug 9
3:28.93			Ngeny			1	GPF	München	11 Sep 9
3:28.95		Fermín	Cacho	ESP	16.2.69	2rA	WK	Zürich	13 Aug 9
3:28.98		Mehdi	Baala	FRA	17.8.78	2	VD	Bruxelles	5 Sep 0
		(31/6)							
3:29.18		Vénuste	Niyongabo	BUR	9.12.73	2	VD	Bruxelles	22 Aug 9
3:29.29		William	Chirchir	KEN	6.2.79	3	VD	Bruxelles	24 Aug 0
3:29.46	WR	Saïd	Aouita	MAR	2.11.59	1	ISTAF	Berlin	23 Aug 8
3:29.46		Daniel	Komen	KEN	17.5.76	1	Herc	Monaco	16 Aug 9
		(10)							
3:29.51		Ali	Saïdi-Sief ¶	ALG	15.3.78	1	Athl	Lausanne	4 Jul 0
3:29.67	WR	Steve	Cram	GBR	14.10.60	1	Nik	Nice	16 Jul 8
3:29.72		Daniel	Kipchirchir Komen	KEN	27.11.84	1	ISTAF	Berlin	4 Sep 0
3:29.77		Sydney	Maree	USA	9.9.56	1	ASV	Köln	25 Aug 8
3:29.77		Sebastian	Coe	GBR	29.9.56	1		Rieti	7 Sep 8
3:29.91		Laban	Rotich	KEN	20.1.69	2rA	WK	Zürich	12 Aug 9
3:30.00		Rashid	Ramzi	BRN	17.7.80	1	GGala	Roma	8 Jul 0
3:30.04		Timothy	Kiptanui	KEN	5.1.80	2	GP	Saint-Denis	23 Jul 0
3:30.07		Rui	Silva	POR	3.8.77	3	Herc	Monaco	19 Jul 0
3:30.18		John	Kibowen	KEN	21.4.69	3rA	WK	Zürich	12 Aug 9
		(20)							
3:30.24		Cornelius	Chirchir	KEN	5.6.83	4	Herc	Monaco	19 Jul 0
3:30.33		Ivan	Geshko	UKR	19.8.79	2	VD	Bruxelles	3 Sep 0
3:30.46		Alex	Kipchirchir	KEN	26.11.84	3	VD	Bruxelles	3 Sep 0
3:30.55		Abdi	Bile	SOM	28.12.62	1		Rieti	3 Sep 8
3:30.57		Reyes	Estévez	ESP	2.8.76	3	WCh	Sevilla	24 Aug 9
3:30.58		William	Tanui	KEN	22.2.64	3	Herc	Monaco	16 Aug 9
3:30.67		Benjamin	Kipkurui	KEN	28.12.80	2	Herc	Monaco	20 Jul 0
3:30.72		Paul	Korir	KEN	15.7.77	3	VD	Bruxelles	5 Sep 0
3:30.77	WR	Steve	Ovett	GBR	9.10.55	1		Rieti	4 Sep 8
3:30.83		Fouad	Chouki ¶	FRA	15.10.78	3	WK	Zürich	15 Aug 0
		(30)							
3:30.92		José Luis	González	ESP	8.12.57	3	Nik	Nice	16 Jul 8
3:30.94		Isaac	Viciosa	ESP	26.12.69	5	Herc	Monaco	8 Aug 9
3:30.99		Robert	Rono	KEN	11.10.74	3	VD	Bruxelles	30 Aug 0
3:30.99		Isaac	Songok	KEN	25.4.84	3rA	WK	Zürich	6 Aug 0
3:31.01		Jim	Spivey	USA	7.3.60	1	R-W	Koblenz	28 Aug 8
3:31.04		Daham Najim	Bashir (David Nyaga)	QAT	8.11.78	2	SGP	Doha	13 May 0
3:31.13		José Manuel	Abascal	ESP	17.3.58	1		Barcelona	16 Aug 8
3:31.13		Mulugueta	Wondimu	ETH	28.2.85	2rA	NA	Heusden	31 Jul 0
3:31.17		Robert K.	Andersen	DEN	12.12.72	5rA	WK	Zürich	13 Aug 9
3:31.21		José Antonio	Redolat	ESP	17.2.76	1	DNG	Stockholm	17 Jul 0
		(40)							
3:31.28		Enock	Koech	KEN	4.4.81	3rA	WK	Zürich	17 Aug 0
3:31.40		William	Kemei	KEN	22.2.69	2	Nik	Nice	12 Jul 9
3:31.45		Driss	Maazouzi	FRA	15.10.69	6	Herc	Monaco	19 Jul 0
3:31.48		Azzedine	Sediki	MAR	21.5.70	3rA	ASV	Köln	18 Aug 9
3:31.48		Andrés	Díaz	ESP	12.7.69	2	Herc	Monaco	18 Aug 0
3:31.52		Steve	Holman	USA	2.3.70	6	VD	Bruxelles	22 Aug 9
3:31.53		David	Lelei	KEN	10.5.71	3		Stuttgart	19 Jul 9
3:31.58		Thomas	Wessinghage	FRG	22.2.52	2		Koblenz	27 Aug 8
3:31.61		Juan Carlos	Higuero	ESP	3.8.78	6	VD	Bruxelles	5 Sep 0
3:31.70		Ali	Hakimi	TUN	24.4.76	7	VD	Bruxelles	22 Aug 9
		(50)	100th man 3:33.28, 200th 3:34.91, 300th 3:35.93						

1 MILE

Mark	Wind	Name		Nat	Born	Pos	Meet	Venue	Date
3:43.13	WR	Hicham	El Guerrouj	MAR	14.9.74	1	GGala	Roma	7 Jul 9
3:43.40		Noah	Ngeny	KEN	2.11.78	2	GGala	Roma	7 Jul 9
3:44.39	WR	Noureddine	Morceli	ALG	28.2.70	1		Rieti	5 Sep 9
3:44.60			El Guerrouj			1	Nik	Nice	16 Jul 9
3:44.90			El Guerrouj			1	Bisl	Oslo	4 Jul 9
3:44.95			El Guerrouj			1	GGala	Roma	29 Jun 0
3:45.19			Morceli			1	WK	Zürich	16 Aug 9
3:45.64			El Guerrouj			1	ISTAF	Berlin	26 Aug 9
3:45.96			El Guerrouj			1	BrGP	London (CP)	5 Aug 0

Mark	Wind	Name		Nat	Born	Pos	Meet	Venue	Date
3:46.24			El Guerrouj			1	Bisl	Oslo	28 Jul 00
3:46.32	WR	Steve	Cram	GBR	14.10.60	1	Bisl	Oslo	27 Jul 85
3:46.38		Daniel	Komen	KEN	17.5.76	2	ISTAF	Berlin	26 Aug 97
3:46.70		Vénuste	Niyongabo	BUR	9.12.73	3	ISTAF	Berlin	26 Aug 97
3:46.76		Saïd	Aouita	MAR	2.11.59	1	WG	Helsinki	2 Jul 87
3:46.78			Morceli			1	ISTAF	Berlin	27 Aug 93
3:46.92			Aouita			1	WK	Zürich	21 Aug 85
3:47.10			El Guerrouj			1	BrGP	London (CP)	7 Aug 99
3:47.28		Bernard	Lagat	KEN/USA	12.12.74	2	GGala	Roma	29 Jun 01
3:47.30			Morceli			1	VD	Bruxelles	3 Sep 93
3:47.33	WR	Sebastian	Coe	GBR	29.9.56	1	VD	Bruxelles	28 Aug 81
3:47.65		Laban	Rotich	KEN	20.1.69	2	Bisl	Oslo	4 Jul 97
		(21/10)							
3:47.69		Steve	Scott	USA	5.5.56	1	OsloG	Oslo	7 Jul 82
3:47.79		José Luis	González	ESP	8.12.57	2	Bisl	Oslo	27 Jul 85
3:47.88		John	Kibowen	KEN	21.4.69	3	Bisl	Oslo	4 Jul 97
3:47.94		William	Chirchir	KEN	6.2.79	2	Bisl	Oslo	28 Jul 00
3:47.97		Daham Najim	Bashir (David Nyaga)	QAT	8.11.78	1	Bisl	Oslo	29 Jul 05
3:48.17		Paul	Korir	KEN	15.7.77	1	GP	London (CP)	8 Aug 03
3:48.23		Ali	Saïdi-Sief ¶	ALG	15.3.78	1	Bisl	Oslo	13 Jul 01
3:48.38		Andrés	Díaz	ESP	12.7.69	3	GGala	Roma	29 Jun 01
3:48.40	WR	Steve	Ovett	GBR	9.10.55	1	R-W	Koblenz	26 Aug 81
3:48.49		Daniel	Kipchirchir Komen	KEN	27.11.84	3	Bisl	Oslo	29 Jul 05
		(20)							
3:48.80		William	Kemei	KEN	22.2.69	1	ISTAF	Berlin	21 Aug 92
3:48.83		Sydney	Maree	USA	9.9.56	1		Rieti	9 Sep 81
3:48.92		Alan	Webb	USA	13.1.83	4	Bisl	Oslo	29 Jul 05
3:48.98		Craig	Mottram	AUS	18.6.80	5	Bisl	Oslo	29 Jul 05
3:49.08		John	Walker	NZL	12.1.52	2	OsloG	Oslo	7 Jul 82
3:49.20		Peter	Elliott	GBR	9.10.62	2	Bisl	Oslo	2 Jul 88
3:49.22		Jens-Peter	Herold	GDR	2.6.65	3	Bisl	Oslo	2 Jul 88
3:49.31		Joe	Falcon	USA	23.6.66	1	Bisl	Oslo	14 Jul 90
3:49.34		David	Moorcroft	GBR	10.4.53	3	Bisl	Oslo	26 Jun 82
3:49.34		Benjamin	Kipkurui	KEN	28.12.80	3	VD	Bruxelles	25 Aug 00
		(30)							
3:49.40		Abdi	Bile	SOM	28.12.62	4	Bisl	Oslo	2 Jul 88
3:49.45		Mike	Boit	KEN	6.1.49	2	VD	Bruxelles	28 Aug 81
3:49.50		Rui	Silva	POR	3.8.77	3	GGala	Roma	12 Jul 02
3:49.56		Fermín	Cacho	ESP	16.2.69	2	Bisl	Oslo	5 Jul 96
3:49.60		José Antonio	Redolat	ESP	17.2.76	4	GGala	Roma	29 Jun 01
3:49.75		Leonard	Mucheru	KEN	13.6.78	5	GGala	Roma	29 Jun 01
3:49.77		Ray	Flynn	IRL	22.1.57	3	OsloG	Oslo	7 Jul 82
3:49.77		Wilfred	Kirochi	KEN	12.12.69	2	Bisl	Oslo	6 Jul 91
3:49.80		Jim	Spivey	USA	7.3.60	3	Bisl	Oslo	5 Jul 86
3:49.83		Vyacheslav	Shabunin	RUS	27.9.69	6	GGala	Roma	29 Jun 01
		(40)							
3:49.91		Simon	Doyle	AUS	9.11.66	4	Bisl	Oslo	6 Jul 91
3:49.95		Tarek	Boukensa	ALG	19.11.81	6	Bisl	Oslo	29 Jul 05
3:49.98		Thomas	Wessinghage	FRG	22.2.52	3	ISTAF	Berlin	17 Aug 83
		(43)	50th man 3:50.38, 100th man 3:52.04, 200th man 3:54.56, 300th 3:55.9						
Indoors									
3:49.78		Eamonn	Coghlan	IRL	24.11.52	1		East Rutherford	27 Feb 83

2000 METRES

Mark	Wind	Name		Nat	Born	Pos	Meet	Venue	Date
4:44.79	WR	Hicham	El Guerrouj	MAR	14.9.74	1	ISTAF	Berlin	7 Sep 99
4:46.88		Ali	Saïdi-Sief ¶	ALG	15.3.78	1		Strasbourg	19 Jun 01
4:47.88	WR	Noureddine	Morceli	ALG	28.2.70	1		Paris	3 Jul 95
4:48.36			El Guerrouj			1		Gateshead	19 Jul 98
4:48.69		Vénuste	Niyongabo	BUR	9.12.73	1	Nik	Nice	12 Jul 95
4:48.74		John	Kibowen	KEN	21.4.69	1		Hechtel	1 Aug 98
4:49.00			Niyongabo			1		Rieti	3 Sep 97
4:49.55			Morceli			1	Nik	Nice	10 Jul 96
4:50.08		Noah	Ngeny	KEN	2.11.78	1	DNG	Stockholm	30 Jul 99
4:50.81	WR	Saïd	Aouita	MAR	2.11.59	1	BNP	Paris	16 Jul 87
4:51.17			El Guerrouj			1	ISTAF	Berlin	31 Aug 01
4:51.30		Daniel	Komen	KEN	17.5.76	1		Milano	5 Jun 98
4:51.39	WR	Steve	Cram	GBR	14.10.60	1	BGP	Budapest	4 Aug 85
4:51.52	WR	John	Walker	NZL	12.1.52	1	Bisl	Oslo	30 Jun 76
		(14/10)							
4:52.20		Thomas	Wessinghage	FRG	22.2.52	1		Ingelheim	31 Aug 82

MEN All-time

3000 METRES

Mark Wind	Name		Nat	Born	Pos	Meet	Venue	Date
7:20.67 WR	Daniel	Komen	KEN	17.5.76	1		Rieti	1 Sep
7:23.09	Hicham	El Guerrouj	MAR	14.9.74	1	VD	Bruxelles	3 Sep
7:25.02	Ali	Saïdi-Sief ¶	ALG	15.3.78	1	Herc	Monaco	18 Aug
7:25.09	Haile	Gebrselassie	ETH	18.4.73	1	VD	Bruxelles	28 Aug
7:25.11 WR	Noureddine	Morceli	ALG	28.2.70	1	Herc	Monaco	2 Aug
7:25.16		Komen			1	Herc	Monaco	10 Aug
7:25.54		Gebrselassie			1	Herc	Monaco	8 Aug
7:25.87		Komen			1	VD	Bruxelles	23 Aug
7:26.02		Gebrselassie			1	VD	Bruxelles	22 Aug
7:26.03		Gebrselassie			1	GP II	Helsinki	10 Jun
7:26.5 e		Komen			1	in 2M	Sydney	28 Feb
7:26.62	Mohammed	Mourhit ¶	BEL	10.10.70	2	Herc	Monaco	18 Aug
7:27.18	Moses	Kiptanui	KEN	1.10.70	1	Herc	Monaco	25 Jul
7:27.3+		Komen			1	in 2M	Hechtel	19 Jul
7:27.42		Gebrselassie			1	Bisl	Oslo	9 Jul
7:27.50		Morceli			1	VD	Bruxelles	25 Aug
7:27.59	Luke	Kipkosgei	KEN	27.11.75	2	Herc	Monaco	8 Aug
7:27.67		Saïdi-Sief			1	Gaz	Saint-Denis	23 Jun
7:27.72	Eliud	Kipchoge	KEN	5.11.84	1	VD	Bruxelles	3 Sep
7:27.75	Tom	Nyariki (10)	KEN	27.9.71	2	Herc	Monaco	10 Aug
7:28.04		Kiptanui			1	ASV	Köln	18 Aug
7:28.28		Kipkosgei			2	Bisl	Oslo	9 Jul
7:28.28	James	Kwalia	KEN	12.6.84	2	VD	Bruxelles	3 Sep
7:28.41	Paul	Bitok	KEN	26.6.70	3	Herc	Monaco	10 Aug
7:28.45	Assefa	Mezegebu	ETH	19.6.78	3	Herc	Monaco	8 Aug
7:28.56		Kipchoge			1	SGP	Doha	13 May
7:28.67	Benjamin	Limo	KEN	23.8.74	1	Herc	Monaco	4 Aug
7:28.70	Paul	Tergat	KEN	17.6.69	4	Herc	Monaco	10 Aug
7:28.78	Augustine	Choge	KEN	21.1.87	2	SGP	Doha	13 May
7:28.92	(30/16)	Komen			3	Herc	Monaco	18 Aug
7:28.93	Salah	Hissou	MAR	16.1.72	2	Herc	Monaco	4 Aug
7:28.94	Brahim	Lahlafi	MAR	15.4.68	3	Herc	Monaco	4 Aug
7:29.09	John	Kibowen	KEN	21.4.69	3	Bisl	Oslo	9 Jul
7:29.34	Isaac	Viciosa	ESP	26.12.69	4	Bisl	Oslo	9 Jul
	(20)							
7:29.45 WR	Saïd	Aouita	MAR	2.11.59	1	ASV	Köln	20 Aug
7:29.92	Sileshi	Sihine	ETH	29.1.83	1	GP	Rieti	28 Aug
7:30.09	Ismaïl	Sghyr	MAR/FRA	16.3.72	2	Herc	Monaco	25 Jul
7:30.14	Isaac	Songok	KEN	25.4.84	1	FBK	Hengelo	29 May
7:30.36	Mark	Carroll	IRL	15.1.72	5	Herc	Monaco	4 Aug
7:30.50	Dieter	Baumann ¶	GER	9.2.65	6	Herc	Monaco	8 Aug
7:30.53	El Hassan	Lahssini	MAR	1.1.74	6	Herc	Monaco	10 Aug
7:30.53	Hailu	Mekonnen	ETH	4.4.80	1	VD	Bruxelles	24 Aug
7:30.62	Boniface	Songok	KEN	25.12.80	3	VD	Bruxelles	3 Sep
7:30.67	Kenenisa	Bekele	ETH	13.6.82	2	VD	Bruxelles	24 Aug
	(30)							
7:30.76	Jamal Bilal	Salem	QAT	12.9.78	4	SGP	Doha	13 May
7:30.78	Mustapha	Essaïd	FRA	20.1.70	7	Herc	Monaco	8 Aug
7:30.84	Bob	Kennedy	USA	18.8.70	8	Herc	Monaco	8 Aug
7:30.99	Khalid	Boulami	MAR	7.8.69	1	Nik	Nice	16 Jul
7:31.13	Julius	Gitahi	KEN	29.4.78	6	Bisl	Oslo	9 Jul
7:31.14	William	Kalya	KEN	4.8.74	3	Herc	Monaco	16 Aug
7:31.59	Manuel	Pancorbo	ESP	7.7.66	7	Bisl	Oslo	9 Jul
7:31.98	Daniel	Kipchirchir Komen	KEN	27.11.84	3	FBK	Hengelo	29 May
7:32.1 WR	Henry	Rono	KEN	12.2.52	1	Bisl	Oslo	27 Jun
7:32.23	Richard	Limo	KEN	18.11.80	5	VD	Bruxelles	24 Aug
	(40)							
7:32.32	Enrique	Molina	ESP	25.2.68	5	Bisl	Oslo	4 Jul
7:32.36	Million	Wolde	ETH	17.3.79	3	Gaz	Saint-Denis	23 Jun
7:32.36	Benjamin	Maiyo	KEN	6.10.78	2	GPII	Athína	28 Jun
7:32.36	Abderrahim	Goumri	MAR	21.5.76	6	VD	Bruxelles	24 Aug
7:32.38	Abiyote	Abate	ETH	20.11.80	7	VD	Bruxelles	24 Aug
7:32.79	David	Moorcroft	GBR	10.4.53	1		London (CP)	17 Jul
7:33.13	Shem	Kororia	KEN	25.9.72	7	Herc	Monaco	10 Aug
7:33.2+	Abebe	Dinkesa	ETH	6.3.84	2	in 5k	Saint-Denis	1 Jul
7:33.37	Sydney	Maree	USA	9.9.56	2		London (CP)	17 Jul
7:33.42	Salah	Ghazi	MAR	2.11.75	4	Herc	Monaco	20 Jul
	(50)	100th man 7:37.60, 200th man 7:42.1, 300th 7:44.36, 400th 7:46.33						

Mark Wind		Name	Nat	Born	Pos	Meet	Venue	Date
Indoors								
7:24.90		Komen			1		Budapest	6 Feb 98
7:26.15		Gebrselassie			1		Karlsruhe	25 Jan 98
7:26.80		Gebrselassie			1		Karlsruhe	24 Jan 99
7:28.29		Gebrselassie			1		Karlsruhe	28 Feb 03
7:32.98	Alberto	García ¶	ESP	22.2.71	1		Sevilla	22 Feb 03

2 MILES

Mark Wind		Name	Nat	Born	Pos	Meet	Venue	Date
7:58.61 WR	Daniel	Komen	KEN	17.5.76	1		Hechtel	19 Jul 97
7:58.91		Komen			1		Sydney	28 Feb 98
8:01.08 WR	Haile	Gebrselassie	ETH	18.4.73	1	APM	Hengelo	31 May 97
8:01.72		Gebrselassie			1	BrGP	London (CP)	7 Aug 99
8:01.86		Gebrselassie			1	APM	Hengelo	30 May 99
8:03.54 WR		Komen			1		Lappeenranta	14 Jul 96
8:07.46 WR		Gebrselassie			1		Kerkrade	28 May 95
8:07.68	Eliud	Kipchoge	KEN	5.11.84	1	Pre	Eugene	4 Jun 05
8:09.01 WR	Moses	Kiptanui	KEN	10.10.70	1		Hechtel	30 Jul 94
Indoors								
8:04.69		Gebrselassie			1	GP	Birmingham	21 Feb 03
8:06.61	Hicham	El Guerrouj	MAR	14.9.74	1		Liévin	23 Feb 03
8:08.39	Markos	Geneti	ETH	30.5.84	1		Birmingham	20 Feb 04
8:09.66	Hailu	Mekonnen	ETH	4.4.80	1		Birmingham	20 Feb 00

5000 METRES

Mark Wind		Name	Nat	Born	Pos	Meet	Venue	Date
12:37.35 WR	Kenenisa	Bekele	ETH	13.6.82	1	FBK	Hengelo	31 May 04
12:39.36 WR	Haile	Gebrselassie	ETH	18.4.73	1	GP II	Helsinki	13 Jun 98
12:39.74 WR	Daniel	Komen	KEN	17.5.76	1	VD	Bruxelles	22 Aug 97
12:40.18		K Bekele			1	Gaz	Saint-Denis	1 Jul 05
12:41.86 WR		Gebrselassie			1	WK	Zürich	13 Aug 97
12:44.39 WR		Gebrselassie			1	WK	Zürich	16 Aug 95
12:44.90		Komen			2	WK	Zürich	13 Aug 97
12:45.09		Komen			1	WK	Zürich	14 Aug 96
12:46.53	Eliud	Kipchoge	KEN	5.11.84	1	GGala	Roma	2 Jul 04
12:47.04	Sileshi	Sihine	ETH	29.1.83	2	GGala	Roma	2 Jul 04
12:48.81	Stephen	Cherono	KEN	15.10.82	1	GS	Ostrava	12 Jun 03
	(now Saïf Saaeed Shaheen QAT)							
12:48.98		Komen			1	GGala	Roma	5 Jun 97
12:49.28	Brahim	Lahlafi	MAR	15.4.68	1	VD	Bruxelles	25 Aug 00
12:49.64		Gebrselassie			1	WK	Zürich	11 Aug 99
12:49.71	Mohammed	Mourhit ¶	BEL	10.10.70	2	VD	Bruxelles	25 Aug 00
12:49.87	Paul	Tergat	KEN	17.6.69	3	WK	Zürich	13 Aug 97
12:50.22		Kipchoge			1	VD	Bruxelles	26 Aug 05
12:50.24	Hicham	El Guerrouj (10)	MAR	14.9.74	2	GS	Ostrava	12 Jun 03
12:50.25	Abderrahim	Goumri	MAR	21.5.76	2	VD	Bruxelles	26 Aug 05
12:50.80	Salah	Hissou	MAR	16.1.72	1	GGala	Roma	5 Jun 96
12:50.86	Ali	Saïdi-Sief ¶	ALG	15.3.78	1	GGala	Roma	30 Jun 00
12:51.60		Komen			1	DNG	Stockholm	8 Jul 96
12:52.26		K Bekele			1	Bisl	Oslo	27 Jun 03
12:52.29	Isaac	Songok	KEN	25.4.84	1	GGala	Roma	8 Jul 05
12:52.33	Sammy	Kipketer	KEN	29.9.81	2	Bisl	Oslo	27 Jun 03
12:52.38		Komen			1	GPF	Milano	7 Sep 96
12:52.39		Hissou			2	GGala	Roma	5 Jun 97
12:52.53		Hissou			1		Milano	9 Jun 99
12:52.61		Kipchoge			3	Bisl	Oslo	27 Jun 03
12.52.70		Gebrselassie			2	WK	Zürich	14 Aug 96
	(30/15)							
12:52.80	Gebre-egziabher	Gebremariam	ETH	10.9.84	3	GGala	Roma	8 Jul 05
12:52.99	Abraham	Chebii	KEN	23.12.79	4	Bisl	Oslo	27 Jun 03
12:53.41	Khalid	Boulami	MAR	7.8.69	4	WK	Zürich	13 Aug 97
12:53.66	Augustine	Choge	KEN	21.1.87	4	GGala	Roma	8 Jul 05
12:53.72	Philip	Mosima	KEN	2.1.77	2	GGala	Roma	5 Jun 96
	(20)							
12:53.84	Assefa	Mezegebu	ETH	19.6.78	1	VD	Bruxelles	28 Aug 98
12:54.07	John	Kibowen	KEN	21.4.69	4	WCh	Saint-Denis	31 Aug 03
12:54.15	Dejene	Berhanu	ETH	12.12.80	3	GGala	Roma	2 Jul 04
12:54.58	James	Kwalia	KEN	12.6.84	5	Bisl	Oslo	27 Jun 03
12:54.70	Dieter	Baumann ¶	GER	9.2.65	5	WK	Zürich	13 Aug 97
12:54.85	Moses	Kiptanui	KEN	1.10.70	3	GGala	Roma	5 Jun 96
12:54.99	Benjamin	Limo	KEN	23.8.74	3	Gaz	Saint-Denis	4 Jul 03

Mark Wind	Name		Nat	Born	Pos	Meet	Venue	Date
12:55.58	Abebe	Dinkesa	ETH	6.3.84	2	Gaz	Saint-Denis	1 Jul
12:55.63	Mark	Bett	KEN	22.12.76	2	Bisl	Oslo	28 Jul
12:55.76	Craig	Mottram	AUS	18.6.80	2	GP	London (CP)	30 Jul
	(30)							
12:55.85	Boniface	Songok	KEN	25.12.80	4	VD	Bruxelles	26 Aug
12:55.94	Tom	Nyariki	KEN	27.9.71	1	DNG	Stockholm	7 Jul
12:56.27	Albert	Chepkurui	KEN	4.4.81	6	Bisl	Oslo	27 Jun
	(Abdullah Ahmad Hassan QAT from August 2003)							
12:56.29	Paul	Koech	KEN	25.6.69	6	WK	Zürich	13 Aug
12:56.50	Luke	Kipkosgei	KEN	27.11.75	5	Bisl	Oslo	28 Jul
12:56.72	Richard	Limo	KEN	18.11.80	1	WK	Zürich	17 Aug
12:57.05	Mulugueta	Wondimu	ETH	28.2.85	2	ISTAF	Berlin	12 Sep
12:57.23	Worku	Bikila	ETH	6.5.68	3	GGala	Roma	8 Jun
12:57.79	David	Chelule	KEN	7.7.77	5	GGala	Roma	7 Jul
12:58.21	Bob	Kennedy	USA	18.8.70	5	WK	Zürich	14 Aug
	(40)							
12:58.39WR	Saïd	Aouita	MAR	2.11.59	1	GGala	Roma	22 Jul
12:58.43	Boniface	Kiprop	UGA	12.10.85	6	GGala	Roma	8 Jul
12:58.57	Hailu	Mekonnen	ETH	4.4.80	1	GGala	Roma	29 Jun
12:58.58	Moukhled	Al-Outaibi	KSA	20.6.76	1	NA	Heusden-Zolder	23 Jul
12:58.83	Ismaïl	Sghyr	MAR/FRA	16.3.72	7	Bisl	Oslo	28 Jul
12:58.94	Paul	Bitok	KEN	26.6.70	4	Bisl	Oslo	28 Jun
12:59.03	Tariku	Bekele	ETH	21.1.87	4	Gaz	Saint-Denis	1 Jul
12:59.29	Bernard	Lagat	KEN/USA	12.12.74	1	ISTAF	Berlin	4 Sep
12:59.39	Million	Wolde	ETH	17.3.79	5	WK	Zürich	12 Aug
12:59.67	Hicham	Bellani	MAR	15.9.79	2	NA	Heusden-Zolder	23 Jul
	(50)	100th man 13:06.83, 200th man 13:14.28, 300th 13:18.53, 400th 13:21.61						
Indoors								
12:49.60		Bekele			1		Birmingham	20 Feb
12:50.38		Gebrselassie			1		Birmingham	14 Feb
12:51.48		Komen			1		Stockholm	19 Feb

10,000 METRES

Mark Wind	Name		Nat	Born	Pos	Meet	Venue	Date
26:17.53WR	Kenenisa	Bekele	ETH	13.6.82	1	VD	Bruxelles	26 Aug
26:20.31WR		K Bekele			1	GS	Ostrava	8 Jun
26:22.75WR	Haile	Gebrselassie	ETH	18.4.73	1	APM	Hengelo	1 Jun
26:27.85WR	Paul	Tergat	KEN	17.6.69	1	VD	Bruxelles	22 Aug
26:28.72		K Bekele			1	FBK	Hengelo	29 May
26:29.22		Gebrselassie			1	VD	Bruxelles	5 Sep
26:30.03	Nicholas	Kemboi	KEN/QAT	25.11.83	2	VD	Bruxelles	5 Sep
26:30.74	Abebe	Dinkesa	ETH	6.3.84	2	FBK	Hengelo	29 May
26:31.32WR		Gebrselassie			1	Bisl	Oslo	4 Jul
26:36.26	Paul	Koech	KEN	25.6.69	2	VD	Bruxelles	22 Aug
26:38.08WR	Salah	Hissou	MAR	16.1.72	1	VD	Bruxelles	23 Aug
26:38.76	Abdullah Ahmad	Hassan	QAT	4.4.81	3	VD	Bruxelles	5 Sep
	(Formerly Albert Chepkurui KEN)							
26:39.69	Sileshi	Sihine	ETH	29.1.83	1	FBK	Hengelo	31 May
26:39.77	Boniface	Kiprop (10)	UGA	12.10.85	2	VD	Bruxelles	26 Aug
26:41.58		Gebrselassie			2	FBK	Hengelo	31 May
26:41.75	Samuel	Wanjiru	KEN	10.11.86	3	VD	Bruxelles	26 Aug
26:43.53WR		Gebrselassie			1	APM	Hengelo	5 Jun
26:46.44		Tergat			1	VD	Bruxelles	28 Aug
26:47.89		Koech			2	VD	Bruxelles	28 Aug
26:49.38	Sammy	Kipketer	KEN	29.9.81	1	VD	Bruxelles	30 Aug
26:49.57		Bekele			1	WCh	Saint-Denis	24 Aug
26:49.90	Assefa	Mezegebu	ETH	19.6.78	2	VD	Bruxelles	30 Aug
26:50.20	Richard	Limo	KEN	18.11.80	3	VD	Bruxelles	30 Aug
26:50.67		Chepkurui			4	VD	Bruxelles	30 Aug
26:50.77		Gebrselassie			2	WCh	Saint-Denis	24 Aug
26:51.49	Charles	Kamathi	KEN	18.5.78	1	VD	Bruxelles	3 Sep
26:51.87		Kemboi			4	VD	Bruxelles	26 Aug
26:52.23WR	William	Sigei	KEN	11.10.69	1	Bisl	Oslo	22 Jul
26:52.30	Mohammed	Mourhit ¶	BEL	10.10.70	2	VD	Bruxelles	3 Sep
26:52.60		Kipketer			5	VD	Bruxelles	26 Aug
	(30/17)							
26:52.87	John Cheruiyot	Korir	KEN	13.12.81	5	VD	Bruxelles	30 Aug
26:52.93	Mark	Bett	KEN	22.12.76	6	VD	Bruxelles	26 Aug
26:53.73	Gebre-egziabher	Gebremariam	ETH	10.9.84	2	GS	Ostrava	8 Jun
	(20)							

Mark	Wind	Name		Nat	Born	Pos	Meet	Venue	Date
26:58.38WR		Yobes	Ondieki	KEN	21.2.61	1	Bisl	Oslo	10 Jul 93
27:02.62		Abderrahim	Goumri	MAR	21.5.76	3	FBK	Hengelo	29 May 05
27:04.20		Abraham	Chebii	KEN	23.12.79	1		Stanford	4 May 01
27:04.45		Bernard Kipyego	Kiprop	KEN	16.7.86	4	FBK	Hengelo	29 May 05
27:04.54		Felix	Limo	KEN	22.8.80	2	VD	Bruxelles	25 Aug 00
27:04.70		Zersenay	Tadesse	ERI	8.2.82	7	VD	Bruxelles	26 Aug 05
27:05.88		Patrick	Ivuti	KEN	30.6.78	6	VD	Bruxelles	30 Aug 02
27:06.17		John	Yuda	TAN	9.6.79	7	VD	Bruxelles	30 Aug 02
27:06.44		Worku	Bikila	ETH	6.5.68	1	VD	Bruxelles	25 Aug 95
27:06.45		Habte	Jifar	ETH	29.1.76	1	APM	Hengelo	30 May 99
		(30)							
27:06.59		Ismael	Kirui	KEN	20.2.75	2	VD	Bruxelles	25 Aug 95
27:07.29		Moses	Masai	KEN	31.5.86	7	VD	Bruxelles	3 Sep 04
27:07.55		Benjamin	Maiyo	KEN	6.10.78	2		Stanford	4 May 01
27:07.91WR		Richard	Chelimo	KEN	21.4.72	1	DNG	Stockholm	5 Jul 93
27:08.23WR		Arturo	Barrios	MEX	12.12.63	1	ISTAF	Berlin	18 Aug 89
27:08.42		Martin	Irungu Mathathi	KEN	25.12.85	1		Kobe	24 Apr 05
27:08.96		Moses	Mosop	KEN	17.7.85	3	WCh	Helsinki	8 Aug 05
27:10.34		Josphat	Machuka	KEN	12.12.73	4	VD	Bruxelles	25 Aug 95
27:11.17		Julius	Gitahi	KEN	29.4.78	1		Kobe	26 Apr 98
27:11.62		John	Ngugi ¶	KEN	10.5.62	1	VD	Bruxelles	13 Sep 91
		(40)							
27:12.22		Dejene	Berhanu	ETH	12.12.80	2	GP II	Stanford	29 May 05
27:12.37		Luke	Kipkosgei	KEN	27.11.75	3		Stanford	4 May 01
27:12.39		Ismaïl	Sghyr	MAR/FRA	16.3.72	2	DNG	Stockholm	30 Jul 99
27:12.47		António	Pinto	POR	22.3.66	3	DNG	Stockholm	30 Jul 99
27:13.38		Girma	Tola	ETH	13.10.75	2	APM	Hengelo	30 May 99
27:13.81WR		Fernando	Mamede	POR	1.11.51	1	DNG	Stockholm	2 Jul 84
27:13.98		Mebrahtom	Keflezighi	USA	5.5.75	4		Stanford	4 May 01
27:14.26		Fita	Bayissa	ETH	15.12.72	1	Bisl	Oslo	4 Jul 92
27:14.44		Fabián	Roncero	ESP	19.10.70	1rA	EChall	Lisboa	4 Apr 98
27:14.53		Khalid	Skah	MAR	29.1.67	2	WCh	Göteborg	8 Aug 95
		(50)	100th man 27:30.04, 200th 27:42.8, 300th 27:50.17						

HALF MARATHON

Included are the slightly downhill courses: Newcastle to South Shields 30.5m, Tokyo 33m. Lisboa (Spring) 69m

Mark	Wind	Name		Nat	Born	Pos	Meet	Venue	Date
59:05	dh	Zersenay	Tadesse	ERI	8.2.82	1	GNR	South Shields	18 Sep 05
59:06	dh	Paul	Tergat	KEN	17.6.69	1		Lisboa	26 Mar 00
59:10	dh		Tergat			1		Lisboa	13 Mar 05
59:16		Samuel	Wanjiru	KEN	10.11.86	1		Rotterdam	11 Sep 05
59:17			Tergat			1		Milano	4 Apr 98
59:20	dh	Hendrick	Ramaala	RSA	2.2.72	2		Lisboa	26 Mar 00
59:21	dh	Robert Kipkoech	Cheruiyot	KEN	26.9.78	2		Lisboa	13 Mar 05
59:22			Tergat			1	Stra	Milano	17 Apr 99
59:27	dh	Wilson	Kiprotich Kebenei	KEN	20.7.80	3		Lisboa	13 Mar 05
59:31	dh	Patrick	Ivuti	KEN	30.6.78	3		Lisboa	26 Mar 00
59:37	dh	Dejene	Berhanu	ETH	12.12.80	1	GNR	South Shields	26 Sep 04
59:38	dh	Faustin	Baha	TAN	30.5.82	4		Lisboa	26 Mar 00
59:41	dh	Haile	Gebrselassie (10)	ETH	18.4.73	1		Lisboa	24 Mar 02
59:42	dh		Ramaala			2		Lisboa	24 Mar 02
59:42	dh	Martin	Lel	KEN	29.10.78	4		Lisboa	13 Mar 05
59:43	dh	António	Pinto	POR	22.3.66	1		Lisboa	15 Mar 98
59:43			Wanjiru			1		Sendai	10 Jul 05
59:45			Ivuti			1	NC	Udine	29 Sep 02
59:46	dh		Tergat			3		Lisboa	24 Mar 02
59:47		Moses	Tanui	KEN	20.8.65	1		Milano	3 Apr 93
59:47			Ivuti			2		Rotterdam	11 Sep 05
59:49	dh	Rodgers	Rop	KEN	16.2.76	1		Lisboa	28 Mar 04
59:51	dh	William	Kiplagat	KEN	21.6.72	5		Lisboa	26 Mar 00
59:51	w	Tesfaye	Tola	ETH	19.10.74	1		Malmö	12 Jun 00
59:51	dh		Lel			2		Lisboa	28 Mar 04
59:52		Fabián	Roncero	ESP	19.10.70	1		Berlin	1 Apr 01
59:53		Philip	Rugut	KEN	18.5.77	2	NC	Udine	29 Sep 02
59:54	dh		R K Cheruiyot			3		Lisboa	28 Mar 04
59:56			Tergat			1		Milano	1 Apr 95
59:56		Shem	Kororia	KEN	25.9.72	1	WCh	Kosice	4 Oct 97
59:56	dh	Jaouad	Gharib	MAR	22.5.72	4		Lisboa	28 Mar 04
		(31/20)							
59:58	dh	Paul	Kosgei	KEN	22.4.78	1	GNR	South Shields	6 Oct 02

Mark	Wind	Name		Nat	Born	Pos	Meet	Venue	Date
60:00		Kenneth	Cheruiyot	KEN	2.8.74	3	WCh	Kosice	4 Oct
60:00	dh	Luke	Kibet	KEN	19.6.73	6		Lisboa	28 Mar
60:01		Paul	Koech	KEN	25.6.69	1	WCh	Uster	27 Sep
60:01	dh	Japhet	Kosgei	KEN	68	1		Lisboa	21 Mar
60:02		Benson	Masya	KEN	14.5.70	1	GNR	South Shields	18 Sep
60:02		Darren	Wilson	AUS	9.8.68	1		Tokyo	19 Jan
60:02		John	Yuda	TAN	9.6.79	2	GNR	South Shields	6 Oct
60:04		Joseph	Kimani	KEN	21.9.72	2		Lisboa	15 Mar
60:04		Tesfaye	Jifar	ETH	23.4.76	2	WCh	Bristol	7 Oct
		(30)							
60:05		Jackson	Koech	KEN	26.12.78	2	GNR	South Shields	21 Sep
60:06		Steve	Moneghetti	AUS	26.9.62	1		Tokyo	24 Jan
60:09	Sh?	Paul	Evans	GBR	13.4.61	1		Marrakesh	15 Jan
60:11		Matthews	Temane	RSA	14.12.60	1	NC	East London	25 Jul
60:11		Zithulele	Sinqe	RSA	9.6.63	2	NC	East London	25 Jul
60:11		Todd	Williams	USA	7.3.69	2		Tokyo	24 Jan
60:12	Sh?	Laban	Chege	KEN	70	2		Marrakesh	15 Jan
60:14		Armando	Quintanilla	MEX	19.4.68	1		Tokyo	21 Jan
60:14		Daniel	Rono	KEN	13.7.78	1		Groningen	11 May
60:15		Sammy	Korir	KEN	12.12.71	1	RdVin	Grevenmacher	27 Sep
		(40)							
60:15		Paul Kimaiyo	Kimugul	KEN	4.3.80	3		Rotterdam	11 Sep
60:17		Dionicio	Cerón	MEX	9.10.65	3		Tokyo	24 Jan
60:18		Mohamed	Mourhit ¶	BEL	10.10.70	5	WCh	Kosice	4 Oct
60:20		Rachid	Berradi	ITA	29.8.75	1	Stram	Milano	13 Apr
60:21		David	Kosgei	KEN	.77	1		Gargnano	29 Sep
60:21		Zakayo	Ngatho	KEN	18.3.78	1		Marugame	2 Feb
60:22		Charles	Kamathi	KEN	18.5.78	2	Stram	Milano	13 Apr
60:22		Paul	Kirui	KEN	5.2.80	1		Ostia	29 Feb
60:22		Robert	Kipchumba	KEN	24.2.84	1	Stra	Milano	3 Apr
60:22		James	Kwambai	KEN	.76	1		Udine	26 Sep
		(50)	100th man 60:48, 200th 61:13, 300th 61:28, 400th 61:38						
Short course									
58:51		Paul	Tergat	KEN	17.6.69	1	Stra	Milano 49m sh	30 Mar
59:24		Sammy	Lelei	KEN	14.8.64	1		Lisboa 97m	13 Mar
59:46		Josephat	Kiprono	KEN	12.12.73	2	Stra	Milano 49m	30 Mar

MARATHON

Note Boston marathon is downhill overall (139m) and, as a point-to-point course, in some years, such as 1994, has been strongly wind-aided - next bests are shown if to standard as a supplement.

In second column: L = loop course or start and finish within 30%, P = point-to-point or start and finish more than 30 apart, D = point-to-point and downhill over 1/1000

Mark		Name		Nat	Born	Pos	Meet	Venue	Date
2:04:55	L WR	Paul	Tergat	KEN	17.6.69	1		Berlin	28 Sep
2:04:56	L	Sammy	Korir	KEN	12.12.71	2		Berlin	28 Sep
2:05:38	L WR	Khalid	Khannouchi	MAR/USA	22.12.71	1		London	14 Apr
2:05:42	L WR		Khannouchi			1		Chicago	24 Oct
2:05:48	L		Tergat			2		London	14 Apr
2:05:50	L	Evans	Rutto	KEN	8.4.78	1		Chicago	12 Oct
2:05:56	L		Khannouchi			1		Chicago	13 Oct
2:06:05	L WR	Ronaldo da	Costa	BRA	7.6.70	1		Berlin	20 Sep
2:06:14	L	Felix	Limo	KEN	22.8.80	1		Rotterdam	4 Apr
2:06:15	L	Titus	Munji	KEN	.79	3		Berlin	28 Sep
2:06:16	L	Moses	Tanui	KEN	20.8.65	2		Chicago	24 Oct
2:06:16	L	Daniel	Njenga	KEN	7.5.76	2		Chicago	13 Oct
2:06:16	L	Toshinari	Takaoka (10)	JPN	24.9.70	3		Chicago	13 Oct
2:06:16	L		Rutto			1		Chicago	10 Oct
2:06:18	L		Tergat			4		Chicago	13 Oct
2:06:18	L		Rutto			1		London	18 Apr
2:06:20	L	Haile	Gebrselassie	ETH	18.4.73	1		Amsterdam	16 Oct
2:06:23	L	Robert	Cheboror	KEN	9.9.78	1		Amsterdam	17 Oct
2:06:33	L	Gert	Thys	RSA	12.11.71	1		Tokyo	14 Feb
2:06:33	L	Michael	Rotich	KEN	26.10.82	1		Paris	6 Apr
2:06:35	L		Gebrselassie			3		London	14 Apr
2:06:36	L	António	Pinto	POR	22.3.66	1		London	16 Apr
2:06:36	L	Benoit	Zwierzchlewski	FRA	19.8.76	2		Paris	6 Apr
2:06:39	L	William	Kipsang	KEN	.77	1		Amsterdam	19 Oct
2:06:42	L		F Limo			2		Amsterdam	19 Oct
2:06:44	L	Josephat	Kiprono	KEN	12.12.73	1		Berlin	26 Sep
2:06:44	L		F Limo			1		Berlin	26 Sep
2:06:46	L	Abdelkader	El Mouaziz	MAR	1.1.69	5		Chicago	13 Oct

Mark	Wind	Name		Nat	Born	Pos	Meet	Venue	Date
2:06:47	L	Fred	Kiprop (20)	KEN	3.6.74	1		Amsterdam	17 Oct 99
2:06:47	L	Raymond	Kipkoech	KEN	.75	1		Berlin	29 Sep 02
2:06:47	L	Wilson	Onsare	KEN	15.6.76	3		Paris	6 Apr 03
		(30/22)							
2:06:48	L	Driss	El Himer	FRA	4.4.74	4		Paris	6 Apr 03
2:06:49	L	Tesfaye	Jifar	ETH	23.4.76	2		Amsterdam	17 Oct 99
2:06:49	L	Simon	Biwott	KEN	3.3.70	2		Berlin	29 Sep 02
2:06:49	L	Joseph	Riri	KEN	.73	2		Berlin	26 Sep 04
2:06:50	L WR	Belayneh	Dinsamo	ETH	28.6.65	1		Rotterdam	17 Apr 88
2:06:50	L	William	Kiplagat	KEN	21.6.72	3		Amsterdam	17 Oct 99
2:06:51	L	Atsushi	Fujita	JPN	6.11.76	1		Fukuoka	3 Dec 00
2:06:52	L	Vincent	Kipsos	KEN	22.6.76	3		Berlin	29 Sep 02
		(30)							
2:06:54	L	Ondoro	Osoro	KEN	3.12.67	1		Chicago	11 Oct 98
2:06:57	L	Takayuki	Inubishi	JPN	11.8.72	2		Berlin	26 Sep 99
2:06:57	L	Tesfaye	Tola	ETH	19.10.74	4		Amsterdam	17 Oct 99
2:07:02	L	Sammy	Lelei	KEN	14.8.64	1		Berlin	24 Sep 95
2:07:02	L	Jaouad (:12?)	Gharib	MAR	22.5.72	3		London	18 Apr 04
2:07:05	L	Joshua	Chelanga	KEN	7.4.73	3		Berlin	26 Sep 04
2:07:06	L	Ian	Syster	RSA	20.1.76	5		London	14 Apr 02
2:07:07	L	Ahmed	Salah	DJI	31.12.56	2		Rotterdam	17 Apr 88
2:07:07	L	Paul	Koech	KEN	25.6.69	2		Chicago	12 Oct 03
2:07:09	L	Japheth	Kosgei	KEN	28.12.68	1		Rotterdam	18 Apr 99
		(40)							
2:07:09	L	Benjamin	Maiyo	KEN	6.10.78	2		Chicago	9 Oct 05
2:07:12	L WR	Carlos	Lopes	POR	18.2.47	1		Rotterdam	20 Apr 85
2:07:13	L	Steve	Jones	GBR	4.8.55	1		Chicago	20 Oct 85
2:07:15	D	Cosmas	Ndeti	KEN	24.11.71	1		Boston	18 Apr 94
2:07:18	L	Kenneth	Cheruiyot	KEN	2.8.74	2		Rotterdam	22 Apr 01
2:07:19	D	Andrés	Espinosa	MEX	4.2.63	2		Boston	18 Apr 94
2:07:20	L	Vincent	Rousseau	BEL	29.7.62	2		Berlin	24 Sep 95
2:07:20	L		Lee Bong-ju	KOR	11.10.70	2		Tokyo	13 Feb 00
2:07:23	L	Fabián	Roncero	ESP	19.10.70	2		Rotterdam	18 Apr 99
2:07:26	L	Benjamin Kimutai	Kosgei	KEN	5.9.71	1		Amsterdam	20 Oct 02
		(50)	100th man 2:08:08, 200th 2:08:59, 300th 2:09:46, 400th 2:10:38, 500th 2:10:53						

2000 METRES STEEPLECHASE

Mark	Name		Nat	Born	Pos	Meet	Venue	Date
5:14.43	Julius	Kariuki	KEN	12.6.61	1		Rovereto	21 Aug 90
5:14.53	Saïf Saeed	Shaheen	QAT	15.10.82	1	SGP	Doha	13 May 05
5:15.96	Bouabdallah	Tahri	FRA	20.12.78	1		Tomblaine	19 Jun 02
5:16.22	Phillip	Barkutwo	KEN	6.10.66	2		Rovereto	21 Aug 90
5:16.46	Wesley	Kiprotich	KEN	31.7.79	2	SGP	Doha	13 May 05
5:16.85	Eliud	Barngetuny	KEN	20.5.73	1		Parma	13 Jun 95
5:18.28	Richard	Kosgei	KEN	29.12.70	2		Parma	13 Jun 95
5:18.36	Alessandro	Lambruschini	ITA	7.1.65	1		Verona	12 Sep 89
5:18.38	Azzedine	Brahmi	ALG	13.9.66	1		Verona	17 Jun 92
5:18.51	John	Langat	KEN	27.11.74	1		Rovereto	29 Aug 01

3000 METRES STEEPLECHASE

Mark	Name		Nat	Born	Pos	Meet	Venue	Date
7:53.63 WR	Saïf Saaeed	Shaheen	QAT	15.10.82	1	VD	Bruxelles	3 Sep 04
	(Formerly Stephen	Cherono KEN)						
7:55.28 WR	Brahim	Boulami ¶	MAR	20.4.72	1	VD	Bruxelles	24 Aug 01
7:55.51		Shaheen			1	VD	Bruxelles	26 Aug 05
7:55.72 WR	Bernard	Barmasai	KEN	6.5.74	1	ASV	Köln	24 Aug 97
7:56.16	Moses	Kiptanui	KEN	1.10.70	2	ASV	Köln	24 Aug 97
7:56.34		Shaheen			1	GGala	Roma	8 Jul 05
7:56.37	Paul Kipsiele	Koech	KEN	10.11.81	2	GGala	Roma	8 Jul 05
7:56.94		Shaheen			1	WAF	Monaco	19 Sep 04
7:57.28		Shaheen			1	SGP	Athína	14 Jun 05
7:57.29	Reuben	Kosgei	KEN	2.8.79	2	VD	Bruxelles	24 Aug 01
7:57.38		Shaheen			1	WAF	Monaco	14 Sep 03
7:57.42		P K Koech			2	WAF	Monaco	14 Sep 03
7:58.09		Boulami			1	Herc	Monaco	19 Jul 02
7:58.10		Cherono			2	Herc	Monaco	19 Jul 02
7:58.50		Boulami			1	WK	Zürich	17 Aug 01
7:58.66		S Cherono			3	VD	Bruxelles	24 Aug 01
7:58.98		Barmasai			1	Herc	Monaco	4 Aug 99
7:59.08 WR	Wilson	Boit Kipketer	KEN	6.10.73	1	WK	Zürich	13 Aug 97
7:59.18 WR		Kiptanui			1	WK	Zürich	16 Aug 95
7.59.52		Kiptanui			1	VD	Bruxelles	25 Aug 95

MEN All-time

Mark	Wind	Name		Nat	Born	Pos	Meet	Venue	Date
7:59.65			P K Koech			1	GGala	Roma	2 Jul
8:00.06			Shaheen			1	VD	Bruxelles	5 Sep
8:00.35			Barmasai			2	WK	Zürich	13 Aug
8:00.42			P K Koech			2	VD	Bruxelles	5 Sep
8:00.54			Kiptanui			1		Rieti	3 Sep
8:00.56			Boit Kipketer			1	DNG	Stockholm	16 Jul
8:00.60			Shaheen			1	WK	Zürich	6 Aug
8:00.67			Barmasai			1	Herc	Monaco	8 Aug
8:00.77			Boulami			2	DNG	Stockholm	16 Jul
8:00.78			Kiptanui			3	WK	Zürich	13 Aug
		(30/7)							
8:01.69		Kipkirui	Misoi	KEN	23.12.78	4	VD	Bruxelles	24 Aug
8:02.49		Ezekiel	Kemboi	KEN	25.5.82	2	WK	Zürich	15 Aug
8:03.41		Patrick	Sang	KEN	11.4.64	3	ASV	Köln	24 Aug
		(10)							
8:03.57		Ali	Ezzine	MAR	3.9.78	1	Gaz	Saint-Denis	23 Jun
8:03.74		Raymond	Yator	KEN	7.4.81	3	Herc	Monaco	18 Aug
8:03.89		John	Kosgei	KEN	13.7.73	3	Herc	Monaco	16 Aug
8:04.22		Brimin	Kipruto	KEN	31.7.85	3	GGala	Roma	8 Jul
8:04.95		Simon	Vroemen	NED	11.5.69	2	VD	Bruxelles	26 Aug
8:05.01		Eliud	Barngetuny	KEN	20.5.73	1	Herc	Monaco	25 Jul
8:05.35	WR	Peter	Koech	KEN	18.2.58	1	DNG	Stockholm	3 Jul
8:05.37		Philip	Barkutwo	KEN	6.10.66	2		Rieti	6 Sep
8:05.4	WR	Henry	Rono	KEN	12.2.52	1		Seattle	13 May
8:05.43		Christopher	Kosgei	KEN	14.8.74	2	WK	Zürich	11 Aug
		(20)							
8:05.51		Julius	Kariuki	KEN	12.6.61	1	OG	Seoul	30 Sep
8:05.68		Wesley	Kiprotich	KEN	1.8.79	4	VD	Bruxelles	3 Sep
8:05.96		Richard	Matelong	KEN	14.10.83	6	VD	Bruxelles	3 Sep
8:05.99		Joseph	Keter	KEN	13.6.69	1	Herc	Monaco	10 Aug
8:06.77		Gideon	Chirchir	KEN	24.2.66	2	WK	Zürich	16 Aug
8:06.88		Richard	Kosgei	KEN	29.12.70	2	GPF	Monaco	9 Sep
8:06.91		Bouabdellah	Tahri	FRA	20.12.78	3	Gaz	Saint-Denis	4 Jul
8:07.13		Paul	Kosgei	KEN	22.4.78	2	GP II	Saint-Denis	3 Jul
8:07.18		Moussa	Omar Obaid	QAT	18.4.85	4	OG	Athína	24 Aug
8:07.44		Luis Miguel	Martín	ESP	11.1.72	2	VD	Bruxelles	30 Aug
		(30)							
8:07.59		Julius	Nyamu	KEN	1.12.77	5	VD	Bruxelles	24 Aug
8:07.62		Joseph	Mahmoud	FRA	13.12.55	1	VD	Bruxelles	24 Aug
8:07.96		Mark	Rowland	GBR	7.3.63	3	OG	Seoul	30 Sep
8:08.02	WR	Anders	Gärderud	SWE	28.8.46	1	OG	Montreal	28 Jul
8:08.12		Matthew	Birir	KEN	5.7.72	3	GGala	Roma	8 Jun
8:08.14		Sa'ad Shaddad	Al-Asmari	KSA	24.9.68	4	DNG	Stockholm	16 Jul
8:08.57		Francesco	Panetta	ITA	10.1.63	1	WCh	Roma	5 Sep
8:08.78		Alessandro	Lambruschini	ITA	7.1.65	3	WCh	Stuttgart	21 Aug
8:09.02		Abdelaziz	Sahere	MAR	18.9.67	5	GGala	Roma	8 Jun
8:09.03		Elarbi	Khattabi	MAR	16.5.67	3	GGala	Roma	7 Jul
		(40)							
8:09.09		Eliseo	Martín	ESP	5.11.73	3	WCh	Saint-Denis	26 Aug
8:09.11		Bronislaw	Malinowski	POL	4.6.51	2	OG	Montreal	28 Jul
8:09.17		Henry	Marsh	USA	15.3.54	1	R-W	Koblenz	28 Aug
8:09.18		Boguslaw	Maminski	POL	18.12.55	2	VD	Bruxelles	24 Aug
8:09.09		David	Chemweno	KEN	18.12.81	2	NA	Heusden-Zolder	23 Jul
8:09.37		Abel	Cheruiyot Yagut	KEN/BRN	26.12.84	2	NA	Heusden	2 Aug
			(now Abel Yagoot Jowhar Salem)						
8:09.48		Damian	Kallabis	GER	10.6.73	4	WK	Zürich	11 Aug
8:09.54		Johnstone	Kipkoech	KEN	20.12.68	2	VD	Bruxelles	25 Aug
8:09.76		Mark	Croghan	USA	8.1.68	5	WCh	Stuttgart	21 Aug
8:10.01		William	van Dijck	BEL	24.1.61	1	VD	Bruxelles	5 Sep
		(50)	100th man 8:14.68, 200th man 8:20.66						
Drugs disqualification: 7:53.17			Brahim Boulami ¶	MAR	20.4.72	1	WK	Zürich	16 Aug

110 METRES HURDLES

Mark	Wind	Name		Nat	Born	Pos	Meet	Venue	Date
12.91	WR 0.5	Colin	Jackson	GBR	18.2.67	1	WCh	Stuttgart	20 Aug
12.91	WR 0.3		Liu Xiang	CHN	13.7.83	1	OG	Athína	27 Aug
12.92	WR -0.1	Roger	Kingdom	USA	26.8.62	1	WK	Zürich	16 Aug
12.92	0.9	Allen	Johnson	USA	1.3.71	1	NC	Atlanta	23 Jun
12.92	0.2		Johnson			1	VD	Bruxelles	23 Aug
12.93	WR -0.2	Renaldo	Nehemiah	USA	24.3.59	1	WK	Zürich	19 Aug
12.93	0.0		Johnson			1	WCh	Athína	7 Aug
12.94	1.6	Jack	Pierce	USA	23.9.62	1s2	NC	Atlanta	22 Jun

Mark	Wind	Name		Nat	Born	Pos	Meet	Venue	Date
2.95	0.6		Johnson			1	OG	Atlanta	29 Jul 96
2.97A	2.0		Kingdom			1		Sestriere	11 Aug 88
2.97A	-1.6		Jackson			1A		Sestriere	28 Jul 93
2.97	-0.5		Johnson			1		Stuttgart	13 Jul 97
2.97	1.5		Johnson			1	NC	Sacramento	23 Jul 00
2.97	0.0		Johnson			1	Gaz	Saint-Denis	4 Jul 03
2.97	1.0	Ladji	Doucouré	FRA	28.3.83	1	NC	Angers	15 Jul 05
2.98	1.5		Kingdom			1	OG	Seoul	26 Sep 88
2.98	0.2		Jackson			1	TOTO	Tokyo	15 Sep 94
2.98	0.2		Johnson			1	ASV	Köln	18 Aug 95
2.98	-0.3		Johnson			1rA	WK	Zürich	12 Aug 98
2.98	0.6	Mark	Crear	USA	2.10.68	1		Zagreb	5 Jul 99
2.99	1.2		Jackson			1	VD	Bruxelles	3 Sep 93
2.99	-0.3		Jackson			1		Madrid	6 Sep 94
2.99	0.2		Johnson			1	NC	Carson	24 Jun 05
3.00	WR 0.9		Nehemiah			1	Pepsi	Los Angeles (Ww)	6 May 79
3.00	0.5	Anthony	Jarrett	GBR	13.8.68	2	WCh	Stuttgart	20 Aug 93
3.00	-0.1		Johnson			1	WCh	Göteborg	12 Aug 95
3.00	-0.3		Crear			2rA	WK	Zürich	12 Aug 98
3.00	0.6	Anier	García (10)	CUB	9.3.76	1	OG	Sydney	25 Sep 00
3.00	-0.1		Doucouré			1	Bisl	Oslo	29 Jul 05
3.01	0.3	Larry	Wade ¶	USA	22.11.74	1rA	Athl	Lausanne	2 Jul 99
3.01	0.8		Johnson			1	GGala	Roma	7 Jul 99
3.01	0.2	Dominique	Arnold	USA	14.9.73	2	NC	Carson	24 Jun 05
		(32/12)							
3.02	0.2	Terrence	Trammell	USA	23.11.78	3	NC	Carson	24 Jun 05
3.03	-0.2	Greg	Foster	USA	4.8.58	2	WK	Zürich	19 Aug 81
3.03	1.0	Reggie	Torian	USA	22.4.75	1	NC	New Orleans	21 Jun 98
3.05	1.4	Tony	Dees ¶	USA	6.8.63	1		Vigo	23 Jul 91
3.05	-0.8	Florian	Schwarthoff	GER	7.5.68	1	NC	Bremen	2 Jul 95
3.08	1.2	Mark	McKoy	CAN	10.12.61	1	BNP	Villeneuve d'Ascq	2 Jul 93
3.08	0.0	Stanislav	Olijar	LAT	22.3.79	2	Athl	Lausanne	1 Jul 03
3.12	1.5	Falk	Balzer ¶	GER	14.12.73	2	EC	Budapest	22 Aug 98
		(20)							
3.12	1.0	Duane	Ross	USA	5.12.72	3	WCh	Sevilla	25 Aug 99
3.13	1.6	Igor	Kovác	SVK	12.5.69	1	DNG	Stockholm	7 Jul 97
3.15	0.3	Robin	Korving	NED	29.7.74	5rA	Athl	Lausanne	2 Jul 99
3.17	-0.4	Sam	Turner	USA	17.6.57	2	Pepsi	Los Angeles (Ww)	15 May 83
3.17	0.0	Tonie	Campbell	USA	14.6.60	3	WK	Zürich	17 Aug 88
3.17	0.5	Courtney	Hawkins	USA	11.7.67	1		Ingolstadt	26 Jul 98
3.17	0.4	Mike	Fenner	GER	24.4.71	1		Leverkusen	9 Aug 98
3.17	-0.1	Maurice	Wignall	JAM	17.4.76	1s1	OG	Athína	26 Aug 04
3.18	0.5	Emilio	Valle	CUB	21.4.67	3s1	OG	Atlanta	29 Jul 96
3.19	1.9	Steve	Brown	USA/TRI	6.1.69	1h4	NC	Atlanta	21 Jun 96
		(30)							
3.20	2.0	Stéphane	Caristan	FRA	31.5.64	1	EC	Stuttgart	30 Aug 86
3.20	1.8	Aleksandr	Markin ¶	RUS	8.9.62	1	Znam	Leningrad	11 Jun 88
3.20	1.7	Larry	Harrington	USA	24.11.70	2s1	NC	Atlanta	22 Jun 96
3.21	WR 0.6	Alejandro	Casañas	CUB	29.1.54	1	WUG	Sofiya	21 Aug 77
3.21	1.8	Vladimir	Shishkin	RUS	12.1.64	2	Znam	Leningrad	11 Jun 88
3.21	0.9	Eugene	Swift	USA	14.9.64	3	NC	Atlanta	23 Jun 96
3.22	-0.2	Terry	Reese	USA	20.6.67	2	ASV	Köln	24 Aug 97
3.22	1.5	Dawane	Wallace	USA	30.12.76	4	NC	Sacramento	23 Jul 00
3.22	-0.1	Joel	Brown	USA	31.1.80	2	Bisl	Oslo	29 Jul 05
3.23	-0.1	Charles	Allen	CAN	29.3.77	4s1	OG	Athína	26 Aug 04
		(40)							
3.23	0.8	Anwar	Moore	USA	5.3.79	1	CalR	Modesto	8 May 05
3.23	0.1	Arend	Watkins	USA	23.5.79	1	SGP	Ath na	14 Jun 05
3.24	WR 0.3	Rod	Milburn	USA	18.5.50	1	OG	München	7 Sep 72
3.24	2.0	Arthur	Blake	USA	19.8.66	2	Athl	Lausanne	24 Jun 88
3.24	1.1	Yoel	Hernández	CUB	12.12.77	2	PAm	Winnipeg	30 Jul 99
3.25	0.1	Andre	Phillips	USA	5.9.59	1	USOF	Baton Rouge	28 Jul 85
3.25	-0.1		Li Tong	CHN	6.5.67	2rA	Gugl	Linz	4 Jul 94
3.25	1.9	Jonathan	N'senga	BEL	21.4.73	3s1	EC	Budapest	22 Aug 98
3.25	-0.3	Dudley	Dorival	HAI	1.9.75	3	WCh	Edmonton	9 Aug 01
3.26		eight men: W Gault, I Kazanov, E Batte, D Philibert, Yun. Hernández, S Bownes , C Phillips , R Bramlett							
		(57)	100th man 13.37, 200th 13.49, 300th 13.59						

Rolling start but accepted by race officials

Mark	Wind	Name		Nat	Born	Pos	Meet	Venue	Date
3.10A	2.0	Falk	Balzer ¶	GER	14.12.73	1	WCp	Johannesburg	13 Sep 98

Mark	Wind	Name		Nat	Born	Pos	Meet	Venue	Date
Doubtful timing									
13.06	1.3	Mike	Fenner	GER	24.4.71	1		Scheessel	4 Jun 9
13.08	1.3	Eric	Kaiser ¶	GER	7.3.71	2		Scheessel	4 Jun 9
Wind-assisted marks			*Performances to 13.00, performers to 13.24*						
12.87	2.6	Roger	Kingdom	USA	26.8.62	1	WCp	Barcelona	10 Sep 8
12.91	3.5	Renaldo	Nehemiah	USA	24.3.59	1	NCAA	Champaign	1 Jun 7
12.94A	2.8		Jackson			1rA		Sestriere	31 Jul 9
12.95	2.6		Jackson			2	WCp	Barcelona	10 Sep 8
12.99	2.7		Jackson			1	v3N	Birmingham	23 Jun 8
13.00	3.5		Nehemiah			1	USOF	Syracuse	26 Jul 8
13.00	2.7		Kingdom			1		Sacramento	21 Jul 8
13.00	3.8		Johnson			1s1	NC	Sacramento	17 Jun 9
13.06	2.1	Mark	McKoy	CAN	10.12.61	1	Gugl	Linz	13 Aug 9
13.14	2.9	Igor	Kazanov	LAT	24.9.63	1r1	Znam	Leningrad	8 Jun 8
13.15	2.1	Courtney	Hawkins	USA	11.7.67	1		Salamanca	10 Jul 9
13.18	4.7	Robert	Reading	USA	9.6.67	1		Azusa	23 Apr 9
13.20	2.4	Arthur	Blake	USA	19.8.66	2	IAC	Edinburgh	6 Jul 9
13.20	3.1	Yoel	Hernández	CUB	12.12.77	2		Camagüey	10 Mar 0
13.21A	2.5	Eric	Cannon	USA	2.3.67	2	NCAA	Provo	3 Jun 8
13.24	2.4	Glenn	Terry	USA	10.2.71	1s2	WUG	Buffalo	18 Jul 9
13.24	3.3	Yuniel	Hernández	CUB	28.3.81	1		Getafe	8 Jul 0
Hand timing									
12.8	1.0	Renaldo	Nehemiah	USA	24.3.59	1		Kingston	11 May 7
13.0 WR	1.8	Guy	Drut	FRA	6.12.50	1	ISTAF	Berlin	22 Aug 7
13.0	1.0	Greg	Foster	USA	4.8.58	2		Kingston	11 May 7
13.0	0.8	Mark	McKoy	CAN	10.12.61	1	Nik	Nice	16 Jul 8
13.0		Stéphane	Caristan	FRA	25.1.64	1		Creteil	3 May 8
13.0		Vladimir	Shishkin	RUS	12.1.64	1		Stayki	7 May 8
13.0* WR	2.0	Rod	Milburn	USA	18.5.50	1s1	AAU	Eugene	25 Jun 7
13.0	0.4	Tomasz	Scigaczewski	POL	18.11.78	1	NC	Wroclaw	28 Jun 9
Wind-assisted									
12.8	2.4	Colin	Jackson	GBR	18.2.67	1		Sydney	10 Jan 9
12.9	4.1	Mark	Crear	USA	2.10.68	1rA	S&W	Modesto	8 May 9
13.0		Alejandro	Casañas	CUB	29.1.54	1	Barr	La Habana	22 May 7
13.0		Tonie	Campbell	USA	14.6.60	1		Los Angeles	16 Jul 8
13.0		Keith	Talley	USA	28.1.64	1		Tuscaloosa	26 Mar 8
13.0	4.1		Li Tong	CHN	6.5.67	2rA	S&W	Modesto	8 May 9

400 METRES HURDLES

Mark	Name		Nat	Born	Pos	Meet	Venue	Date
46.78 WR	Kevin	Young	USA	16.9.66	1	OG	Barcelona	6 Aug 9
47.02 WR	Edwin	Moses	USA	31.8.55	1		Koblenz	31 Aug 8
47.03	Bryan	Bronson	USA	9.9.72	1	NC	New Orleans	21 Jun 9
47.10	Samuel	Matete	ZAM	27.7.68	1rA	WK	Zürich	7 Aug 9
47.13 WR		Moses			1		Milano	3 Jul 8
47.14		Moses			1	Athl	Lausanne	14 Jul 8
47.17		Moses			1	ISTAF	Berlin	8 Aug 8
47.18		Young			1	WCh	Stuttgart	19 Aug 9
47.19	Andre	Phillips	USA	5.9.59	1	OG	Seoul	25 Sep 8
47.23	Amadou	Dia Bâ	SEN	22.9.58	2	OG	Seoul	25 Sep 8
47.24	Kerron	Clement	USA	31.10.85	1	NC	Carson	26 Jun 0
47.25	Félix	Sánchez	DOM	30.8.77	1	WCh	Saint-Denis	29 Aug 0
47.27		Moses			1	ISTAF	Berlin	21 Aug 8
47.30	Bershawn	Jackson	USA	8.5.83	1	WCh	Helsinki	9 Aug 0
47.32		Moses			1		Koblenz	29 Aug 8
47.35		Sánchez			1rA	WK	Zürich	16 Aug 0
47.37		Moses			1	WCp	Roma	4 Sep 8
47.37		Moses			1	WK	Zürich	24 Aug 8
47.37		Moses			1	OT	Indianapolis	17 Jul 8
47.37		Young			1	Athl	Lausanne	7 Jul 9
47.37	Stéphane	Diagana (10)	FRA	23.7.69	1	Athl	Lausanne	5 Jul 9
47.38		Moses			1	Athl	Lausanne	2 Sep 8
47.38	Danny	Harris ¶	USA	7.9.65	1	Athl	Lausanne	10 Jul 9
47.38		Sánchez			1rA	WK	Zürich	17 Aug 0
47.40		Young			1	WK	Zürich	19 Aug 9
47.42		Young			1	ASV	Köln	16 Aug 9
47.43		Moses			1	ASV	Köln	28 Aug 8
47.43	James	Carter	USA	7.5.78	2	WCh	Helsinki	9 Aug 0
47.45 WR		Moses			1	AAU	Los Angeles (Ww)	11 Jun 7
47.46		Moses			1	WCh	Roma	1 Sep 8
	(30/12)							

Mark	Wind	Name		Nat	Born	Pos	Meet	Venue	Date
47.48		Harald	Schmid	FRG	29.9.57	1	EC	Athína	8 Sep 82
47.50		Angelo	Taylor	USA	29.12.78	1	OG	Sydney	27 Sep 00
47.53		Hadi Soua'an	Al-Somaily	KSA	21.8.76	2	OG	Sydney	27 Sep 00
47.54		Derrick	Adkins	USA	2.7.70	2	Athl	Lausanne	5 Jul 95
47.54		Fabrizio	Mori	ITA	28.6.69	2	WCh	Edmonton	10 Aug 01
47.57		James	Carter	USA	7.5.78	2rA	WK	Zürich	16 Aug 02
47.60		Winthrop	Graham	JAM	17.11.65	1	WK	Zürich	4 Aug 93
47.67		Bennie	Brazell	USA	2.6.82	2	NCAA	Sacramento	11 Jun 05
47.75		David	Patrick	USA	12.6.60	4	OT	Indianapolis	17 Jul 88
		(20)							
47.81		Llewellyn	Herbert	RSA	21.7.77	3	OG	Sydney	27 Sep 00
47.82	WR	John	Akii-Bua	UGA	3.12.49	1	OG	München	2 Sep 72
47.82		Kriss	Akabusi	GBR	28.11.58	3	OG	Barcelona	6 Aug 92
47.84		Bayano	Kamani	PAN	17.4.80	2s1	WCh	Helsinki	7 Aug 05
47.89		Dai	Tamesue	JPN	3.5.78	3	WCh	Edmonton	10 Aug 01
47.91		Calvin	Davis	USA	2.4.72	1s2	OG	Atlanta	31 Jul 96
47.92		Aleksandr	Vasilyev	BLR	26.7.61	2	ECp	Moskva	17 Aug 85
47.94		Eric	Thomas	USA	1.12.73	1	GGala	Roma	30 Jun 00
47.97		Maurice	Mitchell	USA	14.5.71	2rA	WK	Zürich	14 Aug 96
47.97		Joey	Woody	USA	22.5.73	3	NC	New Orleans	21 Jun 98
		(30)							
47.98		Sven	Nylander	SWE	1.1.62	4	OG	Atlanta	1 Aug 96
48.00		Danny	McFarlane	JAM	14.2.72	1s2	OG	Athína	24 Aug 04
48.02A		Ockert	Cilliers	RSA	21.4.81	1		Pretoria	20 Feb 04
48.04		Eronilde	de Araújo	BRA	31.12.70	2	Nik	Nice	12 Jul 95
48.05		Ken	Harnden	ZIM	31.3.73	1	GP	Paris	29 Jul 98
48.05		Kemel	Thompson	JAM	25.9.74	1	GP	London (CP)	8 Aug 03
48.06		Oleg	Tverdokhleb	UKR	3.11.69	1	EC	Helsinki	10 Aug 94
48.06		Ruslan	Mashchenko	RUS	11.11.71	1	GP II	Helsinki	13 Jun 98
48.09		Alwyn	Myburgh	RSA	13.10.80	1	WUG	Beijing	31 Aug 01
48.09		Kenji	Narisako	JPN	25.7.84	1	NSF	Okayama	24 Oct 05
		(40)							
48.11		L.J. (Louis)	van Zyl	RSA	20.7.85	3	WAF	Monaco	10 Sep 05
48.12A	WR	David	Hemery	GBR	18.7.44	1	OG	Ciudad de México	15 Oct 68
48.13		Dinsdale	Morgan	JAM	19.11.72	2	GGala	Roma	14 Jul 98
48.13		Marcel	Schelbert	SUI	26.2.76	3	WCh	Sevilla	27 Aug 99
48.14		Chris	Rawlinson	GBR	19.5.72	1rB	WK	Zürich	11 Aug 99
48.16		Tony	Rambo	USA	30.5.60	3s1	OT	Los Angeles	17 Jun 84
48.16		Marek	Plawgo	POL	25.2.81	1	GP	Osaka	12 May 01
48.16		Rickey	Harris	USA	29.9.81	1	NCAA	Baton Rouge	31 May 02
48.17		Pawel	Januszewski	POL	2.1.72	1	EC	Budapest	20 Aug 98
48.17A		Mubarak	Al-Nubi	QAT	30.12.77	2	WCp	Johannesburg	11 Sep 98
48.17		Periklis	Iakovákis	GRE	24.3.79	1s1	WCh	Saint-Denis	27 Aug 03
48.17		Naman	Keïta	FRA	9.4.78	2	Gaz	Saint-Denis	23 Jul 04
		(52)	100th man 48.64, 200th man 49.13, 300th man 49.46						
Drugs Disqualification		47.15	Bronson			1	GWG	Uniondale, NY	19 Jul 98

HIGH JUMP

Mark	Wind	Name		Nat	Born	Pos	Meet	Venue	Date
2.45	WR	Javier	Sotomayor	CUB	13.10.67	1		Salamanca	27 Jul 93
2.44	WR		Sotomayor			1	CAC	San Juan	29 Jul 89
2.43	WR		Sotomayor			1		Salamanca	8 Sep 88
2.43i			Sotomayor			1	WI	Budapest	4 Mar 89
2.42	WR	Patrik	Sjöberg	SWE	5.1.65	1	DNG	Stockholm	30 Jun 87
2.42i	WR	Carlo	Thränhardt	FRG	5.7.57	1		Berlin	26 Feb 88
2.42			Sotomayor			1		Sevilla	5 Jun 94
2.41	WR	Igor	Paklin	KGZ	15.6.63	1	WUG	Kobe	4 Sep 85
2.41i			Sjöberg			1		Pireás	1 Feb 87
2.41i			Sotomayor			1	WI	Toronto	14 Mar 93
2.41			Sotomayor			1	NC	La Habana	25 Jun 94
2.41			Sotomayor			1	TSB	London (CP)	15 Jul 94
2.40	WR	Rudolf	Povarnitsyn	UKR	13.6.62	1		Donetsk	11 Aug 85
2.40i			Thränhardt			1		Simmerath	16 Jan 87
2.40i			Sjöberg			1		Berlin	27 Feb 87
2.40			Sotomayor			1	NC	La Habana	12 Mar 89
2.40			Sjöberg			1	ECp-B	Bruxelles	5 Aug 89
2.40			Sotomayor			1	AmCp	Bogota	13 Aug 89
2.40		Sorin	Matei	ROM	6.7.63	1	PTS	Bratislava	20 Jun 90
2.40i		Hollis	Conway	USA	8.1.67	1	WI	Sevilla	10 Mar 91
2.40			Sotomayor			1		Saint Denis	19 Jul 91

Mark	Wind	Name		Nat	Born	Pos	Meet	Venue	Date
2.40		Charles	Austin	USA	19.12.67	1	WK	Zürich	7 Aug
2.40			Sotomayor			1	Barr	La Habana	22 May
2.40			Sotomayor			1	TSB	London (CP)	23 Jul
2.40			Sotomayor			1	WCh	Stuttgart	22 Aug
2.40i			Sotomayor			1		Wuppertal	4 Feb
2.40i			Sotomayor			1	TSB	Birmingham	26 Feb
2.40			Sotomayor			1		Eberstadt	10 Jul
2.40			Sotomayor			1	Nik	Nice	18 Jul
2.40			Sotomayor			1	GWG	Sankt-Peterburg	29 Jul
2.40			Sotomayor			1	WCp	London (CP)	11 Sep
2.40			Sotomayor			1	PAm	Mar del Plata	25 Mar
2.40		Vyacheslav	Voronin	RUS	5.4.74	1	BrGP	London (CP)	5 Aug
2.40i		Stefan	Holm	SWE	25.5.76	1	EI	Madrid	6 Mar
		(34/10)							
2.39	WR		Zhu Jianhua	CHN	29.5.63	1		Eberstadt	10 Jun
2.39i		Dietmar	Mögenburg	FRG	15.8.61	1		Köln	24 Feb
2.39i		Ralf	Sonn	GER	17.1.67	1		Berlin	1 Mar
2.38i		Gennadiy	Avdeyenko	UKR	4.11.63	2	WI	Indianapolis	7 Mar
2.38		Sergey	Malchenko	RUS	2.11.63	1		Banská Bystrica	4 Sep
2.38		Dragutin	Topic ¶	YUG	12.3.71	1		Beograd	1 Aug
2.38i		Steve	Smith	GBR	29.3.73	2		Wuppertal	4 Feb
2.38i		Wolf-Hendrik	Beyer	GER	14.2.72	1		Weinheim	18 Mar
2.38		Troy	Kemp	BAH	18.6.66	1	Nik	Nice	12 Jul
2.38		Artur	Partyka	POL	25.7.69	1		Eberstadt	18 Aug
		(20)							
2.38i		Matt	Hemingway	USA	24.10.72	1	NC	Atlanta	4 Mar
2.38i		Yaroslav	Rybakov	RUS	22.11.80	1		Stockholm	15 Feb
2.38		Jacques	Freitag	RSA	11.6.82	1		Oudtshoorn	5 Mar
2.38		Andrey	Sokolovskiy	UKR	16.7.78	1	GGala	Roma	8 Jul
2.37		Valeriy	Sereda	RUS	30.6.59	1		Rieti	2 Sep
2.37		Tom	McCants	USA	27.11.62	1	Owens	Columbus	8 May
2.37		Jerome	Carter	USA	25.3.63	2	Owens	Columbus	8 May
2.37		Sergey	Dymchenko	UKR	23.8.67	1		Kiyev	16 Sep
2.37i		Dalton	Grant	GBR	8.4.66	1	EI	Paris	13 Mar
2.37i		Jaroslav	Bába	CZE	2.9.84	2		Arnstadt	5 Feb
		(30)							
2.36	WR	Gerd	Wessig	GDR	16.7.59	1	OG	Moskva	1 Aug
2.36		Sergey	Zasimovich	KZK	6.9.62	1		Tashkent	5 May
2.36		Eddy	Annys	BEL	15.12.58	1		Ghent	26 May
2.36i		Jim	Howard	USA	11.9.59	1		Albuquerque	25 Jan
2.36i		Jan	Zvara	CZE	12.2.63	1	vGDR	Jablonec	14 Feb
2.36i		Gerd	Nagel	FRG	22.10.57	1		Sulingen	17 Mar
2.36		Nick	Saunders	BER	14.9.63	1	CG	Auckland	1 Feb
2.36		Doug	Nordquist	USA	20.12.58	2	TAC	Norwalk	15 Jun
2.36		Georgi	Dakov	BUL	21.10.67	2	VD	Bruxelles	10 Aug
2.36		Lábros	Papakóstas	GRE	20.10.69	1	NC	Athína	21 Jun
		(40)							
2.36i		Steinar	Hoen	NOR	8.2.71	1		Balingen	12 Feb
2.36		Tim	Forsyth	AUS	17.8.73	1	NC	Melbourne	2 Mar
2.36		Sergey	Klyugin	RUS	24.3.74	1	WK	Zürich	12 Aug
2.36		Konstantin	Matusevich	ISR	25.2.71	1		Perth	5 Feb
2.36		Martin	Buss	GER	7.4.76	1	WCh	Edmonton	8 Aug
2.36		Aleksander	Walerianczyk	POL	1.9.82	1	EU23	Bydgoszcz	20 Jul
2.36		Michal	Bieniek	POL	17.5.84	1		Biala Podlaska	28 May
2.35		eleven men: V Yashchenko UKR (i) 1978, J Wszola POL 1980, A Kotovich UKR (i) 1985, B Harken USA 1991, D Plab USA 1992, J-C Gicquel FRA (i) 1994, M Boswell CAN 1999, N Leeper USA 2000, C Clinger USA 2001, S Strand SWE (i) 2002, V Moya CUB 2005							
		(57)	100th man 2.32, 200th man 2.33, 300th man 2.28						

Best outdoor marks for athletes with indoor bests

Mark	Name	Pos	Meet	Venue	Date
2.39	Conway	1	USOF	Norman	30 Jul 89
2.38	Avdeyenko	2=	WCh	Roma	6 Sep 87
2.37	Thranhärdt	2		Rieti	2 Sep 84
2.37	Smith	1	WJ	Seoul	20 Sep 92
2.36	Mögenburg	3		Eberstadt	10 Jun 84
2.36	Howard	1		Rehlingen	8 Jun 87
2.36	Zvara	1		Praha	23 Aug 8
2.36	Grant	4	WCh	Tokyo	1 Sep 9
2.36	Hoen	1		Oslo	1 Jul 9
2.36	Holm	1		Eberstadt	18 Jul 0
2.36	Bába	2=	GGala	Roma	8 Jul 0
2.35	Nagel	1		Forbach	7 Aug 8

Ancillary jumps – en route to final marks

2.40 Sotomayor 8 Sep 88 2.40 Sotomayor 29 Jul 89 2.40 Sotomayor 5 Jun 94

A mark made at an altitude of 1000m or higher, i – indoors, Q – in qualifying competition, WR - world record

POLE VAULT

Mark Wind	Name		Nat	Born	Pos	Meet	Venue	Date
6.15i	Sergey	Bubka	UKR	4.12.63	1		Donetsk	21 Feb 93
6.14i		Bubka			1		Liévin	13 Feb 93
6.14A WR		Bubka			1		Sestriere	31 Jul 94
6.13i		Bubka			1		Berlin	21 Feb 92
6.13 WR		Bubka			1	TOTO	Tokyo	19 Sep 92
6.12i		Bubka			1	Mast	Grenoble	23 Mar 91
6.12 WR		Bubka			1		Padova	30 Aug 92
6.11i		Bubka			1		Donetsk	19 Mar 91
6.11 WR		Bubka			1		Dijon	13 Jun 92
6.10i		Bubka			1		San Sebastián	15 Mar 91
6.10 WR		Bubka			1	MAI	Malmö	5 Aug 91
6.09 WR		Bubka			1		Formia	8 Jul 91
6.08i		Bubka			1	NC	Volgograd	9 Feb 91
6.08 WR		Bubka			1	Znam	Moskva	9 Jun 91
6.07 WR		Bubka			1	Super	Shizuoka	6 May 91
6.06 WR		Bubka			1	Nik	Nice	10 Jul 88
6.05 WR		Bubka			1	PTS	Bratislava	9 Jun 88
6.05i		Bubka			1		Donetsk	17 Mar 90
6.05i		Bubka			1		Berlin	5 Mar 93
6.05		Bubka			1	GPF	London (CP)	10 Sep 93
6.05i		Bubka			1	Mast	Grenoble	6 Feb 94
6.05		Bubka			1	ISTAF	Berlin	30 Aug 94
6.05		Bubka			1	GPF	Fukuoka	13 Sep 97
6.05	Maksim	Tarasov	RUS	2.12.70	1	GP II	Athína	16 Jun 99
6.05	Dmitriy	Markov (ex BLR)	AUS	14.3.75	1	WCh	Edmonton	9 Aug 01
6.03 WR		Bubka			1	Ros	Praha	23 Jun 87
6.03i		Bubka			1		Osaka	11 Feb 89
6.03	Okkert	Brits	RSA	22.8.73	1	ASV	Köln	18 Aug 95
6.03	Jeff	Hartwig	USA	25.9.67	1		Jonesboro	14 Jun 00
6.02i	Rodion	Gataullin	RUS	23.11.65	1	NC	Gomel	4 Feb 89
6.02		Bubka			1	GP	Atlanta	18 May 96
6.02		Hartwig			1	NC	Eugene	27 Jun 99
6.02		Tarasov			1	WCh	Sevilla	26 Aug 99
6.02i		Hartwig			1	IHS	Sindelfingen	10 Mar 02
	(34/6)							
6.01	Igor	Trandenkov	RUS	17.8.66	1	NC	Sankt Peterburg	4 Jul 96
6.01	Tim	Mack	USA	15.9.72	1	WAF	Monaco	18 Sep 04
6.00	Tim	Lobinger	GER	3.9.72	1	ASV	Köln	24 Aug 97
6.00i	Jean	Galfione	FRA	9.6.71	1	WI	Maebashi	6 Mar 99
	(10)							
6.00i	Danny	Ecker	GER	21.7.77	1		Dortmund	11 Feb 01
6.00	Toby	Stevenson	USA	19.11.76	1eA	CalR	Modesto	8 May 04
6.00	Paul	Burgess	AUS	14.8.79	1		Perth	25 Feb 05

Most competitions at 6 metres or more: S Bubka 44, Hartwig 8, Gataullin & Tarasov 7, Brits 3, Markov & Lobinger 2

Mark Wind	Name		Nat	Born	Pos	Meet	Venue	Date
5.98	Lawrence	Johnson	USA	7.5.74	1		Knoxville	25 May 96
5.97	Scott	Huffman	USA	30.11.64	1	NC	Knoxville	18 Jun 94
5.96	Joe	Dial	USA	26.10.62	1		Norman	18 Jun 87
5.96	Brad	Walker	USA	21.6.81	1	GP	Rieti	28 Aug 05
5.95	Andrei	Tivontchik	GER	13.7.70	1	ASV	Köln	16 Aug 96
5.95	Michael	Stolle	GER	17.12.74	1	Herc	Monaco	18 Aug 00
5.95	Romain	Mesnil	FRA	13.7.77	1		Castres	6 Aug 03
	(20)							
5.94i	Philippe	Collet	FRA	13.12.63	1	Mast	Grenoble	10 Mar 90
5.93i	Billy	Olson	USA	19.7.58	1		East Rutherford	8 Feb 86
5.93i	Tye	Harvey	USA	25.9.74	2	NC	Atlanta	3 Mar 01
5.93	Aleksandr	Averbukh	ISR	1.10.74	1	GP	Madrid (C)	19 Jul 03
5.92	István	Bagyula	HUN	2.1.69	1	Gugl	Linz	5 Jul 91
5.92	Igor	Potapovich	KZK	6.9.67	2		Dijon	13 Jun 92
5.92	Dean	Starkey	USA	27.3.67	1	Banes	São Paulo	21 May 94
5.91 WR	Thierry	Vigneron	FRA	9.3.60	2	GGala	Roma	31 Aug 84
5.91i	Viktor	Ryzhenkov	UZB	25.8.66	2		San Sebastián	15 Mar 91
5.91A	Riaan	Botha	RSA	8.11.70	1		Pretoria	2 Apr 97
	(30)							
5.90	Pierre	Quinon	FRA	20.2.62	2	Nik	Nice	16 Jul 85
5.90i	Ferenc	Salbert	FRA	5.8.60	1	Mast	Grenoble	14 Mar 87
5.90	Miroslaw	Chmara	POL	9.5.64	1	BNP	Villeneuve d'Ascq	27 Jun 88
5.90i	Grigoriy	Yegorov	KZK	12.1.67	1		Yokohama	11 Mar 90
5.90	Denis	Petushinskiy ¶	RUS	29.1.67	1	Znam	Moskva	13 Jun 93

Mark	Wind		Name	Nat	Born	Pos	Meet	Venue	Date
5.90i		Pyotr	Bochkaryov	RUS	3.11.67	1	EI	Paris	12 Mar
5.90		Jacob	Davis	USA	29.4.78	1	Tex R	Austin	4 Apr
5.90		Viktor	Chistiakov	RUS/AUS	9.2.75	1		Salamanca	15 Jul
5.90		Pavel	Gerasimov	RUS	29.5.79	1		Rüdlingen	12 Aug
5.90		Nick	Hysong	USA	9.12.71	1	OG	Sydney	29 Sep
		(40)							
5.90		Giuseppe	Gibilisco	ITA	5.1.79	1	WCh	Saint-Denis	28 Aug
5.90i		Igor	Pavlov	RUS	18.7.79	1	EI	Madrid	5 Mar
5.89		Kory	Tarpenning ¶	USA	27.2.62	1	OT	Indianapolis	21 Jul
5.87		Earl	Bell	USA	25.8.55	1		Jonesboro	14 May
5.87		Oscar	Janson	SWE	22.7.75	1		Somero	29 Jun
5.87		Steve	Hooker	AUS	16.7.82	1		Melbourne	12 Mar
5.86		Vasiliy	Bubka	UKR	26.11.60	1		Chelyabinsk	16 Jul
5.86		Bill	Payne	USA	21.12.67	1	SWC	Houston	19 May
5.86		Valeri	Bukrejev	EST	15.6.64	1		Somero	3 Jul 9
5.86A		Pavel	Burlachenko	RUS	7.4.76	1		Pretoria	23 Mar
		(50)	100th man 5.78, 200th man 5.70, 300th man 5.60						

Best outdoor marks for athletes with lifetime bests indoors

6.00	Gataullin	1	Tokyo	16 Sep 89	5.90	Yegorov	2	WCh	Stuttgart	19 Aug
5.98	Galfione	1	Amiens	23 Jul 99	5.86	Bochkaryov	5	OG	Atlanta	2 Aug
5.93	Ecker	1	Ingolstadt	26 Jul 98						

Ancillary jump: 6.05i Bubka 13 Feb 93

Outdoors on built-up runway

5.90	Pyotr	Bochkaryov	RUS	3.11.67	1	Karlskrona	28 Jun

Exhibition or Market Square competitions

6.00	Jean	Galfione	FRA	9.6.71	1	Besançon	23 May
5.95	Viktor	Chistiakov	AUS	9.2.75	1	Chiari	8 Sep
5.86	Gennadiy	Sukharev	BLR	3.2.65	1	Bisceglie	23 Jul 9
5.86i	Larry	Jessee	USA	31.3.52	1	Newcastle	16 Oct 8

LONG JUMP

Mark	Wind		Name	Nat	Born	Pos	Meet	Venue	Date
8.95 WR	0.3	Mike	Powell	USA	10.11.63	1	WCh	Tokyo	30 Aug 9
8.90A WR	2.0	Bob	Beamon	USA	29.8.46	1	OG	Ciudad de México	18 Oct 6
8.87	-0.2	Carl	Lewis	USA	1.7.61	*	WCh	Tokyo	30 Aug 9
8.86A	1.9	Robert	Emmiyan	ARM	16.2.65	1		Tsakhkadzor	22 May 8
8.79	1.9		Lewis			1	TAC	Indianapolis	19 Jun 8
8.79i	-		Lewis			1		New York	27 Jan 8
8.76	1.0		Lewis			1	USOF	Indianapolis	24 Jul 8
8.76	0.8		Lewis			1	OT	Indianapolis	18 Jul 8
8.75	1.7		Lewis			1	PAm	Indianapolis	16 Aug 8
8.74	1.4	Larry	Myricks ¶	USA	10.3.56	2	OT	Indianapolis	18 Jul 8
8.74A	2.0	Erick	Walder	USA	5.11.71	1		El Paso	2 Apr 9
8.72	-0.2		Lewis			1	OG	Seoul	26 Sep 8
8.71	-0.4		Lewis			1	Pepsi	Los Angeles (Ww)	13 May 8
8.71	0.1		Lewis			1	OT	Los Angeles	19 Jun 8
8.71	1.9	Iván	Pedroso	CUB	17.12.72	1		Salamanca	18 Jul 9
8.70	0.8		Myricks			1	TAC	Houston	17 Jun 8
8.70	0.7		Powell			1		Salamanca	27 Jul 9
8.70	1.6		Pedroso			1	WCh	Göteborg	12 Aug 9
8.68	1.0		Lewis			Q	OG	Barcelona	5 Aug 9
8.68	1.6		Pedroso			1		Lisboa	17 Jun 9
8.67	0.4		Lewis			1	WCh	Roma	5 Sep 8
8.67	-0.7		Lewis			1	OG	Barcelona	6 Aug 9
8.66	0.8		Lewis			*	MSR	Walnut	26 Apr 8
8.66	1.0		Myricks			1		Tokyo	23 Sep 8
8.66	0.9		Powell			1	BNP	Villeneuve d'Ascq	29 Jun 9
8.66A	1.4		Lewis			*		Sestriere	31 Jul 9
8.66	0.3		Pedroso			1		Linz	22 Aug 9
8.65	0.2		Lewis			1	VD	Bruxelles	24 Aug 8
8.65	0.7		Lewis			1	TAC	San José	26 Jun 8
8.65	1.5		Pedroso			1	OD	Jena	3 Jun 0
		(30/7)							
8.63	0.5	Kareem	Streete-Thompson	CAY/USA	30.3.73	1	GP II	Linz	4 Jul 9
8.62	0.7	James	Beckford	JAM	9.1.75	1		Orlando	5 Apr 9
8.60	0.5	Dwight	Phillips	USA	1.10.77	1	GP	Linz	2 Aug 0
		(10)							
8.59i		Miguel	Pate	USA	13.6.79	1	NC	New York	1 Mar 0
8.56i	-	Yago	Lamela	ESP	24.7.77	2	WI	Maebashi	7 Mar 9
8.54	0.9	Lutz	Dombrowski	GDR	25.6.59	1	OG	Moskva	28 Jul 8
8.53	1.2	Jaime	Jefferson	CUB	17.1.62	1	Barr	La Habana	12 May 9

Mark	Wind	Name		Nat	Born	Pos	Meet	Venue	Date
8.52	0.7	Savanté	Stringfellow	USA	6.11.78	1	NC	Stanford	21 Jun 02
8.51	1.7	Roland	McGhee	USA	15.10.71	2		São Paulo	14 May 95
8.50	0.2	Llewellyn	Starks	USA	10.2.67	2		Rhede	7 Jul 91
8.49	2.0	Melvin	Lister	USA	29.8.77	1	SEC	Baton Rouge	13 May 00
8.49	0.6	Jai	Taurima	AUS	26.6.72	2	OG	Sydney	28 Sep 00
8.48	0.8	Joe	Greene	USA	17.2.67	3		São Paulo	14 May 95
		(20)							
8.47	1.9	Kevin	Dilworth	USA	14.2.74	1		Abilene	9 May 96
8.47	0.9	John	Moffitt	USA	12.12.80	2	OG	Athína	26 Aug 04
8.46	1.2	Leonid	Voloshin	RUS	30.3.66	1	NC	Tallinn	5 Jul 88
8.46	1.6	Mike	Conley	USA	5.10.62	2		Springfield	4 May 96
8.46	1.8	Cheikh Tidiane	Touré	SEN	25.1.70	1		Bad Langensalza	15 Jun 97
8.45	2.0	Nenad	Stekic	YUG	7.3.51	1	PO	Montreal	25 Jul 75
8.44	1.7	Eric	Metcalf	USA	23.1.68	1	TAC	Tampa	17 Jun 88
8.44	-0.2	Mohamed Salim	Al-Khuwalidi	KSA	19.6.81	1	Is.Sol	Makkah	13 Apr 05
8.43	0.8	Jason	Grimes	USA	10.9.59	•	TAC	Indianapolis	16 Jun 85
8.43	1.8	Giovanni	Evangelisti	ITA	11.9.61	1		San Giovanni Valdarno	16 May 87
		(30)							
8.43i	-	Stanislav	Tarasenko	RUS	23.7.66	1		Moskva	26 Jan 94
8.43	0.1	Luis	Meliz	CUB	11.8.79	2	OD	Jena	3 Jun 00
8.41	1.5	Craig	Hepburn	BAH	10.12.69	1	NC	Nassau	17 Jun 93
8.41i	-	Kirill	Sosunov	RUS	1.11.75	2	WI	Paris (B)	8 Mar 97
8.40	1.4	Douglas de	Souza	BRA	6.8.72	1		São Paulo	15 Feb 95
8.40	0.4	Robert	Howard	USA	26.11.75	1	SEC	Auburn	17 May 97
8.40	2.0	Gregor	Cankar	SLO	25.1.75	1		Celje	18 May 97
8.40	0.0		Lao Jianfeng	CHN	24.5.75	1	NC	Zhaoqing	28 May 97
8.39	0.8	Dion	Bentley	USA	26.8.71	2	NCAA	New Orleans	3 Jun 93
8.38	0.4	Konstantin	Semykin	RUS	26.5.60	1	Drz	Moskva	17 Aug 84
		(40)							
8.38	1.1		Huang Geng	CHN	10.7.70	1	NC	Taiyuan	18 May 95
8.38i	–	Vitaliy	Shkurlatov	RUS	25.5.79	1		Samara	30 Jan 00
8.37A	0.4	Leroy	Burrell	USA	21.2.67	2	NCAA	Provo	2 Jun 89
8.37	1.5	Bogdan	Tudor	ROM	1.2.70	2		Bad Cannstatt	9 Jul 95
8.37i		Joan Lino	Martínez	ESP	17.1.78	1	EI	Madrid	6 Mar 05
8.37A	1.1	Khotso	Mokoena	RSA	6.3.85	1		Johannesburg	22 Apr 05
8.36	1.0	João Carlos	de Oliveira	BRA	28.5.54	1		Rieti	21 Jul 79
8.36	1.6	Frank	Paschek	GDR	25.6.56	1	OD	Berlin	28 May 80
8.36	1.5		Chen Zunrong	CHN	20.10.62	*		Shizuoka	5 May 92
8.36	1.6	Konstadinos	Koukodímos	GRE	14.9.69	1		Hania	5 Jun 94
8.36A	0.8	Nelson	Ferreira Jr	BRA	1.1.73	*	IbAm	Medellín	10 May 96
8.36	1.2	Carlos	Calado	POR	5.10.75	1		Lisboa	20 Jun 97
		(52)	100th man 8.28, 200th 8.20, 300th 8.14						

Sand layer insufficient: 8.37i Sean Robbins USA 9.10.72 1 Bowling Green 10 Feb 96

Irregular conditions: 8.39 1.2 Joan Lino Martínez CUB 17.1.78 1 La Habana 5 Feb 99

Wind-assisted marks performances to 8.68, performers to 8.38

Mark	Wind	Name		Nat	Born	Pos	Meet	Venue	Date
8.99A	4.4	Mike	Powell	USA	10.11.63	1		Sestriere	21 Jul 92
8.96A	1.2+	Iván	Pedroso	CUB	17.12.72	1		Sestriere	29 Jul 95
8.95A	3.9		Powell			1		Sestriere	31 Jul 94
8.91	2.9	Carl	Lewis	USA	1.7.61	2	WCh	Tokyo	30 Aug 91
8.90	3.7		Powell			1	S&W	Modesto	16 May 92
8.79	3.0		Pedroso			1	Barr	La Habana	21 May 92
8.77	3.9		Lewis			1	Pepsi	Los Angeles (Ww)	18 May 85
8.77	3.4		Lewis			1	MSR	Walnut	26 Apr 87
8.73	4.6		Lewis			Q	TAC	Sacramento	19 Jun 81
8.73	3.2		Lewis			Q	TAC	Indianapolis	17 Jun 83
8.73A	2.6		Powell			1		Sestriere	31 Jul 91
8.73	4.8		Pedroso			1		Madrid	20 Jun 95
8.72	2.2		Lewis			1	NYG	New York	24 May 92
8.72A	3.9		Lewis			2		Sestriere	31 Jul 94
8.70	2.5		Pedroso			1		Padova	16 Jul 95
8.68	4.1		Powell			1	NC	Knoxville	18 Jun 94
8.68	4.9	James	Beckford	JAM	9.1.75	1	JUCO	Odessa, Tx	19 May 95
8.66A	4.0	Joe	Greene	USA	17.2.67	2		Sestriere	21 Jul 92
8.64	3.5	Kareem	Streete-Thompson	CAY/USA	30.3.73	2	NC	Knoxville	18 Jun 94
8.63	3.9	Mike	Conley	USA	5.10.62	2	TAC	Eugene	20 Jun 86
8.57	5.2	Jason	Grimes	USA	10.9.59	1	vFRG,AFR	Durham	27 Jun 82
8.53	4.9	Kevin	Dilworth	USA	14.2.74	1		Fort-de-France	27 Apr 02
8.51	2.3	Irving	Saladino	PAN	23.1.83	1		São Paulo	2 Apr 05
8.49	2.6	Ralph	Boston	USA	9.5.39	1	FOT	Los Angeles	12 Sep 64
8.49	4.5	Stanislav	Tarasenko	RUS	23.7.66	2		Madrid	20 Jun 95

Mark	Wind	Name		Nat	Born	Pos	Meet	Venue	Date
8.48	2.8	Kirill	Sosunov	RUS	1.11.75	1		Oristano	18 Sep 95
8.48	3.4	Peter	Burge	AUS	3.7.74	1		Gold Coast (RB)	10 Sep 00
8.46	3.4	Randy	Williams	USA	23.8.53	1		Eugene	18 May 73
8.46		Vernon	George	USA	6.10.64	1		Houston	21 May 89
8.44		Keith	Talley	USA	28.1.64	Q		Odessa, Tx	16 May 85
8.42		Anthony	Bailous	USA	6.4.65	Q		Odessa, Tx	16 May 85
8.42A	4.5	Milan	Gombala	CZE	29.1.68	3		Sestriere	21 Jul 92
8.41	4.3	Shamil	Abbyasov	KGZ	16.4.57	2	vUSA	Indianapolis	3 Jul 82
8.41	3.3	Andre	Ester	USA	27.4.65	1	TexR	Austin	4 Apr 87
8.41A	3.2	Nelson	Ferreira Jr	BRA	1.1.73	1	IbAm	Medellín	10 May 96
8.41w	2.6	Hussein	Al-Sabee	KSA	14.11.79	1		Carson	22 May 04
8.40	4.3	Henry	Hines	USA	12.2.49	1	CalR	Modesto	27 May 72
8.40	2.1	Anthuan	Maybank	USA	30.12.69	1	DrakeR	Des Moines	24 Apr 93
8.40	3.4	Konstadínos	Koukodímos	GRE	14.9.69	1	ECp I	Valencia	11 Jun 94
8.39	6.2	Gary	Honey	AUS	26.7.59	2		Sacramento	21 Jul 84
8.39	3.5	Edrick	Floreal	CAN	5.10.66	1		Fayetteville	22 Apr 89
8.39	5.7	Yusuf	Alli	NGR	28.7.60	1	CG	Auckland	1 Feb 90
8.39	2.4		Chen Zunrong	CHN	20.10.62	1		Shizuoka	5 May 92
Exhibition: 8.46		Yuriy	Naumkin	RUS	4.11.68	1		Iglesias	6 Sep 96

Best outdoors

8.56 1.3 Lamela 1 Torino 24 Jun 99 8.38 1.1 Sosunov 1 ECp Sankt-Peterburg 27 Jun 98

8.46A 0.0 Pate 1 Cd. de México 3 May 03 and 8.45 1.5 2 NC Stanford 21 Jun 02, 8.48w 5.6 1 Fort Worth 21 Apr 01

Ancillary marks – other marks during series (to 8.66/8.71w)

Mark	Wind	Name	Date	Mark	Wind	Name	Date	Mark	Wind	Name	Date
8.84	1.7	Lewis	30 Aug 91	8.84Aw	3.8	Powell	21 Jul 92	8.73w	2.4	Lewis	18 May 85
8.71	0.6	Lewis	19 Jun 83	8.83w	2.3	Lewis	30 Aug 91	8.73w		Powell	16 May 92
8.68	0.3	Lewis	18 Jul 88	8.80Aw	4.0	Powell	21 Jul 92	8.71Aw		Powell	31 Jul 91
8.68	0.0	Lewis	30 Aug 91	8.78Aw		Powell	21 Jul 92	8.68w	3.7	Lewis	16 Aug 87
8.67	-0.2	Lewis	5 Sep 87	8.75w	2.1	Lewis	16 Aug 87	8.68w	4.1	Lewis	16 Aug 87
8.66		Lewis	26 Apr 87	8.75A	3.4	Powell	21 Jul 92				

TRIPLE JUMP

Mark	Wind	Name		Nat	Born	Pos	Meet	Venue	Date
18.29 WR	1.3	Jonathan	Edwards	GBR	10.5.66	1	WCh	Göteborg	7 Aug 95
18.09	-0.4	Kenny	Harrison	USA	13.2.65	1	OG	Atlanta	27 Jul 96
18.01	0.4		Edwards			1	Bisl	Oslo	9 Jul 98
18.00	1.3		Edwards			1	McD	London (CP)	27 Aug 95
17.99	0.5		Edwards			1	EC	Budapest	23 Aug 98
17.98 WR	1.8		Edwards			1		Salamanca	18 Jul 95
17.97 WR	1.5	Willie	Banks	USA	11.3.56	1	TAC	Indianapolis	16 Jun 85
17.93	1.6		Harrison			1	DNG	Stockholm	2 Jul 90
17.92	1.6	Khristo	Markov	BUL	27.1.65	1	WCh	Roma	31 Aug 87
17.92	1.9	James	Beckford	JAM	9.1.75	1	JUCO	Odessa, Tex	20 May 95
17.92	0.7		Edwards			1	WCh	Edmonton	6 Aug 01
17.90	1.0	Vladimir	Inozemtsev	UKR	25.5.64	1	GPB	Bratislava	20 Jun 90
17.89A WR	0.0	João Carlos	de Oliveira	BRA	28.5.54	1	PAm	Ciudad de México	15 Oct 75
17.88	0.9		Edwards			2	OG	Atlanta	27 Jul 96
17.87	1.7	Mike	Conley	USA	5.10.62	1	TAC	San José	27 Jun 87
17.86	1.3	Charles	Simpkins	USA	19.10.63	1	WUG	Kobe	2 Sep 85
17.86	0.3		Conley			1	WCh	Stuttgart	16 Aug 93
17.86	0.7		Edwards			1	CG	Manchester	28 Jul 02
17.85	0.9	Yoelbi	Quesada (10)	CUB	4.8.73	1	WCh	Athína	8 Aug 97
17.84	0.7		Conley			1		Bad Cannstatt	4 Jul 93
17.83i	-	Aliecer	Urrutia	CUB	22.9.74	1		Sindelfingen	1 Mar 97
17.83i		Christian	Olsson	SWE	25.1.80	1	WI	Budapest	7 Mar 04
17.82	1.6		Edwards			1	WG	Helsinki	25 Jun 96
17.81	2.0		Markov			1	Nar	Sofia	31 May 87
17.81	1.0	Marian	Oprea	ROM	6.6.82	1	Athl	Lausanne	5 Jul 05
17.80	0.6		Markov			1	BGP	Budapest	11 Aug 86
17.80i			Olsson			1		Göteborg	5 Mar 02
17.79	-0.8		Harrison			1	OD	Berlin	4 Jul 90
17.79	-0.7		Edwards			1	WK	Zürich	14 Aug 96
17.79	1.4		Olsson			1	OG	Athína	22 Aug 04
		(30/13)							
17.78	1.0	Nikolay	Musiyenko	UKR	16.12.59	1	Znam	Leningrad	7 Jun 86
17.78	0.6	Lázaro	Betancourt ¶	CUB	18.3.63	1	Barr	La Habana	15 Jun 86
17.78	0.8	Melvin	Lister	USA	29.8.77	1	NC/OT	Sacramento	17 Jul 04
17.77	1.0	Aleksandr	Kovalenko	RUS	8.5.63	1	NC	Bryansk	18 Jul 87
17.77i	-	Leonid	Voloshin	RUS	30.3.66	1		Grenoble	6 Feb 94
17.75	0.3	Oleg	Protsenko	RUS	11.8.63	1	Znam	Moskva	10 Jun 90
17.73	1.0	Jadel	Gregório	BRA	16.9.80	1	NC	São Paulo	19 Jun 05
		(20)							

Mark	Wind	Name		Nat	Born	Pos	Meet	Venue	Date
17.72i		Brian	Wellman	BER	8.9.67	1	WI	Barcelona	12 Mar 95
17.69	1.5	Igor	Lapshin	BLR	8.8.63	1		Stayki	31 Jul 88
17.68	1.2	Phillips	Idowu	GBR	30.12.78	2	CG	Manchester	28 Jul 02
17.66	1.7	Ralf	Jaros	GER	13.12.65	1	ECp	Frankfurt-am-Main	30 Jun 91
17.68	0.4	Danila	Burkenya	RUS	20.7.78	1	NC	Tula	31 Jul 04
17.65	1.0	Aleksandr	Yakovlev	UKR	8.9.57	1	Znam	Moskva	6 Jun 87
17.65	0.8	Denis	Kapustin	RUS	5.10.70	2	Bisl	Oslo	9 Jul 98
17.64	1.4	Nathan	Douglas	GBR	4.12.82	1	NC	Manchester (SC)	10 Jul 05
17.63	0.9	Kenta	Bell	USA	16.3.77	1c2	MSR	Walnut	21 Apr 02
17.63	-0.4	Walter	Davis	USA	2.7.79	2	NC/OT	Sacramento	17 Jul 04
		(30)							
17.62i	-	Yoel	García	CUB	25.11.73	2		Sindelfingen	1 Mar 97
17.60	0.6	Vladimir	Plekhanov	RUS	11.4.58	2	NC	Leningrad	4 Aug 85
17.60	1.9	Fabrizio	Donato	ITA	14.8.76	1		Milano	7 Jun 00
17.59i	-	Pierre	Camara	FRA	10.9.65	1	WI	Toronto	13 Mar 93
17.59	0.3	Vasiliy	Sokov	RUS	7.4.68	1	NC	Moskva	19 Jun 93
17.59	0.8	Charles	Friedek	GER	26.8.71	1		Hamburg	23 Jul 97
17.58	1.5	Oleg	Sakirkin	KZK	23.1.66	2	NC	Gorkiy	23 Jul 89
17.57A	0.0	Keith	Connor	GBR	16.9.57	1	NCAA	Provo	5 Jun 82
17.57	0.2	Dmitriy	Valyukevich	BLR	31.5.81	1	EU23	Bydgoszcz	19 Jul 03
		Valukevich of SVK from 2005							
17.56	1.9	Maris	Bruziks	LAT	25.8.62	1		Riga	3 Sep 88
		(40)							
17.55	0.3	Vasiliy	Grishchenkov	RUS	23.1.58	1	Spart	Moskva	19 Jun 83
17.55	0.9	Serge	Hélan	FRA	24.2.64	2	EC	Helsinki	13 Aug 94
17.53	1.0	Aleksandr	Beskrovniy	RUS	5.4.60	2	Spart	Moskva	19 Jun 83
17.53	1.6	Zdzislaw	Hoffmann	POL	27.8.59	1		Madrid	4 Jun 85
17.53	1.0	Gennadiy	Valyukevich	BLR	1.6.58	1		Erfurt	1 Jun 86
17.53	1.6	Al	Joyner	USA	19.1.60	Q	TAC	San José	26 Jun 87
17.53	0.9	Milán	Mikulás	CZE	1.4.63	1	NC	Praha	17 Jul 88
17.53	1.9	Oleg	Denishchik	BLR	10.11.69	2	NC	Kiyev	12 Jul 91
17.53	0.5	Aleksandr	Glavatskiy	BLR	2.5.70	2	WK	Zürich	12 Aug 98
17.53	-0.4	Yoandri	Betanzos	CUB	15.2.82	Q	OG	Athína	20 Aug 04
		(50)	100th man 17.30, 200th man 17.06						

Wind-assisted marks – performances to 17.79, performers to 17.54

Mark	Wind	Name		Nat	Born	Pos	Meet	Venue	Date
18.43	2.4	Jonathan	Edwards	GBR	10.5.66	1	ECp	Villeneuve d'Ascq	25 Jun 95
18.20	5.2	Willie	Banks	USA	11.3.56	1	OT	Indianapolis	16 Jul 88
18.17	2.1	Mike	Conley	USA	5.10.62	1	OG	Barcelona	3 Aug 92
18.08	2.5		Edwards			1	BUPA	Sheffield	23 Jul 95
18.03	2.9		Edwards			1	GhG	Gateshead	2 Jul 95
18.01	3.7		Harrison			1	NC	Atlanta	15 Jun 96
17.97	7.5	Yoelbi	Quesada	CUB	4.8.73	1		Madrid	20 Jun 95
17.93	5.2	Charles	Simpkins	USA	19.10.63	2	OT	Indianapolis	16 Jul 88
17.92	3.4	Christian	Olsson	SWE	25.1.80	1	GP	Gateshead	13 Jul 03
17.91	3.2		Simpkins			1	TAC	Eugene	21 Jun 86
17.86	3.9		Simpkins			1	OT	New Orleans	21 Jun 92
17.86	5.7	Denis	Kapustin	RUS	5.10.70	1		Sevilla	5 Jun 94
17.84	2.3		Conley			2	TAC	Eugene	21 Jun 86
17.82	3.6		Banks			1	Jen	San José	31 May 86
17.81	4.6	Keith	Connor	GBR	16.9.57	1	CG	Brisbane	9 Oct 82
17.79	3.3		Edwards			1	ECp	Madrid	2 Jun 96
17.76A	2.2	Kenta	Bell	USA	16.3.77	1		El Paso	10 Apr 04
17.75		Gennadiy	Valyukevich	BLR	1.6.58	1		Uzhgorod	27 Apr 86
17.75	7.1	Brian	Wellman	BER	8.9.67	2		Madrid	20 Jun 95
17.73	4.1	Vasiliy	Sokov	RUS	7.4.68	1		Riga	3 Jun 89
17.63	4.3	Robert	Cannon	USA	9.7.58	3	OT	Indianapolis	16 Jul 88
17.59	2.1	Jerome	Romain	DMN	12.6.71	3	WCh	Göteborg	7 Aug 95
17.58	5.2	Al	Joyner	USA	19.1.60	5	OT	Indianapolis	16 Jul 88
17.56	3.7	Ron	Livers	USA	20.7.55	1	AAU	Walnut	17 Jun 79
17.55	3.6	Zdzislaw	Hoffmann	POL	27.8.59	1	Kuso	Warszawa	9 Jun 84
17.54	3.2	Ken	Lorraway	AUS	6.2.56	2	CG	Brisbane	9 Oct 82
17.54	3.4	Rodrigo	Mendes	BRA	21.6.68	Q	NCAA	Sacramento	10 Jun 05
17.53	4.8	Ray	Kimble	USA	19.4.53	7	OT	Indianapolis	16 Jul 88

Best outdoor marks for athletes with indoor bests

Mark	Wind	Name	Pos	Meet	Venue	Date	Mark	Wind	Name	Pos	Meet	Venue	Date
17.79	1.4	Olsson	1	OG	Athína	22 Aug 04	17.70	1.7	Urrutia	1	GP II	Sevilla	6 Jun 96
17.75	1.0	Voloshin	2	WCh	Tokyo	26 Aug 91	17.62A		Wellman	1		El Paso	15 Apr 95

Ancillary marks – other marks during series (to 17.78/17.84w)

Mark	Wind	Name	Date	Mark	Wind	Name	Date	Mark	Wind	Name	Date
18.16 WR	1.3	Edwards	7 Aug 95	18.39	3.7	Edwards	25 Jun 95	17.90	2.5	Edwards	25 Jun 95
17.99	0.1	Harrison	27 Jul 96	18.06	4.9	Banks	16 Jul 88	17.84	2.1	Edwards	23 Aug 98

Mark	Wind	Name		Nat	Born	Pos	Meet	Venue	Date

SHOT

Mark	Wind	Name		Nat	Born	Pos	Meet	Venue	Date
23.12	WR	Randy	Barnes ¶	USA	16.6.66	1		Los Angeles (Ww)	20 May 90
23.10			Barnes			1	Jen	San José	26 May 90
23.06	WR	Ulf	Timmermann	GDR	1.11.62	1		Hania	22 May 88
22.91	WR	Alessandro	Andrei	ITA	3.1.59	1		Viareggio	12 Aug 87
22.86		Brian	Oldfield	USA	1.6.45	1	ITA	El Paso	10 May 75
22.75		Werner	Günthör	SUI	1.6.61	1		Bern	23 Aug 88
22.67		Kevin	Toth	USA	29.12.67	1	Kans R	Lawrence	19 Apr 03
22.66i			Barnes			1	Sunkist	Los Angeles	20 Jan 89
22.64	WR	Udo	Beyer	GDR	9.8.55	1		Berlin	20 Aug 86
22.62	WR		Timmermann			1		Berlin	22 Sep 85
22.61			Timmermann			1		Potsdam	8 Sep 88
22.60			Timmermann			1	vURS	Tallinn	21 Jun 86
22.56			Timmermann			1		Berlin	13 Sep 88
22.55i			Timmermann			1	NC	Senftenberg	11 Feb 89
22.54		Christian	Cantwell	USA	30.9.80	1	GP II	Gresham	5 Jun 04
22.52		John	Brenner	USA	4.1.61	1	MSR	Walnut	26 Apr 87
22.51			Timmermann			1		Erfurt	1 Jun 86
22.51		Adam	Nelson	USA	7.7.75	1		Gresham	18 May 02
22.47			Timmermann			1		Dresden	17 Aug 86
22.47			Günthör			1	WG	Helsinki	2 Jul 87
22.47			Timmermann			1	OG	Seoul	23 Sep 88
22.45			Oldfield			1	ITA	El Paso	22 May 76
22.43			Günthör			1	v3-N	Lüdenscheid	18 Jun 87
22.42			Barnes			1	WK	Zürich	17 Aug 88
22.40			Barnes			1		Rüdlingen	13 Jul 96
22.39			Barnes			2	OG	Seoul	23 Sep 88
22.36	@		Timmermann			1		Athína	16 May 88
22.35			Cantwell			1		Carson	22 May 04
22.31			Beyer			1	NC	Potsdam	20 Aug 87
22.28			Oldfield			1	ITA	Edinburgh	18 Jun 75
22.28			Barnes			1	MSR	Walnut	22 Apr 90
		(31/10)							
22.24		Sergey	Smirnov	RUS	17.9.60	2	vGDR	Tallinn	21 Jun 86
22.20		John	Godina	USA	31.5.72	1		Carson	22 May 05
22.10		Sergey	Gavryushin	RUS	27.6.59	1		Tbilisi	31 Aug 86
22.09		Sergey	Kasnauskas	BLR	20.4.61	1		Stayki	23 Aug 84
22.09i		Mika	Halvari	FIN	13.2.70	1		Tampere	7 Feb 00
22.02i		George	Woods	USA	11.2.43	1	LAT	Inglewood	8 Feb 74
22.02		Dave	Laut	USA	21.12.56	1		Koblenz	25 Aug 82
22.00	WR	Aleksandr	Baryshnikov	RUS	11.11.48	1	vFRA	Colombes	10 Jul 76
21.98		Gregg	Tafralis ¶	USA	9.4.58	1		Los Gatos	13 Jun 92
21.97		Janus	Robberts	RSA	10.3.79	1	NCAA	Eugene	2 Jun 01
		(20)							
21.96		Mikhail	Kostin	RUS	10.5.59	1		Vitebsk	20 Jul 86
21.93		Remigius	Machura ¶	CZE	3.7.60	1		Praha	23 Aug 87
21.92		Carl	Myerscough ¶	GBR	21.10.79	1	NCAA	Sacramento	13 Jun 03
21.87		C.J.	Hunter ¶	USA	14.12.68	2	NC	Sacramento	15 Jul 00
21.85	WR	Terry	Albritton	USA	14.1.55	1		Honolulu	21 Feb 76
21.83i		Aleksandr	Bagach ¶	UKR	21.11.66	1		Brovary	21 Feb 99
21.82	WR	Al	Feuerbach	USA	14.1.48	1		San José	5 May 73
21.82		Andy	Bloom	USA	11.8.73	1	GPF	Doha	5 Oct 00
21.81		Yuriy	Belonog	UKR	9.3.74	1	NC	Kiev	3 Jul 03
21.78	WR	Randy	Matson	USA	5.3.45	1		College Station	22 Apr 67
		(30)							
21.77i		Mike	Stulce ¶	USA	21.7.69	1	v GBR	Birmingham	13 Feb 93
21.77		Dragan	Peric	YUG	8.5.64	1		Bar	25 Apr 98
21.76		Mike	Carter	USA	29.10.60	2	NCAA	Eugene	2 Jun 84
21.74		Janis	Bojars	LAT	12.5.56	1		Riga	14 Jul 84
21.74i		Reese	Hoffa	USA	8.10.77	2	NC	Boston (R)	26 Feb 05
21.73		Augie	Wolf ¶	USA	3.9.61	1		Leverkusen	12 Apr 84
21.69		Reijo	Ståhlberg	FIN	21.9.52	1	WCR	Fresno	5 May 79
21.69		Andrey	Mikhnevich ¶	BLR	12.7.76	1	WCh	Saint-Denis	23 Aug 03
21.68		Geoff	Capes	GBR	23.8.49	1	4-N	Cwmbrân	18 May 80
21.68		Edward	Sarul	POL	16.11.58	1		Sopot	31 Jul 83
		(40)							
21.67		Hartmut	Briesenick	GDR	17.3.49	1		Potsdam	1 Sep 73
21.63i		Joachim	Olsen	DEN	31.5.77	1		Tallinn	25 Feb 04
21.61		Kevin	Akins	USA	27.1.60	1	S&W	Modesto	14 May 83

Mark	Wind	Name		Nat	Born	Pos	Meet	Venue	Date
21.60		Jim	Doehring ¶	USA	27.1.62	2		Los Gatos	13 Jun 92
21.58		Vladimir	Kiselyov	UKR	1.1.57	3	Drz	Moskva	17 Aug 84
21.53		Yevgeniy	Mironov ¶	RUS	1.11.49	1	NC	Kiyev	24 Jun 76
21.51		Ralf	Reichenbach	FRG	31.7.50	1	ISTAF	Berlin	8 Aug 80
21.47		Brent	Noon ¶	USA	29.8.71	1	SEC	Tuscaloosa	21 May 95
21.47i		Oliver-Sven	Buder	GER	23.6.66	1	EI	Valencia	28 Feb 98
21.47		Manuel	Martínez	ESP	7.12.74	2		Salamanca	10 Jul 02
		(50)	100th man 20.98, 200th 20.52	@ competitive meeting but unsanctioned by GDR federation					

Not recognised by GDR authorities

Mark	Wind	Name		Nat	Born	Pos	Meet	Venue	Date
22.11		Rolf	Oesterreich	GDR	24.8.49	1		Zschopau	12 Sep 76

Drugs disqualification

Mark	Wind	Name		Nat	Born	Pos	Meet	Venue	Date
22.84			Barnes			1		Malmö	7 Aug 90
21.82		Mike	Stulce ¶	USA	21.7.69	1		Brenham	9 May 90

Best outdoor marks for athletes with lifetime bests indoors

Mark	Name	Pos	Meet	Venue	Date	Mark	Name	Pos	Meet	Venue	Date
21.70	Stulce ¶	1	OG	Barcelona	31 Jul 92	21.67	Hoffa	2		Carson	22 May 04
21.63	Woods	2	CalR	Modesto	22 May 76	21.57	Olsen	2	NCAA	Baton Rouge	1 Jun 02
21.50	Halvari	1		Hämeenkyrö	9 Jul 95	21.47	Bagach ¶	1	Veniz	Haniá	31 May 97

Ancillary marks – other marks during series (to 22.42)

Mark	Name	Date	Mark	Name	Date	Mark	Name	Date
22.84 WR	Andrei	12 Aug 87	22.72 WR	Andrei	12 Aug 87	22.55	Barnes	20 May 90
22.76	Barnes	20 May 90	22.70	Günthör	23 Aug 88	22.45	Timmermann	22 May 88
22.74	Andrei	12 Aug 87	22.58	Beyer	20 Aug 86	22.44	Barnes	20 May 90

DISCUS

Mark	Wind	Name		Nat	Born	Pos	Meet	Venue	Date
74.08	WR	Jürgen	Schult	GDR	11.5.60	1		Neubrandenburg	6 Jun 86
73.88		Virgilijus	Alekna	LTU	13.2.72	1	NC	Kaunas	3 Aug 00
71.86	WR	Yuriy	Dumchev	RUS	5.8.58	1		Moskva	29 May 83
71.70		Róbert	Fazekas ¶	HUN	18.8.75	1		Szombathely	14 Jul 02
71.50		Lars	Riedel	GER	28.6.67	1		Wiesbaden	3 May 97
71.32		Ben	Plucknett ¶	USA	13.4.54	1	Pre	Eugene	4 Jun 83
71.26		John	Powell	USA	25.6.47	1	TAC	San José	9 Jun 84
71.26		Rickard	Bruch	SWE	2.7.46	1		Malmö	15 Nov 84
71.26		Imrich	Bugár	CZE	14.4.55	1	Jen	San José	25 May 85
71.25			Fazekas			1	WCp	Madrid (C)	21 Sep 02
71.18		Art	Burns (10)	USA	19.7.54	1		San José	19 Jul 83
71.16	WR	Wolfgang	Schmidt	GDR	16.1.54	1		Berlin	9 Aug 78
71.14			Plucknett			1		Berkeley	12 Jun 83
71.14		Anthony	Washington	USA	16.1.66	1eA		Salinas	22 May 96
71.12			Alekna			1	WK	Zürich	11 Aug 00
71.06		Luis M.	Delís ¶	CUB	6.12.57	1	Barr	La Habana	21 May 83
71.06			Riedel			1	WK	Zürich	14 Aug 96
71.00			Bruch			1		Malmö	14 Oct 84
70.99			Alekna			1		Stellenbosch	30 Mar 01
70.98		Mac	Wilkins	USA	15.11.50	1	WG	Helsinki	9 Jul 80
70.98			Burns			1	Pre	Eugene	21 Jul 84
70.97			Alekna			1		Réthimno	23 Jun 04
70.92			Schmidt	FRG		1		Norden	9 Sep 89
70.86	WR		Wilkins			1		San José	1 May 76
70.83			Fazekas			2		Réthimno	23 Jun 04
70.82			Plucknett			1		Salinas	1 Jun 83
70.78			Fazekas			1		Budapest	10 May 03
70.72			Bugár			1	vHUN,AUT	Schwechat	18 Jun 83
70.67			Alekna			1	GP	Madrid	16 Jul 05
70.66			Wilkins			1	AAU	Walnut	16 Jun 79
		(30/14)	62 performances over 70m						
70.54		Dmitriy	Shevchenko ¶	RUS	13.5.68	1		Krasnodar	7 May 02
70.38	WRU	Jay	Silvester	USA	27.8.37	1		Lancaster	16 May 71
70.32		Frantz	Kruger	RSA	22.5.75	1		Salon-de-Provence	26 May 02
70.10		Gerd	Kanter	EST	6.5.79	1		Chula Vista	27 Apr 05
70.06		Romas	Ubartas ¶	LIT	26.5.60	1		Smalininkay	8 May 88
70.00		Juan	Martínez ¶	CUB	17.5.58	2	Barr	La Habana	21 May 83
		(20)							
69.91		John	Godina	USA	31.5.72	1		Salinas	19 May 98
69.70		Géjza	Valent	CZE	3.10.53	2		Nitra	26 Aug 84
69.62		Knut	Hjeltnes ¶	NOR	8.12.51	2	Jen	San José	25 May 85
69.62		Timo	Tompuri	FIN	9.6.69	1		Helsingborg	8 Jul 01
69.46		Al	Oerter	USA	19.9.36	1	TFA	Wichita	31 May 80
69.44		Georgiy	Kolnootchenko	BLR	7.5.59	1	vUSA	Indianapolis	3 Jul 82
69.40		Art	Swarts ¶	USA	14.2.45	1		Scotch Plains	8 Dec 79
69.36		Mike	Buncic	USA	25.7.62	1		Fresno	6 Apr 91

Mark	Wind	Name		Nat	Born	Pos	Meet	Venue	Date
69.28		Vladimir	Dubrovshchik	BLR	7.1.72	1	NC-w	Stayki	3 Jun
69.26		Ken	Stadel	USA	19.2.52	2	AAU	Walnut	16 Jun 7
		(30)							
68.94		Adam	Setliff	USA	15.12.69	1		Atascadero	25 Jul 0
68.93		Zoltán	Kövágó	HUN	10.4.79	3	WK	Zürich	6 Aug
68.90		Jean-Claude	Retel	FRA	11.2.68	1		Salon-de-Provence	17 Jul
68.88		Vladimir	Zinchenko	UKR	25.7.59	1		Dnepropetrovsk	16 Jul 8
68.64		Dmitriy	Kovtsun ¶	UKR	29.9.55	1		Riga	6 Jul 8
68.58		Attila	Horváth	HUN	28.7.67	1		Budapest	24 Jun 9
68.52		Igor	Duginyets	UKR	20.5.56	1	NC	Kiyev	21 Aug 8
68.50		Armin	Lemme	GDR	28.10.55	1	vUSA	Karl-Marx-Stadt	10 Jul 8
68.48	WR	John	van Reenen	RSA	26.3.47	1		Stellenbosch	14 Mar 7
68.48		Aleksander	Tammert	EST	2.2.73	1		Arlington	27 Mar
		(40)							
68.44		Vaclovas	Kidykas	LIT	17.10.61	1		Sochi	1 Jun 8
68.30		Stefan	Fernholm	SWE	2.7.59	1		Västerås	15 Jul
68.12		Markku	Tuokko ¶	FIN	24.6.51	1	WCR	Fresno	5 May 7
68.12		Iosif	Nagy	ROM	20.11.46	2		Zaragoza	22 May 8
68.12		Erik	de Bruin ¶	NED	25.5.63	1		Sneek	1 Apr 9
68.08		Hein-Direck	Neu ¶	FRG	13.2.44	1		Bremerhaven	27 May 7
68.00		Svein Inge	Valvik	NOR	20.9.56	1		Juarez	31 May 8
68.00		Mario	Pestano	ESP	8.4.78	1		Zaragoza	8 Jun 0
67.90		Vitaliy	Sidorov	UKR	23.3.70	1		Kiev	3 May 9
67.89		Nick	Sweeney	IRL	26.3.68	1		Helsingborg	4 Sep 9
		(50)	100th man 66.58, 200th man 64.82						

Subsequent to or at drugs disqualification ! recognised as US record

Mark	Wind	Name		Nat	Born	Pos	Meet	Venue	Date
72.34!		Ben	Plucknett ¶	USA	13.4.54	1	DNG	Stockholm	7 Jul 8
71.20			Plucknett			1	CalR	Modesto	16 May 8
70.84		Kamy	Keshmiri ¶	USA	23.1.69	1		Salinas	27 May 9

Sloping ground

Mark	Wind	Name		Nat	Born	Pos	Meet	Venue	Date
72.08		John	Powell	USA	25.6.47	1		Klagshamn	11 Sep 8
69.80		Stefan	Fernholm	SWE	2.7.59	1		Klagshamn	13 Aug 8
69.44		Adam	Setliff	USA	15.12.69	1		La Jolla	21 Jul 0
68.46		Andy	Bloom	USA	11.8.73	2cA		La Jolla	25 Mar 0

Ancillary marks – other marks during series (to 70.70)

72.35 Alekna 3 Aug 00 71.08 Plucknett 4 Jun 83 70.84 Riedel 3 May 9

HAMMER

Mark	Wind	Name		Nat	Born	Pos	Meet	Venue	Date
86.74	WR	Yuriy	Sedykh	RUS	11.6.55	1	EC	Stuttgart	30 Aug 8
86.73		Ivan	Tikhon	BLR	24.7.76	1	NC	Brest	3 Jul 0
86.66	WR		Sedykh			1	vGDR	Tallinn	22 Jun 8
86.34	WR		Sedykh			1		Cork	3 Jul 8
86.04		Sergey	Litvinov	RUS	23.1.58	1	OD	Dresden	3 Jul 8
85.74			Litvinov			2	EC	Stuttgart	30 Aug 8
85.68			Sedykh			1	BGP	Budapest	11 Aug 8
85.60			Sedykh			1	PTG	London (CP)	13 Jul 8
85.60			Sedykh			1	Drz	Moskva	17 Aug 8
85.20			Litvinov			2		Cork	3 Jul 8
85.14			Litvinov			1	PTG	London	11 Jul 8
85.14			Sedykh			1	Kuts	Moskva	4 Sep 8
85.02			Sedykh			1	BGP	Budapest	20 Aug 8
84.92			Sedykh			2	OD	Dresden	3 Jul 8
84.90		Vadim	Devyatovskiy ¶	BLR	20.3.77	1		Staiki	21 Jul 0
84.88			Litvinov			1	GP-GG	Roma	10 Sep 8
84.86		Koji	Murofushi	JPN	8.10.74	1	Odlozil	Praha	29 Jun 0
84.80			Litvinov			1	OG	Seoul	26 Sep 8
84.80			Tikhon			1	WCh	Helsinki	8 Aug 0
84.72			Sedykh			1	GWG	Moskva	9 Jul 8
84.64			Litvinov			2	GWG	Moskva	9 Jul 8
84.62		Igor	Astapkovich	BLR	4.1.63	1	Expo	Sevilla	6 Jun 9
84.60			Sedykh			1	8-N	Tokyo	14 Sep 8
84.58			Sedykh			1	Znam	Leningrad	8 Jun 8
84.48		Igor	Nikulin	RUS	14.8.60	1	Athl	Lausanne	12 Jul 9
84.46			Sedykh			1		Vladivostok	14 Sep 8
84.46			Tikhon			1		Minsk	7 May 0
84.40		Jüri	Tamm	EST	5.2.57	1		Banská Bystrica	9 Sep 8
84.36			Litvinov			2	vGDR	Tallinn	22 Jun 8
84.32			Tikhon			1		Staiki	8 Aug 0
		(30/8)							
84.19		Adrián	Annus ¶	HUN	28.6.73	1		Szombathely	10 Aug 0

Mark Wind		Name	Nat	Born	Pos	Meet	Venue	Date
83.68	Tibor	Gécsek ¶	HUN	22.9.64	1		Zalaegerszeg	19 Sep 98
	(10)							
83.46	Andrey	Abduvaliyev TJK/	UZB	30.6.66	1		Adler	26 May 90
83.43	Aleksey	Zagornyy	RUS	31.5.78	1		Adler	10 Feb 02
83.40 @	Ralf	Haber	GDR	18.8.62	1		Athína	16 May 88
	82.54				1		Potsdam	9 Sep 88
83.38	Szymon	Ziólkowski	POL	1.7.76	1	WCh	Edmonton	5 Aug 01
83.30	Olli-Pekka	Karjalainen	FIN	7.3.80	1		Lahti	14 Jul 04
83.04	Heinz	Weis	GER	14.7.63	1	NC	Frankfurt	29 Jun 97
83.00	Balázs	Kiss	HUN	21.3.72	1	GP II	Saint-Denis	4 Jun 98
82.78	Karsten	Kobs	GER	16.9.71	1		Dortmund	26 Jun 99
82.64	Günther	Rodehau	GDR	6.7.59	1		Dresden	3 Aug 85
82.62	Sergey	Kirmasov ¶	RUS	25.3.70	1		Bryansk	30 May 98
	(20)	@ competitive meeting but unsanctioned by GDR federation						
82.62	Andrey	Skvaruk	UKR	9.3.67	1		Koncha-Zaspa	27 Apr 02
82.54	Vasiliy	Sidorenko	RUS	1.5.61	1		Krasnodar	13 May 92
82.52	Lance	Deal	USA	21.8.61	1	GPF	Milano	7 Sep 96
82.40	Plamen	Minev	BUL	28.4.65	1	NM	Plovdiv	1 Jun 91
82.38	Gilles	Dupray	FRA	2.1.70	1		Chelles	21 Jun 00
82.28	Ilya	Konovalov	RUS	4.3.71	1	NC	Tula	10 Aug 03
82.24	Benjaminas	Viluckis	LIT	20.3.61	1		Klaipeda	24 Aug 86
82.24	Vyacheslav	Korovin	RUS	8.9.62	1		Chelyabinsk	20 Jun 87
82.23	Vladislav	Piskunov ¶	UKR	7.6.78	2		Koncha-Zaspa	27 Apr 02
82.22	Holger	Klose	GER	5.12.72	1		Dortmund	2 May 98
	(30)							
82.16	Vitaliy	Alisevich	BLR	15.6.67	1		Parnu	13 Jul 88
82.08	Ivan	Tanev	BUL	1.5.57	1	NC	Sofia	3 Sep 88
82.00	Sergey	Alay	BLR	11.6.65	1		Stayki	12 May 92
81.88	Jud	Logan ¶	USA	19.7.59	1		State College	22 Apr 88
81.81	Libor	Charfreitag	SVK	11.9.77	3	Odlozil	Praha	29 Jun 03
81.79	Christophe	Épalle	FRA	23.1.69	1		Clermont-Ferrand	30 Jun 00
81.78	Christoph	Sahner	FRG	23.9.63	1		Wemmetsweiler	11 Sep 88
81.70	Aleksandr	Seleznyov	RUS	25.1.63	2		Sochi	22 May 93
81.66	Aleksandr	Krykun	UKR	1.3.68	1		Kiev	29 May 04
81.64	Enrico	Sgrulletti	ITA	24.4.65	1		Ostia	9 Mar 97
	(40)							
81.56	Sergey	Gavrilov	RUS	22.5.70	1	Army	Rostov	16 Jun 96
81.56	Zsolt	Németh	HUN	9.11.71	1		Veszprém	14 Aug 99
81.52	Juha	Tiainen	FIN	5.12.55	1		Tampere	11 Jun 84
81.45	Esref	Apak	TUR	3.1.82	1	Cezmi	Istanbul	4 Jun 05
81.44	Yuriy	Tarasyuk	BLR	11.4.57	1		Minsk	10 Aug 84
81.35	Wojciech	Kondratowicz	POL	18.4.80	1		Bydgoscz	13 Jul 03
81.33	Miloslav	Konopka	SVK	23.1.79	1		Banská Bystrica	29 May 04
81.32	Klaus	Ploghaus	FRG	31.1.56	1		Paderborn	25 May 86
81.28	Vladimir	Maska	CZE	6.2.73	1		Pacov	25 Sep 99
81.26	Vadim	Khersontsev	RUS	8.7.74	1		Bryansk	3 Jul 01
	(50)	100th man 79.36, 200th man 76.80						

Ancillary marks – other marks during series (to 84.85)

86.68	Sedykh	30 Aug 86	85.52	Sedykh	13 Jul 84	85.24	Sedykh	11 Aug 86
86.62	Sedykh	30 Aug 86	85.46	Sedykh	30 Aug 86	85.20	Sedykh	3 Jul 84
86.00	Sedykh	3 Jul 84	85.42	Sedykh	11 Aug 86	85.04	Sedykh	13 Jul 84
86.00	Sedykh	22 Jun 86	85.42	Litvinov	3 Jul 86	84.98	Sedykh	4 Sep 88
85.82	Sedykh	22 Jun 86	85.28	Sedykh	30 Aug 86	84.92	Litvinov	3 Jul 86
			85.26	Sedykh	11 Aug 86			

JAVELIN

Mark		Name	Nat	Born	Pos	Meet	Venue	Date
98.48 WR	Jan	Zelezny	CZE	16.6.66	1		Jena	25 May 96
95.66 WR		Zelezny			1	McD	Sheffield	29 Aug 93
95.54A WR		Zelezny			1		Pietersburg	6 Apr 93
94.64		Zelezny			1	GS	Ostrava	31 May 96
94.02		Zelezny			1		Stellenbosch	26 Mar 97
93.09	Aki	Parviainen	FIN	26.10.74	1		Kuortane	26 Jun 99
92.80		Zelezny			1	WCh	Edmonton	12 Aug 01
92.61	Sergey	Makarov	RUS	19.3.73	1		Sheffield	30 Jun 02
92.60	Raymond	Hecht	GER	11.11.68	1	Bisl	Oslo	21 Jul 95
92.42		Zelezny			1	GS	Ostrava	28 May 97
92.41		Parviainen			1	ECp-1A	Vaasa	24 Jun 01
92.28		Zelezny			1	GPF	Monaco	9 Sep 95
92.28		Hecht			1	WK	Zürich	14 Aug 96
92.12		Zelezny			1	McD	London (CP)	27 Aug 95
92.12		Zelezny			1	TOTO	Tokyo	15 Sep 95

Mark	Wind	Name		Nat	Born	Pos	Meet	Venue	Date
91.82			Zelezny			1	McD	Sheffield	4 Sep 9
91.69		Kostadínos	Gatsioúdis	GRE	17.12.73	1		Kuortane	24 Jun 0
91.68			Zelezny			1	GP	Gateshead	1 Jul 9
91.53		Tero	Pitkämaki	FIN	19.12.82	1		Kuortane	26 Jun 0
91.50			Zelezny			1	Kuso	Lublin	4 Jun 9
91.50A			Zelezny			1		Pretoria	8 Apr 9
91.50			Hecht			1		Gengenbach	1 Sep 9
91.46	WR	Steve	Backley	GBR	12.2.69	1		Auckland	25 Jan 9
91.40			Zelezny			1	BNP	Villeneuve d'Ascq	2 Jul 9
91.34			Zelezny			1		Cape Town	8 Apr 9
91.33			Pitkämaki			1	WAF	Monaco	10 Sep 0
91.31			Parviainen			2	WCh	Edmonton	12 Aug 0
91.30			Zelezny			1	ISTAF	Berlin	1 Sep 9
91.28			Zelezny			1	BNP	Villeneuve d'Ascq	8 Jul 9
91.27			Gatsioúdis			1	ECCp	Madrid	26 May 0
		(30/6)	59 performances over 90m, further 15 by Zelezny						
90.60		Seppo	Räty	FIN	27.4.62	1		Nurmijärvi	20 Jul 9
90.44		Boris	Henry	GER	14.12.73	1	Gugl	Linz	9 Jul 9
89.60		Andreas	Thorkildsen	NOR	1.4.82	2	WAF	Monaco	10 Sep 0
89.16A		Tom	Petranoff	USA	8.4.58	1		Potchefstroom	1 Mar 9
		(10)							
89.10	WR	Patrik	Bodén	SWE	30.6.67	1		Austin	24 Mar 9
88.90		Aleksandr	Ivanov	RUS	25.5.82	1	Znam	Tula	7 Jun 0
88.75		Marius	Corbett	RSA	26.9.75	1	CG	Kuala Lumpur	21 Sep 9
88.70		Peter	Blank	GER	10.4.62	1	NC	Stuttgart	30 Jun 0
88.24		Matti	Närhi	FIN	17.8.75	1		Soini	27 Jul 9
88.22		Juha	Laukkanen	FIN	6.1.69	1		Kuortane	20 Jun 9
88.20		Gavin	Lovegrove	NZL	21.10.67	1	Bisl	Oslo	5 Jul 9
88.00		Vladimir	Ovchinnikov	RUS	2.8.70	1		Tolyatti	14 May 9
87.83		Andrus	Värnik	EST	27.9.77	1		Valga	19 Aug 0
87.82		Harri	Hakkarainen	FIN	16.10.69	1		Kuortane	24 Jun 9
		(20)							
87.68		Breaux	Greer	USA	19.10.76	1	WAF	Monaco	19 Sep 0
87.60		Kazuhiro	Mizoguchi	JPN	18.3.62	1	Jen	San José	27 May 8
87.40		Vladimir	Sasimovich	BLR	14.9.68	2		Kuortane	24 Jun 9
87.34		Andrey	Moruyev	RUS	6.5.70	1	ECp	Birmingham	25 Jun 9
87.20		Viktor	Zaytsev	UZB	6.6.66	1	OT	Moskva	23 Jun 9
87.20		Peter	Esenwein	GER	7.12.67	1		Rehlingen	31 May 0
87.17		Dariusz	Trafas	POL	16.5.72	1		Gold Coast (RB)	17 Sep 0
87.12		Tom	Pukstys	USA	28.5.68	2	OD	Jena	25 May 9
87.12		Emeterio	González	CUB	11.4.73	1	OD	Jena	3 Jun 0
86.98		Yuriy	Rybin	RUS	5.3.63	1		Nitra	26 Aug 9
		(30)							
86.94		Mick	Hill	GBR	22.10.64	1	NC	London (CP)	13 Jun 9
86.80		Einar	Vihljálmsson	ISL	1.6.60	1		Reykjavik	29 Aug 9
86.74		Pål Arne	Fagernes	NOR	8.6.74	q	OG	Sydney	22 Sep 0
86.67		Andrew	Currey	AUS	7.2.71	1		Wollongong	22 Jul 0
86.64		Klaus	Tafelmeier	FRG	12.4.58	1	NC	Gelsenkirchen	12 Jul 8
86.63		Harri	Haatainen	FIN	5.1.78	2	GP II	Gateshead	19 Aug 0
86.50		Tapio	Korjus	FIN	10.2.61	1		Lahti	25 Aug 8
86.47		Eriks	Rags	LAT	1.6.75	2	BrGP	London	22 Jul 0
85.96		Kimmo	Kinnunen	FIN	31.3.68	3	NC	Seinäjoki	8 Aug 9
85.74		Dmitriy	Polyunin ¶	UZB	6.4.69	2	OT	Moskva	23 Jun 9
		(40)							
85.74A		Miroslav	Guzdek	CZE	3.8.75	1		Germiston	5 Apr 0
85.70		Andrey	Shevchuk	RUS	8.3.70	2	Slovn	Bratislava	1 Jun 9
85.67		Mark	Roberson	GBR	13.3.67	2		Gateshead	19 Jul 9
85.60		William	Hamlyn-Harris	AUS	14.1.78	1		Canberra	31 Jan 0
85.42		Andreas	Linden	GER	20.2.65	2		Mülheim-Kärlich	17 Sep 9
85.28		Donald-Aik	Sild	EST	3.10.68	2		St Denis	10 Jun 9
85.21		Björn	Lange	GER	15.6.79	4	GP II	Gateshead	19 Aug 0
85.18		Ari	Pakarinen	FIN	14.5.69	Q		Lapua	22 Jul 9
85.16		Viktor	Yevsyukov	KZK	6.10.56	1	vGDR	Karl-Marx-Stadt	21 Jun 8
85.09		Nick	Nieland	GBR	31.1.72	2	NC	Birmingham	13 Aug 0
		(50)	100th man 83.00, 200th man 80.06						

Ancillary marks – other marks during series (to 91.40)

95.34	Zelezny	29 Aug 93	92.26	Zelezny	26 Mar 97	91.44	Zelezny	25 May 96
92.88	Zelezny	25 May 96	91.88	Zelezny	27 Aug 95	91.44	Zelezny	26 Mar 97
92.30	Zelezny	26 Mar 97	91.48	Zelezny	15 Sep 95			

Mark	Wind	Name		Nat	Born	Pos	Meet	Venue	Date
Javelins with roughened tails, now banned by the IAAF									
96.96	WR	Seppo	Räty	FIN	27.4.62	1		Punkalaidun	2 Jun 91
94.74	Irreg		Zelezny			1	Bisl	Oslo	4 Jul 92
91.98	WR		Räty			1	Super	Shizuoka	6 May 91
90.82		Kimmo	Kinnunen	FIN	31.3.68	1	WCh	Tokyo	26 Aug 91
87.00		Peter	Borglund	SWE	29.1.64	1		Stockholm	13 Aug 91
85.52		Dag	Wennlund	SWE	9.10.63	1	NC	Helsingborg	27 Jul 91

DECATHLON

Mark	Wind	Name		Nat	Born	Pos	Meet	Venue	Date
9026	WR	Roman	Sebrle	CZE	26.11.74	1		Götzis	27 May 01
10.64/0.0	8.11/1.9	15.33	2.12	47.79	13.92/-0.2	47.92	4.80	70.16	4:21.98
8994	WR	Tomás	Dvorák	CZE	11.5.72	1	ECp	Praha	4 Jul 99
10.54/-0.1	7.90/1.1	16.78	2.04	48.08	13.73/0.0	48.33	4.90	72.32	4:37.20
8902			Dvorák			1	WCh	Edmonton	7 Aug 01
10.62/1.5	8.07/0.9	16.57	2.00	47.74	13.80/-0.4	45.51	5.00	68.53	4:35.13
8900			Dvorák			1		Götzis	4 Jun 00
10.54/1.3	8.03/0.0	16.68	2.09	48.36	13.89/-1.0	47.89	4.85	67.21	4:42.33
8893			Sebrle			1	OG	Athína	24 Aug 04
10.85/1.5	7.84/0.3	16.36	2.12	48.36	14.05/1.5	48.72	5.00	70.52	4:40.01
8891	WR	Dan	O'Brien	USA	18.7.66	1		Talence	5 Sep 92
10.43w/2.1	8.08/1.8	16.69	2.07	48.51	13.98/-0.5	48.56	5.00	62.58	4:42.10
8847	WR	Daley	Thompson	GBR	30.7.58	1	OG	Los Angeles	9 Aug 84
10.44/-1.0	8.01/0.4	15.72	2.03	46.97	14.33/-1.1	46.56	5.00	65.24	4:35.00
8844w			O'Brien			1	TAC	New York	13 Jun 91
10.23	7.96	16.06	2.08	47.70	13.95W/4.2	48.08	5.10	57.40	4:45.54
8842			Sebrle			1		Götzis	30 May 04
10.92/0.5	7.86w/3.3	16.22	2.09	48.59	14.15/0.3	47.44	5.00	71.10	4:34.09
8837			Dvorák			1	WCh	Athína	6 Aug 97
10.60/0.8	7.64/-0.7	16.32	2.00	47.56	13.61/0.8	45.16	5.00	70.34	4:35.40
8832	WR	Jürgen	Hingsen	FRG	25.1.58	1	OT	Mannheim	9 Jun 84
10.70w/2.9	7.76/	16.42	2.07	48.05	14.07/0.2	49.36	4.90	59.86	4:19.75
8825	WR		Hingsen			1		Bernhausen	5 Jun 83
10.92/0.0	7.74	15.94	2.15	47.89	14.10	46.80	4.70	67.26	4:19.74
8824			O'Brien			1	OG	Atlanta	1 Aug 96
10.50/0.7	7.57/1.4	15.66	2.07	46.82	13.87/0.3	48.78	5.00	66.90	4:45.89
8820		Bryan	Clay	USA	3.1.80	2	OG	Athína	24 Aug 04
10.44w/2.2	7.96/0.2	15.23	2.06	49.19	14.13/1.5	50.11	4.90	69.71	4:41.65
8817			O'Brien			1	WCh	Stuttgart	20 Aug 93
10.57/0.9	7.99/0.4	15.41	2.03	47.46	14.08/0.0	47.92	5.20	62.56	4:40.08
8815		Erki	Nool	EST	25.6.70	2	WCh	Edmonton	7 Aug 01
10.60/1.5	7.63/2.0	14.90	2.03	46.23	14.40/0.0	43.40	5.40	67.01	4:29.58
8812			O'Brien			1	WCh	Tokyo	30 Aug 91
10.41/-1.6	7.90/0.8	16.24	1.91	46.53	13.94/-1.2	47.20	5.20	60.66	4:37.50
8811			Thompson			1	EC	Stuttgart	28 Aug 86
10.26/2.0	7.72/1.0	15.73	2.00	47.02	14.04/-0.3	43.38	5.10	62.78	4:26.16
8807			Sebrle			1		Götzis	1 Jun 03
10.78/-0.2	7.86/1.2	15.41	2.12	47.83	13.96/0.0	43.42	4.90	69.22	4:28.63
8800			Sebrle			1		Götzis	2 Jun 02
10.95/0.5	7.79/1.8	15.50	2.12	48.35	13.89/1.6	48.02	5.00	68.97	4:38.16
8800			Sebrle			1	EC	München	8 Aug 02
10.83/1.3	7.92/0.8	15.41	2.12	48.48	14.04/0.0	46.88	5.10	68.51	4:42.94
8792		Uwe	Freimuth	GDR	10.9.61	1	OD	Potsdam	21 Jul 84
11.06/	7.79/	16.30	2.03	48.43	14.66/	46.58	5.15	72.42	4:25.19
8784		Tom	Pappas	USA	6.9.76	1	NC	Stanford	22 Jun 03
10.78/0.2	7.96/1.4	16.28	2.17	48.22	14.13/1.7	45.84	5.20	60.77	4:48.12
8774	WR		Thompson			1	EC	Athína	8 Sep 82
10.51/0.3	7.80/0.8	15.44	2.03	47.11	14.39/0.9	45.48	5.00	63.56	4:23.71
8762		Siegfried	Wentz	FRG	7.3.60	2		Bernhausen	5 Jun 83
10.89	7.49/	15.35	2.09	47.38	14.00	46.90	4.80	70.68	4:24.90
8757			Sebrle			2		Götzis	4 Jun 00
10.64/1.3	7.88/1.6	15.19	2.15	49.05	13.99/-1.0	47.21	4.75	67.23	4:35.06
8755			O'Brien			1	GWG	Uniondale, NY	20 Jul 98
10.71/-2.3	7.78w/2.2	15.67	2.11	48.04	13.67/0.4	48.87	5.20	66.31	5:08.77
8750			Pappas			1	WCh	Saint-Denis	27 Aug 03
10.80/-0.5	7.62/1.1	16.11	2.09	47.58	13.99/0.0	46.94	5.10	65.90	4:44.31
8744			Dvorák			1	WCh	Sevilla	25 Aug 99
10.60/0.1	7.98/0.1	16.49	2.00	48.42	13.75/0.7	46.26	4.60	70.11	4:39.87
8742			Nool			3		Götzis	4 Jun 00
10.69/1.3	7.78/1.8	14.14	1.97	47.18	14.37/-0.1	44.16	5.55	69.10	4:35.59

(30/10)

Mark Wind	Name		Nat	Born	Pos	Meet	Venue			Date
8735	Eduard	Hämäläinen	FIN/BLR	21.1.69	1		Götzis			29 May 94
	10.50w/2.1	7.26/1.0	16.05	2.11	47.63	13.82/-3.0	49.70	4.90	60.32	4:35.09
8727	Dave	Johnson	USA	7.4.63	1		Azusa			24 Apr 92
	10.96/0.4	7.52w/4.5	14.61	2.04	48.19	14.17/0.3	49.88	5.28	66.96	4:29.38
8725	Dmitriy	Karpov	KAZ	23.7.81	3	OG	Athína			24 Aug 04
	10.50w/2.2	7.81/-0.9	15.93	2.09	46.81	13.97/1.5	51.65	4.60	55.54	4:38.11
8709	Aleksandr	Apaychev	UKR	6.5.61	1	vGDR	Neubrandenburg			3 Jun 84
	10.96/	7.57/	16.00	1.97	48.72	13.93/	48.00	4.90	72.24	4:26.51
8706	Frank	Busemann	GER	26.2.75	2	OG	Atlanta			1 Aug 96
	10.60/0.7	8.07/0.8	13.60	2.04	48.34	13.47/0.3	45.04	4.80	66.86	4:31.41
8698	Grigoriy	Degtyaryov	RUS	16.8.58	1	NC	Kiyev			22 Jun 84
	10.87/0.7	7.42/0.1	16.03	2.10	49.75	14.53/0.3	51.20	4.90	67.08	4:23.09
8694	Chris	Huffins	USA	15.4.70	1	NC	New Orleans			20 Jun 98
	10.31w/3.5	7.76w/2.5	15.43	2.18	49.02	14.02/1.0	53.22	4.60	61.59	4:59.43
8680	Torsten	Voss	GDR	24.3.63	1	WCh	Roma			4 Sep 87
	10.69/-0.3	7.88/1.2	14.98	2.10	47.96	14.13/0.1	43.96	5.10	58.02	4:25.93
8667 WR	Guido	Kratschmer	FRG	10.1.53	1		Bernhausen			14 Jun 80
	10.58w/2.4	7.80/	15.47	2.00	48.04	13.92/	45.52	4.60	66.50	4:24.15
8644	Steve	Fritz	USA	1.11.67	4	OG	Atlanta			1 Aug 96
	10.90/0.8	7.77/0.9	15.31	2.04	50.13	13.97/0.3	49.84	5.10	65.70	4:38.26
	(20)									
8634 WR	Bruce	Jenner	USA	28.10.49	1	OG	Montreal			30 Jul 76
	10.94/0.0	7.22/0.0	15.35	2.03	47.51	14.84/0.0	50.04	4.80	68.52	4:12.61
8627	Robert	Zmelík	CZE	18.4.69	1		Götzis			31 May 92
	10.62w/2.1	8.02/0.2	13.93	2.05	48.73	13.84/1.2	44.44	4.90	61.26	4:24.83
8626	Michael	Smith	CAN	16.9.67	1		Götzis			26 May 96
	11.23/-0.6	7.72/0.6	16.94	1.97	48.69	14.77/-2.4	52.90	4.90	71.22	4:41.95
8603	Dean	Macey	GBR	12.12.77	3	WCh	Edmonton			7 Aug 01
	10.72/-0.7	7.59/0.4	15.41	2.15	46.21	14.34/0.0	46.96	4.70	54.61	4:29.05
8583w	Jón Arnar	Magnússon	ISL	28.7.69	1	ECp-2	Reykjavik			5 Jul 98
	10.68/2.0	7.63/2.0	15.57	2.07	47.78	14.33W/5.2	44.53	5.00	64.16	4:41.60
8574	Christian	Plaziat	FRA	28.10.63	1	EC	Split			29 Aug 90
	10.72/-0.6	7.77/1.1	14.19	2.10	47.10	13.98/0.7	44.36	5.00	54.72	4:27.83
8574	Aleksandr	Yurkov	UKR	21.7.75	4		Götzis			4 Jun 00
	10.69/0.9	7.93/1.8	15.26	2.03	49.74	14.56/-0.9	47.85	5.15	58.92	4:32.49
8571	Lev	Lobodin	RUS	1.4.69	3	EC	Budapest			20 Aug 98
	10.66w/2.2	7.42/0.2	15.67	2.03	48.65	13.97/0.9	46.55	5.20	56.55	4:30.27
8566	Sebastian	Chmara	POL	21.11.71	1		Alhama de Murcia			17 May 98
	10.97w/2.9	7.56/1.2	16.03	2.10	48.27	14.32/1.8	44.39	5.20	57.25	4:29.66
8554	Attila	Zsivoczky	HUN	29.4.77	5		Götzis			4 Jun 00
	10.64w/2.1	7.24/-1.0	15.72	2.18	48.13	14.87/-0.9	45.64	4.65	63.57	4:23.13
	(30)									
8548	Paul	Meier	GER	27.7.71	3	WCh	Stuttgart			20 Aug 93
	10.57/0.9	7.57/1.1	15.45	2.15	47.73	14.63/0.0	45.72	4.60	61.22	4:32.05
8547	Igor	Sobolevskiy	UKR	4.5.62	2	NC	Kiyev			22 Jun 84
	10.64/0.7	7.71/0.2	15.93	2.01	48.24	14.82/0.3	50.54	4.40	67.40	4:32.84
8534	Siegfried	Stark	GDR	12.6.55	1		Halle			4 May 80
	11.10w	7.64	15.81	2.03	49.53	14.86w	47.20	5.00	68.70	4:27.7
8534w/8478	Antonio	Peñalver	ESP	1.12.68	1		Alhama			24 May 92
	10.76w/3.9	7.42W/6.2 (7.19w/4.0)	16.50	2.12	49.50	14.32/0.8	47.38	5.00	59.32	4:39.94
8526	Francisco Javier	Benet	ESP	25.3.68	2		Alhama de Murcia			17 May 98
	10.72w/2.9	7.45/-1.2	14.57	1.92	48.10	13.83/1.8	46.12	5.00	65.37	4:26.81
8526	Kristjan	Rahnu	EST	29.8.79	1		Arles			5 Jun 05
	10.52w/2.2	7.58/1.6	15.51	1.99	48.60	14.04w/3.1	50.81	4.95	60.71	4:52.18
8524	Sébastien	Levicq	FRA	25.6.71	4	WCh	Sevilla			25 Aug 99
	11.05/0.2	7.52/-0.4	14.22	2.00	50.13	14.48/0.6	44.65	5.50	69.01	4:26.81
8519	Yuriy	Kutsenko	RUS	5.3.52	3	NC	Kiyev			22 Jun 84
	11.07/0.5	7.54/-0.1	15.11	2.13	49.07	14.94/0.3	50.38	4.60	61.70	4:12.68
8506	Valter	Külvet	EST	19.2.64	1		Stayki			3 Jul 88
	11.05/-1.4	7.35/0.4	15.78	2.00	48.08	14.55/-0.8	52.04	4.60	61.72	4:15.93
8500	Christian	Schenk	GER	9.2.65	4	WCh	Stuttgart			20 Aug 93
	11.22/-0.9	7.63/0.0	15.72	2.15	48.78	15.29/0.0	46.94	4.80	65.32	4:24.44
	(40)									
8491	Aleksandr	Nevskiy	UKR	21.2.58	2		Götzis			20 May 84
	10.97/-1.6	7.24/1.2	15.04	2.08	48.44	14.67/1.0	46.06	4.70	69.56	4:19.62
8490	Jagan	Hames	AUS	31.10.75	1	CG	Kuala Lumpur			18 Sep 98
	10.77/0.0	7.64/0.8	14.73	2.19	49.67	14.07/0.4	46.40	5.00	64.67	5:02.68
8485	Konstantin	Akhapkin	RUS	19.1.56	1	NC	Moskva			2 Aug 82
	11.10/0.2	7.72/0.2	15.25	2.02	49.14	14.38/1.8	45.68	4.90	62.42	4:19.60

Mark Wind	Name		Nat	Born	Pos	Meet	Venue	Date
8485	Stefan	Schmid	GER	6.5.70	1	OT	Ratingen	23 Jul 00
	10.82/0.0 7.59/-0.6 14.14 2.01 48.99 14.20/-1.6 44.24 5.06 67.63 4:31.76							
8466 WR	Nikolay	Avilov	UKR	6.8.48	1	OG	München	8 Sep 72
	11.00/ 7.68/ 14.36 2.12 48.45 14.31/ 46.98 4.55 61.66 4:22.82							
8462w	Kip	Janvrin	USA	8.7.65	1	vGER	Edwardsville	18 Jul 96
	10.61W/4.1 7.34w/3.1 14.64 1.96 48.20 14.48W/5.7 45.84 5.00 61.82 4:20.12							
8461	Mike	Maczey	GER	28.9.72	7		Götzis	4 Jun 00
	10.99/0.9 7.59/0.3 14.75 2.06 49.83 14.16/-1.0 44.56 5.15 62.27 4:29.93							
8453	Alain	Blondel	FRA	7.12.62	1	EC	Helsinki	13 Aug 94
	11.12/0.6 7.50w/3.2 13.78 1.99 48.91 14.18/0.9 45.08 5.40 60.64 4:20.48							
8447	Robert	de Wit	NED	7.8.62	1	NC	Eindhoven	22 May 88
	11.07/0.5 6.98/0.2 15.88 2.04 48.80 14.32/0.7 46.20 5.00 63.94 4:20.98							
8445	Ramil	Ganiyev	UZB	23.9.68	5	WCh	Athína	6 Aug 97
	10.94/0.2 7.58/0.7 14.76 2.06 48.34 14.34/-0.1 46.04 5.30 55.14 4:36.78							
	(50)	100th man 8256, 200th man 8104						

4 x 100 METRES RELAY

Mark	Nat	Team	Pos	Meet	Venue	Date
37.40 WR	USA	Marsh, Burrell, Mitchell, C Lewis	1	OG	Barcelona	8 Aug 92
37.40 WR	USA	Drummond, Cason, D Mitchell, L Burrell	1s1	WCh	Stuttgart	21 Aug 93
37.48	USA	Drummond, Cason, D Mitchell, L Burrell	1	WCh	Stuttgart	22 Aug 93
37.50 WR	USA	Cason, Burrell, Mitchell, C Lewis	1	WCh	Tokyo	1 Sep 91
37.59	USA	Drummond, Montgomery, B Lewis, Greene	1	WCh	Sevilla	29 Aug 99
37.61	USA	Drummond, Williams, B Lewis, Greene	1	OG	Sydney	30 Sep 00
37.65	USA	Drummond, Williams, C Johnson, Greene	1	ISTAF	Berlin	1 Sep 00
37.67 WR	USA	Marsh, Burrell, Mitchell, C Lewis	1	WK	Zürich	7 Aug 91
37.69	CAN	Esmie 10.47, Gilbert 9.02, Surin 9.25, Bailey 8.95	1	OG	Atlanta	3 Aug 96
37.73	GBR	Gardener, Campbell, Devonish, Chambers	2	WCh	Sevilla	29 Aug 99
37.75	USA	Cason, Burrell, Mitchell, Marsh	1h2	WCh	Tokyo	31 Aug 91
37.77	GBR	Jackson, Jarrett, Regis, Christie	2	WCh	Stuttgart	22 Aug 93
37.77	USA A	Drummond, B Williams, Patton, Greene	1	ISTAF	Berlin (P)	10 Aug 03
37.79 WR	FRA	Morinière, Sangouma, Trouabal, Marie-Rose	1	EC	Split	1 Sep 90
37.79 WR	Santa Monica TC/USA	Marsh, Burrell, Heard, C Lewis	1	Herc	Monaco	3 Aug 91
37.79	USA - Santa Monica TC	Marsh, Burrell, Heard, C Lewis	1	MSR	Walnut	17 Apr 94
37.82	USA	Drummond, Williams, B.Lewis, Greene	1s1	OG	Sydney	29 Sep 00
37.83 WR	USA	Graddy, R Brown, C Smith, C Lewis	1	OG	Los Angeles	11 Aug 84
37.83	CAN	Esmie, Gilbert, Surin, Mahorn	3	WCh	Stuttgart	22 Aug 93
37.86 WR	USA	E King, Gault, C Smith, C Lewis	1	WCh	Helsinki	10 Aug 83
37.86	CAN	Esmie, Gilbert, Surin, Bailey	1	WCh	Athína	10 Aug 97
37.87	FRA	Morinière, Sangouma, Trouabal, Marie-Rose	2	WCh	Tokyo	1 Sep 91
37.88	USA (HSI)	Drummond, B Williams, C.Johnson, Greene	1	TexR	Austin	7 Apr 01
37.89	Santa Monica TC (USA)	Marsh, Burrell, Heard, C Lewis	1	TexR	Austin	9 Apr 94
37.90	USA	McRae, L McNeill, Glance, C Lewis	1	WCh	Roma	6 Sep 87
37.90	USA	Drummond, Harden, Mitchell, Greene	1	GWG	Uniondale, NY.	22 Jul 98
37.90	BRA	de Lima, Ribeiro, A da Silva, Cl da Silva	2	OG	Sydney	30 Sep 00
37.92	USA	Crawford, Gatlin, Miller, Greene	1	3N	München	8 Aug 04
37.94	NGR	O Ezinwa, Adeniken, Obikwelu, D Ezinwa	1s2	WCh	Athína	9 Aug 97
		(29 by 6 nations) Further bests by nations:				
38.00	CUB	Simón, Lamela, Isasi, Aguilera	3	OG	Barcelona	8 Aug 92
38.02	URS	Yevgenyev, Bryzgin, Muravyov, Krylov	2	WCh	Roma	6 Sep 87
38.10	TRI	Pierre, Burns, Harper, Brown	2	WCh	Helsinki	13 Aug 05
38.12	GHA	Duah, Nkansah, Zakari, Tuffour	1s1	WCh	Athína	9 Aug 97
	(10)					
38.17	AUS	Henderson, Jackson, Brimacombe, Marsh	1s2	WCh	Göteborg	12 Aug 95
38.20	JAM	L Frater, D Thomas, C Williams, Bredwood	4	OG	Sydney	30 Sep 00
38.29	GDR	Schröder, Kübeck, Prenzler, Emmelmann	2	vUSA	Karl-Marx-Stadt	9 Jul 82
38.31	JPN	Inoue, K Ito, Tsuchie, Asahara	5s2	WCh	Athína	9 Aug 97
38.33	POL	Zwolinski, Licznerski, Dunecki, Woronin	2	OG	Moskva	1 Aug 80
38.37	ITA	Tilli, Simionato, Pavoni, Mennea	2	WCh	Helsinki	10 Aug 83
38.45	AHO	Goeloe, Raffaela, Duzant, Martina	6	WCh	Helsinki	13 Aug 05
38.46	URS/RUS	Zharov, Krylov, Fatun, Goremykin	4	EC	Split	1 Sep 90
38.47	RSA	Nagel, du Plessis, Newton, Quinn	1	WCh	Edmonton	12 Aug 01
38.53	UKR	Rurak, Osovich, Kramarenko, Dologodin	1	ECp	Madrid	1 Jun 96
38.54	FRG	Heer, Haas, Klein, Schweisfurth	1	R-W	Koblenz	28 Aug 88
		(20, with RUS and UKR for USSR)				
38.60	ESP	Feo, José, Mayoral, Berlanga	3s1	WCh	Athína	9 Aug 97
38.60	CIV	Meité, Douhou, Sonan, N'Dri	3s1	WCh	Edmonton	12 Aug 01
38.61	GRE	Séggos, Alexópoulos, Panayiotópoulos, Hoídis	2	ECp	Paris (C)	19 Jun 99
38.63	SWE	Karlsson, Mårtensson, Hedner, Strenius	3s2	OG	Atlanta	2 Aug 96
38.63	NED	Beck, T Douglas, van Balkom, C Douglas	5s1	WCh	Saint-Denis	30 Aug 03
38.67	HUN	Karaffa, Nagy, Tatár, Kovács	1	BGP	Budapest	11 Aug 86

Mark	Wind	Name	Nat	Born	Pos	Meet	Venue	Date
38.80		THA Natenee, Sophanich, Janthana, Suwonprateep			1	AsiC	Jakarta	31 Aug 00
38.81		CHN Li Xiaoping, Lin Wei, Huang Danwei, Chen Wenzhong			2h3	WCh	Göteborg	12 Aug 95
38.81		ISR Jaar, Jablonka, Kafri, Porkhomovskiy			3h2	WCh	Sevilla	28 Aug 99
38.82		TCH/CZE Matousek, Demec, Kynos, Bohman			4	OG	München	10 Sep 72
Multi-nation teams								
37.82		Drummond/USA, Jarrett/GBR, Regis/GBR, Mitchell/USA			2	MSR	Walnut	17 Apr 94
37.93		HSI (USA) Drummond, B Williams, Bolden TRI, Greene			1	BrGP	London (CP)	22 Jul 01
Drugs dsqualification								
37.91		NGR Asonze ¶, Obikwelu, Effiong, Aliu			(3)	WCh	Sevilla	29 Aug 99

4 x 200 METRES RELAY

Mark	Team / Names	Pos	Meet	Venue	Date
1:18.68 WR	USA - Santa Monica Track Cluc Marsh 20.0, Burrell 19.6, Heard 19.7, C Lewis 19.4	1	MSR	Walnut	17 Apr 94
1:19.10	World All-Stars Drummond USA 20.4, Mitchell USA 19.3, Bridgewater USA 20.3, Regis GBR 19.1	2	MSR	Walnut	17 Apr 94
1:19.11 WR	Santa Monica TC/USA M.Marsh, L Burrell, Heard, C Lewis	1	Penn	Philadelphia	25 Apr 92
1:19.16	USA Red Team Crawford, Clay, Patton, Gatlin	1	PennR	Philadelphia	26 Apr 03
1:19.38 WR	Santa Monica TC/USA Everett, Burrell, Heard, C Lewis	1	R-W	Koblenz	23 Aug 89
1:19.39	USA Blue Drummond, Crawford, B Williams, Greene	1	PennR	Philadelphia	28 Apr 01
1:19.45	Santa Monica TC/USA DeLoach, Burrell, C.Lewis, Heard	1	Penn	Philadelphia	27 Apr 91
1:19.47	Nike Int./USA Brokenburr, A Harrison, Greene, M Johnson	1	Penn	Philadelphia	24 Apr 99
Best non-US nations					
1:20.79	Central Arizona DC/Jamaica Bucknor, Campbell, O'Connor, Davis)	1		Walnut	24 Apr 88
1:21.10	ITA Tilli, Simionato, Bongiorno, Mennea	1		Cagliari	29 Sep 83
1:21.22	POL Tulin, Balcerzak, Pilarczyk, Urbas	2		Gdansk	14 Jul 01
1:21.29	GBR Adam, Mafe, Christie, Regis	1		Birmingham	23 Jun 89
1:21.32	UKR Vanyaykin, Tverdokhleb, Streltsov, Dologodin	1	EurR	Portsmouth	5 Jun 93

4 x 400 METRES RELAY

Mark	Team / Names	Pos	Meet	Venue	Date
2:54.20 WR	USA Young 44.3, Pettigrew 43.2, Washington 43.5, M Johnson 43.2	1	GWG	Uniondale, NY	22 Jul 98
2:54.29 WR	USA Valmon 44.43, Watts 43.59, Reynolds 43.36, Johnson 42.91	1	WCh	Stuttgart	22 Aug 93
2:55.74 WR	USA Valmon 44.6, Watts 43.00, M.Johnson 44.73, S Lewis 43.41	1	OG	Barcelona	8 Aug 92
2:55.91	USA O Harris 44.5, Brew 43.6, Wariner 43.98, Williamson 43.83	1	OG	Athína	28 Aug 04
2:55.99	USA L Smith 44.62, A Harrison 43.84, Mills 43.66, Maybank 43.87	1	OG	Atlanta	3 Aug 96
2:56.16A WR	USA Matthews 45.0, Freeman 43.2, James 43.9, Evans 44.1	1	OG	Ciu. México	20 Oct 68
2:56.16 WR	USA Everett 43.79, S Lewis 43.69, Robinzine 44.74, Reynolds 43.94	1	OG	Seoul	1 Oct 88
2:56.35	USA A Harrison 44.36, Pettigrew 44.17, C Harrison 43.53, Johnson 44.29	1	OG	Sydney	30 Sep 00
2:56.45	USA J Davis 45.2, Pettigrew 43.9, Taylor 43.92, M Johnson 43.49	1	WCh	Sevilla	29 Aug 99
2:56.47	USA Young 44.6, Pettigrew 43.1, Jones 44.80, Washington 44.80	1	WCh	Athína	10 Aug 97
2:56.60	GBR I Thomas 44.92, Baulch 44.19, Richardson 43.62, Black 43.87	2	OG	Atlanta	3 Aug 96
2:56.60	USA Red Taylor 45.0, Pettigrew 44.2, Washington 43.7, Johnson 43.7	1	PennR	Philadelphia	29 Apr 00
2:56.65	GBR Thomas 44.8, Black 44.2, Baulch 44.08, Richardson 43.57	2	WCh	Athína	10 Aug 97
2:56.75	JAM McDonald 44.5, Haughton 44.4, McFarlane 44.37, Clarke 43.51	3	WCh	Athína	10 Aug 97
2:56.91	USA Rock 44.7, Brew 44.3, Williamson 44.40, Wariner 43.49	1	WCh	Helsinki	14 Aug 05
2:57.29	USA Everett 45.1, Haley 44.0, McKay 44.20, Reynolds 44.00	1	WCh	Roma	6 Sep 87
2:57.32	USA Ramsey 44.9, Mills 44.6, Reynolds 43.74, Johnson 44.11	1	WCh	Göteborg	13 Aug 95
2:57.32	BAH McKinney 44.9, Moncur 44.6, A.Williams 44.43, Brown 43.42	2	WCh	Helsinki	14 Aug 05
2:57.53	GBR Black 44.7, Redmond 44.0, Regis 44.22, Akabusi 44.59	1	WCh	Tokyo	1 Sep 91
2:57.54	USA Byrd 45.9, Pettigrew 43.9, Brew 44.03, Taylor 43.71	1	WCh	Edmonton	12 Aug 01
2:57.57	USA Valmon 44.9, Watts 43.4, D.Everett 44.31, Pettigrew 44.93	2	WCh	Tokyo	1 Sep 91
2:57.87	USA L Smith 44.59, Rouser 44.33, Mills 44.32, Maybank 44.63	1s2	OG	Atlanta	2 Aug 96
2:57.91	USA Nix 45.59, Armstead 43.97, Babers 43.75, McKay 44.60	1	OG	Los Angeles	11 Aug 84
2:57.97	JAM McDonald , Haughton , McFarlane, D Clarke	1	PAm	Winnipeg	30 Jul 99
2:58.00	POL Rysiukiewicz 45.6, Czubak 44.2, Haczek 44.0, Mackowiak 44.2	2	GWG	Uniondale, NY	22 Jul 98
2:58.07	JAM Ayre 44.9, Simpson 44.9, Spence 44.48, Clarke 43.81	3	WCh	Helsinki	14 Aug 05
2:58.19	BAH Moncur 45.1, C Brown 44.5, McIntosh 44.42, Munnings 44.13	2	WCh	Edmonton	12 Aug 01
2:58.22	GBR Sanders 45.85, Akabusi 44.48, Regis 43.93, Black 43.96	1	EC	Split	1 Sep 90
2:58.23	USA Ramsey 44.6, Mills 44.0, Lyles 44.41, Hall 45.22	1h1	WCh	Göteborg	12 Aug 95
2:58.29	JAM McDonald 45.1, D Clarke 43.8, Blake 44.80, McFarlane 44.60	2h1	WCh	Göteborg	12 Aug 95
(30/5)	Further bests by nations:				
2:58.56	BRA Parrela, da Silva, dos Santos, de Araújo	2	PAm	Winnipeg	30 Jul 99
2:58.68	NGR Chukwu 45.18, Monye 44.49, Bada 44.70, Udo-Obong 44.31	2	OG	Sydney	30 Sep 00
2:58.96	FRA Djhone 45.4, Keita 44.7, Diagana 44.69, Raquil 44.15	2	WCh	Saint-Denis	31 Aug 03
2:59.13	CUB Martínez 45.6, Herrera 44.38, Tellez 44.81, Hernández 44.34	1h2	OG	Barcelona	7 Aug 92
2:59.63	KEN D Kitur 45.4, S Kitur 45.13, Kipkemboi 44.76, Kemboi 44.34	3h2	OG	Barcelona	7 Aug 92
(10)					
2:59.70	AUS Frayne 45.38, Clark 43.86, Minihan 45.07, Mitchell 45.39	4	OG	Los Angeles	11 Aug 84
2:59.86	GDR Möller 45.8, Schersing 44.8, Carlowitz 45.3, Schönlebe 44.1	1	vURS	Erfurt	23 Jun 85
2:59.95	YUG Jovkovic, Djurovic, Macev, Brankovic 44.3	2h3	WCh	Tokyo	31 Aug 91

Mark Wind	Nat	Name	Pos	Meet	Venue	Date
2:59.96	FRG	Dobeleit 45.7, Henrich 44.3, Itt 45.12, Schmid 44.93	4	WCh	Roma	6 Sep 87
3:00.16	URS	Lovachov, Lomtyev, Kurochkin, Markin 43.9	1	Drz	Moskva	18 Aug 84
3:00.20	RSA		4	WCh	Sevilla	29 Aug 99
		van Oudtshoorn 46.5, Mokganyetsi 44.5, A Botha 45.43, Malherbe 43.78				
3:00.44	RUS	Kliger 45.71, Kosov 45.14, Vdovin 44.66, Golovastov 44.93	5	WCh	Stuttgart	22 Aug 93
3:00.64	SEN	Diarra 46.53, Dia 44.94, Ndiaye 44.70, Faye 44.47	4	OG	Atlanta	3 Aug 96
3:00.76	JPN	Karube 45.88, Ito 44.86, Osakada 45.08, Omori 44.94	5	OG	Atlanta	3 Aug 96
3:00.79	ZIM	Chiwira 46.2, Mukomana 44.6, Ngidhi 45.79, Harnden 44.20	2h3	WCh	Athína	9 Aug 97
3:01.05	TRI	Delice, A Daniel, De Silva, Morris	1h1	OG	Barcelona	7 Aug 92
		(20 inc. RUS/URS)				
3:01.12	FIN	Lönnqvist 46.7, Salin 45.1, Karttunen 44.8, Kukkoaho 44.5	6	OG	München	10 Sep 72
3:01.37	ITA	Bongiorni 46.2, Zuliani 45.0, Petrella 45.3, Ribaud 44.9	4	EC	Stuttgart	31 Aug 86
3:01.42	ESP	I Rodríguez 46.0, Canal 44.1, Andrés 45.88, Reina 45.48	4h1	WCh	Edmonton	11 Aug 01
3:01.60	BAR	Louis 46.67, Peltier 44.97, Edwards 45.04, Forde 44.92	6	OG	Los Angeles	11 Aug 84
3:01.61	BUL	Georgiev 45.9, Stankulov 46.0, Raykov 45.07, Ivanov 44.66	2h1	WCh	Stuttgart	21 Aug 93
3:02.02	DOM	Peguero, Santa, Vidal, Sánchez	3	PAm	Santo Domingo	9 Aug 03
3:02.09	UGA	Govile 46.72, Kyeswa 44.60, Rwamu 46.40, Okot 44.37	7	OG	Los Angeles	11 Aug 84
3:02.11	MAR	Kasbane, Dahane, Belcaid, Lahlou 44.5	1h2	WCh	Tokyo	31 Aug 91
3:02.24	BOT	Molefe, Kilego, Moseki, Kubisa	1	AfG	Abuja	15 Oct 03
3:02.31	GRE	Dimótsios 46.7, Goúsis 45.6, Sarrís 45.08, Iakovákis 44.93	2h2	WCh	Saint-Denis	30 Aug 03
Multi-nation team						
2:58.52	Adidas	McDonald JAM, Pettigrew, Campbell, Young USA	1	PennR	Philadelphia	24 Apr 99

4 x 800 METRES RELAY

Mark	Nat	Name	Pos	Meet	Venue	Date
7:03.89 WR	GBR	Elliott 1:49.14, Cook 1:46.20, Cram 1:44.54, Coe 1:44.01	1		London (CP)	30 Aug 82
7:04.70	RSA		1		Stuttgart	6 Jun 99
		G van Oudtshoorn 1:46.9, Sepeng 1:45.2, J Kotze 1:48.3, J, Botha 1:44.3				
7:04.89	KEN/ex-St Patrick's School		2		Stuttgart	6 Jun 99
		D Kiptoo 1:46.4, Tengelei 1:48.2, W Chirchir 1:45.7, Kimutai 1:44.6				
7:06.5	Santa Monica TC/USA)		1	MSR	Walnut	26 Apr 86
		J Robinson 1:49.8, Mack 1:46.7, E Jones 1:45.2, Gray 1:44.8				
7:07.40	URS	Masunov, Kostetskiy, Matvetev, Kalinkin	1		Moskva	5 Aug 84

4 x 1500 METRES RELAY

Mark	Nat	Name	Pos	Meet	Venue	Date
14:38.8 WR	FRG		1		Köln	16 Aug 77
		Wessinghage 3:38.8, Hudak 3:40.2, Lederer 3:42.6, Fleschen 3:37.3				
14:40.4 WR	NZL	Polhill 3:42.9, Walker 3:40.4, Dixon 3:41.2, Quax 3:35.9	1		Oslo	22 Aug 73
14:45.63	URS	Kalutskiy, Yakovlev, Legeda, Lotarev	1		Leningrad	4 Aug 85
14:46.16	Larios, ESP		1		Madrid	5 Sep 97
		Jiménez 3:40.9, Pancorbo 3:41.2, A García 3:43.9, Viciosa 3:40.2				
14:46.3	USA	Aldridge, Clifford, Harbour, Duits	1	Int	Bourges	23 Jun 79
14:48.2	FRA	Begouin, Lequement, Philippe 3:42.2, Dien 3:37.2	2	Int	Bourges	23 Jun 79

4 x 1 MILE RELAY

Mark	Nat	Name	Pos	Meet	Venue	Date
15:49.08	IRL	Coghlan 4:00.2, O'Sullivan 3:55.3, O'Mara 3:56.6, Flynn 3:56.98	1		Dublin	17 Aug 85
15:59.57	NZL	Rodhers 3:57.2, VBowden 4:02.5, Gilchrist 4:02.8, Walker 3:57.07	1		Auckland	2 Mar 83

3000 METRES TRACK WALK

Mark		Name	Nat	Born	Pos	Meet	Venue	Date
10:47.11	Giovanni	De Benedictis	ITA	8.1.68	1		S.Giovanni Valdarno	19 May 90
10:56.22	Andrew	Jachno	AUS	13.4.62	1		Melbourne	7 Feb 91
10:56.34+	Roman	Mrázek	SVK	21.1.62	1k	PTS	Bratislava	14 Jun 89
11:00.2+	Jozef	Pribilinec	SVK	6.7.60	1k		Banská Bystrica	30 Aug 85
11:00.56	David	Smith	AUS	24.7.55	1		Perth	24 Jan 87
11:03.01	Vladimir	Andreyev	RUS	7.9.66	2		Formia	13 Jul 97
Indoors								
10:31.42	Andreas	Erm	GER	12.3.76	1		Halle	4 Feb 01
10:54.61	Carlo	Mattioli	ITA	23.10.54	1		Milano	6 Feb 80
10:56.88	Reima	Salonen	FIN	19.11.55	1		Turku	5 Feb 84
11:00.86+	Frants	Kostyukevich	BLR	4.4.63	1k	EI	Genova	28 Feb 92

5000 METRES TRACK WALK

Mark		Name	Nat	Born	Pos	Meet	Venue	Date
18:05.49	Hatem	Ghoula	TUN	7.6.73	1		Tunis	1 May 97
18:17.22	Robert	Korzeniowski	POL	30.7.68	1		Reims	3 Jul 92
18:28.80	Roman	Mrázek	SVK	21.1.62	1	PTS	Bratislava	14 Jun 89
18:30.43	Maurizio	Damilano	ITA	6.4.57	1		Caserta	11 Jun 92
18:31.76	Frants	Kostyukevich	BLR	4.4.63	1	BNP	Villeneuve d'Ascq	2 Jul 93
18:33.16	João	Vieira	POR	20.2.76	1		Rio Maior	10 May 00
ndoors								
18:07.08	Mikhail	Shchennikov	RUS	24.12.67	1		Moskva	14 Feb 95
18:11.41	Ronald	Weigel	GDR	8.8.59	1mx		Wien	13 Feb 88

Mark	Wind	Name		Nat	Born	Pos	Meet	Venue	Date
18:15.25		Grigoriy	Kornev	RUS	14.3.61	1		Moskva	7 Feb 92
18:16.54 ?		Frants	Kostyukevich	BLR	4.4.63	2	NC	Gomel	4 Feb 89
18:19.97		Giovanni	De Benedictis	ITA	8.1.68	1	EI	Genova	28 Feb 92
18:22.25		Andreas	Erm	GER	12.3.76	1	NC	Dortmund	25 Feb 01
18:23.18		Rishat	Shafikov	RUS	23.1.70	1		Samara	1 Mar 97
18:27.15		Alessandro	Gandellini	ITA	30.4.73	1	NC	Genova	12 Feb 00
18:27.80		Jozef	Pribilinec	SVK	6.7.60	2	WI	Indianapolis	7 Mar 87
18:27.95		Stefan	Johansson	SWE	11.4.67	3	EI	Genova	28 Feb 92
18:31.63		Vladimir	Andreyev	RUS	7.9.66	2		Moskva	7 Feb 92
18:32.32		Mikhail	Orlov	RUS	25.6.67	3	CISCh	Moskva	2 Feb 92

10,000 METRES TRACK WALK

Mark	Wind	Name		Nat	Born	Pos	Meet	Venue	Date
37:58.6		Ivano	Brugnetti	ITA	1.9.76	1		Sesto San Gioavnni	23 Jul 05
38:02.60		Jozef	Pribilinec	SVK	6.7.60	1		Banská Bystrica	30 Aug 85
38:06.6		David	Smith	AUS	24.7.55	1		Sydney	25 Sep 86
38:12.13		Ronald	Weigel	GDR	8.8.59	1		Potsdam	10 May 86
38:18.0+		Valdas	Kazlauskas	LTU	23.2.58	1		Moskva	18 Sep 83
38:24 0+		Bernardo	Segura	MEX	11.2.70	1	SGP	Fana	7 May 94
38:24.31		Hatem	Ghoula	TUN	7.6.73	1		Tunis	30 May 98
38:26.4		Daniel	García	MEX	28.10.71	1		Sdr Omme	17 May 97
38:26.53		Robert	Korzeniowski	POL	30.7.68	1		Riga	31 May 02
38:37.6+		Jefferson	Pérez (10)	ECU	1.7.74	1	in 20k	Fana	9 May 98
38:38.0		Walter	Arena	ITA	30.5.64	1		Catania	13 Apr 90
38:40.18		Giovanni	De Benedictis	ITA	8.1.68	1	NC	Cesenatico	1 Jul 95
38:41.17		Andrey	Yurin	UKR	20.1.84	1		Kiev	22 Jun 05
38:42.38		Francisco	Fernández	ESP	6.3.77	1	NC-23	Torremolinos	11 Jul 99
Indoors									
38:31.4		Werner	Heyer	GDR	14.11.56	1		Berlin	12 Jan 80

20 KILOMETRES WALK

Mark	Wind	Name		Nat	Born	Pos	Meet	Venue	Date
1:17:21	WR	Jefferson	Pérez	ECU	1.7.74	1	WCh	Saint-Denis	23 Aug 03
1:17:22	WR	Francisco Javier	Fernández	ESP	5.3.77	1		Turku	28 Apr 02
1:17:23		Vladimir	Stankin	RUS	2.1.74	1	NC-w	Adler	8 Feb 04
1:17:25.6t		Bernardo	Segura	MEX	11.2.70	1	SGP	Fana	7 May 94
1:17:33		Nathan	Deakes	AUS	17.8.77	1		Cixi	23 Apr 05
1:17:41			Zhu Hongjun	CHN	18.8.83	2		Cixi	23 Apr 05
1:17:46		Julio	Martínez	GUA	27.9.73	1		Eisenhüttenstadt	8 May 99
1:17:46		Roman	Rasskazov	RUS	28.4.79	1	NC	Moskva	19 May 00
1:17:52			Fernández			1		La Coruña	4 Jun 05
1:17:53			Cui Zhide	CHN	11.1.83	3		Cixi	23 Apr 05
1:17:56		Alejandro	López (10)	MEX	9.2.75	2		Eisenhüttenstadt	8 May 99
1:18:00			Fernández			2	WCh	Saint-Denis	23 Aug 03
1:18:04	WR		Bo Lingtang	CHN	12.8.70	1	NC	Beijing	7 Apr 94
1:18:05		Dmitriy	Yesipchuk	RUS	17.11.74	1	NC-w	Adler	4 Mar 01
1:18:06		Viktor	Burayev	RUS	23.2.82	2	NC-w	Adler	4 Mar 01
1:18:06		Vladimir	Parvatkin	RUS	10.10.84	1	NC-w	Adler	12 Mar 05
1:18:07			Rasskazov			1	NC-w	Adler	20 Feb 00
1:18:07			Rasskazov			3	WCh	Saint-Denis	23 Aug 03
1:18:07			Li Gaobo	CHN	23.7.89	4		Cixi	23 Apr 05
1:18:12		Artur	Meleshkevich	BLR	11.4.75	1		Brest	10 Mar 01
1:18:13	WR	Pavol	Blazek	SVK	9.7.58	1		Hildesheim	16 Sep 90
1:18:14		Mikhail	Khmelnitskiy	BLR	24.7.69	1	NC	Soligorsk	13 May 00
1:18:14		Nathan	Deakes	AUS	17.8.77	1		Dublin	16 Jun 01
1:18:14		Noé	Hernández	MEX	15.3.78	4	WCh	Saint-Denis	23 Aug 03
1:18:16		Vladimir	Andreyev	RUS	7.9.66	2	NC	Moskva	19 May 00
1:18:17			Parvatkin			2	NC-w	Adler	8 Feb 04
1:18:17		Ilya	Markov	RUS	19.6.72	2	NC-w	Adler	12 Mar 05
1:18:18		Yevgeniy	Misyulya	BLR	13.3.64	1		Eisenhüttenstadt	11 May 96
1:18:20	WR	Andrey	Perlov	RUS	12.12.61	1	NC	Moskva	26 May 90
1:18:20		Denis	Nizhegorodov	RUS	26.7.80	3	NC-w	Adler	4 Mar 01
		(30/24)							
1:18:22		Robert	Korzeniowski	POL	30.7.68	1		Hildesheim	9 Jul 00
1:18:23		Andrey	Makarov	BLR	2.1.71	2	NC	Soligorsk	13 May 00
1:18:27		Daniel	García	MEX	28.10.71	2	WCp	Podebrady	19 Apr 97
1:18:27			Xing Shucai	CHN	4.8.84	5		Cixi	23 Apr 05
1:18:30			Yu Chaohong	CHN	12.12.76	6		Cixi	23 Apr 05
1:18:31			Han Yucheng	CHN	16.12.78	7		Cixi	23 Apr 05
		(30)							
1:18:32			Li Zewen	CHN	5.12.73	4	WCp	Podebrady	19 Apr 97

Mark	Wind	Name		Nat	Born	Pos	Meet	Venue	Date
1:18:33			Liu Yunfeng	CHN	3.8.79	8		Cixi	23 Apr 05
1:18:35.2t		Stefan	Johansson	SWE	11.4.67	1	SGP	Fana	15 May 92
1:18:36		Mikhail	Shchennikov	RUS	24.12.67	1	NC	Sochi	20 Apr 96
1:18:37		Aleksandr	Pershin	RUS	4.9.68	2	NC	Moskva	26 May 90
1:18:37		Ruslan	Shafikov	RUS	27.6.75	1	NC-w23	Adler	11 Feb 95
1:18:39			Lu Ronghua	CHN	21.2.83	9		Cixi	23 Apr 05
1:18:40.0t	WR	Ernesto	Canto	MEX	18.10.59	1	SGP	Fana	5 May 84
1:18:41		Igor	Kollár	SVK	26.6.65	3		Eisenhüttenstadt	11 May 96
1:18:42		Andreas	Erm	GER	12.3.76	2	ECp	Eisenhüttenstadt	17 Jun 00
		(40)							
1:18:45		Stepan	Yudin	RUS	3.4.80	4	NC-w	Adler	12 Mar 05
1:18:46			Tan Mingjun	CHN	17.7.70	2	NC	Beijing	7 Apr 94
1:18:48		Rishat	Shafikov	RUS	23.1.70	2		Cheboksary	30 Aug 98
1:18:51		Frants	Kostyukevich	BLR	4.4.63	3	NC	Moskva	26 May 90
1:18:54		Maurizio	Damilano	ITA	6.4.57	1	7N	La Coruña	6 Jun 92
1:18:56		Grigoriy	Kornev	RUS	14.3.61	4	NC	Moskva	26 May 90
1:18:56			Yu Chaohong	CHN	12.12.76	2	NC	Yangzhou	12 Apr 03
1:19:00		Joel	Sánchez	MEX	15.9.66	3		Eisenhüttenstadt	8 May 99
1:19:02		Hatem	Ghoula	TUN	7.6.73	2		Eisenhüttenstadt	10 May 97
1:19:02		Andrey	Stadnichuk	RUS	14.12.73	1	NC-w	Sochi	17 Feb 02
1:19:02		Eder	Sánchez	MEX	21.5.86	11		Cixi	23 Apr 05
		(50)	100th man 1:19:59, 200th 1:21:14, 300th 1:22:02						
Probable short course									
1:18:33		Mikhail	Shchennikov	RUS	24.12.67	1	4-N	Livorno	10 Jul 93
1:18:49	WR?	Daniel	Bautista	MEX	4.8.52	1	LT	Eschborn	29 Sep 79

30 KILOMETRES WALK

Mark		Name		Nat	Born	Pos	Meet	Venue	Date
2:01:44.1t		Maurizio	Damilano	ITA	6.4.57	1		Cuneo	4 Oct 92
2:01:47+		Vladimir	Kanaykin	RUS	21.3.85	1	in 35k	Adler	13 Mar 05
2:02:27+			Kanaykin			1	in 35k	Adler	8 Feb 04
2:02:41		Andrey	Perlov	RUS	12.12.61	1	NC-w	Sochi	19 Feb 89
2:02:45		Yevgeniy	Misyulya	BLR	13.3.64	1		Mogilyov	28 Apr 91
2:03:06		Daniel	Bautista	MEX	4.8.52	1		Cherkassy	27 Apr 80
2:03:56.5t		Thierry	Toutain	FRA	14.2.62	1		Héricourt	24 Mar 91
2:04:00		Aleksandr	Potashov	BLR	12.3.62	1		Adler	14 Feb 93
2:04:24		Valeriy	Spitsyn	RUS	5.12.65	1	NC-w	Sochi	22 Feb 92
2:04:30		Vitaliy	Matsko	RUS	8.6.60	2	NC-w	Sochi	19 Feb 89
2:04:49+		Semyon	Lovkin	RUS	14.7.77	1=	in 35k	Adler	1 Mar 03
2:04:49+		Stepan	Yudin	RUS	3.4.80	1=	in 35k	Adler	1 Mar 03
2:04:50+		Sergey	Kirdyapkin (10)	RUS	16.1.80	2	in 35k	Adler	13 Mar 05
2:04:55.5t		Guillaume	Leblanc	CAN	14.4.62	1		Sept-Iles	16 Jun 90
2:05:01		Sergey	Katureyev	RUS	29.9.67	2	NC-w	Sochi	22 Feb 92
2:05:05		Pyotr	Pochenchuk	UKR	26.7.54	2		Cherkassy	27 Apr 80

35 KILOMETRES WALK

Mark		Name		Nat	Born	Pos	Meet	Venue	Date
2:23:17		Vladimir	Kanaykin	RUS	21.3.85	1	NC-w	Adler	8 Feb 04
2:23:17			Kanaykin			1	NC-w	Adler	13 Mar 05
2:24:25		Semyon	Lovkin	RUS	14.7.77	1	NC-w	Adler	1 Mar 03
2:25:38		Stepan	Yudin	RUS	3.4.80	2	NC-w	Adler	1 Mar 03
2:25:57		Sergey	Kirdyapkin	RUS	16.1.80	2	NC-w	Adler	13 Mar 05
2:25:58		German	Skurygin ¶	RUS	15.9.63	1	NC-w	Adler	20 Feb 98
2:26:25		Aleksey	Voyevodin	RUS	9.8.70	2	NC-w	Adler	8 Feb 04
2:26:46		Oleg	Ishutkin	RUS	22.7.75	1	NC-w	Adler	9 Feb 97
2:27:02		Yevgeniy	Shmalyuk	RUS	14.1.76	1	NC-w	Adler	20 Feb 00
2:27:07		Dmitriy	Dolnikov	RUS	19.11.72	2	NC-w	Adler	20 Feb 98
2:27:21		Pavel	Nikolayev (10)	RUS	18.12.77	3	NC-w	Adler	20 Feb 98
2:27:29		Nikolay	Matyukhin	RUS	13.12.68	2	NC-w	Adler	9 Feb 97
2:27:51		Oleg	Merkulov	RUS	1.8.70	5	NC-w	Adler	20 Feb 98
2:27:54		Valeriy	Spitsyn	RUS	5.12.65	2	NC-w	Adler	20 Feb 00

50 KILOMETRES WALK

Mark		Name		Nat	Born	Pos	Meet	Venue	Date
3:35:29		Denis	Nizhegorodov	RUS	26.7.80	1	NC	Cheboksary	13 Jun 04
3:36:03	WR	Robert	Korzeniowski	POL	30.7.68	1	WCh	Saint-Denis	27 Aug 03
3:36:06			Yu Chaohong	CHN	12.12.76	1	NG	Nanjing	22 Oct 05
3:36:13			Zhao Chengliang	CHN	1.6.84	2	NG	Nanjing	22 Oct 05
3:36:20			Han Yucheng	CHN	16.12.78	1	NC	Nanning	27 Feb 05
3:36:39	WR		Korzeniowski			1	EC	München	8 Aug 02
3:36:42		German	Skurygin ¶	RUS	15.9.63	2	WCh	Saint-Denis	27 Aug 03
3:37:26	WR	Valeriy	Spitsyn	RUS	5.12.65	1	NC	Moskva	21 May 00
3:37:41	WR	Andrey	Perlov	RUS	12.12.61	1	NC	Leningrad	5 Aug 89

Mark	Wind	Name		Nat	Born	Pos	Meet	Venue	Date
3:37:46		Andreas	Erm	GER	12.3.76	3	WCh	Saint-Denis	27 Aug 03
3:37:58			Xing Shucai (10)	CHN	4.8.84	2	NC	Nanning	27 Feb 05
3:38:01		Aleksey	Voyevodin	RUS	9.8.70	4	WCh	Saint-Denis	27 Aug 03
3:38:08		Sergey	Kirdyapkin	RUS	16.1.80	1	WCh	Helsinki	12 Aug 05
3:38:17	WR	Ronald	Weigel	GDR	8.8.59	1	IM	Potsdam	25 May 86
3:38:23			Nizhegorodov			5	WCh	Saint-Denis	27 Aug 03
3:38:29		Vyacheslav	Ivanenko	RUS	3.3.61	1	OG	Seoul	30 Sep 88
3:38:31	WR		Weigel			1		Berlin	20 Jul 84
3:38:43		Valentin	Massana (10)	ESP	5.7.70	1	NC	Orense	20 Mar 94
3:38:46			Korzeniowski			1	OG	Athína	27 Aug 04
3:38:56			Weigel			2	OG	Seoul	30 Sep 88
3:38:56			Zhao Chengliang			3	NC	Nanning	27 Feb 05
3:39:10			Han Yucheng			1	NC-w	Guangzhou	22 Mar 04
3:39:17			Dong Jimin	CHN	10.10.85	4	NC	Nanning	27 Feb 05
3:39:21		Vladimir	Potemin	RUS	15.1.80	2	NC	Moskva	21 May 00
3:39:22		Sergey	Korepanov	KAZ	9.5.64	1	WCp	Mézidon-Canon	2 May 99
3:39:34		Valentin	Kononen	FIN	7.3.69	1		Dudince	25 Mar 00
3:39:34			Potemin			2	NC	Cheboksary	13 Jun 04
3:39:43		Nathan	Deakes	AUS	17.8.77	1		Melbourne	7 Dec 03
3:39:45		Hartwig	Gauder	GDR	10.11.54	3	OG	Seoul	30 Sep 88
3:39:47			Perlov			1		Leningrad	3 Aug 85
3:39:54		Jesús Angel	García	ESP	17.10.69	1	WCp	Podebrady	20 Apr 97
		(31/21)							
3:40:02		Aleksandr	Potashov	BLR	12.3.62	1	NC	Moskva	27 May 90
3:40:07		Andrey	Plotnikov	RUS	12.8.67	2	NC	Moskva	27 May 90
3:40:08		Tomasz	Lipiec ¶	POL	10.5.71	2	WCp	Mézidon-Canon	2 May 99
3:40:12		Oleg	Ishutkin	RUS	22.7.75	2	WCp	Podebrady	20 Apr 97
3:40:13		Nikolay	Matyukhin	RUS	13.12.68	3	WCp	Mézidon-Canon	2 May 99
3:40:23			Gadasu Alatan	CHN	27.1.84	3	NG	Nanjing	22 Oct 05
3:40:40		Vladimir	Kanaykin	RUS	21.3.85	1	NC	Saransk	12 Jun 05
3:40:46	WR	José	Marin	ESP	21.1.50	1		Valencia	13 Mar 83
3:40:57.9t		Thierry	Toutain	FRA	14.2.62	1		Héricourt	29 Sep 96
3:41:20	WR	Raul	González	MEX	29.2.52	1		Podebrady	11 Jun 78
		(30)							
3:41:20			Zhao Yongsheng	CHN	16.4.70	1	WCp	Beijing	30 Apr 95
3:41:28.2t		René	Piller	FRA	23.4.65	1	SGP	Fana	7 May 94
3:41:30			Ni Liang	CHN	26.7.86	4	NG	Nanjing	22 Oct 05
3:41:47		Mikel	Odriozola	ESP	25.5.73	1	NC	El Prat de Llobregat	27 Feb 05
3:41:51		Venyamin	Nikolayev	RUS	7.10.58	2		Leningrad	3 Aug 85
3:41:54		Alex	Schwazer	ITA	26.12.84	3	WCh	Helsinki	12 Aug 05
3:41:56		Yevgeniy	Shmalyuk	RUS	14.1.76	6	WCp	Mézidon-Canon	2 May 99
3:42:00		Stanislav	Vezhel	BLR	11.10.58	3	NC	Moskva	27 May 90
3:42:03		Carlos	Mercenario	MEX	3.5.67	1	WCp	San José	2 Jun 91
3:42:04		Yevgeniy	Yevsyukov	RUS	2.1.50	3		Leningrad	3 Aug 85
		(40)							
3:42:06		Yuriy	Andronov	RUS	6.11.71	2	NC	Cheboksary	26 May 02
3:42:20		Pavel	Szikora	SVK	26.3.52	1		Dudince	4 Apr 87
3:42:20		Viktor	Ginko	BLR	7.12.65	2		Palma	5 Mar 95
3:42:36		Reima	Salonen	FIN	19.11.55	1	NC	Vantaa	24 May 86
3:42:37		Valeriy	Suntsov	RUS	10.7.55	4		Leningrad	3 Aug 85
3:42:45		Miguel Angel	Rodríguez	MEX	15.1.67	6	WCp	Podebrady	20 Apr 97
3:42:52		Stepan	Yudin	RUS	3.4.80	3	NC	Cheboksary	26 May 02
3:42:55			Si Tianfeng	CHN	17.6.84	5	NG	Nanjing	22 Oct 05
3:43:13		Simon	Baker	AUS	6.2.58	1	LT	L'Hospitalet	28 May 89
3:43:14		Dietmar	Meisch	GDR	10.2.59	3	LT	New York	2 May 87
		(50)	100th man 3:47:34						

100 KILOMETRES WALK

Mark	Name		Nat	Born	Pos	Meet	Venue	Date
8:38.07	Viktor	Ginko	BLR	7.12.65	1		Scanzorosciate	27 Oct 02
8:43:30		Ginko			1		Scanzorosciate	29 Oct 00
8:44:28		Ginko			1		Scanzoroscaite	19 Oct 03
8:48:28	Modris	Liepins	LAT	3.8.66	1		Scanzorosciate	28 Oct 01
8:54:35	Aleksey	Rodionov	RUS	5.3.57	1		Scanzorosciate	15 Nov 98
8:55:12	Pascal	Kieffer	FRA	6.5.61	1		Besançon	18 Oct 92
8:55:40	Vitaliy	Popovich	UKR	22.10.62	1		Scanzorosciate	31 Oct 99
8:57:29		Kieffer			1	NC	Perpignan	15 Oct 95
8:58:12	Gérard	Lelievre	FRA	13.11.49	1		Laval	7 Oct 84
8:58:47	Zóltan	Czukor	HUN	18.12.62	2		Scanzorosciate	27 Oct 02
	(10/7)							

JUNIOR MEN'S ALL-TIME LISTS

100 METRES

Mark	Wind	Name		Nat	Born	Pos	Meet	Venue	Date
10.01	0.0	Darrel	Brown	TRI	11.10.84	1q3	WCh	Saint-Denis	24 Aug 03
10.05		Davidson	Ezinwa	NGR	22.11.71	1		Bauchi	4 Jan 90
10.06	2.0	Dwain	Chambers	GBR	5.4.78	1	EJ	Ljubljana	25 Jul 97
10.06	1.5	Walter	Dix	USA	31.1.86	1h1	NCAA-r	New York	27 May 05
10.07	2.0	Stanley	Floyd	USA	23.6.61	1		Austin	24 May 80
10.07	1.1	DaBryan	Blanton	USA	3.7.84	1h2	NCAA-r	Lincoln, NE	30 May 03
10.07	0.2	Tamunosiki	Atorudibo	NGR	21.3.85	1s2	NC	Abuja	9 Jul 04
10.08	0.0	Andre	Cason	USA	13.1.69	1	NC-j	Tallahassee	24 Jun 88
10.08	0.0	Justin	Gatlin	USA	10.2.82	1	NCAA	Eugene	2 Jun 01
10.08A	1.9	Obadele	Thompson	BAR	30.3.76	3		El Paso	16 Apr 94
10.08	0.7	J-Mee	Samuels	USA	20.5.87	1		Greensboro	24 Jul 05
10.09A	1.8	Mel	Lattany	USA	10.8.59	2r2	USOF	USAF Academy	30 Jul 78
Wind assisted to 10.07									
9.83	7.1	Leonard	Scott	USA	19.1.80	1		Knoxville	9 Apr 99
9.96	4.5	Walter	Dix	USA	31.1.86	1rA	TexR	Austin	9 Apr 05
9.97	??	Mark	Lewis-Francis	GBR	4.9.82	1q3	WCh	Edmonton	4 Aug 01
10.05	2.1	J-Mee	Samuels	USA	20.5.87	1s2		Greensboro	23 Jul 05
10.07	2.9	Lee	McRae	USA	23.1.66	2h5	NCAA	Austin	30 May 85

200 METRES

Mark	Wind	Name		Nat	Born	Pos	Meet	Venue	Date
19.93	1.4	Usain	Bolt	JAM	21.8.86	1		Hamilton, BER	11 Apr 04
20.07	1.5	Lorenzo	Daniel	USA	23.3.66	1	SEC	Starkville	18 May 85
20.13	1.7	Roy	Martin	USA	25.12.66	1		Austin	11 May 85
20.16A	-0.2	Riaan	Dempers	RSA	4.3.77	1	NC-j	Germiston	7 Apr 95
20.18	1.0	Walter	Dix	USA	31.1.86	1s2	NCAA	Sacramento	9 Jun 05
20.22	1.7	Dwayne	Evans	USA	13.10.58	2	OT	Eugene	22 Jun 76
20.23	0.5	Michael	Timpson	USA	6.6.67	1		State College	16 May 86
20.24	0.2	Joe	DeLoach	USA	5.6.67	3		Los Angeles	8 Jun 85
20.24	0.2	Francis	Obikwelu	NGR	22.11.78	2rB		Granada	29 May 96
20.28	0.1	Andrew	Howe	ITA	12.5.85	1	WJ	Grosseto	16 Jul 04
20.29 four men: Clinton Davis USA 1983, Christian Malcolm GBR 1998, Justin Gatlin USA & Yusuke Omae JPN 2001									
Wind assisted									
19.86	4.0	Justin	Gatlin	USA	10.2.82	1h2	NCAA	Eugene	30 May 01
20.01	2.5	Derald	Harris	USA	5.4.58	1		San José	9 Apr 77
20.08	9.2	Leonard	Scott	USA	19.1.80	2r2		Knoxville	9 Apr 99
20.10	4.6	Stanley	Kerr	USA	19.6.67	2r2	SWC	Houston	18 May 86
Hand timing: 19.9		Davidson	Ezinwa	NGR	22.11.71	1		Bauchi	18 Mar 89

400 METRES

Mark	Name		Nat	Born	Pos	Meet	Venue	Date
43.87	Steve	Lewis	USA	16.5.69	1	OG	Seoul	28 Sep 88
44.66	Hamdam Odha	Al-Bishi	KSA	5.5.81	1	WJ	Santiago de Chile	20 Oct 00
44.66	LaShawn	Merritt	USA	27.6.86	1		Kingston	7 May 05
44.69	Darrell	Robinson	USA	23.12.63	2	USOF	Indianapolis	24 Jul 82
44.73A	James	Rolle	USA	2.2.64	1	USOF	USAF Academy	2 Jul 83
44.75	Darren	Clark	AUS	6.9.65	4	OG	Los Angeles	8 Aug 84
44.75	Deon	Minor	USA	22.1.73	1s1	NCAA	Austin	5 Jun 92
44.93	Nagmeldin	El Abubakr	SUD	22.2.86	1	Is.Sol	Makkah	14 Apr 05
45.01	Thomas	Schönlebe	GDR	6.8.65	1		Berlin	15 Jul 84
45.01	Jerome	Young	USA	14.8.76	1	NC-j	Walnut	24 Jun 95
45.04A	Wayne	Collett	USA	20.10.49	1q2	OT	Echo Summit	13 Sep 68
45.04	Brandon	Couts	USA	17.2.79	1	DrakeR	Des Moines	25 Apr 98
44.9+A	Steve	Williams	USA	13.11.53	1	WAC	El Paso	13 May 72

800 METRES

Mark	Name		Nat	Born	Pos	Meet	Venue	Date
1:43.64	Japheth	Kimutai	KEN	20.12.78	3rB	WK	Zürich	13 Aug 97
1:44.27	Majid Saeed	Sultan	QAT	3.11.86	1	AsiC	Inchon	4 Sep 05
1:44.3*	Jim	Ryun	USA	29.4.47	1	USTFF	Terre Haute	10 Jun 66
1:44.3	Joaquim	Cruz	BRA	12.3.63	1		Rio de Janeiro	27 Jun 81
1:44.33	Yuriy	Borzakovskiy	RUS	12.4.81	2s2	OG	Sydney	25 Sep 00
1:44.39	Mohammed	Al-Salhi	KSA	11.5.86	1		Lapinlahti	3 Jul 05
1:44.45	Alfred	Kirwa Yego	KEN	28.11.86	3rA	Bisl	Oslo	29 Jul 05
1:44.46	Nicholas	Wachira	KEN	19.11.82	5	GP II	Rieti	2 Sep 01
1:44.56	Benjamin	Kipkurui	KEN	28.12.80	2		Rehlingen	24 May 99
1:44.69	William	Chirchir	KEN	6.2.79	6	Herc	Monaco	8 Aug 98
1:44.77	Benson	Koech	KEN	10.11.74	1	WJ	Seoul	19 Sep 92
1:44.98	Cornelius	Chirchir	KEN	5.6.83	4		Rovereto	29 Aug 01

Mark	Wind	Name		Nat	Born	Pos	Meet	Venue	Date

1000 METRES

Mark	Name		Nat	Born	Pos	Meet	Venue	Date
2:15.00	Benjamin	Kipkurui	KEN	28.12.80	5	Nik	Nice	17 Jul 99
2:16.84	Ali	Hakimi	TUN	24.4.76	1		Lindau	28 Jul 95
2:16.86	Japheth	Kimutai	KEN	20.12.78	1	VD	Bruxelles	22 Aug 97
2:17.10	Julius	Achon	UGA	12.12.76	1		Rhede	30 Jul 95

1500 METRES

Mark	Name		Nat	Born	Pos	Meet	Venue	Date
3:30.24	Cornelius	Chirchir	KEN	5.6.83	4	Herc	Monaco	19 Jul 02
3:31.13	Mulugueta	Wondimu	ETH	28.2.85	2rA	NA	Heusden	31 Jul 04
3:31.42	Alex	Kipchirchir	KEN	26.11.84	5	VD	Bruxelles	5 Sep 03
3:31.54	Isaac	Songok	KEN	25.4.84	1	NA	Heusden	2 Aug 03
3:32.91	Noah	Ngeny	KEN	2.11.78	9	Herc	Monaco	16 Aug 97
3:33.16	Benjamin	Kipkurui	KEN	28.12.80	1rB	WK	Zürich	11 Aug 99
3:33.24	William	Chirchir	KEN	6.2.79	8rA	WK	Zürich	12 Aug 98
3:33.99	Augustine	Choge	KEN	21.1.87	4rA	GP	Sevilla	4 Jun 05
3:34.03	Bernard	Kiptum	KEN	8.10.86	8	ISTAF	Berlin	4 Sep 05
3:34.17	Michael	Too	KEN	3.8.83	4	GP	Doha	15 May 02
3:34.63	Daniel	Komen	KEN	17.5.76	2	Znam	Moskva	5 Jun 95
3:34.92	Kipkoech	Cheruiyot	KEN	2.12.64	1		München	26 Jul 83

1 MILE

Mark	Name		Nat	Born	Pos	Meet	Venue	Date
3:50.25	Alex	Kipchirchir	KEN	26.11.84	2	GP II	Rieti	7 Sep 03
3:50.39	James	Kwalia	KEN	12.6.84	1	FBK	Hengelo	1 Jun 03
3:50.41	Noah	Ngeny	KEN	2.11.78	2	Nik	Nice	16 Jul 97
3:50.69	Cornelius	Chirchir	KEN	5.6.83	5	GGala	Roma	12 Jul 02
3:51.3	Jim	Ryun	USA	29.4.47	1		Berkeley	17 Jul 66

2000 METRES

Mark	Name		Nat	Born	Pos	Meet	Venue	Date
4:56.86	Isaac	Songok	KEN	25.4.84	6	ISTAF	Berlin	31 Aug 01
4:59.11	James	Kwalia	KEN	12.6.84	5		Naimette	2 Sep 03
4:59.14	Ali	Saïdi-Sief	ALG	15.3.78	9	Gaz	Villeneuve d'Ascq	29 Jun 97
5:00.0+	Sammy	Kipketer	KEN	29.9.81	8	in3k	Monaco	4 Aug 99

3000 METRES

Mark	Name		Nat	Born	Pos	Meet	Venue	Date
7:28.78	Augustine	Choge	KEN	21.1.87	2	SGP	Doha	13 May 05
7:30.67	Kenenisa	Bekele	ETH	13.6.82	2	VD	Bruxelles	24 Aug 01
7:30.91	Eliud	Kipchoge	KEN	5.11.84	2	VD	Bruxelles	5 Sep 03
7:33.00	Hailu	Mekonnen	ETH	4.4.80	2		Stuttgart	6 Jun 99
7:34.32	Richard	Limo	KEN	18.11.80	4	VD	Bruxelles	3 Sep 99
7:34.58	Sammy	Kipketer	KEN	29.9.81	5	VD	Bruxelles	3 Sep 99
7:35.52	Philip	Mosima	KEN	2.1.77	1	GP	London (CP)	12 Jul 96
7:35.53	James	Kwalia	KEN	12.6.84	5	VD	Bruxelles	5 Sep 03
7:36.63	Tariku	Bekele	ETH	21.1.87	2		Shanghai	17 Sep 05
7:38.09	Daniel	Komen	KEN	17.5.76	7	GPF	Monaco	9 Sep 95

5000 METRES

Mark	Name		Nat	Born	Pos	Meet	Venue	Date
12:52.61	Eliud	Kipchoge	KEN	5.11.84	3	Bisl	Oslo	27 Jun 03
12:53.66	Augustine	Choge	KEN	21.1.87	4	GGala	Roma	8 Jul 05
12:53.72	Philip	Mosima	KEN	2.1.77	2	GGala	Roma	5 Jun 96
12:54.07	Sammy	Kipketer	KEN	29.9.81	2	GGala	Roma	30 Jun 00
12:54.58	James	Kwalia	KEN	12.6.84	5	Bisl	Oslo	27 Jun 03
12:56.15	Daniel	Komen	KEN	17.5.76	2	GG	Roma	8 Jun 95
12:57.05	Mulugueta	Wondimu	ETH	28.2.85	2	ISTAF	Berlin	12 Sep 04
12:58.08	Gebre-egziabher	Gebremariam	ETH	10.9.84	6	WCh	Saint-Denis	31 Aug 03
12:59.03	Tariku	Bekele	ETH	21.1.87	4	Gaz	Saint-Denis	1 Jul 05
12:58.15	Richard	Limo	KEN	18.11.80	6	GGala	Roma	7 Jul 99
12:59.39	Million	Wolde	ETH	17.3.79	5	WK	Zürich	12 Aug 98

10,000 METRES

Mark	Name		Nat	Born	Pos	Meet	Venue	Date
26:41.75	Samuel	Wanjiru	KEN	10.11.86	3	VD	Bruxelles	26 Aug 05
27:04.00	Boniface	Kiprop	UGA	12.10.85	5	VD	Bruxelles	3 Sep 04
27:04.45	Bernard Kipyego	Kiprop	KEN	16.7.86	4	FBK	Hengelo	29 May 05
27:07.29	Moses	Masai	KEN	1.6.86	7	VD	Bruxelles	3 Sep 04
27:11.18	Richard	Chelimo	KEN	21.4.72	1	APM	Hengelo	25 Jun 91
27:13.66	Moses	Mosop	KEN	17.7.85	7	VD	Bruxelles	5 Sep 03
27:15.88	Boniface	Kiprop	UGA	12.10.85	9	VD	Bruxelles	5 Sep 03
27:17.82	Addis	Abebe	ETH	5.9.70	2	WG	Helsinki	29 Jun 89
27:22.46	Martin Irung	Mathathi	KEN	25.12.85	1rA		Kobe	25 Apr 04
27:24.75	John Cheruiyot	Korir	KEN	13.12.81	5	OG	Sydney	25 Sep 00
27:25.01	Assefa	Mezegebu	ETH	19.6.78	1	APM	Hengelo	31 May 97

3000 METRES STEEPLECHASE

ark	Wind	Name		Nat	Born	Pos	Meet	Venue	Date
:58.66		Stephen	Cherono	KEN	15.10.82	3	VD	Bruxelles	24 Aug 01
:03.74		Raymond	Yator	KEN	7.4.81	3	Herc	Monaco	18 Aug 00
:05.52		Brimin	Kipruto	KEN	31.7.85	1	FBK	Hengelo	31 May 04
:07.18		Moussa	Omar Obaid	QAT	18.4.85	4	OG	Athína	24 Aug 04
:07.69		Paul	Kosgei	KEN	22.4.78	5	DNG	Stockholm	7 Jul 97
:09.37		Abel	Cheruiyot/Yugut	KEN	26.12.84	2	NA	Heusden	2 Aug 03
:12.91		Thomas	Kiplitan	KEN	15.6.83	7	GP	Doha	15 May 02
:16.69		Ronald	Kipchumba Rutto	KEN	8.10.87	4	FBK	Hengelo	29 May 05
:16.76		Kipkirui	Misoi	KEN	23.10.78	2		Dortmund	8 Jun 97
:18.71		Julius	Chelule	KEN	25.12.78	4	Slovn	Bratislava	10 Jun 97
:18.52		Moustafa Ahmad	Shebto	QAT	4.7.86	14	VD	Bruxelles	3 Sep 04

110 METRES HURDLES

ark	Wind	Name		Nat	Born	Pos	Meet	Venue	Date
3.12	1.6		Liu Xiang	CHN	13.7.83	1rB	Athl	Lausanne	2 Jul 02
3.23	0.0	Renaldo	Nehemiah	USA	24.3.59	1r2	WK	Zürich	16 Aug 78
3.40	-1.0		Shi Dongpeng	CHN	6.1.84	1	NC	Shanghai	14 Sep 03
3.44	-0.8	Colin	Jackson	GBR	18.2.67	1	WJ	Athína	19 Jul 86
3.46	1.8	Jon	Ridgeon	GBR	14.2.67	1	EJ	Cottbus	23 Aug 85
3.46	-1.6	Dayron	Robles	CUB	19.11.86	1	PAm-J	Windsor	29 Jul 05
3.47	1.9	Holger	Pohland	GDR	5.4.63	2	vUSA	Karl-Marx-Stadt	10 Jul 82
3.47	1.2	Aries	Merritt	USA	24.7.85	4	NCAA	Austin	12 Jun 04
3.49	0.6	Stanislav	Olijar	LAT	22.3.79	1		Valmiera	11 Jul 98
3.50	0.7	Jason	Richardson	USA	4.4.86	3	NCAA	Sacramento	10 Jun 05
Vind assisted									
3.41	2.6	Dayron	Robles	CUB	19.11.86	2	CAC	Nassau	10 Jul 05
3.42	4.5	Colin	Jackson	GBR	18.2.67	2	CG	Edinburgh	27 Jul 86
3.42	2.6	Antwon	Hicks	USA	12.3.83	1	WJ	Kingston	21 Jul 02
3.47	2.1	Frank	Busemann	GER	26.2.75	1	WJ	Lisboa	22 Jul 94

400 METRES HURDLES

ark	Wind	Name		Nat	Born	Pos	Meet	Venue	Date
48.02		Danny	Harris	USA	7.9.65	2s1	OT	Los Angeles	17 Jun 84
48.51		Kerron	Clement	USA	31.10.85	1	WJ	Grosseto	16 Jul 04
48.62		Brandon	Johnson	USA	6.3.85	2	WJ	Grosseto	16 Jul 04
48.68		Bayano	Kamani	USA	17.4.80	1	NCAA	Boise	4 Jun 99
48.72		Angelo	Taylor	USA	29.12.78	2	NCAA	Bloomington	6 Jun 97
48.74		Vladimir	Budko	BLR	4.2.65	2	DRZ	Moskva	18 Aug 84
48.76A		Llewellyn	Herbert	RSA	21.7.77	1		Pretoria	7 Apr 96
48.79		Kenneth	Ferguson	USA	22.3.84	1	SEC	Knoxville	18 May 03
48.89		Louis	van Zyl	RSA	20.7.85	1	WJ	Kingston	19 Jul 02
48.94		Ibrahim	Al-Hamaidi	KSA	28.8.85	3	WJ	Grosseto	16 Jul 04
49.07		Mubarak	Al-Nubi	QAT	30.12.77	1	WJ	Sydney	23 Aug 96
49.09		Dai	Tamesue	JPN	3.5.78	1		Hiroshima	14 Oct 96

HIGH JUMP

ark	Wind	Name		Nat	Born	Pos	Meet	Venue	Date
2.37		Dragutin	Topic	YUG	12.3.71	1	WJ	Plovdiv	12 Aug 90
2.37		Steve	Smith	GBR	29.3.73	1	WJ	Seoul	20 Sep 92
2.36		Javier	Sotomayor	CUB	13.10.67	1		Santiago de Cuba	23 Feb 86
2.35i		Vladimir	Yashchenko	UKR	12.1.59	1	EI	Milano	12 Mar 78
		2.34				1	Prv	Tbilisi	16 Jun 78
2.35		Dietmar	Mögenburg	FRG	15.8.61	1		Rehlingen	26 May 80
2.34		Tim	Forsyth	AUS	17.8.73	1	Bisl	Oslo	4 Jul 92
2.33			Zhu Jianhua	CHN	29.5.63	1	AsiG	New Delhi	1 Dec 82
2.33		Patrik	Sjöberg	SWE	5.1.65	1	OsloG	Oslo	9 Jul 83
2.32i		Jaroslav	Bába	CZE	2.9.84	3		Arnstadt	8 Feb 03
2.31		Jörg	Freimuth	GDR	10.9.61	3	OG	Moskva	1 Aug 80
2.31		Lochsley	Thomson	AUS	20.8.73	3	NC	Adelaide	8 Mar 92
2.31i		Andrey	Chubsa	BLR	29.11.82	1		Vitebsk	12 Jan 01
2.31		Jacques	Freitag	RSA	11.6.82	1		Rehlingen	4 Jun 01
2.31		Andra	Manson	USA	30.4.84	1	WJ	Kingston	18 Jul 02

POLE VAULT

ark	Wind	Name		Nat	Born	Pos	Meet	Venue	Date
5.80		Maksim	Tarasov	RUS	2.12.70	1	vGDR-j	Bryansk	14 Jul 89
5.75		Konstadínos	Filippídis	GRE	26.11.86	2	WUG	Izmir	18 Aug 05
5.71		Lawrence	Johnson	USA	7.5.74	1		Knoxville	12 Jun 93
5.70		Viktor	Chistyakov	RUS	9.2.75	1		Leppävirta	7 Jun 94
5.70		Artyom	Kuptsov	RUS	22.4.84	1	Znam	Tula	7 Jun 03
5.65		Radion	Gataullin	UZB	23.11.65	2	NC	Donetsk	8 Sep 84
5.65		István	Bagyula	HUN	2.1.69	1	WJ	Sudbury	28 Jul 88
5.65i		Jacob	Davis	USA	29.4.78	1	Big 12	Lincoln	21 Feb 97
		5.62				2		Austin	5 Apr 97

Mark	Wind	Name		Nat	Born	Pos	Meet	Venue	Date
5.62		Gérald	Baudouin	FRA	15.11.72	1	NC-j	Dreux	7 Jul 9
5.62		Lars	Börgeling	GER	16.4.79	1		Mannheim	13 Jun 9

5.61 four men: Thierry Vigneron FRA 79, (i) Grigoriy Yegorov KAZ 86, Danny Ecker GER 96, Vasiliy Petrov RUS 01

LONG JUMP

Mark	Wind	Name		Nat	Born	Pos	Meet	Venue	Date
8.34	0.0	Randy	Williams	USA	23.8.53	Q	OG	München	8 Sep 7
8.28	0.8	Luis A	Bueno	CUB	22.5.69	1		La Habana	16 Jul 8
8.24	0.2	Eric	Metcalf	USA	23.1.68	1	NCAA	Indianapolis	6 Jun 8
8.24	1.8	Vladimir	Ochkan	UKR	13.1.68	1	vGDR-j	Leningrad	21 Jun 8
8.22		Larry	Doubley	USA	15.3.58	1	NCAA	Champaign	3 Jun 7
8.22		Ivan	Pedroso	CUB	17.12.72	1		Santiago de Cuba	3 May 9
8.22i		Viktor	Kuznetsov	UKR	14.7.86	1		Brovary	22 Jan 0
8.21A	2.0	Vance	Johnson	USA	13.3.63	1	NCAA	Provo	4 Jun 8
8.20	1.5	James	Stallworth	USA	29.4.71	Q	WJ	Plovdiv	9 Aug 9
8.18		LaMonte	King	USA	18.12.59	2	CalR	Modesto	20 May 7
8.18		Petr	Lampart	CZE	31.3.83	1		Brno	15 Sep 0

Wind assisted

Mark	Wind	Name		Nat	Born	Pos	Meet	Venue	Date
8.40	3.2	Kareem	Streete-Thompson	CAY	30.3.73	1		Houston	5 May 9
8.35	2.2	Carl	Lewis	USA	1.7.61	1	NCAA	Austin	6 Jun 8
8.29	2.3	James	Beckford	JAM	9.1.75	1		Tempe	2 Apr 9
8.23	4.4	Peller	Phillips	USA	23.6.70	1		Sacramento	11 Jun 8
8.21	2.8	Masaki	Morinaga	JPN	27.3.72	1		Hamamatsu	7 Sep 9

TRIPLE JUMP

Mark	Wind	Name		Nat	Born	Pos	Meet	Venue	Date
17.50	0.4	Volker	Mai	GDR	3.5.66	1	vURS	Erfurt	23 Jun 8
17.42	1.3	Khristo	Markov	BUL	27.1.65	1	Nar	Sofiya	19 May 8
17.40A	0.4	Pedro	Pérez	CUB	23.2.52	1	PAm	Cali	5 Aug 7
17.31	-0.2	David	Giralt Jr.	CUB	26.8.84	Q	WCh	Saint-Denis	23 Aug 0
17.29	1.3	James	Beckford	JAM	9.1.75	1		Tempe	2 Apr 9
17.27		Aliecer	Urrutia	CUB	22.9.74	1		Artemisa	23 Apr 9
17.23	0.2	Yoelbi	Quesada	CUB	4.8.73	1	NC	La Habana	13 May 9
17.23	0.0		Gu Junjie	CHN	5.5.85	1		Hefei	26 Sep 0
17.11	1.4	Marian	Oprea	ROM	6.6.82	2	WUG	Beijing	31 Aug 0
17.03	0.6	Osiris	Mora	CUB	3.10.73	2	WJ	Seoul	19 Sep 9
17.13w	4.1	Marian	Oprea	ROM	6.6.82	1	ECp-1B	Budapest	24 Jun 0
17.13w	4.6	Kenneth	Hall	USA	17.4.86	1		Eugene	29 Jul 0

SHOT

Mark	Wind	Name		Nat	Born	Pos	Meet	Venue	Date
21.05i		Terry	Albritton	USA	14.1.55	1	AAU	New York	22 Feb 7
		20.38				2	MSR	Walnut	27 Apr 7
20.65		Mike	Carter	USA	29.10.60	1	vSU-j	Boston	4 Jul 7
20.39		Janus	Robberts	RSA	10.3.79	1	NC	Germiston	7 Mar 9
20.20		Randy	Matson	USA	5.3.45	2	OG	Tokyo	17 Oct 64
20.20		Udo	Beyer	GDR	9.8.55	2	NC	Leipzig	6 Jul 74
20.13		Jeff	Chakouian	USA	20.4.82	2		Atlanta	18 May 01
19.99		Karl	Salb	USA	19.5.49	4	OT	Echo Summit	10 Sep 68
19.95		Edis	Elkasevic	CRO	18.2.83	1		Velenje	15 Jun 02
19.74		Andreas	Horn	GDR	31.1.62	2	vSU-j	Cottbus	24 Jun 81
19.71		Vladimir	Kiselyov -1	UKR	1.1.57	1		Yalta	15 May 76
19.69		Mikulás	Konopka	SVK	23.1.79	2	NC	Nitra	11 Jul 98

DISCUS

Mark	Wind	Name		Nat	Born	Pos	Meet	Venue	Date
65.62		Werner	Reiterer	AUS	27.1.68	1		Melbourne	15 Dec 87
63.64		Werner	Hartmann	FRG	20.4.59	1	vFRA	Strasbourg	25 Jun 78
63.26		Sergey	Pachin	UKR	24.5.68	2		Moskva	25 Jul 87
63.22		Brian	Milne	USA	7.1.73	1		State College	28 Mar 92
62.52		John	Nichols	USA	23.8.69	1		Baton Rouge	23 Apr 88
62.36		Nuermaimaiti	Tulake	CHN	8.3.82	2	NG	Guangzhou	21 Nov 01
62.16		Zoltán	Kövágó	HUN	10.4.79	1		Budapest	9 May 97
62.04		Kenth	Gardenkrans	SWE	2.10.55	2		Helsingborg	11 Aug 74
62.04			Wu Tao	CHN	3.10.83	1	NGP	Shanghai	18 May 02
61.84		Attila	Horváth	HUN	28.7.67	2		Budapest	18 May 85
61.84		Andreas	Seelig	GDR	6.7.70	1		Halle	15 May 88

HAMMER

Mark	Wind	Name		Nat	Born	Pos	Meet	Venue	Date
78.33		Olli-Pekka	Karjalainen	FIN	7.3.80	1	NC	Seinäjoki	5 Aug 99
78.14		Roland	Steuk	GDR	5.3.59	1	NC	Leipzig	30 Jun 78
78.00		Sergey	Dorozhon	UKR	17.2.64	1		Moskva	7 Aug 83
76.54		Valeriy	Gubkin	BLR	3.9.67	2		Minsk	27 Jun 86
76.42		Ruslan	Dikiy	TJK	18.1.72	1		Togliatti	7 Sep 91

Mark	Wind	Name		Nat	Born	Pos	Meet	Venue	Date
75.52		Sergey	Kirmasov	RUS	25.3.70	1		Kharkov	4 Jun 89
75.42		Szymon	Ziolkowski	POL	1.7.76	1	EJ	Nyíregyhazá	30 Jul 95
75.24		Christoph	Sahner	FRG	23.9.63	1	vPOL-j	Göttingen	26 Jun 82
75.22		Yaroslav	Chmyr	UKR	29.11.66	1		Kiyev	9 Sep 85
75.20		Igor	Nikulin	RUS	14.8.60	2		Leselidze	1 Jun 79

JAVELIN

Mark	Wind	Name		Nat	Born	Pos	Meet	Venue	Date
83.87		Andreas	Thorkildsen	NOR	1.4.82	1		Fana	7 Jun 01
83.55		Aleksandr	Ivanov	RUS	25.5.82	2	NC	Tula	14 Jul 01
82.52		Harri	Haatainen	FIN	5.1.78	4		Leppävirta	25 May 96
81.80		Sergey	Voynov	UZB	26.2.77	1		Tashkent	6 Jun 96
80.94		Aki	Parviainen	FIN	26.10.74	4	NC	Jyväskylä	5 Jul 92
80.57		Teemu	Wirkkala	FIN	14.1.84	1		Espoo	14 Sep 03
80.43		Tero	Järvenpää	FIN	2.10.84	3	NC	Helsinki	11 Aug 03
80.30		Konstadínos	Gatsioúdis	GRE	17.12.73	1	NC	Athína	20 Jun 92
80.26		Vladimir	Ovchinnikov	RUS	2.8.70	Q	OG	Seoul	24 Sep 88
80.03		Lohan	Rautenbach	RSA	6.2.86	1	NC	Durban	16 Apr o5

DECATHLON

Mark	Wind	Name		Nat	Born	Pos	Meet	Venue	Date
8397		Torsten	Voss	GDR	24.3.63	1	NC	Erfurt	7 Jul 82
		10.76 7.66 14.41 2.09 48.37 14.37 41.76 4.80 62.90 4:34.04							
8114		Michael	Kohnle	FRG	3.5.70	1	EJ	Varazdin	26 Aug 89
		10.95 7.09/0.1 15.27 2.02 49.91 14.40 45.82 4.90 60.82 4:49.43							
8104		Valter	Külvet	EST	19.2.64	1		Viimsi	23 Aug 81
		10.7 7.26 13.86 2.09 48.5 14.8 47.92 4.50 60.34 4:37.8							
8082		Daley	Thompson	GBR	30.7.58	1	ECp/s	Sittard	31 Jul 77
		10.70/0.8 7.54/0.7 13.84 2.01 47.31 15.26/2.0 41.70 4.70 54.48 4:30.4							
8041			Qi Haifeng	CHN	7.8.83	1	AsiG	Busan	10 Oct 02
		11.09/0.2 7.22/0.0 13.05 2.06 49.09 14.54/0.0 43.16 4.80 61.04 4:35.17							
8036		Christian	Schenk	GDR	9.2.65	5		Potsdam	21 Jul 84
		11.54 7.18 14.26 2.16 49.23 15.06 44.74 4.20 65.98 4:24.11							
7938		Frank	Busemann	GER	26.2.75	1		Zeven	2 Oct 94
		10.68/1.6 7.37/1.1 13.08 2.03 50.41 14.34/-1.1 39.84 4.40 63.00 4:37.31)							
7913		Raul	Duany	CUB	4.1.75	2		La Habana	26 May 94
		11.50 7.13 13.99 2.10 49.70 14.77 37.76 4.50 65.58 4:24.03							
7906		Mikhail	Romanyuk	UKR	6.2.62	1	EJ	Utrecht	21 Aug 81
		11.26/1.8 7.11w/3.7 13.50 1.98 49.98 14.72w/4.0 42.94 4.90 59.74 4:30.63							
7897		Dennis	Leyckes	GER	20.4.82	1	WJ	Santiago de Chile	19 Oct 00
		10.98/1.6 7.22/0.4 13.46 1.95 47.59 14.61/-0.1 39.52 4.80 54.76 4:33.10							

10,000 METRES WALK

Mark	Wind	Name		Nat	Born	Pos	Meet	Venue	Date
38:46.4		Viktor	Burayev	RUS	23.8.82	1	NC-j	Moskva	20 May 00
38:54.75		Ralf	Kowalsky	GDR	22.3.62	1		Cottbus	24 Jun 81
39:28.45		Andrey	Ruzavin	RUS	28.9.86	1	EJ	Kaunas	23 Jul 05
39:44.71		Giovanni	De Benedictis	ITA	8.1.68	1	EJ	Birmingham	7 Aug 87
39:49.22			Pei Chuang	CHN	5.12.81	2	NSG	Chengdu	8 Sep 00
39:50.73		Jefferson	Pérez	ECU	1.7.74	1	PAmJ	Winnipeg	15 Jul 93
39:55.52		Ilya	Markov	RUS	19.6.72	1	WJ	Plovdiv	10 Aug 90
39:56.49		Alberto	Cruz	MEX	6.6.72	2	WJ	Plovdiv	10 Aug 90
39:59.58		Sergey	Tyulenyev	RUS	14.3.71	1		Kharkov	4 Jun 90
40:05.62		Michele	Didoni	ITA	7.3.74	1	EJ	San Sebastián	30 Jul 93

4 x 100 METRES RELAY

Mark	Nat	Team	Pos	Meet	Venue	Date
38.66	USA	Kimmons, Omole, I Williams, L Merritt	1	WJ	Grosseto	18 Jun 04
39.05	GBR	Edgar, Grant, Benjamin, Lewis-Francis	1	WJ	Santiago de Chile	22 Oct 00
39.15	JAM	Hutton, Nicely, Plummer, Bolt	2	WJ	Kingston	21 Jul 02
39.17	TRI	Simpson, Burns, Holder, Brown	3	WJ	Kingston	21 Jul 02
39.25	FRG	Dobeleit, Klameth, Evers, Lübke	1	EJ	Schwechat	28 Aug 83
39.30	JPN	Matsumaga, Noda, Takahira, Aikawa	1	AsiC-j	Bangkok	28 Oct 02
39.33	FRA	Pognon, Calligny, Doucoure, Djhone	2	WJ	Santiago de Chile	22 Oct 00
39.47	JPN	Mogi, Kitamura, Omaer, Miyazaki	3	WJ	Santiago de Chile	22 Oct 00

4 x 400 METRES RELAY

Mark	Nat	Team	Pos	Meet	Venue	Date
3:01.09	USA	B Johnson, L Merritt, Craig, Clement	1	WJ	Grosseto	18 Jul 04
3:03.80	GBR	Grindley, Patrick, Winrow, Richardson	2	WJ	Plovdiv	12 Aug 90
3:04.06	JAM	S Clarke, Bolt, Myers, Gonzales	2	WJ	Kingston	21 Jul 02
3:04.22	CUB	Cadogan, Mordoche, González, Hernández	2	WJ	Athína	20 Jul 86
3:04.50	RSA	Le Roux, Gebhardt, Julius, van Zyl	2	WJ	Grosseto	18 Jul 04
3:04.58	GDR	Preusche, Löper, Trylus, Carlowitz	1	EJ	Utrecht	23 Aug 81
3:04.74	AUS	McFarlane, Batman, Thom, Vincent	1	WJ	Annecy	2 Aug 98
3:05.33	JPN	Ota, Noda, Suzuki, Sasaki	3	WJ	Grosseto	18 Jul 04

WOMEN'S ALL-TIME WORLD LISTS

100 METRES

Mark	Wind	Name		Nat	Born	Pos	Meet	Venue	Date
10.49WR	0.0	Florence	Griffith-Joyner	USA	21.12.59	1q1	OT	Indianapolis	16 Jul 88
		@ Probably strongly wind-assisted, but recognised as a US and world record							
10.61	1.2		Griffith-Joyner			1	OT	Indianapolis	17 Jul 88
10.62	1.0		Griffith-Joyner			1q3	OG	Seoul	24 Sep 88
10.65A	1.1	Marion	Jones	USA	12.10.75	1	WCp	Johannesburg	12 Sep 98
10.70	1.6		Griffith-Joyner			1s1	OT	Indianapolis	17 Jul 88
10.70	-0.1		Jones			1	WCh	Sevilla	22 Aug 99
10.71	0.1		Jones			1		Chengdu	12 May 98
10.71	2.0		Jones			1s2	NC	New Orleans	19 Jun 98
10.72	2.0		Jones			1	NC	New Orleans	20 Jun 98
10.72	0.0		Jones			1	Herc	Monaco	8 Aug 98
10.72	0.0		Jones			1	Athl	Lausanne	25 Aug 98
10.73	2.0	Christine	Arron	FRA	13.9.73	1	EC	Budapest	19 Aug 98
10.74	1.3	Merlene	Ottey	JAM	10.5.60	1	GPF	Milano	7 Sep 96
10.75	0.6		Jones			1	GGala	Roma	14 Jul 98
10.75	-0.4		Jones			1	OG	Sydney	23 Sep 00
10.76WR	1.7	Evelyn	Ashford	USA	15.4.57	1	WK	Zürich	22 Aug 84
10.76	0.9		Jones			1	VD	Bruxelles	22 Aug 97
10.76	0.3		Jones			1q4	WCh	Sevilla	21 Aug 99
10.77	0.9	Irina	Privalova	RUS	22.11.68	1rA	Athl	Lausanne	6 Jul 94
10.77	-0.9		Jones			1rA	WK	Zürich	12 Aug 98
10.77	0.7	Ivet	Lalova	BUL	18.5.84	1	ECp-1A	Plovdiv	19 Jun 04
10.78A	1.0	Dawn	Sowell	USA	27.3.66	1	NCAA	Provo	3 Jun 89
10.78	1.7		Ottey			1	Expo	Sevilla	30 May 90
10.78	0.4		Ottey			1	GPF	Paris	3 Sep 94
10.78	1.1		Jones			1	BrGP	London (CP)	5 Aug 00
10.78	0.1		Jones			1	ISTAF	Berlin	1 Sep 00
10.79AWR	0.6		Ashford			1	USOF	USAF Academy	3 Jul 83
10.79	1.7		Ottey			1		Vigo	23 Jul 91
10.79	0.0		Li Xuemei	CHN	5.1.77	1	NG	Shanghai	18 Oct 97
10.79	-0.6		Jones			1		Osaka	9 May 98
10.79	-0.1	Inger	Miller	USA	12.6.72	2	WCh	Sevilla	22 Aug 99
		(31 performances by 10 athletes)							
10.81WR	1.7	Marlies	Göhr'	GDR	21.3.58	1	OD	Berlin	8 Jun 83
10.82	-1.0	Gail	Devers	USA	19.11.66	1	OG	Barcelona	1 Aug 92
10.82	0.4	Gwen	Torrence	USA	12.6.65	2	GPF	Paris	3 Sep 94
10.82	-0.3	Zhanna	Pintusevich-Block	UKR	6.7.72	1	WCh	Edmonton	6 Aug 01
10.83	1.7	Marita	Koch	GDR	18.2.57	2	OD	Berlin	8 Jun 83
10.83	0.0	Sheila	Echols	USA	2.10.64	1q2	OT	Indianapolis	16 Jul 88
10.83	-1.0	Juliet	Cuthbert	JAM	9.4.64	2	OG	Barcelona	1 Aug 92
10.83	0.1	Ekateríni	Thánou	GRE	1.2.75	2s1	WCh	Sevilla	22 Aug 99
10.84	1.3	Chioma	Ajunwa ¶	NGR	25.12.70	1		Lagos	11 Apr 92
10.84	1.9	Chandra	Sturrup	BAH	12.9.71	1	Athl	Lausanne	5 Jul 05
		(20)							
10.85	2.0	Anelia	Nuneva	BUL	30.6.62	1h1	NC	Sofiya	2 Sep 88
10.85	0.4	Veronica	Campbell	JAM	15.5.82	1	WK	Zürich	19 Aug 05
10.86	0.6	Silke	Gladisch/Möller	GDR	20.6.64	1	NC	Potsdam	20 Aug 87
10.86@	0.0	Diane	Williams	USA	14.12.60	2q1	OT	Indianapolis	16 Jul 88
		10.94A	0.6			2	USOF	USAF Academy	3 Jul 83
10.86	1.2	Chryste	Gaines	USA	14.9.70	1	WAF	Monaco	14 Sep 03
10.88	0.4	Lauryn	Williams	USA	11.9.83	2	WK	Zürich	19 Aug 05
10.89	1.8	Katrin	Krabbe ¶	GDR	22.11.69	1		Berlin	20 Jul 88
10.89	0.0		Liu Xiaomei	CHN	11.1.72	2	NG	Shanghai	18 Oct 97
10.90	1.4	Glory	Alozie	NGR/ESP	30.12.77	1		La Laguna	5 Jun 99
10.91	0.2	Heike	Drechsler'	GDR	16.12.64	2	GWG	Moskva	6 Jul 86
		(30)							
10.91	1.1	Savatheda	Fynes	BAH	17.10.74	2	Athl	Lausanne	2 Jul 99
10.91	1.5	Debbie	Ferguson	BAH	16.1.76	1	CG	Manchester	27 Jul 02
10.92	0.0	Alice	Brown	USA	20.9.60	2q2	OT	Indianapolis	16 Jul 88
10.92	1.1	D'Andre	Hill	USA	19.4.73	3	NC	Atlanta	15 Jun 96
10.92	0.1	Yulia	Nesterenko	BLR	15.6.79	1s1	OG	Athína	21 Aug 04
10.93	1.8	Ewa	Kasprzyk	POL	7.9.57	1	NC	Grudziadz	27 Jun 86
10.93	1.0	Tayna	Lawrence	JAM	17.9.75	3	VD	Bruxelles	30 Aug 02
10.93	0.9	Torri	Edwards ¶	USA	31.1.77	1	WCh	Saint-Denis	24 Aug 03
10.94	1.0	Carlette	Guidry	USA	4.9.68	1	TAC	New York	14 Jun 91
10.95	1.0	Bärbel	Wöckel'	GDR	21.3.55	2	NC	Dresden	1 Jul 82
		(40)							

Mark	Wind	Name		Nat	Born	Pos	Meet	Venue	Date
10.96	1.2	Marie-José	Pérec	FRA	9.5.68	1	NC	Dijon	27 Jul 91
10.96	2.0	Galina	Malchugina	RUS	17.12.62	2	CIS Ch	Moskva	22 Jun 92
10.96	1.0	Eldece	Clarke-Lewis	BAH	13.2.65	1	Conseil	Fort-de-France	29 Apr 00
10.96	0.4	Muriel	Hurtis	FRA	25.3.79	1	ECp-S	Annecy	22 Jun 02
10.97	0.0	Angella	Issajenko' ¶	CAN	28.9.58	3	ASV	Köln	16 Aug 87
10.97	0.2	Mary	Onyali	NGR	3.2.68	1q2	WCh	Stuttgart	15 Aug 93
10.97	0.1	Pauline	Davis-Thompson	BAH	9.7.66	3	NC	Nassau	21 Jul 00
10.97	0.1	LaTasha	Colander	USA	23.8.76	1	NC/OT	Sacramento	10 Jul 04
10.97	0.4	Sherone	Simpson	JAM	12.8.84	2	NC	Kingston	25 Jun 05
10.98	0.1	Marina	Zhirova	RUS	6.6.63	2	ECp	Moskva	17 Aug 85
10.98	0.8	Angela	Bailey	CAN	28.2.62	2	BGP	Budapest	6 Jul 87
10.98	1.6	Natalya	Pomoshchnikova'	RUS	9.7.65	2q2	OG	Seoul	24 Sep 88
10.98	0.6	Léonie Myriam	Mani	CMR	21.5.77	2rA	GP	Athína	11 Jun 01
		(53)	100th women 11.08, 200th 11.19, 300th 11.26						

Probably semi-automatic timing

Mark	Wind	Name		Nat	Born	Pos	Meet	Venue	Date
10.87	1.9	Lyudmila	Kondratyeva	RUS	11.4.58	1		Leningrad	3 Jun 80

Low altitude best: 10.91 1.6 Sowell 1 TAC Houston 16 Jun 89

Wind-assisted to 10.78 performances and 10.96 performers

Mark	Wind	Name		Nat	Born	Pos	Meet	Venue	Date
10.54	3.0		Griffith-Joyner			1	OG	Seoul	25 Sep 88
10.60	3.2		Griffith-Joyner			1h1	OT	Indianapolis	16 Jul 88
10.68	2.2		Jones			1	DNG	Stockholm	1 Aug 00
10.70	2.6		Griffith-Joyner			1s2	OG	Seoul	25 Sep 88
10.75	4.1		Jones			1h3	NC	New Orleans	19 Jun 98
10.77	2.3	Gail	Devers	USA	19.11.66	1	Jen	San José	28 May 94
10.77	2.1		Jones			1	Pre	Eugene	31 May 98
10.77	2.3	Ekateríni	Thánou	GRE	1.2.75	1		Rethymno	28 May 99
10.78	3.1		Ashford			1		Modesto	12 May 84
10.78	5.0	Gwen	Torrence	USA	12.6.65	1q3	OT	Indianapolis	16 Jul 88
10.78	2.3		Ottey			1s2	WCh	Tokyo	27 Aug 91
10.79	3.3	Marlies	Göhr'	GDR	21.3.58	1	NC	Cottbus	16 Jul 80
10.80	2.9	Pam	Marshall	USA	16.8.60	1	TAC	Eugene	20 Jun 86
10.80	2.8	Heike	Drechsler'	GDR	16.12.64	1	Bisl	Oslo	5 Jul 86
10.82	2.2	Silke	Gladisch/Möller	GDR	20.6.64	1s1	WCh	Roma	30 Aug 87
10.84	2.9	Alice	Brown	USA	20.9.60	2	TAC	Eugene	20 Jun 86
10.87	3.0	Me'Lisa	Barber	USA	4.10.80	1s1	NC	Carson	25 Jun 05
10.89	3.1	Kerstin	Behrendt	GDR	2.9.67	2		Berlin	13 Sep 88
10.91	4.6	Carlette	Guidry	USA	4.9.68	1s1	NCAA	Eugene	31 May 91
10.92	3.3	Bärbel	Wöckel'	GDR	21.3.55	2	NC	Cottbus	16 Jul 80
10.92	3.4	Angella	Taylor' ¶	CAN	28.9.58	1s2	CG	Brisbane	4 Oct 82
10.92	3.4	Torri	Edwards ¶	USA	31.1.77	1	MAI	Malmö	7 Aug 00
10.93	3.8	Sonia	Lannaman	GBR	24.3.56	1	ECp/sf	Dublin	17 Jul 77
10.93	3.3	Ingrid	Auerswald'	GDR	2.9.57	3	NC	Cottbus	16 Jul 80
10.93	4.2	Holli	Hyche	USA	6.9.71	2h2	NC	Eugene	16 Jun 93
10.94	3.9	Jackie	Washington	USA	17.7.62	1		Houston	18 May 86
10.94A	3.0	Evette	de Klerk'	RSA	21.8.65	1h	NC	Germiston	20 Apr 90
10.96	2.9	Brenda	Morehead	USA	5.10.57	1s2	AAU	Walnut	16 Jun 79
10.96	4.2	Olga	Naumkina'	RUS	20.5.64	1	Znam	Volgograd	11 Jun 89
10.96A	2.5	Michelle	Finn	USA	8.5.65	1		Sestriere	8 Aug 90
10.96	3.7	Angela	Williams	USA	30.1.80	1		Las Vegas	3 Apr 99
10.96	5.5	Kelli	White ¶	USA	1.4.77	1		Knoxville	9 Apr 99

Hand timing

Mark	Wind	Name		Nat	Born	Pos	Meet	Venue	Date
10.6	0.1	Zhanna	Pintusevich	UKR	6.7.72	1		Kiev	12 Jun 97
10.7		Merlene	Ottey	JAM	10.5.60	1h		Kingston	15 Jul 88
10.7	1.1	Juliet	Cuthbert	JAM	9.4.64	1	NC	Kingston	4 Jul 92
10.7		Mary	Onyali	NGR	3.2.68	1	NC	Lagos	22 Jun 96
10.7	-0.2	Svetlana	Goncharenko	RUS	28.5.71	1		Rostov	30 May 98
10.7w	2.6	Savatheda	Fynes	BAH	17.10.74	1		Nassau	22 Jun 95

Drugs disqualification

Mark	Wind	Name		Nat	Born	Pos	Meet	Venue	Date
10.85	0.9	Kelli	White ¶	USA	1.4.77	1	WCh	Saint-Denis	24 Aug 03
10.79w	2.3	Kelli	White ¶	USA	1.4.77	1		Carson/Los Angeles	1 Jun 03

200 METRES

Mark	Wind	Name		Nat	Born	Pos	Meet	Venue	Date
21.34WR	1.3	Florence	Griffith-Joyner	USA	21.12.59	1	OG	Seoul	29 Sep 88
21.56WR	1.7		Griffith-Joyner			1s1	OG	Seoul	29 Sep 88
21.62A	-0.6	Marion	Jones	USA	12.10.75	1	WCp	Johannesburg	11 Sep 98
21.64	0.8	Merlene	Ottey	JAM	10.5.60	1	VD	Bruxelles	13 Sep 91
21.66	-1.0		Ottey			1	WK	Zürich	15 Aug 90
21.71WR	0.7	Marita	Koch	GDR	18.2.57	1	v Can	Karl-Marx-Stadt	10 Jun 79
21.71WR	0.3		Koch			1	OD	Potsdam	21 Jul 84
21.71WR	1.2	Heike	Drechsler'	GDR	16.12.64	1	NC	Jena	29 Jun 86
21.71WR	-0.8		Drechsler			1	EC	Stuttgart	29 Aug 86

Mark	Wind	Name		Nat	Born	Pos	Meet	Venue	Date
21.72	1.3	Grace	Jackson	JAM	14.6.61	2	OG	Seoul	29 Sep 88
21.72	-0.1	Gwen	Torrence	USA	12.6.65	1s2	OG	Barcelona	5 Aug 92
21.74	0.4	Marlies	Göhr'	GDR	21.3.58	1	NC	Erfurt	3 Jun 84
21.74	1.2	Silke	Gladisch'	GDR	20.6.64	1	WCh	Roma	3 Sep 87
21.75	-0.1	Juliet	Cuthbert (10)	JAM	9.4.64	2s2	OG	Barcelona	5 Aug 92
21.76	0.3		Koch			1	NC	Dresden	3 Jul 82
21.76	0.7		Griffith-Joyner			1q1	OG	Seoul	28 Sep 88
21.76	-0.8		Jones			1	WK	Zürich	13 Aug 97
21.77	-0.1		Griffith-Joyner			1q2	OT	Indianapolis	22 Jul 88
21.77	1.0		Ottey			1	Herc	Monaco	7 Aug 93
21.77	-0.3		Torrence			1	ASV	Köln	18 Aug 95
21.77	0.6	Inger	Miller	USA	12.6.72	1	WCh	Sevilla	27 Aug 99
21.78	-1.3		Koch			1	NC	Leipzig	11 Aug 85
21.79	1.7		Gladisch			1	NC	Potsdam	22 Aug 87
21.80	-1.1		Ottey			1	Nik	Nice	10 Jul 90
21.80	0.4		Jones			1	GWG	Uniondale, NY	20 Jul 98
21.81	-0.1	Valerie	Brisco	USA	6.7.60	1	OG	Los Angeles	9 Aug 84
21.81	0.4		Ottey			1	ASV	Köln	19 Aug 90
21.81	-0.6		Torrence			1	OG	Barcelona	6 Aug 92
21.81	0.0		Torrence			1	Herc	Monaco	25 Jul 95
21.81	1.6		Jones			1	Pre	Eugene	30 May 99
		(30/12)							
21.83	-0.2	Evelyn	Ashford	USA	15.4.57	1	WCp	Montreal	24 Aug 79
21.85	0.3	Bärbel	Wöckel'	GDR	21.3.55	2	OD	Potsdam	21 Jul 84
21.87	0.0	Irina	Privalova	RUS	22.11.68	2	Herc	Monaco	25 Jul 95
21.93	1.3	Pam	Marshall	USA	16.8.60	2	OT	Indianapolis	23 Jul 88
21.95	0.3	Katrin	Krabbe ¶	GDR	22.11.69	1	EC	Split	30 Aug 90
21.97	1.9	Jarmila	Kratochvílová	CZE	26.1.51	1	PTS	Bratislava	6 Jun 81
21.99	0.9	Chandra	Cheeseborough	USA	10.1.59	2	TAC	Indianapolis	19 Jun 83
21.99	1.1	Marie-José	Pérec	FRA	9.5.68	1	BNP	Villeneuve d'Ascq	2 Jul 93
		(20)							
22.01	-0.5	Anelia	Nuneva'	BUL	30.6.62	1	NC	Sofiya	16 Aug 87
22.01	0.0		Li Xuemei	CHN	5.1.77	1	NG	Shanghai	22 Oct 97
22.04A	0.7	Dawn	Sowell	USA	27.3.66	1	NCAA	Provo	2 Jun 89
22.05	1.8	Veronica	Campbell	JAM	15.5.82	1	OG	Athína	25 Aug 04
22.06A	0.7	Evette	de Klerk'	RSA	21.8.65	1		Pietersburg	8 Apr 89
22.07	-0.1	Mary	Onyali	NGR	3.2.68	1	WK	Zürich	14 Aug 96
22.10	-0.1	Kathy	Cook'	GBR	3.5.60	4	OG	Los Angeles	9 Aug 84
22.11A	-0.5	Allyson	Felix	USA	18.11.85	1		Ciudad de México	3 May 03
		22.13	0.3			1	NC	Carson	26 Jun 05
22.13	1.2	Ewa	Kasprzyk	POL	7.9.57	2	GWG	Moskva	8 Jul 86
22.14	-0.6	Carlette	Guidry	USA	4.9.68	1	NC	Atlanta	23 Jun 96
		(30)							
22.17A	-2.3	Zhanna	Pintusevich	UKR	6.7.72	1		Monachil	9 Jul 97
		22.24	-0.3			2	VD	Bruxelles	30 Aug 02
22.18	-0.6	Dannette	Young-Stone	USA	6.10.64	2	NC	Atlanta	23 Jun 96
22.18	0.9	Galina	Malchugina	RUS	17.12.62	1s2	NC	Sankt Peterburg	4 Jul 96
22.18	0.5	Merlene	Frazer	JAM	27.12.73	1s2	WCh	Sevilla	25 Aug 99
22.19	1.5	Natalya	Bochina	RUS	4.1.62	2	OG	Moskva	30 Jul 80
22.19	0.0	Debbie	Ferguson	BAH	16.1.76	1	GP II	Saint-Denis	3 Jul 99
22.21 WR	1.9	Irena	Szewinska'	POL	24.5.46	1		Potsdam	13 Jun 74
22.22	-0.9	Falilat	Ogunkoya	NGR	12.5.68	1	AfCh	Dakar	22 Aug 98
22.22	0.6	Beverly	McDonald	JAM	15.2.70	2	WCh	Sevilla	27 Aug 99
22.22	0.3	Rachelle	Smith (Boone)	USA	30.6.81	2	NC	Carson	26 Jun 05
		(40)							
22.23	0.8	Melinda	Gainsford-Taylor	AUS	1.10.71	1		Stuttgart	13 Jul 97
22.24	0.3	Gesine	Walther	GDR	6.10.62	2	NC	Dresden	3 Jul 82
22.24	0.1	Maya	Azarashvili	GEO	6.4.64	1		Kiyev	16 Aug 88
22.25A	0.8	Angella	Taylor'	CAN	28.9.58	1		Colorado Springs	20 Jul 82
22.25	1.3	Cathy	Freeman	AUS	16.2.73	1	CG	Victoria	26 Aug 94
22.25	1.8	Andrea	Philipp	GER	29.7.71	2s1	WCh	Sevilla	25 Aug 99
22.26	0.0	Christine	Arron	FRA	13.9.73	2	GP II	Saint-Denis	3 Jul 99
22.27	1.2	Elvira	Barbashina'	UZB	25.2.63	3	GWG	Moskva	8 Jul 86
22.27	0.7	Pauline	Davis-Thompson	BAH	9.7.66	2	OG	Sydney	28 Sep 00
22.27	1.2	Lauryn	Williams	USA	11.9.83	2		Carson	22 May 05
		(50)	100th woman 22.46, 200th 22.73, 300th 22.87						
Wind-assisted			*Performers listed to 22.25*						
21.82	3.1	Irina	Privalova	RUS	22.11.68	1	Athl	Lausanne	6 Jul 94
22.16	3.1	Dannette	Young-Stone	USA	6.10.64	2	Athl	Lausanne	6 Jul 94
22.16	3.2	Nanceen	Perry	USA	19.4.77	1		Austin	6 May 00

Mark	Wind	Name		Nat	Born	Pos	Meet	Venue	Date
22.18A	2.8	Melinda	Gainsford-Taylor	AUS	1.10.71	1		Pietersburg	18 Mar 00
22.19A	3.1	Angella	Taylor'	CAN	28.9.58	1		Colorado Springs	21 Jul 82
22.22	2.7	LaTasha	Jenkins	USA	19.12.77	1s1	NCAA	Boise	4 Jun 99
22.22	4.0	Muna	Lee	USA	30.10.81	1	NCAA-r	Baton Rouge	29 May 04
22.25	3.8	Peta-Gaye	Dowdie	JAM	18.1.77	1		Baton Rouge	17 Apr 99
Hand timing									
21.9	-0.1	Svetlana	Goncharenko	RUS	28.5.71	1		Rostov-na-Donu	31 May 98
22.0	-0.6	Marina	Molokova	RUS	24.8.62	1	Ros	Praha	23 Jun 87
21.6w	2.5	Pam	Marshall	USA	16.8.60	1	TAC	San José	26 Jun 87
Drugs disqualification									
22.05	-0.3	Kelli	White ¶	USA	1.4.77	1	WCh	Saint-Denis	28 Aug 03
22.18i		Michelle	Collins ¶	USA	12.2.71	1	WI	Birmingham	15 Mar 03

300 METRES

Times in 300m races only

Mark	Wind	Name		Nat	Born	Pos	Meet	Venue	Date
35.30A		Ana Gabriela	Guevara	MEX	4.3.77	1		Ciudad de México	3 May 03
35.46		Kathy	Cook'	GBR	3.5.60	1	Nike	London (CP)	18 Aug 84
35.46		Chandra	Cheeseborough	USA	10.1.59	2	Nike	London (CP)	18 Aug 84
35.68		Marion	Jones	USA	12.10.75	1	MSR	Walnut	22 Apr 01
Indoors									
35.45		Irina	Privalova	RUS	22.11.68	1		Moskva	17 Jan 93
35.48	#	Svetlana	Goncharenko	RUS	28.5.71	1		Tampere	4 Feb 98

400 METRES

Mark	Wind	Name		Nat	Born	Pos	Meet	Venue	Date
47.60 WR		Marita	Koch	GDR	18.2.57	1	WCp	Canberra	6 Oct 85
47.99 WR		Jarmila	Kratochvílová	CZE	26.1.51	1	WCh	Helsinki	10 Aug 83
48.16 WR			Koch			1	EC	Athína	8 Sep 82
48.16			Koch			1	Drz	Praha	16 Aug 84
48.22			Koch			1	EC	Stuttgart	28 Aug 86
48.25		Marie-José	Pérec	FRA	9.5.68	1	OG	Atlanta	29 Jul 96
48.26			Koch			1	GO	Dresden	27 Jul 84
48.27		Olga	Vladykina'	UKR	30.6.63	2	WCp	Canberra	6 Oct 85
48.45			Kratochvílová			1	NC	Praha	23 Jul 83
48.59		Tatána	Kocembová'	CZE	2.5.62	2	WCh	Helsinki	10 Aug 83
48.60 WR			Koch			1	ECp	Torino	4 Aug 79
48.60			Vladykina			1	ECp	Moskva	17 Aug 85
48.61			Kratochvílová			1	WCp	Roma	6 Sep 81
48.63		Cathy	Freeman	AUS	16.2.73	2	OG	Atlanta	29 Jul 96
48.65			Bryzgina'			1	OG	Seoul	26 Sep 88
48.73			Kocembová			2	Drz	Praha	16 Aug 84
48.77			Koch			1	v USA	Karl-Marx-Stadt	9 Jul 82
48.82			Kratochvílová			1	Ros	Praha	23 Jun 83
48.83		Valerie	Brisco	USA	6.7.60	1	OG	Los Angeles	6 Aug 84
48.83			Pérec			1	OG	Barcelona	5 Aug 92
48.85			Kratochvílová			2	EC	Athína	8 Sep 82
48.86			Kratochvílová			1	WK	Zürich	18 Aug 82
48.86			Koch			1	NC	Erfurt	2 Jun 84
48.87			Koch			1	VD	Bruxelles	27 Aug 82
48.88			Koch			1	OG	Moskva	28 Jul 80
48.89 WR			Koch			1		Potsdam	29 Jul 79
48.89			Koch			1		Berlin	15 Jul 84
48.89		Ana Gabriela	Guevara	MEX	4.3.77	1	WCh	Saint-Denis	27 Aug 03
48.92		Sanya	Richards	USA	26.2.85	1	WK	Zürich	19 Aug 05
48.94 WR			Koch			1	EC	Praha	31 Aug 78
		(30/9)							
49.05		Chandra	Cheeseborough	USA	10.1.59	2	OG	Los Angeles	6 Aug 84
			(10)						
49.07		Tonique	Williams-Darling	BAH	17.1.76	1	ISTAF	Berlin	12 Sep 04
49.10		Falilat	Ogunkoya	NGR	12.5.68	3	OG	Atlanta	29 Jul 96
49.11		Olga	Nazarova ¶	RUS	1.6.65	1s1	OG	Seoul	25 Sep 88
49.19		Mariya	Pinigina'	UKR	9.2.58	3	WCh	Helsinki	10 Aug 83
49.24		Sabine	Busch	GDR	21.11.62	2	NC	Erfurt	2 Jun 84
49.28 WR		Irena	Szewinska'	POL	24.5.46	1	OG	Montreal	29 Jul 76
49.28		Pauline	Davis	BAH	9.7.66	4	OG	Atlanta	29 Jul 96
49.29		Charity	Opara ¶	NGR	20.5.72	1	GGala	Roma	14 Jul 98
49.30		Petra	Müller'	GDR	18.7.65	1		Jena	3 Jun 88
49.30		Lorraine	Fenton'	JAM	8.9.73	2	Herc	Monaco	19 Jul 02
		(20)							
49.40		Jearl	Miles-Clark	USA	4.9.66	1	NC	Indianapolis	14 Jun 97
49.42		Grit	Breuer ¶	GER	16.2.72	2	WCh	Tokyo	27 Aug 91
49.43		Kathy	Cook'	GBR	3.5.60	3	OG	Los Angeles	6 Aug 84

Mark	Wind	Name		Nat	Born	Pos	Meet	Venue	Date
49.43A		Fatima	Yusuf	NGR	2.5.71	1		Harare	15 Sep 9
49.47		Aelita	Yurchenko	UKR	1.1.65	2	Kuts	Moskva	4 Sep 8
49.56		Bärbel	Wöckel'	GDR	21.3.55	1		Erfurt	30 May 8
49.56		Monique	Hennagan	USA	26.5.76	1	NC/OT	Sacramento	17 Jul 0
49.57		Grace	Jackson	JAM	14.6.61	1	Nik	Nice	10 Jul 8
49.58		Dagmar	Rübsam'	GDR	3.6.62	3	NC	Erfurt	2 Jun 8
49.59		Marion	Jones	USA	12.10.75	1r6	MSR	Walnut	16 Apr 0
		(30)							
49.59		Katharine	Merry	GBR	21.9.74	1	GP	Athína	11 Jun 0
49.61		Ana Fidelia	Quirot	CUB	23.3.63	1	PAm	Habana	5 Aug 9
49.64		Gwen	Torrence	USA	12.6.65	2	Nik	Nice	15 Jul 9
49.64		Ximena	Restrepo	COL	10.3.69	3	OG	Barcelona	5 Aug 9
49.65		Natalya	Nazarova	RUS	26.5.79	1	NC	Tula	31 Jul 0
49.66		Christina	Lathan'	GDR	28.2.58	3	OG	Moskva	28 Jul 8
49.66		Lillie	Leatherwood	USA	6.7.64	1	TAC	New York	15 Jun 9
49.67		Sandra	Myers	ESP	9.1.61	1	Bisl	Oslo	6 Jul 9
49.74		Anja	Rücker	GER	20.12.72	2	WCh	Sevilla	26 Aug 9
49.75		Gaby	Bussmann	FRG	8.10.59	4	WCh	Helsinki	10 Aug 8
		(40)							
49.77		Olga	Kotlyarova	RUS	12.4.76	3	GGala	Roma	2 Jul 0
49.79		Sandie	Richards	JAM	6.11.68	2	WCh	Athína	4 Aug 9
49.79		Donna	Fraser	GBR	7.11.72	4	OG	Sydney	25 Sep 0
49.80		Svetlana	Pospelova ¶	RUS	24.12.79	1	NC	Tula	11 Jul 0
49.81			Ma Yuqin	CHN	11.9.72	1	NG	Beijing	11 Sep 9
49.84		Diane	Dixon	USA	23.9.64	3s1	OG	Seoul	25 Sep 8
49.85		Natalya	Antyukh	RUS	26.6.81	2	NC	Tula	31 Jul 0
49.86		Ami Mbacké	Thiam	SEN	10.11.76	1	WCh	Edmonton	7 Aug 0
49.87		Denean	Howard/Hill	USA	5.10.64	4s1	OG	Seoul	25 Sep 8
49.87		LaTasha	Colander	USA	23.8.76	1	NC	Sacramento	16 Jul 0
		(50)	100th woman 50.46, 200th woman 51.02						
Low altitude best: 49.77			Yusuf			6	OG	Atlanta	29 Jul 9
Hand timing									
48.9		Olga	Nazarova ¶	RUS	1.6.65	1	NP	Vladivostok	13 Sep 8
49.2A		Ana Fidelia	Quirot	CUB	23.3.63	1	AmCp	Bogotá	13 Aug 8

600 METRES

Mark	Wind	Name		Nat	Born	Pos	Meet	Venue	Date
1:22.63		Ana Fidelia	Quirot	CUB	23.3.63	1		Guadalajara	25 Jul 9
1:22.87		Maria Lurdes	Mutola	MOZ	27.10.72	1		Liège (NX)	27 Aug 0
1:23.5		Doina	Melinte	ROM	27.12.56	1		Poiana Brasov	27 Jul 8
1:23.78		Natalya	Khrushchelyova	RUS	30.5.73	2		Liège (NX)	2 Sep 0

800 METRES

Mark	Wind	Name		Nat	Born	Pos	Meet	Venue	Date
1:53.28 WR		Jarmila	Kratochvílová	CZE	26.1.51	1		München	26 Jul 8
1:53.43 WR		Nadezhda	Olizarenko'	UKR	28.11.53	1	OG	Moskva	27 Jul 8
1:54.44		Ana Fidelia	Quirot	CUB	23.3.63	1	WCp	Barcelona	9 Sep 8
1:54.68			Kratochvílová			1	WCh	Helsinki	9 Aug 8
1:54.81		Olga	Mineyeva	RUS	1.9.52	2	OG	Moskva	27 Jul 8
1:54.82			Quirot			1	ASV	Köln	24 Aug 9
1:54.85 WR			Olizarenko			1	Prav	Moskva	12 Jun 8
1:54.94 WR		Tatyana	Kazankina ¶	RUS	17.12.51	1	OG	Montreal	26 Jul 7
1:55.04			Kratochvílová			1	OsloG	Oslo	23 Aug 8
1:55.05		Doina	Melinte	ROM	27.12.56	1	NC	Bucuresti	1 Aug 8
1:55.1 '			Mineyeva			1	Znam	Moskva	6 Jul 8
1:55.19		Maria Lurdes	Mutola	MOZ	27.10.72	1	WK	Zürich	17 Aug 9
1:55.19		Jolanda	Ceplak	SLO	12.9.76	1rA	NA	Heusden	20 Jul 0
1:55.26		Sigrun	Wodars/Grau	GDR	7.11.65	1	WCh	Roma	31 Aug 8
1:55.29			Mutola			2	ASV	Köln	24 Aug 9
1:55.32		Christine	Wachtel (10)	GDR	6.1.65	2	WCh	Roma	31 Aug 8
1:55.41			Mineyeva			1	EC	Athína	8 Sep 8
1:55.42		Nikolina	Shtereva	BUL	25.1.55	2	OG	Montreal	26 Jul 7
1:55.43			Mutola			1	WCh	Stuttgart	17 Aug 9
1:55.46		Tatyana	Providokhina	RUS	26.3.53	3	OG	Moskva	27 Jul 8
1:55.5			Mineyeva			1	Kuts	Podolsk	21 Aug 8
1:55.54		Ellen	van Langen	NED	9.2.66	1	OG	Barcelona	3 Aug 9
1:55.54			Liu Dong	CHN	24.12.73	1	NG	Beijing	9 Sep 9
1:55.55			Mutola			1	GP	Madrid (C)	19 Jul 0
1:55.56		Lyubov	Gurina	RUS	6.8.57	3	WCh	Roma	31 Aug 8
1:55.60		Elfi	Zinn	GDR	24.8.53	3	OG	Montreal	26 Jul 7
1:55.62			Mutola			1A	WK	Zürich	4 Aug 9
1:55.68		Ella	Kovacs	ROM	11.12.64	1	RomIC	Bucuresti	2 Jun 8

Mark Wind	Name		Nat	Born	Pos	Meet	Venue	Date
1:55.69	Irina	Podyalovskaya	RUS	19.10.59	1	Izv	Kiyev	22 Jun 84
1:55.70		Wodars			2	WCp	Barcelona	9 Sep 89
	(30/18)							
1:55.74	Anita	Weiss'	GDR	16.7.55	4	OG	Montreal	26 Jul 76
1:55.87	Svetlana	Masterkova	RUS	17.1.68	1	Kuts	Moskva	18 Jun 99
	(20)							
1:55.96	Lyudmila	Veselkova	RUS	25.10.50	2	EC	Athína	8 Sep 82
1:55.96	Yekaterina	Podkopayeva'	RUS	11.6.52	1		Leningrad	27 Jul 83
1:55.99	Liliya	Nurutdinova ¶	RUS	15.12.63	2	OG	Barcelona	3 Aug 92
1:56.0 WR	Valentina	Gerasimova	KAZ	15.5.48	1	NC	Kiyev	12 Jun 76
1:56.0	Inna	Yevseyeva	UKR	14.8.64	1		Kiyev	25 Jun 88
1:56.07	Tatyana	Andrianova	RUS	10.12.79	1	NC	Tula	11 Jul 05
1:56.09	Zulia	Calatayud	CUB	9.11.79	1	Herc	Monaco	19 Jul 02
1:56.1	Ravilya	Agletdinova'	BLR	10.2.60	2	Kuts	Podolsk	21 Aug 82
1:56.2 '	Totka	Petrova ¶	BUL	17.12.56	1		Paris	6 Jul 79
1:56.2	Tatyana	Mishkel	UKR	10.6.52	3	Kuts	Podolsk	21 Aug 82
	(30)							
1:56.21	Martina	Kämpfert'	GDR	11.11.59	4	OG	Moskva	27 Jul 80
1:56.21	Zamira	Zaytseva	UZB	16.2.53	2		Leningrad	27 Jul 83
1:56.21	Kelly	Holmes	GBR	19.4.70	2	GPF	Monaco	9 Sep 95
1:56.24		Qu Yunxia	CHN	25.12.72	2	NG	Beijing	9 Sep 93
1:56.40	Jearl	Miles-Clark	USA	4.9.66	3	WK	Zürich	11 Aug 99
1:56.42	Paula	Ivan	ROM	20.7.63	1	Balk	Ankara	16 Jul 88
1:56.43	Hasna	Benhassi	MAR	1.6.78	2	OG	Athína	23 Aug 04
1:56.44	Svetlana	Styrkina	RUS	1.1.49	5	OG	Montreal	26 Jul 76
1:56.51	Slobodanka	Colovic	YUG	10.1.65	1		Beograd	17 Jun 87
1:56.53	Patricia	Djaté	FRA	3.1.71	3	GPF	Monaco	9 Sep 95
	(40)							
1:56.56	Ludmila	Formanová	CZE	2.1.74	4	WK	Zürich	11 Aug 99
1:56.57	Zoya	Rigel	RUS	15.10.52	3	EC	Praha	31 Aug 78
1:56.59	Natalya	Khrushchelyova	RUS	30.5.73	2	NC	Tula	31 Jul 04
1:56.60	Natalya	Tsyganova	RUS	7.2.71	1	NC	Tula	25 Jul 00
1:56.6	Tamara	Sorokina'	RUS	15.8.50	5	Kuts	Podolsk	21 Aug 82
1:56.61	Yelena	Afanasyeva	RUS	1.3.67	3	WK	Zürich	13 Aug 97
1:56.62	Tina	Paulino	MOZ	7.7.73	2	NYG	New York	22 May 93
1:56.64	Nadezhda	Loboyko	KAZ	30.6.61	1	NC	Kiyev	7 Jul 90
1:56.64	Stephanie	Graf	AUT	26.4.73	2	OG	Sydney	25 Sep 00
1:56.67	Fita	Lovin'	ROM	14.1.51	2	Prav	Moskva	12 Jun 80
	(50)	100th woman 1:57.8, 200th woman 1:59.0						
Indoors: 1:55.85	Stephanie	Graf	AUT	26.4.73	2	EI	Wien	3 Mar 02

1000 METRES

Mark Wind	Name		Nat	Born	Pos	Meet	Venue	Date
2:28.98 WR	Svetlana	Masterkova	RUS	17.1.68	1	VD	Bruxelles	23 Aug 96
2:29.34 WR	Maria Lurdes	Mutola	MOZ	27.10.72	1	VD	Bruxelles	25 Aug 95
2:30.6 WR	Tatyana	Providokhina	RUS	26.3.53	1		Podolsk	20 Aug 78
2:30.67 WR	Christine	Wachtel	GDR	6.1.65	1	ISTAF	Berlin	17 Aug 90
2:30.85	Martina	Kämpfert'	GDR	11.11.59	1		Berlin	9 Jul 80
2:31.50	Natalya	Artyomova ¶	RUS	5.1.63	1	ISTAF	Berlin	10 Sep 91
2:31.5	Maricica	Puica	ROM	29.7.50	1		Poiana Brasov	1 Jun 86
2:31.51	Sandra	Gasser ¶	SUI	27.7.62	1		Jerez de la Frontera	13 Sep 89
2:31.6 '	Beate	Liebich	GDR	21.2.58	2		Berlin	9 Jul 80
2:31.65	Olga	Dvirna	RUS	11.2.53	1		Athína	1 Sep 82

1500 METRES

Mark Wind	Name		Nat	Born	Pos	Meet	Venue	Date
3:50.46 WR		Qu Yunxia	CHN	25.12.72	1	NG	Beijing	11 Sep 93
3:50.98		Jiang Bo	CHN	13.3.77	1	NG	Shanghai	18 Oct 97
3:51.34		Lang Yinglai	CHN	22.8.79	2	NG	Shanghai	18 Oct 97
3:51.92		Wang Junxia	CHN	9.1.73	2	NG	Beijing	11 Sep 93
3:52.47 WR	Tatyana	Kazankina ¶	RUS	17.12.51	1	WK	Zürich	13 Aug 80
3:53.91		Yin Lili ¶	CHN	11.11.79	3	NG	Shanghai	18 Oct 97
3:53.96	Paula	Ivan'	ROM	20.7.63	1	OG	Seoul	1 Oct 88
3:53.97		Lan Lixin	CHN	14.2.79	4	NG	Shanghai	18 Oct 97
3:54.23	Olga	Dvirna	RUS	11.2.53	1	NC	Kiyev	27 Jul 82
3:54.52		Zhang Ling (10)	CHN	13.4.80	5	NG	Shanghai	18 Oct 97
3:55.0 ' WR		Kazankina ¶			1	Znam	Moskva	6 Jul 80
3:55.01		Lan Lixin			1h2	NG	Shanghai	17 Oct 97
3:55.07		Dong Yanmei	CHN	16.2.77	6	NG	Shanghai	18 Oct 97
3:55.30	Hassiba	Boulmerka	ALG	10.7.68	1	OG	Barcelona	8 Aug 92
3:55.33	Süreyya	Ayhan ¶	TUR	6.9.78	1	VD	Bruxelles	5 Sep 03
3:55.38		Qu Yunxia			2h2	NG	Shanghai	17 Oct 97
3:55.47		Zhang Ling			3h2	NG	Shanghai	17 Oct 97

Mark Wind		Name	Nat	Born	Pos	Meet	Venue	Date
3:55.60		Ayhan			1	WK	Zürich	15 Aug 0
3:55.82		Dong Yanmei			4h2	NG	Shanghai	17 Oct 9
3:56.0 WR		Kazankina ¶			1		Podolsk	28 Jun 7
3:56.14	Zamira	Zaytseva	UZB	16.2.53	2	NC	Kiyev	27 Jul 8
3:56.22		Ivan			1	WK	Zürich	17 Aug 8
3:56.31		Liu Dong	CHN	24.12.73	5h2	NG	Shanghai	17 Oct 9
3:56.50	Tatyana	Pozdnyakova	RUS	4.3.56	3	NC	Kiyev	27 Jul 8
3:56.56		Kazankina ¶			1	OG	Moskva	1 Aug 8
3:56.63	Nadezhda	Ralldugina	UKR	15.11.57	1	Drz	Praha	18 Aug 8
3:56.65	Yekaterina	Podkopayeva'	RUS	11.6.52	1		Rieti	2 Sep 8
3:56.7 '	Lyubov	Smolka	UKR	29.11.52	2	Znam	Moskva	6 Jul 8
3:56.7	Doina	Melinte (20)	ROM	27.12.56	1		Bucuresti	12 Jul 8
3:56.77+	Svetlana	Masterkova	RUS	17.1.68	1	WK	Zürich	14 Aug 9
	(30/21)							
3:56.79	Maryam	Jamal	BRN	16.9.84	1	GP	Rieti	28 Aug 0
3:56.8 '	Nadezhda	Olizarenko'	UKR	28.11.53	3	Znam	Moskva	6 Jul 8
3:56.91	Lyudmila	Rogachova	RUS	30.10.66	2	OG	Barcelona	8 Aug 9
3:56.97	Gabriela	Szabo	ROM	14.11.75	1	Herc	Monaco	8 Aug 9
3:57.03		Liu Jing	CHN	.2.71	6h2	NG	Shanghai	17 Oct 9
3:57.05	Svetlana	Guskova	MDA	19.8.59	4	NC	Kiyev	27 Jul 8
3:57.12	Mary	Decker/Slaney	USA	4.8.58	1	vNord	Stockholm	26 Jul 8
3:57.22	Maricica	Puica	ROM	29.7.50	1		Bucuresti	1 Jul 8
3:57.40	Suzy	Favor Hamilton	USA	8.8.68	1	Bisl	Oslo	28 Jul 0
	(30)							
3:57.4 '	Totka	Petrova ¶	BUL	17.12.56	1	Balk	Athína	11 Aug 7
3:57.41	Jackline	Maranga	KEN	16.12.77	3	Herc	Monaco	8 Aug 9
3:57.46		Zhang Linli	CHN	6.3.73	3	NG	Beijing	11 Sep 9
3:57.71	Christiane	Wartenberg'	GDR	27.10.56	2	OG	Moskva	1 Aug 8
3:57.71	Carla	Sacramento	POR	10.12.71	4	Herc	Monaco	8 Aug 9
3:57.72	Galina	Zakharova	RUS	7.9.56	1	NP	Baku	14 Sep 8
3:57.73	Natalya	Yevdokimova	RUS	17.3.78	2	GP	Rieti	28 Aug 0
3:57.90	Kelly	Holmes	GBR	19.4.70	1	OG	Athína	28 Aug 0
3:57.92	Tatyana	Dorovskikh ¶	UKR	12.8.61	4	OG	Barcelona	8 Aug 9
3:58.12	Naomi	Mugo	KEN	2.1.77	5	Herc	Monaco	8 Aug 9
	(40)							
3:58.12	Tatyana	Tomashova	RUS	1.7.75	2	OG	Athína	28 Aug 0
3:58.20	Anita	Weyermann	SUI	8.12.77	6	Herc	Monaco	8 Aug 9
3:58.2 '	Natalia	Marasescu' ¶	ROM	3.10.52	1	NC	Bucuresti	13 Jul 7
3:58.28	Elvan	Abeylegesse	TUR	11.9.82	1	ECCp-A	Moskva	28 May 0
3:58.29	Violeta	Szekely' ¶	ROM	26.3.65	1	Herc	Monaco	18 Aug 0
3:58.37	Tatyana	Providokhina	RUS	26.3.53	1	Kuts	Podolsk	22 Aug 8
3:58.38	Kutre	Dulecha	ETH	22.8.78	7	Herc	Monaco	8 Aug 9
3:58.39	Maria	Cioncan	ROM	19.6.77	3	OG	Athína	28 Aug 0
3:58.40	Ravilya	Agletdinova'	BLR	10.2.60	1	ECp	Moskva	18 Aug 8
3:58.5 '	Ileana	Silai ¶	ROM	14.10.41	2	NC	Bucuresti	13 Jul 7
	(50)	100th woman 4:00.49, 200th woman 4:03.9						

1 MILE

Mark Wind		Name	Nat	Born	Pos	Meet	Venue	Date
4:12.56 WR	Svetlana	Masterkova	RUS	17.1.68	1	WK	Zürich	14 Aug 9
4:15.61 WR	Paula	Ivan'	ROM	20.7.63	1	Nik	Nice	10 Jul 8
4:15.8	Natalya	Artyomova ¶	RUS	5.1.63	1		Leningrad	5 Aug 8
4:16.71 WR	Mary	Slaney (Decker)	USA	4.8.58	1	WK	Zürich	21 Aug 8
4:17.25	Sonia	O'Sullivan	IRL	28.11.69	1	Bisl	Oslo	22 Jul 9
4:17.33	Maricica	Puica	ROM	29.7.50	2	WK	Zürich	21 Aug 8
4:17.57	Zola	Budd'	GBR	26.5.66	3	WK	Zürich	21 Aug 8
4:18.13	Doina	Melinte	ROM	27.12.56	1	Bisl	Oslo	14 Jul 9
Indoors								
4:17.14	Doina	Melinte	ROM	27.12.56	1		East Rutherford	9 Feb 9

2000 METRES

Mark Wind		Name	Nat	Born	Pos	Meet	Venue	Date
5:25.36 WR	Sonia	O'Sullivan	IRL	28.11.69	1	TSB	Edinburgh	8 Jul 9
5:26.93	Yvonne	Murray	GBR	4.10.64	2	TSB	Edinburgh	8 Jul 9
5:28.69 WR	Maricica	Puica	ROM	29.7.50	1	PTG	London (CP)	11 Jul 8
5:28.72 WR	Tatyana	Kazankina ¶	RUS	17.12.51	1		Moskva	4 Aug 8
5:29.43+		Wang Junxia	CHN	9.1.73	1h2	NG	Beijing	12 Sep 9
5:29.64	Tatyana	Pozdnyakova	UKR	4.3.56	2		Moskva	4 Aug 8
5:30.19	Zola	Budd'	GBR	26.5.66	3	PTG	London (CP)	11 Jul 8
5:30.92	Galina	Zakharova	RUS	7.9.56	3		Moskva	4 Aug 8
5:32.7 ' WR	Mary	Slaney	USA	4.8.58	1		Eugene	3 Aug 8
Indoors: 5:30.53	Gabriela	Szabo	ROM	14.11.75	1		Sindelfingen	8 Mar 9

3000 METRES

Mark	Wind	Name		Nat	Born	Pos	Meet	Venue	Date
8:06.11	WR		Wang Junxia	CHN	9.1.73	1	NG	Beijing	13 Sep 93
8:12.18			Qu Yunxia	CHN	25.12.72	2	NG	Beijing	13 Sep 93
8:12.19	WR		Wang Junxia			1h2	NG	Beijing	12 Sep 93
8:12.27			Qu Yunxia			2h2	NG	Beijing	12 Sep 93
8:16.50			Zhang Linli	CHN	6.3.73	3	NG	Beijing	13 Sep 93
8:19.78			Ma Liyan	CHN	6.9.68	3h2	NG	Beijing	12 Sep 93
8:21.26			Ma Liyan			4	NG	Beijing	13 Sep 93
8:21.42		Gabriela	Szabo	ROM	14.11.75	1	Herc	Monaco	19 Jul 02
8:21.64		Sonia	O'Sullivan	IRL	28.11.69	1	TSB	London (CP)	15 Jul 94
8:21.84			Zhang Lirong	CHN	3.3.73	5	NG	Beijing	13 Sep 93
8:22.06	WR		Zhang Linli			1h1	NG	Beijing	12 Sep 93
8:22.20		Paula	Radcliffe	GBR	17.12.73	2	Herc	Monaco	19 Jul 02
8:22.44			Zhang Lirong			2h1	NG	Beijing	12 Sep 93
8:22.62	WR	Tatyana	Kazankina ¶	RUS	17.12.51	1		Leningrad	26 Aug 84
8:23.23		Edith	Masai (10)	KEN	4.4.67	3	Herc	Monaco	19 Jul 02
8:23.26		Olga	Yegorova	RUS	28.3.72	1	WK	Zürich	17 Aug 01
8:23.75			Yegorova			1	GP	Saint-Denis	6 Jul 01
8:23.96			Yegorova			1	GGala	Roma	29 Jun 01
8:24.19			Szabo			2	WK	Zürich	17 Aug 01
8:24.31			Szabo			1	GP	Paris	29 Jul 98
8:25.03			Szabo			1	WK	Zürich	11 Aug 99
8:25.40		Yelena	Zadorozhnaya	RUS	3.12.77	2	GGala	Roma	29 Jun 01
8:25.56		Tatyana	Tomashova	RUS	1.7.75	3	GGala	Roma	29 Jun 01
8:25.59			Szabo			1	GP	Paris (C)	21 Jul 99
8:25.62		Berhane	Adere	ETH	21.7.73	3	WK	Zürich	17 Aug 01
8:25.82			Szabo			1	VD	Bruxelles	3 Sep 99
8:25.83		Mary	Slaney	USA	4.8.58	1	GGALA	Roma	7 Sep 85
8:26.14			Adere			1	VD	Bruxelles	30 Aug 02
8:26.15			Szabo			2	VD	Bruxelles	30 Aug 02
8:26.35			Szabo			1	WK	Zürich	11 Aug 00
		(30/15)							
8:26.48		Zahra	Ouaziz	MAR	20.12.69	2	WK	Zürich	11 Aug 99
8:26.53		Tatyana	Samolenko' ¶	UKR	12.8.61	1	OG	Seoul	25 Sep 88
8:26.78	WR	Svetlana	Ulmasova	UZB	4.2.53	1	NC	Kiyev	25 Jul 82
8:27.12	WR	Lyudmila	Bragina	RUS	24.7.43	1	v USA	College Park	7 Aug 76
8:27.15		Paula	Ivan'	ROM	20.7.63	2	OG	Seoul	25 Sep 88
		(20)							
8:27.62		Gete	Wami	ETH	11.12.74	4	WK	Zürich	17 Aug 01
8:27.83		Maricica	Puica	ROM	29.7.50	2	GGALA	Roma	7 Sep 85
8:28.80		Marta	Domínguez	ESP	3.11.75	3	WK	Zürich	11 Aug 00
8:28.83		Zola	Budd'	GBR	26.5.66	3	GGALA	Roma	7 Sep 85
8:28.87		Maryam	Jamal	BRN	16.9.84	1	Bisl	Oslo	29 Jul 05
8:29.02		Yvonne	Murray	GBR	4.10.64	3	OG	Seoul	25 Sep 88
8:29.14		Lydia	Cheromei	KEN	11.5.77	5	WK	Zürich	11 Aug 00
8:29.36		Svetlana	Guskova	MDA	19.8.59	2	NC	Kiyev	25 Jul 82
8:30.18		Mariya	Pantyukhova	RUS	14.8.74	4	WK	Zürich	11 Aug 99
		(30)							
8:30.22		Carla	Sacramento	POR	10.12.71	2	Herc	Monaco	4 Aug 99
8:30.39		Irina	Mikitenko	GER	23.8.72	6	WK	Zürich	11 Aug 00
8:30.45		Yelena	Romanova	RUS	20.3.63	4	OG	Seoul	25 Sep 88
8:30.59		Daniela	Yordanova	BUL	8.3.76	5	GP	Saint-Denis	6 Jul 01
8:30.66		Fernanda	Ribeiro	POR	23.6.69	3	Herc	Monaco	4 Aug 99
8:30.95		Tegla	Loroupe	KEN	9.5.73	2	Herc	Monaco	18 Aug 00
8:31.27		Joanne	Pavey	GBR	20.9.73	4	VD	Bruxelles	30 Aug 02
8:31.32		Isabella	Ochichi	KEN	28.10.79	1	Gaz	Saint-Denis	23 Jul 04
8:31.67		Natalya	Artyomova ¶	RUS	5.1.63	5	OG	Seoul	25 Sep 88
8:31.69		Lidia	Chojecka	POL	25.1.77	5	VD	Bruxelles	30 Aug 02
8:31.75		Grete	Waitz'	NOR	1.10.53	1	OsloG	Oslo	17 Jul 79
		(40)							
8:31.94		Elvan	Abeylegesse	TUR	11.9.82	6	VD	Bruxelles	30 Aug 02
8:32.00		Elana	Meyer'	RSA	10.10.66	1		Durban	29 Apr 91
8:32.0		Tatyana	Pozdnyakova	UKR	4.3.56	1		Ryazan	11 Aug 84
8:32.17		Angela	Chalmers	CAN	6.9.63	1	CG	Victoria	23 Aug 94
8:32.70		Katalin	Szentgyörgyi	HUN	1.1.79	6	GP	Saint-Denis	6 Jul 01
8:32.80		Ayelech	Worku	ETH	12.6.79	7	VD	Bruxelles	30 Aug 02
8:32.89		Alesya	Turova	BLR	6.12.79	7	GP	Saint-Denis	6 Jul 01
8:33.07			Dong Yanmei	CHN	16.2.77	1	GP	Athína	28 Jun 00
8:33.40		Galina	Zakharova	RUS	7.9.56	3	NC	Kiyev	25 Jul 82

Mark	Wind	Name		Nat	Born	Pos	Meet	Venue	Date
8:33.53		Natalia	Marasescu' ¶	ROM	3.10.52	2	EC	Praha	29 Aug 7
8:33.53		Yelena	Sipatova	RUS	7.6.55	1		Moskva	12 Jul 8
		(51)	100th woman 8:39.36, 200th 8:46.16						
Indoors: 8:30.05		Meseret	Defar	ETH	19.11.83	1		Boston (R)	29 Jan 0

5000 METRES

Mark	Wind	Name		Nat	Born	Pos	Meet	Venue	Date
14:24.68	WR	Elvan	Abeylegesse	TUR	11.9.82	1	Bisl	Bergen (Fana)	11 Jun 0
14:28.09	WR		Jiang Bo	CHN	13.3.77	1	NG	Shanghai	23 Oct 9
14:28.98		Meseret	Defar	ETH	19.11.83	1	VD	Bruxelles	26 Aug 0
14:29.11		Paula	Radcliffe	GBR	17.12.73	1	ECpS	Bydgoszcz	20 Jun 0
14:29.32		Olga	Yegorova	RUS	28.3.72	1	ISTAF	Berlin	31 Aug 0
14:29.32		Berhane	Adere	ETH	21.7.73	1	Bisl	Oslo	27 Jun 0
14:29.82			Dong Yanmei	CHN	16.2.77	2	NG	Shanghai	23 Oct 9
14:30.88		Gete	Wami	ETH	11.12.74	1	NA	Heusden	5 Aug 0
14:30.88		Tirunesh	Dibaba	ETH	2.6.85	2	Bisl	Bergen (Fana)	11 Jun 0
14:31.09			Adere			2	VD	Bruxelles	26 Aug 0
14:31.27	WR		Dong Yanmei			1h1	NG	Shanghai	21 Oct 9
14:31.30			Jiang Bo			2h1	NG	Shanghai	21 Oct 9
14:31.42			Radcliffe			1	CG	Manchester	28 Jul 0
14:31.48		Gabriela	Szabo (10)	ROM	14.11.75	1	ISTAF	Berlin	1 Sep 9
14:31.69			Wami			2	ISTAF	Berlin	31 Aug 0
14:32.08		Zahra	Ouaziz	MAR	20.12.69	2	ISTAF	Berlin	1 Sep 9
14:32.33			Liu Shixiang ¶	CHN	13.1.71	3h1	NG	Shanghai	21 Oct 9
14:32.42			T Dibaba		5	1		New York (RI)	11 Jun 0
14:32.44			Radcliffe			3	ISTAF	Berlin	31 Aug 0
14:32.57			T Dibaba			1	GGala	Roma	8 Jul 0
14:32.74		Ejagayehu	Dibaba	ETH	25.6.82	3	Bisl	Bergen (Fana)	11 Jun 0
14:32.79			Adere			2	GGala	Roma	8 Jul 0
14:32.90			Defar			3	GGala	Roma	8 Jul 0
14:33.04		Werknesh	Kidane	ETH	21.11.81	2	Bisl	Oslo	27 Jun 0
14:33.65			Adere			1	BrGP	London (CP)	23 Aug 0
14:34.29			Szabo			2	BrGP	London (CP)	23 Aug 0
14:35.18		Sentayehu	Ejigu	ETH	21.6.85	4	Bisl	Bergen (Fana)	11 Jun 0
14:36.08			Wami		4	3	ISTAF	Berlin	1 Sep 9
14:36.45	WR	Fernanda	Ribeiro	POR	23.6.69	1		Hechtel	22 Jul 9
14:36.92			Adere			1		Milano	2 Jun 0
		(30/16)							
14:37.20		Edith	Masai	KEN	4.4.67	4	GGala	Roma	8 Jul 0
14:37.33	WR	Ingrid	Kristiansen'	NOR	21.3.56	1		Stockholm	5 Aug 8
14:38.21		Isabella	Ochichi	KEN	28.10.79	4	VD	Bruxelles	26 Aug 0
14:38.97		Meselech	Melkamu	ETH	19.4.85	6	GGala	Roma	8 Jul 0
		(20)							
14:39.22		Tatyana	Tomashova	RUS	1.7.75	4	ISTAF	Berlin	31 Aug 0
14:39.83		Leah	Malot	KEN	7.6.72	1	ISTAF	Berlin	1 Sep 0
14:39.96			Yin Lili ¶	CHN	11.11.79	4	NG	Shanghai	23 Oct 9
14:40.41			Sun Yingjie ¶	CHN	3.10.77	1	AsiG	Busan	12 Oct 0
14:40.47		Yelena	Zadorozhnaya	RUS	3.12.77	1	ECp-S	Bremen	24 Jun 0
14:40.71		Jo	Pavey	GBR	20.9.73	7	GGala	Roma	8 Jul 0
14:41.02		Sonia	O'Sullivan	IRL	28.11.69	2	OG	Sydney	25 Sep 0
14:41.23		Ayelech	Worku	ETH	12.6.79	1	BrGP	London (CP)	5 Aug 0
14:42.03		Irina	Mikitenko	GER	23.8.72	3	ISTAF	Berlin	7 Sep 9
14:42.53		Zhor	El Kamch	MAR	15.3.73	5	GGala	Roma	11 Jul 0
		(30)							
14:43.64			Xing Huina	CHN	25.2.84	5	WCh	Helsinki	13 Aug 0
14:43.87		Zakia	Mrisho	TAN	19.2.84	6	WCh	Helsinki	13 Aug 0
14:43.90		Margaret	Maury	FRA	15.5.74	2	VD	Bruxelles	3 Sep 0
14:44.00		Priscila	Jepleting	KEN	26.6.80	7	WCh	Helsinki	13 Aug 0
14:44.05		Elana	Meyer	RSA	10.10.66	2		Hechtel	22 Jul 9
14:44.22		Derartu	Tulu	ETH	21.3.72	1	VD	Bruxelles	5 Sep 0
14:44.50		Roberta	Brunet	ITA	20.5.65	2	ASV	Köln	16 Aug 9
14:44.95		Julia	Vaquero	ESP	18.9.70	3	Bisl	Oslo	5 Jul 9
14:45.33			Lan Lixin	CHN	14.2.79	2h2	NG	Shanghai	21 Oct 9
14:45.35		Regina	Jacobs ¶	USA	28.8.63	1	NC	Sacramento	21 Jul 0
		(40)							
14:45.71			Song Liqing ¶	CHN	.1.80	3h2	NG	Shanghai	21 Oct 9
14:45.95		Tegla	Loroupe	KEN	9.5.73	3	BrGP	London (CP)	5 Aug 0
14:46.41		Rose	Cheruiyot	KEN	21.7.76	3	ASV	Köln	16 Aug 9
14:46.71		Sally	Barsosio	KEN	21.3.78	3	VD	Bruxelles	22 Aug 9
14:46.72		Lydia	Cheromei	KEN	11.5.77	2	ISTAF	Berlin	26 Aug 9
14:47.06		Alice	Timbilil	KEN	16.6.83	8	GGala	Roma	8 Jul 0

Mark Wind		Name	Nat	Born	Pos	Meet	Venue	Date
14:47.07	Liliya	Shobukhova	RUS	13.11.77	9	WCh	Helsinki	13 Aug 05
14:47.20		Dong Zhaoxia	CHN	13.11.74	5	NG	Shanghai	23 Oct 97
14:47.51	Pauline	Konga	KEN	10.4.70	6	ASV	Köln	16 Aug 96
14:47.60	Benita	Johnson	AUS	6.5.79	3	ISTAF	Berlin (P)	6 Sep 02
	(50)	100th woman 15:01.79, 200th 15:13,22, 300th 15:21.01						
Indoors: 14:32.93		T Dibaba			1		Boston (R)	29 Jan 05

10,000 METRES

Mark Wind		Name	Nat	Born	Pos	Meet	Venue	Date
29:31.78 WR		Wang Junxia	CHN	9.1.73	1	NG	Beijing	8 Sep 93
30:01.09	Paula	Radcliffe	GBR	17.12.73	1	EC	München	6 Aug 02
30:04.18	Berhane	Adere	ETH	21.7.73	1	WCh	Saint-Denis	23 Aug 03
30:07.15	Werknesh	Kidane	ETH	21.11.81	2	WCh	Saint-Denis	23 Aug 03
30:07.20		Sun Yingjie ¶	CHN	3.10.77	3	WCh	Saint-Denis	23 Aug 03
30:12.53	Lornah	Kiplagat (KEN)	NED	20.3.74	4	WCh	Saint-Denis	23 Aug 03
30:13.37		Zhong Huandi	CHN	28.6.67	2	NG	Beijing	8 Sep 93
30:13.74 WR	Ingrid	Kristiansen'	NOR	21.3.56	1	Bisl	Oslo	5 Jul 86
30:15.67	Tirunesh	Dibaba	ETH	1.6.85	1		Sollentuna	28 Jun 05
30:17.15		Radcliffe			1	GP	Gateshead	27 Jun 04
30:17.49	Derartu	Tulu (10)	ETH	21.3.72	1	OG	Sydney	30 Sep 00
30:18.39	Ejegayehu	Dibaba	ETH	25.6.82	2		Sollentuna	28 Jun 05
30:19.39		Kidane			1	GP II	Stanford	29 May 05
30:22.48	Gete	Wami	ETH	11.12.74	2	OG	Sydney	30 Sep 00
30:22.88	Fernanda	Ribeiro	POR	23.6.69	3	OG	Sydney	30 Sep 00
30:23.07	Alla	Zhilyayeva	RUS	5.2.69	5	WCh	Saint-Denis	23 Aug 03
30:23.25		Kristiansen			1	EC	Stuttgart	30 Aug 86
30:24.02		T Dibaba			1	WCh	Helsinki	6 Aug 05
30:24.36		Xing Huina	CHN	25.2.84	1	OG	Athína	27 Aug 04
30:24.56		Wami			1	WCh	Sevilla	26 Aug 99
30:24.98		E Dibaba			2	OG	Athína	27 Aug 04
30:25.41		Adere			2	WCh	Helsinki	6 Aug 05
30:26.00		E Dibaba			3	WCh	Helsinki	6 Aug 05
30:26.20	Galina	Bogomolova	RUS	15.10.77	6	WCh	Saint-Denis	23 Aug 03
30:26.42		Tulu			3	OG	Athína	27 Aug 04
30:26.97		Radcliffe			4	OG	Sydney	30 Sep 00
30:27.13		Radcliffe			2	WCh	Sevilla	26 Aug 99
30:27.18		Xing Huina			4	WCh	Helsinki	6 Aug 05
30:28.26		Sun Yingjie			1	AsiG	Busan	8 Oct 02
30:28.30		Kidane			4	OG	Athína	27 Aug 04
	(30/16)							
30:30.26	Edith	Masai	KEN	4.4.67	5	WCh	Helsinki	6 Aug 05
30:32.03	Tegla	Loroupe	KEN	9.5.73	3	WCh	Sevilla	26 Aug 99
30:37.68	Benita	Johnson	AUS	6.5.79	8	WCh	Saint-Denis	23 Aug 03
30:38:09		Dong Yanmei	CHN	16.2.77	1	NG	Shanghai	19 Oct 97
	(20)							
30:39.41		Lan Lixin	CHN	14.2.79	2	NG	Shanghai	19 Oct 97
30:39.98		Yin Lili ¶	CHN	11.11.79	3	NG	Shanghai	19 Oct 97
30:47.22		Dong Zhaoxia	CHN	13.11.74	4	NG	Shanghai	19 Oct 97
30:47.59	Sonia	O'Sullivan	IRL	28.11.69	2	EC	München	6 Aug 02
30:47.72		Wang Dongmei	CHN	3.12.72	5	NG	Shanghai	19 Oct 97
30:48.89	Yoko	Shibui	JPN	14.3.79	1		Stanford	3 May 02
30:50.32	Deena	Drossin/Kastor	USA	14.2.73	2		Stanford	3 May 02
30:51.81	Kayoko	Fukushi	JPN	25.3.82	2	AsiG	Busan	8 Oct 02
30:52.51	Elana	Meyer	RSA	10.10.66	1	WCp	London (CP)	10 Sep 94
30:55.67	Irene	Kwambai	KEN	25.10.78	2		Utrecht	17 Jun 05
	(30)							
30:55.83		Liu Shixiang ¶	CHN	13.1.71	6	NG	Shanghai	19 Oct 97
30:57.07	Liz	McColgan	GBR	24.5.64	1	APM	Hengelo	25 Jun 91
30:57.21	Olga	Bondarenko'	RUS	2.6.60	2	EC	Stuttgart	30 Aug 86
30:57.70	Leah	Malot	KEN	7.6.72	2	NA	Heusden	5 Aug 00
30:57.83	Lydiya	Grigoryeva	RUS	21.1.74	3	NC	Tula	3 Aug 03
30:59.92	Merima	Hashim	ETH	.81	3	NA	Heusden	5 Aug 00
31:03.60	Marleen	Renders	BEL	24.12.68	4	NA	Heusden	5 Aug 00
31:03.62	Kathrin	Ullrich'	GER	14.8.67	1	ECp	Frankfurt-am-Main	30 Jun 91
31:04.00	Lyudmila	Biktasheva	RUS	25.7.74	3	EC	München	6 Aug 02
31:04.10	Jelena	Prokopcuka	LAT	21.9.76	7	OG	Athína	27 Aug 04
	(40)							
31:04.34	Jane	Wanjiku	KEN	14.6.79	1		Kobe	25 Apr 04
31:04.49	Derebe	Alemu	ETH	5.6.83	1		Uden	3 Jul 04
31:05.57	Maura	Viceconte	ITA	3.10.67	5	NA	Heusden	5 Aug 00
31:05.90	Lucy	Wangui	KEN	24.3.84	9	OG	Athína	27 Aug 04

WOMEN All-time

Mark	Wind	Name		Nat	Born	Pos	Meet	Venue	Date
31:06.63		Helena	Javornik	SLO	26.3.66	10	OG	Athína	27 Aug 0
31:06.94			Li Ji ¶	CHN	19.9.79	7	OG	Sydney	30 Sep 0
31:07.88		Jill	Hunter	GBR	14.10.66	2	ECp	Frankfurt-am-Main	30 Jun 9
31:08.41		Catherina	McKiernan	IRL	30.11.69	1		Villeneuve d'Ascq	17 Jun 9
31:08.89		Natalya	Berkut	UKR	30.5.75	3	Rus Ch	Tula	25 Jun 0
31:09.03			Zhou Chunxiu	CHN	8.3.79	2	NG	Nanjing	17 Oct 0
		(50)	100th woman 31:32.02, 200th 31:52.09, 300th 32:07.25, 400th 32:18.62						

HALF MARATHON

Slightly downhill courses included: Newcastle-South Shields 30.5m, Tokyo 33m (to 1998), Lisboa (Spring) 69m

Mark	Wind	Name		Nat	Born	Pos	Meet	Venue	Date
65:40	dh	Paula	Radcliffe	GBR	17.12.73	1	GNR	South Shields	21 Sep 0
65:44	dh	Susan	Chepkemei	KEN	25.6.75	1		Lisboa	1 Apr 0
66:34	dh	Lornah	Kiplagat	KEN	20.3.74	2		Lisboa	1 Apr 0
66:40*		Ingrid	Kristiansen	NOR	21.3.56	1	NC	Sandnes	5 Apr 8
66:43	dh	Masako	Chiba	JPN	18.7.76	1		Tokyo	19 Jan 9
66:44		Elana	Meyer	RSA	10.10.66	1		Tokyo	15 Jan 9
66:47			Radcliffe			1	WCh	Bristol	7 Oct 0
66:49		Esther	Wanjiru	KEN	27.3.77	2		Tokyo	15 Jan 9
66:56			L Kiplagat			1	City-Pier	Den Haag	25 Mar 0
67:03	dh	Derartu	Tulu	ETH	21.3.72	3		Lisboa	1 Apr 0
67:07	dh		Radcliffe			1	GNR	South Shields	22 Oct 0
67:11	dh	Liz	McColgan	GBR	24.5.64	1		Tokyo	26 Jan 9
67:12	dh	Tegla	Loroupe (10)	KEN	9.5.73	1		Lisboa	10 Mar 9
67:19	dh	Sonia	O'Sullivan	IRL	28.11.69	1	GNR	South Shields	6 Oct 0
67:22			Meyer			1		Tokyo	24 Jan 9
67:23		Margaret	Okayo	KEN	30.5.76	1		Udine	28 Sep 0
67:24	dh		Loroupe			1		Lisboa	26 Mar 0
67:29			Meyer			1		Kyoto	8 Mar 9
67:32			Loroupe			1		Den Haag	28 Mar 9
67:32	dh	Berhane	Adere	ETH	21.7.73	2	GNR	South Shields	21 Sep 0
67:33			Meyer			1		Tokyo	10 Jan 0
67:33	dh		Tulu			1	GNR	South Shields	18 Sep 0
67:35			Radcliffe			1	WCh	Vilamoura	4 Oct 0
67:36			Meyer			1		Kyoto	9 Mar 9
67:36			Chepkemei			2	WCh	Bristol	7 Oct 0
67:37			Kiplagat			1		Zaandam	17 Sep 0
67:41			Wanjiru			2		Tokyo	10 Jan 0
67:43	dh		Loroupe			2		Tokyo	19 Jan 9
67:47		Mizuki	Noguchi	JPN	3.7.78	1		Miyazaki	6 Jan 0
67:48		Kerryn	McCann	AUS	2.5.67	3		Tokyo	10 Jan 0
67:50	dh	Catherina	McKiernan	IRL	30.11.69	1		Lisboa	15 Mar 9
		(31/16)							
67:53		Edith	Masai	KEN	4.4.67	1		Nice	22 Apr 0
67:53		Deena	Kastor	USA	14.2.73	1		Philadelphia	18 Sep 0
67:54		Catherine	Ndereba	KEN	21.7.72	1		Den Haag	24 Mar 0
67:55	dh	Benita	Johnson	AUS	6.5.79	1	GNR	South Shields	26 Sep 0
		(20)							
67:56	dh	Susie	Power	AUS	26.3.75	2	GNR	South Shields	6 Oct 0
67:58		Uta	Pippig ¶	GER	7.9.65	1		Kyoto	19 Mar 9
67:59	w	Restituta	Joseph	TAN	30.7.71	1		Malmö	12 Jun 0
68:09	dh	Cristina	Pomacu	ROM	15.9.73	2		Lisboa	15 Mar 9
68:09	dh	Werknesh	Kidane	ETH	21.11.81	2	GNR	South Shields	18 Sep 0
68:10		Constantina	Tomescu'	ROM	23.1.70	1	NC	Turnu-Severin	14 Sep 0
68:11	dh	Joyce	Chepchumba	KEN	6.11.70	1		Lisboa	28 Mar 0
68:11	dh	Jelena	Prokopcuka	LAT	21.9.76	3	GNR	South Shields	18 Sep 0
68:18	dh	Izumi	Maki	JPN	10.12.68	2		Tokyo	21 Jan 9
68:18	dh	Yoshiko	Ichikawa	JPN	18.4.76	3		Tokyo	19 Jan 9
		(30)							
68:21	dh	Albertina	Dias	POR	26.4.65	3		Lisboa	10 Mar 9
68:23	dh	Fernanda	Ribeiro	POR	23.6.69	3		Lisboa	26 Mar 0
68:30	dh	Maria	Guida	ITA	23.1.66	4		Lisboa	10 Mar 9
68:32		Mikie	Takanaka	JPN	6.10.80	2		Miyazaki	6 Jan 0
68:33	dh	Lisa	Ondieki	AUS	12.5.60	2		Tokyo	26 Jan 9
68:34		Joan	Benoit	USA	16.5.57	1		Philadelphia	16 Sep 8
68:34	dh	Olga	Appell	MEX	2.8.63	2		Tokyo	24 Jan 9
68:34		Asmae	Leghzaoui ¶	MAR	30.8.76	1		Marrakech	31 Jan 9
68:34		Lidia	Simon	ROM	4.9.73	4		Tokyo	10 Jan 0
68:35		Takako	Kotorida	JPN	2.4.77	2		Yamaguchi	9 Mar 0
		(40)							
68:38		Colleen	de Reuck	RSA	13.4.64	1	NC	Durban	23 Jul 8

Mark	Wind	Name		Nat	Born	Pos	Meet	Venue	Date
68:38		Isabella	Ochichi	KEN	79	2		Nice	22 Apr 01
68:40			Sun Yingjie ¶	CHN	3.10.77	1	WCh	New Delhi	3 Oct 04
68:41	dh	Junko	Kataoka	JPN	13.6.70	1		Tokyo	23 Jan 94
68:45	w	Lyubov	Morgunova	RUS	14.1.71	3		Malmö	12 Jun 00
68:45		Hiromi	Ominami	JPN	15.11.75	1		Sapporo	4 Jul 04
68:48	w	Abebe	Tola	ETH	3.6.77	4		Malmö	12 Jun 00
68:49	dh	Grete	Waitz	NOR	1.10.53	1	GNR	South Shields	24 Jul 88
68:54		Miwako	Yamanaka	JPN	24.5.78	1		Kobe	16 Dec 01
68:54		Lenah	Cheruiyot	KEN	1.3.73	1		Den Haag	23 Mar 02
68:54	dh	Ines	Chenonge	KEN	1.2.82	4		Lisboa	24 Mar 02
		(51)	100th woman 69:32, 200th 70:15, 300th 70:53						
Downhill			* uncertain course measurement						
68:12		Claudia	Metzner	GER	5.5.66	1		Las Vegas (260m)	4 Feb 95
68:13		Petra	Wassiluk	GER	27.10.69	1		Las Vegas	9 Feb 97
Drugs disqualification:		68:50	Yasuko Kimura #	JPN	6.1.76	(3)		Tokyo	21 Jan 96

MARATHON

Note Boston times included, but course is downhill overall (139m) and sometimes, as in 1994, strongly wind-aided
In second column: first character: L = loop course or start and finish within 30%, P = point-to-point or start and finish more than 30% apart, D + point-to-point and downhil over 1/1000
Second character: M mixed marathon (men and women), W women only race or separated start by time

Mark		Name		Nat	Born	Pos	Meet	Venue	Date
2:15:25	LM	Paula	Radcliffe	GBR	17.12.73	1		London	13 Apr 03
2:17:18	LM		Radcliffe			1		Chicago	13 Oct 02
2:17:42	LW		Radcliffe			1		London	17 Apr 05
2:18:47	LM	Catherine	Ndereba	KEN	21.7.72	1		Chicago	7 Oct 01
2:18:56	LW		Radcliffe			1		London	14 Apr 02
2:19:12	LM	Mizuki	Noguchi	JPN	3.7.78	1		Berlin	25 Sep 05
2:19:26	LM		Ndereba			2		Chicago	13 Oct 02
2:19:39	LM		Sun Yingjie ¶	CHN	3.10.77	1		Beijing	19 Oct 03
2:19:41	LM	Yoko	Shibui	JPN	14.3.79	1		Berlin	26 Sep 04
2:19:46	LM	Naoko	Takahashi	JPN	6.5.72	1		Berlin	30 Sep 01
2:19:55	LM		Ndereba			2		London	13 Apr 03
2:20:43	LM	Tegla	Loroupe	KEN	9.5.73	1		Berlin	26 Sep 99
2:20:43	DM	Margaret	Okayo	KEN	30.5.76	1		Boston	15 Apr 02
2:20:47	LM		Loroupe			1		Rotterdam	19 Apr 98
2:20:57	LW		Radcliffe			1	WCh	Helsinki	14 Aug 05
2:21:01	LM		Sun Yingjie ¶			1	NG	Beijing	16 Oct 05
2:21:06	LM	Ingrid	Kristiansen	NOR	21.3.56	1		London	21 Apr 85
2:21:11	LM	(10)	Zhou Chunxiu	CHN	8.3.79	2	NG	Beijing	16 Oct 05
2:21:12	DM		Ndereba			2		Boston	15 Apr 02
2:21:16	LM	Deena	Drossin/Kastor	USA	14.2.73	3		London	13 Apr 03
2:21:18	LW		Noguchi			1		Osaka	26 Jan 03
2:21:21	LM	Joan	Benoit'	USA	16.5.57	1		Chicago	20 Oct 85
2:21:21	LM		Sun Yingjie			2		Beijing	20 Oct 02
2:21:22	LM		Shibui			3		Chicago	13 Oct 02
2:21:25	LM		Kastor			1		Chicago	9 Oct 05
2:21:30	LM	Constantina	Dita/Tomescu	ROM	23.1.70	2		Chicago	9 Oct 05
2:21:31	LM	Svetlana	Zakharova	RUS	15.9.70	4		Chicago	13 Oct 02
2:21:33	LM		Ndereba			1		Chicago	22 Oct 00
2:21:45	DM	Uta	Pippig ¶	GER	7.9.65	1		Boston	18 Apr 94
2:21:45	LW	Masako	Chiba	JPN	18.7.76	2		Osaka	26 Jan 03
		(30/17)							
2:21:51	LW	Naoko	Sakamoto	JPN	14.11.80	3		Osaka	26 Jan 03
2:22:12	LW	Eri	Yamaguchi	JPN	14.1.73	1		Tokyo	22 Nov 99
2:22:20	LM	Gete	Wami (20)	ETH	11.12.74	1		Amsterdam	20 Oct 02
2:22:22	LW	Lornah	Kiplagat	KEN	20.3.74	4		Osaka	26 Jan 03
2:22:23	LM	Catherina	McKiernan	IRL	30.11.69	1		Amsterdam	1 Nov 98
2:22:33	LW	Lyudmila	Petrova	RUS	7.10.68	3		London	14 Apr 02
2:22:46	LW	Reiko	Tosa	JPN	11.6.76	4		London	14 Apr 02
2:22:54	LW	Lidia	Simon	ROM	4.9.73	1		Osaka	30 Jan 00
2:22:56	LW	Harumi	Hiroyama	JPN	2.9.68	2		Osaka	30 Jan 00
2:22:56	LW	Jelena	Prokopcuka	LAT	21.9.76	1		Osaka	30 Jan 05
2:23:05	LM	Marleen	Renders	BEL	24.12.68	1		Paris	7 Apr 02
2:23:12	LM	Susan	Chepkemei	KEN	25.6.75	4		London	13 Apr 03
2:23:17	LM		Zhang Shujing	CHN	13.9.78	3		Beijing	20 Oct 02
		(30)							
2:23:21	DM	Fatuma	Roba	ETH	18.12.73	1		Boston	20 Apr 98
2:23:22	LW	Joyce	Chepchumba	KEN	6.11.70	1		London	18 Apr 99
2:23:26	LM	Hiromi	Ominami	JPN	15.11.75	2		Berlin	26 Sep 04
2:23:29	LM	Rosa	Mota	POR	29.6.58	3		Chicago	20 Oct 85

Mark	Wind	Name		Nat	Born	Pos	Meet	Venue	Date
2:23:30	LW	Mari	Ozaki	JPN	16.7.75	5		Osaka	26 Jan 03
2:23:30	LW	Derartu	Tulu	ETH	21.3.72	4	WCh	Helsinki	14 Aug 05
2:23:31	LW	Esther	Wanjiru	KEN	27.3.77	3		Osaka	30 Jan 00
2:23:33	DM	Valentina	Yegorova	RUS	16.2.64	2		Boston	18 Apr 94
2:23:37	LM		Liu Min	CHN	29.11.83	1		Beijing	14 Oct 01
2:23:43	DM	Olga	Markova	RUS	6.8.68	1		Boston	20 Apr 92
		(40)							
2:23:43	LM	Takami	Ominami	JPN	15.11.75	1		Rotterdam	21 Apr 02
2:23:47	LM	Maura	Viceconte	ITA	3.10.67	1		Wien	21 May 00
2:23:51	LW	Lisa	Martin/Ondieki	AUS	12.5.60	1		Osaka	31 Jan 88
2:23:57	LM		Zhu Xiaolin	CHN	20.4.84	4		Beijing	20 Oct 02
2:24:02	LM		Wei Yanan¶	CHN	6.12.81	2		Beijing	14 Oct 01
2:24:06	LW	Adriana	Fernández	MEX	4.4.71	2		London	18 Apr 99
2:24:07	LW		Wang Junxia	CHN	9.1.73	1		Tianjin	4 Apr 93
2:24:18	DM	Wanda	Panfil	POL	26.1.59	1		Boston	15 Apr 91
2:24:19	LW	Yumiko	Hara	JPN	9.1.82	1		Nagoya	13 Mar 05
2:24:22	LM		Ren Xiujuan	CHN	14.9.74	3		Beijing	14 Oct 01
2:24:22	LW	Rita	Jeptoo	KEN	15.2.81	7	WCh	Helsinki	14 Aug 05
		(51)	100th woman 2:26:03, 200th 2:27:57, 300th 2:29:23, 400th 2:30:31, 500th 2:31:49						
Drugs dq: 2:20:23	LM		Wei Yanan ¶	CHN	6.12.81	1		Beijing	20 Oct 02

2000 METRES STEEPLECHASE

Mark	Name		Nat	Born	Pos	Meet	Venue	Date
6:04.46	Dorcus	Inzikuru	UGA	2.2.82	1	GP II	Milano	1 Jun 05
6:11.84	Marina	Pluzhnikova	RUS	25.2.63	1	GWG	Sankt-Peterburg	25 Jul 94
6:14.52	Svetlana	Rogova	RUS	4.8.67	1	Znam	Moskva	11 Jun 92
6:16.49	Yelena	Motalova	RUS	28.1.71	1	NC	Moskva	2 Aug 98
6:16.58	Cristina	Casandra	ROM	1.2.77	2	GP II	Milano	1 Jun 05

3000 METRES STEEPLECHASE

$ short water jump (3.06m, standard is now 3.66m)

Mark		Name		Nat	Born	Pos	Meet	Venue	Date
9:01.59	WR	Gulnara	Samitova	RUS	9.7.78	1		Iráklio	4 Jul 04
9:08.33	WR		Samitova			1	NC	Tula	10 Aug 03
9:09.84			Samitova			1		Réthimno	23 Jun 04
9:15.04		Dorcus	Inzikuru	UGA	2.2.82	1	SGP	Athína	14 Jun 05
9:16.46			Inzikuru			1	GP	Rieti	28 Aug 05
9:16.51	WR	Alesya	Turova	BLR	6.12.79	1		Gdansk	27 Jul 02
9:18.24			Inzikuru			1	WCh	Helsinki	8 Aug 05
9:20.28			Turova			1	GS	Ostrava	12 Jun 03
9:20.33			Inzikuru			1	GP	Rieti	28 Aug 05
9:20.49		Yekaterina	Volkova	RUS	16.2.78	2	WCh	Helsinki	8 Aug 05
9:21.40			Samitova			1	GP	Rieti	5 Sep 04
9:21.72	WR		Turova			1	GS	Ostrava	12 Jun 02
9:21.80			Inzikuru			1	WAF	Monaco	9 Sep 05
9:22.29	WR	Justyna	Bak	POL	1.8.74	1		Milano	5 Jun 02
9:23.91			Turova			1	NA	Heusden	20 Jul 02
9:24.78		Lyubov	Ivanova	RUS	2.3.81	2	NC	Tula	10 Aug 03
9:25.09		Wioletta	Janowska	POL	9.6.77	2	SGP	Athína	14 Jun 05
9:25.31	WR$		Bak			1	Nik	Nice	9 Jul 01
9:25.47			Janowska			1	WAF	Monaco	9 Sep 05
9:25.87			Samitova			1		Réthimno	6 Jul 03
		(20/7)							
9:26.95		Jeruto	Kiptum	KEN	12.12.81	3	WCh	Helsinki	8 Aug 05
9:27.21		Mardrea	Hyman	JAM	22.12.72	3	WAF	Monaco	9 Sep 05
9:29.32		Brianna	Shook	USA	6.1.81	1	NA	Heusden	31 Jul 04
		(10)							
9:29.81		Salome	Chepchumba	KEN	29.9.82	2	NA	Heusden	31 Jul 04
9:30.12		Korine	Hinds	JAM	18.1.76	3	GP	Rieti	28 Aug 05
9:30.20		Livia	Tóth	HUN	7.1.80	4	WAF	Monaco	9 Sep 05
9:30.35		Bouchra	Chaabi	MAR	22.9.80	3		Iráklio	4 Jul 04
9:30.70	$	Melissa	Rollison	AUS	13.4.83	1	GWG	Brisbane	4 Sep 01
9:31.96		Cristina	Casandra	ROM	1.2.77	4		Iráklio	4 Jul 04
9:32.41		Yelena	Zadorozhnaya	RUS	3.12.77	5	WAF	Monaco	9 Sep 05
9:33.12		Élodie	Olivarès	FRA	22.5.76	2	NA	Heusden	20 Jul 02
9:35.28		Sigrid	Vanden Bempt	BEL	10.2.81	3	NA	Heusden	31 Jul 04
9:35.51		Natalya	Izmodenova	RUS	1.1.81	5	SGP	Athína	14 Jun 05
		(20)							
9:38.31		Melanie	Schulz	GER	27.8.79	1	NC	Wattenscheid	6 Jul 02
9:38.31		Fatiha Bahi	Azzouhoum	ALG	8.3.83	6	SGP	Athína	14 Jun 05
9:39.20		Inês	Monteiro	POR	18.5.80	7	SGP	Athína	14 Jun 05
9:39.35		Ann	Gaffigan	USA	5.10.81	1	NC/OT	Sacramento	15 Jul 04
9:39.51	$	Irene	Limika	KEN	28.8.79	2	Nik	Nice	9 Jul 01

Mark	Wind	Name		Nat	Born	Pos	Meet	Venue	Date
9:39.68		Carrie	Messner	USA	7.6.77	3h2	WCh	Helsinki	6 Aug 05
9:39.78		Elizabeth	Jackson	USA	27.10.77	1	NC	Carson	26 Jun 05
9:40.58		Lisa	Galaviz	USA	30.11.79	2	NC	Carson	26 Jun 05
9:41.21		Minori	Hayakari	JPN	29.11.72	4h1	WCh	Helsinki	6 Aug 05
9:42.01		Michaela	Mannová	CZE	11.1.82	2	EU23	Bydgoszcz	19 Jul 03
		(30)							
9:42.18		Yamina	Bouchaouante	FRA	31.7.80	5h3	WCh	Helsinki	6 Aug 05
9:42.70		Yelena	Sidorchenkova	RUS	30.5.80	1	GP II	Thessaloníki	17 Jul 05
9:43.00		Analia	Rosa	POR	28.2.76	6		Iráklio	4 Jul 04
9:43.25		Ida	Nilsson	SWE	8.2.81	1		Northridge	29 May 04
9:43.89		Laurence	Duquénoy	FRA	29.9.69	3	GS	Ostrava	12 Jun 02
9:44.68		Kassi	Andersen	USA	25.6.83	2		Northridge	29 May 04
9:45.21		Susanne	Wigene	NOR	12.2.78	1		Königs-Wusterhausen	10 Sep 04
9:45.60		Roisin	McGettigan	IRL	23.8.80	4	NA	Heusden	31 Jul 04
9:45.7A		Jackline Chemutai	Chemwok	KEN	13.9.83	1	WCT	Nairobi	25 Jun 05
9:46.76		Alina	Proca	ROM	24.10.83	3		Pírgos	27 Jul 03
		(40)	50th woman 9:49.24, 100th woman 10:00.32						

100 METRES HURDLES

Mark	Wind	Name		Nat	Born	Pos	Meet	Venue	Date
12.21 WR	0.7	Yordanka	Donkova	BUL	28.9.61	1		Stara Zagora	20 Aug 88
12.24	0.9		Donkova			1h		Stara Zagora	28 Aug 88
12.25 WR	1.4	Ginka	Zagorcheva	BUL	12.4.58	1	v TCH,GRE	Drama	8 Aug 87
12.26 WR	1.5		Donkova			1	Balk	Ljubljana	7 Sep 86
12.26	1.7	Lyudmila	Narozhilenko ¶	RUS	21.4.64	1rB		Sevilla	6 Jun 92
		(now Ludmila Engquist SWE)							
12.27	-1.2		Donkova			1		Stara Zagora	28 Aug 88
12.28	1.8		Narozhilenko			1	NC	Kiyev	11 Jul 91
12.28	0.9		Narozhilenko			1rA		Sevilla	6 Jun 92
12.29 WR	-0.4		Donkova			1	ASV	Köln	17 Aug 86
12.32	1.6		Narozhilenko			1		Saint-Denis	4 Jun 92
12.33	1.4		Donkova			1		Fürth	14 Jun 87
12.33	-0.3	Gail	Devers	USA	19.11.66	1	NC	Sacramento	23 Jul 00
12.34	-0.5		Zagorcheva			1	WCh	Roma	4 Sep 87
12.35 WR	0.1		Donkova			1h2	ASV	Köln	17 Aug 86
12.36 WR	1.9	Grazyna	Rabsztyn	POL	20.9.52	1	Kuso	Warszawa	13 Jun 80
12.36 WR	-0.6		Donkova			1	NC	Sofiya	13 Aug 86
12.36	1.1		Donkova			1		Schwechat	15 Jun 88
12.37	1.4		Donkova			1	ISTAF	Berlin	15 Aug 86
12.37	0.7		Devers			1	WCh	Sevilla	28 Aug 99
12.37	1.5	Joanna	Hayes	USA	23.12.76	1	OG	Athína	24 Aug 04
12.38	0.0		Donkova			1	BGP	Budapest	11 Aug 86
12.38	-0.7		Donkova			1	EC	Stuttgart	29 Aug 86
12.38	0.2		Donkova			1	OG	Seoul	30 Sep 88
12.39	1.5	Vera	Komisova'	RUS	11.6.53	1	GGala	Roma	5 Aug 80
12.39	1.5		Zagorcheva			2	Balk	Ljubljana	7 Sep 86
12.39	1.8	Natalya	Grigoryeva ¶	UKR	3.12.62	2	NC	Kiyev	11 Jul 91
12.39	-0.7		Devers			1	WK	Zürich	11 Aug 00
12.40	0.4		Donkova			1	GWG	Moskva	8 Jul 86
12.40	1.2		Devers			1rA	Athl	Lausanne	2 Jul 02
		(29/8) – 7 performances at 12.42							
12.42	1.8	Bettine	Jahn	GDR	3.8.58	1	OD	Berlin	8 Jun 83
12.42	2.0	Anjanette	Kirkland (10)	USA	24.2.74	1	WCh	Edmonton	11 Aug 01
12.43	-0.9	Lucyna	Kalek (Langer)	POL	9.1.56	1		Hannover	19 Aug 84
12.43	-0.3	Michelle	Perry	USA	1.5.79	1s1	NC	Carson	26 Jun 05
12.44	-0.5	Gloria	Uibel (-Siebert)	GDR	13.1.64	2	WCh	Roma	4 Sep 87
12.44	-0.8	Olga	Shishigina ¶	KAZ	23.12.68	1		Luzern	27 Jun 95
12.44	0.4	Glory	Alozie	NGR/ESP	30.12.77	1	Herc	Monaco	8 Aug 98
12.45	1.3	Cornelia	Oschkenat'	GDR	29.10.61	1		Neubrandenburg	11 Jun 87
12.45	1.4	Brigitte	Foster-Hylton	JAM	7.11.74	1	Pre	Eugene	24 May 03
12.45	1.5	Yelena	Krasovskaya	UKR	17.8.76	2	OG	Athína	24 Aug 04
12.46	0.7	Perdita	Felicien	CAN	29.8.80	1	Pre	Eugene	19 Jun 04
12.47	1.1	Marina	Azyabina	RUS	15.6.63	1s2	NC	Moskva	19 Jun 93
		(20)							
12.50	0.0	Vera	Akimova'	RUS	5.6.59	1		Sochi	19 May 84
12.51	1.4	Miesha	McKelvy	USA	26.7.76	2	Pre	Eugene	24 May 03
12.51	0.0	Delloreen	Ennis-London	JAM	5.3.75	1	NC	Kingston	27 Jun 04
12.52	-0.4	Michelle	Freeman	JAM	5.5.69	1s1	WCh	Athína	10 Aug 97
12.53	0.2	Tatyana	Reshetnikova	RUS	14.10.66	1rA	GP II	Linz	4 Jul 94
12.53	-0.4	Svetla	Dimitrova ¶	BUL	27.1.70	1	Herc	Stara Zagora	16 Jul 94
12.53	1.0	Melissa	Morrison	USA	9.7.71	1	DNG	Stockholm	5 Aug 98

Mark	Wind	Name		Nat	Born	Pos	Meet	Venue	Date
12.54	0.4	Kerstin	Knabe	GDR	7.7.59	3	EC	Athína	9 Sep 82
12.54	0.9	Sabine	Paetz/John'	GDR	16.10.57	1		Berlin	15 Jul 84
12.56	1.2	Johanna	Klier'	GDR	13.9.52	1		Cottbus	17 Jul 80
		(30)							
12.56	1.2	Monique	Ewanje-Epée	FRA	11.7.67	1	BNP	Villeneuve d'Ascq	29 Jun 90
12.56	0.7	Danielle	Carruthers	USA	22.12.79	2	Pre	Eugene	19 Jun 04
12.59 WR	-0.6	Anneliese	Ehrhardt	GDR	18.6.50	1	OG	München	8 Sep 72
12.59	0.0	Natalya	Shekhodanova ¶	RUS	29.12.71	1	NC	Sankt Peterburg	3 Jul 96
12.59	1.0	Patricia	Girard ¶	FRA	8.4.68	2s2	OG	Atlanta	31 Jul 96
12.59	0.2	Brigita	Bukovec	SLO	21.5.70	2	OG	Atlanta	31 Jul 96
12.59	0.4	Kirsten	Bolm	GER	4.3.75	1	LGP	London (CP)	22 Jul 05
12.60	1.7	Maria	Koroteyeva	RUS	10.11.81	4s1	OG	Athína	23 Aug 04
12.61	0.3	Svetlana	Gusarova	KAZ	29.5.59	2	NC	Leningrad	3 Aug 85
12.61	0.2	Jackie	Joyner-Kersee	USA	3.3.62	1	Jenn	San José	28 May 88
		(40)							
12.61	1.4	Katie	Anderson	CAN	9.1.68	1		Villeneuve d'Ascq	13 Jun 99
12.61	-0.3	Virginia	Powell	USA	7.9.83	2s1	NC	Carson	26 Jun 05
12.62	1.2	Mihaela	Pogacian'	ROM	27.1.58	2	BNP	Villeneuve d'Ascq	29 Jun 90
12.62	1.1	Yuliya	Graudyn	RUS	13.11.70	1A	ISTAF	Berlin	30 Aug 94
12.62	1.7	Nichole	Denby	USA	10.10.82	1	NCAA	Austin	11 Jun 04
12.63	1.8	Zofia	Bielczyk	POL	22.9.58	1h1	Kuso	Warszawa	18 Jun 79
12.63	1.4	Heike	Terpe/Theele	GDR	4.10.64	2	NC	Jena	27 Jun 86
12.63	0.0	Angie	Vaughn	USA	4.11.76	1	GP	Edwardsville	25 Jul 98
12.63	2.0	Jenny	Adams	USA	8.7.78	5	WCh	Edmonton	11 Aug 01
12.64		four women: P Patoulídou GRE 1992, Zhang Yu CHN 1993, D Rose-Henley JAM 1996, P Lopes CAN 2004							
		(50)	100th woman 12.76, 200th 12.94, 300th 13.09						
Wind assisted performances to 12.39, performers to 12.63									
12.28	2.7	Cornelia	Oschkenat'	GDR	29.10.61	1		Berlin	25 Aug 87
12.29	3.5		Donkova			1	Athl	Lausanne	24 Jun 88
12.29	2.7	Gail	Devers	USA	19.11.66	1	Pre	Eugene	26 May 02
12.35	2.4	Bettine	Jahn	GDR	3.8.58	1	WCh	Helsinki	13 Aug 83
12.37	2.7	Gloria	Uibel/Siebert'	GDR	13.1.64	2		Berlin	25 Aug 87
12.39	2.8		Rabsztyn			1	4-N	Bremen	24 Jun 79
12.40	2.1	Michelle	Freeman	JAM	5.5.69	1	GPF	Fukuoka	13 Sep 97
12.41	2.2	Olga	Shishigina ¶	KAZ	23.12.68	1rA	Athl	Lausanne	5 Jul 95
12.42	2.4	Kerstin	Knabe	GDR	7.7.59	2	WCh	Helsinki	13 Aug 83
12.44	2.6	Melissa	Morrison	USA	9.7.71	1		Carson	22 May 04
12.45	2.1	Perdita	Felicien	CAN	29.8.80	1	NC	Victoria	10 Jul 04
12.50	2.7	Svetla	Dimitrova ¶	BUL	27.1.70	1		Saint-Denis	10 Jun 94
12.51	3.2	Johanna	Klier'	GDR	13.9.52	1	NC	Cottbus	17 Jul 80
12.51	3.6	Sabine	Paetz/John'	GDR	16.10.57	1		Dresden	27 Jul 84
12.51A	3.3	Yuliya	Graudyn	RUS	13.11.70	1		Sestriere	31 Jul 94
12.53	2.2	Mihaela	Pogacian	ROM	27.1.58	1	IAC	Edinburgh	6 Jul 90
12.61	4.0	Jenny	Adams	USA	8.7.78	1h1	NC	Eugene	23 Jun 01
12.62	2.9	Eunice	Barber	FRA	17.11.74	1H		Arles	4 Jun 05
12.63	2.8	Eva	Sokolova	RUS	25.3.62	1s1	NC	Moskva	19 Jun 93
Probably hand timed									
12.4	0.7	Svetla	Dimitrova ¶	BUL	27.1.70	1		Stara Zagora	9 Jul 97
		Officially 12.36, but subsequent investigations showed this unlikely to have been auto-timed							
12.63		Angela	Atede	NGR	8.2.72	1	NC	Lagos	28 Jun 97
Hand timed									
12.3 WR	1.5	Anneliese	Ehrhardt	GDR	18.6.50	1	NC	Dresden	22 Jul 73
12.3		Marina	Azyabina	RUS	15.6.63	1		Yekaterinburg	30 May 93
12.0w	2.1	Yordanka	Donkova	BUL	28.9.61	1		Sofiya	3 Aug 86
12.1w	2.1	Ginka	Zagorcheva	BUL	12.4.58	2		Sofiya	3 Aug 86

400 METRES HURDLES

Mark	Name		Nat	Born	Pos	Meet	Venue	Date
52.34 WR	Yuliya	Nosova-Pechonkina'	RUS	21.4.78	1	NC	Tula	8 Aug 03
52.61 WR	Kim	Batten	USA	29.3.69	1	WCh	Göteborg	11 Aug 95
52.62	Tonja	Buford-Bailey	USA	13.12.70	2	WCh	Göteborg	11 Aug 95
52.74 WR	Sally	Gunnell	GBR	29.7.66	1	WCh	Stuttgart	19 Aug 93
52.74		Batten			1	Herc	Monaco	8 Aug 98
52.77	Faní	Halkiá	GRE	2.2.79	1s2	OG	Athína	22 Aug 04
52.79	Sandra	Farmer-Patrick	USA	18.8.62	2	WCh	Stuttgart	19 Aug 93
52.82	Deon	Hemmings	JAM	9.10.68	1	OG	Atlanta	31 Jul 96
52.82		Halkiá			1	OG	Athína	25 Aug 04
52.84		Batten			1	WK	Zürich	12 Aug 98
52.89	Daimí	Pernía	CUB	27.12.76	1	WCh	Sevilla	25 Aug 99
52.90		Buford			1	WK	Zürich	16 Aug 95
52.90	Nezha	Bidouane	MAR	18.9.69	2	WCh	Sevilla	25 Aug 99

Mark Wind		Name		Nat	Born	Pos	Meet	Venue	Date
52.90			Pechonkina			1	WCh	Helsinki	13 Aug 05
52.94	WR	Marina	Styepanova' (10)	RUS	1.5.50	1s	Spart	Tashkent	17 Sep 86
52.95		Sheena	Johnson	USA	1.10.82	1	NC/OT	Sacramento	11 Jul 04
52.96A			Bidouane			1	WCp	Johannesburg	11 Sep 98
52.97			Batten			1	NC	Indianapolis	14 Jun 97
52.97			Bidouane			1	WCh	Athína	8 Aug 97
52.98			Hemmings			1rA	WK	Zürich	13 Aug 97
52.99			Hemmings			1s1	OG	Atlanta	29 Jul 96
53.01			Pechonkina			1	NC	Tula	11 Jul 05
53.02		Irina	Privalova	RUS	22.11.68	1	OG	Sydney	27 Sep 00
53.03A			Hemmings			2	WCp	Johannesburg	11 Sep 98
53.05			Bidouane			1	GGala	Roma	7 Jul 99
53.05			Pechonkina			1		Tula	13 Jun 05
53.06			Batten			1	Herc	Monaco	16 Aug 97
53.06			Batten			1	Gaz	Paris	29 Jul 98
53.08			Batten			2	OG	Atlanta	31 Jul 96
53.08			Bidouane			1	Athl	Lausanne	2 Jul 99
		(30/12)							
53.11		Tatyana	Ledovskaya	BLR	21.5.66	1	WCh	Tokyo	29 Aug 91
53.17		Debbie	Flintoff-King	AUS	20.4.60	1	OG	Seoul	28 Sep 88
53.21		Marie-José	Pérec	FRA	9.5.68	2	WK	Zürich	16 Aug 95
53.22		Jana	Pittman	AUS	9.11.82	1	WCh	Saint-Denis	28 Aug 03
53.24		Sabine	Busch	GDR	21.11.62	1	NC	Potsdam	21 Aug 87
53.25		Ionela	Tîrlea-Manolache	ROM	9.2.76	2	GGala	Roma	7 Jul 99
53.27		Lashinda	Demus	USA	10.3.83	2	WCh	Helsinki	13 Aug 05
53.32		Sandra	Glover	USA	30.12.68	3	WCh	Helsinki	13 Aug 05
		(20)							
53.36		Andrea	Blackett	BAR	24.1.76	4	WCh	Sevilla	25 Aug 99
53.36		Brenda	Taylor	USA	9.2.79	2	NC/OT	Sacramento	11 Jul 04
53.37		Tatyana	Tereshchuk	UKR	11.10.69	3s2	OG	Athína	22 Aug 04
53.47		Janeene	Vickers	USA	3.10.68	3	WCh	Tokyo	29 Aug 91
53.48		Margarita	Ponomaryova'	RUS	19.6.63	3	WCh	Stuttgart	19 Aug 93
53.58		Cornelia	Ullrich'	GDR	26.4.63	2	NC	Potsdam	21 Aug 87
53.63		Ellen	Fiedler'	GDR	26.11.58	3	OG	Seoul	28 Sep 88
53.65A		Myrtle	Bothma'	RSA	18.2.64	mx		Pretoria	12 Mar 90
		53.74A				1		Johannesburg	18 Apr 86
53.72		Yekaterina	Bikert	RUS	13.5.80	2	NC	Tula	29 Jul 04
53.88		Debbie-Ann	Parris	JAM	24.3.73	3s1	WCh	Edmonton	6 Aug 01
		(30)							
53.96			Han Qing ¶	CHN	4.3.70	1	NG	Beijing	9 Sep 93
53.96			Song Yinglan	CHN	14.9.75	1	NG	Guangzhou	22 Nov 01
53.96		Anna	Jesien	POL	10.12.78	2	Gaz	Saint Denis	1 Jul 05
54.02	WR	Anna	Ambraziené'	LTU	14.4.55	1	Znam	Moskva	11 Jun 83
54.02A		Judit	Szekeres ¶	HUN	18.11.66	1		Roodepoort	23 Jan 98
54.02		Natasha	Danvers	GBR	19.9.77	2	GGala	Roma	11 Jul 03
54.03		Heike	Meissner	GER	29.1.70	5	OG	Atlanta	31 Jul 96
54.04		Gudrun	Abt	FRG	3.8.62	6	OG	Seoul	28 Sep 88
54.05A		Surita	Febbraio	RSA	27.12.73	1		Pretoria	4 Apr 03
54.11		Anna	Knoroz	RUS	30.7.70	3	Nik	Nice	18 Jul 94
		(40)							
54.14		Yekaterina	Fesenko/Grun	RUS	10.8.58	1	WCh	Helsinki	10 Aug 83
54.15		Ann-Louise	Skoglund	SWE	28.6.62	4	EC	Stuttgart	30 Aug 86
54.15		Michelle	Johnson	USA	12.4.74	5	WK	Zürich	11 Aug 99
54.16		Raasin	McIntosh	USA	29.4.82	5	NC/OT	Sacramento	11 Jul 04
54.17		Tonya	Williams	USA	5.10.74	3	Athl	Lausanne	3 Jul 96
54.18			Huang Xiaoxiao	CHN	3.3.83	1	NG	Nanjing	21 Oct 05
54.21		Ryan	Tolbert	USA	16.6.76	3	NC	Indianapolis	14 Jun 97
54.21		Shauna	Smith	USA	10.9.83	2	NC	Carson	25 Jun 05
54.22A		Silvia	Rieger	GER	14.11.70	5	WCp	Johannesburg	11 Sep 98
54.23		Judi	Brown King	USA	14.7.61	1	PAm	Indianapolis	12 Aug 87
		(50)	100th woman 55.03, 200th woman 55.80, 300th woman 56.39						
Drugs disqualification: 53.38			Jiang Limei ¶	CHN	.3.70	(1)	NG	Shanghai	22 Oct 97

HIGH JUMP

Mark Wind		Name		Nat	Born	Pos	Meet	Venue	Date
2.09	WR	Stefka	Kostadinova	BUL	25.3.65	1	WCh	Roma	30 Aug 87
2.08	WR		Kostadinova			1	NM	Sofiya	31 May 86
2.07	WR	Lyudmila	Andonova ¶	BUL	6.5.60	1	OD	Berlin	20 Jul 84
2.07	WR		Kostadinova			1		Sofiya	25 May 86
2.07			Kostadinova			1		Cagliari	16 Sep 87
2.07			Kostadinova			1	NC	Sofiya	3 Sep 88

Mark Wind	Name		Nat	Born	Pos	Meet	Venue	Date
2.07i	Heike	Henkel'	GER	5.5.64	1	NC	Karlsruhe	8 Feb 92
2.06		Kostadinova			1	ECp	Moskva	18 Aug 85
2.06		Kostadinova			1		Fürth	15 Jun 86
2.06		Kostadinova			1		Cagliari	14 Sep 86
2.06		Kostadinova			1		Wörrstadt	6 Jun 87
2.06		Kostadinova			1		Rieti	8 Sep 87
2.06i		Kostadinova			1		Pireás	20 Feb 88
2.06	Kajsa	Bergqvist	SWE	12.10.76	1		Eberstadt	26 Jul 03
2.06	Hestrie	Cloete	RSA	26.8.78	1	WCh	Saint-Denis	31 Aug 03
2.06	Yelena	Slesarenko	RUS	28.2.82	1	OG	Athína	28 Aug 04
2.05 WR	Tamara	Bykova	RUS	21.12.58	1	Izv	Kiyev	22 Jun 84
2.05		Kostadinova			1		Wörrstadt	14 Jun 86
2.05		Kostadinova			1		Rieti	7 Sep 86
2.05i		Kostadinova			1	WI	Indianapolis	8 Mar 87
2.05		Kostadinova			1	Bisl	Oslo	4 Jul 87
2.05		Kostadinova			1		Padova	13 Sep 87
2.05		Kostadinova			1	BGP	Budapest	12 Aug 88
2.05		Henkel			1	WCh	Tokyo	31 Aug 91
2.05i		Kostadinova			1	NC	Sofiya	1 Feb 92
2.05		Kostadinova			1		San Marino	4 Jul 92
2.05		Kostadinova			1	Toto	Fukuoka	18 Sep 93
2.05	Inga	Babakova	UKR	27.6.67	1		Tokyo	15 Sep 95
2.05		Kostadinova			1	OG	Atlanta	3 Aug 96
2.05		Bergqvist			1		Poznan	18 Aug 02
2.05		Cloete			1	ISTAF	Berlin (P)	10 Aug 03
	(31/8)							
2.04	Silvia	Costa	CUB	4.5.64	1	WCp	Barcelona	9 Sep 89
2.04i	Alina	Astafei	GER	7.6.69	1		Berlin	3 Mar 95
	(10)							
2.04	Venelina	Veneva	BUL	13.6.74	1		Kalamáta	2 Jun 01
2.04i	Anna	Chicherova	RUS	22.7.82	1		Yekaterinburg	7 Jan 03
2.03 WR	Ulrike	Meyfarth	FRG	4.5.56	1	ECp	London (CP)	21 Aug 83
2.03	Louise	Ritter	USA	18.2.58	1		Austin	8 Jul 88
2.03	Tatyana	Motkova	RUS	23.11.68	2		Bratislava	30 May 95
2.03	Níki	Bakoyiánni	GRE	9.6.68	2	OG	Atlanta	3 Aug 96
2.03i	Monica	Iagar/Dinescu	ROM	2.4.73	1		Bucuresti	23 Jan 99
2.03i	Marina	Kuptsova	RUS	22.12.81	1	EI	Wien	2 Mar 02
2.03	Blanka	Vlasic	CRO	8.11.83	1		Ljubljana	10 Aug 04
2.02i	Susanne	Beyer'	GDR	24.6.61	2	WI	Indianapolis	8 Mar 87
	(20)							
2.02	Yelena	Yelesina	RUS	4.4.70	1	GWG	Seattle	23 Jul 90
2.02	Viktoria	Styopina	UKR	21.2.76	3	OG	Athína	28 Aug 04
2.01 WR	Sara	Simeoni	ITA	19.4.53	1	v Pol	Brescia	4 Aug 78
2.01	Olga	Turchak	UKR	5.3.67	2	GWG	Moskva	7 Jul 86
2.01	Desiré	du Plessis	RSA	20.5.65	1		Johannesburg	16 Sep 86
2.01i	Gabriele	Günz	GDR	8.9.61	2		Stuttgart	31 Jan 88
2.01	Heike	Balck	GDR	19.8.70	1	vSU-j	Karl-Marx-Stadt	18 Jun 89
2.01i	Ioamnet	Quintero	CUB	8.9.72	1		Berlin	5 Mar 93
2.01	Hanne	Haugland	NOR	14.12.67	1	WK	Zürich	13 Aug 97
2.01i	Tisha	Waller	USA	1.12.70	1	NC	Atlanta	28 Feb 98
	(30)							
2.01	Yelena	Gulyayeva	RUS	14.8.67	2		Kalamata	23 May 98
2.01	Vita	Palamar	UKR	12.10.77	2=	WK	Zürich	15 Aug 03
2.01	Amy	Acuff	USA	14.7.75	4	WK	Zürich	15 Aug 03
2.01	Irina	Mikhalchenko	UKR	20.1.72	1		Eberstadt	18 Jul 04
2.00 WR	Rosemarie	Ackermann'	GDR	4.4.52	1	ISTAF	Berlin	26 Aug 77
2.00i	Coleen	Sommer'	USA	6.6.60	1		Ottawa	14 Feb 82
2.00	Charmaine	Gale/Weavers	RSA	27.2.64	1		Pretoria	25 Mar 85
2.00i	Emilia	Dragieva'	BUL	11.1.65	3	WI	Indianapolis	8 Mar 87
2.00	Lyudmila	Avdyeyenko'	UKR	14.12.63	1	NC	Bryansk	17 Jul 87
2.00	Svetlana	Isaeva/Leseva	BUL	18.3.67	2	v TCH,GRE	Drama	8 Aug 87
	(40)							
2.00i	Larisa	Kositsyna	RUS	14.12.63	2	NC	Volgograd	11 Feb 88
2.00	Jan	Wohlschlag'	USA	14.7.58	1	Bisl	Oslo	1 Jul 89
2.00	Yolanda	Henry	USA	2.12.64	1	Expo	Sevilla	30 May 90
2.00	Biljana	Petrovic ¶	YUG	28.2.61	1		St. Denis	22 Jun 90
2.00	Tatyana	Shevchik ¶	BLR	11.6.69	1		Gomel	14 May 93
2.00i	Britta	Bilac'	SLO	4.12.68	1		Frankfurt	9 Feb 94
2.00i	Yuliya	Lyakhova	RUS	8.7.77	1		Wuppertal	5 Feb 99
2.00	Zuzana	Hlavonová	CZE	16.4.73	1	Odlozil	Praha	5 Jun 00

Mark Wind	Name		Nat	Born	Pos	Meet	Venue	Date
2.00	Dóra	Györffy	HUN	23.2.78	1	NC	Nyíregyháza	26 Jul 01
2.00	Viktoriya	Seryogina	RUS	22.5.73	1	Univ Ch	Bryansk	11 Jun 02
2.00i	Svetlana	Lapina	RUS	12.4.78	3=	NC	Moskva	26 Feb 03
2.00	Daniela	Rath	GER	6.5.77	1	ECp-S	Firenze	22 Jun 03
2.00	Ruth	Beitia	ESP	1.4.79	1		Avilés	26 Jul 03
2.00	Chaunte	Howard	USA	12.1.84	1		Liège (NX)	20 Jul 05
	(54)	100th woman 1.97, 200th 1.93, 300th woman 1.92						

Best outdoor marks

Mark	Name	Pos	Meet	Venue	Date	Mark	Name	Pos	Meet	Venue	Date
2.02	Iagar/Dinescu	1		Budapest	6 Jun 98	2.00	Kositsyna	1		Chelyabinsk	16 Jul 88
2.02	Kuptsova	1	FBK	Hengelo	1 Jun 03	2.00	Bilac	1	EC	Helsinki	14 Aug 94
2.01	Astafei	2		Wörrstadt	27 May 95	2.00	Waller	1	MSR	Walnut	18 Apr 99
2.00	Quintero	1	Herc	Monaco	7 Aug 93	2.00	Chicherova	1		Moskva	15 Jul 03

Ancillary jumps – 2.06 Kostadinova 30 Aug 87   2.05i Henkel 8 Feb 92

POLE VAULT

Mark Wind	Name		Nat	Born	Pos	Meet	Venue	Date
5.01 WR	Yelena	Isinbayeva	RUS	3.6.82	1	WCh	Helsinki	12 Aug 05
5.00 WR		Isinbayeva			1	LGP	London (CP)	22 Jul 05
4.95 WR		Isinbayeva			1	GP	Madrid	16 Jul 05
4.93 WR		Isinbayeva			1	Athl	Lausanne	5 Jul 05
4.93		Isinbayeva			1	VD	Bruxelles	26 Aug 05
4.92 WR		Isinbayeva			1	VD	Bruxelles	3 Sep 04
4.91 WR		Isinbayeva			1	OG	Athína	24 Aug 04
4.90 WR		Isinbayeva			1	GP	London (CP)	30 Jul 04
4.90i		Isinbayeva			1	EI	Madrid	6 Mar 05
4.89 WR		Isinbayeva			1		Birmingham	25 Jul 04
4.89i		Isinbayeva			1		Liévin	26 Feb 05
4.88 WR	Svetlana	Feofanova	RUS	16.7.80	1		Iráklio	4 Jul 04
4.88i		Isinbayeva			1	GP	Birmingham	18 Feb 05
4.87 WR		Isinbayeva			1	GP	Gateshead	27 Jun 04
4.87i		Isinbayeva			1		Donetsk	12 Feb 05
4.86i WR		Isinbayeva			1	WI	Budapest	6 Mar 04
4.85i WR		Feofanova			1		Athína (P)	20 Feb 04
4.83i WR		Isinbayeva			1		Donetsk	15 Feb 04
4.83	Stacy	Dragila	USA	25.3.71	1	GS	Ostrava	8 Jun 04
4.83		Isinbayeva			1	WAF	Monaco	19 Sep 04
4.83	Anna	Rogowska	POL	21.5.81	2	VD	Bruxelles	26 Aug 05
4.82 WR		Isinbayeva			1	GP	Gateshead	13 Jul 03
4.82		Rogowska			1		Beckum	21 Aug 05
4.81 WR		Dragila			1	GP	Palo Alto	9 Jun 01
4.81i		Dragila			2	WI	Budapest	6 Mar 04
4.80i		Feofanova			1	WI	Birmingham	16 Mar 03
4.80		Feofanova			1	SGP	Madrid	17 Jul 04
4.80		Feofanova			2	GP	London (CP)	30 Jul 04
4.80		Rogowska			2	LGP	London (CP)	22 Jul 05
4.79		Isinbayeva			1	DNG	Stockholm	26 Jul 05
	(30/4)							
4.78	Tatyana	Polnova	RUS	20.4.79	2	WAF	Monaco	19 Sep 04
4.77	Annika	Becker	GER	12.11.81	1	NC	Wattenscheid	7 Jul 02
4.72	Monika	Pyrek	POL	11.8.80	2=	VD	Bruxelles	3 Sep 04
4.70	Yvonne	Buschbaum	GER	14.7.80	1	NC	Ulm	29 Jun 03
4.67	Kellie	Suttle	USA	9.5.73	1		Jonesboro	16 Jun 04
4.66i	Christine	Adams	GER	28.2.74	1	IHS	Sindelfingen	10 Mar 02
	(10)							
4.66	Carolin	Hingst	GER	18.9.80	1		Karlsruhe	21 Jul 04
4.65	Mary	Sauer	USA	31.10.75	2		Madrid (C)	3 Jul 02
4.60 WR	Emma	George	AUS	1.11.74	1		Sydney	20 Feb 99
4.60Ai	Mel	Mueller	USA	16.11.72	1		Flagstaff	9 Feb 02
4.60	Pavla	Hamácková	CZE	20.5.78	1	ECp-1B	Velenje	21 Jun 03
4.60	Yelena	Belyakova	RUS	7.4.76	1	NC	Tula	10 Aug 03
4.60i	Jillian	Schwartz	USA	19.9.79	4	WI	Budapest	6 Mar 04
4.60A	Andrea	DuToit	USA	28.2.78	1		Albuquerque	1 May 04
4.60	Thórey Edda	Elisdóttír	ISL	30.6.77	2	SGP	Madrid	17 Jul 04
4.60	Tracy	O'Hara	USA	20.7.80	1	GP II	Stanford	30 May 05
	(20)							
4.60	Vanessa	Boslak	FRA	11.6.82	1	NC	Angers	15 Jul 05
4.57	Chelsea	Johnson	USA	20.12.83	1		Stanford	26 Mar 04
4.57	Anzhela	Balakhonova	UKR	18.12.72	1	NC	Yalta	4 Jul 04
4.57i	Jennifer	Stuczynski	USA	6.2.82	1		Rochester	31 Dec 05
	4.57 ?				1		New York	7 Jun 05

Mark	Wind	Name		Nat	Born	Pos	Meet	Venue	Date
4.56i		Nicole	Rieger/Humbert	GER	5.2.72	1		Stockholm	25 Feb 99
4.56		Tatiana	Grigorieva	AUS	8.10.75	1		Yokohama	15 Sep 01
4.55		Anastasia	Ivanova	RUS	3.5.79	1	NC	Tula	1 Aug 04
4.53i		Amy	Linnen	USA	15.7.82	1	NCAA	Fayetteville	8 Mar 02
4.53		Krisztina	Molnár	HUN	8.4.76	3	GP II	Rieti	8 Sep 02
4.53			Gao Shuying	CHN	28.10.79	1	AsiC	Inchon	2 Sep 05
		(30)							
4.52		Katerina	Badurová	CZE	18.12.82	1		Praha	7 Aug 04
4.51		Daniela	Bártová	CZE	6.5.74	1	Slovn	Bratislava	9 Jun 98
4.51i		Zsuzsanna	Szabó	HUN	6.5.73	1		Budapest	4 Feb 99
4.51		Kirsten	Belin	SWE	2.5.81	1		Göteborg	27 Aug 02
4.51		Dana	Ellis (-Buller)	CAN	7.12.79	1	NC	Winnipeg	15 Jul 05
4.50i		Nastja	Ryshich	GER	19.9.77	1	WI	Maebashi	5 Mar 99
4.50		Vala	Flosadóttir	ISL	16.2.78	3	OG	Sydney	25 Sep 00
4.50		Alicia	Warlick	USA	11.10.77	1		Houston	24 Mar 01
4.50		Natalya	Kushch	UKR	5.3.83	1		Mariupol	22 Jun 04
		(40)							
4.50i		Natalya	Belinskaya	RUS	21.1.83	3		Stuttgart	29 Jan 05
4.50i		Tanya	Stefanova	BUL	8.3.72	1	Balk I	Athína (P)	16 Feb 05
4.48		Afrodíti	Skafída	GRE	20.3.82	1	NC	Athína	11 Jun 05
4.48i		Silke	Spiegelburg	GER	17.3.86	2		Münster	25 Aug 05
4.47		Becky	Holliday	USA	12.3.80	1	NCAA-r	Stanford	30 May 03
4.47		Naroa	Agirre	ESP	15.5.79	2		Rivas	10 Jun 04
4.47		Yeoryía	Tsiliggíri	GRE	21.6.72	1		Spárti	7 Jul 04
4.47		Janine	Whitlock ¶	GBR	11.8.73	3=	LGP	London (CP)	22 Jul 05
4.46		Marie	Poissonnier	FRA	4.5.79	1	NC	Saint-Étienne	13 Jul 02
4.46i		Dana Elvira	Cervantes	ESP	18.8.78	1		Zaragoza	31 Jan 04
4.46		Kelsie	Hendry	CAN	29.6.82	1		Saskatoon	12 Jul 05
		(51)	100th woman 4.30, 200th 4.20						

Outdoor bests

Mark	Name	Pos	Venue	Date
4.60	Mueller	1	Atascadero	9 Jul 03
4.60	Schwartz	1	Phoenix	14 May 04
4.51	Humbert	1	Salamanca	13 Jul 01
4.46sq	Koleva/Stefanova	1	Praha	16 Jun 04
4.45		2 ECp1B	Velenje	21 Jun 03

Ancillary jumps – (to 4.80)

Mark	Name	Date
4.96 WR	Isinbayeva	22 Jul 05
4.85	Isinbayeva	24 Aug 04
4.82	Isinbayeva	3 Sep 04
4.81i	Isinbayeva	6 Mar 04
4.80	Isinbayeva	27 Jun 04
4.80	Isinbayeva	30 Jul 04
4.80	Isinbayeva	24 Aug 04
4.80i	Isinbayeva	26 Feb 05
4.80i	Isinbayeva	6 Mar 05
4.80	Isinbayeva	22 Jul 05

Street competition, raised runway, slightly uphill

Mark	Name		Nat	Born	Pos	Venue	Date
4.62	Melissa	Mueller	USA	16.11.72	1	Clovis	4 Aug 01

LONG JUMP

Mark	Wind	Name		Nat	Born	Pos	Meet	Venue	Date
7.52 WR	1.4	Galina	Chistyakova	RUS	26.7.62	1	Znam	Leningrad	11 Jun 88
7.49	1.3	Jackie	Joyner-Kersee	USA	3.3.62	1	NYG	New York	22 May 94
7.49A	1.7		Joyner-Kersee			1		Sestriere	31 Jul 94
7.48	1.2	Heike	Drechsler	GER	16.12.64	1	v ITA	Neubrandenburg	9 Jul 88
7.48	0.4		Drechsler			1	Athl	Lausanne	8 Jul 92
7.45 WR	0.9		Drechsler'			1	v URS	Tallinn	21 Jun 86
7.45 WR	1.1		Drechsler			1	OD	Dresden	3 Jul 86
7.45 WR	0.6		Joyner-Kersee			1	PAm	Indianapolis	13 Aug 87
7.45	1.6		Chistyakova			1	BGP	Budapest	12 Aug 88
7.44 WR	2.0		Drechsler			1		Berlin	22 Sep 85
7.43 WR	1.4	Anisoara	Cusmir/Stanciu	ROM	28.6.62	1	RomIC	Bucuresti	4 Jun 83
7.42	2.0	Tatyana	Kotova	RUS	11.12.76	1	ECp-S	Annecy	23 Jun 02
7.40	1.8		Daute' (Drechsler)			1		Dresden	26 Jul 84
7.40	0.7		Drechsler			1	NC	Potsdam	21 Aug 87
7.40	0.9		Joyner-Kersee			1	OG	Seoul	29 Sep 88
7.39	0.3		Drechsler			1	WK	Zürich	21 Aug 85
7.39	0.5	Yelena	Byelevskaya'	BLR	11.10.63	1	NC	Bryansk	18 Jul 87
7.39			Joyner-Kersee			1		San Diego	25 Jun 88
7.37i	-		Drechsler			1	v2N	Wien	13 Feb 88
7.37A	1.8		Drechsler			1		Sestriere	31 Jul 91
7.37		Inessa	Kravets ¶	UKR	5.10.66	1		Kiyev	13 Jun 92
7.36	0.4		Joyner			1	WCh	Roma	4 Sep 87
7.36	1.8		Byelevskaya			2	Znam	Leningrad	11 Jun 88
7.36	1.8		Drechsler			1		Jena	28 May 92
7.35	1.9		Chistyakova			1	GPB	Bratislava	20 Jun 90
7.34	1.6		Daute'			1		Dresden	19 May 84
7.34	1.4		Chistyakova			2	v GDR	Tallinn	21 Jun 86
7.34			Byelevskaya			1		Sukhumi	17 May 87

Mark	Wind		Name	Nat	Born	Pos	Meet	Venue	Date
7.34	0.7		Drechsler			1	v URS	Karl-Marx-Stadt	20 Jun 87
7.33	0.4		Drechsler			1	v URS	Erfurt	22 Jun 85
7.33	2.0		Drechsler			1		Dresden	2 Aug 85
7.33	-0.3		Drechsler			1	Herc	Monaco	11 Aug 92
7.33	0.4	Tatyana	Lebedeva	RUS	21.7.76	1	NC	Tula	31 Jul 04
		(33/8)							
7.31	1.5	Yelena	Kokonova'	UKR	4.8.63	1	NP	Alma-Ata	12 Sep 85
7.31	1.9	Marion	Jones	USA	12.10.75	1	Pre	Eugene	31 May 98
		(10)							
7.27	-0.4	Irina	Simagina	RUS	25.5.82	2	NC	Tula	31 Jul 04
7.26A	1.8	Maurren	Maggi ¶	BRA	25.6.76	1	SACh	Bogotá	26 Jun 99
7.24	1.0	Larisa	Berezhnaya	UKR	28.2.61	1		Granada	25 May 91
7.21	1.6	Helga	Radtke	GDR	16.5.62	2		Dresden	26 Jul 84
7.20 WR	-0.5	Valy	Ionescu	ROM	31.8.60	1	NC	Bucuresti	1 Aug 82
7.20	2.0	Irena	Ozhenko'	LTU	13.11.62	1		Budapest	12 Sep 86
7.20	0.8	Yelena	Sinchukova'	RUS	23.1.61	1	BGP	Budapest	20 Jun 91
7.20	0.7	Irina	Mushayilova	RUS	6.1.67	1	NC	Sankt-Peterburg	14 Jul 94
7.17	1.8	Irina	Valyukevich	BLR	19.11.59	2	NC	Bryansk	18 Jul 87
7.16		Iolanda	Chen	RUS	26.7.61	1		Moskva	30 Jul 88
		(20)							
7.16A	-0.1	Elva	Goulbourne	JAM	21.1.80	1		Ciudad de México	22 May 04
7.14	1.8	Niole	Medvedyeva ¶	LTU	20.10.60	1		Riga	4 Jun 88
7.14	1.2	Mirela	Dulgheru	ROM	5.10.66	1	Balk G	Sofiya	5 Jul 92
7.12	1.6	Sabine	Paetz/John'	GDR	16.10.57	2		Dresden	19 May 84
7.12	0.9	Chioma	Ajunwa ¶	NGR	25.12.70	1	OG	Atlanta	2 Aug 96
7.11	0.8	Fiona	May	ITA	12.12.69	2	EC	Budapest	22 Aug 98
7.09 WR	0.0	Vilma	Bardauskiene	LTU	15.6.53	Q	EC	Praha	29 Aug 78
7.09	1.5	Ljudmila	Ninova	AUT	25.6.60	1	GP II	Sevilla	5 Jun 94
7.08	0.5	Marieta	Ilcu ¶	ROM	16.10.62	1	RumIC	Pitesti	25 Jun 89
7.07	0.0	Svetlana	Zorina	RUS	2.2.60	1		Krasnodar	15 Aug 87
		(30)							
7.06	0.4	Tatyana	Kolpakova	KGZ	18.10.59	1	OG	Moskva	31 Jul 80
7.06	-0.1	Niurka	Montalvo	CUB/ESP	4.6.68	1	WCh	Sevilla	23 Aug 99
7.06		Tatyana	Ter-Mesrobyan	RUS	12.5.68	1		Sankt Peterburg	22 May 02
7.05	0.6	Lyudmila	Galkina	RUS	20.1.72	1	WCh	Athína	9 Aug 97
7.05	-0.4	Eunice	Barber	FRA	17.11.74	1	WAF	Monaco	14 Sep 03
7.04	0.5	Brigitte	Künzel/Wujak	GDR	6.3.55	2	OG	Moskva	31 Jul 80
7.04	0.9	Tatyana	Proskuryakova'	RUS	13.1.56	1		Kiyev	25 Aug 83
7.04	2.0	Yelena	Yatsuk	UKR	16.3.61	1	Znam	Moskva	8 Jun 85
7.04	0.3	Carol	Lewis	USA	8.8.63	5	WK	Zürich	21 Aug 85
7.03	0.6	Níki	Xánthou	GRE	11.10.73	1		Bellinzona	18 Aug 97
		(40)							
7.03i	-	Dawn	Burrell	USA	1.11.73	1	WI	Lisboa	10 Mar 01
7.01	-0.4	Tatyana	Skachko	UKR	18.8.54	3	OG	Moskva	31 Jul 80
7.01	-0.3	Eva	Murková	SVK	29.5.62	1	PTS	Bratislava	26 May 84
7.01	-1.0	Marina	Kibakina'	RUS	2.8.60	1		Krasnoyarsk	10 Aug 85
7.01	1.4		Yao Weili	CHN	6.5.68	1	NC	Jinan	5 Jun 93
7.01	1.1	Shana	Williams	USA	7.4.72	Q	NC	Atlanta	21 Jun 96
7.00	2.0	Jodi	Anderson	USA	10.11.57	1	OT	Eugene	28 Jun 80
7.00		Margarita	Butkiene	LTU	19.8.49	1		Vilnius	25 May 83
7.00	-0.2	Birgit	Grosshennig	GDR	21.2.65	2		Berlin	9 Jun 84
7.00	0.6	Silvia	Khristova'	BUL	22.8.65	1		Sofiya	3 Aug 86
7.00		Susen	Tiedtke ¶	GER	23.1.69	2		Seoul	18 Aug 91
7.00	1.8	Bronwyn	Thompson	AUS	29.1.78	1	GP II	Melbourne	7 Mar 02
		(52)	100th woman 6.87, 200th woman 6.77						
Drugs dq: 7.03	0.1		Xiong Qiying	CHN	14.10.67	Q	NG	Shanghai	21 Oct 97
Wind assisted			*Performances to 7.35, performers to 7.01*						
7.63A	2.1	Heike	Drechsler	GER	16.12.64	1		Sestriere	21 Jul 92
7.45	2.6		Joyner-Kersee			1	OT	Indianapolis	23 Jul 88
7.39	2.6		Drechsler			1		Padova	15 Sep 91
7.39	2.9		Drechsler			1	Expo	Sevilla	6 Jun 92
7.39A	3.3		Drechsler			2		Sestriere	31 Jul 94
7.36	2.2		Chistyakova			1	Znam	Volgograd	11 Jun 89
7.35	3.4		Drechsler			1	NC	Jena	29 Jun 86
7.23A	4.3	Fiona	May	ITA	12.12.69	1		Sestriere	29 Jul 95
7.19A	3.7	Susen	Tiedtke ¶	GER	23.1.69	1		Sestriere	28 Jul 93
7.17	3.6	Eva	Murková	SVK	29.5.62	1		Nitra	26 Aug 84
7.14A	4.5	Marieke	Veltman	USA	18.9.71	2		Sestriere	29 Jul 95
7.12A	5.8	Níki	Xánthou	GRE	11.10.73	3		Sestriere	29 Jul 95
7.12A	4.3	Nicole	Boegman	AUS	5.3.67	4		Sestriere	29 Jul 95

Mark	Wind	Name		Nat	Born	Pos	Meet	Venue	Date
7.09	2.9	Renata	Nielsen	DEN	18.5.66	2		Sevilla	5 Jun 94
7.08	2.2	Lyudmila	Galkina	RUS	20.1.72	1		Thessaloniki	23 Jun 99
7.07A	5.6	Valentina	Uccheddu	ITA	26.10.66	5		Sestriere	29 Jul 95
7.07A	2.7	Sharon	Couch	USA	13.9.67	1		El Paso	12 Apr 97
7.07A	w	Erica	Johansson	SWE	5.2.74	1		Vygieskraal	15 Jan 00
7.06	3.4		Ma Miaolan	CHN	18.1.70	1	NG	Beijing	10 Sep 93
7.01	2.2	Olga	Rublyova	RUS	28.10.74	1	NC	Moskva	16 Jun 95

Best at low altitude:

7.06 0.8 Maggi ¶ 1 Milano 3 Jun 03 | 7.12w 3.4 May 1 NC Bologna 25 May 96
7.17w 2.6 1 São Paulo 13 Apr 02

Ancillary marks – other marks during series (to 7.34/7.36w)

7.45 1.0 Chistyakova 11 Jun 88 / 7.47Aw 3.1 Drechsler 21 Jul 92 \ 7.38w 2.2 Chistyakova 11 Jun 88
7.37 Drechsler 9 Jul 88 / 7.39Aw 3.1 Drechsler 21 Jul 92 \ 7.36w Joyner-Kersee 31 Jul 94

TRIPLE JUMP

Mark	Wind	Name		Nat	Born	Pos	Meet	Venue	Date
15.50 WR	0.9	Inessa	Kravets ¶	UKR	5.10.66	1	WCh	Göteborg	10 Aug 95
15.36i		Tatyana	Lebedeva	RUS	21.7.76	1	WI	Budapest	6 Mar 04
15.34	-0.5		Lebedeva			1		Iráklio	4 Jul 04
15.33	-0.1		Kravets			1	OG	Atlanta	31 Jul 96
15.33	1.2		Lebedeva			1		Lausanne	6 Jul 04
15.32	0.5		Lebedeva			1	Super	Yokohama	9 Sep 00
15.32	0.9	Hrisopiyi	Devetzí	GRE	2.1.76	Q	OG	Athína	21 Aug 04
15.30	0.6	Françoise	Mbango-Etone	CMR	14.4.76	1	OG	Athína	23 Aug 04
15.29	0.3	Yamilé	Aldama	CUB/SUD	14.8.72	1	GGala	Roma	11 Jul 03
15.28	0.3		Aldama			1	GP	Linz	2 Aug 04
15.27	1.3		Aldama			1	GP	London (CP)	8 Aug 03
15.25	-0.8		Lebedeva			1	WCh	Edmonton	10 Aug 01
15.25	-0.1		Devetzí			2	OG	Athína	23 Aug 04
15.23	0.8		Lebedeva			1		Réthimno	23 Jun 04
15.21	1.2		Aldama			2		Réthimno	23 Jun 04
15.20	0.0	Sarka	Kaspárková	CZE	20.5.71	1	WCh	Athína	4 Aug 97
15.20	-0.3	Tereza	Marinova	BUL	5.9.77	1	OG	Sydney	24 Sep 00
15.18	0.3	Iva	Prandzheva ¶	BUL	15.2.72	2	WCh	Göteborg	10 Aug 95
15.18	-0.2		Lebedeva			1	WCh	Saint-Denis	26 Aug 03
15.16	0.1	Rodica	Mateescu ¶	ROM	13.3.71	2	WCh	Athína	4 Aug 97
15.16i	-	Ashia	Hansen (10)	GBR	5.12.71	1	EI	Valencia	28 Feb 98
15.16	0.7	Trecia	Smith	JAM	5.11.75	2	GP	Linz	2 Aug 04
15.15	1.7		Hansen			1	GPF	Fukuoka	13 Sep 97
15.14	-0.1		Mateescu			1	RomIC	Bucuresti	14 Jun 97
15.14	0.3		Lebedeva			1	VD	Bruxelles	5 Sep 03
15.13	0.1		Lebedeva			1	WAF	Monaco	13 Sep 03
15.14	0.7		Lebedeva			3	OG	Athína	23 Aug 04
15.12	2.0		Prandzheva			1	TOTO	Tokyo	19 Sep 98
15.12	-0.9		Lebedeva			1	GL	Saint-Denis	4 Jul 03
15.11	0.1		Aldama			1	Bisl	Oslo	27 Jun 03
15.11	-0.2		Lebedeva			1	Gaz	Saint Denis	1 Jul 05
15.11	0.8		Smith			1	WCh	Helsinki	7 Aug 05
		(32/11)							
15.09 WR	0.5	Anna	Biryukova	RUS	27.9.67	1	WCh	Stuttgart	21 Aug 93
15.09	-0.5	Inna	Lasovskaya	RUS	17.12.69	1	ECCp-A	Valencia	31 May 97
15.07	-0.6	Paraskeví	Tsiamíta	GRE	10.3.72	Q	WCh	Sevilla	22 Aug 99
15.03i		Iolanda	Chen	RUS	26.7.61	1	WI	Barcelona	11 Mar 95
15.03	1.9	Magdelin	Martinez	ITA	10.2.76	1		Roma	26 Jun 04
15.00	1.2	Kène	Ndoye	SEN	20.11.78	2		Iráklio	4 Jul 04
14.98	1.8	Sofiya	Bozhanova ¶	BUL	4.10.67	1		Stara Zagora	16 Jul 94
14.98	0.2	Baya	Rahouli	ALG	27.7.79	1	MedG	Almeria	1 Jul 05
14.96	0.7	Yelena	Govorova	UKR	18.9.73	4	OG	Sydney	24 Sep 00
		(20)							
14.94i	–	Cristina	Nicolau	ROM	9.8.77	1	NC	Bucuresti	5 Feb 00
14.83i	-	Yelena	Lebedenko	RUS	16.1.71	1		Samara	1 Feb 01
14.88	1.2	Anna	Pyatykh	RUS	4.4.81	2	Athl	Lausanne	5 Jul 05
14.83	0.5	Yelena	Oleynikova	RUS	9.12.76	1	Odlozil	Praha	17 Jun 02
14.82	0.7	Yargelis	Savigne	CUB	13.11.84	2	WCh	Helsinki	7 Aug 05
14.79	1.7	Irina	Mushayilova	RUS	6.1.67	1	DNG	Stockholm	5 Jul 93
14.76	0.9	Galina	Chistyakova	RUS	26.7.62	1		Luzern	27 Jun 95
		later Cistjaková SVK							
14.76	1.1	Gundega	Sproge	LAT	12.12.72	3		Sheffield	29 Jun 97
14.76i		Adelina	Gavrila	ROM	26.11.78	1	NC	Bucuresti	22 Feb 03
14.74i		Viktoriya	Gurova	RUS	22.5.82	1	EI	Madrid	6 Mar 05
		(30)							

Mark	Wind		Name	Nat	Born	Pos	Meet	Venue	Date
14.72	1.8		Huang Qiuyan	CHN	25.1.80	1	NG	Guangzhou	22 Nov 01
14.70i		Oksana	Rogova	RUS	7.10.78	1		Volgograd	6 Feb 02
14.69	1.2	Anja	Valant	SLO	8.9.77	3		Kalamáta	4 Jun 00
14.67	1.2	Ólga	Vasdéki	GRE	26.9.73	1		Haniá	28 Jul 99
14.66	1.9		Ren Ruiping	CHN	1.2.76	1	Oda	Hiroshima	29 Apr 97
14.65	0.3	Fiona	May	ITA	12.12.69	1	ECp	Sankt-Peterburg	27 Jun 98
14.65	2.0	Natalya	Safronova	BLR	11.4.74	1	NCp	Stayki	3 Jun 00
14.65i		Nadezhda	Bazhenova	RUS	22.9.78	1		Pireás	20 Feb 02
14.61	2.0	Yusmay	Bicet	CUB	8.12.83	1		La Habana	4 Mar 04
14.60	0.7	Niurka	Montalvo	CUB/ESP	4.6.68	1	NC	La Habana	24 Jun 94
		(40)							
14.60	0.4	Carlota	Castrejana	ESP	25.4.73	2	MedG	Almeria	1 Jul 05
14.58	0.3	Yelena	Donkina	RUS	15.3.73	2	NC	Tula	10 Jul 97
14.57		Irina	Vasilyeva	RUS	9.4.79	2		Moskva	23 Jun 01
14.57i		Mabel	Gay	CUB	5.5.83	Q	WI	Budapest	5 Mar 04
14.55	0.9		Li Huirong	CHN	14.4.65	1	Nambu	Sapporo	19 Jul 92
14.55	-0.3	Jelena	Blazevica	LAT	11.5.70	1	NC	Riga	8 Jun 96
14.55	1.8	Anastasiya	Zhuravlyeva	UZB	9.10.81	1		Haniá	6 Jun 05
14.54i		Mariya	Sokova	RUS	2.9.70	1	NC	Volgograd	24 Feb 95
14.53	0.7	Maurren	Maggi ¶	BRA	25.6.76	1		São Caetano do Sul	27 Apr 03
14.52	0.6	Anastasiya	Ilyina	RUS	16.1.82	Q	WJ	Santiago de Chile	20 Oct 00
14.52	0.8	Mariya	Dimitrova	BUL	7.8.76	1	NC	Plovdiv	6 Jun 04
		(51)	100th woman 14.19, 200th woman 13.93						

Wind assisted *Performances to 15.12, performers to 14.55*

Mark	Wind		Name	Nat	Born	Pos	Meet	Venue	Date
15.24Aw	4.2	Magdelin	Martinez	ITA	10.2.76	1		Sestriere	1 Aug 04
14.99	6.8	Yelena	Govorova	UKR	18.9.73	1	WUG	Palma de Mallorca	11 Jul 99
14.88	3.8	Trecia	Smith	JAM	5.11.75	1	Kans R	Lawrence	21 Apr 01
14.84	4.1	Galina	Chistyakova	RUS	26.7.62	1		Innsbruck	28 Jun 95
14.83	8.3		Ren Ruiping	CHN	1.2.76	1	NC	Taiyuan	21 May 95
14.83	2.2	Heli	Koivula	FIN	27.6.75	2	EC	München	10 Aug 02
14.75	4.2	Jelena	Blazevica	LAT	11.5.70	1	v2N	Kaunas	23 Aug 97
14.71	2.5	Simona	La Mantia	ITA	14.4.83	1		Roma	25 Jun 04
14.67	3.0	Yusmay	Bicet	CUB	8.12.83	2		Zaragoza	8 Jun 04
14.66	3.2	Sheila	Hudson	USA	30.6.67	1	NC	Sacramento	17 Jun 95
14.55	5.5		Wu Lingmei	CHN	16.2.73	2	WUG	Palma de Mallorca	11 Jul 99

Best outdoor mark for athlete with all-time best indoors

Mark	Wind	Name	Pos	Meet	Venue	Date
14.97WR	0.9	Chen	1	NC	Moskva	18 Jun 93
14.75	1.1	Gavrila	3	GP II	Rieti	7 Sep 03
14.70	1.3	Nicolau	1	EU23	Göteborg	1 Aug 99
14.65	0.4	Gurova	2	NC	Tula	1 Aug 04
14.60		Bazhenova	1		Moskva	23 Jun 01
14.59	1.1	Rogova	*	EU23	Göteborg	1 Aug 99
14.65w	2.6		2	EU23	Göteborg	1 Aug 99
14.52	0.0	Gay	5	WCh	Saint-Denis	26 Aug 03

Ancillary marks – other marks during series (to 15.16)

Mark	Wind	Name	Date
15.30	0.5	Mbango	23 Aug 04
15.21	-0.2	Mbango	23 Aug 04
15.16		Lebedeva	9 Sep 00
15.28	-0.3	Ledebeva	4 Jul 04
15.17		Aldama	2 Aug 04
15.16	-0.2	Ledebeva	26 Aug 03
15.25i		Ledebeva	6 Mar 04
15.17	-0.1	Mbango	23 Aug 04
15.16i		Ledebeva	6 Mar 04

SHOT

Mark		Name	Nat	Born	Pos	Meet	Venue	Date
22.63 WR	Natalya	Lisovskaya	RUS	16.7.62	1	Znam	Moskva	7 Jun 87
22.55		Lisovskaya			1	NC	Tallinn	5 Jul 88
22.53 WR		Lisovskaya			1		Sochi	27 May 84
22.53		Lisovskaya			1		Kiyev	14 Aug 88
22.50i	Helena	Fibingerová	CZE	13.7.49	1		Jablonec	19 Feb 77
22.45 WR	Ilona	Slupianek' ¶	GDR	24.9.56	1		Potsdam	11 May 80
22.41		Slupianek			1	OG	Moskva	24 Jul 80
22.40		Slupianek			1		Berlin	3 Jun 83
22.38		Slupianek			1		Karl-Marx-Stadt	25 May 80
22.36 WR		Slupianek			1		Celje	2 May 80
22.34		Slupianek			1		Berlin	7 May 80
22.34		Slupianek			1	NC	Cottbus	18 Jul 80
22.32 WR		Fibingerová			1		Nitra	20 Aug 77
22.24		Lisovskaya			1	OG	Seoul	1 Oct 88
22.22		Slupianek			1		Potsdam	13 Jul 80
22.19	Claudia	Losch	FRG	10.1.60	1		Hainfeld	23 Aug 87
22.14i		Lisovskaya			1	NC	Penza	7 Feb 87
22.13		Slupianek			1		Split	29 Apr 80
22.06		Slupianek			1		Berlin	15 Aug 78
22.06		Lisovskaya			1		Moskva	6 Aug 88
22.05		Slupianek			1	OD	Berlin	28 May 80
22.05		Slupianek			1		Potsdam	31 May 80
22.04		Slupianek			1		Potsdam	4 Jul 79

Mark Wind		Name	Nat	Born	Pos	Meet	Venue	Date
22.04		Slupianek			1		Potsdam	29 Jul 79
21.99 WR		Fibingerová			1		Opava	26 Sep 76
21.98		Slupianek			1		Berlin	17 Jul 79
21.96		Fibingerová			1	GS	Ostrava	8 Jun 77
21.96		Lisovskaya			1	Drz	Praha	16 Aug 84
21.96		Lisovskaya			1		Vilnius	28 Aug 88
21.95		Lisovskaya			1	IAC	Edinburgh	29 Jul 88
	(30/4)							
21.89 WR	Ivanka	Khristova	BUL	19.11.41	1		Belmeken	4 Jul 76
21.86	Marianne	Adam	GDR	19.9.51	1	v URS	Leipzig	23 Jun 79
21.76		Li Meisu	CHN	17.4.59	1		Shijiazhuang	23 Apr 88
21.73	Natalya	Akhrimenko	RUS	12.5.55	1		Leselidze	21 May 88
21.69	Viktoriya	Pavlysh ¶	UKR	15.1.69	1	EC	Budapest	20 Aug 98
21.66		Sui Xinmei ¶	CHN	29.1.65	1		Beijing	9 Jun 90
	(10)							
21.61	Verzhinia	Veselinova	BUL	18.11.57	1		Sofiya	21 Aug 82
21.60i	Valentina	Fedyushina	UKR	18.2.65	1		Simferopol	28 Dec 91
21.58	Margitta	Droese/Pufe	GDR	10.9.52	1		Erfurt	28 May 78
21.57 @	Ines	Müller'	GDR	2.1.59	1		Athína	16 May 88
	21.45				1		Schwerin	4 Jun 86
21.53	Nunu	Abashidze ¶	UKR	27.3.55	2	Izv	Kiyev	20 Jun 84
21.52		Huang Zhihong	CHN	7.5.65	1	NC	Beijing	27 Jun 90
21.46	Larisa	Peleshenko ¶	RUS	29.2.64	1	Kuts	Moskva	26 Aug 00
21.45 WR	Nadezhda	Chizhova	RUS	29.9.45	1		Varna	29 Sep 73
21.43	Eva	Wilms	FRG	28.7.52	2	HB	München	17 Jun 77
21.42	Svetlana	Krachevskaya'	RUS	23.11.44	2	OG	Moskva	24 Jul 80
		@ competitive meeting, but unsanctioned by GDR federation						
	(20)							
21.31 @	Heike	Hartwig'	GDR	30.12.62	2		Athína	16 May 88
	21.27				1		Haniá	22 May 88
21.27	Liane	Schmuhl	GDR	29.6.61	1		Cottbus	26 Jun 82
21.22	Astrid	Kumbernuss	GER	5.2.70	1	WCh	Göteborg	5 Aug 95
21.21	Kathrin	Neimke	GDR	18.7.66	2	WCh	Roma	5 Sep 87
21.19	Helma	Knorscheidt	GDR	31.12.56	1		Berlin	24 May 84
21.15i	Irina	Korzhanenko ¶	RUS	16.5.74	1	NC	Moskva	18 Feb 99
21.10	Heidi	Krieger	GDR	20.7.65	1	EC	Stuttgart	26 Aug 86
21.09	Nadezhda	Ostapchuk	BLR	12.10.80	1		Staiki	21 Jul 05
21.06	Svetlana	Krivelyova	RUS	13.6.69	1	OG	Barcelona	7 Aug 92
21.05	Zdenka	Silhavá' ¶	CZE	15.6.54	2	NC	Praha	23 Jul 83
	(30)							
21.01	Ivanka	Petrova-Stoycheva	BUL	3.2.51	1	NC	Sofiya	28 Jul 79
21.00	Mihaela	Loghin	ROM	1.6.52	1		Formia	30 Jun 84
21.00	Cordula	Schulze	GDR	11.9.59	4	OD	Potsdam	21 Jul 84
20.96	Belsy	Laza	CUB	5.6.67	1		Ciudad de México	2 May 92
20.95	Elena	Stoyanova ¶	BUL	23.1.52	2	Balk	Sofiya	14 Jun 80
20.91	Svetla	Mitkova	BUL	17.6.64	1		Sofiya	24 May 87
20.80	Sona	Vasícková	CZE	14.3.62	1		Praha	2 Jun 88
20.72	Grit	Haupt/Hammer	GDR	4.6.66	3		Neubrandenburg	11 Jun 87
20.61	María Elena	Sarría	CUB	14.9.54	1		Habana	22 Jul 82
20.61	Yanina	Korolchik ¶	BLR	26.12.76	1	WCh	Edmonton	5 Aug 01
	(40)							
20.60	Marina	Antonyuk	RUS	12.5.62	1		Chelyabinsk	10 Aug 86
20.54		Zhang Liuhong	CHN	16.1.69	1	NC	Beijing	5 Jun 94
20.53	Iris	Plotzitzka	FRG	7.1.66	1	ASV	Köln	21 Aug 88
20.50i	Christa	Wiese	GDR	25.12.67	2	NC	Senftenberg	12 Feb 89
20.47	Nina	Isayeva	RUS	6.7.50	1		Bryansk	28 Aug 82
20.47		Cong Yuzhen	CHN	22.1.63	2	IntC	Tianjin	3 Sep 88
20.44	Tatyana	Orlova	BLR	19.7.55	1		Staiki	28 May 83
20.40		Zhou Tianhua ¶	CHN	10.4.66	1		Beijing	5 Sep 91
20.34	Stephanie	Storp	FRG	28.11.68	1		Wolfsburg	1 Jul 90
20.32	Irina	Khudoroshkina ¶	RUS	13.10.68	1		Sochi	25 May 96
	(50)	100th woman 19.51, 200th woman c.18.58						

Best outdoor marks

21.08	Fedyushina	1		Leselidze	15 May 88
20.82	Korzhanenko ¶	1		Rostov na Donu	30 May 98
	21.06 drugs dq	(1)	OG	Athína	18 Aug 04

Ancillary marks – other marks during series (to 22.09)

22.60	Lisovskaya (WR)	7 Jun 87	22.20	Slupianek	13 Jul 80	22.12	Slupianek	13 Jul 80
22.40	Lisovskaya	14 Aug 88	22.19	Lisovskaya	5 Jul 88	22.11	Slupianek	7 May 80
22.34	Slupianek	11 May 80	22.14	Slupianek	25 May 80	22.10	Slupianek	25 May 80
22.33	Slupianek	2 May 80	22.14	Slupianek	13 Jul 80	22.09	Slupianek	7 May 80

Mark	Wind	Name		Nat	Born	Pos	Meet	Venue	Date

DISCUS

Mark	Wind	Name		Nat	Born	Pos	Meet	Venue	Date
76.80	WR	Gabriele	Reinsch	GDR	23.9.63	1	v ITA	Neubrandenburg	9 Jul 88
74.56	WR	Zdenka	Silhavá' ¶	CZE	15.6.54	1		Nitra	26 Aug 84
74.56		Ilke	Wyludda	GDR	28.3.69	1	NC	Neubrandenburg	23 Jul 89
74.44			Reinsch			1		Berlin	13 Sep 88
74.40			Wyludda			2		Berlin	13 Sep 88
74.08		Diana	Gansky'	GDR	14.12.63	1	v URS	Karl-Marx-Stadt	20 Jun 87
73.90			Gansky			1	ECp	Praha	27 Jun 87
73.84		Daniela	Costian ¶	ROM	30.4.65	1		Bucuresti	30 Apr 88
73.78			Costian			1		Bucuresti	24 Apr 88
73.42			Reinsch			1		Karl-Marx-Stadt	12 Jun 88
73.36	WR	Irina	Meszynski	GDR	24.3.62	1	Drz	Praha	17 Aug 84
73.32			Gansky			1		Neubrandenburg	11 Jun 87
73.28		Galina	Savinkova'	RUS	15.7.53	1	NC	Donetsk	8 Sep 84
73.26	WR		Savinkova			1		Leselidze	21 May 83
73.26			Sachse/Gansky			1		Neubrandenburg	6 Jun 86
73.24			Gansky			1		Leipzig	29 May 87
73.22		Tsvetanka	Khristova ¶	BUL	14.3.62	1		Kazanlak	19 Apr 87
73.10		Gisela	Beyer	GDR	16.7.60	1	OD	Berlin	20 Jul 84
73.04			Gansky			1		Potsdam	6 Jun 87
73.04			Wyludda			1	ECp	Gateshead	5 Aug 89
72.96			Savinkova			1	v GDR	Erfurt	23 Jun 85
72.94			Gansky			2	v ITA	Neubrandenburg	9 Jul 88
72.92		Martina	Opitz/Hellmann	GDR	12.12.60	1	NC	Potsdam	20 Aug 87
72.90			Costian			1		Bucuresti	14 May 88
72.78			Hellmann			2		Neubrandenburg	11 Jun 87
72.78			Reinsch			1	OD	Berlin	29 Jun 88
72.72			Wyludda			1		Neubrandenburg	23 Jun 89
72.70			Wyludda			1	NC-j	Karl-Marx-Stadt	15 Jul 88
72.54			Gansky			1	NC	Rostock	25 Jun 88
72.52			Hellmann			1		Frohburg	15 Jun 86
72.52			Khristova			1	BGP	Budapest	11 Aug 86
		(31/10)							
72.14		Galina	Murashova	LTU	22.12.55	2	Drz	Praha	17 Aug 84
71.80	WR	Maria	Vergova/Petkova	BUL	3.11.50	1	NC	Sofiya	13 Jul 80
71.68			Xiao Yanling ¶	CHN	27.3.68	1		Beijing	14 Mar 92
71.58		Ellina	Zvereva' ¶	BLR	16.11.60	1	Znam	Leningrad	12 Jun 88
71.50	WR	Evelin	Schlaak/Jahl	GDR	28.3.56	1		Potsdam	10 May 80
71.30		Larisa	Korotkevich	RUS	3.1.67	1	RusCp	Sochi	29 May 92
71.22		Ria	Stalman	NED	11.12.51	1		Walnut	15 Jul 84
70.88		Hilda	Ramos ¶	CUB	1.9.64	1		Habana	8 May 92
70.80		Larisa	Mikhalchenko	UKR	16.5.63	1		Kharkov	18 Jun 88
70.68		Maritza	Martén	CUB	16.8.63	1	Ib Am	Sevilla	18 Jul 92
		(20)							
70.50	WR	Faina	Melnik	RUS	9.6.45	1	Znam	Sochi	24 Apr 76
70.34	@	Silvia	Madetzky	GDR	24.6.62	3		Athína	16 May 88
		69.34				1		Halle	26 Jun 87
70.02		Natalya	Sadova	RUS	15.6.72	1		Thessaloniki	23 Jun 99
69.86		Valentina	Kharchenko	RUS	.49	1		Feodosiya	16 May 81
69.72		Svetla	Mitkova	BUL	17.6.64	2	NC	Sofiya	15 Aug 87
69.68		Mette	Bergmann	NOR	9.11.62	1		Florø	27 May 95
69.51		Franka	Dietzsch	GER	22.1.68	1		Wiesbaden	8 May 99
69.50		Florenta	Craciunescu'	ROM	7.5.55	1	Balk	Stara Zagora	2 Aug 85
69.14		Irina	Yatchenko	BLR	31.10.65	1		Staiki	31 Jul 04
69.08		Carmen	Romero	CUB	6.10.50	1	NC	Habana	17 Apr 76
		(30)							
69.08		Mariana	Ionescu/Lengyel	ROM	14.4.53	1		Constanta	19 Apr 86
68.92		Sabine	Engel	GDR	21.4.54	1	v URS,POL	Karl-Marx-Stadt	25 Jun 77
68.80		Nicoleta	Grasu	ROM	11.9.71	1		Poiana Brasov	7 Aug 99
68.64		Margitta	Pufe'	GDR	10.9.52	1	ISTAF	Berlin	17 Aug 79
68.62			Yu Hourun	CHN	9.7.64	1		Beijing	6 May 88
68.62			Hou Xuemei	CHN	27.2.62	1	IntC	Tianjin	4 Sep 88
68.60		Nadezhda	Kugayevskikh	RUS	19.4.60	1		Oryol	30 Aug 83
68.58		Lyubov	Zverkova	RUS	14.6.55	1	Izv	Kiyev	22 Jun 84
68.52		Beatrice	Faumuiná	NZL	23.10.74	1	Bisl	Oslo	4 Jul 97
68.38		Olga	Burova'	RUS	17.9.63	2	RusCp	Sochi	29 May 92
		(40)							
68.18		Tatyana	Lesovaya	KAZ	24.4.56	1		Alma-Ata	23 Sep 82
68.18		Irina	Khval	RUS	17.5.62	1		Moskva	8 Jul 88

Mark	Wind	Name		Nat	Born	Pos	Meet	Venue	Date
68.18		Barbara	Hechevarría	CUB	6.8.66	2		Habana	17 Feb 89
67.96		Argentina	Menis	ROM	19.7.48	1	RomIC	Bucuresti	15 May 76
67.90		Petra	Sziegaud	GDR	17.10.58	1		Berlin	19 May 82
67.82		Tatyana	Belova	RUS	12.2.62	1		Irkutsk	10 Aug 87
67.80		Stefenia	Simova ¶	BUL	5.6.63	1		Stara Zagora	27 Jun 92
67.72		Ekateríni	Vóggoli	GRE	30.10.70	1	NC	Athína	10 Jun 04
67.71		Vera	Pospísilová/Cechlová	CZE	19.11.78	1		Réthimno	6 Jul 03
67.70		Anastasía	Kelesídou	GRE	28.11.72	2		Réthimno	29 May 99
		(50)	100th woman 65.33, 200th woman c.63.00						

Unofficial meeting

Mark	Wind	Name		Nat	Born	Pos	Meet	Venue	Date
78.14		Martina	Hellmann	GDR	12.12.60	1		Berlin	6 Sep 88
75.36		Ilke	Wyludda	GDR	28.3.69	2		Berlin	6 Sep 88

Downhill: 69.44 Suzy Powell USA 3.9.76 1 La Jolla 27 Apr 02

Ancillary marks – other marks during series (to 72.92)

73.32 Reinsch 13 Sep 88 | 73.28 Gansky 27 Jun 87 | 73.10 Reinsch 9 Jul 88
73.28 Gansky 11 Jun 87 | 73.16 Wyludda 13 Sep 88 | 73.06 Gansky 27 Jun 87
72.92 Hellmann 20 Aug 87

HAMMER

Mark	Wind	Name		Nat	Born	Pos	Meet	Venue	Date
77.06	WR	Tatyana	Lysenko	RUS	9.10.83	1	Kuts	Moskva	15 Jul 05
76.66		Olga	Tsander	BLR	18.5.76	1		Staiki	21 Jul 05
76.07	WR	Mihaela	Melinte ¶	ROM	27.3.75	1		Rüdlingen	29 Aug 99
75.97	WR		Melinte			1		Clermont-Ferrand	13 May 99
75.95			Lysenko			1		Moskva	29 Jun 05
75.95			Lysenko			1	NC	Tula	13 Jul 05
75.68		Olga	Kuzenkova	RUS	4.10.70	1	NCp	Tula	4 Jun 00
75.21			Melinte			1c1		Rüdlingen	28 Aug 99
75.20			Melinte			1	WCh	Sevilla	24 Aug 99
75.18		Yipsi	Moreno	CUB	19.11.80	1	NC	La Habana	23 Apr 04
75.14			Moreno			1		Savona	17 Jul 03
75.10			Kuzenkova			1	WCh	Helsinki	12 Aug 05
75.06			Moreno			1		Padova	3 Jul 04
75.02			Kuzenkova			1	OG	Athína	25 Aug 04
74.98			Kuzenkova			1	NC	Tula	9 Aug 03
74.95			Moreno			1		Banská Bystrica	28 Aug 05
74.90			Melinte			1		Bucuresti	4 Jul 99
74.77			Melinte			1		Nürnberg	13 Jun 99
74.75			Moreno			1	WAF	Szombathely	3 Sep 05
74.72			Tsander			1	NC	Minsk	10 Jul 04
74.69			Moreno			1		Guadalajara	16 Jun 04
74.66		Manuèla	Montebrun	FRA	13.11.79	1	GP II	Zagreb	11 Jul 05
74.54			Kuzenkova			1	NC	Tula	25 Jul 04
74.50			Montebrun			1		Villeneuve d'Ascq	15 Jun 03
74.48			Melinte			1	ECp	Paris (C)	20 Jun 99
74.43			Montebrun			1	ECpS	Firenze	22 Jun 03
74.43			Moreno			1		La Habana	11 Mar 04
74.30			Kuzenkova			1	Znam	Moskva	4 Jun 99
74.27		Kamila	Skolimowska	POL	4.11.82	1	GP II	Madrid	16 Jul 05
74.25			Moreno			1	PAm	Santo Domingo	5 Aug 03
		(30/7)							
74.16		Irina	Sekachova	UKR	21.7.76	1		Kiev	12 Jun 04
73.87		Erin	Gilreath	USA	11.10.80	1	NC	Carson	25 Jun 05
73.68		Yelena	Konevtsova'	RUS	11.3.81	2	NC	Tula	25 Jul 04
		(10)							
73.59		Ester	Balassini	ITA	20.10.77	1	NC	Bressanone	25 Jun 05
73.24			Zhang Wenxiu	CHN	22.3.86	1	NC	Changsha	24 Jun 05
73.16		Yunaika	Crawford	CUB	2.11.82	3	OG	Athína	25 Aug 04
73.08		Yekaterina	Khoroshkikh	RUS	21.1.83	1	NC-23	Tula	14 Jun 05
72.73		Betty	Heidler	GER	14.10.83	4	OG	Athína	25 Aug 04
72.74		Susanne	Keil	GER	18.5.78	1		Nikiti	15 Jul 05
72.71		Gulfiya	Khanafeyeva	RUS	12.6.82	1	Znam	Kazan	9 Jul 04
72.51			Liu Yinghui	CHN	29.6.79	2	WUG	Izmir	16 Aug 05
72.36			Gu Yuan	CHN	9.5.82	2		Padova	3 Jul 04
72.09		Tatyana	Konstantinova	RUS	18.11.70	2	Znam	Moskva	4 Jun 99
		(20)							
72.01		Anna	Norgren-Mahon	USA	19.12.74	1		Walnut	27 Jul 02
71.45		Candice	Scott	TRI	17.9.80	1		Marietta	15 May 05
71.12		Bronwyn	Eagles	AUS	23.8.80	1		Adelaide	6 Feb 03
71.08		Darya	Pchelnik	BLR	20.12.81	2		Staiki	21 Jul 05
71.00		Ivana	Brkljacic	CRO	25.1.83	1A	EThCp	Mersin	13 Mar 05
70.91		Kathrin	Klaas	GER	8.2.84	2		Mannheim	18 Jun 05

Mark Wind	Name		Nat	Born	Pos	Meet	Venue	Date
70.79	Katalin	Divós ¶	HUN	11.5.74	2	GP	Doha	18 May 01
70.73	Andrea	Bunjes	GER	5.2.76	Q	OG	Athína	23 Aug 04
70.67		Zhao Wei	CHN	27.1.79	1		Nanning	5 Apr 03
70.62	Dawn	Ellerbe	USA	3.4.74	1	Penn R	Philadelphia	28 Apr 01
	(30)							
70.59	Clarissa	Claretti	ITA	7.10.80	1		Savona	15 Jun 05
70.39	Mariya	Smolyachkova	BLR	10.2.85	1		Staiki	26 Jun 04
70.23	Oksana	Menkova	BLR	28.3.82	1		Minsk	23 May 04
70.03	Loree	Smith	USA	6.11.82	1		Fort Collins	13 May 05
69.98	Alexándra	Papayeoryíou	GRE	17.12.80	1	ROM Ch	Bucuresti	9 Aug 03
69.92	Lyudmila	Gubkina	BLR	13.8.73	1		Staiki	19 Aug 00
69.80	Svetlana	Sudak	BLR	20.3.71	4		Staiki	21 Jul 05
69.73	Natalya	Zolotukhina	UKR	4.1.85	1		Kiev	24 Jul 04
69.72	Aldenay	Vasallo	CUB	25.2.77	1		La Habana	21 Jun 03
69.65	Bethany	Hart	USA	10.4.77	1		New Haven	11 Jul 05
	(40)							
69.63	Mia	Strömmer	FIN	26.2.74	1		Potchefstroom	24 Mar 01
69.52	Amber	Campbell	USA	5.6.81	1		Wilmington	14 Jun 05
69.36	Eileen	O'Keefe	IRL	31.5.81	1		Dublin (S)	30 Jul 05
69.28	Kirsten	Münchow/Klose	GER	21.1.77	3	OG	Sydney	29 Sep 00
69.24	Lisa	Misipeka	ASA	3.1.75	1	Jerome	Burnaby	8 Jun 03
69.24	Martina	Danisová ¶	SVK	21.3.83	1		Ostrava	3 Sep 05
69.17	Alla	Davydova	RUS	21.5.66	1	ECCp	Valencia	24 May 03
69.16	Sini	Pöyry	FIN	3.2.80	1		Kaustinen	1 Jul 04
68.93	Lorraine	Shaw	GBR	2.4.68	1		Loughborough	8 Jun 03
68.87	Berta	Castells	ESP	24.1.84	1eB	GP	Sevilla	5 Jun 04
	(50)	100th woman 66.13, 200th 62.52						

Downhill: 75.20 Manuéla Montebrun FRA 13.11.79 1 Vineuil 18 May 03

Irregular circle: 74.31 Yekaterina Khoroshkikh RUS 21.3.83 1 Znam Kazan 24 Jun 05

Ancillary marks – other marks during series to 74.80

76.05 Melinte	29 Aug 99	75.29	Melinte	13 May 99	75.04	Lysenko	13 Jul 05
76.05 Lysenko	15 Jul 05	75.17	Lysenko	13 Jul 05	75.00	Lysenko	29 Jun 05
75.81 Lysenko	15 Jul 05	75.16	Kuzenkova	4 Jun 00	74.97	Lysenko	29 Jun 05
					74.92	Kuzenkova	25 Aug 04

Drugs disqualification

74.80 Melinte 1 Rüdlingen 12 Aug 00 | 74.32 Melinte 1 Nitra 26 Aug 00

70.34 Melissa Price ¶ USA 5.9.79 1 NC Stanford 19 Jun 03

JAVELIN

Mark Wind	Name		Nat	Born	Pos	Meet	Venue	Date
71.70 WR	Osleidys	Menéndez	CUB	14.11.79	1	WCh	Helsinki	14 Aug 05
71.54 WR		Menéndez			1		Réthimno	1 Jul 01
71.53		Menéndez			1	OG	Athína	27 Aug 04
70.03	Christina	Obergföll	GER	22.8.81	2	WCh	Helsinki	14 Aug 05
69.82		Menéndez			1	WUG	Beijing	29 Aug 01
69.53		Menéndez			1	WCh	Edmonton	7 Aug 01
69.48 WR	Trine	Hattestad	NOR	18.4.66	1	Bisl	Oslo	28 Jul 00
68.91		Hattestad			1	OG	Sydney	30 Sep 00
68.47		Menéndez			1	GP	Helsinki	25 Jul 05
68.40		Menéndez			1		Tartu	19 Jun 01
68.32		Hattestad			1	ISTAF	Berlin	1 Sep 00
68.23		Menéndez			1		La Habana	5 Mar 04
68.22 WR		Hattestad			1	GGala	Roma	30 Jun 00
68.19 WRu		Hattestad			1		Fana	28 Jul 99
67.99		Menéndez			1		Iráklio	4 Jul 04
67.92		Hattestad			1	DNG	Stockholm	1 Aug 00
67.87		Menéndez			1	SGP	Madrid	17 Jul 04
67.83		Menéndez			2	ISTAF	Berlin	1 Sep 00
67.76		Hattestad			1	VD	Bruxelles	25 Aug 00
67.67	Sonia	Bisset	CUB	1.4.71	1		Salamanca	6 Jul 05
67.51 WR	Miréla	Manjani/Tzelíli	GRE	21.12.76	2	OG	Sydney	30 Sep 00
67.47		Manjani			1	EC	München	8 Aug 02
67.40		Menéndez			1	Athl	Lausanne	2 Jul 02
67.34		Menéndez			Q	OG	Sydney	29 Sep 00
67.24		Menéndez			1	WAF	Monaco	9 Sep 05
67.20	Tatyana	Shikolenko	RUS	10.5.68	1	Herc	Monaco	18 Aug 00
67.14		Menéndez			1	NC	La Habana	10 Mar 02
67.09		Tzelíli			1	WCh	Sevilla	28 Aug 99
66.99		Menéndez			1	IbAm	Huelva	8 Aug 04
66.96		Hattestad			1	ECp1A	Nadderud	8 Jul 00
	(30/6)							

Mark	Wind	Name		Nat	Born	Pos	Meet	Venue	Date
66.91		Tanja	Damaske	GER	16.11.71	1	NC	Erfurt	4 Jul 99
66.80		Louise	Currey	AUS	24.1.69	1		Gold Coast (RB)	5 Aug 00
66.52		Steffi	Nerius	GER	1.7.72	Q	WCh	Helsinki	12 Aug 05
65.91		Nikola	Brejchová'	CZE	25.6.74	1	GP	Linz	2 Aug 04
		(10)							
65.74		Barbora	Spotáková	CZE	30.6.81	1		Ústí nad Labem	25 Sep 05
65.30		Claudia	Coslovich	ITA	26.4.72	1		Ljubljana	10 Jun 00
65.29		Xiomara	Rivero	CUB	22.11.68	1		Santiago de Cuba	17 Mar 01
65.17		Karen	Forkel	GER	24.3.70	2	NC	Erfurt	4 Jul 99
65.08		Ana Mirela	Termure ¶	ROM	13.1.75	1	NC	Bucuresti	10 Jun 01
64.90		Paula	Huhtaniemi	FIN	17.2.73	1	NC	Helsinki	10 Aug 03
64.89		Yekaterina	Ivakina	RUS	4.12.64	4	Bisl	Oslo	28 Jul 00
64.87		Kelly	Morgan	GBR	17.6.80	1	NC	Birmingham	14 Jul 02
64.62		Joanna	Stone	AUS	4.10.72	2		Gold Coast (RB)	5 Aug 00
64.62		Nikolett	Szabó	HUN	3.3.80	1		Pátra	22 Jul 01
		(20)							
64.61		Oksana	Makarova	RUS	21.7.71	2	ECp	Paris (C)	19 Jun 99
64.49		Valeriya	Zabruskova	RUS	29.7.75	1	Znam	Tula	7 Jun 03
64.46		Dörthe	Friedrich	GER	21.6.73	1	NC	Wattenscheid	7 Jul 02
64.06		Taina	Uppa/Kolkkala	FIN	24.10.76	1		Pihtipudas	23 Jul 00
64.03		Mikaela	Ingberg	FIN	29.7.74	6	ISTAF	Berlin	1 Sep 00
63.92			Wei Jianhua	CHN	23.3.79	1		Beijing	18 Aug 00
63.89		Felicia	Tilea-Moldovan ¶	ROM	29.9.67	2	WK	Zürich	16 Aug 02
63.73		Laverne	Eve	BAH	16.6.65	1		Nashville	22 Apr 00
63.69			Li Lei	CHN	4.5.74	1	OT	Jinzhou	8 Jun 00
63.43		Christina	Scherwin	DEN	11.7.76	4	WCh	Helsinki	14 Aug 05
		(30)							
63.32		Khristina	Georgieva	BUL	3.1.72	3	GP	Athína	28 Jun 00
63.32		Nora Aída	Bicet	CUB	29.10.77	2		Tallinn	21 Jul 04
63.14		Aggelikí	Tsiolakoúdi	GRE	10.5.76	5	EC	München	8 Aug 02
63.07		Tatyana	Lyakhovich	UKR	20.5.79	Q	OG	Athína	25 Aug 04
63.03		Barbara	Madejczyk	POL	30.9.76	1	Déca	Paris (C)	3 Sep 05
62.93			Xue Juan	CHN	10.2.86	1	NG	Changsha	27 Oct 03
62.89		Voisávva	Líka	GRE	27.6.70	1	NC	Athína	11 Jun 04
		(37)	50th best 61.82						

Ancillary marks – other marks during series (to 66.70)

69.42	Menéndez	7 Aug 01	67.51	Tzelíli	30 Sep 00	66.83	Menéndez	19 Jun 01
67.61	Hattestad	28 Jul 99	67.04	Hattestad	28 Jul 99			

Specification changed from 1 May 1999. See ATHLETICS 2000 for Old specification all-time list. Top five:

Mark	Wind	Name		Nat	Born	Pos	Meet	Venue	Date
80.00	WR	Petra	Felke	GDR	30.7.59	1		Potsdam	9 Sep 88
77.44	WR	Fatima	Whitbread	GBR	3.3.61	Q	EC	Stuttgart	28 Aug 86
74.76	WR	Tiina	Lillak	FIN	15.4.61	1		Tampere	13 Jun 83
74.20	WR	Sofía	Sakorafa	GRE	29.4.57	1	NC	Haniá	26 Sep 82
73.58		Tessa	Sanderson	GBR	14.3.56	1		Edinburgh	26 Jun 83

HEPTATHLON

Mark		Name		Nat	Born	Pos	Meet	Venue	Date
7291 WR		Jackie	Joyner-Kersee	USA	3.3.62	1	OG	Seoul	24 Sep 88
		12.69/0.5	1.86	15.80	22.56/1.6	7.27/0.7		45.66	2:08.51
7215 WR			Joyner-Kersee			1	OT	Indianapolis	16 Jul 88
		12.71/-0.9	1.93	15.65	22.30/ 0.0	7.00/-1.3		50.08	2:20.70
7158 WR			Joyner-Kersee			1	USOF	Houston	2 Aug 86
		13.18/-0.5	1.88	15.20	22.85/1.2	7.03/2.9		50.12	2:09.69
7148 WR			Joyner-Kersee			1	GWG	Moskva	7 Jul 86
		12.85/0.2	1.88	14.76	23.00/0.3	7.01/-0.5		49.86	2:10.02
7128			Joyner-Kersee			1	WCh	Roma	1 Sep 87
		12.91/0.2	1.90	16.00	22.95/1.2	7.14/0.9		45.68	2:16.29
7044			Joyner-Kersee			1	OG	Barcelona	2 Aug 92
		12.85/-0.9	1.91	14.13	23.12/0.7	7.10/1.3		44.98	2:11.78
7007		Larisa	Nikitina ¶	RUS	29.4.65	1	NC	Bryansk	11 Jun 89
		13.40/1.4	1.89	16.45	23.97/1.1	6.73/4.0		53.94	2:15.31
7001		Carolina	Klüft	SWE	2.2.83	1	WCh	Saint-Denis	24 Aug 03
		13.18/-0.4	1.94	14.19	22.98/1.1	6.68/1.0		49.90	2:12.12
6985		Sabine	Braun	GER	19.6.65	1		Götzis	31 May 92
		13.11/-0.4	1.93	14.84	23.65/2.0	6.63/2.9		51.62	2:12.67
6979			Joyner-Kersee			1	TAC	San José	24 Jun 87
		12.90/2.0	1.85	15.17	23.02/0.4	7.25/2.3		40.24	2:13.07
6952			Klüft			1	OG	Athína	21 Aug 04
		13.21/0.2	1.91	14.77	23.27/-0.1	6.78/0.4		48.89	2:14.15
6946 WR		Sabine	Paetz'	GDR	16.10.57	1	NC	Potsdam	6 May 84
		12.64/0.3	1.80	15.37	23.37/0.7	6.86/-0.2		44.62	2:08.93

Mark Wind		Name	Nat	Born	Pos	Meet	Venue	Date
6942	Ghada	Shouaa	SYR	10.9.72	1		Götzis	26 May 96
	13.78/0.3	1.87	15.64	23.78/0.6	6.77/0.6	54.74	2:13.61	
6935 WR	Ramona	Neubert	GDR	26.7.58	1	v URS	Moskva	19 Jun 83
	13.42/1.7	1.82	15.25	23.49/0.5	6.79/0.7	49.94	2:07.51	
6910		Joyner			1	MSR	Walnut	25 Apr 86
	12.9/0.0	1.86	14.75	23.24/2.8	6.85/2.1	48.30	2:14.11	
6897		John'			2	OG	Seoul	24 Sep 88
	12.85/0.5	1.80	16.23	23.65/1.6	6.71/ 0.0	42.56	2:06.14	
6889	Eunice	Barber	FRA	17.11.74	1		Arles	5 Jun 05
	12.62w/2.9	1.91	12.61	24.12/1.2	6.78w/3.4	53.07	2:14.66	
6887		Klüft			1	WCh	Helsinki	7 Aug 05
	13.19/-0.4	1.82	15.02	23.70/-2.5	6.87/0.2	47.20	2:08.89	
6878		Joyner-Kersee			1	TAC	New York	13 Jun 91
	12.77	1.89	15.62	23.42	6.97/0.4	43.28	2:22.12	
6875		Nikitina			1	ECp-A	Helmond	16 Jul 89
	13.55/-2.1	1.84	15.99	24.29/-2.1	6.75/-2.5	56.78	2:18.67	
6861		Barber			1	WCh	Sevilla	22 Aug 99
	12.89/-0.5	1.93	12.37	23.57/0.5	6.86/-0.3	49.88	2:15.65	
6859	Natalya	Shubenkova	RUS	25.9.57	1	NC	Kiyev	21 Jun 84
	12.93/1.0	1.83	13.66	23.57/-0.3	6.73/0.4	46.26	2:04.60	
6858	Anke	Vater/Behmer (10)	GDR	5.6.61	3	OG	Seoul	24 Sep 88
	13.20/0.5	1.83	14.20	23.10/1.6	6.68/0.1	44.54	2:04.20	
6847		Nikitina			1	WUG	Duisburg	29 Aug 89
	13.47	1.81	16.12	24.12	6.66	59.28	2:22.07	
6845 WR		Neubert			1	v URS	Halle	20 Jun 82
	13.58/1.8	1.83	15.10	23.14/1.4	6.84w/2.3	42.54	2:06.16	
6845	Irina	Belova ¶	RUS	27.3.68	2	OG	Barcelona	2 Aug 92
	13.25/-0.1	1.88	13.77	23.34/0.2	6.82/0.0	41.90	2:05.08	
6842		Barber			1		Götzis	4 Jun 00
	12.97/0.2	1.88	12.23	23.84/0.5	6.85/-0.1	51.91	2:11.55	
6841		Joyner			1		Götzis	25 May 86
	13.09/-1.3	1.87	14.34	23.63/-0.8	6.76/-0.3	48.88	2:14.58	
6837		Joyner-Kersee			1	WCh	Stuttgart	17 Aug 93
	12.89/0.1	1.81	14.38	23.19/0.0	7.04/1.4	43.76	2:14.49	
6831	Denise	Lewis	GBR	27.8.72	1		Talence	30 Jul 00
	13.13/1.0	1.84	15.07	24.01w/3.6	6.69/-0.4	49.42	2:12.20	
	(30/12)							
6803	Jane	Frederick	USA	7.4.52	1		Talence	16 Sep 84
	13.27/1.2	1.87	15.49	24.15/1.6	6.43/0.2	51.74	2:13.55	
6765	Yelena	Prokhorova	RUS	16.4.78	1	NC	Tula	23 Jul 00
	13.54/-2.8	1.82	14.30	23.37/-0.2	6.72/1.0	43.40	2:04.27	
6750		Ma Miaolan	CHN	18.1.70	1	NG	Beijing	12 Sep 93
	13.28/1.5	1.89	14.98	23.86/	6.64/	45.82	2:15.33	
6741	Heike	Drechsler	GER	16.12.64	1		Talence	11 Sep 94
	13.34/-0.3	1.84	13.58	22.84/-1.1	6.95/1.0	40.64	2:11.53	
6703	Tatyana	Blokhina	RUS	12.3.70	1		Talence	11 Sep 93
	13.69/-0.6	1.91	14.94	23.95/-0.4	5.99/-0.3	52.16	2:09.65	
6702	Chantal	Beaugeant ¶	FRA	16.2.61	2		Götzis	19 Jun 88
	13.10/1.6	1.78	13.74	23.96/3.5	6.45/0.2	50.96	2:07.09	
6695	Jane	Flemming	AUS	14.4.65	1	CG	Auckland	28 Jan 90
	13.21/1.4	1.82	13.76	23.62/2.4	6.57/1.6	49.28	2:12.53	
6660	Ines	Schulz	GDR	10.7.65	3		Götzis	19 Jun 88
	13.56/0.4	1.84	13.95	23.93/2.8	6.70/0.7	42.82	2:06.31	
	(20)							
6658	Svetla	Dimitrova ¶	BUL	27.1.70	2		Götzis	31 May 92
	13.41/-0.7	1.75	14.72	23.06/2.4	6.64/1.9	43.84	2:09.60	
6646	Natalya	Grachova	UKR	21.2.52	1	NC	Moskva	2 Aug 82
	13.80	1.80	16.18	23.86	6.65/3.5	39.42	2:06.59	
6635	Sibylle	Thiele	GDR	6.3.65	2	GWG	Moskva	7 Jul 86
	13.14/0.6	1.76	16.00	24.18	6.62/1.0	45.74	2:15.30	
6635	Svetlana	Buraga	BLR	4.9.65	3	WCh	Stuttgart	17 Aug 93
	12.95/0.1	1.84	14.55	23.69/0.0	6.58/-0.2	41.04	2:13.65	
6633	Natalya	Roshchupkina	RUS	13.1.78	2	NC	Tula	23 Jul 00
	14.05/-2.8	1.88	14.28	23.47/-0.2	6.45/0.4	44.34	2:07.93	
6623	Judy	Simpson'	GBR	14.11.60	3	EC	Stuttgart	30 Aug 86
	13.05/0.8	1.92	14.73	25.09/0.0	6.56/2.5	40.92	2:11.70	
6619	Liliana	Nastase	ROM	1.8.62	4	OG	Barcelona	2 Aug 92
	12.86/-0.9	1.82	14.34	23.70/0.2	6.49/-0.3	41.30	2:11.22	
6616	Malgorzata	Nowak'	POL	9.2.59	1	WUG	Kobe	31 Aug 85
	13.27/4.0	1.95	15.35	24.20/0.0	6.37/3.9	43.36	2:20.39	

Mark Wind Name Nat Born Pos Meet Venue Date

6604 Remigija Nazaroviene' LTU 2.6.67 2 URSCh Bryansk 11 Jun 89
13.26/1.4 1.86 14.27 24.12/0.7 6.58/0.9 40.94 2:09.98
6604 Irina Tyukhay RUS 14.1.67 3 Götzis 28 May 95
13.20/-0.7 1.84 14.97 24.33/1.7 6.71/0.5 43.84 2:17.64
(30)
6598 Svetlana Moskalets RUS 22.1.69 1 NC Vladimir 17 Jun 94
13.20/0.8 1.82 13.78 23.56/0.1 6.74/0.8 42.48 2:14.54
6591 Svetlana Sokolova RUS 9.1.81 1 NC Tula 23 Jun 04
13.56/1.1 1.82 15.09 24.02/0.6 6.26/0.3 45.07 2:07.23
6577 DeDee Nathan USA 20.4.68 1 Götzis 30 May 99
13.28/-0.1 1.76 14.74 24.23/0.2 6.59/1.6 50.08 2:16.92
6573 Rita Ináncsi HUN 6.1.71 3 Götzis 29 May 94
13.66/2.0 1.84 13.94 24.20/2.5 6.78/1.4 46.28 2:16.02
6572 Heike Tischler GDR 4.2.64 2 EC Split 31 Aug 90
14.08/-0.9 1.82 13.73 24.29/0.9 6.22/-0.7 53.24 2:05.50
6563 Natalya Sazanovich BLR 15.8.73 2 OG Atlanta 28 Jul 96
13.56/-1.6 1.80 14.52 23.72/-0.3 6.70/1.1 46.00 2:17.92
6552 Nadezhda Vinogradova' RUS 1.5.58 2 NC Kiyev 21 Jun 84
13.92/1.0 1.80 15.19 23.84/0.2 6.67/0.1 38.60 2:06.80
6551 Yelena Martsenyuk RUS 21.2.61 2 Staiki 2 Jul 88
13.54/-0.4 1.82 15.32 24.25/0.3 6.25/0.7 47.56 2:12.72
6547 Kelly Sotherton GBR 13.11.76 2 Götzis 29 May 05
13.27/1.1 1.85 13.84 23.77/1.7 6.67/-0.6 37.21 2:10.29
6546 Mona Steigauf GER 17.1.70 1 WUG Catania 27 Aug 97
13.13/1.6 1.85 12.83 24.14/1.7 6.56/1.3 43.86 2:11.15
(40)
6542 Urszula Wlodarczyk POL 22.12.65 4 WCh Athína 4 Aug 97
13.55/0.3 1.81 14.16 24.48/0.1 6.63/0.6 44.18 2:09.59
6541 Mila Kolyadina RUS 31.12.60 4 v GDR Moskva 19 Jun 83
14.05 1.82 16.28 24.81 6.48/0.8 48.26 2:15.26
6539 Tatyana Shpak UKR 17.11.60 3 Staiki 2 Jul 88
13.57/-0.4 1.76 15.30 23.61/0.5 6.52/-0.6 39.28 2:07.25
6536 Yekaterina Smirnova RUS 22.10.56 3 v GDR Moskva 19 Jun 83
13.41 1.82 14.82 24.84 6.56/1.1 45.66 2:13.38
6531 Peggy Beer GDR 15.9.69 3 EC Split 31 Aug 90
13.27/-0.2 1.82 13.46 23.99/0.4 6.38/0.9 42.10 2:05.79
6527 Diane Guthrie-Gresham JAM 24.10.71 1 NCAA Knoxville 3 Jun 95
13.86w/2.5 1.86 13.80 24.91/-1.3 6.92w/2.5 49.04 2:20.82
6523 Sabine Everts FRG 4.3.61 1 v URS Mannheim 10 Jun 82
13.45 1.89 12.39 23.73 6.75 36.02 2:07.73
6502 Hyleas Fountain USA 14.1.81 3 Götzis 29 May 05
13.09/1.1 1.88 12.13 23.87/1.7 6.67/-0.9 46.90 2:22.81
6500 Birgit Clarius GER 18.3.65 1 NC Vaterstetten 20 Jun 93
13.61/1.3 1.81 15.22 24.69w/2.1 6.08/-0.6 50.20 2:11.29
6493 Svetlana Filatyeva ' RUS 3.4.64 1 Kiyev 14 Aug 88
13.77 1.89 13.89 24.94 6.30 48.44 2:11.89
(50) 100th woman 6336, 200th 6128, 300th 5997

DECATHLON

8358 WR Austra Skujyte LTU 12.8.79 1 Columbia, MS 15 Apr 05
12.49/1.6 46.19 3.10 48.78 57.19 14.22w/2.4 6.12/1.6 16.42 1.78 5:15.86
8150 WR Marie Collonvillé FRA 23.11.73 1 Talence 26 Sep 04
12.48/0.4 34.69 3.50 47.19 56.15 13.96/0.4 6.18/1.0 11.90 1.80 5:06.09
7885 Mona Steigauf GER 17.1.70 1 Ahlen 21 Sep 97
12.15/1.2 5.93 12.49 1.73 55.34 13.75/0.2 34.68 3.10 42.24 5:07.95
7798 Irina Naumenko KAZ 13.2.80 2 Talence 26 Sep 04
12.58/0.4 34.63 3.30 37.57 55.91 14.42/0.4 5.98/1.0 12.51 1.77 4:59.03
7742 Anna Snetkova RUS 25.2.79 1 Krasnodar 20 Sep 03
12.66 36.90 3.70 37.50 58.88 14.19 5.98 13.48 1.69 5:17.67

IAAF approved order: 100m, DT, PV, JT, 400m / 100mh, LJ, SP, HJ, 1500m, 1997/2000 events used men's order

4 x 100 METRES RELAY

41.37 WR GDR Gladisch, Rieger, Auerswald, Göhr 1 WCp Canberra 6 Oct 85
41.47 USA Gaines, Jones, Miller, Devers 1 WCh Athína 9 Aug 97
41.49 RUS Bogoslovskaya, Malchugina, Voronova, Privalova 1 WCh Stuttgart 22 Aug 93
41.49 USA Finn, Torrence, Vereen, Devers 2 WCh Stuttgart 22 Aug 93
41.52 USA Gaines, Jones, Miller, Devers 1h1 WCh Athína 8 Aug 97
41.53 WR GDR Gladisch, Koch, Auerswald, Göhr 1 Berlin 31 Jul 83
41.55 USA Brown, Williams, Griffith, Marshall 1 ISTAF Berlin 21 Aug 87
41.58 USA Brown, Williams, Griffith, Marshall 1 WCh Roma 6 Sep 87
41.60 WR GDR Müller, Wöckel, Auerswald, Göhr 1 OG Moskva 1 Aug 80

Mark Wind	Nat	Name	Pos	Meet	Venue	Date
1.61A	USA	Brown, Williams, Cheeseborough, Ashford	1	USOF	USAF Academy	3 Jul 83
1.63	USA	Brown, Williams, Cheeseborough, Ashford	1	v GDR	Los Angeles	25 Jun 83
1.65	USA	Brown, Bolden, Cheeseborough, Ashford	1	OG	Los Angeles	11 Aug 84
1.65	GDR	Gladisch, Koch, Auerswald, Göhr	1	ECp	Moskva	17 Aug 85
1.67	USA	A Williams, Jones, L Williams, Colander	1	3-N	München	8 Aug 04
1.67	USA	A Williams, Jones, L Williams, Colander	1h1	OG	Athína	26 Aug 04
1.68	GDR	Möller, Krabbe, Behrendt, Günther	1	EC	Split	1 Sep 90
1.69	GDR	Gladisch, Koch, Auerswald, Göhr	1	OD	Potsdam	21 Jul 84
1.73	GDR	Möller, Behrendt, Lange, Göhr	1		Berlin	13 Sep 88
1.73	JAM	Lawrence, Simpson, Bailey, Campbell	1	OG	Athína	27 Aug 04
1.76	GDR	Gladisch, Koch, Auerswald, Göhr	1	WCh	Helsinki	10 Aug 83
		(20 performances by 4 nations) from here just best by nation				
1.78	FRA	Girard, Hurtis, Félix, Arron	1	WCh	Saint-Denis	30 Aug 03
1.92	BAH	Fynes, Sturrup, Davis-Thompson, Ferguson	1	WCh	Sevilla	29 Aug 99
2.08mx	BUL	Pavlova, Nuneva, Georgieva, Ivanova	mx		Sofiya	8 Aug 84
	42.29	Pencheva, Nuneva, Georgieva, Donkova	1		Sofiya	26 Jun 88
2.23	CHN	(Sichuan) Xiao Lin, Li Yali, Liu Xiaomei, Li Xuemei	1	NG	Shanghai	23 Oct 97
2.39	NGR	Utondu, Idehen, Opara-Thompson, Onyali	2h2	OG	Barcelona	7 Aug 92
2.43	GBR	Hunte, Smallwood, Goddard, Lannaman	3	OG	Moskva	1 Aug 80
	(10)					
2.56	BLR	Nesterenko, Sologub, Nevmerzhitskaya, Dragun	3	WCh	Helsinki	13 Aug 05
2.59	FRG	Possekel, Helten, Richter, Kroniger	2	OG	Montreal	31 Jul 76
2.71	POL	Tomczak, Pakula, Pisiewicz, Kasprzyk	3	ECp	Moskva	17 Aug 85
2.77	CAN	Bailey, Payne, Taylor, Gareau	2	OG	Los Angeles	11 Aug 84
2.89	CUB	Ferrer, López, Duporty, Allen	6	WCh	Stuttgart	22 Aug 93
2.96	UKR	Tkalich, Kravchenko, Pastushenko, Maydanova	1		Kiev	6 Jul 03
2.97A	BRA	K Santos, de Moura, Neto, L dos Santos	1	SAm-r	Bogotá	10 Jul 04
2.98	CZE/TCH	Sokolová, Soborová, Kocembová, Kratochvilová	1	WK	Zürich	18 Aug 82
2.99A	AUS	Massey, Broadrick, Lambert, Gainsford-Taylor	1		Pietersburg	18 Mar 00
3.03	COL	M.Murillo, Palacios, Obregón, N.González	3h2	WCh	Helsinki	12 Aug 05
	(20)					
3.07	GRE	Tsóni, Kóffa, Vasarmídou, Thánou	2	MedG	Bari	18 Jun 97
3.08	BEL	De Caluwé, Huyghebaert, Ouédraogo, Gevaert	3h1	OG	Athína	26 Aug 04
3.19	GHA	Akoto, Twum, Anim, Nsiah	5s1	OG	Sydney	29 Sep 00
3.25A	RSA	Hartman, Moropane, Holtshausen, Seyerling	2		Pietersburg	18 Mar 00
3.35	KAZ	Aleksandrova, Kvast, Miljauskiene, Sevalnikova	2	SPART	Taskent	16 Sep 86
3.37	FIN	Pirtimaa, Hanhijoki, Hernesniemi, Salmela	7	WCh	Stuttgart	22 Aug 93
3.44A WR	NED	van den Berg, Sterk, Hennipman, Bakker	4	OG	Ciudad de México	20 Oct 68
3.44	ITA	Pistone, Graglia, Grillo, Levorato	1		Barletta	26 Jul 00
3.61	MAD	Rahanitraniriana, Ratsimbazafy, Rakotozafy, Rakotondrabé	4h4	OG	Sydney	29 Sep 00
3.61	SWE	Rienas, Klüft, J.Kallur, S.Kallur (30)	1	v FIN	Göteborg	27 Aug 05
est at low altitude						
2.99	BRA	da Costa, de Moura, Ignâcio, L.dos Santos	5	WCh	Helsinki	13 Aug 05
3.18	AUS	Wilson, Wells, Robertson, Boyle	5	OG	Montreal	31 Jul 76
3.48	NED	Cooman, Tromp, Olyslager, Vader	5s1	OG	Seoul	1 Oct 88

4 x 200 METRES RELAY

Mark	Team	Pos	Meet	Venue	Date
:27.46 WR	USA Blue Jenkins, Colander-Richardson, Perry, Jones	1	Penn	Philadelphia	29 Apr 00
:28.15 WR	GDR Göhr, R.Müller, Wöckel, Koch	1		Jena	9 Aug 80
:29.24	Nike International USA Roberts, Miller, Green, M Jones	1	Penn	Philadelphia	25 Apr 98
:29.40	USA Red Colander, Gaines, Miller, M Jones	1	PennR	Philadelphia	24 Apr 04
:29.78	Louisiana State University USA Davy, Hall, Durst, Lee	1	PennR	Philadelphia	26 Apr 03

4 x 400 METRES RELAY

Mark	Nat	Team	Pos	Meet	Venue	Date
:15.17 WR	URS		1	OG	Seoul	1 Oct 88
		Ledovskaya 50.12, O.Nazarova 47.82, Pinigina 49.43, Bryzgina 47.80				
:15.51	USA		2	OG	Seoul	1 Oct 88
		D.Howard 49.82, Dixon 49.17, Brisco 48.44, Griffith-Joyner 48.08				
:15.92 WR	GDR	G.Walther 49.8, Busch 48.9, Rübsam 49.4, Koch 47.8	1	NC	Erfurt	3 Jun 84
:16.71	USA		1	WCh	Stuttgart	22 Aug 93
		Torrence 49.0, Malone 49.4, Kaiser-Brown 49.48, Miles 48.78				
:16.87	GDR	Emmelmann 50.9, Busch 48.8, Müller 48.9, Koch 48.21	1	EC	Stuttgart	31 Aug 86
:18.29	USA		1	OG	Los Angeles	11 Aug 84
		Leatherwood 50.50, S.Howard 48.83, Brisco-Hooks 49.23, Cheeseborough 49.73				
:18.29	GDR	Neubauer 50.58, Emmelmann 49.89, Busch 48.81, Müller 48.99	3	OG	Seoul	1 Oct 88
:18.38	RUS		2	WCh	Stuttgart	22 Aug 93
		Ruzina 50.8, Alekseyeva 49.3, Ponomaryova 49.78, Privalova 48.47				
:18.43	URS		1	WCh	Tokyo	1 Sep 91
		Ledovskaya 51.7, Dzhigalova 49.2, Nazarova 48.87, Bryzgina 48.67				
:18.58	URS	I.Nazarova, Olizarenko, Pinigina, Vladykina	1	ECp	Moskva	18 Aug 85
:18.63	GDR	Neubauer 51.4, Emmelmann 49.1, Müller 48.64, Busch 49.48	1	WCh	Roma	6 Sep 87

Mark	Wind	Nat	Name	Pos	Meet	Venue	Date
3:19.01		USA	Trotter 49.8, Henderson 49.7, Richards 49.81, Hennagan 49.73	1	OG	Athína	28 Aug 04
3:19.04	WR	GDR	Siemon' 51.0, Busch 50.0, Rübsam 50.2, Koch 47.9	1	EC	Athína	11 Sep 82
3:19.12		URS	Baskakova, I.Nazarova, Pinigina, Vladykina	1	Drz	Praha	18 Aug 84
3:19.23	WR	GDR	Maletzki 50.05, Rohde 49.00, Streidt 49.51, Brehmer 49.79	1	OG	Montreal	31 Jul 76
3:19.49		GDR	Emmelmann, Busch, Neubauer, Koch 47.9	1	WCp	Canberra	4 Oct 85
3:19.50		URS	Yurchenko 51.2, O.Nazarova 50.2, Pinigina 49.09, Bryzgina 49.03	2	WCh	Roma	6 Sep 87
3:19.60		USA	Leatherwood, S.Howard, Brisco-Hooks, Cheeseborough	1		Walnut	25 Jul 84
3:19.62		GDR	Kotte, Brehmer, Köhn, Koch 48.3	1	ECp	Torino	5 Aug 79
3:19.66		GDR	Busch, Emmelmann, Neubauer, Müller 48,69	1	v FRG	Düsseldorf	20 Jun 88
			(20/4 with USSR and Russia counted separately)				
3:20.32		CZE/TCH		2	WCh	Helsinki	14 Aug 83
			Kocembová 48.93, Matejkovicová 52.13, Moravcíková 51.51, Kratochvílová 47.75				
3:20.65		JAM	Richards 50.9, Scott 50.1, Parris 49.70, Fenton 49.95	1	WCh	Edmonton	12 Aug 01
3:21.04		NGR	Afolabi 51.13, Yusuf 49.72, Opara 51.29, Ogunkoya 48.90	2	OG	Atlanta	3 Aug 96
3:21.21		CAN	Crooks 50.30, Richardson 50.22, Killingbeck 50.62, Payne 50.07	2	OG	Los Angeles	11 Aug 84
3:21.94		UKR	Dzhigalova, Olizarenko, Pinigina, Vladykina	1	URSCh	Kiyev	17 Jul 86
3:22.01		GBR	Hanson 51.8, Smith 51.0, Gunnell 49.46, Keough 49.71	4	WCh	Tokyo	1 Sep 91
		(10)					
3:22.34		FRA	Landre 51.3, Dorsile 51.1, Elien 50.54, Pérec 49.36	1	EC	Helsinki	14 Aug 94
3:22.49		FRG	Thimm 50.81, Arendt 49.95, Thomas 51.50, Abt 50.23	4	OG	Seoul	1 Oct 88
3:23.81		AUS	Peris-K 51.71, Lewis 51.69, Gainsford-T 51.06, Freeman 49.35	5	OG	Sydney	30 Sep 00
3:24.23		CUB	Bonne 51.91, Duporty 50.92, Morales 51.31, Quirot 50.09	2h2	OG	Atlanta	2 Aug 96
3:24.28		CHN	(Hebei) An X, Bai X, Cao C, Ma Y	1	NG	Beijing	13 Sep 93
3:24.49		POL	Guzowska 52.2, Bejnar 50.2, Prokopek 50.47, Jesien 51.59	4	WCh	Helsinki	14 Aug 05
3:25.68		ROM	Ruicu 52.69, Rîpanu 51.09, Barbu 52.64, Tîrlea 49.26	2	ECp	Paris (C)	20 Jun 99
3:25.7a		FIN	Eklund 53.6, Pursiainen 50.6, Wilmi 51.6, Salin 49.9	2	EC	Roma	8 Sep 74
3:25.81		BUL	Ilieva, Stamenova, Penkova, Damyanova	1	v Hun,Pol	Sofiya	24 Jul 83
3:26.31		BLR	Sologub 52.06, Budnik 51.11, Khlyustova 52.05, Kozak 50.09	3h1	OG	Sydney	29 Sep 00
		(20)					
3:26.33		GRE	Kaidantzi 53.2, Goudenoúdi 51.6, Boudá 51.76, Halkiá 49.75	3	ECpS	Bydgoszcz	20 Jun 04
3:26.69		ITA	Perpoli 51.81, Spuri 51.62, Carbone 52.61, De Angeli 50.65	5	ECp	Paris (C)	20 Jun 99
3:26.82		BRA	Almirão 52.3, Coutinho 52.1, Tito 51.56, Teodoro 50.82	2h2	WCh	Helsinki	13 Aug 05
3:26.89		IND	R Kaur 53.1, Beenamol 51.4, Soman 52.51, M Kaur 49.85	3h2	OG	Athína	27 Aug 04
3:27.08		CMR	Nguimgo 51.7, Kaboud 52.1, Atangana 51.98, Béwouda 51.35	7	WCh	Saint-Denis	31 Aug 03
3:27.54		LTU	Navickaite, Valiuliene, Mendzoryte, Ambraziene	3	SPART	Moskva	22 Jun 83
3:27.57		ESP	Merino 52.2, Lacambra 52.0, Myers 50.85, Ferrer 52.56	7	WCh	Tokyo	1 Sep 91
3:27.86		HUN	Orosz, Forgács, Tóth, Pál	5	OG	Moskva	1 Aug 80
3:27.88		MEX	Allen 53.5, Yanez 52.0, Guevara 50.27, González 52.16	5h2	OG	Athína	27 Aug 04
3:28.02		SEN	Diop 51.27, M T Diouf 51.70, A Diouf 52.53, Thiam 51.52	4h3	OG	Sydney	29 Sep 00

5000 METRES WALK (TRACK)

Mark	Wind	Name		Nat	Born	Pos	Meet	Venue	Date
20:02.60	WR	Gillian	O'Sullivan	IRL	21.8.76	1	NC	Dublin (S)	13 Jul 02
20:03.0	WR	Kerry	Saxby-Junna	AUS	2.6.61	1		Sydney	11 Feb 96
20:07.52	WR	Beate	Anders/Gummelt	GDR	4.2.68	1	vURS	Rostock	23 Jun 90
20:11.45		Sabine	Zimmer	GER	6.2.81	1	NC	Wattenscheid	2 Jul 05
20:12.41		Elisabetta	Perrone	ITA	9.7.68	1	NC	Rieti	2 Aug 03
20:18.87		Melanie	Seeger	GER	8.1.77	1	NC	Braunschweig	10 Jul 04
20:21.69		Annarita	Sidoti	ITA	25.7.69	1	NC	Cesenatico	1 Jul 95
20:27.59	WR	Ileana	Salvador	ITA	16.1.62	1		Trento	3 Jun 89
20:28.62		Sari	Essayah	FIN	21.2.67	1	NC	Tuusula	9 Jul 94
20:29.63		Claudia	Iovan/Stef ¶	ROM	25.2.78	1		Istanbul	19 Jun 99

10 KILOMETRES WALK

Mark	Wind	Name		Nat	Born	Pos	Meet	Venue	Date
41:04	WR	Yelena	Nikolayeva	RUS	1.2.66	1	NC	Sochi	20 Apr 96
41:16			Wang Yan	CHN	3.5.71	1		Eisenhüttenstadt	8 May 99
41:16		Kjersti	Plätzer (Tysse)	NOR	18.1.72	1	NC	Os	11 May 02
41:17		Irina	Stankina	RUS	25.3.77	1	NC-w	Adler	9 Feb 97
41:24		Olimpiada	Ivanova ¶	RUS	5.5.70	2	NC-w	Adler	9 Feb 97
41:29	WR	Larisa	Ramazanova	RUS	23.9.71	1	NC	Izhevsk	4 Jun 95
41:30	WR	Kerry	Saxby-Junna	AUS	2.6.61	1	NC	Canberra	27 Aug 88
41:30			O Ivanova			2	NC	Izhevsk	4 Jun 95
41:31		Yelena	Gruzinova	RUS	24.12.67	2	NC	Sochi	20 Apr 96
41:38			Gao Hongmiao	CHN	17.3.74	1	NC	Beijing	7 Apr 94
41:38		Rossella	Giordano (10)	ITA	1.12.72	1		Naumburg	25 May 97
41:41			Nikolayeva			2		Naumburg	25 May 97
41:45			Liu Hongyu	CHN	11.1.75	2		Eisenhüttenstadt	8 May 99
41:46		Annarita	Sidoti	ITA	25.7.69	1		Livorno	12 Jun 94
41:46			O Ivanova			1	NC/w	Adler	11 Feb 96
41:47			Saxby-Junna			1		Eisenhüttenstadt	11 May 96
41:48			Li Chunxiu	CHN	13.8.69	1	NG	Beijing	8 Sep 93

Mark	Wind	Name		Nat	Born	Pos	Meet	Venue	Date
41:49			Ramazanova			3	NC	Sochi	20 Apr 96
41:49			Nikolayeva			1	OG	Atlanta	29 Jul 96
41:50		Yelena	Arshintseva	RUS	5.4.71	1	NC-w	Adler	11 Feb 95
41:51		Beate	Anders/Gummelt	GER	4.2.68	2		Eisenhüttenstadt	11 May 96
41:52			Stankina			1	WCp	Podebrady	19 Apr 97
41:54			Plätzer			3		Eisenhüttenstadt	8 May 99
41:55			Stankina			1	NC-wj	Adler	11 Feb 95
41:56		Yelena	Sayko	RUS	24.12.67	2	NC/w	Adler	11 Feb 96
41:56			Khmelnitskaya	(Ramazanova)		1		Eisenhüttenstadt	10 May 97
41:56			Plätzer			1		Hildesheim	25 Aug 02
41:56.23t		Nadezhda	Ryashkina	RUS	22.1.67	1	GWG	Seattle	24 Jul 90
41:57			Gao Hongmiao			2	NG	Beijing	8 Sep 93
41:57.22t			Saxby-Junna			2	GWG	Seattle	24 Jul 90
		(30/17)							
42:01		Tamara	Kovalenko	RUS	5.6.64	3	NC-w	Adler	11 Feb 95
42:01		Olga	Panfyorova	RUS	21.8.77	1	NC-23	Izhevsk	16 May 98
42:05+		Margarita	Turova	BLR	28.12.80	1+	in 20k	Adler	12 Mar 05
		(20)							
42:06		Valentina	Tsybulskaya	BLR	19.2.68	4		Eisenhüttenstadt	8 May 99
42:07		Ileana	Salvador	ITA	16.1.62	1		Sesto San Giovanni	1 May 92
42:09		Elisabetta	Perrone	ITA	9.7.68	4		Eisenhüttenstadt	11 May 96
42:11		Nina	Alyushenko	RUS	29.5.68	3	NC	Izhevsk	4 Jun 95
42:13		Natalya	Misyulya	BLR	16.4.66	5		Eisenhüttenstadt	8 May 99
42:13.7t		Madelein	Svensson	SWE	20.7.69	2	SGP	Fana	15 May 92
42:15			Gu Yan	CHN	17.3.74	3	WCp	Podebrady	19 Apr 97
42:15		Erica	Alfridi	ITA	22.2.68	5		Naumburg	25 May 97
42:15		Jane	Saville	AUS	5.11.74	6		Eisenhüttenstadt	8 May 99
42:16		Alina	Ivanova	RUS	16.3.69	1		Novopolotsk	27 May 89
		(30)							
42:16		Norica	Cîmpean	ROM	22.3.72	1		Calella	9 May 99
42:17		Katarzyna	Radtke	POL	31.8.69	5		Eisenhüttenstadt	11 May 96
42:19+		Iraida	Pudovkina	RUS	2.11.80	2	in 20k	Adler	12 Mar 05
42:20		Sari	Essayah	FIN	21.2.67	4	WCh	Göteborg	7 Aug 95
42:29		Olga	Kardopoltseva	BLR	11.9.66	4		Eisenhüttenstadt	10 May 97
42:31		Vera	Nacharkina'	RUS	17.2.66	1	NC	Izhevsk	16 May 98
42:32		Maya	Sazonova	KAZ	28.5.68	4	Rus Ch	Sochi	20 Apr 96
42:34		Mária	Rosza/Urbaník	HUN	12.2.67	7	WCh	Göteborg	7 Aug 95
42:35		Claudia	Iovan/Stef ¶	ROM	25.2.78	2	NC	Alba Iulia	15 Sep 02
42:37		Olga	Lukyanchuk	UKR	7.12.76	1		Mukachevo	21 Oct 00
		(40)	50th woman 42:46.7, 100th 43:36, 200th 44:32, 300th 45:07						
42:39		Susana	Feitor	POR	28.1.75	1		Lanciano	11 Mar 01
Probable short course									
41:30		Ileana	Salvador	ITA	16.1.62	1	4-N	Livorno	10 Jul 93
41:56		Elisabeta	Perrone	ITA	9.7.68	2	4-N	Livorno	10 Jul 93
Best track times									
41:57.22		Kerry	Saxby-Junna	AUS	2.6.61	2	GWG	Seattle	24 Jul 90
42:11.5		Beate	Anders/Gummelt	GER	4.2.68	1	SGP	Fana	15 May 92
42:23.7		Ileana	Salvador	ITA	16.1.62	2	SGP	Fana	8 May 93
42:30.13			Gao Hongmiao	CHN	17.3.74	1		Nanjing	24 Oct 95
42:30.31		Olimpiada	Ivanova ¶	RUS	5.5.70	1	GWG	Sankt-Peterburg	26 Jul 94
42:37.0		Sari	Essayah	FIN	21.2.67	3	SGP	Fana	8 May 93
42:38.24			Liu Hongyu	CHN	11.1.75	2		Nanjing	24 Oct 95

20 KILOMETRES WALK

Mark	Wind	Name		Nat	Born	Pos	Meet	Venue	Date
1:24:50		Olimpiada	Ivanova ¶	RUS	5.5.70	1	NC-w	Adler	4 Mar 01
1:25:18		Tatyana	Gudkova	RUS	23.1.78	1	NC	Moskva	19 May 00
1:25:20		Olga	Polyakova	RUS	23.9.80	2	NC	Moskva	19 May 00
1:25:29		Irina	Stankina	RUS	25.3.77	3	NC	Moskva	19 May 00
1:25:41	WR		O Ivanova			1	WCh	Helsinki	7 Aug 05
1:25:59		Tamara	Kovalenko	RUS	5.6.64	4	NC	Moskva	19 May 00
1:26:08			Ivanova			5	NC	Moskva	19 May 00
1:26:22	WR		Wang Yan	CHN	3.5.71	1	NG	Guangzhou	19 Nov 01
1:26:22	WR	Yelena	Nikolayeva	RUS	1.2.66	1	ECp	Cheboksary	18 May 03
1:26:23			Wang Liping	CHN	8.7.76	2	NG	Guangzhou	19 Nov 01
1:26:28		Iraida	Pudovkina	RUS	2.11.80	1	NC-w	Adler	12 Mar 05
1:26:35		(10)	Liu Hongyu	CHN	11.1.75	3	NG	Guangzhou	19 Nov 01
1:26:42			O Ivanova			1	EC	München	7 Aug 02
1:26:46			Song Hongjuan	CHN	4.7.84	1	NC	Guangzhou	20 Mar 04
1:26:48			Ivanova			1	ECp	Eisenhüttenstadt	17 Jun 00

Mark	Wind	Name		Nat	Born	Pos	Meet	Venue	Date
1:26:48			Ivanova			1	ECp	Dudince	19 May 01
1:26:50		Natalya	Fedoskina	RUS	25.6.80	2	ECp	Dudince	19 May 01
1:26:52			Nikolayeva			1	WCh	Saint-Denis	24 Aug 03
1:26:52.3 t			Ivanova			1	GWG	Brisbane	6 Sep 01
1:26:54			Ivanova			1	NC	Cheboksary	12 Jun 04
1:27:02			Nikolayeva			1	NC	Cheboksary	25 May 02
1:27:05			Turova			2	WCh	Helsinki	7 Aug 05
1:27:09		Elisabetta	Perrone	ITA	9.7.68	3	ECp	Dudince	19 May 01
1:27:14		Antonina	Petrova	RUS	25.1.77	1	NC-w	Adler	1 Mar 03
1:27:16			Song Hongjuan			1	NC	Yangzhou	14 Apr 03
1:27:19			Jiang Jing	CHN	23.10.85	1	NC	Nanning	25 Feb 05
1:27:19			Turova			1		Rio Maior	2 Apr 05
1:27:22		Gillian	O'Sullivan	IRL	21.8.76	1		Sesto San Giovanni	1 May 03
1:27:23		Larisa	Yemelyanova (Safronova)	RUS	6.1.80	2	NC-w	Adler	1 Mar 03
1:27:24			Nikolayeva			1	WCp	Naumburg	2 May 04
1:27:24			Wang Liping			2	NC	Nanning	25 Feb 05
		(31/18)							
1:27:29		Erica	Alfridi	ITA	22.2.68	4	ECp	Dudince	19 May 01
1:27:30	WB	Nadezhda	Ryashkina	RUS	22.1.67	1	NC-w	Adler	7 Feb 99
		(20)							
1:27:30		Tatyana	Kozlova	RUS	2.9.83	2	NC-w	Adler	12 Mar 05
1:27:33		Tatyana	Sibilyeva	RUS	17.5.80	2	NC-w	Adler	4 Mar 01
1:27:35		Tatyana	Korotkova	RUS	24.4.80	2	NC	Cheboksary	12 Jun 04
1:27:36		María	Vasco	ESP	26.12.75	3	WCp	Naumburg	2 May 04
1:27:37			Bai Yanmin	CHN	29.6.87	1	NG	Nanjing	20 Oct 05
1:27:41		Claudia	Iovan/Stef ¶	ROM	25.2.78	1		La Coruña	5 Jun 04
1:27:44		Jane	Saville	AUS	5.11.74	4	WCp	Naumburg	2 May 04
1:27:46		Norica	Cîmpean	ROM	22.3.72	1		Békéscsaba	28 Mar 99
1:27:49		Elisa	Rigaudo	ITA	17.6.80	5	WCp	Naumburg	2 May 04
1:27:51		Lyudmila	Yefimkina	RUS	22.8.81	2	NC	Cheboksary	25 May 02
		(30)							
1:27:53		Kjersti	Tysse Plätzer	NOR	18.1.72	3	ECp	Eisenhüttenstadt	17 Jun 00
1:27:53		Yuliya	Voyevodina	RUS	17.10.71	7	WCp	Naumburg	2 May 04
1:27:54			Song Lijuan	CHN	9.2.75	2		Beijing	1 May 95
1:27:55		Susana	Feitor	POR	28.1.75	1		Rio Maior	7 Apr 01
1:27:56		Sabine	Zimmer	GER	6.2.81	1		Hildesheim	5 Jun 04
1:27:58			Yang Yawei	CHN	16.10.83	2		Cixi	23 Apr 05
1:28:01			Jiang Qiuyan	CHN	5.7.83	3		Cixi	23 Apr 05
1:28:07			Tang Yinghua	CHN	18.5.73	4		Cixi	23 Apr 05
1:28:10		Valentina	Tsybulskaya	BLR	19.2.68	3	WCh	Saint-Denis	24 Aug 03
1:28:11		Yelena	Ginko	BLR	30.7.76	5	RUS-w	Adler	12 Mar 05
		(40)							
1:28:13		Marina	Smyslova	RUS	25.2.66	3	NC	Cheboksary	12 Jun 04
1:28:17		Melanie	Seeger	GER	8.1.77	9	WCp	Naumburg	2 May 04
1:28:18			Kong Yan	CHN	6.7.73	3		Beijing	1 May 95
1:28:19		Vera	Zozulya	UKR	31.8.70	1	NC-w	Yevpatoriya	23 Feb 03
1:28:22			Shi Na	CHN	17.2.81	5		Cixi	23 Apr 05
1:28:24		Natalya	Misyulya	BLR	16.4.66	1	NC	Soligorsk	13 May 00
1:28:24		Margarita	Nazarova	RUS	1.10.76	6	NC	Cheboksary	25 May 02
1:28:35			He Dan	CHN	22.7.84	6		Cixi	23 Apr 05
1:28:38		Annarita	Sidoti	ITA	25.7.69	5	ECp	Eisenhüttenstadt	17 Jun 00
1:28:38		Svetlana	Tolstaya	KAZ	9.8.71	7	NC	Cheboksary	25 May 02
		(50)	100th best woman 1:31:05, 200th 1:33:59						

50 KILOMETRES WALK

Mark	Name		Nat	Born	Pos	Meet	Venue	Date
4:12:16	Yelena	Ginko	BLR	30.7.76	1		Scanzoroscaite	17 Oct 04
4:19:13		Ginko			1		Scanzorosciate	27 Oct 02
4:22:00		Ginko			1		Scanzoroscaite	19 Oct 03
4:28:13	Evaggelía	Xinoú	GRE	22.11.81	2		Scanzoroscaite	17 Oct 04
4:29:56	Natalia	Bruniko	ITA	23.2.73	2		Scanzorosciate	27 Oct 02
4:33:45	Lyudmila	Yegorova	UKR	4.10.74	3		Scanzoroscaite	17 Oct 04
4:36:45	Yelena	Krivokhizha	UKR	10.3.79	3		Scanzorosciate	28 Oct 01
4:39:45	Susan	Armenta	USA	19.9.73	1	NC	Chula Vista	17 Feb 02
4:41:57	Kora	Boufflért	FRA	23.4.66	1		Ay-Champagne	17 Sep 95

100 KILOMETRES WALK

Mark	Name		Nat	Born	Pos	Meet	Venue	Date
10:13:56	Kora	Boufflért	FRA	23.4.66	1		Roubaix	9 Oct 94
10:20:02	Lyudmila	Lyubomirova	RUS	13.11.62	1		Perpignan	15 Oct 95
10:23:47	Anita	Liepina	LAT	17.11.67	1		Scanzoroscaite	19 Oct 03

Mark	Wind	Name		Nat	Born	Pos	Meet	Venue	Date

JUNIOR WOMEN'S ALL-TIME LISTS

Based on the age regulations introduced for 1988, that is under 20 in year of competition.

100 METRES

Mark	Wind	Name		Nat	Born	Pos	Meet	Venue	Date
10.88	2.0	Marlies	Oelsner	GDR	21.3.58	1	NC	Dresden	1 Jul 77
10.89	1.8	Katrin	Krabbe	GDR	22.11.69	1rB		Berlin	20 Jul 88
11.03	1.7	Silke	Gladisch	GDR	20.6.64	3	OD	Berlin	8 Jun 83
11.04	1.4	Angela	Williams	USA	30.1.80	1	NCAA	Boise	5 Jun 99
11.08	2.0	Brenda	Morehead	USA	5.10.57	1	OT	Eugene	21 Jun 76
11.11	0.2	Shakedia	Jones	USA	15.3.79	1		Los Angeles (Ww)	2 May 98
11.11	1.1	Joan Uduak	Ekah	NGR	16.12.80	5	Athl	Lausanne	2 Jul 99
11.12	2.0	Veronica	Campbell	JAM	15.5.82	1	WJ	Santiago de Chile	18 Oct 00
11.13	2.0	Chandra	Cheeseborough	USA	10.1.59	2	OT	Eugene	21 Jun 76
11.13	-1.0	Grit	Breuer	GDR	16.2.72	1		Jena	6 Jun 90
11.13	1.5	Ashley	Owens	USA	19.11.85	1	WJ	Grosseto	14 Jul 04
Uncertain timing: 10.99	1.9	Natalya	Bochina	RUS	4.1.62	2		Leningrad	3 Jun 80
Wind assisted to 11.11									
10.96	3.7	Angela	Williams	USA	30.1.80	1		Las Vegas	3 Apr 99
10.97	3.3	Gesine	Walther	GDR	6.10.62	4	NC	Cottbus	16 Jul 80
11.02	2.1	Nikole	Mitchell	JAM	5.6.74	1	Mutual	Kingston	1 May 93
11.04	5.6	Kelly-Ann	Baptiste	TRI	14.10.86	1rB	TexR	Austin	9 Apr 05
11.06	2.2	Brenda	Morehead	USA	5.10.57	1s	OT	Eugene	21 Jun 76
11.09		Angela	Williams	TRI	15.5.65	1		Nashville	14 Apr 84

200 METRES

Mark	Wind	Name		Nat	Born	Pos	Meet	Venue	Date
22.11A	-0.5	Allyson	Felix	USA	18.11.85	1		Ciudad de México	3 May 03
		22.18	0.8			2	OG	Athína	25 Aug 04
22.19	1.5	Natalya	Bochina	RUS	4.1.62	2	OG	Moskva	30 Jul 80
22.37	1.3	Sabine	Rieger	GDR	6.11.63	2	vURS	Cottbus	26 Jun 82
22.42	0.4	Gesine	Walther	GDR	6.10.62	1		Potsdam	29 Aug 81
22.45	0.5	Grit	Breuer	GER	16.2.72	2	ASV	Köln	8 Sep 91
22.51	2.0	Katrin	Krabbe	GDR	22.11.69	3		Berlin	13 Sep 88
22.52	1.2	Mary	Onyali	NGR	3.2.68	6	WCh	Roma	3 Sep 87
22.58	0.8	Marion	Jones	USA	12.10.75	4	TAC	New Orleans	28 Jun 92
22.70		Marita	Koch	GDR	18.2.57	1		Halle	16 May 76
22.70A	1.9	Kathy	Smallwood	GBR	3.5.60	2	WUG	Ciudad de México	12 Sep 79
Indoors: 22.49i		Sanya	Richards	USA	26.2.85	2rA	NCAA	Fayetteville	12 Mar 04
Wind assisted to 22.66									
22.34	2.3	Katrin	Krabbe	GDR	22.11.69	1	WJ	Sudbury	30 Jul 88
22.49	2.3	Brenda	Morehead	USA	5.10.57	1	OT	Eugene	24 Jun 76
22.53	2.5	Valerie	Brisco	USA	6.7.60	2	AAU	Walnut	17 Jun 79
22.64	2.3	Chandra	Cheeseborough	USA	16.1.59	2	OT	Eugene	24 Jun 76
22.65	3.5	Shakedia	Jones	USA	15.3.79	1	NC-j	Edwardsville IL	27 Jun 98
22.66	5.0	Lauren	Hewitt	AUS	25.11.78	3	NC	Melbourne	2 Mar 97

400 METRES

Mark	Wind	Name		Nat	Born	Pos	Meet	Venue	Date
49.42		Grit	Breuer	GER	16.2.72	2	WCh	Tokyo	27 Aug 91
49.77		Christina	Brehmer	GDR	28.2.58	1		Dresden	9 May 76
49.89		Sanya	Richards	USA	26.2.85	2	NC/OT	Sacramento	17 Jul 04
50.01			Li Jing	CHN	14.2.80	1	NG	Shanghai	18 Oct 97
50.19		Marita	Koch	GDR	18.2.57	3	OD	Berlin	10 Jul 76
50.58		Sanya	Richards	USA	26.2.85	1	NCAA	Sacramento	14 Jun 03
50.59		Fatima	Yusuf	NGR	2.5.71	1	HGP	Budapest	5 Aug 90
		50.5 hand				1	NC	Lagos	25 Aug 90
50.74		Monique	Henderson	USA	18.2.83	1		Norwalk	3 Jun 00
50.86		Charity	Opara	NGR	20.5.72	2		Bologna	7 Sep 91
50.87		Denean	Howard	USA	5.10.64	1	TAC	Knoxville	20 Jun 82
50.87		Magdalena	Nedelcu	ROM	12.5.74	1	NC-j	Bucuresti	31 Jul 92

800 METRES

Mark	Wind	Name		Nat	Born	Pos	Meet	Venue	Date
1:57.18			Wang Yuan	CHN	8.4.76	2h2	NG	Beijing	8 Sep 93
1:57.45		Hildegard	Ullrich	GDR	20.12.59	5	EC	Praha	31 Aug 78
1:57.62			Lang Yinglai	CHN	22.8.79	1	NG	Shanghai	22 Oct 97
1:57.63		Maria	Mutola	MOZ	27.10.72	4	WCh	Tokyo	26 Aug 91
1:57.77			Lu Yi	CHN	10.4.74	4	NG	Beijing	9 Sep 93
1:57.86		Katrin	Wühn	GDR	19.11.65	1		Celje	5 May 84
1:58.16			Lin Nuo	CHN	.1.80	3	NG	Shanghai	22 Oct 97
1:58.18		Marion	Hübner	GDR	29.9.62	2		Erfurt	2 Aug 81
1:58.24		Christine	Wachtel	GDR	6.1.65	3		Potsdam	25 May 84
1:58.37		Gabriela	Sedláková	SVK	2.3.68	4	ISTAF	Berlin	21 Aug 87

Mark	Wind	Name		Nat	Born	Pos	Meet	Venue	Date

1500 METRES

Mark	Wind	Name		Nat	Born	Pos	Meet	Venue	Date
3:51.34			Lang Yinglai	CHN	22.8.79	2	NG	Shanghai	18 Oct 97
3:53.91			Yin Lili	CHN	11.11.79	3	NG	Shanghai	18 Oct 97
3:53.97			Lan Lixin	CHN	14.2.79	4	NG	Shanghai	18 Oct 97
3:54.52			Zhang Ling	CHN	13.4.80	5	NG	Shanghai	18 Oct 97
3:59.60		Gelete	Burka	ETH	15.2.86	5	GP	Rieti	28 Aug 05
3:59.81			Wang Yuan	CHN	8.4.76	7	NG	Beijing	11 Sep 93
3:59.96		Zola	Budd	GBR	26.5.66	3	VD	Bruxelles	30 Aug 85
4:00.05			Lu Yi	CHN	10.4.74	8	NG	Beijing	11 Sep 93
4:01.71			Li Ying	CHN	24.6.75	4h2	NG	Beijing	10 Sep 93
4:03.45		Anita	Weyermann	SUI	8.12.77	1	Athl	Lausanne	3 Jul 96
1 MILE:		4:17.57 Zola	Budd	GBR	26.5.66	3	WK	Zürich	21 Aug 85
2000 METRES:		5:33.15 Zola	Budd	GBR	26.5.66	1		London	13 Jul 84

3000 METRES

Mark	Wind	Name		Nat	Born	Pos	Meet	Venue	Date
8:28.83		Zola	Budd	GBR	26.5.66	3	GG	Roma	7 Sep 85
8:35.89		Sally	Barsosio	KEN	21.3.78	2	Herc	Monaco	16 Aug 97
8:36.45			Ma Ningning	CHN	1.6.76	4	NC	Jinan	6 Jun 93
8:39.90		Gelete	Burka	ETH	15.2.86	3	SGP	Doha	13 May 05
8:40.08		Gabriela	Szabo	ROM	14.11.75	3	EC	Helsinki	12 Aug 94
8:40.28		Meseret	Defar	ETH	19.11.83	10	VD	Bruxelles	30 Aug 02
8:41.86		Tirunesh	Dibaba	ETH	2.6.85	11	VD	Bruxelles	30 Aug 02
8:42.39			Li Ying	CHN	24.6.75	8	NG	Beijing	13 Sep 93
8:42.63		Sentayehu	Ejigu	ETH	21.6.85	5	WAF	Monaco	19 Sep 04
8:44.1mx		Donna	Gould	AUS	10.6.66	-		Eugene	13 Jul 84

5000 METRES

Mark	Wind	Name		Nat	Born	Pos	Meet	Venue	Date
14:30.88		Tirunesh	Dibaba	ETH	2.6.85	2	Bisl	Bergen (Fana)	11 Jun 04
14:35.18		Sentayehu	Ejigu	ETH	21.6.85	4	Bisl	Bergen (Fana)	11 Jun 04
14:39.96			Yin Lili	CHN	11.11.79	4	NG	Shanghai	23 Oct 97
14:45.33			Lan Lixin	CHN	14.2.79	2h2	NG	Shanghai	21 Oct 97
14:45.71			Song Liqing	CHN	20.1.80	3h2	NG	Shanghai	21 Oct 97
14:45.90			Jiang Bo	CHN	13.3.77	1		Nanjing	24 Oct 95
14:46.71		Sally	Barsosio	KEN	21.3.78	3	VD	Bruxelles	22 Aug 97
14:47.40		Worknesh	Kidane	ETH	21.11.81	7	OG	Sydney	25 Sep 00
14:48.07		Zola	Budd	GBR	26.5.66	1	McV	London (CP)	26 Aug 85
14:51.47		Gelete	Burka	ETH	15.2.86	10	GGala	Roma	8 Jul 05
14:53.44		Lydia	Cheromei	KEN	11.5.77	3	ISTAF	Berlin	1 Sep 95

10,000 METRES

Mark	Wind	Name		Nat	Born	Pos	Meet	Venue	Date
30:31.55			Xing Huina	CHN	25.2.84	7	WCh	Saint-Denis	23 Aug 03
30:39.41			Lan Lixin	CHN	14.2.79	2	NG	Shanghai	19 Oct 97
30:39.98			Yin Lili	CHN	11.11.79	3	NG	Shanghai	19 Oct 97
30:59.92		Merima	Hashim	ETH	.81	3	NA	Heusden	5 Aug 00
31:06.20		Lucy	Wangui	KEN	24.3.84	1rA		Okayama	27 Sep 03
31:11.26			Song Liqing	CHN	20.1.80	7	NG	Shanghai	19 Oct 97
31:15.38		Sally	Barsosio	KEN	21.3.78	3	WCh	Stuttgart	21 Aug 93
31:27.35			Bao Guiying	CHN	20.1.86	3	NG	Nanjing	17 Oct 05
31:28.88			Bai Xue	CHN	13.12.88	4	NG	Nanjing	17 Oct 05
31:32.15			Feng Wenhui	CHN	21.1.74	9	NG	Beijing	8 Sep 93
31:39.89		Julia	Mombi	KEN	25.1.85	1		Yokohama	23 Dec 04

MARATHON

Mark	Wind	Name		Nat	Born	Pos	Meet	Venue	Date
2:23:37			Liu Min	CHN	29.11.83	1		Beijing	14 Oct 01
2:23:57			Zhu Xiaolin	CHN	20.4.84	4		Beijing	20 Oct 02
2:25:48			Jin Li	CHN	29.5.83	6		Beijing	14 Oct 01
2:26:34			Wei Yanan	CHN	6.12.81	1		Beijing	15 Oct 00
2:27:30			Ai Dongmei	CHN	15.10.79	3	NG	Beijing	4 Oct 97
2:27:37			Lu Cui	CHN	26.3.85	10		Beijing	20 Oct 02
2:29:12		Chika	Horie	JPN	15.2.81	4		Nagano	9 Apr 00
2:29:33			Wang Linan	CHN	26.11.85	4		Beijing	19 Oct 03

3000 METRES STEEPLECHASE

Mark	Wind	Name		Nat	Born	Pos	Meet	Venue	Date
9:30.70		Melissa	Rollison	AUS	13.4.83	1	GWG	Brisbane	4 Sep 01
9:47.26		Gladys Jerotich	Kipkemboi	KEN	15.10.86	1	WJ	Grosseto	15 Jul 04
9:49.03		Ancuta	Bobocel	ROM	3.10.87	2	WJ	Grosseto	15 Jul 04
9:50.63		Mercy	Njoroge	KEN	10.6.86	1	Afr-J	Radès	4 Sep 05
9:52.25		Mercy	Wanjiku	KEN	10.6.86	4	WJ	Grosseto	15 Jul 04
9:54.01			Ju Yinglan	CHN	10.10.84	2	NC	Shanghai	13 Sep 03

Mark	Wind	Name		Nat	Born	Pos	Meet	Venue	Date
9:59.33		Verena	Dreier	GER	15.1.85	5	WJ	Grosseto	15 Jul 04
10:00.32		Yuliya	Mochalova	RUS	26.5.87	1		Cheboksary	28 Jun 04
10:01.56		Galina	Yegorova	RUS	5.8.83	1		Cheboksary	27 Jul 02
10:02.07			Zhang Chong	CHN	5.1.86	2	NGPF	Tiantai	27 Oct 02

100 METRES HURDLES

Mark	Wind	Name		Nat	Born	Pos	Meet	Venue	Date
12.84	1.5	Aliuska	López	CUB	29.8.69	2	WUG	Zagreb	16 Jul 87
12.88	1.5	Yelena	Ovcharova	UKR	17.6.76	2	ECp	Villeneuve d'Ascq	25 Jun 95
12.89	1.3	Anay	Tejeda	CUB	3.4.83	1		Padova	1 Sep 02
12.92	0.0		Sun Hongwei	CHN	24.11.79	6	NG	Shanghai	18 Oct 97
12.95	1.5	Candy	Young	USA	21.5.62	2	AAU	Walnut	16 Jun 79
12.95A	1.5	Cinnamon	Sheffield	USA	8.3.70	2	NCAA	Provo	3 Jun 89
13.00	0.7	Gloria	Kovarik	GDR	13.1.64	3h2	NC	Karl-Marx-Stadt	16 Jun 83
13.00	2.0	Lyudmila	Khristosenko	UKR	14.10.66	1	NC-j	Krasnodar	16 Jul 85
13.01	0.4	Sally	McLellan	AUS	19.9.86	1		Brisbane	27 Nov 05
13.02	-1.7	Susanna	Kallur	SWE	16.2.81	1	WJ	Santiago de Chile	19 Oct 00
13.02	0.5	Gergana	Stoyanova	BUL	3.1.82	1h3	NC-j	Sofia	15 Jun 01

Wind assisted to 13.00

Mark	Wind	Name		Nat	Born	Pos	Meet	Venue	Date
12.81	3.4	Anay	Tejeda	CUB	3.4.83	1	WJ	Kingston	21 Jul 02
12.90	3.0	Adrianna	Lamalle	FRA-J	27.9.82	1		Fort-de-France	28 Apr 01
13.00	3.5	Gergana	Stoyanova	BUL	3.1.82	1h1	EJ	Grosseto	20 Jul 01

400 METRES HURDLES

Mark	Wind	Name		Nat	Born	Pos	Meet	Venue	Date
54.40			Wang Xing	CHN	30.11.86	2	NG	Nanjing	21 Oct 05
54.70		Lashinda	Demus	USA	10.3.83	1	WJ	Kingston	19 Jul 02
54.93			Li Rui	CHN	22.11.79	1	NG	Shanghai	22 Oct 97
55.15			Huang Xiaoxiao	CHN	3.3.83	2	NG	Guangzhou	22 Nov 01
55.20		Lesley	Maxie	USA	4.1.67	2	TAC	San Jose	9 Jun 84
55.20A		Jana	Pittman	AUS	9.11.82	1		Pietersburg	18 Mar 00
55.22		Tiffany	Ross	USA	5.2.83	2	NCAA	Baton Rouge	31 May 02
55.26		Ionela	Tîrlea	ROM	9.2.76	1	Nik	Nice	12 Jul 95
55.43			Li Shuju	CHN	20.7.81	1h2	NG	Shanghai	21 Oct 97
55.53		Radostina	Dimitrova	BUL	1.6.66	3	OD	Potsdam	21 Jul 84

Drugs disqualification: 54.54 Peng Yinghua ¶ CHN 21.2.79 (2) NG Shanghai 22 Oct 97

HIGH JUMP

Mark	Wind	Name		Nat	Born	Pos	Meet	Venue	Date
2.01		Olga	Turchak	KZK	5.3.67	2	GWG	Moskva	7 Jul 86
2.01		Heike	Balck	GDR	19.8.70	1	vURS-j	Karl-Marx-Stadt	18 Jun 89
2.00		Stefka	Kostadinova	BUL	25.3.65	1		Sofiya	25 Aug 84
2.00		Alina	Astafei	ROM	7.6.69	1	WJ	Sudbury	29 Jul 88
1.98		Silvia	Costa	CUB	4.5.64	2	WUG	Edmonton	11 Jul 83
1.98		Yelena	Yelesina	RUS	5.4.70	1	Druzh	Nyiregyháza	13 Aug 88
1.97		Svetlana	Isaeva	BUL	18.3.67	2		Sofiya	25 May 86
1.96A		Charmaine	Gale	RSA	27.2.64	1	NC-j	Bloemfontein	4 Apr 81
1.96i		Desislava	Aleksandrova	BUL	27.10.75	2	EI	Paris	12 Mar 94
1.96		Marina	Kuptsova	RUS	22.12.81	1	NC	Tula	26 Jul 00
1.96		Blanka	Vlasic	CRO	8.11.83	1	WJ	Kingston	20 Jul 02

POLE VAULT

Mark	Wind	Name		Nat	Born	Pos	Meet	Venue	Date
4.48i		Silke	Spiegelburg	GER	17.3.86	2		Münster	25 Aug 05
		4.42				3		Beckum	21 Aug 05
4.47i		Yelena	Isinbayeva	RUS	3.6.82	1		Budapest	10 Feb 01
		4.46				2	ISTAF	Berlin	31 Aug 01
4.45i			Zhao Yingying	CHN	15.2.86	3		Madrid	24 Feb 05
		4.40				1		Nanjing	1 May 04
4.42		Yvonne	Buschbaum	GER	14.7.80	1		Rheinau-Freistett	27 Jun 99
4.41		Floé	Kühnert	GER	6.3.84	1		Mannheim	15 Jun 02
4.37i		Ekateríni	Stefanídi	GRE	4.2.90	1		Athína (P)	20 Feb 05
4.35		Yuliya	Golubchikova	RUS	27.3.83	2	Mos Ch	Moskva	28 Jun 02
4.33i		Vanessa	Boslak	FRA	11.6.82	5		Liévin	25 Feb 01
		4.32				1		La Roche-sur-Yon	23 Sep 00
4.32i		Mary	Saxer	USA	21.6.87	1		Landover	13 Mar 05
4.31		Monika	Götz	GER	15.6.81	1		Troisdorf	9 May 98
4.31		Amandine	Homo	FRA	24.12.80	3	GP-II	Saint-Denis	3 Jul 99

LONG JUMP

Mark	Wind	Name		Nat	Born	Pos	Meet	Venue	Date
7.14	1.1	Heike	Daute	GDR	16.12.64	1	PTS	Bratislava	4 Jun 83
7.00	-0.2	Birgit	Grosshennig	GDR	21.2.65	2		Berlin	9 Jun 84
6.94	-0.5	Magdalena	Khristova	BUL	25.2.77	2		Kalamata	22 Jun 96
6.91	0.0	Anisoara	Cusmir	ROM	29.6.62	1		Bucuresti	23 May 81
6.90	1.4	Beverly	Kinch	GBR	14.1.64	*	WCh	Helsinki	14 Aug 83

Jnr WOMEN All-time

Mark	Wind	Name	Nat	Born	Pos	Meet	Venue	Date
6.88	0.6	Natalya Shevchenko	RUS	28.12.66	2		Sochi	26 May 84
6.84		Larisa Baluta	UKR	13.8.65	2		Krasnodar	6 Aug 83
6.82	1.8	Fiona May	GBR	12.12.69	*	WJ	Sudbury	30 Jul 88
6.81	1.6	Carol Lewis	USA	8.8.63	1	TAC	Knoxville	20 Jun 82
6.81	1.4	Yelena Davydova	KZK	16.11.67	1	NC-j	Krasnodar	17 Jul 85
Wind assisted								
7.27	2.2	Heike Daute	GDR	16.12.64	1	WCh	Helsinki	14 Aug 83
6.93	4.6	Beverly Kinch	GBR	14.1.64	5	WCh	Helsinki	14 Aug 83
6.88	2.1	Fiona May	GBR	12.12.69	1	WJ	Sudbury	30 Jul 88
6.84	2.8	Anu Kaljurand	EST	16.4.69	2		Riga	4 Jun 88

TRIPLE JUMP

Mark	Wind	Name	Nat	Born	Pos	Meet	Venue	Date
14.62	1.0	Teresa Marinova	BUL	5.9.77	1	WC	Sydney	25 Aug 96
14.57	0.2	Huang Qiuyan	CHN	25.1.80	1	NG	Shanghai	19 Oct 97
14.52	0.6	Anastasiya Ilyina	RUS	16.1.82	q	WJ	Santiago de Chile	20 Oct 00
14.46	1.0	Peng Fengmei	CHN	2.7.79	1		Chengdu	18 Apr 98
14.38	-0.7	Xie Limei	CHN	27.6.86	1	AsiC	Inchon	1 Sep 05
14.37i	-	Ren Ruiping	CHN	1.2.76	3	WI	Barcelona	11 Mar 95
		14.36 0.0			1	NC	Beijing	1 Jun 94
14.32	-0.1	Yelena Lysak ¶	RUS	19.10.75	1		Voronezh	18 Jun 94
14.29	1.2	Mabel Gay	CUB	5.5.83	1		La Habana	5 Apr 02
14.23		Li Jiahui	CHN	8.8.79	1	Asi-J	Bangkok	6 Nov 97
14.22	1.2	Yusmay Bicet	CUB	8.12.83	2		La Habana	23 Feb 02
14.19	2.0	Anna Pyatkh	RUS	4.4.81	1		Lapinlahti	16 Jul 00
Wind assisted								
14.83A	8.3	Ren Ruiping	CHN	1.2.76	1	NC	Taiyuan	21 May 95
14.43	2.7	Yelena Lysak ¶	RUS	19.10.75	1	WJ	Lisboa	21 Jul 94

SHOT

Mark	Wind	Name	Nat	Born	Pos	Meet	Venue	Date
20.54		Astrid Kumbernuss	GDR	5.2.70	1	vFIN-j	Orimattila	1 Jul 89
20.51i		Heidi Krieger	GDR	20.7.65	2		Budapest	8 Feb 84
		20.24			5		Spilt	30 Apr 84
20.23		Ilke Wyludda	GDR	28.3.69	1	NC-j	Karl-Marx-Stadt	16 Jul 88
20.12		Ilona Schoknecht	GDR	24.9.56	2	NC	Erfurt	23 Aug 75
20.02		Cheng Xiaoyan	CHN	30.11.75	3	NC	Beijing	5 Jun 94
19.90		Stephanie Storp	FRG	28.11.68	1		Hamburg	16 Aug 87
19.63		Wang Yawen	CHN	23.8.73	1		Shijiazhuang	25 Apr 92
19.57		Grit Haupt	GDR	4.6.66	1		Gera	7 Jul 84
19.48		Ines Wittich	GDR	14.11.69	5		Leipzig	29 Jul 87
19.42		Simone Michel	GDR	18.12.60	3	vSU	Leipzig	23 Jun 79

DISCUS

Mark	Wind	Name	Nat	Born	Pos	Meet	Venue	Date
74.40		Ilke Wyludda	GDR	28.3.69	2		Berlin	13 Sep 88
67.38		Irina Meszynski	GDR	24.3.62	1		Berlin	14 Aug 81
67.00		Jana Günther	GDR	7.1.68	6	NC	Potsdam	20 Aug 87
66.80		Svetla Mitkova	BUL	17.6.64	1		Sofiya	2 Aug 83
66.60		Astrid Kumbernuss	GDR	5.2.70	1		Berlin	20 Jul 88
66.34		Franka Dietzsch	GDR	22.1.68	2		St Denis	11 Jun 87
66.30		Jana Lauren	GDR	28.6.70	1	vURS-j	Karl-Marx-Stadt	18 Jun 89
66.08		Cao Qi	CHN	15.1.74	1	NG	Beijing	12 Sep 93
65.96		Grit Haupt	GDR	4.6.66	3		Leipzig	13 Jul 84
65.22		Daniela Costian	ROM	30.4.65	3		Nitra	26 Aug 84

HAMMER

Mark	Wind	Name	Nat	Born	Pos	Meet	Venue	Date
73.24		Zhang Wenxiu	CHN	22.3.86	1	NC	Changsha	24 Jun 05
71.71		Kamila Skolimowska	POL	4.11.82	1	GPF	Melbourne	9 Sep 01
70.39		Mariya Smolyachkova	BLR	10.2.85	1		Staiki	26 Jun 04
69.73		Natalya Zolotukhina	UKR	4.1.85	1		Kiev	24 Jul 04
68.74		Arasay Thondike	CUB	28.5.86	2	Barr	La Habana	2 May 05
68.50		Martina Danisová	SVK	21.3.83	1		Kladno	16 Jun 01
68.40		Bianca Achilles	GER	17.4.81	1		Dortmund	25 Sep 99
68.18		Ivana Brkljacic	CRO	25.1.83	1		Pula	28 Apr 00
66.97		Gu Yuan	CHN	9.5.82	1	NG	Guangzhou	22 Nov 01
66.97		Liliya Razinkova	UKR	27.11.85	1		Donetsk	17 Apr 04
66.34		Yipsi Moreno	CUB	19.11.80	1		Ciudad de México	29 May 99

JAVELIN

Mark	Wind	Name	Nat	Born	Pos	Meet	Venue	Date
62.93		Xue Juan	CHN	10.2.86	1	NG	Changsha	27 Oct 03
61.99		Wang Yaning	CHN	4.1.80	1	NC	Huizhou	14 Oct 99
61.79		Nikolett Szabó	HUN	3.3.80	1		Schwechat	23 May 99
61.49		Liang Lili	CHN	16.11.83	1	NC	Benxi	1 Jun 02

Mark	Wind	Name		Nat	Born	Pos	Meet	Venue	Date
Pre 1999 specification									
71.88		Antoaneta	Todorova	BUL	8.6.63	1	ECp	Zagreb	15 Aug 81
71.82		Ivonne	Leal	CUB	27.2.66	1	WUG	Kobe	30 Aug 85
70.12		Karen	Forkel	GDR	24.9.70	1	EJ	Varazdin	26 Aug 89
68.94		Trine	Solberg	NOR	18.4.66	1	vURS	Oslo	16 Jul 85
68.38		Antje	Kempe	GDR	23.6.63	Q	EC	Athína	8 Sep 82
68.17		Osleidys	Menéndez	CUB	14.11.79	1	WJ	Annecy	29 Jul 98

HEPTATHLON

Mark	Name		Nat	Born	Pos	Meet	Venue	Date
6542	Carolina	Klüft	SWE	2.2.83	1	EC	München	10 Aug 02
	13.33/-0.3 1.89 13.16 23.71/-0.3 6.36/1.1 47.61 2:17.99							
6465	Sibylle	Thiele	GDR	6.3.65	1	EJ	Schwechat	28 Aug 83
	13.49 1.90 14.63 24.07 6.65 36.22 2:18.36							
6436	Sabine	Braun	FRG	19.6.65	1	vBUL	Mannheim	9 Jun 84
	13.68 1.78 13.09 23.88 6.03 52.14 2:09.41							
6428	Svetla	Dimitrova ¶	BUL	27.1.70	1	NC	Sofiya	18 Jun 89
	13.49/-0/7 1.77 13.98 23.59/-0.2 6.49/0.7 40.10 2:11.10							
6403	Emilia	Dimitrova	BUL	13.11.67	6	GWG	Moskva	7 Jul 86
	13.73 1.76 13.46 23.17 6.29 43.30 2:09.85							
6276	Larisa	Nikitina	RUS	29.4.65	8	URS Ch	Kiyev	21 Jun 84
	13.87/1.6 1.86 14.04 25.26/-0.7 6.31/0.1 48.62 2:22.76							
6218	Jana	Sobotka	GDR	3.10.65	6	OD	Potsdam	21 Jul 84
	14.40 1.74 13.28 24.19 6.27 43.64 2:06.83							
6198	Anke	Schmidt	GDR	5.2.68	7		Götzis	24 May 87
	13.80/0.9 1.72 13.32 23.82/0.3 6.63/2.0 35.78 2:12.44							
6194	Camelia	Cornateanu	ROM	23.1.67	2	NC	Pitesti	8 Aug 86
	14.35 1.86 14.70 24.97 6.15 38.94 2:11.93							
6187	Ionica	Domniteanu	ROM	8.1.69	1	Bal-j	Pitesti	26 Jul 87
	13.51 1.77 14.56 24.66 6.00 43.86 2:17.60							
Drugs disqualification: 6534	Svetla	Dimitrova	BUL	27.1.70	H	ECp	Helmond	16 Jul 89
	13.30/1.0 1.84 14.35 23.33/-2.2 6.47/-1.4 39.20 2:13.56							

10 KILOMETRES WALK

Mark	Name		Nat	Born	Pos	Meet	Venue	Date
41:55	Irina	Stankina	RUS	25.3.77	1	NCw-j	Adler	11 Feb 95
41:57		Gao Hongmiao	CHN	17.3.74	2	NG	Beijing	8 Sep 93
42:44		Long Yuwen	CHN	1.8.75	3	NC	Shenzen	18 Feb 93
42:45		Li Yuxin	CHN	4.12.74	4		Shenzhen	18 Feb 93
42:47		Liu Hongyu	CHN	1.12.75	5	NC	Shenzen	18 Feb 93
42:50		Gu Yan	CHN	17.3.74	4	NG	Beijing	8 Sep 93
42:53.9t		Tan Lihong	CHN	13.2.73	6	NC	Jinan	15 Mar 92
43:07		Song Lijuan	CHN	1.2.76	6	NG	Beijing	8 Sep 93
43:10.4		Zhang Qinghua	CHN	6.3.73	8	NC	Jinan	15 Mar 92
43:11.34t	Vera	Sokolova	RUS	8.6.87	1	EJ	Kaunas	21Jul 05

20 KILOMETRES WALK

Mark	Name		Nat	Born	Pos	Meet	Venue	Date
1:27:16		Song Hongjuan	CHN	4.7.84	1	NC	Yangzhou	14 Apr 03
1:27:34		Jiang Jing	CHN	23.10.85	2	WCp	Naumburg	2 May 04
1:27:35	Natalya	Fedoskina	RUS	25.6.80	2	WCp	Mézidon-Canon	2 May 99
1:27:37		Bai Yanmin	CHN	29.6.87	1	NG	Nanjing	20 Oct 05
1:29:09	Olga	Polyakova	RUS	23.9.80	5	NC-w	Adler	7 Feb 99

4 X 100 METRES RELAY

Mark	Nat	Team	Pos	Meet	Venue	Date
43.38	USA	Joyce, A.Williams, Robinson, Buchanan	1	PAm-J	Tampa	11 Jul 99
43.40	JAM	Simpson, Stewart, McLaughlin, Facey	1	WJ	Kingston	20 Jul 02
43.44A	NGR	Utondu, Iheagwam, Onyali, Ogunkoya	1	AfrG	Nairobi	9 Aug 87
43.48	GDR	Breuer, Krabbe, Dietz, Henke	1	WJ	Sudbury	31 Jul 88
	Unsanctioned race 43.33	Breuer, Krabbe, Dietz, Henke	1		Berlin	20 Jul 88
43.68	FRA	Vouaux, Jacques-Sebastien, Kamga, Banco	3	WJ	Grosseto	18 Jul 04
43.87	URS	Lapshina, Doronina, Bulatova, Kovalyova	1	vGDR-j	Leningrad	20 Jun 87
44.04	CUB	Riquelme, Allen, López, Valdivia	2	WJ	Sudbury	31 Jul 88
44.14	TRI	Francis, Hutson, Cabral, Baptiste	4	WJ	Grosseto	18 Jul 04

4 X 400 METRES RELAY

Mark	Nat	Team	Pos	Meet	Venue	Date
3:27.60	USA	Anderson, Kidd, Smith, Hastings	1	WJ	Grosseto	18 Jul 04
3:28.39	GDR	Derr, Fabert, Wöhlk, Breuer	1	WJ	Sudbury	31 Jul 88
3:29.66	JAM	Stewart, Morgan, Walker, Hall	1	PennR	Philadelphia	28 Apr 01
3:30.03	RUS	Talko, Shapayeva, Soldatova, Kostetskaya	2	WJ	Grosseto	18 Jul 04
3:30.38	AUS	Scamps, R Poetschka, Hanigan, Andrews	1	WJ	Plovdiv	12 Aug 90
3:30.46	GBR	Wall, Spencer, James,. Miller	2	WJ	Kingston	21 Jul 02
3:30.72	BUL	Kireva, Angelova, Rashova, Dimitrova	3	v2N	Sofiya	24 Jul 83
3:31.57	ROM	Petrea, Florea, Tîrlea, Nedelcu	1	WJ	Seoul	20 Sep 92

ALL-TIME INDOOR LISTS

60 METRES MEN

Mark Wind	Name		Nat	Born	Pos	Meet	Venue	Date
6.39	Maurice	Greene	USA	23.7.74	1rA		Madrid	3 Feb 98
6.41	Andre	Cason	USA	20.1.69	1		Madrid	14 Feb 92
6.43	Tim	Harden	USA	27.1.74	2	WI	Maebashi	7 Mar 99
6.45	Bruny	Surin	CAN	12.7.67	1		Liévin	13 Feb 93
6.45A	Leonard	Myles-Mills	GHA	5.9.73	1	WAC	Air Force Academy	20 Feb 99
6.45A	Terrence	Trammell	USA	23.11.78	1		Pocatello	17 Feb 01
6.45	Justin	Gatlin	USA	10.2.82	1	NC	Boston	1 Mar 03
6.45	Ronald	Pognon	FRA	16.11.82	1		Karlsruhe	13 Feb 05
6.46	Jon	Drummond	USA	9.9.68	2rA	Spark	Stuttgart	1 Feb 98
6.46A	Marcus	Brunson	USA	24.4.78	1		Flagstaff	30 Jan 99
6.46	Jason	Gardener	GBR	17.9.75	3	WI	Maebashi	7 Mar 99
6.46	Tim	Montgomery	USA	28.1.75	2	WI	Lisboa	11 Mar 01
6.46	Leonard	Scott	USA	19.1.80	1		Liévin	26 Feb 05

60 METRES HURDLES MEN

Mark Wind	Name		Nat	Born	Pos	Meet	Venue	Date
7.30	Colin	Jackson	GBR	18.2.67	1		Sindelfingen	6 Mar 94
7.36r?	Greg	Foster	USA	4.8.58	1	Sunk	Los Angeles	6 Jan 87
	7.42				1		San Sebastián	15 Mar 91
7.36	Allen	Johnson	USA	1.3.71	1	WI	Budapest	6 Mar 04
7.37	Roger	Kingdom	USA	26.8.62	1		Pireas	8 Mar 89
7.37	Anier	García	CUB	9.3.76	1		Pireás	9 Feb 00
7.37	Tony	Dees	USA	6.8.63	1		Chemnitz	18 Feb 00
7.38	Mark	Crear	USA	2.10.68	1		Sindelfingen	8 Mar 98
7.38	Reggie	Torian	USA	22.4.75	1	NC	Atlanta	27 Feb 99
7.41	Courtney	Hawkins	USA	11.7.67	2	WI	Barcelona	12 Mar 95
7.41	Falk	Balzer	GER	14.12.73	1h2		Chemnitz	29 Jan 99
7.42	Igor	Kazanov	LAT	24.9.63	1		Moskva	25 Feb 89
7.42	Anthony	Jarrett	GBR	13.8.68	2		Liévin	19 Feb 95
7.42	Terrence	Trammell	USA	23.11.78	1	Tyson	Fayetteville	15 Feb 03

60 METRES WOMEN

Mark Wind	Name		Nat	Born	Pos	Meet	Venue	Date
6.92	Irina	Privalova	RUS	12.11.68	1		Madrid	11 Feb 93
6.95	Gail	Devers	USA	19.11.66	1	WI	Toronto	12 Mar 93
6.95	Marion	Jones	USA	12.10.75	1		Maebashi	7 Mar 98
6.96	Merlene	Ottey	JAM	10.5.60	1		Madrid	14 Feb 92
6.96	Ekateríni	Thánou	GRE	1.2.75	1	WI	Maebashi	7 Mar 99
7.00	Nelli	Cooman	NED	6.6.64	1	EI	Madrid	23 Feb 86
7.01	Savatheda	Fynes	BAH	17.10.74	2s1	WI	Maebashi	7 Mar 99
7.02	Gwen	Torrence	USA	12.6.65	1	Mill	New York	2 Feb 96
7.02	Christy	Opara-Thompson	NGR	2.5.70	2		Gent	12 Feb 97
7.02	Chioma	Ajunwa	NGR	25.12.70	1		Liévin	22 Feb 98
7.02	Philomenah	Mensah	CAN	11.5.75	1h2	WI	Maebashi	7 Mar 99
7.03	Anelia	Nuneva	BUL	30.6.62	2s1	EI	Liévin	22 Feb 87
7.04	Marita	Koch	GDR	18.2.57	1	NC	Senftenberg	16 Feb 85
7.04	Silke	Möller'	GDR	20.6.64	1s1	EI	Budapest	6 Mar 88
7.04	Carlette	Guidry	USA	4.9.68	2	NC	Atlanta	4 Mar 95
7.04	Petya	Pendareva	BUL	20.1.71	1s1	WI	Lisboa	11 Mar 01
7.04	Zhanna	Block'	UKR	6.7.72	1	WI	Birmingham	14 Mar 03

60 METRES HURDLES WOMEN

Mark Wind	Name		Nat	Born	Pos	Meet	Venue	Date
7.69	Lyudmila	Narozhilenko ¶	RUS	21.4.64	1	NC	Chelyabinsk	4 Feb 90
7.73	Cornelia	Oschkenat'	GDR	29.10.61	1		Wien	25 Feb 89
7.74	Yordanka	Donkova	BUL	28.9.61	1	NC	Sofia	14 Feb 87
7.74	Michelle	Freeman	JAM	5.5.69	1		Madrid	3 Feb 98
7.74	Gail	Devers	USA	19.11.66	1h1	NC	Boston	1 Mar 03
7.75	Bettine	Jahn	GDR	3.8.58	1	EI	Budapest	5 Mar 83
7.75	Perdita	Felicien	CAN	29.8.80	1	WI	Budapest	7 Mar 04
7.76	Gloria	Siebert'	GDR	13.1.64	1		Sindelfingen	5 Feb 88
7.77	Zofia	Bielczyk	POL	22.9.58	1	EI	Sindelfingen	1 Mar 80
7.78	Brigita	Bukovec	SLO	21.5.70	1		Stuttgart	7 Feb 99
7.80	Susanna	Kallur	SWE	16.2.81	1	EI	Madrid	6 Mar 05
7.81	Jackie	Joyner-Kersee	USA	3.3.62	1		Fairfax	5 Feb 89
7.82	Yelizaveta	Chernyshova	RUS	26.1.58	1	WI	Budapest	5 Mar 89
7.82	Monique	Ewanje-Epée	FRA	11.7.67	1	6N	Paris	23 Feb 91
7.82	Glory	Alozie	ESP	30.12.77	1h1		Madrid	16 Feb 99
7.82	Olga	Shishigina ¶	KZK	23.12.68	1		Liévin	21 Feb 99
7.82	Linda	Ferga-Khodadin	FRA	24.12.76	3	WI	Budapest	7 Mar 04

MEN'S WORLD LISTS 2005

100 METRES

Mark	Wind		Name	Nat	Born	Pos	Meet	Venue	Date
9.77	1.6	Asafa	Powell	JAM	11.11.82	1	SGP	Athína	14 Jun
9.84	1.8		Powell			1		Kingston	7 May
9.85	0.6		Powell			1	GS	Ostrava	9 Jun
9.88	0.4	Justin	Gatlin	USA	10.2.82	1	WCh	Helsinki	7 Aug
9.89	1.0		Gatlin			1	LGP	London (CP)	22 Jul
9.94	1.0	Leonard	Scott	USA	19.1.80	2	LGP	London (CP)	22 Jul
9.96	1.0	Marc	Burns	TRI	7.1.83	1	NC	Port of Spain	25 Jun
9.96	0.6		Gatlin			1	GGala	Roma	8 Jul
9.98	1.9		Powell			1h2	SGP	Athína	14 Jun
9.99	1.6	Abdul Aziz	Zakari	GHA	2.9.76	2	GP	Athína	14 Jun
9.99	1.0	Darrel	Brown	TRI	11.10.84	2	NC	Port of Spain	25 Jun
9.99	1.0	Shawn	Crawford	USA	14.1.78	1s1	NC	Carson	25 Jun
9.99	1.8	Ronald	Pognon	FRA	16.11.82	1	Athl	Lausanne	5 Jul
9.99	-1.0		Gatlin			1s2	WCh	Helsinki	7 Aug
9.99	0.0		Gatlin			1	VD	Bruxelles	26 Aug
9.99	0.5		Zakari			1	GP	Rieti	28 Aug
10.00	1.0		Gatlin			2s1	NC	Carson	25 Jun
10.00	1.0	Kim	Collins	SKN	5.4.76	3	LGP	London (CP)	22 Jul
10.00	-1.0		Zakari			2s2	WCh	Helsinki	7 Aug
10.00	0.5	Dwight	Thomas (10)	JAM	23.9.80	1	Gugl	Linz	23 Aug
10.00	-0.6		Burns			1	WAF	Monaco	10 Sep
10.01	1.9	Maurice	Greene	USA	23.7.74	1s3	NC	Carson	25 Jun
10.01	0.5		Gatlin			1h2	LGP	London (CP)	22 Jul
10.01	1.1		Collins			1	BrGP	Sheffield	21 Aug
10.01	0.6		Thomas			1	ISTAF	Berlin	4 Sep
10.01	-0.6		Zakari			2	WAF	Monaco	10 Sep
10.01	-0.6		Thomas			3	WAF	Monaco	10 Sep
10.01	-0.4		Gatlin			1		Shanghai	17 Sep
10.02	1.8		Zakari			2	Athl	Lausanne	5 Jul
10.02	1.9	Mark	Jelks	USA	10.4.84	1		Salamanca	6 Jul
10.02	1.9		Brown			1	CAC	Nassau	9 Jul
10.02	1.9		Burns			2	CAC	Nassau	9 Jul
10.02	-0.3		Powell			1h1	LGP	London (CP)	22 Jul
10.02	0.1		Zakari			1	Bisl	Oslo	29 Jul
		(34 performances by 12 men)							
10.03	1.6	Michael	Frater	JAM	6.10.82	3	SGP	Athína	14 Jun
10.04	1.6	Francis	Obikwelu	POR	22.11.78	4	SGP	Athína	14 Jun
10.04	1.0	Aaron	Armstrong	TRI	14.10.77	3	NC	Port of Spain	25 Jun
10.06	1.5	Walter	Dix	USA-J	31.1.86	1h1	NCAA-r	New York	27 May
10.08	1.3	John	Capel	USA	27.10.78	1	GP II	Stanford	30 May
10.08	0.7	J-Mee	Samuels	USA-J	20.5.87	1		Greensboro	24 Jul
10.08	-1.0	Jason	Gardener	GBR	18.9.75	5s2	WCh	Helsinki	7 Aug
10.08	1.4	Monzavous Rae	Edwards	USA	7.5.81	1	MAI	Malmö	16 Aug
		(20)							
10.08	0.5	Tyson	Gay	USA	9.9.82	2	GP	Rieti	28 Aug
10.09A		Olusoji	Fasuba	NGR	9.7.84	1		Nairobi	7 May
10.09	1.8	Joshua 'J.J'	Johnson	USA	10.5.76	1	GP II	Rio de Janeiro	15 May
10.10	1.0	Jacey	Harper	TRI	20.5.80	4	NC	Port of Spain	25 Jun
10.10	1.9	Mardy	Scales	USA	10.9.81	2s3	NC	Carson	25 Jun
10.10	1.9	Churandy	Martina	AHO	3.7.84	3	CAC	Nassau	9 Jul
10.12	1.1	Joshua	Ross	AUS	9.2.81	1		Perth	22 Jan
10.12	1.7	DaBryan	Blanton	USA	3.7.84	2s2	NC	Carson	25 Jun
10.13	1.8	Mark	Lewis-Francis	GBR	4.9.82	5		Kingston	7 May
10.13	1.6	Jason	Smoots	USA	13.7.80	2h1		Atlanta	14 May
		(30)							
10.13		Uchenna	Emedolu	NGR	17.9.76	1	NC	Abuja	9 Jul
10.13	1.1	Marlon	Devonish	GBR	1.6.76	5	BrGP	Sheffield	21 Aug
10.13	1.2	Chris	Williams	JAM	15.3.72	3		Yokohama	19 Sep
10.14	1.4	Dwight	Phillips	USA	1.10.77	3	GP II	Fort-de-France	30 Apr
10.15	1.5	Shingo	Suetsugu	JPN	2.6.80	1	Oda	Hiroshima	29 Apr
10.15	1.6	Patrick	Jarrett	JAM	2.10.77	5	SGP	Athína	14 Jun
10.16	1.6	Coby	Miller	USA	19.10.76	6		Kingston	7 May
10.16	1.3	Brian	Lewis	USA	5.12.74	3	GP II	Stanford	30 May
10.16	1.6	Aaron	Egbele	NGR	29.1.79	6	SGP	Athína	14 Jun
10.16	1.7	Josh	Norman	USA	26.7.80	3s2	NC	Carson	25 Jun
		(40)							

MEN 2005

Mark	Wind	Name		Nat	Born	Pos	Meet	Venue	Date
10.16	0.3	Tobias	Unger	GER	10.7.79	1	NC	Wattenscheid	2 Jul
10.16	0.9	Ainsley	Waugh	JAM	17.9.81	2h2	WCh	Helsinki	6 Aug
10.17	1.8	Vicente	de Lima	BRA	4.6.77	3	GP II	Rio de Janeiro	15 May
10.17	-1.3	Terrence	Trammell	USA	23.11.78	2		Carson	22 May
10.19	1.1	Daniel	Batman	AUS	20.3.81	2		Perth	22 Jan
10.19	1.1	James	McSwain	USA	20.1.84	1rB	MSR	Walnut	17 Apr
10.19	1.5	Leroy	Dixon	USA	20.6.83	2h1	NCAA-r	New York	27 May
10.19	1.0	Deji	Aliu	NGR	22.11.75	1		Lugano	4 Jun
10.20	1.1	Joseph	Batangdon	CMR	29.7.78	3		Perth	22 Jan
10.20	1.9	Henry	Vizcaíno	CUB	16.5.80	4	CAC	Nassau	9 Jul
		(50)							
10.20	0.9	Patrick	Johnson	AUS	26.9.72	2h3	WCh	Helsinki	6 Aug
10.21	1.0	Idrissa	Sanou	BUR	12.6.77	2		Bamako	6 Apr
10.21	0.8	Salem Mubarak	Al-Yami	KSA	9.2.82	1	Is.Sol	Makkah	13 Apr
10.21	1.9	Derrick	Atkins	BAH	5.1.84	5	CAC	Nassau	9 Jul
10.22	1.1	Ambrose	Ezenwa	NGR/AUS	10.4.77	4		Perth	22 Jan
10.22	0.0	Trell	Kimmons	USA	13.7.85	1		Athens, GA	7 May
10.22	1.5	Chris	Johnson	USA	28.4.82	1		New Orleans	15 May
10.22	1.1	Craig	Pickering	GBR-J	16.10.86	1	LI	Loughborough	22 May
10.22	0.9	Michael	Mitchell	USA	16.5.81	1rB		Carson	22 May
10.22	1.0	Kevon	Pierre	TRI	30.3.82	5	NC	Port of Spain	25 Jun
		(60)							
10.22	0.6	Simone	Collio	ITA	27.12.79	7	GGala	Roma	8 Jul
10.23	1.5	Wes	Felix	USA	21.7.83	1		Los Angeles	30 Apr
10.23	1.6		Jin Ke	CHN	13.1.84	1s2	NC	Shijiazhuang	19 Jun
10.23	1.2	Eddy	De Lepine	FRA	30.3.84	1		Bondoufle	2 Jul
10.24	1.5	Phil	Francis	USA	26.4.83	2		Los Angeles	30 Apr
10.24	1.1	Simeon	Williamson	GBR-J	16.1.86	1	NC-j	Bedford	2 Jul
10.24	1.9	Lerone	Clarke	JAM	2.10.81	6	CAC	Nassau	9 Jul
10.24	0.3	Lueyi	Dovy	FRA	10.11.75	1	NC	Angers	15 Jul
10.24	1.3	Matic	Osovnikar	SLO	19.1.80	1h1	NC	Maribor	23 Jul
10.25	1.9	Rodney	Martin	USA	22.12.82	1		Knoxville	15 Apr
		(70)							
10.25	1.3	Mark	Findlay	GBR	20.3.78	1	CAU	Bedford	29 May
10.25A	-0.3	Cláudio Roberto	Sousa	BRA	14.10.73	1h1		Cochabamba	29 May
10.25	-0.1	Christian	Malcolm	GBR	3.6.79	1r1	ECp-S	Firenze	17 Jun
10.25	1.1	Guus	Hoogmoed	NED	27.9.81	2	ECp-1B	Leiria	18 Jun
10.25	1.0	Demi	Omole	USA	29.7.85	5s1	NC	Carson	25 Jun
10.25	1.7	John	Woods	USA	19.6.82	5s2	NC	Carson	25 Jun
10.26	0.7	Kelly	Willie	USA	7.9.82	1h1	TexR	Austin	8 Apr
10.26	1.9	Derrick	Johnson	USA	7.3.82	2		Knoxville	15 Apr
10.26	1.5	Gregory	Bolden	USA	30.6.84	1h3	NCAA-II	Abilene	26 May
10.26	1.9	Freddy	Mayola	CUB	1.11.77	3r3		Salamanca	6 Jul
		(80)							
10.26	0.1	Bernard	Williams	USA	19.1.78	4rB	GGala	Roma	8 Jul
10.26	0.7	Justyn	Warner	CAN-J	28.6.87	2	PAm-J	Windsor	30 Jul
10.27	-3.5	Morné	Nagel	RSA	23.2.78	1		Stellenbosch	11 Mar
10.27	??	Yhann	Plummer	JAM	3.2.83	1h		New Orleans	10 Apr
10.27	1.8	Darvis	Patton	USA	4.12.77	7		Kingston	7 May
10.27	0.9	Kaaron	Conwright	USA	8.8.76	3rB		Carson	22 May
10.27A	-0.3	Basiílo	de Morães	BRA	14.10.73	2h1		Cochabamba	29 May
10.27	0.8	Pierre	Browne	CAN	14.1.80	2		Kassel	10 Jun
10.27	-0.8		Hu Kai	CHN	4.8.82	1	NC	Shijiazhuang	19 Jun
10.27	1.9	Leigh	Julius	RSA	25.3.85	1h3		Lapinlahti	3 Jul
		(90)							
10.27	2.0	Tatsuro	Yoshino	JPN	11.9.82	1h4		Sapporo	10 Jul
10.28	-3.5	Sherwin	Vries	RSA	22.3.80	2		Stellenbosch	11 Mar
10.28	1.6	Jacob	Norman	USA	7.11.85	1r7		Waco	26 Mar
10.28	-0.3	Marvin	Anderson	JAM	12.5.82	1h3	Pac-10	Los Angeles (Ww)	14 May
10.28	1.6	Brian	Johnson	USA	25.3.80	7	GP II	Stanford	30 May
10.28	-0.9	Stéphane	Buckland	MRI	20.1.77	1		Avellino	15 Jun
10.28	1.3	Hank	Palmer	CAN	16.3.85	1		St Laurent	22 Jun
10.28	1.3	Alexander	Kosenkow	GER	14.3.77	2h3	NC	Wattenscheid	2 Jul
10.28	1.1	Yahya Saeed	Al-Kahes	KSA-J	19.2.86	1	PArab	Radès	16 Sep
10.29	1.5	Jeff	Laynes	USA	3.10.70	2		Sacramento	28 May
		(100)							
10.29A	-1.7	Raphael R.	de Oliveira	BRA	5.2.79	1		Cochabamba	1 Jun
10.29	1.1	Kazuyoshi	Hidaka	JPN	7.7.80	1h3	NC	Tokyo	4 Jun
10.29	0.2	Nobuharu	Asahara	JPN	21.6.72	1h4	NC	Tokyo	4 Jun
10.29	1.2	Andre Domingos	da Silva	BRA	26.11.72	2	NC	São Paulo	19 Jun

Mark	Wind	Name		Nat	Born	Pos	Meet	Venue	Date
10.29	0.3	Marc	Blume	GER	28.12.73	2	NC	Wattenscheid	2 Jul

Mark	Wind	Name		Nat	Born	Date
10.30	1.5	Shigeyuki	Kojima	JPN	25.9.79	29 Apr
10.30 ?		Michael	Rodgers	USA	24.4.85	7 May
10.30	1.0	Obadele	Thompson	BAR	30.3.76	7 May
10.30	1.8	Kenneth	Baxter	USA	17.4.82	14 May
10.30	1.7	Ron	Richards	LBR	13.5.83	27 May
10.30	-0.2	Kyle	Farmer	USA	15.4.83	8 Jun
10.30	1.0	Chinedu	Oriala	NGR	17.12.81	11 Jun
10.30	0.5	Tyrone	Edgar	GBR	29.3.82	22 Jul
10.30	1.7	Oudere	Kankarafou	FRA	2.12.83	21 Aug
10.30	0.8	Anil	Kumar	IND	28.5.73	24 Aug
10.31	1.8	Anthony	Buchanan	USA	10.9.81	30 Apr
10.31	-2.8	Ernest	Wiggins	USA	18.6.82	21 May
10.31	1.8	Carlos	Moore	USA	8.5.84	29 May
10.31	-1.4	Jaysuma	Saidy Ndure	GAM	1.1.84	12 Jun
10.31	0.0	Alex	Nelson	GBR-Y	21.3.88	18 Jun
10.31	1.2	Eric	Pacôme N'Dri	CIV	24.3.78	25 Jun
10.31	0.3	Marius	Broening	GER	24.10.83	3 Jul
10.31	2.0	Shingo	Kawabata	JPN	15.5.78	10 Jul
10.31	1.3	Thierry	Lubin	FRA	10.11.70	15 Jul
10.31	1.6	Alanzo	Barrett	JAM	8.11.83	30 Jul
10.31	1.9	Marcus	Brunson	USA	24.4.78	4 Sep
10.32	1.1	Matthew	Shirvington	AUS	25.10.78	22 Jan
10.32	0.2	Jeffrey	Fourth	USA	19.6.79	19 Mar
10.32	1.9	Bradley	Reed	USA	31.7.85	26 Mar
10.32		Larry	Crawford	USA	23.3.79	7 May
10.32	1.1	Konstantin	Vasyukov	UKR	10.1.81	7 May
10.32	1.2	Rondrick	Parker	USA		14 May
10.32	0.6		Liu Dapeng	CHN	5.8.83	21 May
10.32	1.4	Marvin	Bien-Aime	USA	20.10.83	26 May
10.32	1.6	Cyril	Bapte	FRA	10.1.83	10 Jun
10.32	0.8	Anatoliy	Dovgal	UKR	29.1.76	15 Jun
10.32	0.1	Kurt	Watson	JAM	78	25 Jun
10.32	0.7	Andrey	Yepishin	RUS	10.6.81	10 Jul
10.32	0.7	Aleksandr	Smirnov	RUS	25.2.74	10 Jul
10.32	1.1	Lukasz	Chyla	POL	31.3.81	21 Jul
10.32	0.8	Winston	Smith	JAM	22.11.82	23 Jul
10.32	2.0	Yuzo	Kanemaru	JPN-J	18.9.87	23 Oct
10.33A	0.4	Tyree	Gailes	USA	24.2.83	2 Apr
10.33	0.5	Jimmie	Hackley	USA	11.9.75	9 Apr
10.33	0.8	Adam	Wooten	USA	18.3.82	14 May
10.33	-1.3	Shin-ya	Saburi	JPN-J	3.6.86	2 Jul
10.33	0.7	Rafael	Ribeiro	BRA-J	23.6.86	30 Jul
10.33	1.9	Naohiro	Shinada	JPN-J	10.2.86	18 Sep
10.33	-0.5	Adam	Miller	AUS	22.6.84	26 Nov
10.33	1.2	Adam	Basil	AUS	14.4.75	26 Nov
10.34	1.7	Cleavon	Dillon	TRI	5.10.82	2 Apr
10.34	0.3	Juma Mubarak	Al-Jabri	OMA	9.5.85	12 Apr
10.34	1.9	Johann	Jack	TRI	6.3.75	17 Apr
10.34	1.8	Oliver	Williams	USA	10.5.84	7 May
10.34	1.5	Van-Tonio	Fraley	USA	20.1.80	15 May
10.34	0.4	Ryan	Shields	JAM	12.5.83	21 May
10.34	1.3	Nick	Smith	GBR	6.12.82	29 May
10.34	-0.8	Panayiótis	Sarrís	GRE	14.9.75	10 Jun
10.34	-1.2	Jorge Célio	Sena	BRA	31.1.85	19 Jun
10.34	1.4	Wade	Bennett-Jackson	GBR-J	27.2.87	2 Jul
(160)						

Wind assisted

Mark	Wind	Name		Nat	Born	Pos	Meet	Venue	Date
9.84	3.4	Justin	Gatlin	USA	10.2.82	1	Pre	Eugene	4 Jun
9.84	3.4		Powell			2	Pre	Eugene	4 Jun
9.93A	2.2	Churandy	Martina	AHO	3.7.84	1		El Paso	16 Apr
9.94	3.4		Scott			3	Pre	Eugene	4 Jun
9.96	4.5	Walter	Dix	USA-J	31.1.86	1rA	TexR	Austin	9 Apr
9.98	3.4	Shawn	Crawford	USA	14.1.78	4	Pre	Eugene	4 Jun
9.99	2.3	Monzavous Rae	Edwards	USA	7.5.81	1		Wichita	16 Apr
10.00	3.3	Aaron	Armstrong	TRI	14.10.77	1rA	MSR	Walnut	17 Apr
10.01	3.6	Mark	Jelks	USA	10.4.84	1rB	TexR	Austin	9 Apr
10.01	3.5		Pognon			1		Tomblaine	6 Sep
10.01	2.4	Patrick	Johnson	AUS	26.9.72	1		Perth	18 Dec
10.05	2.1	J-Mee	Samuels	USA-J	20.5.87	1s2		Greensboro	23 Jul
10.07	4.2	DaBryan	Blanton	USA	3.7.84	1rB	TexR	Austin	9 Apr
10.08	2.6	Olusoji	Fasuba	NGR	9.7.84	2		Dakar	3 Apr
10.08	3.3	Coby	Miller	USA	19.10.76	2rA	MSR	Walnut	17 Apr
10.08	2.9	Ivory	Williams	USA	2.5.85	1	JUCO	Levelland	18 May
10.10	2.2	Josh	Norman	USA	26.7.80	1rB	MSR	Walnut	17 Apr
10.10	2.1	Mark	Lewis-Francis	GBR	4.9.82	2	ECp-S	Firenze	18 Jun
10.11	4.5	Ernest	Wiggins	USA	18.6.82	2rC	TexR	Austin	9 Apr
10.11	2.5	Kelly	Willie	USA	7.9.82	2rB	TexR	Austin	9 Apr
10.11	3.5	Tobias	Unger	GER	10.7.79	1		Ettlingen	4 Jun
10.13	4.9	Jabari	Fields	USA	10.9.81	1		Abilene	12 May
10.14	3.1	Joseph	Batangdon	CMR	29.7.78	1h1		Perth	22 Jan
10.14	5.0	Dusty	Stamer	USA	28.4.82	1h3	Big 8	Manhattan	14 May
10.14	3.2	Daniel	Batman	AUS	20.3.81	1h2		Perth	18 Dec
10.15	2.8	Gregory	Bolden	USA	30.6.84	1		Albany	16 Apr
10.15	3.3	Anson	Henry	CAN	9.3.79	4rA	MSR	Walnut	17 Apr
10.15	2.1	Simone	Collio	ITA	27.12.79	3	ECp-S	Firenze	18 Jun
10.16A	3.3	John	Woods	USA	19.6.82	1		Colorado Springs	6 May
10.16	4.9	Steve	Slowly	JAM	18.4.79	1		Arlington	7 May
10.16	3.3	Trell	Kimmons	USA	13.7.85	1h4	JUCO	Levelland	17 May
10.17	3.4	Kaaron	Conwright	USA	8.8.76	1		Azusa	16 Jul
10.18	2.6	Idrissa	Sanou	BUR	12.6.77	4		Dakar	3 Apr
10.18	4.5	Tyree	Gailes	USA	24.2.83	3rC	TexR	Austin	9 Apr
10.18	4.2	Brian	Johnson	USA	25.3.80	3rB	TexR	Austin	9 Apr
10.18	2.8	Jaysuma	Saidy Ndure	GAM	1.1.84	2		Cork	2 Jul
10.19	2.3	Tyrone	Edgar	GBR	29.3.82	1		Houston	26 Mar
10.19	4.2	Pierre	Browne	CAN	14.1.80	4rB	TexR	Austin	9 Apr
10.19	3.6	Yhann	Plummer	JAM	3.2.83	2rCol	TexR	Austin	9 Apr
10.19	2.2	Kevon	Pierre	TRI	30.3.82	1		Coral Gables	16 Apr
10.19A	2.2	Jairo	Duzant	AHO	1.8.79	2		El Paso	16 Apr
10.20	5.3	Christie	van Wyk	NAM	12.10.77	1		Abilene	2 Apr
10.20	2.4	Cleavon	Dillon	TRI	5.10.82	2		Fort Worth	23 Apr

MEN 2005

Mark	Wind	Name		Nat	Born	Pos	Meet	Venue	Date
10.20	4.9		Yang Yaozu	CHN	9.1.81	2		Arlington	7 May
10.20	3.2	Basiíio	de Morães	BRA	11.5.82	1		Sertãozinho	21 May
10.20	2.7	Oudere	Kankarafou	FRA	8.12.83	1h1	NC-23	Bondoufle	2 Jul
10.20	3.7	Wade	Bennett-Jackson	GBR-J	27.2.87	1		Abingdon	28 Aug
10.21		Jacoby	Ford	USA-J	27.7.87	1		Palm Beach	7 Apr
10.21	3.1	Wallace	Spearmon	USA	24.12.84	1		Fayetteville	23 Apr
10.21	4.0	Guus	Hoogmoed	NED	27.9.81	1		Leiden	11 Jun
10.21	2.9	Ambrose	Ezenwa	NGR/AUS	10.4.77	1		La Laguna	30 Jul
10.21	3.2	Adam	Basil	AUS	14.4.75	2h1		Perth	18 Dec
10.22	4.2	Brendan	Christian	ANT	11.12.83	4rB	TexR	Austin	9 Apr
10.22A	2.2	Eric	Pacôme Ndri	CIV	24.3.78	4		El Paso	16 Apr
10.22	2.2	Jeff	Laynes	USA	3.10.70	2rC	MSR	Walnut	17 Apr
10.22	3.2	Takashi	Miyata	JPN	24.5.79	1s1	NC	Tokyo	5 Jun
10.22	2.1	Simeon	Williamson	GBR-J	16.1.86	1J	BrGP	Sheffield	21 Aug
10.23	4.5	Desmond	Bynum	USA	9.9.80	5rC	TexR	Austin	9 Apr
10.23	2.2	Lamont	Johnson	USA	19.12.76	3rC	MSR	Walnut	17 Apr
10.24	3.0	Ron	Richards	LBR	13.5.83	2		Atlanta	2 Apr
10.24	2.5	Kyle	Farmer	USA	15.4.83	3rB	TexR	Austin	9 Apr
10.24	2.1	Derrick	Johnson	USA	7.3.82	1h2		Greensboro	9 Apr
10.24	4.9	Shomari	Wilson	USA	6.6.76	3		Arlington	7 May
10.24	3.5	Marius	Broening	GER	24.10.83	2		Ettlingen	4 Jun
10.24	3.2	Shigeyuki	Kojima	JPN	25.9.79	2s1	NC	Tokyo	5 Jun
10.24	2.5		Gong Wei	CHN	3.1.79	1	NG	Nanjing	18 Oct
10.25	4.2	Michael	Rodgers	USA	24.4.85	1h4	Kans R	Lawrence	22 Apr
10.25	3.3	Dion	Rodriguez	TRI	9.6.84	2h5	JUCO	Levelland	18 May
10.25	3.2	Kazuyoshi	Hidaka	JPN	7.7.80	3s1	NC	Tokyo	5 Jun
10.25A	5.2	Morné	Nagel	RSA	23.2.78	1		Windhoek	11 Jun
10.25	3.4	Tatsuro	Yoshino	JPN	11.9.82	2		Sapporo	10 Jul
10.26	2.8	Kris	Neofytou	AUS	3.5.84	1h3		Perth	22 Jan
10.26	2.5	Jonathan	Holland	USA	18.2.85	4rA	TexR	Austin	9 Apr
10.26	4.5	Tim	Walls	USA	30.9.80	6rC	TexR	Austin	9 Apr
10.26	3.2	Shingo	Kawabata	JPN	15.5.78	4s1	NC	Tokyo	5 Jun
10.26	3.6	Harry	Aikines-Aryeetey	GBR-Y	29.8.88	2		London (CP)	10 Jun
10.26	2.1	Andrey	Yepishin	RUS	10.6.81	4	ECp-S	Firenze	18 Jun
10.26	3.2	Xavier	Brown	JAM	.83	1		Gent	20 Jul
10.27	2.8	Anthony	Buchanan	USA	10.9.81	1h2		Tampa	1 Apr
10.27	7.2	Matthieu	Pritchett	USA-J	8.4.86	1		Atlanta	2 Apr
10.27	4.0	Chris	Berrian	USA	17.4.83	1		San Luis Obispo	30 Apr
10.27	4.6	Ronald	Hill	USA	17.5.84	2h1	Big 12	Manhattan, KS	14 May
10.27	3.2	Rafael	Ribeiro	BRA-J	23.6.86	2		Sertaozhino	21 May
10.27A	5.2	Tlhalosang	Molapisi	BOT	15.3.73	2		Windhoek	11 Jun
10.27	4.8	Stefano	Anceschi	ITA	18.6.84	1		Bellinzona	30 Jul

Mark	Wind	Name		Nat	Born	Date
10.28	3.6	Ronald	Wright	USA	4.4.85	9 Apr
10.28	2.1	Carlos	Moore	USA	8.5.84	5 Jun
10.28	3.2	Kazuki	Ishikura	JPN	1.10.80	5 Jun
10.28	3.4	Nobuharu	Asahara	JPN	21.6.72	10 Jul
10.29	2.8	Matthew	Shirvington	AUS	25.10.78	22 Jan
10.29	2.5	Seth	Amoo	GHA	20.3.83	9 Apr
10.29	4.2	Quincy	Boles	USA	7.10.83	9 Apr
10.29	2.4	DeMario	Wesley	USA	20.4.80	23 Apr
10.29	3.2	Hiroyasu	Tsuchie	JPN	14.6.74	5 Jun
10.29	2.3	Daniel	Plummer	GBR	4.1.81	30 Jul
10.29	3.0		Liu Yuan-Kai	TPE	2.12.81	16 Oct
10.30	2.5	Todd	Dutch	USA	10.4.83	7 Apr
10.30	4.2	Trey	Griffin	USA	20.4.82	9 Apr
10.30	3.4	Naohiro	Shinada	JPN-J	10.2.86	13 May
10.30	2.8	Tim	Abeyie	GBR	7.11.82	29 May
10.30	4.8	Alessandro	Rocco	ITA	10.7.83	30 Jul
10.31	5.0	Greg	Bracey	USA	10.7.85	14 May
10.31	3.4	Anatoliy	Dovgal	UKR	29.1.76	12 Jun
10.31	2.1	Lukasz	Chyla	POL	31.3.81	18 Jun
10.32	2.2	Lee-Roy	Newton	RSA	19.12.78	15 Apr
10.32	2.1	Leo	Bookman	USA	3.1.82	23 Apr
10.32	2.3	Kareem	Streete-Thompson	CAY	30.3.73	29 Apr
10.32	4.0	Travis	Morse	USA		30 Apr
10.32	2.5	Joel	Brown	USA	31.1.80	7 May
10.32	2.2	Heber	Viera	URU	29.4.79	8 May
10.32	4.4	Robert	Amedee	USA	4.9.85	17 May
10.32	2.1	Carl	Barrett	JAM	21.4.75	28 May
10.32	4.1	Panayiótis	Sarrís	GRE	14.9.75	28 May
10.32	3.8	Yuichi	Tsutsumi	JPN	14.11.84	18 Oct
10.32	2.8	Iván Carlos	Altamirano	ARG	26.12.78	2 Jul
10.32	2.4	Stefan	Wieser	GER	8.12.84	16 Jul
10.32	2.5		Pang Guibin	CHN	2.2.83	18 Oct
10.32	3.2	Paul	Di Bella	AUS	12.2.77	18 Dec
10.33	2.3	Preston	Perry	USA	13.9.83	26 Mar
10.33	2.9	Chauncey	Harris	USA	21.9.83	9 Apr
10.33	3.4	Shinji	Takahira	JPN	18.7.84	13 May
10.33	3.2	Eliezer	de Almeida	BRA	31.3.83	21 May
10.33	2.6	Alessandro	Attene	ITA	10.9.77	28 May
10.33	2.7	Caimin	Douglas	NED	11.5.77	4 Sep
10.33	4.7	Khaled Yousef	Al Obaidli	QAT	17.8.81	15 Sep
10.33	2.5		Wang Peng	CHN	16.12.78	18 Oct
10.33	3.2	Steven	Tucker	AUS	3.12.82	18 Dec
10.34	2.1	Abraham	Morlu	LBR	5.1.81	9 Apr
10.34	2.5	Jean	du Randt	RSA	13.12.85	16 Apr
10.34	2.2	Bob	Colville	CRC	28.7.81	16 Apr
10.34	2.8	Cameron	Dayne	USA		16 Apr
10.34	2.3	Masaya	Aikawa	JPN	6.4.84	29 Apr
10.34	2.8	Jermaine	Carpenter	USA		7 May
10.34	4.9	Bryan	Davenport	USA		7 May
10.34	2.8	Matthew	Thomas	GBR	27.4.76	29 May
10.34	3.4	Ryo	Matsuda	JPN	26.12.79	25 Jun
10.34	2.4	Koura	Kaba Fantoni	ITA	28.8.84	16 Jul
10.34	2.7	Morten	Jensen	DEN	2.12.82	4 Sep
10.34	6.2	James	Dolphin	NZL	17.6.83	5 Nov

Best at low altitude

10.13 1.3 Fasuba 2 Yokohama 19 Sep

10.32 0.8 R.de Oliveira 3 São Paulo 2 Apr

+ intermediate time in longer race, A made at an altitude of 1000m or higher, D made in a decathlon, h made in a heat, qf quarter-final, sf semi-final, i indoors, Q qualifying round, r race number, -J juniors, -Y youths (b. 1988 or later)

Mark	Wind		Name	Nat	Born	Pos	Meet	Venue	Date

IAAF drugs disqualification (Mullings allowed to compete by NCAA)

Mark	Wind		Name	Nat	Born	Pos	Meet	Venue	Date
10.13	-0.4	Steve	Mullings ¶	JAM	29.11.82	1	NCAA-r	Bloomington	28 May
		10.06w	3.8			1B		Starkville	2 Apr
10.14	1.4	Tim	Montgomery ¶	USA	28.1.75	4	GP II	Fort-de-France	30 Apr
		10.10w	3.4			7	Pre	Eugene	4 Jun

Hand timing

Mark	Wind		Name	Nat	Born	Pos	Meet	Venue	Date
9.8A		Olusoji	Fasuba	NGR	9.7.84	1h2		Nairobi	7 May
10.0	2.0	Vicente	de Lima	BRA	4.6.77	1		Londrina	7 May
10.0	2.0	Claudinei Q	da Silva	BRA	19.11.70	2		Londrina	7 May

Mark	Wind		Name	Nat	Born	Date
10.1	1.5	Eddy	De Lepine	FRA	30.3.84	26 Feb
10.1		Michael	Grant	USA-J	30.3.86	15 Apr
10.1A		Tom	Masinde	KEN		7 May
10.1	2.0	Rafael	Ribeiro	BRA-J	23.6.86	7 May
10.1A		Kipkemboi	Soi	KEN		28 May
10.1	2.0	Ahmed	Awesu	GHA	.84	12 Jun

Wind assisted

Mark	Wind		Name	Nat	Born	Pos	Meet	Venue	Date
9.8w	2.2	Mark	Jelks	USA	10.4.84	1r1		Salamanca	6 Jul
9.9w	2.2	Hank	Palmer	CAN	16.3.85	2r1		Salamanca	6 Jul

Mark	Wind		Name	Nat	Born	Date
10.1		Cannon	McWilliams	USA-J		8 Apr
10.1	2.6	Ralph Waldy	Soguilon	PHI	3.10.83	14 Apr
10.1		Paul	Chaney	USA-J	22.6.87	30 Apr
10.1		J.R.	Rogers	USA-J	23.8.86	14 May
10.1		Clinton	Allen	USA-J		20 May
10.1		John	Beals	USA-J		20 May
10.1	2.2	Freddy	Mayola	CUB	1.11.77	6 Jul
10.1		Sergio	Mullins	RSA	12.5.80	11 Oct

JUNIORS

See main list for top 6 juniors. 11 performances by 3 men to 10.23. Additional marks and further juniors:

Name	Mark	Wind	Pos	Meet	Venue	Date	Mark	Wind	Pos	Meet	Venue	Date
Dix	10.12	1.6	1h1		Atlanta	13 May	10.22	0.9	1		Tallahassee	23 Apr
	10.14	1.9	3s3	NC	Carson	25 Jun	10.22	1.3	1	NCAA-r	New York	28 May
	10.21	-0.4	1	NCAA	Sacramento	10 Jun	10.23	0.8	1h2		Tallahassee	22 Apr
Samuels	10.20	0.7	1	PAm-J	Windsor	30 Jul	10.22	0.9	1		Greensboro	24 Jul

Mark	Wind		Name	Nat	Born	Pos	Meet	Venue	Date
10.31	0.0	Alex	Nelson	GBR-Y	21.3.88	1Y		Mannheim	18 Jun
10.32	2.0	Yuzo	Kanemaru	JPN	18.9.87	1	NSF	Okayama	23 Oct
10.33	-1.3	Shin-ya	Saburi	JPN	3.6.86	1		Tokyo	2 Jul
10.33	0.7	Rafael	Ribeiro (10)	BRA	23.6.86	3	PAm-J	Windsor	30 Jul
10.33	1.9	Naohiro	Shinada	JPN	10.2.86	1h1		Gotenba	18 Sep
10.34	1.4	Wade	Bennett-Jackson	GBR	27.2.87	1s2	NC-j	Bedford	2 Jul
10.35	0.8	Harry	Aikines-Aryeetey	GBR-Y	29.8.88	1	WY	Marrakesh	14 Jul
10.36	1.7	Daniel	Bailey	ANT	9.9.86	1	Carifta	Bacolet	26 Mar
10.37	2.0	Desislav	Gunev	BUL	21.1.86	1s1	NC-j	Sofia	28 May
10.37	0.8	Daniel	Schnelting	GER	9.3.86	1	NC-j	Braunschweig	29 Jul
10.38	-1.4	Matthieu	Pritchett	USA	8.7.86	4r1		Knoxville	9 Apr
10.38	0.6		Yin Hualong	CHN	22.8.87	1h4		Chongqing	14 May
10.38	2.0	Jamere	Holland	USA-Y	6.3.88	1h		Lake Balboa	19 May
10.38	0.6	Greg	Rutherford	GBR	17.11.86	1A		Mannheim	18 Jun

Wind assisted see main list for top 8 juniors. 7 performances by 5 men to 10.22w. Additional marks and further juniors.

Mark	Wind		Name	Nat	Born	Pos	Meet	Venue	Date
Samuels		10.07A	4.1	1				Albuquerque	4 Jun
Dix		10.13	3.0	1				Atlanta	2 Apr
10.30	3.4	Naohiro	Shinada	JPN	10.2.86	1s1		Tokyo	13 May
10.35A	4.1	Jerek	Hewett	USA	13.12.86	2		Albuquerque	4 Jun
10.37		Ahmad	Rashad	USA	12.12.87	1		Wooster	3 Jul
10.37	2.1	Julian	Thomas	GBR	28.12.86	4J	BrGP	Sheffield	21 Aug

200 METRES

Mark	Wind		Name	Nat	Born	Pos	Meet	Venue	Date
19.89	1.8	Wallace	Spearmon	USA	24.12.84	1	LGP	London (CP)	22 Jul
19.91	-0.7		Spearmon			1	NCAA	Sacramento	11 Jun
19.93	0.6	Tyson	Gay	USA	9.9.82	1s1	NCAA	Sacramento	9 Jun
19.96	-1.5		Gay			1	WAF	Monaco	9 Sep
19.97	1.7		Spearmon			1	MSR	Walnut	17 Apr
19.99	1.8	Usain	Bolt	JAM-J	21.8.86	2	LGP	London (CP)	22 Jul
19.99	1.8		Gay			3	LGP	London (CP)	22 Jul
20.00	0.0	Justin	Gatlin	USA	10.2.82	1		Monterrey	11 Jun
20.02	0.0	Xavier	Carter	USA	8.12.85	1rA	NCAA-r	Bloomington	28 May
20.03	1.8		Bolt			1	CAC	Nassau	11 Jul
20.04	-0.9		Gatlin			1	NC	Carson	26 Jun
20.04	-0.5		Gatlin			1	WCh	Helsinki	11 Aug
20.04	1.4		Gatlin			1	BrGP	Sheffield	21 Aug
20.06	-0.9		Gay			2	NC	Carson	26 Jun
20.08	-0.7		Carter			2	NCAA	Sacramento	11 Jun
20.09	1.4		Gay			2	BrGP	Sheffield	21 Aug
20.10	0.0		Gay			2rA	NCAA-r	Bloomington	28 May
20.12	-0.9	Shawn	Crawford	USA	14.1.78	3	NC	Carson	26 Jun
20.14	0.9		Bolt			1		Kingston	7 May
20.14	0.6		Carter			2s1	NCAA	Sacramento	9 Jun

Mark	Wind	Name		Nat	Born	Pos	Meet	Venue	Date
20.15	-0.6	Christian	Malcolm	GBR	3.6.79	1	ECp-S	Firenze	19 Jun
20.16	0.0		Spearmon			1h5	SEC	Nashville	13 May
20.16	1.3		Carter			1	SEC	Nashville	15 May
20.16	-0.7		Gay			3	NCAA	Sacramento	11 Jun
20.16	-0.9		Spearmon			4	NC	Carson	26 Jun
20.18	1.0	Walter	Dix	USA-J	31.1.86	1s2	NCAA	Sacramento	9 Jun
20.19	-1.5	Chris	Williams	JAM	15.3.72	2	WAF	Monaco	9 Sep
20.20	0.7	Tobias	Unger	GER	10.7.79	1	NC	Wattenscheid	3 Jul
20.20	-0.5		Spearmon			1	WCh	Helsinki	11 Aug
20.21	-1.5		Spearmon			3	WAF	Monaco	9 Sep
		(30/10)							
20.27	1.0	Ronald	Pognon	FRA	16.11.82	1	GP	Rieti	28 Aug
20.28	0.3	Stéphane	Buckland	MRI	20.1.77	1		Avellino	15 Jun
20.30	0.0	Joshua 'J.J'	Johnson	USA	10.5.76	2		Monterrey	11 Jun
20.31	-0.5	John	Capel	USA	27.10.78	3	WCh	Helsinki	11 Aug
20.32		Churandy	Martina	AHO	3.7.84	1		Hermosillo	21 May
20.32A	1.1	J-Mee	Samuels	USA-J	20.5.87	1		Albuquerque	4 Jun
20.33	1.0	Brian	Dzingai	ZIM	29.4.81	1		Tallahassee	7 May
20.34	0.6	Rodney	Martin	USA	22.12.82	3s1	NCAA	Sacramento	9 Jun
20.35	-0.3	Morné	Nagel	RSA	23.2.78	1		Stellenbosch	11 Mar
20.35		Leo	Bookman	USA	3.1.82	2		Hermosillo	21 May
		(20)							
20.35	1.8	Aaron	Armstrong	TRI	14.10.77	2	CAC	Nassau	11 Jul
20.36	1.0	Seth	Amoo	GHA	20.3.83	3s2	NCAA	Sacramento	9 Jun
20.36	1.0	Ainsley	Waugh	JAM	17.9.81	3	GP	Rieti	28 Aug
20.38	0.3	LaShawn	Merritt	USA-J	27.6.86	1		Knoxville	15 Apr
20.38	0.2	Leonard	Scott	USA	19.1.80	1		Réthimno	10 Jul
20.41	1.8	Marlon	Devonish	GBR	1.6.76	5	LGP	London (CP)	22 Jul
20.43	-0.3	Omar	Brown	JAM	21.6.82	3	NA	Heusden-Zolder	23 Jul
20.43	0.6	Tyree	Washington	USA	28.8.76	2	ISTAF	Berlin	4 Sep
20.44	1.2	Daniel	Batman	AUS	20.3.81	1s1		Darwin	17 May
20.44	0.6	Kyle	Farmer	USA	15.4.83	4s1	NCAA	Sacramento	9 Jun
		(30)							
20.44	0.7	Vicente	de Lima	BRA	4.6.77	1	NC	São Paulo	17 Jun
20.45	1.8	Coby	Miller	USA	19.10.76	3s2	NC	Carson	26 Jun
20.45	-0.2	Kristof	Beyens	BEL	13.7.83	1	NC	Bruxelles	10 Jul
20.45	1.8	Sebastian	Ernst	GER	11.10.84	3h3	WCh	Helsinki	9 Aug
20.46	1.8	Trell	Kimmons	USA	13.7.85	1		Athens, GA	7 May
20.46	-1.6	Monzavous Rae	Edwards	USA	7.5.81	2h3	NC	Carson	25 Jun
20.46	1.1	Johan	Wissman	SWE	2.11.82	1		Karlstad	18 Jul
20.47	-0.3	Leigh	Julius	RSA	25.3.85	2		Stellenbosch	11 Mar
20.47	-0.5	Kevon	Pierre	TRI	30.3.82	1h1	NC	Port of Spain	26 Jun
20.47	1.8	Dominic	Demeritte	BAH	22.2.78	3	CAC	Nassau	11 Jul
		(40)							
20.47	1.3	David	Alerte	FRA	18.9.84	1	EU23	Erfurt	17 Jul
20.48	0.0	Francis	Obikwelu	POR	22.11.78	1	ECp-1B	Leiria	19 Jun
20.49	0.0	Ambrose	Ezenwa	NGR/AUS	10.4.77	1		Canberra	5 Feb
20.49	1.3	Tyler	Christopher	CAN	3.10.83	1		Claremont	15 Apr
20.49	0.0	Jimmie	Hackley	USA	11.9.75	1	GP	Belém	22 May
20.51	0.5	Jaysuma	Saidy Ndure	GAM	1.1.84	1	MAI	Malmö	16 Aug
20.52	-0.2	Fernada	Blakely	USA	28.9.81	1		Oxford, MS	9 Apr
20.52	-1.6	Rubin	Williams	USA	9.7.83	3h3	NC	Carson	25 Jun
20.52	-0.5	Julien	Raeburn	TRI	18.9.78	2h1	NC	Port of Spain	26 Jun
20.52	1.0	Andrew	Howe	ITA	12.5.85	1	v2N	Viareggio	27 Jul
		(50)							
20.53	0.7	André Domingos	da Silva	BRA	26.11.72	2	NC	São Paulo	17 Jun
20.53	1.8	Obadele	Thompson	BAR	30.3.76	4	CAC	Nassau	11 Jul
20.54	1.7	Chris	Berrian	USA	17.4.83	1		Azusa	17 Jul
20.55	1.8	Shingo	Suetsugu	JPN	2.6.80	1h3		Shizuoka	3 May
20.55	0.5	Joel	Brown	USA	31.1.80	1	Owens	Columbus	7 May
20.55A	0.0	Basíío	de Morães	BRA	11.5.82	1		Cochabamba	29 May
20.55	1.6	Shinji	Takahira	JPN	18.7.84	1		Tokyo	3 Jul
20.55	0.2	Uchenna	Emedolu	NGR	17.9.76	3	GP II	Thessaloníki	17 Jul
20.56	0.0	Joseph	Batangdon	CMR	29.7.78	2		Canberra	5 Feb
20.56	1.5	Gary	Kikaya	COD	4.2.78	1		Atlanta	2 Apr
		(60)							
20.56	1.8	Patrick	Johnson	AUS	26.9.72	4h3	WCh	Helsinki	9 Aug
20.57	-1.0	Tyree	Gailes	USA	24.2.83	1	Big 12	Manhattan, KS	15 May
20.57		Marc	Burns	TRI	7.1.83	3		Hermosillo	21 May
20.57	0.0	Bruno	Pacheco	BRA	20.4.83	3	GP	Belém	22 May
20.58		Haddow	Weatherborne	USA	19.5.80	1		Lamoni	7 May

Mark	Wind	Name		Nat	Born	Pos	Meet	Venue	Date
20.58	-0.1	Leroy	Dixon	USA	20.6.83	2h2	NCAA-r	New York	27 May
20.58	0.0	Wes	Felix	USA	21.7.83	1	NCAA-r	Eugene	28 May
20.58	1.0	Carey	LaCour	USA	17.2.85	5s2	NCAA	Sacramento	9 Jun
20.58	0.1	Koura Kaba	Fantoni	ITA	28.8.84	1	NC	Bressanone	26 Jun
20.58	0.2	Guus	Hoogmoed	NED	27.9.81	4	GP II	Thessaloníki	17 Jul
		(70)							
20.58	0.5	Mark	Jelks	USA	10.4.84	2	MAI	Malmö	16 Aug
20.59	1.0	Nate	Probasco	USA	10.7.83	6s2	NCAA	Sacramento	9 Jun
20.59	1.8	Tommi	Hartonen	FIN	12.5.77	5h3	WCh	Helsinki	9 Aug
20.60	1.6	Kris	Neofytou	AUS	3.5.84	1		Canberra	5 Feb
20.60	-0.1	Olusoji	Fasuba	NGR	9.7.84	1		Dakar	3 Apr
20.60	0.8	James	Dolphin	NZL	17.6.83	2=		Brisbane	27 Nov
20.61	1.0	Kenneth	Baxter	USA	17.4.82	7s2	NCAA	Sacramento	9 Jun
20.61	0.8	Darrel	Brown	TRI	11.10.84	1		Lappeenranta	21 Jul
20.62	-0.2	Chris	Johnson	USA	28.4.82	2		Oxford, MS	9 Apr
20.62	1.0	Adam	Wooten	USA	18.3.82	1		Huntsville	15 May
		(80)							
20.62	0.4	Bernard	Williams	USA	19.1.78	2		Gent	20 Jul
20.62	0.5	Mardy	Scales	USA	10.9.81	3	MAI	Malmö	16 Aug
20.63	0.2	Dwight	Thomas	JAM	23.9.80	2		Réthimno	10 Jul
20.64	1.6	Ron	Richards	LBR	13.5.83	1		Clemson	9 Apr
20.64	1.0	Ben B.J.	Henderson	USA	5.4.83	4	NCAA-r	New York	28 May
20.65	1.0	Kelvin	Love	USA-J	18.5.86	1		Tempe	30 Apr
20.65	0.7	Jacey	Harper	TRI	20.5.80	3	Gugl	Linz	23 Aug
20.66	-0.6	Jirí	Vojtík	CZE	2.7.81	3	ECp-S	Firenze	19 Jun
20.66	0.7	Till	Helmke	GER	6.5.84	2	NC	Wattenscheid	3 Jul
20.66	1.8	Hamed Hamadan	Al-Bishi	KSA	15.5.80	1	AsiC	Inchon	4 Sep
		(90)							
20.67	1.9	Michael	Mitchell	USA	16.5.81	1		Claremont	14 May
20.67	1.3	Tatsuro	Yoshino	JPN	11.9.82	1		Marugame	24 Sep
20.68	-0.2	Leo	Settle	USA	19.10.75	3		Oxford, MS	9 Apr
20.68	0.7	Daniel	Schnelting	GER-J	9.3.86	3	NC	Wattenscheid	3 Jul
20.68	0.4	Lueyi	Dovy	FRA	10.11.75	2	NC	Angers	16 Jul
20.69A	1.9	Jan	van der Merwe	RSA	16.3.84	1		Bloemfontein	5 Mar
20.69	1.0	Robin	Edwards	USA	12.11.83	2		Tallahassee	7 May
20.69	1.0	Panayiótis	Sarrís	GRE	14.9.75	1	BalkC	Novi Sad	24 Jul
20.69	1.4	Alex	Nelson	GBR-Y	21.3.88	1		Stoke-on-Trent	30 Jul
20.70	-0.9	Eric	Milazar	MRI	1.6.75	2		Bamako	6 Apr
		(100)							
20.70	0.9	Jamel	Ashley	USA	17.4.79	2h1	SEC	Nashville	13 May
20.70A	1.2	Jeremy	Dodson	USA-J	30.8.87	1		Aurora	21 May
20.70	1.6	Alessandro	Attene	ITA	10.9.77	1		Fabriano	29 May
20.70	1.0	Florin	Suciu	ROM	18.5.83	2	BalkC	Novi Sad	24 Jul

Mark	Wind	Name		Nat	Born	Date
20.71	0.6	Preston	Perry	USA	13.9.83	15 May
20.71	0.0	Alexander	Kosenkow	GER	14.3.77	9 Jul
20.72	0.0	Domenik	Peterson	USA	12.12.84	16 Apr
20.72	-0.7	Heber	Viera	URU	29.4.79	8 May
20.72	0.3	Luis Alexander	Reyes	CUB	22.10.77	20 May
20.72	0.5	Marvin	Bien-Aime	USA	20.10.83	28 May
20.72	1.0	Yordan	Ilinov	BUL	28.5.85	24 Jul
20.72	-0.3		Yang Yaozu	CHN	9.1.81	17 Sep
20.72	1.5	Adam	Miller	AUS	22.6.84	12 Nov
20.73	0.6	Sherwin	Vries	RSA	22.3.80	5 Mar
20.73	1.3	Rikki	Fifton	GBR	17.6.85	17 Jul
20.73	0.2	Juan Pedro	Toledo	MEX	17.6.78	30 Jul
20.75	1.3	Jorge Celio	Sena	BRA	31.1.85	24 Apr
20.75	1.5	Marvin	Anderson	JAM	12.5.82	30 Apr
20.75	0.6	Derrick	Johnson	USA	7.3.82	15 May
20.75	0.3	Troy	McIntosh	BAH	29.3.73	20 May
20.75	-0.3	Steve	Slowly	JAM	18.4.79	3 Jun
20.75	-0.6	Marcin	Urbas	POL	17.9.76	19 Jun
20.75	0.6	Matic	Osovnikar	SLO	19.1.80	29 Jun
20.75	1.3	DeWayne	Barrett	JAM	27.12.81	10 Jul
20.75A	0.4	Daniel	Grueso	COL	30.7.85	20 Aug
20.76	-0.9	Idrissa	Sanou	BUR	12.6.77	6 Apr
20.77	1.0	Abidemi	Omole	USA	29.7.85	7 May
20.78	1.0	Dirk	Homewood	USA	21.1.82	7 May
20.79	1.6	Dmitriy	Glushchenko	UKR	17.2.81	27 May
20.79	0.4	Cláudio	Sousa	BRA	14.10.73	4 Jun
20.79	1.4	Chris	Lambert	GBR	6.4.81	12 Jun
20.79	0.8	Marc	Schneeberger	SUI	5.7.81	5 Jul
20.79	-0.1	Yusuke	Ishizuka	JPN-J	19.6.87	5 Aug
20.79	-1.0	Yuzo	Kanemaru	JPN-J	18.9.87	3 Nov
20.80	-0.5	Joshua	Ross	AUS	9.2.81	6 Mar
20.80	1.6	Chauncey	Harris	USA	21.9.83	9 Apr
20.80	1.9	Andre	Ammons	USA	12.11.78	28 May
20.80A	1.1	Trey	Harts	USA-J	17.10.87	4 Jun
20.80	0.4	Christophe	Cheval	FRA	25.2.71	16 Jul
20.81		Derrick	Atkins	BAH	5.1.84	6 Apr
20.81	0.6	Oumar	Loum	SEN	31.12.73	30 Apr
20.81	2.0		Jin Ke	CHN	13.1.84	15 May
20.81	1.0	J.D.	Henry	USA		15 May
20.82	1.2	Lancford	Davis	JAM	11.10.78	7 May
20.82	-0.5	Jordan	Kent	USA	24.7.84	14 May
20.82	0.7	Chris	Lawson	USA	12.3.83	28 May
20.82	-0.4	Jordan	Vaden	USA	15.9.78	3 Jun
20.82	-0.4	Kaaron	Conwright	USA	8.8.76	5 Jun
20.82	0.0	Marcin	Jedrusinski	POL	28.9.81	9 Jul
20.83	0.5	Todd	Dutch	USA	10.4.83	7 Apr
20.83		Xavier	Brown	JAM	.83	8 May
20.83	1.6	Mark	Findlay	GBR	20.3.78	27 May
20.83	1.3	Eddy	De Lepine	FRA	30.3.84	10 Jun
20.84	1.1	Lewis	Banda	ZIM	16.8.82	19 Mar
20.84A	-0.5	John	Woods	USA	19.6.82	6 Apr
20.84	0.9	Josip	Soprek	CRO	30.8.81	25 May
20.84	0.3	Michael	Lawrence	USA		28 May
20.84	1.0	Alanzo	Barrett	JAM	8.11.83	27 Aug
20.85	-0.3	Young Talkmore	Nyangani	ZIM	2.9.83	11 Mar
20.85	1.9	Pierre	Browne	CAN	14.1.80	2 Apr
20.85	1.8	James	McSwayn	USA	20.1.84	17 Apr
20.85	1.8	Yusuke	Omae	JPN	6.4.82	3 May
20.85	0.8	Jeff	Laynes	USA	3.10.70	7 May
20.85	0.6	Milton	Campbell	USA	15.5.76	14 May
20.85	0.1	Julian	Thomas	GBR-J	28.12.86	19 Jun
20.85	0.9	Enefiok	Udo-Obong (166)	NGR	22.5.82	9 Jul

Mark	Wind	Name		Nat	Born	Pos	Meet	Venue	Date

Wind assisted

Mark	Wind	Name		Nat	Born	Pos	Meet	Venue	Date
19.98	2.1	Aaron	Armstrong	TRI	14.10.77	1	NC	Port of Spain	26 Jun
19.99	4.3		Gay			1h6	WCh	Helsinki	9 Aug
20.14	4.3	Marcin	Jedrusinski	POL	28.9.81	2h6	WCh	Helsinki	9 Aug
20.14	4.3	Jaysuma	Saidy Ndure	GAM	1.1.84	3h6	WCh	Helsinki	9 Aug
20.22	4.3	Uchenna	Emedolu	NGR	17.9.76	4h6	WCh	Helsinki	9 Aug
20.26	4.3	Johan	Wissman	SWE	2.11.82	5h6	WCh	Helsinki	9 Aug
20.31A	2.4	Churandy	Martina	AHO	3.7.84	1		El Paso	16 Apr
20.32	3.1	Trell	Kimmons	USA	13.7.85	1	JUCO	Levelland	18 May
20.33	3.1	Ivory	Williams	USA	2.5.85	2	JUCO	Levelland	18 May
20.33A	4.9	André Domingos	da Silva	BRA	26.11.72	1	SACh	Cali	23 jul
20.34	2.8	Marlon	Devonish	GBR	1.6.76	1		Cork	2 Jul
20.36	3.6	Marvin	Anderson	JAM	12.5.82	1rA	MSR	Walnut	17 Apr
20.37	4.3	Leigh	Julius	RSA	25.3.85	6h6	WCh	Helsinki	9 Aug
20.39	3.1	Preston	Perry	USA	13.9.83	2h1	NCAA	Sacramento	9 Jun
20.40	4.3	Paul	Hession	IRL	27.1.83	7h6	WCh	Helsinki	9 Aug
20.41	2.4	Guus	Hoogmoed	NED	27.9.81	1	NC	Amsterdam	10 Jul
20.44A	2.4	Basílio	de Morães	BRA	11.5.82	2		Bogotá	3 Jul
20.45	3.0	Kelly	Willie	USA	7.9.82	2		Baton Rouge	23 Apr
20.47	4.5	Chris	Berrian	USA	17.4.83	1		San Luis Obispo	30 Apr
20.49	3.1	Nate	Probasco	USA	10.7.83	3h1	NCAA	Sacramento	9 Jun
20.52	4.3	Jeremy	Wariner	USA	31.1.84	1rA		Arlington	2 Apr
20.54	3.2	Till	Helmke	GER	6.5.84	1		Dublin (S)	30 Jul
20.55	2.1	Jacey	Harper	TRI	20.5.80	3=	NC	Port of Spain	26 Jun
20.61	5.0	Marvin	Bien-Aimé	USA	20.10.83	1		Abilene	2 Apr
20.62A	4.9	Heber	Viera	URU	29.4.79	2	SACh	Cali	23 Jul
20.63	2.7		Yang Yaozu	CHN	9.1.81	1rB		Arlington	2 Apr
20.63	4.0	Robert	Staten	USA	19.5.77	1		Beaumont	28 Apr
20.63	3.1	Jirí	Vojtík	CZE	2.7.81	1		Litomysl	30 Jul
20.64	3.7	DaBryan	Blanton	USA	3.7.84	1h2	Big 12	Manhattan, KS	14 May
20.66	3.7	Andrae	Williams	BAH	11.7.83	2h2	Big 12	Manhattan, KS	14 May
20.67	2.5	Ricardo	Williams	JAM	29.9.76	1		Fort Worth	23 Apr
20.67	2.5	Otis	McDaniel	USA-J	30.6.86	1	PAm-J	Windsor	31 Jul
20.69	4.8	John	Woods	USA	19.6.82	1rB	MSR	Walnut	17 Apr

Mark	Wind	Name		Nat	Born	Date
20.71	2.3	Derrick	Johnson	USA	7.3.82	13 May
20.73		Ahmad	Rashad	USA-J	12.12.87	3 Jul
20.73A	2.4	Jorge Célio	Sena	BRA	31.1.85	3 Jul
20.78	3.1	Jamil	Hubbard	USA-J	12.5.86	18 May
20.78	2.8	Mark	Lewis-Francis	GBR	4.9.82	24 Jun
20.78	2.5	Tremaine	Smith	USA-J	16.4.86	31 Jul
20.79	2.7	Ronald	Wright	USA	4.4.85	23 Apr
20.79	2.7	Christophe	Cheval	FRA	25.2.71	21 Aug
20.80	3.8	LaChristopher	Lewis	USA	28.10.82	2 Apr
20.80A	2.4	Éric	Pacôme N'Dri	CIV	24.3.78	16 Apr
20.80	3.3	Starr	Roberts	USA	24.7.79	17 Apr
20.80A	3.3	Hitjivirue	Kaanjuka	NAM-J	29.12.87	11 Jun
20.80	4.9	Geronimo	Goeloe	AHO	18.11.81	23 Jul
20.80	2.5	Daniel	Bailey	ANT-J	9.9.86	31 Jul
20.81	3.5	Ato	Modibo	TRI	19.6.79	23 Apr
20.82	5.2	Donald	MacDonald	NZL	6.1.77	5 Feb
20.85	4.1	Kendrick	Singleton	USA		2 Apr
20.85	3.6	Michael	Lawrence	USA		17 Apr
20.85	3.5	Sanjay	Ayre	JAM	19.6.80	23 Apr

Indoors

Mark	Wind	Name		Nat	Born	Pos	Meet	Venue	Date
20.40i		Kerron	Clement	USA	31.10.85	3rA	SEC	Fayetteville	27 Feb
20.43i		Domenik	Peterson	USA	12.12.84	2rA	NCAA	Fayetteville	11 Mar
20.68i		Kelly	Willie	USA	7.9.82	1h3	SEC	Fayetteville	26 Feb
20.69i		Chris	Lambert	GBR	6.4.81	2	EI	Madrid	6 Mar
20.80i		Paul	Hession	IRL	27.1.83	2h4	EI	Madrid	5 Mar

Best at low altitude

Mark	Wind	Name		Nat	Born	Pos	Meet	Venue	Date
20.61	1.2	J-Mee	Samuels	USA-J	20.5.87	1		Greensboro	21 May
20.66	0.7	Basílio	de Morães	BRA	11.5.82	3	NC	São Paulo	13 Jul

Hand timing

Mark	Wind	Name		Nat	Born	Pos	Meet	Venue	Date
20.3	2.0	Daniel	Batman	AUS	20.3.81	1	LEAP	Loughborough	16 Jul
20.5	0.1	Bruno	Pacheco	BRA	20.4.83	1		São Paulo	13 Mar

Mark	Wind	Name		Nat	Born	Date
20.6	0.5	Claudinei Q da Silva		BRA	19.11.70	7 May
20.6w		David	Gettis	USA-J	27.8.87	11 Mar

IAAF drugs disqualification (Mullings allowed to compete by NCAA)

Mark	Wind	Name		Nat	Born	Pos	Meet	Venue	Date
20.31	0.9	Steve	Mullings ¶	JAM	29.11.82	1h1	SEC	Nashville	13 May
20.34	0.9	Leo	Bookman #	USA	3.1.82	2		Kingston	7 May

JUNIORS

See main list for top 8 juniors. 15 performances by 4 men to 20.49. Additional marks and further juniors:

Name	Mark	Wind	Pos	Meet	Venue	Date	Mark	Wind	Pos	Meet	Venue	Date
Bolt 3+	20.27	0.5	1	NC	Kingston	26 Jun	20.31	-0.6	1		New York (RI)	11 Jun
Dix	20.23	1.0	1	NCAA-r	New York	28 May	20.37i		1r1	NCAA	Fayetteville	12 Mar
	20.41	1.7	2		Tallahassee	23 Apr	20.41	-0.1	1h2	NCAA-r	New York	27 May
	20.44	-0.7	4	NCAA	Scramento	11 Jun						
Merritt	20.40i		1		Fayetteville	12 Feb	20.49	2.0	1		Greensboro	7 Jul

Mark	Wind	Name		Nat	Born	Pos	Meet	Venue	Date
20.79	-0.1	Yusuke	Ishizuka	JPN	19.6.87	1		Chiba	5 Aug
20.79	-1.0	Yuzo	Kanemaru (10)	JPN	18.9.87	1		Kitakyushu	3 Nov
20.80A	1.1	Trey	Harts	USA	17.10.87	2		Albuquerque	4 Jun
20.85	0.1	Julian	Thomas	GBR	28.12.86	2		Mannheim	19 Jun

Mark	Wind	Name		Nat	Born	Pos	Meet	Venue	Date
0.86	1.8	Tremaine	Smith	USA	16.4.86	1	NC-j	Carson	24 Jun
0.90	1.7	Jacob	Scheuerman	USA-Y	15.5.88	2		Aurora	17 Jul
0.91	0.7	Harry	Aikines Aryeetsey	GBR-Y	29.8.88	1	WY	Marrakesh	17 Jul
0.92	1.7	Jamere	Holland	USA-Y	6.3.88	1h3		Sacramento	3 Jun
0.92	1.2	Dominique	Worsley	USA	5.1.87	2		Greensboro	18 Jun
0.94	0.6		Tang Yik Chun	HKG	23.6.86	1h1		Hong Kong	16 Apr
0.95	-0.7	Andrés	Silva	URU	27.3.86	2		Santa Fe	17 Apr
0.95	1.0	Johnny	Thacker (20)	USA	26.8.86	3		Huntsville	15 May
0.95	-1.5	Ali Abubaker	Nagmeldin	SUD	22.2.86	1	Afr-J	Radès	4 Sep

Wind assisted see main list for top 1 junior – more:

Mark	Wind	Name		Nat	Born	Pos	Meet	Venue	Date
0.73		Ahmad	Rashad	USA	12.12.87	1		Wooster	3 Jul
0.78	3.1	Jamil	Hubbard	USA	12.5.86	3	JUCO	Levelland	18 May
0.78	2.5	Tremaine	Smith	USA	16.4.86	2	PAm-J	Windsor	31 Jul
0.80A	3.3	Hitjivirue	Kaanjuka	NAM	29.12.87	1		Windhoek	11 Jun
0.80	2.5	Daniel	Bailey	ANT	9.9.86	3	PAm-J	Windsor	31 Jul
0.88	3.0	Jamere	Holland	USA-Y	6.3.88	1		Sacramento	4 Jun
0.93A	4.9	José Eduardo	Acevedo	VEN	30.3.86	5	SACh	Cali	23 Jul
0.93	2.5	Hawer Andrés	Murillo	COL	1.10.86	4	PAm-J	Windsor	31 Jul

Hand timing

Mark	Wind	Name		Nat	Born	Pos	Meet	Venue	Date
0.7		Yoan Manuel	Frías	CUB	4.7.86	1		La Habana	14 May

300 METRES

Mark	Wind	Name		Nat	Born	Pos	Meet	Venue	Date
1.95		Gary	Kikaya	COD	4.2.78	1		Villeneuve d'Ascq	12 Jun
2.24		Leslie	Djhone	FRA	18.3.81	2		Villeneuve d'Ascq	12 Jun
2.28		Young Talkmore	Nyangani	ZIM	2.9.83	2		Villeneuve d'Ascq	12 Jun
2.49A		Nagmeldin	El Abubakr	SUD-J	22.2.86	1		Sestriere	23 Jul
2.57		ric	Milazar	MRI	1.6.75	4		Villeneuve d'Ascq	12 Jun
2.65		Joseph	Batangdon	CMR	29.7.78	5		Villeneuve d'Ascq	12 Jun
2.68		Jun	Osakada	JPN	2.4.74	1		Taisha	24 Apr
2.79		Godday	James	NGR	9.1.84	1		Praha	25 May

During 400m races

1 Jun NCAA Sacramento: 32.2 Darold Williamson USA, 32.5 Jamel Ashley USA

5 Jun NC Carson: 32.5 Derrick Brew USA, LaShawn Merritt USA

2 Aug WCh Helsinki: 31.9 Jeremy Wariner, 32.2 Tyler Christopher, 32.4 Andrew Rock, 32.5 Tim Benjamin, Chris Brown

400 METRES

Mark	Wind	Name		Nat	Born	Pos	Meet	Venue	Date
3.93		Jeremy	Wariner	USA	31.1.84	1	WCh	Helsinki	12 Aug
4.20			Wariner			1	NC	Carson	25 Jun
4.27		Darold	Williamson	USA	19.2.83	1s1	NCAA	Sacramento	10 Jun
4.35		Andrew	Rock	USA	23.1.82	2	WCh	Helsinki	12 Aug
4.44		Tyler	Christopher	CAN	3.10.83	3	WCh	Helsinki	12 Aug
4.48		Chris	Brown	BAH	15.10.78	4	WCh	Helsinki	12 Aug
4.51			Williamson			1	NCAA	Sacramento	11 Jun
4.51		Tyree	Washington	USA	28.8.76	1	WAF	Monaco	9 Sep
4.53			Wariner			1		Carson	22 May
4.56		Tim	Benjamin	GBR	2.5.82	2	WAF	Monaco	9 Sep
4.60		Alleyne	Francique	GRN	7.6.76	1		Monterrey	11 Jun
4.62			Williamson			2	NC	Carson	25 Jun
4.66		LaShawn	Merritt	USA-J	27.6.86	1		Kingston	7 May
4.67			Wariner			1	WK	Zürich	19 Aug
4.68			Brown			3	WAF	Monaco	9 Sep
4.69			Christopher			1	Gaz	Saint-Denis	1 Jul
4.70			Rock			3	NC	Carson	25 Jun
4.70		Brandon	Simpson (10)	JAM	6.9.81	1	VD	Bruxelles	26 Aug
4.72			Christopher			1	GP	Belém	22 May
4.73			Merritt			4	NC	Carson	25 Jun
4.74			Benjamin			2	VD	Bruxelles	26 Aug
4.75			Rock			2		Kingston	7 May
4.75		Jamel	Ashley	USA	17.4.79	2	NCAA	Sacramento	11 Jun
4.75			Benjamin			1	LGP	London (CP)	22 Jul
4.76			Williamson			1	NCAA-r	Norman	28 May
4.77		Lansford	Spence	JAM	15.12.82	1	NC	Kingston	26 Jun
4.81		Gary	Kikaya	COD	4.2.78	1	Bisl	Oslo	29 Jul
4.82			Wariner			1s2	NC	Carson	24 Jun
4.83			Williamson			1s1	NC	Carson	24 Jun
4.83			Simpson			2	NC	Kingston	26 Jun
		(30/13)							
4.84		Michael	Blackwood	JAM	29.8.76	4	VD	Bruxelles	26 Aug
4.87		Ricardo	Chambers	JAM	7.10.84	1rA		Atlanta	14 May

MEN 2005

Mark	Name		Nat	Born	Pos	Meet	Venue	Date
44.90	Andrae	Williams	BAH	11.7.83	3	NCAA	Sacramento	11 Ju
44.92	Davian	Clarke	JAM	30.4.76	2	GP	Belém	22 Ma
44.93	Nagmeldin	El Abubakr	SUD-J	22.2.86	1	Is.Sol	Makkah	14 Ap
44.93	Terry	Gatson	USA	23.8.82	2s1	NCAA	Sacramento	10 Ju
44.96A	Young Talkmore	Nyangani	ZIM	2.9.83	1		Pretoria	18 Ma
	(20)							
44.96	Derrick	Brew	USA	28.12.77	3		Monterrey	11 Ju
44.97	Kelly	Willie	USA	7.9.82	1		Tempe	16 Ap
44.97	Sanjay	Ayre	JAM	19.6.80	4	NC	Kingston	26 Ju
45.01	Robert	Tobin	GBR	20.12.83	1		Génève	11 Ju
45.02	Ato	Modibo	TRI	19.6.79	2rA		Atlanta	14 Ma
45.06	Carlos	Santa	DOM	7.1.78	6	WAF	Monaco	9 Se
45.09	Leonard	Byrd	USA	17.3.75	3	GP	Belém	22 Ma
45.15	Domenik	Peterson	USA	12.12.84	2		Tempe	16 Ap
45.16	Miles	Smith	USA	24.9.84	1	NCAA-r	Bloomington	28 Ma
45.19	Yeimar	López	CUB	20.8.82	1	Barr	La Habana	19 Ma
	(30)							
45.21	Michael	McDonald	JAM	17.3.75	4	GP	Belém	22 Ma
45.22	Kedar	Inico	USA	29.8.83	4s2	NCAA	Sacramento	10 Ju
45.25	Fernada	Blakely	USA	28.9.81	1		Starkville	16 Ap
45.30	Godday	James	NGR	9.1.84	3h1	WCh	Helsinki	9 Au
45.31	John	Steffensen	AUS	30.8.82	1r2		Réthimno	10 Ju
45.31	Kerron	Clement	USA	31.10.85	3	DNG	Stockholm	26 Ju
45.34	Dirk	Homewood	USA	21.1.82	3	NCAA-r	Norman	28 Ma
45.34	California	Molefe	BOT	2.5.80	4h1	WCh	Helsinki	9 Au
45.38A	Andrés	Silva	URU-J	27.3.86	1	SACh	Cali	22 Ju
45.41	Anderson J.	dos Santos	BRA	23.4.72	5	GP	Belém	22 Ma
	(40)							
45.42A	Ofentse	Mogawane	RSA	20.2.82	2		Pretoria	18 Ma
45.42	Reggie	Witherspoon	USA	31.5.85	5s2	NCAA	Sacramento	10 Ju
45.45	Bershawn	Jackson	USA	8.5.83	2r2		Réthimno	10 Ju
45.47	Prasanna	Amarasekara	SRI	21.3.81	1		Colombo	4 Ju
45.47	Yuzo	Kanemaru	JPN-J	18.9.87	1		Yokohama	19 Se
45.49	Marvin	Essor	JAM	27.8.81	1	NCAA-II	Abilene	28 Ma
45.49	Pierre	Lavanchy	SUI	30.9.82	1	NC	Bern (W)	3 Ju
45.50	Williams	Collazo	CUB-J	31.8.86	2	Barr	La Habana	19 Ma
45.51	Sofiane	Labidi	TUN	29.9.77	1		Göteborg	14 Ju
45.53	Milton	Campbell	USA	15.5.76	1		Athens, GA	7 Ma
	(50)							
45.54	Éric	Milazar	MRI	1.6.75	3	GP II	Torino	3 Ju
45.55	Damion	Barry	TRI	3.3.82	1	NC	Port of Spain	26 Ju
45.56	Leslie	Djhone	FRA	18.3.81	3		Strasbourg	23 Ju
45.57	Hamdan Odha	Al-Bishi	KSA	5.5.81	2	Is.Sol	Makkah	14 Ap
45.57	Marc	Raquil	FRA	2.4.77	5	Gaz	Saint-Denis	1 Ju
45.59	Cédric	Van Branteghem	BEL	13.3.79	1	NC	Bruxelles	10 Ju
45.60	Avard	Moncur	BAH	2.11.78	2		Atlanta	14 Ma
45.60	Malachi	Davis	GBR	13.9.77	1		Szombathely	24 Ju
45.60	Piotr	Klimczak	POL	18.1.80	1		Poznan	31 Ju
45.60	Chris	Troode	AUS	10.2.83	1		Perth	18 De
	(60)							
45.62	Daniel	Dabrowski	POL	23.9.83	2		Yokohama	19 Se
45.62	Mark	Ormrod	AUS	1.12.82	1		Melbourne (OP)	1 De
45.63	Lancford	Davis	JAM	11.10.78	6	NC	Kingston	26 Ju
45.64A	Sanderlei Claro	Parrela	BRA	7.10.74	1		Cochabamba	29 Ma
45.65	Xavier	Carter	USA	8.12.85	1		Baton Rouge	23 Ap
45.69A	Thomas	Musembi	KEN	26.4.77	1	WCT	Nairobi	25 Ju
45.69	Marcin	Marciniszyn	POL	7.9.82	1	NC	Biala Podlaska	25 Ju
45.70	Matt	Scherer	USA	21.11.83	6s1	NCAA	Sacramento	10 Ju
45.70	Andrea	Barberi	ITA	15.1.79	3h4	WCh	Helsinki	9 Au
45.71A	Marcus	la Grange	RSA	12.12.77	3		Pretoria	18 Ma
	(70)							
45.71	Clinton	Hill	AUS	19.4.80	2		Sydney	17 De
45.73A	Jan	van der Merwe	RSA	16.3.84	4		Pretoria	18 Ma
45.77	Yevgeniy	Lebedev	RUS	19.2.81	1	NCp	Tula	23 Ju
45.78	Lionel	Larry	USA-J	14.9.86	1		Los Angeles	30 Ap
45.78	Mitsuhiro	Sato	JPN	8.1.80	5h4	WCh	Helsinki	9 Au
45.80	Simon	Kirch	GER	26.9.79	1h1	NC	Wattenscheid	2 Ju
45.80	Arizmendi	Peguero	DOM	7.8.80	3h3	WCh	Helsinki	9 Au
45.82	Jerry	Harris	USA	29.10.81	1		Atlanta	3 Ju
45.82	Renny	Quow	TRI-J	25.8.87	2	NC	Port of Spain	26 Ju

Mark	Name		Nat	Born	Pos	Meet	Venue	Date
45.84A	Ezra	Sambu	KEN	4.9.78	1		Nairobi	7 May
	(80)							
45.84	David	Gettis	USA-J	27.8.87	1		Sacramento	4 Jun
45.87A	Hendrik	Mokganyetsi	RSA	7.9.75	5		Pretoria	18 Mar
45.87	Craig	Everhart	USA	13.9.83	1h2	Pac-10	Los Angeles (Ww)	14 May
45.88	Glauder	Garzón	CUB	13.2.82	1h1	CAC	Nassau	9 Jul
45.88	Graham	Hedman	GBR	6.2.79	3	NC	Manchester (SC)	10 Jul
45.89	David	Neville	USA	1.6.84	1	Big 10	Columbus	15 May
45.89	Yoshihiro	Horigome	JPN	2.1.81	4		Yokohama	19 Sep
45.90	Aaron	Cleare	BAH	31.1.83	3	NC	Freeport	25 Jun
45.90	Zeljko	Vincek	CRO-J	16.6.86	2	MedG	Almeria	1 Jul
45.91 ?	Wilan	Louis	BAR	1.3.83	1		Waterford	18 Jun
	45.97				4	NC	Port of Spain	25 Jun
	(90)							
45.92	Marek	Plawgo	POL	25.2.81	1		Biala Podlaska	28 May
45.93	David	Gillick	IRL	9.7.83	5	GP II	Torino	3 Jun
45.94	Lewis	Banda	ZIM	16.8.82	2		Tucson	21 May
45.94	Mohammed	Al-Salhi	KSA-J	11.5.86	2	PArab	Radès	16 Sep
45.95	James	Davis	USA	19.3.76	2	MSR	Walnut	17 Apr
45.95	Jonathan	Johnson	USA	5.3.82	1		Fort Worth	23 Apr
45.95	Bobby	Young	LBR	6.8.84	1		Waverly, IA	28 May
45.95	Ridha	Ghali	TUN	7.5.83	3	MedG	Almeria	1 Jul
45.98	Daniel	Batman	AUS	20.3.81	2		Adelaide	19 Feb
45.98	E.J.	Falkner	USA	.85	2	NCAA-II	Abilene	28 May
	(100)							
45.98	Antonio Manuel	Reina	ESP	13.6.81	2	Déca	Paris (C)	3 Sep

Mark	Name		Nat	Born	Date
45.99	Julien	Raeburn	TRI	18.9.78	26 Jun
45.99	Saul	Weigopwa	NGR	14.6.84	27 Jun
45.99	Dimítrios	Grávalos	GRE	18.4.84	15 Jul
46.00	Omar	Brown	JAM	21.6.82	17 Apr
46.00A	Themba	Ncube	ZIM	23.11.77	20 Apr
46.00A	Sammy	Rono	KEN	2.4.82	25 Jun
46.01A	Chris	Gebhardt	RSA	10.2.85	18 Mar
46.01	Rohan	Pradeep Kumara	SRI	10.3.75	24 Jun
46.01	Robert	Mackowiak	POL	13.5.70	31 Jul
46.02	Kellen	Blassingame	USA	2.3.84	23 Apr
46.02	Carey	LaCour	USA	17.2.85	14 May
46.02	Kenji	Narisako	JPN	25.7.84	26 Oct
46.03	Rafal	Wieruszewski	POL	24.2.81	17 Jul
46.04A	Vincent	Mumo	KEN	3.8.82	7 May
46.05	Schefer	Sherrer	USA	27.8.85	18 May
46.06	Jun	Osakada	JPN	2.4.74	7 May
46.06	Michael	Mathieu	BAH	24.6.84	28 May
46.06	Andrey	Rudnitskiy	RUS	12.10.79	18 Jun
46.07	Robert	Daly	IRL	26.1.78	11 Jun
46.07	Sekou	Clarke	JAM	7.10.83	26 Jun
46.07	Andrey	Tverdostup	UKR	18.6.77	3 Jul
46.08	Michael	Mitchell	USA	16.5.81	17 Apr
46.08	Bryan	Kelley	USA	22.1.84	28 May
46.08	Aleksey	Rachkovskiy	UKR	13.3.84	14 Jun
46.08	Musa	Audu	NGR	18.6.80	9 Jul
46.09	Piotr	Rysiukiewicz	POL	14.7.74	25 Jun
46.09	Konstantin	Svechkar	RUS	17.7.84	15 Jul
46.11	Justin	Oliver	USA-J	7.11.87	18 Jun
46.12	David	Geddes	AUS	26.1.82	4 Mar
46.12	Obakeng	Ngwigwe	BOT	9.7.85	21 May
46.12	DeWayne	Barrett	JAM	27.12.81	25 Jun
46.12	Nathan	Vadeboncoeur	CAN	6.11.84	16 Jul
46.13	Peter	Coley	JAM	21.2.81	26 Mar
46.15	Yuki	Yamaguchi	JPN	22.2.84	17 Aug
46.15		Wang Liangyu	CHN	9.8.84	18 Oct
46.16	Themba	Ncube	ZIM	23.11.77	16 Apr
46.16	Nathan	Daniels	USA	22.8.85	15 May
46.17	Arthur	Davis	USA	11.11.83	16 Apr
46.17	Jason	Barton	USA	9.4.82	30 Apr
46.17	Jimisola	Laursen	SWE	13.7.77	6 Jul
46.17	Abderrahim	El Haouzy	FRA	1.1.75	16 Jul
46.19	Naman	Keïta	FRA	9.4.78	3 Apr
46.19	Johnny	Jacob	USA	6.1.82	15 May
46.19	Bolaji	Lawal	NGR	26.6.76	8 Jul
46.20	Gakologelwane	Masheto	BOT	1.11.84	21 May
46.21	Vladimir	Demchenko	UKR	16.4.81	3 Jul
46.22	Adam	Steele	USA	8.10.80	14 May
46.23	Cedric	Goodman	USA-J	17.3.86	28 May
46.23	Ahmed	Douhou	FRA	14.12.76	15 Jul
46.23	Johan	Wissman	SWE	2.11.82	26 Jul
46.24	Erison	Hurtault	USA	29.12.84	28 May
46.24	Kamghe	Gaba	GER	13.1.84	15 Jul
46.24A	Javier	Mosquera	COL	29.1.83	22 Jul
46.25	Ivory	Williams	USA	2.5.85	16 Apr
46.27	Bernard	Middleton	USA	21.12.85	27 May
46.27A	David	Kirui	KEN	15.12.74	18 Jun
46.27	Piotr	Zrada	POL	3.1.84	15 Jul
46.28A	L.J.	van Zyl	RSA	20.7.85	30 Mar
46.28A	Daniel	Ward	NED	4.1.84	16 Apr
46.28	Nate	Olson	USA	31.5.83	28 May
46.28	Dmitriy	Forshev	RUS	30.5.76	11 Jul
46.29	Randy	Curry	USA		9 Apr
46.29	Justin	Byron	USA	9.7.84	29 Apr
46.29	Godfrey	Herring	USA	18.5.78	7 May
46.29	David	Dickens 166)	USA	19.3.85	7 May

Hand timed

Mark	Name		Nat	Born	Date
46.0A	Themba	Ncube	ZIM	23.11.77	20 Apr
46.0A	Vincent	Mumo	KEN	3.8.82	28 May
46.1A	Gakologelwane	Masheto	BOT	1.11.84	3 Jul
46.2A	David	Kirui	KEN	15.12.74	28 May
46.2A	Nelton	Ndebele	ZIM	6.6.85	19 Jun

Indoors

Mark	Name		Nat	Born	Pos	Meet	Venue	Date
44.57i	Kerron	Clement	USA	31.10.85	1	NCAA	Fayetteville	12 Mar
45.93i	David	Canal	ESP	7.12.78	1	NC	Madrid	20 Feb

Mark	Name		Nat	Born	Date
46.16	Wallace	Spearmon	USA	24.12.84	14 Jan
46.26	Bayano	Kamani	PAN	17.4.80	29 Jan

Low altitude best

Mark	Name	Pos	Meet	Venue	Date
45.10	Nyangani	2		Strasbourg	23 Jun
45.87	van der Merwe	2		Göteborg	14 Jun
45.92	Parrela	1	NC	São Paulo	17 Jun
45.98	Mogawane	1		Oudtshoorn	5 Mar
46.01	la Grange	1		Durban	18 Feb

JUNIORS

See main list for top 10 juniors. 12 performances by 5 men to 45.60. Additional marks and further juniors:

Name	Mark	Pos	Meet	Venue	Date	Mark	Pos	Meet	Venue	Date
Merritt 2+	44.93i	1		Fayetteville	11 Feb	45.34	6	GGala	Roma	8 Jul
	45.31	2s2	NC	Carson	24 Jun	45.54	4	DNG	Stockholm	26 Jul
El Abubakr	45.47	1		Villeneuve d'Ascq	12 Jun	45.52	2	GP II	Torino	3 Jun

Mark	Name		Nat	Born	Pos	Meet	Venue	Date
(Abubakr) 45.52					1	GP	Doha	13 May
46.11	Justin	Oliver	USA	7.11.87	1		Greensboro	18 Jun
46.23	Cedric	Goodman	USA	17.3.86	3	NCAA-r	New York	28 May
46.33	Rabah	Yusif	SUD	11.12.86	4	AAA	Manchester (SC)	10 Jul
46.37	Ben	Offereins	AUS	12.3.86	1	NC	Sydney	5 Mar
46.39	Quentin	Summers	USA	15.6.87	1		New Orleans	6 Aug
46.42	LaJerald	Betters	USA	6.2.88	2r3		Greensboro	18 Jun
46.44	Martyn	Rooney	GBR	3.4.87	1	NC-j	Bedford	3 Jul
46.47	Claudio	Licciardello	ITA	11.1.86	1	NC-j	Grosseto	4 Jun
46.47	Nate	Anderson	USA	28.9.87	2	NC-j	Carson	25 Jun
46.47	Richard	Buck (20)	GBR	14.11.86	1j	BrGP	Sheffield	21 Aug

600 METRES

Mark	Name		Nat	Born	Pos	Meet	Venue	Date
1:15.23	Khadevis	Robinson	USA	19.7.76	1		Liège (NX)	20 Jul
1:15.62	Joseph	Mutua	KEN	10.12.78	2		Liège (NX)	20 Jul
1:15.77	Sherridan	Kirk	TRI	11.2.81	3		Liège (NX)	20 Jul
1:16.03	Marek	Plawgo	POL	25.2.81				30 Apr
1:16.08	Grzegorz	Krzosek	POL	10.1.76				30 Apr
1:16.50	Oabona	Onalenna	BOT	6.5.84				20 Jul
1:16.52A	James	McIlroy	GBR	30.12.76				24 Jan
Indoors								
1:15.60	Dmitrijs	Milkevics	LAT	6.12.81	1		Lincoln, NE	5 Feb

800 METRES

Mark	Name		Nat	Born	Pos	Meet	Venue	Date
1:43.70	Wilfred	Bungei	KEN	24.7.80	1	GP	Rieti	28 Aug
1:43.96	Youssef Saad	Kamel	BRN	29.3.83	1		Rovereto	31 Aug
1:44.08	Mbulaeni	Mulaudzi	RSA	8.9.80	1	GP	Helsinki	25 Jul
1:44.11A		Bungei			1	WCT	Nairobi	25 Jun
1:44.12		Mulaudzi			1	SGP	Athína	14 Jun
1:44.15		Mulaudzi			1rA	Bisl	Oslo	29 Jul
1:44.18	Yuriy	Borzakovskiy	RUS	12.4.81	2rA	Bisl	Oslo	29 Jul
1:44.18	Antonio Manuel	Reina	ESP	13.6.81	2	GP	Rieti	28 Aug
1:44.22	Amine	Laâlou	MAR	13.5.82	1	GP	Sevilla	4 Jun
1:44.24	Rashid	Ramzi	BRN	17.7.80	1	WCh	Helsinki	14 Aug
1:44.26		Kamel			2	GP	Sevilla	4 Jun
1:44.26		Borzakovskiy			1s1	WCh	Helsinki	12 Aug
1:44.26		Mulaudzi			1	ISTAF	Berlin	4 Sep
1:44.27	Majid Saeed	Sultan	QAT-J	3.11.86	1	AsiC	Inchon	4 Sep
1:44.29		Bungei			2	SGP	Athína	14 Jun
1:44.30		Ramzi			2s1	WCh	Helsinki	12 Aug
1:44.30		Reina			2	ISTAF	Berlin	4 Sep
1:44.31		Bungei			3	GP	Sevilla	4 Jun
1:44.32		Reina			1rB	WK	Zürich	19 Aug
1:44.33	Gary	Reed	CAN	25.10.81	1s3	WCh	Helsinki	12 Aug
1:44.34	Bilal	Mansour Ali (10)	BRN	17.10.83	1		Conegliano	17 Jun
1:44.36		Kamel			3	ISTAF	Berlin	4 Sep
1:44.39	Mohammed	Al-Salhi	KSA-J	11.5.86	1		Lapinlahti	3 Jul
1:44.41		Bungei			2s3	WCh	Helsinki	12 Aug
1:44.42		Bungei				GP	Madrid	16 Jul
1:44.45	Alfred	Kirwa Yego	KEN-J	28.11.86	3rA	Bisl	Oslo	29 Jul
1:44.46	Mouhcine	Chéhibi	MAR	28.1.78	2rB	WK	Zürich	19 Aug
1:44.51	William	Yiampoy	KEN	17.5.74	3s1	WCh	Helsinki	12 Aug
1:44.51		Borzakovskiy			2	WCh	Helsinki	14 Aug
1:44.54		Kamel			3	SGP	Athína	14 Jun
1:44.54		Reed			4rA	Bisl	Oslo	29 Jul
1:44.54		Borzakovskiy			1	VD	Bruxelles	26 Aug
	(32/14)							
1:44.62	Khadevis	Robinson	USA	19.7.76	4rB	WK	Zürich	19 Aug
1:44.65	James	McIlroy	GBR	30.12.76	3	GP	Rieti	28 Aug
1:44.71	René	Herms	GER	17.7.82	1		Cuxhaven	9 Jul
1:44.73	Abdulrahman	Suleiman	QAT	10.1.84	2	AsiC	Inchon	4 Sep
1:44.74	Dmitrijs	Milkevics	LAT	6.12.81	1	NCAA	Sacramento	11 Jun
1:44.74	Mehdi	Baala	FRA	17.8.78	1		Villeneuve d'Ascq	12 Jun
	(20)							
1:44.74	Sadjad	Moradi	IRI	30.3.83	3	AsiC	Inchon	4 Sep
1:44.80	Djabir	Saïd-Guerni	ALG	29.3.77	4s1	WCh	Helsinki	12 Aug
1:44.86	Jonathan	Johnson	USA	5.3.82	1	Big 12	Manhattan, KS	15 May
1:44.86	John	Litei	KEN	2.6.83	3		Villeneuve d'Ascq	12 Jun
1:44.94	Kevin	Hicks	USA	7.11.84	2	NCAA	Sacramento	11 Jun
1:45.04	David	Krummenacker	USA	24.5.75	5rB	WK	Zürich	19 Aug
1:45.19	Eugenio	Barrios	ESP	3.11.76	5	GP	Sevilla	4 Jun

Mark	Name		Nat	Born	Pos	Meet	Venue	Date
1:45.20	André	Bucher	SUI	19.10.76	7rA	Bisl	Oslo	29 Jul
1:45.24	Cosmas	Rono	KEN	12.12.84	1rA	NA	Heusden-Zolder	23 Jul
1:45.25	Nicolas	Aïssat	FRA	24.7.80	3		Strasbourg	23 Jun
	(30)							
1:45.28	Samwel	Mwera	TAN	3.6.85	1	GP II	Rio de Janeiro	15 May
1:45.30	Dmitriy	Bogdanov	RUS	11.4.79	7	SGP	Athína	14 Jun
1:45.32	Ismail Ahmed	Ismail	SUD	10.9.84	1rB	GP	Madrid	16 Jul
1:45.36	Osmar B.	dos Santos	BRA	20.10.68	1	GP II	Torino	3 Jun
1:45.37	Florent	Lacasse	FRA	21.1.81	1		Castres	26 Jul
1:45.39	Pawel	Czapiewski	POL	30.3.78	3	GP	Helsinki	25 Jul
1:45.40	Fabiano	Peçanha	BRA	5.6.82	1	GP	Belém	22 May
1:45.43	Sherridan	Kirk	TRI	11.2.81	3	NCAA	Sacramento	11 Jun
1:45.48	Manuel	Olmedo	ESP	17.5.83	7	GP	Sevilla	4 Jun
1:45.5A	Suleiman	Simotwo	KEN	21.4.80	1	NC	Nairobi	18 Jun
	(40)							
1:45.51	Hezekiél	Sepeng	RSA	30.6.74	2	NC	Durban	16 Apr
1:45.54	Alexis	Kipkirchir	KEN	26.11.84	1rB	Bisl	Oslo	29 Jul
1:45.58	Joseph	Mutua	KEN	10.12.78	2rB	GP	Madrid	16 Jul
1:45.62A	Werner	Botha	RSA	31.1.78	2		Pretoria	18 Mar
1:45.65	Achraf	Tadili	CAN	8.7.80	4	GP	Belém	22 May
1:45.67	Antoine	Martiak	FRA	29.1.83	3		Castres	26 Jul
1:45.73	Justus	Koech	KEN	19.3.80	3rB	GP	Madrid	16 Jul
1:45.79	Miguel	Quesada	ESP	18.9.79	8	GP	Sevilla	4 Jun
1:45.86	Jeremy	Mims	USA	15.2.83	4	NCAA	Sacramento	11 Jun
1:45.88A	William	Chirchir	KEN	6.2.79	2		Nairobi	7 May
	(50)							
1:45.89	Yassine	Bensghir	MAR	3.1.83	1		Rabat	18 Jun
1:45.9A	Gilbert	Kipchoge	KEN	4.5.83	1		Nairobi	14 May
1:46.03	Jebreh	Harris	USA	22.9.78	2	CalR	Modesto	7 May
1:46.05	Ådne Svahn	Dæhlin	NOR	26.6.82	8rA	Bisl	Oslo	29 Jul
1:46.05	Andrea	Longo	ITA	26.6.75	3		Rovereto	31 Aug
1:46.06A	Michael	Too	KEN	3.8.83	1B		Nairobi	7 May
1:46.06	Oabona	Onalenna	BOT	6.5.84	1		Covilhã	16 Jul
1:46.07	Kamel	Boulahfane	ALG	1.7.76	2		Rabat	18 Jun
1:46.09	Derrick	Peterson	USA	28.11.77	2		Lignano Sabbiadoro	17 Jul
1:46.13	Johan	Cronje	RSA	13.4.82	2		Lapinlahti	3 Jul
	(60)							
1:46.15	Maurizio	Bobbato	ITA	17.2.79	9rA	GGala	Roma	8 Jul
1:46.15	Willy	Rotich	KEN	23.3.76	1		Lappeenranta	21 Jul
1:46.19	Ivan	Heshko	UKR	19.8.79	1	NC	Kiev	3 Jul
1:46.19	Christian	Obrist	ITA	20.11.80	1		Pergine Valsugana	22 Jul
1:46.19	Jason	Stewart	NZL	21.11.81	1rB	NA	Heusden-Zolder	23 Jul
1:46.20	Edwin	Letting	KEN-J	.86	1		Nijmegen	20 May
1:46.25	Andrew	Ellerton	CAN	18.11.83	5	NCAA	Sacramento	11 Jun
1:46.25	Moise	Joseph	HAI	27.12.81	3rA	NA	Heusden-Zolder	23 Jul
1:46.28	Grzegorz	Krzosek	POL	10.1.76	1		Bydgoszcz	5 Jun
1:46.3A	Elkanah	Angwenyi	KEN	5.2.83	1		Kakamega	19 Mar
	(70)							
1:46.3A	Linus	Ndiwa	KEN		3	NC	Nairobi	18 Jun
1:46.44	Jacob	Koczman	USA	21.11.78	2		Bloomington	12 Jul
1:46.49	Glody	Dube	BOT	2.7.78	3		Cuxhaven	9 Jul
1:46.53	Benson	Esho	KEN-J	2.2.87	3		Conegliano	17 Jun
1:46.55A	Michael	Rotich	KEN	14.7.78	3rA		Nairobi	7 May
1:46.56	Anter	Zerguelaïne	ALG	4.1.85	3		Rabat	18 Jun
1:46.59	Christian	Neunhäuserer	ITA	21.6.78	3		Pergine Valsugana	22 Jul
1:46.60	Tom	Omey	BEL	24.4.75	1		Arnhem	22 Jun
1:46.6A	Michael	Chepkonga	KEN	.79	2		Nairobi	14 May
1:46.61	Yeimar	López	CUB	20.8.82	1	NC	La Habana	18 Mar
	(80)							
1:46.63	Livio	Sciandra	ITA	23.9.80	4		Conegliano	17 Jun
1:46.65	Kleberson	Davide	BRA	20.7.85	5	GP	Belém	22 May
1:46.65	Richard	Smith	USA	10.2.83	6	Pre	Eugene	4 Jun
1:46.67	Mohamed Mutlak	Al-Azimi	KUW	16.6.82	5	AsiC	Inchon	4 Sep
1:46.67	Ghamanda	Ram	IND	1.7.84	1	NC	Hyderabad	9 Nov
1:46.68	Juha	Kukkamo	FIN	1.4.76	8	GP	Helsinki	25 Jul
1:46.70	Sam	Burley	USA	13.2.81	3	GP II	Stanford	30 May
1:46.70	Courtney	Jaworski	USA	7.5.84	7	NCAA	Sacramento	11 Jun
1:46.7A	Remi	Limo Ndiwa	KEN-Y	3.2.88	3		Nairobi	14 May
1:46.75	Diego	Gomes	BRA	19.4.85	5	GP II	Rio de Janeiro	15 May
	(90)							
1:46.75	Nabil	Madi	ALG	9.6.81	4		Rabat	18 Jun

Mark	Name		Nat	Born	Pos	Meet	Venue	Date
1:46.75	Isaac	Sang	KEN	24.8.78	2		Tomblaine	6 Sep
1:46.80	Peter	Etoot	KEN	17.4.84	8	NCAA	Sacramento	11 Jun
1:46.8A	Isaac	Kombich	KEN	16.10.85	2rB		Nairobi	7 May
	1:46.83				2		Nuoro	13 Jul
1:46.84	Jackson	Langat	KEN	15.12.80	1		Arlington	2 Apr
1:46.85	Abdoulaye	Wagne	SEN	30.1.81	3		Tomblaine	6 Sep
1:46.86	Benjamin	Kipkurui	KEN	28.12.80	1		Kingston	7 May
1:46.86	Arnoud	Okken	NED	20.4.82	5	NA	Heusden-Zolder	23 Jul
1:46.87	Isaiah	Nkuna	RSA	5.3.77	4	NC	Durban	16 Apr
1:46.87	Salem Amer	Al-Badri	QAT	12.12.85	3		Lignano Sabbiadoro	17 Jul
	(100)							

Mark	Name		Nat	Born	Date
1:46.91	Walid	Meliani	ALG	18.3.84	18 Jun
1:46.93A	Johan	Pretorius	RSA	23.9.82	18 Mar
1:46.94	Michal	Sneberger	CZE	23.6.78	3 Jul
1:46.95	Juan de Dios	Jurado	ESP	9.4.81	16 Jul
1:46.97	Ramil	Aritkulov	RUS	1.3.78	30 May
1:46.97	Jimmy	Lomba	FRA	30.6.78	23 Jun
1:46.98A	Charles	Jantjies	RSA	21.7.82	4 Feb
1:47.01	Prince	Mumba	ZAM	28.8.84	12 Jul
1:47.03	Dave	Paulsen	USA	18.3.81	12 Jul
1:47.04	Maury Surel	Castillo	CUB	19.10.84	18 Mar
1:47.05A	Paul	Korir	KEN	15.7.77	7 May
1:47.05	Tim	Clerbout	BEL	13.10.81	2 Jul
1:47.05	Jaroslav	Ruza	CZE	26.9.83	3 Jul
1:47.06	Rashid	Mohamed	BRN	9.11.79	27 May
1:47.06	Charles	Gruber	USA	6.8.78	17 Jul
1:47.07	Bernard	Lagat	USA	12.12.74	7 May
1:47.09	Andrew	Baddeley	GBR	20.6.82	6 Aug
1:47.09	Adnan Taees	Akkar	IRQ	24.3.80	4 Sep
1:47.10	Philemon	Kimutai	KEN		31 Aug
1:47.10	Geoffrey	Rono	KEN-J	21.4.87	4 Sep
1:47.1A	Moses	Barmasai	KEN		14 May
1:47.11	Jonathan	Rankin	USA	9.2.82	17 Apr
1:47.13	Kevin	Hautcoeur	FRA	17.1.85	23 Jun
1:47.13	Alan	Webb	USA	13.1.83	16 Aug
1:47.14	Mohamed	Moro	ITA	5.3.84	17 Jun
1:47.15	Miroslaw	Formela	POL	31.10.78	5 Jun
1:47.16	Timothy	Dunne	USA	22.5.79	4 Jun
1:47.19	Christian	Smith	USA	31.10.83	17 Apr
1:47.20	Mounir	Yemmouni	FRA	12.10.83	6 Sep
1:47.21	Fadil	Bellaabouss	FRA-J	15.6.86	23 Jun
1:47.22	Joeri	Jansen	BEL	28.5.79	9 Jun
1:47.26	Jamel	Ahrass	FRA	15.11.81	29 May
1:47.26	Maksim	Adamovich	RUS	24.6.80	11 Jul
1:47.28	Zach	Glavash	USA	14.6.84	16 Apr
1:47.29	Rickard	Pell	SWE	24.3.79	27 May
1:47.30	Elliott	Blount	USA	25.6.79	17 Apr
1:47.30	Nahashon	Ruto	KEN	23.9.77	30 May
1:47.3A	Daniel	Kipchirchir Komen	KEN	27.11.84	30 Apr
1:47.3A	Dedan	Maina Macharia	KEN	.78	28 May
1:47.31	Ryan	Brown	USA	17.9.84	15 May
1:47.34	Rizak	Dirshe	SWE	5.1.72	1 Jun
1:47.35	James	Hatch	USA	27.9.82	15 May
1:47.35	David	Gill	CAN	28.12.78	17 Jul
1:47.37	Berhanu	Alemu	ETH	16.7.82	11 Aug
1:47.38	Paul	Cross	USA	19.8.83	15 May
1:47.38		Lee Jae-hoon	KOR	28.11.76	30 Jul
1:47.4	Réda	Aït Douida	MAR	.82	8 May
	1:47.43				21 May
1:47.4A	Bernard	Kisilu Musyoka	KEN	6.12.74	18 Jun
1:47.42	Mohamed	Moustaoui	MAR	2.4.85	18 Jun
1:47.43	Aaron	Nasers	USA	25.11.83	15 May
1:47.44A	Victor	Kibet	KEN	.81	7 May
1:47.44	Ricardo	Bell	USA	17.1.81	12 Jul
1:47.45	Gareth	Hyett	NZL	13.2.80	9 Jul
1:47.45	Stephan	Frosch	GER	4.1.77	9 Jul
1:47.47	Will	Fitts	USA	18.9.83	15 May
1:47.48	Neville	Miller	USA	22.12.82	4 Jun
1:47.49	Selahattin	Cobanoglu	TUR	20.8.85	20 Aug
1:47.50	Erkin	Isakov	UZB	25.11.74	16 Jul
1:47.51	Andrey	Osipov	RUS	6.3.83	16 Jul
1:47.57A	Bonolo	Maboa	RSA	24.8.85	18 Mar
1:47.57	Soufiane	Zahafi	MAR	27.9.78	2 Jul
1:47.59	Ehsan	Mohajershojaei	IRI	21.3.83	21 Jun
1:47.59	José Manuel	Cortés	ESP	10.6.83	20 Aug
1:47.59	Lukas	Rifesser	ITA-J	17.7.86	31 Aug
1:47.62	Adil	Hadjhamou	MAR	22.3.79	29 May
1:47.65	Moritz	Höft	GER	3.12.80	9 Jul
1:47.66	Mike	Inge	USA	31.1.84	27 May
1:47.67	Shaun	Abrahams	RSA	4.7.70	16 Apr
1:47.67	Tom	Vanchaze	BEL	22.12.82	27 May
1:47.69	Sam	Ellis	GBR	23.6.82	22 May
1:47.69	Pávlos	Faroúggias	GRE	6.6.77	14 Jun
1:47.7	Jimmy	Watkins	GBR	30.10.82	11 Sep
1:47.71	Vitaliy	Voloshin	UKR	12.1.85	3 Jul
1:47.75	Christopher	Lukezic	USA	24.4.84	17 Apr
1:47.76A	Gerrit	Woest	RSA	15.3.79	18 Mar
1:47.78	Marcus	Mayes	USA	10.3.85	15 May
1:47.78	Elkana	Chepsiror	KEN		4 Jun
1:47.79	Nick	Bromley	AUS	23.3.83	7 May
1:47.82	Mohamed	Battani	MAR	7.3.83	15 Jul
1:47.83	Yared	Shegumo	POL	10.1.83	31 Jul
1:47.84	Duane	Solomon	USA	28.12.84	26 Mar
1:47.86	Samir	Khadar	ALG-J	10.6.86	4 Sep
1:47.88	Raphael	Asafo-Agyei	GHA	20.10.83	15 May
1:47.88	Stefan	Eberhardt	GER	12.1.85	9 Jul
1:47.90	Erik	Sproll	CAN	22.2.83	15 May
1:47.90	Abdeslam	Kennouche	ALG	7.10.80	7 Jun
1:47.91	Youssef	Baba	MAR	7.8.79	4 Jun
1:47.91	Ali	Yiampoy	KEN		1 Jun
1:47.93	Maurizio	Angius	ITA	27.7.83	17 Jun
1:47.93	Davide	Rodia	ITA	14.8.81	17 Jun
1:47.93	Kevin	Elliott	USA	7.11.78	9 Jul
1:47.94	Thomas	Matthys	BEL	4.9.85	20 May
1:47.94	Rui	Silva	POR	3.8.77	24 Jul
1:47.95	Pavel	Pikovets	UKR	11.12.76	3 Jul
1:47.95	Mattias	Claesson	SWE-J	26.7.86	16 Aug
1:47.96	Jacob	Hernandez	USA	8.9.85	14 May
1:47.96	Andreas	Freimann	GER	19.8.83	10 Jun
1:47.96	Tim	Rogge	BEL	3.2.77	10 Jul
1:47.97		Li Xiangyu	CHN	21.10.85	19 Aug
1:47.99	Massimo	De Meo	ITA	21.2.73	16 Jul
	(200)				

Indoors

Mark	Name		Nat	Born	Pos	Venue	Date
1:46.27i	Arnoud	Okken	NED	20.4.82	1	Stuttgart	29 Jan
1:46.43i	Joel	Williams	USA	23.6.80?	1	Ames	5 Mar

Mark	Name		Nat	Born	Date
1:47.43i	Aldwyn	Sappleton	JAM	21.12.81	12 Feb
1:47.49i	Shaun	Smith	JAM	19.4.83	5 Mar
1:47.51	Nathan	Brannen	CAN	8.9.82	5 Mar
1:47.58	Wolfram	Müller	GER	8.7.81	4 Feb
1:47.84	Jeffrey	Fisher	USA	8.5.82	5 Mar
1:47.90	Nicholas	Wachira	KEN	19.11.82	24 Feb

JUNIORS

See main list for top 6 juniors. 14 performances by 3 men to 1:45.99. Additional marks and further juniors:

Name	Mark	Pos	Meet	Venue	Date	Mark	Pos	Meet	Venue	Date
Sultan	1:45.58	1		Covilhã	16 Jul					
Al-Salhi	1:45.50	5	GP	Helsinki	25 Jul	1:45.78	4	AsiC	Inchon	4 Sep
	1:45.64	1	GP	Doha	13 May	1:45.87	1B	GGala	Roma	8 Jul
Kirwa Yego	1:44.55	3B	WK	Zürich	19 Aug	1:45.68	2	GP	Doha	13 May
	1:44.62	1	GGala	Roma	8 Jul	1:45.85	3	GP II	Torino	3 Jun
	1:44.63A	2	WCT	Nairobi	25 Jun	1:45.94	6	VD	Bruxelles	26 Aug

Mark	Name		Nat	Born	Pos	Meet	Venue	Date
1:47.10	Geoffrey	Rono	KEN	21.4.87	1	Afr-J	Radès	4 Sep
1:47.21	Fadil	Bellaabouss	FRA	15.6.86	6		Strasbourg	23 Jun
1:47.59	Lukas	Rifesser	ITA-	17.7.86	4B		Rovereto	31 Aug
1:47.86	Samir	Khadar (10)	ALG	10.6.86	2	Afr-J	Radès	4 Sep
1:47.95	Mattias	Claesson	SWE	26.7.86	5	MAI	Malmö	16 Aug
1:48.21A	Isaac	Mboyaza	RSA	26.9.86	5		Potchefstroom	4 Feb
1:48.26	Steven	Fennell	GBR	4.4.86	2		Manchester (Str)	5 Jul
1:48.26	Nasser Shams	Kareem	QAT	30.1.86	4		Tessenderlo	20 Aug
1:48.29	Haillu	Ashenafi	ETH	17.6.87	7		Padova	3 Jul
1:48.31	Dávid	Takács	HUN	15.2.86	2		Budapest	30 Jul
1:48.32	Dmitrijs	Jurkevics	LAT	7.1.87	6		Tallinn	17 Aug
1:48.41	Michael	Rimmer	GBR	3.2.86	2		Watford	11 Jun
1:48.42	Gilbert	Keter	KEN-Y	15.1.88	1	WY	Marrakesh	15 Jul
1:48.43	Alvaro	Rodriguez (20)	ESP	25.5.87	5		Huelva	7 Jun

1000 METRES

Mark	Name		Nat	Born	Pos	Meet	Venue	Date
2:16.94	Alex	Kipchirchir	KEN	26.11.84	1		New York (RI)	11 Jun
2:17.13	Elkanah	Angwenyi	KEN	5.2.83	2		New York (RI)	11 Jun
2:17.57	David	Krummenacker	USA	24.5.75	3		New York (RI)	11 Jun
2:17.81	Pawel	Czapiewski	POL	30.3.78	1		Krakōw	27 Aug

2:19.06 Moise Joseph HAI 27.12.81 11 Jun | 2:19.11 Mehdi Baala FRA 17.8.78 6 Sep
2:19.06 Samuel Burley USA 13.2.81 11 Jun | 2:19.36 Rob Myers USA 5.8.80 11 Jun

Indoors: 2:17.01 Mehdi Baala FRA 17.8.78 1 Karlsruhe 13 Feb
2:19.33 Abdelati Iguider MAR-J 25.3.87 13 Feb | 2:19.49 James McIlroy GBR 30.12.76 29 Jan

1500 METRES

Mark	Name		Nat	Born	Pos	Meet	Venue	Date
3:29.30	Bernard	Lagat	USA	12.12.74	1	GP	Rieti	28 Aug
3:29.72	Daniel	Kipchirchir Komen	KEN	27.11.84	1	ISTAF	Berlin	4 Sep
3:30.00	Rashid	Ramzi	BRN	17.7.80	1	GGala	Roma	8 Jul
3:30.01		K Komen			1	Gaz	Saint-Denis	1 Jul
3:30.37		K Komen			2	GGala	Roma	8 Jul
3:30.49		K Komen			1	WK	Zürich	19 Aug
3:30.64		Lagat			2	Gaz	Saint-Denis	1 Jul
3:30.77		K Komen			1	SGP	Doha	13 May
3:30.80	Mehdi	Baala	FRA	17.8.78	3	Gaz	Saint-Denis	1 Jul
3:30.82	Alex	Kipchirchir	KEN	26.11.84	4	Gaz	Saint-Denis	1 Jul
3:31.04	Daham Najim	Bashir	QAT	8.11.79?	2	SGP	Doha	13 May
3:31.04		Lagat			2	WK	Zürich	19 Aug
3:31.09		Lagat			3	GGala	Roma	8 Jul
3:31.10		Kipchirchir			3	SGP	Doha	13 May
3:31.13		K Komen			1	VD	Bruxelles	26 Aug
3:31.46		K Komen			1rA	GP	Sevilla	4 Jun
3:31.72	Isaac	Songok	KEN	25.4.84	4	ISTAF	Berlin	4 Sep
3:31.85	Suleiman	Simotwo	KEN	21.4.80	4	ISTAF	Berlin	4 Sep
3:31.91	Ivan	Heshko	UKR	19.8.79	4	ISTAF	Berlin	4 Sep
3:31.94		I Songok			4	SGP	Doha	13 May
3:31.95	Anter	Zerguelaïne (10)	ALG	4.1.85	5	ISTAF	Berlin	4 Sep
3:32.00		Zerguelaïne			2	GP	Rieti	28 Aug
3:32.13		Heshko			5	Gaz	Saint-Denis	1 Jul
3:32.38	Nick	Willis	NZL	25.4.83	6	Gaz	Saint-Denis	1 Jul
3:32.47		Heshko			4	GGala	Roma	8 Jul
3:32.52	Alan	Webb	USA	13.1.83	3	GP	Rieti	28 Aug
	Uncertain split:	3:32.1+			3	Bisl	Oslo	29 Jul
3:32.81		Heshko			2rA	GP	Sevilla	4 Jun
3:32.81		Ramzi			2	VD	Bruxelles	26 Aug
3:32.91	Rui	Silva	POR	3.8.77	5	GGala	Roma	8 Jul
3:32.93	William	Chirchir	KEN	6.2.79	6	ISTAF	Berlin	4 Sep
3:32.95		Heshko			3	VD	Bruxelles	26 Aug

(31/14) plus 6 uncertain split times at Bislett Games, Oslo 29 Jul: 1, Komen 3:31.7, 2, Bashir 3:31.8 3. Webb 3:32.1, 4. Lagat 3:32.2, 5. Mottram 3:32.7, 6, Boukensa 3:32.7

Mark	Name		Nat	Born	Pos	Meet	Venue	Date
3:33.25	Hudson	de Souza	BRA	25.2.77	5	GP	Rieti	28 Aug
3:33.32	Michael	East	GBR	20.1.78	3	LGP	London (CP)	22 Jul
3:33.39	Mounir	Yemmouni	FRA	12.10.83	3rA	GP	Sevilla	4 Jun
3:33.43	Elkanah	Angwenyi	KEN	5.2.83	7	VD	Bruxelles	26 Aug
3:33.68	Mark	Fountain	AUS	10.3.82	6	GP	Rieti	28 Aug
3:33.72	Juan Carlos (20)	Higuero	ESP	3.8.78	8	VD	Bruxelles	26 Aug
3:33.75	Youssef	Baba	MAR	7.8.79	5	SGP	Doha	13 May
3:33.80	Eliud	Kipchoge	KEN	5.11.84	4	LGP	London (CP)	22 Jul

Mark	Name		Nat	Born	Pos	Meet	Venue	Date
3:33.83	Markos	Geneti	ETH	30.5.84	4rA	DNG	Stockholm	26 Jul
3:33.83	Laban	Rotich	KEN	20.1.69	7	ISTAF	Berlin	4 Sep
3:33.86	Bilal Mansour Ali	(John Yego)	BRN	17.10.83	1	GP II	Milano	1 Jun
3:33.99	Augustine	Choge	KEN-J	21.1.87	4rA	GP	Sevilla	4 Jun
3:34.03	Bernard	Kiptum	KEN-J	8.10.86	8	ISTAF	Berlin	4 Sep
3:34.48	Ali	Saïdi Sief	ALG	15.3.78	5	SGP	Athína	14 Jun
3:34.68	Tarek	Boukensa	ALG	19.11.81	6	SGP	Athína	14 Jun
	Uncertain split:	3:32.7+			6	Bisl	Oslo	29 Jul
3:34.80	Craig	Mottram	AUS	18.6.80	2	GP	Madrid	16 Jul
	Uncertain split:	3:32.7+			5	Bisl	Oslo	29 Jul
	(30)							
3:34.89	Rob	Myers	USA	5.8.80	6	LGP	London (CP)	22 Jul
3:35.04	Yassine	Bensghir	MAR	3.1.83	6rA	GP	Sevilla	4 Jun
3:35.07	Vyacheslav	Shabunin	RUS	27.9.69	7	SGP	Athína	14 Jun
3:35.11	Kevin	Sullivan	CAN	20.3.74	7	LGP	London (CP)	22 Jul
3:35.20	Boaz	Cheboiywo	KEN	2.8.78	2	GP II	Stanford	30 May
3:35.22	Chris	Lukezic	USA	24.4.84	8	LGP	London (CP)	22 Jul
3:35.22	Kamel	Boulahfane	ALG	1.7.76	5rA	DNG	Stockholm	26 Jul
3:35.26	Jonathan	Rankin	USA	9.2.82	2rB	DNG	Stockholm	26 Jul
3:35.29	Gert-Jan	Liefers	NED	26.9.78	7rA	GP	Sevilla	4 Jun
3:35.50	Adrian	Blincoe	NZL	4.11.79	10	GP	Rieti	28 Aug
	(40)							
3:35.52	Ali	Maataoui	MAR	15.12.80	1		Kassel	10 Jun
3:35.57	Alvaro	Fernández	ESP	7.4.81	12	VD	Bruxelles	26 Aug
3:35.58	Johan	Cronje	RSA	13.4.82	7	SGP	Doha	13 May
3:35.63	Abdelati	Iguider	MAR-J	25.3.87	1		Rabat	18 Jun
3:35.64	Arturo	Casado	ESP	26.1.83	8rA	GP	Sevilla	4 Jun
3:35.72	Nathan	Brannen	CAN	8.9.82	11	GP	Rieti	28 Aug
3:35.74	Nick	McCormick	GBR	11.9.81	9	LGP	London (CP)	22 Jul
	Uncertain split:	3:33.9+			10	Bisl	Oslo	29 Jul
3:35.84	Paul	Korir	KEN	15.7.77	3	GP II	Stanford	30 May
3:35.97	Joeri	Jansen	BEL	28.5.79	9	GP	Sevilla	4 Jun
3:36.10	Sergio	Gallardo	ESP	22.3.79	10rA	GP	Sevilla	4 Jun
	(50)							
3:36.17	Benjamin	Kipkurui	KEN	28.12.80	10	SGP	Athína	14 Jun
3:36.20	Mohammed	Moustaoui	MAR	2.4.85	1		Alger	23 Jun
3:36.24	José Antonio	Redolat	ESP	17.2.76	11rA	GP	Sevilla	4 Jun
3:36.33	Abdeslam	Kennouche	ALG	7.10.80	11	SGP	Athína	14 Jun
3:36.43	Andrew	Baddeley	GBR	20.6.82	10	LGP	London (CP)	22 Jul
3:36.44	Bouabdellah	Tahri	FRA	20.12.78	8	Athl	Lausanne	5 Jul
3:36.45	Robert	Rono	KEN	11.10.74	3rA	NA	Heusden-Zolder	23 Jul
3:36.58	David	Krummenacker	USA	24.5.75	10	Athl	Lausanne	5 Jul
3:36.60	Manuel	Damião	POR	19.7.78	12rA	GP	Sevilla	4 Jun
3:36.95	Churchill	Kipsang	KEN	.85	1rB	GP	Sevilla	4 Jun
	(60)							
3:36.97	Michael	Too	KEN	3.8.83	3	GP II	Milano	1 Jun
3:37.00	Mulugeta	Wondimu	ETH	28.2.85	8	SGP	Doha	13 May
3:37.09	James	Mwangi Murigi	KEN-J	15.7.86	1		Yokohama	19 Sep
3:37.13	Leonel	Manzano	USA	12.9.84	1	NCAA	Sacramento	11 Jun
3:37.18	Driss	Maazouzi	FRA	15.10.69	11	Athl	Lausanne	5 Jul
3:37.2A	Alfred	Kiprop	KEN		1		Nairobi	4 Jun
3:37.28	Musir Salem	Jawher	BRN	13.6.78	4		Zaragoza	24 Jun
3:37.36	Chris	Mulvaney	GBR	25.5.81	11	LGP	London (CP)	22 Jul
3:37.45	Ali Abubaker	Kamal	QAT	.83	4	WK-23	Zürich	19 Aug
3:37.59	Tim	Clerbout	BEL	13.10.81	5rA	NA	Heusden-Zolder	23 Jul
	(70)							
3:37.72	Eugenio	Barrios	ESP	3.11.76	3		Huelva	7 Jun
3:37.78	James	Nolan	IRL	27.1.77	6rA	NA	Heusden-Zolder	23 Jul
3:37.99	Scott	McGowan	USA	27.1.81	2		Bloomington	9 Jul
3:38.00	Adil	Kaouch	MAR	1.1.79	2	WCh	Helsinki	10 Aug
3:38.02	Michal	Sneberger	CZE	23.6.78	8rA	NA	Heusden-Zolder	23 Jul
3:38.07	Paul	Hamblyn	NZL	27.8.80	1rA	NA	Heusden-Zolder	23 Jul
3:38.10	Reyes	Estévez	ESP	2.8.76	6	GP	Madrid	16 Jul
3:38.1A	Benjamin	Limo	KEN	23.8.74	5		Nairobi	7 May
3:38.29	Chris	Estwanik	USA	4.4.80	6	GP II	Stanford	30 May
3:38.3A	Timothy	Kiptanui	KEN	5.1.80	6	WCT	Nairobi	25 Jun
	(80)							
3:38.31	Remi	Limo Ndiwa	KEN-Y	3.2.88	6	GP II	Milano	1 Jun
3:38.31	Bryan	Lindsay	USA	28.6.80	2	NCAA	Sacramento	11 Jun
3:38.34	Roberto	García	ESP	20.8.75	4		Huelva	7 Jun
3:38.42	Corey	Tucker	AUS	19.11.78	2	GP II	Melbourne	17 Feb

Mark	Name		Nat	Born	Pos	Meet	Venue	Date
3:38.44	Sergey	Lebid	UKR	15.7.75	1	NC	Kiev	2 Jul
3:38.46	Sean	Duffy	USA	23.3.83	3	NCAA	Sacramento	11 Jun
3:38.52	Eliud	Njubi	KEN	27.7.79	2rB	NA	Heusden-Zolder	23 Jul
3:38.54	Adam	Perkins	USA	7.5.84	4	NCAA	Sacramento	11 Jun
3:38.57	Jesús	España	ESP	21.8.78	5		Huelva	7 Jun
3:38.57	Shane	Stroup	USA	6.9.84	5	NCAA	Sacramento	11 Jun
	(90)							
3:38.62	Mohamed	Farah	GBR	23.3.83	3	WK-23	Zürich	19 Aug
3:38.8A	Job	Tanui	KEN	26.8.74	8	WCT	Nairobi	25 Jun
3:38.84	Marius	Bakken	NOR	27.3.78	13	GP	Rieti	28 Aug
3:38.86	Victor	Riobo	ESP	6.4.80	2rB	GP	Sevilla	4 Jun
3:38.90	Brimin	Kipruto	KEN	31.7.85	10rA	DNG	Stockholm	26 Jul
3:38.91	Pedro Antonio	Esteso	ESP	13.10.76	13	GP	Sevilla	4 Jun
3:38.91	Sean	Jefferson	USA	30.12.82	7	NCAA	Sacramento	11 Jun
3:38.92	Tom	Lancashire	GBR	2.7.85	8	NCAA	Sacramento	11 Jun
3:38.95	Lachlan	Chisholm	AUS	4.5.80	1		Solihull	25 Jun
3:39.05	Samir	Khadar	ALG-J	10.6.86	3		Alger	20 Jul
	(100)							

Mark	Name		Nat	Born	Date
3:39.09	Abdelghani	Hamoumraoui	ALG	.83	20 Jul
3:39.2A	Charles	Bett	KEN	21.7.84	7 May
3:39.22	Youcef	Abdi	AUS	7.12.77	13 Jul
3:39.28A	Jonathan	Komen	KEN	4.12.82	7 May
3:39.3	Edward	Mutai Kibet	KEN	28.8.84	19 Mar
3:39.38	Miroslaw	Formela	POL	31.10.78	9 Jul
3:39.40	Matt	Tegenkamp	USA	19.1.82	11 Jul
3:39.41	Charles	Gruber	USA	6.8.78	23 Jun
3:39.42A	Michael	Ndiwa	KEN-J		7 May
3:39.47	Jason	Lunn	USA	19.9.74	26 Jul
3:39.48	Adam	Goucher	USA	18.2.75	9 Jul
3:39.50	Chris	Warburton	GBR	23.8.83	11 Jun
3:39.52	Aléxis	Abraham	FRA	14.2.76	28 May
3:39.54A	Cosmas	Rono Kipkorir	KEN	12.12.84	7 May
3:39.55	Christian	Obrist	ITA	20.11.80	8 Jul
3:39.59	Juan	van Deventer	RSA	26.3.83	4 Jun
3:39.6	Benson	Esho	KEN-J	2.2.87	17 Jul
3:39.63	Paul	Hoffman	AUS	17.6.82	9 Jun
3:39.70	Daniel	Wambugu	KEN	83	7 Jun
3:39.71	Drew	Griffin	USA	21.12.76	30 May
3:39.89	Zakaria	Maazouzi	MAR	15.6.85	18 Jun
3:39.9	Abdelhalim	Zahraoui	MAR	18.2.83	29 May
3:39.91	Vickson	Polonet	KEN	2.7.85	27 Jun
3:39.93	Michael	Kipyego	KEN	2.10.83	20 May
3:39.93	Evans	Ndungu	KEN	22.2.79	7 Jun
3:39.95	Guillaume	Éraud	FRA	1.7.81	27 Jul
3:39.96	Tom	Carter	GBR	20.8.82	9 Jul
3:39.98	Paul	Melly	KEN		7 May
3:40.0A	Joseph	Kosgei	KEN	25.8.74	19 Mar
3:40.0	Louis	Rowan	AUS	9.8.78	8 Dec
3:40.01	Abdelkadir	Bakhtache	FRA	31.1.82	6 Jul
3:40.03	Salah	Ghazi	MAR	2.11.75	8 Jun
3:40.05	Ryan	McKenzie	CAN	1.1.78	9 Jul
3:40.11	Enock	Koech	KEN	4.4.81	20 May
3:40.13A	Andrew	Kangogo	KEN		7 May
3:40.14	Pawel	Czapiewski	POL	30.3.78	26 Jun
3:40.15	Fumikazu	Kobayashi	JPN	21.3.78	4 Jun
3:40.2A	Nicholas	Kemboi	KEN/QAT	25.11.83	19 Mar
3:40.21	Zbigniew	Graczyk	POL	4.7.78	4 Jun
3:40.23	Johan	Pretorius	RSA	23.9.82	18 Feb
3:40.28	Yuriy	Borzakovskiy	RUS	12.4.81	13 Jul
3:40.32	Ireneusz	Sekretarski	POL	25.5.84	26 Jun
3:40.33	Cornelius	Chirchir	KEN	5.6.83	6 Jul
3:40.35	Willy	Rotich	KEN	23.3.76	9 Jul
3:40.36	Sébastien	Cosson	FRA	15.3.80	17 Jun
3:40.39	Franek	Haschke	GER	28.3.80	3 Jul
3:40.42	Sean	O'Brien	USA	4.8.80	30 May
3:40.45	José Manuel	Cerezo	ESP	23.6.73	23 Jul
3:40.46	James	Thie	GBR	27.6.78	9 Jul
3:40.48	Emmanuel	Balliat	KEN		17 Jun
3:40.50	Abdea	Zbairi	FRA	11.9.80	8 Jun
3:40.50	Tom	Compernolle	BEL	13.11.75	30 Jul
3:40.51	Stephen	Pifer	USA	7.12.84	9 Jun
3:40.53	Mustapha	Kilou	MAR	12.1.82	18 Jun
3:40.58	Julius	Achon	UGA	12.12.76	9 Jul
3:40.59	Yasunori	Murakami	JPN	30.12.83	4 Jun
3:40.59	Jason	Jabaut	USA	13.3.82	23 Jun
3:40.61	Halil	Akkas	TUR	1.7.83	14 May
3:40.62	Neil	Speaight	GBR	9.9.78	4 Jun
3:40.62	Nasser Shams	Kareem	QAT-J	30.1.86	13 Jul
3:40.67	Philemon	Kimutai	KEN		15 May
3:40.7A	Youssef Saad	Kamel	BRN	29.3.83	19 Mar
3:40.7A	Alfred	Kirwa Yego	KEN-J	28.11.86	7 May
3:40.7A	Geoffrey	Rono	KEN-J	21.4.87	14 May
3:40.7A	Vincent	Rono	KEN		17 Jun
3:40.74	Francisco Javier	Alves	ESP	2.9.80	19 Jul
3:40.75	Maurizio	Bobbato	ITA	17.2.79	13 Jul
3:40.79	Lee	Merrien	GBR	24.4.79	11 Jun
3:40.79	Carsten	Schlangen	GER	31.12.80	3 Jul
3:40.83	Adam	Bowden	GBR	5.8.82	25 Jun
3:40.86	Stefan	Eberhardt	GER	12.1.85	27 May
3:40.88		Dou Zhaobo	CHN	23.9.83	19 Oct
3:40.91	Nikolay	Trubachov	UKR	28.9.79	2 Jul
3:40.92	Adil	Ould Lidam	MAR	2.2.81	21 May
3:40.95	Shadrack	Lagat	KEN	22.7.78	16 May
3:41.00	Collis	Birmingham	AUS	27.12.84	3 Nov
3:41.0A	Bernard Kipyegon	Kirui	KEN	.85	14 May
3:41.0	Daniel	Wilson	USA	19.2.79	12 Jul
3:41.01	Abdulrahman	Suleiman	QAT	10.1.84	4 Jun
3:41.01	Yared	Shegumo	POL	10.1.83	26 Jun
3:41.02	Jeremy	Roff	AUS	11.10.84	17 Feb
3:41.02	Gary	Murray	IRL	31.1.80	11 Jul
3:41.04	Hassan	Khallouki	MAR	4.2.79	28 May
3:41.05	Radoslaw	Poplawski	POL	16.1.83	12 Jun
3:41.10		Tang Baojun	CHN	17.10.81	19 Oct
3:41.11	Juan Luis	Barrios	MEX	24.6.83	14 May
3:41.15	Nicolas	Aïssat	FRA	24.7.80	28 May
3:41.15	Diego	Ruíz	ESP	5.2.82	4 Jun
3:41.15	Jonas	Cheruiyot	KEN	.84	16 Jul
3:41.20	David	Kirwa Chepkwony	KEN	29.12.78	13 Jul
3:41.2A	Richard	Geemi	KEN	23.8.78	25 Jun
3:41.21	Mark	Tucker	AUS	15.8.79	3 Nov
3:41.22	Ben	Ruthe	NZL	17.2.80	17 Feb
3:41.22	Philo	Saunders	AUS	31.10.76	17 Feb
3:41.25	Bartosz	Nowicki	POL	26.2.84	26 Jun
3:41.27	Sergey	Ivanov	RUS	12.1.79	13 Jul
3:41.29	Ed	Jackson	GBR	2.1.82	24 Jul
3:41.30	Mariano	Villarrubia	ESP	20.11.80	4 Jun
3:41.3A	Yusuf	Biwott	KEN		25 Jun
3:41.34	Emilio	Martín (200)	ESP	22.6.82	7 Jun

Indoors

Mark	Name		Nat	Born	Pos	Venue	Date
3:36.51	Reyes	Estévez	ESP	2.8.76	2	Madrid	24 Feb
3:39.47	Wolfram	Müller	GER	8.7.81			4 Feb
3:39.54	James	Thie	GBR	27.6.78			13 Feb

JUNIORS

See main list for top 6 juniors. 10 performances by 4 men to 3:38.3. Additional marks and further juniors:

Name	Mark	Pos	Meet	Venue	Date	Mark	Pos	Venue	Date
Choge	3:34.74	1	GP	Madrid	16 Jul	3:34.8A	1	Nairobi	7 May
Kiptum	3:35.50	9	GP	Rieti	28 Aug	3:38.25	8	Stanford	30 May

MEN 2005

Mark	Name		Nat	Born	Pos	Meet	Venue	Date
	3:35.52 1 WK23 Zürich 19 Aug							
Iguider	3:36.00 7 GGala Roma 8 Jul							

Note: Bilal Mansour Ali (entered by BRN as b. 17.10.88 at WY) also
3:34.33 4 SGP Athína 14 Jun 3:35.98 2 Zaragoza 24 Jun

Mark	Name		Nat	Born	Pos	Meet	Venue	Date
3:39.42A	Michael	Ndiwa	KEN		3B		Nairobi	7 May
3:39.6	Benson	Esho	KEN	2.2.87	4		Thessaloníki	17 Jul
3:40.62	Nasser Shams	Kareem	QAT	30.1.86	4		Nuoro	13 Jul
3:40.7A	Alfred	Kirwa Yego (10)	KEN	28.11.86	8A		Nairobi	7 May
3:40.7A	Geoffrey	Rono	KEN	21.4.87	2		Nairobi	14 May
3:41.43+	Mike	Woods	CAN	12.10.86	2	in 1M	Windsor	28 Jul
3:41.63	Barnabás	Bene	HUN	27.8.86	5		Florø	4 Jun
3:41.7	Jimmy	Adar	UGA	1.11.87	1	NC	Kampala	30 Jul
3:41.74	Abdallah	Abdelgader	SUD	.87	2	PArab	Radès	18 Sep
3:41.79	Alvaro	Rodriguez	ESP	25.5.87	9r2	GP	Sevilla	4 Jun
3:42.34	Hatem	Hamdi	TUN	2.9.86	5		Rabat	18 Jun
3:42.57	Moses	Kipsiro	UGA	2.9.86	10r1		Watford	11 Jun
3:42.62	Abdelaziz Naji	El Idrissi	ITA	8.12.86	10		Nuoro	13 Jul
3:42.91	Abreham Cherkos	Feleke (20)	ETH-Y	23.9.89	12	WK-23	Zürich	19 Aug

1 MILE

Mark	Name		Nat	Born	Pos	Meet	Venue	Date
3:47.97	Daham Najim	Bashir	QAT	8.11.78	1	Bisl	Oslo	29 Jul
3:48.38	Bernard	Lagat	USA	12.12.74	2	Bisl	Oslo	29 Jul
3:48.49	Daniel	Kipchirchir Komen	KEN	27.11.84	3	Bisl	Oslo	29 Jul
3:48.92	Alan	Webb	USA	13.1.83	4	Bisl	Oslo	29 Jul
3:48.98	Craig	Mottram	AUS	18.6.80	5	Bisl	Oslo	29 Jul
3:49.95	Tarek	Boukensa	ALG	19.11.81	6	Bisl	Oslo	29 Jul
3:50.82	Suleiman	Simotwo	KEN	21.4.80	7	Bisl	Oslo	29 Jul
3:50.91	Alex	Kipchirchir	KEN	26.11.84	1	Pre	Eugene	4 Jun
3:51.05	Hudson	de Souza	BRA	25.2.77	8	Bisl	Oslo	29 Jul
3:51.33	Rashid	Ramzi	BRN	17.7.80	2	Pre	Eugene	4 Jun
3:51.53		Lagat			3	Pre	Eugene	4 Jun
	(11/10)							
3:52.02	Nick	McCormick	GBR	11.9.81	9	Bisl	Oslo	29 Jul
3:52.13	Rui	Silva	POR	3.8.77	10	Bisl	Oslo	29 Jul
3:52.50	Michael	East	GBR	20.1.78	1	BrGP	Sheffield	21 Aug
3:52.55	Laban	Rotich	KEN	20.1.69	2	BrGP	Sheffield	21 Aug
3:53.05	Elkanah	Angwenyi	KEN	5.2.83	4	Pre	Eugene	4 Jun
3:53.24	Mark	Fountain	AUS	10.3.82	4	BrGP	Sheffield	21 Aug
3:53.43	Nick	Willis	NZL	25.4.83	11	Bisl	Oslo	29 Jul
3:54.48	Kevin	Sullivan	CAN	20.3.74	5	BrGP	Sheffield	21 Aug
3:54.87	Rob	Myers	USA	5.8.80	5	Pre	Eugene	4 Jun
3:55.62	Paul	Korir	KEN	15.7.77	6	BrGP	Sheffield	21 Aug
	(20)							
3:55.63	Jonathan	Rankin	USA	9.2.82	2	MAI	Malmö	16 Aug
3:55.84	Joeri	Jansen	BEL	28.5.79	12	Bisl	Oslo	29 Jul
3:56.08	Benjamin	Kipkurui	KEN	28.12.80	1	MSR	Walnut	17 Apr
3:56.15	Adam	Goucher	USA	18.2.75	1		Windsor	28 Jul
3:56.16	Nathan	Brannen	CAN	8.9.82	7	BrGP	Sheffield	21 Aug
3:56.27	Lachlan	Chisholm	AUS	4.5.80	1		Brisbane	6 May
3:56.49	Mohamed	Farah	GBR	23.3.83	1		London (CP)	6 Aug

Mark	Name		Nat	Born	Date	Mark	Name		Nat	Born	Date
3:56.92	Charlie	Gruber	USA	6.8.78	4 Jun	3:58.63	James	Thie	GBR	27.6.78	6 Aug
3:56.99	Youcef	Abdi	AUS	7.12.77	6 May	3:58.66	Matthew	Shone	GBR	10.7.75	6 Aug
3:57.21	Scott	McGowan	USA	27.1.81	4 Jun	3:58.80	Chris	Estwanik	USA	4.4.80	17 Apr
3:57.30	Tom	Carter	GBR	20.8.82	6 Aug	3:58.81	John	Cronje	RSA	13.4.82	16 Dec
3:57.48	Mike	Woods	CAN-J	12.10.86	28 Jul	3:58.99	Mark	Christie	IRL	12.1.85	6 Aug
3:58.23	Anthony	Famiglietti	USA	8.11.78	4 Jun	3:59.16	Bryan	Lindsay	USA	28.6.80	9 Apr
3:58.35	Chris	Mulvaney	GBR	25.5.81	14 Jun	3:59.18	Lee	Merrien	GBR	24.4.79	6 Aug
3:58.37	Mark	Tucker	AUS	15.8.79	23 Feb	3:59.44	Robert	Rono	KEN	16.8.78	16 Aug
3:58.41	Paul	Hamblyn	NZL	27.8.80	23 Feb	3:59.52	Gary	Murray	IRL	31.1.80	6 Aug
3:58.45	Juan Luis	Barrios	MEX	24.6.83	14 Jun	3:59.81	Alejandro	Suárez	MEX	30.11.80	14 Jun
3:58.54	James	Nolan	IRL	27.1.77	21 Aug	3:59.88	Jonah	Maiyo (49)	KEN	5.4.79	17 Apr

Indoors

Mark	Name		Nat	Born	Pos	Meet	Venue	Date
3:49.89		Lagat			1		Fayetteville	11 Feb
3:55.11	Nathan	Brannen	CAN	8.9.82	5		Boston (R)	29 Jan
3:56.44	Sean	Jefferson	USA	30.12.82	1		Notre Dame	5 Feb

Mark	Name		Nat	Born	Date	Mark	Name		Nat	Born	Date
3:57.04	Saïd	Ahmed	USA	10.12.82	5 Mar	3:58.75	Kurt	Benninger	CAN	1.1.85	5 Feb
3:57.85	John	Jefferson	USA	30.12.82	5 Feb	3:59.08	Jonah	Maiyo	KEN	5.4.79	26 Feb
3:58.59	Luke	Watson	USA	20.8.80	5 Feb	3:59.23	Robert	Cheseret	KEN	8.10.83	26 Feb

JUNIORS

Mark	Name		Nat	Born	Pos	Meet	Venue	Date
3:57.48	Mike	Woods	CAN	12.10.86	2		Windsor	28 Jul
4:00.34	Bernard	Kiptum	KEN	8.10.86	11	Pre	Eugene	4 Jun

2000 METRES

Mark	Name		Nat	Born	Pos	Meet	Venue	Date
4:53.12	Mehdi	Baala	FRA	17.8.78	1		Strasbourg	23 Jun
5:00.76+	Kenenisa	Bekele	ETH	13.6.82	1	in 3k	Lausanne	5 Jul

Mark	Name		Nat	Born	Date
5:02.03+	Robert	Rono	KEN	11.10.74	28 Aug
5:02.2+_	Sileshi	Sihine	ETH	29.1.83	28 Aug
5:02.42+	Shadrack	Korir	KEN	14.12.78	13 May
5:02.5+	Eliud	Kipchoge	KEN	5.11.84	13 May

3000 METRES

Mark	Name		Nat	Born	Pos	Meet	Venue	Date
7:28.56	Eliud	Kipchoge	KEN	5.11.84	1	SGP	Doha	13 May
7:28.78	Augustine	Choge	KEN-J	21.1.87	2	SGP	Doha	13 May
7:29.60	Benjamin	Limo	KEN	23.8.74	3	SGP	Doha	13 May
7:29.92	Sileshi	Sihine	ETH	29.1.83	1	GP	Rieti	28 Aug
7:30.14	Isaac	Songok	KEN	25.4.84	1	FBK	Hengelo	29 May
7:30.56		Kipchoge			2	FBK	Hengelo	29 May
7:30.76	Jamal Bilal	Salem	QAT	12.9.78	4	SGP	Doha	13 May
7:31.98	Daniel	Kipchirchir Komen	KEN	27.11.84	3	FBK	Hengelo	29 May
7:32.59	Kenenisa	Bekele	ETH	13.6.82	1	WK	Zürich	19 Aug
7:32.71+		K Bekele			1	in 5k	Saint-Denis	1 Jul
7:33.2+	Abebe	Dinkesa	ETH	6.3.84	2	in 5k	Saint-Denis	1 Jul
7:33.93	Paul Kipsiele	Koech (10)	KEN	10.11.81	5	SGP	Doha	13 May
7:34.57		K Bekele			1	Athl	Lausanne	5 Jul
7:35.44+		Kipchoge			1	in 2M	Eugene	4 Jun
7:35.84		I Songok			1	DNG	Stockholm	26 Jul
7:36.36		K Bekele			1		Shanghai	17 Sep
7:36.63	Tariku	Bekele	ETH-J	21.1.87	2		Shanghai	17 Sep
7:36.79		B Limo			2	DNG	Stockholm	26 Jul
7:37.24		Choge			3	DNG	Stockholm	26 Jul
7:37.48	Gert-Jan	Liefers	NED	26.9.78	4	FBK	Hengelo	29 May
7:37.56	Ali	Saïdi Sief	ALG	15.3.78	2	WK	Zürich	19 Aug
7:37.70	Boniface	Songok	KEN	25.12.80	3		Shanghai	17 Sep
7:37.97	Mulugeta	Wondimu	ETH	28.2.85	5	FBK	Hengelo	29 May
	(22/15)							
7:38.00	Bernard	Lagat	USA	12.12.74	1	WAF	Monaco	9 Sep
7:38.03	Craig	Mottram	AUS	18.6.80	3	WK	Zürich	19 Aug
7:38.11	Markos	Geneti	ETH	30.5.84	1		Carson	22 May
7:39.04	Boaz	Cheboiywo	KEN	2.8.78	2		Carson	22 May
7:39.28	Alan	Webb	USA	13.1.83	3+	Pre	Eugene	4 Jun
	(20)							
7:39.46	Khalid	El Amri	TUN	20.3.77	5	DNG	Stockholm	26 Jul
7:39.47	Shadrack	Korir	KEN	14.12.78	1		Villeneuve d'Ascq	12 Jun
7:39.48	Gebre-egziabher	Gebremariam	ETH	10.9.84	1		New York (RI)	11 Jun
7:39.66	Paul	Bitok	KEN	26.6.70	2		Villeneuve d'Ascq	12 Jun
7:39.72	John	Kibowen	KEN	21.4.69	5	WK	Zürich	19 Aug
7:39.93	Zersenay	Tadesse	ERI	8.2.82	6	SGP	Doha	13 May
7:40.09	Adam	Goucher	USA	18.2.75	1		Lignano Sabbiadoro	17 Jul
7:40.28	Tim	Broe	USA	20.6.77	3		Carson	22 May
7:40.47	Robert Kipngetich	Sigei	KEN	3.1.82	6	DNG	Stockholm	26 Jul
7:40.7+	Abderrahim	Goumri	MAR	21.5.76	2	VD	Bruxelles	26 Aug
	(30)							
7:40.75	Musir Salem	Jawher	BRN	13.6.78	4		Villeneuve d'Ascq	12 Jun
7:41.83	Daham Najim	Bashir	QAT	8.11.78	1	GP	Madrid	16 Jul4
7:42.16	Carlos	de la Ossa	ESP	25.11.76	1		Huelva	7 Jun
7:42.22	Shadrack	Kosgei	KEN	24.11.84	8	WK	Zürich	19 Aug
7:42.30	Badi	Worku	ETH-Y	22.7.88	2	GP	Rieti	28 Aug
7:42.49	Bouabdellah	Tahri	FRA	20.12.78	6	FBK	Hengelo	29 May
7:42.50	Meshack	Sang	KEN	24.7.78	4		Carson	22 May
7:42.92	Shadrack	Langat	KEN	22.7.78	5		Villeneuve d'Ascq	12 Jun
7:42.94	Sergey	Lebid	UKR	15.7.75	1	GP II	Torino	3 Jun
	(40)							
7:42.96	Moses	Mosop	KEN	17.7.85	3	GP	Madrid	16 Jul
7:43.00	Abreham Cherkos	Feleke	ETH-Y	23.9.89	3	GP	Rieti	28 Aug
7:43.15	Hicham	Bellani	MAR	15.9.79	4		Shanghai	17 Sep
7:43.23	Tarek	Boukensa	ALG	19.11.81	6		Villeneuve d'Ascq	12 Jun
7:43.27	Sahle	Warga	ETH	.84	2		Huelva	7 Jun
7:43.33	Matt	Tegenkamp	USA	19.1.82	8	DNG	Stockholm	26 Jul
7:43.45	James	Kwalia	QAT	12.6.84	8	Athl	Lausanne	5 Jul
7:43.48	Dennis	Ndiso Musembi	KEN	31.12.83	4	GP	Madrid	16 Jul
7:43.67	David Kirwa	Chepkwony	KEN	29.12.78	7		Villeneuve d'Ascq	12 Jun
7:43.83	Charles	Kamathi	KEN	18.5.78	6	GP	Madrid	16 Jul
7:43.88	Hillary	Chenonge	KEN	30.5.85	5		Shanghai	17 Sep
	(50)							

Mark	Name		Nat	Born	Pos	Meet	Venue	Date
7:43.95	Dathan	Ritzenhein	USA	30.12.82	5		Carson	22 May
7:44.15	Sergio	Gallardo	ESP	22.3.79	3		Huelva	7 Jun
7:44.21	Tessema	Absher	ETH-J	9.12.86	8		Villeneuve d'Ascq	12 Jun
7:44.47	Kiprono	Menjo	KEN	.79	8	GP	Madrid	16 Jul
7:44.57	Moses	Kipsiro	UGA-J	2.9.86	1	GP II	Zagreb	11 Jul
7:44.58	Joseph	Kosgei	KEN	25.8.74	4	GP II	Torino	3 Jun
7:44.6+	Joseph	Ebuya	KEN-J	20.6.87	5=	in 5k	Bruxelles	26 Aug
7:44.97	Edwin	Soi	KEN-J	3.3.86	4		Huelva	7 Jun
7:45.09	Pius	Muli	KEN	15.12.82	6	GP II	Torino	3 Jun
	(60)							
7:45.41	Wilson	Boit Kipketer	KEN	6.10.73	9		Villeneuve d'Ascq	12 Jun
7:45.55	Ayad	Landassem	MAR	11.10.81	5		Huelva	7 Jun
7:45.7+	Jesús	España	ESP	21.8.78	8	in 5k	Bruxelles	26 Aug
7:45.76	Nathan	Lagat	KEN	.77	7		Huelva	7 Jun
7:45.82	Mohammed	Amyn	MAR	25.3.76	5	GP II	Zagreb	11 Jul
7:45.89	Moussa	Omar Obaid	QAT	18.4.85	6	GP II	Zagreb	11 Jul
7:45.97	Nick	Willis	NZL	25.4.83	9	Athl	Lausanne	5 Jul
7:45.98	Alemayehu	Bezabeh	ETH-J	.86	6		Huelva	7 Jun
7:46e	Sammy	Kipketer	KEN	29.9.81	-	ISTAF	Berlin	4 Sep
7:46.49	Adrian	Blincoe	NZL	4.11.79	7	GP II	Zagreb	11 Jul
	(70)							
7:46.92	David	Kilel	KEN	21.5.84	10		Villeneuve d'Ascq	12 Jun
7:47.13	Manuel Angel	Penas	ESP	9.11.77	8		Huelva	8 Jun
7:47.71	Khalid	Zoubaa	FRA	27.4.77	10		Villeneuve d'Ascq	12 Jun
7:47.98	Khoudir	Aggoune	ALG	5.1.81	11		Villeneuve d'Ascq	12 Jun

Mark	Name		Nat	Born	Date	Mark	Name		Nat	Born	Date
7:48.2A	David	Chemweno	KEN	18.12.81	7 May	7:51.64	Vickson	Polonet	KEN	2.7.85	5 Jun
7:48.35	Stephen	Koech	KEN	16.12.76	20 Jul	7:51.70	Steve	Slattery	USA	14.8.80	11 Jun
7:48.71	Richard	Matelong	KEN	14.10.83	16 May	7:51.79	Juan Luis	Barrios	MEX	24.6.83	21 May
7:48.79	Dan	Lincoln	USA	20.10.80	17 Jul	7:52.00	Collins	Kosgei	KEN-Y	4.8.88	16 May
7:49.04	Essa Ismail	Rasheed	QAT-J	14.12.86	13 May	7:52.05	Adil	El Kaouch	MAR	1.1.79	4 Jun
7:49.1A	Moses	Masai	KEN-J	1.6.86	7 May	7:52.34	Slavko	Petrovic	CRO	23.9.80	11 Jul
7:49.16	Galen	Rupp	USA-J	8.5.86	17 Jul	7:52.55	Alejandro	Suárez	MEX	30.11.80	21 May
7:49.43	Vyacheslav	Shabunin	RUS	27.9.69	5 Jun	7:52.55	Anas	Selmouni	MAR	15.3.79	4 Jun
7:49.46+	Micah	Kogo	KEN-J	3.6.86	23 Aug	7:52.62	Ian	Dobson	USA	6.2.82	28 Aug
7:49.57	Mohammed	Moustaoui	MAR	2.4.85	13 May	7:53.03	Mounir	Yemmouni	FRA	12.10.83	12 Jun
7:49.72+	Roberto	García	ESP	20.8.75	23 Aug	7:53.10	Bisluke	Kiplagat Kipkorir	KEN-Y	8.8.88	10 Sep
7:49.87	Mark	Bett	KEN	22.12.76	17 Sep	7:53.11	Justus	Kiprono	KEN-J	28.2.87	3 Jun
7:49.94	Aléxis	Abraham	FRA	14.2.76	12 Jun	7:53.12	Patrick	Kimeli	KEN-Y	.88	5 Jun
7:50.01	Salah	Ghazi	MAR	2.11.75	8 Jul	7:53.18	Michael	Kipyego	KEN	2.10.83	5 Jun
7:50.14+	Mike	Kigen	KEN-J	15.1.86	23 Aug	7:53.18	Solomon	Tsige Asfav	ETH	23.1.85	5 Jun
7:50.22	Frederick	Yegon	KEN-J	.86	28 May	7:53.25	Pablo	Villalobos	ESP	20.5.78	7 Jun
7:50.33	Enock	Koech	KEN	4.4.81	5 Jun	7:53.33	Abdelhalim	Zahraoui	MAR	18.2.83	21 May
7:50.39	Geoffrey	Kipngeno	KEN	10.4.84	20 Jul	7:53.52	Nordine	Gezzar	FRA	17.2.80	8 Jul
7:50.61	Martin	Keino	KEN	20.6.72	22 May	7:53.56	Luke	Kipkosgei	KEN	27.11.75	22 May
7:50.65	Christian	Belz	SUI	11.9.74	5 Jun	7:53.57	Badre Din	Zioini	FRA	25.3.76	12 Jun
7:50.68+	Gunther	Weidlinger	AUT	5.4.78	23 Aug	7:53.69	Ahmed	Baday	MAR	12.1.79	21 May
7:50.92+	Hudson	de Souza	BRA	25.2.77	23 Aug	7:54.01	Henry	Sugut	KEN	4.5.85	5 Jul
7:50.99	Nicholas	Kemboi	QAT	25.11.83	13 May	7:54.09	Mark	Tucker	AUS	15.8.79	11 Jul
7:51.08	Mohamed	Khaldi	ALG	3.5.75	23 Jun	7:54.2A	Bernard	Chepkok	KEN	17.1.84	7 May
7:51.29	Cuthbert	Nyasango	ZIM	17.9.82	25 May	7:54.22	Chris	Estwanik	USA	4.4.80	17 Jul
7:51.41	Jonathon	Riley (100)	USA	29.12.78	17 Jul	7:54.30	Gordon	Mugi Mahugu	KEN	27.11.81	28 May
7:51.62	Samir	Moussaoui	ALG	15.5.75	23 Jun	7:54.48	Mokhtar	Benhari (128)	FRA	22.5.74	16 May

Indoors

Mark	Name		Nat	Born	Pos	Venue	Date
7:39.89i	Alistair	Cragg	IRL	13.6.80	1	Boston (R)	29 Jan
7:43.80i	Reyes	Estévez	ESP	2.8.76	1	Stockholm	15 Feb
7:44.32i	Günther	Weidlinger	AUT	5.4.78	2	Stockholm	15 Feb
7:46.60i	Mark	Carroll	IRL	15.1.72	1	Boston	28 Jan

Mark	Name		Nat	Born	Date	Mark	Name		Nat	Born	Date
7:48.36i	Mark	Bett	KEN	22.12.76	15 Feb	7:52.32i	Richard	Kiplagat	KEN	5.1.81	25 Feb
7:48.46i	Juan Carlos	Higuero	ESP	3.8.78	7 Feb	7:52.38i	Mark	Fountain	AUS	10.3.82	11 Feb
7:50.11i	Erik	Sjöqvist	SWE	4.12.72	15 Feb	7:52.48i	Mokhtar	Benhari	FRA	22.5.74	5 Feb
7:50.44i	Bolota	Asmerom	USA	12.10.78	11 Feb	7:52.78i	Vincent	Le Dauphin	FRA	28.6.76	15 Feb
7:50.75i	Kevin	Sullivan	CAN	20.3.74	29 Jan	7:53.14i	Chris	Solinsky	USA	5.12.84	5 Feb
7:50.94i	Antonio	Jiménez	ESP	18.2.77	29 Jan	7:53.40i	César	Pérez	ESP	7.4.75	12 Feb
7:51.00i	Stephen	Haas	USA	18.4.83	5 Feb	7:53.90i	Bryan	Lindsay	USA	28.6.80	29 Jan
7:51.28i	Joshua	Rohatinsky	USA	7.3.82	29 Jan	7:54.08i	Mohamed	Farah	GBR	23.3.83	5 Mar
7:51.46i	John	Mayock	GBR	26.10.70	5 Mar	7:54.18i	Daniel	Wilson	USA	19.2.79	28 Jan
7:51.61i	Pavel	Shapovalov	RUS	10.10.75	23 Jan	7:54.29i	Eric	Logsdon	USA	4.5.82	29 Jan
7:51.66i	Robert	Cheseret	KEN	8.10.83	26 Feb	7:54.45i	Peter	Kosgei	KEN	3.2.83	12 Mar
7:51.77i	Henrik	Skoog	SWE	17.4.79	15 Feb						

Symbols/Abbreviations

+ intermediate time in longer race, A made at an altitude of 1000m or higher, D made in a decathlon, h made in a heat, qf quarter-final, sf semi-final, i indoors, Q qualifying round, r race number, -J juniors, -Y youths (b. 1988 or later

Mark	Name		Nat	Born	Pos	Meet	Venue	Date

JUNIORS

See main list for top 9 juniors. 15 performances by 7 men to 7:45.0. Additional marks and further juniors:

Choge	7:37.24	3	DNG	Stockholm	26 Jul	7:39.99	3	WAF	Monaco	9 Sep
T Bekele	7:38.18	2	Athl	Lausanne	5 Jul	7:43.47	9	WK	Zürich	19 Aug
	7:40.30	5	WAF	Monaco	9 Sep					
Worku	7:43.81	5	GP	Madrid	16 Jul	7:44.83	2		Zagreb	11 Jul
Feleke	7:44.27	6		Shanghai	17 Sep					

Mark	Name		Nat	Born	Pos	Meet	Venue	Date
7:49.04	Essa Ismail	Rasheed (10)	QAT	14.12.86	9	SGP	Doha	13 May
7:49.1A	Moses	Masai	KEN	1.6.86	1rB		Nairobi	7 May
7:49.16	Galen	Rupp	USA	8.5.86	4		Lignano Sabbiadoro	17 Jul
7:49.46+	Micah	Kogo	KEN	3.6.86	1+	Gugl	Linz	23 Aug
7:50.14+	Mike	Kigen	KEN	15.1.86	3	in 2M	Linz	23 Aug
7:50.22	Frederick	Yegon	KEN	.86	2		Avilés	28 May
7:52.00	Collins	Kosgei	KEN-Y	4.8.88	3		Rehlingen	16 May
7:53.10	Bisluke	Kiplagat Kipkorir	KEN-Y	8.8.88	1		Nuraminis	10 Sep
7:53.11	Justus	Kiprono	KEN	28.2.87	11	GP II	Torino	3 Jun
7:53.12	Patrick	Kimeli	KEN-Y	.88	6		Cottbus	5 Jun
7:58.04	Mike	Woods (20)	CAN	12.10.86	1		Ottawa	29 Jun
Best European: 8:03.48	Marcin	Chabowski	POL	28.5.86	5	Kuso	Warszawa	12 Jun

2 MILES

Mark	Name		Nat	Born	Pos	Meet	Venue	Date
8:07.68	Eliud	Kipchoge	KEN	5.11.84	1	Pre	Eugene	4 Jun
8:11.27	Craig	Mottram	AUS	18.6.80	1	BrGP	Sheffield	21 Aug
8:11.48	Alan	Webb	USA	13.1.83	2	Pre	Eugene	4 Jun
8:11.62	Boaz	Cheboiywo	KEN	2.8.78	3	Pre	Eugene	4 Jun
8:12.86	Boniface	Songok	KEN	25.12.80	2	BrGP	Sheffield	21 Aug
8:16.02	Shadrack	Kosgei	KEN	24.11.84	4	Pre	Eugene	4 Jun
8:19.53	Shadrack	Korir	KEN	14.12.78	3	BrGP	Sheffield	21 Aug
8:19.81	Mulugeta	Wondimu	ETH	28.2.85	5	Pre	Eugene	4 Jun
8:20.09	Mike	Kigen	KEN-J	15.1.86	1	Gugl	Linz	23 Aug
8:20.65	Mark (10)	Bett	KEN	22.12.76	2	Gugl	Linz	23 Aug
8:20.88	Micah	Kogo	KEN-J	3.6.86	3	Gugl	Linz	23 Aug
8:21.00	Adrian	Blincoe	NZL	4.11.79	4	BrGP	Sheffield	21 Aug
8:21.41	Joseph	Kosgei	KEN	25.8.74	4	Gugl	Linz	23 Aug
8:21.67	Hudson	de Souza	BRA	25.2.77	5	Gugl	Linz	23 Aug
8:21.88	Günther	Weidlinger	AUT	5.4.78	6	Gugl	Linz	23 Aug
8:23.21	Joseph	Ebuya	KEN-J	20.6.87	5	BrGP	Sheffield	21 Aug

8:23.45	Dathan	Ritzenhein	USA	30.12.82	4 Jun	8:29.02	Robert Kipngetich	Sigei	KEN	3.1.82	23 Aug
8:26.59	Meshack	Sang	KEN	24.7.78	4 Jun	8:29.30	Ian	Dobson	USA	6.2.82	21 Aug
8:27.80	Luke	Kipkosgei	KEN	27.11.75	4 Jun	8:31.87	Paul	Morrison	CAN	25.9.80	21 Aug
						8:32.62	Dan	Lincoln	USA	20.10.80	4 Jun

Indoors

Mark	Name		Nat	Born	Pos	Meet	Venue	Date
8:14.28	Markos	Geneti	ETH	30.5.84	1	GP	Birmingham	18 Feb
8:15.49	Kenenisa	Bekele	ETH	13.6.82	2	GP	Birmingham	18 Feb

8:24.22	Paul	Bitok	KEN	26.6.70	18 Feb	8:27.23	Monder	Rizki	BEL	16.8.79	18 Feb
8:26.49	Mohammed	Moustaoui	MAR	2.4.85	18 Feb	8:27.91	John	Mayock	GBR	26.10.70	18 Feb

5000 METRES

Mark	Name		Nat	Born	Pos	Meet	Venue	Date
12:40.18	Kenenisa	Bekele	ETH	13.6.82	1	Gaz	Saint-Denis	1 Jul
12:50.22	Eliud	Kipchoge	KEN	5.11.84	1	VD	Bruxelles	26 Aug
12:50.25	Abderrahim	Goumri	MAR	21.5.76	2	VD	Bruxelles	26 Aug
12:52.29	Isaac	Songok	KEN	25.4.84	1	GGala	Roma	8 Jul
12:52.76		Kipchoge			2	GGala	Roma	8 Jul
12:52.80	Gebre-egziabher	Gebremariam	ETH	10.9.84	3	GGala	Roma	8 Jul
12:53.66	Augustine	Choge	KEN-J	21.1.87	4	GGala	Roma	8 Jul
12:55.26	Benjamin	Limo	KEN	23.8.74	3	VD	Bruxelles	26 Aug
12:55.55		K Bekele			1	LGP	London (CP)	22 Jul
12:55.58	Abebe	Dinkesa	ETH	6.3.84	2	Gaz	Saint-Denis	1 Jul
12:55.85	Boniface	Songok	KEN	25.12.80	4	VD	Bruxelles	26 Aug
12:56.13	Craig	Mottram (10)	AUS	18.6.80	2	LGP	London (CP)	22 Jul
12:56.24	Dejene	Berhanu	ETH	12.12.80	5	GGala	Roma	8 Jul
12:58.43	Boniface	Kiprop	UGA	12.10.85	6	GGala	Roma	8 Jul
12:58.58	Moukhled	Al-Outaibi	KSA	20.6.76	1	NA	Heusden-Zolder	23 Jul
12:58.60		Gebremariam			3	Gaz	Saint-Denis	1 Jul
12:58.66		B Limo			7	GGala	Roma	8 Jul
12:59.03	Tariku	Bekele	ETH-J	21.1.87	4	Gaz	Saint-Denis	1 Jul
12:59.19		Kiprop			5	Gaz	Saint-Denis	1 Jul
12:59.29	Bernard	Lagat	USA	12.12.74	1	ISTAF	Berlin	4 Sep
12:59.67	Hicham	Bellani	MAR	15.9.79	2	NA	Heusden-Zolder	23 Jul

Mark	Name		Nat	Born	Pos	Meet	Venue	Date
12:59.79	Musir Salem	Jawher	BRN	13.6.78	6	Gaz	Saint-Denis	1 Jul
13:00.25	Markos	Geneti	ETH	30.5.84	7	Gaz	Saint-Denis	1 Jul
13:01.06	Shadrack	Kosgei	KEN	24.11.84	3	NA	Heusden-Zolder	23 Jul
13:01.15		Berhanu			8	Gaz	Saint-Denis	1 Jul
13:01.45		B Limo			2	ISTAF	Berlin	4 Sep
13:01.55	Sammy	Kipketer	KEN	29.9.81	3	ISTAF	Berlin	4 Sep
13:01.62		Choge			4	ISTAF	Berlin	4 Sep
13:02.30		Dinkesa			8	GGala	Roma	8 Jul
13:02.85		Geneti			5	ISTAF	Berlin	4 Sep
	(30/20)							
13:03.40	Mulugeta	Wondimu	ETH	28.2.85	9	Gaz	Saint-Denis	1 Jul
13:03.79	Joseph	Ebuya	KEN-J	20.6.87	4	NA	Heusden-Zolder	23 Jul
13:04.43	Stephen	Koech	KEN	16.12.76	5	NA	Heusden-Zolder	23 Jul
13:04.70	Hillary	Chenonge	KEN	30.5.85	6	NA	Heusden-Zolder	23 Jul
13:05.05	James	Mwangi Murigi	KEN-J	15.7.86	1	JPN Ch	Tokyo	3 Jun
13:05.33	Josphat	Muchiri Ndambiri	KEN	12.2.85	2	JPN Ch	Tokyo	3 Jun
13:05.99	Martin	Irungu Mathathi	KEN	25.12.85	3	JPN Ch	Tokyo	3 Jun
13:06.83	Moses	Mosop	KEN	17.7.85	3	GP	Sevilla	4 Jun
13:07.63	Marius	Bakken	NOR	27.3.78	7	NA	Heusden-Zolder	23 Jul
13:07.74	John	Kibowen	KEN	21.4.69	1	Bisl	Oslo	29 Jul
	(30)							
13:09.5e+	Samuel	Wanjiru	KEN-J	10.11.86	3	VD	Bruxelles	26 Aug
13:09.52	Richard	Limo	KEN	18.11.80	12	GGala	Roma	8 Jul
13:09.92	Shadrack	Korir	KEN	14.12.78	4		Oslo	29 Jul
13:09.96	Bernard Kipyego	Kiprop	KEN-J	16.7.86	5	Bisl	Oslo	29 Jul
13:10.19	Adam	Goucher	USA	18.2.75	8	NA	Heusden-Zolder	23 Jul
13:10.36	Nicholas	Kemboi	QAT	25.11.83	7	ISTAF	Berlin	4 Sep
13:10.58	Juan Carlos	de la Ossa	ESP	25.11.76	7	GP	Sevilla	4 Jun
13:10.73	Alberto	García	ESP	22.2.71	13	GGala	Roma	8 Jul
13:10.78	Edwin	Soi	KEN-J	3.3.86	8	GP	Sevilla	4 Jun
13:10.86	Alan	Webb	USA	13.1.83	8	ISTAF	Berlin	4 Sep
	(40)							
13:11.18	Jonas	Cheruiyot	KEN	.84	9	NA	Heusden-Zolder	23 Jul
13:11.26	Paul Kipsiele	Koech	KEN	10.11.81	7	VD	Bruxelles	26 Aug
13:11.74	Mohammed	Mourhit	BEL	10.10.70	10	NA	Heusden-Zolder	23 Jul
13:11.77	Tim	Broe	USA	20.6.77	6	Bisl	Oslo	29 Jul
13:11.98	Charles	Kamathi	KEN	18.5.78	2	Oda	Hiroshima	29 Apr
13:12.12	John	Kariuki	KEN-J	10.11.86	3	Oda	Hiroshima	29 Apr
13:12.23	Zersenay	Tadesse	ERI	8.2.82	9	GP	Sevilla	4 Jun
13:12.33	Jamal Bilal	Salem (Kip. Katui)	QAT	12.9.78	11	Gaz	Saint-Denis	1 Jul
13:12.35	Sergey	Lebid	UKR	15.7.75	15	GGala	Roma	8 Jul
13:13.04	Sileshi	Sihine	ETH	29.1.83	3h2	WCh	Helsinki	11 Aug
	(50)							
13:13.23	Robert	Cheseret	KEN	8.10.83	8	Bisl	Oslo	29 Jul
13:13.32	Abdi	Abdirahman	USA	1.1.77	4	LGP	London (CP)	22 Jul
13:13.44	Günther	Weidlinger	AUT	5.4.78	5	LGP	London (CP)	22 Jul
13:13.50	Ali	Saïdi Sief	ALG	15.3.78	4h2	WCh	Helsinki	11 Aug
13:13.81	Moses	Kipsiro	UGA-J	2.9.86	10	Bisl	Oslo	29 Jul
13:14.38	Kiprono	Menjo	KEN	.79	1		Gavá	12 Jun
13:15.33	Ian	Dobson	USA	6.2.82	2	NC	Carson	24 Jun
13:15.44	Jesús	España	ESP	21.8.78	11	GP	Sevilla	4 Jun
13:16.03	Ryan	Hall	USA	14.10.82	3	NC	Carson	24 Jun
13:16.2e+	Mark	Bett	KEN	22.12.76	8	in 10km	Bruxelles	26 Aug
	(60)							
13:16.31	Micah	Kogo	KEN-J	3.6.86	1		Lappeenranta	21 Jul
13:17.10	Essa Ismail	Rasheed	QAT-J	14.12.86	4	FBK	Hengelo	29 May
13:17.41	Sahle	Warga	ETH	.84	1	EChall	Barakaldo	2 Apr
13:18.08	Badi	Worku	ETH-Y	22.7.88	12	Bisl	Oslo	29 Jul
13:18.18	Fabiano	Joseph	TAN	24.12.85	6h2	WCh	Helsinki	11 Aug
13:18.21	Daniel	Mwangi	KEN	1.1.84	6	Oda	Hiroshima	29 Apr
13:19.56	Boaz	Cheboiywo	KEN	2.8.78	13	Bisl	Oslo	29 Jul
13:19.69	Nathan	Lagat	KEN	.77	6	FBK	Hengelo	29 May
13:19.73	Peter	Kamais	KEN	.77	2	EChall	Barakaldo	2 Apr
13:19.95	Joseph	Kosgei	KEN	25.8.74	1		Rovereto	31 Aug
	(70)							
13:20.26	Meshack	Sang	KEN	24.7.78	2	GP II	Stanford	29 May
13:20.40	Khalid	El Amri	MAR	20.3.77	8	LGP	London (CP)	22 Jul
13:20.57	Jorge	Torres	USA	22.8.80	3	GP II	Stanford	29 May
13:20.71	Mebrahtom	Keflezighi	USA	5.5.75	14	Bisl	Oslo	29 Jul
13:21.01	Robert Kipngetich	Sigei	KEN	3.1.82	2	GS	Ostrava	9 Jun
13:21.36	James	Kwalia	QAT	12.6.84	5h1	WCh	Helsinki	11 Aug

Mark	Name		Nat	Born	Pos	Meet	Venue	Date
13:21.52	Linus	Chumba	KEN	9.2.80	2		London (CP)	6 Aug
13:21.6+	Eshetu	Gezahegne	ETH	20.9.82	2	in 10k	Praha	27 Jun
13:21.89	Wilson	Busienei	KEN	18.8.81	3		Rovereto	31 Aug
13:22.17	Gebo	Burka	ETH-J	27.9.87	4	GS	Ostrava	9 Jun
	(80)							
13:22.23	Dathan	Ritzenhein	USA	30.12.82	1		Eugene	7 May
13:22.26	Gert-Jan	Liefers	NED	26.9.78	1		Luzern	14 Jun
13:22.40	David	Kirwa Chepkwony	KEN	1.8.85	5	GS	Ostrava	9 Jun
13:22.48	Mike	Kigen	KEN-J	15.1.86	4		London (CP)	6 Aug
13:22.53	Abraham	Chebii	KEN	23.12.79	6	GS	Ostrava	9 Jun
13:22.61	Mohammed	Moustaoui	MAR	2.4.85	17	GGala	Roma	8 Jul
13:22.91	Sultan Khamis	Zaman	QAT	23.7.85	4		Rovereto	31 Au
13:23.08	Tessema	Absher	ETH-J	9.12.86	12	NA	Heusden-Zolder	23 Jul
13:23.30	Reid	Coolsaet	CAN	29.7.79	10	LGP	London (CP)	22 Jul
13:23.7A	William	Tarus	KEN-J	7.6.87	2	NC	Nairobi	17 Jun
	(90)							
13:24.0A	Mangata	Ndiwa Kimai	KEN-J	.87	3	NC	Nairobi	17 Jun
13:24.19	Ndirangu	Simon	KEN	1.11.85	1		Yokohama	24 Sep
13:24.36	Moses	Masai	KEN-J	1.6.86	7	GS	Ostrava	9 Jun
13:24.98	Yegezu	Zenbaba	ETH	26.9.83	8	GS	Ostrava	9 Jun
13:25.04	Jonathon	Riley	USA	29.12.78	5	NC	Carson	24 Jun
13:25.36	Matt	Tegenkamp	USA	19.1.82	6	NC	Carson	24 Jun
13:25.55	Moses	Kigen	KEN	22.4.73	2		Castleisland	18 Aug
13:25.65	Abreham Cherkos	Feleke	ETH-Y	23.9.89	11	ISTAF	Berlin	4 Sep
13:25.66	Monder	Rizki	BEL	16.8.79	5		Rovereto	31 Aug
13:25.68	Roberto	García	ESP	20.8.75	14	GP	Sevilla	4 Jun
	(100)							

Mark	Name		Nat	Born	Date
13:25.75	Alan	Culpepper	USA	15.9.72	22 Jul
13:25.87	Ed	Moran	USA	27.5.81	24 Jun
13:26.81	Shadrack	Langat	KEN	22.7.78	25 Jun
13:26.82	Christian	Belz	SUI	11.9.74	15 Apr
13:27.06	Tesfaye	Mesfin	ERI	24.11.74	4 Jun
13:27.14	Mekubo	Mogusu	KEN-J	25.12.86	15 May
13:27.29	Kevin	Sullivan	CAN	20.3.74	15 Apr
13:27.43	Damian Paul	Chopa	TAN-J	28.11.86	2 Apr
13:27.54	Nick	Willis	NZL	25.4.83	11 Jun
13:27.61	Abdullah	Hassan	QAT	4.4.81	14 Jun
13:28.37	Loïc	Letellier	FRA	1.10.76	23 Jul
13:29.10	Abere	Chane	ETH	16.6.85	17 Sep
13:29.14	Samuel	Mwera	TAN	3.6.85	17 Feb
13:29.27	William	Kirui	KEN	5.8.82	3 Jun
13:29.32	Tesfaye	Girma	ETH	25.9.82	17 Sep
13:29.37	Jan	Fitschen	GER	2.5.77	14 Jun
13:29.50	Takayuki	Matsumiya	JPN	21.2.80	21 May
13:30.48	Simon	Maina Munyi	KEN	18.3.78	3 Jun
13:30.50	Mohammed	Amyn	MAR	25.3.76	18 Jun
13:30.53	Mohamed	Farah	GBR	23.3.83	25 Jun
13:30.54	Khoudir	Aggoune	ALG	5.1.81	2 Jul
13:31.05	Samson	Kiflemariam	ERI	23.11.84	11 Aug
13:31.30	Yu	Mitsuya	JPN	18.12.84	21 May
13:31.63	Denis	Ndiso Musembi	KEN	31.12.83	25 Jun
13:31.63	Alejandro	Suárez	MEX	30.11.80	11 Aug
13:31.72	Yuki	Sato	JPN-J	26.11.86	21 May
13:32.07	Ayad	Lamdassen	MAR	11.10.81	4 Jun
13:32.2A	Henry	Kipchirchir	KEN	5.2.83	17 Jun
13:32.34	Bouabdellah	Tahri	FRA	20.12.78	17 Jun
13:32.38	Yonas	Kifle	ERI	24.3.77	10 Jun
13:32.43	Henrik	Skoog	SWE	17.4.79	6 Aug
13:32.61	Ahmed	Baday	MAR	12.1.79	18 Jun
13:32.74	Mokhtar	Benhari	FRA	22.5.74	9 Jun
13:32.98	Joseph	Kipkemboi	KEN	29.11.80	28 Apr
13:33.04	Luke	Kipkosgei	KEN	27.11.75	22 Jul
13:33.05	Kurt	Benninger	CAN	1.1.85	25 Mar
13:33.09	James	Mwangi Macharia	KEN	23.6.84	6 Jul
13:33.26	Arne	Gabius	GER	22.3.81	23 Jul
13:33.27	Khalid	Zoubaa	FRA	27.4.77	9 Jun
13:33.32	Bernard	Chepkok	KEN	17.1.84	29 May
13:33.39	Davis	Kabiru	KEN	1.5.83	9 Apr
13:33.42	David	Kilel	KEN	21.5.84	1 Jun
13:33.62	Pablo	Villalobos	ESP	20.5.78	4 Jun
13:34.01	Shadrack	Hoff	RSA	19.5.73	18 Feb
13:34.16	Terukazu	Omori	JPN	3.9.79	23 Jul
13:34.32	Masayuki	Obata	JPN	5.4.80	6 Jul
13:34.53	Pavel	Shapovalov	RUS	10.10.75	12 Jun
13:34.78	Isaac	Sang	KEN	24.8.78	25 Jun
13:34.8A	Henry	Sugut	KEN	4.5.85	25 Jun
13:34.95	Ryuji	Ono	JPN	27.1.85	23 Jul
13:35.32	Matt	Withrow	USA	26.12.85	1 May
13:35.41	Nicholas	Manza Kamayka	KEN	2.3.85	25 Jun
13:35.44	Samuel	Muturi	KEN-J	2.5.86	21 May
13:35.96	Karim	El Mabchour	MAR	8.7.82	18 Jun
13:36.12	Geoffrey	Kipngeno	KEN	10.4.84	23 Jul
13:36.25	Carles	Castillejo	ESP	18.8.78	8 Jul
13:36.28	Yuki	Nakamura	JPN	21.6.81	23 Jul
13:36.32	Hendrick	Ramaala	RSA	2.2.72	18 Feb
13:36.39	James	Ndungu	KEN	30.4.79	21 May
13:36.40	Patrick	Nyangero	TAN-J	2.5.86	17 Feb
13:36.56	Tomohiro	Seto	JPN	19.10.76	6 Jul
13:36.85	Matt	Gonzales	USA	9.10.81	24 Jun
13:36.95	Charles	Nyamongo	KEN	5.12.75	21 May
13:37.10	Atsushi	Sato	JPN	8.5.78	25 Jun
13:37.14	Bolota	Asmerom	USA	12.10.78	1 May
13:37.23	Takeshi	Hamano	JPN	30.7.74	21 May
13:37.45	Nicodemus	Malakwen	KEN		18 May
13:37.55	Chris	Solinsky	USA	5.12.84	24 Jun
13:37.56	Julius	Maina	KEN	14.10.77	8 May
13:37.57	David	Ruschena	AUS	17.2.74	17 Feb
13:37.68	Hillary	Kipchumba	KEN		1 Jul
13:37.70	Toshinari	Takaoka	JPN	24.9.70	29 Apr
13:37.71	Guy	Fays	BEL	15.9.69	23 Jul
13:37.77	Matthew	Cheboi	KEN	82	1 Jul
13:37.99	Yoshitaka	Iwamizu	JPN	20.6.79	21 May
13:38.00	Vasiliy	Matviychuk	UKR	13.1.82	2 Jul
13:38.15	Juan Luis	Barrios	MEX	24.6.83	11 Jun
13:38.53	Koichiro	Nagata	JPN	19.12.78	6 Jul
13:38.59	Evans	Cheruiyot	KEN	.82	18 May
13:38.65	Peter	Kosgei	KEN	3.2.83	15 Apr
13:38.92	Aleksandr	Orlov	RUS	23.2.81	25 Jun
13:39.18	Alvaro	Jiménez	ESP	29.3.79	13 Jul
13:39.28	Rabah	Aboud	ALG	81	18 Jun
13:39.37	Nicodemus	Naimadu	KEN	24.4.84	25 Mar
13:39.69	Brent	Vaughn	USA	1.10.84	1 May
13:39.69	James	Getanda	KEN	5.7.82	6 Jul
13:39.77	Obed	Mutanya	ZAM	10.8.81	25 Mar
13:40.21	Eric	Logsdon	USA	4.5.82	1 May
13:40.23	José Manuel	Martinez	ESP	22.10.71	4 Jun
13:40.56	Enos	Matelane	RSA	11.8.79	18 Feb
13:40.6A	Philip	Tarus	KEN	11.9.74	25 Jun
13:40.8	Marilson	dos Santos	BRA	6.8.77	9 Dec
13:40.90	Benjamin	Bruce	USA	10.9.82	25 Mar
13:40.97	Abraham	Cherono	KEN	21.7.80	25 Jun
13:41.09	Paul	Morrison	CAN	25.9.80	31 Aug
13:41.41	Filmon	Ghirmai	GER	25.1.79	18 May
13:41.60	Kyle	King	USA	28.7.81	29 May
13:41.80	Tomoaki	Kunichika	JPN	22.7.73	21 May

Mark	Name		Nat	Born	Pos	Meet	Venue	Date
13:41.83	Eric	Gillis	CAN	8.3.80				23 Jul
13:42.03	Chris	Estwanik (200)	USA	4.4.80				1 May

Indoors

Mark	Name		Nat	Born	Date
13:38.30	Brent	Vaughn	USA	1.10.84	12 Feb
13:39.27	Jim	Carney	USA	24.5.78	12 Feb
13:41.42	Stephen	Haas	USA	18.4.83	12 Feb

JUNIORS

See main list for top 19 juniors. 22 performances by 11 men to 13:18.0. Additional marks and further juniors:

Choge 2+	13:12.83	1	APM	Hengelo	29 May					
T Bekele	13:09.19+	1	in 10k	Bruxelles	26 Aug	13:14.15	2	APM	Hengelo	29 May
Ebuya	13:07.06	6	VD	Bruxelles	26 Aug	13:17.61	2		Lappeenranta	21 Jul
M. Murigi	13:14.00	5	Bisl	Oslo	29 Jun					
Wanjiru	13:12.40	4	Oda	Hiroshima	29 Apr	13:17.28	1D		Nobeoka	21 May
Kiprop K	13:12.47	3	LGP	London (CP)	22 Jul					
Kariuki	13:12.55	4	JPN Ch	Tokyo	3 Jun					
Kipsiro	13:13.96	11	NA	Heusden-Zolder	23 Jul					

Mark	Name		Nat	Born	Pos	Meet	Venue	Date
13:27.14	Mekubo	Mogusu	KEN	25.12.86	2		Tokyo	15 May
13:27.43	Damian Paul	Chopa (21)	TAN	28.11.86	4	EChall	Barakaldo	2 Apr
Top non-African/Asian	13:44.72	Galen Rupp	USA	8.5.86	17	NA	Heusden-Zolder	23 Jul
Top European:	13:59.1	Barnabás Bene	HUN	27.8.86	1		Budapest	6 Oct

10,000 METRES

Mark	Name		Nat	Born	Pos	Meet	Venue	Date
26:17.53	Kenenisa	Bekele	ETH	13.6.82	1	VD	Bruxelles	26 Aug
26:28.72		K Bekele			1	FBK	Hengelo	29 May
26:30.74	Abebe	Dinkesa	ETH	6.3.84	2	FBK	Hengelo	29 May
26:39.77	Boniface	Kiprop	UGA	12.10.85	2	VD	Bruxelles	26 Aug
26:41.75	Samuel	Wanjiru	KEN-J	10.11.86	3	VD	Bruxelles	26 Aug
26:51.87	Nicholas	Kemboi	QAT	25.11.83	4	VD	Bruxelles	26 Aug
26:52.60	Sammy	Kipketer	KEN	29.9.81	5	VD	Bruxelles	26 Aug
26:52.93	Mark	Bett	KEN	22.12.76	6	VD	Bruxelles	26 Aug
26:57.27	Sileshi	Sihine	ETH	29.1.83	1	Odlozil	Praha	27 Jun
27:02.62	Abderrahim	Goumri	MAR	21.5.76	3	FBK	Hengelo	29 May
27:04.45	Bernard Kipyego	Kiprop (10)	KEN-J	16.7.86	4	FBK	Hengelo	29 May
27:04.70	Zersenay	Tadesse	ERI	8.2.82	7	VD	Bruxelles	26 Aug
27:08.00		Wanjiru			1		Shizuoka	3 May
27:08.33		K Bekele			1	WCh	Helsinki	8 Aug
27:08.42	Martin	Irungu Mathathi	KEN	25.12.85	1		Kobe	24 Apr
27:08.87		Sihine			2	WCh	Helsinki	8 Aug
27:08.96	Moses	Mosop	KEN	17.7.85	3	WCh	Helsinki	8 Aug
27:10.98		Kiprop			4	WCh	Helsinki	8 Aug
27:11.57	Gebre-egziabher	Gebremariam	ETH	10.9.84	1	GP II	Stanford	29 May
27:12.22	Dejene	Berhanu	ETH	12.12.80	2	GP II	Stanford	29 May
27:12.51		Irungu Mathathi			5	WCh	Helsinki	8 Aug
27:12.82		Tadessee			6	WCh	Helsinki	8 Aug
27:13.09		Dinkesa			7	WCh	Helsinki	8 Aug
27:14.64		Goumri			8	WCh	Helsinki	8 Aug
27:16.22		Kemboi			9	WCh	Helsinki	8 Aug
27:19.19	Josphat	Muchiri Ndambiri	KEN	12.2.85	2		Kobe	24 Apr
27:22.67	Mohammed	Amyn	MAR	25.3.76	5	FBK	Hengelo	29 May
27:25.12		Kiprop			6	FBK	Hengelo	29 May
27:26.24	Khalid	El Amri	MAR	20.3.77	7	FBK	Hengelo	29 May
27:26.29		Kipyego			8	VD	Bruxelles	26 Aug
27:27.80	Juan Carlos	de la Ossa	ESP	25.11.76	1	E.Chall	Barakaldo	2 Apr
27:28.35	Charles	Kamathi	KEN	18.5.78	3		Kobe	24 Apr
27:28.69	John	Kariuki	KEN-J	10.11.86	4		Kobe	24 Apr
	(33/21)							
27:30.46	John Cheruiyot	Korir	KEN	13.12.81	9	VD	Bruxelles	26 Aug
27:31.29	Ndirang	Simon	KEN	1.11.85	1		Tokyo	13 May
27:31.89	Tesfaye	Girma	ETH	25.9.82	2		Fukuroi	22 Oct
27:32.02	Assefa	Mezgebu	ETH	19.6.78	8	FBK	Hengelo	29 May
27:33.47	Abdi	Abdirahman	USA	1.1.77	9	FBK	Hengelo	29 May
27:33.84	John	Yuda	TAN	9.6.79	10	FBK	Hengelo	29 May
27:35.55	Samuel	Muturi	KEN-J	2.5.86	5		Kobe	24 Apr
27:35.72	Yonas	Kifle	ERI	24.3.77	11	WCh	Helsinki	8 Aug
27:38.11	Julius	Gitahi	KEN	29.4.78	2		Shizuoka	3 May
	(30)							
27:38.49	Eshetu	Gezahegne	ETH	20.9.82	2	Odlozil	Praha	27 Jun
27:40.94	James	Mwangi Murigi	KEN-J	15.7.86	1		Maebashi	9 Oct
27:41.10	Yu	Mitsuya	JPN	18.12.84	2		Fukugawa	29 Jun
27:41.78	Geoffrey	Kipngeno	KEN	10.4.84	3	Odlozil	Praha	27 Jun
27:42.90	José Manuel	Martínez	ESP	22.10.71	1	NC	Avilés	17 Jul
27:44.12	Girma	Assefa	ETH-J	20.6.86	1		Hachioji	30 Nov

Mark	Name		Nat	Born	Pos	Meet	Venue	Date
27:44.47	Sultan Khamis	Zaman	QAT	23.7.85	12	FBK	Hengelo	29 May
27:45.14	Demissie	Girma	ETH-J	20.6.86	4		Shizuoka	3 May
27:45.56	Abiyote	Abate	ETH	20.11.80	13	FBK	Hengelo	29 May
27:46.16	Dennis	Ndiso Musembi	KEN	31.12.83	4	Odlozil	Praha	27 Jun
	(40)							
27:47.90	Abere	Chane	ETH	16.6.85	3		Fukuroi	22 Oct
27:48.85	Ahmed Ibrahim	Baday	MAR	12.1.79	14	FBK	Hengelo	29 May
27:50.20	Takayuki	Matsumiya	JPN	21.2.80	1		Stanford	1 May
27:53.16	Christian	Belz	SUI	11.9.74	14	WCh	Helsinki	8 Aug
27:53.51	Dieudonné	Disi	RWA	24.4.78	17	WCh	Helsinki	8 Aug
27:54.75	Mekubo	Mogusu	KEN-J	25.12.86	2		Kobe	23 Apr
27:55.92	Stephen	Koech	KEN	16.12.76	11	VD	Bruxelles	26 Aug
27:56.02	Craig	Mottram	AUS	18.6.80	3		Stanford	1 May
27:56.57	Terukazu	Omori	JPN	3.9.79	4		Stanford	1 May
27:57.98	Henry	Kipchirchir	KEN	18.3.83	5	Odlozil	Praha	27 Jun
	(50)							
27:59.39	Ayad	Lamdassem	MAR	11.10.81	12	VD	Bruxelles	26 Aug
27:59.72	Ian	Dobson	USA	6.2.82	5		Stanford	1 May
28:00.1A	Moses	Kimeli	KEN	.84	1		Eldoret	4 Jun
28:00.29	Tomohiro	Seto	JPN	19.10.76	7		Kobe	24 Apr
28:02.18	Ryuji	Ono	JPN	27.1.85	8		Kobe	24 Apr
28:03.11	Christopher	Graff	USA	5.10.75	6		Stanford	1 May
28:04.08	Boaz	Cheboiywo	KEN	2.8.78	7		Stanford	1 May
28:04.5A	Augustine	Togom	KEN	6.12.73	2		Eldoret	4 Jun
28:04.75	Simon	Bairu	CAN	8.8.83	8		Stanford	1 May
28:04.80	Toshinari	Takaoka	JPN	24.9.70	9		Kobe	24 Apr
	(60)							
28:05.6A	Barnabas	Kosgei Kiplagat	KEN-J	20.8.86	1	NC	Nairobi	16 Jun
28:06.88	Carles	Castillejo	ESP	18.8.78	2	E.Chall	Barakaldo	2 Apr
28:07.0A	Peter	Ndegwa	KEN	.82	2	NC	Nairobi	16 Jun
28:07.06	John	Kanyi	KEN	6.9.80	10		Kobe	24 Apr
28:07.27	Josphat	Boit	KEN	26.11.83	1		Stanford	25 Mar
28:07.33	Michael	Aish	NZL	24.7.76	9		Stanford	1 May
28:08.40	Wilson	Busienei	UGA	18.8.81	6	Odlozil	Praha	27 Jun
28:08.45	Cyrus Gichobi	Njui	KEN-J	11.2.86	3		Kobe	24 Apr
28:08.6A	Moses	Masai	KEN-J	1.6.86	5	WCT	Nairobi	25 Jun
28:08.97	Peter	Kosgei	KEN	3.2.83	2		Stanford	25 Mar
	(70)							
28:08.97	Samson	Kiflemariam	ERI	23.1.84	7	Odlozil	Praha	27 Jun
28:09.2A	Elijah	Mutai	KEN	1.4.78	3		Eldoret	4 Jun
28:09.61	James	Getanda	KEN	5.7.82	2	JPN Ch	Tokyo	5 Jun
28:09.62	Takashi	Ota	JPN	27.4.76	3=		Hachioji	30 Nov
28:09.85	Andrew	Letherby	AUS	19.9.73	3		Stanford	25 Mar
28:10.57	Mebrahtom	Keflezighi	USA	5.5.75	2	NC	Carson	23 Jun
28:11.0A	Gilbert	Okari	KEN	2.7.78	3	NC	Nairobi	16 Jun
28:11.0A	Hosea	Macharinyang	KEN	12.6.85	7	WCT	Nairobi	25 Jun
28:11.45	Bernard	Chepkok	KEN	17.1.84	14	VD	Bruxelles	26 Aug
28:14.03	Takeshi	Makabe	JPN	3.2.82	5		Hachioji	30 Nov
	(80)							
28:14.05	Nathan	Lagat	KEN	.77	8	Odlozil	Praha	27 Jun
28:14.26	Atsushi	Sato	JPN	8.5.78	6		Shizuoka	3 May
28:14.90	Fernando	Rey	ESP	16.4.80	9	Odlozil	Praha	27 Jun
28:14.92	Takanobu	Otsubo	JPN	15.6.76	6		Hachioji	30 Nov
28:15.52	Galen	Rupp	USA-J	8.5.86	1		Eugene	7 May
28:16.40		Chen Mingfu	CHN	26.1.85	1	NG	Nanjing	17 Oct
28:16.7A	Richard	Limo	KEN	18.11.80	8	WCT	Nairobi	25 Jun
28:17.46	Matt	Gonzales	USA	9.10.81	10		Stanford	1 May
28:19.20	Ricardo	Serrano	ESP	29.10.80	3	E.Chall	Barakaldo	2 Apr
28:19.65	Nicholas Manza	Kamakya	KEN	2.3.85	10	Odlozil	Praha	27 Jun
	(90)							
28:19.89	Toshihiro	Iwasa	JPN	18.5.76	12		Kobe	24 Apr
28:20.11	Robert	Cheseret	KEN	8.10.83	1	NCAA	Sacramento	9 Jun
28:20.52	Tsuyoshi	Ogata	JPN	11.5.73	13		Kobe	24 Apr
28:20.53	Toshihide	Kato	JPN	4.7.73	14		Kobe	24 Apr
28:20.87	Kazuhiro	Maeda	JPN	19.4.81	1		Isahaya	3 Dec
28:21.30	Stanley	Nganga	KEN-J	30.6.86	7		Hachioji	30 Nov
28:21.62	Willy	Kimutai Kangoo	KEN	12.2.84	2B		Kitakyushu	14 May
28:22.1A	Linus	Maiyo	KEN	11.12.83	5	NC	Nairobi	16 Jun
28:22.46	Ombeche	Mokamba	KEN	6.4.82	1		Yokohama	23 Oct
28:22.85	David	Kariuki	KEN	23.5.82	2		Isahaya	3 Dec
	(100)							

Mark	Name		Nat	Born	Date
28:23.56	Masatoshi	Ibata	JPN	20.8.72	15 Jun
28:23.73	Dmitriy	Maksimov	RUS	6.5.77	2 Apr
28:23.74	Keita	Akiba	JPN	27.11.79	30 Nov
28:24.00	Yoshinori	Oda	JPN	5.12.80	29 Jun
28:24.32	Slavko	Petrovic	CRO	23.9.80	2 Apr
28:24.55	Kazuo	Ietani	JPN	25.8.77	5 Jun
28:24.92	Koji	Watanabe	JPN	20.2.78	16 Oct
28:25.05	Yuki	Matsuoka	JPN-J	14.1.86	13 May
28:25.27	Solomon	Molla	ETH-J	.87	29 May
28:27.50	Yuki	Sato	JPN-J	26.11.86	24 Apr
28:27.94	Hiromichi	Ueki	JPN	11.11.84	3 Dec
28:28.7A	Philemon	Kisang	KEN		14 May
28:28.78	Michitane	Noda	JPN	25.3.75	14 May
28:29.08	Pierre	Joncheray	FRA	9.9.82	2 Apr
28:29.37		Du Pengyuan	CHN	30.9.84	17 Oct
28:29.61	Takeshi	Hamano	JPN	30.7.74	29 Jun
28:29.76	Tetsuo	Nishimura	JPN	27.10.78	16 Oct
28:29.89	Hiromu	Nishizawa	JPN	27.8.75	30 Nov
28:30.15	Abel	Kirui	KEN	.82	17 Aug
28:30.27	Atsushi	Fujita	JPN	6.11.76	14 May
28:30.45	Takasahi	Horiguchi	JPN	26.9.79	30 Nov
28:30.54	Keisuke	Nakatani	JPN	6.4.81	14 May
28:30.65	Daniel	Mwangi Muchunu	KEN	1.1.84	23 Sep
28:30.80	Driss	El Himer	FRA	4.4.74	4 Jun
28:31.12	Masayuki	Kobayashi	JPN	4.4.74	14 May
28:31.39	Matthew	Lane	USA	5.9.77	25 Mar
28:31.86	Fadil	Mohamed	MAR	15.11.81	16 Aug
28:32.82	Wataru	Okutani	JPN	9.1.75	14 May
28:33.31	Bret	Schoolmeester	USA	12.5.84	15 Apr
28:33.44	Fabiano	Joseph	TAN	24.12.85	26 Jul
28:33.96	Takamasa	Uchida	JPN	17.10.81	26 Nov
28:34.2A	Solomon	Bushendich	KEN	10.1.84	25 Jun
28:34.65	Matt	Downin	USA	10.2.77	23 Jun
28:34.75	William	Kirui	KEN	5.8.82	15 Jun
28:35.06	Yuki	Nakamura	JPN	21.6.81	24 Apr
28:35.18	Keizo	Maruyama	JPN	20.4.83	13 May
28:35.24	Noriaki	Takahashi	JPN	26.7.82	29 Jun
28:35.33	Toshinari	Fujimoto	JPN	2.10.75	16 Oct
28:35.40	Koichiro	Nagata	JPN	19.12.78	29 Jun
28:35.48	Mathew	Chesang	KEN	29.12.81	25 Mar
28:35.73		Han Gang	CHN	10.11.78	17 Oct
28:35.81	Kenji	Noguchi	JPN	23.2.75	26 Nov
28:35.86	Radwan	Koborsi	USA	4.10.83	25 Mar
28:35.95	Jim	Carney	USA	24.5.78	23 Jun
28:36.20	Satoshi	Iijima	JPN	22.12.78	26 Nov
28:36.2A	William	Chebon	KEN	.81	16 Jun
28:36.39	Essa Ismail	Rasheed	QAT-J	14.12.86	15 Sep
28:36.57	Daisuke	Isomatsu	JPN	17.12.73	14 May
28:36.58		Zhang Yunshan	CHN	16.3.83	17 Oct
28:36.75	Takashi	Arisumi	JPN	5.7.73	14 May
28:36.76	Satoshi	Irifune	JPN	14.12.75	24 Apr
28:36.88	Khaled	Kamal Khaled	BRN		15 Sep
28:37.11	Takashi	Maeda	JPN	3.10.77	29 Jun
28:37.35	Shuichi	Fujii	JPN	14.2.82	26 Nov
28:37.64	Jason	Hubbard	USA	20.1.75	15 Apr
28:37.75	Kensuke	Takezawa	JPN-J	11.10.86	26 Nov
28:37.97	Joe	Driscoll	USA	2.11.79	23 Jun
28:38.20	Masayoshi	Kuroda	JPN	22.11.81	26 Nov
28:38.29		Chen Fuchun	CHN	23.5.78	17 Oct
28:38.36	Yoshihiro	Yamamoto	JPN	20.4.83	15 Jun
28:38.53	Satoshi	Harada	JPN	29.6.81	26 Nov
28:38.72	Patrick	Gildea	USA	26.1.80	15 Apr
28:38.72	Yusei	Nakao	JPN	28.2.84	16 Oct
28:39.00	Shinji	Matsumura	JPN	21.5.72	14 May
28:39.15	Shigeru	Aburaya	JPN	8.2.77	26 Nov
28:39.26	Giuliano	Battocletti	ITA	1.8.75	22 May
28:39.52	Ryoji	Matsushita	JPN	7.11.80	23 Apr
28:39.54	Reid	Coolsaet	CAN	29.7.79	1 May
28:39.93	Joshua	Rohatinsky	USA	7.3.82	15 Apr
28:40.0A	Fred	Kosgei	KEN		16 Jun
28:40.00	Tomoya	Shirayanagi	JPN	7.7.81	23 Apr
28:40.25	James	Ndungu	KEN	30.4.79	23 Apr
28:40.27	Akinori	Shibutani	JPN	5.12.77	23 Apr
28:40.40	Mark	Carroll	IRL	15.1.72	18 Jun
28:40.58	Gavin	Thompson	GBR	9.4.80	11 Jun
28:40.62	Kenji	Kubo	JPN	1.5.75	26 Nov
28:40.99	Jamal Bilal	Salem	QAT	12.9.78	7 Dec
28:41.19	Keith	Cullen	GBR	13.6.72	11 Jun
28:41.24	Toru	Sakasai	JPN	24.2.82	14 May
28:41.32	Tomoyuki	Honda	JPN	20.1.83	14 May
28:41.33	Yoshinori	Suzuki	JPN	14.4.80	23 Apr
28:41.35	Yoshikazu	Kubo	JPN	18.2.84	23 Apr
28:41.81	Moukhled	Al-Outaibi	KSA	20.6.76	12 Apr
28:42.07	Kosaku	Hoshina	JPN	31.8.84	23 Apr
28:42.24	Daniel	Muryu	KEN	23.4.85	29 Jun
28:42.5A	Salim	Kipsang	KEN	22.12.79	27 May
28:42.50	Tadashi	Shitamori (187)	JPN	29.12.77	23 Apr

JUNIORS

See main list for top 13 juniors. 13 performances by 5 men to 27:50.0. Additional marks and further juniors:

	Mark	Pos	Meet	Venue	Date	Mark	Pos	Venue	Date
Wanjiru 2+	27:32.43	1r2		Kobe	23 Apr	27:39.34	1	Fukagawa	29 Jun
	27:41.64	1	JPN Ch	Tokyo	5 Jun				
Kariuki	27:31.10	1		Fukuroi	22 Oct				
Muturi	27:40.19	3		Shizuoka	3 May	27:47.59	2	Maebashi	9 Oct

Mark	Name		Nat	Born	Pos	Meet	Venue	Date
28:25.05	Yuki	Matsuoka	JPN-	14.1.86	3		Tokyo	13 May
28:25.27	Solomon	Molla	ETH	.87	3	GP II	Stanford	29 May
28:27.50	Yuki	Sato	JPN	26.11.86	15		Kobe	24 Apr
28:36.39	Essa Ismail	Rasheed	QAT	14.12.86	1	PArab	Radès	15 Sep
28:37.75	Kensuke	Takezawa	JPN	11.10.86	6		Yokohama	26 Nov
28:45.64	Cosmas	Ondiba	KEN-Y	13.12.89	1r3		Fukuroi	22 Oct
28:45.84	Japheth	Ng'ojoy	USA	31.12.87	11		Stanford	25 Mar
Top European: 29:37.70	Barnabás	Bene	HUN	27.8.86	1	NC	Budapest	8 May

10 KILOMETRES ROAD

Mark	Name		Nat	Born	Pos	Meet	Venue	Date
27:25	Haile	Gebrselassie	ETH	18.4.73	1		Manchester	22 May
27:34	Eliud	Kipchoge	KEN	5.11.84	1		Madrid	31 Dec
27:35+		Gebrselassie			1		Tilburg	4 Sep
27:39	Gilbert	Okari	KEN	2.7.78	1		Cape Elizabeth	1 Aug
27:45	Wilson Kiprotich	Kebenei	KEN	20.7.80	2		Cape Elizabeth	1 Aug
27:47	Sammy	Kipketer	KEN	29.9.81	1	Cres C	New Orleans	26 Mar
27:49	John Cheruiyot	Korir	KEN	13.12.81	2	Cres C	New Orleans	26 Mar
27:50	John	Kibowen	KEN	21.4.69	1		Brunssum	3 Apr
27:53	John	Kipchumba	KEN	9.12.74	1		Stadskanaal	28 Mar
27:55	Juan Carlos	de la Ossa	ESP	25.11.76	2		Manchester	22 May
27:56	John	Korir	KEN	15.12.75	1		San Juan, PUR	27 Feb
27:56	Jason	Mbote	KEN	.77	1		Zevenaar	28 Aug
28:00	Samuel	Rongo Olengura	KEN	.72	2		Brunssum	3 Apr
28:00	Paul Kimaiyo	Kimugul	KEN	4.3.80	1		Trento	8 Oct

Mark	Name		Nat	Born	Pos	Meet	Venue	Date
Others where superior to track bests								
28:05	Robert Kipkoech	Cheruiyot	KEN	26.9.78	3		San Juan, PUR	27 Feb
28:06	Nicodemus	Malakwen	KEN	.80	1		Strasbourg	15 May
28:06	Tom	Nyariki	KEN	27.9.71	3		Cape Elizabeth	1 Aug
28:06	Peter	Kiprotich	KEN	.79	3		Zevenaar	28 Aug
28:07	Musa Kipkemboi	Cherutich	KEN	.75	1		Hilversum	17 Apr
28:07	Rui	Silva	POR	3.8.77	3		Madrid	31 Dec
28:08	Martin	Lel	KEN	29.10.78	4		San Juan, PUR	27 Feb
28:09	Shadrack	Kosgei	KEN	24.11.84	4	Cres C	New Orleans	26 Mar
28:10	Solomon	Bushendich	KEN	10.1.84	1		Gualtieri	28 Mar
28:10	David	Kogo	KEN-J	.86	1		Marseille	20 Nov
28:11	Enock	Mitei	KEN	26.11.80	2		Marseille	1 May
28:11	Dathan	Ritzenhein	USA	30.12.82	1	NC	Mobile	5 Nov
28:12	Chengere	Tolossa	ETH	.75	1		Carouge	24 Sep
28:13	Evans	Cheruiyot	KEN	.82	2		Strasbourg	15 May
28:13	Joseph	Maregu	KEN	.77	1		Tours	9 Sep
28:13	Joseph	Ebuya	KEN-J	20.6.87	2		Marseille	20 Nov
28:14	Sergiy	Lebid	UKR	15.7.75	3		Manchester	22 May
28:15	Wesley	Kipsang	KEN	.70	2		Tours	9 Sep
28:16	Wesley	Ochoro	KEN	.78	1		Kisii	26 Aug
28:16	Stefano	Baldini	ITA	25.5.71	2		Trento	8 Oct
28:17	Nicholas Manza	Kamakya	KEN	2.3.85	3		Tours	9 Sep
28:17+	Kimwole	Kimutai	KEN		1	in 20k	Paris	16 Oct
28:19	Aïssa	Dghoughi	MAR	10.12.81	1		Issy-les-Moulineaux	11 Dec
28:20	Eliud	Tanui	KEN	.83	1		Würzburg	24 Apr
28:20	Benson	Barus	KEN	4.7.80	3		Marseille	1 May
28:20	Adam Ismael	Khamis	BRN-Y	12.2.89	2		Issy-les-Moulineaux	11 Dec
28:22	Moses	Kigen	KEN	22.4.73	2		Würzburg	24 Apr
28:22	Peter	Kamais	KEN	.77	3		Issy-les-Moulineaux	11 Dec

Mark	Name		Nat	Born	Date
28:23	James	Koskei	KEN	23.11.68	1 Aug
28:24	Luke	Kipkosgei	KEN	27.11.75	26 Mar
28:24	David	Langat	KEN	.77	9 Sep
28:25	Francis	Kiprop	KEN	4.6.82	1 May
28:25	William Chebon	Chebor	KEN	.81	1 Aug
28:25 A	Ketema	Negussie	ETH		27 Nov
28:26 A	Nathan Kibet	Naibei	KEN	22.2.86	27 Nov
28:27	Peter	Githuka	KEN	14.2.69	9 Oct
28:28	Gebo	Burka	ETH	17.9.87	11 Jun
28:28	Meshack	Sang	KEN	24.7.78	1 Aug
28:28	Stanley	Kipkosgei Salil	KEN	2.4.86	4 Sep
28:29	Tewodros	Shiferaw	ETH	21.9.80	30 Jan
28:29	Jefferson	Nyanusi	ITA		20 Nov
28:29	Silas	Sang	KEN	21.8.78	11 Dec
28:30	Benjamin	Limo	KEN	23.8.74	28 Mar
28:30+	Fabiano	Joseph	TAN	24.12.85	10 Apr
28:30+	Lawrence Kiprotich	Saina	KEN	.85	10 Apr
28:30	Marilson	dos Santos	BRA	6.8.77	15 May
28:30	Duncan	Kibet	KEN	.70	9 Sep
28:30	Wilson	Chebet	KEN	.85	9 Oct
28:31+	Luke	Kibet	KEN	19.6.83	4 Sep
28:32	Wilfred	Taragon	KEN	15.2.85	22 May
28:32+	Simon	Maina	KEN	18.3.78	3 Jul
28:33	James Kibocha	Theuri	KEN	30.11.78	1 May
28:33	Ronald	Kipchumba	KEN	.86	27 Nov
28:34	Francis	Kibiwott	KEN	15.9.78	26 Mar
28:34	John	Kipchumba	KEN	8.12.74	17 Apr
28:34	Shadrack	Hoff	RSA	19.5.73	23 Oct
28:35	Sahle	Warga	ETH	.84	3 Apr
28:35	Marcel	Ionescu	ROM	4.8.84	10 Apr
28:35	David	Plimo	KEN	.76	24 Apr
28:35	Yegezu	Zenbaba	ETH	26.9.83	11 Jun
28:35	Pius	Muli	KEN	15.12.82	1 Oct
28:35	Günther	Weidlinger	AUT	5.4.78	26 Nov
28:35 A	Deriba	Mergia	ETH		27 Nov
28:36	Jackson Kirwa	Kiprono	KEN	.86	1 Oct
28:36+	Hillary	Kipchumba	KEN		16 Oct
28:36	Jesús	España	ESP	21.8.78	31 Dec
28:37	Chris	Davies	GBR	19.10.76	22 May
28:37	Tesfaye	Eticha	ETH	27.6.74	24 Sep
28:37	Joseph	Keino	KEN		1 Oct
28:38	Charles	Ngolebus	KEN		10 Apr
28:38+	Abiyote	Guta	ETH	.85	18 Sep
28:38	Kassa	Tadesse	GBR	21.8.74	24 Sep
28:38	Richard	Mavuso	RSA	30.3.78	23 Oct
28:38	Viktor	Röthlin	SUI	14.10.74	30 Oct
28:39	Rômulo	da Silva	BRA	26.5.77	6 Jan
28:39	John	Gwako	KEN	4.9.78	19 Mar
28:39	Douglas	Momanyi	KEN	1.12.80	19 Mar
28:39+	William	Kipsang	KEN	.77	18 Sep
28:39	David Kiptum	Kipruto	KEN	2.11.75	8 Oct
28:39	Tshamano	Setone	RSA	7.5.87	23 Oct
28:40	Samuel	Ndereba	KEN	.76	19 Mar
28:40	Thomas	Pkemoi	KEN		11 Jun
28:40	Jamal	Baligha	MAR	11.12.73	9 Sep
28:40+	Felix	Limo	KEN	22.8.80	18 Sep
28:40	Georges	Towet Kipketer	KEN	.85	24 Sep
28:40+	Henry	Githuka	KEN		16 Oct
28:40+	David	Lagat	KEN	.83	16 Oct
28:40+	Girma	Tola	ETH	13.10.75	16 Oct

Downhill courses

Mark	Name		Nat	Born	Pos	Meet	Venue	Date
27:38+	Dejene	Berhanu	ETH	12.12.80	1	in HMar	South Shields	18 Sep

Mark	Name		Nat	Born	Date
28:24	Fabiano	Joseph	TAN	24.12.85	4 Jul
28:39	Wilson Kipkemboi	Kigen	KEN	15.9.80	4 Jul

Very Downhill (157m Salt Lake City)

Mark	Name		Nat	Born	Date
28:32A	Teren	Jameson	USA	26.4.77	25 Jul

15 KILOMETRES ROAD

Mark	Name		Nat	Born	Pos	Meet	Venue	Date
41:22+	Haile	Gebrselassie	ETH	18.4.73	1	in 10M	Tilburg	4 Sep
41:57		Gebrselassie			1		Nijmegen	20 Nov
42:08+	Samuel	Wanjiru	KEN	10.11.86	1	in HMar	Rotterdam	11 Sep
42:17	Zersenay	Tadesse	ERI	8.2.82	2		Nijmegen	20 Nov
42:43+ dh	Mekubo	Mogusu	KEN-J	25.12.86	1	in HMar	Sapporo	3 Jul
42:58+ dh	Demissie	Girma	ETH-J	20.6.86	2	in HMar	Sapporo	3 Jul
42:59+ dh	Simon	Maina	KEN	18.3.78	3	in HMar	Sapporo	3 Jul
	43:42+				2	in HMar	Nagoya	23 Nov
43:00+	Abiyote	Guta	ETH	.85	1	in 10M	Zaandam	18 Sep

MEN 2005

Mark	Name		Nat	Born	Pos	Meet	Venue	Date
43:01+	Francis	Kibiwott	KEN	15.9.78	2	in 10M	Zaandam	18 Sep
43:02+	William	Kipsang	KEN	.77	3	in 10M	Zaandam	18 Sep
43:09	Hailu	Mekonnen	ETH	4.4.80	1		Heerenberg	4 Dec
43:16	John Ekiru	Kelai	KEN	29.12.76	1		Maastricht	24 Apr
43:18+ dh	Josephat	Muchiri Ndambiri	KEN	12.2.85	4	in HMar	Sapporo	3 Jul
43:22	Gilbert	Okari	KEN	2.7.78	1		Utica	10 Jul
43:26	Bernard Kiprop	Kipyego	KEN	16.7.86	3		Nijmegen	20 Nov
43:28+	Yonas	Kifle	ERI	5.11.77	1=	in HMar	Edmonton	1 Oct
43:28+	Fabiano	Joseph	TAN	24.12.85	1=	in HMar	Edmonton	1 Oct
43:28+	Abebe	Dinkesa	ETH	6.3.84	1=	in HMar	Edmonton	1 Oct
43:28+	Mubarak Hassan	Shami	QAT	2.12.80	1=	in HMar	Edmonton	1 Oct
43:28+	Sileshi	Sihine	ETH	29.1.83	1=	in HMar	Edmonton	1 Oct
43:30+	Larbi	Zéroual	FRA	10.1.71	-	in 10M	Zaandam	18 Sep

Mark	Name		Nat	Born	Date
43:32+	Felix	Limo	KEN	22.8.80	18 Sep
43:32+	John	Yuda	TAN	9.6.79	1 Oct
43:34A	Elijah	Birgen Kipkorir	KEN	28.2.80	27 Nov
43:35A	Paul	Limo	KEN		27 Nov
43:38	Moses	Masai	KEN	1.6.86	24 Apr
	or Moses	Ndiema	KEN	1.6.78 ?	
43:38+dh	Cyrus	Njiri	KEN-J	11.2.86	3 Jul
43:40	Tessema	Absher	ETH	9.12.86	20 Nov
43:42	James	Moiben	KEN	20.4.77	18 Jun
43:42	Nephat	Kinyanjui	KEN	30.6.77	10 Jul
43:47+	James Mwangi	Macharia	KEN	23.6.84	1 Oct
43:48	David	Kyeng	KEN		18 Jun
43:49	William Chebon	Chebor	KEN	.81	10 Jul
43:50+dh	Julius	Gitahi	KEN	29.4.78	3 Jul
43:52	Ryan	Shay	USA	4.5.79	12 Mar
43:54	Stanley	Kipkosgei Salil	KEN	2.4.86	19 Mar
43:55+	Julius	Maina	KEN	14.10.77	23 Nov

Uncertain measurement: 8 Jan Eldoret: 42:03A Clement Kibor Koech KEN .81, 42:28A Wilson Chebet KEN, 42:54A Philip Manyim KEN 24.3.78, 43:08A Thomas Chepkwony KEN, 43:23A Julius Limo KEN

10 MILES ROAD

Mark	Name		Nat	Born	Pos	Meet	Venue	Date
44:24	Haile	Gebrselassie	ETH	18.4.73	1		Tilburg	4 Sep
45:10	Samuel	Wanjiru	KEN-J	10.11.86	1r1		Kosa	11 Dec
45:47	Josephat	Muchiri Ndambiri	KEN	12.2.85	2r2		Kosa	11 Dec
46:04	William	Kipsang	KEN	.77	1		Zaandam	18 Sep
46:05	Francis	Kibiwott	KEN	15.9.78	2		Zaandam	18 Sep
46:09	Abiyote	Guta	ETH	.85	3		Zaandam	18 Sep
46:23	Terukazu	Omori	JPN	3.9.79	1		Himeji	11 Feb
46:28	Yu	Mitsuya	JPN	18.12.84	1r2		Kosa	11 Dec
46:29	Michitaka	Hosokawa	JPN	26.4.76	2		Himeji	11 Feb
46:29	Kazuo	Ietani	JPN	25.8.77	2r2		Kosa	11 Dec

Mark	Name		Nat	Born	Date
46:32	Ryoji	Matsushita	JPN	7.11.80	11 Feb
46:33	Tomoaki	Kunichika	JPN	22.4.73	11 Feb
46:41+	James	Mwangi Macharia	KEN	23.6.84	4 Sep
46:41+	James	Kwambai	KEN	.76	4 Sep
46:42	Larbi	Zéroual	FRA	10.1.71	18 Sep
46:45/55?	John	Yuda	TAN	9.6.79	9 Oct
46:48	Tetsuo	Nishimura	JPN	27.10.78	11 Feb
46:48	Felix	Limo	KEN	22.8.80	18 Sep
46:51	Takashi	Maeda	JPN	3.10.77	13 Feb
46:51	Tomoyuki	Sato	JPN	31.1.81	11 Dec
46:53	Keita	Akiba	JPN	27.11.79	13 Feb
46:53	Luke	Kibet	KEN	19.6.83	4 Sep
46:53	Abere	Chane	ETH	16.6.85	11 Dec
46:53	Masayuki	Kobayashi	JPN	4.4.74	11 Dec
46:55	John	Korir	KEN	15.12.75	3 Apr
46:55	Takashi	Tokunaga	JPN	6.6.81	11 Dec
46:56	Hiromichi	Ueki	JPN	11.11.84	11 Dec
46:58	Reuben Kibet	Chebii	KEN	.82	3 Apr

20 KILOMETRES ROAD

Mark	Name		Nat	Born	Pos	Meet	Venue	Date
56:18+	Samuel	Wanjiru	KEN-J	10.11.86	1	in HMar	Rotterdam	11 Sep
	56:42+				1	in HMar	Sendai	7 Oct
57:19	Evans	Cheruiyot	KEN	.82	1		Paris	16 Oct
57:22	Mekubo	Mogusu	KEN-J	25.12.86	1		Tachikawa	22 Oct
57:31	Kimwole	Kimutai	KEN	.84	2		Paris	16 Oct
57:42	Girma	Tola	ETH	13.10.75	3		Paris	16 Oct
57:43	James Kibocha	Theuri	KEN	30.11.78	4		Paris	16 Oct
57:48	David	Lagat	KEN	.83	5		Paris	16 Oct

Most top 20km times (not always recorded) would come during half marathons

HALF MARATHON

Mark	Name		Nat	Born	Pos	Meet	Venue	Date
59:05 dh	Zersenay	Tadesse	ERI	8.2.82	1	GNR	South Shields	18 Sep
59:10 dh	Paul	Tergat	KEN	17.6.69	1		Lisboa	13 Mar
59:16	Samuel	Wanjiru	KEN-J	10.11.86	1		Rotterdam	11 Sep
59:21 dh	Robert Kipkoech	Cheruiyot	KEN	26.9.78	2		Lisboa	13 Mar
59:27 dh	Wilson	Kiprotich Kebenei	KEN	20.7.80	3		Lisboa	13 Mar
59:42 dh	Martin	Lel	KEN	29.10.78	4		Lisboa	13 Mar
59:43		Wanjiru			1		Sendai	10 Jul
59:47	Patrick	Ivuti	KEN	30.6.78	2		Rotterdam	11 Sep
60:11		Kiprotich Kebenei			1	Stra	Milano	10 Apr
60:15	Paul Kimaiyo	Kimugul	KEN	4.3.80	3		Rotterdam	11 Sep
60:25	John	Yuda	TAN	9.6.79	2	Stra	Milano	10 Apr
60:30	Lawrence Kiprotich	Saina (10)	KEN	.85	3	Stra	Milano	10 Apr
60:42	James	Mwangi Macharia	KEN	23.6.84	1		Virginia Beach	4 Sep

Mark		Name		Nat	Born	Pos	Meet	Venue	Date
60:44	dh	Dejene	Berhanu	ETH	12.12.80	2	GNR	South Shields	18 Sep
60:45		James	Kwambai	KEN	.76	1		Ostia	27 Feb
60:46	dh	Rodgers	Rop	KEN	16.2.76	5		Lisboa	13 Mar
60:47		David	Lagat	KEN	.83	1		Billancourt	6 Nov
60:51	dh	Jaouad	Gharib	MAR	22.5.72	6		Lisboa	13 Mar
60:53		Duncan Kipkemboi	Kibet	KEN	.78	2		Billancourt	6 Nov
60:54		James Kibocha	Theuri	KEN	30.11.78	1		Lille	3 Sep
60:56			Rop			4		Rotterdam	11 Sep
60:59		Luke	Kibet	KEN	19.6.83	5		Rotterdam	11 Sep
61:00		Fabiano	Joseph (20)	TAN	24.12.85	4	Stra	Milano	10 Apr
61:01		Evans	Cheruiyot	KEN	.82	1		Vitry-sur-Seine	17 Apr
61:04			Kimugul			1		Berlin	3 Apr
61:05			Kwambai			2		Virginia Beach	4 Sep
61:07		Silas	Kirui	KEN	.81	1		Praha	2 Apr
61:07			Kimugul			2		Vitry-sur-Seine	17 Apr
61:07			Joseph			6		Rotterdam	11 Sep
61:08			Joseph			1	WCh	Edmonton	1 Oct
61:09		Mubarak Hassan (31/23)	Shami	QAT	2.12.80	2	WCh	Edmonton	1 Oct
61:10/18?		Eliud	Kurgat	KEN	20.8.73	1		Riva del Garda	13 Nov
61:13		Robert	Kipchumba	KEN	24.2.84	1		Udine	25 Sep
61:13		Yonas	Kifle	ERI	24.3.77	3	WCh	Edmonton	1 Oct
61:14		Benson	Barus	KEN	4.7.80	1		Nice	24 Apr
61:14		Sileshi	Sihine	ETH	29.1.83	4	WCh	Edmonton	1 Oct
61:15	dh	Paul	Kirui	KEN	5.2.80	7		Lisboa	13 Mar
61:16		Joseph (30)	Ngolebus	KEN	10.4.75	2		Berlin	3 Apr
61:17	dh	Stefano	Baldini	ITA	25.5.71	8		Lisboa	13 Mar
61:18	dh	Ambese	Tolosa	ETH	28.8.77	9		Lisboa	13 Mar
61:18		Jairus	Chanchaima	KEN		3		Vitry-sur-Seine	17 Apr
61:22		William Todoo	Rotich	KEN	.80	2		Ostia	27 Feb
61:23		Matthew	Sigei Kipkorir	KEN	.83	2		Udine	25 Sep
61:27		Dennis	Ndiso Musembi	KEN	31.12.83	4		Vitry-sur-Seine	17 Apr
61:28		Mekubo	Mogusu	KEN-J	25.12.86	1		Sapporo	3 Jul
61:30		Driss	El Himer	FRA	4.4.74	3		Lille	3 Sep
61:31		Daniel	Njenga	KEN	7.5.76	1		Yamaguchi	13 Mar
61:32		Takayuki (40)	Matsumiya	JPN	21.2.80	2		Yamaguchi	13 Mar
61:32		Francis	Kiprop	KEN	4.6.82	3		Udine	25 Sep
61:33		Haile	Gebrselassie	ETH	18.4.73	1		Granollers	6 Feb
61:33		Philip	Kirui	KEN	11.9.73	2		Nice	24 Apr
61:33		Hendrick	Ramaala	RSA	2.2.72	1	NC	Durban	10 Jul
61:34A		Charles	Munyeki Kiama	KEN		1		Nairobi	23 Oct
61:36		Laban	Kagika	KEN	17.7.78	1		Marugame	6 Feb
61:36		Toshihiro	Iwasa	JPN	18.5.76	3		Yamaguchi	13 Mar
61:37A		Slomon	Tsige	ETH	23.1.85	1	NC	Addis Ababa	28 Aug
61:37		Benson	Cherono	KEN	30.6.84	7		Rotterdam	11 Sep
61:38		Kazuo (50)	Ietani	JPN	25.8.77	4		Yamaguchi	13 Mar
61:38		Wilson Kemei	Kiprono	KEN	6.11.74	4		Udine	1 Sep
61:39		Ombeche	Mokamba	KEN	7.4.82	2		Marugame	6 Feb
61:39		Moses	Kigen	KEN	22.4.73	3		Berlin	3 Apr
61:39		Wilson	Busienei	UGA	18.8.81	5		Vitry-sur-Seine	17 Apr
61:40		Demissie	Girma	ETH-J	20.6.86	2		Sapporo	3 Jul
61:42A		Lishan	Yegezu	ETH-J	1.1.86	2	NC	Addis Ababa	28 Aug
61:43		Julius	Maina	KEN	14.10.77	1		Nagoya	23 Nov
61:44		Simon	Maina	KEN	18.3.78	2		Nagoya	23 Nov
61:45		Stanley	Kipkosgei Salil	KEN-J	2.4.86	2		Praha	2 Apr
61:46		Sammy (60)	Chumba	KEN	9.8.78	2		Den Haag	19 Mar
61:47A		Raji	Assefa	ETH-J	18.2.86	3	NC	Addis Ababa	28 Aug
61:48		Philip	Biwott Kiplagat	KEN-J	.87	3		Ostia	27 Feb
61:48		Jacob	Yator	KEN		1		Málaga	3 Apr
61:49		Cyrus Gichoni	Njui	KEN-J	11.2.86	3		Marugame	6 Feb
61:49		Jason	Mbote	KEN	.77	3		Den Haag	19 Mar
61:49		Elijah	Kipruto Sang	KEN	.83	1		Paderborn	26 Mar
61:51		Julius	Kimutai	KEN	4.4.74	1		Reading	6 Mar
61:51		Christopher	Cheboiboch	KEN	3.3.77	4		Den Haag	19 Mar
61:52		Mark	Tanui	KEN		5		Den Haag	19 Mar
61:53		Hironori (70)	Arai	JPN	19.9.79	5		Yamaguchi	13 Mar

Mark	Name		Nat	Born	Pos	Meet	Venue	Date
61:53	Simon Kipyego	Kiprop	KEN	11.11.78	1		Azpeitia	19 Mar
61:53	Rachid	Amor	TUN	10.4.78	1		Brugnera	16 Apr
61:53	Abebe	Dinkesa	ETH	6.3.84	5	WCh	Edmonton	1 Oct
61:54	Mohammed	Mourhit	BEL	10.10.70	6		Den Haag	19 Mar
61:54	Paul Kipkemei	Kogo	KEN	.83	2		Brugnera	17 Apr
61:54A	Nasir	Abdisa	ETH		4	NC	Addis Ababa	28 Aug
61:54	Jackson	Koech	KEN	26.12.78	4		Lille	3 Sep
61:54	Kensuke	Takahashi	JPN	30.5.78	3		Nagoya	23 Nov
61:55	Takanobu	Otsubo	JPN	15.6.76	6		Yamaguchi	13 Mar
61:55	Robert	Cheboror	KEN	9.9.78	7		Den Haag	19 Mar
	(80)							
61:55	Philip	Rugut	KEN	18.5.77	1		New Delhi	16 Oct
61:56	Joseph	Ngeny Kiprotich	KEN	.78	3		Praha	2 Apr
61:56	Tesfaye	Tola	ETH	19.10.74	1		Vilamoura	10 Apr
61:56	Yusuf	Songoka	KEN	5.2.79	3		Virginia Beach	4 Sep
61:57	Ryoji	Matsushita	JPN	7.11.80	7		Yamaguchi	13 Mar
61:57	Getulo	Bayo	TAN	.80	8		Den Haag	19 Mar
61:57A	Tadesse	Tola	ETH		5	NC	Addis Ababa	28 Aug
61:58	Yoichiro	Akiyama	JPN	25.12.79	8		Yamaguchi	13 Mar
61:58	Ernest	Kipyego	KEN	6.10.78	4		Berlin	3 Apr
61:58	Festus	Langat	KEN		1		Los Palacios	18 Dec
	(90)							
61:59	Malack	Ole Mangira	TAN	.84	2		Reading	6 Mar
61:59	Hailu	Mesfin	ETH	.84	6		Vitry-sur-Seine	17 Apr
61:59	Shadrack	Hoff	RSA	19.5.73	2		Durban	10 Jul
62:00	Sammy Kipkoech	Tum	KEN	18.5.78	2		Vilamoura	10 Apr
62:00	Joseph	Maregu	KEN	.77	2		Saint-Denis	2 Oct
62:02	Larbi	Zéroual	FRA	10.1.71	9		Den Haag	19 Mar
62:02A	Tefera	Tola	ETH		6	NC	Addis Ababa	28 Aug
62:02+	Daniel	Yego	KEN	.71	2	in Mar	Amsterdam	16 Oct
62:03	George	Okworo	KEN	12.5.79	1		Monterrey	17 May
62:04	Joseph	Koech	KEN		2		Monterrey	17 May
	(100)							

Mark	Name		Nat	Born	Date
62:05A	Philemon	Kipchumba	KEN	.77	21 Oct
62:08A	Terefe	Jifar	ETH		28 Aug
62:09	Hillary Kipkering	Koech	KEN	.78	17 Apr
62:10	Josephat Muchiri	Ndambiri	KEN	12.2.85	3 Jul
62:10	Nicholas	Kemboi	QAT	25.11.83	18 Sep
62:10	Alphonse	Yatich	KEN		18 Dec
62:11	Samson	Kiflemariam	ERI	23.1.84	17 Apr
62:11A	Abiyote	Guta	ETH	.85	28 Aug
62:13	Satoshi	Irifune	JPN	14.12.75	13 Mar
62:13	Daniel	Cheribo	KEN	.81	28 Mar
62:13	Nicholas Manza	Kamakya	KEN	2.3.85	3 Sep
62:14	Christopher	Kandie	KEN	.69	3 Apr
62:14	Wilfred	Taragon	KEN	15.2.85	11 Sep
62:14	Fekadu	Degefu	ETH	.74	2 Oct
62:15A	Simion	Kiprop	KEN	5.11.78	21 Oct
62:16	Bellor Miningwo	Yator	KEN	.78	26 Mar
62:16	Luke	Metto	KEN	.76	17 Apr
62:16	Samson	Ramadhani	TAN	25.12.82	24 Jul
62:18	David	Makori	KEN	6.11.73	28 Mar
62:19	Isaya	Deengw	TAN	30.11.85	24 Jul
62:19	Wilson	Chebet	KEN		25 Sep
62:20	Luc	Krotwaar	NED	25.1.68	19 Mar
62:20+	Enock	Mitei	KEN	26.11.80	8 May
62:20	John	Ngeno	KEN	12.9.77	25 Sep
62:22	Koji	Kannan	JPN	8.11.81	13 Mar
62:22	John	Kipruto Korir	KEN	15.12.75	4 Sep
62:22	Munehiro	Sugaya	JPN	2.9.78	23 Nov
62:23	Solomon	Bushendich	KEN	10.1.84	10 Apr
62:23	John	Stephen Rogarth	TAN	26.4.84	24 Jul
62:23A	Eshetu	Gezahegne	ETH	20.9.82	28 Aug
62:23	Gudisa	Shentema	ETH	19.6.80	18 Sep
62:23	Vincent	Kiprop	KEN	1.1.83	25 Sep
62:23	Joseph	Lomala Kimosop	KEN	.82	30 Oct
62:24+	Julius	Sugut	KEN	.78	8 May
62:24	Norman	Dlomo	RSA	18.4.75	10 Jul
62:24	Takeshi	Hamano	JPN	30.7.74	23 Nov
62:25 dh	Kamiel	Maase	NED	20.10.71	13 Mar
62:25	Charles	Ngolebus	KEN	.84	3 Apr
62:25A	Yegazu	Zembaba	ETH	26.9.83	28 Aug
62:25	Silas	Sang	KEN	21.8.78	18 Dec
62:27	Kimwole	Kimutai	KEN	.84	23 Oct
62:27	David	Kipruto	KEN	2.11.75	30 Oct
62:27	Kensuke	Takezawa	JPN-J	11.10.86	20 Nov
62:28	James	Rotich	KEN	.80	2 Oct
62:28	Sammy	Kipruto	KEN	22.11.78	2 Oct
62:29	Reuben	Cheruiyot	KEN	13.3.74	16 Oct
62:30	Mohammed	Amyn	MAR	25.3.76	4 Sep
62:30	Francis	Kibiwott	KEN	15.9.78	2 Oct
62:30	Kenjiro	Jitsui	JPN	16.12.68	23 Nov
62:31	Sander	Schutgens	NED	31.12.75	19 Mar
62:31	Isaac	Kimaiyo	KEN		23 Nov
62:32	Kentaro	Hayashi	JPN	1.1.79	6 Feb
62:32 dh	Abdelkader	El Mouaziz	MAR	1.1.69	18 Sep
62:33	Jacob	Kitur	KEN	.73	24 Apr
62:33	Kani	Simons	RSA	2.8.74	10 Jul
62:34	Koichi	Mitsuyuki	JPN	12.12.81	13 Mar
62:34A	Francis	Komu	KEN	5.5.74	21 Oct
62:35	Keita	Akiba	JPN	27.11.79	13 Mar
62:35	Elijah	Nyambuti	KEN	10.10.79	10 Apr
62:35	Khaled	Kamal Khaled	BRN		27 Apr
62:35A	Elijah	Kirui	KEN		21 Oct
62:36 dh	Mark	Carroll	IRL	15.1.72	18 Sep
62:37	Masato	Imai	JPN	2.4.84	6 Feb
62:37	Ken	Konishi	JPN	29.3.79	6 Feb
62:37	Ismaïl	Sghyr	FRA	16.3.72	6 Mar
62:37	Kosuke	Nakahigashi	JPN	13.6.82	13 Mar
62:37A	Jynocel	Basweti	KEN		21 Oct
62:38	Takayuki	Ota	JPN	29.11.82	6 Feb
62:38	Katsunori	Itakura	JPN	6.8.83	6 Mar
62:38	Antoni	Peña	ESP	26.8.70	11 Sep
62:38	John	Kanda	KEN	.71	2 Oct
62:38	Hideaki	Date	JPN	11.4.85	20 Nov
62:39	Takyuki	Tagami	JPN	29.5.84	13 Mar
62:39	Tesfaye	Jifar	ETH	23.4.76	10 Apr
62:39	Salah	Hissou	MAR	16.1.72	10 Apr
62:39	Jamal	Baligha	MAR	11.12.73	8 May
62:39	Yoji	Yamaguchi	JPN	12.6.75	20 Nov
62:40	Linus	Maiyo	KEN	11.12.83	18 Sep
62:40A	Christopher	Mwinamo	KEN		21 Oct
62:41	Sahle	Warga	ETH	.84	6 Feb
62:41	Abdelkebir	Lamachi	MAR	12.6.80	27 Feb
62:41	Eduardo	Henriques	POR	24.3.68	10 Apr
62:41	Jeffrey	Gwebu	RSA	15.2.81	10 Jul
62:41	Sajji	Bouazza	MAR	.82	2 Oct

Mark	Name		Nat	Born	Date
62:42	Martin Hhaway	Sulle	TAN	28.12.82	16 Oct
62:44	Geoffrey	Kiplagat	KEN		13 Feb
62:44	Julius	Gitahi	KEN	29.4.78	3 Jul
62:44	Yared	Asmerom	ERI	3.2.79	1 Oct
62:44	Yusuke	Ichinoi	JPN	6.1.84	20 Nov
62:45	Nicholas	Murei	KEN	.81	6 Mar
62:45	Benjamin	Itok	KEN	.72	3 Apr
62:45	Giuliano	Battocletti	ITA	1.8.75	10 Apr
62:45	Paul	Atodonyang	KEN	.77	17 Apr
62:45	Cuthbert	Nyasango	ZIM	17.9.82	29 May
62:45	Moses	Kemboi	KEN	.78	4 Sep
62:45	Wilberforce (196)	Talel Kapkeny	KEN	10.1.80	16 Oct

Short course: 61:32A Lusapho April RSA 24.5.82 1 Johannesburg 22 Apr

Best non downhill: at Lisboa 25 Sep: 1. Martin Lel 61:37, 2, Robert Kipkoech Cheruiyot 61:45

JUNIORS

See main list for top 8 juniors. 11 performances by 10 juniors to 62:27. Further juniors:

Mark	Name		Nat	Born	Pos	Meet	Venue	Date
62:27	Kensuke	Takezawa	JPN-J	11.10.86	1		Ageo	20 Nov
62:52	Masatomo	Sugimoto (10)	JPN	24.4.86	6		Ageo	20 Nov
62:56	Samuel	Muturi	KEN	2.5.86	9		Sapporo	3 Jul
63:03	Ernest	Kimeli	KEN	27.4.86	8		Philadelphia	18 Sep
63:08	Yuichi	Takaku	JPN	30.3.86	17		Marugame	6 Feb
63:11	Leshane	Yegezu	ETH	86	13	WCh	Edmonton	1 Oct
63:23	Solomon	Tsege	ETH	24.10.87	18	WCh	Edmonton	1 Oct
63:27	Masatoshi	Kikuchi	JPN	12.2.86	16		Ageo	20 Nov
63:34	Satoru	Kitamura	JPN	4.2.86	17		Ageo	20 Nov
63:35	Patrick	Nyangelo	TAN	2.5.86	1		Gold Coast	3 Jul
63:36	Toyoyuki	Abe	JPN	28.7.86	19		Ageo	20 Nov

25 KILOMETRES ROAD

Mark	Name		Nat	Born	Pos	Meet	Venue	Date
1:13:14+	Takayuki	Matsumiya	JPN	21.2.80	1	in 30k	Kumamoto	27 Feb
1:13:27	Simon	Wangai	KEN	12.11.78	1		Grand Rapids	14 May
1:13:50	Julius Kibet	Koskei	KEN	6.4.82	2		Grand Rapids	14 May
1:13:51	Luke	Kibet	KEN	12.4.83	1		Berlin	8 May
1:13:52	Simon Kipyego	Kiprop	KEN	11.11.78	2		Berlin	8 May
1:13:56	Enock	Mitei	KEN	26.11.80	3		Berlin	8 May
1:13:57+	Haile	Gebrselassie	ETH	18.4.73	1=	in Mar	Amsterdam	16 Oct
1:13:57+	Daniel	Yego	KEN	.71	1=	in Mar	Amsterdam	16 Oct

Further marks at 25k/30k made in major marathons

30 KILOMETRES ROAD

Mark	Name		Nat	Born	Pos	Meet	Venue	Date
1:28:00	Takayuki	Matsumiya	FPN	21.2.80	1		Kumamoto	27 Feb
1:28:57+	Haile	Gebrselassie	ETH	18.4.73	1	in Mar	Amsterdam	16 Oct
1:29:00+	Daniel	Yego	KEN	.71	2	in Mar	Amsterdam	16 Oct
1:29:31+	William	Kipsang	KEN	.77	1=	in Mar	Seoul	13 Mar
1:29:31+	Gert	Thys	RSA	12.11.71	1=	in Mar	Seoul	13 Mar
1:29:54+	Philip	Manyim	KEN	24.3.78	1	in Mar	Berlin	25 Sep
1:29:55+	Faustin	Buha	TAN	30.5.82	3	in Mar	Seoul	13 Mar

MARATHON

L = loop course, P = point-to-point, D = downhill over 1/1000

Mark		Name		Nat	Born	Pos	Venue	Date
2:06:20	L	Haile	Gebrselassie	ETH	18.4.73	1	Amsterdam	16 Oct
2:07:02	L	Felix	Limo	KEN	22.8.80	1	Chicago	9 Oct
2:07:09	L	Benjamin	Maiyo	KEN	6.10.78	2	Chicago	9 Oct
2:07:14	L	Daniel	Njenga	KEN	7.5.76	3	Chicago	9 Oct
2:07:26	L	Martin	Lel	KEN	29.10.78	1	London	17 Apr
2:07:28	L	Evans	Rutto	KEN	8.4.78	4	Chicago	9 Oct
2:07:38	L	Julio	Rey	ESP	13.1.72	1	Hamburg	24 Apr
2:07:41	L	Toshinari	Takaoka	JPN	24.9.70	1	Tokyo	13 Feb
2:07:41	L	Philip	Manyim	KEN	24.3.78	1	Berlin	25 Sep
2:07:46	L	Patrick	Ivuti (10)	KEN	30.6.78	5	Chicago	9 Oct
2:07:49	L	Jaouad	Gharib	MAR	22.5.72	2	London	17 Apr
2:07:50	L	Jimmy	Muindi	KEN	14.8.73	1	Rotterdam	10 Apr
2:08:02	L	Alberico	Di Cecco	ITA	19.4.74	1	Roma	13 Mar
2:08:02	L	Jackson	Koech	KEN	26.12.78	2	Rotterdam	10 Apr
2:08:04	L	Salim	Kipsang	KEN	22.12.79	1	Paris	10 Apr
2:08:07	L		Manyim			2	Roma	13 Mar
2:08:16	L	Daniel	Yego	KEN	.71	3	Roma	13 Mar
2:08:17	L	Paul	Biwott	KEN	18.4.78	2	Paris	10 Apr
2:08:27	L	William	Kiplagat	KEN	21.6.72	1	Seoul	6 Nov
2:08:29	L	Wilfred	Kigen	KEN	23.2.75	1	Frankfurt-am-Main	30 Oct
2:08:29	L	Dmitriy	Baranovskiy (20)	UKR	28.7.79	1	Fukuoka	4 Dec
2:08:30	L	Jason	Mbote	KEN	.77	2	Frankfurt	30 Oct
2:08:32	L	Hendrick	Ramaala	RSA	2.2.72	3	London	17 Apr
2:08:34	L	Wilson	Kigen	KEN	15.9.80	3	Frankfurt-am-Main	30 Oct
2:08:36	L	Charles E	Kibiwott	KEN	8.8.74	4	Frankfurt-am-Main	30 Oct
2:08:45	L	Boniface	Usisivu	KEN	5.9.74	1	Eindhoven	9 Oct

Mark		Name		Nat	Born	Pos	Meet	Venue	Date
2:08:45	L	Philip	Singoei	KEN	31.12.75	2		Eindhoven	9 Oct
2:08:52	L	Luke	Kibet	KEN	12.4.83	3		Eindhoven	9 Oct
2:08:53	L	William	Kipsang	KEN	.77	1		Seoul	13 Mar
2:08:58	L	Peter	Chebet	KEN	24.6.76	2		Berlin	25 Sep
2:08:58	L		Yego			2		Amsterdam	16 Oct
2:09:00	L	Joseph	Riri	KEN	21.10.73	1		Otsu	6 Mar
		(32/30)							
2:09:03	L	José	Rios	ESP	15.3.74	2		Otsu	6 Mar
2:09:03	L	Abdelkader	El Mouaziz	MAR	1.1.69	4		London	17 Apr
2:09:09	L	John Ekiru	Kelai	KEN	29.12.76	4		Eindhoven	9 Oct
2:09:10	L	Michitaka	Hosokawa	JPN	26.4.76	3		Otsu	6 Mar
2:09:10	L	Joshua	Chelanga	KEN	7.4.73	4		Berlin	25 Sep
2:09:13	L	Wataru	Okutani	JPN	9.1.75	4		Otsu	6 Mar
2:09:17	D	Christopher	Cheboiboch	KEN	3.3.77	1		San Diego (76m dh)	5 Jun
		2:10:14	L			5		Rotterdam	10 Apr
2:09:17	L	Tesfaye	Tola	ETH	19.10.74	3		Amsterdam	16 Oct
2:09:18	L	Yuko	Matsumiya	JPN	21.2.80	5		Otsu	6 Mar
2:09:20	L	Noah	Bor	KEN	28.7.77	5		Eindhoven	9 Oct
		(40)							
2:09:21	L	Thomas	Chemitei	KEN	22.5.78	6		Eindhoven	9 Oct
2:09:22	L	Laban	Kipkemboi	KEN	30.12.77	6		Chicago	9 Oct
2:09:22	P	Mubarak Hassan	Shami	QAT	2.12.80	1		Venezia	23 Oct
2:09:24	L	Gashaw	Melesse	ETH	26.9.78	3		Paris	10 Apr
2:09:25	L	Stefano	Baldini	ITA	25.5.71	5		London	17 Apr
2:09:27	L	Elijah Chemwelo	Mutai	KEN	1.4.78	1		Chunchon	23 Oct
2:09:30	L	Paul	Tergat	KEN	17.6.69	1		New York	6 Nov
2:09:31	L	Jon	Brown	GBR	27.2.71	6	1 AAA	London	17 Apr
2:09:35	L	Mark	Saina	KEN	10.11.70	1		Los Angeles	6 Mar
2:09:46	L	Gudisa	Shentema	ETH	19.6.80	4		Rotterdam	10 Apr
		(50)							
2:09:48	L	Atsushi	Fujita	JPN	6.11.76	3		Fukuoka	4 Dec
2:09:49	L	Raymond	Kipkoech Chemwelo	KEN	19.4.78	1		Xiamen	26 Mar
2:09:51	D	Stephen	Kiogora	KEN	10.11.74	2		San Diego (76m dh)	5 Jun
		2:11:58	L			1		Las Vegas	4 Aug
2:09:56	L	Mebrahtom	Keflezighi	USA	5.5.75	3		New York	6 Nov
2:09:58	L	Satoshi	Irifune	JPN	14.12.75	1	Beppu	Oita	6 Feb
2:10:00	L	Helder	Ornelas	POR	6.5.74	1		Milano	4 Dec
2:10:01	D	Benson	Cherono	KEN	30.6.84	3		San Diego (76m dh)	5 Jun
2:10:05	L	Leonid	Shvetsov	RUS	28.3.69	5		Frankfurt-am-Main	30 Oct
2:10:10	L	Takashi	Tokunaga	JPN	6.6.81	6		Otsu	6 Mar
2:10:10	L	Joseph	Ngolepus	KEN	10.4.75	5		Berlin	25 Sep
		(60)							
2:10:11	L	Shimelis	Molla	ETH		6		Berlin	25 Sep
2:10:12	L	Toshiya	Katayama	JPN	23.4.73	7		Otsu	6 Mar
2:10:12	L	Ottaviano	Andriani	ITA	4.1.74	4		Roma	13 Mar
2:10:12	L	Tereje	Wodajo	ETH	27.1.82	7		Eindhoven	9 Oct
2:10:12	L	Joel Kipkemei	Rono	KEN		8		Eindhoven	9 Oct
2:10:13	L	Daniel	Cheribo	KEN	.81	5		Paris	10 Apr
2:10:13	L	Moses	Masai	KEN-J	1.6.86	1		Essen	17 Apr
2:10:17	L	Stanley	Leleito	KEN	.84	1		Zürich	3 Apr
2:10:18	P	Paul	Lokira	KEN	1.1.83	2		Venezia	23 Oct
2:10:21	L	Christopher	Isegwe	TAN	22.2.76	2	WCh	Helsinki	13 Aug
		(70)							
2:10:23	L	Toshinari	Suwa	JPN	29.1.77	7		London	17 Apr
2:10:25	L	Patrick (Oliver)	Tambwé (Nsimba)	COD	5.5.75	6		Paris	10 Apr
2:10:25	P	Francesco	Ingargiola	ITA	15.2.73	3		Venezia	23 Oct
2:10:31	L	Rodgers	Rop	KEN	16.2.76	7		Paris	10 Apr
2:10:34	L	Erick	Nzioki	KEN	22.7.78	2		Zürich	3 Apr
2:10:34	L	Timothy	Cherigat	KEN	29.12.76	8		Chicago	9 Oct
2:10:40	L	Ashebir	Demissie	ETH	.77	3		Hamburg	24 Apr
2:10:42	L	Stephen Matebo	Cheptot	KEN	30.3.74	1		Praha	22 May
2:10:45	L	Getulo	Bayo	TAN	.80	3		Zürich	3 Apr
2:10:48	L	Migidio	Bourifa	ITA	31.1.69	1		Trieste	5 Aug
		(80)							
2:10:49	L	Dejene	Guta	ETH	5.8.81	1		Dubai	7 Jan
2:10:51	L	Zebedayo	Bayo	TAN	20.5.76	2		Tokyo	13 Feb
2:10:52	L	Bernard	Barmasai	KEN	6.5.74	4		Amsterdam	16 Oct
2:10:53	L	Michael	Rotich	KEN	26.10.82	7		Berlin	25 Sep
2:10:53	L	Sammy	Korir	KEN	12.12.71	9		Chicago	9 Oct
2:10:54	P	Aleksandr	Kuzin	UKR	21.10.74	4		Venezia	23 Oct
2:10:59	L	Isaac	Macharia	KEN	25.11.80	1		Nagano	17 Apr

Mark		Name		Nat	Born	Pos	Meet	Venue	Date
2:11:00	L	Viktor	Röthlin	SUI	14.10.74	4		Zürich	3 Apr
2:11:01	L	Robert Kipkoech	Cheruiyot	KEN	26.9.78	4		New York	6 Nov
2:11:02	L	Dawit (90)	Terefa	ETH	23.10.84	5		Roma	13 Mar
2:11:06	L	El Hassan	Lahssini	FRA	1.1.75	8		Paris	10 Apr
2:11:07	L	Titus	Munji	KEN	20.12.79	7		Rotterdam	10 Apr
2:11:13	L	Ruggero	Pertile	ITA	8.8.74	8		Otsu	6 Mar
2:11:13	L	Danilo	Goffi	ITA	3.12.72	1		Torino	17 Apr
2:11:16	L	Francesco	Bennici	ITA	3.10.71	2		Torino	17 Apr
2:11:16	L	Tsuyoshi	Ogata	JPN	11.5.73	3	WCh	Helsinki	13 Aug
2:11:16	D	Stephen Kipkosgei	Biwott	KEN	.74	1		Carpi (100m dh)	16 Oct
2:11:19	L	Gert	Thys	RSA	12.11.71	2		Seoul	13 Mar
2:11:20	L	Dmitriy	Burmakin	RUS	8.1.81	5		Zürich	3 Apr
2:11:20	L	Grigoriy (100)	Andreyev	RUS	7.1.76	2		Nagano	17 Apr

Mark	Name		Nat	Born	Date
2:11:22 L	Joseph	Kadon	KEN	.70	3 Apr
2:11:24 L	Willy	Cheruiyot	KEN	2.8.74	6 Jan
2:11:24 L	Abdi	Abdirahman	USA	1.1.77	6 Nov
2:11:26 L	Giday	Amha	ETH	16.9.77	7 Jan
2:11:27 L	Samson	Kosgei	KEN	.74	27 Nov
2:11:28 L	Johnstone Kipkoror	Changwony	KEN	5.5.84	7 Jan
2:11:29 L	Dejene	Negussie	ETH	.85	13 Mar
2:11:29 L	Paul	Kirui	KEN	5.2.80	4 Dec
2:11:32 L	Tomoaki	Kunichika	JPN	22.4.73	13 Mar
2:11:36 L	Scott	Westcott	AUS	25.9.75	6 Feb
2:11:36 L		Ri Kyong-chol	PRK	8.3.79	10 Apr
2:11:37 L	Denis	Curzi	ITA	14.5.75	6 Mar
2:11:39 L	Augustine	Kavutu	KEN	.77	7 Jan
2:11:40 L	David	Makori	KEN	6.11.73	17 Apr
2:11:41 L	Ambese	Tolosa	ETH	28.8.77	10 Apr
2:11:42 L	Yusuf	Songoka	KEN	5.2.79	10 Apr
2:11:42 L	Andrew	Letherby	AUS	19.9.73	25 Sep
2:11:45 D	Hailu	Negussie	ETH	16.4.78	18 Apr
2:11:47 L	George	Okworo	KEN	12.5.79	6 Mar
2:11:47 L	Richard	Kiprono Maiyo	KEN	24.12.76	20 Mar
2:11:47 L	Dereje	Tesfaye	ETH		30 Oct
2:11:48 L	Yoshiteru	Morishita	JPN	26.5.71	6 Feb
2:11:48 L	Dejene	Berhanu	ETH	12.12.80	4 Dec
2:11:49 L	Jacob	Losian	KEN	6.6.71	24 Apr
2:11:51 L	Shadrack	Hoff	RSA	19.5.73	8 May
2:11:53 L	Joseph	Mutunga Mbithi	KEN	12.12.75	7 Jan
2:11:55 L	Abdelkebir	Lamachi	MAR	16.2.80	17 Apr
2:11:56 L	José Manuel	Martínez	ESP	22.10.71	10 Apr
2:11:57 L	Simon	Bor	KEN	13.2.69	25 Sep
2:11:57 L	James	Rotich	KEN	.80	6 Nov
2:11:59 L	Giuliano	Battocletti	ITA	1.8.75	4 Dec
2:12:01 L	Gebremedhn	Gebremariam	ETH	.80	7 Jan
2:12:02 L	Kasine	Adillo	ETH		23 Oct
2:12:03 L	Kebede	Tekeste	ETH	.82	26 Mar
2:12:03 L	Rômulo	da Silva	BRA	26.5.77	25 Sep
2:12:07 L	Terefe	Yae	ETH	.81	25 Sep
2:12:08 L	Johnson	Kemboi	KEN	.70	1 May
2:12:08 L	Samson	Ramadhani	TAN	25.12.82	13 Aug
2:12:10 L	Bedane	Derba Medeska	ETH	.82	23 Apr
2:12:12 L	Alex	Malinga	UGA	27.7.74	13 Aug
2:12:12 L	Pavel	Loskutov	EST	2.12.69	6 Nov
2:12:13 L	Benson	Ogato	KEN	2.5.80	17 Apr
2:12:13 L	Andrew	Limo	KEN	15.3.84	16 Oct
2:12:14 L	Robert	Cheruiyot	KEN	20.12.74	22 May
2:12:15 L	Andrew	Sambu	TAN	5.10.72	13 Mar
2:12:15 L	James	Moiben	KEN	20.5.77	16 Oct
2:12:15AL	Samson	Barmao	KEN		21 Oct
2:12:16 L	Shin-ichi	Watanabe	JPN	16.11.76	6 Mar
2:12:17 L	Eliud	Kurgat	KEN	20.8.73	27 Nov
2:12:18 L	Nelson	Lebo	KEN	27.12.77	25 Sep
2:12:19 L		Lee Bong-ju	KOR	11.10.70	25 Sep
2:12:21 D	Wilson	Onsare	KEN	15.6.76	18 Apr
2:12:21 P	David	Kirui	KEN	29.12.77	23 Oct
2:12:29 L	David	Chepkwony	KEN	29.12.78	23 Apr
2:12:29 L	Daniel	Rono	KEN	13.7.78	24 Apr
2:12:29 L	Yukinobu	Nakazaki	JPN	4.4.79	16 Oct
2:12:30 L	John	Gwako	KEN	4.9.78	9 Oct
2:12:33 L	Shane	Nankervis	AUS	6.5.74	25 Sep
2:12:33 L	Philip	Tarus	KEN	11.9.74	30 Oct
2:12:34 D	Vasil	Matviychuk	UKR	13.1.82	16 Oct
2:12:36 L	William	Kwambai	KEN	.78	13 Mar
2:12:36 L	Hosea	Kiptanui	KEN	.78	20 Mar
2:12:38 D	Mikhail	Khobotov	RUS	2.2.73	13 Feb
2:12:38 L	Girma	Tola	ETH	13.10.75	10 Apr
2:12:38AL	Benedict	Kimondiu	KEN	30.11.77	21 Oct
2:12:38 L	Philip	Kirui	KEN	11.9.73	23 Oct
2:12:41 L	Tesfaye	Eticha	ETH	16.9.74	23 Oct
2:12:41 L	Matthew	Birir	KEN	5.7.72	30 Oct
2:12:42 L	Sita	Kasirai	ZIM	29.7.78	9 Oct
2:12:43 L	Tefere	Bacha	ETH	.85	8 May
2:12:44 L	Tesfaye	Jifar	ETH	23.4.76	8 May
2:12:44 L	Peter	Kimeli	KEN	24.2.72	11 Sep
2:12:45 L	Pablo	Olmedo	MEX	8.5.75	9 Oct
2:12:45 L	Fekadu	Degefu	ETH	.74	23 Oct
2:12:46 P	Henry	Tarus	KEN	6.12.78	23 Oct
2:12:47 L	Henry	Serem	KEN	21.6.77	9 Oct
2:12:48 L	Tomonori	Onitsuka	JPN	21.3.80	6 Feb
2:12:48 L	Nephat	Kinyaniui	KEN	30.6.77	25 Sep
2:12:50 L	David	Kipkorir	KEN	15.12.74	17 Apr
2:12:51 L	Kamiel	Maase	NED	20.10.71	10 Apr
2:12:52 L	Abebe	Halefom Tsegay	ETH	.85	6 Mar
2:12:52 L	Samuel	Chemweno	KEN	.78	13 Mar
2:12:52 L	Kamel	Ziani	ESP	20.2.72	10 Apr
2:12:55 L	Yukiyasu	Nagao	JPN	25.4.74	6 Mar
2:12:56 L	Simon	Maiyo	KEN	22.2.82	23 Oct
2:13:00 L	David	Maiyo	KEN	5.11.76	13 Mar
2:13:02 L	Collins	Edep	KEN	24.7.77	23 Apr
2:13:04 L		Kim Yi-yong	KOR	20.9.73	8 Apr
2:13:04 L	Abraham	Tandoi	KEN	12.12.74	30 Oct
2:13:09 L	Kodai	Fukunaga	JPN	26.8.80	20 Feb
2:13:10 L	Ernest	Kipyego	KEN	6.10.78	17 Apr
2:13:11 L	Moses	Kemboi	KEN	23.3.84	17 Apr
2:13:12 L	Ahmed	Ezzobayry	FRA	6.6.78	10 Apr
2:13:12 L	Clodoaldo	da Silva	BRA	19.8.76	24 Apr
2:13:14 L	Sisay	Bezabeh	AUS	9.9.77	6 Feb
2:13:14 L	Dmitriy	Osadchiy	UKR	9.10.77	31 Oct
2:13:16 L	Masaki	Iwahara	JPN	18.2.77	6 Feb
2:13:18 P	Wesley	Ngetich	KEN	.77	18 Jun
2:13:19 L	Simon	Wangai	KEN	12.11.78	6 Nov
2:13:20 L	Julius	Sugut	KEN	.78	16 Jan
2:13:20 L	Alan	Culpepper	USA	15.9.72	9 Oct
2:13:20	Henry	Kapkyai (202)	KEN	83	9 Oct

Drugs disqualification

Mark	Name		Nat	Born	Date
2:12:47	Artur	Osman ¶	POL	1.3.70	24 Apr

JUNIORS

Mark		Name		Nat	Born	Pos	Meet	Venue	Date
2:10:13	L	Moses Ndiema	Masai	KEN	1.6.86	1		Essen	17 Apr
2:15:06	L		Zhang Qingle	CHN	11.1.87	7	NG	Beijing	16 Oct

50 KILOMETRES ROAD

Mark	Name		Nat	Born	Pos	Meet	Venue	Date
2:44.03	Josiah	Thugwane	RSA	15.4.71	1		Middelburg	25 Apr
2:46.38+	Marco	Mambo	ZIM		1	in 56k	Cape Town	26 Mar

Mark	Name		Nat	Born	Date
2:47.49+	Sipho	Ngomane	RSA	14.1.82	26 Mar
2:48.41+	Graham	Malinga	RSA	7.3.77	26 Mar
2:49:00	Sipho	Ngcube	ZIM		25 Apr

Mark	Name		Nat	Born	Pos	Meet	Venue	Date

100 KILOMETRES

Mark	Name		Nat	Born	Pos	Meet	Venue	Date
6:23:48	Grigoriy	Murzin	RUS	23.6.70	1		S. Cruz de Bezaña	1 Oct
6:24:15		Murzin			1	WCp	Yubetsu	26 Jun
6:30:31	Oleg	Kharitonov	RUS	13.4.68	1	EC	Winschoten	10 Sep
6:33:03	Jorge	Aubeso	ESP	5.12.66	2	WCp	Yubetsu	26 Jun
6:35:10	Jaroslaw	Janicki	POL	6.7.66	1		Madrid	6 Mar
6:40:20	Tsutomu	Sassa	JPN	26.7.74	3	WCp	Yubetsu	26 Jun
6:40:39	Mario	Ardemagni	ITA	2.4.63	2	EC	Winschoten	10 Sep
6:42:49		Aubeso			2		Madrid	6 Mar
6:44:45	Sándor	Barcza	FRA	15.1.67	4	WCp	Yubetsu	26 Jun
6:48:44	Ildar	Akhmetsin	RUS	.70	2		S. Cruz de Bezaña	1 Oct
6:49:04	Masanori	Yoshida	JPN		5	WCp	Yubetsu	26 Jun
6:49:43	Yoshiaki	Kobayashi	JPN	7.11.72	6	WCp	Yubetsu	26 Jun
6:50:22	Pascal	Fétizon	FRA	30.8.62	3	EC	Winschoten	10 Sep

Mark	Name		Nat	Born	Date	Mark	Name		Nat	Born	Date
6:52:37	Dmitriy	Bula	BLR	5.1.72	10 Sep	6:56:56	Igor	Tyazhkorob	RUS	4.12.67	10 Sep
6:52:50	Miguel Ángel	Jiménez	ESP	9.9.70	10 Sep	6:57:35	Michael	Sommer	GER	2.3.64	26 Jun
6:53:13	Jean-Jacques	Moros	FRA	8.10.70	27 Aug	6:58:55	Lorenzo	Trincheri	ITA	2.5.70	10 Sep
6:54:40	Aleksey	Izmailov	RUS	17.5.75	10 Sep	6:59:07	Oscar	Alarcón	ARG	22.5.63	1 Oct
6:56:29	Mikhail	Kokorev	RUS	1.3.65	10 Sep	6:59:20	Howard	Nippert	USA	15.7.65	26 Jun

24 HOURS

Mark	Name		Nat	Born	Pos	Meet	Venue	Date
268.065	Anatoliy	Kruglikov	RUS	9.10.57	1	WCh	Wörschach	16 Jul
264.410 t	Ryoichi	Sekiya	JPN	12.2.67	1		Soochow	4 Mar
263.810	Ewald	Eder	AUT	27.12.56	2	WCh	Wörschach	16 Jul
256.936		Kruglikov			1		Sankt-Peterburg	3 Sep
256.368	Jens	Lukas	GER	13.4.66	3	WCh	Wörschach	16 Jul
255.070	Mohamed	Magroun	FRA	15.7.59	1	NC	Mulhouse	1 Oct
254.400+t	Yiannis	Kouros	GRE	13.2.56	1	in 6 day	Colac	20 Nov
253.005	Roman	Saliy	RUS		2		Sankt-Peterburg	3 Sep
251.276	Fabien	Hobléa	FRA	5.3.65	2	NC	Mulhouse	1 Oct
250.873 t	Muneharu	Kuroda	JPN	24.7.49	2		Soochow	4 Mar
250.618		Sekiya			4	WCh	Wörschach	16 Jul
249.876	Sergio	Orsi	ITA		5	WCh	Wörschach	16 Jul

Mark	Name		Nat	Born	Date	Mark	Name		Nat	Born	Date
246.405	Osvaldo	Beltramino	ITA		16 Jul	**Track best**					
246.383	Ivan	Seriy	UKR		16 Jul	241.378	Sergio	Orsi	ITA		9 Apr
246.184	Vladimir	Bychkov	RUS	13.5.67	16 Jul	**Indoors**					
245.628	Masayuki	Otaki	JPN	11.7.65	16 Jul	241.800	Kenji	Okiyama	JPN	3.6.65	18 Mar
241.020	Maksim	Vorobyov	RUS		3 Sep						

2000 METRES STEEPLECHASE

Mark	Name		Nat	Born	Pos	Meet	Venue	Date
5:14.53	Saïf Saeed	Shaheen	QAT	15.10.82	1	SGP	Doha	13 May
5:16.46	Wesley	Kiprotich	KEN	31.7.79	2	SGP	Doha	13 May
5:18.65	Antonio	Jiménez	ESP	18.2.77	1		Huelva	7 Jun
5:20.44	Ronald	Kipchumba Rutto	KEN-J	8.10.87	3	SGP	Doha	13 May
5:23.95	Tareq	Mubarak Taher	BRN	24.3.84	1	WY	Marrakech	15 Jul
5:24.69	Abel	Mutai	KEN-Y	2.10.88	2	WY	Marrakech	15 Jul
5:24.79	Eliseo	Martín	ESP	5.11.73	2		Huelva	7 Jun
5:24.87	Bisluke	Kiplagat Kipkorir	KEN-Y	8.8.88	3	WY	Marrakech	15 Jul
5:25.25	José Luis	Blanco	ESP	3.6.75	3		Huelva	7 Jun
5:26.52	Abdelghani	Aït Bahmad	MAR-Y	28.7.89	4	WY	Marrakech	15 Jul
5:28.56	Alexander	Greaux	PUR	22.9.77	4		Huelva	7 Jun

Mark	Name		Nat	Born	Date	Mark	Name		Nat	Born	Date
5:28.58	Krijn	Van Koolwyk	BEL	30.8.81	13 May	5:31.23	Andrey	Farnosov	RUS	9.7.80	5 Jun
5:29.51	Nahom	Mesfin Tariku	ETH-Y	3.6.89	15 Sep	5:31.97	Francisco Javier	Lara	ESP	24.6.76	7 Jun

JUNIORS

Four in main list above plus:

Mark	Name		Nat	Born	Pos	Meet	Venue	Date
5:29.51	Nahom	Mesfin Tariku	ETH-Y	3.6.89	5		Marrakech	15 Sep
5:32.13	Kamal Ali	Thamer	QAT-Y	12.11.88	5	SGP	Doha	13 May
5:33.5 A	Patrick	Kimeli Lagat	KEN-Y	.88	3		Neirobi	15 Jun
5:34.53	Marcin	Chabowski	POL	28.5.86	1		Gdansk	14 May
5:37.52	Mousa Youssef	Idriss	SUD-Y	17.6.88	6	SGP	Doha	13 May

3000 METRES STEEPLECHASE

Mark	Name		Nat	Born	Pos	Meet	Venue	Date
7:55.51	Saïf Saeed	Shaheen	QAT	15.10.82	1	VD	Bruxelles	26 Aug
7:56.34		Shaheen			1	GGala	Roma	8 Jul
7:56.37	Paul Kipsiele	Koech	KEN	10.11.81	2	GGala	Roma	8 Jul
7:57.28		Shaheen			1	SGP	Athína	14 Jun
8:02.69		Shaheen			1	WK	Zürich	19 Aug
8:04.22	Brimin	Kipruto	KEN	31.7.85	3	GGala	Roma	8 Jul
8:04.92	Brahim	Boulami	MAR	20.4.72	4	GGala	Roma	8 Jul
8:04.95	Simon	Vroemen	NED	11.5.69	2	VD	Bruxelles	26 Aug

Mark		Name	Nat	Born	Pos	Meet	Venue	Date
8:06.26		Koech			1	GP	Sevilla	4 Jun
8:07.48		Boulami			3	VD	Bruxelles	26 Aug
8:07.91		Koech			1	WAF	Monaco	9 Sep
8:08.15	Kipkirui	Misoi	KEN	23.12.78	1	NA	Heusden-Zolder	23 Jul
8:08.56		Koech			1	DNG	Stockholm	26 Jul
8:09.04	Ezekiel	Kemboi	KEN	25.5.82	2	WAF	Monaco	9 Sep
8:09.09	David	Chemweno	KEN	18.12.81	2	NA	Heusden-Zolder	23 Jul
8:09.14		Kemboi			1	Gaz	Saint-Denis	1 Jul
8:09.20		Kipruto			3	WAF	Monaco	9 Sep
8:09.32	Wilson	Boit Kipketer	KEN	6.10.73	2	SGP	Athína	14 Jun
8:09.43	Wesley	Kiprotich (10)	KEN	1.8.79	4	WAF	Monaco	9 Sep
8:09.46		Kiprotich			2	Gaz	Saint-Denis	1 Jul
8:09.53		Kipruto			1	FBK	Hengelo	29 May
8:09.58	Bouabdellah	Tahri	FRA	20.12.78	5	GGala	Roma	8 Jul
8:09.71		Tahri			2	DNG	Stockholm	26 Jul
8:09.73		Kemboi			4	VD	Bruxelles	26 Aug
8:09.83		Koech			2	FBK	Hengelo	29 May
8:10.02		Misoi			3	Gaz	Saint-Denis	1 Jul
8:10.13		Tahri			5	WAF	Monaco	9 Sep
8:10.22		Tahri			5	VD	Bruxelles	26 Aug
8:10.66	Michael	Kipyego	KEN	2.10.83	6	GGala	Roma	8 Jul
8:10.69		Kipruto			1	WK	Zürich	19 Aug
8:10.97	Richard	Matelong	KEN	14.10.83	6	VD	Bruxelles	26 Aug
	(31/13)							
8:11.67	Jamal Bilal	Salem	QAT	12.9.78	3	FBK	Hengelo	29 May
8:11.75	Moussa	Omar Obaid	QAT	18.4.85	7	GGala	Roma	8 Jul
8:11.98	Linus	Chumba	KEN	9.2.80	8	GGala	Roma	8 Jul
8:12.26	Günther	Weidlinger	AUT	5.4.78	4	Gaz	Saint-Denis	1 Jul
8:12.57	Reuben	Kosgei	KEN	2.8.79	1	GP II	Milano	1 Jun
8:12.65	Dan	Lincoln	USA	20.10.80	10	GGala	Roma	8 Jul
8:13.74	Martin	Pröll	AUT	21.3.81	3	NA	Heusden-Zolder	23 Jul
	(20)							
8:14.05	Antonio	Jiménez	ESP	18.2.77	6	GP	Sevilla	4 Jun
8:14.68	César	Pérez	ESP	7.4.75	5	Gaz	Saint-Denis	1 Jul
8:15.29	Julius	Nyamu	KEN	1.12.77	6	Gaz	Saint-Denis	1 Jul
8:15.51	Mustafa	Mohamed	SWE	1.3.79	7	Gaz	Saint-Denis	1 Jul
8:16.11	Eliseo	Martín	ESP	5.11.73	9	GP	Sevilla	4 Jun
8:16.26	Tareq	Mubarak Taher	BRN	24.3.84	6	NA	Heusden-Zolder	23 Jul
8:16.69	Ronald	Kipchumba Rutto	KEN-J	8.10.87	4	FBK	Hengelo	29 May
8:17.11	Krijn	Van Koolwyk	BEL	30.8.81	9	NA	Heusden-Zolder	23 Jul
8:17.32	Vincent	Le Dauphin	FRA	28.6.76	5	FBK	Hengelo	29 May
8:17.47	Luís Miguel	Martín	ESP	11.1.72	5h1	WCh	Helsinki	7 Aug
	(30)							
8:17.49	Jakub	Czaja	POL	12.9.80	8	Gaz	Saint-Denis	1 Jul
8:17.87	Radoslaw	Poplawski	POL	16.1.83	1		Bydgoszcz	5 Jun
8:17.87	Steve	Slattery	USA	14.8.80	10	NA	Heusden-Zolder	23 Jul
8:18.18	Gaël	Pencréach	FRA	5.8.77	1		Strasbourg	23 Jun
8:19.46	Anthony	Famiglietti	USA	8.11.78	2	GP	Rieti	28 Aug
8:19.56	Brian	Olinger	USA	2.6.83	11	NA	Heusden-Zolder	23 Jul
8:19.68	Andrey	Olshanskiy	RUS	24.1.78	3		Bydgoszcz	5 Jun
8:20.14	Matthew	Kerr	CAN	3.5.76	12	NA	Heusden-Zolder	23 Jul
8:20.31	Pieter	Desmet	BEL	7.6.83	13	NA	Heusden-Zolder	23 Jul
8:20.40	Ruben	Ramolefi	RSA	17.7.78	12	GGala	Roma	8 Jul
	(40)							
8:21.04	José Luis	Blanco	ESP	3.6.75	3h3	WCh	Helsinki	7 Aug
8:21.38	Hamid	Ezzine	MAR	5.10.83	1		Rabat	18 Jun
8:22.00	Halil	Akkas	TUR	1.7.83	9	SGP	Athína	14 Jun
8:22.37	Filmon	Ghirmai	GER	25.1.79	4	ECp-S	Firenze	17 Jun
8:22.54	Yoshitaka	Iwamizu	JPN	20.6.79	14	GGala	Roma	8 Jul
8:22.82	Vincent	Zouaoui Dandrieux	FRA	12.10.80	2		Strasbourg	23 Jun
8:22.91	Bostjan	Buc	SLO	13.4.80	1	NC	Maribor	24 Jul
8:23.30	Caleb	Ngetich	KEN	.82	10	Gaz	Saint-Denis	1 Jul
8:23.93	Peter	Nowill	AUS	15.6.79	4	GP	Osaka	7 May
8:24.16	Robert	Gary	USA	5.4.73	15	NA	Heusden-Zolder	23 Jul
	(50)							
8:25.14	Jukka	Keskisalo	FIN	27.3.81	7h2	WCh	Helsinki	7 Aug
8:25.48	Irba	Lakhal	FRA	12.12.75	11	Gaz	Saint-Denis	1 Jul
8:25.67	Pavel	Potapovich	RUS	26.11.80	8	GS	Ostrava	9 Jun
8:25.72	Justus	Kiprono	KEN-J	28.2.87	5	GP II	Milano	1 Jun
8:26.79	Abdelgafour	El Asri	MAR	79	2		Pézenas	28 May

Mark	Name		Nat	Born	Pos	Meet	Venue	Date
8:26.96	Roman	Usov	RUS	4.6.78	1	NC	Tula	11 Jul
8:27.06	Tewodros	Shiferaw	ETH	21.9.80	8h2	WCh	Helsinki	7 Aug
8:27.17	Brahim	Taleb	MAR	16.2.85	2		Pézenas	28 May
8:27.29	Mircea	Bogdan	ROM	6.5.82	1	NCAA	Sacramento	10 Jun
8:27.62	Nordine	Gezzar	FRA	17.2.80	4		Strasbourg	23 Jun
	(60)							
8:28.12	Collins	Kosgei	KEN-Y	4.8.88	1		Melbourne	17 Feb
8:28.62	Elijah	Chelimo	KEN-J	.87	1		Cottbus	5 Jun
8:28.85	Vadim	Slobodenyuk	UKR	17.3.81	1		Kiev	24 Jul
8:28.86	Jim	Svenøy	NOR	22.4.72	12	FBK	Hengelo	29 May
8:29.00	Emmanuel	Mkhabela	RSA	19.7.79	2	NC	Durban	16 Apr
8:29.13	Peter	Kosgei	KEN	3.2.83	2	NCAA	Sacramento	10 Jun
8:29.62	Abel	Yagout	BRN	26.12.84	4		Sotteville	8 Jul
8:29.63	Richard	Jeremiah	AUS	3.12.82	2		Melbourne	17 Feb
8:29.66	Andy	Smith	USA	1.5.82	3	NCAA	Sacramento	10 Jun
8:29.69	Jan	Zakrzewski	POL	21.12.70	2	NC	Biala Podlaska	24 Jun
	(70)							
8:29.96	Tomasz	Szymkowiak	POL	5.7.83	3	NC	Biala Podlaska	24 Jun
8:30.10	Henrik	Skoog	SWE	17.4.79	11	DNG	Stockholm	26 Jul
8:30.12	Andrew	Lemoncello	GBR	12.10.82	4	NCAA	Sacramento	10 Jun
8:30.19	Andrey	Farnosov	RUS	9.7.80	3	NC	Tula	11 Jul
8:30:20	Gari	Roba	ETH		12	DNG	Stockholm	26 Jul
8:30.40	Marcin	Chabowski	POL-J	28.5.86	7		Bydgoszcz	5 Jun
8:30.64	Stephan	Hohl	GER	23.2.80	4		Cottbus	5 Jun
8:30.66	Ivan	Luchianov	MDA	31.1.81	2	WUG	Izmir	17 Aug
8:30.86	Per	Jacobsen	SWE	30.12.77	2		Sollentuna	28 Jun
8:31.16	Raphael	Schäfer	GER	6.3.81	5		Cottbus	5 Jun
	(80)							
8:31.18	Lukasz	Parszczynski	POL	4.5.85	4	NC	Biala Podlaska	24 Jun
8:31.22	Boaz	Cheboiywo	KEN	2.8.78	2	Owens	Columbus	6 May
8:31.29	Petrus	Monyani (Sithole)	RSA	29.3.76	3	NC	Durban	16 Apr
8:31.33	Badre Din	Zioini	FRA	25.3.76	4		Pézenas	28 May
8:31.93	Patrick	Mutai	KEN	31.12.83	5	NCAA	Sacramento	10 Jun
8:32.17	Stuart	Stokes	GBR	5.12.76	18	NA	Heusden-Zolder	23 Jul
8:32.24	Sergey	Redko	UKR	24.1.73	1		Yalta	27 May
8:32.36		Sun Wenli	CHN	9.2.78	1	NG	Nanjing	17 Oct
8:32.53	Solomon	Kandie	KEN	28.8.78	3	Owens	Columbus	6 May
8:32.78	Abderrahmane	Mouatassim	MAR		2		Rabat	18 Jun
	(90)							
8:32.81	Mário	Teixeira	POR	20.9.74	1		Gavá	12 Jun
8:32.87	Luke	Gunn	GBR	22.3.85	4	WUG	Izmir	17 Aug
8:33.00	Moustafa	Shebto	QAT-J	4.7.86	9h3	WCh	Helsinki	7 Aug
8:33.0A	Patrick	Nthiwa	KEN	30.6.83	3		Nairobi	28 May
8:33.03	Kamal Ali	Thamer	QAT-J	12.11.88	2	WAsG	Doha	7 Dec
8:33.06	Max	King	USA	24.2.80	5	NC	Carson	25 Jun
8:33.1A	Nathan	Kibet Naibei	KEN-J	22.2.86	2	NC	Nairobi	18 Jun
8:33.14	Lyle	Weese	USA	26.10.79	2	Jerome	Burnaby	14 Jun
8:33.17	John	Langat	KEN	27.11.74	1		Karlstad	18 Jul
8:33.37		Sun Wenyong	CHN	9.2.78	2	NG	Nanjing	17 Oct
	(100)							

Mark	Name		Nat	Born	Date
8:33.70	Benjamin	Bruce	USA	10.9.82	5 Mar
8:33.94		Shi Linzhong	CHN	16.1.81	17 Oct
8:34.09	Mariusz	Gizynski	POL	26.6.81	24 Jun
8:34.1A	James	Cheptuyon	KEN		17 Dec
8:34.12	Itai	Maggidi	ISR	9.1.81	10 Jun
8:34.3A	Nicholas	Lemeto	UGA	.85	1 May
8:34.37	Anatoliy	Kharkovets	UKR	7.7.83	27 May
8:34.38	Kim	Bergdahl	FIN	5.3.78	18 Jul
8:34.39	Joseph	Lomala Kimosop	KEN	.82	9 Jun
8:34.4A	Isaac	Tanui	KEN-J	.86	19 Mar
8:34.45	Mahiedin	Mekhissi Benabbad	FRA	15.3.85	23 Jun
8:34.72	Frederic	Yegon	KEN-J	.86	18 Jun
8:34.80	Erik	Emilsson	SWE	10.3.82	10 Jun
8:34.84	Joshua	McAdams	USA	26.3.80	8 Jun
8:34.89	Henrik	Ahnström	SWE	1.7.81	8 Jun
8:34.91	Jacques	Sallberg	USA	24.9.74	1 May
8:34.94	Mohamed	Abdellaoui	FRA	22.4.79	28 May
8:35.03	Mikael	Talasjoki	FIN	27.3.79	18 Jul
8:35.05	Jakub	Wisniewski	POL	3.11.77	5 Jun
8:35.18	Aaron	Fisher	USA	23.2.83	8 Jun
8:35.4A	Elijah	Kibwalei	KEN		28 May
8:35.82	Adil	El Oualidi	FRA	3.9.81	7 Jun
8:35.82	Willy	Komen	KEN-J	22.12 87	1 Sep
8:36.0A	Abraham	Chirchir	KEN		18 Jun
8:36.10	Abdelhakim	Maazouz	ALG	28.8.75	18 Jun
8:36.1A	Joel	Kiplimo	UGA		1 May
8:36.36	Adam	Bowden	GBR	5.8.82	10 Jul
8:36.39	Lucas	Meyer	USA	1.8.83	8 Jun
8:36.4A	David	Kirwa Chepkwony	KEN	1.8.85	19 Mar
8:36.77	Abraham	Cherono	KEN	21.7.80	23 Jun
8:36.79	Philip	Tarus	KEN	11.9.74	7 Jun
8:36.95	Merzak	Ould Bouchiba	ALG	27.4.75	21 Jul
8:37.08	Rubén	Palomeque	ESP	14.8.80	14 Jul
8:37.13	Adil	Manssouri	MAR	.81	7 Jun
8:37.2A	James	Cheruiyot Melly	KEN		19 Mar
8:37.42	Youcef	Abdi	AUS	7.12.77	4 Mar
8:37.56	Antonio	Lagares	ESP	26.12.82	13 Jul
8:37.6A	John	Kosgei	KEN	13.7.72	28 May
8:37.60	Angelo	Iannelli	ITA	27.7.76	28 Aug
8:37.65		Bai Jie	CHN	24.2.84	17 Oct
8:37.83	Alexandre	Genest	CAN-J	30.6.86	14 Jun
8:37.83	Francisco Javier	Lara	ESP	24.6.76	13 Jul
8:37.85	Kevin	Sheppard	GBR	27.1.79	25 Jun
8:37.90	Abdelghani	Aït Bahmad	MAR-Y	28.7.89	28 Aug
8:37.97	Hubert	Pokrop	POL	2.11.85	24 Jun
8:38.08	Christian	Knoblich	GER	1.10.76	2 Jul

Mark	Wind	Name		Nat	Born	Pos	Meet	Venue	Date
8:38.15		Yasunori	Uchitomi	JPN	29.10.72				2 Jun
8:38.16		Aaron	Aguayo	USA	27.7.84				8 Jun
8:38.24		Yuriy	Gichun	UKR	10.2.77				2 Jul
8:38.25		Mark	Warmby	GBR	12.12.78				25 Jun
8:38.26		Alexander	Greaux	PUR	22.9.77				23 Jul
8:38.32		Steffen	Uliczka	GER	17.7.84				2 Jul
8:38.34		Mark	Buckingham	GBR	4.5.85				11 Jun
8:38.5A		Henry	Kipkosgei	KEN	.78				28 May
8:38.56		Pedro	Ribeiro	POR	25.3.81				8 Jul
8:38.85		Andrew	Robinson	GBR	20.4.78				10 Jul
8:38.97		Bjørnar	Ustad Kristensen	NOR	26.1.82				18 Jul
8:39.0A		Collins	Ngeno	KEN					18 Jun
8:39.1		Benjamin	Kiplagat	UGA					30 Jul
8:39.24		Sivuyile	Dlongwana	RSA	21.8.81				18 Feb
8:39.30		David	Cheromei	KEN					4 Jun
8:39.31		Christian	Klein	GER	19.9.83				2 Jul
8:39.42		Nick	Talbot	GBR	14.12.77				25 Jun
8:39.59			Lin Xiangqian	CHN-J	27.1.87				17 Oct
8:39.8A		David	Lagat	KEN	.83				18 Jun
8:39.96		Rafal	Wojcik (166)	POL	18.9.72				24 Jun

JUNIORS

See main list for top 8 juniors. 8 performances by 3 men to 8:27.0. Additional marks and further juniors:

Kipchumba	8:19.85	3	GP II	Milano	1 Jun	
	8:20.80	4	GP	Rieti	28 Aug	
	8:20.94	14	NA	Heusden-Zolder	23 Jul	
	8:23.23	9	Gaz	Saint-Denis	1 Jul	
	8:24.53	5		Bydgoszcz	5 Jun	
	8:24.76	4	Gugl	Linz	23 Aug	

Tareq Mubarak Taher – we have date of birth as 24.3.84, but entered as b. 1.2.89 by BRN for WY. Further performance:

8:21.68 5h2 WCh Helsinki 7 Aug

Mark	Name		Nat	Born	Pos	Meet	Venue	Date
8:34.4A	Isaac	Tanui	KEN	.86	2		Kakamega	19 Mar
8:34.72	Frederic	Yegon (10)	KEN	.86	2		Alcalá de Henares	18 Jun
8:35.82	Willy	Komen	KEN	22.12 87	1	Afr-J	Radès	1 Sep
8:37.83	Alexandre	Genest	CAN	30.6.86	4	Jerome	Burnaby	14 Jun
8:37.90	Abdelghani	Aït Bahmad	MAR-Y	28.7.89	9	GP	Rieti	28 Aug
8:39.59		Lin Xiangqian	CHN	27.1.87	5	NG	Nanjing	17 Oct
8:40.01	Nahom Masfin	Tariku	ETH-Y	3.6.89	2	Afr-J	Radès	1 Sep
8:40.3 A	Patrick	Kimeli Lagat	KEN-Y	.88	1		Neirobi	5 Nov
8:40.40	Said	El-Medouly	MAR	.87	5		Noisy-le-Grand	7 Jun
8:41.21	Ezekyas	Sisay	ETH-Y	5.12.88	3	Afr-J	Radès	1 Sep
8:41.46	Dieudonné	Gahungu	BDI	16.4.86	20	NA	Heusden-Zolder	23 Jul
8:43.32	Rabia	Makhloufi (20)	ALG	.86	4	Afr-J	Radès	1 Sep

110 METRES HURDLES

Mark	Wind	Name		Nat	Born	Pos	Meet	Venue	Date
12.97	1.0	Ladji	Doucouré	FRA	28.3.83	1	NC	Angers	15 Jul
12.99	0.2	Allen	Johnson	USA	1.3.71	1	NC	Carson	24 Jun
13.00	-0.1		Doucouré			1	Bisl	Oslo	29 Jul
13.01	0.2	Dominique	Arnold	USA	14.9.73	2	NC	Carson	24 Jun
13.02	0.2	Terrence	Trammell	USA	23.11.78	3	NC	Carson	24 Jun
13.02	-0.3		Doucouré			1	Gaz	Saint-Denis	1 Jul
13.03	0.8		Johnson			1		New York (RI)	11 Jun
13.03	-0.2		Arnold			1	WK	Zürich	19 Aug
13.04	-0.3		Johnson			2	Gaz	Saint-Denis	1 Jul
13.05	0.8		Arnold			2		New York (RI)	11 Jun
13.05	1.1		Liu Xiang	CHN	13.7.83	1rA	Athl	Lausanne	5 Jul
13.05	1.1		Trammell			2rA	Athl	Lausanne	5 Jul
13.05	-0.1		Liu			1		Shanghai	17 Sep
13.06	0.0		Liu			1	Pre	Eugene	4 Jun
13.06	-0.3		Liu			3	Gaz	Saint-Denis	1 Jul
13.07	-0.2		Doucouré			1	WCh	Helsinki	12 Aug
13.08	-0.2		Liu			2	WCh	Helsinki	12 Aug
13.08	0.6		Liu			1		Yokohama	19 Sep
13.09	-1.4		Johnson			1	WAF	Monaco	10 Sep
13.10	-0.3		Arnold			4	Gaz	Saint-Denis	1 Jul
13.10	-0.2		Johnson			3	WCh	Helsinki	12 Aug
13.10	-1.4		Arnold			1	WAF	Monaco	10 Sep
13.10	0.4		Liu			1	NG	Nanjing	20 Oct
13.11	0.1	Stanislav	Olijar	LAT	22.3.79	1	SGP	Doha	13 May
13.11	0.8		Liu			3		New York (RI)	11 Jun
13.11	0.0		Arnold			1	GGala	Roma	8 Jul
13.12	1.1		Liu			1	GP	Osaka	7 May
13.12	0.0		Trammell			2	Pre	Eugene	4 Jun
13.12	-0.2		Liu			2	WK	Zürich	19 Aug
13.13	-0.2		Arnold			4	WCh	Helsinki	12 Aug
		(30/6)							
13.20	-1.4	Maurice	Wignall	JAM	17.4.76	5	WAF	Monaco	10 Sep
13.22	-0.1	Joel	Brown	USA	31.1.80	2	Bisl	Oslo	29 Jul
13.23	0.8	Anwar	Moore	USA	5.3.79	1	ModR	Modesto	8 May
13.23	0.1	Arend	Watkins	USA	23.5.79	1	SGP	Athína	14 Jun
		(10)							
13.29	0.0		Shi Dongpeng	CHN	6.1.84	2	NC	Shijiazhuang	20 Jun
13.29	0.6	David	Oliver	USA	24.4.82	2		Cuxhaven	9 Jul
13.30	0.1	Redelen	dos Santos	BRA	24.4.76	3	SGP	Doha	13 May

Mark	Wind	Name		Nat	Born	Pos	Meet	Venue	Date
13.31A	-0.5	Anselmo	da Silva	BRA	22.3.81	1		Cochabamba	29 May
13.31	1.1	Ron	Bramlett	USA	22.10.79	4rA	Athl	Lausanne	5 Jul
13.31	1.5	Thomas	Blaschek	GER	5.4.81	1h1		Cuxhaven	9 Jul
13.33	0.2	David	Payne	USA	24.7.82	5	NC	Carson	24 Jun
13.34	0.7	Matheus	Inocêncio	BRA	17.5.81	1	NC	São Paulo	17 Jun
13.35	0.2	Antwon	Hicks	USA	12.3.83	6	NC	Carson	24 Jun
13.36	0.6	Dawane	Wallace	USA	30.12.76	4		Cuxhaven	9 Jul
		(20)							
13.38	0.9	Aries	Merritt	USA	24.7.85	1	SEC	Nashville	15 May
13.38	0.1	Sergey	Demidyuk	UKR	5.6.82	2	SGP	Athína	14 Jun
13.39	0.7	Josh	Walker	USA	6.5.82	1	NCAA	Sacramento	10 Jun
13.39	1.9	Yoel	Hernández	CUB	12.12.77	2		Zaragoza	23 Jun
13.41	1.1	Duane	Ross	USA	5.12.72	1		Ulm	12 Jun
13.42	0.8	Micah	Harris	USA	30.4.79	2	CalR	Modesto	8 May
13.43	1.4	Marcel	van der Westen	NED	1.8.76	1	ECp-1B	Leiria	19 Jun
13.43	-0.1	Robert	Kronberg	SWE	15.8.76	7	Bisl	Oslo	29 Jul
13.44A	-0.1	Paulo	Villar	COL	28.7.78	1	Bolivar	Armenia/COL	19 Aug
13.45	1.9	Jackson	Quiñónez	ECU	12.6.80	3		Zaragoza	23 Jun
		(30)							
13.46	-1.6	Dayron	Robles	CUB-J	19.11.86	1	PAm-J	Windsor	29 Jul
13.48	1.0	Márcio	de Souza	BRA	24.1.75	3		San Carlos	8 Apr
13.48	1.0	Igor	Peremota	RUS	14.1.81	1	Znam	Kazan	24 Jun
13.48	1.5	Elmar	Lichtenegger	AUT	25.5.74	3rB	Athl	Lausanne	5 Jul
13.50	0.7	Jason	Richardson	USA-J	4.4.86	3	NCAA	Sacramento	10 Jun
13.51	0.8	Tim	Bogdanof	USA	9.11.79	4	CalR	Modesto	8 May
13.51	2.0	Cédric	Lavanne	FRA	13.11.80	1		Castres	26 Jul
13.52	0.8	Karl	Jennings	CAN	14.5.79	6	CalR	Modesto	8 May
13.52	2.0	Andrea	Giaconi	ITA	11.4.74	3	ECp-S	Firenze	19 Jun
13.52	1.9	Ivan	Bitzi	SUI	4.8.75	1		Meilen	10 Jul
		(40)							
13.53	1.1	Masato	Naito	JPN	31.7.80	2	GP	Osaka	7 May
13.53	0.7	Eric	Mitchum	USA	2.8.84	4	NCAA	Sacramento	10 Jun
13.53	0.3	Felipe	Vivancos	ESP	16.6.80	1	MedG	Almeria	29 Jun
13.54	2.0	Jonathan	Nsenga	BEL	21.4.73	2		Castres	26 Jul
13.54	2.0	Jared	MacLeod	CAN	3.4.80	1s2	WUG	Izmir	15 Aug
13.55	1.2		Wu Youjia	CHN	6.5.83	1	AsiGP	Sidoarjo	18 Jun
13.57	0.6	Yevgeniy	Pechonkin	RUS	9.10.73	3	GS	Ostrava	9 Jun
13.57	-0.1	Yuji	Ohashi	JPN	5.9.83	1s1		Ageo	25 Jun
13.57	0.0	Gregory	Sedoc	NED	16.10.81	1		Hilversum	4 Sep
13.58	1.2	Dudley	Dorival	HAI	1.9.75	1	Oda	Hiroshima	29 Apr
		(50)							
13.59	1.7	Damien	Greaves	GBR	19.9.77	1	LI	Loughborough	22 May
13.59	2.0	Dominique	DeGrammont	HAI	13.3.79	1		Azusa	16 Jul
13.60	0.4	Mike	Fenner	GER	24.4.71	1		Mannheim	18 Jun
13.60	1.4	Andrea	Alterio	ITA	11.6.73	1		Fribourg	27 Aug
13.61	0.0	Robby	Hughes	USA	10.10.78	2		Knoxville	16 Apr
13.61	0.7	Sultan	Tucker	LBR	24.10.78	2	PennR	Philadelphia	30 Apr
13.61	0.0	Anier	García	CUB	9.3.76	3	Barr	La Habana	19 May
13.61	1.0	Satoru	Tanigawa	JPN	5.7.72	1=	NC	Tokyo	4 Jun
13.62	0.1	Chris	Pinnock	JAM	26.3.79	1		Houston	26 Mar
13.62	0.0	Jermaine	Cooper	USA	31.8.80	5	GP II	Stanford	30 May
		(60)							
13.62	0.4	Alexandros	Theofánov	GRE	25.2.81	1	NC	Athína	10 Jun
13.62	0.8	Aubrey	Herring	USA	19.9.78	6		New York (RI)	11 Jun
13.62	0.6	Florian Peter	Seibold	GER	27.6.79	2	NC	Wattenscheid	2 Jul
13.62		Allan	Scott	GBR	27.12.82	1	NC	Manchester (SC)	9 Jul
13.63	0.4		Liu Lilu	CHN	6.2.85	2		Yixing	22 May
13.63	0.0	Brandon	Hon	USA	7.7.79	6	GP II	Stanford	30 May
13.63	-0.1	Dexter	Faulk	USA	14.4.84	5h1	NC	Carson	23 Jun
13.63	1.5	Andrew	Turner	GBR	19.9.80	1		Dublin (S)	30 Jul
13.64A	1.3	Hennie	Kotze	RSA	4.2.84	1		Potchefstroom	6 Apr
13.64	1.0	Willi	Mathiszik	GER	17.6.84	4		Kassel	10 Jun
		(70)							
13.64	0.6	Tasuku	Tanonaka	JPN	23.9.78	4		Yokohama	19 Sep
13.65A	-0.1	Shaun	Bownes	RSA	24.10.70	1		Potchefstroom	8 Feb
13.65	0.1	Todd	Matthews Jouda	SUD	28.6.79	5	SGP	Doha	13 May
13.65	1.0	Kai	Doskoczynski	GER	15.7.84	1h1		Mannheim	18 Jun
13.65	-0.9	Dániel	Kiss	HUN	12.2.82	1	NC	Debrecen	6 Jul
13.66	0.6	Chris	Thomas	USA	9.2.81	1		Tucson	21 May
13.66	0.4	Jan	Schindzielorz	GER	8.8.78	2		Mannheim	18 Jun
13.66	1.7	Tomasz	Scigaczewski	POL	18.11.78	1	NC	Biala Podlaska	26 Jun

Mark	Wind	Name		Nat	Born	Pos	Meet	Venue	Date
13.66	1.0	Joseph-Berlioz	Randriamihaja	MAD	30.11.75	3	FRA Ch	Angers	15 Jul
13.67	1.7	David	Hughes	GBR	31.5.84	2	LI	Loughborough	22 May
		(80)							
13.68	0.6	Alleyne	Lett	GRN	7.1.83	1h3	PennR	Philadelphia	29 Apr
13.68	1.4	Adrian	Ray	USA	9.10.81	1		Huntsville	15 May
13.68	1.5	Peter	Coghlan	IRL	27.3.75	2		Dublin (S)	30 Jul
13.69	1.1	Marlon	Odom	USA	4.12.82	1	NCAA-r	Norman	28 May
13.69	1.3	Thiago	Castelo Branco	BRA	4.11.79	1		So Paulo	28 Aug
13.70	1.3	Linnie	Yarbrough	USA	9.9.82	1h3	TexR	Austin	8 Apr
13.70	1.2	Mubarak Ata	Mubarak	KSA	17.12.81	1	Is.Sol	Makkah	15 Apr
13.70	1.4	Alexandru	Mihailescu	ROM	16.8.82	2		Nantes	1 Jun
13.70	2.0	Frikkie	van Zyl	RSA	30.7.81	1		Donnas	19 Jun
13.70	2.0	Artur	Kohutek	POL	1.5.71	5	ECp-S	Firenze	19 Jun
		(90)							
13.70	0.4		Chen Ming	CHN	8.3.84	3	NG	Nanjing	20 Oct
13.71	1.2	Montrell	Person	USA	28.11.81	1h1		Atlanta	13 May
13.71	-0.3	Unyime	Akpan	USA	7.12.81	1	NCAA-II	Abilene	28 May
13.71	-0.7	Jurica	Grabusic	CRO	28.3.83	1		Velenje	23 Jun
13.72	0.3	Eric	Keddo	USA	85	1		Atlanta	14 May
13.72	0.0	Damjan	Zlatnar	SLO	16.12.77	1		Ljubljana	21 May
13.72	0.8	Enrique	Llanos	PUR	7.5.80	1h3	NCAA-II	Abilene	27 May
13.72	0.1	Yasunori	Yoshioka	JPN	19.5.75	2		Nagoya	17 Jul
13.73	1.6	Terry	Reese	USA	20.6.67	2h2		Greensboro	9 Apr
13.73	1.6	Ivo	Burkhardt	GER	7.12.77	2h3	NC	Wattenscheid	2 Jul
		(100)							
13.73	1.6	Garfield	Darien	FRA-J	22.12.87	2		Bron	5 Jul
13.73	2.0	Yevgeniy	Borisov	RUS	7.3.84	5s2	WUG	Izmir	15 Aug

Mark	Wind	Name		Nat	Born	Date
13.74	1.6	Sébastien	Denis	FRA	4.5.71	5 Jul
13.75	1.4	Richard	Davidson	USA	8.4.82	7 May
13.75	1.5	Nolan	Jackson	USA	23.10.84	14 May
13.76	1.6	Andrey	Shalonko	BLR	20.3.83	19 Jun
13.76	0.4		Xing Yanan	CHN	17.6.83	20 Oct
13.77	0.0	Stefan	Wieser	GER	8.12.84	14 May
13.77	1.6		Wang Hui	CHN	12.6.83	15 May
13.77	-1.1	Claude	Edorh	GER	27.2.72	16 Jul
13.78	-0.8	Yuniel	Hernández	CUB	28.3.81	17 Mar
13.78	1.4	Selim	Nurudeen	USA	1.2.83	8 Apr
13.78	1.7	Bryan	Clay	USA	3.1.80	9 Apr
13.78	1.8	Andrew	Carruthers	USA	8.3.83	14 May
13.78	1.8	Héctor	Cotto	PUR-J	8.8.84	14 May
13.78	-0.1	Konstadínos	Douvalídis	GRE-J	10.3.87	22 Jul
13.79	0.4	Anthony	Golston	USA	3.5.82	15 May
13.79A	-0.2	Éder Antônio	de Souza	BRA-J	15.10.86	1 Jun
13.80	1.5	Clarence	Glenn	USA	.85	14 May
13.80	0.9	Shamar	Sands	BAH	30.4.85	15 May
13.80	1.0	Alexander	John	GER-J	3.5.86	18 Jun
13.80	1.0	Bashir	Ramzy	USA	4.5.79	30 Jul
13.81		Daryl	Burgess	USA	14.6.85	16 Apr
13.81	2.0	Anthony	Acklin	USA	26.7.82	15 May
13.81	0.5	Jonathon	Williams	USA	29.8.83	15 May
13.81	1.1	Maksim	Linsha	BLR	6.4.85	26 Jun
13.81	0.2	Decosma	Wright	JAM	1.9.82	26 Jun
13.81	1.4	Matti	Niemi	FIN	15.11.76	30 Jun
13.81	1.5	Yakov	Petrov	RUS	16.5.83	10 Jul
13.81	0.3	Jens	Werrmann	GER	29.5.85	23 Jul
13.81	0.0	Rouhollah	Ashgari	IRI	8.1.82	15 Aug
13.81	-0.3	Philip	Nossmy	SWE	6.12.82	21 Aug
13.82A	-0.8	Ruan	de Vries	RSA-J	1.2.86	4 Feb
13.82	0.3	Yukito	Irie	JPN-	8.6.83	3 Jun
13.82	0.9	Gergely	Palágyi	HUN	19.2.79	11 Jun
13.82	0.6	Dirk	Riekmann	GER	14.4.72	12 Jun
13.82	1.6	Damir	Haracic	BIH	5.5.82	19 Jun
13.83	1.4	Nenad	Loncar	SCG	6.3.81	7 May
13.83	0.1	Tommy	Moore	USA	30.4.82	27 May
13.83	0.8	Courtney	Jones	USA	3.7.84	27 May
13.83	1.3	Obiamlam	Ikwuakor	USA	13.8.84	27 May
13.83	1.5	Charles	Allen	CAN	29.3.77	5 Jul
13.84	0.0	Blake	Frazier	USA	11.10.83	27 May
13.84		Pavel	Onishchenko	RUS	15.4.85	4 Jun
13.84	0.2	Emiliano	Pizzoli	ITA	29.6.74	4 Jun
13.84	0.2	Andreas	Dengler	GER	22.12.80	23 Jul
13.84	0.3	Christopher	Baillie	GBR	21.4.81	13 Aug
13.84	0.0	Andreas	Kundert	SUI	1.10.84	16 Aug
13.85	0.3	Tarmo	Jallai	EST	30.1.79	23 Apr
13.85	0.9	Virgil	Spier	NED	8.1.81	3 Jul
13.85	1.8	Kenji	Yahata	JPN	4.11.80	18 Jul

Mark	Wind	Name		Nat	Born	Date
13.85	1.1	Juha	Sonck	FIN	15.4.81	28 Aug
13.86	0.4	LaRon	Bennett	USA	25.11.82	14 May
13.86	1.1	Jerome	Miller	USA-J	14.8.86	15 May
13.86	1.5	Dwayne	Robinson	JAM	31.3.83	27 May
13.86	-1.5	Aleksey	Davydikov	RUS	23.9.83	13 Jun
13.86	0.5	Martin	Hoffmann	GER	7.4.84	18 Jun
13.87	-1.0	Dominic	Berger	USA-J	19.5.86	23 Jun
13.87	-0.2	Mariusz	Kubaszewski	POL	11.7.82	26 Jun
13.88	0.1	Hideki	Nomoto	JPN	13.3.84	9 Apr
13.88		Dior	Lowry	USA		30 Apr
13.88		Ronaldo	Andrews	USA	12.10.79	20 May
13.88		Pavel	Filev	RUS	5.3.85	4 Jun
13.88	1.2	Stanislav	Sajdok	CZE	22.7.83	27 Jun
13.88		William	Sharman	GBR	12.9.84	9 Jul
13.88	0.4		Ji Wei	CHN	5.2.84	20 Oct
13.89	2.0	Yuriy	Volkov	RUS	16.8.77	24 Jun
13.89	-0.9	Kota	Kumamoto	JPN	5.11.83	2 Nov
13.90	0.3	Jacoby	DuBose	USA	11.12.82	14 May
13.90	0.4	Hristos	Ikonomópoulos	GRE	7.11.80	10 Jun
13.90	0.4	Nikólaos	Filandarákis	GRE-J	1.6.86	10 Jun
13.90	-0.5	Artur	Pereverzev	RUS	3.9.81	16 Jul
13.90	-0.7		Park Tae-kyong	KOR	30.7.80	23 Sep
13.91		Andrew	Oyer	USA	14.7.85	23 Apr
13.91	0.0	Javier	Culson	PUR	25.7.84	12 Jun
13.91	-1.5	Jerome	Crews	GER	20.2.77	10 Jul
13.92		Carlos	Patterson	CUB	20.2.78	20 May
13.92	1.3	Jeff	Hunter	USA	19.2.83	27 May
13.92	2.0	Séléké	Samaké	SEN-J	5.2.86	19 Jun
13.93		J.D.	Henry	USA		11 Mar
13.93	1.2	Mohd Robani	Hassan	MAS	18.1.83	15 Apr
13.93		Ryan	Harlan	USA	25.4.81	29 May
13.93	0.3	Yuto	Aoki	JPN	11.7.84	3 Jun
13.93	-1.9	David	Ilariani	GEO	20.1.81	5 Jun
13.93	1.5	Thomas	Martin	FRA	19.2.80	7 Jun
13.93	-0.6	Dwight	Ruff	USA	31.3.83	8 Jun
13.94	0.9	James	Mortimer	NZL	1.3.83	8 Apr
13.94	1.4	Luiz André	Balcers	BRA	18.10.73	7 Jun
13.94	-0.8	Julius	Jiles-Tindall	USA-J	14.2.86	8 Jun
13.94	1.3	Hamdi	Mhirsi	TUN	13.8.81	23 Jun
13.94	1.3	Damien	Broothaerts	BEL	13.3.83	25 Jun
13.95	0.6	Pat	Brown	USA	.82	29 Apr
13.95	0.8	Julien	Fenes	FRA	17.7.84	8 May
13.95	1.1	Kerron	Clement	USA	31.10.85	14 May
13.95	1.2	Roy	Cheney	USA	7.10.83	14 May
13.95	2.0		Jin Jianfeng	CHN	11.10.80	15 May
13.95	0.0	Carlos B.	Navarro	CUB	14.3.83	19 May
13.95	1.4	Luis	Sá	POR	17.3.81	19 Jun
13.95	0.2	Cédric	Beyera	FRA	3.6.83	29 Jul
		(197)				

Mark	Wind	Name		Nat	Born	Pos	Meet	Venue	Date
Wind assisted									
13.11	2.2		Trammell			1		Carson	22 May
13.20	2.1	Anwar	Moore	USA	5.3.79	1	DNG	Stockholm	26 Jul
13.23	2.1	David	Oliver	USA	24.4.82	2	DNG	Stockholm	26 Jul
13.32	2.6	Yoel	Hernández	CUB	12.12.77	1	CAC	Nassau	10 Jul
13.33	2.1	Dawane	Wallace	USA	30.12.76	3	DNG	Stockholm	26 Jul
13.34	2.1	Aries	Merritt	USA	24.7.85	4	DNG	Stockholm	26 Jul
13.41	2.6	Dayron	Robles	CUB-J	19.11.86	2	CAC	Nassau	10 Jul
13.44	4.0	Adrian	Ray	USA	9.10.81	1		Houston	7 May
13.46	2.8	Daryl	Burgess	USA	.85	1	JUCO	Levelland	18 May
13.48	2.3	Andrea	Giaconi	ITA	11.4.74	1		Lagos/POR	29 May
13.49	2.6	Alleyne	Lett	GRN	7.1.83	3	CAC	Nassau	10 Jul
13.50	2.6	Dudley	Dorival	HAI	1.9.75	4	CAC	Nassau	10 Jul
13.52	2.5	Yevgeniy	Pechonkin	RUS	9.10.73	3h1	GS	Ostrava	9 Jun
13.53	2.2	Jermaine	Cooper	USA	31.8.80	4		Carson	22 May
13.55	2.6	Chris	Pinnock	JAM	26.3.79	5	CAC	Nassau	10 Jul
13.56	3.0	Gregory	Sedoc	NED	16.10.81	2		Leiden	11 Jun
13.56	2.9	David	Hughes	GBR	31.5.84	1	EU23	Erfurt	17 Jul
13.57	4.8	Linnie	Yarbrough	USA	9.9.82	2		Atlanta	2 Apr
13.58	2.9	Willi	Mathiszik	GER	17.6.84	2	EU23	Erfurt	17 Jul
13.65	4.8	Selim	Nurudeen	USA	1.2.83	1		Piscataway	8 May
13.65	3.7	Chris	Thomas	USA	9.2.81	1		Abilene	12 May
13.66	2.9	Stanislav	Sajdok	CZE	22.7.83	3	EU23	Erfurt	17 Jul
13.67	2.2	Marlon	Odom	USA	4.12.82	1rB	MSR	Walnut	17 Apr
13.69	2.8	Dior	Lowry	USA	2.10.85	2	JUCO	Levelland	18 May
13.69	2.6	Enrique	Llanos	PUR	7.5.80	6	CAC	Nassau	10 Jul
13.70	3.7	Tarmo	Jallai	EST	30.1.79	2		Abilene	14 May
13.70	2.3	Maksim	Linsha	BLR	6.4.85	1h1	EU23	Erfurt	15 Jul
13.70	2.8	Christopher	Baillie	GBR	21.4.81	2	Scot	Glasgow (S)	28 Aug
13.71	4.0	Lewis	Edmondson	USA	26.2.79	4	TexR	Austin	9 Apr
13.72	4.8	David	Klics	USA	.83	2		Piscataway	8 May
13.72	2.9	William	Sharman	GBR	12.9.84	4	EU23	Erfurt	17 Jul

Mark	Wind	Name		Nat	Born	Date
13.74	2.2	Ronaldo	Andrews	USA	12.10.79	17 Apr
13.76	2.4	Dominic	Berger	USA-J	19.5.86	29 Jul
13.77	2.9	Andreas	Kundert	SUI	1.10.84	17 Jul
13.78	2.2	Blake	Frazier	USA	11.10.83	17 Apr
13.79	2.6	Robin	Korving	NED	29.7.74	11 Jun
13.80	3.0	Virgil	Spier	NED	8.1.81	11 Jun
13.80	2.9	Luis	Sá	POR	17.3.81	2 Jul
13.82	2.3	Bano	Traoré	FRA	25.4.85	15 Jul
13.82	4.2	Hamdi	Mhirsi	TUN	13.8.81	15 Sep
13.84	4.4	Dominic	Girdler	GBR	6.3.82	12 Jun
13.84	3.4	Markus	Vilén	FIN	19.12.83	30 Jun
13.85	2.3	Andrey	Kislykh	RUS	24.11.76	29 May
13.86	3.4	Marko	Ritola	FIN	29.1.79	30 Jun
13.86	4.2	Aymen	Ben Ahmed	TUN-J	1.3.86	15 Sep
13.86	2.3	Greg	Eyears	AUS	21.8.81	1 Dec
13.87	2.7	Willie	Gault	USA	5.9.60	26 Jun
13.89	4.4	Duncan	Malins	GBR	12.6.78	12 Jun
13.89	3.8	James	Mortimer	NZL	1.3.83	12 Nov
13.90	4.0	Ryan	Harlan	USA	25.4.81	9 Apr
13.91	4.1	Ryan	Fontenot	USA-J	4.5.86	23 Apr
13.91	3.2	Rui	Palma	POR	4.1.78	23 Jul
13.92	3.0	Elton	Bitincka	ALG	26.5.85	21 May
13.92	3.2	Naoya	Hisada	JPN	29.8.80	16 Oct
13.93	3.9	Kyle	Vander-Kuyp	AUS	30.5.71	18 Dec
13.94A	3.3	Ryan	Dowling	RSA	15.5.79	29 Jan
13.94	2.2	Greg	Belger	USA	21.8.81	9 Apr
13.95	3.1	Mohammed	Sillah-Freckleton	GBR	11.9.80	27 May
13.95	3.4	Olli	Talsi	FIN	27.11.82	30 Jun

Low altitude bests

13.50 0.6 da Silva 1 Bielsko Biala 9 Jul | 13.51 0.5 Villar 5 GP Belém 22 May

13.85 1.4 E de Souza 5 Mar | 13.91 1.3 de Vries 25 Jun | 13.95 -2.1 H Kotze 11 Mar

13.85 0.8 Bownes 29 May | 13.75w 2.8 15 Apr

Doubtful wind: 7 May Jonesboro: +2.0? 1. Daniel Kiss HUN 12.2.82 13.49, 2. Greg Belger USA 21.8.81 13.68

Hand timing

Mark	Wind	Name		Nat	Born	Pos	Meet	Venue	Date
13.2		Dayron	Robles	CUB-J	19.11.86	1		La Habana	24 Feb
13.3	1.0	Frikkie	van Zyl	RSA	30.7.81	1		Parow	29 Jan
13.5	0.0	Carlos	Patterson	CUB	20.2.78	1D	Barr	La Habana	24 Jun
13.5	-0.6	David	Ilariani	GEO	20.1.81	1		Tbilisi	9 Jul

Mark	Wind	Name		Nat	Born	Date
13.6A	1.2	Janko	Kotze	RSA	3.3.82	26 Feb
13.6		Yuniel	Hernández	CUB	28.3.81	5 May
13.6		Frédéric	Demaneche	FRA	14.2.75	4 Jun
13.7		Jesús	Costa	CUB	15.3.83	24 Feb
13.6w	2.4	Andrew	Turner	GBR	19.9.80	16 Jul
13.6w	2.4	Christopher	Baillie	GBR	21.4.81	16 Jul

JUNIORS

See main list for top 3 juniors. 11 performances by 3 men to 13.73. Additional marks and further juniors:

Name	Mark	Wind	Pos	Meet	Venue	Date	Mark	Wind	Pos	Meet	Venue	Date
Robles	13.47	0.0	2	Barr	La Habana	19 May	13.55	-0.1	1h1	PAm-J	Windsor	29 Jul
	13.50	1.9	4		Zaragoza	24 Jun	13.59	-0.7	1h2	CAC	Nassau	10 Jul
	13.66	-0.5	5		Padova	3 Jul						
Richardson	13.66	0.0	2	NCAA-r	New York	28 May	13.73	0.6	1h1	NCAA-r	New York	28 May
	13.68	-1.1	2s1	NCAA	Sacramento	8 Jun						

Mark	Wind	Name		Nat	Born	Pos	Meet	Venue	Date
13.78	1.8	Héctor	Cotto	PUR		2		Houston	14 May
13.78	-0.1	Konstadínos	Douvalídis	GRE	10.3.87	1h1	EJ	Kaunas	22 Jul
13.79A	-0.2	Éder Antônio	de Souza	BRA	15.10.86	3		Cochabamba	1 Jun
		13.85	1.4			4		São Paulo	5 Mar
13.80	1.0	Alexander	John	GER	3.5.86	1		Mannheim	18 Jun

Mark		Name		Nat	Born	Pos	Meet	Venue	Date
13.82A	-0.8	Ruan	de Vries	RSA	1.2.86	1		Potchestroom	4 Feb
		13.91	1.3			2		Nivelles	25 Jun
13.86	1.1	Jerome	Miller	USA	14.8.86	3	Big 12	Manhattan, KS	15 May
13.87	-1.0	Dominic	Berger (10)	USA	19.5.86	1	NC-j	Carson	23 Jun
13.90	0.4	Nikólaos	Filandarákis	GRE	1.6.86	3	NC	Athína	10 Jun
13.92	2.0	Séleké	Samaké	SEN	5.2.86	2		Donnas	19 Jun
13.94	-0.8	Julius	Jiles-Tindall	USA	14.2.86	5s2	NCAA	Sacramento	8 Jun
13.99	0.0	Kai	Kelly	USA	8.11.86	2h1	NCAA-r	Eugene	27 May
14.00	-1.6	Tyrone	Akins	USA	6.1.86	2	PAm-J	Windsor	29 Jul
14.01	1.0	Samuel	Coco-Viloin	FRA	10.3.87	1B		Mannheim	18 Jun
14.03	0.4	Drew	Brunson	USA	4.4.86	3h2	SEC	Nashville	14 May
14.07	1.1	Denis	Byvakin	RUS	9.6.86	1		Sochi	22 May
14.09		Dayron	Capetillo	CUB	11.9.87	3r1		La Habana	3 Mar
13.7A hand		Lohann	Fourie	RSA	16.2.87	1		Naboomspruit	15 Oct
Wind assisted: 1 in main list plus									
13.76	2.4	Dominic	Berger	USA	19.5.86	1h2	PAm-J	Windsor	29 Jul
13.86	4.2	Aymen	Ben Ahmed	TUN	1.3.86	2	PArab	Radès	15 Sep
13.91	4.1	Ryan	Fontenot	USA	4.5.86	1		Baton Rouge	23 Apr
13.98	2.4	Markino	Buckley	JAM	16.4.86	2h2	PAm-J	Windsor	29 Jul

300 METRES HURDLES

Mark	Name		Nat	Born	Pos	Meet	Venue	Date
34.8	Ockert	Cilliers	RSA	21.4.81	1		Pliezhausen	8 May

Pliezhausen 8 May: 2. Christian Duma GER 5.2.82 35.7, 2. Henning Kuschewitz GER 9.4.81 35.9
Indoors: Tampere 12 Feb: 1. Llewellyn Herbert RSA 21.7.77 35.43, 2. Jussi Heikkilä FIN 21.3.83 35.96

400 METRES HURDLES

Mark	Name		Nat	Born	Pos	Meet	Venue	Date
47.24	Kerron	Clement	USA	31.10.85	1	NC	Carson	26 Jun
47.30	Bershawn	Jackson	USA	8.5.83	1	WCh	Helsinki	9 Aug
47.43	James	Carter	USA	7.5.78	2	WCh	Helsinki	9 Aug
47.56		Clement			1	NCAA	Sacramento	11 Jun
47.62		Jackson			1		Carson	22 May
47.67	Bennie	Brazell	USA	2.6.82	2	NCAA	Sacramento	11 Jun
47.78		Carter			1s1	WCh	Helsinki	7 Aug
47.80		Jackson			2	NC	Carson	26 Jun
47.84	Bayano	Kamani	PAN	17.4.80	2s1	WCh	Helsinki	7 Aug
47.91		Jackson			1	Pre	Eugene	4 Jun
47.92		Jackson			1	GP	Madrid	16 Jul
47.95		Carter			2	Pre	Eugene	4 Jun
47.97		Jackson			1		Monterrey	11 Jun
47.98		Jackson			1	SGP	London (CP)	22 Jul
48.03		Carter			3	NC	Carson	26 Jun
48.05		Carter			1	Gaz	Saint-Denis	1 Jul
48.05		Jackson			1	WAF	Monaco	10 Sep
48.07		Jackson			1	DNG	Stockholm	26 Jul
48.09		Brazell			4	NC	Carson	26 Jun
48.09	Kemel	Thompson	JAM	25.9.74	2	WAF	Monaco	10 Sep
48.09	Kenji	Narisako	JPN	25.7.84	1	NSF	Okayama	24 Oct
48.10	Dai	Tamesue	JPN	3.5.78	3	WCh	Helsinki	9 Aug
48.11	L.J. (Louis)	van Zyl	RSA	20.7.85	3	WAF	Monaco	10 Sep
48.14		Thompson			1	NC	Kingston	25 Jun
48.14		Jackson			1	WK	Zürich	19 Aug
48.16		van Zyl			1	SGP	Athína	14 Jun
48.16		van Zyl			1s2	WCh	Helsinki	7 Aug
48.16		Thompson			1	GP	Rieti	28 Aug
48.18		Clement			4	WCh	Helsinki	9 Aug
48.19		Jackson			1s3	WCh	Helsinki	7 Aug
	(30/9)							
48.24	Periklis	Iakovákis	GRE	24.3.79	2	SGP	Athína	14 Jun
48.24	Félix	Sánchez	DOM	30.8.77	3s1	WCh	Helsinki	7 Aug
48.27	Naman	Keïta	FRA	9.4.78	2	Gaz	Saint-Denis	1 Jul
48.46	Pieter	de Villiers	RSA	13.7.82	2rB	Athl	Lausanne	5 Jul
48.51	Kenneth	Ferguson	USA	22.3.84	2		Carson	22 May
48.53	Danny	McFarlane	JAM	14.2.72	2	GGala	Roma	8 Jul
48.55	Micheal	Tinsley	USA	21.4.84	3	NCAA	Sacramento	11 Jun
48.57	Llewellyn	Herbert	RSA	21.7.77	2	NC	Durban	16 Apr
48.58	Ian	Weakley	JAM	24.2.74	2	GP	Osaka	7 May
48.59	Brandon	Johnson	USA	6.3.85	4	NCAA	Sacramento	11 Jun
48.66	Masahira	Yoshikata	JPN	23.8.82	3		Yokohama	19 Sep
	(20)							

Mark	Name		Nat	Born	Pos	Meet	Venue	Date
48.74	LaRon	Bennett	USA	25.11.82	5	NCAA	Sacramento	11 Jun
48.75	Alwyn	Myburgh	RSA	13.10.80	1		Stellenbosch	11 Mar
48.78	Marek	Plawgo	POL	25.2.81	4	SGP	Athína	14 Jun
48.78	Dean	Griffiths	JAM	27.1.80	3	NC	Kingston	25 Jun
48.79	Lueroy	Colquhoun	JAM	1.3.80	4	NC	Kingston	25 Jun
48.83	Jirí	Muzík	CZE	1.9.76	6	SGP	Athína	14 Jun
48.84	Gianni	Carabelli	ITA	30.5.79	8	GGala	Roma	8 Jul
48.93	Ockert	Cilliers	RSA	21.4.81	2	GS	Ostrava	9 Jun
48.95	Gregory	Little	JAM	20.2.83	3	GP	Rieti	28 Aug
48.95	Kazuya	Shogata	JPN	8.7.83	5		Yokohama	19 Sep
	(30)							
49.02	Hadi Soua'an	Al-Somaily	KSA	21.8.76	2	GP	Helsinki	25 Jul
49.11	Sergio	Hierrezuelo	CUB	15.3.82	1	Barr	La Habana	20 May
49.12	Yacnier	Luis	CUB	24.1.82	2	CAC	Nassau	9 Jul
49.17	Christian	Duma	GER	5.2.82	4	ECp-S	Firenze	18 Jun
49.18	Yevgeniy	Meleshenko	KAZ	19.1.81	2	AsiC	Inchon	4 Sep
49.19	Osiris	Martínez	CUB	31.12.79	1		Alcalá de Henares	18 Jun
49.19		Meng Yan	CHN	30.9.80	1	NG	Nanjing	21 Oct
49.21	Rickey	Harris	USA	29.9.81	2		Kingston	7 May
49.23	Takayuki	Koike	JPN	12.10.84	2		Tokyo	3 Jul
49.25A	Wouter	le Roux	RSA-J	17.1.86	3		Potchefstroom	4 Feb
	(40)							
49.26	Bryan	Steele	JAM	23.3.84	5	NC	Kingston	25 Jun
49.26	Edivaldo	Monteiro	POR	28.4.76	1		Annecy	3 Jul
49.33	Sherman	Armstrong	USA	22.9.78	4	Pre	Eugene	4 Jun
49.41	Laurent	Ottoz	ITA	10.4.70	2	MedG	Almeria	2 Jul
49.43	Michal	Uhlík	CZE	9.3.80	1	NC	Kladno	3 Jul
49.43	Naohiro	Kawakita	JPN	18.11.80	3	NSF	Okayama	24 Oct
49.47	Mikael	Jakobsson	SWE	9.1.81	1		Göteborg	14 Jun
49.51A	Francois	Malan	RSA	11.5.81	4		Bloemfontein	11 Feb
49.51	Pat	Brown	USA	.82	1		Louisville	28 May
49.51	Joey	Woody	USA	22.5.73	1		Eagle Rock	5 Jun
	(50)							
49.52	Minás	Alozídis	GRE	7.7.84	1		Szombathely	24 Jul
49.55	Ibrahim	Al-Hamaidi	KSA	28.8.85	1	Is.Sol	Makkah	13 Apr
49.55	Ken	Garrett	USA	9.11.76	3		Kingston	7 May
49.55	O'Neil	Wright	LBR	3.5.80	2		Atlanta	14 May
49.59	Thiago	Bueno	BRA	21.2.83	1	NC	São Paulo	19 Jun
49.60	Rhys	Williams	GBR	27.2.84	1	EU23	Erfurt	16 Jul
49.61	Thomas	Goller	GER	28.10.77	1		Rhede	29 May
49.61	Chris	Rawlinson	GBR	19.5.72	7	SGP	Athína	14 Jun
49.61	Orentheus	Hutcherson	USA	18.11.76	5s1	NC	Carson	25 Jun
49.65	Sébastien	Maillard	FRA	2.5.81	2	NC	Angers	16 Jul
	(60)							
49.65		Zhang Shibao	CHN	12.3.84	3	AsiC	Inchon	4 Sep
49.67	Jonathan	Williams	USA	29.8.83	2	Pac-10	Los Angeles (Ww)	15 May
49.67	kos	Dezsö	HUN	27.4.83	1	NC-23	Budapest	26 Jun
49.67	Matthew	Elias	GBR	25.4.79	1	NC	Manchester (SC)	10 Jul
49.67	Ari-Pekka	Lattu	FIN	22.6.78	1		Lapua	30 Jul
49.69	Ken	Yoshizawa	JPN	7.7.78	2s3	NCAA	Tokyo	3 Jun
49.69	Fred	Sharpe	USA	21.8.78	3		Monterrey	11 Jun
49.72	Cleverson	da Silva	BRA	5.9.73	2	NC	São Paulo	19 Jun
49.78	Aleksandr	Derevyagin	RUS	24.3.79	4	WUG	Izmir	20 Aug
49.80	Quinton	Milner	USA	20.12.74	2		Azusa	17 Jul
	(70)							
49.82	Abraham	Reed-Jones	USA	3.6.82	3	NCAA-r	Bloomington	28 May
49.82	Reuben	McCoy	USA-J	16.3.86	8	NCAA	Sacramento	11 Jun
49.84	Yoshihiro	Chiba	JPN	29.4.79	3		Shizuoka	3 May
49.84	Kyle	Erickson	USA	11.1.81	4		Monterrey	11 Jun
49.84	Mikhail	Lipskiy	RUS	6.3.82	6	WUG	Izmir	20 Aug
49.85	Ondrej	Danek	CZE	26.11.81	2	NC	Kladno	3 Jul
49.85	Dale	Garland	GBR	13.10.80	2rB	LGP	London (CP)	22 Jul
49.86	Bryan	Scott	USA	1.3.85	1	Big 12	Manhattan, KS	15 May
49.86	Yaubel	Poll	CUB	30.7.83	3	Barr	La Habana	20 May
49.88		Zhu Zhi	CHN	25.8.82	3	NG	Nanjing	21 Oct
	(80)							
49.89	Raphael	Fernandes	BRA	8.11.84	2s1	NC	São Paulo	18 Jun
49.89	Matthew	Douglas	GBR	26.11.76	1		La Chaux-de-Fonds	21 Aug
49.90	Hideaki	Kawamura	JPN	15.9.74	7	GP	Osaka	7 May
49.90	Adam	Kunkel	CAN	21.2.81	1	NC	Winnipeg	17 Jul
49.94	William	Porter	USA	15.4.73	1		Houston	3 Jun

Mark	Name		Nat	Born	Pos	Meet	Venue	Date
49.95	Janne	Mäkelä	FIN	2.2.79	2	NC	Pori	17 Jul
49.95	Leonid	Vershinin	BLR	23.6.77	2s1	WUG	Izmir	19 Aug
49.96	Isa	Phillips	JAM	22.4.84	1		Arlington	7 May
49.96	Adrian	Findlay	JAM	1.10.82	4h2	NC	Kingston	24 Jun
49.97	Eduardo Iván	Rodríguez	ESP	7.4.78	7s1	WCh	Helsinki	7 Aug
	(90)							
49.99	Pláton	Gavélas	GRE	21.5.80	3	MedG	Almeria	2 Jul
50.01	Diego	Venâncio	BRA	10.5.85	3	NC	São Paulo	19 Jun
50.02A	Pieter	Koekemoer	RSA	12.1.82	2		Johannesburg	23 Apr
50.03	Mahau	Sugimachi	JPN	13.11.84	1		Maebashi	27 Aug
50.06	Fabrizio	Mori	ITA	28.6.69	6	GP II	Torino	3 Jun
50.06		Tan Chunhua	CHN	13.3.77	2	NC	Shijiazhuang	21 Jun
50.08	Christian	Grossenbacher	SUI	28.1.80	1	NC	Bern (W)	3 Jul
50.08	Heni	Kéchi	FRA	31.8.80	2		Annecy	3 Jul
50.10	Jaret	Campisi	USA	7.2.83	1	Big 10	Columbus	15 May
50.10	Mauricio	Teixeira	BRA	22.3.82	4	NC	São Paulo	19 Jun
	(100)							

Mark	Name		Nat	Born	Date
50.11	Kazuki	Kiriyama	JPN	20.9.83	3 Jul
50.11	Akihiro	Morita	JPN	1.9.83	24 Oct
50.15	Milan	Kotur	CRO-J	15.4.86	23 Jul
50.16	Ibrahima	Maïga	MLI	14.3.79	3 Apr
50.16	LaBoris	Bean	USA	24.10.78	24 Jun
50.18	Eric	Dudley	USA	18.4.80	21 May
50.21	Dwight	Ruff	USA	31.3.83	15 May
50.23	Stepán	Tesarík	CZE	6.7.78	24 May
50.23	Michael	Brown	USA	9.1.79	11 Jun
50.24	Dinsdale	Morgan	JAM	19.11.72	7 May
50.24	Scott	Kautz	USA	12.4.83	10 Jun
50.24A	Julius	Bungei	KEN	16.6.84	18 Jun
50.26	Stéphane	Borloz	SUI	6.12.79	5 Jul
50.26	Cédric	El-Idrissi	SUI	24.3.77	23 Jul
50.28	Henning	Hackelbusch	GER	23.2.82	28 May
50.28	Aleksandr	Borshchenko	RUS	8.6.82	11 Jul
50.29	Andrew	Carruthers	USA	8.3.83	10 Jun
50.29	Salah Eddine	Ghaidi	FRA	12.5.79	16 Jul
50.29	Nick	Stewart	GBR	6.4.79	22 Jul
50.32	Yves	N'Dabian	FRA	28.7.83	28 Aug
50.33	Ben	Clark	USA	25.11.80	7 May
50.35	Ibou	Faye	SEN	13.12.69	12 Apr
50.36	Martin	Leiser	SUI	17.6.78	5 Jul
50.37	Mubarak	Al Nubi	QAT	30.12.77	28 Apr
50.38	Andreas	Wickert	GER	15.2.80	10 Jun
50.38	José Maria	Romera	ESP	2.9.80	24 Jul
50.39	Jussi	Heikkilä	FIN	21.3.83	16 Jul
50.42		Qian Chunbo	CHN	5.7.82	21 Jun
50.42	Brendan	Cole	AUS	29.5.81	1 Dec
50.43	Yosuke	Tsushima	JPN	24.12.81	9 Oct
50.45	Denis	de Santana	BRA	8.12.82	18 Jun
50.46	Shane	Charles	GRN	23.8.83	15 May
50.46	Piet	Deveughele	BEL	3.6.77	11 Jun
50.46	Liam	Collins	GBR	23.10.78	10 Jul
50.46	Mitsuo	Otsuka	JPN	24.12.83	18 Sep
50.47	Eronilde	de Araújo	BRA	31.12.70	11 Jun
50.50	Seth	Mbow	SEN	2.4.85	12 Apr
50.50	John	Cassleman	USA	16.8.84	15 May
50.51	Naoki	Ihara	JPN	22.4.82	24 Oct
50.51	Dane	Richter	AUS	6.1.81	13 Nov
50.54A	Ben	Gardner	USA	14.9.84	14 May
50.54	Eric	Thomas	USA	1.12.73	5 Jun
50.54	Corrado	Agrillo	ITA	31.10.74	19 Jun
50.56	Andrés	Silva	URU-J	27.3.86	8 May
50.57	Adrian	Walker	USA	1.10.83	28 May
50.57	Susumu	Saito	JPN	5.5.84	2 Jun
50.57	Shuhei	Takabayashi	JPN	5.12.84	3 Jul
50.58	Claudio	Citterio	ITA	1.8.79	21 Jul
50.59	Tomohide	Ninagawa	JPN	6.7.82	15 May
50.60	Abderahmane	Hamadi	ALG	.84	12 Apr
50.60	Nick	O'Brien	NZL	3.1.80	17 Dec
50.61	Obiamlam	Ikwuakor	USA	13.8.84	15 May
50.61	Andrey	Kozlovskiy	BLR	29.12.83	1 Jun
50.61	Burke	Bockman	USA	2.9.79	5 Jun
50.61	Greg	Offerman	USA-J	6.9.86	18 Jun
50.61A	Paulo	Villar	COL	28.7.78	20 Aug
50.62	Brian	Derby	USA	18.2.81	2 Apr
50.62	Javier	Culson	PUR	25.7.84	12 Jun
50.62	Bram	Kempkens	NED	19.9.78	25 Jun
50.63	Maurice	Bridges	USA	19.11.80	17 Apr
50.63		Gao Hai	CHN	9.4.85	23 Apr
50.63		Chen Tien-Wen	TPE	1.6.78	19 Oct
50.64	Nathaniel	Garcia	USA	18.3.82	23 Apr
50.64	Terry	Beard	USA	16.2.84	15 May
50.64	Derek	Toshner	USA	20.2.82	5 Jun
50.64	João Carlos	dos Santos	BRA	28.4.75	18 Jun
50.66	Gennadiy	Gorbenko	UKR	22.9.75	28 May
50.66	Tomoyuki	Sumizawa	JPN	9.10.84	16 Jul
50.67	Douglas	Lynes-Bell	BAH	2.1.82	10 Jun
50.69	Yevgeniy	Mikheyko	BLR	24.4.81	28 May
50.73A	Jake	Garlick	USA	12.2.82	14 May
50.73	Jaromír	Odvárka	CZE	3.7.82	3 Jul
50.74	Regan	Nichols	USA	26.7.73	7 May
50.74	Terry	Thornton	USA	.85	14 May
50.74	Fadil	Bellaabouss	FRA-J	15.6.86	3 Jul
50.74	Henning	Kuschewitz	GER	9.4.81	3 Jul
50.75	Mark	Harrison	USA	7.12.82	28 May
50.77	Alonzo	Nelson	USA	29.8.84	14 May
50.78		Liu Xiang	CHN	1.5.83	15 May
50.78	Hamza	Deyaf	USA	4.12.85	28 May
50.78	Javier	Fidalgo	ESP	6.7.77	24 Jul
50.80	Shingo	Akimoto	JPN	7.4.82	3 Jun
50.80	Eelco	van Veldhuijzen	NED	19.7.84	11 Jun
50.83	Kurt	Couto	MOZ	14.5.85	12 Apr
50.83	Laroussi	Titi	TUN	3.5.82	15 Jun
50.83	Abdulgadir	Idriss	SUD-Y	25.5.88	12 Apr
50.84		Chen Zhiwei	CHN	10.2.83	24 Apr
50.84	Elliot	Wood	AUS	6.10.83	14 May
50.84	Badr	El Amine	MAR	21.1.84	2 Jul
50.84	Nick	Brown	USA	5.5.83	16 Jul
50.85	Adrian	Ray	USA	9.10.81	15 May
50.85	Justin	Gaymon (192)	USA-J	13.12.86	18 Jun

Hand timed

Mark	Name		Nat	Born	Date
49.9	Sotirios	Iakovákis	GRE	20.9.82	16 Jul
50.4	Yasser	Lismet	CUB	10.3.85	14 May
50.5	Andrey	Kozlovskiy	BLR	29.12.83	24 May

Best at low altitude: 49.95 Francois Malan RSA 11.5.81 6 NC Durban 16 Apr

JUNIORS

See main list for top 2 juniors. 10 performances by 5 men to 50.67. Additional marks and further juniors:

le Roux	50.60A	4		Krugersdorp	15 Jan					
McCoy	50.02	4	NCAA-r	Bloomington	28 May	50.28	1	PAm-J	Windsor	30 Jul
	50.19	4s2	NCAA	Sacramento	10 Jun	50.67	2h4	NCAA-r	Bloomington	27 May

Mark	Name		Nat	Born	Pos	Meet	Venue	Date
50.15	Milan	Kotur	CRO	15.4.86	1	EJ	Kaunas	23 Jul
50.56	Andrés	Silva	URU	27.3.86	3		Santiago	8 May
50.61	Greg	Offerman	USA	6.9.86	1r4		Greensboro	18 Jun
50.74	Fadil	Bellaabouss	FRA	15.6.86	1		Bondoufle	3 Jul

Mark Name Nat Born Pos Meet Venue Date

50.84 Abdulgadir Idriss SUD-Y 25.5.88 3h2 Is.Sol Makkah 12 Apr
50.85 Justin Gaymon USA 13.12.86 2r4 Greensboro 18 Jun
50.89 Tuncay rs TUR 19.2.86 3h1 MedG Almeria 10 Jul
50.93 Víctor Solarte (10) VEN 6.1.86 1 Caracas 30 Jul
51.06 Jason Richardson USA 4.4.86 2h1 SEC Nashville 13 May
51.08A Johann Hanekom RSA 3.12.86 6 Bloemfontein 11 Feb
51.08 Julius Jiles-Tisdall USA 14.2.86 3 Big12 Manhattan 15 May
51.10 Tavaris Washington USA 18.3.87 1 Indianapolis 31 Jul
51.14 David Greene GBR 11.4.86 2 EJ Kaunas 23 Jul
51.15 Yuki Iwataki JPN 29.11.86 3r2 Tsukuba 11 Jun
51.15 Jun-ya Imai JPN 23.6.87 1 Okayama 24 Oct
51.17 Joseff Robertson JAM 14.5.87 1 Kingston 18 Mar
51.17 Shogo Shimizu JPN 1.10.87 1 Chiba 4 Aug
51.23 Frank Gómez (20) CUB .86 3 La Habana 18 Mar

HIGH JUMP

2.40i Stefan Holm SWE 25.5.76 1 EI Madrid 6 Mar
2.20/1 2.24/1 2.27/1 2.30/1 2.32/1 2.34/1 2.38/2 2.40/2 2.42/xxx
2.36 2= GGala Roma 8 Jul 2.20/1 2.24/1 2.27/1 2.30/1 2.33/2 2.36/2 2.40/xxx
2.35i 3 Arnstadt 5 Feb 2.20/1 2.25/2 2.28/1 2.31/1 2.33/1 2.35/1 2.39/x
2.33i 2 Göteborg 3 Feb 2.16/1 2.21/1 2.25/1 2.28/1 2.31/1 2.33/1 2.35/x 2.37/xx
2.33 1 DNG Stockholm 26 Jul 2.20/1 2.24/1 2.27/1 2.30/2 2.33/3 2.37/xxx
2.38i Yaroslav Rybakov RUS 22.11.80 1 Stockholm 15 Feb
2.21/1 2.26/1 2.29/1 2.32/1 2.34/1 2.38/3
2.38i 2 EI Madrid 6 Mar 2.24/1 2.27/1 2.30/1 2.32/1 2.34/1 2.36/1 2.38/2 2.40xx
2.42/x
2.37i 1 Arnstadt 5 Feb 2.20/1 2.25/1 2.28/1 2.31/1 2.33/1 2.35/1 2.37/1 2.39/xxx
2.35i 1 Göteborg 3 Feb 2.21/1 2.25/1 2.28/1 2.31/2 2.33/1 2.35/1 2.37/xxx
2.35i 1 Karlstad 24 Feb 2.24/1 2.30/1 2.33/2 2.35/2 2.40/xxx
2.33i 1 Chelyabinsk 9 Jan
2.33 4 GGala Roma 8 Jul 2.20/1 2.24/1 2.27/1 2.30/1 2.33/2 2.36/xxx
2.38 Jacques Freitag RSA 11.6.82 1 Oudtshoorn 5 Mar
2.10/1 2.15/1 2.20/1 2.25/2 2.30/2 2.33/1 2.38/3
2.35 1 NC Durban 16 Apr 2.15/1. 2.20/1 2.25/1 2.30/2 2.35/2 2.40/xxx
2.38 Andrey Sokolovskiy UKR 16.7.78 1 GGala Roma 8 Jul
2.15/1 2.20/1 2.24/1 2.27/1 2.30/2 2.33/1 2.36/1 2.38/1 2.40/xxx
2.33i 1 Wuppertal 21 Jan 2.14/1 2.21/2 2.24/1 2.27/1 2.30/3 2.33/3 2.37/xxx
2.33i 4 Arnstadt 5 Feb 2.20/1 2.25/2 2.28/1 2.31/3 2.33/1 2.35/xxx
2.33 2 Langen 26 Jun
2.37i Jaroslav Bába CZE 2.9.84 2 Arnstadt 5 Feb
2.20/1 2.25/1 2.28/1 2.33/2 2.35/1 2.37/3 2.39/xxx
2.36 2= GGala Roma 8 Jul 2.20/1 2.24/1 2.27/1 2.30/1 2.33/2 2.36/2 2.38/x 2.40/xx
2.35i 1 Hustopece 22 Jan 2.15/1 2.20/1 2.25/2 2.27/1 2.31/3 2.35/2 2.37/xxx
2.34i 2 Stockholm 15 Feb 2.21/1 2.26/2 2.29/2 2.32/x 2.34/2 2.38/xxx
2.34i 1 Jablonec nad Nisou 11 Mar 2.20/1 2.27/1 2.30/2 2.34/3 2.38/xxx
2.33i 1 Banská Bystrica 8 Feb 2.20/1 2.25/1 2.31/2 2.33/1 2.38/xxx
2.36 Michal Bieniek POL 17.5.84 1 Biala Podlaska 28 May
2.18/1 2.24/1 2.28/3 2.32/3 2.36/1 2.39/x
2.34 1 NC Biala Podlaska 26 Jun 2.18/1 2.22/1 2.28/1 2.30/1 2.34/1
2.35 Víctor Moya CUB 24.10.82 1 WAF Monaco 10 Sep
2.15/1 2.20/1 2.25/1 2.29/1 2.32/3 2.35/1
2.34i Aleksey Dmitrik RUS 12.4.84 1 5N Glasgow 29 Jan
2.10/1 2.15/1 2.20/1 2.23/1 2.26/1 2.29/1 2.32/3 2.34/3 2.36/x
2.33i Svatoslav Ton CZE 20.10.78 1 Brno 22
2.15/1 2.19/1 2.23/1 2.27/1 2.30/3 2.33/1 2.35/xx2.38/x
2.33 Yuriy Krimarenko (10) UKR 11.8.83 1 Langen 26 Jun
2.33 Vyacheslav Voronin RUS 5.4.74 1 Eberstadt 21 Aug
... 2.24/1 2.27/1 2.33/3
(31/11)
2.32i Alessandro Talotti ITA 7.10.80 3 5N Glasgow 29 Jan
2.32i Pavel Fomenko RUS 29.6.76 3 EI Madrid 6 Mar
2.32 Andrey Tereshin RUS 15.12.82 2 NC Tula 13 Jul
2.31i Matt Hemingway USA 24.10.72 5 Arnstadt 5 Feb
2.31i Linus Thörnblad SWE 6.3.85 1 NC Malmö 12 Feb
2.31i Dragutin Topic SCG 12.3.71 1 Balk Athína 16 Feb
2.31A Kyle Lancaster USA 15.8.83 1 El Paso 2 Apr
2.30i Tora Harris USA 21.9.78 1 Trinec 26 Jan
2.30i Andrea Bettinelli ITA 6.10.78 Q EI Madrid 5 Mar
(20)
2.30 Ramsey Carelse RSA 30.10.85 2 Oudtshoorn 5 Mar
2.30 Adam Shunk USA 29.8.79 1 Santo Domingo 14 May

Mark	Name		Nat	Born	Pos	Meet	Venue	Date
2.30	Grzegorz	Sposób	POL	12.2.76	2		Biala Podlaska	28 May
2.30	Nicola	Ciotti	ITA	5.10.76	2	ECp-S	Firenze	17 Jun
2.30	Roman	Fricke	GER	23.3.77	1		Bühl	24 Jun
2.30	Ivan	Ukhov	RUS-J	29.3.86	1	NC-j	Tula	4 Jul
2.30	James	Nieto	USA	2.11.76	6	GGala	Roma	8 Jul
2.30	Jesse	Williams	USA	27.12.83	2	DNG	Stockholm	26 Jul
2.30	Aleksander	Walerianczyk	POL	1.9.82	1	WUG	Izmir	18 Aug
2.29	Lisvany	Pérez	CUB	24.1.82	1	NC	La Habana	18 Mar
	(30)							
2.29	Gennadiy	Moroz	BLR	27.5.78	1		Dudelange	3 Jul
2.29	Mark	Boswell	CAN	28.7.77	4	WCh	Helsinki	14 Aug
2.29	Giulio	Ciotti	ITA	5.10.76	2	Déca	Paris (C)	3 Sep
2.28i	Robert	Wolski	POL	8.12.82	2	NC	Spala	20 Feb
2.28A	Mickaël	Hanany	FRA	25.3.83	1		El Paso	16 Apr
2.28	Aleksandr	Nartov	UKR-Y	21.5.88	1		Kiev	28 May
2.28	Marko	Aleksejev	EST	14.2.79	2		Bühl	24 Jun
2.28	Andrey	Silnov	RUS	9.9.84	2	Znam	Kazan	24 Jun
2.28	László	Boros	HUN	3.2.82	1	NC	Debrecen	6 Jul
2.28	Sergey	Klyugin	RUS	24.3.74	4	NC	Tula	13 Jul
	(40)							
2.28	Grégory	Gabella	FRA	22.6.80	1	NC	Angers	15 Jul
2.27i	Stefan	Vasilache	ROM	9.5.79	1	NC	Bucuresti	12 Feb
2.27i	Tomás	Janku	CZE	27.12.74	2		Brno	22 Feb
2.27i	Ben	Challenger	GBR	7.3.78	3		Brno	22 Feb
2.27i	Kyriacos	Ioannou	CYP	26.7.84	2		Weinheim	23 Feb
2.27i	Javier	Bermejo	ESP	23.12.78	9Q	EI	Madrid	5 Mar
2.27		Zhang Shufeng	CHN	14.11.85	1	NC	Shijiazhuang	21 Jun
2.27	Naoyuki	Daigo	JPN	18.1.81	1		Osaka	26 Jun
2.27	Keith	Moffatt	USA	20.6.84	3	NC	Carson	26 Jun
2.27	Germaine	Mason	JAM	1.4.83	10	GGala	Roma	8 Jul
	(50)							
2.27	Cedric	Norman	USA	5.10.81	1		Viersen	10 Jul
2.27		Huang Haiqiang	CHN-Y	8.2.88	1	WY	Marrakech	16 Jul
2.27	Oskari	Frösén	FIN	24.1.76	1	NC	Pori	17 Jul
2.27	Heikki	Taneli	FIN	12.6.80	2	NC	Pori	17 Jul
2.27	Artyom	Zaytsev	BLR	7.12.84	2	EU23	Erfurt	17 Jul
2.27	Manjula Kumara	Wijesekara	SRI	30.1.84	1	AsiC	Inchon	4 Sep
2.26i	Andra	Manson	USA	30.4.84	1	Big 12	Lincoln	12 Feb
2.26i	Scott	Sellers	USA-J	16.8.86	1		Houston	12 Feb
2.26	Yunier	Carrillo	CUB	1.10.81	3	NC	La Habana	18 Mar
2.26	Steve	Wolf	USA	19.7.82	3	NCAA	Sacramento	11 Jun
	(60)							
2.26	Eike	Onnen	GER	3.8.82	1	NC	Wattenscheid	3 Jul
2.26A	Gilmar	Mayo	COL	30.9.69	1	Bolivar	Armenia/COL	20 Aug
2.26sq	Dimitriy	Demyanyuk	UKR	30.6.83	1		Berdichev	21 Sep
	2.25				1		Tarvisio	31 Jul
2.25i	Artyom	Kozbanov	UKR	18.7.83	4		Ostrava	29 Jan
2.25i	Stéphane	Toinon	FRA	16.10.83	1	NC-23	Paris	13 Feb
2.25i	Michael	Morrison	USA	4.3.84	1	SEC	Fayetteville	26 Feb
2.25	Gerardo	Martínez	MEX	9.3.79	3=	MSR	Walnut	17 Apr
2.25	Niki	Palli	ISR-J	28.5.87	1	Macc	Tel Aviv	12 Jul
2.25	Matthias	Haverney	GER	21.7.85	5	EU23	Erfurt	17 Jul
2.25	Ondrej	Balcar	CZE	2.3.81	1		Litomysl	30 Jul
	(70)							
2.25	Nick	Moroney	AUS	3.8.72	1		Sydney	12 Nov
2.24i	Rozle	Prezelj	SLO	26.9.79	1		Ljubljana	29 Jan
2.24i	Andrey	Chubsa	BLR	29.11.82	1		Minsk	13 Feb
2.24i	Filippo	Campioli	ITA	21.2.82	3	NC	Ancona	20 Feb
2.24	Wilbert	Pennings	NED	12.2.75	1		Herentals	8 Jun
2.24		Wang Hao	CHN	2.2.85	1	Asi GP	Sidoarjo	18 Jun
2.24	Dusty	Jonas	USA-J	19.4.86	1	NC-j	Carson	23 Jun
2.24	Jan-Peter	Larsen	NED	18.3.79	3		Langen	26 Jun
2.24	Martyn	Bernard	GBR	15.12.84	1	NC-23	Bedford	2 Jul
2.24	Aleksandr	Veryutin	BLR	18.11.79	1	NC	Brest	3 Jul
	(80)							
2.24	Wojciech	Theiner	POL-J	25.6.86	1		Kraków	1 Oct
2.24	Mustapha	Raïfak	FRA	9.9.75	1	Franc	Niamey	16 Dec
2.23i	Michael	Diaz	FRA	28.10.86	1		Mayenne	16 Jan
2.23i	Jan	Janku	CZE	10.8.71	2		Hustopece	22 Jan
2.23i	Stanislav	Malyarenko	RUS	19.5.85	2		Hustopece	22 Jan
2.23	Dailén	Ortega	CUB	24.7.83	3		La Habana	27 Jan

Mark	Name		Nat	Born	Pos	Meet	Venue	Date
2.23i	Marcus	Harris	USA	5.5.83	1		Houston	29 Jan
2.23i	Terrance	Woods	USA	18.4.79	2	Mill	New York	4 Feb
2.23i	Shane	Lavy	USA	15.2.76	1		Lincoln	5 Feb
2.23i	Henry (90)	Patterson	USA	27.5.75	1		Akron	5 Feb
2.23i	Aaron	Plas	USA	10.1.84	2		Lincoln	26 Feb
2.23	Tomasz	Smialek	POL	16.1.81	2		Athens, OH	14 May
2.23	Tom	Parsons	GBR	5.5.84	1		Birmingham	19 Jun
2.23	Daniel	Rodríguez	VEN	21.9.83	1		La Habana	24 Jun
2.23	Viktor	Shapoval	UKR	17.10.79	1		Kiev	24 Jul
2.23sq	Aleksandr	Shustov	RUS	13.8.84	3=		Berdichev	21 Sep

Mark	Name		Nat	Born	Date
2.22i	Ivan	Varbanov	BUL	27.2.77	22 Jan
2.22i	Rainer	Piirimets	EST	29.9.83	20 Feb
2.22	William	Littleton	USA	14.10.83	10 Mar
2.22i	Jim	Dilling (100)	USA		28 Apr
2.22	Robbie	Grabarz	GBR-J	3.10.87	19 Jun
2.22	Stefan	Häfner	GER	30.1.84	24 Jun
2.22	Osku	Torro	FIN	21.8.79	7 Jul
2.22	Kwaku	Boateng	CAN	30.6.74	16 Jul
2.22	Sylwester	Bednarek	POL-Y	28.4.89	18 Sep
2.21i	Andrey	Karmelyuk	UKR	9.2.79	29 Jan
2.21i	Sergey	Goleshev	BLR	30.6.84	19 Feb
2.21i	Vladimir	Kisil	RUS	3.5.84	27 Feb
2.21	Fábio	Baptista	BRA	19.10.84	13 Mar
2.21	Alex	Marbley	USA	29.4.83	30 Apr
2.21	Dimitrios	Sirrákos	GRE	26.1.74	11 Jun
2.21	Yiannis	Constantinou	CYP	23.3.78	22 Jun
2.21	Zoltán	Vaskó	HUN	17.4.84	15 Jul
2.21	Martin	Günther	GER-J	8.10.86	20 Aug
2.21		Liang Tong	CHN	30.5.78	19 Oct
2.21	Pyotr	Brayko	RUS	27.3.77	4 Dec
2.21i	Robert	DeVaul	USA		10 Dec
2.20A	Zieg	Veenemans	RSA	13.5.83	15 Jan
2.20i	Mark	Dillon	CAN	6.10.84	22 Jan
2.20i	Kevin	Netzer	USA	22.8.81	22 Jan
2.20i	Peter	Horák	SVK	7.12.83	29 Jan
2.20i	Robert	Mitchell	GBR	14.9.80	12 Feb
2.20i	Marat	Rakipov	RUS	7.6.79	12 Feb
2.20i	Mikhail	Tsvetkov	RUS	4.5.80	12 Feb
2.20i	Branko	Djuricic	SCG	5.1.81	16 Feb
2.20i	Mihail	Tomarás	GRE	3.9.81	20 Feb
2.20	Rodrigo	Santos	BRA	6.5.81	26 Feb
2.20i		Xu Xin	CHN	20.10.83	6 Mar
2.20	Omar Moussa	Al-Masrahi	KSA	17.2.78	15 Apr
2.20	Tristian	Whitley	USA	17.11.77	16 Apr

Mark	Name		Nat	Born	Date
2.20	Lawrence	Hutchinson	USA		16 Apr
2.20		Hu Tong	CHN-J	28.1.86	23 Apr
2.20		Li Bing	CHN	1.2.79	23 Apr
2.20		Chen Hung-Chieh	TPE	10.12.80	3 May
2.20A	Kabelo	Mmono	BOT	4.2.80	7 May
2.20	Stijn	Stroobants	BEL	15.4.84	7 May
2.20A	Jaswinder	Gill	CAN	23.12.81	14 May
2.20	Michael	Mason	CAN-J	30.9.86	14 May
2.20		Wang Zhouzhou	CHN	20.4.77	21 May
2.20	Matthias	Franta	GER	4.12.84	26 May
2.20	Ruslan	Glivinskiy	UKR	7.2.75	28 May
2.20	Nikólaos	Giósis	GRE	22.9.80	30 May
2.20	Olivér	Harsányi	HUN-J	20.3.87	4 Jun
2.20	Enrique	Márquez	ESP	4.3.77	8 Jun
2.20A	Onnanye	Ramohube	BOT	2.3.79	11 Jun
2.20	Marios	Iacovou	CYP	6.7.84	11 Jun
2.20	Sandro	Finesi	ITA	5.4.80	12 Jun
2.20	Vadim	Kolesnikov	RUS	24.5.85	15 Jun
2.20	Jean-Claude	Rabbath	LIB	12.7.77	18 Jun
2.20	Henderson	Dottin	BAR	4.1.80	19 Jun
2.20		Liu Yang	CHN-J	4.1.86	21 Jun
2.20	Abderrahmane	Hammad	ALG	27.5.77	23 Jun
2.20	Martin	Buss	GER	7.4.76	3 Jul
2.20	Samson	Oni	GBR	25.6.81	10 Jul
2.20	Darryl	Stone	GBR	6.6.83	10 Jul
2.20	Trevor	Barry	BAH	.83	11 Jul
2.20	Ivan	Sorokin	RUS	24.8.81	13 Jul
2.20	Yeóryios	Bóhtsos	GRE	5.12.81	24 Jul
2.20	Jovan	Vukicevic	SCG-J	23.10.87	28 Aug
2.20		Lee Hup Wei	MAS-J	5.5.87	26 Sep
2.20	Yoshihiko	Edo	JPN	25.7.83	16 Oct
2.20	Eduard	Sebestyén (162)	ROM	11.3.81	16 Dec

Exhibition

Mark	Name		Nat	Born	Date
2.20	Dalibor	Hon	CZE	2.8.78	14 Sep

Best outdoor marks

Mark	Name	Pos	Meet	Venue	Date
2.36	Bába	2=	GGala	Roma	8 Jul
2.36	Holm	2=	GGala	Roma	8 Jul
2.33	Rybakov	4	GGala	Roma	8 Jul
2.30	Ton	1		Turnov	24May
2.30	Dmitrik	1	ECp-S	Firenze	17 Jun
2.30	Topic	1		Réthimno	10 Jul
2.29	T Harris	2		Shanghai	17 Sep
2.28	Fomenko	1	Znam	Kazan	24 Jun
2.27	Ioannou	5	SGP	Athína	14 Jun
2.27	Hemingway	1	NC	Carson	26 Jun

Mark	Name	Pos	Meet	Venue	Date
2.27	Bettinelli	9	GGala	Roma	8 Jul
2.27	Challenger	1	NC	Manchester (SC)	10Jul
2.26	Sellers	1	TexR	Austin	8 Apr
2.26	Wolski	1		Poznan	21May
2.26	Thrnblad	1		Vellinge	3Aug
2.25	Kozbanov	1		Yalta	28May
2.24	T Janku	3		Viersen	10 Jul
2.23	Morrison	1	SEC	Nashville	14May
2.23	Manson	1	Big 12	Manhattan, KS	15May
2.23	Plas	1	Big 12	Manhattan, KS	15May

Mark	Name	Date
2.22	Vasilache	2 Jul
2.22	Talotti	27 Jul
2.21	J Janku	26 Jun
2.21	Toinon	6 Aug
2.20	M Harris	26 Mar
2.20	Woods	7 May
2.20	Goleshev	23 May
2.20	Chubsa	1 Jun
2.20	Shustov	15 Jun
2.20	Malyarenko	15 Jun
2.20	Bermejo	17 Jun
2.21 exh		26 Aug
2.20	Campioli	26 Jun
2.20	Tsvetkov	13 Jul
2.20	Mitchell	24 Jul
2.20	Prezelj	24 Jul
2.20	Piirimets	16 Aug
2.20	Horák	15 Sep

JUNIORS

See main list for top 7 juniors. 10 performances by 5 men to 2.25. Additional marks and further juniors:

	Mark	Pos	Meet	Venue	Date	Mark	Pos	Venue	Date
Ukhov	2.30	3	NC	Tula	13 Jul	2.27	6	Eberstadt	21 Aug
	2.29i	1		Yekaterinburg	7 Jan	2.25	2	Zhukovskiy	24 Sep

Mark	Name		Nat	Born	Pos	Meet	Venue	Date
2.22	Robbie	Grabarz	GBR	3.10.87	1		Ware	19 Jun
2.22	Sylwester	Bednarek	POL-Y	28.4.89	1		Warszawa	18 Sep
2.21	Martin	Günther (10)	GER	8.10.86	1		Eberstadt	20 Aug
2.20		Hu Tong	CHN	28.1.86	2		Zhongshan	23 Apr
2.20	Michael	Mason	CAN	30.9.86	2	SEC	Nashville	14 May
2.20	Olivér	Harsányi	HUN	20.3.87	1		Budapest	4 Jun
2.20		Liu Yang	CHN	4.1.86	5	NC	Shijiazhuang	21 Jun
2.20	Jovan	Vukicevic	SCG	23.10.87	2	SER Ch	Kragujevac	28 Aug
2.20		Lee Hup Wei	MAS	5.5.87	1		Paroi	26 Sep

Mark	Name		Nat	Born	Pos	Meet	Venue	Date	
2.19i	Andrey	Kravchenko	BLR	4.1.86	1H		Tallinn	5 Feb	
2.19	Torlarp	Sudjinda	THA-Y	1.2.89	1		Bangkok	3 Jun	
2.18i	Ivan	Ilyichev	RUS	12.8.86	1		Moskva	19 Jan	
	2.18				2	NC-j	Tula	4 Jul	
2.18	Sergey	Milokumov (20)	RUS	13.11.87	3	NC-j	Tula	4 Jul	
2.18	Alex	Soto	ESP	25.9.88	3	WY	Marrakesh	16 Jul	
2.18	Mikael	Rajala	FIN	12.3.87	4	NC	Pori	17 Jul	

POLE VAULT

Mark	Name		Nat	Born	Pos	Meet	Venue	Date	Series
6.00	Paul	Burgess	AUS	14.8.79	1		Perth	26 Feb	5.85/1 6.00/1 6.06/x
5.95					1		Perth	12 Feb	5.70/1 5.85/1 5.95/1 6.00/xx
5.91					1		Perth	15 Jan	5.60/1 5.80/2 5.91/3 6.00/xxx
5.85					1		Perth	18 Jun	5.70/2 5.85/3 5.95/xxx
5.96	Brad	Walker	USA	21.6.81	1	GP	Rieti	28 Aug	5.66/1 5.81/3 5.96/3 6.04/xxx
5.90					1	Pre	Eugene	4 Jun	5.50/1 5.60/2 5.70/1 5.80/1 5.90/3 6.04/xxx
5.90					1	BrGP	Sheffield	21 Aug	5.50/3 5.70/xx5.75/1 5.85/x 5.90/2 6.04/xxx
5.86					1	WAF	Monaco	9 Sep	5.60/1 5.70/1 5.86/1 6.04/xxx
5.83i					1		Reno	21 Jan	5.45/2 5.60/1 5.70/3 5.83/2 5.92/xxx
5.93	Tim	Lobinger	GER	3.9.72	1	ISTAF	Berlin	4 Sep	5.63/2 5.73/3 5.83/2 5.93/2 6.01/xx6.16/x
5.85					1		Düsseldorf	17 Sep	
5.82					1	FBK	Hengelo	29 May	5.50/3 5.65/1 5.75/2 5.82/2 5.88/xxx
5.90i	Igor	Pavlov	RUS	18.7.79	1	EI	Madrid	5 Mar	5.50/1 5.70/2 5.75/1 5.80/1 5.85/2 5.90/1 5.95/x 6.00/x
5.90	Toby	Stevenson	USA	19.11.76	2	Pre	Eugene	4 Jun	5.50/1 5.60/2 5.70/1 5.80/3 5.90/3 6.04/xxx
5.90					1		Monterrey	11 Jun	
5.85					1	ModR	Modesto	7 May	5.50/2 5.65/2 5.75/2 5.85/3 6.04/xxx
5.81					1	GGala	Roma	8 Jul	5.51/1 5.71/3 5.81/1 5.95/xxx
5.87	Steve	Hooker	AUS	16.7.82	1		Melbourne	12 Mar	
5.85i	Derek	Miles	USA	28.9.72	1		Donetsk	12 Feb	5.50/1 5.60/1 5.70/1 5.80/3 5.85/1 5.90/xxx
5.81i					1		Stockholm	15 Feb	5.56/1 5.66/2 5.76/x 5.81/1 5.93/xxx
5.81					2	GP	Rieti	28 Aug	5.56/1 5.66/1 5.76/1 5.81/3 5.91/xxx
5.85i	Denis	Yurchenko	UKR	27.1.78	2	EI	Madrid	5 Mar	5.60/2 5.75/1 5.85/2 5.90/x 5.95/xx
5.85	Tim	Mack	USA	15.9.72	1		Chula Vista	21 May	5.55/1 5.65/1 5.75/2 5.85/2 6.02/xxx
5.85i	Daniel	Ryland (10)	USA	6.8.79	1		Jonesboro	24 Jul	
5.81i					1		Jonesboro	17 Jul	
5.84i	Ruslan	Yeremenko	UKR	31.7.78	1		Stuttgart	29 Jan	5.50/2 5.70/2 5.84/3
5.83	Daichi	Sawano	JPN	16.9.80	1		Shizuoka	3 May	5.53/3 5.63/1 5.73/2 5.83/1 5.93/xxx
5.83	Giuseppe	Gibilisco	ITA	5.1.79	2	ISTAF	Berlin	4 Sep	
5.81					1		Rovereto	31 Aug	5.61/1 5.81/2 5.91/xxx
5.81	Aleksandr	Korchmid	UKR	22.1.82	2		Rovereto	31 Aug	5.41/2 5.61/2 5.71/2 5.81/2
	(30/14)								
5.80	Rens	Blom	NED	1.3.77	1		Rechberghausen	1 May	
5.80	Vladislav	Revenko	UKR	15.11.84	1	ECp-1B	Leiria	19 Jun	
5.80	Björn	Otto	GER	16.10.77	1	WUG	Izmir	18 Aug	
5.77	Lars	Börgeling	GER	16.4.79	1	SGP	Athína	14 Jun	
5.76i	Jeff	Hartwig	USA	25.9.67	1		Karlstad	24 Feb	
5.75	Dmitriy	Markov	AUS	14.3.75	1		Adelaide	12 Feb	
	(20)								
5.75i	Danny	Ecker	GER	21.7.77	1	NC	Sindelfingen	20 Feb	
5.75i	Richard	Spiegelburg	GER	12.8.77	1		Chemnitz	25 Feb	
5.75	Russ	Buller	USA	10.9.78	2	CalR	Modesto	7 May	
5.75	Jacob	Pauli	USA	15.6.79	1	GP II	Stanford	30 May	
5.75	Justin	Norberg	USA	18.7.77	1		Atascadero	15 Jun	
5.75	Jean	Galfione	FRA	9.6.71	1		Saint-Etienne	10 Jul	
5.75	Damiel	Dossévi	FRA	3.2.83	1	EU23	Erfurt	16 Jul	
5.75	Romain	Mesnil	FRA	13.7.77	1		Castres	26 Jul	
5.75	Konstadínos	Filippídis	GRE-J	26.11.86	2	WUG	Izmir	18 Aug	
5.75sq	Alhaji	Jeng	SWE	13.12.81	1		Chiari	6 Sep	
	(30)								
5.73	Patrik	Kristiansson	SWE	3.6.77	1	MAI	Malmö	16 Aug	

Mark	Name		Nat	Born	Pos	Meet	Venue	Date
5.71Ai	Nick	Hysong	USA	9.12.71	1		Flagstaff	19 Jan
5.71i	Bubba	McLean	USA	2.9.79	1=		Jonesboro	12 Jun
5.70i	Spas	Bukhalov	BUL	14.11.80	1		Sofia	12 Feb
5.70i	Fabian	Schulze	GER	7.3.84	2	NC	Sindelfingen	20 Feb
5.70i	Artyom	Kuptsov	RUS	22.4.84	Q	EI	Madrid	4 Mar
5.70	Adam	Keul	USA	27.1.80	1		Nacogdoches	16 Apr
5.70		Liu Feiliang	CHN	27.3.85	4	Pre	Eugene	4 Jun
5.70	Charles	Andureu	FRA	13.2.85	1		Bron	5 Jul
5.70	Ilian	Efremov	BUL	2.8.70	1		Sofia	7 Jul
	(40)							
5.70	Pavel	Gerasimov	RUS	29.5.79	1	Déca	Paris (C)	3 Sep
5.66i	Tommy	Skipper	USA	19.9.84	1		Seattle	12 Feb
5.65i	Maksim	Mazurik	UKR	2.4.83	3	NC	Donetsk	12 Feb
5.65	Giovanni	Lanaro	MEX	27.9.81	1		Fullerton	12 Mar
5.65	Aleksandr	Averbukh	ISR	1.10.74	1		Kuortane	26 Jun
5.65	Dmitriy	Kuptsov	RUS	9.11.82	2	NC	Tula	11 Jul
5.65	Przemyslaw	Czerwinski	POL	28.7.83	2	Déca	Paris (C)	3 Sep
5.65	Okkert	Brits	RSA	22.8.73	1		Bellville	10 Dec
5.63	Jérôme	Clavier	FRA	3.5.83	1		Pierre-Benité	10 Jun
5.62i	Kevin	Rans	BEL	19.8.82	1	NC	Gent	20 Feb
	(50)							
5.61i		Kim Yoo-suk	KOR	19.1.82	1		Seattle	26 Feb
5.61	Róbison	Pratt	MEX	25.2.80	1		Atascadero	20 Jul
5.60iA	Paul	Litchfield	USA	27.11.80	1		Pocatello	4 Feb
5.60i	Mikko	Latvala	FIN	8.7.80	1		Kuortane	6 Feb
5.60i	Adam	Kolasa	POL	2.8.75	1		Spala	12 Feb
5.60i	Jeremy	Scott	USA	1.5.81	1		Fayetteville	12 Feb
5.60i	Igor	Alekseyev	BLR	7.4.83	7		Donetsk	12 Feb
5.60i	Vesa	Rantanen	FIN	2.12.75	11=Q	EI	Madrid	4 Mar
5.60i	Javier	Gazol	ESP	27.10.80	13Q	EI	Madrid	4 Mar
5.60	Michael	Stolle	GER	17.12.74	1		Dessau	27 May
	(60)							
5.60sq	Adam	Ptácek	CZE	8.10.80	1		Praha	15 Jun
	5.60				2	ECp-S	Firenze	19 Jun
5.60	Leonid	Andreyev	UZB	6.11.83	1		Dushanbe	24 Jun
5.60	Matti	Mononen	FIN	25.11.83	1		Somero	3 Jul
5.60	Vincent	Favretto	FRA	5.4.84	2		Bron	5 Jul
5.60	Pierre-Charles	Peuf	FRA	27.4.79	1	NC	Angers	16 Jul
5.60	Nick	Buckfield	GBR	5.6.73	9	BrGP	Sheffield	21 Aug
5.55i	Laurens	Looije	NED	12.1.73	1		Luxembourg	29 Jan
5.55i	Jesper	Fritz	SWE	13.9.85	1		Malmö	5 Feb
5.55	Ray	Scotten	USA	20.5.83	1		Norman	16 Apr
5.55	Gabe	Baldwin	USA	9.1.85	1	DrakeR	Des Moines	29 Apr
	(70)							
5.55	Guillaume	Savary	FRA	11.2.81	1		La Roche-sur-Yon	11 Jun
5.55	Sébastien	Homo	FRA	27.4.82	2	NC	La Roche-sur-Yon	20 Jul
5.55	Germán	Chiaraviglio	ARG-J	16.4.87	1		Santa Fe	4 Sep
5.53i	Piotr	Buciarski	DEN	22.11.75	6		Münster	25 Aug
5.51	Dennis	Kholev	ISR	21.10.75	1		Tel Aviv	7 May
5.51	John	Russell	USA	9.10.83	1	NCAA-r	Bloomington	28 May
5.51	Stepán	Janácek	CZE	12.6.77	1		Pardubice	7 Sep
5.51i	Joël	Soler	FRA	15.2.82	1		Aulnay-sous-Bois	10 Dec
5.50i	Scott	Martin	USA	8.3.84	1eB		Reno	21 Jan
5.50i	Mark	Zilch	USA	.82	1		Ames	29 Jan
	(80)							
5.50i	Tye	Harvey	USA	25.9.74	5	Mill	New York	4 Feb
5.50i	Thibaut	Duval	BEL	1.2.79	2		Carrières-sous-Poissy	5 Feb
5.50i	Andrey	Chemov	RUS	13.7.83	1		Moskva	8 Feb
5.50i	Alexandre	Barbaud	FRA	15.2.80	2		Aubière	11 Feb
5.50i	Yevgeniy	Mikhaylichenko	RUS	13.2.79	2	NC	Vologograd	11 Feb
5.50i	Paul	Gensic	USA	27.6.82	3	NCAA	Fayetteville	11 Mar
5.50A	Trent	Powell	USA	25.6.78	1		Provo	1 Apr
5.50A	Pat	Manson	USA	29.11.67	1		Colorado Springs	2 Apr
5.50	Rocky	Danners	USA	21.6.81	1		Knoxville	15 Apr
5.50	Eric	Eshbach	USA	4.2.81	1		Wichita	16 Apr
	(90)							
5.50	Mike	Westlund	USA	24.3.80	1		Arlington	7 May
5.50	Kurt	Hanna	USA	23.4.75	3		Phoenix	13 May
5.50		Zhang Hongwei	CHN	26.4.75	1		Chongqing	15 May
5.50	Randy	Flach	USA	.84	1		Huntsville	15 May
5.50	Nicolas	Guigon	FRA	10.10.80	6=	GP II	Milano	1 Jun

Mark	Name		Nat	Born	Pos	Meet	Venue	Date
5.50	Pavel	Burlachenko	RUS	7.4.76	1B		Tula	14 Jun
5.50	Nicolas	Durand	FRA	23.1.79	2		Clermont-Ferrand	18 Jun
5.50	Yevgeniy	Smiryagin	RUS	17.5.76	1		Sankt-Peterburg	30 Jun
5.50	Dmitriy	Starodubtsev	RUS-J	3.1.86	1	NC-j	Tula	3 Jul
5.50	Fábio (100)	Gomes da Silva	BRA	4.8.83	1		Porto Alegre	9 Jul
5.50	Chris	Tamminga	NED	30.4.74	1	LEAP	Loughborough	16 Jul
5.50	Fabrice	Fortin	FRA	2.2.80	1		Castres	26 Jul
5.50	Alexander	Straub	GER	14.10.83	1		Fribourg	27 Aug

Mark	Name		Nat	Born	Date
5.45i	Aleksandr	Gripich	RUS-J	29.9.86	20 Jan
5.45	Luke	Vedelago	AUS	13.6.80	22 Jan
5.45	Chris	Chappell	USA	24.12.81	16 Apr
5.45	Ben	Allen	USA	1.2.82	16 Apr
5.45	Andrej	Poljanec	SLO	10.11.84	15 May
5.45	Bobby	Most	USA	13.12.82	15 May
5.45	Mohamed	Karbib	MAR	5.6.84	12 Jun
5.45	Takehito	Ariki	JPN	15.1.82	18 Jun
5.45	Giorgio	Piantella	ITA	6.7.81	1 Jul
5.45	Mikhail	Golovtsov	RUS-J	8.6.86	24 Jul
5.45	Olivier	Frey	SUI	11.2.79	18 Aug
5.45		Yang Yansheng	CHN-Y	5.1.88	18 Oct
5.45	Fanie	Jacobs	RSA	21.4.76	19 Nov
5.43i	Johan	Carlsson	SWE	20.2.85	12 Feb
5.42i	Sage	Thames	USA	23.5.82	25 Feb
5.42	Tobias	Scherbarth	GER	17.8.85	23 Jul
5.41i	Chris	Smith	USA	30.12.82	29 Jan
5.41	Makisi	Haleck	ASA		28 May
5.40i	Matt	Phillips	USA	28.12.77	21 Jan
5.40i	Richard	Möcks	GER	15.10.81	22 Jan
5.40i	Nikolay	Ostapenko	RUS-J	21.6.86	24 Jan
5.40i	Pavel	Prokopenko	RUS-J	4.9.87	8 Feb
5.40i	Ralf	Bender	GER	11.6.80	20 Feb
5.40i	Michal	Balner	CZE	12.9.82	26 Feb
5.40i	Brian	Mondschein	USA	9.1.83	5 Mar
5.40i	Brandon	Glenn	USA	30.7.85	11 Mar
5.40	Derek	Mackel	USA	18.11.82	9 Apr
5.40	Spencer	Stephens	USA	3.10.81	16 Apr
5.40	Jon	Takahashi	USA	21.10.82	17 Apr
5.40	Fabian	Mores	LUX	26.9.82	15 May
5.40	Jeff	Ryan	USA	8.12.80	21 May
5.40	Denis	Fedas	UKR	24.8.85	28 May
5.40	Mathieu	Boisrond	FRA	8.1.77	1 Jun
5.40	Satoru	Yasuda	JPN	27.7.75	4 Jun
5.40		Yang Quan	CHN-J	8.12.86	4 Jun
5.40	Brad	Smith	USA	15.10.82	10 Jun
5.40	Tyson	Byers	USA	18.5.83	10 Jun
5.40	Artyom	Matiyenko	UKR	30.8.82	14 Jun
5.40	Yevgeniy	Lukyanenko	RUS	23.1.85	15 Jun
5.40	Jason	Wurster	CAN	23.9.84	21 Jun
5.40	Keith	Higham	GBR	7.11.85	25 Jun
5.40	Björn	Venghaus	GER	5.5.85	25 Jun
5.40	Ales	Honcl	CZE	6.8.75	3 Jul
5.40	Ruslan	Shturkhalyov	UKR	19.10.84	2 Jul
5.40	Artyom	Pilipenko	KAZ-J	9.3.86	8 Jul
5.40	Nikolay	Lavrinenko	RUS	16.5.84	11 Jul
5.40	Julien	Costes	FRA	11.2.79	16 Jul
5.40i	Conrad	Rapp	USA-J	10.1.86	10 Dec
5.39	Chip	Heuser	USA	9.2.85	3 Jul
5.36i	Kevin	Poest	USA	15.8.81	5 Mar
5.35	Alexandr	Miroshnichenko	AUS	28.8.78	26 Jan
5.35i	Erki	Nool	EST	25.6.70	6 Feb
5.35i	Rory	Quiller	USA	14.4.84	18 Feb
5.35i	Jarno	Kivioja	FIN	7.10.82	5 Mar
5.35i	Jon	Derby	USA	16.12.82	5 Mar
5.35	David	Sullivan	USA	20.7.83	23 Apr
5.35	Jurij	Rovan	SLO	23.1.75	30 Apr
5.35	Nicolas	Morent	FRA	15.9.79	10 Jul
5.35	Aleksey	Khanafin	RUS	12.4.81	15 Jul
5.35	Rudy	Bourguignon	FRA	16.7.79	15 Jul
5.35	Joan	Planas	ESP	21.5.81	29 Jul
5.35	Xavier	Tromp	FRA	3.3.84	30 Jul
5.35	Gustaf	Hultgren	SWE	18.8.83	7 Aug
5.35	Steven	Lewis (167)	GBR-J	20.5.86	21 Aug

Best outdoor marks

Mark	Name	Pos	Meet	Venue	Date
5.81	Miles	2	GP	Rieti	28 Aug
5.80	Pavlov	1	NC	Tula	11 Jul
5.75	Ecker	2	NC	Wattenscheid	2 Jul
5.75	Yurchenko	4	BrGP	Sheffield	21 Aug
5.70	Hysong	3		Monterrey	11 Jun
5.70	Schulze	2		Ulm	12 Jun
5.70	Spiegelburg	1		Ingolstadt	25 Jun
5.70	Ryland	2	Gugl	Linz	23 Aug
5.65	Hartwig	5	CalR	Modesto	7 May
5.65	Mazurik	1		Villeneuve d'Ascq	12 Jun
5.60	Latvala	1		Lappeenranta	2 Jun
5.60	Kolasa	2		Barcelona	3 Jun
5.60	Yeremenko	1		Kiev	21 Jun
5.60	Bukhalov	2		Sofia	7 Jul
5.60	Rantanen	1		Lappeenranta	21 Jul
5.60	Rans	3	NA	Heusden-Zolder	23 Jul
5.60	Skipper	4	NA	Heusden-Zolder	23 Jul
5.55	A Kuptsov	2		Moskva	29 Jun
5.55	Looije	2	NC	Amsterdam	10 Jul
5.50	Chemov	1		Schwechat	15May
5.50	Buciarski	1		Fortaleza	18May
5.50	Barbaud	1		Villeneuve-sur-Lot	4 Jun
5.50	Mikhaylichenko	3	ECp-S	Firenze	19 Jun
5.50	Soler	3		Strasbourg	23 Jun
5.50	Alekseyev	1	NC	Brest	3 Jul
5.50	Gazol	1		Zaragoza	9 Jul

Mark	Name	Date
5.46A	Gensic	6 May
5.45	Martin	15 May
5.41	Kim Yoo-suk	14 May
5.40	Möcks	21 May
5.40	Mondschein	10 Jun
5.40	Gripich	25 Jun
5.40	Harvey	23 Jun
5.40	McLean	25 Jun
5.40	Litchfield	25 Jun
5.40	Fritz	16 Jul
5.35	Smith	9 Apr
5.35	Derby	16 Apr

Exhibition

Mark	Name		Nat	Born	Pos	Venue	Date
5.80sq-ex	Ruslan	Yeremenko	UKR	31.7.78	1	Treviso	18 Sep
5.68 ??	Jeff	Hartwig	USA	25.9.67	1	Recklinghausen	28 May
5.60	Stepán	Janácek	CZE	12.6.77	1	Kozienice	23 Sep
5.40	Matteo	Rubbiani	ITA	31.8.78	4	Treviso	18 Sep

JUNIORS

See main list for top 3 juniors. 11 performances by 1 man to 5.60. Additional marks and further juniors:

Name	Mark	Pos	Meet	Venue	Date
Filippídis	5.72	3=	SGP	Athína	14 Jun
	5.71	2	Veniz	Haniá	6 Jun
	5.70	2	GP II	Milano	1 Jun
	5.70	1	v2N	Barcelona	3 Jun
	5.66	6	GP	Rieti	28 Aug
	5.65	2	ECp1B	Leiria	19 Jun
	5.63	4=	ISTAF	Berlin	4 Sep
	5.61i	1		Athína (P)	29 Jan
	5.60i	9=Q	EI	Madrid	4 Mar
	5.60	1	Med G	Almeria	1 Jul

Mark	Name		Nat	Born	Pos	Meet	Venue	Date
5.45i	Aleksandr	Gripich	RUS	29.9.86	1		Shakhty	20 Jan
	5.40				1		Tula	25 Jun
5.45	Mikhail	Golovtsov	RUS	8.6.86	2=	EJ	Kaunas	24 Jul

Mark	Wind	Name		Nat	Born	Pos	Meet	Venue	Date
5.45			Yang Yansheng	CHN-Y	5.1.88	2	NG	Nanjing	18 Oct
5.40i		Nikolay	Ostapenko	RUS	21.6.86	1		Sankt-Peterburg	24 Jan
5.40i		Pavel	Prokopenko	RUS	4.9.87	2		Moskva	8 Feb
5.40			Yang Quan	CHN	8.12.86	1		Bangkok	4 Jun
5.40		Artyom	Pilipenko (10)	KAZ	9.3.86	1	NC	Almaty	8 Jul
5.40i		Conrad	Rapp	USA	10.1.86	1		Kent	10 Dec
5.35		Steven	Lewis	GBR	20.5.86	13	BrGP	Sheffield	21 Aug
5.30i		Leonid	Kivalov	RUS-Y	1.4.88	1		Shakhty	20 Jan
5.30i		Mihaíl	Pástos	GRE	5.10.86	3	Balk	Athína (P)	16 Feb
5.30i		Malte	Mohr	GER	24.7.86	1		Saarbrücken	26 Feb
		5.30				1		Potsdam	28 May
5.30		Robbie	Johnson	USA	.86				7 May
5.30		Albert	Velez	ESP-Y	26.10.88	1	NC-y	Valladolid	4 Jun
5.30		Artyom	Burya	RUS	11.4.86	4	NC-j	Tula	3 Jul
5.25		Lukasz	Michalski	POL-Y	17.8.88	1	NC-j	Bydgoszcz	6 Jul
5.25		Scott	Roth (20)	USA-Y	25.6.88	2	WY	Marrakesh	17 Jul

LONG JUMP

Mark	Wind	Name		Nat	Born	Pos	Meet	Venue	Date	Series
8.60	1.6	Dwight	Phillips	USA	1.10.77	1	WCh	Helsinki	13 Aug	
										8.60 x x x x
8.57	0.5					1	Gugl	Linz	23 Aug	8.57 x x x x p
8.47	1.1					1	GP	Madrid	16 Jul	x 8.47 8.34/2.0 8.44/1.3 p x
8.46	0.8					1	WAF	Monaco	10 Sep	8.46 x x 8.33/0.2
8.44	1.3					1	GP	Helsinki	25 Jul	8.44 x x p p x
8.39	0.5					1	GGala	Roma	8 Jul	8.18 x 8.39 x x p
8.39	0.3					1		Shanghai	17 Sep	x 8.02/-0.6 8.11/0.1 8.39 p x
8.38	0.3					2	BrGP	Sheffield	21 Aug	8.36/0.8 x x 8.38 x 8.29/1.6
8.28	0.0					2	NC	Carson	23 Jun	x x 8.23/-0.4 x 8.28 8.23/-0.1
8.26	1.2					1	v2N	Glasgow (S)	5 Jun	x x 8.26 p p
8.59w	1.6					Q	WCh	Helsinki	12 Aug	8.59w only jump
8.45	1.9	Miguel	Pate	USA	13.6.79	1	BrGP	Sheffield	21 Aug	
										x 7.79 8.45 2.92 8.25/0.9 p
8.35	-0.4					1	NC	Carson	23 Jun	x 8.35 p x 8.13/-0.5 p
8.30	1.6					2	WAF	Monaco	10 Sep	8.30 7.94 8.00 x
8.24	0.6					3	GP	Madrid	16 Jul	x 8.16/0.7 8.24 8.13 8.18/0.5 x
8.23	0.2					2		Réthimno	10 Jul	8.00 8.23 8.05 x 8.06 x
8.44	-0.2	Mohamed Salim	Al-Khuwalidi	KSA	19.6.81	1	Is.Sol	Makkah	13 Apr	
										x 8.10/0.3 x x 8.44 x
8.37i		Joan Lino	Martínez	ESP	17.1.78	1	EI	Madrid	6 Mar	
										x 8.04 7.95 8.37 x p
8.37A	1.1	Khotso	Mokoena	RSA	6.3.85	1		Johannesburg	22 Apr	
										8.18 p p 8.37 p p
8.27A	-2.0					1		Pretoria	29 Oct	8.08 8.08 8.27 x p p
8.26w	2.2					1	NC	Durban	15 Apr	8.14w 8.26w x p p p
8.34	0.2	Ignisious	Gaisah	GHA	20.6.83	2	WCh	Helsinki	13 Aug	
										7.76 8.11w/2.8 8.34 8.17w/2.2 8.05/-0.9 p
8.34	0.4					2		Shanghai	17 Sep	8.05/-0.4 8.16/0.3 7.97 8.34 7.92 8.01/0.8
8.23	0.5					3	BrGP	Sheffield	21 Aug	8.03 x 7.94 8.20/1.9 8.23 x
8.23	1.2					4	WAF	Monaco	10 Sep	8.23 8.11w/2.3 x 6.56
8.33	2.0	Brian	Johnson	USA	25.3.80	1		Bad Langensalza	11 Jun	
8.32	0.4					1		Réthimno	10 Jul	x 8.23/0.1 x 8.32 x 6.35
8.31	2.0	Vladimir	Zyuskov	UKR	29.8.81	1	NC	Kiev	3 Jul	
										8.31 x x x p p
8.29	0.0	Irving	Saladino	PAN	23.1.83	1	GP	Sevilla	4 Jun	
										x 8.25/-0.3 8.05/0.0 8.18/-0.2 8.06/0.0 8.29
8.26	0.3					1		Santiago	8 May	8.09/-1.1 8.13/-0.2 8.22/-0.4 8.26 p 7.73
8.28	0.3	James	Beckford (10)	JAM	9.1.75	3	WAF	Monaco	10 Sep	
										7.82 8.20/2.0 8.17/2.0 8.28
8.25	0.5	Morten	Jensen	DEN	2.12.82	1		Göteborg	3 Jul	
										x 8.25 x p p p
8.25	1.0	Salim	Sdiri	FRA	26.10.78	1	NC	Angers	15 Jul	
										8.19/-0.3 7.79w x x 8.05/1.5 8.25
8.24i						1	NC	Liévin	19 Feb	x 8.15 8.24 8.15 5.84 x
		(32/12)								
8.22i		Viktor	Kuznetsov	UKR-J	14.7.86	1		Brovary	22 Jan	
8.22	2.0	Iván	Pedroso	CUB	17.12.72	1	GP II	Fort-de-France	30 Apr	
8.21	1.2	Nils	Winter	GER	27.3.77	2		Bad Langensalza	11 Jun	
8.20		Ibrahím	Camejo	CUB	28.6.82	1		La Habana	25 Feb	
8.19	1.5	Tommi	Evilä	FIN	6.4.80	*	v SWE	Göteborg	27 Aug	
8.18	1.7	Tim	Parravicini	AUS	25.4.81	1		Canberra	5 Feb	
8.18	1.6	Yahya	Berrabah	MAR	13.10.81	1		Alger	23 Jun	

Mark	Wind	Name		Nat	Born	Pos	Meet	Venue	Date
8.17i		Aarik	Wilson	USA	25.10.82	1	NCAA	Fayetteville	11 Mar
		(20)							
8.17	1.9	Trevell	Quinley	USA	16.1.83	1	TexR	Austin	8 Apr
8.16i		John	Moffitt	USA	12.12.80	1	SEC	Baton Rouge	18 Feb
8.15i		Loúis	Tsátoumas	GRE	12.2.82	1		Athína (P)	29 Jan
8.15	1.7	Rogério	Bispo	BRA	16.11.85	3		São Paulo	2 Apr
8.15	0.0	Vitaliy	Shkurlatov	RUS	25.5.79	1		Rivas	14 Jun
8.15A	0.3	Erivaldo	Vieira	BRA	18.11.80	1	SACh	Cali	23 Jul
8.15	1.6	Dimítrios	Filíndras	GRE	9.2.73	1		Spárti	27 Jul
8.14i		Savanté	Stringfellow	USA	6.11.78	2		Fayetteville	11 Feb
8.14i		Bogdan	Tarus	ROM	1.8.75	2	EI	Madrid	6 Mar
8.14	0.0	Greg	Rutherford	GBR-J	17.11.86	1	EJ	Kaunas	22 Jul
		(30)							
8.13i		Povilas	Mykolaitis	LTU	23.2.83	1	NC	Kaunas	11 Feb
8.13	1.7	Leevan	Sands	BAH	16.8.81	1	CAC	Nassau	10 Jul
8.13	1.7	Issam	Nima	ALG	8.4.79	Q	WCh	Helsinki	12 Aug
8.12	0.9	Arnaud	Casquette #	MRI	16.4.78	2		Pierre-Benité	10 Jun
8.12	0.8	Danut Marian	Simion	ROM	25.1.83	1	EU23	Erfurt	16 Jul
8.12	0.7	Dimítrios	Diamadáras	GRE	18.7.84	2		Spárti	27 Jul
8.11	1.9	Bashir	Ramzy	USA	4.5.79	2		Azusa	17 Jul
8.11		Stepán	Wagner	CZE	5.10.81	1		Brno	18 Sep
8.10i		Roman	Shchurenko	UKR	14.9.76	1		Kiev	14 Jan
8.08Ai		Tony	Allmond	USA	8.10.82	2		Flagstaff	5 Feb
		(40)							
8.07A	1.1	Nicola	Trentin	ITA	20.6.74	*		Krugersdorp	15 Jan
8.07		Vladimir	Malyavin	RUS	4.3.73	1		Moskva	19 May
8.07	1.9	Gable	Garenamotse	BOT	28.2.77	2		Rhede	29 May
8.07	1.3	Gaspar	Araújo	POR	17.12.81	7	GP	Madrid	16 Jul
8.07	1.4	Ciaran	McDonagh	IRL	20.5.76	1		La Chaux-de-Fonds	21 Aug
8.06	0.7	Jadel	Gregório	BRA	16.9.80	Q	NC	São Paulo	16 Jun
8.05i		Yann	Doménech	FRA	17.3.79	2	NC	Liévin	19 Feb
8.05A	0.8	Martin	McClintock	RSA	30.6.75	1		Pretoria	18 Mar
8.05	0.4		Zhou Can	CHN	20.5.79	1		Zhongshang	24 Apr
8.04	0.0	Nelson	Ferreira Junior	BRA	1.1.73	1		Rio de Janeiro	19 Feb
		(50)							
8.04	1.4	Wilfredo	Martínez	CUB	9.1.85	2	GP II	Fort-de-France	30 Apr
8.03	0.2	Kirill	Sosunov	RUS	1.11.75	1	Kuts	Moskva	15 Jul
8.02i		Valeriy	Vasilyev	UKR	21.4.76	2		Kiev	14 Jan
8.02	-1.3	Vytautas	Seliukas	LTU	21.4.82	1		Tartu	11 Jun
8.02	0.3	Andrew	Howe	ITA	12.5.85	1		Eboli	17 Sep
8.01i		Aleksey	Lukashevich	UKR	11.1.77	1		Tallinn	20 Feb
8.01	1.9	Rodrigo	de Araújo	BRA	12.11.79	*		São Paulo	2 Apr
8.01	0.3	Aleksey	Mekerin	RUS	26.2.78	2	Kuts	Moskva	15 Jul
8.01	1.1	Dmitriy	Sapinskiy	RUS	13.10.83	2	EU23	Erfurt	16 Jul
8.01	0.7	Ahmad Fayez	Marzouk Al-Dosari	KSA	6.9.79	Q	AsiC	Inchon	1 Sep
		(60)							
8.00Ai		Víctor	Castillo	VEN	8.6.81	3		Flagstaff	5 Feb
8.00	1.4	Peter	Rapp	GER	29.5.83	1		Ettlingen	5 Jun
8.00	0.7	Oliver	Koenig	GER	31.1.81	2	NCAA	Sacramento	9 Jun
8.00	0.1	Nathan	Morgan	GBR	30.6.78	1		Génève	11 Jun
8.00	0.3	Aleksandr	Patselya	UKR	3.7.83	2	NC	Kiev	3 Jul
7.99	0.0	Osbourne	Moxey	BAH	27.8.78	1	Towns	Athens, GA	23 Apr
7.99		Tarik	Bougtaïb	MAR	30.4.81	1		Casablanca	8 May
7.99	0.4		Gu Junjie	CHN	5.5.85	1		Chongqing	15 May
7.99	0.8	Atanas	Rusenov	BUL	30.8.81	1		Plovdiv	12 Jun
7.99	0.8	Maha	Singh	IND	4.3.82	1	Asi GP	Singapore	21 Jun
		(70)							
7.99	1.6		Zhang Xin	CHN	24.4.83	1	NG	Nanjing	18 Oct
7.98i		Bogdan	Tudor	ROM	1.2.70	2	NC	Bucuresti	13 Feb
7.98	0.0	Walter	Davis	USA	2.7.79	4	NC	Carson	23 Jun
7.98	0.1		Song Jian	CHN	7.5.83	1	Asi GP	Songkhla	24 Jun
7.98	1.8	Kafétien	Gomis	FRA	20.3.80	3	NC	Angers	15 Jul
7.97i		Jonathan	Chimier	MRI	6.8.82	1		Stuttgart	29 Jan
7.96i		Isagani	Pëychar	AUT	23.3.81	1		München	5 Feb
7.96	0.0	Sinisa	Ergotic	CRO	14.9.68	1		Dolenjske Toplice	10 Jun
7.95i		Chris	Tomlinson	GBR	15.9.81	1	GP	Birmingham	18 Feb
7.95	-0.3	Ruslan	Gataullin	RUS	1.12.79	4	NC	Tula	11 Jul
		(80)							
7.95	0.8	Chris	Noffke	AUS-Y	6.1.88	*	WY	Marrakech	15 Jul
7.95	0.4	Stefano	Dacastello	ITA	17.2.80	3	WUG	Izmir	18 Aug
7.94i		Sergey	Pavlushchenko ¶	UKR	23.1.80	3		Kiev	14 Jan

Mark	Wind	Name		Nat	Born	Pos	Meet	Venue	Date
7.94	1.6	Michal	Lukasiak	POL	7.3.84	1		Poznan	21 May
7.94	2.0	Leonidas	Watson	USA	27.5.80	1	NCAA-r	Eugene	27 May
7.94	-0.9	Michel	Tornéus	SWE-J	26.5.86	1-j		Göteborg	2 Jul
7.93i		Denis	Sinyavskiy	RUS	13.8.79	1		Moskva	26 Feb
7.93	-0.3	John	Thornell	AUS	22.4.85	2	NC	Sydney	5 Mar
7.93	1.2	Juaune	Armon	USA	6.5.82	1	CalR	Modesto	7 May
7.93	0.0	Dmitriy	Belotserkevskiy	UKR	25.3.85	3	NC	Kiev	3 Jul
		(90)							
7.93A	0.8	Thiago	Dias	BRA	2.3.84	2	SACh	Cali	23 Jul
7.92	0.9	Matt	Mason	USA	30.6.82	2	Towns	Athens, GA	23 Apr
7.92A	1.3	Esteban	Copland	VEN	12.10.79	3	SACh	Cali	23 Jul
7.91i		Astérios	Noúsios	GRE	25.2.79	2		Athína (P)	29 Jan
7.91	0.7	Aleksandr	Soldatkin	UKR-J	26.4.86	1		Kiev	2 Jun
7.91	0.0	Tomasz	Mateusiak	POL	12.5.80	1	NC	Biala Podlaska	26 Jun
7.90i		Ivan	Pucelj	CRO	11.7.81	1	NC	Zagreb	19 Feb
7.90i			Cai Xiaobao	CHN	11.3.80	2		Tianjin	2 Mar
7.90i		Fabrice	Lapierre	AUS	17.10.83	3	NCAA	Fayetteville	11 Mar
7.90		Petr	Lampart	CZE	31.3.83	1		Tábor	14 Aug
		(100)							

Mark	Wind	Name		Nat	Born	Date
7.89	-0.3	Nikolay	Atanasov	BUL	11.12.74	7 Jul
7.89	0.0	Marcin	Starzak	POL	20.10.85	9 Sep
7.89	-1.9		Li Runrun	CHN	24.2.83	18 Oct
7.88i		Ndiss Kaba	Badji ¶	SEN	21.9.83	18 Feb
7.88		Hatem	Mersal	EGY	20.1.75	30 Mar
7.88	1.9	Dmitriy	Abramov	RUS	1.1.82	11 Jul
7.87i		Alberto	Sanz	ESP	9.9.77	20 Feb
7.87	1.3	Masaki	Morinaga	JPN	27.3.72	15 May
7.87	0.3	Niklas	Rorarius	FIN	7.6.78	28 May
7.87	0.9	Hideaki	Suzuki	JPN-J	31.5.87	17 Jun
7.87	0.2		Oh Sang-won	KOR	10.8.83	2 Sep
7.87	0.0	Robert	Crowther	AUS-J	2.8.87	19 Nov
7.86i		Michael	Morrison	USA	4.3.84	11 Feb
7.86i		Tomas	Bardauskas	LTU	22.3.75	11 Feb
7.86i			Ding Jie	CHN-J	21.4.87	2 Mar
7.86	1.8	Hussein Taber	Al Sabee	KSA	14.11.79	24 Mar
7.86	1.0	Mihail	Mertzanídis	GRE-J	21.8.87	22 Apr
7.86	-0.8	Brian	Veal	USA	4.1.82	27 May
7.86	1.7	Simon	Sundsten	FIN	27.5.78	15 Jun
7.86	0.8	Yochai	Halevi	ISR	10.5.82	13 Jul
7.86	1.2	Roman	Sebrle	CZE	26.11.74	9 Aug
7.86	1.5	Dmitrij	Valukevic	SVK	31.5.81	15 Sep
7.85i		Marko	Milinkov	SCG	12.3.77	16 Feb
7.85	0.9	Yaw	Fosu-Amoah	RSA	8.10.81	5 Mar
7.85	-3.2	Allen	Simms	PUR	26.7.82	2 Apr
7.85		Yevgeniy	Plotnir	RUS	26.6.77	19 May
7.84i		Roman	Valiyev	KAZ	27.3.84	13 Nov
7.83	1.6	Saleh	Al Haddad	KUW-J	7.4.86	10 Mar
7.83	1.5	Schahriar	Bigdeli	GER	26.3.80	5 Jun
7.83	1.4	Mickaël	Loria	FRA	9.6.73	10 Jun
7.83	1.6	Andrejs	Maskancevs	LAT-J	11.10.86	21 Jul
7.83	0.9	Jan	Zumer	SLO	9.6.82	23 Jul
7.83	0.3	Kenneth	Kastrén	FIN	8.11.75	27 Aug
7.83	0.0	Scott	Crowe	AUS	7.10.83	10 Dec
7.82i		Sebastian	Bayer	GER-J	11.6.86	26 Feb
7.82	2.0	Fukutaro	Shimakawa	JPN	15.10.80	16 Apr
7.82		Yevgeniy	Tretyak	RUS	18.7.71	4 Jun
7.82	1.9	Fabien	Faucher	FRA	3.1.85	25 Jun
7.82	0.2	Tomás	Pour	CZE	25.1.83	15 Jul
7.82	2.0	Gregory	Sedoc	NED	16.10.81	4 Sep
7.81i		Melvin	Lister	USA	29.8.77	14 Jan
7.81		Reinier	Reyes	CUB	15.7.82	24 Feb
7.81i		Titus	Ryan	USA		4 Mar
7.81		Ferhat	içek	TUR	13.6.81	14 May
7.81	0.5	Henry	Dagmil	PHI	7.12.81	22 May
7.81	1.9	Pál	Babicz	HUN	18.3.80	7 Jun
7.81	0.0		Yu Zhenwei	CHN-J	18.3.86	20 Jun
7.81	0.9	Jurgen	Cools	NED	16.9.75	25 Jun
7.81	0.2	Tamás	Margl	HUN	18.6.76	27 Jun
7.81	0.4	Shiv Shankar	Yadav	IND	10.1.85	9 Nov
7.80i		Juan	Walker	USA		15 Jan
7.80i		Andreas	Pohle	GER	6.4.81	20 Feb
7.80	1.6	Daisuke	Arakawa	JPN	19.9.81	29 Apr
7.80		Toy Dany	Moody	CUB-J	21.11.87	12 May
7.80	0.7		Wang Cheng	CHN	4.11.80	15 May
7.80	1.8	Petko	Petrov (156)	BUL	1.7.85	10 Jul

Wind assisted

Mark	Wind	Name		Nat	Born	Pos	Meet	Venue	Date
8.51	2.3	Irving	Saladino	PAN	23.1.83	1		São Paulo	2 Apr
					8.39w/2.9	7.97	7.98	8.18/0.3 8.51w	x
8.36	3.1	James	Beckford	JAM	9.1.75	1	Sco Ch	Glasgow	27 Aug
					7.74w	8.10w	7.99w	8.13w 7.78w	8.36w
8.28w	3.0	2 GP	Madrid	16 Jul	x	8.14/0.3	8.28w	8.13/0.9 8.16w/2.2	x
8.28A	4.1	Arnaud	Casquette	MRI	16.4.78	1		Sestriere	24 Jul
8.27	2.4	Tommi	Evilä	FIN	6.4.80	1		Lapinlahti	3 Jul
					8.04	8.01	x	8.04 7.90	8.27w
8.25	3.3	Martin	McClintock	RSA	30.6.75	2	NC	Durban	15 Apr
8.23	2.5	Tony	Allmond	USA	8.10.82	1		Azusa	17 Jul
8.20	4.1	Tim	Parravicini	AUS	25.4.81	1		Brisbane	13 Feb
8.17	3.5	Okoineme	Giwa-Agbomeirele	USA	30.11.78	1	Owens	Columbus	7 May
8.16	3.5	Rodrigo	de Araújo	BRA	12.11.79	2		São Paulo	2 Apr
8.15	2.8	Fabrice	Lapierre	AUS	17.10.83	1	NCAA	Sacramento	9 Jun
8.11A	2.2	Nicola	Trentin	ITA	20.6.74	1		Krugersdorp	15 Jan
8.09	3.9	Mattias	Nuara	ITA	21.12.81	1		Donnas	19 Jun
8.09	2.3	Ciaran	McDonagh	IRL	20.5.76	2		Cork	2 Jul
8.08	3.9	Ahmad Fayez	Marzouk Al-Dosari	KSA	6.9.79	2	PArab	Radès	15 Sep
8.05	2.8	John	Thornell	AUS	22.4.85	1		Perth	22 Jan
8.03	4.1	Jaakko	Ojaniemi	FIN	28.8.80	1D		Arles	4 Jun
8.03	3.5	Osbourne	Moxey	BAH	27.8.78	2	CAC	Nassau	10 Jul
8.01	2.8	Konstantinos	Vasiliádis	GRE	9.3.77	1		Édessa	25 May
8.01	4.6	Marcin	Starzak	POL	20.10.85	2		Donnas	19 Jun
8.00	2.2	Chris	Noffke	AUS-Y	6.1.88	1	NC	Sydney	5 Mar
7.98	2.7	Herbert	McGregor	JAM	.81	1		Spanish Town	8 Apr

Mark	Wind	Name		Nat	Born	Pos	Meet	Venue	Date
7.96	2.9	Alberto	Sanz	ESP	9.9.77	9	GP	Madrid	16 Jul
7.93	3.6	Ivan	Pucelj	CRO	11.7.81	1		Zagreb	15 Jun
7.92	6.4	Hrístos	Hatzivasilíou	GRE	23.3.84	1		Athína (E)	6 May

Mark	Wind	Name		Nat	Born	Date
7.90	3.6	Nikolay	Atanasov	BUL	11.12.74	2 Jul
7.90	2.2	Darren	Ritchie	GBR	14.2.75	22 Jul
7.88		Alain	Bailey	JAM-J	14.8.87	16 Mar
7.88	2.8	Daisuke	Arakawa	JPN	19.9.81	29 Apr
7.87	2.8	Sébastien	Pincemail	FRA	21.2.79	3 Apr
7.85	2.2	Pieter	Smit	RSA-J	23.3.86	11 Mar
7.85	4.6	Jason	Romero	USA	12.1.81	17 Apr
7.85	2.4	Yevgeniy	Tretyak	RUS	18.7.71	26 May
7.85	3.0	Bostjan	Fridrih	SLO	20.9.79	18 Jun
7.85	2.9	Jurgen	Cools	NED	16.9.75	10 Jul
7.85	3.0		Wang Minsheng	CHN	7.4.85	3 Sep
7.84	3.4	David	Frykholm	SWE	8.1.80	27 Aug
7.84	4.4	Leigh	Smith	GBR	24.9.82	3 Sep
7.83	2.2	Sebastian	Bayer	GER-J	11.6.86	5 Jun
7.83	2.3	Tamás	Margl	HUN	18.6.76	30 Jul
7.82	2.8	Dimítrios	Tzimayióryis	GRE	15.9.78	25 May
7.82	2.4	Aleksandr	Vasyukov	RUS	1.12.81	26 May
7.82	4.6	Ferhat	içek	TUR	13.6.81	4 Jun
7.81	3.8	Yoshinori	Yamaguchi	JPN	.85	10 Oct
7.80	2.1	Cleavon	Dillon	TRI	5.10.82	2 Apr

Best outdoor marks

Mark	Wind	Name	Pos	Meet	Venue	Date
8.17	1.4	Martínez	1	NC	Málaga	24 Jul
		8.24w 2.9	4	WCh	Helsinki	13 Aug
8.14	0.8	Tsátoumas	1	Odlozil	Praha	27 Jun
8.09	1.8	Mykolaitis	2	ECp2A	Tallinn	18 Jun
8.02	0.3	Stringfellow	3		Santo Domingo	14 May
7.98	2.0	Allmond	*		Azusa	17 Jul
7.96	0.8	Tarus	2	RomIC	Bucuresti	11 Jun
7.96	1.8	Moffitt	5	BrGP	Sheffield	21 Aug
		8.01w 2.2	3	GP II	Stanford	30 May
7.95	0.1	Lukashevich	1		Yalta	27 May
7.94	0.7	Chimier	1		Réduit	15 May
7.94	1.1	Pëychar	1		Innsbrück	15 May
7.93	0.4	Shchurenko	3	NC	Kiev	3 Jul
7.91	0.3	Wilson	3	NCAA	Sacramento	9 Jun
		8.00w 3.7	2	Big10	Columbus	14 May
7.91	1.3	Noúsios	3	NC	Athína	11 Jun

Mark	Wind	Name	Date
7.89	0.0	Vasilyev	4 Jun
7.89	-0.2	Pucelj	2 Jul
7.89	0.4	Sinyavskiy	15 Jul
7.87		Pavlushchenko ¶	6 May
7.86		Tudor	11 Jun
		7.92w 2.3	11 Jun
7.84	1.0	Cai Xiaobao	24 Apr
7.83	1.8	Lapierre	8 Apr
7.83	0.3	Sanz	18 Jun
7.82	1.6	Tomlinson	21 Aug
		7.83w 2.6	12 Aug
7.80	1.7	Doménech	25 Jun
7.83	2.2	Morrison	8 Apr

Low altitude best

Mark	Wind	Name	Pos	Meet	Venue	Date
8.22la	0.2	Mokoena	Q	WCh	Helsinki	12 Aug
		8.26w 2.2	1	NC	Durban	15 Apr
8.04	1.9	Trentin	*		Isili	27 Aug
		8.07w 3.5	1		Isili	27 Aug
7.98	-0.7	Vieira	1	NC	São Paulo	17 Jun
7.96	0.0	McClintock	3	Odlozil	Praha	27 Jun
7.88	1.3	Dias	2	NC-23	São Paulo	23 Apr

Questionable measurement

Mark	Wind	Name		Nat	Born	Pos	Meet	Venue	Date
7.92	-4.5	Scott	Mayle	USA	14.10.83	1	NCAA-r	Bloomington	27 May

Drugs disqualification

Mark	Wind	Name		Nat	Born	Pos	Meet	Venue	Date
8.06		Ndiss Kaba	Badji ¶	SEN	21.9.83	1		Bamako	6 Apr
		8.30w 3.4				1		Dakar	3 Apr
8.01w	5.1	Sergey	Pavlushchenko ¶	UKR	23.1.80	2		La Laguna	30 Jul
		7.88 0.2				1		Covilha	16 Jul

JUNIORS

See main list for top 5 juniors. 11 performances by 9 men to 7.86. Additional marks and further juniors:

Name	Mark	Wind	Pos	Meet	Venue	Date	Mark	Wind	Pos	Venue	Date
Rutherford	7.90	0.5	1		Mannheim	19 Jun	7.99w		1	Milton Keynes	14 May
Soldatkin	7.90		3		Donetsk	7 May					
Noffke	7.97w	2.2	1	WY	Marrakech	15 Jul	7.90w	2.9	1	Brisbane	13 Feb

Mark	Wind	Name		Nat	Born	Pos	Meet	Venue	Date
7.87	0.9	Hideaki	Suzuki	JPN	31.5.87	1		Chiba	17 Jun
7.87	0.0	Robert	Crowther	AUS-	2.8.87	1		Canberra	19 Nov
7.86i			Ding Jie	CHN	21.4.87	3		Tianjin	2 Mar
7.86	1.0	Mihail	Mertzanídis	GRE	21.8.87	1		Thessaloníki	22 Apr
7.83	1.6	Saleh	Al Haddad (10)	KUW	7.4.86	1		Al Kuwait	10 Mar
7.83	1.6	Andrejs	Maskancevs	LAT	11.10.86	Q	EJ	Kaunas	21 Jul
7.82i		Sebastian	Bayer	GER	11.6.86	1		Sindelfingen	26 Feb
7.81	0.0		Yu Zhenwei	CHN	18.3.86	2	NC	Shijiazhuang	20 Jun
7.80		Toy Dany	Moody	CUB	21.11.87	1		La Habana	12 May
7.79	0.4		Lin Huadeng	CHN-Y	15.1.88	2		Yixing	22 May
7.78	1.7	Nikólaos	Filandarákis	GRE	1.7.86	6	Veniz	Haniá	6 Jun
7.76i		Nils	Sammert	GER	12.8.87	2		Saarbrücken	26 Feb
7.75i		Norris	Frederick	USA	17.2.86	6	NCAA	Fayetteville	12 Mar
7.75	1.7	Adrian	Vasile	ROM	9.4.86	5	RomIC	Bucuresti	11 Jun
7.74	0.4		Jin Zutao	CHN	9.1.87	4	Yixing	22	May

Wind assisted – see main list for top junior, additional:

Mark	Wind	Name		Nat	Born	Pos	Meet	Venue	Date
7.88		Alain	Bailey	JAM	14.8.87	1		Kingston	16 Mar
7.85	2.2	Pieter	Smit	RSA	23.3.86	1		Stellenbosch	11 Mar
7.83	2.2	Sebastian	Bayer	GER	11.6.86	1-J		Bad Camberg	5 Jun
Best out: 7.77	2.9		Ding Jie	CHN	21.4.87	Q	NC	Shijiazhuang	19 Jun

TRIPLE JUMP

Mark	Wind	Name		Nat	Born	Pos	Meet	Venue	Date
17.81	1.0	Marian	Oprea	ROM	6.6.82	1	Athl	Lausanne	5 Jul

						x	17.81	x	p	p	x
17.52	0.9	1	SGP	Athína	14 Jun	17.52	17.44/0.9	15.02	p	p	x
17.46	-0.3	1	Rom IC	Bucuresti	11 Jun	17.33/0.5	x	17.46	p	p	x
17.44	-0.7	2	DNG	Stockholm	26 Jul	17.44	17.33/0.4	p	17.01/0.2	p	17.00/0.3

MEN 2005

Mark	Wind	Name		Nat	Born	Pos	Meet	Venue	Date
	17.40 0.7 1 NC	Bucuresti		2 Jul	x 17.24 17.40 p p p				
	17.40 2.0 3 WCh	Helsinki		11 Aug	17.15/0.9 16.81/1.5 17.22/0.9 x x 17.40				
	17.37 0.5 1 GP II	Torino		3 Jun	17.32/0.3 17.37 16.96 p p 16.84				
17.73	1.0	Jadel	Gregório	BRA	16.9.80	1	NC	São Paulo	19 Jun
					17.01/-0.5 17.16/-1.0 p x x 17.73				
	17.71 1.3 1	São Paulo		29 Apr	17.71 x x 17.05/1.2 p p				
	17.58 -0.5 1	Rio de Janeiro		15 May	17.58 only jump				
	17.48 0.4 1 DNG	Stockholm		26 Jul	17.48 17.07/0.1 x p p 17.00/-0.1				
	17.46 -0.8 1	Fortaleza		18 May	17.46 x x 16.97 p 17.06/1.4				
	17.40 -0.3 1 GP	Belém		22 May	17.40 p x p 16.10 x				
	17.34 0.8 3 Athl	Lausanne		5 Jul	17.34 17.27/1.5 x 17.08 p 17.26/1.3				
	17.32 1.0 2 WAF	Monaco		9 Sep	17.08/0.0 17.32 x 16.87				
17.64	1.4	Nathan	Douglas	GBR	4.12.82	1	NC	Manchester (SC)	10 Jul
					17.36/0.9 17.64 p p p p				
	17.32 1.4 1 LGP	London (CP)		22 Jul	16.86/-0.3 17.00/-0.2 17.21/0.1 17.32 p 15.78				
17.62i		Walter	Davis	USA	2.7.79	1		Baton Rouge	18 Feb
					17.62 x x p p p				
	17.57 0.3 1 WCh	Helsinki		11 Aug	17.22w/2.5 16.84w 17.57 17.03/1.0 p x				
	17.40 1.3 2 BrGP	Sheffield		21 Aug	14.65 16.68 16.94 17.19/1.1 17.19/0.6 17.40				
	17.31i 1 NC	Boston (R)		27 Feb	14.88 17.06 x p p 17.31				
	17.30 0.0 1	Banská Bystrica		28 Aug	16.80 17.30				
17.51	1.4	Alexander	Martínez	CUB	23.8.77	1		Bern (N)	23 Jul
	17.44 1.0 1 BrGP	Sheffield		21 Aug	16.45 16.72 p 16.42 16.82 17.44				
17.46	0.1	Yoandri	Betanzos	CUB	15.2.82	1	WAF	Monaco	9 Sep
					16.98 17.21/0.3 17.15/0.4 17.46				
	17.42 1.2 2 WCh	Helsinki		11 Aug	15.67w 17.03/1.9 17.01/0.5 17.42/1.2 15.09 17.42				
	17.39 1	La Habana		24 Feb	x 17.17 17.00 17.39 x 17.29				
	17.40w 4.2 Q WCh	Helsinki		10 Aug	17.40w only jump				
	17.33w 3.0 1 CAC	Nassau		11 Jul	17.33w 16.66w? 16.97w 17.09w x x				
17.45	1.0	Karl	Taillepierre	FRA	13.8.76	1	NC	Angers	16 Jul
					16.66 x 16.80 17.00w/2.5 x 17.45				
17.40		Igor	Spasovkhodskiy	RUS	1.8.79	1		Moskva	18 Jun
					17.21 17.40 p p p p				
	17.32 1	Moskva		30 Jun	x 17.32 16.50 p x p				
	17.30 -0.1 1 NC	Tula		13 Jul	16.68 16.93 17.15 16.70 17.07 17.30				
17.39	1.6	Charles-Michael	Friedek	GER	26.8.71	1		Bad Schwalbach	10 Jun
					15.87 16.44 17.39 x p p				
17.30i		Phillips	Idowu (10)	GBR	30.12.78	1	NC	Sheffield	13 Feb
					15.86 16.73 16.67 16.74 16.30 17.30				
17.30	0.3	Leevan	Sands	BAH	16.8.81	*	WCh	Helsinki	11 Aug
		(34/11)			17.11/0.1 17.39w 17.18/0.9 x 17.30/0.0 x				
17.29	1.1	Konstadínos	Zalaggítis	GRE	13.12.80	1	Veniz	Haniá	6 Jun
17.25	1.3	Khotso	Mokoena	RSA	6.3.85	1	NC	Durban	16 Apr
17.21	1.8	Colomba	Fofana	FRA	11.4.77	1	ECCp	Lagos/POR	29 May
17.19	0.7	Momchil	Karailiev	BUL	21.5.82	1	NC	Sofia	7 Jun
17.19	1.4	Dmitrij	Valukevic	SVK	31.5.81	3	BrGP	Sheffield	21 Aug
17.15	0.6		Li Yanxi	CHN	26.6.84	2	Pre	Eugene	4 Jun
17.15	1.7	Viktor	Yastrebov	UKR	13.1.82	5	Athl	Lausanne	5 Jul
17.14	-0.3	David	Giralt	CUB	26.8.84	2		Alcalá de Henares	18 Jun
17.11	0.0	Aleksandr	Sergeyev	RUS	29.7.83	1	EU23	Erfurt	17 Jul
		(20)							
17.11	2.0	Kenta	Bell	USA	16.3.77	7	WCh	Helsinki	11 Aug
17.10	-0.7	Viktor	Gushchinskiy	RUS	12.8.78	2	NC	Tula	13 Jul
17.10	0.0	Danila	Burkenya	RUS	20.7.78	4	WAF	Monaco	9 Sep
17.08		Osniel	Tosca	CUB	30.6.84	1		La Habana	19 Feb
17.06	1.2	Julien	Kapek	FRA	12.1.79	2	NC	Angers	16 Jul
17.04	0.8	Vitaliy	Moskalenko	RUS	30.6.74	1		Tula	14 Jun
17.03		Yoelbi	Quesada	CUB	4.8.73	2		La Habana	27 Jan
17.03	1.6	Allen	Simms	PUR	26.7.82	2	NCAA	Sacramento	11 Jun
17.03	1.9	Larry	Achike	GBR	31.1.75	5	SGP	Athína	14 Jun
17.03	0.6	Aleksandr	Petrenko	RUS	8.2.83	2	EU23	Erfurt	17 Jul
		(30)							
17.01i		Nikolay	Savolainen	UKR	25.3.80	2	EI	Madrid	5 Mar
17.00	-0.9	Rodrigo	Mendes	BRA	21.6.78	2	NC	São Paulo	19 Jun
17.00	0.5	Tarik	Bougtaïb	MAR	30.4.81	2	MedG	Almeria	29 Jun
17.00	0.6	Yevgeniy	Plotnir	RUS	26.6.77	1	Kuts	Moskva	16 Jul
16.96i			Gu Junjie	CHN	5.5.85	1	v JPN	Tianjin	1 Mar
16.95		Alexei	Copello	CUB	12.8.85	1		La Habana	4 Mar
16.94	1.6	Aarik	Wilson	USA	25.10.82	3	NCAA	Sacramento	11 Jun
16.92		Dennis	Fernández	CUB-J	23.1.86	1	NC-j	Santiago de Cuba	24 May
16.92	0.4	Kazuyoshi	Ishikawa	JPN	6.11.82	1	NC	Tokyo	4 Jun

Mark	Wind	Name		Nat	Born	Pos	Meet	Venue	Date
16.91	1.1	Sébastien	Pincemail	FRA	21.2.79	2	Veniz	Haniá	6 Jun
		(40)							
16.90i		Michael	Velter	BEL	21.3.81	1		Gent	29 Jan
16.90	1.1	Chris	Hercules	USA	14.5.79	2		Carson	22 May
16.89	1.9	Nelson	Évora	POR	20.4.84	3	EU23	Erfurt	17 Jul
16.88	0.5	Randy	Lewis	GRN	14.10.80	3	Veniz	Haniá	6 Jun
16.86	0.3		Lin Mujie	CHN	25.9.85	1		Zhongshang	23 Apr
16.86	0.5	Paolo	Camossi	ITA	6.1.74	1	NC	Bressanone	26 Jun
16.82	0.4	Emanuele	Sardano	ITA	16.2.79	4	GP II	Torino	3 Jun
16.80	1.9	Younès	Moudrik	MAR	1.10.77	2		Marrakech	21 May
16.79	1.2		Kim Duk-hyung	KOR	8.12.85	1	EAsG	Macau	4 Nov
16.78	0.8		Zhu Shujing	CHN	24.5.85	1	NC	Shijiazhuang	21 Jun
		(50)							
16.76	1.6	Anders	Møller	DEN	5.9.77	1		Århus	24 Jul
16.75	0.2	Jefferson	Dias Sabino	BRA	4.11.82	3	NC	São Paulo	19 Jun
16.74	1.9	Hrístos	Melétoglu	GRE	2.1.72	*	MedG	Almeria	29 Jun
16.72	1.6	Sergey	Oleinik	RUS	28.11.80	1		Olomouc	13 Jul
16.71	1.7	Steve	Shalders	GBR	24.12.81	1		Manchester (SC)	3 Sep
16.70	1.2	Dimítrios	Tsiámis	GRE	12.1.82	4	LGP	London (CP)	22 Jul
16.67i		Péter	Tölgyesi	HUN	9.6.81	1		Budapest	19 Feb
16.67	1.1	Jacob	McReynolds	AUS	8.12.78	1		Adelaide	19 Feb
16.67	0.5	Mohamed	Hazouri	SYR	.83	4	MedG	Almeria	29 Jun
16.67	0.8	Roman	Valiyev	KAZ	27.3.84	Q	AsiC	Inchon	2 Sep
		(60)							
16.67	1.2	Michael	Perry	AUS	30.9.77	1		Brisbane	27 Nov
16.66i		Jacek	Kazmierowski	POL	7.2.74	1	NC	Spala	19 Feb
16.65i		Salvatore	Morello	ITA	5.9.74	1	NC	Ancona	20 Feb
16.65	-0.7	Fabrizio	Donato	ITA	14.8.76	2		Lignano Sabbiadoro	17 Jul
16.63	1.4	Héctor	Fuentes	CUB-Y	19.5.88	1	WY	Marrakech	16 Jul
16.62	1.0	Arnis	Filet	FRA	17.12.77	3		Forbach	29 May
16.59	1.8	Ibrahim Mohd	Aboubaker	QAT	10.12.82	1	PArab	Radès	17 Sep
16.58i		Carlos	Calado	POR	5.10.75	1	ESP Ch	Madrid	20 Feb
16.58	0.5	Brandon	Atkinson	USA	11.6.83	2	NCAA-r	Bloomington	28 May
16.57	1.3	Marcus	Jones	USA	13.8.76	2	GP II	Stanford	30 May
		(70)							
16.55	-0.6	Daniel	Donovici	ROM	5.3.80	1	BalkC	Novi Sad	24 Jul
16.55	1.6	Kenneth	Hall	USA-J	17.4.86	2	PAm-J	Windsor	31 Jul
16.52	-0.8	Alwyn	Jones	AUS	28.2.85	1		Adelaide	8 Jan
16.52	-0.2	Tim	Rusan	USA	25.6.77	3	DrakeR	Des Moines	30 Apr
16.51i		Viktor	Kuznetsov	UKR-J	14.7.86	3		Samara	2 Feb
16.51i		Marcus	Thomas	USA	22.3.79	3		Baton Rouge	18 Feb
16.50	1.6	Brian	Veal	USA	4.1.82	1		Huntsville	15 May
16.50	0.9	Robert	Michniewski	POL	16.2.74	1		Kladno	21 May
16.50	1.8	Johan	Meriluoto	FIN	22.3.74	2		Kuortane	26 Jun
16.49		René L.	Mola	CUB-J	15.2.87	2	NC-j	Santiago de Cuba	24 May
		(80)							
16.49A	-0.7	Johnny	Rodríguez	VEN	4.8.78	2		Cochabamba	1 Jun
16.49	-0.1	Rudolf	Helpling	GER	23.2.81	2	NC	Wattenscheid	3 Jul
16.48	0.3	Tomás	Cholensky	CZE	25.4.78	6	ECp-S	Firenze	19 Jun
16.48	1.9	Brandon	Evans	USA	30.10.79	4	NC	Carson	25 Jun
16.47i		Rafeeq	Curry	USA	19.8.83	1		Fayetteville	12 Feb
16.47	1.2	Thomas	Moede	GER	26.7.77	1		Garbsen	22 May
16.46	0.5	Leonardo	dos Santos	BRA	7.5.84	1		São Paulo	13 Mar
16.46		Tuan	Wreh	LBR	23.11.79	1		Princeton	23 Apr
16.46	0.0	Vladimir	Letnicov	MDA	7.10.81	2	ECp-2B	Istanbul	19 Jun
16.46	-0.4		Li Ming	CHN	21.3.85	3	NG	Nanjing	22 Oct
		(90)							
16.45		Lamont	Dagen	USA					18 Jun
16.45	1.5	Ilya	Yeferemov	RUS-Y	20.3.88	2	WY	Marrakech	16 Jul
16.45	1.7	Yohei	Kajikawa	JPN	8.11.83	2	EAsG	Macau	4 Nov
16.44	-1.5	Yahya	Berrabah	MAR	13.10.81	2	Franc	Niamey	14 Dec
16.43	-0.1	Andrew	Murphy	AUS	18.12.69	2	NC	Sydney	6 Mar
16.43	1.2	Anton	Andersson	SWE	12.3.81	2	ECp-1A	Gävle	19 Jun
16.43	-0.1	Dmitriy	Nikonov	RUS-J	17.10.87	1	NC-j	Tula	4 Jul
16.43	2.0	Alassane	Diarra	FRA	22.1.81	1		Cerizay	13 Jul
16.42i		Jaanus	Uudmäe	EST	24.12.80	2		Fayetteville	12 Feb
16.42	0.8	Henágio	Galvão	BRA	18.11.84	1	NC-23	São Paulo	24 Apr
		(100)							
16.42	2.0	Davy	Manga	FRA	6.5.83	2		Pierre-Benite	10 Jun
16.42	-0.4		Li Xin	CHN	9.12.82	5	NG	Nanjing	22 Oct
16.42		Renjith	Maheshwary	IND-J	30.1.86	1		Bhubaneshwar	23 Oct

Mark	Wind	Name		Nat	Born	Date
16.41i		Andreas	Pohle	GER	6.4.81	19 Feb
16.40i		Alonzo	Moore	USA	17.1.83	12 Mar
16.39i		Melvin	Lister	USA	29.8.77	12 Feb
16.39i		Andrés	Capellan	ESP	10.6.85	20 Feb
16.38	1.5	Petar	Ivanov	BUL	5.9.85	7 Jun
16.38	0.5		Wu Liqiang	CHN	14.11.85	21 Jun
16.38	1.5	Pere	Joseph	ESP	4.2.85	29 Jun
16.37	1.0	Leonidas	Watson	USA	27.5.80	15 May
16.37		Yandy	Posada	CUB-J	6.3.86	24 May
16.37	1.7	LeJuan	Simon	TRI	7.2.81	30 May
16.36		Salem Mouled	Al Ahmadi	KSA	12.9.69	28 Apr
16.36	2.0	Konrad	Katarzynski	POL	16.7.80	26 Jun
16.35	0.0		Wu Bo	CHN	17.6.84	23 Apr
16.35A	-0.8	Hugo	Chila	ECU-J	22.7.87	10 Jul
16.34i		Keeter	Sylvain	FRA	29.4.82	20 Feb
16.34	2.0	Mantas	Dilys	LTU	30.3.84	4 Jun
16.34	1.7	Samyr	Laine	USA	17.7.84	10 Jun
16.33i		Bostjan	Simunic	SLO	28.12.74	19 Feb
16.31		Aleksandr	Vorobey	BLR	.81	23 May
16.31	1.6	Dmitriy	Mashtakov	UZB	19.1.82	24 Jun
16.31	0.7	Yevgeniy	Ektov	KAZ-J	1.9.86	7 Jul
16.30		Yordanis	Durañona	CUB-Y	16.6.88	25 May
16.30	0.2	Pávlos	Galaktiádis	GRE	15.5.84	18 Jun
16.29	0.4	Stávros	Yeoryíou	GRE	23.4.80	10 Jun
16.29	1.4	Fabrizio	Schembri	ITA	27.1.81	16 Jun
16.29	1.9	Stevens	Marie-Sainte	FRA-J	6.4.86	24 Jul
16.28i		Andrey	Yakovchik	BLR	.80	5 Mar
16.27	1.5	Takanori	Sugibayashi	JPN	14.3.76	4 Jun
16.26i		Maksim	Molokov	RUS	24.5.77	12 Feb
16.26	0.4		Wu Ji	CHN	14.8.78	21 Jun
16.26	0.2	Lauri	Leis	EST	7.10.78	1 Jul
16.25	1.1	Gavin	Manoharan	AUS	4.9.80	29 Jan
16.25i			Jiang Wei	CHN	26.7.82	2 Mar
16.25	0.7	Julian	Golley	GBR	12.9.71	29 May
16.25	-0.1	Mateusz	Parlicki (137)	POL	14.4.84	26 Jun

Wind assisted

Mark	Wind	Name		Nat	Born	Pos	Meet	Venue	Date
17.54	3.4	Rodrigo	Mendes	BRA	21.6.68	Q	NCAA	Sacramento	10 Jun
17.39	2.3	Leevan	Sands	BAH	16.8.81	4	WCh	Helsinki	11 Aug
17.36	2.3	Momchil	Karailiev	BUL	21.5.82	2	Athl	Lausanne	5 Jul
					16.79	17.36w	x	x p	16.24
17.33	3.0		Betanzos			1	CAC	Nassau	11 Jul
17.19	2.7	Allen	Simms	PUR	26.7.82	2	CAC	Nassau	11 Jul
17.09	2.5	Hrístos	Melétoglu	GRE	2.1.72	1	MedG	Almeria	29 Jun
17.09	2.6	Alexei	Copello	CUB	12.8.85	4	CAC	Nassau	11 Jul
17.00	2.2	Steve	Shalders	GBR	24.12.81	2	NC	Manchester (SC)	10 Jul
16.80	2.4	Bostjan	Simunic	SLO	28.12.74	1		Ljubljana	22 May
16.78	2.1	LeJuan	Simon	TRI	7.2.81	1		Baton Rouge	23 Apr
16.75	3.8	Rafeeq	Curry	USA	19.8.83	1	NCAA-r	New York	28 May
16.69	3.2	Jaanus	Uudmäe	EST	24.12.80	1	ECp-1A	Gävle	19 Jun
16.68	3.0	Fabrizio	Donato	ITA	14.8.76	2		Cesenatico	12 Jun
16.48	2.3		Wu Bo	CHN	17.6.84	4	NC	Shijiazhuang	21 Jun
16.47	2.3	Takanori	Sugibayashi	JPN	14.3.76	2		Yamaguchi	9 Oct

Mark	Wind	Name		Nat	Born	Date
16.38	2.2	Andrés	Capellán	ESP	10.6.85	29 Jun
16.35	2.9	Yevgeniy	Inozemtsev	RUS	14.4.74	12 Jul
16.31	2.3	Fabrizio	Schembri	ITA	27.1.81	16 Jun
16.30	2.5	Tosin	Oke	GBR	1.10.80	3 Sep
16.29	2.1	Marcelo	da Costa	BRA	1.5.81	19 Mar
16.27	2.1	Mohd Abdou	Al-Majrashi	KSA-J	5.3.86	17 Sep
16.25	6.3	Marat	Safiullin	AUS	3.4.75	22 Jan
16.25	2.5	Mohamed	Hamimid	FRA	16.11.73	16 Jul

Best outdoor marks

Mark	Wind	Name	Pos	Meet	Venue	Date
17.57	0.3	Davis	1	WCh	Helsinki	11 Aug
16.96	0.9	Idowu	6	SGP	Athína	14 Jun
16.78	1.7	Savolainen	2	ECp1B	Leiria	19 Jun
16.65	0.9	Velter	3		Liège (NX)	20 Jul
16.52	0.4	Kazmierowski	1	NC	Biala Podlaska	26 Jun
16.46	0.7	Morello	1		Cesenatico	11 Jun
16.44	-1.4	Gu Junjie	4	NG	Nanjing	22 Oct
		16.90w 2.6	1	AsiC	Inchon	3 Sep

Mark	Wind	Name	Date
16.40	1.6	Curry	11 Jun
16.37	0.0	Capellán	14 May
16.33	0.2	Uudmäe	28 May
16.28	1.5	Simunic	22 May
16.44w	2.2	Thomas	30 May

Drugs disqualification

Mark	Wind	Name		Nat	Born	Pos	Meet	Venue	Date
17.15	1.7	Ndiss Kaba	Badji ¶	SEN	21.9.83	1		Dakar	30 Apr

JUNIORS

See main list for top 8 juniors. 10 performances by 6 men to 16.45. Additional marks and further juniors:

Name	Mark	Wind	Pos	Meet	Venue	Date	Mark	Wind	Pos	Meet	Venue	Date
Fernández	16.60	1.2	*	PAm-J	Windsor	31 Jul	16.48		5		La Habana	23 Jun
	16.52	0.7	3		La Habana	23 Jun	16.80w	2.1	1	PAm-J	Windsor	31 Jul
Fuentes	16.58		1	NC-y	Santiago de C	25 May						

Mark	Wind	Name		Nat	Born	Pos	Meet	Venue	Date
16.37		Yandy	Posada	CUB	6.3.86	3	NC-j	Santiago de Cuba	24 May
16.35A	-0.8	Hugo	Chila (10)	ECU	22.7.87	1	NC	Quito	10 Jul
16.31	0.7	Yevgeniy	Ektov	KAZ	1.9.86	2	NC	Almaty	7 Jul
16.30		Yordanis	Durañona	CUB-Y	16.6.88	2	NC-y	Santiago de Cuba	25 May
16.29	1.9	Stevens	Marie-Sainte	FRA	6.4.86	1	EJ	Kaunas	24 Jul
16.23		Eliecer	Martínez	CUB	87	4	NC-j	Santiago de Cuba	24 May
16.23	1.8	Zhivko	Kolev Petkov	BUL-Y	28.1.88	2	NC-j	Sofia	28 May
16.23	0.7	Stanislav	Ionov	RUS-Y	27.11.88	1	NC-j	Chelyabinsk	23 Jun
16.23	1.2	Mohamed A.	Al-Majrashi	KSA	5.3.86	*		Radès	17 Sep
16.20			Jiang Li	CHN		1		Zhengzhou	31 Aug
16.19		Yasser	Herrera	CUB		5	NC-j	Santiago de Cuba	24 May
16.18	1.2	Sherif	El-Sherif (20)	UKR-Y	2.1.89	5	WY	Marrakesh	16 Jul

Wind assisted

Mark	Wind	Name		Nat	Born	Pos	Meet	Venue	Date
16.27	2.1	Mohd Abdou	Al-Majrashi	KSA	5.3.86	3	PArab	Radès	17 Sep
16.18w	2.2	Mohamed Youssef	Al-Sahabi	BRN-Y	26.7.89	4	WY	Marrakesh	16 Jul

A made at an altitude of 1000m or higher, D made in a decathlon, h made in a heat, qf quarter-final, sf semi-final, i indoors, Q qualifying round, r race number, -J juniors (born 1986 or later), -Y youths (born 1988 or later)

SHOT

Mark			Name	Nat	Born	Pos	Meet	Venue		Date
22.20	John		Godina	USA	31.5.72	1		Carson		22 May
					22.20	x	21.61	21.70	x	x
21.93	1	GP II	Stanford	30 May	21.23	21.84	21.93	x	x	21.37
21.83i	1	NC	Boston (R)	26 Feb	21.83	21.33	21.31	20.73	21.47	21.12
21.46	1		La Jolla	23 Apr	21.22	21.46	x	x	x	x
21.40	2		New York (RI)	11 Jun	x	21.40	p	p		
21.17i	2	Mill	New York	4 Feb	21.17	x	x	x		
21.92	Adam		Nelson	USA	7.7.75	1	WAF	Monaco		10 Sep
					21.92	x	x	x		
21.73	1	WCh	Helsinki	6 Aug	21.73	21.28	21.68	x	21.04	x
21.66i	1		Boston (R)	29 Jan	20.34	20.97	21.66	20.84	20.41	20.63
21.59i	3	NC	Boston (R)	26 Feb	x	x	20.15	21.59	19.75	x
21.58	1		New York (RI)	11 Jun	21.25	21.58	x	x		
21.52	2	NC	Carson	26 Jun	21.11	x	20.95	x	21.52	x
21.51	1		Lapua	30 Jul						
21.74i	Reese		Hoffa	USA	8.10.77	2	NC	Boston (R)		26 Feb
					x	20.36	20.24	20.16	21.74	20.98
21.62i	1	Mill	New York	4 Feb	x	20.19	x	21.62		
21.29	1	SGP	Doha	13 May						
21.67	Christian		Cantwell	USA	30.9.80	1	GP	Sevilla		4 Jun
					20.66	20.60	20.52	20.72	21.18	21.67
21.64	1	NC	Carson	26 Jun	20.98	21.46	21.64	x	x	21.61
21.60	1	LGP	London (CP)	22 Jul	20.71	21.01	x	20.51	x	21.60
21.32	1		Huelva	7 Jun	20.45	21.32	x	x	x	x
21.30	1		Tallinn	16 Aug	19.81	19.72	20.06	21.30	x	p
21.41	Rutger		Smith	NED	9.7.81	1	Cooman	Stadskanaal		3 Jul
					20.55	20.58	20.83	21.41	20.60	20.26
21.29	2	WCh	Helsinki	6 Aug	21.29	21.04	21.23	20.87	x	20.66
21.36	Ralf		Bartels	GER	21.2.78	1		Engers		29 May
21.17	1		Gotha	10 Jun	x	21.06	21.17	20.86	x	20.37
21.32	Joachim		Olsen	DEN	31.5.77	1	GP	Madrid		16 Jul
					20.23	21.32	20.65	p	p	p
21.28	1		København	25 Aug	19.67	20.85	20.58	20.95	20.88	21.28
21.27	1		Kuortane	26 Jun	21.27	x	20.68	20.43	20.85	20.37
21.24	2	Coom	Stadskanaal	3 Jul	19.77	21.11	x	21.24	21.13	20.89
21.19i	1	EI	Madrid	5 Mar	21.19	20.76	20.52	20.81	x	x
21.16i	1		Nordhausen	28 Jan	20.84	21.16	x	x	20.73	20.46
	(31/7)									
21.13	Jamie		Beyer	USA	29.12.76	2	GP II	Stanford		30 May
21.08	Andrey		Mikhnevich	BLR	12.7.76	1	NC	Brest		3 Jul
20.94	Edis		Elkasevic	CRO	18.2.83	1		Velenje		23 Jun
	(10)									
20.94	Sheldon		Battle	USA	23.6.83	4	NC	Carson		26 Jun
20.93i	Gheorghe		Guset	ROM	28.5.68	1	NC	Bucuresti		12 Feb
20.93	Yuriy		Belonog	UKR	9.3.74	1		Århus		24 Jul
20.80	Petr		Stehlik	CZE	15.4.77	1		Turnov		24 May
20.75	Dan		Taylor	USA	12.5.82	2	CalR	Modesto		7 May
20.72	Detlef		Bock	GER	15.8.74	2		Engers		29 May
20.71	Anton		Lyuboslavskiy	RUS	26.6.84	1	Znam	Kazan		24 Jun
20.64	Ville		Tiisanoja	FIN	24.12.75	1		Eurajoki		15 Jun
20.64	Tomasz		Majewski	POL	30.8.81	1		Poznan		31 Jul
20.62	Carl		Myerscough	GBR	21.10.79	1		Lincoln, NE		4 Jun
	(20)									
20.61	Mikulás		Konopka	SVK	23.1.79	1		Palafrugell		28 May
20.57	Ivan		Yushkov	RUS	15.1.81	1	NC	Tula		10 Jul
20.54	Khaled Habash		Al-Suwaidi	QAT	10.10.84	1	Klim	Staiki		25 Jun
20.51i	Manuel		Martínez	ESP	7.12.74	1		Madrid		24 Feb
20.44	Garrett		Johnson	USA	24.5.84	7	NC	Carson		26 Jun
20.43	Janus		Robberts	RSA	10.3.79	4	GP	Sevilla		4 Jun
20.43	Tepa		Reinikainen	FIN	16.3.76	4	GP	Helsinki		25 Jul
20.38	Pavel		Lyzhin	BLR	24.3.81	1		Brest		30 Apr
20.38	Andy		Dittmar	GER	5.7.74	2		Schapbach		25 Jun
20.30	Miran		Vodovnik	SLO	11.9.77	1		Slovenska Bistrica		15 May
	(30)									
20.30	Andrey		Borodkin	UKR	18.4.78	1		Kiev		21 Jun
20.25	Dragan		Peric	SCG	8.5.64	1		Sofia		7 Jul
20.23	Taavi		Peetre	EST	5.7.83	1		Tartu		1 Aug
20.21	Dorian		Scott	JAM	1.2.82	1	CAC	Nassau		10 Jul

Mark	Name		Nat	Born	Pos	Meet	Venue	Date
20.21	Arsi	Harju	FIN	18.3.74	2	NC	Pori	15 Jul
20.18	Jeff	Chakouian	USA	20.4.82	1		Knoxville	9 Apr
20.17	Pavel	Chumachenko	RUS	5.4.71	1		Tula	13 Jun
20.15		Zhang Qi	CHN	2.4.84	1	NG	Nanjing	20 Oct
20.14	Clint	Prange	USA	21.10.81	1	NCAA-II	Abilene	27 May
20.13	Conny	Karlsson	FIN	30.12.75	3	NC	Pori	15 Jul
	(40)							
20.10	Scott	Martin	AUS	12.10.82	1		Melbourne (BH)	3 Dec
20.09	Chris	Figures	USA	8.10.81	2	NCAA-II	Abilene	27 May
20.09	Aleksandr	Salnikov	RUS	27.9.71	2	Znam	Kazan	24 Jun
20.05	Russ	Winger	USA	2.8.84	9	NC	Carson	26 Jun
20.05	Pavel	Sofin	RUS	4.9.81	2	NC	Tula	10 Jul
20.04	Marco Antonio	Verni	CHI	27.2.76	3		Salamanca	6 Jul
20.04	Mark	Proctor	GBR	15.1.63	1		Manchester (Str)	30 Aug
20.03i	Magnus	Lohse	SWE	28.7.84	1		Laramie	29 Jan
20.01	Sean	Shields	USA	10.2.83	1		Los Angeles (Ww)	9 Apr
19.94i	Nedzad	Mulabegovic	CRO	4.2.81	1		West Lafayette	19 Feb
	(50)							
19.90	Vince	Mosca	USA	23.1.80	4		New York (RI)	11 Jun
19.89	Ranvijay	Singh	IND	2.10.84	1		New Delhi	10 May
19.88i	Peter	Sack	GER	27.7.79			Chemnitz	22 Jan
19.87	Yuriy	Belov	BLR	20.3.81	4		Bydgoszcz	5 Jun
19.85i	Marco	Dodoni	ITA	5.9.72	1		Schio	27 Jan
19.84	Mika	Vasara	FIN	22.10.83	3	EU23	Erfurt	17 Jul
19.83	Dylan	Armstrong	CAN	15.1.81	1		Claremont	15 Apr
19.83	Zsolt	Biber	HUN	31.5.76	2	Cezmi	Istanbul	4 Jun
19.82	Navpreet	Singh	IND	15.6.78	1		Ludhiana	24 May
19.80i	Oleg	Korotkov	RUS	16.3.80	1	NC	Volgograd	10 Feb
	(60)							
19.76	Leszek	Sliwa	POL	20.9.79	1		Kutno	8 Sep
19.74i	Steven	Manz	USA	19.9.81	1		Ypsilanti	12 Feb
19.74i	Tony	Thompson	USA	12.3.80	2		Reno	19 Feb
19.74	Jimmy	Nordin	SWE	19.10.79	1	MAI	Malmö	16 Aug
19.72	Grigoriy	Panfilov	RUS	17.5.80	2		Irkutsk	19 Aug
19.70	Brian	Robison	USA	27.4.83	1	Big 12	Manhattan, KS	14 May
19.69i	Gaëtan	Bucki	FRA	9.5.80	1	NC	Liévin	20 Feb
19.69	Robert	Häggblom	FIN	9.8.82	1		Vaasa	25 Aug
19.66	Jesse	Roberge	USA	2.10.78	1		Claremont	14 May
19.65	Alexis	Paumier	CUB	21.1.75	1		La Habana	5 Jul
	(70)							
19.64	Timo	Aaltonen	FIN	11.4.69	1		Keuruu	24 Jun
19.60i	Vikas	Gowda	IND	5.7.83	1		Chapel Hill	19 Feb
19.59	Gunnar	Pfingsten	GER	24.3.75	1eB		Halle	21 May
19.57	Rhuben	Williams	USA	14.2.82	2	Pac10	Los Angeles (Ww)	14 May
19.51	Georgi	Ivanov	BUL	13.3.85	4	EU23	Erfurt	17 Jul
19.50	Rene	Sack	GER	14.7.76	5		Engers	29 May
19.49		Jia Peng	CHN	12.1.84	1	NC	Shijiazhuang	19 Jun
19.49	Hamza	Alic	BIH	20.1.79	3	MedG	Almeria	2 Jul
19.48	Jeremy	Silverman	USA	28.1.83	4		San Diego	23 Apr
19.47	Van	Mounts	USA	5.1.80	3	NCAA II	Abilene	27 May
	(80)							
19.46i	Galin	Kostadinov	BUL	25.12.79	1	NC	Sofia	5 Feb
19.46	Ivan	Emelianov	MDA	19.2.77	1		Onesti	21 May
19.46	Edhem	Kacevic	BIH	18.5.70	2		Novo Mesto	25 May
19.43i	Dmitriy	Goncharuk	BLR	17.7.70	1	NC	Minsk	28 Jan
19.41	Rhys	Jones	AUS	19.3.81	1		Canberra	5 Feb
19.41	Conrad	Woolsey	USA	20.2.81	3	Big 12	Manhattan, KS	14 May
19.37i	Andrey	Sinyakov	BLR	6.1.82	2	NC	Minsk	28 Jan
19.28	Raigo	Toompuu	EST	17.7.81	1	3-N	Tartu	27 Jul
19.25	Burger	Lambrechts	RSA	3.4.73	2		Oudtshoorn	5 Mar
19.25		Tian Yingchun	CHN	29.5.79	2	NG	Nanjing	20 Oct
	(90)							
19.23	Tomasz	Chrzanowski	POL	12.7.81	2		Poznan	31 Jul
19.23i	Justin	Clickett	USA	12.4.85	1		Pittsburgh	2 Dec
19.22	Seppo	Kujala	FIN	24.9.80	3	Nurmi	Turku	5 Jun
19.22	Mihaíl	Stamatóyiannis	GRE	20.5.82	1		Thessaloníki	2 Jul
19.21	Antonín	Zalsky	CZE	7.8.80	3		Turnov	24 May
19.21	Milan	Jotanovic	SCG	11.1.84	3	NCAA-r	New York	27 May
19.18	Eddy	Cardol	NED	6.5.78	1	ECp-1B	Leiria	18 Jun
19.16	Sven-Eric	Hahn	GER	17.10.80	2		Atlanta	13 May
19.09	Kresimir	Radja	CRO	3.11.81	1		Rijeka	7 Jun

Mark	Name		Nat	Born	Pos	Meet	Venue	Date
19.08	Yves (100)	Niaré	FRA	20.7.77	1		Pézenas	28 May

Mark		Name	Nat	Born	Date
19.05	Zack	Lloyd	USA	10.10.84	4 May
19.05		Zhang Heng	CHN	18.5.83	25 Jul
19.03	David	Nichols	USA	13.1.85	14 May
19.03	Joe	Thomas	USA	4.12.84	15 May
19.02	Dominic	Zielinski	POL	25.4.80	1 May
19.02	Andrey	Semyonov	UKR	4.7.84	18 May
19.02	Tilman	Northoff	GER	18.6.69	5 Jul
19.01i	Brian	Hallett	USA	20.5.79	19 Feb
18.98	Andrey	Nemchaninov	UKR	27.11.66	2 Jul
18.98	Andréas	Anastasópoulos	GRE	2.4.76	27 Jul
18.97i	John	Newell	USA	20.5.79	27 Feb
18.97	Sultan Mubarak	Al-Hebshi	KSA	23.2.83	12 Apr
18.97	Ken	Kemeny	USA	16.4.82	27 May
18.97	Scott	Rider	GBR	22.9.77	4 Jun
18.96	Tucker	Woolsey	USA	7.2.79	4 Jun
18.95	Wim	Blondeel	BEL	25.12.73	28 May
18.94	John	Caulfield	USA	22.8.84	18 May
18.91	Will	Denbo	USA	24.2.84	9 Apr
18.88i	Derek	Anderson	USA	7.7.83	9 Jan
18.88	Andy	Banse	USA	13.3.81	2 Apr
18.87	Mark	Edwards	GBR	2.12.74	8 Jun
18.85	Cory	Martin	USA	22.5.85	27 May
18.85	Mehdi	Shahrokhi	IRI	23.5.85	4 Sep
18.84i	Gerhard	Zillner	AUT	22.1.71	15 Jan
18.84	Kuldeep	Singh Mann	IND	16.10.82	17 May
18.84	Luka	Rujevic	SCG	14.10.85	25 Jun
18.83	Kevin	Bookout	USA	12.2.83	10 Jun
18.82	Cody	Brotherton	USA	12.7.84	16 Apr
18.81	Sam	Segond	USA	4.4.83	7 May
18.81	Robert	Dippl	GER	21.10.83	15 Jul
18.80	Shakti	Singh	IND	14.5.62	4 Jul
18.79i	Jarkko	Haukijärvi	FIN	10.6.77	19 Feb
18.78	Clay	Cross	AUS	26.11.77	5 Mar
18.75i	Paolo	Dal Soglio	ITA	29.7.70	20 Feb
18.74i	Ryan	Norwood	USA	5.9.81	3 Mar
18.74	Roelie	Potgieter	RSA	20.3.80	11 Mar
18.74	Yoger	Medina	VEN	5.9.73	21 Aug
18.73	Amin	Nikfar	IRI	2.1.81	12 Apr
18.73	Fatih	Yazici	TUR	4.11.79	11 May
18.73	Maris	Urtans	LAT	9.2.81	21 May
18.73	Jakub	Giza	POL	26.4.85	28 May

Mark		Name	Nat	Born	Date
18.70	Tyler	Custis	USA	22.10.84	9 Apr
18.69	Jake	Knight	USA	10.3.83	8 Apr
18.68i		Abudula Yubulayin	CHN	8.1.81	5 Mar
18.68	Soslan	Tsirikhov	RUS	24.11.84	5 Jun
18.64	Kimani	Kirton	JAM	16.5.84	13 May
18.64	Gjøran	Sørli	NOR	3.6.78	21 Aug
18.63i	Simon	Stewart	USA	28.1.80	28 Jan
18.61	Ioánnis	Vasilópoulos	GRE	16.1.75	2 Jul
18.60	Richard	Harrison	USA	13.5.70	19 Apr
18.60	Borja	Vivas	ESP	26.5.84	14 Jun
18.59	Germán	Millán	ESP	21.5.79	23 Jul
18.58i	Niklas	Arrhenius	SWE	10.9.82	12 Feb
18.58	Tuomo	Tihinen	FIN	12.12.77	20 Aug
18.58	Yasser Fathi	Ibrahim	EGY	2.5.84	25 Aug
18.57	Yioser	Toledo	CUB	24.4.83	11 Mar
18.57		Hui Zhenbao	CHN	10.1.82	20 Oct
18.56	Jaiveer	Singh	IND	1.11.70	21 May
18.55i	Ryan	Ketchum	USA	12.3.83	12 Feb
18.54	Shawn	Best	USA	9.4.84	1 May
18.52	Philipp	Barth	GER	26.12.83	21 May
18.51i	dinn Björn	Thorsteinsson	ISL	3.12.81	3 May
18.50i	Andre	Reid	JAM	26.8.82	6 Mar
18.50	Jiovanny	García	COL	19.12.84	21 Aug
18.49i	Aleksandr	Grekov	RUS	6.5.85	18 Feb
18.49	Chad	McClendon	USA	2.10.83	7 May
18.49	Ian	Waltz	USA	15.4.77	30 May
18.46		Li Wenkui	CHN	31.12.71	20 Oct
18.45	Nikolay	Umrikhin	RUS	1.1.84	10 Jul
18.45i	Brent	Shelby	USA	13.12.82	10 Dec
18.41	Jaroslav	Pittner	SVK	20.4.84	15 May
18.40	Adam	Kuehl	USA	19.1.84	21 May
18.40	Jhonny	Rodríguez	COL	12.11.79	23 Jun
18.39i	Bubba	Kramer	USA	25.10.84	26 Feb
18.39	Dragan	Mustapic	CRO	23.3.63	14 May
18.37		Shon Hyun	KOR	27.5.79	17 Oct
18.36		Zhang Jun	CHN	11.4.83	19 Jun
18.35i	Aukusitino	Hoatau	FRA	27.8.81	16 Jan
18.33	Andy	Fryman	USA	3.2.85	27 May
18.32i	David	Adamek	CAN	6.2.84	3 Dec
18.30	Jarred (180)	Rome	USA	21.12.76	30 May

Best outdoor marks

Mark	Name	Pos	Meet	Venue	Date
21.29	Hoffa	1	SGP	Doha	13 May
20.75	Guset	2	EThCp	Mersin	13 Mar
20.32	Martínez	1		Salamanca	6 Jul
19.68	P Sack	4		Gotha	10 Jun
19.58	Dodoni	1		Savona	22 May
19.55	Mulabegovic	1		Bloomington	6 May
19.31	Sinyakov	3	Klim	Staiki	25 Jun
19.12	Lohse	1	NC-23	Söderhamn	12 Aug

Mark	Name	Date
18.96	Hallett	17 Apr
18.96	Bucki	8 May
18.95	Goncharuk	1 Jun
18.93	Manz	16 Apr
18.78	Kostadinov	20 May
18.77	Zillner	22 Jun
18.71	Clickett	27 May
18.67	Newell	27 May
18.66	Dal Soglio	12 Jun
18.59	Thompson	2 Apr
18.57	Stewart	17 Apr
18.53	Ketchum	15 May
18.52	Norwood	23 Apr
18.39	Abudula Yubulayin	19Jun
18.31	Reid	15 Apr
18.30	Korotkov	24 Jun

JUNIORS

Mark	Name		Nat	Born	Pos	Meet	Venue	Date
18.28	Remigius	Machura	CZE	7.1.86	1	NC-23	Olomouc	25 Aug
	18.14 3 Ostrava 3 Sep			18.03	3	NC	Kladno	2 Jul
18.07i	Amin Atia	Al-Aradi	KSA	13.5.86	2		Tehran	9 Feb
18.05	Satinder	Kumar	IND	19.5.86	1		New Delhi	11 Mar
17.65	Carlos	Véliz	CUB	12.8.87	5	Barr	La Habana	19 May
17.61	Nate	Englin	USA	24.4.86	9	NCAA-r	Bloomington	27 May
17.61	Lajos	Kürthy	HUN	22.10.86	1		Pécs	2 Oct
17.45	Harrison	Benjamin	USA	25.2.86	1		El Paso	2 Apr

6kg Shot

Mark	Name		Nat	Born	Pos	Meet	Venue	Date
20.55	Lajos	Kürthy	HUN	22.10.86	1		Mohács	14 Oct
	19.77 1 Kaposvár 5 Oct			19.65	2	EJ	Kaunas	22 Jul
	19.73 1 Budapest 21 May							
20.20	Saurabh	Vij	IND	14.6.87	1		New Delhi	25 Aug
20.09	Remigius	Machura	CZE	7.1.86	1	EJ	Kaunas	22 Jul
	19.69 1 Mannheim 18 Jun			19.64	1	NC-j	Pardubice	25 Jun
19.75	Ryan	Whitting	USA	24.11.86	1	PAm-J	Windsor	29 Jul
	19.74 1 NC-j Carson 23 Jun							
19.61	Nate	Englin	USA	24.4.86	2	PAM-J	Windsor	29 Jul
19.56	Viktor	Samolyuk	UKR	5.9.86	1		Tula	24 Jun
19.42		Wang Guangtu	CHN	15.11.87	1		Zhengzhou	28 Aug
19.32	Maksim	Sidorov	RUS	13.5.86	3		Kaunas	22 Jul
19.25	Piotr	Golba	POL	7.7.86	1		Bydgoszcz	5 Jul

Mark	Name			Nat	Born	Pos	Meet	Venue		Date
19.21	Marko		Hübenbecker (10)	GER	14.6.86			Zeven		14 May
19.20	Péter		Kovács	HUN	3.1.86	2		Budapest		19 Jun
19.20	Kamil		Zbroszczyk	POL	24.1.87	2	NC-j	Bydgoszcz		5 Jul
19.08	Damianós		Kaloyerákis	GRE	6.9.86	1	NC-j	Thessaloníki		10 Jul
19.08	Om		Prakash	IND	.87	2		New Delhi		25 Aug
19.00	Mamuka		Tugushi	GEO	19.4.86	4	EJ	Kaunas		22 Jul
18.98	Chris		Gearing	GBR	30.9.86	1		Abingdon		4 Sep
18.97i	Piotr		Radziwon	POL	26.9.87	2		Spala		28 Jan
18.95i	Maicol		Spallanzani	ITA	14.9.87	1		Genova		6 Feb
18.92	Mostafa Abdul		El-Moaty	EGY	14.1.87	1		Cairo		8 May
18.89	Candy		Bauer	GER	31.7.86	2		Mannheim		18 Jun

DISCUS

Mark	Name			Nat	Born	Pos	Meet	Venue		Date
70.67	Virgilijus		Alekna	LTU	13.2.72	1	GP	Madrid		16 Jul
					66.49	68.60	x	69.97	70.67	x
70.61	1		Talinn	16 Sep	66.03	68.35	65.21	68.97	68.10	70.61
70.58	1		Réthimno	10 Jul	67.80	x	67.84	69.86	70.58	67.25
70.53	1	Athl	Lausanne	5 Jul	67.92	67.79	68.69	70.53	x	x
70.17	1	WCh	Helsinki	7 Aug	63.93	67.90	68.10	66.75	x	70.17
69.57	1	FBK	Hengelo	29 May	68.92	69.54	x	69.10	68.02	69.57
69.22	1	BrGP	Sheffield	21 Aug	64.40	69.22	65.04	x	x	68.88
69.21	1	NC	Kaunas	8 Jul	67.40	67.30	65.44	66.83	x	69.21
69.06	1		Vilnius	22 Apr	66.10	64.04	66.79	x	65.33	69.06
68.94	1	Sule	Tartu	11 Jun	68.94	65.41	x	x	68.56	x
68.79	Q	WCh	Helsinki	6 Aug	68.79		only throw			
68.05	1	GP	Sevilla	4 Jun		62.34	65.62	68.05	67.01	x
68.04	1		Halle	21 May	65.54	66.04	65.37	68.04	67.22	x
68.03	1		Põltsmaa	17 Sep	62.67	65.76	68.03	63.26	65.09	64.42
68.00	1	WK	Zürich	19 Aug	66.69	68.00	x	67.83	64.83	67.71
67.91	1		Turnov	24 May	67.39	66.27	67.23	67.91	x	x
67.81	1		Vilnius	9 Jun	66.37	66.13	x	64.83	67.81	67.30
67.64	1	WAF	Monaco	9 Sep	64.59	67.16	x	67.64		
70.10	Gerd		Kanter	EST	6.5.79	1		Chula Vista		27 Apr
					65.96	70.10	x	x	x	x
69.35	2		Tallinn	16 Sep	66.14	67.80	69.35	66.58	x	65.85
68.61	1		La Jolla	23 Apr	68.61	?	?	x	x	65.01
68.57	2	WCh	Helsinki	7 Aug	x	64.69	65.10	68.57	65.53	62.64
68.32	2	Athl	Lausanne	5 Jul	x	x	68,32	65.37	63.61	x
68.16	1	ECp1A	Gävle	19 Jun	64.85	x	68.16	x		
67.92	2	WK	Zürich	19 Aug	x	65.62	x	67.92	66.28	p
67.51	2	BrGP	Sheffield	21 Aug	x	67.51	x	x	x	x
67.47	2		Vilnius	9 Jun	66.42	67.47	64.84	63.65	x	x
67.93	Aleksander		Tammert	EST	2.2.73	1		Denton		28 Apr
					62.70	x	62.70	67.93	x	x
67.45	Lois Maikel		Martínez	CUB	3.6.81	1		La Habana		8 Jul
					58.49	60.08	x	64.22	67.45	63.04
67.39	Jarred		Rome	USA	21.12.76	1eA		Salinas		18 May
	(30/5)									
67.30	Frantz		Kruger	RSA	22.5.75	3	WK	Zürich		19 Aug
66.95	Ian		Waltz	USA	15.4.77	1		La Jolla		18 Jun
66.59	Jason		Tunks	CAN	7.5.75	1		Leiden		11 Jun
66.57	Mario		Pestano	ESP	8.4.78	4	WK	Zürich		19 Aug
66.56	Michael		Möllenbeck	GER	12.12.69	1		Wiesbaden		28 May
	(10)									
66.39	Lars		Riedel	GER	28.6.67	1		Thum		16 Aug
66.02	Robert		Harting	GER	18.10.84	2		Wiesbaden		28 May
66.00	Zoltán		Kövágó	HUN	10.4.79	6	WK	Zürich		19 Aug
65.56	Andrzej		Krawczyk	POL	11.4.76	1		Norrtälje		11 Jul
65.51	Rutger		Smith	NED	9.7.81	1	NC	Amsterdam		10 Jul
65.42	Gábor		Máté	HUN	9.2.79	3	GP	Sevilla		4 Jun
65.32	Frank		Casañas	CUB	18.10.78	1		La Habana		29 Apr
65.25	Ehsan		Hadadi	IRI	21.1.85	1	AsiC	Inchon		1 Sep
65.24	Roland		Varga	HUN	22.10.77	1		Szombathely		24 Jul
65.12	Timo		Tompuri	FIN	9.6.69	1		Eurajoki		15 Jun
	(20)									
65.11	Kibwe		Johnson	USA	17.7.81	1		Berea		20 May
64.95	Carl		Brown	USA	11.2.70	4		San Diego		23 Apr
64.79	Yuriy		Belonog	UKR	9.3.74	1		Kiev		19 May
64.74	Piotr		Malachowski	POL	7.6.83	1	NC	Biala Podlaska		26 Jun
64.69	Vikas		Gowda	IND	5.7.83	1		Charlotte		2 Apr

Mark	Name		Nat	Born	Pos	Meet	Venue	Date
64.69	Jorge	Balliengo	ARG	5.1.78	1		Rosario	3 May
64.36	Omar	El-Ghazaly	EGY	9.2.84	1		Cairo	10 Aug
64.28		Wu Tao	CHN	3.10.83	1		Chongqing	15 May
64.08	Bogdan	Pishchalnikov	RUS	26.8.82	1	NC-w	Adler	18 Feb
63.65	Benn	Harradine	AUS	14.10.82	3eA		Salinas	18 May
	(30)							
63.62	Dmitriy	Shevchenko	RUS	13.5.68	1	Znam	Kazan	25 Jun
63.38	Abbas	Samimi	IRI	9.6.77	1		Shiraz	20 May
63.32	Gaute	Myklebust	NOR	29.4.79	1		Helsingborg	23 Jul
63.27	Mikko	Kyyrö	FIN	12.7.80	1		Oulu	28 May
63.17	Mart	Israel	EST	23.9.83	4		Chula Vista	27 Apr
63.11	Libor	Malina	CZE	14.6.73	3		Salon-de-Provence	29 May
63.10	Janne	Hummastenniemi	FIN	3.10.79	2		Oulu	28 May
63.10	Jo	Van Daele	BEL	6.4.72	1		Berlin	1 Jun
63.05	Gjøran	Sørli	NOR	3.6.78	2		Helsingborg	23 Jul
62.99	Dariusz	Slowik	CAN	15.8.77	5eA		Salinas	18 May
	(40)							
62.85	Gerhard	Mayer	AUT	20.5.80	3		Helsingborg	23 Jul
62.85		Li Shaojie	CHN	26.11.75	1	NG	Nanjing	20 Oct
62.80	Dragan	Mustapic	CRO	23.3.63	1		Split	15 May
62.80	Vasiliy	Kaptyukh	BLR	27.6.67	1		Staiki	21 Jul
62.76	Aleksandr	Malasevich	BLR	7.4.77	2		Staiki	21 Jul
62.73	Torsten	Schmidt	GER	9.12.74	1		Schwerin	5 Jun
62.72	Hannes	Kirchler	ITA	22.12.78	1	GP II	Milano	1 Jun
62.62	Pertti	Hynni	FIN	14.2.60	1		Helsinki	26 Jun
62.59	Stanislav	Nesterovskiy	UKR	31.7.80	1		Kiev	5 Jun
62.58	Cristiano	Andrei	ITA	14.5.73	1		Donnas	19 Jun
	(50)							
62.58	Scott	Martin	AUS	12.10.82	1		Melbourne (BH)	10 Dec
62.52	Kiril	Chuprinin	UKR	22.7.75	2		Kiev	19 May
62.46	Aleksey	Semyonov	UKR	27.6.82	3		Kiev	5 Jun
62.46	Nick	Petrucci	USA	10.11.75	2		La Jolla	18 Jun
62.35i	Mika	Loikkanen	FIN	20.2.74	1		Helsinki	26 Feb
62.30	Diego	Fortuna	ITA	14.2.68	1		Pergine Valsugana	22 Jul
62.07	Olgierd	Stanski	POL	4.4.73	2		Lublin	11 Jun
62.01	Michael	Lischka	GER	23.12.73	5		Wiesbaden	28 May
61.87	Casey	Malone	USA	6.4.77	6	Athl	Lausanne	5 Jul
61.77	Graham	Hicks	AUS	14.12.78	1eB		Salinas	18 May
	(60)							
61.76	Aleksandr	Borichevskiy	RUS	25.6.70	3	Znam	Kazan	25 Jun
61.70	Michael	Robertson	USA	19.12.83	5	MSR	Walnut	17 Apr
61.66	Anil	Kumar	IND	20.6.75	3		Szombathely	24 Jul
61.59	Daniel	Vanek	SVK	18.1.83	1	JUCO	Levelland	17 May
61.53	Carl	Myerscough	GBR	21.10.79	1		Lincoln, NE	4 Jun
61.26	Johannes	van Wyk	RSA	16.3.80	2		Donnas	19 Jun
61.20	Vadim	Hranovschi	MDA	14.2.83	1		Chisinau	29 Apr
61.18	Emeka	Udechuku	GBR	10.7.79	1		Carshalton	7 May
61.11	Sultan M.	Al-Dawoodi	KSA	16.6.77	1		Manama	28 Apr
61.06	Adam	Kuehl	USA	19.1.84	3		La Jolla	18 Jun
	(70)							
60.94	Hannes	Hopley	RSA	26.1.81	7	GP	Sevilla	4 Jun
60.87	Sam	Segond	USA	4.4.83	1	PennR	Philadelphia	29 Apr
60.79	Ercüment	Olgundeniz	TUR	7.7.76	1	BalkC	Novi Sad	24 Jul
60.77	Garrett	Johnson	USA	24.5.84	1	NCAA-r	New York	27 May
60.68	Matt	Schwinn	USA	14.1.80	1		Vancouver	2 Apr
60.62	Dmitriy	Sivakov	BLR	15.2.83	3	EU23	Erfurt	16 Jul
60.61	Paulo	Bernardo	POR	21.11.74	2	1 NC	Lisboa (U)	24 Jul
60.55	Sergey	Pruglo	UKR	18.11.83	4		Kiev	5 Jun
60.55	Yuriy	Seskin	RUS	7.7.66	3	NC	Tula	11 Jul
60.54	Edis	Elkasevic	CRO	18.2.83	6		La Jolla	23 Apr
	(80)							
60.51	Stefano	Lomater	ITA	23.4.74	2		Pergine Valsugana	22 Jul
60.39	Vyacheslav	Ivashkin	RUS	6.3.74	5	Znam	Kazan	25 Jun
60.33	Niklas	Arrhenius	SWE	10.9.82	8eA		Salinas	18 May
60.33	Stéfanos	Kónstas	GRE	16.5.77	1	NC	Athína	11 Jun
60.28	Yunio	Lastre	CUB	26.10.81	2		La Habana	23 Jun
60.27i	Jouni	Helppikangas	FIN	10.2.71	2		Helsinki	26 Feb
60.27	Erik	Cadée	NED	15.2.84	2	NC	Amsterdam	10 Jul
60.11	Rasheed	Al-Dosari	QAT	8.5.81	2	WAsG	Doha	7 Dec
60.08	Cameron	Bolles	USA	24.3.76	2	CalR	Modesto	7 May
60.04	Aléxandros	Ganotákis	GRE	3.12.74	2		Athína (E)	7 May
	(90)							

Mark	Name		Nat	Born	Pos	Meet	Venue	Date
59.96	Sergey	Lyakhov	RUS	1.3.68	6	Znam	Kazan	25 Jun
59.88	Michal	Hodun	POL	17.2.83	4	NC	Biala Podlaska	26 Jun
59.77	Luke	Sullivan	USA	4.6.76	3eB		Salinas	18 May
59.76	Reedus	Thurmond	USA	15.12.79	4eB		Salinas	18 May
59.76	Dan	Austin	USA	12.4.83	1		Waverly	26 May
59.73	Nuermaimaiti Tulake		CHN	8.3.82	2		Chongqing	15 May
59.63	Ruslan	Khlebov	BLR	15.2.83	4	NC	Brest	3 Jul
59.61	Bertrand	Vili	FRA	6.9.83	Q	NC-23	Paris (C)	28 Jul
59.54	Marcelo	Pugliese	ARG	2.9.68	2	NC	Santa Fe	2 Jul
59.50	Henrik (100)	Wennberg	SWE	11.3.66	1		Austin	8 Oct

Mark	Name		Nat	Born	Date
59.49	Brian	Trainor	USA	14.3.80	2 Apr
59.49	Mike	van der Bilt	NED	23.10.76	10 Jul
59.45		Zhang Cunbiao	CHN	11.2.69	21 Jun
59.45	Dragan	Peric	SCG	8.5.64	24 Jul
59.36	Nate	Meckes	USA	27.6.83	28 May
59.29	Igor	Primc	SLO	8.1.66	19 Jun
59.29	Tim	Driesen	AUS	27.3.84	30 Sep
59.26	Tony	Thompson	USA	2.3.80	16 Apr
59.23	Jean-Claude	Retel	FRA	11.2.68	29 Jun
59.13	Andy	Bloom	USA	11.8.73	19 Apr
59.10		Xu Yongyi	CHN	28.7.84	22 May
59.04	Eric	Forshaw	CAN	14.9.68	25 Jun
58.97	Spirídon	Arabatzís	GRE	2.6.78	22 May
58.88	Jamal	Cann	USA	12.7.82	11 Jun
58.84	Sascha	Hördt	GER	27.4.84	18 Jun
58.82	Shaka	Sola	SAM	14.3.77	12 Feb
58.82	Jorge	Grave	POR	1.9.82	20 Jul
58.77	Raigo	Toompuu	EST	17.7.81	13 May
58.66	Derek	Anderson	USA	7.7.83	1 Apr
58.64	Yannick	Gunzle	FRA	30.11.81	29 May
58.62	Aaron	Neighbour	AUS	2.12.77	19 Feb
58.61	Stanislav	Alekseyev	RUS	10.2.82	19 May
58.56	Yves	Niaré	FRA	20.7.77	2 Jul
58.52	Ryan	Ketchum	USA	12.3.83	2 Apr
58.49	Chima	Ugwu	NGR	19.7.73	23 Apr
58.49	Clint	Prange	USA	21.10.81	28 May
58.48	Stephen	Boozer	USA	17.5.85	9 Apr
58.41	Arnost	Holovsky	CZE	10.4.82	4 Jun
58.40	Petr	Vuklisevic	CZE	25.2.82	18 Sep
58.31	Luka	Rujevic	SCG	14.10.85	1 Aug
58.21	Ilya	Kostin	RUS	1.4.79	12 Jul
58.17	Sean	Shields	USA	10.2.83	26 Mar
58.12	Tim	Brodersen	USA	15.12.82	9 Apr
58.11	Aukusitino	Hoatau	FRA	27.8.81	5 Jul
58.00	Shigeo	Hatakeyama	JPN	9.3.77	14 May
57.98	Joachim	Olsen	DEN	31.5.77	11 Jun
57.89	Mickaël	Conjungo	FRA	6.5.69	2 Jun
57.88	dinn Björn	Thorsteinsson	ISL	3.12.81	19 May
57.88	Sergey	Gribkov	RUS	30.4.85	19 May
57.80	Sheldon (140)	Battle	USA	23.6.83	29 Apr

Best outdoors

Mark	Name		Nat	Born	Date
60.16	Jouni	Helppikangas	FIN	10.2.71	30 Jul
60.08	Mika	Loikkanen	FIN	20.2.74	17 Jul

JUNIORS

Mark	Name		Nat	Born	Pos	Meet	Venue	Date
56.88		Wu Jian	CHN	25.5.86	5		Chongqing	15 May
56.80	Margus	Hunt	EST	14.7.87	10	Sule	Tartu	11 Jun
56.35	Westley	Stockbarger	USA	28.11.86	1		Coral Gables	16 Apr
56.10	Leif	Arrhenius	SWE	15.7.86	3		Helsingborg	10 Jul
55.38	Martin	Wierig	GER	10.6.87			Magdeburg	29 Apr
54.82	Ronnie	Buckley	AUS	15.6.86	4		Perth	22 Jan
54.60	Kamil	Grzegorczyk	POL	1.7.86	1		Slubice	11 Oct
54.58	Lajos	Kürthy	HUN	22.10.86	2		Budapest	14 May
54.57		Xin Jin	CHN-Y	1.3.88	5		Yixing	22 May
54.26	Mousaeb	Al-Momani	JOR	28.8.86	8	Isl.Sol	Makkah	13 Apr
54.19	Mihai-Liviu	Grasu	ROM	21.4.87	1	NC	Bucuresti	3 Jul
54.08	Eki	Faagai	USA	6.2.86	7		La Jolla	18 Jun
53.69	Jorge Y.	Fernández	CUB	2.10.87	3	NC	La Habana	17 Mar

1.75kg Discus

Mark	Name		Nat	Born	Pos	Meet	Venue	Date
62.21	Margus	Hunt	EST	14.7.87	1		Tartu	1 Oct
	62.19 1 EJ Kaunas 23 Jul						60.81 1 Viljandi	25 May
	60.92 1 Frauenfeld 24 Sep							
61.40	Ryan	Whitting	USA	24.11.86	1		Windsor	31 Jul
60.96	Martin	Wierig	GER	10.6.87	1		Halle	21 May
	60.82 1 Wiesbaden 28 May						60.11 1 Mannheim	18 Jun
60.14	Leif	Arrhenius	SWE	15.7.86	1		Helsingborg	10 Jul
59.92	Kamil	Grzegorczyk	POL	1.7.86	1		Wrocław	14 May
59.76	Mihai	Grasu	ROM	21.4.87	1		Bucuresti	7 Aug
59.75	Lajos	Kürthy	HUN	22.10.86	2	EJ	Kaunas	23 Jul
59.16	Maxim	Malymon	UKR	5.1.86	1		Kiev	19 May
58.87	Pavlo	Karsak	UKR	11.11.87	1		Kiev	5 Jun
58.25	Patrick	Werner (10)	GER	9.8.86			Karlstadt	4 Jun
58.12	Jorge Y.	Fernández	CUB	2.10.87	1	NC-j	Santiago de Cuba	23 May
58.06	Mohammad	Samimi	IRI	18.9.88	1		Sari	3 Aug
57.95	Oleg	Frankov	UKR	13.11.86	2		Kiev	5 Jun
57.89	Oleg	Rogonov	BLR	.86	1		Tula	26 Jun
57.74	Ronnie	Buckley	AUS	15.6.86	1		Melbourne	-13 Feb
57.60	Martin	Richter	GER	6.1.86			Schönebeck	9 Jul

HAMMER

Mark	Name		Nat	Born	Pos	Meet	Venue	Date
86.73	Ivan	Tikhon	BLR	24.7.76	1	NC	Brest	3 Jul
				83.81	83.62	84.80	recx 83.84	86.73
	84.80 1 WCh Helsinki		8 Aug	x	x	80.97	83.89 x	81.52

Mark	Name		Nat	Born	Pos	Meet	Venue	Date
	83.64 1 Klim	Staiki	25 Jun	? 78.62 x 83.64 82.96 81.88				
	82.53 1	Dubnica nad Váhom	29 Aug	77.78. 80.83 82.53 79.87				
	81.70 1 WAF	Szombathely	3 Sep	76.87 81.70 78.98 80.65 x 80.35				
	81.13 1	Yokohama	19 Sep	78.66 78.21 78.68 77.48 80.43 81.13				
	80.79 1 EThCp	Mersin	13 Mar	76.56 77.88 78.49 80.79 x x				
	80.56 1	Banská Bystrica	28 Aug	80.04 80.56 79.90 80.45				
84.90	Vadim	Devyatovskiy	BLR	20.3.77	1		Staiki	21 Jul
				83.55 x x 83.29 84.90 84.58				
	83.69 2 NC	Brest	3 Jul	79.65 81.12 83.69 81.60 82.62 82.07				
	82.60 2 WCh	Helsinki	8 Aug	78.11 80.45 82.60 x 80.47 82.19				
	82.14 2 Klim	Staiki	3 Jul	? 82.14 79.71 80.54 76.79 80.25				
	80.17 1 GP	Osaka	7 May					
	81.31 Q NC	Brest	3 Jul					
	81.20 Q WCh	Helsinki	6 Aug	76.86 81.20 two throws				
	79.68 2	Yokohama	19 Sep	75.08 77.94 77.42 x 76.32 79.68				
	79.64 1	Halle	21 May	76.85 79.64 x 78.45 77.00 x				
81.45	Esref	Apak	TUR	3.1.82	1	Cezmi	Istanbul	4 Jun
				77.23 x 79.03 x 79.79 81.45				
81.00	Andrey	Skvaruk	UKR	9.3.67	1	NC	Kiev	3 Jul
				x 79.80 79.78 81.00 79.00 x				
80.85	Libor	Charfreitag	SVK	11.9.77	1		Arlington	2 Apr
	80.30 1 MSR	Walnut	17 Apr	x 78.32 80.16 78.21 79.41 80.30				
80.81	Aleksey	Zagornyi	RUS	31.5.78	1	NC-w	Adler	19 Feb
				79.26 x 80.81 x x x				
80.63	Chris	Harmse	RSA	31.5.73	1	NC	Durban	15 Apr
				x 80.63 x x 78.50 78.00				
80.41	András	Haklits	CRO	23.9.77	1		Marietta	29 May
80.03	Krisztián	Pars	HUN	18.2.82	2		Dubnica	29 Aug
				x 78.09 x 80.03				
80.00	Markus	Esser (10)	GER	3.2.80	1		Leichlingen	4 Jun
	79.66 1	Leverkusen	23 Jul	x x 77.69 x 79.66 75.13				
79.92	Ilya	Konovalov	RUS	4.3.71	1		Sochi	26 May
				77.13 77.30 76/60 77.42 78.79 79.92				
79.81	Olli-Pekka	Karjalainen	FIN	7.3.80	2	WAF	Szombathely	3 Sep
				78.77 x 77.62 77.29 79.81 78.77				
	79.69 1	Lapua	30 Jul					
	(30/12)							
79.56	Artyom	Rubanko	UKR	21.3.74	1		Kiev	12 May
79.47	Vadim	Khersontsev	RUS	8.7.74	1	Kuts	Moskva	15 Jul
79.46	Karsten	Kobs	GER	16.9.71	1		Wattenscheid	5 Jun
79.36	Lukás	Melich	CZE	16.9.80	1		Turnov	13 Jul
79.35	Szymon	Ziólkowski	POL	1.7.76	3	WCh	Helsinki	8 Aug
79.23	Holger	Klose	GER	5.12.72	1		Mannheim	18 Jun
78.97	Sergey	Kirmasov	RUS	25.3.70	2	Kuts	Moskva	15 Jul
78.93	Andrey	Vorontsov	BLR	24.7.75	Q	NC	Brest	3 Jul
	(20)							
78.85	Igor	Tugay	UKR	22.3.75	2	NC	Kiev	3 Jul
78.72	Vladislav	Piskunov ¶	UKR	7.6.78	2		Kiev	4 Jun
78.43	Patric	Suter	SUI	17.5.77	1		Zug	29 May
78.28	Aléxandros	Papadimitríou	GRE	18.6.73	1		Athína (E)	6 May
78.25	Kibwe	Johnson	USA	17.7.81	2		Marietta	29 May
77.71	Pavel	Sedlácek	CZE	5.4.68	1		Kladno	28 May
77.63	Dilshod	Nazarov	TJK	6.5.82	1		Almaty	5 Jun
77.59	Dmitriy	Shako	BLR	25.3.79	1		Brest	30 Apr
77.51	Pavel	Krivitskiy	BLR	17.4.84	4	Klim	Staiki	25 Jun
76.89	David	Söderberg	FIN	11.8.79	1		Kaustinen	30 Jun
	(30)							
76.77	Vladimír	Maska	CZE	6.2.73	1		Jablonec nad Nisou	11 May
76.74	Miloslav	Konopka	SVK	23.1.79	1		Gavá	12 Jun
76.66	Nicolas	Figère	FRA	19.5.79	1		Chelles	14 Sep
76.47	Koji	Murofushi	JPN	8.10.74	1	NC	Tokyo	4 Jun
76.31	Valeriy	Svyatokho	BLR	20.7.81	2		Staiki	21 Jul
76.25	Ali Mohamed	Al-Zinkawi	KUW	27.2.84	1	WAsG	Doha	7 Dec
76.11	Stuart	Rendell	AUS	30.6.72	1		Sydney	12 Feb
76.07	Marco	Lingua	ITA	4.6.78	1		Génève	11 Jun
76.06	Vitor	Costa	POR	28.5.74	1		Bugeat	14 Jun
76.03	Aleksandr	Vashchilo	BLR	30.8.81	2		Brest	30 Apr
	(40)							
75.80	Roman	Rozna	MDA	25.3.76	1	Rom IC	Bucuresti	11 Jun
75.78	Dorian	Collaku	ALB	2.6.77	1		Tirana	19 May
75.57	A.G.	Kruger	USA	18.2.79	2		Grand Rapids	16 Jun

Mark	Name		Nat	Born	Pos	Meet	Venue	Date
75.54	Steve	Harnapp	GER	30.7.75	4		Schönebeck	29 Jul
75.38	Erik	Jiménez	CUB	17.9.81	1		La Habana	13 May
75.31	Mohsen	Anani	EGY	21.5.85	1		El Maadi	22 Jul
75.03	Grigoriy	Khatantsev	RUS	2.4.78	3	Kuts	Moskva	15 Jul
74.86	Travis	Nutter	USA	9.2.75	1		Walnut	16 Jul
74.82	Nicola	Vizzoni	ITA	4.11.73	4	ECp-S	Firenze	17 Jun
74.78	Juan Ignacio	Cerra	ARG	16.10.76	1		Santa Fé	17 Apr
	(50)							
74.67	James	Parker	USA	3.12.75	5		Lapua	30 Jul
74.50	Cosmin	Sorescu	ROM	11.7.75	1	Rom IC	Bucuresti	11 Jun
74.38	Yevgeniy	Vinogradov	UKR	30.4.84	3		Kiev	14 Jun
74.28	Aleksandr	Kozulko	BLR	8.12.83	5	Klim	Staiki	25 Jun
74.19	Scott	Boothby	USA	9.4.73	1		Vancouver	19 Jun
74.03	Frédéric	Pouzy	FRA	18.2.83	3		Reims	21 Jul
73.98	Sergey	Litvinov	BLR-J	27.1.86	2		Minsk	23 May
73.79	Derek	Woodske	CAN	22.10.76	1		Bloomington	11 Jun
73.73	Jens	Rautenkrantz	GER	11.4.82	1		Vellmar	24 Jun
73.66	Kristóf	Páli	HUN	29.12.80	1		Veszprém	26 May
	(60)							
73.54	Werner	Smit	RSA	14.9.84	2		Krugersdorp	3 Dec
73.37	Jarkko	Paljakka	FIN	7.2.79	2		Saarijärvi	25 Jun
73.35	Nikolay	Avlasevich	BLR	18.2.76	5	NC	Brest	3 Jul
73.20	Ahmed Abderraouf	Mohamed	EGY	12.2.80	1		El Maadi	10 Aug
73.17	Maciej	Palyszko	POL	4.1.78	4	Kuso	Warszawa	12 Jun
73.02	Oleg	Sinkevich	BLR	16.1.83	Q	NC	Brest	2 Jul
72.90	Aleksandr	Krikun	UKR	1.3.68	4		Kiev	4 Jun
72.89	Andrey	Azarenkov	RUS	26.9.85	1		Adler	6 Feb
72.89	Christophe	Épalle	FRA	23.1.69	2	NC	Angers	16 Jul
72.83	Jim	Steacy	CAN	29.5.84	1		Lethbridge	20 May
	(70)							
72.78	Vadim	Grabovoy	UKR	5.4.73	4		Kiev	14 Jun
72.68	Spirídon	Zoullién	GRE	21.6.81	1		Clemson	9 Apr
72.60	Jacob	Freeman	USA	5.11.80	2	NC	Carson	24 Jun
72.56	Aleksey	Korolyov	RUS	5.4.82	5		Adler	6 Feb
72.46	Igors	Sokolovs	LAT	17.8.74	1		Riga	5 Jun
72.43	Iosvany	Surez	CUB	20.12.72	2		La Habana	13 May
72.33	Saber	Souid	TUN	9.3.81	2		Praha	23 Aug
72.10	Moises	Campeny	ESP	27.5.79	1		Benidorm	25 Jun
72.09	Andy	Frost	GBR	17.4.81	1	NC	Manchester (SC)	9 Jul
71.96	Pellegrino	Delli Carri	ITA	4.8.76	1		Viterbo	30 Apr
	(80)							
71.93		Ye Kuigang	CHN	10.1.75	1	NG	Nanjing	18 Oct
71.87	Markus	Kahlmeyer	GER	20.1.82	1		Bad Lauterberg	28 Aug
71.86	Noleysi	Vicet	CUB	6.2.81	2		La Habana	6 May
71.70	Aleksey	Yeliseyev	RUS	12.3.82	5	NC-w	Adler	19 Feb
71.64	Yosmel	Monte	CUB	26.6.77	2		La Habana	23 Jun
71.62	Hiroaki	Doi	JPN	2.12.78	1		Maebashi	9 Oct
71.55	Jan	Bielecki	DEN	20.2.71	1		Franconville	22 May
71.41	Benjamin	Boruschewski	GER	23.4.80	4		Mannheim	18 Jun
71.37	Marin	Fernówka	POL	23.7.82	1		Bydgoszcz	29 Apr
71.35	Xavier	Dallet	FRA	24.12.79	6		Reims	21 Jul
	(90)							
71.35	Dusan	Král	CZE	12.6.83	1		Hradec Králove	4 Jun
71.34	Roland	Ciofani	FRA	29.9.71	2		Franconville	8 May
71.33	Dmitriy	Velikopolskiy	RUS	27.11.84	1		Tula	14 Jun
71.20	Giovanni	Sanguin	ITA	14.5.69	1		Marcon	15 May
71.19	Pavel	Azarenkov	RUS	.82	1	v2N	Adler	12 Feb
71.05	Ruslan	Kravchuk	BLR	.81	7	NC	Brest	3 Jul
71.03	Igor	Vinichenko	RUS	11.4.84	4		Moskva	20 May
70.99	Kristóf	Németh	HUN-J	17.9.87	1		Szombathely	27 Aug
70.90	Dário	Manso	POR	1.7.82	1		Lisboa (U)	13 Jul
70.72		Ma Liang	CHN	22.7.83	1		Chongqing	14 May
	(100)							

Mark	Name		Nat	Born	Date
70.69	Lorenzo	Povegliano	ITA	11.11.84	4 Jun
70.67	Dameion	Smith	USA	3.8.79	6 May
70.54	Jérôme	Bortoluzzi	FRA	20.5.82	24 Jun
70.54	Michael	Jones	GBR	23.7.63	20 Jul
70.48	Sergey	Karpovich	UKR	23.4.81	14 Jun
70.47	Yuriy	Kravchuk	BLR	81	29 May
70.33		Liu Fuxiang	CHN	24.3.75	18 Oct
70.30	Kirill	Ikonnikov	RUS	5.3.84	6 Feb
70.23	Aleksey	Sokirskiy	UKR	16.3.85	21 Jun
70.20	Lasse	Luotonen	FIN	16.6.83	30 Jun
70.19	József	Horváth	HUN	3.4.84	26 Feb
69.94		Zhao Yihai	CHN	29.3.85	19 Jun
69.85	Petri	Rautio	FIN	28.6.82	24 Sep
69.65	Fatih	Eryildirim	TUR	1.3.79	24 Jul
69.64	Lucais	MacKay	USA	13.4.80	29 May
69:58	Samir	Haouam	ALG	20.6.68	5 Jul
69.50	Matko	Tesija	CRO	4.3.85	30 Apr
69.45	Mattias	Jons	SWE	19.11.82	23 Apr

Mark	Name		Nat	Born	Date
69.42	Bengt	Johansson	SWE	7.7.73	27 Aug
69.19	Luke	Woydziak	USA	13.4.77	24 Jun
69.14	Igor	Tsitsorin	BLR-Y	.88	2 Jul
69.12	Michal	Fiala	CZE	22.6.85	18 Jun
69.07	Yamen Hussein	Abdel Moneim	EGY	19.6.78	31 Mar
69.04	Arnaldo	Cueto	USA	5.5.81	9 Apr
68.93	Vitaliy	Baukh	RUS	29.1.83	11 Jul
68.93	Aleksandr	Rizhkevich	BLR	81	21 Jul
68.92	Stamátios	Papadoníou	GRE	3.5.84	17 Jul
68.87	Daniel	Abramovic	GER	10.12.82	15 May
68.75	Guram	Feroyev	RUS	8.10.83	19 Feb
68.71	Viktor	Ustinov	UZB	20.7.74	19 May
68.52	Sándor	Végh	HUN	10.3.77	30 Jul
68.38	Yegor	Agafonov	RUS	7.2.83	14 Jun
68.34	Ralf	Jossa	GER	2.11.66	3 Jul
68.14	Andrey	Volkov	RUS	.85	23 Apr
68.09		Wang Zhen	CHN	1.2.80	23 Apr
68.05	Kamilius	Bethke (136)	GER	21.5.85	13 Aug

Doubtful mark: 79.01 Christophe Épalle FRA 23.1.69 1 Aubière 20 Jul

JUNIORS

Mark	Name		Nat	Born	Pos	Meet	Venue	Date
73.98	Sergey	Litvinov	BLR	27.1.86	2		Minsk	23 May
70.99	Kristóf	Németh	HUN	17.9.87	1		Szombathely	27 Aug
	69.85 3	Zalaegerszeg	28 May	69.54	1		Veszprém	13 Aug
	69.82 2	Tapolca	30 Jul	67.89	2		Szombathely	21 Sep
69.14	Igor	Tsitsorin	BLR-Y	.88	9	NC	Brest	2 Jul
67.35		Qi Dakai	CHN	23.5.87	3	NG	Nanjing	18 Oct
64.66	Juha	Kauppinen	FIN	16.8.86	4		Saarijärvi	25 Jun
64.49	Tuomas	Seppänen	FIN	16.5.86	1		Jyväskylä	7 Sep
64.27	Marcel	Lomnický	SVK	6.7.87	2		Kladno	21 May
64.02		Xu Di	CHN-Y	10.7.88	3		Yichun	16 Apr
63.93	Aleksey	Fedotov	RUS	28.12.86	7		Adler	6 Feb
63.65	Sándor	Pálhegyi	HUN-Y	4.11.88	6		Debrecen	6 Jul

6kg Hammer

Mark	Name		Nat	Born	Pos	Meet	Venue	Date
79.67	Yevgeniy	Aydamirov	RUS	18.6.87	1		Tula	25 Jun
	76.97 2 NC-j	Tula	3 Jul	76.73	2	EJ	Kaunas	24 Jul
78.85	Kristóf	Németh	HUN	17.9.87	1		Kaunas	24 Jul
	77.39 1	Szombathely	1 Jun	76.70	1		Szombathely	4 May
	77.27 1	Varazdin	2 Jul	76.59	1		Uherske Hradiste	29 Jun
	77.10 1	Szombathely	30 Apr	76.58	1	NC-j	Budapest	25 Jun
75.09	Tuomas	Seppänen	FIN	16.5.86	1		Pori	10 Sep
74.78	Yury	Shayunov	BLR	22.10.87	3	EJ	Kaunas	24 Jul
74.73	Mikhail	Levin	RUS	10.4.86	1	NC-wj	Adler	19 Feb
74.53	Juha	Kauppinen	FIN	16.8.86	2		Pori	10 Sep
74.38	Marcel	Lomnický	SVK	6.7.87	1		Reims	10 May
73.20	Anatoliy	Pozdnyakov	RUS	1.2.87	3	NC-j	Tula	3 Jul
73.08	Benjamin	Hedermann	GER	20.1.87	1		Leverkusen	13 Aug
72.41	Aleksey	Fedotov (10)	RUS	28.12.86	2	NC-wj	Adler	19 Feb
72.31	Aleksey	Kochetkov	RUS	23.3.86	5	NC-j	Tula	3 Jul
71.96	Sven	Möhsner	GER	30.1.86	1		Wiesbaden	29 May
71.86	Vyacheslav	Zaykin	RUS	17.2.86	6	NC-j	Tula	3 Jul
71.85	Artyom	Vynnyk	UKR	1.1.88	1		Kiev	4 Jun
71.70	Alex	Smith	GBR-Y	6.3.88	2		Mannheim	18 Jun
71.53	Petr	Mättölä	FIN	1.7.86	2		Kaustinen	30 Jun
71.19	Sándor	Pálhegyi	HUN-Y	4.11.88	2		Szombathely	4 May

JAVELIN

Mark										
91.53	Tero		Pitkämaki	FIN	19.12.82	1		Kuortane		26 Jun
					80.45	x	79.60	82.36	91.53	p
91.33	1	WAF	Monaco	10 Sep	83.54	91.33	85.14	87.66		
90.54	1	Bisl	Oslo	29 Jul	80.93	79.91	82.50	90.54	x	p
89.32	1	ISTAF	Berlin	4 Sep	78.88	85.35	84.91	86.96	87.69	89.32
88.71	1	WK	Zürich	19 Aug	88.71	87.22	x	p	x	p
88.61	1		Seinajöki	15 Aug	86.12	81.45	88.61	79.30	88.01	87.44
87.83	1	NC	Pori	17 Jul	81.20	84.00	x	79.17	87.83	82.61
86.90	1	v SWE	Göteborg	28 Aug	83.93	86.90	p	p	p	p
85.95	1	Gaz	Saint-Denis	1 Jul	80.08	85.95	x	82.57	x	82.01
85.90	3	VD	Bruxelles	26 Aug	84.51	79.99	82.28	85.90	82.57	x
85.90	1	ECp1A	Gävle	19 Jun	85.90	79.77	83.28	x		
85.66	1	GP	Helsinki	25 Jul						
90.33	Sergey		Makarov	RUS	19.3.73	1	NC	Tula		11 Jul
					87.10	86.72	83.37	79.81	83.83	90.33
88.84	1	GS	Ostrava	9 Jun	88.84	87.73	80.14	82.69	84.47	84.90
88.14	2	ISTAF	Berlin	4 Sep	85.21	84.81	83.81	86.91	88.14	84.97
87.76	2	Bisl	Oslo	29 Jul	83.38	81.10	x	80.83	83.47	87.76
86.89	2	WK	Zürich	19 Aug	81.08	82.12	82.58	83.55	83.45	86.89
86.88	1	VD	Bruxelles	26 Aug	85.61	86.88	85.84	86.41	81.72	p
86.69	3	WAF	Monaco	10 Sep	84.85	86.50	84.85	86.69		
86.43	1		Dessau	27 May	82.84	86.43	80.63	x	p	p
89.60	Andreas		Thorkildsen	NOR	1.4.82	2	WAF	Monaco		10 Sep
					83.30	81.58	89.60	85.54		

MEN 2005

Mark	Name		Nat	Born	Pos	Meet	Venue		Date
	87.75 3 ISTAF	Berlin	4 Sep	82.51	81.66	85.92	87.04	86.76	87.75
	87.66 3 Bisl	Oslo	29 Jul	82.31	x	87.66	82.59	86.05	82.26
	86.82 2	Kuortane	26 Jun	86.81	85.29	86.82	p	p	85.36
	86.18 2 WCh	Helsinki	10 Aug	78.36	81.52	83.41	85.71	86.18	x
	86.13 2 VD	Bruxelles	26 Aug	84.63	84.65	86.13	84.88	x	83.17
87.65	Breaux	Greer	USA	19.10.76	1	MSR	Walnut		17 Ap
				79.76	87.65	87.25	79.87	x	83.21
	85.75 1	Athens, GA	7 May	85.75	81.27	79.65	79.69	p	78.10
87.19	Andrus	Värnik	EST	27.9.77	1		Tallinn		25 May
	87.17 1 WCh	Helsinki	10 Aug	79.06	x	76.47	87.17	85.29	x
	(30/5)								
84.88	Mark	Frank	GER	21.6.77	4	ISTAF	Berlin		4 Sep
84.41	Scott	Russell	CAN	16.1.79	1		Ottawa		20 Ju
84.24	Aleksandr	Ivanov	RUS	25.5.82	3	Gaz	Saint-Denis		1 Ju
84.12	Jarko	Koski-Vähäla	FIN	21.11.78	1		änekoski		27 Ju
84.06	Guillermo	Martínez	CUB	28.6.81	1		Bilbao		18 Jur
	(10)								
84.05	Tero	Järvenpää	FIN	2.10.84	2	v SWE	Göteborg		28 Aug
83.98	Jan	Zelezny	CZE	16.6.66	4	WAF	Monaco		10 Sep
83.79	Aki	Parviainen	FIN	26.10.74	1	SGP	Doha		13 May
83.20	Christian	Nicolay	GER	4.3.76	1		Zeulenroda		29 May
83.07	Stefan	Wenk	GER	13.3.81	1		Sindelfingen		12 Feb
82.35	Eriks	Rags	LAT	1.6.75	1		Riga		27 May
82.22	Ainars	Kovals	LAT	21.11.81	1	NC	Riga		9 Ju
82.14	Esko	Mikkola	FIN	14.2.75	1		Lapua		30 Ju
82.04	Tomas	Intas	LTU	15.9.81	2		Riga		27 May
81.80	Andis	Anskins	LAT	25.1.79	3		Riga		27 May
	(20)								
81.67	Francesco	Pignata	ITA	14.2.78	3	ECp-S	Firenze		19 Jur
81.61		Li Rongxiang	CHN	8.1.72	1		Chengdu		10 Apr
81.47	Björn	Lange	GER	15.6.79	1		Berlin		12 Ju
81.30	Vadims	Vasilevskis	LAT	5.1.82	4		Riga		27 May
81.14	Vladislav	Shkurlatov	RUS	30.3.83	Q	EU23	Erfurt		15 Ju
81.01	Manuel	Nau	GER	2.7.77	1		Gengenbach		10 Sep
80.91	Gergely	Horváth	HUN	5.6.75	1		Veszprém		23 Ju
80.68	Teemu	Wirkkala	FIN	14.1.84	1		Saarijärvi		25 Jur
80.53	Voldemars	Lusis	LAT	7.12.74	1		Bangor/GBR		24 Jur
80.50	Emeterio	González	CUB	11.4.73	2	NC	La Habana		19 Mar
	(30)								
80.45	Brian	Chaput	USA	9.4.81	1		Princeton		23 Apr
80.31	Gabriel	Wallin	SWE	14.10.81	2	ECp-1A	Gävle		19 Jur
80.03	Lohan	Rautenbach	RSA-J	6.2.86	1	NC	Durban		16 Apr
80.02	Igor	Sukhomlinov	RUS	13.2.77	2	Euro	Mersin		12 Mar
79.79	Yukifumi	Murakami	JPN	23.12.79	1	NC	Tokyo		5 Jur
79.75	Antti	Ruuskanen	FIN	21.2.84	2		Saarijärvi		25 Jur
79.70	Elefthérios	Karasmanákis	GRE	16.8.78	1		Édessa		25 May
79.68	Risto	Mätas	EST	30.4.84	1		Rakvere		24 Sep
79.56	Nick	Nieland	GBR	31.1.72	1	CAU	Bedford		30 May
79.44A	Luiz Fernando	da Silva	BRA	2.7.71	1	SACh	Cali		24 Ju
	(40)								
79.42	Yervásios	Filippídis	GRE-J	24.7.87	1		dessa		7 May
79.37	Leigh	Smith	USA	28.8.81	2		Lapua		30 Ju
79.31		Chen Qi	CHN	10.3.82	1	NC	Shijiazhuang		21 Jur
79.23	Isbel	Luaces	CUB	20.7.75	1		La Habana		24 Jur
79.15	Mike	Hazle	USA	22.3.79	2		Dubnica nad Váhom		29 Aug
78.98	Stefan	Müller	SUI	20.9.79	3	ECp-1A	Gävle		19 Jur
78.97	Oliver	Dziubak	AUS	30.3.82	1		Perth		18 Dec
78.96	Vitoli	Tipotio	FRA	17.7.75	1		Toulouse		26 Feb
78.93	Ronny	Nilsen	NOR	7.5.71	6		Riga		27 May
78.88	Yéoryios	Itsios	GRE	28.11.81	1		Athína (E)		8 May
	(50)								
78.87		Park Jae-myong	KOR	15.12.81	1	NG	Ulsan		17 Oct
78.62	Pekka	Alaräisänen	FIN	27.12.75	1		Rovaniemi		19 Aug
78.59	Máximo	Rigondeaux	CUB	17.10.76	2		La Habana		24 Jun
78.56	Marcel	Plautz	GER	1.7.80	1		Berlin		25 Jun
78.54	Daniel	Ragnvaldsson	SWE	3.1.76	1	NC	Helsingborg		20 Aug
78.45	Rajmund	Kólko	POL	1.3.71	1		Tønsberg		21 May
78.23	John	Hetzendorf	USA	27.1.77	2	NC	Carson		24 Jun
78.07	Yudel	Moreno	CUB	24.2.83	3	NC	La Habana		19 Mar
78.05	Kristo	Galeta	EST	9.4.83	1		Tallinn		14 Sep

Mark	Name		Nat	Born	Pos	Meet	Venue	Date
78.02	Oleg	Statsenko	UKR	22.10.80	1	NC	Kiev	3 Jul
	(60)							
77.83	Magnus	Arvidsson	SWE	20.2.83	1		Hilversum	3 Sep
77.79	Marián	Bokor	SVK	17.4.77	4	GS	Ostrava	9 Jun
77.79	Dominique	Pausé	FRA	11.1.76	2		Sotteville	8 Jul
77.74	Janis	Liepa	LAT	14.3.81	1		Riga	26 Feb
77.73		Jung Sang-jin	KOR	16.4.84	1		Kwangju	20 Apr
77.64	David	Brisseault	FRA	7.3.69	2		La Roche-sur-Yon	20 Jul
77.57	Vadim	Bavikin	ISR	4.10.70	1		Jerusalem	17 Jul
77.55	Dariusz	Trafas	POL	16.5.72	1	NC	Biala Podlaska	25 Jun
77.37A	Noraldo	Palacios	COL	8.7.80	1	Bolivar	Armenia/COL	21 Aug
77.36	Tomasz	Damszel	POL	25.3.72	2	NC	Biala Podlaska	25 Jun
	(70)							
77.31		An Hyuk-yun	KOR	23.3.79	3	NG	Ulsan	17 Oct
77.25	Igor	Janik	POL	18.1.83	1	EU23	Erfurt	17 Jul
77.25	Ioánnis-Yeóryios	Smaliõs	GRE-J	17.2.87	1	EC-j	Kaunas	23 Jul
77.20	Peter	Esenwein	GER	7.12.67	5	GS	Ostrava	9 Jun
77.20	Raymond	Hecht	GER	11.11.68	1		Wilhelmshaven	10 Jul
77.18	Sebastian	Jachimowicz-Giogowski	POL-J	2.8.86	2	Kuso	Warszawa	12 Jun
77.17	Jagdish Singh	Bishnoi	IND	20.5.72	1		New Delhi	24 Aug
77.09		Liu Yanhong	CHN	20.4.83	3	NG	Nanjing	19 Oct
77.07A	Hardus	Pienaar	RSA	10.8.81	2		Potchefstroom	4 Feb
77.04		Chu Ki-young	KOR	4.3.77	2		Kwangju	21 Apr
	(80)							
76.95	David	Parker	GBR	28.2.80	1		Bedford	27 Aug
76.81	Júlio César	de Oliveira	BRA-J	4.2.86	1	NC-j	Curitiba	18 Sep
76.76	Kari	Vinni	FIN	19.3.83	1	NC-23	Pihtipudas	8 Jul
76.66		Lin Dong	CHN	7.4.81	2	NC	Shijiazhuang	21 Jun
76.62	Christian	Fusenig	GER	9.5.78	1		Rehlingen	5 May
76.56	Manuel	Fuenmayor	VEN	3.12.80	1		Santiago	8 May
76.50	Marko	Kantanen	FIN	17.4.78	6		Tampere	12 Jun
76.43	Vadim	Yevtukhovich	BLR	24.5.81	1		Minsk	23 May
76.40	Ari	Mannio	FIN-J	23.7.87	4		Seinäjoki	15 Aug
76.39	Edi	Ponos	CRO	10.4.76	1		Split	30 Apr
	(90)							
76.31	Ilya	Korotkov	RUS	6.12.83	4		Florø	4 Jun
76.31	Anil	Kumar Yadav	IND	4.3.85	1	NC	Hyderabad	7 Nov
76.30	Petteri	Leinonen	FIN	22.4.80	1		Joensuu	5 Jul
76.26	Anier	Boué	CUB	3.4.84	5	NC	La Habana	19 Mar
76.26	Jan	Syrovátko	CZE	11.2.85	1		Pardubice	19 Oct
76.18		Chou Yi-Chen	TPE	9.7.84	1		Chiayi	3 May
76.17	Mattias	Eriksson	SWE	29.8.80	1		Stockholm	15 May
76.16	Andreas	Wulff	SWE	28.3.80	3	NC	Helsingborg	20 Aug
76.12	Sergey	Voynov	UZB	26.2.77	1		Tashkent	19 May
76.10	Nikolay	Vasiltsov	BLR	24.5.82	1	NC	Brest	3 Jul
	(100)							

Mark	Name		Nat	Born	Date
76.04	Matija	Kranjc	SLO	12.6.84	26 Feb
76.03	Trevor	Snyder	CAN	2.6.82	10 Jun
76.03	Alan	Puuste	EST	26.9.80	24 Aug
76.00	Peter	Blank	GER	10.4.62	12 Jun
75.98	Daniel	Kratzmann	AUS	19.2.81	13 Feb
75.94	Robert	Oosthuizen	RSA-J	23.1.87	3 Sep
75.93	Heiko	Väät	EST	25.8.75	19 Jun
75.85	Alexander	Vieweg	GER-J	28.6.86	23 Jul
75.84	Alexon	Maximiano	BRA	12.10.82	9 Jul
75.79	Tino	Häber	GER	6.10.82	11 Jun
75.72A	Willie	Human	RSA	8.3.82	23 Apr
75.72	Eric	Brown	USA	7.6.84	23 Apr
75.60	Teemu	Pasanen	FIN	24.5.77	8 Sep
75.50	Vladimir	Kozlov	BLR	.85	21 Jul
75.48	Adrian	Markowski	POL	14.10.78	16 Jul
75.38	Felix	Loretz	SUI	13.11.75	3 Jul
75.37	Toyofumi	Muronaga	JPN	10.12.79	14 May
75.35	Matthew	Outzen	AUS-J	10.12.87	30 Nov
75.29		Sun Shipeng	CHN	10.3.76	21 Jun
75.13	Gustavo	Dacal	ESP	30.3.77	29 Jul
75.12	Mohamed Fazal	Ansari	IND	1.2.78	3 Jun
75.08	Petr	Belunek	CZE	5.4.79	9 Jun
75.06	Ken	Arai	JPN	22.12.81	26 Oct
74.99	Rob	Minnitti	USA	6.9.79	24 Jun
74.97	Tom	Engwall	USA	2.9.80	9 Apr
74.93	Dominik	Sadowski	POL	14.12.82	18 Jun
74.88	Levente	Bartha	ROM	8.3.77	24 Jul
74.78	Richard A.	Knudsen	DEN	28.7.72	31 Jul
74.77	Ayoub	Arokhi	IRI	23.5.82	3 Sep
74.74A	Gerbrandt	Grobler	RSA	26.1.83	4 Feb
74.66	Sunil	Kumar Goswami	IND	1.7.78	17 May
74.65	Viljo	Toivanen	FIN	18.8.84	14 Sep
74.61	Justin	St.Clair	USA	17.5.79	30 May
74.50	Muhammad Hussein	Irfan	PAK	8.7.76	29 Dec
74.39	Harri	Haatainen	FIN	5.1.78	27 Jul
74.35	Om	Narayan	IND	17.4.82	17 May
74.35	Pauli	Piiparinen	FIN	21.8.79	2 Aug
74.21	Mika	Aalto	FIN	11.3.82	6 Jul
74.18	Waled	Mohamed	EGY	4.4.73	18 Sep
74.16		Qin Qiang	CHN	18.4.83	24 Apr
74.16	Laurent	Dorique	FRA	10.7.76	25 Jun
74.14		Song Dong-hyun	KOR	17.11.81	4 Jun
74.11	Harri	Hakkarainen	FIN	16.10.69	14 Sep
74.01	Noël	Meyer	RSA-Y	20.4.88	30 Nov
74.00	Kobus	Smit	RSA	31.3.83	2 Apr
74.00	Bérenger	Demerval	FRA	29.4.82	22 May
	(146)				

JUNIORS

See main list for top 6 juniors. 8 performances by 6 men to 76.00. Additional marks and further juniors:

Rautenbach	78.76	1		Äänekoski	27 Jul	78.14	1	Oudtshoorn	5 Mar
	78.59	Q	WUG	Izmir	15 Aug	77.99	1	Réduit	15 May

Mark	Name		Nat	Born	Pos	Meet	Venue	Date
73.98	Keita	Yamada	JPN	1.6.87	1		Chiba	5 Aug
73.50	Fabian	Heinemann	GER	17.5.86	2		Sindelfingen	13 Feb
73.45	Vladimir	Gubskiy	UKR	19.4.87	1		Kiev	5 Jun
71.95		Li Yu	CHN	9.3.87	3		Zhongshan	24 Apr
71.48	Pawe	Rozi ski	POL	11.7.87	1	NC-j	Bydgoszcz	5 Jul
71.03	Arun	Kumar Patel	IND	9.5.86	1	NC-j	Bhubaneshwar	19 Oct
70.54	Matt	Maloney	USA	24.7.87	1		Hartford	15 May
70.53	Anuj	Kumar	IND	26.11.87	1		Chennai	28 Nov
70.47	Sevket	Tas	TUR	28.2.86	1		Istanbul	9 Jul
70.37	Thomas	Lange (20)	GER	1.10.87			Haldensleben	12 Jun
70.37	Mikko	Kankaanpää	FIN	17.4.87	1	Nord-j	Kristiansand	27 Aug

PENTATHLON

3807	7.04w	62.58	22.97w	43.89	4:40.83	Olav Røe	Steinjker	NOR	3.7.82	1	Trondheim	31 May
3806	7.52w	60.92	23.09	45.32	4:59.33	Mikk	Pahapil	EST	18.7.83	1	Tallinn	14 May
3675	6.64	56.00	22.99	43.41	4:29.50	Andrei	Stepanov	EST	14.2.85	2	Tallinn	14 May
3673	6.72	55.14	23.05	43.34	4:29.74	Päärn	Brauer	EST	21.11.82	3	Tallinn	14 May
3621	7.44w	54.03	22.32	39.76	5:03.12	Andres	Raja	EST	2.6.82	4	Tallinn	14 May

DECATHLON

8732	Bryan	Clay	USA	3.1.80	1	WCh	Helsinki	10 Aug		
	10.43w/3.2	7.54/0.6	16.25	2.00	47.78	14.43/-2.6	53.68	4.90	72.00	5:03.77
8534	Roman	Sebrle	CZE	26.11.74	1		Götzis	29 May		
	11.06/0.4	7.85/0.0	15.36	2.06	49.17	14.50/-1.2	47.77	4.80	66.57	4:33.74
8526	Kristjan	Rahnu	EST	29.8.79	1		Arles	5 Jun		
	10.52w/2.2	7.58/1.6	15.51	1.99	48.60	14.04w/3.1	50.81	4.95	60.71	4:52.18
8521		Sebrle			2	WCh	Helsinki	10 Aug		
	10.91/1.2	7.86/1.2	16.29	2.06	48.62	14.71/-2.6	46.85	4.80	63.21	4:39.54
8506		Clay			1	NC	Carson	24 Jun		
	10.70/-1.8	7.44/0.3	14.88	2.06	49.62	14.06/-1.4	55.87	5.00	60.02	4:57.11
8480	Attila	Zsivoczky	HUN	29.4.77	2		Götzis	29 May		
	10.90/0.9	7.15/0.9	15.96	2.15	49.46	14.63/-1.4	47.90	4.90	62.79	4:31.89
8429	Aleksandr	Pogorelov	RUS	10.1.80	3		Götzis	29 May		
	10.91/0.9	7.64/0.6	16.03	2.09	50.16	14.14/-1.2	48.44	5.10	58.23	4:55.90
8385		Zsivoczky			3	WCh	Helsinki	10 Aug		
	10.90w/3.2	7.03/1.6	15.72	2.15	49.29	15.15/-1.9	49.58	4.80	63.02	4:32.17
8326		Sebrle			1		Talence	18 Sep		
	11.09/1.2	7.60w/2.4	15.65	2.04	49.03	14.47/0.8	45.15	4.80	66.05	4:47.79
8320		Zsivoczky			2		Arles	5 Jun		
	11.02w/2.2	7.06/1.4	15.21	2.11	48.98	14.52w/3.1	47.83	4.85	59.17	4:30.33
8316	André	Niklaus	GER	30.8.81	4	WCh	Helsinki	10 Aug		
	11.04/1.2	7.20w/2.6	14.24	2.03	49.42	14.78/-1.9	46.13	5.30	61.74	4:28.93
8290		Qi Haifeng	CHN	7.8.83	4		Götzis	29 May		
	10.87/0.9	7.40/0.1	13.41	2.03	48.72	14.63/-1.4	48.57	4.70	64.53	4:32.02
8247		Pogorelov			2		Talence	18 Sep		
	10.99w/3.4	7.53w/2.2	16.07	2.07	51.10	14.25/0.8	45.83	5.10	58.24	4:57.40
8246		Pogorelov			5	WCh	Helsinki	10 Aug		
	10.86/1.2	7.49/-0.4	15.90	2.09	50.58	14.45/-2.6	46.68	5.00	59.79	5:03.62
8232	Maurice	Smith	JAM	28.9.80	1	NACAC	San Juan	29 May		
	10.71w/2.5	7.22w/3.2	15.80	1.98	48.54	14.17	50.62	4.30	56.76	4:36.00
8223		Rahnu			6	WCh	Helsinki	10 Aug		
	10.59w/2.5	7.36/-1.1	15.79	2.03	48.58	14.87/-1.6	47.13	4.70	61.65	4:59.73
8196	Aleksey	Drozdov	RUS	3.12.83	1	EU23	Erfurt	15 Jul		
	11.18/0.5	7.29/0.1	15.38	2.07	50.67	14.86/0.6	49.10	4.70	63.97	4:38.33
8193		Niklaus			1		Ratingen	26 Jun		
	11.20/0.2	7.42/-0.5	13.92	1.99	50.19	14.54/0.6	43.76	5.30	59.57	4:28.21
8185	Romain	Barras (10)	FRA	1.8.80	5		Götzis	29 May		
	11.32/0.1	7.26w/2.6	14.54	2.00	49.24	14.44/-1.4	43.95	4.90	65.84	4:31.52
8149	Mikk	Pahapill	EST	18.7.83	1	ECp-S	Bydgoszcz	3 Jul		
	11.11/-0.4	7.30/0.3	13.88	2.13	50.62	14.87/0.0	48.65	4.80	65.60	4:50.25
8127		Barras			1	MedG	Almeria	30 Jun		
	11.40/-1.1	7.19/0.8	14.76	1.96	48.84	14.35/-0.9	42.22	4.90	64.67	4:28.48
8124		Rahnu			3		Talence	18 Sep		
	10.72/1.2	7.19w/2.8	14.58	1.92	49.18	14.26/0.8	47.72	4.90	63.95	5:01.35
8120		Drozdov			1	NC	Tula	15 Jun		
	11.31/0.1	7.15/0.5	15.46	2.03	51.06	15.13/0.9	51.68	4.60	65.44	4:34.85
8114	Eugene	Martineau	NED	14.5.80	6		Götzis	29 May		
	10.96/1.6	7.39/0.8	13.80	2.03	49.25	15.01/-1.2	41.89	5.00	61.82	4:34.69
8107	Phil	McMullen	USA	3.2.75	1		Salò	8 May		
	11.53/-1.8	6.69/-1.3	14.83	1.94	48.91	14.86/-1.7	50.54	5.10	58.57	4:18.77

Mark	Name		Nat	Born	Pos	Meet	Venue	Date
8105	Tomás	Dvorák	CZE	11.5.72	1	ECp-1	Jyväskyla	3 Jul
	11.22/0.9 7.25/-0.1 15.92 1.95 50.24 14.56/1.0 42.75 4.70 69.11 4:38.12							
8105		Zsivoczky			2	ECp-1	Jyväskyla	3 Jul
	11.25/0.9 6.84/0.7 15.27 2.10 49.57 14.93/1.0 45.41 4.80 61.53 4:30.18							
8090	Aleksey	Sysoyev	RUS	8.3.85	1		Sochi	18 May
	10.89/0.5 6.73/-1.4 15.61 2.06 49.60 15.34/-1.4 53.49 4.40 59.60 4:33.68							
8089		Sysoyev			2	EU23	Erfurt	15 Jul
	10.93/0.9 6.95/0.4 15.45 2.16 50.62 14.84/0.6 51.73 4.30 59.30 4:44.63							
8087		Barras			7	WCh	Helsinki	10 Aug
	11.15/1.2 7.35/0.5 14.62 1.94 48.63 14.65/-2.6 44.24 4.80 60.39 4:31.94							
	(30/15)							
8076w	Jaakko	Ojaniemi	FIN	28.8.80	3		Arles	5 Jun
	10.73w/2.2 8.03w/4.1 15.19 1.93 49.74 14.75w/3.6 37.46 4.45 62.95 4:37.31							
8051	Aleksandr	Parkhomenko	BLR	22.3.81	1	WUG	Izmir	19 Aug
	11.26/-0.6 7.14/0.1 15.98 2.01 50.32 14.92/-0.8 40.94 4.80 63.75 4:28.99							
8025	Rudy	Bourguignon	FRA	16.7.79	6		Talence	18 Sep
	10.91w/3.4 7.28w/2.7 14.30 1.89 50.31 15.03/1.7 42.55 5.20 59.70 4:30.19							
8023	Hamdi	Dhouibi	TUN	24.1.82	11	WCh	Helsinki	10 Aug
	10.67w/3.2 7.43/0.5 12.85 1.94 47.04 14.56/-1.9 41.17 4.80 52.83 4:31.24							
7997	Ryan	Harlan	USA	25.4.81	2	NACAC	San Juan	29 May
	11.05w/2.5 6.97w/3.5 15.79 2.07 49.65 13.93 42.80 4.60 57.75 4:52.56							
	(20)							
7989	Norman	Müller	GER	7.8.85	3	EU23	Erfurt	15 Jul
	10.96/0.9 7.48/0.8 14.16 1.95 47.68 14.73/0.6 40.99 4.80 53.06 4:34.01							
7976	Paul	Terek	USA	20.10.79	2	NC	Carson	24 Jun
	11.17/-0.6 7.05/0.1 14.97 2.00 49.05 15.21/0.0 44.22 5.20 54.05 4:39.92							
7975	Roland	Schwarzl	AUT	10.12.80	8		Götzis	29 May
	11.09/1.6 7.44/0.0 14.48 1.97 50.28 14.70/-1.4 46.15 4.80 54.71 4:37.96							
7950	François	Gourmet	BEL	28.12.82	10		Talence	18 Sep
	10.61/1.2 7.19/1.9 14.16 1.89 47.77 14.81/1.7 37.37 4.80 56.31 4:27.02							
7920	Lars	Albert	GER	9.2.82	10		Götzis	29 May
	11.05/-0.2 7.53w/2.9 15.36 1.94 51.81 15.12/-1.4 45.71 4.70 63.70 4:52.36							
7902	Frédéric	Xhonneux	BEL	11.5.83	6		Arles	5 Jun
	11.31w/3.6 7.18w/3.0 13.03 1.99 49.07 14.57w/4.0 40.66 4.75 56.61 4:17.27							
7892	Stephen	Harris	USA	5.12.80	1		Clemson	11 May
	10.89/0.0 7.52/0.0 12.62 2.12 49.09 14.40/1.0 39.85 4.45 54.80 4:43.34							
7881	Trey	Hardee	USA	7.2.84	1	NCAA	Sacramento	9 Jun
	10.86/-1.6 7.01w/2.2 13.14 1.85 48.33 14.09/0.3 48.33 4.80 56.28 4:52.46							
7877	Claston	Bernard	JAM	22.3.79	1	CAC	Nassau	10 Jul
	10.89/0.3 7.13/0.5 13.50 2.12 49.94 14.55/0.4 47.44 4.30 54.15 4:45.97							
7854	Jason	Dudley	AUS	10.11.84	1		Townsville	24 Sep
	11.23/0.5 7.33/1.4 14.90 1.89 49.26 14.68/-1.7 48.48 4.50 63.03 5:03.25							
	(30)							
7845	Benjamin	Jensen	NOR	13.4.75	2	ECp-C	Maribor	3 Jul
	11.39/-0.6 7.18/1.6 13.43 2.00 49.40 14.63/-1.4 38.06 4.70 62.15 4:26.84							
7842	Pascal	Behrenbruch	GER	19.1.85	2	v USA	Bernhausen	24 Jul
	11.32/0.0 6.90/0.1 16.11 2.00 49.94 14.94/-0.6 42.12 4.60 65.37 4:51.57							
7836	Chiel	Warners	NED	2.4.78	12		Götzis	29 May
	10.96/0.4 7.61/1.1 14.03 1.94 48.46 14.55/-1.2 41.00 4.60 52.12 4:46.77							
7833	Andrey	Kravchenko	BLR-J	4.1.86	13		Götzis	29 May
	11.06/1.6 7.57/1.1 12.96 2.15 49.43 14.59/-1.4 33.50 4.20 58.26 4:26.89							
7832	Vitaliy	Smirnov	UZB	25.10.78	7		Arles	5 Jun
	11.01w/2.2 7.21/1.6 13.84 1.93 49.09 14.43w/3.6 44.14 4.35 55.80 4:31.69							
7831	Oscar	González	ESP	8.8.76	4	MedG	Almeria	30 Jun
	11.26/-1.1 7.50/1.5 12.86 2.08 49.06 14.78/-0.9 40.43 4.50 50.18 4:22.12							
7803	Aki	Heikkinen	FIN	24.2.80	1		Woerden	28 Aug
	11.25w/2.2 6.89/1.8 14.16 1.96 50.50 15.26/0.0 41.20 4.80 68.57 4:38.85							
7801A	Andrew	Levin	USA	9.3.80	1		Flagstaff	12 May
	10.93/0.7 7.10w/2.5 14.20 2.04 50.41 14.42/1.7 42.65 4.76 52.90 4:52.88							
7794	Donovan	Kilmartin	USA	11.6.84	3	v GER	Bernhausen	24 Jul
	11.27/0.0 7.52/0.5 14.37 2.03 51.28 14.89/1.4 42.07 5.00 51.47 4:49.12							
7780	Chris	Helwick	USA	18.3.85	1	SEC	Nashville	13 May
	11.36/0.8 6.97/0.0 13.49 2.04 49.22 15.06/1.4 40.95 4.75 59.08 4:34.00							
	(40)							
7774		Kim Kun-woo	KOR	29.2.80	1	NC	Daegu	4 Jun
	11.19 7.25 12.68 1.96 48.51 15.25 37.60 4.80 53.50 4:13.78							
7771		Hong Qingyang	CHN	4.2.83	2	NC	Shijiazhuang	20 Jun
	10.93/0.0 7.25/0.5 14.18 1.91 50.59 15.03/0.8 44.14 4.70 64.58 5:01.70							
7767	Nikolay	Tishchenko	RUS	4.2.77	2	ECp-S	Bydgoszcz	3 Jul
	11.02/0.9 7.63/0.6 13.53 1.98 50.45 14.45/1.0 43.97 4.50 47.95 4:39.35							

Mark	Name		Nat	Born	Pos	Meet	Venue	Date
7767	Darius	Draudvila	LTU	29.3.83	1	Kudu	Rakvere	17 Jul
	10.93w/3.4 7.08w/3.9 14.13 2.05 48.92 14.82/0.5 44.46 4.35 50.21 4:41.39							
7764	Sergey	Androsovich	UKR	27.5.83	1		Kiev	25 Jul
	11.01/-0.7 7.19/0.8 13.95 1.94 49.21 15.41/-0.4 42.00 4.70 52.63 4:26.33							
7752	Hans Olav	Uldal	NOR	16.12.82	1	NC	Drammen	24 Jul
	11.29/0.5 7.27/1.0 14.46 1.86 51.25 14.76/-0.2 45.96 4.65 58.93 4:38.35							
7744	Pavel	Andreyev	UZB	24.11.78	1	AsiC	Inchon	4 Sep
	11.71/0.3 6.99/0.0 14.87 2.05 51.83 15.78/-0.3 46.04 4.80 60.80 4:34.53							
7739	Mustafa	Abdur-Rahim	USA	29.9.82	2	NCAA	Sacramento	9 Jun
	10.96/-1.5 6.92/1.8 13.72 1.82 49.01 14.35/0.5 45.51 4.20 57.61 4:25.30							
7724	Nadir	El Fassi	FRA	23.9.83	3	WUG	Izmir	19 Aug
	11.22/-0.6 7.16/-1.8 13.13 2.01 50.59 14.93/-0.2 39.23 4.60 56.24 4:20.76							
7716	Andres	Raja	EST	2.6.82	1		Brezice	25 Sep
	11.10/-0.7 7.40/-0.2 14.00 2.00 49.94 14.39/0.9 40.90 4.50 55.57 4:56.29							
(50)								
7711	Iván	Scolfaro da Silva	BRA	30.7.82	1	NC	São Paulo	19 Jun
	11.10/0.3 7.31/0.7 12.95 1.96 48.87 14.66/1.2 40.52 4.50 56.57 4:40.82							
7705	Anders	Black	DEN	6.11.79	14		Götzis	29 May
	11.25/-0.2 7.46/0.3 14.12 2.15 50.84 15.32/-1.2 40.20 4.10 57.92 4:39.05							
7705		Yu Bin	CHN	26.11.85	2	NG	Nanjing	21 Oct
	11.15/0.4 7.36w/2.6 14.53 1.96 50.00 15.08/0.4 36.83 4.60 66.41 4:58.16							
7698	David	Gómez	ESP	13.2.81	3	ECp-S	Bydgoszcz	3 Jul
	11.09/0.9 7.29/1.6 13.11 1.86 48.49 14.46/1.0 40.15 4.20 62.73 4:37.02							
7690	Lassi	Raunio	FIN	11.10.83	1	v2N	Turku	29 May
	10.85w/4.0 7.07/0.4 14.47 2.00 51.41 14.57/1.9 45.13 4.26 57.76 4:55.22							
7690	Damien	Camberlein	FRA	5.2.80	8		Arles	5 Jun
	11.07w/3.6 7.04w/4.0 13.19 1.96 51.21 14.98w/4.0 40.84 4.35 64.43 4:27.49							
7679	Chris	Boyles	USA	2.5.80	4	NACAC	San Juan	29 May
	11.11w/3.2 7.17w/2.4 14.75 2.01 50.75 14.75 41.10 4.70 53.95 4:55.01							
7673	Nicolas	Moulay	FRA	20.1.79	4	NC	Angers	15 Jul
	11.10/-0.1 7.33w/2.1 12.68 2.04 48.20 15.54/-0.1 40.25 4.65 49.82 4:35.37							
7672	Alberto	Juantorena	CUB	27.6.77	2	CAC	Nassau	10 Jul
	10.95/1.2 7.35/-0.1 12.23 2.09 49.59 14.80/0.4 40.03 4.40 53.57 4:45.09							
7671	Kip	Janvrin	USA	8.7.65	1	DrakeR	Des Moines	28 Apr
	11.19/0.3 6.68/1.9 13.98 1.83 48.43 15.14w/2.1 42.77 4.65 59.65 4:28.62							
(60)								
7667	Christopher	Hallmann	GER	6.6.83	15		Götzis	29 May
	10.81/0.4 7.15/1.2 12.82 1.91 49.11 15.03/-1.4 39.15 4.70 54.55 4:35.15							
7661	Madis	Kallas	EST	22.4.81	3	Kudu	Rakvere	17 Jul
	10.99w/3.4 7.11w/2.8 14.16 1.96 51.71 15.00/0.5 44.79 4.55 56.59 4:46.27							
7655	Stephen	Moore	USA	13.8.75	5	NC	Carson	24 Jun
	11.22/-1.8 6.82/-0.5 12.87 2.00 48.21 14.96/-1.4 42.09 4.70 55.68 4:43.58							
7652	Jacob	Minah	GER	3.4.82	1	NC	Lage	27 Aug
	10.73/0.6 7.35/0.4 13.13 2.00 48.78 14.52/0.6 38.17 4.60 44.54 4:44.96							
7642	Knut Harald	Sommerfeldt	NOR	13.7.79	2	NC	Drammen	24 Jul
	11.27/0.5 7.18w/2.6 14.16 1.89 51.87 14.89/-0.2 40.71 4.65 64.79 4:44.09							
7641	Travis	Brandstatter	USA	10.3.82	1	MSR	Azusa	14 Apr
	11.27 6.55 12.44 2.01 50.42 14.21w/2.2 40.89 4.80 59.58 4:40.40							
7641	Andrew	Aakre	USA	15.6.81	1		Fargo	26 May
	10.78w/2.4 7.14 12.09 1.97 47.88 15.39/-1.0 48.87 4.05 46.60 4:27.41							
7641	Mikk	Joorits	EST	12.2.81	4	Kudu	Rakvere	17 Jul
	10.59w/3.4 7.35/1.4 13.21 1.90 48.34 15.77/0.5 37.65 4.45 50.96 4:25.15							
7632		Hsiao Szu-Pin	TPE	18.12.80	1	NG	Yunlin	17 Oct
	10.84w/2.6 7.02/1.4 13.54 2.00 50.19 14.91/1.8 39.42 4.80 57.56 5:02.62							
7630	Victor	Ruíz	ESP	24.10.74	5	MedG	Almeria	30 Jun
	11.23/-1.1 7.00/0.7 12.89 1.90 49.00 14.72/-0.9 41.91 4.50 54.25 4:26.02							
(70)								
7624	Alexis	Chivás	CUB	7.11.83	3	CAC	Nassau	10 Jul
	11.16/0.3 7.24/0.1 14.75 1.94 53.28 14.80/0.4 50.83 4.00 61.89 4:54.85							
7621	Erik	Surjan	AUS	22.6.83	1	NC	Sydney	5 Mar
	10.93/-0.4 7.17/0.5 13.55 2.00 50.94 14.56/-0.2 47.23 4.40 57.21 5:15.84							
7616	Marian	Geisler	GER	10.8.84	1	NC-23	Bernhausen	5 Jun
	11.40/0.0 7.43/0.5 13.20 1.96 50.05 15.48/-0.8 39.43 4.70 53.29 4:26.98							
7607	Julien	Choffart	FRA	5.11.78	10		Arles	5 Jun
	11.01w/2.5 7.47w/3.0 13.52 1.96 50.61 14.84w/3.6 39.97 4.45 53.87 4:45.86							
7603	Joost	van Bennekom	NED	18.1.81	2		Woerden	28 Aug
	10.86/1.3 7.29w/2.1 13.45 2.08 50.05 14.88/0.0 34.66 4.50 53.42 4:49.23							
7598	Aleksandr	Kislov	RUS	4.11.84	3	NC	Tula	15 Jun
	11.40/1.0 7.33/0.7 14.08 2.00 50.34 14.62/0.1 37.73 4.70 45.85 4:31.50							
7587	Mike	Marsh	USA	20.3.80	1		Claremont	14 May
	10.88/1.4 6.89 12.94 1.99 50.27 14.73/1.2 40.75 4.85 50.06 4:47.24							

Mark	Name			Nat	Born	Pos	Meet	Venue			Date
7577	Marzio	Viti		ITA	10.8.73	4	ECp-S	Bydgoszcz			3 Jul
	11.56/1.6	7.36/-0.1	14.05	2.01	52.05	15.21/1.1		45.57	4.70	52.62	4:49.67
7571	Bruno	Lambèse		FRA	11.4.69	13		Talence			18 Sep
	11.21w/3.2	7.09/1.3	14.25	2.01	51.58	14.79/1.7		41.34	4.70	46.08	4:36.06
7570	Mikhail	Logvinenko		RUS	19.4.84	4	NC	Tula			15 Jun
	11.46/1.1	7.08/0.8	12.14	2.00	49.60	14.65/0.1		40.37	5.00	44.46	4:30.03
	(80)										
7567	Mikko	Halvari		FIN	4.3.83	6	EU23	Erfurt			15 Jul
	11.15/0.4	6.93/-0.4	14.08	1.89	51.49	15.05/-0.3		47.89	4.70	54.65	4:51.23
7553	Pavel	Dubitskiy		KAZ	27.8.82	1	NC	Almaty			8 Jul
	11.24/2.0	7.25/0.2	13.42	2.08	52.07	15.22/2.0		42.88	4.70	58.32	5:10.67
7552	Will	Thomas		USA	11.8.81	3	TexR	Austin			7 Apr
	11.15w/3.8	6.67w/3.2	15.20	2.07	50.18	15.56w/2.9		41.72	4.45	52.35	4:43.14
7550	Alleyne	Lett		GRN	7.1.83	2	SEC	Nashville			13 May
	10.82/0.8	7.29/1.3	14.62	1.79	50.30	13.88w/2.8		49.86	3.65	58.43	5:12.98
7550	Mattias	Cerlati		FRA	25.10.83	8	EU23	Erfurt			15 Jul
	11.11/0.5	7.48/0.3	14.75	1.95	52.00	16.02/-0.5		42.61	4.60	55.87	4:50.95
7547	William	Frullani		ITA	21.9.79	17		Götzis			29 May
	11.00/0.4	7.45/0.8	14.05	2.09	51.23	15.01/-1.4		43.92	4.50	49.15	5:18.49
7546	Jukka	Väkeväinen		FIN	12.9.78	12		Arles			5 Jun
	11.26w/3.6	7.07w/3.1	13.72	1.96	49.76	14.77w/4.0		39.65	4.35	52.81	4:32.70
7546	Yuriy	Blonskiy		UKR	9.7.79	1	NC	Kiev			15 Jun
	11.00/1.8	7.16/0.4	14.52	1.94	51.00	14.99/-0.3		39.01	5.30	53.70	5:27.68
7535	Nikolay	Averyanov		RUS	4.2.80	2		Sochi			18 May
	10.87/0.5	6.68/1.4	13.05	1.97	50.17	15.04/-1.4		39.49	4.60	51.72	4:29.15
7531	Darion	Powell		USA	14.6.82	1	Pac10	Los Angeles (Ww)			8 May
	11.13/0.0	7.02/0.5	14.41	1.89	50.73	14.90/1.2		46.83	4.35	59.07	5:04.39
	(90)										
7530	Matthew	McEwen		AUS	16.10.71	2		Townsville			24 Sep
	11.17/0.5	6.86w/2.5	14.84	1.92	50.52	15.59/-1.7		42.65	4.60	58.82	4:50.59
7525	Travis	Geopfert		USA	20.8.78	7	v GER	Bernhausen			24 Jul
	11.19/0.0	6.85/0.0	14.91	1.82	49.16	15.67/-0.6		44.49	4.50	53.31	4:33.45
7519	David	Gervasi		SUI	1.8.83	18		Götzis			29 May
	11.30/0.1	7.17w/2.2	13.60	1.97	51.25	14.73/-1.4		38.57	4.60	54.15	4:41.00
7515	Damjan	Sitar		SLO	17.8.81	1		Maribor			29 May
	11.04/0.0	7.09/1.4	12.49	2.09	49.62	14.66/1.3		38.36	4.40	45.31	4:36.71
7502	Atis	Vaisjuns		LAT	27.9.82	6	ECp-1	Jyväskyla			3 Jul
	11.31/0.7	6.92/-0.1	14.03	1.95	50.81	15.21/0.4		38.60	4.80	58.31	4:48.62
7497	Tatu	Pussila		FIN	25.5.82	3	v2N	Turku			29 May
	11.00w/4.0	7.25/0.0	14.73	1.91	52.19	14.43/1.9		38.44	4.46	69.19	5:35.69
7497	Lionel	Marceny		FRA	17.7.74	13		Arles			5 Jun
	11.10w/2.5	7.68w/3.8	12.71	1.84	51.70	14.32w/4.0		37.61	4.85	49.65	4:47.74
7494	Schahriar	Bigdeli		GER	26.3.80	2	NC	Lage			27 Aug
	10.76/0.6	7.58/-0.4	12.16	1.91	50.20	15.44/0.0		37.26	4.50	52.05	4:37.63
7493	Santiago	Lorenzo		ARG	4.4.78	4	TexR	Austin			7 Apr
	11.20/1.4	6.94w/3.6	12.84	1.83	49.33	14.85w/3.1		38.23	4.75	54.82	4:32.31
7490	Ludo	van der Plaat		NED	3.7.83	1	NC	Emmeloord			15 May
	11.50/0.2	7.18/1.5	12.27	1.87	49.81	15.26/-0.2		38.36	4.80	62.34	4:40.64
	(100)										

Mark	Name		Nat	Born	Date
7489A	Jorge	Naranjo	CHI	18.1.82	23 Jul
7488	Lukasz	Placzek	POL	4.7.83	3 Jul
7481	Stéphane	Bamboux	FRA	28.2.74	5 Jun
7477	Hiromasa	Tanaka	JPN	28.9.81	3 Jun
7475	Peter	Cox	NZL	6.7.83	20 Nov
7470	Marek	Görlich	GER	7.2.79	5 Jun
7468	Wilfried	Gouacide	FRA	5.9.82	5 Jun
7467	Nikolay	Khrenkov	RUS	15.7.84	18 May
7464	Richard	Allan	AUS	1.12.79	25 Sep
7457	Andrey	Kharlamov	RUS	10.3.80	3 Jul
7453	Zsolt	Kürtösi	HUN	21.3.71	3 Jul
7445	Josef	Karas	CZE	20.8.78	3 Jul
7440	Sergey	Ryabchun	UKR	8.2.78	15 Jun
7439	Yevgeniy	Nikitin	UKR	9.1.85	25 Jul
7437	Takuro	Hirata	JPN	4.7.80	25 Jun
7433	Paolo	Mottadelli	ITA	7.6.79	8 May
7433	Tim	Golomski	GER	4.2.84	19 Jun
7431	Agustin	Felix	ESP	14.3.79	3 Jul
7427	Chris	Staton	USA	11.2.82	14 Apr
7427	Janis	Karlivans	LAT	2.6.82	3 Jul
7426	Carlos Eduardo	Chinin	BRA	3.5.85	19 Jun
7425	Carlos	Patterson	CUB	20.2.78	20 May
7422	Dmitriy	Sobolev	BLR	19.4.84	3 Jul
7401	Attila	Szabó	HUN	16.7.84	15 May
7400	Andrey	Klimarchuk	UKR	20.1.85	15 Jun
	(125)				

Best non wind-assisted

Mark	Name			Nat	Born	Pos	Meet	Venue			Date
8042	Jaakko	Ojaniemi		FIN	28.8.80	9	WCh	Helsinki			10 Aug
	10.67w/3.2	7.57/0.8	14.95	1.91	50.29	15.04/-1.6		42.41	4.50	66.27	4:38.18

Best at low altitude

Mark	Name			Nat	Born	Pos	Meet	Venue			Date
7558	Andrew	Levin		USA	9.3.80	6	NCAA	Sacramento			9 Jun
	11.19/-1.6	7.24/1.5	13.59	2.03	50.34	14.46/0.3		40.38	4.50	43.48	4:37.90

JUNIORS

Mark	Name			Nat	Born	Pos	Meet	Venue			Date
7833	Andrey	Kravchenko		BLR	4.1.86	13		Götzis			29 May
	11.06/1.6	7.57/1.1	12.96	2.15	49.43	14.59/-1.4		33.50	4.20	58.26	4:26.89

Mark	Name		Nat	Born	Pos	Meet	Venue			Date
7267	Leonel	Suárez	CUB	1.9.87	2	NC	La Habana			18 Mar
	11.75	7.04	11.85	2.07	50.1	14.97	35.48	3.80	63.02	4:36.37
7234	Sami	Itani	FIN	24.3.87	15	ECp-1	Jyväskylä			3 Jul
	11.41/0.8	6.71/1.2	11.93	2.04	51.50	15.37/0.0	40.81	4.10	58.99	4:40.93
7162	Michael	Bingham	USA	13.4.86	1		Tallahassee			22 Apr
	10.93/-0.3	7.13/2.0	11.40	1.83	47.13	14.66/0.7	34.52	4.25	45.35	4:51.02
7161	Yunior	Díaz	CUB	21.4.87	4	NC	La Habana			18 Mar
	11.32	7.26	12.45	1.98	48.1	15.37	38.34	3.50	47.24	4:35.16
7106		Chen Tao	CHN	8.1.87	7	NG	Nanjing			21 Oct
	11.28/0.0	6.81/1.5	12.62	1.93	51.16	15.24/0.6	33.50	4.80	47.87	4:48.03
7087	Raven	Cepeda	USA	26.6.86	2		Cedar Falls			14 May
	11.38/3.2	6.43/0.1	13.06	1.87	51.68	15.29/0.5	36.18	5.05	49.01	4:48.45
7045	Aigar	Kukk	EST	22.8.87	10		Rakvere			17 Jul
	11.28/1.9	7.00w/3.7	12.08	1.93	53.50	16.70/0.0	38.32	4.65	58.65	4.51.00
Junior Implements 6kg SP, 1.75kg DT (* with 0.99m hurdles in 110mh)										
7997	Andrey	Kravchenko	BLR-J	4.1.86	1	EJ	Kaunas			22 Jul
	11.38/-2.4	7.72w/2.4	13.83	2.11	49.45	14.62/-0.6	41.66	4.30	60.62	4:33.42
7641	Andrés	Silva	URU	27.3.86	1	PAm-J	Windsor			30 Jul
	10.67/-0.7	7.22/-0.2	13.39	1.87	46.80	14.5/-2.3	37.44	4.40	52.02	4:44.90
	7546	1	Rosario	5 Jun						
7634	Arthur	Abele	GER	30.7.86		EJ	Kaunas			22 Jul
	11.32/-2.4	6.98/1.8	14.35	1.84	49.91	14.96/-0.6	46.25	4.50	55.51	4:32.91
	7401	1	Alzenau	15 May						
7427	Mauri	Kaattari	FIN	6.2.86	3	EJ	Kaunas			22 Jul
	11.92/-0.2	6.88/1.0	14.65	2.17	54.73	15.52/1.2	42.47	4.80	61.71	5:07.36
7409	Arkadiy	Vasilyev	RUS	19.1.87	1	NC-j	Tula			3 Jul
	11.33/-1.0	6.88/0.0	13.38	1.90	49.78	14.95/0.1	40.42	4.50	55.28	4:44.79
7331w	Tero	Ojala	FIN	12.5.86	1	NC-j	Kannus			10 Sep
	11.44w/4.5	6.82w/6.9	14.20	1.81	52.95	16.31/-1.0	45.01	4.50	68.36	4:45.70
7304	Gonzalo	Barroilhet	CHI	19.8.86	1	SAm-J	Rosario			2 Oct
	11.24/1.3	7.02/0.5	14.38	1.91	52.58	14.56/1.2	41.99	4.70	47.85	5:07.18
7297*	Michael	Schrader	GER	.87	1	NC-j	Lage			28 Aug
	11.26/0.4	7.12/0.7	14.20	1.87	49.95	14.99/-0.3*	37.23	4.30	49.88	4:43.63
7290	Yunior	Díaz	CUB	28.4.87	2	PAm-J	Windsor			30 Jul
	11.01/-0.2	7.20/-0.2	14.49	1.93	48.35	15.2/-2.3	39.45	3.50	50.20	4:43.97
7285	Sami	Itani (10)	FIN	24.3.87	4	EJ	Kaunas			22 Jul
	11.52/-1.4	6.78/0.8	13.21	2.02	51.79	15.66/-0.6	44.65	4.30	54.95	4:45.98
7279	Edgars	Erinš	LAT	18.6.86	1		Rakvere			23 May
	11.17w/2.5	7.19/0.7	14.74	1.88	49.59	15.43w/2.3	42.09	3.80	45.74	4.36.82
7267	Luiz Alberto	de Araújo	BRA	27.6.87	2	SAm-J	Rosario			2 Oct
	10.84/1.3	6.97/0.5	14.20	1.91	50.72	14.42/1.2	41.15	3.40	50.24	4:43.35
7262	Vasiliy	Kharlamov	RUS	28.8.86	2	NC-j	Tula			3 Jul
	11.78/-1.0	6.87/0.0	15.70	1.84	51.88	15.16/0.1	40.36	4.60	53.78	4.49.29
7239*	Alexej	Bogdaschin	GER	.86	2	NC-j	Lage			28 Aug
	11.69/0.3	6.81/1,4	14.62	2.02	53.13	15.34/-0.3*	41.56	4.40	50.95	4:44.18
7214	Tomasz	Durasiewicz	POL	9.3.86	1	NC-j	Kielce			5 Jun
	11.48/-0.5	6.58/-0.3	14.64	1.95	51.47	15.47/1.6	50.45	4.10	48.74	4:56.47
7201*	Ingmar	Vos	NED	28.5.86	1		Bernhausen			5 Jun
	11.44/0.9	6.76/1.8	13.83	1.90	51.96	15.72/0.7*	41.40	4.00	59.13	4:33.69
7198*	Ole	Lepthin	GER	17.8.86	2		Alzenau			15 May
	10.92/0.0	6.94/1.0	13.05	1.94	50.64	14.86/0.0*	36.90	3.90	53.36	4:49.77
7190	Heigo	Nurmsalu	EST	15.8.86	6	EJ	Kaunas			22 Jul
	11.63/-2.4	7.07/0.4	14.62	1.93	52.41	16.46/1.2	42.63	4.60	54.09	4:55.14
Best non-wa										
7189	Tero	Ojala	FIN	12.5.86	7	EJ	Kaunas			22 Jul
	11.78/-0.2	6.75/0.3	14.63	1.78	52.77	16.23/1.2	43.86	4.30	68.28	4:43.02
Drugs disqualification										
7471	Aleksandr	Zyabrev ¶	RUS	16.5.87	1		Sochi			18 May
	11.13/0.1	7.16/-1.4	14.49	1.82	49.29	15.34/-1.4	41.83	4.40	49.75	4.35.31)

4 X 100 METRES RELAY

Mark	Nat	Team	Pos	Meet	Venue	Date
38.08	FRA	Doucouré, Pognon, De Lépine, Dovy	1	WCh	Helsinki	13 Aug
38.10	TRI	Pierre, Burns, Harper, Brown	2	WCh	Helsinki	13 Aug
38.27	GBR	Gardener, Devonish, Malcolm, Lewis-Francis	3	WCh	Helsinki	13 Aug
38.28	TRI	Pierre, Burns, Harper, Brown	1h2	WCh	Helsinki	12 Aug
38.28	JAM	L.Clarke, Thomas, Waugh, Frater	4	WCh	Helsinki	13 Aug
38.32	GBR	Gardener, Devonish, Malcolm, Lewis-Francis	2h2	WCh	Helsinki	12 Aug
38.32	AUS	Batman, Ross, Neofytou, P.Johnson	5	WCh	Helsinki	13 Aug
38.34	FRA	Kankarafou, Pognon, De Lépine, Dovy	1h1	WCh	Helsinki	12 Aug
38.37	JAM	L.Clarke, Thomas, Waugh, Frater	2h1	WCh	Helsinki	12 Aug

Mark	Nat	Name	Pos	Meet	Venue	Date
38.38	TRI	Harper, Burns, Armstrong, Brown	1	GP	Helsinki	25 Jul
38.45	AHO	Goeloe, Raffaela, Duzant, Martina	6	WCh	Helsinki	13 Aug
38.46	JPN	Asahara, Takahira, Yoshino, Suetsugu	3h2	WCh	Helsinki	12 Aug
38.47	TRI	Armstrong, Burns, Harper, Brown	1	CAC	Nassau	10 Jul
38.48	USA (HSI)	Capel, Scott, Conwright, Greene	1	TexR	Austin	9 Apr
38.48	GER	Kosenkov, M Blume, Unger, Broening	7	WCh	Helsinki	13 Aug
38.50	USA Red	Edwards, Spearmon, Gay, Jelks	2	GP	Helsinki	25 Jul
38.58	USA Red	Miller, Scott, Crawford, Gatlin	1	PennR	Philadelphia	30 Apr
38.58	GER	Kosenkov, M Blume, Unger, Broening	3h1	WCh	Helsinki	12 Aug
		18 performances by teams from 9 nations				
38.67	CAN	Adu-Bobie, Browne, Henry, Macrozonaris	5h2	WCh	Helsinki	12 Aug
38.69	ITA	Verdecchio, Collio, Torrieri , Kaba Fantoni	2	ECp-S	Firenze	18 Jun
38.92	BRA	Sousa, Pacheco, de Morães, A D da Silva	5h1	WCh	Helsinki	12 Aug
38.96	POL	Chyla, Nowak, Jedrusinski, Tulin	1	GP	Madrid	16 Jul
38.99	NZL	Roberts, Falealili, Dolphin, Donaldson	1		Sydney	20 Nov
39.08	BAH	J.Rolle, Demeritte, Ifill, Atkins	3	CAC	Nassau	10 Jul
39.23	THA	Wongsala, Sondee, Janthana, Suwonprateep	2	AsiC	Inchon	4 Sep
39.24	CHN (Guangxi)	Yang G, Pan G, Zhang Y, Gong W	1	NC	Shijiazhuang	21 Jun
39.25	KSA	Al-Dosari, Al-Mubarak, Al-Kahes, Al-Bishi	3	AsiC	Inchon	4 Sep
39.29	NGR	Fasuba, Emedolu, Oriala, Aliu	6h2	WCh	Helsinki	12 Aug
39.30	FIN	Pöyhönen, Tran, Ruostekivi, Hartonen	6h1	WCh	Helsinki	12 Aug
		(20)				
39.37	NED	Beck, Hoogmoed, Heisen, C.Douglas	4	GP	Helsinki	25 Jul
39.40	CUB	César, Yoel Hernández, Herrera, Vizcaíno	4	CAC	Nassau	10 Jul
39.53	GRE	Halastáras, Voyiatzákis, Petrídis, Papadiás	2	SGP	Athína	14 Jun
39.53	RUS	Volkov, Ryabov, Smirnov, Yegorichev	2		Moskva	4 Sep
39.57	SLO	Borovina, Osovnikar, Fridrikh, Zumer	3	MedG	Almeria	1 Jul
39.60	POR	Pacheco, Santos, Jorge, Ferreira,	2	GP	Madrid	16 Jul
39.69	SWE	Persson, Strandquist, Sandin, Wahn	2	v FIN	Göteborg	27 Aug
39.74	IND	Kumar, Sarkaria, Neelagund, Jayachandran	5	AsiC	Inchon	4 Sep
39.75	HKG	Leung, To, Tang, Chiang	2h2	NG	Nanjing	19 Oct
39.78	ESP	Maestra, Rodríguez, García-Borreguero, Mayoral	1		Guadalajara	15 Jun
		(30)				

39.79	CIV	13 Dec	40.00	EST	18 Jun	40.24	PUR	16 Apr	40.39	KOR	1 Sep	**Hand timed**		
39.80	SUI	18 Jun	40.09	OMA	1 Sep	40.24	UKR	27 May	40.42	RSA	19 Aug	40.1A	ECU	9 Jul
39.80A	COL	20 Aug	40.11	CZE	9 Jun	40.28	DOM	24 Jun	40.45A	ECU	23 Jul	40.4A	MRI	3 Jul
39.89	TPE	3 Mov	40.12	BEL	2 Jul	40.31	CRO	18 Jun	40.48	KAZ	1 Sep	**Drugs Disq.**		
39.97	QAT	26 Jul	40.12	CMR	2 Jul	40.35	HUN	18 Jun	40.48	KUW	8 Dec	40.28	MRI	13 Dec
39.97A	VEN	20 Aug	40.14	IRL	18 Jun	40.36	SEN	13 Dec	40.49	SRI	1 Sep			

Mixed nationality teams

Mark	Team	Pos	Meet	Venue	Date
38.49	University of Arkansas Grant USA, Spearmon USA, Gay USA, O Brown JAM	1	NCAA	Sacramento	10 Jun
38.54	University of Florida Adu-Bobie CAN, Morrison USA, Farmer USA, Clement USA	2	NCAA	Sacramento	10 Jun

JUNIORS

Mark	Nat	Name	Pos	Meet	Venue	Date
39.36	USA	Osaisai, McDaniel, Smith, Samuels	1	PAm-J	Windsor	31 Jul
39.90	GER	Sewald, Blum, Müller, Schnelting	1	EJ	Kaunas	24 Jul
40.03	POL	Lewa ski, Ku , Drapała, Sienkiewicz	2	EJ	Kaunas	24 Jul
40.09	JPN	Goto, Kimura, Kumamoto, Kurokawa	1		Niigata	16 Oct
40.25	CAN	Newton, Smith, Smellie, Warner	2	PAm-J	Windsor	31 Jul
40.27	JAM	Jervis, Mullings, Grant, Brown	3	PAm-J	Windsor	31 Jul
40.29	FIN	Vilén, Hongisto, Salonen, Viiala	3	EJ	Kaunas	24 Jul
40.33	SUI	Dünki, Mancini, Gallay, Schenkel	4		Kaunas	24 Jul
40.47	GBR	Aikines-Aryeetey, Nelson, J Thomas, Williamson	2		Mannheim	18 Jun
40.48	BRA	Gabriel, J E dos Santos, A André, R da Silva	1	SAm-J	Rosario	1 Oct
40.60	RSA	Clement, Tempies, de Vries, Fourie	1	Afr-J	Radès	3 Sep

4 X 200 METRES RELAY

Mark	Team	Pos	Meet	Venue	Date
1:20.94	Univerity of Florida (USA) Witherspoon, Morrison, Framer, Clement	1	PennR	Philadelphia	30 Apr
1:21.06	Louisiana State Univerity (USA) Dardie, Brazell, Willie, Carter	2	PennR	Philadelphia	30 Apr
1:21.31	Mississippi State University Mullings ¶ JAM, Ashley, Davis, Lewis	1h1	PennR	Philadelphia	30 Apr

4 X 400 METRES RELAY

Mark	Nat	Team	Pos	Meet	Venue	Date
2:56.91	USA	Rock 44.7, Brew 44.3, Williamson 44.40, Wariner 43.49	1	WCh	Helsinki	14 Aug
2:57.32	BAH	McKinney 44.9, Moncur 44.6, A.Williams 44.43, Brown 43.42	2	WCh	Helsinki	14 Aug
2:58.07	JAM	Ayre 44.9, Simpson 44.9, Spence 44.48, Clarke 43.81	3	WCh	Helsinki	14 Aug
2:58.82	GBR	Benjamin 45.0, Rooney 44.9, Tobin 44.52, M.Davis 44.40	4	WCh	Helsinki	14 Aug
2:59.59		Louisiana St Un, USA Dardar 46.4 Willie 44.4, Brazell 44.8 X.Carter 44.0	1	NCAA	Sacramento	11 Jun
2:59.73	BAH	McKinney 45.3, Moncur 44.7, McIntosh 45.72, Brown 44.05	1h1	WCh	Helsinki	13 Aug
2:59.75	JAM	Blackwood 45.5, Ayre 45.6, Spence 44.33, Clarke 44.33	2h1	WCh	Helsinki	13 Aug

Mark		Name	Nat	Born	Pos	Meet	Venue	Date
3:00.38	POL	Klimczak 45.7, Marciniszyn 45.5, Mackowiak 44.50, Wieruszewski 44.70			3h1	WCh	Helsinki	13 Aug
3:00.48	USA	M.Smith 45.2, Brew 44.5, Merritt 45.41, Williamson 45.34			1h2	WCh	Helsinki	13 Aug
3:00.51	GBR	Tobin 45.4, Hedman 45.0, M.Davis 45.30, Benjamin 44.73			1	ECp-S	Firenze	19 Jun
3:00.58	POL				5	WCh	Helsinki	14 Aug
		Marciniszyn 46.8, Mackowiak 44.1, Rysukiewicz 45.15, Klimczak 44.50						
3:00.81	Un of Oregon, USA	Kent 46.3, Inico 44.3, Ikwuakor 45.6, Scherer 44.6			3	NCAA	Sacramento	11 Jun
3:01.08	BAH	Cleare, A.Williams, McKinney, Brown			1	CAC	Nassau	11 Jul
3:01.33	POL	Klimczak 46.0, Marciniszyn 45.0, Mackowiak 44.99, Plawgo 45.35			2	ECp-S	Firenze	19 Jun
3:01.36	University of Florida, USA				4	NCAA	Sacramento	11 Jun
		Middleton 45.4, Witherspoon 44.8, Pastor, 45.4 Clement 44.8						
3:01.43	TRI	Modibo, Quow, Kirk, Barry			2	CAC	Nassau	11 Jul
3:01.63	Mississsippi State University USA				5	NCAA	Sacramento	11 Jun
		Coleman, 46.3 A.Davis 46.0, Lewis 44.8, Ashley 44.5						
3:01.65	FRA	El Haouzy 46.68, Keïta 44.45, Maunier 45.73, Raquil 44.79			3	ECp-S	Firenze	19 Jun
3:01.83	Baylor Univ, USA	Mutai 46.7, Teter 45.5, Fitts 46.1, Williamson 43.49			6	NCAA	Sacramento	11 Jun
	19 performances by teams from 7 nations							
3:01.96	ITA	Licciardello 46.3, Vallet 45.2, Galletti 45.23, Barberi 45.22			4	ECp-S	Firenze	19 Jun
3:02.05	RUS	Forshev 46.1, Rudnitskiy 45.3, Polukeyev 45.84, Lebedev 44.81			3h2	WCh	Helsinki	13 Aug
3:02.33	CUB	Collazo, D Martínez, Garzón, López			3	CAC	Nassau	11 Jul
	(10)							
3:02.94	GER	Kirch 46.4, Seitz 45.4, Riester 45.23, Swillims 45.89			6	ECp-S	Firenze	19 Jun
3:03.20	JPN	Ota, Horigome, Yamaguchi, Narisako			2	WUG	Izmir	20 Aug
3:03.41	UKR	Rachovskiy 46.6, Tverdostup 45.5, Knysh 45.89, Dubonosov 45.44			4h2	WCh	Helsinki	13 Aug
3:03.57	DOM	Peguero 45.7, Santa 45.1, Garcia 46.66, Side 46.09			3h3	WCh	Helsinki	13 Aug
3:03.62	SWE	Claesson 46.7, Laursen 45.3, Wissman 45.19, Nikitin 46.42			5h1	WCh	Helsinki	13 Aug
3:03.65	ESP	Canal, Testa, Barrios, Reina			1	MedG	Almeria	2 Jul
3:04.12	SRI	Kumara, Pushpakumara, Perera, Amarasekera			2	AsiC	Inchon	4 Sep
3:04.15A	BRA	Ambrósio, Parrela, Pereira, W dos Santos			1	SACh	Cali	24 Jul
3:04.35	KSA	Al-Hamaidi, Al-Somaily, Al-Bishi, Al-Salhi			1	Is.Sol	Makkah	15 Apr
3:04.64	RSA	van der Merwe 46.8, Cilliers 46.1, de Villiers 46.98, van Zyl 44.76			5h3	WCh	Helsinki	13 Aug
	(20)							
3:04.99	NED U23	Ward, de Wild, Kampen, Lathouwers			3	EU23	Erfurt	17 Jul
3:05.02	CZE	Muzík 46.7, Vojtík 46.3, Götz 46.60, K Bláha 45.39			8	ECp-S	Firenze	19 Jun
3:05.19	TUN	Ghali, Tit, Tabbal, Labidi			1		Rabat	18 Jun
3:05.20A	KEN (Armed Forces)				1		Nairobi	18 Jun
3:05.29	ROM U23	Vîlcu, Cîmpeanu, Bobos, Suciu			4	EU23	Erfurt	17 Jul
3:05.39	CHN (Guangdong)				1	NC	Shijiazhuang	21 Jun
3:05.42	GRE	Dimótsios, Doúpis, Grávalos, Iakovákis			1	ECp1B	Leiria	19 Jun
3:05.48	CAN	Vadeboncеur, Nelson, Reed, Christopher			1	Jerome	Burnaby	14 Jun
3:05.94A	COL	Peña, Mosquera, López-Murillo, Torres			2	SACh	Cali	24 Jul
3:06.08	IRL	Daly, Kennedy, Burke, Gillick			4	ECp1B	Leiria	19 Jun
	(30)							

3:06.20	SUI	19 Jun	3:07.45	IND	4 Sep	3:08.26	ZIM	12 Aug	3:08.89	BEL	19 Jun	3:09.63	SVK	19 Jun
3.06.39	BOT	12 Aug	3:07.76	SUD-J18	Sep	3:08.27	BLR	19 Aug	3:09.06	TPE	4 Nov	3:09.79	NOR	19 Jun
3:06.69	MAR	18 Jun	3:07.91	NGR	12 Aug	3:08.39	NZL	13 Mar	3:09.15	PHI	30 Nov	3:09.81	QAT	9 Dec
3:06.99	HUN	19 Jun	3:08.14	POR	19 Jun	3:08.61	ARG	24 Jul	3:09.25	LBR	14 Jun	3:09.92	KAZ	20 Aug
3:07.18	MRI	16 Dec	3:08.16A	VEN	21 Aug	3:08.75	IRI	4 Sep	3:09.50	CRO	19 Jun	**Best at low altitude**		
												3:06.57	BRA	19 Jun

Mixed nationality teams

Mark	Name	Pos	Meet	Venue	Date
3:00.57	Arizona State University	2	NCAA	Sacramento	11 Jun
	Allen USA 46.7, Amoo/GHA 44.3, Peterson USA 45.2, Banda/ZIM 44.4				
3:01.69	Texas Tech University	1h3	NCAA	Sacramento	9 Jun
	Jacob 46.5, Mathieu xxx 45.6, Beard 45.5, A Williams BAH 44.1				

JUNIORS

Mark	Nat	Name	Pos	Meet	Venue	Date
3:05.34	USA	Larry, Reid, Anderson, Oliver	1	PAm-J	Windsor	31 Jul
3:06.67	GBR	Buck, Osho, Strachan, Rooney	1	EJ	Kaunas	24 Jul
3:07.19	RUS	Sigalovskiy, Buryak, Kokorin, Sergiyenko	2	EJ	Kaunas	24 Jul
3:07.76	SUD	Al-Noor, Koudi, Nagmeldin, Edam	2	Afr-J	Radès	18 Sep
3:08.64	JAM	Gardener, Green, Robinson, Edwards	2	PAm-J	Windsor	31 Jul
3:09.25	POL	Wojty ski, Dobek, Ry , Baranowski	2h2	EJ	Kaunas	23 Jul
3:09.50	CAN	Smellie, White, Cummings, Barnett	3	PAm-J	Windsor	31 Jul
3:09.53	UKR	Bodrov, Myhalin, Melnykov, Ostrovskiy	3h2	EJ	Kaunas	23 Jul
3:09.95	BRA	A R Blanco, N V da Silva, Bargas, J A Silva	1	SAm-J	Rosario	2 Oct
3:10.05	ITA	Turchi, Magi, Quirico, Licciardello	4h2	EJ	Kaunas	23 Jul
3:10.29	GRE	Klisiáris, Papadópoulos, Anastasíou, Régas	5h2	EJ	Kaunas	23 Jul
3:10.32	TRI	James, Douglas, Alleyne, Quow	2		Bacolet	28 Mar
3:10.55	FRA	Sorimoutou, Silou, Matos, Ballaabouss	4	EJ	Kaunas	24 Jul
3:10.66	GER	Wiebe, Schäfer, Ilg, Grothkopp	1h1	EJ	Kaunas	23 Jul
3:11.13	SWE	Johansson, Kageman, Johansson, Jaako	4h1	EJ	Kaunas	23 Jul

4 x 1 MILE

Mark	Name	Pos	Meet	Venue	Date
16:04.54	Univerity of Michigan (USA)	1	PennR	Philadelphia	30 Apr
	Ellerton CAN 4:05.9, Woods CAN 4:03.0, Willis NZL 3:56.2, Brannen CAN 3:59.4				

Mark	Name		Nat	Born	Pos	Meet	Venue	Date

4 x 110 METRES HURDLES

Mark	Team	Pos	Meet	Venue	Date
54.97	University of Tennessee USA Bounware, Brunson, Campbell, Merritt	1	PennR	Philadelphia	29 Apr
55.12	University of Nebraska USA Davidson, Jones, Ross, Loncar SCG	2	PennR	Philadelphia	29 Apr

3000 METRES TRACK WALK

Mark	Name		Nat	Born	Pos	Meet	Venue	Date
11:21.04	Jared	Tallent	AUS	17.10.84	1		Canberra	29 Oct
11:26.29+	Beniamin	Kucinski	POL	1.6.82	1	in 5k	Kraków	3 Sep
11:27.6	Robert	Heffernan	IRL	28.2.78	1		Tullamore	21 Aug
11:29.20+	Grzegorz	Sudol	POL	28.8.78	1	in 5k	Biala Podlaska	28 May
11:32.0+	Aleksandr	Yargunkin	RUS	6.1.81	1=	in 10k	Saransk	19 Jun
11:32.0+	Igor	Yerokhin	RUS	4.9.85	1=	in 10k	Saransk	19 Jun

Mark	Name		Nat	Born	Date	Mark	Name		Nat	Born	Date
11:34.62	Daniel	King	GBR	30.5.83	29 May	11:43.08	Adam	Rutter	AUS-J	24.12.86	4 Jan
11:38.5+	Matej	Tóth	SVK	10.2.83	7 May	11:44.0+	Vladimir	Potemin	RUS	24.1.79	19 Jun

Indoors

Mark	Name		Nat	Born	Pos	Meet	Venue	Date
11:15.19	Robert	Heffernan	IRL	28.2.78	1		Nenagh	16 Jan
11:25.93	Grzegorz	Sudol	POL	28.8.78	1+	in 5k	Spala	19 Feb
11:31.76+	André	Höhne	GER	10.3.78	1	in 5k	Sindelfingen	19 Feb

5000 METRES TRACK WALK

Mark	Name		Nat	Born	Pos	Meet	Venue	Date
18:41.83	Erik	Tysse	NOR	4.12.80	1	NC	Bergen (Fana)	20 Aug
18:44.86	Yohan	Diniz	FRA	1.1.78	1		Lomme	8 May
18:51.60		Diniz			1		Reims	21 Jul
19:06.12		Diniz			1		Bugeat	14 Jun
19:07.27	Ilya	Markov	RUS	19.6.72	1		Kraków	3 Sep
19:09.65		Markov			1		Biala Podlaska	28 May
19:10.53	Grzegorz	Sudol	POL	28.8.78	2		Kraków	3 Sep
19:11.77		Sudol	POL	28.8.78	2		Biala Podlaska	28 May
19:12.5	Juan Manuel	Molina	ESP	15.3.79	1		Lorca	5 Mar
19:13.95	Jared	Tallent	AUS	17.10.84	1		Geelong	17 Dec
	(10/7)							
19:18.47	Denis	Langlois	FRA	10.10.68	2		Nantes	1 Jun
19:21.63	José Ignacio	Díaz	ESP	22.11.79	1		Zaragoza	9 Jul
19:23.80	Matej	Tóth	SVK	10.2.83	1		Banská Bystrica	7 May
19:29.0	Igor	Yerokhin	RUS	4.9.85	1		Saransk	19 Jun
19:29.85+	Andrey	Ruzavin	RUS-J	28.9.86	1	in 10k	Kaunas	23 Jul

Mark	Name		Nat	Born	Date	Mark	Name		Nat	Born	Date
19:35.08	Beniamin	Kucinski	POL	1.6.82	3 Sep	19:40.65	José David	Domínguez	ESP	29.7.80	9 Jul
19:36.82	Rafal	Augustyn	POL	14.5.84	3 Jun	19:41.61	Tim	Berrett	CAN	23.1.65	29 Jul
19:38.1	João	Vieira	POR	20.2.76	12 Mar	19:41.98		Chen Chuanzhan	CHN-J		29 Aug
19:38.20	José Antonio	González	ESP	15.6.79	12 May	19:42.59	Mikel	Odriozola	ESP	25.5.73	9 Jul
19:39.26		Cao Yanjun	CHN-J		29 Aug	19:43.62	Jesús Ángel	García	ESP	17.10.69	9 Jul

Indoors

Mark	Name		Nat	Born	Pos	Meet	Venue	Date
18:45.83	Ilya	Markov	RUS	19.6.72	1		Yekaterinburg	7 Jan
18:49.32	Ivan	Kuznetsov	RUS	11.9.83	2		Yekaterinburg	7 Jan
18:50.63	Francisco J	Fernández	ESP	6.3.77	3		Yekaterinburg	7 Jan
18:55.01	Grzegorz	Sudol	POL	28.8.78	4		Yekaterinburg	7 Jan
19:03.38	Alessandro	Gandellini	ITA	30.4.73	1	NC	Ancona	19 Feb
19:09.48		Markov			1		Samara	3 Feb
19:09.60	Jan	Albrecht	GER	23.7.81	1	NC	Sindelfingen	19 Feb
19:14.45	Yuriy	Andronov	RUS	6.11.71	2		Samara	3 Feb
19:20.00	Michele	Didoni	ITA	7.3.74	2	NC	Ancona	19 Feb
19:20.8	Robert	Heffernan	IRL	28.2.78	1	NC	Nenagh	6 Feb
19:23.0	Vasiliy	Ivanov	RUS	26.12.77	1		Chelyabinsk	6 Jan
19:23.32	Stepan	Yudin	RUS	3.4.80	5		Yekaterinburg	7 Jan
19:26.51	Giorgio	Rubino	ITA	30.4.73	3	NC	Ancona	19 Feb
19:26.9	Aleksandr	Prokhorov	RUS-J	22.1.86	2		Chelyabinsk	6 Jan
19:28.1	Gian Piero	Palumbo	ITA	14.7.81	1		Napoli	22 Jan
19:28.85	Lorenzo	Civallero	ITA	8.8.75	4	NC	Ancona	19 Feb
19:30.6	Dmitriy	Yesipchuk	RUS	17.11.74	3		Chelyabinsk	6 Jan

Mark	Name		Nat	Born	Date	Mark	Name		Nat	Born	Date
19:31.39	Andrea	Manfredini	ITA	9.5.78	19 Feb	19:34.9	Sergey	Lystsov	RUS	14.11.82	6 Jan
19:32.19	André	Höhne	GER	10.3.78	19 Feb	19:38.20	Gian Luca	Trombetti	ITA	28.4.77	19 Feb
19:34.01	Andrey	Stepanchuk	BLR	12.6.79	13 Feb	19:41.35	Enrico	Lang	ITA	31.3.72	19 Feb
19:34.13	Roman	Magdziarczyk	POL	5.7.77	19 Feb	19:43.50	Nikolay	Seredovich	BLR	25.1.84	13 Feb

10,000 METRES TRACK WALK

Mark	Name		Nat	Born	Pos	Meet	Venue	Date
37:58.6	Ivano	Brugnetti	ITA	1.9.76	1		Sesto San Gioavnni	23 Jul
38:41.17	Andrey	Yurin	UKR	20.1.84	1		Kiev	22 Jun
39:26.3	Aleksandr	Yargunkin	RUS	6.1.81	1		Saransk	19 Jun
39:27.3	Igor	Yerokhin	RUS	4.9.85	2		Saransk	19 Jun
39:28.45	Andrey	Ruzavin	RUS-J	28.9.86	1	EJ	Kaunas	23 Jul

Mark	Name		Nat	Born	Pos	Meet	Venue	Date
39:31.35		Brugnetti			1		Cesenatico	11 Jun
39:39.4		Yurin	(7/5)		1		Valga	30 Apr
39:41.94		Kim Hyun-sup	KOR	31.5.85	1		Mokpo	6 Apr
39:46.1	Vladimir	Potemin	RUS	24.1.79	3		Saransk	19 Jun
39:48.94	Jan	Albrecht	GER	23.7.81	1	NC	Wattenscheid	2 Jul
39:51.6	Vasiliy	Ivanov	RUS	26.12.77	4		Saransk	19 Jun
39:57.3	Pyotr	Trofimov	RUS	18.12.83	5		Saransk	19 Jun
40:04.88	Luke	Adams	AUS	22.10.76	1		Adelaide	19 Feb

Mark	Name		Nat	Born	Date
40:24.21	Alessandro	Gandellini	ITA	30.4.73	11 Jun
40:26.2	Vladimir	Parvatkin	RUS	10.10.84	19 Jun
40:32.74	Robert	Heffernan	IRL	28.2.78	24 Jul
40:35.2	Andrey	Krivov	RUS	14.11.85	19 Jun
40:35.46	Juan Manuel	Molina	ESP	15.3.79	15 Apr
40:39.23	Gian Luca	Trombetti	ITA	28.4.77	11 Jun
40:41.27		Lee Dae-ro	KOR	12.3.80	6 Apr
40:43.67	Aleksandr	Prokhorov	RUS-J	22.1.86	23 Jul

Indoors

Mark	Name		Nat	Born	Pos	Meet	Venue	Date
39:55.01	Sergey	Chernov	BLR	5.2.79	1		Minsk	11 Feb

Minsk 11 Feb: (BLR) 2. Andrey Stepanchuk 40:26.80, 3. Aleksandr Kuzmin 40:33.8, 3. Nikolay Seredovich 40:32.5

JUNIORS

Mark	Name		Nat	Born	Pos	Meet	Venue	Date
39:28.45	Andrey	Ruzavin	RUS	28.3.86	1	EJ	Kaunas	23 Jul
40:43.67	Aleksandr	Prokhorov	RUS	22.1.86	2	EJ	Kaunas	23 Jul
40:46.95	Giorgio	Rubino	ITA	15.4.86	3	EJ	Kaunas	23 Jul
40:53.5	Aleksey	Grigoryev	RUS	19.6.87	8		Saransk	19 Jun
40:57.91	Orest	Laniku	ALB	14.7.87	1		Torino	14 May
40:59.7	Vasiliy	Trofimov	RUS	4.1.86	9		Saransk	19 Jun
41:17.1	Ingus	Janevics	LAT	29.4.86	1		Murjani	16 Apr
41:19.82	Carsten	Schmidt	GER	29.5.86	4	EJ	Kaunas	23 Jul
41:28.2	Vyacheslav	Golovin	RUS	14.4.86	1	NC-j	Saransk	11 Jun
41:28.56		Cao Yanjun (10)	CHN		1		Zhengzhou	31 Aug
41:30.5	Sergey	Bakulin	RUS	13.11.86	1	NC-j	Izhevsk	17 Sep
41:32.26		Cui Yang	CHN		2		Zhengzhou	31 Aug
41:35.64		Chen Yingding	CHN		3		Zhengzou	31 Aug
41:37.0R?	Sergey	Morozov	RUS	21.3.88	1		Adler	12 Mar
41:37.67	Denis	Simanovich	BLR	20.4.87	5	EJ	Kaunas	23 Jul
41:38.5	Mikhail	Volkov	RUS	16.2.86	2	NC-j	Izhevsk	17 Sep
41:44.88		Wu Guosong	CHN	21.4.87	4		Zhengzhou	31 Aug
41:47.4	Aleksey	Kanayev	RUS	30.5.86	11	NC-j	Saransk	19 Jun
41:47.44	Adam	Rutter	AUS	24.12.86	3		Adelaide	19 Feb
41:49.6	Aleksey	Kolomytov	RUS	10.3.87	3	NC-j	Izhevsk	17 Sep

20 KILOMETRES WALK

Mark	Name		Nat	Born	Pos	Meet	Venue	Date
1:17:33	Nathan	Deakes	AUS	17.8.77	1		Cixi	23 Apr
1:17:41		Zhu Hongjun	CHN	18.8.83	2		Cixi	23 Apr
1:17:52	Francisco J	Fernández	ESP	6.3.77	1		La Coruña	4 Jun
1:17:53		Cui Zhide	CHN	11.1.83	3		Cixi	23 Apr
1:18:06	Vladimir	Parvatkin	RUS	10.10.84	1	NC-w	Adler	12 Mar
1:18:07		Li Gaobo	CHN-Y	23.7.89	4		Cixi	23 Apr
1:18:17	Ilya	Markov	RUS	19.6.72	2	NC-w	Adler	12 Mar
1:18:22	Vladimir	Stankin	RUS	2.1.74	3	NC-w	Adler	12 Mar
1:18:22		Li Gaobo			1	NG	Nanjing	19 Oct
1:18:27		Xing Shucai	CHN	4.8.84	5		Cixi	23 Apr
1:18:30		Yu Chaohong (10)	CHN	12.12.76	6		Cixi	23 Apr
1:18:31		Han Yucheng	CHN	16.12.78	7		Cixi	23 Apr
1:18:33		Liu Yunfeng	CHN	3.8.79	8		Cixi	23 Apr
1:18:35	Jefferson	Pérez	ECU	1.7.74	1	WCh	Helsinki	6 Aug
1:18:37		Zhu Hongjun			1		Dudince	26 Mar
1:18:39		Lu Ronghua	CHN	21.2.83	9		Cixi	23 Apr
1:18:45	Stepan	Yudin	RUS	3.4.80	4	NC-w	Adler	12 Mar
1:18:48	Viktor	Burayev	RUS	23.2.82	5	NC-w	Adler	12 Mar
1:18:50		Lu Ronghua			2		Dudince	26 Mar
1:18:51	Noé	Hernández	MEX	15.3.78	10		Cixi	23 Apr
1:19:00		Zhu Hongjun			2	NG	Nanjing	19 Oct
1:19:02		Fernández			1		Rio Maior	2 Apr
1:19:02	der	Sánchez	MEX-J	21.5.86	11		Cixi	23 Apr
1:19:08		Yu Chaohong			1	NC	Nanning	25 Feb
1:19:08		Fang Pengfei	CHN	16.2.83	12		Cixi	23 Apr
1:19:08		Yu Chaohong			3	NG	Nanjing	19 Oct
1:19:09		Liu Yunfeng			2	NC	Nanning	25 Feb
1:19:15		Deakes			2		Rio Maior	2 Apr
1:19:19	Luke	Adams (20)	AUS	22.10.76	13		Cixi	23 Apr
1:19:21		Pei Chuang	CHN	5.12.81	3	NC	Nanning	25 Feb
1:19:21	Rolando	Saquipay	ECU	21.7.79	1	PAmCp	Lima	7 May
	(31/22)							

Mark	Name		Nat	Born	Pos	Meet	Venue	Date
1:19:22	Cristian D.	Berdeja	MEX	21.6.81	14		Cixi	23 Apr
1:19:29		Bai Xuejin	CHN-J	6.6.87	15		Cixi	23 Apr
1:19:34		Li Jianbo	CHN-J	14.11.86	16		Cixi	23 Apr
1:19:44	Juan Manuel	Molina	ESP	15.3.79	3	WCh	Helsinki	6 Aug
1:19:51		Bian Aiguo	CHN	10.6.80	17		Cixi	23 Apr
1:19:58	Andrey	Yurin	UKR	20.1.84	1	NC-w	Yevpatoriya	5 Mar
1:20:00	André	Höhne	GER	10.3.78	4	WCh	Helsinki	6 Aug
1:20:05		Si Tianfeng	CHN	17.6.84	18		Cixi	23 Apr
	(30)							
1:20:08	Dmitriy	Yesipchuk	RUS	17.11.74	6	NC-w	Adler	12 Mar
1:20:08		Wang Zhiping	CHN	11.12.83	19		Cixi	23 Apr
1:20:15		Li Hongguang	CHN	10.2.80	20		Cixi	23 Apr
1:20:16	Igor	Yerokhin	RUS	4.9.85	7	NC-w	Adler	12 Mar
1:20:19	Hatem	Ghoula	TUN	7.6.73	5	WCh	Helsinki	6 Aug
1:20:20	Yohan	Diniz	FRA	1.1.78	1		Podebrady	9 Apr
1:20:20		Zhao Chengliang	CHN	1.6.84	6	NG	Nanjing	19 Oct
1:20:25	Omar	Segura	MEX	24.3.81	21		Cixi	23 Apr
1:20:26	Luís Fernando	López	COL	3.6.79	2	PAmCp	Lima	7 May
1:20:27	Aleksandr	Yargunkin	RUS	6.1.81	8	NC-w	Adler	12 Mar
	(40)							
1:20:28		Xu Xingde	CHN	12.6.84	6	NC	Nanning	25 Feb
1:20:28		Liu Wenjun	CHN-J	8.1.87	22		Cixi	23 Apr
1:20:33	Andrey	Talashko	BLR	31.5.82	1	NC	Brest	2 Jul
1:20:34	Beniamin	Kucinski	POL	1.6.82	7	WCh	Helsinki	6 Aug
1:20:41		Dong Jimin	CHN	10.10.85	23		Cixi	23 Apr
1:20:45		Shi Yong	CHN-J	7.2.87	24		Cixi	23 Apr
1:20:47	Roman	Magdziarczyk	POL	5.7.77	2	NC	Rumia	12 Jun
1:20:55	Aigars	Fadejevs	LAT	27.12.75	5		Rio Maior	2 Apr
1:20:59		Meng Ke	CHN-J	8.12.87	26		Cixi	23 Apr
1:20:59		Sun Chao	CHN-J	8.1.87	7	NG	Nanjing	19 Oct
	(50)							
1:21:00	Ivan	Kuznetsov	RUS	11.9.83	9	NC-w	Adler	12 Mar
1:21:01		Zhang Ronglong	CHN	2.11.84	27		Cixi	23 Apr
1:21:03	Grzegorz	Sudol	POL	28.8.78	3	NC	Rumia	12 Jun
1:21:06	Takayuki	Tanii	JPN	14.2.83	1		Kobe	30 Jan
1:21:11+	Vladimir	Kanaykin	RUS	21.3.85	1	in 35k	Adler	13 Mar
1:21:11	Erik	Tysse	NOR	4.12.80	1		Tukums	10 Sep
1:21:13		Liu Guangjun	CHN-Y	7.9.89	28		Cixi	23 Apr
1:21:14	Sergey	Lystsov	RUS	14.11.82	10	NC-w	Adler	12 Mar
1:21:15	Ivan	Trotskiy	BLR	27.5.76	11	NC-w	Adler	12 Mar
1:21:26	Vladimir	Shults	RUS	17.4.82	12	NC-w	Adler	12 Mar
	(60)							
1:21:29	Sérgio	Galdino	BRA	7.5.69	3	PAmCp	Lima	7 May
1:21:36	Rafal	Augustyn	POL	14.5.84	1		Zaniemysl	23 Apr
1:21:36	Kamil	Kalka	POL	28.5.81	4	NC	Rumia	12 Jun
1:21:38	Matej	Tóth	SVK	10.2.83	2		Podebrady	9 Apr
1:21:45		Zhang Tianping	CHN	11.1.82	10	NC	Nanning	25 Feb
1:21:46	Bernardo	Segura	MEX	11.2.70	3		Tijuana	19 Mar
1:21:46	Rafal	Dys	POL	14.1.82	6	NC	Rumia	12 Jun
1:21:51	Andrey	Ruzavin	RUS-J	28.3.86	13	NC-w	Adler	12 Mar
1:21:53	Andrey	Kovenko	UKR	25.11.73	2	NC-w	Yevpatoriya	5 Mar
1:21:56	João	Vieira	POR	20.2.76	4		La Coruña	4 Jun
	(70)							
1:21:57	Michal	Jarosz	POL	30.3.82	3		Zaniemysl	23 Apr
1:22:01	Gustavo	Restrepo	COL	27.7.82	4	PAmCp	Lima	7 May
1:22:02	Sergey	Safarov	RUS	26.1.83	14	NC-w	Adler	12 Mar
1:22:04	Konstantin	Maksimov	RUS	17.6.82	15	NC-w	Adler	12 Mar
1:22:06	Aleksandr	Kuzmin	BLR	24.3.81	16	RUS-w	Adler	12 Mar
1:22:07		Pei Lingjie	CHN-J	3.1.87	12	NC	Nanning	25 Feb
1:22:09		Liu Yong	CHN	1.3.83	30		Cixi	23 Apr
1:22:14	Silviu	Casandra	ROM	27.10.75	10		Rio Maior	2 Apr
1:22:14	Sergey	Chernov	BLR	5.2.79	1		Brest	1 Jun
1:22:15		Kim Hyun-sup	KOR	31.5.85	1	NG	Ulsan	16 Oct
	(80)							
1:22:16		Lee Dae-ro	KOR	12.3.80	1	NC	Daegu	4 Jun
1:22:17		Ao Xinli	CHN	26.1.81	31		Cixi	23 Apr
1:22:18		Chu Yafei	CHN-Y	5.9.88	32		Cixi	23 Apr
1:22:18		Bai Liansheng	CHN	28.7.78	33		Cixi	23 Apr
1:22:21	Akihiro	Sugimoto	JPN	20.10.81	2		Kobe	30 Jan
1:22:21	Andrey	Krivov	RUS	14.11.85	17	NC-w	Adler	12 Mar
1:22:23		Park Chil-sung	KOR	8.7.82	1		Koyang	13 Nov

Mark	Name		Nat	Born	Pos	Meet	Venue	Date
1:22:29	Pyotr	Trofimov	RUS	18.12.83	18	NC-w	Adler	12 Mar
1:22:31	Milos	Holusa	CZE	2.5.65	19	RUS-w	Adler	12 Mar
1:22:35	Daniel	García	MEX	28.10.71	35		Cixi	23 Apr
	(90)							
1:22:36	Omar	Zepeda	MEX	8.6.77	36		Cixi	23 Apr
1:22:36	José Ignacio	Díaz	ESP	22.11.79	7		La Coruña	4 Jun
1:22:39		Zeng Guoqiang	CHN	25.10.84	38		Cixi	23 Apr
1:22:39	Ivaro	García	MEX	18.10.83	39		Cixi	23 Apr
1:22:40	Andrey	Stadnichuk	RUS	14.12.73	19	NC-w	Adler	12 Mar
1:22:45		Miao Yanxi	CHN	3.8.84	40		Cixi	23 Apr
1:22:46		Zhao Jianguo	CHN-Y	19.1.88	3	NC-j	Nanning	25 Feb
1:22:47	Denis	Langlois	FRA	10.10.68	3		Podebrady	9 Apr
1:22:48	Andrey	Makarov	BLR	2.1.71	21	RUS-w	Adler	12 Mar
1:22:48		Wang Hongsheng	CHN		41		Cixi	23 Apr
	(100)							

Mark	Name		Nat	Born	Date
1:22:50	Ivano	Brugnetti	ITA	1.9.76	2 Apr
1:22:52	Koichiro	Morioka	JPN	2.4.85	17 Apr
1:22:52	Lorenzo	Civallero	ITA	8.8.75	6 Aug
1:22:53	Jorge	Segura	MEX	23.4.75	23 Apr
1:22:53	Jared	Tallent	AUS	17.10.84	23 Apr
1:22:55		Gao Lianzuo	CHN	30.8.85	25 Feb
1:23:02	José Alejandro	Cambil	ESP	26.1.75	4 Jun
1:23:03	Rafal	Fedaczynski	POL	3.12.80	23 Apr
1:23:04		Fu Caogen	CHN	5.8.85	25 Feb
1:23:05	Artyom	Valchenko	UKR	3.4.84	5 Mar
1:23:06	Fausto	Quinde	ECU	13.2.76	7 May
1:23:07+	Sergey	Kirdyapkin	RUS	16.1.80	13 Mar
1:23:08	Vitaliy	Talankov	BLR	29.4.82	1 Jun
1:23:09	Jesús Ángel	García	ESP	17.10.69	4 Jun
1:23:09		Byun Young-joon	KOR	20.3.84	15 Oct
1:23:10	Yusuke	Yachi	JPN	2.1.80	30 Jan
1:23:10		Wei Ke	CHN-J	21.4.87	23 Apr
1:23:10		Shin Il-yong	KOR	17.2.79	6 Aug
1:23:14	Andrés	Chocho	ECU	4.11.83	19 Mar
1:23:14	Nikolay	Seredovich	BLR	25.1.84	16 Apr
1:23:18		Chang Chunhu	CHN	1.5.82	25 Feb
1:23:20	Mikel	Odriozola	ESP	25.5.73	30 Jan
1:23:20	Michele	Didoni	ITA	7.3.74	2 Apr
1:23:21	Gabriel	Ortiz	MEX	2.12.81	7 May
1:23:22	Yevgeniy	Apanasenko	RUS	4.5.81	12 Mar
1:23:26	Jan	Albrecht	GER	23.7.81	24 Apr
1:23:27	Alessandro	Gandellini	ITA	30.4.73	2 Apr
1:23:30	Benjamin	Sánchez	ESP	10.3.85	16 Jul
1:23:33		Kang Wenduo	CHN	9.10.83	23 Apr
1:23:37		Cao Guotao	CHN	8.1.83	25 Feb
1:23:45	Andrey	Stepanchuk	BLR	12.6.79	9 Apr
1:23:45.4t	José Alessandro	Bagio	BRA	16.4.81	17 Jun
1:23:46	José David	Domínguez	ESP	29.7.80	10 Apr
1:23:52		Gadasu Alatan	CHN	27.1.84	23 Apr
1:23:55	Diego	Cafagna	ITA	9.7.75	2 Apr
1:23:57	Enrico	Lang	ITA	31.3.72	2 Apr
1:23:57	Yuki	Yamazaki	JPN	16.1.84	2 Oct
1:23:58	Giorgio	Rubino	ITA-J	15.4.86	2 Apr
1:24:00	Aleksey	Kazanin	UKR	22.5.82	1 Oct
1:24:01.8t	Edwin	Centeno	PER	27.6.81	26 Jun
1:24:07	Aleksey	Shelest	UKR	27.3.73	2 Jul
1:24:09	Gian Luca	Trombetti	ITA	28.4.77	2 Apr
1:24:10	Naoki	Ikeya	JPN	7.6.82	30 Jan
1:24:12	Trond	Nymark	NOR	28.12.76	4 Jun
1:24:20	Robert	Heffernan	IRL	28.2.78	21 May
1:24:22	Vasiliy	Ivanov	RUS	26.12.77	12 Mar
1:24:23		Geng Zhiyao	CHN-J	15.8.87	23 Apr
1:24:27		Lee Kil-young	KOR	8.4.84	4 Jun
1:24:28		Wang Yieying	CHN-J	12.12.86	23 Apr
1:24:29		Wang Xiaohong	CHN	15.5.83	25 Feb
1:24:34	Aleksey	Kronin	RUS	23.10.70	11 Jun
1:24:35		Liu Dashan	CHN	10.5.80	23 Apr
1:24:36	Pavel	Nartov	RUS	12.6.84	12 Mar
1:24:45	Rustam	Kuvatov	KAZ	9.11.77	12 Mar
1:24:45	Maik	Berger	GER	17.2.79	9 Apr
1:24:46	Adam	Rutter	AUS-J	24.12.86	6 Mar
1:24:46.0t	Freddy	Hernández	COL	24.4.78	23 Jun
1:24:51	Viktor	Ginko	BLR	7.12.65	2 Jul
1:24:55		Zhao Yang	CHN-Y	23.2.89	23 Apr
1:24:56	Darren	Bown	AUS	30.6.74	6 Mar
1:24:58	Hassanine	Sbai	TUN	21.1.84	4 Jun
1:24:58	Francisco	Arcilla (162)	ESP	14.1.84	4 Jun

Best track times

Mark		Name		Nat	Born	Date
1:22:54.4	A	Jefferson	Pérez	ECU	1.7.74	22 Jul
1:22:55.4	A	Rolando	Saquipay	ECU	21.7.79	22 Jul
1:23:31.6		Sérgio	Galdino	BRA	7.5.69	17 Jun
1:23:43.2	A	Luis Fernando	López	COL	3.6.79	22 Jul
1:23:46.7		João	Vieira	POR	20.2.76	23 Jul
1:24:46.7	A	Gustavo	Restrepo	COL	27.7.82	22 Jul

JUNIORS

See main list for top 3 juniors. 16 performances by 10 men to 1:22:00. Additional marks and further juniors:

E Sánchez	1:20:45	8	WCh	Helsinki	6 Aug					
Shi Yong	1:20:50	1	NC-j	Nanning	25 Feb					
Sun Chao	1:21:36	2	NC-j	Nanning	25 Feb					
Li Jianbo	1:21:51	5		Dudince	26 Mar	1:21:55	8	NG	Nanjing	19 Oct

Mark	Name		Nat	Born	Pos	Meet	Venue	Date
1:23:10		Wei Ke	CHN	21.4.87	44		Cixi	23 Apr
1:23:58	Giorgio	Rubino	ITA	15.4.86	1J		Pomigliano d'Arco	2 Apr
1:24:23		Geng Zhiyao	CHN	15.8.87	49		Cixi	23 Apr
1:24:28		Wang Yieying	CHN	12.12.86	50		Cixi	23 Apr
1:24:46	Adam	Rutter	AUS	24.12.86	3	NC	Sydney	6 Mar
1:24:55		Zhao Yang	CHN-Y	23.2.89	53		Cixi	23 Apr
1:25:20		Yan Changhui	CHN	20.3.87	7	NC-j	Nanning	25 Feb

30 KILOMETRES WALK

Mark	Name		Nat	Born	Pos	Meet	Venue	Date
2:01:47+	Vladimir	Kanaykin	RUS	21.3.85	1	in 35k	Adler	13 Mar
2:04:50+	Sergey	Kirdyapkin	RUS	16.1.80	2	in 35k	Adler	13 Mar
2:08:45+	Yuriy	Andronov	RUS	6.11.71	3	in 35k	Adler	13 Mar
2:09:01	Aleksey	Shelest	UKR	27.3.73	1	NC-w	Yevpatoriya	4 Mar
2:10:05+	Sergey	Yerokhin	RUS	30.12.80	4	in 35k	Adler	13 Mar
2:11:10+	Gennadiy	Kanayev	RUS	17.7.85	5	in 35k	Adler	13 Mar
2:11:18+	Sergey	Melentyev	RUS	5.12.76	6	in 35k	Adler	13 Mar
2:11:53+	Vladimir	Potemin	RUS	15.1.80	2	in 50k	Saransk	12 Jun

Mark		Name	Nat	Born	Pos	Meet	Venue	Date
2:12:13+	Aleksey	Voyevodin	RUS	9.8.70	2	in 50k	Helsinki	12 Aug
2:12:32+		Zhao Chengliang	CHN	1.6.84	3	in 50k	Helsinki	12 Aug
2:12:33+	Jared	Tallent	AUS	17.10.84	1	in 20M	Canberra	12 Jun
2:12:39+		Han Yucheng	CHN	16.12.78	1	in 50k	Dudince	26 Mar
2:13:02+	Mikel	Odriozola	ESP	25.5.73	1	in 50k	El Prat de Llobregat	27 Feb
2:13:27	João	Vieira	POR	20.2.76	1		Beja	29 Jan

35 KILOMETRES WALK

Mark		Name	Nat	Born	Pos	Meet	Venue	Date
2:23:17	Vladimir	Kanaykin	RUS	21.3.85	1	NC-w	Adler	13 Mar
2:25:57	Sergey	Kirdyapkin	RUS	16.1.80	2	NC-w	Adler	13 Mar
2:30:22	Yuriy	Andronov	RUS	6.11.71	3	NC-w	Adler	13 Mar
2:32:06		Andronov			1		Chelyabinsk	6 Sep
2:32:45	Sergey	Yerokhin	RUS	30.12.80	2		Chelyabinsk	6 Sep
2:32:50+		Kanaykin			1	in 50k	Saransk	12 Jun
2:32:50.4 t		Yerokhin			1	NC	Izhevsk	18 Sep
2:33:00		Yerokhin			4	NC-w	Adler	13 Mar
2:33:09+		Kirdyapkin			1	in 50k	Helsinki	12 Aug
2:34:12+	Aleksey	Voyevodin	RUS	9.8.70	2	in 50k	Helsinki	12 Aug
2:34:33+		Zhao Chengliang			3	in 50k	Helsinki	12 Aug
2:34:57.6 t	Sergey	Petrov	RUS	25.11.80	2	NC	Izhevsk	18 Sep
2:35:29	Sergey	Melentyev	RUS	5.12.76	5	NC-w	Adler	13 Mar
2:35:51	Gennadiy	Kanayev	RUS	17.7.85	6	NC-w	Adler	13 Mar
2:35:53+	Vladimir	Potemin	RUS	15.1.80	2	in 50k	Saransk	12 Jun
2:36:40+	Trond	Nymark	NOR	28.12.76	4=	in 50k	Helsinki	12 Aug
2:36:40+	Alex	Schwazer	ITA	26.12.84	4=	in 50k	Helsinki	12 Aug

Mark		Name	Nat	Born	Date
2:36:41+	Jesús Ángel	García	ESP	17.10.69	12 Aug
2:36:43+	Roman	Magdziarczyk	POL	5.7.77	12 Aug
2:36:45	Omar	Zepeda	MEX	8.6.77	12 Aug
2:36:50+	Yohan	Diniz	FRA	1.1.78	21 May
2:36:52	Aleksey	Kronin	RUS	23.10.70	6 Sep
2:37:04+	Andreas	Erm	GER	12.3.76	20 Mar
2:37:10.5t	Aleksandr	Pimenov	RUS	22.7.79	18 Sep
2:37:24.9t	Yuriy	Chesnokov	RUS	29.12.79	18 Sep
2:37:54	Viktor	Ginko	BLR	7.12.65	13 Mar
2:37:55	Andrey	Stepanchuk	BLR	12.6.79	13 Mar

50 KILOMETRES WALK

Mark		Name	Nat	Born	Pos	Meet	Venue	Date
3:36:06		Yu Chaohong	CHN	12.12.76	1	NG	Nanjing	22 Oct
3:36:13		Zhao Chengliang	CHN	1.6.84	2	NG	Nanjing	22 Oct
3:36:20		Han Yucheng	CHN	16.12.78	1	NC	Nanning	27 Feb
3:37:58		Xing Shucai	CHN	4.8.84	2	NC	Nanning	27 Feb
3:38:08	Sergey	Kirdyapkin	RUS	16.1.80	1	WCh	Helsinki	12 Aug
3:38:56		Zhao Chengliang			3	NC	Nanning	27 Feb
3:39:17		Dong Jimin	CHN	10.10.85	4	NC	Nanning	27 Feb
3:40:23		Gadasu Alatan	CHN	27.1.84	3	NG	Nanjing	22 Oct
3:40:30		Han Yucheng			1		Dudince	26 Mar
3:40:40	Vladimir	Kanaykin	RUS	21.3.85	1	NC	Saransk	12 Jun
3:41:03	Aleksey	Voyevodin	RUS	9.8.70	1	ECp	Miskolc	21 May
3:41:11		Kirdyapkin			2	ECp	Miskolc	21 May
3:41:25		Voyevodin			2	WCh	Helsinki	12 Aug
3:41:30		Ni Liang (10)	CHN-J	26.7.86	4	NG	Nanjing	22 Oct
3:41:47	Mikel	Odriozola	ESP	25.5.73	1	NC	El Prat de Llobregat	27 Feb
3:41:54	Alex	Schwazer	ITA	26.12.84	3	WCh	Helsinki	12 Aug
3:42:34	Yuriy	Andronov	RUS	6.11.71	3	ECp	Miskolc	21 May
3:42:55		Si Tianfeng	CHN	17.6.84	5	NG	Nanjing	22 Oct
3:44:04	Trond	Nymark	NOR	28.12.76	4	WCh	Helsinki	12 Aug
3:44:20		Cui Zhide	CHN	11.1.83	5	NC	Nanning	27 Feb
3:44:45		Yu Chaohong			6	NC	Nanning	27 Feb
3:44:45		Zhao Chengliang			5	WCh	Helsinki	12 Aug
3:45:05		Lu Ronghua	CHN	21.2.83	7	NC	Nanning	27 Feb
3:45:13		Li Jianbo	CHN-J	14.11.86	8	NC	Nanning	27 Feb
3:45:17		Gadasu			9	NC	Nanning	27 Feb
3:45:17	Yohan	Diniz	FRA	1.1.78	4	ECp	Miskolc	21 May
3:45:23		Wang Zhiping (20)	CHN	11.12.83	10	NC	Nanning	27 Feb
3:46:05		Nymark			1		Tijuana	20 Mar
3:46:44		Yang Yongjian	CHN	28.4.73	11	NC	Nanning	27 Feb
3:47:02		Zhao Jianguo	CHN-Y	19.1.88	6	NG	Nanjing	22 Oct
	(30/22)							
3:47:19		Chang Chunhu	CHN	1.5.82	12	NC	Nanning	27 Feb
3:47:31	Denis	Langlois	FRA	10.10.68	5	ECp	Miskolc	21 May
3:47:51	Nathan	Deakes	AUS	17.8.77	1	NC	Melbourne	1 May
3:48:15	Santiago	Pérez	ESP	15.1.72	2	NC	El Prat de Llobregat	27 Feb
3:48:19	Jesús Ángel	García	ESP	17.10.69	2		Tijuana	20 Mar
3:49:01	Omar	Zepeda	MEX	8.6.77	6	WCh	Helsinki	12 Aug
3:49:20	José Antonio	González	ESP	15.6.79	4	NC	El Prat de Llobregat	27 Feb

Mark	Name		Nat	Born	Pos	Meet	Venue	Date
3:49:55	Roman	Magdziarczyk	POL	5.7.77	7	WCh	Helsinki	12 Aug
	(30)							
3:50:39	Yuki	Yamazaki	JPN	16.1.84	1	NC	Wajima	17 Apr
3:51:09	José Ignacio	Díaz	ESP	22.11.79	5	NC	El Prat de Llobregat	27 Feb
3:51:30	Peter	Korcok	SVK	12.8.74	7	ECp	Miskolc	21 May
3:51:34	Vladimir	Potemin	RUS	15.1.80	2	NC	Saransk	12 Jun
3:51:40	Francisco José	Pinardo	ESP	15.3.75	6	NC	El Prat de Llobregat	27 Feb
3:51:40	Andrey	Stepanchuk	BLR	12.6.79	8	ECp	Miskolc	21 May
3:51:46		Liu Guangjun	CHN-Y	7.9.89	15	NC	Nanning	27 Feb
3:52:03		Shi Yong	CHN-J	7.2.87	16	NC	Nanning	27 Feb
3:53:57	Horacio	Nava	MEX	20.1.82	9	WCh	Helsinki	12 Aug
3:54:24	Miguel	Solís	MEX	30.9.70	1	PAmCp	Lima	8 May
	(40)							
3:54:40		Wang Yinhang	CHN	15.2.77	17	NC	Nanning	27 Feb
3:54:41		Bai Xuejin	CHN-J	6.6.87	18	NC	Nanning	27 Feb
3:54:49	Milos	Bátovsky	SVK	26.5.79	9	ECp	Miskolc	21 May
3:54:59		Zhang Defu	CHN	5.6.84	8	NG	Nanjing	22 Oct
3:55:11	David	Boulanger	FRA	11.12.74	10	ECp	Miskolc	21 May
3:55:18	Diego	Cafagna	ITA	9.7.75	11	ECp	Miskolc	21 May
3:55:22	Viktor	Ginko	BLR	7.12.65	12	ECp	Miskolc	21 May
3:55:30	Marco	De Luca	ITA	12.5.81	13	ECp	Miskolc	21 May
3:55:35		Yu Guoping	CHN-J	13.6.86	20	NC	Nanning	27 Feb
3:55:48	Tim	Berrett	CAN	23.1.65	11	WCh	Helsinki	12 Aug
	(50)							
3:56:00		Ao Xinli	CHN	26.1.81	21	NC	Nanning	27 Feb
3:56:13	Rafal	Fedaczynski	POL	3.12.80	14	ECp	Miskolc	21 May
3:56:15	Mario	Avellaneda	ESP	12.11.74	7	NC	El Prat de Llobregat	27 Feb
3:56.23	Aleksey	Shelest	UKR	27.3.73	1	NC	Ivano-Frankivsk	2 Oct
3:56:32	Alessandro	Mistretta	ITA	6.3.71	15	ECp	Miskolc	21 May
3:56:44	Aleksey	Kazanin	UKR	22.5.82	16	ECp	Miskolc	21 May
3:57:10	Sergey	Melentyev	RUS	5.12.76	3		Dudince	26 Mar
3:57:11		Xu Xingde	CHN	12.6.84	23	NC	Nanning	27 Feb
3:57:16	Fredrik	Svensson	SWE	10.9.73	17	ECp	Miskolc	21 May
3:57:30	Aleksandar	Rakovic	SCG	13.4.68	18	ECp	Miskolc	21 May
	(60)							
3:57:46		Li Hongguang	CHN	10.2.80	24	NC	Nanning	27 Feb
3:57:56	Julio	Martínez	GUA	27.9.73	12	WCh	Helsinki	12 Aug
3:58:02	Luis	García	GUA	13.9.74	4		Tijuana	20 Mar
3:58:07		Ouyang Shuiping	CHN-J	23.1.86	25	NC	Nanning	27 Feb
3:58:13		Han Guodong	CHN	8.5.84	26	NC	Nanning	27 Feb
3:58:39	Craig	Barrett	NZL	16.11.71	2		Melbourne	1 May
3:58:49		Xu Hongpu	CHN	16.9.79	27	NC	Nanning	27 Feb
3:59:01	Antti	Kempas	FIN	3.10.80	19	ECp	Miskolc	21 May
3:59:11	Ken	Akashi	JPN	6.11.76	3	NC	Wajima	17 Apr
3:59:12		Liang Zhenggan	CHN	27.8.83	28	NC	Nanning	27 Feb
	(70)							
3:59:31	Sergey	Budza	UKR	6.12.84	2	NC	Ivano-Frankivsk	2 Oct
3:59:36		Wang Weijun	CHN	31.12.80	29	NC	Nanning	27 Feb
3:59:51		Wu Guosong	CHN-J	21.4.87	30	NC	Nanning	27 Feb
3:59:53	German	Skurygin	RUS	15.9.63	4	NC	Saransk	12 Jun
3:59:59		Zhang Jiawei	CHN-J	27.10.86	31	NC	Nanning	27 Feb
4:00:19		Hou Yang	CHN	8.7.85	32	NC	Nanning	27 Feb
4:00:26		Li Yi	CHN	19.1.81	33	NC	Nanning	27 Feb
4:01:21	Jorge Ignacio	Silva	ESP	19.4.79	8	NC	El Prat de Llobregat	27 Feb
4:01:25		Kim Dong-young	KOR	6.3.80	16	WCh	Helsinki	12 Aug
4:01:41		Liu Yong	CHN	1.3.83	34	NC	Nanning	27 Feb
	(80)							
4:01:53	János	Tóth	HUN	15.4.78	4	1 NC	Dudince	26 Mar
4:01:54	Modris	Liepins	LAT	30.8.66	17	WCh	Helsinki	12 Aug
4:02:11		He Lin	CHN	1.3.83	35	NC	Nanning	27 Feb
4:02:14	Yusuke	Yachi	JPN	2.1.80	4	NC	Wajima	17 Apr
4:03:03	Claudio	Vargas	MEX	9.12.74	3	PAmCp	Lima	8 May
4:03:09	Pedro	Martins	POR	12.1.68	1	NC	Baixa da Banheira	26 Feb
4:03:28		Zhang Huabing	CHN	28.9.83	36	NC	Nanning	27 Feb
4:03:35		Li Guoqing	CHN	1.10.79	37	NC	Nanning	27 Feb
4:03:42	Milos	Holusa	CZE	2.5.65	5		Dudince	26 Mar
4:03:42	Chris	Erickson	AUS	1.12.81	3	NC	Melbourne	1 May
	(90)							
4:03:53		Wang Pu	CHN	6.1.83	38	NC	Nanning	27 Feb
4:04:05	Rogelio	Sánchez	MEX	26.10.73	4	PAmCp	Lima	8 May
4:04:22	António	Pereira	POR	10.7.75	21	ECp	Miskolc	21 May

Mark		Name	Nat	Born	Pos	Meet	Venue	Date
4:04:23	Kamil	Kalka	POL	28.5.81	1	NC	Wien	2 Oct
4:04:35	Duane	Cousins	AUS	13.7.73	4	NC	Melbourne	1 May
4:04:43	Daugvinas	Zujus	LTU	16.10.75	1		Dublin	26 Jun
4:04:54		Wang Yieying	CHN-J	12.12.86	39	NC	Nanning	27 Feb
4:04:57		Su Lin	CHN	18.3.84	40	NC	Nanning	27 Feb
4:05:01		Zhang Haofu	CHN	28.10.83	41	NC	Nanning	27 Feb
4:05:04	Martin	Pupis	SVK	19.10.78	6		Dudince	26 Mar
	(100)							

Mark		Name	Nat	Born	Date
4:05:10	Maciej	Rosiewicz	POL	31.7.77	2 Oct
4:05:38	Xavier	Moreno	ECU	15.11.79	8 May
4:05:45		Zhang Yuan	CHN-J	6.5.87	27 Feb
4:05:58	Augusto	Cardoso	POR	13.12.70	21 May
4:05:59	Tony	Sargisson	NZL	24.6.75	23 Oct
4:06:21		Guo Chao	CHN	5.2.83	27 Feb
4:06:23	Sergey	Korepanov	KAZ	9.5.64	12 Aug
4:06:24	Donatas	Skarnulis	LTU	21.10.77	2 Oct
4:07:03		Zhang Tianping	CHN	11.1.82	27 Feb
4:07:22	Darren	Bown	AUS	30.6.74	1 May
4:07:39	Zoltán	Czukor	HUN	18.12.62	21 May
4:07:51	Jorge	Costa	POR	20.3.61	26 Feb
4:07:54	Cristian	Bascuñán	CHI	8.3.83	8 May
4:08:05	Juan Antonio	Porras	ESP	19.2.72	27 Feb
4:08:07	Michele	Didoni	ITA	7.3.74	30 Jan
4:08:07	Jesús	Sánchez	MEX	7.2.76	20 Mar
4:08:12	Michal	Jarosz	POL	30.3.82	2 Oct
4:08:21	Gyula	Dudás	HUN	20.8.66	26 Mar
4:08:48	Konstadínos	Stefanópoulos	GRE	11.7.84	16 Oct
4:09:28	David	Mateos	ESP	29.12.81	27 Feb
4:09:32	Curt	Clausen (21)	USA	9.10.67	13 Feb

JUNIORS

See main list for top 11 juniors. 12 performances by 10 men to 4:00:00. Additional marks and further juniors:

Ni Liang	3:50:29	14	NC	Nanning	27 Feb
Zhao Jianguo	3:54:56	19	NC	Nanning	27 Feb

Mark		Name	Nat	Born	Pos	Meet	Venue	Date
4:10:26		Liu Wenjun	CHN	8.1.87	45	NC	Nanning	27 Feb
4:13:28		Sun Chao	CHN	8.1.87	5		Wajima	17 Apr
4:18:25	Andrey	Trofimov	RUS	3.6.87	6	NC	Saransk	12 Jun
4:19:33	Ingus	Janevics	LAT	29.4.86	1	NC	Ogre	3 Apr

100 KILOMETRES WALK

Mark		Name	Nat	Born	Pos	Meet	Venue	Date
9:08:49	Viktor	Ginko	BLR	7.12.65	1		Scanzoroscaite	16 Oct
9:17:58	Ugis	Bruvelis	LAT	28.6.71	2		Scanzoroscaite	16 Oct
9:32:48	Zoltán	Czukor	HUN	18.12.62	2		Scanzoroscaite	16 Oct
9:36:54	Sergey	Dvoretskiy	RUS	25.8.69	4		Scanzoroscaite	16 Oct
9:39:26	Peter	Tichy	SVK	12.3.69	5		Scanzoroscaite	16 Oct
9:57:18	Aleksey	Shelest	UKR	27.3.73	6		Scanzoroscaite	16 Oct
9:57:29	David	Régy	FRA	1.5.69	1	NC	Roubaix	16 Oct
9:59:19	Roberto	Defendeti	ITA	30.5.68	7		Scanzoroscaite	16 Oct
10:06:31	Yuriy	Burban	UKR	18.4.80	8		Scanzoroscaite	16 Oct

WOMEN'S WORLD LISTS 2005

100 METRES

Mark	Wind		Name	Nat	Born	Pos	Meet	Venue	Date
10.84	1.9	Chandra	Sturrup	BAH	12.9.71	1	Athl	Lausanne	5 Jul
10.85	0.4	Veronica	Campbell	JAM	15.5.82	1	WK	Zürich	19 Aug
10.88	0.4	Lauryn	Williams	USA	11.9.83	2	WK	Zürich	19 Aug
10.91	1.9		Williams			2	Athl	Lausanne	5 Jul
10.92	-0.2		Campbell			1	WAF	Monaco	9 Sep
10.93	1.3		Williams			1	WCh	Helsinki	8 Aug
10.93	-0.2	Christine	Arron	FRA	13.9.73	2	WAF	Monaco	9 Sep
10.94	1.9		Arron			3	Athl	Lausanne	5 Jul
10.95	1.7		Arron			1	Déca	Paris (C)	3 Sep
10.95	1.3		Campbell			2	WCh	Helsinki	8 Aug
10.96	0.4		Arron			1s1	WCh	Helsinki	8 Aug
10.96	-0.3		Campbell			1	WAF	Monaco	9 Sep
10.97	0.4		Campbell			1	NC	Kingston	25 Jun
10.97	0.4	Sherone	Simpson	JAM	12.8.84	2	NC	Kingston	25 Jun
10.97	0.4		Sturrup			4	WK	Zürich	19 Aug
10.97	0.3		Arron			1	VD	Bruxelles	26 Aug
10.98	1.3		Arron			2	WCh	Helsinki	8 Aug
10.99	0.4		Arron			4	WK	Zürich	19 Aug
11.00	0.4		Campbell			2s1	WCh	Helsinki	8 Aug
11.01	0.3		Sturrup			1	Gugl	Linz	23 Aug
11.01	1.1		Arron			1	ISTAF	Berlin	4 Sep
11.02	1.1		Sturrup			1	CAC	Nassau	9 Jul
11.02	1.1		Sturrup			2	ISTAF	Berlin	4 Sep
11.02	1.1		Sturrup			1		Shangahi	17 Sep
11.03	0.8		Simpson			1		Kingston	7 May
11.03	1.1	Ivet	Lalova	BUL	18.5.84	1	GS	Ostrava	9 Jun
11.03	0.0		Arron			1	Gaz	Saint-Denis	1 Jul

Mark	Wind	Name		Nat	Born	Pos	Meet	Venue	Date
11.03	-0.3		Arron			1	GGala	Roma	8 Jul
11.03	1.5	Maria	Karastamáti	GRE	10.12.84	1	EU23	Erfurt	16 Jul
11.03	-0.8		Arron			1q2	WCh	Helsinki	7 Aug
11.03	1.3		Williams			1s2	WCh	Helsinki	8 Aug
		(31/7)							
11.04	1.4	Me'Lisa	Barber	USA	4.10.80	1h3	NC	Carson	24 Jun
11.05	0.7	Allyson	Felix	USA	18.11.85	1		Yokohama	19 Sep
11.06	0.1	LaTasha	Colander	USA	23.8.76	1		Santo Domingo	14 May
		(10)							
11.07	1.6	Geraldine	Pillay	RSA	25.8.77	1	NC	Durban	16 Apr
11.07	0.8	Aleen	Bailey	JAM	25.11.80	2		Kingston	7 May
11.08	0.4	Yuliya	Nesterenko	BLR	15.6.79	5	WK	Zürich	19 Aug
11.09	1.3	Muna	Lee	USA	30.10.81	7	WCh	Helsinki	8 Aug
11.12	0.2	Marshevet	Hooker	USA	25.9.84	1	Big 12	Manhattan, KS	15 May
11.12	1.4	Kim	Gevaert	BEL	5.8.78	1	NA	Heusden-Zolder	23 Jul
11.13	1.8	Sylvie	Mballa Eloundou	CMR	21.4.77	1	FRA Ch	Angers	15 Jul
11.17	0.6	Kelly-Ann	Baptiste	TRI-J	14.10.86	1	NC	Port of Spain	25 Jun
11.17	-0.3	Rachelle	Smith (Boone)	USA	30.6.81	4	GGala	Roma	8 Jul
11.18	1.3	Zhanna	Block	UKR	6.7.72	5s2	WCh	Helsinki	8 Aug
		(20)							
11.18A	1.6	Felipa	Palacios	COL	1.12.75	1	Bolivar	Armenia/COL	19 Aug
11.20	0.8	Mariya	Bolikova	RUS	23.5.77	1s2	NC	Tula	10 Jul
11.20	1.8	Sylviane	Félix	FRA	31.10.77	2	NC	Angers	15 Jul
11.21A	0.9	Beverly	McDonald	JAM	15.2.70	1		El Paso	16 Apr
11.21	1.3	Olga	Fyodorova	RUS	14.7.83	2	ECp-S	Firenze	18 Jun
11.22A	1.6	Melisa	Murillo	COL	13.1.82	2	Bolivar	Armenia/COL	19 Aug
11.23	0.2	Tayna	Lawrence	JAM	17.9.75	3		New York (RI)	11 Jun
11.23	2.0	Angela	Daigle	USA	28.5.76	1		Azusa	17 Jul
11.24	1.3	Sheri-Ann	Brooks	JAM	11.2.83	1		Coral Gables	16 Apr
11.24	0.9	Lucimar	de Moura	BRA	22.3.74	1s1	NC	São Paulo	19 Jun
		(30)							
11.24	0.6	Cydonie	Mothersill	CAY	19.3.78	2	TRI Ch	Port of Spain	25 Jun
11.24	0.2	Stephanie	Durst	USA	6.1.82	1		Réthimno	10 Jul
11.25	0.6	Cleo	Tyson	USA-J	1.5.86	1	SEC	Nashville	15 May
11.26	0.1	Monique	Hennagan	USA	26.5.76	3		Santo Domingo	14 May
11.28	1.3	Marion	Jones	USA	12.10.75	1	GP II	Fort-de-France	30 Apr
11.28	-0.1	Virginia	Powell	USA	7.9.83	1	Pac-10	Los Angeles (Ww)	15 May
11.28	-0.1	Oksana	Dragun	BLR	19.4.81	1		Staiki	21 Jul
11.29	0.4	Amandi	Rhett	USA	29.6.82	1rB	MSR	Walnut	17 Apr
11.29	0.6	Shalonda	Solomon	USA	19.12.85	2	SEC	Nashville	15 May
11.29	-0.3	Angela	Williams	USA	30.1.80	5		Carson	22 May
		(40)							
11.29	0.6	Fana	Ashby	TRI	15.6.81	3	NC	Port of Spain	25 Jun
11.29		Endurance	Ojokolo	NGR	29.9.75	1	NC	Abuja	9 Jul
11.29	1.1	Tahesia	Harrigan	IVB	15.2.82	2	CAC	Nassau	9 Jul
11.29	2.0	Tremedia	Brice	USA	22.7.81	2		Azusa	17 Jul
11.30	1.8	Natalya	Sologub	BLR	31.3.75	1	NC	Brest	2 Jul
11.31	0.6	Irina	Shtangeyeva	UKR	6.2.82	1		Donetsk	7 May
11.31	2.0	Olga	Khalandyreva	RUS	13.11.81	1h1		Tula	13 Jun
11.31	1.0	Irina	Khabarova	RUS	18.3.66	1		Moskva	4 Sep
11.32A	0.9	Savatheda	Fynes	BAH	17.10.74	2		El Paso	16 Apr
11.32	0.2	Lakadron	Ivery	USA	23.6.83	2	Big 12	Manhattan, KS	15 May
		(50)							
11.32	2.0	Juanita	Broaddus	USA	12.5.85	1	JUCO	Levelland	18 May
11.32	1.6	Svetlana	Pospelova	RUS	24.12.79	1		Tallinn	16 Aug
11.33	0.5	Yeoryia	Koklóni	GRE	7.5.81	3	SGP	Athína	14 Jun
11.33	0.0		Qin Wangping	CHN	16.6.82	1	NC	Changsha	24 Jun
11.33	1.1	Birgit	Rockmeier	GER	29.11.73	1	NC	Wattenscheid	2 Jul
11.33	0.5	Manuela	Levorato	ITA	16.3.77	2rB	GGala	Roma	8 Jul
11.33	-0.1	Larisa	Kruglova	RUS	27.10.72	3	NC	Tula	10 Jul
11.33	1.8	Patricia	Buval	FRA	22.1.76	3	NC	Angers	14 Jul
11.34		Virgen	Benavídes	CUB	31.12.74	1r2		La Habana	3 Mar
11.34	0.0	Monique	Henderson	USA	18.2.83	2		Tempe	16 Apr
		(60)							
11.34	1.9	Alexis	Weatherspoon	USA	27.7.83	1h1	Pac-10	Los Angeles (Ww)	14 May
11.34	1.7	Véronique	Mang	FRA	15.12.84	1h2	Franc	Niamey	11 Dec
11.35	1.3	Wyllesheia	Myrick	USA	21.11.79	2	GP II	Fort-de-France	30 Apr
11.35	-0.1	Yekaterina	Butusova	RUS	10.1.84	3		Tula	13 Jun
11.35	-0.1	Yekaterina	Grigoryeva	RUS	21.4.74	4	NC	Tula	10 Jul
11.35	0.6	Oluwatoyin	Olupona	CAN	29.1.83	1	NC	Winnipeg	15 Jul
11.35	1.7	Emma	Ania	GBR	7.2.79	3	Déca	Paris (C)	3 Sep

Mark	Wind	Name		Nat	Born	Pos	Meet	Venue	Date
11.36A	0.1	Janice	Josephs	RSA	31.3.82	2		Pretoria	18 Mar
11.36	1.4	Andriane	Lapsley	USA	18.12.83	1h3		Tallahassee	22 Apr
11.36	0.6	Ayanna	Hutchinson	TRI	18.2.78	4	NC	Port of Spain	25 Jun
		(70)							
11.37	0.6	Vukosava	Djapic	SCG	21.1.78	1		Nis	5 Jun
11.37	0.0	Yelena	Novikova	RUS	27.10.85	s		Tula	13 Jun
11.37	0.6	Yelena	Nevmerzhitskaya	BLR	27.7.80	2	ECp-1A	Leiria	18 Jun
11.37	1.1	Glory	Alozie	ESP	30.12.77	6		Shanghai	17 Sep
11.38	0.4	Erica	Whipple	USA	4.12.82	1h1	NCAA-r	New York	27 May
11.38	1.8	Bianca	Knight	USA-Y	2.1.89	1h9	WY	Marrakech	13 Jul
11.38A	1.9	Amandine	Allou Affoué	CIV	29.8.80	1		Sestriere	23 Jul
11.39	1.0	Alexandria	Anderson	USA-J	28.1.87	1		Greensboro	17 Jun
11.39	1.9	LaShauntea	Moore	USA	31.7.83	1		Salamanca	6 Jul
11.39	-0.3	Magdalena	Khristova	BUL	25.2.77	1		Sofia	7 Jul
		(80)							
11.39	1.1	Franciela	Krasucki	BRA-Y	26.4.88	1h5	WY	Marrakech	13 Jul
11.40	0.9	Maryann	Erigha	USA	3.11.84	1		Claremont	15 Apr
11.40	2.0	Elodie	Ouédraogo	BEL	27.2.81	1		Gent	8 May
11.40	1.3	Schillonie	Calvert	JAM-Y	27.7.88	1h12	WY	Marrakech	13 Jul
11.41	0.1	Tianna	Madison	USA	30.8.85	3		Knoxville	9 Apr
11.41	1.5	Amber	Robinson	USA	5.6.80	1h2		Clermont, FL	23 Apr
11.41	1.6	Daria	Onysko	POL	30.7.81	1h1	NC	Biala Podlaska	24 Jun
11.41	1.1	Katja	Wakan	GER	27.6.81	2	NC	Wattenscheid	2 Jul
11.41	0.9	Joice	Maduaka	GBR	30.9.73	1s1	NC	Manchester (SC)	9 Jul
11.41	-0.1	Vida	Anim	GHA	7.12.83	5q4	WCh	Helsinki	7 Aug
		(90)							
11.41	1.1	Sally	McLellan	AUS-J	19.9.86	1		Brisbane	26 Nov
11.42	0.1	Amberly	Nesbitt	USA-J	9.8.86	4		Knoxville	9 Apr
11.42	0.0	Irina	Kozhemyakina	UKR	16.6.80	1		Yalta	27 May
11.42	2.0	Halima	DeCree	USA	27.7.82	1h2	NCAA-r	Eugene	27 May
11.42	0.4	Danielle	Browning	JAM	29.8.81	7	NC	Kingston	25 Jun
11.42		Mercy	Nku	NGR	17.7.76	2	NC	Abuja	9 Jul
11.42	-0.1	Yelena	Bolsun	RUS	25.6.82	6	NC	Tula	10 Jul
11.42	1.8	Delphine	Atangana	CMR	16.8.84	4	FRA Ch	Angers	15 Jul
11.42	1.8	Carima	Louami	FRA	12.5.79	5	NC	Angers	15 Jul
11.42	1.3	Susanna	Kallur	SWE	16.2.81	1	vFIN	Göteborg	28 Aug
		(100)							

Mark	Wind	Name		Nat	Born	Date
11.43	0.7	Laverne	Jones	ISV	16.9.81	16 Apr
11.43A	1.2	Wendy	Seegers	RSA	28.2.76	22 Apr
11.43	1.9	Antonette	Carter	USA	16.2.84	14 May
11.43	0.0	Yelena	Yakovleva	RUS	18.3.83	13 Jun
11.43	0.0		Shu Yan	CHN	25.1.84	24 Jun
11.43	0.4	Peta-Gaye	Dowdie	JAM	18.1.77	25 Jun
11.44	0.1	Khalilah	Carpenter	USA	27.7.83	9 Apr
11.44	0.0	Porchea	Carroll	USA	23.10.83	16 Apr
11.44	2.0	Tracy-Ann	Rowe	JAM	17.9.85	18 May
11.44	2.0	Gloria	Kemasuode	NGR	30.12.79	6 Jun
11.44	-0.1	Ebony	Collins	USA-Y	11.3.89	14 Jul
11.44	1.7	Anyika	Onuora	GBR	28.10.84	30 Jul
11.45	0.2	Connie	Moore	USA	29.8.81	16 Apr
11.45	1.6	Linda	Khodadin	FRA	24.12.76	22 May
11.45	0.9	Guzel	Khubbieva	UZB	2.5.76	18 Jun
11.45	-0.1	Tameka	Clarke	BAH	9.11.80	25 Jun
11.45	1.6	Erica	Broomfield	CAN	17.10.77	2 Jul
11.45	0.5	Vincenza	Calì	ITA	15.10.83	8 Jul
11.45	0.4	Rosemar	Coelho Neto	BRA	2.1.77	7 Aug
11.46	0.8	Inger	Miller	USA	12.6.72	7 May
11.46	1.2		Chen Lisha	CHN	10.4.81	14 May
11.46	1.6	Monika	Ivanova	BUL	8.5.85	28 May
11.46A	-0.2	Thatiana	Ignácio	BRA	2.7.83	1 Jun
11.46	1.5	Lina	Jacques-Sébastien	FRA	10.4.85	16 Jul
11.46A	0.5	Luciana	dos Santos	BRA	10.2.70	22 Jul
11.47	0.0	Ashley	Owens	USA	19.11.85	14 May
11.47	2.0	Sherry	Fletcher	GRN-J	17.1.86	18 May
11.47	2.0	Janice	Davis	USA	27.10.84	27 May
11.47	1.9	Laura	Turner	GBR	12.8.82	7 Jun
11.47	0.0	Esther	Möller	GER	13.9.77	10 Jun
11.47	1.3	Angela	Morosanu	ROM-J	26.7.86	18 Jun
11.47	1.8	Matharie	Diarrassouba	CIV	27.12.79	15 Jul
11.48	0.0	Kadiatou	Camara	MLI	4.5.81	30 Apr
11.48	1.5	Irina	Shepetyuk	UKR	13.2.82	2 Jul
11.48	1.4	Lauren	Hewitt	AUS	25.11.78	23 Jul
11.49		Christine	Amertil	BAH	18.8.79	9 Apr
11.49	1.4	Sakie	Nobuoka	JPN	24.8.77	29 Apr
11.49	0.0	Yelena	Pastushenko	UKR	14.7.79	27 May
11.49	0.8	Yekaterina	Kondratyeva	RUS	8.4.82	17 Jun
11.49	1.5	Karin	Mayr-Krifka	AUT	4.6.71	18 Jun
11.49	1.2	Raquel	Martins da Costa	BRA	30.12.83	19 Jun
11.49	0.7	Jacqueline	Poelman	NED	5.10.73	3 Jul
11.49	1.9	Anika	Baptiste	ANT-Y	30.3.90	13 Jul
11.49	1.1	Melanie	Kleeberg	AUS	27.12.81	26 Nov
11.49	1.2		Vu Thi Huong	VIE-J	7.10.86	28 Nov
11.50	0.1	Alexis	Joyce	USA	5.9.83	9 Apr
11.50	1.3	Fabienne	Béret-Martinel	FRA	22.12.77	30 Apr
11.50	1.5	Yomara	Hinestroza	COL-Y	20.5.88	13 Jul
11.50	-0.9	Natalya	Pigida	UKR	30.1.81	25 Jul
11.50	1.6	Yuliya	Gushchina	RUS	4.3.83	16 Aug
11.50	1.3	Jenny	Kallur	SWE	16.2.81	28 Aug
11.51	1.3	Alenka	Bikar	SLO	7.1.74	30 Apr
11.51	0.0	Anzhela	Kravchenko	UKR	25.1.71	27 May
11.51	1.9	Virgil	Hodge	SKN	17.11.83	3 Jun
11.51	0.0	Heidi	Hannula	FIN	26.2.80	26 Jun
11.51	0.5	Verena	Sailer	GER	16.10.85	2 Jul
11.51	0.0	Damola	Osayomi	NGR-J	26.6.86	7 Jul
11.51	1.9		Liu Li	CHN	5.11.84	18 Oct
11.52	0.5	Elizabeth	Wilson	USA	6.11.82	28 May
11.53	1.5	Rosalind	Holmes	USA	7.1.83	19 Mar
11.53	-0.1	India	Ransom	USA	24.1.84	19 Mar
11.53	1.0	Olga	Andreyeva	UKR	14.5.85	6 May
11.53	0.1	Roxana	Díaz	CUB	17.5.81	23 Jun
11.53	2.0	Anna	Boyle	IRL	29.3.83	24 Jul
11.54	0.0	Latonia	Wilson	USA	30.11.84	23 Apr
11.54	0.4	Natalya	Pogrebnyak	UKR-Y	19.2.88	28 May
11.54	0.5	Kristina	Zumer	SLO	2.9.80	17 Jun
11.54	0.8	Fabé	Dia	FRA	14.2.77	17 Jun
11.54	1.9	Aïda	Diop	SEN	27.4.70	23 Jul
11.54	2.0	Derval	O'Rourke	IRL	28.5.81	24 Jul
11.54	-0.2		Zou Hua (171)	CHN	7.1.79	17 Oct

Drugs disqualification

Mark	Wind	Name		Nat	Born	Pos	Meet	Venue	Date
11.45	0.6	Lyubov	Perepelova ¶	UZB	26.2.79	1		Songkhla	24 Jun
11.48	0.0	Natasha	Mayers ¶	VIN	10.3.79	5	GP II	Stanford	30 May

Mark	Wind	Name		Nat	Born	Pos	Meet	Venue	Date
Wind assisted									
10.82	3.5	Christine	Arron	FRA	13.9.73	1h1		Castres	26 Jul
10.87	3.0	Me'Lisa	Barber	USA	4.10.80	1s1	NC	Carson	25 Jun
10.89	2.4		Campbell			1	BrGP	Sheffield	21 Aug
10.98	2.8		Campbell			1	MSR	Walnut	17 Apr
10.99	3.0	Muna	Lee	USA	30.10.81	2s1	NC	Carson	25 Jun
11.00	5.7	Tremedia	Brice	USA	22.7.81	1rA	TexR	Austin	9 Apr
11.02	2.1	Rachelle	Smith (Boone)	USA	30.6.81	1s2	NC	Carson	25 Jun
11.03	5.7	Marshevet	Hooker	USA	25.9.84	2rA	TexR	Austin	9 Apr
11.04	5.6	Kelly-Ann	Baptiste	TRI-J	14.10.86	1rB	TexR	Austin	9 Apr
11.08	5.7	Ashley	Owens	USA	19.11.85	3rA	TexR	Austin	9 Apr
11.09	2.1	Angela	Daigle	USA	28.5.76	2s2	NC	Carson	25 Jun
11.12	5.7	Fana	Ashby	TRI	15.6.81	4rA	TexR	Austin	9 Apr
11.14	3.7	Yelena	Nevmerzhitskaya	BLR	27.7.80	1		Cork	2 Jul
11.15	2.5	Virginia	Powell	USA	7.9.83	2		Los Angeles (Ww)	30 Apr
11.17	5.6	Savatheda	Fynes	BAH	17.10.74	2rB	TexR	Austin	9 Apr
11.20	2.5	Ayanna	Hutchinson	TRI	18.2.78	1h	NC	Port of Spain	25 Jun
11.21	3.3	Yekaterina	Grigoryeva	RUS	21.4.74	1	Znam	Kazan	24 Jun
11.22	5.6	LaVerne	Jones	ISV	16.9.81	3rB	TexR	Austin	9 Apr
11.22	5.6	Virgil	Hodge	SKN	17.11.83	4rB	TexR	Austin	9 Apr
11.23	5.7	Sheri-Ann	Brooks	JAM	11.2.83	1		Tampa	2 Apr
11.25	2.8	Halima	DeCree	USA	27.7.82	2	MSR	Walnut	17 Apr
11.25	3.0	Lakadron	Ivery	USA	23.6.83	1h2	Big 12	Manhattan, KS	14 May
11.25	3.0	Angela	Williams	USA	30.1.80	4s1	NC	Carson	25 Jun
11.25	3.0	LaShauntea	Moore	USA	31.7.83	5s1	NC	Carson	25 Jun
11.26	2.8	Aminata	Diouf	SEN	18.2.77	1		Donnas	19 Jun
11.28	3.5	Maryann	Erigha	USA	11.11.84	1rB	MSR	Walnut	17 Apr
11.28	3.2	Tahesia	Harrigan	IVB	15.2.82	1h3	CAC	Nassau	9 Jul
11.29	2.4	Wyllesheia	Myrick	USA	21.11.79	3	Kans R	Lawrence	23 Apr
11.30	3.8	Oluwatoyin	Olupona	CAN	29.1.83	1h3	NC	Winnipeg	15 Jul
11.30	3.5	Glory	Alozie	ESP	30.12.77	1		La Laguna	30 Jul
11.31	5.7	Porchea	Carroll	USA	23.10.83	6rA	TexR	Austin	9 Apr
11.31	2.5	Alexis	Weatherspoon	USA	27.7.83	2		Los Angeles (Ww)	30 Apr
11.31	4.1	Gloria	Kemasuode	NGR	30.12.79	1		Elvas	8 May
11.33	5.6	Nicole	Whitman	USA	9.11.80	5rB	TexR	Austin	9 Apr
11.33	3.5	Jasmine	Baldwin	USA-J	27.9.86	2r6	MSR	Walnut	17 Apr
11.33		Yolanda	Goff	USA	14.1.85	2		Arlington	7 May
11.33	3.7	Joice	Maduaka	GBR	30.9.73	3		Cork	3 Jul
11.34	4.9	LaDedra	Guy	USA	16.11.84	1		Beaumont	28 Apr
11.35	4.0	Sherry	Fletcher	GRN-J	17.1.86	1h1	JUCO	Levelland	17 May
11.35	3.3	Yelena	Bolsun	RUS	25.6.82	4	Znam	Kazan	24 Jun
11.36	2.1	Connie	Moore	USA	29.8.81	5s2	NC	Carson	25 Jun
11.36	3.0	Donna	Fraser	GBR	7.11.72	1		Manchester (SC)	3 Sep
11.38		Alexandria	Anderson	USA-J	28.1.87	1		Charleston	20 May
11.38	3.7	Erica	Broomfield	CAN	17.10.77	1		Ottawa	2 Jul
11.38A		Kenyanna	Wilson	USA-Y	27.10.88	1		Aurora	17 Jul
11.38	3.6	Sally	McLellan	AUS-J	19.9.86	1		Perth	18 Dec
11.39	3.4	Lolo	Jones	USA	5.8.82	1		Baton Rouge	23 Apr
11.40	2.8	Kristina	Zumer	SLO	2.2.80	2		Donnas	19 Jun
11.40	3.1	Emily	Maher	IRL	2.5.81	2	LEAP	Loughborough	16 Jul
11.41	5.6	India	Ransom	USA	23.1.84	6rB	TexR	Austin	9 Apr
11.41	2.5	Sierra	Hauser-Price	USA	17.12.83	1h1	Big 10	Columbus	14 May
11.41	3.3	Yekaterina	Kondratyeva	RUS	8.4.82	6	Znam	Kazan	24 Jun

Mark	Wind	Name		Nat	Born	Date
11.42	2.3	Wendy	Seegers	RSA	28.2.76	15 Apr
11.42	2.4	Anyika	Onuora	GBR	28.10.84	21 Aug
11.43	2.5	Jessica	Onyepunuka	USA-J	3.5.86	30 Apr
11.43	3.7	Ailis	McSweeney	IRL	4.10.83	2 Jul
11.43	3.1	Lauren	Hewitt	AUS	25.11.78	16 Jul
11.43	3.5	Fabé	Dia	FRA	14.2.77	26 Jul
11.44	5.7	Nina	Mayes	USA	10.8.83	9 Apr
11.44		LaShawndra	Ratcliff	USA	9.4.82	4 Jun
11.44	2.1	Cherrelle	Garrett	USA-Y	7.5.89	12 Jun
11.44	3.4	Matharie	Diarrassouba	CIV	27.12.79	25 Jun
11.45	5.8	Rosemar	Coelho Neto	BRA	2.1.77	2 Apr
11.45	3.0	Marcia	Fenton	USA	8.9.73	8 Apr
11.45	5.6	Wanda	Hutson	TRI	8.1.85	9 Apr
11.45	2.8	Joanna	Hayes	USA	23.12.76	17 Apr
11.45	3.2	Alenka	Bikar	SLO	7.1.74	25 May
11.46	2.9	Laura	Turner	GBR	12.8.82	12 Jun
11.47	2.4	Katherine	Endacott	GBR	29.1.80	30 May
11.47	4.5	Belén	Recio	ESP	11.8.80	9 Jul
11.48	3.0	Tezdzhyan	Naimova	BUL-J	1.5.87	2 Jul
11.48	3.7	Genevieve	Thibault	CAN-J	25.10.86	2 Jul
11.49A	3.4	Sarah	Matthews	USA-Y	19.7.88	18 Jun
11.50	5.4	Nicole	Brown	USA	28.10.85	1 Apr
11.50		Loni	Forsythe	USA		16 Apr
11.50	3.1	Eleftheria	Kobídou	GRE	10.2.85	7 May
11.50	3.5	Gloria	Asumnu	USA	22.5.85	13 May
11.50	4.5	Céline	Thélamon	FRA	1.3.79	29 May
11.50	4.7	Pascal	van Assendelft	NED	6.10.79	11 Jun
11.50	3.6	Amy	Harris	AUS	7.10.80	18 Dec
11.51	2.3	Rosalind	Holmes	USA	7.1.83	19 Mar
11.51	3.7	Elizabeth	Wilson	USA	6.11.82	14 May
11.51	4.7	Esther	Dankwah	GHA	25.6.82	11 Jun
11.52		Donita	Harmon	USA	1.3.83	7 May
11.52	2.5	Yvonne	Mensah	CAN	15.5.85	14 May
11.52	2.2	Fabienne	Feraez	BEN	6.8.76	6 Sep
11.53		Krystin	Lacy	USA-J	8.7.87	13 Mar
11.53		Porscha	Lucas	USA-Y	18.6.88	24 Mar
11.53	3.4	Donesha	Spivey	USA	20.8.83	23 Apr
11.53	3.7	Kerri-Ann	Mitchell	CAN	29.3.83	14 May

Mark	Wind	Name		Nat	Born	Pos	Meet	Venue	Date
11.53	3.7	Priscilla	Lopes	CAN	26.8.82				14 May
11.53	3.0	Montell	Douglas	GBR-J	24.1.86				3 Sep
11.54	4.1	Jennifer	Morgan	USA					23 Apr
11.54	2.4	Yuliya	Timofeyeva	RUS	3.5.72				10 Jul
11.54	3.9	Fabienne	Weyermann	SUI	3.3.85				21 Aug

Best at low altitude

11.30 0.4 McDonald 4 NC Kingston 25 Jun

11.50 0.1 M Murillo 14 May | 11.52 -2.7 Josephs 11 Mar | 11.54 -1.1 L dos Santos 19 Jun

11.41w 3.6 26 Feb | 11.42w 2.3 Seegers 15 Apr

11.39 1.0 Fynes 2 Hermosillo 21 May

11.42 -0.4 Palacios 1 Getafe 14 Jul

Hand timed

Mark	Wind	Name		Nat	Born	Date
11.2	1.3	Amandine	Allou Affoué	CIV	29.8.80	9 Apr
11.2	-0.5	Franciela	Krasucki	BRA-Y	26.4.88	7 May
11.2		Funmiloa	Ogundana	NGR	26.2.80	15 Nov
11.3	1.3	Kadiatou	Camara	MLI	4.5.81	9 Apr
11.3		Yailin	Morell	CUB-J	22.9.87	23 May
11.3		Natalya	Sologub	BLR	31.3.75	24 May
11.3A	0.2	Estie	Wittstock	RSA	15.9.80	3 Dec

Wind assisted

Mark	Wind	Name		Nat	Born	Date
11.3	2.3	Nongnuch	Sanrat	THA	26.8.83	14 Apr

JUNIORS

See main list for top 8 juniors. 11 performances by 3 women to 11.38. Additional marks and further juniors:

Name	Mark	Wind	Pos	Meet	Venue	Date
Baptiste	11.26	-0.4	1	NCAA-r	Bloomington	28 May
	11.37	0.0	4	NCAA	Sacramento	10 Jun
Tyson	11.29	-0.4	1	NCAA-r	Bloomington	28 May
	11.29	0.0	2	NCAA	Sacramento	10 Jun
	11.33	-0.3	1h1	PAm-J	Windsor	29 Jul
	11.35	1.1	1h1	PAm-J	Windsor	29 Jul
	11.38	0.0	2h3	SEC	Nashville	14 May
Knight	11.38	-0.1	1	WY	Marrakech	14 Jul

Mark	Wind	Name		Nat	Born	Pos	Meet	Venue	Date
11.44	-0.1	Ebony	Collins	USA-Y	11.3.89	2	WY	Marrakech	14 Jul
11.47	2.0	Sherry	Fletcher (10)	GRN	17.1.86	3	JUCO	Levelland	18 May
11.47	1.3	Angela	Morosanu	ROM	26.7.86	5	ECp-S	Firenze	18 Jun
11.49	1.9	Anika	Baptiste	ANT-Y	30.3.90	1h10	WY	Marrakech	13 Jul
11.49	1.2		Vu Thi Huong	VIE-J	7.10.86	1	SEAG	Manila	28 Nov
11.50	1.5	Yomara	Hinestroza	COL-Y	20.5.88	1h8	WY	Marrakech	13 Jul
11.51	0.0	Damola	Osayomi	NGR	26.6.86	1h4	NC	Abuja	7 Jul
11.54	0.4	Natalya	Pogrebnyak	UKR-Y	19.2.88	1		Kiev	28 May
11.55	1.6	Genevieve	Thibault	CAN	25.10.86	2h2		Ottawa	2 Jul
11.56A	1.8	Sarah	Matthews	USA-Y	19.7.88	1		Aurora	21 May
11.56	1.3	Porscha	Lucas	USA-Y	18.6.88	1		Fort Worth	16 Jul
11.56	2.0	Kristina	Davis (20)	USA-Y	28.3.88	4r1		Azusa	17 Jul
11.56	0.5	Montell	Douglas	GBR	24.1.86	1		Cardiff	29 Aug

Wind assisted – see main list for top 6 juniors. Additional marks:

Mark	Wind	Name		Nat	Born	Pos	Meet	Venue	Date
11.43w	2.5	Jessica	Onyepunuka	USA-J	3.5.86	3		Los Angeles (Ww)	30 Apr
11.44	2.1	Cherrelle	Garrett	USA-Y	7.5.89	1		Folsom	12 Jun
11.48	3.0	Tezdzhyan	Naimova	BUL-J	1.5.87	1h1	NC-j	Plovdiv	2 Jul
11.48	3.7	Genevieve	Thibault	CAN-J	25.10.86	2		Ottawa	2 Jul
11.49A	3.4	Sarah	Matthews	USA-Y	19.7.88	1		Aurora	18 Jun
11.53		Krystin	Lacy	USA-J	8.7.87	1		Arlington	13 Mar
11.53		Porscha	Lucas	USA-Y	18.6.88	1		Plano	24 Mar
11.53	3.0	Montell	Douglas	GBR-J	24.1.86	3		Manchester (SC)	3 Sep

Hand timed

Mark	Wind	Name		Nat	Born	Pos	Meet	Venue	Date
11.2	-0.5	Franciela	Krasucki	BRA-Y	26.4.88	1h3		Londrina	7 May
11.3		Yailin	Morell	CUB-J	22.9.87	1s1	NC-j	Santiago de Cuba	23 May

200 METRES

Mark	Wind	Name		Nat	Born	Pos	Meet	Venue	Date
22.13	0.3	Allyson	Felix	USA	18.11.85	1	NC	Carson	26 Jun
22.14	1.2		Felix			1		Carson	22 May
22.16	0.2		Felix			1	WCh	Helsinki	12 Aug
22.22	0.3	Rachelle	Smith (Boone)	USA	30.6.81	2	NC	Carson	26 Jun
22.27	1.2	Lauryn	Williams	USA	11.9.83	2		Carson	22 May
22.27	-0.6		Felix			1	WAF	Monaco	10 Sep
22.31	-0.9		Felix			1		Monterrey	11 Jun
22.31	0.2		Smith			2	WCh	Helsinki	12 Aug
22.31	0.2	Christine	Arron	FRA	13.9.73	3	WCh	Helsinki	12 Aug
22.34	0.3	LaTasha	Colander	USA	23.8.76	3	NC	Carson	26 Jun
22.35	0.0	Veronica	Campbell	JAM	15.5.82	1	GP	Torino	3 Jun
22.37	1.0		Felix			1s2	NC	Carson	26 Jun
22.37	0.3	Me'Lisa	Barber	USA	4.10.80	4	NC	Carson	26 Jun
22.37	-0.6		Campbell			2	WAF	Monaco	10 Sep
22.38	1.0		Barber			2s2	NC	Carson	26 Jun
22.38	0.7		Arron			1	NC	Angers	16 Jul
22.38	0.2		Campbell			4	WCh	Helsinki	12 Aug
22.39	1.2		Colander			3		Carson	22 May
22.39	1.1	Cydonie	Mothersill	CAY	19.3.78	1h1	CAC	Nassau	10 Jul
22.39	0.6		Arron			1h1	NC	Angers	16 Jul
22.39	0.0	Svetlana	Pospelova	RUS	24.12.79	1	NC	Tula	24 Jul
22.41	0.5		Smith			1s1	NC	Carson	26 Jun
22.43	-0.6		Arron			3	WAF	Monaco	10 Sep

Mark	Wind	Name		Nat	Born	Pos	Meet	Venue	Date
22.45	-2.7		Arron			1s1	WCh	Helsinki	11 Aug
22.46	0.3	Muna	Lee	USA	30.10.81	5	NC	Carson	26 Jun
22.53	-0.1		Campbell			1		Kingston	7 May
22.53	0.0		Smith			1		Hermosillo	21 May
22.53	0.9	Sanya	Richards (10)	USA	26.2.85	2		Monterrey	11 Jun
22.53	1.4		Smith			1h2	NC	Carson	25 Jun
22.53	-0.2		Campbell			1	NC	Kingston	26 Jun
22.53	-1.1	Yuliya	Gushchina	RUS	4.3.83	1h2	WCh	Helsinki	10 Aug
		(31/12)							
22.54	1.0	Sherone	Simpson	JAM	12.8.84	1		Santo Domingo	14 May
22.55	0.0	Olesya	Zykina	RUS	7.10.80	2		Tula	24 Jul
22.58	-0.2	Christine	Amertil	BAH	18.8.79	1h2	CAC	Nassau	10 Jul
22.59	1.2	Angela	Daigle	USA	28.5.76	4		Carson	22 May
22.64	1.2	Stephanie	Durst	USA	6.1.82	5		Carson	22 May
22.68	-1.2	Kim	Gevaert	BEL	5.8.78	1	NC	Bruxelles	10 Jul
22.68	0.0	Yekaterina	Kondratyeva	RUS	8.4.82	3		Tula	24 Jul
22.69	-0.2	Irina	Khabarova	RUS	18.3.66	2	NC	Tula	12 Jul
		(20)							
22.70	0.0	Yelena	Bolsun	RUS	25.6.82	4		Tula	24 Jul
22.74	1.0	Shalonda	Solomon	USA	19.12.85	1	SEC	Nashville	15 May
22.75	0.4	Lucimar	de Moura	BRA	22.3.74	1	NC	São Paulo	17 Jun
22.76	1.1	Ivet	Lalova	BUL	18.5.84	2	ECCp	Lagos	29 May
22.78	1.8	Geraldine	Pillay	RSA	25.8.77	1	NC	Durban	16 Apr
22.80	0.0	Marshevet	Hooker	USA	25.9.84	1	Big 12	Manhattan, KS	15 May
22.80	-0.2	Sheri-Ann	Brooks	JAM	11.2.83	2	NC	Kingston	26 Jun
22.81	0.7	Fabienne	Féraez	BEN	6.8.76	2	FRA Ch	Angers	16 Jul
22.82		Natalya	Sologub	BLR	31.3.75	1	NC	Brest	4 Jul
22.84	1.9	Tremedia	Brice	USA	22.7.81	1		Houston	26 Mar
		(30)							
22.85	0.7	Charlette	Greggs	USA	20.10.83	1s1	NCAA	Sacramento	9 Jun
22.85A	0.7	Felipa	Palacios	COL	1.12.75	1	Bolivar	Armenia/COL	20 Aug
22.86	0.5	Monique	Henderson	USA	18.2.83	1		Los Angeles (Ww)	30 Apr
22.87	1.2	Monique	Hennagan	USA	26.5.76	6		Carson	22 May
22.88	1.0	Cleo	Tyson	USA-J	1.5.86	2	SEC	Nashville	15 May
22.90A	0.7	Norma	González	COL	11.8.82	2	Bolivar	Armenia/COL	20 Aug
22.92	0.7	Kaltouma	Nadjina	CHA	16.11.76	1	Franc	Niamey	16 Dec
22.93	0.7	Kelly-Ann	Baptiste	TRI-J	14.10.86	2	NCAA-r	Bloomington	28 May
22.93	1.6	Aminata	Diouf	SEN	18.2.77	1		Alger	23 Jun
22.93	1.0	LaShauntea	Moore	USA	31.7.83	3s2	NC	Carson	26 Jun
		(40)							
22.94	2.0		Chen Lisha	CHN	10.4.81	1		Chongqing	15 May
22.96	0.6	Alexandria	Anderson	USA-J	28.1.87	2	NC-j	Carson	24 Jun
22.97	0.1	Marina	Maydanova	UKR	22.8.82	1	GP II	Zagreb	11 Jul
22.97	-0.2	Natalya	Ivanova	RUS	25.6.81	5	NC	Tula	12 Jul
22.98	1.0	Wyllesheia	Myrick	USA	21.11.79	2		Santo Domingo	14 May
22.98	0.0	Beverly	McDonald	JAM	15.2.70	3	GP II	Belém	22 May
22.98	-0.4	Zhanna	Block	UKR	6.7.72	1		Bydgoszcz	5 Jun
22.99	0.7	Aymeé	Martínez	CUB-Y	17.11.88	1	WY	Marrakech	17 Jul
22.99	0.7	Yelena	Yakovleva	RUS	18.3.83	1	EU23	Erfurt	17 Jul
22.99	0.0	Natalya	Antyukh	RUS	26.6.81	5		Tula	24 Jul
		(50)							
23.00	-0.2	Aleen	Bailey	JAM	25.11.80	3	NC	Kingston	26 Jun
23.00	2.0	Anneisha	McLaughlin	JAM-J	6.1.86	1	PAm-J	Windsor	31 Jul
23.01	0.1	Manuela	Levorato	ITA	16.3.77	2	GP II	Zagreb	11 Jul
23.02	0.7	Solen	Désert	FRA	2.8.82	1		Lamballe	26 Jun
23.02	2.0	Anna	Guzowska	POL	15.1.80	1	NC	Biala Podlaska	26 Jun
23.03	-2.9	Tonique	Williams-Darling	BAH	17.1.76	1	NC	Freeport	25 Jun
23.03	1.0	Vida	Anim	GHA	7.12.83	2	Odlozil	Praha	27 Jun
23.03	0.7	Sylviane	Félix	FRA	31.10.77	3	NC	Angers	16 Jul
23.04	0.0	Peta-Gaye	Dowdie	JAM	18.1.77	2	GP II	Torino	3 Jun
23.04	1.2	Olga	Zaytseva	RUS	10.11.84	2	Znam	Kazan	25 Jun
		(60)							
23.05	0.0	Julian	Clay	USA	2.11.77	2		Hermosillo	21 May
23.05	0.6	Antonette	Carter	USA	16.2.84	4h1	NC	Carson	25 Jun
23.05	1.5	Birgit	Rockmeier	GER	29.11.73	1	NC	Wattenscheid	3 Jul
23.06	0.7	Yuliya	Chermoshanskaya	RUS-J	6.1.86	1	NC-j	Tula	4 Jul
23.08	1.5	Shericka	Williams	JAM	17.9.85	2		Spanish Town	9 Apr
23.08	0.0	Lakadron	Ivery	USA	23.6.83	2	Big 12	Manhattan, KS	15 May
23.08A	1.7	Amandine	Allou Affoué	CIV	29.8.80	1		Sestriere	23 Jul
23.09	0.0	Olesya	Krasnomovets	RUS	8.7.79	7		Tula	24 Jul
23.10	-0.7	Ami Mbacké	Thiam	SEN	10.11.76	3	SGP	Doha	13 May

Mark	Wind	Name		Nat	Born	Pos	Meet	Venue	Date
23.10	0.3	Lauren	Hewitt	AUS	25.11.78	3	NA	Heusden-Zolder	23 Jul
		(70)							
23.10A	0.7	Darlenis	Obregón	COL-J	21.2.86	3	Bolivar	Armenia/COL	20 Aug
23.11	0.7	Alexis	Weatherspoon	USA	27.7.83	3s1	NCAA	Sacramento	9 Jun
23.12		Amber	Robinson	USA	5.6.80	1		Clermont	23 Apr
23.12	0.3	Dee Dee	Trotter	USA	8.12.82	4	NA	Heusden-Zolder	23 Jul
23.13	-1.2	Erica	Whipple	USA	4.12.82	2h4	NCAA-r	New York	27 May
23.13	0.8	Yelena	Nevmerzhitskaya	BLR	27.7.80	1		Brest	1 Jun
23.13	0.9	Brittany	Jones	USA-Y	6.3.89	2		Greensboro	18 Jun
23.14	1.0	LaVerne	Jones	ISV	16.9.81	1		Norman	16 Apr
23.17A	-0.3	Janice	Josephs	RSA	31.3.82	2		Pretoria	18 Mar
23.18	0.1	Natalie	Knight	USA-J	24.10.86	1h6	SEC	Nashville	14 May
		(80)							
23.18	-0.7	Mariya	Lisnichenko	RUS	27.12.80	3		Sochi	27 May
23.18A	1.7	Fatou Binetou	Fall	SEN	23.8.81	2		Sestriere	23 Jul
23.19	1.1	Elodie	Ouédraogo	BEL	27.2.81	2		Rhede	29 May
23.19	0.7	Nikolett	Listár	HUN	6.12.83	2	EU23	Erfurt	17 Jul
23.21	0.0	Irina	Shtangeyeva	UKR	6.2.82	1		Donetsk	8 May
23.21	2.0	Virgil	Hodge	SKN	17.11.83	1		Houston	3 Jun
23.21	-0.6	Donna	Fraser	GBR	7.11.72	1h3	NC	Manchester (SC)	9 Jul
23.21	0.1	Crystal	Cox	USA	28.3.79	3	GP II	Zagreb	11 Jul
23.21	0.9	Damayanthi	Dharsha	SRI	13.2.75	1	AsiC	Inchon	4 Sep
23.22	1.3	Michelle	Perry	USA	1.5.79	2		Los Angeles	9 Apr
		(90)							
23.22	0.6	Francena	McCorory	USA-Y	20.10.88	3	NC-j	Carson	24 Jun
23.22	-0.1	Lee	McConnell	GBR	9.10.78	1		Uden	25 Jun
23.22	1.2	Vincenza	Calì	ITA	15.10.83	1	NC	Bressanone	26 Jun
23.25A	-0.1	Jessica	Fox	USA	10.1.82	1		Fort Collins	14 May
23.25	0.7	Tahesia	Harrigan	IVB	15.2.82	3	NCAA-r	Bloomington	28 May
23.25	0.5	Moushami	Robinson	USA	13.4.81	6	BrGP	Sheffield	21 Aug
23.26	-0.6	Ionela	Tîrlea-Manolache	ROM	9.2.76	5	ECp-S	Firenze	19 Jun
23.27	1.9	Connie	Moore	USA	29.8.81	2		Knoxville	16 Apr
23.28	0.6	Carolina	Klüft	SWE	2.2.83	1		Karlstad	22 Jun
23.29	-0.7	Kadiatou	Camara	MLI	4.5.81	4	SGP	Doha	13 May
		(100)							
23.29A	1.7	Aïda	Diop	SEN	27.4.70	3		Sestriere	23 Jul

Mark	Wind	Name		Nat	Born	Date
23.30	1.0	Juanita	Broaddus	USA	12.5.85	16 Apr
23.31	-0.2	Irina	Rosikhina	RUS	11.5.75	13 Jul
23.32	-0.2	Porchea	Carroll	USA	23.10.83	15 May
23.32	-0.2	Roxana	Díaz	CUB	17.5.81	10 Jul
23.32	-0.3	Susanna	Kallur	SWE	16.2.81	27 Aug
23.33	0.7	Bianca	Knight	USA-Y	2.1.89	17 Jul
23.34	0.0	Shereefa	Lloyd	JAM	2.9.82	15 May
23.34	1.7	Kia	Davis	USA	23.5.76	17 Jul
23.34	1.7	Sarah	Tondé	BUR	30.10.83	24 Jul
23.35	1.8	Ayanna	Hutchinson	TRI	18.2.78	26 Jun
23.35	0.9	Jacqueline	Poelman	NED	5.10.73	2 Jul
23.35	0.9	Joice	Maduaka	GBR	30.9.73	30 Jul
23.36	0.0	Yelena	Chebanu	UKR	4.1.81	7 May
23.36	0.5	Yvonne	Umeh	USA	28.6.83	14 May
23.36	1.1	Ciara	Sheehy	IRL	12.8.80	27 Aug
23.37	1.3	Maryann	Erigha	USA	3.11.84	15 Apr
23.37	0.4	Latonia	Wilson	USA	30.11.84	13 May
23.38A	-1.9	Heide	Seyerling	RSA	19.8.76	11 Feb
23.38	-0.1	Shellene	Williams	JAM	19.2.81	7 May
23.38	2.0	Sa'de	Williams	USA-Y	2.12.89	21 May
23.38	-0.9	Rosalind	Holmes	USA	7.1.83	27 May
23.38	0.7	Candace	Tucker	USA	12.4.84	9 Jun
23.38	0.7		Qin Wangping	CHN	16.6.82	26 Jun
23.38	1.5	Jala	Gangnus	GER-J	5.9.86	3 Jul
23.38			Kay Khine Lwin	MYA	28.8.78	24 Sep
23.39	0.1	Shandria	Brown	JAM	7.7.83	28 May
23.39	1.0	Olga	Andreyeva/Daniv	UKR	14.5.85	25 Jun
23.39	1.7	Angela	Morosanu	ROM-J	26.7.86	3 Jul
23.39	-0.4	Emily	Maher	IRL	2.5.81	23 Jul
23.39	0.2	Monika	Bejnar	POL	10.3.81	18 Aug
23.39	0.3	Rosemar	Coelho Neto	BRA	2.1.77	28 Aug
23.40	-0.1	Tatyana	Levina	RUS	28.2.77	30 Jun
23.40	0.2	Natalya	Pigida	UKR	30.1.81	18 Aug
23.41	0.1	Tiandra	Ponteen	SKN	9.11.84	9 Apr
23.41A?	0.7	Ruth	Grajeda	MEX	31.7.80	9 Apr
23.41	0.5	Erica	Whipple	USA	4.12.82	13 May
23.41	0.5	Véronique	Mang	FRA	15.12.84	4 Jun
23.41	1.0	Yekaterina	Grigoryeva	RUS	21.4.74	25 Jun
23.41	0.6	Doris	Jacob	NGR	16.12.81	12 Jul
23.41	0.2		Hou Xiufen	CHN	11.5.78	21 Oct
23.42	0.7	Sierra	Hauser-Price	USA	17.12.83	28 May
23.42	1.9	Shareese	Woods	USA	20.2.85	9 Jun
23.42	0.9	Ebony	Collins	USA-Y	11.3.89	18 Jun
23.43	1.9	Ashley	Purnell	CAN	25.5.83	14 May
23.43	0.1	Alenka	Bikar	SLO	7.1.74	23 Jun
23.43	0.9	Guzel	Khubbieva	UZB	2.5.76	4 Sep
23.44	0.0	Schillonie	Calvert	JAM-Y	27.7.88	19 Mar
23.44	0.4	Raquel	Martins da Costa	BRA	30.12.83	17 Jun
23.44	0.4	Vanda	Gomes	BRA-Y	7.11.88	17 Jun
23.44	-0.3	Adri	Schoeman	RSA	13.7.70	16 Dec
23.45	-0.6	Sally	McLellan	AUS-J	19.9.86	26 Nov
23.46	2.0		Zhu Juanhong	CHN	5.12.85	15 May
23.47	1.6	Adriane	Lapsley	USA	18.12.83	23 Apr
23.47	-1.0	Jenny	Kallur	SWE	16.2.81	19 Jun
23.47	-1.6	Angelique	Smith	USA-J	22.2.86	23 Jun
23.47	0.0	Mercy	Nku	NGR	17.7.76	9 Jul
23.47	0.2	Lena	Aruhn	SWE	22.4.70	13 Jul
23.47	0.0	Erica	Broomfield	CAN	17.10.77	24 Jul
23.47	1.1	Melanie	Kleeberg	AUS	27.12.81	26 Nov
23.48	0.9	Aliann	Pompey	GUY	9.3.78	9 Apr
23.48	1.0	Stephanie	Smith	USA	27.6.85	15 May
23.49	1.8	Donita	Harmon	USA	1.3.83	14 May
23.49	2.0	Grazyna	Prokopek	POL	20.4.77	26 Jun
23.49	0.6	Fabé	Dia	FRA	14.2.77	16 Jul
23.50	2.0		Liu Li	CHN	5.11.84	15 May
23.50	-0.2	Olga	Kuzekmayeva	RUS	28.11.79	13 Jul
23.51A	-0.1	Halima	Decree	USA	27.7.83	14 May
23.51	-0.1	Stacey	Clausing	USA		15 May
23.51	1.8	Wendy	Seegers	RSA	28.2.76	19 Jun
23.52	-0.3	Nadine	Palmer	JAM	19.2.83	27 May
23.52	0.5	Lizet	Assegbede	UKR	18.10.85	22 Jun
23.52	1.0	Yelena	Migunova	RUS	4.1.84	25 Jun
23.52	1.2	Franciela	Krasucki	BRA-Y	26.4.88	21 Aug
23.53	0.0	Anasthasia	Leroy	JAM-J	11.9.87	19 Mar
23.53	0.0	Grit	Breuer	GER	16.2.72	27 May
23.53	0.0	Yelena	Novikova	RUS	27.10.85	14 Jun
23.53	1.1	Kirsi	Mykkänen	FIN	7.2.78	17 Jul
		(178)				

Mark	Wind		Name	Nat	Born	Pos	Meet	Venue	Date
Indoors									
22.38			Campbell			1	GP	Birmingham	18 Feb
22.91		Fana	Ashby	TRI	15.6.81	1rB	NCAA	Fayetteville	11 Ma
22.94		Karin	Mayr-Krifka	AUT	4.6.71	2	EI	Madrid	6 Ma
22.98		Courtney	Champion	USA-J	10.6.86	2rB	NCAA	Fayetteville	11 Ma
23.02		Hazel-Ann	Regis	GRN	1.2.81	1	SEC	Fayetteville	27 Feb
23.08		Natasha	Hastings	USA-J	23.7.86	1		Clemson	22 Jan
23.24		Anna	Pacholak	POL	15.1.80	2h4	EI	Madrid	5 Ma
23.26		Yuliya	Pechonkina	RUS	21.4.78	1h3		Moskva	22 Jan
23.27		Tatyana	Levina	RUS	28.2.77	1		Moskva	31 Jan
23.29		Khalilah	Carpenter	USA	27.7.83	2	SEC	Fayetteville	27 Feb

23.41 Lina Jacques-Sébastien FRA 10.4.85 5 Mar | 23.45 LaTonya Loche USA 8.10.85 11 Mar
23.42 Fabé Dia FRA 14.2.77 20 Feb | 23.48 Shana Cox USA 22.1.85 29 Jan
23.43 Simone Facey JAM 7.5.85 12 Feb | 23.53 Liz Wilson USA 6.11.82 26 Feb
23.54 Krysha Bayley CAN 21.1.84 25 Feb

Mark	Wind		Name	Nat	Born	Pos	Meet	Venue	Date
Wind assisted									
22.16			Felix			1	LGP	London (CP)	22 Ju
22.26	3.8	Cydonie	Mothersill	CAY	19.3.78	1	CAC	Nassau	11 Ju
22.29	2.2	Veronica	Campbell	JAM	15.5.82	2	LGP	London (CP)	22 Ju
22.30	2.2	LaTasha	Colander	USA	23.8.76	3	LGP	London (CP)	22 Ju
22.52	w?		Colander			1		Clemson	16 Ap
22.72	2.7	Shalonda	Solomon	USA	19.12.85	1		Knoxville	9 Ap
22.72	2.3	Monique	Henderson	USA	18.2.83	1	NCAA-r	Eugene	28 Ma
22.72	3.8	Peta-Gaye	Dowdie	JAM	18.1.77	3	CAC	Nassau	11 Ju
22.73	2.4	Marshevet	Hooker	USA	25.9.84	1h3	Big 12	Manhattan, KS	14 May
22.74	2.8	Charlette	Greggs	USA	20.10.83	1	NCAA-r	New York	28 May
22.74	2.8	Sheri-Ann	Brooks	JAM	11.2.83	2	NCAA-r	New York	28 May
22.75	2.2	Aleen	Bailey	JAM	25.11.80	5	LGP	London (CP)	22 Ju
22.80	2.2	Donna	Fraser	GBR	7.11.72	1		Manchester (SC)	3 Sep
22.84	3.9	Tonette	Dyer	USA	28.3.82	1	MSR	Walnut	17 Ap
22.99	2.2	Kandice	Bell	USA	7.8.83	1		Fort Worth	23 Ap
23.05	2.7	Virgil	Hodge	SKN	17.11.83	2h3	CAC	Nassau	10 Ju
23.06	3.3	Jacqueline	Poelman	NED	5.10.73	1	NC	Amsterdam	10 Ju
23.10	2.8	Erica	Whipple	USA	4.12.82	4	NCAA-r	New York	28 May
23.11	4.4	Elodie	Ouédraogo	BEL	27.2.81	1		Leiden	11 Jun
23.12	2.8	Natalie	Knight	USA-J	24.10.86	5	NCAA-r	New York	28 May
23.14	3.8	Roxana	Díaz	CUB	17.5.81	5	CAC	Nassau	11 Ju
23.14A	5.0	Wilmary	Ivarez	VEN	13.5.84	3	SACh	Cali	23 Ju
23.17	2.8	Juanita	Broaddus	USA	12.5.85	1	JUCO	Levelland	18 Ma
23.18	3.9	Kia	Davis	USA	23.5.76	3	MSR	Walnut	17 Ap
23.22	3.9	Sakie	Nobuoka	JPN	24.8.77	4	MSR	Walnut	17 Ap
23.22A	3.9	Jessica	Fox	USA	10.1.82	1h2		Fort Collins	13 Ma
23.22	2.3	Porchea	Carroll	USA	23.10.83	3	NCAA-r	Eugene	28 May
23.23	3.0	Andriane	Lapsley	USA	18.12.83	1		Atlanta	2 Ap
23.23A	2.9	Kineke	Alexander	VIN-J	21.2.86	1		Albuquerque	4 Ju
23.27	2.6	Joice	Maduaka	GBR	30.9.73	5		Cork	2 Ju
23.28	2.7	Maryann	Erigha	USA	3.11.84	1C	MSR	Walnut	17 Ap
23.28	3.5	LaDedra	Guy	BAH	16.11.84	1h3		Houston	13 Ma

23.29 2.3 Emma Ania GBR 7.2.79 27 Aug | 23.45 2.6 Latonia Wilson USA 30.11.84 2 Ap
23.32 2.7 Khalilah Carpenter USA 27.7.83 9 Apr | 23.45A w Kenyanna Wilson USA-Y 27.10.88 17 Ju
23.32 2.4 Olga Daniv UKR 14.1.85 15 Jun | 23.46 4.2 Jerrika Chapple USA 11.9.84 14 May
23.34 2.7 Stephanie Smith USA 27.6.85 9 Apr | 23.46 2.8 Kerron Stewart JAM 16.4.84 18 May
23.34 2.2 Shereefa Lloyd JAM 2.9.82 23 Apr | 23.47 3.6 Hazel-Ann Regis GRN 1.2.81 23 Ap
23.36 2.4 Amandi Rhett USA 29.6.82 17 Apr | 23.47 3.4 Barbara Petráhn HUN 16.9.78 14 May
23.39 2.8 Shareese Woods USA 20.2.85 28 May | 23.50 5.8 Lashinda Demus USA 10.3.83 9 Ap
23.41 2.6 Beau Walker USA 25.3.83 2 Apr | 23.51 2.9 Elizabeth Olear USA-Y 16.11.88 4 Jun
23.41 2.4 Adrienne Power CAN 11.11.81 17 Jul | 23.53 2.1 Sherry Fletcher GRN-J 17.1.86 17 May
23.44 2.9 Khrystal Carter USA-Y 19.9.88 4 Jun | 23.54 4.1 Rosalind Holmes USA 7.1.83 26 Ma

Best at low altitude

23.02 1.0 González 3 Santo Domingo 14 May | 23.44 1.8 Palacios 18 Jun
23.54 -4.9 Josephs 11 Mar

Hand timing

22.9 Ayanna Hutchinson TRI 18.2.78 1 Port of Spain 8 Ma
23.1 Monique Cabral TRI-J 9.12.86 8 May | 23.3 Lai Lai Win MYA 9.2.77 14 Feb
23.2 Irina Shepetyuk UKR 13.2.82 4 Jun | 23.3 Yelizaveta Yashina RUS 17.7.84 4 Jun

Unknown Irregularity: 23.38 Jernail Hayes USA-Y 8.7.88 1 Glasgow, DE 23 Ap
Drugs Disqualifiaction: 23.18w 3.7 Lyubov Perepelova ¶ UZB 26.2.79 1 Kaohsiung 22 Ma

JUNIORS

See main list for top 10 juniors. 11 performances by 6 women to 23.01 (inc. 1 indoor). Additional marks:

Tyson 22.91 0.7 1 NCAA-r Bloomington 28 May | 23.01 -0.6 3 NCAA Sacramento 11 Ju
22.93 0.6 1 NC Carson 24 Jun

Mark	Wind	Name		Nat	Born	Pos	Meet	Venue	Date
Baptiste	22.94	1.8	1	NC	Port of Spain				26 Jun
Anderson	23.01	-0.8	1h3	NC	Carson				24 Jun
23.33	0.7	Bianca	Knight	USA-Y	2.1.89	2	WY	Marrakech	17 Jul
23.38	2.0	Sa'de	Williams	USA-Y	2.12.89	1		Norwalk	21 May
23.38	1.5	Jala	Gangnus	GER	5.9.86	2	NC	Wattenscheid	3 Jul
23.39	1.7	Angela	Morosanu	ROM	26.7.86	1	NC	Bucuresti	3 Jul
23.42	0.9	Ebony	Collins	USA-Y	11.3.89	5		Greensboro	18 Jun
23.44	0.0	Schillonie	Calvert	JAM-Y	27.7.88	1		Kingston	19 Mar
23.44	0.4	Vanda	Gomes	BRA-Y	7.11.88	3	NC	São Paulo	17 Jun
23.45	-0.6	Sally	McLellan	AUS	19.9.86	1		Brisbane	26 Nov
23.47	-1.6	Angelique	Smith	USA	22.2.86	1h1	NC	Carson	23 Jun
23.52	1.2	Franciela	Krasucki (20)	BRA-Y	26.4.88	1		São Paulo	21 Aug

Wind assisted – see main list for top 2 juniors. Additional marks:

Mark	Wind	Name		Nat	Born	Pos	Meet	Venue	Date
23.44	2.9	Khrystal	Carter	USA-Y	19.9.88	1		Sacramento	4 Jun
23.45A	w	Kenyanna	Wilson	USA-Y	27.10.88	1		Aurora	17 Jul
23.51	2.9	Elizabeth	Olear	USA-Y	16.11.88	2		Sacramento	4 Jun

300 METRES

During 400m races: 11 Jun NCAA Sacramento: 35.8 Monique Henderson

10 Aug WCh Helsinki: 35.6 Sanya Richards, 35.7 Tonique W-Darling, 35.8 Svetlana Pospelova, 36.1 Ana Guevara

Indoors

Mark	Name		Nat	Born	Pos	Meet	Venue	Date
37.09i	Yuliya	Pechonkina	RUS	21.4.78	1		Moskva	7 Jan
37.09i	Kaltouma	Nadjina	CHA	16.11.76	1		Winnipeg	29 Jan
37.35i	Adrienne	Power	CAN	11.11.81	1		Winnipeg	11 Mar

400 METRES

Mark	Name		Nat	Born	Pos	Meet	Venue	Date
48.92	Sanya	Richards	USA	26.2.85	1	WK	Zürich	19 Aug
49.28		Richards			1	NC	Carson	25 Jun
49.30	Tonique	Williams-Darling	BAH	17.1.76	2	WK	Zürich	19 Aug
49.52		Richards			1	WAF	Monaco	10 Sep
49.54		Williams-Darling			2	WAF	Monaco	10 Sep
49.55		Williams-Darling			1	WCh	Helsinki	10 Aug
49.69		Williams-Darling			1	Gaz	Saint-Denis	1 Jul
49.69		Williams-Darling			1s3	WCh	Helsinki	8 Aug
49.74		Richards			2	WCh	Helsinki	10 Aug
49.77		Richards			1	BrGP	Sheffield	21 Aug
49.80	Svetlana	Pospelova	RUS	24.12.79	1	NC	Tula	11 Jul
49.81	Ana Gabriela	Guevara	MEX	4.3.77	3	WCh	Helsinki	10 Aug
49.82		Richards			1	GGala	Roma	8 Jul
49.85		Williams-Darling			1		Monterrey	11 Jun
49.88	Dee Dee	Trotter	USA	8.12.82	2	NC	Carson	25 Jun
49.95		Williams-Darling			1	Pre	Eugene	4 Jun
49.95		Richards			1	Athl	Lausanne	5 Jul
49.96		Richards			1		Kingston	7 May
49.96	Monique	Henderson	USA	18.2.83	3	NC	Carson	25 Jun
49.96		Pospelova			1h4	NC	Tula	10 Jul
49.98		Richards			2	Pre	Eugene	4 Jun
50.00		Richards			1		Carson	22 May
50.02		Williams-Darling			2	BrGP	Sheffield	21 Aug
50.03		Trotter			1		Yokohama	19 Sep
50.05		Guevara			2		Monterrey	11 Jun
50.05		Richards			1s1	WCh	Helsinki	8 Aug
50.06	Olga	Zaytseva	RUS	10.11.84	1	NC-23	Tula	14 Jun
50.09	Christine	Amertil	BAH	18.8.79	2		Yokohama	19 Sep
50.10		Henderson			1	NCAA	Sacramento	11 Jun
50.11		Pospelova			4	WCh	Helsinki	10 Aug
	(30/8)							
50.24	Monique	Hennagan	USA	26.5.76	3	WK	Zürich	19 Aug
50.38	Moushami	Robinson	USA	13.4.81	4	NC	Carson	25 Jun
	(10)							
50.41	Tatyana	Firova	RUS	10.10.82	1		Tula	23 Jul
50.67	Natalya	Antyukh	RUS	26.6.81	1	ECp-S	Firenze	18 Jun
50.69	Ami Mbacké	Thiam	SEN	10.11.76	4	WAF	Monaco	10 Sep
50.73	Christine	Ohuruogu	GBR	17.5.84	2	EU23	Erfurt	16 Jul
50.73	Olesya	Zykina	RUS	7.10.80	3s3	WCh	Helsinki	8 Aug
50.77	Olesya	Krasnomovets	RUS	8.7.79	1		Dubnica nad Váhom	29 Aug
50.83	Tiandra	Ponteen	SKN	9.11.84	2	NCAA	Sacramento	11 Jun
50.85	Mariya	Lisnichenko	RUS	27.12.80	2		Sochi	26 May
50.93	Stephanie	Smith	USA	27.6.85	3	NCAA	Sacramento	11 Jun

Mark	Name		Nat	Born	Pos	Meet	Venue	Date
50.93	Yelena	Migunova	RUS	4.1.84	2	NC-23	Tula	14 Jun
	(20)							
50.95	Lorraine	Fenton	JAM	8.9.73	3rA	GP	Madrid	16 Jul
50.96	Ilona	Usovich	BLR	14.11.82	5s3	WCh	Helsinki	8 Aug
50.97	Shericka	Williams	JAM	17.9.85	1	NC	Kingston	26 Jun
51.07	Tatyana	Roslanova	KAZ	28.9.80	1		Almaty	4 Jun
51.09	Novlene	Williams	JAM	26.4.82	5	GP	Helsinki	25 Jul
51.10	Anastasiya	Ovchinnikova	RUS	16.10.84	3	NC-23	Tula	14 Jun
51.12	Allyson	Felix	USA	18.11.85	1	v2N	Glasgow (S)	5 Jun
51.15	Lee	McConnell	GBR	9.10.78	6s2	WCh	Helsinki	8 Aug
51.19	Nawal	El Jak	SUD-Y	17.10.88	1	WY	Marrakech	15 Jul
51.23	Ronetta	Smith	JAM	2.5.80	2		Carson	22 May
	(30)							
51.23	Lucimar	Teodoro	BRA	1.5.81	1	NC	São Paulo	17 Jun
51.27	Donna	Fraser	GBR	7.11.72	1	NC	Manchester (SC)	10 Jul
51.29	Anna	Guzowska	POL	15.1.80	1	NC	Biala Podlaska	25 Jun
51.30	Maria Laura	Almirão	BRA	20.9.77	2	NC	São Paulo	17 Jun
51.30	Daniela	Grgic	CRO-Y	28.9.88	2	WY	Marrakech	15 Jul
51.31	Natalya	Nazarova	RUS	26.5.79	1	WUG	Izmir	17 Aug
51.33	Kaltouma	Nadjina	CHA	16.11.76	5rA	GP	Madrid	16 Jul
51.33	Fatou Binetou	Fall	SEN	23.8.81	2	WUG	Izmir	17 Aug
51.34	Natasha	Hastings	USA-J	23.7.86	1	NC-j	Carson	25 Jun
51.36	Anna	Kozak	BLR	22.6.74	2		Minsk	25 Jun
	(40)							
51.39	Shereefa	Lloyd	JAM	2.9.82	4	NCAA	Sacramento	11 Jun
51.40	Julian	Clay	USA	2.11.77	5		New York (RI)	11 Jun
51.40	Antonina	Yefremova	UKR	19.7.81	1rB	GP	Madrid	16 Jul
51.43	Aliann	Pompey	GUY	9.3.78	2	GP	Belém	22 May
51.45	Kim	Gevaert	BEL	5.8.78	1		Gent	8 May
51.45	Suziann	Reid	USA	14.1.77	6	NC	Carson	25 Jun
51.47	Heide	Seyerling	RSA	19.8.76	1	NC	Durban	15 Apr
51.48	Yelena	Ildeykina	RUS	16.6.83	4	NC-23	Tula	14 Jun
51.50	Manjeet	Kaur	IND	4.4.82	1	AsiC	Inchon	3 Sep
51.51	Moya	Thompson	JAM	19.2.81	2		Atlanta	14 May
	(50)							
51.52	Solen	Désert	FRA	2.8.82	2	NC	Angers	16 Jul
51.53	Libania	Grenot	CUB	12.7.83	3	CAC	Nassau	10 Jul
51.54	Anastasiya	Kochetova	RUS	18.9.83	5	NC-23	Tula	14 Jun
51.57	Mariya	Dryakhlova	RUS	24.4.84	6	NC-23	Tula	14 Jun
51.58	Zuzanna	Radecka	POL	2.4.75	2	NC	Biala Podlaska	25 Jun
51.59	Karen	Shinkins	IRL	15.10.76	3	GP	Belém	22 May
51.66	Tatyana	Levina	RUS	28.2.77	1	Veniz	Haniá	6 Jun
51.68	Monika	Bejnar	POL	10.3.81	3	NC	Biala Podlaska	25 Jun
51.69	Kia	Davis	USA	23.5.76	2		Eagle Rock	5 Jun
51.69	Natalya	Pigida	UKR	30.1.81	2	NC	Kiev	3 Jul
	(60)							
51.71	Kineke	Alexander	VIN-J	21.2.86	3s1	NCAA	Sacramento	10 Jun
51.72A	Jessica	Fox	USA	10.1.82	1		Fort Collins	14 May
51.75	Sathi	Geetha	IND	5.7.83	2	AsiC	Inchon	2 Sep
51.78	Zulia	Calatayud	CUB	9.11.79	1	Barr	La Habana	20 May
51.79	Lashinda	Demus	USA	10.3.83	2	MSR	Walnut	17 Apr
51.80	Asami	Tanno	JPN	25.9.85	4		Yokohama	19 Sep
51.85	Liliya	Pilyugina	UKR	14.10.85	3		Minsk	25 Jun
51.87	Ashlee	Kidd	USA	26.7.85	5	NCAA	Sacramento	11 Jun
51.87	Svetlana	Usovich	BLR	14.10.80	1	Kuso	Warszawa	12 Jun
51.89	Dímitra	Dóva	GRE	2.7.74	3	ECp-S	Firenze	18 Jun
	(70)							
51.92	Crystal	Cox	USA	28.3.79	6	GGala	Roma	8 Jul
51.95	Nicola	Sanders	GBR	23.6.82	1		Namur	1 Jul
51.95		Huang Xiaoxiao	CHN	3.3.83	1	NG	Nanjing	18 Oct
51.96		Tang Xiaoyin	CHN	29.4.85			Zhongshan	24 Apr
51.97	Ginou	Etienne	USA/HAI	12.1.85	3		Atlanta	14 May
52.00	Olga	Kotlyarova	RUS	12.4.76	4		Sochi	26 May
52.00	Geisa	Coutinho	BRA	1.6.80	3	NC	São Paulo	17 Jun
52.00	Irina	Rosikhina	RUS	11.5.75	2h3	NC	Tula	10 Jul
52.03	Shellene	Williams	JAM	19.2.81	5	NC	Kingston	26 Jun
52.04	Aymeé	Martínez	CUB-Y	17.11.88	3	WY	Marrakech	15 Jul
	(80)							
52.05	Natalya	Sologub	BLR	31.3.75	1		Bangor	24 Jun
52.06	Barbara	Petráhn	HUN	16.9.78	3		Eagle Rock	5 Jun
52.07	Sandie	Richards	JAM	6.11.68	5		Kingston	7 May

Mark	Name		Nat	Born	Pos	Meet	Venue	Date
52.07	Claudia	Marx	GER	16.9.78	3		Leverkusen	23 Jul
52.08	Charlette	Greggs	USA	20.10.83	1		Tallahassee	23 Apr
52.09	Ionela	Tirlea-Manolache	ROM	9.2.76	4	ECp-S	Firenze	18 Jun
52.09	Christy	Ekpukpon	NGR	6.2.85	1		Forbach	29 May
52.09	Grazyna	Prokopek	POL	20.4.77	4	NC	Biala Podlaska	25 Jun
52.10	Sonita	Sutherland	JAM-J	9.7.87	1		Kingston	19 Mar
52.11	Keisha	Howard	USA	13.5.84	1		Houston	14 May
	(90)							
52.14	Yevgeniya	Isakova	RUS	27.11.78	2		Tula	23 Jul
52.17	Shana	Cox	USA	22.1.85	1h3	NCAA-r	New York	27 May
52.17	Amanda	Fontes Dias	BRA	11.11.84	4	NC	São Paulo	17 Jun
52.17	Mariyana	Dimitrova	BUL	29.7.82	1		Sofia	7 Jul
52.18	Jerrika	Chapple	USA	11.9.84	2	Big 12	Manhattan, KS	14 May
52.20	Kim	Wall	GBR	21.4.83	1		Gèneve	11 Jun
52.21	Estie	Wittstock	RSA	15.9.80	2	NC	Durban	15 Apr
52.22	Wiande	Moore	USA	24.11.83	4	NCAA-r	New York	28 May
52.24	Patricia	Hall	JAM	16.10.82	2	SEC	Nashville	15 May
52.30	Nadia	Davy	USA	24.12.80	2		Santo Domingo	14 May
	(100)							

Mark	Name		Nat	Born	Date	Mark	Name		Nat	Born	Date
52.32	Natalya	Ivanova	RUS	25.6.81	10 Jul	52.69	Perla	dos Santos	BRA	29.1.82	17 Jun
52.33	Jana	Pittman	AUS	9.11.82	17 Apr	52.69		Yin Yin Khine	MYA	15.6.77	29 Nov
52.33	Debbie	Dunn	JAM	26.3.78	21 May	52.72	Larisa	Chzhao	RUS	4.2.71	13 Jun
52.34		Bu Fanfang	CHN	10.2.78	18 Oct	52.72	Jaimee-Lee	Hoebergen	AUS-Y	17.2.88	26 Nov
52.35	Sa'de	Williams	USA-Y	2.12.89	4 Jun	52.73	Irina	Khlyustova	BLR	14.6.78	2 Jul
52.36	Hazel-Ann	Regis	GRN	1.2.81	14 May	52.73	Fabienne	Féraez	BEN	6.8.76	24 Jun
52.36	Jane	Arnott	NZL	3.1.76	27 Nov	52.76	Svetlana	Cherkasova	RUS	20.5.78	13 Jun
52.38	Carline	Muir	CAN-Y	1.10.87	30 Jul	52.77	Cassandra	Reed	USA	13.9.83	16 Apr
52.40	Lena	Aruhn	SWE	22.4.70	18 Jun	52.77	Debbie-Ann	Parris	JAM	24.3.73	23 Apr
52.41	Tonette	Dyer	USA	28.3.82	17 Apr	52.77	Ahandrea	Allen	USA	3.6.81	15 May
52.42	Ieva	Zunda	LAT	20.7.78	2 Jul	52.80	Nadezhda	Shlyapnikova	RUS-J	15.3.86	3 Jul
52.43	Anna	Jesien	POL	10.12.78	20 May	52.83		Zhang Hongzhe	CHN	13.11.78	18 Oct
52.43	Johnsie	Liles	USA	25.5.85	25 Jun	52.84	Surita	Febbraio	RSA	27.12.73	5 Mar
52.44	Tamsyn	Lewis	AUS	20.7.78	5 Mar	52.84A	Mayra	González	MEX	24.11.73	21 May
52.44	Brittany	Jones	USA-Y	6.3.89	18 Jun	52.87	Olabisi	Afolabi	NGR	31.10.75	9 Jul
52.44	Phara	Anacharsis	FRA	17.12.83	16 Jul	52.88	Caitlin	Willis	AUS	18.12.82	26 Nov
52.46	Brandi	Cross	USA-Y	20.1.88	14 May	52.91	Davita	Prendergast	JAM	16.12.84	9 Apr
52.47	Shareese	Woods	USA	20.2.85	14 May	52.91	Nathandra	John	SKN	6.11.84	14 May
52.48	Chitra K.	Soman	IND	10.7.83	17 May	52.91	Lesley	Owusu	GBR	21.12.78	24 Jul
52.48	Lauren	McNary	USA-J	9.5.86	25 Jun	52.92	Yekaterina	Bobrik	BLR	15.11.83	25 Jun
52.48	Angela	Morosanu	ROM-J	26.7.86	2 Jul	52.92	Anasthasia	Leroy	JAM-J	11.9.87	26 Jun
52.49	Yuliya	Sotnikova	RUS	18.11.70	26 May	52.93	Nina	Gilbert	USA	17.4.84	14 May
52.50	Natalya	Lavshuk	RUS	22.2.80	26 May	52.93	Jessica	Beard	USA-Y	8.1.89	18 Jun
52.50mx	Jenny	Meadows	GBR	17.4.81	19 Jul	52.94	Latonia	Wilson	USA	30.11.84	14 May
	52.69				18 Jun	52.94	Egle	Uljas	EST	18.12.84	7 Aug
52.50	Claudia	Hoffmann	GER	10.12.82	23 Jul	52.95	Deonna	Lawrence	USA-J	21.3.86	15 May
52.52	Natalya	Peryakova	RUS	4.3.83	10 Jul	52.95	LaTonya	Loche	USA	8.10.85	28 May
52.54	Josiane	Tito	BRA	8.8.79	17 Jun	52.99	Vanya	Stambolova	BUL	28.11.83	28 May
52.55	Shunte	Thomas	USA	5.7.84	28 May	52.99	Virginie	Fouquet	FRA	9.9.75	19 Jun
52.58	Yuliana	Zhalneryuk	BLR	14.8.84	1 Jun	52.99	Mary	Danner	USA	3.1.80	23 Jun
52.58	Ksenia	Karandyuk	UKR-J	21.6.86	26 Jun	52.99	Olga	Tereshkova	KAZ	26.10.84	3 Sep
52.59	Amantle	Montsho	BOT	4.7.83	2 Jul	53.01	Mabel	Madojemu	NGR	26.6.83	11 Mar
52.63	Alexandria	Anderson	USA-J	28.1.87	20 May	53.01	Bozena	Lukasik	POL	16.2.85	25 Jun
52.64	Lorena	Franco de Oliveira	BRA	5.5.78	17 Jun	53.01	Natalya	Makukh	UKR	24.1.75	3 Jul
52.64	Kirsi	Mykkänen	FIN	7.2.78	18 Jun	53.01	Helen	Karagounis	GBR	28.9.81	10 Jul
52.64A	Elizabeth	Muthoka	KEN		25 Jun	53.01	Julia	Alba	ESP	30.5.72	16 Jul
52.64	Ksenia	Zadorina	RUS-J	2.3.87	3 Jul	53.02	Nedyalka	Nedkova	BUL	15.3.77	7 Jun
52.64	Catherine	Murphy	GBR	21.9.75	9 Jul	53.02	Rajwinder	Kaur Gill	IND	24.1.80	5 Jul
52.65		Zhang Xiaoyuan	CHN	17.8.82	18 Oct	53.03	Kudirat	Akhigbe	NGR	29.12.81	25 Jun
52.67	Norma	González	COL	11.8.82	18 May	53.07	Martina	Naef	SUI	23.4.80	5 Jul
52.68	Sherene	Pinnock	JAM-J	30.3.87	5 Mar		(181)				

Hand timing

Mark	Name		Nat	Born	Pos	Meet	Venue	Date
52.1	Yulyana	Zhalneryuk	BLR	14.8.84	1		Minsk	23 May

Mark	Name		Nat	Born	Date	Mark	Name		Nat	Born	Date
52.3	Irina	Khlyustova	BLR	14.6.78	23 May	52.4	Yekaterina	Bobrik	BLR	15.11.83	23 May
						52.6A	Elizabeth	Muthoka	KEN		4 Jun

Indoors

Mark	Name		Nat	Born	Pos	Meet	Venue	Date
50.55	Svetlana	Usovich	BLR	14.10.80	2	EI	Madrid	5 Mar
50.92	Hazel-Ann	Regis	GRN	1.2.81	2	NCAA	Fayetteville	12 Mar
51.58	Irina	Rosikhina	RUS	11.5.75	2	NC	Volgograd	11 Feb
51.77	Grit	Breuer	GER	16.2.72	2		Karlsruhe	13 Feb
51.91	Yuliya	Pechonkina	RUS	21.4.78	3	NC	Volgograd	11 Feb
51.95	Claudia	Marx	GER	16.9.78	3		Karlsruhe	13 Feb
52.24	Veronica	Campbell	JAM	15.5.82	2		Fayetteville	22 Jan

Mark	Name		Nat	Born	Date	Mark	Name		Nat	Born	Date
52.38	Shauna	Smith	USA	10.9.83	11 Mar	52.83	Nadine	Balkow	GER	20.6.82	4 Feb
52.41 o/s	Licretia	Sibley	USA	3.8.83	5 Feb	52.98	Melanie	Purkiss	GBR	11.3.79	18 Feb
52.43	Tiffany	Ross-Williams	USA	5.2.83	27 Feb	53.04	Nicole	Leach	USA-J	18.7.87	13 Mar
52.55	Shevon	Stoddart	JAM	21.11.82	11 Mar	53.19	Marina	Shiyan	RUS	22.1.80	23 Jan

Mark	Name		Nat	Born	Pos	Meet	Venue	Date
Drugs disqualification	51.93	Sun Hongfeng	CHN	11.4.79	(6)		Shanghai	17 Sep

JUNIORS

See main list for top 6. 10 (inc.1 indoors) performances by 5 women to 51.90. Additional marks and further juniors:

El Jak 51.61 3h3 WCh Helsinki 7 Aug 51.85 4s1 WCh Helsinki 8 Aug
51.83 1s2 WY Marrakech 14 Jul 51.90 3 Tallinn 16 Aug
Hastings 51.85i 2 Fayetteville 12 Feb 51.87 6 NCAA Sacramento 11 Jun

Mark	Name		Nat	Born	Pos	Meet	Venue	Date
52.35	Sa'de	Williams	USA-Y	2.12.89	1		Sacramento	4 Jun
52.38	Carline	Muir	CAN-Y	1.10.87	2	PAm-J	Windsor	30 Jul
52.44	Brittany	Jones	USA-Y	6.3.89	1		Greensboro	18 Jun
52.46	Brandi	Cross (10)	USA-Y	20.1.88	1		Austin	14 May
52.48	Lauren	McNary	USA	9.5.86	2	NC	Carson	25 Jun
52.48	Angela	Morosanu	ROM	26.7.86	1	NC	Bucuresti	2 Jul
52.58	Ksenia	Karandyuk	UKR	21.6.86	1		Tula	26 Jun
52.63	Alexandria	Anderson	USA	28.1.87	1		Charleston	20 May
52.64	Ksenia	Zadorina	RUS	2.3.87	1	NC-j	Tula	3 Jul
52.68	Sherene	Pinnock	JAM	30.3.87	1		Kingston	5 Mar
52.72	Jaimee-Lee	Hoebergen	AUS-Y	17.2.88	2		Brisbane	26 Nov
52.80	Nadezhda	Shlyapnikova	RUS	15.3.86	2	NC-j	Tula	3 Jul
52.92	Anasthasia	Leroy	JAM	11.9.87	1	NC-j	Kingston	26 Jun
52.93	Jessica	Beard (20)	USA-Y	8.1.89	3		Greensboro	18 Jun

600 METRES

Indoors

Mark	Name		Nat	Born	Pos	Meet	Venue	Date
1:27.03+	Brigita	Langerholc	SLO	23.7.76	1	in 800m	Karlsruhe	13 Feb
1:27.1+	Maria	Mutola	MOZ	27.10.72	2	in 800m	Karlsruhe	13 Feb

800 METRES

Mark	Name		Nat	Born	Pos	Meet	Venue	Date
1:56.07	Tatyana	Andrianova	RUS	10.12.79	1	NC	Tula	11 Jul
1:56.91		Andrianova			1	Bisl	Oslo	29 Jul
1:56.93	Svetlana	Cherkasova	RUS	20.5.78	1rA	Znam	Kazan	25 Jun
1:57.33	Larisa	Chzhao	RUS	4.2.71	2	NC	Tula	11 Jul
1:57.35	Svetlana	Klyuka	RUS	27.12.78	3	NC	Tula	11 Jul
1:57.42		Cherkasova			4	NC	Tula	11 Jul
1:57.52		Cherkasova			1	Gaz	Saint Denis	1 Jul
1:57.55	Olga	Kotlyarova	RUS	12.4.76	2	Bisl	Oslo	29 Jul
1:57.71		Kotlyarova			5	NC	Tula	11 Jul
1:57.80		Andrianova			1	DNG	Stockholm	26 Jul
1:57.82	Janeth	Jepkosgei	KEN	13.12.83	1		Rovereto	31 Aug
1:57.86		Cherkasova			3	Bisl	Oslo	29 Jul
1:57.92	Zulia	Calatayud	CUB	9.11.79	1s2	WCh	Helsinki	7 Aug
1:57.99	Hazel	Clark	USA	3.10.77	4	Bisl	Oslo	29 Jul
1:58.07		Calatayud			2rA	Znam	Kazan	25 Jun
1:58.17	Svetlana	Usovich	BLR	14.10.80	1	Agl M	Minsk	25 Jun
1:58.35		Chzhao			3rA	Znam	Kazan	25 Jun
1:58.37		Calatayud			2	Gaz	Saint Denis	1 Jul
1:58.41	Hasna	Benhassi (10)	MAR	1.6.78	1rA	GGala	Roma	8 Jul
1:58.44		Klyuka			5	Bisl	Oslo	29 Jul
1:58.46		Andrianova			4rA	Znam	Kazan	25 Jun
1:58.47		Cherkasova			2rA	GGala	Roma	8 Jul
1:58.58		Cherkasova			2s2	WCh	Helsinki	7 Aug
1:58.58		Benhassi			1		Shanghai	17 Sep
1:58.59		Clark			2	DNG	Stockholm	26 Jul
1:58.72	Natalya	Lavshuk	RUS	20.2.80	5rA	Znam	Kazan	25 Jun
1:58.81		Calatayud			1	GP	Madrid	16 Jul
1:58.82		Calatayud			1	WCh	Helsinki	9 Aug
1:58.88	Kenia	Sinclair	JAM	14.7.80	3rA	GGala	Roma	8 Jul
1:58.95		Calatayud			1		Réthimno	10 Jul
	(30/12)							
1:58.96	Maria	Mutola	MOZ	27.10.72	3	Gaz	Saint Denis	1 Jul
1:59.29	Alice	Schmidt	USA	3.10.81	1		Lignano Sabbiadoro	17 Jul
1:59.33	Zhanna	Smolina	RUS	19.1.78	1	Kuts	Moskva	16 Jul
1:59.40	Mayte	Martínez	ESP	17.5.76	4s1	WCh	Helsinki	7 Aug
1:59.54	Laetitia	Valdonado	FRA	4.8.77	7rA	GGala	Roma	8 Jul
1:59.59	Treniere	Clement	USA	27.10.81	2		New York (RI)	11 Jun
1:59.69	Maryam	Jamal	BRN	16.9.84	1		Génève	11 Jun
1:59.74		Liu Qing	CHN-J	28.4.86	1	NG	Nanjing	21 Oct
	(20)							
1:59.75	Hind	Dehiba	FRA	17.3.79	2		Shanghai	17 Sep
1:59.78	Mihaela	Neacsu	ROM	3.5.79	1	GP II	Thessaloníki	17 Jul
1:59.79	Maria	Papadopoúlou	GRE	15.12.74	2	SGP	Athína	14 Jun

Mark	Name		Nat	Born	Pos	Meet	Venue	Date
1:59.91	Agnes	Samaria	NAM	11.8.72	6	DNG	Stockholm	26 Jul
1:59.91	Amina	Aït Hammou	MAR	18.7.78	4	GP	Rieti	28 Aug
1:59.96	Jennifer	Toomey	USA	19.12.71	3		New York (RI)	11 Jun
1:59.98	Jolanda	Ceplak	SLO	12.9.76	1		Velenje	23 Jun
1:59.99	Kameisha	Bennett	USA	13.1.81	4		New York (RI)	11 Jun
2:00.10	Diane	Cummins	CAN	19.1.74	4s2	WCh	Helsinki	7 Aug
2:00.26	Virginie	Fouquet	FRA	9.9.75	8	Gaz	Saint Denis	1 Jul
	(30)							
2:00.26	Natalya	Tsyganova	RUS	7.2.71	6	NC	Tula	11 Jul
2:00.29	Bouchra	Ghézielle	FRA	18.5.79	1	NC	Angers	15 Jul
2:00.34	Natalya	Yevdokimova	RUS	17.3.78	1	v USA	Moskva	4 Sep
2:00.38	Olesya	Chumakova	RUS	23.7.81	2h1	NC	Tula	10 Jul
2:00.45	Miho	Sugimori	JPN	14.4.78	1	NC	Tokyo	5 Jun
2:00.54	Seltana	Aït Hammou	MAR	10.5.80	2		Réthimno	10 Jul
2:00.56	Oksana	Zbrozhek	RUS	12.1.78	3h1	NC	Tula	10 Jul
2:00.59	Marian	Burnett	GUY	22.2.76	5		New York (RI)	11 Jun
2:00.59	Yelena	Soboleva	RUS	3.8.82	2		Tallinn	16 Aug
2:00.64	Lucia	Klocová	SVK	20.11.83	7s1	WCh	Helsinki	7 Aug
	(40)							
2:00.71	Ewelina	Setowska	POL	5.3.80	2	GP II	Thessaloníki	17 Jul
2:00.72	Elisabeth	Grousselle	FRA	6.2.73	1		Villeneuve d'Ascq	12 Jun
2:00.75	Aleksandra	Proshina	RUS	17.3.81	1rB		Tula	23 Jul
2:00.76	Irina	Vashentseva	RUS	30.9.80	6	GP	Sevilla	4 Jun
2:00.78	Yevgeniya	Zolotova	RUS	28.4.83	2		Moskva	5 Jun
2:00.84	Anastasiya	Fesenko	RUS	17.6.82	2h6	NC	Tula	10 Jul
2:00.88	Maria	Cioncan	ROM	19.6.77	1	ECp-S	Firenze	18 Jun
2:00.90	Élodie	Guégan	FRA	19.2.85	4rB	GGala	Roma	8 Jul
2:00.96	Elisa	Cusma	ITA	24.7.81	2		Lignano Sabbiadoro	17 Jul
2:01.00	Monika	Gradzki	GER	21.9.79	2	ECp-S	Firenze	18 Jun
	(50)							
2:01.03	Irina	Krakoviak	LTU	16.11.77	1	ECp-2A	Tallinn	18 Jun
2:01.05	Michelle	Ballentine	JAM	31.8.75	3h5	WCh	Helsinki	6 Aug
2:01.07	Lilya	Bikbulatova	RUS	25.2.84	3h6	NC	Tula	10 Jul
2:01.07	Neisha	Bernard-Thomas	GRN	21.1.81	1	CAC	Nassau	11 Jul
2:01.08	Yuliya	Chizhenko	RUS	30.8.79	4		Shanghai	17 Sep
2:01.14	Teodora	Kolarova	BUL	29.5.81	1		Plovdiv	12 Jun
2:01.17	Susan	Scott	GBR	26.9.77	8s1	WCh	Helsinki	7 Aug
2:01.25	Juliana Paula	de Azevedo	BRA	12.7.83	2	GP II	Rio de Janeiro	15 May
2:01.35	Tatyana	Roslanova	KAZ	28.9.80	3	SGP	Doha	13 May
2:01.41	Brigita	Langerholc	SLO	23.7.76	2		Nuoro	13 Jul
	(60)							
2:01.42	Binnaz	Uslu	TUR	12.3.85	2	WUG	Izmir	20 Aug
2:01.44	Frances	Santin	USA	27.7.80	1	GP II	Stanford	30 May
2:01.45	Kathleen	Friedrich	GER	13.7.77	1		Cuxhaven	9 Jul
2:01.48	Natalya	Kutkina	RUS	4.2.77	2rB	Znam	Kazan	25 Jun
2:01.56A	Nadiha	Touhami	ALG	10.2.78	9	GP	Rieti	28 Aug
2:01.57A	Rosibel	García	COL	13.2.81	1	Bolivar	Armenia/COL	20 Aug
2:01.65	Letitia	Vriesde	SUR	5.10.64	6h5	WCh	Helsinki	6 Aug
2:01.66	Aneita	Denton	JAM	9.6.83	2	CAC	Nassau	11 Jul
2:01.68	Éléni	Filándra	GRE	12.1.84	12	SGP	Athína	14 Jun
2:01.78	Tatyana	Petlyuk	UKR	22.2.82	5h4	WCh	Helsinki	6 Aug
	(70)							
2:01.79	Natalya	Gorelova	RUS	18.4.73	3	GP II	Thessaloníki	17 Jul
2:01.8		Myint Myint Aye	MYA	18.11.77	1	NC	Yangon	13 Feb
2:01.90	Aimee	Teteris	CAN	24.6.79	2	GP II	Stanford	30 May
2:01.90	Jemma	Simpson	GBR	10.2.84	3	WK-23	Zürich	19 Aug
2:01.90	Marilyn	Okoro	GBR	23.9.84	3	WUG	Izmir	20 Aug
2:01.94	Carmo	Tavares	POR	27.4.74	4	GP II	Thessaloníki	17 Jul
2:01.98	Rebecca	Lyne	GBR	4.7.82	1		Watford	11 Jun
2:02.01	Svetlana	Klimkovich	BLR	26.8.80	1	NC	Brest	4 Jul
2:02.05	Jenny	Meadows	GBR	17.4.81	2	LGP	London (CP)	22 Jul
2:02.08	Faith	Macharia	KEN	9.2.76	6	GP II	Thessaloníki	17 Jul
	(80)							
2:02.1	Natalya	Zorkova	RUS	15.6.81	1		Chelyabinsk	26 Jun
2:02.13	Christiane	dos Santos	BRA	6.10.81	4	GP II	Rio de Janeiro	15 May
2:02.17	Kate	Vermeulen	CAN	5.10.76	1		Victoria	14 May
2:02.20	Sasha	Spencer	USA	4.8.79	4		Lignano Sabbiadoro	17 Jul
2:02.24	Esther	Desviat	ESP	27.1.82	8	GP	Sevilla	4 Jun
2:02.27	Melissa	de Leon	TRI	9.4.81	1		Atlanta	14 May
2:02.28	Tamara	Tverdostup (Volkova)	UKR	17.7.79	6	ECp-S	Firenze	18 Jun
2:02.28	Nelya	Neporadna	UKR	29.7.85	1	NC	Kiev	3 Jul

Mark	Name		Nat	Born	Pos	Meet	Venue	Date
2:02.35	Alexia	Oberstoltz	ITA	2.6.80	7	ECp-S	Firenze	18 Jun
2:02.36	Oksana	Dekhtyarchuk	RUS	3.2.80	4	Kuts	Moskva	16 Jul
	(90)							
2:02.38	Yuneysi	Santiusty	CUB	24.12.84	3	CAC	Nassau	11 Jul
2:02.39	Anna	Jakubczak	POL	2.2.73	1		Biala Podlaska	28 May
2:02.43	Mona Jabir	Ahmed	SUD-J	6.1.87	5	WK-23	Zürich	19 Aug
2:02.44	Corina	Dumbravean	ROM	15.4.84	1	BalkC	Novi Sad	23 Jul
2:02.46	Yekaterina	Martynova	RUS-J	12.6.86	1	NC-j	Tula	4 Jul
2:02.48	Sandra	Teixeira	POR	13.3.78	2		La Laguna	30 Jul
2:02.51	Nancy	Lagat Chebet	KEN	22.8.81	1		Kalamáta	30 May
2:02.51	Olga	Cristea	MDA-J	13.12.87	1		Tula	26 Jun
2:02.55	Hilary	Edmondson	CAN	7.8.81	2		Ninove	30 Jul
2:02.58	Olga	Gorshkova	RUS	9.3.83	6	Znam	Kazan	25 Jun
	(100)							

Mark	Name		Nat	Born	Date
2:02.63	Mardrea	Hyman	JAM	22.12.72	7 May
2:02.64	Kay-Ann	Thompson	JAM	30.1.85	26 Jun
2:02.64		Yang Xiaocui	CHN-J	24.1.87	21 Oct
2:02.66	Natalya	Lupu	UKR-J	4.11.87	26 Jun
2:02.68	Karen	Harewood	GBR	19.8.75	11 Jun
2:02.7	Nadezhda	Kosyakova	RUS	30.5.77	26 Jun
2:02.74	Eleonora	Berlanda	ITA	6.4.76	31 Aug
2:02.75	Liliana	Barbulescu/Popescu	ROM	5.2.82	15 May
2:02.75	Fotiní	Dagglí-Paggóto	GRE	13.8.85	10 Jul
2:02.77	Mariya	Shapayeva	RUS-J	7.11.86	26 Jun
2:02.77	Sarah	Ali-Kahn	CAN	9.5.73	16 Aug
2:02.82	Adriana	Muñoz	CUB	16.3.82	20 May
2:02.83		Yang Wei	CHN	24.7.83	21 Oct
2:02.84	Lydia	Wafula	KEN-Y	15.2.88	1 Sep
2:02.92	Sandra	Stals	BEL	5.6.75	13 May
2:02.92	Egle	Uljas	EST	18.12.84	5 Jul
2:02.93	Mishael	Bertrand	USA	3.5.79	30 May
2:02.96	Jenelle	Deatherage	USA	25.9.77	13 Jul
2:02.99	Carmen	Douma-Hussar	CAN	12.3.77	22 Jul
2:03.00	Kristina	Bratton	USA	7.5.81	14 May
2:03.02	Natalya	Dukhnova	BLR	16.7.66	25 Jun
2:03.02	Maria	Zayichenko	RUS	8.4.81	16 Jul
2:03.06	Elisabetta	Artuso	ITA	25.4.74	28 Aug
2:03.07		Huang Xiaofeng	CHN-J	17.10.87	21 Oct
2:03.08	Lisa	Dobriskey	GBR	23.12.83	11 Jun
2:03.10	Maggie	Vessey	USA	23.12.81	11 Jun
2:03.14	Tiffany	McWilliams	USA	20.10.82	14 May
2:03.14	Beata	Rudzinska	POL	22.9.82	11 Jun
2:03.18	Jana	Hartmann	GER	23.10.81	23 Jul
2:03.20	Natalya	Pantelyeva	RUS	18.8.83	14 Jun
2:03.2A	Chanelle	Olivier	RSA-J	15.9.86	3 Dec
2:03.24	Saida	El Mehdi	MAR	21.9.81	15 May
2:03.25	Johanna	Risku/Lehtinen	FIN	21.2.79	21 Jul
2:03.28	Tatyana	Paliyenko	RUS	18.11.83	10 Jul
2:03.29	Charlene	Snelgrove	GBR	6.5.82	21 May
2:03.36	Janina	Goldfuss	GER	22.7.83	19 Jun
2:03.36	Anna	Alminova	RUS	17.1.85	17 Jul
2:03.39	Tatyana	Yegorova	RUS	23.10.80	10 Jul
2:03.41	Svetlana	Kazakova	RUS	20.10.83	10 Jul
2:03.42	Rikke	Rønholt	DEN	1.1.76	9 Jul
2:03.42	Lyudmila	Kuvshinova	RUS	13.3.82	10 Jul
2:03.45	Miriam	Bravo	ESP	29.9.74	16 Jul
2:03.45	Lotte	Visschers	NED	2.8.79	30 Jul
2:03.49	Anita	Brägger	SUI	6.10.72	19 Aug
2:03.5mx	Rachael	Ogden	GBR	23.7.79	17 Aug
	2:03.73				25 Jun
2:03.53	Helen	Clitheroe	GBR	2.1.74	22 Jul
2:03.54	Natalia	Rodríguez	ESP	2.6.79	30 Jul
2:03.55	Olga	Titova	RUS	8.4.79	10 Jul
2:03.57	Rachael	Thompson	GBR	15.11.85	30 Aug
2:03.59	Sheena	Gooding	BAR	1.8.81	11 Jul
2:03.6A	Caroline	Chepkwony	KEN	18.4.84	25 Jun
2:03.62	Yelena	Bondar	UKR	7.6.85	3 Jul
2:03.64	Sandra	Moya	PUR	3.1.75	2 Jul
2:03.65		Do Thi Bong	VIE	4.9.85	28 Nov
2:03.67	Joanna	Ross	GBR	18.1.81	9 Jul
2:03.69	Olesya	Syreva	RUS	25.11.83	24 Jul
2:03.73	Rebekah	Noble	USA-J	15.6.87	24 Jun
2:03.76	Viktoriya	Yalovtseva	KAZ	4.11.78	29 May
2:03.77	Joanna	Buza	POL	15.4.81	25 Jun
2:03.78	Ivonne	Teichmann	GER	11.4.77	9 Jul
2:03.81	Yevgenia	Khaliullina	RUS	22.1.84	14 Jun
2:03.82	Mari	Järvenpää	FIN	29.11.81	30 May
2:03.83	Georgie	Clarke	AUS	17.6.84	22 Jul
2:03.83		Liu Xiaoping	CHN	14.1.78	21 Oct
2:03.85	Natalya	Shipitsyna	RUS	6.5.81	10 Jul
2:03.85	Amanda	Pritchard	GBR	18.3.80	29 Aug
2:03.86	Katie	Erdman	USA	24.8.83	11 Jun
2:03.90	Aneta	Lemiesz	POL	17.1.81	28 May
2:03.93	Treany	Swain	USA	14.6.85	30 Apr
2:03.93	Joy Amechi	Eze	NGR-J	23.4.87	9 Jul
2:03.94	Zoya	Nesterenko	UKR	10.3.83	3 Jul
2:03.97	Joanna	Kus	POL	4.1.84	24 Jun
2:03.99	Ayako	Jinnouchi	JPN-J	21.1.87	5 Jun
2:04.00	Lindsey	Gallo (174)	USA	29.11.81	13 Jul

Indoors

Mark	Name		Nat	Born	Pos	Meet	Venue	Date
1:57.53		Chzhao			1		Moskva	23 Jan
1:58.48	Irina	Vashentseva	RUS	30.9.80	2		Moskva	23 Jan
1:58.49	Maria	Mutola	MOZ	27.10.72	1		Karlsruhe	13 Feb
2:00.75	Nicole	Cook	USA	16.12.82	1	SEC	Fayetteville	27 Feb
2:01.03	Sandra	Stals	BEL	5.6.75	2		Erfurt	4 Feb
2:01.72	Claudia	Gesell	GER	18.12.77	1	NC	Sindelfingen	20 Feb
2:01.99	Marina	Shiyan	RUS	22.1.80	2		Volgograd	15 Jan

Mark	Name		Nat	Born	Date
2:02.65	Malgorzata	Pskit	POL	25.5.76	6 Feb
2:02.67	Janina	Goldfuss	GER	22.7.83	13 Feb
2:03.02	Elena	Iagar	ROM	16.1.75	13 Feb
2:03.41	Margarita	Plaksina	RUS	1.10.77	30 Jan
2:03.77	Névia	Semedo	POR	14.11.78	4 Mar

JUNIORS

See main list for top 4 juniors. 10 performances by 7 women to 2:02.77. Additional marks and further juniors:

Liu Qing 2:00.11 1 EAsG Macao 2 Oct 2:02.34 2s2 WUG Izmir 19 Aug
2:02.27 4 WUG Izmir 20 Aug

Mark	Name		Nat	Born	Pos	Meet	Venue	Date
2:02.64		Yang Xiaocui	CHN	24.1.87	2	NG	Nanjing	21 Oct
2:02.66	Natalya	Lupu	UKR	4.11.87	2		Tula	26 Jun
2:02.77	Mariya	Shapayeva	RUS	7.11.86	3		Tula	26 Jun
2:02.84	Lydia	Wafula	KEN-Y	15.2.88	1	Afr-J	Radès	1 Sep
2:03.07		Huang Xiaofeng	CHN	17.10.87	4	NG	Nanjing	21 Oct
2:03.2A	Chanelle	Olivier (10)	RSA	15.9.86	1		Krugersdorp	3 Dec
2:03.73	Rebekah	Noble	USA	15.6.87	1	NC	Carson	24 Jun

Mark	Name		Nat	Born	Pos	Meet	Venue	Date
2:03.93	Joy Amechi	Eze	NGR	23.4.87	1	NC	Abuja	9 Jul
2:03.99	Ayako	Jinnouchi	JPN	21.1.87	2	NC	Tokyo	5 Jun
2:04.02	Laura	Finucane	GBR	3.8.86	5		Solihull	25 Jun
2:04.12	Heidi	Magill	USA	15.2.86	2	PAm-J	Windsor	30 Jul
2:04.15	Larisa-Elena	Arcip	ROM	19.2.86	4	EJ	Kaunas	23 Jul
2:04.30	Pinki	Parmanik	IND	10.4.86	1	NC	Hyderabad	9 Nov
2:04.48	Meskerem	Legese	ETH	28.9.86	6	WK-23	Zürich	19 Aug
2:04.54	Anzhelika	Shevchenko	UKR	29.10.87	2	NC-j	Kiev	3 Jun
2:04.60	Truong Thanh Hang (20)		VIE	1.5.86	3	SEAG	Manila	28 Nov

1000 METRES

Mark	Name		Nat	Born	Pos	Meet	Venue	Date
2:34.91	Tatyana	Tomashova	RUS	1.7.75	1	Gugl	Linz	23 Aug
2:35.20	Yuliya	Chizhenko	RUS	30.8.79	2	Gugl	Linz	23 Aug
2:36.26	Carmen	Douma-Hussar	CAN	12.3.77	3	Gugl	Linz	23 Aug
2:36.33	Jolanda	Ceplak	SLO	12.9.76	1	GP II	Zagreb	11 Jul
2:36.34	Nelya	Neporadna	UKR	29.7.85	2	GP II	Zagreb	11 Jul
2:36.46	Jennifer	Toomey	USA	19.12.71	3	GP II	Zagreb	11 Jul
2:36.50	Yelena	Soboleva	RUS	3.8.82	4	Gugl	Linz	23 Aug
2:37.37	Kenia	Sinclair	JAM	14.7.80	5	Gugl	Linz	23 Aug
2:37.63	Diane	Cummins	CAN	19.1.74	6	Gugl	Linz	23 Aug

Mark	Name		Nat	Born	Date	Mark	Name		Nat	Born	Date
2:38.37	Nadiha	Touhami	ALG	10.2.78	23 Aug	2:39.97	Sandra	Moya	PUR	14.2.74	11 Jul
2:38.91	Maria	Cioncan	ROM	19.6.77	25 Jun	2:40.48	Irina	Krakoviak	LTU	16.11.77	9 Jun
2:38.91	Anne	Shadle	USA	1.12.82	11 Jul	2:40.57	Kathleen	Friedrich	GER	13.7.77	11 May
2:39.21	Lindsey	Gallo	USA	29.11.81	23 Aug	2:40.61	Liliana	Popescu	ROM	5.2.82	9 Jun
						2:40.64	Anna	Jakubczak	POL	2.2.73	23 Aug

Indoors

Mark	Name		Nat	Born	Pos	Meet	Venue	Date
2:35.34	Larisa	Chzhao	RUS	4.2.72	1		Yekaterinburg	7 Jan
2:35.39	Kelly	Holmes	GBR	19.4.70	1	GP	Birmingham	18 Feb
2:36.99	Agnes	Samaria	NAM	11.8.72	2	GP	Birmingham	18 Feb
2:37.57	Lidia	Chojecka	POL	25.1.77	1		Liévin	26 Feb
2:37.98	Irina	Vashentseva	RUS	30.9.80	2		Yekaterinburg	7 Jan

Mark	Name		Nat	Born	Date	Mark	Name		Nat	Born	Date
2:38.07	Maria	Mutola	MOZ	27.10.72	24 Feb	2:39.61	Amina	At Hammou	MAR	18.7.78	18 Feb
2:38.68	Svetlana	Cherkasova	RUS	20.5.78	7 Jan	2:39.66	Seltana	Aït Hammou	MAR	10.5.80	18 Feb
2:38.80	Mayte	Martínez	ESP	17.5.76	24 Feb	2:39.68	Sandra	Stals	BEL	5.6.75	26 Feb
2:39.39	Oksana	Zbrozhek	RUS	12.1.78	7 Jan	2:40.67	Virginie	Fouquet	FRA	9.9.75	26 Feb

JUNIORS

Mark	Name		Nat	Born	Pos	Meet	Venue	Date
2:43.40i	Sarah	Bowman	USA	15.10.86	1		Blacksburg	26 Feb

1500 METRES

Mark	Name		Nat	Born	Pos	Meet	Venue	Date
3:56.79	Maryam	Jamal	BRN	16.9.84	1	GP	Rieti	28 Aug
3:57.73	Natalya	Yevdokimova	RUS	17.3.78	2	GP	Rieti	28 Aug
3:58.68	Yuliya	Chizhenko	RUS	30.8.79	1	NC	Tula	13 Jul
3:59.05	Tatyana	Tomashova	RUS	1.7.75	3	GP	Rieti	28 Aug
3:59.13		Jamal			1	SGP	Athína	14 Jun
3:59.35		Jamal			1	WAF	Monaco	9 Sep
3:59.47	Olga	Yegorova	RUS	28.3.72	1	Znam	Kazan	25 Jun
3:59.51	Natalia	Rodríguez	ESP	2.6.79	4	GP	Rieti	28 Aug
3:59.60	Gelete	Burka	ETH-J	15.2.86	5	GP	Rieti	28 Aug
3:59.66		Chizhenko			6	GP	Rieti	28 Aug
4:00.09		Chizhenko			2	Znam	Kazan	25 Jun
4:00.28		Tomashova			2	WAF	Monaco	9 Sep
4:00.35		Tomashova			1	WCh	Helsinki	14 Aug
4:00.49	Hind	Dehiba	FRA	17.3.79	7	GP	Rieti	28 Aug
4:00.59	Anna	Jakubczak	POL	2.2.73	8	GP	Rieti	28 Aug
4:00.60		Yevdokimova			3	WAF	Monaco	9 Sep
4:00.63		Yegorova			2	NC	Tula	13 Jul
4:00.93 dq		Chizhenko			(2)	WCh	Helsinki	14 Aug
4:01.14	Yelena	Soboleva (10)	RUS	3.8.82	3	NC	Tula	13 Jul
4:01.28	Bouchra	Ghézielle	FRA	18.5.79	4	WAF	Monaco	9 Sep
4:01.46		Yegorova			2	WCh	Helsinki	14 Aug
4:01.73		Jamal			1	Athl	Lausanne	5 Jul
4:01.85		Yegorova			1	Gaz	Saint Denis	1 Jul
4:01.90		Ghézielle			2	SGP	Athína	14 Jun
4;02.08		Dehiba			5	WAF	Monaco	9 Sep
4:02.17		Ghézielle			9	GP	Rieti	28 Aug
4:02.21	Alesya	Turova	BLR	6.12.79	3	SGP	Athína	14 Jun
4:02.29	Carmen	Douma-Hussar	CAN	12.3.77	10	GP	Rieti	28 Aug
4:02.31	Nancy	Lagat Chebet	KEN	22.8.81	4	SGP	Athína	14 Jun
4:02.45		Ghézielle			3	WCh	Helsinki	14 Aug

Mark	Name		Nat	Born	Pos	Meet	Venue	Date
4:02.48		Soboleva			4	WCh	Helsinki	14 Aug
	(31/14)							
4:02.55	Olesya	Chumakova	RUS	23.7.81	11	GP	Rieti	28 Aug
4:02.66	Yelena	Kanales	RUS	7.2.76	4	NC	Tula	13 Jul
4:03.19	Irina	Krakoviak	LTU	16.11.77	5	SGP	Athína	14 Jun
4:03.65	Yelena	Zadorozhnaya	RUS	3.12.77	6	SGP	Athína	14 Jun
4:03.68	Wioletta	Janowska	POL	9.6.77	4	Gaz	Saint Denis	1 Jul
4:03.73	Nelya	Neporadna	UKR	29.7.85	7	SGP	Athína	14 Jun
	(20)							
4:03.98dq		Xing Huina	CHN	25.2.84	(1)	NG	Nanjing	19 Oct
	disqualified for obstruction							
4:04.00		Liu Qing	CHN-J	28.4.86	1	NG	Nanjing	19 Oct
4:04.56	Corina	Dumbravean	ROM	15.4.84	1	BalkC	Novi Sad	24 Jul
4:04.95	Mestawet	Tadesse	ETH	19.7.85	1	GGala	Roma	8 Jul
4:05.05	Mayte	Martínez	ESP	17.5.76	13	GP	Rieti	28 Aug
4:05.19	Helen	Clitheroe	GBR	2.1.74	10	WCh	Helsinki	14 Aug
4:05.42mx	Lisa	Dobriskey	GBR	23.12.83	1mx		Manchester (Str)	30 Aug
	4:07.47				3	Déca	Paris (C)	3 Sep
4:05.67	Liliya	Bikbulatova	RUS	25.2.84	7	NC	Tula	13 Jul
4:05.75	Lindsey	Gallo	USA	29.11.81	14	GP	Rieti	28 Aug
4:05.76	Olga	Kravtsova	BLR	25.6.81	1	NC	Brest	3 Jul
	(30)							
4:05.77	Treniere	Clement	USA	27.10.81	6	GGala	Roma	8 Jul
4:05.79	Maria	Martins	FRA	1.4.74	7	Gaz	Saint Denis	1 Jul
4:06.24	Jennifer	Toomey	USA	19.12.71	8	GGala	Roma	8 Jul
4:06.37	Tatyana	Krivobok	UKR	17.1.72	1		Kiev	24 Jul
4:06.50	Georgie	Clarke	AUS	17.6.84	9	GGala	Roma	8 Jul
4:06.52	Kelly	Holmes	GBR	19.4.70	1	4N	Glasgow (S)	5 Jun
4:06.80	Sarah	Jamieson	AUS	24.3.75	1		Melbourne	17 Feb
4:06.85	Johanna	Risku/Lehtinen	FIN	21.2.79	10	GGala	Roma	8 Jul
4:07.03	Liliya	Shobukhova	RUS	13.11.77	5	Znam	Kazan	25 Jun
4:07.08	Shayne	Culpepper	USA	3.12.73	1		Carson	22 May
	(40)							
4:07.11	Kenia	Sinclair	JAM	14.7.80	1	GP II	Stanford	30 May
4:07.13	Anastasiya	Fesenko	RUS	17.6.82	1		Moskva	29 Jun
4:07.21	Natalya	Gorelova	RUS	18.4.73	8	NC	Tula	13 Jul
4:07.25	Tatyana	Golovchenko	UKR	13.2.80	2	NC	Kiev	2 Jul
4:07.39	Maria	Cioncan	ROM	19.6.77	2	ECp-S	Firenze	19 Jun
4:07.54	Eleonora	Berlanda	ITA	6.4.76	11	GGala	Roma	8 Jul
4:07.57	Nuria	Fernández	ESP	16.8.76	12	GGala	Roma	8 Jul
4:07.58	Amy	Mortimer	USA	16.8.81	3	NC	Carson	25 Jun
4:07.76	Trine	Pilskog	NOR	1.12.72	13	GGala	Roma	8 Jul
4:07.77	Kate	Vermeulen	CAN	5.10.76	3		Carson	22 May
	(50)							
4:07.78	Olesya	Syreva	RUS	25.11.83	6	Znam	Kazan	25 Jun
4:07.86	Sarah	Schwald	USA	2.1.73	1	GP II	Zagreb	11 Jul
4:07.96	Mardrea	Hyman	JAM	22.12.72	4	GP	Helsinki	25 Jul
4:08.16	Oksana	Zbrozhek	RUS	12.1.78	5	GP	Madrid	16 Jul
4:08.17	Natalya	Pavlovskaya	RUS	30.4.75	7	Znam	Kazan	25 Jun
4:08.30	Meryem Alaoui	Selsouli	MAR	8.4.84	4	GP	Sevilla	4 Jun
4:08.46	Latifa	Essarokh	FRA	11.12.73	2		Cuxhaven	9 Jul
4:08.54	Suzy	Walsham	AUS	22.11.73	1		Sydney	26 Nov
4:08.60	Anne	Shadle	USA	1.12.82	5	WG	Helsinki	25 Jul
4:08.70	Veerle	Dejaeghere	BEL	1.8.73	3		Villeneuve d'Ascq	12 Jun
	(60)							
4:08.76	Christy	Wurth-Thomas	USA	11.7.80	5	GP II	Stanford	30 May
4:08.78	Yelena	Sidorchenkova	RUS	30.5.80	4		Sochi	26 May
4:08.81	Antje	Möldner	GER	13.6.84	1		Dessau	27 May
4:08.88	Kathleen	Friedrich	GER	13.7.77	1		Kassel	10 Jun
4:08.91	Sinead	Delahunty-Evans	IRL	12.2.71	3		Cuxhaven	9 Jul
4:08.92	Naomi	Mugo	KEN	2.1.77	5		Villeneuve d'Ascq	12 Jun
4:08.94	Hilary	Edmondson	CAN	7.8.81	6	GP II	Stanford	30 May
4:08.94	Irene	Alfonso	ESP	6.2.81	6	GP	Sevilla	4 Jun
4:09.00	Susan	Scott	GBR	26.9.77	3		Zaragoza	23 Jun
4:09.03	Yekaterina	Volkova	RUS	16.2.78	2		Tula	24 Jul
	(70)							
4:09.06	Jenelle	Deatherage	USA	25.9.77	3	GP II	Zagreb	11 Jul
4:09.17	Sonja	Stolic	SCG	21.4.80	2	ECp-1B	Leiria	19 Jun
4:09.30	Miho	Sugimori	JPN	14.4.78	1		Kumamoto	9 Apr
4:09.56	Konstadina	Efedáki	GRE	1.10.78	11	SGP	Athína	14 Jun
4:09.71	Larisa	Chzhao	RUS	4.2.71	5		Sochi	26 May

Mark	Name		Nat	Born	Pos	Meet	Venue	Date
4:09.73	Sonja	Roman	SLO	11.3.79	4		Cuxhaven	9 Jul
4:10.13		Huang Jing	CHN-J	4.4.87	2	NG	Nanjing	19 Oct
4:10.14	Galina	Bogomolova	RUS	15.10.77	3		Tula	24 Jul
4:10.28	Sandra	Teixeira	POR	13.3.78	3	ECp-1B	Leiria	19 Jun
4:10.32	Fatima	Lanouar	TUN	14.3.78	2		Braaschaat	24 Jul
	(80)							
4:10.47	Zakia	Mrisho	TAN	19.2.84	5		Cuxhaven	9 Jul
4:10.50	Amy	Rudolph	USA	18.9.73	8		Carson	22 May
4:10.55	Carrie	Tollefson	USA	18.1.77	1		Padova	3 Jul
4:10.61	Tiffany	McWilliams	USA	20.10.82	9		Carson	22 May
4:10.69	Lisa	Corrigan	AUS	2.12.84	5		Kassel	10 Jun
4:11.07	Julie	Coulaud	FRA	7.8.82	7		Villeneuve d'Ascq	12 Jun
4:11.08	Christina	Carruzzo	SUI	9.1.81	6		Kassel	10 Jun
4:11.11		Xie Sainan	CHN-J	3.11.86	3	NG	Nanjing	19 Oct
4:11.29	Birhane	Hirpassa	ETH	30.7.83	2		Padova	3 Jul
4:11.42	Svetlana	Klimkovich	BLR	26.8.80	2	NC	Brest	3 Jul
	(90)							
4:11.58	Nouria	Mérah-Benida	ALG	19.10.70	4		Braaschaat	24 Jul
4:11.64	Daniela	Yordanova	BUL	8.3.76	9h2	WCh	Helsinki	12 Aug
4:11.67	Mihaela	Olaru	ROM	7.2.82	1		Kalamáta	30 May
4:11.72	Jolene	Byrne	IRL	26.10.77	1	NC	Dublin (S)	24 Jul
4:11.73	Maria	McCambridge	IRL	10.7.75	2	NC	Dublin (S)	24 Jul
4:11.79	Yelena	Samokhvalova	RUS	21.11.80	4		Tula	24 Jul
4:11.89	Rachael	Ogden	GBR	23.7.79	2		London (CP)	6 Aug
4:12.02	Tatyana	Andrianova	RUS	10.12.79	2		Moskva	29 Jun
4:12.09	Saida	El Mehdi	MAR	21.9.81	1	NC	Rabat	26 Jun
4:12.12	Alice	Schmidt	USA	3.10.81	10		Carson	22 May
	(100)							

Mark	Name		Nat	Born	Date
4:12.14	Ragnhild	Kvarberg	NOR	23.3.81	24 Jul
4:12.15		Sun Qiuhong	CHN	13.10.78	18 Oct
4:12.26	Krisztina	Papp	HUN	17.12.82	7 Jul
4:12.29	Angela	Rinicella	ITA	7.5.82	1 Jun
4:12.29	Sheila	Chepkirui	KEN-Y	27.12.90	15 Jul
4:12.31	Kara	Goucher	USA	9.7.78	17 Jul
4:12.4	Anastasiya	Starovoytova	BLR	4.11.82	23 May
4:12.58	Liana	Gabdullina	RUS	24.4.81	24 Jul
4:12.67	Hayley	Tullett	GBR	17.2.73	10 Jul
4:12.71	Chanelle	Olivier	RSA-J	15.9.86	16 Dec
4:12.73		Zhu Xiaolin	CHN	20.2.84	18 Oct
4:12.77	Nicole	Teter	USA	8.11.73	26 Mar
4:12.79		Lin Yuan	CHN-Y	11.2.88	18 Oct
4:12.81		Zhuang Yanmei	CHN	27.12.84	18 Oct
4:12.85	Olga	Komyagina	RUS	10.2.74	13 Jul
4:12.85	Yuriko	Kobayashi	JPN-Y	12.12.88	19 Sep
4:12.86	Minori	Hayakari	JPN	29.11.72	19 Sep
4:12.93	Livia	Tóth	HUN	7.1.80	27 May
4:12.97A	Viola	Kibiwott	KEN	22.12.83	25 Jun
4:13.01	Susanne	Wigene	NOR	12.2.78	4 Jun
4:13.02	Malindi	Elmore	CAN	13.3.80	22 May
4:13.07	Elena	Iagar	ROM	16.1.75	4 Jun
4:13.07		Li Lihua	CHN-J	7.2.86	19 Oct
4:13.13	Paula	Radcliffe	GBR	17.12.73	4 Jun
4:13.20	Margarita	Plaksina	RUS	1.10.77	13 Jul
4:13.21	Mary Jayne	Harrelson	USA	17.6.78	22 May
4:13.26	Justyna	Lesman	POL	6.11.80	9 Jul
4:13.34	Eva	Arias	ESP	1.1.80	4 Jun
4:13.36	Johanna	Nilsson	SWE	27.3.83	11 Jun
4:13.44	Natalya	Kutkina	RUS	4.2.77	13 Jul
4:13.55		Wang Shijuan	CHN-J	9.7.86	19 Oct
4:13.59	Tatyana	Borisova	KGZ	3.6.76	18 Jun
4:13.63	Lauren	Fleshman	USA	26.9.81	1 May
4:13.64	Arianna	Lambie	USA	12.6.85	11 Jun
4:13.79	Yukari	So	JPN	20.4.84	25 Jun
4:13.83	Svetlana	Lukashova	KAZ	2.5.77	1 Sep
4:13.84	Natalya	Pantelyeva	RUS	18.8.83	13 Jun
4:13.87	Philes	Ongori	KEN-J	19.7.86	21 Aug
4:13.93	Roisin	McGettigan	IRL	23.8.80	24 Jul
4:13.99	Binnaz	Uslu	TUR	12.3.85	19 Jun
4:14.2A	Mary	Wangari	KEN-J	4.10.86	17 Jun
4:14.29	Fatiha Bahi	Azzouhoum	ALG	8.3.83	18 Jun
4:14.41	Natalie	Harvey	GBR	19.1.75	25 Jun
4:14.5A	Isabella	Ochichi	KEN	28.10.79	17 Jun
4:14.57	Erin	Donohue	USA	8.5.83	11 Jun
4:14.62	Yimenashu	Taye	ETH	79	11 Jul
4:14.7A	Ines	Chenonge	KEN	1.2.82	17 Jun
4:14.75	Kelly	Reid	IRL	17.6.78	24 Jul
4:14.77	Natalya	Korneyeva	RUS	22.3.77	13 Jul
4:14.79	Natalie	Lewis	GBR	25.5.82	25 Jun
4:14.80	Beth	Brewster	USA	18.2.80	10 Jun
4:14.81	Shannon	Rowbury	USA	14.9.84	23 Apr
4:14.82	Isabel	Macias	ESP	11.8.84	23 Jun
4:14.87	Emma	Rilen	AUS	3.11.84	12 Feb
4:14.87	Safa	Issaoui	TUN	23.1.85	18 Jun
4:14.92	Dorcus	Inzikuru	UGA	2.2.82	11 Jun
4:14.93	Emily	Morris	AUS	23.10.78	9 Jul
4:14.93	Sabrina	Mockenhaupt	GER	6.12.80	9 Jul
4:15.00	Hayley	Ovens	GBR	5.12.75	3 Sep
4:15.01	Jane	Wanjiku	KEN	14.6.79	6 Jul
4:15.12	Morag	MacLarty	GBR-J	10.2.86	24 Jul
4:15.21	Marina	Muncan	SCG	6.11.82	9 Jun
4:15.26	Margaret	Chirchir	KEN	5.12.78	27 May
4:15.3	Yuneysi	Santiusty	CUB	24.12.84	24 Feb
4:15.30	Tatyana	Pashnina	RUS	27.8.80	30 May
4:15.33	Sara	Palmas	ITA	7.7.77	26 Jun
4:15.40	Lisa	Labrecque	CAN	22.2.77	10 Jun
4:15.45	Mihaela	Neacsu	ROM	3.5.79	30 May
4:15.46	Yekaterina	Martynova	RUS-J	12.6.86	24 Jul
	(169)				

Indoors

Mark	Name		Nat	Born	Pos	Meet	Venue	Date
4:03.09	Elena	Iagar	ROM	16.1.75	1	EI	Madrid	5 Mar
4:04.84	Lidia	Chojecka	POL	25.1.77	1		Karlsruhe	13 Feb
4:07.59	Anna	Alminova	RUS	17.1.85	4		Karlsruhe	13 Feb
4:08.73	Konstadina	Efedáki	GRE	1.10.78	3		Stuttgart	29 Jan
4:10.98	Tezeta	Desalegn-Dengersa	TUR	8.4.80	4		Madrid	24 Feb
4:11.14	Carmen	Rüdiger	GER	15.8.73	4		Stuttgart	29 Jan

Mark	Name		Nat	Born	Date
4:13.10	Margarita	Plaksina	RUS	1.10.77	30 Jan
4:14.71	Irina	Lishchinska	UKR	15.1.76	20 Feb

Symbols/Abbreviations

+ intermediate time in longer race, A made at altitude of 1000m or higher, H made in a heptathlon, h made in a heat, qf quarter-final, sf semi-final, i indoors, Q qualifying round, r race number, -J juniors, -Y youths (born 1988 or later)

JUNIORS

See main list for top 4 juniors. 10 performances by 4 women to 4:11.69. Additional marks and further juniors:

Name	Mark	Pos	Meet	Venue	Date	Mark	Pos	Meet	Venue	Date
Burka	4:04.77	8	WCh	Helsinki	14 Aug	4:07.62	4	GP	Sevilla	4 Jun
	4:04.97	1	FBK	Hengelo	29 May	4:10.1A	1	NC	Addis Ababa	3 May
	4:07.35	2h2	WCh	Helsinki	12 Aug					
Liu Qing	4:11.69	1h2	NG	Nanjing	18 Oct					

Mark	Name		Nat	Born	Pos	Meet	Venue	Date
4:12.29	Sheila	Chepkirui	KEN-Y	27.12.90	1	WY	Marrakech	15 Jul
4:12.71	Chanelle	Olivier	RSA	15.9.86	1		Parow	16 Dec
4:12.79		Lin Yuan	CHN-Y	11.2.88	5h2	NG	Nanjing	18 Oct
4:12.85	Yuriko	Kobayashi	JPN-Y	12.12.88	4		Yokohama	19 Sep
4:13.07		Li Lihua	CHN	7.2.86	6	NG	Nanjing	19 Oct
4:13.55	(10)	Wang Shijuan	CHN	9.7.86	7	NG	Nanjing	19 Oct
4:13.87	Philes	Ongori	KEN-	19.7.86	1		Sapporo	21 Aug
4:14.2A	Mary	Wangari	KEN-	4.10.86	1	NC	Nairobi	17 Jun
4:15.12	Morag	MacLarty	GBR	10.2.86	1	EJ	Kaunas	24 Jul
4:15.46	Yekaterina	Martynova	RUS-	12.6.86	2	EJ	Kaunas	24 Jul
4:15.57	Heidi	Magill	USA	15.2.86	5	NCAA	Sacramento	11 Jun
4:15.68	Jelena	Stina	LAT	11.5.86	1		Valmiera	1 Jul
4:15.77	Azra	Eminovic	SCG-Y	14.4.88	3	EJ	Kaunas	24 Jul
4:16.2 A	Irene	Chelagat	KEN-Y	89	2		Nairobi	7 May
4:16.20	Rebecca	Forlong	NZL	13.7.86	4		Dublin	30 Jul
4:16.26	Maggie	Infeld (0)	USA	10.4.86	6h2	NCAA	Sacramento	9 Jun

1 MILE

Mark	Name		Nat	Born	Pos	Meet	Venue	Date
4:28.29	Yelena	Kanales	RUS	7.2.76	1	NC	Tula	14 Jun
4:28.90	Natalya	Pavlovskaya	RUS	30.4.75	2	NC	Tula	14 Jun
4:29.60	Yekaterina	Volkova	RUS	16.2.78	3	NC	Tula	14 Jun
4:31.17	Olesya	Chumakova	RUS	23.7.81	4	NC	Tula	14 Jun
4:32.00	Olesya	Syreva	RUS	25.11.83	5	NC	Tula	14 Jun
4:32.25	Carrie	Tollefson	USA	18.1.77	1		Falmouth	13 Aug
4:32.68	Jenelle	Deatherage	USA	25.9.77	2		Falmouth	13 Aug

Mark	Name		Nat	Born	Date	Mark	Name		Nat	Born	Date
4:32.81	Lindsey	Gallo	USA	29.11.81	13 Aug	4:35.07	Treniere	Clement	USA	27.10.81	30 Apr
4:33.73	Oksana	Zbrozhek	RUS	12.1.78	15 Jun	4:35.24	Margarita	Plaksina	RUS	1.10.77	15 Jun
4:34.50	Nadezhda	Rakhimkulova	RUS	5.11.79	15 Jun	4:35.55	Collette	Liss	USA	29.4.73	13 Aug

Indoors

Mark	Name		Nat	Born	Pos	Meet	Venue	Date
4:28.43	Carmen	Douma-Hussar	CAN	12.3.77	1		New York	22 Jan
4:31.91	Hilary	Edmondson	CAN	7.8.81	3		New York	22 Jan
4:31.92	Amy	Rudolph	USA	18.9.73	1		Boston	12 Feb
4:32.33	Kenia	Sinclair	JAM	14.7.80	1		Gainesville	4 Mar
4:32.35	Roisín	McGettigan	IRL	23.8.80	2		Boston	12 Feb

Mark	Name		Nat	Born	Date	Mark	Name		Nat	Born	Date
4:33.69	Sarah	Schwald	USA	2.1.73	4 Feb	4:35.61	Amy	Mortimer	USA	16.8.81	22 Jan
4:34.53	Susanne	Pumper	AUT	1.9.70	5 Feb	4:35.69	Lisa	Labrecque	CAN	22.2.77	22 Jan

2000 METRES

Mark	Name		Nat	Born	Pos	Meet	Venue	Date
5:41.01+	Naomi	Mugo	KEN	2.1.77	1	in 3k	Oslo	29 Jul
5:41.6+	Jo	Pavey	GBR	20.9.73	2	in 3k	Oslo	29 Jul
5:41.9+	Maryam	Jamal	BRN	16.9.84	3	in 3k	Oslo	29 Jul
5:42.0+	Getenesh	Wami	ETH	11.12.74	4	in 3k	Oslo	29 Jul
5:42.3+	Isabella	Ochichi	ETH	28.10.79	5	in 3k	Oslo	29 Jul
5:42.7+	Tirunesh	Dibaba	ETH	1.6.85	1	in 3k	New York (RI)	11 Jun
5:42.9+	Ines	Chenonge	KEN	1.2.82	6	in 3k	Oslo	29 Jul
5:43.0+	Derebe	Alemu	ETH	5.6.83	7	in 3k	Oslo	29 Jul
5:45.45+	Olga	Komyagina	RUS	10.2.74	1	in 5k	Sheffield	21 Aug
5:46.6+	Ejegayehu	Dibaba	ETH	25.6.82	4	in 5k	Sheffield	21 Aug

Indoors

Mark	Name		Nat	Born	Pos	Meet	Venue	Date
5:40.86+i	Meseret	Defar	ETH	19.11.83	1	In 3k	Boston (R)	29 Jan
5:41.4+	Jo	Pavey	GBR	20.9.73	2	in 3k	Birmingham	18 Feb
5:43.80+i	Berhane	Adere	ETH	21.7.73	1	in 3k	Stuttgart	29 Jan
5:44.98i	Sabrina	Mockenhaupt	GER	6.12.80	1		Leipzig	6 Feb

Mark	Name		Nat	Born	Date	Mark	Name		Nat	Born	Date
5:48.80i	Carmen	Rüdiger	GER	15.8.73	6 Feb	5:49.89i	Yelena	Kanales	RUS	7.2.76	7 Jan

3000 METRES

Mark	Name		Nat	Born	Pos	Meet	Venue	Date
8:28.87	Maryam	Jamal	BRN	16.9.84	1	Bisl	Oslo	29 Jul
8:29.45		Jamal			1	WK	Zürich	19 Aug
8:31.27	Edith	Masai	KEN	4.4.67	1	Gaz	Saint Denis	1 Jul
8:31.42	Isabella	Ochichi	KEN	28.10.79	2	Bisl	Oslo	29 Jul
8:31.89	Berhane	Adere	ETH	21.7.73	2	WK	Zürich	19 Aug
8:33.57	Meseret	Defar	ETH	19.11.83	1		New York (RI)	11 Jun
8:33.59		Ochichi			2	Gaz	Saint Denis	1 Jul

Mark	Name		Nat	Born	Pos	Meet	Venue	Date
8:33.79	Jo	Pavey	GBR	20.9.73	3	Bisl	Oslo	29 Jul
8:34.51		Ochichi			3	WK	Zürich	19 Aug
8:34.66		Pavey			3	Gaz	Saint Denis	1 Jul
8:34.73	Meselech	Melkamu	ETH	19.4.85	4	WK	Zürich	19 Aug
8:35.11	Yelena	Zadorozhnaya	RUS	3.12.77	4	Gaz	Saint Denis	1 Jul
8:35.41	Bouchra	Ghézielle	FRA	18.5.79	5	Gaz	Saint Denis	1 Jul
8:36.22	Getenesh	Wami (10)	ETH	11.12.74	4	Bisl	Oslo	29 Jul
8:36.39	Werknesh	Kidane	ETH	21.11.81	2		New York (RI)	11 Jun
8:38.9+	Tirunesh	Dibaba	ETH	1.6.85	1		New York (RI)	11 Jun
8:39.53		Ghzielle			5	WK	Zürich	19 Aug
8:39.75		Defar			1	SGP	Doha	13 May
8:39.87		Adere			2	SGP	Doha	13 May
8:39.90	Gelete	Burka	ETH-J	15.2.86	3	SGP	Doha	13 May
8:39.91	Zakia	Mrisho	TAN	19.2.84	6	WK	Zürich	19 Aug
	(21/14)							
8:40.23	Susanne	Wigene	NOR	12.2.78	7	WK	Zürich	19 Aug
8:40.76	Alice	Timbilil	KEN	16.6.83	6	Gaz	Saint Denis	1 Jul
8:40.82	Liliya	Shobukhova	RUS	13.11.77	7	Gaz	Saint Denis	1 Jul
8:41.85	Priscila	Jepleting	KEN	26.6.80	4	SGP	Doha	13 May
8:42.03	Galina	Bogomolova	RUS	15.10.77	8	Gaz	Saint Denis	1 Jul
8:42.10	Derebe	Alemu	ETH	5.6.83	6	Bisl	Oslo	29 Jul
	(20)							
8:42.38	Ines	Chenonge	KEN	1.2.82	7	Bisl	Oslo	29 Jul
8:42.8+e	Ejegayehu	Dibaba	ETH	25.6.82	3	VD	Bruxelles	26 Aug
8:43.95	Lauren	Fleshman	USA	26.9.81	1		Lappeenranta	21 Jul
8:44.22	Wioletta	Janowska	POL	9.6.77	8	Bisl	Oslo	29 Jul
8:45.50	Krisztina	Papp	HUN	17.12.82	9	Bisl	Oslo	29 Jul
8:46.38	Sabrina	Mockenhaupt	GER	6.12.80	10	Bisl	Oslo	29 Jul
8:49.02	Amy	Rudolph	USA	18.9.73	11	Bisl	Oslo	29 Jul
8:50.18	Paula	Radcliffe	GBR	17.12.73	1	ECp-1B	Leiria	18 Jun
8:50.40	Maria	McCambridge	IRL	10.7.75	3	GP	Madrid	16 Jul
8:50.43	Kim	Smith	NZL	19.11.81	2		Lappeenranta	21 Jul
	(30)							
8:51.12	Sarah	Jamieson	AUS	24.3.75	1		Canberra	5 Feb
8:51.85	Kayoko	Fukushi	JPN	25.3.82	9	Gaz	Saint Denis	1 Jul
8:52.06	Kathy	Butler	GBR	22.10.73	3		Lappeenranta	21 Jul
8:52.16	Benita	Johnson	AUS	6.5.79	4	GP	Madrid	16 Jul
8:52.21	Hind	Dehiba	FRA	17.3.79	10	WK	Zürich	19 Aug
8:52.31	Evelyne	Wambui	KEN-J	4.4.86	1		Kobe	13 Oct
8:52.33	Yuriko	Kobayashi	JPN-Y	12.12.88	1		Kobe	13 Oct
8:52.62+		Sun Yingjie ¶	CHN	3.10.77	1+	WCh	Helsinki	13 Aug
8:52.9A	Veronica	Nyarwai Wanjiru	KEN-Y	29.10.89	1	NC-j	Nairobi	16 Jun
8:53.46	Emily	Chebet	KEN-J	18.2.86	11	Gaz	Saint Denis	1 Jul
	(40)							
8:53.5+		Xing Huina	CHN	25.2.84	8	in 5k	Helsinki	13 Aug
8:53.83	Carmen	Douma-Hussar	CAN	12.3.77	9	WAF	Monaco	10 Sep
8:53.9+	Olga	Kravtsova	BLR	25.6.81	9=	in 5k	Helsinki	13 Aug
8:54.00	Elvan	Abeylegesse	TUR	11.9.82	1	ECCp	Lagos	28 May
8:54.43	Shalane	Flanagan	USA	7.8.81	5		New York (RI)	11 Jun
8:54.49	Irene	Kwambai	KEN	25.10.78	4	Gugl	Linz	23 Aug
8:54.64	Yekaterina	Volkova	RUS	16.2.78	2	Znam	Kazan	24 Jun
8:54.84	Shayne	Culpepper	USA	3.12.73	1		Eugene	7 May
8:55.13	Alesya	Turova	BLR	6.12.79	2	ECp-1B	Leiria	18 Jun
8:55.77	Konstadína	Efedáki	GRE	1.10.78	5	Gugl	Linz	23 Aug
	(50)							
8:55.87	Naomi	Mugo	KEN	2.1.77	9	SGP	Doha	13 May
8:55.89	Yelena	Soboleva	RUS	3.8.82	3		Sochi	27 May
8:56.07	Jen	Rhines	USA	1.7.74	6		New York (RI)	11 Jun

Mark	Name		Nat	Born	Date
8:56.38	Alla	Zhilyayeva	RUS	5.2.69	24 Jun
8:58.53	Viktoriya	Klimina	RUS	1.3.76	27 May
8:58.87	Tatyana	Krivobok	UKR	17.1.72	27 May
8:59.83	Missy	Buttry	USA	14.12.82	21 Jul
8:59.87	Rose	Chepchumba	KEN	14.3.79	3 Jun
9:00.0 A	Pauline	Korikwang	KEN-Y	1.3.88	15 Jun
9:00.34	Belainesh	Gebre Zemedkun	ETH-J	23.12.87	13 May
9:00.61	Yimenashu	Taye	ETH	.79	11 Jun
9:00.71	Maria	Martins	FRA	1.4.74	18 Jun
9:00.71	Sara	Bei	USA	15.4.83	21 Jul
9:00.74	Antje	Möldner	GER	13.6.84	27 Apr
9:00.87	Yelena	Sidorchenkova	RUS	30.5.80	5 Jun
9:01.61	Nuria	Fernández	ESP	16.8.76	18 Jun
9:01.86	Mestawet	Tadesse	ETH	19.7.85	11 Jun
9:02.29	Jolene	Byrne	IRL	26.10.77	2 Jul
9:02.43	Ashu	Kasim	ETH	.85	7 Jun
9:02.44	Olesya	Syreva	RUS	25.11.83	5 Jun
9:02.84	Mihaela	Botezan	ROM	21.11.76	18 Jun
9:02.85	Lisa	Dobriskey	GBR	23.12.83	15 Jun
9:03.09	Yumi	Sato	JPN	22.12.76	29 Jun
9:03.09	Mary	Cullen	IRL	17.8.82	21 Jul
9:03.09	Susanne	Pumper	AUT	1.9.70	23 Aug
9:03.74	Nancy	Kiprop	KEN	12.12.79	7 Jun
9:04.12+	Margaret	Maury	FRA	15.5.74	17 Jun
9:04.20	Fernanda	Ribeiro	POR	23.6.69	11 Jun
9:04.33	Sharon	Dickie-Thompson	USA	1.8.79	5 Jun

Mark	Name		Nat	Born	Date	Mark	Name		Nat	Born	Date
9:04.6A	Agnes	Chenonge	KEN		7 May	9:05.02	Sarah	Schwald	USA	2.1.73	23 Aug
9:04.60	Marina	Ivanova	RUS	30.6.83	24 Jun	9:05.06	Liana	Gabdullina	RUS	24.4.81	24 Jun
9:04.69	Etalemahu	Kidane	ETH	14.2.83	4 Jun	9:05.49	Sally	Barsosio	KEN	21.3.78	13 May
9:04.70	Regina	Rakhimkulova	RUS	5.11.79	24 Jun	9:05.56	Marta	Domínguez	ESP	3.11.75	16 Jul
9:04.88	Olga	Rosseyeva	RUS	1.8.81	24 Jun	9:05.94	Sonia	O'Sullivan	IRL	28.11.69	2 Jul

Unconfirmed: 8:49.7 Khadidja Touati ALG .79 Constantine 9 Jun

Indoors

Mark	Name		Nat	Born	Pos	Meet	Venue	Date
8:30.05	Meseret	Defar	ETH	19.11.83	1		Boston (R)	29 Jan
8:33.05		Defar			1	GP	Birmingham	18 Feb
8:37.91		Adere			1		Stuttgart	29 Jan
8:43.76	Lidia	Chojecka	POL	25.1.77	1	EI	Madrid	6 Mar
8:46.65	Tezeta	Desalegn-Dengersa	TUR	8.4.80	2	EI	Madrid	6 Mar
8:46.67	Sentayehu	Ejigu	ETH	21.6.85	2		Boston (R)	29 Jan
8:47.51	Susanne	Pumper	AUT	1.9.70	3		Stuttgart	29 Jan
8:49.61	Kim	Smith	NZL	19.11.81	3		Boston (R)	29 Jan
8:49.80	Tatyana	Golovchenko	UKR	13.2.80	5		Stuttgart	29 Jan
8:51.75	Marina	Bastos	POR	7.7.71	6		Stuttgart	29 Jan
8:51.76	Maria	Martins	FRA	1.4.74	2		Gent	6 Feb
8:53.57	Veerle	Dejaeghere	BEL	1.8.73	4		Gent	6 Feb
8:53.80	Yuliya	Chizhenko	RUS	30.8.79	2	NC	Volgograd	10 Feb
8:53.95	Konstadína	Efedáki	GRE	1.10.78	5	GP	Birmingham	18 Feb
8:54.42	Sarah	Schwald	USA	2.1.73	4		Boston (R)	29 Jan
8:56.27	Silvia	Weissteiner	ITA	13.7.79	5	EI	Madrid	6 Mar

Mark	Name		Nat	Born	Date	Mark	Name		Nat	Born	Date
8:56.83	Yelena	Kanales	RUS	7.2.76	10 Feb	9:00.78	Siham	Hilali	MAR-J	2.5.86	18 Feb
8:57.65	Jessica	Augusto	POR	8.11.81	6 Feb	9:00.90	Lyubov	Ivanova	RUS	2.3.81	10 Feb
8:58.17	Inês	Monteiro	POR	18.5.80	6 Feb	9:01.24	Marina	Ivanova	RUS	30.6.83	10 Feb
8:58.17	Megan	Metcalfe	CAN	27.1.82	25 Feb	9:02.90	Amy	Mortimer	USA	16.8.81	29 Jan
8:59.20	Carmen	Douma-Hussar	CAN	12.3.77	29 Jan	9:03.82	Teyiba	Erkesso	ETH	28.9.82	29 Jan
9:00.37	Regina	Rakhimkulova	RUS	5.11.79	10 Feb	9:04.32	Helen	Clitheroe	GBR	2.1.74	18 Feb

JUNIORS

See main list for top 5 juniors. 6 performances by 4 women under 9:00.0. Additional marks and further juniors:

Name	Mark	Pos	Meet	Venue	Date
Burka	8:48.65	2	WAF	Monaco	10 Sep
Chebet	8:53.69	5	GP	Madrid	16 Jul

Mark	Name		Nat	Born	Pos	Meet	Venue	Date
9:00.0 A	Pauline	Korikwang	KEN-Y	1.3.88	2	NC-j	Nairobi	15 Jun
9:00.34	Belainesh	Gebre Zemedkun	ETH	23.12.87	10	SGP	Doha	13 May
9:00.78i	Siham	Hilali	MAR	2.5.86	7	GP	Birmingham	18 Feb
9:06.3A	Beatrice	Chepngeno	KEN-Y	26.1.88	3	NC-j	Nairobi	15 Jun
9:08.86	Hitomi	Niiya	JPN-Y	26.2.88	1		Okayama	18 Jun
9:08.93	Emily	Pluck-Brichacek	AUS-Y	7.7.90	1		Canberra	29 Oct
9:10.7	Daniela	Fetcere	LAT-Y	18.8.90	1		Valmiera	25 May

5000 METRES

Mark	Name		Nat	Born	Pos	Meet	Venue	Date
14:28.98	Meseret	Defar	ETH	19.11.83	1	VD	Bruxelles	26 Aug
14:31.09	Berhane	Adere	ETH	21.7.73	2	VD	Bruxelles	26 Aug
14:32.42	Tirunesh	Dibaba	ETH	1.6.85	1		New York (RI)	11 Jun
14:32.57		T Dibaba			1	GGala	Roma	8 Jul
14:32.79		Adere			2	GGala	Roma	8 Jul
14:32.90		Defar			3	GGala	Roma	8 Jul
14:37.20	Edith	Masai	KEN	4.4.67	4	GGala	Roma	8 Jul
14:37.34	Ejegayehu	Dibaba	ETH	25.6.82	3	VD	Bruxelles	26 Aug
14:38.07		E Dibaba			5	GGala	Roma	8 Jul
14:38.21	Isabella	Ochichi	KEN	28.10.79	4	VD	Bruxelles	26 Aug
14:38.59		T Dibaba			1	WCh	Helsinki	13 Aug
14:38.97	Meselech	Melkamu	ETH	19.4.85	6	GGala	Roma	8 Jul
14:39.54		Defar			2	WCh	Helsinki	13 Aug
14:40.71	Jo	Pavey	GBR	20.9.73	7	GGala	Roma	8 Jul
14:42.47		E Dibaba			3	WCh	Helsinki	13 Aug
14:43.47		Melkamu			4	WCh	Helsinki	13 Aug
14:43.64		Xing Huina	CHN	25.2.84	5	WCh	Helsinki	13 Aug
14:43.87	Zakia	Mrisho (10)	TAN	19.2.84	6	WCh	Helsinki	13 Aug
16:00.46- 04								
14:44.00	Priscila	Jepleting	KEN	26.6.80	7	WCh	Helsinki	13 Aug
14:45.14		Ochichi			8	WCh	Helsinki	13 Aug
14:45.87		Defar			1	WAF	Monaco	9 Sep
14:46.37		E Dibaba			2		New York (RI)	11 Jun
14:46.84		T Dibaba			2	WAF	Monaco	9 Sep
14:46.91		Adere			3	WAF	Monaco	9 Sep
14:47.06	Alice	Timbilil	KEN	16.6.83	8	GGala	Roma	8 Jul
14:47.07	Liliya	Shobukhova	RUS	13.11.77	9	WCh	Helsinki	13 Aug

Mark	Name		Nat	Born	Pos	Meet	Venue	Date
14:47.56		Adere			1	ISTAF	Berlin	4 Sep
14:47.75	Olga	Kravtsova	BLR	25.6.81	10	WCh	Helsinki	13 Aug
14:48.53	Susanne	Wigene	NOR	12.2.78	5	VD	Bruxelles	26 Aug
14:50.96		Ochichi			1	FBK	Hengelo	29 May
	(30/15)							
14:51.11	Sentayehu	Ejigu	ETH	21.6.85	9	GGala	Roma	8 Jul
14:51.19		Sun Yingjie ¶	CHN	3.10.77	11	WCh	Helsinki	13 Aug
14:51.47	Gelete	Burka	ETH-J	15.2.86	10	GGala	Roma	8 Jul
14:51.68	Maryam	Jamal	BRN	16.9.84	2	FBK	Hengelo	29 May
14:53.22	Kayoko	Fukushi	JPN	25.3.82	12	GGala	Roma	8 Jul
	(20)							
14:54.43	Ines	Chenonge	KEN	1.2.82	4	WAF	Monaco	9 Sep
14:54.98	Marta	Domínguez	ESP	3.11.75	13	GGala	Roma	8 Jul
14:56.76	Irene	Kwambai	KEN	25.10.78	6	VD	Bruxelles	26 Aug
14:58.58	Getenesh	Wami	ETH	11.12.74	2	NA	Heusden-Zolder	23 Jul
14:59.07	Margaret	Maury	FRA	15.5.74	3	NA	Heusden-Zolder	23 Jul
15:00.20	Lucy	Wangui	KEN	24.3.84	5	WAF	Monaco	9 Sep
15:00.56	Derebe	Alemu	ETH	5.6.83	4	NA	Heusden-Zolder	23 Jul
15:01.6+	Werknesh	Kidane	ETH	21.11.81	1+	GP II	Stanford	29 May
15:02.52	Lauren	Fleshman	USA	26.9.81	15	GGala	Roma	8 Jul
15:03.10	Jelena	Prokopcuka	LAT	21.9.76	3	DNG	Stockholm	26 Jul
	(30)							
15:03.59	Amy	Rudolph	USA	18.9.73	5	DNG	Stockholm	26 Jul
15:05.68	Kim	Smith	NZL	19.11.81	6	DNG	Stockholm	26 Jul
15:06.49	Bezunesh	Bekele	ETH	18.9.83	4	FBK	Hengelo	29 May
15:06.74	Evelyne	Wambui	KEN-J	4.4.86	1		Kobe	15 Oct
15:07.17	Workitu	Ayanu	ETH-J	19.4.87	5	NA	Heusden-Zolder	23 Jul
15:07.89	Jane	Wanjiku	KEN	14.6.79	2		Nobeoka	21 May
15:08.03	Maria	Protópappa	GRE	5.5.73	6	NA	Heusden-Zolder	23 Jul
15:08.28	Mary Mureithi	Wangari	KEN	9.4.78	3		Nobeoka	21 May
15:08.38	Wioletta	Janowska	POL	9.6.77	2	ECp-S	Firenze	17 Jun
15:08.59	Elvan	Abeylegesse	TUR	11.9.82	1	ECCp	Lagos	29 May
	(40)							
15:08.65	Krisztina	Papp	HUN	17.12.82	8	VD	Bruxelles	26 Aug
15:09.39	Sabrina	Mockenhaupt	GER	6.12.80	1	NC	Wattenscheid	2 Jul
15:09.49	Philes	Ongori	KEN-J	19.7.86	3	GP II	Osaka	7 May
15:10.26	Lornah	Kiplagat	NED	20.3.74	6	FBK	Hengelo	29 May
15:10.96	Shalane	Flanagan	USA	7.8.81	1	NC	Carson	23 Jun
15:11.17	Yukiko	Akaba	JPN	18.10.79	2		Yokohama	27 Nov
15:11.42	Minori	Hayakari	JPN	29.11.72	7	NA	Heusden-Zolder	23 Jul
15:11.70	Kathy	Butler	GBR	22.10.73	7	DNG	Stockholm	26 Jul
15:12.39	Jen	Rhines	USA	1.7.74	8	DNG	Stockholm	26 Jul
15:13.1A	Veronica	Nyarwai Wanjiru	KEN-Y	29.10.89	2	WCT	Nairobi	25 Jun
	(50)							
15:13.36	Mihaela	Botezan	ROM	21.11.76	3	ECp-S	Firenze	17 Jun
15:14.15	Evelyne	Kimwei	KEN-J	25.8.87	4		Nobeoka	21 May
15:15.78	Renee	Metivier	USA	25.12.81	8	NA	Heusden-Zolder	23 Jul
15:15.85	Yelena	Zadorozhnaya	RUS	3.12.77	7	ISTAF	Berlin	4 Sep
15:16.26	Etalemahu	Kidane	ETH	14.2.83	7	FBK	Hengelo	29 May
15:16.29+	Paula	Radcliffe	GBR	17.12.73	1+	WCh	Helsinki	6 Aug
15:16.44	Hayley	Yelling	GBR	3.1.74	9	NA	Heusden-Zolder	23 Jul
15:17.55	Kara	Goucher	USA	9.7.78	10	NA	Heusden-Zolder	23 Jul
15:17.92	Alla	Zhilyayeva	RUS	5.2.69	2	NC	Tula	12 Jul
15:18.69	Simret	Sultan	ERI	20.7.84	19	GGala	Roma	8 Jul
	(60)							
15:19.68	Yumi	Sato	JPN	22.12.76	2		Sapporo	6 Jul
15:19.73	Veerle	Dejaeghere	BEL	1.8.73	21	GGala	Roma	8 Jul
15:20.10	Souad	Aït Salem	ALG	6.1.79	9	DNG	Stockholm	26 Jul
15:20.45	Jessica	Augusto	POR	8.11.81	11	NA	Heusden-Zolder	23 Jul
15:21.02	Benita	Johnson	AUS	6.5.79	1		Melbourne	17 Feb
15:21.23	Anikó	Kálovics	HUN	13.5.77	22	GGala	Roma	8 Jul
15:21.70	Yuri	Kano	JPN	27.10.78	4		Sapporo	6 Jul
15:22.35		Zhu Xiaolin	CHN	20.2.84	2	NG	Nanjing	22 Oct
15:23.24	Katie	McGregor	USA	2.9.77	10	DNG	Stockholm	26 Jul
15:23.30	Asmae	Leghzaoui	MAR	30.8.76	2	MedG	Almeria	30 Jun
	(70)							
15:23.31	Shayne	Culpepper	USA	3.12.73	4	NC	Carson	23 Jun
15:23.61	Terumi	Asoshina	JPN	2.8.82	2	Oda	Hiroshima	29 Apr
15:24.13	Carrie	Tollefson	USA	18.1.77	5	NC	Carson	23 Jun
15:24.74	Sara	Bei	USA	15.4.83	6	NC	Carson	23 Jun

Mark		Name	Nat	Born	Pos	Meet	Venue	Date
15:24.88	Amy	Begley	USA	11.1.78	7	NC	Carson	23 Jun
15:25.21	Julia	Mombi	KEN	25.1.85	3		Marugame	23 Sep
15:25.36		Xi Qiuhong	CHN	4.9.84	3	NG	Nanjing	22 Oct
15:25.47	Natalie	Harvey	GBR	19.1.75	13	NA	Heusden-Zolder	23 Jul
15:25.52	Hitomi	Miyai	JPN	18.3.85	2		Naka	15 May
15:25.59	Hiromi	Ominami	JPN	15.11.75	4	NC	Tokyo	4 Jun
	(80)							
15:25.67	Ruth	Wanjiru	KEN	11.9.81	4		Marugame	23 Sep
15:26.21		Sun Weiwei	CHN	13.1.85	4	NG	Nanjing	22 Oct
15:26.50		Jiang Yuanyuan	CHN-J	20.12.86	5	NG	Nanjing	22 Oct
15:26.60	Blake	Russell	USA	24.7.75	2	GP II	Stanford	29 May
15:27.06		Zhang Chong	CHN-J	5.1.86	6	NG	Nanjing	22 Oct
15:27.18	Doris	Changeywo	KEN	12.12.84	11	FBK	Hengelo	29 May
15:27.60	Kayo	Sugihara	JPN	24.2.83	6	NC	Tokyo	4 Jun
15:27.84		Dai Yanyan	CHN	8.1.80	7	NG	Nanjing	22 Oct
15:28.23	Michiko	Ogawa	JPN	30.12.83	5		Sapporo	6 Jul
15:28.26	Win	Fridam	KEN	16.4.85	6		Marugame	23 Sep
	(90)							
15:28.51	Kiyomi	Ogawa	JPN	15.9.81	6		Sapporo	6 Jul
15:28.55	Silvia	Weissteiner	ITA	13.7.79	3	MedG	Almeria	30 Jun
15:28.70	Hitomi	Niiya	JPN-Y	26.2.88	1		Isahaya	3 Dec
15:28.93	Megumi	Yoshino	JPN	26.6.84	7	NC	Tokyo	4 Jun
15:29.06		Bai Xue	CHN-Y	13.12.88	8	NG	Nanjing	22 Oct
15:29.19		Bao Guiying	CHN-J	20.1.86	9	NG	Nanjing	22 Oct
15:29.45	Yukari	So	JPN	20.4.84	5		Nobeoka	21 May
15:29.82	Takako	Kotorida	JPN	2.4.77	7		Sapporo	6 Jul
15:29.88	Sarah	Jamieson	AUS	24.3.75	1		Melbourne (N)	19 Nov
15:29.96	Yoshiko	Fujinaga	JPN	15.8.81	8	NC	Tokyo	4 Jun
	(100)							

Mark		Name	Nat	Born	Date
15:31.18	Tomoko	Hatori	JPN	28.5.81	21 May
15:31.80	Amane	Gobena	ETH	1.9.82	9 Jun
15:31.81		Zhu Yanmei	CHN-J	16.10.86	22 Oct
15:31.91	Yoshimi	Ozaki	JPN	1.7.81	29 Apr
15:32.05	Sara	Slattery	USA	2.10.81	23 Jun
15:32.72	Yelena	Samokhvalova	RUS	21.11.80	12 Jul
15:32.74	Marie	Davenport	IRL	24.1.75	1 May
15:33.17	Nicole	Aish	USA	8.3.76	23 Jun
15:33.60	Noriko	Matsuoka	JPN	2.5.79	21 May
15:33.65		Cha Caijuan	CHN	21.1.85	22 Oct
15:33.66	Saori	Nejyo	JPN	16.5.82	27 Nov
15:33.98	Chiaki	Iwamoto	JPN	6.3.85	7 May
15:34.07	Mika	Okunaga	JPN	27.10.82	21 May
15:34.35	Kaori	Oyama	JPN	6.12.82	10 Dec
15:34.40	Mari	Ozaki	JPN	16.7.75	9 Apr
15:34.41	Yurika	Nakamura	JPN-J	1.4.86	10 Dec
15:34.47	Catherine	Berry	GBR	8.10.75	1 May
15:34.71	Yumiko	Okamoto	JPN	28.3.78	21 May
15:34.79		Zhou Chunxiu	CHN	8.3.79	11 Jun
15:35.41		Dong Xiaoqin	CHN	2.1.83	22 Oct
15:35.45	Inês	Monteiro	POR	18.5.80	23 Jul
15:35.83	Tatyana	Golovchenko	UKR	13.2.80	23 Jul
15:35.84	Natalya	Berkut	UKR	30.5.75	17 Jun
15:35.90	Madoka	Ogi	JPN	26.10.83	21 May
15:36.01	Adriana	Pîrtea	ROM	31.1.80	24 Jul
15:36.29	Tomoko	Ishii	JPN	14.10.83	6 Jul
15:36.74	Miki	Ohira	JPN	28.6.81	29 Apr
15:37.08	Sonia	Bejarano	ESP	2.8.81	30 Jun
15:37.59	Eri	Sato	JPN-J	5.4.86	23 Oct
15:37.72	Miriam	Wangari	KEN	22.2.79	1 Jun
15:38.03	Miwako	Yamanaka	JPN	24.5.78	7 May
15:38.34	Fernanda	Ribeiro	POR	23.6.69	19 Jun
15:38.34		Jin Man	CHN	5.12.84	22 Oct
15:38.63	Ayako	Suzuki	JPN	17.12.80	6 Jul

Mark		Name	Nat	Born	Date
15:38.72	Marina	Dubrova	UKR	9.12.78	2 Jul
15:39.31	Mizuho	Nasukawa	JPN	22.11.79	23 Oct
15:39.38	Yukari	Takahashi	JPN	15.2.80	23 Oct
15:39.45	Ida	Nilsson	SWE	8.2.81	15 Apr
15:39.50	Mestawet	Tufa	ETH	14.9.83	29 May
15:39.54	Miki	Oyama	JPN	22.10.79	15 May
15:40.03	Kumi	Tsuguma	JPN	23.8.81	23 Sep
15:40.22	Marie	Yamagishi	JPN	16.10.85	10 Dec
15:40.74		Chen Xiaofang	CHN	28.10.81	22 Oct
15:40.79+	Mersha	Alemayehu	ETH		2 Apr
15:41.20	Yuka	Izumi	JPN	18.1.85	10 Dec
15:41.67		Lee Eun-jung	KOR	21.4.81	3 Sep
15:41.76	Kerryn	McCann	AUS	2.5.67	17 Feb
15:41.83	Yuka	Kakimi	JPN-J	4.4.86	15 Oct
15:42.22	Dorcus	Inzikuru	UGA	2.2.82	12 Jun
15:42.24	Beatrice	Chepchumba	KEN	25.11.83	9 Jun
15:42.52	Harumi	Hiroyama	JPN	2.9.68	29 Apr
15:42.53	Mizuki	Noguchi	JPN	3.7.78	11 Jun
15:42.70	Vera	Notz-Umberg	SUI	3.1.76	23 Jul
15:42.99	Yoko	Shibui	JPN	14.3.79	15 May
15:43.18	Siri Merete	Alfheim Espin	NOR	6.7.76	21 Aug
15:43.2A	Sally	Barsosio	KEN	21.3.78	17 Jun
15:43.31	Olga	Rosseyeva	RUS	1.8.81	12 Jul
15:43.39	Yoko	Miyauchi	JPN	19.6.83	6 Jul
15:43.42	Reiko	Tosa	JPN	11.6.76	15 May
15:43.57	Ikuko	Nagao	JPN	7.1.82	15 Oct
15:43.73	Yuki	Saito	JPN	25.9.80	25 Jun
15:43.88	Jesica	Obare	KEN		2 Jun
15:44.10	Noriko	Takayama	JPN	27.8.85	15 May
15:44.34	Fatiha	Fauvel-Klilech	FRA	1.2.75	30 Jun
15:44.65	Dulce M	Rodríguez	MEX	14.8.72	10 Aug
15:45.03	Renate	Rungger	ITA	6.9.79	15 May
15:45.22	Sakura	Sato	JPN	17.11.84	15 May
15:45.69	Akemi	Ozaki	JPN	12.10.77	23 Jul
15:45.86mx	Charlotte	Dale (169)	GBR	23.3.84	15 May

Indoors

Mark		Name	Nat	Born	Pos	Venue	Date
14:32.93i		T Dibaba			1	Boston (R)	29 Jan
14:50.46i	Kim	Smith	NZL	19.11.81	1	Boston (A)	11 Feb
15:42.81i	Lindsey	Scherf	USA-J	13.9.86			3 Dec

Drugs Disqualification: 15:33.17 Zhang Yuhong ¶ CHN 15.1.83 16 Apr

JUNIORS

See main list for top 11 juniors. 12 performances by 6 women under 15:17.0. Additional marks and further juniors:

Burka	15:01.84	3		Shanghai	17 Sep				
Wambui	15:09.3	1		Takamatsu	8 Oct	15:16.69	3	Sapporo	6 Jul
Ongori	15:10.58	1	JPN Ch	Tokyo	4 Jun	15:14.6	1	Kofu	16 Jul
	15:10.97	3		Yokohama	27 Nov				

Mark		Name	Nat	Born	Pos	Meet	Venue	Date
15:31.81		Zhu Yanmei	CHN-J	16.10.86	10	NG	Nanjing	22 Oct
15:34.41	Yurika	Nakamura	JPN-J	1.4.86	2		Himeji	10 Dec
15:37.59	Eri	Sato	JPN-J	5.4.86	3	NSF	Okayama	23 Oct
15:41.83	Yuka	Kakimi	JPN-J	4.4.86	4		Kobe	15 Oct
15:42.81i	Lindsey	Scherf	USA-J	13.9.86	1		Boston	3 Dec
15:46.3 A	Esther	Chemutai	KEN	6.6.87	2	NC	Nairobi	17 Jun
15:48.0 A	Mercy	Wanjiru Njoroge	KEN	10.6.86	3	NC	Nairobi	17 Jun
15:48.37	Risa	Shigemoto	JPN	29.8.87	2r2		Isahaya	3 Dec
15:49.21	Yuka	Takashima	JPN-Y	12.5.88	3r2		Isahaya	3 Dec
Top European: 16:04.46	Emily	Pidgeon	GBR-Y	1.6.89	1		Manchester (C)	21 May

10,000 METRES

Mark		Name	Nat	Born	Pos	Meet	Venue	Date
30:15.67	Tirunesh	Dibaba	ETH	1.6.85	1		Sollentuna	28 Jun
30:18.39	Ejegayehu	Dibaba	ETH	25.6.82	2		Sollentuna	28 Jun
30:19.39	Werknesh	Kidane	ETH	21.11.81	1	GP II	Stanford	29 May
30:24.02		T Dibaba			1	WCh	Helsinki	6 Aug
30:25.41	Berhane	Adere	ETH	21.7.73	2	WCh	Helsinki	6 Aug
30:26.00		E Dibaba			3	WCh	Helsinki	6 Aug
30:27.18		Xing Huina	CHN	25.2.84	4	WCh	Helsinki	6 Aug
30:30.26	Edith	Masai	KEN	4.4.67	5	WCh	Helsinki	6 Aug
30:32.47		Kidane			6	WCh	Helsinki	6 Aug
30:33.53		Sun Yingjie ¶	CHN	3.10.77	7	WCh	Helsinki	6 Aug
30:33.75	Galina	Bogomolova	RUS	15.10.77	8	WCh	Helsinki	6 Aug
30:42.75	Paula	Radcliffe	GBR	17.12.73	9	WCh	Helsinki	6 Aug
30:51.99		Masai			1		Utrecht	17 Jun
30:55.67	Irene	Kwambai (10)	KEN	25.10.78	2		Utrecht	17 Jun
30:55.80		Kwambai			10	WCh	Helsinki	6 Aug
31:00.73		Xing			1	NG	Nanjing	17 Oct
31:03.75	Kayoko	Fukushi	JPN	25.3.82	11	WCh	Helsinki	6 Aug
31:03.90		Sun			2	NG	Nanjing	17 Oct
31:04.55	Jelena	Prokopcuka	LAT	21.9.76	12	WCh	Helsinki	6 Aug
31:04.61		Bogomolova			1	NC	Tula	14 Jun
31:09.03		Zhou Chunxiu	CHN	8.3.79	2	NG	Nanjing	17 Oct
31:10.68	Bezunesh	Bekele	ETH	18.9.83	3		Utrecht	17 Jun
31:12.57	Yelena	Samokhvalova	RUS	21.11.80	2	NC	Tula	14 Jun
31:14.27	Alla	Zhilyayeva	RUS	5.2.69	3	NC	Tula	14 Jun
31:17.97		Zhilyayeva			13	WCh	Helsinki	6 Aug
31:18.96	Amy	Rudolph	USA	18.9.73	1		Stanford	1 May
31:20.58	Lydiya	Grigoryeva	RUS	21.1.74	4	NC	Tula	14 Jun
31:21.00	Kim	Smith	NZL	19.11.81	2		Stanford	1 May
31:21.20	Katie	McGregor (20)	USA	2.9.77	14	WCh	Helsinki	6 Aug
31:21.28	Sabrina	Mockenhaupt	GER	6.12.80	1	EChall	Barakaldo	2 Apr
	(30/21)							
31:21.92	Elva	Dryer	USA	26.9.71	3		Stanford	1 May
31:22.37	Lucy	Wangui	KEN	24.3.84	1		Kobe	24 Apr
31:23.55	Terumi	Asoshina	JPN	2.5.82	2		Kobe	24 Apr
31:24.33	Yumiko	Hara	JPN	9.1.82	3		Kobe	24 Apr
31:25.33	Dulce M	Rodríguez	MEX	14.8.72	4		Stanford	1 May
31:26.66	Jen	Rhines	USA	1.7.74	16	WCh	Helsinki	6 Aug
31:27.35		Bao Guiying	CHN-J	20.1.86	3	NG	Nanjing	17 Oct
31:28.88		Bai Xue	CHN-Y	13.12.88	4	NG	Nanjing	17 Oct
31:29.81	Rose	Chepchumba	KEN	14.3.79	4		Utrecht	17 Jun
	(30)							
31:30.71	Derebe	Alemu	ETH	5.6.83	5		Utrecht	17 Jun
31:31.64		Xi Qiuhong	CHN	4.9.84	5	NG	Nanjing	17 Oct
31:34.15	Mari	Ozaki	JPN	16.7.75	4		Kobe	24 Apr
31:34.79	Harumi	Hiroyama	JPN	2.9.68	2	NC	Tokyo	2 Jun
31:35.18	Hiromi	Ominami	JPN	15.11.75	3	NC	Tokyo	2 Jun
31:35.25	Blake	Russell	USA	24.7.75	2	NC	Carson	24 Jun
31:37.24	Hitomi	Miyai	JPN	18.3.85	4	NC	Tokyo	2 Jun
31:38.81	Mary Mureithi	Wangari	KEN	9.4.78	1		Shizuoka	3 May
31:38.84	Jane	Wanjiku	KEN	14.6.79	2		Shizuoka	3 May
31:40.34	Kazue	Ogoshi	JPN	2.3.81	5	NC	Tokyo	2 Jun
	(40)							
31:42.51	Evelyne	Kimwei	KEN-J	25.8.87	1		Kobe	15 Oct
31:42.67	Julia	Mombi	KEN	25.1.85	7		Kobe	24 Apr
31:43.02	Miki	Ohira	JPN	28.6.81	8		Kobe	24 Apr
31:44.29	Mizuki	Noguchi	JPN	3.7.78	1		Naruto	13 May
31:45.08	Deena	Kastor	USA	14.2.73	4	NC	Carson	24 Jun

Mark	Name		Nat	Born	Pos	Meet	Venue	Date
31:45.4A	Alice	Timbilil	KEN	16.6.83	1	WCT	Nairobi	25 Jun
31:46.53	Kathy	Butler	GBR	22.10.73	1	NC	Watford	11 Jun
31:47.23	Yoshimi	Ozaki	JPN	1.7.81	9		Kobe	24 Apr
31:48.95	Yumi	Sato	JPN	22.12.76	6	NC	Tokyo	2 Jun
31:53.61	Hayley	Yelling	GBR	3.1.74	2	NC	Watford	11 Jun
	(50)							
31:55.15	Benita	Johnson	AUS	6.5.79	19	WCh	Helsinki	6 Aug
31:56.07	Viktoriya	Klimina	RUS	1.3.76	5	NC	Tula	14 Jun
31:58.49	Tomoko	Hatori	JPN	28.5.81	7	NC	Tokyo	2 Jun
31:59.18	Michiko	Ogawa	JPN	30.12.83	9	NC	Tokyo	2 Jun
31:59.37	Adanech	Zekiros	ETH	26.3.82	3		Sollentuna	28 Jun
31:59.56	Kiyomi	Ogawa	JPN	15.9.81	10	NC	Tokyo	2 Jun
31:59.94	Workitu	Ayanu	ETH-J	19.4.87	6		Utrecht	17 Jun
32:00.08	Tomoko	Ishii	JPN	14.10.83	1		Fukagawa	29 Jun
32:03.22	Fernanda	Ribeiro	POR	23.6.69	2	EChall	Barakaldo	2 Apr
32:07.66	Reiko	Tosa	JPN	11.6.76	4		Shizuoka	3 May
	(60)							
32:08.19	Mika	Okunaga	JPN	27.10.82	12	NC	Tokyo	2 Jun
32:09.67	Megumi	Oshima	JPN	4.9.75	13	NC	Tokyo	2 Jun
32:09.94	Yuki	Saito	JPN	25.9.80	14	NC	Tokyo	2 Jun
32:09.95	Yoko	Yagi	JPN	14.4.80	7		Utrecht	17 Jun
32:10.24	Yuri	Kano	JPN	27.10.78	15	NC	Tokyo	2 Jun
32:10.28	Doris	Changeywo	KEN	12.12.84	8		Utrecht	17 Jun
32:10.72	Madoka	Ogi	JPN	26.10.83	16	NC	Tokyo	2 Jun
32:11.14	Maya	Nishio	JPN	19.12.78	17	NC	Tokyo	2 Jun
32:11.40	Noriko	Matsuoka	JPN	2.5.79	9		Utrecht	17 Jun
32:12.33	Susanne	Pumper	AUT	1.9.70	1	NC	Salzburg	7 May
	(70)							
32:12.67	Akane	Taira	JPN	3.11.82	13		Kobe	24 Apr
32:13.70	Souad	Aït Salem	ALG	6.1.79	10		Utrecht	17 Jun
32:14.18	Merima	Hashim	ETH	.81	2	GP II	Stanford	29 May
32:15.70	Laura	O'Neill	USA	29.7.80	6	NC	Carson	24 Jun
32:17.49	Tatyana	Petrova	RUS	8.4.83	6	NC	Tula	14 Jun
32:17.59	Yumiko	Okamoto	JPN	28.3.78	2		Naka	14 May
32:18.03	Megumi	Yoshino	JPN	26.6.84	4		Fukagawa	29 Jun
32:18.05	Yoko	Miyauchi	JPN	19.6.83	5		Fukagawa	29 Jun
32:19.48		Sun Wenqing	CHN	2.6.81	6	NG	Nanjing	17 Oct
32:22.12	Hiroko	Miyauchi	JPN	19.6.83	2		Kitakyushu	14 May
	(80)							
32:23.87	Margaret	Maury	FRA	15.5.74	4	EChall	Barakaldo	2 Apr
32:24.5A	Susan	Chepkemei	KEN	25.6.75	3	WCT	Nairobi	25 Jun
32:25.21	Miki	Oyama	JPN	22.10.79	21	NC	Tokyo	2 Jun
32:25.83	Inga	Abitova	RUS	6.3.82	7	NC	Tula	14 Jun
32:27.79	Ruth	Wanjiru	KEN	11.9.81	5		Marugame	24 Sep
32:27.8A	Caroline	Cheptanui	KEN	13.5.83	5	WCT	Nairobi	25 Jun
32:28.02	Aya	Manome	JPN	30.8.82	23	NC	Tokyo	2 Jun
32:28.10		Zhang Chong	CHN-J	5.1.86	7	NG	Nanjing	17 Oct
32:28.29	Mihaela	Botezan	ROM	21.11.76	23	WCh	Helsinki	6 Aug
32:28.96	Natalya	Berkut	UKR	30.5.75	8	RUS Ch	Tula	14 Jun
	(90)							
32:29.29	Kayo	Sugihara	JPN	24.2.83	6		Fukagawa	29 Jun
32:29.79	Olga	Romanova	RUS	23.5.80	9	NC	Tula	14 Jun
32:30.48	Zivile	Balciunaite	LTU	3.4.79	10	RUS Ch	Tula	14 Jun
32:30.83	Philes	Ongori	KEN-J	19.7.86	18		Kobe	24 Apr
32:31.14	Kiragu	Wanguru	KEN	26.8.80	7		Fukagawa	29 Jun
32:32.42	Kaori	Oyama	JPN	6.12.82	9		Fukagawa	29 Jun
32:32.55	Win	Fridam	KEN	16.4.85	3		Kobe	15 Oct
32:33.22	Sylvia	Mosqueda	USA	8.4.66	1	MSR	Walnut	15 Apr
32:33.89	Yoshiko	Fujinaga	JPN	15.8.81	5		Shizuoka	3 May
32:34.11	Yoko	Shibui	JPN	14.3.79	24	NC	Tokyo	2 Jun
	(100)							

Mark	Name		Nat	Born	Date
32:34.17	Eyerusalem	Kuma	ETH	4.11.81	28 Jun
32:35.00	Irina	Timofeyeva	RUS	5.4.70	14 Jun
32:36.57	Mara	Yamauchi	GBR	13.8.73	11 Jun
32:37.00	Yasuyo	Iwamoto	JPN	8.9.76	14 May
32:38.66		Jiang Chengcheng	CHN-J	5.11.86	17 Oct
32:39.61	Krisztina	Papp	HUN	17.12.82	8 May
32:42.42	Norie	Takahashi	JPN	22.4.80	3 May
32:43.20	Miwako	Yamanaka	JPN	24.5.78	1 May
32:43.35		Lee Eun-jeong	KOR	21.4.81	29 Jun
32:43.54	Tara	Quinn	CAN	19.9.79	1 May
32:43.77	Jolene	Byrne	IRL	28.10.77	2 Apr
32:43.87	Josephine	Wairimu	KEN		15 Oct
32:44.19	Teresa	Recio	ESP	7.7.63	17 Jul
32:44.51	Caroline	Bierbaum	USA	7.11.83	7 May
32:45.62	Rina	Fujioka	JPN	18.10.83	24 Apr
32:46.62	Kaoru	Nishi	JPN	28.11.83	29 Jun
32:47.79	Kim	Fitchen-Young	USA	3.9.68	25 Mar
32:47.98	Miho	Notagashira	JPN	17.8.83	13 May
32:49.02	Miho	Ichikawa	JPN	20.5.73	29 Jun
32:49.16	Yoshiko	Hosokawa	JPN	17.8.81	29 Jun
32:49.44	Ayako	Suzuki	JPN	17.12.80	2 Jun
32:49.68	Natalie	Harvey	GBR	19.1.75	1 May

Mark		Name	Nat	Born	Date
32:51.20	Lindsey	Scherf	USA-J	13.9.86	7 May
32:51.56	Yesenia	Centeno	ESP	27.6.71	17 Jul
32:52.59	Kana	Yoshida	JPN	27.4.84	24 Apr
32:52.94	Yurika	Nakamura	JPN-J	1.4.86	14 May
32:53.38	Mayumi	Yoshida	JPN-J	7.1.86	29 Jun
32:53.46	Nami	Kurosawa	JPN	26.12.78	13 May
32:56.0A	Monica	Wangare	KEN-J	4.10.86	30 Apr
32:56.18	Yuki	Sato	JPN	28.5.84	14 May
32:56.50		Dong Xiaoqin	CHN	2.1.83	17 Oct
32:57.03	Ryoko	Eda	JPN	12.6.76	29 Jun
32:57.61	Mary	Cullen	IRL	17.8.82	15 Apr
32:58.60	Elza	Kireyeva	RUS	26.3.77	14 Jun
32:58.68	Kayoko	Obata	JPN	18.9.71	24 Sep
32:59.2A	Dinah	Kipkoech	KEN		30 Apr
32:59.24	Asmae	Leghzaoui	MAR	30.8.76	29 Jun
32:59.54	Alevtina	Ivanova	RUS	22.5.75	14 Jun
32:59.97	Keiko	Isogai	JPN	22.7.81	14 May
33:00.77	Mika	Kawamura	JPN	9.11.79	14 May
33:01.57	Viktoria	Zuyeva	RUS	9.6.83	14 Jun
33:02.13	Annie	Bersagel	USA	30.3.81	25 Mar
33:02.21	Sara	Slattery	USA	2.10.81	9 Jun
33:02.35	Yuko	Machida	JPN	11.8.80	14 May
33:02.80	Masami	Sakata	JPN	11.10.84	24 Sep
33:04.34	Annemari	Hyvärinen (Sandell)	FIN	2.1.77	28 Aug
33:05.28	Sabrina	Monroe	USA	5.6.80	25 Mar
33:05.36	Mónica	Rosa	POR	5.5.78	2 Apr
33:05.71	Jennifer	Crain	USA	12.2.68	15 Apr
33:06.83	Elena	Moreno	ESP	14.3.79	17 Jul
33:07.94	Silvia	Skvortsova	RUS	16.11.74	14 Jun
33:08.75	Dolores	Pulido	ESP	1.10.74	2 Apr
33:09.33		Zhang Yuhong	CHN	15.1.83	17 Apr
33:10.33	Ayumi	Nakayama	JPN	10.9.85	24 Sep
33:10.61	Rodica	Moroianu	FRA	18.11.70	17 Jun
33:12.01	Alessandra	Aguilar	ESP	1.7.78	2 Apr
33:12.71	Shiori	Ishiyama	JPN	28.6.84	24 Apr
33:13.25	Mai	Endo	JPN-J	22.12.86	15 Oct
33:13.27	M.Luisa	Larraga	ESP	10.12.70	17 Jul
33:14.02	Yukiko	Matsuo	JPN	10.9.84	24 Sep
33:14.76		Zhu Yanmei	CHN-J	16.10.86	17 Apr
(161)					

JUNIORS

See main list for top 6 juniors. 10 performances by 6 women under 32:48.0. Additional marks and further juniors:

Bao Guiying 32:35.07 1 EAsG Macao 1 Oct 32:43.71 1 Yichin 17 Apr

Ongori 32:47.05 1 Marugame 24 Sep

Mark		Name	Nat	Born	Pos	Meet	Venue	Date
32:38.66		Jiang Chengcheng	CHN	5.11.86	8	NG	Nanjing	17 Oct
32:51.20	Lindsey	Scherf	USA	13.9.86	2		New York	7 May
32:52.94	Yurika	Nakamura	JPN	1.4.86	1		Miyoshi	14 May
32:53.38	Mayumi	Yoshida (10)	JPN	7.1.86	15		Fukagawa	29 Jun
32:56.0A	Monica	Wangare	KEN	4.10.86	1		Nakuru	30 Apr
33:13.25	Mai	Endo	JPN	22.12.86	5		Kobe	15 Oct
33:14.76		Zhu Yanmei	CHN	16.10.86	5		Yichun	17 Apr
33:15.06		Chen Rong	CHN-Y	18.5.88	6		Yichun	17 Apr
33:23.41		Zhang Yingjie	CHN	6.10.86	12	NG	Nanjing	17 Oct
33:32.58	Eri	Sato	JPN	5.4.86	1		Yokohama	28 May
33:55.41	Veronicah	Kanyi	KEN	6.2.88	1		Yuwa	3 Sep
33:56.13	Andrea	Walkonen	USA	25.9.86	10	MSR	Walnut	15 Apr
33:58.34	Yuki	Kogochi	JPN	86	1		Tokyo	13 May
34:01.64	Yumi	Sumida (20)	JPN	86	2		Tokyo	13 May

10 KILOMETRES ROAD

Mark		Name	Nat	Born	Pos	Meet	Venue	Date
30:27	Isabella	Ochichi	ETH	28.10.79	1	Cres C	New Orleans	26 Mar
30:45	Paula	Radcliffe	GBR	17.12.73	2	Cres C	New Orleans	26 Mar
31:10	Asmae	Leghzaoui	MAR	30.8.76	1		Cleveland	22 May
31:16		Radcliffe			1		Madrid	31 Dec
31:25	Irene	Kwambai	KEN	25.10.78	1		Barcelona	3 Apr
31:25	Grace	Momanyi	KEN	3.3.82	1		Ottawa	22 May
Others where superior to track bests								
31:28	Lornah	Kiplagat	NED	20.3.74	1		Manchester	22 May
31:38	Benita	Johnson	AUS	6.5.79	2		Barcelona	3 Apr
31:45	Luminita	Zaituc	GER	9.10.68	1		Ottendorf	11 Sep
31:46	Hilda	Kibet	KEN	.81	3		Manchester	22 May
31:57	Alevtina	Ivanova	RUS	22.5.75	2		Cape Elizabeth	6 Aug
31:58	Anikó	Kálovics	HUN	13.5.77	1		Budapest	16 Oct
31:59	Michiko	Ogawa	JPN	30.12.83	3		Karatsu	13 Feb
32:02	Helen	Kiprop	KEN	.85	1		Caen	24 Sep
32:05	Doris	Chengeywo	KEN	12.12.84	3		Glasgow	15 May
32:07+	Constantina	Tomescu	ROM	23.1.70	1	in HMar	Edmonton	1 Oct
32:08	Sally	Barsosio	KEN	21.3.78	3	Cres C	New Orleans	26 Mar
32:10+	Derartu	Tulu	ETH	21.3.72	1	in HMar	Newcastle	18 Sep
32:13	Charlotte	Dale	GBR	23.3.84	1		Ashford	6 Feb
32:13	Kana	Yoshida	JPN	27.4.84	4		Karatsu	13 Feb
32:16	Eunice	Chepkorir	KEN	.81	1		Paderborn	26 Mar
32:18	Sonia	O'Sullivan	IRL	28.11.69	2		Dublin	9 Apr
32:20	Tatyana	Petrova	RUS	8.4.83	4	Cres C	New Orleans	26 Mar
32:20	Helen	Clitheroe	GBR	2.1.74	1		Clitheroe	27 Dec
32:21	Jolene	Byrne	IRL	26.10.77	3		Dublin	9 Apr
32:22	Yuka	Kakimi	JPN-J	4.4.86	2		Otawara	23 Nov
32:25	Teyiba	Erkiso	ETH	.82	1		Ratingen	2 Jan
32:25	Rose	Cheruiyot	KEN	21.7.76	1		Marseille	1 May
32:27	Masako	Chiba	JPN	18.7.76	2		Cleveland	22 May
32:28	Marie	Davenport	IRL	24.1.75	2		Boston	10 Oct
32:30	Lydia	Cheromei	KEN	11.5.77	1		Punta del Este	6 Jan

Mark	Name		Nat	Born	Pos	Meet	Venue	Date
32:30	Nicole	Stevenson	CAN	13.9.74	1		Vancouver	17 Apr
32:32	Albina	Ivanova	RUS	16.5.77	3		Cleveland	22 May
32:33	Teresa	Wanjuku	KEN	7.4.74	3		Ottawa	28 May

Mark	Name		Nat	Born	Date
32:37	Winfridah	Kebaso	JPN	16.4.85	23 Dec
32:40	Nancy	Kiprop	KEN	7.7.79	3 Apr
32:40	Tegla	Loroupe	KEN	9.5.73	15 May
32:40	Aster	Demissie	ETH	.84	10 Oct
32:41	Tatyana	Gladyr	UKR	17.4.75	26 Mar
32:43	Silvia	Skvortsova	RUS	16.11.74	27 Feb
32:43	Miriam	Wangari	KEN	22.2.79	5 May
32:43	Samira	Chellah	ALG	29.12.79	20 Nov
32:45	Kelly	Keane	USA	25.8.72	19 Mar
32:45	Olga	Kimaiyo	KEN		21 Aug
32:45	Amy	Begley	USA	11.1.78	10 Oct
32:46	Amina	Godana	ETH-J	.86	2 Jan
32:46	Eriko	Iwata	JPN	5.12.84	23 Nov
32:47	Asha	Gigi	ETH	15.10.73	26 Jun
32:48	Teresa	Wangui	KEN-J		23 Dec
32:49	Zakia	Mrisho	TAN	19.2.84	22 May
32:50	Yukiko	Akaba	JPN	18.10.79	13 Feb
32:53	Joyce	Chepchumba	KEN	6.11.70	15 May
32:56	Yelena	Burykina	RUS	7.5.72	19 Mar
32:57	Fatiha	Fauvel-Klilech	FRA	1.2.75	1 May
32:59	Maria	McCambridge	IRL	10.7.75	22 May
32:59+	Evelyne	Kimwei	KEN-J	25.8.87	23 Dec
33:00	Julia	Bleasdale	GBR	9.9.81	3 Apr
33:00	Christelle	Daunay	FRA	5.12.74	9 Sep
33:00	Carrie	Tollefson	USA	18.1.77	10 Oct

Downhill courses

Mark	Name		Nat	Born	Pos	Meet	Venue	Date
31:17	Lornah	Kiplagat	NED	20.3.74	1	Peach	Atlanta	4 Jul
31:52	Sally	Barsosio	KEN	21.3.78	2	Peach	Atlanta	4 Jul
32:32	Luminita	Talpos	ROM	9.10.72	4	Peach	Atlanta	4 Jul

Morlaix, Oct 30: 1. Jesica Obare KEN 32:17, 2. Alice Mogire KEN-J .87 32:35, 3. Esther Wanjiru KEN 27.3.77 32:49

15 KILOMETRES ROAD

Mark	Name		Nat	Born	Pos	Meet	Venue	Date
47:48+ dh	Derartu	Tulu	ETH	21.3.72	1	in HMar	Newcastle	18 Sep
47:48	Berhane	Adere	ETH	21.7.73	1		Nijmegen	20 Nov
48:00	Rose	Cheruiyot	KEN	21.7.76	2		Nijmegen	20 Nov
48:32	Bezunesh	Bekele	ETH	18.9.83	1		s'Heerenberg	4 Dec
48:34+ dh	Paula	Radcliffe	GBR	17.12.73	1	in Mar	London	17 Apr
48:41	Isabella	Ochichi	KEN	28.10.79	1		Puy-en-Velay	1 May
48:42+	Constantina	Tomescu	ROM	23.1.70	1	in HMar	Edmonton	1 Oct
49:00+	Terumi	Asoshina	JPN	2.5.82	1	in HMar	Yamaguchi	13 Mar
49:00+	Catherine	Ndereba	KEN	21.7.72	1	in HMar	Sapporo	3 Jul
49:00	Mestawet	Tufa	ETH	14.9.83	3		Nijmegen	20 Nov
49:02+ dh	Yasuyo	Iwamoto	JPN	8.9.76	2	in HMar	Sapporo	3 Jul
49:04+ dh	Mizuki	Noguchi	JPN	3.7.78	3	in HMar	Sapporo	3 Jul
	49:22+				1	in Mar	Berlin	25 Sep
49:12	Margaret	Okayo	KEN	30.5.76	1		Luanda	31 Dec
49:18+ dh	Megumi	Oshima	JPN	4.9.75	4	in HMar	Sapporo	3 Jul
49:20+ dh	Hiromi	Ominami	JPN	15.11.75	5	in HMar	Sapporo	3 Jul
49:21	Jen	Rhines	USA	1.7.74	1	NC	Jacksonville	12 Mar
49:34+	Kana	Yoshida	JPN	27.4.84	2	in HMar	Yamaguchi	13 Mar
49:42	Elva	Dryer	USA	26.9.71	2	NC	Jacksonville	12 Mar
49:43+	Susan	Chepkemei	KEN	25.6.75	2=	in HMar	Edmonton	1 Oct
49:43+	Lornah	Kiplagat	NED	2.5.74	2=	in HMar	Edmonton	1 Oct
49:46	Blake	Russell	USA	24.7.75	3	NC	Jacksonville	12 Mar
49:48+ dh	Eri	Hayakawa	JPN	15.11.81	6=	in HMar	Sapporo	3 Jul
49:48+ dh	Yoko	Yagi	JPN	14.4.80	6=	in HMar	Sapporo	3 Jul
49:49+	Madoka	Ogi	JPN	26.10.83	3=	in HMar	Yamaguchi	13 Mar
49:49+	Hitomi	Miyai	JPN	18.3.85	3=	in HMar	Yamaguchi	13 Mar
49:51	Colleen	de Reuck	USA	13.4.64	4	NC	Jacksonville	12 Mar
49:52+	Evelyne	Kimwei	KEN-J	25.8.87	1	in HMar	Okayama	23 Dec
49:53	Elizabeth	Rumokol	KEN	.84	1		Porto	15 Jun
49:54+	Yumiko	Hara	JPN	9.1.82	5	in HMar	Yamaguchi	13 Mar
49:56+	Akane	Taira	JPN	3.11.82	6	in HMar	Yamaguchi	13 Mar
49:56+	Fumi	Murata	JPN	13.3.75	7	in HMar	Yamaguchi	13 Mar
49:56+	Galina	Bogomolova	RUS	15.10.77	4	in HMar	Edmonton	1 Oct
50:02+ dh	Masako	Chiba	JPN	18.7.76	8	in HMar	Sapporo	3 Jul
50:03	Emily	Chebet	KEN-J	18.2.86	2		Porto	15 Jun
50:05+	Lidia	Simon	ROM	4.9.73	1	in HMar	Miyazaki	6 Jan
50:06+	Harumi	Hiroyama	JPN	2.9.68	2	in HMar	Miyazaki	6 Jan
50:07+	Yoko	Miyauchi	JPN	19.6.83	3	in HMar	Miyazaki	6 Jan
50:07+	Miho	Notagashira	JPN	17.8.83	5	in HMar	Miyazaki	6 Jan

Mark	Name		Nat	Born	Date
50:11	Sally	Barsosio	KEN	21.3.78	10 Jul
50:15+	Ayoko	Suzuki	JPN	17.12.80	6 Jan
50:17+	Hiroko	Miyauchi	JPN	19.6.83	6 Jan
50:18	Rose	Chepchumba	KEN	14.3.79	31 Dec
50:20+	Yuko	Machida	JPN	11.8.80	6 Jan
50:23+	Ruth	Wanjiru	KEN	11.9.81	13 Mar
50:24	Fatima	Baouf	BEL	15.7.70	24 Apr
50:25	Ana	Dias	POR	15.1.74	15 Jun
50:27+	Rie	Ueno	JPN	11.6.76	13 Mar
50:29+	Michiko	Ogawa	JPN	30.12.83	13 Mar

10 MILES ROAD

Mark	Name		Nat	Born	Pos	Meet	Venue	Date
51:08	Isabella	Ochichi	KEN	28.10.79	1		Zaandam	18 Sep
51:13	Susan	Chepkemei	KEN	25.6.75	2		Zaandam	18 Sep
51:18+ dh	Derartu	Tulu	ETH	21.3.72	1	GNR	Newcastle	18 Sep

Mark	Name		Nat	Born	Pos	Meet	Venue	Date
51:27		Tulu			1	GSR	Portsmouth	9 Oct
51:30	Gete	Wami	ETH	11.12.74	3		Zaandam	18 Sep
51:33	Rose	Cheruiyot	KEN	21.7.76	4		Zaandam	18 Sep
51:36+	Deena	Kastor	USA	14.2.73	1	in HMar	Philadelphia	18 Sep
52:01	Nuta	Olaru	ROM	18.8.70	1		Washington, DC	3 Apr
52:06+ dh	Paula	Radcliffe	GBR	17.12.73	1	in Mar	London	17 Apr
52:18	Derebe	Alemu	ETH	5.6.83	2	GSR	Portsmouth	9 Oct
52:28	Anikó	Kálovics	HUN	13.5.77	3	GSR	Portsmouth	9 Oct
53:03	Hayley	Yelling	GBR	3.1.74	4	GSR	Portsmouth	9 Oct
53:08	Hilda	Kibet	KEN	.81	5		Zaandam	18 Sep
53:17	Alevtina	Ivanova	RUS	22.5.75	2		Washington, DC	3 Apr
53:21	Charlotte	Dale	GBR	23.3.84	1		Folkestone	2 Mar
53:46	Olga	Kimaiyo	KEN		5	GSR	Portsmouth	9 Oct
53:48+	Werknesh	Kidane	ETH	21.11.81	1	in HMar	Virginia Beach	4 Sep
53:49+	Asha	Gigi	ETH	15.10.73	2=	in HMar	Virginia Beach	4 Sep
53:49+	Naoko	Takahashi	JPN	6.5.72	2=	in HMar	Virginia Beach	4 Sep
53:50+	Selina	Kosgei	KEN	16.11.76	4=	in HMar	Virginia Beach	4 Sep
53:50+	Ikuko	Nagao	JPN	7.1.82	4=	in HMar	Virginia Beach	4 Sep
53:50+	Mihaela	Botezan	ROM	21.11.76	4=	in HMar	Virginia Beach	4 Sep
53:55	Liz	Yelling	GBR	5.12.74	6	GSR	Portsmouth	9 Oct
54:16	Tatyana	Gladyr	UKR	17.4.75	3		Washington, DC	3 Apr

20 KILOMETRES ROAD

Mark	Name		Nat	Born	Pos	Meet	Venue	Date
64:06+ dh	Derartu	Tulu	ETH	21.3.72	1	in HMar	South Shields	18 Sep
64:55+ dh	Paula	Radcliffe	GBR	17.12.73	1	in Mar	London	17 Apr
65:43+	Mizuki	Noguchi	JPN	3.7.78	1	in Mar	Berlin	25 Sep
65:51+	Catherine	Ndereba	KEN	21.7.72	1	in HMar	Sapporo	3 Jul
66:08+		Noguchi			2	in HMar	Sapporo	3 Jul
66:13+	Yasuyo	Iwamoto	JPN	8.9.76	3	in HMar	Sapporo	3 Jul
66:15+	Masako	Chiba	JPN	18.7.76	1	in Mar	Chicago	9 Oct
66:17+	Terumi	Asoshina	JPN	2.5.82	1	in HMar	Yamaguchi	13 Mar
66:28+	Megumi	Oshima	JPN	4.9.75	4	in HMar	Sapporo	3 Jul
66:31+	Lidia	Simon	ROM	4.9.73	1=	in HMar	Miyazaki	6 Jan
66:31+	Harumi	Hiroyama	JPN	2.9.68	1=	in HMar	Miyazaki	6 Jan
66:34+	Yoko	Miyauchi	JPN	19.6.83	3	in HMar	Miyazaki	6 Jan
66:43	Blake	Russell	USA	24.7.75	1	NC	New Haven	5 Sep
66:45+	Eri	Hayakawa	JPN	15.11.81	5	in HMar	Sapporo	3 Jul
66:46+	Yumiko	Hara	JPN	9.1.82	6+	in Mar	Helsinki	14 Aug

Most quality marks at this distance made during longer races, especially half marathons

HALF MARATHON

Slightly downhill courses: Lisboa 69m, South Shields 30.5m

Mark	Name		Nat	Born	Pos	Meet	Venue	Date
67:33 dh	Derartu	Tulu	ETH	21.3.72	1	GNR	South Shields	18 Sep
67:53	Deena	Kastor	USA	14.2.73	1		Philadelphia	18 Sep
68:09 dh	Werknesh	Kidane	ETH	21.11.81	2	GNR	South Shields	18 Sep
68:11 dh	Jelena	Prokopcuka	LAT	21.9.76	3	GNR	South Shields	18 Sep
68:19 dh	Edith	Masai	KEN	4.4.67	4	GNR	South Shields	18 Sep
68:27+ dh	Paula	Radcliffe	GBR	17.12.73	1		London	17 Apr
68:47 dh	Susan	Chepkemei	KEN	25.6.75	1		Lisboa	13 Mar
69:09	Pamela	Chepchumba	KEN	28.2.78	1		Udine	25 Sep
69:17	Constantina	Tomescu	ROM	23.1.70	1	WCh	Edmonton	1 Oct
69:17 dh	Margaret	Okayo (10)	KEN	30.5.76	2		Lisboa	13 Mar
69:17+		Kastor			1	in Mar	Chicago	9 Oct
69:18+		Tomescu			2	in Mar	Chicago	9 Oct
69:19+	Mizuki	Noguchi	JPN	3.7.78	1	in Mar	Berlin	25 Sep
69:24	Catherine	Ndereba	KEN	21.7.72	1		Sapporo	3 Jul
69:34	Takako	Kotorida	JPN	2.4.77	1		Marugame	6 Feb
69:34	Rosaria	Console	ITA	17.12.79	1		Ostia	27 Feb
69:43	Yasuko	Hashimoto	JPN	12.8.75	2		Marugame	6 Feb
69:45	Yasuyo	Iwamoto	JPN	8.9.76	2		Sapporo	3 Jul
69:46		Noguchi			3		Sapporo	3 Jul
69:47 dh	Berhane	Adere	ETH	21.7.73	5	GNR	South Shields	18 Sep
69:49+		Radcliffe			1	in Mar	Helsinki	14 Aug
69:51 dh	Mara	Yamauchi	GBR	13.8.73	6	GNR	South Shields	18 Sep
69:52+	Hellen	Kimutai	KEN	28.12.77	2=	in Mar	Helsinki	14 Aug
69:52+		Ndereba			2=	in Mar	Helsinki	14 Aug
69:53	Helena	Javornik (20)	SLO	26.3.66	1		Ferrara	20 Feb
69:53 dh	Asha	Gigi	ETH	15.10.73	3		Lisboa	13 Mar
69:53+		Tomescu			4	in Mar	Helsinki	14 Aug
69:54	Terumi	Asoshina	JPN	2.5.82	1		Yamaguchi	13 Mar

Mark		Name		Nat	Born	Pos	Meet	Venue	Date
69:55	dh		Console			4		Lisboa	13 Mar
69:55		Margaret	Atodonyang	KEN	10.10.78	2		Philadelphia	18 Sep
69:58		Lidia	Simon	ROM	4.9.73	1		Miyazaki	6 Jan
69:59		Megumi	Oshima	JPN	4.9.75	4		Sapporo	3 Jul
		(32/25)							
70:00		Teyiba	Erkesso	ETH	28.9.82	1		Reims	23 Oct
70:02		Harumi	Hiroyama	JPN	2.9.68	2		Miyazaki	6 Jan
70:02		Rie	Ueno	JPN	11.6.76	3		Philadelphia	18 Sep
70:02+		Masako	Chiba	JPN	18.7.76		in Mar	Chicago	9 Oct
70:03		Selina	Kosgei	KEN	16.11.76	2		Virginia Beach	4 Sep
		(30)							
70:13		Ikuko	Nagao	JPN	7.1.82	3		Virginia Beach	4 Sep
70:14		Eri	Hayakawa	JPN	15.11.81	5		Sapporo	3 Jul
70:15		Yoko	Miyauchi	JPN	19.6.83	3		Miyazaki	6 Jan
70:15		Rose	Chepchumba	KEN	14.3.79	2		Udine	25 Sep
70:18		Mary	Ptikany	KEN	.78	1		Den Haag	19 Mar
70:19		Lornah	Kiplagat	NED	20.3.74	2	WCh	Edmonton	1 Oct
70:19+			Zhou Chunxiu	CHN	8.3.79	5+	in Mar	Helsinki	14 Aug
70:20		Grace	Momanyi	KEN	3.3.82	1		Monterrey	17 Apr
70:22		Genoveva	Kigen Chelagat	KEN	.80	1		Mazatlán	4 Dec
70:23		Zivile	Balciunaite	LTU	3.4.79	1		Budapest	6 Nov
		(40)							
70:25		Miho	Notagashira	JPN	17.8.83	3		Marugame	6 Feb
70:25		Caroline	Kiptoo	KEN	.76	1		Breda	2 Oct
70:26		Akane	Taira	JPN	3.11.82	4		Miyazaki	6 Jan
70:27+		Yumiko	Hara	JPN	9.1.82	6+	in Mar	Helsinki	14 Aug
70:28		Hiromi	Ominami	JPN	15.11.75	6		Sapporo	3 Jul
70:30		Naoko	Takahashi	JPN	6.5.72	4		Virginia Beach	4 Sep
70:30		Dulce M	Rodríguez	MEX	14.8.72	2		Mazatlán	4 Dec
70:31		Madoka	Ogi	JPN	26.10.83	3		Yamaguchi	13 Mar
70:34		Galina	Bogomolova	RUS	15.10.77	4	WCh	Edmonton	1 Oct
70:35		Fumi	Murata	JPN	13.3.75	4		Yamaguchi	13 Mar
		(50)							
70:35		Irina	Timofeyeva	RUS	5.4.70	1		New Delhi	16 Oct
70:36		Madaí	Pérez	MEX	2.2.80	2		Monterrey	17 Apr
70:36		Mihaela	Botezan	ROM	21.11.76	5	WCh	Edmonton	1 Oct
70:37	dh	Merima	Denboba	ETH	21.8.74	5		Lisboa	13 Mar
70:39		Jane	Ekimat	KEN	12.6.74	1		Vitry-sur-Seine	17 Apr
70:39	dh	Joyce	Chepchumba	KEN	6.11.70	6		Lisboa	13 Mar
70:41		Rita	Jeptoo	KEN	15.2.81	2		New Delhi	16 Oct
70:47		Ayako	Suzuki	JPN	17.12.80	6		Miyazaki	6 Jan
70:47		Evelyne	Kimwei	KEN-J	25.8.87	1		Okayama	23 Dec
70:49		Kana	Yoshida	JPN	27.4.84	5		Yamaguchi	13 Mar
		(60)							
70:49		Nina	Rillstone	NZL	15.4.75	1		Christchurch	5 Jun
70:54		Kaori	Yoshida	JPN	4.8.81	4		Marugame	6 Feb
70:54		Hitomi	Miyai	JPN	18.3.85	6		Yamaguchi	13 Mar
70:54		Kutre	Dulecha	ETH	22.8.78	2		Den Haag	19 Mar
71:01		Anikó	Kálovics	HUN	13.5.77	3		Udine	25 Sep
71:01		Lydiya	Grigoryeva	RUS	21.1.74	7	WCh	Edmonton	1 Oct
71:02		Yoko	Yagi	JPN	14.4.80	7		Sapporo	3 Jul
71:03		Yuko	Machida	JPN	11.8.80	8		Miyazaki	6 Jan
71:04		Luminita	Zaituc	GER	9.10.68	1		Berlin	3 Apr
71:06		Nuta	Olaru	ROM	28.8.70	7		Virginia Beach	4 Sep
		(70)							
71:06		Inga	Abitova	RUS	6.3.82	2		Novosibirsk	9 Sep
71:07		Miki	Ohira	JPN	28.6.81	1		Matsue	20 Mar
71:09		Merima	Hashim	ETH	.81	9	WCh	Edmonton	1 Oct
71:10		Adriana	Pîrtea	ROM	31.1.80	10	WCh	Edmonton	1 Oct
71:14		Alevtina	Ivanova	RUS	22.5.75	8		Virginia Beach	4 Sep
71:15			Lee Eun-jung	KOR	21.4.81	2		Berlin	3 Apr
71:15+		Rose	Cheruiyot	KEN	21.7.76	+	in 25km	Berlin	8 May
71:16+		Dire	Tune	ETH	.85	+	in 25km	Berlin	8 May
71:18		Beatrice	Omwanza	KEN	24.2.74	3		Berlin	3 Apr
71:18		Yurika	Nakamura	JPN-J	1.4.86	3		Okayama	23 Dec
		(80)							
71:19		Gladys	Cherono	KEN		1		Santa Pola	23 Jan
71:20		Penninah	Arusei	KEN	1.1.79	4		Den Haag	19 Mar
71:21		Hiroko	Miyauchi	JPN	19.6.83	9		Miyazaki	6 Jan
71:22		Bruna	Genovese	ITA	24.9.76	1		Cremona	16 Oct
71:23		Selma	Borst	NED	6.9.83	5	1 NC	Den Haag	19 Mar

Mark	Name		Nat	Born	Pos	Meet	Venue	Date
71:24	Miwako	Ueki	JPN	27.6.78	10		Miyazaki	6 Jan
71:26	Ruth	Wanjiru	KEN	11.9.81	8		Yamaguchi	13 Mar
71:27	Malika	Assahsah	MAR	24.9.82	1		Torrevieja	27 Feb
71:28+	Elfenesh	Alemu	ETH	10.6.75	4	in Mar	Tokyo	20 Nov
71:30	Chieko	Yamasaki	JPN	28.5.77	5		Marugame	6 Feb
	(90)							
71:30+	Svetlana	Zakharova	RUS	15.9.70	6	in Mar	Tokyo	20 Nov
71:33	Miho	Ichikawa	JPN	20.5.73	9		Virginia Beach	4 Sep
71:36	Lenah	Cheruiyot	KEN	1.3.73	2		Vitry-sur-Seine	17 Apr
71:39	Yuri	Kano	JPN	27.10.78	2		Matsue	20 Mar
71:39	Mie	Ueda	JPN	9.6.82	1		Nagoya	23 Nov
71:40	Takami	Nishiyama	JPN	17.10.80	6		Marugame	6 Feb
71:41+	Mari	Ozaki	JPN	16.7.75		in Mar	Osaka	30 Jan
71:41+	Miki	Oyama	JPN	22.10.79		in Mar	Osaka	30 Jan
71:41	Luminita	Talpos	ROM	9.10.72	10		Virginia Beach	4 Sep
71:42	Kei	Terada	JPN	27.3.85	1		Okayama	27 Oct
	(100)							

Mark	Name		Nat	Born	Date
71:43+	Kazue	Ogoshi	JPN	2.3.81	30 Jan
71:43	Ryoko	Kizaki	JPN	21.6.85	20 Mar
71:47	Pauline	Wangui	KEN		2 Oct
71:47	Susan	Muthoni	KEN		16 Oct
71:49	Susan	Kirui	KEN	4.4.80	19 Mar
71:51+	Ryoko	Eda	JPN	12.6.76	13 Mar
71:51+	Yoko	Shibui	JPN	14.3.79	13 Mar
71:52	Junko	Ochi	JPN	18.8.82	6 Jan
71:52+	Takami	Ominami	JPN	15.11.75	13 Mar
71:52+	Kiyomi	Ogawa	JPN	15.9.81	13 Mar
71:52	Florence	Chepkorir	KEN		4 Sep
71:52+	Worknesh	Tola	ETH	6.6.77	25 Sep
71:52+	Asale	Megersa Tafa	ETH	84	25 Sep
71:52	Sonia	O'Sullivan	IRL	28.11.69	23 Dec
71:53	Kathy	Butler	GBR	22.10.73	18 Sep
71:54	Miriam	Wangari	KEN	22.2.79	23 Oct
71:54+	Marleen	Renders	BEL	24.12.68	30 Oct
71:56	Bezunesh	Bekele	ETH	18.9.83	11 Sep
71:56	Nadezhda	Wijenberg	NED	2.4.64	19 Mar
71:56	Irene	Kwambai	KEN	25.10.78	10 Apr
71:57	Junko	Ogawa	JPN	3.12.82	6 Feb
71:59	Alina	Ivanova	RUS	16.3.69	8 May
71:59+	Tegla	Loroupe	KEN	9.5.73	14 Aug
72:00	Leah	Malot	KEN	7.6.72	13 Mar
72:04A	Eyerusalem	Kuma	ETH	4.11.81	28 Aug
72:05	Emi	Takagi	JPN	11.2.82	6 Jan
72:05	Olga	Kimayio	KEN		11 Sep
72:05 dh	Sally	Barsosio	KEN	21.3.78	18 Sep
72:06	Fujiko	Takahashi	JPN	196.83	13 Mar
72:06	Yuka	Izumi	JPN	18.1.85	13 Mar
72:06	Mai	Ito	JPN	23.5.84	20 Mar
72:06A	Adanech	Zekiros	ETH	26.3.82	28 Aug
72:06	Tegla	Loroupe	KEN	9.5.73	17 Sep
72:06	Dorota	Gruca	POL	5.12.70	17 Sep
72:08	Nami	Kosugi	JPN	6.2.84	13 Mar
72:09	Yoshiko	Ichikawa	JPN	18.4.76	6 Jan
72:10	Mizuho	Nasukawa	JPN	22.11.79	6 Jan
72:10A	Letay	Negash	ETH		28 Aug
72:12	Yuki	Sato	JPN	28.5.84	6 Jan
72:13	Miho	Watanabe	JPN	19.6.82	13 Mar
72:13	Irene	Cherotich	KEN	.82	3 Apr
72:13	Caroline	Cheptanui	KEN	13.5.83	1 Oct
72:14	Akemi	Ozaki	JPN	12.10.77	6 Jan
72:14	Mayumi	Fujita	JPN	26.5.83	20 Mar
72:14	Yesenia	Centeno	ESP	27.6.71	11 Sep
72:15	Masayo	Kobayashi	JPN	4.2.80	6 Feb
72:15	Adriana	Fernández	MEX	4.4.71	16 Oct
72:16	Junko	Akagi	JPN	3.12.75	6 Jan
72:16	Tomoe	Yokoyama	JPN	9.8.76	23 Nov
72:17	Neriah	Asiba	KEN	.81	16 Oct
72:17	Agnes	Ngunjiri	KEN	.75	6 Nov
72:18	Reiko	Satake	JPN	4.11.81	23 Jan
72:19	Yuko	Sato	JPN	17.1.82	6 Feb
72:20	Irina	Permitina	RUS	3.2.68	24 Apr
72:20	Irina	Safarova	RUS	19.6.69	5 Jun
72:20A	Sisay	Measo	ETH	.80	28 Aug
72:20	Jesica	Obare	KEN		2 Oct
72:21	Grazyna	Syrek	POL	9.1.72	6 Mar
72:21A	Derebe	Alemu	ETH	5.6.83	28 Aug
72:21	Nataliya	Berkut	UKR	30.5.75	9 Oct
72:22	Asuka	Kato	JPN	7.3.80	13 Mar
72:22+	Galina	Karnatsevich	BLR	2.11.69	14 Aug
72:24+	Albina	Ivanova	RUS	16.5.77	9 Oct
72:26	Juri	Ide	JPN		23 Jan
72:27	Minori	Hayakari	JPN	29.11.72	27 Nov
72:30	Kumi	Tsuguma	JPN	23.8.81	20 Mar
72:30	María Dolores	Pulido	ESP	1.10.74	11 Sep
72:31	Liliya	Yadzhak	RUS	14.11.70	9 Sep
72:31	Miyuki	Ando	JPN	25.3.80	23 Dec
72:32	Hayley	Haining	GBR	6.3.72	26 Jun
72:32	Susan	Kihara	KEN		3 Sep
72:33	Jane	Kariuki Nymabura	KEN	12.12.74	17 Apr
72:33	Hanan	Farhoun	FRA	26.5.74	3 Sep
72:34	Fatiha	Fauvel-Klilech	FRA	1.2.75	2 Oct
72:36	Kaori	Tanabe	JPN	30.4.75	6 Jan
72:36	Olga	Romanova	RUS	23.5.80	16 Jan
72:36	Mariko	Horimoto	JPN	28.12.84	27 Feb
72:38+	Lyubov	Morgunova	RUS	14.1.71	18 Apr
72:38	Haley	McGregor	AUS	27.5.79	22 May
72:39	Vincenza	Sicari	ITA	19.3.79	10 Apr
72:41	Ionelia	Vasile	ROM	29.2.76	3 Sep
72:42	Yuko	Shimizu	JPN	13.7.85	27 Feb
72:42	Norie	Kawashima	JPN-J	.86	26 Nov
72:43	Ayaka	Kawata	JPN	28.9.81	6 Feb
72:44	Reiko	Tosa	JPN	11.6.76	20 Mar
72:48	Svetlana	Ponomarenko	RUS	28.11.69	5 Jun
72:49	Shizuka	Marumo	JPN	11.1.84	13 Mar
72:49	Mika	Kawamura	JPN	9.11.79	13 Mar
72:51	Sachiyo	Yamada	JPN	30.12.83	3 Jul
72:52+	Shitaye	Gemechu	ETH	17.6.80	14 Aug
72:53	Birhan	Dagne	GBR	8.4.78	2 Oct
72:54	Eri	Kojina	JPN	3.3.83	6 Jan
72:54	Hiroko	Watanabe	JPN	23.5.83	13 Mar
72:54	Asami	Obi	JPN	22.3.76	3 Jul
72:54+	Leila	Aman	ETH	24.11.77	23 Oct
72:55	Lioudmila	Kortchaguina	CAN	26.7.71	16 Jan
72:55	Sylvia	Mosqueda	USA	8.4.66	3 Dec
72:56	Rika	Tabashi	JPN	12.11.81	6 Feb
72:56	Noriko	Matsuoka	JPN	2.5.79	13 Mar
72:56	Jen	Rhines	USA	1.7.74	9 Oct
	(200)				

Uncertified course: 71:37 Joan Ayabei KEN 17.5.79 1 Valladolid 18 Sep

JUNIORS

Mark	Name		Nat	Born	Pos	Venue	Date
70:47	Evelyne	Kimwei	KEN-J	25.8.87	1	Okayama	23 Dec
71:18	Yurika	Nakamura	JPN-J	1.4.86	3	Okayama	23 Dec
	72:59 12	Sapporo	3 Jul	4 performances by 3 women under 74:00			
72:42	Norie	Kawashima	JPN	.86	1	Shanghai	26 Nov
74:03	Farida	Makula	TAN	11.7.87	5	Vitry-sur-Seine	17 Apr

WOMEN 2005

25 KILOMETRES ROAD

Mark	Name		Nat	Born	Pos	Meet	Venue	Date
1:21:03++dh	Paula	Radcliffe	GBR	17.12.73	1	in Mar	London	17 Apr
1:21:57+	Deena	Kastor	USA	14.2.73	1	in Mar	Chicago	9 Oct
1:22:13+	Mizuki	Noguchi	JPN	3.7.78	1	in Mar	Berlin	25 Sep
1:24:46	Rose	Cheruiyot	KEN	21.7.76	1		Berlin	8 May
1:24:47	Dire	Tune	ETH	.85	2		Berlin	8 May
1:25:15	Colleen	de Reuck	USA	13.4.64	1	NC	Grand Rapids	14 May

30 KILOMETRES ROAD

Further marks at 25k/30k made in major marathons

Mark	Name		Nat	Born	Pos	Meet	Venue	Date
1:37:27++dh	Paula	Radcliffe	GBR	17.12.73	1	in Mar	London	17 Apr
1:38:29+	Deena	Kastor	USA	14.2.73	1	in Mar	Chicago	9 Oct
1:38:49++	Mizuki	Noguchi	JPN	3.7.78	1	in Mar	Berlin	25 Sep

MARATHON

L = loop course, P = point-to-point, D = downhill over 1/1000, W women only race

Mark		Name		Nat	Born	Pos	Meet	Venue	Date
2:17:42	LW	Paula	Radcliffe	GBR	17.12.73	1		London	17 Apr
2:19:12	LM	Mizuki	Noguchi	JPN	3.7.78	1		Berlin	25 Sep
2:20:57	LW		Radcliffe			1	WCh	Helsinki	14 Aug
2:21:01	LM		Sun Yingjie ¶	CHN	3.10.77	1	NG	Beijing	16 Oct
2:21:11	LM		Zhou Chunxiu	CHN	8.3.79	2	NG	Beijing	16 Oct
2:21:25	LM	Deena	Kastor	USA	14.2.73	1		Chicago	9 Oct
2:21:30	LM	Constantina	Tomescu	ROM	23.1.70	2		Chicago	9 Oct
2:22:01	LW	Catherine	Ndereba	KEN	21.7.72	2	WCh	Helsinki	14 Aug
2:22:50	LW		Tomescu			2		London	17 Apr
2:22:56	LW	Jelena	Prokopcuka	LAT	21.9.76	1		Osaka	30 Jan
2:23:19	LW		Tomescu			3	WCh	Helsinki	14 Aug
2:23:24	LM		Zhou			1		Seoul	13 Mar
2:23:30	LW	Derartu	Tulu	ETH	21.3.72	4	WCh	Helsinki	14 Aug
2:23:59	LW	Mari	Ozaki (10)	JPN	16.7.75	2		Osaka	30 Jan
2:24:00	LW	Susan	Chepkemei	KEN	25.6.75	3		London	17 Apr
2:24:12	LW		Zhou			5	WCh	Helsinki	14 Aug
2:24:19	LW	Yumiko	Hara	JPN	9.1.82	1		Nagoya	13 Mar
2:24:20	LW		Hara			6	WCh	Helsinki	14 Aug
2:24:22	LW	Rita	Jeptoo	KEN	15.2.81	7	WCh	Helsinki	14 Aug
2:24:25	LW	Megumi	Oshima	JPN	4.9.75	2		Nagoya	13 Mar
2:24:39	LW	Naoko	Takahashi	JPN	6.5.72	1		Tokyo	20 Nov
2:24:41	LW		Prokopcuka			1		New York	6 Nov
2:24:54	LW	Ryoko	Eda	JPN	12.6.76	3		Nagoya	13 Mar
2:24:55	LW		Chepkemei			2		New York	6 Nov
2:25:12	LM	Alevtina	Biktimirova	RUS	10.9.82	1		Frankfurt-am-Main	30 Oct
2:25:13	DW		Ndereba			1		Boston	18 Apr
2:25:15	LW	Zivile	Balciunaite	LTU	3.4.79	2		Tokyo	20 Nov
2:25:21	LW	Yasuko	Hashimoto	JPN	12.8.75	4		Nagoya	13 Mar
2:25:21	LW		Tulu			3		New York	6 Nov
2:25:22	LW	Margaret (30/20)	Okayo	KEN	30.5.76	4		London	17 Apr
2:25:30	LW	Selina	Kosgei	KEN	16.11.76	4		New York	6 Nov
2:25:46	LW	Harumi	Hiroyama	JPN	2.9.68	8	WCh	Helsinki	14 Aug
2:25:46	LM	Masako	Chiba	JPN	18.7.76	1		Sapporo	28 Aug
2:25:55	LM		Wei Yanan	CHN	6.12.81	2		Seoul	13 Mar
2:26:02	LW	Kiyomi	Ogawa	JPN	15.9.81	5		Nagoya	13 Mar
2:26:11	LM	Lyubov	Denisova	RUS	6.10.71	1		Los Angeles	6 Mar
2:26:14	LW	Hellen	Kimutai	KEN	28.12.77	9	WCh	Helsinki	14 Aug
2:26:14	LM	Kiyoko	Shimahara	JPN	22.12.76	2		Sapporo	28 Aug
2:26:26	LM	Marleen	Renders	BEL	24.12.68	2		Frankfurt-am-Main	30 Oct
2:26:29	LW	Lyudmila (30)	Petrova	RUS	7.10.68	5		London	17 Apr
2:26:32	LW	Benita	Johnson	AUS	6.5.79	6		London	17 Apr
2:26:46	L	Luminita	Zaituc	GER	9.10.68	1		Düsseldorf	8 May
2:26:50	LW	Madaí	Pérez	MEX	2.2.80	11	WCh	Helsinki	14 Aug
2:26:50	LW	Elfenesh	Alemu	ETH	10.6.75	3		Tokyo	20 Nov
2:26:55	LW	Miki	Oyama	JPN	22.10.79	4		Osaka	30 Jan
2:26:55	LW	Svetlana	Zakharova	RUS	15.9.70	4		Tokyo	20 Nov
2:27:01	LW	Lidia	Simon	ROM	4.9.73	5		Osaka	30 Jan
2:27:01	LW	Lydiya	Grigoryeva	RUS	21.1.74	1		Paris	10 Apr
2:27:01	LW	Joyce	Chepchumba	KEN	6.11.70	7		London	17 Apr
2:27:06	L	Edith (40)	Masai	KEN	4.4.67	1		Hamburg	24 Apr

Mark		Name		Nat	Born	Pos	Meet	Venue	Date
2:27:14	LW	Galina	Karnatsevich	BLR	2.11.69	12	WCh	Helsinki	14 Aug
2:27:15	LW	Bruna	Genovese	ITA	24.9.76	5		New York	6 Nov
2:27:18	LW	Florence	Barsosio	KEN	11.8.76	2		Paris	10 Apr
2:27:22	LW	Chieko	Yamasaki	JPN	28.5.77	6		Nagoya	13 Mar
2:27:35	L		Sun Weiwei	CHN	13.1.85	3	NG	Beijing	16 Oct
2:27:36	L	Lornah	Kiplagat	NED	20.3.74	1	NC	Rotterdam	10 Apr
2:27:38	LW	Asha	Gigi	ETH	15.10.73	3		Paris	10 Apr
2:27:38	LW	Mara	Yamauchi	GBR	13.8.73	5		Tokyo	20 Nov
2:27:40	LW	Yoko	Shibui	JPN	14.3.79	7		Nagoya	13 Mar
2:27:40	LW	Getenesh	Wami	ETH	11.12.74	7		New York	6 Nov
		(50)							
2:27:41	L		Zhang Shujing	CHN	13.9.78	4	NG	Beijing	16 Oct
2:27:46	LW	Dorota	Gruca	POL	5.12.70	13	WCh	Helsinki	14 Aug
2:28:01	L	Silviya	Skvortsova	RUS	16.11.74	1		Roma	13 Mar
2:28:04	LW	Rosaria	Console	ITA	17.12.79	4		Paris	10 Apr
2:28:07	LW	Hiromi	Ominami	JPN	15.11.75	6		Osaka	30 Jan
2:28:21	xL	Albina	Ivanova	RUS	16.5.77	1		Nagano	17 Apr
2:28:27	L	Assale	Tafa	ETH	.84	3		Berlin	25 Sep
2:28:34	LW	Mihaela	Botezan	ROM	21.11.76	7		Osaka	30 Jan
2:28:40	L	Colleen	de Reuck	USA	13.4.64	4		Chicago	9 Oct
2:28:42	P	Emily	Kimuria	KEN	10.6.75	1		Venezia	23 Oct
		(60)							
2:28:46	L	Malgorzata	Sobanska	POL	25.4.69	2		Hamburg	24 Apr
2:28:48	LW	Corinne	Raux	FRA	16.8.76	5		Paris	10 Apr
2:28:50	L	Eri	Hayakawa	JPN	15.11.81	5		Chicago	9 Oct
2:29:00	L	Dulce M	Rodríguez	MEX	14.8.72	1		Torreón	6 Mar
2:29:01	LW	Sonia	O'Sullivan	IRL	28.11.69	8		London	17 Apr
2:29:10	L	Blake	Russell	USA	24.7.75	6		Chicago	9 Oct
2:29:15	LM	Chika	Horie	JPN	15.2.81	3		Sapporo	28 Aug
2:29:18	LM	Helena	Javornik	SLO	26.3.66	3		Seoul	13 Mar
2:29:30	LM	Roba	Tola	ETH		3		Frankfurt-am-Main	30 Oct
2:29:34	LW	Tatyana	Gladyr	UKR	17.4.75	11		New York	6 Nov
		(70)							
2:29:35	LW	Olesya	Nurgalyeva	RUS	9.1.76	12		New York	6 Nov
2:29:43	LW		Jong Yong-ok	PRK	24.1.81	14	WCh	Helsinki	14 Aug
2:29:44	LW	Irina	Permitina	RUS	3.2.68	6		Paris	10 Apr
2:29:45	LM	Mary	Ptikany	KEN	.78	4		Frankfurt-am-Main	30 Oct
2:29:49	L	Claudia	Dreher	GER	2.5.71	3		Hamburg	24 Apr
2:29:54	LM	Worknesh	Tola	ETH	3.6.77	4		Seoul	13 Mar
2:29:56	L	Lyudmila	Pushkina	UKR	2.10.65	1		Columbus	16 Oct
2:30:01	L	Kathy	Butler	GBR	22.10.73	7		Chicago	9 Oct
2:30:03	L	Lioudmila	Kortchaguina	CAN	26.7.71	1		Dallas	11 Dec
2:30:06	L	Kutre	Dulecha	ETH	22.8.78	1		Amsterdam	16 Oct
		(80)							
2:30:11	LW	Irina	Timofeyeva	RUS	5.4.70	7		Paris	10 Apr
2:30:14	L	Larisa	Zyusko	RUS	27.4.69	2		Praha	22 May
2:30:15	LW	Mizuho	Nasukawa	JPN	22.11.79	8		Osaka	30 Jan
2:30:41	L	Beatrice	Omwanza	KEN	24.2.74	1		Torino	17 Apr
2:30:45	LW	Anastasha	Ndereba	KEN	27.9.74	9		Osaka	30 Jan
2:30:46	L	Alice	Chelangat	KEN	27.12.76	1		Firenze	27 Nov
2:30:48	LM	Dire	Tune	ETH	.85	4		Los Angeles	6 Mar
2:30:54	LW	Mulu	Seboka	ETH	13.1.84	9		London	17 Apr
2:31:01	D	Tatyana	Borisova	KGZ	3.6.76	1		Austin (dh 137m)	13 Feb
2:31:03	L	Tatyana	Petrova	RUS	8.4.83	8		Chicago	9 Oct
		(90)							
2:31:05	LM	Tatyana	Pozdnyakova	UKR	4.3.56	5		Los Angeles	6 Mar
2:31:10	P	Leila	Aman	ETH	24.11.77	2		Venezia	23 Oct
2:31:16	LW	Takami	Ominami	JPN	15.11.75	8		Nagoya	13 Mar
2:31:22	L	Alina	Ivanova	RUS	16.3.69	4		Hamburg	24 Apr
2:31:23	L	Margaret	Torotoich	KEN		2		Torreón	6 Mar
2:31:26	LM	Svetlana	Ponomarenko	RUS	28.11.69	5		Frankfurt-am-Main	30 Oct
2:31:27	L	Ana	Dias	POR	15.1.74	2		Rotterdam	10 Apr
2:31:28	L	Hellen	Cherono	KEN	22.2.84	3		Praha	22 May
2:31:41	LM		Oh Jung-hee	KOR	4.12.78	6		Seoul	13 Mar
		(100)							

Mark		Name		Nat	Born	Date
2:31:43	LW	Olivera	Jevtic	SCG	24.7.77	30 Jan
2:31:46	L	Tiziana	Alagia	ITA	8.3.73	13 Mar
2:31:46	L		Ham Bong-sil	PRK	24.7.74	10 Apr
2:31:51	L		Dai Yanyan	CHN	8.1.80	16 Oct
2:31:53	L	Lidiya	Vasilevskaya	RUS	1.4.73	29 May
2:31:54	L	Adriana	Fernández	MEX	4.4.71	4 Dec
2:31:54	L	Galina	Bogomolova	RUS	15.10.77	4 Dec
2:31:57	L	Nuta	Olaru	ROM	28.8.70	4 Dec
2:32:11	LW	Kazue	Ogoshi	JPN	2.3.81	30 Jan
2:32:14	LW	Rie	Matsuoka	JPN	9.3.77	20 Nov
2:32:16	L		Wang Ling	CHN-J	22.9.87	26 Mar
2:32:27	L	Kelly	Keane	USA	25.8.72	16 Jan

Mark			Name	Nat	Born	Date
2:32:27	L		Zhu Xiaolin	CHN	20.2.84	16 Oct
2:32:29	D	Kerryn	McCann	AUS	2.5.67	5 Jun
2:32:35	L		Jin Man	CHN	5.12.84	16 Oct
2:32:36	L	Asami	Obi	JPN	22.3.76	16 Octy
2:32:36	LW	Yelena	Nurgaliyeva	RUS	9.1.76	6 Nov
2:32:39	LW	Kaoru	Nishi	JPN	28.11.83	13 Mar
2:32:41	DW	Madina	Biktagirova	RUS	20.9.64	18 Apr
2:32:44	L	Svetlana	Demidenko	RUS	16.2.76	18 Jun
2:32:51	L	Shitaye	Gemechu	ETH	17.6.80	9 Jan
2:32:53	L	Zinayida	Semyonova	RUS	19.3.62	31 Oct
2:33:01	L	Tigist	Abedi	ETH	.85	8 May
2:33:02	LM	Anna	Pichrtová	CZE	19.5.73	6 Mar
2:33:03	L	Ramilya	Burangulova	RUS	11.7.61	18 Jun
2:33:05	L	Mindaye	Gishu	ETH		30 Oct
2:33:09	L		Oh Song-suk	PRK	2.9.77	10 Apr
2:33:09	L	Kirsten	Melkevik Otterbu	NOR	29.5.70	24 Apr
2:33:13	L		Li Fenjin	CHN	11.2.83	26 Mar
2:33:14	LW	Monika	Drybulska	POL	15.5.80	13 Mar
2:33:14	L	Isabel	Eizmendi	ESP	15.6.70	10 Apr
2:33:15	L	Irina	Safarova	RUS	19.6.69	4 Dec
2:33:16	L		Wang Linan	CHN	26.11.85	26 Mar
2:33:17	L	Marcella	Mancini	ITA	5.9.71	17 Apr
2:33:20	L	Anna	Thompson	AUS	11.12.76	10 Apr
2:33:20	LW	Aura	Buia	ROM	16.2.70	14 Aug
2:33:24	DW	Lyubov	Morgunova	RUS	14.1.71	18 Apr
2:33:27	L	Larisa	Malikova	RUS	2.4.69	24 Apr
2:33:28	L	Kristijna	Loonen	NED	26.7.70	10 Apr
2:33:29	L		Choi Kyung-hee	KOR	13.9.81	13 Mar
2:33:31	LW	Miwako	Ueki	JPN	27.6.78	13 Mar
2:33:33	L	Margaret	Atodonyang	KEN	10.10.78	5 Jun
2:33:37	L	Ayumi	Hayashi	JPN	7.6.82	13 Mar
2:33:37	L		Ryang Gum-hwa	PRK	27.10.80	10 Apr
2:33:39	L	Jane	Ekimat	KEN	12.6.74	18 Dec
2:33:42	L	Kate	Smyth	AUS	22.9.72	9 Oct
2:33:42	LW	Lauren	Shelley	AUS	2.12.76	20 Nov
2:33:47	L	Haley	McGregor	AUS	27.5.79	10 Jan
2:33:47	LW	Yumiko	Okamoto	JPN	28.3.78	13 Mar
2:33:48	D	Fátima	Silva	POR	6.5.70	17 Apr
2:33:51	L	Liza	Hunter-Galvan	NZL	25.6.69	11 Dec
2:33:52	L	Angélica	Sánchez	MEX	11.12.75	4 Dec
2:33:52	L	Merima	Hashim	ETH	.81	4 Dec
2:33:59	LW	Marie	Davenport	IRL	24.1.75	6 Nov
2:34:06	L	Albina	Gallyamova	RUS	8.5.64	11 Dec
2:34:08	L	Caroline	Cheptanui	KEN	13.5.83	24 Apr
2:34:10	LW	Jackie	Fairweather	AUS	10.11.67	13 Mar
2:34:11	L	Abebe	Tola	ETH	3.6.77	13 Mar
2:34:21	L		Kim Sun-yong	PRK	5.8.80	10 Apr
2:34:23	L	Melanie	Kraus	GER	24.10.74	25 Sep
2:34:30	LW	Junko	Akagi	JPN	3.12.75	30 Jan
2:34:37	L		Jong Song-ok	PRK	18.8.74	10 Apr
2:34:39	L	Claudia	Oberlin	SUI	29.1.79	3 Apr
2:34:41	LM	Fabiola	William John	TAN	26.12.84	12 Jun
2:34:41	LW	Hayley	Haining	GBR	6.3.72	14 Aug
2:34:42	LW	Elena	Fétizon	FRA	4.3.75	10 Apr
2:34:42	LW	Tegla	Loroupe	KEN	9.5.73	17 Apr
2:34:43	LW	Aki	Negoro	JPN	10.9.81	13 Mar
2:34:43	L		Mu Shuixian	CHN	10.9.84	26 Mar
2:34:43	LW	Turena	Johnson Lane	USA	20.7.75	14 Aug
2:34:50		Elizabeth	Chemweno	KEN	13.7.78	27 Nov
2:34:51	L	Lucy	Muhami	KEN		4 Dec
2:34:53	L	Nina	Kolyaseva	RUS	4.7.75	18 Sep
2:34:59	L	Anne	Chelagat Kibor	KEN	4.6.69	31 Oct
2:35:05	L	Tsege	Worku	ETH	19.1.82	28 Aug
2:35:05	L	Aki	Fujikawa	JPN	14 11.78	28 Aug
2:35:06	LW	Tomoko	Kai	JPN	5.11.76	13 Mar
2:35:07	L		Pyo Un-suk	PRK	13.6.81	10 Apr
2:35:24	LW	Yuki	Saito	JPN	25.9.80	30 Jan
2:35:25	L	Wioletta	Kryza	POL	10.8.68	16 Jan
2:35:25	L	Mika	Hikita	JPN	4.8.76	28 Aug
2:35:28	LW	Emi	Takagi	JPN	11.2.82	13 Mar
2:35:30	L		Shawuti Nuerguli	CHN	20.3.83	26 Mar
2:35:35	L	Maria	Portillo-Cruz	PER	10.4.72	11 Dec
2:35:43	L	Edyta	Lewandowska	POL	22.11.80	13 Mar
2:35:45	L	Neriah	Asiba	KEN	.81	4 Dec
2:35:48	L	Meseret	Kotu	ETH	20.1.81	17 Apr
2:35:55	L	Ivana	Iozzia	ITA	18.2.73	24 Apr
2:35:55	L	Adanech	Zekiros	ETH	26.3.82	23 Oct
2:35:58	L	Yoshimi	Hoshino	JPN	17.6.66	23 Nov
2:36:02	LW	Carmen	Olivéras	FRA	29.6.71	10 Apr
2:36:09	LW	Rose	Nyangacha	KEN	28.10.76	13 Mar
2:36:12	L	Gladys	Asiba	KEN	31.5.77	17 Apr
2:36:13	L		Kim Chol-sun	PRK		16 Oct
2:36:14	LM	Yelena	Burykina	RUS	7.5.72	6 Mar
2:36:19	L	Alicia	Rodríguez (196)	MEX	12.6.68	6 Mar

Downhill: Las Vegas 20 Mar (dh 207m): 1, Olga Kovpotina RUS 10.1.68 2:31:54, 2. Firiya Zhdanova RUS 29.4.61 2:36:08

JUNIORS

Mark			Name	Nat	Born	Pos	Meet	Venue	Date
2:32:16	L		Wang Ling	CHN	22.9.87	4	NC	Xiamen	26 Mar
		2:33:35 9 NG Beijing 16 Oct			2:37:58	8		Pyongyang	10 Apr
2:36:31	L		Wang Xiaoshu	CHN	15.11.86	13	NG	Beijing	16 Oct
2:39:29	L		Zeng Guang	CHN	9.5.86	14	NC	Xiamen	26 Mar
2:39:31			Liu Hong	CHN	17.10.87	2		Qingdao	15 May
2:41:31	L		Gao Yanli	CHN	7.3.86	15	NC	Xiamen	26 Mar
2:41:40	L	Josephine	Deemay	TAN	13.6.86	9		Las Vegas	4 Dec
2:42:08	L		Ji Cui	CHN	10.3.87	17	NC	Xiamen	26 Mar
2:42.33	L		Liu Hongyan	CHN	3.10.86	18	NC	Xiamen	26 Mar

50 KILOMETRES

Mark		Name	Nat	Born	Pos	Meet	Venue	Date
3:15.51	Olesya	Nurgalyeva	RUS	9.1.76	1	in 56k	Cape Town	26 Mar
3:15.51	Yelena	Nurgalyeva	RUS	9.1.76	2	in 56k	Cape Town	26 Mar
3:18.29	Marina	Bychkova	RUS	18.12.75	3	in 56k	Cape Town	26 Mar
3:19.50	Gladys	Lukhwareni ¶	RSA	25.7.80	4	in 56k	Cape Town	26 Mar
3:21.09	Yolande	Maclean	RSA	10.3.78	1		Middelburg	25 Apr

100 KILOMETRES

Mark		Name	Nat	Born	Pos	Meet	Venue	Date
7:53:25	Monica	Casiraghi	ITA	4.4.69	1	EC	Winschoten	10 Sep
7:53:28	Birgit	Schönherr-Hölscher	GER	16.8.68	2	EC	Winschoten	10 Sep
7:53:41	Hiroko	Sho	JPN	.70	1	WCp	Yubetsu	26 Jun
7:54:22	Anne	Riddle Lundblad	USA	21.6.66	2	WCp	Yubetsu	26 Jun
7:55:53	Karine	Herry	FRA	2.1.68	3	EC	Winschoten	10 Sep
7:56:14	Susan	Bruce	GBR	23.7.64	4	EC	Winschoten	10 Sep
7:57:13		Herry			1	NC	Nouvion-en-Ponthieu	5 Jun
8:00:45	Laurence	Fricotteaux	FRA	22.1.69	5	EC	Winschoten	10 Sep
8:00:51	Sonja	Knöpfli	SUI	11.7.77	1		Biel	17 Jun
8:01:20	Svetlana	Ivanova	LAT	4.4.81	6	EC	Winschoten	10 Sep
8:03:49	Emi	Iwasaki	JPN		3	WCp	Yubetsu	26 Jun
8:08:53	Christine	Lelan	FRA	14.9.73	2	NC	Nouvion-en-Ponthieu	5 Jun

Mark		Name	Nat	Born	Pos	Meet	Venue	Date
8:10:27	Yoko	Yamazawa	JPN		4	WCp	Yubetsu	26 Jun

Mark		Name	Nat	Born	Date	Mark		Name	Nat	Born	Date
8:12:02		Fricotteaux			26 Jun	8:19:43	Marion	Braun	GER	2.7.57	10 Sep
8:14:46	Magali	Reymonenq	FRA	21.5.69	10 Sep	8:19:49		Kim Yong-ok	KOR	17.3.78	26 Jun
8:17:42	Brigitte	Bec	FRA	7.4.64	10 Sep	8:19:55	Carmen	Hildebrand	GER	3.5.69	13 Aug

24 HOURS

Mark		Name	Nat	Born	Pos	Meet	Venue	Date
242,228k	Lyudmila	Kalinina	RUS	30.8.68	1	WCh	Wörschach	16 Jul
241.521 t		Kalinina			1		Moskva	7 May
239.874	Galina	Yeremina	RUS	15.2.53	2	WCh	Wörschach	16 Jul
234.803	Sumie	Inagaki	JPN	6.4.66	3	WCh	Wörschach	16 Jul
227.469	Irina	Koval	RUS	19.11.58	4	WCh	Wörschach	16 Jul
225.660		Koval			1		Sankt-Peterburg	3 Sep
224.264	Irina	Reutovich	RUS	21.1.50	2		Sankt-Peterburg	3 Sep
223.942	Brigitte	Bec	FRA	7.4.64	1	NC	Gravigny	2 Apr
223.933 t		Yeremina			2		Moskva	7 May
223.763 t	Naomii	Fujita	JPN	28.5.58	1		Soochow	4 Mar
223.109		Kim Jung-ok	KOR	.75	5	WCh	Wörschach	16 Jul
221.300 t		Hur Sookhoe ?	KOR		1		Seoul	15 May
219.859 t	Edit	Bérces	HUN	16.5.64	1		Surgères	13 May
219.283	Irina	Rysina	RUS		3		Sankt-Peterburg	3 Sep
216.343	Pam	Reed	USA		2		San Diego	12 Nov
214.422	Sandy	Powell	USA		6	WCh	Wörschach	16 Jul
214.293	Kimie	Noto	JPN	10.1.52	7	WCh	Wörschach	16 Jul
214.194	Nadezhda	Tarasova	RUS	7.4.52	8	WCh	Wörschach	16 Jul
213.208	Masae	Kamura	JPN	4.4.58	3		San Diego	12 Nov
213.181	M.Auxiliadora	Venâncio	BRA	2.5.58	1		São Caetano do Sul	11 Dec
210.678	Rebecca	Johnson	USA		4		San Diego	12 Nov

Mark		Name	Nat	Born	Date	Mark		Name	Nat	Born	Date
206.427	Ilona	Schlegel	GER	9.6.66	15 Jul	200.824	Anke	Drescher	GER	14.12.67	6 May
206.399	Nathalie	Firmin	FRA	2.4.66	2 Apr	200.513	Sharon	Gayter	GBR	30.10.63	16 Jul
206.083	Carolyn	Smith	USA	4.6.65	1 Jan	200.405	Martine	Bertin	FRA	10.5.51	16 Jul
205.597	Michaela	Dimitriadu	CZE		16 Jul	200.063	Laura	Nelson	USA		12 Nov
205.218 t	Fumi	Sata	JPN	25.6.62	4 Mar	**Track best**					
201.877 t	Stephanie	Ehret	USA	21.1.63	4 Mar	210.600	Irina	Rysina	RUS		7 May
201.810	Véronique	Jehanno	FRA	27.12.62	1 Oct	204.650	Nadezhda	Tarasova	RUS	7.4.52	7 May
201.695	Rimma	Paltseva	RUS	10.10.48	16 Jul	203.573	Irina	Koval	RUS	19.11.58	13 May

2000 METRES STEEPLECHASE

Mark		Name	Nat	Born	Pos	Meet	Venue	Date
6:04.46	Dorcus	Inzikuru	UGA	2.2.82	1	GP II	Milano	1 Jun
6:16.58	Cristina	Casandra	ROM	1.2.77	2	GP II	Milano	1 Jun
6:18.77	Johanna	Risku/Lehtinen	FIN	21.2.79	3	GP II	Milano	1 Jun
6:20.14	Stephanie	De Croock	BEL	3.4.79	1		Beveren	3 Sep
6:20.23	Bouchra	Chaabi	MAR	22.9.80	4	GP II	Milano	1 Jun
6:21.93	Salome	Chepchumba	KEN	29.9.82	5	GP II	Milano	1 Jun
6:22.61	Livia	Tóth	HUN	7.1.80	6	GP II	Milano	1 Jun
6:23.04	Lyubov	Ivanova	RUS	2.3.81	1		Moskva	5 Jun
6:25.54	Ancuta	Bobocel	ROM-J	3.10.87	7	GP II	Milano	1 Jun
6:25.81	Ida	Nilsson	SWE	8.2.81	1		Göteborg	14 Jun
6:28.01	Clarisse	Cruz	POR	9.7.78	8	GP II	Milano	1 Jun
6:28.26	Yuliya	Mochalova	RUS-J	26.5.87	1	NC-j	Tula	3 Jul
6:28.98	Polina	Jelizarova	LAT-Y	1.5.89	1		Riga	22 Jun
6:29.2	Ann	Gaffigan	USA	5.10.81	1		Eugene	28 Jul

Mark		Name	Nat	Born	Date	Mark		Name	Nat	Born	Date
6:31.63	Julia	Hiller	GER-J	24.7.87	29 Jul	6:33.81	Louise	Mørch	DEN	2.5.82	14 Jun
6:33.71	Susi	Lutz	GER-J	26.3.87	29 Jul						

JUNIORS

Three above plus:

Mark		Name	Nat	Born	Pos	Meet	Venue	Date
6:31.63	Julia	Hiller	GER	24.7.87	1	NC-j	Braunschweig	29 Jul
6:33.71	Susi	Lutz	GER	26.3.87	2	NC-j	Braunschweig	29 Jul
6:35.60	Yelena	Kundush	RUS-Y	27.11.88	1	NC-y	Chelyabinsk	23 Jun
6:39.60	Lindsey	Ferguson	USA-Y	12.8.88	1r2		Greensboro	18 Jun
6:41.98	Oksana	Juravel	MDA	23.2.86	1	NC-j	Chisinau	4 Jun
6:43.13A	Emily	Pidgeon	GBR-Y	1.6.89	2		Potchefstroom	6 Apr

3000 METRES STEEPLECHASE

Mark		Name	Nat	Born	Pos	Meet	Venue	Date
9:15.04	Dorcus	Inzikuru	UGA	2.2.82	1	SGP	Athína	14 Jun
9:16.46		Inzikuru			1	GP	Rieti	28 Aug
9:18.24		Inzikuru			1	WCh	Helsinki	8 Aug
9:20.33		Inzikuru			1	GP	Rieti	28 Aug
9:20.49	Yekaterina	Volkova	RUS	16.2.78	2	WCh	Helsinki	8 Aug
9:21.80		Inzikuru			1	WAF	Monaco	9 Sep
9:25.09	Wioletta	Janowska	POL	9.6.77	2	SGP	Athína	14 Jun
9:25.47		Janowska			1	WAF	Monaco	9 Sep
9:26.95	Jeruto	Kiptum	KEN	12.12.81	3	WCh	Helsinki	8 Aug

Mark	Name		Nat	Born	Pos	Meet	Venue	Date
9:27.21	Mardrea	Hyman	JAM	22.12.72	3	WAF	Monaco	9 Sep
9:27.85		Inzikuru			1h3	WCh	Helsinki	6 Aug
9:28.50		Inzikuru			1	SGP	Doha	13 May
9:29.21		Kiptum			2h3	WCh	Helsinki	6 Aug
9:29.88		Volkova			3h3	WCh	Helsinki	6 Aug
9:29.94		Volkova			2	GP	Rieti	28 Aug
9:30.12	Korine	Hinds	JAM	18.1.76	3	GP	Rieti	28 Aug
9:30.20	Livia	Tóth	HUN	7.1.80	4	WAF	Monaco	9 Sep
9:31.44	Salome	Chepchumba	KEN	29.9.82	3	SGP	Athína	14 Jun
9:32.41	Yelena	Zadorozhnaya	RUS	3.12.77	5	WAF	Monaco	9 Sep
9:32.52		Tóth			4	SGP	Athína	14 Jun
9:32.96		Zadorozhnaya			1h1	WCh	Helsinki	6 Aug
9:33.30		Hinds			4	WCh	Helsinki	8 Aug
9:33.46		Hinds			6	WAF	Monaco	9 Sep
9:33.99		Hyman			4	GP	Rieti	28 Aug
9:35.51	Natalya	Izmodenova (10)	RUS	1.1.81	5	SGP	Athína	14 Jun
9:35.66		Janowska			1h2	WCh	Helsinki	6 Aug
9:35.95	Cristina	Casandra	ROM	1.2.77	1	ECp-S	Firenze	17 Jun
9:36.08		Zadorozhnaya			5	GP	Rieti	28 Aug
9:36.12		Volkova			1	NC	Tula	11 Jul
9:36.14		Hyman			1	NC	Kingston	26 Jun
	(30/11)							
9:36.23		Hinds			2	NC	Kingston	26 Jun
9:36.76		Hinds			2h1	WCh	Helsinki	6 Aug
9:38.31	Fatiha Bahi	Azzouhoum	ALG	8.3.83	6	SGP	Athína	14 Jun
9:39.20	Inês	Monteiro	POR	18.5.80	7	SGP	Athína	14 Jun
9:39.68	Carrie	Messner	USA	7.6.77	3h2	WCh	Helsinki	6 Aug
9:39.78	Elizabeth	Jackson	USA	27.10.77	1	NC	Carson	26 Jun
9:40.47	Elodie	Olivarès	FRA	22.5.76	1		Paris	13 Jul
9:40.58	Lisa	Galaviz	USA	30.11.79	2	NC	Carson	26 Jun
9:41.21	Minori	Hayakari	JPN	29.11.72	4h1	WCh	Helsinki	6 Aug
9:41.82	Bouchra	Chaabi	MAR	22.9.80	5h1	WCh	Helsinki	6 Aug
9:42.18	Yamina	Bouchaouante	FRA	31.7.80	5h3	WCh	Helsinki	6 Aug
	(20)							
9:42.70	Yelena	Sidorchenkova	RUS	30.5.80	1	GP II	Thessaloníki	17 Jul
9:45.7A	Jackline Chemutai	Chemwok	KEN	13.9.83	1	WCT	Nairobi	25 Jun
9:45.91	Brianna	Shook	USA	6.1.81	4	NC	Carson	26 Jun
9:46.12	Roisín	McGettigan	IRL	23.8.80	9	WAF	Monaco	9 Sep
9:46.63	Lyubov	Ivanova	RUS	2.3.81	2	ECp-S	Firenze	17 Jun
9:47.47	Rasa	Troup-Michniovaite	LTU	1.3.77	5h2	WCh	Helsinki	6 Aug
9:47.54	Victoria	Mitchell	AUS	25.4.82	2	WUG	Izmir	17 Aug
9:47.9	Clarisse	Cruz	POR	9.7.78	2	ECp-1B	Leiria	19 Jun
9:48.57	Tina	Brown	GBR	22.8.76	8	GP	Rieti	28 Aug
9:48.65	Stephanie	De Croock	BEL	3.4.79	1		Ninove	30 Jul
	(30)							
9:48.85	Ida	Nilsson	SWE	8.2.81	2	ECp-1A	Gävle	18 Jun
9:49.50	Ann	Gaffigan	USA	5.10.81	3	GP II	Thessaloníki	17 Jul
9:49.73	Valentyna	Gorpinich	UKR	12.3.83	1	NC	Kiev	2 Jul
9:50.10	Jo	Ankier	GBR	5.8.83	4		Liège (N-X)	20 Jul
9:50.21	Svetlana	Ivanova	RUS	18.8.83	1	NC-23	Tula	14 Jun
9:50.32	Türkan	Erismis	TUR	5.1.84	3	WUG	Izmir	17 Aug
9:50.63	Mercy	Njoroge	KEN-J	10.6.86	1	Afr-J	Radès	4 Sep
9:51.05	Anália	Rosa	POR	28.2.76	5	SGP	Doha	13 May
9:51.3	Miranda	Boonstra	NED	29.8.72	4	ECp-1B	Leiria	19 Jun
9:51.49	Habiba	Ghribi	TUN	9.4.84	8h3	WCh	Helsinki	6 Aug
	(40)							
9:51.51	Justyna	Bak	POL	1.8.74	3	ECp-S	Firenze	17 Jun
9:51.60	Donna	MacFarlane	AUS	18.6.77	1		Melbourne (OP)	1 Dec
9:53.48	Tatyana	Vilisova	RUS	27.11.79	4	GP II	Thessaloníki	17 Jul
9:54.17	Katarzyna	Kowalska	POL	7.4.85	1	EU23	Erfurt	16 Jul
9:54.20	Rosa	Morató	ESP	19.6.79	3	ECp-1A	Gävle	18 Jun
9:56.54	Esther	Chebor Tuwei	KEN	21.4.81	5	Odlozil	Praha	27 Jun
9:56.70	Verena	Dreier	GER	15.1.85	3h1	EU23	Erfurt	14 Jul
9:56.74	Valeriya	Mara	UKR	22.2.83	2	NC	Kiev	2 Jul
9:56.75	Dobrinka	Shalamanova	BUL	1.5.83	5h1	EU23	Erfurt	16 Jul
9:56.78	Andrea	Mayr	AUT	15.10.79	1		Ulm	12 Jun
	(50)							
9:56.88	Irene	Limika	KEN	28.8.79	7	SGP	Doha	13 May
9:57.12	Ancuta	Bobocel	ROM-J	3.10.87	9	SGP	Athína	14 Jun
9:58.24	Marina	Ivanova	RUS	30.6.83	2	v2N	Viareggio	27 Jul

Mark	Name		Nat	Born	Pos	Meet	Venue	Date
9:59.82	Cassie	Hunt	USA	6.3.85	2	NCAA	Sacramento	10 Jun
10:00.54	Michele	da Costa	BRA	23.1.79	1	NC	São Paulo	17 Jun
10:01.09	Agnes	Tschurtschentaler	ITA	12.1.82	3	v2N	Viareggio	27 Jul
10:01.49	Sigrid	Van den Bempt	BEL	10.2.81	1	NC	Vilvoorde	6 Jul
10:01.84	Zenaide	Vieira	BRA	25.6.85	1		Rio de Janeiro	18 Nov
10:01.89	Fiona	Crombie	NZL	15.8.82	2		Oordegem	30 Jul
10:02.21	Renata	Williams-Chesser	USA	17.5.83	3	NCAA	Sacramento	10 Jun
	(60)							
10:02.41	Nancy	Kiprop	KEN	7.7.79	1		Gava	12 Jun
10:02.43	Kelly	Strong	USA	27.9.78	4	MSR	Walnut	15 Apr
10:02.91	Claudia	Colita	ROM	20.11.77	2	NC	Bucuresti	3 Jul
10:03.33	Daneja	Grandovec	SLO	2.7.84	4	ECp-1A	Gävle	18 Jun
10:04.39	Dawn	Cromer (Cleary)	USA	24.11.79	2		Waltham	11 Jun
10:04.65	Louise	Mørch	DEN	2.5.82	7	Odlozil	Praha	27 Jun
10:04.71	Sabine	Heitling	BRA-J	2.7.87	1	PAm-J	Windsor	30 Jul
10:05.39	Liz	Wort	USA	.84	4	NCAA	Sacramento	10 Jun
10:05.57	Polina	Jelizarova	LAT-Y	1.5.89	1	ECp-2A	Tallinn	18 Jun
10:05.76	Elena	Romagnolo	ITA	5.10.82	4	v2N	Viareggio	27 Jul
	(70)							
10:05.84	Helen	Hofstede	NED	31.12.80	1		Uden	25 Jun
10:06.0A	Genoveva	Kigen	KEN	.80	3	NC	Nairobi	18 Jun
10:06.05	Tebogo	Masehla	RSA	6.10.79	5	WUG	Izmir	17 Aug
10:06.10	Jane	Rudkin	USA	15.5.80	7		St.Paul	21 May
10:06.12	Emily	Pidgeon	GBR-Y	1.6.89	1	NC-j	Bedford	3 Jul
10:06.26	Fionualla	Britton	IRL	24.9.84	2		Palafrugell	28 May
10:06.44	Christin	Johansson	SWE	26.1.78	1		Sävedalen	4 Jun
10:06.45	Dina	Malheiro	POR	11.10.83	2	NC	Lisboa (U)	23 Jul
10:06.88	Delilah	DiCrescenzo	USA	28.2.83	1		Princeton	9 Apr
10:06.91	Tamara	Sanfabio	ESP	14.3.78	3		Oordegem	30 Jul
	(80)							
10:07.11	Diana	Martín	ESP	1.4.81	2		Matarõ	14 Jul
10:07.14	Shannon	Wommack	USA	9.4.83	5	NCAA	Sacramento	10 Jun
10:07.16	Irene	Pelayo	ESP	16.2.80	1		Santander	22 Jun
10:07.31	Barbora	Kuncová	CZE	26.4.82	2h1	NCAA	Sacramento	8 Jun
10:07.51	Natalie	Florence	USA	25.12.81	6	NC	Carson	26 Jun
10:07.73	Sophie	Duarte	FRA	31.7.81	5	v2N	Viareggio	27 Jul
10:07.90	Elizabeth	Hall	GBR	28.4.85	6h1	EU23	Erfurt	14 Jul
10:08.45	Agnieszka	Fulbiszewska	POL	9.3.80	4	Kuso	Warszawa	12 Jun
10:08.59	María	Pardaloú	GRE	21.4.84	8	ECp-S	Firenze	17 Jun
10:08.70	Cassie	King	USA	28.3.84	3h2	NCAA	Sacramento	8 Jun
	(90)							
10:08.79	Brianna	Dahm	USA	13.3.82	7	NCAA	Sacramento	10 Jun
10:09.78	Mercy Chelimo	Kosgei	KEN-Y	10.10.89	2	Afr-J	Radès	4 Sep
10:09.85	Kristina	Roth	USA	5.8.83	4h1	NCAA	Sacramento	8 Jun
10:10.5A	Rachel	Murkomen	KEN		4	NC	Nairobi	18 Jun
10:11.5A	Beatrice	Chepchumba	KEN	25.11.83	4	WCT	Nairobi	25 Jun
10:12.0A	Ruth	Nyagau	KEN		5	NC	Nairobi	18 Jun
10:12.13	Iwona	Lewandowska	POL	19.2.85	6	Kuso	Warszawa	12 Jun
10:12.35	Biljana	Jovic	SCG	2.3.85	2	BalkC	Novi Sad	23 Jul
10:12.66	Maria Teresa	Urbina	ESP	20.3.85	7h1	EU23	Erfurt	14 Jul
10:13.00	Yamilka	González	ESP	1.8.72	1		Benidorm	25 Jun
	(100)							

Mark	Name		Nat	Born	Date
10:13.21	Kara	June	USA	10.8.82	1 May
10:13.80	Renee	Metivier	USA	25.12.81	15 Apr
10:13.88	Andrea	Parker	USA	10.10.82	8 Jun
10:13.92	Aurélie	Casado	FRA	6.6.80	16 Jul
10:14.3A	Evaline	Chebichi	KEN		18 Jun
10:14.55	Lisa	Pratt	USA		8 Jun
10:14.64	Yuliya	Mochalova	RUS-J	26.5.87	14 Jun
10:14.68	Xénia	Kazimírova	GRE	17.9.84	10 Jun
10:14.81	Hanne	Lyngstad	NOR	5.12.75	17 Jul
10:14.90	Galina	Saykina	RUS-Y	27.11.88	14 Jun
10:14.96	Susi	Lutz	GER-J	26.3.87	24 Jul
10:15.15	Yoanna	Parusheva	BUL	23.5.82	7 Apr
10:15.24	Sonia	Thomas	GBR	16.5.79	11 Jun
10:15.38	Fanny	Pruvost	FRA	21.5.79	30 Jul
10:15.47	Olga	Derevyeva	RUS	28.5.85	26 May
10:15.59	Tara	Krzywicki	GBR	9.3.74	11 Jun
10:16.26	Jolanda	Verstraten	NED	26.6.83	25 Jun
10:16.5	Patrícia	Lobo	BRA	6.11.83	9 Dec
10:16.59	Christine	Bardelle	FRA	16.8.74	8 Jun
10:16.6A	Ruth	Waithera	KEN-Y	.90	18 Jun
10:16.71	Lucinda	Hull	USA	2.10.81	26 Jun
10:16.81	Claire	Entwistle	GBR	9.12.76	10 Jul
10:17.31	Rebecca	Forlong	NZL-J	13.7.86	6 Aug
10:17.38	Anna	Hay	USA		22 Apr
10:17.40	Eszter	Erdélyi	HUN	22.5.82	6 Jul
10:17.51	Jeane	Goff	USA	1.12.83	28 May
10:17.56	Anni	Tuimala	FIN	27.4.82	16 Jul
10:17.70	Maureen	Scott	USA	8.10.83	8 Jun
10:17.76	Mihaela	Botezan	ROM	21.11.76	13 May
10:18.15	Kathleen	Trotter	USA	4.5.85	23 Apr
10:18.3	Eunice	Chepkirui	KEN	20.5.84	19 Mar
10:18.31	Tegla	Loroupe	KEN	9.5.73	14 Jun
10:18.57	Angelina	Stanek	POL	5.4.85	28 Aug
10:18.59	Kelly	Siefker	USA	29.3.84	8 Jun
10:18.62	Yulia	Ignatova	UKR	30.7.83	2 Jul
10:19.0A	Eunice	Chepkorir	KEN	17.2.82	18 Jun
10:19.03	A Havahla	Haynes	USA	1.3.84	8 Jun
10:19.21	Jessa	Chance	USA	26.8.82	25 Mar
10:19.72	Gwendoline	Desprès	FRA	27.11.83	14 Jul
10:19.73	Sarah	Becker	USA	23.1.84	8 Jun
10:19.87	Anna	Kadziela	POL	27.4.80	26 Jun
10:19.95	Malika	Assahsah	MAR	24.9.82	4 Jun

Mark	Name		Nat	Born	Pos	Meet	Venue	Date

JUNIORS

See main list for top 6 juniors. 11 performances by 7 women to 10:14.7. Additional marks and further juniors:

Bobocel 10:09.11 9 SGP Doha 13 May 10:14.29 2 EJ Kaunas 24 Jul
10:10.71 1 Bucuresti 7 Aug
Jelizarova 10:05.57 1 ECp-2A Tallinn 18 Jun

Mark	Name		Nat	Born	Pos	Meet	Venue	Date
10:14.64	Yuliya	Mochalova	RUS	26.5.87	3	NC-j	Tula	14 Jun
10:14.90	Galina	Saykina	RUS-Y	27.11.88	4		Tula	14 Jun
10:14.96	Susi	Lutz	GER	26.3.87	3	EJ	Kaunas	24 Jul
10:16.6A	Ruth	Waithera (10)	KEN-Y	.90	7	NC	Nairobi	18 Jun
10:17.31	Rebecca	Forlong	NZL	13.7.86	1		London (CP)	6 Aug
10:21.00	Linda	Byrne	IRL	13.5.86	4	EJ	Kaunas	24 Jul
10:22.82	Oksana	Juravel	MDA	23.2.86	2		Bucuresti	7 Aug
10:23.82	Julia	Hiller	GER	24.7.87	5		Ulm	12 Jun
10:24.35	Natalia	Jarawka	POL	13.7.86	6	EJ	Kaunas	24 Jul
10:24.39	Kalameya	Durka Muna	SUD-Y	19.6.88	3	Afr-J	Radès	4 Sep
10:26.71	Lindsay	Allen	USA	30.6.86	6r1		Stanford	25 Mar
10:27.44	Marie	Lawrence	USA-Y	29.8.89	2	PAm-J	Windsor	30 Jul
10:28.63	Stacie	Lifferth	USA	17.6.86	6r2	NCAA-r	Eugene	28 May
10:28.64	Lilian Priscila	Leonel (20)	BRA	19.11.86	4	PAm-J	Windsor	30 Jul

100 METRES HURDLES

Mark	Wind	Name		Nat	Born	Pos	Meet	Venue	Date
12.43	-0.3	Michelle	Perry	USA	1.5.79	1s1	NC	Carson	26 Jun
12.45	1.7		Perry			1		New York (RI)	11 Jun
12.45	0.8		Perry			1		Réthimno	10 Jul
12.47	1.7	Joanna	Hayes	USA	23.12.76	2		New York (RI)	11 Jun
12.52	-0.9		Perry			1h1	NC	Carson	25 Jun
12.54	-0.8		Perry			1	WAF	Monaco	10 Sep
12.55	-0.6		Perry			1	WK	Zürich	19 Aug
12.55	-0.8	Brigitte	Foster-Hylton	JAM	7.11.74	2	WAF	Monaco	10 Sep
12.57	0.1	Anjanette	Kirkland	USA	24.2.74	1	GGala	Roma	8 Jul
12.57	-0.8	Delloreen	Ennis-London	JAM	5.3.75	3	WAF	Monaco	10 Sep
12.58	-0.6	Perdita	Felicien	CAN	29.8.80	1	Pre	Eugene	4 Jun
12.58	1.7		Kirkland			3		New York (RI)	11 Jun
12.59	-0.1		Hayes			1s2	NC	Carson	26 Jun
12.59	0.4	Kirsten	Bolm	GER	4.3.75	1	LGP	London (CP)	22 Jul
12.60	1.1		Ennis-London			1		New York (RI)	11 Jun
12.60	0.5		Foster-Hylton			1=	NC	Kingston	26 Jun
12.60	0.5		Ennis-London			1=	NC	Kingston	26 Jun
12.60	0.4		Hayes			1	Gaz	Saint-Denis	1 Jul
12.61	-0.3	Virginia	Powell	USA	7.9.83	2s1	NC	Carson	26 Jun
12.61	1.2		Perry			1rA	Athl	Lausanne	5 Jul
12.62	1.2		Hayes			1h2	NC	Carson	25 Jun
12.62	0.4		Kirkland			2	LGP	London (CP)	22 Jul
12.63	0.2		Foster-Hylton			1	ISTAF	Berlin	4 Sep
12.64	0.1		Hayes			1		Carson	22 May
12.64	-2.1		Perry			1h1	WCh	Helsinki	9 Aug
12.64	0.5		Foster-Hylton			1h4	WCh	Helsinki	9 Aug
12.65	0.7	Susanna	Kallur	SWE	16.2.81	1	FBK	Hengelo	29 May
12.65	-0.4		Perry			1	GP II	Stanford	30 May
12.65	1.2		Kirkland			2rA	Athl	Lausanne	5 Jul
12.65	1.2		Ennis-London			1h2	WCh	Helsinki	9 Aug
12.65	0.5		Foster-Hylton			1s2	WCh	Helsinki	10 Aug
12.65	1.3		Foster-Hylton			1	Gugl	Linz	23 Aug
		(32/9)							
12.66	0.9	Linda	Khodadin (10)	FRA	24.12.76	1	NCAA	Angers	15 Jul
12.67	1.1	Vonette	Dixon	JAM	26.11.75	3	NC	Kingston	26 Jun
12.68	1.1	Lacena	Golding-Clarke	JAM	20.3.75	4	NC	Kingston	26 Jun
12.71	1.2	Glory	Alozie	ESP	30.12.77	2h2	WCh	Helsinki	9 Aug
12.72	0.0	Danielle	Carruthers	USA	22.12.79	2	GP II	Zagreb	11 Jul
12.73	1.2	Maria	Koroteyeva	RUS	10.11.81	3h2	WCh	Helsinki	9 Aug
12.75	0.6	Yelena	Krasovska	UKR	17.8.76	1	GP	Sevilla	4 Jun
12.75	0.9	Reïna-Flor	Okori	FRA	2.5.80	2	NC	Angers	15 Jul
12.76	-0.1	Lolo	Jones	USA	5.8.82	3s2	NC	Carson	26 Jun
12.76	0.5	Irina	Shevchenko	RUS	2.9.75	3h4	WCh	Helsinki	9 Aug
12.77	0.8	Aurelia	Trywianska	POL	9.5.76	2		Réthimno	10 Jul
		(20)							
12.79	1.4	Nichole	Denby	USA	10.10.82	3rA	MSR	Walnut	17 Apr
12.82	-0.6	Priscilla	Lopes	CAN	26.8.82	2	NCAA	Sacramento	10 Jun
12.83	0.8	Ashlee	Williams	USA	27.3.84	1rB	TexR	Austin	9 Apr

Mark	Wind	Name		Nat	Born	Pos	Meet	Venue	Date
12.83	0.8	Ashlee	Williams	USA	27.3.84	1rB	TexR	Austin	9 Apr
12.83	1.1	Andrea	Bliss	JAM	5.10.80	5	NC	Kingston	26 Jun
12.83	1.5	Nadine	Faustin-Parker	HAI	14.4.76	1	CAC	Nassau	10 Jul
12.84	1.5	Michelle	Freeman	JAM	5.5.69	4		Kingston	7 May
12.85	1.2	Natalya	Rusakova	RUS	12.12.80	2	Znam	Kazan	24 Jun
12.85	0.9	Adrianna	Lamalle	FRA	27.9.82	3	NC	Angers	15 Jul
12.85	-0.5	Jenny	Kallur	SWE	16.2.81	3s1	WCh	Helsinki	10 Aug
12.86	0.2	Melissa	Morrison-Howard	USA	9.7.71	2		Santo Domingo	14 May
		(30)							
12.88	0.3	Angela	Whyte	CAN	22.5.80	4h5	WCh	Helsinki	9 Aug
12.89	-0.7	Maiía Paula	Machado	BRA	22.1.81	1	NC	São Paulo	19 Jun
12.89	0.8	Jenny	Adams	USA	8.7.78	4		Réthimno	10 Jul
12.89	0.6	Eunice	Barber	FRA	17.11.74	1		Nancy	6 Sep
12.91	0.0	Dawn	Harper	USA	13.5.84	2	Pac10	Los Angeles (Ww)	15 May
12.92	1.7		Feng Yun	CHN	23.2.76	8		New York (RI)	11 Jun
12.93	0.9	Mirjam	Liimask	EST	25.10.83	1	EU23	Erfurt	17 Jul
12.94	-0.2	Antoinette	Wilks	JAM	14.10.80	1h1		Atlanta	3 Jun
12.95	-0.3	Ebony	Foster	USA	26.7.83	5s1	NC	Carson	26 Jun
12.95	0.8	Anay	Tejeda	CUB	3.4.83	5		Réthimno	10 Jul
		(40)							
12.96	1.0	Sarah	Claxton	GBR	23.9.79	1	NC	Manchester (SC)	9 Jul
12.96	1.4		Liu Jing	CHN	8.8.77	1	NG	Nanjing	18 Oct
12.97	0.2	Tatyana	Pavliy	RUS	18.5.78	3=	NC	Tula	12 Jul
12.97	0.9	Tina	Klein	GER	24.4.83	2	EU23	Erfurt	17 Jul
12.99	1.4	Beau	Walker	USA	25.3.83	4rA	MSR	Walnut	17 Apr
12.99	1.4	Tiffany	Ross-Williams	USA	5.2.83	2	Towns	Athens, GA	23 Apr
13.00	0.5	Derval	O'Rourke	IRL	28.5.81	6h3	WCh	Helsinki	9 Aug
13.01	0.4	Sally	McLellan	AUS-J	19.9.86	1		Brisbane	27 Nov
13.03	-1.3	Flóra	Redoúmi	GRE	11.9.76	3	ECp-S	Firenze	19 Jun
13.04	0.7	Juliane	Sprenger-Afflerbach	GER	22.3.77	1		Dudelange	22 May
		(50)							
13.04	1.7	Yolanda	McCray	USA	11.9.76	9		New York (RI)	11 Jun
13.05	0.0		Su Yiping	CHN	4.8.79	1		Zhongshan	24 Apr
13.07	1.4	Lucie	Martincová	CZE	4.1.82	1		Praha	23 Jun
13.08	0.9	Nicole	Ramalalanirina	FRA	5.3.72	4	NC	Angers	15 Jul
13.09	-0.1	Lashinda	Demus	USA	10.3.83	1		Clemson	7 May
13.09	1.1	Hyleas	Fountain	USA	14.1.81	1H		Götzis	28 May
13.09	1.5	Yaumara	Neyra	CUB	18.4.76	3	CAC	Nassau	10 Jul
13.09	0.9	Patricia	Girard	FRA	8.4.68	5	NC	Angers	15 Jul
13.11	1.8	Lynnsey	Dailey	USA	5.3.83	1h1		Albany	16 Apr
13.11	1.4		Zhang Rong	CHN	5.1.83	4	NG	Nanjing	18 Oct
		(60)							
13.12	0.9	Anna	Yevdokimova	RUS	27.5.83	3	EU23	Erfurt	17 Jul
13.12	1.6	Gi-Gi	Miller	USA	12.1.79	H		Talence	17 Sep
13.13	0.8	Kasia	Williams	JAM	14.12.84	3rB	TexR	Austin	9 Apr
13.13	0.7	Sharifa	Jones	USA	16.11.82	2h1	NCAA-r	Eugene	27 May
13.13	0.2	Hanna	Korell	FIN	16.3.79	1		Lappeenranta	21 Jul
13.14	1.5	Joanna	Bujak	FRA	30.8.79	3		La Chaux-de-Fonds	21 Aug
13.15	1.1	Carolina	Klüft	SWE	2.2.83	2H		Götzis	28 May
13.15	1.5	Aliuska	López	ESP	29.8.69	2		Kalamáta	30 May
13.16	1.1	Monique	Morgan	JAM	10.10.85	1s1	IC4A	Princeton	15 May
13.17	-0.6	Ashley	Lodree	USA	22.10.85	3s2	NCAA	Sacramento	8 Jun
		(70)							
13.19	0.1		He Liyuan	CHN	14.1.83	2h3	NG	Nanjing	17 Oct
13.20		Natalya	Ivoninskaya	KAZ	22.2.85	2h3	WUG	Izmir	15 Aug
13.21	0.8	Raquel	Washington	USA	26.9.82	4rB	TexR	Austin	9 Apr
13.21	0.2	Candice	Davis	USA	26.10.85	3		Los Angeles (Ww)	30 Apr
13.21	0.3	Melaine	Walker	JAM	1.1.83	3	PennR	Philadelphia	30 Apr
13.21	1.0	Diane	Allahgreen	GBR	21.2.75	2	NC	Manchester (SC)	9 Jul
13.22	0.6	Ronetta	Alexander	USA	8.5.85	1h3	SEC	Nashville	14 May
13.22	1.5	Irina	Lenskiy	ISR	12.6.71	4		Kalamáta	30 May
13.22	0.2	Patricia	Buval	FRA	22.1.76	1h1		Argentan	10 Jun
13.23	0.2	Johanna	Halkoaho	FIN	13.1.77	2		Lappeenranta	21 Jul
		(80)							
13.23	0.4	Fiona	Cullen	AUS	31.8.79	2		Brisbane	27 Nov
13.24	0.9	Elisabeth	Maurer	AUT	10.2.83	4	EU23	Erfurt	17 Jul
13.24	0.8	Natalya	Davydenko	RUS	13.4.75	5		Tallinn	16 Aug
13.24	0.8	Toyin	Augustus	NGR	24.12.79	2		Hilversum	4 Sep
13.25	-0.6	Heather	Heron	USA	20.6.82	5s2	NCAA	Sacramento	8 Jun
13.25	1.1	Toni Ann	D'Oyley	JAM	25.10.81	8	NC	Kingston	26 Jun
13.26	0.8	Karin	Ruckstuhl	NED	2.11.80	3	ECp-1B	Leiria	19 Jun

Mark	Wind	Name		Nat	Born	Pos	Meet	Venue	Date
13.26	1.0	Jessica	Ennis	GBR-J	28.1.86	3	NC	Manchester (SC)	9 Jul
13.27	1.1	Kelly	Sotherton	GBR	13.11.76	3H		Götzis	28 May
13.27	0.0	Judith	Ritz	GER	16.6.83	2h1		Mannheim	18 Jun
		(90)							
13.27	0.9	Kumiko	Ikeda	JPN	10.1.81	1		Marugame	25 Sep
13.28	0.9	Carolin	Nytra	GER	26.2.85	3	NC	Wattenscheid	2 Jul
13.28	1.6	Radmila	Vukmirovic	SLO	23.11.79	1	NC	Maribor	23 Jul
13.29	1.6	Julie	Pratt	GBR	20.3.79	1	CAU	Bedford	29 May
13.29	-1.1	Yenima	Arencibia	CUB	25.12.84	1		La Habana	23 Jun
13.30	0.8	Olga	Korsunova	RUS	20.5.81	1H		Sochi	17 May
13.30	0.0	Shameka	Marshall	USA	9.9.83	3	NCAA-r	New York	28 May
13.31	1.7	Micol	Cattaneo	ITA	14.5.82	1		Bellinzona	30 Jul
13.31	0.8	Kadri	Viigipuu	EST	4.2.82	1		Tartu	1 Aug
13.32	0.2	Fatmata	Fofanah	USA	26.6.85	1h1		Tallahassee	23 Apr
		(100)							
13.32	1.4	Polina	Roslavtseva	RUS	17.3.78	3s1	NC	Tula	12 Jul

Mark	Wind	Name		Nat	Born	Date
13.33	0.2		Lee Yeon-kyong	KOR	15.4.81	3 Jun
13.33	0.9	Mami	Ishino	JPN	10.1.83	25 Sep
13.34	1.2	Deanna	Lane	USA	10.10.83	24 Mar
13.34	-0.4	Lela	Nelson	USA	19.5.83	14 May
13.34	0.0	Bertha	Peñalver	CUB	3.10.81	19 May
13.34	0.0	Marina	Tomic	SLO	30.4.83	21 May
13.34	-0.7	Daniela	Wöckinger	AUT	9.5.81	9 Jul
13.35	1.4	MaKeatha	Cooper	USA	19.7.85	14 May
13.36	0.0	Josephine	Onyia	NGR-J	15.7.86	23 Apr
13.36	0.0	Tamera	Thomas	JAM		23 Apr
13.36	1.6	Yevgenia	Snigur	UKR	7.3.84	6 May
13.36	1.4	Alicia	Cave	TRI	4.2.82	14 May
13.36	1.3	Tatyana	Degtyarova	RUS	8.5.81	24 Jun
13.36	1.4	Alexandra	Antonova	RUS	24.3.80	12 Jul
13.37	0.8	Ranysha	LeBlanc	USA	11.1.83	9 Apr
13.37		Shantrell	Moss	USA-J	27.10.86	27 May
13.37	1.2	Cécile	Michot	FRA	2.6.74	26 Jun
13.37	1.8	Arantza	Loureiro	ESP	22.2.81	9 Jul
13.38	-0.8	Katja	Keller	GER	9.8.80	28 May
13.38	0.0	Lyudmila	Blonska	UKR	9.11.77	27 Aug
13.39	1.4	Doria	Appleberry	USA	5.2.83	14 May
13.39	0.4	Eline	Berings	BEL-J	28.5.86	2 Jul
13.39	1.9	Dora	Jémaa	FRA	15.7.85	5 Jul
13.40	1.1	Dominique	Darden	USA	9.12.83	16 Apr
13.40	1.0	Josanne	Lucas	TRI	14.5.84	15 May
13.40			Ji Fangqian	CHN	18.7.84	15 Aug
13.41	1.0	Shevon	Stoddart	JAM	21.11.82	15 May
13.41	-0.8	Margaret	Simpson	GHA	31.12.81	28 May
13.41	0.9	Aurore	Ruet	FRA	14.2.84	17 Jul
13.42	0.7	Elisabeth	Davin	BEL	3.6.81	22 May
13.42	1.1	Jessica	Zelinka	CAN	3.9.81	28 May
13.42	1.6	Stephanie	Lichtl	GER	12.7.85	5 Jun
13.42	0.8	Yeoryía	Stoyiannídou	GRE	3.1.82	10 Jun
13.42	1.7	Vasilíki	Delinikóla	GRE	9.2.81	16 Jul
13.43	1.2	Kim	Jones	USA	13.6.81	15 May
13.43	0.0	Jessica	Czaikowski	CAN	20.4.84	28 May
13.43	-0.3	Rosina	Hodde	NED	10.2.83	15 Jul
13.44	0.3	Lindsay	Eck	USA	14.9.81	27 May
13.45		Tamara	McGill	USA	11.1.83	2 Apr
13.45A	1.1	Nevin	Yanit	TUR-J	16.2.86	3 Aug
13.46	0.0	Jessica	Ohanaja	USA-J	6.12.86	14 May
13.46	0.0	Raasin	McIntosh	USA	29.4.82	12 Jun
13.47	1.1	Sonja	Kesselschläger	GER	20.1.78	28 May
13.47	1.5	Jacquie	Munro	AUS	4.10.81	2 Jul
13.47	0.3		Xu Jia	CHN	23.9.79	17 Oct
13.48	-1.6	Lauren	Smith	USA	27.8.81	3 Jun
13.48	1.2	Mariya	Solovyova	RUS	11.5.83	24 Jun
13.48	-0.7	Victoria	Schreibeis	AUT	9.1.79	3 Jul
13.49	0.9	Aniko	Bozsik	GER	12.1.82	2 Jul
13.49	1.8	Raquel	Fraguas	ESP	2.3.76	9 Jul
13.49	0.5	Veronica	Borsi	ITA-J	13.6.87	6 Aug
13.50	1.8	Yvonne	Mensah	CAN	15.5.85	14 May
13.50	-0.6	Frances	Keating	CAN	21.6.85	15 May
13.50	0.5	Ryanne	Dupree	USA	13.4.84	28 May
13.50	2.0	Justyna	Oleksy	POL	19.9.83	26 Jun
13.50	1.5	Zolymar	Febles	PUR	30.3.83	10 Jul
13.50	0.8	Naide	Gomes	POR	10.11.79	23 Jul
13.51	0.3	Funmi	Jimoh	USA	29.5.84	27 May
13.51A	1.1	Shalina	Clarke	USA-Y	8.8.88	4 Jun
13.51	0.0	Joanna	Grzesiak	POL	15.8.80	4 Jun
13.51	0.5	Lucile	Berliat	FRA	7.12.82	18 Jun
13.51A	0.4	Kira	Robinson	USA-J	25.5.87	18 Jun
13.51	0.1	Tracye	Lawyer-Thomas	USA	28.8.77	25 Jun
13.51A	0.1	Princesa	Oliveros	COL	10.8.75	22 Jul
13.51	0.6	Fanny	Gérance	FRA	4.1.81	6 Sep
13.52	0.3	Dana	Rogers	USA	18.2.83	30 Apr
13.52A	0.3	Amy	Menlove	USA	23.7.85	13 May
13.52	-1.1	Yvette	Lewis	USA	16.3.85	14 May
13.52	1.9	Sharon-Louise	Walls	GBR	9.10.84	18 Jun
13.52	-1.8	Joanna	Kocielnik	POL	11.3.83	15 Jul
13.52	0.2	Yevgeniya	Likhuta	BLR	24.3.81	21 Jul
13.52	0.6	Sabrina	Altermatt	SUI	6.3.85	15 Aug
13.53	0.2	Adriane	Lapsley	USA	18.12.83	22 Apr
13.53	2.0	Kamilah	Tyson	USA	8.9.77	14 May
13.53	0.0	Laurien	Hoos	NED	18.8.83	22 May
13.54	0.8	Yanique	Booth	JAM	3.5.84	27 May
13.54	0.6	Marzia	Caravelli	ITA	23.10.81	4 Jun
13.54	1.6	LaToya	Greaves	JAM-J	31.5.86	29 Jul
13.54	-1.4		Moh Siew Wei	MAS	30.4.78	28 Nov
		(180)				

Wind assisted

Mark	Wind	Name		Nat	Born	Pos	Meet	Venue	Date
12.62	2.4	Glory	Alozie	ESP	30.12.77	1rA	Athl	Lausanne	5 Jul
12.62	2.9	Eunice	Barber	FRA	17.11.74	1H		Arles	4 Jun
12.63	2.9	Danielle	Carruthers	USA	22.12.79	1		Karlstad	18 Jul
12.66	2.3	Nichole	Denby	USA	10.10.82	1rA	TexR	Austin	9 Apr
12.67	2.4	Lacena	Golding-Clarke	JAM	20.3.75	3rA	Athl	Lausanne	5 Jul
12.85	3.6	Tatyana	Pavliy	RUS	18.5.78	2		Sochi	27 May
12.88	2.9	Jenny	Adams	USA	8.7.78	2		Karlstad	18 Jul
12.93	3.9	Lashinda	Demus	USA	10.3.83	1	Kans R	Lawrence	23 Apr
12.95	4.1	Derval	O'Rourke	IRL	28.5.81	1	NC	Dublin (S)	24 Jul
13.01	2.3	Natalya	Davydenko	RUS	13.4.75	3s2	NC	Tula	12 Jul
13.03	2.3	Gi-Gi	Miller	USA	12.1.79	1H	NC	Carson	25 Jun
13.03	2.1	Patricia	Girard	FRA	8.4.68	2s2	NC	Angers	15 Jul
13.09	3.8	Aliuska	López	ESP	29.8.69	1		Bilbao	18 Jun
13.10	3.7	Susanne	Dickerson	JAM	12.2.78	1		Arlington	7 May
13.10	2.1	Dora	Jémaa	FRA	15.7.85	1		Bron	5 Jul
13.13	2.6	Patricia	Buval	FRA	22.1.76	2		Noisy-le-Grand	7 Jun
13.13	2.2	Candice	Davis	USA	26.10.85	1rB	MSR	Walnut	17 Apr
13.15	2.9	Jessica	Zelinka	CAN	3.9.81	2H		Arles	4 Jun

Mark	Wind	Name		Nat	Born	Pos	Meet	Venue	Date
13.17	3.3	Melaine	Walker	JAM	1.1.83	2h2	Big 12	Manhattan, KS	14 May
13.18	2.9	Julie	Pratt	GBR	20.3.79	1		Bedford	27 Aug
13.20	0.4	Fiona	Cullen	AUS	31.8.79	2		Perth	18 Dec
13.22	2.5	Dana	Rogers	USA	18.2.83	1		Atlanta	2 Apr
13.23	2.4	Ranysha	LeBlanc	USA	11.1.83	1		Baton Rouge	23 Apr
13.26	2.7	Josephine	Onyia	NGR-J	15.7.86	1		Alfaz del Pi	16 Apr
13.26	3.4	Lauren	Smith	USA	27.8.81	2		Houston	7 May
13.28	2.4	Doria	Appleberry	USA	5.2.83	2		Baton Rouge	23 Apr
13.29	2.9	Kellie	Wells	USA	16.7.82	1		Durham	9 Apr
13.29	2.9	Janice	Josephs	RSA	31.3.82	3H		Arles	4 Jun
13.30	2.3	Tatyana	Degtyarova	RUS	8.5.81	4s2	NC	Tula	12 Jul

Mark	Wind	Name		Nat	Born	Date
13.34A	4.5	Ryanne	Dupree	USA	13.4.84	16 Apr
13.36	2.3	Veronica	Borsi	ITA-J	13.6.87	29 May
13.37	3.9	Lindsay	Eck	USA	14.9.81	23 Apr
13.38	6.2	Jessica	Ohanaja	USA-J	6.12.86	23 Apr
13.38	2.6	Eline	Berings	BEL-J	28.5.86	28 May
13.38	2.1	LaToya	Greaves	JAM-J	31.5.86	29 Jul
13.39	2.3	Amy	Menlove	USA	23.7.85	14 May
13.42	2.1	Natasha	Ruddock	JAM-Y	24.1.89	29 Jul
13.43	3.1	Antoinette	Djimou	FRA	2.8.85	4 Jun
13.44	3.3	Alandra	Sherman	USA	25.11.85	14 May
13.45	2.9	Anzhela	Atroshchenko	TUR	14.11.70	4 Jun
13.47	2.1	Sabrina	Altermatt	SUI	6.3.85	3 Jul
13.49	2.4	Funmi	Jimoh	USA	29.5.84	23 Apr
13.49	3.7	Yvonne	Wisse	NED	6.6.82	18 Sep
13.50	2.1	Christine	Spence	USA	25.11.81	13 May
13.50	2.1	Genevieve	Thibault	CAN-J	25.10.86	29 Jul
13.51	2.2	Keisha	Brown	JAM	17.3.85	18 May
13.51	3.1	Amandine	Constantin	FRA	12.2.84	4 Jun
13.52	2.4		Liu Haili	CHN	24.12.84	17 Oct
13.53	2.3	Natalya	Kotova	RUS	13.5.83	12 Jul
13.53	3.5	Elizabeth	García	ESP	30.10.83	24 Jul
13.53	2.9	Elizabeth	Fairs	GBR	1.12.77	27 Aug
13.54	2.3	Doris	Kratt	USA		7 May
13.54	2.4	Desislava	Mutafchieva	BUL	23.11.84	28 May
13.54	3.4	Heather	Jones	GBR-J	10.9.86	7 Jun
13.54	2.1	Edith	Vári	HUN	31.5.75	11 Jun

Best at low altitude

Mark	Wind	Name		Nat	Born	Date
13.53w	2.1	Kira	Robinson	USA-J	25.5.87	29 Jul

Hand timed

Mark	Wind	Name		Nat	Born	Date
13.2	0.3	Radmila	Vukmirovic	SLO	23.11.79	15 Jul
13.3	0.3	Elisa	Trevisan	ITA	5.3.80	15 Jul
13.3	0.2	Jacquie	Munro	AUS	4.10.81	16 Jul

JUNIORS

Mark	Wind	Name		Nat	Born	Pos	Meet	Venue	Date
13.01	0.4	Sally	McLellan	AUS	19.9.86	1		Brisbane	27 Nov
		13.16 1.3 1	Perth		18 Dec	13.41	0.7 1= NC	Sydney	6 Mar
		13.39 0.4 1=	Brisbane		4 Nov	13.41	-1.5 1	Brisbane	11 Nov
13.26	1.0	Jessica	Ennis	GBR	28.1.86	3	NC	Manchester (SC)	9 Jul
13.36	0.0	Josephine	Onyia	NGR	15.7.86	1		Alicante	23 Apr
13.37		Shantrell	Moss	USA	27.10.86	2h2	NCAA-r	New York	27 May
13.39	0.4	Eline	Berings	BEL	28.5.86	1		Oordegem	2 Jul
		13.41 -1.5 1	EJ Kaunas		23 Jul	13.42	1.0 1	Kortrijk	16 Jul
13.45A	1.1	Nevin	Yanit	TUR	16.2.86	1		Konya	3 Aug
13.46	0.0	Jessica	Ohanaja	USA	6.12.86	2h2	SEC	Nashville	14 May
13.49	0.5	Veronica	Borsi	ITA	13.6.87	1		Marseille	6 Aug
13.51A	1.1	Shalina	Clarke	USA-Y	8.8.88	1		Albuquerque	4 Jun
13.51A	0.4	Kira	Robinson (10)	USA-	25.5.87	1		Aurora	18 Jun
13.54	1.6	LaToya	Greaves	JAM	31.5.86	1h1	PAm-J	Windsor	29 Jul
13.56	0.0		Wang Jindan	CHN	1.4.87	h		Zhongshan	23 Apr
13.56	-1.5	Christina	Vukicevic	NOR	18.6.87	2	EJ	Kaunas	23 Jul
13.57	0.0	Cindy	Billaud	FRA	11.3.86	1	NC-j	Paris	29 Jul
13.57	2.0	Nadine	Hildebrand	GER	20.9.87	2	NC-23	Rostock	21 Aug
13.57	-0.1	Azusa	Ichiki	JPN	2.5.86	1		Tokyo	2 Sep
13.62	1.6	Anne-Kathrin	Elbe	GER	24.2.87	2A		Mannheim	18 Jun
13.64	1.3	Theresa	Lewis	USA-Y	23.3.88	1h2		Baltimore	27 May
13.65	1.4	Heather	Jones	GBR	10.9.86	5		Loughborough	22 May
13.67	0.5	Yekaterina	Kostetskaya (10)	RUS	31.12.86	3		Huntsville	15 May

Wind assisted

Mark	Wind	Name		Nat	Born	Pos	Meet	Venue	Date
13.26	2.7	Josephine	Onyia	NGR	15.7.86	1		Alfaz del Pi	16 Apr
13.36	2.3	Veronica	Borsi	ITA	13.6.87	3	ECCp	Lagos/POR	29 May
13.38	6.2	Jessica	Ohanaja	USA	6.12.86	1B		Baton Rouge	23 Apr
13.38	2.6	Eline	Berings	BEL	28.5.86	1h1		Den Haag	28 May
13.38	2.1	LaToya	Greaves	JAM	31.5.86	1	PAm-J	Windsor	29 Jul
13.42	2.1	Natasha	Ruddock	JAM-Y	24.1.89	2	PAm-J	Windsor	29 Jul
13.50	2.1	Genevieve	Thibault	CAN	25.10.86	3	PAm-J	Windsor	29 Jul
13.54	3.4	Heather	Jones	GBR	10.9.86	4		Bratislava	7 Jun
13.57	2.9	Piia	Roslund	FIN	2.4.86	2h1		Jämsänkoski	30 Jun
13.58	2.2	Leslie	Mercado	USA	8.6.87	1		Sacramento	4 Jun
13.59	2.8	Rena	Joshita	JPN	2.4.86	1		Toyama	26 Jun
13.59	3.7	Johanna	Bloch	GER	11.4.86	1	NC-j	Braunschweig	31 Jul

200 METRES HURDLES

Mark	Wind	Name		Nat	Born	Pos	Meet	Venue	Date
26.99	0.0	Yvonne	Wisse	NED	6.6.82	1		Hilversum	4 Sep
27.37	0.4	Marjolein	De Jong	NED	12.6.81	1		Krommenie	3 Jul

400 METRES HURDLES

Mark	Wind	Name		Nat	Born	Pos	Meet	Venue	Date
52.90		Yuliya	Nosova-Pechonkina	RUS	21.4.78	1	WCh	Helsinki	13 Aug

WOMEN 2005

Mark	Wind	Name		Nat	Born	Pos	Meet	Venue	Date
53.01			Pechonkina			1	NC	Tula	11 Jul
53.05			Pechonkina			1		Tula	13 Jun
53.27		Lashinda	Demus	USA	10.3.83	2	WCh	Helsinki	13 Aug
53.30			Pechonkina			1	WK	Zürich	19 Aug
53.31			Pechonkina			1h3	NC	Tula	10 Jul
53.32		Sandra	Glover	USA	30.12.68	3	WCh	Helsinki	13 Aug
53.35			Demus			1	NC	Carson	25 Jun
53.37			Demus			1	WAF	Monaco	9 Sep
53.44		Jana	Pittman	AUS	9.11.82	1	SGP	Athína	14 Jun
53.56			Demus			1	GP	Belém	22 May
53.61			Demus			1	VD	Bruxelles	26 Aug
53.68			Demus			1	GGala	Roma	8 Jul
53.73			Glover			2	VD	Bruxelles	26 Aug
53.74			Pittman			2	GGala	Roma	8 Jul
53.77			Pechonkina			1h1	WCh	Helsinki	10 Aug
53.80			Pechonkina			2	WAF	Monaco	9 Sep
53.83			Demus			2	WK	Zürich	19 Aug
53.85			Demus			1	Gaz	Saint-Denis	1 Jul
53.86			Pechonkina			1s3	WCh	Helsinki	11 Aug
53.87			Pechonkina			3	VD	Bruxelles	26 Aug
53.89			Pechonkina			1	Znam	Kazan	25 Jun
53.91			Glover			3	WK	Zürich	19 Aug
53.92			Glover			1	GP	Rieti	28 Aug
53.93			Glover			1	Bisl	Oslo	29 Jul
53.96		Anna	Jesien	POL	10.12.78	2	Gaz	Saint Denis	1 Jul
54.01			Glover			1		Atlanta	14 May
54.09			Glover			2	GP	Belém	22 May
54.09			Glover			3	WAF	Monaco	9 Sep
54.15			Pittman			3	Gaz	Saint-Denis	1 Jul
		(30/5)							
54.18			Huang Xiaoxiao	CHN	3.3.83	1	NG	Nanjing	21 Oct
54.21		Shauna	Smith	USA	10.9.83	2	NC	Carson	25 Jun
54.39		Yevgeniya	Isakova	RUS	27.11.78	2	NC	Tula	11 Jul
54.40			Wang Xing	CHN-J	30.11.86	2	NG	Nanjing	21 Oct
54.47		Shevon	Stoddart	JAM	21.11.82	2	NCAA	Sacramento	11 Jun
		(10)							
54.56		Tiffany	Ross-Williams	USA	5.2.83	3	NCAA	Sacramento	11 Jun
54.60		Surita	Febbraio	RSA	27.12.73	1	NC	Durban	16 Apr
54.72		Sheena	Johnson	USA	1.10.82	4	GGala	Roma	8 Jul
54.79		Andrea	Blackett	BAR	24.1.76	3s1	WCh	Helsinki	11 Aug
54.79		Benedetta	Ceccarelli	ITA	23.1.80	3	GP	Rieti	28 Aug
54.96		Debbie-Ann	Parris	JAM	24.3.73	4	SGP	Athína	14 Jun
55.03		Malgorzata	Pskit	POL	25.5.76	6	VD	Bruxelles	26 Aug
55.09		Melaine	Walker	JAM	1.1.83	1	Big 12	Manhattan, KS	15 May
55.09		Tatyana	Tereshchuk	UKR	11.10.69	7	WCh	Helsinki	13 Aug
55.14		Marina	Shiyan	RUS	22.1.80	1	WUG	Izmir	20 Aug
		(20)							
55.16		Oksana	Gulumyan	RUS	8.12.82	3	NC	Tula	11 Jul
55.27		Cora	Olivero	ESP	28.8.78	1h1	MedG	Almeria	29 Jun
55.40		Brenda	Taylor	USA	9.2.79	3	GP II	Thessaloníki	17 Jul
55.49		Marta	Chrust-Rozej	POL	29.9.78	3	WUG	Izmir	20 Aug
55.51		Dominique	Darden	USA	9.12.83	1	NCAA-r	New York	28 May
55.57		TaNisha	Mills	USA	2.11.74	1		Carson	22 May
55.58		Kim	Batten	USA	29.3.69	3s2	NC	Carson	24 Jun
55.58		Tawa	Dortch (Babatunde)	CAN	19.12.79	4s2	WCh	Helsinki	11 Aug
55.59		Claudia	Marx	GER	16.9.78	1		Kassel	10 Jun
55.59		Josanne	Lucas	TRI	14.5.84	5	NCAA	Sacramento	11 Jun
		(30)							
55.61		Nicola	Sanders	GBR	23.6.82	1	NC	Manchester (SC)	10 Jul
55.64		Marjolein	de Jong	NED	12.6.81	1		Breda	20 Aug
55.72		Yekaterina	Bikert	RUS	13.5.80	1		Tula	24 Jul
55.86		Yelena	Ildeykina	RUS	16.6.83	1rB	Znam	Kazan	25 Jun
55.87		Alena	Rücklová	CZE	7.10.81	4	WUG	Izmir	20 Aug
55.89		Zuzana	Hejnová	CZE-J	19.12.86	1	EJ	Kaunas	23 Jul
55.89		Yekaterina	Kostetskaya	RUS-J	31.12.87	2	EJ	Kaunas	23 Jul
55.91			Zhang Rongrong	CHN	27.1.84	3	NG	Nanjing	21 Oct
55.94		Ulrike	Urbansky	GER	6.4.77	1		Zeulenroda	29 May
55.94			Yao Yuehua	CHN	27.8.80	4	NG	Nanjing	21 Oct
		(40)							
55.95		Monika	Niederstätter	ITA	2.3.74	2	NC	Bressanone	26 Jun

Mark	Name		Nat	Born	Pos	Meet	Venue	Date
55.96	Ebony	Collins	USA-Y	11.3.89	1	WY	Marrakech	15 Jul
55.99	Yekaterina	Bakhvalova	RUS	29.10.72	3rA	Znam	Kazan	25 Jun
56.06	Lee	McConnell	GBR	9.10.78	2	NC	Manchester (SC)	10 Jul
56.10	Christina	Kron	GER	3.4.81	7	WUG	Izmir	20 Aug
56.12	Lucimar	Teodoro	BRA	1.5.81	1	NC	São Paulo	19 Jun
56.12	Christine	Spence	USA	25.11.81	7	NC	Sacramento	11 Jun
56.13	Anastasiya	Trifonova	RUS	17.12.84	1	NC-23	Tula	14 Jun
56.14	Anastasiya	Rabchenyuk	UKR	14.9.83	2		Luzern	14 Jun
56.15	Hristina	Hantzí-Neag	GRE	26.12.76	3h1	WCh	Helsinki	10 Aug
	(50)							
56.18	Anja	Neupert	GER	10.10.78	2	NC	Wattenscheid	3 Jul
56.20	Louise	Gundert	SWE	31.7.80	1		Sollentuna	28 Jun
56.22	Sylvanie	Morandais	FRA	14.7.79	1	NC	Angers	16 Jul
56.29	Vanya	Stambolova	BUL	28.11.83	1		Plovdiv	12 Jun
56.29	Melinda	Sallins	USA	30.6.73	3h3	NC	Carson	23 Jun
56.33	Yuliya	Mulyukova	RUS	1.12.85	2	NC-23	Tula	14 Jun
56.39	Norasheela Mohd	Khalid	MAS	27.9.79	2	AsiC	Inchon	4 Sep
56.41		He Yu	CHN-J	26.6.86	3		Zhongshan	24 Apr
56.42	Sian	Scott	GBR	20.3.84	4h1	WUG	Izmir	18 Aug
56.43	Beau	Walker	USA	25.3.83	1	MSR	Walnut	17 Apr
	(60)							
56.43	Natalya	Alimzhanova	KAZ	4.10.68	1	Asi GP	Songkhla	24 Jun
56.43	Aurore	Kassambara	FRA	26.10.79	2	NC	Angers	16 Jul
56.45	Aïssata	Soulama	BUR	11.2.79	3	FRA Ch	Angers	16 Jul
56.48	Klodiana	Shala	ALB	22.8.79	3s1	MedG	Almeria	29 Jun
56.50	Perla	dos Santos	BRA	29.1.82	2	NC	São Paulo	19 Jun
56.51	Oksana	Volosyuk	UKR	28.11.81	1		Yalta	28 May
56.58	Satomi	Kubokura	JPN	27.4.82	2	Asi GP	Songkhla	24 Jun
56.62	Silja	Ulfarsdóttir	ISL	20.6.81	2		Tallahassee	23 Apr
56.65	Liz	Fairs	GBR	1.12.77	1	ECp-1B	Leiria	18 Jun
56.67	Makiko	Yoshida	JPN	16.7.76	3	Asi GP	Singapore	21 Jun
	(70)							
56.69	Mariya	Menshchikova	RUS	26.2.83	3	NC-23	Tula	14 Jun
56.71		Song Yinglan	CHN	14.9.75	2		Chongqing	15 May
56.83	Krystal	Cantey	USA-J	27.6.87	1		Greensboro	18 Jun
56.84	Ieva	Zunda	LAT	20.7.78	1	ECp-2A	Tallinn	18 Jun
56.99	Raasin	McIntosh	USA	29.4.82	4		Kassel	10 Jun
57.01	Olga	Adamovich	RUS	30.8.84	4	NC-23	Tula	14 Jun
57.02	Tatyana	Azarova	KAZ	2.12.85	2		Almaty	4 Jun
57.03	Amanda	Fontes Dias	BRA	11.11.84	2h2	NC	São Paulo	18 Jun
57.06	Erin	Crawford	USA	14.8.85	3		Tallahassee	23 Apr
57.06	Emma	Duck	GBR	9.2.81	1		Portsmouth	15 May
	(80)							
57.11	Laia	Forcadell	ESP	6.6.82	2	NC	Málaga	24 Jul
57.15	Isabel	Rocha Silva	BRA	15.6.79	3	GP II	Rio de Janeiro	15 May
57.18	Sherene	Pinnock	JAM-J	30.3.87	1	Carifta	Bacolet	26 Mar
57.18	Luciana	França	BRA	19.5.77	1		São Paulo	13 Jul
57.20	Vassanee	Vinatho	THA	30.6.80	1	SEAG	Manila	29 Nov
57.23	Irina	Anashkina	RUS	31.1.72	2		Moskva	20 May
57.24	Ilona	Ranta	FIN	28.10.82	3		Lappeenranta	21 Jul
57.25	Nicole	Leach	USA-J	18.7.87	1	NC-j	Carson	24 Jun
57.26	Camille	Robinson	JAM	30.3.84	5s2	NCAA	Sacramento	10 Jun
57.29	Katie	Jones	GBR	4.1.77	2		Annecy	3 Jul
	(90)							
57.31	Elisa	Scardanzan	ITA	15.7.85	3	NC	Bressanone	26 Jun
57.33	Tawana	Watkins	USA	27.3.84	1h3	SEC	Nashville	13 May
57.37	Michelle	Carey	IRL	20.2.81	1		Genève	11 Jun
57.37	Houria	Moussa	ALG	14.5.82	2		Braaschaat	24 Jul
57.38	Nickeisha	Wilson	JAM-J	28.7.86	2	Carifta	Bacolet	27 Mar
57.41	Janet	Wienand	RSA	15.5.85	2	NC	Durban	16 Apr
57.41	Markita	James	USA	28.6.83	5s1	NCAA	Sacramento	10 Jun
57.42	Rika	Sakurai	JPN	15.5.85	1		Tokyo	3 Jul
57.46	Maren	Schott	GER	11.2.76	1		Kevelaer	19 Jun
57.47	Oksana	Ilyushkina	UKR	25.5.74	1		Mykolaiv	13 Jun
	(100)							
57.47	Natasha	Danvers-Smith	GBR	19.9.77	3	LGP	London (CP)	22 Jul

Mark	Name		Nat	Born	Date
57.48	Galina	Pedan	KGZ	29.5.83	24 Jun
57.48	Irina	Obedina	RUS	1.7.85	11 Jul
57.50	Doria	Appleberry	USA	5.2.83	28 May
57.52	Marina	Ivanova	UKR	19.8.82	28 May
57.55	Danielle	Myricks	USA	25.10.83	9 Apr
57.58	Crystal	Dooley	USA	3.7.82	9 Jun
57.58A	Lucy	Jaramillo	ECU	23.2.83	20 Aug
57.59		Chen Yumei	CHN-Y	10.1.88	20 Oct
57.61	Meta	Macus	SLO	23.3.75	30 Jun
57.61	Agniezska	Karpiesiuk	POL	17.4.82	28 Aug

Mark		Name	Nat	Born	Date
57.65	Elodie	Cruchant	FRA	22.12.80	3 Jul
57.67	Alicia	Cave	TRI	4.2.82	14 May
57.67	Melissa	Steele	USA	15.7.82	15 May
57.70	Chitra K.	Soman	IND	10.7.83	24 May
57.71	Yelena	Golovankova	RUS	12.5.84	25 Jun
57.71	Nadja	Petersen	SWE	14.7.78	20 Aug
57.72		Chen Lin	CHN	8.3.81	25 Jun
57.73A	Florence	Wasike	KEN	20.3.79	18 Jun
57.73	Manuela	Gentili	ITA	7.2.78	26 Jun
57.73	Caroline	Mebam Kaboud	CMR	17.9.78	3 Jul
57.84	Sara	Oresnik	SLO	3.6.84	29 Jun
57.85	Lakendra	McColumn	USA	20.5.84	23 Apr
57.85	Olga	Tereshkova	KAZ	26.10.84	18 Aug
57.86	Nawal	El Jak	SUD-Y	17.10.88	18 Jun
57.87	Frances	Keating	CAN	21.6.85	15 May
57.88	Muna	Jabir Ahmed	SUD-J	6.1.87	17 Sep
57.89	Lynnsey	Dailey	USA	5.3.83	28 May
57.89	Olivia	Abderrhamane	FRA	2.8.79	5 Jun
57.89	Sayaka	Aoki	JPN-J	15.12.86	3 Jul
57.89	Sonia	Brito	AUS	10.6.79	1 Dec
57.90	Anneli	Melin	SWE	26.8.76	27 Aug
57.97	Maiteland	Marks	USA	19.9.76	6 Jul
57.98	zge	Gürler	TUR	17.6.85	15 May
57.99	Shonda	Brown	USA	30.1.83	15 May
57.99	Inna	Kalinina	BLR	10.4.77	1 Jun
58.00		Wang Hui	CHN-J	1.6.87	24 Apr
58.00	Mariana	Dimitrova	BUL	29.7.82	21 May
58.04	Ewelina	Setowska	POL	5.3.80	3 Jun
58.05	Hanane	Skhayi	MAR	1.7.83	22 May
58.05		Xiao Hongfan	CHN	6.1.83	20 Oct
58.06		Li Yun	CHN	20.7.83	25 Jun
58.07	Gaia	Biella	ITA	25.1.80	26 Jun
58.08	Meka	Rembert-Thompson	USA	10.1.74	30 Apr
58.08	Aya	Miyahara	JPN-Y	12.3.88	24 Oct
58.09	Erica	Mårtensson	SWE	24.6.79	22 Jun
58.09A	Patricia	Lopes	POR	11.7.82	27 Jul
58.09	Mary Grace	Milgar	PHI	10.3.81	4 Sep
58.12	Yuliya	Bychkova	RUS-J	11.8.86	23 Jul
58.13	Teodora	Kolarova	BUL	29.5.81	7 Jul
58.14		Wang Jia	CHN	17.7.83	20 Oct
58.15	Julianna	Reed	USA	29.7.85	27 May
58.19	Lauren	Boden	AUS-Y	3.8.88	14 Jul
58.21	Sara	Petersen	DEN-J	9.4.87	31 Jul
58.22	Celia	Medina	ESP	10.7.77	23 Jul
58.23	Birsen	Bezgöz-Yavuz	TUR	18.10.80	15 May
58.23	Zahra	Lachgar	MAR	8.6.78	21 May
58.27	Gladys	Stephens	NGR	.84	25 Jun
58.27	Salhate	Djamaldine	COM	23.12.78	16 Jul
58.29	Stiliani	Dímoglou	GRE	18.11.84	3 Jun
58.31	Alison	Erzinger	USA	18.6.83	28 May
58.33	Yaniuska	Pérez	CUB	12.3.81	20 May
58.35A	Princesa	Oliveros	COL	10.8.75	20 Aug
58.36	Aminata	Sylla	SEN	19.4.84	18 Jun
58.38	Nyoka	Cole	JAM	7.10.85	18 Mar
58.38	Tiffany	Abney	USA	15.10.84	27 May
58.38	Martina	Naef	SUI	23.4.80	3 Jul
58.39	Ramona	Modeste	TRI	21.11.83	27 May
58.43	Lise Margareth	Jensen	NOR	21.12.79	21 Aug
58.45	Shereta	Jones	USA	12.9.83	9 Apr
58.46	Lauren	Jauncey	AUS	19.10.81	5 Feb
58.47	Dora	Jémaa	FRA	15.7.85	15 Jul
58.49	Tamara	Ruben (172)	NED	11.6.82	16 Jul

Hand timed

Mark		Name	Nat	Born	Date
58.4	Dalelque	Ferreira	BRA-J	12.4.87	26 Aug

Best at low altitude

Mark		Name	Nat	Born	Date
58.20	Patricia	Lopes	POR	11.7.82	8 Jun

JUNIORS

See main list for top 9 juniors. 10 performances by 5 women to 56.67. Additional mark and further juniors:

	Mark	Pos	Meet	Venue	Date	Mark	Pos	Meet	Venue	Date
Wang Xing	55.39	1	NC	Changsha	26 Jun	56.54	2	EAsG	Macao	2 Nov
	56.47	1h1	NG	Nanjing	20 Oct					
Kostetskaya	56.20	7	Bisl	Oslo	29 Jul	56.67	6	NC	Tula	11 Jul

Mark		Name	Nat	Born	Pos	Meet	Venue	Date
57.59		Chen Yumei (10)	CHN-Y	10.1.88	3h2	NG	Nanjing	20 Oct
57.86	Nawal	El Jak	SUD-Y	17.10.88	1		Rabat	18 Jun
57.88	Muna	Jabir Ahmed	SUD-J	6.1.87	1	PArab	Radès	17 Sep
57.89	Sayaka	Aoki	JPN-J	15.12.86	2		Tokyo	3 Jul
58.00		Wang Hui	CHN-J	1.6.87	6		Zhongshan	24 Apr
58.08	Aya	Miyahara	JPN-Y	12.3.88	1	NSF	Okayama	24 Oct
58.12	Yuliya	Bychkova	RUS-J	11.8.86	3	EJ	Kaunas	23 Jul
58.19	Lauren	Boden	AUS-Y	3.8.88	1h1	WY	Marrakech	14 Jul
58.21	Sara	Petersen	DEN-J	9.4.87	1	NC	Odense	31 Jul
58.62		Wu Haili	CHN	12.12.86	4h2	NC	Changsha	25 Jun
58.69	Irina	Gornova (20)	RUS	3.11.86	h	NC-j	Tula	2 Jul

HIGH JUMP

2.03 Kajsa Bergqvist SWE 12.10.76 1 GP Sheffield 21 Aug
1.84/1 1.88/1 1.91/1 1.94/1 1.97/2 2.00/1 2.03/1
2.02 1 WCh Helsinki 8 Aug 1.85/1 1.89/1 1.93/1 1.96/1 1.98/1 2.00/2 2.02/1 2.10/xxx
2.01 1 ECp1A Gävle 19 Jun 1.86/1 1.90/1 1.94/1 1.96/1 1.98/1 2.01/1 2.03/xxx
2.00 1 Málaga 19 May 1.86/1 1.92/1 1.96/1 2.00/1 2.04/xx
2.00 1 Sollentuna 28 Jun 1.83/1 1.90/1 1.93/1 1.86/1 2.00/1 2.02/xxx
2.00 1 GP II Zagreb 11 Jul 1.85/1 1.90/1 1.95/1 1.98/1 2.00/1 2.02/xxx
2.00 1 WAF Monaco 9 Sep 1.85/1 1.93/1 1.96/1 2.00/3 2.07/xxx
1.99 1 Salamanca 6 Jul 1.85/1 1.91/1 1.94/1 1.96/2 1.99/3 2.02/xx
1.99 1 Rovereto 31 Aug 1.85/1 1.90/1 1.93/1 1.96/1 1.99/xxx 1.99/1
1.98 1 GP Madrid 16 Jul 1.85-1 1.92-1 1.95-1 1.98-1 2.01-xxx

2.01i Anna Chicherova RUS 22.7.82 1 EI Madrid 6 Mar
1.80/1 1.85/1 1.89/1 1.92/1 1.95/1 1.97/1 1.99/2 2.01/3
2.00i 1 Arnstadt 5 Feb 1.80/1 1.85/1 1.88/1 1.91/2 1.94/2 1.97/2 2.00/3 2.03/xxx
1.99 1 Déca Paris (C) 3 Sep 1.83/3 1.87/1 1.90/2 1.93/2 1.95/1 1.97/x 1.99/1
1.98i 1 NC Volgograd 11 Feb 1.80/1 1.85/1 1.89/2 1.92/1 1.95/1 1.98/1 2.01/xxx
1.98 1 Tula 24 Jul 1.80/1 1.85/1 1.89/1 1.92/1 1.95/1 1.98/2 2.01/xxx

2.00 Yelena Slesarenko RUS 28.2.82 1 NC Tula 12 Jul
1.80/1 1.85/1 1.89/1 1.92/1 1.95/2 1.98/1 2.00/2 2.02/xxx

2.00 Chaunte Howard USA 12.1.84 1 Liège (NX) 20 Jul
2.00 1 NA Heusden-Zolder 23 Jul
2.00 2 WCh Helsinki 8 Aug 1.80/1 1.85/1 1.89/1 1.93/1 1.96/2 1.98/2 2.00/3 2.02/xxx
1.97 1 Azusa 16 Jul

Mark	Name		Nat	Born	Pos	Meet	Venue	Date
1.99i	Ruth	Beitia	ESP	1.4.79	2	EI	Madrid	6 Mar
	1.80/1 1.85/1 1.89/1 1.92/1 1.95/1 1.97/1 1.99/1 2.01/xxx							
	1.97 2 Déca Paris (C) 3 Sep 1.78/1 1.83/1 1.87/1 1.90/1 1.93/3 1.95/x 1.97/1 1.99/x 2.01/xx							
1.98	Venelina	Veneva	BUL	13.6.74	1	Cezmi	Istanbul	4 Jun
	1.80/1 1.86/1 1.88/1 1/90/1 1.92/2 1.95/1 1.98/2 2.01/xxx							
	1.97i 3 EI Madrid 6 Mar 1.85/1 1.89/1 1.92/2 1.95/1 1.97/2 1.99/xxx							
1.98	Tatyana	Kivimyagi	RUS	23.6.84	1	ECp-S	Firenze	19 Jun
	1.80/1 1.85/1 1.89/1 1.92/1 1.95/3 1.98/2 2.00/xxx							
1.97	Yekaterina	Aleksandrova/Savchenko	RUS	3.6.77	1		Tula	14 Jun
	1.75/1 1.79/1 1.82/1 1.85/1 1.88/1 1.91/1 1.94/1 1.97/3 2.00/xxx							
1.97	Irina	Mikhalchenko	UKR	20.1.72	1	NC	Kiev	2 Jul
	1.80/1 1.83/1 1.86/1 1.89/1 1.92/1 1.95/1 1.97/3 1.99/xx							
1.97	Emma	Green	SWE	8.12.84	1	NC	Helsingborg	20 Aug
	1.81/1 1.86/1 1.90/1 1.94/2 1.97/1 2.00/xxx							
	(28/10) (Performances at 1.96: Chicherova 2i/3, Bergqvist 1, Beitia 1i, Green 1, Dubnova 1)							
1.96	Romana	Dubnova	CZE	4.11.78	1		Cáslav	30 Aug
1.95i	Olga	Kaliturina	RUS	9.3.76	1		Hustopece	22 Jan
1.95i	Viktoria	Styopina	UKR	21.2.76	1		Cottbus	26 Jan
1.95i	Oana	Pantelimon	ROM	27.9.72	1	NC	Bucuresti	13 Feb
1.95i	Marta	Mendía	ESP	18.5.75	4	EI	Madrid	6 Mar
1.95	Tatyana	Efimenko	KGZ	2.1.81	1		Bishkek	28 May
1.95	Erin	Aldrich	USA	27.12.77	1	Pre	Eugene	4 Jun
1.95	Mélanie	Skotnik	FRA	8.11.82	1		Strasbourg	23 Jun
1.95	Olga	Kychanova	RUS	14.7.75	1		Sankt-Peterburg	29 Jun
1.95	Vita	Palamar	UKR	12.10.77	2	NC	Kiev	2 Jul
	(20)							
1.95	Viktoriya	Seryogina	RUS	22.5.73	1		Dudelange	3 Jul
1.95	Blanka	Vlasic	CRO	8.11.83	1	NC	Zagreb	30 Jul
1.94i	Iva	Straková	CZE	4.8.80	1		Ostrava	29 Jan
1.94		Bui Thi Nhung	VIE	21.1.83	1	THA Ch	Bangkok	4 May
1.94	Carolina	Klüft	SWE	2.2.83	1H		Götzis	28 May
1.94	Lavern	Spencer	LCA	23.6.84	1	CAC	Nassau	10 Jul
1.93	Amy	Acuff	USA	14.7.75	1	MSR	Walnut	17 Apr
1.93	Dóra	Gy rffy	HUN	23.2.78	1		Budapest	21 May
1.93	Corinne	Müller	SUI	20.11.75	1		Zug	28 May
1.93	Sharon	Day	USA	9.6.85	1	NCAA	Sacramento	11 Jun
	(30)							
1.93A	Caterine	Ibargüen	COL	12.2.84	1	SACh	Cali	22 Jul
1.93	Ifoma	Jones (-Olausson)	USA	4.9.77	2	Bisl	Oslo	29 Jul
1.93	Tia	Hellebaut	BEL	16.2.78	Q	WCh	Helsinki	6 Aug
1.92i	Irina	Kovalenko	UKR-J	12.6.86	2		Göteborg	3 Feb
1.92i	Anna	Ustinova	KAZ	8.12.85	1	NC	Karaganda	5 Feb
1.92i	Diana	Láznicková	SVK	14.8.74	1		Bratislava	13 Feb
1.92i	Monica	Iagar	ROM	2.4.73	2	NC	Bucuresti	13 Feb
1.92i	Svetlana	Shkolina	RUS-J	9.3.86	1	NC-23	Moskva	20 Feb
1.92i	Gaëlle	Niaré	FRA	12.3.82	2	NCAA	Fayetteville	11 Mar
1.92		Zheng Xingyuan	CHN-J	29.3.89	1		Zhongshan	24 Apr
	(40)							
1.92	Inna	Gliznutsa	MDA	18.4.73	1	NC	Chisinau	5 Jun
1.92	Hanna	Mikkonen	FIN	15.1.81	1		Tampere	12 Jun
1.92	Marina	Kuptsova	RUS	22.12.81	2=	NC	Tula	12 Jul
1.92		Jing Xuezhu	CHN	20.4.75	2	AsiC	Inchon	4 Sep
1.91	Sheena	Gordon	USA	26.9.83	2		Tallahassee	23 Apr
1.91	Juana	Arrendel	DOM	16.6.78	1	Barr	La Habana	20 May
1.91	Eunice	Barber	FRA	17.11.74	1H		Arles	4 Jun
1.90i	Annett	Engel	GER-J	6.11.87	1		Unna	23 Jan
1.90i	Deirdre	Ryan	IRL	1.6.82	1		Glasgow	23 Jan
1.90i	Susan	Jones/Moncrieff	GBR	8.6.78	1	NC	Sheffield	13 Feb
	(50)							
1.90i	Julie	Crane	GBR	26.9.76	1		Loughborough	19 Feb
1.90i	Barbora	Laláková	CZE	2.5.81	1		Brno	22 Feb
1.90	Yariadnis	Argüelles	CUB	18.4.84	1	NC	La Habana	17 Mar
1.90	Romary	Rifka	MEX	23.12.70	1		Xalapa	7 May
1.90	Antonietta	Di Martino	ITA	1.6.78	1		Marano di Napoli	22 May
1.90	Anne Gerd	Eieland	NOR	28.12.82	3	ECp-1A	Gävle	19 Jun
1.90	Daniela	Rath	GER	6.5.77	3=		Bühl	24 Jun
1.90	Ariane	Friedrich	GER	10.1.84	6=		Bühl	24 Jun
1.90	Birgit	Kähler	GER	14.8.70	6=		Bühl	24 Jun
1.90	Nicole	Forrester	CAN	17.11.76	8		Bühl	24 Jun
	(60)							

WOMEN 2005

Mark	Name		Nat	Born	Pos	Meet	Venue	Date
1.90		Gu Biwei	CHN-Y	17.2.88	1	NG	Nanjing	17 Oct
1.90	Ellen	Pettitt	AUS-J	13.2.86	1		Perth	13 Nov
1.90i	Yekaterina	Kuntsevich	RUS	13.7.84	2		Omsk	24 Dec
1.89	Raffaella	Lamera	ITA	13.4.83	1		Roma	14 May
1.89	María	Papayeoryíou	GRE	8.8.79	4	ECp-S	Firenze	19 Jun
1.89		Jiang Haiyan	CHN	19.12.79	1	Asi GP	Singapore	21 Jun
1.89	Stefania	Cadamuro	ITA	23.2.79	1	NC	Bressanone	25 Jun
1.89	Sheree	Francis	JAM	20.10.83	1	NC	Kingston	26 Jun
1.89	Anika	Smit	RSA-J	26.5.86	1	Afr-J	Radès	3 Sep
1.88i	Darya	Kuntsevich	RUS	2.11.85	3		Yekaterinburg	7 Jan
	(70)							
1.88i	Anna	Ksok	POL	29.9.83	2		Cottbus	26 Jan
1.88i	Gwen	Wentland	USA	29.4.72	1		Lincoln	5 Feb
1.88i	Andrea	Ispan	ROM	2.6.78	3	NC	Bucuresti	13 Feb
1.88i	Anna	Visigalli	ITA	24.2.81	1	NC	Ancona	19 Feb
1.88i	Alina	Budnikova	RUS	22.10.83	2	NC-23	Moskva	20 Feb
1.88i	Irina	Glavatskikh	RUS	29.12.84	3		Moskva	20 Feb
1.88	Angela	McKee	NZL	11.12.74	1		Wanganui	12 Mar
1.88		Ma Bei	CHN	28.8.84	1		Zhaoqing	10 Apr
1.88	Deirdre	Mullen	USA	21.5.82	3=	MSR	Walnut	17 Apr
1.88	Kaylene	Wagner	USA	15.11.84	3=	MSR	Walnut	17 Apr
	(80)							
1.88	Inika	McPherson	USA-J	29.9.86	1		Humble	29 Apr
1.88	Bernadett	Bódi	HUN	14.4.80	2		Budapest	21 May
1.88	Irina	Gordeyeva	RUS-J	9.10.86	1		Sochi	22 May
1.88	Hyleas	Fountain	USA	14.1.81	2H		Götzis	28 May
1.88	Candeger	Oguz	TUR	16.7.80	2	Cezmi	Istanbul	4 Jun
1.88	Julia	Bennett	GBR	26.3.70	1	BIG	Bedford	12 Jun
1.88A	Solange	Witteveen	ARG	6.2.76	1	SACh	Cali	22 Jul
1.88i	Noengruthai	Chaipetch	THA	1.12.82	1	Asi-I	Pattaya	15 Nov
1.88	Sophia	Begg	AUS-Y	14.6.88	1	N.Sch	Sydney	11 Dec
1.87	Viktoriya	Andonova	USA-J	19.11.86	1		Coral Gables	11 Mar
	(90)							
1.87	Debra	Vento	USA	17.12.85	3		Tallahassee	23 Apr
1.87	Eliana Renata	da Silva	BRA	14.2.78	1		Santiago de Chile	8 May
1.87	Viktoria	Leks	EST-J	28.9.87	1		Tallinn	21 May
1.87	Persefóni	Hatzinákou	GRE	6.6.84	5	EU23	Erfurt	16 Jul
1.87	Julia	Hartmann	GER-J	10.4.86	2	EJ	Kaunas	24 Jul
1.87	Jonna	Anias	FIN	12.5.84	1		Lapua	30 Jul
1.87	Jessica	Ennis	GBR-J	28.1.86	1H	WUG	Izmir	15 Aug

Mark	Name		Nat	Born	Date
1.86i	Olga	Chuprova	BLR	6.4.81	25 Jan
1.86i	Soultána	Papasotiríou	GRE	11.11.79	13 Feb
1.86	Marizca	Gertenbach	RSA	20.10.82	18 Feb
	(100)				
1.86i	Natalie	Clark	GBR	4.9.82	27 Feb
1.86i	Yekaterina	Yevseyeva	KAZ-Y	22.6.88	12 Mar
1.86	Claire	Mallett	AUS	29.12.84	10 Apr
1.86	Whitney	Evans	CAN	10.4.80	15 Apr
1.86	Yelena	Kholosha	UKR	26.1.82	6 May
1.86	Valentina	Lyashenko	UKR	30.1.81	6 May
1.86	Marta	Borkowska	POL	26.12.82	21 May
1.86	Yoko	Hunnicutt	JPN	14.1.75	4 Jun
1.86	Svetlana	Stavskaya	KAZ	10.5.77	4 Jun
1.86	Yekaterina	Bolshova	RUS-Y	2.12.88	21 Jun
1.86	Kamila	Stepaniuk	POL-J	22.3.86	24 Jun
1.86	Karen	Beautle	JAM	13.6.71	26 Jun
1.86 sq	Natalya	Gapchuk	UKR-Y	15.11.88	21 Sep
1.86	Nguyen Thi Ngoc Tam		VIE	21.4.84	18 Oct
1.86		Shen Shengfei	CHN	21.1.81	18 Oct
1.86i	Olga Rypakova (Alekseyeva)		KAZ	30.11.84	14 Nov
1.86	Kylie	Wheeler	AUS	17.1.80	26 Nov
1.86	Marierlis	Rojas	VEN-J	30.4.86	20 Dec
1.85i	Olga	Pinakina	RUS	16.2.85	23 Jan
1.85i	Michelle	Dunkley	GBR	26.1.78	29 Jan
1.85i	Karol	Rovelto	USA	20.12.69	29 Jan
1.85i	Alexandra	Shamsutdinova	RUS-J	6.6.87	5 Feb
1.85i	Peaches	Roach	JAM	21.12.84	5 Feb
1.85i	Alina	Mattila	FIN	27.12.82	20 Feb
1.85i	Lucie	Finez	FRA	25.11.76	26 Feb
1.85i	Svetlana	Radzivil	UZB-J	17.1.87	1 Mar
1.85	Lacy	Wilson	USA	3.11.84	23 Apr
1.85	Mariya	Nestseruk	BLR-Y	14.8.89	11 May
1.85	Miruna	Mataoanu	ROM	4.6.83	13 May
1.85	Kelly	Sotherton	GBR	13.11.76	28 May

Mark	Name		Nat	Born	Date
1.85	Margaret	Simpson	GHA	31.12.81	28 May
1.85	Anja	Iljustsenko	EST	12.10.85	3 Jun
1.85	Natalya	Dobrinska	UKR	29.5.82	4 Jun
1.85	Tatyana	Gordeyeva	RUS	3.6.73	4 Jun
1.85	Svetlana	Lapina	RUS	12.4.78	5 Jun
1.85	Elena	Brambilla	ITA	23.4.83	11 Jun
1.85	Valentina	Khomitskaya	UKR	30.1.81	14 Jun
1.85	Adonía	Steryíou	GRE	7.7.85	18 Jun
1.85	Beatrice	Lundmark	SUI	26.4.80	18 Jun
1.85	Tatyana	Grigoryeva	RUS	13.5.81	25 Jun
1.85	Sarah	Bouaoudia	ALG	13.8.83	1 Jul
1.85	Yelena	Tsolan	RUS	24.6.80	12 Jul
1.85	Ruky	Abdulai	GHA	8.8.82	24 Jul
1.85	Marie	Collonvillé	FRA	23.11.73	6 Aug
1.85	Oldriska	Maresová	CZE-J	14.10.86	20 Aug
1.85	Miyuki	Aoyama	JPN	4.1.77	11 Sep
1.84i	Stephanie	Linz	USA	1.11.82	15 Jan
1.84i	Lindsey	Metcalf	USA	14.5.82	22 Jan
1.84i	Mária	Henkelová	SVK	21.10.75	22 Jan
1.84i	Juliane	Urban	GER-J	20.1.87	29 Jan
1.84i	Anett	Jambor	GER	27.7.83	20 Feb
1.84i	Gema	Martin-Pozuelo	ESP-J	21.6.87	24 Feb
1.84i		Zhao Jing	CHN-Y	20.7.88	2 Mar
1.84i	Sonja	Kesselschläger	GER	20.1.78	4 Mar
1.84i		Shen Qinli	CHN-Y	9.2.88	6 Mar
1.84i		Gu Xuan	CHN-J	19.11.87	6 Mar
1.84i		Liu Shuang	CHN-J	8.1.87	6 Mar
1.84	Destinee	Hooker	USA-Y	.88	19 Mar
1.84	Caroline	Wolf	USA	13.2.85	23 Apr
1.84A	Chelsea	Taylor	USA-J	27.10.86	21 May
1.84		He Yanhong	CHN	17.4.84	22 May
1.84		Li Rong	CHN	14.9.83	22 May
1.84	Viktorija	Zemaityte	LTU	11.3.85	27 May
1.84	Magdalena	Drop	POL-J	21.9.86	12 Jun

Mark		Name		Nat	Born	Pos	Meet	Venue	Date
1.84		Yanisleidi	Fern ndez	CUB	10.5.78				23 Jun
1.84		Zhanna	Melnichenko	UKR	23.4.83				2 Jul
1.84		Jana	Kersevan	SLO-Y	16.6.88				7 Jul
1.84		Simone	Oberer	SUI	8.4.80				15 Aug
1.84		Erika	Wiklund	SWE-Y	10.3.88				20 Aug
1.84		Øyunn	Grindem (170)	NOR-J	11.11.87				4 Sep

Best outdoor marks

1.99 Chicherova 1 Déca Paris (C) 3 Sep
1.97 Beitia 2 Déca Paris (C) 3 Sep
1.95 Pantelimon 4 GP Madrid 16 Jul
1.94 Mendía 1 NC Málaga 24 Jul
1.93 Styopina 1 GP Sevilla 4 Jun
1.93 Straková 2 Bühl 24 Jun
1.92 Shkolina 1 Mannheim 19 Jun
1.86 Yevseyeva 26 Apr
1.86 Wentland 14 May
1.86 Chaipetch 21 Jun
1.86 Budnikova 30 Jun
1.86 Jones/Moncrieff 9 Jul
1.86 Ispan 24 Jul
1.85 Chuprova 1 Jun
1.85 Glavatskikh 15 Jun
1.92 Iagar 1 NC Bucuresti 4 Jul
1.90 Kovalenko 1 Tula 24 Jun
1.90 Laláková 2 Cáslav 30 Aug
1.88 Ksok 1 Poznan 21 May
1.88 Engel 1 Berlin 21 May
1.87 Kaliturina 3 Herzogenbuchsee5 Jun
1.87 Ustinova 3 Asi GP Sidoarjo 18 Jun
1.87 Láznicková 2 Formia 16 Jul
1.85 Kuntsevich 15 Jun
1.85 Rovelto 23 Jun
1.85 Radzivil 24 Jun
1.84 Zhao Jing 17 Apr
1.84 Shen Qinli 17 Apr
1.84 Jambor 24 Jun
1.84 Gu Xuan 17 Oct

JUNIORS

See main list for 14 top juniors. 12 (inc. 4 indoors) performances by 6 women to 1.90. Additional mark and further juniors:

Kovalenko 2+ 1.90i 2 Moskva 15 Feb
Shkolina 2+ 1.91 1 EJ Kaunas 24 Jul 1.90 1 NC-j Tula 3 Jul
Zheng X 1.90 1 Yixing 22 May

Mark		Name		Nat	Born	Pos	Meet	Venue	Date
1.86i		Yekaterina	Yevseyeva	KAZ-Y	22.6.88	1		Tashkent	12 Mar
		1.86				1		Shimkent	26 Apr
1.86		Yekaterina	Bolshova	RUS-Y	2.12.88	1		Chelyabinsk	21 Jun
1.86		Kamila	Stepaniuk	POL	22.3.86	2	NC	Biala Podlaska	24 Jun
1.86	sq	Natalya	Gapchuk	UKR-Y	15.11.88	2		Berdichev	21 Sep
1.86		Marierlis	Rojas	VEN	30.4.86	1	NG	San Cristóbal	20 Dec
1.85i		Alexandra	Shamsutdinova	RUS	6.6.87	1		Saransk	5 Feb
1.85i		Svetlana	Radzivil	UZB	17.1.87	2		Tianjin	1 Mar
		1.85				2		Tula	24 Jun
1.85		Mariya	Nestseruk	BLR-Y	14.8.89			Gomel	11 May
1.85		Oldriska	Maresová (23)	CZE	14.10.86	1		Jablonec nad Nisou	20 Aug

POLE VAULT

5.01 WR Yelena Isinbayeva RUS 3.6.82 1 WCh Helsinki 12 Aug
4.50/1 4.60/1 4.70/1 5.01/2
WR 5.00 1 LGP London (CP) 22 Jul 4.70/1 4.80/1 4.96/2 WR 5.00/1
WR 4.95 1 GP Madrid 16 Jul 4.65/3 4.95/2
WR 4.93 1 Athl Lausanne 5 Jul 4.60/2 4.70/1 4.93/1
WR 4.93 1 VD Bruxelles 26 Aug 4.73/1 4.83/x. 4.93/1 5.02/xxx
WIR 4.90i 1 EI Madrid 6 Mar 4.60/x 4.70/1 4.80/1 4.90/1
WIR 4.89i 1 Liévin 26 Feb 4.60/x 4.70/1 4.80/1 4.89/1 5.05/x
WIR 4.88i 1 GP Birmingham 18 Feb 4.60/1 4.79/1 4.88/2
WIR 4.87i 1 Donetsk 12 Feb 4.50/1 4.70/1 4.75/1 4.87/2
4.79 1 DNG Stockholm 26 Jul 4.72/1 4.79/2 5.01/xxx
4.74 1 WAF Monaco 10 Sep 4.62/1 4.74/2 5.02/xxx
4.70 1 Réthimno 10 Jul 4.60/x 4.70/1 4.94/xxx
4.83 Anna Rogowska POL 21.5.81 2 VD Bruxelles 26 Aug
4.43/1 4.63/1 4.73/1 4.83/1 4.93/xxx
4.82 1 Beckum 21 Aug 4.32/1 4.52/1 4.62/1 4.82/2 4.90/xxx
4.80 2 LGP London (CP) 22 Jul 4.32/1 4.47/1 4.60/1 4.70/1 4.80/1 4.96/xxx
4.77 1 Sopot 2 Jun 4.30/2 4.50/1 4.77/2 4.86/xx
4.76 1 Gdansk 28 May 4.30/1 4.50/2 4.70/2 4.76/1 4.86/xxx
4.75i 2 Donetsk 12 Feb 4.20/1 4.40/2 4.50/1 4.60/1 4.70/1 4.75/2 4.80/xxx
4.75i 2 EI Madrid 6 Mar 4.20/1 4.45/1 4.55/1 4.65/1 4.70/1 4.75/2 4.80/xxx
4.73i 1 Bydgoszcz 26 Jan 4.23/2 4.43/2 4.53/1 4.63/3 4.73/2 4.80/xxx
4.70i 1 Spala 22 Jan 4.20/1 4.40/1 4.50/1 4.60/3 4.70/3 4.80/x
4.70i Monika Pyrek POL 11.8.80 3 Donetsk 12 Feb
4.20/1 4.40/1 4.60/1 4.70/3 4.75/xxx
4.70i 1 NC Spala 20 Feb 4.40/1 4.60/x 4.70/
4.70i 1 Madrid 24 Feb 4.30/1 4.45/1 4.60/1 4.70/1 4.80/xxx
4.70i 2 Liévin 26 Feb 4.35/2 4.55/1 4.70/2 4.80/xxx
4.70i 3 EI Madrid 6 Mar 4.35/1 4.55/1 4.70/1 4.75/xx 4.80/x
4.70 1 NC Biala Podlaska 25 Jun 4.40/2 4.55/1 4.65/1 4.70/1 4.80/xxx
4.70i Svetlana Feofanova RUS 16.7.80 2 GP Birmingham 18 Feb
4.45/1 4.60/1 4.70/2 4.79/xxx
(28/4) (4.65 performances: Pyrek 2i/3, Hingst 1i, Isinbayeva 1, Rogowska)
4.65i Carolin Hingst GER 18.9.80 4 EI Madrid 6 Mar
4.60i Tatyana Polnova RUS 20.4.79 4= Donetsk 12 Feb
4.60 Tracy O'Hara USA 20.7.80 1 GP II Stanford 30 May

WOMEN 2005

Mark	Name		Nat	Born	Pos	Meet	Venue	Date
4.60	Mary	Sauer	USA	31.10.75	1		Atascadero	29 Jun
4.60	Stacy	Dragila	USA	25.3.71	2	Athl	Lausanne	5 Jul
4.60	Vanessa	Boslak	FRA	11.6.82	1	NC	Angers	15 Jul
	(10)							
4.57i	Jennifer	Stuczynski	USA	6.2.82	1		Rochester	31 Dec
	4.57 ?				1		New York	7 Jun
4.55i	Pavla	Hamácková	CZE	20.5.78	6	EI	Madrid	6 Mar
4.55	Jillian	Schwartz	USA	19.9.79	1	CalR	Modesto	7 May
4.53		Gao Shuying	CHN	28.10.79	1	AsiC	Inchon	2 Sep
4.51	Dana	Ellis (-Buller)	CAN	7.12.79	1	NC	Winnipeg	15 Jul
4.50i	Natalya	Belinskaya	RUS	21.1.83	3		Stuttgart	29 Jan
4.50i	Kellie	Suttle	USA	9.5.73	1		Jonesboro	8 Feb
4.50i	Tanya	Stefanova	BUL	8.3.72	1	Balk I	Athína (P)	16 Feb
4.50	Thórey Edda	Elisdóttir	ISL	30.6.77	1		Mannheim	18 Jun
4.48	Afrodíti	Skafída	GRE	20.3.82	1	NC	Athína	11 Jun
	(20)							
4.48i	Silke	Spiegelburg	GER-J	17.3.86	2		Münster	25 Aug
4.47	Janine	Whitlock	GBR	11.8.73	3=	LGP	London (CP)	22 Jul
4.47	Tatyana	Grigorieva	AUS	8.10.75	6	LGP	London (CP)	22 Jul
4.46	Kelsie	Hendry	CAN	29.6.82	1		Saskatoon	12 Jul
4.45i		Zhao Yingying	CHN-J	15.2.86	3		Madrid	24 Feb
4.45	April	Steiner	USA	22.4.80	1		New York (RI)	11 Jun
4.45	Kirsten	Belin	SWE	2.5.81	1		Sollentuna	28 Jun
4.45	Krisztina	Molnár	HUN	8.4.76	1	NC	Debrecen	6 Jul
4.45	Naroa	Agirre	ESP	15.5.79	4	Déca	Paris (C)	3 Sep
4.40i	Anna	Fitidou	CYP	22.4.77	1		Athína (P)	29 Jan
	(30)							
4.40i	Natalya	Kushch	UKR	5.3.83	9		Donetsk	12 Feb
4.40i	Martina	Strutz	GER	4.11.81	2	NC	Sindelfingen	19 Feb
4.40	Lindsay	Taylor	USA	9.2.79	4		Carson	22 May
4.40	Anzhela	Balakhonova	UKR	18.12.72	2		Villeneuve d'Ascq	12 Jun
4.40	Fabiana	Murer	BRA	16.3.81	1		Porto Alegre	9 Jul
4.40	Yuliya	Golubchikova	RUS	27.3.83	2	NC	Tula	10 Jul
4.40	Anastasiya	Kiryanova	RUS	26.7.82	1		Tula	23 Jul
4.40		Yang Jing	CHN	1.1.84	2	NG	Nanjing	20 Oct
4.40	Kym	Howe-Nadin	AUS	12.6.80	1		Perth	10 Dec
4.37i	Ekateríni	Stefanídi	GRE-Y	4.2.90	1		Athína (P)	20 Feb
	(40)							
4.36i	Kate	Soma	USA	13.2.83	1		Seattle	12 Feb
4.36i	Becky	Holliday	USA	12.3.80	2		Seattle	12 Feb
4.36Ai	Erica	Bartolina	USA	15.5.80	2		Pocatello	18 Feb
4.36	Hanna-Mia	Persson	SWE	11.2.78	1	NC	Helsingborg	20 Aug
4.36	Anna	Schultze	GER	26.5.85	1		Rostock	20 Aug
4.35i	Mar	Sánchez	ESP	25.12.79	1		Valencia	12 Feb
4.35	Nastja	Ryshich	GER	19.9.77	2	NC	Wattenscheid	3 Jul
4.32i	Mary	Saxer	USA-J	21.6.87	1		Landover	13 Mar
4.31	Melina	Hamilton	NZL	15.6.76	1	NC	Wanganui	13 Mar
4.31	Joana	Ribeiro Costa	BRA	15.8.81	1		São Paulo	12 Jun
	(50)							
4.30i	Aleksandra	Kiryashova	RUS	21.8.85	1		Sankt-Peterburg	23 Jan
4.30i	Lacy	Janson	USA	20.2.83	1		Gainesville	6 Feb
4.30i		Wu Sha	CHN-J	21.10.87	1		Shanghai	19 Feb
4.30i	Elisabete	Tavares	POR	7.3.80	Q	EI	Madrid	4 Mar
4.30i	Amy	Linnen	USA	15.7.82	1	NCAA	Fayetteville	12 Mar
4.30	Chelsea	Johnson	USA	20.12.83	1		Los Angeles	30 Apr
4.30	Shayla	Balentine	USA	8.8.82	2	NCAA	Sacramento	11 Jun
4.30	Breanna	Eveland	USA	25.1.84	4	NCAA	Sacramento	11 Jun
4.30	Julia	Hütter	GER	26.7.83	2		Mannheim	18 Jun
4.30	Floé	Kühnert	GER	6.3.84	3		Mannheim	18 Jun
	(60)							
4.30	Róza	Kasprzak	POL	9.4.82	3	NC	Biala Podlaska	25 Jun
4.30	Alejandra	García	ARG	13.6.73	1		Buenos Aires	25 Jun
4.30	Nadine	Rohr	SUI	29.6.77	2		Rheinau-Freistett	26 Jun
4.30	Keisa	Monterola	VEN-Y	26.2.88	2	WY	Marrakech	16 Jul
4.30	Yelena	Belyakova	RUS	7.4.76	4=	GP	Madrid	16 Jul
4.30	Ikuko	Nishikori	JPN	5.1.80	3	EAsG	Macau	2 Nov
4.30	Alana	Boyd	AUS	10.5.84	1		Brisbane	26 Nov
4.30i	Anastasiya	Shvedova (Ivanova)	RUS	3.5.79	1		Sankt-Peterburg	25 Dec
4.27	Ebby	Metzinger	USA	16.6.79	1		Eagle Rock	5 Jun
4.27	Tiffany	Maskulinski	USA-J	26.9.86	1		Elma	6 Aug
	(70)							

Mark	Name		Nat	Born	Pos	Meet	Venue	Date
4.26i	Aurore	Pignot	FRA	24.12.79	1		Lingolsheim	26 Feb
4.25Ai	Connie	Jerz	USA	26.4.82	4		Reno	22 Jan
4.25i	Linda	Persson	SWE	22.9.81	1		Malmö	13 Feb
4.25	Fanni	Juhász	HUN	31.3.81	1	Towns	Athens, GA	23 Apr
4.25	Chloë	Mourand	FRA-J	20.10.87	1		Aix-les-Bains	25 Jun
4.25	Adigóni	Asteríou	GRE	2.11.76	1		Athína (E)	26 Jun
4.25	Amélie	Delzenne	FRA	4.8.83	1		Bondoufle	2 Jul
4.25	Katiuska	Pérez	CUB	21.12.75	1	CAC	Nassau	9 Jul
4.23i	Zsuzsanna	Olgyay (Szabó)	HUN	6.5.73	1		Budapest	5 Mar
4.22	Beth	Hinshaw-Spearman	USA	30.7.81	1		Houston	20 May
	(80)							
4.22	Kristina	Gadschiew	GER	3.7.84	1		Eisenberg	21 May
4.21i	Dana	Cervantes	ESP	18.8.78	2	NC	Madrid	19 Feb
4.21i	Sandra	Tavares	POR	29.5.82	3		Lingolsheim	25 Feb
4.21A	Milena	Agudelo	COL	15.4.85	1	Bolivar	Armenia/COL	19 Aug
4.20i	Sabine	Schulte	GER	29.1.76	4		Wuppertal	21 Jan
4.20i	Teja	Melink	SLO	23.3.80	1		Budapest	28 Jan
4.20i	Nadine	Sonnabend	GER	28.1.81	3		Potsdam	4 Feb
4.20i		Liang Dan	CHN-Y	21.6.88	2		Shanghai	19 Feb
4.20i		Feng Lingjian	CHN	28.4.83	1		Beijing	5 Mar
4.20i		Zhang Na	CHN	27.9.80	2		Beijing	5 Mar
	(90)							
4.20i		Yu Shuo	CHN-Y	14.1.88	3=		Beijing	5 Mar
4.20i	Ashley	Wildhaber	USA	29.10.83	5	NCAA	Fayetteville	12 Mar
4.20i	Laura	Chmielewski	USA	13.9.83	6	NCAA	Fayetteville	12 Mar
4.20	Andrea	Wildrick	USA	23.12.79	1		Lynchburg	2 Apr
4.20	Karla Rosa	da Silva	BRA	12.11.84	1		São Paulo	28 Apr
4.20	Anna	Battke	GER	3.1.85	7		Saulheim	22 May
4.20	Lyudmila	Vaylenko	UKR	18.3.74	2		Yalta	27 May
4.20	Erin	Asay	USA	17.3.83	8		San Diego	4 Jun
4.20	Katerina	Badurová	CZE	18.12.82	4	GS	Ostrava	9 Jun
4.20	Jackie	Rodgers	USA	2.3.83	5	NCAA	Sacramento	11 Jun
	(100)							
4.20	Carly	Dockendorf	CAN	31.12.83	6	NCAA	Sacramento	11 Jun
4.20	Roslinda	Samsu	MAS	9.6.82	1		Torrent	18 Jun
4.20	Elise	Genévrier	FRA	27.6.83	4	u-23	Mannheim	18 Jun
4.20	Simone	Langhirt	GER	19.1.84	5	u-23	Mannheim	18 Jun
4.20	Justyna	Ratajczak	POL	29.6.85	4	NC	Biala Podlaska	25 Jun
4.20	Paulina	Debska	POL	27.9.85	5	NC	Biala Podlaska	25 Jun
4.20	Stephanie	McCann	CAN	22.4.77	1	Cooman	Stadskanaal	3 Jul
4.20	Amandine	Homo	FRA	24.12.80	1		Aulnay-sous-Bois	4 Jul
4.20	Iréna	Dufour	BEL	1.6.78	1	NC	Bruxelles	10 Jul
4.20	Zoë	Brown	GBR	15.9.83	5	EU23	Erfurt	17 Jul
4.20	Svetlana	Makarevich	BLR-J	5.3.86	2	EJ	Kaunas	23 Jul
4.20	Anna	Giordano Bruno	ITA	13.12.80	3	v2N	Viareggio	27 Jul
4.20	Dimitra	Emmanouíl	GRE	13.5.84	3	WUG	Izmir	17 Aug

Mark	First	Last	Nat	Born	Date
4.17i	Tamara	Diles	USA	11.5.82	26 Feb
4.16i	Yekaterina	Sultanova	RUS	31.12.84	5 Feb
4.16	Sarah	Landau	USA	9.10.85	27 May
4.15iA	Denisse	Orengo	PUR	18.8.81	21 Jan
4.15i	Stevie	Marshalek	USA	1.6.85	5 Mar
4.15	Jennie	Sewell	USA	21.2.84	9 Apr
4.15	Katrina	Miroshnichenko	AUS-J	12.1.86	14 May
4.15	Julie	Vigourt	FRA	19.10.79	7 Jun
4.15	Ellie	Spain	GBR	23.8.82	12 Jun
4.15	Nicole	Büchler	SUI	17.12.83	14 Jun
4.15	Lisa	Ryshich	GER-Y	27.9.88	18 Jun
4.15	Camille	Simon	FRA-J	24.4.86	18 Jun
4.15		Huang Yu	CHN	15.1.83	25 Jun
4.15	Vicky	Parnov	AUS-Y	24.10.90	5 Jul
4.15	Maria	Rendin	SWE	28.7.82	11 Jul
4.15	Sue	Kupper	CAN	28.8.84	15 Jul
4.15	Elena	Scarpellini	ITA-J	14.1.87	23 Jul
4.15	Jirina	Ptácniková	CZE-J	20.5.86	6 Aug
4.15	Takayo	Kondo	JPN	17.11.75	7 Aug
4.15	Slavica	Semenjuk	SCG	25.10.84	17 Aug
4.15		Sun Lei	CHN	30.4.83	20 Oct
4.15		Zhou Yang	CHN-Y	16.5.88	20 Oct
4.14i	Caroline	Bocquet	FRA	22.9.76	19 Mar
4.13	Kierney	Hiteshew	USA	12.4.83	15 May
4.13	Marta	Plewa	POL	17.12.83	16 Jul
4.12A	Alejandra	Meza	MEX	18.7.78	13 Feb
4.12	Randalene	Sergent	USA	2.5.81	25 Mar
4.12	Annelise	Pradal	FRA-Y	22.6.88	1 Jun
4.12	Brittany	Parker	USA-J	29.10.87	26 Jun
4.12	Minna	Nikkanen	FIN-Y	9.4.88	27 Aug
4.12i	Kate	Dennison	GBR	7.5.84	17 Dec
4.11i	Enikö	Erös	HUN-J	8.9.86	27 Feb
4.11i	Stacie	Manuel	USA	6.12.83	5 Mar
4.11	Allison	Stokke	USA-Y	22.3.89	26 Mar
4.11	Lindsay	Regan	USA-Y	10.1.88	19 May
4.11	Brysun	Stately	USA-J	22.11.86	20 May
4.11	Sara	Bruzzese	ITA	7.10.82	19 Jun
4.11	Mami	Nakano	JPN	12.3.79	3 Nov
4.10i	Yuliya	Lukinskaya	RUS	3.5.76	7 Jan
4.10i	Shannon	Gallagher	USA	10.3.75	21 Jan
4.10i	Yeoryía	Tsiliggíri	GRE	21.6.72	29 Jan
4.10i	Valeriya	Volik	RUS-Y	11.5.89	16 Feb
4.10i	Nina	Vezjak	SLO	20.9.79	19 Feb
4.10i		Huo Zhiting	CHN-J	12.1.87	19 Feb
4.10i	Katarzyna	Sowa	POL	19.11.85	20 Feb
4.10i	Sirine	Balti	TUN	31.10.83	20 Feb
4.10i	Melanie	Buczko	USA	30.4.85	25 Feb
4.10i	Christi	Lehman	USA	8.8.83	26 Feb
4.10i	Kim	Marino	USA	23.4.81	26 Feb
4.10i		Li Gaoqun	CHN-J	29.6.86	5 Mar
4.10	Maryoris	Sánchez	CUB	3.10.85	17 Mar
4.10	Charmaine	Lucock	AUS-J	8.4.87	20 Mar
4.10A	Kelley	Schulz	USA	14.6.85	2 Apr
4.10	Kara	Stoughton	USA		15 Apr

Mark	Name		Nat	Born	Date
4.10	Aurélie	Clerc	FRA	13.4.83	30 Apr
4.10	Angela	Tavlarides	USA	17.9.81	30 Apr
4.10	Chaunte	Mitchell	USA		7 May
4.10	Zsuzsanna	Lendvai	HUN	16.10.84	14 May
4.10	Yarisley	Silva	CUB-J	1.6.87	20 May
4.10	Béatrice	Denis	FRA	18.6.72	28 May
4.10	Joanna	Piwowarska	POL	4.11.83	5 Jun
4.10	Michelle	Rzepka	USA	4.8.83	9 Jun
4.10	Nikolía	Kyriakopoúlou	GRE-J	21.3.86	11 Jun
4.10	Tina	Sutej	SLO-Y	7.11.88	12 Jun
4.10	Karen	Pollefeyt	BEL	15.12.79	12 Jun
4.10	Aino-Maija	Karvinen	FIN-J	17.9.86	18 Jun
4.10	Rianna	Galiart	NED	22.11.85	18 Jun
4.10	Irie	Hill	GBR	16.1.69	26 Jun
4.10	Anna	Zhidkova	RUS-J	14.3.87	2 Jul
4.10	Alevtina	Ruyeva	UKR-Y	13.3.88	3 Jul
4.10	Elise	Duboquet	FRA	18.11.81	15 Jul
4.10		Chang Ko-Hsin	TPE	20.6.80	2 Sep
4.10	Petra	Pechstein	SUI	26.7.71	10 Sep
4.10		Le Thi Phuong	VIE	12.11.83	17 Oct
4.10	Samantha	Dodd	RSA	13.8.79	12 Nov
4.09i	Chelo	Canino	USA	13.7.82	4 Mar
4.08i	Jackie	Nguyen	USA	20.4.84	12 Feb
4.06i	Molly	Lederman	USA	5.6.84	12 Feb
4.06	April	Kubishta	USA	5.7.85	23 Apr
4.06	Cheryl	Terrio	USA	6.5.84	27 May
4.06	Amanda	Storck	USA		27 May
4.06	Rachel	Greff	USA-J	5.4.86	27 May
4.06	Kelly	DiVesta (196)	USA	20.10.85	27 May
4.05	17 women				

Best outdoor marks

Mark	Name	Pos	Meet	Venue	Date
4.70	Pyrek	1	NC	Biala Podlaska	25 Jun
4.55	Polnova	3	Déca	Paris (C)	3 Sep
4.51	Hamácková	1		Praha	27 Jun
4.50	Hingst	2	ECp-S	Firenze	18 Jun
4.42	Spiegelburg	3		Beckum	21 Aug
4.41	Suttle	1		Oxford, MS	9 Apr
4.40	Kushch	1		Yalta	27 May
4.40	Zhao Yingying	1	NG	Nanjing	20 Oct
4.35	Stefanova	1	NC	Sofia	7 Jun
4.35	Strutz	1		Rheinau-Freistett	26 Jun
4.30	Holliday	1		Eugene	7 May
4.30	Linnen	3	NCAA	Sacramento	11 Jun
4.30	Soma	1	NCAA	Sacramento	11 Jun
4.30	Stefanídi	1	WY	Marrakech	16 Jul
4.30	Kiryashova	1	v2N	Viareggio	27 Jul
4.26	Stuczynski	1		Cedarville	22 Apr
4.25	E Tavares	2	ECp-1B	Leiria	18 Jun
4.25	Fitidou	2	MedG	Almeria	29 Jun
4.25	L Persson	2		Göteborg	3 Jul
4.21	Sánchez	1		Mataró	14 Jul
4.20	Belinskaya	2		Sochi	26 May
4.30ex		2		Sopot	2 Jun
4.20	Pignot	5=	ECp-S	Firenze	18 Jun
4.20	Yu Shuo	3	WY	Marrakech	16 Jul
4.20	Melink	1	NC	Maribor	24 Jul
4.19	Saxer	1		Lancaster	14 May

Mark	Name	Date
4.18	Schulte	28 May
4.16	Sultanova	27 May
4.15	Wu Sha	23 Apr
4.15	Diles	30 Apr
4.15	Zhang Na	20 Oct
4.15	Liang Dan	20 Oct
4.13	S Tavares	23 Jul
4.11	Janson	9 Apr
4.11	Dennison	27 Aug
4.10	Wildhaber	17 Apr
4.10	Manuel	28 Apr
4.10	Orengo	7 May
4.10	Sonnabend	29 May
4.10	Vezjak	12 Jun
4.10	Volik	21 Jun
4.10	Lukinskaya	10 Jul
4.10	Bocquet	21 Jul
4.06	Lederman	27 May
4.06	Lehman	27 May

Exhibition: 4.20 Susan DeNigris USA 28.5.80 1 Hot Springs 4 Jun

JUNIORS

See main list for 11 top juniors. 12 (inc. 4 indoors) perfs by 3 women to 4.35. Additional mark and further juniors:

Name	Mark	Pos	Meet	Venue	Date
Spiegelburg 2+	4.40	1		Saulheim	22 May
	4.40	1	NC	Wattenscheid	3 Jul
	4.35	1		Luzern	14 Jun
	4.35	1		Mannheim	18 Jun
	4.35	1	EJ	Kaunas	23 Jul
Zhao Y 2+	4.40i	1		Karlsruhe	13 Feb
	4.40	1	EAsG	Macao	2 Nov

Mark	Name		Nat	Born	Pos	Meet	Venue	Date
4.15	Katrina	Miroshnichenko	AUS	12.1.86	3		Chongqing	14 May
4.15	Lisa	Ryshich	GER-Y	27.9.88	1		Mannheim	18 Jun
4.15	Camille	Simon	FRA	24.4.86	3		Mannheim	18 Jun
4.15	Vicky	Parnov	AUS-Y	24.10.90	1		Gold Coast	5 Jul
4.15	Elena	Scarpellini	ITA	14.1.87	3	EJ	Kaunas	23 Jul
4.15	Jirina	Ptácniková	CZE	20.5.86	1	v3N-23	Manchester (SC)	6 Aug
4.15		Zhou Yang	CHN-Y	16.5.88	5	NG	Nanjing	20 Oct
4.12	Annelise	Pradal	FRA-Y	22.6.88	1		Clermont-Ferrand	1 Jun
4.12	Brittany	Parker (20)	USA	29.10.87	1		Dallas	26 Jun
4.12	Minna	Nikkanen	FIN-Y	9.4.88	4	vSWE	Göteborg	27 Aug

Best out

Mark	Name	Pos	Meet	Venue	Date
4.15	Wu Sha	2		Zhongshan	23 Apr
4.15	Liang Dan	9	NG	Nanjing	20 Oct
4.10	Volik	1	NC-y	Chelyabinsk	21 Jun

LONG JUMP

Mark	Wind	Name		Nat	Born	Pos	Meet	Venue	Date
7.04	1.2	Irina	Simagina	RUS	25.5.82	1		Sochi	26 May

7.00/1.2 6.70 7.04 6.67 p p

Mark	Wind	Pos	Meet	Venue	Date	Series
7.01	0.4	1	Kuts	Moskva	15 Jul	x x 6.82/0.4 6.90/0.7 6.86/0.3 7.01
6.86	1.8	*	v2N	Glasgow (S)	5 Jun	6.75/1.2 6.79w/2.8 6.86/1.8 6.88w/2.2 6.81w/2.9 6.85w/2.4
6.76	1.1	1	ECp-S	Firenze	17 Jun	x 6.76 6.46 x

Mark	Wind	Name		Nat	Born	Pos	Meet	Venue	Date
6.96	0.2	Tatyana	Kotova	RUS	11.12.76	1	NC	Tula	13 Jul

6.78/0.6 6.94/-0.7 6.85/0.1 x p 6.96

Mark	Wind	Pos	Meet	Venue	Date	Series
6.87	-0.7	1	VD	Bruxelles	26 Aug	x x 6.87 x 6.31 x
6.83	0.8	1	WAF	Monaco	9 Sep	6.78/-0.2 x 6.69/0.6 6.83
6.80	1.1	1	Pre	Eugene	4 Jun	6.59/2.0 6.74/1.3 6.32/-0.7 6.57/0.9 6.80 6.79/1.5
6.79	1.5	2	WCh	Helsinki	10 Aug	6.76/0.5 6.69/0.7 6.79 6.59 6.59 6.53

Mark	Wind	Name		Nat	Born	Pos	Meet	Venue	Date
6.92	1.7	Concepción	Montaner	ESP	14.1.81	2	GP	Madrid	16 Jul

6.41w/3.3 6.65/1.7 6.84w/2.5 6.92 6.79/1.7 6.72/1.4

Mark	Wind	Name		Nat	Born	Pos	Meet	Venue	Date
6.89	1.1	Tianna	Madison	USA	30.8.85	1	WCh	Helsinki	10 Aug

x 6.69/1.5 6.35 x 6.89 x

Mark	Wind	Pos	Meet	Venue	Date	Series
6.83	1.2	Q	WCh	Helsinki	9 Aug	6.83 only jump

Mark	Wind	Name		Nat	Born	Pos	Meet	Venue	Date
	6.82 0.0 1		Knoxville	9 Apr	6.82	6.53	6.56	p p	p
	6.78i 1 NCAA		Fayetteville	11 Mar	6.49	6.72	6.78	p p	p
6.87	0.2	Carolina	Klüft	SWE	2.2.83	1H	WCh	Helsinki	7 Aug
					6.87	6.75/0.3	x		
	6.84i 1		Göteborg	3 Feb	6.59	x	4.96	6.66 x	6.84
	6.79 0.8 1 EU23		Erfurt	17 Jul	6.65/-0.2	6.62/0.8	6.63/1.0	6.69/0.3 6.79	x
6.86	1.1	Oksana	Udmurtova	RUS	1.2.82	1	Znam	Kazan	25 Jun
					5.90	6.73/0.9	6.39	x 6.86	x
	6.85 -0.1 1 NC		Tula	13 Jul	6.59	6.61	6.71	6.85 x	6.64
	6.81 -0.8 2 VD		Bruxelles	26 Aug	6.81	6.72/0.9	x	6.76/0.8 x	6.31
	6.82w 3.4 5 GP		Madrid	16 Jul	6.22	6.61w	6.82w	x 5.65	x
6.81i		Viktoriya	Molchanova	UKR	26.5.82	1		Kharkov	19 Jan
6.80	-1.8	Ineta	Radevica	LAT	13.7.81	1	ECp-2A	Tallinn	19 Jun
					6.52	6.15	6.80	x	
6.80	0.8	Eunice	Barber	FRA	17.11.74	1	Déca	Paris (C)	3 Sep
					6.14	6.80	6.44	6.53	
	6.75 0.7 2H WCh		Helsinki	7 Aug	6.65	6.75	6.69w		
	6.76w 2.3 3 WCh		Helsinki	10 Aug	6.44	x	6.31	6.70/-1.4 x	6.76w
6.79	0.1	Lyudmila	Kolchanova (10)	RUS	1.10.79	1	WUG	Izmir	16 Aug
					6.48	6.60	6.50	6.62 6.52	6.79
6.78	0.0		Guan Yingnan	CHN	25.4.77	1		Zhongshan	24 Apr
6.78	0.6	Natalya	Lebusova	RUS	4.4.78	3	NC	Tula	13 Jul
					6.61	6.60	x	6.70 6.78	6.50
6.77	0.9	Yargelis	Savigne	CUB	13.11.84	1	Barr	La Habana	19 May
					6.48	6.77	4.64	x x	6.55
6.77	1.5	Yuliya	Zinovyeva	RUS	18.5.84	2		Sochi	26 May
					6.30	6.45	6.77	6.58 p	p
6.76	-0.7	Lyudmila	Blonska	UKR	9.11.77	1		Kiev	25 Jul
					x	6.76	6.26	x 6.38	x
6.75	0.2	Tatyana	Ivanova	RUS	16.10.81	2	Kuts	Moskva	15 Jul
					x	6.51	x	6.75 6.69	x
6.75	0.5	Anju Bobby	George	IND	19.4.77	2	WAF	Monaco	9 Sep
					x	x	6.75	x	
		(32/17)							
6.74	0.2	Tatyana	Ter-Mesrobyan	RUS	12.5.68	5	NC	Tula	13 Jul
6.73	1.4	Rose	Richmond	USA	29.1.81	1	GP II	Fort-de-France	30 Apr
6.73	2.0	Grace	Upshaw	USA	22.9.75	1	GP II	Stanford	30 May
		(20)							
6.72i		Angelica	Badea	ROM	1.10.75	1	NC	Bucuresti	13 Feb
6.72	2.0	Stilianí	Pilátou	GRE	28.3.80	1		Thessaloníki	2 Jul
6.72	0.0	Naide	Gomes	POR	10.11.79	1		Salamanca	6 Jul
6.72A	1.3	Niurka	Montalvo	ESP	4.6.68	1		Monachil	25 Jul
6.70		Yudelkis	Fernández	CUB	28.2.85	1		La Habana	25 Feb
6.70	-0.8	Tatyana	Lebedeva	RUS	21.7.76	1	SGP	Doha	13 May
6.69	1.1	Kumiko	Ikeda	JPN	10.1.81	1	NC	Tokyo	5 Jun
6.69	-0.1	Maho	Hanaoka	JPN	3.8.76	2	NC	Tokyo	5 Jun
6.69	1.3	Tünde	Vaszi	HUN	18.4.72	1	NC	Debrecen	6 Jul
6.68	0.5	Brianna	Glenn	USA	18.4.80	3	NC	Carson	24 Jun
		(30)							
6.67i		Amy	Menlove	USA	23.7.85	1P	NCAA	Fayetteville	12 Mar
6.67	-0.9	Hyleas	Fountain	USA	14.1.81	2=H		Götzis	29 May
6.67	-0.6	Kelly	Sotherton	GBR	13.11.76	2=H		Götzis	29 May
6.66	0.2	Bianca	Kappler	GER	8.8.77	1		Wesel	25 Jun
6.66	0.5	Martina	Darmovzalová	CZE	12.10.78	1	NC	Kladno	2 Jul
6.65i		Adina	Anton	ROM	6.10.84	1		Bucuresti	5 Feb
6.65	1.7	Marshevet	Hooker	USA	25.9.84	1	TexR	Austin	8 Apr
6.65	0.9	Olga	Balayeva	RUS	30.6.84	2	NC-23	Tula	13 Jun
6.65	-3.2	Jackie	Edwards	BAH	14.4.71	1	NC	Freeport	25 Jun
6.64i		Denisa	Scerbová	CZE-J	21.8.86	1		Bratislava	6 Feb
		(40)							
6.64i		Irina	Melnikova	RUS	14.5.75	1	NC	Volgograd	12 Feb
6.64	1.6	Elva	Goulbourne	JAM	21.1.80	2	Pre	Eugene	4 Jun
6.64	1.3	Veronika	Shutkova	BLR-J	26.5.86	1		Tula	24 Jun
6.64	0.5	Fiona	May	ITA	12.12.69	1	MedG	Almeria	30 Jun
6.63i		Anastasiya	Ilyina	RUS	16.1.82	2	NC	Volgograd	12 Feb
6.63	0.6		Wang Lina	CHN	28.2.83	1		Chongqing	15 May
6.63	2.0	Zita	Ajkler	HUN	9.6.75	1		Györ	7 Jun
6.63	1.3	Keila	Silva Costa	BRA	6.2.83	1	NC	São Paulo	17 Jun
6.63	0.0		Liu Huahua	CHN	20.9.84	Q	NC	Changsha	24 Jun
6.63	0.0	Alina	Militaru	ROM	10.4.82	2	Odlozil	Praha	27 Jun
		(50)							

WOMEN 2005

Mark	Wind	Name		Nat	Born	Pos	Meet	Venue	Date
6.63	0.5	Marestella	Torres	PHI	20.2.81	2	AsiC	Inchon	4 Sep
6.62	0.2	Aleksandra	Shishlyuk	UKR	16.4.80	2	Veniz	Haniá	6 Jun
6.62	1.4	Ioánna	Kafetzí	GRE	30.5.76	1	NC	Athína	11 Jun
6.62	0.5	Urzula	Gutowicz-Westhof	GER	13.7.77	1		Cuxhaven	9 Jul
6.60	1.2	Malgorzata	Trybanska	POL	21.6.81	1		Biala Podlaska	28 May
6.60	1.9	Olga	Rypakova (Alekseyeva)	KAZ	30.11.84	1		Almaty	4 Jun
6.60	1.2	Claudia	Tonn	GER	18.4.81	1H		Ratingen	26 Jun
6.59	1.6	Akiba	McKinney	USA	9.3.79	4	NC	Carson	24 Jun
6.59	0.3	Jana	Veldáková	SVK	3.6.81	1		Kosice	10 Jul
6.59	0.8	Bronwyn	Thompson	AUS	29.1.78	*		Brisbane	26 Nov
		(60)							
6.58	1.5	Natalia	Kilpeläinen	FIN	19.7.70	1		Tampere	12 Jun
6.58	1.1	Karin	Ruckstuhl	NED	2.11.80	1	ECp-1B	Leiria	19 Jun
6.57i		Krysha	Bayley	CAN	21.1.84	1		Clemson	21 Jan
6.57i		Anna	Pyatykh	RUS	4.4.81	1		Moskva	23 Jan
6.57i		Olivia	Wöckinger	AUT	23.5.79	1		Linz	12 Feb
6.57	1.0	Shameka	Marshall	USA	9.9.83	1	IC4A	Princeton	15 May
6.57	0.8		Zhong Mei	CHN	7.1.77	2		Chongqing	15 May
6.56	1.5	Tanika	Liburd	SKN	20.5.82	1		Baton Rouge	23 Apr
6.56	1.1	Hrisopiyi	Devetzí	GRE	2.1.76	2	NC	Athína	11 Jun
6.56	0.8	Oksana	Zubkovska	UKR	15.7.81	1		Kiev	15 Jun
		(70)							
6.56i		Olga	Kucherenko	RUS	14.2.85	1		Volgograd	22 Dec
6.54	1.9	Esther	Aghatise	NGR	15.4.85	1		Argentan	10 Jun
6.54	-0.4	Sofia	Schulte	GER	8.4.76	1		Kassel	10 Jun
6.54A	0.7	Caterine	Ibargüen	COL	12.2.84	1	Bolivar	Armenia/COL	19 Aug
6.53	0.0	Yuliya	Ignatkina	RUS	13.9.82	3	Kuts	Moskva	15 Jul
6.52i		Jesenija	Volzankina	LAT	28.11.83	1		Moskva	15 Feb
6.52i		Jade	Johnson	GBR	7.6.80	2	GP	Birmingham	18 Feb
6.52	0.0	Tina	Harris	USA	17.11.84	2	SEC	Nashville	14 May
6.52	0.8	Natalya	Sorokina	UKR	24.3.75	2		Kiev	15 Jun
6.52	0.5	Inna	Kazantseva	RUS	19.1.85	3	NC-23	Tula	15 Jun
		(80)							
6.52		Lerma Elvira	Gabito	PHI	17.10.74	1	Asi GP	Singapore	21 Jun
6.51i		Inna	Ivlyeva	RUS	27.6.71	Q	NC	Volgograd	11 Feb
6.51	0.8	Alexandra	Zelenina	MDA-J	21.11.86	1	NC	Chisinau	4 Jun
6.51	0.0	Yelena	Shchors	UKR	6.3.84	1		Kiev	21 Jun
6.51	1.5	Chantal	Brunner	NZL	5.11.70	1		Auckland (MS)	15 Oct
6.50i		Anna	Nazarova	RUS-J	14.3.86	1		Sankt-Peterburg	22 Jan
6.50	0.9	Antonette	Carter	USA	16.2.84	-	NCAA-r	Eugene	27 May
6.50	1.2	Panayióta	Koutsioumári	GRE	23.8.81	2	ECCp	Lagos/POR	29 May
6.50		Olga	Denisova	RUS	25.10.83	1		Moskva	4 Jun
6.50	0.7		Zhang Yuan	CHN-J	9.2.87	2	NG	Nanjing	19 Oct
		(90)							
6.50	-0.2	Janice	Josephs	RSA	31.3.82	1		Parow	16 Dec
6.50i		Oksana	Potapova	RUS	12.9.84	1		Moskva	25 Dec
6.49i		Kathrin	van Bühren	GER	29.5.82	1	NC	Sindelfingen	19 Feb
6.49i		Kristel	Berendsen	EST	25.8.77	2		Tallinn	20 Feb
6.49i		Tabia	Charles	CAN	6.4.85	1		Blacksburg	5 Mar
6.49	0.8	Dawn	Burrell	USA	1.11.73	1		Houston	20 May
6.49	0.8	Lela	Nelson	USA	19.5.83	3	NCAA	Sacramento	9 Jun
6.48	0.0	Simona	La Mantia	ITA	14.4.83	1		Palermo	21 May
6.48	-0.1	Jovanee	Jarrett	JAM	15.1.83	3	NCAA-r	Bloomington	28 May
6.48	1.1	Yuliya	Pidluzhnaya	RUS-Y	1.10.88	1		Chelyabinsk	30 Jul
		(100)							

Mark	Wind	Name		Nat	Born	Date
6.47	1.9	Lynn	Hernandez	USA	6.10.81	15 May
6.47i		Olesya	Kazanovskaya	RUS	12.7.82	24 Dec
6.46i		Kierra	Foster	USA	22.2.84	15 Jan
6.46i		Barbara	Leuthard	SUI	4.12.81	19 Feb
6.46i		Ksenija	Balta	EST-J	1.11.86	20 Feb
6.46	0.9	Kim	Jones	USA	13.6.81	7 May
6.46		Natalya	Safronova	BLR	11.7.74	25 May
6.46	1.0	Anastasiya	Zhuravlyeva	UZB	9.10.81	21 Jun
6.46	1.1	Sarah	Claxton	GBR	23.9.79	27 Aug
6.45i		Annika	Becker	GER	12.11.81	4 Feb
6.45	-0.7	Katja	Keller	GER	9.8.80	16 May
6.45	1.1	Tatyana	Dyachenko	UKR-J	25.1.86	28 May
6.45A	1.5	Sarah	Matthews	USA-Y	19.7.88	4 Jun
6.45	-0.5	Gi-Gi	Miller	USA	12.1.79	4 Sep
6.44i		Zhanna	Demidova	UKR-J	8.4.87	5 Jan
6.44	1.8	Kerrie	Taurima	AUS	2.4.79	6 Mar
6.44	-0.3	Valentina	Gotovska	LAT	3.9.65	11 Jun
6.44	1.1	Yelena	Sviridenko	UKR	11.4.81	15 Jun
6.44	-1.3	Luciana	dos Santos	BRA	10.2.70	17 Jun
6.44	1.2	Elise	Vésanes	FRA	25.1.84	17 Jul
6.43	-0.4	April	Holliness	USA	27.5.82	16 Apr
6.43	1.5	Candice	Baucham	USA	22.2.83	14 May
6.43	1.2	Lucie	Komrsková	CZE	24.10.77	10 Jun
6.43	1.7	Ivana	Spanovic	SCG-Y	10.5.90	30 Jul
6.42i		Yekaterina	Chernyavska	UKR	31.1.83	12 Feb
6.42	1.9	Ola	Sesay	USA	30.5.79	23 Apr
6.42A	-2.8	Chelsea	Taylor	USA-J	27.10.86	21 May
6.42	1.2	Simone	Oberer	SUI	8.4.80	16 Aug
6.42	0.4	Dana	Veldáková	SVK	3.6.81	3 Sep
6.41i			Huang Jianfen	CHN	10.10.78	2 Mar
6.41	0.0		Jung Soon-ok	KOR	23.4.83	19 Apr
6.41A	1.4	Delia	Visser	RSA	9.4.83	22 Apr
6.41	?0.0	Silvia	Otto	GER	21.1.79	4 Jun
6.41A	1.2	Karin	Mey	RSA	31.5.83	11 Jun

Mark	Wind	Name		Nat	Born	Date
6.41	0.4	Olesya	Rybakova	RUS-J	1.2.88	15 Jul
6.41	0.9	Emma	Green	SWE	8.12.84	21 Aug
6.41	1.8	Julie	Hollman	GBR	16.2.77	28 Aug
6.41	1.6	Eliane	Martins	BRA-J	26.5.86	1 Oct
6.40i		Antonia	Yordanova	BUL	17.8.76	16 Feb
6.40	1.7	Ilaria	Beltrami	ITA	16.7.81	15 May
6.40	0.0	Alice	Falaiye	CAN	24.12.78	11 Jun
6.40	1.6	Kaire	Leibak	EST-Y	21.5.88	5 Jul
6.40	2.0	Eloyse	Lesueur	FRA-Y	15.7.88	16 Jul
6.40i		Natalya	Mamysheva	RUS	9.12.84	25 Dec
6.39i		Nolle	Graham	USA	12.9.81	29 Jan
6.39i		Austra	Skujyte	LTU	12.8.79	15 Feb
6.39	0.0		Zhang Chunxiao	CHN	3.5.83	15 May
6.39	1.5	Kène	Ndoye	SEN	20.11.78	12 Jun
6.39	2.0	Arantxa	King	BER-Y	27.11.89	17 Jul
6.39	-1.0		Kim Su-yeon	KOR	2.5.77	15 Oct
6.38i		Bianca	Dürr	AUT	12.11.76	5 Feb
6.38	0.7	Narayane	Dossevi	FRA	3.2.83	17 Jul
6.37i		Panayióta	Alexándrou	GRE	30.7.75	22 Jan
6.37i		Julia	Machtig	GER-J	1.1.86	30 Jan
6.37		Starlie	Graves	USA	25.10.70	3 Jun
6.37	1.3	Christiane	Mendy	FRA	25.8.82	25 Jun
6.37	1.6	Sandra	Chukwu	POL-J	13.3.87	5 Jul
6.37	1.0	Niina	Saarman-Bartholdi	FIN	28.2.77	16 Jul
6.37	-0.6		Zhu Yanyan	CHN	3.12.78	19 Oct
6.36i		Marquita	Aldridge	USA	7.8.83	14 Jan
6.36i		Olga	Timofeyeva	RUS-Y	8.11.88	15 Jan
6.36	0.5	Toni	Smith	USA	13.10.84	30 Apr
6.36		LaShonda	Davis	USA		13 May
6.35i		Svetlana	Zaytseva	RUS	14.8.81	2 Feb
6.35		Peta-Gaye	Beckford	JAM	17.4.85	19 Feb
6.35i		Shana	Woods	USA-J	7.7.88	12 Mar
6.35	0.3	Aisha Onika	James	TRI	12.3.81	26 Mar
6.35	-0.2	Natalya	Dobrinska	UKR	29.5.82	29 May
6.35	0.7	Olga	Levenkova	RUS	11.1.84	15 Jun
6.35	0.6	Manuela	Galtier	FRA-Y	22.5.88	19 Jun
6.35	0.5	Kylie	Wheeler	AUS	17.1.80	26 Jun
6.35	1.2	Amy	Harris	GBR-J	14.9.87	24 Jul
6.34	0.8		Wang Ying	CHN	24.7.83	24 Apr
6.34	0.7	Yuka	Sato	JPN	6.7.81	5 Jun
6.34	0.3	Olesya	Belyayeva	KAZ	29.6.80	23 Sep
6.34	0.6	Jacinta	Boyd	AUS-J	10.2.86	26 Nov
6.33i		Laura	Gatto	ITA	4.3.77	19 Feb
6.33i			Gu Ying	CHN	26.5.80	6 Mar
6.33	1.9	Kadiatou	Camara	MLI	4.5.81	6 Apr
6.33	1.5	Tameisha	King	USA	24.8.81	17 Apr
6.33	0.8	Liubov	Malla	MDA	20.8.83	28 Apr
6.33	0.5	Sirkka-Liisa	Kivine	EST	22.6.77	27 May
6.33	1.2	Lúzia Maria	Teodoro	BRA	25.7.78	17 Jun
6.33	0.0	Viorica	Tigau	ROM	12.8.79	27 Jun
6.33	1.6	Gillian	Cooke	GBR	3.10.82	30 Jul
6.33	1.0	Jenni	Dryburgh	NZL	30.8.78	22 Oct
		(186)				

Wind assisted

Mark	Wind	Name		Nat	Born	Pos	Meet	Venue	Date
7.20	2.3	Tatyana	Kotova	RUS	11.12.76	1	GP	Madrid	16 Jul
					7.01w/4.0 7.06w/2.8 7.15w/5.5 6.84w/3.9 x 7.20w				
	6.93w 2.2 1 ECCp Lagos			28 May	6.93w x 6.74/1.0 x				
6.92	2.2	Tianna	Madison	USA	30.8.85	1	SEC	Nashville	14 May
					6.92w 6.79w/2.9 6.60w p p p				
6.92	3.0	Carolina	Klüft	SWE	2.2.83	1	v FIN	Göteborg	28 Aug
					6.49 x p p 6.71w/2.3 6.92w				
	6.91w 2.1 1 ECp-1A Gävle			19 Jun	6.48w/3.1 6.51w/2.7 6.60/1.8 6.91w				
6.89	4.7	Marshevet	Hooker	USA	25.9.84	1	Big 12	Manhattan, KS	14 May
					6.52w 6.59w 6.89w p p p				
6.88	4.6	Yargelis	Savigne	CUB	3.11.84	1	CAC	Nassau	11 Jul
					6.68w 6.43w x 6.88w x 6.59w				
6.87	2.1	Grace	Upshaw	USA	22.9.75	3	GP	Madrid	16 Jul
					x 6.87w/3.7 x 5.16w 6.87w/4.1 6.87w/2.1				
6.87	2.8	Niurka	Montalvo	ESP	4.6.68	4	GP	Madrid	16 Jul
					x 6.74w/3.5 6.66w/2.5 x 6.87w 6.75w/2.3				
6.82	2.3	Maho	Hanaoka	JPN	3.8.76	1	GP	Osaka	7 May
					6.34 5.99w 6.61w 6.39 6.82w 6.60/0.8				
6.81	2.2	Elva	Goulbourne	JAM	21.1.80	6	GP	Madrid	16 Jul
					6.17w 6.71w 6.81w 6.51w x 6.45				
6.79	3.8	Rose	Richmond	USA	29.1.81	7	GP	Madrid	16 Jul
					6.79w 6.74w x 6.64w 6.54w x				
6.77	5.7	Stilianí	Pilátou	GRE	28.3.80	1		Réthimno	7 May
6.73	2.1	Bronwyn	Thompson	AUS	29.1.78	1		Brisbane	26 Nov
6.72	2.9	Tünde	Vaszi	HUN	18.4.72	1		Szombathely	24 Jul
6.71	3.5	Jackie	Edwards	BAH	14.4.71	3	CAC	Nassau	11 Jul
6.70	3.1	Brianna	Glenn	USA	18.4.80	1		Azusa	14 Apr
6.69	2.1	Bianca	Kappler	GER	8.8.77	10		Madrid	16 Jul
6.64A	4.7	Alice	Falaiye	CAN	24.12.78	1		El Paso	16 Apr
6.62	3.3	Tanika	Liburd	SKN	20.5.82	1		Baton Rouge	23 Apr
6.61	4.3	Lakadron	Ivery	USA	23.6.83	2	Big 12	Manhattan, KS	14 May
6.61	3.6	Akiba	McKinney	USA	9.3.79	1		Chula Vista	21 May
6.59	3.1	Kerrie	Taurima	AUS	2.4.79	1	NC	Sydney	6 Mar
6.56	2.3	Antonette	Carter	USA	16.2.84	1	NCAA-r	Eugene	27 May
6.54	3.1	Lucie	Komrsková	CZE	24.10.77	1		Praha	10 Jun
6.53	2.9	Candice	Baucham	USA	22.2.83	1		Los Angeles	30 Apr
6.52	2.5	Chantal	Brunner	NZL	5.11.70	2	Aus Ch	Sydney	6 Mar
6.51	5.0	Candice	Mills	USA	13.11.84	3	Big 12	Manhattan, KS	14 May
6.51	3.2	Cornelia	Deiac	ROM-Y	20.3.88	3	Rom IC	Bucuresti	11 Jun
6.49	5.3	Natalya	Dobrinska	UKR	29.5.82	2H		Arles	5 Jun

Mark	Wind	Name		Nat	Born	Date
6.47	4.2	Erika	Fano	ESP	11.7.82	9 Jul
6.46	3.6	Kedine	Geddes	JAM	28.2.84	9 Apr
6.46	4.2		Kim Su-yeon	KOR	2.5.77	19 Apr
6.46	3.1	Erica	McLain	USA-J	24.1.86	14 May
6.46	2.7	Ilaria	Beltrami	ITA	16.7.81	15 May
6.45	3.5	Valentina	Gotovska	LAT	3.9.65	2 Jul
6.43	4.2	Janay	DeLoach	USA		9 Apr
6.43	2.5	Sirkka-Liisa	Kivine	EST	22.6.77	27 May
6.43	5.1	Peta-Gaye	Beckford	JAM	17.4.85	11 Jul
6.43	2.2	Manuela	Galtier	FRA-Y	22.5.88	16 Jul
6.41	5.1	Charisse	Bacchus	TRI	26.4.84	14 May
6.41	2.6	Dominika	Miszczak	POL	12.4.85	27 Aug
6.39	3.7	Yuliya	Akulenko	UKR	3.6.77	5 Jun
6.39	5.3	Amy	Harris	GBR-J	14.9.87	8 Jul

Mark Wind Name Nat Born Pos Meet Venue Date

6.38 3.0 Panayióta Alexándrou GRE 30.7.75 11 Jun
6.38 5.6 Carlota Castrejana ESP 25.4.73 16 Jul
6.38 4.6 Svetlana Gnezdilov ISR 20.7.69 19 Jul
6.38 5.1 Jessica Penney NZL-J 21.12.87 11 Dec
6.37 2.9 Jacinta Boyd AUS-J 10.2.86 18 Dec
6.36 2.9 Naroa Agirre ESP 15.5.79 30 Apr
6.36 2.1 Tameisha King USA 24.8.81 21 May
6.36 3.6 Clélia Reuse SUI-Y 1.8.88 5 Jul
6.36 3.1 Shevell Quinley USA-J 26.6.87 16 Jul
6.34 2.2 Zhanna Melnichenko UKR 24.4.83 11 Jun
6.34 2.1 Céline Nyanga FRA 27.12.81 16 Jul
6.33 2.6 Tori Polk USA 21.9.83 23 Apr
6.33 3.6 Chelsea Hammond JAM 2.8.83 28 Apr
6.33 2.4 Daniela Lincoln-Saavedra SWE 4.8.84 28 Aug

Best outdoor marks

6.61 0.0 Molchanova 2 Kiev 25 Jul
6.57 1.0 Melnikova 3 Tula 23 Jul
6.57 0.3 Scerbová 3 EJ Kaunas 24 Jul
6.62w 2.3 11 GP Madrid 16 Jul
6.55 1.8 Anton 3 EU23 Erfurt 17 Jul
6.53 0.4 Pyatykh Q NC Tula 12 Jul
6.48 1.8 van Bühren 1 Kevelaer 19 Jun

6.41 0.3 Menlove 27 May
6.52Aw 2.6 13 May
6.39 0.7 Huang Jianfen 26 Jun
6.38 0.2 Chernyavskaya 6 Jun
6.38 Potapova 15 Jun
6.36 1.0 Badea 30 Apr
6.39w 2.3 1 Jun
6.35 1.4 Demidova 24 Jun
6.34 1.3 Kucherenko 26 May
6.34 1.5 Becker 29 May
6.41w 2.4 Balta 28 Aug
6.35w 2.5 Wöckinger 21 May

Low altitude bests

6.55 0.6 Montalvo 2 MedG Almeria 30 Jun
6.56w 5.1 Falaiye 2 Baton Rouge 23 Apr

JUNIORS

See main list for top 6 juniors. 12 performances (inc. 3 indoors) by 7 women to 6.45 Additional marks and further juniors:

Scerbová 2+ 6.56 1.7 4 ECp1A Gävle 19 Jun 6.54 1.1 1 Kladno 21 May
6.46i Ksenija Balta EST 1.11.86 3 Tallinn 20 Feb
6.41w 2.4 1H NC Rakvere 28 Aug
6.45 1.1 Tatyana Dyachenko UKR 25.1.86 3 Yalta 28 May
6.45A 1.5 Sarah Matthews USA-Y 19.7.88 1 Albuquerque 4 Jun
6.44i Zhanna Demidova (10) UKR 8.4.87 1 Kiev 5 Jan
6.35 1.4 3 Tula 24 Jun
6.43 1.7 Ivana Spanovic SCG-Y 10.5.90 1 Trípoli 30 Jul
6.42A -2.8 Chelsea Taylor USA 27.10.86 1 Aurora 21 May
6.41 0.4 Olesya Rybakova RUS 1.2.88 4 Kuts Moskva 15 Jul
6.41 1.6 Eliane Martins BRA 26.5.86 1 SAm-J Rosario 1 Oct
6.40 1.6 Kaire Leibak EST-Y 21.5.88 1 EY Lignano 5 Jul
6.40 2.0 Eloyse Lesueur FRA-Y 15.7.88 Q WY Marrakech 16 Jul
6.39 2.0 Arantxa King BER-Y 27.11.89 1 WY Marrakech 17 Jul
6.37i Julia Machtig GER 1.1.86 1P Halle 30 Jan
6.37 1.6 Sandra Chukwu POL 13.3.87 1 NC-j Bydgoszcz 5 Jul
6.36i Olga Timofeyeva (20) RUS-Y 8.11,88 1 Sankt-Peterburg 15 Jan

Wind assisted see main lists for 6.51w Deiac, plus to 6.38w:

6.46 3.1 Erica McLain USA 24.1.86 1 Pac10 Los Angeles (Ww) 14 May
6.43 2.2 Manuela Galtier FRA-Y 22.5.88 Q WY Marrakech 16 Jul
6.39 5.3 Amy Harris GBR 14.9.87 1 NSch Birmingham 8 Jul
6.38 5.1 Jessica Penney NZL 21.12.87 1 Auckland (MS) 11 Dec

TRIPLE JUMP

15.11 -0.2 Tatyana Lebedeva RUS 21.7.76 1 Gaz Saint Denis 1 Jul
15.11 14.97/-0.7 x p 15.07/0.7 15.08/0.3
15.05 0.9 1 Athl Lausanne 5 Jul 15.05 x 14.62 p 14.51 14.86
15.03 0.6 1 GGala Roma 8 Jul 14.51 14.87 15.03 15.01 14.48 14.86
14.94 -0.9 1 WK Zürich 19 Aug 14.63/-0.3 14.57/0.7 x 14.73/0.1 14.94 x
14.94 -0.2 1 VD Bruxelles 26 Aug 14.80/-0.3 14.78/-0.2 x 14.53/0.1 14.94 x
14.89 0.1 1 Bisl Oslo 29 Jul 14.58/-0.5 x x 14.89 p p
14.86 0.8 2 WAF Monaco 10 Sep 14.52/-0.4 14.70/1.7 14.61/1.1 14.86
14.85 0.8 1 ISTAF Berlin 4 Sep 13.95 14.85 14.68/0.2 14.76/0.4 p 14.33/0.2
15.11 0.8 Trecia Smith JAM 5.11.75 1 WCh Helsinki 7 Aug
x 14.67/0.2 14.51/0.9 14.91/1.5 15.11 15.01/-0.1
14.91 0.6 1 Fortaleza 18 May 14.91 x p p p p
14.85 -0.1 2 GGala Roma 8 Jul 14.51 x 14.85 x 14.82 14.55
14.81 0.7 1 GP Belém 22 May 14.63/1.7 14.81 p p p p
14.81 1.3 3 Athl Lausanne 5 Jul x 14.81 x 14.60 14.68 14.71
14.76 0.8 2 VD Bruxelles 26 Aug x x 14.11 14.25 x 14.76
14.69 0.5 4 WAF Monaco 10 Sep x 14.69 x 14.26
14.98 0.2 Baya Rahouli ALG 27.7.79 1 MedG Almeria 1 Jul
14.28 14.88/0.0 14.98 14.76/-0.3 x x
14.72 -0.6 1 SGP Athína 14 Jun 13.96 14.66/-0.9 x 14.72/-0.6 x x
14.83w 3.5 1 Alger 23 Jun also 14.29/1.9
14.89 1.7 Hrisopiyi Devetzí GRE 2.1.76 1 WAF Monaco 10 Sep
14.52/1.4 14.89 14.38/0.4 14.37/0.5
14.72 0.7 Q WCh Helsinki 6 Aug 14.10 x 14.72
14.88 1.2 Anna Pyatykh RUS 4.4.81 2 Athl Lausanne 5 Jul
14.23 14.53 14.72 14.39 x 14.88

Mark	Wind	Name		Nat	Born	Pos	Meet	Venue	Date	
14.78	-0.5					3	WCh	Helsinki	7 Aug	14.38/0.2 14.75/0.4 14.31 14.66/0.1 14.77/0.5 14.78
14.75						1		Moskva	5 Jun	14.48 14.50 14.78 p
14.72	0.9					1	ECp-S	Firenze	18 Jun	x 14.72/0.9 x 14.70w
14.72	1.2					1	GP	Rieti	28 Aug	x 14.67 14.62 x 14.55 14.72
14.70	0.8					2	Gaz	Saint Denis	1 Jul	14.20 14.55 x 14.45 14.46 14.70
14.82	0.7	Yargelis	Savigne	CUB	13.11.84	2	WCh	Helsinki	7 Aug	
										13.09 14.73/0.7 14.36 14.71/0.8 14.82 14.73/-0.1
14.81	1.5					3	WAF	Monaco	10 Sep	14.50/0.9 14.41/1.5 14.59/1.3 14.81
14.82	0.8	Yamilé	Aldama	SUD	14.8.72	2	ISTAF	Berlin	4 Sep	
										x x 14.13 14.26 14.75/0.7 14.82
14.72	0.8					4	WCh	Helsinki	7 Aug	14.72 14.56/0.7 14.56/0.3 14.47/0.4 14.69/0.5 14.64/-0.1
14.74i		Viktoriya	Gurova	RUS	22.5.82	1	EI	Madrid	6 Mar	
										14.37 14.35 14.74 x x x
14.69	1.2	Simona	La Mantia	ITA	14.4.83	1		Palermo	22 May	
										14.40 x 13.98 14.49 14.69 x
14.69	1.4	Magdelin	Martinez	ITA	10.2.76	1		Padova	3 Jul	
										14.38w 14.46 14.69 14.54w x 14.57w
		(32/10)								
14.61		Yusmay	Bicet	CUB	8.12.83	1		La Habana	24 Feb	
14.60	0.4	Carlota	Castrejana	ESP	25.4.73	2	MedG	Almeria	1 Jul	
14.58i		Adelina	Gavrila	ROM	26.11.78	1	NC	Bucuresti	12 Feb	
14.58	0.3		Huang Qiuyan	CHN	25.1.80	1		Zhongshan	23 Apr	
14.55	1.8	Anastasiya	Zhuravlyeva	UZB	9.10.81	1	Veniz	Haniá	6 Jun	
14.47	0.5	Kène	Ndoye	SEN	20.11.78	6	WCh	Helsinki	7 Aug	
14.38	-0.7		Xie Limei	CHN-J	27.6.86	1	AsiC	Inchon	1 Sep	
14.34i		Sárka	Kaspárková	CZE	20.5.71	4	EI	Madrid	6 Mar	
14.33i		Yelena	Oleynikova	RUS	9.12.76	2	NC	Volgograd	11 Feb	
14.31i		Natalya	Safronova	BLR	11.7.74	6	EI	Madrid	6 Mar	
		(20)								
14.31	1.4	Nadezhda	Bazhenova	RUS	22.9.78	1	GP II	Thessaloníki	17 Jul	
14.29i		Mariana	Solomon	ROM	8.9.80	1		Bucuresti	29 Jan	
14.27i		Yelena	Ivanova	RUS	16.3.79	1		Sankt-Peterburg	23 Jan	
14.27i		Athanasía	Pérra	GRE	2.2.83	2		Athína (P)	20 Feb	
14.25i		Oksana	Rogova	RUS	7.10.78	3	NC	Volgograd	11 Feb	
14.23i		Iríni	Dimitráki	GRE	8.8.80	3		Athína (P)	20 Feb	
14.23		Yelena	Parfyonova	KAZ	26.1.74	1	NC	Almaty	7 Jul	
14.21	1.6	Mabel	Gay	CUB	5.5.83	3		Padova	3 Jul	
14.20	-0.3	Anastasiya	Taranova	RUS	6.9.85	1	NC-23	Tula	15 Jun	
14.18		Yarianna	Martínez	CUB	20.9.84	1	CAC	Nassau	9 Jul	
		(30)								
14.18	0.6	Snezana	Vukmirovic	SLO	19.8.82	3	GP	Rieti	28 Aug	
14.16	1.1	Suzette	Lee	JAM	6.3.75	1		Baton Rouge	23 Apr	
14.16	1.2	Dana	Veldáková	SVK	3.6.81	3	GP II	Thessaloníki	17 Jul	
14.13	1.1	Mariya	Dimitrova	BUL	7.8.76	8	Athl	Lausanne	5 Jul	
14.12	0.4		Wang Ying	CHN	24.7.83	1	WUG	Izmir	19 Aug	
14.11i		Constanta	Stucan	ROM	12.7.81	2		Bucuresti	29 Jan	
14.11	1.4		Qiu Huijing	CHN	4.2.85	3		Zhongshan	23 Apr	
14.11	0.7	Svetlana	Bolshakova	RUS	14.10.84	2	EU23	Erfurt	16 Jul	
14.10	1.0	Tatyana	Dyachenko	UKR-J	25.1.86	1		Tula	26 Jun	
14.09	1.6	Aleksandra	Shishlyuk	UKR	16.4.80	4	ECp-S	Firenze	18 Jun	
		(40)								
14.07	0.7	Candice	Baucham	USA	22.2.83	1	NCAA	Sacramento	11 Jun	
14.07	-0.1	Françoise	Mbango	CMR	14.4.76	6	WK	Zürich	19 Aug	
14.04	0.6	Olga	Saladukha	UKR	4.6.83	1		Kiev	21 Jun	
14.03	1.5	Theresa	Nzola	FRA	30.11.83	1		Castres	26 Jul	
14.02	1.8	Svetlana	Semyonova	RUS	24.8.80	2	Kuts	Moskva	16 Jul	
14.02	1.1	Irina	Vasilyeva	RUS	9.4.79	*	Kuts	Moskva	15 Jul	
14.01	0.0		Wu Xueli	CHN	5.1.78	Q	NC	Changsha	25 Jun	
14.01	1.8	Erica	McLain	USA-J	24.1.86	1	NC	Carson	26 Jun	
13.98	0.0	Betty	Lise	FRA	5.9.72	1		Forbach	29 May	
13.97	1.4	Thaimi	O'Reilly	ITA	20.7.76	1		Pierre-Benité	10 Jun	
		(50)								
13.96	1.9	Tatyana	Shchurenko	UKR	26.2.76	2		Yalta	27 May	
13.95	1.1	Martina	Darmovzalová	CZE	12.10.78	2		Kladno	21 May	
13.95	1.3	Keila	Silva Costa	BRA	6.2.83	4	Veniz	Haniá	6 Jun	
13.95	0.0		Wu Lingmei	CHN	16.2.73	3	NC	Changsha	26 Jun	
13.95A	-1.6	Gisele	Lima de Oliveira	BRA	1.8.80	1		Bogotá	2 Jul	
13.94	-0.3	Darinka	Yotova	BUL	14.2.85	1	NC-j	Sofia	29 May	
13.93	1.2	Silvia	Otto	GER	21.1.79	1		Ohrdruf	5 Jun	
13.91	1.0	Silvia	Biondini	ITA	24.1.76	3	GP II	Torino	3 Jun	
13.91	1.9	Natalya	Tomashevska/Yastrebova	UKR	12.10.84	2	NC	Kiev	3 Jul	

Mark	Wind	Name		Nat	Born	Pos	Meet	Venue	Date
13.90	0.9	Aneta	Sadach	POL	22.4.75	1		Bielsko-Biala	9 Jul
		(60)							
13.90A	2.0	Johana	Triviño	COL	24.3.81	1	Bolivar	Armenia/COL	20 Aug
13.87		Yahyma	Kindelán	CUB	25.9.82	2		La Habana	4 Mar
13.87	0.0		Zhang Hao	CHN	26.2.78	4	NC	Changsha	26 Jun
13.86	1.8	Natalia	Kilpeläinen	FIN	19.7.70	1		Lapinlahti	3 Jul
13.85	1.1		Li Mingli	CHN-J	23.1.87	2		Zhaoqing	9 Apr
13.85	1.5	Yuliana	Perez	USA	21.7.81	1	MSR	Walnut	17 Apr
13.85	0.7		Lin Baohua	CHN	12.6.83	Q	NC	Changsha	25 Jun
13.83i		Dímitra	Márkou	GRE	28.7.80	5		Athína (P)	20 Feb
13.83	1.5		Sha Li	CHN-Y	14.8.88	5		Zhongshan	23 Apr
13.83	-0.5	Tatyana	Titova	RUS	2.1.83	3	NC-23	Tula	15 Jun
		(70)							
13.81		Chinoye	Ohadugba	NGR-J	24.3.86	1	NC	Abuja	9 Jul
13.79	0.0	Alexandra	Zelenina	MDA-J	21.11.86	1	NC	Chisinau	5 Jun
13.79	0.0	Olga	Pankova	RUS	13.8.76	1	Znam	Kazan	24 Jun
13.79	0.7	Amy	Zongo	FRA	4.10.80	5	MedG	Almeria	1 Jul
13.78	-1.9	Nicole	Whitman	USA	9.11.80	3	NC	Carson	26 Jun
13.75	1.4	Nelly	Tchayem	FRA	4.8.83	4		Pierre-Benité	10 Jun
13.74i		Tiombé	Hurd	USA	17.8.73	1		Blacksburg	11 Feb
13.74	-0.5	Camilla	Johansson	SWE	3.11.76	1		Göteborg	14 Jun
13.74	0.3	Kaire	Leibak	EST-Y	21.5.88	2	WY	Marrakech	14 Jul
13.73	0.8	Aleksandra	Fila	POL	17.8.83	6	EU23	Erfurt	16 Jul
		(80)							
13.72	1.3	Cristina	Bujin	ROM-Y	12.4.88	2	EJ	Kaunas	22 Jul
13.70	-0.6	Agata	Kosuda	POL	1.8.84	1	Big 12	Manhattan, KS	15 May
13.70	1.0	Shakeema	Walker	USA	10.11.76	7	FBK	Hengelo	29 May
13.70	1.2	Cristina	Nicolau	ROM	9.8.77	1	Rom IC	Bucuresti	11 Jun
13.70	1.3	Teija	Hannila	FIN	2.8.80	2		Lapinlahti	3 Jul
13.70	0.7	Irina	Beskrovnaja	SVK	28.12.82	1		Bratislava	6 Sep
13.69	1.1	Fernanda	Delfino	BRA	7.11.82	3	NC	São Paulo	19 Jun
13.69	0.9	Liliana	Zagacka	POL	28.1.77	1		Norrtälje	11 Jul
13.69	1.1	Brittany	Daniels	USA-J	22.9.87	3		Azusa	16 Jul
13.69	0.5	Veera	Baranova	EST	12.2.84	7	EU23	Erfurt	16 Jul
		(90)							
13.68A	1.1	Chaytan	Hill	USA	13.10.82	*		El Paso	2 Apr
13.67i		Katja	Demut	GER	21.12.83	2	NC	Sindelfingen	20 Feb
13.67		Olesya	Bufalova	RUS	6.10.82	1		Krasnodar	5 Jun
13.66A	-0.8	Caterine	Ibargüen	COL	12.2.84	3		Bogotá	3 Jul
13.66	1.6	Olesya	Belyayeva	KAZ	29.6.80	2	NC	Almaty	7 Jul
13.66		Domike	Nkiruka	NGR	28.8.85	2	NC	Abuja	9 Jul
13.65i		Shani	Marks	USA	24.8.80	1	NC	Boston	27 Feb
13.64		Latifa	Ezziraoui	MAR	26.10.85	1		Marrakech	22 May
13.62i		Tatyana	Yakovleva	RUS-J	9.9.86	2		Minsk	26 Feb
13.62	0.9	Taneisha	Scanlon	IRL	19.11.77	1		Bratislava	7 Jun
		(100)							
13.62	1.2	Kamila	Rywelska	POL	15.11.83	Q	NCAA	Sacramento	10 Jun
13.62	2.0	Patricia	Sarrapio	ESP	16.11.82	2	NC	Málaga	24 Jul
13.62	-0.6		Liu Yanan	CHN-J	18.1.87	1		Zhengzhou	30 Aug

Mark	Wind	Name		Nat	Born	Date
13.61	0.2		Tang Zhimin	CHN	26.6.79	14 May
13.61	0.5		Ngew Sin Mei	MAS	4.6.83	29 Nov
13.60		Elena	Denkova	BUL	7.1.85	25 Jul
13.58i		Andreja	Ribac	SLO	14.1.76	16 Feb
13.58	1.1	Luciana	dos Santos	BRA	10.2.70	2 Apr
13.55i		Zinaida	Lifintseva	RUS	19.6.84	20 Feb
13.54	1.1		Lu Bin	CHN	23.2.83	23 Apr
13.54	1.7	Yanelis	Veranes	CUB-J	20.7.87	31 Jul
13.53i		Anastasiya	Nazarova	RUS	13.1.83	20 Feb
13.53		Viktoriya	Molchanova	UKR	26.5.82	8 May
13.53	1.8	Maria	Høgheim	NOR	16.7.81	11 Jul
13.52	0.8	Zita	Ajkler	HUN	9.6.75	7 Jul
13.52	0.0	Yennifer	Arveláez	VEN	28.10.82	29 Jul
13.51	-1.2		Cho Eun-jung	KOR	10.3.81	16 Oct
13.50i		Irina	Malkina	RUS	14.1.80	27 Feb
13.50	1.3	Rosalind	Goodwin	GHA	6.6.83	11 Jun
13.50	0.7	Tabia	Charles	CAN	6.4.85	11 Jun
13.50	-0.2	Rakhima	Sardi	KGZ-J	11.4.86	26 Jun
13.50	0.5	Yekaterina	Kayukova	RUS-J	9.10.86	4 Jul
13.49	0.0	Thitima	Muangian	THA	3.11.84	3 May
13.49		Svetlana	Zubcova	MDA	3.6.80	5 Jun
13.48	1.8	Elina	Sorsa	FIN-J	22.7.86	21 Jul
13.47	1.2	Giovanna	Franzon	ITA	26.5.81	26 Jun
13.47	-0.1	Liliya	Kulik	UKR-J	27.1.87	26 Jun
13.46i		Rebeca	Azcona	ESP	31.5.80	19 Feb
13.46	1.0		Lin Nuai	CHN	6.1.84	25 Jun
13.44i		Laura	Tosoni	ITA	10.10.79	20 Feb
13.44	1.8		Qu Lei	CHN	28.1.83	22 May
13.43i		Olga	Timofeyeva	RUS-Y	8.11,88	16 Jan
13.43	1.4		Kim Su-yeon	KOR	2.5.77	1 Sep
13.42A	0.6	Ludmila	Reyes	VEN	22.3.76	24 Jul
13.41	0.3	Laurice	Félix	BRA	28.5.81	2 Apr
13.40		Béatrice	Kamboulé	BUR	25.2.80	9 Apr
13.40	1.2	Wibke	Walter	GER	17.1.79	29 May
13.40		Olesya	Lesun	BLR	18.10.82	3 Jul
13.39	0.3		Hu Qian	CHN-Y	14.1.89	13 May
13.39	0.2		Jung Hye-kyung	KOR	13.4.81	4 Jun
13.39	0.1	Sirkka-Liisa	Kivine	EST	22.6.77	19 Jul
13.38i		Colleen	Ramharak	CAN	14.6.82	5 Mar
13.38		Liubov	Malla	MDA	20.8.83	5 Jun
13.38	-1.1	Aleksandra	Ocheretko	UKR	10.11.83	21 Jun
13.38A	1.8	Victoria	Mayo	ESP	9.3.77	17 Jul
13.38	0.5	Lyudmila	Kolchanova	RUS	1.10.79	19 Aug
13.37	0.9		Luo Wen	CHN-Y	2.10.88	23 Apr
13.37	0.6		Zhang Chunxiao	CHN	3.5.83	23 Apr
13.37	1.1		Li Qian	CHN	20.10.85	25 Jun
13.37	-0.7	Jeanette	Bowles	AUS	14.1.79	1 Dec
13.36	0.7	Suanly	Larrinaga	CUB	6.10.85	20 May

Mark	Wind		Name	Nat	Born	Pos	Meet	Venue	Date
13.36	-0.7	Tánia	da Silva	BRA-J	17.12.86				28 Aug
13.36	1.1	Irina	Pak	UZB	25.3.80				30 Sep
13.35i		Margarita	Dobrobobova	UKR	24.6.85				13 Feb
13.35	1.0		Sha Liyuan	CHN-Y	23.5.88				23 Apr
13.34i		Mariya	Samborska	UKR	6.4.77				13 Feb
13.34	0.2		Yu Shaohua	CHN	4.1.85				23 Apr
13.34	-1.4	Fabrícia	da Silva	BRA	9.5.82				19 Jun
13.34	1.7	Aminata	Koné	FRA	1.8.83				25 Jun
13.34		Anna	Nazarova	RUS-J	14.3.86				14 Jun
13.34		Olga	Permyakova	RUS-J	8.6.86				14 Jun
13.34	1.9	Fumiyo	Yoshida	JPN	25.4.81				25 Sep
13.33	1.1	Lúzia Maria	Teodoro	BRA	25.7.78				30 Apr
13.33	0.6	Shayla	Moore	USA	20.8.83				28 May
13.33	0.6	Chasity	Johnson	USA	14.9.85				28 May
13.32i		Maria	Diikiti	CYP	6.11.82				13 Feb
13.32i		Malgorzata	Trybanska	POL	21.6.81				20 Feb
13.32	0.1	Courtney	Stafford	USA					9 Apr
13.32	0.0	Ewelina	Wilk	POL	29.11.84				28 May
13.31	1.9	Yasmina	Soualhia	FRA	7.3.80				17 Jun
13.31	0.3	Nadia	Williams	GBR	17.11.81				18 Jun
13.31		Anisha	Vijayvan	IND	2.5.80				24 Nov
13.30	1.3	Miladys	Velázquez	CUB-J	25.5.87				17 Mar
13.30	0.0	Julia	Dubina (174)	GEO	23.6.84				9 Jul

Wind assisted

Mark	Wind		Name	Nat	Born	Pos	Meet	Venue	Date
14.83	3.5		Rahouli			1		Alger	23 Jun
14.44	4.2	Mabel	Gay	CUB	5.5.83	2		Zaragoza	23 Jun
14.34A	7.7	Suzette	Lee	JAM	6.3.75	1		El Paso	16 Apr
14.05	2.2	Irina	Vasilyeva	RUS	9.4.79	1	Kuts	Moskva	16 Jul
14.02	5.3	Silvia	Biondini	ITA	24.1.76	1		Bilbao	18 Jun
14.01	2.2	Silvia	Otto	GER	21.1.79	6	ECp-S	Firenze	18 Jun
13.90	3.8	Brittany	Daniels	USA-J	22.9.87	1		Sacramento	27 May
13.88	2.3	Amy	Zongo	FRA	4.10.80	1	NC	Angers	14 Jul
13.84A	2.2	Chaytan	Hill	USA	13.10.82	1		El Paso	2 Apr
13.84	3.1	Camilla	Johansson	SWE	3.11.76	2	ECp-1A	Gävle	18 Jun
13.82	2.6	Irina	Beskrovnaja	SVK	28.12.82	1		Bratislava	18 Jun
13.72	w?	Lúzia Maria	Teodoro	BRA	25.7.78	1		Botucatu	16 Oct
13.58	2.9	Laurice	Félix	BRA	28.5.81				2 Mar
13.57	2.4	Simidele	Adeagbo	USA	29.7.81				19 Mar
13.53	4.4	Susana	Costa	POR	22.9.84				2 Jul
13.51	2.5	Nina	Simunic	SLO	5.6.84				4 Jun
13.51	3.0	Rebecca	White	GBR	5.6.80				3 Sep
13.49	4.7	Michelle	Vaughn	GUY	23.1.83				18 May
13.48	2.5	Sirkka-Liisa	Kivine	EST	22.6.77				23 Jul
13.44	3.1	Courtney	Stafford	USA					17 Apr
13.42	2.7	Zita	vári	HUN	1.5.84				26 Jun
13.39	6.4	Emma	Green	SWE	8.12.84				8 Sep
13.38	2.5		Yu Shaohua	CHN	4.1.85				9 Apr
13.38	2.2	Tánia	da Silva	BRA-J	17.12.86				31 Jul
13.30	2.6	Henny	Gastel	GER	1.7.79				29 May
13.30	2.5	Verónica	Davis	VEN-J	22.5.87				31 Jul

Best outdoor marks

Mark	Wind	Name	Pos	Meet	Venue	Date
14.38	1.5	Gurova	Q	WCh	Helsinki	6 Aug
14.29	1.3	Oleynikova	2		Huelva	7 Jun
14.29	1.5	Safronova	3		Zaragoza	23 Jun
14.23	0.3	Gavrila	2	FBK	Hengelo	29 May
14.21	-0.2	Ivanova	2	NC	Tula	13 Jul
14.15	1.4	Dimitráki	3	Veniz	Haniá	6 Jun
14.12	0.4	Pérra	2	NC	Athína	10 Jun
14.06	0.9	Solomon	5	ECp-S	Firenze	18 Jun
13.86	0.4	Kaspárková	6	Bisl	Oslo	29 Jul
13.75	0.2	Lima de Oliveira	2	NC	São Paulo	19 Jun
		13 86w 3.7	1		São Paulo	13 Jul
13.72	1.0	Stucan	2	NC	Bucuresti	2 Jul
13.71	0.7	Márkou	6	GP II	Thessaloníki	17 Jul
13.67	0.5	Demut	1		Wesel	16 May
13.55	0.9	Hurd				26 Jun
13.40	0.4	Tosoni				26 Jun
13.34	0.5	Dobrobobova				8 May
13.30		Lifintseva				15 Jun

Best at low altitude

Mark	Wind	Name	Pos	Meet	Venue	Date
13.75	0.2	L de Oliveira	2	NC	São Paulo	19 Jun
		13.86w 3.7	1		São Paulo	13 Jul
13.60	0.0	Triviño				30 Jul
13.36	0.0	Reyes				30 Jul

JUNIORS

See main list for top 12 juniors. 12 performances (inc. 1 indoors) by 4 women to 13.85. Additional marks and further juniors:

Name	Mark	Wind	Pos	Meet	Venue	Date
Xie Limei	14.26	1.4	2		Zhongshan	23 Apr
	14.09	0.7	1		New York (RI)	11 Jun
Dyachenko	14.04	0.7	1	EJ	Kaunas	27 Jul
McLain	13.90i		1		Seattle	26 Feb
	14.05	0.0	2	NC	Changsha	26 Jun
	14.23w	2.5	1		Yixing	22 May
	14.03	1.4	1	NCp	Yalta	27 May
	13.85	2.0	1		Azusa	16 Jul

Mark	Wind		Name	Nat	Born	Pos	Meet	Venue	Date
13.54	1.7	Yanelis	Veranes	CUB	20.7.87	1	PAm-J	Windsor	31 Jul
13.50	-0.2	Rakhima	Sardi	KGZ	11.4.86	4		Tula	26 Jun
13.50	0.5	Yekaterina	Kayukova	RUS	9.10.86	1	NC-j	Tula	4 Jul
13.48	1.8	Elina	Sorsa	FIN	22.7.86	Q	EJ	Kaunas	21 Jul
13.47	-0.1	Liliya	Kulik	UKR	27.1.87	5		Tula	26 Jun
13.43i		Olga	Timofeyeva	RUS-Y	8.11,88	1		Sankt-Peterburg	16 Jan
13.39	0.3		Hu Qian	CHN-Y	14.1.89	1	NC-y	Huainan	13 May
13.37	0.9		Luo Wen (20)	CHN-Y	2.10.88	11		Zhongshan	23 Apr
13.38w	2.2	Tánia	da Silva	BRA	17.12.86	2	PAm-J	Windsor	31 Jul

SHOT

Mark		Name	Nat	Born	Pos	Meet	Venue	Date
21.09	Nadezhda	Ostapchuk	BLR	12.10.80	1		Staiki	21 Jul

					19.42	20.36	21.09	p	p	p
20.93	1	NC	Brest	3 Jul	20.93	x	x	p	20.01	x
20.60	1	Klim	Staiki	25 Jun						
20.51	1	WCh	Helsinki	13 Aug	20.30	20.13	x	x	20.23	20.51
20.44	1	WAF	Monaco	9 Sep	19.55	x	x	20.44		
20.12	1		Yokohama	19 Sep	20.12	p	p	p	p	p
20.09	1		Ulm	12 Jun	19.73	19.95	20.09	x	x	19.44
19.76	1		Shanghai	17 Sep	19.13	19.32	x 19.76	x	x	
19.65	Q	WCh	Helsinki	12 Aug	19.65	only throw				

WOMEN 2005

Mark Name Nat Born Pos Meet Venue Date

19.57 1 ECCp Lagos 29 May x 18.22 19.57 x
19.37i 1 EI Madrid 5 Mar x 17.99 18.99 18.97 19.37 x
20.24 Svetlana Krivelyova RUS 13.6.69 1 Tula 24 Jul
19.20 19.60 19.39 19.79 19.82 20.24
20.06 Nadine Kleinert GER 20.10.75 1 Hannover 10 Jul
19.86 20.00 20.06
19.39 1 Gotha 10 Jun 19.39 x x x 18.99 18.67
19.37 2 Ulm 12 Jun 18.73 x 19.37 x 19.18 19.15
19.87 Valerie Vili NZL 6.10.84 Q WCh Helsinki 12 Aug
19.87 only throw
19.62 3 WCh Helsinki 13 Aug x 18.23 19.62 19.33 x 19.62
19.55 2 WAF Monaco 9 Sep 19.24 19.55 19.31 x
19.52 1 GP II Rio de Janeiro 15 May 18.22 19.52 18.80 18.79 18.47,
19.47 2 Shanghai 17 Sep 18.89 19.47 19.18 19.41 x 19.37
19.46 1 Vigo 12 Jul 19.44 19.46 19.25 19.46 x 18.98
19.44 1 Auckland (NS) 17 Dec 19.44 18.85 x x x x
19.41 1 GP Belém 22 May 18.85 19.41 18.59 19.15 18.53 18.11
19.38 1 Hamilton 14 Dec 19.05 18.95 x x 19.38 19.02
19.32 1 NC Wanganui 12 Mar 19.21 19.32 19.12 19.23 19.09 18.95
19.81 Petra Lammert GER 3.3.84 1 Schapbach 25 Jun
19.81 x 18.76 18.97 x 18.31
19.78 Natalya Khoroneko BLR 25.5.82 2 NC Brest 3 Jul
18.81 x 19.14 18.82 19.18 19.78
19.65 Olga Ryabinkina RUS 24.9.76 1 ECp-S Firenze 19 Jun
18.69 x 19.65 x
19.64 2 WCh Helsinki 13 Aug x 19.34 19.64 x 19.06 18.76
19.60 1 NC Tula 10 Jul 19.05 19.60 x x 18.86 p
(30/7)
19.16 Astrid Kumbernuss GER 5.2.70 2 Hannover 10 Jul
19.06 Yumileidi Cumbá CUB 11.2.75 2 GP Belém 22 May
19.05 Li Meiju CHN 23.1.81 1 NC Changsha 24 Jun
(10)
18.96i Krystyna Zabawska POL 14.1.68 2 EI Madrid 5 Mar
18.92 Misleydis González CUB 19.6.78 1 GP II Zagreb 11 Jul
18.84 Christina Schwanitz GER 24.12.85 1 Rechberghausen 1 May
18.80 Assunta Legnante ITA 14.5.78 1 v2N Viareggio 27 Jul
18.71 Chiara Rosa ITA 28.1.83 1 NC Bressanone 25 Jun
18.69i Oksana Chibisova RUS 31.3.77 1 Shakhty 19 Jan
18.68 Kristin Heaston USA 23.11.75 1 NC Carson 24 Jun
18.68 Li Ling CHN 7.2.85 2 NG Nanjing 17 Oct
18.59 Cristiana Checchi ITA 8.7.77 1 MedG Almeria 30 Jun
18.59 Lieja Tunks NED 10.3.76 1 Cooman Stadskanaal 3 Jul
(20)
18.58 Liz Wanless USA 18.11.81 1 Clermont 21 May
18.58 Qian Chunhua CHN 11.2.79 3 NG Nanjing 17 Oct
18.57 Zhang Guirong SIN 5.2.78 2 AsiC Inchon 1 Sep
18.56 Olga Ivanova RUS 6.4.79 2 Tula 24 Jul
18.44 Cleopatra Borel-Brown TRI 3.10.79 1 Knoxville 16 Apr
18.33 Vivian Chukwuemeka NGR 4.5.77 1 Azusa 9 Apr
18.29 Adriane Blewitt USA 24.5.80 1 Tempe 26 Mar
18.28 Zhang Chunjing CHN 19.5.83 4 NG Nanjing 17 Oct
18.26 Michelle Carter USA 12.10.85 2 NC Carson 24 Jun
18.22i Nadine Beckel GER 27.5.77 3 NC Sindelfingen 19 Feb
(30)
18.20 Kimberly Barrett JAM 18.11.81 1 NCAA Sacramento 11 Jun
18.19 Li Fengfeng CHN 9.1.79 1 Yixing 22 May
18.05i Denise Hinrichs GER-J 7.6.87 1J Magdeburg 17 Dec
18.02 Elena Hila ROM 20.5.74 1 Onesti 21 May
18.01 Tatyana Ilyushchenko BLR 18.4.83 2 Klim Staiki 25 Jun
17.94 Jill Camarena USA 2.8.82 1 Tucson 21 May
17.91 Yuliya Leontyuk BLR 31.1.84 4 NC-23 Erfurt 16 Jul
17.87i Wang Lihong CHN 9.1.83 2 Shanghai 21 Feb
17.85 Wang Yawen CHN 23.8.73 5 NG Nanjing 17 Oct
17.80 Tatyana Nasonova UKR 15.12.76 1 Kiev 18 May
(40)
17.78 Vera Yepimashko BLR 10.7.76 2 Brest 30 Apr
17.69 Becky Breisch USA 16.3.83 5 NC Carson 24 Jun
17.68 Kristin Marten GER 23.5.83 3 Mersin 12 Mar
17.67 Laurence Manfrédi FRA 20.5.74 1 Amiens 22 Jun
17.65i Candice Scott TRI 17.9.80 3 NCAA Fayetteville 11 Mar
17.65 Martina de la Puente ESP 4.4.75 1 Oviedo 8 May

Mark	Name		Nat	Born	Pos	Meet	Venue	Date
17.63	Jessica	Cosby	USA	31.5.82	1		Los Angeles	30 Apr
17.62		Lee Mi-young	KOR	19.8.79	1		Kwangju	19 Apr
17.61		Yang Cui	CHN	15.8.84	6	NG	Nanjing	17 Oct
17.57		Cheng Xiaoyan	CHN	30.11.75	1		Chengdu	10 Apr
	(50)							
17.57		Jiang Ping	CHN	10.1.79	7	NG	Nanjing	17 Oct
17.55	Elisângela	Adriano	BRA	27.7.72	1		São Caetano do Sul	26 Feb
17.52	Amarachi	Ukabam	USA	14.3.84	1	NCAA-r	Bloomington	28 May
17.49		Li Li	CHN-J	24.2.87	1		Zhaoqing	10 Apr
17.39	Anna	Avdeyeva	RUS	6.4.85	1	NC-23	Tula	15 Jun
17.37		Du Xianhui	SIN	4.1.81	2	SEAG	Manila	28 Nov
17.33		Liu Yingfan	CHN-J	9.2.87	6		Zhongshan	23 Apr
17.31	Mailín	Vargas	CUB	24.3.83	1		La Habana	12 May
17.14i	Loree	Smith	USA	6.11.82	1		Air Force Academy	26 Feb
17.14	Marli	Knoetze	RSA-J	2.10.87	1		Naboomspruit	14 Oct
	(60)							
17.13	Simoné	du Toit	RSA-Y	27.9.88	2		Naboomspruit	14 Oct
17.10	Melinda	Lincoln	USA	20.1.77	2		Azusa	16 Jul
17.09	Filiz	Kadogan	TUR	12.2.82	1	NC	Ankara	14 May
17.08i		Zhang Qiang	CHN-J	14.2.87	5		Tianjin	2 Mar
17.07	Magnolia	Iglesias	ESP	26.5.79	1		Avilés	9 Apr
17.07	Yoko	Toyonaga	JPN	15.4.77	4	AsiC	Inchon	1 Sep
17.05	Jessica	Pressley	USA	27.12.84	1	NCAA-r	Eugene	28 May
17.05		Lee Myung-sun	KOR	12.2.76	1	NG	Ulsan	14 Oct
17.04i	Anna	Omarova	RUS	3.10.81	4		Moskva	22 Jan
17.03	Austra	Skujyté	LTU	12.8.79	1	NC	Kaunas	8 Jul
	(70)							
17.01	Aubrey	Martin	USA	16.1.84	2	NCAA-r	Bloomington	28 May
16.97	Anca	Heltne	ROM	1.1.78	2	NC	Bucuresti	3 Jul
16.93i	Radoslava	Mavrodieva	BUL-J	13.3.87	1		Sofia	29 Jan
16.92	Ana	Po'uhila	TGA	12.10.79	1		Koror	27 Jul
16.91	Chandra	Brewer	USA	26.7.81	Q	NCAA	Sacramento	9 Jun
16.90	Sarah	Stevens	USA-J	2.4.86	1	NC-j	Carson	24 Jun
16.89		Lu Ying	CHN	30.10.85	10	NC	Changsha	24 Jun
16.89	Oksana	Gaus	RUS	9.7.81	4	NC	Tula	10 Jul
16.87	Jessica	Cérival	FRA	20.1.82	2		Bron	5 Jul
16.84	Magdalena	Sobieszek	POL-J	4.5.86	1		Barcelona	3 Jun
	(80)							
16.83i	Janae	Strickland	USA	19.8.82	1		Ames	12 Feb
16.83	Svetlana	Sakun	UKR	1.3.81	1		Donetsk	6 May
16.81	Jana	Kárníková	CZE	14.2.81	1		Bangor	24 Jun
16.80	Amanda	Walker	USA	12.9.82	1	IC4A	Princeton	15 May
16.79i	Irina	Tarasova	RUS-J	15.4.87	5		Moskva	22 Jan
16.78	Aymara	Albury	BAH	25.7.85	2		Oxford, MS	9 Apr
16.75	Laura	Bordignon	ITA	26.3.81	3	ECCp	Lagos, POR	29 May
16.75	Iolanta	Ulyeva	KAZ	27.7.76	3	Asi GP	Sidoarjo	18 Jun
16.72i	Aleksandra	Kopaneva	RU	5.12.80	2		Shakhty	19 Jan
16.71		Jiang Limin	CHN-Y	20.2.88	1		Zhengzhou	31 Aug
	(90)							
16.70	Agnieszka	Bronisz	POL-J	16.3.86	3		Biala Podlaska	28 May
16.69	Breann	Smith	USA	29.1.83	1		Akron	7 May
16.67	Kacey	Onwuchekwa	USA	22.11.85	4	NCAA	Sacramento	11 Jun
16.62i	Julia	Wiechmann	GER	28.3.84	7	NC	Sindelfingen	19 Feb
16.60	Kamaiya	Warren	USA	10.3.84	2		La Jolla	23 Apr
16.60	Andréa Maria	Pereira	BRA	8.12.73	1	SACh	Cali	23 Jul
16.58	Kathleen	Kluge	GER	17.11.81	1		Wiesbaden	28 May
16.56	Zara	Northover	JAM	6.3.84	1		Tampa	2 Apr
16.56	Julia	Pedersen	USA	12.4.83	3	Pac10	Los Angeles (Ww)	14 May
16.55	Megan	Howard	USA-J	9.4.86	Q	NCAA	Sacramento	10 Jun
	(100)							

Mark	Name		Nat	Born	Date
16.54	Sivan	Jean	ISR	25.6.85	14 May
16.54	Joanne	Duncan	GBR	27.12.66	22 May
16.54	Luz Dary	Castro	COL	30.5.78	2 Jul
16.52	Beth	Mallory	USA	31.5.84	15 May
16.52	Mara	Rosolen	ITA	27.7.65	25 Jun
16.52i	Jennifer	Gilson	USA	29.10.82	10 Dec
16.47	Anja	Burkhardt	GER	13.10.81	8 May
16.45	Fotíni	Kiriakídou	GRE	6.1.71	7 May
16.44	Bree	Fuqua	USA	19.3.82	9 Apr
16.43	Dana	Lawson	USA	13.7.79	18 May
16.43i	Svetlana	Ladokhina	RUS	21.2.79	24 Dec
16.40i	Helena	Engman	SWE	16.6.76	12 Feb
16.40i		Li Bo	CHN-Y	4.9.88	21 Feb
16.38	Oksana	Zakharchuk	UKR	3.4.80	12 Mar
16.37	Aline	Schäffel	GER	15.5.80	25 Jun
16.32i	Kenitra	Woods	USA	18.5.80	22 Jan
16.29		Ma Qiao	CHN-Y	28.9.89	13 May
16.22i	Veerle	Blondeel	BEL	14.1.75	19 Feb
16.21	Halee	Prickett	USA	14.11.82	14 May
16.18i	Christina	Ochs	GER-J	14.3.86	23 Jan
16.18	Yaniuvis	López	CUB-J	1.2.86	29 Apr
16.18	Melissa	Boekelman	NED-Y	11.5.89	20 Jun
16.18	Mariam	Kevkhishvili	GEO	17.9.85	9 Jul
16.17i	Jutaporn	Krasaeyan	THA	13.2.72	1 Mar

Mark	Name		Nat	Born	Date	Mark	Name		Nat	Born	Date
16.17	Melissa	Faubus	USA-J	17.3.86	23 Apr	16.02i	Irache	Quintanal	ESP	18.9.78	18 Feb
16.14	Julie	Dunkley	GBR	11.9.79	10 Jul	16.02	Jennifer	Leatherman	USA	26.9.83	7 May
16.13	Linda-Marie	Mårtensson	SWE	22.6.71	18 Jul	16.01	Kelli	Burton	USA	5.7.84	21 May
16.11	Stiliani	Papadopoúlou	GRE	15.3.82	11 Jun	15.99i	Ilona	Rutjes	NED	28.5.80	5 Mar
16.09i	Leann	Boerema	USA	25.8.80	29 Jan	15.97	Melissa	Yunghans	USA-J	21.8.86	1 May
16.09i	Katja	Kròl	GER	5.2.80	19 Feb	15.96	Adrienne	Moss	USA	15.11.81	10 Jun
16.09	Amanda	Barnes	USA	15.9.83	23 Apr	15.93	Seilala	Sua	USA	25.2.78	5 Mar
16.07	Liz	Podominick	USA	5.12.84	10 Jun	15.90i	Ursula	Ruíz	ESP	11.8.83	12 Feb
16.06	Zhanna	Samolyuk	UKR-Y	13.1.88	23 Apr	15.90	April	Burton	USA	4.4.81	7 May
16.06	Kerri	McClung	USA	5.2.83	7 May	15.87	Jacqueline	Wells	USA		10 May
16.04i	Cassandra	Lee	USA		22 Jan	15.86		Liu Mingxing	CHN-J	22.2.87	31 Aug
16.03	Stephanie	Horton	USA-J	11.8.87	27 Apr	15.85i	Jennifer	Kowacz	USA	8.3.83	5 Feb
16.03	Marie-Patrice	Calabre	FRA	19.1.83	5 Jun	15.85	Catarina	Andersson (150)	SWE	17.11.77	28 Aug

Best outdoor marks

Mark	Name	Pos	Meet	Venue	Date	Mark	Name	Pos	Meet	Venue	Date
18.79	Zabawska	1		Biala Podlaska	28 May	17.23	Wang Lihong	7	NC	Changsha	24 Jun
18.62	Chibisova	2	NC	Tula	10 Jul	16.95	C Scott	2		Tempe	16 Apr
17.95	Beckel	3		Gotha	10 Jun	16.70	L Smith	1		Fort Collins	14 May
17.55	Hinrichs	1	EJ	Kaunas	21 Jul	16.70	Omarova	3		Tula	24 Jul

16.53 Zhang Qiang 22 May | 16.44 Strickland 16 Apr | 16.19 Wiechmann 4 Jun | 15.97 Engman 20 Aug
16.53 Tarasova 21 Jul | 16.40 Mavrodieva 29 May | 15.98 Krasaeyan 10 Apr | 15.92 Li Bo 16 Jul
15.88 Blondeel 28 May

JUNIORS

See main list for top 13 juniors. 11 perfs (inc. 1 indoor) by 5 women to 17.13. Additional marks and further juniors:

	Mark	Pos	Meet	Venue	Date	Mark	Pos	Meet	Venue	Date
Hinrichs 2+	17.42	4	NC	Wattenscheid	2 Jul	17.31	1	NC-j	Braunschweig	30 Jul
	17.35	3	NC-23	Rostock	21 Aug	17.19	1		Mannheim	18 Jun
Li Li	17.32	6	NC	Changsha	24 Jun					

Mark	Name		Nat	Born	Pos	Meet	Venue	Date
16.40i		Li Bo	CHN-Y	4.9.88	11		Shanghai	21 Feb
	15.92				2	WY	Marrakech	16 Jul
16.29		Ma Qiao	CHN-Y	28.9.89	1	NC-y	Huainan	13 May
16.18i	Christina	Ochs	GER	14.3.86	1		Bad Segeberg	23 Jan
16.18	Yaniuvis	López	CUB	1.2.86	1		La Habana	29 Apr
16.18	Melissa	Boekelman	NED-Y	11.5.89	2		Arnhem	20 Jun
16.17	Melissa	Faubus	USA	17.3.86	1		Stanford	23 Apr
16.06	Zhanna	Samolyuk	UKR-Y	13.1.88	1		Odessa	23 Apr

Best outdoors

16.53 Zhang Qiang 10 Yixing 22 May | 16.53 Tarasova 2 EJ Kaunas 21 Jul
16.40 Mavrodieva 1 NC-23 Sofia 29 May

DISCUS

66.81 Vera Cechlová-Pospisilová CZE 19.11.78 1 Odlozil Praha 27 Jun
57.36 64.34 66.81 64.58 x x
65.98 1 GS Ostrava 9 Jun x 64.71 65.97 x 62.22 65.98
65.35 1 NC Kladno 3 Jul 60.56 63.00 62.57 62.43 60.74 65.35
64.69 2 GP II Torino 3 Jun 63.98 64.69 62.66 63.88 61.89 64.11
66.56 Franka Dietzsch GER 22.1.68 1 WCh Helsinki 11 Aug
64.89 64.08 64.36 66.56 65.29 p
66.29 1 Halle 21 May 66.29 x x 65.01 61.52 x
65.81 1 Schönebeck 29 Jul x 65.81 57.65 63.64 x x
64.92 1 SGP Athína 14 Jun x 64.92 64.42 x 63.37 x
64.50 1 Wiesbaden 28 May 64.50 62.68 x 63.55 63.98 62.85
64.38 2 GP Doha 13 May
64.38 1 ECp-S Firenze 17 Jun 64.38 63.84 64.00 64.13
66.29 Natalya Sadova RUS 15.6.72 1 Dessau 27 May
x 64.21 61.46 64.25 65.39 66.29
65.84 1 Kuso Warszawa 12 Jun x 65.84 64.84 65.43 64.50 63.18
65.66 2 GS Ostrava 9 Jun 61.34 63.23 64.86 64.32 65.66 64.53
65.63 1 NC Tula 11 Jul 60.91 65.63 63.70 64.20 64.70 x
65.10 1 GP Doha 13 May
64.54 1 Salon-de-Provence 29 May 63.58 64.54 x x x x
64.33 2 WCh Helsinki 11 Aug 64.33 60.63 61.28 62.31 62.68 61.59
65.89 Yelena Antonova UKR 16.6.72 1 Kiev 5 Jun
65.89 64.55 x 63.40 61.45 65.89
64.50 1 Kiev 19 May 59.14 64.50 62.20 61.91 63.65 64.10
65.23 Song Aimin CHN 15.3.78 1 Asi GP Sidoarjo 18 Jun
61.19 63.97 62.28 64.49 57.97 65.23
65.15 1 AsiC Inchon 2 Sep 62.14 x 62.31 61.95 65.15 64.51
65.09 Beatrice Faumuina NZL 23.10.74 1 Hamilton 9 Feb
65.09 x 63.30 62.11 61.83 59.68
64.89 Nicoleta Grasu ROM 11.9.71 1 GP II Torino 3 Jun
63.74 61.00 59.24 58.57 x 64.89
64.89 Li Qiumei CHN 26.9.74 1 NG Nanjing 18 Oct
62.25 x x 59.94 63.73 64.89

Mark	Name		Nat	Born	Pos	Meet	Venue	Date
64.57	Marzena	Wysocka	POL	17.2.69	2	Kuso	Warszawa	12 Jun
				64.57	x	63.85	61.52 x	x
64.56	Aretha	Hill-Thurmond (10)	USA	14.8.76	1		Lapua	30 Jul
64.53		Huang Qun	CHN	12.4.79	2	NG	Nanjing	18 Oct
				62.64	62.35	60.65	x 64.53	64.49
64.52	Yania	Ferrales	CUB	28.7.77	2	Odlozil	Praha	27 Jun
				x	64.52	60.69	x x	x
64.40	1	La Habana	19 Feb	56.60	64.40	64.00	57.10 x	x
	(30/12)							
63.67	Wioletta	Potepa	POL	13.12.80	3	Kuso	Warszawa	12 Jun
63.53	Becky	Breisch	USA	16.3.83	1		Lincoln, NE	7 May
63.42	Natalya	Ampleyeva	RUS	25.9.72	1	Kuts	Moskva	15 Jul
63.17A	Elizna	Naude	RSA	14.9.78	1		Bloemfontein	4 Mar
62.89	Harwant	Kaur	IND	5.7.80	1	Asi GP	Singapore	21 Jun
62.80	Natalya	Fokina	UKR	7.7.82	1		Donetsk	7 May
62.50		Ma Shuli	CHN	20.1.78	1		Zhongshan	23 Apr
62.50	Joanna	Wisniewska	POL	24.5.72	1		Gdansk	1 Jul
	(20)							
62.43	Dragana	Tomasevic	SCG	4.6.82	1	BalkC	Novi Sad	23 Jul
62.38	Ellina	Zvereva	BLR	16.11.60	1		Brest	1 Jun
62.35	Suzy	Powell-Roos	USA	3.9.76	1		La Jolla	23 Apr
62.18	Oksana	Yesipchuk	RUS	13.12.76	1		Tula	24 Jul
61.87		Ma Xuejun	CHN	26.3.85	4	NG	Nanjing	18 Oct
61.82	Seilala	Sua	USA	25.2.78	2	NC	Carson	23 Jun
61.78	Olga	Chernyavskaya	RUS	17.9.63	1		Salamanca	13 Jun
61.61		Li Yanfeng	CHN	15.5.79	4eA		Halle	21 May
61.56		Xu Shaoyang	CHN	9.2.83	5	NG	Nanjing	18 Oct
61.26	Anna	Söderberg	SWE	11.6.73	6	Odlozil	Praha	27 Jun
	(30)							
61.08		Sun Tanfeng	CHN	26.8.82	2		Chongqing	14 May
61.06	Oksana	Tuchak	RUS	27.3.73	1		Adler	6 Feb
60.75	Sabine	Rumpf	GER	18.3.83	1	EU23	Erfurt	17 Jul
60.65	Neelam J	Singh ¶	IND	8.1.71	1		Patiala	21 May
60.63	Ulrike	Giesa	GER	16.8.84	1		Halle	22 May
60.62	Darya	Pishchalnikova	RUS	19.7.85	1		Krasnodar	4 Jun
60.61	Yarelis	Barrios	CUB	12.7.83	2	Barr	La Habana	19 May
60.31	Jana	Tucholke	GER	20.5.81	3		Wiesbaden	28 May
60.30	Kristin	Kuehl	USA	30.7.70	2	DrakeR	Des Moines	29 Apr
60.25	Irina	Yatchenko	BLR	31.10.65	1	Klim	Staiki	25 Jun
	(40)							
60.17	Lyudmila	Kupriyanova (Starovoytova)	BLR	8.4.74	2	Klim	Staiki	25 Jun
59.95	Olga	Chernogorova	BLR	30.1.82	2	NC	Brest	3 Jul
59.85		Wang Yu	CHN	22.9.85	7	NG	Nanjing	18 Oct
59.71	Ileana	Brîndusoiu	ROM	9.5.79	1	GP II	Thessaloníki	17 Jul
59.35	Nadine	Müller	GER	21.11.85	2eB		Halle	21 May
59.35	Beth	Mallory	USA	31.5.84	1	NCAA	Sacramento	10 Jun
59.08		Xiao Yanling	CHN	27.3.68	8	NG	Nanjing	18 Oct
58.90		Tao Hongbo	CHN	20.9.79	9	NG	Nanjing	18 Oct
58.88		Liu Linpeng	CHN-J	22.2.87	4	WUG	Izmir	18 Aug
58.65	Yekaterina	Korsak	UKR	26.12.85	2		Kiev	5 Jun
	(50)							
58.52		Pan Seili	CHN-Y	4.12.88	1		Zhaoqing	9 Apr
58.52	Daniele	Samuels	AUS-Y	26.5.88	1		Brisbane	26 Nov
58.47	Cecilia	Barnes	USA	24.7.80	1		Chico	7 May
58.42	Vera	Begic	CRO	17.3.82	1		Rijeka	7 Jun
58.33	Krishna	Poonia	IND	5.5.77	2		Patiala	21 May
58.23	Aretí	Abatzí	GRE	14.5.74	1		Trípoli	28 May
58.23	Grete	Snyder (Etholm)	NOR	25.1.76	2	NC	Helsingborg	23 Jul
58.07	Philippa	Roles	GBR	1.3.78	3	BIG	Bedford	12 Jun
58.01	Melina	Robert-Michon	FRA	18.7.79	1		Les Abymes	15 Jan
58.00		Cao Liping	CHN	8.11.78	7		Zhongshan	23 Apr
	(60)							
57.98	Laura	Bordignon	ITA	26.3.81	2	MedG	Almeria	2 Jul
57.83	Ilona	Rutjes	NED	28.5.80	1		Tempe	30 Apr
57.81	Olga	Olshevskaya	RUS	5.7.82	3		Adler	6 Feb
57.62	Svetlana	Ivanova	RUS	10.7.85	5	NC	Tula	11 Jul
57.57	Veerle	Blondeel	BEL	14.1.75	1		Eeklo	1 Jul
57.47	Summer	Pierson	USA	3.9.78	1		La Jolla	19 Mar
57.46	Melinda	Lincoln	USA	20.1.77	1		Claremont	14 May
57.43	Rhonda	Gullatte	USA	10.2.84	1		Marietta	12 Jun
57.30	Laura	Saye	USA	27.11.81	3		La Jolla	23 Apr

Mark	Name		Nat	Born	Pos	Meet	Venue	Date
57.30	Romy	Logsch	GER	5.2.82	4	NC	Wattenscheid	3 Jul
	(70)							
57.29	Elisângela	Adriano	BRA	27.7.72	1		São Paulo	2 Apr
57.27	Monique	Nacsa	AUS	26.10.76	1		Brisbane	29 Jan
57.27	Kara	Nwidobie/Sharpe	GBR	13.4.81	1		Manchester (SC)	18 Jun
57.04		Lin Xiaojing	CHN-J	8.1.86	7		Yixing	21 May
57.03	Rachelle	Longfors	USA	6.6.83	2	NCAA	Sacramento	10 Jun
57.01		Tan Jian	CHN-Y	22.1.88	1		Sydney	21 Jan
56.96	Seema	Antil	IND	27.7.83	4	Asi GP	Singapore	21 Jun
56.95	Viktoriya	Boyko	UKR	20.1.74	3	NC	Kiev	2 Jul
56.90	Monia	Kari	TUN	14.4.71	1		Radès	12 Jun
56.84	Stiliani	Tsikoúna	GRE	19.10.72	1		Athína (E)	7 May
	(80)							
56.71	Dace	Ruskule	LAT	20.9.81	1	NCAA-r	Norman	28 May
56.70	Laura	Gerraughty	USA	29.7.83	1		Los Angeles	14 Apr
56.66	Izabela	Koralewska	POL	29.1.85	4	NC	Biala Podlaska	26 Jun
56.59		Tang Jinling	CHN		1		Qingdao	21 Jul
56.59	Alice	Matejková	ESP	11.1.69	1	NC	Málaga	23 Jul
56.39	Nadine	Beckel	GER	27.5.77	9eA		Halle	21 May
56.34	Vasilisa	Zelenska	UKR	31.8.85	3		Kiev	5 Jun
56.26	Olga	Ryabinkina	RUS	24.9.76	1		Bryansk	4 Jun
56.23	Olesya	Korotkova	RUS	20.11.83	4		Tula	24 Jul
56.23	Yuka	Murofushi	JPN	11.2.77	4	AsiC	Inchon	2 Sep
	(90)							
56.18	Amarachi	Ukabam	USA	14.3.84	2	NCAA-r	Bloomington	28 May
56.16	Jessica	Kolotzei	GER	6.4.85	3		Rostock	21 Aug
56.15	Zaneta	Glanc	POL	11.3.83	1		Poznan	4 Jun
56.13		Cao Qi	CHN	15.1.74	12	NG	Nanjing	18 Oct
56.12	Cristiana	Checchi	ITA	8.7.77	1		Savona	15 Jun
56.11	Veronka	Watzek	AUT	13.8.85	1		Wien	16 May
56.10		Lin Qingping	CHN-J	3.5.86	8		Yixing	21 May
56.08	Olga	Goncharenko	BLR	13.7.81	3		Bielsko-Biala	9 Jul
55.95	Elin	Isane	NOR	18.4.75	1		Spikkestad	16 Sep
55.93	Yelena	Machkanova	RUS	24.1.81	2		Moskva	4 Jun
	(100)							
55.93	Claire	Smithson	GBR	3.8.83	1		Hoo	20 Aug

Mark	Name		Nat	Born	Date
55.86	Kamaiya	Warren	USA	10.3.84	15 May
55.82	Anaelys	Fernández	CUB	15.12.79	23 Jun
55.82A	Ahu	Sulak	TUR	27.8.81	31 Jul
55.75	Rachel	Varner	USA	20.7.83	23 Apr
55.58	Julia	Pedersen	USA	12.4.83	30 Apr
55.58	Lieja	Tunks	NED	10.3.76	10 Jul
55.54	Lisandra	Rodríguez	CUB-J	14.10.86	19 May
55.51	Vladimíra	Racková	CZE	15.5.67	9 Jul
55.50		Wang Jinxiang	CHN	14.8.84	18 Oct
55.47		Wang Bin	CHN-J	7.1.87	23 Apr
55.35	Stephanie	Brown	USA	1.12.79	29 May
55.30		Cheng Xianhong	CHN	24.10.68	21 May
55.26	Dayana	Octavien	USA	10.6.82	16 Apr
55.25	Zinaida	Sendriute	LTU	20.12.84	3 May
55.23	Teresa	Machado	POR	22.7.69	27 Feb
55.17	Tomoko	Yamaguchi	JPN	14.2.72	2 Oct
55.16	Saroj	Kumari Sihag	IND	13.6.80	8 Nov
55.09	Katja	Kròl	GER	5.2.80	5 Feb
55.09	Heike	Koderisch	GER	27.5.85	22 May
55.07	Jessica	Pressley	USA	27.12.84	2 Apr
55.00	Olga	Ivanova	RUS	6.4.79	4 Jun
54.99		Luo Xiaorong	CHN	4.11.83	23 Apr
54.83	Eha	Rünne	EST	25.5.63	18 Jun
54.78	Melissa	Bickett	USA	16.4.82	20 May
54.73		Wang Ying	CHN-J		28 Aug
54.71	DeShaya	Williams	USA	8.7.80	7 May
54.70	Giorgia	Baratella	ITA	8.1.75	19 Jun
54.62	Kristal	Robinson	USA		14 May
54.58		Liu Fengying	CHN	26.1.79	9 Apr
54.50	Magdalini	Komótoglou	GRE	13.11.85	7 May
54.48	April	Burton	USA	4.4.81	7 May
54.47	Karin	Hagmann	SUI	9.3.74	10 Jul
54.46	Yarisley	Collado	CUB	30.4.85	5 May
54.46	Katalin	Máté	HUN	3.8.84	8 May
54.46	Tereapii	Tapoki	COK	19.4.84	19 Sep
54.45	Novelle	Murray	CAN	31.8.84	3 May
54.44	Katalin	Divós	HUN	11.5.74	7 Jul
54.40	Fanta	Diarra	FRA	11.3.82	4 Jun
54.32	Anna	Brel	BLR	4.6.85	1 Jun
54.16	Tsvetanka	Khristova	BUL	14.3.62	7 Jul
54.09		Azi Guli	CHN	31.10.81	9 Apr
54.09	Austrite	Mikelyte	LTU	5.5.69	30 Apr
54.03	Alifatou	Djibril	TOG	13.2.80	5 Mar
54.02	Anita	Hietalahti	FIN	17.2.77	8 Jul
53.98A	Loree	Smith	USA	6.11.82	13 May
53.98	Jocelyn	White	USA-J	26.9.86	10 Jun
53.96	Yaima	Vives	CUB	16.12.85	19 May
53.96	Eva	Kürti	HUN	21.7.76	7 Jul
53.93	Annika	Larsson	SWE	10.7.70	3 Aug
53.92	Irache	Quintanal	ESP	18.9.78	25 Jun
53.89	Sivan	Jean	ISR	25.6.85	27 Feb
53.88	Liliana	Cá	POR-J	5.11.86	20 Mar
53.82		Zhang Hongxia	CHN-J	10.1.87	21 Jul
53.76	Rita	Lora	ESP	23.3.73	26 Feb
53.74	Kalthoum	Saadaoui	TUN	17.9.80	1 Jun
53.70	Shanna	Dickenson	USA-J	19.9.86	23 Jun
53.69	Melehifo	Uhi	TGA	2.3.79	21 Sep
53.68	Hediye	Gürbüzgullan	TUR	78	12 May
53.66	Agnieszka	Jarmuzek	POL	3.2.84	26 Jun
53.61	Yuneimy	Soria	CUB-J	15.11.87	5 May
53.61	Agnieszka	Krawczak	POL	14.2.83	28 May
53.60A	Rosario	Ramos	VEN	8.12.79	19 Aug
53.55	Breann	Smith	USA	29.1.83	28 May
53.55	Veronica	Karlsson	SWE	5.10.80	28 May
53.52	Ivona	Tomanová	SVK	24.10.72	5 Jun
53.51	Precious	Akins	USA	18.5.85	7 May
53.50	Niina	Kelo	FIN	26.3.80	12 Jun
	(167)				

JUNIORS

See main list for top 6 juniors. 11 performances by 6 women to 56.10. Additional marks and further juniors:

Liu Linpeng	56.93	Q	WUG	Izmir	17 Aug
Pan Saoli	56.77	9		Zhongshan	23 Apr

Mark	Name		Nat	Born	Pos	Meet	Venue		Date
Tan Jian	56.71 10	Zhongshan	23 Apr	56.56 8			Chongqing		14 May
	56.58 7	Chengdu	9 Apr						
55.54	Lisandra	Rodríguez	CUB	14.10.86	3	Barr	La Habana		19 May
55.47		Wang Bin	CHN	7.1.87	14		Zhongshan		23 Apr
54.73		Wang Ying	CHN		1		Zhengzhou		28 Aug
53.98	Jocelyn	White	USA	26.9.86	5	NCAA	Sacramento		10 Jun
53.88	Liliana	Cá	POR	5.11.86	1		Quinta do Anjo		20 Mar
53.82		Zhang Hongxia	CHN	10.1.87	1		Qingdao		21 Jul
53.70	Shanna	Dickenson	USA	19.9.86	1	NC	Carson		23 Jun
53.61	Yuneimy	Soria	CUB	15.11.87	2c2		La Habana		5 May
53.29	Oksana	Kot	UZB	4.10.87	1		Tashkent		19 May
53.24		Ma Yanjie	CHN-Y	16.4.88	2		Zhengzhou		28 Aug
52.99	Christina	Gehrig	GER	21.6.87	1		Erding		8 May
52.72A	Simoné	du Toit	RSA-Y	27.9.88	1		Germiston		5 Mar
52.66	Emily	Strot (20)	USA	12.5.86	1		Stanford		1 May
52.66	Marina	Yekimova	BLR	27.5.86			Brest		28 May

HAMMER

Mark	Name		Nat	Born	Pos	Meet	Venue		Date
77.06	Tatyana	Lysenko	RUS	9.10.83	1	Kuts	Moskva		15 Jul
				74.20	74.39	76.05	75.81	x	77.06
75.95	1	Moskva	29 Jun	74.41	74.97	75.00	73.11	75.95	74.64
75.95	1 NC	Tula	13 Jul	74.17	75.04	75.95	75.17	71.91	x
72.64	1	Tula	23 Jul	x	69.34	71.10	71.76	x	72.64
72.46	3 WCh	Helsinki	12 Aug	x	70.30	68.44	68.92	72.46	71.68
76.66	Olga	Tsander	BLR	18.5.76	1		Staiki		21 Jul
				73.48	x	x	x	76.66	x
75.10	Olga	Kuzenkova	RUS	4.10.70	1	WCh	Helsinki		12 Aug
				x	68.94	70.70	70.80	74.03	75.10
73.59	2 NC	Tula	13 Jul	72.16	x	70.88	73.52	73.59	x
72.46	3 WAF	Szombathely	3 Sep	72.19	72.08	x	72.06	x	72.46
72.63	2 Znam	Kazan (irregular)	24 Jun	69.56	71.79	69.92	72.63	x	72.06
74.95	Yipsi	Moreno	CUB	19.11.80	1		Banská Bystrica		28 Aug
				69.73	72.57	74.95	74.40		
74.75	1 WAF	Szombathely	3 Sep	72.11	72.64	x	x	74.75	74.40
73.88	2 GP II	Zagreb	11 Jul	71.15	73.22	73.88	71.58	x	x
73.36	1	Dubnica nad Váhom	29 Aug	71.17	71.77	73.36	72.13		
73.08	2 WCh	Helsinki	12 Aug	70.39	x	70.88	71.26	73.08	73.04
72.67	Q WCh	Helsinki	10 Aug	72.67		only throw			
74.66	Manuèla	Montebrun	FRA	13.11.79	1	GP II	Zagreb		11 Jul
				74.17	73.12	x	74.66	74.61	72.86
73.96	1	Chelles	6 Jul	72.90	72.02	71.02	73.96	71.70	70.80
73.20	1	Padova	2 Jul	71.68	69.85	73.20	72.19	71.85	72.36
72.92	1	Castres	26 Jul	70.73	72.26	x	72.55	72.53	72.92
74.27	Kamila	Skolimowska	POL	4.11.82	1	GP II	Madrid		16 Jul
				68.91	68.63	x	67.36	x	74.27
72.75	1 WUG	Izmir	16 Aug	69.98	68.81	x	67.25	67.79	72.75
72.73	2 WAF	Szombathely	3 Sep	x	67.01	72.73	71.41	x	x
72.43	1 NC	Biala Podlaska	25 Jun	x	60.00	65.54	68.47	72.43	70.98
73.87	Erin	Gilreath	USA	11.10.80	1	NC	Carson		25 Jun
				67.73	68.42	70.97	71.76	69.42	73.87
73.59	Ester	Balassini	ITA	20.10.77	1	NC	Bressanone		25 Jun
				x	66.51	70.27	x	66.91	73.59
73.24		Zhang Wenxiu	CHN-J	22.3.86	1	NC	Changsha		24 Jun
73.08	Yekaterina	Khoroshkikh (10)	RUS	21.1.83	1	NC-23	Tula		14 Jun
				71.39	73.08	71.73	x	71.67	71.34
72.45	1	Sochi	26 May	67.14	71.67	72.45	69.89	67.49	x
72.74	Susanne	Keil	GER	18.5.78	1		Nikiti		15 Jul
				71.55	x	71.06	69.43	72.74	72.54
72.51		Liu Yinghui	CHN	29.6.79	2	WUG	Izmir		16 Aug
	(30/12)			65.35	69.85	72.19	x	72.04	72.51
72.19	Betty	Heidler	GER	14.10.83	1		Schönebeck		29 Jul
71.95	Mihaela	Melinte	ROM	27.3.75	1		Mersin		26 Feb
71.45	Candice	Scott	TRI	17.9.80	1		Marietta		15 May
71.08	Darya	Pchelnik	BLR	20.12.81	2		Staiki		21 Jul
71.00	Ivana	Brkljacic	CRO	25.1.83	1A	EThCp	Mersin		13 Mar
70.91	Kathrin	Klaas	GER	8.2.84	2		Mannheim		18 Jun
70.76	Gulfiya	Khanafayeva	RUS	12.6.82	2		Tula		23 Jul
70.59	Clarissa	Claretti	ITA	7.10.80	1		Savona		15 Jun
	(20)								
70.30	Irina	Sekachova	UKR	21.7.76	1	NC	Kiev		2 Jul

Mark	Name		Nat	Born	Pos	Meet	Venue	Date
70.15	Oksana	Menkova	BLR	28.3.82	3		Staiki	21 Jul
70.03	Loree	Smith	USA	6.11.82	1		Fort Collins	13 May
69.85	Mariya	Smolyachkova	BLR	10.2.85	2	NC	Brest	3 Jul
69.80	Svetlana	Sudak	BLR	20.3.71	4		Staiki	21 Jul
69.69		Gu Yuan	CHN	9.5.82	2		Zhongshan	24 Apr
69.65	Bethany	Hart	USA	10.4.77	1		New Haven	11 Jul
69.52	Amber	Campbell	USA	5.6.81	1		Wilmington	14 Jun
69.36	Eileen	O'Keefe	IRL	31.5.81	1		Dublin (S)	30 Jul
69.30	Yunaika	Crawford	CUB	2.11.82	1	NC	La Habana	18 Mar
	(30)							
69.24	Martina	Danisová	SVK	21.3.83	1		Ostrava	3 Sep
68.90	Sini	Pöyry	FIN	3.2.80	1		Töysä	8 Jun
68.74	Arasay	Thondike	CUB-J	28.5.86	2	Barr	La Habana	20 May
68.70	Éva	Orbán	HUN	29.11.84	4		Padova	2 Jul
68.49	Andrea	Bunjes	GER	5.2.76	2		Frankisch-Crumbach	15 May
68.48	Marwa Ahmed	Hussein	EGY	19.6.78	1		Cairo	18 Feb
68.48	Jennifer	Joyce	CAN	25.9.80	1		Burnaby	9 Jul
68.44	Cecilia	Nilsson	SWE	22.6.79	1		Nyköping	5 Jun
68.31	Berta	Castells	ESP	24.1.84	1		Sabadell	3 Jul
68.25	Brooke	Krueger-Billett	AUS	9.7.80	1		Sydney	26 Nov
	(40)							
68.20	Amélie	Perrin	FRA	30.3.80	2		Nantes	1 Jun
68.17	Britney	Henry	USA	17.10.84	2	GP II	Stanford	29 May
68.14	Stiliani	Papadopoúlou	GRE	15.3.82	1	NC-23	Athína	10 Jun
68.09		Yang Meiping	CHN	23.10.85	3	NG	Nanjing	17 Oct
67.75	Natalya	Zolotukhina	UKR	4.1.85	3	EU23	Erfurt	17 Jul
67.58	Shirley	Webb	GBR	28.9.81	1	LEAP	Loughborough	16 Jul
67.56	Sanja	Gavrilovic	CRO	20.9.82	1		Bar	7 May
67.51	Yelena	Konevtsova	RUS	11.9.81	2		Adler	6 Feb
67.40	Nadezhda	Pavlyukovskaya	BLR	6.6.85	5		Staiki	21 Jul
67.33	Merja	Korpela	FIN	15.5.81	2		Töysä	8 Jun
	(50)							
67.14	Katalin	Divós	HUN	11.5.74	1	NC-w	Budapest	26 Feb
67.13	Alexándra	Papayeoryíou	GRE	17.12.80	3	MedG	Almeria	29 Jun
67.07	Jennifer	Dahlgren	ARG	27.8.84	1	Towns	Athens, GA	23 Apr
66.84	Yelena	Matoshko	BLR	23.6.82	4	NC	Brest	3 Jul
66.81	Jessica	Cosby	USA	31.5.82	5	NC	Carson	25 Jun
66.75	Simone	Mathes	GER	13.3.75	3		Frankisch-Crumbach	15 May
66.42	Sultana	Frizell	CAN	24.10.84	2		Athens, GA	7 May
66.39	Inna	Sayenko	UKR	8.3.82	1		Kiev	4 Jun
66.14	Vânia	Silva	POR	8.6.80	1		Quinta do Anjo	20 Mar
66.13	Yelena	Priyma	RUS	2.12.83	3	NC-23	Tula	14 Jun
	(60)							
65.86	Cari	Soong	USA	11.7.81	5	MSR	Walnut	17 Apr
65.75	Bronwyn	Eagles	AUS	23.8.80	1		Sydney	6 Aug
65.70	Marina	Rezanova	UKR	28.8.74	3		Kiev	21 Jun
65.60		Yang Qiaoyu	CHN	14.9.85	4	NG	Nanjing	17 Oct
65.53		Liao Xiaoyan	CHN-J	8.1.87	5	NG	Nanjing	17 Oct
65.52	Olivia	Waldet	FRA	23.5.84	2		Castres	26 Jul
65.48	Zoe	Derham	GBR	24.11.80	1		Birmingham	23 Jul
65.39	LaQuanda	Cotten	USA	30.12.80	1		Marietta	5 Jun
65.38	Yuka	Murofushi	JPN	11.2.77	1		Toyota	2 Apr
65.33	Lorraine	Shaw	GBR	2.4.68	1		Birmingham	19 Jun
	(70)							
65.29		Zhao Wenjiang	CHN	10.7.81	7	NG	Nanjing	17 Oct
65.19	Bianca	Achilles	GER	17.4.81	1		Leverkusen	9 Apr
65.13	Bianca	Perie	ROM-Y	1.6.90	1		Bucuresti	18 Mar
65.12	Stéphanie	Falzon	FRA	7.1.83	1	Franc	Niamey	13 Dec
65.04	Kirsten	Klose	GER	21.1.77	4		Frankisch-Crumbach	15 May
64.96	Silvia	Salis	ITA	17.9.85	6		Padova	2 Jul
64.85	Tracey	Andersson	SWE	5.12.84	1	NC	Helsingborg	19 Aug
64.69	Delisa	McClain	USA	24.9.81	2	NCAA-r	Norman	27 May
64.67	M.Dolores	Pedrares	ESP	17.1.73	2		Jaén	6 Jul
64.59	Maria José	Conde	POR	26.8.80	1		Porto	12 Mar
	(80)							
64.54	Lucie	Vrbenská	CZE	12.5.77	1		Praha	4 Jun
64.43	Karyne	DiMarco	AUS	14.3.78	1		Sydney	13 Feb
64.43	Anna	Bulgakova	RUS-Y	17.1.88	1eB	NC-w	Adler	20 Feb
64.43		Hao Shuai	CHN-J	19.7.87	1		Tula	25 Jun
64.31	Sónia	Alves	POR	3.6.79	3eB	EThCp	Mersin	13 Mar

Mark	Name		Nat	Born	Pos	Meet	Venue	Date
64.24	Malwina	Sobierajska	POL	22.4.85	1		Bialystok	3 May
64.13	Malgorzata	Zadura	POL	3.10.82	1		Warszawa	18 Jun
64.11	Vanda	Nickl	HUN	4.9.85	3	NC-w	Budapest	26 Feb
64.09	Noemi	Németh	HUN-J	7.4.86	2		Szombathely	1 Jun
64.01	Laura (90)	Gibilisco	ITA-J	17.1.86	1		Palermo	18 Jun
63.94	Jenny	Leatherman	USA	26.9.83	8	NC	Carson	25 Jun
63.60		Wei Xioyan	CHN	13.3.83	3		Chengdu	9 Apr
63.58	Manuela	Priemer	GER	29.11.78	8eA		Halle	21 May
63.51	Jessica	Pressley	USA	27.12.84	1		Tempe	30 Apr
63.45	Georgiana	Artenie	ROM-J	14.8.86	2	NC-w	Mersin	26 Feb
63.44	Liliya	Razinkova	UKR	29.11.85	5		Kiev	21 Jun
63.40	Tatyana	Chikina	UKR	16.11.82	6	NC	Kiev	2 Jul
63.36	Beth	Mallory	USA	31.5.84	3	SEC	Nashville	13 May
63.30	Yelena	Kiselyova	RUS	24.3.79	4		Tula	23 Jul
63.14	April (100)	Burton	USA	4.4.81	1		Claremont	15 Apr

Mark	Name		Nat	Born	Date
63.12	Valentina	Srsa	CRO-J	16.1.86	23 Jul
63.03	Crystal	Smith	CAN	6.3.81	29 May
62.87	Nathalie	Grant	JAM	25.5.81	16 Apr
62.85	Rosa	Rodríguez	VEN-J	2.7.86	19 Dec
62.84	Larisa	Tarasyuk	RUS	14.6.70	19 Feb
62.82	Kelly	Godsey	USA-J	1.1.86	20 May
62.82	Mona	Holm	NOR	5.8.83	20 Aug
62.65	Amarilys	Alméstica	PUR	12.2.81	28 Jun
62.62	Lyudmila	Gubkina	BLR	13.8.73	25 Jun
62.55	Evaggelia	Dervéni	GRE	2.5.80	10 Jun
62.53	Tatyana	Khatantseva	RUS	18.2.81	20 Feb
62.52	Melanie	Motzenbäcker	GER-J	2.3.86	17 Sep
62.50	Katarzyna	Kita	POL	4.7.84	25 Jun
62.44	Polina	Vashukova	RUS-J	10.8.87	3 Jul
62.36	Karina	Moya	ARG	28.9.73	3 Jul
62.35	Maris	Rongelepp	EST	17.3.84	26 Jun
62.28	Kristal	Kostiew	USA	8.1.82	25 Jun
62.26	Shelaine	Larson	USA	26.6.82	6 Apr
62.24	Oksana	Kondratyeva	RUS	22.11.85	23 Jul
62.23	Sarah	Hopping	USA	5.8.83	27 May
62.20	Kimberly	Barrett	JAM	18.11.81	21 Apr
62.13	Kristen	Callan	USA	5.4.85	21 Apr
62.12	Zübeyde	Yildiz	TUR	7.9.80	10 Jul
61.92	Lenka	Ledvinová	CZE	11.8.85	27 Jun
61.91A	Johana	Ramírez	COL	7.6.82	19 Aug
61.90	Yuliya	Rozenfeld	RUS	5.4.84	12 Mar
61.84		Zhao Wei	CHN	27.1.79	16 Apr
61.80	Zalina	Marghiev	MDA-Y	6.2.88	5 Jun
61.76	Ashley	Jones	USA		6 Apr
61.75	Laura	Douglas	GBR	4.1.83	10 Jul
61.75	Marie	Hilmersson	SWE	14.1.81	19 Aug
61.73	Mariya	Bespalova	RUS-J	21.5.86	20 Feb
61.67	Laetetia	Bambara	FRA	30.3.84	7 May
61.65	Johana	Moreno	COL	15.4.85	24 Jul
61.55	Florence	Ezeh	FRA	29.12.77	29 May
61.55	Lesley	Brannan	GBR	13.9.76	24 Jul
61.54		Huang Chih-Feng	TPE	9.5.77	16 Oct
61.52	Laci	Heller	USA	21.3.85	15 Apr
61.52	Svetlana	Kovalchuk	UKR	3.1.84	2 Jul
61.43	Irina	Novozhilova	UKR-J	4.5.86	6 May
61.43	Rebecka	Kvist	SWE	17.2.83	19 Aug
61.42	Michelle	Fournier	CAN	9.9.75	8 May
61.35	Josiane	Soares	BRA	21.6.76	18 Mar
61.34	Laura	Gerraughty	USA	29.7.83	15 Apr
61.16	Megan	Reid	CAN	18.4.83	3 Aug
61.07	Agnieszka	Pogroszewska	POL	20.2.77	28 May
61.03	Karin	Engström	SWE	10.8.83	5 Jun
61.00	Elisa	Palmieri	ITA	18.9.83	22 May
60.80	Faith	Thompson	USA	4.4.82	27 May
60.77	Chisato	Ohashi	JPN	31.5.77	1 Nov
60.76	Tuba	Kayhan	TUR-J	.86	5 Jun
60.74	Courtney	Magnuson	USA	1.5.82	6 Apr
60.74	Carys	Parry	GBR	24.7.81	22 May
60.71	Brittany	Hinchcliffe	USA	24.7.82	9 Apr
60.57	Suzanne	Roberts	GBR	19.12.78	22 May
60.54	Amy	Moses	CAN	8.12.82	16 Apr
60.51	Anita	Wlodarczyk	POL	8.8.85	14 May
60.51	Ekateríni	Maslatzídou	GRE	17.8.83	18 Jun
60.50	Vanessa	Mortensen	DEN	15.9.82	1 Apr
60.40	Gabrielle	Neighbour	AUS	22.11.83	3 Dec
60.36	Masumi	Aya	JPN	1.1.80	9 Oct
60.22	Ariannys	Vichy	CUB-Y	18.5.89	23 Jun
60.20	Kate	Burton	USA	12.4.85	7 May
60.09	Jenn	Wynn	USA	10.12.83	13 May
59.98	Daimara	Rovira	CUB	9.5.85	18 Mar
59.98	Terje	Matsik	EST	28.12.76	17 May
59.97	Monika	Královenská	SVK	31.12.82	29 Aug
59.95	Irini	Míliou	GRE	12.4.85	4 Jun
59.94		Yang Jie	CHN	10.12.83	16 Apr
59.83	Odette	Palma	CHI	7.8.82	23 Oct
59.76	Anna	Dolegiewicz	CAN		25 Jun
59.72	Brittany	Riley	USA-J	26.8.86	31 Jul
59.70	Stefanía	Zoryez	URU	14.11.83	19 Nov
59.70	Dorotea	Habazin	CRO-Y	14.6.88	29 Jun
59.69	Hayat	El Ghazi	MAR	1.1.79	18 Jun
59.63	Adriana	Benaventa	VEN	19.10.84	18 Apr
59.60	Dana	Posey	USA		23 Apr
59.60	Violeta	Guzmán	MEX	14.5.77	20 May
59.59	Tamara	Burns	USA	21.12.81	21 Apr
59.58	Debby (180)	van der Schilt	NED	24.11.81	13 Mar

Irregular circle

74.31ic	Yekaterina	Khoroshkikh	RUS	21.3.83	1	Znam	Kazan	24 Jun
				x	x	66.03	71.32 72.32	74.31
72.63		Kuzenkova			2	Znam	Kazan	24 Jun

JUNIORS

See main list for top 9 juniors. 11 performances by 2 women to 66.70. Additional marks and further juniors:

Zhang W+	72.34	1	GP	Osaka	7 May	70.50	1		Zhongshan	24 Apr
	72.23	1	EAsG	Macao	1 Nov	70.05	1	AsiC	Inchon	3 Sep
	71.84	2	NG	Nanjing	17 Oct	69.82	5	WCh	Helsinki	12 Aug
	70.88	1		Chongqing	14 May	66.73	Q	WCh	Helsinki	10 Aug
	70.81	1		Yixing	22 May					

63.12	Valentina	Srsa (10)	CRO	16.1.86	2	EJ	Kaunas	23 Jul
62.85	Rosa	Rodríguez	VEN	2.7.86	1	NG	San Cristóbal	19 Dec
62.82	Kelly	Godsey	USA	1.1.86	1		Houston	20 May
62.52	Melanie	Motzenbäcker	GER	2.3.86	1		Karlsruhe	17 Sep
62.44	Polina	Vashukova	RUS	10.8.87	2	NC-j	Tula	3 Jul
61.80	Zalina	Marghiev	MDA-Y	6.2.88	1	NC	Chisinau	5 Jun

Mark	Name			Nat	Born	Pos	Meet	Venue		Date
61.73	Mariya		Bespalova	RUS	21.5.86	6	NC-w	Adler		20 Feb
61.43	Irina		Novozhilova	UKR	4.5.86	4		Donetsk		6 May
60.76	Tuba		Kayhan	TUR	.86	1		Istanbul		5 Jun
60.22	Ariannys		Vichy	CUB-Y	18.5.89	2		La Habana		23 Jun
59.72	Brittany		Riley (20)	USA	26.8.86	2	PAm-J	Windsor		31 Jul

JAVELIN

Mark	Name			Nat	Born	Pos	Meet	Venue		Date
71.70	Osleidys		Menéndez	CUB	14.11.79	1	WCh	Helsinki		14 Aug
					71.70	x	p	65.53	63.80	p
68.47	1	GP	Helsinki	25 Jul	68.47	62.26	62.93	60.42	x	64.53
67.24	1	WAF	Monaco	9 Sep	64.58	63.30	63.21	67.24		
66.28	1		Rovereto	31 Aug	62.68	x	60.28	61.71	66.28	p
66.02	1		Salamanca	6 Jul	x	61.95	63.96	x	66.02	61.92
65.77	Q	WCh	Helsinki	12 Aug	65.77		only throw			
65.01	2	SGP	Athína	14 Jun	63.92	63.15	x	60.66	64.63	65.01
64.53	1		Zaragoza	23 Jun	x	64.53	x	61.11	x 60.61	
64.29	1	NC	La Habana	19 Mar	64.29	x	62.70	x	x	x
64.29	1	GP	Madrid	16 Jul	62.60	x	63.19	64.29	x	63.44
70.03	Christina		Obergföll	GER	22.8.81	2	WCh	Helsinki		14 Aug
					61.55	70.03	p	p	p	59.67
64.59	2		Halle	21 May	62.51	64.59	60.82	61.24	x	60.07
67.67	Sonia		Bisset	CUB	1.4.71	1		Salamanca		6 Jul
					x	58.33	61.16	x	67.67	x
64.50	Q	WCh	Helsinki	12 Aug	64.50		only throw			
64.21	2	GP	Madrid	16 Jul	x	x	64.21	x	x	57.81
66.52	Steffi		Nerius	GER	1.7.72	Q	WCh	Helsinki		12 Aug
					66.52		only throw			
66.43	1		Leverkusen	23 Jul	63.74	66.43	65.61	p	p	p
66.35	2	WAF	Monaco	9 Sep	63.27	63.53	66.35	x		
65.96	3	WCh	Helsinki	14 Aug	65.96	x	x	64.26	64.35	x
65.84	1		Zeulenroda	29 May	61.38	x	x	65.84	x	63.17
65.49	1		Halle	21 May	59.28	65.49	65.35	x	64.10	65.45
65.08	1	SGP	Athína	14 Jun	65.08	62.62	x	p	x	63.30
64.59	1	ECp-S	Firenze	18 Jun	63.20	64.59	62.73	x		
64.56	1		Ulm	12 Jun	63.47	63.58	64.56	63.18	64.19	x
64.54	1	NC	Wattenscheid	3 Jul	64.54		only throw			
64.45	1		Bad Köstritz	28 Aug	64.45	61.90	x	61.18	p	x
64.14	1		Sondershausen	17 Aug						
63.97	1		Kassel	10 Jun	63.68	x	63.97	x	62.36	63.30
65.74	Barbora		Spotáková	CZE	30.6.81	1		Ústí nad Labem		25 Sep
64.08	1		Cáslav	30 Aug						
	(30/5)									
63.43	Christina		Scherwin	DEN	11.7.76	4	WCh	Helsinki		14 Aug
63.03	Barbara		Madejczyk	POL	30.9.76	1	Déca	Paris (C)		3 Sep
62.75	Zahra		Bani	ITA	31.12.79	5	WCh	Helsinki		14 Aug
62.72	Aggelikí		Tsiolakoúdi	GRE	10.5.76	4	SGP	Athína		14 Jun
62.64	Paula		Tarviainen	FIN	17.2.73	6	WCh	Helsinki		14 Aug
	(10)									
62.27	Inga		Stasiulionyte	LTU	29.6.81	1	NC	Kaunas		9 Jul
61.96	Laverne		Eve	BAH	16.6.65	4	WAF	Monaco		9 Sep
61.95			Ma Ning	CHN	4.11.83	1	EAsG	Macau		2 Nov
61.68	Nikolett		Szabó	HUN	3.3.80	1		Kalamáta		30 May
61.65	Felicia		Moldovan	ROM	29.9.67	1		Pontevedra		17 Apr
61.45	Goldie		Sayers	GBR	16.7.82	1	LI	Loughborough		22 May
61.42			Xue Juan	CHN-J	10.2.86	2	EAsG	Macau		2 Nov
61.10	Olivia		McKoy	JAM	1.12.73	2	CAC	Nassau		10 Jul
61.08	Jarmila		Klimesová	CZE	9.2.81	2		Turnov		24 May
61.06	Mikaela		Ingberg	FIN	29.7.74	Q	WCh	Helsinki		12 Aug
	(20)									
60.83	Mariya		Yakovenko	RUS	6.1.82	1	NC	Tula		12 Jul
60.74	Olga		Ivankova	UKR	7.1.73	1		Kiev		5 Jun
60.69	Rumyana		Karapetrova	BUL	7.2.82	1		Sofia		20 May
60.59	Indre		Jakubaitite	LTU	24.1.76	1		Tartu		11 Jun
60.22	Mercedes		Chilla	ESP	19.1.80	1	ECp-1A	Gävle		18 Jun
60.05	Lada		Chernova	RUS	1.1.70	1eB	EThCp	Mersin		13 Mar
59.97	Inga		Kozarenoka	LAT	16.3.82	1		Murjani		15 Jun
59.69	Taina		Kolkkala	FIN	24.10.76	1		Lapinlahti		3 Jul
59.53	Mariya		Abakumova	RUS-J	15.1.86	1-j	NC-w	Adler		19 Feb
59.46A	Justine		Robbeson	RSA	15.5.85	1		Potchefstroom		7 Sep
	(30)									

Mark	Name		Nat	Born	Pos	Meet	Venue	Date
59.24	Kim	Kreiner	USA	26.7.77	1		Baton Rouge	23 Apr
59.22	Miréla	Manjani	GRE	21.12.76	1	NC	Athína	11 Jun
59.20	Nora Aída	Bicet	CUB	29.10.77	2	Barr	La Habana	20 May
59.04		Geng Aihua	CHN	29.6.83	3	NG	Nanjing	17 Oct
58.74	Vivian	Zimmer	GER-J	22.7.87	3eA	EThCp	Mersin	13 Mar
58.74	Ilze	Gribule	LAT	25.1.84	1		Riga	14 May
58.43	Tatyana	Lyakhovich	UKR	20.5.79	4		Kalamáta	30 May
58.39	Annika	Suthe	GER	15.10.85	3		Ulm	12 Jun
58.38	Claudia	Coslovich	ITA	26.4.72	4eA	EThCp	Mersin	13 Mar
58.36		Zhang Li	CHN	19.10.78	4	NG	Nanjing	17 Oct
	(40)							
58.16	Kimberley	Mickle	AUS	28.12.84	1		Perth	18 Dec
58.09	María de la Caridad	Álvarez	CUB	30.8.75	3	NC	La Habana	19 Mar
57.97		Chu Chunxia	CHN	28.1.78	5	NG	Nanjing	17 Oct
57.92	María	Zérva	GRE-J	10.8.87	Q	EJ	Kaunas	23 Jul
57.88	Voisávva	Líka	GRE	27.6.70	2	NC	Athína	11 Jun
57.86	Lindy	Leveau-Agricole	SEY	14.11.79	1		Victoria	25 Jun
57.80		Zhang Li	CHN-Y	17.1.89	3	NC	Changsha	25 Jun
57.70	Natalya	Shimchuk	BLR	1.10.81	1		Staiki	21 Jul
57.62	Sarah	Walter	FRA	5.5.78	1		La Roche-sur-Yon	20 Jul
57.53	Kirsi	Ahonen	FIN	8.4.76	3		Kuortane	26 Jun
	(50)							
57.53	Zuleima	Araméndiz	COL	23.9.75	7	GP II	Madrid	16 Jul
57.52	Dana	Pounds	USA	5.6.84	2	MSR	Walnut	17 Apr
57.48	Vera	Rebrik	UKR-Y	25.2.89	2		Kiev	19 May
57.45	Panayióta	Touoloumtzí	GRE-J	26.9.86	1	NC-23	Lárisa	19 Jun
57.37	Sephora	Bissoly	FRA	6.11.81	1		Les Sables d'Olonne	7 Aug
57.36	Jana	Woytkowska	GER	7.8.77	1		Regensburg	11 Jun
57.31	Sunette	Viljoen	RSA	6.10.83	1		Parow	16 Dec
57.29	Ynthie	Coetzee	RSA-Y	31.12.88	1	NC	Durban	16 Apr
57.23		Liang Lili	CHN	16.11.83	6	NG	Nanjing	17 Oct
57.14	Teodora	Petras	ROM	5.2.82	1		Onesti	21 May
	(60)							
57.14	Aïda	Sellam	TUN	13.9.77	1		Jablonec nad Nisou	8 Jun
57.10	sdis	Hjálmsdóttir	ISL	28.10.85	1		Reykjavik	28 May
57.01	Katharina	Molitor	GER	8.11.83	2	EU23	Erfurt	16 Jul
56.94	Sarah	Malone	USA	14.9.81	1	NCAA-r	Eugene	28 May
56.91	Brenda-Grace	Hunt	JAM	9.9.81	1	TexR	Austin	9 Apr
56.79	Esther	Eisenlauer	GER	29.10.77	3	NC	Wattenscheid	3 Jul
56.78	Monika	Aava	EST	19.6.79	6	FBK	Hengelo	29 May
56.36	Margaret	Simpson	GHA	31.12.81	1H	WCh	Helsinki	7 Aug
56.27		Liu Chunhua	CHN-J	1.10.86	7	NG	Nanjing	17 Oct
56.24	Annika	Pettersson	SWE	10.1.79	5	ECp-1A	Gävle	18 Jun
	(70)							
56.20	Zhanna	Slastina	UKR	4.9.77	1	NC-w	Yalta	5 Feb
56.20	Mareike	Rittweg	GER	1.6.84	1		Rostock	20 Aug
56.14	Elisabetta	Marin	ITA	5.11.77	1	NC-w	Roma (Vigna di Valle)	27 Feb
56.12	Linda	Brivule	LAT	9.9.83	3	EU23	Erfurt	16 Jul
56.06A	Alessandra	Rezende	BRA	5.3.75	1	SACh	Cali	23 Jul
55.98		Lee Young-sun	KOR	21.2.74	1	NG	Ulsan	16 Oct
55.97		Zheng Ruixia	CHN	14.3.83	1		Zhaoqing	10 Apr
55.91	Jana	Trakmann	EST	17.2.82	1		Tallinn	25 May
55.83	Barbara	Vontein	GER	7.6.78	3		Zeulenroda	29 May
55.70	Izabela	Wojczakowska	POL	24.3.74	1		Kraków	3 Sep
	(80)							
55.67	Nadine	Vigliano	FRA	24.6.77	4	v2N	Viareggio	27 Jul
55.63	Katy	Doyle	USA	1.8.80	2	TexR	Austin	9 Apr
55.60	Anne Maheshi	De Silva	SRI	15.11.77	1		Trincomalee	16 May
55.60		Chang Jeong-yeon	KOR	6.4.77	1		Daegu	23 Sep
55.60	Emika	Yoshida	JPN	10.12.85	1		Kitakyushu	3 Nov
55.58		Park Ho-hyun	KOR	21.3.78	1	AsiC	Inchon	4 Sep
55.49	Sandra	Schaffarzik	GER-J	22.6.87	3	EJ	Kaunas	24 Jul
55.41	Yelena	Makarova	RUS	21.12.81	3	NC	Tula	12 Jul
55.32	Margarita	Dorozhon	UKR-J	4.9.87	1		Kiev	5 Jun
55.32	Susanne	Rosenbauer	GER	2.8.84	1		Regensberg	23 Jul
	(90)							
55.31	Yekaterina	Rybko	RUS	5.6.82	1		Moskva	5 Jun
55.30		Ha Xiaoyan	CHN	30.1.72	9	NG	Nanjing	17 Oct
55.24	Marina	Novik	BLR	19.1.84	2		Staiki	21 Jul
55.15	Rita	Ramanauskaite	LTU	22.2.70	1		Riga	27 May
55.14	Shelley	Holroyd	GBR	17.5.73	2	NC	Manchester (SC)	10 Jul

Mark	Name		Nat	Born	Pos	Meet	Venue	Date
55.06	Natalya	Davydova	RUS	24.11.78	2		Moskva	5 Jun
55.06	Buaban	Phamang	THA-J	27.12.86	1	SEAG	Manila	28 Nov
55.04	Stefanie	Hessler	GER	16.3.83	6		Ulm	12 Jun
54.99	Laura	Cornford	AUS-Y	11.6.88	1		Sydney	17 Dec
54.91	Kateema (100)	Riettie	JAM	5.12.73	2		New York (RI)	11 Jun

Mark	Name		Nat	Born	Date
54.90	Neely	Falgout	USA	24.3.82	13 May
54.90		Zhao Hongxia	CHN	25.2.81	17 Oct
54.87	Kathryn	Mitchell	AUS	10.7.82	18 Dec
54.72	Misa	Nakano	JPN	27.11.81	13 May
54.61	Urszula	Jasinska	POL	6.12.83	21 May
54.56	Marina	Maksimova	RUS	20.5.85	12 Jul
54.53	Momoko	Matsumoto	JPN-J	7.12.87	24 Oct
54.52	Liliya	Dusmetova	UZB	11.2.81	4 Sep
54.48		Zhang Cuiduo	CHN	18.3.85	24 Apr
54.44	Marina	Buksa	BLR-J	19.10.87	27 May
54.41	Silvia	Cruz	POR	29.12.80	6 Jul
54.36	Suman	Devi	IND	15.7.84	24 Aug
54.35	Ana Érika	Gutiérrez	MEX	27.7.83	10 Jul
54.25	Inge	Jorgensen	USA	6.10.80	19 Mar
54.25	Yanelis	Riveaux	CUB-J	30.12.87	25 May
54.24	Maria	Negoita	ROM-J	6.12.86	11 Jun
54.23	Alexándra	Násta	GRE/CYP	2.7.81	10 Jun
54.23	Galina	Kakhova	BLR	26.3.82	3 Jul
54.13	Berna	Demirci	TUR-J	13.5.86	14 May
54.08		Chen Yu-Hsun	TPE-J	9.7.87	18 Oct
54.00	Nadeeka	Lakmali	SRI	19.9.81	15 Jul
53.99		Yi Chunmei	CHN	15.3.83	25 Jun
53.94	Linda	Stahl	GER	2.10.85	15 Jan
53.90	Serafina	Akeli	SAM	7.12.78	8 Oct
53.88	Roshunda	Betts	USA		25 Mar
53.88	Elodie	Masset	FRA	2.7.84	30 Apr
53.87	Olga	Gamza	BLR	2.10.85	30 Apr
53.80	Bregje	Crolla	NED-J	31.1.86	15 May
53.77	Rachel	Yurkovich	USA-J	10.10.86	30 Apr
53.77	Gurmeet	Kaur	IND	20.6.70	10 Nov
53.69		Zhang Ying	CHN-Y	5.1.88	15 May
53.65	Hanaa	Hassan Omar	EGY	3.1.83	3 May
53.64	Tatyana	Alisevich	BLR	22.1.69	3 Jul
53.63	Dominique	Bilodeau	CAN	14.5.79	15 Jul
53.61		Chang Chunfeng	CHN-J		28 Aug
53.56		Wu Meihong	CHN	5.6.84	10 Apr
53.55	Rosemary	Hooper	AUS	4.8.78	1 Dec
53.53	Panayióta	Tsiála	GRE	30.6.84	19 Jun
53.46	Romina	Ugatai	FRA-J	10.10.86	18 Mar
53.41		Zhu Jingya	CHN-J	15.12.87	17 Oct
53.39	Ivana	Vukovic	CRO-J	18.5.86	22 May
53.24	Karine	Hervieu	FRA	24.2.82	22 May
53.20	Yanet	Cruz	CUB-Y	8.2.88	23 May
53.15A	Linda	Smit	RSA	15.8.85	14 Sep
53.15		Kim Kyong-ae	KOR-Y	5.3.88	18 Oct
53.13	Kayla	Wilkinson	USA	20.4.84	29 Apr
53.13	Silke	Bachmann	GER	21.6.79	3 Jul
53.10	Eunice	Barber	FRA	17.11.74	15 Jul
53.08	Natalya	Kostyukovskaya	BLR	.71	3 Mar
53.07	Dörthe	Friedrich	GER	21.6.73	10 Jul
53.06	Daniela (151)	Janke	GER	21.5.84	29 May

Old specification javelin: 57.56 Joanna Nixon (Stone)	AUS	4.10.72	1		Gold Coast	4 Dec
700 grams: 57.60 Osleidys Menéndez	CUB	14.11.79	1		La Habana	25 Feb

JUNIORS

See main list for top 13 juniors. 11 performances by 3 women to 58.80. Additional marks and further juniors:

Name	Mark	Pos	Meet	Venue	Date	Mark	Pos	Meet	Venue	Date
Xue Juan	59.87	2	NG	Nanjing	17 Oct	59.25	Q	NC	Changsha	24 Jun
	59.72	1	NC	Changsha	25 Jun	58.81	1		Yixing	21 May
Abakumova	59.53	1	NC-j	Tula	30 Jul	59.06	2eA	EThCp	Mersin	13 Mar
	59.12	4		Halle	21 May	58.90	1		Sochi	27 May

Mark	Name		Nat	Born	Pos	Meet	Venue	Date
54.53	Momoko	Matsumoto	JPN	7.12.87	1	NSF	Okayama	24 Oct
54.44	Marina	Buksa	BLR	19.10.87			Brest	27 May
54.25	Yanelis	Riveaux	CUB	30.12.87	1	NC-j	Santiago de Cuba	25 May
54.24	Maria	Negoita	ROM	6.12.86	1	Rom IC	Bucuresti	11 Jun
54.13	Berna	Demirci	TUR	13.5.86	1	NC	Ankara	14 May
54.08		Chen Yu-Hsun	TPE	9.7.87	1		Yunlin	18 Oct
53.80	Bregje	Crolla (20)	NED	31.1.86	1H		Emmeloord	15 May

HEPTATHLON

Mark	Name		Nat	Born	Pos	Meet	Venue	Date
6889	Eunice	Barber	FRA	17.11.74	1		Arles	5 Jun
	12.62w/2.9 1.91 12.61 24.12/1.2			6.78w/3.4	53.07	2:14.66		
6887	Carolina	Klüft	SWE	2.2.83	1	WCh	Helsinki	7 Aug
	13.19/-0.4 1.82 15.02 23.70/-2.5			6.87/0.2	47.20	2:08.89		
6824		Klüft			1		Götzis	29 May
	13.15/1.1 1.94 13.33 23.34/1.7			6.68/0.5	44.08	2:10.46		
6824		Barber			2	WCh	Helsinki	7 Aug
	12.94/-0.4 1.91 13.20 24.01/-1.0			6.75/0.7	48.24	2:11.94		
6688		Klüft			1	ECp-1	Jyväskylä	3 Jul
	13.26/0.9 1.90 13.84 23.62/0.8			6.37/1.6	46.32	2:11.54		
6675		Barber			1		Talence	18 Sep
	12.96/1.6 1.87 13.65 24.08/-1.2			6.72w/3.2	47.66	2:18.79		
6547	Kelly	Sotherton	GBR	13.11.76	2		Götzis	29 May
	13.27/1.1 1.85 13.84 23.77/1.7			6.67/-0.6	37.21	2:10.29		
6502	Hyleas	Fountain	USA	14.1.81	3		Götzis	29 May
	13.09/1.1 1.88 12.13 23.87/1.7			6.67/-0.9	46.90	2:22.81		
6423	Margaret	Simpson	GHA	31.12.81	4		Götzis	29 May
	13.41/-0.8 1.85 13.01 24.55/1.0			6.32/0.7	52.71	2:21.71		
6386	Austra	Skujyte	LTU	12.8.79	5		Götzis	29 May
	14.16/-0.6 1.82 16.92 25.22/1.0			6.12/-0.1	48.79	2:18.32		
6378	Lyudmila	Blonska	UKR	9.11.77	1		Woerden	28 Aug
	13.38/0.0 1.78 12.91 24.31/1.8			6.54/1.9	45.13	2:14.56		

Mark	Name		Nat	Born	Pos	Meet	Venue	Date
6375		Simpson			3	WCh	Helsinki	7 Aug
	13.55/-0.4	1.79	13.33	24.94/-1.0	6.09/0.0	56.36	2:17.02	
6360		Skujyte			4	WCh	Helsinki	7 Aug
	14.22/-1.2	1.82	16.61	25.31/0.3	6.12/0.8	48.82	2:17.48	
6325		Sotherton			5	WCh	Helsinki	7 Aug
	13.33/-0.4	1.82	13.38	23.94/-2.5	6.41/0.0	33.09	2:07.96	
6318	Karin	Ruckstuhl	NED	2.11.80	6		Götzis	29 May
	13.38/-0.8	1.76	13.55	24.27/1.0	6.34/-0.5	43.61	2:13.76	
6299	Natalya	Dobrinska	UKR	29.5.82	7		Götzis	29 May
	13.95/1.1	1.82	15.34	24.95/1.0	6.35/-0.2	43.52	2:18.63	
6297		Blonska			1	WUG	Izmir	16 Aug
	13.47/-1.3	1.78	13.03	24.25/-0.4	6.38/0.4	44.57	2:15.97	
6291	Laurien	Hoos (10)	NED	18.8.83	1	EU23	Erfurt	15 Jul
	13.53/1.2	1.77	15.03	24.61/-1.7	6.04/0.6	49.77	2:21.76	
6279w		Dobrinska			2		Arles	5 Jun
	13.74w/2.9	1.85	14.72	24.84/1.2	6.49w/5.3	40.39	2:21.76	
6278		Sotherton			2		Talence	18 Sep
	13.32/1.6	1.75	13.91	23.64/-1.2	6.39/0.0	34.79	2:11.60	
6278		Blonska			3		Talence	18 Sep
	13.62/1.6	1.78	12.19	24.58/1.7	6.49/1.1	45.57	2:13.48	
6248	Marie	Collonvillé	FRA	23.11.73	6	WCh	Helsinki	7 Aug
	13.73/-0.8	1.85	12.36	25.44/-1.4	6.30/1.4	45.65	2:11.74	
6235		Dobrinska			4		Talence	18 Sep
	13.71w/3.7	1.78	14.95	25.22/1.7	6.17w/2.3	45.70	2:17.50	
6231	Kylie	Wheeler	AUS	17.1.80	1		Ratingen	26 Jun
	13.88/0.2	1.82	13.19	24.24/-0.7	6.35/0.5	37.06	2:09.98	
6230	Naide	Gomes	POR	10.11.79	1		Logroño	17 Jul
	13.54/0.0	1.79	13.87	24.87/0.0	6.39/0.0	41.66	2:17.00	
6221	Sonja	Kesselschläger	GER	20.1.78	8		Götzis	29 May
	13.47/1.1	1.79	12.99	24.94/-0.4	6.22/-0.2	44.35	2:13.63	
6214		Hoos			9		Götzis	29 May
	13.58/-0.8	1.76	15.22	23.97/1.0	5.78/1.1	50.22	2:26.29	
6208		Fountain			1	NC	Carson	26 Jun
	13.28/0.1	1.81	11.22	24.35/-2.2	6.25/0.0	46.05	2:16.88	
6206		Skujyte			2	ECp-1	Jyväskylä	3 Jul
	14.32/0.9	1.78	16.69	25.66/0.8	6.04/1.4	47.87	2:19.00	
6199	Christine	Schulz	GER	30.1.84	1		Wesel	22 May
	13.67/1.8	1.80	12.99	24.88/0.4	6.30w/2.6	44.96	2:17.03	
(30/15)								
6196	Lilli	Schwarzkopf	GER	28.8.83	2	EU23	Erfurt	15 Jul
	13.72/1.3	1.77	13.21	25.87/-1.7	6.12/-0.5	50.21	2:11.94	
6192	Gi-Gi	Miller	USA	12.1.79	2	NC	Carson	26 Jun
	13.03w/2.3	1.69	13.05	23.68/1.7	6.13w/3.3	43.04	2:16.55	
6173	Tatyana	Alisevich	BLR	22.1.69	1	ECp-S	Bydgoszcz	3 Jul
	13.88/0.7	1.66	14.63	24.51/0.6	6.10/1.9	53.64	2:22.23	
6165		Shen Shengfei	CHN	21.1.81	1	NG	Nanjing	18 Oct
	14.40/0.5	1.86	14.22	26.08/-0.5	6.22/0.4	49.68	2:20.46	
6163	Karin	Ertl	GER	23.6.74	2		Ratingen	26 Jun
	13.57/0.2	1.79	13.35	25.11/-0.7	6.32/1.4	43.40	2:18.26	
(20)								
6137	Jessica	Zelinka	CAN	3.9.81	11		Götzis	29 May
	13.42/1.1	1.70	13.41	24.49/1.7	6.14/0.9	42.74	2:13.20	
6132		Liu Haili	CHN	24.12.84	2	NG	Nanjing	18 Oct
	13.52w/2.4	1.71	13.06	24.21w/2.5	6.22/-0.4	42.98	2:15.68	
6130	Katja	Keller	GER	9.8.80	12		Götzis	29 May
	13.38/-0.8	1.79	13.06	24.78/-0.4	6.10/-0.6	41.41	2:15.64	
6128		Wang Hailan	CHN	6.4.76	3	NG	Nanjing	18 Oct
	13.89w/2.4	1.71	13.66	24.84w/2.5	6.12/-0.6	48.49	2:16.21	
6103	Yuliya	Akulenko	UKR	3.6.77	1	NC	Kiev	15 Jun
	14.09/0.5	1.71	13.43	24.75/0.2	6.30/1.9	48.10	2:18.92	
6090	Magdalena	Szczepanska	POL	25.1.80	1	NC	Kielce	5 Jun
	14.03/0.0	1.78	13.85	25.27w/3.8	5.89/1.2	49.47	2:17.98	
6090	Julie	Hollman	GBR	16.2.77	2		Woerden	28 Aug
	13.94/0.0	1.81	12.79	24.75/1.8	6.41/1.8	38.54	2:16.46	
6089w	Antoinette	Djimou	FRA	2.8.85	3		Arles	5 Jun
	13.43w/3.1	1.73	13.49	24.52w/3.1	6.29w/4.9	44.46	2:25.23	
6054	Claudia	Tonn	GER	18.4.81	3		Ratingen	26 Jun
	14.12/0.2	1.70	12.11	24.97/-0.7	6.60/1.2	40.24	2:09.80	
6052	Simone	Oberer	SUI	8.4.80	13		Götzis	29 May
	13.76/-0.6	1.82	12.08	25.03/-0.4	6.25/1.4	38.85	2:13.47	

Mark	Name		Nat	Born	Pos	Meet	Venue	Date
	(30)							
6026	Karolina	Tyminska	POL	4.10.84	2	NC	Kielce	5 Jun
	14.26/0.0 1.69 14.60 24.43w/3.8 6.16/1.6 37.00 2:10.40							
6026	Yvonne	Wisse	NED	6.6.82	2	ECp-S	Bydgoszcz	3 Jul
	13.72/0.2 1.78 12.81 24.02/1.2 5.89/1.3 36.35 2:11.17							
6003	Natalya	Roshchupkina	RUS	13.1.78	1	NC	Tula	15 Jun
	14.59/1.7 1.79 14.22 25.09/0.3 5.99 39.76 2:11.51							
5999	Larisa	Netseporuk	EST	24.12.70	5		Arles	5 Jun
	13.98w/2.5 1.73 13.57 24.84w/2.3 6.14w/4.0 46.11 2:23.08							
5994w	Diana	Koritskaya	RUS	22.2.75	6		Arles	5 Jun
	13.97w/2.5 1.64 13.73 24.84/1.2 6.13w/5.0 44.81 2:14.47							
5994	Fiona	Asigbee	USA	18.5.81	3	NC	Carson	26 Jun
	13.56w/2.3 1.81 12.64 24.68/-2.2 6.09/1.8 37.45 2:18.29							
5991	Irina	Naumenko	KAZ	13.2.80	14	WCh	Helsinki	7 Aug
	14.07/-1.2 1.76 13.74 25.24/0.3 6.15/0.6 39.30 2:14.27							
5982	Joanna	Grzesiak	POL	15.8.80	3	NC	Kielce	5 Jun
	13.51/0.0 1.69 12.59 23.76w/3.8 5.95/1.7 35.96 2:10.13							
5973	Olga	Levenkova	RUS	11.1.84	2	NC	Tula	15 Jun
	13.95/0.0 1.73 12.65 24.85/0.3 6.35/0.7 37.66 2:13.71							
5958	Janice	Josephs	RSA	31.3.82	2		Salò	8 May
	13.66/0.1 1.70 12.68 24.02/-3.3 6.14/1.6 37.31 2:15.79							
	(40)							
5943	Aryiró	Stratáki	GRE	3.8.75	2	MedG	Almeria	2 Jul
	14.04/-1.8 1.76 13.47 25.00/0.3 5.85/-0.2 43.51 2:17.53							
5939	Tatyana	Gordeyeva	RUS	3.6.73	7		Arles	5 Jun
	14.30w/2.5 1.85 13.88 25.97w/2.3 6.08w/2.7 38.38 2:16.93							
5931	Yuliya	Ignatkina	RUS	13.9.82	3	NC	Tula	15 Jun
	14.38/0.0 1.82 12.32 25.40/0.3 6.20/0.9 38.63 2:13.19							
5921	Silke	Bachmann	GER	21.6.79	5	ECp-S	Bydgoszcz	3 Jul
	14.79/-0.4 1.75 12.21 25.28w/2.3 6.15w/2.3 53.13 2:23.11							
5916	Anna	Kryazheva	RUS	17.7.84	5	NC	Tula	15 Jun
	14.14/1.7 1.76 13.98 25.31/0.3 5.98/0.1 38.08 2:14.18							
5913	Viktorija	Zemaityte	LTU	11.3.85	4	EU23	Erfurt	15 Jul
	14.32/0.3 1.83 12.40 25.39/-0.5 6.18/-0.7 42.45 2:21.34							
5910	Tracy	Lawyer-Thomas	USA	28.8.77	4	NC	Carson	26 Jun
	13.51/0.1 1.75 13.57 24.21/1.0 5.91/0.6 45.29 2:35.30							
5910	Jessica	Ennis	GBR-J	28.1.86	3	WUG	Izmir	16 Aug
	13.56/-1.1 1.87 12.26 24.43/0.6 6.22/-1.0 28.94 2:21.08							
5905	Yuki	Nakata	JPN	10.3.77	1	NC	Tokyo	5 Jun
	13.95/-1.2 1.75 12.22 25.41w/2.2 6.16/0.9 43.46 2:18.45							
5899	Tiia	Hautala	FIN	3.4.72	1		Turku	29 May
	13.98/-1.1 1.77 12.51 25.34w/2.2 6.22w/3.0 42.79 2:22.7h							
	(50)							
5896w	Svetlana	Gnezdilov	ISR	20.7.69	1		Tel Aviv	19 Jul
	13.71/0.9 1.61 12.55 24.83/0.9 6.38w/4.6 34.19 2:07.34							
5894	Gertrud	Bacher	ITA	28.2.71	17		Götzis	29 May
	14.32/-0.6 1.70 13.43 25.30/1.2 5.77w/2.2 46.26 2:12.96							
5878	Lela	Nelson	USA	19.5.83	1	NCAA	Sacramento	11 Jun
	13.49/1.0 1.66 12.15 23.78/0.6 6.45/-1.1 34.87 2:22.71							
5873w	Anzhela	Atroshchenko	TUR	14.11.70	9		Arles	5 Jun
	13.45w/2.9 1.70 12.69 24.65w/2.3 6.11w/4.7 41.45 2:25.05							
5865w	Julie	Martin	FRA	28.10.79	10		Arles	5 Jun
	14.00w/2.5 1.82 11.33 25.08w/2.3 5.98w/4.3 43.82 2:21.41							
5835	Maren	Schwerdtner	GER	3.10.85	1	NC-23	Bernhausen	5 Jun
	13.93w/2.5 1.83 12.60 24.40w/2.4 5.90/1.8 37.84 2:26.16							
5830	Julia	Mächtig	GER-J	1.1.86	2	EJ	Kaunas	24 Jul
	15.00/0.1 1.73 13.60 25.41/-2.1 6.27/0.4 40.13 2:16.16							
5819	Vera	Yepimashko	BLR	10.7.76	11		Arles	5 Jun
	13.73w/2.5 1.67 16.90 25.58w/2.3 6.14w/2.3 38.42 2:35.06							
5809	Zhanna	Melnichenko	UKR	23.4.83	9	ECp-S	Bydgoszcz	3 Jul
	13.75/0.7 1.84 11.64 24.85/0.6 5.85/1.2 40.58 2:25.85							
5808	Niina	Kelo	FIN	26.3.80	10	ECp-S	Bydgoszcz	3 Jul
	14.15/0.7 1.66 14.77 25.94/0.6 5.67/0.0 49.61 2:22.10							
	(60)							
5794	Jessica	Stockard	USA	2.3.84	2	NCAA	Sacramento	11 Jun
	14.04/1.0 1.81 11.89 24.47/0.0 6.03/1.3 32.60 2:17.70							
5794	Vasilikí	Delinikóla	GRE	9.2.81	6	ECp-1	Jyväskylä	3 Jul
	13.49/1.2 1.72 12.88 24.82/1.3 5.78/0.1 45.52 2:30.68							
5794	Ksenja	Balta	EST-J	1.11.86	1	NC	Rakvere	28 Aug
	13.89/1.6 1.73 10.02 24.03/0.0 6.41w/2.4 32.75 2:15.01							

Mark	Name		Nat	Born	Pos	Meet	Venue	Date
5786	Nadezhda	Sergeyeva	RUS-J	13.6.87	7	NC	Tula	15 Jun
	14.22/0.3 1.73	12.57	24.94/0.3	6.03/0.3		36.95	2:15.24	
5782	Lyudmila	Yosipenko	UKR	24.9.84	11	ECp-S	Bydgoszcz	3 Jul
	14.39/0.4 1.75	11.12	24.80/1.1	5.74/0.7		47.72	2:18.28	
5780	Anastasia	Kivelídou	GRE	23.9.79	1	NCAA-II	Abilene	27 May
	13.78w/3.7 1.66	11.96	25.30w/3.3	6.07/1.9		45.38	2:21.40	
5776	Tatyana	Zhevnova	BLR	17.10.77	12	ECp-S	Bydgoszcz	3 Jul
	13.88/0.2 1.72	13.45	25.76/1.2	5.79w/2.3		40.76	2:17.38	
5775	Ashley	Selig	USA	23.2.84	3	NCAA	Sacramento	11 Jun
	13.94/0.4 1.75	11.54	25.01/0.0	5.91/-1.5		35.87	2:11.36	
5773		Cao Lan	CHN	25.1.82	4	NG	Nanjing	18 Oct
	13.94/0.5 1.65	12.18	25.17/1.5	6.01/-0.4		48.14	2:24.03	
5766	Amandine	Constantin	FRA	12.2.84	12		Arles	5 Jun
	13.51w/3.1 1.79	11.57	24.34w/3.1	6.06/2.0		37.25	2:30.45	
	(70)							
5762	Yelena	Ivlyeva	RUS	31.7.74	3		Sochi	18 May
	14.17/0.8 1.73	12.01	25.15	6.04/1.7		39.14	2:16.88	
5760	Marina	Goncharova	RUS-J	26.4.86	1	NC-j	Tula	3 Jul
	14.45/-0.4 1.65	12.78	25.66/0.4	6.27/1.4		42.34	2:17.13	
5760	Juana	Castillo	DOM	17.6.84	1	CAC	Nassau	11 Jul
	14.17/1.1 1.72	13.01	25.30w/2.2	5.59w/2.2		44.59	2:17.45	
5760	Jolanda	Keizer	NED	5.4.85	6	EU23	Erfurt	15 Jul
	14.40/-0.2 1.80	13.06	24.87/-0.6	5.83/1.0		40.88	2:25.75	
5754	Fiona	Harrison	GBR	30.11.81	14	ECp-S	Bydgoszcz	3 Jul
	14.11/-0.4 1.75	11.62	24.55w/2.3	5.91w/2.3		36.66	2:15.54	
5753	Kaie	Kand	EST	31.3.84	7	ECp-1	Jyväskylä	3 Jul
	14.05/1.0 1.75	11.58	25.20/1.4	6.03/0.3		34.94	2:12.10	
5744	Elisa	Trevisan	ITA	5.3.80	1	NC	Forlì	2 Oct
	13.85/0.7 1.69*	12.91	24.91/1.0	5.90/0.7		41.85	2:24.45	
5743		Dong Wangwei	CHN	28.6.81	5	NG	Nanjing	18 Oct
	14.06/0.5 1.71	12.41	25.51/-0.5	6.08/0.5		42.93	2:23.35	
5736	Olga	Karas	RUS	9.7.82	8	NC	Tula	15 Jun
	14.91/1.7 1.67	13.33	25.32/0.7	6.17/0.6		39.03	2:14.07	
5730	Jackie	Poulson	USA	22.2.81	7		Salò	8 May
	14.16/1.3 1.70	12.23	25.33/-3.3	5.84/0.9		43.94	2:18.63	
	(80)							
5718	Natalya	Kotova	RUS	13.5.83	9	NC	Tula	15 Jun
	13.99/0.0 1.79	13.64	24.79/0.3	6.11/0.4		36.44	2:36.45	
5714	Manuela	Kurrat	GER	25.12.81	4	NCAA	Sacramento	11 Jun
	14.23/1.0 1.63	13.17	25.53/-0.9	5.53/0.4		43.99	2:09.89	
5711	Tacita	Bass	USA	28.10.79	6	NC	Carson	26 Jun
	13.75w/2.3 1.69	12.31	23.97/1.0	5.80w/2.1		32.85	2:16.70	
5706	Sylvie	Dufour	SUI	24.1.79	1	NC	Payenne	7 Aug
	14.33/-1.2 1.72	13.41	25.45/1.6	5.60/1.7		40.60	2:15.51	
5705	Maike	Goldkuhle	GER	10.3.80	15	ECp-S	Bydgoszcz	3 Jul
	13.97/0.7 1.66	13.62	24.94/0.6	5.85w/3.1		37.06	2:18.81	
5695	Michaela	Hejnová	CZE	10.4.80	8	ECp-1	Jyväskylä	3 Jul
	13.91/0.9 1.66	12.36	25.64/0.8	5.80/1.3		47.62	2:23.13	
5691	Sarah	Bouaoudia	ALG	13.8.83	5	MedG	Almeria	2 Jul
	14.04/-1.8 1.85	9.12	24.85/0.3	6.18/0.5		30.84	2:14.03	
5689	Svetlana	Sokolova	RUS	9.1.81	10	NC	Tula	15 Jun
	14.38/0.0 1.73	13.73	25.27/0.2	5.83/0.2		37.69	2:20.72	
5684	Céline	Laporte	SEY	7.12.84	1	FRA-23	Saint-Cyr-sur-Loire	3 Jul
	14.07/-0.7 1.72	10.87	25.30/1.1	6.28/1.1		40.34	2: 23.26	
5682	Beata	Lukaszewska	POL	19.2.80	4	NC	Kielce	5 Jun
	14.76/0.0 1.72	14.81	26.21w/3.8	5.59/1.9		46.14	2:22.40	
	(90)							
5663	Kathrin	Geissler	GER	10.6.85	17	ECp-S	Bydgoszcz	3 Jul
	14.38/0.2 1.78	10.70	24.58/1.2	6.21/1.3		34.15	2:20.72	
5662	Olga	Zinovyeva	RUS-J	29.10.86	1-j		Sochi	18 May
	14.59/0.1 1.70	13.06	24.76	6.20/1.8		32.21	2:18.90	
5658	Yuliya	Cherey	RUS	15.11.83	12	NC	Tula	15 Jun
	13.97/0.3 1.70	11.82	24.92/0.2	5.86/0.2		33.74	2:12.96	
5657	Aleksandra	Kasitskaya	RUS	15.3.85	13	NC	Tula	15 Jun
	14.38/0.9 1.61	11.35	25.11/0.7	6.11/0.3		39.19	2:10.63	
5656	Maija	Kovalainen	FIN	23.8.81	3	v2N	Turku	29 May
	13.94/1.1 1.71	14.55	25.37/0.6	6.04/1.9		41.13	2: 40.5	
5654	LaToya	McBride	USA	15.12.82	2	SEC	Nashville	13 May
	14.30/-0.6 1.78	11.21	24.19/0.0	6.01/0.4		34.79	2:23.82	
5654	Ewa	Nowakowska	POL	20.12.81	5	NC	Kielce	5 Jun
	13.90/0.0 1.72	12.50	25.15w/3.8	5.83w/2.3		37.37	2:21.75	

Mark	Name		Nat	Born	Pos	Meet	Venue	Date
5653	Salla	Käppi	FIN	22.5.80	4	v2N	Turku	29 May
	13.82/-1.1 1.71 13.67 25.71w/2.2			5.83/1.7		42.18	2:31.0h	
5652		Fu Pengcheng	CHN	15.1.80	3	NC	Changsha	25 Jun
	14.80/1.3 1.75 12.87 24.60/0.9			5.82/0.0		41.02	2: 26.09	
5650	Julie	Pickler	USA	9.12.83	5	NCAA	Sacramento	11 Jun
	14.07/0.1 1.72 11.95 24.46/-0.9			5.86/0.9		38.11	2: 23.98	
	(100)							

5647	Emilie	Boulleret	FRA	23.5.73	15 Jul	5518	Beyonka	McDowell	USA	19.9.82	13 May
5646	Danielle	Ayers-Stamper	USA	29.3.84	26 Jun	5512	Yasmiany	Pedroso	CUB	5.8.74	19 Mar
5637	Jennifer	Oeser	GER	29.11.83	26 Jun	5509	Sanna	Saarman	FIN	14.5.81	17 Jul
5636	Annett	Wichmann	GER	4.5.84	26 Jun	5507h	Natalya	Germanyuk	BLR	30.3.75	21 Jul
5633	Jessica	Samuelsson	SWE	14.3.85	17 Jul	5504	Danielle	McNaney	USA	1.5.83	26 Apr
5629	Sara	Aerts	BEL	25.1.84	8 May	5502	Marlen	Buder	GER-J	4.2.87	5 Jun
5616	Jesenija	Volzankina	LAT	28.11.83	15 Jul	5494	Panayióta	Alexándrou	GRE	30.7.75	15 May
5615		Shi Wei	CHN	7.7.83	18 Oct	5490	Amber	Williams	USA	15.12.85	22 Apr
5611	Brooke	Meredith	USA	3.2.82	26 Jun	5486	Beata	Lewicka	POL	21.1.84	5 Jun
5610	Cecilia	Ricali	ITA	20.1.85	15 Jul	5486	Amy	Menlove	USA	23.7.85	11 Jun
5607	Marina	Brezgina	UKR	16.1.77	15 Jun	5483	Anastasiya	Arsenova	RUS-J	3.3.86	3 Jul
5605	Annelie	Schrader	GER	9.12.79	27 Jun	5480	Aléna-María	Padi	GRE	21.6.84	3 Jul
5595	Diana	Pickler	USA	9.12.83	11 Jun	5479	Melissa	Talbot	USA	23.4.84	14 May
5595		Chen Jing	CHN	16.8.84	18 Oct	5469	Sara Jane	Baker	USA	26.5.84	15 Apr
5595		Zhang Weijia	CHN	3.3.81	18 Oct	5461A	Thaimara	Rivas	VEN	23.7.82	20 Aug
5582	Linda	Züblin	SUI-J	21.3.86	7 Aug	5460	Luzia	Häberli	SUI	24.1.79	12 Jun
5578w	Rosalyn	Gonse	GBR	1.3.82	5 Jun	5448		Song Lijuan	CHN-J	2.2.87	25 Jun
5575	Ryanne	Dupree	USA	13.4.84	11 Jun	5432h	Mariya	Malashitskaya	BLR	28.5.81	21 Jul
5575	Maria	Peinado	ESP	8.2.77	2 Jul	5431	Liane	Weber	GER-J	24.2.86	27 Aug
5573	Gillian	Ragus	AUS	5.4.76	16 Jan	5429A	Elizete	da Silva	BRA	2.5.71	24 Jul
5566	Rebecca	Wardell	NZL	21.12.77	16 Aug	5419	Sushmita	Singha Roy	IND	26.3.84	2 Aug
5554	Bregje	Crolla	NED-J	31.1.86	24 Jul	5415	Ida	Marcussen	NOR-J	1.11.87	24 Jul
5542	Cheilín	Povea	CUB	6.12.85	20 May	5413	Yulia	Tarasova	UZB-J	13.3.86	30 Sep
5542	Ulrike	Hebestreit	GER	19.3.81	26 Jun	5413	Tamara	McGill	USA	11.1.83	11 Jun
5539	Zita	vári	HUN	1.5.84	18 Sep	5407	Anu	Teesaar	EST	15.2.83	3 Jul
5536	Krystal	Ward	USA	1.5.83	13 May	5405	Ana	Capdevila	ESP	5.9.81	17 Jul
5525	Louise	Hazel	GBR	6.10.85	5 Jun	5404	Marisa	De Aniceto	FRA-J	11.11.86	3 Jul
5519	Natalya	Khamidulina	RUS	26.11.81	15 Jun		(155)				

Best non wind-assisted

Mark	Name		Nat	Born	Pos	Meet	Venue	Date
5981	Diana	Koritskaya	RUS	22.2.75	3	ECp-S	Bydgoszcz	3 Jul
	14.22/-0.4 1.66 13.70 24.43w/2.3			5.83/1.4		47.80	2:14.65	
5965	Antoinette	Djimou	FRA	2.8.85	*		Arles	5 Jun
	13.43w/3.1 1.73 13.49 24.52w/3.1			5.89/1.5		44.46	2:25.23	
5870	Anzhela	Atroshchenko	TUR	14.11.70	3	MedG	Almeria	2 Jul
	14.15/-1.8 1.70 13.22 25.26/0.3			6.17/0.0		40.73	2:16.61	
5845	Svetlana	Gnezdilov	ISR	20.7.69	*		Tel Aviv	19 Jul
	13.71/0.9 1.61 12.55 24.83/0.9			6.22/0.9		34.19	2:07.34	
5775	Julie	Martin	FRA	28.10.79	*		Arles	5 Jun
	14.00w/2.5 1.82 11.33 25.08w/2.3			5.68w/3.3		43.82	2:21.41	
5465	Rosalyn	Gonse	GBR	1.3.82	23	ECp-S	Bydgoszcz	3 Jul

JUNIORS

See main list for top 6 juniors. 10 performances by 5 women over 5740. Additional marks and further juniors:

Ennis	5891	1	EJ	Kanuas	24 Jul	5827	4	Saló	8 May
Mächtig	5777	6		Ratingen	26 Jun				
Balta	5747	3	EJ	Kanuas	24 Jul				
Sergeyeva	5740	4	EJ	Kanuas	24 Jul				

Mark	Name		Nat	Born	Pos	Meet	Venue	Date
5582	Linda	Züblin	SUI	21.3.86	1	NC-j	Payerne	7 Aug
	14.05/0.0 1.57 11.64 24.97/1.1			5.73/0.2		47.74	2:21.81	
5554	Bregje	Crolla	NED	31.1.86	5	EJ	Kaunas	24 Jul
	14.75/0.1 1.67 12.06 26.67/-2.1			5.46/0.0		52.04	2:16.74	
5502	Marlen	Buder	GER	4.2.87	1		Bernhausen	5 Jun
	14.56w/2.4 1.59 12.93 25.45/1.5			5.51/0.5		47.19	2:21.84	
5483	Anastasiya	Arsenova (10)	RUS	3.3.86	3	NC-j	Tula	3 Jul
	14.65/-2.9 1.68 12.72 25.25/0.4			5.77/-0.6		35.93	2:20.04	
5448		Song Lijuan	CHN	2.2.87	7	NC	Changsha	25 Jun
	13.80/-0.9 1.72 10.84 24.83/1.1			5.96/0.6		30.34	2:25.16	
5431	Liane	Weber	GER	24.2.86	1	NC-J	Lage	27 Aug
	14.55/-0.8 1.66 11.81 25.92/0.0			5.52/-0.6		43.70	2:19.78	
5415	Ida	Marcussen	NOR	1.11.87	6	EJ	Kaunas	24 Jul
	15.15/0.1 1.64 13.26 25.91/-2.1			5.50/0.0		45.58	2:22.84	
5413	Yulia	Tarasova	UZB	13.3.86	1		Tashkent	30 Sep
	14.86 1.70 11.73 25.33			6.28		36.91	2:33.47	
5404	Marisa	De Aniceto	FRA	11.11.86	1	NC-j	Saint-Cyr-sur-Loire	3 Jul
	14.56/0.4 1.60 11.17 26.22/-0.8			5.96/1.1		42.24	2:19.07	
5389	Chinami	Yasuda	JPN	7.11.86	1		Toyama	26 Jun
	14.32/0/3 1.66 10.33 25.52/0.5			5.89/1.0		37.60	2:20.15	

Mark	Name		Nat	Born	Pos	Meet	Venue	Date
5381	Yana	Panteleyeva	RUS-Y	16.6.88	1	v2N-j	Stoke-on-Trent	31 Jul
	15.50/-0.9 1.72 10.07 25.63/1.1			5.99w/2.7		39.21	2:17.14	
5372	Irina	Ilkevych	UKR	6.3.87	1	NC-j	Kiev	15 Jun
	14.56/2.0 1.68 9.91 24.87/-0.1			5.94/1.0		32.18	2:16.66	
5333	Lauren	Stewart	USA	8.1.87	1	PAm-J	Windsor	31 Jul
	14.28/0.5 1.75 10.20 25.48/0.8			5.84w/2.2		30.44	2:21.31	
5331	Ellen	Sprunger (20)	SUI	5.8.86	2	NC-j	Payerne	7 Aug
	14.63/0.0 1.60 10.96 24.65/1.1			5.55/1.0		38.29	2:18.56	

DECATHLON

Mark	Name		Nat	Born	Pos	Meet	Venue	Date
8358	Austra	Skujyte	LTU	12.8.79	1		Columbia, MS	15 Apr
	12.49/1.6 46.19 3.10 48.78 57.19			14.22w/2.4		6.12/1.6	16.42 1.78	5:15.86

4 X 100 METRES RELAY

Mark	Nat	Team	Pos	Meet	Venue	Date
41.78	USA	Daigle, Lee, Barber, L.Williams	1	WCh	Helsinki	13 Aug
41.99	JAM	Browning, Simpson, Bailey, Campbell	2	WCh	Helsinki	13 Aug
42.16	USA	Daigle, Lee, Barber, L.Williams	1h1	WCh	Helsinki	12 Aug
42.56	BLR	Nesterenko, Sologub, Nevmerzhitskaya, Dragun	3	WCh	Helsinki	13 Aug
42.65	USA Red	Daigle, Lee, L.Williams, Colander	1	GP	Helsinki	25 Jul
42.68	USA Red	Daigle, L.Williams, I.Miller, Colander	1	PennR	Philadelphia	30 Apr
42.73	RUS	Fyodorova, Gushchina, Khabarova, Kondratyeva	1	ECp-S	Firenze	18 Jun
42.80	BLR	Nesterenko, Sologub, Nevmerzhitskaya, Dragun	1h3	WCh	Helsinki	12 Aug
42.85	FRA	Buval, Jacques-Sébastien, Dia, Arron	4	WCh	Helsinki	13 Aug
42.86	FRA	Buval, Jacques-Sébastien, Dia, Arron	1h2	WCh	Helsinki	12 Aug
42.97	USA Blue	R Smith, V.Powell, L.Moore, M.Robinson	2	GP	Helsinki	25 Jul
42.97	JAM	Browning, Simpson, McDonald, Bailey	2h2	WCh	Helsinki	12 Aug
42.99	BRA	da Costa, de Moura, Ignâcio, L.dos Santos	5	WCh	Helsinki	13 Aug
43.00		University of South Carolina, USA	2	NCAA	Sacramento	10 Jun
		Ross-Williams, Whipple, Joyce, Solomon				
43.03	COL	M.Murillo, Palacios, Obregón, N.González	3h2	WCh	Helsinki	12 Aug
43.07	COL	M.Murillo, Palacios, Obregón, N.González	6	WCh	Helsinki	13 Aug
43.15	USA Blue	A.Williams, Felix, Durst, Lee	2	PennR	Philadelphia	30 Apr
43.17A	COL	M.Murillo, Palacios, Obregón, N.González	1	SACh	Cali	23 Jul
		18 performances by teams from 7 nations				
43.25	NGR	Kemasuode, Ojokolo, Osayomi, Nku	7	WCh	Helsinki	13 Aug
43.37	POL	Dorobisz, Onysko, Dydo, Brzezinska	2h3	WCh	Helsinki	12 Aug
43.40	BEL	De Caluwe, Callaerts, Ouédraogo, Gevaert	3h3	WCh	Helsinki	12 Aug
	(10)					
43.48	BAH	Clarke, Arnette-Willie, Fynes, Sturrup	2	CAC	Nassau	10 Jul
43.58	GER	Wakan, Möller, B.Rockmeier, Sailer	2	ECp-S	Firenze	18 Jun
43.61	SWE	Rienas, Klüft, J.Kallur, S.Kallur	1	v FIN	Göteborg	27 Aug
43.62	UKR		4h3	WCh	Helsinki	12 Aug
		Kozhemyakina, Shtangyeyeva, Shepetyuk, Pastushenko-Sinyavina				
43.83	ITA	Sordelli, Calì, Grillo, Levorato	3	ECp-S	Firenze	18 Jun
43.83	GBR	Freeman, Ania, Turner, Endacott	4h1	WCh	Helsinki	12 Aug
44.00	NED	van Assendelft, Poelman, Kramer, Baarssen	1		Leiden	11 Jun
44.02	CHN (Guangxi)	Huang N, Yan J, Huang M, Han L	1h1	NG	Nanjing	19 Oct
44.11	GRE	Kobidou, Koklóni, Kopsiá, Karastamáti	5	ECp-S	Firenze	18 Jun
44.18	THA	Jaksunin, Klomdee, Thavoncharoen, Saenrat	1	AsiC	Inchon	4 Sep
	(20)					
44.33	ESP	Blay, Recio, Sanz, Alozie	1		Guadalajara	15 Jun
44.33	FIN	Ranta, Salivaara, Keskitalo, Hannula	3	GP	Helsinki	25 Jul
44.35	ROM	Tudorache, Morosanu, Lisenco, Tigau	7	ECp-S	Firenze	18 Jun
44.51	CAN	Mensah, Dortch, George, Muir	1	Jerome	Burnaby	14 Jun
44.52	JPN	Ishida, Suzuki, Sato, Nobuoka	5h3	WCh	Helsinki	12 Aug
44.58	CUB	Bience, Díaz, Lazo, Benavides	1	GP II	Fort-de-France	30 Apr
44.68	IRL	O'Rourke, Boyle, McSweeney, Sheehy	5	ECp1B	Leiria	18 Jun
44.76	TRI-J		2	Carifta	Bacolet	27 Mar
45.05	HUN	Szakács, Listár, Rózsa, Petráhn	3	ECp1A	Gävle	18 Jun
	(30)					

45.11	VIE	29 Nov	45.24	SLO	18 Jun	45.37A	CHI	23 Jul	45.45	PUR	16 Apr	45.65	TUR	18 Jun
45.12	DOM	10 Jul	45.34	CZE	2 Jul	45.40	CYP	4 Jun	45.46	LTU	18 Jun	45.75	EST	18 Jun
45.17	SUI	18 Jun	45.36	CIV	13 Dec	45.41	GRN-J	27 Mar	45.56	BUL	18 Jun	45.75	NOR	18 Jun
						45.42	RSA	16 Apr	45.58	AUT	18 Jun	45.85	POR	18 Jun

Mixed nationality teams

Mark	Team	Pos	Meet	Venue	Date
42.87	University of Texas, USA/JAM	1	NCAA	Sacramento	10 Jun
	A.Williams, M.Walker JAM, Chapple, Hooker				
43.11	Tiger Olympians ??	1		Baton Rouge	26 Mar
43.18	University of Tennessee, USA/CAN	3	NCAA	Sacramento	12 Aug
	Madison, Champion, Olupona CAN, Tyson				

JUNIORS

Mark	Nat	Team	Pos	Meet	Venue	Date
43.97	USA	Nesbitt, Anderson, Davis, Tyson	1	PAm-J	Windsor	31 Jul
44.25	JAM		1		Kingston	19 Mar
44.43	GER	Börner, Heinrich, Dix, Gangnus	1	NC	Wattenscheid	2 Jul
44.65	POL	Ceglarek, Popowicz, Jeschke, Brzezinska	1	EJ	Kaunas	24 Jul
44.70	RUS	Mekhri-Zade, Dashina, Kashina, Chernoshanskaya	2	EJ	Kaunas	24 Jul
44.72	ITA	Pacini, Salvagno, Arcioni, Borsi	1h1	EJ	Kaunas	24 Jul
44.76	TRI	Francis, Hackett, Cabral, Baptiste	2	Carifta	Bacolet	27 Mar
44.79	FRA	Monne, Banco, Behi, Distel	3	EJ	Kaunas	24 Jul
44.94	GBR	Hopeson, Duck, Sargent, Gibbons	2h1	EJ	Kaunas	24 Jul
45.25	BRA	Ferraz, Valentim, Venáncio, Krasucki	1	SAm-j	Rosario	1 Oct
45.41	GRN	Francis, Mitchell, George, Fletcher	3	Carifta	Bacolet	27 Mar
45.47	LTU	Valetova, Andrijauskaite, Tamosaityte, Grincikaite	6	EJ	Kaunas	24 Jul
45.59	CZE	Mazácová, Dostálová, Hrivnová, Šcerbová	2		Kladno	2 Jul
45.73	ESP	García, Riba, San MartínGarrantxo	2		Guadalajara	15 Jun
45.89	BAH		4	Carifta	Bacolet	27 Mar

4 X 200 METRES RELAY

Mark	Team	Pos	Meet	Venue	Date
1:31.57	University of South Carolina, USA	1	PennR	Philadelphia	30 Apr
	Smith, Whipple, Carpenter, Solomon				

4 X 400 METRES RELAY

Mark	Nat	Team	Pos	Meet	Venue	Date
3:20.32	RUS	Krasnomovets 50.1, Antyukh 49.4, Fireva, 50.09, Zykina 50.78	1h1	WCh	Helsinki	13 Aug
3:20.95	RUS		1	WCh	Helsinki	14 Aug
		Pechonkina 51.3, Krasnomovets 49.5, Antyukh 49.72, Pospelova 50.42				
3:22.93	USA Red	Trotter 52.4, Demus 50.1, Richards 49.9, Hennagan 50.5	1	PennR	Philadelphia	30 Apr
3:23.29	JAM	S.Williams 51.38, N.Williams 49.92, R.Smith 51.57, Fenton 50.42	2	WCh	Helsinki	14 Aug
3:23.56	RUS	Gushchina 51.4, Levina 51.5, Lisnichenko 50.85, Antyukh 49.85	1	ECp-S	Firenze	19 Jun
3:24.44	GBR	McConnell 51.4, Fraser 51.0, Sanders 50.80, Ohuruogu 51.27	3	WCh	Helsinki	14 Aug
3:24.49	POL	Guzowska 52.2, Bejnar 50.2, Prokopek 50.47, Jesien 51.59	4	WCh	Helsinki	14 Aug
3:24.61	POL	Radecka 52.0, Bejnar 51.2, Prokopek 50.90, Jesien 50.50	2	ECp-S	Firenze	19 Jun
3:25.64	RUS	Pospelova 52.2, Pechonkina 51.0, Kotlyarova 50.9, Zykina 51.5	2	PennR	Philadelphia	30 Apr
3:26.04	POL	Guzowska 52.6, Bejnar 50.6, Prokopek 51.02, Radecka 51.80	2h1	WCh	Helsinki	13 Aug
3:26.19	GBR	McConnell 51.3, Fraser 51.9, Sanders 51.38, Ohuruogu 51.56	1h2	WCh	Helsinki	13 Aug
3:26.72	UKR	Yefremova 52.4, Ilyushkina 51.6, Pilyugina 51.21, Pigida 51.48	3	ECp-S	Firenze	19 Jun
3:26.82	BRA	Almirão 52.3, Coutinho 52.1, Tito 51.56, Teodoro 50.82	2h2	WCh	Helsinki	13 Aug
3:27.03	GBR	Ohuruogu, Wall, Fraser, McConnell	1	ECp1B	Leiria	19 Jun
3:27.22		University of South Carolina, USA	2	NCAA	Sacramento	11 Jun
		Stoddart 53.4, Hastings 51.4, Ross-Williams 52.1, S.Smith 50.3				
3:27.23	UKR	Yefremova 52.6, Ilyushkina 52.4, Pilyugina 50.95, Pigida 51.44	3h2	WCh	Helsinki	13 Aug
3:27.27	RUS-23	Ovchinnikova, Kochetova, Migunov, Zaytseva	1	EU23	Erfurt	17 Jul
		17 performances by teams from 7 nations				
3:27.65	BLR	Sologub 51.9, Zhalneryuk 54.0, Kozak 51.73, I.Usovich 50.02	3h1	WCh	Helsinki	13 Aug
3:27.78	ROM	Morosanu 51.9, Neacsu 52.8, Rîpanu 52.52, Manolache 50.61	4	ECp-S	Firenze	19 Jun
3:27.92	GER	Urbansky 53.7, Hoffmann 50.8, Fink 52.31, Marx 51.08	5	ECp-S	Firenze	19 Jun
	(10)					
3:28.92	FRA	Anacharsis 52.3, Grouselle 52.2, Morandais 52.63, Désert 51.77	6	ECp-S	Firenze	19 Jun
3:29.03	SEN	Diop 53.8, Fall 51.0, Diouf 53.72, Thiam 50.51	5h1	WCh	Helsinki	13 Aug
3:30.51	CHN	(Guangdong) Zhong S, Yang Y, Gao L, Tang X	1	NG	Nanjing	22 Oct
3:30.93	IND	Kaur Gill, Geetha , Soman, M.Kaur	1	AsiC	Inchon	4 Sep
3:31.28	SWE	Björkman, Klüft, Stuhrmann, Aruhn	1	ECp1A	Gävle	19 Jun
3:31.36	CUB	Calatayud, Grenot, Peña, Terrero	1	Barr	La Habana	20 May
3:31.41	MEX	Grajeda 54.3, Medina 52.8, González 52.01, Yañez 52.32	5h2	WCh	Helsinki	13 Aug
3:31.45	ESP	Alba, Recio, Olivero, Martínez	1	MedG	Almeria	2 Jul
3:31.71	RSA	A Kotze 53.9, Koster 53.4, Febbriao 52.45, Wittstock 51.92	6h2	WCh	Helsinki	13 Aug
3:32.61	KAZ	Gavrushenko, Alimzhanova, Roslanova, Tereshkova	2	AsiC	Inchon	4 Sep
	(20)					
3:33.14	BAH	Rolle, Amertil, Henfield, Williams-Darling	2	CAC	Nassau	11 Jul
3:33.17	ITA	Graglia 54.50, Ceccarelli 52.46, Niederstätter 53.06, De Angeli 53.15	7	ECp-S	Firenze	19 Jun
3:33.54	JPN	Kubokura, Tanno, Kida, Yoshida	3	AsiC	Inchon	4 Sep
3:34.38	BUL	Gachevska, Dimitrova, Nedkova, Ivanova	2	ECp1B	Leiria	19 Jun
3:35.25A	COL	García, Idrovo, Palacios, González	1	Bolivar	Armenia	21 Aug
3:35.55	TRI	Charles, Toussaint, Cabral, Lucas	4	CAC	Nassau	11 Jul
3:35.68	MYA	Yin Yin Khine, Myint Myint Aye, Lai Lai Win, Kay Khine Lwin	1	SEAG	Manila	30 Nov
3:35.60	GRE	Pahatouridou 55.4, Filándra 53.5, Hantzi 54.05, Dóva 52.61	8	ECp-S	Firenze	19 Jun
3:35.97	HUN	Rózsa, Bobcsek, B Varga, Petráhn	3	ECp1A	Gävle	19 Jun
3:35.98	FIN	Bosco, Myllymäki, Jarvenpää, Mykkänen	1	v SWE	Göteborg	28 Aug
	(30)					

Mark	Nat	Date	Mark	Nat	Date	Mark	Nat	Date	Mark	Nat	Date	Mark	Nat	Date
3:36.10	IRL	20 Aug	3:36.57	NED	19 Jun	3:37.45	CZE	19 Jun	3:38.9 A	SUD	? 5 May	3:40.49A	CHI	24 Jul
3:36.28	BEL	19 Jun	3:36.82	LAT	19 Jun	3:37.47	SUI	19 Jun	3:39.49	THA	30 Nov	3:40.59	VEN	24 Jun
3:36.30	LTU	19 Aug	3:37.31	CAN	30 Apr	3:38.63	CRO	19 Jun	3:39.53	EST	19 Jun	3:41.15	NGR	9 Jul
3:36.49	TUR	19 Jun	3:37.43	POR	19 Jun	3:38.8A	KEN	18 Jun	3:40.03	NOR	19 Jun	3:41.7A	ETH	?5 May

Mark	Nat	Date	Mark	Nat	Date	Mark	Nat	Date	Mark	Nat	Date	Mark	Nat	Date
3:42.05	SVK	19 Jun	3:42.48	MAR	16 Dec	3:43.16	SLO	19 Jun	3:43.97	PUR	16 Apr	3:44.50	DEN	19 Jun
3:42.4	VIE-J	8 Jul	3:42.60	SRI	4 Sep	3:43.20	DOM	11 Jul	3:44.0	AUS	15 Jan			

Team of mixed nationality

Mark	Name	Pos	Meet	Venue	Date
3:27.13	University of Texas, USA/JAM	1	NCAA	Sacramento	11 Jun
	S.Jones 53.5, M.Walker/JAM 51.5, Kerr 51.0, Chapple 51.1				

JUNIORS

Mark	Nat	Name	Pos	Meet	Venue	Date
3:32.63	RUS	Kuznetsova, Zadorina, Shlyapnikova, Kostetskaya	1	EJ	Kaunas	24 Jul
3:32.82	USA	Leach, Lawrence, Jones, Hastings	1	PAm-J	Windsor	31 Jul
3:36.33	JAM		1		Kingston	7 May
3:36.63	GER	Ullmann, Meyer, Müller-Foell, Lindenberg	2	EJ	Kaunas	24 Jul
3:36.64	UKR	Peycheva, Shevchenko, Lupu, Karandyuk	3	EJ	Kaunas	24 Jul
3:37.12	POL	Jurowska, Pura, Młynarczyk, Tomza	4	EJ	Kaunas	24 Jul
3:37.37	GBR	Nicol, Flower, Kodilinye-Sims, Finucane	5	EJ	Kaunas	24 Jul
3:39.77	SWE	Martin, Björkman, Holmroos, Persson	6	EJ	Kaunas	24 Jul
3:40.23	FRA	Soumaré, Moh, Sountoura, Lacordelle	4h2	EJ	Kaunas	23 Jul
3:40.24	SUD	Omer, Jaber, Musa, El-Jak	1	Afr-J	Radès	4 Sep
		unconfirmed 3:38.9A Omar, El-Jak, Musa, Adam	1		Addis Ababa	? ?
3:40.61	ROM	Banyai, Banut, Ionit , Moro anu	3h1	EJ	Kaunas	23 Jul
3:41.29	CAN	Lewis, Campbell-Fell, Omoye, Muir	3	PAm-J	Windsor	31 Jul
3:41.91	NED	Wijnker, Krommendijk, Mulder, R.Boddy			Leiden	11 Jun
3:42.15	ITA	Milani, Anello, Apollo, Spacca	4h1	EJ	Kaunas	23 Jul
3:42.20	CUB	Videaux, Isaac, Valazco, Clement	2		La Habana	24 Jun
3:42.4	VIE	Ng.Thi Tham, Ngu Thi Bac, Duong Thi Hien, Le Thi Hong Anh	1		Ho-Chi-Minh	8 Jul

4 X 100 METRES HURDLES

Mark	Name	Pos	Meet	Venue	Date
53.19	University of South Carolina, USA	1	PennR	Philadelphia	29 Apr
	Martin, Alexander, Stoddart JAM, Ross-Williams				
53.70	Georgia Tech University USA Moss, Fofanah, Lapsley, Howard	2	PennR	Philadelphia	29 Apr

3000 METRES WALK

Mark		Name	Nat	Born	Pos	Meet	Venue	Date
12:10.31		Chen Zhuo	CHN-J		1		Zhengzhou	28 Aug
12:11.70		Yu Miao	CHN-J		2		Zhengzhou	28 Aug
12:18.18		Liu Hong	CHN-J	12.5.87	3		Zhengzhou	28 Aug
12:22.2+	Irina	Petrova	RUS	26.5.85	1	in 5k	Saransk	19 Jun
12:23.5+	Olga	Kaniskina	RUS	19.1.85	2	in 5k	Saransk	19 Jun
12:24.0+	Tatyana	Korotkova	RUS	24.4.80	3	in 5k	Saransk	19 Jun
12:24.70		Zhai Lijuan	CHN-J	28.11.86	4		Zhengzhou	28 Aug
12:25.5+	Iraida	Pudovkina	RUS	2.11.80	4	in 5k	Saransk	19 Jun
12:28.5+	Raisa	Shiviryova	RUS	31.8.78	5	in 5k	Saransk	19 Jun
12:30.1	Jolanta	Dukure	LAT	20.9.79	1		Murjani	15 Jun
12:34.5+	Lyudmila	Arkhipova	RUS	12.9.78	6	in 5k	Saransk	19 Jun
12:34.71	Gillian	O'Sullivan	IRL	21.8.76	1		Ringsend	22 May

Mark		Name	Nat	Born	Date	Mark		Name	Nat	Born	Date
12:36.0+	Yevdokiya	Korotkova	RUS	28.2.79	19 Jun	12:40.2	Elmira	Alembekova	RUS-J	30.6.90	19 Jun
12:38.0+	Vera	Sokolova	RUS-J	8.6.87	19 Jun	12:41.1	Aleksandra	Kudryashova	RUS-J	18.7.90	19 Jun
12:390+	Larisa	Yemelyanova	RUS	6.1.80	19 Jun	12:42.80	Ana	Cabecinha	POR	29.4.84	10 Jun
12:39.28	Sonata	Milusauskaite	LTU	31.8.73	10 Jun	12:45.0+	Oksana	Kirillova	RUS-Y	18.7.88	19 Jun
						12:45.05	Fatiha	Ouali	FRA	58.10.74	21 Jul

Indoors

Mark		Name	Nat	Born	Pos	Meet	Venue	Date
12:04.86	Sabine	Zimmer	GER	6.2.81	1	NC	Sindelfingen	19 Feb
12:09.57	Elisa	Rigaudo	ITA	17.6.80	1	NC	Ancona	19 Feb
12:27.16	Melanie	Seeger	GER	8.1.77	2	NC	Sindelfingen	19 Feb

Mark		Name	Nat	Born	Date	Mark		Name	Nat	Born	Date
12:37.8	Sylwia	Korzeniowska	POL	25.4.80	30 Jan	12:40.88	Cristiana	Pellino	ITA	21.9.70	19 Feb

JUNIORS

See main list for top 4 juniors plus:

Mark		Name	Nat	Born	Pos	Meet	Venue	Date
12:38.0+	Vera	Sokolova	RUS	8.6.87	8	in 5k	Saransk	19 Jun
12:40.2	Elmira	Alembekova	RUS	30.6.90	1		Saransk	19 Jun
12:41.1	Aleksandra	Kudryashova	RUS	18.7.90	2		Saransk	19 Jun
12:45.0+	Oksana	Kirillova	RUS-Y	18.7.88	10	in 5k	Saransk	19 Jun
12:47.93		Han Jie	CHN	21.12.87	5		Zhengzhou	28 Aug
12:48.4	Tanya	Holliday	AUS-Y	21.9.88	1		Adelaide	19 Nov

5000 METRES WALK

Mark		Name	Nat	Born	Pos	Meet	Venue	Date
20:11.45	Sabine	Zimmer	GER	6.2.81	1	NC	Wattenscheid	2 Jul
20:36.2	Irina	Petrova	RUS	26.5.85	1		Saransk	19 Jun
20:38.2	Olga	Kaniskina	RUS	19.1.85	2		Saransk	19 Jun
20:40.3	Tatyana	Korotkova	RUS	24.4.80	3		Saransk	19 Jun
20:42.9	Iraida	Pudovkina	RUS	2.11.80	4		Saransk	19 Jun
20:48.3	Natalya	Shiviryova	RUS	31.8.78	5		Saransk	19 Jun
20:58.8	Lyudmila	Arkhipova	RUS	12.9.78	6		Saransk	19 Jun
21:00.9	Yevdokiya	Korotkova	RUS	28.2.79	7		Saransk	19 Jun

Mark	Name		Nat	Born	Pos	Meet	Venue	Date
21:05.7	Vera	Sokolova	RUS-J	8.6.87	8		Saransk	19 Jun
21:06.1	Larisa	Yemelyanova	RUS	6.1.80	9		Saransk	19 Jun
21:10.85		Chen Zhuo	CHN-J		1		Zhengzhou	30 Aug
21:15.9	Oksana	Kirillova	RUS-Y	18.7.88	10		Saransk	19 Jun
21:18.05		Yu Miao	CHN-J		2		Zhengzhou	30 Aug
21:21.14		Zhai Lijuan	CHN-J	28.11.86	3		Zhengzhou	30 Aug
21:25.44	Susana	Feitor	POR	28.1.75	1		Rio Maior	16 Jul
21:30.03		Liu Hong	CHN-J	12.5.87	4		Zhengzhou	28 Aug
21:35.47	María	Vasco	ESP	26.12.75	1		Barcelona	3 Jun
21:37.05	Zuzana	Maliková	SVK	2.8.83	1		Banská Bystrica	7 May
21:37.89	Maria	Gáliková	SVK	21.8.80	2		Banská Bystrica	7 May

Mark	Name		Nat	Born	Date	Mark	Name		Nat	Born	Date
21:49.1	Anisya	Kornikova	RUS-J	23.10.89	19 Jun	21:53.8	Vera	Santos	POR	3.12.81	12 Mar
21:49.8	Natalya	Kolotukhina	RUS	12.6.83	19 Jun	21:55.5	Yekaterina	Yezhova	RUS	18.2.82	19 Jun
21:50.0	Aleksandra	Kudryashova	RUS-Y	18.7.90	12 Mar	21:55.73	Gisella	Orsini	ITA	9.12.71	11 Jun
21:52.56	Olive	Loughnane	IRL	14.1.76	23 Jul	21:58.0	Jolanta	Dukure	LAT	20.9.79	16 Apr

Indoors

Mark	Name		Nat	Born	Pos	Venue	Date
20:37.77	Margarita	Turova	BLR	28.12.80	1	Minsk	13 Feb
21:26.7	Alena	Zenkova	RUS	1.1.82	1	Chelyabinsk	6 Jan
21:37.54	Larisa	Khmelnitskaya	BLR	23.9.71	2	Minsk	13 Feb

Mark	Name		Nat	Born	Date	Mark	Name		Nat	Born	Date
21:55.0	Yelena	Ladanova	RUS-J	17.11.87	30 Dec	21:57.3	Svetlana	Vasilyeva	RUS	17.8.85	23 Jan

JUNIORS

See main list for top 6 juniors. 10 performances by 10 women over 21:50.00. Additional marks and further juniors:

Sokolova 21:22.92+1 in 10k Kaunas 21 Jul 21:30.1i 2 Chelyabinsk 6 Jan

Kirillova 21:41.8 1j Saransk 19 Jun

Mark	Name		Nat	Born	Pos	Meet	Venue	Date
21:49.1	Anisya	Kornikova	RUS	23.10.89	2rB		Saransk	19 Jun
21:50.0	Aleksandra	Kudryashova	RUS-Y	18.7.90	1	NC-wy	Adler	12 Mar
22:05.0	Yelena	Alembekova	RUS-Y	30.6.90	2	NC-wy	Adler	12 Mar
22:06.65		Hie Jingjing	CHN-Y	1.3.88	5		Zhengzhou	30 Aug
22:07.0	Yelena	Kostromitina	RUS-Y	30.10.89	3	NC-wy	Adler	12 Mar
22:07.5mx	Tanya	Holliday	AUS-Y	21.9.88	1		Adelaide	26 Nov

10 KILOMETRES WALK

Mark	Name		Nat	Born	Pos	Meet	Venue	Date
42:05+	Margarita	Turova	BLR	28.12.80	1+	in 20k	Adler	12 Mar
42:19+	Iraida	Pudovkina	RUS	2.11.80	2	in 20k	Adler	12 Mar
42:27		Turova			1		Kraków	17 Sep
42:53	Yelena	Ginko	BLR	30.7.76	2		Kraków	17 Sep
42:54+	Olimpiada	Ivanova	RUS	26.8.70	1	in 20k	Helsinki	7 Aug
43:09		Turova			1		Nesvizh	16 Apr
43:11.34t	Vera	Sokolova	RUS-J	8.6.87	1	EJ	Kaunas	21 Jul
43:16	Olga	Kaniskina	RUS	19.1.85	1=	in 20k	Saransk	11 Jun
43:16+	Irina	Petrova	RUS	26.5.85	1=	in 20k	Saransk	11 Jun
43:17	Sabine	Zimmer	GER	6.2.81	1		Naumburg	11 May
43:25+		Ivanova			1	in 20k	Miskolc	21 May
43:26	Elisa	Rigaudo	ITA	17.6.80	1		Lloret de Mar	10 Apr
43:26.39t	Ana-Maria	Groza (10)	ROM	1.6.76	1	NC-w	Bucuresti	20 Mar
43:37		Ginko			2		Nesvizh	16 Apr
43:40+		Turova			1	in 20k	Rio Maior	2 Apr
43:42	Lyudmila	Yefimkina	RUS	22.8.81	3		Kraków	17 Sep
43:51	Rossella	Giordano	ITA	1.12.72	2		Lloret de Mar	10 Apr
43:56+	Lyudmila	Arkhipova	RUS	12.9.78	3	in 20k	Adler	12 Mar
43:56	Valentina	Tsybulskaya	BLR	19.2.68	3		Nesvizh	16 Apr
43:59	María	Vasco	ESP	26.12.75	3		Lloret de Mar	10 Apr
43:59+		Turova			2=	in 20k	Helsinki	7 Aug
43:59+		Song Hongjuan	CHN	4.7.84	2=	in 20k	Helsinki	7 Aug
	(22/16)							
44:04+	Cristina	López	ESA	19.9.82	4	in 20k	Helsinki	7 Aug
44:05+	Athanasía	Tsoumeléka	GRE	2.1.82	5	in 20k	Helsinki	7 Aug
44:08.9t		Qin Aihua	CHN-Y	22.9.88	1		Nanjing	26 Feb
44:12+	Athína	Papayiánni	GRE	18.8.80	8	in 20k	Helsinki	7 Aug
	(20)							
44:18+	Tatyana	Kozlova	RUS	2.9.83	4=	in 20k	Adler	12 Mar
44:18+	Raisa	Shiviryova	RUS	31.8.78	4=	in 20k	Adler	12 Mar
44:18+	Irina	Stankina	RUS	25.3.77	4=	in 20k	Adler	12 Mar
44:18+	Yuliya	Voyevodina	RUS	17.10.71	4=	in 20k	Adler	12 Mar
44:18+	Larisa	Yemelyanova	RUS	6.1.80	4=	in 20k	Adler	12 Mar
44:19+	Tatyana	Gudkova	RUS	23.12.78	4	in 20k	Saransk	11 Jun
44:23+	Tatyana	Korotkova	RUS	24.4.80	5	in 20k	Saransk	11 Jun
44:25+	Susana	Feitor	POR	28.1.75	10	in 20k	Helsinki	7 Aug
44:25.36t	Ana	Cabecinha	POR	29.4.84	1	NC	Lisboa	23 Jul
44:27+	Alena	Zenkova	RUS	1.1.82	9	in 20k	Adler	12 Mar

Mark		Name	Nat	Born	Pos	Meet	Venue	Date
	(30)							
44:29	Veronica	Budileanu	ROM	27.2.76	2	NC	Alba Iulia	4 Sep
44:31+	Melanie	Seeger	GER	8.1.77	12	in 20k	Helsinki	7 Aug
44:36	Tatyana	Kalmykova	RUS-Y	10.1.90	2	NC-w-j	Adler	12 Mar
44:41+	Tatyana	Sibilyeva	RUS	17.5.80	9	in 20k	Saransk	11 Jun
44:41	Zuzana	Maliková	CZE	2.8.83	4		Kraków	17 Sep
44:43+	Claudia	Stef	ROM	25.2.78	5+	ECp	Miskolc	21 May
44:50+	Barbora	Dibelková	CZE	26.5.83	14	in 20k	Helsinki	7 Aug
44:53+	Yevdokiya	Korotkova	RUS	28.2.79	10	in 20k	Saransk	11 Jun
44:58	Jane	Saville	AUS	5.11.74	16	in 20k	Helsinki	7 Aug
45:00.1t	Yelena	Ladanova	RUS	17.11.87	1	NC-j	Saransk	11 Jun
	(40)							
45:02	Norica	Cîmpean	ROM	22.3.72	3		Alba Iulia	4 Sep
45:05+	Vera	Santos	POR	3.12.81	3=+		Rio Maior	2 Apr
45:05+		Wang Liping	CHN	8.7.76	3=+		Rio Maior	2 Apr
45:06+	Svetlana	Tolstaya	KAZ	9.8.71	+	RUS-w	Adler	12 Mar
45:06.16 t	Inês	Henriques	POR	1.5.80	2	NC	Lisboa	23 Jul
45:07+	Mayumi	Kawasaki	JPN	10.5.80	1	in 20k	Kobe	30 Jan
45:07+	Irina	Balakley	RUS	6.10.81	1	in 20k	Izhevsk	17 Aug
45:08+		Jiang Jing	CHN	23.10.85	2=+		Dudince	26 Mar
45:08+		Bai Yanmin	CHN-J	29.6.87	2=+		Dudince	26 Mar
45:17	Maria	Gáliková	SVK	21.8.80	1		Borsky Mikulás	11 Jun
	(50)							
45:19	Rocio	Florido	ESP	16.1.76	1		Almeria	13 Feb
45:19	Beatriz	Pascual	ESP	9.5.82	1		Santa Eulalia del Rio	19 Mar
45:20+	Yekaterina	Yezhova	RUS	18.2.82	+		Chelyabinsk	28 Jul
45:21	Sonata	Milusauskaite	LTU	31.8.73	1		Olhâo	23 Apr
45:21+	Kristina	Saltanovic	LTU	20.2.75	19	in 20k	Helsinki	7 Aug
45:22	Geovana	Irusta	BOL	26.9.75	21=	in 20k	Helsinki	7 Aug
45:22+	Maite	Gargallo	ESP	15.10.69	21=	in 20k	Helsinki	7 Aug
45:23+	Sachiko	Konishi	JPN	4.2.82	2	in 20k	Kobe	30 Jan
45:23	Aleksandra	Kubasova	RUS-J	19.8.86	3	NC-w-j	Adler	12 Mar
45:24.12t	Maribel	Gonçalves	POR	1.4.78	3	NC	Lisboa (U)	23 Jul
	(60)							
45:25+	Olive	Loughnane	IRL	14.1.76	23	in 20k	Helsinki	7 Aug
45:26+	Marina	Smyslova	RUS	20.2.66	11	in 20k	Saransk	11 Jun
45:27+	Gisella	Orsini	ITA	9.12.71	8	ECp	Miskolc	21 May
45:28+	Natalya	Misyulya	BLR	16.4.66	10	ECp	Miskolc	21 May
45:29+	Daniela	Cîrlan	ROM	18.9.80	4+		La Coruña	4 Jun
45:31.49t	Olga	Mikhailova	RUS-J	7.12.86	2	EC-j	Kaunas	21 Jul
45:32+	Miriam	Ramón	ECU	10.2.73	2+	PAmCp	Lima	7 May
45:41+	Maria José	Poves	ESP	16.3.78	1	NC	El Prat de Llobregat	27 Feb
45:41		Pang Yingting	CHN-J	28.1.87	1		Gyeonggi-Do	11 Jun
45:42	Jolanta	Dukure	LAT	20.9.79	1		Druskininkai	3 Sep
	(70)							
45:47	Tatyana	Shemyakina	RUS-J	3.9.87	1		Chelyabinsk	6 Sep
45:53+	Svetlana	Vasilyeva	RUS	17.8.85	6	in 20k	Chelyabinsk	6 Sep
45:56	Teresa	Vaill	USA	20.11.62	1		Ocean Township	11 Sep
45:57+	Ryoko	Sakakura	JPN	9.5.76	1	in 20k	Wajima	17 Apr
45:58+	Galina	Kolpakova	RUS	14.6.83	14	in 20k	Saransk	11 Jun
45:58.1t	Irina	Yezhova	RUS-J	25.6.86	3	NC-j	Saransk	11 Jun

Mark		Name	Nat	Born	Date
46:03+	Tatyana	Metlevskaya	BLR	14.9.84	12 Mar
46:03+	Svetlana	Bogdanova	RUS-J	6.11.86	12 Mar
46:03.10tmx	Cheryl	Webb	AUS	3.10.76	19 Feb
46:04.0+t	Yekaterina	Yezhova	RUS	3.7.82	17 Sep
46:04+	Graciela	Mendoza	MEX	23.3.63	7 May
46:05	Alexandra	Kudryashova	RUS-Y	18.7.90	13 Mar
46:07	Sumiko	Suzuki	JPN-J	10.3.86	13 Mar
46:10.54t		Kim Mi-jung	KOR	10.6.79	7 Apr
46:10.99tmx	Natalie	Saville	AUS	7.9.78	12 Feb
46:12+	Vera	Zozulya	UKR	31.8.70	26 Mar
46:12.4 t	Oksana	Kirillova	RUS-Y	18.7.88	17 Sep
46:13	Yelena	Shumkina	RUS-Y	24.1.88	13 Mar
46:17	Yekaterina	Popova	RUS-J	10.12.87	13 Mar
46:19.20	Nadezhda	Prokopuk	UKR	25.2.81	7 May
46:20+	Svetlana	Trifonova	RUS	24.3.82	12 Mar
46:21	Simone	Wolowiec	AUS	12.2.74	17 Jul
46:22.20t	María	Hatzipanayiotídou	GRE	17.1.82	7 May
46:23	Snezhana	Yurchenko	BLR	8.3.84	16 Oct
46:25.91t	Chihiro	Fukunaka	JPN-J	7.1.86	26 Oct
46:34	Anastasia	Yatsevich	BLR	18.1.85	16 Oct
46:37	Yelena	Rusak	BLR-J	16.5.86	21 May
46:38	Teresa	Linares	ESP	29.4.69	6 Feb
46:38.53t	Martina	Gabrielli	ITA-J	15.2.86	21 Jul
46:44	Fatiha	Ouali	FRA	25.10.74	25 Sep

133m short: 44:49 Jolanta Dukure LAT 20.9.79 1 Valmiera 7 Feb

Best track times

Mark	Name	Pos	Meet	Venue	Date
45:09.3	Sibilyeva	1		Ankara	6 Feb
45:16.67	Vasco	1	NC	Málaga	24 Jul
45:26.94	Florido	2	NC	Málaga	24 Jul
45:27.25	mxJ Saville	1		Adelaide	19 Feb
45:34.30	Santos	4	NC	Lisboa (U)	23 Jul
45:47.10	Cîrlan	2		Bucuresti	19 Mar
45:52.32	C López	1	CAC	Nassau	10 Jul
45:56.34	Kalmykova	2		Tula	25 Jun

Mark	Name	Date
46:04.0+	Smyslova	17 Sep
46:04.0+	Y Yezhova	17 Sep
46:10.0+	Yemelyanova	17 Sep
46:10.0+	Shiviryeva	17 Sep
46:19.05	Kawasaki	26 Oct
46:22.06	Konishi	26 Oct
46:29.0+	N Kozlova	17 Sep
46:31.32	Gargallo	24 Jul

Mark		Name	Nat	Born	Pos	Meet	Venue	Date

46:33.76 Milusauskaite 23 Jul | 46:35.0+ Arkhipova 17 Sep | 46:38.2 Shemyakina 11 Jun

Indoors
46:10.7 Yurchenko 28 Jan

JUNIORS

See main list for top 9 juniors. 12 performances by 8 women to 45:50. Additional mark and further juniors:

Sokolova 44:09 1 ECp-J Miskolc 21 May | 45:31.91t 1 Tula 26 Jun
44:25 1 NC-wj Adler 13 Mar
Kalmykova 45:02 2 ECp-J Miskolc 21 May

Mark		Name	Nat	Born	Pos	Meet	Venue	Date
46:03+	Svetlana	Bogdanova (10)	RUS-J	6.11.86	17=	in 20k	Adler	12 Mar
46:05	Alexandra	Kudryashova	RUS-Y	18.7.90	4	NC-w-j	Adler	13 Mar
46:07	Sumiko	Suzuki	JPN	10.3.86	1		Savona	13 Mar
46:12.4 t	Oksana	Kirillova	RUS-Y	18.7.88	1		Izhevsk	17 Sep
46:13	Yelena	Shumkina	RUS-Y	24.1.88	5	NC-w-j	Adler	13 Mar
46:17	Yekaterina	Popova	RUS	10.12.87	6	NC-w-j	Adler	13 Mar
46:25.91 t	Chihiro	Fukunaka	JPN	7.1.86	3	NSF	Okayama	26 Oct
46:37	Yelena	Rusak	BLR	16.5.86	3	ECp	Miskolc	21 May
46:38.53 t	Martina	Gabrielli	ITA	15.2.86	3	EJ	Kaunas	21 Jul
47:02	Anna	Drabenya	BLR	15.8.87	1		Ivano-Frankivsk	1 Oct
47:06	Yekaterina	Nigametzhanova	RUS	18.1.88	10	NC-wj	Adler	13 Mar
47:06.08 t	Kanami	Suzuki (21)	JPN	16.12.86	4	NSF	Okayama	26 Oct
Best track times								
46:29.0+	Natalya	Kozlova	RUS	17.4.87	5	in 20k	Izhevsk	17 Sep
46:38.2	Tatyana	Shemyakina	RUS	3.9.87	4	NC	Saransk	11 Jun

20 KILOMETRES WALK

Mark		Name	Nat	Born	Pos	Meet	Venue	Date
1:25:41	Olimpiada	Ivanova	RUS	26.8.70	1	WCh	Helsinki	7 Aug
1:26:28	Iraida	Pudovkina	RUS	2.11.80	1	NC-w	Adler	12 Mar
1:27:05	Margarita	Turova	BLR	28.12.80	2	WCh	Helsinki	7 Aug
1:27:19		Jiang Jing	CHN	23.10.85	1	NC	Nanning	25 Feb
1:27:19		Turova			1		Rio Maior	2 Apr
1:27:24		Wang Liping	CHN	8.7.76	2	NC	Nanning	25 Feb
1:27:30	Tatyana	Kozlova	RUS	2.9.83	2	NC-w	Adler	12 Mar
1:27:37		Bai Yanmin	CHN-J	29.6.87	1	NG	Nanjing	20 Oct
1:27:56	Irina	Stankina	RUS	25.3.77	3	NC-w	Adler	12 Mar
1:27:56		Jiang Jing			1		Cixi	23 Apr
1:27:58		Yang Yawei	CHN	16.10.83	2		Cixi	23 Apr
1:28:01		Jiang Qiuyan (10)	CHN	5.7.83	3		Cixi	23 Apr
1:28:02	Yuliya	Voyevodina	RUS	17.10.71	4	NC-w	Adler	12 Mar
1:28:07		Tang Yinghua	CHN	18.5.73	4		Cixi	23 Apr
1:28:11	Yelena	Ginko	BLR	30.7.76	5	RUS-w	Adler	12 Mar
1:28:14		Jiang Jing			2	NG	Nanjing	20 Oct
1:28:18		Ivanova			1	ECp	Miskolc	21 May
1:28:22		Shi Na	CHN	17.2.81	5		Cixi	23 Apr
1:28:24		Shi Na			3	NG	Nanjing	20 Oct
1:28:26		Song Hongjuan	CHN	4.7.84	3	NC	Nanning	25 Feb
1:28:35		He Dan	CHN	22.7.84	6		Cixi	23 Apr
1:28:37		Song Hongjuan			1		Dudince	26 Mar
1:28:43		Turova			1		Sesto San Giovanni	1 May
1:28:44	Susana	Feitor	POR	28.1.75	3	WCh	Helsinki	7 Aug
1:28:51		Gao Kelian	CHN	15.8.83	7		Cixi	23 Apr
1:28:51	María	Vasco	ESP	26.12.75	4	WCh	Helsinki	7 Aug
1:28:52	Lyudmila	Arkhipova	RUS	12.9.78	6	NC-w	Adler	12 Mar
1:28:58		Bai Yanmin			8		Cixi	23 Apr
1:29:01		Song Hongjuan			2		Rio Maior	2 Apr
1:29:01		Feitor			2	ECp	Miskolc	21 May
	(30/20)							
1:29:02	Tatyana	Gudkova	RUS	23.1.78	1	NC	Saransk	11 Jun
1:29:05	Barbora	Dibelková	CZE	26.5.83	5	WCh	Helsinki	7 Aug
1:29:07	Sabine	Zimmer	GER	6.2.81	1		Dresden	24 Apr
1:29:21	Athína	Papayiánni	GRE	18.8.80	6	WCh	Helsinki	7 Aug
1:29:25	Olga	Kanishkina	RUS	19.1.85	2	NC	Saransk	11 Jun
1:29:26	Elisa	Rigaudo	ITA	17.6.80	3	ECp	Miskolc	21 May
1:29:33	Jane	Saville	AUS	5.11.74	9		Cixi	23 Apr
1:29:33		Yang Sha	CHN-J	16.1.86	6	NG	Nanjing	20 Oct
1:29:39		Liu Hong	CHN-J	12.5.87	10		Cixi	23 Apr
1:29:40		Pang Yingting	CHN-J	28.1.87	11		Cixi	23 Apr
	(30)							
1:29:43	Larisa	Yemelyanova	RUS	6.1.80	7	NC-w	Adler	12 Mar
1:29:50	Natalya	Shiviryova	RUS	31.8.78	8	NC-w	Adler	12 Mar
1:29:51		Zhang Nan	CHN-J	18.4.86	5	NC	Nanning	25 Feb

Mark	Name		Nat	Born	Pos	Meet	Venue	Date
1:29:51	Lyudmila	Yefimkina	RUS	22.8.81	1		Chelyabinsk	6 Sep
1:29:54	Claudia	Stef	ROM	25.2.78	3		Sesto San Giovanni	1 May
1:30:03	Tatyana	Korotkova	RUS	24.4.80	9	NC-w	Adler	12 Mar
1:30:08	Cristina	Lõpez	ESP	19.9.82	1		La Coruña	4 Jun
1:30:13	Svetlana	Tolstaya	KAZ	9.8.71	10	RUS-w	Adler	12 Mar
1:30:14		Ha Mingming	CHN	15.4.82	7	NG	Nanjing	20 Oct
1:30:15		Song Xiaoling	CHN-J	21.12.87	12		Cixi	23 Apr
	(40)							
1:30:16		Sun Lihua	CHN	30.9.83	13		Cixi	23 Apr
1:30:18	Irina	Petrova	RUS	26.5.85	11	NC-w	Adler	12 Mar
1:30:19		Zhai Lijun	CHN-J	28.11.86	14		Cixi	23 Apr
1:30:21	Melanie	Seeger	GER	8.1.77	4		La Coruña	4 Jun
1:30:35		Zhou Tongmei	CHN		15		Cixi	23 Apr
1:30:39		Sun Limin	CHN-J	6.2.87	16		Cixi	23 Apr
1:30:45	Lyudmila	Yegorova	UKR	4.10.74	1	BLR Ch	Brest	1 Jul
1:30:49		Liu Xiaoyan	CHN	4.9.85	18		Cixi	23 Apr
1:31:18	Tatyana	Sibilyeva	RUS	17.5.80	5	NC	Saransk	11 Jun
1:31:19	Yevdokiya	Korotkova	RUS	28.2.79	14	NC-w	Adler	12 Mar
	(50)							
1:31:23	Kristina	Saltanovic	LTU	20.2.75	12	WCh	Helsinki	7 Aug
1:31:25	Miriam	Ramón	ECU	10.2.73	2	PAmCp	Lima	7 May
1:31:30	Vera	Santos	POR	3.12.81	8		Rio Maior	2 Apr
1:31:37		Chai Xue	CHN-Y	21.1.88	10	NG	Nanjing	20 Oct
1:31:38	Vera	Zozulya	UKR	31.8.70	1	NC-w	Yevpatoriya	4 Mar
1:31:38	Marina	Smyslova	RUS	25.2.66	4		Chelyabinsk	6 Sep
1:31:39		Kim Mi-jung	KOR	10.6.79	1	NG	Ulsan	15 Oct
1:31:45		Zou Ying	CHN	20.8.82	20		Cixi	23 Apr
1:31:45	Natalya	Misyulya	BLR	16.4.66	15	RUS-w	Adler	12 Mar
1:31:48	Ana-Maria	Groza	ROM	1.6.76	14	WCh	Helsinki	7 Aug
	(60)							
1:31:51	Mayumi	Kawasaki	JPN	10.5.80	1		Kobe	30 Jan
1:31:55	Maria José	Poves	ESP	16.3.78	1	NC	El Prat de Llobregat	27 Feb
1:31:57	Gisella	Orsini	ITA	9.12.71	21		Cixi	23 Apr
1:32:04	Yekaterina	Yezhova	RUS	18.2.82	5		Chelyabinsk	6 Sep
1:32:06		Liu Feifei	CHN-J	16.9.86	22		Cixi	23 Apr
1:32:08	Norica	Cîmpean	ROM	22.3.72	7		La Coruña	4 Jun
1:32:18	Maite	Gargallo	ESP	15.10.69	9	ECp	Miskolc	21 May
1:32:20		Li Cui	CHN-J	18.1.87	24		Cixi	23 Apr
1:32:21	Sachiko	Konishi	JPN	4.2.82	2		Kobe	30 Jan
1:32:24		Hu Ming	CHN	8.10.84	25		Cixi	23 Apr
	(70)							
1:32:25	Svetlana	Vasilyeva	RUS-J	17.8.86	16	NC-w	Adler	12 Mar
1:32:28	Olive	Loughnane	IRL	14.1.76	1		Dublin	26 Jun
1:32:31		Yang Liping	CHN	12.9.84	26		Cixi	23 Apr
1:32:34	Tatyana	Metlevskaya	BLR	14.9.84	17	RUS-w	Adler	12 Mar
1:32:34	Daniela	Cîrlan	ROM	18.9.80	8		La Coruña	4 Jun
1:32:41	Valentina	Tsybulskaya	BLR	19.2.68	6		Sesto San Giovanni	1 May
1:32:47		Xu Aihui	CHN	25.4.78	12	NG	Nanjing	20 Oct
1:32:48	Zuzana	Malíková	SVK	2.8.83	12	ECp	Miskolc	21 May
1:32:49	Beatriz	Pascual	ESP	9.5.82	3	NC	El Prat de Llobregat	27 Feb
1:32:53	Sonata	Milusauskaite	LTU	31.8.73	9		La Coruña	4 Jun
	(80)							
1:32:57	Rossella	Giordano	ITA	1.12.72	13	ECp	Miskolc	21 May
1:33:04	Graciela	Mendoza	MEX	23.3.63	3	PAmCp	Lima	7 May
1:33:11	Olga	Povalyayeva	RUS	19.10.84	18	NC-w	Adler	12 Mar
1:33:14	Cheryl	Webb	AUS	3.10.76	2		Canberra	6 Feb
1:33:19	Geovanna	Irusta	BOL	26.9.75	19	WCh	Helsinki	7 Aug
1:33:20		Jian Xingli	CHN	4.12.83	27		Cixi	23 Apr
1:33:24	Inês	Henriques	POR	1.5.80	11		Rio Maior	2 Apr
1:33:28		Jiang Kun	CHN	18.5.85	12	NC	Nanning	25 Feb
1:33:28.15t	Teresa	Vaill	USA	20.11.62	1	NC	Carson	25 Jun
1:33:31		Song Jinzhao	CHN-Y	16.1.88	28		Cixi	23 Apr
	(90)							
1:33:38		Xue Ailing	CHN	12.2.79	29		Cixi	23 Apr
1:33:50		Li Yanhong	CHN	2.6.84	14	NC	Nanning	25 Feb
1:33:51	Snezhana	Yurchenko	BLR	8.3.84	19	RUS-w	Adler	12 Mar
1:33:58	Larisa	Khmelnitskaya	BLR	23.9.71	30		Cixi	23 Apr
1:34:00	Svetlana	Bogdanova	RUS-J	6.11.86	20	NC-w	Adler	12 Mar
1:34:04	Ryoko	Sakakura	JPN	9.5.76	1		Wajima	17 Apr
1:34:05		Zang Yan	CHN	13.12.83	15	NC	Nanning	25 Feb
1:34:07	Maribel	Gonçalves	POR	1.4.78	16	ECp	Miskolc	21 May

Mark	Name		Nat	Born	Pos	Meet	Venue	Date
1:34:07	Anastasiya	Yatsevich	BLR	18.1.85	2		Brest	1 Jun
1:34:11		Li Shuang	CHN	4.1.85	31		Cixi	23 Apr
	(100)							
1:34:11	Irina	Balakley	RUS	6.10.81	8		Chelyabinsk	6 Sep

Mark	Name		Nat	Born	Date
1:34:13	Ana	Cabecinha	POR	29.4.84	4 Jun
1:34:24	Jolanta	Dukure	LAT	20.9.79	7 Aug
1:34:38	Maria	Gáliková	SVK	21.8.80	7 Aug
1:34:40	Galina	Kolpakova	RUS	14.6.83	12 Mar
1:34:46	Alina	Olaru	ROM	13.10.82	11 Jun
1:34:48	Alla	Bozhko	BLR	12.11.84	1 Jun
1:34:49	Simone	Wolowiec	AUS	12.2.74	1 May
1:35:01	Natalie	Saville	AUS	7.9.78	19 Mar
1:35:11	Athanasía	Tsoumeléka	GRE	2.1.82	2 Apr
1:35:13	Evelyn	Nuñez	GUA	9.4.71	26 Jun
1:35:14	Nadezhda	Prokopuk	UKR	25.2.81	2 Oct
1:35:17		Lu Yanmei	CHN	29.6.85	23 Apr
1:35:27	Monica	Svensson	SWE	26.12.78	26 Jun
1:35:33	Yelena	Rusak	BLR-J	16.5.86	1 Jun
1:35:34	Svetlana	Trifonova	RUS	24.3.82	12 Mar
1:35:35	Evaggelía	Xinoú	GRE	22.11.81	23 Apr
1:35:45	Carolina	Jiménez	ESP	2.2.80	4 Jun
1:35:49	Christine	Guinaudeau	FRA	20.6.78	26 Jun
1:35:54	Rocio	Florido	ESP	16.1.76	27 Feb
1:36:03.3t	Amber	Antonia	USA	4.11.79	25 Jun
1:36:06		Feng Rui	CHN-J	1.4.87	23 Apr
1:36:11	Natalya	Kozlova	RUS-J	17.4.87	6 Sep
1:36:14	Maria	Hatzipanayiotídou	GRE	17.1.82	23 Apr
1:36:16	Teresa	Linares	ESP	29.4.69	27 Feb
1:36:21	Claire	Woods	AUS	6.7.81	23 Jul
1:36:22.6t	Fatiha	Ouali	FRA	25.10.74	28 May
1:36:24	Natalya	Khlimashevska	UKR	12.1.83	4 Mar
1:36:28	Tatyana	Zuyeva	BLR	22.3.83	1 Jun
1:36:34	Natalya	Kolotukhina	RUS	12.6.83	12 Mar
1:36:49	Tatiana	Denize	FRA	13.7.73	9 Apr
1:36:50	Déspina	Zapounídou	GRE	5.10.85	2 Oct
1:36:58	Marie	Polli	SUI	28.11.80	9 Apr
1:36:59	Olga	Mikhaylova	RUS-J	7.12.86	6 Sep
1:37:00	Mariya	Shorokhova	RUS	24.12.85	12 Mar
1:37:04	Joanne	Dow	USA	19.3.64	3 Apr
1:37:05	Yarelis	Sánchez	CUB	2.1.82	20 May
1:37:09		Zuo Yan	CHN	18.8.83	25 Feb
1:37:09	Alena	Zenkova	RUS	1.1.82	11 Jun
1:37:13	Olga	Kardopoltseva	BLR	11.9.66	16 Apr
1:37:16	Chihiro	Fukunaka	JPN-J	7.1.86	13 Nov
1:37:34	Outi	Sillanpää	FIN	2.2.76	24 Apr
1:37:39	Yeliz	Ay	TUR	9.11.77	23 Apr
1:37:39	Lisa	Grant	AUS	26.4.85	23 Jul
1:37:44	Cristiana	Pellino	ITA	21.9.70	17 Apr
1:37:46	Kellie	Wapshott	AUS	23.8.81	7 Aug
1:37:47	Yelena	Miroshnichenko	UKR	1.3.77	4 Mar
1:37:47	Agnieszka	Olesz	POL	27.8.79	12 Jun
1:37:57	Mabel	Oncebay	PER	29.1.82	7 May
1:38:00	Sarah-Jane	Cattermole	GBR	29.1.77	2 Jan
1:38:01	Iratxe	Pérez	ESP	5.7.83	2 Apr
1:38:05	Lynette	Ventris	AUS	2.10.66	24 Jul
1:38:06	Daisy	González	MEX	15.11.84	7 May
1:38:13	Kumi	Otoshi	JPN	29.7.85	17 Apr
1:38:19	Sakiko	Tadokoro	JPN	18.11.84	30 Jan
1:38:20	Lidia	Mongelli	ITA	3.8.80	2 Oct
1:38:34	Nadia	Moreno	COL	15.3.78	7 May
1:38:35		Cao Xue	CHN	2.3.82	25 Feb
1:38:43	Agnieszka	Dygacz	POL	18.7.85	23 Apr
1:38:48.3t	Jolene	Moore	USA	14.3.66	25 Jun
1:39:07	Natalya	Ivanova	RUS	10.11.85	6 Sep
1:39:09	Laura	Polli	SUI	7.9.83	20 Mar
1:39:09	Alexia	Triadafíllou	GRE	3.9.85	5 Jun
1:39:16	Brigita	Virbalyte	LTU	1.2.85	9 Apr
1:39:22	Patricia	Garnier	FRA	13.5.67	9 Apr
1:39:26	Annarita	Fidanza	ITA	3.8.77	15 Aug
1:39:28	Carmen	Bone	ESP	20.12.80	27 Feb
1:39:35	Anna	Pudovkina	RUS	29.3.85	6 Sep
1:39:41		Han Jie	CHN-J	31.12 87	25 Feb
1:39:47	Bobbi Jo	Chapman	USA	31.10.73	7 May
1:39:48	Ann	Loughnane	IRL-J	8.4.86	17 Dec
1:39:54	Emanuela	Perilli	ITA	19.5.73	2 Oct
1:39:55	Esther	Serra	ESP	27.5.84	27 Feb
1:39:56	(174)	Park Ha-na	KOR-J	17.2.87	15 Oct

Best track times

Mark	Name		Nat	Born	Pos	Meet	Venue	Date
1:33:20.2	Larisa	Yemelyanova	RUS	6.1.80	1	NC	Izhevsk	18 Sep
1:33:29.9	Yekaterina	Yezhova	RUS	18.2.82	2	NC	Izhevsk	18 Sep
1:33:38.3	Marina	Smyslova	RUS	25.2.66	3	NC	Izhevsk	18 Sep

Mark	Name		Nat	Born	Date
1:34:50.9	Iraida	Pudovkina	RUS	2.11.80	18 Sep
1:35:17.3	Natalya	Shiviryova	RUS	31.8.78	18 Sep
1:35:36.4	Galina	Kolpakova	RUS	14.6.83	18 Sep
1:36:28.0	Lyudmila	Arkhipova	RUS	12.9.78	18 Sep
1:36:40.0	Irina	Balakley	RUS	6.10.81	18 Sep
1:37:14.9	Joanne	Dow	USA	19.3.64	25 Jun
1:38:01.0	Christine	Guinaudeau	FRA	20.6.78	16 Jul
1:39:14.5	Natalya	Ivanova	RUS	10.11.85	18 Sep
1:39:38.3	Olga	Povalyayeva	RUS	19.10.84	18 Sep

JUNIORS

See main list for top 14 juniors. 14 performances by 9 women to 1:32:00. Additional marks and further juniors:

Bai Y 2+	1:30:16	4		Rio Maior	2 Apr
Liu Hong	1:30:22	8	NG	Nanjing	20 Oct
Zhang Nan	1:31:21	19		Cixi	23 Apr
Zhai Lijun	1:30:44	9	NG	Nanjing	20 Oct

Mark	Name		Nat	Born	Pos	Meet	Venue	Date
1:35:33	Yelena	Rusak	BLR	16.5.86	4		Brest	1 Jun
1:36:06		Feng Rui	CHN	1.4.87	35		Cixi	23 Apr
1:36:11	Natalya	Kozlova	RUS	17.4.87	10		Chelyabinsk	6 Sep
1:36:59	Olga	Mikhaylova	RUS	7.12.86	12		Chelyabinsk	6 Sep
1:37:16	Chihiro	Fukunaka	JPN	7.1.86	1		Koyang	13 Nov
1:39:41		Han Jie (20)	CHN	31.12 87	11	NC-j	Nanning	25 Feb

50 KILOMETRES WALK

Mark	Name		Nat	Born	Pos	Meet	Venue	Date
4:41:03	Lyudmila	Yegorova	UKR	4.10.74	1		Scanzoroscaite	16 Oct
4:45:57	Laura	Polli	SUI	7.9.83	2		Scanzoroscaite	16 Oct
4:49:39	Déspina	Zapounídou	GRE-J	5.10.85	3		Scanzoroscaite	16 Oct
4:50:37	Monica	Gardini	ITA	3.11.73	4		Scanzoroscaite	16 Oct
5:04:00	Henrieta	Rusnáková	SVK	17.10.71	5		Scanzoroscaite	16 Oct
5:09:14	Kora	Boufflert	FRA	23.4.66	1	NC	Roubaix	16 Oct

100 KILOMETRES WALK

Mark	Name		Nat	Born	Pos	Meet	Venue	Date
10:48:49	Anita	Liepina	LAT	17.11.67	1		Scanzoroscaite	16 Oct

WORLD LIST TRENDS – MEN

This table shows the 10th and 100th bests in the year lists for 1988, 1992, 1996 and the last seven years.

Men 10th Bests	*1988*	*1992*	*1996*	*1999*	*2000*	*2001*	*2002*	*2003*	*2004*	*2005*
100m	10.06	10.07	10.01	10.00	10.03	10.05	9.99	10.00	10.01	10.00
200m	20.18	20.15	20.17	20.08	**20.03**	20.19	20.21	20.15	20.17	20.21
400m	44.61	44.52	**44.51**	44.59	44.70	44.80	44.84	44.78	44.72	44.70
800m	1:44.10	1:44.33	**1:43.66**	1:43.98	1:44.06	1:43.98	1:43.93	1:44.22	1:44.09	1:44.34
1500m	3:34.61	3:33.80	3:33.00	3:31.60	3:32.01	**3:31.49**	3:32.37	3:31.61	3:31.10	3:31.95
5000m	13:17.48	13:10.47	12:59.19	12:59.09	12:58.70	13:01.64	13:01.98	**12:54.99**	12:59.04	12:56.13
10000m	27:40.36	27:45.46	27:30.37	27:18.28	27:23.65	27:25.55	27:26.12	27:14.61	27:05.14	27:04.45
Marathon	2:08:49	2:09:30	2:09:15	2:07:09	2:07:47	2:07:52	2:07:06	**2:06:48**	2:07:43	2:07:46
3000mSt	8:16.04	8:13.65	8:12.54	8:10.56	8:10.23	8:09.23	**8:08.14**	8:09.37	8:11.44	8:09.43
110mh	13.36	13.33	13.24	13.21	13.24	13.26	13.30	13.28	13.22	13.23
400mh	48.65	48.60	48.28	48.22	48.40	48.40	48.25	48.50	**48.16**	48.24
HJ	**2.36**	2.34	2.34	2.32	2.34	2.33	2.32	2.32	2.32	2.33
PV	5.80	5.85	**5.90**	5.85	5.85	5.85	5.81	5.81	5.81	5.85
LJ	8.31	8.28	8.34	8.26	8.33	8.22	8.26	8.30	8.28	8.28
TJ	17.43	17.30	17.20	17.27	17.26	17.22	17.35	17.28	17.41	17.30
SP	21.16	20.93	20.78	20.84	21.27	20.88	21.11	21.14	21.14	20.94
DT	67.38	66.64	66.70	66.95	66.93	67.57	66.90	66.35	66.73	66.56
HT	**81.88**	80.46	79.52	80.51	81.36	80.88	81.59	80.89	80.90	80.00
JT	82.70	85.74	**87.12**	87.11	86.65	86.63	85.74	84.54	85.83	84.06
Decathlon	8387	8237	8462	8379	8467	8307	8175	8203	8285	8185
20kmW	1:20:10	1:20:32	1:19:31	1:19:55	1:19:18	1:19:45	1:20:36	1:19:35	1:19:30	**1:18:30**
50kmW	3:46:30	3:50:01	3:44:19	3:46:36	3:44:33	3:46:12	3:45:45	3:44:53	3:44:42	**3:41:30**

Peak years shown in bold. Other peaks: 100m 9.98 (1997), 110mh 13.20 (1998), PV 5.90 (1998), TJ 17.48 (1985), SP 21.63 (1984), DT 68.20 (1982), Dec 8526 (1998)

Men 100th Bests	*1988*	*1992*	*1996*	*1999*	*2000*	*2001*	*2002*	*2003*	*2004*	*2005*
100m	10.34	10.32	10.27	10.26	**10.24**	10.26	10.27	10.26	10.26	10.29
200m	20.79	20.78	**20.66**	20.66	20.66	20.72	20.74	20.69	20.67	20.70
400m	45.99	45.98	45.91	45.88	**45.78**	45.90	45.99	45.83	45.86	45/98
800m	1:46.91	1:46.95	1:46.82	**1:46.54**	1:46.71	1:47.00	1:47.12	1:46.91	1:46.67	1:46.87
1500m	3:39.46	3:39.11	3:38.66	3:39.05	3:38.68	3:38.94	3:39.70	3:39.49	3:38.50	3:30.05
5000m	13:37.20	13:31.44	13:34.29	13:32.94	13:28.62	13:30.56	13:31.61	13:30.06	**13:25.52**	13:25.68
10000m	28:27.28	28:30.42	28:20.9	28:19.07	**28:15.98**	28:27.33	28:27.17	28:22.29	28:21.4	28:22.85
Marathon	2:13:08	2:13:22	2:12:25	2:11:26	2:11:24	2:11:18	**2:11:08**	**2:10:38**	2:11:13	2:11:20
3000mSt	8:35.24	8:34.43	8:34.91	8:34.04	**8:33.37**	8:35.17	8:34.18	8:33.58	**8:31.06**	8:33.37
110mh	13.83	13.78	13.72	13.80	13.76	13.78	13.79	13.75	**13.70**	13.73
400mh	50.52	50.50	50.17	50.10	**50.06**	50.12	50.19	50.20	50.14	50.10
HJ	**2.24**	**2.24**	**2.24**	2.22	2.23	2.22	2.23	2.22	2.23	2.22
PV	5.50	5.50	5.50	5.50	**5.55**	5.45	5.50	5.50	5.50	5.50
LJ	7.93	7.93	7.94	7.92	7.93	7.89	7.90	7.92	**7.96**	7.90
TJ	**16.60**	16.59	16.56	16.37	16.48	16.45	16.41	16.43	16.55	16.42
SP	19.17	18.79	18.81	18.81	19.05	19.00	19.11	19.02	19.28	19.08
DT	60.84	59.80	59.82	59.87	60.16	59.60	59.72	59.62	60.05	59.50
HT	72.34	70.70	70.88	70.93	71.28	70.62	69.88	70.63	71.12	70.72
JT	76.48	76.40	76.20	75.78	76.06	76.12	76.60	76.17	76.31	76.10
Decathlon	**7702**	7567	7701	7592	7633	7562	7537	7512	7572	7490
20kmW	1:24:54	1:24:09	1:23:55	1:24:31	1:24:22	1:24:08	1:24:41	1:24:04	1:23:25	**1:22.48**
50kmW	4:06:34	4:07:33	4:06:31	**4:03:49**	4:04:34	4:05:45	4:07:43	4:06:54	4:05:13	4:05:04

Other peaks: 1500m 3:38.42 (1997), HJ 2.24 (also 1984, 1989), SP 19.48 (1984), DT 60.96 (1984), HT 73.06 (1984), JT 77.14 (1991)

Number of athletes achieving base level standards for world lists:

Men		2000	2001	2002	2003	2004	2005			2000	2001	2002	2003	2004	2005
100m	10.34	212	195	178	196	204	160	HJ	2.20	193	167	173	165	177	162
200m	20.85	194	164	153	177	179	166	PV	5.35	199	156	157	173	180	167
400m	46.29	209	158	169	188	203	166	LJ	7.80	172	154	160	157	167	156
800m	1:47.99	212	168	177	200	218	200	TJ	16.30	135	132	122	125	148	138
1500m	3:41.4	202	165	155	156	204	206	SP	18.25	198	184	180	186	209	190
5000m	13:42.0	205	165	182	185	205	199	DT	57.80	166	139	142	140	150	140
10000m	28:42.0	220	179	168	174	195	183	HT	68.00	161	153	147	147	157	136
HMar	62:45	193	174	165	194	197	196	JT	74.00	148	147	153	147	155	146
Mar	2:13:15	174	201	204	199	213	196	Dec	7400	156	147	131	130	147	125
3000St	8:40.0	163	137	151	154	166	167	20kmW	1:25:00	116	122	112	133	149	162
110mh	13.95	185	177	166	185	202	199	50kmW	4:10:00	123	119	109	112	125	121
400mh	50.85	201	197	185	187	189	192								

Notes: Standards in 2005 were generally down on 2004, particularly in depth
2004 marks were better than 2005 in 12-9 (1=) for 10th best, 18-3 (1=) at 100th best, 19-4 on numbers at base levels

WOMEN'S WORLD LIST TRENDS

This table shows the 10th and 100th bests in the year lists for 1988, 1992, 1996 and the last seven years.

10th Bests	*1988*	*1992*	*1996*	*1999*	*2000*	*2001*	2002	*2003*	*2004*	*2005*
100m	**10.92**	11.07	11.03	10.98	10.99	11.06	11.05	11.05	11.04	11.05
200m	**22.24**	22.44	22.27	22.31	22.49	22.63	22.54	22.60	22.46	22.46
400m	49.90	50.30	50.32	50.34	50.04	50.63	50.80	50.59	50.19	50.38
800m	**1:56.91**	1:57.93	1:58.22	1:58.24	1:58.34	1:58.60	1:58.90	1:58.86	1:57.96	1:58.41
1500m	4:01.02	4:01.23	4:02.38	4:03.14	4:01.23	4:03.20	4:01.28	4:01.69	4:01.29	4:01.14
5000m	15:17.89	15:19.20	14:48.36	14:56.00	14:45.35	14:51.58	14:48.29	14:46.73	14:44.81	**14:43.87**
10000m	31:42.02	31:28.06	31:24.08	31:32.63	31:03.60	31:38.18	31:27.83	31:01.07	31:04.34	**30:55.67**
Marathon	2:28:40	2:27:42	2:27:41	2:25:29	2:24:33	2:24:21	**2:22:33**	2:23:07	2:24:27	2:23:59
3000mSt				10:09.83	10:02.60	9:52.71	9:47.87	9:44.95	9:39.84	**9:35.51**
100mh	12.73	12.76	12.69	12.73	12.70	12.71	12.75	12.72	**12.60**	12.66
400mh	54.49	54.70	54.40	54.15	54.41	54.47	54.72	54.60	**53.99**	54.47
HJ	1.98	1.96	1.98	1.99	1.98	1.96	1.97	**2.01**	2.00	1.97
PV	-	3.70	4.15	4.46	4.50	4.52	**4.60**	**4.60**	**4.60**	**4.60**
LJ	**7.07**	6.92	6.92	6.93	6.93	6.87	6.79	6.79	6.83	6.79
TJ	13.07	14.07	14.55	14.70	14.52	14.57	14.56	14.76	**14.78**	14.69
SP	20.81	19.78	19.46	19.21	19.32	19.30	19.20	19.10	19.29	19.05
DT	**70.34**	67.08	64.90	64.68	65.41	65.12	64.55	65.38	65.25	64.56
HT	-	56.40	61.84	67.24	69.36	68.50	68.70	71.12	72.57	**73.08**
JT *	**68.42**	65.02	66.14	63.52*	64.89	64.30	63.89	62.89	63.07	62.64
Heptathlon	**6540**	6460	6406	6287	6396	6270	6151	6209	6287	6291
20kmW	Previously 10km standard			1:28:51	1:28:06	1:27:55	1:28:46	1:28:17	**1:27:52**	1:28:01

Other peaks: 400m 49.74 (1984), 1500m 3:58.07 (1997), SP 20.85 (1987). 5000m succeeded 3000m as standard from 1995.

100th Bests	1988	1992	1996	1999	2000	2001	2002	2003	2004	2005
100m	11.43	11.45	11.44	11.41	**11.36**	11.43	11.43	11.43	11.38	11.42
200m	23.32	23.36	23.32	23.22	23.21	23.27	23.35	23.31	**23.20**	23.29
400m	52.50	52.60	52.29	52.46	52.25	52.49	52.55	52.34	**52.14**	52.30
800m	2:01.66	2:02.80	2:02.96	2:02.53	2:02.51	2:03.02	2:02.65	2:02.38	2:01.98	2:02.58
1500m	4:11.70	4:11.80	4:11.87	4:11.79	4:11.18	4:12.13	4:12.37	4:11.37	4:10.34	4:12.12
5000m			15:35.62	15:37.76	15:29.36	15:34.49	15:36.99	15:43.15	**15:26.01**	15:29.96
10000m	33:11.31	33:05.80	32:56.63	32:59.05	**32:32.47**	32:35.90	32:46.11	32:43.76	32:37.88	32:34.11
Marathon	2:35:29	2:36:14	2:33:24	2:33:05	2:32:25	**2:31:05**	2:31:29	2:31:21	2:31:53	2:31:43
3000mSt								10:23.76	10:18.55	**10:13.00**
100mh	13.39	13.35	13.31	13.32	**13.22**	13.31	13.33	13.26	13.26	13.32
400mh	57.50	57.60	57.63	57.59	57.48	57.50	57.88	57.61	57.33	57.47
HJ	**1.88**	**1.88**	1.87	1.86	1.87	1.86	1.86	1.87	1.87	1.86
PV			3.60	4.00	4.10	4.08	4.10	4.15	**4.20**	**4.20**
LJ	**6.53**	6.45	6.50	6.48	6.49	6.45	6.43	6.46	6.50	6.48
TJ		13.16	13.45	13.64	13.68	13.60	13.64	13.67	**13.70**	13.62
SP	17.02	16.40	16.34	16.53	16.46	16.57	16.49	16.58	16.76	16.55
DT	57.40	56.20	56.86	56.02	56.22	55.54	55.20	55.15	56.32	55.93
HT			53.84	59.08	60.66	61.46	61.50	63.23	**63.73**	63.14
JT *	**58.14**	56.36	56.16	54.54*	55.55	54.56	54.97	54.27	55.09	54.91
Heptathlon	**5741**	5661	5649	5596	5647	5640	5580	5622	5631	5650
20kmW				1:36:59	1:34:44	1:35:15	1:37:08	1:35:46	1:34:32	**1:34:11**

All-time record levels indicated in bold. * Note new javelin from 1999.

Other peaks: 800m 2:01.50 (1984), 1500m 4:10.22 (1984), 3000m 9:00.65 (1993), HJ 1.88 (also 1986, 1987, 1993), SP 17.19 (1987), DT 58.50 (1984)

Number of athletes achieving base level standards for world lists:

Women		2000	2001	2002	2003	2004	2005
100m	11.54	217	185	168	181	212	171
200m	23.54	192	166	148	180	198	177
400m	53.19	190	174	183	198	208	191
800m	2:04.0	169	145	159	183	210	174
1500m	4:15.5	188	175	155	193	191	169
5000m	15:45.0	193	154	151	156	187	165
10000m	33:15.0	203	140	152	166	153	161
HMar	72:59	170	193	179	194	183	205
Mar	2:36:00	169	182	185	198	182	189
3000mSt	10:20.0	28	63	70	84	107	142
100mh	13.54	193	184	177	183	221	180

Women		2000	2001	2002	2003	2004	2005
400mh	58.44	168	163	141	164	179	169
HJ	1.85	148	120	123	130	146	146
PV	4.05	106	114	139	151	179	213
LJ	6.33	200	159	169	191	201	186
TJ	13.30	171	167	173	185	201	174
SP	15.85	156	151	153	172	181	150
DT	53.65	151	144	143	136	147	160
HT	59.60	119	122	144	172	193	178
JT	53.00	157	138	148	130	156	151
Hep	5450	180	168	128	145	141	144
20kmW	1:40:00	171	157	144	164	175	173

Notes: As for the men, standards were generally down on 2004, particularly in depth
2004 marks were better than 2005 in 12-7 (2=) for 10th best, 15-5 (1=) at 100th best, 14-7 (1=) on numbers at base levels.

IAAF WORLD CUP IN ATHLETICS

THE 10th edition of this meeting will be hel at the Olympc Stadium, Athens, Greece, on 16-17 September 2006.The idea of having a competition between teams representing the continents and top athletics nations was conceived in 1975 and the first World Cup was staged in Düsseldorf FRG on 2-4 Sep 1977.

The aims of the IAAF for these events have been to provide a great athletics meeting, to offer additional world-class competition for the sport's elite, to stimulate the continental areas not only in the World Cup competition itself but also by the staging of trial meetings to determine the teams, and not least to provide additional revenue for the development of athletics throughout the world. The competing teams represent each of the five continents, with national teams from the USA, the top two men's and women's teams from the European Cup Super League final 2006 and the host nation of Greece. From 1994 the event has been staged every four years.

Meeting Best Performances – Men

100m	9.87	Obadele Thompson BAR/AME	1998
200m	19.97	Frank Fredericks NAM/AFR	1998
400m	44.47	Mike Franks USA	1985
800m	1:43.83	Antonio Reina ESP	2002
1500m	3:31.20	Bernard Lagat KEN/AFR	2002
3000m	7:41.37	Craig Mottram AUS/OCE	2002
5000m	13:13.82	Miruts Yifter ETH/AFR	1977
10000m	27:38.43	Werner Schildhauer GDR	1981
3000mSt	8:19.89	Boguslaw Maminski POL/EUR	1981
110mh	13.07	Colin Jackson GBR	1992
	12.87w	Roger Kingdom USA	1989
400mh	47.31	Edwin Moses USA	1981
HJ	2.40	Javier Sotomayor CUB	1994
PV	5.90	Okkert Brits RSA/AFR	1994
LJ	8.52	Larry Myricks USA	1979
TJ	17.61	Yoelbi Quesada CUB/AME	1994
SP	22.00	Ulf Timmermann GDR	1985
DT	71.25	Róbert Fazekas HUN/EUR	2002
HT	82.68	Tibor Gécsek HUN/EUR	1998
JT	88.71	Steve Backley GBR	1998
(old)	96.96	Uwe Hohn GDR	1985
4x100mR	37.95	USA	2002
4x400mR	2:59.12	USA	1981

Women

100m	10.65	Marion Jones USA	1998
200m	21.62	Marion Jones USA	1998
400m	47.60	Marita Koch GDR	1985
800m	1:54.44	Ana Quirot CUB/AME	1989
1500m	4:01.05	Hassiba Boulmerka ALG/AFR	1994
3000m	8:36.32	Svetlana Ulmasova URS	1979
5000m	15:18.15	Olga Yegorova RUS	2002
10000m	30:52.51	Elana Meyer RSA/AFR	1994
100mh	12.60	Cornelia Oschkenat GDR	1989
	12.58w	Glory Alozie NGR/AFR	1998
400mh	52.96	Nezha Bidouane AFR	1998
HJ	2.04	Silvia Costa CUB	1989
PV	4.55	Annika Becker GER	2002
LJ	7.27	Heike Drechsler GDR	1985
TJ	14.64	Olga Vasdeki GRE	1998
SP	20.98	Ilona Slupianek GDR	1979
DT	71.54	Ilke Wyludda GDR	1989
HT	70.75	Gu Yuan CHN/ASI	2002
JT	70.32	Petra Felke GDR	1989
4x100mR	41.37	GDR	1985
4x400mR	3:19.50	GDR	1985

Previous Venues

1977 Düsseldorf, FRG
1979 Montreal, CAN
1981 Rome, ITA
1985 Canberra, AUS
1989 Barcelona, ESP
1992 Havana, CUB
1994 London (Crystal Palace), GBR
1998 Johannesburg, RSA
2002 Madrid, ESP

Previous 1-2-3 Teams

Men	*1*	*2*	*3*
1977	GDR 127	USA 120	FRG 112
1979	USA 119	EUR 112	GDR 108
1981	EUR 147	GDR 130	USA 127
1985	USA 123	USSR 115	GDR 114
1989	USA 133	EUR 127	GBR 119
1992	AFR 115	GBR 103	EUR 99
1994	AFR 116	GBR 111	AME 95
1998	AFR 110	EUR 109	GER 102
2002	AFR 134	EUR 116	USA 114

Women	*1*	*2*	*3*
1977	EUR 109	GDR 93	USSR 90
1979	GDR 106	USSR 98	EUR 88
1981	GDR 120.5	EUR 110	USSR 98
1985	GDR 121.5	USSR 105.5	EUR 86
1989	GDR 124	USSR 106	AME 94
1992	EUN* 102	EUR 94	AME 79
1994	EUR 111	AME 98	GER 79
1998	USA 96	EUR 94	AFR 88
2002	RUS 126	EUR 123	AME 110

* Unified team (ex-USSR)

Most Individual Event Wins

4 Miruts Yifter AFR/ETH 5000m & 10000m 1977 & 1979

4 Evelyne Ashford USA 100m & 200m 1981 & 19083

4 Maria Mutola MOZ/AFR 800m 1992, 1994, 1998 & 2002

Triple winner at one meeting

Marita Koch GDR 200m, 400m, 4x400mR 1985

Ana Fidelia Quirot CUB/AME 400m, 800m and 4x400mR 1989.

MEN'S INDEX 2005

Athletes included are those ranked in the top 100s at standard (World Championships) events (plus shorter lists for 1000m, 1M, 2000m and 3000m). Those with detailed biographical profiles are indicated in first column by:
* in this year's Annual, ^ in a previous year's Annual.

	Name		Nat	Born	Ht/Wt	Event	2005 Mark	Pre-2005 Best
	Aakre	Andrew	USA	15.6.81		Dec	7641	7308- 03
^	Aaltonen	Timo	FIN	11.4.69	189/130	SP	19.64	20.70- 00
*	Abate	Abiyote	ETH	20.11.80	174/56	10000	27:45.56	
	Abdirahman	Abdi	USA	1.1.77	178/60	5000	13:13.32	13:19.82- 01
						10000	27:33.47	27:34.24- 04
	Abdisa	Nasir	ETH			HMar	61:54A	
	Abdur-Rahim	Mustafa	USA	29.9.82	175/85	Dec	7739	7937- 04
	Aboubaker	Ibrahim Mohd	QAT	10.12.82	186/82	TJ	16.59	17.15- 04
	Absher	Tessema	ETH-J	9.12.86		3000	7:46.76	7:54.72- 03
						5000	13:23.08	
^	Achike	Larry	GBR	31.1.75	188/75	TJ	17.03	17.30, 17.31w- 00
*	Adams	Luke	AUS	22.10.76	189/70	20kW	1:19:19	1:19:35- 03
	Aggoune	Khoudir	ALG	5.1.81	175/66	3000	7:47.98	7:43.63- 03
	Aikines-Aryeetey	Harry	GBR-Y	29.8.88	175/68	100	10.26w	10.59, 10.5w- 04
	Aish	Michael	NZL	24.7.76	175/60	10000	28:07.33	27:53.28- 04
	Aïssat	Nicolas	FRA	24.7.80	175/60	800	1:45.25	1:44.98- 01
	Akashi	Ken	JPN	6.11.76	169/59	50kW	3:59:11	3:54:11- 03
	Akiyama	Yoichiro	JPN	25.12.79		HMar	61:58	
	Akkas	Halil	TUR	1.7.83	175/60	3kSt	8:22.00	8:33.68- 03
	Akpan	Unyime	USA	7.12.81	180/66	110H	13.71	14.12- 03
	Alaräisänen	Pekka	FIN	27.12.75	188/111	JT	78.62	83.45- 04
	Al-Azimi	Mohamed Mutlak	KUW	16.6.82	176/70	800	1:46.67	1:45.25- 04
	Al-Badri	Salem Amer	QAT	12.12.85	180/65	800	1:46.87	1:46.63- 02
	Albert	Lars	GER	9.2.82	197/97	Dec	7920	7893- 02
	Al-Bishi	Hamdan Odha	KSA	5.5.81	180/70	400	45.57	44.66- 00
	Al-Bishi	Hamed Hamadan	KSA	15.5.80	185/67	200	20.66	20.55- 03
	Al-Dawoodi	Sultan M.	KSA	16.6.77	183/95	DT	61.11	59.66- 03
	Al-Dosari	Rasheed	QAT	8.5.81	198/120	DT	60.11	64.43- 02
*	Alekna	Virgilijus	LTU	13.2.72	200/130	DT	70.67	73.88- 00
	Aleksejev	Marko	EST	14.2.79	196/80	HJ	2.28	2.27- 04
	Alekseyev	Igor	BLR	7.4.83		PV	5.60i, 5.50	5.65- 03
	Alerte	David	FRA	18.9.84	192/83	200	20.47	20.86, 20.65w- 04
	Al-Hamaidi	Ibrahim	KSA	28.8.85	177/68	400H	49.55	48.94- 04
	Ali	Bilal Mansour	BRN	17.10.83	170/60	1500	3:33.86	
	Alic	Hamza	BIH	20.1.79	192/108	SP	19.49	19.14- 03
^	Aliu	Deji	NGR	22.11.75	187/75	100	10.19	9.95- 03, 9.9- 96
	Al-Kahes	Yahya Saeed	KSA-J	19.2.86	160/70	100	10.28	10.30, 10.24w- 04
	Al-Khuwalidi	Mohamed Salim	KSA	19.6.81	177/67	LJ	8.44	8.12- 04, 8.18w- 02
	Allmond	Tony	USA	8.10.82	193/75	LJ	8.08Ai, 8.23w, 7.98	8.10, 8.35w- 04
	Al-Outaibi	Moukhled	KSA	20.6.76	174/67	5000	12:58.58	13:21.11- 03
	Alozídis	Minás	GRE	7.7.84	185/72	400H	49.52	50.66- 04
^	Al-Salhi	Mohammed	KSA-J	11.5.86	180/70	400	45.94	45.75- 03
						800	1:44.39	1:46.48- 03
^	Al-Somaily	Hadi Soua'an	KSA	21.8.76	191/72	400H	49.02	47.53- 00
	Al-Suwaidi	Khaled Habash	QAT	10.10.84	188/105	SP	20.54	20.07i, 19.93- 04
	Alterio	Andrea	ITA	11.6.73	183/77	110H	13.60	13.69- 97
	Al-Yami	Salem Mubarak	KSA	9.2.82	175/70	100	10.21	10.13- 02
	Al-Zinkawi	Ali Mohamed	KUW	27.2.84	183/95	HT	76.25	76.54- 04
	Amarasekara	Prasanna	SRI	21.3.81	163/57	400	45.47	45.95- 04
	Amoo	Seth	GHA	20.3.83	170/68	200	20.36	20.57- 04
	Amor	Rachid	TUN	10.4.78		HMar	61:53	63:32- 04
*	Amyn	Mohammed	MAR	25.3.76	168/53	3000	7:45.82	7:35.35- 01
						10000	27:22.67	27:44.24- 04
	An Hyuk-yun		KOR	23.3.79	184/90	JT	77.31	75.97- 04
	Anani	Mohsen	EGY	21.5.85	187/117	HT	75.31	72.50- 04
	Anceschi	Stefano	ITA	18.6.84		100	10.27w	
	Anderson	Marvin	JAM	12.5.82	175/69	100	10.28	10.24- 03, 10.1w- 00
						200	20.36w	20.84- 00
	Andersson	Anton	SWE	12.3.81	194/91	TJ	16.43	16.49- 02
	Andrei	Cristiano	ITA	14.5.73	198/112	DT	62.58	64.49- 03
	Andreyev	Grigoriy	RUS	7.1.76		Mar	2:11:20	
	Andreyev	Leonid	UZB	6.11.83	196/80	PV	5.60	5.55- 04
	Andreyev	Pavel	UZB	24.11.78	196/80	Dec	7744	8036- 04
	Andriani	Ottaviano	ITA	4.1.74	172/61	Mar	2:10:12	2:09:07- 01
	Andronov	Yuriy	RUS	6.11.71	180/68	50kW	3:42:34	3:42:06- 02

Name		Nat	Born	Ht/Wt	Event	2005Mark	Pre-2005 Best
Androsovich	Sergey	UKR	27.5.83		Dec	7764	7013- 02
Andureu	Charles	FRA	13.2.85	183/78	PV	5.70	5.22i- 04, 5.20- 03
Angwenyi	Elkanah	KEN	5.2.83	176/62	800	1:46.3A	1:47.5- 04
					1000	2:17.13	
					1500	3:33.43	3:38.66+- 04
					1M	3:53.05	3:54.52- 04
Anskins	Andis	LAT	25.1.79	183/82	JT	81.80	78.43- 02
Ao Xinli		CHN	26.1.81	177/70	20kW	1:22:17	1:27:01- 01
					50kW	3:56:00	3:56:29- 03
* Apak	Esref	TUR	3.1.82	186/100	HT	81.45	80.16- 04
Arai	Hironori	JPN	19.9.79	180/63	HMar	61:53	
Araújo	Gaspar	POR	17.12.81	185/80	LJ	8.07	8.10, 8.15w- 04
de Araújo	Rodrigo	BRA	12.11.79		LJ	8.01, 8.16w	8.08- 04
Armon	Juaune	USA	6.5.82	193/84	LJ	7.93	8.00- 02
* Armstrong	Aaron	TRI	14.10.77	173/78	100	10.04, 10.00w	10.17- 03
					200	20.35, 19.98w	20.08- 99
Armstrong	Dylan	CAN	15.1.81	190/125	SP	19.83	19.55- 04
Armstrong	Sherman	USA	22.9.78	185/75	400H	49.33	48.55A- 04, 48.61- 00
* Arnold	Dominique	USA	14.9.73	185/76	110H	13.01	13.11- 00
Arrhenius	Niklas	SWE	10.9.82	194/108	DT	60.33	63.62- 04
Arvidsson	Magnus	SWE	20.2.83		JT	77.83	73.98- 04
Asahara	Nobuharu	JPN	21.6.72	178/72	100	10.29	10.02- 01
Ashley	Jamel	USA	17.4.79	188/82	200	20.70	20.85- 00
					400	44.75	45.56- 04
Assefa	Girma	ETH-J	20.6.86		10000	27:44.12	29:44.0A- 02
Assefa	Raji	ETH-J	18.2.86		HMar	61:47A	
Atkins	Derrick	BAH	5.1.84		100	10.21	10.30- 03
Atkinson	Brandon	USA	11.6.83	190/75	TJ	16.58	16.15- 04
Attene	Alessandro	ITA	10.9.77	182/81	200	20.70	20.57- 97
Augustyn	Rafal	POL	14.5.84	177/71	20kW	1:21:36	1:23:49- 04
Austin	Dan	USA	12.4.83		DT	59.76	52.40- 02
Avellaneda	Mario	ESP	12.11.74	168/58	50kW	3:56:15	3:49:35- 03
* Averbukh	Aleksandr	ISR	1.10.74	178/76	PV	5.65	5.93- 03
Averyanov	Nikolay	RUS	4.2.80	182/77	Dec	7535	8048- 04
Avlasevich	Nikolay	BLR	18.2.76	191/110	HT	73.35	74.92- 97
Ayre	Sanjay	JAM	19.6.80	188/75	400	44.97	44.92- 02
Azarenkov	Andrey	RUS	26.9.85	191/98	HT	72.89	71.56- 04
Azarenkov	Pavel	RUS	.82		HT	71.19	
* Baala	Mehdi	FRA	17.8.78	183/65	800	1:44.74	1:43.15- 02
					1000	2:17.01i	2:13.96- 03
					1500	3:30.80	3:28.98- 03
					2000	4:53.12	
Baba	Youssef	MAR	7.8.79	173/55	1500	3:33.75	3:33.01- 04
* Bába	Jaroslav	CZE	2.9.84	196/82	HJ	2.37i, 2.36	2.34- 04
Baday	Ahmed Ibrahim	MAR	12.1.79	182/74	10000	27:48.85	28:13.54- 01
Baddeley	Andrew	GBR	20.6.82	185/70	1500	3:36.43	3:39.11- 04
Badji ¶	Ndiss Kaba	SEN	21.9.83	192/79	LJ	8.06dq/8.03wdq	8.20A, 8.03, 8.30Aw- 04
					TJ	17.15dq	16.30- 02
Bai Liansheng		CHN	28.7.78	178/65	20kW	1:22:18	1:20:48- 03
Bai Xuejin		CHN-J	6.6.87		20kW	1:19:29	
					50kW	3:54:41	
Baillie	Christopher	GBR	21.4.81		110H	13.84, 13.70w	
Bairu	Simon	CAN	8.8.83	173/57	10000	28:04.75	28:28.69- 04
* Bakken	Marius	NOR	27.3.78	183/63	1500	3:38.84	3:40.41- 01
					5000	13:07.63	13:06.39- 04
Balcar	Ondrej	CZE	2.3.81		HJ	2.25	2.18- 02
* Baldini	Stefano	ITA	25.5.71	176/60	HMar	61:17 dh	60:56- 97, 60:50w- 00
					Mar	2:09:25	2:07:29- 02
Baldwin	Gabe	USA	9.1.85		PV	5.55	5.20- 03
Balliengo	Jorge	ARG	5.1.78	194/110	DT	64.69	61.36- 04
Banda	Lewis	ZIM	16.8.82	173/67	400	45.94	44.58- 04
Baranovskiy	Dmitriy	UKR	28.7.79	174/59	Mar	2:08:29	2:12:34- 04
Barbaud	Alexandre	FRA	15.2.80	194/82	PV	5.50i, 5.50	5.75- 03
Barberi	Andrea	ITA	15.1.79	178/64	400	45.70	45.79- 03
^ Barmasai	Bernard	KEN	6.5.74	173/55	Mar	2:10:52	
* Barras	Romain	FRA	1.8.80	193/84	Dec	8185	8196- 03
Barrett	Craig	NZL	16.11.71	183/70	50kW	3:58:39	3:48:05- 01
Barrios	Eugenio	ESP	3.11.76	182/75	800	1:45.19	1:46.38- 03
					1500	3:37.72	3:42.95- 02
Barry	Damion	TRI	3.3.82	188/83	400	45.55	45.67- 03
* Bartels	Ralf	GER	21.2.78	186/125	SP	21.36	20.88- 04

Name		Nat	Born	Ht/Wt	Event	2005 Mark	Pre-2005 Best
Barus	Benson	KEN	4.7.80		HMar	61:14	61:31- 04
* Bashir	Daham Najim	QAT	8.11.78	171/60	1500	3:31.04	3:35.47- 02
	(David Nyaga)				1M	3:47.97	
					3000	7:41.83	7:44.37- 04
Basil	Adam	AUS	14.4.75		100	10.33, 10.21w	10.34- 99, 10.22wA- 00
Batangdon	Joseph	CMR	29.7.78	180/75	100	10.20, 10.14w	10.19- 02, 9.9- 00
					200	20.56	20.31A, 20.3- 99, 20.31- 00
Batman	Daniel	AUS	20.3.81	173/73	100	10.19, 10.14w	10.39- 04
					200	20.44, 20.3	20.59- 04
					400	45.98	45.02- 03
Bátovsky	Milos	SVK	26.5.79	178/65	50kW	3:54:49	3:54:08- 04
Battle	Sheldon	USA	23.6.83	188/120	SP	20.94	18.88- 04
Bavikin	Vadim	ISR	4.10.70	188/97	JT	77.57	81.94- 04
Baxter	Kenneth	USA	17.4.82		200	20.61	20.91, 20.86w- 03
Bayo	Getulo	TAN	.80		HMar	61:57	63:22- 01
					Mar	2:10:45	2:15:12- 04
Bayo	Zebedayo	TAN	20.5.76	178/64	Mar	2:10:51	2:08:51- 98
* Beckford	James	JAM	9.1.75	183/73	LJ	8.28, 8.36w	8.62- 97, 8.68w- 95
Behrenbruch	Pascal	GER	19.1.85	195/89	Dec	7842	0
* Bekele	Kenenisa	ETH	13.6.82	160/54	2000	5:00.76+	
					3000	7:32.59	7:30.67- 01
					5000	12:40.18	12:52.26- 03
					10000	26:17.53	26:20.31- 04
* Bekele	Tariku	ETH-J	21.1.87	160/52	3000	7:36.63	7:45.23- 04
					5000	12:59.03	13:11.97- 04
Belger	Greg	USA	21.8.81	183/80	110H	13.68dt	13.84, 13.66w- 04
* Bell	Kenta	USA	16.3.77	183/77	TJ	17.11	17.63- 02
Bellani	Hicham	MAR	15.9.79	180/64	3000	7:43.15	7:37.86- 04
					5000	12:59.67	13:05.72- 04
* Belonog	Yuriy	UKR	9.3.74	200/135	SP	20.93	21.81- 03
					DT	64.79	65.53- 03
Belotserkevskiy	Dmitriy	UKR	25.3.85	192/80	LJ	7.93	7.91- 04
^ Belov	Yuriy	BLR	20.3.81	183/120	SP	19.87	21.14- 03
Belz	Christian	SUI	11.9.74	179/60	10000	27:53.16	0
* Benjamin	Tim	GBR	2.5.82	183/75	400	44.56	45.04- 04
Bennett	LaRon	USA	25.11.82	183/75	400H	48.74	49.04- 04
Bennett-Jackson	Wade	GBR-J	27.2.87	175/68	100	10.20w	10.45- 04
Bennici	Francesco	ITA	3.10.71	171/50	Mar	2:11:16	2:16:04- 93
Bensghir	Yassine	MAR	3.1.83	170/68	800	1:45.89	1:46.89- 03
					1500	3:35.04	3:36.76- 03
Berdeja	Cristian D.	MEX	21.6.81	169/58	20kW	1:19:22	1:21:20- 01
* Berhanu	Dejene	ETH	12.12.80	182/64	5000	12:56.24	12:54.15- 04
					10000	27:12.22	27:14.61-03
					HMar	60:44 dh	59:37- 04
Bermejo	Javier	ESP	23.12.78	191/77	HJ	2.27i	2.28- 04
^ Bernard	Claston	JAM	22.3.79	193/90	Dec	7877	8225- 04
Bernard	Martyn	GBR	15.12.84	195/86	HJ	2.24	2.27- 04
Bernardo	Paulo	POR	21.11.74	184/115	DT	60.61	60.58- 03
Berrabah	Yahya	MAR	13.10.81	186/75	LJ	8.18	8.33- 03
					TJ	16.44	
^ Berrett	Tim	CAN	23.1.65	179/66	50kW	3:55:48	3:50:21- 04
Berrian	Chris	USA	17.4.83	173/70	100	10.27w	
					200	20.54. 20.47w	21.08- 04
* Betanzos	Yoandri	CUB	15.2.82	179/71	TJ	17.46	17.53- 04
* Bett	Mark	KEN	22.12.76	180/64	3000	7:48.36i	7:36.66- 01
					5000	13:16.2e+	12:55.63- 00
					10000	26:52.93	27:02.00- 04
Bettinelli	Andrea	ITA	6.10.78	194/82	HJ	2.30i, 2.27	2.31- 03
Beyens	Kristof	BEL	13.7.83	189/70	200	20.45	20.80- 02
Beyer	Jamie	USA	29.12.76	193/113	SP	21.13	21.00- 02
Bezabeh	Alemayehu	ETH-J	.86		3000	7:45.98	
Bian Aiguo		CHN	10.6.80	178/65	20kW	1:19:51	1:22:29- 01
Biber	Zsolt	HUN	31.5.76	194/104	SP	19.83	20.81i, 20.55- 04
Bielecki	Jan	DEN	20.2.71	188/103	HT	71.55	77.02- 02
Bien-Aimé	Marvin	USA	20.10.83	175/75	200	20.61w	21.21, 20.64w- 04
* Bieniek	Michal	POL	17.5.84	194/72	HJ	2.36	2.30- 03
Bigdeli	Schahriar	GER	26.3.80	182/76	Dec	7494	0
Bishnoi	Jagdish Singh	IND	20.5.72	182/86	JT	77.17	79.67- 00
Bispo	Rogério	BRA	16.11.85		LJ	8.15	7.69- 04
* Bitok	Paul	KEN	26.6.70	173/58	3000	7:39.66	7:28.41- 96
Bitzi	Ivan	SUI	4.8.75	185/73	110H	13.52	13.59- 02

Name		Nat	Born	Ht/Wt	Event	2005Mark	Pre-2005 Best
Biwott	Paul	KEN	18.4.78		Mar	2:08:17	2:10:30- 04
Biwott	Stephen Kipkosgei	KEN	.74		Mar	2:11:16	
Biwott Kiplagat	Philip	KEN-J	.87		HMar	61:48	63:20- 04
Black	Anders	DEN	6.11.79		Dec	7705	7234- 03
* Blackwood	Michael	JAM	29.8.76	190/79	400	44.84	44.60- 02
Blakely	Fernada	USA	28.9.81	185/79	200	20.52	20.82, 20.79w- 04
					400	45.25	46.25- 04, 45.99dq- 00
Blanco	José Luis	ESP	3.6.75	175/61	3kSt	8:21.04	8:13.86- 03
Blanton	DaBryan	USA	3.7.84	179/74	100	10.12, 10.07w	10.07- 03
					200	20.64w	20.37- 01
* Blaschek	Thomas	GER	5.4.81	189/83	110H	13.31	13.62- 04
Blincoe	Adrian	NZL	4.11.79	181/61	1500	3:35.50	3:36.53- 04
					3000	7:46.49	7:47.46- 03
* Blom	Rens	NED	1.3.77	178/75	PV	5.80	5.81- 04
Blonskiy	Yuriy	UKR	9.7.79	187/85	Dec	7546	7890- 01
Blume	Marc	GER	28.12.73	180/74	100	10.29	10.13- 96, 10.12w- 02
Bobbato	Maurizio	ITA	17.2.79	191/77	800	1:46.15	1:47.03- 04
Bock	Detlef	GER	15.8.74	194/135	SP	20.72	20.47- 02
Bogdan	Mircea	ROM	6.5.82	184/60	3kSt	8:27.29	8:41.72- 03
Bogdanof	Tim	USA	9.11.79	190/82	110H	13.51	13.51- 03
Bogdanov	Dmitriy	RUS	11.4.79	190/75	800	1:45.30	1:45.04- 04
Boit	Josphat	KEN	26.11.83	170/57	10000	28:07.27	
* Boit Kipketer	Wilson	KEN	6.10.73	167/52	3000	7:45.41	7:33.96- 97
					3kSt	8:09.32	7:59.08- 97
Bokor	Marián	SVK	17.4.77	193/83	JT	77.79	83.38- 00
Bolden	Gregory	USA	30.6.84	180/87	100	10.26, 10.15w	10.49- 04
Bolles	Cameron	USA	24.3.76		DT	60.08	61.37- 01
* Bolt	Usain	JAM-J	21.8.86	196/86	200	19.99	19.93- 04
Bookman #	Leo	USA	3.1.82	191/95	200	20.35, 20.34 dq	20.37- 03
Boothby	Scott	USA	9.4.73	183/104	HT	74.19	72.28- 04
Bor	Noah	KEN	28.7.77		Mar	2:09:20	2:08:48- 03
* Börgeling	Lars	GER	16.4.79	189/86	PV	5.77	5.85- 02
Borichevskiy	Aleksandr	RUS	25.6.70	195/120	DT	61.76	65.08- 99
Borisov	Yevgeniy	RUS	7.3.84	185/75	110H	13.73	13.98- 03
Borodkin	Andrey	UKR	18.4.78	202/135	SP	20.30	20.38- 04
Boros	László	HUN	3.2.82	190/73	HJ	2.28	2.27- 04
Boruschewski	Benjamin	GER	23.4.80	190/130	HT	71.41	72.73- 02
* Borzakovskiy	Yuriy	RUS	12.4.81	182/72	800	1:44.18	1:42.47- 01
* Boswell	Mark	CAN	28.7.77	189/77	HJ	2.29	2.35- 99
Botha	Werner	RSA	31.1.78	186/73	800	1:45.62A	1:44.41- 00
Boué	Anier	CUB	3.4.84	192/90	JT	76.26	75.54- 04
Bougtaïb	Tarik	MAR	30.4.81	180/75	LJ	7.99	8.21- 04
					TJ	17.00	15.64- 02
Boukensa	Tarek	ALG	19.11.81	178/62	1500	3:34.68/3:32.7+u	3:32.35- 04
					1M	3:49.95	3:52.34- 03
					3000	7:43.23	
Boulahfane	Kamel	ALG	1.7.76	178/63	800	1:46.07	1:46.49- 99
					1500	3:35.22	3:32.44- 04
* Boulami	Brahim	MAR	20.4.72	180/64	3kSt	8:04.92	7:55.28- 01, 7:53.17dq- 02
Boulanger	David	FRA	11.12.74	176/64	50kW	3:55:11	3:51:36- 01
Bourguignon	Rudy	FRA	16.7.79	185/82	Dec	8025	7698- 02
Bourifa	Migidio	ITA	31.1.69	171/55	Mar	2:10:48	2:09:07- 02
^ Bownes	Shaun	RSA	24.10.70	194/90	110H	13.65A	13.26- 01, 13.2A- 98
Boyles	Chris	USA	2.5.80	188/93	Dec	7679	7827w- 04
* Bramlett	Ron	USA	22.10.79	181/68	110H	13.31	13.26- 04
Brandstatter	Travis	USA	10.3.82	188/86	Dec	7641	7736- 04
Brannen	Nathan	CAN	8.9.82	175/59	1500	3:35.72	3:39.05- 04
					1M	3:56.16, 3:55.11i	3:59.85- 01, 3:57.96i- 03
* Brazell	Bennie	USA	2.6.82	185/77	400H	47.67	48.05- 04
* Brew	Derrick	USA	28.12.77	185/82	400	44.96	44.29- 99
Brisseault	David	FRA	7.3.69	185/95	JT	77.64	82.20- 04
^ Brits	Okkert	RSA	22.8.73	198/84	PV	5.65	6.03- 95
Broe	Tim	USA	20.6.77	180/66	3000	7:40.28	7:39.45- 01, 7:39.23i- 02
					5000	13:11.77	13:18.61- 04
Broening	Marius	GER	24.10.83	183/88	100	10.24w	10.37- 03
Brown	Carl	USA	11.2.70	193/105	DT	64.95	66.66, 67.86dh-03
* Brown	Chris	BAH	15.10.78	178/68	400	44.48	44.94A- 03, 45.08- 00
* Brown	Darrel	TRI	11.10.84	184/79	100	9.99	10.01- 03
					200	20.61	20.41- 01
* Brown	Joel	USA	31.1.80	183/75	200	20.55	20.64- 04
					110H	13.22	13.35- 04

Name		Nat	Born	Ht/Wt	Event	2005 Mark	Pre-2005 Best
^ Brown	Jon	GBR	27.2.71	175/57	Mar	2:09:31	2:09:44- 99
* Brown	Omar	JAM	21.6.82	177/70	200	20.43	20.66, 20.36w- 04
Brown	Pat	USA	.82		400H	49.51	50.85- 04
Brown	Xavier	JAM	.83		100	10.26w	10.41- 04
Browne	Pierre	CAN	14.1.80	178/75	100	10.27, 10.19w	10.12, 9.98w- 02
Buc	Bostjan	SLO	13.4.80	178/60	3kSt	8:22.91	8:16.96- 03
Buchanan	Anthony	USA	10.9.81	175/77	100	10.27w	10.21- 04, 10.10w- 03
^ Bucher	André	SUI	19.10.76	185/75	800	1:45.20	1:42.55- 01
Buciarski	Piotr	DEN	22.11.75	183/79	PV	5.53i, 5.50	5.75- 02
Buckfield	Nick	GBR	5.6.73	185/78	PV	5.60	5.81i- 02, 5.80- 98
Bucki	Gaëtan	FRA	9.5.80	195/125	SP	19.69i	19.24- 03
* Buckland	Stéphane	MRI	20.1.77	187/73	100	10.28	10.13- 01, 10.0A- 99
					200	20.28	20.06- 03
Budza	Sergey	UKR	6.12.84	180/72	50kW	3:59:31	
Bueno	Thiago	BRA	21.2.83		400H	49.59	50.04- 03
Bukhalov	Spas	BUL	14.11.80	186/85	PV	5.70i, 5.60	5.70- 03
Buller	Russ	USA	10.9.78	178/72	PV	5.75	5.81- 01
* Bungei	Wilfred	KEN	24.7.80	172/60	800	1:43.70	1:42.34- 02
* Burayev	Viktor	RUS	23.2.82	176/58	20kW	1:18:48	1:18:06- 01
Burgess	Daryl	USA	.85	183/79	110H	13.46w	14.12- 04
* Burgess	Paul	AUS	14.8.79	184/83	PV	6.00	5.77- 04
Burka	Gebo	ETH-J	27.9.87		5000	13:22.17	
* Burkenya	Danila	RUS	20.7.78	198/82	TJ	17.10	17.68- 04
Burkhardt	Ivo	GER	7.12.77	186/81	110H	13.73	13.82- 97
Burlachenko	Pavel	RUS	7.4.76	184/80	PV	5.50	5.81- 98
Burley	Sam	USA	13.2.81	175/68	800	1:46.70	1:45.39- 02
Burmakin	Dmitriy	RUS	8.1.81		Mar	2:11:20	2:14:19- 04
* Burns	Marc	TRI	7.1.83	185/79	100	9.96	10.12, 9.99w- 04
					200	20.57	20.93- 04
Busienei	Wilson	KEN	18.8.81	167/61	5000	13:21.89	13:12.03- 04
					10000	28:08.40	27:29.95- 04
					HMar	61:39	62:55- 04
Bynum	Desmond	USA	9.9.80	183/77	100	10.23w	10.23w- 03
^ Byrd	Leonard	USA	17.3.75	178/64	400	45.09	44.45- 02
Cadée	Erik	NED	15.2.84	200/110	DT	60.27	56.59- 04
Cafagna	Diego	ITA	9.7.75	174/60	50kW	3:55:18	3:57:23- 02
Cai Xiaobao		CHN	11.3.80		LJ	7.90i	
^ Calado	Carlos	POR	5.10.75	186/80	TJ	16.58i	17.09i- 99, 17.08- 96
Camberlein	Damien	FRA	5.2.80	192/85	Dec	7690	7367- 02
Camejo	Ibrahím	CUB	28.6.82	179/74	LJ	8.20	8.24- 02
^ Camossi	Paolo	ITA	6.1.74	176/72	TJ	16.86	17.45- 00
^ Campbell	Milton	USA	15.5.76	178/75	400	45.53	44.67- 97
Campeny	Moises	ESP	27.5.79	186/90	HT	72.10	75.42- 03
Campioli	Filippo	ITA	21.2.82	193/78	HJ	2.24i	2.24- 03
Campisi	Jaret	USA	7.2.83	178/75	400H	50.10	51.23- 04
Canal	David	ESP	7.12.78	183/80	400	45.93i	45.01- 03
* Cantwell	Christian	USA	30.9.80	198/145	SP	21.67	22.54- 04
* Capel	John	USA	27.10.78	180/82	100	10.08	9.95- 04
					200	20.31	19.85- 00
Carabelli	Gianni	ITA	30.5.79	189/79	400H	48.84	49.51- 03
Cardol	Eddy	NED	6.5.78	193/106	SP	19.18	17.77- 03
Carelse	Ramsey	RSA	30.10.85	181/73	HJ	2.30	2.21- 04
Carrillo	Yunier	CUB	1.10.81	186/80	HJ	2.26	2.25- 04
^ Carroll	Mark	IRL	15.1.72	177/66	3000	7:46.60i	7:30.36- 99
* Carter	James	USA	7.5.78	186/77	400H	47.43	47.57- 02
* Carter	Xavier	USA	8.12.85	190/86	200	20.02	20.69- 03
					400	45.65	45.44, 45.3- 04
Casado	Arturo	ESP	26.1.83	185/75	1500	3:35.64	3:38.04- 04
Casañas	Frank	CUB	18.10.78	184/101	DT	65.32	65.08- 03
Casandra	Silviu	ROM	27.10.75	183/64	20kW	1:22:14	1:21:35- 00
Casquette #	Arnaud	MRI	16.4.78	175/70	LJ	8.12, 8.28wA	8.05- 00, 8.13A, 8.23w- 03
Castelo Branco	Thiago	BRA	4.11.79		110H	13.69	13.93- 03
Castillejo	Carles	ESP	18.8.78	171/60	10000	28:06.88	28:11.27- 04
Castillo	Víctor	VEN	8.6.81	180/74	LJ	8.00Ai	8.34A- 04, 7.98, 8.10w- 03
Cerlati	Mattias	FRA	25.10.83	191/84	Dec	7550	7405- 04
Cerra	Juan Ignacio	ARG	16.10.76	180/95	HT	74.78	76.42- 01
Chabowski	Marcin	POL-J	28.5.86	170/50	3kSt	8:30.40	8:37.28- 04
Chakouian	Jeff	USA	20.4.82	185/118	SP	20.18	20.19- 04
Challenger	Ben	GBR	7.3.78	186/75	HJ	2.27i, 2.27	2.30- 99
Chambers	Ricardo	JAM	7.10.84	177/73	400	44.87	46.02- 04
Chanchaima	Jairus	KEN			HMar	61:18	

	Name		Nat	Born	Ht/Wt	Event	2005Mark	Pre-2005 Best
	Chane	Abere	ETH	16.6.85		10000	27:47.90	28:46.99- 04
	Chang Chunhu		CHN	1.5.82	177/63	50kW	3:47:19	3:55:39- 03
	Chaput	Brian	USA	9.4.81	186/93	JT	80.45	79.81- 04
*	Charfreitag	Libor	SVK	11.9.77	191/117	HT	80.85	81.81- 03
	Chebet	Peter	KEN	24.6.76		Mar	2:08:58	2:08:43- 03
*	Chebii	Abraham	KEN	23.12.79	172/63	3000	7:42.49	7:36.11- 02
						5000	13:22.53	12:52.99- 03
	Cheboiboch	Christopher	KEN	3.3.77	168/52	HMar	61:51	60:33- 03
						Mar	2:09:17dh/2:10:14	2:08:17- 02
	Cheboiywo	Boaz	KEN	2.8.78	160/54	1500	3:35.20	3:38.47- 04
						3000	7:39.04	7:47.88, 7:38.30i- 04
						5000	13:19.56	13:29.77, 13:29.26i- 03
						10000	28:04.08	27:46.47- 03
						3kSt	8:31.22	
	Cheboror	Robert	KEN	9.9.78		HMar	61:55	61:42- 02
*	Chéhibi	Mouhcine	MAR	28.1.78	182/70	800	1:44.46	1:44.62- 04
	Chelanga	Joshua	KEN	7.4.73	168/56	Mar	2:09:10	2:07:05- 04
	Chelimo	Elijah	KEN-J	.87		3kSt	8:28.62	
	Chemitei	Thomas	KEN	22.5.78		Mar	2:09:21	2:10:26- 03
	Chemov	Andrey	RUS	13.7.83		PV	5.50i, 5.50	5.50- 03
*	Chemweno	David	KEN	18.12.81	175/58	3000	7:48.2A	7:41.35- 04
						3kSt	8:09.09	8:11.44- 04
	Chen Ming		CHN	8.3.84		110H	13.70	13.96- 03
	Chen Mingfu		CHN	26.1.85		10000	28:16.40	29:06.34- 04
	Chen Qi		CHN	10.3.82	184/79	JT	79.31	81.38- 04
	Chenonge	Hillary	KEN	30.5.85	166/52	3000	7:43.88	7:39.22- 02
						5000	13:04.70	13:06.47- 02
	Chepkok	Bernard	KEN	17.1.84	181/67	10000	28:11.45	
	Chepkonga	Michael	KEN	.79		800	1:46.6A	
	Chepkwony	David Kirwa	KEN	29.12.78		3000	7:43.67	
	Cheptot	Stephen Matebo	KEN	30.3.74		Mar	2:10:42	2:07:59- 02
	Cheribo	Daniel	KEN	.81		Mar	2:10:13	2:08:38- 04
	Cherigat	Timothy	KEN	29.12.76		Mar	2:10:34	2:09:34- 02
	Chernov	Sergey	BLR	5.2.79	178/70	20kW	1:22:14	1:21:56.7t- 04
	Cherono	Benson	KEN	30.6.84	168/52	HMar	61:37	60:28- 04
						Mar	2:10:01 dh	2:11:23- 04
	Cheruiyot	Evans	KEN	.82		HMar	61:01	
	Cheruiyot	Jonas	KEN	.84		5000	13:11.18	
	Cheruiyot	Robert Kipkoech	KEN	26.9.78	168/54	HMar	59:21 dh, 61:45	59:54dh- 04, 60:06- 02
						Mar	2:11:01	2:08:13- 03
	Cheseret	Robert	KEN	8.10.83	180/61	5000	13:13.23	13:22.65- 04
						10000	28:20.11	28:25.62- 04
	Chiaraviglio	Germán	ARG-J	16.4.87	192/77	PV	5.55	5.51- 04
	Chiba	Yoshihiro	JPN	29.4.79	178/65	400H	49.84	48.65- 01
	Chimier	Jonathan	MRI	6.8.82	175/75	LJ	7.97i, 7.94	8.26A, 8.08, 8.29Aw- 03
*	Chirchir	William	KEN	6.2.79	175/55	800	1:45.88A	1:43.33- 99
						1500	3:32.93	3:29.29- 01
	Chisholm	Lachlan	AUS	4.5.80	185/73	1500	3:38.95	3:37.03- 04
						1M	3:56.27	4:03.15- 01
	Chivás	Alexis	CUB	7.11.83	180/84	Dec	7624	7262- 04
	Choffart	Julien	FRA	5.11.78	186/79	Dec	7607	7580- 04
*	Choge	Augustine	KEN-J	21.1.87	162/53	1500	3:33.99	3:36.64- 04
						3000	7:42.78	7:36.82- 04
						5000	12:53.66	12:57.01- 04
	Cholensky	Toms	CZE	25.4.78	177/77	TJ	16.48	16.37- 04
	Chou Yi-Chen		TPE	9.7.84	187/95	JT	76.18	72.78- 02
	Christian	Brendan	ANT	11.12.83	178/70	100	10.22w	10.11, 10.06w- 04, 9.9- 02
*	Christopher	Tyler	CAN	3.10.83	188/84	200	20.49	20.50- 04
						400	44.44	45.25- 04
	Chrzanowski	Tomasz	POL	12.7.81	189/119	SP	19.23	19.47- 03
	Chu Ki-young		KOR	4.3.77	180/80	JT	77.04	78.92- 02
	Chu Yafei		CHN-Y	5.9.88		20kW	1:22:18	1:27:23- 04
	Chubsa	Andrey	BLR	29.11.82	191/75	HJ	2.24i	2.32- 03
^	Chumachenko	Pavel	RUS	5.4.71	189/138	SP	20.17	20.91i, 20.54- 01
	Chumba	Linus	KEN	9.2.80	171/57	5000	13:21.52	
						3kSt	8:11.98	8:19.26- 03
	Chumba	Sammy	KEN	9.8.78		HMar	61:46	63:10- 04
	Chuprinin	Kiril	UKR	22.7.75	197/140	DT	62.52	63.92- 03
^	Cilliers	Ockert	RSA	21.4.81	186/76	400H	48.93	48.02A, 48.23- 04
	Ciofani	Roland	FRA	29.9.71	181/95	HT	71.34	72.18- 03
	Ciotti	Giulio	ITA	5.10.76	188/78	HJ	2.29	2.28- 02

MEN'S INDEX

Name		Nat	Born	Ht/Wt	Event	2005 Mark	Pre-2005 Best
Ciotti	Nicola	ITA	5.10.76	188/78	HJ	2.30	2.30i- 02, 2.30- 03
* Clarke	Davian	JAM	30.4.76	180/77	400	44.92	44.83- 04
Clarke	Lerone	JAM	2.10.81	174/66	100	10.24	10.29, 10.12w- 04
Clavier	Jérôme	FRA	3.5.83	176/60	PV	5.63	5.65i, 5.60- 04
* Clay	Bryan	USA	3.1.80	180/83	Dec	8732	8820- 04
Cleare	Aaron	BAH	31.1.83	185/84	400	45.90	46.61- 04
* Clement	Kerron	USA	31.10.85	188/84	200	20.40i	20.82- 04
					400	45.31, 44.57i	45.90i- 04
					400H	47.24	48.51- 04
Clerbout	Tim	BEL	13.10.81	184/70	1500	3:37.59	3:37.50- 04
Clickett	Justin	USA	12.4.85	191/118	SP	19.23i	17.92- 04
Coghlan	Peter	IRL	27.3.75	186/81	110H	13.68	13.30- 99
Collaku	Dorian	ALB	2.6.77	184/108	HT	75.78	74.41- 04
Collazo	Williams	CUB-J	31.8.86	175/66	400	45.50	46.65- 04
* Collins	Kim	SKN	5.4.76	175/64	100	10.00	9.98- 02, 9.92w- 03
Collio	Simone	ITA	27.12.79	180/74	100	10.22, 10.15w	10.20, 10.14w- 04
Colquhoun	Lueroy	JAM	1.3.80	185/73	400H	48.79	48.91- 02
Conwright	Kaaron	USA	8.8.76	175/73	100	10.27, 10.17w	10.10, 10.05A- 00
Coolsaet	Reid	CAN	29.7.79	175/60	5000	13:23.30	13:31.01- 04
Cooper	Jermaine	USA	31.8.80	178/77	110H	13.62, 13.53w	13.54- 02, 13.52w- 01
Copello	Alexei	CUB	12.8.85	181/74	TJ	16.95, 17.09w	16.90- 04
Copland	Esteban	VEN	12.10.79	179/62	LJ	7.92A	7.97- 00, 8.18Aw- 01
Costa	Vítor	POR	28.5.74	183/105	HT	76.06	76.86- 04
Cousins	Duane	AUS	13.7.73	177/65	50kW	4:04:35	3:54:38- 95
* Cragg	Alistair	IRL	13.6.80	183/59	3000	7:39.89i	7:38.96, 7:38.59i- 04
* Crawford	Shawn	USA	14.1.78	181/86	100	9.99, 9.98w	9.88, 9.86w- 04
					200	20.12	19.79- 04
Cronje	Johan	RSA	13.4.82	180/65	800	1:46.13	1:47.18- 02
					1500	3:35.58	3:37.28- 02
* Cui Zhide		CHN	11.1.83	179/65	20kW	1:17:53	1:20:12- 04
					50kW	3:44:20	3:45:36- 04
Curry	Rafeeq	USA	19.8.83	183/68	TJ	16.47i, 16.75w	16.34i- 03, 16.17, 16.61w- 04
Czaja	Jakub	POL	12.9.80	179/64	3kSt	8:17.49	8:22.51- 04
^ Czapiewski	Pawel	POL	30.3.78	178/57	800	1:45.39	1:43.22- 01
					1000	2:17.81	2:17.22- 02
Czerwinski	Przemyslaw	POL	28.7.83	184/80	PV	5.65	5.55- 04
Dabrowski	Daniel	POL	23.9.83	180/69	400	45.62	46.90- 03
Dacastello	Stefano	ITA	17.2.80	183/72	LJ	7.95	8.17- 04
Dæhlin	dne Svahn	NOR	26.6.82		800	1:46.05	1:49.96- 02
Dagen	Lamont	USA			TJ	16.45	
Daigo	Naoyuki	JPN	18.1.81	182/64	HJ	2.27	2.23- 04
Dallet	Xavier	FRA	24.12.79	183/94	HT	71.35	71.06- 04
Damião	Manuel	POR	19.7.78	174/62	1500	3:36.60	3:34.37- 04
Damszel	Tomasz	POL	25.3.72	188/95	JT	77.36	77.69- 04
Danek	Ondrej	CZE	26.11.81	186/80	400H	49.85	50.49- 03
Danners	Rocky	USA	21.6.81	178/70	PV	5.50	5.51- 02
Darien	Garfield	FRA-J	22.12.87	187/76	110H	13.73	14.03, 13.98w- 04
Davide	Kleberson	BRA	20.7.85		800	1:46.65	1:48.55- 03
Davis	James	USA	19.3.76	185/82	400	45.95	45.21- 02
Davis	Lancford	JAM	11.10.78	187/77	400	45.63	45.87- 01
Davis	Malachi	GBR	13.9.77	180/79	400	45.60	45.52- 04
* Davis	Walter	USA	2.7.79	188/83	LJ	7.98	8.25- 04
					TJ	17.62i, 17.57	17.63- 04
de la Ossa	Carlos	ESP	25.11.76	168/50	3000	7:42.16	7:43.57- 03
* de la Ossa	Juan Carlos	ESP	25.11.76	168/50	5000	13:10.58	13:18.43- 04
					10000	27:27.80	28:07.19- 03
De Lepine	Eddy	FRA	30.3.84	175/65	100	10.23	10.19- 03
De Luca	Marco	ITA	12.5.81	189/72	50kW	3:55:30	4:05:01- 04
de Villiers	Pieter	RSA	13.7.82	179/75	400H	48.46	49.28- 02
* Deakes	Nathan	AUS	17.8.77	183/66	20kW	1:17:33	1:18:14- 01
					50kW	3:47:51	3:39:43- 03
DeGrammont	Dominique	HAI	13.3.79	175/80	110H	13.59	13.66- 02, 13.62w- 03
Delli Carri	Pellegrino	ITA	4.8.76	182/97	HT	71.96	71.48- 04
Demeritte	Dominic	BAH	22.2.78	180/67	200	20.47	20.21- 02
Demidyuk	Sergey	UKR	5.6.82	195/80	110H	13.38	13.37- 04
Demissie	Ashebir	ETH	.77		Mar	2:10:40	2:09:14- 03
Demyanyuk	Dimitriy	UKR	30.6.83	195/68	HJ	2.26sq/2.25	2.26- 04
Derevyagin	Aleksandr	RUS	24.3.79	178/78	400H	49.78	49.50- 04
Desmet	Pieter	BEL	7.6.83	177/57	3kSt	8:20.31	8:32.91- 04
^ Devonish	Marlon	GBR	1.6.76	183/76	100	10.13	10.13- 98
					200	20.41, 20.34w	20.19, 20.18w- 02

Name		Nat	Born	Ht/Wt	Event	2005Mark	Pre-2005 Best
* Devyatovskiy	Vadim	BLR	20.3.77	194/120	HT	84.90	82.91- 04
Dezsö	Ákos	HUN	27.4.83	188/82	400H	49.67	50.09- 04
Dhouibi	Hamdi	TUN	24.1.82	190/85	Dec	8023	7851- 03, 7965w- 02
Di Cecco	Alberico	ITA	19.4.74	174/62	Mar	2:08:02	2:08:53- 03
Diamadáras	Dimítrios	GRE	18.7.84	180/65	LJ	8.12	8.10- 04
Diarra	Alassane	FRA	22.1.81	179/79	TJ	16.43	16.45- 03
Dias	Thiago	BRA	2.3.84	188/71	LJ	7.93A	7.97- 02, 8.03w- 03
Dias Sabino	Jefferson	BRA	4.11.82	188/78	TJ	16.75	16.66- 03
Diaz	Michael	FRA	28.10.86	195/80	HJ	2.23i	2.16- 04
Díaz	José Ignacio	ESP	22.11.79	173/63	20kW	1:22:36	1:22:20- 04
					50kW	3:51:09	3:59:30- 03
Dillon	Cleavon	TRI	5.10.82	186/79	100	10.20w	10.29, 10.23w- 04
Diniz	Yohan	FRA	1.1.78	185/69	20kW	1:20:20	1:24:25- 04
					50kW	3:45:17	3:52:11.0t- 04
* Dinkesa	Abebe	ETH	6.3.84	169/55	3000	7:33.2+	
					5000	12:55.58	13:23.85- 04
					10000	26:30.74	27:23.60- 04
					HMar	61:53	
Disi	Dieudonné	RWA	24.4.78	178/67	10000	27:53.51	28:01.34- 04
Dittmar	Andy	GER	5.7.74	196/120	SP	20.38	20.23- 02
* Dix	Walter	USA-J	31.1.86	170/73	100	10.06, 9.96w	10.28- 04
					200	20.18	20.62, 20.54w- 04
Dixon	Leroy	USA	20.6.83	168/66	100	10.19	10.37- 02
					200	20.58	20.95- 04
* Djhone	Leslie	FRA	18.3.81	187/72	400	45.56	44.64- 04
* Dmitrik	Aleksey	RUS	12.4.84	191/69	HJ	2.34i, 2.30	2.30- 04
Dobson	Ian	USA	6.2.82	188/68	5000	13:15.33	
					10000	27:59.72	28:15.66- 04
Dodoni	Marco	ITA	5.9.72	197/120	SP	19.85i, 19.58	19.81- 04
Dodson	Jeremy	USA-J	30.8.87		200	20.70A	
Doi	Hiroaki	JPN	2.12.78	179/103	HT	71.62	73.33- 03
Dolphin	James	NZL	17.6.83		200	20.60	20.69- 03
Doménech	Yann	FRA	17.3.79	173/61	LJ	8.05i	8.28- 04
* Donato	Fabrizio	ITA	14.8.76	189/82	TJ	16.65. 16.68w	17.60- 00
Dong Jimin		CHN	10.10.85	178/64	20kW	1:20:41	1:24:07- 04
					50kW	3:39:17	3:49:38- 04
Donovici	Daniel	ROM	5.3.80	191/75	TJ	16.55	16.82i, 16.81- 04
* Dorival	Dudley	HAI	1.9.75	185/77	110H	13.58, 13.50w	13.25- 01
Doskoczynski	Kai	GER	15.7.84	184/74	110H	13.65	13.90- 04
Dossévi	Damiel	FRA	3.2.83	182/78	PV	5.75	5.60- 04
* Doucouré	Ladji	FRA	28.3.83	183/75	110H	12.97	13.06- 04
Douglas	Matthew	GBR	26.11.76	190/82	400H	49.89	48.54- 03
* Douglas	Nathan	GBR	4.12.82	183/72	TJ	17.64	16.95- 04
Dovy	Lueyi	FRA	10.11.75	173/65	100	10.24	10.33- 00, 10.32w- 01
					200	20.68	21.08- 00
Draudvila	Darius	LTU	29.3.83	188/87	Dec	7767	
* Drozdov	Aleksey	RUS	3.12.83	184/80	Dec	8196	7805- 04
Dube	Glody	BOT	2.7.78	165/56	800	1:46.49	1:44.59- 01
Dubitskiy	Pavel	KAZ	27.8.82	177/75	Dec	7553	7693- 03
Dudley	Jason	AUS	10.11.84	187/89	Dec	7854	7305- 04
Duffy	Sean	USA	23.3.83	181/66	1500	3:38.46	3:43.09- 04
Duma	Christian	GER	5.2.82	177/76	400H	49.17	49.53- 03
Durand	Nicolas	FRA	23.1.79	176/71	PV	5.50	5.50- 02
Duval	Thibaut	BEL	1.2.79	185/76	PV	5.50i	5.70- 00
Duzant	Jairo	AHO	1.8.79	179/70	100	10.19Aw	10.40A- 03, 10.49- 02
* Dvorák	Tomás	CZE	11.5.72	186/88	Dec	8105	8994- 99
Dys	Rafal	POL	14.1.82	178/63	20kW	1:21:46	1:23:57- 03
Dzingai	Brian	ZIM	29.4.81	168/64	200	20.33	20.12- 04
Dziubak	Oliver	AUS	30.3.82	197/104	JT	78.97	82.79- 04
* East	Michael	GBR	20.1.78	187/68	1500	3:33.32	3:32.37- 04
					1M	3:52.50	3:58.40- 02
Ebuya	Joseph	KEN-J	20.6.87	176/60	3000	7:44.6	
					5000	13:03.79	
* Ecker	Danny	GER	21.7.77	192/80	PV	5.75i, 5.75	6.00i- 01, 5.93- 98
Edgar	Tyrone	GBR	29.3.82	183/73	100	10.19w	10.23, 10.04w- 03
Edmondson	Lewis	USA	26.2.79		110H	13.71w	13.68- 02, 13.59w- 04
Edwards	Monzavous Rae	USA	7.5.81	183/77	100	10.08, 9.99w	10.09- 03, 10.04w- 04
					200	20.46	20.57- 00, 20.37Aw- 04
Edwards	Robin	USA	12.11.83		200	20.69	21.47- 04
Efremov	Ilian	BUL	2.8.70	191/84	PV	5.70	5.73i- 04, 5.70- 98, 5.75sq- 03

Name		Nat	Born	Ht/Wt	Event	2005 Mark	Pre-2005 Best
Egbele	Aaron	NGR	29.1.79	181/79	100	10.16	10.11, 10.03Aw- 04
El Abubakr	Nagmeldin	SUD-J	22.2.86	171/61	400	44.93	45.22- 03
El Amri	Khalid	TUN	20.3.77	163/54	3000	7:28.56	7:47.29- 04
					5000	13:20.40	13:27.59- 03
					10000	27:26.24	28:07.92- 03
El Asri	Abdelgafour	MAR	79		3kSt	8:26.79	8:33.09- 02
El Fassi	Nadir	FRA	23.9.83	180/74	Dec	7724	7437- 04
^ El Himer	Driss	FRA	4.4.74	178/58	HMar	61:30	62:08- 01
* El Mouaziz	Abdelkader	MAR	1.1.69	172/58	Mar	2:09:03	2:06:46- 02
El-Ghazaly	Omar	EGY	9.2.84	196/120	DT	64.36	61.46- 04
Elias	Matthew	GBR	25.4.79	182/62	400H	49.67	49.11- 02
Elkasevic	Edis	CRO	18.2.83	198/118	SP	20.94	19.95- 02, 20.30ex- 04
					DT	60.54	60.05- 04
Ellerton	Andrew	CAN	18.11.83	181/68	800	1:46.25	1:46.56- 04
* Emedolu	Uchenna	NGR	17.9.76	183/79	100	10.13	9.97- 03
					200	20.55, 20.22w	20.31- 02
Emelianov	Ivan	MDA	19.2.77	202/130	SP	19.46	20.26i- 00, 20.08- 03
^ Épalle	Christophe	FRA	23.1.69	194/116	HT	72.89, 79.01dm	81.79- 00
Ergotic	Sinisa	CRO	14.9.68	179/63	LJ	7.96	8.23, 8.25w- 02
Erickson	Chris	AUS	1.12.81	173/63	50kW	4:03:42	4:14:16- 04
Erickson	Kyle	USA	11.1.81	183/70	400H	49.84	49.36- 04
Eriksson	Mattias	SWE	29.8.80	185/93	JT	76.17	73.80- 01
Ernst	Sebastian	GER	11.10.84	180/68	200	20.45	20.36- 04
Esenwein	Peter	GER	7.12.67	188/85	JT	77.20	87.20- 04
Eshbach	Eric	USA	4.2.81	183/84	PV	5.50	5.70- 04
Esho	Benson	KEN-J	2.2.87		800	1:46.53	1:46.25- 04
España	Jesús	ESP	21.8.78	173/56	1500	3:38.57	3:36.53- 02
					3000	7:45.7+	7:42.40- 04
					5000	13:15.44	13:18.31- 04
* Esser	Markus	GER	3.2.80	182/99	HT	80.00	79.01- 04
Essor	Marvin	JAM	27.8.81	173/68	400	45.49	46.87- 03
Esteso	Pedro Antonio	ESP	13.10.76	181/70	1500	3:38.91	3:36.71- 02
* Estévez	Reyes	ESP	2.8.76	187/70	1500	3:38.10, 3:36.51i	3:30.57- 99
					3000	7:43.80i	7:44.87- 99
Estwanik	Chris	USA	4.4.80	183/66	1500	3:38.29	3:40.19- 04
Etoot	Peter	KEN	17.4.84	175/62	800	1:46.80	1:46.83- 04
Evans	Brandon	USA	30.10.79	180/79	TJ	16.48	16.59- 03
Everhart	Craig	USA	13.9.83	180/75	400	45.87	44.89- 04
* Evilä	Tommi	FIN	6.4.80	194/83	LJ	8.19, 8.27w	8.15- 04
Evora	Nelson	POR	20.4.84	181/64	TJ	16.89	16.85i- 04, 16.43-03
Ezenwa	Ambrose	NGR/AUS	10.4.77	179/77	100	10.22, 10.21w	10.25- 04, 10.13w- 03
					200	20.49	20.60- 04, 20.46w- 03
Ezzine	Hamid	MAR	5.10.83	174/60	3kSt	8:21.38	8:25.10- 04
* Fadejevs	Aigars	LAT	27.12.75	175/59	20kW	1:20:55	1:19:25- 02
Falkner	E.J.	USA	.85		400	45.98	47.97- 04
Famiglietti	Anthony	USA	8.11.78	173/57	3kSt	8:19.46	8:17.91- 04
Fang Pengfei		CHN	16.2.83	173/50	20kW	1:19:08	1:24:28- 04
Fantoni	Koura Kaba	ITA	28.8.84	193/78	200	20.58	20.81- 04
Farah	Mohamed	GBR	23.3.83	175/65	1500	3:38.62	3:43.17- 03
					1M	3:56.49	4:00.07- 04
Farmer	Kyle	USA	15.4.83	186/87	100	10.24w	
					200	20.44	20.41- 04
Farnosov	Andrey	RUS	9.7.80		3kSt	8:30.19	8:34.19- 04
* Fasuba	Olusoji	NGR	9.7.84	175/72	100	10.09A, 10.08w, 10.13, 9.8A	10.09- 04
					200	20.60	20.52- 04
Faulk	Dexter	USA	14.4.84	187/75	110H	13.63	13.60, 13.53w- 04
Favretto	Vincent	FRA	5.4.84	188/70	PV	5.60	5.60i- 04, 5.50- 02
Fedaczynski	Rafal	POL	3.12.80	160/50	50kW	3:56:13	4:05:10- 04
Feleke	Abreham Cherkos	ETH-Y	23.9.89	158/52	3000	7:43.00	
					5000	13:25.65	
Felix	Wes	USA	21.7.83	180/75	100	10.23	10.27- 04, 10.24w- 03
					200	20.58	20.43- 04
^ Fenner	Mike	GER	24.4.71	188/92	110H	13.60	13.17- 98, 13.06dt- 95
Ferguson	Kenneth	USA	22.3.84	187/74	400H	48.51	48.79- 03
Fernandes	Raphael	BRA	8.11.84		400H	49.89	50.04- 04
Fernández	Alvaro	ESP	7.4.81	180/67	1500	3:35.57	3:32.88- 04
Fernández	Dennis	CUB-J	23.1.86	178/67	TJ	16.92	16.61- 04
* Fernández	Francisco J	ESP	6.3.77	175/65	20kW	1:17:52	1:17:22- 02
Fernówka	Marin	POL	23.7.82	182/85	HT	71.37	69.67- 04
^ Ferreira Junior	Nelson	BRA	1.1.73	188/82	LJ	8.04	8.36A, 8.32, 8.41Aw- 96
Fields	Jabari	USA	10.9.81	183/75	100	10.13w	10.22- 03

Name		Nat	Born	Ht/Wt	Event	2005Mark	Pre-2005 Best
^ Figère	Nicolas	FRA	19.5.79	177/91	HT	76.66	80.88- 01
Figures	Chris	USA	8.10.81	180/111	SP	20.09	19.34- 04
Filet	Arnis	FRA	17.12.77	182/67	TJ	16.62	17.15- 01
Filíndras	Dimítrios	GRE	9.2.73	174/68	LJ	8.15	8.30- 03
* Filippídis	Konstadínos	GRE-J	26.11.86	187/73	PV	5.75	5.50- 04
Filippídis	Yervásios	GRE-J	24.7.87	184/84	JT	79.42	73.37- 04
Findlay	Adrian	JAM	1.10.82	179/70	400H	49.96	49.64- 04
Findlay	Mark	GBR	20.3.78	188/80	100	10.25	10.35- 99
Flach	Randy	USA	.84	186/82	PV	5.50	5.10- 03
Fofana	Colomba	FRA	11.4.77	186/76	TJ	17.21	17.00- 00, 17.02w- 03
Fomenko	Pavel	RUS	29.6.76	198/76	HJ	2.32i, 2.28	2.32i, 2.31- 02
Ford	Jacoby	USA-J	27.7.87	175/79	100	10.21w	
Fortin	Fabrice	FRA	2.2.80	175/68	PV	5.50	5.55- 00
Fortuna	Diego	ITA	14.2.68	190/116	DT	62.30	64.69- 00
Fountain	Mark	AUS	10.3.82	187/69	1500	3:33.68	3:39.18- 04
					1M	3:53.24	3:59.63- 04
* Francique	Alleyne	GRN	7.6.76	188/75	400	44.60	44.47- 04
Francis	Phil	USA	26.4.83	180/75	100	10.24	10.35- 04
* Frank	Mark	GER	21.6.77	187/91	JT	84.88	83.24- 02
* Frater	Michael	JAM	6.10.82	170/67	100	10.03	10.06- 04, 10.05w- 02
Freeman	Jacob	USA	5.11.80	193/129	HT	72.60	71.72- 03
* Freitag	Jacques	RSA	11.6.82	207/83	HJ	2.38	2.37- 02
Fricke	Roman	GER	23.3.77	192/83	HJ	2.30	2.30- 04
* Friedek	Charles-Michael	GER	26.8.71	184/80	TJ	17.39	17.59- 97
Fritz	Jesper	SWE	13.9.85		PV	5.55i	5.45- 04
Frösén	Oskari	FIN	24.1.76	194/86	HJ	2.27	2.31i- 04, 2.30- 01
Frost	Andy	GBR	17.4.81	189/115	HT	72.09	69.94- 04
Frullani	William	ITA	21.9.79	191/88	Dec	7547	7984- 02
Fuenmayor	Manuel	VEN	3.12.80	190/105	JT	76.56	77.94- 04
Fuentes	Héctor	CUB-Y	19.5.88	183/70	TJ	16.63	15.90- 04
Fujita	Atsushi	JPN	6.11.76	166/52	Mar	2:09:48	2:06:51- 00
Fusenig	Christian	GER	9.5.78	184/88	JT	76.62	79.28- 99
Gabella	Grégory	FRA	22.6.80	190/70	HJ	2.28	2.30- 02
* Gadasu Alatan		CHN	27.1.84	173/60	50kW	3:40:23	3:45:41- 04
Gailes	Tyree	USA	24.2.83	170/67	100	10.33A, 10.18w	10.11- 04, 10.03w- 03
					200	20.57	20.80, 20.57w- 03
* Gaisah	Ignisious	GHA	20.6.83	186/70	LJ	8.34	8.32- 04
Galdino	Sérgio	BRA	7.5.69	169/57	20kW	1:21:29	1:19:56- 95
Galeta	Kristo	EST	9.4.83	190/86	JT	78.05	72.90- 04
^ Galfione	Jean	FRA	9.6.71	184/82	PV	5.75	6.00i, 5.98- 99, 6.00ex- 97
Gallardo	Sergio	ESP	22.3.79	178/67	1500	3:36.10	3:35.24- 03
					3000	7:44.15	7:48.27i- 04
Galvão	Henágio	BRA	18.11.84		TJ	16.42	15.77- 04
Ganotákis	Aléxandros	GRE	3.12.74	197/125	DT	60.04	60.50, 61.80 dh- 03
* García	Alberto	ESP	22.2.71	163/45	5000	13:10.73	13:02.54- 01
García	Ivaro	MEX	18.10.83		20kW	1:22:39	1:26:25- 04
* García	Anier	CUB	9.3.76	189/79	110H	13.61	13.00- 00
Garca	Daniel	MEX	28.10.71	168/56	20kW	1:22:35	1:18:27- 97
* García	Jesús Ángel	ESP	17.10.69	171/62	50kW	3:48:19	3:39:54- 97
García	Luis	GUA	13.9.74	174/62	50kW	3:58:02	3:53:31- 03
García	Roberto	ESP	20.8.75	168/55	1500	3:38.34	3:38.61- 00
					5000	13:25.68	13:16.13- 04
* Gardener	Jason	GBR	18.9.75	178/70	100	10.08	9.98- 99
Garenamotse	Gable	BOT	28.2.77	183/75	LJ	8.07	8.14- 03, 8.26w- 01
Garland	Dale	GBR	13.10.80	185/74	400H	49.85	51.16- 04
Garrett	Ken	USA	9.11.76	181/75	400H	49.55	48.61- 04
Gary	Robert	USA	5.4.73	178/68	3kSt	8:24.16	8:19.26- 96
Garzón	Glauder	CUB	13.2.82	173/69	400	45.88	45.48- 01
Gataullin	Ruslan	RUS	1.12.79	184/77	LJ	7.95	8.11i, 8.09- 03
* Gatlin	Justin	USA	10.2.82	185/79	100	9.88, 9.84w	9.85- 04
					200	20.00	20.01- 04, 19.86w- 01, 19.86dq- 02
Gatson	Terry	USA	23.8.82	183/66	400	44.93	45.36- 04
Gavélas	Pláton	GRE	21.5.80	185/75	400H	49.99	50.13- 04
* Gay	Tyson	USA	9.9.82	183/73	100	10.08	10.06- 04, 10.01w- 03
					200	19.93	20.07- 04
Gazol	Javier	ESP	27.10.80	184/70	PV	5.60i, 5.50	5.60- 04
* Gebremariam	Gebre-egziabher	ETH	10.9.84	178/56	3000	7:39.48	7:46.8+- 03
					5000	12:52.80	12:55.59- 04
					10000	27:11.57	26:53.73- 04
* Gebrselassie	Haile	ETH	18.4.73	164/53	HMar	61:33	59:41- 02
					Mar	2:06:20	2:06:35- 02

	Name		Nat	Born	Ht/Wt	Event	2005 Mark	Pre-2005 Best
	Geisler	Marian	GER	10.8.84	185/74	Dec	7616	7361- 04
*	Geneti	Markos	ETH	30.5.84	175/55	1500	3:33.83	
						3000	7:38.11	7:42.24, 7:37.0i- 04
						5000	13:00.25	13:11.87- 03
	Gensic	Paul	USA	27.6.82	183/82	PV	5.50i	5.50- 04
	Geopfert	Travis	USA	20.8.78	183/86	Dec	7525	7785w, 7732- 04
*	Gerasimov	Pavel	RUS	29.5.79	190/80	PV	5.70	5.90- 00
	Gervasi	David	SUI	1.8.83		Dec	7519	7323- 04
	Getanda	James	KEN	5.7.82	178/66	10000	28:09.61	27:44.73- 04
	Gettis	David	USA-J	27.8.87	190/84	400	45.84	46.39- 04
	Gezahegne	Eshetu	ETH	20.9.82		5000	13:21.6+	
						10000	27:38.49	
	Gezzar	Nordine	FRA	17.2.80	184/60	3kSt	8:27.62	8:30.73- 04
	Ghali	Ridha	TUN	7.5.83		400	45.95	45.81- 04
*	Gharib	Jaouad	MAR	22.5.72	176/66	HMar	60:51 dh	61:36- 02, 59:56dh- 04
						Mar	2:07:49	2:07:12 (2:07:02 off)- 04
	Ghirmai	Filmon	GER	25.1.79	168/52	3kSt	8:22.37	8:20.50- 03
	Ghoula	Hatem	TUN	7.6.73	180/67	20kW	1:20:19	1:19:02- 97
	Giaconi	Andrea	ITA	11.4.74	184/72	110H	13.52, 13.48w	13.35, 13.1- 02
*	Gibilisco	Giuseppe	ITA	5.1.79	183/78	PV	5.83	5.90- 03
	Gillick	David	IRL	9.7.83	188/80	400	45.93	46.29- 04
^	Ginko	Viktor	BLR	7.12.65	186/77	50kW	3:55:22	3:42:20- 95
*	Giralt	David	CUB	26.8.84	182/72	TJ	17.14	17.31- 03
	Girma	Demissie	ETH-J	20.6.86	165/45	10000	27:45.14	27:55.88- 04
						HMar	61:40	61:34- 04
	Giruma	Tesfaye	ETH	25.9.82	168/50	10000	27:31.89	
	Gitahi	Julius	KEN	29.4.78	168/52	10000	27:38.11	27:11.17- 98
	Giwa-Agbomeirele	Okoineme	USA	30.11.78		LJ	8.17w	7.97i- 03, 7.93- 01
*	Godina	John	USA	31.5.72	193/129	SP	22.20	22.02- 99
	Goffi	Danilo	ITA	3.12.72	173/52	Mar	2:11:13	2:08:33- 98
	Goller	Thomas	GER	28.10.77	191/83	400H	49.61	48.54- 99
	Gomes	Diego	BRA	19.4.85		800	1:46.75	1:48.55- 04
	Gomes da Silva	Fábio	BRA	4.8.83	177/70	PV	5.50	5.55- 04
	Gómez	David	ESP	13.2.81	185/85	Dec	7698	7940- 04
	Gomis	Kafétien	FRA	20.3.80	183/67	LJ	7.98	8.21- 04
	Goncharuk	Dmitriy	BLR	17.7.70	190/112	SP	19.43i	20.33- 95
	Gong Wei		CHN	3.1.79	180/65	100	10.24w	10.27- 97
	Gonzales	Matt	USA	9.10.81	168/57	10000	28:17.46	28:22.77- 04
^	González	Emeterio	CUB	11.4.73	184/105	JT	80.50	87.12- 00
	González	José Antonio	ESP	15.6.79	178/73	50kW	3:49:20	3:49:01- 04
	González	Oscar	ESP	8.8.76	193/83	Dec	7831	7949- 01
*	Goucher	Adam	USA	18.2.75	178/64	1M	3:56.15	3:54.17- 99
						3000	7:40.09	7:34.96- 01
						5000	13:10.19	13:11.25- 99
*	Goumri	Abderrahim	MAR	21.5.76	167/60	3000	7:40.7+	7:32.36- 01
						5000	12:50.25	12:59.04- 04
						10000	27:02.62	27:26.01- 01
	Gourmet	François	BEL	28.12.82	179/80	Dec	7950	7628- 04
	Gowda	Vikas	IND	5.7.83	206/125	SP	19.60i	19.10i- 04, 17.63- 02
						DT	64.69	64.35- 04
	Grabovoy	Vadim	UKR	5.4.73	190/108	HT	72.78	79.82- 02
	Grabusic	Jurica	CRO	28.3.83	185/75	110H	13.71	13.54- 03
	Graff	Christopher	USA	5.10.75	178/61	10000	28:03.11	28:07.17- 99
	Greaves	Damien	GBR	19.9.77	185/95	110H	13.59	13.54- 02, 13.50w- 04
*	Greene	Maurice	USA	23.7.74	176/80	100	10.01	9.79- 99, 9.78w- 04
*	Greer	Breaux	USA	19.10.76	188/102	JT	87.65	87.68- 04
*	Gregório	Jadel	BRA	16.9.80	202/102	LJ	8.06	8.22- 04
						TJ	17.73	17.72- 04
	Griffiths	Dean	JAM	27.1.80	180/72	400H	48.78	48.55- 03
	Grossenbacher	Christian	SUI	28.1.80	191/77	400H	50.08	50.78- 03
	Gu Junjie		CHN	5.5.85	184/60	LJ	7.99	7.82- 02
						TJ	16.96i, 16.44, 16.90w	17.23- 04
	Guigon	Nicolas	FRA	10.10.80	181/60	PV	5.50	5.75- 04
	Gunn	Luke	GBR	22.3.85	180/64	3kSt	8:32.87	8:54.56- 04
*	Guset	Gheorghe	ROM	28.5.68	185/142	SP	20.93i, 20.75	20.84- 99
*	Gushchinskiy	Viktor	RUS	12.8.78	202/95	TJ	17.10	17.22- 04
	Guta	Dejene	ETH	5.8.81		Mar	2:10:49	2:17:20- 04
	Hackley	Jimmie	USA	11.9.75	175/69	200	20.49	20.31- 04
	Hadadi	Ehsan	IRI	21.1.85		DT	65.25	54.96- 04
	Häggblom	Robert	FIN	9.8.82	183/110	SP	19.69	19.48- 04
	Hahn	Sven-Eric	GER	17.10.80	202/135	SP	19.16	18.78- 04

Name		Nat	Born	Ht/Wt	Event	2005Mark	Pre-2005 Best
Haklits	András	CRO	23.9.77	189/103	HT	80.41	79.30- 02
Hall	Kenneth	USA-J	17.4.86	188/84	TJ	16.55	16.72, 17.13w- 04
Hall	Ryan	USA	14.10.82	180/64	5000	13:16.03	13:45.00- 04
Hallmann	Christopher	GER	6.6.83	188/84	Dec	7667	8045- 04
^ Halvari	Mikko	FIN	4.3.83	182/85	Dec	7567	7426- 03
Hamblyn	Paul	NZL	27.8.80		1500	3:38.07	3:42.12- 03
Han Guodong		CHN	8.5.84		50kW	3:58:13	4:09:47- 03
* Han Yucheng		CHN	16.12.78	175/63	20kW	1:18:31	1:19:30- 04
					50kW	3:36:20	3:39:10- 04
Hanany	Mickaël	FRA	25.3.83	198/78	HJ	2.28A	2.24- 03
Hanna	Kurt	USA	23.4.75	178/73	PV	5.50	5.75- 01
Hardee	Trey	USA	7.2.84	196/82	Dec	7881	8041- 04
^ Harju	Arsi	FIN	18.3.74	183/125	SP	20.21	21.39- 00
Harlan	Ryan	USA	25.4.81	190/93	Dec	7997	8171- 04
Harmse	Chris	RSA	31.5.73	184/118	HT	80.63	80.21- 04
Harnapp	Steve	GER	30.7.75	180/92	HT	75.54	75.14- 02
Harper	Jacey	TRI	20.5.80	183/77	100	10.10	10.19- 03
					200	20.65, 20.55w	20.71- 01, 20.68w- 03
Harradine	Benn	AUS	14.10.82	198/118	DT	63.65	57.78- 02
Harris	Jebreh	USA	22.9.78	178/66	800	1:46.03	1:46.66- 04
Harris	Jerry	USA	29.10.81	182/68	400	45.82	44.72- 04
Harris	Marcus	USA	5.5.83		HJ	2.23i	2.20- 04
Harris	Micah	USA	30.4.79	190/84	110H	13.42	13.38- 04
^ Harris	Rickey	USA	29.9.81	176/73	400H	49.21	48.16- 02
Harris	Stephen	USA	5.12.80	191/82	Dec	7892	8103w, 8061- 03
Harris	Tora	USA	21.9.78	190/83	HJ	2.30i, 2.29	2.31- 02
Harting	Robert	GER	18.10.84	201/115	DT	66.02	64.05- 04
Hartonen	Tommi	FIN	12.5.77	189/85	200	20.59	20.47- 00
* Hartwig	Jeff	USA	25.9.67	190/82	PV	5.76i, 5.65, 5.68ex?	6.03- 00
^ Harvey	Tye	USA	25.9.74	186/73	PV	5.50i	5.93i- 01, 5.80- 00
Hatzivasilíou	Hrístos	GRE	23.3.84	180/73	LJ	7.92w	7.60- 04
Haverney	Matthias	GER	21.7.85	198/78	HJ	2.25	2.16- 04
Hazle	Mike	USA	22.3.79	183/82	JT	79.15	73.66- 03
Hazouri	Mohamed	SYR	.83	178/65	TJ	16.67	16.58- 04
He Lin		CHN	1.3.83	174/58	50kW	4:02:11	4:05:01- 01
^ Hecht	Raymond	GER	11.11.68	191/95	JT	77.20	92.60- 95
Hedman	Graham	GBR	6.2.79	188/79	400	45.88	46.37- 02
Heikkinen	Aki	FIN	24.2.80	188/76	Dec	7803	8188- 00
Helmke	Till	GER	6.5.84	182/74	200	20.66, 20.54w	20.47- 04
Helpling	Rudolf	GER	23.2.81	195/78	TJ	16.49	16.78- 03
Helppikangas	Jouni	FIN	10.2.71	201/118	DT	60.27i, 60.16	61.72- 01
Helwick	Chris	USA	18.3.85	193/89	Dec	7780	7290- 04
* Hemingway	Matt	USA	24.10.72	201/81	HJ	2.31i, 2.27	2.38i- 00, 2.34- 03
Henderson	Ben B.J.	USA	5.4.83	183/77	200	20.64	20.87- 03
Henry	Anson	CAN	9.3.79	188/79	100	10.15w	10.17, 10.04w- 02
* Herbert	Llewellyn	RSA	21.7.77	185/80	400H	48.57	47.81- 00
Hercules	Chris	USA	14.5.79	188/86	TJ	16.90	16.69i- 01, 16.63- 00
* Herms	René	GER	17.7.82	195/80	800	1:44.71	1:44.14- 04
* Hernández	Noé	MEX	15.3.78	175/64	20kW	1:18:51	1:18:14- 03
* Hernández	Yoel	CUB	12.12.77	184/77	110H	13.39, 13.32w	13.24- 99, 13.20w- 00
Herring	Aubrey	USA	19.9.78	183/77	110H	13.62	13.36- 02
* Heshko	Ivan	UKR	19.8.79	181/70	800	1:46.19	1:45.41- 03
					1500	3:31.91	3:30.33- 04
Hession	Paul	IRL	27.1.83	186/75	200	20.40w	20.61- 04
Hetzendorf	John	USA	27.1.77	183/102	JT	78.23	75.11- 04
Hicks	Antwon	USA	12.3.83	187/73	110H	13.35	13.45- 04, 13.42w- 02
Hicks	Graham	AUS	14.12.78		DT	61.77	60.56- 04
Hicks	Kevin	USA	7.11.84	173/68	800	1:44.94	1:48.02- 04
Hidaka	Kazuyoshi	JPN	7.7.80	172/60	100	10.29, 10.25w	10.45- 04
Hierrezuelo	Sergio	CUB	15.3.82	175/70	400H	49.11	49.31- 04
* Higuero	Juan Carlos	ESP	3.8.78	180/60	1500	3:33.72	3:31.61- 03
					3000	7:48.46i	7:51.56i- 04, 7:59.76- 99
Hill	Clinton	AUS	19.4.80	186/77	400	45.71	45.16- 04
Hill	Ronald	USA	17.5.84	175/76	100	10.27w	10.50- 02
Hodun	Michal	POL	17.2.83	196/115	DT	59.88	58.70- 01
Hoff	Shadrack	RSA	19.5.73	169/51	HMar	61:59	61:11- 00
* Hoffa	Reese	USA	8.10.77	182/133	SP	21.74i, 21.29	21.67- 04
Hohl	Stephan	GER	23.2.80	182/63	3kSt	8:30.64	8:27.72- 04
* Höhne	André	GER	10.3.78	185/72	20kW	1:20:00	1:20:44- 03
Holland	Jonathan	USA	18.2.85	183/85	100	10.26w	10.69- 02

Name		Nat	Born	Ht/Wt	Event	2005 Mark	Pre-2005 Best
* Holm	Stefan	SWE	25.5.76	181/70	HJ	2.40i, 2.36	2.37i, 2.36- 04
Holusa	Milos	CZE	2.5.65	174/62	20kW	1:22:31	1:21:58- 97
					50kW	4:03:42	3:49:08- 96
Homewood	Dirk	USA	21.1.82	188/77	400	45.34	46.10- 02
Homo	Sébastien	FRA	27.4.82	182/70	PV	5.55	5.50- 02
Hon	Brandon	USA	7.7.79	185/77	110H	13.63	13.72- 04
Hong Qingyang		CHN	4.2.83		Dec	7771	7463- 01
Hoogmoed	Guus	NED	27.9.81	187/80	100	10.25. 10.21w	10.38, 10.34w- 04
					200	20.58, 20.41w	20.93- 04
* Hooker	Steve	AUS	16.7.82	187/82	PV	5.87	5.65- 04
^ Hopley	Hannes	RSA	26.1.81	181/105	DT	60.94	67.66- 04
Horigome	Yoshihiro	JPN	2.1.81		400	45.89	46.01- 03
Horváth	Gergely	HUN	5.6.75	186/90	JT	80.91	81.55- 03
Hosokawa	Michitaka	JPN	26.4.76	173/60	Mar	2:09:10	2:10:38- 04
Hou Yang		CHN	8.7.85		50kW	4:00:19	4:08:24- 04
* Howe	Andrew	ITA	12.5.85	184/73	200	20.52	20.28- 04
					LJ	8.02	8.11- 04
Hranovschi	Vadim	MDA	14.2.83	198/110	DT	61.20	62.60- 04
Hsiao Szu-Pin		TPE	18.12.80	188/72	Dec	7632	7465- 04
Hu Kai		CHN	4.8.82		100	10.27	10.29- 04
Huang Haiqiang		CHN-Y	8.2.88	184/65	HJ	2.27	2.21- 04
Hughes	David	GBR	31.5.84	193/87	110H	13.67, 13.56w	14.02- 04
Hughes	Robby	USA	10.10.78	182/80	110H	13.61	13.38, 13.31w- 04
Hummastenniemi	Janne	FIN	3.10.79	196/107	DT	63.10	60.28- 01
Hutcherson	Orentheus	USA	18.11.76		400H	49.61	50.14- 01
Hynni	Pertti	FIN	14.2.60	193/110	DT	62.62	63.25- 98
* Hysong	Nick	USA	9.12.71	183/77	PV	5.71Ai, 5.70	5.90- 00
* Iakovákis	Periklis	GRE	24.3.79	185/76	400H	48.24	48.17- 03
Iakovákis	Sotirios	GRE	20.9.82	184/72	400H	49.9	50.75- 04
* Idowu	Phillips	GBR	30.12.78	192/89	TJ	17.30i, 16.96	17.68- 02
Ietani	Kazuo	JPN	25.8.77	166/53	HMar	61:38	61:30- 01
Iguider	Abdelati	MAR-J	25.3.87	185/75	1500	3:35.63	3:35.53- 04
Ilariani	David	GEO	20.1.81	195/84	110H	13.5	13.69- 04
Itsios	Yéoryios	GRE	28.11.81	187/97	JT	78.88	77.71- 03
Ingargiola	Francesco	ITA	15.2.73	172/60	Mar	2:10:25	2:08:49- 00
Inico	Kedar	USA	29.8.83	183/75	400	45.22	46.39- 03
* Inocêncio	Matheus	BRA	17.5.81	192/93	110H	13.34	13.33- 04
Intas	Tomas	LTU	15.9.81	200/108	JT	82.04	82.94- 04
Ioannou	Kyriacos	CYP	26.7.84	193/66	HJ	2.27i, 2.27	2.28- 04
Irifune	Satoshi	JPN	14.12.75	176/60	Mar	2:09:58	2:11:26- 02
* Irungu Mathathi	Martin	KEN	25.12.85	165/49	5000	13:05.99	13:03.84- 04
					10000	27:08.42	27:22.46- 04
* Isegwe	Christopher	TAN	22.2.76	168/56	Mar	2:10:21	2:10:56- 04
Ishikawa	Kazuyoshi	JPN	6.11.82	179/70	TJ	16.92	16.98- 04
Ismail	Ismail Ahmed	SUD	10.9.84	191/71	800	1:45.32	1:45.17- 04
Israel	Mart	EST	23.9.83	190/115	DT	63.17	58.32, 62.18irr- 04
* Ivanov	Aleksandr	RUS	25.5.82	194/110	JT	84.24	88.90- 03
Ivanov	Georgi	BUL	13.3.85	188/108	SP	19.51	19.15- 04
Ivashkin	Vyacheslav	RUS	6.3.74		DT	60.39	61.09- 04
* Ivuti	Patrick	KEN	30.6.78	165/52	HMar	59:47	59:31- 00
					Mar	2:07:46	0
Iwamizu	Yoshitaka	JPN	20.6.79	174/53	3kSt	8:22.54	8:18.93- 03
Iwasa	Toshihiro	JPN	18.5.76	172/57	10000	28:19.89	28:06.89- 00
					HMar	61:36	62:16- 02
Jachimowicz-Giogowski	Sebastian	POL-J	2.8.86	184/75	JT	77.18	75.96- 04
* Jackson	Bershawn	USA	8.5.83	170/68	400	45.45	46.25- 03
					400H	47.30	47.86- 04
Jacobsen	Per	SWE	30.12.77	174/62	3kSt	8:30.86	8:40.38- 04
Jakobsson	Mikael	SWE	9.1.81	194/90	400H	49.47	49.38- 02
Jallai	Tarmo	EST	30.1.79	192/79	110H	13.70w	13.67- 04
James	Godday	NGR	9.1.84	186/76	400	45.30	45.69- 04
Janácek	Stepán	CZE	12.6.77	189/79	PV	5.51, 5.60ex	5.76- 02
Janik	Igor	POL	18.1.83	201/100	JT	77.25	82.54- 03
Janku	Jan	CZE	10.8.71	193/79	HJ	2.23i	2.30i- 96, 2.29- 97
^ Janku	Tomás	CZE	27.12.74	191/75	HJ	2.27i, 2.24	2.33- 04
Jansen	Joeri	BEL	28.5.79	180/65	1500	3:35.97	3:41.04- 04
					1M	3:55.84	
^ Janvrin	Kip	USA	8.7.65	183/84	Dec	7671	8462w, 8345- 96
Jarosz	Michal	POL	30.3.82	177/69	20kW	1:21:57	1:25:58- 04
Jarrett	Patrick	JAM	2.10.77	186/82	100	10.15	10.12, 10.08dq, 9.89w-rs- 01

	Name		Nat	Born	Ht/Wt	Event	2005Mark	Pre-2005 Best
	Järvenpää	Tero	FIN	2.10.84	186/90	JT	84.05	80.43- 03
*	Jawher	Musir Salem	BRN	13.6.78	182/66	1500	3:37.28	3:33.79+-01
						3000	7:40.75	7:35.35- 01
						5000	12:59.79	13:00.40- 04
	Jaworski	Courtney	USA	7.5.84	192/77	800	1:46.70	1:47.81- 04
	Jedrusinski	Marcin	POL	28.9.81	190/88	200	20.14w	20.31- 02
	Jefferson	Sean	USA	30.12.82	170/61	1500	3:38.91	3:40.90- 04
						1M	3:56.44i	4:00.16i- 04
	Jelks	Mark	USA	10.4.84	170/66	100	10.02, 10.01w, 9.8w	10.45, 10.25w- 02
						200	20.58	21.23- 02
*	Jeng	Alhaji	SWE	13.12.81	186/75	PV	5.75sq	5.61- 04
	Jennings	Karl	CAN	14.5.79	188/82	110H	13.52	13.47- 04
	Jensen	Benjamin	NOR	13.4.75	188/78	Dec	7845	8160- 99
	Jensen	Morten	DEN	2.12.82	189/81	LJ	8.25	8.03- 04
	Jeremiah	Richard	AUS	3.12.82	183/65	3kSt	8:29.63	8:39.70- 03
	Jia Peng		CHN	12.1.84	186/100	SP	19.49	19.33- 04
*	Jiménez	Antonio	ESP	18.2.77	178/63	3kSt	8:14.05	8:11.52- 01
	Jiménez	Erik	CUB	17.9.81	182/83	HT	75.38	71.09- 04
	Jin Ke		CHN	13.1.84		100	10.23	10.48- 05
*	Johnson	Allen	USA	1.3.71	178/70	110H	12.99	12.92- 96
	Johnson	Brandon	USA	6.3.85	175/68	400H	48.59	48.62- 04
	Johnson	Brian	USA	25.3.80	196/91	100	10.28, 10.18w	10.24- 02
						LJ	8.33	8.28i- 03, 8.07A, 8.33w- 02, 8.06- 04
	Johnson	Chris	USA	28.4.82	183/77	100	10.22	10.27- 02, 10.18w- 04
						200	20.62	20.97- 01
	Johnson	Derrick	USA	7.3.82	178/75	100	10.26, 10.24w	10.20w- 02
	Johnson	Garrett	USA	24.5.84	193/122	SP	20.44	19.26i. 18.87- 03
						DT	60.77	55.23- 03
	Johnson	Jonathan	USA	5.3.82	177/73	400	45.95	46.20- 03
						800	1:44.86	1:44.77- 04
*	Johnson	Joshua 'J.J'	USA	10.5.76	191/91	100	10.09	9.95- 02
						200	20.30	19.88- 01
	Johnson	Kibwe	USA	17.8.81	189/100	DT	65.11	61.00- 04
						HT	78.25	69.49- 04
	Johnson	Lamont	USA	19.12.76	175/81	100	10.23w	10.39- 02
*	Johnson	Patrick	AUS	26.9.72	177/73	100	10.20, 10.10w	9.93, 9.88w- 03
						200	20.56	20.50, 20.25w- 03
	Jonas	Dusty	USA-J	19.4.86		HJ	2.24	2.22- 03
	Jones	Alwyn	AUS	28.2.85	189/72	TJ	16.52	16.30- 04
	Jones	Marcus	USA	13.8.76	190/80	TJ	16.57	16.49i- 04, 16.30- 03
	Jones	Rhys	AUS	19.3.81	195/125	SP	19.41	19.54- 04
	Joorits	Mikk	EST	12.2.81	192/79	Dec	7641	7528- 03
						HMar	61:00	60:52- 03
*	Joseph	Fabiano	TAN	24.12.85	158/48	5000	13:18.18	13:15.90- 04
						HMar	61:00	60:52- 03
	Joseph	Moise	HAI	27.12.81	180/67	800	1:46.25	1:45.74- 02
	Jotanovic	Milan	SCG	11.1.84	184/115	SP	19.21	18.37- 04
	Juantorena	Alberto	CUB	27.6.77	186/72	Dec	7672	7769- 04
	Julius	Leigh	RSA	25.3.85	170/66	100	10.27	10.24- 03
						200	20.47, 20.37w	20.44- 04
	Jung Sang-jin		KOR	16.4.84	184/82	JT	77.73	78.61- 04
	Kacevic	Edhem	BIH	18.5.70	189/105	SP	19.46	18.96- 03
	Kagika	Laban	KEN	17.7.78	164/50	HMar	61:36	61:43- 02
	Kahlmeyer	Markus	GER	20.1.82	189/110	HT	71.87	70.01- 04
	Kajikawa	Yohei	JPN	8.11.83	185/69	TJ	16.45	16.11- 04
	Kalka	Kamil	POL	28.5.81	184/64	20kW	1:21:36	1:24:40- 04
						50kW	4:04:23	3:56:29- 04
	Kallas	Madis	EST	22.4.81	189/84	Dec	7661	7763-04
	Kamais	Peter	KEN	.77		5000	13:19.73	13:22.52- 04
	Kamakya	Nicholas Manza	KEN	2.3.85		10000	28:19.65	
	Kamal	Ali Abubaker	QAT	.83	165/56	1500	3:37.45	3:36.98- 04
	Kamani	Bayano	PAN	17.4.80	188/79	400H	47.84	48.23- 04
*	Kamathi	Charles	KEN	18.5.78	165/51	3000	7:43.83	7:41.89- 03
						5000	13:11.98	13:02.51- 02
						10000	27:28.35	26:51.49- 99
*	Kamel	Youssef Saad	BRN	29.3.83	190/73	800	1:43.96	1:43.11- 04
*	Kanaykin	Vladimir	RUS	21.3.85	170/60	20kW	1:21:11+	1:21:23- 03
						50kW	3:40:40	0
	Kandie	Solomon	KEN	28.8.78	173/64	3kSt	8:32.53	8:31.23- 04
	Kanemaru	Yuzo	JPN-J	18.9.87	177/70	400	45.47	45.89- 04
	Kankarafou	Oudere	FRA	8.12.83	188/77	100	10.20w	10.44- 04

MEN'S INDEX

Name		Nat	Born	Ht/Wt	Event	2005 Mark	Pre-2005 Best
Kantanen	Marko	FIN	17.4.78	183/98	JT	76.50	78.08- 04
* Kanter	Gerd	EST	6.5.79	196/120	DT	70.10	68.50- 04
Kanyi	John	KEN	6.9.80	160/50	10000	28:07.06	27:46.87- 03
* Kaouch	Adil	MAR	1.1.79	170/60	1500	3:38.00	3:32.86- 04
Kapek	Julien	FRA	12.1.79	178/70	TJ	17.06	17.12, 17.24w- 03
* Kaptyukh	Vasiliy	BLR	27.6.67	197/120	DT	62.80	67.59- 00
Karailiev	Momchil	BUL	21.5.82	188/75	TJ	17.19, 17.36w	17.16- 04
Karasmanákis	Eleftthérios	GRE	16.8.78	185/98	JT	79.70	77.58- 01
Kariuki	David	KEN	23.5.82	164/53	10000	28:22.85	27:46.53- 03
Kariuki	John	KEN-J	10.11.86	171/55	5000	13:12.12	13:26.94- 04
					10000	27:28.69	27:46.47- 04
* Karjalainen	Olli-Pekka	FIN	7.3.80	194/110	HT	79.81	83.30- 04
Karlsson	Conny	FIN	30.12.75	195/120	SP	20.13	20.78- 01
Katayama	Toshiya	JPN	23.4.73	176/61	Mar	2:10:12	2:11:05- 04
Kato	Toshihide	JPN	4.7.73	174/56	10000	28:20.53	28:16.80- 03
Kawabata	Shingo	JPN	15.5.78	175/70	100	10.26w	10.11- 00
Kawakita	Naohiro	JPN	18.11.80	180/76	400H	49.43	49.70- 01
Kawamura	Hideaki	JPN	15.9.74	175/69	400H	49.90	48.84- 00
Kazanin	Aleksey	UKR	22.5.82	170/58	50kW	3:56:44	3:58:20- 03
Kazmierowski	Jacek	POL	7.2.74	185/76	TJ	16.66i, 16.52	16.77- 02, 16.89w- 04
Kéchi	Heni	FRA	31.8.80	186/75	400H	50.08	49.89- 02
Keddo	Eric	USA	85	186/77	110H	13.72	14.06- 04
* Keflezighi	Mebrahtom	USA	5.5.75	169/58	5000	13:20.71	13:11.77- 00
					10000	28:10.57	27:13.98- 01
					Mar	2:09:56	2:09:53- 04
* Keïta	Naman	FRA	9.4.78	196/86	400H	48.27	48.17- 04
Kelai	John Ekiru	KEN	29.12.76		Mar	2:09:09	2:11:00- 04
* Kemboi	Ezekiel	KEN	25.5.82	175/62	3kSt	8:09.04	8:02.49- 03
* Kemboi	Nicholas	QAT	25.11.83	163/50	5000	13:10.36	13:01.14- 03
					10000	26:51.87	26:30.03- 03
Kempas	Antti	FIN	3.10.80	191/70	50kW	3:59:01	4:02:15- 04
Kennouche	Abdeslam	ALG	7.10.80	183/70	1500	3:36.33	3:33.46- 04
Kerr	Matthew	CAN	3.5.76	186/66	3kSt	8:20.14	8:29.94- 03
Keskisalo	Jukka	FIN	27.3.81	184/66	3kSt	8:25.14	8:17.72- 03
Keul	Adam	USA	27.1.80	193/88	PV	5.70	5.68i, 5.59- 01
Khadar	Samir	ALG-J	10.6.86		1500	3:39.05	
Khatantsev	Grigoriy	RUS	2.4.78		HT	75.03	71.82- 98
* Khersontsev	Vadim	RUS	8.7.74	192/106	HT	79.47	81.26- 01
Khlebov	Ruslan	BLR	15.2.83		DT	59.63	60.28- 04
Kholev	Dennis	ISR	21.10.75	187/80	PV	5.51	5.71- 02
Kibet	Duncan Kipkemboi	KEN	.78		HMar	60:53	61:01- 04
Kibet	Lukas	KEN	19.6.73		Mar	2:08:52	2:10:18- 01
Kibet	Luke	KEN	19.6.83		HMar	60:59	60:00dh- 04, 61:10- 03
Kibet Naibei	Nathan	KEN-J	22.2.86		3kSt	8:33.1A	8:30.77- 04
Kibiwott	Charles E	KEN	8.8.74		Mar	2:08:36	2:10:21- 03
* Kibowen	John	KEN	21.4.69	175/64	3000	7:39.72	7:29.09- 98
					5000	13:07.74	12:54.07- 03
* Kifle	Yonas	ERI	24.3.77	168/55	10000	27:35.72	27;40.92- 04
					HMar	61:13	61:05- 02
Kiflemariam	Samson	ERI	23.1.84		10000	28:08.97	
Kigen	Mike	KEN-J	15.1.86	170/54	5000	13:22.48	
Kigen	Moses	KEN	22.4.73	182/68	5000	13:25.55	13:19.29- 03
					HMar	61:39	61:38- 04
Kigen	Wilfred	KEN	23.2.75		Mar	2:08:29	2:11:52- 04
Kigen	Wilson	KEN	15.9.80		Mar	2:08:34	2:23:39- 04
* Kikaya	Gary	COD	4.2.78	184/75	200	20.56	21.23- 02
					400	44.81	44.53- 02
Kilel	David	KEN	21.5.84	170/59	3000	7:46.92	7:42.49- 02
Kilmartin	Donovan	USA	11.6.84	188/78	Dec	7794	7729- 04
Kim Dong-young		KOR	6.3.80	174/56	50kW	4:01:25	3:58:00- 04
Kim Duk-hyung		KOR	8.12.85		TJ	16.79	16.15- 03
Kim Hyun-sup		KOR	31.5.85	176/56	20kW	1:22:15	1:24:58- 04
Kim Kun-woo		KOR	29.2.80	181/79	Dec	7774	7675- 03
Kim Yoo-suk		KOR	19.1.82	190/81	PV	5.61i	5.60- 04
Kimeli	Moses	KEN	.84		10000	28:00.1A	
Kimmons	Trell	USA	13.7.85	178/77	100	10.22, 10.16w	10.39, 10.0, 10.34w- 04
					200	20.46, 20.32w	21.18, 20.9- 04
Kimugul	Paul Kimaiyo	KEN	4.3.80		HMar	60:15	61:29- 04
Kimutai	Julius	KEN	4.4.74	175/63	HMar	61:51	61:36- 01
Kimutai Kangoo	Willy	KEN	12.2.84		10000	28:21.62	

Name		Nat	Born	Ht/Wt	Event	2005Mark	Pre-2005 Best
King	Max	USA	24.2.80	173/63	3kSt	8:33.06	8:40.12- 02
Kiogora	Stephen	KEN	10.11.74	170/55	Mar	2:09:51dh/2:11:58	2:09:21- 04
* Kipchirchir	Alex	KEN	26.11.84	188/63	1000	2:16.94	
					1500	3:30.82	3:30.46- 04
					1M	3:50.91	3:50.25- 03
Kipchirchir	Henry	KEN	18.3.83	183/60	10000	27:57.98	
* Kipchirchir Komen	Daniel	KEN	27.11.84	175/60	1500	3:29.72	3:34.66- 04
					1M	3:48.49	3:54.02- 04
					3000	7:31.98	
* Kipchoge	Eliud	KEN	5.11.84	167/52	1500	3:33.80	3:33.20- 04
					3000	7:28.56	7:27.72- 04
					5000	12:50.22	12:46.53- 04
Kipchoge	Gilbert	KEN	4.5.83		800	1:45.9A	
Kipchumba	Robert	KEN	24.2.84	170/62	HMar	61:13	60:22- 04
Kipchumba Rutto	Ronald	KEN-J	8.10.87	173/63	3kSt	8:16.69	8:18.51- 04
Kipkemboi	Laban	KEN	30.12.77	172/66	Mar	2:09:22	2:08:39- 02
* Kipketer	Sammy	KEN	29.9.81	166/52	3000	7:46e	7:33.62- 01
					5000	13:01.55	12:52.33- 03
					10000	26:52.60	26:49.38- 02
Kipkirchir	Alexis	KEN	26.11.84	188/63	800	1:45.54	1:45.5A- 02
* Kipkoech Chemwelo	Raymond	KEN	19.4.78		Mar	2:09:49	2:06:47- 02
Kipkosgei Salil	Stanley	KEN-J	2.4.86		HMar	61:45	61:53- 04
* Kipkurui	Benjamin	KEN	28.12.80	174/57	800	1:46.86	1:44.56- 99
					1500	3:36.17	3:30.67- 01
					1M	3:56.08	3:49.34- 00
Kiplagat	William	KEN	21.6.72		Mar	2:08:27	2:06:50- 99
Kipngeno	Geoffrey	KEN	10.4.84	170/55	10000	27:41.78	
Kiprono	Justus	KEN-J	28.2.87		3kSt	8:25.72	8:19.63- 04
Kiprono	Wilson Kemei	KEN	6.11.74		HMar	61:38	62:44- 04
Kiprop	Alfred	KEN			1500	3:37.2A	
* Kiprop	Bernard Kipyego	KEN-J	16.7.86	160/50	5000	13:09.96	13:24.27- 04
					10000	27:04.45	28:18.94- 04
* Kiprop	Boniface	UGA	12.10.85	167/53	5000	12:58.43	13:05.47- 04
					10000	26:39.77	27:04.00- 04
Kiprop	Francis	KEN	4.6.82	172/54	HMar	61:32	
Kiprop	Simon Kipyego	KEN	11.11.78		HMar	61:53	64:00- 03
* Kiprotich	Wesley	KEN	1.8.79	179/64	3kSt	8:09.43	8:05.68- 04
Kiprotich Kebenei	Wilson	KEN	20.7.80		HMar	59:27 dh	60:29- 04
* Kipruto	Brimin	KEN	31.7.85	176/54	1500	3:38.90	3:35.96- 04
					3kSt	8:04.22	8:05.52- 04
Kipruto Sang	Elijah	KEN	.83		HMar	61:49	62:05- 04
Kipsang	Churchill	KEN	.85		1500	3:36.95	3:40.0- 04
Kipsang	Salim	KEN	22.12.79	172/52	Mar	2:08:04	2:12:44- 04
Kipsang	William	KEN	.77		Mar	2:08:53	2:06:39- 03
Kipsiro	Moses	UGA-J	2.9.86	174/59	3000	7:44.57	
					5000	13:13.81	
* Kiptanui	Timothy	KEN	5.1.80	182/60	1500	3:38.3A	3:30.04- 04
Kiptum	Bernard	KEN-J	8.10.86	173/64	1500	3:34.03	3:38.0- 04
Kipyego	Ernest	KEN	6.10.78		HMar	61:58	
Kipyego	Michael	KEN	2.10.83	162/58	3kSt	8:10.66	8:13.02- 03
Kirch	Simon	GER	26.9.79	191/76	400	45.80	46.31- 01
Kirchler	Hannes	ITA	22.12.78	191/98	DT	62.72	62.13- 04
* Kirdyapkin	Sergey	RUS	16.1.80	178/66	50kW	3:38:08	3:43:20- 04
Kirk	Sherridan	TRI	11.2.81	175/72	800	1:45.43	1:46.67- 04
* Kirmasov	Sergey	RUS	25.3.70	180/118	HT	78.97	82.62- 98
* Kirui	Paul	KEN	5.2.80		HMar	61:15 dh, 62:45	60:22- 04
Kirui	Philip	KEN	11.9.73		HMar	61:33	61:07- 00
Kirui	Silas	KEN	.81		HMar	61:07	61:22- 04
Kirwa Chepkwony	David	KEN	1.8.85		5000	13:22.40	
* Kirwa Yego	Alfred	KEN-J	28.11.86	175/56	800	1:44.45	1:47.39- 04
Kislov	Aleksandr	RUS	4.11.84		Dec	7598	
Kiss	Daniel	HUN	12.2.82	195/73	110H	13.65, 13.49dw	13.71- 04
Klics	David	USA	.83		110H	13.72w	13.91- 04
Klimczak	Piotr	POL	18.1.80	182/72	400	45.60	45.90- 04
Klose	Holger	GER	5.12.72	191/117	HT	79.23	82.22- 98
* Klyugin	Sergey	RUS	24.3.74	192/82	HJ	2.28	2.36- 98
* Kobs	Karsten	GER	16.9.71	196/118	HT	79.46	82.78- 99
Koczman	Jacob	USA	21.11.78	188/79	800	1:46.44	1:47.06- 04
Koech	Jackson	KEN	26.12.78	173/55	HMar	61:54	60:05- 03
					Mar	2:08:02	

MEN'S INDEX

Name		Nat	Born	Ht/Wt	Event	2005 Mark	Pre-2005 Best
Koech	Joseph	KEN			HMar	62:04	
* Koech	Justus	KEN	19.3.80	175/60	800	1:45.73	1:44.16A- 03
* Koech	Paul Kipsiele	KEN	10.11.81	168/57	3000	7:33.93	7:39.40- 04
					5000	13:11.26	
					3kSt	7:56.37	7:57.42- 03
Koech	Stephen	KEN	16.12.76	171/55	3000	7:48.35	
					5000	13:04.43	
					10000	27:55.92	
Koekemoer	Pieter	RSA	12.1.82		400H	50.02A	50.14A- 02
Koenig	Oliver	GER	31.1.81	180/78	LJ	8.00	7.84, 8.08w- 02
Kogo	Micah	KEN-J	3.6.86		3000	7:49.46+	
					5000	13:16.31	
Kogo	Paul Kipkemei	KEN	.83		HMar	61:54	
Kohutek	Artur	POL	1.5.71	190/78	110H	13.70	13.27- 97
Koike	Takayuki	JPN	12.10.84	181/69	400H	49.23	50.98- 04
Kojima	Shigeyuki	JPN	25.9.79	173/64	100	10.24w	10.20- 00, 10.12w- 99
Kolasa	Adam	POL	2.8.75	196/91	PV	5.60i, 5.60	5.75- 01
Kólko	Rajmund	POL	1.3.71	188/95	JT	78.45	84.95- 01
Kombich	Isaac	KEN	16.10.85		800	1:46.8A/1:46.83	
* Konopka	Mikulás	SVK	23.1.79	193/110	SP	20.61	20.66- 01, 20.87i-dq- 02
Konopka	Miloslav	SVK	23.1.79	189/102	HT	76.74	81.33- 04
* Konovalov	Ilya	RUS	4.3.71	192/120	HT	79.92	82.28- 03
Kónstas	Stéfanos	GRE	16.5.77	198/119	DT	60.33	61.41- 04
Korchmid	Aleksandr	UKR	22.1.82	188/89	PV	5.81	5.75- 03
Korcok	Peter	SVK	12.8.74	178/64	50kW	3:51:30	3:51:09- 04
* Korir	John Cheruiyot	KEN	13.12.81	172/57	10000	27:30.46	26:52.87- 02
* Korir	Paul	KEN	15.7.77	180/64	1500	3:35.84	3:30.72- 03
					1M	3:55.62	3:48.17- 03
* Korir	Sammy	KEN	12.12.71	160/61	Mar	2:10:53	2:04:56- 03
Korir	Shadrack	KEN	14.12.78	170/54	3000	7:39.47	7:44.57+- 03
					5000	13:09.92	13:14.02- 02
Korolyov	Aleksey	RUS	5.4.82		HT	72.56	71.48- 04
Korotkov	Ilya	RUS	6.12.83		JT	76.31	77.91- 04
Korotkov	Oleg	RUS	16.3.80		SP	19.80i	18.89- 03
Kosenkow	Alexander	GER	14.3.77	178/70	100	10.28	10.14- 03
Kosgei	Collins	KEN-Y	4.8.88		3kSt	8:28.12	8:32.0- 04
Kosgei	Joseph	KEN	25.8.74	173/60	3000	7:44.58	7:39.38- 02
					5000	13:19.95	13:11.32- 04
Kosgei	Peter	KEN	3.2.83	183/65	10000	28:08.97	
					3kSt	8:29.13	8:52.99- 04
* Kosgei	Reuben	KEN	2.8.79	170/55	3kSt	8:12.57	7:57.29- 01
Kosgei	Shadrack	KEN	24.11.84	176/60	3000	7:42.22	7:45.96- 03
					5000	13:01.06	13:12.24- 03
Kosgei Kiplagat	Barnabas	KEN-J	20.8.86		10000	28:05.6A	29:05.9- 04
Koski-Vähala	Jarko	FIN	21.11.78	194/97	JT	84.12	81.46- 03
Kostadinov	Galin	BUL	25.12.79	194/113	SP	19.46i	20.02- 04
Kotze	Hennie	RSA	4.2.84		110H	13.64A	14.18- 03
* Kövágó	Zoltán	HUN	10.4.79	204/127	DT	66.00	68.93- 04
Kovals	Ainars	LAT	21.11.81	192/100	JT	82.22	82.13- 04
Kovenko	Andrey	UKR	25.11.73	174/64	20kW	1:21:53	1:24:36- 04
Kozbanov	Artyom	UKR	18.7.83	185/75	HJ	2.25i, 2.25	2.25- 04
Kozulko	Aleksandr	BLR	8.12.83	200/95	HT	74.28	72.62- 04
Král	Dusan	CZE	12.6.83	189/114	HT	71.35	63.86- 03
Kravchenko	Andrey	BLR-J	4.1.86		Dec	7833	
Kravchuk	Ruslan	BLR	.81		HT	71.05	70.30- 04
* Krawczyk	Andrzej	POL	11.4.76	195/112	DT	65.56	63.67- 02
Krikun	Aleksandr	UKR	1.3.68	194/130	HT	72.90	81.66- 04
* Krimarenko	Yuriy	UKR	11.8.83	187/65	HJ	2.33	2.23- 04
* Kristiansson	Patrik	SWE	3.6.77	192/83	PV	5.73	5.85- 02
Krivitskiy	Pavel	BLR	17.4.84	188/100	HT	77.51	71.29- 04
Krivov	Andrey	RUS	14.11.85	177/64	20kW	1:22:21	
* Kronberg	Robert	SWE	15.8.76	181/86	110H	13.43	13.35- 01
Kruger	A.G.	USA	18.2.79	193/118	HT	75.57	79.26- 04
* Kruger	Frantz	RSA	22.5.75	203/125	DT	67.30	70.32- 02
^ Krummenacker	David	USA	24.5.75	190/79	800	1:45.04	1:43.92- 02
					1000	2:17.57	2:15.97- 02
					1500	3:36.58	3:31.93- 02
Krzosek	Grzegorz	POL	10.1.76	182/67	800	1:46.28	1:45.97- 01
Kucinski	Beniamin	POL	1.6.82	172/51	20kW	1:20:34	1:20:52- 04
Kuehl	Adam	USA	19.1.84	188/116	DT	61.06	56.69- 04
Kujala	Seppo	FIN	24.9.80	186/111	SP	19.22	18.48- 04

Name		Nat	Born	Ht/Wt	Event	2005Mark	Pre-2005 Best
Kukkamo	Juha	FIN	1.4.76	188/75	800	1:46.68	1:47.09- 03
Kumar	Anil	IND	20.6.75	189/99	DT	61.66	64.37- 04
Kumar Yadav	Anil	IND	4.3.85		JT	76.31	74.70- 04
Kunkel	Adam	CAN	21.2.81	180/77	400H	49.90	49.49- 03
Kuptsov	Artyom	RUS	22.4.84	183/64	PV	5.70i, 5.55	5.70- 03
Kuptsov	Dmitriy	RUS	9.11.82		PV	5.65	5.70i- 03, 5.65- 02
Kurgat	Eliud	KEN	20.8.73		HMar	61:10/61:18?	61:23- 99
Kuzin	Aleksandr	UKR	21.10.74	179/63	Mar	2:10:54	2:11:07- 02
Kuzmin	Aleksandr	BLR	24.3.81	178/69	20kW	1:22:06	1:23:49- 02
Kuznetsov	Ivan	RUS	11.9.83	177/64	20kW	1:21:00	1:21:48- 04
Kuznetsov	Viktor	UKR-J	14.7.86	190/67	LJ	8.22i	8.12i- 03
					TJ	16.51i	16.84i, 16.58- 04
* Kwalia	James	QAT	12.6.84	171/59	3000	7:43.45	7:28.28- 04
					5000	13:21.36	12:54.58- 03
Kwambai	James	KEN	.76		HMar	60:45	60:22- 04
Kyyrö	Mikko	FIN	12.7.80	191/106	DT	63.27	63.24- 03
la Grange	Marcus	RSA	12.12.77	186/75	400	45.71A	44.65A, 44.76- 02
Laâlou	Amine	MAR	13.5.82	178/57	800	1:44.22	1:43.68- 04
Labidi	Sofiane	TUN	29.9.77	190/78	400	45.51	45.19- 04
Lacasse	Florent	FRA	21.1.81	185/65	800	1:45.37	1:44.42- 04
LaCour	Carey	USA	17.2.85	180/73	200	20.58	20.84, 20.65w- 04
* Lagat	Bernard	USA	12.12.74	175/61	1500	3:29.30	3:26.34- 01
					1M	3:48.38	3:47.28- 01
					3000	7:38.00	7:33.51- 00
					5000	12:59.29	13:19.14- 02
Lagat	David	KEN	.83		HMar	60:47	
Lagat	Nathan	KEN	.77		3000	7:45.76	8:03.16- 04
					5000	13:19.69	13:19.89- 04
					10000	28:14.05	
^ Lahssini	El Hassan	FRA	1.1.75	175/62	Mar	2:11:06	2:10:10- 04
Lakhal	Irba	FRA	12.12.75	168/61	3kSt	8:25.48	8:20.45- 04
Lambert	Chris	GBR	6.4.81	188/80	200	20.69i	20.34- 03
Lambèse	Bruno	FRA	11.4.69	190/96	Dec	7571	7756- 01
^ Lambrechts	Burger	RSA	3.4.73	200/145	SP	19.25	20.63- 04, 20.90dq- 01
Lamdassem	Ayad	MAR	11.10.81	175/63	10000	27:59.39	
Lampart	Petr	CZE	31.3.83	191/77	LJ	7.90	8.18- 02, 8.3Aw- 04
Lanaro	Giovanni	MEX	27.9.81	183/77	PV	5.65	5.60- 04
Lancashire	Tom	GBR	2.7.85	179/63	1500	3:38.92	3:42.48- 04
Lancaster	Kyle	USA	15.8.83	196/80	HJ	2.31A	2.29- 04
Landassem	Ayad	MAR	11.10.81		3000	7:45.55	
Langat	Festus	KEN			HMar	61:58	
Langat	Jackson	KEN	15.12.80		800	1:46.84	1:46.41- 03, 1:46.09i- 04
Langat	John	KEN	27.11.74	185/72	3kSt	8:33.17	8:15.17- 01
Langat	Shadrack	KEN	22.7.78	168/55	3000	7:42.92	7:52.04- 02
Lange	Björn	GER	15.6.79	193/106	JT	81.47	85.21- 01
Langlois	Denis	FRA	10.10.68	172/60	20kW	1:22:47	1:20:35- 97
					50kW	3:47:31	3:47:38- 00
Lapierre	Fabrice	AUS	17.10.83	178/60	LJ	7.90i, 8.15w	7.74- 02, 7.93w, 7.94Aw- 04
Larry	Lionel	USA-J	14.9.86	175/68	400	45.78	47.28- 04
Larsen	Jan-Peter	NED	18.3.79		HJ	2.24	2.22- 03
Lastre	Yunio	CUB	26.10.81	189/104	DT	60.28	60.00- 04
Lattu	Ari-Pekka	FIN	22.6.78	191/76	400H	49.67	49.36- 03
Latvala	Mikko	FIN	8.7.80	182/82	PV	5.60i, 5.60	5.66- 01
Lavanchy	Pierre	SUI	30.9.82		400	45.49	46.81- 04
Lavanne	Cédric	FRA	13.11.80	183/72	110H	13.51	13.58- 02, 13.47w- 03
Lavy	Shane	USA	15.2.76	185/72	HJ	2.23i	2.32i- 00, 2.30- 99
Laynes	Jeff	USA	3.10.70	178/84	100	10.29, 10.22w	10.01- 96, 9.9- 95
Le Dauphin	Vincent	FRA	28.6.76	190/72	3kSt	8:17.32	8:15.76- 99
le Roux	Wouter	RSA-J	17.1.86	186/77	400H	49.25A	49.45A-04
Lebedev	Yevgeniy	RUS	19.2.81	192/81	400	45.77	46.06- 04
* Lebid	Sergey	UKR	15.7.75	180/65	1500	3:38.44	3:39.95- 98
					3000	7:42.94	7:35.06- 02
					5000	13:12.35	13:10.78- 02
Lee Dae-ro		KOR	12.3.80	170/58	20kW	1:22:16	1:21:52- 03
Leinonen	Petteri	FIN	22.4.80	185/82	JT	76.30	72.42- 03
* Lel	Martin	KEN	29.10.78	171/54	HMar	59:42 dh, 61:37	60:10- 03, 59:51dh- 04
					Mar	2:07:26	2:10:02- 02
Leleito	Stanley	KEN	.84		Mar	2:10:17	2:17:32- 04
Lemoncello	Andrew	GBR	12.10.82	187/68	3kSt	8:30.12	8:47.32- 03
Letherby	Andrew	AUS	19.9.73	165/55	10000	28:09.85	28:25.56- 01
Letnicov	Vladimir	MDA	7.10.81	185/73	TJ	16.46	17.06- 02

Name		Nat	Born	Ht/Wt	Event	2005 Mark	Pre-2005 Best
Lett	Alleyne	GRN	7.1.83	193/97	110H	13.68, 13.49w	13.89- 04
					Dec	7550	6849- 04
Letting	Edwin	KEN-J	.86		800	1:46.20	1:46.04- 04
Levin	Andrew	USA	9.3.80		Dec	7801A, 7558	7390- 04
Lewis	Brian	USA	5.12.74	170/72	100	10.16	9.99- 02, 9.96w- 00
Lewis	Randy	GRN	14.10.80	188/74	TJ	16.88	17.34- 04
Lewis-Francis	Mark	GBR	4.9.82	183/85	100	10.13.10.10w	10.04, 9.97w- 02, 9.97fwg-01
Li Gaobo		CHN-Y	23.7.89		20kW	1:18:07	1:22:41- 04
Li Guoqing		CHN	1.10.79	165/57	50kW	4:03:35	3:54:14- 04
Li Hongguang		CHN	10.2.80	178/70	20kW	1:20:15	1:27:15- 01
					50kW	3:57:46	3:52:18- 03
Li Jianbo		CHN-J	14.11.86		20kW	1:19:34	1:26:21- 04
					50kW	3:45:13	4:03:08- 03
Li Ming		CHN	21.3.85		TJ	16.46	15.86- 04
Li Rongxiang		CHN	8.1.72	180/80	JT	81.61	84.29- 00
Li Shaojie		CHN	26.11.75	194/100	DT	62.85	65.16- 96
Li Xin		CHN	9.12.82	187/77	TJ	16.42	16.48- 03
Li Yanxi		CHN	26.6.84	176/54	TJ	17.15	17.09- 04
Li Yi		CHN	19.1.81		50kW	4:00:26	3:59:00- 01
Liang Zhenggan		CHN	27.8.83	178/60	50kW	3:59:12	4:01:19- 04
Lichtenegger	Elmar	AUT	25.5.74	186/82	110H	13.48	13.33- 99
* Liefers	Gert-Jan	NED	26.9.78	187/71	1500	3:35.29	3:32.89- 01
					3000	7:47.38	7:42.95- 02
					5000	13:22.26	14:04.21- 96
Liepa	Janis	LAT	14.3.81	191/96	JT	77.74	80.87- 04
Liepins	Modris	LAT	30.8.66	178/68	50kW	4:01:54	3:47:48- 98
^ de Lima	Vicente	BRA	4.6.77	165/63	100	10.17, 10.0	10.13- 04,10.08Aw- 02,10.0- 03
					200	20.44	20.39- 04
* Limo	Benjamin	KEN	23.8.74	178/65	1500	3:38.1A	3:37.59- 99
					3000	7:29.60	7:28.67- 99
					5000	12:55.26	12:54.99- 03
* Limo	Felix	KEN	22.8.80	174/58	Mar	2:07:02	2:06:14- 04
* Limo	Richard	KEN	18.11.80	167/53	5000	13:09.52	12:56.72- 01
					10000	28:16.7A	26:50.20- 02
Limo Ndiwa	Remi	KEN-Y	3.2.88		800	1:46.7A	
					1500	3:38.31	
Lin Dong		CHN	7.4.81		JT	76.66	72.08- 02
Lin Mujie		CHN	25.9.85	170/55	TJ	16.86	16.55- 04
Lincoln	Dan	USA	20.10.80	190/70	3000	7:48.79	7:40.17i- 04
					3kSt	8:12.65	8:15.02- 04
Lindsay	Bryan	USA	28.6.80	175/68	1500	3:38.31	3:45.00- 04
Lingua	Marco	ITA	4.6.78	179/110	HT	76.07	76.72- 99
Linsha	Maksim	BLR	6.4.85	190/72	110H	13.70w	13.93- 04
Lipskiy	Mikhail	RUS	6.3.82	183/69	400H	49.84	48.97- 04
Lischka	Michael	GER	23.12.73	197/135	DT	62.01	65.04- 01
Litchfield	Paul	USA	27.11.80		PV	5.60iA	5.50Ai- 03
Litei	John	KEN	2.6.83		800	1:44.86	1:46.70- 03
Little	Gregory	JAM	20.2.83	168/56	400H	48.95	50.04- 03
Litvinov	Sergey	BLR-J	27.1.86	183/93	HT	73.98	60.00- 04
Liu Feiliang		CHN	27.3.85	188/68	PV	5.70	5.60i, 5.55- 04
Liu Guangjun		CHN-Y	7.9.89		20kW	1:21:13	1:32:24- 04
					50kW	3:51:46	
Liu Lilu		CHN	6.2.85	189/79	110H	13.63	13.82- 04
Liu Wenjun		CHN-J	8.1.87		20kW	1:20:28	1:24:13- 04
* Liu Xiang		CHN	13.7.83	189/82	110H	13.05	12.91- 04
Liu Yanhong		CHN	20.4.83		JT	77.09	79.23- 03
Liu Yong		CHN	1.3.83		20kW	1:22:09	1:25:37- 04
					50kW	4:01:41	4:07:50- 03
Liu Yunfeng		CHN	3.8.79	179/65	20kW	1:18:33	1:20:01- 00
Llanos	Enrique	PUR	7.5.80		110H	13.72, 13.69w	13.78- 04
* Lobinger	Tim	GER	3.9.72	193/83	PV	5.93	6.00- 97
Logvinenko	Mikhail	RUS	19.4.84		Dec	7570	7149- 03
Lohse	Magnus	SWE	28.7.84	198/134	SP	20.03i, 19.12	19.25i, 19.12- 04
Loikkanen	Mika	FIN	20.2.74	195/120	DT	62.35i, 60.08	62.93- 01
Lokira	Paul	KEN	1.1.83		Mar	2:10:18	
Lomater	Stefano	ITA	23.4.74	190/115	DT	60.51	62.12- 02
^ Longo	Andrea	ITA	26.6.75	191/82	800	1:46.05	1:43.74- 00
Looije	Laurens	NED	12.1.73	185/80	PV	5.55i, 5.55	5.71- 98
López	Luís Fernando	COL	3.6.79	173/60	20kW	1:20:26	1:22:52- 04
López	Yeimar	CUB	20.8.82	184/73	400	45.19	45.11- 03
					800	1:46.61	1:47.2- 02

Name		Nat	Born	Ht/Wt	Event	2005Mark	Pre-2005 Best
Lorenzo	Santiago	ARG	4.4.78	191/88	Dec	7493	7911w- 03, 7889- 01
Louis	Wilan	BAR	1.3.83	185/66	400	45.91/45.97?	45.91- 01
Love	Kelvin	USA-J	18.5.86	178/75	200	20.65	21.32, 21.18w- 04
Lowry	Dior	USA	2.10.85	185/75	110H	13.69w	14.26- 04
Lu Ronghua		CHN	21.2.83	174/60	20kW	1:18:39	1:20:54- 03
					50kW	3:45:05	3:47:37- 04
Luaces	Isbel	CUB	20.7.75	187/97	JT	79.23	83.63- 02
Luchianov	Ivan	MDA	31.1.81	178/67	3kSt	8:30.66	8:26.17- 04
Luis	Yacnier	CUB	24.1.82	179/75	400H	49.12	48.83- 04
^ Lukashevich	Aleksey	UKR	11.1.77	175/70	LJ	8.01i, 7.95	8.27- 00
Lukasiak	Michal	POL	7.3.84	182/71	LJ	7.94	7.84- 04
Lukezic	Chris	USA	24.4.84	173/58	1500	3:35.22	3:39.90- 04
Lusis	Voldemars	LAT	7.12.74	187/102	JT	80.53	84.19- 03
^ Lyakhov	Sergey	RUS	1.3.68	195/107	DT	59.96	66.78- 95
Lystsov	Sergey	RUS	14.11.82	177/60	20kW	1:21:14	1:21:54- 04
Lyuboslavskiy	Anton	RUS	26.6.84	190/126	SP	20.71	19.63- 04
Lyzhin	Pavel	BLR	24.3.81	189/110	SP	20.38	20.92- 04
Ma Liang		CHN	22.7.83		HT	70.72	71.01- 03
Maataoui	Ali	MAR	15.12.80	180/60	1500	3:35.52	3:35.72- 02
* Maazouzi	Driss	FRA	15.10.69	180/65	1500	3:37.18	3:31.45- 02
Macharia	Isaac	KEN	25.11.80		Mar	2:10:59	2:11:26- 04
Macharinyang	Hosea	KEN	12.6.85		10000	28:11.0A	28:19.6A- 04
* Mack	Tim	USA	15.9.72	188/78	PV	5.85	6.01- 04
MacLeod	Jared	CAN	3.4.80	183/74	110H	13.54	13.65- 04
Madi	Nabil	ALG	9.6.81	180/69	800	1:46.75	1:45.73- 04
Maeda	Kazuhiro	JPN	19.4.81	167/54	10000	28:20.87	28:10.66- 03
* Magdziarczyk	Roman	POL	5.7.77	180/70	20kW	1:20:47	1:22:54- 02
					50kW	3:49:55	3:44:53- 03
Maheshwary	Renjith	IND-J	30.1.86		TJ	16.42	
Maillard	Sébastien	FRA	2.5.81	184/81	400H	49.65	49.10- 03
Maina	Julius	KEN	14.10.77	179/65	HMar	61:43	62:08- 02
^ Maina	Simon	KEN	18.3.78	177/52	HMar	61:44	60:48- 00
* Maiyo	Benjamin	KEN	6.10.78	175/58	Mar	2:07:09	2:13:17- 04
Maiyo	Linus	KEN	11.12.83		10000	28:22.1A	27:49.73- 04
* Majewski	Tomasz	POL	30.8.81	204/132	SP	20.64	20.83i, 20.52- 04
Makabe	Takeshi	JPN	3.2.82	164/53	10000	28:14.03	
Makarov	Andrey	BLR	2.1.71	181/72	20kW	1:22:48	1:18:23- 00
* Makarov	Sergey	RUS	19.3.73	192/100	JT	90.33	92.61- 02
Mäkelä	Janne	FIN	2.2.79	183/77	400H	49.95	49.59- 02
Maksimov	Konstantin	RUS	17.6.82	178/67	20kW	1:22:04	1:22:19- 04
Malachowski	Piotr	POL	7.6.83	192/122	DT	64.74	62.40- 04
Malan	Francois	RSA	11.5.81		400H	49.51A, 49.95	50.48A- 04
Malasevich	Aleksandr	BLR	7.4.77	200/115	DT	62.76	65.80- 04
* Malcolm	Christian	GBR	3.6.79	174/67	100	10.25	10.11, 10.09w?- 01
					200	20.15	20.08- 01
Malina	Libor	CZE	14.6.73	193/120	DT	63.11	67.13- 10
* Malone	Casey	USA	6.4.77	203/109	DT	61.87	66.58A- 02
Malyarenko	Stanislav	RUS	19.5.85		HJ	2.23i	2.11- 04
Malyavin	Vladimir	RUS	4.3.73	188/75	LJ	8.07	8.25- 00
Manga	Davy	FRA	6.5.83	188/79	TJ	16.42	16.38- 03, 16.62w- 04
Mannio	Ari	FIN-J	23.7.87	186/97	JT	76.40	70.63- 04
Manso	Dário	POR	1.7.82		HT	70.90	68.24- 04
Manson	Andra	USA	30.4.84	196/75	HJ	2.26i, 2.23	2.32- 04
^ Manson	Pat	USA	29.11.67	178/75	PV	5.50A	5.85- 94
Mansour Ali	Bilal	BRN	17.10.83	170/60	800	1:44.34	1:46.8 - 04
Manyim	Philip	KEN	24.3.78	175/64	Mar	2:07:41	2:18:17- 04
Manz	Steven	USA	19.9.81	183/120	SP	19.74i	19.80- 04
Manzano	Leonel	USA	12.9.84	165/57	1500	3:37.13	3:52.04- 04
Marceny	Lionel	FRA	17.7.74	184/70	Dec	7497	8094- 00
Marciniszyn	Marcin	POL	7.9.82	185/72	400	45.69	45.75- 04
Maregu	Joseph	KEN	.77		HMar	62:00	
* Markov	Dmitriy	AUS	14.3.75	182/82	PV	5.75	6.05- 01
* Markov	Ilya	RUS	19.6.72	174/65	20kW	1:18:17	1:18:30- 97
Marsh	Mike	USA	20.3.80		Dec	7587	7370- 04
Martiak	Antoine	FRA	29.1.83	185/70	800	1:45.67	1:47.15- 03
Martin	Rodney	USA	22.12.82	180/73	100	10.25	10.48- 02
					200	20.34	20.57w- 03
Martin	Scott	USA	8.3.84		PV	5.50i	5.36- 04
Martin	Scott	AUS	12.10.82	190/130	SP	20.10	19.53- 04
					DT	62.58	63.78- 04
* Martín	Eliseo	ESP	5.11.73	172/61	3kSt	8:16.11	8:09.09- 03

Name		Nat	Born	Ht/Wt	Event	2005 Mark	Pre-2005 Best
* Martín	Luís Miguel	ESP	11.1.72	180/67	3kSt	8:17.47	8:07.44- 02
Martina	Churandy	AHO	3.7.84	180/68	100	10.10, 9.93Aw	10.13- 04
					200	20.32, 20.31Aw	20.81- 02
Martineau	Eugene	NED	14.5.80	180/79	Dec	8114	8082- 04
* Martínez	Alexander	CUB	23.8.77	184/82	TJ	17.51	17.32- 02
Martínez	Gerardo	MEX	9.3.79		HJ	2.25	2.21- 04
* Martínez	Guillermo	CUB	28.6.81	190/101	JT	84.06	81.45- 04
* Martínez	Joan Lino	ESP	17.1.78	176/69	LJ	8.37i, 8.17, 8.24w	8.32- 04, 8.39ic- 99
* Martínez	José Manuel	ESP	22.10.71	176/65	10000	27:42.90	27:30.56- 03
Martínez	Julio	GUA	27.9.73	165/44	50kW	3:57:56	3:56:19- 04
Martínez	Lois Maikel	CUB	3.6.81	185/90	DT	67.45	64.62- 03
* Martínez	Manuel	ESP	7.12.74	185/140	SP	20.51i, 20.32	21.47- 02
Martínez	Osiris	CUB	31.12.79	185/78	400H	49.19	49.83- 02
Martínez	Wilfredo	CUB	9.1.85	184/68	LJ	8.04	7.90- 03
Martins	Pedro	POR	12.1.68	163/60	50kW	4:03:09	3:55:29- 04
Marzouk Al-Dosari	Ahmad Fayez	KSA	6.9.79		LJ	8.01, 8.08w	
Masai	Moses	KEN-J	1.6.86		3000	7:49.1A	
					5000	13:24.36	13:25.5e+- 04
					10000	28:08.6A	27:07.29- 04
					Mar	2:10:13	2:12:28- 04
Maska	Vladimír	CZE	6.2.73	193/120	HT	76.77	81.28- 99
^ Mason	Germaine	JAM	1.4.83	195/80	HJ	2.27	2.34- 03
Mason	Matt	USA	30.6.82	188/79	LJ	7.92	8.08i- 04, 7.80- 02
Mätas	Risto	EST	30.4.84		JT	79.68	73.31- 04
Máté	Gábor	HUN	9.2.79	199/104	DT	65.42	66.54- 00, 66.99dh- 03
Matelong	Richard	KEN	14.10.83	179/65	3000	7:48.71	7:53.13- 04
					3kSt	8:10.97	8:05.96- 04
Mateusiak	Tomasz	POL	12.5.80	170/62	LJ	7.91	8.08, 8.15w- 03
Mathiszik	Willi	GER	17.6.84	185/70	110H	13.64, 13.58w	13.98- 03
Matsumiya	Takayuki	JPN	21.2.80	163/49	10000	27:50.20	27:50.97- 03
					HMar	61:32	61:34- 03
Matsumiya	Yuko	JPN	21.2.80	165/49	Mar	2:09:18	2:09:25- 04
Matsushita	Ryoji	JPN	7.11.80	170/55	HMar	61:57	62:43- 02
Matthews Jouda	Todd	SUD	28.6.79	193/86	110H	13.65	13.36- 02
Mayer	Gerhard	AUT	20.5.80	191/93	DT	62.85	61.81- 03
^ Mayo	Gilmar	COL	30.9.69	190/72	HJ	2.26A	2.33- 94
^ Mayola	Freddy	CUB	1.11.77	176/74	100	10.26	10.10- 99, 10.00rw- 00, 10.08w- 01
Mazurik	Maksim	UKR	2.4.83	190/85	PV	5.65i, 5.65	5.75- 04
Mbote	Jason	KEN	.77		HMar	61:49	61:49- 03
					Mar	2:08:30	
McClintock	Martin	RSA	30.6.75	187/82	LJ	8.05A, 7.96, 8.25w	7.98A- 04, 7.97- 01
McCormick	Nick	GBR	11.9.81	188/72	1500	3:35.74/3:33.9+u	3:39.50- 04
					1M	3:52.02	4:07.45- 01
McCoy	Reuben	USA-J	16.3.86	186/75	400H	49.82	51.39- 04
McDaniel	Otis	USA-J	30.6.86	183/84	200	20.67w	21.15- 04
McDonagh	Ciaran	IRL	20.5.76	183/72	LJ	8.07, 8.09w	8.00- 00, 8.04w- 99
McDonald	Michael	JAM	17.3.75	183/85	400	45.21	44.64A- 96, 44.65- 97
McEwen	Matthew	AUS	16.10.71	194/88	Dec	7530	7825- 01
* McFarlane	Danny	JAM	14.2.72	185/81	400H	48.53	48.00- 04
McGowan	Scott	USA	27.1.81	190/73	1500	3:37.99	3:42.25- 02
McGregor	Herbert	JAM	.81		LJ	7.98w	7.40- 04
McIlroy	James	GBR	30.12.76	180/68	800	1:44.65	1:45.30- 03
McLean	Bubba	USA	2.9.79	175/70	PV	5.71i	5.70- 04
McMullen	Phil	USA	3.2.75	196/93	Dec	8107	8285- 04
McReynolds	Jacob	AUS	8.12.78	184/79	TJ	16.67	16.47, 16.89w- 03
McSwain	James	USA	20.1.84	170/66	100	10.19	10.50- 04, 10.1w- 02
Mekerin	Aleksey	RUS	26.2.78		LJ	8.01	7.87- 01
Melentyev	Sergey	RUS	5.12.76	178/68	50kW	3:57:10	3:57:52- 04
Meleshenko	Yevgeniy	KAZ	19.1.81	185/70	400H	49.18	48.46- 01
Melesse	Gashaw	ETH	26.9.78	170/52	Mar	2:09:24	2:09:47- 04
Melétoglu	Hrístos	GRE	2.1.72	190/80	TJ	16.74, 17.09w	17.19- 01
Melich	Lukás	CZE	16.9.80	186/105	HT	79.36	76.38- 03
Mendes	Rodrigo	BRA	21.6.68	190/77	TJ	17.00, 17.54w	16.78- 00
Meng Ke		CHN-J	8.12.87		20kW	1:20:59	1:33:42- 04
Meng Yan		CHN	30.9.80	188/68	400H	49.19	49.84- 04
Menjo	Kiprono	KEN	.79		3000	7:44.47	
					5000	13:14.38	13:48.7- 04
Meriluoto	Johan	FIN	22.3.74	187/73	TJ	16.50	16.95- 00, 17.04w- 01
Merritt	Aries	USA	24.7.85	188/75	110H	13.38, 13.34w	13.47- 04
* Merritt	LaShawn	USA-J	27.6.86	188/82	200	20.38	20.72, 20.69w- 04
					400	44.66	45.25- 04

	Name		Nat	Born	Ht/Wt	Event	2005Mark	Pre-2005 Best
	Mesfin	Hailu	ETH	.84		HMar	61:59	62:15A- 03
*	Mesnil	Romain	FRA	13.7.77	188/79	PV	5.75	5.95- 03
^	Mezgebu	Assefa	ETH	19.6.78	175/55	10000	27:32.02	26:49.90- 02
	Miao Yanxi		CHN	3.8.84		20kW	1:22:45	
	Michniewski	Robert	POL	16.2.74	188/76	TJ	16.50	16.54- 03
	Mihailescu	Alexandru	ROM	16.8.82	184/78	110H	13.70	13.64- 04
	Mikhaylichenko	Yevgeniy	RUS	13.2.79	185/77	PV	5.50i, 5.50	5.70- 02
*	Mikhnevich	Andrey	BLR	12.7.76	202/127	SP	21.08	21.69- 03
	Mikkola	Esko	FIN	14.2.75	183/95	JT	82.14	84.27- 04
*	Milazar	Eric	MRI	1.6.75	192/80	200	20.70	20.66- 04, 20.2w- 98
						400	45.54	44.69- 01
*	Miles	Derek	USA	28.9.72	191/82	PV	5.85i, 5.84	5.82- 01
	Milkevics	Dmitrijs	LAT	6.12.81	182/72	800	1:44.74	1:45.60- 04
^	Miller	Coby	USA	19.10.76	168/68	100	10.16, 10.08w	9.98, 9.88w- 00
						200	20.45	19.96- 00
	Milner	Quinton	USA	20.12.74	180/75	400H	49.80	49.44- 04
	Mims	Jeremy	USA	15.2.83	193/79	800	1:45.86	1:48.04- 03
	Minah	Jacob	GER	3.4.82		Dec	7652	7374- 04
*	Misoi	Kipkirui	KEN	23.12.78	177/59	3kSt	8:08.15	8:01.69- 01
	Mistretta	Alessandro	ITA	6.3.71	172/58	50kW	3:56:32	3:51:33- 99
	Mitchell	Michael	USA	16.5.81	180/70	100	10.22	10.29, 10.07w- 04
						200	20.67	20.59- 00
	Mitchum	Eric	USA	2.8.84	188/82	110H	13.53	13.38- 04
	Mitsuya	Yu	JPN	18.12.84	166/49	10000	27:41.10	28:00.23- 04
	Miyata	Takashi	JPN	24.5.79	168/66	100	10.22w	10.37- 99
	Mkhabela	Emmanuel	RSA	19.7.79		3kSt	8:29.00	8:28.29- 04
	Modibo	Ato	TRI	19.6.79	188/75	400	45.02	44.87- 01
	Moede	Thomas	GER	26.7.77	184/77	TJ	16.47	16.90- 01
	Moffatt	Keith	USA	20.6.84		HJ	2.27	2.27- 04
*	Moffitt	John	USA	12.12.80	185/75	LJ	8.16i, 7.96, 8.01w	8.47- 04
	Mogawane	Ofentse	RSA	20.2.82		400	45.42A, 45.98	46.72A- 04
	Mogusu	Mekubo	KEN-J	25.12.86	166/48	10000	27:54.75	28:02.96- 04
						HMar	61:28	
	Mohamed	Ahmed Abderraouf	EGY	12.2.80		HT	73.20	69.85- 04
	Mohamed	Mustafa	SWE	1.3.79	172/54	3kSt	8:15.51	8:18.05- 04
	Mokamba	Ombeche	KEN	6.4.82	177/63	10000	28:22.46	
						HMar	61:39	61:56- 02
	Mokganyetsi	Hendrik	RSA	7.9.75	190/76	400	45.87A	44.59- 00
*	Mokoena	Khotso	RSA	6.3.85	190/73	LJ	8.37A, 8.22, 8.26w	8.09- 04
						TJ	17.25	16.96A, 16.77- 04
	Mola	René L.	CUB-J	15.2.87	173/70	TJ	16.49	16.50- 04
	Molapisi	Tlhalosang	BOT	15.3.73		100	10.27wA	10.55A- 04
	Molefe	California	BOT	2.5.80	172/62	400	45.34	45.43- 03
*	Molina	Juan Manuel	ESP	15.3.79	173/67	20kW	1:19:44	1:20:18- 02
	Molla	Shimelis	ETH			Mar	2:10:11	2:13:19- 04
*	Möllenbeck	Michael	GER	12.12.69	200/130	DT	66.56	67.64- 02
	Møller	Anders	DEN	5.9.77	185/81	TJ	16.76	16.09- 04
^	Moncur	Avard	BAH	2.11.78	196/82	400	45.60	44.45- 01
	Mononen	Matti	FIN	25.11.83	177/75	PV	5.60	5.66- 04
	Monte	Yosmel	CUB	26.6.77	189/100	HT	71.64	74.77- 02
	Monteiro	Edivaldo	POR	28.4.76	175/68	400H	49.26	49.10- 04
^	Montgomery ¶	Tim	USA	28.1.75	178/72	100	10.14/10.10w	9.78- 02
	Monyani (Sithole)	Petrus	RSA	29.3.76	160/53	3kSt	8:31.29	8:26.40- 04
*	Moore	Anwar	USA	5.3.79	182/75	110H	13.23, 13.20w	13.35- 04
	Moore	Stephen	USA	13.8.75	180/76	Dec	7655	8085w- 04, 8037- 99
	Moradi	Sadjad	IRI	30.3.83	182/67	800	1:44.74	1:46.07- 04
	de Morães	Basílio	BRA	11.5.82	178/71	100	10.27A, 10.20w	10.44- 04
						200	20.55A, 20.44Aw, 20.66	20.57- 04
	Morello	Salvatore	ITA	5.9.74	176/65	TJ	16.65i, 16.46	16.81- 04
	Moreno	Yudel	CUB	24.2.83	183/83	JT	78.07	76.96- 04
	Morgan	Nathan	GBR	30.6.78	187/86	LJ	8.00	8.26- 03
	Mori	Fabrizio	ITA	28.6.69	175/68	400H	50.06	47.54- 01
	Moroney	Nick	AUS	3.8.72	184/75	HJ	2.25	2.25- 00
^	Moroz	Gennadiy	BLR	27.5.78	200/77	HJ	2.29	2.33- 01
	Morrison	Michael	USA	4.3.84	186/74	HJ	2.25i, 2.23	2.24i, 2.22- 03
	Mosca	Vince	USA	23.1.80	189/127	SP	19.90	20.23- 04
	Moskalenko	Vitaliy	RUS	30.6.74	184/80	TJ	17.04	17.17- 03
*	Mosop	Moses	KEN	17.7.85	172/57	3000	7:42.96	7:41.78- 04
						5000	13:06.83	13:09.68- 04
						10000	27:08.96	27:13.66- 03

	Name		Nat	Born	Ht/Wt	Event	2005 Mark	Pre-2005 Best
*	Mottram	Craig	AUS	18.6.80	188/72	1500	3:34.80/3:32.7+u	3:35.40- 01
						1M	3:48.98	3:52.90- 01
						3000	7:38.03	7:37.30- 02
						5000	12:56.13	12:55.76- 04
						10000	27:56.02	27:50.55- 03
	Mouatassim	Abderrahmane	MAR			3kSt	8:32.78	
^	Moudrik	Younès	MAR	1.10.77	176/72	TJ	16.80	
	Moulay	Nicolas	FRA	20.1.79	187/84	Dec	7673	7452- 04
	Mounts	Van	USA	5.1.80	191/127	SP	19.47	19.87- 02
^	Mourhit	Mohammed	BEL	10.10.70	164/55	5000	13:11.74	12:49.71- 00
						HMar	61:54	60:18- 97
	Moustaoui	Mohammed	MAR	2.4.85	178/62	1500	3:36.20	3:37.44- 04
						5000	13:22.61	
	Moxey	Osbourne	BAH	27.8.78	175/79	LJ	7.99, 8.03w	8.19- 02
*	Moya	Víctor	CUB	24.10.82	196/80	HJ	2.35	2.25- 04
	Mubarak	Mubarak Ata	KSA	17.12.81	175/67	110H	13.70	13.68- 04, 13.60w- 02
	Mubarak Taher	Tareq	BRN	24.3.84		3kSt	8:16.26	
	Muchiri Ndambiri	Josphat	KEN	12.2.85	170/53	5000	13:05.33	13:27.53- 04
						10000	27:19.19	27:46.10- 04
	Muindi	Jimmy	KEN	14.8.73		Mar	2:07:50	2:08:25- 02
	Mulabegovic	Nedzad	CRO	4.2.81	189/100	SP	19.94i, 19.55	20.15- 03, 20.31ex- 04
*	Mulaudzi	Mbulaeni	RSA	8.9.80	171/62	800	1:44.08	1:42.89- 03
	Muli	Pius	KEN	15.12.82	169/54	3000	7:45.09	7:40.82- 03
	Müller	Norman	GER	7.8.85	195/84	Dec	7989	0
	Müller	Stefan	SUI	20.9.79	190/96	JT	78.98	77.95- 03
	Mullings ¶	Steve	JAM	29.11.82	173/68	100	10.13dq/10.06w	10.05, 10.04dq, 9.96w- 04
						200	20.31dq	20.27, 19.90w, 20.22dq- 04
	Mulvaney	Chris	GBR	25.5.81	170/60	1500	3:37.36	3:40.43- 04
	Munji	Titus	KEN	20.12.79		Mar	2:11:07	2:06:15- 03
	Munyeki Kiama	Charles	KEN			HMar	61:34A	
	Murakami	Yukifumi	JPN	23.12.79	185/80	JT	79.79	81.71- 04
*	Murofushi	Koji	JPN	8.10.74	187/97	HT	76.47	84.86- 03
^	Murphy	Andrew	AUS	18.12.69	185/82	TJ	16.43	17.32- 99
	Musembi	Thomas	KEN	26.4.77		400	45.69A	46.28A- 04
	Mustapic	Dragan	CRO	23.3.63	196/110	DT	62.80	64.40- 00
	Mutai	Elijah Chemwelo	KEN	1.4.78		Mar	2:09:27	2:10:41- 02
	Mutai	Emmanuel	KEN	1.4.78		10000	28:09.2A	
	Mutai	Patrick	KEN	31.12.83	178/63	3kSt	8:31.93	
*	Mutua	Joseph	KEN	10.12.78	170/58	800	1:45.58	1:43.33- 02
	Muturi	Samuel	KEN-J	2.5.86	166/51	10000	27:35.55	27:52.83- 04
*	Muzík	Jirí	CZE	1.9.76	181/75	400H	48.83	48.27- 97
	Mwangi	Daniel	KEN	1.1.84	175/62	5000	13:18.21	13:29.18- 04
	Mwangi Macharia	James	KEN	23.6.84	175/58	HMar	60:42	61:28- 04
	Mwangi Murigi	James	KEN-J	15.7.86	176/58	1500	3:37.09	
						5000	13:05.05	13:13.96- 04
						10000	27:40.94	
	Mwera	Samwel	TAN	3.6.85	175/54	800	1:45.28	1:45.30- 04
*	Myburgh	Alwyn	RSA	13.10.80	188/71	400H	48.75	48.09- 01
	Myers	Rob	USA	5.8.80	172/59	1500	3:34.89	3:38.6+- 04
						1M	3:54.87	3:53.78- 04
*	Myerscough	Carl	GBR	21.10.79	209/149	SP	20.62	21.92- 03
						DT	61.53	65.10- 04
	Myklebust	Gaute	NOR	29.4.79	195/120	DT	63.32	61.52- 03
	Mykolaitis	Povilas	LTU	23.2.83	187/79	LJ	8.13i, 8.09	7.96i- 04, 7.80- 03
^	Nagel	Morné	RSA	23.2.78	183/77	100	10.27, 10.25wA	10.13A- 02, 10.13- 03
						200	20.35	20.11A, 20.34- 02
	Naito	Masato	JPN	31.7.80	185/70	110H	13.53	13.47- 03
*	Narisako	Kenji	JPN	25.7.84	185/73	400H	48.09	48.54- 04
	Nartov	Aleksandr	UKR-Y	21.5.88	182/67	HJ	2.28	2.20i- 04, 2.15- 03
	Nau	Manuel	GER	2.7.77	190/90	JT	81.01	83.04- 00
	Nava	Horacio	MEX	20.1.82	175/62	50kW	3:53:57	
	Nazarov	Dilshod	TJK	6.5.82	187/100	HT	77.63	76.58- 04
	Ndegwa	Peter	KEN	.82		10000	28:07.0A	
	Ndiso Musembi	Dennis	KEN	31.12.83	183.63	3000	7:43.48	
						10000	27:46.16	
						HMar	61:27	61:24- 03
	Ndiwa	Linus	KEN			800	1:46.3A	1:49.5A- 04
	Ndiwa Kimai	Mangata	KEN-J	.87		5000	13:24.0A	
*	Nelson	Adam	USA	7.7.75	181/115	SP	21.92	22.51- 02
	Nelson	Alex	GBR-Y	21.3.88	182/75	200	20.69	22.36- 03
	Németh	Kristóf	HUN-J	17.9.87	190/97	HT	70.99	67.43- 04

	Name		Nat	Born	Ht/Wt	Event	2005Mark	Pre-2005 Best
	Neofytou	Kris	AUS	3.5.84	166/66	100	10.26w	10.33- 04
						200	20.60	20.71- 04
	Nesterovskiy	Stanislav	UKR	31.7.80	198/110	DT	62.59	60.33- 04
	Neunhäuserer	Christian	ITA	21.6.78	182/65	800	1:46.59	1:46.07- 02
	Neville	David	USA	1.6.84	193/77	400	45.89	45.05- 04
	Nganga	Stanley	KEN-J	30.6.86	176/55	10000	28:21.30	
	Ngeny Kiprotich	Joseph	KEN	.78		HMar	61:56	61:35- 03
	Ngetich	Caleb	KEN	.82	175/60	3kSt	8:23.30	8:43.4A- 04
	Ngolebus	Joseph	KEN	10.4.75		HMar	61:16	60:56- 03
						Mar	2:10:10	2:07:57- 03
	Ni Liang		CHN-J	26.7.86	173/55	50kW	3:41:30	4:07:56- 04
	Niaré	Yves	FRA	20.7.77	195/100	SP	19.08	19.76- 01
*	Nicolay	Christian	GER	4.3.76	189/88	JT	83.20	84.54- 03
	Nieland	Nick	GBR	31.1.72	190/100	JT	79.56	85.09- 00
*	Nieto	James	USA	2.11.76	193/79	HJ	2.30	2.34- 04
*	Niklaus	André	GER	30.8.81	190/82	Dec	8316	8042- 01
	Nikonov	Dmitriy	RUS-J	17.10.87		TJ	16.43	15.64- 04
	Nilsen	Ronny	NOR	7.5.71	182/90	JT	78.93	84.73- 04
	Nima	Issam	ALG	8.4.79	186/74	LJ	8.13	7.92, 7.97w?, 7.99w- 04
*	Njenga	Daniel	KEN	7.5.76	176/61	HMar	61:31	60:39- 96
						Mar	2:07:14	2:06:16- 02
	Njubi	Eliud	KEN	27.7.79		1500	3:38.52	3:38.18- 02
	Njui	Cyrus Gichobi	KEN-J	11.2.86	169/52	10000	28:08.45	28:46.39- 04
						HMar	61:49	
	Nkuna	Isaiah	RSA	5.3.77		800	1:46.87	1:46.93A- 01
	Noffke	Chris	AUS-Y	6.1.88	188/76	LJ	7.95, 8.00w	7.74- 04
	Nolan	James	IRL	27.1.77	183/71	1500	3:37.78	3:35.69- 03
	Norberg	Justin	USA	18.7.77	190/82	PV	5.75	5.70- 04
	Nordin	Jimmy	SWE	19.10.79	179/115	SP	19.74	20.73- 02
	Norman	Cedric	USA	5.10.81	190/77	HJ	2.27	2.29- 04
	Norman	Jacob	USA	7.11.85	188/82	100	10.28	10.43, 10.37w- 04
	Norman	Josh	USA	26.7.80	188/60	100	10.16, 10.10w	10.09- 04
	Noúsios	Astérios	GRE	25.2.79	185/74	LJ	7.91i, 7.91	8.00- 00
	Nowill	Peter	AUS	15.6.79	179/69	3kSt	8:23.93	8:22.85- 04
	Nsenga	Jonathan	BEL	21.4.73	187/82	110H	13.54	13.25- 98
	Nthiwa	Patrick	KEN	30.6.83		3kSt	8:33.0A	8:27.63- 04
	Nuara	Mattias	ITA	21.12.81	185/67	LJ	8.09w	7.60, 7.76w- 04
	Nurudeen	Selim	USA	1.2.83	183/75	110H	13.65w	13.61, 13.57w- 04
	Nutter	Travis	USA	9.2.75	178/95	HT	74.86	73.53- 04
*	Nyamu	Julius	KEN	1.12.77	178/66	3kSt	8:15.29	8:07.59- 01
	Nyangani	Young Talkmore	ZIM	2.9.83	172/70	400	44.96A, 45.10	45.09, 44.9- 04
*	Nymark	Trond	NOR	28.12.76	180/64	50kW	3:44:04	3:44:55- 04
	Nzioki	Erick	KEN	22.7.78		Mar	2:10:34	2:16:37- 04
*	Obikwelu	Francis	POR	22.11.78	195/79	100	10.04	9.86- 04
						200	20.48	19.84- 99
	Obrist	Christian	ITA	20.11.80	186/66	800	1:46.19	1:46.35- 03
	Odom	Marlon	USA	4.12.82	183/66	110H	13.69, 13.67w	14.22- 03
*	Odriozola	Mikel	ESP	25.5.73	180/62	50kW	3:41:47	3:42:03- 03
*	Ogata	Tsuyoshi	JPN	11.5.73	165/50	10000	28:20.52	28:05.76- 04
						Mar	2:11:16	2:08:37- 03
	Ohashi	Yuji	JPN	5.9.83	185/70	110H	13.57	13.75- 04
^	Ojaniemi	Jaakko	FIN	28.8.80	192/87	LJ	8.03w	7.66- 02
						Dec	8076w, 80.42	8192- 02
	Okari	Gilbert	KEN	2.7.78		10000	28:11.0A	27:40.9, 03
	Okken	Arnoud	NED	20.4.82	182/65	800	1:46.86, 1:46.27i	1:45.64- 01
	Okutani	Wataru	JPN	9.1.75	181/60	Mar	2:09:13	2:11:24- 99
	Okworo	George	KEN	12.5.79		HMar	62:03	
	Ole Mangira	Malack	TAN	.84	165/57	HMar	61:59	
	Oleinik	Sergey	RUS	28.11.80		TJ	16.72	15.97- 02
	Olgundeniz	Ercüment	TUR	7.7.76	203/120	DT	60.79	63.49- 04
*	Olijar	Stanislav	LAT	22.3.79	190/80	110H	13.11	13.08- 03
	Olinger	Brian	USA	2.6.83		3kSt	8:19.56	8:50.02- 04
	de Oliveira	Júlio César	BRA-J	4.2.86		JT	76.81	74.42- 04
	de Oliveira	Raphael R.	BRA	5.2.79	170/68	100	10.29A	10.20A- 00, 10.23, 10.16w- 01
	Oliver	David	USA	24.4.82	190/93	110H	13.29, 13.23w	13.55- 04
	Olmedo	Manuel	ESP	17.5.83	173/53	800	1:45.48	1:45.25- 04
*	Olsen	Joachim	DEN	31.5.77	184/142	SP	21.32	21.63i- 04, 21.57- 02
	Olshanskiy	Andrey	RUS	24.1.78	191/73	3kSt	8:19.68	8:40.53- 01
*	Omar Obaid	Moussa	QAT	18.4.85	185/68	3000	7:45.89	
						3kSt	8:11.75	8:07.18- 04
	Omey	Tom	BEL	24.4.75	186/79	800	1:46.60	1:45.75- 03

Name		Nat	Born	Ht/Wt	Event	2005 Mark	Pre-2005 Best
Omole	Demi	USA	29.7.85	178/73	100	10.25	10.15, 10.12w- 04
Omori	Terukazu	JPN	3.9.79	174/55	10000	27:56.57	27:43.94- 04
Onalenna	Oabona	BOT	6.5.84	185/60	800	1:46.06	1:46.0- 04
Onnen	Eike	GER	3.8.82	194/83	HJ	2.26	2.23- 03
Ono	Ryuji	JPN	27.1.85	160/47	10000	28:02.18	27:59.32- 04
* Oprea	Marian	ROM	6.6.82	190/80	TJ	17.81	17.63- 03
Ormrod	Mark	AUS	1.12.82	185/73	400	45.62	46.07- 01
Ornelas	Helder	POR	6.5.74	176/63	Mar	2:10:00	0
Ortega	Dailén	CUB	24.7.83	196/92	HJ	2.23	2.23- 04
Osovnikar	Matic	SLO	19.1.80	177/75	100	10.24	10.15, 10.08w- 04
Ota	Takashi	JPN	27.4.76	175/57	10000	28:09.62	28:06.22- 04
Otsubo	Takanobu	JPN	15.6.76	180/62	10000	28:14.92	28:38.53- 04
					HMar	61:55	
Otto	Björn	GER	16.10.77	188/84	PV	5.80	5.82i- 04, 5.70- 03
^ Ottoz	Laurent	ITA	10.4.70	180/69	400H	49.41	48.52- 96
Ouyang Shuiping		CHN-J	23.1.86		50kW	3:58:07	4:13:30- 01
Pacheco	Bruno	BRA	20.4.83	178/71	200	20.57	20.54- 02
Pacôme Ndri	ric	CIV	24.3.78	185/83	100	10.22Aw	10.17, 10.11w- 01
Pahapill	Mikk	EST	18.7.83	193/85	Dec	8149	7226- 04
Palacios	Noraldo	COL	8.7.80	173/75	JT	77.37A	77.84- 04
Páli	Kristóf	HUN	29.12.80		HT	73.66	71.84- 03
Paljakka	Jarkko	FIN	7.2.79	186/102	HT	73.37	74.29- 03
Palli	Niki	ISR-J	28.5.87	186/76	HJ	2.25	2.09- 04
Palmer	Hank	CAN	16.3.85	188/80	100	10.28, 9.9w	10.38- 04
Palyszko	Maciej	POL	4.1.78	186/112	HT	73.17	80.89- 03
Panfilov	Grigoriy	RUS	17.5.80		SP	19.72	19.95- 04
* Papadimitríou	Aléxandros	GRE	18.6.73	185/115	HT	78.28	80.45- 00
Park Chil-sung		KOR	8.7.82	173/61	20kW	1:22:23	1:22:38- 03
Park Jae-myong		KOR	15.12.81	181/88	JT	78.87	83.99- 04
Parker	David	GBR	28.2.80	189/93	JT	76.95	78.33A- 01, 78.24- 00
Parker	James	USA	3.12.75	180/107	HT	74.67	79.20- 04
Parkhomenko	Aleksandr	BLR	22.3.81	182/82	Dec	8051	7954- 03
Parravicini	Tim	AUS	25.4.81	190/81	LJ	8.18, 8.20w	8.06- 04
Parrela	Sanderlei Claro	BRA	7.10.74	194/77	400	45.64A, 45.92	44.29- 99
* Pars	Krisztián	HUN	18.2.82	188/104	HT	80.03	80.90- 04
Parsons	Tom	GBR	5.5.84	190/78	HJ	2.23	2.20- 04
Parszczynski	Lukasz	POL	4.5.85	180/64	3kSt	8:31.18	9:01.30- 04
* Parvatkin	Vladimir	RUS	10.10.84	175/65	20kW	1:18:06	1:18:17- 04
* Parviainen	Aki	FIN	26.10.74	191/96	JT	83.79	93.09- 99
* Pate	Miguel	USA	13.6.79	188/84	LJ	8.45	8.59i, 8.45- 02, 8.46A- 03
Patselya	Aleksandr	UKR	3.7.83	184/82	LJ	8.00	8.13- 03
Patterson	Carlos	CUB	20.2.78	186/79	110H	13.92, 13.5	13.70- 04, 13.2- 02
Patterson	Henry	USA	27.5.75	196/86	HJ	2.23i	2.32- 99
* Patton	Darvis	USA	4.12.77	183/75	100	10.27	10.00- 03, 9.89w- 04
Pauli	Jacob	USA	15.6.79	191/86	PV	5.75	5.80- 04
Paumier	Alexis	CUB	21.1.75	191/100	SP	19.65	20.78- 00
Pausé	Dominique	FRA	11.1.76	176/72	JT	77.79	79.66- 02
* Pavlov	Igor	RUS	18.7.79	187/83	PV	5.90i, 5.80	5.80- 04
Pavlushchenko ¶	Sergey	UKR	23.1.80	176/70	LJ	7.94i, 8.01wdq, 7.88dq	7.60- 02
Payne	David	USA	24.7.82	183/75	110H	13.33	13.48, 13.42w- 04
Peçanha	Fabiano	BRA	5.6.82	186/73	800	1:45.40	1:46.12- 04
^ Pechonkin	Yevgeniy	RUS	9.10.73	190/90	110H	13.57, 13.52w	13.38- 96, 13.37w- 00
* Pedroso	Iván	CUB	17.12.72	176/70	LJ	8.22	8.71, 8.96Aw- 95, 8.79w-92
Peetre	Taavi	EST	4.7.83	192/119	SP	20.23	20.30- 04
Peguero	Arizmendi	DOM	7.8.80	173/76	400	45.80	45.63- 04, 45.2- 03
Pei Chuang		CHN	5.12.81	174/58	20kW	1:19:21	1:20:09- 03
Pei Lingjie		CHN-J	3.1.87	175/51	20kW	1:22:07	1:24:26- 04
Penas	Manuel Angel	ESP	9.11.77	172/54	3000	7:47.13	7:44.70- 04
Pencréach	Gaël	FRA	5.8.77	180/68	3kSt	8:18.18	8:13.16- 99
Pennings	Wilbert	NED	12.2.75	194/81	HJ	2.24	2.31i- 02, 2.30- 99
Pereira	António	POR	10.7.75	173/68	50kW	4:04:22	4:07:30- 04
Peremota	Igor	RUS	14.1.81	191/78	110H	13.48	13.52- 04
Pérez	César	ESP	7.4.75	172/63	3kSt	8:14.68	8:19.82- 03
* Pérez	Jefferson	ECU	1.7.74	174/59	20kW	1:18:35	1:17:21- 03
Pérez	Lisvany	CUB	24.1.82	198/76	HJ	2.29	2.28- 04
Pérez	Santiago	ESP	15.1.72	179/70	50kW	3:48:15	3:45:55- 98
^ Peric	Dragan	SCG	8.5.64	186/115	SP	20.25	21.77- 98
Perkins	Adam	USA	7.5.84	178/66	1500	3:38.54	3:49.09- 02
Perry	Michael	AUS	30.9.77	193/80	TJ	16.67	16.25- 03, 16.29w- 02
Perry	Preston	USA	13.9.83	171/68	200	20.39w	21.31- 03, 20.87w- 04
Person	Montrell	USA	28.11.81	189/79	110H	13.71	13.53- 04

Name		Nat	Born	Ht/Wt	Event	2005Mark	Pre-2005 Best
Pertile	Ruggero	ITA	8.8.74	170/55	Mar	2:11:13	2:10:12- 04
* Pestano	Mario	ESP	8.4.78	195/120	DT	66.57	68.00- 04
Peterson	Derrick	USA	28.11.77	182/73	800	1:46.09	1:45.08- 04
Peterson	Domenik	USA	12.12.84	183/75	200	20.43i	20.62, 20.57i, 20.60w- 04
					400	45.15	46.01- 04
Petrenko	Aleksandr	RUS	8.2.83	183/75	TJ	17.03	16.79- 04
Petrucci	Nick	USA	10.11.75	197/129	DT	62.46	66.35- 03
Peuf	Pierre-Charles	FRA	27.4.79	187/82	PV	5.60	5.70- 03
Pëychar	Isagani	AUT	23.3.81	170/70	LJ	7.96i, 7.94	7.91- 04
Pfingsten	Gunnar	GER	24.3.75	196/120	SP	19.59	20.08- 00
* Phillips	Dwight	USA	1.10.77	181/82	100	10.14	10.16- 02, 10.11w- 00
					LJ	8.60	8.60- 04
Phillips	Isa	JAM	22.4.84		400H	49.96	50.39- 04
Pickering	Craig	GBR-J	16.10.86	173/70	100	10.22	10.41- 04
Pienaar	Hardus	RSA	10.8.81	190/88	JT	77.07A	84.50- 03
Pierre	Kevon	TRI	30.3.82	179/73	100	10.22, 10.19w	10.52- 02, 10.3- 03
					200	20.47	21.22- 04
Pignata	Francesco	ITA	14.2.78	190/81	JT	81.67	79.34- 04
Pinardo	Francisco José	ESP	15.3.75	179/64	50kW	3:51:40	3:52:51- 02
Pincemail	Sébastien	FRA	21.2.79	186/84	TJ	16.91	16.95- 03
Pinnock	Chris	JAM	26.3.79	183/82	110H	13.62, 13.55w	13.38- 03
Pishchalnikov	Bogdan	RUS	26.8.82	197/107	DT	64.08	60.89- 04
^ Piskunov ¶	Vladislav	UKR	7.6.78	183/108	HT	78.72	82.23- 02
* Pitkämaki	Tero	FIN	19.12.82	195/92	JT	91.53	84.64- 04
Plas	Aaron	USA	10.1.84		HJ	2.23i, 2.23	2.18- 02
Plautz	Marcel	GER	1.7.80	192/86	JT	78.56	78.02- 02
* Plawgo	Marek	POL	25.2.81	181/72	400	45.92	45.35- 02
					400H	48.78	48.16- 01
Plotnir	Yevgeniy	RUS	26.6.77	196/85	TJ	17.00	16.82- 03
Plummer	Yhann	JAM	3.2.83	178/71	100	10.27, 10.19w	10.56, 10.27w- 02
* Pognon	Ronald	FRA	16.11.82	185/75	100	9.99	10.11- 04
					200	20.27	20.49-04, 20.4w- 01
* Pogorelov	Aleksandr	RUS	10.1.80	201/97	Dec	8429	8163- 02
Poll	Yaubel	CUB	30.7.83	185/83	400H	49.86	50.64- 04
Ponos	Edi	CRO	10.4.76	196/118	JT	76.39	77.95- 04
Poplawski	Radoslaw	POL	16.1.83	176/61	3kSt	8:17.87	8:17.32- 04
Porter	William	USA	15.4.73	193/87	400H	49.94	48.65- 99
Potapovich	Pavel	RUS	26.11.80	185/74	3kSt	8:25.67	8:15.54- 03
* Potemin	Vladimir	RUS	15.1.80	177/69	50kW	3:51:34	3:39:21- 00
Pouzy	Frédéric	FRA	18.2.83	184/88	HT	74.03	72.64- 04
* Powell	Asafa	JAM	11.11.82	190/88	100	9.77	9.87- 04
Powell	Darion	USA	14.6.82		Dec	7531	7511- 03
Powell	Trent	USA	25.6.78	178/68	PV	5.50A	5.45- 03
Prange	Clint	USA	21.10.81	196/116	SP	20.14	17.40- 04
Pratt	Róbison	MEX	25.2.80	197/80	PV	5.61	5.60A- 00, 5.56- 03
Prezelj	Rozle	SLO	26.9.79	193/73	HJ	2.24i	2.31i- 04, 2.27- 03
Pritchett	Matthieu	USA-J	8.4.86	173/75	100	10.27w	10.70- 04
Probasco	Nate	USA	10.7.83	188/90	200	20.59, 20.49w	21.16, 20.97w- 04
Proctor	Mark	GBR	15.1.63	193/131	SP	20.04	20.85i- 98, 20.40- 99
Pröll	Martin	AUT	21.3.81	177/60	3kSt	8:13.74	8:18.53- 04
Pruglo	Sergey	UKR	18.11.83	187/109	DT	60.55	62.74- 04
^ Ptácek	Adam	CZE	8.10.80	178/65	PV	5.60sq	5.81i- 03, 5.80- 02
Pucelj	Ivan	CRO	11.7.81	181/70	LJ	7.90i, 7.93w	7.92- 03
Pugliese	Marcelo	ARG	2.9.68	191/105	DT	59.54	64.23- 02
Pupis	Martin	SVK	19.10.78	175/60	50kW	4:05:04	3:59:13- 00
Pussila	Tatu	FIN	25.5.82	196/88	Dec	7497	7450- 04
* Qi Haifeng		CHN	7.8.83	186/78	Dec	8290	8126- 03
Quesada	Miguel	ESP	18.9.79	180/60	800	1:45.79	1:45.61- 04
* Quesada	Yoelbi	CUB	4.8.73	181/71	TJ	17.03	17.85- 97, 17.97w- 95
Quinley	Trevell	USA	16.1.83	198/82	LJ	8.17	7.72- 04
Quiñónez	Jackson	ECU	12.6.80	186/80	110H	13.45	13.44- 04
Quow	Renny	TRI-J	25.8.87		400	45.82	46.60- 04
Radja	Kresimir	CRO	3.11.81	199/134	SP	19.09	18.67- 04
Raeburn	Julien	TRI	18.9.78	188/82	200	20.52	20.57- 03
Ragnvaldsson	Daniel	SWE	3.1.76		JT	78.54	77.34- 01
* Rags	Eriks	LAT	1.6.75	183/93	JT	82.35	86.47- 01
* Rahnu	Kristjan	EST	29.8.79	192/90	Dec	8526	8203- 03
Raïfak	Mustapha	FRA	9.9.75	184/67	HJ	2.24	2.28- 97
Raja	Andres	EST	2.6.82	186/80	Dec	7716	7095- 04
Rakovic	Aleksandar	SCG	13.4.68	183/75	50kW	3:57:30	3:48:01- 99
Ram	Ghamanda	IND	1.7.84		800	1:46.67	1:48.24- 02

Name		Nat	Born	Ht/Wt	Event	2005 Mark	Pre-2005 Best
* Ramaala	Hendrick	RSA	2.2.72	172/58	HMar	61:33	59:20- 00
					Mar	2:08:32	2:08:58- 03
Ramolefi	Ruben	RSA	17.7.78	174/56	3kSt	8:20.40	8:25.59- 04
* Ramzi	Rashid	BRN	17.7.80	175/58	800	1:44.24	1:46.15i- 04
					1500	3:30.00	3:30.25- 04
					1M	3:51.33	
Ramzy	Bashir	USA	4.5.79	185/86	LJ	8.11	8.15- 04
Randriamihaja	Joseph-Berlioz	MAD	30.11.75	188/75	110H	13.66	13.46- 04, 13.3- 03
Rankin	Jonathan	USA	9.2.82	178/64	1500	3:35.26	3:43.10- 04
					1M	3:55.63	4:03.70- 04
Rans	Kevin	BEL	19.8.82	187/80	PV	5.62i, 5.60	5.60- 01
Rantanen	Vesa	FIN	2.12.75	184/72	PV	5.60i, 5.60	5.72- 01
Rapp	Peter	GER	29.5.83	196/84	LJ	8.00	7.98i, 7.89- 04
* Raquil	Marc	FRA	2.4.77	191/81	400	45.57	44.79- 03
Rasheed	Essa Ismail	QAT-J	14.12.86	178/65	3000	7:49.04	
					5000	13:17.10	
Raunio	Lassi	FIN	11.10.83	195/93	Dec	7690	7326- 04
Rautenbach	Lohan	RSA-J	6.2.86		JT	80.03	74.42- 04
Rautenkrantz	Jens	GER	11.4.82	189/95	HT	73.73	73.06- 04
^ Rawlinson	Chris	GBR	19.5.72	185/82	400H	49.61	48.14- 99
Ray	Adrian	USA	9.10.81	185/77	110H	13.68, 13.44w	13.71- 03
Redko	Sergey	UKR	24.1.73	184/68	3kSt	8:32.24	8:24.35- 99
^ Redolat	José Antonio	ESP	17.2.76	181/66	1500	3:36.24	3:31.21- 01
* Reed	Gary	CAN	25.10.81	175/66	800	1:44.33	1:44.92- 04
Reed-Jones	Abraham	USA	3.6.82	181/81	400H	49.82	50.00- 04
^ Reese	Terry	USA	20.6.67	183/79	110H	13.73	13.22- 97
* Reina	Antonio Manuel	ESP	13.6.81	186/71	400	45.98	46.26- 02
					800	1:44.18	1:43.83- 02
* Reinikainen	Tepa	FIN	16.3.76	198/147	SP	20.43	20.88- 01
Rendell	Stuart	AUS	30.6.72	187/120	HT	76.11	79.29- 02
Restrepo	Gustavo	COL	27.7.82	165/60	20kW	1:22:01	1:23:37- 04
Revenko	Vladislav	UKR	15.11.84	181/76	PV	5.80	5.60i- 03, 5.55- 02
Rey	Fernando	ESP	16.4.80	165/50	10000	28:14.90	29:13.57- 03
* Rey	Julio	ESP	13.1.72	166/51	Mar	2:07:38	2:07:27- 03
Ribeiro	Rafael	BRA-J	23.6.86	178/73	100	10.33, 10.27w	10.53- 03
Richards	Ron	LBR	13.5.83	175/68	100	10.30, 10.24w	10.50-04
					200	20.64	21.14- 04
Richardson	Jason	USA-J	4.4.86	190/75	110H	13.50	13.76- 04
* Riedel	Lars	GER	28.6.67	199/115	DT	66.39	71.50- 97
Rigondeaux	Máximo	CUB	17.10.76	182/85	JT	78.59	81.43- 00
Riley	Jonathon	USA	29.12.78	175/58	5000	13:25.04	13:21.11- 04
Riobo	Victor	ESP	6.4.80		1500	3:38.86	
* Rios	José	ESP	15.3.74	170/49	Mar	2:09:03	2:07:42- 04
Riri	Joseph	KEN	21.10.73		Mar	2:09:00	2:06:49-04
Ritzenhein	Dathan	USA	30.12.82	170/52	3000	7:43.95	
					5000	13:22.23	13:27.77- 02
Rizki	Monder	BEL	16.8.79	176/66	5000	13:25.66	13:15.51- 04
Roba	Gari	ETH			3kSt	8:30:20	
* Robberts	Janus	RSA	10.3.79	196/130	SP	20.43	21.97- 01
Roberge	Jesse	USA	2.10.78	193/136	SP	19.66	19.62- 04
Robertson	Michael	USA	19.12.83	198/111	DT	61.70	64.89- 04
Robinson	Khadevis	USA	19.7.76	183/74	800	1:44.62	1:44.41- 02
Robison	Brian	USA	27.4.83	190/121	SP	19.70	18.74- 04
* Robles	Dayron	CUB-J	19.11.86	189/74	110H	13.46, 13.41w, 13.2	13.75- 04
* Rock	Andrew	USA	23.1.82	188/75	400	44.35	44.66- 04
Rodgers	Michael	USA	24.4.85	183/75	100	10.25w	10.55, 10.31w- 04
Rodriguez	Dion	TRI	9.6.84	180/79	100	10.25w	10.45, 10.42w- 02
Rodríguez	Daniel	VEN	21.9.83		HJ	2.23	
Rodríguez	Eduardo Iván	ESP	7.4.78	179/64	400H	49.97	49.08- 04
Rodríguez	Johnny	VEN	4.8.78		TJ	16.49A	16.41A, 16.45Aw- 99
* Rome	Jarred	USA	21.12.76	196/145	DT	67.39	67.51- 04
Rono	Cosmas	KEN	12.12.84	164/52	800	1:45.24	1:47.4- 02
Rono	Joel Kipkemei	KEN			Mar	2:10:12	
^ Rono	Robert	KEN	11.10.74	172/60	1500	3:36.45	3:30.99- 02
^ Rop	Rodgers	KEN	16.2.76	172/52	HMar	60:46 dh	59:49dh- 04, 60:45- 02
					Mar	2:10:31	2:08:07- 02
* Ross	Duane	USA	5.12.72	183/78	110H	13.41	13.12- 99
Ross	Joshua	AUS	9.2.81	185/81	100	10.12	10.22- 04
Röthlin	Viktor	SUI	14.10.74	174/58	Mar	2:11:00	2:09:56- 04
* Rotich	Laban	KEN	20.1.69	163/45	1500	3:33.83	3:29.91- 98
					1M	3:52.55	3:47.65- 97

	Name		Nat	Born	Ht/Wt	Event	2005Mark	Pre-2005 Best
	Rotich	Michael	KEN	14.7.78	173/58	800	1:46.55A	1:44.09- 04
^	Rotich	Michael	KEN	26.10.82	174/58	Mar	2:10:53	2:06:33- 03
	Rotich	William Todoo	KEN	.80		HMar	61:22	61:45A- 04
	Rotich	Willy	KEN	23.3.76	177/58	800	1:46.15	1:45.33- 02
	Rozna	Roman	MDA	25.3.76	190/105	HT	75.80	76.62- 03
	Rubanko	Artyom	UKR	21.3.74	191/110	HT	79.56	80.44- 04
	Rugut	Philip	KEN	18.5.77	165/50	HMar	61:55	59:53- 02
	Ruíz	Victor	ESP	24.10.74	185/80	Dec	7630	7575- 04
	Rupp	Galen	USA-J	8.5.86	180/62	3000	7:49.16	8:03.67- 04
						10000	28:15.52	29:09.56- 04
^	Rusan	Tim	USA	25.6.77	190/84	TJ	16.52	17.45i- 03, 17.37- 04
	Rusenov	Atanas	BUL	30.8.81	173/67	LJ	7.99	8.06- 04
	Russell	John	USA	9.10.83		PV	5.51	5.50i, 5.40- 04
	Russell	Scott	CAN	16.1.79	206/122	JT	84.41	81.66- 01
	Rutherford	Greg	GBR-J	17.11.86	174/67	LJ	8.14	7.28- 04
*	Rutto	Evans	KEN	8.4.78	168/56	Mar	2:07:28	2:05:50- 03
	Ruuskanen	Antti	FIN	21.2.84	189/86	JT	79.75	75.84- 04
	Ruzavin	Andrey	RUS-J	28.3.86	175/70	20kW	1:21:51	1:25:58- 04
*	Rybakov	Yaroslav	RUS	22.11.80	198/82	HJ	2.38i, 2.33	2.34- 03
	Ryland	Daniel	USA	6.8.79	188/86	PV	5.85i, 5.70	5.75- 04
	Sack	Peter	GER	27.7.79	192/135	SP	19.88i, 19.68	20.32- 04
	Sack	Rene	GER	14.7.76	190/135	SP	19.50	19.84- 02
	Safarov	Sergey	RUS	26.1.83	178/67	20kW	1:22:02	1:26:26- 04
*	Saïd-Guerni	Djabir	ALG	29.3.77	187/70	800	1:44.80	1:43.09- 99
*	Saïdi Sief	Ali	ALG	15.3.78	180/68	1500	3:34.48	3:29.51- 01
						3000	7:37.56	7:25.02- 00
						5000	13:13.50	12:50.86- 00
	Saidy Ndure	Jaysuma	GAM	1.1.84	192/72	100	10.18w	10.26- 04
						200	20.51, 20.14w	20.69- 04
	Saina	Lawrence Kiprotich	KEN	85		HMar	60:30	61:38- 04
	Saina	Mark	KEN	10.11.70	170/53	Mar	2:09:35	2:09:00- 00
	Sajdok	Stanislav	CZE	22.7.83	190/75	110H	13.66w	13.79- 04
*	Saladino	Irving	PAN	23.1.83	183/70	LJ	8.29. 8.51w	8.12A, 7.74- 04
	Salem	Jamal Bilal	QAT	12.9.78	178/62	3000	7:30.76	
	(Kipkemboi Katui)					5000	13:12.33	13:19.92- 04
						3kSt	8:11.67	8:24.26- 04
	Salnikov	Aleksandr	RUS	27.9.71		SP	20.09	20.13- 04
	Sambu	Ezra	KEN	4.9.78	175/70	400	45.84A	44.43A, 44.98- 03
	Samimi	Abbas	IRI	9.6.77	203/110	DT	63.38	64.98- 04
	Samuels	J-Mee	USA-J	20.5.87	165/64	100	10.08, 10.05w	10.25, 10.07w- 04
						200	20.32A, 20.61	20.58- 04
	Sánchez	der	MEX-J	21.5.86		20kW	1:19:02	
*	Sánchez	Félix	DOM	30.8.77	178/73	400H	48.24	47.25- 03
	Sánchez	Rogelio	MEX	26.10.73		50kW	4:04:05	3:51:41- 04
*	Sands	Leevan	BAH	16.8.81	190/75	LJ	8.13	8.10i, 8.04- 04, 8.28w- 03
						TJ	17.30, 17.39w	17.50- 02
	Sang	Isaac	KEN	24.8.78		800	1:46.75	1:46.36- 04
	Sang	Meshack	KEN	24.7.78	174/55	3000	7:42.50	7:57.03- 99
						5000	13:20.26	13:45.10- 99
	Sanguin	Giovanni	ITA	14.5.69	185/100	HT	71.20	74.52- 97
	Sanou	Idrissa	BUR	12.6.77	183/80	100	10.21, 10.18w	10.14, 10.12Aw- 02, 10.0- 04
	Santa	Carlos	DOM	7.1.78	182/68	400	45.06	45.05- 04
	Santos	Anderson J. dos	BRA	23.4.72	186/75	400	45.41	45.39A- 99, 45.47- 01
	dos Santos	Leonardo	BRA	7.5.84	183/65	TJ	16.46	16.29- 04, 16.58w- 03
*	dos Santos	Redelen	BRA	24.4.76	200/96	110H	13.30	13.29- 04
	Santos	Osmar B. dos	BRA	20.10.68	175/65	800	1:45.36	1:44.87- 00
	Sanz	Alberto	ESP	9.9.77	190/72	LJ	7.96w	7.96, 8.03w- 04
	Sapinskiy	Dmitriy	RUS	13.10.83	192/84	LJ	8.01	8.04i, 7.86- 04
	Saquipay	Rolando	ECU	21.7.79	166/57	20kW	1:19:21	1:20:47- 04
	Sardano	Emanuele	ITA	16.2.79	182/78	TJ	16.82	16.46, 16.69w- 04
	Sarrís	Panayiótis	GRE	14.9.75	181/74	200	20.69	20.48- 02
	Sato	Atsushi	JPN	8.5.78	170/55	10000	28:14.26	27:56.86- 04
	Sato	Mitsuhiro	JPN	8.1.80	175/62	400	45.78	45.50- 03
	Savary	Guillaume	FRA	11.2.81	183/68	PV	5.55	5.50- 03
	Savolainen	Nikolay	UKR	25.3.80	189/76	TJ	17.01i, 16.78	17.16i- 04, 17.08- 02
*	Sawano	Daichi	JPN	16.9.80	182/68	PV	5.83	5.80- 04
	Scales	Mardy	USA	10.9.81	173/73	100	10.10	10.07, 10.02w- 04
						200	20.62	20.65- 01, 20.37w- 04
	Schäfer	Raphael	GER	6.3.81	173/59	3kSt	8:31.16	8:26.65- 03
	Scherer	Matt	USA	21.11.83	184/75	400	45.70	45.95- 04
	Schindzielorz	Jan	GER	8.8.78	187/77	110H	13.66	13.50- 02

Name		Nat	Born	Ht/Wt	Event	2005 Mark	Pre-2005 Best
Schmidt	Torsten	GER	9.12.74	207/105	DT	62.73	64.78- 04
Schnelting	Daniel	GER-J	9.3.86		200	20.68	21.32- 04
Schulze	Fabian	GER	7.3.84	192/79	PV	5.70i, 5.70	5.70- 04
Schwarzl	Roland	AUT	10.12.80	199/94	Dec	7975	8102- 04
* Schwazer	Alex	ITA	26.12.84	185/73	50kW	3:41:54	4:00:51- 04
Schwinn	Matt	USA	14.1.80		DT	60.68	59.14- 04
Sciandra	Livio	ITA	23.9.80	187/73	800	1:46.63	1:46.26- 04
Scigaczewski	Tomasz	POL	18.11.78	188/88	110H	13.66	13.29- 99, 13.25w, 13.0- 98
Scolfaro da Silva	Iván	BRA	30.7.82	180/75	Dec	7711	7408- 03
Scott	Allan	GBR	27.12.82	183/82	110H	13.62	13.78, 13.72w- 04
Scott	Bryan	USA	1.3.85		400H	49.86	50.73- 04
Scott	Dorian	JAM	1.2.82	185/136	SP	20.21	19.46- 04
Scott	Jeremy	USA	1.5.81	206/91	PV	5.60i	5.70i- 03, 5.56- 04
* Scott	Leonard	USA	19.1.80	181/84	100	9.94	10.01- 04, 9.83w 99
					200	20.38	20.34- 01, 20.08w- 99
Scotten	Ray	USA	20.5.83		PV	5.55	5.46- 04
* Sdiri	Salim	FRA	26.10.78	185/80	LJ	8.25	8.24- 04, 8.29w- 03
* Sebrle	Roman	CZE	26.11.74	186/88	Dec	8534	9026- 01
Sedlácek	Pavel	CZE	5.4.68	198/111	HT	77.71	79.56- 96
Sedoc	Gregory	NED	16.10.81	179/74	110H	13.57, 13.56w	13.51, 13.46w- 04
Segond	Sam	USA	4.4.83		DT	60.87	58.85- 04
* Segura	Bernardo	MEX	11.2.70	175/62	20kW	1:21:46	1:17:25.6t- 94
Segura	Omar	MEX	24.3.81	170/57	20kW	1:20:25	1:20:43- 04
Seibold	Florian Peter	GER	27.6.79	187/74	110H	13.62	13.67- 03
Seliukas	Vytautas	LTU	21.4.82		LJ	8.02	7.65- 03
Sellers	Scott	USA-J	16.8.86	190/72	HJ	2.26i, 2.26	2.27i, 2.26- 04
Semyonov	Aleksey	UKR	27.6.82	200/120	DT	62.46	59.48- 03
^ Sepeng	Hezekiél	RSA	30.6.74	182/70	800	1:45.51	1:42.69- 99
Sergeyev	Aleksandr	RUS	29.7.83	191/78	TJ	17.11	17.23i, 17.11- 04
Serrano	Ricardo	ESP	29.10.80	180/65	10000	28:19.20	29:59.93- 04
Seskin	Yuriy	RUS	7.7.66	196/110	DT	60.55	64.58- 88
Seto	Tomohiro	JPN	19.10.76	168/53	10000	28:00.29	28:11.56- 04
Settle	Leo	USA	19.10.75	183/73	200	20.68	20.50, 20.17Aw- 00
^ Shabunin	Vyacheslav	RUS	27.9.69	171/56	1500	3:35.07	3:32.28- 00
					3000	7:49.43	7:39.24- 95
* Shaheen	Saïf Saeed	QAT	15.10.82	177/64	3kSt	7:55.51	7:53.63- 04
Shako	Dmitriy	BLR	25.3.79	192/92	HT	77.59	77.39- 04
Shalders	Steve	GBR	24.12.81	184/82	TJ	16.71, 17.00w	16.62- 04
* Shami	Mubarak Hassan	QAT	2.12.80	163/50	HMar	61:09	
	(Richard Yatich)				Mar	2:09:22	
Shapoval	Viktor	UKR	17.10.79	198/75	HJ	2.23	2.26- 03
Sharman	William	GBR	12.9.84		110H	13.88, 13.72w	13.94, 13.86w- 04
Sharpe	Fred	USA	21.8.78	173/70	400H	49.69	48.86- 03
^ Shchurenko	Roman	UKR	14.9.76	187/82	LJ	8.10i, 7.93	8.35- 00
Shebto	Moustafa	QAT-J	4.7.86	176/59	3kSt	8:33.00	8:18.52- 04
Shelest	Aleksey	UKR	27.3.73	173/64	50kW	3:56.23	3:57:12- 03
Shentema	Gudisa	ETH	19.6.80		Mar	2:09:46	2:15:16- 04
^ Shevchenko	Dmitriy	RUS	13.5.68	200/140	DT	63.62	70.54- 02
* Shi Dongpeng		CHN	6.1.84	189/75	110H	13.29	13.40- 03
Shi Yong		CHN-J	7.2.87		20kW	1:20:45	1:27:11- 04
					50kW	3:52:03	
Shields	Sean	USA	10.2.83	196/117	SP	20.01	19.58i, 19.34- 03
Shiferaw	Tewodros	ETH	21.9.80	176/59	3kSt	8:27.06	8:22.22- 04
* Shkurlatov	Vitaliy	RUS	25.5.79	182/80	LJ	8.15	8.38i- 00, 8.23- 03
Shkurlatov	Vladislav	RUS	30.3.83	186/90	JT	81.14	78.39- 03
Shogata	Kazuya	JPN	8.7.83	183/70	400H	48.95	50.41- 04
Shults	Vladimir	RUS	17.4.82	178/67	20kW	1:21:26	1:25:09- 84
Shunk	Adam	USA	29.8.79	183/75	HJ	2.30	2.27- 04
Shustov	Aleksandr	RUS	13.8.84		HJ	2.23sq	2.15- 04
Shvetsov	Leonid	RUS	28.3.69	185/70	Mar	2:10:05	2:09:16- 97
Si Tianfeng		CHN	17.6.84		20kW	1:20:05	1:22:44- 04
					50kW	3:42:55	3:55:37- 04
Sigei	Robert Kipngetich	KEN	3.1.82	165/53	3000	7:40.47	7:48.15, 7:43.09i- 04
					5000	13:21.01	13:19.95- 03
Sigei Kipkorir	Matthew	KEN	.83		HMar	61:23	
* Sihine	Sileshi	ETH	29.1.83	165/48	3000	7:29.92	7:42.6+, 7:41.18i- 04
					5000	13:13.04	12:47.04- 04
					10000	26:57.27	26:39.69- 04
					HMar	61:14	
Silnov	Andrey	RUS	9.9.84		HJ	2.28	2.15- 04

Name		Nat	Born	Ht/Wt	Event	2005Mark	Pre-2005 Best
da Silva	Andre Domingos	BRA	26.11.72	187/78	100	10.29	10.15, 10.0- 04, 10.05dt- 97, 10.10w- 95, 10.06A-99
					200	20.53, 20.33Aw	20.35- 00, 20.15A- 03
Silva	Andrés	URU-J	27.3.86	180/76	400	45.38A	45.80- 04
da Silva	Anselmo	BRA	22.3.81	189/82	110H	13.31A, 13.50	13.52, 13.5- 03
da Silva	Claudinei Q	BRA	19.11.70	186/86	100	10.0	10.12- 99, 10.0w- 96, 10.08dt-97
da Silva	Cleverson	BRA	5.9.73	185/75	400H	49.72	49.10- 99
da Silva	Luiz Fernando	BRA	2.7.71	186/87	JT	79.44A	79.50- 00
Silva	Jorge Ignacio	ESP	19.4.79	175/60	50kW	4:01:21	
* Silva	Rui	POR	3.8.77	175/65	1500	3:32.91	3:30.07- 02
					1M	3:52.13	3:49.50- 02
Silverman	Jeremy	USA	28.1.83	190/117	SP	19.48	19.52- 04
Simion	Danut Marian	ROM	25.1.83	190/78	LJ	8.12	8.12- 03
Simms	Allen	PUR	26.7.82	178/75	TJ	17.03, 17.19w	17.26i, 17.17- 03
Simon	LeJuan	TRI	7.2.81	186/75	TJ	16.78w	17.05i- 04, 16.87, 17.39w- 02
Simon	Ndirang	KEN	1.11.85	174/55	5000	13:24.19	13:52.0- 04
					10000	27:31.29	28:28.20- 04
* Simotwo	Suleiman	KEN	21.4.80	182/70	800	1:45.5A	1:48.96- 03
					1500	3:31.85	3:34.48- 04
					1M	3:50.82	
* Simpson	Brandon	JAM	6.9.81	185/79	400	44.70	44.76- 04
Simunic	Bostjan	SLO	28.12.74	186/73	TJ	16.80w	16.82- 02
Singh	Maha	IND	4.3.82		LJ	7.99	7.70- 04
Singh	Navpreet	IND	15.6.78	186/116	SP	19.82	19.93- 04
Singh	Ranvijay	IND	2.10.84	186/104	SP	19.89	20.26- 04
Singoei	Philip	KEN	31.12.75		Mar	2:08:45	2:10:07- 04
Sinkevich	Oleg	BLR	16.1.83		HT	73.02	68.28- 02
Sinyakov	Andrey	BLR	6.1.82		SP	19.37i, 19.31	18.74- 03
Sinyavskiy	Denis	RUS	13.8.79		LJ	7.93i	7.99- 03
Sitar	Damjan	SLO	17.8.81		Dec	7515	7248- 03
Sivakov	Dmitriy	BLR	15.2.83	194/110	DT	60.62	58.85- 04
Skipper	Tommy	USA	19.9.84	186/86	PV	5.66i, 5.60	5.75- 04
Skoog	Henrik	SWE	17.4.79	186/69	3kSt	8:30.10	8:25.55- 03
^ Skurygin	German	RUS	15.9.63	165/63	50kW	3:59:53	3:36:42- 03
* Skvaruk	Andrey	UKR	9.3.67	184/109	HT	81.00	82.62- 02
Slattery	Steve	USA	14.8.80	180/73	3kSt	8:17.87	8:22.32- 03
Sliwa	Leszek	POL	20.9.79	190/110	SP	19.76	20.02i- 02, 19.90- 04
Slobodenyuk	Vadim	UKR	17.3.81	189/74	3kSt	8:28.85	8:24.84- 04
Slowik	Dariusz	CAN	15.8.77	196/123	DT	62.99	64.56- 04
Slowly	Steve	JAM	18.4.79		100	10.16w	10.37- 99
Smaliõs	Ioánnis-Yeóryios	GRE-J	17.2.87	192/80	JT	77.25	65.02- 04
Smialek	Tomasz	POL	16.1.81	183/60	HJ	2.23	2.22- 04
Smirnov	Vitaliy	UZB	25.10.78	191/86	Dec	7832	8021- 03
^ Smiryagin	Yevgeniy	RUS	17.5.76	184/79	PV	5.50	5.85- 97
Smit	Werner	RSA	14.9.84	187/110	HT	73.54	73.91- 04
Smith	Andy	USA	1.5.82		3kSt	8:29.66	8:40.46- 02
Smith	Leigh	USA	28.8.81	198/95	JT	79.37	81.67- 04
Smith	Maurice	JAM	28.9.80	190/90	Dec	8232	8024- 04
Smith	Miles	USA	24.9.84	190/77	400	45.16	46.49- 04
Smith	Richard	USA	10.2.83	180/67	800	1:46.65	1:47.47- 04
* Smith	Rutger	NED	9.7.81	197/124	SP	21.41	20.94- 04
					DT	65.51	64.69- 02
Smoots	Jason	USA	13.7.80	183/89	100	10.13	10.14A, 10.17- 04, 10.07w- 02
Sneberger	Michal	CZE	23.6.78	185/75	1500	3:38.02	3:36.50- 04
Söderberg	David	FIN	11.8.79	185/105	HT	76.89	78.83- 03
* Sofin	Pavel	RUS	4.9.81	201/120	SP	20.05	20.33- 03
Soi	Edwin	KEN-J	3.3.86		3000	744.97	7:56.3- 04
					5000	13:10.78	13:22.57- 04
Sokolovs	Igors	LAT	17.8.74	185/100	HT	72.46	71.49- 04
* Sokolovskiy	Andrey	UKR	16.7.78	196/80	HJ	2.38	2.36- 02
Soldatkin	Aleksandr	UKR-J	26.4.86	192/84	LJ	7.91	7.40- 03
Soler	Joël	FRA	15.2.82	176/66	PV	5.51i, 5.50	5.50- 04
Solís	Miguel	MEX	30.9.70		50kW	3:54:24	4:06:31- 01
Sommerfeldt	Knut Harald	NOR	13.7.79		Dec	7642	7685w- 03, 7504- 04
Song Jian		CHN	7.5.83		LJ	7.98	7.78- 04
* Songok	Boniface	KEN	25.12.80	172/57	3000	7:37.70	7:30.62- 04
					5000	12:55.85	13:00.62- 04
* Songok	Isaac	KEN	25.4.84	170/54	1500	3:31.72	3:30.99- 04
					3000	7:30.14	
					5000	12:52.29	13:37.3A- 00
Songoka	Yusuf	KEN	5.2.79	170/55	HMar	61:56	60:53- 02

Name		Nat	Born	Ht/Wt	Event	2005 Mark	Pre-2005 Best
Sorescu	Cosmin	ROM	11.7.75	188/95	HT	74.50	76.46- 03
Sørli	Gjøran	NOR	3.6.78	191/125	DT	63.05	65.86- 04
^ Sosunov	Kirill	RUS	1.11.75	195/86	LJ	8.03	8.41i- 97, 8.38- 98, 8.48w- 95
Souid	Saber	TUN	9.3.81	185/112	HT	72.33	71.41- 04
Sousa	Cláudio Roberto	BRA	14.10.73	168/68	100	10.25A	10.19- 02
Souza	Hudson de	BRA	25.2.77	180/65	1500	3:33.25	3:33.99- 01
					1M	3:51.05	3:52.97- 02
Souza	Márcio de	BRA	24.1.75	181/74	110H	13.48	13.38- 99
* Spasovkhodskiy	Igor	RUS	1.8.79	191/91	TJ	17.40	17.44- 01
* Spearmon	Wallace	USA	24.12.84	188/78	100	10.21w	10.38- 04
					200	19.89	20.25, 20.12w- 04
Spence	Lansford	JAM	15.12.82	188/85	400	44.77	45.93- 02
Spiegelburg	Richard	GER	12.8.77	182/77	PV	5.75i, 5.70	5.85- 01
* Sposób	Grzegorz	POL	12.2.76	200/87	HJ	2.30	2.34- 04
Stadnichuk	Andrey	RUS	14.12.73	176/64	20kW	1:22:40	1:19:02- 02
Stamatóyiannis	Mihaíl	GRE	20.5.82	187/97	SP	19.22	19.98- 04
Stamer	Dusty	USA	28.4.82	174/82	100	10.14w	10.24, 10.21w- 04
* Stankin	Vladimir	RUS	2.1.74	184/71	20kW	1:18:22	1:17:23- 04
Stanski	Olgierd	POL	4.4.73	196/98	DT	62.07	64.20- 00
Starodubtsev	Dmitriy	RUS-J	3.1.86	185/80	PV	5.50	5.50- 04
Starzak	Marcin	POL	20.10.85	176/58	LJ	8.01w	8.01i- 04, 7.67- 03
Staten	Robert	USA	19.5.77	178/77	200	20.63w	20.77- 99
Statsenko	Oleg	UKR	22.10.80	189/97	JT	78.02	79.44- 03
Steacy	Jim	CAN	29.5.84	191/111	HT	72.83	70.98- 04
Steele	Bryan	JAM	23.3.84	179/73	400H	49.26	50.18- 04
* Steffensen	John	AUS	30.8.82	179/74	400	45.31	45.63- 04
Stehlik	Petr	CZE	15.4.77	185/102	SP	20.80	20.96- 04
Stepanchuk	Andrey	BLR	12.6.79	175/66	50kW	3:51:40	3:58:31- 04
* Stevenson	Toby	USA	19.11.76	186/79	PV	5.90	6.00- 04
Stewart	Jason	NZL	21.11.81	184/75	800	1:46.19	1:46.24- 04
Stokes	Stuart	GBR	5.12.76	180/70	3kSt	8:32.17	8:26.45- 02
^ Stolle	Michael	GER	17.12.74	192/85	PV	5.60	5.95- 00
Straub	Alexander	GER	14.10.83	180/73	PV	5.50	5.31- 02
* Stringfellow	Savanté	USA	6.11.78	191/84	LJ	8.14i, 8.02	8.52- 02
Stroup	Shane	USA	6.9.84	186/75	1500	3:38.57	3:46.74- 04
Su Lin		CHN	18.3.84		50kW	4:04:57	
Suárez	Iosvany	CUB	20.12.72	181/95	HT	72.43	73.69- 03
Suciu	Florin	ROM	18.5.83	181/69	200	20.70	20.92- 04
* Sudol	Grzegorz	POL	28.8.78	174/60	20kW	1:21:03	1:22:17- 04
* Suetsugu	Shingo	JPN	2.6.80	178/68	100	10.15	10.03- 03
					200	20.55	20.03- 03
Sugibayashi	Takanori	JPN	14.3.76	185/66	TJ	16.47w	16.02- 00
Sugimachi	Mahau	JPN	13.11.84		400H	50.03	
Sugimoto	Akihiro	JPN	20.10.81	162/54	20kW	1:22:21	1:21:09- 04
Sukhomlinov	Igor	RUS	13.2.77		JT	80.02	79.92- 02
Suleiman	Abdulrahman	QAT	10.1.84	177/65	800	1:44.73	1:46.51- 03
^ Sullivan	Kevin	CAN	20.3.74	183/70	1500	3:35.11	3:31.71- 00
					1M	3:54.48	3:50.26- 00
Sullivan	Luke	USA	4.6.76	188/114	DT	59.77	61.06- 99
Sultan	Majid Saeed	QAT-J	3.11.86	190/62	800	1:44.27	1:45.25- 04
Sun Chao		CHN-J	8.1.87	173/63	20kW	1:20:59	1:25:35- 04
Sun Wenli		CHN	9.2.78		3kSt	8:32.36	8:29.57- 97
Sun Wenyong		CHN	9.2.78		3kSt	8:33.37	8:44.17- 00
Surjan	Erik	AUS	22.6.83	191/93	Dec	7621	7362- 04
Suter	Patric	SUI	17.5.77	192/115	HT	78.43	80.51- 03
Suwa	Toshinari	JPN	29.1.77	178/58	Mar	2:10:23	2:07:55- 03
^ Svenøy	Jim	NOR	22.4.72	186/70	3kSt	8:28.86	8:12.05- 97
Svensson	Fredrik	SWE	10.9.73	184/77	50kW	3:57:16	3:53:46- 04
Svyatokho	Valeriy	BLR	20.7.81		HT	76.31	77.25- 04
Syrovátko	Jan	CZE	11.2.85	178/72	JT	76.26	69.89- 04
Sysoyev	Aleksey	RUS	8.3.85	194/96	Dec	8090	0
Szymkowiak	Tomasz	POL	5.7.83	176/58	3kSt	8:29.96	8:36.00- 04
* Tadesse	Zersenay	ERI	8.2.82	160/56	3000	7:39.93	7:43.89- 03
					5000	13:12.23	13:05.57- 03
					10000	27:04.70	27:22.57- 04
					HMar	59:05 dh	61:26- 03
Tadili	Achraf	CAN	8.7.80	180/68	800	1:45.65	1:45.05- 03
* Tahri	Bouabdellah	FRA	20.12.78	190/65	1500	3:36.44	3:34.85- 02
					3000	7:42.49	7:41.41i- 02, 7:46.7- 03
					3kSt	8:09.58	8:06.91- 03

	Name		Nat	Born	Ht/Wt	Event	2005Mark	Pre-2005 Best
*	Taillepierre	Karl	FRA	13.8.76	176/64	TJ	17.45	17.16- 04
	Takahashi	Kensuke	JPN	30.5.78		HMar	61:54	
	Takahira	Shinji	JPN	18.7.84	179/62	200	20.55	20.59- 04
*	Takaoka	Toshinari	JPN	24.9.70	186/64	10000	28:04.80	27:35.09- 01
						Mar	2:07:41	2:06:16- 02
	Talashko	Andrey	BLR	31.5.82	173/65	20kW	1:20:33	1:21:19- 04
	Taleb	Brahim	MAR	16.2.85	182/70	3kSt	8:27.17	8:37.99- 04
	Talotti	Alessandro	ITA	7.10.80	193/79	HJ	2.32i	2.30- 03
	Tambwé (Nsimba)	Patrick (Oliver)	COD	5.5.75		Mar	2:10:25	2:08:55- 04
*	Tamesue	Dai	JPN	3.5.78	170/67	400H	48.10	47.89- 01
*	Tammert	Aleksander	EST	2.2.73	196/126	DT	67.93	68.48- 04
	Tamminga	Chris	NED	30.4.74	172/67	PV	5.50	5.76- 98
	Tan Chunhua		CHN	13.3.77	183/76	400H	50.06	49.25- 98
	Taneli	Heikki	FIN	12.6.80	191/80	HJ	2.27	2.18i- 01, 2.18- 02
	Tanigawa	Satoru	JPN	5.7.72	185/80	110H	13.61	13.39- 04
	Tanii	Takayuki	JPN	14.2.83	166/57	20kW	1:21:06	1:20:39- 04
	Tanonaka	Tasuku	JPN	23.9.78	184/77	110H	13.64	13.63- 04
	Tanui	Job	KEN	26.8.74		1500	3:38.8A	3:35.73- 03
	Tanui	Mark	KEN			HMar	61:52	
^	Tarus	Bogdan	ROM	1.8.75	192/77	LJ	8.14i, 7.96	8.30i- 00, 8.29- 96,
	Tarus	William	KEN-J	7.6.87		5000	13:23.7A	14:08.3A- 04
*	Taylor	Dan	USA	12.5.82	198/145	SP	20.75	21.33i- 03, 20.62- 04
	Tegenkamp	Matt	USA	19.1.82	183/57	3000	7:43.33	7:55.14i- 04
						5000	13:25.36	13:30.90- 04
	Teixeira	Mário	POR	20.9.74	181/67	3kSt	8:32.81	8:25.64- 04
	Teixeira	Mauricio	BRA	22.3.82		400H	50.10	50.87- 03
	Terefa	Dawit	ETH	23.10.84		Mar	2:11:02	2:10:38- 03
*	Terek	Paul	USA	20.10.79	186/83	Dec	7976	8312- 04
*	Tereshin	Andrey	RUS	15.12.82	195/77	HJ	2.32	2.28i- 04, 2.27- 03
*	Tergat	Paul	KEN	17.6.69	183/61	HMar	59:10 dh	59:06- 00, 58:51sc- 96
						Mar	2:09:30	2:04:55- 03
	Thamer	Kamal Ali	QAT-J	12.11.88		3kSt	8:33.03	
	Theiner	Wojciech	POL-J	25.6.86	187/74	HJ	2.24	2.15- 04
	Theofánov	Alexandros	GRE	25.2.81	187/82	110H	13.62	13.94- 04
	Theuri	James Kibocha	KEN	30.11.78		HMar	60:54	
	Thomas	Chris	USA	9.2.81		110H	13.66, 13.65w	14.07- 04
*	Thomas	Dwight	JAM	23.9.80	185/82	100	10.00	10.12- 00
						200	20.63	20.41- 04
	Thomas	Marcus	USA	22.3.79	183/82	TJ	16.51i, 16.44w	16.63- 00
	Thomas	Will	USA	11.8.81	193/91	Dec	7552	7894- 03
*	Thompson	Kemel	JAM	25.9.74	180/75	400H	48.09	48.05- 03
^	Thompson	Obadele	BAR	30.3.76	175/67	200	20.53	19.97- 00
	Thompson	Tony	USA	12.3.80	188/109	SP	19.74i	19.35- 03
*	Thorkildsen	Andreas	NOR	1.4.82	188/90	JT	89.60	86.50- 04
*	Thörnblad	Linus	SWE	6.3.85	180/76	HJ	2.31i, 2.26	2.30- 03
	Thornell	John	AUS	22.4.85	175/60	LJ	7.93, 8.05w	7.99, 8.00w- 04
	Thurmond	Reedus	USA	15.12.79		DT	59.76	62.06, 62.34dh- 00
^	Thys	Gert	RSA	12.11.71	167/55	Mar	2:11:19	2:06:33- 99
	Tian Yingchun		CHN	29.5.79		SP	19.25	18.99- 04
*	Tiisanoja	Ville	FIN	24.12.75	192/119	SP	20.64	21.09- 02
*	Tikhon	Ivan	BLR	24.7.76	186/110	HT	86.73	84.46- 04
	Tinsley	Micheal	USA	21.4.84	182/75	400H	48.55	52.5- 02
	Tipotio	Vitoli	FRA	17.7.75	182/87	JT	78.96	80.34- 02
	Tishchenko	Nikolay	RUS	4.2.77	195/93	Dec	7767	8043- 04
	Tobin	Robert	GBR	20.12.83	187/73	400	45.01	45.89- 04
	Togom	Augustine	KEN	6.12.73		10000	28:04.5A	
	Toinon	Stéphane	FRA	16.10.83	188/70	HJ	2.25i	2.20- 04
	Tokunaga	Takashi	JPN	6.6.81	163/52	Mar	2:10:10	2:13:39- 04
	Tola	Tadesse	ETH			HMar	61:57A	
	Tola	Tefera	ETH			HMar	62:02A	
^	Tola	Tesfaye	ETH	19.10.74	167/60	HMar	61:56	60:24- 01, 59:51w- 00
						Mar	2:09:17	2:06:57- 99
	Tölgyesi	Péter	HUN	9.6.81	199/89	TJ	16.67i	16.74- 03
	Tolosa	Ambese	ETH	28.8.77	171/53	HMar	61:18 dh	
^	Tomlinson	Chris	GBR	15.9.81	197/81	LJ	7.95i	8.27- 02, 8.28w- 04
	Tompuri	Timo	FIN	9.6.69	187/120	DT	65.12	69.62- 01
*	Ton	Svatoslav	CZE	20.10.78	192/75	HJ	2.33i, 2.30	2.33- 04
	Too	Michael	KEN	3.8.83	171/60	800	1:46.06A	1:46.7A- 04
						1500	3:36.97	3:34.17- 02
	Toompuu	Raigo	EST	17.7.81	188/118	SP	19.28	18.20- 04
*	Topic	Dragutin	SCG	12.3.71	197/77	HJ	2.31i, 2.30	2.38- 93

MEN'S INDEX

Name		Nat	Born	Ht/Wt	Event	2005 Mark	Pre-2005 Best
Tornéus	Michel	SWE-J	26.5.86		LJ	7.94	7.41- 04
Torres	Jorge	USA	22.8.80	170/62	5000	13:20.57	13:24.17- 03
Tosca	Osniel	CUB	30.6.84	178/58	TJ	17.08	17.17- 04
Tóth	János	HUN	15.4.78	180/67	50kW	4:01:53	3:59:24- 03
Tóth	Matej	SVK	10.2.83	185/72	20kW	1:21:38	1:23:17- 03
^ Trafas	Dariusz	POL	16.5.72	188/87	JT	77.55	87.17- 00
* Trammell	Terrence	USA	23.11.78	188/84	100	10.17	10.04- 00
					110H	13.02, 13.11w	13.09- 04
Trentin	Nicola	ITA	20.6.74	178/70	LJ	8.07A, 8.11Aw,8.04,8.07w	8.20- 03, 8.32w- 96
Trofimov	Pyotr	RUS	18.12.83	174/63	20kW	1:22:29	1:22:25- 04
Troode	Chris	AUS	10.2.83	184/84	400	45.60	46.40- 04
^ Trotskiy	Ivan	BLR	27.5.76	167/50	20kW	1:21:15	1:19:40- 03
Tsátoumas	Loúis	GRE	12.2.82	187/76	LJ	8.15i, 8.14	8.34- 03, 8.37w- 04
Tsiámis	Dimítrios	GRE	12.1.82	178/67	TJ	16.70	16.84- 02
Tsige	Slomon	ETH	23.1.85		HMar	61:37A	62:42- 04
Tucker	Corey	AUS	19.11.78		1500	3:38.42	3:44.76- 02
Tucker	Sultan	LBR	24.10.78	181/75	110H	13.61	13.54- 04
^ Tudor	Bogdan	ROM	1.2.70	187/70	LJ	7.98i	8.37- 95
Tugay	Igor	UKR	22.3.75	185/108	HT	78.85	76.24- 03
Tulake	Nuermaimaiti	CHN	8.3.82	190/90	DT	59.73	62.36- 01
Tum	Sammy Kipkoech	KEN	18.5.78		HMar	62:00	61:35- 04
* Tunks	Jason	CAN	7.5.75	200/125	DT	66.59	67.88- 98
Turner	Andrew	GBR	19.9.80	183/77	110H	13.63	13.47- 04
Tysse	Erik	NOR	4.12.80	184/59	20kW	1:21:11	1:21:41- 02
Udechuku	Emeka	GBR	10.7.79	176/102	DT	61.18	64.93- 04
Uhlík	Michal	CZE	9.3.80	187/69	400H	49.43	49.96- 04
* Ukhov	Ivan	RUS-J	29.3.86	192/83	HJ	2.30	2.15- 04
Uldal	Hans Olav	NOR	16.12.82	184/86	Dec	7752	7733- 04
* Unger	Tobias	GER	10.7.79	181/70	100	10.16, 10.11w	10.32- 03
					200	20.20	20.30- 04
Usisivu	Boniface	KEN	5.9.74		Mar	2:08:45	2:07:50- 02
Usov	Roman	RUS	4.6.78	176/56	3kSt	8:26.96	8:26.96- 00
Uudmäe	Jaanus	EST	24.12.80	188/75	TJ	16.42i, 16.69w	16.28- 02
Vaisjuns	Atis	LAT	27.9.82	183/80	Dec	7502	7681- 03
Väkeväinen	Jukka	FIN	12.9.78	182/76	Dec	7546	7944- 01
Valiyev	Roman	KAZ	27.3.84	173/67	TJ	16.67	16.62- 04
* Valukevic	Dmitrij	SVK	31.5.81	186/78	TJ	17.19	17.57- 03
van Bennekom	Joost	NED	18.1.81	185/81	Dec	7603	7457- 04
^ Van Branteghem	Cédric	BEL	13.3.79	182/72	400	45.59	45.02- 03
Van Daele	Jo	BEL	6.4.72	191/110	DT	63.10	64.24- 01
van der Merwe	Jan	RSA	16.3.84		200	20.69A	
					400	45.73A, 45.87	46.55A- 04
van der Plaat	Ludo	NED	3.7.83	188/80	Dec	7490	7302- 04
van der Westen	Marcel	NED	1.8.76	192/86	110H	13.43	13.58- 04
Van Koolwyk	Krijn	BEL	30.8.81	181/62	3kSt	8:17.11	8:24.54- 04
van Wyk	Christie	NAM	12.10.77	171/65	100	10.20w	10.09- 04, 9.99w- 01
van Wyk	Johannes	RSA	16.3.80	194/109	DT	61.26	61.70- 04
van Zyl	Frikkie	RSA	30.7.81	189/80	110H	13.70, 13.3	13.58- 04
* van Zyl	L.J. (Louis)	RSA	20.7.85	186/75	400H	48.11	48.89- 02
Vanek	Daniel	SVK	18.1.83		DT	61.59	59.89- 03
* Varga	Roland	HUN	22.10.77	197/102	DT	65.24	67.38- 02
Vargas	Claudio	MEX	9.12.74		50kW	4:03:03	3:51:35- 04
* Värnik	Andrus	EST	27.9.77	182/100	JT	87.19	87.83- 03
Vasara	Mika	FIN	22.10.83	193/115	SP	19.84	19.53- 04
Vashchilo	Aleksandr	BLR	30.8.81	197/108	HT	76.03	78.58- 04
Vasilache	Stefan	ROM	9.5.79	190/70	HJ	2.27i	2.30- 03
* Vasilevskis	Vadims	LAT	5.1.82	187/82	JT	81.30	84.95- 04
Vasiliádis	Konstantinos	GRE	9.3.77	180/68	LJ	8.01w	8.10- 03
Vasiltsov	Nikolay	BLR	24.5.82		JT	76.10	69.18- 04
Vasilyev	Valeriy	UKR	21.4.76	189/82	LJ	8.02i	8.21- 04
Veal	Brian	USA	4.1.82	186/68	TJ	16.50	16.24- 03, 16.51w- 04
Velikopolskiy	Dmitriy	RUS	27.11.84		HT	71.33	68.89- 04
Velter	Michael	BEL	21.3.81	187/73	TJ	16.90i, 16.65	16.86- 02
Venâncio	Diego	BRA	10.5.85	184/70	400H	50.01	50.39- 04
Verni	Marco Antonio	CHI	27.2.76	188/114	SP	20.04	21.14- 04
Vershinin	Leonid	BLR	23.6.77	187/79	400H	49.95	49.76- 04
Veryutin	Aleksandr	BLR	18.11.79	197/77	HJ	2.24	2.28i- 02, 2.25- 01
Vicet	Noleysi	CUB	6.2.81	193/103	HT	71.86	71.02- 04
Vieira	Erivaldo	BRA	18.11.80		LJ	8.15A, 7.98	7.99- 02
Vieira	João	POR	20.2.76	174/58	20kW	1:21:56	1:20:30- 03
Viera	Heber	URU	29.4.79	180/74	200	20.62Aw	20.46A, 20.52- 02

Name		Nat	Born	Ht/Wt	Event	2005Mark	Pre-2005 Best
Vili	Bertrand	FRA	6.9.83	185/108	DT	59.61	58.36- 04
Villar	Paulo	COL	28.7.78	175/64	110H	13.44A, 13.51	13.44- 04
Vincek	Zeljko	CRO-J	16.6.86		400	45.90	46.13- 04
Vinichenko	Igor	RUS	11.4.84		HT	71.03	68.81- 04
Vinni	Kari	FIN	19.3.83	188/92	JT	76.76	76.63- 01
Vinogradov	Yevgeniy	UKR	30.4.84	195/95	HT	74.38	71.51- 04
Viti	Marzio	ITA	10.8.73	187/80	Dec	7577	7861- 02
Vivancos	Felipe	ESP	16.6.80	177/70	110H	13.53	13.47, 13.43w- 04
Vizcaíno	Henry	CUB	16.5.80		100	10.20	10.37- 00
Vizzoni	Nicola	ITA	4.11.73	193/122	HT	74.82	80.50- 01
Vodovnik	Miran	SLO	11.9.77	197/115	SP	20.30	20.56- 04
Vojtík	Jirí	CZE	2.7.81	187/86	200	20.66. 20.63w	20.69- 04
* Voronin	Vyacheslav	RUS	5.4.74	191/78	HJ	2.33	2.40- 00
Vorontsov	Andrey	BLR	24.7.75	191/105	HT	78.93	78.53- 03
* Voyevodin	Aleksey	RUS	9.8.70	178/65	50kW	3:41:03	3:38:01- 03
Voynov	Sergey	UZB	26.2.77	188/89	JT	76.12	84.80- 00
Vries	Sherwin	RSA	22.3.80	179/74	100	10.28	10.08- 03
* Vroemen	Simon	NED	11.5.69	189/68	3kSt	8:04.95	8:06.91- 02
Wagne	Abdoulaye	SEN	30.1.81	180/75	800	1:46.85	1:45.08- 03
Wagner	Stepán	CZE	5.10.81	187/74	LJ	8.11	7.88- 04
* Walerianczyk	Aleksander	POL	1.9.82	195/78	HJ	2.30	2.36- 03
* Walker	Brad	USA	21.6.81	188/86	PV	5.96	5.82- 04
Walker	Josh	USA	6.5.82	185/73	110H	13.39	13.32- 04
* Wallace	Dawane	USA	30.12.76	190/79	110H	13.36, 13.33w	13.22- 00
Wallin	Gabriel	SWE	14.10.81	192/91	JT	80.31	80.71- 04
Walls	Tim	USA	30.9.80	182/73	100	10.26w	10.19- 02, 10.0w- 01
* Waltz	Ian	USA	15.4.77	186/122	DT	66.95	66.14- 04
Wang Hao		CHN	2.2.85		HJ	2.24	2.21- 04
Wang Hongsheng		CHN			20kW	1:22:48	1:23:27- 04
Wang Pu		CHN	6.1.83		50kW	4:03:53	4:30:39- 00
Wang Weijun		CHN	31.12.80	163/62	50kW	3:59:36	4:01:59- 03
Wang Yieying		CHN-J	12.12.86		50kW	4:04:54	4:04:53- 03
Wang Yinhang		CHN	15.2.77	170/54	50kW	3:54:40	3:44:28- 01
Wang Zhiping		CHN	11.12.83	172/56	20kW	1:20:08	1:24:40- 03
					50kW	3:45:23	3:57:23- 04
* Wanjiru	Samuel	KEN-J	10.11.86	163/51	5000	13:09.5e+	13:38.98- 03
					10000	26:41.75	28:00.14- 04
					HMar	59:16	
Warga	Sahle	ETH	.84	182/64	3000	7:43.27	
					5000	13:17.41	
* Wariner	Jeremy	USA	31.1.84	188/67	200	20.52w	20.59- 04, 20.41w- 02
					400	43.93	44.00- 04
Warner	Justyn	CAN-J	28.6.87	174/70	100	10.26	10.63- 04
^ Warners	Chiel	NED	2.4.78	194/85	Dec	7836	8363- 99
* Washington	Tyree	USA	28.8.76	185/84	200	20.43	20.09- 99
					400	44.51	44.28- 01
Watkins	Arend	USA	23.5.79	190/86	110H	13.23	13.27- 04
Watson	Leonidas	USA	27.5.80	178/75	LJ	7.94	7.73- 04
Waugh	Ainsley	JAM	17.9.81	186/75	100	10.16	10.21- 04
					200	20.36	20.60- 04, 20.57w- 03
Weakley	Ian	JAM	24.2.74	180/68	400H	48.58	48.55- 03
Weatherborne	Haddow	USA	19.5.80	180/82	200	20.58	20.72- 01
* Webb	Alan	USA	13.1.83	175/64	1500	3:32.52/3:32.1+u	3:32.73- 04
					1M	3:48.92	3:50.73- 04
					3000	7:39.28	
					5000	13:10.86	13:46.31- 04
Weese	Lyle	USA	26.10.79	188/68	3kSt	8:33.14	8:33.35- 03
* Weidlinger	Günther	AUT	5.4.78	169/54	3000	7:44.32i	7:44.19i- 03, 7:48.46- 04
					5000	13:13.44	13:17.59- 04
					3kSt	8:12.26	8:10.83- 99
Wenk	Stefan	GER	13.3.81	192/83	JT	83.07	82.95- 04
Wennberg	Henrik	SWE	11.3.66	192/114	DT	59.50	62.56- 94
Westlund	Mike	USA	24.3.80	188/82	PV	5.50	5.50- 01
Wiggins	Ernest	USA	18.6.82	183/77	100	10.11w	10.20, 10.18w- 04
* Wignall	Maurice	JAM	17.4.76	186/75	110H	13.20	13.17- 04
Wijesekara	Manjula Kumara	SRI	30.1.84	185/68	HJ	2.27	2.27- 04
Williams	Andrae	BAH	11.7.83	185/82	200	20.66w	21.34- 04
					400	44.90	45.79- 04
* Williams	Bernard	USA	19.1.78	183/81	100	10.26	9.94- 01
					200	20.62	20.01- 01

	Name		Nat	Born	Ht/Wt	Event	2005 Mark	Pre-2005 Best
*	Williams	Chris	JAM	15.3.72	178/68	100	10.13	10.05, 10.04w- 00
						200	20.19	20.02- 00
	Williams	Ivory	USA	2.5.85	173/77	100	10.08w	10.27, 10.12w- 02
						200	20.33w	21.02- 04, 20.70w, 20.5- 02
	Williams	Jesse	USA	27.12.83	184/75	HJ	2.30	2.24- 03
	Williams	Joel	USA	23.6.80?	194/80	800	1:46.43i	1:51.63- 04
	Williams	Jonathan	USA	29.8.83	178/67	400H	49.67	50.14- 04
	Williams	Rhuben	USA	14.2.82	176/102	SP	19.57	19.75- 04
	Williams	Rhys	GBR	27.2.84	185/73	400H	49.60	51.15- 03
	Williams	Ricardo	JAM	29.9.76	183/73	200	20.67w	20.33- 00, 20.20w- 03
	Williams	Rubin	USA	9.7.83	175/70	200	20.52	20.84- 02
*	Williamson	Darold	USA	19.2.83	188/77	400	44.27	44.51- 04
	Williamson	Simeon	GBR-J	16.1.86	184/77	100	10.24, 10.22w	10.53- 04
	Willie	Kelly	USA	7.9.82	177/72	100	10.26, 10.11w	10.24A- 02
						200	20.68i, 20.45w	20.49A, 20.3- 02
						400	44.97	44.63- 04
	Willis	Nick	NZL	25.4.83	183/68	1500	3:32.38	3:32.64- 04
						1M	3:53.43	3:53.51- 04
						3000	7:45.97	7:44.90i- 04
	Wilson	Aarik	USA	25.10.82	190/88	LJ	8.17i, 7.91, 8.00w	7.97- 04
						TJ	16.94	16.99i-03, 16.96A, 16.91, 16.97Aw- 04
	Wilson	Shomari	USA	6.6.76	183/73	100	10.24w	10.23A, 10.19Aw- 00, 10.26- 04
	Winger	Russ	USA	2.8.84	191/120	SP	20.05	17.69- 04
	Winter	Nils	GER	27.3.77	187/84	LJ	8.21	8.17- 04
	Wirkkala	Teemu	FIN	14.1.84	186/84	JT	80.68	80.87- 04
	Wissman	Johan	SWE	2.11.82	180/75	200	20.46, 20.26w	20.43- 03
	Witherspoon	Reggie	USA	31.5.85	173/77	400	45.42	45.53- 04
	Wodajo	Tereje	ETH	27.1.82	157/53	Mar	2:10:12	2:08:11- 04
	Wolf	Steve	USA	19.7.82	185/71	HJ	2.26	2.16- 03
	Wolski	Robert	POL	8.12.82	181/63	HJ	2.28i, 2.26	2.30- 04
*	Wondimu	Mulugeta	ETH	28.2.85	173/57	1500	3:37.00	3:31.13- 04
						3000	7:35.97	7:39.60- 04
						5000	13:03.40	12:57.05- 04
	Woods	John	USA	19.6.82	174/76	100	10.25, 10.16Aw	10.39- 04
						200	20.69w	20.55- 04
	Woods	Terrance	USA	18.4.79	180/76	HJ	2.23i	2.27- 03
	Woodske	Derek	CAN	22.10.76	188/107	HT	73.79	71.35- 04
^	Woody	Joey	USA	22.5.73	188/78	400H	49.51	47.97- 98
	Woolsey	Conrad	USA	20.2.81	180/124	SP	19.41	19.09- 04
	Wooten	Adam	USA	18.3.82	175/73	200	20.62	20.78- 01, 20.56w- 03
	Worku	Badi	ETH-Y	22.7.88	179/63	3000	7:42.30	8:10.97- 04
						5000	13:18.08	13:25.65- 04
	Wreh	Tuan	LBR	23.11.79	175/70	TJ	16.46	16.28- 02
	Wright	O'Neil	LBR	3.5.80		400H	49.55	50.98- 04
	Wu Bo		CHN	17.6.84		TJ	16.48w	16.79- 04
	Wu Guosong		CHN-J	21.4.87		50kW	3:59:51	
	Wu Tao		CHN	3.10.83	190/100	DT	64.28	63.68- 03
	Wu Youjia		CHN	6.5.83	185/72	110H	13.55	13.67- 04
	Wulff	Andreas	SWE	28.3.80		JT	76.16	75.29- 04
	Xhonneux	Frédéric	BEL	11.5.83		Dec	7902	7040- 04
*	Xing Shucai		CHN	4.8.84	172/60	20kW	1:18:27	1:21:53- 04
						50kW	3:37:58	3:40:22- 04
	Xu Hongpu		CHN	16.9.79	174/60	50kW	3:58:49	4:05:03- 02
	Xu Xingde		CHN	12.6.84	168/54	20kW	1:20:28	1:19:14- 03
						50kW	3:57:11	3:46:49- 04
	Yachi	Yusuke	JPN	2.1.80	172/55	50kW	4:02:14	4:02:42- 04
	Yagout (Cheruiyot)	Abel	BRN	26.12.84		3kSt	8:29.62	8:29.62- 04
	Yamazaki	Yuki	JPN	16.1.84	178/63	50kW	3:50:39	3:55:20- 04
	Yang Yaozu		CHN	9.1.81	185/70	100	10.20w	10.32- 04
						200	20.63w	20.58- 02
	Yang Yongjian		CHN	28.4.73	182/68	50kW	3:46:44	3:48:42- 00
	Yarbrough	Linnie	USA	9.9.82	191/82	110H	13.70, 13.57w	13.68- 04
	Yargunkin	Aleksandr	RUS	6.1.81	182/68	20kW	1:20:27	1:20:22- 04
	Yastrebov	Viktor	UKR	13.1.82	185/73	TJ	17.15	17.32- 04
	Yator	Jacob	KEN			HMar	61:48	63:53- 04
	Ye Kuigang		CHN	10.1.75	188/96	HT	71.93	73.67- 00
	Yeferemov	Ilya	RUS-Y	20.3.88	179/68	TJ	16.45	15.40- 04
	Yegezu	Lishan	ETH-J	1.1.86		HMar	61:42A	
	Yego	Daniel	KEN	.71	167/52	HMar	62:02+	
						Mar	2:08:16	

Name		Nat	Born	Ht/Wt	Event	2005Mark	Pre-2005 Best
Yeliseyev	Aleksey	RUS	12.3.82	188/90	HT	71.70	72.15- 02
Yemmouni	Mounir	FRA	12.10.83	184/63	1500	3:33.39	3:32.97- 04
Yepishin	Andrey	RUS	10.6.81	178/82	100	10.26w	10.25- 04
* Yeremenko	Ruslan	UKR	31.7.78	193/78	PV	5.84i, 5.60, 5.80ex	5.80i- 02, 5.70- 01
Yerokhin	Igor	RUS	4.9.85	176/64	20kW	1:20:16	
Yesipchuk	Dmitriy	RUS	17.11.74	178/66	20kW	1:20:08	1:18:05- 01
Yevtukhovich	Vadim	BLR	24.5.81		JT	76.43	74.80- 00
* Yiampoy	William	KEN	17.5.74	183/70	800	1:44.51	1:42.91- 02
Yoshikata	Masahira	JPN	23.8.82	175/65	400H	48.66	49.37- 04
Yoshino	Tatsuro	JPN	11.9.82	170/63	100	10.27, 10.25w	10.32- 03
					200	20.67	20.67, 20.51w- 03
Yoshioka	Yasunori	JPN	19.5.75	181/80	110H	13.72	13.74- 01
Yoshizawa	Ken	JPN	7.7.78	178/69	400H	49.69	48.85- 04
Young	Bobby	LBR	6.8.84		400	45.95	47.30- 03
Yu Bin		CHN	26.11.85	186/80	Dec	7705	7462- 04
* Yu Chaohong		CHN	12.12.76	175/63	20kW	1:18:30	1:18:56- 03
					50kW	3:36:06	3:42:28- 04
Yu Guoping		CHN-J	13.6.86	168/62	50kW	3:55:35	3:45:46- 01
* Yuda	John	TAN	9.6.79	162/53	10000	27:33.84	27:09.83- 03
					HMar	60:25	60:02- 02
Yudin	Stepan	RUS	3.4.80	175/61	20kW	1:18:45	1:21:33- 01
* Yurchenko	Denis	UKR	27.1.78	174/74	PV	5.85i, 5.75	5.81- 03
Yurin	Andrey	UKR	20.1.84	180/66	20kW	1:19:58	1:22:33- 04
Yushkov	Ivan	RUS	15.1.81	193/120	SP	20.57	20.55- 04
* Zagornyi	Aleksey	RUS	31.5.78	197/130	HT	80.81	83.43- 02
* Zakari	Abdul Aziz	GHA	2.9.76	178/73	100	9.99	10.00- 04, 9.98w- 03
Zakrzewski	Jan	POL	21.12.70	187/70	3kSt	8:29.69	8:22.49- 01
Zalaggítis	Konstadínos	GRE	13.12.80	185/78	TJ	17.29	17.43- 02
Zalsky	Antonín	CZE	7.8.80	200/108	SP	19.21	20.71- 04
Zaman	Sultan Khamis	QAT	23.7.85	175/61	5000	13:22.91	13:18.41- 04
(Nkunzimana)					10000	27:44.47	
Zaytsev	Artyom	BLR	7.12.84	202/75	HJ	2.27	2.22- 03
* Zelezny	Jan	CZE	16.6.66	186/88	JT	83.98	98.48- 96
Zenbaba	Yegezu	ETH	26.9.83		5000	13:24.98	
Zeng Guoqiang		CHN	25.10.84	176/65	20kW	1:22:39	1:23:49- 04
Zepeda	Omar	MEX	8.6.77		20kW	1:22:36	1:21:59- 97
					50kW	3:49:01	3:54:26- 98
Zerguelaïne	Anter	ALG	4.1.85	177/60	800	1:46.56	1:47.33- 04
					1500	3:31.95	3:40.99- 04
Zéroual	Larbi	FRA	10.1.71	178/65	HMar	62:02	60:58- 99
Zhang Defu		CHN	5.6.84	176/60	50kW	3:54:59	3:53:10- 03
Zhang Haofu		CHN	28.10.83		50kW	4:05:01	4:07:07- 04
Zhang Hongwei		CHN	26.4.75	199/74	PV	5.50	5.63- 00
Zhang Huabing		CHN	28.9.83	168/50	50kW	4:03:28	3:59:46- 03
Zhang Jiawei		CHN-J	27.10.86		50kW	3:59:59	3:55:15- 01
Zhang Qi		CHN	2.4.84	180/95	SP	20.15	19.03i, 18.95- 04
Zhang Ronglong		CHN	2.11.84	172/60	20kW	1:21:01	1:23:52- 04
Zhang Shibao		CHN	12.3.84	180/80	400H	49.65	50.07- 02
Zhang Shufeng		CHN	14.11.85		HJ	2.27	2.21- 04
Zhang Tianping		CHN	11.1.82	170/56	20kW	1:21:45	1:21:39- 03
Zhang Xin		CHN	24.4.83		LJ	7.99	7.88- 01
* Zhao Chengliang		CHN	1.6.84	170/62	20kW	1:20:20	1:23:03- 04
					50kW	3:36:13	3:43:09- 04
Zhao Jianguo		CHN-Y	19.1.88	170/58	20kW	1:22:46	1:26:55- 04
					50kW	3:47:02	4:04:35- 04
Zhou Can		CHN	20.5.79	184/68	LJ	8.05	8.13i- 04, 8.11- 99
* Zhu Hongjun		CHN	18.8.83	175/68	20kW	1:17:41	1:18:43- 03
Zhu Shujing		CHN	24.5.85	181/74	TJ	16.78	16.83- 04
Zhu Zhi		CHN	25.8.82		400H	49.88	51.45- 04
Zilch	Mark	USA	.82		PV	5.50i	5.20i, 5.10- 04
Zioini	Badre Din	FRA	25.3.76	175/53	3kSt	8:31.33	8:23.97- 02
* Ziólkowski	Szymon	POL	1.7.76	192/120	HT	79.35	83.38- 01
Zlatnar	Damjan	SLO	16.12.77	187/72	110H	13.72	13.62- 04
Zouaoui Dandrieux	Vincent	FRA	12.10.80	188/72	3kSt	8:22.82	8:25.61- 03
Zoubaa	Khalid	FRA	27.4.77	180/58	3000	7:47.71	7:49.48- 03
Zoullién	Spirídon	GRE	21.6.81	187/114	HT	72.68	70.70- 04
* Zsivoczky	Attila	HUN	29.4.77	193/82	Dec	8480	8554- 00
Zujus	Daugvinas	LTU	16.10.75	182/65	50kW	4:04:43	3:55:10- 98
* Zyuskov	Vladimir	UKR	29.8.81	190/75	LJ	8.31	8.23- 04

WOMEN'S INDEX 2005

Athletes included are those ranked in the top 100s at standard (World Champs) events (plus shorter lists for 1000m, 1M, 2000m, 3000m and 3000m St). Those with detailed biographical profiles are indicated in first column by: * in this year's Annual, ^ in a previous year's Annual, # old javelin.

Name		Nat	Born	Ht/Wt	Event	2005 Mark	Pre-2005 Best
Aava	Monika	EST	19.6.79	168/64	JT	56.78	61.42- 04
Abakumova	Mariya	RUS-J	15.1.86		JT	59.53	58.26- 04
Abatzí	Aretí	GRE	14.5.74	183/78	DT	58.23	62.95- 01
* Abeylegesse	Elvan	TUR	11.9.82	159/40	3000	8:54.00	8:31.94- 02
					5000	15:08.59	14:24.68- 04
Abitova	Inga	RUS	6.3.82		10000	32:25.83	
					HMar	71:06	
^ Achilles	Bianca	GER	17.4.81	180/98	HT	65.19	68.40- 99
* Acuff	Amy	USA	14.7.75	188/66	HJ	1.93	2.01- 03
Adamovich	Olga	RUS	30.8.84		400H	57.01	
* Adams	Jenny	USA	8.7.78	165/55	100H	12.89, 12.88w	12.63, 12.61w- 01
* Adere	Berhane	ETH	21.7.73	170/48	3000	8:31.89	8:25.62- 01
					5000	14:31.09	14:29.32- 03
					10000	30:25.41	30:04.18- 03
					HMar	69:47 dh	67:32- 03
^ Adriano	Elisângela	BRA	27.7.72	180/95	SP	17.55	19.30- 01
					DT	57.29	61.96- 98, 62.23dq- 99
Aghatise	Esther	NGR	15.4.85	165/58	LJ	6.54	6.58- 03
Agirre	Naroa	ESP	15.5.79	176/64	PV	4.45	4.47- 04
Agudelo	Milena	COL	15.4.85		PV	4.21A	4.20- 04
Ahmed	Mona Jabir	SUD-J	6.1.87		800	2:02.43	2:07.37- 04
Ahonen	Kirsi	FIN	8.4.76	196.75	JT	57.53	58.59- 04
* Aït Hammou	Amina	MAR	18.7.78	165/49	800	1:59.91	1:57.82- 03
Aït Hammou	Seltana	MAR	10.5.80	165/49	800	2:00.54	1:59.74- 03
Aït Salem	Souad	ALG	6.1.79	158/50	5000	15:20.10	15:15.54- 04
					10000	32:13.70	32:13.15- 04
Ajkler	Zita	HUN	9.6.75	170/56	LJ	6.63	6.76- 04
Akaba	Yukiko	JPN	18.10.79	158/44	5000	15:11.17	15:27.89- 99
Akulenko	Yuliya	UKR	3.6.77	176/64	Hep	6103	6203- 04
Albury	Aymara	BAH	25.7.85		SP	16.78	17.09- 04
* Aldama	Yamil	SUD	14.8.72	173/62	TJ	14.82	15.29- 03
Aldrich	Erin	USA	27.12.77	186/62	HJ	1.95	1.97i- 98, 1.95- 00
* Aleksandrova/Savchenko	Yekaterina	RUS	3.6.77	180/60	HJ	1.97	1.98i- 04, 1.97- 03
Alemu	Derebe	ETH	5.6.83		3000	8:42.10	8:50.74- 04
					5000	15:00.56	15:09.65- 04
					10000	31:30.71	31:04.49- 04
* Alemu	Elfenesh	ETH	10.6.75	171/53	HMar	71:28+	69:46- 00
					Mar	2:26:50	2:24:29- 01
Alexander	Kineke	VIN-J	21.2.86	173/60	200	23.23Aw	
					400	51.71	53.83- 04
Alexander	Ronetta	USA	8.5.85	168/59	100H	13.22	13.22- 04
Alfonso	Irene	ESP	6.2.81	178/58	1500	4:08.94	4:14.80- 04
^ Alimzhanova	Natalya	KAZ	4.10.68	172/60	400H	56.43	54.50- 00
Alisevich	Tatyana	BLR	22.1.69	173/63	Hep	6173	6146- 00
Allahgreen	Diane	GBR	21.2.75	164/63	100H	13.21	12.92- 02
Allou Affoué	Amandine	CIV	29.8.80	160/52	100	11.38A	11.30- 04
					200	23.08A	23.14- 04
Alminova	Anna	RUS	17.1.85	165/50	1500	4:07.59i	4:10.30- 04
Almirão	Maria Laura	BRA	20.9.77	162/50	400	51.30	51.43- 04
* Alozie	Glory	ESP	30.12.77	156/52	100	11.37, 11.30w	10.90- 99
					100H	12.71, 12.62w	12.44, 12.4w- 98
Ivarez	María de la Caridad	CUB	30.8.75	165/62	JT	58.09	61.57- 00, 63.02#- 95
Ivarez	Wilmary	VEN	13.5.84		200	23.14Aw	23.39- 03
Alves	Sónia	POR	3.6.79	174/88	HT	64.31	67.14- 04
Aman	Leila	ETH	24.11.77		Mar	2:31:10	2:27:54- 04
* Amertil	Christine	BAH	18.8.79	168/53	200	22.58	22.88, 22.86w- 03
					400	50.09	50.17- 04
Ampleyeva	Natalya	RUS	25.9.72		DT	63.42	63.58- 02
Anashkina	Irina	RUS	31.1.72		400H	57.23	55.64- 04
Anderson	Alexandria	USA-J	28.1.87	175/60	100	11.39, 11.38w	11.41- 04
					200	22.96	23.45- 04
Andersson	Tracey	SWE	5.12.84	167/68	HT	64.85	60.48- 04
Andonova	Viktoriya	USA-J	19.11.86		HJ	1.87	1.85- 04
* Andrianova	Tatyana	RUS	10.12.79	173/61	800	1:56.07	1:56.23- 04
					1500	4:12.02	
Ania	Emma	GBR	7.2.79		100	11.35	11.59, 11.45w- 04

Name		Nat	Born	Ht/Wt	Event	2005Mark	Pre-2005 Best
Anias	Jonna	FIN	12.5.84	175/60	HJ	1.87	1.77- 04
Anim	Vida	GHA	7.12.83	168/58	100	11.41	11.14- 04, 11.0- 02
					200	23.03	22.90- 03
Ankier	Jo	GBR	5.8.83	170/52	3kSt	9:50.10	10:09.48- 04
Antil	Seema	IND	27.7.83	183/85	DT	56.96	64.84- 04
Anton	Adina	ROM	6.10.84	174/56	LJ	6.65i, 6.55	6.80- 04
* Antonova	Yelena	UKR	16.6.72	182/95	DT	65.89	67.30- 04
* Antyukh	Natalya	RUS	26.6.81	182/73	200	22.99	22.75- 04
					400	50.67	49.85- 04
Appleberry	Doria	USA	5.2.83	170/50	100H	13.28w	13.59- 04
Araméndiz	Zuleima	COL	23.9.75	172/75	JT	57.53	59.09A- 01, 61.72#- 96
Arencibia	Yenima	CUB	25.12.84	169/61	100H	13.29	13.54- 04, 13.13w- 01
Argüelles	Yariadnis	CUB	18.4.84	173/58	HJ	1.90	1.89- 03
Arkhipova	Lyudmila	RUS	12.9.78	167/55	20kW	1:28:52	1:29:38- 04
^ Arrendel	Juana	DOM	16.6.78	191/60	HJ	1.91	1.97- 02
* Arron	Christine	FRA	13.9.73	177/64	100	10.93, 10.82w	10.73- 98
					200	22.31	22.26- 99
Artenie	Georgiana	ROM-J	14.8.86	170/68	HT	63.45	62.01- 04
Arusei	Penninah	KEN	1.1.79		HMar	71:20	
Asay	Erin	USA	17.3.83	168/55	PV	4.20	3.97- 04
Ashby	Fana	TRI	15.6.81	163/64	100	11.29, 11.12w	11.12, 11.03w- 04
					200	22.91i	23.05, 22.69w- 03
Asigbee	Fiona	USA	18.5.81		Hep	5994	5675- 04
Asoshina	Terumi	JPN	2.8.82	157/42	5000	15:23.61	15:22.51- 03
					10000	31:23.55	31:49.59- 03
					HMar	69:54	73:56- 03
Assahsah	Malika	MAR	24.9.82	173/56	HMar	71:27	70:58- 04
Asteríou	Adigóni	GRE	2.11.76	163/52	PV	4.25	4.20- 03
Atangana	Delphine	CMR	16.8.84	170/56	100	11.42	11.24- 03
Atodonyang	Margaret	KEN	10.10.78		HMar	69:55	69:12- 03
Atroshchenko	Anzhela	TUR	14.11.70	178/65	Hep	5873w, 5870	6339- 93
Augusto	Jessica	POR	8.11.81	160/43	5000	15:20.45	15:15.76- 04
Augustus	Toyin	NGR	24.12.79	160/52	100H	13.24	12.89- 04
Avdeyeva	Anna	RUS	6.4.85	170/85	SP	17.39	17.13- 04
Ayanu	Workitu	ETH-J	19.4.87		5000	15:07.17	15:29.21- 04
					10000	31:59.94	
Azarova	Tatyana	KAZ	2.12.85	166/51	400H	57.02	57.44- 04
de Azevedo	Juliana Paula	BRA	12.7.83	165/50	800	2:01.25	2:02.60- 04
Azzouhoum	Fatiha Bahi	ALG	8.3.83	170/55	3kSt	9:38.31	9:48.97- 04
^ Bacher	Gertrud	ITA	28.2.71	180/63	Hep	5894	6185- 99
Bachmann	Silke	GER	21.6.79	172/58	Hep	5921	5505- 01
Badea	Angelica	ROM	1.10.75	175/60	LJ	6.72i	6.62- 04
Badurová	Katerina	CZE	18.12.82	167/50	PV	4.20	4.52- 04
Bai Xue		CHN-Y	13.12.88		5000	15:29.06	15:39.87- 04
					10000	31:28.88	33:23.94- 04
Bai Yanmin		CHN-J	29.6.87		20kW	1:27:37	1:30:44- 04
* Bailey	Aleen	JAM	25.11.80	170/64	100	11.07	11.04- 04
					200	23.00, 22.75w	22.33- 04
^ Bak	Justyna	POL	1.8.74	174/52	3kSt	9:51.51	9:22.29- 02
^ Bakhvalova	Yekaterina	RUS	29.10.72	175/61	400H	55.99	54.65- 99
^ Balakhonova	Anzhela	UKR	18.12.72	162/55	PV	4.40	4.57- 04
Balakley	Irina	RUS	6.10.81	171/57	20kW	1:34:11	1:33:24- 03
* Balassini	Ester	ITA	20.10.77	173/74	HT	73.59	71.28- 04
Balayeva	Olga	RUS	30.6.84		LJ	6.65	6.37- 02
Balciunaite	Zivile	LTU	3.4.79	160/43	10000	32:30.48	32:47.47- 04
					HMar	70:23	72:27- 02
					Mar	2:25:15	2:27:28- 04
Baldwin	Jasmine	USA-J	27.9.86	170/57	100	11.33w	11.33- 04
Balentine	Shayla	USA	8.8.82	168/57	PV	4.30	4.16- 01
Ballentine	Michelle	JAM	31.8.75	178/63	800	2:01.05	1:59.92- 04
Balta	Ksenja	EST-J	1.11.86	167/53	Hep	5794	5344- 04
* Bani	Zahra	ITA	31.12.79	173/71	JT	62.75	59.10- 04
Bao Guiying		CHN-J	20.1.86		5000	15:29.19	15:48.33- 03
					10000	31:27.35	32:15.63- 04
Baptiste	Kelly-Ann	TRI-J	14.10.86	160/54	100	11.17, 11.04w	11.40- 04
					200	22.93	23.22- 03, 22.99w- 04
Baranova	Veera	EST	12.2.84	174/61	TJ	13.69	13.45- 04
* Barber	Eunice	FRA	17.11.74	175/68	100H	12.89, 12.62w	12.78- 01
					HJ	1.91	1.93- 99
					LJ	6.80	7.05- 03
					Hep	6889	6861- 99

Name		Nat	Born	Ht/Wt	Event	2005 Mark	Pre-2005 Best
* Barber	Me'Lisa	USA	4.10.80	160/52	100	11.04, 10.87w	11.35- 02
					200	22.37	23.01- 02
Barnes	Cecilia	USA	24.7.80		DT	58.47	54.79- 04
Barrett	Kimberly	JAM	18.11.81	165/80	SP	18.20	18.28- 04
Barrios	Yarelis	CUB	12.7.83	174/76	DT	60.61	59.51- 04
Barsosio	Florence	KEN	11.8.76	167/52	Mar	2:27:18	2:27:00- 00
Bartolina	Erica	USA	15.5.80	168/57	PV	4.36Ai	4.40- 04
Bass	Tacita	USA	28.10.79		Hep	5711	5742- 04
Bastos	Marina	POR	7.7.71	165/50	3000	8:51.75i	8:38.13- 99
^ Batten	Kim	USA	29.3.69	170/57	400H	55.58	52.61- 95
Battke	Anna	GER	3.1.85	173/58	PV	4.20	4.00- 04
Baucham	Candice	USA	22.2.83	165/57	LJ	6.53w	6.04- 03, 6.14w- 04
					TJ	14.07	13.61- 04
Bayley	Krysha	CAN	21.1.84	170/64	LJ	6.57i	6.52i- 02
* Bazhenova	Nadezhda	RUS	22.9.78	176/63	TJ	14.31	14.65i- 02, 14.60- 01
Beckel	Nadine	GER	27.5.77	190/89	SP	18.22i, 17.95	18.59- 03
					DT	56.39	59.49- 99
Begg	Sophia	AUS-Y	14.6.88	173/50	HJ	1.88	1.82- 04
Begic	Vera	CRO	17.3.82	169/69	DT	58.42	59.04- 04
Begley	Amy	USA	11.1.78	168/52	5000	15:24.88	15:38.60- 02
Bei	Sara	USA	15.4.83	162/52	5000	15:24.74	15:36.21- 04
* Beitia	Ruth	ESP	1.4.79	192/71	HJ	1.99i, 1.97	2.00- 03
Bejnar	Monika	POL	10.3.81	173/57	400	51.68	52.13- 04
Bekele	Bezunesh	ETH	18.9.83	145/38	5000	15:06.49	
					10000	31:10.68	31:29.07- 04
^ Belin	Kirsten	SWE	2.5.81	176/60	PV	4.45	4.51- 02
Belinskaya	Natalya	RUS	21.1.83	176/57	PV	4.50i, 4.20, 4.30ex	4.40- 04
Bell	Kandice	USA	7.8.83		200	22.99w	24.12, 23.24w- 03
Belyakova	Yelena	RUS	7.4.76	177/56	PV	4.30	4.60- 03
Belyayeva	Olesya	KAZ	29.6.80		TJ	13.66	
Benavídes	Virgen	CUB	31.12.74	165/56	100	11.34	11.14, 11.10w- 99
* Benhassi	Hasna	MAR	1.6.78	166/55	800	1:58.41	1:56.43- 04
Bennett	Julia	GBR	26.3.70	177/58	HJ	1.88	1.92i- 90, 1.89- 94
Bennett	Kameisha	USA	13.1.81	163/64	800	1:59.99	2:00.37- 04
Berendsen	Kristel	EST	25.8.77	178/58	LJ	6.49i	6.41- 04
* Bergqvist	Kajsa	SWE	12.10.76	175/59	HJ	2.03	2.06- 03
Berkut	Natalya	UKR	30.5.75	172/53	10000	32:28.96	31:08.89- 04
Berlanda	Eleonora	ITA	6.4.76	172/49	1500	4:07.54	4:12.80- 04
Bernard-Thomas	Neisha	GRN	21.1.81	163/64	800	2:01.07	2:01.32- 04
Beskrovnaja	Irina	SVK	28.12.82	174/66	TJ	13.70, 13.82w	13.71- 01
Bicet	Nora Aída	CUB	29.10.77	178/78	JT	59.20	63.32- 04
Bicet	Yusmay	CUB	8.12.83	183/73	TJ	14.61	14.61, 14.67w- 04
Bikbulatova	Liliya	RUS	25.2.84	170/52	800	2:01.07	2:03.55- 03
					1500	4:05.67	
* Bikert	Yekaterina	RUS	13.5.80	182/68	400H	55.72	53.72- 04
Biktimirova	Alevtina	RUS	10.9.82		Mar	2:25:12	2:32:33- 04
Biondini	Silvia	ITA	24.1.76	166/58	TJ	13.91, 14.02w	14.15- 01
* Bisset	Sonia	CUB	1.4.71	171/69	JT	67.67	66.54- 01, 68.24#- 97
Bissoly	Sephora	FRA	6.11.81	168/66	JT	57.37	53.70- 04
* Blackett	Andrea	BAR	24.1.76	160/54	400H	54.79	53.36- 99
Blewitt	Adriane	USA	24.5.80	178/79	SP	18.29	17.99- 03
Bliss	Andrea	JAM	5.10.80	172/63	100H	12.83	12.94, 12.89w- 04
Block	Zhanna	UKR	6.7.72	164/62	100	11.18	10.82- 01, 10.6- 97
					200	22.98	22.17A, 22.32- 97
Blondeel	Veerle	BEL	14.1.75	179/86	DT	57.57	57.70- 03
Blonska	Lyudmila	UKR	9.11.77	176/68	LJ	6.76	6.51- 03
					Hep	6378	6316, 6425dq- 03
Bobocel	Ancuta	ROM-J	3.10.87	163/52	3kSt	9:57.12	9:49.03- 04
Bódi	Bernadett	HUN	14.4.80	174/57	HJ	1.88	1.92i- 03, 1.86- 01
Bogdanova	Svetlana	RUS-J	6.11.86	164/53	20kW	1:34:00	1:37:09- 04
* Bogomolova	Galina	RUS	15.10.77	159/41	1500	4:10.14	4:10.00- 04
					3000	8:42.03	8:43.45- 00
					10000	30:33.75	30:26.20- 03
					HMar	70:34	72:12- 03
Bolikova	Mariya	RUS	23.5.77	160/58	100	11.20	11.30- 04
* Bolm	Kirsten	GER	4.3.75	181/70	100H	12.59	12.80, 12.66w- 04
Bolshakova	Svetlana	RUS	14.10.84	174/59	TJ	14.11	13.93- 04
Bolsun	Yelena	RUS	25.6.82	167/61	100	11.42, 11.35w	11.36- 04
					200	22.70	22.64- 04
Boonstra	Miranda	NED	29.8.72	175/58	3kSt	9:51.3	9:51.17- 04

	Name		Nat	Born	Ht/Wt	Event	2005Mark	Pre-2005 Best
	Bordignon	Laura	ITA	26.3.81	180/78	SP	16.75	15.71- 02
						DT	57.98	56.61- 04
	Borel-Brown	Cleopatra	TRI	3.10.79	168/93	SP	18.44	19.48i, 18.90- 04
	Borisova	Tatyana	KGZ	3.6.76	176/54	Mar	2:31:01	2:30:39- 04
	Borst	Selma	NED	6.9.83		HMar	71:23	
*	Boslak	Vanessa	FRA	11.6.82	169/57	PV	4.60	4.51- 04
*	Botezan	Mihaela	ROM	21.11.76	162/49	5000	15:13.36	15:08.78- 01
						10000	32:28.29	31:11.24- 04
						HMar	70:36	69:24- 02
						Mar	2:28:34	2:25:32- 03
	Bouaoudia	Sarah	ALG	13.8.83		Hep	5691	5534- 04
	Bouchaouante	Yamina	FRA	31.7.80	164/58	3kSt	9:42.18	9:52.96- 04
	Boyd	Alana	AUS	10.5.84		PV	4.30	3.85- 03
	Boyko	Viktoriya	UKR	20.1.74	180/84	DT	56.95	63.43- 01
	Breisch	Becky	USA	16.3.83	180/104	SP	17.69	17.86- 04
						DT	63.53	63.12- 04
	Breuer	Grit	GER	16.2.72	166/60	400	51.77i	49.42- 91
	Brewer	Chandra	USA	26.7.81		SP	16.91	16.45- 04
	Brice	Tremedia	USA	22.7.81	167/64	100	11.29, 11/00w	11.32, 11.16w- 04
						200	22.84	23.17, 23.00w- 04
	Brîndusoiu	Ileana	ROM	9.5.79	174/77	DT	59.71	59.96- 03
	Britton	Fionualla	IRL	24.9.84	158/40	3kSt	10:06.26	10:33.10- 04
	Brivule	Linda	LAT	9.9.83	184/74	JT	56.12	56.36- 04
*	Brkljacic	Ivana	CRO	25.1.83	170/65	HT	71.00	69.38- 04
	Broaddus	Juanita	USA	12.5.85	170/60	100	11.32	11.49- 04
						200	23.17w	23.53, 23.25w- 04
	Bronisz	Agnieszka	POL-J	16.3.86	174/73	SP	16.70	15.70- 04
*	Brooks	Sheri-Ann	JAM	11.2.83	170/64	100	11.24, 11.23w	11.52- 04
						200	22.80, 22.74w	24.11, 23.98w- 04
	Broomfield	Erica	CAN	17.10.77		100	11.38w	11.57- 04
	Brown	Tina	GBR	22.8.76	174/55	3kSt	9:48.57	10:00.89- 04
	Brown	Zoë	GBR	15.9.83	169/63	PV	4.20	4.26i, 4.15- 04
	Browning	Danielle	JAM	29.8.81	170/62	100	11.42	11.48, 11.30w- 03
	Brunner	Chantal	NZL	5.11.70	168/58	LJ	6.51, 6.52w	6.68- 97, 6.77Aw- 00
	Budnikova	Alina	RUS	22.10.83		HJ	1.88i	1.80- 03
	Bufalova	Olesya	RUS	6.10.82		TJ	13.67	13.09- 01
	Bui Thi Nhung		VIE	21.1.83		HJ	1.94	1.88- 03
	Bujak	Joanna	FRA	30.8.79	170/55	100H	13.14	13.14, 13.06w- 04
	Bujin	Cristina	ROM-Y	12.4.88	171/52	TJ	13.72	13.46- 04
	Bulgakova	Anna	RUS-Y	17.1.88		HT	64.43	63.83- 04
^	Bunjes	Andrea	GER	5.2.76	175/80	HT	68.49	70.73- 04
*	Burka	Gelete	ETH-J	15.2.86	165/45	1500	3:59.60	4:06.10- 04
						3000	8:39.90	8:48.93- 03
						5000	14:51.47	16:23.8A- 00
	Burnett	Marian	GUY	22.2.76	156/50	800	2:00.59	1:59.47- 04
^	Burrell	Dawn	USA	1.11.73	174/58	LJ	6.49	7.03i- 01, 6.98, 6.99w- 00
	Burton	April	USA	4.4.81		HT	63.14	59.62- 02
	Butler	Kathy	GBR	22.10.73	175/55	3000	8:52.06	8:40.97- 01
						5000	15:11.70	15:05.51- 04
						10000	31:46.53	31:36.90- 04
						Mar	2:30:01	0
	Butusova	Yekaterina	RUS	10.1.84		100	11.35	11.54- 04
	Buval	Patricia	FRA	22.1.76	168/57	100	11.33	11.48- 04
						100H	13.22, 13.13w	13.02- 01, 12.92w- 03
	Byrne	Jolene	IRL	26.10.77	172/55	1500	4:11.72	4:23.32- 04
	Cadamuro	Stefania	ITA	23.2.79	178/57	HJ	1.89	1.91- 00
*	Calatayud	Zulia	CUB	9.11.79	169/59	400	51.78	50.87- 01
						800	1:57.92	1:56.09- 02
	Calì	Vincenza	ITA	15.10.83	171/58	200	23.22	23.25- 02
	Calvert	Schillonie	JAM-Y	27.7.88		100	11.40	11.44, 11.33w- 04
	Camara	Kadiatou	MLI	4.5.81	180/53	200	23.29	23.21- 04
	Camarena	Jill	USA	2.8.82	180/91	SP	17.94	18.15- 04
	Campbell	Amber	USA	5.6.81		HT	69.52	67.23- 04
*	Campbell	Veronica	JAM	15.5.82	163/61	100	10.85	10.91- 04
						200	22.35, 22.29w	22.05- 04
						400	52.24i	
	Cantey	Krystal	USA-J	27.6.87	168/60	400H	56.83	60.63- 03
	Cao Lan		CHN	25.1.82		Hep	5773	5519- 03
	Cao Liping		CHN	8.11.78		DT	58.00	58.71- 04
	Cao Qi		CHN	15.1.74	182/83	DT	56.13	66.08- 93
	Carey	Michelle	IRL	20.2.81		400H	57.37	57.95- 04

	Name		Nat	Born	Ht/Wt	Event	2005 Mark	Pre-2005 Best
	Carpenter	Khalilah	USA	27.7.83	173/61	200	23.29i	23.16- 00
	Carroll	Porchea	USA	23.10.83	170/55	100	11.31w	11.60- 00
						200	23.22w	24.15- 00
*	Carruthers	Danielle	USA	22.12.79	173/62	100H	12.72, 12.63w	12.56- 04
	Carruzzo	Christina	SUI	9.1.81	179/58	1500	4:11.08	4:13.62- 02
	Carter	Antonette	USA	16.2.84	170/57	200	23.05	23.26- 04
						LJ	6.50, 6.56w	6.13- 04
	Carter	Michelle	USA	12.10.85	175/104	SP	18.26	17.55- 04
*	Casandra	Cristina	ROM	1.2.77	168/50	3kSt	9:35.95	9:31.96- 04
	Castells	Berta	ESP	24.1.84	174/73	HT	68.31	68.87- 04
	Castillo	Juana	DOM	17.6.84		Hep	5760	5381- 03
	Castrejana	Carlota	ESP	25.4.73	188/70	TJ	14.60	14.51- 02
	Cattaneo	Micol	ITA	14.5.82	174/63	100H	13.31	13.33- 04
	Ceccarelli	Benedetta	ITA	23.1.80	170/51	400H	54.79	55.14- 04
*	Cechlová-Pospisilová	Vera	CZE	19.11.78	178/78	DT	66.81	67.71- 03
*	Ceplak	Jolanda	SLO	12.9.76	168/55	800	1:59.98	1:55.19- 02
						1000	2:36.33	2:31.66- 02
	Cérival	Jessica	FRA	20.1.82	185/100	SP	16.87	17.44- 04
	Cervantes	Dana	ESP	18.8.78	166/63	PV	4.21i	4.46i, 4.40- 04
	Chaabi	Bouchra	MAR	22.9.80	162/50	3kSt	9:41.82	9:30.35- 04
	Chai Xue		CHN-Y	21.1.88	160/50	20kW	1:31:37	1:33:49- 04
	Chaipetch	Noengruthai	THA	1.12.82	165/49	HJ	1.88i	1.91- 04
	Champion	Courtney	USA-J	10.6.86	175/63	200	22.98i	23.53, 23.50w- 03
	Chang Jeong-yeon		KOR	6.4.77	174/74	JT	55.60	56.90- 03
	Changeywo	Doris	KEN	12.12.84		5000	15:27.18	15:31.82- 04
						10000	32:10.28	32:19.5A- 04
	Chapple	Jerrika	USA	11.9.84	169/59	400	52.18	51.75- 04
	Charles	Tabia	CAN	6.4.85		LJ	6.49i	6.37- 04
	Chebet	Emily	KEN-J	18.2.86		3000	8:53.46	9:03.53- 04
	Chebor Tuwei	Esther	KEN	21.4.81		3kSt	9:56.54	
	Checchi	Cristiana	ITA	8.7.77	174/80	SP	18.59	18.64i- 03, 18.27- 04
						DT	56.12	52.35- 04
	Chelangat	Alice	KEN	27.12.76	152/49	Mar	2:30:46	2:28:16- 02
	Chemwok	Jackline Chemutai	KEN	13.9.83	160/48	3kSt	9:45.7A	
	Chen Lisha		CHN	10.4.81		200	22.94	23.39- 01
	Cheng Xiaoyan		CHN	30.11.75	174/100	SP	17.57	20.02- 94
	Chenonge	Ines	KEN	1.2.82	168/54	3000	8:42.38	8:40.02- 02
						5000	14:54.43	15:00.76- 04
	Chepchumba	Beatrice	KEN	25.11.83	/46	3kSt	10:11.5A	
*	Chepchumba	Joyce	KEN	6.11.70	160/52	HMar	70:39 dh	68:11- 04
						Mar	2:27:01	2:23:22- 99
	Chepchumba	Pamela	KEN	28.2.78	155/44	HMar	69:09	69:30- 02
	Chepchumba	Rose	KEN	14.3.79		10000	31:29.81	
						HMar	70:15	71:30- 04
*	Chepchumba	Salome	KEN	29.9.82	174/57	3kSt	9:31.44	9:29.81- 04
*	Chepkemei	Susan	KEN	25.6.75	164/48	10000	32:24.5A	31:32.04- 02
						HMar	68:47 dh	65:44- 01
						Mar	2:24:00	2:23:12- 03
	Cheptanui	Caroline	KEN	13.5.83	156/46	10000	32:27.8A	33:35.4- 04
	Cherey	Yuliya	RUS	15.11.83	176/64	Hep	5658	5652- 02
*	Cherkasova	Svetlana	RUS	20.5.78	170/52	800	1:56.93	1:57.50- 04
	Chermoshanskaya	Yuliya	RUS-J	6.1.86		200	23.06	24.15- 04
	Chernogorova	Olga	BLR	30.1.82	182/90	DT	59.95	58.90- 04
	Chernova	Lada	RUS	1.1.70		JT	60.05	58.88- 01, 61.34#- 96
	Chernyavskaya	Olga	RUS	17.9.63	180/80	DT	61.78	68.38- 92
	Cherono	Gladys	KEN			HMar	71:19	
	Cherono	Hellen	KEN	22.2.84		Mar	2:31:28	2:34:21- 04
	Cheruiyot	Lenah	KEN	1.3.73		HMar	71:36	68:54- 02
	Cheruiyot	Rose	KEN	21.7.76	163/48	HMar	71:15+	69:32- 02
*	Chiba	Masako	JPN	18.7.76	156/39	HMar	70:02+	66:43- 97
						Mar	2:25:46	2:21:45- 03
	Chibisova	Oksana	RUS	31.3.77	178/89	SP	18.69i, 18.62	18.42i- 04, 18.20- 02
*	Chicherova	Anna	RUS	22.7.82	180/56	HJ	2.01i, 1.99	2.04i, 2.00- 03
	Chikina	Tatyana	UKR	16.11.82	170/90	HT	63.40	62.07- 03
	Chilla	Mercedes	ESP	19.1.80	165/54	JT	60.22	62.32- 04
*	Chizhenko	Yuliya	RUS	30.8.79	166/54	800	2:01.08	2:03.08- 03
						1000	2:35.20	
						1500	3:58.68	4:04.58- 04
						3000	8:53.80i	9:01.22- 03
	Chmielewski	Laura	USA	13.9.83		PV	4.20i	4.06- 04

Name		Nat	Born	Ht/Wt	Event	2005Mark	Pre-2005 Best
* Chojecka	Lidia	POL	25.1.77	163/51	1000	2:37.57i	2:36.97i- 03
					1500	4:04.84i	3:59.22- 00
					3000	8:43.76i	8:31.69- 02
Chrust-Rozej	Marta	POL	29.9.78	161/51	400H	55.49	55.97- 04
Chu Chunxia		CHN	28.1.78	182/60	JT	57.97	59.85- 01, 61.91#- 98
Chukwuemeka	Vivian	NGR	4.5.77	178/90	SP	18.33	18.43- 03
Chumakova	Olesya	RUS	23.7.81	167/52	800	2:00.38	2:02.20- 02, 2:01.93I- 04
					1500	4:02.55	4:07.05- 04
					1M	4:31.17	
* Chzhao	Larisa	RUS	4.2.71	175/58	800	1:57.33	1:58.71- 03
					1000	2:35.34i	
					1500	4:09.71	4:16.44- 01
* Cîmpean	Norica	ROM	22.3.72	164/58	20kW	1:32:08	1:27:46- 99*
Cioncan	Maria	ROM	19.6.77	172/51	800	2:00.88	1:59.44- 04
					1500	4:07.39	3:58.39- 04
Cîrlan	Daniela	ROM	18.9.80	162/45	20kW	1:32:34	1:30:19- 04
Claretti	Clarissa	ITA	7.10.80	170/70	HT	70.59	69.40- 04
* Clark	Hazel	USA	3.10.77	178/55	800	1:57.99	1:58.75- 00
Clarke	Georgie	AUS	17.6.84	170/48	1500	4:06.50	4:06.77- 00
Claxton	Sarah	GBR	23.9.79	165/57	100H	12.96	13.01, 12.91w- 04
Clay	Julian	USA	2.11.77	168/54	200	23.05	23.41- 04
					400	51.40	51.98- 03
Clement	Treniere	USA	27.10.81	159/50	800	1:59.59	2:02.35- 04
					1500	4:05.77	4:11.01- 04
Clitheroe	Helen	GBR	2.1.74	168/57	1500	4:05.19	4:01.10- 02
Coetzee	Ynthie	RSA-Y	31.12.88		JT	57.29	
* Colander	LaTasha	USA	23.8.76	168/52	100	11.06	10.97- 04
					200	22.34, 22.30w	22.37- 04
Colita	Claudia	ROM	20.11.77	164/48	3kSt	10:02.91	0
Collins	Ebony	USA-Y	11.3.89	168/52	400H	55.96	60.40- 04
* Collonvillé	Marie	FRA	23.11.73	163/54	Hep	6248	6350- 97
Conde	Maria José	POR	26.8.80	159/64	HT	64.59	63.70- 03
Console	Rosaria	ITA	17.12.79	160/42	HMar	69:34	69:56- 03
					Mar	2:28:04	2:27:48- 03
Constantin	Amandine	FRA	12.2.84	170/58	Hep	5766	5607w- 04, 5564- 02
Cook	Nicole	USA	16.12.82	163/52	800	2:00.75i	2:02.33- 04
Cornford	Laura	AUS-Y	11.6.88		JT	54.99	44.30- 04
Corrigan	Lisa	AUS	2.12.84	165/45	1500	4:10.69	4:10.30mx, 4:12.55- 04
Cosby	Jessica	USA	31.5.82	173/77	SP	17.63	17.38- 02
					HT	66.81	66.88- 04
Coslovich	Claudia	ITA	26.4.72	170/74	JT	58.38	65.30- 00, 65.55#- 98
Cotten	LaQuanda	USA	30.12.80	172/85	HT	65.39	62.60- 04
Coulaud	Julie	FRA	7.8.82	169/53	1500	4:11.07	4:14.36- 04
Coutinho	Geisa	BRA	1.6.80	160/53	400	52.00	51.44- 03
Cox	Crystal	USA	28.3.79	190/73	200	23.21	22.58- 04
					400	51.92	50.52- 04
Cox	Shana	USA	22.1.85		400	52.17	52.43- 03
Crane	Julie	GBR	26.9.76	178/60	HJ	1.90i	1.90i, 1.89- 04
Crawford	Erin	USA	14.8.85		400H	57.06	58.56- 04
* Crawford	Yunaika	CUB	2.11.82	165/75	HT	69.30	73.16- 04
Cristea	Olga	MDA-J	13.12.87	172/60	800	2:02.51	2:01.29- 04
Crombie	Fiona	NZL	15.8.82	173/62	3kSt	10:01.89	
Cromer (Cleary)	Dawn	USA	24.11.79	179/60	3kSt	10:04.39	9:59.30- 03
Cruz	Clarisse	POR	9.7.78	170/52	3kSt	9:47.9	9:55.24- 04
Cullen	Fiona	AUS	31.8.79	172/64	100H	13.23, 13.20w	13.19- 02, 13.0, 13.14w- 03
Culpepper	Shayne	USA	3.12.73	165/55	1500	4:07.08	4:06.33- 04
					3000	8:54.84	8:55.42i- 04, 9:06.86- 97
					5000	15:23.31	15:01.36- 04
* Cumbá	Yumileidi	CUB	11.2.75	183/100	SP	19.06	19.97- 04
* Cummins	Diane	CAN	19.1.74	165/50	800	2:00.10	1:58.39- 01
					1000	2:37.63	2:34.14- 02
Cusma	Elisa	ITA	24.7.81	167/49	800	2:00.96	2:05.97- 03
da Costa	Michele	BRA	23.1.79		3kSt	10:00.54	10:03.56- 04
da Silva	Eliana Renata	BRA	14.2.78		HJ	1.87	1.86- 04
da Silva	Karla Rosa	BRA	12.11.84	168/58	PV	4.20	4.05- 03
Dahlgren	Jennifer	ARG	27.8.84	180/115	HT	67.07	66.12- 04
Dahm	Brianna	USA	13.3.82	164/52	3kSt	10:08.79	10:01.77- 02
Dai Yanyan		CHN	8.1.80	175/55	5000	15:27.84	15:24.71- 01
Daigle	Angela	USA	28.5.76	157/57	100	11.23, 11.09w	11.23, 11.17w- 04
					200	22.59	22.98- 04
Dailey	Lynnsey	USA	5.3.83	172/63	100H	13.11	13.62- 02

Name		Nat	Born	Ht/Wt	Event	2005 Mark	Pre-2005 Best
Daniels	Brittany	USA-J	22.9.87	177/70	TJ	13.69, 13.90w	13.71- 04
Danisová	Martina	SVK	21.3.83	180/100	HT	69.24	68.50- 01
* Danvers-Smith	Natasha	GBR	19.9.77	175/61	400H	57.47	54.02- 03
Darden	Dominique	USA	9.12.83	165/57	400H	55.51	56.59- 04
Darmovzalová	Martina	CZE	12.10.78	172/54	LJ	6.66	6.57i, 6.53- 04
					TJ	13.95	13.98- 02
Davis	Candice	USA	26.10.85	170/62	100H	13.21, 13.13w	13.19- 02
Davis	Kia	USA	23.5.76	168/55	200	23.34, 23.18w	23.45- 04
					400	51.69	51.63- 04
Davy	Nadia	USA	24.12.80	168/55	400	52.30	50.66- 03
Davydenko	Natalya	RUS	13.4.75	168/54	100H	13.24, 13.01w	13.28- 02
Davydova	Natalya	RUS	24.11.78		JT	55.06	56.84- 03
Day	Sharon	USA	9.6.85	173/60	HJ	1.93	1.91- 04
De Croock	Stephanie	BEL	3.4.79	170/55	3kSt	9:48.65	9:54.25- 04
de Jong	Marjolein	NED	12.6.81	184/62	400H	55.64	56.26- 00
de la Puente	Martina	ESP	4.4.75	180/97	SP	17.65	18.17- 99
de Leon	Melissa	TRI	9.4.81	170/63	800	2:02.27	2:03.09- 04
^ de Reuck	Colleen	USA	13.4.64	164/47	Mar	2:28:40	2:26:36- 96
De Silva	Anne Maheshi	SRI	15.11.77	160/58	JT	55.60	54.56- 02
Deatherage	Jenelle	USA	25.9.77	175/59	1500	4:09.06	4:07.87- 04
					1M	4:32.68	4:31.58- 02
Debska	Paulina	POL	27.9.85	163/48	PV	4.20	3.90- 02
DeCree	Halima	USA	27.7.82		100	11.42, 11.25w	11.57- 04, 11.49w- 03
* Defar	Meseret	ETH	19.11.83	155/42	3000	8:33.57, 8:30.05i	8:36.46, 8:33.44i- 04
					5000	14:28.98	14:40.34- 03
* Dehiba	Hind	FRA	17.3.79	162/44	800	1:59.75	2:01.37- 04
					1500	4:00.49	4:03.72- 04
					3000	8:52.21	8:53.86- 04
Deiac	Cornelia	ROM-Y	20.3.88		LJ	6.51w	6.35i, 6.24- 04
Dejaeghere	Veerle	BEL	1.8.73	164/52	1500	4:08.70	4:05.05- 02
					3000	8:53.57i	8:49.31- 01
					5000	15:19.73	
Dekhtyarchuk	Oksana	RUS	3.2.80		800	2:02.36	2:01.55- 04
Dektyareva	Tatyana	RUS	4.6.84		100H	13.30w	
Delahunty-Evans	Sinead	IRL	12.2.71	172/60	1500	4:08.91	4:04.22- 98
Delfino	Fernanda	BRA	7.11.82		TJ	13.69	12.82- 00
Delinikóla	Vasilikí	GRE	9.2.81	175/61	Hep	5794	5909- 03
Delzenne	Amélie	FRA	4.8.83	168/52	PV	4.25	4.10- 04
* Demus	Lashinda	USA	10.3.83	170/62	400	51.79	51.24- 02
					100H	13.09m 12.93w	13.08, 12.99w- 04
					400H	53.27	53.43- 04
Demut	Katja	GER	21.12.83	180/60	TJ	13.67i, 13.67	13.96i- 04, 13.74- 03
^ Denboba	Merima	ETH	21.8.74	168/48	HMar	70:37 dh	69:36- 04
Denby	Nichole	USA	10.10.82	163/52	100H	12.79, 12.66w	12.62- 04
DeNigris	Susan	USA	28.5.80		PV	4.20ex	4.00- 03
Denisova	Lyubov	RUS	6.10.71	152/40	Mar	2:26:11	2:25:18- 04
Denisova	Olga	RUS	25.10.83		LJ	6.50	6.41- 04
Denton	Aneita	JAM	9.6.83	160/58	800	2:01.66	2:05.55- 04
Derham	Zoe	GBR	24.11.80	180/118	HT	65.48	62.27- 02
Desalegn-Dengersa	Tezeta	TUR	8.4.80	160/50	1500	4:10.98i	4:16.40- 04
					3000	8:46.65i	8:57.24- 04
Désert	Solen	FRA	2.8.82	182/62	200	23.02	23.26- 02
					400	51.52	51.56- 04
Desviat	Esther	ESP	27.1.82	162/49	800	2:02.24	2:00.76- 03
* Devetzí	Hrisopiyi	GRE	2.1.76	170/57	LJ	6.56	6.36- 03
					TJ	14.89	15.32- 04
Dharsha	Damayanthi	SRI	13.2.75	168/60	200	23.21	22.48- 98
Di Martino	Antonietta	ITA	1.6.78	169/57	HJ	1.90	1.98- 01
Dias	Ana	POR	15.1.74	169/50	Mar	2:31:27	2:28:49- 03
Díaz	Roxana	CUB	17.5.81	178/60	200	23.14w	22.69- 03
* Dibaba	Ejegayehu	ETH	25.6.82	160/46	3000	8:42.8+e	8:48.7+- 03
					5000	14:37.34	14:32.74- 04
					10000	30:18.39	30:24.98- 04
* Dibaba	Tirunesh	ETH	1.6.85	160/47	3000	8:38.9+	8:41.86- 02, 8:33.56i- 04
					5000	14:32.42	14:30.88- 04
					10000	30:15.67	0
Dibelková	Barbora	CZE	26.5.83	172/58	20kW	1:29:05	1:33:08- 04
Dickerson	Susanne	JAM	12.2.78	168/54	100H	13.10w	13.08- 04
DiCrescenzo	Delilah	USA	28.2.83	168/53	3kSt	10:06.88	10:18.52- 04
* Dietzsch	Franka	GER	22.1.68	183/92	DT	66.56	69.51- 99
DiMarco	Karyne	AUS	14.3.78	168/78	HT	64.43	67.44- 04

Name		Nat	Born	Ht/Wt	Event	2005Mark	Pre-2005 Best
Dimitráki	Iríni	GRE	8.8.80	175/67	TJ	14.23i, 14.15	14.21- 04
Dimitrova	Mariya	BUL	7.8.76	170/55	TJ	14.13	14.52- 04
Dimitrova	Mariyana	BUL	29.7.82	173/62	400	52.17	51.20- 04
Diop	Aïda	SEN	27.4.70	164/59	200	23.29A	22.64A, 22.76- 00
Diouf	Aminata	SEN	18.2.77	172/60	100	11.26w	11.24- 99, 10.9- 98
					200	22.93	22.90- 98
^ Divós	Katalin	HUN	11.5.74	180/84	HT	67.14	70.79- 01
* Dixon	Vonette	JAM	26.11.75	170/62	100H	12.67	12.72- 03
Djapic	Vukosava	SCG	21.1.78	172/57	100	11.37	11.47, 11.30w- 99
Djimou	Antoinette	FRA	2.8.85	177/68	Hep	6089w, 5965	5649- 04
* Dobrinska	Natalya	UKR	29.5.82	182/77	LJ	6.49w	6.27- 03
					Hep	6299	6387- 04
Dobriskey	Lisa	GBR	23.12.83	170/58	1500	4:05.42mx/4:07.47	4:08.14- 04
Dockendorf	Carly	CAN	31.12.83	165/59	PV	4.20	4.05- 04
* Domínguez	Marta	ESP	3.11.75	163/52	5000	14:54.98	14:48.33- 03
Dong Wangwei		CHN	28.6.81		Hep	5743	5651- 04
Dorozhon	Margarita	UKR-J	4.9.87	180/75	JT	55.32	53.90- 04
Dortch (Babatunde)	Tawa	CAN	19.12.79	175/60	400H	55.58	56.38- 03
* Douma-Hussar	Carmen	CAN	12.3.77	172/57	1000	2:36.26	
					1500	4:02.29	4:02.31- 04
					1M	4:28.43i	4:33.62- 03
					3000	8:53.83	9:39.98- 00
Dóva	Dímitra	GRE	2.7.74		400	51.89	52.31- 04
Dowdie	Peta-Gaye	JAM	18.1.77	170/60	200	23.04, 22.72w	22.51- 00, 22.25w- 99
Doyle	Katy	USA	1.8.80	170/68	JT	55.63	56.57- 04
D'Oyley	Toni Ann	JAM	25.10.81	180/64	100H	13.25	12.92- 02
* Dragila	Stacy	USA	25.3.71	173/64	PV	4.60	4.83- 04
Dragun	Oksana	BLR	19.4.81	170/60	100	11.28	11.31- 03
Dreher	Claudia	GER	2.5.71	169/52	Mar	2:29:49	2:27:55- 99
Dreier	Verena	GER	15.1.85	166/52	3kSt	9:56.70	9:59.33- 04
Dryakhlova	Mariya	RUS	24.4.84	174/58	400	51.57	51.66- 04
Dryer	Elva	USA	26.9.71	165/51	10000	31:21.92	31:26.88- 03
du Toit	Simoné	RSA-Y	27.9.88		SP	17.13	15.53- 04
Du Xianhui		SIN	4.1.81	188/90	SP	17.37	18.67- 02
Duarte	Sophie	FRA	31.7.81	170/54	3kSt	10:07.73	10:17.76- 03
Dubnova	Romana	CZE	4.11.78	180/58	HJ	1.96	1.90- 04
Duck	Emma	GBR	9.2.81	167/54	400H	57.06	59.1- 04
Dufour	Iréna	BEL	1.6.78	172/58	PV	4.20	4.20- 04
Dufour	Sylvie	SUI	24.1.79	176/65	Hep	5706	6033- 03
* Dulecha	Kutre	ETH	22.8.78	166/48	HMar	70:54	
					Mar	2:30:06	0
Dumbravean	Corina	ROM	15.4.84	167/50	800	2:02.44	2:01.55- 04
					1500	4:04.56	4:09.10- 04
Durst	Stephanie	USA	6.1.82	168/58	100	11.24	11.39- 02
					200	22.64	22.48, 22.46w- 02
Dyachenko	Tatyana	UKR-J	25.1.86	189/69	TJ	14.10	13.52- 04
Dyer	Tonette	USA	28.3.82	183/66	200	22.84w	22.34- 04
^ Eagles	Bronwyn	AUS	23.8.80	176/95	HT	65.75	71.12- 03
Eda	Ryoko	JPN	12.6.76	158/43	Mar	2:24:54	2:29:20- 02
Edmondson	Hilary	CAN	7.8.81	158/48	800	2:02.55	2:06.88- 03
					1500	4:08.94	4:14.13- 04
					1M	4:31.91i	
Edwards	Jackie	BAH	14.4.71	172/64	LJ	6.65, 6.71w	6.80- 96, 6.89Aw- 95
Efedáki	Konstadina	GRE	1.10.78	162/48	1500	4:09.56, 4:08.73i	4:05.63- 04
					3000	8:55.77, 8:53.95i	8:57.76- 03
Efimenko	Tatyana	KGZ	2.1.81	187/70	HJ	1.95	1.97- 03
Eieland	Anne Gerd	NOR	28.12.82	175/58	HJ	1.90	1.93- 03
Eisenlauer	Esther	GER	29.10.77	180/79	JT	56.79	55.29- 04, 56.02#- 97
* Ejigu	Sentayehu	ETH	21.6.85	160/45	3000	8:46.67i	8:42.63- 04
					5000	14:51.11	14:35.18- 04
Ekimat	Jane	KEN	12.6.74		HMar	70:39	70:18- 00
Ekpukpon	Christy	NGR	6.2.85	168/61	400	52.09	52.03- 04
El Jak	Nawal	SUD-Y	17.10.88		400	51.19	54.37- 04
El Mehdi	Saida	MAR	21.9.81	165/50	1500	4:12.09	4:08.60- 04
* Elisdóttír	Thórey Edda	ISL	30.6.77	181/64	PV	4.50	4.60- 04
* Ellis (-Buller)	Dana	CAN	7.12.79	162/57	PV	4.51	4.47- 04
Emmanouíl	Dimitra	GRE	13.5.84	172/61	PV	4.20	4.20- 04
Engel	Annett	GER-J	6.11.87	192/72	HJ	1.90i, 1.88	1.87- 04
* Ennis	Jessica	GBR-J	28.1.86	166/57	100H	13.26	13.57- 04
					HJ	1.87	1.83- 04
					Hep	5910	5542- 04

Name		Nat	Born	Ht/Wt	Event	2005 Mark	Pre-2005 Best
* Ennis-London	Delloreen	JAM	5.3.75	178/67	100H	12.57	12.51- 04
Erigha	Maryann	USA	3.11.84	170/57	100	11.40, 11.28w	11.75- 02
Erismis	Türkan	TUR	5.1.84	174/50	3kSt	9:50.32	10:25.51- 03
Erkesso	Teyiba	ETH	28.9.82	155/42	HMar	70:00	71:15- 01
^ Ertl	Karin	GER	23.6.74	177/65	Hep	6163	6396- 00
Essarokh	Latifa	FRA	11.12.73	162/48	1500	4:08.46	4:04.69- 04
Etienne	Ginou	USA/HAI	12.1.85	173/64	400	51.97	51.94- 04
* Eve	Laverne	BAH	16.6.65	179/77	JT	61.96	63.73- 00, 64.78#- 89
Eveland	Breanna	USA	25.1.84	175/64	PV	4.30	4.05- 04
Ezziraoui	Latifa	MAR	26.10.85		TJ	13.64	13.64- 04
Fairs	Liz	GBR	1.12.77	170/57	400H	56.65	56.73- 04
Falaiye	Alice	CAN	24.12.78	168/55	LJ	6.64Aw,6.56w	6.63A-00, 6.59-04, 6.67Aw- 03
Fall	Fatou Binetou	SEN	23.8.81	174/57	200	23.18A	23.35- 03
					400	51.33	50.62- 04
Falzon	Stéphanie	FRA	7.1.83	170/66	HT	65.12	65.21- 04
* Faumuina	Beatrice	NZL	23.10.74	185/115	DT	65.09	68.52- 97
Faustin-Parker	Nadine	HAI	14.4.76	160/56	100H	12.83	12.74- 04
^ Febbraio	Surita	RSA	27.12.73	168/58	400H	54.60	54.05A- 03, 54.48- 01
* Feitor	Susana	POR	28.1.75	160/52	20kW	1:28:44	1:27:55- 01
* Felicien	Perdita	CAN	29.8.80	165/63	100H	12.58	12.46, 12.45w- 04
* Felix	Allyson	USA	18.11.85	168/57	100	11.05	11.16- 04, 11.12w- 03
					200	22.13	22.11A- 03, 22.18- 04
					400	51.12	51.83A- 04, 52.26- 03
Félix	Sylviane	FRA	31.10.77	174/58	100	11.20	11.15- 98
					200	23.03	22.56- 97
Feng Lingjian		CHN	28.4.83		PV	4.20i	4.00- 03
Feng Yun		CHN	23.2.76	170/60	100H	12.92	12.85- 99
* Fenton	Lorraine	JAM	8.9.73	174/59	400	50.95	49.30- 02
* Feofanova	Svetlana	RUS	16.7.80	164/52	PV	4.70i	4.88- 04
Féraez	Fabienne	BEN	6.8.76	175/57	200	22.81	23.12- 04
Fernández	Nuria	ESP	16.8.76	168/58	1500	4:07.57	4:03.57- 03
Fernández	Yudelkis	CUB	28.2.85	174/63	LJ	6.70	6.74A- 04, 6.69- 03
* Ferrales	Yania	CUB	28.7.77	180/86	DT	64.52	62.88- 04
Fesenko	Anastasiya	RUS	17.6.82		800	2:00.84	2:01.21- 04
					1500	4:07.13	4:12.61- 03
Fila	Aleksandra	POL	17.8.83	173/60	TJ	13.73	13.32- 04
Filándra	Iéni	GRE	12.1.84	173/60	800	2:01.68	2:04.87- 04
Firova	Tatyana	RUS	10.10.82	178/64	400	50.41	50.44- 04
Fitidou	Anna	CYP	22.4.77	160/57	PV	4.40i, 4.25	4.30- 03
Flanagan	Shalane	USA	7.8.81	165/50	3000	8:54.43	8:55.05- 04
					5000	15:10.96	15:05.08- 04
Fleshman	Lauren	USA	26.9.81	173/54	3000	8:43.95	9:01.58i-03
					5000	15:02.52	15:09.98- 04
Fletcher	Sherry	GRN-J	17.1.86		100	11.35w	11.72- 04
Florence	Natalie	USA	25.12.81	158/50	3kSt	10:07.51	10:28.24- 03
Fofanah	Fatmata	USA	26.6.85	178/64	100H	13.32	13.69- 04
Fokina	Natalya	UKR	7.7.82	178/85	DT	62.80	63.11- 03
Fontes Dias	Amanda	BRA	11.11.84	168/44	400	52.17	54.04- 03
					400H	57.03	57.27- 03
Forcadell	Laia	ESP	6.6.82	173/55	400H	57.11	57.72- 04
Forrester	Nicole	CAN	17.11.76	192/72	HJ	1.90	1.94- 01
Foster	Ebony	USA	26.7.83		100H	12.95	12.81- 04
* Foster-Hylton	Brigitte	JAM	7.11.74	170/62	100H	12.55	12.45- 03
* Fountain	Hyleas	USA	14.1.81	170/60	100H	13.09	13.11- 04
					HJ	1.88	1.83- 00
					LJ	6.67	6.59, 6.61w- 04
					Hep	6502	6035- 04
Fouquet	Virginie	FRA	9.9.75	162/48	800	2:00.26	1:59.78- 02
Fox	Jessica	USA	10.1.82	175/60	200	23.25A, 23.22Aw	23.58- 03
					400	51.72A	51.92A, 51.93- 03
França	Luciana	BRA	19.5.77	167/58	400H	57.18	57.04- 04
Francis	Sheree	JAM	20.10.83	177/63	HJ	1.89	1.86- 00
Fraser	Donna	GBR	7.11.72	181/70	100	11.36w	11.57- 00, 11.32w- 97, 11.2wA-98
					200	23.21, 22.80w	23.05- 04, 22.96i, 22.90w- 97
					400	51.27	49.79- 00
* Freeman	Michelle	JAM	5.5.69	170/63	100H	12.84	12.52, 12.40w- 97
Fridam	Win	KEN	16.4.85		5000	15:28.26	15:40.3- 04
					10000	32:32.55	
Friedrich	Ariane	GER	10.1.84	178/59	HJ	1.90	1.92- 04
Friedrich	Kathleen	GER	13.7.77	174/57	800	2:01.45	2:01.79- 02
					1500	4:08.88	4:04.27- 01

Name		Nat	Born	Ht/Wt	Event	2005Mark	Pre-2005 Best
Frizell	Sultana	CAN	24.10.84	178/100	HT	66.42	63.36- 04
Fu Pengcheng		CHN	15.1.80	180/55	Hep	5652	5802- 04
Fujinaga	Yoshiko	JPN	15.8.81	169/50	5000	15:29.96	15:22.68- 99
					10000	32:33.89	31:47.82- 01
* Fukushi	Kayoko	JPN	25.3.82	161/45	3000	8:51.85	8:44.40- 02
					5000	14:53.22	14:55.19- 02
					10000	31:03.75	30:51.81- 02
Fulbiszewska	Agnieszka	POL	9.3.80	174/60	3kSt	10:08.45	10:27.43- 04
^ Fynes	Savatheda	BAH	17.10.74	165/58	100	11.32A, 11.39, 11.17w	10.91- 99, 10.7w- 95
Fyodorova	Olga	RUS	14.7.83	178/74	100	11.21	11.27- 04
Gabito	Lerma Elvira	PHI	17.10.74	162/52	LJ	6.52	6.56- 04
Gadschiew	Kristina	GER	3.7.84	179/57	PV	4.22	3.90i- 00, 3.70- 01
Gaffigan	Ann	USA	5.10.81	163/50	3kSt	9:49.50	9:39.35- 04
Galaviz	Lisa	USA	30.11.79	160/46	3kSt	9:40.58	9:46.30- 03
Gallo	Lindsey	USA	29.11.81	166/50	1500	4:05.75	4:09.94- 04
Gao Kelian		CHN	15.8.83	165/55	20kW	1:28:51	1:29:39- 01
* Gao Shuying		CHN	28.10.79	180/63	PV	4.53	4.52- 01
^ García	Alejandra	ARG	13.6.73	174/60	PV	4.30	4.43- 04
García	Rosibel	COL	13.2.81		800	2:01.57A	2:02.84- 03
Gargallo	Maite	ESP	15.10.69	162/46	20kW	1:32:18	1:30:41- 03
Gaus	Oksana	RUS	9.7.81		SP	16.89	16.43- 03
* Gavrila	Adelina	ROM	26.11.78	175/56	TJ	14.58i, 14.23	14.76i, 14.75- 03
Gavrilovic	Sanja	CRO	20.9.82	179/69	HT	67.56	67.72- 03
* Gay	Mabel	CUB	5.5.83	186/71	TJ	14.21, 14.44w	14.57i- 04, 14.52- 03
Geetha	Sathi	IND	5.7.83		400	51.75	52.25- 04
Geissler	Kathrin	GER	10.6.85	182/64	Hep	5663	5727- 04
Genévrier	Elise	FRA	27.6.83	165/55	PV	4.20	4.20- 04
Geng Aihua		CHN	29.6.83		JT	59.04	58.86- 04
Genovese	Bruna	ITA	24.9.76	161/50	HMar	71:22	71:45- 02
					Mar	2:27:15	2:25:35- 01
* George	Anju Bobby	IND	19.4.77	170/62	LJ	6.75	6.83- 04
Gerraughty	Laura	USA	29.7.83	175/93	DT	56.70	53.13- 04
^ Gesell	Claudia	GER	18.12.77	170/59	800	2:01.72i	1:58.34- 00
* Gevaert	Kim	BEL	5.8.78	170/60	100	11.12	11.14- 04
					200	22.68	22.48- 04
					400	51.45	52.16- 04
* Ghézielle	Bouchra	FRA	18.5.79	165/47	800	2:00.29	2:06.63- 04
					1500	4:01.28	4:04.19- 04
					3000	8:35.41	8:47.78- 04
Ghribi	Habiba	TUN	9.4.84		3kSt	9:51.49	
Gibilisco	Laura	ITA-J	17.1.86	162/85	HT	64.01	62.66- 04
Giesa	Ulrike	GER	16.8.84	183/90	DT	60.63	58.98- 04
Gigi	Asha	ETH	15.10.73	165/48	HMar	69:53 dh	70:42- 02
					Mar	2:27:38	2:26:05- 04
* Gilreath	Erin	USA	11.10.80	177/92	HT	73.87	72.12- 04
Ginko	Yelena	BLR	30.7.76	165/53	20kW	1:28:11	1:29:02- 04
* Giordano	Rossella	ITA	1.12.72	170/51	20kW	1:32:57	1:29:12- 97
Giordano Bruno	Anna	ITA	13.12.80	171/65	PV	4.20	4.10- 02
^ Girard	Patricia	FRA	8.4.68	162/48	100H	13.09, 13.03w	12.59- 96
Gladyr	Tatyana	UKR	17.4.75	162/48	Mar	2:29:34	2:32:24- 04
Glanc	Zaneta	POL	11.3.83	183/79	DT	56.15	51.30- 04
Glavatskikh	Irina	RUS	29.12.84	180/56	HJ	1.88i	1.90i- 04, 1.87- 03
Glenn	Brianna	USA	18.4.80	168/55	LJ	6.68, 6.70w	6.65A- 00, 6.59- 03
Gliznutsa	Inna	MDA	18.4.73	184/65	HJ	1.92	1.95- 99
* Glover	Sandra	USA	30.12.68	173/59	400H	53.32	53.33- 00
Gnezdilov	Svetlana	ISR	20.7.69	170/58	Hep	5896w, 5845	6031- 03
Goff	Yolanda	USA	14.1.85		100	11.33w	11.88- 04
* Golding-Clarke	Lacena	JAM	20.3.75	168/57	100H	12.68, 12.67w	12.69- 04
Goldkuhle	Maike	GER	10.3.80		Hep	5705	5675- 04
Golovchenko	Tatyana	UKR	13.2.80	164/54	1500	4:07.25	4:05.87- 04
					3000	8:49.80i	8:50.67- 04
Golubchikova	Yuliya	RUS	27.3.83	175/54	PV	4.40	4.35- 02
* Gomes	Naide	POR	10.11.79	181/70	LJ	6.72	6.57- 02
					Hep	6230	6160- 02
Gonçalves	Maribel	POR	1.4.78	167/51	20kW	1:34:07	1:31:19.2t- 04
Goncharenko	Olga	BLR	13.7.81	185/95	DT	56.08	59.06- 01
Goncharova	Marina	RUS-J	26.4.86		Hep	5760	5599- 04
González	Misleydis	CUB	19.6.78	178/80	SP	18.92	18.73- 04
González	Norma	COL	11.8.82	172/53	200	22.90A, 23.02	23.18A, 23.34- 03
González	Yamilka	ESP	1.8.72	156/49	3kSt	10:13.00	9:56.22- 04

	Name		Nat	Born	Ht/Wt	Event	2005 Mark	Pre-2005 Best
	Gordeyeva	Irina	RUS-J	9.10.86		HJ	1.88	1.88- 04
	Gordeyeva	Tatyana	RUS	3.6.73	180/63	Hep	5939	6336- 00
	Gordon	Sheena	USA	26.9.83	180/55	HJ	1.91	1.88- 04
^	Gorelova	Natalya	RUS	18.4.73	173/56	800	2:01.79	1:57.90- 99
						1500	4:07.21	3:59.70- 01
	Gorpinich	Valentyna	UKR	12.3.83	161/48	3kSt	9:49.73	9:56.92- 04
	Gorshkova	Olga	RUS	9.3.83		800	2:02.58	2:05.49- 04
	Goucher	Kara	USA	9.7.78	170/58	5000	15:17.55	15:28.78- 00
*	Goulbourne	Elva	JAM	21.1.80	170/50	LJ	6.64, 6.81w	
								7.16A- 04, 6.86-01, 6.96w- 03, 6.91i- 02
	Gradzki	Monika	GER	21.9.79	172/59	800	2:01.00	2:00.96- 03
	Grandovec	Daneja	SLO	2.7.84	174/58	3kSt	10:03.33	10:42.53- 04
*	Grasu	Nicoleta	ROM	11.9.71	176/88	DT	64.89	68.80- 99
*	Green	Emma	SWE	8.12.84	180/62	HJ	1.97	1.90- 04
	Greggs	Charlette	USA	20.10.83	170/57	200	22.85, 22.74w	23.18- 03
						400	52.08	51.65- 03
	Grenot	Libania	CUB	12.7.83	176/60	400	51.53	51.68- 04
	Grgic	Daniela	CRO-Y	28.9.88		400	51.30	53.65- 03
	Gribule	Ilze	LAT	25.1.84	173/70	JT	58.74	58.58- 04
*	Grigorieva	Tatyana	AUS	8.10.75	172/60	PV	4.47	4.56- 01
*	Grigoryeva	Lydiya	RUS	21.1.74	164/58	10000	31:20.58	30:57.83- 03
						HMar	71:01	69:32- 03
						Mar	2:27:01	2:32:40- 00
	Grigoryeva	Yekaterina	RUS	21.4.74	176/68	100	11.35, 11.21w	11.13- 98
	Grousselle	Elisabeth	FRA	6.2.73	163/49	800	2:00.72	1:59.46- 04
	Groza	Ana-Maria	ROM	1.6.76	167/53	20kW	1:31:48	1:29:31- 04
	Gruca	Dorota	POL	5.12.70	159/46	Mar	2:27:46	2:28:49- 04
	Grzesiak	Joanna	POL	15.8.80	173/56	Hep	5982	5930- 04
	Gu Biwei		CHN-Y	17.2.88		HJ	1.90	1.81- 04
*	Gu Yuan		CHN	9.5.82	171/85	HT	69.69	72.36- 04
*	Guan Yingnan		CHN	25.4.77	177/60	LJ	6.78	6.95- 00
*	Gudkova	Tatyana	RUS	23.1.78	170/60	20kW	1:29:02	1:25:18- 00
	Guégan	lodie	FRA	19.2.85	169/55	800	2:00.90	2:03.19- 04
*	Guevara	Ana Gabriela	MEX	4.3.77	173/61	400	49.81	48.89- 03
	Gullatte	Rhonda	USA	10.2.84		DT	57.43	51.59- 02
	Gulumyan	Oksana	RUS	8.12.82	173/59	400H	55.16	55.69- 04
	Gundert	Louise	SWE	31.7.80	177/58	400H	56.20	57.61- 04
*	Gurova	Viktoriya	RUS	22.5.82	178/63	TJ	14.74i, 14.38	14.65- 04
*	Gushchina	Yuliya	RUS	4.3.83	175/62	200	22.53	23.06- 04
	Gutowicz-Westhof	Urzula	GER	13.7.77	175/60	LJ	6.62	6.53- 03
	Guy	LaDedra	USA	16.11.84	168/56	100	11.34w	11.43- 04
	Guzowska	Anna	POL	15.1.80	174/51	200	23.02	22.87- 03
						400	51.29	51.88- 03
*	Györffy	Dóra	HUN	23.2.78	176/58	HJ	1.93	2.00- 01
	Ha Mingming		CHN	15.4.82	168/51	20kW	1:30:14	1:30:26- 03
	Ha Xiaoyan		CHN	30.1.72	176/73	JT	55.30	59.90- 02, 65.44#- 93
	Halkoaho	Johanna	FIN	13.1.77	165/55	100H	13.23	13.25, 13.24w- 99
	Hall	Elizabeth	GBR	28.4.85	166/	3kSt	10:07.90	-0-
	Hall	Patricia	JAM	16.10.82	170/57	400	52.24	53.00- 04
*	Hamácková	Pavla	CZE	20.5.78	170/68	PV	4.55i, 4.51	4.60- 03
	Hamilton	Melina	NZL	15.6.76	172/64	PV	4.31	4.40- 03
	Hanaoka	Maho	JPN	3.8.76	171/60	LJ	6.69, 6.82w	6.82- 01
	Hannila	Teija	FIN	2.8.80	166/54	TJ	13.70	13.50- 03
	Hantzí-Neag	Hristina	GRE	26.12.76	168/55	400H	56.15	56.67- 02
	Hao Shuai		CHN-J	19.7.87		HT	64.43	58.52- 04
*	Hara	Yumiko	JPN	9.1.82	163/43	10000	31:24.33	31:48.50- 01
						HMar	70:27+	69:28- 02
						Mar	2:24:19	0
	Harper	Dawn	USA	13.5.84	168/57	100H	12.91	13.16, 12.91w- 04
	Harrigan	Tahesia	IVB	15.2.82		100	11.29, 11.28w	11.37- 02
						200	23.25	23.46- 02
	Harris	Tina	USA	17.11.84	180/67	LJ	6.52	6.41- 04
	Harrison	Fiona	GBR	30.11.81	173/63	Hep	5754	6011w- 04, 5598- 03
	Hart	Bethany	USA	10.4.77	172/73	HT	69.65	68.01- 04
	Hartmann	Julia	GER-J	10.4.86	181/62	HJ	1.87	1.82- 04
	Harvey	Natalie	GBR	19.1.75	164/50	5000	15:25.47	15:14.08- 04
^	Hashim	Merima	ETH	.81	162/49	10000	32:14.18	30:59.92- 00
						HMar	71:09	
	Hashimoto	Yasuko	JPN	12.8.75	163/47	HMar	69:43	68:55- 01
						Mar	2:25:21	2:26:32- 03

	Name		Nat	Born	Ht/Wt	Event	2005Mark	Pre-2005 Best
	Hastings	Natasha	USA-J	23.7.86	173/63	200	23.08i	23.66- 04
						400	51.34	52.04- 04
	Hatori	Tomoko	JPN	28.5.81	153/40	10000	31:58.49	31:15.34- 04
	Hatzinákou	Persefóni	GRE	6.6.84		HJ	1.87	1.81i, 1.79- 04
	Hauser-Price	Sierra	USA	17.12.83	173/64	100	11.41w	11.52- 03
	Hautala	Tiia	FIN	3.4.72	171/65	Hep	5899	6369- 99
	Hayakari	Minori	JPN	29.11.72	164/48	5000	15:11.42	15:33.66- 01
						3kSt	9:41.21	0
	Hayakawa	Eri	JPN	15.11.81		HMar	70:14	71:17- 04
						Mar	2:28:50	2:28:11- 04
*	Hayes	Joanna	USA	23.12.76	165/58	100H	12.47	12.37- 04
	He Dan		CHN	22.7.84	167/58	20kW	1:28:35	1:34:18- 04
	He Liyuan		CHN	14.1.83		100H	13.19	13.36- 03
	He Yu		CHN-J	26.6.86	172/55	400H	56.41	57.62- 04
	Heaston	Kristin	USA	23.11.75	180/127	SP	18.68	18.66- 04
*	Heidler	Betty	GER	14.10.83	175/81	HT	72.19	72.73- 04
	Heitling	Sabine	BRA-J	2.7.87		3kSt	10:04.71	10:29.73- 04
	Hejnová	Michaela	CZE	10.4.80	168/62	Hep	5695	6174w- 04, 6032- 02
	Hejnová	Zuzana	CZE-J	19.12.86	170/54	400H	55.89	57.54- 03
*	Hellebaut	Tia	BEL	16.2.78	182/66	HJ	1.93	1.95- 04
	Heltne	Anca	ROM	1.1.78	175/76	SP	16.97	17.51- 99
*	Henderson	Monique	USA	18.2.83	170/54	100	11.34	11.59- 04
						200	22.86, 22.72w	22.71- 04
						400	49.96	50.53- 04
	Hendry	Kelsie	CAN	29.6.82	170/59	PV	4.46	4.30- 04
*	Hennagan	Monique	USA	26.5.76	173/55	100	11.26	11.86- 92, 11.3- 93, 11.69w- 94
						200	22.87	22.97- 04
						400	50.24	49.56- 04
	Henriques	Inês	POR	1.5.80	156/48	20kW	1:33:24	1:31:23.7t- 04
	Henry	Britney	USA	17.10.84		HT	68.17	63.24- 04
	Heron	Heather	USA	20.6.82	170/62	100H	13.25	13.39- 02
	Hessler	Stefanie	GER	16.3.83	166/65	JT	55.04	57.00- 03
^	Hewitt	Lauren	AUS	25.11.78	170/60	200	23.10	22.52- 00
	Hila	Elena	ROM	20.5.74	180/98	SP	18.02	18.73i- 99, 18.73- 02
	Hill	Chaytan	USA	13.10.82	178/64	TJ	13.68A, 13.84Aw	13.67- 03, 14.27w- 04
*	Hill-Thurmond	Aretha	USA	14.8.76	181/98	DT	64.56	65.86- 04, 66.23dh- 03
*	Hinds	Korine	JAM	18.1.76	163/54	3kSt	9:30.12	9:50.64- 04
*	Hingst	Carolin	GER	18.9.80	174/60	PV	4.65i, 4.50	4.66- 04
	Hinrichs	Denise	GER-J	7.6.87	181/81	SP	18.05i, 17.55	15.94i, 15.80- 04
	Hinshaw-Spearman	Beth	USA	30.7.81	165/57	PV	4.22	4.11A- 03
*	Hiroyama	Harumi	JPN	2.9.68	160/47	10000	31:34.79	31:22.72- 97
						HMar	70:02	69:41- 01
						Mar	2:25:46	2:22:56- 00
	Hirpassa	Birhane	ETH	30.7.83		1500	4:11.29	4:07.44- 01
	Hjálmsdóttir	sdis	ISL	28.10.85	175/65	JT	57.10	55.51- 04
	Hodge	Virgil	SKN	17.11.83	168/54	100	11.22w	11.44- 04
						200	23.21, 23.05w	23.52- 04
	Hofstede	Helen	NED	31.12.80	168/54	3kSt	10:05.84	10:09.90- 04
	Holliday	Becky	USA	12.3.80	160/52	PV	4.36i, 4.30	4.47- 03
	Hollman	Julie	GBR	16.2.77	180/69	Hep	6090	6135- 02
^	Holmes	Kelly	GBR	19.4.70	164/55	1000	2:35.39i	2:32.55- 97
						1500	4:06.52	3:57.90- 04
	Holroyd	Shelley	GBR	17.5.73	174/72	JT	55.14	57.48- 04
	Homo	Amandine	FRA	24.12.80	170/58	PV	4.20	4.31- 99
	Hooker	Marshevet	USA	25.9.84	173/67	100	11.12, 11.03w	11.14- 04
						200	22.80, 22.73w	23.59- 01, 23.25w- 02
						LJ	6.65, 6.89w	6.40- 04, 6.50w- 01
	Hoos	Laurien	NED	18.8.83	180/66	Hep	6291	5631- 04
	Horie	Chika	JPN	15.2.81	159/44	Mar	2:29:15	2:26:11- 02
*	Howard	Chaunte	USA	12.1.84	175/59	HJ	2.00	1.98A, 1.95- 04
	Howard	Keisha	USA	13.5.84		400	52.11	53.71- 04
	Howard	Megan	USA-J	9.4.86		SP	16.55	15,33- 04
*	Howe-Nadin	Kym	AUS	12.6.80	177/64	PV	4.40	4.45- 02
	Hu Ming		CHN	8.10.84	161/45	20kW	1:32:24	1:35:02- 03
	Huang Jing		CHN-J	4.4.87		1500	4:10.13	4:19.47- 04
*	Huang Qiuyan		CHN	25.1.80	172/66	TJ	14.58	14.72- 01
	Huang Qun		CHN	12.4.79	180/85	DT	64.53	64.42- 04
*	Huang Xiaoxiao		CHN	3.3.83	181/62	400	51.95	51.93- 03
						400H	54.18	54.83- 04
	Hunt	Brenda-Grace	JAM	9.9.81	170/66	JT	56.91	51.38- 04
	Hunt	Cassie	USA	6.3.85	180/61	3kSt	9:59.82	10:17.55- 04

	Name		Nat	Born	Ht/Wt	Event	2005 Mark	Pre-2005 Best
	Hurd	Tiombé	USA	17.8.73	178/64	TJ	13.74i	14.45- 04
	Hussein	Marwa Ahmed	EGY	19.6.78	168/110	HT	68.48	66.54- 04
	Hutchinson	Ayanna	TRI	18.2.78	165/60	100	11.36, 11.20w	11.26- 00, 11.20w- 04
						200	23.35, 22.9	23.44- 00
	Hütter	Julia	GER	26.7.83	170/54	PV	4.30	4.00- 04
*	Hyman	Mardrea	JAM	22.12.72	168/52	1500	4:07.96	4:05.25- 01
						3kSt	9:27.21	-0-
*	Iagar	Elena	ROM	16.1.75	173/54	1500	4:03.09i	4:02.90- 02
^	Iagar	Monica	ROM	2.4.73	186/68	HJ	1.92i, 1.92	2.03i- 99, 2.02- 98
	Ibargüen	Caterine	COL	12.2.84	181/65	HJ	1.93A	1.91- 04
						LJ	6.54A	6.42- 04
						TJ	13.66A	13.64A- 04
	Ichikawa	Miho	JPN	20.5.73	160/46	HMar	71:33	72:33- 04
	Iglesias	Magnolia	ESP	26.5.79	185/80	SP	17.07	16.20- 04
	Ignatkina	Yuliya	RUS	13.9.82	171/64	LJ	6.53	6.55- 03
						Hep	5931	6120- 04
	Ikeda	Kumiko	JPN	10.1.81	167/55	100H	13.27	13.20, 13.09w- 04
						LJ	6.69	6.78- 01
	Ildeykina	Yelena	RUS	16.6.83	165/52	400	51.48	51.79- 04
						400H	55.86	55.49- 04
	Ilyina	Anastasiya	RUS	16.1.82	172/57	LJ	6.63i	6.66- 04
	Ilyushchenko	Tatyana	BLR	18.4.83	178/85	SP	18.01	16.97- 04
	Ilyushkina	Oksana	UKR	25.5.74	169/56	400H	57.47	
*	Ingberg	Mikaela	FIN	29.7.74	176/74	JT	61.06	64.03- 00, 67.32#- 97
*	Inzikuru	Dorcus	UGA	2.2.82	158/49	3kSt	9:15.04	9:29.30- 04
	Irusta	Geovanna	BOL	26.9.75	157/48	20kW	1:33:19	1:32:06- 04
	Isakova	Yevgeniya	RUS	27.11.78	175/67	400	52.14	53.42- 04
						400H	54.39	55.62- 04
	Isane	Elin	NOR	18.4.75	178/82	DT	55.95	55.55- 99
	Ishii	Tomoko	JPN	14.10.83	154/42	10000	32:00.08	-
*	Isinbayeva	Yelena	RUS	3.6.82	174/65	PV	5.01WR	4.92- 04
	Ispan	Andrea	ROM	2.6.78	189/68	HJ	1.88i	1.85i- 01, 1.82- 99
	Ivankova	Olga	UKR	7.1.73	173/72	JT	60.74	57.75- 00, 60.94#- 96
	Ivanova	Albina	RUS	16.5.77	154/46	Mar	2:28:21	2:25:35- 03
	Ivanova	Alevtina	RUS	22.5.75	160/53	HMar	71:14	72:24- 04
^	Ivanova	Alina	RUS	16.3.69	163/52	Mar	2:31:22	2:25:34- 01
*	Ivanova	Lyubov	RUS	2.3.81		3kSt	9:46.63	9:24.78- 03
	Ivanova	Marina	RUS	30.6.83		3kSt	9:58.24	10:08.81- 02
	Ivanova	Natalya	RUS	25.6.81	184/68	200	22.97	23.26- 04
	Ivanova	Olga	RUS	6.4.79	182/91	SP	18.56	17.60- 03
*	Ivanova	Olimpiada	RUS	26.8.70	160/50	20kW	1:25:41	1:24:50- 01
	Ivanova	Svetlana	RUS	18.8.83	166/55	3kSt	9:50.21	9:49.24- 04
	Ivanova	Svetlana	RUS	10.7.85		DT	57.62	55.70- 04
	Ivanova	Tatyana	RUS	16.10.81		LJ	6.75	6.55i, 6.52, 6.66w- 04
	Ivanova	Yelena	RUS	16.3.79	175/64	TJ	14.27i, 14.21	14.39- 04
	Ivery	Lakadron	USA	23.6.83	170/57	100	11.32, 11.25w	11.28- 03, 11.26w- 04
						200	23.08	22.95- 04, 22.87w- 03
						LJ	6.61w	6.32- 04
	Ivlyeva	Inna	RUS	27.6.71		LJ	6.51i	6.71i, 6.52, 6.59w- 01
	Ivlyeva	Yelena	RUS	31.7.74		Hep	5762	5966- 03
	Ivoninskaya	Natalya	KAZ	22.2.85	176/54	100H	13.20	13.92- 04
	Iwamoto	Yasuyo	JPN	8.9.76	156/43	HMar	69:45	70:06- 01
	Izmodenova	Natalya	RUS	1.1.81	175/62	3kSt	9:35.51	9:58.26- 04
	Jackson	Elizabeth	USA	27.10.77	170/59	3kSt	9:39.78	9:41.94- 01
	Jakubaitite	Indre	LTU	24.1.76	177/70	JT	60.59	59.26- 04
*	Jakubczak	Anna	POL	2.2.73	166/53	800	2:02.39	2:00.78- 99
						1500	4:00.59	4:00.15- 04
*	Jamal	Maryam	BRN	16.9.84	155/44	800	1:59.69	2:02.18- 04
						1500	3:56.79	4:07.78- 04
						3000	8:28.87	8:40.32- 04
						5000	14:51.68	15:19.45mx- 04
	James	Markita	USA	28.6.83	178/62	400H	57.41	58.24- 04
	Jamieson	Sarah	AUS	24.3.75	172/58	1500	4:06.80	4:04.73- 04
						3000	8:51.12	8:49.46- 04
						5000	15:29.88	15:42.17- 04
*	Janowska	Wioletta	POL	9.6.77	176/58	1500	4:03.68	4:03.09- 04
						3000	8:44.22	9:00.77- 03, 8:53.90i- 04
						5000	15:08.38	15:24.25- 04
						3kSt	9:25.09	10:18.10- 99
	Janson	Lacy	USA	20.2.83	178/68	PV	4.30i	4.45i, 4.37- 03
	Jarrett	Jovanee	JAM	15.1.83	170/62	LJ	6.48	6.09- 01

Name		Nat	Born	Ht/Wt	Event	2005Mark	Pre-2005 Best
^ Javornik	Helena	SLO	26.3.66	163/52	HMar	69:53	69:22- 04
					Mar	2:29:18	2:27:33- 04
Jelizarova	Polina	LAT-Y	1.5.89		3kSt	10:05.57	10:55.57- 03
Jémaa	Dora	FRA	15.7.85	154/45	100H	13.10w	13.54- 04
* Jepkosgei	Janeth	KEN	13.12.83	167/47	800	1:57.82	2:00.52- 04
* Jepleting	Priscila	KEN	26.6.80	158/47	3000	8:41.85	8:52.35- 02
					5000	14:44.00	14:54.24- 04
Jeptoo	Rita	KEN	15.2.81		HMar	70:41	71:24- 03
					Mar	2:24:22	2:28:11- 04
Jerz	Connie	USA	26.4.82	165/62	PV	4.25Ai	4.30- 03
* Jesien	Anna	POL	10.12.78	168/56	400H	53.96	55.11- 02
* Jevtic	Olivera	SCG	24.7.77	174/52	Mar	2:31:43	2:25:03- 03
Jian Xingli		CHN	4.12.83	155/50	20kW	1:33:20	1:29:31- 01
Jiang Haiyan		CHN	19.12.79	183/67	HJ	1.89	1.94- 04
* Jiang Jing		CHN	23.10.85	164/51	20kW	1:27:19	1:27:34- 04
Jiang Kun		CHN	18.5.85	160/52	20kW	1:33:28	1:30:52- 01
Jiang Limin		CHN-Y	20.2.88		SP	16.71	17.51- 04
Jiang Ping		CHN	10.1.79		SP	17.57	18.59- 01
Jiang Qiuyan		CHN	5.7.83	160/48	20kW	1:28:01	1:30:03- 03
Jiang Yuanyuan		CHN-J	20.12.86	169/50	5000	15:26.50	15:51.58- 04
Jing Xuezhu		CHN	20.4.75	176/60	HJ	1.92	1.94- 04
Johansson	Camilla	SWE	3.11.76	166/52	TJ	13.74, 13.84w	14.15- 03, 14.17w- 01
Johansson	Christin	SWE	26.1.78		3kSt	10:06.44	10:17.68- 03
* Johnson	Benita	AUS	6.5.79	166/50	3000	8:52.16	8:38.06- 03
					5000	15:21.02	14:47.60- 02
					10000	31:55.15	30:37.68- 03
					Mar	2:26:32	2:38:03- 04
^ Johnson	Chelsea	USA	20.12.83	175/62	PV	4.30	4.57- 04
* Johnson	Jade	GBR	7.6.80	185/72	LJ	6.52i	6.80- 04
* Johnson	Sheena	USA	1.10.82	165/58	400H	54.72	52.95- 04
Jones	Brittany	USA-Y	6.3.89		200	23.13	
Jones	Katie	GBR	4.1.77	172/60	400H	57.29	57.69- 02
Jones	LaVerne	ISV	16.9.81	171/59	100	11.22w	11.25, 11.23w- 04
					200	23.14	22.81- 04
Jones	Lolo	USA	5.8.82	168/60	100	11.39w	11.53- 03
					100H	12.76	12.77- 04, 12.7w- 01
* Jones	Marion	USA	12.10.75	178/64	100	11.28	10.70- 99, 10.65A- 98
Jones	Sharifa	USA	16.11.82	165/55	100H	13.13	13.10- 04
Jones (-Olausson)	Ifoma	USA	4.9.77	168/60	HJ	1.93	1.91i, 1.90A- 03
Jones/Moncrieff	Susan	GBR	8.6.78	179/62	HJ	1.90i	1.95- 01
Jong Yong-ok		PRK	24.1.81	153/40	Mar	2:29:43	2:26:12- 02
Josephs	Janice	RSA	31.3.82	160/60	100	11.36A	11.38A- 03
					200	23.17A	23.15- 04
					100H	13.29w	13.30- 04
					LJ	6.50	6.41- 04
					Hep	5958	6127- 04
Jovic	Biljana	SCG	2.3.85	175/50	3kSt	10:12.35	10:06.96- 04
Joyce	Jennifer	CAN	25.9.80	175/80	HT	68.48	68.22- 04
Juhász	Fanni	HUN	31.3.81	169/58	PV	4.25	4.27- 04
Kadogan	Filiz	TUR	12.2.82	187/95	SP	17.09	17.16- 03
Kafetzí	Ioánna	GRE	30.5.76	165/55	LJ	6.62	6.71- 04
^ Kähler	Birgit	GER	14.8.70	182/60	HJ	1.90	1.94- 91
^ Kaliturina	Olga	RUS	9.3.76	180/57	HJ	1.95i, 1.87	1.98- 04
* Kallur	Jenny	SWE	16.2.81	170/62	100H	12.85	12.88- 04
* Kallur	Susanna	SWE	16.2.81	170/61	100	11.42	11.55- 04
					100H	12.65	12.67- 04
^ Kálovics	Anikó	HUN	13.5.77	175/60	5000	15:21.23	15:10.21- 04
					HMar	71:01	69:16- 02
Kanales	Yelena	RUS	7.2.76	158/48	1500	4:02.66	4:09.94- 04
					1M	4:28.29	4:37.01- 04
					3000	8:56.83i	
Kand	Kaie	EST	31.3.84	175/63	Hep	5753	5143- 03
Kanishkina	Olga	RUS	19.1.85	161/45	20kW	1:29:25	
Kano	Yuri	JPN	27.10.78	152/39	5000	15:21.70	15:41.83- 04
					10000	32:10.24	31:53.07- 04
					HMar	71:38	70:28- 03
Käppi	Salla	FIN	22.5.80	176/64	Hep	5653	5801w- 01, 5766- 02
Kappler	Bianca	GER	8.8.77	180/62	LJ	6.66, 6.69w	6.71- 04
Karapetrova	Rumyana	BUL	7.2.82	171/74	JT	60.69	59.72- 04
Karas	Olga	RUS	9.7.82	174/66	Hep	5736	5745- 01
* Karastamáti	Maria	GRE	10.12.84	172/63	100	11.03	11.48- 04

	Name		Nat	Born	Ht/Wt	Event	2005 Mark	Pre-2005 Best
	Kari	Monia	TUN	14.4.71	172/72	DT	56.90	61.74- 96
	Karnatsevich	Galina	BLR	2.11.69		Mar	2:27:14	2:35:40- 98
	Kárníková	Jana	CZE	14.2.81	187/85	SP	16.81	16.40- 04
	Kasitskaya	Aleksandra	RUS	15.3.85		Hep	5657	5544- 04
*	Kaspárková	Sárka	CZE	20.5.71	187/68	TJ	14.34i, 13.86	15.20- 97
	Kasprzak	Róza	POL	9.4.82	174/60	PV	4.30	4.20- 03
	Kassambara	Aurore	FRA	26.10.79	169/58	400H	56.43	58.60- 04
*	Kastor	Deena	USA	14.2.73	163/48	10000	31:45.08	30:50.32- 02
						HMar	67:53	70:08- 01
						Mar	2:21:25	2:21:16- 03
	Kaur	Harwant	IND	5.7.80	165/70	DT	62.89	63.05- 04
	Kaur	Manjeet	IND	4.4.82	167/59	400	51.50	51.05- 04
	Kawasaki	Mayumi	JPN	10.5.80	167/52	20kW	1:31:51	1:31:19- 04
	Kazantseva	Inna	RUS	19.1.85		LJ	6.52	6.68- 04
*	Keil	Susanne	GER	18.5.78	172/69	HT	72.74	71.93- 03
	Keizer	Jolanda	NED	5.4.85	183/67	Hep	5760	5366- 04
	Keller	Katja	GER	9.8.80	175/62	Hep	6130	6082- 01
	Kelo	Niina	FIN	26.3.80	178/69	Hep	5808	5786- 03
	Kemasuode	Gloria	NGR	30.12.79	164/62	100	11.44, 11.31w	11.21- 02, 11.18w- 03
*	Kesselschläger	Sonja	GER	20.1.78	178/66	Hep	6221	6287- 04
	Khabarova	Irina	RUS	18.3.66	170/65	100	11.31	11.32, 11.19w- 00
						200	22.69	22.34- 04
	Khalandyreva	Olga	RUS	13.11.81	173/60	100	11.31	11.29- 04
	Khalid	Norasheela Mohd	MAS	27.9.79	166/54	400H	56.39	56.63- 04
*	Khanafayeva	Gulfiya	RUS	12.6.82	170/73	HT	70.76	72.71- 04
	Khmelnitskaya	Larisa	BLR	23.9.71	173/60	20kW	1:33:58	1:28:56- 00
*	Khodadin	Linda	FRA	24.12.76	169/51	100H	12.66	12.67- 01
*	Khoroneko	Natalya	BLR	25.5.82	180/81	SP	19.78	20.04- 04
	Khoroshkikh	Yekaterina	RUS	21.1.83	172/73	HT	73.08	68.44- 04
	Khristova	Magdalena	BUL	25.2.77	165/55	100	11.39	11.54- 02
	Kidane	Etalemahu	ETH	14.2.83	156/45	5000	15:16.26	15:04.34- 04
*	Kidane	Werknesh	ETH	21.11.81	158/42	3000	8:36.39	8:39.51- 03
						5000	15:01.6+	14:33.04- 03
						10000	30:19.39	30:07.15- 03
						HMar	68:09 dh	-0-
	Kidd	Ashlee	USA	26.7.85	179/67	400	51.87	51.76- 04
	Kigen	Genoveva	KEN	.80		3kSt	10:06.0A	
						HMar	70:22	
	Kilpeläinen	Natalia	FIN	19.7.70	168/57	LJ	6.58	6.49- 03, 6.50w- 01
						TJ	13.86	14.18- 03
	Kim Mi-jung		KOR	10.6.79	165/56	20kW	1:31:39	1:33:03- 03
	Kimuria	Emily	KEN	10.6.75		Mar	2:28:42	2:28:18- 03
	Kimutai	Hellen	KEN	28.12.77		HMar	69:52+	69:59- 00
						Mar	2:26:14	2:25:42- 03
	Kimwei	Evelyne	KEN-J	25.8.87	150/47	5000	15:14.15	15:48.00- 04
						10000	31:42.51	
						HMar	70:47	
	Kindelán	Yahyma	CUB	25.9.82	165/48	TJ	13.87	14.06- 04
	King	Cassie	USA	28.3.84	175/58	3kSt	10:08.70	
*	Kiplagat	Lornah	NED	20.3.74	166/49	5000	15:10.26	14:51.95mx- 02, 14:56.43- 03
						HMar	70:19	66:34- 01
						Mar	2:27:36	2:22:22- 03
	Kiprop	Nancy	KEN	7.7.79		3kSt	10:02.41	
	Kiptoo	Caroline	KEN	.76		HMar	70:25	73:05- 04
*	Kiptum	Jeruto	KEN	12.12.81	166/50	3kSt	9:26.95	
*	Kirkland	Anjanette	USA	24.2.74	172/66	100H	12.57	12.42- 01
	Kiryanova	Anastasiya	RUS	26.7.82		PV	4.40	4.20- 01
	Kiryashova	Aleksandra	RUS	21.8.85	162/54	PV	4.30i, 4.30	4.25i, 4.20- 04
	Kiselyova	Yelena	RUS	24.3.79		HT	63.30	61.12- 02
	Kivelídou	Anastasia	GRE	23.9.79	168/58	Hep	5780	5625- 02
	Kivimyagi	Tatyana	RUS	23.6.84	185/64	HJ	1.98	1.98- 04
	Kizaki	Ryoko	JPN	21.6.85	156/45	HMar	71:43	
	Klaas	Kathrin	GER	8.2.84	168/72	HT	70.91	68.01- 04
	Klein	Tina	GER	24.4.83	175/57	100H	12.97	13.20- 02
*	Kleinert	Nadine	GER	20.10.75	190/90	SP	20.06	19.86- 01
	Klimesová	Jarmila	CZE	9.2.81	172/78	JT	61.08	62.00- 04
	Klimina	Viktoriya	RUS	1.3.76	166/55	10000	31:56.07	33:07.69- 00
	Klimkovich	Svetlana	BLR	26.8.80		800	2:02.01	2:04.52- 03
						1500	4:11.42	4:18.91- 04
	Klocová	Lucia	SVK	20.11.83	176/53	800	2:00.64	2:00.60- 03
*	Klose	Kirsten	GER	21.1.77	172/75	HT	65.04	69.28- 00

	Name		Nat	Born	Ht/Wt	Event	2005Mark	Pre-2005 Best
*	Klüft	Carolina	SWE	2.2.83	178/64	200	23.28	22.98- 03
						100H	13.15	13.18- 03
						HJ	1.94	1.94- 03
						LJ	6.87, 6.92w	6.97- 04
						Hep	6887	7001- 03
	Kluge	Kathleen	GER	17.11.81	170/100	SP	16.58	17.64- 03
	Klyuka	Svetlana	RUS	27.12.78	172/60	800	1:57.35	1:58.47- 03
	Knight	Bianca	USA-Y	2.1.89	163/60	100	11.38	11.56- 04
	Knight	Natalie	USA-J	24.10.86		200	23.18, 23.12w	23.91- 02
	Knoetze	Marli	RSA-J	2.10.87		SP	17.14	15.67- 04
	Kobayashi	Yuriko	JPN-Y	12.12.88	163/48	3000	8:52.33	9:38.45- 03
	Kochetova	Anastasiya	RUS	18.9.83		400	51.54	54.16- 03
	Koklóni	Yeoryia	GRE	7.5.81	165/55	100	11.33	11.33- 03
	Kolarova	Teodora	BUL	29.5.81		800	2:01.14	2:07.03- 04
	Kolchanova	Lyudmila	RUS	1.10.79		LJ	6.79	6.54- 04
*	Kolkkala	Taina	FIN	24.10.76	173/74	JT	59.69	64.06- 00, 66.00#- 95
	Kolotzei	Jessica	GER	6.4.85	186/86	DT	56.16	49.78- 04
	Komrsková	Lucie	CZE	24.10.77	165/56	LJ	6.54w	6.57- 04, 6.64w- 01
	Kondratyeva	Yekaterina	RUS	8.4.82	160/48	100	11.49, 11.41w	11.40- 04
						200	22.68	22.64- 04
*	Konevtsova	Yelena	RUS	11.9.81	183/95	HT	67.51	73.68- 04
	Konishi	Sachiko	JPN	4.2.82	154/43	20kW	1:32:21	1:36:36- 04
	Kopaneva	Aleksandra	RU	5.12.80		SP	16.72i	17.12- 02
	Koralewska	Izabela	POL	29.1.85	172/85	DT	56.66	50.12- 03
	Korell	Hanna	FIN	16.3.79	164/58	100H	13.13	13.13- 04
	Koritskaya	Diana	RUS	22.2.75	170/65	Hep	5994w, 5981	6401- 00
*	Koroteyeva	Maria	RUS	10.11.81	175/63	100H	12.73	12.60- 04
	Korotkova	Olesya	RUS	20.11.83		DT	56.23	53.00- 04
	Korotkova	Tatyana	RUS	24.4.80	165/57	20kW	1:30:03	1:27:35- 04
	Korotkova	Yevdokiya	RUS	28.2.79	166/54	20kW	1:31:19	1:33:24- 04
	Korpela	Merja	FIN	15.5.81	170/75	HT	67.33	66.41- 04
	Korsak	Yekaterina	UKR	26.12.85	183/88	DT	58.65	56.04- 04
	Korsunova	Olga	RUS	20.5.81	169/60	100H	13.30	13.36-02
	Kortchaguina	Lioudmila	CAN	26.7.71		Mar	2:30:03	2:29:53- 03
	Kosgei	Mercy Chelimo	KEN-Y	10.10.89		3kSt	10:09.78	
*	Kosgei	Selina	KEN	16.11.76	162/58	HMar	70:03	70:32- 04
						Mar	2:25:30	2:24:32- 04
	Kostetskaya	Yekaterina	RUS-J	31.12.87	168/59	400H	55.89	55.55- 04
	Kosuda	Agata	POL	1.8.84	172/61	TJ	13.70	13.17- 03
*	Kotlyarova	Olga	RUS	12.4.76	180/65	400	52.00	49.77- 04
						800	1:57.55	1:57.96- 04
	Kotorida	Takako	JPN	2.4.77	169/50	5000	15:29.82	15:15.16- 03
						HMar	69:34	68:45- 03
	Kotova	Natalya	RUS	13.5.83		Hep	5718	5475- 04
*	Kotova	Tatyana	RUS	11.12.76	182/59	LJ	6.96, 7.20w	7.42- 02
	Koutsioumári	Panayióta	GRE	23.8.81		LJ	6.50	6.61- 04
	Kovalainen	Maija	FIN	23.8.81	177/63	Hep	5656	5512- 03
	Kovalenko	Irina	UKR-J	12.6.86	183/60	HJ	1.92i, 1.90	1.95i- 03, 1.93- 04
	Kovpotina	Olga	RUS	10.1.68	172/50	Mar	2:31:54dh	2:27:37- 01
	Kowalska	Katarzyna	POL	7.4.85	177/57	3kSt	9:54.17	10:24.95- 04
	Kozak	Anna	BLR	22.6.74	172/56	400	51.36	50.94- 96
	Kozarenoka	Inga	LAT	16.3.82	174/70	JT	59.97	58.10- 04
	Kozhemyakina	Irina	UKR	16.6.80	168/60	100	11.42	11.39- 04
	Kozlova	Tatyana	RUS	2.9.83	163/57	20kW	1:27:30	1:28:59- 04
	Krakoviak	Irina	LTU	16.11.77	167/53	800	2:01.03	2:01.04- 98
						1500	4:03.19	4:07.99- 00
*	Krasnomovets	Olesya	RUS	8.7.79	171/60	200	23.09	23.81- 04
						400	50.77	50.19- 04
*	Krasovska	Yelena	UKR	17.8.76	176/65	100H	12.75	12.45- 04
	Krasucki	Franciela	BRA-Y	26.4.88		100	11.39	11.48- 04
	Kravtsova	Olga	BLR	25.6.81	165/48	1500	4:05.76	4:20.18- 04
						3000	8:53.9+	9:13.70- 05
						5000	14:47.75	15:18.92- 04
	Kreiner	Kim	USA	26.7.77	175/76	JT	59.24	60.86- 83
*	Krivelyova	Svetlana	RUS	13.6.69	184/94	SP	20.24	21.06- 92
	Krivobok	Tatyana	UKR	17.1.72	164/50	1500	4:06.37	4:06.31- 01
	Kron	Christina	GER	3.4.81	173/55	400H	56.10	57.29- 04
*	Krueger-Billett	Brooke	AUS	9.7.80	180/125	HT	68.25	68.78- 04
	Kruglova	Larisa	RUS	27.10.72	166/65	100	11.33	11.23- 04
	Kryazheva	Anna	RUS	17.7.84	173/62	Hep	5916	5911w- 04, 5769- 03
	Ksok	Anna	POL	29.9.83	181/68	HJ	1.88i, 1.88	1.94- 02

Name		Nat	Born	Ht/Wt	Event	2005 Mark	Pre-2005 Best
Kubokura	Satomi	JPN	27.4.82	161/52	400H	56.58	56.73- 04
Kucherenko	Olga	RUS	14.2.85		LJ	6.56i	6.30- 04
Kuehl	Kristin	USA	30.7.70	183/89	DT	60.30	65.34- 00
Kühnert	Floé	GER	6.3.84	174/58	PV	4.30	4.41- 02
^ Kumbernuss	Astrid	GER	5.2.70	186/90	SP	19.16	21.22- 95
Kuncová	Barbora	CZE	26.4.82	170/53	3kSt	10:07.31	10:12.10- 03
Kuntsevich	Darya	RUS	2.11.85		HJ	1.88i	1.82- 04
Kuntsevich	Yekaterina	RUS	13.7.84		HJ	1.90i	
Kupriyanova (Starovoytova)	Lyudmila	BLR	8.4.74		DT	60.17	63.55- 01
* Kuptsova	Marina	RUS	22.12.81	185/68	HJ	1.92	2.03i- 02, 2.02- 03
Kurrat	Manuela	GER	25.12.81	178/60	Hep	5714	5512- 98
Kushch	Natalya	UKR	5.3.83	170/56	PV	4.40i, 4.40	4.50- 04
Kutkina	Natalya	RUS	4.2.77		800	2:01.48	2:02.87- 04
* Kuzenkova	Olga	RUS	4.10.70	176/76	HT	75.10	75.68- 00
Kwambai	Irene	KEN	25.10.78	170/52	3000	8:54.49	8:46.38- 03
					5000	14:56.76	15:05.04- 04
					10000	30:55.67	31:57.54- 04
Kychanova	Olga	RUS	14.7.75	182/56	HJ	1.95	1.95- 96
La Mantia	Simona	ITA	14.4.83	177/65	LJ	6.48	6.32, 6.39w- 04
					TJ	14.69	14.49, 14.71w- 04
Lagat Chebet	Nancy	KEN	22.8.81	153/48	800	2:02.51	2:01.26- 00
					1500	4:02.31	4:04.76- 04
Laláková	Barbora	CZE	2.5.81	178/58	HJ	1.90i, 1.90	1.94i, 1.91- 02
* Lalova	Ivet	BUL	18.5.84	168/56	100	11.03	10.77- 04
					200	22.76	22.51, 22.36w- 04
Lamalle	Adrianna	FRA	27.9.82	170/58	100H	12.85	13.08- 00, 12.90w- 01
Lamera	Raffaella	ITA	13.4.83	175/56	HJ	1.89	1.88i, 1.86- 02
* Lammert	Petra	GER	3.3.84	182/85	SP	19.81	17.16- 04
^ Langerholc	Brigita	SLO	23.7.76	170/56	800	2:01.41	1:58.51- 00
Langhirt	Simone	GER	19.1.84	172/55	PV	4.20	4.10- 04
Lanouar	Fatima	TUN	14.3.78	165/52	1500	4:10.32	4:06.91- 00
Laporte	Céline	SEY	7.12.84		Hep	5684	5545- 04
Lapsley	Andriane	USA	18.12.83	175/63	100	11.36	11.65- 04
					200	23,47, 23.23w	23.90w- 04
Lavshuk	Natalya	RUS	20.2.80	172/59	800	1:58.72	1:57.45- 04
^ Lawrence	Tayna	JAM	17.9.75	163/52	100	11.23	10.93- 02
Lawyer-Thomas	Tracy	USA	28.8.77	178/67	Hep	5910	5995w, 5844- 00
Láznicková	Diana	SVK	14.8.74	178/62	HJ	1.92i, 1.87	1.90i- 04, 1.87- 01
Leach	Nicole	USA-J	18.7.87	170/57	400H	57.25	57.56- 04
Leatherman	Jenny	USA	26.9.83		HT	63.94	58.81- 04
* Lebedeva	Tatyana	RUS	21.7.76	171/61	LJ	6.70	7.33- 04
					TJ	15.11	15.36i, 15.34- 04
LeBlanc	Ranysha	USA	11.1.83	165/55	100H	13.23w	13.09- 03, 12.92w- 04
Lebusova	Natalya	RUS	4.4.78		LJ	6.78	6.46- 04
* Lee	Muna	USA	30.10.81	173/50	100	11.09, 10.99w	11.04, 10.97w- 03
					200	22.46	22.36, 22.22w- 04
Lee	Suzette	JAM	6.3.75	180/70	TJ	14.16, 14.34Aw	14.25i-97,14.12-04,14.26w- 03
Lee Eun-jung		KOR	21.4.81	167/50	HMar	71:15	74:42- 03
Lee Mi-young		KOR	19.8.79	174/81	SP	17.62	17.60- 03
Lee Myung-sun		KOR	12.2.76	168/89	SP	17.05	19.36- 00
Lee Young-sun		KOR	21.2.74	165/65	JT	55.98	58.87- 02, 63.32#- 92
* Leghzaoui	Asmae	MAR	30.8.76	155/40	5000	15:23.30	14:48.31- 00
Legnante	Assunta	ITA	14.5.78	187/118	SP	18.80	19.20i- 02, 18.92- 04
Leibak	Kaire	EST-Y	21.5.88	177/58	TJ	13.74	12.86- 04
Leks	Viktoria	EST-J	28.9.87		HJ	1.87	
Lenskiy	Irina	ISR	12.6.71	176/57	100H	13.22	12.80- 02
Leontyuk	Yuliya	BLR	31.1.84	180/82	SP	17.91	17.44- 03
Leveau-Agricole	Lindy	SEY	14.11.79	172/65	JT	57.86	55.83- 02
Levenkova	Olga	RUS	11.1.84	175/63	Hep	5973	5919- 04
Levina	Tatyana	RUS	28.2.77	173/60	200	23.40, 23.27i	22.69- 04
					400	51.66	50.98- 04
^ Levorato	Manuela	ITA	16.3.77	180/66	100	11.33	11.14- 01, 11.13w- 00
					200	23.01	22.60- 99
Lewandowska	Iwona	POL	19.2.85	158/47	3kSt	10:12.13	10:29.67- 04
Li Cui		CHN-J	18.1.87		20kW	1:32:20	1:36:45- 03
Li Fengfeng		CHN	9.1.79	175/100	SP	18.19	18.96- 03
Li Li		CHN-J	24.2.87		SP	17.49	16.73- 04
Li Ling		CHN	7.2.85	179/85	SP	18.68	17.34- 04
* Li Meiju		CHN	23.1.81	173/85	SP	19.05	18.96- 03
Li Mingli		CHN-J	23.1.87		TJ	13.85	13.64- 04

Name		Nat	Born	Ht/Wt	Event	2005Mark	Pre-2005 Best
Li Qiumei		CHN	26.9.74	180/80	DT	64.89	67.50- 04
Li Shuang		CHN	4.1.85	160/46	20kW	1:34:11	1:38:54- 04
Li Yanfeng		CHN	15.5.79	179/85	DT	61.61	64.34- 04
Li Yanhong		CHN	2.6.84		20kW	1:33:50	1:35:53- 03
Liang Dan		CHN-Y	21.6.88	177/60	PV	4.20i	4.00- 04
Liang Lili		CHN	16.11.83	170/75	JT	57.23	61.49- 02, 61.81#- 98
Liao Xiaoyan		CHN-J	8.1.87	175/65	HT	65.53	65.13- 03
Liburd	Tanika	SKN	20.5.82		LJ	6.56, 6.62w	6.22- 04
Liimask	Mirjam	EST	25.10.83	174/61	100H	12.93	13.21- 04
Líka	Voisávva	GRE	27.6.70	168/70	JT	57.88	62.89- 04
Lima de Oliveira	Gisele	BRA	1.8.80		TJ	13.95A, 13.75, 13.86w	13.82A- 04, 13.56- 03
Limika	Irene	KEN	28.8.79		3kSt	9:56.88	9:39.51- 01
Lin Baohua		CHN	12.6.83	163/48	TJ	13.85	14.11- 04
Lin Qingping		CHN-J	3.5.86	180/82	DT	56.10	53.60- 04
Lin Xiaojing		CHN-J	8.1.86		DT	57.04	56.89- 02
Lincoln	Melinda	USA	20.1.77		SP	17.10	17.09- 04
					DT	57.46	55.60- 04
Linnen	Amy	USA	15.7.82	178/64	PV	4.30i, 4.30	4.53i- 02, 4.40- 03
Lise	Betty	FRA	5.9.72	188/69	TJ	13.98	14.50- 97
Lisnichenko	Mariya	RUS	27.12.80	176/63	200	23.18	23.22- 04
					400	50.85	50.83- 04
Listár	Nikolett	HUN	6.12.83	172/54	200	23.19	23.66- 03
Liu Chunhua		CHN-J	1.10.86		JT	56.27	58.03- 03
Liu Feifei		CHN-J	16.9.86	160/48	20kW	1:32:06	1:33:02- 04
Liu Haili		CHN	24.12.84		Hep	6132	5771- 04
Liu Hong		CHN-J	12.5.87	159/46	20kW	1:29:39	1:35:04- 04
Liu Huahua		CHN	20.9.84		LJ	6.63	6.30- 02
Liu Jing		CHN	8.8.77		100H	12.96	12.76- 97
Liu Linpeng		CHN-J	22.2.87		DT	58.88	56.06- 04
Liu Qing		CHN-J	28.4.86	163/53	800	1:59.74	2:02.25- 03
					1500	4:04.00	4:10.51- 04
Liu Xiaoyan		CHN	4.9.85	161/45	20kW	1:30:49	1:32:29- 04
Liu Yanan		CHN-J	18.1.87		TJ	13.62	13.39- 04
Liu Yingfan		CHN-J	9.2.87		SP	17.33	18.70- 04
Liu Yinghui		CHN	29.6.79	180/85	HT	72.51	69.05- 03
Lloyd	Shereefa	JAM	2.9.82	164/53	400	51.39	54.92- 04
Lodree	Ashley	USA	22.10.85	167/54	100H	13.17	13.41- 04
Logsch	Romy	GER	5.2.82	182/87	DT	57.30	58.44- 04
Longfors	Rachelle	USA	6.6.83		DT	57.03	57.48- 04
Lopes	Priscilla	CAN	26.8.82	168/67	100H	12.82	12.64- 04
* López	Aliuska	ESP	29.8.69	169/53	100H	13.15, 13.09w	12.67- 96
Lõpez	Cristina	ESP	19.9.82	169/51	20kW	1:30:08	1:49:01- 01
Louami	Carima	FRA	12.5.79	165/50	100	11.42	11.46, 11.37w- 04
Loughnane	Olive	IRL	14.1.76	160/49	20kW	1:32:28	1:30:29- 03
Lu Ying		CHN	30.10.85	174/115	SP	16.89	16.25- 03
Lucas	Josanne	TRI	14.5.84	170/55	400H	55.59	56.96- 04
Lukaszewska	Beata	POL	19.2.80	174/63	Hep	5682	5551- 04
Lyakhovich	Tatyana	UKR	20.5.79	173/78	JT	58.43	63.07- 04
Lyne	Rebecca	GBR	4.7.82	173/52	800	2:01.98	2:01.26- 04
* Lysenko	Tatyana	RUS	9.10.83	180/85	HT	77.06	71.54- 04
Ma Bei		CHN	28.8.84	185/58	HJ	1.88	1.84- 04
Ma Ning		CHN	4.11.83	173/78	JT	61.95	62.38- 03
Ma Shuli		CHN	20.1.78	178/75	DT	62.50	62.21- 01
Ma Xuejun		CHN	26.3.85	185/90	DT	61.87	60.20- 03
* MacFarlane	Donna	AUS	18.6.77	176/57	3kSt	9:51.60	10:31.10- 00
Machado	Maiía Paula	BRA	22.1.81	167/62	100H	12.89	12.86- 04
^ Macharia	Faith	KEN	9.2.76	165/55	800	2:02.08	1:58.34- 01
Machida	Yuko	JPN	11.8.80	158/44	HMar	71:03	73:29- 04
Machkanova	Yelena	RUS	24.1.81		DT	55.93	59.40- 04
Mächtig	Julia	GER-J	1.1.86	187/75	Hep	5830	5679- 04
Madejczyk	Barbara	POL	30.9.76	179/78	JT	63.03	61.36- 04
* Madison	Tianna	USA	30.8.85	168/60	100	11.41	11.50, 11.35w- 04
					LJ	6.89, 6.92w	6.60- 04
Maduaka	Joice	GBR	30.9.73	172/65	100	11.41, 11.33w	11.24- 99
					200	23.27w	22.83- 99
Maher	Emily	IRL	2.5.81	172/56	100	11.40w	11.58- 00
Makarevich	Svetlana	BLR-J	5.3.86		PV	4.20	4.11- 04
Makarova	Yelena	RUS	21.12.81		JT	55.41	55.35- 02
Malheiro	Dina	POR	11.10.83		3kSt	10:06.45	
Malíková	Zuzana	SVK	2.8.83	175/50	20kW	1:32:48	1:33:02- 04

Name		Nat	Born	Ht/Wt	Event	2005 Mark	Pre-2005 Best
Mallory	Beth	USA	31.5.84		DT	59.35	58.32- 04
					HT	63.36	62.48- 04
Malone	Sarah	USA	14.9.81	173/77	JT	56.94	54.61- 02
Manfrédi	Laurence	FRA	20.5.74	175/92	SP	17.67	18.69i, 18.68- 00
Mang	Véronique	FRA	15.12.84	170/63	100	11.34	11.24- 04
* Manjani	Miréla	GRE	21.12.76	165/64	JT	59.22	67.51- 00
Manome	Aya	JPN	30.8.82	160/46	10000	32:28.02	
Mara	Valeriya	UKR	22.2.83	163/50	3kSt	9:56.74	9:57.35- 04
Marin	Elisabetta	ITA	5.11.77	177/75	JT	56.14	61.77- 04
Márkou	Dímitra	GRE	28.7.80	178/58	TJ	13.83i, 13.71	14.05- 00
Marks	Shani	USA	24.8.80		TJ	13.65i	13.79- 03
Marshall	Shameka	USA	9.9.83		100H	13.30	13.63- 04
					LJ	6.57	6.32- 04
Marten	Kristin	GER	23.5.83	184/90	SP	17.68	17.87- 04
Martin	Aubrey	USA	16.1.84		SP	17.01	16.90- 04
Martin	Julie	FRA	28.10.79	175/57	Hep	5865w, 5775	5876- 04
Martín	Diana	ESP	1.4.81	151/50	3kSt	10:07.11	10:33.47- 03
Martincová	Lucie	CZE	4.1.82	170/64	100H	13.07	13.08- 04
Martínez	Aymeé	CUB-Y	17.11.88	165/55	200	22.99	23.60- 04
					400	52.04	53.63- 04
* Martinez	Magdelin	ITA	10.2.76	178/63	TJ	14.69	15.03, 15.24Aw- 04
* Martínez	Mayte	ESP	17.5.76	168/56	800	1:59.40	1:58.29- 02
					1500	4:05.05	
Martínez	Yarianna	CUB	20.9.84	168/56	TJ	14.18	14.10- 04
Martins	Maria	FRA	1.4.74	162/53	1500	4:05.79	4:04.55- 03
					3000	8:51.76i	8:56.82i- 04, 9:12.80- 03
Martynova	Yekaterina	RUS-J	12.6.86		800	2:02.46	2:05.57- 04
Marx	Claudia	GER	16.9.78	172/61	400	52.07, 51.95i	51.41- 01
					400H	55.59	0
* Masai	Edith	KEN	4.4.67	168/55	3000	8:31.27	8:23.23- 02
					5000	14:37.20	14:42.64- 04
					10000	30:30.26	0
					HMar	68:19 dh	67:53- 01
					Mar	2:27:06	-0-
Masehla	Tebogo	RSA	6.10.79		3kSt	10:06.05	10:15.10- 04
Maskulinski	Tiffany	USA-J	26.9.86		PV	4.27	4.11- 04
Matejková	Alice	ESP	11.1.69	180/74	DT	56.59	62.66- 97
^ Mathes	Simone	GER	13.3.75	171/85	HT	66.75	67.97- 04
Matoshko	Yelena	BLR	23.6.82		HT	66.84	65.88- 04
Matsuoka	Noriko	JPN	2.5.79	156/41	10000	32:11.40	31:50.53- 00
Maurer	Elisabeth	AUT	10.2.83	169/54	100H	13.24	13.31- 02
Maury	Margaret	FRA	15.5.74	165/49	5000	14:59.07	14:43.90- 04
					10000	32:23.87	32:01.01- 04
Mavrodieva	Radoslava	BUL-J	13.3.87		SP	16.93i	17.12- 04
^ May	Fiona	ITA	12.12.69	181/60	LJ	6.64	7.11- 98, 7.23Aw- 95
Maydanova	Marina	UKR	22.8.82	172/69	200	22.97	22.70- 03
Mayr	Andrea	AUT	15.10.79	174/53	3kSt	9:56.78	10:16.20- 04
^ Mayr-Krifka	Karin	AUT	4.6.71	179/69	200	22.94i	22.70i, 22.70- 02
Mballa Eloundou	Sylvie	CMR	21.4.77	175/62	100	11.13	11.31- 03
* Mbango	Françoise	CMR	14.4.76	172/63	TJ	14.07	15.30- 04
McBride	LaToya	USA	15.12.82	173/62	Hep	5654	5189- 04
McCambridge	Maria	IRL	10.7.75	174/55	1500	4:11.73	4:23.21- 03
					3000	8:50.40	8:56.7, 8:56.48i- 04
McCann	Stephanie	CAN	22.4.77	171/59	PV	4.20	4.41- 03
McClain	Delisa	USA	24.9.81		HT	64.69	60.06- 04
* McConnell	Lee	GBR	9.10.78	178/64	200	23.22	23.39mx- 04, 23.66- 01
					400	51.15	50.82- 02
					400H	56.06	0
McCorory	Francena	USA-Y	20.10.88	172/60	200	23.22	24.25- 04
McCray	Yolanda	USA	11.9.76	168/60	100H	13.04	12.78, 12.77w- 99
^ McDonald	Beverly	JAM	15.2.70	169/59	100	11.21A, 11.30	10.99- 98
					200	22.98	22.22- 99
McGettigan	Roisín	IRL	23.8.80	170/55	1M	4:32.35i	
					3kSt	9:46.12	9:45.60- 04
McGregor	Katie	USA	2.9.77	173/52	5000	15:23.24	15:27.20- 04
					10000	31:21.20	31:51.26- 04
McIntosh	Raasin	USA	29.4.82	170/61	400H	56.99	54.16- 04
McKee	Angela	NZL	11.12.74		HJ	1.88	1.85- 04
McKinney	Akiba	USA	9.3.79	160/55	LJ	6.59, 6.61w	6.57- 04
McKoy	Olivia	JAM	1.12.73	165/73	JT	61.10	58.29- 00
McLain	Erica	USA-J	24.1.86	170/62	TJ	14.01	13.44- 04

Name		Nat	Born	Ht/Wt	Event	2005Mark	Pre-2005 Best
McLaughlin	Anneisha	JAM-J	6.1.86	167/59	200	23.00	22.94- 02
McLellan	Sally	AUS-J	19.9.86	166/66	100	11.41, 11.38w	11.40- 04
					100H	13.01	13.30- 04
McPherson	Inika	USA-J	29.9.86		HJ	1.88	1.83- 02
McWilliams	Tiffany	USA	20.10.82	178/58	1500	4:10.61	4:06.75- 03
Meadows	Jenny	GBR	17.4.81	152/47	800	2:02.05	2:03.35i, 2:04.46- 02
Melink	Teja	SLO	23.3.80	168/57	PV	4.20i, 4.20	4.30- 04
* Melinte	Mihaela	ROM	27.3.75	174/92	HT	71.95	76.07- 99
* Melkamu	Meselech	ETH	19.4.85	158/47	3000	8:34.73	8:51.20- 03
					5000	14:38.97	15:00.02- 04
Melnichenko	Zhanna	UKR	23.4.83	178/58	Hep	5809	5720- 04
Melnikova	Irina	RUS	14.5.75	169/57	LJ	6.64i, 6.57	6.76- 03
Mendía	Marta	ESP	18.5.75	172/58	HJ	1.95i, 1.94	1.96i- 04, 1.95- 03
^ Mendoza	Graciela	MEX	23.3.63	156/48	20kW	1:33:04	1:30:03- 99
* Menéndez	Osleidys	CUB	14.11.79	178/80	JT	71.70	71.54- 01
Menkova	Oksana	BLR	28.3.82	183/79	HT	70.15	70.23- 04
Menlove	Amy	USA	23.7.85	168/57	LJ	6.67i, 6.41, 6.52Aw	6.44- 04
Menshchikova	Mariya	RUS	26.2.83		400H	56.69	56.56- 04
Mérah-Benida	Nouria	ALG	19.10.70	162/52	1500	4:11.58	3:59.12- 00
Messner	Carrie	USA	7.6.77	160/52	3kSt	9:39.68	9:49.40- 04
Metivier	Renee	USA	25.12.81	160/50	5000	15:15.78	15:49.08- 04
Metlevskaya	Tatyana	BLR	14.9.84	171/58	20kW	1:32:34	1:35:02- 04
Metzinger	Ebby	USA	16.6.79		PV	4.27	4.30- 04
Mickle	Kimberley	AUS	28.12.84	168/69	JT	58.16	52.77- 02
Migunova	Yelena	RUS	4.1.84	173/65	400	50.93	53.47- 01
* Mikhalchenko	Irina	UKR	20.1.72	179/60	HJ	1.97	2.01- 04
Mikkonen	Hanna	FIN	15.1.81	171/56	HJ	1.92	1.90- 03
Militaru	Alina	ROM	10.4.82	170/53	LJ	6.63	6.73- 04
Miller	Gi-Gi	USA	12.1.79	165/55	100H	13.12, 13.03w	13.12, 13.00A- 04, 13.11w- 01
					Hep	6192	6063- 04
Mills	Candice	USA	13.11.84		LJ	6.51w	6.19- 04
Mills	TaNisha	USA	2.11.74	172/62	400H	55.57	55.82A, 55.94- 04
Milusauskaite	Sonata	LTU	31.8.73	163/53	20kW	1:32:53	1:30:53- 03
^ Misyulya	Natalya	BLR	16.4.66	157/47	20kW	1:31:45	1:28:24- 00
Mitchell	Victoria	AUS	25.4.82	164/48	3kSt	9:47.54	10:09.53- 02
Miyai	Hitomi	JPN	18.3.85	162/43	5000	15:25.52	15:40.94- 04
					10000	31:37.24	-
					HMar	70:54	70:46- 04
Miyauchi	Hiroko	JPN	19.6.83	153/41	10000	32:22.12	32:53.04- 03
					HMar	71:21	71:26- 04
Miyauchi	Yoko	JPN	19.6.83	153/41	10000	32:18.05	32:55.92- 04
					HMar	70:15	71:27- 04
* Mockenhaupt	Sabrina	GER	6.12.80	156/46	3000	8:46.38	8:44.65- 03
					5000	15:09.39	15:03.47- 04
					10000	31:21.28	31:23.35- 04
Molchanova	Viktoriya	UKR	26.5.82	171/55	LJ	6.81i, 6.61	6.60-03
Möldner	Antje	GER	13.6.84	174/55	1500	4:08.81	4:14.27- 04
* Moldovan	Felicia	ROM	29.9.67	169/70	JT	61.65	63.89- 02, 69.26#- 96
Molitor	Katharina	GER	8.11.83	182/76	JT	57.01	50.04- 04
^ Molnár	Krisztina	HUN	8.4.76	168/51	PV	4.45	4.53- 02
Momanyi	Grace	KEN	3.3.82		HMar	70:20	74:17- 04
Mombi	Julia	KEN	25.1.85	164/46	5000	15:25.21	15:17.19- 04
					10000	31:42.67	31:39.89- 04
^ Montalvo	Niurka	ESP	4.6.68	172/57	LJ	6.72A, 6.55, 6.87w	7.06- 99
* Montaner	Concepción	ESP	14.1.81	170/56	LJ	6.92	6.89- 02
* Montebrun	Manuèla	FRA	13.11.79	175/92	HT	74.66	74.50, 75.20dh- 03
Monteiro	Inês	POR	18.5.80	159/46	3kSt	9:39.20	
Monterola	Keisa	VEN-Y	26.2.88		PV	4.30	3.90- 04
Moore	Connie	USA	29.8.81	165/63	100	11.45, 11.36w	11.21- 03
					200	23.27	22.63- 03, 22.60i, 22.45w- 04
Moore	LaShauntea	USA	31.7.83	170/56	100	11.39, 11.25w	11.26- 04
					200	22.93	22.63, 22.37w- 04
Moore	Wiande	USA	24.11.83		400	52.22	53.46- 04
Morandais	Sylvanie	FRA	14.7.79	162/50	400H	56.22	55.49- 01
Morató	Rosa	ESP	19.6.79	158/46	3kSt	9:54.20	9:51.08- 04
Mørch	Louise	DEN	2.5.82	165/53	3kSt	10:04.65	10:22.04- 04
* Moreno	Yipsi	CUB	19.11.80	168/70	HT	74.95	75.18- 04
Morgan	Monique	JAM	10.10.85		100H	13.16	13.59- 04
* Morrison-Howard	Melissa	USA	9.7.71	163/52	100H	12.86	12.53- 98, 12.44w- 04
Mortimer	Amy	USA	16.8.81	175/59	1500	4:07.58	4:12.39- 03
Mosqueda	Sylvia	USA	8.4.66	160/48	10000	32:33.22	31:54.03- 96

	Name		Nat	Born	Ht/Wt	Event	2005 Mark	Pre-2005 Best
*	Mothersill	Cydonie	CAY	19.3.78	170/54	100	11.24	11.26- 03, 11.15w- 04
						200	22.39, 22.26w	22.40- 04
	Mourand	Chloë	FRA-J	20.10.87	167/55	PV	4.25	4.01- 04
	de Moura	Lucimar	BRA	22.3.74	174/60	100	11.24	11.29, 11.17A- 99
						200	22.75	22.60A, 22.75- 99
	Moussa	Houria	ALG	14.5.82		400H	57.37	57.51- 04
*	Mrisho	Zakia	TAN	19.2.84	165/45	1500	4:10.47	4:15.25- 03
						3000	8:39.91	8:46.77- 03
						5000	14:43.87	15:40.00i- 04, 16:00.46- 04
^	Mugo	Naomi	KEN	2.1.77	163/50	1500	4:08.92	3:58.12- 98
						3000	8:55.87	8:43.30+- 02
	Mullen	Deirdre	USA	21.5.82		HJ	1.88	1.88- 04
	Müller	Corinne	SUI	20.11.75	183/68	HJ	1.93	1.92- 04
	Müller	Nadine	GER	21.11.85	192/95	DT	59.35	57.85- 04
	Mulyukova	Yuliya	RUS	1.12.85		400H	56.33	58.78- 04
	Murata	Fumi	JPN	13.3.75	153/40	HMar	70:35	69:26- 00
	Murer	Fabiana	BRA	16.3.81	172/64	PV	4.40	4.25- 04
	Murillo	Melisa	COL	13.1.82	157/51	100	11.22A	11.57- 04, 11.38Aw- 03
	Murkomen	Rachel	KEN			3kSt	10:10.5A	
	Murofushi	Yuka	JPN	11.2.77	170/63	DT	56.23	56.84- 99
						HT	65.38	67.77- 04
*	Mutola	Maria	MOZ	27.10.72	162/61	800	1:58.96, 1:58.49i	1:55.19- 94
	Myint Myint Aye		MYA	18.11.77		800	2:01.8	2:05.43- 03
	Myrick	Wyllesheia	USA	21.11.79	163/54	100	11.35, 11.29w	11.27A, 11.28- 04
						200	22.98	22.94- 04
	Nacsa	Monique	AUS	26.10.76	177/85	DT	57.27	59.91- 03
^	Nadjina	Kaltouma	CHA	16.11.76	171/60	200	22.92	22.73, 22.55w- 02
						400	51.33	50.38- 01
	Nagao	Ikuko	JPN	7.1.82	162/42	HMar	70:13	
	Nakamura	Yurika	JPN-J	1.4.86		HMar	71:18	73:12- 04
	Nakata	Yuki	JPN	10.3.77	167/54	Hep	5905	5962- 04
	Nasonova	Tatyana	UKR	15.12.76	183/87	SP	17.80	17.58- 04
	Nasukawa	Mizuho	JPN	22.11.79	165/43	Mar	2:30:15	2:29:49- 04
	Naude	Elizna	RSA	14.9.78	180/87	DT	63.17A	61.79- 04
	Naumenko	Irina	KAZ	13.2.80	180/63	Hep	5991	6140- 03
	Nazarova	Anna	RUS-J	14.3.86		LJ	6.50i	6.48- 04
*	Nazarova	Natalya	RUS	26.5.79	165/55	400	51.31	49.65- 04
	Ndereba	Anastasha	KEN	27.9.74		Mar	2:30:45	2:29:03- 02
*	Ndereba	Catherine	KEN	21.7.72	160/45	HMar	69:24	67:54- 01
						Mar	2:22:01	2:18:47- 01
*	Ndoye	Kène	SEN	20.11.78	164/58	TJ	14.47	15.00- 04
	Neacsu	Mihaela	ROM	3.5.79	170/58	800	1:59.78	2:03.19- 04
	Nelson	Lela	USA	19.5.83	180/64	LJ	6.49	6.19- 04
						Hep	5878	5290- 04
	Németh	Noemi	HUN-J	7.4.86		HT	64.09	62.09- 04
	Neporadna	Nelya	UKR	29.7.85	164/48	800	2:02.28	2:00.53- 04
						1000	2:36.34	2:35.56- 03
						1500	4:03.73	4:04.24- 03
*	Nerius	Steffi	GER	1.7.72	178/72	JT	66.52	65.82- 04, 69.42#- 96
	Nesbitt	Amberly	USA-J	9.8.86	156/50	100	11.42	11.78, 11.53w- 04
*	Nesterenko	Yuliya	BLR	15.6.79	173/61	100	11.08	10.92- 04
^	Netseporuk	Larisa	EST	24.12.70	171/59	Hep	5999	6331- 00
	Neupert	Anja	GER	10.10.78	176/59	400H	56.18	55.48- 04
	Nevmerzhitskaya	Yelena	BLR	27.7.80	168/55	100	11.37, 11.14w	11.25- 03
						200	23.13	23.35- 04
	Neyra	Yaumara	CUB	18.4.76	158/50	100H	13.09	12.82- 03, 12.7- 02, 12.70w- 01
	Niaré	Gaëlle	FRA	12.3.82	182/72	HJ	1.92i	1.93- 03
	Nickl	Vanda	HUN	4.9.85		HT	64.11	62.59- 04
^	Nicolau	Cristina	ROM	9.8.77	186/66	TJ	13.70	14.94i- 00, 14.70- 99
	Niederstätter	Monika	ITA	2.3.74	168/52	400H	55.95	55.10- 99
	Niiya	Hitomi	JPN-Y	26.2.88	164/43	5000	15:28.70	15:54.99- 03
	Nilsson	Cecilia	SWE	22.6.79	178/87	HT	68.44	66.77- 04
	Nilsson	Ida	SWE	8.2.81	173/58	3kSt	9:48.85	9:43.25- 04
	Nishikori	Ikuko	JPN	5.1.80	165/54	PV	4.30	4.00- 04
	Nishio	Maya	JPN	19.12.78	163/44	10000	32:11.14	32:22.57- 99
	Nishiyama	Takami	JPN	17.10.80	166/49	HMar	71:40	71:07- 01
	Njoroge	Mercy	KEN-J	10.6.86		3kSt	9:50.63	
	Nkiruka	Domike	NGR	28.8.85	165/60	TJ	13.66	13.52- 04
^	Nku	Mercy	NGR	17.7.76	170/67	100	11.42	11.06- 01, 11.03A, 10.98w- 99
	Nobuoka	Sakie	JPN	24.8.77	164/54	200	23.22w	23.33- 04

	Name		Nat	Born	Ht/Wt	Event	2005Mark	Pre-2005 Best
*	Noguchi	Mizuki	JPN	3.7.78	150/41	10000	31:44.29	31:21.03- 04
						HMar	69:19+	67:47- 04
						Mar	2:19:12	2:21:18- 03
	Northover	Zara	JAM	6.3.84		SP	16.56	16.48- 04
*	Nosova-Pechonkina	Yuliya	RUS	21.4.78	180/65	200	23.26i	
						400	51.91i	51.00i- 03
						400H	52.90	52.34- 03
	Notagashira	Miho	JPN	17.8.83	171/49	HMar	70:25	
	Novik	Marina	BLR	19.1.84		JT	55.24	55.15- 04
	Novikova	Yelena	RUS	27.10.85		100	11.37	11.90- 03
	Nowakowska	Ewa	POL	20.12.81	175/59	Hep	5654	5959- 04
	Nurgalyeva	Olesya	RUS	9.1.76		Mar	2:29:35	2:29:48- 04
	Nwidobie/Sharpe	Kara	GBR	13.4.81		DT	57.27	52.98- 04
	Nyagau	Ruth	KEN			3kSt	10:12.0A	
	Nyarwai Wanjiru	Veronica	KEN-Y	29.10.89	165/43	3000	8:52.9A	
						5000	15:13.1A	16:05.7- 04
	Nytra	Carolin	GER	26.2.85	175/61	100H	13.28	13.54- 04
	Nzola	Theresa	FRA	30.11.83	170/53	TJ	14.03	13.82i- 03, 13.60, 13.74w- 04
	Oberer	Simone	SUI	8.4.80	176/61	Hep	6052	5933- 03
*	Obergföll	Christina	GER	22.8.81	175/71	JT	70.03	63.34- 04
	Oberstoltz	Alexia	ITA	2.6.80	167/52	800	2:02.35	2:02.87- 04
	Obregón	Darlenis	COL-J	21.2.86		200	23.10A	23.35A- 04
*	Ochichi	Isabella	KEN	28.10.79	162/48	3000	8:31.42	8:31.32- 04
						5000	14:38.21	14:46.42- 04
	Ogawa	Kiyomi	JPN	15.9.81	157/46	5000	15:28.51	15:26.01- 04
						10000	31:59.56	32:01.43- 01
						Mar	2:26:02	
	Ogawa	Michiko	JPN	30.12.83	155/42	5000	15:28.23	15:26.01- 04
						10000	31:59.18	0
	Ogden	Rachael	GBR	23.7.79		1500	4:11.89	4:19.48- 03
	Ogi	Madoka	JPN	26.10.83	157/42	10000	32:10.72	33:00.20- 03
						HMar	70:31	72:19- 04
	Ogoshi	Kazue	JPN	2.3.81	160/44	10000	31:40.34	31:24.00- 03
						HMar	71:43+	
	Oguz	Candeger	TUR	16.7.80	182/63	HJ	1.88	1.93- 04
	Oh Jung-hee		KOR	4.12.78		Mar	2:31:41	2:33:29- 04
	Ohadugba	Chinoye	NGR-J	24.3.86	175/64	TJ	13.81	13.00- 03
	O'Hara	Tracy	USA	20.7.80	165/55	PV	4.60	4.58- 04
	Ohira	Miki	JPN	28.6.81	170/49	10000	31:43.02	31:54.44- 04
						HMar	71:07	70:13- 04
*	Ohuruogu	Christine	GBR	17.5.84	175/70	400	50.73	50.50- 04
	Ojokolo	Endurance	NGR	29.9.75	178/67	100	11.29	11.06- 01
	Okamoto	Yumiko	JPN	28.3.78	157/43	10000	32:17.59	
*	Okayo	Margaret	KEN	30.5.76	150/39	HMar	69:17 dh	67:23- 03
						Mar	2:25:22	2:20:43- 02
	O'Keefe	Eileen	IRL	31.5.81	170/80	HT	69.36	64.66- 04
	Okori	Reïna-Flor	FRA	2.5.80	165/56	100H	12.75	12.81, 12.71w- 04
	Okoro	Marilyn	GBR	23.9.84	165/64	800	2:01.90	2:03.71- 04
	Okunaga	Mika	JPN	27.10.82	160/43	10000	32:08.19	32:26.11- 04
	Olaru	Mihaela	ROM	7.2.82	167/52	1500	4:11.67	4:08.71- 04
	Olaru	Nuta	ROM	28.8.70	161/40	HMar	71:06	69:00- 02
*	Oleynikova	Yelena	RUS	9.12.76	178/57	TJ	14.33i, 14.29	14.83- 02
	Olgyay (Szabó)	Zsuzsanna	HUN	6.5.73	178/67	PV	4.23i	4.51i, 4.40- 99
	Olivarès	Elodie	FRA	22.5.76	170/55	3kSt	9:40.47	9:33.12- 02
	Olivero	Cora	ESP	28.8.78	170/56	400H	55.27	55.65- 03
	Olshevskaya	Olga	RUS	5.7.82		DT	57.81	57.56- 04
	Olupona	Oluwatoyin	CAN	29.1.83	177/63	100	11.35, 11.30w	11.54- 04
	Omarova	Anna	RUS	3.10.81	178/79	SP	17.04i, 16.70	17.28- 03
	Ominami	Hiromi	JPN	15.11.75	166/46	5000	15:25.59	15:20.75- 04
						10000	31:35.18	31:50.89- 00
						HMar	70:28	68:45- 04
						Mar	2:28:07	2:23:26- 04
	Ominami	Takami	JPN	15.11.75	167/47	Mar	2:31:16	2:23:43- 02
	Omwanza	Beatrice	KEN	24.2.74		HMar	71:18	71:33- 02
						Mar	2:30:41	2:27:19- 04
	O'Neill	Laura	USA	29.7.80	160/45	10000	32:15.70	32:27.89- 04
	Ongori	Philes	KEN-J	19.7.86	158/47	5000	15:09.49	15:08.3mx, 15:25.50- 04
						10000	32:30.83	
	Onwuchekwa	Kacey	USA	22.11.85		SP	16.67	15.20- 04
	Onyia	Josephine	NGR-J	15.7.86		100H	13.36, 13.26w	13.48- 04

	Name		Nat	Born	Ht/Wt	Event	2005 Mark	Pre-2005 Best
	Onysko	Daria	POL	30.7.81	169/54	100	11.41	11.46- 03
	Orbán	va	HUN	29.11.84	173/75	HT	68.70	67.60- 04
	O'Reilly	Thaimi	ITA	20.7.76	174/60	TJ	13.97	13.90- 03
*	O'Rourke	Derval	IRL	28.5.81	168/57	100H	13.00, 12.95w	12.96- 03
	Orsini	Gisella	ITA	9.12.71	161/49	20kW	1:31:57	1:32:19- 04
	Oshima	Megumi	JPN	4.9.75	160/43	10000	32:09.67	31:34.01- 04
						HMar	69:59	
						Mar	2:24:25	2:24:47- 04
*	Ostapchuk	Nadezhda	BLR	12.10.80	180/78	SP	21.09	20.56i- 03, 20.36- 04
^	O'Sullivan	Sonia	IRL	28.11.69	173/53	Mar	2:29:01	2:32:06- 02
	Otto	Silvia	GER	21.1.79	171/55	TJ	13.93, 14.01w	13.73i, 13.68- 04
	Ouédraogo	Elodie	BEL	27.2.81	173/59	100	11.40	11.50- 03
						200	23.19, 23.11w	23.11- 04
	Ovchinnikova	Anastasiya	RUS	16.10.84		400	51.10	52.68- 04
	Owens	Ashley	USA	19.11.85	158/53	100	11.08w	11.13, 11.12w- 04
	Oyama	Kaori	JPN	6.12.82	159/43	10000	32:32.42	32:56.60- 04
	Oyama	Miki	JPN	22.10.79	157/41	10000	32:25.21	32:17.19- 04
						HMar	71:41+	69:54- 04
						Mar	2:26:55	2:27:58- 04
*	Ozaki	Mari	JPN	16.7.75	162/46	10000	31:34.15	31:46.57- 03
						HMar	71:41+	69:33- 02
						Mar	2:23:59	2:23:30- 03
	Ozaki	Yoshimi	JPN	1.7.81	154/41	10000	31:47.23	32:19.30- 04
	Pacholak	Anna	POL	15.1.80	174/51	200	23.24i	22.87- 03
	Palacios	Felipa	COL	1.12.75	168/60	100	11.18A, 11.42	11.31, 11.15Aw- 97
						200	22.85A	22.74Aw, 22.7w-97, 22.8A-98, 23.05-99, 22.92A-01
*	Palamar	Vita	UKR	12.10.77	187/66	HJ	1.95	2.01- 03
	Pan Seili		CHN-Y	4.12.88		DT	58.52	49.96- 04
	Pang Yingting		CHN-J	28.1.87	168/51	20kW	1:29:40	1:36:11- 04
	Pankova	Olga	RUS	13.8.76		TJ	13.79	14.11- 04
	Pantelimon	Oana	ROM	27.9.72	179/61	HJ	1.95i, 1.95	1.99- 00
	Papadopoúlou	Maria	GRE	15.12.74	173/53	800	1:59.79	2:01.00- 02
	Papadopoúlou	Stiliani	GRE	15.3.82	172/86	HT	68.14	68.08- 04
	Papayeoryíou	Alexándra	GRE	17.12.80	176/76	HT	67.13	69.98- 03
	Papayeoryíou	María	GRE	8.8.79	175/67	HJ	1.89	1.85- 03
	Papayiánni	Athína	GRE	18.8.80	170/56	20kW	1:29:21	1:28:58- 04
	Papp	Krisztina	HUN	17.12.82	170/54	3000	8:45.50	8:48.58- 04
						5000	15:08.65	15:20.31- 04
	Pardaloú	María	GRE	21.4.84	162/45	3kSt	10:08.59	10:33.97- 04
	Parfyonova	Yelena	KAZ	26.1.74	176/58	TJ	14.23	14.20- 00
	Park Ho-hyun		KOR	21.3.78	164/58	JT	55.58	54.17- 02, 56.32#- 97
^	Parris	Debbie-Ann	JAM	24.3.73	162/52	400H	54.96	53.88- 01
	Pascual	Beatriz	ESP	9.5.82	163/53	20kW	1:32:49	1:30:22- 04
*	Pavey	Joanne	GBR	20.9.73	162/51	3000	8:33.79	8:31.27- 02
						5000	14:40.71	14:48.66- 02
	Pavliy	Tatyana	RUS	18.5.78	168/63	100H	12.97, 12.85w	13.34- 02
	Pavlovskaya	Natalya	RUS	30.4.75		1500	4:08.17	4:06.20- 04
						1M	4:28.90	4:38.26- 04
	Pavlyukovskaya	Nadezhda	BLR	6.6.85		HT	67.40	63.00- 04
	Pchelnik	Darya	BLR	20.12.81		HT	71.08	69.16- 04
	Pedersen	Julia	USA	12.4.83		SP	16.56	16.04- 04
	Pedrares	M.Dolores	ESP	17.1.73	168/69	HT	64.67	67.14- 04
	Pelayo	Irene	ESP	16.2.80		3kSt	10:07.16	10:38.29- 04
	Pereira	Andréa Maria	BRA	8.12.73		SP	16.60	16.50- 03
	Perepelova ¶	Lyubov	UZB	26.2.79	163/53	200	23.18wdq	22.72- 00
	Pérez	Katiuska	CUB	21.12.75	157/54	PV	4.25	4.20- 03
	Pérez	Madaí	MEX	2.2.80	157/45	HMar	70:36	70:55+- 04
						Mar	2:26:50	2:27:08- 04
	Perez	Yuliana	USA	21.7.81	171/70	TJ	13.85	14.23- 03, 14.29w- 01
	Perie	Bianca	ROM-Y	1.6.90	170/62	HT	65.13	58.67- 04
	Permitina	Irina	RUS	3.2.68	165/49	Mar	2:29:44	2:26:51- 04
	Pérra	Athanasía	GRE	2.2.83	167/55	TJ	14.27i, 14.12	14.39- 04
	Perrin	Amélie	FRA	30.3.80	171/85	HT	68.20	67.12- 04
*	Perry	Michelle	USA	1.5.79	175/67	200	23.22	22.91- 04
						100H	12.43	12.74- 04
	Persson	Hanna-Mia	SWE	11.2.78	178/61	PV	4.36	4.35i- 04, 4.30- 02
	Persson	Linda	SWE	22.9.81	177/55	PV	4.25i, 4.25	4.25sq- 04, 4.20- 03
	Petlyuk	Tatyana	UKR	22.2.82	174/60	800	2:01.78	1:59.48- 04
	Petráhn	Barbara	HUN	16.9.78	170/55	400	52.06	51.85- 01
	Petras	Teodora	ROM	5.2.82	177/68	JT	57.14	55.40- 04
	Petrova	Irina	RUS	26.5.85	174/50	20kW	1:30:18	

Name		Nat	Born	Ht/Wt	Event	2005Mark	Pre-2005 Best
* Petrova	Lyudmila	RUS	7.10.68	160/44	Mar	2:26:29	2:22:33- 02
Petrova	Tatyana	RUS	8.4.83	160/53	10000	32:17.49	31:36.76- 03
					Mar	2:31:03	2:36:44- 04
Pettersson	Annika	SWE	10.1.79	176/74	JT	56.24	56.70- 00
Pettitt	Ellen	AUS-J	13.2.86	182/62	HJ	1.90	1.82- 03
Phamang	Buaban	THA-J	27.12.86		JT	55.06	51.47- 04
Pickler	Julie	USA	9.12.83	178/64	Hep	5650	5338- 02
Pidgeon	Emily	GBR-Y	1.6.89	165/48	3kSt	10:06.12	0
Pidluzhnaya	Yuliya	RUS-Y	1.10.88		LJ	6.48	
Pierson	Summer	USA	3.9.78	180/84	DT	57.47	60.40- 98
Pigida	Natalya	UKR	30.1.81	167/54	400	51.69	51.44- 04
Pignot	Aurore	FRA	24.12.79	172/57	PV	4.26i, 4.20	4.25- 04
Pilátou	Stilianí	GRE	28.3.80	173/57	LJ	6.72, 6.77w	6.80i- 03, 6.75- 02
Pillay	Geraldine	RSA	25.8.77	178/64	100	11.07	11.20- 03
					200	22.78	23.07A, 23.11- 03
Pilskog	Trine	NOR	1.12.72	168/50	1500	4:07.76	4:05.75- 04
Pilyugina	Liliya	UKR	14.10.85	168/54	400	51.85	52.81- 04
Pinnock	Sherene	JAM-J	30.3.87	167/55	400H	57.18	57.54-04
Pîrtea	Adriana	ROM	31.1.80		HMar	71:10	
Pishchalnikova	Darya	RUS	19.7.85	189/95	DT	60.62	58.26- 04
* Pittman	Jana	AUS	9.11.82	181/68	400H	53.44	53.22- 03
Poelman	Jacqueline	NED	5.10.73	171/63	200	23.06w	23.00- 02
* Polnova	Tatyana	RUS	20.4.79	173/64	PV	4.60i, 4.55	4.78- 04
^ Pompey	Aliann	GUY	9.3.78	168/55	400	51.43	50.93- 04
Ponomarenko	Svetlana	RUS	28.11.69		Mar	2:31:26	2:35:15- 99
Ponteen	Tiandra	SKN	9.11.84	173/61	400	50.83	51.00A, 51.17- 04
Poonia	Krishna	IND	5.5.77		DT	58.33	57.19- 04
* Pospelova	Svetlana	RUS	24.12.79	168/65	100	11.32	11.42- 00
					200	22.39	22.80- 00
					400	49.80	50.47- 00
Potapova	Oksana	RUS	12.9.84		LJ	6.50i	5.94- 03
Potepa	Wioletta	POL	13.12.80	186/83	DT	63.67	62.90- 04
Po'uhila	Ana	TGA	12.10.79	180/95	SP	16.92	16.37- 04
Poulson	Jackie	USA	22.2.81		Hep	5730	5640- 04
Pounds	Dana	USA	5.6.84		JT	57.52	53.15- 04
Povalyayeva	Olga	RUS	19.10.84	168/48	20kW	1:33:11	1:34:59- 04
Poves	Maria José	ESP	16.3.78	167/52	20kW	1:31:55	1:32:32- 04
Powell	Virginia	USA	7.9.83	178/66	100	11.28, 11.15w	11.32- 04
					100H	12.61	13.07- 03
* Powell-Roos	Suzy	USA	3.9.76	178/73	DT	62.35	65.48, 69.44dh- 02
Pöyry	Sini	FIN	3.2.80	182/88	HT	68.90	69.16- 04
^ Pozdnyakova	Tatyana	UKR	4.3.56	164/56	Mar	2:31:05	2:29:00- 02
Pratt	Julie	GBR	20.3.79	168/51	100H	13.29, 13.18w	13.08- 02
Pressley	Jessica	USA	27.12.84	178/100	SP	17.05	15.67- 03
					HT	63.51	54.46- 04
Priemer	Manuela	GER	29.11.78	178/75	HT	63.58	67.26- 03
Priyma	Yelena	RUS	2.12.83		HT	66.13	62.21- 03
* Prokopcuka	Jelena	LAT	21.9.76	168/51	5000	15:03.10	14:47.71- 00
					10000	31:04.55	31:04.10- 04
					HMar	68:11 dh	68:43- 01
					Mar	2:22:56	2:24:01- 03
Prokopek	Grazyna	POL	20.4.77	170/51	400	52.09	51.29- 04
Proshina	Aleksandra	RUS	17.3.81		800	2:00.75	2:04.65- 04
Protópappa	Maria	GRE	5.5.73	170/60	5000	15:08.03	15:07.81- 04
* Pskit	Malgorzata	POL	25.5.76	175/61	400H	55.03	54.75- 04
Ptikany	Mary	KEN	.78		HMar	70:18	71:32- 04
					Mar	2:29:45	2:32:04- 00
Pudovkina	Iraida	RUS	2.11.80	173/50	20kW	1:26:28	1:31:46- 04
Pumper	Susanne	AUT	1.9.70	170/50	3000	8:47.51i	8:47.04- 00
					10000	32:12.33	32:49.92- 02
Pushkina	Lyudmila	UKR	2.10.65	168/56	Mar	2:29:56	2:28:15- 03
* Pyatykh	Anna	RUS	4.4.81	176/64	LJ	6.57i, 6.,53	6.43- 00
					TJ	14.88	14.85- 04
* Pyrek	Monika	POL	11.8.80	174/52	PV	4.70i, 4.70	4.72- 04
Qian Chunhua		CHN	11.2.79	170/78	SP	18.58	18.41- 01
Qin Wangping		CHN	16.6.82	164/53	100	11.33	11.30- 00
Qiu Huijing		CHN	4.2.85	169/49	TJ	14.11	13.85- 02
Rabchenyuk	Anastasiya	UKR	14.9.83	177/64	400H	56.14	56.30- 03
* Radcliffe	Paula	GBR	17.12.73	173/54	3000	8:50.18	8:22.20- 02
					5000	15:16.29+	14:29.11- 04
					10000	30:42.75	30:01.09- 02

	Name		Nat	Born	Ht/Wt	Event	2005 Mark	Pre-2005 Best
	(Radcliffe)					HMar	68:27+ dh	65:40- 03
						Mar	2:17:42	2:15:25- 03
	Radecka	Zuzanna	POL	2.4.75	172/58	400	51.58	51.93- 04
	Radevica	Ineta	LAT	13.7.81	173/56	LJ	6.80	6.70- 03
*	Rahouli	Baya	ALG	27.7.79	179/64	TJ	14.98	14.89- 04
^	Ramalalanirina	Nicole	FRA	5.3.72	164/57	100H	13.08	12.76- 00
	Ramanauskaite	Rita	LTU	22.2.70	174/72	JT	55.15	62.69- 00, 65.46#- 96
	Ramón	Miriam	ECU	10.2.73	158/55	20kW	1:31:25	1:37:27- 99
	Ransom	India	USA	23.1.84		100	11.41w	11.48- 03
	Ranta	Ilona	FIN	28.10.82	164/52	400H	57.24	57.99- 04
	Ratajczak	Justyna	POL	29.6.85	165/58	PV	4.20	4.10- 04
^	Rath	Daniela	GER	6.5.77	180/64	HJ	1.90	2.00- 03
	Raux	Corinne	FRA	16.8.76	164/50	Mar	2:28:48	2:29:19- 04
	Razinkova	Liliya	UKR	29.11.85	170/90	HT	63.44	66.97- 04
	Rebrik	Vera	UKR-Y	25.2.89	174/65	JT	57.48	52.47- 04
	Redoúmi	Flóra	GRE	11.9.76	168/64	100H	13.03	12.86- 04
	Regis	Hazel-Ann	GRN	1.2.81	165/50	200	23.02i	24.08- 02, 23.41w- 94
						400	50.92i	50.64- 04
	Reid	Suziann	USA	14.1.77	168/64	400	51.45	50.74- 99
^	Renders	Marleen	BEL	24.12.68	166/47	Mar	2:26:26	2:23:05- 02
	Rezanova	Marina	UKR	28.8.74	180/80	HT	65.70	68.35- 04
	Rezende	Alessandra	BRA	5.3.75		JT	56.06A	57.44- 02
	Rhett	Amandi	USA	29.6.82	168/56	100	11.29	11.32, 11.29w- 04
	Rhines	Jen	USA	1.7.74	160/50	3000	8:56.07	8:50.72- 00
						5000	15:12.39	15:13.26- 01
						10000	31:26.66	31:41.16- 02
*	Ribeiro	Fernanda	POR	23.6.69	161/48	10000	32:03.22	30:22.88- 00
	Ribeiro Costa	Joana	BRA	15.8.81		PV	4.31	3.85- 00
	Richards	Sandie	JAM	6.11.68	175/67	400	52.07	49.79- 97
*	Richards	Sanya	USA	26.2.85	175/63	200	22.53	22.73, 22.49i- 04
						400	48.92	49.89- 04
	Richmond	Rose	USA	29.1.81	168/61	LJ	6.73, 6.79w	6.76- 04
	Riettie	Kateema	JAM	5.12.73		JT	54.91	52.95- 04
	Rifka	Romary	MEX	23.12.70	180/64	HJ	1.90	1.97- 04
*	Rigaudo	Elisa	ITA	17.6.80	168/56	20kW	1:29:26	1:27:49- 04
	Rillstone	Nina	NZL	15.4.75		HMar	70:49	73:29- 04
	Risku/Lehtinen	Johanna	FIN	21.2.79	170/55	1500	4:06.85	4:07.32- 03
	Rittweg	Mareike	GER	1.6.84	175/68	JT	56.20	57.39- 04
	Ritz	Judith	GER	16.6.83	174/62	100H	13.27	13.44- 04
	Robbeson	Justine	RSA	15.5.85	167/58	JT	59.46A	55.82- 04
	Robert-Michon	Melina	FRA	18.7.79	178/87	DT	58.01	65.78- 02
	Robinson	Amber	USA	5.6.80	165/56	100	11.41	11.43- 03
						200	23.12	23.12- 02
	Robinson	Camille	JAM	30.3.84	165/53	400H	57.26	56.14- 02
	Robinson	Moushami	USA	13.4.81	167/55	200	23.25	23.64- 03, 23.54w- 01
						400	50.38	51.54- 04
	Rocha Silva	Isabel	BRA	15.6.79		400H	57.15	56.99A- 02, 57.01- 04
	Rockmeier	Birgit	GER	29.11.73	173/62	100	11.33	11.17- 01
						200	23.05	22.90- 01, 22.89i- 98
	Rodgers	Jackie	USA	2.3.83	168/55	PV	4.20	3.90- 04
	Rodríguez	Dulce M	MEX	14.8.72	157/54	10000	31:25.33	32:26.37- 04
						HMar	70:30	71:08+- 02
						Mar	2:29:00	2:31:45- 01
*	Rodríguez	Natalia	ESP	2.6.79	164/49	1500	3:59.51	4:01.30- 03
	Rogers	Dana	USA	18.2.83		100H	13.22w	13.40- 04
*	Rogova	Oksana	RUS	7.10.78	180/60	TJ	14.25i	14.70i- 02, 14.59, 14.65w- 99
*	Rogowska	Anna	POL	21.5.81	171/55	PV	4.83	4.71- 04
	Rohr	Nadine	SUI	29.6.77	170/56	PV	4.30	4.30- 03
	Roles	Philippa	GBR	1.3.78	180/100	DT	58.07	62.89- 03
	Romagnolo	Elena	ITA	5.10.82	165/50	3kSt	10:05.76	0
	Roman	Sonja	SLO	11.3.79	165/54	1500	4:09.73	4:08.30- 04
	Romanova	Olga	RUS	23.5.80		10000	32:29.79	32:28.91- 03
	Rosa	Anália	POR	28.2.76		3kSt	9:51.05	9:43.00- 04
	Rosa	Chiara	ITA	28.1.83	178/90	SP	18.71	17.76- 04
	Rosenbauer	Susanne	GER	2.8.84		JT	55.32	51.47- 04
*	Roshchupkina	Natalya	RUS	13.1.78	182/70	Hep	6003	6633- 00
	Rosikhina	Irina	RUS	11.5.75	175/65	400	52.00, 51.58i	50.66- 04, 50.5- 98
	Roslanova	Tatyana	KAZ	28.9.80	168/54	400	51.07	50.68- 04
						800	2:01.35	1:59.50- 04
	Roslavtseva	Polina	RUS	17.3.78		100H	13.32	13.35- 01

Name		Nat	Born	Ht/Wt	Event	2005Mark	Pre-2005 Best
Ross-Williams	Tiffany	USA	5.2.83	157/57	100H	12.99	13.12- 03, 13.01w- 02
					400H	54.56	55.22- 02
Roth	Kristina	USA	5.8.83	168/60	3kSt	10:09.85	10:18.33- 04
Rücklová	Alena	CZE	7.10.81	165/65	400H	55.87	56.34- 04
* Ruckstuhl	Karin	NED	2.11.80	181/65	100H	13.26	13.44- 04
					LJ	6.58	6.57i, 6.56- 04
					Hep	6318	6206- 04
Rüdiger	Carmen	GER	15.8.73	175/58	1500	4:11.14i	4:06.7- 99
Rudkin	Jane	USA	15.5.80		3kSt	10:06.10	10:09.75- 04
^ Rudolph	Amy	USA	18.9.73	176/55	1500	4:10.50	4:06.02- 00
					1M	4:31.92i	4:27.66- 99
					3000	8:49.02	8:39.86- 00
					5000	15:03.59	14:56.04- 96
					10000	31:18.96	0
Rumpf	Sabine	GER	18.3.83	176/95	DT	60.75	58.05- 04
Rusakova	Natalya	RUS	12.12.80	178/66	100H	12.85	12.70- 04
Ruskule	Dace	LAT	20.9.81	178/78	DT	56.71	59.68- 04
Russell	Blake	USA	24.7.75	168/51	5000	15:26.60	15:21.37- 00
					10000	31:35.25	32:11.94- 03
					Mar	2:29:10	2:30:32- 04
Rutjes	Ilona	NED	28.5.80	181/76	DT	57.83	59.56- 00
* Ryabinkina	Olga	RUS	24.9.76	190/87	SP	19.65	19.36- 02
					DT	56.26	61.66- 98
Ryan	Deirdre	IRL	1.6.82	183/	HJ	1.90i	1.87- 04
Rybko	Yekaterina	RUS	5.6.82		JT	55.31	52.93- 04
Rypakova (Alekseyeva)	Olga	KAZ	30.11.84	183/64	LJ	6.60	6.53i- 04, 6.26- 02
^ Ryshich	Nastja	GER	19.9.77	170/58	PV	4.35	4.50i, 4.44- 99
Rywelska	Kamila	POL	15.11.83	178/58	TJ	13.62	13.36- 02
Sadach	Aneta	POL	22.4.75	175/56	TJ	13.90	13.99- 03
* Sadova	Natalya	RUS	15.6.72	180/100	DT	66.29	70.02- 99
^ Safronova	Natalya	BLR	11.7.74	176/60	TJ	14.31i, 14.29	14.65- 00
Saito	Yuki	JPN	25.9.80	155/40	10000	32:09.94	31:41.49- 04
Sakakura	Ryoko	JPN	9.5.76	164/47	20kW	1:34:04	1:32:16- 04
Sakun	Svetlana	UKR	1.3.81	176/93	SP	16.83	17.00- 04
Sakurai	Rika	JPN	15.5.85	169/57	400H	57.42	59.35- 03
Saladukha	Olga	UKR	4.6.83	175/55	TJ	14.04	13.66i, 13.63- 02
Salis	Silvia	ITA	17.9.85	179/72	HT	64.96	61.70- 04
Sallins	Melinda	USA	30.6.73	178/64	400H	56.29	56.06- 97
Saltanovic	Kristina	LTU	20.2.75	162/53	20kW	1:31:23	1:30:44- 02
Samaria	Agnes	NAM	11.8.72	166/56	800	1:59.91	1:59.15- 02
					1000	2:36.99i	2:34.19- 02
Samokhvalova	Yelena	RUS	21.11.80	165/51	1500	4:11.79	4:14.75- 02
					10000	31:12.57	31:43.51- 03
Samsu	Roslinda	MAS	9.6.82	160/50	PV	4.20	4.00- 04
Samuels	Daniele	AUS-Y	26.5.88	182/82	DT	58.52	52.21- 04
Sánchez	Mar	ESP	25.12.79	170/60	PV	4.35i, 4.21	4.31- 01
* Sanders	Nicola	GBR	23.6.82	172/60	400	51.95	53.77- 04
					400H	55.61	58.28- 04
Sanfabio	Tamara	ESP	14.3.78	162/50	3kSt	10:06.91	10:09.42- 03
Santin	Frances	USA	27.7.80	175/57	800	2:01.44	2:00.84- 04
Santiusty	Yuneysi	CUB	24.12.84	167/63	800	2:02.38	2:00.92- 04
dos Santos	Christiane	BRA	6.10.81		800	2:02.13	2:00.98- 03
dos Santos	Perla	BRA	29.1.82	155/49	400H	56.50	56.08- 03
Santos	Vera	POR	3.12.81	164/59	20kW	1:31:30	1:32:43- 03
Sarrapio	Patricia	ESP	16.11.82	167/56	TJ	13.62	13.40- 04
Sato	Yumi	JPN	22.12.76	172/55	5000	15:19.68	15:22.86- 97
					10000	31:48.95	33:03.5- 95
^ Sauer	Mary	USA	31.10.75	164/59	PV	4.60	4.65- 02
* Savigne	Yargelis	CUB	13.11.84	165/53	LJ	6.77, 6.88w	6.63- 03
					TJ	14.82	13.03- 01
* Saville	Jane	AUS	5.11.74	164/53	20kW	1:29:33	1:27:44- 04
Saxer	Mary	USA-J	21.6.87		PV	4.32i	4.14i, 3.81- 04
Saye	Laura	USA	27.11.81	175/77	DT	57.30	56.32- 04
Sayenko	Inna	UKR	8.3.82	177/80	HT	66.39	65.90- 04
Sayers	Goldie	GBR	16.7.82	171/69	JT	61.45	60.85- 04
Scanlon	Taneisha	IRL	19.11.77		TJ	13.62	13.23- 03
Scardanzan	Elisa	ITA	15.7.85	174/60	400H	57.31	59.93- 02
Scerbová	Denisa	CZE-J	21.8.86	174/61	LJ	6.64i, 6.57, 6.62w	6.68- 04
Schaffarzik	Sandra	GER-J	22.6.87	175/65	JT	55.49	49.67- 04
* Scherwin	Christina	DEN	11.7.76	176/67	JT	63.43	59.36- 04

	Name		Nat	Born	Ht/Wt	Event	2005 Mark	Pre-2005 Best
	Schmidt	Alice	USA	3.10.81	180/64	800	1:59.29	2:01.16- 03
						1500	4:12.12	418.08- 03
	Schott	Maren	GER	11.2.76	173/62	400H	57.46	55.28- 03
	Schulte	Sabine	GER	29.1.76	169/58	PV	4.20i	4.40, 4.43sq- 02
	Schulte	Sofia	GER	8.4.76	178/58	LJ	6.54	6.72- 00
	Schultze	Anna	GER	26.5.85	173/61	PV	4.36	4.31sq, 4.25- 04
	Schulz	Christine	GER	30.1.84	178/59	Hep	6199	5705- 04
	Schwald	Sarah	USA	2.1.73	165/48	1500	4:07.86	4:04.43- 01
						3000	8:54.42i	8:56.49- 02, 8:51.07i- 03
	Schwanitz	Christina	GER	24.12.85	185/109	SP	18.84	16.98- 04
*	Schwartz	Jillian	USA	19.9.79	173/63	PV	4.55	4.60- 04
	Schwarzkopf	Lilli	GER	28.8.83	174/63	Hep	6196	6161- 04
	Schwerdtner	Maren	GER	3.10.85	180/68	Hep	5835	5603- 04
*	Scott	Candice	TRI	17.9.80	180/100	SP	17.65i, 16.95	17.28- 04
						HT	71.45	69.94- 04
	Scott	Sian	GBR	20.3.84	168/56	400H	56.42	58.36- 03
	Scott	Susan	GBR	26.9.77	168/56	800	2:01.17	1:59.30- 02
						1500	4:09.00	4:09.79- 02
	Seboka	Mulu	ETH	13.1.84		Mar	2:30:54	2:37:29- 04
*	Seeger	Melanie	GER	8.1.77	169/55	20kW	1:30:21	1:28:17- 04
*	Sekachova	Irina	UKR	21.7.76	165/72	HT	70.30	74.16- 04
	Selig	Ashley	USA	23.2.84	175/63	Hep	5775	5587- 04
	Sellam	Aïda	TUN	13.9.77	167/74	JT	57.14	60.87- 04
	Selsouli	Meryem Alaoui	MAR	8.4.84	165/49	1500	4:08.30	4:13.9-02
	Semyonova	Svetlana	RUS	24.8.80		TJ	14.02	13.92- 03
	Sergeyeva	Nadezhda	RUS-J	13.6.87		Hep	5786	5444- 04
*	Seryogina	Viktoriya	RUS	22.5.73	180/60	HJ	1.95	2.00- 02
	Setowska	Ewelina	POL	5.3.80	170/55	800	2:00.71	2:03.21- 03
^	Seyerling	Heide	RSA	19.8.76	168/55	400	51.47	50.05- 00
	Sha Li		CHN-Y	14.8.88		TJ	13.83	13.66- 04
	Shadle	Anne	USA	1.12.82	162/47	1500	4:08.60	
	Shala	Klodiana	ALB	22.8.79	168/59	400H	56.48	57.67- 04
	Shalamanova	Dobrinka	BUL	1.5.83	165/50	3kSt	9:56.75	10:28.55- 04
^	Shaw	Lorraine	GBR	2.4.68	171/90	HT	65.33	68.93- 03
	Shchors	Yelena	UKR	6.3.84	173/62	LJ	6.51	6.46- 03
	Shchurenko	Tatyana	UKR	26.2.76	188/82	TJ	13.96	14.22- 04
	Shen Shengfei		CHN	21.1.81	178/70	Hep	6165	6263- 01
*	Shevchenko	Irina	RUS	2.9.75	175/65	100H	12.76	12.67- 04
	Shi Na		CHN	17.2.81	160/50	20kW	1:28:22	1:29:30- 04
*	Shibui	Yoko	JPN	14.3.79	165/46	10000	32:34.11	30:48.89- 02
						Mar	2:27:40	2:19:41- 04
	Shimahara	Kiyoko	JPN	22.12.76	154/43	Mar	2:26:14	2:26:43- 04
	Shimchuk	Natalya	BLR	1.10.81	179/77	JT	57.70	60.12- 04
	Shinkins	Karen	IRL	15.10.76	165/53	400	51.59	51.07- 99
	Shishlyuk	Aleksandra	UKR	16.4.80	170/57	LJ	6.62	6.64- 04
						TJ	14.09	14.12i- 02, 13.91- 04
	Shiviryova	Natalya	RUS	31.8.78	164/54	20kW	1:29:50	1:31:51- 00
	Shiyan	Marina	RUS	22.1.80	168/52	800	2:01.99i	
						400H	55.14	55.45- 02
	Shkolina	Svetlana	RUS-J	9.3.86		HJ	1.92i, 1.92	1.91- 04
*	Shobukhova	Liliya	RUS	13.11.77	169/50	1500	4:07.03	4:03.78- 04
						3000	8:40.82	8:34.85- 04
						5000	14:47.07	14:52.19- 04
	Shook	Brianna	USA	6.1.81	175/58	3kSt	9:45.91	9:29.32- 04
	Shtangeyeva	Irina	UKR	6.2.82	170/56	100	11.31	11.77- 04
						200	23.21	23.77- 04
	Shutkova	Veronika	BLR-J	26.5.86		LJ	6.64	6.22- 04
	Shvedova (Ivanova)	Anastasiya	RUS	3.5.79	174/63	PV	4.30i	4.55- 04
	Sibilyeva	Tatyana	RUS	17.5.80	164/51	20kW	1:31:18	1:27:33- 01
	Sidorchenkova	Yelena	RUS	30.5.80		1500	4:08.78	4:08.98i- 03, 4:12.47- 04
						3kSt	9:42.70	
	Silva	Vânia	POR	8.6.80	172/79	HT	66.14	68.82- 04
	Silva Costa	Keila	BRA	6.2.83	170/62	LJ	6.63	6.61- 04
						TJ	13.95	14.00, 14.15w- 01
*	Simagina	Irina	RUS	25.5.82	171/60	LJ	7.04	7.27- 04
*	Simon	Lidia	ROM	4.9.73	157/44	HMar	69:58	68:34- 00
						Mar	2:27:01	2:22:54- 00
	Simpson	Jemma	GBR	10.2.84	168/55	800	2:01.90	2:03.42- 03
*	Simpson	Margaret	GHA	31.12.81	162/53	JT	56.36	56.29- 04
						Hep	6423	6306- 04

	Name		Nat	Born	Ht/Wt	Event	2005Mark	Pre-2005 Best
*	Simpson	Sherone	JAM	12.8.84	160/50	100	10.97	11.01- 04
						200	22.54	22.70- 04
*	Sinclair	Kenia	JAM	14.7.80	167/54	800	1:58.88	2:03.21- 03
						1000	2:37.37	
						1500	4:07.11	4:22.42- 04
						1M	4:32.33i	
	Singh ¶	Neelam J	IND	8.1.71	167/85	DT	60.65	64.55- 02
	Skafida	Afrodíti	GRE	20.3.82	167/60	PV	4.48	4.40- 04
*	Skolimowska	Kamila	POL	4.11.82	180/105	HT	74.27	72.60- 02
	Skotnik	Mélanie	FRA	8.11.82	182/59	HJ	1.95	1.97i, 1.91- 03
*	Skujyte	Austra	LTU	12.8.79	188/75	Hep	6386	6435- 04
						Dec	8358	0
						SP	17.03	17.03- 02
	Skvortsova	Silviya	RUS	16.11.74		Mar	2:28:01	2:27:07- 02
	Slastina	Zhanna	UKR	4.9.77	167/64	JT	56.20	59.09- 04
*	Slesarenko	Yelena	RUS	28.2.82	178/57	HJ	2.00	2.06- 04
	Smit	Anika	RSA-J	26.5.86		HJ	1.89	1.86A- 03, 1.85- 02
	Smith	Breann	USA	29.1.83		SP	16.69	15.34- 04
	Smith	Kim	NZL	19.11.81	166/49	3000	8:50.43, 8:49.61i	8:49.18i- 04
						5000	15:05.68, 14:50.46i	15:09.72- 04
						10000	31:21.00	33:45.81- 04
	Smith	Lauren	USA	27.8.81		100H	13.26w	13.04A- 04
	Smith	Loree	USA	6.11.82	168/89	SP	17.14i, 16.70	15.80- 03
						HT	70.03	67.05- 04
	Smith	Ronetta	JAM	2.5.80	172/60	400	51.23	51.35- 03
	Smith	Shauna	USA	10.9.83	178/64	400H	54.21	54.42- 04
	Smith	Stephanie	USA	27.6.85	175/60	400	50.93	51.96- 04
*	Smith	Trecia	JAM	5.11.75	185/77	TJ	15.11	15.16- 04
*	Smith (Boone)	Rachelle	USA	30.6.81	163/59	100	11.17, 11.02w	11.22- 03
						200	22.22	22.69- 04
	Smolina	Zhanna	RUS	19.1.78		800	1:59.33	
	Smolyachkova	Mariya	BLR	10.2.85	179/76	HT	69.85	70.39- 04
	Smyslova	Marina	RUS	25.2.66	163/61	20kW	1:31:38. 1:33:38.3t	1:28:13- 04
	Snyder (Etholm)	Grete	NOR	25.1.76	183/72	DT	58.23	59.48- 03
	So	Yukari	JPN	20.4.84	160/43	5000	15:29.45	15:42.47- 04
^	Sobanska	Malgorzata	POL	25.4.69	165/50	Mar	2:28:46	2:26:08- 01
	Sobierajska	Malwina	POL	22.4.85	174/70	HT	64.24	60.82- 04
	Sobieszek	Magdalena	POL-J	4.5.86	175/75	SP	16.84	15.89- 04
*	Soboleva	Yelena	RUS	3.8.82	176/66	800	2:00.59	2:01.65- 03
						1000	2:36.50	
						1500	4:01.14	4:12.02- 03
						3000	8:55.89	
^	Söderberg	Anna	SWE	11.6.73	177/85	DT	61.26	64.54- 99
*	Sokolova	Svetlana	RUS	9.1.81	176/70	Hep	5689	6594- 04
	Sologub	Natalya	BLR	31.3.75	176/64	100	11.30	11.57- 99, 11.1- 98
						200	22.82	23.00- 98
						400	52.05	51.61, 51.43dq- 01
	Solomon	Mariana	ROM	8.9.80	172/58	TJ	14.29i, 14.06	14.42- 04
	Solomon	Shalonda	USA	19.12.85	169/56	100	11.29	11.35, 11.25w- 03
						200	22.74, 22.72w	22.82- 04
	Soma	Kate	USA	13.2.83	152/55	PV	4.36i, 4.30	4.32- 04
*	Song Aimin		CHN	15.3.78	178/90	DT	65.23	65.33- 03
*	Song Hongjuan		CHN	4.7.84	166/50	20kW	1:28:26	1:26:46- 04
	Song Jinzhao		CHN-Y	16.1.88		20kW	1:33:31	1:46:10- 04
	Song Xiaoling		CHN-J	21.12.87		20kW	1:30:15	
	Song Yinglan		CHN	14.9.75	173/60	400H	56.71	53.96- 01
	Sonnabend	Nadine	GER	28.1.81	179/60	PV	4.20i	4.10- 02
	Soong	Cari	USA	11.7.81	173/89	HT	65.86	65.92- 03
	Sorokina	Natalya	UKR	24.3.75	174/58	LJ	6.52	6.45- 04
*	Sotherton	Kelly	GBR	13.11.76	180/66	100H	13.27	13.29- 04
						LJ	6.67	6.68- 04
						Hep	6547	6424- 04
	Soulama	Aïssata	BUR	11.2.79	172/57	400H	56.45	57.60- 04
	Spence	Christine	USA	25.11.81		400H	56.12	57.20- 04
	Spencer	Lavern	LCA	23.6.84	180/54	HJ	1.94	1.88- 04
	Spencer	Sasha	USA	4.8.79	163/52	800	2:02.20	2:01.56- 03
*	Spiegelburg	Silke	GER-J	17.3.86	173/62	PV	4.48i, 4.42	4.41- 04
*	Spotáková	Barbora	CZE	30.6.81	182/80	JT	65.74	60.95- 04
	Sprenger-Afflerbach	Juliane	GER	22.3.77	163/60	100H	13.04	12.87- 03
	Stals	Sandra	BEL	5.6.75	170/55	800	2:01.03i	1:58.31- 98
*	Stambolova	Vanya	BUL	28.11.83		400H	56.29	61.11- 02

	Name		Nat	Born	Ht/Wt	Event	2005 Mark	Pre-2005 Best
^	Stankina	Irina	RUS	25.3.77	167/50	20kW	1:27:56	1:25:29- 00
	Stasiulionyte	Inga	LTU	29.6.81	176/66	JT	62.27	56.95- 02
*	Stef	Claudia	ROM	25.2.78	160/48	20kW	1:29:54	1:27:41- 04
	Stefanídi	Ekateríni	GRE-Y	4.2.90	171/57	PV	4.37i, 4.30	4.14- 04
	Stefanova	Tanya	BUL	8.3.72	178/62	PV	4.50i, 4.35	4.46- 04
	Steiner	April	USA	22.4.80	175/58	PV	4.45	4.45- 04
	Stevens	Sarah	USA-J	2.4.86	178/83	SP	16.90	15.35- 04
	Stockard	Jessica	USA	2.3.84	178/62	Hep	5794	5378- 04
	Stoddart	Shevon	JAM	21.11.82	165/53	400H	54.47	55.50- 04
	Stolic	Sonja	SCG	21.4.80	167/48	1500	4:09.17	4:13.43- 00
	Straková	Iva	CZE	4.8.80	187/65	HJ	1.94i, 1.93	1.96i- 03, 1.93- 04
	Stratáki	Aryiró	GRE	3.8.75	173/60	Hep	5943	6157- 04
	Strickland	Janae	USA	19.8.82		SP	16.83i	16.92- 04
	Strong	Kelly	USA	27.9.78	168/54	3kSt	10:02.43	9:55.49- 01
	Strutz	Martina	GER	4.11.81	160/53	PV	4.40i, 4.35	4.42- 01
	Stucan	Constanta	ROM	12.7.81	180/60	TJ	14.11i, 13.72	13.98- 03
*	Stuczynski	Jennifer	USA	6.2.82	180/64	PV	4.57i, 4.57?, 4.26	3.49- 04
*	Sturrup	Chandra	BAH	12.9.71	163/55	100	10.84	10.86- 00
*	Styopina	Viktoria	UKR	21.2.76	178/58	HJ	1.95i, 1.93	2.02- 04
	Su Yiping		CHN	4.8.79	174/58	100H	13.05	12.91- 99, 12.70w- 01
*	Sua	Seilala	USA	25.2.78	188/109	DT	61.82	65.90- 00
	Sudak	Svetlana	BLR	20.3.71	174/90	HT	69.80	69.59- 04
	Sugihara	Kayo	JPN	24.2.83	161/44	5000	15:27.60	15:29.09- 04
						10000	32:29.29	32:49.13- 04
	Sugimori	Miho	JPN	14.4.78	156/48	800	2:00.45	2:00.46- 04
						1500	4:09.30	4:13.53- 04
	Sultan	Simret	ERI	20.7.84	169/50	5000	15:18.69	16:09.48- 03
	Sun Hongfeng		CHN	11.4.79		400	51.93dq	51.87- 04
	Sun Lihua		CHN	30.9.83	162/44	20kW	1:30:16	1:33:59- 04
	Sun Limin		CHN-J	6.2.87	174/65	20kW	1:30:39	1:32:43- 04
	Sun Tanfeng		CHN	26.8.82	187/90	DT	61.08	58.09- 04
	Sun Weiwei		CHN	13.1.85	160/45	5000	15:26.21	15:50.67- 04
						Mar	2:27:35	2:25:15- 02
	Sun Wenqing		CHN	2.6.81		10000	32:19.48	33:24.24- 01
*	Sun Yingjie ¶		CHN	3.10.77	165/50	3000	8:52.62+	8:50.34+-03
						5000	14:51.19	14:40.41- 02
						10000	30:33.53	30:07.20- 03
						Mar	2:21:01	2:19:39- 03
	Suthe	Annika	GER	15.10.85	175/68	JT	58.39	61.38- 04
	Sutherland	Sonita	JAM-J	9.7.87	174/64	400	52.10	52.29- 04
*	Suttle	Kellie	USA	9.5.73	170/59	PV	4.50i, 4.41	4.67- 04
	Suzuki	Ayako	JPN	17.12.80	160/44	HMar	70:47	
	Syreva	Olesya	RUS	25.11.83	165/50	1500	4:07.78	4:14.32- 02
						1M	4:32.00	
*	Szab	Nikolett	HUN	3.3.80	168/65	JT	61.68	64.62- 01
	Szczepanska	Magdalena	POL	25.1.80	178/62	Hep	6090	6115- 04
	Tadesse	Mestawet	ETH	19.7.85	164/40	1500	4:04.95	4:05.15- 04
	Tafa	Assale	ETH	.84		Mar	2:28:27	
	Taira	Akane	JPN	3.11.82	161/45	10000	32:12.67	32:46.68- 04
						HMar	70:26	72:04- 04
*	Takahashi	Naoko	JPN	6.5.72	163/46	HMar	70:30	68:55- 00
						Mar	2:24:39	2:19:46- 01
	Talpos	Luminita	ROM	9.10.72		HMar	71:41	70:08- 02
	Tan Jian		CHN-Y	22.1.88		DT	57.01	56.00- 04
	Tang Jinling		CHN			DT	56.59	50.14- 02
	Tang Xiaoyin		CHN	29.4.85	163/47	400	51.96	52.57- 03
	Tang Yinghua		CHN	18.5.73	164/45	20kW	1:28:07	1:30:36- 00
	Tanno	Asami	JPN	25.9.85	162/48	400	51.80	52.88- 04
	Tao Hongbo		CHN	20.9.79		DT	58.90	60.83- 99
	Taranova	Anastasiya	RUS	6.9.85	178/61	TJ	14.20	14.11- 04
	Tarasova	Irina	RUS-J	15.4.87		SP	16.79i	17.05- 04
*	Tarviainen	Paula	FIN	17.2.73	167/68	JT	62.64	64.90- 03
	Taurima	Kerrie	AUS	2.4.79	174/59	LJ	6.59w	6.62, 6.78w- 04
	Tavares	Carmo	POR	27.4.74	168/52	800	2:01.94	
	Tavares	Elisabete	POR	7.3.80	170/54	PV	4.30i, 4.25	4.25- 03
	Tavares	Sandra	POR	29.5.82	166/55	PV	4.21i	4.20- 03
*	Taylor	Brenda	USA	9.2.79	174/63	400H	55.40	53.36- 04
	Taylor	Lindsay	USA	9.2.79		PV	4.40	4.45- 04
	Tchayem	Nelly	FRA	4.8.83	173/60	TJ	13.75	13.28- 03, 13.51w- 04
	Teixeira	Sandra	POR	13.3.78	170/52	800	2:02.48	2:01.81- 04
						1500	4:10.28	4:17.29- 02

Name		Nat	Born	Ht/Wt	Event	2005Mark	Pre-2005 Best
* Tejeda	Anay	CUB	3.4.83	165/59	100H	12.95	12.74- 04, 12.6- 02
Teodoro	Lucimar	BRA	1.5.81	178/67	400	51.23	52.07- 03
					400H	56.12	55.94- 04
Teodoro	Lúzia Maria	BRA	25.7.78		TJ	13.72	13.54- 04
Terada	Kei	JPN	27.3.85		HMar	71:42	70:53- 04
* Tereshchuk	Tatyana	UKR	11.10.69	185/63	400H	55.09	53.37- 04
Ter-Mesrobyan	Tatyana	RUS	12.5.68	180/62	LJ	6.74	7.06- 02
Teteris	Aimee	CAN	24.6.79	163/48	800	2:01.90	2:01.68- 04
* Thiam	Ami Mbacké	SEN	10.11.76	183/70	200	23.10	23.20, 23.0A- 99
					400	50.69	49.86- 01
* Thompson	Bronwyn	AUS	29.1.78	177/68	LJ	6.59, 6.73w	7.00- 02
Thompson	Moya	JAM	19.2.81	178/62	400	51.51	51.80- 03
Thondike	Arasay	CUB-J	28.5.86	168/71	HT	68.74	63.71- 04
* Timbilil	Alice	KEN	16.6.83	155/45	3000	8:40.76	8:42.01- 04
					5000	14:47.06	14:53.17- 04
					10000	31:45.4A	31:23.99- 04
Timofeyeva	Irina	RUS	5.4.70	156/48	HMar	70:35	70:42- 04
					Mar	2:30:11	2:25:29- 01
* Tîrlea-Manolache	Ionela	ROM	9.2.76	169/54	200	23.26	22.35- 99
					400	52.09	49.88- 99
Titova	Tatyana	RUS	2.1.83		TJ	13.83	12.58- 01
Tola	Roba	ETH			Mar	2:29:30	
Tola	Worknesh	ETH	3.6.77	168/50	Mar	2:29:54	2:25:42- 03
Tollefson	Carrie	USA	18.1.77	175/54	1500	4:10.55	4:06.13- 04
					1M	4:32.25	4:33.15- 01
					5000	15:24.13	15:04.07- 04
Tolstaya	Svetlana	KAZ	9.8.71	168/52	20kW	1:30:13	1:28:38- 02
* Tomasevic	Dragana	SCG	4.6.82	175/80	DT	62.43	59.52- 04
Tomashevska/Yastrebova	Natalya	UKR	12.10.84	175/57	TJ	13.91	13.52- 03
* Tomashova	Tatyana	RUS	1.7.75	164/50	1000	2:34.91	
					1500	3:59.05	3:58.12- 04
* Tomescu	Constantina	ROM	23.1.70	165/48	HMar	69:17	68:10- 02
					Mar	2:21:30	2:23:35- 03
Tonn	Claudia	GER	18.4.81	182/72	LJ	6.60	6.46- 04
					Hep	6054	6169- 04
* Toomey	Jennifer	USA	19.12.71	165/51	800	1:59.96	1:59.75- 03, 1:59.63i- 04
					1000	2:36.46	2:39.56- 02, 2:34.19i- 04
					1500	4:06.24	4:06.61- 04
Torotoich	Margaret	KEN			Mar	2:31:23	
Torres	Marestella	PHI	20.2.81		LJ	6.63	6.41- 04
* Tosa	Reiko	JPN	11.6.76	167/45	10000	32:07.66	32:15.63- 00
* Tóth	Livia	HUN	7.1.80	176/57	3kSt	9:30.20	9:39.84- 04
Touhami	Nadiha	ALG	10.2.78	175/60	800	2:01.56A	1:59.65- 04
Touoloumtzí	Panayióta	GRE-J	26.9.86	169/60	JT	57.45	51.76- 04
Toyonaga	Yoko	JPN	15.4.77	164/87	SP	17.07	17.57- 04
Trakmann	Jana	EST	17.2.82		JT	55.91	57.57- 04
Trevisan	Elisa	ITA	5.3.80	166/55	Hep	5744	5844- 04
Trifonova	Anastasiya	RUS	17.12.84	168/57	400H	56.13	57.22- 04
Triviño	Johana	COL	24.3.81		TJ	13.90A	13.57- 04
Triviño	Johana	COL	24.3.81		TJ	13.60	
* Trotter	Dee Dee	USA	8.12.82	178/60	200	23.12	23.42- 03, 23.19i- 04
					400	49.88	50.00- 04
Troup-Michniovaite	Rasa	LTU	1.3.77	176/62	3kSt	9:47.47	9:56.51- 04
Trybanska	Malgorzata	POL	21.6.81	176/61	LJ	6.60	6.59- 03
* Trywianska	Aurelia	POL	9.5.76	174/59	100H	12.77	12.79- 04
* Tsander	Olga	BLR	18.5.76	174/83	HT	76.66	74.72- 04
Tschurtschentaler	Agnes	ITA	12.1.82	160/45	3kSt	10:01.09	0
^ Tsikoúna	Stiliani	GRE	19.10.72	171/75	DT	56.84	65.25- 04
* Tsiolakoúdi	Aggelikí	GRE	10.5.76	167/72	JT	62.72	63.14- 02, 63.32#- 97
* Tsybulskaya	Valentina	BLR	19.2.68	163/54	20kW	1:32:41	1:28:10- 03
^ Tsyganova	Natalya	RUS	7.2.71	162/52	800	2:00.26	1:56.60- 00
Tuchak	Oksana	RUS	27.3.73	187/82	DT	61.06	64.25- 99
Tucholke	Jana	GER	20.5.81	185/90	DT	60.31	60.48- 04
* Tulu	Derartu	ETH	21.3.72	155/45	HMar	67:33 dh	67:03- 01
					Mar	2:23:30	2:23:57- 01
Tune	Dire	ETH	.85		HMar	71:16+	
					Mar	2:30:48	-0-
Tunks	Lieja	NED	10.3.76	183/95	SP	18.59	18.82- 03
* Turova	Alesya	BLR	6.12.79	180/64	1500	4:02.21	3:59.89- 02
					3000	8:55.13	8:32.89- 01
* Turova	Margarita	BLR	28.12.80	174/55	20kW	1:27:05	1:29:06- 04

Name		Nat	Born	Ht/Wt	Event	2005 Mark	Pre-2005 Best
Tverdostup (Volkova)	Tamara	UKR	17.7.79	167/56	800	2:02.28	2:00.76- 04
Tyminska	Karolina	POL	4.10.84	172/68	Hep	6026	5787- 04
Tyson	Cleo	USA-J	1.5.86	168/55	100	11.25	11.42A, 11.35w- 04
					200	22.88	23.36- 04
* Udmurtova	Oksana	RUS	1.2.82	172/56	LJ	6.86	6.78- 03
Ueda	Mie	JPN	9.6.82	158/42	HMar	71:39	72:35- 04
Ueki	Miwako	JPN	27.6.78	157/39	HMar	71:24	72:47- 01
Ueno	Rie	JPN	11.6.76	164/46	HMar	70:02	69:57- 00
Ukabam	Amarachi	USA	14.3.84		SP	17.52	16.65- 04
					DT	56.18	56.21- 03
Ulfarsdóttir	Silja	ISL	20.6.81	174/64	400H	56.62	57.48- 04
Ulyeva	Iolanta	KAZ	27.7.76	172/85	SP	16.75	18.04i- 02, 17.82- 00
* Upshaw	Grace	USA	22.9.75	178/65	LJ	6.73, 6.87w	6.84- 04, 6.99w- 03
^ Urbansky	Ulrike	GER	6.4.77	174/62	400H	55.94	54.57- 00
Urbina	Maria Teresa	ESP	20.3.85		3kSt	10:12.66	10:26.89- 04
Uslu	Binnaz	TUR	12.3.85	160/55	800	2:01.42	2:00.94- 04
Usovich	Ilona	BLR	14.11.82	167/55	400	50.96	52.31- 04
Usovich	Svetlana	BLR	14.10.80	164/52	400	51.87, 50.55i	50.79- 04
					800	1:58.17	2:05.55- 03
Ustinova	Anna	KAZ	8.12.85	178/59	HJ	1.92i, 1.87	1.89- 04
Vaill	Teresa	USA	20.11.62	162/48	20kW	1:33:28.15t	1:33:23- 01
Valdonado	Laetitia	FRA	4.8.77	160/46	800	1:59.54	1:59.35- 04
van Bühren	Kathrin	GER	29.5.82	174/63	LJ	6.49i, 6.48	6.65- 04
Van den Bempt	Sigrid	BEL	10.2.81	173/58	3kSt	10:01.49	9:35.28- 04
Vargas	Mailín	CUB	24.3.83	176/80	SP	17.31	17.12- 04
* Vasco	María	ESP	26.12.75	156/47	20kW	1:28:51	1:27:36- 04
Vashentseva	Irina	RUS	30.9.80	173/58	800	2:00.76, 1:58.48i	1:59.63- 03
					1000	2:37.98i	2:35.71i- 04
Vasilyeva	Irina	RUS	9.4.79	168/54	TJ	14.02, 14.05w	14.57- 01
Vasilyeva	Svetlana	RUS-J	17.8.86	168/50	20kW	1:32:25	
* Vaszi	Tünde	HUN	18.4.72	170/60	LJ	6.69, 6.72w	6.86- 01
Vaylenko	Lyudmila	UKR	18.3.74	169/55	PV	4.20	4.20i- 03, 4.20- 04
Veldáková	Dana	SVK	3.6.81	178/59	TJ	14.16	14.02- 03
Veldáková	Jana	SVK	3.6.81	177/59	LJ	6.59	6.49- 04
* Veneva	Venelina	BUL	13.6.74	179/61	HJ	1.98	2.04- 01
Vento	Debra	USA	17.12.85		HJ	1.87	1.83- 04
Vermeulen	Kate	CAN	5.10.76	175/54	800	2:02.17	2:02.31- 04
					1500	4:07.77	4:06.92- 04
Vieira	Zenaide	BRA	25.6.85		3kSt	10:01.84	10:10.66- 04
Vigliano	Nadine	FRA	24.6.77	181/72	JT	55.67	55.93- 03
Viigipuu	Kadri	EST	4.2.82	174/62	100H	13.31	13.54- 04
* Vili	Valerie	NZL	6.10.84	193/123	SP	19.87	19.29- 04
Vilisova	Tatyana	RUS	27.11.79		3kSt	9:53.48	9:50.14- 04
Viljoen	Sunette	RSA	6.10.83	168/63	JT	57.31	61.15- 04
Vinatho	Vassanee	THA	30.6.80		400H	57.20	56.40- 03
Visigalli	Anna	ITA	24.2.81	182/62	HJ	1.88i	1.90i- 01, 1.89- 04
* Vlasic	Blanka	CRO	8.11.83	192/75	HJ	1.95	2.03- 04
* Volkova	Yekaterina	RUS	16.2.78	169/55	1500	4:09.03	4:21.48- 03
					1M	4:29.60	
					3000	8:54.64	9:20.81- 03
					3kSt	9:20.49	9:32.31- 03
Volosyuk	Oksana	UKR	28.11.81	178/59	400H	56.51	57.11- 04
Volzankina	Jesenija	LAT	28.11.83	173/56	LJ	6.52i	6.28- 04
Vontein	Barbara	GER	7.6.78	182/64	JT	55.83	58.34- 04
Voyevodina	Yuliya	RUS	17.10.71	170/56	20kW	1:28:02	1:27:53- 04
Vrbenská	Lucie	CZE	12.5.77	180/85	HT	64.54	67.86- 03
Vriesde	Letitia	SUR	5.10.64	159/55	800	2:01.65	1:56.68- 95
Vukmirovic	Radmila	SLO	23.11.79	170/62	100H	13.28	13.16- 04
Vukmirovic	Snezana	SLO	19.8.82	180/66	TJ	14.18	13.97- 04
Wagner	Kaylene	USA	15.11.84	186/64	HJ	1.88	1.92- 04
Wakan	Katja	GER	27.6.81	165/58	100	11.41	11.54- 03
Waldet	Olivia	FRA	23.5.84	177/79	HT	65.52	60.03- 04
Walker	Amanda	USA	12.9.82		SP	16.80	15.64- 03
Walker	Beau	USA	25.3.83	174/64	100H	12.99	12.99, 12.96w- 04
					400H	56.43	56.28- 04
Walker	Melaine	JAM	1.1.83	165/53	100H	13.21, 13.17w	13.37- 02
					400H	55.09	55.62- 01
Walker	Shakeema	USA	10.11.76	182/61	TJ	13.70	14.06, 14.07w- 04
Wall	Kim	GBR	21.4.83	175/53	400	52.20	53.07- 04
Walsham	Suzy	AUS	22.11.73	168/50	1500	4:08.54	4:07.78- 03

	Name		Nat	Born	Ht/Wt	Event	2005Mark	Pre-2005 Best
	Walter	Sarah	FRA	5.5.78	173/64	JT	57.62	62.53- 03
	Wambui	Evelyne	KEN-J	4.4.86	162/49	3000	8:52.31	
						5000	15:06.74	
*	Wami	Getenesh	ETH	11.12.74	154/45	3000	8:36.22	8:27.62- 01
						5000	14:58.58	14:30.88- 00
						Mar	2:27:40	2:22:19- 02
	Wang Hailan		CHN	6.4.76	168/59	Hep	6128	5970- 03
	Wang Lihong		CHN	9.1.83		SP	17.87i, 17.23	17.64- 04
	Wang Lina		CHN	28.2.83	168/58	LJ	6.63	6.72- 04
*	Wang Liping		CHN	8.7.76	165/48	20kW	1:27:24	1:26:23- 01
	Wang Xing		CHN-J	30.11.86	169/50	400H	54.40	55.79- 04
	Wang Yawen		CHN	23.8.73	187/90	SP	17.85	19.89- 93
	Wang Ying		CHN	24.7.83	176/68	TJ	14.12	13.83- 04
	Wang Yu		CHN	22.9.85	182/92	DT	59.85	59.08- 03
	Wangari	Mary Mureithi	KEN	9.4.78	163/50	5000	15:08.28	15:20.53- 04
						10000	31:38.81	32:17.79- 04
*	Wangui	Lucy	KEN	24.3.84	155/41	5000	15:00.20	14:57.09- 04
						10000	31:22.37	31:05.90- 04
	Wanguru	Kiragu	KEN	26.8.80		10000	32:31.14	
	Wanjiku	Jane	KEN	14.6.79	158/43	5000	15:07.89	15:04.00- 03
						10000	31:38.84	31:04.34- 04
	Wanjiru	Ruth	KEN	11.9.81	155/44	5000	15:25.67	15:31.99- 03
						10000	32:27.79	31:56.21- 03
						HMar	71:26	70:15- 02
	Wanless	Liz	USA	18.11.81		SP	18.58	17.42i- 04
	Warren	Kamaiya	USA	10.3.84		SP	16.60	16.83- 04
	Washington	Raquel	USA	26.9.82		100H	13.21	13.61- 04
	Watkins	Tawana	USA	27.3.84		400H	57.33	57.48- 01
	Watzek	Veronka	AUT	13.8.85	184/75	DT	56.11	52.95- 04
	Weatherspoon	Alexis	USA	27.7.83	165/55	100	11.34, 11.31w	11.58- 04
						200	23.11	23.76- 04
	Webb	Cheryl	AUS	3.10.76	165/53	20kW	1:33:14	1:31:43- 04
	Webb	Shirley	GBR	28.9.81	178/91	HT	67.58	67.52- 04
	Wei Xioyan		CHN	13.3.83	179/77	HT	63.60	60.90- 03
	Wei Yanan		CHN	6.12.81	160/48	Mar	2:25:55	2:20:23- 02
	Weissteiner	Silvia	ITA	13.7.79	163/46	3000	8:56.27i	8:58.91- 03
						5000	15:28.55	15:35.20- 04
	Wells	Kellie	USA	16.7.82		100H	13.29w	13.25- 04
	Wentland	Gwen	USA	29.4.72	178/64	HJ	1.88i	1.96i- 95, 1.95- 03
*	Wheeler	Kylie	AUS	17.1.80	180/64	Hep	6231	6296- 04
	Whipple	Erica	USA	4.12.82	168/50	100	11.38	11.15- 03, 11.0- 99
						200	23.13, 23.10w	22.82- 03
^	Whitlock	Janine	GBR	11.8.73	164/54	PV	4.47	4.44i, 4.41dq- 02, 4.40- 01
	Whitman	Nicole	USA	9.11.80		100	11.33w	11.65- 03
						TJ	13.78	13.32- 03
*	Whyte	Angela	CAN	22.5.80	170/57	100H	12.88	12.69- 04
	Wiechmann	Julia	GER	28.3.84	187/85	SP	16.62i	16.59- 04
	Wienand	Janet	RSA	15.5.85		400H	57.41	58.83A-03
*	Wigene	Susanne	NOR	12.2.78	168/50	3000	8:40.23	9:01.27- 04
						5000	14:48.53	15:12.27- 04
	Wildhaber	Ashley	USA	29.10.83		PV	4.20i	4.01- 04
	Wildrick	Andrea	USA	23.12.79	170/	PV	4.20	4.35- 02
	Wilks	Antoinette	JAM	14.10.80		100H	12.94	13.53- 03
^	Williams	Angela	USA	30.1.80	156/52	100	11.29, 11.25w	11.04, 10.96w- 99
	Williams	Ashlee	USA	27.3.84	170/54	100H	12.83	12.90- 04
	Williams	Kasia	JAM	14.12.84	165/53	100H	13.13	13.27, 13.08w- 04
*	Williams	Lauryn	USA	11.9.83	157/57	100	10.88	10.96, 10.94w- 04
						200	22.27	22.46- 04
*	Williams	Novlene	JAM	26.4.82	167/55	400	51.09	50.59- 04
	Williams	Shellene	JAM	19.2.81	170/64	400	52.03	51.94- 04
	Williams	Shericka	JAM	17.9.85	170/64	200	23.08	23.90- 03
						400	50.97	53.52- 04
	Williams-Chesser	Renata	USA	17.5.83	163/52	3kSt	10:02.21	10:27.57- 04
*	Williams-Darling	Tonique	BAH	17.1.76	168/59	200	23.03	22.77- 04
						400	49.30	49.07- 04
	Wilson	Kenyanna	USA-Y	27.10.88		100	11.38Aw	11.69- 04
	Wilson	Nickeisha	JAM-J	28.7.86		400H	57.38	
	Wisniewska	Joanna	POL	24.5.72	187/82	DT	62.50	63.97- 99
	Wisse	Yvonne	NED	6.6.82	180/60	Hep	6026	5895- 03
^	Witteveen	Solange	ARG	6.2.76	171/59	HJ	1.88A	1.96- 97

WOMEN'S INDEX

Name		Nat	Born	Ht/Wt	Event	2005 Mark	Pre-2005 Best
Wittstock	Estie	RSA	15.9.80	172/58	400	52.21	51.48- 04
Wöckinger	Olivia	AUT	23.5.79	168/54	LJ	6.57i	6.69- 03, 6.72w- 04
Wojczakowska	Izabela	POL	24.3.74	180/65	JT	55.70	56.32- 01
Wommack	Shannon	USA	9.4.83	173/58	3kSt	10:07.14	10:45.65- 04
Wort	Liz	USA	.84	178/60	3kSt	10:05.39	10:40.99- 04
Woytkowska	Jana	GER	7.8.77	182/64	JT	57.36	59.55- 02
Wu Lingmei		CHN	16.2.73	168/60	TJ	13.95	14.39- 98, 14.55w- 99
Wu Sha		CHN-J	21.10.87	173/64	PV	4.30i	4.30- 03
Wu Xueli		CHN	5.1.78	172/62	TJ	14.01	13.99- 04
Wurth-Thomas	Christy	USA	11.7.80	165/52	1500	4:08.76	4:10.49- 03
Wysocka	Marzena	POL	17.2.69	176/80	DT	64.57	63.60- 03
Xi Qiuhong		CHN	4.9.84	163/47	5000	15:25.36	15:41.46- 04
					10000	31:31.64	33:07.16- 04
Xiao Yanling		CHN	27.3.68	180/92	DT	59.08	71.68- 92
Xie Limei		CHN-J	27.6.86	173/52	TJ	14.38	14.08- 04
Xie Sainan		CHN-J	3.11.86	168/58	1500	4:11.11	4:10.29- 04
* Xing Huina		CHN	25.2.84	166/50	1500	4:03.98dq	4:09.01- 03
					3000	8:53.5+	8:58.61- 01
					5000	14:43.64	14:56.01- 04
					10000	30:27.18	30:24.36- 04
Xu Aihui		CHN	25.4.78	167/54	20kW	1:32:47	1:29:30- 04
Xu Shaoyang		CHN	9.2.83	180/84	DT	61.56	62.54- 02
Xue Ailing		CHN	12.2.79	173/52	20kW	1:33:38	1:30:52- 04
Xue Juan		CHN-J	10.2.86	176/68	JT	61.42	62.93- 03
Yagi	Yoko	JPN	14.4.80	159/43	10000	32:09.95	32:33.64- 04
					HMar	71:02	72:52- 04
Yakovenko	Mariya	RUS	6.1.82	174/85	JT	60.83	59.65- 00
Yakovleva	Tatyana	RUS-J	9.9.86		TJ	13.62i	13.85- 04
Yakovleva	Yelena	RUS	18.3.83		200	22.99	23.99- 03, 23.85i- 04
Yamasaki	Chieko	JPN	28.5.77	155/45	HMar	71:30	71:32- 04
					Mar	2:27:22	
Yamauchi	Mara	GBR	13.8.73	162/52	HMar	69:51 dh	72:33- 03
					Mar	2:27:38	2:39:16- 04
Yang Cui		CHN	15.8.84	177/95	SP	17.61	16.80- 04
Yang Jing		CHN	1.1.84	170/57	PV	4.40	4.20- 04
Yang Liping		CHN	12.9.84	165/49	20kW	1:32:31	1:35:58- 04
Yang Meiping		CHN	23.10.85		HT	68.09	67.21- 04
Yang Qiaoyu		CHN	14.9.85		HT	65.60	64.30- 03
Yang Sha		CHN-J	16.1.86	161/43	20kW	1:29:33	1:32:21- 04
Yang Yawei		CHN	16.10.83	168/51	20kW	1:27:58	1:36:38- 04
Yao Yuehua		CHN	27.8.80	172/60	400H	55.94	55.58- 01
^ Yatchenko	Irina	BLR	31.10.65	186/105	DT	60.25	69.14- 04
Yatsevich	Anastasiya	BLR	18.1.85		20kW	1:34:07	
Yefimkina	Lyudmila	RUS	22.8.81	158/44	20kW	1:29:51	1:27:51- 02
Yefremova	Antonina	UKR	19.7.81	176/60	400	51.40	50.70- 02
Yegorova	Lyudmila	UKR	4.10.74	164/54	20kW	1:30:45	1:32:02- 00
* Yegorova	Olga	RUS	28.3.72	160/48	1500	3:59.47	4:01.00- 03
Yelling	Hayley	GBR	3.1.74	152/45	5000	15:16.44	15:19.12- 01
					10000	31:53.61	31:45.14- 04
Yemelyanova	Larisa	RUS	6.1.80	164/52	20kW	1:29:43, 1:33:20.2t	1:27:23- 03
Yepimashko	Vera	BLR	10.7.76	181/79	SP	17.78	17.54i, 16.90- 04
					Hep	5819	5829- 04
Yesipchuk	Oksana	RUS	13.12.76	182/96	DT	62.18	63.68- 00
Yevdokimova	Anna	RUS	27.5.83		100H	13.12	13.35- 04
* Yevdokimova	Natalya	RUS	17.3.78	174/65	800	2:00.34	1:58.75- 03
					1500	3:57.73	3:59.05- 04
Yezhova	Yekaterina	RUS	18.2.82	166/51	20kW	1:32:04, 1:33:29l9t	1:34:54- 03
* Yordanova	Daniela	BUL	8.3.76	165/52	1500	4:11.64	3:59.10- 04
Yoshida	Emika	JPN	10.12.85	165/60	JT	55.60	53.72- 03
Yoshida	Kana	JPN	27.4.84	167/48	HMar	70:49	71:33- 04
Yoshida	Kaori	JPN	4.8.81	155/38	HMar	70:54	70:18- 01
Yoshida	Makiko	JPN	16.7.76	164/49	400H	56.67	55.89- 03
Yoshino	Megumi	JPN	26.6.84	157/42	5000	15:28.93	15:31.29- 04
					10000	32:18.03	
Yosipenko	Lyudmila	UKR	24.9.84	175/63	Hep	5782	5564- 04
Yotova	Darinka	BUL	14.2.85		TJ	13.94	13.56- 04
Yu Shuo		CHN-Y	14.1.88		PV	4.20i, 4,20	3.90- 04
Yurchenko	Snezhana	BLR	8.3.84	159/51	20kW	1:33:51	1:35:41- 01
* Zabawska	Krystyna	POL	14.1.68	183/92	SP	18.96i, 18.79	19.42- 92
* Zadorozhnaya	Yelena	RUS	3.12.77	157/42	1500	4:03.65	3:59.94- 02
					3000	8:35.11	8:25.40- 01

Name		Nat	Born	Ht/Wt	Event	2005Mark	Pre-2005 Best
(Zadorozhnaya)					5000	15:15.85	14:40.47- 01
					3kSt	9:32.41	-0-
Zadura	Malgorzata	POL	3.10.82	172/75	HT	64.13	63.65- 04
Zagacka	Liliana	POL	28.1.77	168/56	TJ	13.69	14.22- 01
^ Zaituc	Luminita	GER	9.10.68	165/50	HMar	71:04	69:35- 04
					Mar	2:26:46	2:26:01- 01
* Zakharova	Svetlana	RUS	15.9.70	158/48	HMar	71:30+	69:48- 02
					Mar	2:26:55	2:21:31- 02
Zang Yan		CHN	13.12.83		20kW	1:34:05	1:31:04- 03
* Zaytseva	Olga	RUS	10.11.84	176/67	200	23.04	23.43- 04
					400	50.06	51.09- 04
Zbrozhek	Oksana	RUS	12.1.78	167/49	800	2:00.56	1:58.06- 04
					1500	4:08.16	4:14.75i, 4:18.01- 04
Zekiros	Adanech	ETH	26.3.82		10000	31:59.37	
Zelenina	Alexandra	MDA-J	21.11.86		LJ	6.51	6.28- 04
					TJ	13.79	13.59- 04
Zelenska	Vasilisa	UKR	31.8.85	180/80	DT	56.34	52.95- 04
Zelinka	Jessica	CAN	3.9.81	175/61	100H	13.15w	13.26- 04
					Hep	6137	6051w, 5757- 04
Zemaityte	Viktorija	LTU	11.3.85	184/65	Hep	5913	5810- 04
Zérva	María	GRE-J	10.8.87	170/72	JT	57.92	51.19- 04
Zhai Lijun		CHN-J	28.11.86	169/56	20kW	1:30:19	1:39:50- 04
Zhalneryuk	Yulyana	BLR	14.8.84	173/56	400	52.1, 52.58	
Zhang Chong		CHN-J	5.1.86	169/62	5000	15:27.06	15:47.28- 04
					10000	32:28.10	32:35.60- 04
Zhang Chunjing		CHN	19.5.83		SP	18.28	16.90- 03
Zhang Guirong		SIN	5.2.78	182/98	SP	18.57	18.37- 04
Zhang Hao		CHN	26.2.78	172/60	TJ	13.87	14.22- 03
Zhang Li		CHN	19.10.78		JT	58.36	60.02- 00
Zhang Li		CHN-Y	17.1.89		JT	57.80	53.98- 04
Zhang Na		CHN	27.9.80	178/60	PV	4.20i	4.25i, 4.20- 04
Zhang Nan		CHN-J	18.4.86	157/43	20kW	1:29:51	1:31:55- 03
Zhang Qiang		CHN-J	14.2.87		SP	17.08i	17.16- 04
Zhang Rong		CHN	5.1.83	174/65	100H	13.11	13.14- 03, 13.03w- 01
Zhang Rongrong		CHN	27.1.84		400H	55.91	57.00- 04
Zhang Shujing		CHN	13.9.78	158/55	Mar	2:27:41	2:23:17- 02
* Zhang Wenxiu		CHN-J	22.3.86	182/102	HT	73.24	72.42- 04
Zhang Yuan		CHN-J	9.2.87	171/52	LJ	6.50	6.43- 04
Zhao Wenjiang		CHN	10.7.81	184/92	HT	65.29	64.95- 04
Zhao Yingying		CHN-J	15.2.86	167/53	PV	4.45i, 4.40	4.40- 04
Zheng Ruixia		CHN	14.3.83	174/60	JT	55.97	55.04- 04
Zheng Xingyuan		CHN-J	29.3.89		HJ	1.92	1.87- 04
Zhevnova	Tatyana	BLR	17.10.77	173/60	Hep	5776	6077w- 04, 6023- 03
* Zhilyayeva	Alla	RUS	5.2.69	163/50	3000	8:56.38	8:47.46- 04
					5000	15:17.92	14:59.46- 04
					10000	31:14.27	30:23.07- 03
Zhong Mei		CHN	7.1.77	167/63	LJ	6.57	6.76- 97
* Zhou Chunxiu		CHN	8.3.79	162/51	10000	31:09.03	32:13.96- 03
					HMar	70:19+	72:52- 04
					Mar	2:21:11	2:23:28- 04
Zhou Tongmei		CHN			20kW	1:30:35	1:35:43- 04
Zhu Xiaolin		CHN	20.2.84		5000	15:22.35	15:58.24- 02
Zhuravlyeva	Anastasiya	UZB	9.10.81	170/60	TJ	14.55	14.35- 04
Zimmer	Sabine	GER	6.2.81	165/48	20kW	1:29:07	1:27:56- 04
Zimmer	Vivian	GER-J	22.7.87	176/69	JT	58.74	60.14- 04
Zinovyeva	Olga	RUS-J	29.10.86		Hep	5662	
Zinovyeva	Yuliya	RUS	18.5.84		LJ	6.77	5.92- 02
Zolotova	Yevgeniya	RUS	28.4.83	166/59	800	2:00.78	2:04.53- 04
Zolotukhina	Natalya	UKR	4.1.85	180/77	HT	67.75	69.73- 04
Zongo	Amy	FRA	4.10.80	163/49	TJ	13.79, 13.88w	13.77- 04
Zorkova	Natalya	RUS	15.6.81		800	2:02.1	2:06.22- 03
Zou Ying		CHN	20.8.82	171/58	20kW	1:31:45	1:31:32- 04
Zozulya	Vera	UKR	31.8.70	166/56	20kW	1:31:38	1:28:19- 03
Zubkovska	Oksana	UKR	15.7.81	175/63	LJ	6.56	6.53- 04
Zumer	Kristina	SLO	2.2.80	177/63	100	11.40w	11.64- 03
Zunda	Ieva	LAT	20.7.78	164/54	400H	56.84	55.59- 04
^ Zvereva	Ellina	BLR	16.11.60	186/96	DT	62.38	71.58- 88
* Zykina	Olesya	RUS	7.10.80	170/60	200	22.55	22.78- 00, 22.3- 99
					400	50.73	50.15- 01
Zyusko	Larisa	RUS	27.4.69	168/57	Mar	2:30:14	2:28:05- 03

WORLD INDOOR LISTS 2006 – MEN

60 METRES

6.50	Leonard	Scott	USA	19.1.80	1s3	WI	Moskva	10 Mar
6.52	Andrey	Yepishin	RUS	10.6.81	2	WI	Moskva	10 Mar
6.53	Johnie	Drake	USA	28.3.83	1		Mount Pleasant	18 Feb
6.53	Terrence	Trammell	USA	23.11.78	2	NC	Boston (R)	26 Feb
6.53	Trell	Kimmons	USA	13.7.85	1h3	JUCO	Manhattan KS	3 Mar
6.55	Jason	Gardener	GBR	17.9.75	1h2		Karlsruhe	29 Jan
6.55	Freddy	Mayola	CUB	1.11.77	1	GP	Birmingham	18 Feb
6.55	Josh	Norman	USA	26.7.80	1s1	NC	Boston (R)	26 Feb
6.55	Jason	Smoots	USA	13.7.80	3	NC	Boston (R)	26 Feb
6.55	Marcus	Brunson	USA	24.4.78	1s2	NC	Boston (R)	26 Feb
6.55	Olusoji	Fasuba	NGR	9.7.84	1h1	Erdgas	Chemnitz	3 Mar
6.56	Tyson	Gay	USA	9.8.82	2	Tyson	Fayetteville	10 Feb
6.56	Jacob	Norman	USA	7.11.85	1h1	NCAA	Fayetteville	10 Mar
6.58	Mikhail	Yegorychev	RUS	21.7.77	h		Samara	4 Feb
6.58	Matic	Osovnikar	SLO	19.1.80	4	WI	Moskva	10 Mar

6.59	Shawn	Crawford	USA	14.1.78	3 Feb
6.59	Anson	Henry	CAN	9.3.79	4 Feb
6.59	Walter	Dix	USA	31.1.86	10 Mar
6.60	Mardy	Scales	USA	10.9.81	28 Jan
6.60	Ronnie	Pines	USA		4 Feb
6.60	Aleksandr	Volkov	RUS	6.7.76	4 Feb
6.60	Vicente	de Lima	BRA	4.6.77	10 Mar
6.61	Morne	Nagel	RSA	23.2.78	25 Jan
6.61	Aleksandr	Smirnov	RUS	25.2.74	4 Feb
6.61	Marc	Burns	TRI	7.1.83	10 Feb
6.61	Anatoliy	Dovgal	UKR	29.1.76	22 Feb
6.61		Hu Kai	CHN	4.8.82	24 Feb
6.61	Ronald	Pognon	FRA	16.11.82	10 Mar

50m: 5.68+ Freddy Mayola CUB 1.11.77 1h2 Liévin 3 Mar

200 METRES

20.27	Walter	Dix	USA	31.1.86	1r2	NCAA	Fayetteville	10 Mar
20.30	Xavier	Carter	USA	8.12.85	2r2	NCAA	Fayetteville	10 Mar
20.42	Milton	Campbell	USA	15.5.76	1r1		Blacksburg	18 Feb
20.46	Kelly	Willie	USA	7.9.82	3r2	NCAA	Fayetteville	10 Mar
20.57	Wallace	Spearmon	USA	24.12.84	1r1		Fayetteville	20 Jan
20.62	Willie	Perry	USA-J	16.5.87	1r1	NCAA	Fayetteville	10 Mar
20.67	Rubin	Williams	USA	9.7.83	4r2	NCAA	Fayetteville	10 Mar
20.71	Tobias	Unger	GER	10.7.79	1r2		Karlsruhe	29 Jan
20.71	Reggie	Witherspoon	USA	31.5.85	2r1	NCAA	Fayetteville	10 Mar
20.72	LaShawn	Merritt	USA	27.6.86	1r8		State College	28 Jan
20.50 OT	Walter	Dix	USA	31.1.86	1r2		Ames	4 Mar
20.61 OT	Milton	Campbell	USA	15.5.76	1r1		Lexington KY	28 Jan

20.81	David	Neville	USA	1.6.84	10 Mar
20.86	Tim	Abeyie	GBR	7.11.82	18 Feb

300 METRES

31.88	Wallace	Spearmon	USA	24.12.84	1	Tyson	Fayetteville	10 Feb
31.94	Kerron	Clement	USA	31.10.85	2	Tyson	Fayetteville	10 Feb
31.94	LaShawn	Merritt	USA	27.6.86	3	Tyson	Fayetteville	10 Feb
32.61	Johan	Wissman	SWE	2.12.82	1	Gaz	Liévin	3 Mar

400 METRES

45.28	Xavier	Carter	USA	8.12.85	1r2	NCAA	Fayetteville	11 Mar
45.54	Alleyne	Francique	GRN	6.6.76	1	WI	Moskva	12 Mar
45.58	David	Neville	USA	1.6.84	1h1	NCAA	Fayetteville	10 Mar
45.67	Lewis	Banda	ZIM	16.9.82	2h1	NCAA	Fayetteville	10 Mar
45.74	California	Molefe	BOT	2.5.80	1h1	WI	Moskva	10 Mar
45.78	Chris	Brown	BAH	15.10.78	3	WI	Moskva	12 Mar
45.81	Milton	Campbell	USA	15.5.76	1r1		Blacksburg	18 Feb
45.90	Robert	Tobin	GBR	20.12.83	1	NC	Sheffield	12 Feb
45.93	Ricardo	Chambers	JAM	7.10.84	1r2		Blacksburg	25 Feb
45.93	Davian	Clarke	JAM	30.4.76	4	WI	Moskva	12 Mar
46.00	Bershawn	Jackson	USA	8.5.83	1r13	Tyson	Fayetteville	10 Feb
46.01	Aaron	Buzard	USA	11.10.84	1r1	NCAA	Fayetteville	11 Mar
46.02	Micheal	Tinsley	USA	21.4.84	1h2	NCAA	Fayetteville	10 Mar

46.08	Sekou	Clarke	JAM	7.10.83	10 Mar
46.17	LaShawn	Merritt	USA	27.6.86	26 Feb
46.18	Tyree	Washington	USA	28.8.76	26 Feb
46.18	Abe	Jones	USA	3.6.82	10 Mar
46.25	James	Davis	USA	19.3.76	4 Feb
46.28	Dmitriy	Petrov	RUS	4.1.82	18 Feb
46.28	Éric	Milazar	MRI	1.6.75	26 Feb
46.28	Miles	Smith	USA	24.9.84	10 Mar

Oversized track

45.40 OT	Milton	Campbell	USA	15.5.76	1r1	Lexington KY	28 Jan
45.63 OT	Jamel	Ashley	USA	17.4.79	1r1	Lexington KY	14 Jan

46.20	Godfrey	Herring	USA	18.5.78	14 Jan
46.20	Aaron	Buzard	USA	11.10.84	11 Feb

600 Metres: 1:16.63 Ricardo Bell USA 17.1.81 1 Bloomington 17 Feb

Oversized track

800 METRES

1:45.4	Yuriy	Borzakovskiy	RUS	12.4.81	1		Shchelkovo	11 Feb
1:45.60	Wilfred	Bungei	KEN	24.7.80	1	Spark	Stuttgart	4 Feb
1:46.46	Dmitrijs	Milkevics	LAT	6.12.81	1	Big 12	Lincoln NE	25 Feb
1:46.63	Sam	Burley	USA	13.2.81	1		Boston	11 Feb
1:46.80	Zach	Glavash	USA	14.6.84	2	Big 12	Lincoln NE	25 Feb
1:46.82	Mbulaeni	Mulaudzi	RSA	8.9.80	1s1	WI	Moskva	11 Mar
1:46.91	Dmitriy	Bogdanov	RUS	11.4.79	3		Karlsruhe	29 Jan
1:46.98	Khadevis	Robinson	USA	19.7.76	1	NC	Boston (R)	26 Feb
1:47.02	Jackson	Langat	KEN	15.12.80	1	NCAA	Fayetteville	11 Mar
1:47.07	Florent	Lacasse	FRA	21.1.81	4		Karlsruhe	29 Jan
1:47.08	Ramil	Aritkulov	RUS	1.3.78	1	NC	Moskva	18 Feb

1:47.19#	Prince	Mumba	ZAM	28.8.84	11 Feb	1:47.36	Amine	Laâlou	MAR	13.5.82	10 Mar
1:47.23	Jimmy	Watkins	GBR	30.10.82	11 Mar	1:47.38	Manuel	Olmedo	ESP	17.5.83	29 Jan
1:47.25	David	Krummenacker	USA	24.5.75	26 Feb	1:47.38	Juan de Dios	Jurado	ESP	9.4.81	11 Mar
1:47.34	Antoine	Martiak	FRA	28.1.83	2 Feb	1:47.50	Joseph	Mutua	KEN	10.12.78	4 Feb

1000 METRES

2:18.19	Daniel Kipchirchir	Komen	KEN	27.11.84	1		Karlsruhe	29 Jan
2:19.04	William	Yiampoy	KEN	15.5.74	2		Karlsruhe	29 Jan

1500 METRES

3:34.20	Daniel Kipchirchir	Komen	KEN	27.11.84	1	Spark	Stuttgart	4 Feb
3:35.24	Suleiman	Simotwo	KEN	21.4.80	2	Spark	Stuttgart	4 Feb
3:36.25	Eliud	Kipchoge	KEN	5.11.84	2	GP	Birmingham	18 Feb
3:38.65	Neil	Speaight	GBR	9.9.78	3	GP	Birmingham	18 Feb
3:38.88	Mounir	Yemmouni	FRA	12.10.83	3	Spark	Stuttgart	4 Feb
3:39.29	Bouabdellah	Tahri	FRA	20.12.78	1		Karlsruhe	29 Jan
3:39.40+	Bernard	Lagat	USA	12.12.74	1	Mill	New York	3 Feb

3:39.89	James	Nolan	IRL	27.1.77	29 Jan	3:40.15	Guillaume	Éraud	FRA	1.7.81	4 Feb
3:39.97	Laban	Rotich	KEN	20.1.69	18 Feb	3:40.18	Stefan	Eberhardt	GER	12.1.85	4 Feb
3:40.04	Sergio	Gallardo	ESP	22.3.79	10 Mar	3:40.20	Ivan	Heshko	UKR	19.8.79	21 Feb
3:40.05	Driss	Maazouzi	FRA	20.10.69	4 Feb	3:40.73	Abdelati	Iguider	MAR-J	25.3.87	4 Feb
3:40.14	Youssef	Baba	MAR	7.8.79	29 Jan	3:40.97	Chris	Lukezic	USA	24.4.84	10 Mar

1 MILE

3:55.04	Alistair	Cragg	IRL	13.6.80	1		Fayetteville	21 Jan
3:55.87	Jason	Lunn	USA	19.9.74	1	Tyson	Fayetteville	10 Feb
3:55.95	Elkana	Angwenyi	KEN	5.2.83	1	BIG	Boston (R)	28 Jan
3:56.83	Laban	Rotich	KEN	20.1.69	3	BIG	Boston (R)	28 Jan
3:56.85	Bernard	Lagat	USA	12.12.74	1	Mill	New York	3 Feb

3:57.17	Nate	Brannen	CAN	8.9.82	28 Jan	3:58.49	Neil	Speaight	GBR	9.9.78	28 Jan
3:57.40	Richard	Kiplagat	KEN	5.1.81	13 Jan	3:58.52	Tom	Lancashire	GBR	2.7.85	2 Mar
3:57.60	Adam	Goucher	USA	18.2.75	28 Jan	3:58.53	Chris	Lukezic	USA	24.4.84	28 Jan
3:57.87	Mike	Woods	CAN	12.10.86	28 Jan	3:58.54#	Chris	Estwanik	USA	4.4.80	14 Jan
3:58.07	Kevin	Sullivan	CAN	20.3.74	28 Jan	3:58.60	Geoffrey	Rono	KEN-J	21.4.87	21 Jan
3:58.23	Andy	Baddeley	GBR	20.6.82	21 Jan	3:58.77#	Kurt	Benninger	CAN	1.1.85	27 Jan
3:58.24	Rob	Myers	USA	5.8.80	28 Jan	3:58.84#	Leonel	Manzano	USA	12.9.84	11 Feb

2000 METRES

4:59.84	Bouabdellah	Tahri	FRA	20.12.78	1	Gaz	Liévin	3 Mar
5:01.16	Khalid	El Amri	MAR	20.3.77	2	Gaz	Liévin	3 Mar
5:01.61	Laban	Rotich	KEN	20.1.69	3	Gaz	Liévin	3 Mar

3000 METRES

7:33.07	Eliud	Kipchoge	KEN	5.11.84	1		Karlsruhe	29 Jan
7:35.1+	Kenenisa	Bekele	ETH	13.6.82	1	in 2M	Birmingham	18 Feb
7:35.65	Boaz	Cheboiywo	KEN	2.8.78	1	Tyson	Fayetteville	10 Feb
7:37.49	Shadrack	Korir	KEN	14.12.78	2	Spark	Stuttgart	4 Feb
7:39.76	Paul	Bitok	KEN	26.6.70	3	Spark	Stuttgart	4 Feb
7:39.77	Saïf Saeed	Shaheen	QAT	15.10.82	1	AsiC	Pattaya	11 Feb
7:41.59	Adam	Goucher	USA	18.2.75	2	Tyson	Fayetteville	10 Feb
7:41.5+	Tariku	Bekele	ETH	21.1.87	2	in 2M	Birmingham	18 Feb
7:42.17	Kevin	Sullivan	CAN	20.3.74	3	Tyson	Fayetteville	10 Feb
7:42.48	Bouabdellah	Tahri	FRA	20.12.78	4	Spark	Stuttgart	4 Feb
7:44.22	Adil	Kaouch	MAR	1.1.79	1		Gent	26 Feb
7:44.31	Abebe	Dinkesa	ETH	6.3.84	5	Spark	Stuttgart	4 Feb
7:44.64	Moukhled	Al-Outaibi	KSA	20.6.76	3		Valencia	11 Feb
7:44.6+	Markos	Geneti	ETH	30.5.84	4	in 2M	Birmingham	18 Feb
7:44.80	Hicham	Bellani	MAR	15.9.79	2		Gent	26 Feb
7:45.10	Günther	Weidlinger	AUT	5.4.78	4		Valencia	11 Feb
7:46.43	Alistair	Cragg	IRL	13.6.80	4	WI	Moskva	12 Mar

7:46.59	Francisco Javier	Alves	ESP	2.9.80	5		Valencia	11 Feb

7:47.21	Jan	Fitschen	GER	2.5.77	17 Feb
7:47.90	Nate	Brannen	CAN	8.9.82	10 Feb
7:48.18	Sergey	Ivanov	RUS	3.3.79	18 Feb
7:49.05	Chris	Lukezic	USA	24.4.84	10 Feb
7:49.43	César	Pérez	ESP	7.4.75	11 Feb
7:49.45	Daniel	Lincoln	USA	22.10.80	10 Feb
7:49.69	Isaac	Sang	KEN	24.8.78	17 Feb
7:49.84	Tareq Mubarak	Taher	BRN	24.3.84	11 Feb
7:49.98	Richard	Kiplagat	KEN	5.1.81	24 Feb
7:50.10	Adam Ismael	Khamis	BRN-Y	12.2.89	11 Feb
7:50.36#	Chris	Estwanik	USA	4.4.80	28 Jan
7:50.40#	Robert	Cheseret	KEN	8.10.83	28 Jan
7:50.44	Pavel	Naumov	RUS	26.12.79	18 Feb
7:50.46	Ismaïl	Sghyr	FRA	16.3.72	4 Feb
7:50.49+	Sileshi	Sihine	ETH	29.1.83	2 Feb
7:50.50	Anter	Zerguelaine	ALG	4.1.85	26 Feb

2 MILES

8:05.12	Kenenisa	Bekele	ETH	13.6.82	1	GP	Birmingham	18 Feb
8:13.32	Tariku	Bekele	ETH	21.1.87	2	GP	Birmingham	18 Feb
8:14.84	Shadrack	Korir	KEN	14.12.78	3	GP	Birmingham	18 Feb
8:17.39	Markos	Geneti	ETH	30.5.84	4	GP	Birmingham	18 Feb

5000 METRES

13:06.72	Sileshi	Sihine	ETH	29.1.83	1		Stockholm	2 Feb
13:17.46	Mike	Kigen	KEN	15.1.86	2		Stockholm	2 Feb
13:28.39	Halil	Akkas	TUR	1.7.83	3		Stockholm	2 Feb
13:29.55	Abderrahim	Goumri	MAR	21.5.76	4		Stockholm	2 Feb
13:34.43	Ahmed	Baday	MAR	12.1.79	5		Stockholm	2 Feb

60 METRES HURDLES

7.43	Terrence	Trammell	USA	23.11.78	1	WI	Moskva	11 Mar
7.46	Dayron	Robles	CUB	19.11.86	2	WI	Moskva	11 Mar
7.51	Dominique	Arnold	USA	14.9.73	2	NC	Boston (R)	26 Feb
7.51	Aries	Merritt	USA	24.7.85	1	NCAA	Fayetteville	10 Mar
7.52	Anwar	Moore	USA	5.3.79	3	NC	Boston (R)	26 Feb
7.52	Maurice	Wignall	JAM	17.4.76	4=	WI	Moskva	11 Mar
7.52	Stanislav	Olijar	LAT	22.3.79	4=	WI	Moskva	11 Mar
7.54	Joel	Brown	USA	31.1.80	4	NC	Boston (R)	26 Feb
7.54	David	Payne	USA	24.7.82	5	NC	Boston (R)	26 Feb
7.56	Igor	Peremota	RUS	14.1.81	1		Moskva	25 Jan
7.56	Ron	Bramlett	USA	22.10.79	2	Spark	Stuttgart	4 Feb
7.56	Jackson	Quiñonez	ESP	12.6.80	1	NC	San Sebastián	26 Feb
7.57	Thomas	Blaschek	GER	5.4.81	6	WI	Moskva	11 Mar
7.60	Kedrieck	Gibbons	USA	8.6.85	1h2	JUCO	Manhattan KS	3 Mar
7.61	David	Oliver	USA	24.4.82	7	NC	Boston (R)	26 Feb
7.61	Paulo	Villar	COL	28.7.78	4s3	WI	Moskva	11 Mar
7.62	Ladji	Doucouré	FRA	28.3.83	1	ElCp	Liévin	5 Mar
7.62	Yoel	Hernández	CUB	12.12.77	8	WI	Moskva	11 Mar
7.63		Shi Dongpeng	CHN	6.1.84	3s2	WI	Moskva	11 Mar
7.64	Antwon	Hicks	USA	12.3.83	2r2	Mill	New York	3 Feb
7.64	Andy	Turner	GBR	19.9.80	1h3	NC	Sheffield	11 Feb
7.64	Elmar	Lichtenegger	AUT	25.4.74	1		Leipzig	12 Feb

7.65	Redelen	dos Santos	BRA	24.4.76	25 Jan
7.65	Yevgeniy	Borisov	RUS	7.3.84	25 Jan
7.66A	Micah	Harris	USA	30.4.79	21 Jan
7.66	Mike	Fenner	GER	24.4.71	4 Feb
7.66	Robby	Hughes	USA	10.10.78	25 Feb
7.66	Sergey	Demidyuk	UKR	5.6.82	28 Feb
7.66	Jerome	Miller	USA	19.8.83	10 Mar
7.67	Jermaine	Cooper	USA	31.8.80	26 Feb
7.67	Eric	Mitchum	USA	2.8.84	4 Mar
7.67	Mateus	Inocêncio	BRA	17.5.81	11 Mar
7.68	Dániel	Kiss	HUN	12.2.82	27 Jan
7.68	Gregory	Sedoc	NED	16.10.81	18 Feb
7.69	Decosma	Wright	JAM	1.9.82	10 Mar
7.69	Dominic	Berger	USA	19.5.86	10 Mar

HIGH JUMP

2.37	Yaroslav	Rybakov	RUS	22.11.80	1		Arnstadt	4 Feb
2.37	Ivan	Ukhov	RUS	29.3.86	2		Arnstadt	4 Feb
2.36	Andrey	Sokolovskiy	UKR	16.7.78	1		Banská Bystrica	14 Feb
2.36	Andrey	Tereshin	RUS	15.12.82	1	NC	Moskva	17 Feb
2.35	Andrey	Silnov	RUS	9.9.84	3		Arnstadt	4 Feb
2.34	Linus	Thörnblad	SWE	6.3.85	2		Banská Bystrica	14 Feb
2.33	Svatoslav	Ton	CZE	20.10.78	1		Hustopece	21 Jan
2.31	Giulio	Ciotti	ITA	5.10.76	3		Hustopece	21 Jan
2.31	Nicola	Ciotti	ITA	5.10.76	4		Hustopece	21 Jan
2.31	Yuriy	Krimarenko	UKR	11.8.83	4		Arnstadt	4 Feb
2.30*	Tora	Harris	USA	21.9.78	1		Princeton	10 Dec
2.30	Mikhail	Tsvetkov	RUS	4.5.80	2		Chelyabinsk	9 Jan
2.30	Tomás	Janku	CZE	27.12.74	1		Bydgoszcz	25 Jan
2.30	Kyriacos	Ioannou	CYP	26.7.84	3		Banská Bystrica	14 Feb
2.30	Víctor	Moya	CUB	24.10.82	4	WI	Moskva	11 Mar
2.30	Stefan	Holm	SWE	25.5.76	5	WI	Moskva	11 Mar
2.29	Jim	Dilling	USA	23.4.85	1	NCAA-II	Boston	11 Mar
2.29	Keith	Moffatt	USA	20.6.84	2	NCAA-II	Boston	11 Mar

2.29	Jesse	Williams	USA	27.12.83	1	NCAA	Fayetteville	11 Mar
2.28	Pavel	Fomenko	RUS	29.6.76	5		Yekaterinburg	7 Jan
2.28	Andra	Manson	USA	30.4.84	1		Houston	14 Jan
2.28	Jaroslav	Bába	CZE	2.9.84	4		Ostrava	18 Jan
2.28	Jamie	Nieto	USA	2.11.76	7		Arnstadt	4 Feb
2.28	Andrea	Bettinelli	ITA	6.10.78	1		Maromme	4 Feb
2.28	Fyodor	Getov	RUS	14.3.84	1	NC-23	Saransk	9 Feb
2.28	Roman	Fricke	GER	23.3.77	1		Otterberg	11 Feb
2.28	Wojciech	Theiner	POL	25.6.86	1		Slupsk	12 Feb
2.28	Stefan	Vasilache	ROM	9.5.79	1		Bucuresti	12 Feb
2.28	Robert	Wolski	POL	8.12.82	1	NC	Spala	26 Feb
2.28	Mustapha	Raïfak	FRA	9.9.75	1	NC	Aubière	26 Feb
2.28	Ramsay	Carelse	RSA	30.10.85	3		Tallinn	28 Feb

2.27	Kyle	Lancaster	USA	15.8.83	18 Feb	2.25	Adam	Shunk	USA	29.8.79	7 Jan
2.27	Mike	Morrison	USA	4.3.84	26 Feb	2.25	Grzegorz	Sposób	POL	12.2.76	27 Jan
2.26	Javier	Bermejo	ESP	23.12.78	4 Feb	2.25	Gennadiy	Moroz	BLR	27.5.78	5 Feb
2.26	Wilbert	Pennings	NED	12.2.75	14 Feb	2.25	Jan-Peter	Larsen	NED	18.3.79	11 Feb
2.26	Aleksander	Walerianczyk	POL	1.9.82	14 Feb	2.25	Ivan	Ilyichev	RUS	14.10.86	14 Feb
2.26	Marat	Rakipov	RUS	7.6.79	17 Feb	2.25	Dusty	Jonas	USA	19.4.86	17 Feb
2.26	Sergey	Klyugin	RUS	24.3.74	17 Feb	2.25	Oskari	Frösén	FIN	24.1.76	19 Feb
2.26	Aleksey	Dmitrik	RUS	12.4.84	17 Feb	2.25	Artyom	Kozbanov	UKR	18.7.83	22 Feb
2.26	Osku	Torro	FIN	21.8.79	25 Feb						

POLE VAULT

5.85	Jeff	Hartwig	USA	25.9.67	1		Vermillion	18 Feb
5.82	Tim	Lobinger	GER	3.9.72	1	Euro	Göteborg	8 Feb
5.81	Alex	Averbukh	ISR	1.10.74	1		Gent	26 Feb
5.80	Paul	Burgess	AUS	14.8.79	1		Donetsk	12 Feb
5.80	Alhaji	Jeng	SWE	13.12.81	2		Donetsk	12 Feb
5.80	Brad	Walker	USA	21.6.81	1	WI	Moskva	12 Mar
5.76	Aleksandr	Korchmid	UKR	22.1.82	1		Karlsruhe	29 Jan
5.76	Dmitriy	Kuptsov	RUS	9.11.82	1		Stockholm	2 Feb
5.76	Spas	Bukhalov	BUL	14.11.80	1		Sofia	4 Feb
5.75	Romain	Mesnil	FRA	13.7.77	1		Epinal	11 Feb
5.75	Fabian	Schulze	GER	7.3.84	1		Düsseldorf	17 Feb
5.75	Björn	Otto	GER	16.10.77	3	NC	Karlsruhe	26 Feb
5.71A	Russ	Buller	USA	10.9.78	1		Flagstaff	4 Feb
5.71A	Giovanni	Lanaro	MEX	27.9.81	1		Flagstaff	18 Feb
5.71	Tommy	Skipper	USA	14.4.84	1		Seattle	25 Feb
5.70	Ruslan	Yeremenko	UKR	31.7.78	2		Cottbus	25 Jan
5.70A	Robbie	Pratt	MEX	25.2.80	1		Reno	28 Jan
5.70	Denis	Yurchenko	UKR	27.1.78	1	Spark	Stuttgart	4 Feb
5.70	Lars	Börgeling	GER	16.4.79	1		Leipzig	12 Feb
5.70	Przemyslaw	Czerwinski	POL	28.7.83	3		Donetsk	12 Feb
5.70	Kevin	Rans	BEL	19.8.82	6		Donetsk	12 Feb
5.70	Tim	Mack	USA	15.9.72	1		Knoxville	17 Feb
5.70	Maksim	Mazurik	UKR	2.4.83	1	NC	Sumy	22 Feb

5.65	Charles	Andureu	FRA	13.2.85	20 Jan	5.60	Richard	Spiegelburg	GER	12.8.77	4 Feb
5.65	Jérôme	Clavier	FRA	3.5.83	28 Jan	5.60	Giuseppe	Gibilisco	ITA	5.1.79	4 Feb
5.65	Derek	Miles	USA	28.9.72	8 Feb	5.60	Alexander	Straub	GER	14.10.83	4 Feb
5.65	Dmitriy	Starodubtsev	RUS	3.1.86	18 Feb	5.60	Štepán	Janácek	CZE	12.6.77	12 Feb
5.65	Laurens	Looije	NED	12.1.73	18 Feb	5.60	Igor	Pavlov	RUS	18.7.79	18 Feb
5.65	Daichi	Sawano	JPN	16.9.80	11 Mar	5.60	Ilian	Efremov	BUL	2.8.70	22 Feb
5.60	Vladyslav	Revenko	UKR	15.11.84	25 Jan	5.60		Liu Feiliang	CHN	27.3.85	25 Feb
5.60A	Toby	Stevenson	USA	19.11.76	27 Jan	5.60	Michael	Stolle	GER	17.12.74	3 Mar

LONG JUMP

8.36	Ignisious	Gaisah	GHA	20.6.83	1		Stockholm	2 Feb
8.29	Irving	Saladino	PAN	23.1.83	2	WI	Moskva	11 Mar
8.27	Salim	Sdiri	FRA	26.10.78	1		Mondeville	28 Jan
8.23	John	Moffitt	USA	12.12.80	1		Baton Rouge	27 Jan
8.19	Andrew	Howe	ITA	12.5.85	3	WI	Moskva	11 Mar
8.18	Morten	Jensen	DEN	2.12.82	1	Euro	Göteborg	8 Feb
8.16	Miguel	Pate	USA	13.6.79	2	Euro	Göteborg	8 Feb
8.15	Loúis	Tsátoumas	GRE	12.2.82	1	NC	Athína	19 Feb
8.11	Ruslan	Gataullin	RUS	1.12.79	1	NC	Moskva	17 Feb
8.11	Arturs	Abolins	LAT	14.8.84	1	NCAA	Fayetteville	10 Mar
8.10	Walter	Davis	USA	2.7.79	2	Spark	Stuttgart	4 Feb
8.08	Nelson	Évora	POR	20.4.84	1		Espinho	11 Feb
8.06	Aleksey	Lukashevich	UKR	11.1.77	1	UKR Cp	Zaporizhzhya	25 Jan
8.05	Nathan	Morgan	GBR	30.6.78	1	v4N	Glasgow	28 Jan
8.04	Fabrice	Lapierre	AUS	17.10.83	2	NCAA	Fayetteville	10 Mar

Mark	First	Last	Nat	Born	Pos	Meet	Venue	Date
8.03	Valeriy	Vasilyev	UKR	21.4.76	1		Kyiv	13 Jan
8.03		Song Jian	CHN	7.5.83	1	NGP	Beijing	25 Feb

Mark	First	Last	Nat	Born	Date	Mark	First	Last	Nat	Born	Date
8.01	Danut	Simion	ROM	25.1.83	2 Feb	7.99	James	Beckford	JAM	9.1.75	3 Mar
8.01	Nikolay	Atanasov	BUL	11.12.74	4 Feb	7.97	Vitaliy	Shkurlatov	RUS	25.5.79	14 Jan
8.01	Khotso	Mokoena	RSA	6.3.85	11 Mar	7.97	Erivaldo	Vieira	BRA	18.11.80	11 Mar
8.00	Ciaran	McDonagh	IRL	20.5.76	14 Jan	7.95	Sergey	Mikhailovskiy	RUS-J	20.5.87	4 Feb
8.00	Marcin	Starzak	POL	20.10.85	27 Jan	7.95	Brian	Johnson	USA	25.3.80	26 Feb
						7.94	Astérios	Noúsios	GRE	25.2.79	19 Feb

TRIPLE JUMP

Mark	First	Last	Nat	Born	Pos	Meet	Venue	Date
17.31	Igor	Spasovkhodskiy	RUS	1.8.79	Q	WI	Moskva	11 Mar
17.19	Nelson	Évora	POR	20.4.84	1		Moskva	25 Jan
17.19	Dmitrij	Valukevic	SVK	31.5.81	1		Bratislava	29 Jan
17.16	Momchil	Karailiev	BUL	21.5.82	1		Sofia	4 Feb
17.13	Danila	Burkenya	RUS	20.7.78	2		Moskva	25 Jan
17.12	Dimítrios	Tsiámis	GRE	12.1.82	1	NC	Athína (P)	18 Feb
17.10	Leevan	Sands	BAH	16.1.81	1	Tyson	Fayetteville	11 Feb
17.06	Jefferson	Sabino	BRA	4.11.82	3		Samara	4 Feb
17.05	Nathan	Douglas	GBR	4.12.82	7	WI	Moskva	12 Mar
17.04	Vitaliy	Moskalenko	RUS	30.6.74	4	NC	Moskva	18 Feb
17.01	Anders	Møller	DEN	5.9.77	1	NC	Malmö	25 Feb
16.99	Aleksandr	Petrenko	RUS	8.2.83	2		Moskva	25 Jan
16.90	Karl	Taillepierre	FRA	13.8.76	1	NC	Aubière	25 Feb
16.89	Viktor	Yastrebov	UKR	13.1.82	5		Samara	4 Feb
16.89	Konstadínos	Zalaggítis	GRE	15.12.80	2		Athína (P)	4 Feb
16.85	Paolo	Camossi	ITA	6.1.74	2	NC	Ancona	19 Feb
16.84	Randy	Lewis	GRN	14.10.80	4		Karlsruhe	29 Jan
16.82	Allen	Simms	PUR	26.7.82	11Q	WI	Moskva	11 Mar
16.79A	Rodrigo	Mendes	BRA	21.6.78	1		Air Force Academy	4 Feb

Mark	First	Last	Nat	Born	Date	Mark	First	Last	Nat	Born	Date
16.74	Colomba	Fofana	FRA	11.4.77	25 Feb	16.61	Aarik	Wilson	USA	25.10.82	11 Mar
16.72	Pawel	Kruhlik	POL	25.8.83	25 Feb	16.60A	Rafeeq	Curry	USA	19.8.83	21 Jan
16.70	Alexander	Martínez	SUI	23.8.77	26 Feb	16.60	Michaël	Velter	BEL	21.3.80	26 Feb
16.68	Emanuele	Sardano	ITA	16.2.79	19 Feb	16.60	Nikolay	Savolainen	UKR	25.3.80	28 Feb
16.61	Tareq	Bougtaïb	MAR	30.4.81	18 Feb	16.58	Chris	Hercules	TRI	14.5.79	27 Jan

SHOT

Mark	First	Last	Nat	Born	Pos	Meet	Venue	Date
20.99	Adam	Nelson	USA	7.7.75	3	BIG	Boston (R)	28 Jan
20.98	Dan	Taylor	USA	12.5.82	1		Ames	11 Feb
20.75	Anton	Lyuboslavskiy	RUS	26.6.84	1	NC	Moskva	16 Feb
20.68	Pavel	Sofin	RUS	4.9.81	4	WI	Moskva	10 Mar
20.60	Tomasz	Majewski	POL	30.8.81	1	EICp	Liévin	5 Mar
20.59	Peter	Sack	GER	27.7.79	2	NC	Karlsruhe	25 Feb
20.52	Dorian	Scott	JAM	1.2.82	1		Blacksburg	18 Feb
20.50	John	Godina	USA	31.5.72	3	NC	Boston (R)	25 Feb
20.48	Garrett	Johnson	USA	24.5.84	1	NCAA	Fayetteville	10 Mar
20.43	Manuel	Martínez	ESP	7.12.74	6	WI	Moskva	10 Mar
20.41	Miran	Vodovnik	SLO	11.9.77	1		Slovenska Bistrica	22 Feb
20.38	Detlef	Bock	GER	15.8.74	2		Nordhausen	27 Jan
20.34	Carl	Myerscough	GBR	21.10.79	1		Lincoln NE	9 Dec
20.29	Steve	Manz	USA	19.9.81	5	NC	Boston (R)	25 Feb
20.27	Ivan	Yushkov	RUS	15.1.81	1		Moskva	24 Jan
20.09	Khaled Habash	Al-Suwaidi	QAT	10.10.84	1		Schio	11 Feb
20.05	Vince	Mosca	USA	23.1.80	7	NC	Boston (R)	25 Feb
20.02	Sheldon	Battle	USA	23.6.83	1		Lawrence KS	20 Jan
19.96	Ville	Tiisanoja	FIN	24.12.75	1	NC	Tampere	26 Feb

Mark	First	Last	Nat	Born	Date	Mark	First	Last	Nat	Born	Date
19.87	Yuriy	Belov	BLR	20.3.81	24 Feb	19.66	Tony	Thompson	USA	12.3.80	4 Feb
19.87	Sean	Shields	USA	10.2.83	25 Feb	19.65	Chris	Figures	USA	8.10.81	28 Jan
19.81	Taavi	Peetre	EST	5.7.83	8 Feb	19.63	Luka	Rujevic	SCG	14.10.85	4 Feb
19.77	Dmitri	Goncharuk	BLR	17.7.70	28 Jan	19.63	Antonín	Zalsky	CZE	7.8.80	26 Feb
19.76	Mika	Vasara	FIN	22.10.83	28 Feb	19.62	Jarred	Rome	USA	21.12.76	4 Feb
19.75	Robert	Häggblom	FIN	9.8.82	19 Feb	19.61	Russ	Winger	USA	2.8.84	24 Feb
19.74	Pavel	Chumachenko	RUS	5.4.71	24 Jan	19.60	Bryan	Vickers	USA	14.1.85	11 Mar
19.74	Galin	Kostadinov	BUL	25.12.79	11 Feb	19.54	Yves	Niaré	FRA	20.7.77	26 Feb
19.72	Andy	Dittmar	GER	5.7.74	14 Jan	19.52	Jeff	Chakouian	USA	20.4.82	28 Jan
19.70	Gaëtan	Bucki	FRA	9.5.80	26 Feb	19.50	Vince	Mosca	USA	23.1.80	26 Feb

WEIGHT

Mark	First	Last	Nat	Born	Pos	Meet	Venue	Date
25.01	Libor	Charfreitag	SVK	11.9.77	1		Nampa	3 Feb
24.54*	Kibwe	Johnson	USA	17.7.81	1		Findlay	3 Dec
23.74	A.G.	Kruger	USA	18.2.79	1	NC	Boston (R)	24 Feb
23.73	Spirídon	Zoullién	GRE	21.6.81	1	NCAA	Fayetteville	11 Mar
23.48	Jacob	Freeman	USA	5.11.80	3	NC	Boston (R)	24 Feb
23.19	Yegor	Agafonov	RUS	7.2.83	2	NCAA	Fayetteville	11 Mar

22.95	Mohsen	Anani	EGY	21.5.85	1		Blacksburg	24 Feb
22.89	Cory	Martin	USA	22.5.85	3	NCAA	Fayetteville	11 Mar
22.61	Travis	Nutter	USA	9.2.75	4	NC	Boston (R)	24 Feb

22.36	Jake	Dunkleberger	USA	6.10.84	4 Mar
22.09	Leonard	Jatsek	USA	21.6.85	3 Mar
22.06	Mattias	Jons	SWE	19.11.82	3 Feb
22.04	Arnaldo	Cueto	USA	5.5.81	4 Feb
21.88	Mike	Mai	USA	27.9.77	22 Jan
21.87	Pellegrino	Delli Carri	ITA	4.8.76	11 Feb

HEPTATHLON

6229	Aleksandr	Pogorelov		RUS	10.1.80	1	NC	Moskva	5 Feb
	6.90	7.48	15.77	2.10	7.93		5.10	2.55.59	
6225	Aleksey	Drozdov		RUS	3.12.83	2	NC	Moskva	5 Feb
	6.94	7.35	16.98	2.07	8.19		4.90	2.44.14	
6208A	Trey	Hardee		USA	7.2.84	1		Albuquerque	27 Jan
	6.73	7.73	14.31	1.95	7.87		5.30	2:55.16	
6192	André	Niklaus		GER	30.8.81	1	WI	Moskva	12 Mar
	7.06	7.64	14.41	2.07	8.14		5.30	2:47.80	
6187	Bryan	Clay		USA	3.1.80	2	WI	Moskva	12 Mar
	6.67	7.74	13.89	2.10	7.83		4.60	2:50.92	
6161	Roman	Sebrle		CZE	26.11.74	3	WI	Moskva	12 Mar
	7.10	7.76	15.74	2.10	8.08		4.80	2:49.38	
6062	Kristjan	Rahnu		EST	29.8.79	4	WI	Moskva	12 Mar
	6.91	7.33	15.78	2.04	8.01		4.90	2:54.70	
6048	Donovan	Kilmartin		USA	11.6.84	1	NCAA	Fayetteville	11 Mar
	7.13	7.56	13.84	2.06	8.09		5.30	2:54.42	
6047	Konstantin	Smirnov		RUS	8.3.84	3	NC	Moskva	5 Feb
	6.82	7.40	13.59	1.98	7.92		4.80	2.42.05	
5969	Mikk	Pahapill		EST	18.7.83	4	Reval	Tallinn	5 Feb
	7.15	7.41	15.30	2.07	8.34		5.05	2:53.81	
5949	Ryan	Harlan		USA	25.4.81	1	NC	Chapel Hill	5 Mar
	7.07	6.93	16.36	2.08	7.96		4.72	2:53.86	
5917	Chris	Helwick		USA	18.3.85	2	NCAA	Fayetteville	11 Mar
	7.26	7.46	13.88	2.06	8.45		5.20	2:49.03	
5909	Aleksandr	Parkhomenko		BLR	22.3.81	5	Reval	Tallinn	5 Feb
	7.31	7.20	15.67	2.01	8.24		4.95	2:45.75	

5899	Nadir	El Fassi	FRA	23.9.83	12 Feb
5897	Andres	Raja	EST	2.6.82	5 Feb
5896	Maurice	Smith	JAM	28.9.80	28 Jan
5895	Romain	Barras	FRA	1.8.80	12 Feb
5883	Paul	Terek	USA	20.10.79	5 Mar
5869	Stefan	Drews	GER	12.2.79	29 Jan
5848	Nikolay	Tishchenko	RUS	4.2.77	5 Feb
5827	Aleksey	Sysoyev	RUS	8.3.85	5 Feb
5813	Norman	Müller	GER	7.8.85	29 Jan
5806	Madis	Kallas	EST	22.4.81	5 Mar
5801	Rudy	Bourguignon	FRA	16.7.79	25 Feb
5800	François	Gourmet	BEL	28.12.82	5 Feb

3000 METRES WALK

11:26.62	Tim	Seaman	USA	14.5.72	1	NC	Findlay	28 Jan

5000 METRES WALK

18:48.76	Ilya	Markov	RUS	19.6.72	1		Yekaterinburg	7 Jan
18:54.40	Francisco Javier	Fernández	ESP	6.3.77	2		Yekaterinburg	7 Jan
19:04.24	Grzegorz	Sudol	POL	28.8.78	1	NC	Spala	25 Feb
19:05.9	Aleksandr	Yargunkin	RUS	6.10.81	1		Chelyabinsk	6 Jan

19:12.33	André	Höhne	GER	10.3.78
19:15.59	João	Vieira	POR	20.2.76
19:15.88	Tim	Seaman	USA	14.5.72
19:20.6	Aleksandr	Prokhorov	RUS	22.1.86

WORLD INDOOR LISTS 2006 – WOMEN

60 METRES

7.01	Me'Lisa	Barber	USA	4.10.80	1	WI	Moskva	10 Mar
7.01	Lauryn	Williams	USA	11.9.83	2	WI	Moskva	10 Mar
7.04	Mariya	Bolikova	RUS	23.5.77	1		Samara	4 Feb
7.04	Veronica	Campbell	JAM	15.5.82	1	Tyson	Fayetteville	10 Feb
7.06	Christine	Arron	FRA	13.9.73	1	NC	Aubière	26 Feb
7.08	Yuliya	Tabakova	RUS	1.5.80	1		Moskva	25 Jan
7.10	Torri	Edwards	USA	31.1.77	1s2	NC	Boston (R)	26 Feb
7.11	Kim	Gevaert	BEL	5.8.78	3	WI	Moskva	10 Mar
7.12	Larisa	Kruglova	RUS	27.10.72	1h		Samara	4 Feb
7.14	Marina	Kislova	RUS	12.12.78	h		Samara	4 Feb
7.16	Kelliann	Baptiste	TRI	14.10.86	1h2	NCAA	Fayetteville	10 Mar
7.17	Irina	Khabarova	RUS	18.3.66	1h		Omsk	24 Dec
7.18	Olga	Khalandyreva	RUS	13.11.81	h		Samara	4 Feb
7.18	Marshevet	Hooker	USA	25.9.84	1h3	NCAA	Fayetteville	10 Mar
7.19	Tahesia	Harrigan	IVB	15.2.82	1h3	Mill	New York	3 Feb
7.19	Delphine	Atangana	CMR	16.8.84	1s1	NC	Aubière	26 Feb
7.19	Zhanna	Block	UKR	6.7.72	3s1	WI	Moskva	10 Mar

7.20 Svetlana Pospelova RUS 24.12.79 14 Jan
7.20 Michelle Freeman JAM 5.5.69 20 Jan
7.20 Alena Nevmerzhitskaya BLR 27.7.80 25 Feb
7.20A Ashley Owens USA 19.11.85 25 Feb
7.20 Cleo Tyson USA 1.5.86 10 Mar
7.21 Amberly Nesbitt USA 19.8.86 10 Feb
7.21 Shalonda Solomon USA 19.12.85 10 Mar
7.21 Virginia Powell USA 7.9.83 10 Mar
7.21 Chauntae Bayne USA 4.4.84 10 Mar
7.22 Jeanette Kwakye GBR 20.3.83 11 Feb
7.22 Laverne Jones ISV 16.9.81 10 Mar
7.22 Sylvie Mballa Éloundou CMR 21.4.77 10 Mar
7.22 Kerron Stewart JAM 16.4.84 10 Mar
7.24 Heidi Hannula FIN 26.2.80 10 Mar

50m: 6.12+ Christine Arron FRA 13.9.73 1h1 in 60m Liévin 3 Mar

200 METRES

22.57 Shalonda Solomon USA 19.12.85 1r2 NCAA Fayetteville 10 Mar
22.77 Chauntae Bayne USA 4.4.84 2r1 NCAA Fayetteville 10 Mar
22.77 Carol Rodriguez PUR 16.12.85 1r1 NCAA Fayetteville 10 Mar
22.80 Christine Arron FRA 13.9.73 1 Gaz Liévin 3 Mar
22.82 Yuliya Gushchina RUS 4.3.83 Moskva 24 Jan
22.84 Veronica Campbell JAM 15.5.82 1 GP Birmingham 18 Feb
22.84 Brooklyn Morris USA 27.3.86 1h1 NCAA Fayetteville 10 Mar
22.86 Marshevet Hooker USA 25.9.84 2r2 NCAA Fayetteville 10 Mar
22.97 Kerron Stewart JAM 16.4.84 1r2 Tyson Fayetteville 11 Feb
23.02 Peta-Gaye Dowdie JAM 18.1.77 2 GP Birmingham 18 Feb
23.05 Kelliann Baptiste TRI 14.10.86 3r1 NCAA Fayetteville 10 Mar
23.13 Natalya Ivanova RUS 25.6.81 1 NC Moskva 18 Feb
23.19 Yelena Novikova RUS 27.10.85 18 Feb
23.20 Ciara Sheehy IRL 12.8.80 12 Feb
23.22 Tatyana Levina RUS 28.2.77 4 Feb
23.24 Tiandra Ponteen SKN 9.11.84 11 Feb
23.25 Christine Amertil BAH 18.8.79 10 Feb
23.26A Bianca Knight USA-Y 2.1.89 18 Feb
23.26 Janice Davis USA 27.10.84 10 Mar
23.27 Crystal Cox USA 28.3.79 18 Feb
23.28 Lyudmila Zuyenko RUS 6.9.83 18 Feb
23.29 Alena Nevmerzhitskaya BLR 27.7.80 28 Jan

300 Metres: Yekaterinburg 7 Jan: 1. Olesya Krasnomovets RUS 36.30, 2. Svetlana Pospelova RUS 36.64

400 METRES

49.98 Natalya Nazarova RUS 22.5.79 1 NC Moskva 18 Feb
50.04 Olesya Krasnomovets RUS 8.7.79 2 NC Moskva 18 Feb
50.15 Olga Zaytseva RUS 10.11.84 1 Moskva 25 Jan
50.21 Vanya Stambolova BUL 28.11.83 2 WI Moskva 12 Mar
50.34 Christine Amertil BAH 18.8.79 3 WI Moskva 12 Mar
50.37 Natalya Antyukh RUS 26.6.81 3 NC Moskva 18 Feb
50.72 Nicola Sanders GBR 23.6.82 1 NC Sheffield 12 Feb
51.07 Tatyana Veshkurova RUS 23.9.81 2s2 NC Moskva 17 Feb
51.16 Tiandra Ponteen SKN 9.11.84 1 Tyson Fayetteville 10 Feb
51.17 Tatyana Levina RUS 28.2.77 4 NC Moskva 18 Feb
51.22 Olga Kotlyarova RUS 12.4.76 1B Moskva 25 Jan
51.25 Novlene Williams JAM 26.4.82 3s1 WI Moskva 11 Mar
51.26 Yuliya Gushchina RUS 4.3.83 2s1 NC Moskva 17 Feb
51.28 Sanya Richards USA 26.2.85 1 NC Boston (R) 26 Feb
51.41 Tatyana Firova RUS 10.10.82 3r1 Athína (P) 25 Feb
51.53 Ilona Usovich BLR 14.11.82 4s1 WI Moskva 11 Mar
51.85 Tonique Darling BAH 17.1.76 1 GP Birmingham 18 Feb
51.93 Francena McCorory USA-J 20.10.88 1r2 Nike Landover 12 Mar
51.96 Patricia Hall JAM 16.10.82 2 Tyson Fayetteville 10 Feb
52.02 Claudia Hoffmann GER 10.12.82 1h2 NC Karlsruhe 25 Feb
52.07 Mariyana Dimitrova BUL 29.7.82 2h2 WI Moskva 10 Mar
52.09 Claudia Marx GER 16.9.78 2 GP Birmingham 18 Feb
52.16 Kineke Alexander VIN 21.2.86 11 Mar
52.17 Dominique Darden USA 9.12.83 11 Mar
52.36 Monika Bejnar POL 10.3.81 10 Mar
52.38 Monique Henderson USA 18.2.83 10 Feb
52.48 Monica Hargrove USA 30.12.82 28 Jan
52.48 Ami Mbacké Thiam SEN 10.11.76 2 Feb
52.49 Angela Morosanu ROM 26.7.86 10 Mar
52.50 Anastasiya Ovchinnikova RUS 16.10.84 9 Feb
52.53 Clora Williams JAM 26.11.83 10 Mar
52.56 Markita James USA 28.6.83 11 Mar
52.61 Ashlee Kidd USA 26.7.85 25 Feb
52.62 Shana Cox USA 22.1.85 28 Jan
52.62 Kseniya Zadorina RUS-J 2.3.87 16 Feb
52.63 Anastasiya Kochetova RUS 18.9.83 17 Feb
52.68 Olesya Pogorelova RUS 30.3.79 3 Feb
52.69 Tatyana Roslanova KAZ 28.9.80 14 Nov
52.69 Mary Danner USA 3.1.80 26 Feb
52.62 o/s 18 Feb

500 Metres: Yekaterinburg 7 Jan: 1. Olesya Krasnomovets RUS 1:06.31, 2. Olga Zatytseva 1:06.76, 3. Olga Kotlyarova RUS 1:07.74; Moskva 12 Jan: 1, Natalya Nazarova RUS 1:07.79, 2. Kseniya Zadorina RUS-J 1:08.94

600 Metres: Omsk 24 Dec: Olga Kotlyarova RUS 1:26:23

800 METRES

1:57.51 Olga Kotlyarova RUS 12.4.76 1 NC Moskva 18 Feb
1:58.34 Svetlana Cherkasova RUS 20.5.78 1 Moskva 4 Feb
1:58.53 Yelena Soboleva RUS 3.10.82 2 Moskva 4 Feb
1:58.90 Maria Mutola MOZ 27.10.72 1 WI Moskva 12 Mar
1:59.18 Natalya Tsyganova RUS 7.2.71 2r2 Moskva 24 Jan
1:59.54 Kenia Sinclair JAM 14.7.80 2 WI Moskva 12 Mar

2:00.34	Hasna	Benhassi	MAR	1.6.78	3	WI	Moskva	12 Mar
2:00.42	Elisabeth	Grousselle	FRA	6.2.73	3s2	WI	Moskva	11 Mar
2:00.53	Karen	Harewood	GBR	19.8.75	1		Budapest	27 Jan
2:00.67	Irina	Vashentseva	RUS	30.9.80	3r2		Moskva	24 Jan
2:01.55	Tatyana	Petlyuk	UKR	22.2.82	1	Spark	Stuttgart	4 Feb
2:01.70	Maria	Cioncan	ROM	19.6.77	1	NC	Bucuresti	19 Feb
2:01.76	Svetlana	Usovich	BLR	14.10.80	1		Minsk	12 Feb

2:01.83	Mariya	Shapayeva	RUS	7.11.86	18 Feb	2:02.39	Ewelina	Setowska	POL	5.3.80	12 Mar
2:01.86	Zhanna	Smolina	RUS	19.1.78	24 Jan	2:02.40	Yuliya	Chizhenko	RUS	30.8.79	28 Jan
2:01.87	Elisa	Cusma	ITA	24.7.81	31 Jan	2:02.41	Jenny	Meadows	GBR	17.4.81	12 Feb
2:01.93	Alice	Schmidt	USA	3.10.81	26 Feb	2:02.56	Elena	Iagar	ROM	16.1.75	22 Feb
2:01.95	Brigita	Langerholc	SLO	23.7.76	26 Feb	2:02.5	Olesya	Chumakova	RUS	23.7.81	11 Feb
2:01.99	Natalya	Gorelova	RUS	18.4.73	24 Jan	2:02.74	Mariya	Dryakhlova	RUS	24.4.84	18 Feb
2:02.00	Mihaela	Neacsu	ROM	3.5.79	22 Feb	2:02.80	Svetlana	Klyuka	RUS	27.12.78	20 Jan
2:02.03	Teodora	Kolarova	BUL	29.5.81	27 Jan	2:02.83	Yekaterina	Martynova	RUS	12.6.86	17 Feb

1000 METRES

2:32.16	Yuliya	Chizhenko	RUS	30.8.79	1r2		Moskva	25 Jan
2:32.40	Yelena	Soboleva	RUS	3.10.82	2r2		Moskva	25 Jan
2:32.91	Yelena	Kanales	RUS	7.2.76	3r2		Moskva	25 Jan
2:35.67	Tatyana	Petlyuk	UKR	22.2.82	4r2		Moskva	25 Jan
2:35.92	Svetlana	Cherkasova	RUS	20.5.78	5r2		Moskva	25 Jan
2:36.76	Olga	Komyagina	RUS	10.2.74	1	Gaz	Liévin	3 Mar
2:37.06	Olesya	Syreva	RUS	25.11.83	1r1		Moskva	25 Jan
2:37.42	Irina	Vashentseva	RUS	30.9.80	1		Moskva	12 Jan
2:38.50	Anna	Alminova	RUS	17.1.85	2		Moskva	12 Jan

2:38.77	Irina	Krakoviak	LTU	16.11.77	25 Jan	2:39.32	Mayte	Martínez	ESP	17.5.76	3 Mar
2:38.93	Mariya	Shapayeva	RUS	7.11.86	25 Jan	2:39.42	Svetlana	Klyuka	RUS	27.12.78	25 Jan

1500 METRES

3:58.28	Yelena	Soboleva	RUS	3.10.82	1	NC	Moskva	18 Feb
4:01.26	Yuliya	Chizhenko	RUS	30.8.79	2	NC	Moskva	18 Feb
4:01.82	Maryam	Jamal	BRN	16.9.84	1		Valencia	11 Feb
4:03.53	Yelena	Kanales	RUS	7.2.76	3	NC	Moskva	18 Feb
4:04.33	Olga	Komyagina	RUS	10.2.74	1		Athína (P)	25 Feb
4:04.39	Olesya	Chumakova	RUS	23.7.81	4	NC	Moskva	18 Feb
4:04.69	Corina	Dumbravean	ROM	15.4.84	2		Valencia	11 Feb
4:05.67	Hind	Dehiba	FRA	17.3.79	4	WI	Moskva	12 Mar
4:05.75	Anna	Alminova	RUS	17.1.85	2		Athína (P)	25 Feb
4:06.25	Natalya	Gorelova	RUS	18.4.73	5	NC	Moskva	18 Feb
4:06.46	Alesya	Turova	BLR	6.12.79	3		Valencia	11 Feb
4:06.90	Lidia	Chojecka	POL	25.1.77	4		Valencia	11 Feb
4:07.11	Daniela	Yordanova	BUL	8.3.76	1	Balk	Athína (P)	22 Feb
4:07.26	Natalya	Tobias	UKR	22.11.80	4		Athína (P)	25 Feb
4:07.82	Irina	Lishchinska	UKR	15.1.76	5	WI	Moskva	12 Mar
4:08.12	Bouchra	Ghézielle	FRA	18.5.79	1		Eaubonne	10 Feb
4:08.13	Treniere	Clement	USA	27.10.81	1	NC	Boston (R)	25 Feb
4:08.18	Maria	Cioncan	ROM	19.6.77	1	NC	Bucuresti	18 Feb
4:08.55	Hayley	Tullett	GBR	17.2.73	5		Valencia	11 Feb

4:09.17	Tiffany	McWilliams	USA	20.10.82	25 Feb	4:11.39	Susan	Scott	GBR	26.7.78	22 Jan
4:09.28	Yelena	Sidorchenkova	RUS	30.5.80	2 Feb	4:11.72	Hayley	Ovens	GBR	5.12.75	4 Feb
4:09.65	Katrina	Wootton	GBR	2.9.85	2 Feb	4:11.75	Krisztina	Papp	HUN	17.12.82	29 Jan
4:09.78	Helen	Clitheroe	GBR	2.1.74	2 Feb	4:11.75	Jenelle	Deatherage	USA	25.9.77	25 Feb
4:09.91	Elena	Iagar	ROM	16.1.75	11 Feb	4:11.86	Olesya	Syreva	RUS	25.11.83	24 Jan
4:10.74	Irina	Krakoviak	LTU	16.11.77	2 Feb	4:12.03	Antje	Möldner	GER	13.6.84	29 Jan
4:10.76	Nouriah	Mérah-Benida	ALG	19.10.70	4 Feb	4:12.09	Nahida	Touhami	ALG	10.2.78	11 Mar
4:11.20	Maria	Martins	FRA	1.4.74	10 Feb	4:12.15	Nuria	Fernández	ESP	16.8.76	11 Feb

1 MILE

4:29.23	Hayley	Tullett	GBR	17.2.73	1		New York (A)	21 Jan

4:29.52	Carmen	Douma-Hussar	CAN	12.3.77	28 Jan	4:31.03	Malindi	Elmore	CAN	13.3.80	10 Feb
4:29.93	Treniere	Clement	USA	27.10.81	28 Jan	4:31.87#	Courtney	Babcock	CAN	30.6.72	11 Feb
4:30.03	Tiffany	McWilliams	USA	20.10.82	28 Jan	4:31.91	Megan	Metcalfe	CAN	27.1.82	21 Jan
4:30.39	Jen	Toomey	USA	19.12.71	28 Jan	4:32.08	Carrie	Tollefson	USA	18.1.77	10 Feb
4:30.92	Mestawet	Tadesse	ETH	19.7.85	10 Feb	4:32.49	Jenelle	Deatherage	USA	25.9.77	10 Feb

2000 METRES

5:34.74+	Meseret	Defar	ETH	19.11.83	1	in 3k	Stuttgart	4 Feb
5:39.15	Yelena	Kanales	RUS	7.2.76	1		Yekaterinburg	7 Jan
5:40.75	Yelena	Soboleva	RUS	3.10.82	2		Yekaterinburg	7 Jan
5:43.62	Wioletta	Janowska	POL	9.6.77	1		Leipzig	12 Feb
5:45.05	Liliya	Shobukhova	RUS	13.11.77	3		Yekaterinburg	7 Jan

3000 METRES

8:30.72	Meseret	Defar	ETH	19.11.83	1	Spark	Stuttgart	4 Feb
8:35.67	Olga	Komyagina	RUS	10.2.74	3	NC	Moskva	17 Feb
8:41.22	Tirunesh	Dibaba	ETH	1.10.85	1	GP	Birmingham	18 Feb
8:41.67	Meryem Alaoui	Selsouli	MAR	8.4.84	1		Gent	26 Feb
8:42.59	Lidia	Chojecka	POL	25.1.77	3	WI	Moskva	11 Mar
8:43.38	Sentayehu	Ejigu	ETH	21.6.85	4	WI	Moskva	11 Mar
8:43.88	Yelena	Sidorchenkova	RUS	30.5.80	2		Gent	26 Feb
8:45.09	Yekaterina	Volkova	RUS	16.2.78	4	NC	Moskva	17 Feb
8:45.56	Jo	Pavey	GBR	20.9.73	3		Gent	26 Feb
8:48.45	Daniela	Yordanova	BUL	8.3.76	1	NC	Sofia	12 Feb
8:49.02	Berhane	Adere	ETH	21.7.73	2	Spark	Stuttgart	4 Feb
8:49.59	Ejegayehu	Dibaba	ETH	21.3.82	2	GP	Birmingham	18 Feb
8:50.63	Bouchra	Ghézielle	FRA	18.5.79	3	Spark	Stuttgart	4 Feb

8:53.9	Tatyana	Krivobok	UKR	17.1.72	23 Feb
8:56.45	Yuliya	Vinokurova	RUS	17.6.72	17 Feb
8:57.51	Regina	Rakhimkulova	RUS	5.11.79	17 Feb
8:57.65	Maria	McCambridge	IRL	10.7.75	4 Feb
8:57.91	Wioletta	Janowska	POL	9.6.77	18 Feb
8:58.83	Julie	Coulaud	FRA	7.8.82	18 Feb

5000 METRES

14:35.46	Tirunesh	Dibaba	ETH	1.10.85	1	BIG	Boston (R)	28 Jan
15:18.97	Ejegayehu	Dibaba	ETH	21.3.82	2	BIG	Boston (R)	28 Jan

60 METRES HURDLES

7.83	Lacena	Golding-Clarke	JAM	20.3.75	1		Leipzig	12 Feb
7.84	Virginia	Powell	USA	7.9.83	1	NCAA	Fayetteville	10 Mar
7.84	Derval	O'Rourke	IRL	28.5.81	1	WI	Moskva	11 Mar
7.86	Susanna	Kallur	SWE	16.2.81	1	v4N	Glasgow	28 Jan
7.86	Michelle	Perry	USA	1.5.79	2		Leipzig	12 Feb
7.86	Glory	Alozie	ESP	30.12.77	2	WI	Moskva	11 Mar
7.87	Priscilla	Lopes	CAN	26.8.82	2	NCAA	Fayetteville	10 Mar
7.88	Josephine	Onyia	NGR	15.7.86	1h1	Gaz	Liévin	3 Mar
7.88	Danielle	Carruthers	USA	22.12.79	4	WI	Moskva	11 Mar
7.89	Michelle	Freeman	JAM	5.5.69	1	Tyson	Fayetteville	10 Feb
7.89	Lolo	Jones	USA	5.8.82	2		Düsseldorf	17 Feb
7.91	Kirsten	Bolm	GER	4.3.75	1s1	WI	Moskva	11 Mar
7.93	Joanna	Hayes	USA	23.12.76	1	Mill	New York	3 Feb
7.93	Aurelia	Trywianska	POL	9.5.76	3	GP	Birmingham	18 Feb
7.93	Jenny	Kallur	SWE	16.2.81	3s2	WI	Moskva	11 Mar
7.95	Vonette	Dixon	JAM	26.11.75	2h2	Spark	Stuttgart	4 Feb
7.95	Damu	Cherry	USA	29.11.77	2	NC	Boston (R)	26 Feb
7.98	Dawn	Harper	USA	13.5.84	3	NCAA	Fayetteville	10 Mar
7.99	Nadine	Faustin-Parker	HAI	14.4.76	3		Düsseldorf	17 Feb
7.99	Jenny	Adams	USA	8.7.78	4	NC	Boston (R)	26 Feb
8.01	Sarah	Claxton	GBR	23.9.79	2	NC	Sheffield	12 Feb
8.01	Angela	Whyte	CAN	22.5.80	1h1		Moscow ID	17 Feb
8.01	Beau	Walker	USA	25.3.83	4	NCAA	Fayetteville	10 Mar

8.02	Adrianna	Lamalle	FRA	27.9.82	11 Mar
8.03	Nicole	Ramalalanirina	FRA	5.3.72	25 Feb
8.03	Nichole	Denby	USA	10.10.82	26 Feb
8.04		Feng Yun	CHN	23.2.76	11 Mar
8.05	Alexándra	Kómnou	GRE	4.9.79	25 Feb
8.05	Melaine	Walker	JAM	1.1.83	10 Mar
8.05	Anay	Tejeda	CUB	3.4.83	11 Mar
8.06	Tatyana	Pavliy	RUS	18.5.78	14 Jan
8.06	Delloreen	Ennis-London	JAM	5.3.75	4 Feb
8.07	Viorica	Tigau	ROM	12.8.79	18 Feb
8.07	Ebony	Foster	USA	26.7.83	25 Feb
8.07	Sani	Roseby	USA	5.2.82	26 Feb
8.08	Aleksandra	Antonova	RUS	24.3.80	14 Jan
8.08	Andrea	Bliss	JAM	5.10.80	17 Feb
8.08	Kellie	Wells	USA	16.7.82	18 Feb
8.08	Raquel	Washington	USA	26.9.82	10 Mar
8.08	Maíla Paula	Machado	BRA	22.1.81	11 Mar
8.09	Olga	Korsunova	RUS	20.5.81	17 Feb
8.10	Reina-Flor	Okori	FRA	2.5.80	25 Feb
8.10	Candice	Davis	USA	26.10.85	10 Mar

50mh: Mar 3, Liévin: 6.78 Josephine Onyia 1h1, Derval O'Rourke 1h2, 6.84 Glory Alozie 2h1, 6.87 Aurelia Trywianska 3

55mh: Feb 24, Gainesville: 7.49 Andrea Bliss JAM 5.10.80 1, 7.51 Beau Walker USA 25.3.83 1h1

HIGH JUMP

2.08	Kajsa	Bergqvist	SWE	12.10.76	1		Arnstadt	4 Feb
2.05	Blanka	Vlasic	CRO	8.11.83	1		Banská Bystrica	14 Feb
2.02	Yelena	Slesarenko	RUS	28.2.82	1	WI	Moskva	12 Mar
1.99	Viktoriya	Styopina	UKR	21.2.76	3		Arnstadt	4 Feb
1.99	Barbora	Laláková	CZE	2.5.81	2		Banská Bystrica	14 Feb
1.98	Ruth	Beitia	ESP	1.4.79	3	WI	Moskva	12 Mar
1.98	Yekaterina	Savchenko	RUS	3.6.77	4	WI	Moskva	12 Mar
1.97	Tia	Hellebaut	BEL	16.2.78	1		Tallinn	28 Feb
1.96	Anna	Chicherova	RUS	22.7.82	4		Arnstadt	4 Feb
1.96	Iva	Straková	CZE	4.8.80	5		Arnstadt	4 Feb
1.96	Emma	Green	SWE	8.12.84	3		Banská Bystrica	14 Feb
1.96	Antonietta	Di Martino	ITA	1.6.78	5	WI	Moskva	12 Mar

1.95	Chaunte	Howard	USA	12.1.84	1	BIG	Boston (R)	28 Jan
1.95	Tatyana	Efimenko	KGZ	2.1.81	3		Stockholm	2 Feb
1.95	Romana	Dubnova	CZE	4.11.78	1	Iagar	Bucuresti	5 Feb
1.95	Amy	Acuff	USA	14.7.75	1	Tyson	Fayetteville	10 Feb
1.95	Irina	Mikhalchenko	UKR	20.1.72	1	NC	Sumy	22 Feb
1.94	Dóra	Györffy	HUN	23.2.78	1		Budapest	27 Jan
1.93	Marina	Aitova	KAZ	13.9.82	1	AsiC	Pattaya	12 Feb
1.93	Melanie	Skotnik	FRA	8.11.82	4		Banská Bystrica	14 Feb
1.93	Venelina	Veneva	BUL	13.6.74	1	Balk	Athína (P)	22 Feb
1.93	Marta	Mendía	ESP	18.5.75	9Q	WI	Moskva	11 Mar

1.92	Gwen	Wentland	USA	29.4.72	7 Jan
1.92	Marina	Kuptsova	RUS	22.12.81	25 Jan
1.92	Svetlana	Shkolina	RUS	9.3.86	10 Feb
1.92	Iryna	Kovalenko	UKR	12.6.86	22 Feb
1.92	Destinee	Hooker	USA-J	.88	25 Feb
1.91	Svetlana	Radzivil	UZB	17.1.87	12 Feb
1.90	Yekaterina	Kuntsevich	RUS	2.11.85	24 Dec
1.90	Nicole	Forrester	CAN	17.11.76	13 Jan
1.90	Irina	Glavatskikh	RUS	29.12.84	21 Jan
1.90	Olga	Chuprova	BLR	6.4.81	27 Jan
1.90	Oana	Pantelimon	ROM	17.9.72	28 Jan
1.90	Viktoria	Leks	EST-J	28.9.87	3 Feb
1.90		Zheng Xingyuan	CHN-Y	29.3.89	19 Feb
1.90	Ariane	Friedrich	GER	10.1.84	26 Feb
1.89	Austra	Skujyte	LTU	12.8.79	6 Jan
1.89	Viktoriya	Seryogina	RUS	22.5.73	7 Jan
1.89	Julie	Crane	GBR	26.9.76	28 Jan
1.89	Olga	Kychanova	RUS	14.7.75	18 Feb

POLE VAULT

4.91	Yelena	Isinbayeva	RUS	3.6.82	1		Donetsk	12 Feb
4.80	Anna	Rogowska	POL	21.5.81	1	EICp	Liévin	5 Mar
4.76	Monika	Pyrek	POL	11.8.80	2		Donetsk	12 Feb
4.70	Svetlana	Feofanova	RUS	16.7.80	3	WI	Moskva	11 Mar
4.68	Jen	Stuczynski	USA	6.2.82	1		Ypsilanti	14 Jan
4.65	Vanessa	Boslak	FRA	11.6.82	5	WI	Moskva	11 Mar
4.57	Tatyana	Polnova	RUS	20.4.79	4	Gaz	Liévin	3 Mar
4.55A	Jillian	Schwartz	USA	19.9.79	2		Reno	27 Jan
4.55	Kellie	Suttle	USA	9.5.73	1	NC	Boston (R)	26 Feb
4.51	Mary	Sauer	USA	31.10.75	1		Seattle	11 Feb
4.51	Nataliya	Kushch	UKR	5.3.83	6		Donetsk	12 Feb
4.50	Pavla	Hamácková	CZE	5.2.78	1		Dresden	29 Jan
4.50	Martina	Strutz	GER	4.11.81	1		Potsdam	10 Feb
4.50	Krisztina	Molnár	HUN	8.4.76	1	NC	Budapest	26 Feb
4.50	Naroa	Agirre	ESP	15.5.79	Q	WI	Moskva	10 Mar
4.50	Chelsea	Johnson	USA	20.12.83	1	NCAA	Fayetteville	11 Mar
4.50	Lacy	Janson	USA	20.2.83	2	NCAA	Fayetteville	11 Mar
4.45A	Tracy	O'Hara	USA	20.7.80	3		Reno	27 Jan
4.45	Silke	Spiegelburg	GER	17.3.86	2	NC	Karlsruhe	25 Feb
4.41	Fabiana	Murer	BRA	16.3.81	1		Wuppertal	27 Jan
4.41	Becky	Holliday	USA	12.3.80	2		Seattle	11 Feb
4.40A	Dana	Ellis	CAN	7.12.79	1		Flagstaff	21 Jan
4.40	April	Steiner	USA	22.4.80	1		Fayetteville	21 Jan
4.40	Anna	Schultze	GER	26.5.85	3		Karlsruhe	29 Jan
4.40	Tünde	Vaszi	HUN	18.4.72	1		Budapest	4 Feb
4.40	Hanna-Mia	Persson	SWE	11.2.78	1	Euro	Göteborg	8 Feb
4.40	Kirsten	Belin	SWE	2.3.81	2	Euro	Göteborg	8 Feb
4.40	Niki	McEwen	USA	1.4.80	5	NC	Boston (R)	26 Feb
4.40	Nastja	Ryshich	GER	19.9.77	2		Bad Oeynhausen	3 Mar
4.40	Róza	Kasprzak	POL	9.4.82	3		Bad Oeynhausen	3 Mar
4.40	Breanna	Eveland	USA	25.1.84	1		Ames	4 Mar

4.32	Elisabete	Tavares	POR	7.3.80	11 Feb
4.31		Yang Jing	CHN	1.1.84	14 Nov
4.31	Anastasiya	Shvedova	RUS	3.5.79	10 Feb
4.30	Yuliya	Golubchikova	RUS	27.3.83	12 Jan
4.30	Joanna	Piwowarska	POL	4.11.83	20 Jan
4.30	Linda	Persson	SWE	22.9.81	28 Jan
4.30	Beth	Hinshaw-Spearman	USA	30.7.81	3 Feb
4.30	Anastasiya	Kiryanova	RUS	26.7.82	9 Feb
4.30		Gao Shuying	CHN	28.10.79	18 Feb
4.30		Zhao Yingzhu	CHN-J	14.1.88	24 Feb
4.30	Nadine	Rohr	SUI	29.6.77	26 Feb
4.28A	Erin	Asay	USA	17.3.83	11 Feb

LONG JUMP

7.00	Tatyana	Kotova	RUS	11.12.76	1	WI	Moskva	12 Mar
6.80	Tianna	Madison	USA	30.8.85	2	WI	Moskva	12 Mar
6.77	Oksana	Udmurtova	RUS	1.2.82	1	NC	Moskva	18 Feb
6.76	Naide	Gomes	POR	20.11.79	3	WI	Moskva	12 Mar
6.76	Concepción	Montaner	ESP	14.1.81	4	WI	Moskva	12 Mar
6.71	Marshevet	Hooker	USA	25.9.84	1	NCAA	Fayetteville	10 Mar
6.69	Lyudmila	Kolchanova	RUS	1.10.79	2	NC	Moskva	18 Feb
6.68	Tatyana	Shchurenko	UKR	26.2.76	1		Kiev	13 Jan
6.67	Stilianí	Pilátou	GRE	28.3.80	1	NC	Athína (P)	18 Feb
6.66	Viorica	Tigau	ROM	12.8.79	1		Bucuresti	25 Feb
6.66	Shameka	Marshall	USA	9.9.83	2	NCAA	Fayetteville	10 Mar
6.65	Viktoriya	Molchanova	UKR	26.5.82	1		Kharkov	18 Jan
6.65	Viktoriya	Rybalko	UKR	26.10.82	1		Rochester	21 Jan

6.64	Aleksandra	Stadnyuk	UKR	16.4.80	2		Kiev	13 Jan
6.63	Yargelis	Savigne	CUB	13.11.84	1	Gaz	Liévin	3 Mar
6.62	Adina	Anton	ROM	6.10.84	1	NC	Bucuresti	18 Feb
6.62	Akiba	McKinney	USA	9.3.79	1	NC	Boston (R)	25 Feb
6.61	Olga	Kucherenko	RUS	14.2.85	1		Volgograd	14 Jan
6.60	Alina	Militaru	ROM	10.4.82	2	NC	Bucuresti	18 Feb
6.60	Kierra	Foster	USA	22.2.84	1		Blacksburg	24 Feb

6.59	Ineta	Radevica	LAT	13.7.81	3 Mar
6.58	Claudia	Tonn	GER	18.4.81	17 Feb
6.58	Ioánna	Kafetzí	GRE	30.5.76	22 Feb
6.57	Irina	Melnikova	RUS	14.5.75	4 Feb
6.57	Natalya	Mamysheva	RUS	9.12.84	8 Feb
6.55	Elva	Goulbourne	JAM	21.1.80	4 Feb
6.55	Olga	Rypakova	KAZ	30.11.84	10 Feb
6.55	Karin	Ruckstuhl	NED	2.11.80	12 Feb
6.55	Angelica	Badea	ROM	1.10.75	18 Feb
6.54		Guan Yingnan	CHN	25.4.77	15 Nov
6.54	Natalya	Lebusova	RUS	4.4.78	1 Mar
6.53	Martina	Darmovzalová	CZE	12.10.78	4 Feb
6.53	Yelena	Kremneva	RUS	23.7.86	8 Feb
6.53	Kelly	Sotherton	GBR	13.11.76	11 Feb
6.52	Chelsea	Hammond	JAM	2.8.83	14 Jan
6.52	Tatyana	Lebedeva	RUS	21.7.76	14 Jan
6.52	Tabia	Charles	CAN	6.4.85	24 Feb
6.50	Lyudmila	Blonska	UKR	9.11.77	4 Feb

TRIPLE JUMP

14.95	Tatyana	Lebedeva	RUS	21.7.76	1	WI	Moskva	11 Mar
14.93	Anna	Pyatykh	RUS	4.4.81	2	WI	Moskva	11 Mar
14.86	Yamilé	Aldama	SUD	14.8.72	3	WI	Moskva	11 Mar
14.84	Trecia	Smith	JAM	5.11.75	4	WI	Moskva	11 Mar
14.72	Yargelis	Savigne	CUB	13.11.84	5	WI	Moskva	11 Mar
14.49	Tereza	Marinova	BUL	5.9.77	1	Balk	Athína (P)	22 Feb
14.38	Oksana	Rogova	RUS	7.10.78	3	NC	Moskva	17 Feb
14.34	Oleksandra	Stadnyuk	UKR	16.4.80	7	WI	Moskva	11 Mar
14.24	Simona	La Mantia	ITA	14.4.83	1	NC	Ancona	19 Feb
14.24	Anastasiya	Zhuravlyeva	UZB	9.10.81	2		Athína (P)	25 Feb
14.22	Yelena	Oleynikova	RUS	9.12.76	3		Athína (P)	25 Feb
14.21	Dana	Veldáková	SVK	3.6.81	Q	WI	Moskva	10 Mar
14.20	Natallia	Safronava	BLR	11.7.74	1	NC	Mogilyov	27 Jan
14.15	Irina	Vasilyeva	RUS	9.4.79	4	NC	Moskva	17 Feb
14.14	Carlota	Castrejana	ESP	25.4.73	9Q	WI	Moskva	10 Mar
14.12	Olga	Pankova	RUS	13.8.76	5		Samara	4 Feb
14.11	Keila	Costa	BRA	6.2.83	10Q	WI	Moskva	10 Mar
14.10		Xie Limei	CHN	27.6.86	1	NGP	Beijing	24 Feb
14.08	Marija	Sestak-Martinovic	SCG	17.4.79	1		Budapest	27 Jan
14.08	Olga	Saladukha	UKR	4.6.83	5		Athína (P)	25 Feb
14.07	Mabel	Gay	CUB	5.5.83	3		Tallinn	28 Feb

14.06	Cristina	Bujin	ROM-J	12.4.88	28 Jan
14.05	Anastasiya	Taranova	RUS	6.9.85	10 Feb
14.05	Mariana	Solomon	ROM	8.9.80	26 Feb
14.00	Svetlana	Bolshakova	RUS	14.10.84	4 Feb
13.97	Theresa	N'Zola	FRA	30.11.83	5 Mar
13.91	Yelena	Parfyonova	KAZ	26.1.74	10 Feb
13.91	Mariya	Dimitrova	BUL	7.8.76	22 Feb
13.91	Tiombé	Hurd	USA	17.8.73	4 Mar
13.90	Livia	Pruteanu	ROM	22.12.81	19 Feb
13.90	Camilla	Johansson	SWE	3.11.76	26 Feb
13.89	Yelena	Ivanova	RUS	16.3.79	24 Jan
13.88	Kéne	Ndoye	SEN	20.11.78	10 Mar
13.86	Veera	Baranova	EST	12.2.84	11 Feb
13.85	Aneta	Sah	POL	22.4.75	5 Mar
13.84	Elena Alina	Popescu	ROM	27.10.85	19 Feb
13.84	Tatyana	Dyachenko	UKR	25.1.86	23 Feb

SHOT

20.86	Nadzeya	Ostapchuk	BLR	12.10.80	1		Minsk	24 Feb
19.84	Natallia	Khoroneko	BLR	25.5.82	1	WI	Moskva	12 Mar
19.64	Nadine	Kleinert	GER	20.10.75	2	WI	Moskva	12 Mar
19.26	Jill	Camarena	USA	2.8.82	1	NC	Boston (R)	25 Feb
19.25	Petra	Lammert	GER	3.3.84	1	NC	Karlsruhe	25 Feb
19.24	Olga	Ryabinkina	RUS	24.9.76	3	WI	Moskva	12 Mar
18.87	Laura	Gerraughty	USA	29.7.83	1		Blacksburg	25 Feb
18.79	Cleopatra	Borel-Brown	TRI	3.10.79	2		Blacksburg	18 Feb
18.73	Yumileidi	Cumbá	CUB	11.2.75	Q	WI	Moskva	11 Mar
18.56	Michelle	Carter	USA	12.10.85	1	NCAA	Fayetteville	11 Mar
18.41	Chiara	Rosa	ITA	28.1.83	1	NC	Ancona	18 Feb
18.32		Li Fengfeng	CHN	9.1.79	1	NGP	Shanghai	19 Feb
18.24	Kristin	Heaston	USA	23.11.75	2	NC	Boston (R)	25 Feb
18.21	Denise	Hinrichs	GER-J	7.6.87	3	NC	Karlsruhe	25 Feb
18.20		Li Ling	CHN	7.2.85	1	AsG-i	Pattaya	15 Nov
18.14	Oksana	Gaus	RUS	9.7.81	1		Volgograd	14 Jan
18.14	Olga	Ivanova	RUS	6.4.79	2	NC	Moskva	18 Feb
18.13	Vivian	Chukwuemeka	NGR	4.3.75	1		Flagstaff	4 Feb
18.06	Anna	Omarova	RUS	3.10.81	2		Volgograd	14 Jan
18.03	Yuliya	Leontyuk	BLR	31.1.84	2		Minsk	10 Feb

18.02	Krystyna	Zabawska	POL	14.1.68	25 Feb
18.01	Tatyana	Ilyushchenko	BLR	18.4.83	24 Feb
17.99		Zhang Guirong	SIN	5.2.78	15 Nov
17.91	Sarah	Stevens	USA	2.4.86	11 Mar
17.87	Cristiana	Checchi	ITA	8.7.77	4 Feb
17.64	Becky	Breisch	USA	16.3.83	11 Feb
17.61	Nadine	Beckel	GER	27.5.77	25 Feb
17.58	Oksana	Chibisova	RUS	31.3.77	24 Jan

WEIGHT

24.04	Jennifer	Dahlgren	ARG	27.8.84	1	NCAA	Fayetteville	10 Mar
22.99	Brittany	Riley	USA	26.8.86	1		Ames	10 Feb
22.95	Erin	Gilreath	USA	11.8.80	1	NC	Boston (R)	24 Feb
22.82	Jen	Leatherman	USA	26.9.83	1	Big 10	Madison	26 Feb
22.66	Amber	Campbell	USA	5.6.81	2	NC	Boston (R)	24 Feb
22.33*	Tamara	Burns	USA	21.12.83	1		Clemson	3 Dec
22.32	Achi	Ukabam	USA	14.3.84	2	NCAA	Fayetteville	10 Mar
22.08	Loree	Smith	USA	6.11.82	1	Mill	New York (Riverdale)	3 Feb

21.43	Ariel	Brooks	USA	27.11.83	3 Feb	21.39	Jessica	Pressley	USA	27.12.84	4 Feb

PENTATHLON

4713	Olga	Levenkova	RUS	11.1.84	1	NC	Moskva	4 Feb
	8.31	1.82	13.21	6.44	2.19.94			
4685	Lyudmila	Blonska	UKR	9.11.77	1	WI	Moskva	10 Mar
	8.29	1.83	12.43	6.50	2:19.62			
4683	Karin	Ruckstuhl	NED	2.11.80	1	v4N	Praha	12 Feb
	8.41	1.82	13.50	13.50	6.55	2:17.39		
4648	Yuliya	Ignatkina	RUS	23.9.82	2	NC	Moskva	4 Feb
	8.57	1.82	14.56	6.16	2.13.54			
4613*	Svetlana	Ladokhina	RUS	21.2.79			Kemerovo	24 Dec
	8.42	1.75	16.43	6.06	2:18.98			
4586	Sonja	Kesselschläger	GER	20.1.78	1	NC	Frankfurt-Kalbach	29 Jan
	8.56	1.81	13.46	6.34	2:16.15			
4582	Olga	Rypakova	KAZ	30.11.84	1	AsiC	Pattaya	10 Feb
	8.68	1.88	12.90	6.55	2:23.26			
4554	Anna	Kryazheva	RUS	17.7.84	2		Moskva	15 Jan
	8.76	1.76	13.63	6.33	2:11.46			
4549	Marie	Collonvillé	FRA	23.11.73	1	NC	Aubière	25 Feb
	8.49	1.82	12.34	6.39	2:16.58			
4501	Lilli	Schwarzkopf	GER	28.8.83	2	NC	Frankfurt-Kalbach	29 Jan
	8.67	1.81	14.08	6.00	2:15.85			
4498	Julie	Hollman	GBR	16.2.77	2	v4N	Praha	12 Feb
	8.53	1.85	12.23	6.36	2:21.10			
4487	Natalya	Kotova	RUS	13.5.83	3	NC	Moskva	4 Feb
	8.28	1.82	13.89	6.25	2.29.15			
4458	Karolina	Tyminska	POL	4.10.84	1	NC	Spala	25 Feb
	8.66	1.67	13.96	6.27	2:12.19			
4442	Svetlana	Sokolova	RUS	9.1.81	4	NC	Moskva	4 Feb
	8.48	1.73	14.31	6.08	2.18.75			
4430	Viorica	Tigau	ROM	12.8.79	1		Bucuresti	12 Feb
	8.24	1.70	13.15	6.43	2:23.43			
4421	Karin	Ertl	GER	23.6.74	3	NC	Frankfurt-Kalbach	29 Jan
	8.41	1.81	14.05	6.12	2:28.73			
4405	Katja	Keller	GER	9.8.80	4	NC	Frankfurt-Kalbach	29 Jan
	8.47	1.81	12.63	6.09	2:21.03			
4401	Jessica	Ennis	GBR	28.1.86	1	v2N-23	Eaubonne	25 Feb
	8.29	1.87	11.82	5.85	2:20.45			
4392	Denisa	Scerbová	CZE	21.8.86	3	v4N	Praha	12 Feb
	8.49	1.79	11.04	6.38	2:18.80			

4349	Anna	Bogdanova	RUS	21.10.84	4 Feb	4283	Zhanna	Melnichenko	UKR	24.4.83	15 Feb
4336	Ashley	Selig	USA	23.2.84	24 Feb	4270	Vera	Yepimashko	BLR	10.7.76	24 Jan
4315	Marina	Goncharova	RUS	26.4.86	4 Feb	4267	Julie	Pickler	USA	9.12.83	11 Mar
4307	Jennifer	Oeser	GER	29.11.83	29 Jan	4266	Tatyana	Zhevnova	BLR	17.10.77	24 Jan
4287	Jackie	Johnson	USA	8.9.84	11 Mar	4243	Kaie	Kand	EST	31.3.84	17 Feb

3000 METRES WALK

11:59.64	Melanie	Seeger	GER	8.1.77	1	NC	Karlsruhe	25 Feb
12:02.40	Sabine	Zimmer	GER	6.2.81	2	NC	Karlsruhe	25 Feb
12:10.61	Elisa	Rigaudo	ITA	17.6.80	1	NC	Ancona	18 Feb
12:26.23	Sonata	Milusauskaite	LTU	21.8.73	1	NC	Espinho	25 Feb

5000 METRES WALK

21:14.8	Irina	Petrova	RUS	26.5.85	1		Moskva	25 Dec
21:24.3	Natalya	Shivireva	RUS	19.11.78	1		Chelyabinsk	6 Jan
21:30.0	Tatyana	Gudkova	RUS	23.12.78	2		Chelyabinsk	6 Jan
21:43.1	Alena	Zenkova	RUS	1.1.82	3		Chelyabinsk	6 Jan
21:53.07	Vera	Zozulya	UKR	31.8.70	1	NC	Sumy	21 Feb

WORLD INDOOR CHAMPIONSHIPS 2006

At Moscow, Russia 10-12 March

The 11th IAAF World Indoor Championships held in the superbly appointed Olympic Sport Palace (built for the 1980 Games), were an undoubted success. There was plenty of dramatic action and lots of exciting races and close competition for field event medals, although standards at the top and in depth were generally down from the 2004 Championships held in Budapest. The amazing Maria Mutola won a record seventh World Indoor title at 800m and the one championships record came from Olesya Krasnomovets at 400m. The Russians scored 1-2s in the men's high jump and women's 1500m and triple jump, and although the anticipated possible world records from Yelena Isinbayeva and the women's 4x400m relay did not happen, they still won in impressive style.

Apart from Mutola, athletes to successfully defend their titles were Alleyne Francique (400m), Yelena Slesarenko (HJ), Isinbayeva (PV) and Tatyana Lebedeva (TJ), while Terrence Trammell (60mh) and Tatyana Kotova (LJ) regained their titles. Kenenisa Bekele became the first athlete to win Olympic, World, World Cross Country and now World Indoor titles – with a typically devastating finish in the 3000m. Ignisious Gaisah became the first athlete from Ghana to win a world indoor title as he won the log jump by just 1cm from Irving Saladino who set four South American indoor records (8.18, 8.19, 8.27 and 8.29) in the final after one (8.10) in qualifying. Another to impress was Rees Hoffa who added 37cm to his lifetime best to win the shot.

11 nations won gold medals, 33 medals of any colour, and 52 placed athletes in the top eight.

MEN

60 Metres (10)
1. Leonard Scott USA 6.50
2. Andrey Yepishin RUS 6.52
3. Terrence Trammell USA 6.54
4. Matic Osovnikar SLO 6.58
5. Olusoji Fasuba NGR 6.58
6. Ronald Pognon FRA 6.61
7. Vicente de Lima BRA 6.62
8. Henry Vizcaino CUB 6.84

400 Metres (12)
1. Alleyne Francique GRN 45.54
2. California Molefe BOT 45.75
3. Chris Brown BAH 45.78
4. Davian Clarke JAM 45.93
5. Milton Campbell USA 46.15
6. Dmitriy Petrov RUS 47.33

800 Metres (12)
1. Wilfred Bungei KEN 1:47.15
2. Mbulaeni Mulaudzi RSA 1:47.16
3. Yuriy Borzakovskiy RUS 1:47.38
4. Dmitrijs Milkevics LAT 1:48.01
5. Juan de Dios Jurado ESP 1:48.44
6. Jimmy Watkins GBR 1:48.56

1500 Metres (11)
1. Ivan Heshko UKR 3:42.08
2. Daniel Kip. Komen KEN 3:42.55
3. Elkanah Angwenyi KEN 3:42.98
4. Halil Akkas TUR 3:43.61
5. Sergio Gallardo ESP 3:43.77
6. James Nolan IRL 3:43.98
7. Christopher Lukezic USA 3:45.09
8. Yassine Bensghir MAR 3:47.20
9. Youssef Baba MAR 3:49.25

3000 Metres (12)
1. Kenenisa Bekele ETH 7:39.32
2. Saïf Saaeed Shaheen QAT 7:41.28
3. Eliud Kipchoge KEN 7:42.58
4. Alistair Cragg IRL 7:46.43
5. Shadrack Korir KEN 7:47.11
6. Tariku Bekele ETH-J 7:47.67
7. Adil Kaouch MAR 7:48.01
8. Moukheld Al-Outaibi KSA 7:52.91

60 Metres Hurdles (11)
1. Terrence Trammell USA 7.43
2. Dayron Robles CUB 7.46
3. Dominique Arnold USA 7.52
4= Stanislav Olijar LAT 7.52
4= Maurice Wignall JAM 7.52
6. Thomas Blaschek GER 7.57
7. Paulo Villar COL 7.61
8. Yoel Hernández CUB 7.62

High Jump (11)
1. Yaroslav Rybakov RUS 2.37
2. Andrey Tereshin RUS 2.35
3. Linus Thörnblad SWE 2.33
4. Victor Moya CUB 2.30
5. Stefan Holm SWE 2.30
6. Andrey Sokolovskiy UKR 2.26
7. Giulio Ciotti ITA 2.26
8. Robert Wolski POL 2.22

Pole Vault (12)
1. Brad Walker USA 5.80
2. Alhaji Jeng SWE 5.70
3. Tim Lobinger GER 5.60
4= Alex Averbukh ISR 5.50
4= Giovanni Lanaro MEX 5.50
4= Fabian Schulze GER 5.50
nh. Jeff Hartwig USA –
nh. Denys Yurchenko UKR –

Long Jump (11)
1. Ignisious Gaisah GHA 8.30
2. Irving Saladino PAN 8.29
3. Andrew Howe ITA 8.19
4. Loúis Tsátoumas GRE 8.10
5. Godfrey Mokoena RSA 8.01
6. Erivaldo Vieira BRA 7.97
7. Brian Johnson USA 7.90
8. Issam Nima ALG 7.84

Triple Jump (11)
1. Walter Davis USA 17.73
2. Jadel Gregório BRA 17.56
3. Yoandri Betanzos CUB 17.42
4. Marian Oprea ROM 17.34
5. Igor Spasovkhodskiy RUS 17.25
6. Nelson Évora POR 17.14
7. Nathan Douglas GBR 17.05
8. Dimitrios Tsiámis GRE 16.94
9. Momchil Karailiev BUL 16.87

Shot (10)
1. Reese Hoffa USA 22.11
2. Andrey Mikhnevich BLR 21.37
3. Joachim Olsen DEN 21.16
4. Pavel Sofin RUS 20.68
5. Gheorghe Guset ROM 20.60
6. Manuel Martínez ESP 20.43
7. Tomasz Majewski POL 20.07
8. Anton Lyuboslavskiy RUS 19.93

Heptathlon (11-12)
1. André Niklaus GER 6192
2. Bryan Clay USA 6187
3. Roman Sebrle CZE 6161
4. Kristjan Rahnu EST 6062
5. Aleksey Drozdov RUS 6052
6. Aleksandr Pogorelov RUS 5910
7. Konstantin Smirnov RUS 5795

4 x 400 Metres Relay (12)
1. USA (T Washington, L Merritt, M Campbell, W Spearmon) 3:03.24
2. POL (D Dabrowski, M Marciniszyn R Wieruszewski, P Klimczak) 3:04.67
3. RUS (K Svechkar, A Derevyagin, Y Lebedev, D Petrov) 3:06.91
4. SWE 3:07.32 6. FRA 3:09.55
5. DOM 3:08.47

Women – 60 Metres (10)
1. Me'Lisa Barber USA 7.01
2. Lauryn Williams USA 7.01
3. Kim Gevaert BEL 7.11
4. Christine Arron FRA 7.13
5. Mariya Bolikova RUS 7.17
6. Zhanna Block UKR 7.19
7. Larisa Kruglova RUS 7.23
8. Sylvie Mballa Éloundou CMR 7.30

400 Metres (12)
1. Olesya Krasnomovets RUS 50.04*
2. Vanya Stambolova BUL 50.21
3. Christine Amertil BAH 50.34
4. Natalya Nazarova RUS 50.60
5. Novlene Williams JAM 51.82
6. Mariyana Dimitrova BUL 52.66

800 Metres (12)
1. Maria Mutola MOZ 1:58.90
2. Kenia Sinclair JAM 1:59.54
3. Hasna Benhassi MAR 2:00.34
4. Elisabeth Grouselle FRA 2:00.74
5. Olga Kotlyarova RUS 2:01.26
6. Ewelina Setowska POL 2:02.39

1500 Metres (12)
1. Yuliya Chizhenko RUS 4:04.70
2. Yelena Soboleva RUS 4:05.21
3. Maryam Yusuf Jamal BRN 4:05.53
4. Hind Dehiba FRA 4:05.67
5. Irina Lishchynska UKR 4:07.82
6. Corina Dumbravean ROM 4:08.29
7. Treniere Clement USA 4:11.21
8. Maria Martins FRA 4:15.17
9. Nahida Touhami ALG 4:19.44

3000 Metres (11)
1. Meseret Defar ETH 8:38.80
2. Liliya Shobukhova RUS 8:42.18
3. Lidia Chojecka POL 8:42.59
4. Sentayehu Ejigu ETH 8:43.38
5. Olesya Syreva RUS 8:44.10
6. Mariem Selsouli MAR 8:55.97
7. Carrie Tollefson USA 8:59.13

8. Analia Rosa POR 8:59.99

60 Metres Hurdles (11)
1. Derval O'Rourke IRL 7.84
2. Glory Alozie ESP 7.86
3. Susanna Kallur SWE 7.87
4. Danielle Carruthers USA 7.88
5. Kirsten Bolm GER 7.93
6. Lacena Golding-Clarke JAM 7.94
7. Damu Cherry USA 7.95
8. Jenny Kallur SWE 7.98

High Jump (12)
1. Yelena Slesarenko RUS 2.02
2. Blanka Vlasic CRO 2.00
3. Ruth Beitia ESP 1.98
4. Yekaterina Savchenko RUS 1.98
5. Antonietta Di Martino ITA 1.96
6. Tia Hellebaut BEL 1.96
7. Vita Styopina UKR 1.96
8. Chaunte Howard USA 1.94

Pole Vault (11)
1. Yelena Isinbayeva RUS 4.80
2. Anna Rogowska POL 4.75
3. Svetlana Feofanova RUS 4.70
4. Monika Pyrek POL 4.65
5. Vanessa Boslak FRA 4.65
6. Naroa Agirre ESP 4.50
7. Kellie Suttle USA 4.40
8. Silke Spiegelburg GER 4.30

Long Jump (12)
1. Tatyana Kotova RUS 7.00
2. Tianna Madison USA 6.80
3. Naide Gomes POR 6.76
4. Concepción Montaner ESP 6.76
5. Ineta Radevica LAT 6.54
6. Yargelis Savigne CUB 6.51
7. Oksana Udmurtova RUS 6.50
8. Stilianí Pilátou GRE 6.50

Triple Jump (11)
1. Tatyana Lebedeva RUS 14.95
2. Anna Pyatykh RUS 14.93
3. Yamilé Aldama SUD 14.86
4. Trecia Smith JAM 14.84
5. Yargelis Savigne CUB 14.72
6. Tereza Marinova BUL 14.37
7. Oleksandra Stadnyuk UKR 14.34
8. Dana Veldáková SVK 13.76

Shot (12)
1. Natalya Khoroneko BLR 19.84
2. Nadine Kleinert GER 19.64
3. Olga Ryabinkina RUS 19.24
4. Petra Lammert GER 19.21
5. Yumileidi Cumbá CUB 18.28
6. Nadezhda Ostapchuk BLR 18.13
7. Jill Camarena USA 17.60
8. Cleopatra Borel-Brown TRI 17.59

Pentathlon (10)
1. Lyudmila Blonska UKR 4685
2. Karin Ruckstuhl NED 4607
3. Olga Levenkova RUS 4579
4. Sonja Kesselschläger GER 4574
5. Yuliya Ignatkina RUS 4459
6. Svetlana Ladokhina RUS 4374
7. Olga Rypakova KAZ 4368
8. Hyleas Fountain USA 4205

4 x 400 Metres Relay (12)
1. RUS (T Levina, N Nazarova, O Krasnomovets, N Antyukh) 3:24.91
2. USA (D Dunn, T Ross-Williams, M Hargrove, M Danner) 3:28.63
3. BLR (N Sologub, A Kozak, Y Zhalniryuk, I Usovich) 3:28.65
4. POL 3:28.95
5. JAM 3:29.54
6. GBR 3:29.70

Leading Nations – Medals & Points

Nation	1	2	3	Points
Russia	8	5	5	178
USA	7	4	2	122.5
Germany	1	1	1	43
Poland	0	2	1	36
Jamaica	0	1	0	32.5
Spain	0	1	1	32
Ukraine	2	0	0	31.5
Kenya	1	1	2	31
Cuba	0	1	1	31
Sweden	0	1	2	29
France	0	0	0	26
Belarus	1	1	1	24
Ethiopia	2	0	0	24
Kenya	2	0	0	20

COMMONWEALTH GAMES 2006

Melbourne, Australia 19-25 March

The 18th multi-sport Commonwealth Games were a huge success as could confidently be expected in the world's top sporting nation. The track and field events were staged in the Melbourne Cricket Ground, previously used for athletics at the 1956 Olympic Games. The crowd support was fantastic throughout with every appearance by an Australian ecstatically received – and they had plenty to shout about as the host nation swept to overwhelming success with 36 medals, 14 of them gold (not including the EAD events). England came next in the points table, but 6 gold, 4 silver and 8 bronze compared to 12-6-11 in Manchester 2002, and the smaller teams from Jamaica and Kenya had much more reason for satisfaction. Kenya's six gold medals were particularly striking given the priority inevitably given to the World Cross-Country Champs and Jamaicans were totally dominant in the sprints. There was an aggregate total of over 700,000 for all sessions in the stadium including the ceremonies, and some 83,000 was the reported peak figure for the fifth day when Jana Pittman delivered her commanding performance to win the 400m hurdles.

Nathan Deakes repeated the walks double that he had achieved four years earlier, winning both 20k and 50k races by huge margins in championships record times and others to retain titles won in 2002 were Mark Boswell (HJ), Kerryn McCann (Marathon), Pittman (400mh) and Jane Saville (20km walk). Stuart Rendell (HT) regained the title he won in 1998 and perhaps the most amazng winner was Dean Macey, far from fully fit, yet able to win his first major gold medal as he took the decathlon in his first competition (at any event) since the 2004 Olympic Games.

The most unfortunate athletes were the Englishwomen's 4x400m relay team. Christine Ohuruogu, who earlier had a superb world-class victory in the 400m over Tonique Darling, had an easy run in bringing home the team to victory after Jamaica had dropped the baton. Then elation turned to despair as the team was disqualified. The decision was undoubtedly correct as Natasha Danvers-Smith broke the rule (brought in to help prevent the pushing and shoving so often seen at changeovers) by taking the wrong station for the third leg (she walked out in third place as this was the English team's position with 200m to go, but Nicola Sanders ran a superb leg in 50.5 to go into second so Danvers-Smith walked into that position. Can a disqualification ever have be en so less deserved?

MEN

100 Metres (20) +0.9
1. Asafa Powell JAM 10.03
2. Olusoji Fasuba NGR 10.11
3. Marc Burns TRI 10.17
4. Uchenna Emedolu NGR 10.22
5. Aziz Zakari GHA 10.22
6. Patrick Johnson AUS 10.26
7. Anson Henry CAN 10.28
8. Marlon Devonish ENG 10.30

200 Metres (23) +0.5
1. Omar Brown JAM 20.47
2. Stéphan Buckland MRI 20.47
3. Chris Williams JAM 20.52
4. Patrick Johnson AUS 20.59
5. Aaron Armstrong TRI 20.61
6. Uchenna Emedolu NGR 20.66
7. Enefiok Udo-Obong NGR 20.69
8. James Dolphin NZL 20.72

400 Metres (22)
1. John Steffensen AUS 44.73
2. Alleyne Francique GRN 45.09
3. Jermaine Gonzales JAM 45.16
4. Chris Brown BAH 45.19
5. Martyn Rooney ENG-J 45.51
6. California Molefe BOT 45.78
7. Paul Gorries RSA 45.79
8. Lansford Spence JAM 45.79

800 Metres (23)
1. Alex Kipchirchir KEN 1:45.88
2. Achraf Tadili CAN 1:46.93
3. John Litei KEN 1:46.98
4. Sherridan Kirk TRI 1:47.45
5. Jason Stewart NZL 1:47.72
6. Nicholas Bromley AUS 1:50.45
7. Cosmas Rono KEN 1:52.03
8. Oabona Onalenna BOT 1:57.20

1500 Metres (25)
1. Nick Willis NZL 3:38.49
2. Nathan Brannen CAN 3:39.20
3. Mark Fountain AUS 3:39.33
4. Paul Hamblyn NZL 3:39.38

5. Nick McCormick ENG 3:39.55
6. Ismael Kombich KEN 3:40.92
7. Kevin Sullivan CAN 3:41.19
8. Jeremy Roff AUS 3:41.50
9. Craig Mottram AUS (fell) 3:44.37
10. Adrian Blincoe NZL 3:44.88

5000 Metres (20)
1. Augustine Choge KEN 12:56.41*
2. Craig Mottram AUS 12:58.19
3. Ben Limo KEN 13:05.30
4. Joseph Ebuya KEN 13:05.89
5. Fabian Joseph TAN 13:12.76
6. Damian Chopa TAN 13:24.03
7. Moses Kipsiro UGA 13:25.06
8. Dickson Marwa TAN 13:26.49
9. Mohammed Farah ENG 13:40.53
10. Tonny Wamulya ZAM 13:40.78

10000 Metres (25)
1. Boniface Kiprop UGA 27:50.99
2. Geoffrey Kipngeno KEN 27:51.16
3. Fabiano Joseph TAN 27:51.99
4. Paul Langat KEN 27:52.36
5. Wilson Busienei UGA 28:37.38
6. Dickson Marwa TAN 28:47.49
7. Michael Aish NZL 29:05.55
8. Gavin Thompson ENG 29:41.77

Marathon (19)
1. Samson Ramadhani TAN 2:11:29
2. Fred Mogaka KEN 2:12:03
3. Dan Robinson ENG 2:14:50
4. Scott Westcott AUS 2:16:32
5. Andrew Letherby AUS 2:17:11
6. Jacob Yator KEN 2:17:31
7. Shane Nankervis AUS 2:19:15
8. Francis Robert Naali TAN 2:19:39

3000 Metres Steeplechase (24)
1. Ezekiel Kemboi KEN 8:18.17
2. Wesley Kiprotich KEN 8:19.38
3. Reuben Kosgei KEN 8:19.82
4. Martin Dent AUS 8:28.98
5. Stuart Stokes ENG 8:29.94
6. Peter Nowill AUS 8:30.59
7. Ruben Ramolefi RSA 8:35.91
8. Matthew Kerr CAN 8:38.97

110 Metres Hurdles (21) -1.1
1. Maurice Wignall JAM 13.26
2. Chris Baillie SCO 13.61
3. Andrew Turner ENG 13.62
4. Charles Allen CAN 13.66
5. Christopher Pinnock JAM 13.67
6. Shaun Bownes RSA 13.70
7. David Hughes ENG 13.70
8. Jared MacLeod CAN 13.80

400 Metres Hurdles (23)
1. Louis van Zyl RSA 48.05*
2. Alwyn Myburgh RSA 48.23
3. Kemel Thompson JAM 48.65
4. Rhys Williams WAL 49.09
5. Brendan Cole AUS 49.41
6. Dean Griffiths JAM 49.85
7. Pieter de Villiers RSA 50.51
8. Chris Rawlinson ENG 52.89

High Jump (22)
1. Mark Boswell CAN 2.26
2. Martyn Bernard ENG 2.26
3. Kyricos Ioannou CYP 2.23
4. Donald Thomas BAH 2.23
5= Ramsay Carelse RSA 2.20
5= Nick Moroney AUS 2.20
7. Robert Mitchell WAL 2.15
8. Ben Challenger ENG 2.15

Pole Vault (24)
1. Steve Hooker AUS 5.80*
2. Dmitri Markov AUS 5.60
3. Steve Lewis ENG 5.50
4. Nick Buckfield ENG 5.35
5. Dominic Johnson LCA 5.35
6. Scott Simpson WAL 5.20
nh. Paul Burgess AUS –

Long Jump (22)
1. Ignisious Gaisah GHA 8.20/0.2
2. Gable Garenamotse BOT 8.17/0.2
3. Fabrice Lapierre AUS 8.10/-0.1
4. Khotso Mokoena RSA 8.04/0.4
5. John Thornell AUS 7.98/0.8
6. Chris Tomlinson ENG 7.96/0.1
7. Tom Parravicini AUS 7.91/0.6
8. Greg Rutherford ENG 7.85/0.2

Triple Jump (25)
1. Phillips Idowu ENG 17.45/0.2
2. Khotso Mokoena RSA 16.95/0.7
3. Alwyn Jones AUS 16.75/0.4
4. Andrew Murphy AUS 16.70/0.7
5. LeJuan Simon TRI 16.59/0.6
6. Randy Lewis GRN 16.53/1.9
7. Chris Hercules TRI 16.47/1.7
8. Wilbert Walker JAM 16.33/1.1

Shot (20)
1. Janus Robberts RSA 19.76
2. Dorian Scott JAM 19.75
3. Scott Martin AUS 19.48
4. Carl Myerscough ENG 19.07
5. Vikas Gowda IND 18.46
6. Clay Cross AUS 18.44
7. Hannes Hopley RSA 18.44
8. Mark Proctor ENG 17.59

Discus (20)
1. Scott Martin AUS 63.48
2. Jason Tunks CAN 63.07
3. Dariusz Slowik CAN 61.49
4. Hannes Hopley RSA 60.99
5. Carl Myerscough ENG 60.64
6. Vikas Gowda IND 60.08
7. Emeka Udechuku ENG 59.36
8. Benn Harradine AUS 58.87

Hammer (24)
1. Stuart Rendell AUS 77.53*
2. James Steacy CAN 74.75
3, Chris Harmse RSA 73.81
4. Andrew Frost ENG 72.62
5. Mick Jones ENG 70.09
6. Simon Bown ENG 65.42
7. Derek Woodske CAN 64.42
8. John Osazuwa NGR 62.71

Javelin (25)
1. Nick Nieland ENG 80.10
2. William Hamlyn-Harris AUS 79.89
3. Oliver Dziubak AUS 79.89
4. Gerhardus Pienaar RSA 78.91
5. Johan Oosthuizen RSA 78.32
6. Jarrod Bannister AUS 78.06
7. Stuart Farquhar NZL 77.40
8. Scott Russell CAN 73.88

Decathlon (20-21)
1. Dean Macey ENG 8143
2. Maurice Smith JAM 8074
3. Jason Dudley AUS 8001
4. Brent Newdick NZL 7566
5. Dale Garland GUE 7413
6. Richard Allan AUS 7367
7. Matt McEwen AUS 7277
8. Guillaume Thierry MRI 6746

20 Kilometres Walk (20)
1. Nathan Deakes AUS 1:19:55*
2. Luke Adams AUS 1:21:38
3. Jared Tallent AUS 1:23:32
4. David Kimutai KEN 1:25:42
5. Parayil Jalal IND 1:30:43
6. Daniel King ENG 1:31:17
7. Dominic King ENG 1:32:21
8. Andrew Penn ENG 1:32:54

50 Kilometres Walk (24)
1. Nathan Deakes AUS 3:42:53*
2. Tony Sargisson NZL 3:58:05
3. Chris Erickson AUS 3:58:22
4. Craig Barrett NZL 4:02:27
5. Tim Berrett CAN 4:08:18
6. Steve Partington IOM 4:25:39
7. Abd. M Sharrulhaizy MAS 5:07:32

4 x 100 Metres Relay (25)
1. JAM (M Frater, A Waugh, C Williams, A Powell) 38.36
2. RSA (L Newton, L Julius, S Prinsloo, S Vries) 38.98
3. CAN (C Allen, A Henry, N Taylor, E Parris) 39.21
4. MRI 39.97 5. ANT 40.76
dnf. AUS, GHA, NZL –

4 x 400 Metres Relay (25)
1. AUS (J Steffensen, C Troode, M Ormrod, C Hill) 3:00.93
2. RSA (J van der Merwe, I Mogawane, P Gorries, L van Zyl) 3:01.84
3. JAM (L Davis, D Clarke, L Spence, J Gonzales) 3:01.94
4. ENG 3:02.01 dq. TRI (3:03.43)
5. NGR 3:02.16 dnf. BAH –
6. SRI 3:06.42

WOMEN

100 Metres (20) 0.2
1. Sheri-Ann Brooks JAM 11.19
2. Geraldine Pillay RSA 11.31
3. Deplhine Atangana CMR 11.39
4. Laura Turner ENG 11.46
5. Tahesia Harrigan IVB 11.48
6. Erica Broomfield CAN 11.49
7. Sally McLellan AUS 11.50
8. Emma Ania ENG 11.51

200 Metres (23) 0.6
1. Sherone Simpson JAM 22.59
2. Veronica Campbell JAM 22.72
3. Geraldine Pillay RSA 22.92
4. Cydonie Mothersill CAY 23.01
5. Sherri-Ann Brooks JAM 23.07
6. Vida Anim GHA 23.34
7. Delphine Atangana CMR 23.45
8. Myriam Mani CMR 23.78

400 Metres (21)
1. Christine Ohuruogu ENG 50.28
2. Tonique Darling BAH 50.76
3. Novlene Williams JAM 51.12
4. Christine Amertil BAH 51.52
5. Shericka Williams JAM 51.81
6. Hazel-Ann Regis GRN 52.35
7. Manjit Kaur IND 52.58
8. Rosemary Hayward AUS 52.81

800 Metres (24)
1. Janeth Jepkosgei KEN 1:57.88
2. Kenia Sinclair JAM 1:58.16
3. Maria Mutola MOZ 1:58.77
4. Susan Scott SCO 1:59.02
5. Diane Cummins CAN 1:59.31
6. Jemma Simpson ENG 2:01.11

7. Marilyn Okoro ENG 2:01.65
8. N. Bernard-Thomas GRN 2:01.96

1500 Metres (21)
1. Lisa Dobriskey ENG 4:06.21
2. Sarah Jamieson AUS 4:06.64
3. Hayley Tullett WAL 4:06.76
4. Helen Clitheroe ENG 4:06.81
5. Car. Douma-Hussar CAN 4:07.48
6. Suzanne Walsham AUS 4:08.42
7. Viola Kibiwot KEN 4:08.74
8. Malindi Elmore CAN 4:09.06
9. Ashley Couper BER 4:10.48
10. Hayley Ovens SCO 4:10.75

5000 Metres (24)
1. Isabella Ochichi KEN 14:57.84
2. Jo Pavey ENG 14:59.08
3. Lucy Wangui KEN 15:00.20
4. Eloise Wellings AUS 15:00.69
5. Sarah Jamieson AUS 15:02.90
6. Ines Chenonge KEN 15:12.34
7. Courtney Babcock CAN 15:44.22
8. Zakia Mrisho TAN 15:50.87
9. Natalie Harvey ENG 15:50.87

10000 Metres (19)
1. Lucy Wangui KEN 31:29.66
2. Evelyne Wambui KEN 31:30.86
3. Mara Yamauchi ENG 31:49.40
4. Benita Johnson AUS 31:58.08
5. Anna Thompson AUS 32:27.74
6. Hayley Yelling ENG 32:32.38
7. Kathy Butler SCO 32:44.29
8. Tara Quinn CAN 33:15.50
9. Catherine Dugdale WAL 34:09.85

Marathon (19)
1. Kerryn McCann AUS 2:30:54
2. Hellen Cherono KEN 2:30:56
3. Liz Yelling ENG 2:32:19
4. Tracey Morris WAL 2:33:13
5. Josephine Akunay TAN 2:36:27
6. Lioud. Kortchaguina CAN 2:36:43
7. Kate Smyth AUS 2:38:30
8. Lauren Shelley AUS 2:39:13

3000 Metres Steeplechase (22)
1. Dorcus Inzikuru UGA 9:19.51*
2. Melissa Rollison AUS 9:24.29
3. Donna MacFarlane AUS 9:25.05
4. Victoria Mitchell AUS 9:34.24
5. Kate McIlroy NZL 9:35.70
6. Jeruto Kiptum KEN 9:49.09
7. Jo Ankier ENG 9:53.12
8. Tina Brown ENG 10:09.14

100 Metres Hurdles (24) -0.3
1. Brigitte Foster-Hylton JAM 12.76 (12.65* in heat)
2. Angela Whyte CAN 12.94
3. Dell. Ennis-London JAM 13.00
4. Lacena Golding-Clark JAM 13.01
5. Fiona Cullen AUS 13.31
6. Julie Pratt ENG 13.48
7. Evmorfia Baourda CYP 13.64
fell. Sally McLellan AUS –

400 Metres Hurdles (23)
1. Jana Pittman AUS 53.82*
2. Tasha Danvers-Smith ENG 55.17
3. Lee McConnell SCO 55.25
4. Nicola Sanders ENG 55.32
5. Shevon Stoddart JAM 56.67
6. Norasheela M Khalid MAS 56.89
7. Sonia Brito AUS 57.23
dq (5) Androula Sialou CYP (55.82)

High Jump (23)
1. Anika Smit RSA 1.91
2. Julie Crane WAL 1.88
3= Karen Beautle JAM 1.83
3= Angela McKee NZL 1.83
5. Lavern Spencer LCA 1.83
6= Claire Mallett AUS 1.83
6= Susan Moncrieff ENG 1.83
6= Ellen Pettitt AUS 1.83

Pole Vault (25)
1. Kym Howe-Nadin AUS 4.62* (also * for 4.35, 4.45, 4.50)
2. Tatiana Grigorieva AUS 4.35
3. Stephanie McCann CAN 4.25
4= Dana Ellis CAN 4.25
4= Rosalinda Samsu MAS 4.25
6. Vicky Parnov AUS-Y 4.25
7. Kate Dennison ENG 4.15
8= Melina Hamilton NZL 4.15
8= Kelsie Hendry CAN 4.15

Long Jump (22)
1. Bronwyn Thompson AUS6.97/1.9*
2. Kerrie Taurima AUS 6.57/1.4
3. Céline Laporte SEY 6.57/0.8
4. Chantal Brunner NZL 6.56/1.7
5. Jade Johnson ENG 6.55/0.6
6. Anju Bobby George IND 6.54/-0.7
7. Esther Aghatise NGR 6.47/1.8
8. Jackie Edwards BAH 6.46/1.9

Triple Jump (21)
1. Trecia Smith JAM 14.39/0.0
2. Otonye Iworima NGR 13.53/-1.0
3. Nadia Williams ENG 13.42/-0.3
4. Chin. Ohadugha NGR 13.26/-0.7
5. Nkiruka Domike NGR 13.24/0.1
6. Jeanette Bowles AUS 13.23/-0.5
7. Michelle Robinson ENG 12.80/-0.3
8. Soko Salaniqiqi FIJ 11.61/0.0

Shot (22)
1. Valerie Vili NZL 19.66*
2. Vivian Chukwuemeka NGR 18.25
3. Cleopatra Borel-Brown TRI 17.87
4. Zhang Guirong SIN 17.39
5. Du Xianhui SIN 16.76
6. Simoné du Toit RSA-J 16.52
7. Ana Po'uhila TON 16.43
8. Joanne Duncan ENG 16.42
9. Marli Knoetze RSA 16.08
10. Julie Dunkley ENG 15.98

Discus (21)
1. Elizna Naude RSA 61.55
2. Seema Antil IND 60.56
3. Dani Samuels AUS-J 59.44
4. Beatrice Faumuina NZL 59.12
5. Krishna Poonia IND 58.65
6. Philippa Roles WAL 58.38
7. Harwant Kaur IND 57.64
8. Claire Smithson ENG 54.34

Hammer (20)
1. Brooke Billett AUS 67.90*
2. Jennifer Joyce CAN 67.29
3. Lorraine Shaw ENG 66.00
4. Karyne DiMarco AUS 62.23
5. Zoe Derham ENG 61.92
6. Carys Parry WAL 61.80
7. Gabrielle Neighbour AUS 61.55
8. Lesley Brannan WAL 61.55
9. Laura Douglas WAL 60.35

Javelin (19)
1. Sunette Viljoen RSA 60.72*
2. Laverne Eve BAH 60.54
3. Olivia McKoy JAM 58.27
4. Kimberley Mickle AUS 58.18
5. Goldie Sayers ENG 57.29
6. Kathryn Mitchell AUS 55.22
7. Lindy Leveau SEY 54.50
8. Rosie Hooper AUS 52.46

Heptathlon (21-22)
1. Kelly Sotherton ENG 6396
2. Kylie Wheeler AUS 6298
3. Jessica Ennis ENG 6269
4. Jessica Zelinka CAN 6213
5. Janice Josephs RSA 6181
6. Julie Hollman ENG 6002
7. Rebecca Wardell NZL 5845
8. Soma Biswas IND 5573
9. Javur J Shobha IND 5533

20 Kilometres Walk (20)
1. Jane Saville AUS 1:32:46*
2. Natalie Saville AUS 1:33:33
3. Cheryl Webb AUS 1:36:03
4. Nicolene Cronje RSA 1:38:19
5. Susanne Erasmus RSA 1:40:54
6. Deepmala L. Devi IND 1:41:54
7. Johanna Jackson ENG 1:42:04
8. Niobe Menendez ENG 1:47:35

4 x 100 Metres Relay (25)
4 x 100 Metres (25th)
1. JAM (D Browning, S Brooks, P Dowdie, S Simpson) 43.10
2. ENG (A Onuora, K Wall, L Turner, E Ania) 43.43
3. AUS (S McLellan, M Kleeberg, L Hewitt, C Attenborough) 44.25
4. NGR 44.37 dnf. GHA –

4 x 400 Metres Relay (25)
1. AUS (J Pittman, C Willis, T Lewis, R Hayward) 3:28.66
2. IND (R Kaur, C Soman, M Kaur, P Parmanik) 3:29.57
3. NGR (K Akhigbe, J Eze, F Abugan, C Ekpukhon) 3:31.83
4. JAM 3:34.91 5. PNG 3:47.88
dq. ENG (Wall, Sanders, N Danvers-Smith, C Ohuruogu) (1-3:27.17)
dq. RSA (4_3:30.06)

Leading Nations – Medals & Points

Nation	1	2	3	Points
Australia	14	10	12	379.5
England	6	4	8	238
Jamaica	9	5	8	185.5
South Africa	5	5	2	134.5
Kenya	6	4	4	131
Canada	1	6	3	114
New Zealand	2	1	1	71
Nigeria	0	3	1	54
India	0	2	0	39
Wales	0	1	1	35
Bahamas	0	2	0	31.5
Tanzania	1	0	1	31
Trinidad & Tobago	0	0	2	28.5
Uganda	2	0	0	22
Scotland	0	1	1	20
Ghana	1	0	0	17

21 nations won medals, with 36 placing athletes in the top eight.

* Championships record

WORLD CROSS-COUNTRY CHAMPIONSHIPS 2006

Fukuoka, Japan 1-2 April

Kenenisa Bekele won both men's races for the fifth successive year to take his collection of World CC medals to 25 team and individual including 11 individual and 7 team golds. Afterwards he said that. although he is only 23, this might be the end of his cross-country career which brought him 26 succcessive individual victories from December 2001. There were senior victories also for his female compatriots Tirunesh Dibaba and Gelete Burka, although Dibaba dropped out of the short-course race on the second day. However, Kenya regained both the senior men's team titles as well as winning both the junior titles while Ethiopia took both the the senior women's team titles. While the amazing success of Kenya and Ethiopia in this event continued, they were split by their smaller East African neighbour Eritrea in the senior men's team contest, and Eritrea also won junior men's team bronze. Kenyan-born Lornah Kiplagat pushed Dibaba hard and won the first ever medal at the IAAF Wold CC Championships for the Netherlands. From 2007 the event reverts to having just one (long) race for men and for women.

Men's 4km (1)
1. Kenenisa Bekele ETH 10:54
2. Isaac Songok KEN 10:55
3. Adil Kaouch MAR 10:57
4. Benjamin Limo KEN 11:00
5. Mohamed Ali Aboosh ETH 11:01
6. Adam Goucher USA 11:02
7. Augustine Choge KEN 11:03
8. Edwin Soi KEN 11:06
9. Saif Saaeed Shaheen QAT 11:08
10. Sultan Khamis Zaman QAT 11:08
11. Craig Mottram AUS 11:10
12. Sileshi Sihine ETH 11:12
13. Kevin Sullivan CAN 11:14
14. Hicham Bellani MAR 11:15
15. Khalid El Amri MAR 11:16
16. Khoudir Aggoune ALG 11:17
17. Wilson Busienei UGA 11:17
18. Brimin Kipruto KEN 11:17
19. Ryan Hall USA 11:18
20. Yusuf Kibet Biwot KEN 11:18

126 of 128 finished

Team 21 completed
1. KEN 21 6. ESP 140
2. ETH 48 7. UGA 142
3. MAR 53 8. ALG 158
4. QAT 66 9. MEX 170
5. USA 80 10. ERI 173

Men's 12km (2)
1. Kenenisa Bekele ETH 35:40
2. Sileshi Sihine ETH 35:43
3. Martin Mathathi KEN 35:44
4. Zersenay Tadesse ERI 35:47
5. Mike Kigen KEN 35:54
6. Hosea Macharinyang KEN 36:02
7. Yonas Kifle ERI 36:05
8. Ali Abdallah ERI 36:18
9. Tesfaye Mesfin ETH 36:18
10. Simon Arusei KEN 36:18
11. Abderrahim Goumri MAR 36:20
12. John Kibowen KEN 36:21
13. Gebre Gebremariam ETH 36:24
14. Abdullah Ahmad Hassan QAT 36:25
15. Mohammed Amyn MAR 36:28
16. Khalid El Amri MAR 36:31
17. Juan C de la Ossa ESP 36:35
18. Camal Belal Salem QAT 36:40
19. Samson Kiflemariam ERI 36:41
20. Aïssa Dghoughi MAR 36:42

132 of 141 finished

Team 20 completed
1. KEN 24 6. QAT 116
2. ERI 28 7. POR 152
3. ETH 42 8. JPN 171
4. MAR 62 9. MEX 199
5. UGA 102 10. ALG 200

Junior Men's 8km (2)
1. Mangata Kimai Ndiwa KEN 23:53
2. Leonard Komon KEN 23:54
3. Tariku Bekele ETH 23:56
4. Joseph Ebuya KEN 23:59
5. Ibrahim Jellan Gashu ETH 24:04
6. Habtamu Fed. Awash ETH 24:04
7. Kamal Ali Thamar QAT 24:05
8. Samuel Tesfamrian ERI 24:06
9. Bernard Matheka KEN 24:08
10. Tadesse Woldegebrel ETH 24:09

92 of 98 finished

Team 15 completed
1. KEN 16 6. QAT 88
2. ETH 24 7. JPN 118
3. ERI 45 8. MAR 132
4. UGA 87 9. USA 178
5. BRN 88 10. ITA 219

Women's 4km (2)
1. Gelete Burka ETH 12:51
2. Priscah Jepleting KEN 12:53
3. Meselech Melkamu ETH 12:54
4. Benita Johnson AUS 12:55
5. Lornah Kiplagat NED 12:55
6. Beatrice Jepchumba KEN 12:58
7. Zhor El Kamch MAR 13:03
8. Vivian Cheruiyot KEN 13:10
9. Bezenesh Bekele ETH 13:10
10. Isabella Ochichi KEN 13:11
11. Melissa Rollison AUS 13:11
12. Teyiba Erkesso ETH 13:12
13. Etalemahu Kisane ETH 13:13
14. Nancy Wambui KEN 13:13
15. Mariem Selsouli MAR 13:14
16. Olga Komyagina RUS 13:16
17. Ruhama Shauri TAN 13:20
18. Blake Russell USA 13:21
19. Malindi Elmore CAN 13:21
20. Bouchra Chaabi MAR 13:32

91 of 92 finished

Teams 14 completed
1. ETH 25 6. RUS 102
2. KEN 26 7. CAN 115
3. AUS 69 8. CHN 156
4. MAR 73 9. TAN 187
5. USA 99 10. BRN 201

Women's 8km (1)
1. Tirunesh Dibaba ETH 25:21
2. Lornah Kiplagat NED 25:26
3. Meselech Melkamu ETH 25:38
4. Benita Johnson AUS 25:43
5. Wude Ayalew Yimer ETH 25:47
6. Kayoko Fukushi JPN 25:51
7. Mestawet Tufa ETH 25:59
8. Evelyne Wambui KEN 26:11
9. Faith Chemutai KEN 26:12
10. Alice Chelangat KEN 26:13
11. Blake Russell USA 26:23
12. Mercy Wanjiku Njorege KEN 26:26
13. Edna Kiplagat KEN 26:32
14. Ejegayehu Dibaba ETH 26:37
15. Nina Rillstone NZL 26:39
16. Kate McIlroy NZL 26:42
17. Simret Sultan ERI 26:43
18. Bao Guiying CHN 26:43
19. Yoshimi Ozaki JPN 26:45
20. Christine Bardelle FRA 26:45

98 of 99 finished

Team 15 completed
1. ETH 16 6. NZL 112
2. KEN 39 7. GBR 134
3. JPN 80 8. CHN 141
4. AUS 87 9. FRA 175
5. USA 91 10. ESP 18

Junior Women's 6km (1)
1. Pauline Korikwiang KEN 19:27
2. Veronica Nyarwai KEN 19:27
3. Mercy Kosgei KEN 19:45
4. Emmy Chepkirui KEN 19:52
5. Belaynesh Zemedkun ETH 19:56
6. Workitu Ayanu ETH 19:57
7. Emedet Bedada ETH 20:05
8. Pamela Lisoreng KEN 20:06
9. Gladys Chemweno KEN 20:09
10. Sian Edwards GBR 20:10

76 of 78 finished

Team 12 completed
1. KEN 19 6. RUS 133
2. ETH 29 7. MAR 145
3. JPN 58 8. USA 146
4. ERI 83 9. AUS 161
5. GBR 116 10. CAN 199